Department of Economic and Social Affairs
Département des affaires économiques et sociales

ST/ESA/STAT/SER.R/36

2005
Demographic Yearbook
Annuaire démographique

Fifty-seventh issue/Cinquante-septième édition

United Nations/Nations Unies
New York, 2008

The Department of Economic and Social Affairs of the United Nations Secretariat is a vital interface between global policies in the economic, social and environmental spheres and national action. The Department works in three main interlinked areas: (i) it compiles, generates and analyses a wide range of economic, social and environmental data and information on which States Members of the United Nations draw to review common problems and to take stock of policy options; (ii) it facilitates the negotiations of Member States in many intergovernmental bodies on joint courses of action to address ongoing or emerging global challenges; and (iii) it advises interested Governments on the ways and means of translating policy frameworks developed in United Nations conferences and summits into programmes at the country level and, through technical assistance, helps build national capacities.

Le Département des affaires économiques et sociales du Secrétariat de l'Organisation des Nations Unies sert de relais entre les orientations arrêtées au niveau international dans les domaines économiques, sociaux et environnementaux et les politiques exécutées à l'échelon national. Il intervient dans trois grands domaines liés les uns aux autres : i) il compile, produit et analyse une vaste gamme de données et d'éléments d'information sur des questions économiques, sociales et environnementales dont les États Membres de l'Organisation se servent pour examiner des problèmes communs et évaluer les options qui s'offrent à eux; ii) il facilite les négociations entre les États Membres dans de nombreux organes intergouvernementaux sur les orientations à suivre de façon collective afin de faire face aux problèmes mondiaux existants ou en voie d'apparition; iii) il conseille les gouvernements intéressés sur la façon de transposer les orientations politiques arrêtées à l'occasion des conférences et sommets des Nations Unies en programmes exécutables au niveau national et aide à renforcer les capacités nationales au moyen de programmes d'assistance technique.

NOTE

Symbols of United Nations documents are composed of capital letters combined with figures. Mention of such a symbol indicates reference to a United Nations document.

The designations employed and the presentation of material in this publication do not imply the expression of any opinion whatsoever on the part of the Secretariat of the United Nations concerning the legal status of any country, territory, city or area, or of its authorities, or concerning the delimitation of its frontiers or boundaries.

Where the designation "country or area" appears in the headings of tables, it covers countries, territories, cities or areas. In prior issues of this publication, where the designation "country" appears in the headings of tables, it should be interpreted to cover countries, territories, cities or areas.

NOTE

Les cotes des documents de l'Organisation des Nations Unies se composent de lettres majuscules et de chiffres. La simple mention d'une cote dans un texte signifie qu'il s'agit d'un document de l'Organisation.

Les appellations employées dans cette publication et la présentation des données qui y figurent n'impliquent de la part du Secrétariat de l'Organisation des Nations Unies aucune prise de position quant au statut juridique des pays, territoires, villes ou zones, ou de leurs autorités, ni quant au tracé de leurs frontières ou limites.

L'appellation "pays ou zone" figurant dans les titres des rubriques des tableaux désigne des pays, des territoires, des villes ou des zones. L'appellation "pays" figurant dans certaines rubriques des tableaux de numéros antérieurs de cette publication doit être interprétée comme désignant des pays, des territoires, des villes ou des zones.

ST/ESA/STAT/SER.R/36

UNITED NATIONS PUBLICATION
Sales number: E/F.08.XIII.1

PUBLICATION DES NATIONS UNIES
Numéro de vente: E/F.08.XIII.1

ISBN 978-92-1-051099-8
ISSN 0082-8041

Topics of the Demographic Yearbook series: 1948 - 2005

Sujets des diverses éditions de l'Annuaire démographique: 1948 - 2005

Year Année	Sales No. - Numéro de vente	Issue - Edition	Special topic - Sujet spécial
1948	49.XIII.1	First-Première	General demography-Démographie générale
1949-50	51.XIII.1	Second-Deuxième	Natality statistics-Statistiques de la natalité
1951	52.XIII.1	Third-Trosième	Mortality statistics-Statistiques de la mortalité
1952	53.XIII.1	Fourth-Quatrième	Population distribution-Répartition de la population
1953	54.XIII.1	Fifth-Cinquième	General demography-Démographie générale
1954	55.XIII.1	Sixth-Sixième	Natality statistics -Statistiques de la natalité
1955	56.XIII.1	Seventh-Septième	Population censuses-Recensement de population
1956	57.XIII.1	Eighth-Huitième	Ethnic and economic characteristics of population-Caractéristiques ethniques et économiques de la population
1957	58.XIII.1	Ninth-Neuvième	Mortality statistics- Statistiques de la mortalité
1958	59.XIII.1	Tenth-Dixième	Marriage and divorce statistics- Statistiques de la nuptialité et de la divortialité
1959	60.XIII.1	Eleventh-Onzième	Natality statistics- Statistiques de la natalité
1960	61.XIII.1	Twelfth-Douzième	Population trends- l' évolution de la population
1961	62.XIII.1	Thirteenth-Treizième	Mortality Statistics- Statistiques de la mortalité
1962	63.XIII.1	Fourteenth-Quatorzième	Population census statistics I- Statistiques des recensements de population I
1963	64.XIII.1	Fifteenth-Quinzième	Population census statistics II- Statistiques des recensements de population II
1964	65.XIII.1	Sixteenth-Seizième	Population census statistics III- Statistiques des recensements de population III
1965	66.XIII.1	Seventeenth-Dix-septième	Natality statistics- Statistiques de la natalité
1966	67.XIII.1	Eighteenth-Dix-huitième	Mortality statistics I- Statistiques de la mortalité I
1967	E/F.68.XIII.1	Nineteenth-Dix-neuvième	Mortality statistics II - Statistiques de la mortalité II
1968	E/F.69.XIII.1	Twentieth-Vingtième	Marriage and divorce statistics-Statistiques de la nuptialité et de la divortialité
1969	E/F.70.XIII.1	Twenty-first-Vingt et unième	Natality statistics-Statistiques de la natalité
1970	E/F.71.XIII.1	Twenty-second-Vingt-deuxième	Population trends-l' évolution de la population
1971	E/F.72.XIII.1	Twenty-third-Vingh-troisième	Population census statistics I- Statistiques de recensements de population I
1972	E/F.73.XIII.1	Twenty-fourth-Vingt-quatrième	Population census statistics II- Statistiques des recensements de population II
1973	E/F.74.XIII.1	Twenty-fifth-Vingt-cinquième	Population census statistics III- Statistiques des recensements de population III
1974	E/F.75.XIII.1	Twenty-sixth-Vingt-sixième	Mortality statistics - Statistiques de la mortalité
1975	E/F.76.XIII.1	Twenty-seventh-Vingt-septième	Natality statistics- Statistiques de la natalité
1976	E/F.77.XIII.1	Twenty-eighth-Vingt-huitième	Marriage and divorce statistics- Statistiques de la nuptialité et de la divortialité
1977	E/F.78.XIII.1	Twenty-ninth-Vingt-neuvième	International Migration Statistics- internationales
1978	E/F.79.XIII.1	Thirtieth-Trentième	General tables- Tableaux de caractère général
1978	E/F.79.XIII.8	Special issue-Edition spéciale	Historical supplement-Supplément rétrospectif
1979	E/F.80.XIII.1	Thirty-first-Trente et unième	Population census statistics-Statistiques des recensements de population
1980	E/F.81.XIII.1	Thirty-second-Trente-deuxième	Mortality statistics- Statistiques de la mortalité
1981	E/F.82.XIII.1	Thirty-third-Trente-troisième	Natality statistics-Statistiques de la natalité
1982	E/F.83.XIII.1	Thirty-fourth-	Marriage and divorce statistics-

Topics of the Demographic Yearbook series: 1948 - 2005

Sujets des diverses éditions de l'Annuaire démographique: 1948 - 2005

Year Année	Sales No. - Numéro de vente	Issue - Edition	Special topic - Sujet spécial
		Trente-quatrième	Statistiques de la nuptialité et de la divortialité
1983	E/F.84.XIII.1	Thirty fifth- Trente-cinquième	Population census statistics I- Statistiques des recensements de population I
1984	E/F.85.XIII.1	Thirty-sixth- Trente-sixième	Population census statistics II- Statistiques des recensements de population II
1985	E/F.86.XIII.1	Thirty-seventh- Trente-septième	Mortality statistics- Statistiques de la mortalité
1986	E/F.87.XIII.1	Thirty-eightth- Trente-Hiutième	Natality statistics- Statistiques de la natalité
1987	E/F.88.XIII.1	Thirty-ninth- Trente-neuvième	Household composition- Les éléments du ménage
1988	E/F.89.XIII.1	Fortieth- Quarantième	Population census statistics- Statistiques des recensements de population
1989	E/F.90.XIII.1	Forty-first- Quarante-et-unième	International Migration Statistics- Statistiques des migration internationales
1990	E/F.91.XIII.1	Forty-second- Quarante-deuxième	Marriage and divorce statistics- Statistiques de la nuptialité et de la divortialité
1991	E/F.92.XIII.1	Forty-third- Quarante-troisième	General tables- Tableaux de caractère général
1991	E/F.92.XIII.8	Special issue- Edition spéciale	Population ageing and the situation of elderly persons- Vieillissement de la population et situation des personnes agées
1992	E/F.94.XIII.1	Forty-forth- Quarante-quatrième	Fertility and mortality statistics- Statistiques de la fecondité et de la mortalité
1993	E/F.95.XIII.1	Forty-fifth- Quarante-cinquième	Population census statistics I- Statistiques des recensements de population I
1994	E/F.96.XIII.1	Forty-sixth- Quarante-sixième	Population census statistics II- Statistiques des recensements de population II
1995	E/F.97.XIII.1	Forty-seventh- Quarante-septième	Household composition-Les éléments du ménage
1996	E/F.98.XIII.1	Forty-eighth- Quarante-hutième	Mortality statistics- Statistiques de la mortalité
1997	E/F.99.XIII.1	Forty-ninth- Quarante-neuvième	General tables- Tableaux de caractère général
1997	E/F.99.XIII.12	Special issue- Edition spéciale (CD)	Historical supplement- Supplément rétrospectif
1998	E/F.00.XIII.1	Fiftieth- Cinquantième	General tables- Tableaux de caractère général
1999	E/F.01.XIII.1	Fifty-first- Cinquante-et-unième	General tables- Tableaux de caractère général
1999	E/F.02.XIII.6	Special issue- Edition spéciale (CD)	Natality Statistics- Statistiques de la natalité
2000	E/F.02.XIII.1	Fifty-second- Cinquante-deuxième	General tables- Tableaux de caractère général
2001	E/F.03.XIII.1	Fifty-third- Cinquante- troisième	General tables- Tableaux de caractère général
2002	E/F.05.XIII.1	Fifty-fourth- Cinquante-quatrième	General tables- Tableaux de caractère général
2003	E/F.06.XIII.1	Fifty-fifth- Cinquante-cinquième	General tables- Tableaux de caractère général
2004	E/F.07.XIII.1	Fifty-sixth- Cinquante- sixième	General tables- Tableaux de caractère général
2005	E/F.08.XIII.1	Fifty-seventh- Cinquante- septième	General tables- Tableaux de caractère général

CONTENTS - TABLE DES MATIERES

EXPLANATIONS OF SYMBOLS

Category not applicable	..
Data not available	...
Magnitude zero or less than half of unit employed	-
Provisional	*
Data tabulated by year of registration rather than occurrence	+
Based on less than specified minimum	◆
Relatively reliable data	Roman type
Data of lesser reliability	*Italics*

EXPLICATION DES SIGNES

Sans objet	..
Données non disponibles	...
Néant ou chiffre inférieur à la moitié de l'unité employée	-
Données provisoires	*
Donnée exploitées selon l'année de l'enregistrement et non l'année de l'événement	+
Rapport fondé sur un nombre inférieur à celui spécifié	◆
Données relativement sûres	Caractères romains
Données dont l'exactitude est moindre	*Italiques*

INTRODUCTION

The *Demographic Yearbook* is an international compendium of national demographic statistics, provided by national statistical authorities to the Statistics Division of the United Nations Department of Economic and Social Affairs. The *Yearbook* is part of the set of coordinated and interrelated publications issued by the United Nations and its specialized agencies,[1] designed to supply basic statistical data for such users as demographers, economists, public-health workers and sociologists. Through the co-operation of national statistical services, official demographic statistics are compiled in the *Yearbook*, as available, for more than 230 countries or areas throughout the world.

The *Demographic Yearbook 2005* is the fifty-seventh in a series published by the United Nations since 1948. It contains general tables including a world summary of selected demographic statistics, statistics on the size, distribution and trends in national populations, natality, foetal mortality, infant and maternal mortality, general mortality, nuptiality and divorce. Data are shown by urban/rural residence, as available. In addition, the volume provides Technical Notes, a synoptic table, a historical index and a listing of the issues of the *Yearbook* published to date.

The Technical Notes on the Statistical Tables are provided to assist the reader in using the tables. Table A, the synoptic table, provides a glance of the completeness of data coverage of the current *Yearbook*. The cumulative historical index is a guide on content and coverage of all fifty-seven issues, and indicates for each of the topics that have been published, the issues in which they are presented and the years covered. A list of the *Demographic Yearbook* issues, with their corresponding sales number and the special topics featured in each issue are shown on pages iii and iv.

Until the 48th issue (1996), each issue consisted of two parts, the general tables and special topic tables, published in the same volume with the regular topics.[2] Beginning with the 49th issue (1997), the special topic tables were being disseminated on CD-ROMs as supplements to the regular issues. Two CD-ROMs have so far been issued: the *Demographic Yearbook Historical Supplement*, which presents a wide panorama of basic demographic statistics for the period 1948 to 1997, and the *Demographic Yearbook: Natality Statistics*, which contains a series of detailed tables dedicated to natality and covering the period from 1980 to 1998. Three volumes of a new Demographic Yearbook Special Census Topics have now been prepared and are presented at: http://unstats.un.org/unsd/demographic/products/dyb/default.htm

Population statistics are not available for all countries or areas, for a variety of reasons. In an effort to provide estimates of mid-year population and of selected vital statistics for all countries and areas, two annexes have been introduced since the 53rd issue of the *Demographic Yearbook*. Annex 1 presents United Nations population estimates for the period 1996-2005 and the second presents the medium variant estimates of crude birth and death rates, infant mortality and total fertility rates, as well as expectation of life at birth over the period 2000-2005. These data are produced by the United Nations Population Division and are published in the *World Population Prospects - The 2006 Revision*.[3]

Demographic statistics shown in this issue of the *Yearbook* are available online at the *Demographic Yearbook* website http://unstats.un.org/unsd/demographic/products/dyb/default.htm. Information about the Statistics Division's data collection and dissemination programme is also available on the same website. Additional information can be made available by contacting the Statistics Division of the United Nations Secretariat, at demostat@un.org.

TECHNICAL NOTES ON THE STATISTICAL TABLES

1. GENERAL REMARKS

1.1 Arrangement of Technical Notes

These Technical Notes are designed to provide the reader with relevant information for using the statistical tables. Information pertaining to the *Yearbook* in general is presented in the sections dealing with geographical aspects, population and vital statistics. In addition, preceding each table are notes describing the variables, remarks on the reliability and limitation of the data, countries and areas covered, and information on the presentation of earlier data. When appropriate, details on computation of rates, ratios or percentages are presented.

1.2 Arrangement of tables

This issue contains general tables only. Since the numbering of the tables does not correspond exactly to those in previous issues, the reader is advised to use the historical index that appears at the end of this book to find the reference to data in earlier issues.

1.3 Source of data

The statistics presented in the *Demographic Yearbook* are national data provided by official statistical authorities unless otherwise indicated. The primary source of data for the *Yearbook* is a set of questionnaires sent annually by the United Nations Statistics Division to over 230 national statistical services and other appropriate government offices. Data reported on these questionnaires are supplemented, to the extent possible, with data taken from official national publications, official websites and through correspondence with national statistical services. In the interest of comparability, rates, ratios and percentages have been calculated by the Statistics Division of the United Nations, except for the life table functions, the total fertility rate, and also crude birth rate and crude death rate for some countries or areas as appropriately noted. The methods used by the Statistics Division to calculate these rates and ratios are described in the Technical Notes for each table. The population figures used for these computations are those pertaining to the corresponding years published in this or previous issues of the *Yearbook*.

In cases when data in this issue of the *Demographic Yearbook* differ from those published in earlier issues or related publications, statistics in this issue may be assumed to reflect revisions to these data received by September 2007.

2. GEOGRAPHICAL ASPECTS

2.1 Coverage

Data are shown for all individual countries or areas that provided the information. Table 3 is the most comprehensive in geographical coverage, presenting data on population and surface area for all countries or areas with a population of at least 50 persons. Not all of these countries or areas appear in subsequent tables. In many cases the data required for a particular table are not available. In general, the more detailed the data required for a table, the fewer the number of countries or areas that can provide them.

In addition, rates and ratios are presented only for countries or areas reporting at least a minimum number of relevant events. The minimums are stated in the Technical Notes to individual tables.

Except for summary data shown for the world and by major areas and regions in tables 1 and 2 and data shown for capital city and cities with a population of 100 000 or more in table 8, all data are presented at the national level. The number of countries shown in each table is provided in table A, the synoptic table.

2.2 Territorial composition

To the extent possible, all data, including time series data, relate to the territory within 2005 boundaries, when the data were requested from the countries or areas. Exceptions are footnoted in individual tables. Additionally, in table 3, recent changes and other relevant clarifications are specified.

Data relating to the People's Republic of China generally do not include those for Taiwan Province except in tables 1 and 2.

2.3 Nomenclature

Because of space limitations, the country or area names listed in the tables are generally the commonly employed short titles in use in the United Nations as of September 2007[4], the full titles being used only when a short form is not available. The latest version of the *Standard Country or Area Codes for Statistics Use* can be accessed at http://unstats.un.org/unsd/methods/m49/m49.htm.

2.3.1 Order of presentation

Countries or areas are listed in English alphabetical order within the following continents: Africa, North America, South America, Asia, Europe and Oceania.

The designations and presentation of the material in this publication were adopted solely for the purpose of providing a convenient geographical basis for the accompanying statistical series. The same qualification applies to all notes and explanations concerning the geographical units for which data are presented.

2.4 Surface area data

Surface area data, shown in tables 1 and 3, represent the total surface area, comprising land area and inland waters (assumed to consist of major rivers and lakes) and excluding only Polar Regions and uninhabited islands. The surface area given is the most recent estimate available. They are presented in square kilometres, a conversion factor of 2.589988 having been applied to surface areas originally reported in square miles.

2.4.1 Comparability over time

Comparability over time in surface area estimates for any given country or area may be affected by changes in the surface area estimation procedures, increases in actual land surface by reclamation, boundary changes, changes in the concept of "land surface area" used or a change in the unit of measurement used. In most cases it was possible to ascertain the reason for a revision; otherwise, the latest figures have generally been accepted as correct and substituted for those previously on file.

2.4.2 International comparability

Lack of international comparability between surface area estimates arises primarily from differences in definition. In particular, there is considerable variation in the treatment of coastal bays, inlets and gulfs, rivers and lakes. International comparability is also impaired by the variation in methods employed to estimate surface area. These range from surveys based on modern scientific methods to conjectures based on diverse types of information. Some estimates are recent while others may not be. Since neither the exact method of determining the surface area nor the precise definition of its composition and time reference is known for all countries or areas, the estimates in table 3 should not be considered strictly comparable from one country or area to another.

3. POPULATION

Population statistics, that is, those pertaining to the size, geographical distribution and demographic characteristics of the population, are presented in a number of tables of the *Demographic Yearbook*.

Data for countries or areas include population census figures, estimates based on results of sample surveys (in the absence of a census), postcensal or intercensal estimates and those derived from continuous population registers. In the present issue of the *Yearbook*, the latest available census figure of the total population of each country or area and mid-year estimates for 2000 and 2005 are presented in table 3. Mid-year estimates of total population for 10 years (1996-2005) are shown in table 5 and mid-year estimates of urban and total population by sex for 10 years (1996-2005) are shown in table 6. The latest available data on population by age, sex and urban/rural residence are given in table 7. The latest available figures on the population of capital cities and of cities or urban agglomerations of 100 000 or more inhabitants are presented in table 8.

Summary estimates of the mid-year population of the world, major areas and regions for selected years and of its age and sex distribution in 2005 are set forth in tables 1 and 2, respectively.

The statistics on total population, population by age, sex and urban/rural distribution are used in the calculation of rates in the *Yearbook*. Vital rates by age and sex were calculated using data that appear in table 7 in this issue or the corresponding tables of previous issues of the *Demographic Yearbook*.

3.1 Sources of variation of data

The comparability of data is affected by several factors, including (1) the definition of total population; (2) the definition used to classify the population into its urban/rural components; (3) the accuracy of age reporting; (4) the extent of over-enumeration or under-enumeration in the most recent census or other source of benchmark population statistics; and (5) the quality of population estimates. These five factors will be discussed in some detail in sections 3.1.1 to 3.2.2 below. Other relevant problems are discussed in the technical notes to the individual tables. Readers interested in more detail, relating in particular to the basic concepts of population size, distribution and characteristics as elaborated by the United Nations, should consult the *Principles and Recommendations for Population and Housing Censuses, Revision 2.*[5]

3.1.1 Total population

The most important impediment to comparability of total populations is the difference between the concept of a de facto and de jure population. A de facto population should include all persons physically present in the country or area at the reference date. The de jure population, by contrast, should include all usual residents of the given country or area, whether or not they were physically present in the area at the reference date. By definition, therefore, a de facto total and a de jure total are not entirely comparable.

Comparability of even two de facto or de jure totals is often affected by the fact that strict conformity to either of these concepts is rare. For example, some so-called de facto counts do not include foreign military, naval and diplomatic personnel present in the country or area on official duty, and their accompanying family members and servants; some do not include foreign visitors in transit through the country or area or transients on ships in the harbour. On the other hand, they may include such persons as merchant seamen and fishermen who are temporarily out of the country or area working at their trade.

The de jure population figure presents even greater variations in comparability, in part because it depends in the first place on the concept of "usual residence", which varies from one country or area to another and is difficult to apply consistently in a census or survey enumeration. For example, non-national civilians temporarily in a country or area as short-term workers may officially be considered residents after a stay of a specified period of time or they may be considered as non-residents throughout the duration of their stay; at the same time, these individuals may be officially considered as residents or non-residents of the country or area from which they came, depending on the duration and/or purpose of their absence. Furthermore, regardless of the official treatment, individual respondents may apply their own interpretation of residence in responding to the inquiry. In addition, there may be considerable differences in the accuracy with which countries or areas are informed about the number of their residents temporarily out of the country or area.

As far as possible, the population statistics presented in the tables of the *Yearbook* refer to the de facto population. Those reported to have been based on the de jure concept are identified as such. Figures not otherwise qualified may, therefore, be assumed to have been reported by countries or areas as being based on a de facto definition of the population. In an effort to overcome, to the extent possible, the effect of the lack of strict conformity to either the de facto or the de jure concept given above, significant exceptions with respect to inclusions and exclusions of specific population groups, are footnoted when they are known.

It should be remembered, however, that the necessary detailed information has not been available in many cases. It cannot, therefore, be assumed that figures not thus qualified reflect strict de facto or de jure definitions.

A possible source of variation within the statistics of a single country or area may arise from the fact that some countries or areas collect information on both the de facto and the de jure population in, for example, a census, but prepare detailed tabulations for only the de jure population. Hence, even though the total population shown in table 3 is de facto, the figures shown in the tables presenting various characteristics of the population, for example, urban/rural distribution, age and sex distribution, may be de jure.

4

3.1.2 Urban/rural classification

International comparability of urban/rural distributions is seriously impaired by the wide variation among national definitions of the concept of "urban". The definitions used by individual countries or areas and their implications are shown at the end of technical notes for table 6.

3.1.3 Age distribution

The classification of population by age is a core element of most analyses, estimation and projection of population statistics. Unfortunately, age data are subject to a number of sources of error and non-comparability. Accordingly, the reliability of age data should be of concern to users of these statistics.

3.1.3.1 Collection and compilation of age data

Age is the estimated or calculated interval of time between the date of birth and the date of the census or survey, expressed in completed solar years.[6] There are two methods of collecting information on age. The first is to obtain the date of birth for each member of the population in a census or survey and then to calculate the completed age of the individual by subtracting the date of birth from the date of enumeration.[7] The second method is to record the individual's completed age at the time of the census or survey, that is to say, age at last birthday.

The recommended method is to calculate age at last birthday by subtracting the exact date of birth from the date of the census. Some practices, however, do not use this method but instead calculate the difference between the year of birth and the year of the census. Classifications of this type are footnoted whenever possible. They can be identified to a certain extent by a smaller than expected population under one year of age. However, an irregular number of births from one year to the next or age selective omission of infants may also obscure the expected population under one year of age.

3.1.3.2 Errors in age data

Errors in age data may be due to a variety of causes, including ignorance of the correct age; reporting years of age in terms of a calendar concept other than completed solar years since birth;[8] carelessness in reporting and recording age; a general tendency to state age in figures ending in certain digits (such as zero, two, five and eight); a tendency to exaggerate length of life at advanced ages; a subconscious aversion to certain numbers; and wilful misrepresentations.

These reasons for errors in reported age data are common to most investigations of age and to most countries or areas, and they may significantly impair comparability of the data.

As a result of the above-mentioned difficulties, the age-sex distribution of population in many countries or areas shows irregularities which may be summarized as follows: (1) a deficiency in the number of infants and young children; (2) a concentration at ages ending with zero and five (that is, 5, 10, 15, 20...); (3) heaping at even ages (for example, 10, 12, 14...) relative to odd ages (for example, 11, 13, 15...); (4) unexpectedly large differences between the frequency of males and females at certain ages; and (5) unaccountably large differences between the frequencies in adjacent age groups. Comparing of identical age-sex cohorts from successive censuses, as well as studying the age-sex composition of each census, may reveal these and other inconsistencies, some of which in varying degree are characteristic of even the most modern censuses.

3.1.3.3 Evaluation of accuracy

To measure the accuracy of data by age, based on the evidence of irregularities in 5-year groups, an index was devised for presentation in the *Demographic Yearbook 1949-1950*[9]. Although this index was sensitive to various sources of inaccuracy in the data, it could also be affected considerably by real fluctuations in past demographic processes. It could not, therefore, be applied indiscriminately to all types of statistics, unless certain adjustments were made and caution used in the interpretation of results.

The publication of population statistics by single years of age in the *Demographic Yearbook 1955* made it possible to apply a simple, yet highly sensitive, index known as Whipple's Index, or the Index of Concentration[10], the interpretation of which is relatively free from consideration of factors not connected with the accuracy of age reporting. More refined methods for the measurement of accuracy of distributions by single year of age have been devised, but this particular index was selected for presentation in the *Demographic Yearbook* for its simplicity and the wide use it has already found in other sources.

Whipple's Index is obtained by summing the age returns between 23 and 62 years inclusive and finding what percentage is borne by the sum of the returns of years ending with 5 and 0 to one-fifth of the total sum.

The results would vary between a minimum of 0, if no returns were recorded ending with 0 or 5, and a maximum of 500, if no returns were recorded ending with any digits other than 0 or 5. If there is no age heaping at ages ending 0 or 5, the Whipple's index is 100.[11]

The index is applicable to all age distributions for which single years are given at least to the age of 62, with the following exceptions: (1) where the data presented are the result of graduation, no irregularity is scored by Whipple's Index, even though the graduated data may still be affected by inaccuracies of a different type; and (2) where statistics on age have been derived by reference to the year of birth, and tendencies to round off the birth year would result in an excessive number of ages ending in odd numbers, the frequency of age reporting with terminal digits 5 and 0 is not an adequate measure of their accuracy.

Most recently, the index has been computed for all the single-year age distributions from censuses held between 1985 and 2003, with the exception of those excluded on the criteria set forth above. Such data are published in the special issue of the *Demographic Yearbook* special topic on population censuses, Volume 1, which is available online at http://unstats.un.org/unsd/demographic/products/dyb/dybcens.htm.

Although Whipple's Index measures only the effects of preferences for ages ending in 5 and 0, it can be assumed that such digit preference is usually connected with other sources of inaccuracy in age statements and the index can be accepted as a fair measure of the general reliability of the age distribution.

3.2 Methods used to indicate quality of published statistics

To the extent possible, efforts have been made to give the reader an indication of reliability of the statistics published in the *Demographic Yearbook*. This has been approached in several ways. Any information regarding a possible under-enumeration or over-enumeration, coming from a postcensal survey, for example, has been noted in the footnotes to table 3. Any deviation from full national coverage, as explained in section 2.1 under Geographical Aspects, has also been noted. In addition, national statistical offices have been asked to evaluate the estimates of total population they submit to the Statistics Division of the United Nations.

3.2.1 Treatment of time series of population estimates

When a series of mid-year population estimates are presented, the same indication of quality is shown for the entire series as was determined for the latest estimate. The quality is indicated by the type face employed.

No attempt has been made to split the series even though it is evident that in cases where the data are now considered reliable, in earlier years, many may have been considerably less reliable than the current classification implies. Thus it will be evident that this method overstates the probable reliability of the time series in many cases. It may also understate the reliability of estimates for years immediately preceding or following a census enumeration.

3.2.2 Treatment of estimated distributions by age and other demographic characteristics

Estimates of the age-sex distribution of population may be constructed by two major methods: (1) by applying the specific components of population change to each age-sex group of the population as enumerated at the time of the census, and (2) by distributing the total estimated for a postcensal year proportionately according to the age-sex structure at the time of the census. Estimates constructed by the latter method are not published in the *Demographic Yearbook*.

Estimated age-sex distributions are categorized as "reliable" or otherwise, according to the method of construction established for the latest estimate of total mid-year population. Hence, the quality designation of the total figure, as indicated by the code, is considered to apply also to the whole distribution by age and sex, and the data are set in *italic* or roman type, as appropriate, on this basis alone. Further evaluation of detailed age structure data has not been undertaken to date.

6

4. VITAL STATISTICS

For purposes of the *Demographic Yearbook*, vital statistics have been defined as statistics of live birth, death, foetal death, marriage and divorce.

This volume of the *Yearbook* presents general tables on natality, nuptiality and divorce as well as tables on mortality referring to: foetal mortality, infant and maternal mortality and general mortality.

4.1 Sources of variation of data

Most of the vital statistics data published in this *Yearbook* come from national civil registration systems. The completeness and the accuracy of the data that these systems produce vary from one country or area to another.

The provision for a national civil registration system is not universal, and in some cases, the registration system covers only certain vital events. For example, in some countries or areas only births and deaths are registered. There are also differences in the effectiveness with which national laws pertaining to civil registration operate in the various countries or areas. The manner in which the law is implemented and the degree to which the public complies with the legislation determine the reliability of the vital statistics obtained from the civil registers.

It should be noted that some statistics on marriage and divorce are obtained from sources other than civil registers. For example, in some countries or areas, the only source for data on marriages is church registers. Divorce statistics, on the other hand, are obtained from court records and/or civil registers according to national practice. The actual compilation of these statistics may be the responsibility of the civil registrar, the national statistical office or other government offices.

Other factors affecting international comparability of vital statistics are much the same as those that must be considered in evaluating the variations in other population statistics. Differences in statistical definitions of vital events, differences in geographical and ethnic coverage of the data and diverse tabulation procedures may also influence comparability.

In addition to vital statistics from civil registers, some vital statistics published in the *Yearbook* are official estimates. These estimates are frequently from population censuses and sample surveys. As such, their comparability may be affected by the national completeness of reporting in population censuses and household surveys, whether a de facto or de jure based census, non-sampling and sampling errors and other sources of bias.

Readers interested in more detailed information on standards for vital statistics should consult the *Principles and Recommendations for a Vital Statistics System Revision 2* [12]; *Handbook on Civil Registration and Vital Statistics Systems: Preparation of a Legal Framework* [13]; *Handbook on Civil Registration and Vital Statistics Systems: Management, Operation and Maintenance;* [14] *Handbook on Civil Registration and Vital Statistics Systems: Developing Information, Education and Communication* [15]; *Handbook on Civil Registration and Vital Statistics Systems: Policies and Protocols for the Release and Archiving of Individual Records* [16]; and *Handbook on Civil Registration and Vital Statistics Systems: Computerization* [17]. The *Handbook on the Collection of Fertility and Mortality Data* [18] provides information in collection and evaluation of data on fertility and mortality collected in population censuses and household surveys. These publications are also available on the website at http://unstats.un.org/unsd/demographic/standmeth/handbooks/default.htm.

4.1.1 Statistical definition of events

An important source of variation lies in the statistical definition of each vital event. The *Demographic Yearbook* attempts to collect data on vital events, using the standard definitions put forth in paragraph 57 of *Principles and Recommendations for a Vital Statistics System Revision 2.* [12] These are as follows:

LIVE BIRTH is the complete expulsion or extraction from its mother of a product of conception, irrespective of the duration of pregnancy, which after such separation breathes or shows any other evidence of life such as beating of the heart, pulsation of the umbilical cord, or definite movement of voluntary muscles, whether or not the umbilical cord has been cut or the placenta is attached; each product of such a birth is considered live-born regardless of gestational age.

DEATH is the permanent disappearance of all evidence of life at any time after live birth has taken place (postnatal cessation of vital functions without capability of resuscitation). This definition therefore excludes foetal deaths.

FOETAL DEATH is death prior to the complete expulsion or extraction from its mother of a product of conception, irrespective of the duration of pregnancy; the death is indicated by the fact that after such separation the foetus does not breathe or show any other evidence of life, such as beating of the heart, pulsation of the umbilical cord, or definite movement of voluntary muscles. Late foetal deaths are those of twenty-eight or more completed weeks of gestation. These are synonymous with the events reported under the pre-1950 term stillbirth [19].

MARRIAGE is an act, ceremony or process by which the legal relationship of husband and wife is constituted. The legality of the union may be established by civil, religious or other means as recognized by the laws of each country or area.

DIVORCE is a final legal dissolution of a marriage, that is, that separation of husband and wife which confers on the parties the right to remarriage under civil, religious and/or other provisions, according to the laws of each country.

In addition to these recommended definitions, the *Demographic Yearbook* collects and presents data on abortions, defined as:

ABORTION is defined, with reference to the woman, as any interruption of pregnancy before 28 weeks of gestation with a dead foetus. There are two major categories of abortion: spontaneous and induced. Induced abortions are those initiated by deliberate action undertaken with the intention of terminating pregnancy; all other abortions are considered spontaneous.

4.1.2 Problems relating to standard definitions

A basic problem affecting international comparability of vital statistics is deviations from the standard definitions of vital events. An example of this can be seen in the cases of live births and foetal deaths.[20] In some countries or areas, an infant must survive for at least 24 hours, to be inscribed in the live-birth register. Infants who die before the expiration of the 24-hour period are classified as late foetal deaths and, barring special tabulation procedures, they would not be counted either as live births or as deaths. Similarly, in several other countries or areas, those infants who are born alive but die before registration of their birth, are also considered late foetal deaths.

Unless special tabulation procedures are adopted in such cases, the live-birth and death statistics will both be deficient by the number of these infants, while the incidence of late foetal deaths will be increased by the same amount. Hence the infant mortality rate is underestimated. Although both components (infant deaths and live births) are deficient by the same absolute amount, the deficiency is proportionately greater in relation to the infant deaths, causing greater errors in the infant mortality rate than in the birth rate.

Moreover, the practice exaggerates the late foetal death ratios. Some countries or areas make provision for correcting this deficiency (at least in the total frequencies) at the tabulation stage. Data for which the correction has not been made are indicated by footnote whenever possible.

The definitions used for marriage and divorce also present problems for international comparability. Unlike birth and death, which are biological events, marriage and divorce are defined only in terms of law and custom and as such are less amenable to universally applicable statistical definitions. They have therefore been defined for statistical purposes in general terms referring to the laws of individual countries or areas. Laws pertaining to marriage and particularly to divorce, vary from one country or area to another. With respect to marriage, the most widespread requirement relates to the minimum age at which persons may marry but frequently other requirements are specified.

When known the minimum legal age of men and women at which marriage can occur with (or in some cases without) parental consent is presented in table 24-1. Laws and regulations relating to the dissolution of marriage by divorce range from total prohibition, through a wide range of grounds upon which divorces may be granted, to the granting of divorce in response to a simple statement of desire or intention by husbands.

4.1.3 Fragmentary geographical or ethnic coverage

Ideally, vital statistics for any given country or area should cover the entire geographical area and include all ethnic groups. Fragmentary coverage is, however, not uncommon. In some countries or areas, registration is compulsory for only a small part of the population, limited to certain ethnic groups, for example. In other places there is no national provision for compulsory registration, but only municipal or state ordinances that do not cover the entire geographical area. Still others have developed a registration area that comprises only a part of the country or area, the remainder being excluded because of inaccessibility or for economic and cultural considerations that make regular registration practically impossible.

4.1.4 Tabulation procedures

4.1.4.1 By place of occurrence

Vital statistics presented at the national level relate to the de facto, that is, the present-in-area population. Thus, unless otherwise noted, vital statistics for a given country or area cover all the events that occur within its present boundaries and among all segments of the population therein. They may be presumed to include events among nomadic tribes and indigenous peoples, and among nationals and foreigners. When known, deviations from the de facto concept are footnoted.

Urban/rural differentials in vital rates for some countries may vary considerably depending on whether the relevant vital events were tabulated on the basis of place of occurrence or place of usual residence. For example, if a substantial number of women residing in rural areas near major urban centres travel to hospitals or maternity homes located in a city to give birth, urban fertility and neo-natal and infant mortality rates will usually be higher (and the corresponding rural rates will usually be lower) if the events are tabulated on the basis of place of occurrence rather than on the basis of place of usual residence. A similar process will affect general mortality differentials if substantial numbers of persons residing in rural areas use urban health facilities when seriously ill.

4.1.4.2 By date of occurrence versus by date of registration

To the extent possible, the vital statistics presented in the *Demographic Yearbook* refer to events that occurred during the specified year, rather than to those that were registered during that period. However, a considerable number of countries or areas tabulate their vital statistics not by date of occurrence, but by date of registration. Because such statistics can be very misleading, the countries or areas known to tabulate vital statistics by date of registration are identified in the tables by a plus sign (+). Since information on the method of tabulating vital statistics is not available for all countries and areas, tabulation by date of registration may be more prevalent than the symbols on the vital statistics tables would indicate.

Because quality of data is inextricably related to the timeliness of registration, this must always be considered in conjunction with the quality code description in section 4.2.1 below. If registration of births is complete and timely (code C), the ill effects of tabulating by date of registration, are, for all practical purposes, nullified. Similarly, with respect to death statistics, the effect of tabulating events by date of registration may be minimized in many countries or areas in which the sanitary code requires that a death must be registered before a burial permit can be issued, and this regulation tends to make registration prompt. With respect to foetal death, registration is usually done right away or not at all. Therefore, if registration is prompt, the difference between statistics tabulated by date of occurrence and those tabulated by date of registration may be negligible. In many cases, the length of the statutory time period allowed for registering various vital events plays an important part in determining the effects of tabulation by date of registration on comparability of data.

With respect to marriage and divorce, the practice of tabulating data by date of registration does not generally pose serious problems. In many countries or areas marriage is a civil legal contract which, to establish its legality, must be celebrated before a civil officer. It follows that for these countries or areas registration would tend to be almost automatic at the time of, or immediately following, the marriage ceremony. Because the registration of a divorce in many countries or areas is the responsibility solely of the court or the authority which granted it, and since the registration record in such cases is part of the records of the court proceedings, it follows that divorces are likely to be registered soon after the decree is granted.

On the other hand, if registration is not prompt, vital statistics by date of registration will not produce internationally comparable data. Under the best circumstances, statistics by date of registration will include primarily events that occurred in the immediately preceding year; in countries or areas with less developed systems, tabulations will include some events that occurred many years in the past. Examination of available information reveals that delays of many years are not uncommon for birth registration, though the majority is recorded between two to four years after birth.

As long as registration is not prompt, statistics by date of registration will not be internationally comparable either among themselves or with statistics by date of occurrence.

It should also be mentioned that lack of international comparability is not the only limitation introduced by date-of-registration tabulation. Even within the same country or area, comparability over time may be lost by the practice of counting registrations rather than occurrences. If the number of events registered from year to year fluctuates because of ad hoc incentives to stimulate registration, or to the sudden need, for example, for proof of (unregistered) birth or death to meet certain requirements, vital statistics tabulated by date of registration are not useful in measuring and analyzing demographic levels and trends. All they can give is an indication of the fluctuations in the need for a birth, death or marriage certificate and the work-load of the registrars. Therefore, statistics tabulated by date of registration may be of very limited use for either national or international studies.

4.2 Methods used to indicate quality of published vital statistics

The quality of vital statistics can be assessed in terms of a number of factors. Most fundamental is the completeness of the civil registration system on which the statistics are based. In some cases, the incompleteness of the data obtained from civil registration systems is revealed when these events are used to compute rates. However, this technique applies only where the data are markedly deficient, where they are tabulated by date of occurrence and where the population base is correctly estimated. Tabulation by date of registration will often produce rates which appear correct, simply because the numerator is artificially inflated by the inclusion of delayed registrations and, conversely, rates may be of credible magnitude because the population at risk has been underestimated. Moreover, it should be remembered that knowledge of what is credible in regard to levels of fertility, mortality and nuptiality is extremely scanty for many parts of the world, and borderline cases, which are the most difficult to appraise, are frequent.

4.2.1 Quality code for vital statistics from registers.

In the *Demographic Yearbook* annual "Questionnaire on Vital Statistics" national statistical offices are asked to provide their own estimates of the completeness of the births, deaths, late foetal deaths, marriages and divorces recorded in their civil registers.

On the basis of information from the questionnaires, from direct correspondence and from relevant official publications, it has been possible to classify current national statistics from civil registers of birth, death, infant death, late foetal death, marriage and divorce into three broad quality categories, as follows:

C: Data estimated to be virtually complete, that is, representing at least 90 per cent of the events occurring each year.

U: Data estimated to be incomplete, that is representing less than 90 per cent of the events occurring each year.

|: Data not derived from civil registration systems but considered reliable, such as estimates derived from projections, other estimation techniques or population and housing census.

...: Data for which no specific information is available regarding completeness.

These quality codes appear in the first column of the tables which show total frequencies and crude rates (or ratios) over a period of years for all tables on live births, late foetal deaths, infant deaths, deaths, marriages, and divorces. Reliability of maternal mortality statistics is provided by the World Health Organisation and instead of indicating data quality in the first column, reliable data are shown in roman type while unreliable data are shown in italics.

The classification of countries and areas in terms of these quality codes may not be uniform. Nevertheless, it was felt that national statistical offices were in the best position to judge the quality of their data. It was considered that even the very broad categories that could be established on the basis of the available information would provide useful indicators of the quality of the vital statistics presented in this *Yearbook*.

In the past, the bases of the national estimates of completeness were usually not available. In connection with the *Demographic Yearbook 1977*, countries were asked, for the first time, to provide some indication of the basis of their completeness estimates. They were requested to indicate whether the completeness estimates reported for registered live births, deaths, and infant deaths were prepared on the basis of demographic analysis, dual record checks or some other specified method. Relatively few countries or areas have responded to this new question; therefore, no attempt has been made to revise the system of quality codes used in connection with the vital statistics data presented in the *Yearbook*. It is hoped that, in the future, more countries will be able to provide this information so that the system of quality codes used in connection with the vital statistics data presented in the *Yearbook* may be revised.

Among the countries or areas indicating that the registration of live births was estimated to be 90 per cent or more complete (and hence classified as C in table 9), the following countries or areas provided information on the basis of this completeness estimate:

(a) Demographic analysis -- Argentina, Australia, Canada, Chile, Croatia, Cuba, Czech Republic, Egypt, French Guiana, Guadeloupe, Guernsey, Iceland, Ireland, Israel, Republic of Korea, Kuwait, Latvia, Mauritius, Puerto Rico, Romania, San Marino, Singapore, Sweden, Switzerland and United States.

(b) Dual record check -- Barbados, Belgium, Bulgaria, Cook Islands, Cuba, Cyprus, Denmark, Estonia, Fiji, Finland, France, French Guiana, Greece, Guam, Guadeloupe, Guernsey, Hungary, Iceland, Isle of Man, Japan, Kyrgyzstan, Lithuania, Maldives, New Zealand, Malaysia, Romania, Saint Kitts and Nevis, Saint Lucia, Singapore, Sri Lanka, Sweden, Switzerland, Uruguay and Venezuela.

(c) Other specified methods -- Belgium, Bermuda, Cayman Islands, China Hong Kong SAR, China Macao SAR, Germany, Greenland, Iceland, Japan, Luxembourg, Netherlands, Norway, Poland, Singapore and Slovenia.

Among the countries or areas indicating that the registration of deaths was estimated to be 90 per cent or more complete (and hence classified as C in table 18), the following countries or areas provided information on the basis of this completeness estimate:

(a) Demographic analysis -- Argentina, Australia, Canada, Chile, Cuba, Egypt, French Guiana, Guadeloupe, Guernsey, Iceland, Ireland, Israel, Kuwait, Latvia, Mauritius, Puerto Rico, Romania, San Marino, Singapore, Switzerland and United States.

(b) Dual record check -- Bahamas, Bulgaria, Cook Islands, Cuba, Denmark, Fiji, Finland, France, Greece, Greenland, Guam, Guernsey, Iceland, Isle of Man, Maldives, New Zealand, Romania, Saint Kitts and Nevis, Saint Lucia, Singapore, Sri Lanka, Sweden, Switzerland and Uruguay.

(c) Other specified methods -- Belgium, Bermuda, Cayman Islands, Germany, Hong Kong SAR, Iceland, Ireland, Japan, Luxembourg, Netherlands, Norway, Poland, Singapore and Slovenia.

Among the countries or areas indicating that the registration of infant deaths was estimated to be 90 per cent or more complete (and hence classified as C in table 15), the following countries or areas provided information on the basis of this completeness estimate:

(a) Demographic analysis -- Argentina, Australia, Canada, Chile, Cuba, Egypt, Iceland, Ireland, Israel, Kuwait, Latvia, Mauritius, Puerto Rico, Romania, San Marino, Singapore, Sri Lanka, Switzerland and United States.

(b) Dual record check -- Bahamas, Bulgaria, Cook Islands, Cuba, Denmark, Fiji, Finland, France, Greece, Greenland, Guam, Guernsey, Iceland, Isle of Man, Japan, Maldives, New Zealand, Romania, Saint Kitts and Nevis, Saint Lucia, Singapore, Sweden, Switzerland and Uruguay.

(c) Other specified methods -- Belgium, Bermuda, Cayman Islands, Germany, Hong Kong SAR, Iceland, Japan, Luxembourg, Netherlands, Norway, Poland, Singapore and Slovenia.

4.2.2 Treatment of vital statistics from registers

On the basis of the quality code described above, the vital statistics shown in all tables of the *Yearbook* are treated as either reliable or unreliable. Data coded C are considered reliable and appear in roman type. Data coded U or ... are considered unreliable and appear in *italics*. Although the quality code itself appears only in certain tables, the indication of reliability (that is, the use of *italics* to indicate unreliable data) is shown in all tables presenting vital statistics data.

In general, the quality code for deaths shown in table 18 is used to determine whether data on deaths in other tables appear in roman or *italic* type. However, for some of the maternal deaths data shown in *italics* in table 17, the known quality code differs from that ascribed on the basis of the completeness of registration of the total number of deaths. In cases where the quality code in table 18 does not correspond with the quality level implied by the typeface used in table 17, relevant information regarding the completeness of maternal mortality is given in a footnote.

The same indication of reliability used in connection with tables showing the frequencies of vital events is also used in connection with tables showing the corresponding vital rates. For example, death rates computed using deaths from a register that is incomplete or of unknown completeness are considered unreliable and appear in *italics*. Strictly speaking, to evaluate vital rates more precisely, one would have to also take into account the accuracy of population data used in the denominator of these rates. The quality of population data is discussed in section 3.2 of the Technical Notes.

It should be noted that the indications of reliability used for infant mortality rates, maternal mortality rates and late foetal death ratios (all of which are calculated using the number of live births in the denominator) are determined on the basis of the quality codes for infant deaths, deaths and late foetal deaths respectively. To evaluate these rates and ratios more precisely, one would have to take into account the quality of the live-birth data used in the denominator of these rates and ratios. The quality codes for live births are shown in table 9 and described more fully in the text of the technical notes for that table.

4.2.3 Treatment of time series of vital statistics from registers

The quality of a time series of vital statistics is more difficult to determine than the quality of data for a single year. Since a time series of vital statistics is usually generated only by a system of continuous civil registration, it was assumed that the quality of the entire series was the same as that for the latest year's data obtained from the civil register. The entire series is treated as described in section 4.2.2 above. That is, if the quality code for the latest registered data is C, the frequencies and rates for earlier years are also considered reliable and appear in roman type. Conversely, if the latest registered data are coded as U or ... then data for earlier years are considered unreliable and appear in *italics*. It is recognized that this method is not entirely satisfactory because it is known that data from earlier years in many of the series were considerably less reliable than the current code implies.

4.2.4 Treatment of estimated vital statistics

In addition to data from vital registration systems, estimated frequencies and rates of the events, usually ad hoc official estimates that have been derived either from the results of a sample survey or by demographic analyses, also appear in the *Demographic Yearbook*. Estimated frequencies and rates have been included in the tables because it is assumed that they provide information that is more accurate than that from existing civil registration systems. By implication, they are assumed to be reliable and as such they are set in roman type. Estimated frequencies and rates continue to be treated in this manner even when they are interspersed in a time series with data from civil registers.

In tables showing the quality code, the code applies only to data from civil registers. If a series of data for a country or area contains both data from a civil register and estimated data, the code applies only to the registered data; if only estimated data are shown, the symbol (|) is shown.

4.3 Cause of death

World Health Organization (WHO) Member States are bound by the International Nomenclature Regulations to provide the Organization with cause of death data coded in accordance with the current revision of the International Statistical Classification of Diseases and Related Health Problems (ICD) as adopted from time to time by the World Health Assembly [21]. The data are collected by the WHO using the ICD. In order to promote international comparability of cause of death statistics, the World Health Organization organizes and conducts an international Conference for the revision of the ICD on a regular basis in order to ensure that the Classification is kept current with the most recent clinical and statistical concepts. The data are now usually submitted to WHO at the full four-character level of detail provided by the ICD and are stored in the WHO Mortality Database at the level of detail as provided by the country. For earlier versions, however, the data are only available according to the ICD's list of 150 causes. Data from the WHO Mortality Database are available in electronic format at http://www3.who.int/whosis/menu.cfm.

Although revisions provide an up-to-date version of the ICD, such revisions create several problems related to the comparability of cause of death statistics. The first is the lack of comparability over time that inevitably accompanies the use of a new classification. The second problem affects comparability between countries and areas because they may adopt a new classification at different times. The more refined the classification becomes the greater is the need for expert clinical diagnosis of cause of death. In many countries or areas, few of the deaths occur in the presence of an attendant, who is medically trained, i.e., most deaths are certified by a lay attendant. Because the ICD contains many diagnoses that cannot be identified by a non-medical person, the ICD does not always promote international comparability particularly between countries and areas where the level of medical services differ widely.

The chapters of the tenth revision [22], the latest revision of the ICD, consist of an alphanumeric coding scheme of one letter followed by three numbers at the four-character level. Chapter one contains infectious and parasitic diseases, chapter two refers to all neoplasms, chapter three to disorders of the immune mechanism including diseases of the blood and blood-forming organs; and chapter four to endocrine, nutritional and metabolic diseases. The remaining chapters group diseases according to the anatomical site affected, except for chapters that refer to mental disorders; complications of pregnancy, childbirth and the puerperium; congenital malformations; and conditions originating in the perinatal period. Finally, an entire chapter is devoted to symptoms, signs, and abnormal findings.

4.3.1 Maternal mortality

According to the tenth revision of the ICD, "Maternal death" is defined as the death of a woman while pregnant or within 42 days of termination of pregnancy, irrespective of the duration and the site of the pregnancy, from any cause related to or aggravated by the pregnancy or its management but not from accidental or incidental causes.

"Maternal deaths should be subdivided into direct and indirect obstetric deaths. Direct obstetric deaths are those resulting from obstetric complications of the pregnant state (pregnancy, labour and puerperium), from interventions, omissions, incorrect treatment, or from a chain of events resulting from any of the above. Indirect obstetric deaths are those resulting from previous existing disease or disease that developed during pregnancy and which was not due to direct obstetric causes, but which was aggravated by physiologic effects of pregnancy".

While the denominator maternal rate should be the number of pregnant women, it is impossible to determine the number of pregnant women. A further recommendation by the tenth revision conference is therefore that maternal mortality rates be expressed per 100,000 live births or per 100,000 total births (live births and foetal deaths). [23] The maternal mortality rate calculated here is expressed per 100,000 live births. Although live births do not represent an unbiased estimate of pregnant women, this figure is more reliable than other estimates in particular, live births are more accurately registered than live births plus foetal deaths.

NOTES

[1] The data on maternal mortality are from the World Health Organization, and are available at http://www3.who.int/whosis/menu.cfm, as one cause of death.

[2] There are two exceptions – the 1978 and 1991 issues, which were disseminated in separate volumes from the respective regular issues.

[3] *World Population Prospects - The 2006 Revision*, Sales No. E.07.XIII.7,. United Nations, New York. Highlights and selected output are available by following links at www.unpopulation.org,.

[4] ST/ESA/STAT/SER.M/49/Rev.4/WWW ; http://unstats.un.org/unsd/methods/m49/m49.htm; see also Standard Country or Area Codes for Statistical Use, Sales No. M.98.XVII.9, United Nations, New York, 1999.

[5] Forthcoming, Sales No. E.07.XVII.8, United Nations, New York, 2007. Until this is published, the publication is available online at http://unstats.un.org/unsd/demographic/sources/census/docs/P&R_%20Rev2.pdf

[6] Ibid, para. 2.135.

[7] Alternatively, if a population register is used, completed ages are calculated by subtracting the date of birth of individuals listed in the register from a reference date to which the age data pertain.

[8] A source of non-comparability may result from differences in the method of reckoning age, is for example, the Western versus the Eastern or, as it is usually known, the English versus the Chinese system. By the latter, a child is considered one year old at birth and advances an additional year at each Chinese New Year. The effect of this system is most obvious at the beginning of the age span, where the frequencies in the under-one-year category are markedly understated. The effect on higher age groups is not so apparent. Distributions constructed on this basis are often adjusted before publication, but the possibility of such aberrations should not be excluded when census data by age are compared.

[9] In this index, differences were scored from expected values of ratios between numbers of either sex in the same age group, and numbers of the same sex in adjoining age group. In compounding the score, allowance had to be made for certain factors such as the effects of past fluctuations in birth rates, of heavy war casualties, and of the smallness of the population itself. A detailed description of the index, with results from its application to the data presented in the 1949-1950 and 1951 issues of the *Demographic Yearbook*, is furnished in *Population Bulletin, No. 2* (United Nations publication, Sales No. 52.XIII.4), pp. 59-79. The scores obtained from statistics presented in *Demographic Yearbook 1952* are presented in that issue, and the index has also been briefly explained in that issue, as well as those of 1953 and 1954.

[10] United States, Bureau of the Census, Thirteenth Census, Vol. I (Washington, D.C., U.S. Government Printing Office), pp. 291-292.

[11] J. T. Marten, Census of India, 1921, vol. I, part I (Calcutta, 1924), pp. 126-127.

[12] Sales No. E. 01.XVII.10, United Nations, New York, 2001.

[13] Sales No. E. 98.XVII.7, United Nations, New York, 1998.

[14] Sales No. E.98.XVII.11, United Nations, New York, 1998.

[15] Sales No. E.98.XVII.4, United Nations, New York, 1998.

[16] Sales No. E.98.XVII.6, United Nations, New York, 1998;

[17] Sales No. E.98.XVII.10, United Nations, New York, 1998.

[18] *Handbook on the Collection of Fertility and Mortality data*, Sales No. 03.XVII.11, United Nations, New York, 2003.

[19] For more detailed discussion on this issue, refer to *Principles and Recommendations for a Vital Statistics System Revision 2,* Sales No. E. 01.XVII.10, United Nations, New York, 2001, para 57.

[20] For more information on historical and legal background on the use of differing definitions of live births and foetal deaths, comparisons of definitions used as of 1 January 1950, and evaluation of the effects of these differences on the calculation of various rates, see *Handbook of Vital Statistics Systems and Methods Volume 2, Review of National Practices*, Sales No. E.84.XVII.11, United Nations, New York, 1985, Chapter IV.

[21] The World Health Assembly is the annual meeting of the Member States of the World Health Organization and its highest governing body.

[22] *International Statistical Classification of Diseases and Related Health Problems*, Tenth Revision, Volume 2, World Health Organization, Geneva, 1992.

[23] *International Statistical Classification of Diseases and Related Health Problems*, Tenth Revision, Volume 2, World Health Organization, Geneva, 1992, pp. 129-136.

INTRODUCTION

L'*Annuaire démographique* est un recueil de statistiques démographiques internationales qui est établi par la Division de statistique du Département des affaires économiques et sociales de l'Organisation des Nations Unies. Il fait partie d'un ensemble de publications complémentaires publiées par l'Organisation des Nations Unies et les institutions spécialisées[1], qui ont pour objet de fournir des statistiques de base aux démographes, aux économistes, aux spécialistes de la santé publique et aux sociologues. Grâce à la coopération des services nationaux de statistique, il a été possible de faire figurer dans la présente édition des statistiques démographiques officielles pour plus de 230 pays ou zones du monde entier.

L'*Annuaire démographique 2005* est le cinquante-septième d'une série que publie l'ONU depuis 1948. Le présent volume contient des tableaux à caractère général, y compris un aperçu mondial des statistiques démographiques de base et des tableaux qui regroupent des statistiques sur la dimension, la répartition et les tendances de la population, la natalité, la mortalité fœtale, la mortalité infantile et la mortalité liée à la maternité, la mortalité générale, la nuptialité et la divortialité. Des données classées selon le lieu de résidence (zone urbaine ou rurale) sont présentées dans un grand nombre de tableaux. En outre, l'*Annuaire* contient des notes techniques, un tableau synoptique, un index historique et une liste des éditions de l'*Annuaire* publiées jusqu'à présent.

Les notes techniques sur les tableaux statistiques sont destinées à aider le lecteur. Le tableau A, qui correspond au tableau synoptique, permet de se rendre compte en un coup d'oeil du niveau d'exhaustivité des données publiées dans le présent *Annuaire* et l'index thématique facilite le repérage des sujets abordés. Un index cumulatif donne des renseignements sur les matières traitées dans chacune des 56 éditions et sur les années sur lesquelles portent les données. Les numéros de vente des éditions antérieures et une liste des sujets spéciaux traités dans les différentes éditions sont indiqués aux pages iii et iv.

Jusqu'à la 48ème édition (1996), chaque édition se composait de deux parties : les tableaux de caractère général et ceux sur des sujets spéciaux[2]. À partir de 49ème édition (1997), les tableaux sur les sujets spéciaux ont été publiés sur CD-ROM sous forme de suppléments à l'*Annuaire*. Deux CD-ROM ont été produits jusqu'à présent : l'*Annuaire démographique : Supplément historique*, qui présente un grand nombre de statistiques démographiques pour la période allant de 1948 à 1997, et l'*Annuaire démographique : Statistiques de la natalité*, qui contient des tableaux détaillés sur la natalité pour la période allant de 1980 à 1998. Trois volumes concernant un nouvel Annuaire démographique consacré à des thèmes de recensement spéciaux ont été produits et sont présentés à l'adresse suivante : http://unstats.un.org/unsd/demographic/products/dyb/default.htm.

Les statistiques sur la population ne sont pas disponibles pour tous les pays et zones pour plusieurs raisons. Deux annexes ont été ajoutées à partir de la 53ème édition afin d'offrir des estimations sur la population en milieu d'année et un aperçu des statistiques de l'état civil. La première porte sur des estimations concernant la population pour chaque pays ou zone pour la période 1995-2004. La seconde présente les estimations des variantes moyennes concernant les taux bruts de natalité et de mortalité, la mortalité infantile, les indicateurs synthétiques de fécondité et l'espérance de vie à la naissance pour la période 2000-2005. Ces données ont été établies par la Division de la population de l'ONU et publiées dans *World Population Prospects - The 2006 Revision*[3].

Les statistiques démographiques figurant dans la présente édition de l'*Annuaire* sont disponibles en ligne sur les pages Web consacrées à l'Annuaire :
http://unstats.un.org/unsd/demographic/products/dyb/default.htm.
On trouvera également des renseignements sur le programme de collecte et de diffusion des données de la Division de statistique sur le même site. Il est possible de se procurer d'autres données en contactant la Division de statistique de l'Organisation des Nations Unies à l'adresse suivante : demostat@un.org.

NOTES TECHNIQUES SUR LES TABLEAUX STATISTIQUES

1. REMARQUES D'ORDRE GÉNÉRAL

1.1 Notes techniques

Les notes techniques ont pour but de donner au lecteur tous les renseignements dont il a besoin pour se servir des tableaux statistiques. Les renseignements qui concernent l'*Annuaire* en général sont présentés dans des sections portant sur diverses considérations géographiques, sur la population et sur les statistiques de natalité et de mortalité. Les tableaux sont ensuite commentés séparément et l'on trouvera pour chacun une description des variables et des observations sur la fiabilité et les lacunes des données ainsi que sur les pays et zones visés et sur les données publiées antérieurement. Des détails sont également donnés, le cas échéant, sur le mode de calcul des taux, quotients et pourcentages.

1.2 Tableaux

La présente édition contient seulement des tableaux de caractère général. Comme la numérotation des tableaux ne correspond pas exactement à celle des éditions précédentes, il est recommandé de se reporter à l'index qui figure à la fin du présent ouvrage pour trouver les données publiées dans les précédentes éditions.

1.3 Origine des données

Sauf indication contraire, les statistiques présentées dans l'*Annuaire démographique* sont des données nationales fournies par les organismes de statistique officiels. Elles sont recueillies essentiellement au moyen de questionnaires qui sont envoyés tous les ans à plus de 230 services nationaux de statistique et autres services gouvernementaux compétents. Les données communiquées en réponse à ces questionnaires sont complétées, dans toute la mesure possible, par des données tirées de publications nationales officielles et des sites web d'organismes officiels et des renseignements communiqués par les services nationaux de statistique à la demande de l'ONU. Pour que les données soient comparables, les taux, rapports et pourcentages ont été calculés par la Division de statistique de l'ONU, à l'exception des paramètres des tables de mortalité et des indicateurs synthétiques de fécondité ainsi que des taux bruts de natalité et de mortalité pour certains pays et zones, qui ont été dûment signalés en note. Les méthodes suivies par la Division pour le calcul des taux et rapports sont décrites dans les notes techniques relatives à chaque tableau. Les chiffres de population utilisés pour ces calculs sont ceux qui figurent dans la présente édition de l'*Annuaire* ou qui ont paru dans des éditions antérieures.

Chaque fois que l'on constatera des différences entre les données du présent volume et celles des éditions antérieures de l'*Annuaire démographique*, ou de certaines publications apparentées, on pourra en conclure que les statistiques publiées cette année sont des chiffres révisés communiqués à la Division de statistique avant septembre 2007.

2. CONSIDÉRATIONS GÉOGRAPHIQUES

2.1 Portée

La portée géographique des tableaux du présent *Annuaire* est aussi complète que possible. Des données sont présentées sur tous les pays ou zones qui en ont communiquées. Le tableau 3, le plus complet, contient des données sur la population et la superficie de chaque pays ou zone ayant une population d'au moins 50 habitants. Ces pays ou zones ne figurent pas tous dans les tableaux qui suivent. Dans bien des cas, les données requises pour un tableau particulier n'étaient pas disponibles. En général, les pays ou zones qui peuvent fournir des données sont d'autant moins nombreux que les données demandées sont plus détaillées.

De plus les taux et rapports ne sont présentés que pour les pays ou zones ayant communiqué des chiffres correspondant à un nombre minimal de faits considérés. Les minimums sont indiqués dans les notes techniques relatives à chacun des tableaux.

À l'exception des données récapitulatives présentées dans les tableaux 1 et 2 pour l'ensemble du monde et les grandes zones et régions et des données relatives aux capitales et aux villes de 100 000 habitants ou plus dans le tableau 8, toutes les données se rapportent aux pays. Le nombre de pays sur lequel porte chacun des tableaux est indiqué dans le tableau A.

2.2 Composition territoriale

Autant que possible, toutes les données, y compris les séries chronologiques, se rapportent au territoire de 2005. Les exceptions à cette règle sont signalées en note à la fin des tableaux. On trouve dans le tableau 3 des renseignements concernant les changements intervenus récemment et d'autres précisions intéressantes.

Les données relatives à la République populaire de Chine ne comprennent généralement pas celles de la province de Taiwan ; à l'exception de celles des tableaux 1 et 2.

2.3 Nomenclature

En règle générale, pour gagner de la place, on a jugé commode de désigner dans les tableaux les pays ou zones par les noms abrégés couramment utilisés par l'Organisation des Nations Unies en septembre 2007[4], les désignations complètes n'étant utilisées que lorsqu'il n'existait pas de forme abrégée. La liste des désignations des pays ou zones est disponible à l'adresse suivante : http://unstats.un.org/unsd/methods/m49/m49alphaf.htm.

2.3.1 Ordre de présentation

Les pays ou zones sont classés dans l'ordre alphabétique anglais et regroupés par continent comme ci-après : Afrique, Amérique du Nord, Amérique du Sud, Asie, Europe et Océanie.

Les appellations employées dans la présente édition et la présentation des données qui y figurent n'ont d'autre objet que de donner un cadre géographique commode aux séries statistiques. La même observation vaut pour toutes les notes et précisions concernant les unités géographiques pour lesquelles des données sont présentées.

2.4 Superficie

Les données relatives à la superficie qui figurent dans les tableaux 1 et 3 représentent la superficie totale, c'est-à-dire qu'elles englobent les terres émergées et les eaux intérieures (qui sont censées comprendre les principaux lacs et cours d'eau) mais excluent les régions polaires et les îles inhabitées. Les données relatives à la superficie correspondent aux chiffres estimatifs les plus récents. Les superficies sont toutes exprimées en kilomètres carrés ; les chiffres qui avaient été communiqués en miles carrés ont été convertis au moyen d'un coefficient de 2,589988.

2.4.1 Comparabilité dans le temps

La révision des estimations antérieures de la superficie, des augmentations effectives de la superficie terrestre due par exemple à des travaux d'assèchement, à des rectifications de frontières, à des changements d'interprétation du concept de « terres émergées » ou à l'utilisation de nouvelles unités de mesure peut avoir des incidences sur la comparabilité dans le temps des estimations relatives à la superficie d'un pays ou d'une zone donnés. Dans la plupart des cas, il a été possible de déterminer la raison de ces révisions; toutefois, même lorsque la raison n'était pas connue, on a remplacé les anciens chiffres par les nouveaux et on a généralement admis que ce sont ces derniers qui sont exacts.

2.4.2 Comparabilité internationale

Le manque de comparabilité internationale entre les données relatives à la superficie est dû principalement à des différences de définition. En particulier, la définition des golfes, baies et criques, lacs et cours d'eau varie sensiblement d'un pays à l'autre. La diversité des méthodes employées pour estimer les superficies nuit elle aussi à la comparabilité internationale. Certaines données proviennent de levés effectués selon des méthodes scientifiques modernes ; d'autres ne représentent que des conjectures reposant sur diverses catégories de renseignements. Certains chiffres sont récents, d'autres pas. Étant donné que ni la méthode de calcul de la superficie ni la composition du territoire et la date à laquelle se rapportent les données ne sont connues avec précision pour tous les pays ou zones, les estimations figurant dans le tableau 3 ne doivent pas être considérées comme rigoureusement comparables d'un pays ou d'une zone à une autre.

3. POPULATION

Les statistiques de la population, c'est-à-dire celles qui se rapportent à la dimension, à la répartition géographique et aux caractéristiques démographiques de la population, sont présentées dans un certain nombre de tableaux de l'*Annuaire démographique*.

Les données concernant les pays ou les zones représentent les résultats de recensements de population, des estimations fondées sur les résultats d'enquêtes par sondage (s'il n'y a pas eu recensement), des estimations postcensitaires ou intercensitaires, ou des estimations établies à partir de données provenant des registres permanents de population. Dans la présente édition, le tableau 3 indique pour chaque pays ou zone le chiffre le plus récent de la population totale issu du dernier recensement et des estimations établies au milieu de l'année 2000 et de l'année 2004. Le tableau 5 contient des estimations de la population totale au milieu de chaque année pendant 10 ans (1996-2005), et le tableau 6 des estimations de la population urbaine et de la population totale, par sexe, au milieu de chaque année pendant 10 ans (1996-2005). Les dernières données disponibles sur la répartition de la population selon l'âge, le sexe et le lieu de résidence (zone urbaine ou rurale) sont présentées dans le tableau 7. Les derniers chiffres disponibles sur la population des capitales et des villes de 100 000 habitants ou plus sont regroupés dans le tableau 8.

Les tableaux 1 et 2 présentent respectivement des estimations récapitulatives de la population du monde, des grandes zones et des régions en milieu d'année, pour certaines années, ainsi que des estimations récapitulatives, pour 2005, concernant la population répartie selon l'âge et le sexe.

On a utilisé pour le calcul des taux les statistiques de la population totale et de la population répartie selon l'âge, le sexe et le lieu de résidence (zone urbaine ou rurale). Les taux démographiques selon l'âge et le sexe ont été calculés à partir des données qui figurent dans le tableau 7 de la présente édition ou dans les tableaux correspondants d'éditions précédentes de l'*Annuaire démographique*.

3.1 Sources de variation des données

Plusieurs facteurs influent sur la comparabilité des données : 1) la définition de la population totale ; 2) les définitions utilisées pour faire la distinction entre population urbaine et population rurale ; 3) les difficultés liées aux déclarations d'âge ; 4) l'étendue du sur-dénombrement ou du sous-dénombrement dans le recensement le plus récent ou dans une autre source de statistiques de référence sur la population ; 5) la qualité des estimations relatives à la population. Ces cinq facteurs sont analysés en détail aux sections 3.1.1 à 3.2.2 ci-après. D'autres questions seront traitées dans les notes techniques relatives à chaque tableau. Pour plus de précisions concernant, notamment, les notions fondamentales de dimension, de répartition et de caractéristiques de la population qui ont été élaborées par l'Organisation des Nations Unies, le lecteur est invité à se reporter aux *Principes et recommandations concernant les recensements de la population et de l'habitat. Révision 2*[5].

3.1.1 Population totale

Le principal obstacle à la comparabilité des données relatives à la population totale est la différence qui existe entre population de fait et population de droit. La population de fait comprend toutes les personnes présentes dans le pays ou la zone à la date de référence, tandis que la population de droit comprend toutes celles qui résident habituellement dans le pays ou la zone, qu'elles y aient été ou non présentes à la date de référence. Par définition, la population totale de fait et la population totale de droit ne sont donc pas rigoureusement comparables entre elles.

Même lorsque l'on veut comparer deux totaux qui se rapportent à des populations de fait ou deux totaux qui se rapportent à des populations de droit, on risque souvent de faire des erreurs pour cette raison qu'il est rare que l'une et l'autre notions soient appliquées strictement. Pour citer quelques exemples, certains chiffres qui sont censés porter sur la population de fait ne tiennent pas compte du personnel militaire, naval et diplomatique étranger en fonction dans le pays ou la zone, ni des membres de leurs familles et de leurs domestiques les accompagnant; d'autres ne comprennent pas les visiteurs étrangers de passage dans le pays ou la zone ni les personnes à bord de navires ancrés dans les ports. En revanche, il arrive que l'on compte des personnes, inscrits maritimes et marins pêcheurs par exemple, qui, en raison de leur activité professionnelle, se trouvent hors du pays ou de la zone de recensement.

Les risques de disparités sont encore plus grands quand il s'agit de comparer des populations de droit, car les comparaisons dépendent au premier chef de la définition que l'on donne à l'expression « lieu de résidence habituel », qui varie d'un pays ou d'une zone à l'autre et qu'il est, de toute façon, difficile d'appliquer uniformément pour le dénombrement lors d'un recensement ou d'une enquête. Par exemple, les civils étrangers qui se trouvent temporairement dans un pays ou une zone comme travailleurs à court terme peuvent officiellement être considérés comme résidents après un séjour d'une durée déterminée, mais ils peuvent aussi être considérés comme non-résidents pendant toute la durée de leur séjour ; ailleurs, ces mêmes personnes peuvent être considérées officiellement comme résidents ou comme non-résidents du pays ou de la zone d'où elles viennent, selon la durée et, éventuellement, la raison de leur absence. Qui plus est, quel que soit son statut officiel, chacun des recensés peut, au moment de l'enquête, interpréter à sa façon la notion de résidence. De plus, les autorités nationales ou les entités responsables des zones ne savent pas toutes avec la même précision combien de leurs résidents se trouvent temporairement à l'étranger.

Les chiffres de population présentés dans les tableaux de l'*Annuaire* représentent, autant qu'il a été possible, la population de fait. Sauf indication contraire, on peut supposer que les chiffres présentés ont été communiqués par les pays ou les zones comme se rapportant à la population de fait. Les chiffres qui ont été communiqués comme se rapportant à la population de droit sont indiqués comme tels. Lorsque l'on savait que les données avaient été recueillies selon une définition de la population de fait ou de la population de droit qui s'écartait sensiblement de celle exposée plus haut, on l'a signalé en note, de manière à compenser dans toute la mesure possible les conséquences des divergences.

Il ne faut pas oublier néanmoins que l'on ne disposait pas toujours de renseignements détaillés à ce sujet. On ne peut donc partir du principe que les chiffres qui ne sont pas accompagnés d'une note signalant une divergence correspondent exactement aux définitions de la population de fait ou de la population de droit.

Il peut y avoir hétérogénéité dans les statistiques d'un même pays ou d'une même zone dans le cas des pays ou zones qui ne font une exploitation statistique détaillée des données que pour la population de droit alors qu'ils recueillent des données sur la population de droit et sur la population de fait à l'occasion d'un recensement, par exemple. Ainsi, tandis que les chiffres relatifs à la population totale qui figurent au tableau 3 se rapportent à la population de fait, ceux des tableaux qui présentent des données sur diverses caractéristiques de la population, par exemple le lieu de résidence (zone urbaine ou rurale), l'âge et le sexe, peuvent n'avoir trait qu'à la population de droit.

3.1.2 Lieu de résidence (zone urbaine ou rurale)

L'hétérogénéité des définitions nationales du terme « urbain » nuit considérablement à la comparabilité internationale des données concernant la répartition selon le lieu de résidence. Les définitions utilisées par les différents pays ou zones et leurs implications sont exposées à la fin des notes techniques correspondant au tableau 6.

3.1.3 Répartition par âge

La répartition de la population selon l'âge est un paramètre fondamental de la plupart des analyses, estimations et projections relatives aux statistiques de la population. Malheureusement, ces données sont sujettes à un certain nombre d'erreurs et difficilement comparables. C'est pourquoi pratiquement tous les utilisateurs de ces statistiques doivent considérer ces répartitions avec la plus grande circonspection.

3.1.3.1 Collecte et exploitation des données sur l'âge

L'âge est l'intervalle de temps déterminé par calcul ou par estimation qui sépare la date de naissance de la date du recensement et qui est exprimé en années solaires révolues.[6] Les données sur l'âge peuvent être recueillies selon deux méthodes : la première consiste à obtenir la date de naissance de chaque personne à l'occasion d'un recensement ou d'un sondage, puis à calculer l'âge en années révolues en soustrayant la date de naissance de celle du dénombrement[7]. La seconde consiste à enregistrer l'âge en années révolues au moment du recensement, c'est-à-dire l'âge au dernier anniversaire.

La méthode recommandée consiste à calculer l'âge au dernier anniversaire en soustrayant la date exacte de la naissance de la date du recensement. Toutefois, on n'a pas toujours recours à cette méthode ; certains pays ou zones calculent l'âge en faisant la différence entre l'année du recensement et l'année de la naissance. Lorsque les données sur l'âge ont été établies de cette façon, on l'a signalé chaque fois que possible par une note. On peut d'ailleurs s'en rendre compte dans une certaine mesure, car les chiffres dans la catégorie des moins d'un an sont plus faibles qu'ils ne devraient l'être. Cependant, un nombre irrégulier de naissances d'une année à l'autre ou l'omission de certains âges parmi les moins d'un an peut aussi fausser les chiffres de la population de moins d'un an.

3.1.3.2 Erreurs dans les données sur l'âge

Les causes d'erreurs dans les données sur l'âge sont diverses : on peut citer notamment l'ignorance de l'âge exact, la déclaration d'années d'âge correspondant à un calendrier différent de celui des années solaires révolues depuis la naissance[8], la négligence dans les déclarations et dans la façon dont elles sont consignées, la tendance générale à déclarer des âges se terminant par certains chiffres tels que 0, 2, 5 ou 8, la tendance pour les personnes âgées à exagérer leur âge, une aversion subconsciente pour certains nombres, et les fausses déclarations faites délibérément.

Les causes d'erreurs mentionnées ci-dessus, communes à la plupart des enquêtes sur l'âge et à la plupart des pays ou zones, peuvent nuire sensiblement à la comparabilité.

À cause des difficultés indiquées ci-dessus, les répartitions par âge et par sexe de la population d'un grand nombre de pays ou de zones font apparaître les irrégularités suivantes : 1) sous-estimation des groupes d'âge correspondant aux enfants de moins d'un an et aux jeunes enfants ; 2) polarisation des déclarations sur les âges se terminant par les chiffres 0 ou 5 (c'est-à-dire 5, 10,15, 20...) ; 3) prépondérance des âges pairs (par exemple 10, 12, 14...) au détriment des âges impairs (par exemple 11, 13, 15...) ; 4) écart considérable et surprenant entre le rapport masculin/féminin à certains âges ; 5) différences importantes et difficilement explicables entre les données concernant des groupes d'âge voisins. En comparant les statistiques provenant de recensements successifs pour des cohortes identiques sur le plan de l'âge et de la répartition par sexe et en étudiant la répartition par âge et par sexe de la population à chaque recensement, on peut déceler l'existence de ces incohérences et de quelques autres, un certain nombre d'entre elles se retrouvant à des degrés divers même dans les recensements les plus modernes.

3.1.3.3 Évaluation de l'exactitude

Pour déterminer, sur la base des anomalies relevées dans les groupes d'âge quinquennaux, le degré d'exactitude des statistiques par âge, on avait mis au point un indice spécial[9] pour l'Annuaire démographique 1949-1950. Cet indice était sensible à l'influence des différents facteurs qui limitent l'exactitude des données et il n'échappait pas non plus à celle des véritables fluctuations démographiques du passé. On ne pouvait donc l'appliquer indistinctement à tous les types de données à moins d'effectuer les ajustements nécessaires et de faire preuve de prudence dans l'interprétation des résultats.

La publication dans l'Annuaire démographique 1955 de statistiques de la population par année d'âge a permis d'utiliser un indice simple, mais très sensible, connu sous le nom d'indice de Whipple ou indice de concentration[10], dont l'interprétation échappe pratiquement à l'influence des facteurs sans rapport avec l'exactitude des déclarations d'âge. Il existe des méthodes plus perfectionnées pour évaluer l'exactitude des répartitions de population par année d'âge, mais on a décidé de se servir ici de l'indice de Whipple à cause de sa simplicité et de la large utilisation dont il a déjà fait l'objet dans d'autres publications.

L'indice de Whipple s'obtient en additionnant les déclarations d'âge comprises entre 23 et 62 ans inclusivement et en calculant le pourcentage des âges déclarés se terminant par 0 ou 5 par rapport au cinquième du nombre total de déclarations.

Les résultats varient entre 0, si aucun âge déclaré ne se termine par 0 ou 5, et un maximum de 500, si aucun âge déclaré ne se termine par un chiffre autre que 0 ou 5. S'il n'y a pas de concentration sur les âges se terminant par 0 et 5, l'indice de Whipple est de 100[11].

Cet indice est applicable à toutes les répartitions par âge pour lesquelles les années d'âge sont données au moins jusqu'à 62 ans, sauf dans les cas suivants : 1) lorsque les données présentées ont déjà fait l'objet d'un ajustement, l'indice de Whipple ne révèle aucune irrégularité bien que des inexactitudes d'un type différent puissent fausser ces données ; 2) lorsque les statistiques relatives à l'âge sont établies sur la base de l'année de naissance et que la tendance à arrondir l'année de naissance se traduit par une fréquence excessive des âges impairs, on ne peut utiliser la méthode reposant sur les déclarations d'âge se terminant par 5 et 0 pour évaluer l'exactitude des données recueillies.

L'indice a dernièrement été calculé pour toutes les distributions par année d'âge des recensements effectués entre 1985 et 2003, à l'exception de celles que l'on a écartées pour les motifs indiqués plus haut. Ces données sont publiées dans l 'édition spéciale de l'*Annuaire démographique* consacrée aux recensements de la population, volume I , que l'on peut consulter en ligne à l'adresse http://unstats.un.org/unsd/demographic/products/dyb/dybcens.htm .

Bien que l'indice de Whipple ne mesure que les effets de la préférence pour les âges se terminant par 5 et 0, il semble que l'on puisse admettre qu'il existe généralement certains liens entre cette préférence et d'autres sources d'inexactitudes dans les déclarations d'âge, de telle sorte que l'on peut dire qu'il donne une assez bonne idée de l'exactitude de la répartition par âge en général.

3.2 Méthodes utilisées pour indiquer la qualité des statistiques publiées

On a cherché dans toute la mesure possible à donner au lecteur une indication du degré de fiabilité des statistiques publiées dans *l'Annuaire démographique*. Pour ce faire, on a procédé de diverses façons. Chaque fois que l'on savait, grâce par exemple à une enquête post censitaire, qu'il y avait eu sous-dénombrement ou surdénombrement, on l'a signalé dans les notes qui accompagnent le tableau 3. Comme on l'a indiqué à la section 2.1 sous la rubrique « Considérations géographiques », chaque fois que les données ne portaient pas sur la totalité du pays, on l'a également signalé en note. De plus, les services nationaux de statistique ont été invités à fournir une évaluation des estimations de la population totale qu'ils communiquaient à la Division de statistique de l'ONU.

3.2.1 Traitement des séries chronologiques d'estimations de la population

En ce qui concerne les séries d'estimations de la population en milieu d'année, on considère que la qualité de la série tout entière est la même que celle de la dernière estimation. La qualité de la série est indiquée par le caractère d'imprimerie utilisé.

On n'a pas cherché à subdiviser les séries, mais il est évident que les données qui sont jugées sûres actuellement n'ont pas toutes le même degré de fiabilité et que, pour les premières années, nombre d'entre elles étaient peut-être bien moins sûres que la classification actuelle ne le laisse supposer. Ainsi, il apparaît clairement que cette méthode tend, dans bien des cas, à surestimer la fiabilité probable des séries chronologiques. Elle peut aussi inciter à sous-estimer la fiabilité des estimations pour les années qui précèdent ou qui suivent immédiatement un recensement.

3.2.2 Traitement des séries estimatives selon l'âge et d'autres caractéristiques démographiques

Des estimations de la répartition de la population par âge et par sexe peuvent être obtenues selon deux grandes méthodes : 1) en appliquant les composantes spécifiques du mouvement de la population, pour chaque groupe d'âge et pour chaque sexe, à la population dénombrée lors du recensement ; 2) en répartissant proportionnellement le chiffre total estimé pour une année postcensitaire d'après la composition par âge et par sexe au moment du recensement. Les estimations obtenues par la seconde méthode ne sont pas publiées dans *l'Annuaire démographique*.

Les séries estimatives selon l'âge et le sexe qui sont publiées sont classées en deux catégories, « sûres » ou « moins sûres », selon la méthode retenue pour le plus récent calcul estimatif de la population totale en milieu d'année. Ainsi, l'appréciation de la qualité du chiffre total, telle qu'elle ressort des signes de code, est censée s'appliquer aussi à l'ensemble de la répartition par âge et par sexe, et c'est sur cette seule base que l'on décide si les données figureront en caractères italiques ou romains. On n'a pas encore procédé à une évaluation plus poussée des données détaillées concernant la composition par âge.

4. STATISTIQUES DE L'ÉTAT CIVIL

Aux fins de *l'Annuaire démographique*, on entend par statistiques de l'état civil les statistiques des naissances vivantes.

Dans le présent volume de l'*Annuaire*, on n'a présenté que les tableaux de caractère général sur la natalité, la mortalité, la nuptialité et la divortialité. Les tableaux consacrés à la mortalité sont groupés sous les rubriques suivantes : mortalité fœtale, mortalité infantile, mortalité liée à la maternité et mortalité générale, y compris des tableaux portant sur la cause des décès.

4.1 Sources de variations des données

La plupart des statistiques de l'état civil publiées dans le présent *Annuaire* émanent des systèmes nationaux d'enregistrement des faits d'état civil. Le degré d'exhaustivité et d'exactitude de ces données varie d'un pays ou d'une zone à l'autre.

Il n'existe pas partout de système national d'enregistrement des faits d'état civil et, dans quelques cas, seuls certains faits sont enregistrés. Par exemple, dans certains pays ou zones, seuls les naissances et les décès sont enregistrés. Il existe également des différences quant au degré d'efficacité avec lequel les lois relatives à l'enregistrement des faits d'état civil sont appliquées dans les divers pays ou zones. La fiabilité des statistiques provenant des registres d'état civil dépend des modalités d'application de la loi et de la mesure dans laquelle le public s'y soumet.

Il est à signaler que dans certains cas les statistiques de la nuptialité et de la divortialité sont tirées d'autres sources que les registres d'état civil. Dans certains pays ou zones, par exemple, les seules données disponibles sur la nuptialité proviennent des registres des églises. Selon la pratique suivie par chaque pays, les statistiques de la divortialité sont tirées des actes des tribunaux et/ou des registres d'état civil. L'officier de l'état civil, le service national de statistique ou d'autres services administratifs peuvent être chargés d'établir ces statistiques.

Les autres facteurs qui influent sur la comparabilité internationale des statistiques de l'état civil sont à peu près les mêmes que ceux qu'il convient de prendre en considération pour interpréter les variations observées dans les statistiques de la population. La définition des faits d'état civil aux fins de statistique, la portée des données du point de vue géographique et ethnique ainsi que les méthodes d'exploitation des données sont autant d'éléments qui peuvent influer sur la comparabilité.

En plus des statistiques tirées des registres d'état civil, l'*Annuaire* présente des statistiques de l'état civil qui sont des estimations officielles nationales, fondées souvent sur les résultats de sondages. Aussi leur comparabilité varie-t-elle en fonction du degré d'exhaustivité des déclarations recueillies lors d'enquêtes sur les ménages, des erreurs d'échantillonnage ou autres, et des distorsions d'origines diverses.

Pour plus de détails au sujet des pratiques nationales relatives au rassemblement des statistiques d'état civil, le lecteur pourra se reporter aux : *Principes et recommandations pour un système de statistiques de l'état civil, deuxième révision*[12] ; *Manuel des systèmes d'enregistrement des faits d'état civil et de statistiques de l'état civil : Élaboration d'un cadre juridique*[13] ; *Manuel des systèmes d'enregistrement des faits d'état civil et de statistiques de l'état civil : Gestion, fonctionnement et tenue*[14]; *Manuel des systèmes d'enregistrement des faits d'état civil et de statistiques de l'état civil : Élaboration de programmes d'information, d'éducation et de communication*[15] ; *Manuel des systèmes d'enregistrement des faits d'état civil et de statistiques de l'état civil : Principes et protocoles concernant la communication et l'archivage des documents individuels*[16]; *Manuel des systèmes d'enregistrement des faits d'état civil et de statistiques de l'état civil : Informatisation*[17]. Le *Manuel de collecte de données sur la fécondité et la mortalité*[18] fournit des informations ayant trait à la collecte et à l'évaluation des données sur la fécondité, sur la mortalité et sur d'autres faits d'état civil, qui ont été recueillies au cours des enquêtes sur les ménages. Ces publications sont également disponibles sur le Web à partir de l'adresse suivante : http://unstats.un.org/unsd/demographic/sources/civilreg/default.htm.

4.1.1 Définition des faits d'état civil aux fins de la statistique

Une cause importante d'hétérogénéité dans les données est le manque d'uniformité des définitions des différents faits d'état civil. Aux fins de l'*Annuaire démographique*, il est recommandé de recueillir les données relatives aux faits d'état civil en utilisant les définitions établies au paragraphe 57 des *Principes et recommandations pour un système de statistiques de l'état civil, deuxième révision*[12]. Ces définitions sont les suivantes :

La NAISSANCE VIVANTE est l'expulsion ou l'extraction complète du corps de la mère, indépendamment de la durée de la gestation, d'un produit de la conception qui, après cette séparation, respire ou manifeste tout autre signe de vie, tel que battement de cœur, pulsation du cordon ombilical ou contraction effective d'un muscle soumis à l'action de la volonté, que le cordon ombilical ait été coupé ou non et que le placenta soit ou non demeuré attaché; tout produit d'une telle naissance est considéré comme « enfant né vivant ».

Le DÉCÈS est la disparition permanente de tout signe de vie à un moment quelconque postérieur à la naissance vivante (cessation des fonctions vitales après la naissance sans possibilité de réanimation). Cette définition ne comprend donc pas les morts fœtales.

La MORT FŒTALE est le décès d'un produit de la conception lorsque ce décès est survenu avant l'expulsion ou l'extraction complète du corps de la mère, indépendamment de la durée de la gestation; le décès est indiqué par le fait qu'après cette séparation le fœtus ne respire ni ne manifeste aucun signe de vie, tel que battement de cœur, pulsation du cordon ombilical ou contraction effective d'un muscle soumis à l'action de la volonté. Les morts fœtales tardives sont celles qui sont survenues après 28 semaines de gestation ou plus. Il n'y a aucune différence entre ces « morts fœtales tardives » et les faits désignés, avant 1950, par le terme « mortinatalité[19] ».

Le MARIAGE est l'acte, la cérémonie ou la procédure qui établit un rapport légal entre mari et femme. L'union peut être rendue légale par une procédure civile ou religieuse, ou par toute autre procédure, conformément à la législation du pays.

Le DIVORCE est la dissolution légale et définitive des liens du mariage, c'est-à-dire la séparation de l'époux et de l'épouse qui confère aux parties le droit de se remarier civilement ou religieusement, ou selon toute autre procédure, conformément à la législation du pays.

Des données concernant les avortements sont également recueillies et présentées dans l'*Annuaire démographique*, la définition retenue étant la suivante :

Par référence à la femme, l'AVORTEMENT se définit comme toute interruption de grossesse qui est survenue avant 28 semaines de gestation et dont le produit est un fœtus mort. Il existe deux grandes catégories d'avortement : l'avortement spontané et l'avortement provoqué. L'avortement provoqué a pour origine une action délibérée entreprise en vue d'interrompre une grossesse. Tout autre avortement est considéré comme spontané.

4.1.2 Problèmes posés par les définitions établies

Les variations par rapport aux définitions établies des faits d'état civil sont le principal obstacle à la comparabilité internationale des statistiques de l'état civil. Un exemple en est fourni par le cas des naissances vivantes et celui des morts fœtales[20]. Dans certains pays ou zones, il faut que le nouveau-né ait vécu 24 heures pour pouvoir être inscrit sur le registre des naissances vivantes. Les décès d'enfants qui surviennent avant l'expiration du délai de 24 heures sont classés parmi les morts fœtales tardives et, en l'absence de méthodes spéciales d'exploitation des données, ne sont comptés ni dans les naissances vivantes ni dans les décès. De même, dans plusieurs autres pays ou zones, les décès d'enfants nés vivants et décédés avant l'enregistrement de leur naissance sont également comptés parmi les morts fœtales tardives.

À moins que des méthodes spéciales n'aient été adoptées pour l'exploitation de ces données, les statistiques des naissances vivantes et des décès ne tiendront pas compte de ces cas, qui viendront en revanche accroître d'autant le nombre des morts fœtales tardives. Le taux de mortalité infantile sera donc sous-estimé. Bien que les éléments constitutifs du taux (décès d'enfants de moins d'un an et naissances vivantes) accusent exactement la même insuffisance en valeur absolue, les lacunes sont proportionnellement plus fortes pour les décès de moins d'un an, ce qui cause des erreurs plus importantes dans les taux de mortalité infantile.

De plus, cette pratique augmente les rapports de mortinatalité. Quelques pays ou zones effectuent les ajustements nécessaires pour corriger cette anomalie (du moins dans les fréquences totales) au moment de l'établissement des tableaux. Si aucun ajustement n'a été effectué, cela est indiqué dans les notes chaque fois que possible.

Les définitions du mariage et du divorce posent aussi un problème du point de vue de la comparabilité internationale. Contrairement à la naissance et au décès, qui sont des faits biologiques, le mariage et le divorce sont uniquement déterminés par la législation et la coutume et, de ce fait, il est moins facile d'en donner une définition statistique qui ait une application universelle. À des fins statistiques, ces notions ont donc été définies de manière générale par référence à la législation de chaque pays ou zone. La législation relative au mariage et plus particulièrement au divorce varie d'un pays ou d'une zone à l'autre. En ce qui concerne le mariage, l'âge de nubilité est la condition la plus fréquemment requise mais il arrive souvent que d'autres conditions soient exigées.

Lorsqu'il est connu, l'âge minimum auquel le mariage peut avoir lieu avec le consentement des parents (et dans certains cas sans le consentement des parents) est indiqué au tableau 24-1 as part of the technical notes for table 24. Les lois et règlements relatifs à la dissolution du mariage par le divorce vont de l'interdiction absolue, en passant par diverses conditions requises pour l'obtention du divorce, jusqu'à la simple déclaration, par l'époux, de son désir ou de son intention de divorcer.

4.1.3 Portée géographique ou ethnique restreinte

En principe, les statistiques de l'état civil devraient s'étendre à l'ensemble du pays ou de la zone auxquels elles se rapportent et englober tous les groupes ethniques. En fait, il n'est pas rare que les données soient fragmentaires. Dans certains pays ou zones, l'enregistrement n'est obligatoire que pour une petite partie de la population, par exemple pour certains groupes ethniques. Dans d'autres, il n'existe pas de disposition qui prescrive l'enregistrement obligatoire sur le plan national, mais seulement des règlements ou décrets des municipalités ou des États, qui ne s'appliquent pas à l'ensemble du territoire. Il en est encore autrement dans d'autres pays ou zones où les autorités ont institué une zone d'enregistrement comprenant seulement une partie du territoire, le reste étant exclu en raison des difficultés d'accès ou parce qu'il est pratiquement impossible, pour des raisons d'ordre économique ou culturel, d'y procéder à un enregistrement régulier.

4.1.4 Exploitation des données

4.1.4.1 Selon le lieu de l'événement

Les statistiques de l'état civil qui sont présentées pour l'ensemble du territoire national se rapportent à la population de fait ou population présente. En conséquence, sauf indication contraire, les statistiques de l'état civil relatives à une zone ou à un pays donné portent sur tous les faits survenus dans l'ensemble de la population, à l'intérieur des frontières actuelles de la zone ou du pays considéré. On peut donc estimer qu'elles englobent les faits d'état civil survenus dans les tribus nomades et parmi les populations autochtones ainsi que parmi les ressortissants du pays et les étrangers. Des notes signalent les exceptions lorsque celles-ci sont connues.

Pour certains pays, les écarts entre les taux démographiques pour les zones urbaines et pour les zones rurales peuvent varier notablement selon que les faits d'état civil ont été exploités sur la base du lieu de l'événement ou du lieu de résidence habituel. Par exemple, si un nombre appréciable de femmes résidant dans des zones rurales proches de grands centres urbains accouchent dans les hôpitaux ou maternités d'une ville, les taux de fécondité ainsi que les taux de mortalité néo-natale et infantile seront généralement plus élevés dans les zones urbaines (et par conséquent plus faibles dans les zones rurales) si les faits sont exploités en se fondant sur le lieu de l'événement et non sur le lieu de résidence habituel. Le phénomène sera le même dans le cas de la mortalité générale si un bon nombre de personnes résidant dans des zones rurales font appel aux services de santé des villes lorsqu'elles sont gravement malades.

4.1.4.2 Selon la date de l'événement ou la date de l'enregistrement

Autant que possible, les statistiques de l'état civil figurant dans l'*Annuaire démographique* se rapportent aux faits survenus pendant l'année considérée et non aux faits enregistrés au cours de ladite année. Bon nombre de pays ou zones, toutefois, exploitent leurs statistiques de l'état civil selon la date de l'enregistrement et non selon la date de l'événement. Comme ces statistiques risquent d'induire gravement en erreur, les pays ou zones dont on sait qu'ils établissent leurs statistiques d'après la date de l'enregistrement sont signalés dans les tableaux par un signe plus (+). On ne dispose toutefois pas pour tous les pays ou zones de renseignements complets sur la méthode d'exploitation des statistiques de l'état civil et les données sont peut-être exploitées selon la date de l'enregistrement plus souvent que ne le laisserait supposer l'emploi des signes.

Étant donné que la qualité des données est inextricablement liée aux retards dans l'enregistrement, il faudra toujours considérer en même temps le code de qualité qui est décrit à la section 4.2.1 ci-après. Évidemment, si l'enregistrement des naissances est complet et effectué en temps voulu (code 'C'), les effets perturbateurs de la méthode consistant à exploiter les données selon la date de l'enregistrement seront pratiquement annulés. De même, s'agissant des statistiques des décès, les effets pourront bien souvent être réduits au minimum dans les pays ou zones où le code sanitaire subordonne la délivrance du permis d'inhumer à l'enregistrement du décès, ce qui tend à hâter l'enregistrement. Quant aux morts fœtales, elles sont généralement déclarées immédiatement ou ne sont pas déclarées du tout. En conséquence, si l'enregistrement se fait dans un délai très court, la différence entre les statistiques établies selon la date de l'événement et celles qui sont établies selon la date de l'enregistrement peut être négligeable. Dans bien des cas, la durée des délais légaux accordés pour l'enregistrement des faits d'état civil est un facteur dont dépend dans une large mesure l'incidence sur la comparabilité de l'exploitation des données selon la date de l'enregistrement.

En ce qui concerne le mariage et le divorce, la pratique consistant à exploiter les statistiques selon la date de l'enregistrement ne pose généralement pas de graves problèmes. Le mariage étant, dans de nombreux pays ou zones, un contrat juridique civil qui, pour être légal, doit être conclu devant un officier de l'état civil, il s'ensuit que dans ces pays ou zones l'enregistrement a lieu presque systématiquement au moment de la cérémonie ou immédiatement après. De même, dans de nombreux pays ou zones, le tribunal ou l'autorité qui a prononcé le divorce est seul habilité à enregistrer cet acte, et comme l'acte d'enregistrement figure alors sur les registres du tribunal l'enregistrement suit généralement de peu le jugement.

En revanche, si l'enregistrement n'a lieu qu'avec un certain retard, les statistiques de l'état civil établies selon la date de l'enregistrement ne sont pas comparables sur le plan international. Au mieux, les statistiques par date de l'enregistrement prendront surtout en considération des faits survenus au cours de l'année précédente ; dans les pays ou zones où le système d'enregistrement n'est pas très développé, il y entrera des faits datant de plusieurs années. Il ressort des documents dont on dispose que des retards de plusieurs années dans l'enregistrement des naissances ne sont pas rares, encore que, dans la majorité des cas, les retards ne dépassent pas deux à quatre ans.

Tant que l'enregistrement se fera avec retard, les statistiques fondées sur la date d'enregistrement ne seront comparables sur le plan international ni entre elles ni avec les statistiques établies selon la date de fait d'état civil.

Il convient également de noter que l'exploitation des données selon la date de l'enregistrement ne nuit pas seulement à la comparabilité internationale des statistiques. Même à l'intérieur d'un pays ou d'une zone, le procédé qui consiste à compter les enregistrements et non les faits peut compromettre la comparabilité des chiffres sur une longue période. Si le nombre des faits d'état civil enregistrés varie d'une année à l'autre (par suite de l'application de mesures visant tout particulièrement à encourager l'enregistrement ou parce qu'il est subitement devenu nécessaire de produire le certificat d'une naissance ou d'un décès non enregistré pour l'accomplissement de certaines formalités), les statistiques de l'état civil établies d'après la date de l'enregistrement ne permettent pas de quantifier ni d'analyser l'état et l'évolution de la population. Tout au plus peuvent-elles révéler l'évolution des conditions d'exigibilité du certificat de naissance, de décès ou de mariage et les fluctuations du volume de travail des bureaux d'état civil. Les statistiques établies selon la date de l'enregistrement peuvent donc ne présenter qu'une utilité très réduite pour des études nationales ou internationales.

4.2 Méthodes utilisées pour indiquer la qualité des statistiques de l'état civil qui sont publiées

La qualité des statistiques de l'état civil peut être évaluée en se fondant sur plusieurs facteurs. Le facteur essentiel est la complétude du système d'enregistrement des faits d'état civil d'après lequel les statistiques sont établies. Dans certains cas, on constate que les données tirées de l'enregistrement ne sont pas complètes lorsque l'on les utilise pour le calcul des taux. Toutefois, cette observation est valable uniquement lorsque les statistiques présentent des lacunes évidentes, qu'elles sont exploitées d'après la date de l'événement et que l'estimation du chiffre de population pris pour base est exacte. L'exploitation des données d'après la date de l'enregistrement donne souvent des taux qui paraissent exacts, tout simplement parce que le numérateur est artificiellement gonflé par suite de l'inclusion d'un grand nombre d'enregistrements tardifs ; inversement, il arrive que des taux paraissent vraisemblables parce que l'on a sous-évalué la population étudiée. Il ne faut pas non plus oublier que les renseignements dont on dispose sur les taux de fécondité, de mortalité et de nuptialité considérés comme normaux sont extrêmement sommaires dans un grand nombre de régions du monde et que les cas limites, qui sont les plus difficiles à évaluer, sont fréquents.

4.2.1 Codage qualitatif des statistiques provenant des registres de l'état civil

Dans le questionnaire relatif au mouvement de la population qui leur est envoyé chaque année dans le cadre de l'établissement de *l'Annuaire démographique*, les services nationaux de statistique sont invités à donner leur propre évaluation du degré de complétude des données sur les naissances, les décès, les décès d'enfants de moins d'un an, les morts fœtales tardives, les mariages et les divorces figurant dans leurs registres d'état civil.

D'après les renseignements directement communiqués par les gouvernements ou extraits des questionnaires ou de publications officielles pertinentes, il a été possible de classer les statistiques de l'enregistrement des faits d'état civil (naissances, décès, décès d'enfants de moins d'un an, morts fœtales tardives, mariages et divorces) en trois grandes catégories, selon leur qualité :

C : Données jugées pratiquement complètes, c'est-à-dire représentant au moins 90 p. 100 des faits d'état civil survenant chaque année.

U : Données jugées incomplètes, c'est-à-dire représentant moins de 90 p. 100 des faits survenant chaque année.

| : Données ne provenant pas des systèmes nationaux d'enregistrement des faits d'état civil mais jugées fiables, telles que les estimations dérivées des projections, d'autres techniques d'estimation ou recensements de population ou du logement.

... : Données dont le degré de complétude ne fait pas l'objet de renseignements précis.

Ces codes de qualité figurent dans la deuxième colonne des tableaux qui présentent, pour un nombre d'années déterminé les chiffres absolus et les taux (ou rapports) bruts concernant les naissances vivantes (tableau 9), les morts fœtales tardives (tableau 12), les décès d'enfants de moins d'un an (tableau 15), les décès (tableau 18), les mariages (tableau 23) et les divorces (tableau 25).

La classification des pays ou zones selon ces codes de qualité peut ne pas être uniforme. On a estimé néanmoins que les services nationaux de statistique étaient les mieux placés pour juger de la qualité de leurs données. On a pensé que les catégories que l'on pouvait distinguer sur la base des renseignements disponibles, bien que très larges, permettaient cependant de se faire une idée de la qualité des statistiques de l'état civil publiées dans l'*Annuaire*.

Par le passé, les bases sur lesquelles les pays évaluaient l'exhaustivité de leurs données n'étaient généralement pas connues. À l'occasion de l'établissement de l'*Annuaire démographique 1977*, les pays ont été invités, pour la première fois, à donner des indications à ce sujet. On leur a demandé de préciser si leurs estimations du degré d'exhaustivité des données d'enregistrement des naissances vivantes, des décès et de la mortalité infantile reposaient sur une analyse démographique, un double contrôle des registres ou d'autres méthodes qu'ils devaient spécifier. Relativement peu de pays ou zones ont jusqu'à présent répondu à cette nouvelle question ; on n'a donc pas cherché à réviser le système de codage qualitatif utilisé pour les statistiques de l'état civil présentées dans l'*Annuaire*. Il faut espérer qu'à l'avenir davantage de pays pourront fournir ces renseignements afin que l'on puisse adapter le système de codage qualitatif.

Sur les pays ou zones qui ont estimé à 90 p. 100 ou plus le degré d'exhaustivité de leur enregistrement des naissances vivantes (classé 'C' dans le tableau 9), les pays ou zones suivants ont communiqué des renseignements concernant les bases sur lesquelles leur estimation reposait :

a) Analyse démographique : Argentine, Australie, Canada, Chili, Croatie, Cuba, Égypte, États-Unis, Guadeloupe, Guernesey, Guyane française, Irlande, Islande, Israël, Koweït, Lettonie, Maurice, Porto Rico, République de Corée, République tchèque, Roumanie, Saint-Marin, Singapour, Suède et Suisse.

b) Double contrôle des registres : Barbade, Belgique, Bulgarie, Chypre, Cuba, Danemark, Estonie, Fidji, Finlande, France, Guadeloupe, Guam, Guyane française, Grèce, Guernesey, Hongrie, Île de Man, Îles Cook, Islande, Kirghizistan, Lituanie, Japon, Malaisie, Maldives, Nouvelle-Zélande, Saint-Kitts-et-Nevis, Sainte-Lucie, Roumanie, Singapour, Sri Lanka, Suède, Suisse, Uruguay et Venezuela (République bolivarienne du).

c) Autre méthode : Allemagne, Belgique, Bermudes, Chine, Groenland, région administrative spéciale de Hong Kong (Chine), région administrative spéciale de Macao (Chine), Îles Caïmanes, Islande, Japon, Luxembourg, Norvège, Pays-Bas, Pologne, Singapour et Slovénie.

Sur les pays ou zones qui ont estimé à 90 p. 100 ou plus le degré d'exhaustivité de leur enregistrement des décès (classé 'C' dans le tableau 18), les pays ou zones suivants ont donné des indications touchant la base de cette estimation :

a) Analyse démographique : Argentine, Australie, Canada, Chili, Cuba, Égypte, États-Unis, Guadeloupe, Guernesey, Guyane française, Irlande, Islande, Israël, Koweït, Lettonie, Maurice, Porto Rico, Roumanie, Saint-Marin, Singapour et Suisse.

b) Double contrôle des registres : Bahamas, Bulgarie, Cuba, Danemark, Fidji, Finlande, France, Grèce, Groenland, Guam, Guernesey, Îles Cook, Île de Man, Islande, Maldives, Nouvelle-Zélande, Roumanie, Saint-Kitts-et-Nevis, Sainte-Lucie, Singapour, Sri Lanka, Suède, Suisse,et Uruguay.

c) Autre méthode : Allemagne, Belgique, Bermudes, région administrative spéciale de Hong Kong, Îles Caïmanes, Irlande, Islande, Japon, Luxembourg, Norvège, Pays-Bas, Pologne, Singapour et Slovénie.

Sur les pays ou zones qui ont estimé à 90 p. 100 ou plus le degré d'exhaustivité de leur enregistrement des décès à moins d'un an (classé 'C' dans le tableau 15), les pays ou zones suivants ont donné des indications touchant la base de cette estimation :

a) Analyse démographique : Argentine, Australie, Canada, Chili, Cuba, Égypte, États-Unis, Irlande, Islande, Israël, Koweït, Lettonie, Maurice, Porto Rico, Roumanie, Saint-Marin, Singapour, Sri Lanka et Suisse.

b) Double contrôle des registres : Bahamas, Bulgarie, Cuba, Danemark, Fidji, Finlande, France, Grèce, Groenland, Guam, Guernesey, Île de Man, Îles Cook, Islande, Japon, Maldives, Nouvelle-Zélande, Roumanie, Saint-Kitts-et-Nevis, Sainte-Lucie, Singapour, Suède, Suisse,et Uruguay.

c) Autre méthode : Allemagne, Belgique, Bermudes, région administrative spéciale de Hong Kong, Îles Caïmanes, Islande, Japon, Luxembourg, Norvège, Pays-Bas, Pologne, Singapour et Slovénie.

4.2.2 Traitement des statistiques tirées des registres d'état civil

Dans tous les tableaux de l'*Annuaire*, on a indiqué le degré de fiabilité des statistiques de l'état civil en se fondant sur le codage qualitatif décrit ci-dessus. Les statistiques codées 'C', jugées sûres, sont imprimées en caractères romains. Celles qui sont codées 'U' ou '...', jugées douteuses, sont reproduites en *italique*. Bien que le codage qualitatif proprement dit n'apparaisse que dans certains tableaux, l'indication du degré de fiabilité (c'est-à-dire l'emploi des caractères italiques pour désigner les données douteuses) se retrouve dans tous les tableaux présentant des statistiques de l'état civil.

En général, le code de qualité pour les décès utilisé au tableau 18 sert à déterminer si, dans les autres tableaux, les données relatives aux décès apparaissent en caractères romains ou en italique. Toutefois, le code associé à certaines données sur les décès liés à la maternité dans le tableau 17 diffère de celui employé dans le tableau 18 lorsque l'on sait que le degré d'exhaustivité des données diffère grandement de celui du nombre total des décès. Dans les cas où le code de qualité du tableau 18 ne correspond pas aux caractères utilisés dans le tableau 17, les renseignements concernant l'exhaustivité des statistiques des décès selon la cause sont indiqués en note à la fin du tableau.

On a utilisé la même indication de fiabilité dans les tableaux des taux démographiques et dans ceux des fréquences correspondantes. Par exemple, les taux de mortalité calculés d'après les décès figurant sur un registre incomplet ou d'exhaustivité indéterminée sont jugés douteux et apparaissent en italique. Au sens strict, pour évaluer de façon plus précise les taux démographiques, il faudrait tenir compte de la précision des données sur la population figurant au dénominateur dans les taux. La qualité des données sur la population est étudiée à la section 3.2 des notes techniques.

Il convient de noter que, pour les taux de mortalité infantile, les taux de mortalité liée à la maternité et les rapports de morts fœtales tardives (calculées en utilisant au dénominateur le nombre de naissances vivantes), les indications relatives à la fiabilité sont déterminées sur la base des codes de qualité utilisés pour les décès d'enfants de moins d'un an, les décès totaux et les morts fœtales tardives, respectivement.

Pour évaluer ces taux et rapports de façon plus précise, il faudrait tenir compte de la qualité des données relatives aux naissances vivantes, utilisées au dénominateur dans leur calcul. Les codes de qualité pour les naissances vivantes figurent au tableau 9 et sont décrits plus en détail dans les notes techniques se rapportant à ce tableau.

4.2.3 Traitement des séries chronologiques de statistiques tirées des registres d'état civil

Il est plus difficile de déterminer la qualité des séries chronologiques de statistiques de l'état civil que celle des données pour une seule année. Étant donné qu'une série chronologique de statistiques de l'état civil ne peut généralement avoir pour source qu'un système permanent d'enregistrement des faits d'état civil, on a arbitrairement supposé que le degré d'exactitude de la série tout entière était le même que celui de la dernière tranche annuelle de données tirées du registre d'état civil. La série tout entière est traitée de la manière décrite à la section 4.2.2 ci-dessus : lorsque le code de qualité relatif aux données d'enregistrement les plus récentes est 'C', les fréquences et les taux relatifs aux années antérieures sont eux aussi considérés comme sûrs et figurent en caractères romains. Inversement, si les données d'enregistrement les plus récentes sont codées 'U' ou '...', les données des années antérieures sont jugées douteuses et figurent en italique. Cette méthode n'est certes pas entièrement satisfaisante, car les données des premières années de la série sont souvent beaucoup moins sûres que le code actuel ne le laisse supposer.

4.2.4 Traitement des estimations fondées sur les statistiques de l'état civil

En plus des données provenant des systèmes d'enregistrement des faits d'état civil, l'*Annuaire démographique* contient aussi des estimations relatives aux fréquences et aux taux. Il s'agit d'estimations officielles, généralement calculées à partir des résultats d'un sondage ou par analyse démographique. Si des estimations concernant les fréquences et les taux figurent dans les tableaux, c'est parce que l'on considère qu'elles fournissent des renseignements plus exacts que les systèmes existants d'enregistrement des faits d'état civil. En conséquence, elles sont également jugées sûres et sont donc imprimées en caractères romains, même si elles sont entrecoupées dans une série chronologique de données tirées des registres d'état civil.

Dans les tableaux qui indiquent le code de qualité, ce code ne s'applique qu'aux données tirées des registres d'état civil. Si une série pour un pays ou une zone comprend à la fois des données tirées d'un registre d'état civil et des données estimatives, le code ne s'applique qu'aux données d'enregistrement. Si seules des données estimatives apparaissent, le symbole '|' est utilisé.

4.3 Causes de décès

Les États membres de l'Organisation mondiale de la santé (OMS) sont tenus de communiquer à celle-ci les données sur les causes de décès codifiées selon la révision en vigueur de la Classification internationale des maladies et des problèmes de santé connexes (CIM) adoptée par l'Assemblé mondiale de la santé[21]. Les données sont collectées par l'OMS sur la base de la CIM. Pour assurer la comparabilité internationale des statistiques des causes de décès, l'OMS organise régulièrement des conférences internationales de révision de la Classification internationale des maladies afin de suivre, au fur et à mesure, les progrès les plus récents de la médecine clinique et de la statistique. Les données sont généralement envoyées à l'OMS selon la classification à 4 caractères prévue par la CIM et sont archivées dans la base de données sur la mortalité de l'OMS telles qu'elles ont été présentées par le pays. Pour les versions antérieures, par contre, les données sont disponibles seulement selon la liste A de 150 causes de la CIM. Les données de l'OMS sont disponibles sur le site Internet suivant: http://www3.who.int/whosis/menu.cfm.

Les révisions de la CIM permettent certes de disposer d'une version actualisée, mais elles posent plusieurs problèmes de comparabilité des statistiques des causes de décès. Le premier tient au manque de comparabilité dans le temps, qui accompagne inévitablement la mise en oeuvre d'une classification nouvelle. Le deuxième est celui de la comparabilité entre pays ou zones, car les différents pays peuvent adopter la nouvelle classification à des époques différentes. Établir la cause des décès exige des compétences de plus en plus poussées à mesure que la classification devient plus précise. Or, dans beaucoup de pays ou zones, il est rare que les décès se produisent en présence d'un témoin possédant une formation médicale et le certificat de décès est le plus souvent établi par quelqu'un qui n'est pas qualifié sur le plan médical. Étant donné que la CIM répertorie de nombreux diagnostics qu'il est impossible d'établir si l'on n'a pas de formation en médecine, elle ne favorise pas toujours la comparabilité internationale, notamment entre pays ou zones où la qualité des services médicaux est très disparate.

La dixième révision[22] est la dernière qu'ait connue la CIM. Les chapitres de la dixième révision se fondent sur un système de codification alphanumérique à une lettre suivie de trois chiffres pour les catégories à quatre caractères. Le chapitre 1 concerne les maladies infectieuses et parasitaires et le chapitre 2 l'ensemble des néoplasmes. Le chapitre 3 a trait aux troubles du système immunitaire, aux maladies du sang et aux organes hématopoïétiques. Le chapitre 4 porte sur les maladies du système endocrinien, de la nutrition et du métabolisme. Les autres chapitres groupent les maladies selon leur site anatomique, à l'exception de ceux qui concernent les affections mentales, les complications de la grossesse, de l'accouchement et des suites de couches, les malformations congénitales et les affections de la période périnatale. Enfin, un chapitre entier est consacré aux symptômes, manifestations et résultats anormaux.

4.3.1 Mortalité liée à la maternité

D'après la dixième révision de la CIM, la « mortalité liée à la maternité » est définie comme le décès d'une femme survenu au cours de la grossesse ou dans un délai de 42 jours après sa terminaison, quelle qu'en soit la durée et la localisation, pour une cause quelconque déterminée ou aggravée par la grossesse ou les soins qu'elle a motivés, mais ni accidentelle ni fortuite.

Les décès liés à la maternité se répartissent en deux groupes :

1) Décès par cause obstétricale directe qui résultent de complications obstétricales (grossesse, travail et suites de couches), d'interventions, d'omissions, d'un traitement incorrect ou d'un enchaînement d'événements de l'un quelconque des facteurs ci-dessus ;
2) Décès par cause obstétricale indirecte qui résultent d'une maladie préexistante ou d'une affection apparue au cours de la grossesse, sans qu'elle soit due à des causes obstétricales directes, mais qui a été aggravée par les effets physiologiques de la grossesse.

Il est recommandé dans la dixième révision d'exprimer les taux de mortalité liée à la maternité sur la base de 100 000 naissances vivantes ou 100 000 naissances totales (naissances vivantes et morts fœtales)[23]. Le nombre de femmes enceintes aurait dû être pris comme dénominateur, mais étant donné qu'il est impossible de le déterminer, le taux de mortalité liée à la maternité est ici calculé par 100 000 naissances vivantes. Bien que les naissances vivantes ne permettent pas d'évaluer sans distorsion le nombre des femmes enceintes, leur nombre est plus fiable que d'autres estimations car le nombre des naissances vivantes est plus exactement enregistré que celui des naissances vivantes et des morts fœtales.

NOTES

[1] Les données relatives à la mortalité liée à la maternité et aux taux de mortalité selon la cause émanent de l'Organisation mondiale de la santé et sont disponibles à l'adresse suivante : http://www3.who.int/whosis/menu.cfm.

[2] Les éditions de 1978 et de 1991 font exception à la règle, puisque les tableaux sur des sujets spéciaux ont été publiés séparément.

[3] *World Population Prospects: The 2006 Revision.* Nations Unies, New York, numéro de vente : E.07.XIII.7, 2007. Dans l'intervalle, on peut consulter des extraits et certaines données sur le site www.unpopulation.org.

[4] ST/ESA/STAT/SER.M/49/Rev.4/WWW ; http://unstats.un.org/unsd/methods/m49/m49.htm; voir également *Code standard des pays et des zones à usage statistique*, numéro de vente : M.98.XVII.9, Nations Unies, New York, 1999.

[5] À paraître, F.07.XVII.8, Nations Unies, New York, 2007. Avant d'être publiée, cette publication est disponible en ligne à l'adresse suivante : http://unstats.un.org/unsd/demographic/sources/census/docs/P&R_%20Rev2.pdf

[6] Ibid., par. 2.135

[7] Lorsque l'on utilise un registre de la population, on peut également calculer l'âge en années révolues en soustrayant la date de naissance de chaque personne inscrite sur le registre de la date de référence à laquelle se rapportent les données sur l'âge.

[8] L'emploi de méthodes différentes de calcul de l'âge, par exemple la méthode occidentale et la méthode orientale, ou, comme on les désigne plus communément, la méthode anglaise et la méthode chinoise, représente une cause de non-comparabilité. Selon la méthode chinoise, on considère que l'enfant est âgé d'un an à sa naissance et qu'il avance d'un an à chaque nouvelle année chinoise. Les répercussions de cette méthode sont particulièrement apparentes dans les données pour le premier âge : les données concernant les enfants de moins d'un an sont nettement inférieures à la réalité. Les effets sur les chiffres relatifs aux groupes d'âge suivants sont moins visibles. Les séries ainsi établies sont souvent ajustées avant d'être publiées, mais il ne faut pas exclure la possibilité d'aberrations de ce genre lorsque l'on compare des données censitaires sur l'âge.

[9] Dans cet indice, on déterminait les différences à partir des rapports prévus de masculinité dans un groupe d'âge et dans les groupes d'âge adjacents. Il fallait pour cela tenir compte de l'influence de facteurs tels que les mouvements passés des taux de natalité, les pertes de guerre élevées et, le cas échéant, le faible effectif de la population. On trouvera dans le *Bulletin démographique*, no 2 (publication des Nations Unies, numéro de vente : 52.XIII.4), p. 64 à 87, un exposé détaillé sur cet indice ainsi que les résultats de son application aux données présentées dans les éditions de 1949-1950 et de 1951 de l'*Annuaire démographique*. On a fait les mêmes calculs sur les statistiques publiées dans l'*Annuaire démographique 1952* et les résultats obtenus sont indiqués dans l'édition correspondante de l'*Annuaire*, qui, comme celles de 1953 et de 1954, donne de brèves explications sur l'indice en question.

[10] United States Bureau of the Census, Thirteenth Census, vol. I (Washington, D.C., U.S. Government Printing Office), p. 291 et 292.

[11] J.T. Marten, Census of India, 1921, vol. I, partie I (Calcutta, 1924), p. 126 et 127.

[12] Numéro de vente : F.01.XVII.10, publication des Nations Unies, New York, 2003.

[13] Numéro de vente : F. 98.XVII.7, publication des Nations Unies, New York, 1998.

[14] Numéro de vente : F.98.XVII.11, publication des Nations Unies, New York, 1998.

[15] Numéro de vente : F.98.XVII.4, publication des Nations Unies, New York, 1998.

[16] Numéro de vente : F.98.XVII.6, publication des Nations Unies, New York, 1998.

[17] Numéro de vente : F.98.XVII.10, publication des Nations Unies, New York, 1998.

[18] *Manuel de Collecte de données sur la fécondité et la mortalité*, Numéro de vente 03.XVII.11, United Nations, New York, 2003.

[19] Pour plus de précisions, voir *Principes et recommandations pour un système de statistiques de l'état civil, deuxième révision*, numéro de vente : F.01.XVII.10, publication des Nations Unies, New York, 2001, par. 57.

[20] Pour plus de précisions au sujet des considérations historiques et juridiques auxquelles se rattachent les différentes définitions correspondant aux naissances vivantes et aux morts fœtales, pour une comparaison des définitions utilisées depuis le 1er janvier 1950 et pour une évaluation des effets de ces différences de définition sur le calcul de divers taux, voir le *Manuel de statistique de l'état civil, Volume II, Étude des pratiques nationales*, numéro de vente : F.84.XVII.11, publication des Nations Unies, New York, 1985, chap. IV.

[21] Les États membres de l'Organisation mondiale de la santé se réunissent annuellement dans le cadre de l'Assemblée mondiale de la santé, qui est l'organe directeur de l'Organisation.

[22] Organisation mondiale de la santé, *Classification statistique internationale des maladies et problèmes de santé connexes*, dixième révision, vol. 2, Genève, 1992.

[23] Organisation mondiale de la santé, *Classification statistique internationale des maladies et problèmes de santé connexes*, dixième révision, vol. 2, Genève, 1992, pp. 129-136.

Table A. *Demographic Yearbook 2005* synoptic table: Availability of data by country/area, table and sex, where applicable
Tableau A. Tableau synoptique de l'*Annuaire démographique 2005*: Disponibilité des données par pays ou zone, tableau et le sexe , si disponible

Continent, country or area / Continent, pays ou zone	Table totals	Summary - Apercu 3 Total	3 M/F	4	5	Population 6 Total	6 M/F	7 Total	7 M/F	8 Total	8 M/F	9	Natality - Natalité 10 Total	10 M/F	11	Foetal mortality - Mortalité foetale 12	13	14
Total number of countries or areas - Total des pays ou zones	..	232	220	178	215	218	211	197	192	218	120	169	136	97	104	88	61	43
AFRICA — AFRIQUE																		
Algeria - Algérie	18	•	•	•	•	•	•	•	•	•	...	•	...	...	•	•	...	...
Angola	3	•	•	•	...	•	...	•	...	•	...	...	...	...	...	...	...	...
Benin - Bénin	13	•	•	•	•	•	•	•	•	•	•	•	•	...	...	...	...	...
Botswana	18	•	•	•	•	•	•	•	•	•	•	•	•	...	...	...	...	...
Burkina Faso	9	•	•	...	•	•	•	•	•	•	•	•	...	...	...	...	...	...
Burundi	7	•	•	...	•	•	•	•	•	•	•	•	...	...	...	...	...	...
Cameroon - Cameroun	4	•	...	...	•	•	•	•	•	•	...	...	...	...	...	...	...	...
Cape Verde - Cap-Vert	10	•	•	•	•	•	•	•	•	•	...	•	...	...	...	...	...	...
Central African Republic - République centrafricaine	7	•	•	...	•	•	•	•	•	•	...	•	...	...	...	...	...	...
Chad - Tchad	6	•	•	...	•	•	•	•	•	•	...	•	...	...	...	...	...	...
Comoros - Comores	3	•	...	...	•	•	...	•	...	•	...	...	...	...	...	...	...	...
Congo	6	•	•	...	•	•	...	•	...	•	...	•	...	...	...	...	...	...
Côte d'Ivoire	6	•	•	•	•	•	•	•	...	•	...	...	...	...	...	...	...	...
Democratic Republic of the Congo - République démocratique du Congo	2	•	•	...	...	•	...	...	...	...	...	...	...	...	...	...	...	...
Djibouti	4	•	•	...	•	•	...	•	...	•	...	...	...	...	...	...	...	...
Egypt - Égypte	27	•	•	•	•	•	•	•	•	•	•	•	•	•	•	•	•	...
Equatorial Guinea - Guinée équatoriale	4	•	•	...	...	•	...	•	...	•	...	...	...	...	...	...	...	...
Eritrea - Érythrée	3	•	•	...	...	•	...	•	...	•	...	...	...	...	...	...	...	...
Ethiopia - Éthiopie	8	•	•	...	•	•	•	•	•	•	•	•	...	...	...	...	...	...
Gabon	4	•	...	...	•	•	...	•	...	•	...	•	...	...	...	...	...	...
Gambia - Gambie	7	•	•	•	•	•	•	•	•	•	...	•	...	...	...	...	...	...
Ghana	14	•	•	...	•	•	•	•	•	•	•	•	...	...	...	...	...	...
Guinea - Guinée	7	•	•	...	•	•	•	•	•	•	...	•	...	...	...	...	...	...
Guinea-Bissau - Guinée-Bissau	4	•	•	...	•	•	...	•	...	•	...	...	...	...	...	...	...	...
Kenya	17	•	•	•	•	•	•	•	•	•	•	•	•	•	...	...	...	...
Lesotho	10	•	•	•	•	•	•	•	•	•	•	•	...	...	...	...	...	...
Liberia - Libéria	4	•	•	...	•	•	...	•	...	•	...	...	...	...	...	...	...	...
Libyan Arab Jamahiriya - Jamahiriya arabe libyenne	17	•	•	•	•	•	•	•	•	•	•	•	•	...	...	...	...	...
Madagascar	8	•	•	•	•	•	•	•	•	•	...	•	...	...	...	...	...	...
Malawi	17	•	•	•	•	•	•	•	•	•	•	•	•	...	...	...	...	...
Mali	11	•	•	•	•	•	•	•	•	•	•	•	...	...	...	...	...	...
Mauritania - Mauritanie	8	•	•	...	•	•	•	•	•	•	•	•	...	...	...	...	...	...
Mauritius - Maurice	28	•	•	•	•	•	•	•	•	•	•	•	•	•	•	•	...	...
Morocco - Maroc	18	•	•	•	•	•	•	•	...	•	•	•	•	•	...	...	...	...
Mozambique	16	•	•	•	•	•	•	•	•	•	•	•	•	...	...	...	...	...
Namibia - Namibie	18	•	•	•	•	•	•	•	•	•	•	•	•	...	...	...	...	...
Niger	9	•	•	...	•	•	•	•	•	•	...	•	...	...	...	...	...	...
Nigeria - Nigéria	8	•	•	...	•	•	•	•	•	•	...	...	...	...	...	...	...	...
Réunion	29	•	•	•	•	•	•	•	•	•	•	•	•	•	•	•	•	•
Rwanda	8	•	•	...	•	•	•	•	•	•	•	...	...	...	...	...	...	...
Saint Helena ex. dep. - Sainte-Hélène sans dép.	22	•	•	•	•	•	•	•	•	•	•	•	•	•	•	...	...	...
Saint Helena: Ascension - Sainte-Hélène: Ascension	6	•	•	...	...	•	...	...	...	...	...	...	...	...	...	...	...	...
Saint Helena: Tristan da Cunha - Sainte-Hélène: Tristan da Cunha	7	•	•	...	•	•	•	•	•	•	...	...	...	...	...	...	...	...
Sao Tome and Principe - Sao Tomé-et-Principe	8	•	•	•	•	•	•	•	•	•	...	•	...	...	...	...	...	...
Senegal - Sénégal	6	•	•	...	•	•	•	•	...	•	...	...	...	...	...	...	...	...
Seychelles	18	•	•	•	•	•	•	•	•	•	•	•	•	•	...	•	...	...
Sierra Leone	7	•	•	...	•	•	•	•	•	•	...	...	...	...	...	...	...	...
Somalia - Somalie	7	•	•	...	•	•	...	•	...	•	•	...	...	...	...	...	...	...
South Africa - Afrique du Sud	21	•	•	•	•	•	•	•	•	•	•	•	•	•	...	...	•	...
Sudan - Soudan	6	•	•	...	•	•	•	•	•	•	...	...	...	...	...	...	...	...

Table A. *Demographic Yearbook 2005* synoptic table: Availability of data by country/area, table and sex, where applicable
Tableau A. Tableau synoptique de l'*Annuaire démographique 2005:* Disponibilité des données par pays ou zone, tableau et le sexe , si disponible (continued — suite)

Continent, country or area / Continent, pays ou zone	General topic and table number- Suject général et numéro de tableau													
	Infant and maternal mortality - Mortalité infantile et mortalité liée à la maternité				General mortality - Mortalité générale							Nuptiality and divorces - Nuptialité et divortialité		
	15	16 Total	16 M/F	17	18	19 Total	19 M/F	20 Total	20 M/F	21	22	23	24	25
Total number of countries or areas - Total des pays ou zones	142	105	...	107	171	148	145	94	94	107	129	134	90	117
AFRICA — AFRIQUE														
Algeria - Algérie	•	...	...	...	•	•	•	...	...	•	•	•	...	...
Angola	•	...	...	...	•	...	...	...	...	...	...	...	...	...
Benin - Bénin	•	...	...	...	•	•	...	...	...	...	•	...	...	...
Botswana	•	...	...	...	•	•	•	...	•	•	...	•	...	...
Burkina Faso	...	...	...	...	...	...	...	...	...	...	•	...	...	...
Burundi	...	...	...	...	...	...	...	...	...	...	...	...	...	...
Cameroon - Cameroun	...	...	...	...	...	...	...	...	...	...	...	...	...	...
Cape Verde - Cap-Vert	...	...	...	...	...	...	...	...	...	...	...	...	...	...
Central African Republic - République centrafricaine	...	...	...	...	...	...	...	...	...	...	...	...	...	...
Chad - Tchad	...	...	...	...	...	...	...	...	...	...	...	...	...	...
Comoros - Comores	...	...	...	...	...	...	...	...	...	...	...	...	...	...
Congo	...	...	...	...	...	...	...	...	...	...	...	...	...	...
Côte d'Ivoire	...	...	...	...	...	...	...	...	...	...	...	...	...	...
Democratic Republic of the Congo - République démocratique du Congo	...	...	...	...	...	...	...	...	...	...	...	...	...	...
Djibouti	...	...	...	...	...	...	...	...	...	...	...	•	...	...
Egypt - Égypte	•	•	...	...	•	•	•	...	•	•	•	•	...	•
Equatorial Guinea - Guinée équatoriale	...	...	...	...	...	...	...	...	...	...	...	...	...	...
Eritrea - Érythrée	...	...	...	...	...	...	...	...	...	...	...	...	...	...
Ethiopia - Éthiopie	...	...	...	...	...	...	...	...	...	...	...	...	...	...
Gabon	...	...	...	...	...	...	...	...	...	...	...	...	...	...
Gambia - Gambie	...	...	...	...	...	...	...	...	...	...	...	...	...	...
Ghana	•	...	...	...	...	...	...	...	...	...	...	...	...	...
Guinea - Guinée	...	...	...	...	...	...	...	...	...	...	...	...	...	...
Guinea-Bissau - Guinée-Bissau	...	...	...	...	...	...	...	...	...	...	...	...	...	...
Kenya	•	...	...	...	•	•	•	...	...	...	...	...	...	...
Lesotho	...	...	...	...	...	...	...	...	...	...	...	•	...	...
Liberia - Libéria	•	...	...	...	•	•	...	...	...	•	...	•	...	•
Libyan Arab Jamahiriya - Jamahiriya arabe libyenne	•	...	...	...	•	•	...	...	...	•	...	•	...	...
Madagascar	...	...	...	...	...	...	...	...	...	...	...	...	...	...
Malawi	...	...	...	...	•	•	•	...	...	...	...	...	...	...
Mali	...	...	...	...	...	...	...	...	...	...	...	...	...	...
Mauritania - Mauritanie	•	•	...	...	•	•	•	...	...	...	...	•	...	•
Mauritius - Maurice	•	•	...	...	•	•	•	...	...	•	•	•	...	•
Morocco - Maroc	•	...	...	...	•	•	•	...	...	...	...	...	...	...
Mozambique	•	...	...	...	•	•	•	...	...	...	...	...	...	...
Namibia - Namibie	...	...	...	...	•	•	•	...	...	...	...	...	...	...
Niger	...	...	...	...	...	...	...	...	...	...	...	...	...	...
Nigeria - Nigéria	•	•	...	•	•	•	•	...	...	•	...	•	...	•
Réunion	...	...	...	...	...	...	...	...	...	...	...	...	...	...
Rwanda	...	...	...	...	•	...	•	...	...	...	...	...	...	•
Saint Helena ex. dep. - Sainte-Hélène sans dép.	•	•	...	...	•	...	...	...	...	...	...	...	...	•
Saint Helena: Ascension - Sainte-Hélène: Ascension	...	...	...	...	...	...	...	...	...	...	...	...	...	...
Saint Helena: Tristan da Cunha - Sainte-Hélène: Tristan da Cunha	...	...	...	...	...	...	...	...	...	...	...	...	...	...
Sao Tome and Principe - Sao Tomé-et-Principe	...	...	...	...	...	...	...	...	...	...	...	...	...	...
Senegal - Sénégal	...	...	...	...	...	...	...	...	...	...	...	...	...	...
Seychelles	•	...	...	...	•	•	•	...	...	...	...	•	...	•
Sierra Leone	...	...	...	...	...	...	...	...	...	...	...	...	...	...
Somalia - Somalie	...	...	...	...	...	...	...	...	...	...	...	•	...	•
South Africa - Afrique du Sud	...	•	...	•	•	•	...	...	...	•	...	•	...	•
Sudan - Soudan	...	...	...	...	...	...	...	...	...	...	...	...	...	...

Table A. *Demographic Yearbook 2005* synoptic table: Availability of data by country/area, table and sex, where applicable
Tableau A. Tableau synoptique de l'*Annuaire démographique 2005*: Disponibilité des données par pays ou zone, tableau et le sexe , si disponible (continued — suite)

General topic and table number- Suject général et numéro de tableau

Continent, country or area / Continent, pays ou zone	Table totals	3 Total	3 M/F	4	5	6 Total	6 M/F	7 Total	7 M/F	8 Total	8 M/F	9	10 Total	10 M/F	11	12	13	14
AFRICA — AFRIQUE																		
Swaziland	15	•	•	…	•	•	•	•	•	•	•	…	…	•	•	…	…	…
Togo	4	•	•	…	•	•	…	•	…	•	…	…	…	…	…	…	…	…
Tunisia - Tunisie	16	•	…	•	•	•	•	•	•	•	•	…	•	•	…	…	…	…
Uganda - Ouganda	9	•	•	…	•	•	•	•	•	•	•	…	…	…	…	…	…	…
United Republic of Tanzania - République Unie de Tanzanie	9	•	•	…	•	•	•	•	•	•	•	…	…	…	…	…	…	…
Western Sahara - Sahara occidental	3	•	•	…	•	…	…	…	…	…	…	…	…	…	…	…	…	…
Zambia - Zambie	9	•	•	…	•	•	•	•	•	•	•	…	…	…	…	…	…	…
Zimbabwe	16	•	•	•	•	•	•	•	•	•	•	…	…	…	…	…	…	…
AMERICA, NORTH — AMERIQUE DU NORD																		
Anguilla	21	•	•	•	•	•	•	•	•	•	•	…	•	•	•	•	•	…
Antigua and Barbuda - Antigua-et-Barbuda	13	•	•	•	•	•	•	•	•	•	•	…	•	•	•	…	…	…
Aruba	22	•	•	•	•	•	•	•	•	•	•	•	•	•	•	•	…	…
Bahamas	23	•	•	•	•	•	•	•	•	•	•	•	•	•	•	•	…	…
Barbados - Barbade	15	•	•	•	•	•	•	•	•	•	•	…	•	•	•	…	…	…
Belize	20	•	•	•	•	•	•	•	•	•	•	…	•	•	•	…	…	…
Bermuda - Bermudes	22	•	•	•	•	•	•	•	•	•	•	…	•	•	•	•	…	…
British Virgin Islands - Îles Vierges britanniques	17	•	•	•	•	•	•	•	•	•	•	…	•	•	•	…	…	…
Canada	29	•	•	•	•	•	•	•	•	•	•	•	•	•	•	•	•	…
Cayman Islands - Îles Caïmanes	17	•	•	•	•	•	•	•	•	•	•	…	•	•	•	…	…	…
Costa Rica	27	•	•	•	•	•	•	•	•	•	•	•	•	•	•	…	…	…
Cuba	28	•	•	•	•	•	•	•	•	•	•	•	•	•	•	•	…	…
Dominica - Dominique	15	•	•	•	•	•	•	•	•	•	•	…	•	•	…	…	…	…
Dominican Republic - République dominicaine	21	•	•	•	•	•	•	•	•	•	•	…	•	•	•	…	…	…
El Salvador	28	•	•	•	•	•	•	•	•	•	•	…	•	•	•	…	…	…
Greenland - Groenland	22	•	•	•	•	•	•	•	•	•	•	•	•	•	…	…	…	…
Grenada - Grenade	18	•	•	•	•	•	•	•	•	•	•	…	•	•	•	…	…	…
Guadeloupe	28	•	•	•	•	•	•	•	•	•	•	…	•	•	•	•	…	…
Guatemala	24	•	…	•	•	•	•	•	•	•	•	…	•	•	•	…	…	…
Haiti - Haïti	12	•	•	•	•	•	•	•	•	•	•	…	…	…	…	…	…	…
Honduras	8	•	•	…	•	•	•	•	…	•	…	…	…	…	…	…	…	…
Jamaica - Jamaïque	22	•	•	•	•	•	•	•	•	•	•	…	•	•	•	…	…	…
Martinique	28	•	•	•	•	•	•	•	•	•	•	…	•	•	•	•	…	…
Mexico - Mexique	28	•	•	•	•	•	•	•	•	•	•	•	•	•	•	•	•	•
Montserrat	12	•	•	…	•	•	•	•	•	•	•	…	•	•	…	…	…	…
Netherlands Antilles - Antilles néerlandaises	24	•	•	•	•	•	•	•	•	•	•	…	•	•	•	…	…	…
Nicaragua	22	•	•	•	•	•	•	•	•	•	•	…	•	•	•	…	…	…
Panama	28	•	•	•	•	•	•	•	•	•	•	•	•	•	•	•	•	…
Puerto Rico - Porto Rico	29	•	•	•	•	•	•	•	•	•	•	…	•	•	•	•	•	…
Saint Kitts and Nevis - Saint-Kitts-et-Nevis	16	•	•	•	•	•	•	•	•	•	•	…	•	•	…	…	…	…
Saint Lucia - Sainte-Lucie	28	•	•	•	•	•	•	•	•	•	•	…	•	•	•	…	…	…
Saint Pierre and Miquelon - Saint Pierre-et-Miquelon	6	•	•	…	•	•	…	…	…	…	…	…	…	…	…	…	…	…
Saint Vincent and the Grenadines - Saint Vincent-et-les Grenadines	24	•	•	•	•	•	•	•	•	•	•	…	•	•	•	…	…	…
Trinidad and Tobago - Trinité-et-Tobago	26	•	•	•	•	•	•	•	•	•	•	…	•	•	•	…	…	…
Turks Caicos Islands - Îles Turques et Caïques	25	•	•	•	•	•	•	•	•	•	•	…	•	•	•	…	…	…
United States - États-Unis	24	•	•	•	•	•	•	•	•	•	•	…	•	•	•	…	…	…
United States Virgin Islands - Îles Vierges américaines	13	•	•	•	•	•	…	•	…	•	…	…	•	…	…	…	…	…
AMERICA, SOUTH — AMERIQUE DU SUD																		
Argentina - Argentine	23	•	•	•	•	•	•	•	•	•	•	…	•	•	•	•	…	…
Bolivia - Bolivie	10	•	•	…	•	•	•	•	•	•	•	…	…	…	…	…	…	…

34

Table A. *Demographic Yearbook 2005* synoptic table: Availability of data by country/area, table and sex, where applicable

Tableau A. Tableau synoptique de l'*Annuaire démographique 2005:* Disponibilité des données par pays ou zone, tableau et le sexe , si disponible (continued — suite)

Continent, country or area / Continent, pays ou zone	Infant and maternal mortality - Mortalité infantile et mortalité liée à la maternité				General mortality - Mortalité générale							Nuptiality and divorces - Nuptialité et divortialité		
	15	16 Total	16 M/F	17	18	19 Total	19 M/F	20 Total	20 M/F	21	22	23	24	25
AFRICA — AFRIQUE														
Swaziland	…	…	…	…	…	•	•	•	•	…	•	…	…	…
Togo	…	…	…	…	…	…	…	…	…	…	…	…	…	…
Tunisia - Tunisie	…	•	…	…	•	•	…	•	…	…	…	•	…	…
Uganda - Ouganda	…	…	…	…	…	…	…	…	…	…	…	…	…	…
United Republic of Tanzania - République Unie de Tanzanie	…	…	…	…	…	…	…	…	…	…	…	…	…	…
Western Sahara - Sahara occidental	…	…	…	…	…	…	…	…	…	…	…	…	…	…
Zambia - Zambie	…	…	…	…	…	…	…	…	…	…	…	…	…	…
Zimbabwe	…	…	…	…	•	•	•	•	…	…	•	…	…	…
AMERICA, NORTH — AMERIQUE DU NORD														
Anguilla	•	…	…	•	•	•	•	…	…	…	…	•	•	•
Antigua and Barbuda - Antigua-et-Barbuda	•	…	…	•	•	•	…	…	…	…	…	•	•	•
Aruba	•	…	…	•	•	•	•	•	…	…	…	•	•	…
Bahamas	•	•	…	•	•	•	•	•	•	…	•	•	•	…
Barbados - Barbade	•	…	…	•	•	•	•	•	…	…	…	•	•	…
Belize	•	…	…	•	•	•	•	…	…	…	…	•	•	•
Bermuda - Bermudes	•	•	…	•	•	•	•	•	…	…	…	•	•	•
British Virgin Islands - Îles Vierges britanniques	…	•	…	•	•	•	•	•	•	…	…	•	•	•
Canada	…	•	…	•	•	•	•	•	•	…	…	•	•	…
Cayman Islands - Îles Caïmanes	…	•	…	•	•	•	•	•	…	…	…	•	•	…
Costa Rica	•	•	…	•	•	•	•	•	•	…	…	•	•	•
Cuba	•	•	…	•	•	•	•	•	•	…	•	•	•	…
Dominica - Dominique	•	…	…	•	•	•	•	…	…	…	…	…	…	…
Dominican Republic - République dominicaine	…	…	…	•	•	•	•	•	•	…	…	•	•	•
El Salvador	•	…	…	•	•	•	•	…	…	…	…	•	•	…
Greenland - Groenland	•	•	…	…	•	•	•	•	…	…	…	•	•	…
Grenada - Grenade	•	…	…	•	•	•	•	…	…	…	…	•	•	•
Guadeloupe	•	•	…	•	•	•	•	•	•	…	…	•	•	•
Guatemala	•	•	…	•	•	•	•	•	•	…	…	•	•	…
Haiti - Haïti	…	…	…	•	•	•	•	…	…	…	…	…	…	…
Honduras	…	…	…	•	•	•	…	…	…	…	…	…	…	…
Jamaica - Jamaïque	•	…	…	•	•	•	•	…	…	…	…	•	•	•
Martinique	•	•	…	•	•	•	•	•	•	…	…	•	•	•
Mexico - Mexique	•	•	…	•	•	•	•	•	•	…	…	•	•	•
Montserrat	…	•	…	•	•	•	…	…	…	…	…	…	…	•
Netherlands Antilles - Antilles néerlandaises	•	•	…	•	•	•	•	•	•	…	…	•	•	•
Nicaragua	•	•	…	•	•	•	•	…	…	…	…	•	•	•
Panama	•	•	…	•	•	•	•	•	•	…	…	•	•	•
Puerto Rico - Porto Rico	•	•	…	•	•	•	•	•	•	…	…	•	•	•
Saint Kitts and Nevis - Saint-Kitts-et-Nevis	…	…	…	•	•	•	•	…	…	…	…	…	…	…
Saint Lucia - Sainte-Lucie	•	•	…	•	•	•	•	•	…	…	…	…	…	…
Saint Pierre and Miquelon - Saint Pierre-et-Miquelon	…	…	…	…	…	…	…	…	…	…	…	…	…	…
Saint Vincent and the Grenadines - Saint Vincent-et-les Grenadines	•	•	…	•	•	•	•	…	…	•	•	•	•	•
Trinidad and Tobago - Trinité-et-Tobago	•	•	…	•	•	•	•	•	•	…	•	•	•	•
Turks Caicos Islands - Îles Turques et Caïques	•	…	…	•	•	•	•	…	…	•	•	•	•	•
United States - États-Unis	•	•	…	•	•	•	•	•	•	…	•	•	•	•
United States Virgin Islands - Îles Vierges américaines	…	…	…	…	•	•	•	…	…	…	…	…	…	…
AMERICA, SOUTH — AMERIQUE DU SUD														
Argentina - Argentine	•	•	…	•	•	•	•	•	•	…	•	•	…	…
Bolivia - Bolivie	…	…	…	…	…	…	…	…	…	…	•	…	…	…

Table A. *Demographic Yearbook 2005* synoptic table: Availability of data by country/area, table and sex, where applicable

Tableau A. Tableau synoptique de l'*Annuaire démographique 2005:* Disponibilité des données par pays ou zone, tableau et le sexe , si disponible (continued — suite)

Continent, country or area / Continent, pays ou zone	Table totals	Summary - Aperçu 3 Total	3 M/F	4	5	Population 6 Total	6 M/F	7 Total	7 M/F	8 Total	8 M/F	Natality 9	10 Total	10 M/F	11	Foetal mortality 12	13	14
AMERICA, SOUTH — AMERIQUE DU SUD																		
Brazil - Brésil	24	•	•	•	•	•	•	•	•	•	...	•	•	•	•	•	...	...
Chile - Chili	27	•	•	•	•	•	•	•	•	•	•	•	•	•	•	•	...	...
Colombia - Colombie	21	•	•	•	•	•	•	•	•	•	•	•	•	•	...	...	...	...
Ecuador - Équateur	23	•	•	•	•	•	•	•	•	•	•	•	•	•	...	...	...	...
Falkland Islands (Malvinas) - Îles Falkland (Malvinas)	8	•	•	...	...	•	•	•	•	•	•	...	...	...	...	...	...	...
French Guiana - Guyane française	26	•	•	•	•	•	•	•	•	•	•	•	...	...	•	•	...	...
Guyana	13	•	•	•	•	•	•	•	•	•	...	•	...	...	...	...	...	...
Paraguay	19	•	•	•	•	•	•	•	•	•	•	•	...	...	...	...	...	...
Peru - Pérou	19	•	•	•	•	•	•	•	•	•	•	•	...	...	...	...	...	...
Suriname	24	•	•	•	•	•	•	•	•	•	•	•	...	...	•	•	...	...
Uruguay	27	•	•	•	•	•	•	•	•	•	•	•	•	•	...	•	...	...
Venezuela (Bolivarian Republic of) - Venezuela (République bolivarienne du)	26	•	•	•	•	•	•	•	•	•	•	•	•	•	•	•	...	...
ASIA — ASIE																		
Afghanistan	8	•	•	•	•	•	•	...	...	•		•		...	...	...	...	...
Armenia - Arménie	27	•	•	•	•	•	•	•	•	•	•	•	•	•	...	...	...	...
Azerbaijan - Azerbaïdjan	30	•	•	•	•	•	•	•	•	•	•	•	•	•	...	...	...	•
Bahrain - Bahreïn	27	•	•	•	•	•	•	•	•	•	•	•	•	•	...	...	...	...
Bangladesh	11	•	•	•	•	•	•	•	•	•	...	•	...	...	...	...	...	...
Bhutan - Bhoutan	20	•	•	•	•	•	•	•	•	•	•	•	•	•	...	...	...	...
Brunei Darussalam - Brunéi Darussalam	25	•	•	•	•	•	•	•	•	•	•	•	•	•	...	...	...	...
Cambodia - Cambodge	15	•	•	•	•	•	•	•	•	•	•	•	...	...	...	...	...	...
China - Chine[1]	17	•	•	•	•	•	•	•	•	•	•	•	•	•	...	...	...	...
China: Hong Kong SAR - Chine: Hong Kong RAS	30	•	•	•	•	•	•	•	•	•	•	•	•	•	...	...	...	•
China: Macao SAR - Chine: Macao RAS	27	•	•	•	•	•	•	•	•	•	•	•	•	•	...	...	...	•
Cyprus - Chypre	25	•	•	•	•	•	•	•	•	•	...	•	•	•	...	...	...	...
Georgia - Géorgie	25	•	•	•	•	•	•	•	•	•	...	•	•	•	•	•	...	...
India - Inde[2]	14	•	•	•	•	•	•	•	•	•	•	•	...	...	...	...	...	...
Indonesia - Indonésie	8	•	•	...	...	•	•	•	•	•		•		...	...	...	...	...
Iran (Islamic Republic of) - Iran (République islamique d')	15	•	•	•	•	•	•	•	•	•	•	•	•	•	...	...	...	...
Iraq	15	•	•	•	•	•	•	•	•	•	•	•	...	...	•	•	...	...
Israel - Israël[3]	30	•	•	•	•	•	•	•	•	•	•	•	•	•	...	•	•	•
Japan - Japon	30	•	•	•	•	•	•	•	•	•	•	•	•	•	...	•	•	•
Jordan - Jordanie	14	•	•	•	•	•	•	•	•	•	•	•	...	...	...	...	...	...
Kazakhstan	30	•	•	•	•	•	•	•	•	•	•	•	•	•	...	...	...	...
Korea (Dem. People's Republic of) - Corée (Rép. populaire dém. de)	4	•	•	...	...	...	...	•				•			...	...	...	...
Korea (Republic of) - Corée (République de)	26	•	•	•	•	•	•	•	•	•	•	•	•	•	...	...	...	...
Kuwait - Koweït	27	•	•	•	•	•	•	•	•	•	•	•	•	•	...	...	...	...
Kyrgyzstan - Kirghizistan	30	•	•	•	•	•	•	•	•	•	•	•	•	•	•	•	...	•
Lao People's Democratic Republic - République démocratique populaire lao	10	•	•	•	•	•	•	•	•	•	•	...	...	...	...	...	...	...
Lebanon - Liban	9	•	•	•	•	•	...	...	...	•		•		...	...	...	...	...
Malaysia - Malaisie	18	•	•	•	•	•	•	•	•	•	•	•	...	...	...	...	...	...
Maldives	26	•	•	•	•	•	•	•	•	•	•	•	•	•	...	•	•	...
Mongolia - Mongolie	26	•	•	•	•	•	•	•	•	•	•	•	•	•	...	...	...	...
Myanmar	7	•	•	...	...	•	•	•	•	○		•		...	...	...	...	...
Nepal - Népal	17	•	•	•	•	•	•	•	•	•	•	•	...	...	...	...	...	...
Occupied Palestinian Territory - Territoire palestinien occupé	20	•	•	•	•	•	•	•	•	○		•		...	...	...	...	...
Oman	17	•	•	•	•	•	•	•	•	•	•	•	...	...	•	•	...	...
Pakistan[4]	23	•	•	•	•	•	•	•	•	•	•	•	•	•	•	...	...	...

Table A. *Demographic Yearbook 2005* synoptic table: Availability of data by country/area, table and sex, where applicable

Tableau A. Tableau synoptique de l'*Annuaire démographique 2005:* Disponibilité des données par pays ou zone, tableau et le sexe , si disponible (continued — suite)

Continent, country or area / Continent, pays ou zone	Infant and maternal mortality - Mortalité infantile et mortalité liée à la maternité				General mortality - Mortalité générale							Nuptiality and divorces - Nuptialité et divortialité		
	15	16 Total	16 M/F	17	18	19 Total	19 M/F	20 Total	20 M/F	21	22	23	24	25
AMERICA, SOUTH — AMERIQUE DU SUD														
Brazil - Brésil	•	•	...	•	•	•	•	...	...	•	•	•	•	•
Chile - Chili	•	•	...	•	•	•	•	•	•	•	•	•	•	...
Colombia - Colombie	•	•	...	•	•	•	•	•	...	•	•	...	...	...
Ecuador - Équateur	•	•	...	•	•	•	•	...	...	•	•	•	•	•
Falkland Islands (Malvinas) - Îles Falkland (Malvinas)	...	...	...	...	...	...	...	...	...	...	...	•	•	•
French Guiana - Guyane française	•	•	...	•	•	•	•	•	...	•	•	•	•	•
Guyana	•	...	...	•	•	•	•	•	...	•	•	•	•	•
Paraguay	•	•	...	•	•	•	•	•	...	•	•	•	•	•
Peru - Pérou	•	•	...	•	•	•	•	•	...	•	•	•	•	•
Suriname	•	•	...	•	•	•	•	•	...	•	•	•	•	•
Uruguay	•	•	...	•	•	•	•	•	...	•	•	•	•	•
Venezuela (Bolivarian Republic of) - Venezuela (République bolivarienne du)	•	•	...	•	•	•	•	...	...	•	•	•	•	•
ASIA — ASIE														
Afghanistan	...	...	...	...	...	...	...	...	...	•	...	...	...	...
Armenia - Arménie	•	...	...	•	•	•	•	•	...	•	•	•	•	•
Azerbaijan - Azerbaïdjan	•	•	...	•	•	•	•	•	...	•	•	•	•	•
Bahrain - Bahreïn	•	•	...	•	•	•	•	•	...	•	•	•	•	•
Bangladesh	•	•	...	•	•	•	•	...	...	•	...	...	...	...
Bhutan - Bhoutan	•	...	...	...	•	•	•	...	...	•	...	...	...	...
Brunei Darussalam - Brunéi Darussalam	•	...	...	...	•	•	•	...	...	•	...	•	•	•
Cambodia - Cambodge	...	...	...	...	•	•	•	...	...	•	•	•	•	•
China - Chine[1]	...	...	...	...	•	•	•	•	...	•	•	•	•	•
China: Hong Kong SAR - Chine: Hong Kong RAS	•	•	...	•	•	•	•	•	...	•	•	•	•	•
China: Macao SAR - Chine: Macao RAS	•	•	...	•	•	•	•	•	...	•	•	•	•	•
Cyprus - Chypre	•	•	...	•	•	•	•	•	...	•	•	•	•	•
Georgia - Géorgie	•	•	...	•	•	•	•	•	...	•	•	•	•	•
India - Inde[2]	...	...	...	...	...	...	...	...	...	•	...	...	...	...
Indonesia - Indonésie	...	...	...	...	...	...	...	...	...	...	...	...	...	...
Iran (Islamic Republic of) - Iran (République islamique d')	...	...	...	...	•	•	•	...	...	•	...	...	...	•
Iraq	•	...	...	...	•	...	...	...	...	•	•	•	•	•
Israel - Israël[3]	•	•	...	•	•	•	•	•	...	•	•	•	•	•
Japan - Japon	•	•	...	•	•	•	•	•	...	•	•	•	•	•
Jordan - Jordanie	...	...	...	...	•	...	...	...	...	•	•	•	•	•
Kazakhstan	•	•	...	•	•	•	•	•	...	•	•	•	•	•
Korea (Dem. People's Republic of) - Corée (Rép. populaire dém. de)	...	...	...	...	...	...	...	...	...	...	...	...	...	...
Korea (Republic of) - Corée (République de)	•	...	...	•	•	•	•	•	...	•	•	•	•	•
Kuwait - Koweït	•	•	...	•	•	•	•	•	...	•	•	•	•	•
Kyrgyzstan - Kirghizistan	•	•	...	•	•	•	•	•	...	•	•	•	•	•
Lao People's Democratic Republic - République démocratique populaire lao	...	...	...	...	...	...	...	...	...	•	...	•	•	•
Lebanon - Liban	...	...	...	...	•	•	•	...	...	•	...	•	•	•
Malaysia - Malaisie	•	...	...	...	•	•	•	•	...	•	•	•	•	•
Maldives	•	•	...	•	•	•	•	•	...	•	•	•	•	•
Mongolia - Mongolie	•	•	...	•	•	•	•	•	...	•	•	•	•	•
Myanmar	...	...	...	...	...	...	...	...	...	•	...	•	•	•
Nepal - Népal	•	...	...	...	•	•	•	...	...	•	...	...	...	...
Occupied Palestinian Territory - Territoire palestinien occupé	•	•	...	•	•	•	•	...	...	•	•	•	•	•
Oman	•	...	...	...	•	•	•	...	...	...	...	...	...	...
Pakistan[4]	•	•	...	•	•	•	•	...	...	•	•	...	...	...

Table A. *Demographic Yearbook 2005* synoptic table: Availability of data by country/area, table and sex, where applicable
Tableau A. Tableau synoptique de l'*Annuaire démographique 2005:* Disponibilité des données par pays ou zone, tableau et le sexe , si disponible (continued — suite)

Continent, country or area / Continent, pays ou zone	Table totals	Summary - Apercu 3 Total	3 M/F	4	5	Population 6 Total	6 M/F	7 Total	7 M/F	8 Total	8 M/F	9	Natality 10 Total	10 M/F	11	12	13	14
ASIA — ASIE																		
Philippines	26	•	•	•	•	•	•	•	•	•	•	•	•	•	•	•	…	…
Qatar	29	•	•	•	•	•	•	•	•	•	•	•	•	•	•	•	•	…
Saudi Arabia - Arabie saoudite	22	•	•	•	•	•	•	•	•	•	•	•	•	•	•	•	…	…
Singapore - Singapour	29	•	•	•	•	•	•	•	•	•	…	•	•	•	•	•	•	•
Sri Lanka	22	•	•	•	•	•	•	•	•	•	•	•	•	•	•	•	…	…
Syrian Arab Republic - République arabe syrienne	14	•	•	•	•	•	•	•	•	•	…	•	…	…	…	•	…	…
Tajikistan - Tadjikistan	17	•	•	•	•	•	•	…	•	•	•	•	•	•	•	•	•	•
Thailand - Thaïlande	19	•	•	•	•	•	•	•	•	•	•	•	•	•	•	•	…	…
Timor-Leste	5	•	•	…	…	•	•	•	•	…	…	…	…	…	…	…	…	…
Turkey - Turquie	19	•	•	•	•	•	•	•	•	•	•	•	•	•	•	•	…	…
Turkmenistan - Turkménistan	5	•	•	…	…	•	•	…	…	…	…	…	…	…	…	…	…	…
United Arab Emirates - Émirats arabes unis	7	•	•	•	•	•	•	•	•	•	•	•	…	…	…	…	…	…
Uzbekistan - Ouzbékistan	25	•	•	•	•	•	•	•	•	•	•	•	•	•	•	•	•	•
Viet Nam	10	•	•	•	•	•	•	•	•	•	•	•	…	…	…	…	…	…
Yemen - Yémen	15	•	•	•	•	•	•	•	•	•	•	•	•	…	…	…	…	…
EUROPE																		
Albania - Albanie	27	•	•	•	•	•	…	•	•	•	•	•	•	•	•	•	…	•
Andorra - Andorre	21	•	•	•	•	•	•	•	•	•	•	•	•	•	•	•	…	…
Austria - Autriche	28	•	•	•	•	•	•	•	•	•	•	•	•	•	•	•	•	…
Belarus - Bélarus	29	•	•	•	•	•	•	•	•	•	•	•	•	•	…	•	…	•
Belgium - Belgique	26	•	•	•	•	•	•	•	•	•	•	•	•	•	•	•	•	•
Bosnia and Herzegovina - Bosnie-Herzégovine	20	•	•	•	•	•	•	•	•	•	•	…	•	•	•	•	•	•
Bulgaria - Bulgarie	30	•	•	•	•	•	•	•	•	•	•	•	•	•	•	•	•	•
Channel Islands: Guernsey - Îles Anglo-Normandes: Guernesey	15	•	•	…	•	•	•	•	•	•	•	…	…	•	•	•	•	•
Channel Islands: Jersey - Îles Anglo-Normandes: Jersey	14	•	•	•	•	•	•	•	•	•	•	…	…	…	•	•	…	…
Croatia - Croatie	29	•	•	•	•	•	•	•	•	•	•	•	•	•	•	•	•	•
Czech Republic - République tchèque	30	•	•	•	•	•	•	•	•	•	•	•	•	•	•	•	•	•
Denmark - Danemark	30	•	•	•	•	•	•	•	•	•	•	•	•	•	•	•	•	•
Estonia - Estonie	29	•	•	•	•	•	•	•	•	•	•	•	•	•	•	•	•	•
Faeroe Islands - Îles Féroé	11	•	…	•	…	•	•	…	…	•	•	•	•	•	•	•	•	•
Finland - Finlande	30	•	•	•	•	•	•	•	•	•	•	•	•	•	•	•	•	•
France	30	•	•	•	•	•	•	•	•	•	•	•	•	•	•	•	•	•
Germany - Allemagne	30	•	•	•	•	•	•	•	•	•	•	•	•	•	•	•	•	•
Gibraltar	18	•	•	•	•	•	•	•	•	•	•	•	•	•	•	…	…	…
Greece - Grèce	29	•	•	•	•	•	•	•	•	•	•	•	•	•	•	•	•	•
Holy See - Saint-Siège	6	•	•	•	•	•	•	•	•	•	…	…	…	…	…	…	…	…
Hungary - Hongrie	30	•	•	•	•	•	•	•	•	•	•	•	•	•	•	•	•	•
Iceland - Islande	30	•	•	•	•	•	•	•	•	•	•	•	•	•	•	•	•	•
Ireland - Irlande	28	•	•	•	•	•	•	•	•	•	•	•	•	•	•	•	…	•
Isle of Man - Îles de Man	20	•	•	•	•	•	•	•	•	•	•	•	•	•	•	…	…	…
Italy - Italie	30	•	•	•	•	•	•	•	•	•	•	•	•	•	•	•	•	•
Latvia - Lettonie	30	•	•	•	•	•	•	•	•	•	•	•	•	•	•	•	•	•
Liechtenstein	21	•	•	•	•	•	•	•	•	•	•	•	•	•	•	•	…	…
Lithuania - Lituanie	30	•	•	•	•	•	•	•	•	•	•	•	•	•	•	•	•	•
Luxembourg	27	•	•	•	•	•	•	•	•	•	•	•	•	•	•	•	…	…
Malta - Malte	27	•	•	•	•	•	•	•	•	•	•	•	•	•	•	•	…	…
Monaco	14	•	•	•	•	•	•	•	•	•	•	…	…	…	•	•	…	…
Netherlands - Pays-Bas	29	•	•	•	•	•	•	•	•	•	•	•	•	•	•	•	•	…
Norway - Norvège	30	•	•	•	•	•	•	•	•	•	•	•	•	•	•	•	•	•
Poland - Pologne	30	•	•	•	•	•	•	•	•	•	•	•	•	•	•	•	•	•
Portugal	28	•	•	•	•	•	•	•	•	•	•	•	•	•	•	•	…	…
Republic of Moldova - République de Moldova	28	•	•	•	•	•	•	•	•	•	…	•	•	•	•	•	…	•

Table A. *Demographic Yearbook 2005* synoptic table: Availability of data by country/area, table and sex, where applicable
Tableau A. Tableau synoptique de l'*Annuaire démographique 2005:* Disponibilité des données par pays ou zone, tableau et le sexe , si disponible (continued — suite)

Continent, country or area / Continent, pays ou zone	General topic and table number - Suject général et numéro de tableau													
	Infant and maternal mortality - Mortalité infantile et mortalité liée à la maternité			General mortality - Mortalité générale							Nuptiality and divorces - Nuptialité et divortialité		
	15	16 Total	16 M/F	17	18	19 Total	19 M/F	20 Total	20 M/F	21	22	23	24	25
ASIA — ASIE														
Philippines	•	•	...	•	•	•	•	•	•	•	...	•	•	...
Qatar	•	•	...	•	•	•	•	•	•	•	•	•	•	•
Saudi Arabia - Arabie saoudite	•	...	...	•	•	•	•	•	•	•	...	•	•	•
Singapore - Singapour	•	•	...	•	•	•	•	•	•	•	•	•	•	•
Sri Lanka	•	...	...	•	•	•	•	•	•	•	...	•	•	•
Syrian Arab Republic - République arabe syrienne	...	...	...	•	...	...	...	...	...	...	...	•	•	•
Tajikistan - Tadjikistan	...	...	...	•	•	•	•	•	•	...	...	•	•	•
Thailand - Thaïlande	...	...	...	•	•	•	...	•	...	...	...	•	...	•
Timor-Leste	...	...	...	...	...	...	...	...	...	...	...	...	...	...
Turkey - Turquie	•	•	...	•	•	...	...	...	...	•	...	•	•	•
Turkmenistan - Turkménistan	...	...	...	•	•	•	...	•	...	...	...	•	...	•
United Arab Emirates - Émirats arabes unis	...	...	...	•	•	•	...	•	...	...	...	•	...	•
Uzbekistan - Ouzbékistan	...	...	...	•	•	...	...	...	...	...	...	•	...	•
Viet Nam	...	...	...	...	...	...	...	...	...	...	...	•	...	•
Yemen - Yémen	...	...	...	•	...	...	...	•	...	...	...	•	...	•
EUROPE														
Albania - Albanie	•	•	...	•	•	•	•	•	•	•	•	•	•	•
Andorra - Andorre	•	•	...	•	•	•	•	•	•	•	•	•	•	...
Austria - Autriche	•	•	•	•	•	•	•	•	•	•	•	•	•	•
Belarus - Bélarus	•	•	•	•	•	•	•	•	•	•	•	•	•	•
Belgium - Belgique	•	•	•	•	•	•	•	•	•	•	•	•	•	•
Bosnia and Herzegovina - Bosnie-Herzégovine	•	•	•	•	•	•	•	•	•	•	•	•	•	•
Bulgaria - Bulgarie	•	•	•	•	•	•	•	•	•	•	•	•	•	•
Channel Islands: Guernsey - Îles Anglo-Normandes: Guernesey	...	...	...	•	•	...	...	...	...	...	...	...	...	...
Channel Islands: Jersey - Îles Anglo-Normandes: Jersey	...	...	...	•	•	...	...	...	...	...	...	•	•	•
Croatia - Croatie	•	•	...	•	•	•	•	•	•	•	•	•	•	•
Czech Republic - République tchèque	•	•	•	•	•	•	•	•	•	•	•	•	•	•
Denmark - Danemark	•	•	•	•	•	•	•	•	•	•	•	•	•	•
Estonia - Estonie	•	•	•	•	•	•	•	•	•	•	•	•	•	•
Faeroe Islands - Îles Féroé	•	•	•	•	•	•	•	•	•	•	•	•	•	•
Finland - Finlande	•	•	•	•	•	•	•	•	•	•	•	•	•	•
France	•	•	•	•	•	•	•	•	•	•	•	•	•	•
Germany - Allemagne	•	•	•	•	•	•	•	•	•	•	•	•	•	•
Gibraltar	•	...	...	•	•	...	...	...	...	•	•	•	•	•
Greece - Grèce	•	•	...	•	•	•	•	•	•	•	•	•	•	•
Holy See - Saint-Siège	...	...	...	...	...	...	...	...	...	...	...	...	...	...
Hungary - Hongrie	•	•	•	•	•	•	•	•	•	•	•	•	•	•
Iceland - Islande	•	•	•	•	•	•	•	•	•	•	•	•	•	•
Ireland - Irlande	•	•	...	•	•	•	•	...	...	•	•	•	•	•
Isle of Man - Îles de Man	•	•	...	•	•	•	•	...	...	•	•	•	•	•
Italy - Italie	•	•	•	•	•	•	•	•	•	•	•	•	•	•
Latvia - Lettonie	•	•	•	•	•	•	•	•	•	•	•	•	•	•
Liechtenstein	•	...	...	•	•	•	•	•	•	•	•	•	...	•
Lithuania - Lituanie	•	•	•	•	•	•	•	•	•	•	•	•	•	•
Luxembourg	•	•	•	•	•	•	•	•	•	•	•	•	•	•
Malta - Malte	•	•	...	•	•	•	•	•	•	•	•	•	•	...
Monaco	...	...	...	•	...	...	...	...	...	•	...	•	•	•
Netherlands - Pays-Bas	•	•	•	•	•	•	•	•	•	•	•	•	•	•
Norway - Norvège	•	•	•	•	•	•	•	•	•	•	•	•	•	•
Poland - Pologne	•	•	...	•	•	•	•	•	•	•	•	•	•	•
Portugal	•	•	...	•	•	•	•	•	•	•	•	•	•	•
Republic of Moldova - République de Moldova	•	•	...	•	•	•	•	•	•	•	•	•	•	•

Table A. *Demographic Yearbook 2005* synoptic table: Availability of data by country/area, table and sex, where applicable
Tableau A. Tableau synoptique de l'*Annuaire démographique 2005*: Disponibilité des données par pays ou zone, tableau et le sexe , si disponible (continued — suite)

Continent, country or area / Continent, pays ou zone	Table totals	Summary - Apercu				Population							Natality - Natalité			Foetal mortality - Mortalité foetale		
		3 Total	3 M/F	4	5	6 Total	6 M/F	7 Total	7 M/F	8 Total	8 M/F	9	10 Total	10 M/F	11	12	13	14
EUROPE																		
Romania - Roumanie	30	•	•	•	•	•	•	•	•	•	•	•	•	•	•	•	•	•
Russian Federation - Fédération de Russie	29	•	•	•	•	•	•	•	•	•	•	•	•	•	…	•	•	•
San Marino - Saint-Marin	25	•	•	•	•	•	•	•	•	•	•	•	•	•	…	•	•	•
Serbia and Montenegro - Serbie-et-Montenegro	30	•	•	•	•	•	•	•	•	•	•	•	•	•	•	•	•	•
Slovakia - Slovaquie	30	•	•	•	•	•	•	•	•	•	•	•	•	•	•	•	•	•
Slovenia - Slovénie	30	•	•	•	•	•	•	•	•	•	•	•	•	•	•	•	•	•
Spain - Espagne	30	•	•	•	•	•	•	•	•	•	•	•	•	•	•	•	•	•
Sweden - Suède	30	•	•	•	•	•	•	•	•	•	•	•	•	•	•	•	•	•
Switzerland - Suisse	28	•	•	•	•	•	•	•	•	•	•	•	•	•	…	•	•	…
The Former Yugoslav Rep. of Macedonia - L'ex-République yougoslave de Macédoine	29	•	•	•	•	•	•	•	•	•	•	•	•	•	•	•	•	•
Ukraine	30	•	•	•	•	•	•	•	•	•	•	•	•	•	•	•	•	•
United Kingdom - Royaume-Uni	28	•	•	•	•	•	•	•	•	•	•	•	•	•	•	•	•	…
OCEANIA — OCEANIE																		
American Samoa - Samoas américaines	19	•	•	•	•	•	•	•	•	•	•	…	•	•	…	…	…	…
Australia - Australie	28	•	•	•	•	•	•	•	•	•	•	•	•	•	…	•	•	…
Cook Islands - Îles Cook	12	•	•	•	•	•	…	•	•	•	…	…	•	…	…	…	…	…
Fiji - Fidji	16	•	•	•	•	•	•	•	•	•	•	…	•	…	…	…	…	…
French Polynesia - Polynésie française	13	•	…	•	•	•	•	•	•	•	•	…	•	…	…	…	…	…
Guam	16	•	•	•	•	•	•	•	•	•	•	•	•	…	…	…	…	…
Kiribati	10	•	…	…	•	•	•	…	•	•	…	…	•	…	…	…	…	…
Marshall Islands - Îles Marshall	17	•	•	•	•	•	•	•	•	•	•	…	•	…	…	…	…	…
Micronesia, Federated States of - Micronésie (États fédérés de)	13	•	•	•	•	•	•	•	•	•	•	…	•	…	…	…	…	…
Nauru	8	•	•	•	•	…	•	…	•	…	…	…	•	…	…	…	…	…
New Caledonia - Nouvelle-Calédonie	27	•	•	•	•	•	•	•	•	•	•	•	•	•	•	•	•	•
New Zealand - Nouvelle-Zélande	30	•	•	•	•	•	•	•	•	•	•	•	•	•	•	•	•	•
Niue - Nioué	13	•	•	•	•	•	•	•	•	•	•	…	•	…	…	…	…	…
Norfolk Island - Île Norfolk	7	•	•	•	•	…	•	…	•	…	…	…	•	…	…	…	…	…
Northern Mariana Islands - Îles Mariannes septentrionales	15	•	•	•	•	•	…	•	…	•	…	•	•	…	…	…	…	…
Palau - Palaos	17	•	•	•	•	•	•	•	•	•	•	…	•	…	•	…	…	…
Papua New Guinea - Papouasie-Nouvelle-Guinée	15	•	•	•	•	•	•	•	•	•	•	…	•	…	•	…	…	…
Pitcairn	2	•	…	…	…	…	…	…	•	…	…	…	…	…	…	…	…	…
Samoa	14	•	•	•	…	•	•	…	•	•	•	…	•	…	…	…	…	…
Solomon Islands - Îles Salomon	6	•	•	…	•	…	…	…	•	…	…	…	•	…	…	…	…	…
Tokelau - Tokélaou	8	•	•	•	…	•	…	…	•	…	…	…	•	…	…	…	…	…
Tonga	21	•	•	•	•	•	•	•	•	•	•	•	•	…	•	…	…	…
Tuvalu	18	•	•	•	•	•	•	•	•	•	•	•	•	…	…	…	…	…
Vanuatu	9	•	•	•	•	…	•	…	•	…	…	…	•	…	…	…	…	…
Wallis and Futuna Islands - Îles Wallis et Futuna	14	•	•	•	…	•	•	…	•	•	…	…	•	…	…	…	…	…

Table A. *Demographic Yearbook 2005* synoptic table: Availability of data by country/area, table and sex, where applicable
Tableau A. Tableau synoptique de l'*Annuaire démographique 2005:* Disponibilité des données par pays ou zone, tableau et le sexe , si disponible (continued — suite)

Continent, country or area / Continent, pays ou zone	15	16 Total	16 M/F	17	18	19 Total	19 M/F	20 Total	20 M/F	21	22	23	24	25
EUROPE														
Romania - Roumanie	•	•	…	•	•	•	•	•	•	•	•	•	•	•
Russian Federation - Fédération de Russie	•	•	…	•	•	•	•	•	•	•	•	•	•	•
San Marino - Saint-Marin	•	•	…	•	•	•	•	…	…	•	•	•	•	•
Serbia and Montenegro - Serbie-et-Montenegro	•	•	…	•	•	•	•	•	•	•	•	•	•	•
Slovakia - Slovaquie	•	•	…	•	•	•	•	•	•	•	•	•	•	•
Slovenia - Slovénie	•	•	…	•	•	•	•	•	•	•	•	•	•	•
Spain - Espagne	•	•	…	•	•	•	•	•	•	•	•	•	•	•
Sweden - Suède	•	•	…	•	•	•	•	•	•	•	•	•	•	•
Switzerland - Suisse	•	•	…	•	•	•	•	•	•	•	•	•	•	•
The Former Yugoslav Rep. of Macedonia - L'ex-République yougoslave de Macédoine	•	•	…	•	•	•	•	•	•	•	•	•	•	•
Ukraine	•	•	…	•	•	•	•	•	•	•	•	•	•	•
United Kingdom - Royaume-Uni	•	•	…	•	•	•	•	•	•	•	•	•	•	•
OCEANIA — OCEANIE														
American Samoa - Samoas américaines	•	…	…	…	•	…	…	…	…	•	…	…	…	…
Australia - Australie	•	•	…	•	•	•	•	•	•	•	•	•	•	•
Cook Islands - Îles Cook	•	…	…	…	•	•	…	…	…	•	…	…	…	…
Fiji - Fidji	•	…	…	…	•	•	…	…	…	•	…	…	…	…
French Polynesia - Polynésie française	•	…	…	…	•	•	…	…	…	•	…	…	…	…
Guam	•	…	…	…	•	•	…	…	…	•	…	…	…	…
Kiribati	…	…	…	…	…	…	…	…	…	•	…	…	…	…
Marshall Islands - Îles Marshall	…	…	…	…	•	•	…	…	…	•	…	…	…	…
Micronesia, Federated States of - Micronésie (États fédérés de)	…	…	…	…	…	…	…	…	…	•	…	…	…	…
Nauru	…	…	…	…	…	…	…	…	…	•	…	…	…	…
New Caledonia - Nouvelle-Calédonie	•	•	…	…	•	•	…	…	…	•	•	•	•	…
New Zealand - Nouvelle-Zélande	•	•	…	•	•	•	•	•	•	•	•	•	•	•
Niue - Nioué	…	…	…	…	…	…	…	…	…	•	…	…	…	…
Norfolk Island - Île Norfolk	…	…	…	…	…	…	…	…	…	•	…	…	…	…
Northern Mariana Islands - Îles Mariannes septentrionales	•	…	…	…	•	•	…	…	…	•	…	•	•	…
Palau - Palaos	•	…	…	…	•	…	…	…	…	•	…	•	•	…
Papua New Guinea - Papouasie-Nouvelle-Guinée	•	…	…	…	…	…	…	…	…	•	…	…	…	…
Pitcairn	…	…	…	…	…	…	…	…	…	•	…	…	…	…
Samoa	…	…	…	…	•	•	…	…	…	•	…	•	•	…
Solomon Islands - Îles Salomon	…	…	…	…	…	…	…	…	…	•	…	…	…	…
Tokelau - Tokélaou	…	…	…	…	…	…	…	…	…	•	…	…	…	…
Tonga	•	•	…	…	•	•	…	…	…	•	…	•	…	•
Tuvalu	•	…	…	…	•	•	…	…	…	•	…	•	•	…
Vanuatu	…	…	…	…	•	•	…	…	…	•	…	…	…	…
Wallis and Futuna Islands - Îles Wallis et Futuna	…	…	…	…	•	•	…	•	…	•	…	…	…	…

FOOTNOTES - NOTES

• Data presented in the table - Les données présentées dans le tableau.

… Data not available - Données pas disponibles.

[1] For statistical purposes, the data for China do not include those for the Hong Kong Special Administrative Region (Hong Kong SAR), Macao special Administrative Region (Macao SAR) and Taiwan province of China. - Pour la présentation des statistiques, les données pour Chine ne comprend pas la Région Administrative Spéciale de Hong Kong (Hong Kong RAS), la Région Administrative Spéciale de Macao (Macao RAS) et Taïwan province de Chine.

[2] Including data for the Indian-held part of Jammu and Kashmir, the final status of which has not yet been determined. - Y compris les données pour la partie du Jammu et du Cachemire occupée par l'Inde dont le statut définitif n'a pas encore été déterminé.

[3] Including data for East Jerusalem and Israeli residents in certain other territories under occupation by Israeli military forces since June 1967. - Y compris les données pour Jérusalem-Est et les résidents israéliens dans certains autres territoires occupés depuis 1967 par les forces armées israéliennes.

[4] Excluding data for the Pakistan-held part of Jammu and Kashmir, the final status of which has not yet been determined. - Non compris les données concernant la partie du Jammu et Cachemire occupée par le Pakistan dont le statut définitif n'a pas été déterminé.

Table 1

Table 1 presents for the world, major areas and regions estimates of the order of magnitude of population size, rates of population increase, crude birth and death rates, surface area as well as population density.

Description of variables: Estimates of world population by major areas and by regions are presented for 1950, 1960, 1970, 1980, 1990, 2000 and 2005. The average annual percentage rates of population growth, the crude birth and crude death rates are shown for the period 2000 to 2005. Surface area in square kilometers and population density estimates relate to 2005.

All population estimates and rates presented in this table were prepared by the Population Division of the United Nations, Department of Economic and Social Affairs, and have been published in *World Population Prospects: The 2006 Revision, CD Rom Edition – Extended Dataset*[1].

The scheme of regionalization used for these estimates is described below. Although some continental totals are given, and all can be derived, the basic scheme presents six major areas that are so drawn as to obtain greater homogeneity in sizes of population, types of demographic circumstances and accuracy of demographic statistics. Five of the major areas are subdivided into a total of 20 regions, which are arranged within the major areas; these regions together with Northern America, which is not subdivided, make a total of 21 regions.

The major areas of Northern America and Latin America are distinguished, rather than the conventional continents of North America and South America, because population trends in the middle American mainland and the Caribbean region more closely resemble those of South America than those of America north of Mexico. Data for the traditional continents of North and South America can be obtained by adding Central America and Caribbean region to Northern America and deducting from Latin America. Latin America, as defined here, has somewhat wider limits than it would be if defined only to include the Spanish-speaking, French-speaking and Portuguese-speaking countries.

The average annual percentage rates of population growth are calculated by the Population Division, United Nations Department of Economic and Social Affairs, using an exponential rate of increase.

Crude birth and crude death rates are expressed in terms of the average annual number of births and deaths, respectively, per 1 000 mid-year population. These rates are estimated.

Surface area totals are estimated by Population Division, United Nations Department of Economic and Social Affairs.

Computation: Density, calculated by the Statistics Division of the United Nations Department of Social and Economic Affairs, is the number of persons in the 2005 total population per square kilometer of total surface area.

Reliability of data: With the exception of surface area, all data are set in *italic* type to indicate their conjectural quality.

Limitations: The estimated orders of magnitude of population and surface area are subject to all the basic limitations set forth in connection with table 3, and to the same qualifications set forth for population and surface area statistics in sections 3 and 2.4 of the Technical Notes, respectively.

Likewise, the rates of population increase and the density index are affected by the limitations of the original figures. However, it may be noted that, in compiling data for regional and major areas totals, errors in the components may tend to compensate each other and the resulting aggregates may be more reliable than the quality of the individual components would imply.

Because of their estimated character, many of the birth and death rates shown should also be considered only as orders of magnitude, and not as measures of the true level of natality or mortality.

In interpreting the population densities, one should consider that some of the regions include large segments of land that are uninhabitable or barely habitable, and density values calculated as described make no allowance for this, nor for differences in patterns of land settlement.

Composition of macro geographical regions and sub-regions

AFRICA

Eastern Africa
Burundi
Comoros
Djibouti
Eritrea
Ethiopia
Kenya
Madagascar
Malawi
Mauritius
Mozambique
Réunion
Rwanda
Seychelles
Somalia
Uganda
United Republic of Tanzania
Zambia
Zimbabwe

Middle Africa
Angola
Cameroon
Central African Republic
Chad
Congo
Democratic Republic of the
  Congo
Equatorial Guinea
Gabon
Sao Tome and Principe

Northern Africa
Algeria
Egypt
Libyan Arab Jamahiriya
Morocco
Sudan
Tunisia
Western Sahara

Southern Africa
Botswana
Lesotho
Namibia
South Africa
Swaziland

Western Africa

Benin
Burkina Faso
Cape Verde
Côte d'Ivoire
Gambia
Ghana

Guinea
Guinea-Bissau
Liberia
Mali
Mauritania
Niger
Nigeria
Saint Helena
Senegal
Sierra Leone
Togo

ASIA

Eastern Asia
China
China - Hong Kong SAR
China - Macao SAR
Japan
Korea, Democratic People's
  Republic of
Korea, Republic of
Mongolia

South-central Asia
Afghanistan
Bangladesh
Bhutan
India
Iran (Islamic Republic of)
Kazakhstan
Kyrgyzstan
Maldives
Nepal
Pakistan
Sri Lanka
Tajikistan
Turkmenistan
Uzbekistan

South-eastern Asia
Brunei Darussalam
Cambodia
Indonesia
Lao People's Democratic
  Republic
Malaysia
Myanmar
Philippines
Singapore
Thailand
Timor Leste
Viet Nam

Western Asia
Armenia
Azerbaijan
Bahrain

Cyprus
Georgia
Iraq
Israel
Jordan
Kuwait
Lebanon
Occupied Palestinian Territory
Oman
Qatar
Saudi Arabia
Syrian Arab Republic
Turkey
United Arab Emirates
Yemen

EUROPE

Eastern Europe
Belarus
Bulgaria
Czech Republic
Hungary
Poland
Republic of Moldova
Romania
Russian Federation
Slovakia
Ukraine

Northern Europe
Channel Islands
Denmark
Estonia
Faeroe Islands
Finland
Iceland
Ireland
Isle of Man
Latvia
Lithuania
Norway
Sweden
United Kingdom of Great Britain
  and Northern Ireland

Southern Europe
Albania
Andorra
Bosnia and Herzegovina
Croatia
Gibraltar
Greece
Holy See
Italy
Malta
Portugal

San Marino
Serbia and Montenegro
Slovenia
Spain
The Former Yugoslav Republic
of Macedonia

Western Europe
Austria
Belgium
France
Germany
Liechtenstein
Luxembourg
Monaco
Netherlands
Switzerland

LATIN AMERICA
and the CARIBBEAN

Caribbean
Anguilla
Antigua and Barbuda
Aruba
Bahamas
Barbados
British Virgin Islands
Cayman Islands
Cuba
Dominica
Dominican Republic
Grenada
Guadaloupe
Haiti
Jamaica
Martinique
Montserrat
Netherlands Antilles
Puerto Rico

Saint Kitts and Nevis
Saint Lucia
Saint Vincent and the
Grenadines
Trinidad and Tobago
Turks and Caicos Islands
United States Virgin
Islands

Central America
Belize
Costa Rica
El Salvador
Guatemala
Honduras
Mexico
Nicaragua
Panama

South America
Argentina
Bolivia
Brazil
Chile
Colombia
Ecuador
Falkland Islands (Malvinas)
French Guiana
Guyana
Paraguay
Peru
Suriname
Uruguay
Venezuela (Bolivarian Republic
of)

NORTHERN AMERICA

Bermuda

Canada
Greenland
Saint Pierre and Miquelon
United States of America

OCEANIA

Australia and New Zealand
Australia
New Zealand
Norfolk Island

Melanesia
Fiji
New Caledonia
Papua New Guinea
Solomon Islands
Vanuatu

Micronesia
Guam
Kiribati
Marshall Islands
Micronesia (Federated States of)
Nauru
Northern Mariana Islands
Palau

Polynesia
American Samoa
Cook Islands
French Polynesia
Niue
Pitcairn
Samoa
Tokelau
Tonga
Tuvalu
Wallis and Futuna Islands

NOTES

[1] *World Population Prospects: The 2006 Revision, CD Rom Edition – Extended Dataset in Excel and ASCII formats* (United Nations publication, Sales No. E.07.XIII.7), New York 2007.

Tableau 1

Le tableau 1 présente, pour l'ensemble du monde et les grandes zones et régions, des estimations concernant l'ordre de grandeur de la population, les taux d'accroissement démographique, les taux bruts de natalité et de mortalité, la superficie et la densité de peuplement.

Description des variables : des estimations de la population mondiale par grandes zones et régions sont présentées pour 1950, 1960, 1970, 1980, 1990 et 2000 ainsi que pour 2005. Les taux annuels moyens d'accroissement de la population et les taux bruts de natalité et de mortalité portent sur la période allant de 2000 à 2005. Les indications concernant la superficie exprimée en kilomètres carrés et les estimations de la densité de population se rapportent à 2005.

Toutes les estimations de population et les taux de natalité, taux de mortalité et taux annuels d'accroissement de la population qui sont présentés dans le tableau 1 ont été établis par la Division de la population du Département des affaires économiques et sociales (Secrétariat de l'Organisation des Nations Unies), et ont été publiés dans *World Population Prospects: The 2006 Revision, CD Rom Edition – Extended Dataset*[1].

Bien que l'on ait donné certains totaux pour les continents (tous les autres pouvant être calculés), on a réparti le monde en huit grandes zones qui ont été découpées de manière à obtenir une plus grande homogénéité du point de vue des dimensions de population, des types de situations démographiques et de l'exactitude des statistiques démographiques.

Cinq de ces huit grandes zones ont été subdivisées en 20 régions. Avec l'Amérique septentrionale, qui n'est pas subdivisée, on arrive à un total de 21 régions.

Au lieu de faire la distinction classique entre l'Amérique du Nord et l'Amérique du Sud, on a choisi d'opérer une comparaison entre l'Amérique septentrionale et l'Amérique latine, parce que les tendances démographiques dans la partie continentale de l'Amérique centrale et dans la région des Caraïbes se rapprochent davantage de celles de l'Amérique du Sud que de celles de l'Amérique au nord du Mexique. On obtient les données pour les continents traditionnels de l'Amérique du Nord et de l'Amérique du Sud en extrayant les données concernant l'Amérique centrale et les Caraïbes de celles relatives à l'Amérique latine et en les regroupant avec celles relatives à l'Amérique septentrionale. L'Amérique latine ainsi définie a par conséquent des limites plus larges que celles des pays ou zones de langues espagnole, portugaise et française qui constituent l'Amérique latine au sens le plus strict du terme.

La Division de la population a calculé les taux annuels moyens d'accroissement de la population en appliquant un taux d'accroissement exponentiel.

Les taux bruts de natalité et de mortalité représentent respectivement le nombre annuel moyen de naissances et de décès par millier d'habitants en milieu d'année. Ces taux sont estimatifs.

La superficie totale a été estimée par la Division de la population du Département des affaires économiques et sociales.

Calculs : la densité, calculée par la Division de statistique du Département des affaires économiques et sociales, est égale au rapport entre l'effectif total de la population en 2004 et la superficie totale exprimée en kilomètres carrés.

Fiabilité des données : á l'exception des données concernant la superficie, toutes les données sont reproduites en *italique* pour en faire ressortir le caractère conjectural.

Insuffisance des données : les estimations concernant l'ordre de grandeur de la population et la superficie reposent en partie sur les données du tableau 3 ; elles appellent donc toutes les réserves fondamentales formulées à propos de ce tableau, et celles qui ont été respectivement formulées aux sections 3 et 2.4 des Notes techniques en ce qui concerne les statistiques relatives à la population et à la superficie.

Les taux d'accroissement et les indices de densité de la population se ressentent eux aussi des insuffisances inhérentes aux données de base. Toutefois, il est à noter que, lorsque l'on additionne des données par territoire pour obtenir des totaux régionaux et par grandes zones, les erreurs qu'elles comportent arrivent parfois à s'équilibrer, de sorte que les agrégats obtenus peuvent être un peu plus exacts que chacun des éléments dont on est parti.

Vu leur caractère estimatif, nombre des taux de natalité et de mortalité du tableau 1 doivent être considérés uniquement comme des ordres de grandeur et ne sont pas censés mesurer exactement le niveau de la natalité ou de la mortalité.

Parce que les totaux des superficies ont été obtenus en additionnant les chiffres pour chaque pays ou zones, qui apparaissent dans le tableau 3, ils ne comprennent pas les lieux où la population est inférieure à 50 personnes, tels que les régions polaires inhabitées.

Pour interpréter les valeurs de la densité de population, on se souviendra qu'il existe dans certaines des régions de vastes étendues de terres inhabitables ou à peine habitables et que les chiffres calculés selon la méthode indiquée ne tiennent compte ni de ce fait ni des différences de dispersion de la population selon le mode d'habitat.

Composition des grandes zones et régions

AFRIQUE

Afrique orientale
Burundi
Comores
Djibouti
Érythrée
Éthiopie
Kenya
Madagascar
Malawi
Maurice
Mozambique
Ouganda
République-Unie de Tanzanie
Réunion
Rwanda
Seychelles
Somalie
Zambie
Zimbabwe

Afrique centrale
Angola
Cameroun
Congo
Gabon
Guinée équatoriale
République centrafricaine
République démocratique du Congo
Sao Tomé-et-Principe
Tchad

Afrique septentrionale
Algérie
Égypte
Jamahiriya arabe libyenne
Maroc
Sahara occidental
Soudan
Tunisie

Afrique australe
Afrique du Sud
Botswana
Lesotho
Namibie
Swaziland

Afrique occidentale
Bénin
Burkina Faso
Cap-Vert
Côte d'Ivoire
Gambie
Ghana
Guinée
Guinée-Bissau
Libéria
Mali
Mauritanie
Niger
Nigéria
Sainte-Hélène
Sénégal
Sierra Leone
Togo

AMÉRIQUE LATINE ET CARAÏBES

Caraïbes
Anguilla
Antigua-et-Barbuda
Antilles néerlandaises
Aruba
Bahamas
Barbade
Cuba
Dominique
Grenade
Guadeloupe

Haïti
Îles Caïmanes
Îles Turques et Caïques
Îles Vierges américaines
Îles Vierges britanniques
Jamaïque
Martinique
Montserrat
Porto Rico
République dominicaine
Saint-Kitts-et-Nevis
Sainte-Lucie
Saint-Vincent-et-les Grenadines
Trinité-et-Tobago

Amérique centrale
Belize
Costa Rica
El Salvador
Guatemala
Honduras
Mexique
Nicaragua
Panama

Amérique du Sud
Argentine
Bolivie
Brésil
Chili
Colombie
Équateur
Guyana
Guyane française
Îles Falkland (Malvinas)
Paraguay
Pérou
Suriname
Uruguay
Venezuela (République bolivarienne du)

AMÉRIQUE SEPTENTRIONALE

Bermudes
Canada
États-Unis d'Amérique
Groenland
Saint-Pierre-et-Miquelon

ASIE

Asie orientale
Chine
Chine - Région administrative spéciale de Hong Kong
Chine - Région administrative spéciale de Macao
Japon
Mongolie
République de Corée
République populaire démocratique de Corée

Asie centrale et Asie du Sud
Afghanistan
Bangladesh
Bhoutan
Inde
Iran (République Islamique d')
Kazakhstan
Kirghizistan
Maldives
Népal
Ouzbékistan
Pakistan
Sri Lanka
Tadjikistan
Turkménistan

Asie du Sud-Est
Brunéi Darussalam
Cambodge
Indonésie
Malaisie
Myanmar
Philippines
République démocratique populaire lao
Singapour
Thaïlande
Timor-Leste
Viet Nam

Asie occidentale
Arabie saoudite
Arménie
Azerbaïdjan
Bahreïn
Chypre
Émirats arabes unis
Géorgie
Iraq
Israël
Jordanie
Koweït
Liban
Oman
Qatar
République arabe syrienne
Territoire palestinien occupé
Turquie
Yémen

EUROPE

Europe orientale
Bélarus
Bulgarie
Fédération de Russie
Hongrie
Pologne
République de Moldova
République tchèque
Roumanie
Slovaquie
Ukraine

Europe septentrionale
Danemark
Estonie
Finlande
Île de Man
Îles Anglo-Normandes
Îles Féroé
Îles Svalbard et Jan Mayen
Irlande
Islande
Lettonie
Lituanie
Norvège
Royaume-Uni de Grande-Bretagne et d'Irlande du Nord
Suède

Europe méridionale
Albanie
Andorre
Bosnie-Herzégovine
Croatie
Espagne
Ex-République yougoslave de Macédoine
Gibraltar
Grèce
Italie
Malte
Portugal
Saint-Marin
Saint-Siège
Serbie-et-Monténégro
Slovénie

Europe occidentale
Allemagne
Autriche
Belgique
France
Liechtenstein
Luxembourg
Monaco
Pays-Bas
Suisse

OCÉANIE

Australie et Nouvelle-Zélande
Australie
Île Norfolk
Nouvelle-Zélande

Mélanésie
Fidji
Îles Salomon
Nouvelle-Calédonie
Papouasie-Nouvelle-Guinée
Vanuatu

Micronésie
Guam
Îles Mariannes septentrionales
Îles Marshall
Kiribati
Micronésie (États fédérés de)
Nauru
Palaos

Polynésie
Îles Cook
Îles Wallis et Futuna
Nioué
Pitcairn
Polynésie française
Samoa
Samoa américaines
Tokélaou
Tonga
Tuvalu

---

[1] *World Population Prospects, The 2006 Revision, CD Rom Edition – Extended Dataset in Excel and ASCII formats* (numéro de vente : E.07.XIII.7, publication des Nations Unies, New York, 2007).

1. Population, rate of increase, birth and death rates, surface area and density for the world, major areas and regions: selected years
Population, taux d'accroissement, taux de natalité et taux de mortalité, superficie et densité pour l'ensemble du monde, les régions macro géographiques et les composantes géographiques: diverses années

Major areas and regions / Régions macro géographiques et composantes	Mid-year population estimates - Estimations de population au milieu de l'année (millions)							Annual rate of increase - Taux d'accroissement annuel (%)	Crude birth rate - Taux bruts de natalité	Crude death rate - Taux bruts de mortalité	Surface area (km2) - Superficie (km2) (000s)	Density - Densité[1]
	1950	1960	1970	1980	1990	2000	2005	2000 - 2005			2005	
WORLD TOTAL - ENSEMBLE DU MONDE	2 520	3 024	3 697	4 442	5 280	6 086	6 515	1.2	21	9	136 127	48
AFRICA - AFRIQUE	224	282	364	479	636	812	922	2.2	38	15	30 312	30
Eastern Africa - Afrique orientale	65	82	109	146	198	256	292	2.4	41	17	6 361	46
Middle Africa - Afrique centrale	26	32	41	54	73	96	112	2.6	46	20	6 613	17
Northern Africa - Afrique septentrionale	53	67	86	112	144	175	190	1.7	26	7	8 525	22
Southern Africa - Afrique méridionale	16	20	26	33	42	52	55	0.7	24	17	2 675	21
Western Africa - Afrique occidentale	64	80	102	134	178	234	272	2.4	42	18	6 138	44
LATIN AMERICA AND CARIBBEAN - AMERIQUE LATINE ET CARAIBES	167	219	285	362	444	523	558	1.4	22	6	20 546	27
Caribbean - Caraïbes	17	20	25	29	34	38	40	0.9	20	8	234	173
Central America - Amérique centrale	37	50	68	91	113	136	144	1.6	24	5	2 480	58
South America - Amérique du Sud	113	148	192	242	297	349	374	1.4	21	6	17 832	21
NORTHERN AMERICA - AMERIQUE SEPTENTRIONALE[2]	172	204	232	256	283	315	332	1.0	14	8	21 776	15
ASIA - ASIE[3]	1 396	1 699	2 140	2 630	3 169	3 676	3 938	1.2	20	8	31 880	124
Eastern Asia - Asie orientale	671	792	987	1 178	1 350	1 479	1 522	0.6	13	7	11 763	129
South Central Asia - Asie centrale méridionale	496	617	780	978	1 226	1 485	1 646	1.6	26	9	10 791	153
South Eastern Asia - Asie méridionale orientale	178	223	286	358	440	519	558	1.4	21	7	4 495	124
Western Asia - Asie occidentale[3]	51	67	88	116	154	193	212	2.1	26	6	4 831	44
EUROPE[3]	547	604	656	692	721	728	731	0.0	10	12	23 049	32
Eastern Europe - Europe orientale	220	254	276	295	311	305	298	-0.5	10	14	18 814	16
Northern Europe - Europe septentrionale	77	81	86	89	92	94	96	0.3	11	10	1 810	53
Southern Europe - Europe méridionale	109	118	127	138	143	146	150	0.4	10	10	1 317	114
Western Europe - Europe occidentale	141	152	166	170	176	184	187	0.2	10	10	1 108	168
OCEANIA - OCEANIE[2]	12.8	15.9	19.6	22.9	26.7	30.9	33.4	1.3	17	7	8 564	4
Australia and New Zealand - Australie et Nouvelle-Zélande	10.1	12.6	15.5	17.8	20.3	22.9	24.4	1.1	13	7	8 012	3
Melanesia - Melanésie	2.3	2.7	3.4	4.4	5.5	6.9	7.8	2.0	31	10	541	14
Micronesia - Micronésie	0.1	0.2	0.2	0.3	0.4	0.5	0.5	1.9	26	5	3	167
Polynesia - Polynésie	0.2	0.3	0.4	0.5	0.5	0.6	0.6	1.2	24	5	8	75

FOOTNOTES - NOTES

[1] Population per square kilometre of surface area. Figures are estimates of population divided by surface area and are not to be considered as either reflecting density in the urban sense or as indicating the supporting power of a territory's land and resources. — Habitants par kilomètre carré. Il s'agit simplement du quotient calculé en divisant la population par la superficie et n'est par considéré comme indiquant la densité au sens urbain du terme ni l'effectif de population que les terres et les ressources du territoire sont capables de nourrir.

[2] Hawaii, a state of the United States of America, is included in Northern America rather than in Oceania. — Hawaii, un Etat des Etats-Unis d'Amérique, est compris en Amérique septentrionale plutôt qu'en Océanie.

[3] The European part of Turkey is included in Western Asia rather than Europe. — La partie européenne de la Turquie est comprise en Asie Occidentale plutôt qu'en Europe.

Table 2

Table 2 presents estimates of population and the percentage distribution by age and sex as well as the sex ratio for all ages; data are presented for the world, the six major areas and the 20 regions for 2005.

Description of variables: All population estimates presented in this table are prepared by the Population Division of the United Nations Department of Economic and Social Affairs. These estimates were published (using more detailed age groups) in the *World Population Prospects: The 2006 Revision, CD Rom Edition – Extended Dataset*[1].

The scheme of regionalization used for these estimates is discussed in detail in the technical notes for table 1. Age groups presented in this table are: under 15 years, 15-64 years and 65 years and over. Sex ratio refers to the number of males per 100 females of all ages.

The percentage distributions and the sex ratios that appear in this table were calculated by the Statistics Division of the United Nations Department of Economic and Social Affairs using the Population Division estimates.

Reliability of data: All data are set in *italic* type to indicate their conjectural quality.

Limitations: The data presented in this table are from the same series of estimates, prepared by the Population Division, presented in table 1. The estimated orders of magnitude of population are subject to all the basic limitations set forth for population statistics in section 3 of the Technical Notes. In brief, because they are estimates, these distributions by broad age groups and sex should be considered only as orders of magnitude. However, in compiling data for regional and macro region totals, errors in the components tend to compensate each other and the resulting aggregates may be somewhat more reliable than the quality of the individual components would imply.

In addition, data in this table are limited by factors affecting data by age. These factors are described in the technical notes for table 7. Because the age groups presented in this table are so broad, these problems are minimized.

NOTES

[1] *World Population Prospects: The 2006 Revision, CD Rom Edition – Extended Dataset in Excel and ASCII formats* (United Nations publication, Sales No. E.07.XIII.7), New York 2007

Tableau 2

Le tableau 2 présente, pour l'ensemble du monde, les six grandes zones et les 20 régions, des estimations concernant la population en 2005 ainsi que sa répartition en pourcentage selon l'âge et le sexe, et le rapport de masculinité pour tous les âges.

Description des variables : Toutes les données figurant dans le tableau 2 ont été établies par la Division de la population du Département des affaires économiques et sociales (Secrétariat de l'Organisation des Nations Unies) et ont été publiées dans l'ouvrage intitulé *World Population Prospects: The 2006 Revision, CD Rom Edition – Extended Dataset* [1].

La classification géographique utilisée pour établir ces estimations est exposée en détail dans les notes techniques relatives au tableau 1. Les groupes d'âge présentés dans ce tableau sont définis comme suit : moins de 15 ans, de 15 à 64 ans et 65 ans et plus. Le rapport de masculinité correspond au nombre d'individus de sexe masculin pour 100 individus de sexe féminin sans considération d'âge.

Les pourcentages et les rapports de masculinité qui sont présentés dans le tableau 2 ont été calculés par la Division de statistique de l'ONU à partir des estimations établies par la Division de la population.

Fiabilité des données : toutes les données figurant dans ce tableau sont reproduites en *italique* pour en faire ressortir le caractère conjectural.

Insuffisance des données : Les données de ce tableau appartiennent à la même série d'estimations, établie par la Division de la population, que celles qui figurent au tableau 1. Les estimations concernant l'ordre de grandeur de la population appellent donc toutes les réserves fondamentales qui ont été formulées à la section 3 des Notes techniques à propos des statistiques relatives à la population. Sans entrer dans le détail, il convient de préciser que les données relatives à la répartition par grand groupe d'âge et par sexe doivent être considérées uniquement comme des ordres de grandeur en raison de leur caractère estimatif. Toutefois, il est à noter que, lorsque l'on additionne des données par territoire pour obtenir des totaux régionaux et par grandes zones, les erreurs qu'elles comportent arrivent parfois à s'équilibrer, de sorte que les agrégats obtenus peuvent être un peu plus exacts que chacun des éléments dont on est parti.

En outre, les donnés figurant dans le tableau 2 comportent certaines imprécisions en raison des facteurs influant sur les données par âge (voir à ce propos les notes techniques relatives au tableau 7). Ces imprécisions sont cependant atténuées du fait de l'étendue des groupes d'âge présentés dans le tableau 2.

NOTE

[1] *World Population Prospects: The 2006 Revision, CD Rom Edition – Extended Dataset in Excel and ASCII formats* (United Nations publication, Sales No. E.07.XIII.7), New York 2007

2. Estimates of population and its percentage distribution, by age and sex and sex ratio for all ages for the world, major areas and regions: 2005
Estimations de la population et pourcentage de répartition selon l'âge et le sexe et rapport de masculinité pour l'ensemble du monde, les grandes regions et les régions géographiques: 2005

Major areas and regions / Grandes régions et régions	Population (millions)											
	Both sexes - Les deux sexes				Male - Masculin				Female - Féminin			
	All ages - Tous âges	-15	15-64	65+	All ages - Tous âges	-15	15-64	65+	All ages - Tous âges	-15	15-64	65+
WORLD TOTAL - ENSEMBLE DU MONDE	6 515	1 845	4 192	477	3 283	951	2 122	210	3 232	894	2 071	268
AFRICA - AFRIQUE	922	382	509	31	459	193	252	14	463	189	256	17
Eastern Africa - Afrique orientale	293	130	154	8	145	65	76	4	148	65	78	5
Middle Africa - Afrique centrale	113	51	58	3	56	26	29	1	57	26	29	2
Northern Africa - Afrique septentrionale	190	63	118	9	95	32	59	4	95	31	59	5
Southern Africa - Afrique méridionale	55	18	35	2	27	9	17	1	28	9	18	1
Western Africa - Afrique occidentale	273	120	144	8	136	61	72	4	136	59	72	5
LATIN AMERICA AND CARIBBEAN - AMERIQUE LATINE ET CARAIBES	558	166	356	35	275	85	175	15	283	82	181	20
Caribbean - Caraïbes	41	11	26	3	20	6	13	1	20	6	13	2
Central America - Amérique centrale	144	47	89	8	70	24	43	4	73	23	46	4
South America - Amérique du Sud	374	108	242	24	185	55	119	10	189	53	122	14
NORTHERN AMERICA - AMERIQUE SEPTENTRIONALE[2]	332	68	223	41	164	35	111	17	169	33	112	24
ASIA - ASIE[3]	3 938	1 104	2 583	250	2 016	575	1 325	116	1 922	529	1 259	134
Eastern Asia - Asie orientale	1 522	318	1 071	133	781	169	551	62	741	149	521	71
South Central Asia - Asie centrale méridionaie	1 646	552	1 016	77	848	287	524	37	798	265	492	41
South Eastern Asia - Asie méridionale orientale	558	164	364	30	278	83	181	13	280	80	183	17
Western Asia - Asie occidentale	212	70	132	10	109	36	69	4	103	34	63	5
EUROPE[3]	731	116	499	116	352	60	247	45	379	57	252	71
Eastern Europe - Europe orientale	298	46	210	42	140	23	102	15	158	22	108	28
Northern Europe - Europe septentrionale	96	17	64	15	47	9	32	6	49	8	32	9
Southern Europe - Europe méridionale	150	23	101	26	74	12	51	11	77	11	50	15
Western Europe - Europe occidentale	187	30	124	32	91	16	62	13	95	15	62	19
OCEANIA - OCEANIE[2]	33.41	8.31	21.67	3.43	16.69	4.27	10.87	1.55	16.72	4.04	10.80	1.88
Australia and New Zealand - Australie et Nouvelle Zélande	24.41	4.84	16.40	3.16	12.12	2.49	8.21	1.42	12.29	2.36	8.19	1.74
Melanesia - Melanésie	7.82	3.08	4.53	0.21	3.98	1.59	2.29	0.10	3.84	1.49	2.24	0.11
Micronesia - Micronésie	0.54	0.17	0.34	0.02	0.27	0.09	0.17	0.01	0.27	0.08	0.17	0.01
Polynesia - Polynésie	0.65	0.22	0.39	0.03	0.33	0.11	0.20	0.02	0.31	0.11	0.19	0.02

2. Estimates of population and its percentage distribution, by age and sex and sex ratio for all ages for the world, major areas and regions: 2005
Estimations de la population et pourcentage de répartition selon l'âge et le sexe et rapport de masculinité pour l'ensemble du monde, les grandes régions et les régions géographiques: 2005 (continued — suite)

Major areas and regions / Grandes régions et régions	Percent - Pourcentage												Sex ratio - Rapport de masculinité[1]
	Both sexes - Les deux sexes				Male - Masculin				Female - Féminin				
	All ages - Tous âges	-15	15-64	65+	All ages - Tous âges	-15	15-64	65+	All ages - Tous âges	-15	15-64	65+	
WORLD TOTAL - ENSEMBLE DU MONDE	100.0	28.3	64.4	7.3	100.0	29.0	64.6	6.4	100.0	27.7	64.1	8.3	102
AFRICA - AFRIQUE	100.0	41.4	55.2	3.4	100.0	42.0	55.0	3.0	100.0	40.9	55.4	3.7	99
Eastern Africa - Afrique orientale	100.0	44.4	52.7	2.9	100.0	45.0	52.4	2.6	100.0	43.8	53.0	3.2	98
Middle Africa - Afrique centrale	100.0	45.6	51.5	2.9	100.0	46.2	51.3	2.5	100.0	45.1	51.7	3.2	98
Northern Africa - Afrique septentrionale	100.0	33.1	62.2	4.6	100.0	33.7	62.1	4.2	100.0	32.6	62.4	5.1	101
Southern Africa - Afrique méridionale	100.0	32.9	62.9	4.2	100.0	33.8	62.9	3.3	100.0	32.1	62.9	5.0	96
Western Africa - Afrique occidentale	100.0	43.9	53.0	3.1	100.0	44.4	52.7	2.9	100.0	43.4	53.2	3.4	100
LATIN AMERICA AND CARIBBEAN - AMERIQUE LATINE ET CARAIBES	100.0	29.8	63.9	6.3	100.0	30.7	63.7	5.6	100.0	28.9	64.1	6.9	97
Caribbean - Caraïbes	100.0	28.4	63.8	7.8	100.0	29.2	63.5	7.3	100.0	27.6	64.0	8.4	98
Central America - Amérique centrale	100.0	32.6	61.8	5.5	100.0	33.7	61.2	5.1	100.0	31.6	62.4	5.9	96
South America - Amérique du Sud	100.0	28.9	64.7	6.4	100.0	29.8	64.6	5.6	100.0	28.1	64.8	7.2	98
NORTHERN AMERICA - AMERIQUE SEPTENTRIONALE[2]	100.0	20.5	67.2	12.3	100.0	21.3	68.1	10.6	100.0	19.7	66.2	14.1	97
ASIA - ASIE[3]	100.0	28.0	65.6	6.4	100.0	28.5	65.7	5.8	100.0	27.5	65.5	7.0	105
Eastern Asia - Asie orientale	100.0	20.9	70.4	8.8	100.0	21.6	70.5	7.9	100.0	20.1	70.2	9.6	105
South Central Asia - Asie centrale méridionale	100.0	33.6	61.8	4.7	100.0	33.8	61.8	4.3	100.0	33.3	61.7	5.1	106
South Eastern Asia - Asie méridionale orientale	100.0	29.3	65.2	5.4	100.0	30.0	65.1	4.8	100.0	28.7	65.3	6.0	99
Western Asia - Asie occidentale	100.0	33.1	62.3	4.6	100.0	32.8	63.1	4.0	100.0	33.4	61.4	5.2	106
EUROPE[3]	100.0	15.9	68.2	15.9	100.0	16.9	70.2	12.9	100.0	14.9	66.4	18.7	93
Eastern Europe - Europe orientale	100.0	15.3	70.4	14.2	100.0	16.7	72.8	10.5	100.0	14.1	68.3	17.6	89
Northern Europe - Europe septentrionale	100.0	18.0	66.2	15.8	100.0	18.8	67.6	13.6	100.0	17.1	64.9	18.0	96
Southern Europe - Europe méridionale	100.0	15.1	67.4	17.6	100.0	15.8	69.1	15.1	100.0	14.3	65.7	19.9	96
Western Europe - Europe occidentale	100.0	16.3	66.4	17.2	100.0	17.1	68.5	14.4	100.0	15.6	64.5	19.9	96
OCEANIA - OCEANIE[2]	100.0	24.9	64.8	10.3	100.0	25.6	65.1	9.3	100.0	24.2	64.6	11.3	100
Australia and New Zealand - Australie et Nouvelle Zélande	100.0	19.8	67.2	12.9	100.0	20.5	67.8	11.7	100.0	19.2	66.6	14.2	99
Melanesia - Melanésie	100.0	39.4	57.9	2.7	100.0	39.9	57.5	2.6	100.0	38.8	58.3	2.9	103
Micronesia - Micronésie	100.0	32.1	63.7	4.3	100.0	33.2	62.9	3.9	100.0	30.9	64.5	4.6	99
Polynesia - Polynésie	100.0	34.1	60.7	5.2	100.0	34.4	61.0	4.7	100.0	33.8	60.5	5.7	105

FOOTNOTES - NOTES

[1] Males per 100 females of all ages - Hommes pour 100 femmes de tous âges

[2] Hawaii, a state of the United States of America, is included in Northern America rather than in Oceania. — Hawaii, un Etat des Etats-Unis d'Amérique, est compris en Amérique septentrionale plutôt qu'en Océanie.

[3] The European part of Turkey is included in Western Asia rather than Europe. — La partie européenne de la Turquie est comprise en Asie Occidentale plutôt qu'en Europe.

Table 3

Table 3 presents for each country or area of the world the total, male and female population enumerated at the latest population census, estimates of the mid-year total population for 2000 and 2005, the average annual exponential rate of increase (or decrease) for the period 2000 to 2005 the surface area and the population density for 2005.

Description of variables: The total, male and female population is, unless otherwise indicated, the *de facto* (present-in-area) population enumerated at the most recent census for which data are available. The date of this census is given. Population census data are usually the results of a nation-wide enumeration (traditional census). Alternatively other approaches for generating reliable statistics on population and housing can be used by countries, such as the use of population registers. Data that are the result of such an alternative approach are also coded as census and are footnoted accordingly. Also, the results of sample surveys, essentially national in character, may be presented showing the appropriate code. However, results of surveys referring to less than 50 percent of the total territory or population are not included.

Mid-year population estimates refer to the population on 1 July. Otherwise, a footnote is appended. Mid-year estimates of the total population are those provided by national statistical offices.

Surface area, expressed in square kilometres, refers to the total surface area, comprising land area and inland waters (assumed to consist of major rivers and lakes) and excluding Polar Regions as well as uninhabited islands. Exceptions to this are noted. Surface areas, originally reported in square miles by the country or area, have been converted to square kilometres using a conversion factor of 2.589988.

Computation: The annual rate of increase is the average annual percentage rate of population growth between 2000 and 2005, computed by the Statistics Division of the United Nations Department of Economic and Social Affairs using the unrounded mid-year estimates as presented in this table.

Density is the number of persons in the 2005 total population per square kilometre of total surface area.

Reliability of data: Reliable mid-year population estimates are those that are based on a complete census (or a sample survey) and have been adjusted by a continuous population register or on the basis of the calculated balance of births, deaths and migration. Mid-year estimates of this type are considered reliable and appear in roman type. Mid-year estimates not calculated on this basis are considered less reliable and are shown in italics. Estimates for years prior to 2005 are considered reliable or less reliable on the basis of the 2005 code and appear in roman type or in *italics*, accordingly.

Census data and sample survey results are considered reliable and, therefore, appear in roman type.

Rates of population increase that were calculated using population estimates considered less reliable, as described above, are set in italics rather than roman type.

All surface area data are assumed to be reliable and therefore appear in roman type.

Population density data, however, are considered reliable or less reliable on the basis of the reliability of the 2005 population estimates used as the numerator.

Limitations: Statistics on the total population enumerated at the time of the census, estimates of the mid-year total population and surface area data are subject to the same qualifications as have been set forth for population and surface area statistics in sections 3 and 2.4 of the Technical Notes, respectively.

Regarding the limitations of census data, it should be noted that although census data are considered reliable, and therefore appear in roman type, the actual quality of census data varies widely from one country or area to another. When known, an estimate of the extent of over-enumeration or under-enumeration is given in footnotes. In the case of sample surveys, a description of the population covered is provided.

Because the reliability of the population estimates for any given country or area is based on the quality of the 2005 estimate, the reliability of estimates prior to 2005 may be overstated.

Rates of population increase are subject to all the qualifications of the population estimates mentioned above. In some cases, they simply reflect the rate calculated or assumed in constructing the estimates themselves when adequate measures of natural increase and net migration were not available. Despite their shortcomings, these rates provide a useful index for studying population change and can be useful also in evaluating the accuracy of vital and migration statistics.

Population density data as shown in this table give only an indication of actual population density as they do not take account of the dispersion or concentration of population within countries or areas nor the proportion of habitable land. They should not be interpreted as reflecting density in the urban sense or as indicating the supporting power of a territory's land and resources.

Tableau 3

Le tableau 3 indique pour chaque pays ou zone du monde la population totale selon le sexe d'après les derniers recensements effectués, les estimations concernant la population totale au milieu de l'année 2000 et de l'année 2005, le taux moyen d'accroissement annuel exponentiel positif ou négatif pour la période allant de 2000 à 2005, ainsi que la superficie et la densité de population en 2005.

Description des variables : la population masculine et féminine totale est, sauf indication contraire, la population de fait (c'est-à-dire présente) enregistrée lors du recensement le plus récent sur lequel on dispose de données. La date de ce recensement est indiquée. Les données des recensements de la population sont habituellement obtenues au moyen d'un enregistrement à l'échelle nationale (recensement traditionnel). Les pays peuvent recourir à d'autres moyens pour établir des statistiques fiables sur la population et le logement, tels que des registres de la population. Les données obtenues par ce moyen sont présentées comme celles d'un recensement et sont annotées en conséquence. Par ailleurs, les résultats des enquêtes par sondage, réalisées habituellement à l'échelle nationale, peuvent être présentés à l'aide du code correspondant. En revanche, les résultats des enquêtes portant sur moins de 50 % du territoire total ou de la population ne sont pas indiqués.

Les estimations de la population en milieu d'année sont celles de la population au 1er juillet. Lorsque la date est différente, cela est signalé par une note. Les estimations de la population totale en milieu d'année sont celles qui ont été communiquées par les services nationaux de statistique.

La superficie - exprimée en kilomètres carrés - représente la superficie totale, c'est-à-dire qu'elle englobe les terres émergées et les eaux intérieures (qui sont censées comprendre les principaux lacs et cours d'eau) mais exclut les régions polaires et certaines îles inhabitées. Les exceptions à cette règle sont signalées en note. Les superficies initialement exprimées en miles carrés par les pays ou les zones ont été transformées en kilomètres carrés au moyen d'un coefficient de conversion de 2,589988.

Calculs : le taux d'accroissement annuel est le taux annuel moyen de variation (en pourcentage) de la population entre 2000 et 2005, calculé par la Division de statistique du Département des affaires économiques et sociales (Secrétariat de l'Organisation des Nations Unies) à partir des estimations en milieu d'année non arrondies qui figurent dans le tableau.

La densité est égale au rapport de l'effectif total de la population en 2005 à la superficie totale, exprimée en kilomètres carrés.

Fiabilité des données : les estimations en milieu d'année qui sont considérées sûres sont fondées sur un recensement complet (ou sur une enquête par sondage) et ont été ajustées en fonction des données provenant d'un registre permanent de population ou en fonction de la balance établie par le calcul des naissances, des décès et des migrations. Les estimations de ce type sont considérées comme sûres et apparaissent en caractères romains. Les estimations en milieu d'année dont le calcul n'a pas été effectué sur cette base sont considérées comme moins sûres et apparaissent en italique. Les estimations relatives aux années antérieures à 2005 sont jugées plus ou moins sûres en fonction du codage de 2005 et indiquées, selon le cas, en caractères romains ou en italique.

Les données de recensements ou les résultats d'enquêtes par sondage sont considérés comme sûrs et apparaissent par conséquent en caractères romains.

Les taux d'accroissement de la population, calculés à partir d'estimations jugées moins sûres d'après les normes décrites ci-dessus, sont indiqués en italique plutôt qu'en caractères romains.

Toutes les données de superficie sont présumées sûres et apparaissent par conséquent en caractères romains. En revanche, les données relatives à la densité de la population sont considérées plus ou moins sûres en fonction de la fiabilité des estimations de la population en 2005 ayant servi de numérateur.

Insuffisance des données : les statistiques portant sur la population totale dénombrée lors d'un recensement, les estimations de la population totale en milieu d'année et les données de superficie appellent les mêmes réserves que celles formulées aux sections 3 et 2.4 des Notes techniques à propos des statistiques relatives à la population et à la superficie.

S'agissant de l'insuffisance des données obtenues par recensement, il convient d'indiquer que, bien que ces données soient considérées comme sûres et apparaissent par conséquent en caractères romains, leur qualité réelle varie considérablement d'un pays ou d'une région à l'autre. Lorsque l'on possédait les renseignements voulus, on a donné une estimation du degré de sur-dénombrement ou de sous-dénombrement. Dans le cas des enquêtes par sondage, une description de la population considérée est fournie.

La fiabilité des estimations de la population d'un pays ou zone quelconque reposant sur la qualité des estimations de 2005, il se peut que la fiabilité des estimations antérieures à 2005 soit surévaluée.

Les taux d'accroissement appellent toutes les réserves formulées plus haut à propos des estimations concernant la population. Dans certains cas, ils représentent seulement le taux calculé ou que l'on a pris pour base pour établir les estimations elles-mêmes lorsque l'on ne disposait pas de mesures appropriées de l'accroissement naturel et des migrations nettes. Malgré leurs imperfections, ces taux fournissent des indications intéressantes pour l'étude du mouvement de la population et, utilisés avec les précautions nécessaires, ils peuvent également servir à évaluer l'exactitude des statistiques de l'état civil et des migrations.

Les données relatives à la densité de population figurant dans le tableau 3 n'ont qu'une valeur indicative en ce qui concerne la densité de population effective, car elles ne tiennent compte ni de la dispersion ou de la concentration de la population à l'intérieur des pays ou zones, ni de la proportion du territoire qui est habitable. Il ne faut donc y voir d'indication ni de la densité au sens urbain du terme ni du nombre d'habitants qui pourraient vivre sur les terres et avec les ressources naturelles du territoire considéré.

3. Population by sex, rate of population increase, surface area and density
Population selon le sexe, taux d'accroissement de la population, superficie et densité

| Continent, country or area and census date / Continent, pays ou zone et date du recensement | Census type[1] | Latest available census — Dernier recensement disponible (in units — en unités) | | | Estimate type[1] | Mid-year estimates - Estimations au milieu de l'année (in thousands — en milliers) | | Annual rate of increase Taux d' accrois sement annuel 2000-05 | Surface area Superficie (km2) 2005 | Density Densité 2005[2] |
		Both sexes Les deux sexes	Male Masculin	Female Feminin		2000	2005			
AFRICA — AFRIQUE										
Algeria - Algérie										
25 VI 1998	DJ	29 100 867	14 698 589	14 402 278	DJ	30 416	32 906	1.6	2 381 741	14
Angola[3]										
15 XII 1970	DF	5 646 166	2 943 974	2 702 192	...	...	...	...	1 246 700	...
Benin - Bénin										
11 II 2002	DJ	6 769 914	3 284 119	3 485 795	DF	6 169	...	...	112 622	...
Botswana										
17 VIII 2001	DF	1 680 863	813 488	867 375	DF	1 653	...	...	581 730	...
Burkina Faso[4]										
10 XII 1996	DF	10 862 075	5 355 982	5 506 093	DJ	11 347	12 802	2.4	274 200	47
Burundi										
16 VIII 1990	DF	5 139 073	2 473 599	2 665 474	...	...	...	...	27 834	...
Cameroon - Cameroun[5]										
10 IV 1987	DF	10 493 655	...	...	DF	15 292	...	...	475 442	...
Cape Verde - Cap-Vert										
16 VI 2000	DF	436 863	211 479	225 384	DF	435	...	...	4 033	...
Central African Republic - République centrafricaine										
8 XII 2003	DF	3 151 072	1 569 446	1 581 626	...	...	...	...	622 984	...
Chad - Tchad[6]										
8 IV 1993	DF	6 279 931	...	...	...	...	...	...	1 284 000	...
Comoros - Comores[7]										
1 IX 2003	DF	575 660	...	...	...	...	...	...	2 235	...
Congo										
6 VI 1996	DF	*2 600 000	...	...	DF	2 893	...	...	342 000	...
Côte d'Ivoire										
21 XI 1998	DF	15 366 672	7 844 621	7 522 050	DF	16 402	19 097	3.0	322 463	59
Democratic Republic of the Congo - République démocratique du Congo										
1 VII 1984	DF	29 916 800	14 543 800	15 373 000	...	...	...	...	2 344 858	...
Djibouti										
11 XII 1960	DF	81 200	...	...	...	...	...	...	23 200	...
Egypt - Égypte[8]										
11 XI 2006	DF	*72 579 030	*37 100 853	*35 478 177	DF	63 976	71 898	2.3	1 002 000	72
Equatorial Guinea - Guinée équatoriale[9]										
1 II 2002	DF	1 014 999	501 387	513 612	...	...	...	...	28 051	...
Eritrea - Érythrée										
9 V 1984	DF	2 748 304	1 374 452	1 373 852	...	...	...	...	117 600	...
Ethiopia - Éthiopie										
11 X 1994	DF	53 477 265	26 910 698	26 566 567	DF	63 495	...	...	1 104 300	...
Gabon										
1 XII 2003	DF	*1 269 000	...	...	DF	1 206	...	...	267 668	...
Gambia - Gambie										
15 IV 2003	DF	*1 364 507	*676 726	*687 781	DF	1 393	...	...	11 295	...
Ghana										
26 III 2000	DF	18 912 079	9 357 382	9 554 697	DF	18 412	...	...	238 533	...
Guinea - Guinée										
1 XII 1996	DF	7 156 406	3 497 979	3 658 427	...	...	...	...	245 857	...
Guinea-Bissau - Guinée-Bissau[5]										
1 XII 1991	DF	983 367	476 210	507 157	DF	...	1 326	...	36 125	37
Kenya										
24 VIII 1999	DF	28 686 607	14 205 589	14 481 018	DF	30 150	35 267	3.1	580 367	61
Lesotho[10]										
9 IV 2006	DJ	*1 872 721	*911 847	*960 874	DF	2 144	...	...	30 355	...

3. Population by sex, rate of population increase, surface area and density
Population selon le sexe, taux d'accroissement de la population, superficie et densité
(continued — suite)

Continent, country or area and census date / Continent, pays ou zone et date du recensement	Census type[1]	Latest available census — Dernier recensement disponible (in units — en unités)			Estimate type[1]	Mid-year estimates - Estimations au milieu de l'année (in thousands — en milliers)		Annual rate of increase Taux d'accrois sement annuel 2000-05	Surface area Superficie (km²) 2005	Density Densité 2005[2]
		Both sexes Les deux sexes	Male Masculin	Female Feminin		2000	2005			
AFRICA — AFRIQUE										
Liberia - Libéria										
1 II 1984	DF	2 101 628	1 063 127	1 038 501	...	...	...	...	111 369	...
Libyan Arab Jamahiriya - Jamahiriya arabe libyenne[11]										
11 VIII 1995	DF	4 404 986	2 236 943	2 168 043	DF	5 125	...	...	1 759 540	...
Madagascar										
1 VIII 1993	DF	12 238 914	6 088 116	6 150 798	DF	15 085	17 730	3.2	587 041	30
Malawi[5]										
1 IX 1998	DF	9 933 868	4 867 563	5 066 305	DF	10 475	*12 341	3.3	118 484	104
Mali										
1 IV 1998	DJ	9 790 492	4 847 436	4 943 056	DJ	10 243			1 240 192	...
Mauritania - Mauritanie										
1 XI 2000	DF	2 548 157	1 240 414	1 307 743	DF	2 645	2 906	1.9	1 025 520	3
Mauritius - Maurice										
2 VII 2000	DJ	1 178 848	583 756	595 092	DJ	1 187	1 243	0.9	2 040	609
Morocco - Maroc										
1 IX 2004	DF	29 680 069	14 640 662	15 039 407	DF	28 705	*30 172	1.0	446 550	68
Mozambique[12,13]										
1 VIII 1997	DF	16 099 246	7 714 306	8 384 940	DF	17 691	*19 420	1.9	801 590	24
Namibia - Namibie[14]										
27 VIII 2001	DF	1 830 330	887 721	942 572	DF	*1 817	...	...	824 292	...
Niger										
20 V 2001	DF	*10 790 352	*5 380 287	*5 410 065	DJ	10 493	12 628	3.7	1 267 000	10
Nigeria - Nigéria[5]										
21 III 2006	DF	*140 003 542	*71 709 859	*68 293 683	DF	115 224	133 767	3.0	923 768	145
Réunion										
8 III 1999	DJ	706 180	347 076	359 104	DF	722	779	1.5	2 510	310
Rwanda										
16 VIII 2002	DJ	8 128 553	3 879 448	4 249 105	...	...	...	...	26 338	...
Saint Helena ex. dep. - Sainte-Hélène sans dép.										
8 III 1998	DF	5 157	2 612	2 545	...	...	...	...	122	...
Saint Helena: Ascension - Sainte-Hélène: Ascension										
8 III 1998	DJ	712	458	254	...	...	...	...	88	...
Saint Helena: Tristan da Cunha - Sainte-Hélène: Tristan da Cunha										
31 XII 1988	DF	296	139	157	...	...	...	...	98	...
Sao Tome and Principe - Sao Tomé-et-Principe										
25 VIII 2001	DJ	137 599	68 236	69 363	DF	135	149	1.9	964	155
Senegal - Sénégal										
8 XII 2002	DJ	*9 956 202	*4 886 485	*5 069 717	DJ	9 427	10 848	2.8	196 722	55
Seychelles[15]										
26 VIII 2002	DJ	81 755	40 751	41 004	DF	81	83	0.4	455	182
Sierra Leone										
4 XII 2004	DF	*4 963 298	*2 412 860	*2 550 438	DF	4 944	...	...	71 740	...
Somalia - Somalie										
15 II 1987	DF	7 114 431	3 741 664	3 372 767	...	...	...	...	637 657	...
South Africa - Afrique du Sud[12]										
10 X 2001	DF	*44 819 778	*21 434 041	*23 385 737	DF	43 686	46 888	1.4	1 221 037	38

3. Population by sex, rate of population increase, surface area and density
Population selon le sexe, taux d'accroissement de la population, superficie et densité
(continued — suite)

Continent, country or area and census date / Continent, pays ou zone et date du recensement	Census type[1]	Latest available census — Dernier recensement disponible (in units — en unités) — Both sexes Les deux sexes	Male Masculin	Female Feminin	Estimate type[1]	Mid-year estimates - Estimations au milieu de l'année (in thousands — en milliers) 2000	2005	Annual rate of increase Taux d'accroissement annuel 2000-05	Surface area Superficie (km²) 2005	Density Densité 2005[2]
AFRICA — AFRIQUE										
Sudan - Soudan 15 IV 1993	DF	24 940 683	12 518 638	12 422 045	DF	31 081	35 397	2.6	2 505 813	14
Swaziland 11 V 1997	DF	929 718	440 154	489 564	DF	1 003	1 126	2.3	17 364	65
Togo 22 XI 1981	DF	2 719 567	1 325 641	1 393 926	DF	4 629	5 337	2.8	56 785	94
Tunisia - Tunisie 28 IV 2004	DF	9 932 400	...	...	DF	9 564	10 029	1.0	163 610	61
Uganda - Ouganda 12 IX 2002	DF	24 442 084	11 929 803	12 512 281	DF	22 972	...	...	241 038	...
United Republic of Tanzania - République Unie de Tanzanie 24 VIII 2002	DF	*34 443 603	*16 829 861	*17 613 742	DF	...	37 379	...	945 087	40
Western Sahara - Sahara occidental[16] 31 XII 1970	DF	76 425	43 981	32 444	...	...	...	...	266 000	...
Zambia - Zambie 25 X 2000	DF	9 885 591	4 946 298	4 939 293	DF	9 337	...	...	752 618	...
Zimbabwe 17 VIII 2002	DF	11 631 657	5 634 180	5 997 477	...	...	...	...	390 757	...
AMERICA, NORTH — AMERIQUE DU NORD										
Anguilla 9 V 2001	DF	11 430	5 628	5 802	DF	11	14	3.8	91	150
Antigua and Barbuda - Antigua-et-Barbuda 28 V 2001	DF	77 426	37 002	40 424	DF	72	83	2.7	442	187
Aruba 14 X 2000	DJ	90 508	43 435	47 073	DJ	91	101	2.1	180	559
Bahamas 1 V 2000	DF	303 611	147 715	155 896	DF	303	...	...	13 878	...
Barbados - Barbade 1 V 2000	DF	250 010	119 926	130 084	DF	269	273	0.3	430	635
Belize 12 V 2000	DF	240 204	121 278	118 926	DF	250	292	3.1	22 966	13
Bermuda - Bermudes[17] 20 V 2000	DJ	62 059	29 802	32 257	DJ	63	64	0.2	54	1 177
British Virgin Islands - Îles Vierges britanniques 21 V 2001	DF	20 647	10 627	10 020	DF	20	...	...	151	...
Canada[18] 15 V 2001	DJ	30 007 095	14 706 850	15 300 245	DJ	30 689	32 312	1.0	9 984 670	3
Cayman Islands - Îles Caïmanes 10 X 1999	DF	39 020	19 033	19 987	DJ	40	48	3.7	264	183
Costa Rica 26 VI 2000	DJ	3 810 179	1 902 614	1 907 565	DJ	3 810	4 266	2.3	51 100	83
Cuba 6 IX 2002	DJ	11 177 743	5 597 233	5 580 510	DF	11 130	11 243	0.2	109 886	102
Dominica - Dominique[10] 12 V 2001	DF	69 625	35 073	34 552	DF	72	...	...	751	...
Dominican Republic - République dominicaine 20 X 2002	DJ	8 562 541	4 265 215	4 297 326	DF	8 552	9 028	1.1	48 671	185

3. **Population by sex, rate of population increase, surface area and density**
Population selon le sexe, taux d'accroissement de la population, superficie et densité
(continued — suite)

Continent, country or area and census date / Continent, pays ou zone et date du recensement	Census type[1]	Latest available census — Dernier recensement disponible (in units — en unités)			Estimate type[1]	Mid-year estimates - Estimations au milieu de l'année (in thousands — en milliers)		Annual rate of increase Taux d'accroissement annuel 2000-05	Surface area Superficie (km²) 2005	Density Densité 2005[2]
		Both sexes Les deux sexes	Male Masculin	Female Feminin		2000	2005			
AMERICA, NORTH — AMERIQUE DU NORD										
El Salvador										
27 IX 1992	DF	5 118 599	2 485 613	2 632 986	DF	6 276	6 875	1.8	21 041	327
Greenland - Groenland[19]										
1 VII 2000	DJ	56 124	29 989	26 135	DJ	56	...	...	2 166 086	...
Grenada - Grenade[20]										
25 V 2001	DF	102 632	50 481	52 151	DF	101	...	...	344	...
Guadeloupe[21]										
8 III 1999	DJ	422 222	203 146	219 076	DJ	428	*446	0.8	1 705	261
Guatemala[12]										
24 XI 2002	DJ	11 237 196	...	...	DF	11 385	12 701	2.2	108 889	117
Haiti - Haïti										
11 I 2003	DJ	8 373 750	...	...	DJ	7 959	...	...	27 750	...
Honduras										
28 VII 2001	DF	6 071 200	3 000 530	3 070 670	DF	6 369	...	...	112 088	...
Jamaica - Jamaïque										
10 IX 2001	DJ	2 607 632	1 283 547	1 324 085	DJ	2 589	2 661	0.5	10 991	242
Martinique										
8 III 1999	DJ	381 325	180 910	200 415	DJ	385	398	0.7	1 102	361
Mexico - Mexique										
14 II 2000	DJ	97 483 412	47 592 253	49 891 159	DJ	98 439	103 947	1.1	1 964 375	53
Montserrat										
12 V 2001	DF	4 491	2 418	2 073	DF	5	...	...	102	...
Netherlands Antilles - Antilles néerlandaises[22]										
29 I 2001	DJ	175 653	82 521	93 132	DJ	179	...	...	800	...
Nicaragua										
4 VI 2005	DJ	5 144 553	2 535 461	2 609 092	DJ	5 106	5 457	1.3	120 340	45
Panama										
14 V 2000	DF	2 839 177	1 432 566	1 406 611	DF	2 856	3 228	2.5	75 517	43
Puerto Rico - Porto Rico[23]										
1 IV 2000	DJ	3 808 610	1 833 577	1 975 033	DJ	3 816	3 912	0.5	8 870	441
Saint Kitts and Nevis - Saint-Kitts-et-Nevis										
14 V 2001	DF	45 841	22 784	23 057	DF	40	...	...	261	...
Saint Lucia - Sainte-Lucie										
22 V 2001	DF	157 164	76 741	80 423	DF	156	165	1.1	539	306
Saint Pierre and Miquelon - Saint Pierre-et-Miquelon										
8 III 1999	DF	6 316	3 147	3 169	...	...	...	...	242	...
Saint Vincent and the Grenadines - Saint Vincent-et-les Grenadines[24,25]										
14 V 2001	DF	109 022	55 456	53 566	DF	110	104	-1.1	389	267
Trinidad and Tobago - Trinité-et-Tobago										
15 V 2000	DF	1 262 366	633 051	629 315	DF	1 290	...	...	5 130	...
Turks Caicos Islands - Îles Turques et Caïques										
20 VIII 2001	DF	19 886	9 896	9 990	DJ	18	31	10.1	948	32
United States - États-Unis[26]										
1 IV 2000	DJ	281 421 906	138 053 563	143 368 343	DJ	282 193	296 410	1.0	9 629 091	31

3. Population by sex, rate of population increase, surface area and density
Population selon le sexe, taux d'accroissement de la population, superficie et densité
(continued — suite)

Continent, country or area and census date / Continent, pays ou zone et date du recensement	Census type[1]	Latest available census — Dernier recensement disponible (in units — en unités)			Estimate type[1]	Mid-year estimates - Estimations au milieu de l'année (in thousands — en milliers)		Annual rate of increase Taux d'accrois sement annuel 2000-05	Surface area Superficie (km²) 2005	Density Densité 2005[2]
		Both sexes Les deux sexes	Male Masculin	Female Feminin		2000	2005			
AMERICA, NORTH — AMERIQUE DU NORD										
United States Virgin Islands - Îles Vierges américaines[23] 1 IV 2000	DJ	108 612	51 864	56 748	DJ	109	...	...	347	...
AMERICA, SOUTH — AMERIQUE DU SUD										
Argentina - Argentine 18 XI 2001	DF	36 260 130	17 659 072	18 601 058	DF	36 784	38 592	1.0	2 780 400	14
Bolivia - Bolivie 5 IX 2001	DF	8 280 184	4 130 342	4 149 842	DF	8 428	9 427	2.2	1 098 581	9
Brazil - Brésil[27] 1 VIII 2000	DJ	169 799 170	83 576 015	86 223 155	DF	171 280	184 184	1.5	8 514 877	22
Chile - Chili 24 IV 2002	DF	15 116 435	7 447 695	7 668 740	DF	15 398	16 267	1.1	756 102	22
Colombia - Colombie 22 V 2005	DF	41 468 384	20 336 117	21 132 267	DF	42 299	46 045	1.7	1 138 914	40
Ecuador - Équateur[28] 25 XI 2001	DF	12 156 608	6 018 353	6 138 255	DF	12 299	13 215	1.4	283 561	47
Falkland Islands (Malvinas) - Îles Falkland (Malvinas)[29,30] 8 X 2006	DF	2 955	1 569	1 386	...	...	...	...	12 173	...
French Guiana - Guyane française 8 III 1999	DJ	156 790	78 963	77 827	DJ	164	*200	4.0	90 000	2
Guyana 15 IX 2002	DF	751 223	376 034	375 189	DF	742	758	0.4	214 969	4
Paraguay 28 VIII 2002	DF	5 163 198	2 603 242	2 559 956	DF	5 346	5 899	2.0	406 752	15
Peru - Pérou[12,31,32] 18 VII 2005	DF	*26 152 265	*13 061 026	*13 091 239	DF	25 939	27 947	1.5	1 285 216	22
Suriname[33,34] 2 VIII 2004	DJ	492 829	247 846	244 618	DJ	464	499	1.5	163 820	3
Uruguay[12,35] 1 VI 2004	DF	3 241 003	1 565 533	1 675 470	DF	3 301	3 306	0.0	176 215	19
Venezuela (Bolivarian Republic of) - Venezuela (République bolivarienne du)[31] 30 X 2001	DF	23 054 210	11 402 869	11 651 341	DF	24 311	26 577	1.8	912 050	29
ASIA — ASIE										
Afghanistan[36] 23 VI 1979	DF	13 051 358	6 712 377	6 338 981	DF	21 770	...	...	652 090	...
Armenia - Arménie[37] 10 X 2001	DF	3 002 594	1 407 220	1 595 374	DJ	3 221	3 218	0.0	29 800	108
Azerbaijan - Azerbaïdjan 27 I 1999	DJ	7 953 438	3 883 155	4 070 283	DF	8 049	*8 392	0.8	86 600	97
Bahrain - Bahreïn 7 IV 2001	DF	650 604	373 649	276 955	DF	638	725	2.6	694	1 044
Bangladesh[38] 22 I 2001	DF	130 522 598	67 731 320	62 791 278	DF	129 300	138 600	1.4	143 998	963
Bhutan - Bhoutan 30 V 2005	DF	634 982	333 595	301 387	DF	678	...	...	47 000	...

3. Population by sex, rate of population increase, surface area and density
Population selon le sexe, taux d'accroissement de la population, superficie et densité
(continued — suite)

Continent, country or area and census date / Continent, pays ou zone et date du recensement	Census type[1] / Census type[1]	Latest available census — Dernier recensement disponible (in units — en unités)			Estima-te type[1]	Mid-year estimates - Estimations au milieu de l'année (in thousands — en milliers)		Annual rate of increase Taux d' accrois sement annuel 2000-05	Surface area Superficie (km²) 2005	Density Densité 2005[2]
		Both sexes Les deux sexes	Male Masculin	Female Feminin		2000	2005			
ASIA — ASIE										
Brunei Darussalam - Brunéi Darussalam										
21 VIII 2001	DF	*332 844	*168 974	*163 870	DF	325	370	2.6	5 765	64
Cambodia - Cambodge[39]										
3 III 1998	DF	11 437 656	5 511 408	5 926 248	DF	12 688	*13 661	1.5	181 035	75
China - Chine[40,41,42]										
1 XI 2000	DJ	1 242 612 226	640 275 969	602 336 257	DF	1 262 645	1 303 720	0.6	9 596 961	136
China: Hong Kong SAR - Chine: Hong Kong RAS										
14 VII 2006	DJ	6 864 346	3 272 956	3 591 390	DJ	6 665	6 813	0.4	1 104	6 171
China: Macao SAR - Chine: Macao RAS[43]										
19 VIII 2006	DJ	502 113	245 167	256 946	DJ	431	473	1.9	29	16 326
Cyprus - Chypre[44,45]										
1 X 2001	DJ	689 565	338 497	351 068	DJ	694	758	1.8	9 251	82
Georgia - Géorgie										
17 I 2002	DJ	4 371 535	2 061 753	2 309 782	DF	4 418	4 361	-0.3	69 700	63
India - Inde[46,47]										
1 III 2001	DF	1 028 610 328	532 156 772	496 453 556	DF	1 016 320	*1 101 000	1.6	3 287 263	335
Indonesia - Indonésie[48]										
30 VI 2000	DF	206 264 595	103 417 180	102 847 415	DJ	...	*219 898	...	1 904 569	115
Iran (Islamic Republic of) - Iran (République islamique d')[49]										
23 X 1996	DJ	60 055 488	30 515 159	29 540 329	DJ	63 664	68 467	1.5	1 648 195	42
Iraq[50]										
16 X 1997	DF	19 184 543	9 536 570	9 647 973	DF	24 086	27 963	3.0	438 317	64
Israel - Israël[51]										
4 XI 1995	DJ	5 548 523	2 738 175	2 810 348	DJ	6 289	6 930	1.9	22 072	314
Japan - Japon[52]										
1 X 2005	DF	*127 756 815	*62 340 864	*65 415 951	DF	126 843	127 773	0.1	377 873	338
Jordan - Jordanie[53]										
1 X 2004	DF	5 103 639	2 626 287	2 477 352	DF	4 857	*5 473	2.4	89 342	61
Kazakhstan										
26 II 1999	DJ	14 953 126	7 201 785	7 751 341	DF	14 884	15 147	0.4	2 724 900	6
Korea (Dem. People's Republic of) - Corée (Rép. populaire dém. de)										
31 XII 1993	DF	21 213 378	10 329 699	10 883 679	DF	22 963	...	...	120 538	...
Korea (Republic of) - Corée (République de)[54,55]										
1 XI 2000	DF	46 136 101	23 158 582	22 977 519	DF	47 008	48 294	0.5	99 538	485
Kuwait - Koweït										
20 IV 2005	DF	*2 213 403	*1 310 067	*903 336	DF	2 138	2 457	2.8	17 818	138
Kyrgyzstan - Kirghizistan										
24 III 1999	DJ	4 822 938	2 380 465	2 442 473	DF	4 915	5 144	0.9	199 951	26
Lao People's Democratic Republic - République démocratique populaire lao[56]										
1 III 2005	DJ	5 621 982	2 800 551	2 821 431	DF	5 218	5 679	1.7	236 800	24
Lebanon - Liban[57]										
15 XI 1970	SDF	2 126 325	1 080 015	1 046 310	...	...	...	...	10 400	...

3. Population by sex, rate of population increase, surface area and density
Population selon le sexe, taux d'accroissement de la population, superficie et densité
(continued — suite)

Continent, country or area and census date / Continent, pays ou zone et date du recensement	Census type[1]	Latest available census — Dernier recensement disponible (in units — en unités)			Estimate type[1]	Mid-year estimates - Estimations au milieu de l'année (in thousands — en milliers)		Annual rate of increase Taux d'accrois sement annuel 2000-05	Surface area Superficie (km²) 2005	Density Densité 2005[2]
		Both sexes Les deux sexes	Male Masculin	Female Feminin		2000	2005			

ASIA — ASIE

Malaysia - Malaisie[58,59] 5 VII 2000	DJ	23 274 690	11 853 432	11 421 258	DF	23 495	26 128	2.1	329 847	79
Maldives 21 III 2006	DF	298 968	151 459	147 509	DF	271	294	1.6	298	986
Mongolia - Mongolie 5 I 2000	DF	2 373 493	1 177 981	1 195 512	DF	2 390	2 548	1.3	1 564 100	2
Myanmar 31 III 1983	DF	35 307 913	17 518 255	17 789 658	...	...	...	...	676 578	...
Nepal - Népal[60] 22 VI 2001	DJ	23 151 423	11 563 921	11 587 502	DJ	*22 904	25 343	2.0	147 181	172
Occupied Palestinian Territory - Territoire palestinien occupé[61] 9 XII 1997	DF	2 601 669	1 322 264	1 279 405	DF	3 149	3 762	3.6	6 020	625
Oman 7 XII 2003	DF	2 340 815	1 313 239	1 027 576	DF	2 401	2 509	0.9	309 500	8
Pakistan[62] 2 III 1998	DF	130 579 571	67 840 137	62 739 434	DF	138 945	153 455	2.0	796 095	193
Philippines 1 V 2000	DJ	76 504 077	38 524 267	37 979 810	DJ	76 348	*85 237	2.2	300 000	284
Qatar 16 III 2004	DF	744 029	496 382	247 647	DF	617	796	5.1	11 493	69
Saudi Arabia - Arabie saoudite 15 IX 2004	DF	22 678 262	12 557 240	10 121 022	DF	20 476	23 119	2.4	2 149 690	11
Singapore - Singapour[63] 1 VII 2000	DF	4 017 700	2 061 800	1 955 900	DF	4 028	4 342	1.5	699	6 208
Sri Lanka[64] 17 VII 2001	DF	*16 864 544	*8 343 964	*8 520 580	DF	19 359	*19 668	0.3	65 610	300
Syrian Arab Republic - République arabe syrienne[65] 3 IX 1994	DF	13 782 315	7 048 906	6 733 409	DF	16 320	18 138	2.1	185 180	98
Tajikistan - Tadjikistan 20 I 2000	DF	*6 127 000	*3 082 000	*3 045 000	DF	6 188	6 850	2.0	143 100	48
Thailand - Thaïlande 1 IV 2000	DJ	60 617 200	29 850 100	30 767 100	DJ	61 770	64 839	1.0	513 120	126
Timor-Leste 11 VII 2004	DF	*924 642	*467 757	*456 885	...	...	...	...	14 874	...
Turkey - Turquie 22 X 2000	DF	67 803 927	34 346 735	33 457 192	DF	67 420	72 065	1.3	783 562	92
Turkmenistan - Turkménistan 10 I 1995	DF	4 483 251	2 225 331	2 257 920	...	...	...	...	488 100	...
United Arab Emirates - Émirats arabes unis[66] 17 XII 1995	DF	2 411 041	1 606 804	804 237	...	...	...	...	83 600	...
Uzbekistan - Ouzbékistan 12 I 1989	DJ	19 810 077	9 784 156	10 025 921	DF	24 650	...	...	447 400	...
Viet Nam 1 IV 1999	DF	76 323 173	37 469 117	38 854 056	DF	77 635	83 106	1.4	331 689	251
Yemen - Yémen 16 XII 2004	DF	19 685 161	10 036 953	9 648 208	DF	18 261	...	...	527 968	...

3. Population by sex, rate of population increase, surface area and density
Population selon le sexe, taux d'accroissement de la population, superficie et densité
(continued — suite)

Continent, country or area and census date / Continent, pays ou zone et date du recensement	Census type[1]	Latest available census — Dernier recensement disponible (in units — en unités)			Estimate type[1]	Mid-year estimates - Estimations au milieu de l'année (in thousands — en milliers)		Annual rate of increase Taux d' accrois sement annuel 2000-05	Surface area Superficie (km²) 2005	Density Densité 2005[2]
		Both sexes Les deux sexes	Male Masculin	Female Feminin		2000	2005			
EUROPE										
Albania - Albanie										
1 IV 2001	DF	3 069 300	1 530 500	1 538 800	DF	3 061	3 142	0.5	28 748	109
Andorra - Andorre[19]										
1 VII 2000	DF	66 089	34 344	31 745	DJ	66	79	3.5	468	168
Austria - Autriche										
15 V 2001	DJ	8 032 926	3 889 189	4 143 737	DJ	8 012	8 233	0.5	83 858	98
Belarus - Bélarus										
16 II 1999	DJ	10 045 237	4 717 621	5 327 616	DF	10 005	9 775	-0.5	207 600	47
Belgium - Belgique										
1 X 2001	DJ	10 296 350	5 035 446	5 260 904	DJ	10 251	10 479	0.4	30 528	343
Bosnia and Herzegovina - Bosnie-Herzégovine										
31 III 1991	DJ	4 377 033	2 183 795	2 193 238	DF	3 781	3 843	0.3	51 197	75
Bulgaria - Bulgarie										
1 III 2001	DF	7 928 901	3 862 465	4 066 436	DF	8 170	7 740	-1.1	110 912	70
Channel Islands: Guernsey - Îles Anglo-Normandes: Guernesey										
29 IV 2001	DJ	59 807	29 138	30 669	DF	60	...	...	78	...
Channel Islands: Jersey - Îles Anglo-Normandes: Jersey										
11 III 2001	DJ	87 186	42 485	44 701	DF	...	88	...	116	756
Croatia - Croatie										
31 III 2001	DJ	4 437 460	2 135 900	2 301 560	DJ	4 381	4 442	0.3	56 538	79
Czech Republic - République tchèque										
1 III 2001	DJ	10 230 060	4 982 071	5 247 989	DJ	10 273	10 234	-0.1	78 866	130
Denmark - Danemark[19,67]										
1 I 2001	DJ	5 349 212	2 644 319	2 704 893	DJ	5 337	5 416	0.3	43 094	126
Estonia - Estonie										
31 III 2000	DJ	1 370 052	631 851	738 201	DF	1 370	1 346	-0.3	45 228	30
Faeroe Islands - Îles Féroé[19]										
1 VII 2002	DJ	47 350	...	...	DJ	46	48	1.1	1 393	35
Finland - Finlande[19]										
31 XII 2000	DJ	5 181 115	2 529 341	2 651 774	DJ	5 176	5 246	0.3	338 145	16
France[68,69]										
8 III 1999	DJ	58 520 688	28 419 419	30 101 269	DJ	59 049	*60 996	0.6	551 500	111
Germany - Allemagne[70,71,72]										
28 III 2004	SDJ	82 491 000	40 330 000	42 161 000	DJ	82 188	82 464	0.1	357 022	231
Gibraltar[73]										
12 XI 2001	DF	27 495	13 644	13 851	DF	27	29	1.2	6	4 804
Greece - Grèce[74,75]										
18 III 2001	DF	10 964 020	5 431 816	5 532 204	DF	10 917	11 104	0.3	131 957	84
Holy See - Saint-Siège[19,76]										
1 VII 2000	DF	*798	*529	*269	...	...	...	...	-	...
Hungary - Hongrie										
1 II 2001	DF	10 198 315	4 850 650	5 347 665	DF	10 024	10 087	0.1	93 032	108
Iceland - Islande[19]										
1 VII 2000	DJ	281 154	140 718	140 436	DJ	281	296	1.0	103 000	3
Ireland - Irlande[77]										
28 IV 2002	DF	3 917 203	1 946 164	1 971 039	DF	3 790	4 131	1.7	70 273	59

3. Population by sex, rate of population increase, surface area and density
Population selon le sexe, taux d'accroissement de la population, superficie et densité
(continued — suite)

Continent, country or area and census date / Continent, pays ou zone et date du recensement	Census type[1]	Latest available census — Dernier recensement disponible (in units — en unités)			Estimate type[1]	Mid-year estimates - Estimations au milieu de l'année (in thousands — en milliers)		Annual rate of increase Taux d'accrois sement annuel 2000-05	Surface area Superficie (km²) 2005	Density Densité 2005[2]
		Both sexes Les deux sexes	Male Masculin	Female Feminin		2000	2005			
EUROPE										
Isle of Man - Îles de Man										
23 IV 2006	DJ	80 058	39 523	40 535	DJ	75	78	0.8	572	136
Italy - Italie										
21 X 2001	DF	57 110 144	27 617 335	29 492 809	DJ	56 942	58 607	0.6	301 318	195
Latvia - Lettonie										
31 III 2000	DJ	2 377 383	1 094 964	1 282 419	DJ	2 373	2 301	-0.6	64 600	36
Liechtenstein										
5 XII 2000	DF	33 307	16 420	16 887	DF	33	35	1.2	160	217
Lithuania - Lituanie										
6 IV 2001	DJ	3 483 972	1 629 148	1 854 824	DJ	3 500	3 414	-0.5	65 300	52
Luxembourg										
15 II 2001	DJ	439 539	216 541	222 998	DJ	436	457	0.9	2 586	177
Malta - Malte[78]										
26 XI 1995	DJ	378 132	186 836	191 296	DJ	383	404	1.1	316	1 277
Monaco										
21 VI 2000	DJ	32 020	15 544	16 476	...	...	...	...	2	...
Netherlands - Pays-Bas[79]										
1 I 2002	DJ	16 105 285	7 971 967	8 133 318	DJ	15 926	16 320	0.5	41 528	393
Norway - Norvège[19,80,81]										
3 XI 2001	DJ	4 520 947	2 240 281	2 280 666	DJ	4 491	4 623	0.6	323 802	14
Poland - Pologne[82,83,84]										
20 V 2002	DF	38 230 080	18 516 403	19 713 677	DF	38 256	38 161	0.0	312 685	122
Portugal[85]										
12 III 2001	DF	*10 148 259	*4 862 699	*5 285 560	DJ	10 226	10 549	0.6	92 090	115
Republic of Moldova - République de Moldova[86]										
5 X 2004	DF	*3 388 071	*1 632 519	*1 755 549	DJ	3 639	3 595	-0.2	33 851	106
Romania - Roumanie										
18 III 2002	DJ	21 680 974	10 568 741	11 112 233	DJ	22 435	21 624	-0.7	238 391	91
Russian Federation - Fédération de Russie[87]										
9 X 2002	DJ	145 166 731	67 605 133	77 561 598	DJ	146 597	*143 150	-0.5	17 098 242	8
San Marino - Saint-Marin[19]										
1 VII 2000	DF	26 941	13 185	13 756	DF	27	31	2.7	61	506
Serbia and Montenegro - Serbie-et-Montenegro[88]										
31 III 1991	DJ	10 394 026	5 157 120	5 236 906	DJ	10 634	...	...	102 173	...
Slovakia - Slovaquie										
25 V 2001	DJ	5 379 455	2 612 515	2 766 940	DJ	5 401	5 387	0.0	49 033	110
Slovenia - Slovénie										
31 III 2002	DJ	*1 964 036	*958 576	*1 005 460	DJ	1 990	2 001	0.1	20 256	99
Spain - Espagne[89]										
1 XI 2001	DF	40 847 371	20 012 882	20 834 489	DJ	40 264	43 398	1.5	505 992	86
Svalbard and Jan Mayen Islands - Îles Svalbard et Jan Mayen[90]										
1 XI 1960	DF	3 431	2 545	886	...	...	...	...	62 422	...
Sweden - Suède[19]										
1 VII 2000	DJ	8 872 110	4 386 436	4 485 674	DJ	8 872	9 030	0.4	449 964	20

3. Population by sex, rate of population increase, surface area and density
Population selon le sexe, taux d'accroissement de la population, superficie et densité
(continued — suite)

| Continent, country or area and census date / Continent, pays ou zone et date du recensement | Census type[1] | Latest available census — Dernier recensement disponible (in units — en unités) | | | Estimate type[1] | Mid-year estimates - Estimations au milieu de l'année (in thousands — en milliers) | | Annual rate of increase Taux d' accrois sement annuel 2000-05 | Surface area Superficie (km²) 2005 | Density Densité 2005[2] |
		Both sexes Les deux sexes	Male Masculin	Female Feminin		2000	2005			
EUROPE										
Switzerland - Suisse[91]										
5 XII 2000	DJ	7 204 055	3 519 698	3 684 357	DJ	7 204	7 459	0.7	41 277	181
The Former Yugoslav Rep. of Macedonia - L'ex-République yougoslave de Macédoine										
1 XI 2002	DJ	2 022 547	1 015 377	1 007 170	DF	2 024	2 037	0.1	25 713	79
Ukraine										
5 XII 2001	DF	48 240 902	22 316 317	25 924 585	DJ	49 176	*47 075	-0.9	603 700	78
United Kingdom - Royaume-Uni[92,93]										
29 IV 2001	DF	58 789 187	28 579 867	30 209 320	DF	58 886	60 209	0.4	242 900	248
OCEANIA — OCEANIE										
American Samoa - Samoas américaines[23]										
1 IV 2000	DJ	57 291	29 264	28 027	DJ	58	66	2.5	199	329
Australia - Australie[12,94]										
7 VIII 2001	DF	18 769 249	9 270 466	9 498 783	DJ	19 153	20 409	1.3	7 692 024	3
Cook Islands - Îles Cook[95]										
1 XII 2001	DF	18 027	9 303	8 724	DF	18	20	2.3	236	86
Fiji - Fidji										
25 VIII 1996	DF	775 077	393 931	381 146	DF	808	*842	0.8	18 274	46
French Polynesia - Polynésie française[96]										
7 XI 2002	DF	245 516	...	...	DF	235	255	1.6	4 000	64
Guam[23]										
1 IV 2000	DJ	154 805	79 181	75 624	DJ	...	*169	...	549	307
Kiribati[97]										
7 XII 2005	DF	*92 533	*45 612	*46 921	...	...	...	...	726	...
Marshall Islands - Îles Marshall										
1 VI 1999	DF	50 848	26 034	24 814	DF	53	...	...	181	...
Micronesia, Federated States of - Micronésie, États Fédérés de La										
1 IV 2000	DJ	107 008	54 191	52 817	DJ	119	...	...	702	...
Nauru										
17 IV 1992	DF	9 919	5 079	4 840	DF	12	...	...	21	...
New Caledonia - Nouvelle-Calédonie[98]										
31 VIII 2004	DF	*230 789	*116 485	*114 304	DF	213	...	...	18 575	...
New Zealand - Nouvelle-Zélande[99]										
6 III 2001	DJ	3 820 749	1 863 309	1 957 440	DJ	3 858	4 099	1.2	270 534	15
Niue - Nioué										
7 IX 2001	DF	1 788	897	891	...	...	...	...	260	...
Norfolk Island - Île Norfolk										
8 VIII 2006	DF	2 523	1 218	1 305	...	...	...	...	36	...

3. Population by sex, rate of population increase, surface area and density
Population selon le sexe, taux d'accroissement de la population, superficie et densité
(continued — suite)

Continent, country or area and census date / Continent, pays ou zone et date du recensement	Census type[1]	Latest available census — Dernier recensement disponible (in units — en unités)			Estimate type[1]	Mid-year estimates - Estimations au milieu de l'année (in thousands — en milliers)		Annual rate of increase Taux d'accrois sement annuel 2000-05	Surface area Superficie (km²) 2005	Density Densité 2005[2]
		Both sexes Les deux sexes	Male Masculin	Female Feminin		2000	2005			
OCEANIA — OCEANIE										
Northern Mariana Islands - Îles Mariannes septentrionales										
1 IV 2000	DF	69 221	31 984	37 237	DF	72	...	...	464	...
Palau - Palaos										
1 IV 2005	DF	19 907	10 699	9 208	DF	19	...	...	459	...
Papua New Guinea - Papouasie-Nouvelle-Guinée[100]										
9 VII 2000	DF	5 190 786	2 691 744	2 499 042	DF	5 100	...	...	462 840	...
Pitcairn										
31 XII 1991	DF	66	...	...	...	...	...	...	5	...
Samoa										
5 XI 2001	DF	176 710	92 050	84 660	DF	171	183	1.4	2 831	65
Solomon Islands - Îles Salomon[101]										
21 XI 1999	DF	409 042	211 381	197 661	DF	415	471	2.5	28 896	16
Tokelau - Tokélaou										
11 X 2001	DF	1 537	761	776	...	...	...	...	12	...
Tonga[102]										
30 XI 2006	DF	*101 134	*51 197	*49 937	DF	100	...	...	747	...
Tuvalu										
1 XI 2002	DF	9 561	4 729	4 832	DF	9	...	...	26	...
Vanuatu										
16 XI 1999	DJ	186 678	95 682	90 996	...	...	...	...	12 189	...
Wallis and Futuna Islands - Îles Wallis et Futuna										
22 VII 2003	DF	14 944	7 494	7 450	...	...	...	...	142	...

FOOTNOTES - NOTES

* Provisional. — Données provisoires.

[1] 'Code' indicates the source of data, as follows:
DF - De facto
DJ - De jure
SDF - Sample survey, de facto
SDJ - Sample survey, de jure
Le 'Code' indique la source des données, comme suit:
DF - Population de fait
DJ - Population de droit
SDF - Enquête par sondage, population de fait
SDJ - Enquête par sondage, Population de droit

[2] Population per square kilometre of surface area in 2005. Figures are estimates of population divided by surface area and are not to be considered either as reflecting density in the urban sense or as indicating the supporting power of a territory's land and resources. — Nombre d'habitants au kilomètre carré en 2005. Il s'agit simplement d'éstimations de la population divisé par celui de la superficie: il ne faut pas y voir d'indication de la densité au sens urbain du terme ni de l'effectif de population que les terres et les ressources du territoire sont capables de nourrir.

[3] Including the enclave of Cabinda. -Y compris l'enclave de Cabinda.

[4] Census result, including emigrants. -Les résultat du recensement, y compris les émigrants.

[5] Data for estimates refer to national projections. -Les estimations se données se réfèrent aux projections nationales.

[6] Census results have been adjusted for underenumeration, estimated at 1.4 per cent. -Les résultat du recensement ont été ajustées pour compenser les lacunes du dénombrement, estimées à 1;4 p. 100.

[7] Census result, excluding Mayotte. -Résultat du recensement, non compris Mayotte.

[8] Census result, exclude border population. -Les résultat du recensement, à l'exception de la population frontalière.

[9] Comprising Bioko (which includes Pagalu) and Rio Muni (which includes Corisco and Elobeys). -Comprend Bioko (qui comprend Pagalu) et Rio Muni (qui comprend Corisco et Elobeys).

[10] Census data excluding the institutional population. -Les données de recensement non compris la population dans les institutions.

[11] Data refer to Libyan nationals only. -Les données se raportent aux nationaux libyens seulement.

[12] Mid-year estimates have been adjusted for underenumeration, at latest census. -Les estimations au millieu de l'année tiennent compte d'un ajustement destiné à compenser les lacunes du dénombrement lors du dernier recensement.

[13] Census results have been adjusted for underenumeration, estimated at 5.1 per cent. -Les résultats du recensement ont été ajustées pour compenser les lacunes du dénombrement, estimées à 5,1 p. 100.

[14] The number of males and / or females excludes persons whose sex is not stated (18 urban, 19 rural). -Il n'est pas tenu compte dans le nombre d'hommes et de femmes des personnes dont le sexe n'est pas indiqué (18 en zone urbaine et 19 en zone rurale).

[15] Data exclude adjustment for underenumeration, estimated at 2.4 per cent. -Les données n'ont pas été ajustées pour compenser les lacunes du dénombrement, estimées à 2,4 p. 100.

[16] Comprising the Northern Region (former Saguia el Hamra) and Southern Region (former Rio de Oro). -Comprend la région septentrionale (ancien Saguia-el-Hamra) et la région méridionale (ancien Rio de Oro).

[17] Excluding the institutional population. -Non compris la population dans les institutions.

[18] For 2000, final intercensal estimates. For 2005, Updated postcensal estimates. -Pour 2000, estimations inter censitaires finales.Pour 2005, estimations post censitaires mises à jour.

[19] Population statistics are compiled from registers. -Les statistiques de la population sont compilées à partir des registres.

[20] Including Carriacou and other dependencies in the Grenadines. -Y compris Carriacou et les autres dépendances du groupe des îles Grenadines.

[21] Including dependencies: Marie-Galante, la Désirade, les Saintes, Petite-Terre, St. Barthélemy and French part of St. Martin. -Y compris les dépendances: Marie-Galante, la Désirade, les Saintes, Petite-Terre, Saint-Barthélemy et la partie française de Saint-Martin.

[22] Comprising Bonaire, Curaçao, Saba, St. Eustatius and Dutch part of St. Martin. -Comprend Bonaire, Curaçao, Saba, Saint-Eustache et la partie néederlandaise de Saint-Martin.

[23] Including armed forces stationed in the area. -Y compris les militaires en garnison sur le territoire.

[24] Including Bequia and other islands in the Grenadines. -Y compris Bequia et autres îles dans les Grenadines.

[25] Census data exclude adjustment for underenumeration. Excluding persons residing in institutions. -Les données de recensement n'ont pas été ajustées pour compenser les lacunes du dénombrement. Non compris les personnes dans les institutions.

[26] Excluding armed forces overseas and civilian citizens absent from country for an extended period of time. -Non compris les militaires à l'étranger, et les civils hors du pays pendant une période prolongée.

[27] Data include persons in remote areas, military personnel outside the country, merchant seamen at sea, civilian seasonal workers outside the country, and other civilians outside the country, and exclude nomads, foreign military, civilian aliens temporarily in the country, transients on ships and Indian jungle population. -Y compris les personnes dans des régions éloignées, le personel militaire en dehors du pays, les marins marchands, les ouvriers saisonniers en dehors du pays, et autres civils en dehors du pays, et non compris les nomades, les militaires étrangers, les étrangers civils temporairement dans le pays, les personnes en transit sur des bateaux et les Indiens de la jungle.

[28] Excluding nomadic Indian tribes. -Non compris les tribus d'Indiens nomades.

[29] Excluding dependencies, of which South Georgia (area 3 755 km2) had an estimated population of 499 in 1964 (494 males, 5 females). The other dependencies namely, the South Sandwich group (surface area 337 km2) and a number of smaller islands, are presumed to be uninhabited. -Non compris les dépendances, parmi lesquelles figure la Georgie du Sud (3 755 km2) avec une population estimée à 499 personnes en 1964 (494 du sexe masculin et 5 du sexe féminin). Les autres dépendances, c'est-à-dire le groupe des Sandwich du Sud (superficie: 337 km2) et certaines petites-îles, sont présumées inhabitées.

[30] A dispute exists between the governments of Argentina and the United Kingdom of Great Britain and Northern Ireland concerning sovereignty over the Falkland Islands (Malvinas). -La souveraineté sur les îles Falkland (Malvinas) fait l'objet d'un différend entre le Gouvernement argentin et le Gouvernement du Royaume-Uni de Grande-Bretagne et d'Irlande du Nord.

[31] Excluding Indian jungle population. -Non compris les Indiens de la jungle.

[32] The population for the year 2005 corresponds to the population actually enumerated in the census conducted between 18 July and 20 August 2005. The total (adjusted) population is 27 219 264 inhabitants. -La population pour 2005 correspond à la population effectivement dénombrée lors du recensement réalisé entre le 18 juillet et le 20 août 2005. La population totale (après ajustement) compte 27 219 264 habitants.

[33] The previous census was conducted only 16 months earlier (on 31 Mar 2003) but it was repeated because all of its data were destroyed in a fire before they could be fully processed, analyzed, and reported. -Le recensement précédent a eu lieu seulement 16 mois auparavant (le 31 mars 2003), mais a dû être refait parce que toutes les données ont été détruites dans un incendie avant que l'on n'ait pu les traiter et les analyser.

[34] Figures for male and female population do not add up to the figure for total population, because they exclude 365 persons of unknown sex. -Les chiffres relatifs à la population masculine et féminine ne correspondent pas au chiffre de la population totale, parce que l'on en a exclu 365 personnes de sexe inconnu.

[35] Data refer to resident population in Uruguay according to Census Phase 1, carried out between the months of June and July 2004. -Les données se rapportent à la population résidente en Uruguay d'après la phase 1 du recensement, qui a eu lieu entre juin et juillet 2004.

[36] Census result, excluding nomad population. -Les résultat du recensement, non compris les nomades.

[37] The methodology used for calculating the number of the de facto and de jure population in the 2001 census data differs as follows from the methodology used in previous censuses: the duration that defines a person as being 'temporary present' or 'temporary absent' is now 'under one year'. The previously applied definition was for '6 months'. -La méthode utilisée pour dénombrer la population présente et la population légale dans le contexte du recensement de 2001 diffère de celle qui a été appliquée lors des recensements antérieurs en ce que la durée considérée pour définir la 'présence temporaire 'ou' l'absence temporaire' était dorénavant fixée à 'moins d'un an' alors qu'elle était de '6 mois' auparavant.

[38] Census results have been adjusted for underenumeration, estimated at 4.96 per cent. -Les données ont été ajustées pour compenser les lacunes du dénombrement, estimées à 4,96 %.

[39] Excluding foreign diplomatic personnel and their dependants. Data for estimates based on 1998 census result. -Non compris le personnel diplomatique étranger et les membres de leur famille les accompagnant. Les estimations se réfèrent aux des résultats 1998 de recensement.

[40] For statistical purposes, the data for China do not include those for the Hong Kong Special Administrative Region (Hong Kong SAR), Macao Special Administrative Region (Macao SAR) and Taiwan province of China. -Pour la présentation des statistiques, les données pour la Chine ne comprennent pas la Région Administrative Spéciale de Hong Kong (Hong Kong RAS), la Région Administrative Spéciale de Macao (Macao RAS) et Taïwan province de Chine.

[41] Census data for the civilian population of 31 provinces, municipalities and autonomous regions. -Les données du recensement, pour la population civile seulement de 31 provinces, municipalités et régions autonomes.

[42] Estimates for 2000 have been adjusted on the basis of the Population Census of 2000. Data for 2005 are estimated from the National Sample Survey of 1 Per cent population. -Les estimations pour 2000 ont été ajustées à partir des résultats du recensement de la population de 2000. Les données pour 2005 ont été estimées à partir de l'enquête nationale qui a porté sur un échantillon de 1 % de la population.

[43] Data derived from the By-Census 2006 held during 19 to 31 of August 2006. -Donnes dérivées du recensement partiel de 2006 organisé entre les 19 et 31 août 2006.

[44] Data refer to government controlled areas. -Les données se rapportent aux zones contrôlées par le Gouvernement.

[45] Data include all population irrespective of citizenship, who at the time of the census resided in the country or intended to reside for a period of at least one year. It does not distinguish between those present or absent at the time of census. -Les chiffres comprennent toute la population, quelle que soit la nationalité, qui à l'époque de recensement avait résidé dans le pays, ou avait l'intention de résider, pendant une période d'au moins un an. Il n'y a pas de distinction entre les personnes présentes ou absentes au moment du recensement.

[46] Including data for the Indian-held part of Jammu and Kashmir, the final status of which has not yet been determined. -Y compris les données pour la partie du Jammu et du Cachemire occupée par l'Inde dont le statut définitif n'a pas encore été déterminé.

[47] Census data exclude Mao-Maram, Paomata and Purul sub-divisions of Senapati district of Manipur. The population of Manipur including the estimated population of the three sub-divisions of Senapati district is 2,291,125 (Males 1,161,173 and females 1,129,952). -Les données du recensement, non compris les subdivisions Mao-Maram Paomata et Purul du district de Senapati dans l'État du Manipur. Cet État compte 2 291 125 habitants (1 161 173 hommes et 1 129 952 femmes), y compris la population estimative des trois subdivisions du district de Senapati.

[48] Census data include an estimated population of 459 557 persons in urban and 1 857 659 persons in rural areas that were not directly enumerated, and a population of 566 403 persons in urban and 1 717 578 persons in rural areas that decline the participation. Also included are 421 399 non permanent residents (the homeless, the crew of ships carrying national flag, boat/floating house people, remote located tribesmen and refugees.) -Les données du recensement, y compris la population estimée a 459 557 personnes dans les zones urbaines et de 1 857 659 personnes dans les zones rurales qui n'ont pas été énumérées directement, aussi que 566 403 personnes qui non pas répondu dans les zones urbaines et de 1 717 578 personnes dans les zones rurales. Y compris 421 399 résidants non permanents (les sans abri, l'équipage des bateaux portant le drapeau national, les habitants des embarcations ou des maisons flottantes, les habitants des tribus isolées et les réfugies.)

[49] Estimates relate to the Iranian Year which begins on 21 March and ends on 20 March of the following year. For 2005, data relate to the population for the Iranian Year 1384 (21 March 2005-20 March 2006). -Les estimations concernent l'année iranienne, qui commence le 21 mars et se termine le 20 mars de l'année suivante. Pour 2005, les données concernent la population pour l'année iranienne 1384 (21 mars 2005-20 mars 2006).

[50] For the 1997 population census, data exclude population in three autonomous provinces in the north of the country. -Pour le recensement de 1997, la population des trois provinces autonomes dans le nord du pays

est exclue.

51 Including data for East Jerusalem and Israeli residents in certain other territories under occupation by Israeli military forces since June 1967. -Y compris les données pour Jérusalem-Est et les résidents israéliens dans certains autres territoires occupés depuis 1967 par les forces armées israéliennes.

52 Excluding diplomatic personnel outside the country and foreign military and civilian personnel and their dependants stationed in the area. - Non compris le personnel diplomatique hors du pays ni les militaires et agents civils étrangers en poste sur le territoire et les membres de leur famille les accompagnant.

53 Excluding data for Jordanian territory under occupation since June 1967 by Israeli military forces. Excluding foreigners, including registered Palestinian refugees. -Non compris les données pour le territoire jordanien occupé depuis juin 1967 par les forces armées israéliennes. Non compris les étrangers, mais y compris les réfugiés de Palestine enregistrés.

54 Census result, excluding foreigners. -Les résultat du recensement, non compris étrangers.

55 Including diplomats and their families abroad, but excluding foreign diplomats, foreign military personal, and their families in the country. -Y compris le personnel diplomatique et les membres de leurs familles à l'étranger, mais sans tenir compte du personnel diplomatique et militaire étranger et des membres de leurs familles.

56 For 2000, calculated base on Population census 1995 structure and growth rate at year 2000. -Pour 2000, on a pris pour base la structure issue du recensement de population de 1995 et le taux de croissance de 2000.

57 Excluding Palestinian refugees in camps. -Non compris les réfugiés de Palestine dans les camps.

58 Excluding Malaysian citizens and permanent residents who were away or intended to be away from the country for more than six months. Excluding Malaysian military, naval and diplomatic personnel and their families outside the country, and tourists, businessman who intended to be in Malaysia for less than six months. -Non compris les citoyens malaisiens et les résidents permanents qui étaient ou qui ont prévu d'être hors du pays pour six mois ou plus. Non compris le personnel militaire Malaisien, le personnel naval ou diplomatique et leurs familles hors du pays, et les touristes et les hommes d'affaires qui avaient l'intention de rester en Malaisie moins de six mois.

59 Census results have been adjusted for underenumeration. -Les résultats du recensement ont été ajustées pour compenser les lacunes du dénombrement

60 Data including estimated population from household listing from Village Development Committees and Wards which could not be enumerated at the time of census. -Les données incluent la population estimée par les listes des ménages des comités de développement des villages et des circonscriptions qui n'ont pas pu être énumérée au moment du recensement.

61 Total population does not include Palestinian population living in those parts of Jerusalem governorate which were annexed by Israel in 1967, amounting to 210 209 persons. Likewise, the results does not include the estimates of not enumerated population based on the findings of the post enumeration study, i.e 83 805 persons. -Les données relatives à la population totale ne comprennent pas la population palestinienne -équivalent à 210 209 personnes - habitant dans les territoires du gouvernorat de Jérusalem qui ont été annexés par Israël en 1967. Egalement, les données ne tiennent pas compte des estimations de la population calculée sur la base des résultats de l'enquête postcensitaire, équivalent à 83 805 personnes.

62 Excluding data for the Pakistan-held part of Jammu and Kashmir, the final status of which has not yet been determined. -Non compris les données concernant la partie du Jammu et Cachemire occupée par le Pakistan dont le statut définitif n'a pas été déterminé.

63 Census result, excluding transients afloat and non-locally domiciled military and civilian services personnel and their dependants and visitors. - Les résultats du recensement, non compris les personnes de passage à bord de navires ni les militaires et agents civils non-résidents et les membres de leur famille les accompagnants et visiteurs.

64 The Population and Housing Census 2001 did not cover the whole area of the country due to the security problems; the Census was complete in 18 districts only; in three districts it was not possible to conduct it; and in four districts it was partially conducted. -Le recensement de la population et de l'habitat en 2001 n'a pas couvert la totalité du pays pour des problèmes de sécurité ; le recensement a été complété seulement en 18 districts ; dans 3 districts ça n'a pas été possible de conduire le recensement et dans 4 districts il a été partiellement conduit.

65 Including Palestinian refugees. -Y compris les réfugiés de Palestine.

66 Comprising 7 sheikdoms of Abu Dhabi, Dubai, Sharjah, Ajaman, Umm al Qaiwain, Ras al Khaimah and Fujairah, and the area lying within the modified Riyadh line as announced in October 1955. -Comprend les sept cheikhats de Abou Dhabi, Dabai, Ghârdja, Adjmân, Oumm-al-Quiwaïn, Ras al Khaîma et Foudjaïra, ainsi que la zone délimitée par la ligne de Riad modifiée comme il a été annoncé en octobre 1955.

67 Excluding Faeroe Islands and Greenland. -Non compris les Iles Féroé et le Grôenland.

68 Excluding diplomatic personnel outside the country and including members of alien armed forces not living in military camps and foreign diplomatic personnel not living in embassies or consulates. -Non compris le personnel diplomatique hors du pays et y compris les militaires étrangers ne vivant pas dans des camps militaires et le personnel diplomatique étranger ne vivant pas dans les ambassades ou les consulats.

69 Excluding Overseas Departments, namely, French Guiana, Guadeloupe, Martinique and Reunion, shown separately. -Non compris les départements d'outre-mer, c'est-à-dire la Guyane française, la Guadeloupe, la Martinique et la Réunion, qui font l'objet de rubriques distinctes.

70 Data of the microcensus - a 1% household sample survey - refer to a single reference week in spring (usually last week in April). -Les données du microrecensement (enquête sur les ménages, réalisée sur un échantillon de 1 %) concernent une seule semaine de référence au printemps (habituellement la dernière semaine d'avril).

71 Excluding homeless persons. -Non compris les personnes sans domicile fixe.

72 Excluding foreign military personnel and foreign diplomatic and consular personnel and their family members in the country. -Non compris le personnel militaire étranger, le personnel diplomatique et consulaire étranger et les membres de leur famille se trouvant dans le pays.

73 Excluding families of military personnel, visitors and transients. -Non compris les familles des militaires, ni les visiteurs et transients.

74 Census data including armed forces stationed outside the country, but excluding alien armed forces stationed in the area. -Les données de recensement comprennent les militaires se trouvant hors du pays, mais ne comprennent pas les militaires étrangers en poste sur le territoire.

75 Mid-year population excludes armed forces stationed outside the country, but includes alien armed forces stationed in the area. -Les estimations au milieu de l'année non compris les militaires en garnison hors du pays, mais y compris les militaires étrangers en garnison sur le territoire.

76 Data refer to the Vatican City State. -Les données se rapportent à l'Etat de la Cité du Vatican.

77 Estimates refer to 15th of April.-Les estimations se rapportent au 15 avril.

78 Census data including foreigners residing in Malta for 12 months before the census date and excluding foreign diplomatic personnel. -Les données du recensement, y compris les étrangers habitant à Malte pour 12 mois avant le recensement et le personnel diplomatique étrangers.

79 Census result, based on compilation of continuous accounting and sample surveys. -Les résultat du recensement, d'après les résultats des dénombrements et enquêtes par sondage continue.

80 Including residents temporarily outside the country. -Y compris les résidents se trouvant temporairement hors du pays.

81 Excluding Svalbard and Jan Mayen Island shown separately. -Non compris Svalbard et Jan Mayen qui font l'objet de rubriques distinctes.

82 Excluding civilian aliens within country, but including civilian nationals temporarily outside country. -Non compris les civils étrangers dans le pays, mais y compris les civils nationaux temporairement hors du pays.

83 Surface area includes inland waters as well as part of internal waters. -Superficie comprend les eaux intérieures et une partie des eaux situées en deçà de la ligne de base de la mer territoriale.

84 Average year data for 2000 contain revised data according to the final results of population census 2002. -Les données annuelles moyennes pour 2000 comportent des données révisées en fonction des résultats du recensement de 2002.

85 Including the Azores and Madeira Islands. -Y compris les Açores et Madère.

86 Data do not include information for Transnistria and the municipality of Bender. -Les données ne tiennent pas compte de l'information sur la Transnistria et la municipalité de Bender.

87 Figures were updated taking into account the results of the 2002 All-Russian population census. -Les chiffres ont été calculés compte tenu des résultats du recensement de la population de la Fédération de Russie de 2002.

88 For 2000, estimates of Kosovo and Metohia computed on the basis of natural increases from year 1997. -Pour 2000, les estimations pour le Kosovo et la Metohia ont été calculées sur la base des accroissements naturels depuis 1997.

89 Including the Balearic and Canary Islands, and Alhucemas, Ceuta, Chafarinas, Melilla and Penon de Vélez de la Gomera. -Y compris les Baléares et les Canaries, Al Hoceima, Ceuta, les îles Zaffarines, Melilla et Penon de Vélez de la Gomera.

90 Inhabited only during the winter season. Census data are for total population while estimates refer to Norwegian population only. Included also in the de jure population of Norway. -N'est habitée pendant la saison d'hiver. Les données de recensement se rapportent à la population totale,

mais les estimations ne concernent que la population norvégienne, comprise également dans la population de droit de la Norvège.

[91] Surface area do not include state forests and communanzas (7.15 km2). -Superficie ne comprend pas les forêts domaniales et communanzas (7,15 km2) non comprises.

[92] Excluding Channel Islands and Isle of Man, shown separately. -Non compris les îles Anglo-Normandes et l'île de Man, qui font l'objet de rubriques distinctes.

[93] Population estimates for 2000 were revised in light of the local studies. -Les estimations de la population pour les années 2000 ont été révisées en fonction d'études locales.

[94] Census result, exclude visitors. -Les résultat du recensement, non compris des visiteurs.

[95] Excluding Niue, shown separately, which is part of Cook Islands, but because of remoteness is administered separately. -Non compris Nioué, qui fait l'objet d'une rubrique distincte et qui fait partie des îles Cook, mais qui, en raison de son éloignement, est administrée séparément.

[96] Comprising Austral, Gambier, Marquesas, Rapa, Society and Tuamotu Islands. -Comprend les îles Australes, Gambier, Marquises, Rapa, de la Societé et Tuamotou.

[97] Including Christmas, Fanning, Ocean and Washington Islands. -Y compris les îles Christmas, Fanning, Océan et Washington.

[98] Including the islands of Huon, Chesterfield, Loyalty, Walpole and Belep Archipelago. -Y compris les îles Huon, Chesterfield, Loyauté et Walpole, et l'archipel Belep.

[99] Including Campbell and Kermadec Islands (population 20 in 1961, surface area 148 km2) as well as Antipodes, Auckland, Bounty, Snares, Solander and Three Kings island, all of which are uninhabited. -Y compris les îles Campbell et Kermadec (20 habitants en 1961, superficie: 148 km2) ainsi que les îles Antipodes, Auckland, Bounty, Snares, Solander et Three Kings, qui sont toutes inhabitées.

[100] Comprising the eastern part of New Guinea, the Bismarck Archipelago, Bougainville and Buka of Solomon Islands group and about 600 smaller islands. -Comprend l'est de la Nouvelle-Guinée, l'archipel Bismarck, Bougainville et Buka (ces deux dernières du groupe des Salomon) et environ 600 îlots.

[101] Comprising the Solomon Islands group (except Bougainville and Buka which are included with Papua New Guinea shown separately), Ontong, Java, Rennel and Santa Cruz Islands. -Comprend les îles Salomon(à l'exception de Bougainville et de Buka dont la population est comprise dans celle de Papouasie-Nouvelle Guinée qui font l'objet d'une rubrique distincte), ainsi que les îles Ontong, Java, Rennel et Santa Cruz.

[102] Data for estimates based on the results of the 1996 population census not necessarily mid year estimated. -Les estimations d'aprés les résultats du recensement de la population de 1996, pas nécessairement des estimations en milieu d'année.

Table 4

Table 4 presents, for each country or area of the world, basic vital statistics including: live births, crude birth rate, deaths, crude death rate, rate of natural increase, infant deaths, infant death rate, expectation of life at birth by sex and total fertility rate.

Description of variables: The vital events and rates shown in this table are defined as follows[1]:

Live birth is the complete expulsion or extraction from its mother of a product of conception, irrespective of the duration of pregnancy, which after such separation breathes or shows any other evidence of life such as beating of the heart, pulsation of the umbilical cord, of definite movement of voluntary muscles, whether or not the umbilical cord has been cut or the placenta is attached. Each product of such a birth is considered live-born regardless of gestational age.

Death is the permanent disappearance of all evidence of life at any time after live birth has taken place (post-natal cessation of vital functions without capability of resuscitation).

Infant deaths are deaths of live-born infants under one year of age.

Expectation of life at birth is defined as the average number of years of life for males and females if they continued to be subject to the same mortality experienced in the year(s) to which these life expectancies refer.

The total fertility rate is the average number of children that would be born alive to a hypothetical cohort of women if, throughout their reproductive years, the age-specific fertility rates remained unchanged. The standard method of calculating the total fertility rate is the sum of the age-specific fertility rates.

Crude birth rates and crude death rates presented in this table are calculated using the number of live births and the number of deaths obtained from civil registers. These civil registration data are used only if they are considered reliable (estimated completeness of 90 per cent or more).

Similarly, infant mortality rates presented in this table are calculated using the number of live births and the number of infant deaths obtained from civil registers. If, however, the registration of births or infant deaths for any given country or area is estimated to be less than 90 per cent complete, the rates are not calculated.

Rate computation: The crude birth and death rates are the annual number of each of these vital events per 1 000 mid-year population.

Infant mortality rate is the annual number of deaths of infants under one year of age per 1 000 live births in the same year.

Rates of natural increase are the difference between the crude birth rate and the crude death rate. It should be noted that the rates of natural increase presented here may differ from the population growth rates presented in table 3 as rates of natural increase do not take net international migration into account while the population growth rates do.

Rates that appear in this table have been calculated by the Statistics Division of the United Nations Department of Economic and Social Affairs, unless otherwise noted. Exceptions include official estimated rates for Bangladesh and India, which were based on sample registration system in these countries.

Rates calculated by the Statistics Division of the United Nations presented in this table have been limited to those countries or areas having a minimum number of 30 events (for life births and deaths) or 100 events (for infant deaths) in a given year.

Reliability of data: Rates calculated on the basis of registered vital statistics which are considered unreliable (estimated to be less than 90 per cent complete) are not calculated. Estimated rates, prepared by individual countries or areas, are presented whenever applicable.

The designation of vital statistics as being either reliable or unreliable is discussed in general in section 4.2 of the Technical Notes. The technical notes for tables 9, 15 and 18 provide specific information on reliability of statistics on live births, infant deaths and deaths, respectively.

The values shown for life expectancy in this table come from official life tables. It is assumed that, if necessary, the basic data (population and deaths classified by age and sex) have been adjusted for deficiencies before their use in constructing the life tables.

Limitations: Statistics on births, deaths and infant deaths are subject to the same qualifications as have been set forth for vital statistics, in general, in section 4 of the Technical Notes and in the technical notes for individual tables presenting detailed data on these events (table 9, live births; table 15, infant deaths; table 18, deaths).

In assessing comparability it is important to take into account the reliability of the data used to calculate the rates, as discussed above.

The problem of obtaining precise correspondence between numerator (births and deaths) and denominator (population for crude birth and death rates) as regards the inclusion or exclusion of armed forces, refugees, displaced persons and other special groups is particularly difficult where vital rates are concerned. This is the case for Japan and Malta. For Japan, births and deaths refer to Japanese nationals only while the population include foreigners except foreign military and civilian personnel and their dependants stationed in the area. Similarly for Malta, births and deaths are for Maltese nationals only while the population include foreigners who hold work and resident permit and reside in the country.

It should also be noted that crude rates are particularly affected by the age-sex structure of the population. Infant mortality rates, and to a much lesser extent crude birth rates and crude death rates, are affected by the variation in the definition of a live birth and tabulation procedures.

_____

NOTES

[1] *Principles and Recommendations for a Vital Statistics System, Revision 2,* United Nations publication, Sales No. E.01.XVII.10, United Nations, New York, 2001.

Tableau 4

Le tableau 4 présente, pour chaque pays ou zone du monde, des statistiques de base de l'état civil comprenant, dans l'ordre, les naissances vivantes, le taux brut de natalité, les décès, le taux brut de mortalité et le taux d'accroissement naturel de la population, les décès d'enfants de moins d'un an et le taux de mortalité infantile, l'espérance de vie à la naissance par sexe et l'indice synthétique de fécondité.

Description des variables : Les faits d'état civil utilisés aux fins du calcul des taux présentés dans le tableau 4 sont définis comme suit[1] :

La naissance vivante est l'expulsion ou l'extraction complète du corps de la mère, indépendamment de la durée de la gestation, d'un produit de la conception qui après cette séparation, respire ou manifeste tout autre signe de vie, tel que battement de cœur, pulsation du cordon ombilical ou contraction effective d'un muscle soumis à l'action de la volonté, que le cordon ombilical ait été coupé ou non et que le placenta soit ou non demeuré attaché ; tout produit d'une telle naissance est considéré comme « enfant né vivant ».

Le décès est la disparition permanente de tout signe de vie à un moment quelconque postérieur à la naissance vivante (cessation des fonctions vitales après la naissance sans possibilité de réanimation).

Il convient de préciser que les chiffres relatifs aux décès d'enfants de moins d'un an se rapportent aux naissances vivantes.

L'espérance de vie à la naissance est le nombre moyen d'années que vivraient les individus de sexe masculin et de sexe féminin s'ils continuaient d'être soumis aux mêmes conditions de mortalité que celles qui existaient pendant les années auxquelles se rapportent les valeurs indiquées.

L'indice synthétique de fécondité représente le nombre moyen d'enfants que mettrait au monde une cohorte hypothétique de femmes qui seraient soumises, tout au long de leur vie, aux mêmes conditions de fécondité par âge que celles auxquelles sont soumises les femmes, dans chaque groupe d'âge, au cours d'une année ou d'une période donnée. La méthode standard pour calculer l'indice synthétique de fécondité consiste à additionner les taux de fécondité par âge simple.

Les taux bruts de natalité et de mortalité ont été établis sur la base du nombre de naissances vivantes et du nombre de décès inscrits sur les registres de l'état civil. Ces données n'ont été utilisées que lorsqu'elles étaient considérées comme sûres (degré estimatif de complétude égal ou supérieur à 90 p. 100).

De même, les taux de mortalité infantile présentés dans le tableau 4 ont été établis à partir du nombre de naissances vivantes et du nombre de décès d'enfants de moins d'un an inscrits sur les registres de l'état civil. Toutefois, lorsque les données relatives aux naissances ou aux décès d'enfants de moins d'un an pour un pays ou zone quelconque n'étaient pas considérées complètes à 90 p. 100 au moins, les indices n'ont pas été calculés.

Calcul des taux : Les taux bruts de natalité et de mortalité, représentent le nombre annuel de chacun de ces faits d'état civil pour 1 000 habitants au milieu de l'année considérée.

Les taux de mortalité infantile correspondent au nombre annuel de décès d'enfants de moins d'un an pour 1 000 naissances vivantes survenues pendant la même année.

Le taux d'accroissement naturel est égal à la différence entre le taux brut de natalité et le taux brut de mortalité. Il y a lieu de noter que les taux d'accroissement naturel indiqués dans le tableau 4 peuvent différer des taux d'accroissement de la population figurant dans le tableau 3, les taux d'accroissement naturel ne tenant pas compte des taux nets de migration internationale, alors que ceux-ci sont inclus dans les taux d'accroissement de la population.

Sauf indication contraire, les taux figurant dans le tableau 4 ont été calculés par la Division de statistique du Département des affaires économiques et sociales (Secrétariat de l'Organisation des Nations Unies). Les exceptions comprennent le Bangladesh et l'Inde, pour lesquels les taux estimatifs officiels ont été fournis sur la base d'un système d'enregistrement par échantillonnage.

Les taux calculés par la Division de statistique de l'ONU qui sont présentés dans le tableau 4 se rapportent aux seuls pays ou zones où l'on a enregistré au moins 30 événements (pour les naissances

73

vivantes et les décès) ou 100 événements (pour les décès d'enfants de moins d'un an) au cours d'une année donnée.

Fiabilité des données : Les taux n'ont pas été calculés lorsque les statistiques de l'état civil issues de systèmes d'enregistrement d'état civil étaient jugées douteuses (degré estimatif de complétude inférieur à 90 p.100) et des taux estimatifs, calculés par les pays ou zones, ont été présentés lorsqu'ils étaient disponibles.

On trouve à la section 4.2 des Notes techniques des explications générales concernant la façon dont les statistiques de l'état civil ont été classées selon leur degré de fiabilité. Les notes techniques relatives aux tableaux 9, 15 et 18 ont trait respectivement à la fiabilité des statistiques des naissances vivantes, des décès d'enfants de moins d'un an et des décès.

Les valeurs relatives à l'espérance de vie figurant dans le tableau 4 proviennent de tables officielles de mortalité. On présume que les données de base (population t décès par sexe et âge) ont été rectifiées d'éventuelles insuffisances avant d'être utilisées pour construire les tables de mortalité.

Insuffisance des données : les statistiques des naissances, décès et décès d'enfants de moins d'un an appellent toutes les réserves qui ont été formulées à propos des statistiques de l'état civil en général à la section 4 des Notes techniques et dans les notes techniques relatives aux différents tableaux présentant des données détaillées sur ces événements [tableau 9 (naissances vivantes), tableau 15 (décès d'enfants de moins d'un an) et tableau 18 (décès)].

Pour évaluer la comparabilité des divers taux, il importe de tenir compte de la fiabilité des données utilisées pour calculer ces taux, comme il a été indiqué précédemment.

Le calcul des taux est particulièrement affecté par la difficulté à obtenir une correspondance parfaite entre le numérateur (naissances et décès) et le dénominateur (population, pour les taux bruts de natalité et de mortalité) en raison de l'inclusion ou non dans la population des forces armées, des réfugiés, des personnes déplacées ou d'autres groupes sociaux. C'est le cas pour le Japon et Malte. Pour le Japon, les naissances et les décès se réfèrent aux seuls nationaux japonais tandis que la population inclus les étrangers, à l'exception toutefois des militaires étrangers ainsi que des personnels civils et leurs familles stationnés sur le territoire. De même, pour Malte, les naissances et les décès ne sont comptabilisés que pour les nationaux maltais alors que la population inclus les étrangers titulaires d'un permis de travail et de résidence et qui résident dans le pays.

Il y a lieu de noter que la structure par âge et par sexe de la population influe de façon particulière sur les taux bruts. Le manque d'uniformité dans la définition des naissances vivantes et dans les procédures de mise en tableaux a une incidence sur les taux de mortalité infantile et, à un moindre degré, sur les taux bruts de natalité et les taux bruts de mortalité.

NOTE

[1] *Principes et recommandations pour un système de statistiques de l'état civil, deuxième révision*, numéro de vente : F.01.XVII.10, publication des Nations Unies, New York, 2001.

4. Vital statistics summary and expectation of life at birth: 2001 - 2005
Aperçu des statistiques de l'état civil et espérance de vie à la naissance: 2001 - 2005

Continent, country or area and year / Continent, pays ou zone et année	Code[a]	Live births / Naissances vivantes — Number Nombre	Live births — Crude birth rate Taux brut de natalité	Code[a]	Deaths / Décès — Number Nombre	Deaths — Crude death rate Taux brut de mortalité	Rate of natural increase Taux d'accroissement naturel	Code[a]	Infant deaths / Décès d'enfants de moins d'un an — Number Nombre	Infant deaths — Rate (per 1000 births) Taux (par 1000 naissances)	Expectation of life at birth / Espérance de vie à la naissance — Male[b] Masculin[b]	Expectation of life — Female[b] Féminin[b]	Total fertility rate L'indice synthétique de fécondité
AFRICA - AFRIQUE													
Algeria - Algérie													
2001	C	618 380[1]	20.0	U	129 092[1]	...	...	U	21 622[1]	...	...	...	2.570
2002	C	616 963[1]	19.7	U	126 557[1]	...	...	U	19 850[1]	...	...	...	...
Benin - Bénin[2]													
2001	I	263 726	41.1	I	83 417	13.0	28.1	I	25 001	94.8	...	...	...
Botswana													
2001	I	53 735[2]	32.0	I	20 823[3]	12.4	19.6	I	1 576[3]	29.3	...	...	...
Cape Verde - Cap-Vert													
2001	C	12 926	29.1		...	...	...		...	...	...	...	...
2002	C	13 123	29.0		...	...	...		...	...	...	...	...
2003	C	13 334	28.9		...	...	...		...	...	...	...	...
Chad - Tchad													
2001	...	397 896	...	...	138 025	...	...		...	...	...	...	...
Congo[4]													
2001	+U	41 312	...	...	...	...	...		...	...	...	...	...
2002	+U	40 708	...	...	...	...	...		...	...	...	...	...
2003	+U	44 132	...	...	...	...	...		...	...	...	...	...
2004	+U	44 473	...	...	...	...	...		...	...	...	...	...
Egypt - Égypte													
2001	C	1 741 308	26.7	C	404 531	6.2	20.5	C	49 149	28.2	65.6	67.4	...
2002	C	1 766 589	26.5	C	424 034	6.4	20.2	C	37 904	21.5	67.5	71.9	...
2003	C	1 777 418	26.1	C	440 149	6.5	19.7	C	38 859	21.9	67.9	72.3	3.200
2004	C	1 779 500	25.0	C	440 790	6.2	18.8	C	40 177	22.6	...	...	3.100
2005	C	1 800 972	25.0	C	450 646	6.3	18.8	C	36 146	20.1	...	...	...
Ghana													
2001	...	433 202	...	...	52 332	...	...	...	51 639	...	...	...	...
2002		...	...	...	34 682	...	...	...	34 293	...	...	...	...
2003		...	...		...	...	...		...	...	...	...	4.400
Kenya													
2001	U	468 249	...	U	168 500	...	...	U	36 289	...	...	...	5.060
2002	U	494 941	...	U	171 800	...	...	U	35 940	...	...	...	4.896
2003	U	495 433	...	U	174 950	...	...	U	35 515	...	...	...	4.900
2004		...	...	U	178 051	...	...	U	35 321	...	...	...	...
2005		...	...	U	168 919	...	...	U	35 252	...	...	...	...
Lesotho													
2001		...	...		...	...	...		...	...	48.7	56.3	...
Libyan Arab Jamahiriya - Jamahiriya arabe libyenne													
2001	C	99 187	18.7	U	18 334	...	...	U	2 568	...	...	...	...
2002	C	111 053	20.2	U	19 362	...	...		...	...	...	...	...
Madagascar													
2003		...	...		...	...	...		...	...	...	...	5.200
2004		...	...		...	...	...		...	...	...	...	5.200
Malawi													
2001	I	555 558[2]	51.4	I	221 963[2]	20.5	30.8		...	...	42.3[5]	44.9[5]	...
2002	I	567 241[2]	50.8	I	217 205[2]	19.4	31.3		...	...	42.8[5]	45.5[5]	...
2003	I	578 978[2]	50.1	I	213 705[2]	18.5	31.6		...	...	43.4[5]	46.0[5]	...
Mali													
2001	U	525 685	...		...	...	...		...	...	...	...	...
Mauritius - Maurice													
2001	+C	19 696	16.4	+C	7 983	6.7	9.8	+C	282	14.3	III68.2	75.3	1.910
2002	+C	19 983	16.5	+C	8 310	6.9	9.6	+C	297	14.9	...	...	1.940
2003	+C	19 343	15.8	+C	8 520	7.0	8.9	+C	250	12.9	68.6	75.3	1.870
2004	+C	19 230	15.6	+C	8 475	6.9	8.7	+C	277	14.4	III68.4	75.3	1.870
2005	+C	18 820	15.1	+C	8 646	7.0	8.2	+C	248	13.2	...	...	1.820
Morocco - Maroc													
2001	C	541 298	18.6	U	95 612	...	...	U	7 379	...	...	...	...
Mozambique													
2001	I	753 252[2]	42.7	I	331 162[2]	18.8	23.9	I	99 164[2]	131.6	...	...	5.700
2002		...	...		...	...	...		...	...	...	...	5.500

Continent, country or area and year — Continent, pays ou zone et année	Live births — Naissances vivantes			Deaths — Décès			Rate of natural increase Taux d'accroissement naturel	Infant deaths — Décès d'enfants de moins d'un an			Expectation of life at birth — Espérance de vie à la naissance		Total fertility rate L'indice synthétique de fécondité
	Code[a]	Number Nombre	Crude birth rate Taux brut de natalité	Code[a]	Number Nombre	Crude death rate Taux brut de mortalité		Code[a]	Number Nombre	Rate (per 1000 births) Taux (par 1000 naissances)	Male[b] Masculin[b]	Female[b] Féminin[b]	
AFRICA - AFRIQUE													
Namibia - Namibie													
2001	I	45 157[3]	24.7	U	25 061[6]	...	...		...	...	...	...	...
Réunion													
2001	C	14 541[7]	19.8	C	3 829[7]	5.2	14.6	C	103	7.1	71.0	79.4	2.460
2002	C	14 789[7]	19.8	C	4 004[7]	5.4	14.4	C	91	...	...	...	2.500
2003	C	14 427[7]	18.9	C*	4 022[7]	5.3	13.6	C*	107	7.4	71.3	79.8	2.430
2004	C	14 545[7]	18.9	C	3 884[7]	5.1	13.9		...	...	...	...	...
2005	C*	14 799[7]	19.0	C	4 357[7]	5.6	13.4		...	...	...	...	...
Saint Helena ex. dep. - Sainte-Hélène sans dép.													
2001	C	36	...	C	41	...	...	C	-		...	...	...
2002	C	39	...	C	52	...	...		...		...	...	...
2003	C	37	...	C	44	...	...	C	1		...	...	...
2004	C	34	...	C	33	...	...		...		×71.9	79.1	...
2005	C	34	...	C	39	...	...	C	1		...	...	...
Seychelles													
2001	+C	1 440	17.7	+C	554	6.8	10.9	+C	19	...	...	...	1.980
2002	+C	1 481	17.7	+C	647	7.7	10.0	+C	26	...	...	...	...
2003	+C	1 498	18.1	+C	668	8.1	10.0	+C	25	...	...	...	...
2004	+C	1 435	17.4	+C	611	7.4	10.0	+C	17	...	...	...	...
2005	+C*	1 536	18.5	+C*	673	8.1	10.4	+C*	16	...	...	...	...
South Africa - Afrique du Sud													
2001	U	896 200	...	...	451 279[8]	...	...		...	...	51.8	56.7	2.800
2002	U	899 286	...	...	497 577[8]	...	...		...	...	...	...	...
2003	U	875 748	...	...	550 904[8]	...	...		...	...	...	...	2.820
2004	U	897 514	...	...	565 954[8]	...	...		...	...	49.9	52.9	2.800
2005	U	848 043	...	...	...	...	...		...	...	...	...	2.780
Tunisia - Tunisie													
2001	C*	163 300	16.9	U	53 300	...	...		...	...	...	...	...
Zimbabwe													
2002		...	...	I	200 294[9]	17.2			...	...	‖42.7	45.9	...
2005		...	...		...	...	...		...	...	...	...	3.800
AMERICA, NORTH - AMÉRIQUE DU NORD													
Anguilla													
2001	+C	183	15.8	+C	50	4.3	11.5	+C	-	...	...	...	...
2002	+C	169	14.2	+C	52	4.4	9.8	+C	2	...	...	...	...
2003	+C	139	11.4	+C	65	5.3	6.1	+C	2	...	...	...	...
2004	+C	164	13.1	+C	53	4.2	8.9	+C	-	...	...	...	...
2005	+C	167	12.2	+C	62	4.5	7.7	+C	3	...	...	...	...
Antigua and Barbuda - Antigua-et-Barbuda[10]													
2001		...	...	+C	462	6.0	...		...	...	...	...	...
2002		...	...	+C	444	5.7	...		...	...	...	...	...
Aruba													
2001	C	1 263	13.7	C	435	4.7	9.0	+U	4	...	...	...	3.150
2002	C	1 228	13.2	C	492	5.3	7.9	+U	3	...	...	...	2.990
2003	C	1 244	13.1	C	501	5.3	7.8	+U	3	...	...	...	1.627
2004	C	1 193	12.2	C	502	5.1	7.1	+U	3	...	...	...	1.749
2005	C	1 234	12.3	C	482	4.8	7.5	+U	6	...	...	...	1.739
Bahamas													
2001	U	5 353	...	C	1 609	5.2	...	C	37	...	...	...	1.995
2003	U	5 054	...	C	1 649	5.2	...	C	87	...	...	...	...

Continent, country or area and year / Continent, pays ou zone et année	Live births / Naissances vivantes			Deaths / Décès			Rate of natural increase Taux d'accrois-sement naturei	Infant deaths / Décès d'enfants de moins d'un an			Expectation of life at birth / Espérance de vie à la naissance		Total fertility rate / L'indice synthétique de fécondité
	Code[a]	Number Nombre	Crude birth rate Taux brut de natalité	Code[a]	Number Nombre	Crude death rate Taux brut de mortalité		Code[a]	Number Nombre	Rate (per 1000 births) Taux (par 1000 naiss-ances)	Male[b] Masculin[b]	Female[b] Féminin[b]	
AMERICA, NORTH - AMÉRIQUE DU NORD													
Barbados - Barbade													
2001		...	...	+C	1 712[10]	6.3	...		...	...	...	...	...
2002	+C*	3 812	14.1	+C*	2 285	8.4	5.6	+C*	54	...	...	...	...
Belize													
2001	U	7 215	...	U	1 261	...	...	U	120	...	...	...	...
2002	U	7 553	...	U	1 284	...	...	U	145	...	...	...	...
2003	U	7 440	...	U	1 277	...	...		...	...	...	...	...
2004	U	8 083	...	U	1 298	...	...	U	112	...	...	...	...
2005	U	8 396	...	U	1 369	...	...	U	137	...	...	...	...
Bermuda - Bermudes													
2001	C	831	13.3	C	442	7.1	6.2	C	3	...	...	...	...
2002	C	830	13.2	C	404	6.4	6.8	C	-	...	...	...	...
2003	C	834	13.2	C	434	6.9	6.3	C	2	...	...	...	...
2004	C	831	13.1	C	406	6.4	6.7		...	...	...	...	...
2005	C*	835	13.1	C*	437	6.9	6.3	C*	2	...	...	...	...
British Virgin Islands - Îles Vierges britanniques													
2001	C	314	15.2	C	101	4.9	10.3		...	...	73.2	77.7	1.970
2002	C	253	12.1	C	97	4.6	7.4		...	...	76.6	75.4	1.620
2003	C	269	12.6	C	104	4.9	7.7		...	...	73.8	78.9	1.700
2004	C	318	14.7	C	120	5.5	9.1		...	...	69.9	78.5	1.990
Canada													
2001	C	333 744[11]	10.8	C	219 538[11]	7.1	3.7	C	1 739[11]	5.2	77.0	82.2	1.510
2002	C	328 802[11]	10.5	C	223 603[11]	7.1	3.4	C	1 762[11]	5.4	77.2	82.1	1.501
2003	C	335 202[11]	10.6	C	226 169[11]	7.1	3.4	C	1 765[11]	5.3	77.4	82.4	1.525
2004	C	337 422[11]	10.5	C	226 584[11]	7.1	3.5	C	1 775[11]	5.3	77.8	82.6	1.526
2005	C	342 176[11]	10.6	C	231 240[11]	7.2	3.4		...	...	...	...	...
Cayman Islands - Îles Caïmanes													
2001	C	622	15.0	C	132	3.2	11.9		...	...	...	...	...
2002	C	583	13.7	C	120	2.8	10.9		...	...	...	...	...
2003	C	623	14.3	C	153	3.5	10.8		...	...	...	...	...
2004	C	611	13.8	C	196	4.4	9.4		...	...	...	...	...
2005	C	699	14.5	C	170	3.5	10.9		...	...	...	...	...
Costa Rica													
2001	C	76 401	19.6	C	15 609	4.0	15.6	C	827	10.8	...	...	...
2002	C	71 144	17.8	C	15 004	3.8	14.0	C	793	11.1	...	...	...
2003	C	72 938	17.8	C	15 800	3.9	14.0	C	737	10.1	...	...	2.100
2004	C	72 247	17.3	C	15 949	3.8	13.5	C	668	9.2	...	...	2.000
2005	C	71 548	16.8	C	16 139	3.8	13.0	C	700	9.8	...	...	2.000
Cuba													
2001	C	138 718	12.4	C	79 395	7.1	5.3	C	861	6.2	...	...	...
2002	C	141 276	12.6	C	73 882	6.6	6.0	C	922	6.5	...	...	1.675
2003	C	136 795	12.2	C	78 434	7.0	5.2	C	859	6.3	[III]75.1	79.0	1.628
2004	C	127 192	11.3	C*	81 095	7.2	4.1	C*	736	5.8	...	...	1.543
2005	C	120 716	10.7	C	84 824	7.5	3.2	C	746	6.2	...	...	1.493
Dominica - Dominique													
2001	+C	1 213	17.1	+C	510	7.2	9.9	+C	24	...	...	...	...
2002	+C	1 081	15.4	+C	594[10]	8.4	6.9		...	...	...	...	...
2003		...	...	+C	557[10]	...	...		...	...	...	...	...
Dominican Republic - République dominicaine													
2001	+U	161 733	...	+U	26 636	...	...		...	...	...	...	...
2002	+U	147 027	...	+U	26 166	...	...		...	...	...	...	...
2003	+U	142 051	...	+U	28 343	...	...		...	...	...	...	...
2004	+U	112 630	...	+U	30 118	...	...		...	...	...	...	...
El Salvador													
2001	C	138 354	21.6	C	29 559	4.6	17.0	C	1 682	12.2	...	...	...
2002	C	129 363	19.8	C	27 458	4.2	15.6	C	1 284	9.9	...	...	...

Continent, country or area and year / Continent, pays ou zone et année	Live births / Naissances vivantes			Deaths / Décès			Rate of natural increase / Taux d'accrois-sement naturel	Infant deaths / Décès d'enfants de moins d'un an			Expectation of life at birth / Espérance de vie à la naissance		Total fertility rate / L'indice synthétique de fécondité
	Code[a]	Number Nombre	Crude birth rate Taux brut de natalité	Code[a]	Number Nombre	Crude death rate Taux brut de mortalité		Code[a]	Number Nombre	Rate (per 1000 births) Taux (par 1000 naissances)	Male[b] Masculin[b]	Female[b] Féminin[b]	
AMERICA, NORTH - AMÉRIQUE DU NORD													
El Salvador													
2003	C	124 476	18.8	C	29 377	4.4	14.3	C	1 322	10.6	...	...	...
2004	C	119 710	17.7	C	30 058	4.4	13.3	C	1 255	10.5	...	...	...
2005	C	112 769	16.4	C	...	...	...		...	...	VI67.7	73.7	...
Greenland - Groenland													
2001	C	937	16.6	C	438	7.8	8.8	C	10	...	...	...	2.451
2002	C	940	16.6	C	435	7.7	8.9	C	10	...	...	...	2.488
2003	C	895	15.8	C	412	7.3	8.5	C	8	...	V64.1	69.5	2.361
2004	C	893	15.7		...	...	...		...	...	...	...	...
2005	C	887	...		...	...	...		...	...	...	...	...
Grenada - Grenade													
2001	+C	1 899	18.8	+C	727	7.2	11.6	+C	33	...	...	...	...
Guadeloupe													
2001	C	7 503[7]	17.3	C	2 765[7]	6.4	11.0	C	49[7]	...	...	...	2.300
2002	C	6 995[7]	16.0	C	2 584[7]	5.9	10.1	C	45[7]	...	74.6	81.5	2.200
2003	C	7 047[7]	16.1	C	2 636[7]	6.0	10.1	C	56[7]	...	...	...	...
2004	C	7 273[7]	16.4	C	2 676[7]	6.0	10.3	C	50[7]	...	...	...	...
2005	C	7 551[7]	16.9	C	2 904[7]	6.5	10.4		...	...	...	...	...
Guatemala													
2001	C	415 338	35.6	C	68 041	5.8	29.7		...	...	...	...	...
2002	C	387 287	32.3	C	66 089	5.5	26.8		...	...	...	...	...
2003	C	375 092	31.0	C	66 695	5.5	25.5	C	11 022	29.4	...	...	...
2004	C	383 704	31.0	C	66 991	5.4	25.6	C	10 038	26.2	...	...	...
2005	C*	374 066	29.5	C*	71 039	5.6	23.9	C*	9 947	26.6	...	...	...
Haiti - Haïti[10]													
2001		...	...	U	9 599	...	...		...	...	...	...	...
2002		...	...	U	7 657	...	...		...	...	...	...	...
2003		...	...	U	8 011	...	...		...	...	...	...	...
Jamaica - Jamaïque													
2001	C	48 065[12]	18.5	U	14 473	...	...	U	833	...	...	...	2.215
2002	C	44 331[12]	16.9	U	15 711	...	...	U	809	...	III72.8	76.5	2.044
2003	C	43 407[12]	16.5	U	15 581	...	...	U	753	...	71.3	77.1	2.067
2004	C	42 448[12]	16.1	U	15 389	...	...	U	695	...	...	...	...
2005	C	41 836[12]	15.7	U	15 523	...	...		...	...	...	...	...
Martinique													
2001	C	5 908[7]	15.3	C	2 754[7]	7.1	8.1	C	43	...	...	...	2.000
2002	C	5 446[7]	14.0	C	2 681[7]	6.9	7.1	C	33	...	75.4	82.2	1.900
2003	C	5 430[7]	13.9	C	2 725[7]	7.0	6.9	C	33	...	...	...	...
2004	C	5 255[7]	13.3	C	2 647[7]	6.7	6.6	C	27	...	...	...	...
2005	C	5 032[7]	12.7	C	2 610[7]	6.6	6.1		...	...	...	...	...
Mexico - Mexique													
2001	+U	2 767 610	...	C	443 127	4.4	...	U	35 911	...	...	...	2.453
2002	+U	2 699 084	...	C	459 687	4.6	...	U	36 567	...	...	...	2.285
2003	+U	2 655 894	...	C	472 140	4.6	...	U	33 355	...	...	...	2.333
2004	+U	2 625 056	...	C	473 417	4.6	...	U	32 764	...	...	...	2.242
2005	+U	2 567 906	...	C	495 240	4.8	...	U	32 603	...	71.9	77.4	2.198
Netherlands Antilles - Antilles néerlandaises													
2001	C	2 705[13]	15.5	C	1 215[14]	7.0	8.6	C	24	...	...	...	2.256
2002	C	2 442[13]	14.0	C	1 220[14]	7.0	7.0	C	17	...	V72.1	78.7	2.068
2003	C	2 488[13]	13.9	C	1 374[14]	7.7	6.2	C	19	...	...	...	2.059
2004	C	2 357[13]	12.9	C	1 412[14]	7.7	5.2	C	20	...	III70.6	79.0	1.879
Nicaragua													
2001	+U	121 310	...	+U	14 236	...	...	+U	2 031	...	...	...	...
2002	+U	121 361	...	+U	15 070	...	...	+U	2 217	...	...	...	...
2003	+U	120 784	...	+U	15 379	...	...	+U	2 008	...	...	...	...
2004	+U	121 402	...	+U	14 975	...	...	+U	1 827	...	...	...	...
2005	+U	121 380	...	+U	16 770	...	...	+U	1 970	...	VI67.2	71.9	...

Continent, country or area and year — Continent, pays ou zone et année	Code[a]	Number Nombre	Crude birth rate Taux brut de natalité	Code[a]	Number Nombre	Crude death rate Taux brut de mortalité	Rate of natural increase Taux d'accrois-sement naturel	Code[a]	Number Nombre	Rate (per 1000 births) Taux (par 1000 naissances)	Male[b] Masculin[b]	Female[b] Féminin[b]	Total fertility rate L'indice synthétique de fécondité
AMERICA, NORTH - AMÉRIQUE DU NORD													
Panama													
2001	C	63 900	22.1	U	12 442	...	...	U	1 053	...	...	...	2.495
2002	C	61 671	20.2	U	12 428	...	...	U	885	...	...	...	...
2003	C	61 753	19.8	U	13 248	...	...	U	940	...	...	...	...
2004	C	62 743	19.8	U	13 475	...	...	U	932	...	...	...	...
2005	C*	63 645	19.7	U	14 180	...	...	U	980	...	...	...	...
Puerto Rico - Porto Rico													
2001	C	55 982	14.6	C	28 794	7.5	7.1	C	515	9.2	...	...	1.916
2002	C	52 871	13.7	C	28 098	7.3	6.4	C	516	9.8	73.2	80.9	1.817
2003	C	50 803	13.1	C	28 356	7.3	5.8	C	498	9.8	...	...	1.760
2004		...	...		...	...	...		...	...	[III]73.7	81.1	...
2005	C	50 687	13.0	C	29 701	7.6	5.4	C	472	9.3	...	...	1.749
Saint Kitts and Nevis - Saint-Kitts-et-Nevis													
2001	+C	803	17.4	+C	352	7.6	9.8		...	...	...	...	...
Saint Lucia - Sainte-Lucie													
2001	C	2 788	17.7	C	998	6.3	11.3	C	37	...	...	...	...
2002	C	2 598	16.3	C	960	6.0	10.3	C	36	...	72.0	76.7	...
2003	C	2 486	15.5	C	1 046	6.5	9.0	C	37	...	...	...	...
2004	C*	2 322	14.3	C*	1 114	6.9	7.4	C*	45	...	...	...	...
Saint Vincent and the Grenadines - Saint Vincent-et-les Grenadines													
2001	+C	2 109	19.3	+C	765	7.0	12.3	+C	39	...	66.9	72.9	...
2002	+C	1 985	18.4	+C	766	7.1	11.3	+C	35	...	...	...	...
2003	+C	1 923	18.3	+C	790	7.5	10.8	+C	35	...	...	...	...
2004	+C	1 804	17.3	+C	812	7.8	9.5	+C	33	...	...	...	...
2005	+C	1 779	17.1	+C	813	7.8	9.3	+C	29	...	...	...	...
Trinidad and Tobago - Trinité-et-Tobago													
2001	C	18 078	14.3	C	9 753	7.7	6.6	C	335	18.5	...	...	...
2002	C	16 990	13.3	C	9 797	7.7	5.6	C	412	24.2	...	...	...
Turks Caicos Islands - Îles Turques et Caïques													
2001	C	271	13.6	C	69	3.5	10.2	C	2	...	79.0	77.4	...
2002	C	153	7.3	C	48	2.3	5.0	C	2	...	...	...	...
2003	C	213	8.5	C	61	2.4	6.0	C	2	...	...	...	...
2004	C	300	10.9	C	46	1.7	9.2	C	-	...	...	...	...
2005	C	318	10.4	C	53	1.7	8.7	C	1	...	...	...	...
United States - États-Unis													
2001	C	4 025 933	14.1	C	2 416 425	8.5	5.6	C	27 568	6.8	74.4	79.8	2.034
2002	C	4 021 726	14.0	C	2 443 387	8.5	5.5	C	28 034	7.0	74.5	79.9	2.013
2003	C	4 089 950	14.1	C	2 448 288	8.4	5.6	C	28 025	6.9	74.8	80.1	2.043
2004	C*	4 115 590	14.0	C*	2 398 343	8.2	5.8	C*	27 838	6.8	...	...	2.049
2005	C	4 138 349	14.0		...	...	...		...	...	...	...	...
United States Virgin Islands - Îles Vierges américaines[10]													
2001		...	...	C	605	5.6	...		...	...	...	...	...
2002		...	...	C	617	5.7	...		...	...	...	...	...
AMERICA, SOUTH - AMÉRIQUE DU SUD													
Argentina - Argentine													
2001	C	683 495	18.4	C	285 941	7.7	10.7	C	11 111	16.3	[II]70.0	77.5	...
2002	C	694 684	18.5	C	291 190	7.8	10.8	C	11 703	16.8	...	...	...
2003	C	697 952	18.4	C	302 064	8.0	10.5	C	11 494	16.5	...	...	2.406

4. Vital statistics summary and expectation of life at birth: 2001 - 2005
Aperçu des statistiques de l'état civil et espérance de vie à la naissance: 2001 - 2005 (continued - suite)

Continent, country or area and year / Continent, pays ou zone et année	Live births / Naissances vivantes Code[a]	Number Nombre	Crude birth rate Taux brut de natalité	Deaths / Décès Code[a]	Number Nombre	Crude death rate Taux brut de mortalité	Rate of natural increase Taux d'accroissement naturel	Infant deaths / Décès d'enfants de moins d'un an Code[a]	Number Nombre	Rate (per 1000 births) Taux (par 1000 naissances)	Expectation of life at birth Male[b] Masculin[b]	Female[b] Féminin[b]	Total fertility rate L'indice synthétique de fécondité
AMERICA, SOUTH - AMÉRIQUE DU SUD													
Argentina - Argentine													
2004	C	736 261	19.3	C	294 051	7.7	11.6	C	10 576	14.4	...	...	2.501
2005	C	712 220	18.5	C	293 529	7.6	10.8	C	9 507	13.3	...	...	2.389
Brazil - Brésil[15]													
2001	U	2 509 354	...	U	931 017	...	...	U	47 171	...	...	...	2.180
2002	U	2 581 055	...	U	958 475	...	...	U	45 243	...	67.3	74.9	2.160
2003	U	2 822 462	...	U	977 717	...	...	U	48 039	...	...	...	2.330
2004	U	2 813 704	...	U	998 725	...	...	U	41 851	...	...	...	2.310
2005	U	2 874 542	...	U	979 854	...	...	U	39 259	...	68.1	75.8	2.290
Chile - Chili													
2001	C	246 116	15.8	C	81 873	5.3	10.5	C	2 159	8.8	...	...	2.000
2002	C	238 981	15.2	C	81 079	5.1	10.0	C	1 964	8.2	[II]74.4	80.4	2.000
2003	C	234 486	14.7	C	83 672	5.3	9.5	C	1 935	8.3	...	...	1.900
2004	C	230 352	14.3	C	86 138	5.4	9.0	C	2 034	8.8	...	...	1.910
Colombia - Colombie													
2001	U	724 319[16]	...	U	191 513[16]	...	...	U	14 430[16]	...	...	...	...
2002	U	700 455[16]	...	U	192 262[16]	...	...	U	12 640[16]	...	...	...	...
2003	U	710 702[16]	...	U	193 267[16]	...	...	U	12 335[16]	...	...	...	...
2004	U	723 099[16]	...	U	188 933[16]	...	...	U	11 772[16]	...	...	...	...
2005	U	719 533[16]	...	U	188 795[16]	...	...	U	11 441[16]	...	[VI]69.2	75.3	...
Ecuador - Équateur[17]													
2001	U	192 786	...	U	55 214	...	...	U	4 800	...	...	...	...
2002	U	183 792	...	U	55 549	...	...	U	4 530	...	...	...	...
2003	U	178 549	...	U	53 521	...	...	U	3 985	...	...	...	...
2004	U	168 893	...	U	54 729	...	...	U	3 942	...	...	...	...
2005	U	168 324	...	U	56 825	...	...	U	3 717	...	[VI]71.3	77.2	...
French Guiana - Guyane française													
2001	C	5 114[7]	30.1	C	668[7]	3.9	26.2	C	70[7]	...	...	...	3.900
2002	C	5 249[7]	29.9	C	656[7]	3.7	26.2	C	52[7]	...	72.5	79.2	3.900
2003	C	5 553[7]	30.7	C	692[7]	3.8	26.8	C	58[7]	...	71.3	79.7	...
2004	C	5 312[7]	28.4	C	719[7]	3.8	24.9	C	55[7]	...	...	...	...
2005	C	5 998[7]	30.0	C	705[7]	3.5	26.5			...	...	...	...
Guyana													
2001		...	...	+C	4 629	6.2	...		...	...	...	...	...
2002		...	...	+C	5 003	6.7	...		...	...	...	...	...
2003		...	...	+C	4 986	6.6	...		...	...	...	...	...
2004		...	...	+C	5 141	6.8	...		...	...	...	...	...
Paraguay													
2001		...	...	U	18 400[10]	...	...	I	3 898[18]	...	...	...	...
2003	U	45 669	...	U	19 593	...	...	U	674	...	...	...	...
2004	U	49 857	...	U	20 283	...	...	U	647	...	...	...	...
2005	U	51 444	...	U	17 360	...	...	U	539	...	[VI]68.6	73.1	...
Peru - Pérou[15]													
2001	+U	354 618[19]	...	+U	79 966[20]	...	...	+U	6 604[21]	...	...	...	2.960
2002	+U	355 870[19]	...	+U	80 862[20]	...	...	+U	6 511[21]	...	...	...	2.890
2003	+U	373 600[19]	...	+U	85 198[20]	...	...	+U	7 122[21]	...	...	...	2.830
2004		...	...	+U	94 149[20]	...	...		...	...	...	...	...
Suriname													
2001	C	9 717	20.7	C	3 099	6.6	14.1	C	133	13.7	...	...	...
2002	C	10 188	21.4	C	3 125	6.6	14.8	C	148	14.5	...	...	...
2003	C	9 634	20.0	C	3 154	6.6	13.5	C	109	11.3	...	...	...
2004	C	9 062	18.6	C	3 319	6.8	11.8	C	120	13.2	...	...	2.530
2005	C	8 657	17.3	C	3 392	6.8	10.6		...	...	...	...	...
Uruguay													
2001	C	51 959	15.7	C	31 228	9.4	6.3	C	721	13.9	...	...	2.230
2002	C	51 953	15.7	C	31 628	9.6	6.1	C	708	13.6	...	...	2.210
2003	C*	50 631	15.3	C	32 587	9.9	5.5	C*	757	15.0	71.3	79.2	...

Continent, country or area and year / Continent, pays ou zone et année	Code[a]	Live births Number Nombre	Crude birth rate Taux brut de natalité	Code[a]	Deaths Number Nombre	Crude death rate Taux brut de mortalité	Rate of natural increase Taux d'accroiss-ement naturel	Code[a]	Infant deaths Number Nombre	Rate (per 1000 births) Taux (par 1000 naissances)	Male[b] Masculin[b]	Female[b] Féminin[b]	Total fertility rate L'indice synthétique de fécondité
AMERICA, SOUTH - AMÉRIQUE DU SUD													
Uruguay													
2004	C*	50 052	15.2	C*	32 222	9.8	5.4	C*	660	13.2	71.7	78.9	...
2005	C	47 334	14.3	C*	33 319	10.1	4.2	C*	601	12.7	...	...	...
Venezuela (Bolivarian Republic of) - Venezuela (République bolivarienne du)[15]													
2001	C	529 552	21.4	C	107 867	4.4	17.0	C	8 158	15.4	70.6	76.4	...
2002	C	492 678	19.5	C	105 388	4.2	15.4	C	7 645	15.5	70.8	76.6	...
2003	C	555 614	21.6	C	118 562	4.6	17.0		...	...	...	...	...
2004	C	637 799	24.4	C	110 946	4.2	20.2		...	...	...	...	...
2005	C	665 997	25.1	C	110 301	4.2	20.9		...	...	...	...	2.650
ASIA - ASIE													
Afghanistan													
2001		...	...		...	...	...		...	...	43.0	43.0	...
2002		...	...		...	...	...		...	...	43.0	43.0	...
Armenia - Arménie													
2001	C	32 065[22]	10.0	C	24 003[22]	7.5	2.5	C	497[22]	15.5	70.0	76.1	1.107
2002	C	32 229[22]	10.0	C	25 554[22]	8.0	2.1	C	450[22]	14.0	69.8	75.9	1.208
2003	C	35 793[22]	11.1	C	26 014[22]	8.1	3.0	C	422[22]	11.8	69.9	75.8	1.349
2004	C	37 520[22]	11.7	C	25 679[22]	8.0	3.7	C	430[22]	11.5	70.3	76.4	1.383
2005	C	37 499[22]	11.7	C	26 379[22]	8.2	3.5	C	460[22]	12.3	70.3	76.5	1.365
Azerbaijan - Azerbaïdjan													
2001	+C	110 356[22]	13.6	+C	45 284[22]	5.6	8.0	+C	1 382[22]	12.5	68.7	75.2	1.830
2002	+C	110 715[22]	13.5	+C	46 522[22]	5.7	7.9	+C	1 422[22]	12.8	69.4	75.0	1.840
2003	+C	113 467[22]	13.8	+C	49 001[22]	6.0	7.8	+C	1 451[22]	12.8	69.5	75.1	1.910
2004	+C	131 609[22]	15.8	+C	49 568[22]	6.0	9.9	+C	1 287[22]	9.8	69.6	75.2	2.050
2005	+C	141 901[22]	16.9	+C	51 962[22]	6.2	10.7	+C	1 321[22]	9.3	69.6	75.2	...
Bahrain - Bahreïn													
2001	C	13 468	20.6	C	1 979	3.0	17.6	C	117	8.7	73.2	76.2	2.576
2002	C	13 576	20.2	C	2 035	3.0	17.2	C	94	...	...	...	2.528
2003	C	14 560	21.1	C	2 114	3.1	18.1	C	107	7.3	...	...	2.600
2004	C	14 968	21.2	C	2 215	3.1	18.0	C	135	9.0	...	...	2.600
2005	C	15 198	21.0	C	2 222	3.1	17.9	C	134	8.8	73.1	77.3	2.600
Bangladesh													
2001	I	...	18.9 [23]	I	...	4.8 [23]	...	I	...	56.0 [23]	64.0	64.5	2.560
2002	I	...	20.1 [23]	I	...	5.1 [23]	...	I	...	53.0 [23]	64.5	65.4	2.550
2003	I	...	20.9 [23]	I	...	5.9 [23]	...	I	...	53.0 [23]	64.3	65.4	2.570
2004	I	...	20.8 [2]	I	...	5.8 [23]	...	I	...	52.0 [23]	64.4	65.7	2.510
2005		...	...		...	...	...		...	...	64.5	65.7	...
Bhutan - Bhoutan[24]													
2005	I	12 538	19.7	I	4 498	7.1	12.7	I	503	40.1	...	...	...
Brunei Darussalam - Brunéi Darussalam													
2001	+C	7 363	22.1	+C	1 014	3.0	19.1	+C	50	...	...	...	2.238
2002	+C	7 464	21.7	+C	1 041	3.0	18.7	+C	62	...	...	...	...
2003	+C	7 047	20.2	+C	1 010	2.9	17.3	+C	67	...	...	...	...
2004	+C	7 163	19.9	+C	1 010	2.8	17.1	+C	63	...	...	...	...
2005	+C*	6 933	18.7	+C*	1 072	2.9	15.8	+C*	51	...	...	...	...
Cambodia - Cambodge													
2001	U	359 678	...	U	126 257	...	...		87	...	...	...	3.830
2002	U	367 569	...	U	125 617	...	...		83	...	...	...	3.780
2003	U	375 799	...	U	124 981	...	...		80	...	...	...	3.780
2004	U	384 267	...	U	124 391	...	...		76	...	...	...	3.680

Continent, country or area and year / Continent, pays ou zone et année	Code[a]	Live births — Naissances vivantes — Number / Nombre	Crude birth rate Taux brut de natalité	Code[a]	Deaths — Décès — Number / Nombre	Crude death rate Taux brut de mortalité	Rate of natural increase Taux d'accrois-sement naturel	Code[a]	Infant deaths — Décès d'enfants de moins d'un an — Number / Nombre	Rate (per 1000 births) Taux (par 1000 naiss-ances)	Male[b] Masculin[b]	Female[b] Féminin[b]	Total fertility rate L'indice synthétique de fécondité
ASIA - ASIE													
China - Chine[26]													
2001	I	17 020 000[27]	13.4	I	8 180 000[27]	6.4	7.0		...	...	...	...	...
2002	I	16 470 000[27]	12.9	I	8 210 000[27]	6.4	6.5		...	...	...	...	...
2003	I	15 990 000[27]	12.4	I	8 250 000[27]	6.4	6.0		...	...	...	...	...
2004	I	15 930 000[27]	12.3	I	8 320 000[27]	6.4	5.9		...	...	...	...	...
2005	I	16 170 000[28]	12.4	I	8 490 000[28]	6.5	5.9		...	...	...	...	...
China: Hong Kong SAR - Chine: Hong Kong RAS													
2001	C	48 219	7.2	C	33 378	5.0	2.2	C	124	2.6	78.4	84.6	0.931[25]
2002	C	48 209	7.1	C	34 267	5.1	2.1	C	110	2.3	78.5	84.5	0.941[25]
2003	C	46 965	7.0	C	36 971	5.5	1.5	C	109	2.3	78.5	84.4	0.901[25]
2004	C	49 796	7.3	C	36 918	5.4	1.9	C	132	2.7	79.0	84.8	0.922[25]
2005	C	57 098	8.4	C	38 830	5.7	2.7	C	131	2.3	78.8	84.6	0.959[25]
China: Macao SAR - Chine: Macao RAS													
2001	C	3 241	7.5	C	1 327	3.1	4.4	C	14	...	...	...	0.818
2002	C	3 162	7.2	C	1 415	3.2	4.0	C	11	...	...	...	0.813
2003	C	3 212	7.2	C	1 474	3.3	3.9	C	2	...	...	...	0.837
2004	C	3 308	7.3	C	1 533	3.4	3.9	C	10	...	[IV]77.5	82.1	0.855
2005	C	3 671	7.8	C	1 615	3.4	4.3	C	12	...	[IV]77.6	82.3	0.912
Cyprus - Chypre[29]													
2001	C	8 167	11.6	C	4 827	6.9	4.8	C	37	...	...	...	1.559
2002	C	7 883	11.1	C	5 168	7.3	3.8	C	37	...	...	...	1.491
2003	C	8 088	11.2	C	5 200	7.2	4.0	C	33	...	[II]77.0	81.4	1.498
2004	C	8 309	11.3	C	5 225	7.1	4.2	C	29	...	...	...	1.487
2005	C	8 243	10.9	C	5 425	7.2	3.7	C	33	...	[II]77.0	81.7	1.420
Georgia - Géorgie													
2001	C	47 589[22]	10.8	C	46 218[22]	10.5	0.3	C	1 098[22]	23.1	68.0	74.8	1.440
2002	C	46 605[22]	10.7	C	46 446[22]	10.7	0.0	C	1 102[22]	23.6	68.0	74.8	1.420
2003	C	46 194[22]	10.7	C	46 055[22]	10.6	0.0	C	1 144[22]	24.8	69.1	74.7	1.370
2004	C	49 572[22]	11.5	C	48 793[22]	11.3	0.2	C	1 178[22]	23.8	67.8	74.9	1.440
2005	C	46 512[22]	10.7	C	42 984[22]	9.9	0.8	C	916[22]	19.7	69.3	76.7	1.350
India - Inde[30]													
2001	I	...	25.4[31]	I	...	8.4[31]	...	I	...	66.0[31]	...	...	3.100
2002	I	...	25.0[31]	I	...	8.1[31]	...	I	...	63.0[31]	...	...	3.000
2003	I	...	24.8[31]	I	...	8.0[31]	...	I	...	60.0[31]	[V]61.8	63.5	3.000
2004	I	...	24.1[31]	I	...	7.5[31]	...	I	...	58.0[31]	[V]62.1	63.7	2.900
2005	I	...	23.8[31]	I	...	7.6[31]	...	I	...	58.0[31]	...	...	2.900
Iran (Islamic Republic of) - Iran (République islamique d')													
2001	C	1 112 193[32]	17.2	C	421 525[32]	6.5	10.7		...	...	67.6	70.4	2.500
2002	C	1 122 104[32]	17.1	C	337 237[32]	5.1	12.0		...	...	...	...	...
2003	C	1 171 573[32]	17.6	C	368 518[32]	5.5	12.1		...	...	...	...	...
2004	C	1 154 368[32]	17.1	C	355 213[32]	5.3	11.8		...	...	...	...	...
2005	C	1 233 873[32]	18.0	C	361 326[32]	5.3	12.7		...	...	...	...	...
Iraq													
2003	U*	691 269	...	U*	95 935	...	...		...	...	...	...	...
2004	U*	840 257	...	U*	101 820	...	...	U*	10 972	...	...	...	...
2005	U*	896 340	...	U*	115 775	...	...	U*	12 460	...	...	...	...
Israel - Israël[33]													
2001	C	136 638	21.2	C	37 186	5.8	15.4	C	700	5.1	77.3	81.2	2.887
2002	C	139 535	21.2	C	38 409[34]	5.8	15.4	C	752[35]	5.4	77.5	81.5	2.888
2003	C	144 936	21.7	C	38 499[36]	5.8	15.9	C	717[35]	4.9	77.7	81.9	2.945
2004	C	145 207	21.3	C	37 939[37]	5.6	15.8	C	670[35]	4.6	78.1	82.4	2.904
2005	C	143 913	20.8	C	38 911[38]	5.6	15.2	C	627[35]	4.4	78.3	82.3	2.836

4. Vital statistics summary and expectation of life at birth: 2001 - 2005
Aperçu des statistiques de l'état civil et espérance de vie à la naissance: 2001 - 2005 (continued - suite)

Continent, country or area and year / Continent, pays ou zone et année	Code[a]	Live births Naissances vivantes Number Nombre	Live births Crude birth rate Taux brut de natalité	Code[a]	Deaths Décès Number Nombre	Deaths Crude death rate Taux brut de mortalité	Rate of natural increase Taux d'accrois-sement naturel	Code[a]	Infant deaths Décès d'enfants de moins d'un an Number Nombre	Infant deaths Rate (per 1000 births) Taux (par 1000 naiss-ances)	Expectation of life at birth Espérance de vie à la naissance Male[b] Masculin[b]	Expectation of life at birth Female[b] Féminin[b]	Total fertility rate L'indice synthétique de fécondité
ASIA - ASIE													
Japan - Japon[39]													
2001	C	1 170 662	9.2	C	970 331	7.6	1.6	C	3 599	3.1	78.1	84.9	1.330
2002	C	1 153 855	9.1	C	982 379	7.7	1.4	C	3 497	3.0	78.3	85.2	1.319
2003	C	1 123 610	8.8	C	1 014 951	7.9	0.9	C	3 364	3.0	78.4	85.3	1.290
2004	C	1 110 721	8.7	C	1 028 602	8.1	0.7	C	3 122	2.8	78.6	85.6	1.289
2005	C	1 062 530	8.3	C	1 083 796	8.5	-0.2	C	2 958	2.8	78.5	85.5	1.260
Jordan - Jordanie[40]													
2001	C	142 956	28.7	U	16 164	...	...		...	...	68.8	71.1	3.500
2002	C	146 077	28.7	U	17 220	...	...		...	...	70.6	72.4	3.700
2003	C	148 294	28.4	U	16 937	...	...		...	...	70.6	72.4	3.700
2004	C	150 248[41]	28.1	U	17 896[41]	...	...		...	...	70.6	72.4	3.700
2005	C	152 276[41]	27.8	U	17 883[41]	...	...		...	...	70.6	72.4	3.700
Kazakhstan													
2001	C	221 487[22]	14.9	C	147 876[22]	10.0	5.0	C	4 239[22]	19.1	60.5	71.3	1.840
2002	C	227 171[22]	15.3	C	149 381[22]	10.1	5.2	C	3 850[22]	16.9	60.7	71.5	1.880
2003	C	247 946[22]	16.6	C	155 277[22]	10.4	6.2	C	3 824[22]	15.4	60.5	71.5	2.030
2004	C	273 028[22]	18.2	C	152 250[22]	10.1	8.0	C	3 901[22]	14.3	60.6	72.0	2.210
2005	C	278 977[22]	18.4	C	157 121[22]	10.4	8.0	C	4 213[22]	15.1	60.3	71.8	...
Korea (Republic of) - Corée (République de)													
2001	C	557 228[42]	11.8	C	242 730[42]	5.1	6.6	C	3 008[42]	5.4	72.8	80.0	1.300
2002	C	494 625[42]	10.4	C	246 515[42]	5.2	5.2	C	2 545[42]	5.1	73.4	80.4	1.170
2003	C	493 471[42]	10.3	C	245 817[42]	5.1	5.2	C	2 470[42]	5.0	73.9	80.8	1.190
2004	C	476 052[42]	9.9	C	245 771[42]	5.1	4.8	C	2 209[42]	4.6	...	...	1.160
2005	C	438 062[42]	9.1	C	245 511[42]	5.1	4.0		...	...	...	...	...
Kuwait - Koweït													
2001	C	41 342	18.9	C	4 364	2.0	16.9	C	420	10.2	...	...	4.042
2002	C	43 490	19.2	C	4 342	1.9	17.3	C	418	9.6	...	...	4.146
2003	C	43 982	18.9	C	4 424	1.9	17.0	C	412	9.4	...	...	4.064
2004	C	47 274	19.8	C	4 793	2.0	17.8	C	422	8.9	...	...	4.101
2005	C	50 941	20.7	C	4 784	1.9	18.8	C	420	8.2	...	...	4.155
Kyrgyzstan - Kirghizistan													
2001	C	98 138[22]	19.8	C	32 677[22]	6.6	13.2	C	2 123[22]	21.6	65.0	72.6	2.383
2002	C	101 012[22]	20.2	C	35 235[22]	7.1	13.2	C	2 128[22]	21.1	64.4	72.1	2.465
2003	C	105 490[22]	20.9	C	35 941[22]	7.1	13.8	C	2 186[22]	20.7	...	...	2.521
2004	C	109 939[22]	21.6	C	35 061[22]	6.9	14.7	C	2 812[43]	25.6	64.4	72.3	2.582
2005	C	109 839[22]	21.4	C	36 992[22]	7.2	14.2	C	3 258[22]	29.7	64.2	71.9	2.531
Lao People's Democratic Republic - République démocratique populaire lao[44]													
2005		...	...		...	...	...		...	...	55.0	63.0	4.500
Lebanon - Liban													
2001	C	83 693	...	C	17 568	...	...		...	...	...	...	...
2002	C	76 405	...	C	17 294	...	...		...	...	...	...	...
2003	C	71 465	...	C	17 187	...	...		...	...	...	...	...
2004	C	73 900	19.7	C	17 774	4.7	14.9		...	...	...	...	...
2005	C	73 770	...	C	18 012	...	...		...	...	...	...	...
Malaysia - Malaisie													
2001	C	516 000[7]	21.5	C	104 600	4.4	17.1	C	2 900	5.6	70.0	73.9	...
2002	C	482 600[7]	19.7	C	105 900	4.3	15.4	C	3 100	6.4	70.7	75.3	...
2003	C*	516 300[7]	20.6	C*	111 700	4.5	16.2	C*	3 000	5.8	71.1	75.6	...
2004	C*	514 500[7]	20.1	C*	113 900	4.5	15.7	C*	2 700	5.2	71.7	76.1	...
2005	C*	512 700[7]	19.6	C*	116 200	4.4	15.2	C*	2 600	5.1	70.6	76.4	...
Maldives													
2001	C	4 897	17.7	C	1 081	3.9	13.8	C	85	...	70.2	70.7	...
2002	C	5 003	17.8	C	1 113	4.0	13.9	C	89	...	70.1	71.2	...
2003	C	5 154	18.1	C	1 026	3.6	14.5	C	72	...	70.4	71.3	...

4. Vital statistics summary and expectation of life at birth: 2001 - 2005
Aperçu des statistiques de l'état civil et espérance de vie à la naissance: 2001 - 2005 (continued - suite)

Continent, country or area and year / Continent, pays ou zone et année	Code[a]	Live births / Naissances vivantes Number Nombre	Crude birth rate Taux brut de natalité	Code[a]	Deaths / Décès Number Nombre	Crude death rate Taux brut de mortalité	Rate of natural increase Taux d'accrois-sement naturel	Code[a]	Infant deaths / Décès d'enfants de moins d'un an Number Nombre	Rate (per 1000 births) Taux (par 1000 naiss-ances)	Expectation of life at birth / Espérance de vie à la naissance Male[b] Masculin[b]	Female[b] Féminin[b]	Total fertility rate L'indice synthétique de fécondité
ASIA - ASIE													
Maldives													
2004	C	5 198	18.0	C	1 007	3.5	14.5	C	76	...	71.1	72.1	...
2005	C	5 518	18.8	C	1 015	3.5	15.3	C	67	...	71.7	72.7	...
Mongolia - Mongolie													
2001	C	49 685	20.5	C	15 999	6.6	13.9	C	1 464	29.5	...	...	2.200
2002	C	46 922	19.1	C	15 857	6.4	12.6	C	1 390	29.6	...	...	2.100
2003	C	45 723	18.4	C	16 006	6.4	11.9	C	1 051	23.0	...	...	2.000
2004	C	45 501	18.1	C	16 404	6.5	11.6	C	1 016	22.3	...	...	2.000
2005	C	45 326	17.8	C	16 480	6.5	11.3	C	938	20.7	...	...	1.948
Nepal - Népal													
2001		...	...	I	106 789[45]	4.6	...	I	13 037[45]	...	60.1	60.7	4.100
2005		...	...		...	...	...		...	...	62.3	63.1	3.600
Occupied Palestinian Territory - Territoire palestinien occupé													
2001	U	103 780	...	U	9 177	...	...	U	1 138	...	70.5	73.6	...
2002	U	106 511	...	U	10 316	...	...	U	1 126	...	...	...	...
2003	U	106 355	...	U	10 207	...	...	U	1 150	...	...	...	4.600
2004	U	111 245	...	U	10 029	...	...	U	1 103	...	...	...	...
2005	U	109 439	...	U	9 645	...	...	U	1 057	...	...	...	4.600
Oman													
2001	U	39 297[46]	...	U	2 550[46]	...	...	U	335[46]	...	72.4	75.3	4.200
2002	U	40 222[46]	...	U	2 564[46]	...	...	U	332[46]	...	72.2	75.4	3.600
2003	U	40 062[46]	...	U	2 701[46]	...	...	U	335[46]	...	73.1	75.4	3.560
2004	U	40 584[46]	...	U	2 743[46]	...	...	U	336[46]	...	73.2	75.4	3.190
2005	U	42 065[46]	...	U	2 849[46]	...	...	U	315[46]	...	73.2	74.4	3.130
Pakistan[47]													
2001	I	3 719 694[48]	26.2	I	956 515[48]	6.7	19.5	I	286 609[48]	77.1	64.5[48]	66.1[48]	4.100[48]
2003	I	3 683 290[49]	25.0	I	970 428[49]	6.6	18.4	I	280 729[49]	76.2	64.7[49]	65.6[49]	3.900[49]
2005	I	3 772 494[50]	24.6	I	1 019 467[50]	6.6	17.9	I	289 169[50]	76.7	...	...	3.800[50]
Philippines													
2001	C	1 714 093	22.0	C	381 834	4.9	17.1	C	26 129	15.2	...	...	2.753
2002	C	1 666 773	21.0	C	396 297	5.0	16.0	C	23 778	14.3	...	...	2.500
2003	C	1 669 442	20.6	C	396 331	4.9	15.7	C	22 844	13.7	...	...	2.600
Qatar													
2001	C	12 118	18.7	C	1 210	1.9	16.8	C	111	9.2	...	...	...
2002	C	12 200	17.9	C	1 220	1.8	16.1	C	107	8.8	...	...	2.766
2003	C	12 856	17.9	C	1 311	1.8	16.1	C	137	10.7	...	...	2.864
2004	C	13 190	17.4	C	1 341	1.8	15.7	C	113	8.6	76.1	75.6	2.780
2005	C	13 401	16.8	C	1 545	1.9	14.9	C	110	8.2	III75.1	75.6	2.600
Saudi Arabia - Arabie saoudite													
2001	...	559 680	...	...	87 125	...	...	...	11 669	...	...	...	...
2002	...	564 483	...	...	88 476	...	...	...	11 498	...	...	...	...
2003	...	569 326	...	...	89 849	...	...	...	11 330	...	...	...	...
2004	...	574 211	...	...	91 243	...	...	...	11 164	...	...	...	3.320
2005	...	582 582	...	...	92 487	...	...	...	11 078	...	...	...	3.280
Singapore - Singapour													
2001	C	41 451	10.0	+C	15 367	3.7	6.3	+C	100	2.4	76.4	80.3	1.406
2002	C	40 760	9.8	+C	15 820	3.8	6.0	+C	123	3.0	76.6	80.7	1.370
2003	C	37 485	9.0	+C	16 036	3.8	5.1	+C	100	2.7	77.0	80.9	1.250
2004	C	37 174	8.8	+C	15 860	3.7	5.0	+C	82	...	77.4	81.3	1.240
2005	C	37 492	8.6	+C	16 215	3.7	4.9	+C	95	...	77.9	81.6	1.240
Sri Lanka													
2001	+C	358 583	19.1	+C	112 858	6.0	13.1	+C*	4 323	12.1	...	...	...
2002	+C*	363 549	19.1	+C*	110 637	5.8	13.3		...	...	...	...	...
2003	+C*	363 343	18.9	+C*	114 310	5.9	12.9		...	...	...	...	...
2004	+C*	360 220	18.5	+C*	112 568	5.8	12.7		...	...	...	...	...

4. Vital statistics summary and expectation of life at birth: 2001 - 2005
Aperçu des statistiques de l'état civil et espérance de vie à la naissance: 2001 - 2005 (continued - suite)

Continent, country or area and year / Continent, pays ou zone et année	Code[a]	Live births Number	Crude birth rate	Code[a]	Deaths Number	Crude death rate	Rate of natural increase	Code[a]	Infant deaths Number	Rate (per 1000 births)	Male[b]	Female[b]	Total fertility rate
ASIA - ASIE													
Syrian Arab Republic - République arabe syrienne[51]													
2001	U	524 212	...	U	60 814	...	...		...	...	...	...	...
2002	U	471 970	...	U	53 252	...	...		...	...	...	...	...
2003	U	492 639	...	U	53 778	...	...		...	...	...	...	...
2004	U	491 476	...	U	57 855	...	...		...	...	...	...	...
Tajikistan - Tadjikistan[22]													
2001	I	171 623[52]	27.2	C	32 015	5.1	22.1		...	...	...	...	...
2002	I	175 599[52]	27.3	C	31 142	4.8	22.4		...	...	...	...	...
2003	I	177 938[52]	27.1	C	33 185	5.0	22.0		...	...	...	...	...
2004	I	179 600[52]	26.8	C	29 700	4.4	22.3		...	...	...	...	...
2005	I	180 800[52]	26.4	C	31 500	4.6	21.8		...	...	...	...	...
Thailand - Thaïlande													
2001	+U	790 425	...	+U	369 493	...	...	+U	5 105	...	...	...	...
2002	+U	782 911	...	+U	380 364	...	...	+U	5 105	...	...	...	...
2003	+U	742 183	...	+U	384 131	...	...	+U	5 349	...	...	...	...
2004	+U	813 069	...	+U	393 592	...	...	+U	6 061	...	...	...	...
2005	+U	809 485	...	+U	395 374	...	...	+U	6 183	...	...	...	...
Turkey - Turquie													
2001	I	1 486 000[53]	21.7	I	485 000[53]	7.1	14.6	I	60 332[54]	40.6	...	...	2.250
2002	I	1 362 000[53]	19.7	I	429 000[53]	6.2	13.5	I	36 365[53]	26.7	...	...	2.240
2003	I	1 361 000[53]	19.4	I	436 000[53]	6.2	13.2	I	34 842[53]	25.6	...	...	2.220
2004	I	1 360 000[53]	19.1	I	443 000[53]	6.2	12.9	I	33 456[53]	24.6	68.8[53]	73.6[53]	2.210
2005	I	1 361 000[53]	18.9	I	450 000[53]	6.2	12.6		...	...	...	...	...
Uzbekistan - Ouzbékistan[22]													
2001	C	512 950	20.5	C	132 542	5.3	15.2	C	9 427	18.4	...	...	...
Yemen - Yémen													
2002	...	189 341	...	...	21 157	...	...		...	...	...	...	...
2003	...	130 112	...	...	20 346	...	...		...	...	...	...	6.200
2004	...	153 945	...	...	22 255	...	...		...	...	60.2	62.0	6.100
2005	...	152 792	...	...	19 653	...	...		...	...	...	...	...
EUROPE													
Albania - Albanie													
2001	C	54 283	17.7	C	15 813	5.1	12.5	C	603	11.1	...	...	2.374
2002	C	45 515	14.7	C	16 248	5.3	9.5	C	466	10.2	...	...	1.946
2003	C	47 012	15.1	C	17 967	5.8	9.3	C	395	8.4	...	...	1.980
2004	C	43 022	13.8	C	17 749	5.7	8.1	C	336	7.8	...	...	1.788
2005	C	39 612	12.6	C	17 427	5.5	7.1	C	303	7.6	...	...	...
Andorra - Andorre													
2001	C	777	11.8	C	237	3.6	8.2	C	2	...	...	...	1.420
2002	C	749	11.3	C	218	3.3	8.0	C	-	...	...	...	1.370
2003	C	721	10.3	C	221	3.2	7.2	C	-	...	...	...	1.190
2004	C	814	10.9	C	281	3.8	7.1	C	2	...	...	...	1.210
2005	C	828	10.5	C	276	3.5	7.0	C	5	...	...	...	1.231
Austria - Autriche													
2001	C	75 458	9.4	C	74 767	9.3	0.1	C	365	4.8	75.9	81.7	1.329
2002	C	78 399	9.7	C	76 131	9.4	0.3	C	318	4.1	75.8	81.7	1.393
2003	C	76 944	9.5	C	77 209	9.5	0.0	C	343	4.5	75.9	81.6	1.378
2004	C	78 968	9.7	C	74 292	9.1	0.6	C	353	4.5	76.4	82.1	1.419
2005	C	78 190	9.5	C	75 189	9.1	0.4	C	327	4.2	75.5	81.5	1.407
Belarus - Bélarus													
2001	C	91 720[22]	9.2	C	140 299[22]	14.1	-4.9	C	839[22]	9.1	...	...	1.650
2002	C	88 743[22]	8.9	C	146 655[22]	14.8	-5.8	C	695[22]	7.8	62.3	74.1	1.222
2003	C	88 512[22]	9.0	C	143 200[22]	14.5	-5.5	C	685[22]	7.7	62.7	74.7	1.206
2004	C	88 943[22]	9.1	C	140 064[22]	14.3	-5.2	C	614[22]	6.9	63.2	75.0	1.201
2005	C	90 508[22]	9.3	C	141 857[22]	14.5	-5.3	C	640[22]	7.1	...	...	1.210

Continent, country or area and year / Continent, pays ou zone et année	Code[a] / Code[a]	Live births / Naissances vivantes Number / Nombre	Crude birth rate / Taux brut de natalité	Code[a] / Code[a]	Deaths / Décès Number / Nombre	Crude death rate / Taux brut de mortalité	Rate of natural increase / Taux d'accrois-sement naturel	Code[a] / Code[a]	Infant deaths / Décès d'enfants de moins d'un an Number / Nombre	Rate (per 1000 births) / Taux (par 1000 naiss-ances)	Expectation of life at birth / Espérance de vie à la naissance Male[b] / Masculin[b]	Female[b] / Féminin[b]	Total fertility rate / L'indice synthétique de fécondité
EUROPE													
Belgium - Belgique													
2001	C	114 014[55]	11.1	C	103 447[55]	10.1	1.0	C	518[55]	4.5	...	...	...
2002	C	111 225[55]	10.8	C	105 642[55]	10.2	0.5	C	551[55]	5.0	...	...	...
2003	C	112 591[55]	10.9	C	107 628[55]	10.4	0.5	C	538[55]	4.8	...	...	...
2004	C	116 048[55]	11.1	C	101 929[55]	9.8	1.4	C	549[55]	4.7	76.5	82.4	...
2005	C	117 799[55]	11.2	C	102 963[55]	9.8	1.4	C	515[55]	4.4	...	...	...
Bosnia and Herzegovina - Bosnie-Herzégovine													
2001	C	37 717	9.9	C	30 325	8.0	1.9	C	287	7.6	71.3	76.7	1.230
2002	C	35 587	9.3	C	30 155	7.9	1.4	C	335	9.4	71.3	76.7	1.230
2003	C	35 234	9.2	C	31 757	8.3	0.9	C	268	7.6	71.3	76.7	1.215
2004	C	35 151	9.1	C	32 616	8.5	0.7	C	253	7.2	...	...	1.217
2005	C	34 627	9.0	C	34 402	9.0	0.1	C	233	6.7	...	...	1.214
Bulgaria - Bulgarie													
2001	C	68 180	8.6	C	112 368	14.2	-5.6	C	982	14.4	III68.5	75.2	1.243
2002	C	66 499	8.5	C	112 617	14.3	-5.9	C	887	13.3	68.5	75.4	1.212
2003	C	67 359	8.6	C	111 927	14.3	-5.7	C	831	12.3	III68.7	75.6	1.232
2004	C	69 886	9.0	C	110 110	14.2	-5.2	C	814	11.6	III69.1	76.2	1.290
2005	C	71 075	9.2	C	113 374	14.6	-5.5	C	739	10.4	III69.0	76.3	1.310
Channel Islands: Jersey - Îles Anglo-Normandes: Jersey													
2001	+C	973	11.2	+C	784	9.0	2.2		...	...	...	...	...
2002	+C	930	10.6	+C	841	9.6	1.0		...	...	...	...	...
2003	+C	1 005	11.5	+C	760	8.7	2.8		...	...	...	...	...
2004	+C	971	11.1	+C	748	8.5	2.5		...	...	...	...	...
2005	+C	969	11.0	+C	752	8.6	2.5		...	...	...	...	...
Croatia - Croatie													
2001	C	40 993	9.2	C	49 552	11.2	-1.9	C	315	7.7	...	...	1.380
2002	C	40 094	9.0	C	50 569	11.4	-2.4	C	282	7.0	...	...	1.340
2003	C	39 668	8.9	C	52 575	11.8	-2.9	C	251	6.3	...	...	1.327
2004	C	40 307	9.1	C	49 756	11.2	-2.1	C	245	6.1	...	...	1.346
2005	C	42 492	9.6	C	51 790	11.7	-2.1	C	242	5.7	...	...	1.420
Czech Republic - République tchèque													
2001	C	90 715	8.9	C	107 755	10.5	-1.7	C	360	4.0	72.1	78.5	1.146
2002	C	97 878	9.6	C	108 243	10.6	-1.0	C	385	3.9	72.1	78.5	1.171
2003	C	93 685	9.2	C	111 288	10.9	-1.7	C	365	3.9	72.0	78.5	1.179
2004	C	97 664	9.6	C	107 177	10.5	-0.9	C	366	3.7	72.5	79.0	1.226
2005	C	102 211	10.0	C	107 938	10.5	-0.6	C	347	3.4	72.9	79.1	1.282
Denmark - Danemark[56]													
2001	C	65 458	12.2	C	58 338	10.9	1.3	C	320	4.9	74.6	79.2	1.747
2002	C	64 075	11.9	C	58 610	10.9	1.0	C	284	4.4	74.8	79.4	1.723
2003	C	64 599	12.0	C	57 574	10.7	1.3	C	286	4.4	II74.9	79.5	1.758
2004	C	64 609	12.0	C	55 806	10.3	1.6	C	283	4.4	II75.2	79.9	1.784
2005	C	64 282	11.9	C	54 962	10.1	1.7	C	280	4.4	II75.6	80.2	1.799
Estonia - Estonie													
2001	C	12 632	9.3	C	18 516	13.6	-4.3	C	111	8.8	II65.1	76.0	1.337
2002	C	13 001	9.6	C	18 355	13.5	-3.9	C	74	...	64.8	76.3	1.372
2003	C	13 036	9.6	C	18 152	13.4	-3.8	C	91	...	66.1	77.1	1.371
2004	C	13 992	10.4	C	17 685	13.1	-2.7	C	90	...	66.4	77.8	1.465
2005	C	14 350	10.7	C	17 316	12.9	-2.2	C	78	...	67.2	78.1	1.497
Faeroe Islands - Îles Féroé													
2001	C	632	13.6	C	358	7.7	5.9		...	...	...	...	...
2002	C	709	15.0	C	392	8.3	6.7		...	...	...	...	...
2003	C	705	14.7	C	404	8.4	6.3		...	...	...	...	...
2004	C	713	14.8	C	379	7.9	6.9		...	...	...	...	...
2005	C	712	14.8	C	419	8.7	6.1		...	...	...	...	...

Continent, country or area and year / Continent, pays ou zone et année	Code[a]	Live births Naissances vivantes Number Nombre	Crude birth rate Taux brut de natalité	Code[a]	Deaths Décès Number Nombre	Crude death rate Taux brut de mortalité	Rate of natural increase Taux d'accroissement naturel	Code[a]	Infant deaths Décès d'enfants de moins d'un an Number Nombre	Rate (per 1000 births) Taux (par 1000 naissances)	Expectation of life at birth Espérance de vie à la naissance Male[b] Masculin[b]	Female[b] Féminin[b]	Total fertility rate L'indice synthétique de fécondité
EUROPE													
Finland - Finlande													
2001	C	56 189[57]	10.8	C	48 550[57]	9.4	1.5	C	181[57]	3.2	74.6	81.5	1.726
2002	C	55 555[57]	10.7	C	49 418[57]	9.5	1.2	C	168[57]	3.0	74.9	81.5	1.718
2003	C	56 630[57]	10.9	C	48 996[57]	9.4	1.5	C	176[57]	3.1	75.1	81.8	1.760
2004	C	57 758[57]	11.0	C	47 600[57]	9.1	1.9	C	191[57]	3.3	75.3	82.3	1.800
2005	C	57 745[57]	11.0	C	47 928[57]	9.1	1.9	C	174[57]	3.0	75.5	82.3	1.803
France[58]													
2001	C	770 945[59]	13.0	C	531 073[59]	8.9	4.0	C	3 438[59]	4.5	75.5	82.9	1.879
2002	C	761 630[59]	12.7	C	535 144[59]	8.9	3.8	C	3 114[59]	4.1	75.8	83.0	1.868
2003	C	761 464[59]	12.6	C	552 339[59]	9.2	3.5	C	3 053[59]	4.0	75.9	82.9	1.875
2004	C	767 816[59]	12.7	C	509 429[59]	8.4	4.3	C	2 988[59]	3.9	76.7	83.8	1.900
2005	C	774 355[59]	12.7	C	527 533[59]	8.6	4.0	C	2 775[59]	3.6	...	...	1.923
Germany - Allemagne													
2001	C	734 475	8.9	C	828 541	10.1	-1.1	C	3 163	4.3	75.6	81.4	1.349
2002	C	719 250	8.7	C	841 686	10.2	-1.5	C	3 036	4.2	75.7	81.3	1.341
2003	C	706 721	8.6	C	853 946	10.3	-1.8	C	2 990	4.2	75.8	81.3	1.340
2004	C	705 622	8.6	C	818 271	9.9	-1.4	C	2 918	4.1	III75.9	81.5	1.355
2005	C	685 795	8.3	C	830 227	10.1	-1.8	C	2 696	3.9	III76.2	81.8	1.340
Gibraltar													
2001	+C	374[60]	13.6	C	249[60]	9.1	4.5		...	...	78.5	83.3	...
2002	+C	371[60]	13.0	C	242[60]	8.5	4.5		...	...	...	...	...
2003	+C	372[60]	13.0	C	234[60]	8.2	4.8	C	2	...	...	...	...
2004	+C	421[60]	14.7	C	242[60]	8.4	6.2		...	...	...	...	...
2005	+C	418[60]	14.5	C	249[60]	8.6	5.9	C	1	...	...	...	...
Greece - Grèce													
2001	C	102 282	9.3	C	102 559	9.4	0.0	C	522	5.1	75.9	81.0	1.290
2002	C	103 838	9.5	C	103 915	9.5	0.0	C	600	5.8	76.2	81.1	1.270
2003	C	104 420	9.5	C	105 529	9.6	-0.1	C	420	4.0	76.5	81.3	1.288
2004	C	105 655	9.6	C	104 942	9.5	0.1	C	429	4.1	76.6	81.3	1.300
2005	C	107 545	9.7	C	105 091	9.5	0.2	C	409	3.8	76.8	81.7	1.338
Hungary - Hongrie													
2001	C	97 047	9.5	C	132 183	13.0	-3.4	C	789	8.1	68.2	76.5	1.313
2002	C	96 804	9.5	C	132 833	13.1	-3.5	C	693	7.2	68.3	76.6	1.305
2003	C	94 647	9.3	C	135 823	13.4	-4.1	C	690	7.3	68.3	76.5	1.276
2004	C	95 137	9.4	C	132 492	13.1	-3.7	C	628	6.6	68.6	76.9	1.285
2005	C	97 496	9.7	C	135 732	13.5	-3.8	C	607	6.2	68.6	76.9	1.317
Iceland - Islande													
2001	C	4 091	14.4	C	1 725	6.1	8.3	C	11	...	78.4	82.6	1.948
2002	C	4 049	14.1	C	1 821	6.3	7.7	C	9	...	78.6	82.5	1.932
2003	C	4 143	14.3	C	1 827	6.3	8.0	C	10	...	II79.0	82.4	1.990
2004	C	4 234	14.5	C	1 824	6.2	8.2	C	12	...	78.9	83.2	2.040
2005	C	4 280	14.5	C	1 838	6.2	8.3	C	10	...	II79.2	83.3	2.052
Ireland - Irlande													
2001	+C	57 854[61]	15.0	+C	30 212[61]	7.9	7.2	+C	331[61]	5.7	74.7	79.7	1.961
2002	+C	60 521[61]	15.5	+C	29 348[61]	7.5	8.0	+C	306[61]	5.1	75.1	80.3	1.978
2003	+C	61 529[61]	15.5	+C	29 074[61]	7.3	8.2	+C	326[61]	5.3	...	...	1.980
2004	+C*	61 684[61]	15.3	+C*	28 151[61]	7.0	8.3	+C*	300[61]	4.9	...	...	1.945
2005	+C*	61 042[61]	14.8	+C*	27 441[61]	6.6	8.1	+C*	244[61]	4.0	...	...	1.882
Isle of Man - Îles de Man													
2001	+C	863	11.3	+C	855	11.2	0.1	+C	-	...	...	...	...
2002	+C	903	11.7	+C	877	11.4	0.3	+C	3	...	...	...	...
2003	+C	860	11.1	+C	852	11.0	0.1	+C	6	...	...	...	...
2004	+C	862	11.1	+C	798	10.3	0.8	+C	2	...	...	...	...
2005	+C	901	11.6	+C	775	9.9	1.6		...	...	...	...	...
Italy - Italie													
2001	C	535 282	9.4	C	556 892	9.8	-0.4	C	2 482	4.6	...	...	1.251
2002	C	530 443	9.3	C	560 390	9.8	-0.5	C	2 337	4.4	77.1	83.0	1.270
2003	C	544 063	9.4	C	586 468	10.2	-0.7	C	2 482	4.6	77.2	82.8	1.285

4. Vital statistics summary and expectation of life at birth: 2001 - 2005
Aperçu des statistiques de l'état civil et espérance de vie à la naissance: 2001 - 2005 (continued - suite)

Continent, country or area and year / Continent, pays ou zone et année	Live births — Naissances vivantes Code[a]	Number Nombre	Crude birth rate Taux brut de natalité	Deaths — Décès Code[a]	Number Nombre	Crude death rate Taux brut de mortalité	Rate of natural increase Taux d'accroissement naturel	Infant deaths — Code[a]	Number Nombre	Rate (per 1000 births) Taux (par 1000 naissances)	Expectation of life at birth Male[b] Masculin[b]	Female[b] Féminin[b]	Total fertility rate L'indice synthétique de fécondité
EUROPE													
Italy - Italie													
2004	C	562 599	9.7	C	545 051	9.4	0.3	C*	2 289	4.1	...	...	1.333
2005	C	554 022	9.5	C	567 304	9.7	-0.2	C*	2 554	4.6	...	...	1.344
Latvia - Lettonie													
2001	C	19 664[22]	8.3	C	32 991[22]	14.0	-5.7	C	217[22]	11.0	65.2	76.6	1.207
2002	C	20 044[22]	8.6	C	32 498[22]	13.9	-5.3	C	197[22]	9.8	65.4	76.8	1.232
2003	C	21 006[22]	9.0	C	32 437[22]	13.9	-4.9	C	198[22]	9.4	65.9	76.9	1.290
2004	C	20 334[22]	8.8	C	32 024[22]	13.8	-5.1	C	191[22]	9.4	67.1	77.2	1.240
2005	C	21 497[22]	9.3	C	32 777[22]	14.2	-4.9	C	168[22]	7.8	65.6	77.4	1.309
Liechtenstein													
2001	C	401	12.1	C	220	6.6	5.5	C	-	...	...	...	1.527
2002	C	395	11.7	C	215	6.4	5.3	C	1	...	...	...	1.492
2003	C	347	10.2	C	217	6.4	3.8	C	1	...	...	...	1.357
2004	C	372	10.8	C	198	5.7	5.0	C	1	...	...	...	1.458
2005	C*	381	11.0	C*	215	6.2	4.8	C*	1	...	...	...	1.510
Lithuania - Lituanie													
2001	C	31 546[22]	9.1	C	40 399[22]	11.6	-2.5	C	250[22]	7.9	65.9	77.4	1.296
2002	C	30 014[22]	8.7	C	41 072[22]	11.8	-3.2	C	238[22]	7.9	66.2	77.6	1.236
2003	C	30 598[22]	8.9	C	40 990[22]	11.9	-3.0	C	206[22]	6.7	66.5	77.8	1.262
2004	C	30 419[22]	8.9	C	41 340[22]	12.0	-3.2	C	240[22]	7.9	66.4	77.7	1.260
2005	C	30 541[22]	8.9	C	43 799[22]	12.8	-3.9	C	209[22]	6.8	65.4	77.4	1.272
Luxembourg													
2001	C	5 459	12.4	C	3 719	8.4	3.9	C	32	...	...	...	1.654
2002	C	5 345	12.0	C	3 744	8.4	3.6	C	27	...	III74.8	81.0	1.625
2003	C	5 303	11.8	C	4 053	9.0	2.8	C	26	...	...	...	1.634
2004	C	5 452	12.0	C	3 578	7.9	4.1	C	21	...	...	...	1.704
2005	C	5 371	11.7	C	3 621	7.9	3.8	C	14	...	...	...	1.697
Malta - Malte													
2001	C	3 859[62]	10.0	C	2 935[63]	7.6	2.4	C	17	...	76.1	80.9	1.720
2002	C	3 805[62]	9.8	C	3 031[63]	7.8	2.0	C	23	...	75.8	80.5	1.460
2003	C	4 036[62]	10.1	C	3 072[63]	7.7	2.4	C	23	...	76.4	80.4	1.480
2004	C	3 887[62]	9.7	C	2 903[63]	7.2	2.5	C	23	...	76.7	80.5	1.370
2005	C	3 858[62]	9.6	C	3 130[63]	7.8	1.8	C	23	...	77.7	81.4	1.370
Monaco													
2001	C	748	...	C	636	...	...		...	...	...	...	...
2002	C	771	...	C	564	...	...		...	...	...	...	...
2003	C	842	...	C	617	...	...		...	...	...	...	...
2004	C	825	...	C	525	...	...		...	...	...	...	...
2005	C	894	...	C	601	...	...		...	...	...	...	...
Netherlands - Pays-Bas													
2001	C	202 603[64]	12.6	C	140 377[64]	8.7	3.9	C	1 088[64]	5.4	75.8	80.7	1.710
2002	C	202 083[64]	12.5	C	142 355[64]	8.8	3.7	C	1 014[64]	5.0	76.0	80.7	1.731
2003	C	200 297[64]	12.3	C	141 936[64]	8.7	3.6	C	962[64]	4.8	76.2	80.9	1.747
2004	C	194 007[64]	11.9	C	136 553[64]	8.4	3.5	C	852[64]	4.4	76.9	81.4	1.726
2005	C	187 910[64]	11.5	C	136 402[64]	8.4	3.2	C	928[64]	4.9	77.2	81.6	1.708
Norway - Norvège													
2001	C	56 696	12.6	C	43 981[65]	9.7	2.8	C	223[65]	3.9	76.2	81.5	1.784
2002	C	55 434	12.2	C	44 465[65]	9.8	2.4	C	192[65]	3.5	76.5	81.5	1.754
2003	C	56 458	12.4	C	42 478[65]	9.3	3.1	C	190[65]	3.4	77.0	81.9	1.797
2004	C	56 951	12.4	C	41 200[65]	9.0	3.4	C	185[65]	3.2	77.5	82.3	1.828
2005	C	56 756	12.3	C	41 232[65]	8.9	3.4	C	175[65]	3.1	77.7	82.5	1.836
Poland - Pologne													
2001	C	368 205	9.6	C	363 220	9.5	0.1	C	2 823	7.7	70.2	78.4	1.315
2002	C	353 765	9.3	C	359 486	9.4	-0.1	C	2 662	7.5	70.4	78.8	1.249
2003	C	351 072	9.2	C	365 230	9.6	-0.4	C	2 470	7.0	70.5	78.9	1.222
2004	C	356 131	9.3	C	363 522	9.5	-0.2	C	2 423	6.8	70.7	79.2	1.227
2005	C	364 383	9.5	C	368 285	9.7	-0.1	C	2 340	6.4	70.8	79.4	1.243

4. Vital statistics summary and expectation of life at birth: 2001 - 2005
Aperçu des statistiques de l'état civil et espérance de vie à la naissance: 2001 - 2005 (continued - suite)

Continent, country or area and year / Continent, pays ou zone et année	Live births / Naissances vivantes			Deaths / Décès			Rate of natural increase / Taux d'accrois-sement naturel	Infant deaths / Décès d'enfants de moins d'un an			Expectation of life at birth / Espérance de vie à la naissance		Total fertility rate / L'indice synthétique de fécondité
	Code[a]	Number Nombre	Crude birth rate Taux brut de natalité	Code[a]	Number Nombre	Crude death rate Taux brut de mortalité		Code[a]	Number Nombre	Rate (per 1000 births) Taux (par 1000 naiss-ances)	Male[b] Masculin[b]	Female[b] Féminin[b]	
EUROPE													
Portugal													
2001	C	112 774	11.0	C	105 092	10.2	0.7	C	567	5.0	73.5	80.3	1.460
2002	C	114 383	11.0	C	106 258	10.2	0.8	C	574	5.0	II73.4	80.4	1.473
2003	C	112 515	10.8	C	108 795	10.4	0.4	C	466	4.1	II73.7	80.6	1.444
2004	C	109 298	10.4	C	102 010	9.7	0.7	C	418	3.8	II74.5	81.0	1.403
2005	C	109 399	10.4	C	107 462	10.2	0.2	C	382	3.5	II74.9	81.4	1.408
Republic of Moldova - République de Moldova													
2001	C	36 448[22]	10.0	C	40 075[22]	11.0	-1.0	C	597[22]	16.4	64.5	71.8	1.249
2002	C	35 705[22]	9.9	C	41 852[22]	11.6	-1.7	C	528[22]	14.8	64.4	71.7	1.211
2003	C	36 471[22]	10.1	C	43 079[22]	11.9	-1.8	C	522[22]	14.3	64.5	71.6	1.219
2004	C	38 272[22]	10.6	C	41 668[22]	11.6	-0.9	C	464[22]	12.1	64.5	72.2	1.257
2005	C	37 695[22]	10.5	C	44 689[22]	12.4	-1.9	C	468[22]	12.4	...	...	1.219
Romania - Roumanie													
2001	C	220 368	9.8	C	259 603	11.6	-1.8	C	4 057	18.4	67.7	74.8	1.232
2002	C	210 529	9.7	C	269 666	12.4	-2.7	C	3 648	17.3	67.6	74.9	1.254
2003	C	212 459	9.8	C	266 575	12.3	-2.5	C	3 546	16.7	67.4	74.8	1.270
2004	C	216 261	10.0	C	258 890	11.9	-2.0	C	3 641	16.8	...	...	...
2005	C	221 020	10.2	C	262 101	12.1	-1.9	C	3 310	15.0	68.2	75.5	1.319
Russian Federation - Fédération de Russie													
2001	C	1 311 604[22]	9.0	C	2 254 856[22]	15.4	-6.5	C	19 104[22]	14.6	58.9	72.2	1.249
2002	C	1 396 967[22]	9.6	C	2 332 272[22]	16.1	-6.4	C	18 407[22]	13.2	58.7	71.9	1.322
2003	C	1 477 301[22]	10.2	C	2 365 826[22]	16.4	-6.1	C	18 142[22]	12.3	58.6	71.8	1.319
2004	C	1 502 477[22]	10.4	C	2 295 402[22]	16.0	-5.5	C	17 339[22]	11.5	58.9	72.3	1.341
2005	C*	1 457 400[22]	10.2	C	2 303 935[22]	16.1	-5.9		...	...	58.9	72.4	...
San Marino - Saint-Marin													
2001	+C	315	11.4	+C	195	7.1	4.3	+C	1	...	...	...	1.317
2002	+C	295	10.4	+C	203	7.1	3.2	+C	2	...	...	...	1.206
2003	+C	300	10.3	+C	216	7.5	2.9	+C	2	...	...	...	1.250
2004	+C	306	10.4	+C	185	6.3	4.1	+C	1	...	...	...	1.255
2005	+C	284	9.2	+C	219	7.1	2.1	+C	-	...	...	...	...
Serbia and Montenegro - Serbie-et-Montenegro													
2001	C	130 194	12.2	C	113 063	10.6	1.6	C	1 709	13.1	70.1	75.2	1.693[66]
2002	C	86 600[66]	10.7	C	108 298[66]	13.3	-2.7	C	882[66]	10.2	69.9[66]	75.2[66]	1.575[66]
2003	C	87 370[66]	10.7	C	109 650[66]	13.4	-2.7	C	803[66]	9.2	70.0[66]	75.2[66]	1.577[66]
2004	C*	88 406[66]	10.9	C*	110 148[66]	13.5	-2.7	C*	660[66]	7.5	...	...	...
Slovakia - Slovaquie													
2001	C	51 136	9.5	C	51 980	9.7	-0.2	C	319	6.2	69.5	77.5	1.205
2002	C	50 841	9.5	C	51 532	9.6	-0.1	C	388	7.6	69.9	77.6	1.190
2003	C	51 713	9.6	C	52 230	9.7	-0.1	C	406	7.9	69.8	77.6	1.199
2004	C	53 747	10.0	C	51 852	9.6	0.4	C	365	6.8	70.3	77.8	1.241
2005	C	54 430	10.1	C	53 475	9.9	0.2	C	392	7.2	70.1	77.9	1.253
Slovenia - Slovénie													
2001	C	17 477	8.8	C	18 508	9.3	-0.5	C	74	...	72.1	79.6	1.211
2002	C	17 501	8.8	C	18 701	9.4	-0.6	C	67	...	73.2	80.7	1.212
2003	C	17 321	8.7	C	19 451	9.7	-1.1	C	69	...	72.5	80.3	1.202
2004	C	17 961	9.0	C	18 523	9.3	-0.3	C	66	...	II73.5	81.1	1.247
2005	C	18 157	9.1	C	18 825	9.4	-0.3	C	75	...	II74.1	81.3	1.262
Spain - Espagne													
2001	C	406 380	10.0	C	360 131	8.8	1.1	C	1 657	4.1	76.4	83.1	1.244
2002	C	418 846	10.1	C	368 618	8.9	1.2	C	1 737	4.1	II76.3	83.0	1.263
2003	C	441 881	10.5	C	384 828	9.2	1.4	C	1 733	3.9	...	...	1.310
2004	C	454 591	10.6	C	371 934	8.7	1.9	C	1 813	4.0	II76.7	83.2	1.329
2005	C*	465 616	10.7	C	387 355	8.9	1.8	C*	1 765	3.8	...	...	1.342*
Sweden - Suède													
2001	C	91 466	10.3	C	93 752	10.5	-0.3	C	334	3.7	77.6	82.1	1.570
2002	C	95 815	10.7	C	95 009	10.6	0.1	C	313	3.3	77.7	82.1	1.650

4. Vital statistics summary and expectation of life at birth: 2001 - 2005
Aperçu des statistiques de l'état civil et espérance de vie à la naissance: 2001 - 2005 (continued - suite)

Continent, country or area and year / Continent, pays ou zone et année	Code[a]	Live births Naissances vivantes Number Nombre	Crude birth rate Taux brut de natalité	Code[a]	Deaths Décès Number Nombre	Crude death rate Taux brut de mortalité	Rate of natural increase Taux d'accrois-sement naturel	Code[a]	Infant deaths Décès d'enfants de moins d'un an Number Nombre	Rate (per 1000 births) Taux (par 1000 naiss-ances)	Expectation of life at birth Espérance de vie à la naissance Male[b] Masculin[b]	Female[b] Féminin[b]	Total fertility rate L'indice synthétique de fécondité
EUROPE													
Sweden - Suède													
2003	C	99 157	11.1	C	92 961	10.4	0.7	C	308	3.1	77.9	82.4	1.720
2004	C	100 928	11.2	C	90 532	10.1	1.2	C	314	3.1	78.4	82.7	1.752
2005	C	101 346	11.2	C	91 710	10.2	1.1	C	246	2.4	78.4	82.8	1.769
Switzerland - Suisse													
2001	C	73 509	10.1	C	61 287	8.4	1.7	C	365	5.0	77.2	82.8	1.382
2002	C	72 372	9.9	C	61 768	8.4	1.4	C	326	4.5	77.6	83.0	1.390
2003	C	71 848	9.8	C	63 070	8.6	1.2	C	311	4.3	77.9	83.0	1.385
2004	C	73 082	9.9	C	60 180	8.1	1.7	C	309	4.2	78.2	83.3	1.416
2005	C	72 903	9.8	C	61 124	8.2	1.6	C	308	4.2	[II]78.6	83.7	1.420
The Former Yugoslav Rep. of Macedonia - L'ex-République yougoslave de Macédoine													
2001	C	27 010	13.3	C	16 919	8.3	5.0	C	321	11.9	[II]70.7	75.2	1.700
2002	C	27 761	13.7	C	17 962	8.8	4.8	C	283	10.2	70.8	75.7	...
2003	C	27 011	13.3	C	18 006	8.9	4.4	C	305	11.3	71.1	75.7	1.540
2004	C	23 361	11.5	C	17 944	8.8	2.7	C	308	13.2	71.4	75.9	1.520
2005	C	22 482	11.0	C	18 406	9.0	2.0	C	287	12.8	...	...	1.457
Ukraine													
2001	C	376 478[22]	7.7	C	745 952[22]	15.3	-7.6	C	4 283[22]	11.4	62.8	74.1	1.080
2002	C	390 688[22]	8.1	C	754 911[22]	15.7	-7.6	C	4 023[22]	10.3	...	...	1.095
2003	C	408 589[22]	8.5	C	765 408[22]	16.0	-7.5	C	3 882[22]	9.5	[II]62.6	74.1	1.147
2004	C	427 259[22]	9.0	C	761 261[22]	16.1	-7.1	C	4 024[22]	9.4	[II]62.6	74.1	1.192[67]
2005	C	426 086[22]	9.1	C	781 961[22]	16.6	-7.6	C	4 259[22]	10.0	...	...	...
United Kingdom - Royaume-Uni													
2001	C	669 123[68]	11.3	C	602 268	10.2	1.1	C	3 664	5.5	...	...	1.630
2002	C	668 777[68]	11.3	C	606 283	10.2	1.1	C	3 499	5.2	...	...	1.640
2003	C	695 549[68]	11.7	C*	611 188	10.3	1.4	C	3 686	5.3	...	...	1.710
2004	C*	715 996[69]	12.0	C*	584 600	9.8	2.2	C	3 606	5.0	...	...	1.780
2005	C*	722 600[69]	12.0	C*	582 900	9.7	2.3	C*	3 670	5.1	...	...	1.840
OCEANIA - OCÉANIE													
American Samoa - Samoas américaines													
2001	C	1 655	27.9	C	239	4.0	23.8	C	14	...	...	...	...
2002	C	1 629	26.8	C	295	4.9	21.9	C	27	...	...	...	...
2003	C	1 608	25.7	C	257	4.1	21.6	C	20	...	...	...	...
2004	C	1 713	26.7	C	289	4.5	22.2	C	26	...	...	...	...
2005	C	1 720	26.3	C	279	4.3	22.0	C	12	...	...	...	...
Australia - Australie													
2001	+C	246 394	12.7	+C	128 544	6.6	6.1	+C	1 309	5.3	[III]77.0	82.4	1.729
2002	+C	250 988	12.8	+C	133 707	6.8	6.0	+C	1 264	5.0	[III]77.4	82.6	1.759
2003	+C	251 161	12.6	+C	132 292	6.6	6.0	+C	1 199	4.8	[III]77.8	82.8	1.754
2004	+C	254 246	12.6	+C	132 508	6.6	6.0	+C	1 184	4.7	[III]78.1	83.0	1.774
2005	+C	259 791	12.7	+C	130 714	6.4	6.3	+C	1 302	5.0	[III]78.5	83.3	1.806
Cook Islands - Îles Cook[70]													
2001	+C	313	17.2	+C	88	4.8	12.4	+C	4	...	...	...	...
2002	+C	292	15.9	+C	97	5.3	10.6	+C	2	...	...	...	...
2003	+C	298	16.2	+C	86	4.7	11.5	+C	4	...	...	...	...
2004	+C	295	14.5	+C	99	4.9	9.7	+C	5	...	...	...	...
Fiji - Fidji													
2001	+C	16 689	20.5	+C	4 929	6.1	14.5	+C	342	20.5	...	...	2.500
2002	+C	16 990	20.7	+C	5 133	6.3	14.5	+C	320	18.8	...	...	2.500
2003	+C	17 701	21.4	+C	5 068	6.1	15.2	+C	304	17.2	...	...	2.600

Continent, country or area and year / Continent, pays ou zone et année	Live births Naissances vivantes				Deaths Décès			Rate of natural increase Taux d'accrois-sement naturel	Infant deaths Décès d'enfants de moins d'un an			Expectation of life at birth Espérance de vie à la naissance		Total fertility rate L'indice synthétique de fécondité
	Co-de[a]	Number Nombre	Crude birth rate Taux brut de natalité	Co-de[a]		Number Nombre	Crude death rate Taux brut de mortalité		Co-de[a]	Number Nombre	Rate (per 1000 births) Taux (par 1000 naiss-ances)	Male[b] Masculin[b]	Female[b] Féminin[b]	
OCEANIA - OCÉANIE														
French Polynesia - Polynésie française														
2001	C	4 874	20.4	C		1 171	4.9	15.5	C	36	...	...	...	...
2002	C	4 763	19.6	C		1 127	4.6	14.9	C	32	...	...	...	...
2003	C	4 501	18.2	C		1 122	4.5	13.7	C	31	...	...	...	...
2004	C	4 431	17.7	C		1 130	4.5	13.2	C	20	...	...	...	...
2005	C	4 469	17.6	C		1 265	5.0	12.6	C	28	...	...	...	...
Guam[71]														
2001	C	3 583	22.6	C		691	4.4	18.3	C	35	...	...	...	...
2002	C	3 222	20.0	C		658	4.1	15.9	C	20	...	...	...	...
2003	C	3 298	20.2	C		700	4.3	15.9	C	37	...	...	...	...
2004	C*	3 427	20.6	C*		691	4.2	16.5	C*	41	...	...	...	...
2005	C*	3 203	19.0	C*		697	4.1	14.9			...	...	...	...
Marshall Islands - Îles Marshall														
2001	+U*	1 511	...	+U		271	...	...	+U	40	...	...	...	...
Micronesia, Federated States of - Micronésie, États Fédérés de La														
2001	U	2 620	...	U		482	...	...			...	...	...	...
2002	U	2 446	...	U		539	...	...			...	...	...	...
2003	U	2 483	...	U		427	...	...			...	...	...	...
Nauru														
2001	C	296	25.3	C		92	7.9	17.4			...	...	...	...
2002	C	219	...	C		75	...	...			...	...	...	...
New Caledonia - Nouvelle-Calédonie														
2001	C	4 326	19.9	C		1 131	5.2	14.7	C	24	...	70.5	76.1	...
2002	C	4 194	18.9	C		1 121	5.1	13.9	C	29	...	...	...	...
2003	C	4 102	18.2	C		1 121	5.0	13.2	C	24	...	71.3	77.3	...
2004	C	3 978	17.3	C		1 116	4.9	12.4	C	25	...	...	...	...
New Zealand - Nouvelle-Zélande														
2001	+C	55 799	14.4	+C		27 825[72]	7.2	7.2	+C	296[72]	5.3	III76.0	80.9	1.968
2002	+C	54 021	13.7	+C		28 065[72]	7.1	6.6	+C	300[72]	5.6	III76.3	81.1	1.896
2003	+C	56 134	14.0	+C		28 010[72]	7.0	7.0	+C	277[72]	4.9	III76.7	81.2	1.952
2004	+C	58 073	14.3	+C		28 419[72]	7.0	7.3	+C	324[72]	5.6	III77.0	81.3	2.012
2005	+C	57 745	14.1	+C		27 034[72]	6.6	7.5	+C	295[72]	5.1	III77.5	81.7	2.003
Niue - Nioué														
2001	C	23[73]	...	C		14[74]	...	...			...	...	...	...
2002	C	25[73]	...	C		13[74]	...	...	C	-	...	...	...	...
2003	C	33[73]	...	C		16[74]	...	...			...	...	...	...
2004	C	18[73]	...	C		18[74]	...	...			...	...	...	...
Northern Mariana Islands - Îles Mariannes septentrionales														
2001	U	1 451	...	U		150	...	...	U	11	...	...	...	...
2002	U	1 289	...	U		164	...	...	U	10	...	...	...	...
2003	U	1 355	...			...	...	...			...	...	...	...
2004	U	1 439	...			...	...	...			...	...	...	...
2005	U	1 335	...			...	...	...			...	...	...	...
Palau - Palaos														
2001	C	300	15.3	C		138	7.0	8.3	C	5	...	...	...	...
2002	C	259	13.0	C		134	6.7	6.3	C	6	...	...	...	...
2003	C	312	15.4	C		136	6.7	8.7	C	2	...	...	...	...
2004	C	259	12.6	C		142	6.9	5.7	C	7	...	...	...	...
2005	C	279	14.0	C		134	6.7	7.3	C	6	...	...	...	...

4. Vital statistics summary and expectation of life at birth: 2001 - 2005
Aperçu des statistiques de l'état civil et espérance de vie à la naissance: 2001 - 2005 (continued - suite)

Continent, country or area and year / Continent, pays ou zone et année	Code[a] / Code[a]	Live births / Naissances vivantes Number / Nombre	Crude birth rate Taux brut de natalité	Code[a] / Code[a]	Deaths / Décès Number / Nombre	Crude death rate Taux brut de mortalité	Rate of natural increase Taux d'accroissement naturel	Code[a] / Code[a]	Infant deaths / Décès d'enfants de moins d'un an Number / Nombre	Rate (per 1000 births) Taux (par 1000 naissances)	Expectation of life at birth / Espérance de vie à la naissance Male[b] / Masculin[b]	Female[b] / Féminin[b]	Total fertility rate L'indice synthétique de fécondité
OCEANIA - OCÉANIE													
Papua New Guinea - Papouasie-Nouvelle-Guinée													
2001	U	182 619	...	U	6 737	...	...	U	1 841	...	...	...	...
2002	U	187 645	...	U	7 573	...	...	U	2 230	...	...	...	...
2003	U	192 817	...	U	7 054	...	...	U	2 082	...	...	...	...
Samoa													
2001	C*	3 516	19.9	U	339	...	...	...	...	...	...	...	...
2002	C*	2 826	15.8	U*	355	...	...	...	...	...	...	...	...
2003	C*	2 070	11.5	U*	551	...	...	...	...	...	...	...	...
2004	C*	1 679	9.2	U*	547	...	...	...	...	...	...	...	...
Tokelau - Tokélaou													
2001	...	19		...	...	...	...	...	...	...	...	...	...
2002	...	20		...	...	...	...	...	...	...	...	...	...
Tonga													
2001	+C	2 546	25.3	+C	579	5.8	19.5	+C	33	...	...	...	3.100
2002	+C	2 662	26.4	+C	591	5.9	20.5	+C	26	...	...	...	...
2003	+C	2 781	27.4	+C	617	6.1	21.3	+C	34	...	...	...	3.900
2004	+C*	2 628	...	+C*	559	...	...	+C*	35	...	...	...	...
Tuvalu													
2001	U	197	...	U	86	...	...	U	5	...	...	...	...
2002	U	156	...	U	87	...	...	U	4	...	VI61.7	65.1	3.700
2003	U	185	...	U	83	...	...	U	4	...	...	...	...
2004	U	190	...	U	89	...	...	U	5	...	...	...	...
2005	U	231	...	U	64	...	...	U	6	...	...	...	...
Wallis and Futuna Islands - Îles Wallis et Futuna													
2001	C	266	...	C	69	...	...	...	...	...	...	...	...
2002	C	262	...	C	67	...	...	...	...	...	...	...	...
2003	C	290	19.4	C	88	5.9	13.5	...	...	...	...	...	...
2004	C	241	...	C	72	...	...	...	...	...	...	...	...
2005	C	223	...	C	65	...	...	...	...	...	...	...	...

FOOTNOTES - NOTES

Italics: data from civil registers which are incomplete or of unknown completeness. -
Italiques: données incomplètes ou dont le degré d'exactitude n'est pas connu, provenant des registres de l'état civil.

* Provisional. -
  Données provisoires.

[a] 'Code' indicates the source of data, as follows:
C - Civil registration, estimated over 90% complete
U - Civil registration, estimated less than 90% complete
| - Other source, estimated reliable
+ - Data tabulated by date of registration rather than occurence.
... - Information not available

Le 'Code' indique la source des données, comme suit:
C - Registres de l'état civil considérés complets à 90 p. 100 au moins.
U - Registres de l'état civil qui ne sont pas considérés complets à 90 p. 100 au moins.
| - Autre source, considérée fiable.
+ - Données exploitées selon la date de l'enregistrement et non la date de l'événement.
... - Information non disponible.

[b] A Roman number in front of the data for males specifiies the range of the reference period of life expectancy for males and females presented on the

row. For example, a reference year of 2005 and a range of V years means that the reference period for the life expectancy is 2001 - 2005. The absence of a Roman number means the reference period is one year and the reference period therefore coincides with the reference year.

Un chiffre romain devant la donnée relative aux hommes indique l'étendue de la période de référence concernant l'espérance de vie des hommes et des femmes présentée dans la ligne. Par exemple, une année de référence 2005 et une étendue de V signifie que la période de référence pour l'espérance de vie est 2001-2005. L'absence de chiffre romain signifie que la période de référence est d'un an et donc coïncide avec l'année de référence.

[1] Excluding live-born infants who died before their birth was registered. For Algerian population only. - Non compris les enfants nés vivants décédés avant l'enregistrement de leur naissance. Pour la population algérienne seulement.
[2] Data refer to national projections. - Les données se réfèrent aux projections nationales.
[3] For 2001, data refer to last twelve months preceding census in August 2001. - Pour 2001, les données se rapportent aux douze mois précédant le recensement d'août 2001.
[4] Data from civil registration centers of Brazzaville, Pointe-Noire, Dolisie, Nkayi, Mossendijo and Ouesso communes. - Données issues des centres d'enregistrement des faits d'état-civil des communes de Brazzaville, Pointe-Noire, Dolisie, Nkayi, Mossendijo et Ouesso.
[5] Projections based on the 1998 Malawi Population and Housing Census. - Les projections sont basées sur les résultats du recensement de la population et de l'habitat de Malawi de 1998.

[6] Deaths for 2001 refer to the period January-August 2001. - Le chiffre des décès de 2001 correspond à la période allant de janvier à août 2001.

[7] Excluding live-born infants who died before their birth was registered. - Non compris les enfants nés vivants décédés avant l'enregistrement de leur naissance.

[8] Excluding deaths of unknown sex. - Non compris les décès dont on ignore le sexe.

[9] Data are for 12 months preceding the census date. - Les données portent sur les 12 mois précédant la date du recensement.

[10] Source: World Health Organization. - Source : Organisation mondiale de la santé.

[11] Including Canadian residents temporarily in the United States, but excluding United States residents temporarily in Canada. - Y compris les résidents canadiens se trouvant temporairement aux Etats-Unis, mais ne comprenant pas les résidents des Etats-Unis se trouvant temporairement au Canada.

[12] Including births to non-resident mothers. - Y compris les naissances chez des mères non résidentes.

[13] Data refer to births to mothers resident in the Netherlands Antilles (including births outside the Netherlands Antilles to resident mothers, excluding births to non-resident mothers). - Ces données concernent les enfants nés de femmes qui résidaient aux Antilles néerlandaises (y compris ceux qui sont nés hors des Antilles néerlandaises). Elles ne concernent pas les enfants nés de non-résidentes.

[14] Data refer to deaths of residents of the Netherlands Antilles (including those that died outside the Netherlands Antilles). Data exclude deaths by non-residents. - Ces données concernent les décès de résidents des Antilles néerlandaises (y compris ceux survenus hors des Antilles néerlandaises). Elles ne concernent pas les décès des non-résidents.

[15] Excluding Indian jungle population. - Non compris les Indiens de la jungle.

[16] Data on live births and deaths are based on a civil registration system put in place in January 1998. - Les données sur les naissances et les décès sont basées sur un système d'enregistrement des faits d'état civil mis en place en janvier 1998.

[17] Excluding nomadic Indian tribes. - Non compris les tribus d'Indiens nomades.

[18] For 2001, data were collected from population census held on August 2002, referring to events in calendar year 2001. - Pour 2001, les données sont tirées du recensement de la population réalisé en août 2002, concernant des événements de l'année civile 2001.

[19] Data refer to registered live births only. - Les données concernent les naissances vivantes enregistrées seulement.

[20] Data refer to registered deaths only. - Les données se rapportent aux décès enregistrés seulement.

[21] Data refer to registered infant deaths only. - Les données se rapportent aux décès enregistrés d'enfants de moins de 1 an seulement.

[22] Excluding infants born alive of less than 28 weeks' gestation, of less than 1 000 grams in weight and 35 centimeters in length, who die within seven days of birth. - Non compris les enfants nés vivants après moins de 28 semaines de gestations, pesant moins de 1 000 grammes, mesurant moins de 35 centimètres et décédés dans les sept jours qui ont suivi leur naissance.

[23] Rates were obtained by the Sample Vital Registration System 2004 of Bangladesh. - Taux obtenus au moyen du Sample Vital Registration System 2004 du Bangladesh.

[24] For 2005, data refer to last twelve months preceding census in May 2005. - Pour 2005, les données se rapportent aux douze mois précédant le recensement de mai 2005.

[25] The fertility rates have been compiled using a population denominator which has excluded female foreign domestic helpers. - Les taux de fécondité ont été compilés pour une population (en dénominateur) ne comprenant pas les domestiques étrangères.

[26] For statistical purposes, the data for China do not include those for the Hong Kong Special Administrative Region (Hong Kong SAR), Macao Special Administrative Region (Macao SAR) and Taiwan province of China. - Pour la présentation des statistiques, les données pour la Chine ne comprennent pas la Région Administrative Spéciale de Hong Kong (Hong Kong RAS), la Région Administrative Spéciale de Macao (Macao RAS) et Taïwan province de Chine.

[27] Data have been estimated on the basis of the annual National Sample Surveys on Population Changes. - Les données ont été estimées sur la base de l'enquête annuelle "National Sample Survey on Population Changes".

[28] Data for 2005 are estimated from the National Sample Survey of 1 Per cent population. - Les données pour 2005 ont été estimées à partir de l'enquête nationale qui a porté sur un échantillon de 1 % de la population.

[29] Data refer to government controlled areas. - Les données se rapportent aux zones contrôlées par le Gouvernement.

[30] Including data for the Indian-held part of Jammu and Kashmir, the final status of which has not yet been determined. - Y compris les données pour la partie du Jammu et du Cachemire occupée par l'Inde dont le statut définitif n'a pas encore été déterminé.

[31] Rates were obtained by the Sample Registration System of India, actually a large demographic survey. - Les taux ont été obtenus par le Système de l'enregistrement par échantillon de l'Inde qui est une large enquête démographique.

[32] Data relate to the Iranian Year which begins on 21 March and ends on 20 March of the following year. - Les données concernent l'année iranienne, qui commence le 21 mars et se termine le 20 mars de l'année suivante.

[33] Including data for East Jerusalem and Israeli residents in certain other territories under occupation by Israeli military forces since June 1967. - Y compris les données pour Jérusalem-Est et les résidents israéliens dans certains autres territoires occupés depuis 1967 par les forces armées israéliennes.

[34] As of 2002, data on deaths include deaths abroad of Israeli residents who were out of the country for less than a year (there were 109 deaths of Israelis abroad in 2002). - Depuis 2002, les données sur les décès comprennent les décès à l'étranger de résidents israéliens qui ont quitté le pays depuis moins d'un an (en 2002, 109 Israéliens sont morts à l'étranger).

[35] Data include deaths abroad of Israeli residents who were out of the country for less than a year. - Y compris les décès à l'étranger de résidents israéliens qui ont quitté le pays depuis moins d'un an.

[36] Data include 182 deaths abroad of Israeli residents who were out of the country for less than a year. - Y compris les décès à l'étranger de 182 résidents israéliens qui ont quitté le pays depuis moins d'un an.

[37] Data include 183 deaths abroad of Israeli residents who were out of the country for less than a year. - Y compris les décès à l'étranger de 183 résidents israéliens qui ont quitté le pays depuis moins d'un an.

[38] Data include 30 (preliminary figure) deaths abroad of Israeli residents who were out of the country for less than a year. - Y compris les décès à l'étranger de 30 résidents israéliens (chiffres préliminaires) qui ont quitté le pays depuis moins d'un an.

[39] Data refer to Japanese nationals in Japan only. - Les données se raportent aux nationaux japonais au Japon seulement.

[40] Excluding data for Jordanian territory under occupation since June 1967 by Israeli military forces. Excluding foreigners, including registered Palestinian refugees. - Non compris les données pour le territoire jordanien occupé depuis juin 1967 par les forces armées israéliennes. Non compris les étrangers, mais y compris les réfugiés de Palestine enregistrés.

[41] Published by the United Nations Economic and Social Commission for Western Asia. - Publié par la Commission économique et sociale des Nations Unies pour l'Asie occidentale.

[42] Excluding alien armed forces, civilian aliens employed by armed forces, and foreign diplomatic personnel and their dependants. - Non compris les militaires étrangers, les civils étrangers employés par les forces armées ni le personnel diplomatique étranger et les membres de leur famille les accompagnant.

[43] Excluding infants born alive of less than 28 weeks' gestation, of less than 1 000 grams in weight and 35 centimeters in length, who die within seven days of birth.Since 2004, WHO criteria have been adopted in the country. - Non compris les enfants nés vivants après moins de 28 semaines de gestations, pesant moins de 1 000 grammes, mesurant moins de 35 centimètres et décédés dans les sept jours qui ont suivi leur naissance.Depuis 2004, le pays a adopté les critères de l'OMS.

[44] Data estimated from population and housing census 2005. - Données dérivées du recensement de population et du logement de 2005.

[45] For 2001, data refer to last twelve months preceding census on June 2001. - Pour 2001, les données se rapportent aux douze mois précédant le recensement juin 2001.

[46] Data refer to the recorded events in Ministry of Health hospitals and health centres only. - Les données se rapportent aux faits d'état civil enregistrés dans les hôpitaux et les dispensaires du Ministère de la santé seulement.

[47] Excluding data for the Pakistan-held part of Jammu and Kashmir, the final status of which has not yet been determined. - Non compris les données concernant la partie du Jammu et Cachemire occupée par le Pakistan dont le statut définitif n'a pas été déterminé.

[48] Data based on Pakistan Demographic Survey (PDS 2001) . - Données extraites de l'enquête démographique effectuée par le Pakistan en 2001.

[49] Data based on Pakistan Demographic Survey (PDS 2003) . - Données extraites de l'enquête démographique effectuée par le Pakistan en 2003.

[50] Data based on Pakistan Demographic Survey (PDS 2005) . - Données extraites de l'enquête démographique effectuée par le Pakistan en 2005.

[51] Excluding nomad population and Palestinian refugees.Excluding live-born infants who died before their birth was registered. - Non compris la population nomade et les réfugiés de Palestine.Non compris les enfants nés vivants décédés avant l'enregistrement de leur naissance.

[52] Including an upward adjustment for under-registration. - Y compris un ajustement pour sous-enregistrement.

[53] Based on the results of the Population Demographic Survey. - D'après les résultats de la Population Demographic Survey.

[54] Based on the results of the Population Demographic Survey.Reason for discrepancy between the figure for 2001 and the figures for 2002-2004 not ascertained. - D'après les résultats de la Population Demographic Survey.On ne sait pas comment s'explique la divergence entre les chiffre pour 2001 et les chiffres pour 2002-2004.

[55] Including armed forces stationed outside the country, but excluding alien armed forces stationed in the area. - Y compris les militaires nationaux hors du pays, mais non compris les militaires étrangers en garnison sur le territoire.

[56] Excluding Faeroe Islands and Greenland. - Non compris les Iles Féroé et le Gröenland.

[57] Including nationals temporarily outside the country. - Y compris les nationaux se trouvant temporairement hors du pays.

[58] Excluding Overseas Departments, namely, French Guiana, Guadeloupe, Martinique and Reunion, shown separately. - Non compris les départements d'outre mer, c'est-à-dire la Guyane française, la Guadeloupe, la Martinique et la Réunion, qui font l'objet de rubriques distinctes.

[59] Including armed forces stationed outside the country. - Y compris les militaires nationaux hors du pays.

[60] Excluding armed forces. - Non compris les militaires en garnison.

[61] Events registered within one year of occurrence. - Evénements enregistrés dans l'année qui suit l'événement.

[62] Live births to Maltese parents only. - Naissances vivantes aux parents maltais seulement.

[63] Maltese population only. - Population Maltaise seulement.

[64] Including residents outside the country if listed in a Netherlands population register. - Y compris les résidents hors du pays, s'ils sont inscrits sur un registre de population néerlandais.

[65] Including residents temporarily outside the country. - Y compris les résidents se trouvant temporairement hors du pays.

[66] Without data for Kosovo and Metohia. - Sans les données pour le Kosovo and Metohie.

[67] Data based on fertility for range of two years shown under the year ending. - Données fournies sur la base de la fécondité pour une période de deux années consécutives ; les données qui apparaissent sont celles de l'année finale de cette période.

[68] Data revised to exclude births in Northern Ireland to non-residents of Northern Ireland.Data tabulated by date of occurrence for England and Wales, and by date of registration for Northern Ireland and Scotland. - Données révisées pour exclure les naissances en Irlande du Nord de non-résidents de l'Irlande du Nord.Données exploitées selon la date de l'événement pour l'Angleterre et le pays de Galles, et selon la date de l'enregistrement pour l'Irlande du Nord et l'Ecosse.

[69] Data tabulated by date of occurrence for England and Wales, and by date of registration for Northern Ireland and Scotland. - Données exploitées selon la date de l'événement pour l'Angleterre et le pays de Galles, et selon la date de l'enregistrement pour l'Irlande du Nord et l'Ecosse.

[70] Excluding Niue, shown separately, which is part of Cook Islands, but because of remoteness is administered separately. - Non compris Nioué, qui fait l'objet d'une rubrique distincte et qui fait partie des îles Cook, mais qui, en raison de son éloignement, est administrée séparément.

[71] Including United States military personnel, their dependants and contract employees. - Y compris les militaires des Etats-Unis, les membres de leur famille les accompagnant et les agents contractuels des Etats-Unis.

[72] For resident population only. - Pour la population résidante seulement.

[73] Includes children born in New Zealand to women resident in Niue who chose to travel to New Zealand to give birth. - Y compris les enfants nés en Nouvelle-Zélande de femmes résidant à Nioué qui ont choisi de se rendre en Nouvelle-Zélande pour accoucher.

[74] Includes deaths occurred in New Zealand but buried in Niue and deaths occurred in Niue but buried elsewhere. - Y compris les personnes décédées en Nouvelle-Zélande qui sont enterrées à Nioué et les personnes décédées à Nioué qui sont enterrées ailleurs.

Table 5

Table 5 presents national estimates of mid-year population for all available years between 1996 and 2005.

Description of variables: Mid-year estimates of the total population are those provided by national statistical offices. They refer to the *de facto* or *de jure* population on 1 July. In cases where the national statistical office provided data referring to the beginning or the end of a year the average was calculated by the Statistics Division. The data are presented in thousands, rounded by the Statistics Division.

For certain countries or areas, there is a discrepancy between the mid-year population estimates shown in this table and those shown in subsequent tables for the same year. Usually this discrepancy arises because the estimates for a given year are revised and the remaining tabulations are not.

Unless otherwise indicated, all estimates relate to the population within present geographical boundaries. Major exceptions to this principle are explained in footnotes.

Reliability of data: Reliable mid-year population estimates are those that are based on a complete census (or on a sample survey) and have been adjusted on a basis of a continuous population register or on the balance of births, deaths and migration. Reliable mid-year estimates appear in roman type. Mid-year estimates that are not calculated on this basis are considered less reliable and are shown in *italics.*

Limitations: Statistics on estimates of the mid-year total population are subject to the same qualifications as have been set forth for population statistics in general in section 3 of the Technical Notes.

International comparability of mid-year population estimates is also affected by the fact that some of these estimates refer to the *de jure*, and not the *de facto*, population. These are indicated in the column titled "Code". The difference between the *de facto* and the *de jure* population is discussed in section 3.1.1 of the Technical Notes.

Earlier data: Estimates of mid-year population have been shown in previous issues of the *Demographic Yearbook*. Information on the years and specific topics covered is presented in the Historical Index.

Tableau 5

Le tableau 5 présente des estimations nationales de la population en milieu d'année pour le plus grand nombre possible d'années entre 1996 et 2005.

Description des variables : les estimations de la population totale en milieu d'année sont celles qui ont été communiquées par les services nationaux de statistique. Elles correspondent à la population de fait ou se réfèrent à la population de droit, au 1er juillet. Lorsque la date est différente, cela est signalé par une note. Sauf indication contraire, tous les chiffres sont exprimés en milliers. Les données ont été arrondies par la Division de statistique de l'ONU.

Pour certains pays ou territoires, il existe une différence entre les estimations de la population en milieu d'année et celles présentées dans les tableaux suivants pour la même année. Généralement, les différences apparaissent parce que les estimations de l'année ont été révisées mais que les autres tabulations ne l'ont pas été.

Sauf indication contraire, toutes les estimations se rapportent à la population présente sur le territoire actuel des pays ou zones considérés. Les principales exceptions à cette règle sont expliquées en note.

Fiabilité des données : les estimations de la population en milieu d'année sont considérées sûres quand elles sont fondées sur un recensement complet (ou sur une enquête par sondage) et ont été ajustées en fonction des données provenant d'un registre permanent de population ou en fonction des naissances, décès et mouvements migratoires qui ont eu lieu pendant la période. Les estimations considérées comme sûres et apparaissent en caractères romains. Les estimations dont le calcul n'a pas été effectué sur cette base sont considérées comme moins sûres et apparaissent en italique.

Insuffisance des données : les statistiques concernant les estimations de la population totale en milieu d'année appellent toutes les réserves qui ont été formulées à la section 3 des Notes techniques à propos des statistiques de la population en général.

Le fait que certaines des estimations concernant la population en milieu d'année se réfèrent à la population de droit et non à la population de fait influe sur la comparabilité internationale. Ces cas ont été signalés dans la colonne « Code ». La différence entre la population de fait et la population de droit est expliquée à la section 3.1.1 des Notes techniques.

Données publiées antérieurement : des estimations de la population en milieu d'année ont été publiées dans des éditions antérieures de l'*Annuaire démographique*. Pour plus de précisions concernant les années et les sujets pour lesquels des données ont été publiées, se reporter à l'index.

5. Estimates of mid-year population: 1996 - 2005
Estimations de la population au milieu de l'année: 1996 - 2005

Continent and country or area / Continent et pays ou zone	Code[a]	Population estimates (in thousands) - Estimations (en milliers)									
		1996	1997	1998	1999	2000	2001	2002	2003	2004	2005
AFRICA - AFRIQUE											
Algeria - Algérie	DJ	28 566	29 045	29 507	29 965	30 416	30 872	31 332	31 848	32 364	32 906
Benin - Bénin	DF	5 594	5 639	5 816	5 990	6 169	˙6 417	...	...	...	...
Botswana	DF	1 496	1 533	1 572	1 611	1 653	...	1 667	1 691	1 711	...
Burkina Faso	DJ	...	10 561	10 816	11 078	11 347	11 623	11 906	12 197	12 496	12 802
Burundi	DF	6 088	6 194	6 300	6 483	...	...	...	...	...	...
Cameroon - Cameroun[1]	DF	...	14 298	14 439	...	15 292	15 731	16 170	16 626	17 000	...
Cape Verde - Cap-Vert	DF	396	407	417	428	435	445	453	461		...
Central African Republic - République centrafricaine	DF	...	3 245	...	...	...	...	...	3 151	...	...
Chad - Tchad[1]	DF	6 763	6 932	7 105	7 283	...	8 322				
Congo	DF		2 663	2 738	2 815	2 893	2 974	3 058	3 143	3 231	...
Côte d'Ivoire	DF	14 781	15 383	15 366	15 881	16 402	16 928	17 461	18 001	18 546	19 097
Djibouti	DF	715	755	795	840	...	...	...	...	...	...
Egypt - Égypte	DF	58 755	60 080	61 341	62 652	63 976	65 292	66 628	67 976	71 223	71 898
Ethiopia - Éthiopie	DF	56 372	58 117	59 882	61 672	63 495	65 374	67 220	69 127	71 066	...
Gabon	DF	1 093	1 120	1 148	1 177	1 206	˙1 237	˙1 268	˙1 300	...	...
Gambia - Gambie	DF	...	...	...	1 385	1 393	1 420	...	...	...	...
Ghana	DF	17 742	18 305	18 885	19 484	18 412					
Guinea-Bissau - Guinée-Bissau[1]	DF	...	...	...	...	...	1 211	1 238	1 267	1 296	1 326
Kenya	DF	26 999	27 793	28 611	29 453	30 150	31 121	32 118	33 142	34 191	35 267
Lesotho	DF	...	2 012	2 055	2 100	2 144	...	...	...	...	...
Liberia - Libéria	DF	2 820	2 879	...	...	...	...	...	...	...	...
Libyan Arab Jamahiriya - Jamahiriya arabe libyenne[2]	DF	4 519	4 648	4 772	4 958	5 125	5 300	5 484	...	17 206	17 730
Madagascar	DF	13 393	13 803	14 222	14 650	15 085	15 529	15 981	16 441		
Malawi[1]	DF	10 114	10 441	...	10 153	10 475	10 816	11 175	11 549	˙11 938	˙12 341
Mali	...	8 869	9 325	9 811	9 969	10 243	10 525	...	...	...	2 906
Mauritania - Mauritanie	DF	2 351	2 421	2 493	2 568	2 645	2 724	...	...		
Mauritius - Maurice	DJ	1 134	1 148	1 160	1 175	1 187	1 200	1 210	1 223	1 233	1 243
Morocco - Maroc	DF	26 848	27 310	27 775	28 238	28 705	29 170	29 631	30 088	30 540	˙30 172
Mozambique[3]	DF	16 177	16 543	16 917	17 299	17 691	˙17 656	...	...		˙19 420
Namibia - Namibie	DF	...	...	...	˙1 817	...	...	...	...		
Niger	DJ	9 286	9 574	9 871	10 177	10 493	11 090	11 456	11 834	12 225	12 628
Nigeria - Nigéria[1]	DF	...	...	...	...	115 224	118 801	122 444	126 153	129 175	133 767
Réunion	DF	675	687	698	710	722	735	748	764	769	779
Saint Helena ex. dep. - Sainte-Hélène sans dép.	DF	5	...	...	...	...	...	...	...	...	...
Saint Helena: Tristan da Cunha - Sainte-Hélène: Tristan da Cunha	DF	0	...	...	...	...	...	...	...	...	...
Sao Tome and Principe - Sao Tomé-et-Principe	DF	127	129	131	133	135	...	140	143	146	149
Senegal - Sénégal	DJ	8 525	8 742	8 964	9 193	9 427	9 667	9 913	10 165	10 564	10 848
Seychelles	DF	76	77	79	80	81	81	84	83	82	83
Sierra Leone	DF	4 522	4 625	4 730	4 836	4 944	5 054	5 167	5 280	...	...
South Africa - Afrique du Sud[3]	DF	40 342	41 227	42 131	43 054	43 686	44 561	45 454	46 430	46 587	46 888
Sudan - Soudan	DF	27 747	28 507	29 266	30 326	31 081	31 627	32 468	33 334	34 512	35 397
Swaziland	DF	938	...	952	977	1 003	1 030	1 056	1 081	1 105	1 126
Togo	DF	4 179	4 269	4 406	4 506	4 629	4 740	4 854	4 970	5 090	5 337
Tunisia - Tunisie	DF	9 089	9 215	9 333	9 456	9 564	9 674	9 782	9 840	9 941	10 029
Uganda - Ouganda	DF	19 848	20 752	21 467	22 207	22 972	22 788	...	...	...	...
United Republic of Tanzania - République Unie de Tanzanie	DF	29 086	29 984	...	...	...	...	...	...	...	37 379
Zambia - Zambie	DF	9 454	9 780	10 096	10 407	9 337	10 089	10 409	10 744	11 090	...
Zimbabwe	DF	11 908	12 294	12 685	13 079	...	12 960	...	...	...	...
AMERICA, NORTH - AMÉRIQUE DU NORD											
Anguilla	DF	10	10	11	11	11	12	12	12	13	14
Antigua and Barbuda - Antigua-et-Barbuda	DF	69	69	70	71	72	77	78	80	81	83
Aruba	DJ	83	86	88	90	91	92	93	95	98	101
Bahamas	DF	284	288	293	298	303	309	312	317	...	...
Barbados - Barbade	DF	264	265	265	267	269	270	271	272	272	273
Belize	DF	222	230	239	243	250	257	265	274	283	292

5. Estimates of mid-year population: 1996 - 2005
Estimations de la population au milieu de l'année: 1996 - 2005 (continued - suite)

Continent and country or area Continent et pays ou zone	Code[a]	Population estimates (in thousands) - Estimations (en milliers)									
		1996	1997	1998	1999	2000	2001	2002	2003	2004	2005
AMERICA, NORTH - **AMÉRIQUE DU NORD**											
Bermuda - Bermudes	DJ	62	62	62	63	63	62	63	63	63	64
British Virgin Islands - Îles Vierges britanniques	DF	19	19	19	20	20	21	21	21	22	...
Canada	DJ	29 611[4]	29 907[4]	30 157[4]	30 404[4]	30 689[4]	31 021[5]	31 373[5]	31 676[5]	31 995[5]	32 312[6]
Cayman Islands - Îles Caïmanes	DJ	34	36	38	...	40	41	42	44	44	48
Costa Rica	DJ	3 202	3 271	3 341	3 413	3 810	3 907	3 998	4 089	4 179	4 266
Cuba	DF	10 965	11 009	11 055	11 095	11 130	11 157	11 184	11 215	11 236	11 243
Dominica - Dominique	DF	72	72	72	72	72	71	70	...	71	...
Dominican Republic - République dominicaine	DF	*7 808*	*7 988*	*8 172*	*8 360*	*8 552*	*8 749*	...	*8 715*	*8 870*	*9 028*
El Salvador	DF	5 787	5 908	6 031	6 154	6 276	6 397	6 518	6 638	6 757	6 875
Greenland - Groenland[7]	DJ	56	56	56	56	56	56	57	57	57	...
Grenada - Grenade[8]	DF	99	100	100	101	101	101	...	...	...	...
Guadeloupe[9]	DJ	409	414	419	424	428	432	437	439	445	*446
Guatemala[3]	DF	10 243	10 517	10 799	11 088	11 385	11 678	11 987	12 084	12 390	12 701
Haiti - Haïti	DJ	*7 336*	*7 492*	*7 647*	*7 803*	*7 959*	*8 132*	...	...	...	...
Honduras	DF	*5 755*	*5 908*	*6 057*	*6 211*	*6 369*	*6 530*	*6 695*	*6 861*	*7 028	...
Jamaica - Jamaïque	DJ	2 510	2 534	2 557	2 574	2 589	2 605	2 617	2 629	2 642	2 661
Martinique	DJ	372	376	379	382	385	387	389	391	394	398
Mexico - Mexique	DJ	*93 130*	*94 478*	*95 790*	*97 115*	*98 439*	*99 716*	*100 909*	*102 000*	*103 002*	*103 947*
Montserrat	DF	8[10]	6[10]	4	5	5	...	...	...	...	...
Netherlands Antilles - Antilles néerlandaises[11]	DJ	*191*	*193*	*192*	*186*	*179*	*174*	*175*	*179*	*183*	...
Nicaragua	DJ	*4 549*	*4 674*	*4 803*	*4 936*	*5 106*	*5 174*	*5 243*	*5 314*	*5 385*	*5 457*
Panama	DF	*2 674*	*2 719*	*2 764*	*2 809*	*2 856*	*2 897*	*3 060*	*3 116*	*3 172*	*3 228*
Puerto Rico - Porto Rico[12]	DJ	3 685	3 716	3 748	3 782	3 816	3 840	3 859	3 879	3 895	3 912
Saint Kitts and Nevis - Saint-Kitts-et-Nevis	DF	42	41	40	42	40	*46	...	...	...	...
Saint Lucia - Sainte-Lucie	DF	147	150	152	154	156	158	159	161	162	165
Saint Pierre and Miquelon - Saint Pierre-et-Miquelon	DF	7	...	...	...	...	...	...	...	...	...
Saint Vincent and the Grenadines - Saint Vincent-et-les Grenadines	DF	111	112	112	112	110	...	108	105	105	104
Trinidad and Tobago - Trinité-et-Tobago	DF	1 264	1 275	1 278	1 284	1 290	1 267	1 276	1 282	...	...
Turks Caicos Islands - Îles Turques et Caïques	DJ	*15*	*16*	*17*	*17*	*18*	*20*	*21*	*25*	*27*	*31*
United States - États-Unis[13]	DJ	269 394	272 647	275 854	279 040	282 193	285 108	287 985	290 850	293 623	296 410
United States Virgin Islands - Îles Vierges américaines	DJ	108	108	109	109	109	109	109	109	...	...
AMERICA, SOUTH - **AMÉRIQUE DU SUD**											
Argentina - Argentine	DF	*35 196*	*35 604*	*36 005*	*36 399*	*36 784*	*37 156*	*37 516*	*37 870*	*38 226*	*38 592*
Bolivia - Bolivie	DF	*7 661*	*7 845*	*8 035*	*8 229*	*8 428*	*8 624*	*8 824*	*9 025*	*9 227*	*9 427*
Brazil - Brésil[14]	DF	*161 323*	*163 780*	*166 252*	*168 754*	*171 280*	*173 822*	*176 391*	*178 985*	*181 586*	*184 184*
Chile - Chili	DF	14 596	14 796	14 997	15 197	15 398	15 572	15 746	15 919	16 093	16 267
Colombia - Colombie	DF	*39 281*	*40 019*	*40 773*	*41 539*	*42 299*	*43 035*	*43 776*	*44 531*	*45 295*	*46 045*
Ecuador - Équateur[15]	DF	*11 591*	*11 773*	*11 948*	*12 121*	*12 299*	*12 480*	*12 661*	*12 843*	*13 027*	*13 215*
French Guiana - Guyane française	DJ	142	148	153	158	164	170	175	181	*187	*200
Guyana	DF	770	775	773	771	742	744	748	752[16]	755	758
Paraguay	DF	*4 955*	*5 085*	*5 219*	*5 356*	*5 346*	*5 456*	*5 567*	*5 677*	*5 788*	*5 899*
Peru - Pérou[17]	DF	*24 258*	*24 681*	*25 104*	*25 525*	*25 939*	*26 347*	*26 749*	*27 148*	*27 547*	*27 947*
Suriname	DJ	440	446	452	458	464	470	476	481	487	499
Uruguay[3]	DF	3 236	3 256	3 274	3 289	3 301	3 308	3 309	3 304	3 302	3 306
Venezuela (Bolivarian Republic of) - Venezuela (République bolivarienne du)[18]	DF	22 502	22 959	23 413	23 867	24 311	24 766	25 220	25 674	26 127	26 577

5. Estimates of mid-year population: 1996 - 2005
Estimations de la population au milieu de l'année: 1996 - 2005 (continued - suite)

Continent and country or area / Continent et pays ou zone	Code[a]	Population estimates (in thousands) - Estimations (en milliers)									
		1996	1997	1998	1999	2000	2001	2002	2003	2004	2005
ASIA - ASIE											
Afghanistan	DF	19 820	20 350	20 760	21 200	21 770	22 080	22 930	...	...	...
Armenia - Arménie	DJ	3 247	3 242	3 235	3 229	3 221	3 214	3 212	3 211	3 214	3 218
Azerbaijan - Azerbaïdjan	DF	7 763	7 838	7 913	7 983	8 049	8 111	8 172	8 234	8 307	˙8 392
Bahrain - Bahreïn	DF	574	589	605	621	638	655	672	689	707	725
Bangladesh	DF	122 100	124 300	126 200	˙128 100	129 300	131 100	132 900	134 800	136 700	138 600
Bhutan - Bhoutan	DF	600	619	˙638	658	678	699	716	734	753	...
Brunei Darussalam - Brunéi Darussalam	DF	295	302	310	317	325	333	344	350	360	370
Cambodia - Cambodge[19]	DF	10 340	10 368	12 242[20]	12 462[20]	12 688[20]	12 922[20]	13 164[20]	13 415[20]	13 091[20]	˙13 661[20]
China - Chine[21]	DF	1 217 550[22]	1 230 075[22]	1 241 935[22]	1 252 735[22]	1 262 645[22]	1 271 850[23]	1 280 400[23]	1 288 400[23]	1 296 075[23]	1 303 720[24]
China: Hong Kong SAR - Chine: Hong Kong RAS	DJ	6 436	6 489	6 544	6 607	6 665	6 714	6 744	6 731	6 784	6 813
China: Macao SAR - Chine: Macao RAS	DJ	415	417	422	427	431	434	438	444	455	473
Cyprus - Chypre[25]	DJ	661	670	679	686	694	701	710	721	737	758
Georgia - Géorgie	DF	4 617	4 532	4 487	4 453	4 418	4 387	4 357	4 329	4 318	4 361
India - Inde[26]	DF	942 157	960 550	979 051	997 645	1 016 320	1 035 066	1 050 640	1 068 214	1 085 600	˙1 101 000
Indonesia - Indonésie	DJ	198 320	201 353	204 393	207 437	...	208 643	211 439	214 251	217 077	˙219 898
Iran (Islamic Republic of) - Iran (République islamique d')	DJ	...	60 939[27]	61 836[27]	62 746[27]	63 664[27]	64 528[27]	65 540[27]	66 480[27]	67 477[27]	68 467[28]
Iraq	DF	21 124	22 046	22 702	23 382	24 086	24 813	25 565	26 340	27 139	27 963
Israel - Israël[29]	DJ	5 685	5 829	5 971	6 125	6 289	6 439	6 570	6 690	6 809	6 930
Japan - Japon[30]	DF	125 757	126 057	126 400	126 631	126 843	127 149	127 445	127 718	127 761	127 773
Jordan - Jordanie[31]	DF	4 383	4 506	4 623	4 738	4 857	4 978	5 098	5 230	5 350	˙5 473
Kazakhstan	DF	15 578	15 334	15 073	14 928	14 884	14 858	14 859	14 909	15 013	15 147
Korea (Dem. People's Republic of) - Corée (Rép. populaire dém. de)	DF	22 114	22 355	22 554	22 754	22 963	23 149	23 313	23 464	23 612	...
Korea (Republic of) - Corée (République de)	DF	45 546	45 954	46 287	46 617	47 008	47 354	47 615	47 849	48 082	48 294
Kuwait - Koweït	DF	1 894	1 980	2 027	2 107	2 138	2 183	2 262	2 325	2 391	2 457
Kyrgyzstan - Kirghizistan	DF	4 657	4 725	4 797	4 865	4 915	4 955	4 993	5 039	5 093	5 144
Lao People's Democratic Republic - République démocratique populaire lao	DF	...	...	...	5 091	5 218[32]	5 377[32]	5 526[32]	5 679[32]	5 836[32]	5 679
Lebanon - Liban	DF	...	...	...	...	...	...	...	...	3 755	...
Malaysia - Malaisie	DF	21 169	20 996	21 475	21 852	23 495	24 013	24 527	25 048	25 581	26 128
Maldives	DF	251	259	267	278	271	276	281	285	289	294
Mongolia - Mongolie	DF	2 255	2 273	2 281	2 332	2 390	2 425	2 459	2 490	2 519	2 548
Myanmar	DF	...	˙46 402	...	...	...	...	...	...	...	...
Nepal - Népal	DJ	20 832	21 331	21 843	22 367	˙22 904	23 151	23 701	24 250	24 797	25 343
Occupied Palestinian Territory - Territoire palestinien occupé	DF	2 631	2 783	2 897	3 019	3 149	3 275	3 394	3 515	3 638	3 762
Oman	DF	2 214	2 256	2 288	2 325	2 401	2 478	2 538	...	2 416	2 509
Pakistan[33]	DF	125 380	128 420	131 510	134 510	138 945	141 765	144 560	147 335	150 135	153 455
Philippines	DJ	71 899	73 527	75 155	76 783	76 348	77 926	79 504	81 081	82 664	˙85 237
Qatar	DF	510	530	557	586	617	649	682	718	756	796
Saudi Arabia - Arabie saoudite	DF	18 582	19 039	19 506	19 985	20 476	20 979	21 495	22 023	22 564	23 119
Singapore - Singapour	DF	3 671	3 796	3 927	3 959	4 028	4 138	4 176	4 186	4 238	4 342
Sri Lanka	DF	18 315	18 552	18 774	19 043	19 359	18 732	19 007	19 253	19 462	˙19 668
Syrian Arab Republic - République arabe syrienne[34]	DF	14 619	15 100	15 597	16 110	16 320	16 720	17 130	17 550	17 980	18 138
Tajikistan - Tadjikistan	DF	5 919	...	6 103	6 064	6 188	6 313	6 441	6 573	6 710	6 850
Thailand - Thaïlande	DJ	60 003	60 602	61 156	61 564	61 770	62 914	63 482	64 019	64 177	64 839
Turkey - Turquie	DF	62 909	64 064	65 215	66 350	67 420	68 365	69 302	70 231	71 152	72 065
Turkmenistan - Turkménistan	DF	4 569	...	4 859	...	...	...	...	...	...	...
United Arab Emirates - Émirats arabes unis[35]	DF	2 443	2 624	2 776	2 938	...	...	3 754	4 041	...	...
Uzbekistan - Ouzbékistan	DF	23 130	23 560	24 051	23 954	24 650	24 964	˙25 368	...	...	...
Viet Nam	DF	73 157	74 307	75 456	76 597	77 635	78 686	79 727	80 902	82 032	83 106
Yemen - Yémen	DF	15 915	16 484	17 072	17 671	18 261	˙18 863	˙19 495	...	...	...
EUROPE											
Albania - Albanie	DF	3 076	3 075	3 055	3 054	3 061	3 074	3 093	3 111	3 127	3 142
Andorra - Andorre[7]	DJ	64	66	66	66	66	66	66	70	75	79

5. Estimates of mid-year population: 1996 - 2005
Estimations de la population au milieu de l'année: 1996 - 2005 (continued - suite)

Continent and country or area / Continent et pays ou zone	Code[a]	Population estimates (in thousands) - Estimations (en milliers)									
		1996	1997	1998	1999	2000	2001	2002	2003	2004	2005
EUROPE											
Austria - Autriche	DJ	7 959	7 968	7 977	7 992	8 012	8 043	8 084	8 118	8 175	8 233
Belarus - Bélarus	DF	10 250	10 220	10 191	10 035	10 005	9 971	9 925	9 874	9 825	9 775
Belgium - Belgique	DJ	10 157	10 181	10 203	10 226	10 251	10 287	10 333	10 376	10 421	10 479
Bosnia and Herzegovina - Bosnie-Herzégovine	DF	3 645	3 738	3 653	3 725	3 781	3 798	3 828	3 832	3 843	3 843
Bulgaria - Bulgarie	DF	8 363	8 312	8 257	8 211	8 170	7 910	7 869	7 824	7 781	7 740
Channel Islands: Guernsey - Îles Anglo-Normandes: Guernesey	DF	59	59	59	60	60	...	...	...	60	...
Channel Islands: Jersey - Îles Anglo-Normandes: Jersey	DF	...	...	...	...	...	87	87	88	88	88
Croatia - Croatie	DJ	4 494	4 572	4 501	4 554	4 381	...	4 443	4 442	4 439	4 442
Czech Republic - République tchèque	DJ	10 315	10 304	10 295	10 283	10 273	10 224	10 201	10 202	10 207	10 234
Denmark - Danemark[36]	DJ	5 262	5 284	5 301	5 327	5 337	5 359	5 374	5 387	5 401	5 416
Estonia - Estonie	DF	1 416	1 400	1 386	1 376	1 370	1 364	1 359	1 354	1 349	1 346
Faeroe Islands - Îles Féroé[7]	DJ	44	44	45	45	46	47	47	48	48	48
Finland - Finlande[7]	DJ	5 125	5 140	5 153	5 165	5 176	5 188	5 201	5 213	5 228	5 246
France[37]	DJ	58 026	58 207	58 398	58 673	59 049	59 454	59 863	60 264	60 643	60 996
Germany - Allemagne	DJ	81 896	82 052	82 029	82 087	82 188	82 340	82 482	82 520	82 501	82 464
Gibraltar[38]	DF	27	27	27	27	27	...	29	29	29	29
Greece - Grèce[39]	DF	10 709	10 777	10 835	10 883	10 917	10 950	10 988	11 024	11 062	11 104
Holy See - Saint-Siège[40]	DF	...	...	1	...	...	...	...	...	...	...
Hungary - Hongrie	DF	10 193	10 155	10 114	10 068	10 024	10 188	10 159	10 130	10 107	10 087
Iceland - Islande[7]	DJ	269	271	274	277	281	285	288	289	293	296
Ireland - Irlande[41]	DF	...	3 664	3 703	3 742	3 790	3 847	...	3 979	4 044	4 131
Isle of Man - Îles de Man	DJ	72	72	74	...	75	76	77	77	78	78
Italy - Italie	DJ	56 860	56 890	56 907	56 916	56 942	56 978	57 158	57 605	58 175	58 607
Latvia - Lettonie	DJ	2 457	2 433	2 410	2 390	2 373	2 355	2 339	2 325	2 313	2 301
Liechtenstein	DF	31	31	32	32	33	33	34	34	34	35
Lithuania - Lituanie	DJ	3 602	3 575	3 549	3 524	3 500	3 481	3 469	3 454	3 436	3 414
Luxembourg	DJ	414	419	425	430	436	442	446	450	453	457
Malta - Malte	DJ	374	377	379	380	383	385	387	399	401	404
Monaco	DJ		32		33	...	...	...	...	...	...
Netherlands - Pays-Bas	DJ	15 530	15 611	15 707	15 812	15 926	16 046	16 149	16 225	16 282	16 320
Norway - Norvège[42]	DJ	4 381	4 405	4 431	4 462	4 491	4 514	4 538	4 565	4 592	4 623
Poland - Pologne[43]	DF	38 289	38 292	38 283	38 270	38 256[44]	38 251[44]	38 232	38 195	38 180	38 161
Portugal[45]	DJ	10 058	10 091	10 129	10 172	10 226	10 293	10 368	10 441	10 502	10 549
Republic of Moldova - République de Moldova[46]	DJ	4 327	3 654	3 652	3 646	3 639	3 631	3 623	3 613	3 604	3 595
Romania - Roumanie	DJ	22 608	22 546	22 503	22 458	22 435	22 408	21 795	21 734	21 673	21 624
Russian Federation - Fédération de Russie[47]	DJ	148 160	147 915	147 671	147 215	146 597	145 976	145 306	144 566	143 821	143 150
San Marino - Saint-Marin[7]	DF	25	26	26	26	27	28	28	29	29	31
Serbia and Montenegro - Serbie-et-Montenegro	DJ	10 577	10 600	10 617[48]	10 629[48]	10 634[48]	10 652[48]	8 114[49]	8 153[49]	8 147[49]	...
Slovakia - Slovaquie	DJ	5 374	5 383	5 391	5 395	5 401	5 380	5 379	5 379	5 383	5 387
Slovenia - Slovénie	DJ	1 991	1 987	1 983	1 986	1 990	1 992	1 996	1 997	1 997	2 001
Spain - Espagne[50]	DJ	39 479	39 583	39 722	39 927	40 264	40 721	41 314	42 005	42 692	43 398
Sweden - Suède[7]	DJ	8 841	8 846	8 851	8 858	8 872	8 896	8 925	8 958	8 994	9 030
Switzerland - Suisse	DJ	7 081	7 096	7 124	7 164	7 204	7 256	7 314	7 364	7 415	7 459
The Former Yugoslav Rep. of Macedonia - L'ex-République yougoslave de Macédoine	DF	1 975	1 997	2 008	2 017	2 024	2 035	2 031[51]	2 027[51]	2 033	2 037
Ukraine	...	51 058	50 595	50 144	49 674[52]	49 177[52]	48 690	48 230	47 813	47 271	47 075
United Kingdom - Royaume-Uni	DF	58 164[53]	58 314[53]	58 475[53]	58 684[53]	58 886[53]	59 113[53]	59 322[53]	59 554	59 834	60 209
OCEANIA - OCÉANIE											
American Samoa - Samoas américaines[12]	DJ	54[54]	55[54]	56[54]	57[54]	58	59	61	63	64	66
Australia - Australie[3]	DJ	18 311	18 518	18 711	18 926	19 153	19 413	19 655	19 903	20 140	20 409
Cook Islands - Îles Cook[55]	DF	20	18	17	16	18	18	18	18	20	20
Fiji - Fidji	DF	775	788	788	802	808	813	820	829	835	842
French Polynesia - Polynésie française	DF	219	223	226	228	235	239	243	247	251	255

5. Estimates of mid-year population: 1996 - 2005
Estimations de la population au milieu de l'année: 1996 - 2005 (continued - suite)

Continent and country or area / Continent et pays ou zone	Code[a] / Code[a]	Population estimates (in thousands) - Estimations (en milliers)									
		1996	1997	1998	1999	2000	2001	2002	2003	2004	2005
OCEANIA - OCÉANIE											
Guam[12]	DJ	145	147	150	153	...	158	161	164	166	*169
Kiribati	DF	...	*83	...	...	...	...	...	...	...	...
Marshall Islands - Îles Marshall	DF	57	61	63	51	53	55	57	...	...	...
Micronesia, Federated States of - Micronésie, États Fédérés de La	DJ	110	110	112	113	119	117	120	...	...	...
Nauru	DF	11	11	11	11	12	12	...	...	...	...
New Caledonia - Nouvelle-Calédonie	DF	197	201	204	208	213	217	221	226	230	...
New Zealand - Nouvelle-Zélande	DJ	3 732	3 781	3 815	3 835	3 858	3 881	3 939	4 009	4 061	4 099
Niue - Nioué	DF	...	...	...	...	...	...	*2			
Northern Mariana Islands - Îles Mariannes septentrionales	DF	61	64	67	69	72	75	74	76	...	...
Palau - Palaos	DF	18	18	18	19	19	20	20	20	21	...
Papua New Guinea - Papouasie-Nouvelle-Guinée	DF	...	4 209	4 600	...	5 100	...	5 462	...	...	...
Samoa	DF	...	...	168	169	171	...	178	180	182	183
Solomon Islands - Îles Salomon	DF	...	...	...	405	415	426	437	448	460	471
Tonga[56]	DF	...	99	99	100	100	101	101	101	...	...
Tuvalu	DF	9	9	9	9	9	9	9	...	...	...
Vanuatu	DF	170	174	...	...	...	...	...	...	216[57]	...

FOOTNOTES - NOTES

Italics: estimates which are less reliable. -
Italiques: estimations moins sûres.

* Provisional. - Données provisoires.

[a] 'Code' indicates source of data, as follows:
DF Estimates of population de facto - Population de fait
FJ Estimates of population de jure. - Population de droit

[1] Data refer to national projections. - Les données se réfèrent aux projections nationales.

[2] Data refer to Libyan nationals only. - Les données se raportent aux nationaux libyens seulement.

[3] Mid-year estimates have been adjusted for underenumeration, at latest census. - Les estimations au millieu de l'année tiennent compte d'un ajustement destiné à compenser les lacunes du 'dénombrement lors du dernier recensement.

[4] Final intercensal estimates. - Estimations inter censitaires finales.

[5] Final postcensal estimates. - Évaluations postcensal finales.

[6] Updated postcensal estimates. - Estimations post censitaires mises à jour.

[7] Population statistics are compiled from registers. - Les statistiques de la population sont compilées à partir des registres.

[8] Including Carriacou and other dependencies in the Grenadines. - Y compris Carriacou et les autres dépendances du groupe des îles Grenadines.

[9] Including dependencies: Marie-Galante, la Désirade, les Saintes, Petite-Terre, St. Barthélemy and French part of St. Martin. - Y compris les dépendances: Marie-Galante, la Désirade, les Saintes, Petite-Terre, Saint-Barthélemy et la partie française de Saint-Martin.

[10] Around 1996 - 1997 volcanic activity on Montserrat escalated, forcing people to relocate. - Vers 1996 - 1997 l'activité volcanique a connu une recrudescence à Montserrat, forçant les habitants à s'installer ailleurs.

[11] Comprising Bonaire, Curaçao, Saba, St. Eustatius and Dutch part of St. Martin. - Comprend Bonaire, Curaçao, Saba, Saint-Eustache et la partie néederlandaise de Saint-Martin.

[12] Including armed forces stationed in the area. - Y compris les militaires en garnison sur le territoire.

[13] Excluding armed forces overseas and civilian citizens absent from country for an extended period of time. - Non compris les militaires à l'étranger, et les civils hors du pays pendant une période prolongée.

[14] Data include persons in remote areas, military personnel outside the country, merchant seamen at sea, civilian seasonal workers outside the country, and other civilians outside the country, and exclude nomads, foreign military, civilian aliens temporarily in the country, transients on ships and Indian jungle population. - Y compris les personnes vivant dans des régions éloignées, le personel militaire en dehors du pays, les marins marchands, les ouvriers saisonniers en dehors du pays, et autres civils en dehors du pays, et non compris les nomades, les militaires étrangers, les étrangers civils temporairement dans le pays, les transiteurs sur des bateaux et les Indiens de la jungle.

[15] Excluding nomadic Indian tribes. - Non compris les tribus d'Indiens nomades.

[16] Data for 2003 have been adjusted on the basis of the Population Census of 2002. - Les données de 2003 ont été ajustées sur la base du recensement de population de 2002.

[17] Excluding Indian jungle population. Mid-year estimates have been adjusted for underenumeration, at latest census. - Non compris les Indiens de la jungle. Les estimations au millieu de l'année tiennent compte d'un ajustement destiné à compenser les lacunes du dénombrement lors du dernier recensement.

[18] Excluding Indian jungle population. - Non compris les Indiens de la jungle.

[19] Excluding foreign diplomatic personnel and their dependants. - Non compris le personnel diplomatique étranger et les membres de leur famille les accompagnant.

[20] From 1998 based on census result. - Depuis 1998, à partir des résultats de recensement.

[21] For statistical purposes, the data for China do not include those for the Hong Kong Special Administrative Region (Hong Kong SAR), Macao Special Administrative Region (Macao SAR) and Taiwan province of China. - Pour la présentation des statistiques, les données pour la Chine ne comprennent pas la Région Administrative Spéciale de Hong Kong (Hong Kong RAS), la Région Administrative Spéciale de Macao (Macao RAS) et Taïwan province de Chine.

[22] Data for the period 1990 to 2000 have been adjusted on the basis of the Population Census of 2000. - Les données pour la période allant de 1990 à 2000 ont été ajustées à partir des résultats du recensement de la population de 2000.

[23] Data have been estimated on the basis of the annual National Sample Surveys on Population Changes. - Les données ont été estimées sur la base de l'enquête annuelle "National Sample Survey on Population Changes".

[24] Data for 2005 are estimated from the National Sample Survey of 1 Per cent population. - Les données pour 2005 ont été estimées à partir de l'enquête nationale qui a porté sur un échantillon de 1 % de la population.

[25] Data refer to government controlled areas. - Les données se rapportent aux zones contrôlées par le Gouvernement.

[26] Including data for the Indian-held part of Jammu and Kashmir, the final status of which has not yet been determined. - Y compris les données pour la partie du Jammu et du Cachemire occupée par l'Inde dont le statut définitif n'a pas encore été déterminé.

[27] Data relate to the Iranian Year which begins on 21 March and ends on 20 March of the following year. - Les données concernent l'année iranienne, qui commence le 21 mars et se termine le 20 mars de l'année suivante.

[28] Data relate to the population for the Iranian Year 1384 (21 March 2005-20 March 2006). - Les données concernent la population pour l'année iranienne 1384 (21 mars 2005-20 mars 2006).

[29] Including data for East Jerusalem and Israeli residents in certain other territories under occupation by Israeli military forces since June 1967. - Y compris les données pour Jérusalem-Est et les résidents israéliens dans certains autres territoires occupés depuis 1967 par les forces armées israéliennes.

[30] Excluding diplomatic personnel outside the country and foreign military and civilian personnel and their dependants stationed in the area. - Non compris le personnel diplomatique hors du pays ni les militaires et agents civils étrangers en poste sur le territoire et les membres de leur famille les accompagnant.

[31] Excluding data for Jordanian territory under occupation since June 1967 by Israeli military forces. Excluding foreigners, including registered Palestinian refugees. - Non compris les données pour le territoire jordanien occupé depuis juin 1967 par les forces armées israéliennes. Non compris les étrangers, mais y compris les réfugiés de Palestine enregistrés.

[32] From year 2000-2004, calculated base on Population census 1995 structure and growth rate at year 2000. - Pour les années 2000 à 2004, on a pris pour base la structure issue du recensement de population de 1995 et le taux de croissance de 2000.

[33] Excluding data for the Pakistan-held part of Jammu and Kashmir, the final status of which has not yet been determined. - Non compris les données concernant la partie du Jammu et Cachemire occupée par le Pakistan dont le statut définitif n'a pas été déterminé.

[34] Including Palestinian refugees. - Y compris les réfugiés de Palestine.

[35] Comprising 7 sheikdoms of Abu Dhabi, Dubai, Sharjah, Ajaman, Umm al Qaiwain, Ras al Khaimah and Fujairah, and the area lying within the modified Riyadh line as announced in October 1955. - Comprend les sept cheikhats de Abou Dhabi, Dabai, Ghârdja, Adjmân, Oumm-al-Quiwaïn, Ras al Khaïma et Foudjaïra, ainsi que la zone délimitée par la ligne de Riad modifiée comme il a été annoncé en octobre 1955.

[36] Excluding Faeroe Islands and Greenland. Population statistics are compiled from registers. - Non compris les Iles Féroé et le Gröenland. Les statistiques de la population sont compilées à partir des registres.

[37] Excluding Overseas Departments, namely, French Guiana, Guadeloupe, Martinique and Reunion, shown separately. Excluding diplomatic personnel outside the country and including members of alien armed forces not living in military camps and foreign diplomatic personnel not living in embassies or consulates. - Non compris les départements d'outre mer, c'est-à-dire la Guyane française, la Guadeloupe, la Martinique et la Réunion, qui font l'objet de rubriques distinctes. Non compris le personnel diplomatique hors du pays et y compris les militaires étrangers ne vivant pas dans des camps militaires et le personnel diplomatique étranger ne vivant pas dans les ambassades ou les consulats.

[38] Excluding families of military personnel, visitors and transients. - Non compris les familles des militaires, ni les visiteurs et transients.

[39] Mid-year population excludes armed forces stationed outside the country, but includes alien armed forces stationed in the area. - Les estimations au millieu de l'année non compris les militaires en garnison hors du pays, mais y compris les militaires étrangers en garnison sur le territoire.

[40] Data refer to the Vatican City State. Population statistics are compiled from registers. - Les données se rapportent à l'Etat de la Cité du Vatican. Les statistiques de la population sont compilées à partir des registres.

[41] Data refer to 15th of April. - Données se rapportent au 15 avril.

[42] Including residents temporarily outside the country. - Y compris les résidents se trouvant temporairement hors du pays.

[43] Excluding civilian aliens within country, but including civilian nationals temporarily outside country. - Non compris les civils étrangers dans le pays, mais y compris les civils nationaux temporairement hors du pays.

[44] Average year data for 2000-2001 contain revised data according to the final results of population census 2002. - Les données annuelles moyennes pour 2000 et 2001 comportent des données révisées en fonction des résultats du recensement de 2002.

[45] Including the Azores and Madeira Islands. - Y compris les Açores et Madère.

[46] Data do not include information for Transnistria and the municipality of Bender. - Les données ne tiennent pas compte de l'information sur la Transnistria et la municipalité de Bender.

[47] Figures were updated taking into account the results of the 2002 All-Russian population census. - Les chiffres ont été calculés compte tenu des résultats du recensement de la population de la Fédération de Russie de 2002.

[48] 1998 - 2001, estimates of Kosovo and Metohia computed on the basis of natural increases from year 1997. - 1998 - 2001, les estimations pour le Kosovo et la Metohia ont été calculées sur la base des incréments naturelles depuis 1997.

[49] Without data for Kosovo and Metohia. - Sans les données pour le Kosovo and Metohie.

[50] Including the Balearic and Canary Islands, and Alhucemas, Ceuta, Chafarinas, Melilla and Penon de Vélez de la Gomera. - Y compris les Baléares et les Canaries, Al Hoceima, Ceuta, les îles Zaffarines, Melilla et Penon de Vélez de la Gomera.

[51] Figures for 2002 and 2003 were calculated on the base of census data 2002. - Les chiffres pour 2002 et 2003 ont été calculés à partir des résultats du recensement de 2002.

[52] Starting from 1994 until 1999 data is de facto and from 2000 and later data is de jure. - De 1994 à 1999, les données sont de fait, à partir de 2000 elles sont de jure.

[53] Population estimates for 1994 to 2002 were revised in light of the local studies. - Les estimations de la population pour les années 1994 à 2002 ont été révisées en fonction d'études locales.

[54] Population estimates for the years 1991 to 1999 have been smoothed using the 1995 mid-decade household survey and the year 2000 census. - L'estimation de la population a été lissée pour les années entre 1991 et 1999 en utilisant l'enquête des ménages de 1995 et le recensement de l'année 2000.

[55] Excluding Niue, shown separately, which is part of Cook Islands, but because of remoteness is administered separately. - Non compris Nioué, qui fait l'objet d'une rubrique distincte et qui fait partie des îles Cook, mais qui, en raison de son éloignement, est administrée séparément.

[56] Based on the results of the 1996 population census not necessarily mid year estimated. - À partir des résultats du recensement de la population de 1996, pas nécessairement des estimations en milieu d'année.

[57] Data refer to national projections. Figures for male and female do not add up to the total, reason for discrepancy not ascertained. - Les données se réfèrent aux projections nationales. La some des données pour la population masculine et pour la population féminine n'est pas égale au total, les raisons de cette différence ne sont pas expliquées.

Table 6

Table 6 presents urban and total population by sex for as many years as possible between 1996 and 2005.

Description of variables: Data are from nation-wide population censuses or are estimates, some of which are based on sample surveys of population carried out among all segments of the population. The results of censuses are identified by a code following the date in the stub; sample surveys are further identified by footnotes; other data are generally estimates, the characteristics of which (*de jure* or *de facto*) are also indicated with a code.

Estimates of urban population presented in this table have been limited to countries or areas for which estimates have been based on the results of sample surveys or have been constructed by the component method from the results of a population census or sample survey. Distributions that result from the estimated total population being distributed by urban/rural residence according to percentages in each group at the time of a census or sample survey have not been included in this table.

Urban is defined according to the national census definition. The definition for each country is set forth at the end of the technical notes to this table.

Percentage computation: Percentages urban are the number of persons residing in an area defined as "urban" per 100 total population. They are calculated by the United Nations Statistics Division. In very few cases the data for total population has been revised but the data for the urban and rural population has not been. These data are footnoted accordingly. In these cases, particular caution should be used in interpreting the figures for percentage urban.

Reliability of data: Estimates that are believed to be less reliable are set in *italics* rather than in roman type. Classification in terms of reliability is based on the method of construction of the total population estimate discussed in the technical notes for table 3.

Limitations: Statistics on urban population by sex are subject to the same qualifications as have been set forth for population statistics in general, as discussed in section 3 of the Technical Notes.

The basic limitations imposed by variations in the definition of the total population and in the degree of under-enumeration are perhaps more important in relation to urban/rural than to any other distributions. The classification by urban and rural is affected by variations in defining usual residence for purposes of sub-national tabulations. Likewise, the geographical differentials in the degree of under-enumeration in censuses affect the comparability of these categories throughout the table. The distinction between *de facto* and *de jure* population is also very important with respect to urban/rural distributions. The difference between the *de facto* and the *de jure* population is discussed at length in section 3.1.1 of the Technical Notes.

A most important and specific limitation, however, lies in the national differences in the definition of urban. Because the distinction between urban and rural areas is made in so many different ways, the definitions have been included at the end of this table. The definitions are necessarily brief and, where the classification as urban involves administrative civil divisions, they are often given in the terminology of the particular country or area. As a result of variations in terminology, it may appear that differences between countries or areas are greater than they actually are. On the other hand, similar or identical terms (for example, town, village, district) as used in different countries or areas may have quite different meanings.

It will be seen from an examination of the definitions that they fall roughly into three major types: (1) classification of localities as urban based on size; (2) classification of administrative centres of minor civil divisions as urban and the remainder of the division as rural; and (3) classification of minor civil divisions on a set of criteria, which may include type of local government, number of inhabitants or proportion of population engaged in agriculture.

The designation of areas as urban or rural is so closely bound to historical, political, cultural, and administrative considerations that the process of developing uniform definitions and procedures moves very slowly. Not only do the definitions differ from one country or area to the other, but, they may also no longer reflect the original intention for distinguishing urban from rural. The criteria once established on the basis of administrative subdivisions (as most of these are) become fixed and resistant to change. For this reason, comparisons of time-series data may be severely affected because the definitions used become outdated. Special care must be taken in comparing data from censuses with those from sample surveys because the definitions of urban used may differ.

Despite their shortcomings, however, statistics on urban and rural population are useful in describing the diversity within the population of a country or area.

The definition of urban/rural areas is based on both qualitative and quantitative criteria that may include any combination of the following: size of population, population density, distance between built-up areas, predominant type of economic activity, conformity to legal or administrative status and urban characteristics such as specific services and facilities[1]. Although statistics classified by urban/rural areas are widely available, no international standard definition appears to be possible at this time since the meaning differs from one country or area to another. The urban/rural classification of population used here is reported according to the national definition.

Earlier data: Urban and total population by sex have been shown in previous issues of the Demographic Yearbook. For information on specific years covered, readers should consult the Historical Index.

DEFINITION OF "URBAN"

AFRICA

Botswana: Agglomeration of 5 000 or more inhabitants where 75 per cent of the economic activity is non-agricultural.
Burundi: Commune of Bujumbura.
Comoros: Administrative centres of prefectures and localities of 5 000 or more inhabitants.
Egypt: Governorates of Cairo, Alexandria, Port Said, Ismailia, Suez, frontier governorates and capitals of other governorates, as well as district capitals (Markaz).
Equatorial Guinea: District centres and localities with 300 dwellings and/or 1 500 inhabitants or more.
Ethiopia: Localities of 2 000 or more inhabitants.
Liberia: Localities of 2 000 or more inhabitants.
Malawi: All townships and town planning areas and all district centres.
Mauritius: Towns with proclaimed legal limits.
Niger: Capital city, capitals of the departments and districts
Senegal: Agglomerations of 10 000 or more inhabitants.
South Africa: Places with some form of local authority.
Sudan: Localities of administrative and/or commercial importance or with population of 5 000 or more inhabitants.
Swaziland: Localities proclaimed as urban.
Tunisia: Population living in communes.
United Republic of Tanzania: 16 gazetted townships.
Zambia: Localities of 5 000 or more inhabitants, the majority of whom all depend on non-agricultural activities.

AMERICA, NORTH

Canada: Places of 1 000 or more inhabitants, having a population density of 400 or more per square kilometre.
Costa Rica: Administrative centres of cantons.
Cuba: Population living in a nucleus of 2 000 or more inhabitants.
Dominican Republic: Administrative centres of municipalities and municipal districts, some of which include suburban zones of rural character.
El Salvador: Administrative centres of municipalities.
Greenland: Localities of 200 or more inhabitants.
Guatemala: Municipality of Guatemala Department and officially recognized centres of other departments and municipalities.
Haiti: Administrative centres of communes.
Honduras: Localities of 2 000 or more inhabitants, having essentially urban characteristics.
Mexico: Localities of 2 500 or more inhabitants.
Nicaragua: Administrative centres of municipalities and localities of 1 000 or more inhabitants with streets and electric light.
Panama: Localities of 1 500 or more inhabitants having essentially urban characteristics. Beginning 1970, localities of 1 500 or more inhabitants with such urban characteristics as streets, water supply systems, sewerage systems and electric light.
Puerto Rico: Agglomerations of 2 500 or more inhabitants, generally having population densities of 1 000 persons per square mile or more. Two types of urban areas: urbanized areas of 50 000 or more inhabitants and urban clusters of at least 2 500 and less than 50 000 inhabitants.
United States: Agglomerations of 2 500 or more inhabitants, generally having population densities of 1 000 persons per square mile or more. Two types of urban areas: urbanized areas of 50 000 or more inhabitants and urban clusters of at least 2 500 and less than 50 000 inhabitants.
U.S. Virgin Islands: Agglomerations of 2 500 or more inhabitants, generally having population densities of 1 000 persons per square mile or more. Two types of urban areas: urbanized areas of 50 000 or more inhabitants and urban clusters of

at least 2 500 and less than 50 000 inhabitants. (As of Census 2000, no urbanized areas are identified in the U.S. Virgin Islands.)

AMERICA, SOUTH

Argentina: Populated centres with 2 000 or more inhabitants.
Bolivia: Localities of 2 000 or more inhabitants.
Brazil: Urban and suburban zones of administrative centres of municipalities and districts.
Chile: Populated centres which have definite urban characteristics such as certain public and municipal services.
Ecuador: Capitals of provinces and cantons.
Falkland Islands (Malvinas): Town of Stanley.
Paraguay: Cities, towns and administrative centres of departments and districts.
Peru: Populated centres with 100 or more dwellings.
Suriname: Paramaribo town.
Uruguay: Cities.
Venezuela, Bolivarian Republic: Centres with a population of 1 000 or more inhabitants.

ASIA

Armenia: Cities and urban-type localities, officially designated as such, usually according to the criteria of number of inhabitants and predominance of agricultural, or number of non-agricultural workers and their families.
Azerbaijan: Cities and urban-type localities, officially designated as such, usually according to the criteria of number of inhabitants and predominance of agricultural, or number of non-agricultural workers and their families.
Bahrain: Communes or villages of 2 500 or more inhabitants.
Cambodia: Towns.
China: Cities only refer to the cities proper of those designated by the State Council. In the case of cities with district establishment, the city proper refers to the whole administrative area of the district if its population density is 1 500 people per kilometre or higher; or the seat of the district government and other areas of streets under the administration of the district if the population density is less than 1 500 people per kilometre. In the case of cities without district establishment, the city proper refers to the seat of the city government and other areas of streets under the administration of the city. For the city district with the population density below 1 500 people per kilometre and the city without district establishment, if the urban construction of the district or city government seat has extended to some part of the neighboring designated town(s) or township(s), the city proper does include the whole administrative area of the town(s) or township(s).
Cyprus: Urban areas are those defined by local town plans.
Georgia: Cities and urban-type localities, officially designated as such, usually according to the criteria of number of inhabitants and predominance of agricultural, or number of non-agricultural workers and their families.
India: Towns (places with municipal corporation, municipal area committee, town committee, notified area committee or cantonment board); also, all places having 5 000 or more inhabitants, a density of not less than 1 000 persons per square mile or 400 per square kilometre, pronounced urban characteristics and at least three fourths of the adult male population employed in pursuits other than agriculture.
Indonesia: Places with urban characteristics.
Iran (Islamic Republic of): Every district with a municipality.
Israel: All settlements of more than 2 000 inhabitants, except those where at least one third of households, participating in the civilian labour force, earn their living from agriculture.
Japan: City (shi) having 50 000 or more inhabitants with 60 per cent or more of the houses located in the main built-up areas and 60 per cent or more of the population (including their dependants) engaged in manufacturing, trade or other urban type of business. Alternatively, a shi having urban facilities and conditions as defined by the prefectural order is considered as urban.
Kazakhstan: Cities and urban-type localities, officially designated as such, usually according to the criteria of number of inhabitants and predominance of agricultural, or number of non-agricultural workers and their families.
Korea, Republic of: Population living in cities irrespective of size of population.
Kyrgyzstan: Cities and urban-type localities, officially designated as such, usually according to the criteria of number of inhabitants and predominance of agricultural, or number of non-agricultural workers and their families.
Malaysia: Gazetted areas with population of 10 000 and more.
Maldives: Malé, the capital.
Mongolia: Capital and district centres.
Pakistan: Places with municipal corporation, town committee or cantonment.
Sri Lanka: Urban sector comprises of all municipal and urban council areas.
Syrian Arab Republic: Cities, Mohafaza centres and Mantika centres, and communities with 20 000 or more inhabitants.
Tajikistan: Cities and urban-type localities, officially designated as such, usually according to the criteria of number of inhabitants and predominance of agricultural, or number of non-agricultural workers and their families.
Thailand: Municipal areas.

Turkey: Population of settlement places, 20 001 and over.

Turkmenistan: Cities and urban-type localities, officially designated as such, usually according to the criteria of number of inhabitants and predominance of agricultural, or number of non-agricultural workers and their families.

Uzbekistan: Cities and urban-type localities, officially designated as such, usually according to the criteria of number of inhabitants and predominance of agricultural, or number of non-agricultural workers and their families.

Viet Nam: Urban areas include inside urban districts of cities, urban quarters and towns. All other local administrative units (communes) belong to rural areas.

EUROPE

Albania: Towns and other industrial centres of more than 400 inhabitants.

Austria: Communes of more than 5 000 inhabitants.

Belarus: Cities and urban-type localities, officially designated as such, usually according to the criteria of number of inhabitants and predominance of agricultural, or number of non-agricultural workers and their families.

Bulgaria: Towns, that is, localities legally established as urban.

Czech Republic: Localities with 2 000 or more inhabitants.

Estonia: Cities and urban-type localities, officially designated as such, usually according to the criteria of number of inhabitants and predominance of agricultural, or number of non-agricultural workers and their families.

Finland: Urban communes. 1970: Localities.

France: Communes containing an agglomeration of more than 2 000 inhabitants living in contiguous houses or with not more than 200 metres between houses, also communes of which the major portion of the population is part of a multicommunal agglomeration of this nature.

Greece: Population of municipalities and communes in which the largest population centre has 10 000 or more inhabitants. Including also the population of the 18 urban agglomerations, as these were defined at the census of 1991, namely: Greater Athens, Thessaloniki, Patra, Iraklio, Volos, Chania, Irannina, Chalkida, Agrinio, Kalamata, Katerini, Kerkyra, Salamina, Chios, Egio, Rethymno, Ermoupolis, and Sparti.

Hungary: Budapest and all legally designated towns.

Iceland: Localities of 200 or more inhabitants.

Ireland: Cities and towns including suburbs of 1 500 or more inhabitants.

Latvia: Cities and urban-type localities, officially designated as such, usually according to the criteria of number of inhabitants and predominance of agricultural, or number of non-agricultural workers and their families.

Lithuania: Urban population refers to persons who live in cities and towns, i.e., the population areas with closely built permanent dwellings and with the resident population of more than 3 000 of which 2/3 of employees work in industry, social infrastructure and business. In a number of towns the population may be less than 3 000 since these areas had already the states of "town" before the law was enforced (July 1994)

Netherlands: Urban: Municipalities with a population of 2 000 and more inhabitants. Semi-urban: Municipalities with a population of less than 2 000 but with not more than 20 per cent of their economically active male population engaged in agriculture, and specific residential municipalities of commuters.

Norway: Localities of 200 or more inhabitants.

Poland: Towns and settlements of urban type, e.g. workers' settlements, fishermen's settlements, health resorts.

Portugal: Agglomeration of 10 000 or more inhabitants.

Republic of Moldova: Cities and urban-type localities, officially designated as such, usually according to the criteria of number of inhabitants and predominance of agricultural, or number of non-agricultural workers and their families.

Romania: Cities, municipalities and other towns.

Russian Federation: Cities and urban-type localities, officially designated as such, usually according to the criteria of number of inhabitants and predominance of agricultural, or number of non-agricultural workers and their families.

Slovakia: 138 cities with 5 000 inhabitants or more.

Spain: Localities of 2 000 or more inhabitants.

Switzerland: Communes of 10 000 or more inhabitants, including suburbs.

Ukraine: Cities and urban-type localities, officially designated as such, usually according to the criteria of number of inhabitants and predominance of agricultural, or number of non-agricultural workers and their families.

OCEANIA

American Samoa: Agglomerations of 2 500 or more inhabitants, generally having population densities of 1 000 persons per square mile or more. Two types of urban areas: urbanized areas of 50 000 or more inhabitants and urban clusters of at least 2 500 and less than 50 000 inhabitants. (As of Census 2000, no urbanized areas are identified in American Samoa.)

Guam: Agglomerations of 2 500 or more inhabitants, generally having population densities of 1 000 persons per square mile or more, referred to as "urban clusters".

New Caledonia: Nouméa and communes of Païta, Nouvel Dumbéa and Mont-Dore.

New Zealand: All cities, plus boroughs, town districts, townships and country towns with a population of 1 000 or more.

Northern Mariana Islands: Agglomerations of 2 500 or more inhabitants, generally having population densities of 1 000 persons per square mile or more. Two types of urban areas: urbanized areas of 50 000 or more inhabitants and urban clusters of at least 2 500 and less than 50 000 inhabitants.

Vanuatu: Luganville centre and Vila urban.

NOTES

[1] For further information, see *Social and Demographic Statistics: Classifications of Size and Type of Locality and Urban/Rural Areas.* E/CN.3/551, United Nations, New York, 1980.

Tableau 6

Le tableau 6 présente des données sur la population urbaine et la population totale selon le sexe pour le plus grand nombre possible d'années entre 1996 et 2005.

Description des variables : les données proviennent de recensements de la population ou sont des estimations fondées, dans certains cas, sur des enquêtes par sondage portant sur toute la population. Le code qui figure dans la deuxième colonne du tableau indique comment les données ont été obtenues ; les enquêtes par sondage sont en outre signalées par une note en fin de tableau ; toutes les autres données sont en général des estimations et la colonne « Code » indique si elles portent sur la population de fait ou la population de droit.

Les estimations de la population urbaine qui figurent dans le tableau 6 ne concernent que les pays ou zones pour lesquels les estimations se fondent sur les résultats d'une enquête par sondage ou ont été établies par la méthode des composantes à partir des résultats d'un recensement de la population ou d'une enquête par sondage. Les répartitions selon le lieu de résidence (zone urbaine ou rurale) obtenues en appliquant à l'estimation de la population totale les pourcentages enregistrés pour chaque groupe lors d'un recensement ou d'une enquête par sondage n'ont pas été reproduites dans le tableau 6.

Le sens donné au terme « urbain » est conforme aux définitions utilisées dans les recensements nationaux. La définition pour chaque pays figure à la fin des présentes notes technique.

Calcul des pourcentages : les pourcentages de la population urbaine sont calculés par la Division de statistique de l'Organisation des Nations Unies et représentent le nombre de personnes qui vivent dans des régions considérées comme urbaines pour 100 personnes de la population totale. Dans de très rares cas, les données pour la population totale ont été révisées mais les données pour la population urbaine et la population rurale ne l'ont pas été. Ces données sont indiquées en note. Dans ces cas, les proportions de population urbaine ou rurale sont à interpréter avec précaution.

Fiabilité des données : les estimations considérées comme moins sûres sont indiquées en italique plutôt qu'en caractères romains. Le classement du point de vue de la fiabilité est fondé sur la méthode utilisée pour établir l'estimation de la population totale qui figure au tableau 3 (voir les explications dans les notes techniques relatives à ce même tableau).

Insuffisance des données : les statistiques de la population urbaine selon le sexe appellent toutes les réserves qui ont été formulées à la section 3 des Notes techniques à propos des statistiques de la population en général.

Les limitations fondamentales imposées par les variations de la définition de la population totale et par les lacunes du recensement se font peut-être sentir davantage dans la répartition de la population en population urbaine et population rurale que dans sa répartition suivant toute autre caractéristique. De fait, des différences dans la définition du lieu de résidence habituel utilisée pour l'exploitation des données à l'échelon sous-national influent sur la classification en population urbaine et en population rurale. De même, les différences de degré de sous-dénombrement suivant la zone, à l'occasion des recensements, ont une incidence sur la comparabilité de ces deux catégories dans l'ensemble du tableau. La distinction entre population de fait et population de droit est également très importante du point de vue de la répartition de la population en population urbaine et en population rurale. Cette distinction est expliquée en détail à la section 3.1.1 des Notes techniques.

Toutefois, la difficulté la plus importante tient aux différences de définition du terme « urbain » selon le pays. Les distinctions faites entre « zone urbaine » et « zone rurale » varient tellement que les définitions utilisées ont été reproduites à la fin des notes techniques du tableau 6. Les définitions sont forcément brèves et, lorsque le classement en « zone urbaine » repose sur des divisions administratives, on a souvent désigné celles-ci par le nom qu'elles portent dans la zone ou le pays considéré. Par suite des variations dans la terminologie, les différences entre pays ou zones peuvent sembler plus grandes qu'elles ne le sont réellement. Il se peut aussi que des termes similaires ou identiques, tels que ville, village ou district, aient des significations très différentes selon les pays ou zones.

On constatera, en examinant les définitions adoptées par les différents pays ou zones, qu'elles peuvent être ramenées à trois types principaux : 1) les localités dépassant certaines dimensions sont classées parmi les zones urbaines ; 2) les centres administratifs de petites circonscriptions administratives sont classées parmi les zones urbaines, le reste de la circonscription étant considéré comme zone rurale ; 3) les petites divisions administratives sont classées parmi les zones urbaines selon un critère déterminé, qui peut être soit le type d'administration locale, soit le nombre d'habitants, soit le pourcentage de la population exerçant une activité agricole.

La distinction entre régions urbaines et régions rurales est si étroitement liée à des considérations d'ordre historique, politique, culturel et administratif que l'on ne peut progresser que très lentement vers des définitions et des méthodes uniformes. Non seulement les définitions sont différentes d'une zone ou d'un pays à un autre, mais on n'y retrouve parfois même plus l'intention originale de distinguer les régions rurales des régions urbaines. Lorsque la classification est fondée, en particulier, sur le critère des circonscriptions administratives (comme la plupart le sont), elle a tendance à devenir rigide avec le temps et à décourager toute modification. Pour cette raison, la comparaison des données appartenant à des séries chronologiques risque d'être gravement faussée du fait que les définitions employées sont désormais périmées. Il faut être particulièrement prudent lorsque l'on compare des données issues de recensements avec des données provenant d'enquêtes par sondage, car il se peut que les définitions du terme « urbain » auxquelles ces données se réfèrent respectivement soient différentes.

Malgré leurs insuffisances, les statistiques sur la population urbaine et rurale permettent de mettre en évidence la diversité de la population d'un pays ou d'une zone.

La distinction entre « zone urbaine » et « zone rurale » repose sur une série de critères qualitatifs aussi bien que quantitatifs, notamment l'effectif de la population, la densité de peuplement, la distance entre îlots d'habitations, le type prédominant d'activité économique, le statut juridique ou administratif, et les caractéristiques d'une agglomération urbaine, c'est-à-dire l'existence de services publics et d'équipements collectifs[1]. Bien que les statistiques différenciant les zones urbaines des zones rurales soient très répandues, il ne paraît pas possible pour le moment d'adopter une classification internationale type de ces zones, vu la diversité des interprétations nationales. La classification de la population en population urbaine et population rurale retenue ici est celle qui correspond aux définitions nationales.

Données publiées antérieurement : des statistiques concernant la population urbaine et la population totale selon le sexe ont été publiées dans des éditions antérieures de l'*Annuaire démographique*. Pour plus de précisions concernant les années pour lesquelles ces données ont été publiées, se reporter à l'index historique.

DÉFINITIONS DU TERME « URBAIN »

AFRIQUE

Afrique du Sud : Zones dotées d'une administration locale.

Botswana : Agglomération de 5 000 habitants ou plus dont 75 p. 100 de l'activité économique n'est pas de type agricole.

Burundi : Commune de Bujumbura.

Comores : Chefs-lieux de préfectures et localités de 5 000 habitants ou plus.

Égypte : Chefs-lieux des gouvernorats du Caire, d'Alexandrie, de Port Saïd, d'Ismaïlia, de Suez ; chefs-lieux des gouvernorats frontaliers, autres chefs-lieux de gouvernorat et chefs-lieux de district (Markaz).

Éthiopie : Localités de 2 000 habitants ou plus.

Guinée équatoriale : Chefs-lieux de district et localités comprenant 300 habitations et/ou 1 500 habitants ou plus.

Libéria : Localités de 2 000 habitants ou plus.

Malawi : Toutes les villes et zones urbanisées et tous les chefs-lieux de district.

Maurice : Villes ayant des limites officiellement définies.

Niger : Ville capital, villes capitales de départements ou de districts.

République-Unie de Tanzanie : 16 townships érigées en communes.

Sénégal : Agglomérations de 10 000 habitants ou plus.

Soudan : Centres administratifs et/ou commerciaux ou localités ayant une population de 5 000 habitants ou plus.

Swaziland : Localités déclarées urbaines.

Tunisie : Population vivant dans les communes.

Zambie : Localités de 5 000 habitants ou plus dont l'activité économique prédominant n'est pas de type agricole.

AMÉRIQUE DU NORD

Canada : Agglomérations de 1 000 habitants ou plus ayant une densité de population d'au moins 400 habitants au kilomètre carré.

Costa Rica : Chefs-lieux de canton.

Cuba : Population vivant dans des agglomérations de 2 000 habitants ou plus.

El Salvador : Chefs-lieux de municipios.

États-Unis : Agglomérations de 2 500 habitants ou plus ayant généralement une densité de population d'au moins 1 000 habitants au mile carré. Deux types de zones urbaines : zones urbanisées de 50 000 habitants ou plus et groupements urbains comptant au moins 2 500 habitants mais moins de 50 000.

Groenland : Localités d'au moins 200 habitants.

Guatemala : Municipio du département de Guatemala et centres administratifs officiels d'autres départements et municipios.

Haïti : Chefs-lieux de communes.

Honduras : Localités d'au moins 2 000 habitants ayant des caractéristiques essentiellement urbaines.

Îles Vierges américaines : Agglomérations de 2 500 habitants ou plus ayant généralement une densité de population d'au moins 1 000 habitants au mile carré. Deux types de zones urbaines : zones urbanisées de 50 000 habitants ou plus et groupements urbains comptant au moins 2 500 habitants mais moins de 50 000. (D'après les résultats du recensement de 2000, les Îles Vierges américaines ne comptent aucune zone urbanisée.)

Mexique : Localités d'au moins 2 500 habitants.

Nicaragua : Chefs-lieux de municipios et agglomérations d'au moins 1 000 habitants dotées de rues et de l'éclairage électrique.

Panama : Localités d'au moins 1 500 habitants ayant des caractéristiques essentiellement urbaines. À partir de 1970, localités de 1 500 habitants ou plus présentant des caractéristiques urbaines, telles que rues, éclairage électrique, systèmes d'approvisionnement en eau et réseaux d'égouts.

Porto Rico : Agglomérations de 2 500 habitants ou plus ayant généralement une densité de population d'au moins 1 000 habitants au mile carré. Deux types de zones urbaines : zones urbanisées de 50 000 habitants ou plus et groupements urbains comptant au moins 2 500 habitants mais moins de 50 000.

République dominicaine : Chefs-lieux de municipios et districts municipaux, dont certains comprennent des zones suburbaines ayant des caractéristiques rurales.

AMÉRIQUE DU SUD

Argentine : Centres comptant au moins 2 000 habitants.

Bolivie : Localités de 2 000 habitants ou plus.

Brésil : Zones urbaines et suburbaines des chefs lieux de municipalités et de districts.

Chili : Centres de peuplement ayant des caractéristiques nettement urbaines (présence de certains services publics et municipaux).

Équateur : Capitales des provinces et chefs-lieux de canton.

Îles Falkland (Malvinas) : Ville de Stanley.

Paraguay : Grandes villes, villes et chefs-lieux des départements et des districts.

Pérou : Centres de peuplement comptant plus de 100 logements.

Suriname : Ville de Paramaribo.

Uruguay : Villes.

Venezuela : Centres de 1 000 habitants ou plus.

ASIE

Arménie : Grandes villes et localités de type urbain, officiellement désignées comme telles, généralement sur la base du nombre d'habitants et de la prédominance des travailleurs agricoles ou non agricoles avec leur famille.

Azerbaïdjan : Grandes villes et localités de type urbain, officiellement désignées comme telles, généralement sur la base du nombre d'habitants et de la prédominance des travailleurs agricoles ou non agricoles avec leur famille.

Bahreïn : Communes ou villages comptant au moins 2 500 habitants.

Cambodge : Villes.

Chine : Villes désignées comme telles par le Conseil d'État. Dans le cas de villes ayant rang de district, la ville s'entend comme l'ensemble de la zone administrative qui relève du district si sa densité est d'au moins 1 500 habitants au kilomètre carré ou comme le siège des autorités du district et les rues qui relèvent du district si sa densité est inférieure à 1 500 habitants au kilomètre carré. Dans le cas des villes qui n'ont pas rang de district, la ville s'entend comme le siège des autorités de la commune et les rues qui relèvent des autorités de la commune. Dans le cas des villes ayant rang de district qui comptent moins de 1 500 habitants au kilomètre carré et des villes n'ayant pas rang de district, si l'urbanisation du siège du district ou du siège des autorités de la commune a empiété sur une partie de la ou des localités voisines, la ville inclut alors l'ensemble de la zone administrative desdites localités.

Chypre : Zones désignées comme urbaines dans les plans d'urbanisme locaux.

Géorgie : Grandes villes et localités de type urbain, officiellement désignées comme telles, généralement sur la base du nombre d'habitants et de la prédominance des travailleurs agricoles ou non agricoles avec leur famille.

Inde : Villes [localités dotées d'une charte municipale, d'un comité de zone municipale, d'un comité de zone déclarée urbaine ou d'un comité de zone de regroupement (cantonnement)] ; également toutes les localités qui ont une population de 5 000 habitants au moins, une densité de population d'au moins 1 000 habitants au mile carré ou 400 au kilomètre carré, des caractéristiques urbaines prononcées et où les trois quarts au moins des adultes de sexe masculin ont une occupation non agricole.

Indonésie : Localités présentant des caractéristiques urbaines.

Iran (République islamique d') : Tous les districts comptant une municipalité.

Israël : Tous les lieux comptant au moins 2 000 habitants, à l'exception de ceux où le tiers au moins des chefs de ménage faisant partie de la population civile active vivent de l'agriculture.

Japon : Villes (shi), comptant au moins 50 000 habitants, où 60 p. 100 au moins des logements sont situés dans les principales zones bâties, et dont 60 p. 100 au moins de population (y compris les personnes à charge) exercent un métier dans l'industrie, le commerce et d'autres branches d'activités essentiellement urbaines. Tout shi possédant les équipements et présentant les caractéristiques définies comme urbaines par l'administration préfectorale est également considéré comme zone urbaine.

Kazakhstan : Grandes villes et localités de type urbain, officiellement désignées comme telles, généralement sur la base du nombre d'habitants et de la prédominance des travailleurs agricoles ou non agricoles avec leur famille.

Kirghizistan : Grandes villes et localités de type urbain, officiellement désignées comme telles, généralement sur la base du nombre d'habitants et de la prédominance des travailleurs agricoles ou non agricoles avec leur famille.

Malaisie : Zones déclarées « zones urbaines » et comptant au moins 10 000 habitants.

Maldives : Malé (capitale).

Mongolie : Capitale et chefs-lieux de district.

Ouzbékistan : Grandes villes et localités de type urbain, officiellement désignées comme telles, généralement sur la base du nombre d'habitants et de la prédominance des travailleurs agricoles ou non agricoles avec leur famille.

Pakistan : Localités dotées d'une charte municipale ou d'un comité municipal et regroupements (cantonments).

République arabe syrienne : Villes, chefs-lieux de district (Mohafaza) et chefs-lieux de sous district (Mantika), et communes d'au moins 20 000 habitants.

République de Corée : Population vivant dans des villes, quel qu'en soit le nombre d'habitants.

Sri Lanka : Secteur urbain composé de toutes les zones municipales et zones dotées d'un conseil urbain.

Tadjikistan : Grandes villes et localités de type urbain, officiellement désignées comme telles, généralement sur la base du nombre d'habitants et de la prédominance des travailleurs agricoles ou non agricoles avec leur famille.

Thaïlande : Zones municipales.

Turkménistan : Grandes villes et localités de type urbain, officiellement désignées comme telles, généralement sur la base du nombre d'habitants et de la prédominance des travailleurs agricoles ou non agricoles avec leur famille.

Turquie : Population d'établissements humains s'établissant à plus de 20 000 personnes.

Viet Nam : Zones urbaines comprises à l'intérieur des districts urbains des villes ainsi que des quartiers urbains et des localités. Toutes les autres unités administratives locales (communes) sont considérées comme zones rurales.

Yémen : Définition non communiquée.

EUROPE

Albanie : Villes et autres centres industriels de plus de 400 habitants.

Autriche : Communes de plus de 5 000 habitants.

Bélarus : Grandes villes et localités de type urbain, officiellement désignées comme telles, généralement sur la base du nombre d'habitants et de la prédominance des travailleurs agricoles ou non agricoles avec leur famille.

Bulgarie : Villes, c'est-à-dire localités reconnues comme urbaines.

Espagne : Localités de 2 000 habitants et plus.

Estonie : Grandes villes et localités de type urbain, officiellement désignées comme telles, généralement sur la base du nombre d'habitants et de la prédominance des travailleurs agricoles ou non agricoles avec leur famille.

Fédération de Russie : Grandes villes et localités de type urbain, officiellement désignées comme telles, généralement sur la base du nombre d'habitants et de la prédominance des travailleurs agricoles ou non agricoles avec leur famille.

Finlande : Communes urbaines. 1970 : Localités.

France : Communes comprenant une agglomération de plus de 2 000 habitants vivant dans des habitations contiguës ou qui ne sont pas distantes les unes des autres de plus de 200 mètres et communes où la majeure partie de la population vit dans une agglomération regroupant plusieurs communes de cette nature.

Grèce : Municipalités et communes de 10 000 habitants ou plus pour l'agglomération. Y compris également 18 agglomérations urbaines, selon la définition qui en a été donnée lors du recensement de 1991, à savoir : Athènes et sa banlieue, Thessalonique, Patras, Héraklion, Volos, Chania, Ioannina, Chalkida, Agrinio, Kalamata, Katerini, Kerkyra, Salamine, Chios, Egio, Rethymno, Ermoupolis et Sparte.

Hongrie : Budapest et toutes les autres localités reconnues officiellement comme urbaines.

Irlande : Localités, y compris leur banlieues, comptant 1 500 habitants ou plus.

Islande : Localités de 200 habitants ou plus.

Lettonie : Grandes villes et localités de type urbain, officiellement désignées comme telles, généralement sur la base du nombre d'habitants et de la prédominance des travailleurs agricoles ou non agricoles avec leur famille.

Lituanie : Par population urbaine, on entend les personnes qui vivent dans des villes ou des localités, à savoir les zones habitées comportant des logements permanents proches les uns des autres et dont la population est d'au moins 3 000 habitants, les deux tiers desquels étant employés dans le secteur industriel, l'infrastructure sociale ou le commerce. Un certain nombre de villes peuvent compter moins de 3 000 habitants dans la mesure où elles avaient acquis le statut de ville avant l'entrée en vigueur de la nouvelle loi en juillet 1994.

Norvège : Localités de 200 habitants ou plus.

Pays Bas : Zones urbaines : municipalités comptant au moins 2 000 habitants. Zones semi-urbaines : municipalités comptant moins de 2 000 habitants, mais où 20 p. 100 au maximum de la population active de sexe masculin pratiquent l'agriculture, et certaines municipalités de caractère résidentiel dont les habitants travaillent ailleurs.

Pologne : Villes et zones de type urbain, par exemple groupements de travailleurs ou de pêcheurs et stations climatiques.

Portugal : Agglomérations d'au moins 10 000 habitants.

République de Moldova : Grandes villes et localités de type urbain, officiellement désignées comme telles, généralement sur la base du nombre d'habitants et de la prédominance des travailleurs agricoles ou non agricoles avec leur famille.

République tchèque : Localités d'au moins 2 000 habitants.

Roumanie : Grandes villes, municipalités et autres villes.

Slovaquie : 138 localités comptant 5 000 habitants ou plus.

Suisse : Communes de 10 000 habitants ou plus, et leurs banlieues.

Ukraine : Grandes villes et localités de type urbain, officiellement désignées comme telles, généralement sur la base du nombre d'habitants et de la prédominance des travailleurs agricoles ou non agricoles avec leur famille.

OCÉANIE

Guam : Agglomérations de 2 500 habitants ou plus ayant généralement une densité de population d'au moins 1 000 habitants au mile carré et considérées comme étant des groupements urbains.

Îles Mariannes septentrionales : Agglomérations de 2 500 habitants ou plus ayant généralement une densité de population d'au moins 1 000 habitants au mile carré. Deux types de zones urbaines : zones urbanisées de 50 000 habitants ou plus et groupements urbains comptant au moins 2 500 habitants mais moins de 50 000.

Nouvelle-Calédonie : Nouméa et communes de Païta, Dumbéa et Mont-Dore.

Nouvelle-Zélande : Grandes villes, boroughs, chefs-lieux, municipalités et chefs-lieux de comté d'au moins 1 000 habitants.

Samoa américaines : Agglomérations de 2 500 habitants ou plus ayant généralement une densité de population d'au moins 1 000 habitants au mile carré. Deux types de zones urbaines : zones urbanisées de 50 000 habitants ou plus et groupements urbains comptant au moins 2 500 habitants mais moins de 50 000. (D'après les résultats du recensement de 2000, les Samoa américaines ne comptent aucune zone urbanisée.)

Vanuatu : Centre de Luganville et Port-Vila.

NOTES

[1] Pour plus de précisions, voir *Social and Demographic Statistics: Classifications of Size and Type of Locality and Urban/Rural Areas*, E/CN.3/551, publication des Nations Unies, New York, 1980.

Continent, country or area, and date / Continent, pays ou zone et date	Code[a]	Both sexes - Les deux sexes			Male - Masculin			Female - Féminin		
		Total	Urban - Urbaine		Total	Urban - Urbaine		Total	Urban - Urbaine	
			Number Nombre	Percent P.100		Number Nombre	Percent P.100		Number Nombre	Percent P.100
AFRICA - AFRIQUE										
Algeria - Algérie										
1 VII 1996	ESDJ	28 566 000	...	...	14 479 812	...	...	14 086 188	...	...
1 VII 1997	ESDJ	29 045 000	...	...	14 722 612	...	...	14 322 388	...	...
25 VI 1998	CDJC	29 100 867	16 966 939	58.3	14 698 589	8 563 287	58.3	14 402 278	8 403 652	58.3
1 VII 1998	ESDJ	29 507 000	...	...	14 957 049	...	...	14 550 451	...	...
1 VII 1999	ESDJ	29 965 000	...	...	15 132 000	...	...	14 833 000	...	...
1 VII 2000	ESDJ	30 416 000	...	...	15 357 000	...	...	15 059 000	...	...
1 VII 2001	ESDJ	30 871 734	...	...	15 598 261	...	...	15 273 473	...	...
1 VII 2002	ESDJ	31 332 033	...	...	15 830 343	...	...	15 501 690	...	...
1 VII 2003	ESDJ	31 847 995	...	...	16 090 568	...	...	15 757 427	...	...
Benin - Bénin										
1 VII 1996	ESDF	5 594 499	2 098 699	37.5	2 722 854	1 019 980	37.5	2 871 645	1 078 719	37.6
1 VII 1997	ESDF	5 638 987	2 177 515	38.6	...	...	...	...	...	...
1 VII 1998	ESDF	5 816 488	2 278 190	39.2	...	...	...	...	...	...
1 VII 1999	ESDF	5 990 396	2 383 244	39.8	...	...	...	...	...	...
1 VII 2000	ESDF	6 169 084	2 492 967	40.4	3 013 705	1 220 905	40.5	3 155 379	1 272 062	40.3
1 VII 2001*	ESDF	6 416 692	...	...	3 136 516	...	...	3 280 176	...	...
11 II 2002	CDJC	6 769 914	2 630 133	38.9	3 284 119	1 280 418	39.0	3 485 795	1 349 715	38.7
Botswana										
1 VII 1996	ESDF	1 495 993	720 783[1]	48.2	720 207	...	...	775 786	...	...
1 VII 1997	ESDF	1 533 393	...	...	739 189	...	...	794 204	...	...
1 VII 1998	ESDF	1 571 728	...	...	757 669	...	...	814 059	...	...
1 VII 1999	ESDF	1 611 021	...	...	779 010	...	...	832 011	...	...
1 VII 2000	ESDF	1 653 061	...	...	799 735	...	...	853 326	...	...
17 VIII 2001	CDFC	1 680 863	910 480[1]	54.2	813 488	428 856	52.7	867 375	481 624	55.5
1 VII 2002	ESDF	1 667 487	375 461	22.5	...	...	...	...	...	...
1 VII 2003	ESDF	1 691 390	384 940	22.8	...	...	...	...	...	...
1 VII 2004	ESDF	1 711 334	393 528	23.0	828 082	191 287	23.1	883 252	202 241	22.9
Burkina Faso										
10 XII 1996[2]	CDFC	10 862 075	...	...	5 355 982	...	...	5 506 093	...	...
1 VII 1997	ESDJ	10 561 129	1 647 584	15.6	...	...	...	...	...	...
1 VII 1998	ESDJ	10 816 222	1 695 441	15.7	...	...	...	...	...	...
1 VII 1999	ESDJ	11 078 076	1 744 784	15.7	...	...	...	...	...	...
1 VII 2000	ESDJ	11 346 880	1 795 663	15.8	...	...	...	...	...	...
1 VII 2001	ESDJ	11 622 833	1 848 126	15.9	...	...	...	...	...	...
1 VII 2002	ESDJ	11 906 137	1 902 225	16.0	...	...	...	...	...	...
1 VII 2003	ESDJ	12 197 002	1 958 013	16.1	...	...	...	...	...	...
1 VII 2005	ESDJ	12 802 282	2 074 879	16.2	6 182 079	...	...	6 620 203	...	...
Burundi										
1 VII 1996	ESDF	6 087 951	454 661	7.5	2 960 208	233 221	7.9	3 127 743	221 440	7.1
1 VII 1997	ESDF	6 194 220	473 284	7.6	3 011 678	240 554	8.0	3 182 542	232 730	7.3
1 VII 1998	ESDF	6 300 489	493 297	7.8	3 064 211	...	...	3 236 278	...	...
1 VII 1999	ESDF	6 482 662	...	...	3 152 810	...	...	3 329 852	...	...
Cameroon - Cameroun[3]										
1 VII 1997	ESDF	14 297 617	6 748 475	47.2	...	...	...	...	...	...
1 VII 1998	ESDF	14 439 000	6 960 000	48.2	...	...	...	...	...	...
1 VII 2001	ESDF	15 731 000	8 023 000	51.0	...	...	...	...	...	...
1 VII 2002	ESDF	16 170 000	8 392 000	51.9	...	...	...	...	...	...
1 VII 2003	ESDF	16 626 000	8 779 000	52.8	...	...	...	...	...	...
1 VII 2004	ESDF	17 000 000	9 086 000	53.4	...	...	...	...	...	...
Cape Verde - Cap-Vert										
1 VII 1996	ESDF	396 173	...	...	188 504	...	...	207 669	...	...
1 VII 1997	ESDF	406 513	...	...	193 636	...	...	212 877	...	...
1 VII 1998	ESDF	417 200	...	...	198 946	...	...	218 254	...	...
1 VII 1999	ESDF	428 230	...	...	204 433	...	...	223 797	...	...
16 VI 2000	CDFC	436 863	235 470	53.9	211 479	114 928	54.3	225 384	120 542	53.5
1 VII 2001	ESDF	444 683	242 484	54.5	215 288	118 351	55.0	229 395	124 133	54.1
1 VII 2002	ESDF	452 714	249 794	55.2	219 211	121 924	55.6	233 503	127 870	54.8
1 VII 2003	ESDF	460 968	257 412	55.8	223 253	125 652	56.3	237 715	131 759	55.4

Continent, country or area, and date / Continent, pays ou zone et date	Code[a]	Both sexes - Les deux sexes Total	Urban - Urbaine Number Nombre	Urban - Urbaine Percent P.100	Male - Masculin Total	Urban - Urbaine Number Nombre	Urban - Urbaine Percent P.100	Female - Féminin Total	Urban - Urbaine Number Nombre	Urban - Urbaine Percent P.100
AFRICA - AFRIQUE										
Central African Republic - République centrafricaine										
8 XII 2003 ....CDFC	CDFC	3 151 072	1 194 851	37.9	1 569 446	598 880	38.2	1 581 626	595 969	37.7
Comoros - Comores										
1 IX 2003............CDFC	CDFC	575 660[4]	160 865	27.9	...	...	...	...	...	...
Congo										
1 VII 1997 ....ESDF	ESDF	2 663 354	...	...	1 297 053	...	...	1 366 301	...	...
1 VII 1998 ....ESDF	ESDF	2 737 928	...	...	1 333 371	...	...	1 404 557	...	...
1 VII 1999 ....ESDF	ESDF	2 814 590	...	...	1 370 705	...	...	1 443 885	...	...
1 VII 2000 ....ESDF	ESDF	2 893 398	...	...	1 409 085	...	...	1 484 313	...	...
1 VII 2001 ....ESDF	ESDF	2 974 413	...	...	1 448 539	...	...	1 525 874	...	...
1 VII 2002 ....ESDF	ESDF	3 057 697	...	...	1 489 098	...	...	1 568 599	...	...
1 VII 2003 ....ESDF	ESDF	3 143 313	...	...	1 530 793	...	...	1 612 520	...	...
1 VII 2004 ....ESDF	ESDF	3 231 326	...	...	1 573 656	...	...	1 657 670	...	...
Côte d'Ivoire										
1 VII 1996 ....ESDF	ESDF	14 781 000	...	...	7 523 000	...	...	7 258 000	...	...
21 XI 1998............CDFC	CDFC	15 366 672	6 529 138	42.5	7 844 621	...	...	7 522 050	...	...
1 VII 1999 ....ESDF	ESDF	15 881 066	...	...	8 107 236	...	...	7 773 828	...	...
1 VII 2000 ....ESDF	ESDF	16 401 514	...	...	8 372 518	...	...	8 028 996	...	...
1 VII 2001 ....ESDF	ESDF	16 928 324	...	...	8 640 647	...	...	8 287 679	...	...
1 VII 2002 ....ESDF	ESDF	17 461 446	...	...	8 911 589	...	...	8 549 848	...	...
1 VII 2003 ....ESDF	ESDF	18 000 876	...	...	9 185 374	...	...	8 815 505	...	...
1 VII 2004 ....ESDF	ESDF	18 545 968	...	...	9 461 591	...	...	9 084 374	...	...
1 VII 2005 ....ESDF	ESDF	19 096 988	...	...	9 740 427	...	...	9 356 561	...	...
Egypt - Égypte										
1 VII 1996 ....ESDF	ESDF	58 755 211	25 019 402	42.6	30 063 860	12 801 923	42.6	28 691 351	12 217 479	42.6
19 XI 1996............CDFC	CDFC	59 312 914	25 286 335	42.6	30 351 390	12 957 775	42.7	28 961 524	12 328 560	42.6
1 VII 1997 ....ESDF	ESDF	60 080 063	25 589 396	42.6	30 736 254	13 091 232	42.6	29 343 809	12 498 164	42.6
1 VII 1998 ....ESDF	ESDF	61 340 882	26 123 481	42.6	31 379 023	13 363 507	42.6	29 961 859	12 759 974	42.6
1 VII 1999 ....ESDF	ESDF	62 652 065	26 641 192	42.5	32 059 065	13 632 299	42.5	30 593 000	13 008 893	42.5
1 VII 2000 ....ESDF	ESDF	63 976 000	27 204 000	42.5	32 695 000	...	...	31 281 000	...	...
1 VII 2003 ....ESDF	ESDF	67 976 000	28 912 000	42.5	...	...	...	...	...	...
1 VII 2005 ....ESDF	ESDF	71 897 547	...	...	38 001 000	...	...	36 032 000	...	...
Equatorial Guinea - Guinée équatoriale										
1 II 2002..............CDFC	CDFC	1 014 999	...	...	501 387	...	...	513 612	...	...
Ethiopia - Éthiopie										
1 VII 1996 ....ESDF	ESDF	56 372 000	7 950 000	14.1	28 344 000	3 885 000	13.7	28 028 000	4 065 000	14.5
1 VII 1997 ....ESDF	ESDF	58 117 000	8 315 000	14.3	29 202 000	4 094 000	14.0	28 915 000	4 221 000	14.6
1 VII 1998 ....ESDF	ESDF	59 882 000	8 691 000	14.5	30 071 000	4 299 000	14.3	29 811 000	4 392 000	14.7
1 VII 1999 ....ESDF	ESDF	61 672 000	9 074 000	14.7	30 956 000	4 504 000	14.5	30 716 000	4 570 000	14.9
1 VII 2000 ....ESDF	ESDF	63 494 702	9 472 971	14.9	...	...	...	...	...	...
1 VII 2001 ....ESDF	ESDF	65 374 320	9 883 138	15.1	32 815 082	4 938 725	15.1	32 559 238	4 944 413	15.2
1 VII 2002 ....ESDF	ESDF	67 220 000	10 307 000	15.3	33 707 000	5 134 000	15.2	33 513 000	5 173 000	15.4
1 VII 2003 ....ESDF	ESDF	69 127 000	10 745 000	15.5	34 653 000	5 347 000	15.4	34 474 000	5 398 000	15.7
1 VII 2004 ....ESDF	ESDF	71 066 000	11 199 000	15.8	35 618 000	5 568 000	15.6	35 448 000	5 631 000	15.9
Gambia - Gambie										
15 IV 2003*..........CDFC	CDFC	1 364 507	...	...	676 726	...	...	687 781	...	...
Ghana										
26 III 2000 ....CDFC	CDFC	18 912 079	8 274 270	43.8	9 357 382	4 043 830	43.2	9 554 697	4 230 440	44.3
Guinea - Guinée										
1 XII 1996 ....CDFC	CDFC	7 156 406	...	...	3 497 979	...	...	3 658 427	...	...
Kenya										
1 VII 1997 ....ESDF	ESDF	27 793 345	...	...	14 425 000	...	...	14 520 000	...	...
1 VII 1998 ....ESDF	ESDF	28 611 152	...	...	14 772 000	...	...	14 858 000	...	...
1 VII 1999 ....ESDF	ESDF	29 453 024	5 429 790	18.4	14 342 209	...	...	15 110 815	...	...
24 VIII 1999 ....CDFC	CDFC	28 686 607	3 539 888	12.3	14 205 589	1 933 437	13.6	14 481 018	1 606 451	11.1
1 VII 2000 ....ESDF	ESDF	30 149 656	5 234 577	17.4	14 846 350	3 096 394	20.9	15 303 306	2 138 183	14.0
1 VII 2001 ....ESDF	ESDF	31 120 677	5 421 964	17.4	15 341 600	3 209 419	20.9	15 779 077	2 212 546	14.0
1 VII 2002 ....ESDF	ESDF	32 117 987	5 613 669	17.5	15 850 411	3 325 186	21.0	16 267 576	2 288 483	14.1
1 VII 2003 ....ESDF	ESDF	33 141 617	5 809 612	17.5	16 372 798	3 443 644	21.0	16 768 819	2 365 968	14.1
1 VII 2004 ....ESDF	ESDF	34 191 382	6 009 718	17.6	16 908 648	3 564 746	21.1	17 282 734	2 444 972	14.1
1 VII 2005 ....ESDF	ESDF	35 267 222	6 213 505	17.6	17 457 906	3 688 113	21.1	17 809 316	2 525 392	14.2

Continent, country or area, and date / Continent, pays ou zone et date — Code[a]	Both sexes - Les deux sexes Total	Urban - Urbaine Number Nombre	Urban - Urbaine Percent P.100	Male - Masculin Total	Urban - Urbaine Number Nombre	Urban - Urbaine Percent P.100	Female - Féminin Total	Urban - Urbaine Number Nombre	Urban - Urbaine Percent P.100
AFRICA - AFRIQUE									
Lesotho									
14 IV 1996 ....CDJC	1 960 069	312 444[5]	15.9	964 346	...	...	995 723	...	...
1 VII 1997 ....ESDF	2 011 644	...	...	991 216	...	...	1 020 399	...	...
1 VII 1998 ....ESDF	2 055 449	...	...	1 013 911	...	...	1 041 504	...	...
1 VII 1999 ....ESDF	2 099 646	...	...	1 036 504	...	...	1 063 142	...	...
1 VII 2000 ....ESDF	2 144 146	...	...	1 059 014	...	...	1 085 132	...	...
1 VII 2001 ....SSDJ	2 157 537	288 895	13.4	1 065 484	131 861	12.4	1 092 053	157 034	14.4
Liberia - Libéria									
1 VII 1996 ....ESDF	2 819 540	1 269 668	45.0	...	...	...	...	...	...
1 VII 1997 ....ESDF	2 879 366	1 307 463	45.4	...	...	...	...	...	...
Libyan Arab Jamahiriya - Jamahiriya arabe libyenne[6]									
1 VII 1996 ....ESDF	4 519 367	...	...	2 225 584	...	...	2 293 783	...	...
1 VII 1997 ....ESDF	4 647 520	...	...	2 288 420	...	...	2 359 100	...	...
1 VII 1998 ....ESDF	4 772 430	...	...	2 350 628	...	...	2 421 802	...	...
1 VII 1999 ....ESDF	4 957 663	...	...	2 444 706	...	...	2 512 957	...	...
1 VII 2000 ....ESDF	5 124 519	...	...	2 528 980	...	...	2 595 539	...	...
1 VII 2001 ....ESDF	5 299 943	...	...	2 682 254	...	...	2 617 689	...	...
1 VII 2002 ....ESDF	5 484 426	...	...	2 773 333	...	...	2 711 093	...	...
Madagascar									
1 VII 1996 ....ESDF	13 393 000	3 230 000	24.1	...	...	...	...	...	...
1 VII 1997 ....ESDF	13 803 000	3 391 000	24.6	...	...	...	...	...	...
1 VII 1998 ....ESDF	14 222 000	3 562 000	25.0	7 091 000[7]	1 745 000	24.6	7 132 000[7]	1 817 000	25.5
1 VII 1999 ....ESDF	14 650 000	3 741 000	25.5	7 306 000[7]	1 834 000	25.1	7 343 000[7]	1 907 000	26.0
1 VII 2000 ....ESDF	15 085 000	3 927 000	26.0	7 526 000	1 926 000	25.6	7 559 000	2 001 000	26.5
1 VII 2001 ....ESDF	15 529 000	4 122 000	26.5	...	...	...	...	...	...
1 VII 2002 ....ESDF	15 981 000	4 327 000	27.1	...	...	...	...	...	...
1 VII 2003 ....ESDF	16 441 000	4 544 000	27.6	...	...	...	...	...	...
1 VII 2004 ....ESDF	17 206 280	4 232 745	24.6	...	...	...	...	...	...
Malawi									
1 VII 1996[3] ....ESDF	10 114 257	1 980 700[7]	19.6	...	...	...	...	...	...
1 IX 1998 ....CDFC	9 933 868	1 435 436	14.4	4 867 563	742 839	15.3	5 066 305	692 597	13.7
1 VII 1999*3 ....ESDF	...	...	...	4 978 411	...	...	5 174 342	...	...
1 VII 2000*3 ....ESDF	...	...	...	5 138 486	...	...	5 336 771	...	...
1 VII 2001*3 ....ESDF	...	...	...	5 307 972	...	...	5 503 322	...	...
1 VII 2002*3 ....ESDF	...	...	...	5 486 254	...	...	5 688 394	...	...
1 VII 2003*3 ....ESDF	...	...	...	5 672 569	...	...	5 876 272	...	...
1 VII 2004*3 ....ESDF	11 937 934	...	...	5 866 452	...	...	6 071 472	...	...
1 VII 2005*3 ....ESDF	12 341 170	1 783 289	14.4	6 067 563	...	...	6 273 607	...	...
Mali									
1 VII 1996 ....ESDF	8 868 975	...	...	4 264 475	...	...	4 604 500	...	...
1 IV 1998 ....CDJC	9 790 492	...	...	4 847 436	...	...	4 943 056	...	...
Mauritania - Mauritanie									
1 XI 2000 ....CDFC	2 548 157	...	...	1 240 414	...	...	1 307 743	...	...
1 VII 2005 ....ESDF	2 905 727	...	...	1 450 418	...	...	1 455 309	...	...
Mauritius - Maurice									
1 VII 1996 ....ESDJ	1 133 996	489 793	43.2	...	...	...	...	...	...
1 VII 1997 ....ESDJ	1 148 284	494 446	43.1	571 169	244 867	42.9	577 115	249 579	43.2
1 VII 1998 ....ESDJ	1 160 421	498 138	42.9	576 620	246 388	42.7	583 801	251 750	43.1
1 VII 1999 ....ESDJ	1 175 267	502 958	42.8	583 169	248 362	42.6	592 098	254 596	43.0
1 VII 2000 ....ESDJ	1 186 873	506 357	42.7	588 212	249 678	42.4	598 661	256 679	42.9
2 VII 2000 ....CDJC	1 178 848	503 045	42.7	583 756	247 844	42.5	595 092	255 201	42.9
1 VII 2001 ....ESDJ	1 199 881	510 822	42.6	594 490	251 721	42.3	605 391	259 101	42.8
1 VII 2002 ....ESDJ	1 210 203	513 761	42.5	599 165	252 848	42.2	611 038	260 913	42.7
1 VII 2003 ....ESDJ	1 222 811	518 368	42.4	605 084	255 077	42.2	617 727	263 291	42.6
1 VII 2004 ....ESDJ	1 233 386	521 588	42.3	610 108	256 542	42.0	623 278	265 046	42.5
1 VII 2005 ....ESDJ	1 243 253	524 318	42.2	614 786	257 785	41.9	628 467	266 533	42.4
Morocco - Maroc									
1 VII 1996 ....ESDF	26 848 000	14 100 000	52.5	13 357 000	...	...	13 491 000	...	...
1 VII 1997 ....ESDF	27 310 000	14 524 000	53.2	13 588 000	7 173 000	52.8	13 722 000	7 351 000	53.6
1 VII 1998 ....ESDF	27 775 000	14 957 000	53.9	13 819 000	7 373 000	53.4	13 956 000	7 584 000	54.3
1 VII 1999 ....ESDF	28 238 000	15 401 000	54.5	14 049 000	7 580 000	54.0	14 189 000	7 821 000	55.1
1 VII 2000 ....ESDF	28 705 000	15 849 000	55.2	14 281 000	7 787 000	54.5	14 424 000	8 062 000	55.9

Continent, country or area, and date / Continent, pays ou zone et date	Code[a]	Both sexes - Les deux sexes			Male - Masculin			Female - Féminin		
		Total	Urban - Urbaine		Total	Urban - Urbaine		Total	Urban - Urbaine	
			Number Nombre	Percent P.100		Number Nombre	Percent P.100		Number Nombre	Percent P.100

AFRICA - AFRIQUE

Morocco - Maroc

1 VII 2001 .... ESDF		29 170 000	16 307 000	55.9	14 512 000	8 000 000	55.1	14 658 000	8 307 000	56.7
1 VII 2002 .... ESDF		29 631 000	16 772 000	56.6	14 742 000	8 217 000	55.7	14 889 000	8 555 000	57.5
1 VII 2003 .... ESDF		30 088 000	17 244 000	57.3	14 972 000	8 438 000	56.4	15 116 000	8 806 000	58.3
1 VII 2004 .... ESDF		30 540 000	17 723 000	58.0	...	...	...	...	...	...
1 IX 2004 .... CDFC		29 680 069	16 339 561	55.1	14 640 662	8 022 273	54.8	15 039 407	8 317 288	55.3

Mozambique

1 VII 1996[8] .... ESDF		16 177 291	...	...	7 685 330	...	...	8 491 962	...	...
1 VII 1997[8] .... ESDF		16 542 740	...	...	7 831 001	...	...	8 711 739	...	...
1 VIII 1997[9] .... CDFC		16 099 246	4 601 132	28.6	7 714 306	2 274 116	29.5	8 384 940	2 327 016	27.8
1 VII 1998[8] .... ESDF		16 916 638	...	...	7 979 434	...	...	8 937 204	...	...
1 VII 1999[8] .... ESDF		17 299 184	...	...	8 130 680	...	...	9 168 504	...	...
1 VII 2000[8] .... ESDF		17 690 584	...	...	8 284 793	...	...	9 405 791	...	...
1 VII 2005*[8] .... ESDF		19 420 036	...	...	9 368 425	...	...	10 051 611	...	...

Namibia - Namibie

1 VII 2000* .... ESDF		1 816 600	...	...	886 900	...	...	929 600	...	...
27 VIII 2001 .... CDFC		1 830 330	603 612	33.0	887 721[10]	300 358[10]	33.8	942 572[10]	303 236[10]	32.2

Niger

1 VII 1996 .... ESDJ		9 286 395	1 468 536	15.8	4 625 090	738 926	16.0	4 661 305	729 610	15.7
1 VII 1997 .... ESDJ		9 574 274	1 521 647	15.9	4 769 563	764 464	16.0	4 804 711	757 183	15.8
1 VII 1998 .... ESDJ		9 871 076	1 576 639	16.0	4 918 547	790 858	16.1	4 952 529	785 781	15.9
1 VII 1999 .... ESDJ		10 177 080	1 633 578	16.1	5 072 184	818 138	16.1	5 104 896	815 440	16.0
1 VII 2000 .... ESDJ		10 492 569	1 692 532	16.1	5 230 620	846 331	16.2	5 261 949	846 201	16.1
20 V 2001* .... CDFC		10 790 352	...	...	5 380 287	...	...	5 410 065	...	...
1 VII 2001 .... ESDJ		11 090 256	1 804 243	16.3	5 531 534	902 637	16.3	5 558 722	901 606	16.2
1 VII 2002 .... ESDJ		11 456 235	1 863 783	16.3	5 714 075	932 424	16.3	5 742 160	931 359	16.2
1 VII 2003 .... ESDJ		11 834 290	1 925 288	16.3	5 902 639	963 194	16.3	5 931 651	962 094	16.2
1 VII 2004 .... ESDJ		12 224 822	1 988 822	16.3	6 097 426	994 979	16.3	6 127 396	993 843	16.2
1 VII 2005 .... ESDJ		12 628 241	2 054 453	16.3	6 298 641	1 027 814	16.3	6 329 600	1 026 640	16.2

Nigeria - Nigéria[3]

1 VII 2000 .... ESDF		115 224 312	...	...	57 750 754	...	...	57 473 558	...	...
1 VII 2001 .... ESDF		118 800 696	...	...	59 538 640	...	...	59 262 056	...	...
1 VII 2002 .... ESDF		122 443 748	...	...	61 369 212	...	...	61 074 536	...	...
1 VII 2003 .... ESDF		126 152 844	...	...	63 241 808	...	...	62 911 036	...	...
1 VII 2004 .... ESDF		129 175 000	...	...	64 459 000	...	...	64 716 000	...	...
1 VII 2005 .... ESDF		133 767 000	...	...	67 111 000	...	...	48 531 000	...	...

Réunion

8 III 1999 .... CDJC		706 180	...	...	347 076	...	...	359 104	...	...
1 VII 1999 .... CDSF		709 900	...	...	349 100	...	...	360 800	...	...
1 VII 2000 .... ESDF		722 200	...	...	355 100	...	...	367 100	...	...
1 VII 2001 .... ESDF		734 700	...	...	361 200	...	...	373 500	...	...
1 VII 2002 .... ESDF		747 554	...	...	373 861	...	...	373 693	...	...
1 VII 2003 .... ESDF		764 000	...	...	375 400	...	...	388 600	...	...
1 VII 2004 .... ESDF		768 808	...	...	377 607	...	...	391 201	...	...

Rwanda

16 VIII 2002 .... CDJC		8 128 553	1 372 604	16.9	3 879 448	727 172	18.7	4 249 105	645 432	15.2

Saint Helena ex. dep. - Sainte-Hélène sans dép.

8 III 1998 .... CDFC		5 157	884	17.1	2 612	452	17.3	2 545	432	17.0

Saint Helena: Ascension - Sainte-Hélène: Ascension

8 III 1998 .... CDJC		712	...	...	458	...	...	254	...	...

Saint Helena: Tristan da Cunha - Sainte-Hélène: Tristan da Cunha

1 VII 1996 .... ESDF		286	...	...	137	...	...	149	...	...

Sao Tome and Principe - Sao Tomé-et-Principe

1 VII 1996 .... ESDF		127 154	...	...	62 931	...	...	64 223	...	...
1 VII 1997 .... ESDF		129 178	...	...	63 958	...	...	65 220	...	...
1 VII 1998[8] .... ESDF		131 234	...	...	65 002	...	...	66 232	...	...
1 VII 1999 .... ESDF		133 323	...	...	66 063	...	...	67 260	...	...

6. Total and urban population by sex: 1996 - 2005
Population totale et population urbaine selon le sexe: 1996 - 2005 (continued - suite)

Continent, country or area, and date / Continent, pays ou zone et date	Code[a]	Both sexes - Les deux sexes			Male - Masculin			Female - Féminin		
		Total	Urban - Urbaine		Total	Urban - Urbaine		Total	Urban - Urbaine	
			Number Nombre	Percent P.100		Number Nombre	Percent P.100		Number Nombre	Percent P.100
AFRICA - AFRIQUE										
Sao Tome and Principe - Sao Tomé-et-Principe										
1 VII 2000 ....ESDF		135 445	...	...	67 141	...	...	68 304	...	...
25 VIII 2001 ....CDJC		137 599	75 013	54.5	68 236	36 455	53.4	69 363	38 558	55.6
1 VII 2002 ....ESDF		140 365	...	...	69 515	...	...	70 850	...	...
1 VII 2003 ....ESDF		143 186	...	...	70 821	...	...	72 365	...	...
1 VII 2004 ....ESDF		146 056	...	...	72 153	...	...	73 903	...	...
1 VII 2005 ....ESDF		148 968	...	...	73 506	...	...	75 462	...	...
Senegal - Sénégal										
1 VII 1996 ....ESDJ		8 524 605	...	...	4 107 035	...	...	4 417 571	...	...
1 VII 1997 ....ESDJ		8 741 686	...	...	4 208 744	...	...	4 532 942	...	...
1 VII 1998[8] ....ESDJ		8 964 295	...	...	4 305 771	...	...	4 658 524	...	...
1 VII 1999 ....ESDJ		9 192 572	...	...	4 415 174	...	...	4 777 398	...	...
1 VII 2000 ....ESDJ		9 426 663	...	...	4 619 065	...	...	4 807 598	...	...
1 VII 2001 ....ESDJ		9 666 715	...	...	4 740 557	...	...	4 926 158	...	...
1 VII 2002 ....ESDJ		9 912 880	...	...	4 865 222	...	...	5 047 658	...	...
8 XII 2002* ....CDJC		9 956 202	...	...	4 886 485	...	...	5 069 717	...	...
1 VII 2003 ....ESDJ		10 165 314	...	...	5 000 053	...	...	5 165 260	...	...
1 VII 2004 ....ESDJ		10 564 303	...	...	5 069 869	...	...	5 494 434	...	...
1 VII 2005 ....ESDJ		10 848 051	...	...	5 315 545	...	...	5 532 506	...	...
Seychelles										
1 VII 1996 ....ESDF		76 417	...	...	37 923	...	...	38 494	...	...
29 VIII 1997 ....CDFC		75 876	...	...	37 589	...	...	38 287	...	...
1 VII 2001 ....ESDF		81 202	...	...	39 973	...	...	41 229	...	...
1 VII 2002 ....ESDF		83 723	...	...	41 990	...	...	41 733	...	...
26 VIII 2002[11] ....CDJC		81 755	...	...	40 751	...	...	41 004	...	...
1 VII 2003 ....ESDF		82 781	...	...	40 859	...	...	41 922	...	...
1 VII 2004 ....ESDF		82 475	...	...	40 652	...	...	41 823	...	...
1 VII 2005 ....ESDF		82 852	...	...	41 233	...	...	41 619	...	...
Sierra Leone										
1 VII 1996 ....ESDF		4 522 314	1 594 408	35.3	...	...	...	...	...	...
1 VII 1997 ....ESDF		4 625 013	1 638 198	35.4	...	...	...	...	...	...
1 VII 1998 ....ESDF		4 729 579	1 682 456	35.6	...	...	...	...	...	...
1 VII 1999 ....ESDF		4 836 011	1 727 184	35.7	...	...	...	...	...	...
1 VII 2000 ....ESDF		4 944 310	1 772 379	35.8	...	...	...	...	...	...
1 VII 2001 ....ESDF		5 054 476	1 818 044	36.0	...	...	...	...	...	...
1 VII 2002 ....ESDF		5 166 508	1 864 177	36.1	...	...	...	...	...	...
1 VII 2003 ....ESDF		5 280 406	1 910 779	36.2	...	...	...	...	...	...
4 XII 2004* ....CDFC		4 963 298	...	...	2 412 860	...	...	2 550 438	...	...
Somalia - Somalie[12]										
1 VII 2002 ....SSDF		6 799 079	2 310 817	34.0	3 499 523	1 168 410	33.4	3 299 556	1 142 407	34.6
South Africa - Afrique du Sud										
1 VII 1996[8] ....ESDF		40 342 300	21 659 400	53.7	19 394 900	10 604 600	54.7	20 947 400	11 054 800	52.8
10 X 1996[13] ....CDFC		40 583 573	21 781 807	53.7	19 520 887	10 667 927	54.6	21 062 686	11 113 880	52.8
1 VII 1997[8] ....ESDF		41 226 700	22 107 800	53.6	19 857 000	10 836 700	54.6	21 369 700	11 271 100	52.7
1 VII 1998[8] ....ESDF		42 130 500	22 565 300	53.6	20 330 100	11 073 800	54.5	21 800 400	11 491 500	52.7
1 VII 1999[8] ....ESDF		43 054 306	23 032 381	53.5	20 814 425	11 316 037	54.4	22 239 881	11 716 344	52.7
1 VII 2000[8] ....ESDF		43 685 699	23 125 194	52.9	21 016 530	11 273 108	53.6	22 669 169	11 852 086	52.3
1 VII 2001[8] ....ESDF		44 560 644	23 501 443	52.7	21 438 993	11 439 101	53.4	23 121 651	12 062 342	52.2
10 X 2001* ....CDFC		44 819 778	...	...	21 434 041	...	...	23 385 737	...	...
1 VII 2002[8] ....ESDF		45 454 211	23 888 278	52.6	21 870 730	11 612 775	53.1	23 583 481	12 275 503	52.1
1 VII 2003[8] ....ESDF		46 429 823	...	...	22 150 308	...	...	24 279 515	...	...
1 VII 2004[8] ....ESDF		46 586 607	...	...	22 987 410	...	...	23 599 197	...	...
1 VII 2005[8] ....ESDF		46 888 200	...	...	23 070 300	...	...	23 817 900	...	...
Sudan - Soudan										
1 VII 1996 ....ESDF		27 747 348	...	...	14 063 126	...	...	13 684 222	...	...
1 VII 1997 ....ESDF		28 506 732	...	...	14 444 769	...	...	14 061 963	...	...
1 VII 1998 ....ESDF		29 266 405	...	...	14 738 449	...	...	14 527 956	...	...
1 VII 1999 ....ESDF		30 326 000	...	...	15 276 000	...	...	15 050 000	...	...
1 VII 2000 ....ESDF		31 081 000	...	...	15 602 227	...	...	15 478 773	...	...
1 VII 2001 ....ESDF		31 626 526	...	...	16 014 575	...	...	15 611 951	...	...
1 VII 2002 ....ESDF		32 468 401	...	...	16 440 837	...	...	16 027 564	...	...

Continent, country or area, and date / Continent, pays ou zone et date	Code[a]	Both sexes - Les deux sexes			Male - Masculin			Female - Féminin		
		Total	Urban - Urbaine		Total	Urban - Urbaine		Total	Urban - Urbaine	
			Number Nombre	Percent P.100		Number Nombre	Percent P.100		Number Nombre	Percent P.100
AFRICA - AFRIQUE										
Sudan - Soudan										
1 VII 2003 ....ESDF		33 333 648	...	...	16 793 306	...	...	16 540 342	...	...
1 VII 2004 ....ESDF		34 512 000	...	...	17 390 000	...	...	17 122 000	...	...
Swaziland										
1 VII 1996 ....ESDF		937 747	237 368	25.3	438 334	118 562	27.0	499 413	118 806	23.8
11 V 1997 ....CDFC		929 718	214 428	23.1	440 154	106 256	24.1	489 564	108 172	22.1
Tunisia - Tunisie										
1 VII 1996 ....ESDF		9 089 300	...	...	4 590 300	...	...	4 499 000	...	...
1 VII 1997 ....ESDF		9 214 900	...	...	4 647 000	...	...	4 567 900	...	...
1 VII 1998 ....ESDF		9 333 300	...	...	4 709 000	...	...	4 624 300	...	...
Uganda - Ouganda										
1 VII 1996 ....ESDF		19 847 689	2 764 579	13.9	9 802 558	...	...	10 045 131	...	...
1 VII 1997 ....ESDF		20 752 400	2 732 878	13.2	...	...	...	...	...	...
1 VII 1998 ....ESDF		21 467 200	2 878 135	13.4	...	...	...	...	...	...
1 VII 1999 ....ESDF		22 206 600	3 026 742	13.6	...	...	...	...	...	...
1 VII 2000 ....ESDF		22 971 500	3 178 692	13.8	...	...	...	...	...	...
12 IX 2002...........CDFC		24 442 084	2 999 387	12.3	11 929 803	1 449 684	12.2	12 512 281	1 549 703	12.4
United Republic of Tanzania - République Unie de Tanzanie										
24 VIII 2002* ....CDFC		34 443 603	...	...	16 829 861	...	...	17 613 742	...	...
Zambia - Zambie										
1 VII 1999 ....ESDF		10 406 681	...	...	5 198 440	...	...	5 208 241	...	...
1 VII 2000 ....ESDF		9 337 425	3 347 069	35.8	4 594 290	1 662 739	36.2	4 743 135	1 684 330	35.5
25 X 2000 ....CDFC		9 885 591	3 426 862	34.7	4 946 298	1 725 359	34.9	4 939 293	1 701 503	34.4
Zimbabwe										
1 VII 1997 ....ESDF		12 293 953	...	...	6 000 009	...	...	6 293 944	...	...
18 VIII 1997 ....SSDF		11 789 274	3 826 580	32.5	5 647 090	1 906 476	33.8	6 142 184	1 920 104	31.3
1 VII 1999 ....ESDF		13 079 127	...	...	6 382 092	...	...	6 697 035	...	...
17 VIII 2002 ....CDFC		11 631 657	4 029 707	34.6	5 634 180	1 988 176	35.3	5 997 477	2 041 531	34.0
AMERICA, NORTH - AMÉRIQUE DU NORD										
Anguilla										
9 V 2001 ....CDFC		11 430	...	...	5 628	...	...	5 802	...	...
1 VII 2001 ....ESDF		11 561	...	...	5 701	...	...	5 860	...	...
Antigua and Barbuda - Antigua-et-Barbuda										
1 VII 1996 ....ESDF		68 612	...	...	33 075	...	...	35 537	...	...
1 VII 2000 ....ESDF		72 310	...	...	34 858	...	...	37 452	...	...
28 V 2001 ....CDFC		77 426	...	...	37 002	...	...	40 424	...	...
1 VII 2001 ....ESDF		76 886	...	...	36 107	...	...	40 779	...	...
1 VII 2002 ....ESDF		78 320	...	...	36 780	...	...	41 540	...	...
1 VII 2003 ....ESDF		79 781	...	...	37 467	...	...	42 314	...	...
1 VII 2004 ....ESDF		81 270	...	...	38 166	...	...	43 104	...	...
1 VII 2005 ....ESDF		82 786	...	...	38 878	...	...	43 908	...	...
Aruba										
1 VII 1996 ....ESDJ		83 022	...	...	40 695	...	...	42 325	...	...
1 VII 1997 ....ESDJ		86 302	...	...	42 175	...	...	44 127	...	...
1 VII 1998 ....ESDJ		88 452	...	...	43 027	...	...	45 425	...	...
1 VII 1999 ....ESDJ		89 659	...	...	43 362	...	...	46 297	...	...
1 VII 2000 ....ESDJ		90 600	...	...	43 594	...	...	47 005	...	...
14 X 2000 ....CDJC		90 508	...	...	43 435	...	...	47 073	...	...
1 VII 2001 ....ESDJ		91 870	...	...	44 042	...	...	47 828	...	...
1 VII 2002 ....ESDJ		93 310	...	...	44 651	...	...	48 659	...	...
1 VII 2003 ....ESDJ		95 076	...	...	45 461	...	...	49 615	...	...
1 VII 2004 ....ESDJ		97 658	...	...	46 657	...	...	51 001	...	...
1 VII 2005 ....ESDJ		100 629	...	...	48 030	...	...	52 599	...	...
Bahamas										
1 VII 1996 ....ESDF		283 666	...	...	140 507	...	...	143 459	...	...
1 VII 1997 ....ESDF		288 467	...	...	143 142	...	...	145 714	...	...

6. Total and urban population by sex: 1996 - 2005
Population totale et population urbaine selon le sexe: 1996 - 2005 (continued - suite)

Continent, country or area, and date / Continent, pays ou zone et date	Code[a]	Both sexes - Les deux sexes Total	Urban - Urbaine Number Nombre	Urban - Urbaine Percent P.100	Male - Masculin Total	Urban - Urbaine Number Nombre	Urban - Urbaine Percent P.100	Female - Féminin Total	Urban - Urbaine Number Nombre	Urban - Urbaine Percent P.100
AMERICA, NORTH - AMÉRIQUE DU NORD										
Bahamas										
1 V 2000	CDFC	303 611	...	...	147 715	...	...	155 896	...	...
1 VII 2001	ESDF	308 905	...	...	150 206	...	...	158 699	...	...
Barbados - Barbade										
1 V 2000	CDFC	250 010	...	...	119 926	...	...	130 084	...	...
Belize										
1 VII 1996	ESDF	222 000	113 640	51.2	111 000	54 440	49.0	111 000	59 200	53.3
1 VII 1997	ESDF	230 000	115 975	50.4	114 500	55 350	48.3	115 500	60 625	52.5
1 VII 1998	ESDF	238 500	120 110	50.4	118 500	57 095	48.2	120 000	63 015	52.5
1 VII 1999	ESDF	243 055	118 125	48.6	122 745	58 750	47.9	120 310	59 750	49.7
12 V 2000	CDFC	240 204	114 541	47.7	121 278	56 565	46.6	118 926	57 976	48.7
1 VII 2000	ESDF	249 800	121 455	48.6	126 080	59 985	47.6	123 720	61 470	49.7
1 VII 2001	ESDF	257 310	125 830	48.9	129 890	62 160	47.9	127 420	63 370	49.7
1 VII 2002	ESDF	265 200	130 500	49.2	133 900	64 400	48.1	131 300	66 100	50.3
1 VII 2003	ESDF	273 700	135 600	49.5	138 300	67 000	48.4	135 400	68 600	50.7
1 VII 2004	ESDF	282 600	141 000	49.9	142 700	69 500	48.7	139 900	71 500	51.1
1 VII 2005	ESDF	291 800	146 600	50.2	147 400	72 200	49.0	144 400	74 400	51.5
Bermuda - Bermudes										
1 VII 1996	ESDJ	61 545	...	...	29 920	...	...	31 625	...	...
1 VII 1997	ESDJ	61 957	...	...	30 107	...	...	31 850	...	...
1 VII 1998	ESDJ	62 277	...	...	31 258	...	...	31 019	...	...
1 VII 1999	ESDJ	62 656	...	...	30 433	...	...	32 223	...	...
20 V 2000[14]	CDJC	62 059	...	...	29 802	...	...	32 257	...	...
1 VII 2000	ESDJ	63 023	...	...	30 628	...	...	32 395	...	...
1 VII 2001	ESDJ	62 455	...	...	29 969	...	...	32 486	...	...
1 VII 2002	ESDJ	62 754	...	...	30 092	...	...	32 662	...	...
1 VII 2003	ESDJ	63 042	...	...	30 205	...	...	32 837	...	...
1 VII 2004	ESDJ	63 320	...	...	30 323	...	...	32 997	...	...
1 VII 2005	ESDJ	63 571	...	...	30 424	...	...	33 147	...	...
British Virgin Islands - Îles Vierges britanniques										
21 V 2001	CDFC	20 647	...	...	10 627	...	...	10 020	...	...
Canada										
14 V 1996[15]	CDJC	28 846 760	22 461 210	77.9	14 170 030	10 902 295	76.9	14 676 735	11 558 910	78.8
1 VII 1996[16]	ESDJ	29 610 757	23 056 084	77.9	14 650 764	...	...	14 959 993	...	...
1 VII 1997[16]	ESDJ	29 907 172	23 397 908	78.2	14 800 432	...	...	15 106 740	...	...
1 VII 1998[16]	ESDJ	30 157 082	23 704 015	78.6	14 927 226	...	...	15 229 856	...	...
1 VII 1999[16]	ESDJ	30 403 878	...	...	15 052 451	...	...	15 351 427	...	...
1 VII 2000[16]	ESDJ	30 689 035	...	...	15 196 709	...	...	15 492 326	...	...
15 V 2001	CDJC	30 007 095	23 908 105	79.7	14 706 850	11 594 915	78.8	15 300 245	12 313 190	80.5
1 VII 2001[17]	ESDJ	31 021 251	...	...	15 364 404	...	...	15 656 847	...	...
1 VII 2002[17]	ESDJ	31 372 587	...	...	15 538 572	...	...	15 834 015	...	...
1 VII 2003[17]	ESDJ	31 676 077	...	...	15 688 977	...	...	15 987 100	...	...
Cayman Islands - Îles Caïmanes										
10 X 1999	CDFC	39 020	...	...	19 033	...	...	19 987	...	...
1 VII 2004	ESDJ	44 240	...	...	21 235	...	...	23 005	...	...
Costa Rica										
1 VII 1996	ESDJ	3 202 440	1 392 892	43.5	1 604 305	678 747	42.3	1 598 135	714 145	44.7
1 VII 1997	ESDJ	3 270 700	1 419 407	43.4	1 630 815	689 949	42.3	1 639 885	729 458	44.5
1 VII 1998	ESDJ	3 340 909	1 440 272	43.1	1 662 735	693 376	41.7	1 678 174	746 896	44.5
1 VII 1999	ESDJ	3 412 613	1 576 288	46.2	1 688 946	757 345	44.8	1 723 667	818 943	47.5
26 VI 2000	CDJC	3 810 179	2 249 414	59.0	1 902 614	1 096 248	57.6	1 907 565	1 153 166	60.5
1 VII 2000	ESDJ	3 810 187	2 249 301	59.0	1 890 808	1 100 259	58.2	1 919 379	1 149 042	59.9
1 VII 2001	ESDJ	3 906 742	2 305 723	59.0	1 935 168	1 119 394	57.8	1 971 574	1 186 329	60.2
1 VII 2002	ESDJ	3 997 883	2 359 158	59.0	1 983 715	1 147 227	57.8	2 014 168	1 211 931	60.2
1 VII 2003	ESDJ	4 088 773	2 412 542	59.0	2 017 467	1 167 617	57.9	2 071 306	1 244 925	60.1
1 VII 2004	ESDJ	4 178 755	2 465 255	59.0	2 062 468	1 191 560	57.8	2 116 287	1 273 695	60.2
1 VII 2005	ESDJ	4 266 185	2 516 602	59.0	2 116 648	1 231 912	58.2	2 149 537	1 284 690	59.8
Cuba										
1 VII 1996	ESDF	10 965 222	8 200 237	74.8	...	...	...	...	...	...
1 VII 1997	ESDF	11 008 659	8 263 940	75.1	...	...	...	...	...	...

Continent, country or area, and date / Continent, pays ou zone et date	Code[a]	Both sexes - Les deux sexes			Male - Masculin			Female - Féminin		
		Total	Urban - Urbaine		Total	Urban - Urbaine		Total	Urban - Urbaine	
			Number Nombre	Percent P.100		Number Nombre	Percent P.100		Number Nombre	Percent P.100
AMERICA, NORTH - AMÉRIQUE DU NORD										
Cuba										
1 VII 1998	ESDF	11 055 405	8 325 827	75.3	...	...	...	...	...	...
1 VII 1999	ESDF	11 094 972	8 363 577	75.4	5 509 823	4 059 126	73.7	5 585 149	4 304 451	77.1
1 VII 2000	ESDF	11 129 665	8 417 965	75.6	5 548 671	4 111 545	74.1	5 580 994	4 306 420	77.2
1 VII 2001	ESDF	11 157 364	8 467 052	75.9	5 586 835	4 163 395	74.5	5 570 529	4 303 657	77.3
1 VII 2002	ESDF	11 184 457	8 483 688	75.9	5 601 052	4 172 285	74.5	5 583 405	4 311 403	77.2
6 IX 2002	CDJC	11 177 743	8 479 329	75.9	5 597 233	4 169 722	74.5	5 580 510	4 309 607	77.2
1 VII 2003	ESDF	11 215 229	8 501 628	75.8	5 616 275	4 181 234	74.4	5 598 954	4 320 394	77.2
1 VII 2004	ESDF	11 235 687	8 503 738	75.7	5 626 690	4 183 047	74.3	5 608 997	4 320 691	77.0
1 VII 2005	ESDF	11 242 519	8 497 885	75.6	5 629 843	4 180 296	74.3	5 612 676	4 317 589	76.9
Dominica - Dominique										
1 VII 1996	ESDF	72 490	...	...	37 238	...	...	35 252		...
1 VII 1997	ESDF	72 183	...	...	36 906	...	...	35 277		...
1 VII 1998	ESDF	72 042	...	...	36 678	...	...	35 364		...
1 VII 1999	ESDF	71 814	...	...	36 561	...	...	35 253		...
1 VII 2000	ESDF	71 544	...	...	35 744	...	...	35 800		...
12 V 2001[18]	CDFC	69 625	...	...	35 073	...	...	34 552		...
1 VII 2001	ESDF	70 922	...	...	35 241	...	...	35 681		...
1 VII 2002	ESDF	70 382	...	...	35 472	...	...	34 910		...
Dominican Republic - République dominicaine										
1 VII 1996	ESDF	*7 808 297*	*4 460 894*	*57.1*	...	...	...	...	...	...
1 VII 1997	ESDF	*7 987 888*	*4 590 259*	*57.5*	...	...	...	...	...	...
1 VII 1998	ESDF	*8 171 610*	*4 723 377*	*57.8*	...	...	...	...	...	...
1 VII 1999	ESDF	*8 359 557*	*4 860 355*	*58.1*	...	...	...	...	...	...
1 VII 2000	ESDF	*8 551 826*	*5 001 305*	*58.5*	...	...	...	...	...	...
1 VII 2001	ESDF	*8 748 518*	*5 146 343*	*58.8*	...	...	...	...	...	...
20 X 2002	CDJC	8 562 541	5 446 704	63.6	4 265 215	2 648 064	62.1	4 297 326	2 798 640	65.1
1 VII 2003	ESDF	*8 714 954*	*5 620 999*	*64.5*	...	...	...	...	...	...
1 VII 2004	ESDF	*8 870 080*	*5 800 870*	*65.4*	...	...	...	...	...	...
1 VII 2005	ESDF	*9 027 968*	*5 986 498*	*66.3*	...	...	...	...	...	...
El Salvador										
1 VII 1996	ESDF	5 787 093	3 305 082	57.1	2 835 313	1 585 186	55.9	2 951 780	1 719 896	58.3
1 VII 1997	ESDF	5 908 460	3 394 950	57.5	2 896 114	1 629 017	56.2	3 012 346	1 765 933	58.6
1 VII 1998	ESDF	6 031 326	3 485 465	57.8	2 957 835	1 673 250	56.6	3 073 491	1 812 215	59.0
1 VII 1999	ESDF	6 154 311	3 575 956	58.1	3 019 645	1 717 489	56.9	3 134 666	1 858 467	59.3
1 VII 2000	ESDF	6 276 037	3 665 747	58.4	3 080 704	1 761 327	57.2	3 195 333	1 904 420	59.6
1 VII 2001	ESDF	6 396 890	3 754 903	58.7	3 141 208	1 804 804	57.5	3 255 682	1 950 099	59.9
1 VII 2002	ESDF	6 517 798	3 843 878	59.0	3 201 720	1 848 194	57.7	3 316 078	1 995 684	60.2
1 VII 2003	ESDF	6 638 168	3 932 569	59.2	3 261 938	1 891 429	58.0	3 376 230	2 041 140	60.5
1 VII 2004	ESDF	6 757 408	4 020 878	59.5	3 321 564	1 934 445	58.2	3 435 844	2 086 433	60.7
1 VII 2005	ESDF	6 874 926	4 108 703	59.8	3 380 300	1 977 177	58.5	3 494 626	2 131 526	61.0
Greenland - Groenland[19]										
1 VII 1996	ESDJ	55 917	45 330	81.1	29 828	23 993	80.4	26 089	21 337	81.8
1 VII 1997	ESDJ	56 024	45 420	81.1	29 872	24 043	80.5	26 152	21 378	81.7
1 VII 1998	ESDJ	56 076	45 489	81.1	29 904	24 092	80.6	26 172	21 397	81.8
1 VII 1999	ESDJ	56 087	45 523	81.2	29 941	24 189	80.8	26 146	21 334	81.6
1 VII 2000	CDJC	56 124	45 714	81.5	29 989	24 257	80.9	26 135	21 457	82.1
1 VII 2001	ESDJ	56 394	46 125	81.8	30 102	24 454	81.2	26 292	21 671	82.4
1 VII 2002	ESDJ	56 609	46 462	82.1	30 215	24 626	81.5	26 394	21 836	82.7
1 VII 2003	ESDJ	56 766	46 746	82.3	30 292	24 771	81.8	26 474	21 975	83.0
1 VII 2004	ESDJ	56 912	46 989	82.6	...	...	...	...	...	...
Grenada - Grenade[20]										
1 VII 1996	ESDF	98 900	...	...	48 900	...	...	50 000		...
1 VII 1997	ESDF	99 500	...	...	49 300	...	...	50 200		...
1 VII 1998	ESDF	100 100	...	...	49 600	...	...	50 500		...
1 VII 1999	ESDF	100 700	...	...	49 800	...	...	50 900		...
1 VII 2000	ESDF	101 400	...	...	50 100	...	...	51 300		...
25 V 2001	CDFC	102 632	...	...	50 481	...	...	52 151		...
Guadeloupe[21]										
1 VII 1997	ESDJ	413 824	...	...	199 635	...	...	214 190		...
1 VII 1998	ESDJ	418 876	...	...	201 713	...	...	217 163		...

Continent, country or area, and date / Continent, pays ou zone et date	Code[a]	Both sexes - Les deux sexes			Male - Masculin			Female - Féminin		
		Total	Urban - Urbaine		Total	Urban - Urbaine		Total	Urban - Urbaine	
			Number Nombre	Percent P.100		Number Nombre	Percent P.100		Number Nombre	Percent P.100
AMERICA, NORTH - AMÉRIQUE DU NORD										
Guadeloupe[21]										
8 III 1999 ....CDJC		422 222	...	...	203 146	...	...	219 076	...	...
1 VII 1999 ....ESDJ		423 570	...	...	203 607	...	...	219 963	...	...
1 VII 2000 ....ESDJ		427 928	...	...	205 433	...	...	222 495	...	...
1 VII 2001 ....ESDJ		432 453	...	...	207 453	...	...	225 000	...	...
1 VII 2003 ....ESDJ		438 820	...	...	210 130	...	...	228 690	...	...
Guatemala[8]										
1 VII 1996 ....ESDF		10 243 110	...	...	5 169 718	...	...	5 073 392		
1 VII 1997 ....ESDF		10 517 448	...	...	5 306 910	...	...	5 210 538		
1 VII 1998 ....ESDF		10 799 133	...	...	5 447 743	...	...	5 351 390		
1 VII 1999 ....ESDF		11 088 362	...	...	5 592 313	...	...	5 496 049		
1 VII 2000 ....ESDF		11 385 338	...	...	5 740 720	...	...	5 644 618		
1 VII 2001 ....ESDF		11 678 411	...	...	5 888 426	...	...	5 789 985		
Haïti - Haïti										
1 VII 1996 ....ESDJ		7 336 028	2 433 878	33.2	...	...	...	...	...	...
1 VII 1997 ....ESDJ		7 491 762	2 531 060	33.8	...	...	...	...	...	...
1 VII 1998 ....ESDJ		7 647 496	2 630 383	34.4	...	...	...	...	...	...
1 VII 1999 ....ESDJ		7 803 230	2 731 843	35.0	...	...	...	...	...	...
1 VII 2000 ....ESDJ		7 958 964	2 835 433	35.6	...	...	...	...	...	...
Honduras										
1 VII 1996 ....ESDF		5 754 845	2 488 850	43.2	...	...	...	...	...	...
1 VII 1997 ....ESDF		5 908 069	2 587 337	43.8	...	...	...	...	...	...
1 VII 1998 ....ESDF		6 056 942	2 689 721	44.4	...	...	...	...	...	...
1 VII 1999 ....ESDF		6 211 412	2 796 156	45.0	...	...	...	...	...	...
1 VII 2000 ....ESDF		6 369 188	2 907 091	45.6	...	...	...	...	...	...
1 VII 2001 ....ESDF		6 530 331	3 022 150	46.3	...	...	...	...	...	...
28 VII 2001 ....CDJC		6 071 200	...	...	3 000 530	...	...	3 070 670	...	...
1 VII 2002 ....ESDF		6 694 761	3 140 880	46.9	...	...	...	...	...	...
1 VII 2003 ....ESDF		6 860 842	3 260 934	47.5	3 388 874	1 555 369	45.9	3 471 968	1 705 565	49.1
1 VII 2004* ....ESDF		7 028 389	3 382 254	48.1	...	...	...	...	...	...
Jamaica - Jamaïque										
1 VII 1999 ....ESDJ		2 574 314	1 266 233	49.2	1 338 022	637 675	47.7	1 236 292	628 558	50.8
1 VII 2000 ....ESDJ		2 589 395	1 345 867	52.0	1 274 076	641 652	50.4	1 315 319	704 231	53.5
1 VII 2001 ....ESDJ		2 604 739	1 353 842	52.0	1 282 091	645 688	50.4	1 322 648	708 155	53.5
10 IX 2001..........CDJC		2 607 632	1 353 240[22]	51.9	1 283 547	645 374	50.3	1 324 085	707 866	53.5
1 VII 2002 ....ESDJ		2 616 928	1 360 177	52.0	1 288 532	648 932	50.4	1 328 396	711 232	53.5
1 VII 2003 ....ESDJ		2 628 567	1 366 227	52.0	1 294 572	651 974	50.4	1 333 995	714 230	53.5
1 VII 2004 ....ESDJ		2 641 946	1 373 154	52.0	1 301 385	655 404	50.4	1 340 561	717 750	53.5
Martinique										
1 VII 1997 ....ESDJ		375 547	...	...	178 702	...	...	196 845	...	...
1 VII 1998 ....ESDJ		379 042	...	...	180 005	...	...	199 038	...	...
8 III 1999 ....CDJC		381 325	...	...	180 910	...	...	200 415	...	...
1 VII 1999 ....ESDJ		382 090	...	...	181 140	...	...	200 951	...	...
1 VII 2000 ....ESDJ		384 615	...	...	182 044	...	...	202 571	...	...
1 VII 2001 ....ESDJ		387 135	...	...	182 935	...	...	204 200	...	...
1 VII 2002 ....ESDJ		389 455	...	...	183 727	...	...	205 729	...	...
1 VII 2003 ....ESDJ		390 552	...	...	184 084	...	...	206 468	...	...
Mexico - Mexique										
1 VII 1996 ....ESDJ		93 130 089	73 385 379	78.8	46 282 031	...	...	46 848 058	...	...
1 VII 1997 ....ESDJ		94 478 046	74 760 965	79.1	46 903 095	...	...	47 574 951	...	...
1 VII 1998 ....ESDJ		95 790 135	76 083 002	79.4	47 502 593	...	...	48 287 542	...	...
1 VII 1999 ....ESDJ		97 114 831	77 348 051	79.6	48 111 343	...	...	49 003 488	...	...
14 II 2000 ....CDJC		97 483 412	72 759 822	74.6	47 592 253	35 317 569	74.2	49 891 159	37 442 253	75.0
1 VII 2000 ....ESDJ		98 438 553	75 317 689	76.5	48 722 406	...	...	49 716 147	...	...
1 VII 2001 ....ESDJ		99 715 512	76 408 198	76.6	49 312 378	...	...	50 403 134	...	...
1 VII 2002 ....ESDJ		100 909 383	77 465 861	76.8	49 862 643	...	...	51 046 740	...	...
1 VII 2003 ....ESDJ		101 999 558	78 503 652	77.0	50 361 178	...	...	51 638 380	...	...
1 VII 2004 ....ESDJ		103 001 871	79 520 470	77.2	50 814 582	...	...	52 187 289	...	...
1 VII 2005 ....ESDJ		103 946 866	...	...	51 238 427	...	...	52 708 439	...	...
Montserrat										
1 VII 1996[23] ....ESDF		7 867	...	...	3 781	...	...	4 086	...	...
1 VII 1997[23] ....ESDF		6 094	...	...	3 019	...	...	3 075	...	...
1 VII 1998 ....ESDF		3 595	...	...	1 944	...	...	1 651	...	...

Continent, country or area, and date / Continent, pays ou zone et date	Code[a]	Both sexes - Les deux sexes			Male - Masculin			Female - Féminin		
		Total	Urban - Urbaine		Total	Urban - Urbaine		Total	Urban - Urbaine	
			Number Nombre	Percent P.100		Number Nombre	Percent P.100		Number Nombre	Percent P.100
AMERICA, NORTH - AMÉRIQUE DU NORD										
Montserrat										
1 VII 1999 ....ESDF		4 771	...	...	2 536	...	...	2 235	...	...
1 VII 2000 ....ESDF		5 274	...	...	2 793	...	...	2 481	...	...
12 V 2001 ....CDFC		4 491	...	...	2 418	...	...	2 073	...	...
Netherlands Antilles - Antilles néerlandaises[24]										
1 VII 1996 ....ESDJ		191 444	...	...	91 169	...	...	100 275	...	...
1 VII 1997 ....ESDJ		193 373	...	...	92 010	...	...	101 363	...	...
1 VII 1998 ....ESDJ		192 052	...	...	91 253	...	...	100 800	...	...
1 VII 1999 ....ESDJ		186 176	...	...	88 162	...	...	98 014	...	...
1 VII 2000 ....ESDJ		179 225	...	...	84 459	...	...	94 766	...	...
29 I 2001 ....CDJC		175 653	...	...	82 521	...	...	93 132	...	...
1 VII 2001 ....ESDJ		174 145	...	...	81 747	...	...	92 398	...	...
1 VII 2002 ....ESDJ		174 603	...	...	81 818	...	...	92 793	...	...
1 VII 2003 ....ESDJ		178 681	...	...	83 556	...	...	95 125	...	...
1 VII 2004 ....ESDJ		183 115	...	...	85 456	...	...	97 659	...	...
Nicaragua										
1 VII 1996 ....ESDJ		4 548 755	2 535 091	55.7	2 261 141	1 221 317	54.0	2 287 614	1 313 774	57.4
1 VII 1997 ....ESDJ		4 674 199	2 621 328	56.1	2 324 066	1 264 550	54.4	2 350 133	1 356 778	57.7
1 VII 1998 ....ESDJ		4 803 102	2 710 381	56.4	2 388 742	1 309 236	54.8	2 414 360	1 401 145	58.0
1 VII 1999 ....ESDJ		4 935 559	2 802 340	56.8	2 455 217	1 355 417	55.2	2 480 342	1 446 923	58.3
1 VII 2000 ....ESDJ		5 105 680	2 856 185	55.9	2 551 144	1 374 025	53.9	2 554 536	1 482 160	58.0
1 VII 2001 ....ESDJ		5 173 571	2 910 342	56.3	2 583 831	1 400 209	54.2	2 589 740	1 510 133	58.3
1 VII 2002 ....ESDJ		5 243 082	2 966 357	56.6	2 617 291	1 426 993	54.5	2 625 791	1 539 364	58.6
1 VII 2003 ....ESDJ		5 313 803	3 023 106	56.9	2 651 331	1 454 281	54.9	2 662 472	1 568 825	58.9
1 VII 2004 ....ESDJ		5 385 315	3 082 134	57.2	2 685 742	1 483 453	55.2	2 699 573	1 598 681	59.2
4 VI 2005 ....CDJC		5 144 553	2 877 002	55.9	2 535 461	1 369 108	54.0	2 609 092	1 507 894	57.8
1 VII 2005 ....ESDJ		5 457 208	3 140 854	57.6	2 720 336	1 511 552	55.6	2 736 872	1 629 302	59.5
Panama										
1 VII 1996 ....ESDF		2 674 490	1 476 665	55.2	1 351 574	719 973	53.3	1 322 916	756 692	57.2
1 VII 1997 ....ESDF		2 718 686	1 508 703	55.5	1 373 349	735 709	53.6	1 345 337	772 994	57.5
1 VII 1998 ....ESDF		2 763 612	1 540 742	55.8	1 395 475	751 450	53.8	1 368 137	789 292	57.7
1 VII 1999 ....ESDF		2 809 280	1 572 780	56.0	1 417 957	767 186	54.1	1 391 323	805 594	57.9
14 V 2000 ....CDFC		2 839 177	...	...	1 432 566	...	...	1 406 611	...	...
1 VII 2000 ....ESDF		2 855 703	1 604 823	56.2	1 440 801	782 928	54.3	1 414 902	821 895	58.1
1 VII 2004 ....ESDF		3 172 360	...	...	1 600 879	...	...	1 571 481	...	...
1 VII 2005 ....ESDF		3 228 186	2 050 965	63.5	1 628 720	1 011 700	62.1	1 599 466	1 039 265	65.0
Puerto Rico - Porto Rico[25]										
1 VII 1996 ....ESDJ		3 684 739	...	...	1 778 320	...	...	1 906 419	...	...
1 VII 1997 ....ESDJ		3 715 726	...	...	1 792 139	...	...	1 923 587	...	...
1 VII 1998 ....ESDJ		3 748 150	...	...	1 806 604	...	...	1 941 546	...	...
1 VII 1999 ....ESDJ		3 782 143	...	...	1 821 772	...	...	1 960 371	...	...
1 IV 2000 ....CDJC		3 808 610	3 594 948[26]	94.4	1 833 577	1 723 589	94.0	1 975 033	1 871 359	94.8
1 VII 2000 ....ESDJ		3 815 893	3 604 039[27]	94.4	1 836 799	...	...	1 979 094	...	...
1 VII 2001 ....ESDJ		3 839 810	...	...	1 847 559	...	...	1 992 251	...	...
1 VII 2002 ....ESDJ		3 858 806	...	...	1 855 781	...	...	2 003 025	...	...
1 VII 2003 ....ESDJ		3 878 532	...	...	1 865 170	...	...	2 013 362	...	...
1 VII 2004 ....ESDJ		3 894 855	...	...	1 871 657	...	...	2 023 198	...	...
1 VII 2005 ....ESDJ		3 912 054	...	...	1 879 236	...	...	2 032 818	...	...
Saint Kitts and Nevis - Saint-Kitts-et-Nevis										
1 VII 1996 ....ESDF		42 280	...	...	21 290	...	...	20 990	...	...
1 VII 1997 ....ESDF		40 740	...	...	20 550	...	...	20 190	...	...
1 VII 1998 ....ESDF		40 130	...	...	20 230	...	...	19 900	...	...
1 VII 1999 ....ESDF		42 460	...	...	21 360	...	...	21 100	...	...
1 VII 2000 ....ESDF		40 410	...	...	20 400	...	...	20 010	...	...
14 V 2001 ....CDFC		45 841	...	...	22 784	...	...	23 057	...	...
1 VII 2001* ....ESDF		46 111	...	...	22 919	...	...	23 192	...	...

Continent, country or area, and date / Continent, pays ou zone et date	Code[a]	Both sexes - Les deux sexes			Male - Masculin			Female - Féminin		
		Total	Urban - Urbaine		Total	Urban - Urbaine		Total	Urban - Urbaine	
			Number Nombre	Percent P.100		Number Nombre	Percent P.100		Number Nombre	Percent P.100

AMERICA, NORTH - AMÉRIQUE DU NORD

Saint Lucia - Sainte-Lucie										
1 VII 1996 .... ESDF		147 047	43 486	29.6	71 760	21 219	29.6	75 302	22 267	29.6
1 VII 1997 .... ESDF		149 621	44 256	29.6	73 114	21 620	29.6	76 552	22 636	29.6
1 VII 1998 .... ESDF		151 972	44 932	29.6	74 320	21 976	29.6	77 632	22 956	29.6
1 VII 1999 .... ESDF		153 703	...	...	75 266	...	...	78 437	...	...
1 VII 2000 .... ESDF		155 996	...	...	76 494	...	...	79 502	...	...
22 V 2001 .... CDFC		157 164	43 316	27.6	76 741	20 711	27.0	80 423	22 605	28.1
1 VII 2002 .... ESDF		159 133	...	...	77 868	...	...	81 265	...	...
1 VII 2003 .... ESDF		160 673	...	...	78 618	...	...	82 055	...	...
1 VII 2004 .... ESDF		162 434	...	...	79 407	...	...	83 027	...	...
1 VII 2005 .... ESDF		164 791	...	...	80 595	...	...	84 196	...	...
Saint Pierre and Miquelon - Saint Pierre-et-Miquelon										
8 III 1999 .... CDFC		6 316	...	...	3 147	...	...	3 169	...	...
Saint Vincent and the Grenadines - Saint Vincent-et-les Grenadines										
1 VII 1996 .... ESDF		111 214	48 567	43.7	...	...	...	...	...	...
1 VII 1997 .... ESDF		111 655	48 761	43.7	55 713	...	...	55 942	...	...
1 VII 1998 .... ESDF		111 810	48 839	43.7	55 378	...	...	56 432	...	...
1 VII 1999 .... ESDF		112 030	...	...	55 925	...	...	56 105	...	...
1 VII 2000 .... ESDF		109 790	...	...	54 774	...	...	55 016	...	...
14 V 2001[28] .... CDFC		109 022	49 590	45.5	55 456	24 809	44.7	53 566	24 781	46.3
1 VII 2002 .... ESDF		107 854	48 535	45.0	54 434	...	...	53 420	...	...
1 VII 2003 .... ESDF		105 158	42 063	40.0	53 494	...	...	51 664	...	...
1 VII 2004 .... ESDF		104 555	41 822	40.0	53 187	...	...	51 368	...	...
1 VII 2005 .... ESDF		103 751	...	...	52 778	...	...	50 973	...	...
Trinidad and Tobago - Trinité-et-Tobago										
1 VII 1996 .... ESDF		1 263 618	...	...	635 318	...	...	628 298	...	...
1 VII 1997 .... ESDF		1 274 799	...	...	636 340	...	...	638 459	...	...
1 VII 1998 .... ESDF		1 277 675	...	...	638 096	...	...	639 579	...	...
1 VII 1999 .... ESDF		1 283 863	...	...	640 914	...	...	642 949	...	...
15 V 2000 .... CDFC		1 262 366	...	...	633 051	...	...	629 315	...	...
1 VII 2000 .... ESDF		1 290 000	...	...	643 700	...	...	642 900	...	...
1 VII 2001 .... ESDF		1 266 800	...	...	635 200	...	...	631 600	...	...
1 VII 2002 .... ESDF		1 275 700	...	...	639 700	...	...	636 000	...	...
1 VII 2003 .... ESDF		1 282 400	...	...	642 000	...	...	640 400	...	...
Turks Caicos Islands - Îles Turques et Caïques										
20 VIII 2001 .... CDFC		19 886	...	...	9 896	...	...	9 990	...	...
1 VII 2002 .... ESDJ		*20 900*	...	...	*10 402*	...	...	*10 498*	...	...
1 VII 2003 .... ESDJ		*25 143*	...	...	*12 513*	...	...	*12 630*	...	...
1 VII 2004 .... ESDJ		*27 496*	...	...	*13 684*	...	...	*13 812*	...	...
1 VII 2005 .... ESDJ		*30 602*	...	...	*15 230*	...	...	*15 372*	...	...
United States - États-Unis[29]										
1 VII 1996 .... ESDJ		269 394 284	...	...	131 807 484	...	...	137 586 800	...	...
1 VII 1997 .... ESDJ		272 646 925	...	...	133 473 526	...	...	139 173 399	...	...
1 VII 1998 .... ESDJ		275 854 104	...	...	135 129 904	...	...	140 724 200	...	...
1 VII 1999 .... ESDJ		279 040 168	...	...	136 802 873	...	...	142 237 295	...	...
1 IV 2000 .... CDJC		281 421 906	222 360 539	79.0	138 053 563	108 375 797	78.5	143 368 343	113 984 742	79.5
1 VII 2000 .... ESDJ		282 193 477	...	...	138 469 724	...	...	143 723 753	...	...
1 VII 2001 .... ESDJ		285 107 923	...	...	140 015 885	...	...	145 092 038	...	...
1 VII 2002 .... ESDJ		287 984 799	...	...	141 542 448	...	...	146 442 351	...	...
1 VII 2003 .... ESDJ		290 850 005	...	...	143 057 818	...	...	147 792 187	...	...
1 VII 2004 .... ESDJ		293 622 764	...	...	144 528 730	...	...	149 094 034	...	...
1 VII 2005 .... ESDJ		296 410 404	...	...	145 999 746	...	...	150 410 658	...	...

6. Total and urban population by sex: 1996 - 2005
Population totale et population urbaine selon le sexe: 1996 - 2005 (continued - suite)

Continent, country or area, and date / Continent, pays ou zone et date	Code[a]	Both sexes - Les deux sexes Total	Urban - Urbaine Number Nombre	Urban - Urbaine Percent P.100	Male - Masculin Total	Urban - Urbaine Number Nombre	Urban - Urbaine Percent P.100	Female - Féminin Total	Urban - Urbaine Number Nombre	Urban - Urbaine Percent P.100
AMERICA, NORTH - AMÉRIQUE DU NORD										
United States Virgin Islands - Îles Vierges américaines										
1 IV 2000[25] .... CDJC		108 612	...	...	51 864	...	...	56 748	...	...
1 VII 2000 .... ESDJ		108 637	...	...	51 876	...	...	56 761	...	...
1 VII 2001 .... ESDJ		108 749	...	...	51 920	...	...	56 829	...	...
1 VII 2002 .... ESDJ		108 810	...	...	51 952	...	...	56 858	...	...
AMERICA, SOUTH - AMÉRIQUE DU SUD										
Argentina - Argentine										
1 VII 1996 .... ESDF		35 195 575	...	...	17 264 238	...	...	17 931 337	...	...
1 VII 1997 .... ESDF		35 604 362	...	...	17 459 211	...	...	18 145 151	...	...
1 VII 1998 .... ESDF		36 005 387	...	...	17 650 012	...	...	18 355 375	...	...
1 VII 1999 .... ESDF		36 398 577	...	...	17 837 342	...	...	18 561 235	...	...
1 VII 2000 .... ESDF		36 783 859	32 902 070	89.4	18 021 900	15 957 354	88.5	18 761 959	16 944 716	90.3
1 VII 2001 .... ESDF		37 156 195	33 312 347	89.7	18 201 249	16 161 696	88.8	18 954 946	17 150 651	90.5
18 XI 2001 .... CDFC		36 260 130	32 431 950	89.4	17 659 072	15 629 299	88.5	18 601 058	16 802 651	90.3
1 VII 2002 .... ESDF		37 515 632	33 709 927	89.9	18 374 920	16 361 823	89.0	19 140 712	17 348 104	90.6
1 VII 2003 .... ESDF		37 869 730	34 101 536	90.0	18 546 570	16 559 682	89.3	19 323 160	17 541 854	90.8
1 VII 2004 .... ESDF		38 226 051	34 493 965	90.2	18 719 869	16 758 540	89.5	19 506 182	17 735 425	90.9
1 VII 2005 .... ESDF		38 592 150	34 894 057	90.4	18 898 472	16 961 698	89.8	19 693 678	17 932 359	91.1
Bolivia - Bolivie										
1 VII 1996 .... ESDF		7 660 669	4 576 132	59.7	3 806 863	...	...	3 853 806	...	...
1 VII 1997 .... ESDF		7 845 341	4 751 190	60.6	3 900 250	...	...	3 945 092	...	...
1 VII 1998 .... ESDF		8 035 143	4 931 398	61.4	3 996 143	...	...	4 039 000	...	...
1 VII 1999 .... ESDF		8 229 487	5 116 850	62.2	4 094 229	...	...	4 135 259	...	...
1 VII 2000 .... ESDF		8 427 789	5 208 601	61.8	4 194 195	...	...	4 233 594	...	...
1 VII 2001 .... ESDF		8 624 268	5 375 460	62.3	4 293 344	...	...	4 330 924	...	...
5 IX 2001 .... CDFC		8 280 184	5 153 230	62.2	4 130 342	2 501 256	60.6	4 149 842	2 651 974	63.9
1 VII 2002 .... ESDF		8 823 743	5 543 908	62.8	4 393 968	...	...	4 429 776	...	...
1 VII 2003 .... ESDF		9 024 922	5 713 606	63.3	4 495 426	...	...	4 529 495	...	...
1 VII 2004 .... ESDF		9 226 511	5 884 213	63.8	4 597 081	...	...	4 629 430	...	...
1 VII 2005 .... ESDF		9 427 219	...	...	4 698 293	...	...	4 728 926	...	...
Brazil - Brésil[30]										
1 VII 1996 .... ESDF		161 323 169	...	...	79 579 114	...	...	81 744 055	...	...
1 VIII 1996 .... CDJC		157 070 163	123 076 831	78.4	77 442 865	59 716 389	77.1	79 627 298	63 360 442	79.6
1 VII 1997 .... ESDF		163 779 827	...	...	80 755 823	...	...	83 024 004	...	...
1 VII 1998 .... ESDF		166 252 088	...	...	81 940 241	...	...	84 311 847	...	...
1 VII 1999 .... ESDF		168 753 552	...	...	83 139 277	...	...	85 614 275	...	...
1 VII 2000 .... ESDF		171 279 882	...	...	84 350 720	...	...	86 929 162	...	...
1 VIII 2000 .... CDJC		169 799 170	137 953 959	81.2	83 576 015	66 882 993	80.0	86 223 155	71 070 966	82.4
1 VII 2001 .... ESDF		173 821 934	...	...	85 569 888	...	...	88 252 046	...	...
1 VII 2002 .... ESDF		176 391 015	...	...	86 802 515	...	...	89 588 500	...	...
1 VII 2003 .... ESDF		178 985 306	...	...	88 047 716	...	...	90 937 590	...	...
1 VII 2004 .... ESDF		181 586 030	...	...	89 296 014	...	...	92 290 016	...	...
1 VII 2005 .... ESDF		184 184 264	...	...	90 542 990	...	...	93 641 274	...	...
Chile - Chili										
1 VII 1996 .... ESDF		14 595 504	12 415 178	85.1	7 220 924	6 054 287	83.8	7 374 580	6 360 891	86.3
1 VII 1997 .... ESDF		14 796 076	12 645 610	85.5	7 320 768	6 170 742	84.3	7 475 308	6 474 868	86.6
1 VII 1998 .... ESDF		14 996 647	12 876 051	85.9	7 420 612	6 287 197	84.7	7 576 035	6 588 854	87.0
1 VII 1999 .... ESDF		15 197 213	13 106 477	86.2	7 520 454	6 403 647	85.1	7 676 759	6 702 830	87.3
1 VII 2000 .... ESDF		15 397 784	13 336 913	86.6	7 620 300	6 520 105	85.6	7 777 484	6 816 808	87.6
1 VII 2001 .... ESDF		15 571 679	13 494 230	86.7	7 706 752	6 598 130	85.6	7 864 927	6 896 100	87.7
24 IV 2002 .... CDFC		15 116 435	13 090 113	86.6	7 447 695	6 366 311	85.5	7 668 740	6 723 802	87.7
1 VII 2002 .... ESDF		15 745 583	13 651 558	86.7	7 793 208	6 676 157	85.7	7 952 375	6 975 401	87.7
1 VII 2003 .... ESDF		15 919 479	13 808 880	86.7	7 879 658	6 754 181	85.7	8 039 821	7 054 699	87.7
1 VII 2004 .... ESDF		16 093 378	13 966 203	86.8	7 966 110	6 832 205	85.8	8 127 268	7 133 998	87.8
1 VII 2005 .... ESDF		16 267 278	14 123 527	86.8	8 052 564	6 910 230	85.8	8 214 714	7 213 297	87.8

Continent, country or area, and date / Continent, pays ou zone et date	Code[a]	Both sexes - Les deux sexes			Male - Masculin			Female - Féminin		
		Total	Urban - Urbaine		Total	Urban - Urbaine		Total	Urban - Urbaine	
			Number Nombre	Percent P.100		Number Nombre	Percent P.100		Number Nombre	Percent P.100
AMERICA, SOUTH - AMÉRIQUE DU SUD										
Colombia - Colombie										
1 VII 1996 ....ESDF		39 281 340	27 390 035	69.7	...	...	...	...	...	...
1 VII 1997 ....ESDF		40 018 837	28 048 220	70.1	...	...	...	...	...	...
1 VII 1998 ....ESDF		40 772 995	28 734 719	70.5	...	...	...	...	...	...
1 VII 1999 ....ESDF		41 539 012	29 435 181	70.9	...	...	...	...	...	...
1 VII 2000 ....ESDF		42 299 300	30 125 776	71.2	...	...	...	...	...	...
1 VII 2001 ....ESDF		43 035 393	30 772 485	71.5	...	...	...	...	...	...
1 VII 2002 ....ESDF		43 775 838	31 428 374	71.8	...	...	...	...	...	...
1 VII 2003 ....ESDF		44 531 433	32 101 585	72.1	...	...	...	...	...	...
1 VII 2004 ....ESDF		45 294 952	32 787 008	72.4	...	...	...	...	...	...
22 V 2005 ....CDFC		41 468 384	...	...	20 336 117	...	...	21 132 267	...	...
1 VII 2005 ....ESDF		46 045 111	33 464 183	72.7	...	...	...	...	...	...
Ecuador - Équateur[31]										
1 VII 1996 ....ESDF		11 591 128	6 780 934	58.5	5 877 274[32]	...	...	5 821 222[32]		
1 VII 1997 ....ESDF		11 772 871	6 953 116	59.1	5 914 625	3 433 722	58.1	5 858 242	3 519 394	60.1
1 VII 1998 ....ESDF		11 947 586	7 118 271	59.6	6 001 552	3 517 425	58.6	5 946 036	3 600 846	60.6
1 VII 1999 ....ESDF		12 120 981	7 282 105	60.1	6 087 690	3 600 349	59.1	6 033 294	3 681 756	61.0
1 VII 2000 ....ESDF		12 298 745	7 450 308	60.6	6 175 859	3 685 298	59.7	6 122 886	3 765 010	61.5
1 VII 2001 ....ESDF		12 479 924	7 633 850	61.2	6 265 558	3 778 158	60.3	6 214 366	3 855 692	62.0
25 XI 2001 ....CDFC		12 156 608	7 431 355	61.1	6 018 353	3 625 962	60.2	6 138 255	3 805 393	62.0
1 VII 2002 ....ESDF		12 660 728	7 817 018	61.7	6 354 906	3 870 667	60.9	6 305 821	3 946 351	62.6
1 VII 2003 ....ESDF		12 842 578	8 001 231	62.3	6 444 656	3 963 574	61.5	6 397 920	4 037 657	63.1
1 VII 2004 ....ESDF		13 026 891	8 187 908	62.9	6 535 564	4 057 642	62.1	6 491 327	4 130 266	63.6
1 VII 2005 ....ESDF		13 215 089	...	...	6 628 368	...	...	6 586 721	...	...
Falkland Islands (Malvinas) - Îles Falkland (Malvinas)[33]										
24 IV 1996 ....CDFC		2 564	...	...	1 447	...	...	1 117	...	...
8 IV 2001 ....CDFC		2 913	...	...	1 598	...	...	1 315	...	...
French Guiana - Guyane française										
1 VII 1997 ....ESDJ		147 590	...	...	74 698	...	...	72 892	...	...
1 VII 1998 ....ESDJ		153 001	...	...	77 177	...	...	75 825	...	...
8 III 1999 ....CDJC		156 790	...	...	78 963	...	...	77 827	...	...
1 VII 1999 ....ESDJ		158 444	...	...	79 670	...	...	78 774	...	...
1 VII 2000 ....ESDJ		163 979	...	...	82 200	...	...	81 779	...	...
1 VII 2001 ....ESDJ		169 667	...	...	84 782	...	...	84 885	...	...
1 VII 2002 ....ESDJ		175 426	...	...	87 387	...	...	88 039	...	...
1 I 2004 ....ESDJ		184 451	...	...	91 522	...	...	92 929	...	...
Guyana										
1 VII 1996 ....ESDF		770 139	...	...	379 447	...	...	390 692	...	...
1 VII 1997 ....ESDF		775 137	...	...	381 910	...	...	393 227	...	...
1 VII 1998 ....ESDF		773 432	...	...	381 070	...	...	392 362	...	...
1 VII 1999 ....ESDF		770 584	...	...	379 667	...	...	390 917	...	...
1 VII 2000 ....ESDF		742 000	...	...	365 583	...	...	376 417	...	...
1 VII 2001 ....ESDF		743 600	...	...	366 372	...	...	377 228	...	...
1 VII 2002 ....ESDF		747 712	...	...	371 351	...	...	376 361	...	...
15 IX 2002 ....CDFC		751 223	...	...	376 034	...	...	375 189	...	...
1 VII 2003[34] ....ESDF		752 498	...	...	376 675	...	...	375 823	...	...
1 VII 2004 ....ESDF		755 061	...	...	377 958	...	...	377 103	...	...
1 VII 2005 ....ESDF		757 637	...	...	379 245	...	...	378 393	...	...
Paraguay										
1 VII 1996 ....ESDF		4 955 238	...	...	2 497 197	...	...	2 458 041	...	...
1 VII 2000 ....ESDF		5 346 267	...	...	2 705 524	...	...	2 640 743	...	...
1 VII 2001 ....ESDF		5 456 418	...	...	2 761 141	...	...	2 695 278	...	...
1 VII 2002 ....ESDF		5 566 852	...	...	2 816 687	...	...	2 750 164	...	...
28 VIII 2002 ....CDFC		5 163 198	2 928 437	56.7	2 603 242	1 422 339	54.6	2 559 956	1 506 098	58.8
1 VII 2003 ....ESDF		5 677 448	...	...	2 872 186	...	...	2 805 262	...	...
1 VII 2004 ....ESDF		5 788 088	...	...	2 927 657	...	...	2 860 430	...	...
1 VII 2005 ....ESDF		5 898 651	...	...	2 983 123	...	...	2 915 528	...	...
Peru - Pérou[35]										
1 VII 1996[8] ....ESDF		24 257 671	17 294 032	71.3	12 206 832	8 869 457[32]	72.7	12 050 839	8 906 470[32]	73.9
1 VII 1997[8] ....ESDF		24 681 045	17 640 917	71.5	12 419 397	8 849 804	71.3	12 261 648	8 791 113	71.7

Continent, country or area, and date / Continent, pays ou zone et date	Code[a]	Both sexes - Les deux sexes			Male - Masculin			Female - Féminin		
		Total	Urban - Urbaine		Total	Urban - Urbaine		Total	Urban - Urbaine	
			Number Nombre	Percent P.100		Number Nombre	Percent P.100		Number Nombre	Percent P.100
AMERICA, SOUTH - AMÉRIQUE DU SUD										
Peru - Pérou[35]										
1 VII 1998[8] ....ESDF		25 104 276	17 978 819	71.6	12 631 667	9 017 356	71.4	12 472 609	8 961 463	71.8
1 VII 1999[8] ....ESDF		25 524 613	18 312 557	71.7	12 842 267	9 182 458	71.5	12 682 346	9 130 099	72.0
1 VII 2000[8] ....ESDF		25 939 329	18 647 242	71.9	13 049 847	9 348 264	71.6	12 889 482	9 298 978	72.1
1 VII 2001[8] ....ESDF		26 346 840	18 980 589	72.0	13 253 619	9 513 198	71.8	13 093 221	9 467 391	72.3
1 VII 2002[8] ....ESDF		26 748 972	19 310 309	72.2	13 454 486	9 676 260	71.9	13 294 486	9 634 049	72.5
1 VII 2003[8] ....ESDF		27 148 101	19 638 160	72.3	13 653 636	9 838 166	72.1	13 494 465	9 799 994	72.6
1 VII 2004[8] ....ESDF		27 546 574	19 966 180	72.5	13 852 228	9 999 924	72.2	13 694 346	9 966 256	72.8
1 VII 2005*[8] ....ESDF		27 946 774	20 296 436	72.6	...	...	...	...	...	...
18 VII 2005*[36] ....CDFC		26 152 265	...	...	13 061 026	...	...	13 091 239	...	...
Suriname										
31 III 2003*[37] ....CDJC		481 146	...	...	241 837	...	...	239 292	...	...
2 VIII 2004[38] ....CDJC		492 829	...	...	247 846[39]	...	...	244 618[39]	...	...
1 VII 2005 ....ESDJ		499 009	...	...	251 155	...	...	247 854	...	...
Uruguay										
22 V 1996 ....CDFC		3 163 763	2 872 077	90.8	1 532 288	1 366 092	89.2	1 631 475	1 505 985	92.3
1 VII 1996[8] ....ESDF		3 235 549	2 970 873	91.8	1 569 584	1 417 118	90.3	1 665 965	1 553 755	93.3
1 VII 1997[8] ....ESDF		3 256 182	2 996 846	92.0	1 578 874	1 429 782	90.6	1 677 308	1 567 064	93.4
1 VII 1998[8] ....ESDF		3 273 777	3 019 947	92.2	1 586 775	1 441 116	90.8	1 687 002	1 578 831	93.6
1 VII 1999[8] ....ESDF		3 288 819	3 040 697	92.5	1 593 452	1 451 298	91.1	1 695 368	1 589 399	93.7
1 VII 2000[8] ....ESDF		3 300 847	3 058 437	92.7	1 598 685	1 460 013	91.3	1 702 162	1 598 424	93.9
1 VII 2001[8] ....ESDF		3 308 356	3 071 727	92.8	1 601 593	1 466 408	91.6	1 706 763	1 605 319	94.1
1 VII 2002[8] ....ESDF		3 308 527	3 077 804	93.0	1 600 814	1 469 148	91.8	1 707 713	1 608 656	94.2
1 VII 2003[8] ....ESDF		3 303 540	3 078 812	93.2	1 597 362	1 469 246	92.0	1 706 177	1 609 565	94.3
1 VI 2004[40] ....CDFC		3 241 003	2 974 714	91.8	1 565 533	1 415 362	90.4	1 675 470	1 559 352	93.1
1 VII 2004[8] ....ESDF		3 301 732	3 083 096	93.4	1 595 635	1 471 098	92.2	1 706 097	1 611 998	94.5
1 VII 2005[8] ....ESDF		3 305 723	3 089 988	93.5	1 597 040	1 474 638	92.3	1 708 683	1 615 350	94.5
Venezuela (Bolivarian Republic of) - Venezuela (République bolivarienne du)[35]										
1 VII 1996 ....ESDF		22 501 988	19 710 481	87.6	11 333 607	9 818 511	86.6	11 168 381	9 891 970	88.6
1 VII 1997 ....ESDF		22 958 680	20 123 896	87.7	11 559 949	10 021 295	86.7	11 398 731	10 102 601	88.6
1 VII 1998 ....ESDF		23 412 742	20 534 451	87.7	11 784 967	10 222 629	86.7	11 627 775	10 311 822	88.7
1 VII 1999 ....ESDF		23 867 393	20 945 043	87.8	12 010 280	10 423 959	86.8	11 857 113	10 521 084	88.7
1 VII 2000 ....ESDF		24 310 896	21 345 288	87.8	12 229 953	10 620 092	86.8	12 080 943	10 725 196	88.8
1 VII 2001 ....ESDF		24 765 581	21 754 766	87.8	12 454 204	10 820 038	86.9	12 311 377	10 934 728	88.8
30 X 2001 ....CDFC		23 054 210	...	...	11 402 869	...	...	11 651 341	...	...
1 VII 2002 ....ESDF		25 219 910	22 163 339	87.9	12 678 275	11 021 146	86.9	12 541 635	11 142 193	88.8
1 VII 2003 ....ESDF		25 673 550	...	...	12 901 999	...	...	12 771 551	...	...
1 VII 2004 ....ESDF		26 127 351	...	...	13 125 804	...	...	13 001 547	...	...
1 VII 2005 ....ESDF		26 577 423	...	...	13 347 732	...	...	13 229 691	...	...
ASIA - ASIE										
Afghanistan										
1 VII 2002 ....ESDF		22 930 000	4 463 000[41]	19.5	10 453 500[41]	2 332 600[41]	22.3	9 844 300[41]	2 130 400[41]	21.6
Armenia - Arménie										
1 VII 1996 ....ESDJ		3 247 395	2 143 746	66.0	1 551 295	1 016 135	65.5	1 696 100	1 127 611	66.5
1 VII 1997 ....ESDJ		3 242 100	2 130 651	65.7	1 554 242	1 016 310	65.4	1 687 858	1 114 341	66.0
1 VII 1998 ....ESDJ		3 235 151	2 117 251	65.4	1 553 260	1 011 028	65.1	1 681 891	1 106 223	65.8
1 VII 1999 ....ESDJ		3 229 499	2 103 700	65.1	1 552 362	1 002 727	64.6	1 677 138	1 100 974	65.6
1 VII 2000 ....ESDJ		3 221 106	2 086 054	64.8	1 544 397	988 741	64.0	1 676 709	1 097 313	65.4
1 VII 2001 ....ESDJ		3 214 095	2 070 947	64.4	1 542 728	977 820	63.4	1 671 367	1 093 127	65.4
10 X 2001[42] ....CDFC		3 002 594	1 945 514	64.8	1 407 220	898 977	63.9	1 595 374	1 046 537	65.6
1 VII 2002 ....ESDJ		3 211 593	2 063 913	64.3	1 542 974	974 775	63.2	1 668 619	1 089 138	65.3
1 VII 2003 ....ESDJ		3 211 267	2 061 952	64.2	1 545 168	975 356	63.1	1 666 099	1 086 596	65.2
1 VII 2004 ....ESDJ		3 214 030	2 061 984	64.2	1 548 713	976 728	63.1	1 665 317	1 085 256	65.2
1 VII 2005 ....ESDJ		3 217 535	2 062 472	64.1	1 552 382	978 396	63.0	1 665 153	1 084 076	65.1

6. Total and urban population by sex: 1996 - 2005
Population totale et population urbaine selon le sexe: 1996 - 2005 (continued - suite)

Continent, country or area, and date / Continent, pays ou zone et date	Code[a]	Both sexes - Les deux sexes			Male - Masculin			Female - Féminin		
		Total	Urban - Urbaine		Total	Urban - Urbaine		Total	Urban - Urbaine	
			Number Nombre	Percent P.100		Number Nombre	Percent P.100		Number Nombre	Percent P.100
ASIA - ASIE										
Azerbaijan - Azerbaïdjan										
1 VII 1996 . . . . ESDF	ESDF	7 763 000	4 046 200	52.1	3 824 000	1 988 900	52.0	3 939 000	2 057 300	52.2
1 VII 1997 . . . . ESDF	ESDF	7 838 300	4 070 200	51.9	3 864 300	2 006 500	51.9	3 974 000	2 063 700	51.9
1 VII 1998 . . . . ESDF	ESDF	7 913 000	4 072 600	51.5	3 882 100	1 993 500	51.4	4 030 900	2 079 100	51.6
27 I 1999 . . . . CDJC	CDJC	7 953 438	4 053 584	51.0	3 883 155	1 970 022	50.7	4 070 283	2 083 562	51.2
1 VII 1999 . . . . ESDF	ESDF	7 982 800	4 074 600	51.0	3 899 600	1 981 300	50.8	4 083 200	2 093 300	51.3
1 VII 2000 . . . . ESDF	ESDF	8 048 600	4 096 900	50.9	3 936 400	1 994 300	50.7	4 112 200	2 102 600	51.1
1 VII 2001 . . . . ESDF	ESDF	8 111 200	4 118 800	50.8	3 971 600	2 006 800	50.5	4 139 600	2 112 000	51.0
1 VII 2002 . . . . ESDF	ESDF	8 172 000	4 142 200	50.7	4 005 900	2 020 200	50.4	4 166 100	2 122 000	50.9
1 VII 2003 . . . . ESDF	ESDF	8 234 100	4 242 000	51.5	4 040 800	2 070 800	51.2	4 193 300	2 171 200	51.8
1 VII 2004 . . . . ESDF	ESDF	8 306 500	4 276 300	51.5	4 081 100	2 089 500	51.2	4 225 400	2 186 800	51.8
Bahrain - Bahreïn										
1 VII 1996 . . . . ESDF	ESDF	573 792	...	...	330 855	...	...	242 937	...	...
1 VII 1997 . . . . ESDF	ESDF	589 115	...	...	339 372	...	...	249 743	...	...
1 VII 1998 . . . . ESDF	ESDF	604 842	...	...	348 100	...	...	256 742	...	...
1 VII 1999 . . . . ESDF	ESDF	620 989	...	...	357 056	...	...	263 933	...	...
1 VII 2000 . . . . ESDF	ESDF	637 582	...	...	366 247	...	...	271 335	...	...
7 IV 2001 . . . . CDFC	CDFC	650 604	...	...	373 649	...	...	276 955	...	...
1 VII 2001 . . . . ESDF	ESDF	654 619	...	...	375 674	...	...	278 945	...	...
1 VII 2002 . . . . ESDF	ESDF	672 123	...	...	386 220	...	...	285 903	...	...
1 VII 2003 . . . . ESDF	ESDF	689 140	...	...	396 278	...	...	293 140	...	...
1 VII 2004 . . . . ESDF	ESDF	707 160	...	...	406 617	...	...	300 543	...	...
1 VII 2005 . . . . ESDF	ESDF	724 645	...	...	416 755	...	...	307 890	...	...
Bangladesh										
1 VII 1996 . . . . ESDF	ESDF	122 100 000	...	...	62 700 000	...	...	59 400 000	...	...
1 VII 1997 . . . . ESDF	ESDF	124 300 000	...	...	63 900 000	...	...	60 400 000	...	...
1 VII 1998 . . . . ESDF	ESDF	126 200 000	...	...	64 800 000	...	...	61 400 000	...	...
1 VII 1999* . . . . ESDF	ESDF	128 100 000	...	...	65 900 000	...	...	62 200 000	...	...
1 VII 2000 . . . . ESDF	ESDF	129 300 000	...	...	66 300 000	...	...	63 000 000	...	...
22 I 2001[43] . . . . CDFC	CDFC	130 522 598	31 077 952	23.8	67 731 320	16 844 256	24.9	62 791 278	14 233 696	22.7
1 VII 2002 . . . . ESDF	ESDF	132 900 000	...	...	68 200 000	...	...	64 700 000	...	...
1 VII 2003 . . . . ESDF	ESDF	134 800 000	...	...	69 100 000	...	...	65 700 000	...	...
1 VII 2004 . . . . ESDF	ESDF	136 700 000	...	...	70 100 000	...	...	66 600 000	...	...
1 VII 2005 . . . . ESDF	ESDF	138 600 000	...	...	71 000 000	...	...	67 600 000	...	...
Bhutan - Bhoutan										
1 VII 2000 . . . . ESDF	ESDF	677 934	...	...	342 324	...	...	335 610	...	...
1 VII 2001 . . . . ESDF	ESDF	698 949	...	...	352 935	...	...	346 014	...	...
1 VII 2002 . . . . ESDF	ESDF	716 424	...	...	361 759	...	...	354 665	...	...
1 VII 2003 . . . . ESDF	ESDF	734 340	...	...	370 805	...	...	363 535	...	...
1 VII 2004 . . . . ESDF	ESDF	752 700	...	...	380 090	...	...	372 610	...	...
30 V 2005 . . . . CDFC	CDFC	634 982	...	...	333 595	...	...	301 387	...	...
Brunei Darussalam - Brunéi Darussalam										
1 VII 1997 . . . . ESDF	ESDF	301 700	...	...	155 600	...	...	146 100	...	...
1 VII 1998 . . . . ESDF	ESDF	309 500	...	...	159 000	...	...	150 500	...	...
1 VII 1999 . . . . ESDF	ESDF	316 900	...	...	162 200	...	...	154 700	...	...
1 VII 2000 . . . . ESDF	ESDF	324 800	...	...	165 500	...	...	159 300	...	...
1 VII 2001 . . . . ESDF	ESDF	332 800	...	...	168 900	...	...	163 900	...	...
21 VIII 2001* . . . . CDFC	CDFC	332 844	238 699	71.7	168 974	120 046	71.0	163 870	118 653	72.4
1 VII 2002 . . . . ESDF	ESDF	344 200	...	...	180 600	...	...	163 600	...	...
1 VII 2003 . . . . ESDF	ESDF	349 600	...	...	182 500	...	...	167 100	...	...
1 VII 2004 . . . . ESDF	ESDF	359 700	...	...	189 400	...	...	170 300	...	...
1 VII 2005 . . . . ESDF	ESDF	370 100	...	...	195 300	...	...	174 800	...	...
Cambodia - Cambodge										
1 III 1996 . . . . SSDF	SSDF	10 702 000	1 540 000	14.4	5 119 000	738 000	14.4	5 583 000	802 000	14.4
3 III 1998[44] . . . . CDFC	CDFC	11 437 656	1 795 575	15.7	5 511 408	878 186	15.9	5 926 248	917 389	15.5
1 VII 2004[45] . . . . SSDF	SSDF	12 824 170	1 920 752	15.0	6 197 128	932 126	15.0	6 627 042	988 626	14.9
China - Chine[46]										
1 VII 1996[47] . . . . ESDF	ESDF	1 217 550 000	362 390 000[48]	29.8	620 040 000	...	...	597 510 000	...	...
1 VII 1997[47] . . . . ESDF	ESDF	1 230 075 000	383 765 000[48]	31.2	626 655 000	...	...	603 420 000	...	...
1 VII 1998[47] . . . . ESDF	ESDF	1 241 935 000	405 285 000[48]	32.6	635 355 000	...	...	606 580 000	...	...
1 VII 1999[47] . . . . ESDF	ESDF	1 252 735 000	426 780 000[48]	34.1	643 160 000	...	...	609 575 000	...	...
1 VII 2000[47] . . . . ESDF	ESDF	1 262 645 000	448 270 000[48]	35.5	650 645 000	...	...	612 000 000	...	...
1 XI 2000[49] . . . . CDJC	CDJC	1 242 612 226	458 770 983	36.9	640 275 969	235 264 707	36.7	602 336 257	223 506 276	37.1

Continent, country or area, and date / Continent, pays ou zone et date	Code[a]	Both sexes - Les deux sexes			Male - Masculin			Female - Féminin		
		Total	Urban - Urbaine		Total	Urban - Urbaine		Total	Urban - Urbaine	
			Number Nombre	Percent P.100		Number Nombre	Percent P.100		Number Nombre	Percent P.100

ASIA - ASIE

China - Chine[46]

1 VII 2001[50] ....ESDF		1 271 850 000	469 850 000[48]	36.9	655 545 000	...	...	616 305 000	...	...
1 VII 2002[50] ....ESDF		1 280 400 000	491 380 000[48]	38.4	658 935 000	...	...	621 465 000	...	...
1 VII 2003[50] ....ESDF		1 288 400 000	512 940 000[48]	39.8	663 355 000	...	...	625 045 000	...	...
1 VII 2004[50] ....ESDF		1 296 075 000	533 295 000[48]	41.1	667 660 000	...	...	628 415 000	...	...
1 VII 2005[51] ....ESDF		1 303 720 000	552 475 000[48]	42.4	671 755 000	...	...	631 965 000	...	...

China: Hong Kong SAR - Chine: Hong Kong RAS

15 III 1996............CDFC		6 217 556	...	...	3 108 107	...	...	3 109 449	...	...
1 VII 1996 ....ESDJ		6 435 500	...	...	3 220 000	...	...	3 215 500	...	...
1 VII 1997 ....ESDJ		6 489 300	...	...	3 235 400	...	...	3 253 900	...	...
1 VII 1998 ....ESDJ		6 543 700	...	...	3 249 900	...	...	3 293 800	...	...
1 VII 1999 ....ESDJ		6 606 500	...	...	3 264 700	...	...	3 341 800	...	...
1 VII 2000 ....ESDJ		6 665 000	...	...	3 276 500	...	...	3 388 500	...	...
14 III 2001[52] ....CDJC		6 708 389	...	...	3 285 344	...	...	3 423 045	...	...
1 VII 2001 ....ESDJ		6 714 300	...	...	3 282 000	...	...	3 432 300	...	...
1 VII 2002 ....ESDJ		6 744 100	...	...	3 279 600	...	...	3 464 500	...	...
1 VII 2003 ....ESDJ		6 730 800	...	...	3 259 100	...	...	3 471 700	...	...
1 VII 2004 ....ESDJ		6 783 500	...	...	3 266 800	...	...	3 516 700	...	...
1 VII 2005 ....ESDJ		6 813 200	...	...	3 264 000	...	...	3 549 200	...	...

China: Macao SAR - Chine: Macao RAS

1 VII 1996 ....ESDJ		415 101	...	...	199 711	...	...	215 390	...	...
1 VII 1997 ....ESDJ		417 295	...	...	201 320	...	...	215 975	...	...
1 VII 1998 ....ESDJ		422 304	...	...	203 535	...	...	218 769	...	...
1 VII 1999 ....ESDJ		427 411	...	...	205 322	...	...	222 089	...	...
1 VII 2000 ....ESDJ		430 569	...	...	206 686	...	...	223 883	...	...
1 VII 2001 ....ESDJ		433 903	...	...	208 235	...	...	225 668	...	...
23 VIII 2001 ....CDJC		435 235	...	...	208 865	...	...	226 370	...	...
1 VII 2002 ....ESDJ		438 408	...	...	210 218	...	...	228 190	...	...
1 VII 2003 ....ESDJ		443 600	...	...	212 866	...	...	230 734	...	...
1 VII 2004 ....ESDJ		454 661	...	...	218 122	...	...	236 539	...	...
1 VII 2005 ....ESDJ		473 457	...	...	227 600	...	...	245 857	...	...

Cyprus - Chypre[53]

1 VII 1996 ....ESDJ		660 900	...	...	326 800	...	...	334 100	...	...
1 VII 1997 ....ESDJ		670 400	...	...	330 900	...	...	339 500	...	...
1 VII 1998 ....ESDJ		678 900	...	...	334 600	...	...	344 300	...	...
1 VII 1999 ....ESDJ		686 400	...	...	337 800	...	...	348 600	...	...
1 VII 2000 ....ESDJ		693 600	...	...	341 000	...	...	352 600	...	...
1 VII 2001 ....ESDJ		701 300	...	...	344 300	...	...	357 000	...	...
1 X 2001[54]...........CDJC		689 565	474 450	68.8	338 497	231 128	68.3	351 068	243 322	69.3
1 VII 2002 ....ESDJ		709 600	...	...	347 900	...	...	361 700	...	...
1 VII 2003 ....ESDJ		720 600	...	...	353 700	...	...	366 900	...	...
1 VII 2004 ....ESDJ		737 100	...	...	363 000	...	...	374 100	...	...
1 VII 2005 ....ESDJ		758 000	...	...	373 600	...	...	384 400	...	...

Georgia - Géorgie

1 VII 1996 ....ESDF		4 616 500	2 479 100	53.7	...	...	...	...	...	...
1 VII 1997 ....ESDF		4 531 700	2 389 200	52.7	...	...	...	...	...	...
1 VII 1998 ....ESDF		4 487 400	2 352 000	52.4	...	...	...	...	...	...
1 VII 1999 ....ESDF		4 452 500	2 323 200	52.2	...	...	...	...	...	...
1 VII 2000 ....ESDF		4 418 300	2 294 500	51.9	...	...	...	...	...	...
1 VII 2001 ....ESDF		4 386 500	2 282 800	52.0	2 300 700	...	...	2 085 800	...	...
17 I 2002.............CDJC		4 371 535	2 284 796	52.3	2 061 753	1 048 593	50.9	2 309 782	1 236 203	53.5
1 VII 2002 ....ESDF		4 357 100	2 275 800	52.2	...	...	...	...	...	...
1 VII 2003 ....ESDF		4 328 900	2 259 600	52.2	2 045 500	...	...	2 283 400	...	...
1 VII 2004 ....ESDF		4 318 400	2 255 000	52.2	...	...	...	...	...	...
1 VII 2005 ....ESDF		4 361 400	2 284 000	52.4	...	...	...	...	...	...

India - Inde[55]

1 VII 1996 ....ESDF		942 156 780	252 335 381	26.8	487 475 000[32]	134 819 000[32]	27.7	452 065 000[32]	121 947 000[32]	27.0
1 VII 1997 ....ESDF		960 550 440	259 230 163	27.0	497 960 000[32]	136 329 000[32]	27.4	461 832 000[32]	122 577 000[32]	26.5
1 VII 1998 ....ESDF		979 050 965	266 283 953	27.2	507 167 000[32]	139 952 000[32]	27.6	470 914 000[32]	125 912 000[32]	26.7
1 VII 1999 ....ESDF		997 644 935	273 525 428	27.4	516 309 000[32]	143 671 000[32]	27.8	480 121 000[32]	129 323 000[32]	26.9
1 VII 2000 ....ESDF		1 016 320 137	280 992 154	27.6	525 366 000[32]	147 504 000[32]	28.1	489 459 000[32]	132 826 000[32]	27.1
1 III 2001[56] ....CDFC		1 028 610 328	286 119 689	27.8	532 156 772	150 554 098	28.3	496 453 556	135 565 591	27.3

6. Total and urban population by sex: 1996 - 2005
Population totale et population urbaine selon le sexe: 1996 - 2005 (continued - suite)

Continent, country or area, and date / Continent, pays ou zone et date	Code[a]	Both sexes - Les deux sexes			Male - Masculin			Female - Féminin		
		Total	Urban - Urbaine		Total	Urban - Urbaine		Total	Urban - Urbaine	
			Number Nombre	Percent P.100		Number Nombre	Percent P.100		Number Nombre	Percent P.100

ASIA - ASIE

India - Inde[55]
1 VII 2001 ....ESDF		1 035 066 015	288 732 422	27.9	534 317 000[32]	151 355 000[32]	28.3	498 931 000[32]	136 357 000[32]	27.3
1 VII 2002 ....ESDF		1 050 640 000	294 858 000	28.1	543 188 000	155 043 000	28.5	507 452 000	139 815 000	27.6
1 VII 2003 ....ESDF		1 068 214 000	302 015 000	28.3	552 085 000	158 728 000	28.8	516 129 000	143 287 000	27.8
1 VII 2004 ....ESDF		1 085 600 000	309 189 000	28.5	560 895 000	162 413 000	29.0	524 705 000	146 776 000	28.0

Indonesia - Indonésie
1 VII 1996 ....ESDJ		198 320 000	73 640 300[32]	37.1	...	...	...	...	...	...
1 VII 1997 ....ESDJ		201 353 100	76 914 000[32]	38.2	100 206 800	...	...	101 146 300	...	...
1 VII 1998 ....ESDJ		204 392 500	80 275 300[32]	39.3	101 719 200	...	...	102 673 300	...	...
1 VII 1999 ....ESDJ		207 437 100	83 718 400[32]	40.4	103 234 400	...	...	104 202 700	...	...
30 VI 2000[57] ....CDFC		206 264 595	86 601 850	42.0	103 417 180	43 368 496	41.9	102 847 415	43 233 354	42.0
1 VII 2003 ....ESDJ		214 251 300	...	...	107 335 600	...	...	106 915 700	...	...

Iran (Islamic Republic of) - Iran (République islamique d')
23 X 1996 ....CDJC		60 055 488	36 817 789	61.3	30 515 159	18 805 023	61.6	29 540 329	18 012 766	61.0
1 VII 1997[58] ....ESDJ		60 938 837	37 826 305	62.1	31 011 770	19 249 804	62.1	29 927 067	18 576 501	62.1
1 VII 1998[58] ....ESDJ		61 835 591	38 839 280	62.8	...	...	...	...	...	...
1 VII 1999[58] ....ESDJ		62 745 540	39 856 570	63.5	...	...	...	...	...	...
1 VII 2000[58] ....ESDJ		63 663 942	40 873 494	64.2	...	...	...	...	...	...
1 VII 2001[58] ....ESDJ		64 528 159	42 173 587	65.4	...	...	...	...	...	...
1 VII 2002[58] ....ESDJ		65 540 239	43 054 650	65.7	...	...	...	...	...	...
1 VII 2003[58] ....ESDJ		66 480 365	43 892 714	66.0	...	...	...	...	...	...
1 VII 2004[58] ....ESDJ		67 477 499	44 190 104	65.5	34 350 656	22 669 195	66.0	33 126 843	21 520 909	65.0
1 VII 2005[59] ....ESDJ		68 467 369	45 650 230	66.7	34 801 582	23 316 275	67.0	33 665 787	22 333 955	66.3

Iraq
1 VII 1996 ....ESDF		21 124 000	...	...	10 843 000	...	...	10 281 000	...	...
1 VII 1997 ....ESDF		22 046 000	...	...	10 987 000	...	...	11 059 000	...	...
16 X 1997[60] ....CDFC		19 184 543	12 945 776	67.5	9 536 570	6 466 325	67.8	9 647 973	6 479 451	67.2
1 VII 1998 ....ESDF		22 702 000	...	...	11 328 000	...	...	11 374 000	...	...
1 VII 1999 ....ESDF		23 382 000	...	...	11 682 000	...	...	11 700 000	...	...
1 VII 2000 ....ESDF		24 086 000	...	...	12 047 000	...	...	12 039 000	...	...
1 VII 2001 ....ESDF		24 813 000	...	...	12 424 000	...	...	12 389 000	...	...
1 VII 2002 ....ESDF		25 565 000	...	...	12 814 000	...	...	12 751 000	...	...
1 VII 2003 ....ESDF		26 340 000	...	...	13 216 000	...	...	13 124 000	...	...
1 VII 2004 ....ESDF		27 139 000	...	...	13 629 000	...	...	13 510 000	...	...
1 VII 2005 ....ESDF		27 963 000	...	...	14 055 000	...	...	13 908 000	...	...

Israel - Israël[61]
1 VII 1996 ....ESDJ		5 685 100	5 166 000	90.9	...	...	...	...	...	...
1 VII 1997 ....ESDJ		5 829 000	5 294 100	90.8	2 875 400	2 599 900	90.4	2 953 500	2 694 300	91.2
1 VII 1998 ....ESDJ		5 970 700	5 418 400	90.7	...	...	...	...	...	...
1 VII 1999 ....ESDJ		6 125 300	5 554 200	90.7	3 021 743			3 103 533		
1 VII 2000 ....ESDJ		6 289 200	5 696 100	90.6	3 102 400	2 797 800	90.2	3 186 800	2 898 300	90.9
1 VII 2001 ....ESDJ		6 439 000	5 900 700	91.6	3 176 600	2 900 200	91.3	3 262 500	3 000 500	92.0
1 VII 2002 ....ESDJ		6 569 900	6 017 300	91.6	3 241 700	2 958 200	91.3	3 328 200	3 059 100	91.9
1 VII 2003 ....ESDJ		6 689 700	6 122 400	91.5	3 301 800	3 010 900	91.2	3 387 900	3 111 600	91.8
1 VII 2004 ....ESDJ		6 809 000	6 226 900	91.5	3 362 000	3 063 600	91.1	3 447 000	3 163 300	91.8
1 VII 2005 ....ESDJ		6 930 128	6 359 940	91.8	3 423 132	3 131 229	91.5	3 506 996	3 228 711	92.1

Japan - Japon[62]
1 VII 1996 ....ESDF		125 757 000	...	...	61 646 000	...	...	64 112 000	...	...
1 VII 1997 ....ESDF		126 057 000	...	...	61 782 000	...	...	64 275 000	...	...
1 VII 1998 ....ESDF		126 400 000	...	...	61 910 000	...	...	64 490 000	...	...
1 VII 1999 ....ESDF		126 631 000	...	...	61 996 000	...	...	64 635 000	...	...
1 VII 2000 ....ESDF		126 843 000	...	...	62 063 000	...	...	64 780 000	...	...
1 X 2000 ....CDFC		126 925 843	99 865 289	78.7	62 110 764	49 005 691	78.9	64 815 079	50 859 598	78.5
1 VII 2001 ....ESDF		127 149 000	...	...	62 178 000	...	...	64 971 000	...	...
1 VII 2002 ....ESDF		127 445 000	...	...	62 278 000	...	...	65 167 000	...	...
1 VII 2003 ....ESDF		127 718 000	...	...	62 370 000	...	...	65 348 000	...	...
1 VII 2004 ....ESDF		127 761 000	...	...	62 355 000	...	...	65 406 000	...	...
1 VII 2005 ....ESDF		127 773 000	...	...	62 332 000	...	...	65 441 000	...	...
1 X 2005* ....CDFC		127 756 815	...	...	62 340 864	...	...	65 415 951	...	...

6. Total and urban population by sex: 1996 - 2005
Population totale et population urbaine selon le sexe: 1996 - 2005 (continued - suite)

Continent, country or area, and date / Continent, pays ou zone et date	Code[a]	Both sexes - Les deux sexes Total	Urban - Urbaine Number Nombre	Urban - Urbaine Percent P.100	Male - Masculin Total	Urban - Urbaine Number Nombre	Urban - Urbaine Percent P.100	Female - Féminin Total	Urban - Urbaine Number Nombre	Urban - Urbaine Percent P.100
ASIA - ASIE										
Jordan - Jordanie[63]										
1 VII 1996	ESDF	4 383 000	3 416 655[32]	78.0	...	...	...	...	...	...
1 VII 1997	ESDF	4 506 000	3 549 000[32]	78.8	...	...	...	...	...	...
1 VII 1998	ESDF	4 623 000	3 681 635[32]	79.6	2 445 600[32]	...	...	2 232 275[32]	...	...
1 VII 1999	ESDF	4 738 000	3 799 685[32]	80.2	2 524 000[32]	...	...	2 303 850[32]	...	...
1 VII 2000	ESDF	4 857 000	3 910 997[32]	80.5	2 598 800[32]	...	...	2 370 700[32]	...	...
1 VII 2001	ESDF	4 978 000	4 021 965[32]	80.8	2 672 817[32]	...	...	2 437 682[32]	...	...
1 VII 2002	ESDF	5 098 000	4 136 080[32]	81.1	2 748 675[32]	...	...	2 506 825[32]	...	...
1 VII 2003	ESDF	5 230 000	4 253 935[32]	81.3	2 826 658[32]	...	...	2 577 843[32]	...	...
1 X 2004	CDFC	5 103 639	3 997 383	78.3	2 626 287	2 055 431	78.3	2 477 352	1 941 952	78.4
1 VII 2005*	ESDF	5 473 000	...	...	2 821 100	...	...	2 651 900	...	...
Kazakhstan										
1 VII 1996	ESDF	15 578 228	8 682 790	55.7	7 738 053[32]	4 175 974[32]	54.0	8 182 844[32]	4 606 539[32]	56.3
1 VII 1997	ESDF	15 334 405	8 567 329	55.9	7 393 786	4 014 495	54.3	7 940 619	4 552 834	57.3
1 VII 1998	ESDF	15 072 983	8 434 080	56.0	7 263 077	3 945 189	54.3	7 809 906	4 488 891	57.5
26 II 1999	CDJC	14 953 126	8 377 303	56.0	7 201 785	3 918 556	54.4	7 751 341	4 458 747	57.5
1 VII 1999	ESDF	14 928 373	8 406 019	56.3	7 190 238	3 933 622	54.7	7 738 135	4 472 397	57.8
1 VII 2000	ESDF	14 883 626	8 405 483	56.5	7 168 613	3 933 997	54.9	7 715 013	4 471 486	58.0
1 VII 2001	ESDF	14 858 335	8 421 366	56.7	7 156 582	3 942 353	55.1	7 701 753	4 479 013	58.2
1 VII 2002	ESDF	14 858 948	8 443 242	56.8	7 156 816	3 952 649	55.2	7 702 132	4 490 593	58.3
1 VII 2003	ESDF	14 909 018	8 487 697	56.9	7 179 583	3 971 520	55.3	7 729 435	4 516 177	58.4
1 VII 2004	ESDF	15 012 985	8 566 447	57.1	7 227 960	4 005 199	55.4	7 785 025	4 561 248	58.6
1 VII 2005	ESDF	15 147 029	8 655 586	57.1	7 290 852	4 044 092	55.5	7 856 177	4 611 494	58.7
Korea (Republic of) - Corée (République de)										
1 VII 1996	ESDF	45 545 681	...	...	22 924 512	...	...	22 600 169	...	...
1 VII 1997	ESDF	45 953 580	...	...	23 148 092	...	...	22 805 488	...	...
1 VII 1998	ESDF	46 286 503	...	...	23 295 727	...	...	22 990 776	...	...
1 VII 1999	ESDF	46 616 677	...	...	23 457 837	...	...	23 158 840	...	...
1 VII 2000	ESDF	47 008 111	...	...	23 666 769	...	...	23 341 342	...	...
1 XI 2000[64]	CDFC	46 136 101	36 755 144[65]	79.7	23 158 582	18 484 139[65]	79.8	22 977 519	18 271 005[65]	79.5
1 VII 2001	ESDF	47 353 519	...	...	23 848 450	...	...	23 505 069	...	...
1 VII 2002	ESDF	47 615 132	...	...	23 980 764	...	...	23 634 368	...	...
1 VII 2003	ESDF	47 849 227	...	...	24 105 667	...	...	23 743 560	...	...
1 VII 2004	ESDF	48 082 163	...	...	24 228 209	...	...	23 853 954	...	...
1 VII 2005	ESDF	48 294 143	...	...	24 333 130	...	...	23 961 013	...	...
Kuwait - Koweït										
1 VII 1996	ESDF	1 894 362	...	...	1 142 683	...	...	751 679	...	...
1 VII 1997	ESDF	1 979 689	...	...	1 195 171	...	...	784 518	...	...
1 VII 1998	ESDF	2 027 103	...	...	1 226 774	...	...	800 329	...	...
1 VII 1999	ESDF	2 107 195	...	...	1 278 822	...	...	828 373	...	...
1 VII 2000	ESDF	2 138 115	...	...	1 287 369	...	...	850 746	...	...
1 VII 2001	ESDF	2 182 609	...	...	1 305 391	...	...	877 218	...	...
1 VII 2002	ESDF	2 261 956	...	...	1 355 300	...	...	906 656	...	...
1 VII 2003	ESDF	2 325 440	...	...	1 392 820	...	...	932 620	...	...
1 VII 2004	ESDF	2 390 591	...	...	1 432 051	...	...	958 540	...	...
20 IV 2005*	CDFC	2 213 403	...	...	1 310 067	...	...	903 336	...	...
1 VII 2005	ESDF	2 457 257	...	...	1 472 312	...	...	984 945	...	...
Kyrgyzstan - Kirghizistan										
1 VII 1996	ESDF	4 657 400	1 660 200	35.6	2 293 100	792 300	34.6	2 364 300	867 900	36.7
1 VII 1997	ESDF	4 724 900	1 675 900	35.5	2 328 100	800 500	34.4	2 396 800	875 400	36.5
1 VII 1998	ESDF	4 797 000	1 696 900	35.4	2 365 200	811 200	34.3	2 431 800	885 700	36.4
24 III 1999	CDJC	4 822 938	1 678 623	34.8	2 380 465	802 256	33.7	2 442 473	876 367	35.9
1 VII 1999	ESDF	4 864 600	1 717 100	35.3	2 399 900	821 100	34.2	2 464 700	896 000	36.4
1 VII 2000	ESDF	4 915 300	1 738 800	35.4	2 425 800	831 300	34.3	2 489 500	907 500	36.5
1 VII 2001	ESDF	4 954 800	1 760 600	35.5	2 445 900	841 900	34.4	2 508 900	918 700	36.6
1 VII 2002	ESDF	4 993 200	1 763 600	35.3	2 465 500	843 400	34.2	2 527 700	920 200	36.4
1 VII 2003	ESDF	5 038 600	1 785 700	35.4	2 488 900	854 000	34.3	2 549 700	931 700	36.5
1 VII 2004	ESDF	5 092 800	1 816 400	35.7	2 516 400	868 300	34.5	2 576 400	948 100	36.8
1 VII 2005	ESDF	5 143 500	1 830 400	35.6	2 542 300	875 100	34.4	2 601 200	955 300	36.7

Continent, country or area, and date / Continent, pays ou zone et date	Code[a]	Both sexes - Les deux sexes			Male - Masculin			Female - Féminin		
		Total	Urban - Urbaine		Total	Urban - Urbaine		Total	Urban - Urbaine	
			Number Nombre	Percent P.100		Number Nombre	Percent P.100		Number Nombre	Percent P.100
ASIA - ASIE										
Lao People's Democratic Republic - République démocratique populaire lao										
1 VII 1997[66] ....SSDF		5 087 322	...	...	2 521 009	...	...	2 566 313	...	...
1 VII 1999 ....ESDF		5 091 100	...	...	2 516 100	...	...	2 575 000	...	...
1 VII 2000[67] ....ESDF		5 218 300	...	...	2 579 000	...	...	2 639 300	...	...
1 VII 2001[67] ....ESDF		5 377 000	...	...	2 657 000	...	...	2 720 000	...	...
1 VII 2002[67] ....ESDF		5 526 000	...	...	2 731 000	...	...	2 795 000	...	...
1 VII 2003[67] ....ESDF		5 679 000	...	...	2 807 000	...	...	2 872 000	...	...
1 VII 2004[67] ....ESDF		5 836 000	...	...	2 884 000	...	...	2 952 000	...	...
1 III 2005 ....CDJC		5 621 982	...	...	2 800 551	...	...	2 821 431	...	...
1 VII 2005 ....ESDF		5 679 000	...	...	2 806 400	...	...	2 872 600	...	...
Malaysia - Malaisie										
1 VII 1996 ....ESDF		21 169 048	...	...	10 823 484	...	...	10 345 564	...	...
1 VII 1997 ....ESDF		20 995 951	...	...	10 650 205	...	...	10 345 746	...	...
1 VII 1998 ....ESDF		21 475 488	...	...	10 891 958	...	...	10 583 530	...	...
1 VII 1999 ....ESDF		21 852 454	...	...	11 081 226	...	...	10 771 228	...	...
1 VII 2000 ....ESDF		23 494 891	...	...	11 965 620	...	...	11 529 271	...	...
5 VII 2000[68] ....CDJC		23 274 690	14 426 871	62.0	11 853 432	7 318 396	61.7	11 421 258	7 108 475	62.2
1 VII 2001 ....ESDF		24 012 900	...	...	12 227 400	...	...	11 785 500	...	...
1 VII 2002 ....ESDF		24 526 500	...	...	12 487 100	...	...	12 039 500	...	...
1 VII 2003 ....ESDF		25 048 300	...	...	12 751 900	...	...	12 296 400	...	...
1 VII 2004 ....ESDF		25 580 900	...	...	13 023 300	...	...	12 557 700	...	...
1 VII 2005 ....ESDF		26 127 700	...	...	13 302 800	...	...	12 824 900	...	...
Maldives										
1 VII 1996 ....ESDF		251 152	...	...	127 727	...	...	123 425	...	...
1 VII 1997 ....ESDF		258 678	...	...	131 545	...	...	127 133	...	...
1 VII 1998 ....ESDF		267 464	...	...	135 986	...	...	131 478	...	...
1 VII 1999 ....ESDF		277 579	...	...	141 073	...	...	136 506	...	...
31 III 2000 ....CDFC		270 101	74 069	27.4	137 200	38 559	28.1	132 901	35 510	26.7
1 VII 2000 ....ESDF		271 410	...	...	137 697	...	...	133 713	...	...
1 VII 2001 ....ESDF		275 975	75 680	27.4	140 184	39 398	28.1	135 791	36 282	26.7
1 VII 2002 ....ESDF		280 549	76 934	27.4	142 507	40 051	28.1	138 042	36 884	26.7
1 VII 2003 ....ESDF		285 066	78 173	27.4	144 802	40 695	28.1	140 264	37 477	26.7
1 VII 2004 ....ESDF		289 480	79 383	27.4	147 044	41 326	28.1	142 436	38 058	26.7
1 VII 2005 ....ESDF		293 746	...	...	148 929	...	...	144 817	...	...
Mongolia - Mongolie										
1 VII 1996 ....ESDF		2 255 201	1 166 826	51.7	1 111 715	569 936	51.3	1 143 486	596 890	52.2
1 VII 1997 ....ESDF		2 273 112	1 186 605[69]	52.2	1 119 654	577 519	51.6	1 153 457	609 086	52.8
1 VII 1998 ....ESDF		2 280 750	1 176 278[69]	51.6	1 121 068	568 895	50.7	1 159 682	607 383	52.4
1 VII 1999 ....ESDF		2 332 393	1 264 011	54.2	1 151 534	613 955	53.3	1 180 859	650 057	55.0
5 I 2000 ....CDFC		2 373 493	1 344 516	56.6	1 177 981	657 081	55.8	1 195 512	687 435	57.5
1 VII 2000 ....ESDF		2 390 491	1 360 746	56.9	1 185 039	664 991	56.1	1 205 452	695 756	57.7
1 VII 2001 ....ESDF		2 425 016	1 381 869	57.0	1 195 232	672 397	56.3	1 229 784	709 472	57.7
1 VII 2002 ....ESDF		2 458 963	1 403 859	57.1	1 205 717	679 229	56.3	1 253 245	724 630	57.8
1 VII 2003 ....ESDF		2 489 702	1 442 590	57.9	1 219 870	697 720	57.2	1 269 832	744 870	58.7
1 VII 2004 ....ESDF		2 518 572	1 481 205	58.8	1 231 996	715 111	58.0	1 286 575	766 094	59.5
1 VII 2005 ....ESDF		2 547 751	1 511 600[69]	59.3	1 219 950[70]	726 818	59.6	1 280 883[70]	784 782	61.3
Myanmar										
1 VII 1997* ....ESDF		46 402 000	...	...	23 039 000	...	...	23 363 000	...	...
Nepal - Népal										
1 VII 1996 ....ESDJ		20 831 644	2 207 967	10.6	10 393 913	1 138 641	11.0	10 437 731	1 069 326	10.2
1 VII 1999 ....ESDJ		22 367 048	...	...	11 167 503	...	...	11 199 545	...	...
22 VI 2001[71] ....CDJC		23 151 423	...	...	11 563 921	...	...	11 587 502	...	...
1 VII 2001 ....ESDJ		23 151 423	...	...	11 563 921	...	...	11 587 502	...	...
1 VII 2002 ....ESDJ		23 701 451	...	...	11 845 495	...	...	11 855 956	...	...
1 VII 2003 ....ESDJ		24 249 996	...	...	12 126 262	...	...	12 123 734	...	...
1 VII 2004 ....ESDJ		24 797 059	...	...	12 406 222	...	...	12 390 837	...	...
1 VII 2005 ....ESDJ		25 342 638	...	...	12 685 375	...	...	12 657 263	...	...

Continent, country or area, and date / Continent, pays ou zone et date	Code[a]	Both sexes - Les deux sexes Total	Urban - Urbaine Number Nombre	Urban - Urbaine Percent P.100	Male - Masculin Total	Urban - Urbaine Number Nombre	Urban - Urbaine Percent P.100	Female - Féminin Total	Urban - Urbaine Number Nombre	Urban - Urbaine Percent P.100
ASIA - ASIE										
Occupied Palestinian Territory - Territoire palestinien occupé										
1 VII 1997 ....ESDF		2 783 084	1 992 780[72]	71.6	1 404 481	...	...	1 378 603	...	...
9 XII 1997[73] ....CDFC		2 601 669	...		1 322 264	...	...	1 279 405	...	...
1 VII 1998 ....ESDF		2 897 113	2 074 825[72]	71.6	1 462 821	...	...	1 434 292	...	...
1 VII 1999 ....ESDF		3 019 158	2 162 657[72]	71.6	1 525 297	...	...	1 493 861	...	...
1 VII 2000 ....ESDF		3 149 448	2 256 470[72]	71.6	1 592 028	...	...	1 557 419	...	...
1 VII 2001 ....ESDF		3 275 389	2 346 926[72]	71.7	1 656 513	...	...	1 618 876	...	...
1 VII 2002 ....ESDF		3 394 046	2 432 044[72]	71.7	1 717 239	...	...	1 676 807	...	...
1 VII 2003 ....ESDF		3 514 868	2 519 018[72]	71.7	1 779 088	...	...	1 735 780	...	...
1 VII 2004 ....ESDF		3 637 529	2 607 633[72]	71.7	1 841 894	...	...	1 795 635	...	...
1 VII 2005 ....ESDF		3 762 005	2 697 879[72]	71.7	1 905 642	...	...	1 856 363	...	...
Oman										
1 VII 1997 ....ESDF		2 255 609	...	...	1 320 084	...	...	935 525	...	...
1 VII 1998 ....ESDF		2 287 642	...	...	1 333 557	...	...	954 085	...	...
1 VII 1999 ....ESDF		2 325 438	...	...	1 365 775	...	...	959 663	...	...
1 VII 2000 ....ESDF		2 401 256	...	...	1 401 589	...	...	999 667	...	...
1 VII 2001 ....ESDF		2 477 687	...	...	1 451 041	...	...	1 026 646	...	...
7 XII 2003 ....CDFC		2 340 815	1 673 480	71.5	1 313 239	950 471	72.4	1 027 576	723 009	70.4
1 VII 2004 ....ESDF		2 415 576	...	...	1 360 891	...	...	1 054 685	...	...
1 VII 2005 ....ESDF		2 508 837	...	...	1 458 845	...	...	1 049 992	...	...
Pakistan[74]										
2 III 1998 ....CDFC		130 579 571	42 458 339	32.5	67 840 137	22 419 286	33.0	62 739 434	20 039 053	31.9
1 VII 1998 ....ESDF		131 510 000	42 910 000	32.6	68 290 000	22 100 000	32.4	63 220 000	20 810 000	32.9
1 VII 1999 ....ESDF		138 945 000	...	...	72 300 000	...	...	66 645 000	...	...
1 VII 2001 ....ESDF		141 765 000	...	...	73 770 000	...	...	67 995 000	...	...
1 VII 2002 ....ESDF		144 560 000	...	...	75 225 000	...	...	69 335 000	...	...
1 VII 2003 ....ESDF		147 335 000	...	...	76 670 000	...	...	70 665 000	...	...
1 VII 2004 ....ESDF		150 135 000	...	...	78 125 000	...	...	72 010 000	...	...
1 VII 2005 ....ESDF		153 455 000	...	...	79 745 000	...	...	73 710 000	...	...
Philippines										
1 VII 1996 ....ESDJ		71 899 136	...	...	35 251 544[82]	...	...	34 700 266[82]	...	...
1 VII 1997 ....ESDJ		73 526 941	...	...	36 051 342[82]	...	...	35 498 448[82]	...	...
1 VII 1998 ....ESDJ		75 154 743	...	...	36 851 141[82]	...	...	36 296 635[82]	...	...
1 VII 1999 ....ESDJ		76 782 548	...	...	37 650 939[82]	...	...	37 094 817[82]	...	...
1 V 2000 ....CDJC		76 504 077	...	...	38 524 267	...	...	37 979 810	...	...
1 VII 2000 ....ESDJ		76 348 114	...	...	38 452 927	...	...	37 895 187	...	...
1 VII 2001 ....ESDJ		77 925 894	...	...	39 242 185	...	...	38 683 709	...	...
1 VII 2002 ....ESDJ		79 503 675	...	...	40 031 449	...	...	39 472 226	...	...
1 VII 2003 ....ESDJ		81 081 457	...	...	40 820 706	...	...	40 260 751	...	...
Qatar										
1 VII 1996 ....ESDF		510 401	...	...	340 517	...	...	169 884	...	...
1 III 1997 ....CDFC		522 023	...	...	342 459	...	...	179 564	...	...
1 VII 1997 ....ESDF		529 823	...	...	353 474	...	...	176 349	...	...
1 VII 1998 ....ESDF		557 335	...	...	371 829	...	...	185 506	...	...
1 VII 1999 ....ESDF		586 275	...	...	391 136	...	...	195 139	...	...
1 VII 2000 ....ESDF		616 719	...	...	411 447	...	...	205 272	...	...
1 VII 2001 ....ESDF		648 744	...	...	432 812	...	...	215 932	...	...
1 VII 2002 ....ESDF		682 434	...	...	455 289	...	...	227 145	...	...
1 VII 2003 ....ESDF		717 766	...	...	478 860	...	...	238 906	...	...
16 III 2004 ....CDFC		744 029	...	...	496 382	...	...	247 647	...	...
1 VII 2004 ....ESDF		756 486	...	...	504 693	...	...	251 793	...	...
1 VII 2005 ....ESDF		796 186	...	...	531 056	...	...	265 130	...	...
Saudi Arabia - Arabie saoudite										
1 VII 1996 ....ESDF		18 582 023	...	...	10 360 675	...	...	8 221 349	...	...
1 VII 1997 ....ESDF		19 038 517	...	...	10 606 265	...	...	8 432 251	...	...
1 VII 1998 ....ESDF		19 506 225	...	...	10 857 670	...	...	8 648 555	...	...
1 VII 1999 ....ESDF		19 985 423	...	...	11 115 026	...	...	8 870 397	...	...
1 VII 2000 ....ESDF		20 476 393	...	...	11 378 473	...	...	9 097 920	...	...
1 VII 2001 ....ESDF		20 979 424	...	...	11 648 157	...	...	9 331 268	...	...
1 VII 2002 ....ESDF		21 494 814	...	...	11 924 224	...	...	9 570 590	...	...
1 VII 2003 ....ESDF		22 022 864	...	...	12 206 825	...	...	9 816 039	...	...

Continent, country or area, and date / Continent, pays ou zone et date	Code[a]	Both sexes - Les deux sexes			Male - Masculin			Female - Féminin		
		Total	Urban - Urbaine		Total	Urban - Urbaine		Total	Urban - Urbaine	
			Number Nombre	Percent P.100		Number Nombre	Percent P.100		Number Nombre	Percent P.100
ASIA - ASIE										
Saudi Arabia - Arabie saoudite										
1 VII 2004	ESDF	22 563 886	...	...	12 493 910	...	...	10 069 976	...	...
15 IX 2004	CDFC	22 678 262	...	...	12 557 240	...	...	10 121 022	...	...
1 VII 2005	ESDF	23 118 994	...	...	12 791 330	...	...	10 327 664	...	...
Singapore - Singapour										
1 VII 1996	ESDJ	3 068 100	...	...	1 540 000	...	...	1 528 100	...	...
1 VII 1997	ESDJ	3 123 400	...	...	1 565 800	...	...	1 557 700	...	...
1 VII 1998	ESDJ	3 180 000	...	...	1 591 800	...	...	1 588 200	...	...
1 VII 1999	ESDJ	3 229 700	...	...	1 614 800	...	...	1 614 900	...	...
1 VII 2000[75]	CDFC	4 017 700	...	...	2 061 800	...	...	1 955 900	...	...
1 VII 2000	ESDJ	3 273 400	...	...	1 634 700	...	...	1 638 700	...	...
1 VII 2001	ESDJ	3 325 900	...	...	1 658 600	...	...	1 667 300	...	...
1 VII 2002	ESDJ	3 382 900	...	...	1 684 300	...	...	1 698 600	...	...
1 VII 2004	ESDJ	3 486 900	...	...	1 732 800	...	...	1 754 100	...	...
Sri Lanka										
1 VII 1996	ESDF	*18 315 000*	...	...	*9 336 000*	...	...	*8 979 000*	...	...
1 VII 1997	ESDF	*18 552 000*	...	...	*9 457 000*	...	...	*9 095 000*	...	...
1 VII 1998	ESDF	*18 774 000*	...	...	*9 570 000*	...	...	*9 204 000*	...	...
1 VII 1999	ESDF	*19 043 000*	...	...	*9 707 000*	...	...	*9 336 000*	...	...
1 VII 2001	ESDF	*18 732 400*	...	...	*9 267 300*	...	...	*9 465 100*	...	...
17 VII 2001*[76]	CDFC	16 864 544	2 467 171	14.6	8 343 964	1 246 983	14.9	8 520 580	1 220 188	14.3
1 VII 2002	ESDF	*19 007 410*	...	...	*9 402 966*	...	...	*9 604 444*	...	...
1 VII 2003*	ESDF	*19 252 000*	...	...	*9 510 000*	...	...	*9 742 000*	...	...
1 VII 2004*	ESDF	*19 462 000*	...	...	*9 615 000*	...	...	*9 847 000*	...	...
1 VII 2005*	ESDF	*19 668 000*	...	...	*9 718 000*	...	...	*9 950 000*	...	...
Syrian Arab Republic - République arabe syrienne[77]										
1 VII 1996	ESDF	*14 619 000*	...	...	*7 477 000*	...	...	*7 142 000*	...	...
1 VII 1997	ESDF	*15 100 000*	...	...	*7 723 000*	...	...	*7 377 000*	...	...
1 VII 1998	ESDF	*15 597 000*	...	...	*7 965 000*	...	...	*7 632 000*	...	...
1 VII 1999	ESDF	*16 110 000*	...	...	*8 240 000*	...	...	*7 870 000*	...	...
1 VII 2000	ESDF	*16 320 000*	...	...	*8 343 000*	...	...	*7 977 000*	...	...
1 VII 2001	ESDF	*16 720 000*	*8 376 000*	*50.1*	*8 552 000*	...	...	*8 168 000*	...	...
1 VII 2002	ESDF	*17 130 000*	*8 599 000*	*50.2*	*8 763 000*	*4 439 000*	*50.7*	*8 367 000*	*4 324 000*	*51.7*
1 VII 2003	ESDF	*17 550 000*	*8 806 000*	*50.2*	*8 979 000*	*4 541 000*	*50.6*	*8 571 000*	*4 265 000*	*49.8*
1 VII 2004	ESDF	*17 980 000*	*9 022 000*	*50.2*	*9 199 000*	*4 652 000*	*50.6*	*8 781 000*	*4 370 000*	*49.8*
1 VII 2005	ESDF	*18 138 000*	...	...	*9 268 000*	...	...	*8 870 000*	...	...
Tajikistan - Tadjikistan										
1 VII 1999	ESDF	6 064 048	1 609 723	26.5	3 036 700	800 020	26.3	3 027 349	809 703	26.7
20 I 2000*	CDFC	6 127 000	...	...	3 082 000	...	...	3 045 000	...	...
1 VII 2000	ESDF	6 188 366	1 642 401	26.5	3 099 855	817 233	26.4	3 088 512	825 168	26.7
1 VII 2001	ESDF	6 312 757	1 675 211	26.5	3 163 111	834 679	26.4	3 149 646	840 533	26.7
1 VII 2002	ESDF	6 441 009	1 705 240	26.5	3 228 657	850 898	26.4	3 212 352	854 343	26.6
1 VII 2003	ESDF	6 573 225	1 738 839	26.5	3 296 212	868 891	26.4	3 277 013	869 948	26.5
1 VII 2004	ESDF	6 710 200	1 774 850	26.5	...	...	...	...	...	...
1 VII 2005	ESDF	6 850 350	1 808 350	26.4	...	...	...	...	...	...
Thailand - Thaïlande										
1 VII 1996	ESDJ	*60 003 000*	...	...	*29 963 000*	...	...	*30 040 000*	...	...
1 VII 1997	ESDJ	*60 602 000*	...	...	*30 245 000*	...	...	*30 357 000*	...	...
1 VII 1998	ESDJ	*61 155 888*	...	...	*30 443 716*	...	...	*30 712 172*	...	...
1 VII 1999	ESDJ	*61 563 980*	...	...	*30 620 906*	...	...	*30 943 074*	...	...
1 IV 2000	CDJC	60 617 200	18 833 700	31.1	29 850 100	9 085 400	30.4	30 767 100	9 748 300	31.7
1 VII 2000	ESDJ	*61 770 259*	...	...	*30 687 612*	...	...	*31 082 647*	...	...
1 VII 2001	ESDJ	*62 914 000*	...	...	*31 348 000*	...	...	*31 566 000*	...	...
1 VII 2002	ESDJ	*63 482 287*	*20 731 494*	*32.7*	*31 623 509*	*10 072 055*	*31.8*	*31 858 778*	*10 659 439*	*33.5*
1 VII 2003	ESDJ	*64 018 857*	*20 990 626*	*32.8*	...	...	...	...	...	...
1 VII 2004	ESDJ	*64 177 484*	*19 300 414*	*30.1*	...	...	...	...	...	...
1 VII 2005	ESDJ	*64 838 628*	*19 538 420*	*30.1*	...	...	...	...	...	...

6. Total and urban population by sex: 1996 - 2005
Population totale et population urbaine selon le sexe: 1996 - 2005 (continued - suite)

Continent, country or area, and date / Continent, pays ou zone et date	Code[a]	Both sexes - Les deux sexes			Male - Masculin			Female - Féminin		
		Total	Urban - Urbaine		Total	Urban - Urbaine		Total	Urban - Urbaine	
			Number Nombre	Percent P.100		Number Nombre	Percent P.100		Number Nombre	Percent P.100
ASIA - ASIE										
Timor-Leste										
11 VII 2004*	CDFC	924 642	...	...	467 757	...	...	456 885	...	...
Turkey - Turquie										
1 VII 1996	ESDF	62 909 000	35 627 615	56.6	31 808 000	...	...	31 101 000	...	...
1 VII 1997	ESDF	64 064 000	36 670 310	57.2	32 383 000	...	...	31 682 000	...	...
1 VII 1998	ESDF	65 215 000	37 724 702	57.8	32 956 000	...	...	32 259 000	...	...
1 VII 1999	ESDF	66 350 000	38 783 705	58.5	33 521 000	...	...	32 829 000	...	...
1 VII 2000	ESDF	67 420 000	39 818 088	59.1	34 053 000	...	...	33 367 000	...	...
22 X 2000	CDFC	67 803 927	44 006 274	64.9	34 346 735	22 427 603	65.3	33 457 192	21 578 671	64.5
1 VII 2001	ESDF	68 365 000	40 790 867	59.7	34 519 000	...	...	33 846 000	...	...
1 VII 2002	ESDF	69 302 000	41 770 289	60.3	34 981 000	...	...	34 320 000	...	...
1 VII 2003	ESDF	70 231 000	42 756 206	60.9	35 441 000	...	...	34 790 000	...	...
1 VII 2004	ESDF	71 152 000	43 748 475	61.5	35 897 000	...	...	35 255 000	...	...
1 VII 2005	ESDF	72 065 000	44 746 949	62.1	36 349 000	...	...	35 716 000	...	...
United Arab Emirates - Émirats arabes unis[78]										
1 VII 1996	ESDF	2 443 000	...	...	1 625 000	...	...	818 000	...	...
1 VII 1997	ESDF	2 624 000	...	...	1 755 000	...	...	869 000	...	...
1 VII 1998	ESDF	2 776 000	...	...	1 861 000	...	...	915 000	...	...
1 VII 1999	ESDF	2 938 000	...	...	1 975 000	...	...	963 000	...	...
Uzbekistan - Ouzbékistan										
1 VII 1996	ESDF	23 130 400	8 817 600	38.1	11 487 300	4 335 600	37.7	11 643 100	4 482 000	38.5
1 VII 1997	ESDF	23 560 400	8 931 400	37.9	11 710 400	4 394 700	37.5	11 850 000	4 536 700	38.3
1 VII 1998	ESDF	24 051 000	9 109 700	37.9	...	...	...	...	...	...
1 VII 1999	ESDF	23 953 922	9 037 904	37.7	11 913 994	4 450 641	37.4	12 039 928	4 587 263	38.1
1 VII 2000	ESDF	24 650 415	9 195 435	37.3	12 278 626	4 538 871	37.0	12 371 789	4 656 564	37.6
1 VII 2001	ESDF	24 964 433	9 256 101	37.1	12 442 510	4 573 055	36.8	12 521 923	4 683 046	37.4
Viet Nam										
1 VII 1996	ESDF	73 156 700	15 419 900	21.1	35 857 300	...	...	37 299 400	...	...
1 VII 1997	ESDF	74 306 900	16 835 400	22.7	36 473 100	...	...	37 833 800	...	...
1 VII 1998	ESDF	75 456 300	17 464 600	23.1	37 059 700	...	...	38 366 600	...	...
1 IV 1999	CDFC	76 323 173	18 076 823	23.7	37 469 117	8 825 112	23.6	38 854 056	9 251 711	23.8
1 VII 1999	ESDF	76 596 700	18 081 600	23.6	37 662 100	...	...	38 934 600	...	...
1 VII 2000	ESDF	77 635 400	18 771 900	24.2	38 166 400	...	...	39 469 000	...	...
1 VII 2001	ESDF	78 685 800	19 469 300	24.7	38 684 200	...	...	40 001 600	...	...
1 VII 2002	ESDF	79 727 379	20 022 142	25.1	39 197 378	...	...	40 530 001	...	...
1 VII 2003	ESDF	80 902 400	20 869 500	25.8	39 755 400	...	...	41 147 000	...	...
1 VII 2004	ESDF	82 031 700	21 737 200	26.5	40 310 500	...	...	41 721 200	...	...
1 VII 2005	ESDF	83 106 300	22 336 800	26.9	40 846 200	...	...	42 260 100	...	...
Yemen - Yémen										
1 VII 1996	ESDF	15 915 000	3 913 000	24.6	7 943 000	...	...	7 972 000	...	...
1 VII 1997	ESDF	16 484 000	4 130 000	25.1	8 229 000	...	...	8 255 000	...	...
1 VII 1998	ESDF	17 072 000	...	...	8 532 000	...	...	8 540 000	...	...
1 VII 1999	ESDF	17 671 000	...	...	8 837 000	...	...	8 834 000	...	...
1 VII 2000	ESDF	18 261 000	4 802 000	26.3	9 143 000	2 587 000	28.3	9 118 000	2 215 000	24.3
1 VII 2001*	ESDF	18 863 000	...	...	9 448 000	...	...	9 415 000	...	...
1 VII 2002*	ESDF	19 495 000	...	...	9 772 000	...	...	9 723 000	...	...
16 XII 2004	CDFC	19 685 161	5 637 756	28.6	10 036 953	3 012 256	30.0	9 648 208	2 625 500	27.2
EUROPE										
Albania - Albanie										
1 VII 1996	ESDF	3 075 545	1 186 360	38.6	...	...	...	...	...	...
1 VII 1997	ESDF	3 074 832	1 211 925	39.4	...	...	...	...	...	...
1 VII 1998	ESDF	3 055 331	1 227 208	40.2	...	...	...	...	...	...
1 VII 1999	ESDF	3 053 831	1 234 975	40.4	...	...	...	...	...	...
1 VII 2000	ESDF	3 060 908	1 249 919	40.8	...	...	...	...	...	...
1 IV 2001	CDFC	3 069 300	1 292 800	42.1	1 530 500	...	...	1 538 800	...	...
1 VII 2001	ESDF	3 073 733	1 268 370	41.3	...	...	...	...	...	...
1 VII 2002	ESDF	3 093 465	1 347 871	43.6	1 542 211	625 060	40.5	1 551 254	722 811	46.6
1 VII 2003	ESDF	3 111 163	1 375 367	44.2	1 550 728	636 985	41.1	1 560 435	738 382	47.3

6. Total and urban population by sex: 1996 - 2005
Population totale et population urbaine selon le sexe: 1996 - 2005 (continued - suite)

Continent, country or area, and date / Continent, pays ou zone et date	Code[a]	Both sexes - Les deux sexes Total	Urban - Urbaine Number Nombre	Urban - Urbaine Percent P.100	Male - Masculin Total	Urban - Urbaine Number Nombre	Urban - Urbaine Percent P.100	Female - Féminin Total	Urban - Urbaine Number Nombre	Urban - Urbaine Percent P.100
EUROPE										
Albania - Albanie										
1 VII 2004 ....ESDF		3 127 263	1 406 443	45.0	1 558 376	661 335	42.4	1 568 887	745 108	47.5
1 VII 2005 ....ESDF		3 142 065	1 468 522	46.7	1 565 316	671 848	42.9	1 576 749	796 864	50.5
Andorra - Andorre[19]										
1 VII 1997 ....ESDJ		65 592	...	...	34 387	...	...	32 705	...	...
1 VII 1998 ....ESDJ		65 924	...	...	34 463	...	...	31 461	...	...
1 VII 1999 ....ESDJ		65 908	...	...	34 351	...	...	31 557	...	...
1 VII 2000 ....CDFC		66 089	...	...	34 344	...	...	31 745	...	...
1 VII 2000 ....ESDJ		66 089	...	...	34 344	...	...	31 745	...	...
1 VII 2001 ....ESDJ		66 087	...	...	34 356	...	...	31 731	...	...
1 VII 2002 ....ESDJ		66 120	...	...	34 257	...	...	31 863	...	...
1 VII 2003 ....ESDJ		69 840	...	...	36 258	...	...	33 582	...	...
1 VII 2004 ....ESDJ		74 885	...	...	38 990	...	...	35 895	...	...
Austria - Autriche										
1 VII 1996 ....ESDJ		7 959 016	...	...	3 840 484	...	...	4 118 532	...	...
1 VII 1997 ....ESDJ		7 968 041	...	...	3 846 162	...	...	4 121 879	...	...
1 VII 1998 ....ESDJ		7 976 789	...	...	3 852 166	...	...	4 124 623	...	...
1 VII 1999 ....ESDJ		7 992 323	...	...	3 862 180	...	...	4 130 143	...	...
1 VII 2000 ....ESDJ		8 011 566	...	...	3 874 717	...	...	4 136 849	...	...
15 V 2001 ....CDJC		8 032 926	5 368 693	66.8	3 889 189	2 564 828	65.9	4 143 737	2 803 865	67.7
1 VII 2001 ....ESDJ		8 043 046	...	...	3 894 129	...	...	4 148 917	...	...
1 VII 2002 ....ESDJ		8 083 797	...	...	3 918 990	...	...	4 164 807	...	...
1 VII 2003 ....ESDJ		8 117 754	...	...	3 938 582	...	...	4 179 172	...	...
1 VII 2004 ....ESDJ		8 174 733	...	...	3 969 190	...	...	4 205 543	...	...
1 VII 2005 ....ESDJ		8 233 306	...	...	4 001 861	...	...	4 231 445	...	...
Belarus - Bélarus										
1 VII 1996 ....ESDF		10 250 250	7 080 710	69.1	4 784 616	3 324 087	69.5	5 465 634	3 756 623	68.7
1 VII 1997 ....ESDF		10 219 982	7 106 247	69.5	4 769 223	3 332 777	69.9	5 450 759	3 773 470	69.2
1 VII 1998 ....ESDF		10 191 479	7 140 980	70.1	4 753 951	3 345 660	70.4	5 437 528	3 795 320	69.8
16 II 1999 ....CDJC		10 045 237	6 961 516	69.3	4 717 621	3 279 196	69.5	5 327 616	3 682 320	69.1
1 VII 1999 ....ESDF		10 035 210	6 971 628	69.5	4 711 689	3 282 317	69.7	5 323 521	3 689 311	69.3
1 VII 2000 ....ESDF		10 004 958	6 999 510	70.0	...	...	...	...	...	...
1 VII 2001 ....ESDF		9 970 688	7 022 386	70.4	...	...	...	...	...	...
1 VII 2002 ....ESDF		9 924 766	7 034 721	70.9	4 652 109	3 299 920	70.9	5 272 657	3 734 801	70.8
1 VII 2003 ....ESDF		9 873 826	7 040 950	71.3	4 623 963	3 297 535	71.3	5 249 863	3 743 415	71.3
1 VII 2004 ....ESDF		9 824 568	7 050 685	71.8	4 596 633	3 296 800	71.7	5 227 935	3 753 885	71.8
1 VII 2005 ....ESDF		9 775 307	7 057 463	72.2	4 569 189	3 294 851	72.1	5 206 118	3 762 612	72.3
Belgium - Belgique										
1 VII 1996 ....ESDJ		10 156 637	...	...	4 965 283	...	...	5 191 354	...	...
1 VII 1997 ....ESDJ		10 181 245	...	...	4 977 226	...	...	5 204 019	...	...
1 VII 1998 ....ESDJ		10 203 008	...	...	4 988 195	...	...	5 214 813	...	...
1 VII 1999 ....ESDJ		10 226 419	...	...	4 999 866	...	...	5 226 553	...	...
1 VII 2000 ....ESDJ		10 251 250	...	...	5 012 017	...	...	5 239 233	...	...
1 VII 2001 ....ESDJ		10 286 570	...	...	5 030 154	...	...	5 256 416	...	...
1 X 2001 ....CDJC		10 296 350	...	...	5 035 446	...	...	5 260 904	...	...
1 VII 2002 ....ESDJ		10 332 785	...	...	5 054 587	...	...	5 278 198	...	...
1 VII 2003 ....ESDJ		10 376 133	...	...	5 077 031	...	...	5 299 102	...	...
1 VII 2004 ....ESDJ		10 421 137	...	...	5 099 251	...	...	5 321 886	...	...
1 VII 2005 ....ESDJ		10 478 617	...	...	5 127 573	...	...	5 351 044	...	...
Bosnia and Herzegovina - Bosnie-Herzégovine										
1 VII 2003 ....ESDF		3 832 301	...	...	1 877 827	...	...	1 954 474	...	...
1 VII 2004 ....ESDF		3 842 527	...	...	1 882 838	...	...	1 959 689	...	...
1 VII 2005 ....ESDF		3 842 537	...	...	1 882 843	...	...	1 959 694	...	...
Bulgaria - Bulgarie										
1 VII 1996 ....ESDF		8 362 826	5 661 482	67.7	...	...	...	...	...	...
1 VII 1997 ....ESDF		8 312 068	5 623 899	67.7	4 061 233	2 734 426	67.3	4 250 835	2 889 473	68.0
1 VII 1998 ....ESDF		8 256 786	5 603 501	67.9	4 029 518	...	...	4 227 268	...	...
1 VII 1999 ....ESDF		8 210 624	5 587 165	68.0	4 002 616	...	...	4 208 008	...	...
1 VII 2000 ....ESDF		8 170 172	5 577 216	68.3	3 979 292	2 700 131	67.9	4 190 880	2 877 085	68.7
1 III 2001 ....CDFC		7 928 901	5 474 534	69.0	3 862 465	2 651 312	68.6	4 066 436	2 823 222	69.4
1 VII 2001 ....ESDF		7 910 430	5 477 604	69.2	3 852 034	2 652 367	68.9	4 058 397	2 825 237	69.6
1 VII 2002 ....ESDF		7 868 900	5 467 777	69.5	3 828 882	2 644 285	69.1	4 040 018	2 823 492	69.9
1 VII 2003 ....ESDF		7 823 557	5 459 344	69.8	3 803 501	2 636 908	69.3	4 020 056	2 822 436	70.2

Continent, country or area, and date / Continent, pays ou zone et date	Code[a]	Both sexes - Les deux sexes			Male - Masculin			Female - Féminin		
		Total	Urban - Urbaine Number Nombre	Urban - Urbaine Percent P.100	Total	Urban - Urbaine Number Nombre	Urban - Urbaine Percent P.100	Total	Urban - Urbaine Number Nombre	Urban - Urbaine Percent P.100
EUROPE										
Bulgaria - Bulgarie										
1 VII 2004	ESDF	7 781 161	5 440 536	69.9	3 779 224	2 624 031	69.4	4 001 937	2 816 505	70.4
1 VII 2005	ESDF	7 739 900	5 424 661	70.1	3 755 469	2 613 346	69.6	3 984 431	2 811 315	70.6
Channel Islands: Guernsey - Îles Anglo-Normandes: Guernesey										
13 III 1996	CDJC	58 681	...	...	28 244	...	...	30 437	...	...
1 VII 1998	ESDF	59 050	...	...	28 434	...	...	30 616	...	...
1 VII 1999	ESDF	60 268	...	...	29 042	...	...	31 226	...	...
29 IV 2001	CDJC	59 807	...	...	29 138	...	...	30 669	...	...
1 VII 2004	ESDF	60 382	...	...	29 841	...	...	30 541	...	...
Channel Islands: Jersey - Îles Anglo-Normandes: Jersey										
10 III 1996	CDJC	85 150	...	...	41 394	...	...	43 756	...	...
11 III 2001	CDJC	87 186	...	...	42 485	...	...	44 701	...	...
Croatia - Croatie										
1 VII 1996	ESDJ	4 493 581	...	...	2 159 527	...	...	2 334 054	...	...
1 VII 1997	ESDJ	4 572 474	...	...	2 197 442	...	...	2 375 032	...	...
1 VII 1998	ESDJ	4 501 149	...	...	2 163 164	...	...	2 337 985	...	...
1 VII 1999	ESDJ	4 553 769	...	...	2 188 455	...	...	2 365 314	...	...
1 VII 2000	ESDJ	4 381 000	...	...	2 105 000	...	...	2 276 000	...	...
31 III 2001	CDJC	4 437 460	2 471 328	55.7	2 135 900	1 171 950	54.9	2 301 560	1 299 378	56.5
1 VII 2002	ESDJ	4 442 900	...	...	2 138 400	...	...	2 304 500	...	...
1 VII 2003	ESDJ	4 441 800	...	...	2 137 600	...	...	2 304 100	...	...
1 VII 2004	ESDJ	4 439 400	...	...	2 136 900	...	...	2 302 500	...	...
1 VII 2005	ESDJ	4 441 900	...	...	2 138 600	...	...	2 303 300	...	...
Czech Republic - République tchèque										
1 VII 1996	ESDJ	10 315 353	7 701 911	74.7	5 014 667	...	...	5 300 686	...	...
1 VII 1997	ESDJ	10 303 642	7 692 120	74.7	5 010 531	...	...	5 293 111	...	...
1 VII 1998	ESDJ	10 294 943	7 675 220	74.6	5 007 480	...	...	5 287 463	...	...
1 VII 1999	ESDJ	10 282 784	7 659 954	74.5	5 002 823	...	...	5 279 961	...	...
1 VII 2000	ESDJ	10 272 503	7 641 415	74.4	4 999 326	3 694 433	73.9	5 273 177	3 946 982	74.9
1 III 2001	CDJC	10 230 060	7 564 200	73.9	4 982 071	3 657 775	73.4	5 247 989	3 906 425	74.4
1 VII 2001	ESDJ	10 224 192	7 559 732	73.9	4 978 951	3 655 116	73.4	5 245 241	3 904 616	74.4
1 VII 2002	ESDJ	10 200 774	7 536 154	73.9	4 964 598	3 640 572	73.3	5 236 176	3 895 582	74.4
1 VII 2003	ESDJ	10 201 651	7 533 782	73.8	4 968 189	3 640 805	73.3	5 233 462	3 892 977	74.4
1 VII 2004	ESDJ	10 206 923	7 526 698	73.7	4 971 730	3 637 603	73.2	5 235 193	3 889 095	74.3
1 VII 2005	ESDJ	10 234 092	7 552 515	73.8	4 991 439	3 655 100	73.2	5 242 653	3 897 415	74.3
Denmark - Danemark[79]										
1 VII 1996	ESDJ	5 261 503	...	...	2 597 989	...	...	2 663 514	...	...
1 VII 1997	ESDJ	5 284 220	...	...	2 610 070	...	...	2 674 150	...	...
1 VII 1998	ESDJ	5 301 304	...	...	2 618 854	...	...	2 682 450	...	...
1 VII 1999	ESDJ	5 327 358	...	...	2 632 641	...	...	2 694 717	...	...
1 VII 2000	ESDJ	5 337 344	...	...	2 637 878	...	...	2 699 466	...	...
1 I 2001	CDJC	5 349 212	...	...	2 644 319	...	...	2 704 893	...	...
1 VII 2001	ESDJ	5 358 783	...	...	2 649 233	...	...	2 709 551	...	...
1 VII 2002	ESDJ	5 374 255	...	...	2 657 341	...	...	2 716 914	...	...
1 VII 2003	ESDJ	5 387 174	...	...	2 664 526	...	...	2 722 648	...	...
1 VII 2004	ESDJ	5 401 177	...	...	2 671 907	...	...	2 729 270	...	...
1 VII 2005	ESDJ	5 415 978	...	...	2 679 857	...	...	2 736 121	...	...
Estonia - Estonie										
1 VII 1996	ESDF	1 415 594	1 022 675[32]	72.2	654 423	468 434[32]	71.6	761 171	554 241[32]	72.8
1 VII 1997	ESDF	1 399 535	1 011 012[32]	72.2	646 245	462 004[32]	71.5	753 290	549 008[32]	72.9
1 VII 1998	ESDF	1 386 156	1 003 119[32]	72.4	639 629	457 641[32]	71.5	746 527	545 478[32]	73.1
1 VII 1999	ESDF	1 375 654	997 188[32]	72.5	634 484	454 363[32]	71.6	741 170	542 825[32]	73.2
31 III 2000	CDJC	1 370 052	923 211	67.4	631 851	415 515	65.8	738 201	507 696	68.8
1 VII 2000	ESDF	1 369 515	947 308	69.2	631 579	426 593	67.5	737 936	520 715	70.6
1 VII 2001	ESDF	1 364 101	943 944	69.2	629 020	424 985	67.6	735 081	518 959	70.6
1 VII 2002	ESDF	1 358 644	940 465	69.2	626 276	423 224	67.6	732 368	517 241	70.6
1 VII 2003	ESDF	1 353 557	937 201	69.2	623 705	421 604	67.6	729 852	515 597	70.6

Continent, country or area, and date / Continent, pays ou zone et date	Code[a]	Both sexes - Les deux sexes			Male - Masculin			Female - Féminin		
		Total	Urban - Urbaine		Total	Urban - Urbaine		Total	Urban - Urbaine	
			Number Nombre	Percent P.100		Number Nombre	Percent P.100		Number Nombre	Percent P.100
EUROPE										
Estonia - Estonie										
1 VII 2004	ESDF	1 349 290	934 665	69.3	621 525	420 309	67.6	727 765	514 356	70.7
1 VII 2005	ESDF	1 346 097	932 985	69.3	619 949	419 513	67.7	726 148	513 472	70.7
Faeroe Islands - Îles Féroé										
1 VII 1996	ESDJ	43 540	...	...	22 468	...	...	21 072	...	...
1 VII 1997	ESDJ	43 993	...	...	22 688	...	...	21 305	...	...
1 VII 1998	ESDJ	44 504	...	...	22 983	...	...	21 521	...	...
1 VII 1999	ESDJ	45 063	...	...	23 305	...	...	21 758	...	...
1 VII 2000	ESDJ	45 749	...	...	23 676	...	...	22 073	...	...
1 VII 2001	ESDJ	46 553	...	...	24 116	...	...	22 437	...	...
1 VII 2002	ESDJ	47 315	...	...	24 534	...	...	22 781	...	...
1 VII 2003	ESDJ	47 923	...	...	24 873	...	...	23 051	...	...
1 VII 2004	ESDJ	48 258	...	...	25 070	...	...	23 188	...	...
1 VII 2005	ESDJ	48 260	...	...	25 074	...	...	23 187	...	...
Finland - Finlande[19]										
1 VII 1996	ESDJ	5 124 573	3 323 247	64.8	2 496 149	1 589 993	63.7	2 628 425	1 733 254	65.9
1 VII 1997	ESDJ	5 139 835	3 064 503	59.6	2 504 847	1 451 773	58.0	2 634 988	1 589 177	60.3
1 VII 1998	ESDJ	5 153 498	3 089 077	59.9	2 512 587	1 476 277	58.8	2 640 911	1 612 800	61.1
1 VII 1999	ESDJ	5 165 474	3 112 147	60.2	2 519 551	1 488 063	59.1	2 645 924	1 624 084	61.4
1 VII 2000	ESDJ	5 176 209	3 157 401	61.0	2 526 184	...	...	2 650 025	...	...
31 XII 2000	CDJC	5 181 115	3 167 668	61.1	2 529 341	1 516 812	60.0	2 651 774	1 650 856	62.3
1 VII 2001	ESDJ	5 188 008	3 179 283	61.3	2 533 469	1 523 008	60.1	2 654 539	1 656 275	62.4
1 VII 2002	ESDJ	5 200 598	3 217 447	61.9	2 541 257	1 543 243	60.7	2 659 342	1 674 204	63.0
1 VII 2003	ESDJ	5 213 014	3 234 178	62.0	2 548 905	1 552 734	60.9	2 664 109	1 681 445	63.1
1 VII 2004	ESDJ	5 228 172	3 245 435	62.1	2 557 485	1 559 747	61.0	2 670 687	1 685 689	63.1
1 VII 2005	ESDJ	5 246 096	3 285 197	62.6	2 567 214	1 580 650	61.6	2 678 882	1 704 547	63.6
France[80]										
1 VII 1996	ESDJ	58 025 989	...	...	28 195 599	...	...	29 830 390	...	...
1 VII 1997	ESDJ	58 207 490	...	...	28 275 964	...	...	29 931 526	...	...
1 VII 1998	ESDJ	58 397 788	...	...	28 361 163	...	...	30 036 625	...	...
8 III 1999	CDJC	58 520 688	...	...	28 419 419	...	...	30 101 269	...	...
1 VII 1999	ESDJ	58 673 079	...	...	28 492 821	...	...	30 180 258	...	...
1 VII 2000	ESDJ	59 049 357	...	...	28 677 892	...	...	30 371 465	...	...
1 VII 2001	ESDJ	59 454 461	...	...	28 877 376	...	...	30 577 085	...	...
1 VII 2002	ESDJ	59 863 266	...	...	29 079 470	...	...	30 783 796	...	...
1 VII 2003	ESDJ	60 264 196	...	...	29 279 506	...	...	30 984 690	...	...
1 VII 2004*	ESDJ	60 643 307	...	...	29 466 783	...	...	31 176 524	...	...
1 VII 2005*	ESDJ	60 995 911	...	...	29 638 708	...	...	31 357 203	...	...
Germany - Allemagne										
1 VII 1996	ESDJ	81 895 637	...	...	39 887 683	...	...	42 007 954	...	...
1 VII 1997	ESDJ	82 051 699	...	...	39 997 915	...	...	42 063 284	...	...
1 VII 1998	ESDJ	82 028 948	...	...	39 992 272	...	...	42 036 675	...	...
1 VII 1999	ESDJ	82 086 582	...	...	40 004 142	...	...	42 052 784	...	...
1 VII 2001	ESDJ	82 339 777	...	...	40 215 606	...	...	42 134 319	...	...
1 VII 2002	ESDJ	82 482 309	...	...	40 310 430	...	...	42 171 879	...	...
1 VII 2003	ESDJ	82 520 176	...	...	40 349 200	...	...	42 170 976	...	...
28 III 2004[81]	SSDJ	82 491 000	...	...	40 330 000	...	...	42 161 000	...	...
1 VII 2004	ESDJ	82 501 274	...	...	40 350 091	...	...	42 151 183	...	...
1 VII 2005	ESDJ	82 464 344	...	...	40 348 986	...	...	42 115 358	...	...
Gibraltar[82]										
1 VII 1996	ESDF	27 128	...	...	13 618	...	...	13 510	...	...
1 VII 1997	ESDF	27 139	...	...	13 550	...	...	13 588	...	...
1 VII 1998	ESDF	27 025	...	...	13 419	...	...	13 606	...	...
1 VII 1999	ESDF	27 114	...	...	13 460	...	...	13 654	...	...
1 VII 2000	ESDF	27 118	...	...	13 453	...	...	13 665	...	...
12 XI 2001	CDFC	27 495	...	...	13 644	...	...	13 851	...	...
1 VII 2002	ESDF	28 520	...	...	14 300	...	...	14 220	...	...
1 VII 2003	ESDF	28 562	...	...	14 342	...	...	14 220	...	...
1 VII 2004	ESDF	28 704	...	...	14 410	...	...	14 294	...	...
1 VII 2005	ESDF	28 827	...	...	14 422	...	...	14 406	...	...
Greece - Grèce										
1 VII 1996[83]	ESDF	10 709 150	...	...	5 303 330	...	...	5 405 820	...	...
1 VII 1997[83]	ESDF	10 776 531	...	...	5 337 781	...	...	5 438 750	...	...

Continent, country or area, and date / Continent, pays ou zone et date	Code[a]	Both sexes - Les deux sexes			Male - Masculin			Female - Féminin		
		Total	Urban - Urbaine		Total	Urban - Urbaine		Total	Urban - Urbaine	
			Number Nombre	Percent P.100		Number Nombre	Percent P.100		Number Nombre	Percent P.100
EUROPE										
Greece - Grèce										
1 VII 1998[83] ....ESDF		10 834 910	...	...	5 366 820	...	...	5 468 090	...	...
1 VII 1999[83] ....ESDF		10 882 607	...	...	5 389 881	...	...	5 492 726	...	...
1 VII 2000[83] ....ESDF		10 917 457	...	...	5 406 043	...	...	5 511 414	...	...
18 III 2001[84] ....CDFC		10 964 020	...	...	5 431 816	...	...	5 532 204	...	...
1 VII 2001[83] ....ESDF		10 949 953	...	...	5 421 043	...	...	5 528 910	...	...
1 VII 2002[83] ....ESDF		10 987 559	...	...	5 439 332	...	...	5 548 227	...	...
1 VII 2003[83] ....ESDF		11 023 532	...	...	5 456 496	...	...	5 567 036	...	...
1 VII 2004[83] ....ESDF		11 061 735	...	...	5 475 529	...	...	5 586 206	...	...
1 VII 2005[83] ....ESDF		11 103 929	...	...	5 497 372	...	...	5 606 557	...	...
Holy See - Saint-Siège[85]										
1 VII 1998 ....ESDF		786	...	...	604	...	...	182	...	...
1 VII 2000* ....CDFC		798	...	...	529	...	...	269	...	...
Hungary - Hongrie										
1 VII 1996 ....ESDF		10 193 371	6 403 581[86]	62.8	4 873 597	3 018 697[86]	61.9	5 319 775	3 384 884[86]	63.6
1 VII 1997 ....ESDF		10 154 900	6 402 241[86]	63.0	4 852 592	3 016 070[86]	62.2	5 302 309	3 386 171[86]	63.9
1 VII 1998 ....ESDF		10 113 574	6 431 702[86]	63.6	4 829 734	3 028 148[86]	62.7	5 283 840	3 403 554[86]	64.4
1 VII 1999 ....ESDF		10 067 507	6 385 626[86]	63.4	4 804 690	3 003 675[86]	62.5	5 262 817	3 381 951[86]	64.3
1 VII 2000 ....ESDF		10 024 222	6 364 276[86]	63.5	4 781 701	2 991 619[86]	62.6	5 242 522	3 372 657[86]	64.3
1 II 2001 ....CDFC		10 198 315	6 572 880	64.5	4 850 650	3 091 857	63.7	5 347 665	3 481 023	65.1
1 VII 2001 ....ESDF		10 187 576	6 544 089[86]	64.2	4 843 996	3 073 458[86]	63.4	5 343 580	3 470 631[86]	64.9
1 VII 2002 ....ESDF		10 158 608	6 607 159[86]	65.0	4 827 718	3 101 463[86]	64.2	5 330 890	3 505 696[86]	65.8
1 VII 2003 ....ESDF		10 129 552	6 568 539[86]	64.8	4 811 285	3 079 592[86]	64.0	5 318 268	3 488 947[86]	65.6
1 VII 2004 ....ESDF		10 107 146	6 571 923[86]	65.0	4 798 614	3 078 582[86]	64.2	5 308 532	3 493 342[86]	65.8
1 VII 2005 ....ESDF		10 087 065	6 670 187	66.1	4 788 847	3 125 833	65.3	5 298 218	3 544 354	66.9
Iceland - Islande[19]										
1 VII 1996 ....ESDJ		268 927	246 983	91.8	134 779	123 025	91.3	134 148	123 958	92.4
1 VII 1997 ....ESDJ		270 915	249 293	92.0	135 779	124 196	91.5	135 136	125 097	92.6
1 VII 1998 ....ESDJ		273 794	252 356	92.2	137 092	125 634	91.6	136 702	126 722	92.7
1 VII 1999 ....ESDJ		277 184	255 910	92.3	138 783	127 433	91.8	138 401	128 477	92.8
1 VII 2000 ....CDJC		281 154	259 661	92.4	140 718	129 258	91.9	140 436	130 403	92.9
1 VII 2000 ....ESDJ		281 154	259 661	92.4	140 718	129 258	91.9	140 436	130 403	92.9
1 VII 2001 ....ESDJ		285 054	263 409	92.4	142 660	131 217	92.0	142 308	132 192	92.9
1 VII 2002 ....ESDJ		287 559	266 010	92.5	143 860	132 371	92.0	143 699	133 639	93.0
1 VII 2003 ....ESDJ		289 272	267 957	92.6	144 713	133 340	92.1	144 559	134 617	93.1
1 VII 2004 ....ESDJ		292 587	270 931	92.6	146 697	134 827	91.9	145 890	136 104	93.3
1 VII 2005 ....ESDJ		295 864	275 017	93.0	148 449	137 003	92.3	147 415	138 014	93.6
Ireland - Irlande										
28 IV 1996...........CDFC		3 626 087	2 107 991	58.1	1 800 232	1 018 779	56.6	1 825 855	1 089 212	59.7
15 IV 1997[87].........ESDF		3 664 313	...	...	1 819 394	...	...	1 844 919	...	...
15 IV 1998[87].........ESDF		3 703 082	...	...	1 838 859	...	...	1 864 223	...	...
15 IV 1999[87].........ESDF		3 741 647	...	...	1 858 613	...	...	1 883 034	...	...
15 IV 2000[87].........ESDF		3 789 536	...	...	1 882 946	...	...	1 906 590	...	...
15 IV 2001[87].........ESDF		3 847 198	...	...	1 913 128	...	...	1 934 070	...	...
28 IV 2002...........CDFC		3 917 203	2 334 300	59.6	1 946 164	1 133 500	58.2	1 971 039	1 200 800	60.9
15 IV 2003[87].........ESDF		3 978 862			1 977 208	...	...	2 001 654	...	...
15 IV 2004[87].........ESDF		4 043 763			2 011 159	...	...	2 032 604	...	...
15 IV 2005[87].........ESDF		4 130 722			2 058 952	...	...	2 071 770	...	...
Isle of Man - Îles de Man										
14 IV 1996...........CDJC		71 714	...	...	34 797	...	...	36 917	...	...
1 VII 1996 ....ESDJ		71 714	...	...	34 797	...	...	36 917	...	...
1 VII 1997 ....ESDJ		72 452	...	...	35 166	...	...	37 286	...	...
1 VII 2000 ....ESDJ		74 861	...	...	36 534	...	...	38 327	...	...
29 IV 2001...........CDJC		76 315	...	...	37 372	...	...	38 943	...	...
1 VII 2001 ....ESDJ		76 315			37 372	...	...	38 943	...	...
1 VII 2002 ....ESDJ		77 156			37 827	...	...	39 330	...	...
1 VII 2003 ....ESDJ		77 464			38 019	...	...	39 444	...	...
1 VII 2004 ....ESDJ		77 581			38 111	...	...	39 470	...	...
1 VII 2005 ....ESDJ		78 003			38 360	...	...	39 643	...	...
Italy - Italie										
1 VII 1996 ....ESDJ		56 860 281	...	...	27 563 534	...	...	29 296 747	...	...
1 VII 1997 ....ESDJ		56 890 372	17 459 276	30.7	27 569 176	...	...	29 321 196	...	...
1 VII 1998 ....ESDJ		56 906 744	17 419 059	30.6	27 567 663	...	...	29 339 081	...	...

6. Total and urban population by sex: 1996 - 2005
Population totale et population urbaine selon le sexe: 1996 - 2005 (continued - suite)

Continent, country or area, and date / Continent, pays ou zone et date	Code[a]	Both sexes - Les deux sexes Total	Urban - Urbaine Number Nombre	Urban - Urbaine Percent P.100	Male - Masculin Total	Urban - Urbaine Number Nombre	Urban - Urbaine Percent P.100	Female - Féminin Total	Urban - Urbaine Number Nombre	Urban - Urbaine Percent P.100
EUROPE										
Italy - Italie										
1 VII 1999	ESDJ	56 916 317	17 348 485	30.5	27 563 368	...	...	29 352 949	...	...
1 VII 2000	ESDJ	56 942 108	17 329 002	30.4	27 569 657	...	...	29 372 451	...	...
1 VII 2001	ESDJ	56 978 218	...	...	27 581 654	...	...	29 396 564	...	...
21 X 2001	CDFC	57 110 144	...	...	27 617 335	...	...	29 492 809	...	...
1 VII 2002	ESDJ	57 158 407	...	...	27 676 603	...	...	29 481 805	...	...
1 VII 2003	ESDJ	57 604 658	...	...	27 917 416	...	...	29 687 242	...	...
1 VII 2004	ESDJ	58 175 310	...	...	28 222 706	...	...	29 952 604	...	...
1 VII 2005	ESDJ	58 607 043	...	...	28 451 846	...	...	30 155 197	...	...
Latvia - Lettonie										
1 VII 1996	ESDJ	2 457 222	1 686 975	68.7	1 132 799	766 252	67.6	1 324 423	920 723	69.5
1 VII 1997	ESDJ	2 432 851	1 668 743	68.6	1 121 142	757 156	67.5	1 311 709	911 587	69.5
1 VII 1998	ESDJ	2 410 019	1 649 491	68.4	1 110 461	746 363	67.2	1 299 558	903 128	69.5
1 VII 1999	ESDJ	2 390 482	1 630 335	68.2	1 101 163	735 684	66.8	1 289 319	894 651	69.4
31 III 2000	CDJC	2 377 383	1 618 144	68.1	1 094 964	729 745	66.6	1 282 419	888 399	69.3
1 VII 2000	ESDJ	2 372 985	1 614 159	68.0	1 092 871	727 722	66.6	1 280 114	886 437	69.2
1 VII 2001	ESDJ	2 355 011	1 599 272	67.9	1 084 484	720 359	66.4	1 270 527	878 913	69.2
1 VII 2002	ESDJ	2 338 624	1 586 220	67.8	1 076 587	713 616	66.3	1 262 037	872 604	69.1
1 VII 2003	ESDJ	2 325 342	1 576 965	67.8	1 070 697	709 024	66.2	1 254 645	867 941	69.2
1 VII 2004	ESDJ	2 312 819	1 570 406	67.9	1 065 627	706 082	66.3	1 247 192	864 324	69.3
1 VII 2005	ESDJ	2 300 512	1 563 372[88]	68.0	1 060 101	702 490	66.3	1 240 411	860 882	69.4
Liechtenstein										
1 VII 1996	ESDF	31 143	...	...	15 142	...	...	15 900	...	...
1 VII 1997	ESDF	31 320	...	...	15 192	...	...	16 040	...	...
1 VII 1998	ESDF	32 015	...	...	15 418	...	...	16 250	...	...
1 VII 1999	ESDF	32 426	...	...	15 702	...	...	16 519	...	...
1 VII 2000	ESDF	32 673	...	...	15 912	...	...	16 761	...	...
5 XII 2000	CDFC	33 307	...	...	16 420	...	...	16 887	...	...
1 VII 2001	ESDF	33 104	...	...	16 195	...	...	16 909	...	...
1 VII 2002	ESDF	33 678	...	...	16 514	...	...	17 164	...	...
1 VII 2003	ESDF	34 022	...	...	16 725	...	...	17 297	...	...
1 VII 2004	ESDF	34 477	...	...	16 974	...	...	17 503	...	...
1 VII 2005	ESDF	34 734	...	...	17 100	...	...	17 634	...	...
Lithuania - Lituanie										
1 VII 1996	ESDJ	3 601 613	2 430 778	67.5	1 693 703	1 132 093	66.8	1 907 910	1 298 685	68.1
1 VII 1997	ESDJ	3 575 137	2 413 579	67.5	1 678 748	1 120 359	66.7	1 896 390	1 293 220	68.2
1 VII 1998	ESDJ	3 549 331	2 387 853	67.3	1 664 608	1 105 128	66.4	1 884 724	1 282 726	68.1
1 VII 1999	ESDJ	3 524 238	2 367 146	67.2	1 650 931	1 092 628	66.2	1 873 307	1 274 518	68.0
1 VII 2000	ESDJ	3 499 536	2 345 640	67.0	1 637 616	1 079 945	65.9	1 861 921	1 265 695	68.0
6 IV 2001	CDJC	3 483 972	2 332 098	66.9	1 629 148	1 071 986	65.8	1 854 824	1 260 112	67.9
1 VII 2001	ESDJ	3 481 292	2 330 184	66.9	1 627 704	1 070 901	65.8	1 853 588	1 259 283	67.9
1 VII 2002	ESDJ	3 469 070	2 321 713	66.9	1 620 891	1 065 912	65.8	1 848 179	1 255 801	67.9
1 VII 2003	ESDJ	3 454 205	2 307 326	66.8	1 612 996	1 058 108	65.6	1 841 209	1 249 218	67.8
1 VII 2004	ESDJ	3 435 591	2 289 399	66.6	1 603 421	1 048 397	65.4	1 832 170	1 241 002	67.7
1 VII 2005	ESDJ	3 414 304	2 275 118	66.6	1 592 402	1 040 296	65.3	1 821 902	1 234 822	67.8
Luxembourg										
1 VII 1996	ESDJ	414 225	...	...	204 000	...	...	211 550	...	...
1 VII 1998	ESDJ	424 700	...	...	209 716	...	...	216 734	...	...
1 VII 1999	ESDJ	430 475	...	...	211 978	...	...	218 497	...	...
1 VII 2000	ESDJ	436 300	...	...	214 958	...	...	221 343	...	...
15 II 2001	CDJC	439 539	...	...	216 541	...	...	222 998	...	...
1 VII 2001	ESDJ	441 525	...	...	217 562	...	...	223 963	...	...
1 VII 2002	ESDJ	446 175	...	...	219 916	...	...	226 259	...	...
1 VII 2003	ESDJ	449 950	...	...	222 015	...	...	227 935	...	...
1 VII 2004	ESDJ	453 300	...	...	223 880	...	...	229 420	...	...
1 VII 2005	ESDJ	457 250	...	...	225 775	...	...	231 475	...	...
Malta - Malte										
1 VII 1996	ESDJ	373 958	...	...	185 319	...	...	188 639	...	...
1 VII 1997	ESDJ	376 513	...	...	186 664	...	...	189 849	...	...
1 VII 1998	ESDJ	378 518	...	...	187 689	...	...	190 829	...	...
1 VII 1999	ESDJ	380 201	...	...	188 589	...	...	191 612	...	...
1 VII 2000	ESDJ	382 525	...	...	189 720	...	...	192 805	...	...
31 XII 2001	ESDJ	394 641	...	...	195 363	...	...	199 278	...	...
31 XII 2002	ESDJ	397 296	...	...	196 836	...	...	200 460	...	...
1 VII 2003	ESDJ	398 582	...	...	197 468	...	...	201 114	...	...

Continent, country or area, and date / Continent, pays ou zone et date	Code[a]	Both sexes - Les deux sexes			Male - Masculin			Female - Féminin		
		Total	Urban - Urbaine		Total	Urban - Urbaine		Total	Urban - Urbaine	
			Number Nombre	Percent P.100		Number Nombre	Percent P.100		Number Nombre	Percent P.100
EUROPE										
Malta - Malte										
1 VII 2004 ....ESDJ		401 306	...	...	198 860	...	...	202 446	...	...
1 VII 2005 ....ESDJ		403 509	...	...	200 104	...	...	203 405	...	...
Monaco										
21 VI 2000...........CDJC		32 020	...	...	15 544	...	...	16 476	...	...
Netherlands - Pays-Bas										
1 VII 1996 ....ESDJ		15 530 498	9 545 330	61.5	7 679 546	4 679 415	60.9	7 850 952	4 865 915	62.0
1 VII 1997 ....ESDJ		15 610 650	9 678 486	62.0	7 718 439	4 745 978	61.5	7 892 211	4 932 508	62.5
1 VII 1998 ....ESDJ		15 707 209	9 826 124	62.6	7 766 673	4 820 259	62.1	7 940 536	5 005 865	63.0
1 VII 1999 ....ESDJ		15 812 088	9 974 974	63.1	7 819 794	4 895 583	62.6	7 992 294	5 079 392	63.6
1 VII 2000 ....ESDJ		15 925 513	10 170 596	63.9	7 878 086	4 995 169	63.4	8 047 427	5 175 427	64.3
1 VII 2001 ....ESDJ		16 046 180	10 388 487	64.7	7 940 911	5 106 377	64.3	8 105 269	5 282 110	65.2
1 I 2002[89] ....CDJC		16 105 285	10 447 684	64.9	7 971 967	5 137 422	64.4	8 133 318	5 310 262	65.3
1 VII 2002 ....ESDJ		16 148 928	10 488 796	65.0	7 993 719	5 158 261	64.5	8 155 209	5 330 535	65.4
1 VII 2003 ....ESDJ		16 225 302	10 598 154	65.3	8 030 693	5 212 792	64.9	8 194 610	5 385 362	65.7
1 VII 2004 ....ESDJ		16 281 779	10 708 529	65.8	8 055 947	5 266 567	65.4	8 225 833	5 441 963	66.2
1 VII 2005 ....ESDJ		16 319 868	10 772 189	66.0	8 071 693	5 296 667	65.6	8 248 175	5 475 522	66.4
Norway - Norvège[90]										
1 VII 1996 ....ESDJ		4 381 336		...	2 166 445		...	2 214 891		...
1 VII 1997 ....ESDJ		4 405 157		...	2 178 625		...	2 226 532		...
1 VII 1998 ....ESDJ		4 431 464		...	2 192 333		...	2 239 132		...
1 VII 1999 ....ESDJ		4 461 913		...	2 208 350		...	2 253 564		...
1 VII 2000 ....ESDJ		4 490 967		...	2 224 221		...	2 266 746		...
1 VII 2001 ....ESDJ		4 513 751		...	2 236 618		...	2 277 134		...
3 XI 2001[19] ....CDJC		4 520 947	3 458 699	76.5	2 240 281	1 694 153	75.6	2 280 666	1 764 546	77.4
1 VII 2002 ....ESDJ		4 538 159		...	2 249 021		...	2 289 139		...
1 VII 2003 ....ESDJ		4 564 855		...	2 262 578		...	2 302 277		...
1 VII 2004 ....ESDJ		4 591 910		...	2 276 560		...	2 315 351		...
1 VII 2005 ....ESDJ		4 623 291		...	2 293 026		...	2 330 266		...
Poland - Pologne[91]										
1 VII 1996 ....ESDF		38 289 000	23 683 000	61.9	18 623 000	11 323 000	60.8	19 666 000	12 360 000	62.8
1 VII 1997 ....ESDF		38 292 000	23 693 000	61.9	18 610 000	11 317 000	60.8	19 682 000	12 376 000	62.9
1 VII 1998 ....ESDF		38 283 000	23 689 000	61.9	18 590 000	11 303 000	60.8	19 693 000	12 386 000	62.9
1 VII 1999 ....ESDF		38 270 000	23 668 000	61.8	18 566 000	11 281 000	60.8	19 704 000	12 387 000	62.9
1 VII 2000[92] ....ESDF		38 255 945	23 691 220	61.9	18 541 844	11 284 476	60.9	19 714 101	12 406 744	62.9
1 VII 2001[92] ....ESDF		38 250 790	23 656 606	61.8	18 532 945	11 261 781	60.8	19 717 845	12 394 825	62.9
20 V 2002 ....CDFC		38 230 080	23 610 365	61.8	18 516 403	11 234 165	60.7	19 713 677	12 376 200	62.8
1 VII 2002 ....ESDF		38 232 301	23 607 932	61.7	18 517 179	11 232 736	60.7	19 715 122	12 375 196	62.8
1 VII 2003 ....ESDF		38 195 177	23 543 325	61.6	18 492 950	11 195 269	60.5	19 702 227	12 348 056	62.7
1 VII 2004 ....ESDF		38 180 249	23 490 202	61.5	18 478 368	11 162 807	60.4	19 701 881	12 327 395	62.6
1 VII 2005 ....ESDF		38 161 313	23 450 597	61.5	18 460 730	11 135 706	60.3	19 700 583	12 314 891	62.5
Portugal[93]										
1 VII 1996 ....ESDJ		10 057 861		...	4 847 812		...	5 210 049		...
1 VII 1997 ....ESDJ		10 091 120		...	4 864 760		...	5 226 360		...
1 VII 1998 ....ESDJ		10 129 290		...	4 884 188		...	5 245 102		...
1 VII 1999 ....ESDJ		10 171 949		...	4 906 234		...	5 265 715		...
1 VII 2000 ....ESDJ		10 225 836		...	4 934 468		...	5 291 368		...
12 III 2001* ....CDFC		10 148 259	5 573 842	54.9	4 862 699	2 638 617	54.3	5 285 560	2 935 225	55.5
1 VII 2001 ....ESDJ		10 292 999		...	4 969 817		...	5 323 183		...
1 VII 2002 ....ESDJ		10 368 403		...	5 009 592		...	5 358 811		...
1 VII 2003 ....ESDJ		10 441 075		...	5 048 278		...	5 392 798		...
1 VII 2004 ....ESDJ		10 501 970		...	5 080 324		...	5 421 647		...
1 VII 2005 ....ESDJ		10 549 424		...	5 105 041		...	5 444 383		...
Republic of Moldova - République de Moldova[94]										
1 VII 1996 ....ESDJ		4 327 200	1 999 700	46.2	2 067 700	960 900	46.5	2 259 500	1 038 800	46.0
1 VII 1997 ....ESDJ		3 654 208	1 525 600	41.7	1 749 374	733 792	41.9	1 904 834	791 808	41.6
1 VII 1998 ....ESDJ		3 652 200	1 535 200	42.0	1 748 400	739 800	42.3	1 903 800	795 400	41.8
1 VII 1999 ....ESDJ		3 646 400	1 530 500	42.0	1 745 550	738 850	42.3	1 900 850	791 650	41.6
1 VII 2000 ....ESDJ		3 639 000	1 513 300	41.6	1 742 300	730 800	41.9	1 896 700	782 500	41.3
1 VII 2001 ....ESDJ		3 631 462	1 485 810	40.9	1 739 081	717 661	41.3	1 892 381	768 149	40.6
1 VII 2002 ....ESDJ		3 623 062	1 484 676	41.0	1 735 430	716 822	41.3	1 887 632	767 854	40.7
1 VII 2003 ....ESDJ		3 612 874	1 481 035	41.0	1 730 861	714 970	41.3	1 882 013	766 065	40.7

6. Total and urban population by sex: 1996 - 2005
Population totale et population urbaine selon le sexe: 1996 - 2005 (continued - suite)

Continent, country or area, and date / Continent, pays ou zone et date	Code[a]	Both sexes - Les deux sexes			Male - Masculin			Female - Féminin		
		Total	Urban - Urbaine		Total	Urban - Urbaine		Total	Urban - Urbaine	
			Number Nombre	Percent P.100		Number Nombre	Percent P.100		Number Nombre	Percent P.100

EUROPE

Republic of Moldova - République de Moldova[94]										
1 VII 2004 ....ESDJ		3 603 940	1 476 980	41.0	1 726 630	712 971	41.3	1 877 310	764 009	40.7
5 X 2004*............CDFC		3 388 071	1 308 911	38.6	1 632 519	615 387	37.7	1 755 549	693 521	39.5
1 VII 2005 ....ESDJ		3 595 187	1 472 929	41.0	1 722 105	710 796	41.3	1 873 082	762 133	40.7
Romania - Roumanie										
1 VII 1996 ....ESDJ		22 607 620	12 411 174	54.9	11 080 933	6 016 714	54.3	11 526 687	6 394 460	55.5
1 VII 1997 ....ESDJ		22 545 925	12 404 690	55.0	11 041 414	6 007 827	54.4	11 504 511	6 396 863	55.6
1 VII 1998 ....ESDJ		22 502 803	12 347 886	54.9	11 012 110	5 971 134	54.2	11 490 693	6 376 752	55.5
1 VII 1999 ....ESDJ		22 458 022	12 302 729	54.8	10 984 529	5 943 708	54.1	11 473 493	6 359 021	55.4
1 VII 2000 ....ESDJ		22 435 205	12 244 598	54.6	10 968 854	5 907 848	53.9	11 466 351	6 336 750	55.3
1 VII 2001 ....ESDJ		22 408 393	12 243 748	54.6	10 949 490	5 903 537	53.9	11 458 903	6 340 211	55.3
18 III 2002 ....CDJC		21 680 974	...		10 568 741	...	...	11 112 233	...	...
1 VII 2002 ....ESDJ		21 794 793	11 608 735	53.3	10 642 538	5 579 042	52.4	11 152 255	6 029 693	54.1
1 VII 2003 ....ESDJ		21 733 556	11 600 157	53.4	10 606 245	5 566 401	52.5	11 127 311	6 033 756	54.2
1 VII 2004 ....ESDJ		21 673 328	11 895 598	54.9	10 571 606	5 704 297	54.0	11 101 722	6 191 301	55.8
1 VII 2005 ....ESDJ		21 623 849	11 879 897	54.9	10 543 518	5 692 516	54.0	11 080 331	6 187 381	55.8
Russian Federation - Fédération de Russie[95]										
1 VII 1996 ....ESDJ		148 160 126	108 249 217	73.1	...	...	...	...	...	...
1 VII 1997 ....ESDJ		147 915 373	108 149 293	73.1	...	...	...	...	...	...
1 VII 1998 ....ESDJ		147 670 780	108 082 037	73.2	...	...	...	...	...	...
1 VII 1999 ....ESDJ		147 214 777	107 736 373	73.2	...	...	...	...	...	...
1 VII 2000 ....ESDJ		146 596 870	107 245 609	73.2	...	...	...	...	...	...
1 VII 2001 ....ESDJ		145 976 473	106 899 541	73.2	68 130 465	49 504 490	72.7	77 846 008	57 394 051	73.7
1 VII 2002 ....ESDJ		145 306 497	106 523 307	73.3	67 706 316	49 224 967	72.7	77 600 181	57 298 340	73.8
9 X 2002 ....CDJC		145 166 731	106 429 049	73.3	67 605 133	49 149 510	72.7	77 561 598	57 279 539	73.9
1 VII 2003 ....ESDJ		144 565 934	106 069 837	73.4	67 257 276	48 917 406	72.7	77 308 658	57 152 431	73.9
1 VII 2004 ....ESDJ		143 821 215	105 268 883	73.2	66 813 322	48 452 954	72.5	77 007 893	56 815 929	73.8
San Marino - Saint-Marin[19]										
1 VII 1997 ....ESDF		25 823	23 085	89.4	12 757	11 404	89.4	13 066	11 681	89.4
1 VII 2000 ....CDFC		26 941	22 738	84.4	13 185	11 787	89.4	13 756	10 951	79.6
1 VII 2000 ....ESDF		26 941	22 738	84.4	13 185	11 787	89.4	13 756	10 951	79.6
1 VII 2001 ....ESDF		27 634	...	...	13 548	...	...	14 086	...	...
1 VII 2002 ....ESDF		28 486	...	...	13 946	...	...	14 540	...	...
1 VII 2003 ....ESDF		28 992	...	...	14 207	...	...	14 785	...	...
1 VII 2004 ....ESDF		29 421	...	...	14 422	...	...	14 999	...	...
Serbia and Montenegro - Serbie-et-Montenegro										
1 VII 1996 ....ESDJ		10 577 208	5 440 835	51.4	5 245 109	2 656 349	50.6	5 332 099	2 784 486	52.2
1 VII 1997 ....ESDJ		10 600 067	5 456 379	51.5	5 256 354	2 664 248	50.7	5 343 713	2 792 131	52.3
1 VII 1998[96] ....ESDJ		10 616 886	5 468 037	51.5	5 264 001	2 669 658	50.7	5 352 885	2 798 379	52.3
1 VII 1999[96] ....ESDJ		10 629 358	5 477 426	51.5	5 269 974	2 674 193	50.7	5 359 384	2 803 233	52.3
1 VII 2000[96] ....ESDJ		10 633 508	5 482 862	51.6	...	...	...	...	...	...
1 VII 2001[96] ....ESDJ		10 651 650	5 495 310	51.6	5 280 896	2 683 098	50.8	5 370 754	2 812 212	52.4
1 VII 2002[97] ....ESDJ		8 113 868	4 608 767	56.8	3 948 798	2 206 353	55.9	4 165 070	2 402 414	57.7
1 VII 2003[97] ....ESDJ		8 152 676	4 654 786	57.1	3 967 478	2 227 301	56.1	4 185 198	2 427 485	58.0
1 VII 2004*[97] ....ESDJ		8 146 756	...	...	3 964 380	...	...	4 182 376	...	...
Slovakia - Slovaquie										
1 VII 1996 ....ESDJ		5 373 793	3 062 080	57.0	...	...	...	...	...	...
1 VII 1997 ....ESDJ		5 383 233	3 066 450	57.0	...	...	...	...	...	...
1 VII 1998 ....ESDJ		5 390 866	3 066 457	56.9	...	...	...	...	...	...
1 VII 1999 ....ESDJ		5 395 324	3 061 062	56.7	...	...	...	...	...	...
1 VII 2000 ....ESDJ		5 400 679	3 059 010	56.6	...	...	...	...	...	...
25 V 2001* ....CDJC		5 379 455	3 022 106	56.2	2 612 515	1 453 638	55.6	2 766 940	1 568 468	56.7
1 VII 2001 ....ESDJ		5 379 780	3 017 527	56.1	...	...	...	...	...	...
1 VII 2002 ....ESDJ		5 378 809	3 011 737	56.0	2 611 452	1 447 959	55.4	2 767 357	1 563 778	56.5
1 VII 2003 ....ESDJ		5 378 950	3 001 776	55.8	2 610 872	1 442 174	55.2	2 768 078	1 559 602	56.3
1 VII 2004 ....ESDJ		5 382 574	2 994 284	55.6	2 612 313	1 438 019	55.0	2 770 261	1 556 265	56.2
1 VII 2005 ....ESDJ		5 387 285	2 989 291	55.5	2 614 912	1 435 469	54.9	2 772 373	1 553 822	56.0

Continent, country or area, and date / Continent, pays ou zone et date	Code[a]	Both sexes - Les deux sexes Total	Urban - Urbaine Number Nombre	Urban - Urbaine Percent P.100	Male - Masculin Total	Urban - Urbaine Number Nombre	Urban - Urbaine Percent P.100	Female - Féminin Total	Urban - Urbaine Number Nombre	Urban - Urbaine Percent P.100
EUROPE										
Slovenia - Slovénie										
1 VII 1996	ESDJ	1 991 169	...	...	969 114	...	...	1 022 055	...	...
1 VII 1997	ESDJ	1 986 848	...	...	969 155	...	...	1 017 693	...	...
1 VII 1998	ESDJ	1 982 603	...	...	966 513	...	...	1 016 090	...	...
1 VII 1999	ESDJ	1 985 557	...	...	968 463	...	...	1 017 094	...	...
1 VII 2000	ESDJ	1 990 272	...	...	972 581	...	...	1 017 691	...	...
1 VII 2001	ESDJ	1 992 035	...	...	973 711	...	...	1 018 324	...	...
31 III 2002*	CDJC	1 964 036	997 772[98]	50.8	958 576	479 356	50.0	1 005 460	518 416	51.6
1 VII 2002	ESDJ	1 995 718	975 163[98]	48.9	976 111	462 513	47.4	1 019 607	512 650	50.3
1 VII 2003	ESDJ	1 996 773	971 513[98]	48.7	977 436	460 811	47.1	1 019 337	510 702	50.1
1 VII 2004	ESDJ	1 997 004	968 989[98]	48.5	977 092	459 504	47.0	1 019 912	509 485	50.0
1 VII 2005	ESDJ	2 001 114	965 538[98]	48.3	980 070	457 869	46.7	1 021 044	507 669	49.7
Spain - Espagne[99]										
1 VII 1996	ESDJ	39 479 159	...	...	19 332 882	...	...	20 146 277	...	...
1 VII 1997	ESDJ	39 583 381	...	...	19 382 107	...	...	20 201 274	...	...
1 VII 1998	ESDJ	39 722 075	...	...	19 448 294	...	...	20 273 781	...	...
1 VII 1999	ESDJ	39 927 224	...	...	19 547 393	...	...	20 379 831	...	...
1 VII 2000	ESDJ	40 264 162	...	...	19 719 334[32]	...	...	20 544 828[32]	...	...
1 VII 2001	ESDJ	40 721 447	...	...	19 956 780[32]	...	...	20 764 667[32]	...	...
1 XI 2001	CDFC	40 847 371	...	...	20 012 882	...	...	20 834 489	...	...
1 VII 2002	ESDJ	41 314 019	...	...	20 266 005[32]	...	...	21 048 014[32]	...	...
1 VII 2003	ESDJ	42 004 575	...	...	20 626 192	...	...	21 378 383	...	...
1 VII 2004	ESDJ	42 691 751	...	...	20 987 670	...	...	21 704 081	...	...
1 VII 2005	ESDJ	43 398 190	...	...	21 367 297	...	...	22 030 893	...	...
Sweden - Suède[19]										
1 VII 1996	ESDJ	8 840 998	...	...	4 367 895	...	...	4 473 104	...	...
1 VII 1997	ESDJ	8 846 062	...	...	4 370 816	...	...	4 475 247	...	...
1 VII 1998	ESDJ	8 850 974	...	...	4 373 767	...	...	4 477 208	...	...
1 VII 1999	ESDJ	8 857 874	...	...	4 377 870	...	...	4 480 006	...	...
1 VII 2000	CDJC	8 872 110	...	...	4 386 436	...	...	4 485 674	...	...
1 VII 2000	ESDJ	8 872 110	...	...	4 386 436	...	...	4 485 674	...	...
1 VII 2001	ESDJ	8 895 963	...	...	4 400 600	...	...	4 495 363	...	...
1 VII 2002	ESDJ	8 924 958	...	...	4 417 776	...	...	4 507 182	...	...
1 VII 2003	ESDJ	8 958 229	...	...	4 436 882	...	...	4 521 348	...	...
1 VII 2004	ESDJ	8 993 531	...	...	4 456 484	...	...	4 537 048	...	...
1 VII 2005	ESDJ	9 029 572	...	...	4 476 431	...	...	4 553 142	...	...
Switzerland - Suisse										
1 VII 1996	ESDJ	7 081 346	5 159 238	72.9	3 457 621	2 497 633	72.2	3 623 725	2 661 605	73.4
1 VII 1997	ESDJ	7 096 465	5 168 174	72.8	3 465 243	2 502 892	72.2	3 631 222	2 665 282	73.4
1 VII 1998	ESDJ	7 123 537	5 189 624	72.9	3 478 689	2 513 947	72.3	3 644 848	2 675 677	73.4
1 VII 1999	ESDJ	7 164 444	5 224 102	72.9	3 500 708	2 532 960	72.4	3 663 736	2 691 142	73.5
1 VII 2000	ESDJ	7 204 055	5 261 149	73.0	3 519 698	2 550 876	72.5	3 684 357	2 710 273	73.6
5 XII 2000	CDJC	7 204 055	4 871 949	67.6	3 519 698	2 357 890	67.0	3 684 357	2 514 099	68.2
1 VII 2001	ESDJ	7 255 653	5 306 567	73.1	3 544 349	2 573 237	72.6	3 711 304	2 733 330	73.6
1 VII 2002	ESDJ	7 313 853	5 354 489	73.2	3 575 029	2 598 662	72.7	3 738 824	2 755 827	73.7
1 VII 2003	ESDJ	7 364 148	5 393 811	73.2	3 601 539	2 619 324	72.7	3 762 609	2 774 487	73.7
1 VII 2004	ESDJ	7 415 102	5 434 009	73.3	3 628 696	2 640 781	72.8	3 786 406	2 793 228	73.8
1 VII 2005	ESDJ	7 459 128	5 468 772	73.3	3 652 502	2 660 065	72.8	3 806 626	2 808 707	73.8
The Former Yugoslav Rep. of Macedonia - L'ex-République yougoslave de Macédoine										
1 VII 1997	ESDF	1 996 869	1 189 442	59.6	999 595	590 300	59.1	997 274	599 142	60.1
1 VII 1998	ESDF	2 007 523	...	...	1 004 771	...	...	1 002 752	...	...
1 VII 1999	ESDF	2 017 142	...	...	1 009 369	...	...	1 007 773	...	...
1 VII 2000	ESDF	2 031 153[100]	...	...	1 019 616	...	...	1 019 035	...	...
1 XI 2002	CDJC	2 022 547	...	...	1 015 377	...	...	1 007 170	...	...
1 VII 2003	ESDF	2 026 773[100]	...	...	1 017 274	...	...	1 009 499	...	...
1 VII 2004	ESDF	2 032 544	...	...	1 019 903	...	...	1 012 641	...	...
1 VII 2005	ESDF	2 036 855	...	...	1 021 772	...	...	1 015 083	...	...
Ukraine										
1 VII 1996	ESDF	51 057 750	34 832 500	68.2	...	...	...	...	...	...
1 VII 1997	ESDF	50 594 600	34 521 800	68.2	...	...	...	...	...	...

6. Total and urban population by sex: 1996 - 2005
Population totale et population urbaine selon le sexe: 1996 - 2005 (continued - suite)

Continent, country or area, and date / Continent, pays ou zone et date	Code[a]	Both sexes - Les deux sexes Total	Urban - Urbaine Number Nombre	Urban - Urbaine Percent P.100	Male - Masculin Total	Urban - Urbaine Number Nombre	Urban - Urbaine Percent P.100	Female - Féminin Total	Urban - Urbaine Number Nombre	Urban - Urbaine Percent P.100
EUROPE										
Ukraine										
1 VII 1998	ESDF	50 144 450	34 271 600	68.3	...	...	...	...	...	...
1 VII 1999	ESDF	49 673 950[101]	34 017 400	68.5	...	...	...	...	...	...
1 VII 2000	ESDJ	49 176 500[101]	32 768 879	66.6	22 642 532	15 171 760	67.0	26 246 748	17 597 119	67.0
1 VII 2001	ESDJ	48 690 151	32 448 930	66.6	22 423 360	14 992 532	66.9	26 028 896	17 456 398	67.1
5 XII 2001	CDFC	48 240 902	32 290 729	66.9	22 316 317	14 903 592	66.8	25 924 585	17 387 137	67.1
1 VII 2002	ESDJ	48 230 283	32 181 723	66.7	22 214 426	14 843 215	66.8	25 817 580	17 338 508	67.2
1 VII 2003	ESDJ	47 812 949	31 981 796	66.9	22 019 672	14 732 101	66.9	25 612 922	17 249 695	67.3
1 VII 2004	ESDJ	47 271 271	...	...	21 840 401	...	...	25 430 870		
United Kingdom - Royaume-Uni[102]										
1 VII 1996[102]	ESDF	58 164 374	...	...	28 287 144	...	...	29 877 230	...	...
1 VII 1997[102]	ESDF	58 314 249	...	...	28 371 035	...	...	29 943 214	...	...
1 VII 1998[102]	ESDF	58 474 943	...	...	28 458 360	...	...	30 016 583	...	...
1 VII 1999[102]	ESDF	58 684 427	...	...	28 578 474	...	...	30 105 953	...	...
1 VII 2000[102]	ESDF	58 886 065	...	...	28 690 450	...	...	30 195 615	...	...
29 IV 2001	CDFC	58 789 187	47 007 427	80.0	28 579 867	22 769 606	79.7	30 209 320	24 237 821	80.2
1 VII 2001[102]	ESDF	59 113 497	...	...	28 832 420	...	...	30 281 077	...	...
1 VII 2002[102]	ESDF	59 321 686	...	...	28 963 098	...	...	30 358 588	...	...
1 VII 2003	ESDF	59 553 759	...	...	29 108 023	...	...	30 445 736	...	...
1 VII 2004	ESDF	59 834 314	...	...	29 270 975	...	...	30 563 339	...	...
1 VII 2005	ESDF	60 209 452	...	...	29 479 150	...	...	30 730 302	...	...
OCEANIA - OCÉANIE										
American Samoa - Samoas américaines[25]										
1 IV 2000	CDJC	57 291	...	...	29 264	...	...	28 027		
Australia - Australie										
1 VII 1996[8]	ESDJ	18 310 714	...	...	9 108 055	...	...	9 202 659	...	...
9 VIII 1996	CDFC	17 892 423			8 849 224			9 043 199		
1 VII 1997[8]	ESDJ	18 517 564	...	...	9 203 171	...	...	9 314 393	...	...
1 VII 1998[8]	ESDJ	18 711 271	...	...	9 294 674	...	...	9 416 597	...	...
1 VII 1999[8]	ESDJ	18 925 855	...	...	9 396 548	...	...	9 529 307	...	...
1 VII 2000[8]	ESDJ	19 153 380	...	...	9 505 331	...	...	9 648 049	...	...
1 VII 2001[8]	ESDJ	19 413 240	15 744 532	81.1	9 630 652	7 764 126	80.6	9 782 588	7 980 406	81.6
7 VIII 2001	CDJC	18 769 249	16 344 412	87.1	9 270 466	8 003 865	86.3	9 498 783	8 340 547	87.8
1 VII 2002[8]	ESDJ	19 654 875	...	...	9 756 969	...	...	9 897 906	...	...
1 VII 2003[8]	ESDJ	19 902 738	...	...	9 882 364	...	...	10 020 374	...	...
1 VII 2004[8]	ESDJ	20 139 792	17 503 103	86.9	10 005 472	8 639 350	86.3	10 134 320	8 863 753	87.5
1 VII 2005[8]	ESDJ	20 409 146	...	...	10 144 053	...	...	10 265 093	...	...
Cook Islands - Îles Cook[103]										
1 XII 1996	CDFC	19 103	11 225	58.8	9 842	5 730	58.2	9 261	5 495	59.3
1 XII 2001	CDFC	18 027	...	...	9 303	...	...	8 724	...	...
Fiji - Fidji										
25 VIII 1996	CDFC	775 077	359 495	46.4	393 931	180 119	45.7	381 146	179 376	47.1
French Polynesia - Polynésie française										
3 IX 1996	CDFC	219 521	...	...	113 830	...	...	105 691	...	...
1 VII 1999	ESDF	*227 525*	...	...	*117 738*	...	...	*109 787*	...	...
Guam[25]										
1 VII 1996	ESDJ	145 324	55 445	38.2	...	...	...	...	...	...
1 VII 1997	ESDJ	146 799	56 008	38.2	...	...	...	...	...	...
1 VII 1998	ESDJ	149 724	57 124	38.2	...	...	...	...	...	...
1 VII 1999	ESDJ	152 590	58 217	38.2	...	...	...	...	...	...
1 IV 2000	CDJC	154 805	144 129[26]	93.1	79 181	...	...	75 624	...	...
1 VII 2001	ESDJ	158 330	147 411[26]	93.1	...	...	...	...	...	...
1 VII 2002	ESDJ	161 057	149 950[26]	93.1	...	...	...	...	...	...
1 VII 2003	ESDJ	163 593	152 311[26]	93.1	...	...	...	...	...	...
1 VII 2004	ESDJ	166 090	154 636[26]	93.1	...	...	...	...	...	...

Continent, country or area, and date / Continent, pays ou zone et date	Code[a]	Both sexes - Les deux sexes			Male - Masculin			Female - Féminin		
		Total	Urban - Urbaine		Total	Urban - Urbaine		Total	Urban - Urbaine	
			Number Nombre	Percent P.100		Number Nombre	Percent P.100		Number Nombre	Percent P.100
OCEANIA - OCÉANIE										
Kiribati										
7 XI 2000*	CDFC	84 494	36 717	43.5	41 646	17 822	42.8	42 848	18 895	44.1
7 XII 2005*	CDFC	92 533	...	...	45 612	...	...	46 921	...	...
Marshall Islands - Îles Marshall										
1 VII 1996	ESDF	57 362	...	...	29 323	...	...	28 039	...	...
1 VII 1997	ESDF	60 851	...	...	30 999	...	...	29 852	...	...
1 VII 1998	ESDF	63 301	...	...	32 235	...	...	31 066	...	...
1 VI 1999	CDFC	50 848	...	...	26 034	...	...	24 814	...	...
1 VII 1999	ESDF	50 908	...	...	26 058	...	...	24 850	...	...
1 VII 2000	ESDF	52 671	...	...	26 976	...	...	25 695	...	...
1 VII 2001	ESDF	54 584	...	...	27 960	...	...	26 624	...	...
1 VII 2002	ESDF	56 639	...	...	29 003	...	...	27 636	...	...
Micronesia, Federated States of - Micronésie, États Fédérés de La										
1 VII 1996	ESDJ	109 555	...	...	...	...	...	38 167	...	...
1 VII 1997	ESDJ	110 073	...	...	...	...	...	38 928	...	...
1 IV 2000	CDJC	107 008	...	...	54 191	...	...	52 817	...	...
New Caledonia - Nouvelle-Calédonie										
16 IV 1996	CDFC	196 836	...	...	100 762	...	...	96 074	...	...
1 VII 1996	ESDF	197 389	118 823	60.2	101 030	...	...	96 394	...	...
1 VII 1997	ESDF	200 894	...	...	102 772	...	...	98 158	...	...
1 VII 1998	ESDF	204 316	...	...	104 413	...	...	99 939	...	...
1 VII 1999	ESDF	207 612	...	...	105 996	...	...	101 662	...	...
1 I 2003	ESDF	225 735	...	...	111 314[32]	...	...	107 663[32]	...	...
1 VII 2004	ESDF	230 068	133 815	58.2	112 716	...	...	109 242	...	...
31 VIII 2004*	CDFC	230 789	...	...	116 485	...	...	114 304	...	...
New Zealand - Nouvelle-Zélande										
5 III 1996	CDJC	3 618 303	3 091 740	85.4	1 777 464	1 503 444	84.6	1 840 839	1 588 296	86.3
1 VII 1996	ESDJ	3 732 000	3 191 300	85.5	1 830 300	...	...	1 883 800	...	...
1 VII 1997	ESDJ	3 781 400	3 237 800	85.6	1 863 700	...	...	1 917 700	...	...
1 VII 1998	ESDJ	3 815 000	3 269 700	85.7	1 877 800	...	...	1 937 200	...	...
1 VII 1999	ESDJ	3 835 100	3 289 300	85.8	1 884 900	...	...	1 950 200	...	...
1 VII 2000	ESDJ	3 857 800	3 310 100	85.8	1 893 800	...	...	1 964 000	...	...
6 III 2001	CDJC	3 820 749	...	...	1 863 309	...	...	1 957 440	...	...
1 VII 2001	ESDJ	3 880 500	3 331 400	85.8	1 903 200	...	...	1 977 300	...	...
1 VII 2002	ESDJ	3 939 100	3 385 000	85.9	1 934 000	...	...	2 005 100	...	...
1 VII 2003	ESDJ	4 009 200	3 449 300	86.0	1 971 300	...	...	2 037 900	...	...
1 VII 2004	ESDJ	4 061 400	3 497 100	86.1	1 997 700	...	...	2 063 700	...	...
1 VII 2005	ESDJ	4 098 900	3 530 500	86.1	2 017 100	1 724 600	85.5	2 081 800	1 805 900	86.7
Niue - Nioué										
17 VIII 1997	CDFC	2 088	...	...	1 053	...	...	1 035	...	...
7 IX 2001	CDFC	1 788	...	...	897	...	...	891	...	...
Norfolk Island - Île Norfolk										
6 VIII 1996	CDFC	2 181	...	...	1 039	...	...	1 142	...	...
7 VIII 2001	CDFC	2 037	...	...	1 017	...	...	1 020	...	...
Northern Mariana Islands - Îles Mariannes septentrionales										
1 VII 1996	ESDF	60 960	...	...	30 147	...	...	30 813	...	...
1 VII 1997	ESDF	63 763	...	...	31 311	...	...	32 452	...	...
1 VII 1998	ESDF	66 559	...	...	32 475	...	...	34 084	...	...
1 VII 1999	ESDF	69 341	...	...	33 636	...	...	35 705	...	...
1 IV 2000	CDFC	69 221	...	...	31 984	...	...	37 237	...	...
1 VII 2000	ESDF	72 101	...	...	34 790	...	...	37 311	...	...
1 VII 2001	ESDF	74 847	...	...	35 941	...	...	38 906	...	...
Palau - Palaos										
1 VII 1996	ESDF	17 600	...	...	9 380	...	...	8 220	...	...
1 VII 1997	ESDF	18 061	...	...	9 618	...	...	8 443	...	...
1 VII 1998	ESDF	18 494	...	...	9 842	...	...	8 652	...	...
1 VII 1999	ESDF	18 882	...	...	10 039	...	...	8 843	...	...

Continent, country or area, and date / Continent, pays ou zone et date	Code[a]	Both sexes - Les deux sexes Total	Urban - Urbaine Number Nombre	Urban - Urbaine Percent P.100	Male - Masculin Total	Urban - Urbaine Number Nombre	Urban - Urbaine Percent P.100	Female - Féminin Total	Urban - Urbaine Number Nombre	Urban - Urbaine Percent P.100
OCEANIA - OCÉANIE										
Palau - Palaos										
15 IV 2000	CDFC	19 129	13 303	69.5	10 450	...	...	8 679	...	...
1 VII 2000	ESDF	19 257	...	...	10 229	...	...	9 028	...	...
1 VII 2001	ESDF	19 626	...	...	10 415	...	...	9 211	...	...
1 VII 2002	ESDF	19 976	...	...	10 590	...	...	9 386	...	...
1 IV 2005	CDFC	19 907	15 399	77.4	10 699	...	...	9 208	...	...
Papua New Guinea - Papouasie-Nouvelle-Guinée										
1 VII 1997	ESDF	*4 209 335*	...	...	*2 218 293*	...	...	*1 991 042*	...	...
9 VII 2000	CDFC	5 190 786	686 301	13.2	2 691 744	372 453	13.8	2 499 042	313 848	12.6
1 VII 2002	ESDF	*5 461 940*	...	...	*2 826 212*	...	...	*2 635 722*	...	...
Samoa										
5 XI 2001	CDFC	176 710	38 836	22.0	92 050	19 837	21.6	84 660	18 999	22.4
1 VII 2002	ESDF	*178 329*	*39 192*	*22.0*	*92 893*	*20 019*	*21.6*	*85 436*	*19 173*	*22.4*
1 VII 2003	ESDF	*179 962*	*39 551*	*22.0*	*93 744*	*20 202*	*21.6*	*86 218*	*19 349*	*22.4*
1 VII 2004	ESDF	*181 611*	*39 913*	*22.0*	*94 603*	*20 387*	*21.6*	*87 008*	*19 526*	*22.4*
1 VII 2005	ESDF	*183 275*	*40 279*	*22.0*	*95 470*	*20 574*	*21.6*	*87 805*	*19 705*	*22.4*
Solomon Islands - Îles Salomon										
21 XI 1999	CDFC	409 042	...	...	211 381	...	...	197 661	...	...
1 VII 2003	ESDF	*448 286*	...	...	*231 267*	...	...	*217 019*	...	...
1 VII 2004	ESDF	*460 110*	...	...	*237 626*	...	...	*222 484*	...	...
1 VII 2005	ESDF	*471 266*	...	...	*242 927*	...	...	*228 339*	...	...
Tokelau - Tokélaou										
11 XI 1996	CDFC	1 487	...	...	736	...	...	751	...	...
11 X 2001	CDFC	1 537	...	...	761	...	...	776	...	...
Tonga										
30 XI 1996	CDFC	97 784	22 400	22.9	49 615	...	...	48 169	...	...
1 VII 1997[104]	ESDF	*98 591*	...	...	*50 037*	...	...	*48 553*	...	...
1 VII 1998[104]	ESDF	*99 264*	...	...	*50 406*	...	...	*48 856*	...	...
1 VII 1999[104]	ESDF	*99 821*	...	...	*50 731*	...	...	*49 088*	...	...
1 VII 2000[104]	ESDF	*100 283*	...	...	*51 017*	...	...	*49 264*	...	...
1 VII 2001[104]	ESDF	*100 673*	...	...	*51 272*	...	...	*49 400*	...	...
1 VII 2002[104]	ESDF	*101 002*	...	...	*51 473*	...	...	*49 528*	...	...
1 VII 2003[104]	ESDF	*101 405*	...	...	*51 710*	...	...	*49 694*	...	...
Tuvalu										
1 XI 2002	CDFC	9 561	...	...	4 729	2 281	48.2	4 832	2 211	45.8
Vanuatu										
16 XI 1999	CDJC	186 678	40 094	21.5	95 682	20 726	21.7	90 996	19 368	21.3
1 VII 2004[105]	ESDF	*215 541*	...	...	*110 441*	...	...	*105 399*	...	...
Wallis and Futuna Islands - Îles Wallis et Futuna										
3 X 1996	CDFC	14 166	...	...	6 984	...	...	7 182	...	...
22 VII 2003	CDFC	14 944	...	...	7 494	...	...	7 450	...	...

FOOTNOTES - NOTES

Italics: estimates which are less reliable. - Italiques: estimations moins sûres.

* Provisional. - Données provisoires.

[a] 'Code' indicates the source of data, as follows:
CDFC - Census, de facto, complete tabulation
CDFS - Census, de facto, sample tabulation
CDJC - Census, de jure, complete tabulation
CDJS - Census, de jure, sample tabulation
SSDF - Sample survey, de facto
SSDJ - Sample survey, de jure
ESDF - Estimates, de facto

ESDJ - Estimates, de jure
Le 'Code' indique la source des données, comme suit:
CDFC - Recensement, population de fait, tabulation complète
CDFS - Recensement, population de fait, tabulation par sondage
CDJC - Recensement, population de droit, tabulation complète
CDJS - Recensement, population de droit, tabulation par sondage
SSDF - Enquête par sondage, population de fait
SSDJ - Enquête par sondage, population de droit
ESDF - Données estimées, population de fait
ESDJ - Données estimées, population de droit

[1] Series not strictly comparable due to differences of definitions of "urban". - Les séries ne sont pas strictement comparables en raison de différences existant dans la définition des "regions urbaines".

[2] Including emigrants. - Y compris les émigrants.

[3] Data refer to national projections. - Les données se réfèrent aux projections nationales.

[4] Census result, excluding Mayotte. - Les résultat du recensement, non compris Mayotte.

[5] Data for urban and rural areas are not adjusted for under-enumeration, estimated around 5 per cent for the total country. - Les données pour les zones urbaines et rurales n'ont pas été adjustées pour tenir en compte de la sous-estimation de 5 p. cent approximativement.

[6] Data refer to Libyan nationals only. - Les données se raportent aux nationaux libyens seulement.

[7] Because of rounding, totals are not in all cases the sum of the parts. - Les chiffres étant arrondis, les totaux ne correspondent pas toujours rigoureusement à la somme des chiffres partiels.

[8] Mid-year estimates have been adjusted for underenumeration, at latest census. - Les estimations au millieu de l'année tiennent compte d'un ajustement destiné à compenser les lacunes du dénombrement lors du dernier recensement.

[9] Census results have been adjusted for underenumeration, estimated at 5.1 per cent. - Les résultats du recensement ont été ajustées pour compenser les lacunes du dénombrement, estimées à 5,1 p. 100.

[10] The number of males and/or females excludes persons whose sex is not stated (18 urban, 19 rural). - Il n'est pas tenu compte dans le nombre d'hommes et de femmes des personnes dont le sexe n'est pas indiqué (18 en zone urbaine et 19 en zone rurale).

[11] Data exclude adjustment for underenumeration, estimated at 2.4 per cent. - Les données n'ont pas été ajustées pour compenser les lacunes du dénombrement, estimées à 2,4 p. 100.

[12] Based on results of a Socio Economic Survey. - Basé sur les résultats d'une enquête Socio-Economique.

[13] For 1996, census results have been adjusted for underenumeration estimated at 6.8 per cent. - Les résultat du recensement ont été ajustées pour compenser les lacunes du dénombrement, estimées à 6,8 p. 100.

[14] Excluding the institutional population. - Non compris la population dans les institutions.

[15] Because of rounding, totals are not in all cases the sum of the parts. Census data have not been adjusted for underenumeration. - Les chiffres étant arrondis, les totaux ne correspondent pas toujours rigoureusement à la somme des chiffres partiels. Les données de recensement ne tiennent pas compte de d'une ajustement destiné à compenser les lacunes du dénombrement.

[16] Final intercensal estimates. - Estimations inter censitaires finales.

[17] Final postcensal estimates. - Évaluations postcensal finales.

[18] Census data excluding the institutional population. - Les donnees de recensement non compris la population dans les institutions.

[19] Population statistics are compiled from registers. - Les statistiques de la population sont compilées à partir des registres.

[20] Including Carriacou and other dependencies in the Grenadines. - Y compris Carriacou et les autres dépendances du groupe des îles Grenadines.

[21] Including dependencies: Marie-Galante, la Désirade, les Saintes, Petite-Terre, St. Barthélemy and French part of St. Martin. - Y compris les dépendances: Marie-Galante, la Désirade, les Saintes, Petite-Terre, Saint-Barthélemy et la partie française de Saint-Martin.

[22] Including persons of unknown residence. - Y compris les personnes d'état résidence inconnu.

[23] Around 1996 - 1997 volcanic activity on Montserrat escalated, forcing people to relocate. - Vers 1996 - 1997 l'activité volcanique a connu une recrudescence à Montserrat, forçant les habitants à s'installer ailleurs.

[24] Comprising Bonaire, Curaçao, Saba, St. Eustatius and Dutch part of St. Martin. - Comprend Bonaire, Curaçao, Saba, Saint-Eustache et la partie néederlandaise de Saint-Martin.

[25] Including armed forces stationed in the area. - Y compris les militaires en garnison sur le territoire.

[26] Definition of urban and rural distribution changed from the year 2000. - La définition des régions urbaines et rurales a changée depuis 2000.

[27] Definition of urban and rural distribution changed from the year 2000. Unrevised data. - La définition des régions urbaines et rurales a changée depuis 2000. Les données n'ont pas été révisées.

[28] Excluding persons residing in institutions. - Non compris les personnes dans les institutions.

[29] Excluding armed forces overseas and civilian citizens absent from country for an extended period of time. - Non compris les militaires à l'étranger, et les civils hors du pays pendant une période prolongée.

[30] Data include persons in remote areas, military personnel outside the country, merchant seamen at sea, civilian seasonal workers outside the country, and other civilians outside the country, and exclude nomads, foreign military, civilian aliens temporarily in the country, transients on ships and Indian jungle population. - Y compris les personnes vivant dans des régions éloignées, le personel militaire en dehors du pays, les marins marchands, les ouvriers saisonniers en dehors du

pays, et autres civils en dehors du pays, et non compris les nomades, les militaires étrangers, les étrangers civils temporairement dans le pays, les transiteurs sur des bateaux et les Indiens de la jungle.

[31] Excluding nomadic Indian tribes. - Non compris les tribus d'Indiens nomades.

[32] Unrevised data. - Les données n'ont pas été révisées.

[33] Excluding dependencies, of which South Georgia (area 3 755 km2) had an estimated population of 499 in 1964 (494 males, 5 females). The other dependencies namely, the South Sandwich group (surface area 337 km2) and a number of smaller islands, are presumed to be uninhabited. A dispute exists between the governments of Argentina and the United Kingdom of Great Britain and Northern Ireland concerning sovereignty over the Falkland Islands (Malvinas). - Non compris les dépendances, parmi lesquelles figure la Georgie du Sud (3 755 km2) avec une population estimée à 499 personnes en 1964 (494 du sexe masculin et 5 du sexe féminin). Les autres dépendances, c'est-à-dire le groupe des Sandwich du Sud (superficie: 337 km2) et certaines petites-îles, sont présumées inhabitées. La souveraineté sur les îles Falkland (Malvinas) fait l'objet d'un différend entre le Gouvernement argentin et le Gouvernement du Royaume-Uni de Grande-Bretagne et d'Irlande du Nord.

[34] Data for 2003 have been adjusted on the basis of the Population Census of 2002. - Les données de 2003 ont été ajustées sur la base du recensement de population de 2002.

[35] Excluding Indian jungle population. - Non compris les Indiens de la jungle.

[36] The population for the year 2005 corresponds to the population actually enumerated in the census conducted between 18 July and 20 August 2005. The total (adjusted) population is 27 219 264 inhabitants. - La population pour 2005 correspond à la population effectivement dénombrée lors du recensement réalisé entre le 18 juillet et le 20 août 2005. La population totale (après ajustement) compte 27 219 264 habitants.

[37] Data for the total population include 17 diplomats. - La population totale indiquée comprend 17 diplomates.

[38] The previous census was conducted only 16 months earlier (on 31 Mar 2003) but it was repeated because all of its data were destroyed in a fire before they could be fully processed, analyzed, and reported. - Le recensement précédent a eu lieu seulement 16 mois auparavant (le 31 mars 2003), mais a dû être refait parce que toutes les données ont été détruites dans un incendie avant que l'on n'ait pu les traiter et les analyser.

[39] Figures for male and female population do not add up to the figure for total population, because they exclude 365 persons of unknown sex. - Les chiffres relatifs à la population masculine et féminine ne correspondent pas au chiffre de la population totale, parce que l'on en a exclu 365 personnes de sexe inconnu.

[40] Data refer to resident population in Uruguay according to Census Phase 1, carried out between the months of June and July 2004. - Les données se rapportent à la population résidente en Uruguay d'après la phase 1 du recensement, qui a eu lieu entre juin et juillet 2004.

[41] For 2002 total population was the only figure revised. For urban/rural distribution, data refer to the settled population based on the 1979 Population Census; an estimated 1.5 million nomads was not included. - Pour 2002, l'effectif total de la population est le seul chiffre révisé. Pour la distribution urbaine/rurale, les données se rapportent à la population sédentaire sur la base du recensement de 1979; les nomades, estimées a 1.5 million, ne sont pas inclus.

[42] The methodology used for calculating the number of de facto and de jure population in the 2001 census data differs as follows from the methodology used in previous censuses: the duration that defines a person as being ' temporary present ' or 'temporary absent' is now 'under one year'. The previously applied definition was for '6 months'. - La méthode utilisée pour dénombrer la population de fait et la population de droit dans le contexte du recensement de 2001 diffère de celle qui a été appliquée lors des recensements antérieurs en ce que la durée considérée pour définir la ' présence temporaire 'ou' l'absence temporaire' était dorénavant fixée à 'moins d'un an' alors qu'elle était de '6 mois' auparavant.

[43] Census results have been adjusted for underenumeration, estimated at 4.96 per cent. - Les données ont été ajustées pour compenser les lacunes du dénombrement, estimées à 4,96 %.

[44] Excluding foreign diplomatic personnel and their dependants. - Non compris le personnel diplomatique étranger et les membres de leur famille les accompagnant.

[45] Excluding foreign diplomatic personnel and their dependants. Based on Cambodia Intercensal Population Survey. Data exclude institutional, homeless households and transient poulation. - Non compris le personnel diplomatique étranger et les membres de leur famille les accompagnant. Les données ne comprennent pas la population des institutions, les ménages sans abri et la population de passage.

[46] For statistical purposes, the data for China do not include those for the Hong Kong Special Administrative Region (Hong Kong SAR), Macao Special Administrative Region (Macao SAR) and Taiwan province of China. - Pour la présentation des statistiques, les données pour la Chine ne comprennent pas la

Région Administrative Spéciale de Hong Kong (Hong Kong RAS), la Région Administrative Spéciale de Macao (Macao RAS) et Taïwan province de Chine.

[47] Data for the period 1990 to 2000 have been adjusted on the basis of the Population Census of 2000. - Les données pour la période allant de 1990 à 2000 ont été ajustées à partir des résultats du recensement de la population de 2000.

[48] The military personnel are classified as urban population. - Le personnel militaire est classé dans la population urbaine.

[49] For the civilian population of 31 provinces, municipalities and autonomous regions. - Pour la population civile seulement de 31 provinces, municipalités et régions autonomes.

[50] Data have been estimated on the basis of the annual National Sample Surveys on Population Changes. - Les données ont été estimées sur la base de l'enquête annuelle "National Sample Survey on Population Changes".

[51] Data for 2005 are estimated from the National Sample Survey of 1 Per cent population. - Les données pour 2005 ont été estimées à partir de l'enquête nationale qui a porté sur un échantillon de 1 % de la population.

[52] For 2001, data refer to Hong Kong resident population at the census moment, which covers usual residents and mobile residents. Usual residents refer to two categories of people: (1) Hong Kong permanent residents who had stayed in Hong Kong for at least three months during the six months before or for at least three months during the six months after the census moment, regardless of whether they were in Hong Kong or not at the census moment; and (2) Hong Kong non-permanent residents who were in Hong Kong at the census moment. Mobile Residents, they are Hong Kong permanent residents who had stayed in Hong Kong for at least one month but less than three months during the six months before or for at least one month but less than three months during the six months after the census moment, regardless of whether they were in Hong Kong or not at the census moment. - Pour 2001, les données se rapportent à la population résidente à Hong Kong au moment du recensement. Cette population est composée des résidants habituels et des résidants mobiles. La population résidente est partagée en deux catégories: (1) les résidents permanents qui ont habité à Hong Kong au moins trois mois pendant les six mois précédents ou les six mois suivants le recensement; (2) les habitants non-permanents de Hong Kong qui étaient à Hong Kong au moment du recensement. La population mobile se rapporte aux résidents permanents de Hong Kong qui ont habité à Hong Kong pendant les six mois après le recensement pour une période comprise entre un mois et trois mois, indépendamment du fait qu'ils étaient à Hong Kong au moment du recensement au pays.

[53] Data refer to government controlled areas. - Les données se rapportent aux zones contrôlées par le Gouvernement.

[54] Data include all population irrespective of citizenship, who at the time of the census resided in the country or intended to reside for a period of at least one year. It does not distinguish between those present or absent at the time of census. - Les chiffres comprennent toute la population, quelle que soit la nationalité, qui à l'époque de recensement avait résidé dans le pays, ou avait l'intention de résider, pendant une période d'au moins un an. Il n'y a pas de distinction entre les personnes présentes ou absentes au moment du recensement.

[55] Including data for the Indian-held part of Jammu and Kashmir, the final status of which has not yet been determined. - Y compris les données pour la partie du Jammu et du Cachemire occupée par l'Inde dont le statut définitif n'a pas encore été déterminé.

[56] Data exclude Mao-Maram, Paomata and Purul sub-divisions of Senapati district of Manipur. The population of Manipur including the estimated population of the three sub-divisions of Senapati district is 2,291,125 (Males 1,161,173 and females 1,129,952). - Non compris les subdivisions Mao-Maram Paomata et Purul du district de Senapati dans l'État du Manipur. Cet État compte 2 291 125 habitants (1 161 173 hommes et 1 129 952 femmes), y compris la population estimative des trois subdivisions du district de Senapati.

[57] The figure includes an estimated population of 459 557 persons in urban and 1 857 659 persons in rural areas that were not directly enumerated, and a population of 566 403 persons in urban and 1 717 578 persons in rural areas that decline the participation. Also included are 421 399 non permanent residents (the homeless, the crew of ships carrying national flag, boat/floating house people, remote located tribesmen and refugees.) - Y compris la population estimée a 459 557 personnes dans les zones urbaines et de 1 857 659 personnes dans les zones rurales qui n'ont pas été énumérées directement, aussi que 566 403 personnes qui non pas répondu dans les zones urbaines et de 1 717 578 personnes dans les zones rurales. Y compris 421 399 résidants non permanents (les sans abri, l'équipage des bateaux portant le pavillon national, les habitants des embarcations ou des maisons flottantes, les habitants des tribus isolées et les réfugiés.)

[58] Data relate to the Iranian Year which begins on 21 March and ends on 20 March of the following year. - Les données concernent l'année iranienne, qui commence le 21 mars et se termine le 20 mars de l'année suivante.

[59] Data relate to the population for the Iranian Year 1384 (21 March 2005-20 March 2006). - Les données concernent la population pour l'année iranienne 1384 (21 mars 2005-20 mars 2006).

[60] For the 1997 population census, data exclude population in three autonomous provinces in the north of the country. - Pour le recensement de 1997, la population des trois provinces autonomes dans le nord du pays est exclue.

[61] Including data for East Jerusalem and Israeli residents in certain other territories under occupation by Israeli military forces since June 1967. - Y compris les données pour Jérusalem-Est et les résidents israéliens dans certains autres territoires occupés depuis 1967 par les forces armées israéliennes.

[62] Excluding diplomatic personnel outside the country and foreign military and civilian personnel and their dependants stationed in the area. - Non compris le personnel diplomatique hors du pays ni les militaires et agents civils étrangers en poste sur le territoire et les membres de leur famille les accompagnant.

[63] Excluding data for Jordanian territory under occupation since June 1967 by Israeli military forces. Excluding foreigners, including registered Palestinian refugees. - Non compris les données pour le territoire jordanien occupé depuis juin 1967 par les forces armées israéliennes. Non compris les étrangers, mais y compris les réfugiés de Palestine enregistrés.

[64] Excluding foreigners. Including diplomats and their families abroad, but excluding foreign diplomats, foreign military personnal, and their families in the country. - Non compris étrangers. Y compris le personnel diplomatique et les membres de leurs familles à l'étranger, mais sans tenir compte du personnel diplomatique et militaire étranger et des membres de leurs familles.

[65] Urban/Rural: Places with 50 000 or more inhabitants are usually considered urban in Korea. However, the census results are composed in the basis of the minor administrative divisions such as Dongs (mostly urban areas) and Eups or Myeons (rural areas) rather than urban or rural residences. In this report, urban refers to Dongs and rural refers ro Eups and Myeons. - Urbaine/rurale: les lieux avec 50,000 habitants ou plus sont habituellement considérés urbains en Corée. Cependant, les résultats du recensement ont été préparés sur la base des divisions administratives mineures comme les Dongs (principalement des zones urbaines), et les Eups ou Myeons (des zones rurales) plutôt que sur les résidences urbaines ou rurales. Dans ce rapport urbaine se rapporte aux Dongs et rural aux Eups et aux Myeons.

[66] For 1997, based on Lao expenditure and consumption survey 1997/98. - Les données se rapportent à l'Enquête sur la consommation et les dépenses des ménages du Laos du 1997/98.

[67] From year 2000-2004, calculated base on Population census 1995 structure and growth rate at year 2000. - Pour les années 2000 à 2004, on a pris pour base la structure issue du recensement de population de 1995 et le taux de croissance de 2000.

[68] Excluding Malaysian citizens and permanent residents who were away or intended to be away from the country for more than six months. Excluding Malaysian military, naval and diplomatic personnel and their families outside the country, and tourists, businessman who intended to be in Malaysia for less than six months. Census results have been adjusted for underenumeration. - Non compris les citoyens malaisiens et les résidents permanents qui étaient ou qui ont prévu d'être hors du pays pour six mois ou plus. Non compris le personnel militaire Malaisien, le personnel naval ou diplomatique et leurs familles hors du pays, et les touristes et les hommes d'affaires qui avaient l'intention de rester en Malaisie moins de six mois. Les résultats du recensement ont été ajustées pour compenser les lacunes du dénombrement

[69] Figures for urban and rural areas do not add up to the total; reason for discrepancy not ascertained. - La somme des données pour la résidence urbaine et rurale n'est pas égale au total; on ne sait pas comment s'explique la divergence.

[70] Reason for discrepancy between these figures and corresponding figures shown elsewhere not ascertained. - On ne sait pas comment s'explique la divergence entre ces chiffres et les chiffres correspondants indiqués ailleurs.

[71] Data including estimated population from household listing from Village Development Committees and Wards which could not be enumerated at the time of census. - Les données incluent la population estimée par les listes des ménages des comités de développement des villages et des circonscriptions qui n'ont pas pu être énumérée au moment du recensement.

[72] Data for urban including population in refugee camps. - Les données pour la population urbaine comprennent la population dans les camps réfugiés.

[73] Total population does not include Palestinian population living in those parts of Jerusalem governorate which were annexed by Israel in 1967, amounting to 210 209 persons. Likewise, the results does not include the estimates of not enumerated population based on the findings of the post enumeration study, i.e 83 805 persons. - Les données relatives à la population totale ne comprennent pas la population palestinienne -équivalent à 210 209 personnes - habitant dans les territoires du gouvernorat de Jérusalem qui ont été annexés par Israël en 1967. Egalement, les données ne tiennent pas compte des estimations de la

population calculée sur la base des résultats de l'enquête postcensitaire, équivalent à 83 805 personnes.

[74] Excluding data for the Pakistan-held part of Jammu and Kashmir, the final status of which has not yet been determined. - Non compris les données concernant la partie du Jammu et Cachemire occupée par le Pakistan dont le statut définitif n'a pas été déterminé.

[75] Census result, excluding transients afloat and non-locally domiciled military and civilian services personnel and their dependants and visitors. - Les résultats du recensement, non compris les personnes de passage à bord de navires ni les militaires et agents civils non-résidents et les membres de leur famille les accompagnants et visiteurs.

[76] The Population and Housing Census 2001 did not cover the whole area of the country due to the security problems; the Census was complete in 18 districts only; in three districts it was not possible to conduct it; and in four districts it was partially conducted. - Le recensement de la population et de l'habitat en 2001 n'a pas couvert la totalité du pays pour des problèmes de sécurité ; le recensement a été complété seulement en 18 districts ; dans 3 districts ça n'a pas été possible de conduire le recensement et dans 4 districts il a été partiellement conduit.

[77] Including Palestinian refugees. - Y compris les réfugiés de Palestine.

[78] Comprising 7 sheikdoms of Abu Dhabi, Dubai, Sharjah, Ajaman, Umm al Qaiwain, Ras al Khaimah and Fujairah, and the area lying within the modified Riyadh line as announced in October 1955. - Comprend les sept cheikhats de Abou Dhabi, Dabai, Ghârdja, Adjmân, Oumm-al-Quiwaïn, Ras al Khaïma et Foudjaïra, ainsi que la zone délimitée par la ligne de Riad modifiée comme il a été annoncé en octobre 1955.

[79] Excluding Faeroe Islands and Greenland. Population statistics are compiled from registers. - Non compris les Iles Féroé et le Grœnland. Les statistiques de la population sont compilées à partir des registres.

[80] Excluding Overseas Departments, namely, French Guiana, Guadeloupe, Martinique and Reunion, shown separately. Excluding diplomatic personnel outside the country and including members of alien armed forces not living in military camps and foreign diplomatic personnel not living in embassies or consulates. - Non compris les départements d'outre mer, c'est-à-dire la Guyane française, la Guadeloupe, la Martinique et la Réunion, qui font l'objet de rubriques distinctes. Non compris le personnel diplomatique hors du pays et y compris les militaires étrangers ne vivant pas dans des camps militaires et le personnel diplomatique étranger ne vivant pas dans les ambassades ou les consulats.

[81] Data of the microcensus - a 1% household sample survey - refer to a single reference week in spring (usually last week in April). Excluding homeless persons. Excluding foreign military personnel and foreign diplomatic and consular personnel and their family members in the country. - Les données du microrecensement (enquête sur les ménages, réalisée sur un échantillon de 1 %) concernent une seule semaine de référence au printemps (habituellement la dernière semaine d'avril). Non compris les personnes sans domicile fixe. Non compris le personnel militaire étranger, le personnel diplomatique et consulaire étranger et les membres de leur famille se trouvant dans le pays.

[82] Excluding families of military personnel, visitors and transients. - Non compris les familles des militaires, ni les visiteurs et transients.

[83] Mid-year population excludes armed forces stationed outside the country, but includes alien armed forces stationed in the area. - Les estimations au millieu de l'année non compris les militaires en garnison hors du pays, mais y compris les militaires étrangers en garnison sur le territoire.

[84] Census data including armed forces stationed outside the country, but excluding alien armed forces stationed in the area. - Les données de recensement comprennent les militaires se trouvant hors du pays, mais ne comprennent pas les militaires étrangers en poste sur le territoire.

[85] Data refer to the Vatican City State. Population statistics are compiled from registers. - Les données se rapportent à l'Etat de la Cité du Vatican. Les statistiques de la population sont compilées à partir des registres.

[86] The regional grouping (urban/rural) was made from 1990 to 2000 according to the administrative division of 1 January 2000 and from 2001 according to the administrative division of 1 January 2004. - Pour les années 1990 à 2000, le découpage régional (zone urbaine/rurale) correspond au découpage administratif en vigueur au 1er janvier 2000; à partir de 2001, il correspond à celui en vigueur au 1er janvier 2004.

[87] Data refer to 15th of April. - Données se rapportent au 15 avril.

[88] Urban and rural population is given according to the 2007 administrative division. - Les données sur la population urbaine et la population rurale correspondent aux divisions administratives de 2007.

[89] Census result, based on compilation of continuous accounting and sample surveys. - Les résultat du recensement, d'aprés les résultats des dénombrements et enquêtes par sondage continue.

[90] Including residents temporarily outside the country. - Y compris les résidents se trouvant temporairement hors du pays.

[91] Excluding civilian aliens within country, but including civilian nationals temporarily outside country. - Non compris les civils étrangers dans le pays, mais y compris les civils nationaux temporairement hors du pays.

[92] Average year data for 2000-2001 contain revised data according to the final results of population census 2002. - Les données annuelles moyennes pour 2000 et 2001 comportent des données révisées en fonction des résultats du recensement de 2002.

[93] Including the Azores and Madeira Islands. - Y compris les Açores et Madère.

[94] Data do not include information for Transnistria and the municipality of Bender. - Les données ne tiennent pas compte de l'information sur la Transnistria et la municipalité de Bender.

[95] Figures were updated taking into account the results of the 2002 All-Russian population census. - Les chiffres ont été calculés compte tenu des résultats du recensement de la population de la Fédération de Russie de 2002.

[96] 1998 - 2001, estimates of Kosovo and Metohia computed on the basis of natural increases from year 1997. - 1998 - 2001, les estimations pour le Kosovo et la Metohia ont été calculées sur la base des incréments naturelles depuis 1997.

[97] Without data for Kosovo and Metohia. - Sans les données pour le Kosovo et Metohie.

[98] Because the data by urban/rural residence are available only for citizens of the Republic of Slovenia, excluding citizens temporarily residing abroad, the sum by urban and rural does not add up to the total. - Les données concernant la résidence en zone urbaine ou rurale sont disponibles seulement pour les nationaux slovènes, mais les nationaux se trouvant provisoirement à l'étranger ne sont pas pris en compte. La somme des chiffres disponibles pour les zones urbaines et rurales ne correspond donc pas au total.

[99] Including the Balearic and Canary Islands, and Alhucemas, Ceuta, Chafarinas, Melilla and Penon de Vélez de la Gomera. - Y compris les Baléares et les Canaries, Al Hoceima, Ceuta, les îles Zaffarines, Melilla et Penon de Vélez de la Gomera.

[100] Figures for 2002 and 2003 were calculated on the base of census data 2002. - Les chiffres pour 2002 et 2003 ont été calculés à partir des résultats du recensement de 2002.

[101] Starting from 1994 until 1999 data is de facto and from 2000 and later data is de jure. - De 1994 à 1999, les données sont de fait, à partir de 2000 elles sont de jure.

[102] Population estimates for 1994 to 2002 were revised in light of the local studies. - Les estimations de la population pour les années 1994 à 2002 ont été révisées en fonction d'études locales.

[103] Excluding Niue, shown separately, which is part of Cook Islands, but because of remoteness is administered separately. - Non compris Nioué, qui fait l'objet d'une rubrique distincte et qui fait partie des îles Cook, mais qui, en raison de son éloignement, est administrée séparément.

[104] Based on the results of the 1996 population census not necessarily mid year estimated. - À partir des résultats du recensement de la population de 1996, pas nécessairement des estimations en milieu d'année.

[105] Figures for male and female do not add up to the total, reason for discrepancy not ascertained. Data refer to national projections. - La some des données pour la population masculine et pour la population féminine n'est pas égale au total, les raisons de cette différence ne sont pas expliquées. Les données se réfèrent aux projections nationales.

Table 7

Table 7 presents population by age, sex and urban/rural residence for the latest available year.

Description of variables: Data in this table are either population census figures or estimates, some of which are based on sample surveys. Data refer to the de facto population unless otherwise noted.

The reference date of the census or estimate appears in the stub of the table. In general, the estimates refer to mid-year (1 July).

Age is defined as age at last birthday, that is, the difference between the date of birth and the reference date of the age distribution expressed in completed solar years. The age classification used in this table is the following: under 1 year, 1-4 years, 5-year groups through 95-99 years, and 100 years or over.

Statistics are presented for one year, the most recent available. However, if more complete disaggregation is available for an earlier year, both are displayed.

The urban/rural classification of population by age and sex is that provided by each country or area; it is presumed to be based on the national census definitions of urban population that have been set forth at the end of the technical notes to table 6.

Estimates of population by age and sex presented in this table have been limited to countries or areas for which estimates have been based on the results of a sample survey or have been constructed by the component method from the results of a population census or sample survey. Estimations derived from distributing estimated total population according to percentages in each age-sex group at the time of a census or sample survey are not included in this table.

Reliability of data: Estimates which are believed to be less reliable are set in *italics* rather than in roman type. No attempt has been made to take account of age-reporting accuracy, the evaluation of which has been described in section 3.1.3 of the Technical Notes. However, the Whipple's Index presented in table 1c of the Demographic Yearbook Special Census Topic Volume 1 (Basic population characteristics) provides an assessment of age heaping for 145 countries for censuses being held between 1985 and 2003.

Limitations: Statistics on population by age and sex are subject to the same qualifications as have been set forth for population statistics in general and age distributions in particular, as discussed in sections 3 and 3.1.3, respectively, of the Technical Notes.

Comparability of population data classified by age and sex is limited by variations in the definition of total population, discussed in detail in section 3 of the Technical Notes, and by the accuracy of the original enumeration. Both factors are more important in relation to certain age groups than to others. For example, under-enumeration is known to be more prevalent among infants and young children than among older persons. Similarly, the exclusion from the total population of certain groups that tend to be of selected ages (such as the armed forces) can markedly affect the age structure and its comparability with that for other countries or areas. Consideration should be given to the implications of these basic limitations in using the data.

In addition to these general qualifications are the special problems of comparability that arise in relation to age statistics in particular. Age distributions of population are known to suffer from certain deficiencies that have their origin in irregularities in age reporting. Although some of the irregularities tend to be obscured or eliminated when data are tabulated in five-year age groups rather than by single years, precision still continues to be affected, though the degree of distortion is not always readily seen.

Another factor limiting comparability is the age classification employed by the various countries or areas. Age may be based on the year of birth rather than the age at last birthday, in other words, calculated using the day, month and year of birth. Distributions based only on the year of birth are footnoted when known.

The absence of frequencies in the unknown age group does not necessarily indicate completely accurate reporting and tabulation of the age item. The unknowns may have been eliminated by assigning ages to them before tabulation, or by proportionately distributing the unknown category across the age groups after tabulation.

As noted in connection with table 5, intercensal estimates of total population are usually revised to accord with the results of a census of population if inexplicable discontinuities appear to exist. Postcensal age-sex distributions, however, are less likely to be revised in this way. When it is known that a total population estimate for a given year has been revised and the corresponding age distribution has not been, the age distribution is shown as provisional. Distributions of this type should be used with caution when studying trends over a period of years, though their utility for studying age structure for the specified year is probably unimpaired.

The comparability of data by urban/rural residence is affected by the national definitions of urban and rural used in tabulating these data. When known, the definitions of urban used in national population censuses are presented at the end of the technical notes for table 6. As discussed in detail in the technical notes for table 6, these definitions vary considerably from one country or area to another.

Earlier data: Population by age, sex and urban/rural residence has been shown in previous issues of the *Demographic Yearbook*. For more information on specific topics, and years for which data are reported, readers should consult the Historical Index. In addition, population by single years of age, sex and urban/rural residence are shown in the *Demographic Yearbook* Special Census Topics table 1 available online at http://unstats.un.org/unsd/demographic/products/dyb/dybcens.htm.

Tableau 7

Le tableau 7 présente les données les plus récentes dont on dispose sur la population selon l'âge, le sexe et le lieu de résidence (zone urbaine ou rurale).

Description des variables : les données de ce tableau proviennent de recensements de la population ou correspondent à des estimations fondées, dans certains cas, sur des enquêtes par sondage. Sauf indication contraire, elles se rapportent à la population de fait.

La date du recensement ou de l'estimation figure dans la colonne de gauche du tableau. En général, les estimations se rapportent au milieu de l'année (1er juillet).

L'âge désigne l'âge au dernier anniversaire, c'est-à-dire la différence entre la date de naissance et la date de référence de la répartition par âge exprimée en années solaires révolues. La classification par âge utilisée dans ce tableau est la suivante : moins d'un an, 1 à 4 ans, groupes quinquennaux jusqu'à 95-99 ans et 100 ans ou plus.

Les statistiques portent sur une année, qui correspond à celle pour laquelle on dispose des statistiques les plus récentes. Toutefois, si l'on dispose de répartitions plus complètes pour des années antérieures, les statistiques sont alors présentées pour les deux années.

La classification par zones urbaines et rurales de la population selon l'âge et le sexe est celle qui est communiquée par chaque pays ou zone ; on part du principe qu'elle repose sur les définitions de la population urbaine utilisées pour les recensements de la population nationaux telles qu'elles sont reproduites à la fin des notes techniques du tableau 6.

Les estimations de la population selon l'âge et le sexe qui figurent dans ce tableau ne concernent que les pays ou zones pour lesquels les estimations sont fondées sur les résultats d'une enquête par sondage ou ont été établies par la méthode des composantes à partir des résultats d'un recensement de la population ou d'une enquête par sondage. Les répartitions par âge et par sexe obtenues en appliquant à l'estimation de la population totale les pourcentages enregistrés pour les divers groupes d'âge pour chaque sexe lors d'un recensement ou d'une enquête par sondage n'ont pas été reproduites dans ce tableau.

Fiabilité des données : les estimations considérées comme moins sûres sont indiquées en italique plutôt qu'en caractères romains. On n'a pas tenu compte des inexactitudes dans les déclarations d'âge, dont la méthode d'évaluation est exposée à la section 3.1.3 des Notes techniques. Cependant, l'index de Whipple présenté au tableau 1 c) du volume 1 de l'Annuaire démographique, qui est consacré aux recensements et porte sur les caractéristiques de la population, fournit une évaluation de l'exactitude des déclarations d'âge faites à l'occasion des recensements effectués entre 1985 et 2003 dans 145 pays.

Insuffisance des données : les statistiques de la population selon l'âge et le sexe appellent les mêmes réserves que celles qui ont été formulées aux sections 3 et 3.1.3 des Notes techniques à propos des statistiques de la population en général et des répartitions par âge en particulier.

La comparabilité des statistiques de la population selon l'âge et le sexe pâtit du manque d'uniformité dans la définition de la population totale (voir la section 3 des Notes techniques) et des lacunes des dénombrements. L'influence de ces deux facteurs varie selon les groupes d'âge. Ainsi, le dénombrement des enfants de moins d'un an et des jeunes enfants comporte souvent plus de lacunes que celui des personnes plus âgées. De même, le fait que certains groupes de personnes appartenant souvent à des groupes d'âge déterminés, par exemple les militaires, ne soient pas pris en compte dans la population totale peut influer sensiblement sur la structure par âge et sur la comparabilité des données avec celles d'autres pays ou zones. Il conviendra de tenir compte de ces facteurs fondamentaux lorsque l'on utilisera les données du tableau.

Outre ces difficultés d'ordre général, la comparabilité pose des problèmes particuliers lorsqu'il s'agit des données par âge. On sait que les répartitions de la population selon l'âge présentent certaines imperfections dues à l'inexactitude des déclarations d'âge. Certaines de ces anomalies ont tendance à s'estomper ou à disparaître lorsque l'on classe les données par groupes d'âge quinquennaux et non par années d'âge, mais une certaine imprécision subsiste, même s'il n'est pas toujours facile de voir à quel point il y a distorsion.

Le degré de comparabilité dépend également de la classification par âge employée dans les divers pays ou zones. L'âge retenu peut être défini par date exacte (jour, mois et année) de naissance ou par celle du dernier anniversaire. Lorsqu'elles étaient connues, les répartitions établies seulement d'après l'année de la naissance ont été signalées en note à la fin du tableau.

Si aucun nombre ne figure dans la rangée réservée aux âges inconnus, cela ne signifie pas nécessairement que les déclarations d'âge et l'exploitation des données par âge aient été tout à fait exactes. C'est souvent une indication que l'on a attribué un âge aux personnes d'âge inconnu avant l'exploitation des données ou qu'elles ont été réparties proportionnellement entre les différents groupes après cette opération.

Comme on l'a indiqué à propos du tableau 5, les estimations intercensitaires de la population totale sont d'ordinaire rectifiées d'après les résultats des recensements de population si l'on constate des discontinuités inexplicables. Les données postcensitaires concernant la répartition de la population par âge et par sexe ont toutefois moins de chance d'être rectifiées de cette manière. Lorsque l'on savait qu'une estimation de la population totale pour une année donnée avait été rectifiée sans qu'il en soit de même pour la répartition par âge correspondante, cette dernière a été indiquée comme ayant un caractère provisoire. Les répartitions de ce type doivent être utilisées avec prudence lorsque l'on étudie les tendances sur un certain nombre d'années, quoique leur utilité pour l'étude de la structure par âge de la population pour l'année visée reste probablement entière.

La comparabilité des données selon le lieu de résidence (zone urbaine ou rurale) peut être limitée par les définitions nationales des termes « urbain » et « rural » utilisées pour la mise en tableaux de ces données. Les définitions du terme « urbain » utilisées pour les recensements nationaux de population ont été présentées à la fin des notes techniques du tableau 6 lorsqu'elles étaient connues. Comme on l'a précisé dans les notes techniques relatives au tableau 6, ces définitions varient considérablement d'un pays ou d'une zone à l'autre.

Données publiées antérieurement : des statistiques concernant la population selon l'âge, le sexe et le lieu de résidence (zone urbaine ou rurale) ont été présentées dans des éditions antérieures de l'*Annuaire démographique*. Pour plus de précisions concernant les années et les sujets pour lesquels des données ont été publiées, se reporter à l'index historique.

Continent, country or area, date, code and age (in years)	Total			Urban - Urbaine			Rural - Rurale		
Continent, pays ou zone, date, code et âge (en années)	Both sexes Les deux sexes	Male Masculin	Female Féminin	Both sexes Les deux sexes	Male Masculin	Female Féminin	Both sexes Les deux sexes	Male Masculin	Female Féminin
AFRICA - AFRIQUE									
Algeria - Algérie									
1 VII 2003 (ESDJ)									
Total.....................	31 847 995	16 090 568	15 757 427	...	...	...	...	...	...
0.........................	604 019	308 412	295 607	...	...	...	...	...	...
1 - 4.....................	2 310 513	1 180 730	1 129 783	...	...	...	...	...	...
5 - 9.....................	3 224 819	1 647 090	1 577 729	...	...	...	...	...	...
10 - 14...................	3 642 440	1 856 114	1 786 326	...	...	...	...	...	...
15 - 19...................	3 808 498	1 939 408	1 869 089	...	...	...	...	...	...
20 - 24...................	3 522 547	1 791 140	1 731 407	...	...	...	...	...	...
25 - 29...................	2 959 388	1 493 925	1 465 463	...	...	...	...	...	...
30 - 34...................	2 508 416	1 259 600	1 248 816	...	...	...	...	...	...
35 - 39...................	2 102 178	1 056 627	1 045 551	...	...	...	...	...	...
40 - 44...................	1 680 817	845 183	835 634	...	...	...	...	...	...
45 - 49...................	1 378 726	694 140	684 586	...	...	...	...	...	...
50 - 54...................	1 081 550	545 636	535 914	...	...	...	...	...	...
55 - 59...................	776 901	382 388	394 513	...	...	...	...	...	...
60 - 64...................	659 350	320 650	338 700	...	...	...	...	...	...
65 - 69...................	591 984	286 760	305 224	...	...	...	...	...	...
70 - 74...................	452 969	219 670	233 299	...	...	...	...	...	...
75 - 79...................	282 819	137 992	144 827	...	...	...	...	...	...
80 +.....................	260 063	125 104	134 959	...	...	...	...	...	...
Benin - Bénin									
11 II 2002 (CDJC)									
Total.....................	6 769 914	3 284 119	3 485 795	2 630 133	1 280 418	1 349 715	4 139 781	2 003 701	2 136 080
0.........................	235 342	118 243	117 099	82 945	41 797	41 148	152 397	76 446	75 951
1 - 4.....................	939 907	475 297	464 610	309 993	157 189	152 804	629 914	318 108	311 806
5 - 9.....................	1 155 377	589 653	565 724	380 207	188 422	191 785	775 170	401 231	373 939
10 - 14...................	838 749	438 376	400 373	332 753	162 989	169 764	505 996	275 387	230 609
15 - 19...................	653 251	321 984	331 267	294 811	144 462	150 349	358 440	177 522	180 918
20 - 24...................	563 947	243 515	320 432	262 496	123 275	139 221	301 451	120 240	181 211
25 - 29...................	532 056	228 090	303 966	232 948	107 420	125 528	299 108	120 670	178 438
30 - 34...................	414 166	192 429	221 737	180 416	88 668	91 748	233 750	103 761	129 989
35 - 39...................	340 632	157 551	183 081	143 773	69 970	73 803	196 859	87 581	109 278
40 - 44...................	264 488	125 792	138 696	109 427	54 554	54 873	155 061	71 238	83 823
45 - 49...................	196 056	94 805	101 251	81 020	40 280	40 740	115 036	54 525	60 511
50 - 54...................	167 901	81 461	86 440	63 992	31 615	32 377	103 909	49 846	54 063
55 - 59...................	93 493	46 214	47 279	36 952	18 405	18 547	56 541	27 809	28 732
60 - 64...................	116 796	53 543	63 253	38 629	17 488	21 141	78 167	36 055	42 112
65 - 69...................	63 847	28 630	35 217	22 857	10 048	12 809	40 990	18 582	22 408
70 - 74...................	71 231	32 523	38 708	22 048	9 550	12 498	49 183	22 973	26 210
75 - 79...................	32 158	14 609	17 549	10 617	4 473	6 144	21 541	10 136	11 405
80 - 84...................	41 705	18 397	23 308	11 461	4 501	6 960	30 244	13 896	16 348
85 - 89...................	13 113	6 037	7 076	3 860	1 497	2 363	9 253	4 540	4 713
90 - 94...................	12 256	5 945	6 311	3 413	1 457	1 956	8 843	4 488	4 355
95 +.....................	23 098	10 753	12 345	5 317	2 201	3 116	17 781	8 552	9 229
Unknown - Inconnu.......	345	272	73	198	157	41	147	115	32
Botswana									
1 VII 2004 (ESDF)									
Total.....................	1 711 334	828 082	883 252	393 528	191 287	202 241	1 317 806	636 795	681 011
0 - 4.....................	...	...	...	39 462	19 821	19 641	142 574	71 938	70 636
0.........................	40 211	20 179	20 032	...	...	...	...	...	...
1 - 4.....................	182 036	91 759	90 277	...	...	...	...	...	...
5 - 9.....................	209 001	105 382	103 619	36 523	17 780	18 743	172 478	87 602	84 876
10 - 14...................	206 554	104 108	102 446	35 391	16 470	18 921	171 163	87 638	83 525
15 - 19...................	200 428	100 765	99 663	42 174	18 910	23 264	158 254	81 855	76 399
20 - 24...................	184 195	92 070	92 125	58 457	28 634	29 823	125 738	63 436	62 302
25 - 29...................	160 484	78 938	81 546	54 633	26 777	27 856	105 851	52 161	53 690
30 - 34...................	124 469	61 673	62 796	41 938	21 392	20 546	82 531	40 281	42 250
35 - 39...................	88 744	42 494	46 250	27 627	14 270	13 357	61 117	28 224	32 893
40 - 44...................	68 717	28 867	39 850	19 497	9 029	10 468	49 220	19 838	29 382
45 - 49...................	59 897	23 659	36 238	14 618	6 738	7 880	45 279	16 921	28 358
50 - 54...................	45 006	18 356	26 650	9 248	4 692	4 556	35 758	13 664	22 094
55 - 59...................	33 955	14 131	19 824	5 674	2 896	2 778	28 281	11 235	17 046
60 - 64...................	29 417	12 772	16 645	3 332	1 711	1 621	26 085	11 061	15 024
65 - 69...................	24 103	10 638	13 465	1 995	972	1 023	22 108	9 666	12 442

Continent, country or area, date, code and age (in years) Continent, pays ou zone, date, code et âge (en années)	Total			Urban - Urbaine			Rural - Rurale		
	Both sexes Les deux sexes	Male Masculin	Female Féminin	Both sexes Les deux sexes	Male Masculin	Female Féminin	Both sexes Les deux sexes	Male Masculin	Female Féminin
AFRICA - AFRIQUE									
Botswana									
1 VII 2004 (ESDF)									
70 - 74	16 916	7 281	9 635	1 066	469	597	15 850	6 812	9 038
75 +	37 201	15 010	22 191	1 893	726	1 167	35 308	14 284	21 024
Burkina Faso									
10 XII 1996 (CDJC)									
Total	10 312 609	4 970 882	5 341 727	1 591 469[1]	806 605[1]	784 864[1]	8 680 876[1]	4 144 138[1]	4 536 738[1]
0	346 453	173 583	172 870	44 282[1]	22 630[1]	21 652[1]	379 344[1]	187 107[1]	192 237[1]
1 - 4	1 421 971	715 961	706 010	178 087[1]	90 253[1]	87 835[1]	1 409 665[1]	702 395[1]	707 269[1]
5 - 9	1 798 242	913 006	885 236	224 172[1]	111 929[1]	112 243[1]	1 508 713[1]	768 749[1]	739 963[1]
10 - 14	1 375 393	706 641	668 752	214 312[1]	105 399[1]	108 912[1]	1 133 028[1]	588 567[1]	544 461[1]
15 - 19	1 082 487	534 025	548 462	204 101[1]	101 271[1]	102 829[1]	860 697[1]	419 328[1]	441 368[1]
20 - 24	767 462	340 162	427 300	167 292[1]	86 255[1]	81 038[1]	595 534[1]	249 848[1]	345 687[1]
25 - 29	666 645	285 292	381 353	133 549[1]	69 229[1]	64 320[1]	527 207[1]	213 566[1]	313 641[1]
30 - 34	572 745	250 049	322 696	108 137[1]	56 285[1]	51 852[1]	433 532[1]	182 037[1]	251 495[1]
35 - 39	467 470	205 558	261 912	85 353[1]	45 377[1]	39 976[1]	376 059[1]	157 347[1]	218 712[1]
40 - 44	390 677	173 362	217 315	62 272[1]	33 622[1]	28 650[1]	300 211[1]	129 991[1]	170 220[1]
45 - 49	311 624	145 091	166 533	47 040[1]	25 019[1]	22 021[1]	264 139[1]	118 495[1]	145 644[1]
50 - 54	279 315	127 031	152 284	35 991[1]	18 429[1]	17 563[1]	218 482[1]	100 485[1]	117 997[1]
55 - 59	208 700	102 910	105 790	27 758[1]	14 113[1]	13 645[1]	189 860[1]	90 856[1]	99 004[1]
60 - 64	196 248	93 494	102 754	20 701[1]	10 312[1]	10 389[1]	153 310[1]	74 651[1]	78 659[1]
65 - 69	132 659	66 895	65 764	14 352[1]	6 789[1]	7 563[1]	122 396[1]	61 044[1]	61 352[1]
70 - 74	114 931	54 300	60 631	10 163[1]	4 509[1]	5 654[1]	90 982[1]	44 841[1]	46 141[1]
75 - 79	62 654	31 623	31 031	6 136[1]	2 665[1]	3 471[1]	55 113[1]	27 874[1]	27 239[1]
80 - 84	36 026	15 405	20 621	3 230[1]	1 183[1]	2 047[1]	27 309[1]	12 551[1]	14 759[1]
85 - 89	14 151	6 253	7 898	1 504[1]	515[1]	990[1]	12 960[1]	5 841[1]	7 117[1]
90 +	25 391	9 581	15 810	969[1]	274[1]	693[1]	8 247[1]	3 359[1]	4 886[1]
Unknown - Inconnu	41 365	20 660	20 705	...	...	...	...	...	...
1 VII 2005 (ESDJ)									
Total	12 802 282	6 182 079	6 620 203	...	...	...	...	...	...
0 - 4	2 510 678	1 251 348	1 259 330	...	...	...	...	...	...
5 - 9	2 161 350	1 098 299	1 063 051	...	...	...	...	...	...
10 - 14	1 681 117	865 540	815 577	...	...	...	...	...	...
15 - 19	1 332 664	651 425	681 239	...	...	...	...	...	...
20 - 24	959 180	424 059	535 121	...	...	...	...	...	...
25 - 29	830 284	357 298	472 986	...	...	...	...	...	...
30 - 34	679 849	300 735	379 114	...	...	...	...	...	...
40 - 44	577 757	255 271	322 486	...	...	...	...	...	...
45 - 49	453 009	205 521	247 488	...	...	...	...	...	...
50 - 54	387 808	179 647	208 161	...	...	...	...	...	...
55 - 59	316 611	148 463	168 148	...	...	...	...	...	...
60 - 64	270 079	130 724	139 355	...	...	...	...	...	...
65 - 69	215 896	105 703	110 193	...	...	...	...	...	...
70 - 74	169 261	84 144	85 117	...	...	...	...	...	...
75 - 79	125 232	61 177	64 055	...	...	...	...	...	...
80 - 84	75 746	37 813	37 933	...	...	...	...	...	...
85 +	55 761	24 912	30 849	...	...	...	...	...	...
Cape Verde - Cap-Vert									
1 VII 2003 (ESDF)									
Total	460 968	223 254	237 715	257 412	125 652	131 759	203 556	97 600	105 956
0 - 4	58 940	30 004	28 936	30 116	15 352	14 765	28 823	14 652	14 171
5 - 9	61 218	30 867	30 351	30 927	15 643	15 284	30 291	15 224	15 067
10 - 14	64 803	32 445	32 358	34 166	16 918	17 248	30 636	15 526	15 110
15 - 19	57 898	28 923	28 975	33 909	16 551	17 358	23 990	12 372	11 618
20 - 24	42 677	21 383	21 294	26 883	13 427	13 456	15 794	7 956	7 838
25 - 29	31 691	15 870	15 821	20 027	9 970	10 057	11 664	5 901	5 763
30 - 34	27 198	13 321	13 877	16 627	8 322	8 306	10 570	4 999	5 571
35 - 39	26 745	12 770	13 975	16 748	8 330	8 419	9 996	4 440	5 556
40 - 44	22 729	10 461	12 268	13 844	6 826	7 018	8 886	3 635	5 251
45 - 49	16 084	6 733	9 351	9 359	4 438	4 921	6 726	2 296	4 430
50 - 54	9 378	3 674	5 704	5 496	2 386	3 110	3 882	1 288	2 594
55 - 59	5 466	2 224	3 242	2 921	1 271	1 651	2 545	953	1 592
60 - 64	7 569	2 919	4 650	3 580	1 404	2 176	3 989	1 515	2 474
65 - 69	9 285	3 660	5 625	4 224	1 629	2 595	5 062	2 032	3 030

155

Continent, country or area, date, code and age (in years) / Continent, pays ou zone, date, code et âge (en années)	Total			Urban - Urbaine			Rural - Rurale		
	Both sexes Les deux sexes	Male Masculin	Female Féminin	Both sexes Les deux sexes	Male Masculin	Female Féminin	Both sexes Les deux sexes	Male Masculin	Female Féminin
AFRICA - AFRIQUE									
Cape Verde - Cap-Vert									
1 VII 2003 (ESDF)									
70 - 74	7 654	3 244	4 410	3 316	1 270	2 046	4 338	1 974	2 364
75 - 79	5 041	2 183	2 858	2 264	853	1 410	2 778	1 330	1 448
80 +	6 593	2 573	4 020	3 005	1 064	1 941	3 589	1 510	2 079
Congo									
1 VII 2004 (ESDF)									
Total	3 231 326	...	...	...	...	...	...	...	...
0 - 4	544 478	...	...	...	...	...	...	...	...
5 - 9	484 376	...	...	...	...	...	...	...	...
10 - 14	414 902	...	...	...	...	...	...	...	...
15 - 19	357 708	...	...	...	...	...	...	...	...
20 - 24	291 466	...	...	...	...	...	...	...	...
25 - 29	231 040	...	...	...	...	...	...	...	...
30 - 34	171 583	...	...	...	...	...	...	...	...
35 - 39	142 178	...	...	...	...	...	...	...	...
40 - 44	130 546	...	...	...	...	...	...	...	...
45 - 49	116 005	...	...	...	...	...	...	...	...
50 - 54	95 970	...	...	...	...	...	...	...	...
55 - 59	80 783	...	...	...	...	...	...	...	...
60 - 64	66 565	...	...	...	...	...	...	...	...
65 - 69	48 793	...	...	...	...	...	...	...	...
70 +	54 933	...	...	...	...	...	...	...	...
Egypt - Égypte									
19 XI 1996 (CDFC)									
Total	59 312 914	30 351 390	28 961 524	25 286 335	12 957 775	12 328 560	34 026 579	17 393 615	16 632 964
0	560 622	288 082	272 540	238 653	122 073	116 580	321 969	166 009	155 960
1 - 4	6 294 620	3 223 694	3 070 926	2 257 688	1 152 819	1 104 869	4 036 932	2 070 875	1 966 057
5 - 9	7 626 252	3 939 121	3 687 131	2 852 218	1 464 520	1 387 698	4 774 034	2 474 601	2 299 433
10 - 14	7 864 002	4 076 601	3 787 401	3 116 208	1 602 009	1 514 199	4 747 794	2 474 592	2 273 202
15 - 19	6 901 611	3 602 857	3 298 754	2 930 311	1 510 230	1 420 081	3 971 300	2 092 627	1 878 673
20 - 24	5 075 136	2 642 620	2 432 516	2 273 551	1 167 895	1 105 656	2 801 585	1 474 725	1 326 860
25 - 29	4 370 522	2 105 063	2 265 459	1 916 234	933 765	982 469	2 454 288	1 171 298	1 282 990
30 - 34	3 979 720	1 993 212	1 986 508	1 847 108	917 762	929 346	2 132 612	1 075 450	1 057 162
35 - 39	3 860 105	1 914 367	1 945 738	1 776 094	879 215	896 879	2 084 011	1 035 152	1 048 859
40 - 44	3 173 226	1 616 449	1 556 777	1 573 960	810 931	763 029	1 599 266	805 518	793 748
45 - 49	2 696 169	1 408 498	1 287 671	1 296 912	687 877	609 035	1 399 257	720 621	678 636
50 - 54	2 022 136	994 936	1 027 200	984 817	503 584	481 233	1 037 319	491 352	545 967
55 - 59	1 476 673	776 537	700 136	686 141	372 516	313 625	790 532	404 021	386 511
60 - 64	1 398 994	706 189	692 805	665 441	349 766	315 675	733 553	356 423	377 130
65 - 69	930 576	507 085	423 491	404 645	232 503	172 142	525 931	274 582	251 349
70 - 74	617 669	315 767	301 902	269 065	144 153	124 912	348 604	171 614	176 990
75 +	464 858	240 302	224 556	197 282	106 154	91 128	267 576	134 148	133 428
Unknown - Inconnu	23	10	13	7	3	4	16	7	9
1 VII 2000 (ESDF)									
Total	63 976 000	32 695 000	31 281 000	...	...	...	...	...	...
0 - 4	7 394 000	3 783 000	3 611 000	...	...	...	...	...	...
5 - 9	8 225 000	4 245 000	3 980 000	...	...	...	...	...	...
10 - 14	8 481 000	4 392 000	4 089 000	...	...	...	...	...	...
15 - 19	7 445 000	3 882 000	3 563 000	...	...	...	...	...	...
20 - 24	5 474 000	2 848 000	2 626 000	...	...	...	...	...	...
25 - 29	4 714 000	2 266 000	2 448 000	...	...	...	...	...	...
30 - 34	4 293 000	2 149 000	2 144 000	...	...	...	...	...	...
35 - 39	4 164 000	2 064 000	2 100 000	...	...	...	...	...	...:
40 - 44	3 422 000	1 740 000	1 682 000	...	...	...	...	...	...
45 - 49	2 909 000	1 516 000	1 393 000	...	...	...	...	...	...
50 - 54	2 180 000	1 071 000	1 109 000	...	...	...	...	...	...
55 - 59	1 593 000	835 000	758 000	...	...	...	...	...	...
60 - 64	1 510 000	761 000	749 000	...	...	...	...	...	...
65 - 69	1 003 000	546 000	457 000	...	...	...	...	...	...
70 - 74	667 000	339 000	328 000	...	...	...	...	...	...
75 +	502 000	258 000	244 000	...	...	...	...	...	...

Continent, country or area, date, code and age (in years) / Continent, pays ou zone, date, code et âge (en années)	Total			Urban - Urbaine			Rural - Rurale		
	Both sexes Les deux sexes	Male Masculin	Female Féminin	Both sexes Les deux sexes	Male Masculin	Female Féminin	Both sexes Les deux sexes	Male Masculin	Female Féminin
AFRICA - AFRIQUE									
Ethiopia - Éthiopie[2]									
1 VII 2004 (ESDF)									
Total	71 066 000	35 618 000	35 448 000	11 199 000	5 568 000	5 631 000	59 867 000	30 050 000	29 817 000
0 - 4	11 917 056	6 014 178	5 902 878	1 393 080	725 408	667 672	10 524 357	5 289 011	5 235 347
5 - 9	10 421 979	5 263 051	5 158 928	1 326 399	673 204	653 194	9 095 835	4 590 015	4 505 820
10 - 14	8 339 406	4 231 901	4 107 506	1 211 825	601 515	610 310	7 127 670	3 630 453	3 497 217
15 - 19	7 711 167	3 915 017	3 796 150	1 306 124	633 484	672 639	6 404 983	3 281 509	3 123 475
20 - 24	6 758 895	3 431 134	3 327 761	1 285 452	625 694	659 757	5 473 275	2 805 340	2 667 935
25 - 29	5 671 553	2 854 595	2 816 959	1 118 289	551 599	566 690	4 553 085	2 302 877	2 250 208
30 - 34	4 561 471	2 249 158	2 312 313	893 161	448 377	444 784	3 668 161	1 800 673	1 867 489
35 - 39	3 705 298	1 797 673	1 907 625	704 491	353 537	350 954	3 000 700	1 444 054	1 556 646
40 - 44	2 936 161	1 395 857	1 540 304	516 131	255 593	260 538	2 419 980	1 140 222	1 279 758
45 - 49	2 390 190	1 140 061	1 250 128	400 411	199 348	201 063	1 989 754	940 690	1 049 064
50 - 54	1 940 461	948 128	992 333	311 877	156 709	155 168	1 628 576	791 409	837 166
55 - 59	1 533 568	759 770	773 797	239 310	118 269	121 041	1 294 259	641 502	652 757
60 - 64	1 158 467	583 393	575 075	179 619	85 210	94 409	978 853	498 189	480 664
65 - 69	852 130	432 577	419 552	133 357	61 337	72 020	718 777	371 247	347 529
70 - 74	579 410	295 965	283 445	89 239	39 851	49 388	490 176	256 121	234 055
75 +	588 788	305 542	283 246	90 236	38 864	51 372	498 558	266 687	231 871
Ghana									
26 III 2000 (CDFC)									
Total	18 912 079	9 357 382	9 554 697	8 274 270	4 043 830	4 230 440	10 637 809	5 313 552	5 324 257
0	525 258	262 041	263 217	196 042	98 044	97 998	329 216	163 997	165 219
1 - 4	2 244 163	1 117 729	1 126 434	837 690	415 237	422 453	1 406 473	702 492	703 981
5 - 9	2 775 206	1 390 652	1 384 554	1 053 432	517 610	535 822	1 721 774	873 042	848 732
10 - 14	2 262 216	1 151 131	1 111 085	963 577	461 218	502 359	1 298 639	689 913	608 726
15 - 19	1 883 753	961 162	922 591	918 094	441 479	476 615	965 659	519 683	445 976
20 - 24	1 600 820	763 051	837 769	836 838	407 200	429 638	763 982	355 851	408 131
25 - 29	1 487 299	695 494	791 805	747 897	358 913	388 984	739 402	336 581	402 821
30 - 34	1 206 809	566 439	640 370	582 893	279 843	303 050	623 916	286 596	337 320
35 - 39	1 029 765	490 864	538 901	485 638	231 910	253 728	544 127	258 954	285 173
40 - 44	886 931	443 284	443 647	403 917	201 666	202 251	483 014	241 618	241 396
45 - 49	720 357	377 315	343 042	318 875	167 117	151 758	401 482	210 198	191 284
50 - 54	568 369	279 950	288 419	240 038	120 107	119 931	328 331	159 843	168 488
55 - 59	355 842	182 843	172 999	154 952	80 607	74 345	200 890	102 236	98 654
60 - 64	366 351	177 347	189 004	142 687	70 401	72 286	223 664	106 946	116 718
65 - 69	258 709	129 090	129 619	103 807	51 472	52 335	154 902	77 618	77 284
70 - 74	225 158	106 513	118 645	83 860	38 523	45 337	141 298	67 990	73 308
75 - 79	144 830	74 268	70 562	56 031	27 696	28 335	88 799	46 572	42 227
80 - 84	140 847	66 941	73 906	52 469	24 266	28 203	88 378	42 675	45 703
85 - 89	107 558	58 254	49 304	46 202	25 229	20 973	61 356	33 025	28 331
90 - 94	57 242	28 258	28 984	22 228	10 699	11 529	35 014	17 559	17 455
95 +	64 596	34 756	29 840	27 103	14 593	12 510	37 493	20 163	17 330
Guinea - Guinée									
1 XII 1996 (CDFC)									
Total	7 156 406	3 497 979	3 658 427	...	...	...	...	...	...
0	249 593	126 198	123 395	...	...	...	...	...	...
1 - 4	1 023 234	517 530	505 704	...	...	...	...	...	...
5 - 9	1 213 159	618 249	594 910	...	...	...	...	...	...
10 - 14	778 661	415 215	363 446	...	...	...	...	...	...
15 - 19	662 646	315 248	347 398	...	...	...	...	...	...
20 - 24	518 667	234 435	284 232	...	...	...	...	...	...
25 - 29	553 395	237 650	315 745	...	...	...	...	...	...
30 - 34	427 376	188 867	238 509	...	...	...	...	...	...
35 - 39	372 907	173 506	199 401	...	...	...	...	...	...
40 - 44	305 272	149 956	155 316	...	...	...	...	...	...
45 - 49	231 669	117 477	114 192	...	...	...	...	...	...
50 - 54	195 512	93 711	101 801	...	...	...	...	...	...
55 - 59	142 344	75 899	66 445	...	...	...	...	...	...
60 - 64	159 660	73 113	86 547	...	...	...	...	...	...
65 - 69	108 893	57 077	51 816	...	...	...	...	...	...
70 - 74	87 052	40 047	47 005	...	...	...	...	...	...
75 +	126 366	63 801	62 565	...	...	...	...	...	...

7. Population by age, sex and urban/rural residence: latest available year, 1996 - 2005
Population selon l'âge, le sexe et la résidence, urbaine/rurale: dernière année disponible, 1996 - 2005 (continued - suite)

Continent, country or area, date, code and age (in years) / Continent, pays ou zone, date, code et âge (en annèes)	Total			Urban - Urbaine			Rural - Rurale		
	Both sexes Les deux sexes	Male Masculin	Female Féminin	Both sexes Les deux sexes	Male Masculin	Female Féminin	Both sexes Les deux sexes	Male Masculin	Female Féminin
AFRICA - AFRIQUE									
Kenya									
1 VII 2005 (ESDF)									
Total	35 267 222	17 457 906	17 809 316	6 213 505	3 688 113	2 525 392	29 053 718	13 769 794	15 283 924
0 - 4	6 238 991	3 150 182	3 088 809	982 463	542 222	440 241	5 256 528	2 607 960	2 648 568
5 - 9	4 694 561	2 367 882	2 326 679	634 554	347 165	287 388	4 060 007	2 020 717	2 039 291
10 - 14	3 973 404	2 001 411	1 971 993	471 546	262 014	209 532	3 501 858	1 739 397	1 762 461
15 - 19	4 082 140	2 061 657	2 020 483	631 251	340 802	290 450	3 450 889	1 720 855	1 730 033
20 - 24	3 627 797	1 833 154	1 794 643	910 302	537 287	373 015	2 717 495	1 295 867	1 421 628
25 - 29	2 953 347	1 398 489	1 554 858	812 771	480 022	332 749	2 140 576	918 467	1 222 109
30 - 34	2 387 831	1 119 233	1 268 598	602 678	380 498	222 181	1 785 153	738 735	1 046 417
35 - 39	1 778 184	864 349	913 835	391 067	266 270	124 797	1 387 117	598 079	789 038
40 - 44	1 394 011	685 786	708 225	275 799	191 704	84 096	1 118 212	494 082	624 129
45 - 49	1 038 421	507 834	530 587	177 566	125 206	52 361	860 855	382 628	478 226
50 - 54	829 200	403 131	426 069	122 953	86 594	36 359	706 247	316 537	389 710
55 - 59	681 227	329 709	351 518	76 409	52 171	24 238	604 818	277 538	327 280
60 - 64	546 365	262 036	284 329	50 927	32 721	18 206	495 438	229 315	266 123
65 - 69	420 546	193 429	227 117	30 973	19 350	11 623	389 573	174 079	215 494
70 - 74	300 941	136 132	164 809	21 116	12 614	8 502	279 825	123 518	156 307
75 +	320 257	143 493	176 764	21 129	11 474	9 655	299 128	132 019	167 109
Lesotho									
1 VII 2001 (SSDJ)									
Total	2 157 537	1 065 484	1 092 053	288 895	131 861	157 034	1 868 642	933 623	935 019
0	45 867	24 441	21 426	5 590	3 177	2 413	40 277	21 264	19 013
1 - 4	184 467	92 420	92 047	21 097	10 832	10 265	163 370	81 588	81 782
5 - 9	250 417	127 720	122 697	27 655	13 408	14 247	222 762	114 312	108 450
10 - 14	280 429	141 486	138 943	29 492	14 094	15 398	250 937	127 392	123 545
15 - 19	286 404	145 591	140 813	35 686	14 075	21 611	250 719	131 517	119 202
20 - 24	225 779	116 163	109 616	35 176	14 235	20 941	190 603	101 928	88 675
25 - 29	159 700	79 705	79 995	30 051	12 477	17 574	129 648	67 227	62 421
30 - 34	114 507	56 175	58 332	23 915	11 542	12 373	90 592	44 633	45 959
35 - 39	110 264	55 375	54 889	21 547	11 162	10 385	88 717	44 213	44 504
40 - 44	93 645	43 925	49 720	15 044	7 468	7 576	78 602	36 457	42 145
45 - 49	81 488	41 152	40 336	11 468	5 651	5 817	70 019	35 501	34 518
50 - 54	77 212	33 959	43 253	9 388	3 592	5 796	67 824	30 367	37 457
55 - 59	56 352	28 197	28 155	5 927	2 782	3 145	50 425	25 415	25 010
60 - 64	48 107	21 105	27 002	4 770	1 866	2 904	43 337	19 239	24 098
65 - 69	49 001	21 165	27 836	4 284	1 949	2 335	44 717	19 216	25 501
70 - 74	29 628	11 671	17 957	1 801	843	958	27 828	10 829	16 999
75 +	45 242	14 815	30 427	3 208	982	2 226	42 033	13 832	28 201
Unknown - Inconnu	19 028	10 419	8 609	2 796	1 726	1 070	16 232	8 693	7 539
Malawi									
1 IX 1998 (CDFC)									
Total	9 933 868	4 867 563	5 066 305	1 435 436	742 839	692 597	8 498 432	4 124 724	4 373 708
0	368 325	182 508	185 817	49 018	24 549	24 469	319 307	157 959	161 348
1 - 4	1 292 065	641 117	650 948	166 030	83 011	83 019	1 126 035	558 106	567 929
5 - 9	1 440 370	714 830	725 540	183 924	90 095	93 829	1 256 446	624 735	631 711
10 - 14	1 232 500	616 445	616 055	180 430	84 521	95 909	1 052 070	531 924	520 146
15 - 19	1 087 936	527 865	560 071	179 240	88 044	91 196	908 696	439 821	468 875
20 - 24	979 060	435 138	543 922	185 677	89 626	96 051	793 383	345 512	447 871
25 - 29	792 465	393 913	398 552	152 217	85 808	66 409	640 248	308 105	332 143
30 - 34	601 241	303 080	298 161	105 241	60 855	44 386	496 000	242 225	253 775
35 - 39	484 827	239 043	245 784	75 067	42 734	32 333	409 760	196 309	213 451
40 - 44	360 709	180 167	180 542	50 294	30 145	20 149	310 415	150 022	160 393
45 - 49	332 756	166 258	166 498	38 650	23 268	15 382	294 106	142 990	151 116
50 - 54	238 846	120 193	118 653	24 745	15 195	9 550	214 101	104 998	109 103
55 - 59	175 226	89 909	85 317	14 921	9 171	5 750	160 305	80 738	79 567
60 - 64	153 084	72 251	80 833	10 405	5 973	4 432	142 679	66 278	76 401
65 - 69	139 320	65 655	73 665	7 818	4 226	3 592	131 502	61 429	70 073
70 - 74	98 049	45 310	52 739	4 936	2 407	2 529	93 113	42 903	50 210
75 - 79	65 485	32 151	33 334	2 936	1 489	1 447	62 549	30 662	31 887
80 - 84	45 632	20 495	25 137	1 968	873	1 095	43 664	19 622	24 042
85 - 89	25 214	11 540	13 674	1 042	463	579	24 172	11 077	13 095
90 - 94	11 167	5 180	5 987	521	227	294	10 646	4 953	5 693
95 +	9 591	4 515	5 076	356	159	197	9 235	4 356	4 879

Continent, country or area, date, code and age (in years) / Continent, pays ou zone, date, code et âge (en années)	Total			Urban - Urbaine			Rural - Rurale		
	Both sexes Les deux sexes	Male Masculin	Female Féminin	Both sexes Les deux sexes	Male Masculin	Female Féminin	Both sexes Les deux sexes	Male Masculin	Female Féminin
AFRICA - AFRIQUE									
Malawi									
1 VII 2005 (ESDF)[3]									
Total	12 341 170	6 067 563	6 273 607	1 783 289	...	...	10 557 881	...	...
0	457 583	227 502	230 081	60 897	...	...	396 686	...	...
1 - 4	1 605 175	799 172	806 003	206 265	...	...	1 398 910	...	...
5 - 9	1 789 419	891 057	898 362	228 495	...	...	1 560 924	...	...
10 - 14	1 531 175	768 417	762 758	224 154	...	...	1 307 021	...	...
15 - 19	1 351 579	658 000	693 579	222 676	...	...	1 128 903	...	...
20 - 24	1 216 318	542 413	673 906	230 673	...	...	985 646	...	...
25 - 29	984 505	491 024	493 481	189 104	...	...	795 401	...	...
30 - 34	746 941	377 798	369 143	130 744	...	...	616 197	...	...
35 - 39	602 316	297 974	304 342	93 258	...	...	509 058	...	...
40 - 44	448 121	224 584	223 537	62 482	...	...	385 639	...	...
45 - 49	413 394	207 246	206 148	48 016	...	...	365 378	...	...
50 - 54	296 726	149 824	146 902	30 742	...	...	265 985	...	...
55 - 59	217 689	112 074	105 615	18 537	...	...	199 152	...	...
60 - 64	190 181	90 063	100 118	12 926	...	...	177 255	...	...
65 - 69	173 082	81 841	91 241	9 713	...	...	163 369	...	...
70 - 74	121 809	56 480	65 329	6 132	...	...	115 677	...	...
75 - 79	81 354	40 077	41 277	3 647	...	...	77 707	...	...
80 - 84	56 690	25 548	31 142	2 445	...	...	54 245	...	...
85 - 89	31 324	14 385	16 939	1 295	...	...	30 030	...	...
90 - 94	13 873	6 457	7 416	647	...	...	13 226	...	...
95 +	11 916	5 629	6 287	442	...	...	11 472	...	...
Mali									
1 VII 1996 (ESDF)									
Total	8 868 975	4 264 475	4 604 500	2 500 669	1 229 063	1 271 606	6 644 127	3 173 960	3 470 167
0 - 4	1 682 635	845 920	836 715	440 383	221 684	218 699	1 287 016	646 803	640 213
5 - 9	1 456 460	741 585	714 875	373 794	188 962	184 832	1 119 769	571 260	548 509
10 - 14	1 002 534	522 316	480 218	298 181	147 785	150 396	738 977	390 891	348 086
15 - 19	818 660	383 173	435 487	277 502	129 708	147 794	576 971	270 199	306 772
20 - 24	640 229	272 613	367 616	221 542	106 119	115 423	447 713	181 473	266 240
25 - 29	603 332	245 670	357 662	194 875	90 323	104 552	432 723	167 666	265 057
30 - 34	502 092	215 604	286 488	151 134	72 641	78 493	368 697	152 301	216 396
35 - 39	429 744	194 654	235 090	124 093	61 412	62 681	319 664	140 745	178 919
40 - 44	371 431	173 398	198 033	100 510	50 109	50 401	281 536	128 951	152 585
45 - 49	301 509	147 116	154 393	79 809	41 294	38 515	229 922	110 355	119 567
50 - 54	272 469	131 761	140 708	66 116	33 748	32 368	212 446	101 354	111 092
55 - 59	210 833	108 229	102 604	48 070	25 069	23 001	166 789	85 315	81 474
60 - 64	210 537	102 686	107 851	42 919	20 921	21 998	170 512	83 174	87 338
65 - 69	135 476	69 845	65 631	27 948	14 131	13 817	109 464	56 650	52 814
70 - 74	96 762	46 790	49 972	19 578	9 078	10 500	78 482	38 253	40 229
75 - 79	49 104	24 630	24 474	10 546	5 113	5 433	39 353	19 877	19 476
80 +	62 612	29 269	33 343	12 798	5 415	7 383	50 682	24 134	26 548
Unknown - Inconnu	22 556	9 216	13 340	10 871	5 551	5 320	13 411	4 559	8 852
Mauritania - Mauritanie									
1 VII 2005 (ESDF)									
Total	2 905 727	1 450 418	1 455 309	...	...	...	...	...	...
0 - 4	473 161	242 179	230 982	...	...	...	...	...	...
5 - 9	417 913	214 175	203 738	...	...	...	...	...	...
10 - 14	360 193	185 840	174 353	...	...	...	...	...	...
15 - 19	300 592	153 780	146 812	...	...	...	...	...	...
20 - 24	267 559	130 687	136 872	...	...	...	...	...	...
25 - 29	213 382	100 660	112 722	...	...	...	...	...	...
30 - 34	186 169	87 170	98 999	...	...	...	...	...	...
35 - 39	152 901	72 861	80 040	...	...	...	...	...	...
40 - 44	133 205	63 934	69 271	...	...	...	...	...	...
45 - 49	103 483	51 959	51 524	...	...	...	...	...	...
50 - 54	94 773	46 624	48 149	...	...	...	...	...	...
55 - 59	61 455	30 423	31 032	...	...	...	...	...	...
60 - 64	40 130	20 549	19 581	...	...	...	...	...	...
65 - 69	41 849	20 925	20 924	...	...	...	...	...	...
70 - 74	24 539	12 283	12 256	...	...	...	...	...	...
75 +	34 423	16 369	18 054	...	...	...	...	...	...

Continent, country or area, date, code and age (in years) / Continent, pays ou zone, date, code et âge (en années)	Total			Urban - Urbaine			Rural - Rurale		
	Both sexes Les deux sexes	Male Masculin	Female Féminin	Both sexes Les deux sexes	Male Masculin	Female Féminin	Both sexes Les deux sexes	Male Masculin	Female Féminin

AFRICA - AFRIQUE

Mauritius - Maurice
2 VII 2000 (CDJC)

Total	1 178 848	583 756	595 092	503 045	247 844	255 201	675 803	335 912	339 891
0	18 915	9 574	9 341	7 127	3 608	3 519	11 788	5 966	5 822
1 - 4	75 388	38 066	37 322	29 620	14 938	14 682	45 768	23 128	22 640
5 - 9	105 189	53 037	52 152	42 660	21 428	21 232	62 529	31 609	30 920
10 - 14	97 740	49 428	48 312	41 020	20 818	20 202	56 720	28 610	28 110
15 - 19	102 088	51 671	50 417	41 369	20 985	20 384	60 719	30 686	30 033
20 - 24	110 892	55 108	55 784	44 167	21 778	22 389	66 725	33 330	33 395
25 - 29	93 797	46 749	47 048	36 979	18 021	18 958	56 818	28 728	28 090
30 - 34	99 515	49 964	49 551	40 103	19 977	20 126	59 412	29 987	29 425
35 - 39	101 946	51 621	50 325	44 743	22 491	22 252	57 203	29 130	28 073
40 - 44	90 406	45 798	44 608	40 283	20 482	19 801	50 123	25 316	24 807
45 - 49	77 931	39 133	38 798	35 122	17 793	17 329	42 809	21 340	21 469
50 - 54	56 939	27 790	29 149	25 928	12 558	13 370	31 011	15 232	15 779
55 - 59	40 491	19 228	21 263	19 033	9 016	10 017	21 458	10 212	11 246
60 - 64	33 097	15 301	17 796	16 474	7 711	8 763	16 623	7 590	9 033
65 - 69	25 768	11 758	14 010	13 159	6 067	7 092	12 609	5 691	6 918
70 - 74	21 694	9 491	12 203	11 050	4 886	6 164	10 644	4 605	6 039
75 - 79	14 910	6 047	8 863	7 697	3 128	4 569	7 213	2 919	4 294
80 - 84	7 132	2 584	4 548	3 713	1 372	2 341	3 419	1 212	2 207
85 - 89	3 498	1 049	2 449	1 916	564	1 352	1 582	485	1 097
90 - 94	1 104	272	832	637	163	474	467	109	358
95 +	289	42	247	173	31	142	116	11	105
Unknown - Inconnu	119	45	74	72	29	43	47	16	31

1 VII 2005 (ESDJ)

Total	1 243 253	614 786	628 467	...	...	...	...	...	...
0	18 695	9 463	9 232	...	...	...	...	...	...
1 - 4	77 871	39 584	38 287	...	...	...	...	...	...
5 - 9	98 354	49 898	48 456	...	...	...	...	...	...
10 - 14	108 820	55 050	53 770	...	...	...	...	...	...
15 - 19	97 512	49 290	48 222	...	...	...	...	...	...
20 - 24	101 716	51 432	50 284	...	...	...	...	...	...
25 - 29	110 404	54 768	55 636	...	...	...	...	...	...
30 - 34	93 252	46 345	46 907	...	...	...	...	...	...
35 - 39	98 664	49 337	49 327	...	...	...	...	...	...
40 - 44	100 548	50 591	49 957	...	...	...	...	...	...
45 - 49	88 441	44 410	44 031	...	...	...	...	...	...
50 - 54	75 353	37 396	37 957	...	...	...	...	...	...
55 - 59	53 954	25 828	28 126	...	...	...	...	...	...
60 - 64	37 220	17 275	19 945	...	...	...	...	...	...
65 - 69	29 160	13 008	16 152	...	...	...	...	...	...
70 - 74	21 419	9 248	12 171	...	...	...	...	...	...
75 - 79	16 380	6 644	9 736	...	...	...	...	...	...
80 - 84	9 985	3 666	6 319	...	...	...	...	...	...
85 +	5 505	1 553	3 952	...	...	...	...	...	...

Morocco - Maroc
1 IX 2004 (CDFC)

Total	29 680 069	14 640 662	15 039 407	16 339 561	8 022 273	8 317 288	13 340 508	6 618 389	6 722 119
0 - 4	2 924 464	1 488 631	1 435 833	1 465 885	745 267	720 618	1 458 579	743 364	715 215
5 - 9	3 055 158	1 552 440	1 502 718	1 511 682	766 172	745 510	1 543 476	786 268	757 208
10 - 14	3 281 000	1 666 632	1 614 368	1 642 135	828 764	813 371	1 638 865	837 868	800 997
15 - 19	3 148 590	1 564 900	1 583 690	1 636 889	813 086	823 803	1 511 701	751 814	759 887
20 - 24	2 947 700	1 426 174	1 521 526	1 625 648	787 591	838 057	1 322 052	638 583	683 469
25 - 29	2 482 273	1 190 111	1 292 162	1 424 367	673 033	751 334	1 057 906	517 078	540 828
30 - 34	2 203 371	1 054 069	1 149 302	1 318 733	625 462	693 271	884 638	428 607	456 031
35 - 39	1 891 551	897 812	993 739	1 180 871	554 909	625 962	710 680	342 903	367 777
40 - 44	1 860 474	892 083	968 391	1 159 631	557 317	602 314	700 843	334 766	366 077
45 - 49	1 489 679	758 044	731 635	936 838	480 462	456 376	552 841	277 582	275 259
50 - 54	1 227 188	627 433	599 755	737 394	386 568	350 826	489 794	240 865	248 929
55 - 59	759 563	370 969	388 594	437 721	215 386	222 335	321 842	155 583	166 259
60 - 64	740 891	340 722	400 169	399 888	182 093	217 795	341 003	158 629	182 374
65 - 69	535 064	261 046	274 018	289 607	137 352	152 255	245 457	123 694	121 763
70 - 74	503 367	236 107	267 260	259 229	119 385	139 844	244 138	116 722	127 416

Continent, country or area, date, code and age (in years) Continent, pays ou zone, date, code et âge (en années)	Total			Urban - Urbaine			Rural - Rurale		
	Both sexes Les deux sexes	Male Masculin	Female Féminin	Both sexes Les deux sexes	Male Masculin	Female Féminin	Both sexes Les deux sexes	Male Masculin	Female Féminin
AFRICA - AFRIQUE									
Morocco - Maroc									
1 IX 2004 (CDFC)									
75 + ...	596 301	294 664	301 637	291 761	137 447	154 314	304 540	157 217	147 323
Unknown - Inconnu	33 435	18 825	14 610	21 282	11 979	9 303	12 153	6 846	5 307
Mozambique									
1 VIII 1997 (CDJC)									
Total.....................	15 278 334	7 320 948	7 957 386	4 454 859	2 201 292	2 253 567	10 823 475	5 119 656	5 703 819
0	535 237	263 539	271 698	138 601	68 743	69 858	396 636	194 796	201 840
1 - 4	2 206 319	1 089 667	1 116 652	558 601	277 008	281 593	1 647 718	812 659	835 059
5 - 9	2 225 996	1 112 321	1 113 675	617 241	304 392	312 849	1 608 755	807 929	800 826
10 - 14	1 825 665	947 236	878 429	600 911	301 921	298 990	1 224 754	645 315	579 439
15 - 19	1 628 405	774 327	854 078	564 519	287 073	277 446	1 063 886	487 254	576 632
20 - 24	1 464 727	637 113	827 614	461 071	217 269	243 802	1 003 656	419 844	583 812
25 - 29	1 163 574	509 109	654 465	345 841	161 031	184 810	817 733	348 078	469 655
30 - 34	887 710	410 148	477 562	284 119	137 905	146 214	603 591	272 243	331 348
35 - 39	802 208	373 813	428 395	246 954	126 347	120 607	555 254	247 466	307 788
40 - 44	573 193	270 046	303 147	173 329	90 578	82 751	399 864	179 468	220 396
45 - 49	539 168	257 070	282 098	139 708	72 415	67 293	399 460	184 655	214 805
50 - 54	390 962	178 902	212 060	95 508	48 098	47 410	295 454	130 804	164 650
55 - 59	336 356	162 122	174 234	76 557	39 078	37 479	259 799	123 044	136 755
60 - 64	239 431	114 335	125 096	57 172	27 663	29 509	182 259	86 672	95 587
65 - 69	209 713	100 425	109 288	44 486	20 277	24 209	165 227	80 148	85 079
70 - 74	98 014	47 407	50 607	21 390	9 542	11 848	76 624	37 865	38 759
75 - 79	84 387	41 529	42 858	16 670	7 113	9 557	67 717	34 416	33 301
80 - 84	32 631	15 305	17 326	6 162	2 542	3 620	26 469	12 763	13 706
85 - 89	20 033	9 041	10 992	3 795	1 361	2 434	16 238	7 680	8 558
90 - 94	7 179	3 537	3 642	1 114	430	684	6 065	3 107	2 958
95 + ...	7 426	3 956	3 470	1 110	506	604	6 316	3 450	2 866
1 VII 2000 (ESDF)									
*Total..................... *	*17 690 584*	*8 284 793*	*9 405 791*	*...*	*...*	*...*	*...*	*...*	*...*
*0 - 4 .... *	*3 139 293*	*1 514 640*	*1 624 653*	*...*	*...*	*...*	*...*	*...*	*...*
*5 - 9 .... *	*2 664 689*	*1 282 460*	*1 382 229*	*...*	*...*	*...*	*...*	*...*	*...*
*10 - 14 .... *	*2 208 552*	*1 059 016*	*1 149 536*	*...*	*...*	*...*	*...*	*...*	*...*
*15 - 19 .... *	*1 966 758*	*940 308*	*1 026 450*	*...*	*...*	*...*	*...*	*...*	*...*
*20 - 24 .... *	*1 540 328*	*743 941*	*796 387*	*...*	*...*	*...*	*...*	*...*	*...*
*25 - 29 .... *	*1 312 794*	*598 600*	*714 194*	*...*	*...*	*...*	*...*	*...*	*...*
*30 - 34 .... *	*1 023 631*	*438 932*	*584 699*	*...*	*...*	*...*	*...*	*...*	*...*
*35 - 39 .... *	*858 865*	*372 869*	*485 996*	*...*	*...*	*...*	*...*	*...*	*...*
*40 - 44 .... *	*745 586*	*341 179*	*404 407*	*...*	*...*	*...*	*...*	*...*	*...*
*45 - 49 .... *	*621 564*	*286 675*	*334 889*	*...*	*...*	*...*	*...*	*...*	*...*
*50 - 54 .... *	*496 069*	*226 219*	*269 850*	*...*	*...*	*...*	*...*	*...*	*...*
*55 - 59 .... *	*388 778*	*173 800*	*214 978*	*...*	*...*	*...*	*...*	*...*	*...*
*60 - 64 .... *	*289 060*	*126 794*	*162 266*	*...*	*...*	*...*	*...*	*...*	*...*
*65 - 69 .... *	*201 364*	*86 207*	*115 157*	*...*	*...*	*...*	*...*	*...*	*...*
*70 - 74 .... *	*124 004*	*50 747*	*73 257*	*...*	*...*	*...*	*...*	*...*	*...*
*75 - 79 .... *	*66 792*	*26 277*	*40 515*	*...*	*...*	*...*	*...*	*...*	*...*
*80 + ... *	*42 457*	*16 129*	*26 328*	*...*	*...*	*...*	*...*	*...*	*...*
Namibia - Namibie									
27 VIII 2001 (CDFC)									
Total.....................	1 830 330	887 721	942 572	603 612	300 358[4]	303 236[4]	1 226 718	587 363[4]	639 336[4]
0 - 4	241 229	120 044	121 185	67 484	33 494	33 990	173 745	86 550	87 195
0	46 852	23 281	23 571	...	...	...	...	...	...
1 - 4	194 377	96 763	97 614	...	...	...	...	...	...
5 - 9	246 964	121 785	125 179	59 123	28 683	30 440	187 841	93 102	94 739
10 - 14	230 287	113 081	117 206	55 162	25 564	29 598	175 125	87 517	87 608
15 - 19	202 298	99 307	102 991	55 865	25 383	30 482	146 433	73 924	72 509
20 - 24	174 484	86 382	88 102	70 592	34 483	36 109	103 892	51 899	51 993
25 - 29	150 783	74 304	76 479	73 635	37 316	36 319	77 148	36 988	40 160
30 - 34	118 529	57 125	61 404	58 312	29 851	28 461	60 217	27 274	32 943
35 - 39	96 416	45 083	51 333	46 071	23 521	22 550	50 345	21 562	28 783
40 - 44	74 050	34 170	39 880	33 152	16 966	16 186	40 898	17 204	23 694
45 - 49	57 749	26 942	30 807	23 576	12 615	10 961	34 173	14 327	19 846
50 - 54	47 779	21 999	25 780	16 798	9 193	7 605	30 981	12 806	18 175
55 - 59	35 209	16 600	18 609	10 890	5 893	4 997	24 319	10 707	13 612
60 - 64	34 378	15 569	18 809	8 512	4 192	4 320	25 866	11 377	14 489

Continent, country or area, date, code and age (in years) Continent, pays ou zone, date, code et âge (en années)	Total			Urban - Urbaine			Rural - Rurale		
	Both sexes Les deux sexes	Male Masculin	Female Féminin	Both sexes Les deux sexes	Male Masculin	Female Féminin	Both sexes Les deux sexes	Male Masculin	Female Féminin
AFRICA - AFRIQUE									
Namibia - Namibie									
27 VIII 2001 (CDFC)									
65 - 69	25 262	11 399	13 863	5 458	2 596	2 862	19 804	8 803	11 001
70 - 74	22 052	9 313	12 739	3 707	1 619	2 088	18 345	7 694	10 651
75 - 79	16 007	6 382	9 625	2 531	1 068	1 463	13 476	5 314	8 162
80 - 84	13 818	5 359	8 459	1 753	680	1 073	12 065	4 679	7 386
85 - 89	5 407	2 033	3 374	973	341	632	4 434	1 692	2 742
90 - 94	2 555	927	1 628	376	152	224	2 179	775	1 404
95 +	2 712	897	1 815	262	111	151	2 450	786	1 664
Unknown - Inconnu	32 325	19 020	13 305	9 362	6 637	2 725	22 963	12 383	10 580
Niger									
1 VII 2005 (ESDJ)									
Total	12 546 000	6 272 500	6 270 600	2 203 800	1 105 000	1 098 800	10 342 200	5 169 500	5 172 700
0 - 4	2 434 700	1 248 700	1 186 000	331 800	168 200	163 600	2 102 900	1 080 500	1 022 400
5 - 9	2 122 700	1 092 400	1 030 300	346 000	175 900	170 100	1 776 700	916 500	860 200
10 - 14	1 638 200	826 800	811 400	333 700	167 900	165 800	1 304 500	658 900	645 600
15 - 19	1 181 800	579 000	602 800	255 900	127 200	128 700	925 900	451 800	474 100
20 - 24	960 100	459 100	501 000	180 700	90 400	90 300	779 400	368 700	410 700
25 - 29	832 600	389 500	443 100	152 000	74 700	77 300	680 600	314 800	365 800
30 - 34	721 900	343 800	378 100	134 400	65 300	69 100	587 500	278 500	309 000
35 - 39	642 600	320 200	322 400	118 900	60 200	58 700	523 700	260 000	263 700
40 - 44	521 900	263 400	258 500	94 200	49 200	45 000	427 700	214 200	213 500
45 - 49	385 900	196 000	189 900	69 000	35 900	33 100	316 900	160 100	156 800
50 - 54	315 500	159 300	156 200	55 800	26 700	29 100	259 700	132 600	127 100
55 - 59	261 400	127 500	133 900	45 700	21 100	24 600	215 700	106 400	109 300
60 - 64	188 200	92 200	96 000	31 600	17 000	14 600	156 600	75 200	81 400
65 - 69	110 900	56 300	54 600	18 300	10 100	8 200	92 600	46 200	46 400
70 - 74	79 100	40 800	38 300	13 100	6 300	6 800	66 000	34 500	31 500
75 - 79	59 100	30 800	28 300	10 100	3 500	6 600	49 000	27 300	21 700
80 +	86 500	46 700	39 800	12 600	5 400	7 200	73 900	43 300	33 000
Nigeria - Nigéria[5]									
1 VII 2003 (ESDF)									
Total	126 152 844	63 241 808	62 911 036	...	...	...	...	...	...
0 - 4	22 090 300	11 214 033	10 876 267	...	...	...	...	...	...
5 - 9	18 333 245	9 362 226	8 971 019	...	...	...	...	...	...
10 - 14	15 408 885	7 804 986	7 603 899	...	...	...	...	...	...
15 - 19	12 867 025	6 446 554	6 420 471	...	...	...	...	...	...
20 - 24	10 991 665	5 543 883	5 447 782	...	...	...	...	...	...
25 - 29	9 891 507	4 951 575	4 939 932	...	...	...	...	...	...
30 - 34	8 076 673	3 913 158	4 163 515	...	...	...	...	...	...
35 - 39	6 511 687	3 017 320	3 494 367	...	...	...	...	...	...
40 - 44	5 541 919	2 616 888	2 925 031	...	...	...	...	...	...
45 - 49	4 682 410	2 287 112	2 395 298	...	...	...	...	...	...
50 - 54	3 658 941	1 835 806	1 823 135	...	...	...	...	...	...
55 - 59	2 708 234	1 411 256	1 296 978	...	...	...	...	...	...
60 - 64	1 983 965	1 050 256	933 709	...	...	...	...	...	...
65 - 69	1 357 083	726 454	630 629	...	...	...	...	...	...
70 - 74	950 824	501 708	449 116	...	...	...	...	...	...
75 - 79	612 840	309 402	303 438	...	...	...	...	...	...
80 +	485 641	249 191	236 450	...	...	...	...	...	...
Réunion									
1 VII 2004 (ESDJ)									
Total	768 808	377 607	391 201	...	...	...	...	...	...
0 - 4	71 930	36 411	35 519	...	...	...	...	...	...
5 - 9	65 184	33 594	31 590	...	...	...	...	...	...
10 - 14	70 090	35 753	34 338	...	...	...	...	...	...
15 - 19	69 963	35 471	34 492	...	...	...	...	...	...
20 - 24	63 276	31 776	31 500	...	...	...	...	...	...
25 - 29	51 936	25 236	26 700	...	...	...	...	...	...
30 - 34	54 625	26 227	28 398	...	...	...	...	...	...
35 - 39	64 738	31 385	33 353	...	...	...	...	...	...
40 - 44	60 007	29 454	30 553	...	...	...	...	...	...
45 - 49	48 331	23 682	24 649	...	...	...	...	...	...
50 - 54	39 885	19 654	20 231	...	...	...	...	...	...
55 - 59	29 165	14 336	14 829	...	...	...	...	...	...

Continent, country or area, date, code and age (in years) Continent, pays ou zone, date, code et âge (en années)	Total			Urban - Urbaine			Rural - Rurale		
	Both sexes Les deux sexes	Male Masculin	Female Féminin	Both sexes Les deux sexes	Male Masculin	Female Féminin	Both sexes Les deux sexes	Male Masculin	Female Féminin
AFRICA - AFRIQUE									
Réunion									
1 VII 2004 (ESDJ)									
60 - 64	23 794	11 430	12 364	...	...	...	...	...	...
65 - 69	19 589	8 961	10 628	...	...	...	...	...	...
70 - 74	13 974	6 085	7 890	...	...	...	...	...	...
75 - 79	10 529	4 259	6 270	...	...	...	...	...	...
80 - 84	7 018	2 469	4 549	...	...	...	...	...	...
85 - 89	2 981	874	2 107	...	...	...	...	...	...
90 +	1 796	554	1 242	...	...	...	...	...	...
Rwanda									
16 VIII 2002 (CDJC)									
Total	8 128 553	3 879 448	4 249 105	1 372 604	727 172	645 432	6 755 949	3 152 276	3 603 673
0	325 221	161 653	163 568	46 968	23 496	23 472	278 253	138 157	140 096
1 - 4	995 010	493 437	501 573	147 083	73 621	73 462	847 927	419 816	428 111
5 - 9	1 141 039	563 351	577 688	157 009	77 648	79 361	984 030	485 703	498 327
10 - 14	1 095 225	536 876	558 349	149 787	71 947	77 840	945 438	464 929	480 509
15 - 19	1 078 839	526 563	552 276	184 874	89 576	95 298	893 965	436 987	456 978
20 - 24	810 681	382 561	428 120	177 151	98 145	79 006	633 530	284 416	349 114
25 - 29	555 509	253 180	302 329	130 102	74 049	56 053	425 407	179 131	246 276
30 - 34	448 439	208 742	239 697	100 840	59 871	40 969	347 599	148 871	198 728
35 - 39	382 636	177 816	204 820	76 430	46 117	30 313	306 206	131 699	174 507
40 - 44	363 067	168 934	194 133	63 795	38 834	24 961	299 272	130 100	169 172
45 - 49	268 262	122 615	145 647	43 450	26 007	17 443	224 812	96 608	128 204
50 - 54	193 382	86 925	106 457	30 845	17 673	13 172	162 537	69 252	93 285
55 - 59	123 868	50 480	73 388	18 782	9 561	9 221	105 086	40 919	64 167
60 - 64	111 809	45 221	66 588	15 483	7 293	8 190	96 326	37 928	58 398
65 - 69	84 928	35 178	49 750	11 333	5 166	6 167	73 595	30 012	43 583
70 - 74	71 020	30 970	40 050	8 790	4 025	4 765	62 230	26 945	35 285
75 - 79	37 989	16 255	21 734	4 451	1 923	2 528	33 538	14 332	19 206
80 - 84	26 788	12 081	14 707	3 295	1 378	1 917	23 493	10 703	12 790
85 +	14 841	6 610	8 231	2 136	842	1 294	12 705	5 768	6 937
Saint Helena ex. dep. -									
Sainte-Hélène sans dép.									
8 III 1998 (CDJC)									
Total	4 913	2 481	2 432	...	...	...	...	...	...
0	60	33	27	...	...	...	...	...	...
1 - 4	252	139	113	...	...	...	...	...	...
5 - 9	369	197	172	...	...	...	...	...	...
10 - 14	368	199	169	...	...	...	...	...	...
15 - 19	452	217	235	...	...	...	...	...	...
20 - 24	300	154	146	...	...	...	...	...	...
25 - 29	370	185	185	...	...	...	...	...	...
30 - 34	329	150	179	...	...	...	...	...	...
35 - 39	391	181	210	...	...	...	...	...	...
40 - 44	336	181	155	...	...	...	...	...	...
45 - 49	340	173	167	...	...	...	...	...	...
50 - 54	346	200	146	...	...	...	...	...	...
55 - 59	230	124	106	...	...	...	...	...	...
60 - 64	202	127	75	...	...	...	...	...	...
65 - 69	190	86	104	...	...	...	...	...	...
70 - 74	143	51	92	...	...	...	...	...	...
75 - 79	111	41	70	...	...	...	...	...	...
80 - 84	69	25	44	...	...	...	...	...	...
85 - 89	26	7	19	...	...	...	...	...	...
90 - 94	18	7	11	...	...	...	...	...	...
95 +	1	-	1	...	...	...	...	...	...
Unknown - Inconnu	10	4	6	...	...	...	...	...	...
Saint Helena: Ascension -									
Sainte-Hélène: Ascension									
8 III 1998 (CDJC)									
Total	712	458	254	...	...	...	...	...	...
0	8	4	4	...	...	...	...	...	...
1 - 4	15	9	6	...	...	...	...	...	...
5 - 9	30	11	19	...	...	...	...	...	...
10 - 14	37	21	16	...	...	...	...	...	...

Continent, country or area, date, code and age (in years) — Continent, pays ou zone, date, code et âge (en années)	Total			Urban - Urbaine			Rural - Rurale		
	Both sexes Les deux sexes	Male Masculin	Female Féminin	Both sexes Les deux sexes	Male Masculin	Female Féminin	Both sexes Les deux sexes	Male Masculin	Female Féminin
AFRICA - AFRIQUE									
Saint Helena: Ascension - Sainte-Hélène: Ascension									
8 III 1998 (CDJC)									
15 - 19	30	21	9	...	...	...	...	...	...
20 - 24	93	55	38	...	...	...	...	...	...
25 - 29	115	81	34	...	...	...	...	...	...
30 - 34	105	67	38	...	...	...	...	...	...
35 - 39	68	42	26	...	...	...	...	...	...
40 - 44	67	43	24	...	...	...	...	...	...
45 - 49	63	42	21	...	...	...	...	...	...
50 - 54	49	37	12	...	...	...	...	...	...
55 - 59	25	21	4	...	...	...	...	...	...
60 - 64	5	2	3	...	...	...	...	...	...
65 - 69	1	1	-	...	...	...	...	...	...
70 - 74	1	1	-	...	...	...	...	...	...
75 +	-	-	-	...	...	...	...	...	...
Saint Helena: Tristan da Cunha - Sainte-Hélène: Tristan da Cunha									
1 VII 1996 (ESDF)									
Total	286	137	149	...	...	...	...	...	...
0	1	1	-	...	...	...	...	...	...
1 - 4	10	7	3	...	...	...	...	...	...
5 - 9	14	9	5	...	...	...	...	...	...
10 - 14	17	9	8	...	...	...	...	...	...
15 - 19	13	8	5	...	...	...	...	...	...
20 - 24	17	3	14	...	...	...	...	...	...
25 - 29	35	17	18	...	...	...	...	...	...
30 - 34	12	6	6	...	...	...	...	...	...
35 - 39	19	10	9	...	...	...	...	...	...
40 - 44	14	4	10	...	...	...	...	...	...
45 - 49	24	14	10	...	...	...	...	...	...
50 - 54	18	8	10	...	...	...	...	...	...
55 - 59	22	6	16	...	...	...	...	...	...
60 - 64	18	11	7	...	...	...	...	...	...
65 - 69	12	5	7	...	...	...	...	...	...
70 - 74	22	12	10	...	...	...	...	...	...
75 - 79	10	5	5	...	...	...	...	...	...
80 - 84	6	1	5	...	...	...	...	...	...
85 - 89	1	1	-	...	...	...	...	...	...
90 +	1	-	1	...	...	...	...	...	...
Unknown - Inconnu	-	-	-	...	...	...	...	...	...
Sao Tome and Principe - Sao Tomé-et-Principe									
25 VIII 2001 (CDFC)									
Total	136 554	67 422	69 132	73 907	35 679	38 228	62 647	31 743	30 904
0	4 588	2 299	2 289	2 433	1 221	1 212	2 155	1 078	1 077
1 - 4	16 111	8 149	7 962	8 440	4 325	4 115	7 671	3 824	3 847
5 - 9	18 794	9 587	9 207	9 780	4 972	4 808	9 014	4 615	4 399
10 - 14	18 468	9 416	9 052	9 829	4 883	4 946	8 639	4 533	4 106
15 - 19	17 311	8 663	8 648	9 762	4 701	5 061	7 549	3 962	3 587
20 - 24	13 981	6 870	7 111	7 926	3 783	4 143	6 055	3 087	2 968
25 - 29	9 703	4 795	4 908	5 333	2 564	2 769	4 370	2 231	2 139
30 - 34	7 684	3 700	3 984	4 235	1 960	2 275	3 449	1 740	1 709
35 - 39	6 567	3 050	3 517	3 639	1 632	2 007	2 928	1 418	1 510
40 - 44	5 367	2 465	2 902	3 066	1 413	1 653	2 301	1 052	1 249
45 - 49	3 984	1 864	2 120	2 261	1 026	1 235	1 723	838	885
50 - 54	3 020	1 408	1 612	1 659	758	901	1 361	650	711
55 - 59	2 397	1 119	1 278	1 247	559	688	1 150	560	590
60 - 64	2 710	1 301	1 409	1 288	568	720	1 422	733	689
65 - 69	2 108	1 043	1 065	1 014	482	532	1 094	561	533
70 - 74	1 648	780	868	829	366	463	819	414	405
75 - 79	1 124	513	611	593	251	342	531	262	269
80 - 84	616	262	354	349	140	209	267	122	145
85 +	373	138	235	224	75	149	149	63	86

Continent, country or area, date, code and age (in years) / Continent, pays ou zone, date, code et âge (en années)	Total			Urban - Urbaine			Rural - Rurale		
	Both sexes Les deux sexes	Male Masculin	Female Féminin	Both sexes Les deux sexes	Male Masculin	Female Féminin	Both sexes Les deux sexes	Male Masculin	Female Féminin

AFRICA - AFRIQUE

Seychelles
1 VII 2005 (ESDF)

Total	82 852	41 233	41 619	...	...	...	...	...	...
0 - 4	6 861	3 441	3 420	...	...	...	...	...	...
5 - 9	6 399	3 270	3 129	...	...	...	...	...	...
10 - 14	7 191	3 716	3 475	...	...	...	...	...	...
15 - 19	7 280	3 747	3 533	...	...	...	...	...	...
20 - 24	7 180	3 759	3 421	...	...	...	...	...	...
25 - 29	7 091	3 615	3 476	...	...	...	...	...	...
30 - 34	7 133	3 530	3 603	...	...	...	...	...	...
35 - 39	6 787	3 243	3 544	...	...	...	...	...	...
40 - 44	6 257	3 079	3 178	...	...	...	...	...	...
45 - 49	5 807	3 047	2 760	...	...	...	...	...	...
50 - 54	3 334	1 790	1 544	...	...	...	...	...	...
55 - 59	2 902	1 485	1 417	...	...	...	...	...	...
60 - 64	2 019	987	1 032	...	...	...	...	...	...
65 - 69	2 053	858	1 195	...	...	...	...	...	...
70 - 74	1 762	709	1 053	...	...	...	...	...	...
75 - 79	1 300	503	797	...	...	...	...	...	...
80 +	1 496	454	1 042	...	...	...	...	...	...

Sierra Leone
1 VII 2003 (ESDF)

Total	5 280 406	2 606 045	2 674 361	...	...	...	...	...	...
0	205 242	102 685	102 557	...	...	...	...	...	...
1 - 4	657 985	331 968	326 016	...	...	...	...	...	...
5 - 9	794 093	399 695	394 398	...	...	...	...	...	...
10 - 14	516 752	273 918	242 834	...	...	...	...	...	...
15 - 19	513 263	240 312	272 951	...	...	...	...	...	...
20 - 24	408 352	182 703	225 649	...	...	...	...	...	...
25 - 29	423 009	188 100	234 910	...	...	...	...	...	...
30 - 34	329 828	149 713	180 116	...	...	...	...	...	...
35 - 39	297 142	146 203	150 940	...	...	...	...	...	...
40 - 44	220 272	108 870	111 402	...	...	...	...	...	...
45 - 49	193 199	104 586	88 612	...	...	...	...	...	...
50 - 54	155 484	80 832	74 652	...	...	...	...	...	...
55 - 59	111 025	60 805	50 221	...	...	...	...	...	...
60 - 64	116 884	59 762	57 122	...	...	...	...	...	...
65 - 69	84 034	44 224	39 811	...	...	...	...	...	...
70 - 74	67 884	36 953	30 932	...	...	...	...	...	...
75 - 79	50 153	27 772	22 381	...	...	...	...	...	...
80 - 84	38 623	19 711	18 912	...	...	...	...	...	...
85 - 89	27 246	14 469	12 777	...	...	...	...	...	...
90 +	34 069	17 392	16 677	...	...	...	...	...	...
Unknown - Inconnu	35 894	15 402	20 492	...	...	...	...	...	...

Somalia - Somalie
1 VII 2002 (SSDF)

Total	6 799 079	3 499 523	3 299 556	2 310 817	1 168 410	1 142 407	4 488 262	2 331 113	2 157 149
0 - 4	1 235 105	634 959	600 146	408 646	206 987	201 659	826 459	427 972	398 487
5 - 9	1 049 189	544 431	504 758	352 471	179 293	173 178	696 718	365 138	331 580
10 - 14	870 180	455 323	414 857	297 807	151 845	145 962	572 373	303 478	268 895
15 - 19	725 723	373 328	352 395	250 718	125 641	125 077	475 005	247 687	227 318
20 - 24	581 690	280 786	300 904	202 030	95 671	106 359	379 660	185 115	194 545
25 - 29	491 651	231 254	260 397	170 250	78 983	91 267	321 401	152 271	169 130
30 - 34	428 269	198 101	230 168	146 024	67 081	78 943	282 245	131 020	151 225
35 - 39	366 113	175 050	191 063	123 698	58 860	64 838	242 415	116 190	126 225
40 - 44	311 989	164 941	147 048	104 080	54 778	49 302	207 909	110 163	97 746
45 - 49	248 939	139 351	109 588	82 971	46 198	36 773	- 165 968	93 153	72 815
50 - 54	174 517	105 972	68 545	58 869	35 355	23 514	115 648	70 617	45 031
55 - 59	124 841	79 206	45 635	42 868	26 625	16 243	81 973	52 581	29 392
60 - 64	80 530	51 293	29 237	28 988	17 492	11 496	51 542	33 801	17 741
65 - 69	51 554	32 843	18 711	19 396	11 603	7 793	32 158	21 240	10 918
70 - 74	28 997	17 795	11 202	11 675	6 878	4 797	17 322	10 917	6 405
75 - 79	12 860	6 152	6 708	5 828	3 320	2 508	7 032	2 832	4 200
80 +	16 932	8 738	8 194	4 498	1 800	2 698	12 434	6 938	5 496

Continent, country or area, date, code and age (in years) / Continent, pays ou zone, date, code et âge (en années)	Total			Urban - Urbaine			Rural - Rurale		
	Both sexes Les deux sexes	Male Masculin	Female Féminin	Both sexes Les deux sexes	Male Masculin	Female Féminin	Both sexes Les deux sexes	Male Masculin	Female Féminin
AFRICA - AFRIQUE									
South Africa - Afrique du Sud									
10 X 1996 (CDFC)[6]									
Total....................	40 583 573	19 520 887	21 062 686	21 781 807	10 667 927	11 113 880	18 801 766	8 852 960	9 948 806
0.......................	856 238	426 858	429 380	407 569	204 037	203 532	448 669	222 821	225 848
1 - 4...................	3 587 383	1 789 905	1 797 478	1 608 627	801 912	806 715	1 978 756	987 993	990 763
5 - 9...................	4 668 721	2 333 562	2 335 159	2 038 226	1 016 905	1 021 321	2 630 495	1 316 657	1 313 838
10 - 14.................	4 654 098	2 308 758	2 345 340	2 061 009	1 016 787	1 044 222	2 593 089	1 291 971	1 301 118
15 - 19.................	4 180 717	2 050 214	2 130 503	1 995 798	978 031	1 017 767	2 184 919	1 072 183	1 112 736
20 - 24.................	3 982 354	1 917 919	2 064 435	2 271 339	1 120 919	1 150 420	1 711 015	797 000	914 015
25 - 29.................	3 455 728	1 663 064	1 792 664	2 186 820	1 088 452	1 098 368	1 268 908	574 612	694 296
30 - 34.................	3 074 202	1 463 499	1 610 703	1 970 405	972 890	997 515	1 103 797	490 609	613 188
35 - 39.................	2 653 756	1 284 957	1 368 799	1 709 987	847 993	861 994	943 769	436 964	506 805
40 - 44.................	2 138 626	1 030 597	1 108 029	1 360 825	676 387	684 438	777 801	354 210	423 591
45 - 49.................	1 677 526	813 816	863 710	1 050 144	525 516	524 628	627 382	288 300	339 082
50 - 54.................	1 268 895	600 476	668 419	775 141	383 915	391 226	493 754	216 561	277 193
55 - 59.................	1 069 936	483 678	586 258	621 620	294 100	327 520	448 316	189 578	258 738
60 - 64.................	890 537	352 053	538 484	482 701	208 117	274 584	407 836	143 936	263 900
65 - 69.................	758 886	304 013	454 873	374 423	160 695	213 728	384 463	143 318	241 145
70 - 74.................	482 162	195 119	287 043	254 856	105 173	149 683	227 306	89 946	137 360
75 - 79.................	377 427	141 844	235 583	184 420	70 699	113 721	193 007	71 145	121 862
80 - 84.................	178 903	62 072	116 831	96 886	32 757	64 129	82 017	29 315	52 702
85 +...................	137 284	43 230	94 054	69 901	21 596	48 305	67 383	21 634	45 749
Unknown - Inconnu......	490 194	255 253	234 941	261 110	141 046	120 064	229 084	114 207	114 877
1 VII 2004 (ESDF)[7]									
Total....................	46 586 607	22 987 410	23 599 197	...	...	...	...	...	...
0 - 4...................	5 176 465	2 616 514	2 559 951	...	...	...	...	...	...
5 - 9...................	5 119 465	2 583 940	2 535 525	...	...	...	...	...	...
10 - 14.................	5 051 614	2 545 484	2 506 130	...	...	...	...	...	...
15 - 19.................	4 923 992	2 475 651	2 448 341	...	...	...	...	...	...
20 - 24.................	4 679 210	2 358 355	2 320 855	...	...	...	...	...	...
25 - 29.................	4 291 589	2 179 953	2 111 636	...	...	...	...	...	...
30 - 34.................	3 696 445	1 852 780	1 843 665	...	...	...	...	...	...
35 - 39.................	2 851 312	1 401 549	1 449 763	...	...	...	...	...	...
40 - 44.................	2 538 649	1 226 582	1 312 067	...	...	...	...	...	...
45 - 49.................	2 213 991	1 056 100	1 157 891	...	...	...	...	...	...
50 - 54.................	1 761 981	834 806	927 175	...	...	...	...	...	...
55 - 59.................	1 369 218	636 046	733 172	...	...	...	...	...	...
60 - 64.................	1 050 415	475 193	575 222	...	...	...	...	...	...
65 - 69.................	767 452	329 787	437 665	...	...	...	...	...	...
70 - 74.................	514 517	206 198	308 319	...	...	...	...	...	...
75 - 79.................	312 251	116 808	195 443	...	...	...	...	...	...
80 +...................	268 041	91 664	176 377	...	...	...	...	...	...
Swaziland									
11 V 1997 (CDFC)									
Total....................	929 718	440 154	489 564	214 428	106 256	108 172	715 290	333 898	381 392
0.......................	24 405	12 049	12 356	5 123	2 519	2 604	19 282	9 530	9 752
1 - 4...................	111 992	55 480	56 512	19 744	9 701	10 043	92 248	45 779	46 469
5 - 9...................	139 245	68 976	70 269	22 232	10 663	11 569	117 013	58 313	58 700
10 - 14.................	137 487	68 200	69 287	22 036	9 908	12 128	115 451	58 292	57 159
15 - 19.................	112 356	54 775	57 581	24 504	10 716	13 788	87 852	44 059	43 793
20 - 24.................	85 094	38 807	46 287	27 184	12 804	14 380	57 910	26 003	31 907
25 - 29.................	68 043	30 147	37 896	24 731	12 610	12 121	43 312	17 537	25 775
30 - 34.................	52 156	21 988	30 168	18 103	9 257	8 846	34 053	12 731	21 322
35 - 39.................	45 802	19 645	26 157	15 043	7 841	7 202	30 759	11 804	18 955
40 - 44.................	35 505	16 165	19 340	11 090	6 128	4 962	24 415	10 037	14 378
45 - 49.................	30 371	14 461	15 910	8 627	5 068	3 559	21 744	9 393	12 351
50 - 54.................	23 316	10 799	12 517	5 756	3 413	2 343	17 560	7 386	10 174
55 - 59.................	17 920	8 758	9 162	3 759	2 275	1 484	14 161	6 483	7 678
60 - 64.................	13 866	6 325	7 541	2 349	1 298	1 051	11 517	5 027	6 490
65 - 69.................	10 152	4 645	5 507	1 340	710	630	8 812	3 935	4 877
70 - 74.................	7 301	2 924	4 377	766	343	423	6 535	2 581	3 954
75 - 79.................	5 269	2 175	3 094	527	256	271	4 742	1 919	2 823
80 - 84.................	3 085	1 161	1 924	266	110	156	2 819	1 051	1 768
85 - 89.................	1 765	707	1 058	145	64	81	1 620	643	977
90 - 94.................	731	264	467	61	25	36	670	239	431

Continent, country or area, date, code and age (in years) Continent, pays ou zone, date, code et âge (en années)	Total			Urban - Urbaine			Rural - Rurale		
	Both sexes Les deux sexes	Male Masculin	Female Féminin	Both sexes Les deux sexes	Male Masculin	Female Féminin	Both sexes Les deux sexes	Male Masculin	Female Féminin
AFRICA - AFRIQUE									
Swaziland									
11 V 1997 (CDFC)									
95 + ...	959	371	588	63	34	29	896	337	559
Unknown - Inconnu	2 898	1 332	1 566	979	513	466	1 919	819	1 100
Tunisia - Tunisie									
1 VII 1998 (ESDF)									
Total....................	9 333 300	4 709 000	4 624 300	...	...	...	...	...	...
0 - 4	978 500	500 700	477 800	...	...	...	...	...	...
5 - 9	1 015 200	519 500	495 700	...	...	...	...	...	...
10 - 14	1 058 900	541 400	517 500	...	...	...	...	...	...
15 - 19	1 006 100	514 400	491 700	...	...	...	...	...	...
20 - 24	898 500	455 600	443 000	...	...	...	...	...	...
25 - 29	795 900	395 900	399 900	...	...	...	...	...	...
30 - 34	714 800	351 200	363 600	...	...	...	...	...	...
35 - 39	621 900	310 300	311 600	...	...	...	...	...	...
40 - 44	512 500	257 400	255 100	...	...	...	...	...	...
45 - 49	384 400	190 800	193 700	...	...	...	...	...	...
50 - 54	291 800	142 200	149 600	...	...	...	...	...	...
55 - 59	266 800	131 200	135 600	...	...	...	...	...	...
60 - 64	255 000	127 100	127 900	...	...	...	...	...	...
65 - 69	208 200	105 500	102 700	...	...	...	...	...	...
70 - 74	145 800	74 200	71 600	...	...	...	...	...	...
75 - 79	94 700	48 500	46 200	...	...	...	...	...	...
80 + ...	84 100	43 000	41 000	...	...	...	...	...	...
Uganda - Ouganda									
12 IX 2002 (CDFC)									
Total....................	24 442 084	11 929 803	12 512 281	2 999 387	1 449 684	1 549 703	21 442 697	10 480 119	10 962 578
0	1 007 407	505 006	502 401	104 439	52 481	51 958	902 968	452 525	450 443
1 - 4	3 537 016	1 767 120	1 769 896	347 233	172 444	174 789	3 189 783	1 594 676	1 595 107
5 - 9	4 001 052	1 998 157	2 002 895	399 119	193 271	205 848	3 601 933	1 804 886	1 797 047
10 - 14	3 509 151	1 757 111	1 752 040	391 236	180 572	210 664	3 117 915	1 576 539	1 541 376
15 - 19	2 708 143	1 324 222	1 383 921	407 299	180 461	226 838	2 300 844	1 143 761	1 157 083
20 - 24	2 175 580	981 994	1 193 586	392 217	180 869	211 348	1 783 363	801 125	982 238
25 - 29	1 778 541	831 129	947 412	308 026	152 765	155 261	1 470 515	678 364	792 151
30 - 34	1 420 073	708 138	711 935	215 168	116 304	98 864	1 204 905	591 834	613 071
35 - 39	1 020 968	492 372	528 596	138 208	72 826	65 382	882 760	419 546	463 214
40 - 44	828 317	400 433	427 884	96 870	50 662	46 208	731 447	349 771	381 676
45 - 49	542 862	257 694	285 168	58 821	30 676	28 145	484 041	227 018	257 023
50 - 54	486 060	223 345	262 715	44 728	22 839	21 889	441 332	200 506	240 826
55 - 59	325 875	149 792	176 083	25 198	12 690	12 508	300 677	137 102	163 575
60 - 64	363 765	173 325	190 440	24 371	11 139	13 232	339 394	162 186	177 208
65 - 69	226 029	115 081	110 948	14 175	6 657	7 518	211 854	108 424	103 430
70 - 74	217 160	102 858	114 302	12 538	5 157	7 381	204 622	97 701	106 921
75 - 79	105 318	54 213	51 105	6 582	2 824	3 758	98 736	51 389	47 347
80 - 84	112 785	52 143	60 642	7 542	2 926	4 616	105 243	49 217	56 026
85 - 89	31 184	15 009	16 175	2 146	821	1 325	29 038	14 188	14 850
90 - 94	27 871	13 036	14 835	2 126	786	1 340	25 745	12 250	13 495
95 + ...	16 927	7 625	9 302	1 345	514	831	15 582	7 111	8 471
United Republic of Tanzania - République Unie de Tanzanie									
24 VIII 2002 (CDFC)									
Total....................	34 443 603	16 829 861	17 613 742	...	...	...	...	...	...
0 - 4	5 664 907	2 830 545	2 834 362	...	...	...	...	...	...
5 - 9	5 130 448	2 573 993	2 556 455	...	...	...	...	...	...
10 - 14	4 443 257	2 233 401	2 209 856	...	...	...	...	...	...
15 - 19	3 595 735	1 761 329	1 834 406	...	...	...	...	...	...
20 - 24	3 148 513	1 402 077	1 746 436	...	...	...	...	...	...
25 - 29	2 801 965	1 309 661	1 492 304	...	...	...	...	...	...
30 - 34	2 229 046	1 087 599	1 141 447	...	...	...	...	...	...
35 - 39	1 669 873	824 338	845 535	...	...	...	...	...	...
40 - 44	1 348 508	669 549	678 959	...	...	...	...	...	...
45 - 49	984 823	478 522	506 301	...	...	...	...	...	...
50 - 54	883 820	428 501	455 319	...	...	...	...	...	...
55 - 59	590 667	290 117	300 550	...	...	...	...	...	...

Continent, country or area, date, code and age (in years) / Continent, pays ou zone, date, code et âge (en années)	Total			Urban - Urbaine			Rural - Rurale		
	Both sexes Les deux sexes	Male Masculin	Female Féminin	Both sexes Les deux sexes	Male Masculin	Female Féminin	Both sexes Les deux sexes	Male Masculin	Female Féminin
AFRICA - AFRIQUE									
United Republic of Tanzania - République Unie de Tanzanie									
24 VIII 2002 (CDFC)									
60 - 64	604 956	287 502	317 454	...	...	...	...	...	...
65 - 69	439 671	213 635	226 036	...	...	...	...	...	...
70 - 74	377 852	180 246	197 606	...	...	...	...	...	...
75 - 79	221 354	113 205	108 149	...	...	...	...	...	...
80 +	308 208	145 641	162 567	...	...	...	...	...	...
Zambia - Zambie									
1 VII 2000 (ESDF)									
Total	9 337 425	4 594 290	4 743 135	3 347 069	1 662 739	1 684 330	5 990 356	2 931 551	3 058 805
0	339 228	168 841	170 387	101 775	50 699	51 076	237 453	118 142	119 311
1 - 4	1 317 492	656 948	660 544	420 759	209 814	210 945	896 733	447 134	449 599
5 - 9	1 461 082	729 181	731 901	500 572	247 117	253 455	960 510	482 064	478 446
10 - 14	1 205 646	601 279	604 367	428 831	206 305	222 526	776 815	394 974	381 841
15 - 19	1 069 996	513 320	556 676	415 197	195 518	219 679	654 799	317 802	336 997
20 - 24	908 672	416 083	492 589	376 695	174 331	202 364	531 977	241 752	290 225
25 - 29	741 148	361 901	379 247	308 436	155 070	153 366	432 712	206 831	225 881
30 - 34	557 873	282 439	275 434	225 707	119 524	106 183	332 166	162 915	169 251
35 - 39	429 987	211 356	218 631	169 148	87 763	81 385	260 839	123 593	137 246
40 - 44	325 776	161 179	164 597	125 995	66 050	59 945	199 781	95 129	104 652
45 - 49	245 320	122 486	122 834	91 507	50 128	41 379	153 813	72 358	81 455
50 - 54	203 612	97 850	105 762	65 547	37 513	28 034	138 065	60 337	77 728
55 - 59	144 838	71 905	72 933	39 418	22 860	16 558	105 420	49 045	56 375
60 - 64	131 475	62 678	68 797	29 438	15 308	14 130	102 037	47 370	54 667
65 - 69	100 493	52 499	47 994	20 294	10 642	9 652	80 199	41 857	38 342
70 - 74	68 935	37 066	31 869	12 763	6 634	6 129	56 172	30 432	25 740
75 - 79	40 649	23 301	17 348	7 217	3 793	3 424	33 432	19 508	13 924
80 - 84	24 242	13 311	10 931	4 418	2 206	2 212	19 824	11 105	8 719
85 +	20 961	10 667	10 294	3 352	1 464	1 888	17 609	9 203	8 406
25 X 2000 (CDFC)									
Total	9 885 591	4 946 298	4 939 293	...	...	...	...	...	...
0	344 302	171 621	172 681	...	...	...	...	...	...
1 - 4	1 350 718	674 381	676 337	...	...	...	...	...	...
5 - 9	1 516 952	758 146	758 806	...	...	...	...	...	...
10 - 14	1 266 462	633 357	633 105	...	...	...	...	...	...
15 - 19	1 149 583	557 197	592 386	...	...	...	...	...	...
20 - 24	977 269	458 727	518 542	...	...	...	...	...	...
25 - 29	797 605	400 193	397 412	...	...	...	...	...	...
30 - 34	601 213	314 108	287 105	...	...	...	...	...	...
35 - 39	467 166	238 292	228 874	...	...	...	...	...	...
40 - 44	354 338	182 745	171 593	...	...	...	...	...	...
45 - 49	268 473	140 304	128 169	...	...	...	...	...	...
50 - 54	221 088	111 862	109 226	...	...	...	...	...	...
55 - 59	157 193	82 263	74 930	...	...	...	...	...	...
60 - 64	143 213	72 222	70 991	...	...	...	...	...	...
65 - 69	107 479	58 961	48 518	...	...	...	...	...	...
70 - 74	72 942	40 941	32 001	...	...	...	...	...	...
75 - 79	42 678	25 347	17 331	...	...	...	...	...	...
80 - 84	25 241	14 287	10 954	...	...	...	...	...	...
85 +	21 676	11 344	10 332	...	...	...	...	...	...
Zimbabwe									
17 VIII 2002 (CDFC)									
Total	11 631 657	5 634 180	5 997 477	4 029 707	1 988 176	2 041 531	7 601 950	3 646 004	3 955 946
0	340 331	170 054	170 277	117 756	59 103	58 653	222 575	110 951	111 624
1 - 4	1 335 738	668 008	667 730	422 397	210 186	212 211	913 341	457 822	455 519
5 - 9	1 533 700	764 453	769 247	424 731	207 986	216 745	1 108 969	556 467	552 502
10 - 14	1 512 244	754 587	757 657	381 331	180 444	200 887	1 130 913	574 143	556 770
15 - 19	1 503 576	736 686	766 890	511 394	217 513	293 881	992 182	519 173	473 009
20 - 24	1 222 907	564 034	658 873	566 584	260 105	306 479	656 323	303 929	352 394
25 - 29	987 777	473 984	513 793	474 294	242 497	231 797	513 483	231 487	281 996
30 - 34	730 127	369 836	360 291	345 675	191 527	154 148	384 452	178 309	206 143
35 - 39	504 489	235 692	268 797	222 381	116 670	105 711	282 108	119 022	163 086
40 - 44	434 429	194 702	239 727	168 100	87 760	80 340	266 329	106 942	159 387

Continent, country or area, date, code and age (in years) / Continent, pays ou zone, date, code et âge (en annèes)	Total			Urban - Urbaine			Rural - Rurale		
	Both sexes Les deux sexes	Male Masculin	Female Féminin	Both sexes Les deux sexes	Male Masculin	Female Féminin	Both sexes Les deux sexes	Male Masculin	Female Féminin
AFRICA - AFRIQUE									
Zimbabwe									
17 VIII 2002 (CDFC)									
45 - 49	356 605	165 437	191 168	128 388	70 668	57 720	228 217	94 769	133 448
50 - 54	301 258	128 029	173 229	87 458	48 199	39 259	213 800	79 830	133 970
55 - 59	210 915	98 417	112 498	55 467	31 214	24 253	155 448	67 203	88 245
60 - 64	193 867	94 447	99 420	42 546	23 384	19 162	151 321	71 063	80 258
65 - 69	132 152	64 301	67 851	26 735	14 234	12 501	105 417	50 067	55 350
70 - 74	122 775	60 311	62 464	20 371	10 602	9 769	102 404	49 709	52 695
75 +	328 522	143 900	184 622	23 687	10 598	13 089	140 574	61 352	79 222
75 - 79	64 470	29 997	34 473	...	...	...	...	...	...
80 - 84	59 045	26 764	32 281	...	...	...	...	...	...
85 - 89	19 084	7 727	11 357	...	...	...	...	...	...
90 - 94	9 188	3 752	5 436	...	...	...	...	...	...
95 +	12 474	3 710	8 764	...	...	...	...	...	...
Unknown - Inconnu	44 506	19 252	25 254	10 412	5 486	4 926	34 094	13 766	20 328
AMERICA, NORTH - AMÉRIQUE DU NORD									
Anguilla[8]									
9 V 2001 (CDFC)									
Total	11 430	5 628	5 802	...	...	...	...	...	...
0	252	131	121	...	...	...	...	...	...
1 - 4	821	394	427	...	...	...	...	...	...
5 - 9	993	502	491	...	...	...	...	...	...
10 - 14	1 136	563	573	...	...	...	...	...	...
15 - 19	966	477	489	...	...	...	...	...	...
20 - 24	788	375	413	...	...	...	...	...	...
25 - 29	873	440	433	...	...	...	...	...	...
30 - 34	999	494	505	...	...	...	...	...	...
35 - 39	1 040	507	533	...	...	...	...	...	...
40 - 44	881	429	452	...	...	...	...	...	...
45 - 49	714	364	350	...	...	...	...	...	...
50 - 54	468	236	232	...	...	...	...	...	...
55 - 59	323	166	157	...	...	...	...	...	...
60 - 64	304	144	160	...	...	...	...	...	...
65 - 69	288	159	129	...	...	...	...	...	...
70 - 74	211	82	129	...	...	...	...	...	...
75 - 79	155	65	90	...	...	...	...	...	...
80 - 84	102	52	50	...	...	...	...	...	...
85 - 89	79	31	48	...	...	...	...	...	...
90 - 94	30	15	15	...	...	...	...	...	...
95 +	7	2	5	...	...	...	...	...	...
Antigua and Barbuda - Antigua-et-Barbuda									
1 VII 2005 (ESDF)									
Total	82 786	38 878	43 908	...	...	...	...	...	...
0	1 537	765	772	...	...	...	...	...	...
1 - 4	6 269	3 230	3 039	...	...	...	...	...	...
5 - 9	7 954	3 966	3 988	...	...	...	...	...	...
10 - 14	7 635	3 699	3 937	...	...	...	...	...	...
15 - 19	6 812	3 230	3 582	...	...	...	...	...	...
20 - 24	6 527	3 119	3 408	...	...	...	...	...	...
25 - 29	6 889	3 169	3 719	...	...	...	...	...	...
30 - 34	7 518	3 344	4 174	...	...	...	...	...	...
35 - 39	7 199	3 251	3 948	...	...	...	...	...	...
40 - 44	5 977	2 697	3 280	...	...	...	...	...	...
45 - 49	4 658	2 176	2 482	...	...	...	...	...	...
50 - 54	3 518	1 659	1 859	...	...	...	...	...	...
55 - 59	2 573	1 162	1 411	...	...	...	...	...	...
60 - 64	2 028	929	1 099	...	...	...	...	...	...
65 - 69	1 700	778	922	...	...	...	...	...	...
70 - 74	1 442	633	809	...	...	...	...	...	...
75 - 79	1 100	507	593	...	...	...	...	...	...

Continent, country or area, date, code and age (in years) Continent, pays ou zone, date, code et âge (en années)	Total			Urban - Urbaine			Rural - Rurale		
	Both sexes Les deux sexes	Male Masculin	Female Féminin	Both sexes Les deux sexes	Male Masculin	Female Féminin	Both sexes Les deux sexes	Male Masculin	Female Féminin
AMERICA, NORTH - AMÉRIQUE DU NORD									
Antigua and Barbuda - Antigua-et-Barbuda									
1 VII 2005 (ESDF)									
80 - 84	783	332	451	...	...	...	...	...	...
85 - 89	437	160	278	...	...	...	...	...	...
90 - 94	197	65	132	...	...	...	...	...	...
95 + ...	32	9	23	...	...	...	...	...	...
Aruba									
1 VII 2002 (ESDJ)									
Total....................	94 149	45 019	49 130	...	...	...	...	...	...
0 - 4....................	6 779	3 419	3 361	...	...	...	...	...	...
5 - 9....................	7 299	3 719	3 580	...	...	...	...	...	...
10 - 14	7 078	3 557	3 521	...	...	...	...	...	...
15 - 19	6 366	3 161	3 206	...	...	...	...	...	...
20 - 24	5 098	2 539	2 559	...	...	...	...	...	...
25 - 29	6 027	2 873	3 155	...	...	...	...	...	...
30 - 34	8 000	3 772	4 228	...	...	...	...	...	...
35 - 39	8 871	4 221	4 650	...	...	...	...	...	...
40 - 44	9 159	4 349	4 810	...	...	...	...	...	...
45 - 49	7 685	3 575	4 109	...	...	...	...	...	...
50 - 54	6 097	2 882	3 215	...	...	...	...	...	...
55 - 59	4 635	2 174	2 461	...	...	...	...	...	...
60 - 64	3 624	1 679	1 945	...	...	...	...	...	...
65 - 69	2 913	1 251	1 663	...	...	...	...	...	...
70 - 74	2 075	921	1 154	...	...	...	...	...	...
75 - 79	1 090	461	629	...	...	...	...	...	...
80 - 84	708	288	419	...	...	...	...	...	...
85 - 89	414	125	289	...	...	...	...	...	...
90 - 94	177	49	129	...	...	...	...	...	...
95 + ...	54	6	48	...	...	...	...	...	...
Bahamas									
1 V 2000 (CDFC)									
Total....................	303 611	147 715	155 896	...	...	...	...	...	...
0	5 908	2 929	2 979	...	...	...	...	...	...
1 - 4.....................	23 212	11 737	11 475	...	...	...	...	...	...
5 - 9.....................	31 648	16 014	15 634	...	...	...	...	...	...
10 - 14	28 561	14 149	14 412	...	...	...	...	...	...
15 - 19	26 439	13 355	13 084	...	...	...	...	...	...
20 - 24	24 772	12 140	12 632	...	...	...	...	...	...
25 - 29	26 904	13 110	13 794	...	...	...	...	...	...
30 - 34	26 117	12 601	13 516	...	...	...	...	...	...
35 - 39	25 887	12 438	13 449	...	...	...	...	...	...
40 - 44	21 014	9 971	11 043	...	...	...	...	...	...
45 - 49	15 827	7 617	8 210	...	...	...	...	...	...
50 - 54	11 978	5 749	6 229	...	...	...	...	...	...
55 - 59	10 142	4 768	5 374	...	...	...	...	...	...
60 - 64	8 011	3 750	4 261	...	...	...	...	...	...
65 - 69	5 806	2 651	3 155	...	...	...	...	...	...
70 - 74	4 072	1 689	2 383	...	...	...	...	...	...
75 - 79	2 615	1 039	1 576	...	...	...	...	...	...
80 - 84	1 919	714	1 205	...	...	...	...	...	...
85 - 89	914	293	621	...	...	...	...	...	...
90 + ...	451	137	314	...	...	...	...	...	...
Unknown - Inconnu	1 414	864	550	...	...	...	...	...	...
Barbados - Barbade									
1 V 2000 (CDFC)									
Total....................	250 010	119 926	130 084	...	...	...	...	...	...
0 - 4....................	17 239	8 763	8 476	...	...	...	...	...	...
5 - 9....................	18 749	9 479	9 270	...	...	...	...	...	...
10 - 14	18 613	9 425	9 188	...	...	...	...	...	...
15 - 19	18 636	9 434	9 202	...	...	...	...	...	...
20 - 24	17 804	8 913	8 891	...	...	...	...	...	...
25 - 29	19 738	9 758	9 980	...	...	...	...	...	...
30 - 34	19 588	9 574	10 014	...	...	...	...	...	...

Continent, country or area, date, code and age (in years) Continent, pays ou zone, date, code et âge (en années)	Total			Urban - Urbaine			Rural - Rurale		
	Both sexes Les deux sexes	Male Masculin	Female Féminin	Both sexes Les deux sexes	Male Masculin	Female Féminin	Both sexes Les deux sexes	Male Masculin	Female Féminin
AMERICA, NORTH -									
AMÉRIQUE DU NORD									
Barbados - Barbade									
1 V 2000 (CDFC)									
35 - 39	21 257	10 155	11 102	...	...	...	...	...	...
40 - 44	20 055	9 544	10 511	...	...	...	...	...	...
45 - 49	16 774	8 007	8 767	...	...	...	...	...	...
50 - 54	13 638	6 563	7 075	...	...	...	...	...	...
55 - 59	9 583	4 376	5 207	...	...	...	...	...	...
60 - 64	8 925	3 969	4 956	...	...	...	...	...	...
65 - 69	8 319	3 648	4 671	...	...	...	...	...	...
70 + ...	21 092	8 318	12 774	...	...	...	...	...	...
Belize									
1 VII 2005 (ESDF)									
Total....................	291 800	147 400	144 400	...	...	...	...	...	...
0 - 4	42 080	21 330	20 750	...	...	...	...	...	...
5 - 9	40 080	20 280	19 800	...	...	...	...	...	...
10 - 14	37 410	19 145	18 265	...	...	...	...	...	...
15 - 19	32 090	16 135	15 955	...	...	...	...	...	...
20 - 24	25 990	12 705	13 285	...	...	...	...	...	...
25 - 29	22 800	11 200	11 600	...	...	...	...	...	...
30 - 34	19 710	9 730	9 980	...	...	...	...	...	...
35 - 39	17 280	8 700	8 580	...	...	...	...	...	...
40 - 44	13 705	7 100	6 605	...	...	...	...	...	...
45 - 49	10 430	5 405	5 025	...	...	...	...	...	...
50 - 54	7 570	3 970	3 600	...	...	...	...	...	...
55 - 59	5 565	2 945	2 620	...	...	...	...	...	...
60 - 64	4 840	2 670	2 170	...	...	...	...	...	...
65 - 69	4 270	2 180	2 090	...	...	...	...	...	...
70 - 74	3 320	1 670	1 650	...	...	...	...	...	...
75 - 79	2 200	1 145	1 055	...	...	...	...	...	...
80 - 84	1 315	595	720	...	...	...	...	...	...
85 + ...	1 145	495	650	...	...	...	...	...	...
Bermuda - Bermudes[9]									
20 V 2000 (CDJC)									
Total....................	62 059	29 802	32 257	...	...	...	...	...	...
0	823	404	419	...	...	...	...	...	...
1 - 4	3 166	1 574	1 592	...	...	...	...	...	...
5 - 9	4 031	2 016	2 015	...	...	...	...	...	...
10 - 14	3 827	1 907	1 920	...	...	...	...	...	...
15 - 19	3 542	1 776	1 766	...	...	...	...	...	...
20 - 24	3 222	1 557	1 665	...	...	...	...	...	...
25 - 29	4 661	2 250	2 411	...	...	...	...	...	...
30 - 34	5 461	2 707	2 754	...	...	...	...	...	...
35 - 39	6 228	3 071	3 157	...	...	...	...	...	...
40 - 44	5 618	2 706	2 912	...	...	...	...	...	...
45 - 49	4 735	2 327	2 408	...	...	...	...	...	...
50 - 54	4 146	1 994	2 152	...	...	...	...	...	...
55 - 59	3 260	1 538	1 722	...	...	...	...	...	...
60 - 64	2 617	1 229	1 388	...	...	...	...	...	...
65 - 69	2 332	1 056	1 276	...	...	...	...	...	...
70 - 74	1 845	794	1 051	...	...	...	...	...	...
75 - 79	1 275	473	802	...	...	...	...	...	...
80 - 84	713	249	464	...	...	...	...	...	...
85 - 89	401	125	276	...	...	...	...	...	...
90 - 94	122	43	79	...	...	...	...	...	...
95 - 99	33	6	27	...	...	...	...	...	...
100 + ...	1	-	1	...	...	...	...	...	...
British Virgin Islands - Îles									
Vierges britanniques									
21 V 2001 (CDFC)									
Total....................	20 647	10 627	10 020	...	...	...	...	...	...
0 - 4	1 787	913	874	...	...	...	...	...	...
5 - 9	1 865	946	919	...	...	...	...	...	...
10 - 14	1 768	880	888	...	...	...	...	...	...
15 - 19	1 529	778	751	...	...	...	...	...	...

171

7. Population by age, sex and urban/rural residence: latest available year, 1996 - 2005
Population selon l'âge, le sexe et la résidence, urbaine/rurale: dernière année disponible, 1996 - 2005 (continued - suite)

Continent, country or area, date, code and age (in years) / Continent, pays ou zone, date, code et âge (en années)	Total			Urban - Urbaine			Rural - Rurale		
	Both sexes Les deux sexes	Male Masculin	Female Féminin	Both sexes Les deux sexes	Male Masculin	Female Féminin	Both sexes Les deux sexes	Male Masculin	Female Féminin
AMERICA, NORTH - AMÉRIQUE DU NORD									
British Virgin Islands - Îles Vierges britanniques									
21 V 2001 (CDFC)									
20 - 24	1 465	752	713	...	...	...	...	...	...
25 - 29	1 483	756	727	...	...	...	...	...	...
30 - 34	1 826	913	913	...	...	...	...	...	...
35 - 39	2 085	1 091	994	...	...	...	...	...	...
40 - 44	1 910	991	919	...	...	...	...	...	...
45 - 49	1 501	777	724	...	...	...	...	...	...
50 - 54	1 128	614	514	...	...	...	...	...	...
55 - 59	774	421	353	...	...	...	...	...	...
60 - 64	523	267	256	...	...	...	...	...	...
65 - 69	337	177	160	...	...	...	...	...	...
70 - 74	282	145	137	...	...	...	...	...	...
75 - 79	204	113	91	...	...	...	...	...	...
80 +	180	93	87	...	...	...	...	...	...
Canada									
1 VII 2003 (ESDJ)[10]									
Total	31 629 677	15 661 734	15 967 943	25 212 723	12 355 256	12 854 903	6 416 976	3 306 472	3 113 035
0	330 644	169 512	161 132	266 115	136 475	129 645	64 529	33 037	31 492
1 - 4	1 383 658	707 774	675 884	1 102 100	563 751	538 349	281 558	144 028	137 545
5 - 9	1 949 702	998 569	951 133	1 524 480	780 199	744 285	425 232	218 384	206 833
10 - 14	2 117 613	1 084 753	1 032 860	1 619 935	828 418	791 540	497 678	256 350	241 340
15 - 19	2 120 545	1 088 772	1 031 773	1 645 028	840 027	804 942	475 517	248 740	226 832
20 - 24	2 188 501	1 119 035	1 069 466	1 836 847	928 955	907 537	351 654	190 079	161 946
25 - 29	2 118 132	1 073 969	1 044 163	1 793 207	906 422	886 635	324 930	167 559	157 518
30 - 34	2 228 713	1 124 790	1 103 923	1 841 469	928 696	912 757	387 243	196 101	191 172
35 - 39	2 481 199	1 247 414	1 233 785	1 993 776	999 796	993 876	487 428	247 599	239 908
40 - 44	2 719 324	1 364 310	1 355 014	2 154 925	1 072 864	1 081 808	564 388	291 456	273 212
45 - 49	2 515 743	1 251 593	1 264 150	1 975 279	971 446	1 003 640	540 474	280 153	260 504
50 - 54	2 176 497	1 078 752	1 097 745	1 696 925	831 506	865 385	479 588	247 236	232 350
55 - 59	1 842 459	913 922	928 537	1 410 796	689 298	721 465	431 656	224 617	207 067
60 - 64	1 396 800	684 822	711 978	1 069 033	512 657	556 262	327 784	172 155	155 722
65 - 69	1 147 902	552 166	595 736	892 139	417 080	474 989	255 758	135 080	120 737
70 - 74	1 039 113	484 186	554 927	829 340	373 391	455 502	209 773	110 784	99 420
75 - 79	839 427	358 752	480 675	689 192	283 797	404 920	150 230	74 955	75 759
80 - 84	583 656	221 629	362 027	486 967	178 027	308 751	96 688	43 596	53 281
85 - 89	296 953	97 229	199 724	252 975	79 576	173 340	43 973	17 659	26 378
90 +	153 096	39 785	113 311	132 195	32 875	99 275	20 895	6 904	14 019
1 VII 2005 (ESDJ)									
Total	32 270 507	15 979 460	16 291 047	...	...	...	...	...	...
0	337 099	172 546	164 553	...	...	...	...	...	...
1 - 4	1 361 289	695 887	665 402	...	...	...	...	...	...
5 - 9	1 882 270	963 015	919 255	...	...	...	...	...	...
10 - 14	2 104 798	1 079 124	1 025 674	...	...	...	...	...	...
15 - 19	2 145 807	1 099 655	1 046 152	...	...	...	...	...	...
20 - 24	2 243 341	1 147 505	1 095 836	...	...	...	...	...	...
25 - 29	2 194 272	1 110 468	1 083 804	...	...	...	...	...	...
30 - 34	2 224 845	1 122 426	1 102 419	...	...	...	...	...	...
35 - 39	2 365 752	1 189 818	1 175 934	...	...	...	...	...	...
40 - 44	2 745 901	1 380 123	1 365 778	...	...	...	...	...	...
45 - 49	2 619 498	1 307 008	1 312 490	...	...	...	...	...	...
50 - 54	2 301 756	1 139 132	1 162 624	...	...	...	...	...	...
55 - 59	2 011 464	994 858	1 016 606	...	...	...	...	...	...
60 - 64	1 514 637	743 775	770 862	...	...	...	...	...	...
65 - 69	1 193 521	574 412	619 109	...	...	...	...	...	...
70 - 74	1 042 644	488 605	554 039	...	...	...	...	...	...
75 - 79	864 272	377 744	486 528	...	...	...	...	...	...
80 - 84	625 282	241 692	383 590	...	...	...	...	...	...
85 - 89	322 532	107 095	215 437	...	...	...	...	...	...
90 +	169 527	44 572	124 955	...	...	...	...	...	...

Continent, country or area, date, code and age (in years) / Continent, pays ou zone, date, code et âge (en années)	Total			Urban - Urbaine			Rural - Rurale		
	Both sexes Les deux sexes	Male Masculin	Female Féminin	Both sexes Les deux sexes	Male Masculin	Female Féminin	Both sexes Les deux sexes	Male Masculin	Female Féminin
AMERICA, NORTH - AMÉRIQUE DU NORD									
Cayman Islands - Îles Caïmanes									
10 X 1999 (CDFC)									
Total	39 020	19 033	19 987	...	...	...	...	...	...
0 - 14	7 598	3 830	3 768	...	...	...	...	...	...
15 - 29	8 706	4 218	4 488	...	...	...	...	...	...
30 - 49	15 966	7 703	8 263	...	...	...	...	...	...
50 - 64	4 486	2 268	2 218	...	...	...	...	...	...
65 +	2 195	980	1 215	...	...	...	...	...	...
Unknown - Inconnu	69	34	35	...	...	...	...	...	...
Costa Rica									
1 VII 2003 (ESDJ)									
Total	4 088 773	2 017 467	2 071 306	2 412 542	1 167 617	1 244 925	1 676 231	849 850	826 381
0	60 248	30 527	29 721	32 962	14 647	18 315	27 286	15 880	11 406
1 - 4	279 051	141 252	137 799	148 097	74 961	73 136	130 954	66 291	64 663
5 - 9	402 505	204 375	198 130	217 185	112 057	105 128	185 320	92 318	93 002
10 - 14	442 485	227 753	214 732	239 102	125 816	113 286	203 383	101 937	101 446
15 - 19	440 022	224 939	215 083	252 653	128 173	124 480	187 369	96 766	90 603
20 - 24	389 692	196 190	193 502	244 780	123 374	121 406	144 912	72 816	72 096
25 - 29	299 949	148 956	150 993	181 903	91 509	90 394	118 046	57 447	60 599
30 - 34	290 238	141 083	149 155	168 005	79 878	88 127	122 233	61 205	61 028
35 - 39	310 103	144 944	165 159	180 989	81 049	99 940	129 114	63 895	65 219
40 - 44	286 982	133 450	153 532	174 446	78 374	96 072	112 536	55 076	57 460
45 - 49	223 424	105 944	117 480	144 000	63 925	80 075	79 424	42 019	37 405
50 - 54	188 484	94 698	93 786	122 409	60 119	62 290	66 075	34 579	31 496
55 - 59	115 893	53 403	62 490	72 372	31 030	41 342	43 521	22 373	21 148
60 - 64	106 094	51 800	54 294	66 729	30 719	36 010	39 365	21 081	18 284
65 - 69	80 418	38 330	42 088	49 558	21 979	27 579	30 860	16 351	14 509
70 - 74	66 915	30 475	36 440	45 599	19 369	26 230	21 316	11 106	10 210
75 - 79	49 986	24 345	25 641	33 147	15 502	17 645	16 839	8 843	7 996
80 - 84	28 734	13 082	15 652	19 773	8 212	11 561	8 961	4 870	4 091
85 - 89	14 983	6 075	8 908	9 781	3 049	6 732	5 202	3 026	2 176
90 - 94	7 113	3 237	3 876	5 403	2 092	3 311	1 710	1 145	565
95 +	2 218	857	1 361	1 632	727	905	586	130	456
Unknown - Inconnu	3 236	1 752	1 484	2 017	1 056	961	1 219	696	523
1 VII 2004 (ESDJ)									
Total	4 248 481	2 160 688	2 087 793	...	...	...	...	...	...
0 - 4	389 790	199 755	190 035	...	...	...	...	...	...
5 - 9	409 512	210 641	198 871	...	...	...	...	...	...
10 - 14	430 901	222 118	208 783	...	...	...	...	...	...
15 - 19	439 222	225 554	213 668	...	...	...	...	...	...
20 - 24	400 014	204 931	195 083	...	...	...	...	...	...
25 - 29	348 962	178 412	170 550	...	...	...	...	...	...
30 - 34	309 848	157 640	152 208	...	...	...	...	...	...
35 - 39	317 374	162 360	155 014	...	...	...	...	...	...
40 - 44	296 069	151 463	144 606	...	...	...	...	...	...
45 - 49	243 375	124 335	119 040	...	...	...	...	...	...
50 - 54	185 252	93 233	92 019	...	...	...	...	...	...
55 - 59	136 390	67 900	68 490	...	...	...	...	...	...
60 - 64	101 796	50 008	51 788	...	...	...	...	...	...
65 - 69	81 561	39 494	42 067	...	...	...	...	...	...
70 - 74	62 383	29 572	32 811	...	...	...	...	...	...
75 - 79	46 204	21 435	24 769	...	...	...	...	...	...
80 - 84	27 054	12 009	15 045	...	...	...	...	...	...
85 - 89	14 510	6 382	8 128	...	...	...	...	...	...
90 - 94	6 301	2 573	3 728	...	...	...	...	...	...
95 +	1 963	873	1 090	...	...	...	...	...	...
Cuba									
1 VII 2005 (ESDF)									
Total	11 242 519	5 629 843	5 612 676	8 497 885	4 180 296	4 317 589	2 744 634	1 449 547	1 295 087
0	123 124	63 480	59 644	89 851	46 387	43 464	33 273	17 093	16 180
1 - 4	545 877	280 865	265 012	397 114	204 336	192 778	148 763	76 529	72 234
5 - 9	716 872	369 866	347 006	522 883	269 650	253 233	193 989	100 216	93 773
10 - 14	779 179	399 061	380 118	570 509	291 300	279 209	208 670	107 761	100 909

7. Population by age, sex and urban/rural residence: latest available year, 1996 - 2005
Population selon l'âge, le sexe et la résidence, urbaine/rurale: dernière année disponible, 1996 - 2005 (continued - suite)

Continent, country or area, date, code and age (in years) / Continent, pays ou zone, date, code et âge (en années)	Total			Urban - Urbaine			Rural - Rurale		
	Both sexes Les deux sexes	Male Masculin	Female Féminin	Both sexes Les deux sexes	Male Masculin	Female Féminin	Both sexes Les deux sexes	Male Masculin	Female Féminin
AMERICA, NORTH - AMÉRIQUE DU NORD									
Cuba									
1 VII 2005 (ESDF)									
15 - 19	845 164	434 545	410 619	628 083	320 732	307 351	217 081	113 813	103 268
20 - 24	723 790	373 349	350 441	539 677	276 054	263 623	184 113	97 295	86 818
25 - 29	736 869	379 311	357 558	543 157	278 795	264 362	193 712	100 516	93 196
30 - 34	1 021 831	519 345	502 486	758 656	382 845	375 811	263 175	136 500	126 675
35 - 39	1 070 100	534 916	535 184	807 156	397 599	409 557	262 944	137 317	125 627
40 - 44	1 009 744	501 561	508 183	787 902	385 025	402 877	221 842	116 536	105 306
45 - 49	683 183	335 124	348 059	527 280	252 716	274 564	155 903	82 408	73 495
50 - 54	646 046	316 691	329 355	504 582	240 999	263 583	141 464	75 692	65 772
55 - 59	588 354	285 807	302 547	460 828	218 235	242 593	127 526	67 572	59 954
60 - 64	508 216	248 918	259 298	396 038	187 625	208 413	112 178	61 293	50 885
65 - 69	708 511	344 050	364 461	548 118	253 519	294 599	160 393	90 531	69 862
70 - 74	389 201	180 368	208 833	302 673	130 455	172 218	86 528	49 913	36 615
75 +	146 458	62 586	83 872	113 378	44 024	69 354	33 080	18 562	14 518
Dominica - Dominique									
12 V 2001 (CDFC)									
Total	68 635	34 549	34 086	...	...	...	...	...	...
0 - 4	6 087	3 059	3 028	...	...	...	...	...	...
5 - 9	7 277	3 770	3 507	...	...	...	...	...	...
10 - 14	6 847	3 395	3 452	...	...	...	...	...	...
15 - 19	6 570	3 293	3 277	...	...	...	...	...	...
20 - 24	4 409	2 326	2 083	...	...	...	...	...	...
25 - 29	4 934	2 481	2 453	...	...	...	...	...	...
30 - 34	5 456	2 753	2 703	...	...	...	...	...	...
35 - 39	5 100	2 710	2 390	...	...	...	...	...	...
40 - 44	4 310	2 306	2 004	...	...	...	...	...	...
45 - 49	3 428	1 857	1 571	...	...	...	...	...	...
50 - 54	2 717	1 400	1 317	...	...	...	...	...	...
55 - 59	2 303	1 153	1 150	...	...	...	...	...	...
60 - 64	2 175	975	1 200	...	...	...	...	...	...
65 - 69	2 241	1 041	1 200	...	...	...	...	...	...
70 - 74	1 778	831	947	...	...	...	...	...	...
75 - 79	1 285	568	717	...	...	...	...	...	...
80 - 84	895	347	548	...	...	...	...	...	...
85 +	823	284	539	...	...	...	...	...	...
Dominican Republic - République dominicaine									
20 X 2002 (CDJC)									
Total	8 562 541	4 265 215	4 297 326	5 446 704	2 648 064	2 798 640	3 115 837	1 617 151	1 498 686
0	206 819	105 023	101 796	129 423	65 765	63 658	77 396	39 258	38 138
1 - 4	766 825	389 861	376 964	474 695	240 650	234 045	292 130	149 211	142 919
5 - 9	971 881	492 845	479 036	590 809	297 879	292 930	381 072	194 966	186 106
10 - 14	959 338	485 882	473 456	592 802	295 497	297 305	366 536	190 385	176 151
15 - 19	838 239	418 089	420 150	534 887	260 051	274 836	303 352	158 038	145 314
20 - 24	785 802	387 397	398 405	518 495	248 857	269 638	267 307	138 540	128 767
25 - 29	687 785	331 527	356 258	456 484	215 653	240 831	231 301	115 874	115 427
30 - 34	646 112	318 320	327 792	426 196	205 314	220 882	219 916	113 006	106 910
35 - 39	590 750	287 717	303 033	389 835	185 218	204 617	200 915	102 499	98 416
40 - 44	476 647	240 175	236 472	309 735	151 229	158 506	166 912	88 946	77 966
45 - 49	380 028	188 288	191 740	247 776	118 243	129 533	132 252	70 045	62 207
50 - 54	330 713	166 302	164 411	210 832	102 066	108 766	119 881	64 236	55 645
55 - 59	233 976	115 834	118 142	146 945	69 876	77 069	87 031	45 958	41 073
60 - 64	207 933	104 624	103 309	126 435	60 113	66 322	81 498	44 511	36 987
65 - 69	158 365	77 400	80 965	97 293	44 811	52 482	61 072	32 589	28 483
70 - 74	136 068	68 480	67 588	81 410	38 123	43 287	54 658	30 357	24 301
75 - 79	77 871	37 809	40 062	47 933	21 371	26 562	29 938	16 438	13 500
80 - 84	54 402	26 076	28 326	32 545	14 287	18 258	21 857	11 789	10 068
85 - 89	27 303	12 772	14 531	16 966	7 230	9 736	10 337	5 542	4 795
90 - 94	15 157	6 454	8 703	9 244	3 545	5 699	5 913	2 909	3 004
95 +	10 274	4 192	6 082	5 820	2 209	3 611	4 454	1 983	2 471
Unknown - Inconnu	253	148	105	144	77	67	109	71	38

Continent, country or area, date, code and age (in years) / Continent, pays ou zone, date, code et âge (en annèes)	Total			Urban - Urbaine			Rural - Rurale		
	Both sexes Les deux sexes	Male Masculin	Female Féminin	Both sexes Les deux sexes	Male Masculin	Female Féminin	Both sexes Les deux sexes	Male Masculin	Female Féminin
AMERICA, NORTH - AMÉRIQUE DU NORD									
El Salvador									
1 VII 2003 (ESDF)									
Total	6 638 168	3 261 938	3 376 230	3 932 569	1 891 429	2 041 140	2 705 599	1 370 509	1 335 090
0	162 479	83 082	79 397	87 126	44 566	42 560	75 353	38 516	36 837
1 - 4	644 889	329 352	315 537	342 656	174 855	167 801	302 233	154 497	147 736
5 - 9	777 836	396 371	381 465	438 845	222 691	216 154	338 991	173 680	165 311
10 - 14	720 117	365 942	354 175	404 131	203 433	200 698	315 986	162 509	153 477
15 - 19	661 005	334 785	326 220	358 075	177 949	180 126	302 930	156 836	146 094
20 - 24	660 518	333 143	327 375	374 723	183 684	191 039	285 795	149 459	136 336
25 - 29	638 627	318 847	319 780	380 057	183 630	196 427	258 570	135 217	123 353
30 - 34	509 962	246 818	263 144	324 396	152 402	171 994	185 566	94 416	91 150
35 - 39	387 053	178 680	208 373	259 673	117 642	142 031	127 380	61 038	66 342
40 - 44	309 588	140 553	169 035	210 767	94 677	116 090	98 821	45 876	52 945
45 - 49	268 869	124 218	144 651	176 322	80 071	96 251	92 547	44 147	48 400
50 - 54	225 211	105 929	119 282	143 766	66 453	77 313	81 445	39 476	41 969
55 - 59	186 454	88 100	98 354	116 650	53 968	62 682	69 804	34 132	35 672
60 - 64	146 201	68 603	77 598	90 734	41 238	49 496	55 467	27 365	28 102
65 - 69	122 667	56 429	66 238	76 373	33 785	42 588	46 294	22 644	23 650
70 - 74	97 128	43 336	53 792	61 565	26 420	35 145	35 563	16 916	18 647
75 - 79	64 745	27 429	37 316	42 647	17 583	25 064	22 098	9 846	12 252
80 +	54 819	20 321	34 498	44 063	16 382	27 681	10 756	3 939	6 817
Greenland - Groenland									
1 I 2005 (ESDJ)									
Total	56 969	30 319	26 650	47 086	24 884	22 202	9 883	5 435	4 448
0	797	405	392	639	324	315	158	81	77
1 - 4	3 540	1 793	1 747	2 866	1 449	1 417	674	344	330
5 - 9	4 763	2 419	2 344	3 833	1 969	1 864	930	450	480
10 - 14	5 220	2 638	2 582	4 187	2 128	2 059	1 033	510	523
15 - 19	4 483	2 256	2 227	3 739	1 872	1 867	744	384	360
20 - 24	3 943	2 054	1 889	3 292	1 680	1 612	651	374	277
25 - 29	3 428	1 790	1 638	2 832	1 436	1 396	596	354	242
30 - 34	3 635	2 001	1 634	3 015	1 660	1 355	620	341	279
35 - 39	5 627	3 025	2 602	4 699	2 501	2 198	928	524	404
40 - 44	5 627	3 030	2 597	4 736	2 518	2 218	891	512	379
45 - 49	4 442	2 537	1 905	3 721	2 102	1 619	721	435	286
50 - 54	3 431	1 955	1 476	2 863	1 610	1 253	568	345	223
55 - 59	2 637	1 627	1 010	2 228	1 362	866	409	265	144
60 - 64	2 253	1 291	962	1 862	1 064	798	391	227	164
65 - 69	1 317	699	618	1 056	557	499	261	142	119
70 - 74	970	467	503	806	388	418	164	79	85
75 - 79	575	238	337	483	192	291	92	46	46
80 - 84	188	70	118	152	52	100	36	18	18
85 - 89	68	16	52	54	13	41	14	3	11
90 - 94	23	8	15	22	7	15	1	1	-
95 +	2	-	2	1	-	1	1	-	1
Unknown - Inconnu	-	-	-	-	-	-	-	-	-
Grenada - Grenade									
1 VII 2000 (ESDF)									
Total	101 308	50 200	51 108	...	...	...	...	...	...
0 - 4	10 412	5 292	5 120	...	...	...	...	...	...
5 - 9	11 547	5 798	5 749	...	...	...	...	...	...
10 - 14	13 546	6 837	6 709	...	...	...	...	...	...
15 - 19	11 911	6 077	5 834	...	...	...	...	...	...
20 - 24	9 267	4 686	4 581	...	...	...	...	...	...
25 - 29	7 290	3 883	3 407	...	...	...	...	...	...
30 - 34	5 977	2 999	2 978	...	...	...	...	...	...
35 - 39	6 537	3 294	3 243	...	...	...	...	...	...
40 - 44	5 364	2 628	2 736	...	...	...	...	...	...
45 - 49	3 780	1 955	1 825	...	...	...	...	...	...
50 - 54	2 904	1 371	1 533	...	...	...	...	...	...
55 - 59	2 472	1 160	1 312	...	...	...	...	...	...
60 - 64	2 383	1 078	1 305	...	...	...	...	...	...
65 - 69	2 356	1 010	1 346	...	...	...	...	...	...
70 +	5 562	2 132	3 430	...	...	...	...	...	...

Continent, country or area, date, code and age (in years) / Continent, pays ou zone, date, code et âge (en annèes)	Total			Urban - Urbaine			Rural - Rurale		
	Both sexes Les deux sexes	Male Masculin	Female Féminin	Both sexes Les deux sexes	Male Masculin	Female Féminin	Both sexes Les deux sexes	Male Masculin	Female Féminin
AMERICA, NORTH - AMÉRIQUE DU NORD									
Guadeloupe									
1 I 2004 (ESDJ)									
Total	442 953	211 832	231 121	...	...	...	...	...	...
0	6 918	3 479	3 439	...	...	...	...	...	...
1 - 4	28 700	14 770	13 930	...	...	...	...	...	...
5 - 9	33 521	17 124	16 397	...	...	...	...	...	...
10 - 14	37 037	18 794	18 243	...	...	...	...	...	...
15 - 19	34 828	17 666	17 162	...	...	...	...	...	...
20 - 24	30 258	15 313	14 945	...	...	...	...	...	...
25 - 29	24 245	11 873	12 372	...	...	...	...	...	...
30 - 34	32 983	14 998	17 985	...	...	...	...	...	...
35 - 39	36 262	16 333	19 929	...	...	...	...	...	...
40 - 44	35 808	16 938	18 870	...	...	...	...	...	...
45 - 49	29 796	13 907	15 889	...	...	...	...	...	...
50 - 54	25 806	11 849	13 957	...	...	...	...	...	...
55 - 59	21 525	10 241	11 284	...	...	...	...	...	...
60 - 64	16 754	7 757	8 997	...	...	...	...	...	...
65 - 69	14 621	6 800	7 821	...	...	...	...	...	...
70 - 74	11 500	5 074	6 426	...	...	...	...	...	...
75 - 79	9 590	4 034	5 556	...	...	...	...	...	...
80 - 84	6 741	2 748	3 993	...	...	...	...	...	...
85 - 89	3 626	1 400	2 226	...	...	...	...	...	...
90 +	2 434	734	1 700	...	...	...	...	...	...
Guatemala									
1 VII 2005 (ESDF)									
Total	12 699 780	6 197 399	6 502 381	6 345 918	3 059 570	3 286 348	6 353 862	3 137 829	3 216 033
0 - 4	2 036 312	1 035 549	1 000 763	866 844	447 724	419 120	1 169 468	587 825	581 643
5 - 9	1 823 642	921 924	901 718	790 225	405 750	384 475	1 033 417	516 174	517 243
10 - 14	1 624 119	815 791	808 328	755 292	378 704	376 587	868 827	437 087	431 741
15 - 19	1 379 574	685 359	694 215	715 501	351 554	363 947	664 073	333 805	330 268
20 - 24	1 180 264	571 385	608 879	636 046	306 874	329 172	544 218	264 511	279 707
25 - 29	952 695	446 309	506 386	523 699	243 461	280 237	428 996	202 848	226 149
30 - 34	753 145	340 378	412 767	416 357	184 973	231 384	336 788	155 405	181 383
35 - 39	600 160	270 907	329 253	326 576	144 824	181 752	273 584	126 083	147 501
40 - 44	492 747	225 243	267 504	270 162	120 913	149 248	222 585	104 330	118 256
45 - 49	409 688	191 635	218 053	221 123	100 439	120 685	188 565	91 196	97 368
50 - 54	367 062	175 311	191 751	201 790	92 775	109 014	165 272	82 536	82 737
55 - 59	310 913	149 593	161 320	171 480	79 044	92 436	139 433	70 549	68 884
60 - 64	233 643	113 686	119 957	128 803	58 925	69 878	104 840	54 761	50 079
65 - 69	192 992	94 128	98 864	111 865	51 579	60 285	81 127	42 549	38 579
70 - 74	156 267	74 463	81 804	93 750	42 080	51 669	62 517	32 383	30 135
75 - 79	107 429	50 340	57 089	66 759	29 241	37 519	40 670	21 099	19 570
80 +	79 128	35 398	43 730	49 648	20 709	28 939	29 480	14 689	14 791
Haiti - Haïti									
1 VII 1999 (ESDJ)									
Total	7 803 232	3 834 240	3 968 992	2 731 843	1 234 809	1 497 034	5 071 389	2 599 431	2 471 958
0	242 106	122 835	119 271	68 885	36 499	32 386	173 221	86 336	86 885
1 - 4	913 669	462 018	451 651	252 773	130 783	121 990	660 896	331 235	329 661
5 - 9	1 034 513	521 302	513 211	321 389	154 420	166 969	713 124	366 882	346 242
10 - 14	925 920	466 007	459 913	363 812	161 340	202 472	562 108	304 667	257 441
15 - 19	810 881	407 544	403 337	375 052	156 361	218 691	435 829	251 183	184 646
20 - 24	696 906	347 026	349 880	337 696	153 000	184 696	359 210	194 026	165 184
25 - 29	612 995	301 403	311 592	272 739	124 048	148 691	340 256	177 355	162 901
30 - 34	526 616	255 640	270 976	198 846	88 085	110 761	327 770	167 555	160 215
35 - 39	452 327	216 102	236 225	135 215	57 299	77 916	317 112	158 803	158 309
40 - 44	370 430	173 392	197 038	106 911	42 010	64 901	263 519	131 382	132 137
45 - 49	306 075	141 518	164 557	71 946	29 912	42 034	234 129	111 606	122 523
50 - 54	247 324	114 254	133 070	70 080	31 126	38 954	177 244	83 128	94 116
55 - 59	201 858	93 663	108 195	51 060	22 494	28 566	150 798	71 169	79 629
60 - 64	161 143	74 625	86 518	40 580	18 949	21 631	120 563	55 676	64 887
65 - 69	122 392	56 450	65 942	28 310	12 719	15 591	94 082	43 731	50 351
70 - 74	84 796	38 744	46 052	18 717	7 726	10 991	66 079	31 018	35 061
75 - 79	52 884	23 831	29 053	11 309	5 008	6 301	41 575	18 823	22 752
80 +	40 397	17 886	22 511	6 523	3 030	3 493	33 874	14 856	19 018

Continent, country or area, date, code and age (in years) / Continent, pays ou zone, date, code et âge (en années)	Total			Urban - Urbaine			Rural - Rurale		
	Both sexes Les deux sexes	Male Masculin	Female Féminin	Both sexes Les deux sexes	Male Masculin	Female Féminin	Both sexes Les deux sexes	Male Masculin	Female Féminin
AMERICA, NORTH - AMÉRIQUE DU NORD									
Honduras									
1 VII 2003 (ESDF)									
Total	6 860 842	3 388 874	3 471 968	3 260 934	1 555 369	1 705 565	3 599 908	1 833 505	1 766 403
0	211 122	107 546	103 576	92 446	47 136	45 310	118 676	60 410	58 266
1 - 4	820 813	416 615	404 198	340 186	174 013	166 173	480 627	242 602	238 025
5 - 9	949 750	480 017	469 733	389 928	198 612	191 316	559 822	281 405	278 417
10 - 14	837 102	421 803	415 299	362 885	180 041	182 844	474 217	241 762	232 455
15 - 19	743 031	372 741	370 290	362 858	170 460	192 398	380 173	202 281	177 892
20 - 24	663 253	330 233	333 020	352 858	165 359	187 499	310 395	164 874	145 521
25 - 29	559 428	276 591	282 837	299 286	142 499	156 787	260 142	134 092	126 050
30 - 34	453 592	221 413	232 179	242 678	113 600	129 078	210 914	107 813	103 101
35 - 39	358 774	170 994	187 780	190 971	87 412	103 559	167 803	83 582	84 221
40 - 44	292 742	137 740	155 002	153 583	69 630	83 953	139 159	68 110	71 049
45 - 49	244 002	114 465	129 537	124 151	56 039	68 112	119 851	58 426	61 425
50 - 54	196 270	91 939	104 331	97 646	43 561	54 085	98 624	48 378	50 246
55 - 59	152 017	71 521	80 496	72 441	32 030	40 411	79 576	39 491	40 085
60 - 64	119 860	56 175	63 685	55 043	23 792	31 251	64 817	32 383	32 434
65 - 69	95 844	44 359	51 485	44 728	18 795	25 933	51 116	25 564	25 552
70 - 74	70 413	32 212	38 201	33 351	13 867	19 484	37 062	18 345	18 717
75 - 79	49 736	22 968	26 768	24 076	9 963	14 113	25 660	13 005	12 655
80 +	43 093	19 542	23 551	21 819	8 560	13 259	21 274	10 982	10 292
Jamaica - Jamaïque									
1 VII 2004 (ESDJ)									
Total	2 641 946	1 301 385	1 340 561	1 373 154	655 404	717 750	1 268 792	645 981	622 811
0	53 642	27 332	26 309	27 059	13 808	13 251	26 583	13 524	13 059
1 - 4	222 773	113 511	109 262	112 898	57 611	55 287	109 874	55 899	53 975
5 - 9	298 754	151 734	147 020	146 831	74 087	72 744	151 923	77 647	74 276
10 - 14	279 512	141 307	138 206	137 418	69 066	68 351	142 095	72 240	69 854
15 - 19	255 298	128 220	127 078	130 719	64 190	66 528	124 579	64 030	60 550
20 - 24	218 728	106 447	112 280	121 467	57 243	64 224	97 260	49 204	48 056
25 - 29	209 655	100 490	109 165	118 314	54 477	63 837	91 341	46 013	45 328
30 - 34	200 131	95 433	104 699	112 210	51 344	60 865	87 922	44 088	43 833
35 - 39	187 355	88 841	98 514	104 151	47 097	57 054	83 204	41 743	41 461
40 - 44	157 489	77 360	80 129	85 702	39 809	45 893	71 787	37 551	34 236
45 - 49	115 167	56 634	58 533	62 917	29 290	33 627	52 251	27 344	24 906
50 - 54	98 555	50 363	48 193	52 335	25 312	27 023	46 220	25 051	21 169
55 - 59	76 634	39 183	37 451	38 656	18 731	19 925	37 978	20 452	17 526
60 - 64	66 150	32 266	33 883	32 010	14 806	17 204	34 140	17 461	16 679
65 - 69	60 663	29 306	31 357	28 243	12 905	15 338	32 420	16 401	16 019
70 - 74	52 785	25 200	27 584	24 012	10 827	13 185	28 772	14 373	14 399
75 - 79	39 085	17 953	21 133	17 190	7 249	9 941	21 896	10 704	11 192
80 - 84	24 874	10 446	14 427	10 570	4 096	6 474	14 303	6 350	7 953
85 +	24 696	9 359	15 338	10 453	3 454	6 998	14 244	5 904	8 339
Martinique									
1 I 2004 (ESDJ)									
Total	392 756	184 877	207 879	...	...	...	...	...	...
0	5 348	2 734	2 614	...	...	...	...	...	...
1 - 4	22 112	11 180	10 932	...	...	...	...	...	...
5 - 9	26 268	13 248	13 020	...	...	...	...	...	...
10 - 14	31 293	15 676	15 617	...	...	...	...	...	...
15 - 19	31 576	15 917	15 659	...	...	...	...	...	...
20 - 24	25 844	13 091	12 753	...	...	...	...	...	...
25 - 29	20 030	9 556	10 474	...	...	...	...	...	...
30 - 34	27 167	12 185	14 982	...	...	...	...	...	...
35 - 39	32 249	14 386	17 863	...	...	...	...	...	...
40 - 44	33 178	15 439	17 739	...	...	...	...	...	...
45 - 49	27 437	12 762	14 675	...	...	...	...	...	...
50 - 54	23 531	10 741	12 790	...	...	...	...	...	...
55 - 59	19 693	9 073	10 620	...	...	...	...	...	...
60 - 64	15 768	7 303	8 465	...	...	...	...	...	...
65 - 69	15 599	7 142	8 457	...	...	...	...	...	...
70 - 74	12 522	5 484	7 038	...	...	...	...	...	...
75 - 79	10 256	4 304	5 952	...	...	...	...	...	...
80 - 84	6 821	2 615	4 206	...	...	...	...	...	...

Continent, country or area, date, code and age (in years) / Continent, pays ou zone, date, code et âge (en années)	Total			Urban - Urbaine			Rural - Rurale		
	Both sexes Les deux sexes	Male Masculin	Female Féminin	Both sexes Les deux sexes	Male Masculin	Female Féminin	Both sexes Les deux sexes	Male Masculin	Female Féminin
AMERICA, NORTH - AMÉRIQUE DU NORD									
Martinique									
1 I 2004 (ESDJ)									
85 - 89	3 674	1 301	2 373	...	...	...	...	...	...
90 + ...	2 390	740	1 650	...	...	...	...	...	...
Mexico - Mexique[11]									
1 VII 2003 (ESDJ)									
Total...................	104 213 503	51 844 576	52 368 927	81 801 856	40 688 600	41 113 256	22 411 647	11 155 976	11 255 671
0....................	1 988 104	1 016 141	971 963	1 508 871	771 725	737 146	479 233	244 416	234 817
1 - 4..................	8 224 746	4 200 612	4 024 134	6 165 162	3 150 898	3 014 264	2 059 584	1 049 714	1 009 870
5 - 9..................	11 221 550	5 726 862	5 494 688	8 307 592	4 242 705	4 064 887	2 913 958	1 484 157	1 429 801
10 - 14	11 292 993	5 753 255	5 539 738	8 405 074	4 284 703	4 120 371	2 887 919	1 468 552	1 419 367
15 - 19	10 720 008	5 425 993	5 294 015	8 312 392	4 209 127	4 103 265	2 407 616	1 216 866	1 190 750
20 - 24	10 046 197	5 045 196	5 001 001	8 123 608	4 080 731	4 042 877	1 922 589	964 465	958 124
25 - 29	9 283 984	4 628 632	4 655 352	7 645 051	3 812 091	3 832 960	1 638 933	816 541	822 392
30 - 34	8 342 545	4 131 720	4 210 825	6 897 062	3 416 033	3 481 029	1 445 483	715 687	729 796
35 - 39	7 290 764	3 589 381	3 701 383	6 009 930	2 958 760	3 051 170	1 280 834	630 621	650 213
40 - 44	6 210 837	3 040 035	3 170 802	5 091 720	2 492 046	2 599 674	1 119 117	547 989	571 128
45 - 49	5 039 061	2 452 084	2 586 977	4 071 772	1 981 067	2 090 705	967 289	471 017	496 272
50 - 54	3 904 782	1 887 706	2 017 076	3 103 340	1 499 863	1 603 477	801 442	387 843	413 599
55 - 59	3 020 567	1 447 895	1 572 672	2 354 970	1 128 356	1 226 614	665 597	319 539	346 058
60 - 64	2 397 618	1 135 833	1 261 785	1 840 130	871 137	968 993	557 488	264 696	292 792
65 - 69	1 881 811	876 547	1 005 264	1 433 783	667 181	766 602	448 028	209 366	238 662
70 - 74	1 386 312	632 273	754 039	1 052 714	479 456	573 258	333 598	152 817	180 781
75 - 79	927 909	412 951	514 958	702 566	312 083	390 483	225 343	100 868	124 475
80 - 84	559 212	242 248	316 964	423 247	182 917	240 330	135 965	59 331	76 634
85 - 89	283 944	120 094	163 850	213 331	89 977	123 354	70 613	30 117	40 496
90 - 94	138 894	57 810	81 084	102 913	42 695	60 218	35 981	15 115	20 866
95 - 99	43 932	18 142	25 790	31 387	12 913	18 474	12 545	5 229	7 316
100 + ...	7 733	3 166	4 567	5 241	2 136	3 105	2 492	1 030	1 462
Montserrat									
12 V 2001 (CDFC)									
Total...................	4 491	2 418	2 073	...	...	...	...	...	...
0 - 4..................	311	153	158	...	...	...	...	...	...
5 - 9..................	277	153	124	...	...	...	...	...	...
10 - 14	281	148	133	...	...	...	...	...	...
15 - 19	273	149	124	...	...	...	...	...	...
20 - 24	206	113	93	...	...	...	...	...	...
25 - 29	319	169	150	...	...	...	...	...	...
30 - 34	346	176	170	...	...	...	...	...	...
35 - 39	382	211	171	...	...	...	...	...	...
40 - 44	325	171	154	...	...	...	...	...	...
45 - 49	335	196	139	...	...	...	...	...	...
50 - 54	282	170	112	...	...	...	...	...	...
55 - 59	239	136	103	...	...	...	...	...	...
60 - 64	203	108	95	...	...	...	...	...	...
65 - 69	148	76	72	...	...	...	...	...	...
70 - 74	169	94	75	...	...	...	...	...	...
75 - 79	139	72	67	...	...	...	...	...	...
80 - 84	107	47	60	...	...	...	...	...	...
85 - 89	67	32	35	...	...	...	...	...	...
90 - 94	38	14	24	...	...	...	...	...	...
95 + ...	21	9	12	...	...	...	...	...	...
Unknown - Inconnu	23	21	2	...	...	...	...	...	...
Netherlands Antilles - Antilles néerlandaises									
1 VII 2004 (ESDJ)									
Total...................	183 115	85 456	97 659	...	...	...	...	...	...
0	2 450	1 252	1 198	...	...	...	...	...	...
1 - 4..................	10 781	5 478	5 303	...	...	...	...	...	...
5 - 9..................	13 872	6 983	6 889	...	...	...	...	...	...
10 - 14	15 240	7 606	7 634	...	...	...	...	...	...
15 - 19	13 002	6 492	6 510	...	...	...	...	...	...
20 - 24	9 050	4 310	4 740	...	...	...	...	...	...
25 - 29	10 285	4 830	5 455	...	...	...	...	...	...

Continent, country or area, date, code and age (in years) / Continent, pays ou zone, date, code et âge (en années)	Total			Urban - Urbaine			Rural - Rurale		
	Both sexes Les deux sexes	Male Masculin	Female Féminin	Both sexes Les deux sexes	Male Masculin	Female Féminin	Both sexes Les deux sexes	Male Masculin	Female Féminin
AMERICA, NORTH - AMÉRIQUE DU NORD									
Netherlands Antilles - Antilles néerlandaises									
1 VII 2004 (ESDJ)									
30 - 34	13 980	6 426	7 554	...	...	...	...	...	...
35 - 39	15 792	7 136	8 656	...	...	...	...	...	...
40 - 44	16 660	7 483	9 177	...	...	...	...	...	...
45 - 49	14 691	6 595	8 096	...	...	...	...	...	...
50 - 54	12 472	5 614	6 858	...	...	...	...	...	...
55 - 59	9 982	4 604	5 378	...	...	...	...	...	...
60 - 64	7 299	3 296	4 003	...	...	...	...	...	...
65 - 69	6 094	2 761	3 333	...	...	...	...	...	...
70 - 74	4 601	2 007	2 594	...	...	...	...	...	...
75 - 79	3 099	1 283	1 816	...	...	...	...	...	...
80 - 84	2 032	751	1 281	...	...	...	...	...	...
85 - 89	1 120	376	744	...	...	...	...	...	...
90 - 94	460	124	336	...	...	...	...	...	...
95 - 99	125	39	86	...	...	...	...	...	...
100 +	28	10	18	...	...	...	...	...	...
Nicaragua									
1 VII 2005 (ESDJ)									
Total	5 457 208	2 720 336	2 736 872	3 140 854	1 511 552	1 629 302	2 316 354	1 208 784	1 107 570
0 - 4	672 455	343 130	329 325	347 013	177 124	169 889	325 442	166 006	159 436
5 - 9	693 677	353 907	339 770	372 884	189 029	183 855	320 793	164 878	155 915
10 - 14	703 201	357 159	346 042	390 798	195 006	195 792	312 403	162 153	150 250
15 - 19	623 677	313 155	310 522	353 483	171 662	181 821	270 194	141 493	128 701
20 - 24	560 765	279 115	281 650	324 357	154 423	169 934	236 408	124 692	111 716
25 - 29	458 598	223 079	235 519	276 680	129 399	147 281	181 918	93 680	88 238
30 - 34	373 458	180 491	192 967	234 445	108 580	125 865	139 013	71 911	67 102
35 - 39	306 231	149 402	156 829	191 266	89 647	101 619	114 965	59 755	55 210
40 - 44	256 202	124 889	131 313	160 165	74 579	85 586	96 037	50 310	45 727
45 - 49	215 751	104 592	111 159	131 630	60 632	70 998	84 121	43 960	40 161
50 - 54	167 246	82 212	85 034	101 171	46 410	54 761	66 075	35 802	30 273
55 - 59	119 466	61 751	57 715	71 254	34 215	37 039	48 212	27 536	20 676
60 - 64	95 217	48 028	47 189	57 028	26 492	30 536	38 189	21 536	16 653
65 - 69	74 655	36 888	37 767	45 147	20 405	24 742	29 508	16 483	13 025
70 - 74	58 515	27 772	30 743	35 515	15 150	20 365	23 000	12 622	10 378
75 - 79	39 934	18 622	21 312	24 476	10 144	14 332	15 458	8 478	6 980
80 +	38 160	16 144	22 016	23 542	8 655	14 887	14 618	7 489	7 129
Unknown - Inconnu	-	-	-	-	-	-	-	-	-
Panama									
1 VII 2000 (ESDF)									
Total	2 855 703	1 440 801	1 414 902	1 604 823	782 928	821 895	1 250 880	657 873	593 007
0	59 949	30 595	29 354	30 248	15 460	14 788	29 701	15 135	14 566
1 - 4	241 433	123 553	117 880	121 253	62 069	59 184	120 180	61 484	58 696
5 - 9	300 852	153 986	146 866	150 849	77 061	73 786	150 003	76 925	73 079
10 - 14	291 489	148 579	142 911	148 812	75 471	73 342	142 678	73 109	69 569
15 - 19	271 684	137 805	133 878	146 537	73 631	72 906	125 147	64 174	60 974
20 - 24	254 772	129 237	125 536	146 169	72 295	73 875	108 605	56 944	51 661
25 - 29	250 152	125 922	124 230	150 336	71 923	78 413	99 816	53 999	45 817
30 - 34	230 835	115 884	114 951	141 488	67 582	73 906	89 347	48 302	41 045
35 - 39	203 446	101 421	102 025	126 268	59 890	66 378	77 178	41 531	35 647
40 - 44	170 180	84 702	85 478	105 158	50 101	55 057	65 022	34 601	30 421
45 - 49	140 684	70 369	70 315	86 739	41 477	45 262	53 945	28 892	25 053
50 - 54	115 342	58 278	57 064	69 710	33 225	36 485	45 632	25 053	20 579
55 - 59	93 684	47 379	46 305	53 771	25 760	28 011	39 913	21 619	18 294
60 - 64	73 087	36 664	36 423	40 256	18 795	21 461	32 831	17 869	14 962
65 - 69	55 236	27 712	27 524	30 061	13 914	16 147	25 175	13 798	11 377
70 - 74	43 900	21 495	22 405	24 076	10 692	13 384	19 824	10 803	9 021
75 - 79	30 250	14 158	16 092	17 010	7 216	9 794	13 240	6 942	6 298
80 +	28 727	13 063	15 664	16 083	6 367	9 716	12 644	6 696	5 948
1 VII 2004 (ESDF)									
Total	3 172 360	1 600 879	1 571 481	...	...	...	...	...	...
0 - 4	340 907	174 072	166 835	...	...	...	...	...	...
5 - 9	325 887	166 386	159 501	...	...	...	...	...	...

Continent, country or area, date, code and age (in years) / Continent, pays ou zone, date, code et âge (en années)	Total			Urban - Urbaine			Rural - Rurale		
	Both sexes Les deux sexes	Male Masculin	Female Féminin	Both sexes Les deux sexes	Male Masculin	Female Féminin	Both sexes Les deux sexes	Male Masculin	Female Féminin
AMERICA, NORTH - AMÉRIQUE DU NORD									
Panama									
1 VII 2004 (ESDF)									
10 - 14	306 161	156 219	149 942	...	...	...	...	...	...
15 - 19	296 516	151 046	145 470	...	...	...	...	...	...
20 - 24	275 607	139 984	135 623	...	...	...	...	...	...
25 - 29	264 106	133 531	130 575	...	...	...	...	...	...
30 - 34	258 960	130 360	128 600	...	...	...	...	...	...
35 - 39	233 501	117 367	116 134	...	...	...	...	...	...
40 - 44	197 947	98 917	99 030	...	...	...	...	...	...
45 - 49	162 673	80 921	81 752	...	...	...	...	...	...
50 - 54	132 881	66 324	66 557	...	...	...	...	...	...
55 - 59	107 456	54 039	53 417	...	...	...	...	...	...
60 - 64	85 974	42 919	43 055	...	...	...	...	...	...
65 - 69	64 888	32 179	32 709	...	...	...	...	...	...
70 - 74	49 964	24 451	25 513	...	...	...	...	...	...
75 - 79	35 712	16 978	18 734	...	...	...	...	...	...
80 +	33 220	15 186	18 034	...	...	...	...	...	...
Puerto Rico - Porto Rico[12]									
1 VII 2005 (ESDJ)									
Total	3 912 054	1 879 236	2 032 818	...	...	...	...	...	...
0 - 4	258 735	132 208	126 527	...	...	...	...	...	...
5 - 9	289 841	148 236	141 605	...	...	...	...	...	...
10 - 14	304 169	155 712	148 457	...	...	...	...	...	...
15 - 19	297 283	150 840	146 443	...	...	...	...	...	...
20 - 24	293 657	147 360	146 297	...	...	...	...	...	...
25 - 29	284 625	139 486	145 139	...	...	...	...	...	...
30 - 34	266 299	129 685	136 614	...	...	...	...	...	...
35 - 39	262 367	125 597	136 770	...	...	...	...	...	...
40 - 44	264 719	124 169	140 550	...	...	...	...	...	...
45 - 49	252 133	116 661	135 472	...	...	...	...	...	...
50 - 54	233 479	107 305	126 174	...	...	...	...	...	...
55 - 59	228 467	104 640	123 827	...	...	...	...	...	...
60 - 64	186 461	85 213	101 248	...	...	...	...	...	...
65 - 69	154 036	70 199	83 837	...	...	...	...	...	...
70 - 74	122 664	54 428	68 236	...	...	...	...	...	...
75 - 79	90 702	38 776	51 926	...	...	...	...	...	...
80 +	122 417	48 721	73 696	...	...	...	...	...	...
Saint Kitts and Nevis - Saint-Kitts-et-Nevis									
1 VII 2000 (ESDF)									
Total	40 410	20 400	20 010	...	...	...	...	...	...
0 - 4	4 250	2 130	2 120	...	...	...	...	...	...
5 - 9	4 100	2 140	1 960	...	...	...	...	...	...
10 - 14	4 040	2 120	1 920	...	...	...	...	...	...
15 - 19	3 870	2 000	1 870	...	...	...	...	...	...
20 - 24	3 620	1 880	1 740	...	...	...	...	...	...
25 - 29	3 240	1 640	1 600	...	...	...	...	...	...
30 - 34	3 100	1 550	1 550	...	...	...	...	...	...
35 - 39	2 910	1 430	1 480	...	...	...	...	...	...
40 - 44	2 520	1 270	1 250	...	...	...	...	...	...
45 - 49	1 880	900	980	...	...	...	...	...	...
50 - 54	1 390	710	680	...	...	...	...	...	...
55 - 59	1 100	560	540	...	...	...	...	...	...
60 - 64	820	400	420	...	...	...	...	...	...
65 - 69	840	410	430	...	...	...	...	...	...
70 - 74	810	380	430	...	...	...	...	...	...
75 - 79	700	330	370	...	...	...	...	...	...
80 - 84	470	240	230	...	...	...	...	...	...
85 +	750	310	440	...	...	...	...	...	...
Saint Lucia - Sainte-Lucie									
22 V 2001 (CDFC)									
Total	157 164	76 741	80 423	42 310	20 208	22 102	111 559	54 897	56 662
0	973	458	515	238	120	118	735	338	397
1 - 4	12 958	6 485	6 473	3 203	1 627	1 576	9 755	4 858	4 897

Continent, country or area, date, code and age (in years) / Continent, pays ou zone, date, code et âge (en années)	Total			Urban - Urbaine			Rural - Rurale		
	Both sexes Les deux sexes	Male Masculin	Female Féminin	Both sexes Les deux sexes	Male Masculin	Female Féminin	Both sexes Les deux sexes	Male Masculin	Female Féminin
AMERICA, NORTH - AMÉRIQUE DU NORD									
Saint Lucia - Sainte-Lucie									
22 V 2001 (CDFC)									
5 - 9	16 382	8 260	8 122	3 906	1 963	1 943	12 476	6 297	6 179
10 - 14	16 605	8 323	8 282	4 023	2 005	2 018	12 582	6 318	6 264
15 - 19	16 348	8 051	8 297	4 296	2 116	2 180	12 052	5 935	6 117
20 - 24	13 369	6 635	6 734	3 886	1 947	1 939	9 483	4 688	4 795
25 - 29	12 572	6 112	6 460	3 592	1 788	1 804	8 980	4 324	4 656
30 - 34	11 419	5 652	5 767	2 822	1 481	1 341	8 597	4 171	4 426
35 - 39	11 167	5 397	5 770	3 238	1 576	1 662	7 929	3 821	4 108
40 - 44	9 041	4 410	4 631	2 531	1 193	1 338	6 510	3 217	3 293
45 - 49	6 811	3 401	3 410	2 109	995	1 114	4 702	2 406	2 296
50 - 54	5 830	2 926	2 904	1 958	1 000	958	3 872	1 926	1 946
55 - 59	4 479	2 103	2 376	1 353	599	754	3 126	1 504	1 622
60 - 64	3 856	1 788	2 068	1 030	416	614	2 826	1 372	1 454
65 - 69	3 573	1 661	1 912	1 043	440	603	2 530	1 221	1 309
70 - 74	2 776	1 326	1 450	909	399	510	1 867	927	940
75 - 79	2 217	991	1 226	684	283	401	1 533	708	825
80 - 84	1 570	647	923	483	176	307	1 087	471	616
85 - 89	897	352	545	272	81	191	625	271	354
90 - 94	323	128	195	120	39	81	203	89	114
95 +	143	53	90	54	18	36	89	35	54
1 VII 2005 (ESDF)									
Total	164 791	80 595	84 196	...	...	...	...	...	...
0 - 4	14 223	7 054	7 169	...	...	...	...	...	...
5 - 9	15 158	7 551	7 607	...	...	...	...	...	...
10 - 14	17 429	8 797	8 632	...	...	...	...	...	...
15 - 19	17 483	8 648	8 835	...	...	...	...	...	...
20 - 24	15 900	7 787	8 113	...	...	...	...	...	...
25 - 29	13 468	6 585	6 883	...	...	...	...	...	...
30 - 34	12 556	6 037	6 519	...	...	...	...	...	...
35 - 39	11 755	5 687	6 068	...	...	...	...	...	...
40 - 44	11 050	5 340	5 710	...	...	...	...	...	...
45 - 49	8 724	4 314	4 410	...	...	...	...	...	...
50 - 54	6 446	3 258	3 188	...	...	...	...	...	...
55 - 59	5 041	2 431	2 610	...	...	...	...	...	...
60 - 64	4 077	1 883	2 194	...	...	...	...	...	...
65 - 69	3 606	1 693	1 913	...	...	...	...	...	...
70 - 74	3 043	1 423	1 620	...	...	...	...	...	...
75 - 79	1 954	914	1 040	...	...	...	...	...	...
80 +	2 878	1 193	1 685	...	...	...	...	...	...
Saint Vincent and the Grenadines - Saint Vincent-et-les Grenadines[13]									
14 V 2001 (CDFC)									
Total	106 253	53 626	52 627	...	...	...	...	...	...
0 - 4	9 975	5 128	4 847	...	...	...	...	...	...
5 - 9	11 457	5 739	5 718	...	...	...	...	...	...
10 - 14	11 143	5 650	5 493	...	...	...	...	...	...
15 - 19	11 293	5 676	5 617	...	...	...	...	...	...
20 - 24	9 715	4 975	4 740	...	...	...	...	...	...
25 - 29	8 515	4 350	4 165	...	...	...	...	...	...
30 - 34	7 672	4 018	3 654	...	...	...	...	...	...
35 - 39	8 069	4 194	3 875	...	...	...	...	...	...
40 - 44	6 695	3 447	3 248	...	...	...	...	...	...
45 - 49	4 729	2 415	2 314	...	...	...	...	...	...
50 - 54	3 733	1 938	1 795	...	...	...	...	...	...
55 - 59	2 783	1 393	1 390	...	...	...	...	...	...
60 - 64	2 734	1 310	1 424	...	...	...	...	...	...
65 - 69	2 551	1 226	1 325	...	...	...	...	...	...
70 - 74	1 951	891	1 060	...	...	...	...	...	...
75 - 79	1 514	634	880	...	...	...	...	...	...
80 - 84	943	385	558	...	...	...	...	...	...
85 +	781	257	524	...	...	...	...	...	...
Unknown - Inconnu	-	-	-	...	...	...	...	...	...

Continent, country or area, date, code and age (in years) Continent, pays ou zone, date, code et âge (en années)	Total			Urban - Urbaine			Rural - Rurale		
	Both sexes Les deux sexes	Male Masculin	Female Féminin	Both sexes Les deux sexes	Male Masculin	Female Féminin	Both sexes Les deux sexes	Male Masculin	Female Féminin
AMERICA, NORTH -									
AMÉRIQUE DU NORD									
Trinidad and Tobago -									
Trinité-et-Tobago									
1 VII 1999 (ESDF)									
Total.................	1 283 863	640 914	642 949	...	...	...	...	...	...
0 - 4..................	86 272	43 501	42 771	...	...	...	...	...	...
5 - 9..................	108 030	55 286	52 744	...	...	...	...	...	...
10 - 14................	128 496	65 242	63 254	...	...	...	...	...	...
15 - 19................	125 851	64 835	61 016	...	...	...	...	...	...
20 - 24................	116 913	60 316	56 597	...	...	...	...	...	...
25 - 29................	107 970	54 735	53 235	...	...	...	...	...	...
30 - 34................	102 098	51 124	50 974	...	...	...	...	...	...
35 - 39................	102 869	50 435	52 434	...	...	...	...	...	...
40 - 44................	94 053	47 403	46 650	...	...	...	...	...	...
45 - 49................	79 996	39 595	40 401	...	...	...	...	...	...
50 - 54................	61 988	30 951	31 037	...	...	...	...	...	...
55 - 59................	48 415	23 125	25 290	...	...	...	...	...	...
60 - 64................	34 697	16 917	17 780	...	...	...	...	...	...
65 +...................	86 215	37 449	48 766	...	...	...	...	...	...
Turks Caicos Islands - Îles									
Turques et Caïques									
20 VIII 2001 (CDFC)									
Total.................	19 886	9 896	9 990	...	...	...	...	...	...
0 - 4..................	2 324	1 053	1 271	...	...	...	...	...	...
5 - 14.................	3 369	1 683	1 686	...	...	...	...	...	...
15 - 24................	2 663	1 270	1 393	...	...	...	...	...	...
25 - 49................	9 168	4 688	4 480	...	...	...	...	...	...
50 - 64................	1 605	868	737	...	...	...	...	...	...
65 +...................	757	334	423	...	...	...	...	...	...
United States - États-Unis[14]									
1 IV 2000 (CDJC)									
Total.................	281 421 906	138 053 563	143 368 343	222 360 539	108 375 797	113 984 742	59 061 367	29 677 766	29 383 601
0......................	3 805 648	1 949 017	1 856 631	3 108 179	1 591 301	1 516 878	697 469	357 716	339 753
1 - 4..................	15 370 150	7 861 716	7 508 434	12 426 799	6 352 829	6 073 970	2 943 351	1 508 887	1 434 464
5 - 9..................	20 549 505	10 523 277	10 026 228	16 303 052	8 338 164	7 964 888	4 246 453	2 185 113	2 061 340
10 - 14................	20 528 072	10 520 197	10 007 875	15 865 132	8 114 898	7 750 234	4 662 940	2 405 299	2 257 641
15 - 19................	20 219 890	10 391 004	9 828 886	15 862 692	8 092 790	7 769 902	4 357 198	2 298 214	2 058 984
20 - 24................	18 964 001	9 687 814	9 276 187	16 062 564	8 150 162	7 912 402	2 901 437	1 537 652	1 363 785
25 - 29................	19 381 336	9 798 760	9 582 576	16 247 338	8 210 254	8 037 084	3 133 998	1 588 506	1 545 492
30 - 34................	20 510 388	10 321 769	10 188 619	16 761 355	8 449 017	8 312 338	3 749 033	1 872 752	1 876 281
35 - 39................	22 706 664	11 318 696	11 387 968	17 967 717	8 957 072	9 010 645	4 738 947	2 361 624	2 377 323
40 - 44................	22 441 863	11 129 102	11 312 761	17 434 999	8 608 239	8 826 760	5 006 864	2 520 863	2 486 001
45 - 49................	20 092 404	9 889 506	10 202 898	15 431 618	7 528 331	7 903 287	4 660 786	2 361 175	2 299 611
50 - 54................	17 585 548	8 607 724	8 977 824	13 395 145	6 480 878	6 914 267	4 190 403	2 126 846	2 063 557
55 - 59................	13 469 237	6 508 729	6 960 508	10 060 185	4 791 948	5 268 237	3 409 052	1 716 781	1 692 271
60 - 64................	10 805 447	5 136 627	5 668 820	8 026 903	3 738 462	4 288 441	2 778 544	1 398 165	1 380 379
65 - 69................	9 533 545	4 400 362	5 133 183	7 180 256	3 236 555	3 943 701	2 353 289	1 163 807	1 189 482
70 - 74................	8 857 441	3 902 912	4 954 529	6 865 515	2 943 669	3 921 846	1 991 926	959 243	1 032 683
75 - 79................	7 415 813	3 044 456	4 371 357	5 901 375	2 367 269	3 534 106	1 514 438	677 187	837 251
80 - 84................	4 945 367	1 834 897	3 110 470	3 982 799	1 445 556	2 537 243	962 568	389 341	573 227
85 - 89................	2 789 818	876 501	1 913 317	2 274 316	695 943	1 578 373	515 502	180 558	334 944
90 - 94................	1 112 531	282 325	830 206	920 357	227 019	693 338	192 174	55 306	136 868
95 - 99................	286 784	58 115	228 669	239 942	47 265	192 677	46 842	10 850	35 992
100 +..................	50 454	10 057	40 397	42 301	8 176	34 125	8 153	1 881	6 272
1 VII 2005 (ESDJ)									
Total.................	296 410 404	145 999 746	150 410 658	...	...	...	...	...	...
0......................	4 106 627	2 101 135	2 005 492	...	...	...	...	...	...
1 - 4..................	16 197 097	8 280 211	7 916 886	...	...	...	...	...	...
5 - 9..................	19 538 793	9 993 397	9 545 396	...	...	...	...	...	...
10 - 14................	20 857 743	10 681 835	10 175 908	...	...	...	...	...	...
15 - 19................	21 038 989	10 790 223	10 248 766	...	...	...	...	...	...
20 - 24................	21 037 860	10 856 936	10 180 924	...	...	...	...	...	...
25 - 29................	20 065 702	10 268 169	9 797 533	...	...	...	...	...	...
30 - 34................	20 077 210	10 153 091	9 924 119	...	...	...	...	...	...
35 - 39................	21 001 954	10 563 375	10 438 579	...	...	...	...	...	...

Continent, country or area, date, code and age (in years) / Continent, pays ou zone, date, code et âge (en années)	Total			Urban - Urbaine			Rural - Rurale		
	Both sexes Les deux sexes	Male Masculin	Female Féminin	Both sexes Les deux sexes	Male Masculin	Female Féminin	Both sexes Les deux sexes	Male Masculin	Female Féminin
AMERICA, NORTH - AMÉRIQUE DU NORD									
United States - États-Unis[14]									
1 VII 2005 (ESDJ)									
40 - 44	22 860 510	11 376 664	11 483 846	...	...	...	...	...	...
45 - 49	22 484 523	11 106 575	11 377 948	...	...	...	...	...	...
50 - 54	19 997 742	9 788 780	10 208 962	...	...	...	...	...	...
55 - 59	17 353 678	8 425 070	8 928 608	...	...	...	...	...	...
60 - 64	13 001 863	6 201 648	6 800 215	...	...	...	...	...	...
65 - 69	10 131 444	4 721 791	5 409 653	...	...	...	...	...	...
70 - 74	8 508 369	3 807 605	4 700 764	...	...	...	...	...	...
75 - 79	7 411 813	3 117 774	4 294 039	...	...	...	...	...	...
80 - 84	5 642 549	2 161 671	3 480 878	...	...	...	...	...	...
85 - 89	3 210 503	1 092 012	2 118 491	...	...	...	...	...	...
90 - 94	1 414 938	404 657	1 010 281	...	...	...	...	...	...
95 - 99	400 393	93 114	307 279	...	...	...	...	...	...
100 +	70 104	14 013	56 091	...	...	...	...	...	...
United States Virgin Islands - Îles Vierges américaines[12]									
1 IV 2000 (CDJC)									
Total	108 612	...	...	...	...	...	...	...	...
0 - 4	8 553	...	...	...	...	...	...	...	...
5 - 9	10 176	...	...	...	...	...	...	...	...
10 - 14	9 676	...	...	...	...	...	...	...	...
15 - 19	8 688	...	...	...	...	...	...	...	...
20 - 24	5 916	...	...	...	...	...	...	...	...
25 - 34	13 705	...	...	...	...	...	...	...	...
35 - 44	15 746	...	...	...	...	...	...	...	...
45 - 54	15 521	...	...	...	...	...	...	...	...
55 - 59	6 757	...	...	...	...	...	...	...	...
60 - 64	4 757	...	...	...	...	...	...	...	...
65 - 74	5 845	...	...	...	...	...	...	...	...
75 - 84	2 505	...	...	...	...	...	...	...	...
85 +	767	...	...	...	...	...	...	...	...
AMERICA, SOUTH - AMÉRIQUE DU SUD									
Argentina - Argentine									
1 VII 2005 (ESDF)									
Total	38 592 150	18 898 472	19 693 678	34 894 057	16 961 698	17 932 359	3 698 093	1 936 774	1 761 319
0 - 4	3 329 198	1 693 479	1 635 719	2 918 049	1 488 141	1 429 908	411 149	205 338	205 811
5 - 9	3 419 104	1 738 020	1 681 084	2 993 762	1 525 211	1 468 551	425 342	212 809	212 533
10 - 14	3 456 317	1 755 899	1 700 418	3 060 166	1 556 344	1 503 822	396 151	199 555	196 596
15 - 19	3 361 395	1 705 978	1 655 417	3 022 703	1 527 187	1 495 516	338 692	178 791	159 901
20 - 24	3 225 378	1 629 984	1 595 394	2 938 711	1 477 950	1 460 761	286 667	152 034	134 633
25 - 29	3 268 243	1 641 925	1 626 318	2 999 963	1 501 016	1 498 947	268 280	140 909	127 371
30 - 34	2 732 974	1 367 895	1 365 079	2 506 251	1 248 597	1 257 654	226 723	119 298	107 425
35 - 39	2 398 695	1 195 951	1 202 744	2 196 309	1 086 570	1 109 739	202 386	109 381	93 005
40 - 44	2 261 291	1 117 097	1 144 194	2 065 328	1 009 217	1 056 111	195 963	107 880	88 083
45 - 49	2 119 022	1 024 468	1 094 554	1 933 827	923 523	1 010 304	185 195	100 945	84 250
50 - 54	1 975 521	953 838	1 021 683	1 800 662	857 541	943 121	174 859	96 297	78 562
55 - 59	1 722 476	822 699	899 777	1 570 198	737 371	832 827	152 278	85 328	66 950
60 - 64	1 449 366	680 458	768 908	1 319 570	607 934	711 636	129 796	72 524	57 272
65 - 69	1 221 234	549 019	672 215	1 118 457	493 177	625 280	102 777	55 842	46 935
70 - 74	1 035 416	438 837	596 579	952 950	395 628	557 322	82 466	43 209	39 257
75 - 79	813 712	318 893	494 819	752 951	287 828	465 123	60 761	31 065	29 696
80 +	802 808	264 032	538 776	744 200	238 463	505 737	58 608	25 569	33 039
Bolivia - Bolivie									
1 VII 2003 (ESDF)									
Total	9 024 922	4 495 426	4 529 495	5 713 606	2 780 802	2 932 804	3 311 316	1 714 625	1 596 692
0 - 4	...	...	...	744 336	377 941	366 395	507 820	260 704	247 117
0	254 798	129 963	124 834	...	...	...	...	...	...
1 - 4	997 358	508 681	488 678	...	...	...	...	...	...
5 - 9	1 166 265	594 608	571 657	692 312	349 521	342 790	473 953	245 087	228 866

183

7. Population by age, sex and urban/rural residence: latest available year, 1996 - 2005
Population selon l'âge, le sexe et la résidence, urbaine/rurale: dernière année disponible, 1996 - 2005 (continued - suite)

Continent, country or area, date, code and age (in years) Continent, pays ou zone, date, code et âge (en annèes)	Total			Urban - Urbaine			Rural - Rurale		
	Both sexes Les deux sexes	Male Masculin	Female Féminin	Both sexes Les deux sexes	Male Masculin	Female Féminin	Both sexes Les deux sexes	Male Masculin	Female Féminin
AMERICA, SOUTH - AMÉRIQUE DU SUD									
Bolivia - Bolivie									
1 VII 2003 (ESDF)									
10 - 14	1 073 561	546 244	527 317	675 965	336 689	339 276	397 596	209 555	188 041
15 - 19	932 510	472 358	460 151	630 783	309 369	321 414	301 727	162 989	138 737
20 - 24	814 526	409 846	404 680	572 694	281 691	291 003	241 832	128 155	113 677
25 - 29	721 254	359 771	361 483	494 257	239 881	254 376	226 998	119 890	107 107
30 - 34	624 992	309 212	315 780	427 459	204 574	222 885	197 533	104 638	92 895
35 - 39	512 151	251 779	260 373	334 677	158 910	175 767	177 474	92 868	84 606
40 - 44	432 316	210 816	221 500	280 542	132 378	148 164	151 775	78 438	73 336
45 - 49	366 481	176 834	189 646	229 283	107 308	121 975	137 198	69 526	67 671
50 - 54	302 980	144 864	158 116	182 392	84 279	98 113	120 587	60 584	60 003
55 - 59	243 463	115 925	127 538	140 577	64 747	75 830	102 886	51 178	51 708
60 - 64	191 980	90 333	101 647	103 324	46 382	56 942	88 655	43 950	44 705
65 - 69	155 368	71 595	83 774	82 620	36 420	46 200	72 748	35 175	37 574
70 - 74	116 485	52 380	64 104	60 079	25 772	34 307	56 405	26 608	29 797
75 - 79	73 314	31 963	41 351	39 546	16 287	23 258	33 768	15 676	18 092
80 +	45 120	18 254	26 866	22 759	8 652	14 107	22 361	9 602	12 759
1 VII 2005 (ESDF)									
Total	9 427 219	4 698 293	4 728 926	...	...	...	...	...	...
0	260 417	132 799	127 618	...	...	...	...	...	...
1 - 4	1 018 861	519 518	499 343	...	...	...	...	...	...
5 - 9	1 184 544	603 976	580 568	...	...	...	...	...	...
10 - 14	1 120 715	570 690	550 025	...	...	...	...	...	...
15 - 19	980 559	497 309	483 250	...	...	...	...	...	...
20 - 24	855 044	431 020	424 024	...	...	...	...	...	...
25 - 29	749 965	374 997	374 968	...	...	...	...	...	...
30 - 34	667 439	330 655	336 784	...	...	...	...	...	...
35 - 39	547 366	269 556	277 810	...	...	...	...	...	...
40 - 44	455 786	222 704	233 082	...	...	...	...	...	...
45 - 49	388 216	187 929	200 287	...	...	...	...	...	...
50 - 54	320 255	153 041	167 214	...	...	...	...	...	...
55 - 59	262 279	124 663	137 616	...	...	...	...	...	...
60 - 64	201 661	94 918	106 743	...	...	...	...	...	...
65 - 69	163 270	75 254	88 016	...	...	...	...	...	...
70 - 74	120 939	54 285	66 654	...	...	...	...	...	...
75 - 79	80 278	34 932	45 346	...	...	...	...	...	...
80 +	49 625	20 047	29 578	...	...	...	...	...	...
Brazil - Brésil[15]									
1 VIII 2000 (CDJC)									
Total	169 799 170	83 576 015	86 223 155	137 953 959	66 882 993	71 070 966	31 845 211	16 693 022	15 152 189
0	3 213 310	1 635 916	1 577 394	2 518 464	1 282 941	1 235 523	694 846	352 975	341 871
1 - 4	13 162 418	6 691 010	6 471 408	10 242 356	5 207 423	5 034 933	2 920 062	1 483 587	1 436 475
5 - 9	16 542 327	8 402 353	8 139 974	12 821 519	6 500 814	6 320 705	3 720 808	1 901 539	1 819 269
10 - 14	17 348 067	8 777 639	8 570 428	13 530 190	6 803 898	6 726 292	3 817 877	1 973 741	1 844 136
15 - 19	17 939 815	9 019 130	8 920 685	14 403 539	7 132 822	7 270 717	3 536 276	1 886 308	1 649 968
20 - 24	16 141 515	8 048 218	8 093 297	13 352 132	6 549 365	6 802 767	2 789 383	1 498 853	1 290 530
25 - 29	13 849 665	6 814 328	7 035 337	11 570 969	5 606 425	5 964 544	2 278 696	1 207 903	1 070 793
30 - 34	13 028 944	6 363 983	6 664 961	10 918 396	5 248 443	5 669 953	2 110 548	1 115 540	995 008
35 - 39	12 261 529	5 955 875	6 305 654	10 326 271	4 929 130	5 397 141	1 935 258	1 026 745	908 513
40 - 44	10 546 694	5 116 439	5 430 255	8 913 019	4 249 804	4 663 215	1 633 675	866 635	767 040
45 - 49	8 721 541	4 216 418	4 505 123	7 309 621	3 472 375	3 837 246	1 411 920	744 043	667 877
50 - 54	7 062 601	3 415 678	3 646 923	5 833 659	2 764 708	3 068 951	1 228 942	650 970	577 972
55 - 59	5 444 715	2 585 244	2 859 471	4 387 995	2 032 135	2 355 860	1 056 720	553 109	503 611
60 - 64	4 600 929	2 153 209	2 447 720	3 712 213	1 676 323	2 035 890	888 716	476 886	411 830
65 - 69	3 581 106	1 639 325	1 941 781	2 916 899	1 284 812	1 632 087	664 207	354 513	309 694
70 - 74	2 742 302	1 229 329	1 512 973	2 249 617	966 115	1 283 502	492 685	263 214	229 471
75 - 79	1 779 587	780 571	999 016	1 456 665	610 767	845 898	322 922	169 804	153 118
80 - 84	1 036 034	428 501	607 533	841 798	331 002	510 796	194 236	97 499	96 737
85 - 89	534 871	208 088	326 783	436 121	160 379	275 742	98 750	47 709	51 041
90 - 94	180 426	65 117	115 309	147 784	50 531	97 253	32 642	14 586	18 056
95 - 99	56 198	19 221	36 977	45 682	14 899	30 783	10 516	4 322	6 194
100 +	24 576	10 423	14 153	19 050	7 882	11 168	5 526	2 541	2 985

Continent, country or area, date, code and age (in years) / Continent, pays ou zone, date, code et âge (en années)	Total			Urban - Urbaine			Rural - Rurale		
	Both sexes Les deux sexes	Male Masculin	Female Féminin	Both sexes Les deux sexes	Male Masculin	Female Féminin	Both sexes Les deux sexes	Male Masculin	Female Féminin
AMERICA, SOUTH - AMÉRIQUE DU SUD									
Brazil - Brésil[15]									
1 VII 2005 (ESDF)									
Total	184 184 264	90 542 990	93 641 274	...	...	...	...	...	...
0 - 4	17 970 749	9 123 653	8 847 096	...	...	...	...	...	...
5 - 9	16 992 071	8 616 413	8 375 658	...	...	...	...	...	...
10 - 14	16 463 415	8 333 675	8 129 740	...	...	...	...	...	...
15 - 19	17 357 202	8 757 685	8 599 517	...	...	...	...	...	...
20 - 24	17 782 204	8 929 189	8 853 015	...	...	...	...	...	...
25 - 29	15 735 323	7 851 746	7 883 577	...	...	...	...	...	...
30 - 34	14 144 074	7 022 983	7 121 091	...	...	...	...	...	...
35 - 39	13 479 781	6 597 635	6 882 146	...	...	...	...	...	...
40 - 44	12 626 795	6 045 877	6 580 918	...	...	...	...	...	...
45 - 49	10 485 825	4 982 152	5 503 673	...	...	...	...	...	...
50 - 54	8 351 766	3 934 334	4 417 432	...	...	...	...	...	...
55 - 59	6 508 343	3 058 018	3 450 325	...	...	...	...	...	...
60 - 64	5 044 084	2 326 548	2 717 536	...	...	...	...	...	...
65 - 69	4 137 717	1 898 188	2 239 529	...	...	...	...	...	...
70 - 74	2 940 775	1 303 338	1 637 437	...	...	...	...	...	...
75 - 79	2 119 353	913 000	1 206 353	...	...	...	...	...	...
80 +	2 044 787	848 556	1 196 231	...	...	...	...	...	...
Chile - Chili									
1 VII 2005 (ESDF)									
Total	16 267 278	8 052 564	8 214 714	14 123 527	6 910 230	7 213 297	2 143 751	1 142 334	1 001 417
0 - 4	1 237 463	630 199	607 264	1 086 558	553 080	533 478	150 905	77 119	73 786
5 - 9	1 328 126	675 971	652 155	1 151 784	585 838	565 946	176 342	90 133	86 209
10 - 14	1 488 498	757 261	731 237	1 283 409	651 748	631 661	205 089	105 513	99 576
15 - 19	1 463 158	743 521	719 637	1 261 733	637 990	623 743	201 425	105 531	95 894
20 - 24	1 322 128	670 186	651 942	1 159 247	579 846	579 401	162 881	90 340	72 541
25 - 29	1 171 107	590 486	580 621	1 036 288	517 476	518 812	134 819	73 010	61 809
30 - 34	1 239 874	621 698	618 176	1 090 661	542 326	548 335	149 213	79 372	69 841
35 - 39	1 239 003	618 613	620 390	1 077 489	532 649	544 840	161 514	85 964	75 550
40 - 44	1 261 636	627 266	634 370	1 093 337	534 943	558 394	168 299	92 323	75 976
45 - 49	1 090 382	539 610	550 772	948 821	460 464	488 357	141 561	79 146	62 415
50 - 54	857 796	420 961	436 835	746 764	358 927	387 837	111 032	62 034	48 998
55 - 59	700 924	338 904	362 020	606 275	286 711	319 564	94 649	52 193	42 456
60 - 64	577 002	272 780	304 222	493 954	227 852	266 102	83 048	44 928	38 120
65 - 69	432 884	198 612	234 272	363 926	161 577	202 349	68 958	37 035	31 923
70 - 74	348 283	151 602	196 681	291 667	122 023	169 644	56 616	29 579	27 037
75 - 79	256 350	105 023	151 327	217 163	84 859	132 304	39 187	20 164	19 023
80 +	252 664	89 871	162 793	214 451	71 921	142 530	38 213	17 950	20 263
Colombia - Colombie[16]									
1 VII 2005 (ESDF)									
Total	46 039 144	22 764 130	23 275 014	...	...	...	...	...	...
0	967 264	495 449	471 815	...	...	...	...	...	...
1 - 4	3 820 446	1 949 380	1 871 066	...	...	...	...	...	...
5 - 9	4 756 116	2 427 834	2 328 282	...	...	...	...	...	...
10 - 14	4 709 283	2 400 582	2 308 701	...	...	...	...	...	...
15 - 19	4 330 509	2 200 739	2 129 770	...	...	...	...	...	...
20 - 24	4 104 798	2 072 954	2 031 844	...	...	...	...	...	...
25 - 29	3 883 995	1 941 490	1 942 505	...	...	...	...	...	...
30 - 34	3 482 966	1 714 604	1 768 362	...	...	...	...	...	...
35 - 39	3 433 468	1 669 150	1 764 318	...	...	...	...	...	...
40 - 44	3 039 557	1 465 908	1 573 649	...	...	...	...	...	...
45 - 49	2 504 334	1 194 949	1 309 385	...	...	...	...	...	...
50 - 54	2 053 789	971 389	1 082 400	...	...	...	...	...	...
55 - 59	1 545 169	729 857	815 312	...	...	...	...	...	...
60 - 64	1 105 797	522 861	582 936	...	...	...	...	...	...
65 - 69	824 072	379 510	444 562	...	...	...	...	...	...
70 - 74	613 510	273 043	340 467	...	...	...	...	...	...
75 - 79	425 614	183 054	242 560	...	...	...	...	...	...
80 +	438 457	171 377	267 080	...	...	...	...	...	...

Continent, country or area, date, code and age (in years) / Continent, pays ou zone, date, code et âge (en années)	Total			Urban - Urbaine			Rural - Rurale		
	Both sexes Les deux sexes	Male Masculin	Female Féminin	Both sexes Les deux sexes	Male Masculin	Female Féminin	Both sexes Les deux sexes	Male Masculin	Female Féminin
AMERICA, SOUTH - AMÉRIQUE DU SUD									
Ecuador - Équateur[17]									
1 VII 2004 (ESDF)									
Total....................	13 026 891	6 535 564	6 491 327	8 187 908	4 057 642	4 130 266	4 838 983	2 477 922	2 361 061
0 - 4.....................	...	...	...	845 152	436 348	408 804	603 550	302 713	300 837
0........................	289 789	147 951	141 838	...	...	...	...	...	...
1 - 4.....................	1 158 913	591 110	567 803	...	...	...	...	...	...
5 - 9.....................	1 441 016	734 425	706 591	836 049	427 823	408 226	604 967	306 602	298 365
10 - 14...................	1 388 671	706 484	682 187	823 734	415 692	408 042	564 937	290 792	274 145
15 - 19...................	1 333 679	676 728	656 951	845 605	417 825	427 780	488 074	258 903	229 171
20 - 24...................	1 212 307	612 337	599 970	810 941	400 445	410 496	401 366	211 892	189 474
25 - 29...................	1 078 378	542 390	535 988	747 747	370 239	377 508	330 631	172 151	158 480
30 - 34...................	961 155	481 345	479 810	669 833	332 454	337 379	291 322	148 891	142 431
35 - 39...................	850 352	424 450	425 902	573 835	284 859	288 976	276 517	139 591	136 926
40 - 44...................	732 296	364 669	367 627	477 753	236 161	241 592	254 543	128 508	126 035
45 - 49...................	627 106	310 951	316 155	389 964	191 248	198 716	237 142	119 703	117 439
50 - 54...................	524 929	259 110	265 819	320 750	155 727	165 023	204 179	103 383	100 796
55 - 59...................	388 289	191 007	197 282	232 525	111 128	121 397	155 764	79 879	75 885
60 - 64...................	315 353	153 704	161 649	188 353	88 492	99 861	127 000	65 212	61 788
65 - 69...................	256 073	123 154	132 919	151 767	69 992	81 775	104 306	53 162	51 144
70 - 74...................	196 820	93 022	103 798	115 227	51 777	63 450	81 593	41 245	40 348
75 - 79...................	140 537	65 267	75 270	82 153	36 021	46 132	58 384	29 246	29 138
80 +.....................	131 228	57 460	73 768	76 520	31 411	45 109	54 708	26 049	28 659
1 VII 2005 (ESDF)									
Total....................	13 215 089	6 628 368	6 586 721	...	...	...	...	...	...
0 - 4.....................	1 445 080	737 258	707 822	...	...	...	...	...	...
5 - 9.....................	1 446 824	737 543	709 281	...	...	...	...	...	...
10 - 14...................	1 393 402	709 081	684 321	...	...	...	...	...	...
15 - 19...................	1 341 419	680 849	660 570	...	...	...	...	...	...
20 - 24...................	1 226 894	619 791	607 103	...	...	...	...	...	...
25 - 29...................	1 094 290	550 287	544 003	...	...	...	...	...	...
30 - 34...................	976 014	488 676	487 338	...	...	...	...	...	...
35 - 39...................	867 949	433 025	434 924	...	...	...	...	...	...
40 - 44...................	750 456	373 564	376 892	...	...	...	...	...	...
45 - 49...................	642 240	318 410	323 830	...	...	...	...	...	...
50 - 54...................	548 106	270 440	277 666	...	...	...	...	...	...
55 - 59...................	405 117	199 246	205 871	...	...	...	...	...	...
60 - 64...................	325 144	158 469	166 675	...	...	...	...	...	...
65 - 69...................	264 095	127 014	137 081	...	...	...	...	...	...
70 - 74...................	203 903	96 338	107 565	...	...	...	...	...	...
75 - 79...................	146 633	68 066	78 567	...	...	...	...	...	...
80 +.....................	137 523	60 311	77 212	...	...	...	...	...	...
Falkland Islands (Malvinas) - Îles Falkland (Malvinas)									
8 IV 2001 (CDFC)									
Total....................	2 913	1 598	1 315	...	...	...	...	...	...
0 - 4.....................	137	70	67	...	...	...	...	...	...
5 - 9.....................	146	71	75	...	...	...	...	...	...
10 - 14...................	155	87	68	...	...	...	...	...	...
15 - 19...................	149	69	80	...	...	...	...	...	...
20 - 24...................	223	111	112	...	...	...	...	...	...
25 - 29...................	271	143	128	...	...	...	...	...	...
30 - 34...................	292	173	119	...	...	...	...	...	...
35 - 39...................	277	159	118	...	...	...	...	...	...
40 - 44...................	250	124	126	...	...	...	...	...	...
45 - 49...................	241	152	89	...	...	...	...	...	...
50 - 54...................	233	139	94	...	...	...	...	...	...
55 - 59...................	188	117	71	...	...	...	...	...	...
60 - 64...................	110	68	42	...	...	...	...	...	...
65 - 69...................	90	50	40	...	...	...	...	...	...
70 - 74...................	64	26	38	...	...	...	...	...	...
75 - 79...................	29	15	14	...	...	...	...	...	...
80 +.....................	58	24	34	...	...	...	...	...	...

7. Population by age, sex and urban/rural residence: latest available year, 1996 - 2005
Population selon l'âge, le sexe et la résidence, urbaine/rurale: dernière année disponible, 1996 - 2005 (continued - suite)

Continent, country or area, date, code and age (in years) / Continent, pays ou zone, date, code et âge (en années)	Total			Urban - Urbaine			Rural - Rurale		
	Both sexes Les deux sexes	Male Masculin	Female Féminin	Both sexes Les deux sexes	Male Masculin	Female Féminin	Both sexes Les deux sexes	Male Masculin	Female Féminin
AMERICA, SOUTH - AMÉRIQUE DU SUD									
French Guiana - Guyane française									
1 I 2005 (ESDJ)									
Total....................	197 997	98 956	99 041	...	...	...	...	...	...
0 - 4.....................	26 319	13 398	12 921	...	...	...	...	...	...
5 - 9.....................	23 808	12 008	11 800	...	...	...	...	...	...
10 - 14...................	21 102	10 622	10 480	...	...	...	...	...	...
15 - 19...................	18 148	9 165	8 983	...	...	...	...	...	...
20 - 24...................	14 218	6 993	7 225	...	...	...	...	...	...
25 - 29...................	14 744	7 120	7 624	...	...	...	...	...	...
30 - 34...................	15 644	7 464	8 180	...	...	...	...	...	...
35 - 39...................	14 729	7 229	7 500	...	...	...	...	...	...
40 - 44...................	13 155	6 641	6 514	...	...	...	...	...	...
45 - 49...................	10 610	5 391	5 219	...	...	...	...	...	...
50 - 54...................	8 432	4 337	4 095	...	...	...	...	...	...
55 - 59...................	6 042	3 193	2 849	...	...	...	...	...	...
60 - 64...................	3 695	1 954	1 741	...	...	...	...	...	...
65 - 69...................	2 617	1 294	1 323	...	...	...	...	...	...
70 - 74...................	1 880	924	956	...	...	...	...	...	...
75 - 79...................	1 253	576	677	...	...	...	...	...	...
80 - 84...................	851	374	477	...	...	...	...	...	...
85 - 89...................	449	183	266	...	...	...	...	...	...
90 +.....................	301	90	211	...	...	...	...	...	...
Guyana									
15 IX 2002 (CDFC)									
Total....................	751 223	376 034	375 189	213 705	103 127	110 578	537 518	272 907	264 611
0 - 4.....................	88 996	45 291	43 705	22 436	11 372	11 064	66 560	33 919	32 642
5 - 9.....................	96 671	49 119	47 552	25 254	12 909	12 345	71 416	36 210	35 206
10 - 14...................	81 497	41 218	40 279	22 393	11 215	11 178	59 104	30 002	29 101
15 - 19...................	66 922	33 496	33 426	19 559	9 737	9 822	47 363	23 759	23 604
20 - 24...................	64 409	31 908	32 501	19 443	9 301	10 142	44 966	22 608	22 359
25 - 29...................	61 086	30 232	30 854	18 068	8 439	9 629	43 017	21 792	21 225
30 - 34...................	57 942	29 088	28 854	16 403	7 687	8 717	41 538	21 401	20 137
35 - 39...................	52 735	26 441	26 295	14 716	6 779	7 937	38 020	19 662	18 358
40 - 44...................	46 488	23 338	23 150	13 203	6 194	7 009	33 285	17 144	16 141
45 - 49...................	35 810	17 952	17 859	10 609	4 910	5 699	25 202	13 042	12 160
50 - 54...................	28 149	14 207	13 942	8 459	4 008	4 450	19 690	10 198	9 492
55 - 59...................	18 129	8 980	9 149	5 539	2 628	2 911	12 590	6 352	6 238
60 - 64...................	15 005	7 191	7 813	4 540	2 081	2 459	10 465	5 110	5 354
65 - 69...................	11 741	5 575	6 167	3 671	1 649	2 021	8 071	3 925	4 145
70 - 74...................	8 543	3 965	4 578	2 784	1 212	1 571	5 759	2 753	3 006
75 +.....................	11 746	5 217	6 529	3 977	1 640	2 337	7 769	3 577	4 192
Unknown - Inconnu......	5 354	2 818	2 536	2 699	1 394	1 305	2 655	1 424	1 231
Paraguay									
28 VIII 2002 (CDFC)									
Total....................	5 163 198	2 603 242	2 559 956	2 928 437	1 422 339	1 506 098	2 234 761	1 180 903	1 053 858
0........................	115 558	59 043	56 515	62 098	31 869	30 229	53 460	27 174	26 286
1 - 4.....................	491 743	250 996	240 747	256 692	130 582	126 110	235 051	120 414	114 637
5 - 9.....................	663 294	338 199	325 095	341 612	173 363	168 249	321 682	164 836	156 846
10 - 14...................	644 714	328 120	316 594	331 808	165 636	166 172	312 906	162 484	150 422
15 - 19...................	576 807	292 731	284 076	327 674	156 108	171 566	249 133	136 623	112 510
20 - 24...................	472 545	238 527	234 018	294 654	139 622	155 032	177 891	98 905	78 986
25 - 29...................	359 766	179 299	180 467	221 966	105 928	116 038	137 800	73 371	64 429
30 - 34...................	333 192	167 025	166 167	204 138	98 568	105 570	129 054	68 457	60 597
35 - 39...................	307 521	153 333	154 188	186 657	89 705	96 952	120 864	63 628	57 236
40 - 44...................	284 082	145 797	138 285	170 959	84 148	86 811	113 123	61 649	51 474
45 - 49...................	227 719	116 069	111 650	135 829	66 659	69 170	91 890	49 410	42 480
50 - 54...................	182 317	93 396	88 921	106 049	52 006	54 043	76 268	41 390	34 878
55 - 59...................	135 707	68 353	67 354	78 597	37 878	40 719	57 110	30 475	26 635
60 - 64...................	114 843	56 778	58 065	64 874	29 968	34 906	49 969	26 810	23 159
65 - 69...................	80 528	38 292	42 236	45 618	20 151	25 467	34 910	18 141	16 769
70 - 74...................	70 708	33 286	37 422	40 227	17 320	22 907	30 481	15 966	14 515
75 - 79...................	47 931	21 703	26 228	27 650	11 307	16 343	20 281	10 396	9 885
80 - 84...................	29 287	12 433	16 854	16 753	6 289	10 464	12 534	6 144	6 390

Continent, country or area, date, code and age (in years) / Continent, pays ou zone, date, code et âge (en années)	Total			Urban - Urbaine			Rural - Rurale		
	Both sexes Les deux sexes	Male Masculin	Female Féminin	Both sexes Les deux sexes	Male Masculin	Female Féminin	Both sexes Les deux sexes	Male Masculin	Female Féminin
AMERICA, SOUTH - AMÉRIQUE DU SUD									
Paraguay									
28 VIII 2002 (CDFC)									
85 - 89	16 412	6 750	9 662	9 573	3 548	6 025	6 839	3 202	3 637
90 +	8 524	3 112	5 412	5 009	1 684	3 325	3 515	1 428	2 087
1 VII 2005 (ESDF)									
Total	5 898 651	2 983 123	2 915 528	...	...	...	...	...	...
0 - 4	728 551	371 147	357 404	...	...	...	...	...	...
5 - 9	706 173	359 302	346 871	...	...	...	...	...	...
10 - 14	680 414	345 932	334 482	...	...	...	...	...	...
15 - 19	643 206	326 320	316 886	...	...	...	...	...	...
20 - 24	581 259	294 518	286 741	...	...	...	...	...	...
25 - 29	465 047	235 224	229 823	...	...	...	...	...	...
30 - 34	375 840	188 940	186 900	...	...	...	...	...	...
35 - 39	342 408	172 409	169 999	...	...	...	...	...	...
40 - 44	305 655	154 902	150 753	...	...	...	...	...	...
45 - 49	266 211	135 737	130 474	...	...	...	...	...	...
50 - 54	225 590	115 789	109 801	...	...	...	...	...	...
55 - 59	171 546	87 607	83 939	...	...	...	...	...	...
60 - 64	130 727	65 794	64 933	...	...	...	...	...	...
65 - 69	102 290	50 515	51 775	...	...	...	...	...	...
70 - 74	70 837	33 775	37 062	...	...	...	...	...	...
75 - 79	55 851	25 250	30 601	...	...	...	...	...	...
80 +	47 046	19 962	27 084	...	...	...	...	...	...
Peru - Pérou[18]									
1 VII 2004 (ESDF)[19]									
Total	27 546 574	13 852 228	13 694 346	19 966 180	9 999 924	9 966 256	7 580 394	3 852 304	3 728 090
0	605 682	309 315	296 367	394 239	201 428	192 811	211 443	107 887	103 556
1 - 4	2 406 566	1 226 479	1 180 087	1 566 432	798 689	767 743	840 134	427 790	412 344
5 - 9	3 028 195	1 540 372	1 487 823	2 000 852	1 019 164	981 688	1 027 343	521 208	506 135
10 - 14	2 972 853	1 509 007	1 463 846	1 984 192	1 007 505	976 687	988 661	501 502	487 159
15 - 19	2 776 367	1 407 353	1 369 014	1 950 217	990 386	959 831	826 150	416 967	409 183
20 - 24	2 568 299	1 299 504	1 268 795	1 882 650	935 460	947 190	685 649	364 044	321 605
25 - 29	2 388 323	1 205 444	1 182 879	1 834 973	912 116	922 857	553 350	293 328	260 022
30 - 34	2 081 011	1 050 232	1 030 779	1 607 497	803 450	804 047	473 514	246 782	226 732
35 - 39	1 825 093	918 479	906 614	1 420 666	712 002	708 664	404 427	206 477	197 950
40 - 44	1 582 605	795 015	787 590	1 245 343	625 123	620 220	337 262	169 892	167 370
45 - 49	1 309 304	654 287	655 017	1 034 704	517 979	516 725	274 600	136 308	138 292
50 - 54	1 073 619	534 424	539 195	838 797	419 696	419 101	234 822	114 728	120 094
55 - 59	849 522	420 671	428 851	647 262	323 002	324 260	202 260	97 669	104 591
60 - 64	675 160	330 788	344 372	506 099	248 749	257 350	169 061	82 039	87 022
65 - 69	539 233	259 833	279 400	398 614	191 417	207 197	140 619	68 416	72 203
70 - 74	394 112	185 198	208 914	290 413	135 697	154 716	103 699	49 501	54 198
75 - 79	253 281	114 903	138 378	189 658	85 593	104 065	63 623	29 310	34 313
80 +	217 349	90 924	126 425	173 572	72 468	101 104	43 777	18 456	25 321
18 VII 2005 (CDFC)[20]									
Total	26 152 265	13 061 026	13 091 239	...	...	...	...	...	...
0	511 576	259 802	251 774	...	...	...	...	...	...
1 - 4	1 960 473	996 764	963 709	...	...	...	...	...	...
5 - 9	2 762 560	1 403 316	1 359 244	...	...	...	...	...	...
10 - 14	2 889 331	1 476 327	1 413 004	...	...	...	...	...	...
15 - 19	2 647 138	1 333 164	1 313 974	...	...	...	...	...	...
20 - 24	2 500 008	1 247 083	1 252 925	...	...	...	...	...	...
25 - 29	2 180 629	1 074 853	1 105 776	...	...	...	...	...	...
30 - 34	1 918 842	946 529	972 313	...	...	...	...	...	...
35 - 39	1 814 390	883 449	930 941	...	...	...	...	...	...
40 - 44	1 503 497	748 496	755 001	...	...	...	...	...	...
45 - 49	1 272 823	629 120	643 703	...	...	...	...	...	...
50 - 54	1 079 349	534 119	545 230	...	...	...	...	...	...
55 - 59	811 393	404 439	406 954	...	...	...	...	...	...
60 - 64	672 988	334 163	338 825	...	...	...	...	...	...
65 - 69	542 612	267 957	274 655	...	...	...	...	...	...
70 - 74	423 161	208 888	214 273	...	...	...	...	...	...
75 - 79	316 094	155 765	160 329	...	...	...	...	...	...
80 +	345 401	156 792	188 609	...	...	...	...	...	...

7. Population by age, sex and urban/rural residence: latest available year, 1996 - 2005
Population selon l'âge, le sexe et la résidence, urbaine/rurale: dernière année disponible, 1996 - 2005 (continued - suite)

Continent, country or area, date, code and age (in years) / Continent, pays ou zone, date, code et âge (en années)	Total			Urban - Urbaine			Rural - Rurale		
	Both sexes Les deux sexes	Male Masculin	Female Féminin	Both sexes Les deux sexes	Male Masculin	Female Féminin	Both sexes Les deux sexes	Male Masculin	Female Féminin
AMERICA, SOUTH - AMÉRIQUE DU SUD									
Suriname									
2 VIII 2004 (CDJC)									
Total....................	492 829	247 846[21]	244 618[21]	...	...	...	...	...	...
0	9 872	4 995	4 854	...	...	...	...	...	...
1 - 4	41 965	21 238	20 713	...	...	...	...	...	...
5 - 9	49 409	25 195	24 206	...	...	...	...	...	...
10 - 14	45 143	22 880	22 246	...	...	...	...	...	...
15 - 19	46 508	23 456	23 035	...	...	...	...	...	...
20 - 24	43 843	22 430	21 399	...	...	...	...	...	...
25 - 29	37 901	18 984	18 874	...	...	...	...	...	...
30 - 34	38 994	19 818	19 156	...	...	...	...	...	...
35 - 39	37 279	19 161	18 083	...	...	...	...	...	...
40 - 44	33 985	17 655	16 327	...	...	...	...	...	...
45 - 49	25 635	12 643	12 992	...	...	...	...	...	...
50 - 54	20 420	9 931	10 485	...	...	...	...	...	...
55 - 59	14 982	6 954	8 027	...	...	...	...	...	...
60 - 64	13 259	6 200	7 059	...	...	...	...	...	...
65 - 69	10 602	5 148	5 452	...	...	...	...	...	...
70 - 74	8 659	4 101	4 554	...	...	...	...	...	...
75 - 79	5 152	2 418	2 732	...	...	...	...	...	...
80 - 84	2 853	1 235	1 618	...	...	...	...	...	...
85 - 89	1 075	392	677	...	...	...	...	...	...
90 - 94	460	184	276	...	...	...	...	...	...
95 + ...	129	34	95	...	...	...	...	...	...
Unknown - Inconnu	4 704	2 794	1 758	...	...	...	...	...	...
Uruguay[19]									
1 VII 2005 (ESDF)									
Total....................	3 305 723	1 597 040	1 708 683	3 089 988	1 474 638	1 615 350	215 735	122 402	93 333
0 - 4	247 893	126 694	121 199	232 774	118 853	113 921	15 119	7 841	7 278
5 - 9	272 408	139 170	133 238	255 496	130 416	125 080	16 912	8 754	8 158
10 - 14	270 922	138 415	132 507	254 400	129 670	124 730	16 522	8 745	7 777
15 - 19	264 527	134 712	129 815	248 930	125 969	122 961	15 597	8 743	6 854
20 - 24	247 693	124 517	123 176	232 845	115 930	116 915	14 848	8 587	6 261
25 - 29	246 531	122 064	124 467	231 372	113 438	117 934	15 159	8 626	6 533
30 - 34	226 246	111 815	114 431	211 402	103 280	108 122	14 844	8 535	6 309
35 - 39	206 577	100 793	105 784	192 227	92 586	99 641	14 350	8 207	6 143
40 - 44	211 782	103 211	108 571	197 200	94 697	102 503	14 582	8 514	6 068
45 - 49	195 836	95 216	100 620	182 199	87 180	95 019	13 637	8 036	5 601
50 - 54	180 036	86 319	93 717	166 647	78 358	88 289	13 389	7 961	5 428
55 - 59	153 706	72 774	80 932	141 484	65 401	76 083	12 222	7 373	4 849
60 - 64	142 523	66 066	76 457	131 385	59 238	72 147	11 138	6 828	4 310
65 - 69	123 418	54 768	68 650	114 117	49 154	64 963	9 301	5 614	3 687
70 - 74	118 096	49 471	68 625	110 592	45 005	65 587	7 504	4 466	3 038
75 - 79	90 752	35 877	54 875	85 749	33 028	52 721	5 003	2 849	2 154
80 - 84	60 342	21 694	38 648	57 250	20 090	37 160	3 092	1 604	1 488
85 - 89	30 434	9 519	20 915	28 826	8 767	20 059	1 608	752	856
90 - 94	12 141	3 017	9 124	11 445	2 732	8 713	696	285	411
95 + ...	3 860	928	2 932	3 648	846	2 802	212	82	130
Venezuela (Bolivarian Republic of) - Venezuela (République bolivarienne du)[18]									
1 VII 2002 (ESDF)									
Total....................	25 219 910	12 678 275	12 541 635	22 163 339	11 021 146	11 142 193	3 056 571	1 657 129	1 399 442
0 - 4	...	...	...	2 365 585	1 212 601	1 152 984	431 255	216 828	214 427
0	566 727	289 817	276 910	...	...	...	...	...	...
1 - 4	2 230 113	1 139 612	1 090 501	...	...	...	...	...	...
5 - 9	2 731 128	1 394 224	1 336 904	2 338 027	1 195 058	1 142 969	393 101	199 166	193 935
10 - 14	2 712 386	1 383 578	1 328 808	2 355 253	1 197 602	1 157 651	357 133	185 976	171 157
15 - 19	2 568 391	1 306 597	1 261 794	2 258 881	1 135 863	1 123 018	309 510	170 734	138 776
20 - 24	2 336 801	1 182 579	1 154 222	2 075 006	1 035 987	1 039 019	261 795	146 592	115 203
25 - 29	2 055 341	1 034 449	1 020 892	1 827 634	907 988	919 646	227 707	126 461	101 246
30 - 34	1 871 230	938 046	933 184	1 675 269	828 977	846 292	195 961	109 069	86 892
35 - 39	1 744 170	872 099	872 071	1 567 126	772 287	794 839	177 044	99 812	77 232

Continent, country or area, date, code and age (in years) / Continent, pays ou zone, date, code et âge (en années)	Total			Urban - Urbaine			Rural - Rurale		
	Both sexes Les deux sexes	Male Masculin	Female Féminin	Both sexes Les deux sexes	Male Masculin	Female Féminin	Both sexes Les deux sexes	Male Masculin	Female Féminin
AMERICA, SOUTH - AMÉRIQUE DU SUD									
Venezuela (Bolivarian Republic of) - Venezuela (République bolivarienne du)[18]									
1 VII 2002 (ESDF)									
40 - 44	1 506 179	751 648	754 531	1 358 018	667 128	690 890	148 161	84 520	63 641
45 - 49	1 266 420	631 252	635 168	1 141 806	559 946	581 860	124 614	71 306	53 308
50 - 54	1 044 891	520 661	524 230	935 412	457 944	477 468	109 479	62 717	46 762
55 - 59	800 903	396 302	404 601	708 958	343 000	365 958	91 945	53 302	38 643
60 - 64	590 879	287 629	303 250	516 207	244 396	271 811	74 672	43 233	31 439
65 - 69	450 395	214 998	235 397	391 277	180 798	210 479	59 118	34 200	24 918
70 - 74	344 553	160 308	184 245	299 965	135 041	164 924	44 588	25 267	19 321
75 - 79	232 921	104 448	128 473	203 220	87 769	115 451	29 701	16 679	13 022
80 +	166 482	70 028	96 454	145 695	58 761	86 934	20 787	11 267	9 520
1 VII 2005 (ESDF)									
Total	26 577 423	13 347 732	13 229 691	...	...	...	...	...	...
0 - 4	2 843 098	1 453 604	1 389 494	...	...	...	...	...	...
5 - 9	2 743 832	1 401 035	1 342 797	...	...	...	...	...	...
10 - 14	2 717 359	1 386 638	1 330 721	...	...	...	...	...	...
15 - 19	2 696 867	1 372 425	1 324 442	...	...	...	...	...	...
20 - 24	2 460 836	1 244 694	1 216 142	...	...	...	...	...	...
25 - 29	2 229 999	1 121 329	1 108 670	...	...	...	...	...	...
30 - 34	1 917 948	960 346	957 602	...	...	...	...	...	...
35 - 39	1 819 485	908 310	911 175	...	...	...	...	...	...
40 - 44	1 672 350	833 347	839 003	...	...	...	...	...	...
45 - 49	1 371 781	681 979	689 802	...	...	...	...	...	...
50 - 54	1 168 000	579 762	588 238	...	...	...	...	...	...
55 - 59	929 210	460 272	468 938	...	...	...	...	...	...
60 - 64	678 055	331 052	347 003	...	...	...	...	...	...
65 - 69	491 014	234 292	256 722	...	...	...	...	...	...
70 - 74	374 240	174 245	199 995	...	...	...	...	...	...
75 - 79	271 283	122 475	148 808	...	...	...	...	...	...
80 +	192 066	81 927	110 139	...	...	...	...	...	...
ASIA - ASIE									
Armenia - Arménie									
1 VII 2004 (ESDJ)									
Total	3 214 030	1 548 713	1 665 317	2 061 984	976 728	1 085 256	1 152 046	571 985	580 061
0	36 293	19 569	16 724	22 852	12 214	10 638	13 441	7 355	6 086
1 - 4	146 197	78 259	67 938	88 904	47 013	41 891	57 293	31 246	26 047
5 - 9	224 726	118 042	106 684	131 399	68 815	62 584	93 327	49 227	44 100
10 - 14	302 265	154 661	147 604	177 653	90 648	87 005	124 612	64 013	60 599
15 - 19	319 575	161 108	158 467	196 411	98 248	98 163	123 164	62 860	60 304
20 - 24	291 595	145 748	145 847	192 029	94 506	97 523	99 566	51 242	48 324
25 - 29	240 088	117 731	122 357	161 757	78 772	82 985	78 331	38 959	39 372
30 - 34	205 706	98 812	106 894	135 045	64 027	71 018	70 661	34 785	35 876
35 - 39	213 650	101 241	112 409	131 752	60 072	71 680	81 898	41 169	40 729
40 - 44	270 473	128 610	141 863	172 499	78 415	94 084	97 974	50 195	47 779
45 - 49	240 954	114 040	126 914	165 131	75 447	89 684	75 823	38 593	37 230
50 - 54	178 726	82 841	95 885	130 740	59 412	71 328	47 986	23 429	24 557
55 - 59	107 772	48 612	59 160	80 204	35 974	44 230	27 568	12 638	14 930
60 - 64	102 849	44 772	58 077	70 912	31 000	39 912	31 937	13 772	18 165
65 - 69	130 343	56 313	74 030	83 475	35 997	47 478	46 868	20 316	26 552
70 - 74	99 829	42 669	57 160	59 533	25 104	34 429	40 296	17 565	22 731
75 - 79	70 682	26 461	44 221	41 877	15 337	26 540	28 805	11 124	17 681
80 - 84	22 017	6 511	15 506	13 833	4 073	9 760	8 184	2 438	5 746
85 +	10 290	2 713	7 577	5 978	1 654	4 324	4 312	1 059	3 253
1 VII 2005 (ESDJ)									
Total	3 217 534	1 552 382	1 665 152	...	...	...	...	...	...
0 - 4	180 256	96 696	83 560	...	...	...	...	...	...
5 - 9	215 031	113 729	101 302	...	...	...	...	...	...
10 - 14	284 879	146 101	138 778	...	...	...	...	...	...

Continent, country or area, date, code and age (in years) / Continent, pays ou zone, date, code et âge (en années)	Total			Urban - Urbaine			Rural - Rurale		
	Both sexes Les deux sexes	Male Masculin	Female Féminin	Both sexes Les deux sexes	Male Masculin	Female Féminin	Both sexes Les deux sexes	Male Masculin	Female Féminin
ASIA - ASIE									
Armenia - Arménie									
1 VII 2005 (ESDJ)									
15 - 19	319 609	161 652	157 957	...	...	...	...	...	...
20 - 24	300 542	150 595	149 947	...	...	...	...	...	...
25 - 29	249 794	123 206	126 588	...	...	...	...	...	...
30 - 34	208 639	100 583	108 056	...	...	...	...	...	...
35 - 39	205 300	97 714	107 586	...	...	...	...	...	...
40 - 44	259 695	123 161	136 534	...	...	...	...	...	...
45 - 49	253 174	120 030	133 144	...	...	...	...	...	...
50 - 54	188 844	87 723	101 121	...	...	...	...	...	...
55 - 59	124 911	56 448	68 463	...	...	...	...	...	...
60 - 64	84 802	36 886	47 916	...	...	...	...	...	...
65 - 69	135 765	58 017	77 748	...	...	...	...	...	...
70 - 74	95 341	40 707	54 634	...	...	...	...	...	...
75 - 79	75 168	28 832	46 336	...	...	...	...	...	...
80 - 84	25 929	7 762	18 167	...	...	...	...	...	...
85 +	9 855	2 540	7 315	...	...	...	...	...	...
Azerbaijan - Azerbaïdjan									
1 VII 2004 (ESDF)									
Total	8 306 500	4 081 100	4 225 400	4 276 300	2 089 500	2 186 800	4 030 200	1 991 600	2 038 600
0	122 600	66 200	56 400	55 000	29 900	25 100	67 600	36 300	31 300
1 - 4	445 900	239 600	206 300	200 300	108 600	91 700	245 600	131 000	114 600
5 - 9	674 900	353 600	321 300	303 300	160 500	142 800	371 600	193 100	178 500
10 - 14	906 800	466 100	440 700	444 800	229 400	215 400	462 000	236 700	225 300
15 - 19	906 400	463 500	442 900	468 800	240 200	228 600	437 600	223 300	214 300
20 - 24	768 100	387 900	380 200	402 200	203 000	199 200	365 900	184 900	181 000
25 - 29	650 500	315 400	335 100	334 300	160 000	174 300	316 200	155 400	160 800
30 - 34	620 600	293 500	327 100	308 600	140 300	168 300	312 000	153 200	158 800
35 - 39	670 100	315 500	354 600	342 400	156 800	185 600	327 700	158 700	169 000
40 - 44	693 300	331 300	362 000	382 400	181 300	201 100	310 900	150 000	160 900
45 - 49	542 200	262 600	279 600	314 200	152 500	161 700	228 000	110 100	117 900
50 - 54	347 200	167 200	180 000	212 300	103 100	109 200	134 900	64 100	70 800
55 - 59	203 400	96 100	107 300	126 300	60 400	65 900	77 100	35 700	41 400
60 - 64	182 900	83 300	99 600	102 500	47 200	55 300	80 400	36 100	44 300
65 - 69	248 600	109 400	139 200	124 100	54 800	69 300	124 500	54 600	69 900
70 - 74	167 200	73 300	93 900	78 800	33 700	45 100	88 400	39 600	48 800
75 - 79	92 600	37 800	54 800	46 300	18 300	28 000	46 300	19 500	26 800
80 - 84	38 300	12 400	25 900	19 200	6 300	12 900	19 100	6 100	13 000
85 - 89	13 800	3 800	10 000	6 300	2 000	4 300	7 500	1 800	5 700
90 - 94	7 200	1 700	5 500	2 800	800	2 000	4 400	900	3 500
95 - 99	2 500	600	1 900	800	200	600	1 700	400	1 300
100 +	1 400	300	1 100	600	200	400	800	100	700
Bahrain - Bahreïn									
1 VII 2005 (ESDF)									
Total	724 645	416 755	307 890	...	...	...	...	...	...
0 - 4	62 248	30 331	31 917	...	...	...	...	...	...
5 - 9	69 639	35 260	34 379	...	...	...	...	...	...
10 - 14	65 913	33 962	31 951	...	...	...	...	...	...
15 - 19	57 117	29 494	27 623	...	...	...	...	...	...
20 - 24	65 826	36 094	29 732	...	...	...	...	...	...
25 - 29	77 959	48 157	29 802	...	...	...	...	...	...
30 - 34	81 259	50 351	30 907	...	...	...	...	...	...
35 - 39	73 502	44 889	28 613	...	...	...	...	...	...
40 - 44	62 090	39 850	22 239	...	...	...	...	...	...
45 - 49	42 435	28 118	14 317	...	...	...	...	...	...
50 - 54	23 947	15 834	8 113	...	...	...	...	...	...
55 - 59	13 745	8 011	5 734	...	...	...	...	...	...
60 - 64	10 644	5 534	5 110	...	...	...	...	...	...
65 - 69	7 168	3 532	3 636	...	...	...	...	...	...
70 - 74	5 463	2 795	2 667	...	...	...	...	...	...
75 +	5 690	2 956	2 735	...	...	...	...	...	...
Bhutan - Bhoutan									
30 V 2005 (CDFC)									
Total	634 982	333 595	301 387	196 111	105 559	90 552	438 871	228 036	210 835
0	12 314	6 096	6 218	4 108	2 050	2 058	8 206	4 046	4 160

Continent, country or area, date, code and age (in years) / Continent, pays ou zone, date, code et âge (en années)	Total			Urban - Urbaine			Rural - Rurale		
	Both sexes Les deux sexes	Male Masculin	Female Féminin	Both sexes Les deux sexes	Male Masculin	Female Féminin	Both sexes Les deux sexes	Male Masculin	Female Féminin
ASIA - ASIE									
Bhutan - Bhoutan									
30 V 2005 (CDFC)									
1 - 4	50 239	25 393	24 846	15 095	7 659	7 436	35 144	17 734	17 410
5 - 9	70 399	35 547	34 852	19 254	9 589	9 665	51 145	25 958	25 187
10 - 14	77 007	38 728	38 279	22 332	10 904	11 428	54 675	27 824	26 851
15 - 19	75 236	37 504	37 732	27 628	13 659	13 969	47 608	23 845	23 763
20 - 24	70 574	40 254	30 320	28 922	16 884	12 038	41 652	23 370	18 282
25 - 29	57 358	31 386	25 972	21 766	12 170	9 596	35 592	19 216	16 376
30 - 34	42 806	23 208	19 598	15 161	8 527	6 634	27 645	14 681	12 964
35 - 39	38 729	21 124	17 605	13 061	7 613	5 448	25 668	13 511	12 157
40 - 44	29 900	16 022	13 878	8 475	5 068	3 407	21 425	10 954	10 471
45 - 49	27 662	14 895	12 767	6 664	3 984	2 680	20 998	10 911	10 087
50 - 54	22 047	11 779	10 268	4 509	2 769	1 740	17 538	9 010	8 528
55 - 59	16 392	8 764	7 628	2 700	1 532	1 168	13 692	7 232	6 460
60 - 64	14 574	7 564	7 010	2 134	1 084	1 050	12 440	6 480	5 960
65 - 69	11 361	5 999	5 362	1 621	845	776	9 740	5 154	4 586
70 - 74	8 742	4 493	4 249	1 233	579	654	7 509	3 914	3 595
75 - 79	5 245	2 677	2 568	741	337	404	4 504	2 340	2 164
80 - 84	2 884	1 452	1 432	452	200	252	2 432	1 252	1 180
85 - 89	1 082	528	554	193	80	113	889	448	441
90 - 94	297	121	176	40	19	21	257	102	155
95 - 99	104	48	56	18	6	12	86	42	44
100 +	30	13	17	4	1	3	26	12	14
Brunei Darussalam - Brunéi Darussalam									
21 VIII 2001 (CDFC)									
Total	332 844	168 974	163 870	238 699	120 046	118 653	94 145	48 928	45 217
0 - 14	100 912	52 304	48 608	72 076	37 396	34 680	28 836	14 908	13 928
15 - 19	27 963	14 014	13 949	20 019	10 085	9 934	7 944	3 929	4 015
20 - 24	32 604	15 390	17 214	23 592	10 885	12 707	9 012	4 505	4 507
25 - 29	35 773	17 884	17 889	25 856	12 573	13 283	9 917	5 311	4 606
30 - 34	34 375	16 878	17 497	24 973	11 931	13 042	9 402	4 947	4 455
35 - 39	28 764	14 581	14 183	21 112	10 461	10 651	7 652	4 120	3 532
40 - 44	24 198	12 984	11 214	17 808	9 544	8 264	6 390	3 440	2 950
45 - 49	17 149	9 150	7 999	12 402	6 637	5 765	4 747	2 513	2 234
50 - 54	10 687	5 542	5 145	7 609	4 013	3 596	3 078	1 529	1 549
55 - 59	6 140	3 249	2 891	4 153	2 197	1 956	1 987	1 052	935
60 - 64	4 962	2 432	2 530	3 217	1 544	1 673	1 745	888	857
65 - 69	3 757	1 768	1 989	2 366	1 102	1 264	1 391	666	725
70 - 74	2 441	1 263	1 178	1 530	758	772	911	505	406
75 - 79	1 582	793	789	1 027	492	535	555	301	254
80 - 84	844	423	421	548	264	284	296	159	137
85 - 89	397	188	209	252	98	154	145	90	55
90 - 94	197	86	111	111	47	64	86	39	47
95 - 99	66	33	33	33	14	19	33	19	14
100 +	33	12	21	15	5	10	18	7	11
1 VII 2004 (ESDF)									
Total	*357 800*	*186 200*	*171 600*	...	...	...	...	...	...
0	*7 200*	*3 700*	*3 500*	...	...	...	...	...	...
1 - 4	*45 500*	*23 800*	*21 700*	...	...	...	...	...	...
5 - 9	*34 800*	*18 100*	*16 700*	...	...	...	...	...	...
10 - 14	*32 300*	*16 900*	*15 400*	...	...	...	...	...	...
15 - 19	*28 500*	*14 500*	*14 000*	...	...	...	...	...	...
20 - 24	*33 500*	*16 300*	*17 200*	...	...	...	...	...	...
25 - 29	*37 300*	*19 400*	*17 900*	...	...	...	...	...	...
30 - 34	*35 800*	*18 400*	*17 400*	...	...	...	...	...	...
35 - 39	*29 800*	*15 700*	*14 100*	...	...	...	...	...	...
40 - 44	*25 300*	*14 100*	*11 200*	...	...	...	...	...	...
45 - 49	*17 700*	*9 700*	*8 000*	...	...	...	...	...	...
50 - 54	*10 900*	*5 800*	*5 100*	...	...	...	...	...	...
55 - 59	*6 200*	*3 300*	*2 900*	...	...	...	...	...	...
60 - 64	*5 000*	*2 500*	*2 500*	...	...	...	...	...	...
65 - 69	*3 600*	*1 700*	*1 900*	...	...	...	...	...	...
70 - 74	*2 300*	*1 200*	*1 100*	...	...	...	...	...	...
75 - 79	*1 200*	*600*	*600*	...	...	...	...	...	...

Continent, country or area, date, code and age (in years) / Continent, pays ou zone, date, code et âge (en années)	Total			Urban - Urbaine			Rural - Rurale		
	Both sexes Les deux sexes	Male Masculin	Female Féminin	Both sexes Les deux sexes	Male Masculin	Female Féminin	Both sexes Les deux sexes	Male Masculin	Female Féminin
ASIA - ASIE									
Brunei Darussalam - Brunéi Darussalam									
1 VII 2004 (ESDF)									
80 - 84	700	400	300	...	...	...	...	...	...
85 +	200	100	100	...	...	...	...	...	...
Cambodia - Cambodge									
3 III 1998 (CDFC)									
Total	11 437 656	5 511 408	5 926 248	1 795 575	878 186	917 389	9 642 081	4 633 222	5 008 859
0	231 609	118 075	113 534	32 869	16 851	16 018	198 740	101 224	97 516
1 - 4	1 235 183	629 217	605 966	160 680	82 377	78 303	1 074 503	546 840	527 663
5 - 9	1 772 820	903 976	868 844	239 934	122 652	117 282	1 532 886	781 324	751 562
10 - 14	1 658 196	851 139	807 057	246 998	126 217	120 781	1 411 198	724 922	686 276
15 - 19	1 344 258	664 184	680 074	233 677	113 229	120 448	1 110 581	550 955	559 626
20 - 24	745 687	354 100	391 587	128 884	63 561	65 323	616 803	290 539	326 264
25 - 29	888 540	426 968	461 572	157 736	79 241	78 495	730 804	347 727	383 077
30 - 34	782 682	370 090	412 592	137 139	69 093	68 046	645 543	300 997	344 546
35 - 39	695 868	325 331	370 537	123 310	61 255	62 055	572 558	264 076	308 482
40 - 44	497 067	199 722	297 345	92 433	40 499	51 934	404 634	159 223	245 411
45 - 49	415 931	175 052	240 879	72 681	32 868	39 813	343 250	142 184	201 066
50 - 54	312 463	132 413	180 050	50 505	22 227	28 278	261 958	110 186	151 772
55 - 59	256 930	110 189	146 741	37 186	16 284	20 902	219 744	93 905	125 839
60 - 64	204 994	86 602	118 392	28 433	11 627	16 806	176 561	74 975	101 586
65 - 69	166 928	70 660	96 268	21 891	8 614	13 277	145 037	62 046	82 991
70 - 74	112 213	46 769	65 444	14 851	5 535	9 316	97 362	41 234	56 128
75 - 79	67 528	27 838	39 690	9 135	3 337	5 798	58 393	24 501	33 892
80 - 84	30 652	12 159	18 493	4 288	1 515	2 773	26 364	10 644	15 720
85 - 89	13 368	5 029	8 339	1 874	592	1 282	11 494	4 437	7 057
90 - 94	2 867	1 026	1 841	453	157	296	2 414	869	1 545
95 +	1 872	869	1 003	618	455	163	1 254	414	840
1 VII 2004 (SSDF)[22]									
Total	12 824 170	6 197 128	6 627 042	...	...	...	...	...	...
0	314 512	165 946	148 566	...	...	...	...	...	...
1 - 4	1 105 489	567 442	538 047	...	...	...	...	...	...
5 - 9	1 638 623	847 582	791 040	...	...	...	...	...	...
10 - 14	1 892 316	967 807	924 509	...	...	...	...	...	...
15 - 19	1 499 278	761 411	737 867	...	...	...	...	...	...
20 - 24	1 305 670	633 237	672 433	...	...	...	...	...	...
25 - 29	717 482	345 923	371 559	...	...	...	...	...	...
30 - 34	814 752	388 580	426 172	...	...	...	...	...	...
35 - 39	797 807	372 679	425 128	...	...	...	...	...	...
40 - 44	687 814	305 922	381 893	...	...	...	...	...	...
45 - 49	529 666	213 901	315 765	...	...	...	...	...	...
50 - 54	429 213	174 662	254 552	...	...	...	...	...	...
55 - 59	331 469	140 436	191 033	...	...	...	...	...	...
60 - 64	258 291	109 132	149 159	...	...	...	...	...	...
65 - 69	200 689	84 610	116 079	...	...	...	...	...	...
70 - 74	143 581	54 578	89 003	...	...	...	...	...	...
75 - 79	89 402	35 620	53 782	...	...	...	...	...	...
80 - 84	44 885	19 066	25 820	...	...	...	...	...	...
85 - 89	16 012	5 401	10 612	...	...	...	...	...	...
90 - 94	5 144	2 135	3 009	...	...	...	...	...	...
95 +	2 075	1 058	1 017	...	...	...	...	...	...
China - Chine[23]									
1 XI 2000 (CDJC)									
Total	1242612226	640 275 969	602 336 257	458 770 983	235 264 707	223 506 276	783 841 243	405 011 262	378 829 981
0	13 793 799	7 460 206	6 333 593	4 449 020	2 376 585	2 072 435	9 344 779	5 083 621	4 261 158
1 - 4	55 184 575	30 188 488	24 996 087	17 669 697	9 525 854	8 143 843	37 514 878	20 662 634	16 852 244
5 - 9	90 152 587	48 303 208	41 849 379	26 588 363	14 180 433	12 407 930	63 564 224	34 122 775	29 441 449
10 - 14	125 396 633	65 344 739	60 051 894	35 802 884	18 701 307	17 101 577	89 593 749	46 643 432	42 950 317
15 - 19	103 031 165	52 878 170	50 152 995	42 231 585	21 086 911	21 144 674	60 799 580	31 791 259	29 008 321
20 - 24	94 573 174	47 937 766	46 635 408	41 021 887	20 651 361	20 370 526	53 551 287	27 286 405	26 264 882
25 - 29	117 602 265	60 230 758	57 371 507	48 788 516	24 820 721	23 967 795	68 813 749	35 410 037	33 403 712
30 - 34	127 314 298	65 360 456	61 953 842	49 723 640	25 760 568	23 963 072	77 590 658	39 599 888	37 990 770
35 - 39	109 147 295	56 141 391	53 005 904	44 518 164	23 269 889	21 248 275	64 629 131	32 871 502	31 757 629
40 - 44	81 242 945	42 243 187	38 999 758	33 518 610	17 499 183	16 019 427	47 724 335	24 744 004	22 980 331

Continent, country or area, date, code and age (in years) / Continent, pays ou zone, date, code et âge (en années)	Total			Urban - Urbaine			Rural - Rurale		
	Both sexes Les deux sexes	Male Masculin	Female Féminin	Both sexes Les deux sexes	Male Masculin	Female Féminin	Both sexes Les deux sexes	Male Masculin	Female Féminin
ASIA - ASIE									
China - Chine[23]									
1 XI 2000 (CDJC)									
45 - 49	85 521 045	43 939 603	41 581 442	31 708 706	16 245 324	15 463 382	53 812 339	27 694 279	26 118 060
50 - 54	63 304 200	32 804 125	30 500 075	22 335 748	11 462 314	10 873 434	40 968 452	21 341 811	19 626 641
55 - 59	46 370 375	24 061 506	22 308 869	16 004 389	8 077 159	7 927 230	30 365 986	15 984 347	14 381 639
60 - 64	41 703 848	21 674 478	20 029 370	14 944 552	7 519 377	7 425 175	26 759 296	14 155 101	12 604 195
65 - 69	34 780 460	17 549 348	17 231 112	12 174 470	6 128 605	6 045 865	22 605 990	11 420 743	11 185 247
70 - 74	25 574 149	12 436 154	13 137 995	8 479 487	4 216 193	4 263 294	17 094 662	8 219 961	8 874 701
75 - 79	15 928 330	7 175 811	8 752 519	5 000 134	2 291 543	2 708 591	10 928 196	4 884 268	6 043 928
80 - 84	7 989 158	3 203 868	4 785 290	2 472 016	1 004 359	1 467 657	5 517 142	2 199 509	3 317 633
85 - 89	3 030 698	1 056 941	1 973 757	994 079	347 550	646 529	2 036 619	709 391	1 327 228
90 - 94	783 594	229 758	553 836	276 586	80 189	196 397	507 008	149 569	357 439
95 - 99	169 756	51 373	118 383	62 255	17 827	44 428	107 501	33 546	73 955
100 +	17 877	4 635	13 242	6 195	1 455	4 740	11 682	3 180	8 502
China: Hong Kong SAR - Chine: Hong Kong RAS									
1 VII 2005 (ESDJ)									
Total	6 813 200	3 264 000	3 549 200	...	...	...	...	...	...
0	39 400	20 400	19 000	...	...	...	...	...	...
1 - 4	181 700	94 000	87 700	...	...	...	...	...	...
5 - 9	332 800	171 300	161 500	...	...	...	...	...	...
10 - 14	415 000	213 100	201 900	...	...	...	...	...	...
15 - 19	434 200	220 200	214 000	...	...	...	...	...	...
20 - 24	470 900	226 400	244 500	...	...	...	...	...	...
25 - 29	486 700	220 500	266 200	...	...	...	...	...	...
30 - 34	556 400	241 800	314 600	...	...	...	...	...	...
35 - 39	590 900	256 600	334 300	...	...	...	...	...	...
40 - 44	689 200	318 400	370 800	...	...	...	...	...	...
45 - 49	648 200	319 500	328 700	...	...	...	...	...	...
50 - 54	509 900	253 900	256 000	...	...	...	...	...	...
55 - 59	388 100	198 000	190 100	...	...	...	...	...	...
60 - 64	235 100	125 200	109 900	...	...	...	...	...	...
65 - 69	246 200	126 300	119 900	...	...	...	...	...	...
70 - 74	228 300	112 700	115 600	...	...	...	...	...	...
75 - 79	169 800	77 400	92 400	...	...	...	...	...	...
80 - 84	107 700	42 600	65 100	...	...	...	...	...	...
85 +	82 700	25 700	57 000	...	...	...	...	...	...
China: Macao SAR - Chine: Macao RAS[10]									
1 VII 2005 (ESDJ)									
Total	473 457	227 600	245 857	...	...	...	...	...	...
0 - 4	16 380	8 539	7 841	...	...	...	...	...	...
5 - 9	25 805	13 485	12 320	...	...	...	...	...	...
10 - 14	37 019	19 034	17 985	...	...	...	...	...	...
15 - 19	46 450	23 490	22 960	...	...	...	...	...	...
20 - 24	37 997	17 913	20 084	...	...	...	...	...	...
25 - 29	31 675	14 375	17 300	...	...	...	...	...	...
30 - 34	37 185	16 079	21 106	...	...	...	...	...	...
35 - 39	38 958	16 200	22 758	...	...	...	...	...	...
40 - 44	48 880	22 211	26 669	...	...	...	...	...	...
45 - 49	47 744	24 117	23 627	...	...	...	...	...	...
50 - 54	34 812	18 241	16 571	...	...	...	...	...	...
55 - 59	23 305	12 586	10 719	...	...	...	...	...	...
60 - 64	12 413	6 406	6 007	...	...	...	...	...	...
65 - 69	9 662	4 894	4 768	...	...	...	...	...	...
70 - 74	9 207	3 940	5 267	...	...	...	...	...	...
75 +	15 965	6 090	9 875	...	...	...	...	...	...
Cyprus - Chypre[24]									
1 X 2001 (CDJC)									
Total	689 565	338 497	351 068	474 450	231 128	243 322	215 115	107 369	107 746
0	8 024	4 068	3 956	5 443	2 765	2 678	2 581	1 303	1 278
1 - 4	34 558	17 625	16 933	23 296	11 821	11 475	11 262	5 804	5 458
5 - 9	51 718	26 502	25 216	34 111	17 402	16 709	17 607	9 100	8 507
10 - 14	53 178	27 396	25 782	35 772	18 332	17 440	17 406	9 064	8 342
15 - 19	54 603	28 132	26 471	36 725	18 872	17 853	17 878	9 260	8 618

Continent, country or area, date, code and age (in years) / Continent, pays ou zone, date, code et âge (en annèes)	Total			Urban - Urbaine			Rural - Rurale		
	Both sexes Les deux sexes	Male Masculin	Female Féminin	Both sexes Les deux sexes	Male Masculin	Female Féminin	Both sexes Les deux sexes	Male Masculin	Female Féminin
ASIA - ASIE									
Cyprus - Chypre[24]									
1 X 2001 (CDJC)									
20 - 24	51 803	26 208	25 595	36 231	18 178	18 053	15 572	8 030	7 542
25 - 29	48 272	23 096	25 176	35 248	16 654	18 594	13 024	6 442	6 582
30 - 34	48 233	22 682	25 551	34 899	16 196	18 703	13 334	6 486	6 848
35 - 39	51 561	24 813	26 748	36 645	17 304	19 341	14 916	7 509	7 407
40 - 44	52 289	25 602	26 687	37 070	17 786	19 284	15 219	7 816	7 403
45 - 49	45 580	22 705	22 875	32 005	15 647	16 358	13 575	7 058	6 517
50 - 54	42 587	21 027	21 560	30 186	14 803	15 383	12 401	6 224	6 177
55 - 59	34 554	16 930	17 624	24 216	11 883	12 333	10 338	5 047	5 291
60 - 64	30 747	14 968	15 779	20 763	10 239	10 524	9 984	4 729	5 255
65 - 69	25 445	11 905	13 540	16 669	7 943	8 726	8 776	3 962	4 814
70 - 74	20 965	9 375	11 590	13 157	5 885	7 272	7 808	3 490	4 318
75 - 79	15 974	7 073	8 901	9 899	4 338	5 561	6 075	2 735	3 340
80 - 84	9 802	4 232	5 570	6 010	2 522	3 488	3 792	1 710	2 082
85 - 89	5 861	2 423	3 438	3 523	1 368	2 155	2 338	1 055	1 283
90 - 94	1 975	825	1 150	1 269	532	737	706	293	413
95 - 99	411	148	263	252	89	163	159	59	100
100 +	40	14	26	25	8	17	15	6	9
Unknown - Inconnu	1 385	748	637	1 036	561	475	349	187	162
1 VII 2005 (ESDJ)									
Total	757 795	373 517	384 278	...	...	...	...	...	...
0	8 250	4 226	4 024	...	...	...	...	...	...
1 - 4	32 712	16 832	15 880	...	...	...	...	...	...
5 - 9	46 701	23 872	22 829	...	...	...	...	...	...
10 - 14	54 826	28 140	26 686	...	...	...	...	...	...
15 - 19	56 762	28 953	27 809	...	...	...	...	...	...
20 - 24	63 295	32 220	31 075	...	...	...	...	...	...
25 - 29	59 272	29 940	29 332	...	...	...	...	...	...
30 - 34	55 740	27 397	28 343	...	...	...	...	...	...
35 - 39	53 997	25 977	28 020	...	...	...	...	...	...
40 - 44	56 627	27 737	28 891	...	...	...	...	...	...
45 - 49	53 980	26 487	27 493	...	...	...	...	...	...
50 - 54	47 585	23 467	24 119	...	...	...	...	...	...
55 - 59	42 527	20 685	21 843	...	...	...	...	...	...
60 - 64	34 653	16 758	17 895	...	...	...	...	...	...
65 - 69	29 839	14 306	15 533	...	...	...	...	...	...
70 - 74	23 418	10 686	12 733	...	...	...	...	...	...
75 - 79	17 806	7 725	10 081	...	...	...	...	...	...
80 - 84	11 417	4 824	6 593	...	...	...	...	...	...
85 - 89	5 416	2 206	3 211	...	...	...	...	...	...
90 - 94	2 497	912	1 585	...	...	...	...	...	...
95 - 99	402	153	249	...	...	...	...	...	...
100 +	79	20	59	...	...	...	...	...	...
Georgia - Géorgie									
1 VII 2000 (ESDF)[11]									
Total	4 945 553	2 364 247	2 581 306	2 860 786	1 348 715	1 512 071	2 084 767	1 015 532	1 069 235
0	42 247	22 938	19 309	26 206	14 152	12 054	16 041	8 786	7 255
1 - 4	197 055	104 267	92 788	119 229	63 120	56 109	77 826	41 147	36 679
5 - 9	361 619	185 741	175 878	208 452	107 038	101 414	153 167	78 703	74 464
10 - 14	409 671	209 366	200 305	229 154	116 874	112 280	180 517	92 492	88 025
15 - 19	388 789	198 066	190 723	222 064	113 224	108 840	166 725	84 842	81 883
20 - 24	376 407	191 927	184 480	213 454	108 613	104 841	162 953	83 314	79 639
25 - 29	350 129	181 759	168 370	213 415	110 488	102 927	136 714	71 271	65 443
30 - 34	363 659	175 712	187 947	214 156	100 573	113 583	149 503	75 139	74 364
35 - 39	403 179	191 543	211 636	241 215	109 394	131 821	161 964	82 149	79 815
40 - 44	353 366	168 218	185 148	216 428	98 958	117 470	136 938	69 260	67 678
45 - 49	305 841	143 921	161 920	193 528	88 504	105 024	112 313	55 417	56 896
50 - 54	216 111	100 444	115 667	137 119	62 640	74 479	78 992	37 804	41 188
55 - 59	225 223	99 437	125 786	130 629	56 530	74 099	94 594	42 907	51 687
60 - 64	280 405	126 438	153 967	155 346	68 463	86 883	125 059	57 975	67 084
65 - 69	242 085	102 877	139 208	123 373	51 091	72 282	118 712	51 786	66 926
70 - 74	218 503	85 840	132 663	111 805	41 553	70 252	106 698	44 287	62 411
75 - 79	113 417	34 835	78 582	56 587	16 900	39 687	56 830	17 935	38 895
80 - 84	59 039	24 600	34 439	29 156	12 606	16 550	29 883	11 994	17 889

7. Population by age, sex and urban/rural residence: latest available year, 1996 - 2005
Population selon l'âge, le sexe et la résidence, urbaine/rurale: dernière année disponible, 1996 - 2005 (continued - suite)

Continent, country or area, date, code and age (in years) / Continent, pays ou zone, date, code et âge (en années)	Total			Urban - Urbaine			Rural - Rurale		
	Both sexes Les deux sexes	Male Masculin	Female Féminin	Both sexes Les deux sexes	Male Masculin	Female Féminin	Both sexes Les deux sexes	Male Masculin	Female Féminin
ASIA - ASIE									
Georgia - Géorgie									
1 VII 2000 (ESDF)[11]									
85 - 89	27 302	11 583	15 719	13 332	5 601	7 731	13 970	5 982	7 988
90 - 94	8 410	3 605	4 805	4 432	1 819	2 613	3 978	1 786	2 192
95 - 99	2 730	1 020	1 710	1 510	527	983	1 220	493	727
100 +	366	110	256	196	47	149	170	63	107
1 VII 2005 (ESDF)									
Total	4 361 400	2 067 200	2 294 200	...	...	...	...	...	...
0 - 4	235 850	122 650	113 200	...	...	...	...	...	...
5 - 9	248 700	127 150	121 550	...	...	...	...	...	...
10 - 14	304 600	155 450	149 150	...	...	...	...	...	...
15 - 19	342 150	174 150	168 000	...	...	...	...	...	...
20 - 24	351 950	177 000	174 950	...	...	...	...	...	...
25 - 29	364 250	179 900	184 350	...	...	...	...	...	...
30 - 34	311 950	152 050	159 900	...	...	...	...	...	...
35 - 39	288 450	139 000	149 450	...	...	...	...	...	...
40 - 44	330 350	157 150	173 200	...	...	...	...	...	...
45 - 49	327 000	154 700	172 300	...	...	...	...	...	...
50 - 54	303 350	140 650	162 700	...	...	...	...	...	...
55 - 59	182 600	81 500	101 100	...	...	...	...	...	...
60 - 64	188 750	82 450	106 300	...	...	...	...	...	...
65 - 69	185 650	79 900	105 750	...	...	...	...	...	...
70 - 74	179 450	72 050	107 400	...	...	...	...	...	...
75 - 79	124 200	45 250	78 950	...	...	...	...	...	...
80 - 84	60 750	19 050	41 700	...	...	...	...	...	...
85 +	31 400	7 150	24 250	...	...	...	...	...	...
India - Inde[25]									
1 III 2001 (CDFC)									
Total	1028610328	532 156 772	496 453 556	286 119 689	150 554 098	135 565 591	742 490 639	381 602 674	360 887 965
0 - 4	110 447 164	57 119 612	53 327 552	25 338 754	13 262 414	12 076 340	85 108 410	43 857 198	41 251 212
5 - 9	128 316 790	66 734 833	61 581 957	29 860 545	15 640 135	14 220 410	98 456 245	51 094 698	47 361 547
10 - 14	124 846 858	65 632 877	59 213 981	32 464 536	17 030 132	15 434 404	92 382 322	48 602 745	43 779 577
15 - 19	100 215 890	53 939 991	46 275 899	30 154 067	16 191 573	13 962 494	70 061 823	37 748 418	32 313 405
20 - 24	89 764 132	46 321 150	43 442 982	28 365 228	15 193 668	13 171 560	61 398 904	31 127 482	30 271 422
25 - 29	83 422 393	41 557 546	41 864 847	25 737 253	13 180 373	12 556 880	57 685 140	28 377 173	29 307 967
30 - 34	74 274 044	37 361 916	36 912 128	22 445 165	11 673 137	10 772 028	51 828 879	25 688 779	26 140 100
35 - 39	70 574 085	36 038 727	34 535 358	21 615 541	11 157 103	10 458 438	48 958 544	24 881 624	24 076 920
40 - 44	55 738 297	29 878 715	25 859 582	17 173 126	9 458 276	7 714 850	38 565 171	20 420 439	18 144 732
45 - 49	47 408 976	24 867 886	22 541 090	14 453 974	7 844 213	6 609 761	32 955 002	17 023 673	15 931 329
50 - 54	36 587 559	19 851 608	16 735 951	10 809 961	6 038 917	4 771 044	25 777 598	13 812 691	11 964 907
55 - 59	27 653 347	13 583 022	14 070 325	7 682 278	4 010 268	3 672 010	19 971 069	9 572 754	10 398 315
60 - 64	27 516 779	13 586 347	13 930 432	6 864 810	3 439 621	3 425 189	20 651 969	10 146 726	10 505 243
65 - 69	19 806 955	9 472 103	10 334 852	4 990 199	2 401 397	2 588 802	14 816 756	7 070 706	7 746 050
70 - 74	14 708 644	7 527 688	7 180 956	3 579 168	1 780 696	1 798 472	11 129 476	5 746 992	5 382 484
75 - 79	6 551 225	3 263 209	3 288 016	1 721 085	851 088	869 997	4 830 140	2 412 121	2 418 019
80 +	8 038 718	3 918 980	4 119 738	2 022 345	935 920	1 086 425	6 016 373	2 983 060	3 033 313
Unknown - Inconnu	2 738 472	1 500 562	1 237 910	841 654	465 167	376 487	1 896 818	1 035 395	861 423
Indonesia - Indonésie									
30 VI 2000 (CDJC)[26]									
Total	201 241 999	100 934 962	100 307 037	85 380 627	42 759 571	42 621 056	115 861 372	58 175 391	57 685 981
0	3 492 259	1 799 525	1 692 734	1 529 180	790 207	738 973	1 963 079	1 009 318	953 761
1 - 4	16 810 117	8 496 176	8 313 941	6 642 545	3 361 599	3 280 946	10 167 572	5 134 577	5 032 995
5 - 9	20 494 091	10 433 865	10 060 226	7 962 806	4 034 352	3 928 454	12 531 285	6 399 513	6 131 772
10 - 14	20 453 732	10 460 908	9 992 824	7 951 997	4 017 276	3 934 721	12 501 735	6 443 632	6 058 103
15 - 19	21 149 517	10 649 348	10 500 169	9 501 797	4 656 022	4 845 775	11 647 720	5 993 326	5 654 394
20 - 24	19 258 101	9 237 464	10 020 637	9 394 813	4 528 914	4 865 899	9 863 288	4 708 550	5 154 738
25 - 29	18 640 937	9 130 504	9 510 433	8 720 487	4 321 110	4 399 377	9 920 450	4 809 394	5 111 056
30 - 34	16 399 720	8 204 302	8 195 418	7 499 021	3 795 282	3 703 739	8 900 699	4 409 020	4 491 679
35 - 39	14 904 226	7 432 840	7 471 386	6 430 999	3 230 371	3 200 628	8 473 227	4 202 469	4 270 758
40 - 44	12 467 848	6 433 438	6 034 410	5 322 075	2 767 298	2 554 777	7 145 773	3 666 140	3 479 633
45 - 49	9 656 005	5 087 252	4 568 753	4 015 532	2 137 790	1 877 742	5 640 473	2 949 462	2 691 011
50 - 54	7 384 968	3 791 185	3 593 783	2 905 386	1 500 733	1 404 653	4 479 582	2 290 452	2 189 130
55 - 59	5 678 664	2 883 226	2 795 438	2 235 074	1 145 432	1 089 642	3 443 590	1 737 794	1 705 796
60 - 64	5 321 019	2 597 076	2 723 943	1 951 238	949 193	1 002 045	3 369 781	1 647 883	1 721 898
65 - 69	3 564 926	1 666 191	1 898 735	1 310 805	600 348	710 457	2 254 121	1 065 843	1 188 278

196

Continent, country or area, date, code and age (in years) / Continent, pays ou zone, date, code et âge (en années)	Total			Urban - Urbaine			Rural - Rurale		
	Both sexes Les deux sexes	Male Masculin	Female Féminin	Both sexes Les deux sexes	Male Masculin	Female Féminin	Both sexes Les deux sexes	Male Masculin	Female Féminin
ASIA - ASIE									
Indonesia - Indonésie									
30 VI 2000 (CDJC)[26]									
70 - 74	2 837 037	1 368 190	1 468 847	1 016 304	479 243	537 061	1 820 733	888 947	931 786
75 +	2 716 985	1 257 526	1 459 459	986 136	442 204	543 932	1 730 849	815 322	915 527
Unknown - Inconnu	11 847	5 946	5 901	4 432	2 197	2 235	7 415	3 749	3 666
1 VII 2003 (ESDJ)									
Total	214 251 300	107 335 600	106 915 700	...	...	...	...	...	...
0	4 095 640	2 086 219	2 009 421	...	...	...	...	...	...
1 - 4	16 178 560	8 235 381	7 943 179	...	...	...	...	...	...
5 - 9	20 752 800	10 551 900	10 200 900	...	...	...	...	...	...
10 - 14	21 637 800	11 006 300	10 631 500	...	...	...	...	...	...
15 - 19	21 206 000	10 727 000	10 479 000	...	...	...	...	...	...
20 - 24	20 729 800	10 253 900	10 475 900	...	...	...	...	...	...
25 - 29	19 575 400	9 504 700	10 070 700	...	...	...	...	...	...
30 - 34	18 047 200	8 863 100	9 184 100	...	...	...	...	...	...
35 - 39	16 098 400	8 053 700	8 044 700	...	...	...	...	...	...
40 - 44	13 974 000	7 067 000	6 907 000	...	...	...	...	...	...
45 - 49	11 369 600	5 886 800	5 482 800	...	...	...	...	...	...
50 - 54	8 637 400	4 505 700	4 131 700	...	...	...	...	...	...
55 - 59	6 552 000	3 335 000	3 217 000	...	...	...	...	...	...
60 - 64	5 209 400	2 565 200	2 644 200	...	...	...	...	...	...
65 - 69	4 168 100	1 975 600	2 192 500	...	...	...	...	...	...
70 - 74	2 770 200	1 275 100	1 495 100	...	...	...	...	...	...
75 +	3 249 000	1 443 000	1 806 000	...	...	...	...	...	...
Iran (Islamic Republic of) - Iran (République islamique d')[27]									
1 VII 2005 (ESDJ)									
Total	68 467 369	34 801 582	33 665 787	45 650 230	23 316 275	22 333 955	22 817 140	11 485 308	11 331 832
0	1 184 820	597 647	587 173	727 317	356 467	370 850	457 503	241 180	216 323
1 - 4	4 876 120	2 509 011	2 367 108	3 003 588	1 545 528	1 458 060	1 872 532	963 483	909 049
5 - 9	7 179 426	3 688 505	3 490 921	4 408 829	2 263 160	2 145 669	2 770 597	1 425 345	1 345 251
10 - 14	7 039 567	3 685 380	3 354 187	4 412 828	2 308 219	2 104 609	2 626 739	1 377 162	1 249 578
15 - 19	8 699 798	4 498 984	4 200 814	5 704 368	2 918 032	2 786 336	2 995 431	1 580 952	1 414 478
20 - 24	7 495 211	3 740 990	3 754 221	5 128 370	2 618 524	2 509 846	2 366 842	1 122 466	1 244 375
25 - 29	5 698 538	2 831 638	2 866 900	3 900 751	1 956 914	1 943 837	1 797 788	874 724	923 064
30 - 34	4 780 634	2 393 631	2 387 003	3 295 280	1 657 622	1 637 658	1 485 354	736 009	749 345
35 - 39	4 561 614	2 238 113	2 323 501	3 308 678	1 626 511	1 682 167	1 252 936	611 602	641 334
40 - 44	3 999 313	2 044 606	1 954 707	2 878 480	1 489 784	1 388 696	1 120 833	554 822	566 011
45 - 49	3 489 945	1 778 347	1 711 599	2 546 710	1 305 974	1 240 737	943 235	472 373	470 862
50 - 54	2 834 437	1 414 749	1 419 687	1 986 046	1 023 448	962 598	848 391	391 302	457 089
55 - 59	1 986 428	987 604	998 824	1 384 972	715 765	669 208	601 455	271 839	329 617
60 - 64	1 514 901	773 864	741 037	1 030 604	545 936	484 667	484 298	227 928	256 370
65 - 69	1 099 452	565 387	534 065	692 892	353 353	339 540	406 560	212 034	194 526
70 - 74	982 703	497 599	485 104	600 899	302 576	298 323	381 804	195 023	186 781
75 - 79	584 895	311 253	273 642	365 857	186 541	179 316	219 038	124 712	94 326
80 - 84	342 227	189 024	153 203	201 765	106 905	94 860	140 462	82 119	58 343
85 - 89	73 001	35 896	37 105	46 182	25 040	21 142	26 819	10 855	15 964
90 - 94	24 408	10 967	13 440	14 851	6 065	8 786	9 557	4 902	4 655
95 +	19 932	8 388	11 544	10 964	3 912	7 052	8 968	4 476	4 493
Iraq									
1 VII 2005 (ESDF)									
Total	27 962 968	14 055 166	13 907 802	18 712 777	9 432 869	9 279 908	9 250 191	4 622 297	4 627 894
0 - 4	4 698 930	2 406 976	2 291 954	2 942 197	1 507 115	1 435 082	1 756 733	899 861	856 872
5 - 9	3 971 295	2 033 920	1 937 375	2 522 443	1 291 534	1 230 909	1 448 852	742 386	706 466
10 - 14	3 425 445	1 739 250	1 686 195	2 211 941	1 121 972	1 089 969	1 213 504	617 278	596 226
15 - 19	3 027 695	1 538 875	1 488 820	1 995 479	1 014 481	980 998	1 032 216	524 394	507 822
20 - 24	2 592 603	1 315 057	1 277 546	1 745 198	886 542	858 656	847 405	428 515	418 890
25 - 29	2 207 198	1 113 028	1 094 170	1 513 054	765 525	747 529	694 144	347 503	346 641
30 - 34	1 853 590	927 489	926 101	1 294 727	651 676	643 051	558 863	275 813	283 050
35 - 39	1 512 543	747 725	764 818	1 076 551	537 433	539 118	435 992	210 292	225 700
40 - 44	1 198 580	582 436	616 144	870 729	429 636	441 093	327 851	152 800	175 051
45 - 49	954 109	460 057	494 052	700 073	343 916	356 157	254 036	116 141	137 895
50 - 54	739 296	354 291	385 005	545 922	267 270	278 652	193 374	87 021	106 353
55 - 59	571 222	273 940	297 282	422 322	206 741	215 581	148 900	67 199	81 701

Continent, country or area, date, code and age (in years) / Continent, pays ou zone, date, code et âge (en années)	Total			Urban - Urbaine			Rural - Rurale		
	Both sexes Les deux sexes	Male Masculin	Female Féminin	Both sexes Les deux sexes	Male Masculin	Female Féminin	Both sexes Les deux sexes	Male Masculin	Female Féminin
ASIA - ASIE									
Iraq									
1 VII 2005 (ESDF)									
60 - 64	426 096	205 138	220 958	313 760	153 712	160 048	112 336	51 426	60 910
65 - 69	305 328	144 204	161 124	224 230	107 428	116 802	81 098	36 776	44 322
70 - 74	203 355	92 951	110 404	148 090	68 269	79 821	55 265	24 682	30 583
75 - 79	127 857	56 090	71 767	90 354	39 584	50 770	37 503	16 506	20 997
80 +	147 826	63 739	84 087	95 707	40 035	55 672	52 119	23 704	28 415
Israel - Israël[28]									
1 VII 2005 (ESDJ)									
Total	6 930 128	3 423 132	3 506 996	6 359 940	3 131 229	3 228 711	570 188	291 904	278 285
0	143 483	73 731	69 753	130 589	67 096	63 493	12 894	6 635	6 260
1 - 4	565 787	290 059	275 728	514 510	263 889	250 621	51 278	26 171	25 107
5 - 9	656 116	336 733	319 383	595 720	305 652	290 068	60 396	31 081	29 315
10 - 14	598 722	306 859	291 863	541 687	277 234	264 453	57 035	29 626	27 410
15 - 19	572 629	292 910	279 720	516 243	262 876	253 367	56 387	30 034	26 353
20 - 24	557 116	283 369	273 747	511 343	259 090	252 253	45 774	24 280	21 494
25 - 29	545 734	274 478	271 256	504 223	252 982	251 241	41 511	21 496	20 015
30 - 34	506 930	254 994	251 936	469 054	235 866	233 188	37 876	19 129	18 748
35 - 39	421 898	209 686	212 212	385 812	191 650	194 163	36 086	18 037	18 049
40 - 44	386 971	189 528	197 444	353 661	172 797	180 864	33 310	16 731	16 580
45 - 49	378 511	182 820	195 691	347 420	166 876	180 544	31 091	15 944	15 148
50 - 54	372 228	179 143	193 085	343 349	164 192	179 158	28 879	14 951	13 928
55 - 59	332 286	158 779	173 507	309 056	146 833	162 223	23 230	11 946	11 284
60 - 64	204 280	96 896	107 384	189 310	89 208	100 102	14 970	7 688	7 283
65 - 69	205 755	93 724	112 031	193 904	87 636	106 268	11 851	6 088	5 763
70 - 74	166 298	73 007	93 291	156 884	68 615	88 269	9 415	4 393	5 022
75 - 79	141 838	58 296	83 543	134 272	55 064	79 208	7 567	3 232	4 335
80 - 84	104 279	41 288	62 991	98 333	38 720	59 614	5 946	2 568	3 378
85 - 89	43 868	17 570	26 298	41 165	16 434	24 731	2 703	1 136	1 567
90 +	25 404	9 267	16 138	23 409	8 523	14 886	1 995	744	1 252
Japan - Japon[29]									
1 X 2000 (CDFC)									
Total	126 925 843	62 110 764	64 815 079	99 865 289	49 005 691	50 859 598	27 060 554	13 105 073	13 955 481
0	1 171 652	600 466	571 186	946 482	485 130	461 352	225 170	115 336	109 834
1 - 4	4 732 446	2 422 055	2 310 391	3 771 724	1 930 430	1 841 294	960 722	491 625	469 097
5 - 9	6 021 789	3 083 431	2 938 358	4 686 566	2 399 688	2 286 878	1 335 223	683 743	651 480
10 - 14	6 546 612	3 353 150	3 193 462	5 000 556	2 560 796	2 439 760	1 546 056	792 354	753 702
15 - 19	7 488 165	3 833 984	3 654 181	5 878 320	3 010 056	2 868 264	1 609 845	823 928	785 917
20 - 24	8 421 460	4 307 242	4 114 218	6 989 577	3 582 379	3 407 198	1 431 883	724 863	707 020
25 - 29	9 790 309	4 965 277	4 825 032	8 149 612	4 131 227	4 018 385	1 640 697	834 050	806 647
30 - 34	8 776 610	4 436 818	4 339 792	7 301 831	3 699 586	3 602 245	1 474 779	737 232	737 547
35 - 39	8 114 865	4 096 286	4 018 579	6 578 179	3 330 783	3 247 396	1 536 686	765 503	771 183
40 - 44	7 800 219	3 924 171	3 876 048	6 099 826	3 068 796	3 031 030	1 700 393	855 375	845 018
45 - 49	8 916 008	4 467 772	4 448 236	6 895 939	3 440 338	3 455 601	2 020 069	1 027 434	992 635
50 - 54	10 441 990	5 210 038	5 231 952	8 237 639	4 085 392	4 152 247	2 204 351	1 124 646	1 079 705
55 - 59	8 734 172	4 290 239	4 443 933	6 965 529	3 418 751	3 546 778	1 768 643	871 488	897 155
60 - 64	7 735 833	3 749 528	3 986 305	6 039 491	2 935 344	3 104 147	1 696 342	814 184	882 158
65 - 69	7 105 939	3 357 281	3 748 658	5 374 653	2 546 769	2 827 884	1 731 286	810 512	920 774
70 - 74	5 900 576	2 670 270	3 230 306	4 304 854	1 951 802	2 353 052	1 595 722	718 468	877 254
75 - 79	4 150 600	1 625 822	2 524 778	2 979 368	1 169 120	1 810 248	1 171 232	456 702	714 530
80 - 84	2 614 689	915 268	1 699 421	1 864 830	652 632	1 212 198	749 859	262 636	487 223
85 - 89	1 532 323	477 083	1 055 240	1 089 747	341 275	748 472	442 576	135 808	306 768
90 - 94	570 281	149 295	420 986	401 755	105 381	296 374	168 526	43 914	124 612
95 - 99	118 488	25 070	93 418	82 972	17 454	65 518	35 516	7 616	27 900
100 +	12 256	2 027	10 229	8 403	1 355	7 048	3 853	672	3 181
Unknown - Inconnu	228 561	148 191	80 370	217 436	141 207	76 229	11 125	6 984	4 141
1 VII 2005 (ESDF)[10]									
Total	127 773 000	62 332 000	65 441 000	...	...	...	...	...	...
0 - 4	5 668 000	2 909 000	2 760 000	...	...	...	...	...	...
5 - 9	5 901 000	3 022 000	2 879 000	...	...	...	...	...	...
10 - 14	6 030 000	3 090 000	2 940 000	...	...	...	...	...	...
15 - 19	6 628 000	3 395 000	3 233 000	...	...	...	...	...	...
20 - 24	7 615 000	3 894 000	3 721 000	...	...	...	...	...	...
25 - 29	8 551 000	4 365 000	4 186 000	...	...	...	...	...	...
30 - 34	9 813 000	4 958 000	4 855 000	...	...	...	...	...	...

7. Population by age, sex and urban/rural residence: latest available year, 1996 - 2005
Population selon l'âge, le sexe et la résidence, urbaine/rurale: dernière année disponible, 1996 - 2005 (continued - suite)

Continent, country or area, date, code and age (in years) / Continent, pays ou zone, date, code et âge (en années)	Total			Urban - Urbaine			Rural - Rurale		
	Both sexes Les deux sexes	Male Masculin	Female Féminin	Both sexes Les deux sexes	Male Masculin	Female Féminin	Both sexes Les deux sexes	Male Masculin	Female Féminin
ASIA - ASIE									
Japan - Japon[29]									
1 VII 2005 (ESDF)[10]									
35 - 39	8 753 000	4 402 000	4 351 000	...	...	...	...	...	...
40 - 44	8 019 000	4 028 000	3 991 000	...	...	...	...	...	...
45 - 49	7 768 000	3 890 000	3 879 000	...	...	...	...	...	...
50 - 54	8 911 000	4 438 000	4 473 000	...	...	...	...	...	...
55 - 59	10 074 000	4 978 000	5 096 000	...	...	...	...	...	...
60 - 64	8 525 000	4 126 000	4 399 000	...	...	...	...	...	...
65 - 69	7 389 000	3 508 000	3 880 000	...	...	...	...	...	...
70 - 74	6 574 000	3 002 000	3 573 000	...	...	...	...	...	...
75 - 79	5 199 000	2 224 000	2 975 000	...	...	...	...	...	...
80 - 84	3 360 000	1 197 000	2 163 000	...	...	...	...	...	...
85 +	2 877 000	806 000	2 070 000	...	...	...	...	...	...
Jordan - Jordanie[30]									
1 X 2004 (CDFC)									
Total	5 103 639	2 626 287	2 477 352	3 997 383	2 055 431	1 941 952	1 106 256	570 856	535 400
0	122 757	62 643	60 114	94 974	48 529	46 445	27 783	14 114	13 669
1 - 4	527 574	270 573	257 001	408 893	209 140	199 753	118 681	61 433	57 248
5 - 9	642 871	329 133	313 738	495 583	253 774	241 809	147 288	75 359	71 929
10 - 14	610 129	313 083	297 046	469 321	240 723	228 598	140 808	72 360	68 448
15 - 19	559 838	287 693	272 145	431 275	221 213	210 062	128 563	66 480	62 083
20 - 24	540 193	279 600	260 593	421 400	217 092	204 308	118 793	62 508	56 285
25 - 29	456 261	239 774	216 487	355 950	186 570	169 380	100 311	53 204	47 107
30 - 34	399 169	207 178	191 991	316 235	164 238	151 997	82 934	42 940	39 994
35 - 39	323 426	167 737	155 689	259 736	134 829	124 907	63 690	32 908	30 782
40 - 44	241 400	123 945	117 455	196 923	101 442	95 481	44 477	22 503	21 974
45 - 49	170 456	87 098	83 358	138 372	70 890	67 482	32 084	16 208	15 876
50 - 54	128 240	64 607	63 633	102 179	51 210	50 969	26 061	13 397	12 664
55 - 59	113 721	55 765	57 956	92 893	45 618	47 275	20 828	10 147	10 681
60 - 64	98 787	52 084	46 703	80 269	42 634	37 635	18 518	9 450	9 068
65 - 69	71 823	37 095	34 728	57 484	29 956	27 528	14 339	7 139	7 200
70 - 74	46 820	23 467	23 353	36 958	18 503	18 455	9 862	4 964	4 898
75 - 79	24 268	12 651	11 617	19 160	9 923	9 237	5 108	2 728	2 380
80 +	...	...	...	16 376	7 369	9 007	5 684	2 768	2 916
80 - 84	13 585	6 144	7 441	...	...	...	...	...	...
85 - 89	5 032	2 444	2 588	...	...	...	...	...	...
90 - 94	2 316	1 012	1 304	...	...	...	...	...	...
95 +	1 127	537	590	...	...	...	...	...	...
Unknown - Inconnu	3 846	2 024	1 822	3 402	1 778	1 624	444	246	198
Kazakhstan									
1 VII 2005 (ESDF)									
Total	15 147 029	7 290 852	7 856 177	8 655 586	4 044 092	4 611 494	6 491 443	3 246 760	3 244 683
0	272 684	140 078	132 606	157 919	81 127	76 792	114 765	58 951	55 814
1 - 4	926 575	474 574	452 001	503 912	258 417	245 495	422 663	216 157	206 506
5 - 9	1 103 210	565 008	538 202	541 683	278 121	263 562	561 527	286 887	274 640
10 - 14	1 388 087	707 270	680 817	685 006	348 869	336 137	703 081	358 401	344 680
15 - 19	1 581 625	802 985	778 640	834 855	420 478	414 377	746 770	382 507	364 263
20 - 24	1 390 163	704 249	685 914	788 908	390 477	398 431	601 255	313 772	287 483
25 - 29	1 225 794	613 130	612 664	731 805	350 625	381 180	493 989	262 505	231 484
30 - 34	1 137 510	561 317	576 193	674 263	317 267	356 996	463 247	244 050	219 197
35 - 39	1 054 473	514 627	539 846	631 937	296 018	335 919	422 536	218 609	203 927
40 - 44	1 113 705	534 305	579 400	671 575	311 276	360 299	442 130	223 029	219 101
45 - 49	1 017 412	478 706	538 706	623 403	284 082	339 321	394 009	194 624	199 385
50 - 54	805 688	365 985	439 703	500 470	220 101	280 369	305 218	145 884	159 334
55 - 59	580 808	255 842	324 966	365 289	155 743	209 546	215 519	100 099	115 420
60 - 64	370 662	153 119	217 543	217 994	86 046	131 948	152 668	67 073	85 595
65 - 69	522 572	208 516	314 056	313 973	118 547	195 426	208 599	89 969	118 630
70 - 74	263 858	98 714	165 144	165 044	58 527	106 517	98 814	40 187	58 627
75 - 79	237 770	75 576	162 194	151 086	45 425	105 661	86 684	30 151	56 533
80 - 84	104 256	26 197	78 059	66 167	16 239	49 928	38 089	9 958	28 131
85 - 89	34 147	7 450	26 697	21 386	4 740	16 646	12 761	2 710	10 051
90 - 94	12 918	2 427	10 491	7 434	1 532	5 902	5 484	895	4 589
95 - 99	2 414	555	1 859	1 185	311	874	1 229	244	985
100 +	698	222	476	292	124	168	406	98	308

Continent, country or area, date, code and age (in years) / Continent, pays ou zone, date, code et âge (en années)	Total			Urban - Urbaine			Rural - Rurale		
	Both sexes Les deux sexes	Male Masculin	Female Féminin	Both sexes Les deux sexes	Male Masculin	Female Féminin	Both sexes Les deux sexes	Male Masculin	Female Féminin
ASIA - ASIE									
Korea (Republic of) - Corée (République de)[31]									
1 XI 2000 (CDFC)[32]									
Total	45 985 289	23 068 181	22 917 108	36 642 448	18 417 822	18 224 626	9 342 841	4 650 359	4 692 482
0	599 073	315 765	283 308	490 482	258 602	231 880	108 591	57 163	51 428
1 - 4	2 531 185	1 325 401	1 205 784	2 057 666	1 077 474	980 192	473 519	247 927	225 592
5 - 9	3 444 056	1 831 446	1 612 610	2 829 540	1 506 192	1 323 348	614 516	325 254	289 262
10 - 14	3 064 442	1 615 013	1 449 429	2 519 417	1 331 718	1 187 699	545 025	283 295	261 730
15 - 19	3 691 584	1 913 885	1 777 699	3 039 961	1 576 628	1 463 333	651 623	337 257	314 366
20 - 24	3 848 186	2 028 206	1 819 980	3 198 906	1 644 839	1 554 067	649 280	383 367	265 913
25 - 29	4 096 978	2 057 321	2 039 657	3 448 553	1 710 894	1 737 659	648 425	346 427	301 998
30 - 34	4 093 228	2 068 202	2 025 026	3 405 783	1 708 064	1 697 719	687 445	360 138	327 307
35 - 39	4 186 953	2 117 492	2 069 461	3 469 047	1 735 895	1 733 152	717 906	381 597	336 309
40 - 44	3 996 336	2 029 413	1 966 923	3 321 790	1 672 139	1 649 651	674 546	357 274	317 272
45 - 49	2 952 023	1 496 104	1 455 919	2 407 921	1 221 781	1 186 140	544 102	274 323	269 779
50 - 54	2 350 250	1 185 239	1 165 011	1 843 397	935 327	908 070	506 853	249 912	256 941
55 - 59	1 968 472	959 680	1 008 792	1 434 106	717 315	716 791	534 366	242 365	292 001
60 - 64	1 788 849	836 465	952 384	1 173 089	562 529	610 560	615 760	273 936	341 824
65 - 69	1 376 122	593 974	782 148	834 195	364 346	469 849	541 927	229 628	312 299
70 - 74	918 121	348 226	569 895	544 456	202 747	341 709	373 665	145 479	228 186
75 - 79	600 598	211 347	389 251	349 676	117 488	232 188	250 922	93 859	157 063
80 - 84	303 759	94 135	209 624	175 121	51 314	123 807	128 638	42 821	85 817
85 +	173 206	39 715	133 491	97 893	21 602	76 291	75 313	18 113	57 200
Unknown - Inconnu	1 868	1 152	716	1 449	928	521	419	224	195
1 VII 2004 (ESDF)									
Total	48 082 163	24 228 209	23 853 954	...	...	...	...	...	...
0	481 264	249 891	231 373	...	...	...	...	...	...
1 - 4	2 205 493	1 152 595	1 052 898	...	...	...	...	...	...
5 - 9	3 319 682	1 753 544	1 566 138	...	...	...	...	...	...
10 - 14	3 410 958	1 816 184	1 594 774	...	...	...	...	...	...
15 - 19	3 116 530	1 636 580	1 479 950	...	...	...	...	...	...
20 - 24	3 988 212	2 065 189	1 923 023	...	...	...	...	...	...
25 - 29	3 860 243	2 001 577	1 858 666	...	...	...	...	...	...
30 - 34	4 428 884	2 265 549	2 163 335	...	...	...	...	...	...
35 - 39	4 173 661	2 149 646	2 024 015	...	...	...	...	...	...
40 - 44	4 287 669	2 175 607	2 112 062	...	...	...	...	...	...
45 - 49	3 814 653	1 928 551	1 886 102	...	...	...	...	...	...
50 - 54	2 674 137	1 347 718	1 326 419	...	...	...	...	...	...
55 - 59	2 215 949	1 107 834	1 108 115	...	...	...	...	...	...
60 - 64	1 923 056	912 896	1 010 160	...	...	...	...	...	...
65 - 69	1 660 982	748 545	912 437	...	...	...	...	...	...
70 - 74	1 163 330	472 452	690 878	...	...	...	...	...	...
75 - 79	727 601	259 598	468 003	...	...	...	...	...	...
80 - 84	409 361	130 472	278 889	...	...	...	...	...	...
85 - 89	165 824	43 450	122 374	...	...	...	...	...	...
90 - 94	45 913	9 183	36 730	...	...	...	...	...	...
95 +	8 761	1 148	7 613	...	...	...	...	...	...
Kuwait - Koweït									
1 VII 2005 (ESDF)									
Total	2 457 257	1 472 312	984 945	...	...	...	...	...	...
0	40 594	20 324	20 270	...	...	...	...	...	...
1 - 4	165 576	82 830	82 746	...	...	...	...	...	...
5 - 9	196 268	98 766	97 502	...	...	...	...	...	...
10 - 14	173 895	88 459	85 436	...	...	...	...	...	...
15 - 19	163 833	83 369	80 464	...	...	...	...	...	...
20 - 24	218 493	123 740	94 753	...	...	...	...	...	...
25 - 29	324 139	208 595	115 544	...	...	...	...	...	...
30 - 34	310 399	203 918	106 481	...	...	...	...	...	...
35 - 39	280 178	185 862	94 316	...	...	...	...	...	...
40 - 44	210 080	137 879	72 201	...	...	...	...	...	...
45 - 49	151 117	100 932	50 185	...	...	...	...	...	...
50 - 54	93 824	62 454	31 370	...	...	...	...	...	...
55 - 59	54 612	34 570	20 042	...	...	...	...	...	...
60 - 64	31 577	18 527	13 050	...	...	...	...	...	...
65 - 69	20 495	11 385	9 110	...	...	...	...	...	...

Continent, country or area, date, code and age (in years) Continent, pays ou zone, date, code et âge (en années)	Total			Urban - Urbaine			Rural - Rurale		
	Both sexes Les deux sexes	Male Masculin	Female Féminin	Both sexes Les deux sexes	Male Masculin	Female Féminin	Both sexes Les deux sexes	Male Masculin	Female Féminin
ASIA - ASIE									
Kuwait - Koweït									
1 VII 2005 (ESDF)									
70 - 74	11 250	5 636	5 614	...	...	...	...	...	...
75 - 79	5 972	2 869	3 103	...	...	...	...	...	...
80 - 84	2 915	1 290	1 625	...	...	...	...	...	...
85 +	2 040	907	1 133	...	...	...	...	...	...
Kyrgyzstan - Kirghizistan[33]									
1 VII 2005 (ESDJ)									
Total	5 115 750	2 528 497	2 587 253	1 795 006	857 802	937 204	3 320 744	1 670 695	1 650 049
0	106 654	54 765	51 889	34 712	17 847	16 865	71 942	36 918	35 024
1 - 4	394 563	201 612	192 951	120 615	61 479	59 136	273 948	140 133	133 815
5 - 9	511 019	260 482	250 537	143 335	73 122	70 213	367 684	187 360	180 324
10 - 14	583 981	295 858	288 123	168 819	85 122	83 697	415 162	210 736	204 426
15 - 19	584 970	294 981	289 989	177 707	87 309	90 398	407 263	207 672	199 591
20 - 24	498 705	250 627	248 078	176 508	83 978	92 530	322 197	166 649	155 548
25 - 29	424 759	213 941	210 818	179 853	87 473	92 380	244 906	126 468	118 438
30 - 34	378 373	189 818	188 555	151 001	72 164	78 837	227 372	117 654	109 718
35 - 39	341 593	170 282	171 311	137 965	66 380	71 585	203 628	103 902	99 726
40 - 44	327 935	160 405	167 530	128 417	60 838	67 579	199 518	99 567	99 951
45 - 49	279 628	135 131	144 497	109 725	51 102	58 623	169 903	84 029	85 874
50 - 54	197 091	93 884	103 207	78 518	36 120	42 398	118 573	57 764	60 809
55 - 59	131 372	61 410	69 962	55 530	25 011	30 519	75 842	36 399	39 443
60 - 64	71 407	32 963	38 444	27 944	12 064	15 880	43 463	20 899	22 564
65 - 69	104 622	45 133	59 489	40 506	16 553	23 953	64 116	28 580	35 536
70 - 74	73 365	30 284	43 081	25 392	9 543	15 849	47 973	20 741	27 232
75 - 79	61 758	24 065	37 693	22 088	7 292	14 796	39 670	16 773	22 897
80 - 84	27 827	8 835	18 992	10 476	2 862	7 614	17 351	5 973	11 378
85 - 89	9 969	2 518	7 451	3 769	1 003	2 766	6 200	1 515	4 685
90 - 94	3 978	934	3 044	1 451	354	1 097	2 527	580	1 947
95 - 99	1 661	436	1 225	461	144	317	1 200	292	908
100 +	520	133	387	214	42	172	306	91	215
Lao People's Democratic Republic - République démocratique populaire lao[10]									
1 VII 2005 (ESDF)									
Total	5 679 000	2 806 400	2 872 600	...	...	...	...	...	...
0 - 4	894 000	450 900	443 100	...	...	...	...	...	...
5 - 9	865 500	440 800	424 700	...	...	...	...	...	...
10 - 14	752 200	386 200	366 000	...	...	...	...	...	...
15 - 19	564 700	277 100	287 600	...	...	...	...	...	...
20 - 24	453 000	211 000	242 000	...	...	...	...	...	...
25 - 29	423 500	200 200	223 300	...	...	...	...	...	...
30 - 34	349 600	170 500	179 100	...	...	...	...	...	...
35 - 39	330 300	166 200	164 000	...	...	...	...	...	...
40 - 44	225 800	112 600	113 200	...	...	...	...	...	...
45 - 49	194 800	94 900	99 900	...	...	...	...	...	...
50 - 54	165 300	75 100	90 100	...	...	...	...	...	...
55 - 59	135 900	65 700	70 200	...	...	...	...	...	...
60 - 64	111 500	53 400	58 100	...	...	...	...	...	...
65 - 69	84 400	42 400	42 100	...	...	...	...	...	...
70 - 74	57 200	27 100	30 000	...	...	...	...	...	...
75 +	71 500	32 300	39 100	...	...	...	...	...	...
Malaysia - Malaisie									
5 VII 2000 (CDJC)[34]									
Total	23 274 690	11 853 432	11 421 258	14 426 871	7 318 396	7 108 475	8 847 819	4 535 036	4 312 783
0 - 4	2 612 744	1 347 633	1 265 111	1 574 757	812 456	762 301	1 037 987	535 177	502 810
5 - 9	2 646 527	1 364 984	1 281 543	1 534 452	792 519	741 933	1 112 075	572 465	539 610
10 - 14	2 491 777	1 276 348	1 215 429	1 383 003	709 140	673 863	1 108 774	567 208	541 566
15 - 19	2 367 021	1 195 803	1 171 218	1 408 673	707 968	700 705	958 348	487 835	470 513
20 - 24	2 087 173	1 050 916	1 036 257	1 436 911	708 607	728 304	650 262	342 309	307 953
25 - 29	1 921 052	972 668	948 384	1 315 940	653 627	662 313	605 112	319 041	286 071
30 - 34	1 800 196	915 814	884 382	1 207 148	606 473	600 675	593 048	309 341	283 707
35 - 39	1 705 044	866 212	838 832	1 141 371	577 947	563 424	563 673	288 265	275 408
40 - 44	1 487 498	764 706	722 792	976 771	504 183	472 588	510 727	260 523	250 204
45 - 49	1 168 527	604 844	563 683	743 757	389 417	354 340	424 770	215 427	209 343

Continent, country or area, date, code and age (in years) / Continent, pays ou zone, date, code et âge (en années)	Total			Urban - Urbaine			Rural - Rurale		
	Both sexes Les deux sexes	Male Masculin	Female Féminin	Both sexes Les deux sexes	Male Masculin	Female Féminin	Both sexes Les deux sexes	Male Masculin	Female Féminin
ASIA - ASIE									
Malaysia - Malaisie									
5 VII 2000 (CDJC)[34]									
50 - 54	918 868	480 261	438 607	562 704	298 115	264 589	356 164	182 146	174 018
55 - 59	616 598	320 119	296 479	356 078	186 312	169 766	260 520	133 807	126 713
60 - 64	551 027	274 216	276 811	306 351	153 941	152 410	244 676	120 275	124 401
65 - 69	346 725	164 943	181 782	189 063	89 783	99 280	157 662	75 160	82 502
70 - 74	264 119	125 883	138 236	138 716	64 354	74 362	125 403	61 529	63 874
75 +	289 794	128 082	161 712	151 176	63 554	87 622	138 618	64 528	74 090
1 VII 2005 (ESDF)									
Total	26 127 700	13 302 800	12 824 900	...	...	...	...	...	...
0 - 4	3 054 900	1 575 900	1 479 100	...	...	...	...	...	...
5 - 9	2 827 800	1 456 200	1 371 600	...	...	...	...	...	...
10 - 14	2 642 500	1 362 800	1 279 700	...	...	...	...	...	...
15 - 19	2 527 400	1 288 400	1 239 000	...	...	...	...	...	...
20 - 24	2 362 600	1 197 600	1 165 000	...	...	...	...	...	...
25 - 29	2 106 800	1 064 500	1 042 200	...	...	...	...	...	...
30 - 34	1 927 200	974 400	952 800	...	...	...	...	...	...
35 - 39	1 837 200	931 800	905 400	...	...	...	...	...	...
40 - 44	1 657 900	843 800	814 100	...	...	...	...	...	...
45 - 49	1 432 900	734 700	698 200	...	...	...	...	...	...
50 - 54	1 176 100	604 600	571 500	...	...	...	...	...	...
55 - 59	843 200	435 400	407 800	...	...	...	...	...	...
60 - 64	611 700	312 600	299 100	...	...	...	...	...	...
65 - 69	461 600	223 600	238 000	...	...	...	...	...	...
70 - 74	306 400	141 800	164 600	...	...	...	...	...	...
75 +	351 400	154 500	196 900	...	...	...	...	...	...
Maldives									
1 VII 2005 (ESDF)									
Total	293 746	148 929	144 817	...	...	...	...	...	...
0 - 4	27 200	13 960	13 240	...	...	...	...	...	...
5 - 9	30 886	15 710	15 176	...	...	...	...	...	...
10 - 14	38 200	19 495	18 705	...	...	...	...	...	...
15 - 19	41 412	21 084	20 328	...	...	...	...	...	...
20 - 24	33 513	16 731	16 782	...	...	...	...	...	...
25 - 29	23 676	11 710	11 966	...	...	...	...	...	...
30 - 34	20 212	9 874	10 338	...	...	...	...	...	...
35 - 39	18 253	8 942	9 311	...	...	...	...	...	...
40 - 44	15 738	7 852	7 886	...	...	...	...	...	...
45 - 49	12 379	6 257	6 122	...	...	...	...	...	...
50 - 54	7 384	3 929	3 455	...	...	...	...	...	...
55 - 59	5 815	2 958	2 857	...	...	...	...	...	...
60 - 64	5 699	2 952	2 747	...	...	...	...	...	...
65 - 69	5 756	3 037	2 719	...	...	...	...	...	...
70 - 74	3 944	2 236	1 708	...	...	...	...	...	...
75 +	3 679	2 202	1 477	...	...	...	...	...	...
Mongolia - Mongolie									
5 I 2000 (CDFC)									
Total	2 373 493	1 177 981	1 195 512	1 344 516	657 081	687 435	1 028 977	520 900	508 077
0	49 804	25 356	24 448	23 778	12 119	11 659	26 026	13 237	12 789
1 - 4	196 219	99 126	97 093	91 687	46 096	45 591	104 532	53 030	51 502
5 - 9	285 664	144 315	141 349	150 401	75 700	74 701	135 263	68 615	66 648
10 - 14	317 434	159 294	158 140	179 974	89 670	90 304	137 460	69 624	67 836
15 - 19	263 358	133 327	130 031	154 244	75 040	79 204	109 114	58 287	50 827
20 - 24	235 751	118 023	117 728	135 694	66 010	69 684	100 057	52 013	48 044
25 - 29	216 652	107 962	108 690	125 644	61 274	64 370	91 008	46 688	44 320
30 - 34	187 872	92 473	95 399	113 537	54 332	59 205	74 335	38 141	36 194
35 - 39	172 606	84 846	87 760	108 347	52 275	56 072	64 259	32 571	31 688
40 - 44	127 220	62 619	64 601	79 563	38 840	40 723	47 657	23 779	23 878
45 - 49	82 888	40 562	42 326	50 873	25 089	25 784	32 015	15 473	16 542
50 - 54	57 835	27 707	30 128	35 016	17 094	17 922	22 819	10 613	12 206
55 - 59	55 895	27 379	28 516	30 397	15 011	15 386	25 498	12 368	13 130
60 - 64	42 292	20 778	21 514	21 889	10 658	11 231	20 403	10 120	10 283
65 - 69	35 415	15 982	19 433	18 480	8 145	10 335	16 935	7 837	9 098
70 - 74	20 239	8 766	11 473	10 946	4 579	6 367	9 293	4 187	5 106
75 - 79	14 843	5 832	9 011	7 963	3 197	4 766	6 880	2 635	4 245

Continent, country or area, date, code and age (in years) Continent, pays ou zone, date, code et âge (en années)	Total			Urban - Urbaine			Rural - Rurale		
	Both sexes Les deux sexes	Male Masculin	Female Féminin	Both sexes Les deux sexes	Male Masculin	Female Féminin	Both sexes Les deux sexes	Male Masculin	Female Féminin
ASIA - ASIE									
Mongolia - Mongolie									
5 I 2000 (CDFC)									
80 - 84	7 036	2 329	4 707	3 777	1 281	2 496	3 259	1 048	2 211
85 - 89	3 376	991	2 385	1 746	519	1 227	1 630	472	1 158
90 - 94	869	257	612	441	125	316	428	132	296
95 - 99	196	53	143	104	24	80	92	29	63
100 + ...	29	4	25	15	3	12	14	1	13
1 VII 2005 (ESDF)									
Total....................	2 547 751	1 263 962	1 283 789	...	...	...	...	...	...
0 - 4.....................	235 585	117 366	118 219	...	...	...	...	...	...
5 - 9.....................	273 460	135 990	137 470	...	...	...	...	...	...
10 - 14..................	322 501	161 659	160 842	...	...	...	...	...	...
15 - 19..................	298 216	151 767	146 449	...	...	...	...	...	...
20 - 24..................	270 725	136 373	134 352	...	...	...	...	...	...
25 - 29..................	235 250	116 845	118 405	...	...	...	...	...	...
30 - 34..................	202 334	100 685	101 649	...	...	...	...	...	...
35 - 39..................	184 861	91 476	93 385	...	...	...	...	...	...
40 - 44..................	151 288	74 615	76 673	...	...	...	...	...	...
45 - 49..................	103 670	51 638	52 032	...	...	...	...	...	...
50 - 54..................	70 701	34 504	36 197	...	...	...	...	...	...
55 - 59..................	59 247	28 912	30 335	...	...	...	...	...	...
60 - 64..................	50 367	23 510	26 857	...	...	...	...	...	...
65 - 69..................	37 246	17 080	20 166	...	...	...	...	...	...
70 + ...	52 300	21 542	30 758	...	...	...	...	...	...
Myanmar									
1 VII 1997 (ESDF)									
Total....................	46 402 000	23 039 000	23 363 000	...	...	...	...	...	...
0 - 4.....................	5 786 000	2 879 000	2 907 000	...	...	...	...	...	...
5 - 9.....................	4 959 000	2 558 000	2 401 000	...	...	...	...	...	...
10 - 14..................	4 708 000	2 440 000	2 268 000	...	...	...	...	...	...
15 - 19..................	4 593 000	2 343 000	2 250 000	...	...	...	...	...	...
20 - 24..................	4 299 000	2 165 000	2 134 000	...	...	...	...	...	...
25 - 29..................	3 952 000	1 961 000	1 991 000	...	...	...	...	...	...
30 - 34..................	3 555 000	1 745 000	1 810 000	...	...	...	...	...	...
35 - 39..................	3 060 000	1 496 000	1 564 000	...	...	...	...	...	...
40 - 44..................	2 594 000	1 263 000	1 331 000	...	...	...	...	...	...
45 - 49..................	2 131 000	1 035 000	1 096 000	...	...	...	...	...	...
50 - 54..................	1 747 000	842 000	905 000	...	...	...	...	...	...
55 - 59..................	1 466 000	695 000	771 000	...	...	...	...	...	...
60 - 64..................	1 202 000	561 000	641 000	...	...	...	...	...	...
65 + ...	2 350 000	1 056 000	1 294 000	...	...	...	...	...	...
Nepal - Népal									
1 VII 1996 (ESDJ)									
Total....................	20 831 644	10 393 913	10 437 731	2 207 967	1 138 641	1 069 326	18 623 677	9 255 272	9 368 405
0 - 4.....................	3 235 783	1 658 100	1 577 683	283 174	139 204	143 970	2 952 609	1 518 896	1 433 713
5 - 9.....................	2 838 712	1 447 733	1 390 979	280 407	151 796	128 611	2 558 305	1 295 937	1 262 368
10 - 14..................	2 521 943	1 275 549	1 246 394	241 904	124 110	117 794	2 280 040	1 151 439	1 128 601
15 - 19..................	2 149 812	1 041 495	1 108 317	233 403	110 195	123 208	1 916 408	931 300	985 108
20 - 24..................	1 839 716	882 635	957 081	237 790	118 604	119 186	1 601 926	764 031	837 895
25 - 29..................	1 565 942	766 431	799 511	222 983	122 864	100 119	1 342 960	643 568	699 392
30 - 34..................	1 310 586	648 320	662 266	170 140	93 500	76 640	1 140 446	554 820	585 626
35 - 39..................	1 139 089	570 183	568 906	133 684	73 273	60 411	1 005 405	496 910	508 495
40 - 44..................	983 519	494 106	489 413	105 506	56 085	49 421	878 013	438 021	439 992
45 - 49..................	839 008	423 529	415 479	81 831	44 633	37 198	757 176	378 896	378 280
50 - 54..................	698 161	351 396	346 765	62 770	32 371	30 399	635 391	319 025	316 366
55 - 59..................	566 009	283 271	282 738	49 332	24 253	25 079	516 677	259 019	257 658
60 - 64..................	438 536	216 857	221 679	38 025	17 312	20 713	400 511	199 545	200 966
65 - 69..................	318 278	154 732	163 546	28 023	13 376	14 647	290 255	141 356	148 899
70 - 74..................	208 529	98 933	109 596	19 466	8 853	10 613	189 062	90 079	98 983
75 - 79..................	115 654	53 285	62 369	12 217	4 965	7 252	103 437	48 320	55 117
80 + ...	62 367	27 358	35 009	7 312	3 247	4 065	55 056	24 110	30 946
22 VI 2001 (CDJC)									
Total....................	22 736 934	11 359 378	11 377 556	...	...	...	...	...	...
0	494 813	252 519	242 294	...	...	...	...	...	...
1 - 4.....................	2 260 400	1 143 196	1 117 204	...	...	...	...	...	...

Continent, country or area, date, code and age (in years) / Continent, pays ou zone, date, code et âge (en années)	Total			Urban - Urbaine			Rural - Rurale		
	Both sexes Les deux sexes	Male Masculin	Female Féminin	Both sexes Les deux sexes	Male Masculin	Female Féminin	Both sexes Les deux sexes	Male Masculin	Female Féminin
ASIA - ASIE									
Nepal - Népal									
22 VI 2001 (CDJC)									
5 - 9	3 211 442	1 633 087	1 578 355	...	...	...	...	...	...
10 - 14	2 981 932	1 533 806	1 448 126	...	...	...	...	...	...
15 - 19	2 389 002	1 185 826	1 203 176	...	...	...	...	...	...
20 - 24	2 016 768	946 742	1 070 026	...	...	...	...	...	...
25 - 29	1 725 478	821 014	904 464	...	...	...	...	...	...
30 - 34	1 489 503	726 040	763 463	...	...	...	...	...	...
35 - 39	1 310 653	651 351	659 302	...	...	...	...	...	...
40 - 44	1 088 044	539 993	548 051	...	...	...	...	...	...
45 - 49	923 373	469 695	453 678	...	...	...	...	...	...
50 - 54	766 054	392 659	373 395	...	...	...	...	...	...
55 - 59	602 093	318 610	283 483	...	...	...	...	...	...
60 - 64	520 908	262 255	258 653	...	...	...	...	...	...
65 - 69	387 223	196 053	191 170	...	...	...	...	...	...
70 - 74	273 789	141 678	132 111	...	...	...	...	...	...
75 - 79	165 764	82 335	83 429	...	...	...	...	...	...
80 - 84	84 255	41 192	43 063	...	...	...	...	...	...
85 - 89	27 947	13 630	14 317	...	...	...	...	...	...
90 - 94	11 421	5 082	6 339	...	...	...	...	...	...
95 +	6 072	2 615	3 457	...	...	...	...	...	...
Occupied Palestinian Territory - Territoire palestinien occupé									
1 VII 2005 (ESDF)									
Total	3 762 005	1 905 642	1 856 363	...	...	...	...	...	...
0	136 866	69 788	67 078	...	...	...	...	...	...
1 - 4	523 070	266 825	256 245	...	...	...	...	...	...
5 - 9	580 953	296 298	284 655	...	...	...	...	...	...
10 - 14	490 271	249 044	241 227	...	...	...	...	...	...
15 - 19	402 724	205 220	197 504	...	...	...	...	...	...
20 - 24	327 172	167 774	159 398	...	...	...	...	...	...
25 - 29	276 635	141 110	135 525	...	...	...	...	...	...
30 - 34	233 703	118 819	114 884	...	...	...	...	...	...
35 - 39	195 485	100 227	95 258	...	...	...	...	...	...
40 - 44	160 912	83 436	77 476	...	...	...	...	...	...
45 - 49	120 656	62 146	58 510	...	...	...	...	...	...
50 - 54	84 179	42 510	41 669	...	...	...	...	...	...
55 - 59	64 781	31 093	33 688	...	...	...	...	...	...
60 - 64	49 789	22 064	27 725	...	...	...	...	...	...
65 - 69	41 347	17 788	23 559	...	...	...	...	...	...
70 - 74	33 581	14 303	19 278	...	...	...	...	...	...
75 - 79	21 865	9 227	12 638	...	...	...	...	...	...
80 +	18 016	7 970	10 046	...	...	...	...	...	...
Oman									
1 VII 2005 (ESDF)									
Total	2 508 837	1 458 845	1 049 992	...	...	...	...	...	...
0 - 4	248 958	128 210	120 748	...	...	...	...	...	...
5 - 9	256 966	133 152	123 814	...	...	...	...	...	...
10 - 14	287 312	148 162	139 150	...	...	...	...	...	...
15 - 19	285 711	146 945	138 766	...	...	...	...	...	...
20 - 24	284 114	151 203	132 911	...	...	...	...	...	...
25 - 29	283 770	171 705	112 065	...	...	...	...	...	...
30 - 34	235 172	156 357	78 815	...	...	...	...	...	...
35 - 39	186 743	128 215	58 528	...	...	...	...	...	...
40 - 44	147 660	104 223	43 437	...	...	...	...	...	...
45 - 49	104 526	73 659	30 867	...	...	...	...	...	...
50 - 54	68 820	47 505	21 315	...	...	...	...	...	...
55 - 59	45 441	28 389	17 052	...	...	...	...	...	...
60 - 64	29 240	17 590	11 650	...	...	...	...	...	...
65 - 69	19 153	10 665	8 488	...	...	...	...	...	...
70 - 74	11 754	6 256	5 498	...	...	...	...	...	...
75 - 79	5 859	2 910	2 949	...	...	...	...	...	...
80 +	7 638	3 699	3 939	...	...	...	...	...	...

7. Population by age, sex and urban/rural residence: latest available year, 1996 - 2005
Population selon l'âge, le sexe et la résidence, urbaine/rurale: dernière année disponible, 1996 - 2005 (continued - suite)

Continent, country or area, date, code and age (in years) / Continent, pays ou zone, date, code et âge (en années)	Total			Urban - Urbaine			Rural - Rurale		
	Both sexes Les deux sexes	Male Masculin	Female Féminin	Both sexes Les deux sexes	Male Masculin	Female Féminin	Both sexes Les deux sexes	Male Masculin	Female Féminin
ASIA - ASIE									
Pakistan[35]									
1 VII 2003 (SSDJ)									
Total	138 979 270	71 741 403	67 237 867	49 640 104	25 819 279	23 820 825	89 339 166	45 922 123	43 417 043
0 - 4	18 874 090	9 641 577	9 232 513	5 798 058	2 932 025	2 866 033	13 076 032	6 709 552	6 366 480
5 - 9	20 770 885	10 696 306	10 074 579	6 545 959	3 370 981	3 174 978	14 224 926	7 325 326	6 899 601
10 - 14	19 004 548	9 998 775	9 005 773	6 682 490	3 508 172	3 174 318	12 322 058	6 490 603	5 831 455
15 - 19	16 304 449	8 586 808	7 717 641	6 335 209	3 356 840	2 978 369	9 969 240	5 229 967	4 739 272
20 - 24	12 807 395	6 573 668	6 233 727	5 037 368	2 680 281	2 357 087	7 770 027	3 893 387	3 876 640
25 - 29	9 704 504	4 842 061	4 862 443	3 755 282	1 893 606	1 861 676	5 949 222	2 948 455	3 000 767
30 - 34	7 706 844	3 751 378	3 955 465	2 877 291	1 462 892	1 414 399	4 829 553	2 288 486	2 541 066
35 - 39	7 338 853	3 624 659	3 714 194	2 800 153	1 396 436	1 403 717	4 538 701	2 228 223	2 310 477
40 - 44	6 082 558	3 110 905	2 971 653	2 331 614	1 216 237	1 115 376	3 750 944	1 894 667	1 856 277
45 - 49	5 625 302	2 899 571	2 725 731	2 216 767	1 155 448	1 061 319	3 408 535	1 744 123	1 664 412
50 - 54	4 245 641	2 255 598	1 990 043	1 563 957	850 028	713 930	2 681 684	1 405 570	1 276 114
55 - 59	3 095 898	1 644 139	1 451 759	1 160 460	606 560	553 900	1 935 438	1 037 579	897 859
60 - 64	2 709 743	1 472 941	1 236 802	933 107	513 221	419 886	1 776 636	959 720	816 915
65 - 69	1 903 851	1 059 937	843 915	675 240	371 961	303 279	1 228 611	687 976	540 635
70 - 74	1 336 807	759 803	577 004	450 996	247 618	203 378	885 810	512 185	373 626
75 - 79	645 190	354 323	290 867	215 784	114 212	101 572	429 406	240 111	189 294
80 - 84	474 912	272 801	202 111	157 114	87 558	69 556	317 798	185 244	132 555
85 +	347 801	196 152	151 649	103 256	55 205	48 051	244 545	140 947	103 598
Philippines									
1 VII 2003 (ESDJ)									
Total	81 081 457	40 820 706	40 260 751	...	...	...	...	...	...
0 - 4	9 633 446	4 923 339	4 710 107	...	...	...	...	...	...
5 - 9	9 416 816	4 825 448	4 591 368	...	...	...	...	...	...
10 - 14	9 046 260	4 650 500	4 395 760	...	...	...	...	...	...
15 - 19	8 359 222	4 254 885	4 104 337	...	...	...	...	...	...
20 - 24	7 591 134	3 825 549	3 765 585	...	...	...	...	...	...
25 - 29	6 799 991	3 404 184	3 395 807	...	...	...	...	...	...
30 - 34	6 016 620	3 001 529	3 015 091	...	...	...	...	...	...
35 - 39	5 245 030	2 619 599	2 625 431	...	...	...	...	...	...
40 - 44	4 485 000	2 245 860	2 239 140	...	...	...	...	...	...
45 - 49	3 748 090	1 877 697	1 870 393	...	...	...	...	...	...
50 - 54	3 046 766	1 523 354	1 523 412	...	...	...	...	...	...
55 - 59	2 412 086	1 194 640	1 217 446	...	...	...	...	...	...
60 - 64	1 836 897	895 575	941 322	...	...	...	...	...	...
65 - 69	1 362 119	650 983	711 136	...	...	...	...	...	...
70 - 74	956 336	443 008	513 328	...	...	...	...	...	...
75 - 79	621 662	274 907	346 755	...	...	...	...	...	...
80 +	503 982	209 649	294 333	...	...	...	...	...	...
Qatar									
1 VII 2005 (ESDF)									
Total	796 186	530 685	265 501	...	...	...	...	...	...
0	13 524	6 965	6 559	...	...	...	...	...	...
1 - 4	50 309	25 906	24 403	...	...	...	...	...	...
5 - 9	60 171	30 409	29 762	...	...	...	...	...	...
10 - 14	56 536	28 556	27 980	...	...	...	...	...	...
15 - 19	45 145	23 741	21 404	...	...	...	...	...	...
20 - 24	63 737	42 688	21 049	...	...	...	...	...	...
25 - 29	89 937	63 640	26 297	...	...	...	...	...	...
30 - 34	101 445	71 664	29 781	...	...	...	...	...	...
35 - 39	90 731	65 293	25 438	...	...	...	...	...	...
40 - 44	81 188	60 580	20 608	...	...	...	...	...	...
45 - 49	63 257	49 742	13 515	...	...	...	...	...	...
50 - 54	40 003	31 819	8 184	...	...	...	...	...	...
55 - 59	21 268	16 876	4 392	...	...	...	...	...	...
60 - 64	9 766	7 241	2 525	...	...	...	...	...	...
65 - 69	4 104	2 495	1 609	...	...	...	...	...	...
70 - 74	2 722	1 732	990	...	...	...	...	...	...
75 - 79	1 226	724	502	...	...	...	...	...	...
80 - 84	674	380	294	...	...	...	...	...	...
85 - 89	257	116	141	...	...	...	...	...	...
90 - 94	126	78	48	...	...	...	...	...	...
95 +	60	40	20	...	...	...	...	...	...

Continent, country or area, date, code and age (in years) / Continent, pays ou zone, date, code et âge (en années)	Total			Urban - Urbaine			Rural - Rurale		
	Both sexes Les deux sexes	Male Masculin	Female Féminin	Both sexes Les deux sexes	Male Masculin	Female Féminin	Both sexes Les deux sexes	Male Masculin	Female Féminin
ASIA - ASIE									
Saudi Arabia - Arabie saoudite									
1 VII 2005 (ESDF)									
Total	23 118 994	12 791 330	10 327 664	...	...	...	...	...	...
0 - 4	2 700 530	1 369 520	1 331 010	...	...	...	...	...	...
5 - 9	2 563 188	1 290 580	1 272 608	...	...	...	...	...	...
10 - 14	2 401 439	1 199 627	1 201 812	...	...	...	...	...	...
15 - 19	2 168 666	1 075 444	1 093 222	...	...	...	...	...	...
20 - 24	2 084 441	1 088 249	996 192	...	...	...	...	...	...
25 - 29	2 306 910	1 336 705	970 205	...	...	...	...	...	...
30 - 34	2 244 070	1 347 423	896 647	...	...	...	...	...	...
35 - 39	1 910 695	1 199 250	711 445	...	...	...	...	...	...
40 - 44	1 465 427	945 534	519 893	...	...	...	...	...	...
45 - 49	1 072 377	684 950	387 427	...	...	...	...	...	...
50 - 54	736 658	455 668	280 990	...	...	...	...	...	...
55 - 59	485 925	282 673	203 252	...	...	...	...	...	...
60 - 64	335 795	181 584	154 211	...	...	...	...	...	...
65 - 69	235 483	121 853	113 630	...	...	...	...	...	...
70 - 74	167 150	85 231	81 919	...	...	...	...	...	...
75 - 79	109 693	56 912	52 781	...	...	...	...	...	...
80 +	130 547	70 127	60 420	...	...	...	...	...	...
Singapore - Singapour									
1 VII 2005 (ESDJ)									
Total	3 543 900	1 758 000	1 785 900	...	...	...	...	...	...
0 - 4	201 500	103 700	97 800	...	...	...	...	...	...
5 - 9	241 800	124 700	117 100	...	...	...	...	...	...
10 - 14	263 100	135 300	127 800	...	...	...	...	...	...
15 - 19	237 500	122 000	115 500	...	...	...	...	...	...
20 - 24	221 900	111 900	110 000	...	...	...	...	...	...
25 - 29	253 100	120 500	132 600	...	...	...	...	...	...
30 - 34	302 100	145 100	157 000	...	...	...	...	...	...
35 - 39	308 000	151 100	156 900	...	...	...	...	...	...
40 - 44	329 400	165 700	163 700	...	...	...	...	...	...
45 - 49	313 200	158 100	155 100	...	...	...	...	...	...
50 - 54	259 400	130 800	128 600	...	...	...	...	...	...
55 - 59	201 900	100 700	101 300	...	...	...	...	...	...
60 - 64	120 200	58 700	61 500	...	...	...	...	...	...
65 - 69	103 600	49 500	54 100	...	...	...	...	...	...
70 - 74	78 800	36 100	42 600	...	...	...	...	...	...
75 - 79	55 300	24 100	31 200	...	...	...	...	...	...
80 - 84	29 800	12 300	17 500	...	...	...	...	...	...
85 +	23 300	7 800	15 500	...	...	...	...	...	...
Sri Lanka									
1 VII 1998 (ESDF)									
Total	18 774 000	9 570 000	9 204 000	...	...	...	...	...	...
0 - 4	2 345 000	1 194 000	1 151 000	...	...	...	...	...	...
5 - 9	2 128 000	1 082 000	1 046 000	...	...	...	...	...	...
10 - 14	2 136 000	1 090 000	1 046 000	...	...	...	...	...	...
15 - 19	2 028 000	1 028 000	1 000 000	...	...	...	...	...	...
20 - 24	1 931 000	969 000	962 000	...	...	...	...	...	...
25 - 29	1 612 000	807 000	805 000	...	...	...	...	...	...
30 - 34	1 424 000	721 000	703 000	...	...	...	...	...	...
35 - 39	1 060 000	533 000	527 000	...	...	...	...	...	...
40 - 44	883 000	455 000	428 000	...	...	...	...	...	...
45 - 49	770 000	390 000	380 000	...	...	...	...	...	...
50 - 54	682 000	360 000	322 000	...	...	...	...	...	...
55 - 59	534 000	281 000	253 000	...	...	...	...	...	...
60 - 64	431 000	232 000	199 000	...	...	...	...	...	...
65 - 69	318 000	168 000	150 000	...	...	...	...	...	...
70 +	492 000	260 000	232 000	...	...	...	...	...	...
Syrian Arab Republic - République arabe syrienne [36]									
1 VII 2004 (ESDF)									
Total	17 980 000	9 199 000	8 781 000	9 022 000	4 652 000	4 370 000	8 958 000	4 547 000	4 411 000
0	412 000	202 000	210 000	202 000	102 000	100 000	210 000	100 000	110 000

Continent, country or area, date, code and age (in years) / Continent, pays ou zone, date, code et âge (en années)	Total			Urban - Urbaine			Rural - Rurale		
	Both sexes Les deux sexes	Male Masculin	Female Féminin	Both sexes Les deux sexes	Male Masculin	Female Féminin	Both sexes Les deux sexes	Male Masculin	Female Féminin
ASIA - ASIE									
Syrian Arab Republic - République arabe syrienne[36]									
1 VII 2004 (ESDF)									
1 - 4	1 778 000	915 000	863 000	831 000	433 000	398 000	947 000	482 000	465 000
5 - 9	2 409 000	1 253 000	1 156 000	1 106 000	577 000	529 000	1 303 000	676 000	627 000
10 - 14	2 520 000	1 304 000	1 216 000	1 199 000	619 000	580 000	1 321 000	685 000	636 000
15 - 19	2 325 000	1 226 000	1 099 000	1 150 000	604 000	546 000	1 175 000	622 000	553 000
20 - 24	1 678 000	879 000	799 000	865 000	461 000	404 000	813 000	418 000	395 000
25 - 29	1 264 000	589 000	675 000	645 000	312 000	333 000	619 000	277 000	342 000
30 - 34	1 049 000	491 000	558 000	556 000	265 000	291 000	493 000	226 000	267 000
35 - 39	1 047 000	506 000	541 000	573 000	274 000	299 000	474 000	232 000	242 000
40 - 44	843 000	424 000	419 000	472 000	247 000	225 000	371 000	177 000	194 000
45 - 49	650 000	328 000	322 000	364 000	186 000	178 000	286 000	142 000	144 000
50 - 54	579 000	290 000	289 000	310 000	158 000	152 000	269 000	132 000	137 000
55 - 59	392 000	199 000	193 000	221 000	112 000	109 000	171 000	87 000	84 000
60 - 64	383 000	203 000	180 000	204 000	112 000	92 000	179 000	91 000	88 000
65 +	651 000	390 000	261 000	324 000	190 000	134 000	327 000	200 000	127 000
Thailand - Thaïlande									
1 VII 2005 (ESDJ)									
Total	64 838 628	31 848 905	32 989 723	19 538 420	9 360 642	10 177 778	45 300 208	22 488 263	22 811 945
0 - 4	4 833 681	2 462 564	2 371 117	1 359 798	686 987	672 811	3 473 883	1 775 577	1 698 306
5 - 9	4 810 642	2 465 728	2 344 914	1 280 304	648 863	631 441	3 530 338	1 816 865	1 713 473
10 - 14	5 241 915	2 678 693	2 563 222	1 391 405	701 321	690 084	3 850 510	1 977 372	1 873 138
15 - 19	5 244 833	2 677 722	2 567 111	1 449 555	722 626	726 929	3 795 278	1 955 096	1 840 182
20 - 24	5 335 108	2 703 661	2 631 447	1 681 978	822 305	859 673	3 653 130	1 881 356	1 771 774
25 - 29	5 371 176	2 698 328	2 672 848	1 882 329	908 312	974 017	3 488 847	1 790 016	1 698 831
30 - 34	5 494 169	2 680 164	2 814 005	1 873 463	891 669	981 794	3 620 706	1 788 495	1 832 211
35 - 39	5 520 246	2 651 641	2 868 605	1 773 485	831 929	941 556	3 746 761	1 819 712	1 927 049
40 - 44	5 214 577	2 510 660	2 703 917	1 617 985	758 210	859 775	3 596 592	1 752 450	1 844 142
45 - 49	4 641 782	2 234 127	2 407 655	1 419 676	666 213	753 463	3 222 106	1 567 914	1 654 192
50 - 54	3 659 315	1 755 492	1 903 823	1 098 941	514 005	584 936	2 560 374	1 241 487	1 318 887
55 - 59	2 763 666	1 321 478	1 442 188	810 634	379 827	430 807	1 953 032	941 651	1 011 381
60 - 64	2 174 410	1 021 706	1 152 704	615 012	283 067	331 945	1 559 398	738 639	820 759
65 - 69	1 795 215	821 414	973 801	511 961	228 697	283 264	1 283 254	592 717	690 537
70 - 74	1 303 532	575 811	727 721	360 761	154 218	206 543	942 771	421 593	521 178
75 - 79	815 297	348 118	467 179	232 128	95 368	136 760	583 169	252 750	330 419
80 +	619 064	241 598	377 466	179 005	67 025	111 980	440 059	174 573	265 486
Turkey - Turquie									
22 X 2000 (CDFC)									
Total	67 803 927	34 346 735	33 457 192	44 006 274	22 427 603	21 578 671	23 797 653	11 919 132	11 878 521
0	1 244 675	640 760	603 915	782 345	402 411	379 934	462 330	238 349	223 981
1 - 4	5 340 147	2 755 930	2 584 217	3 305 208	1 705 098	1 600 110	2 034 939	1 050 832	984 107
5 - 9	6 756 617	3 485 746	3 270 871	4 239 171	2 186 546	2 052 625	2 517 446	1 299 200	1 218 246
10 - 14	6 878 656	3 570 657	3 307 999	4 390 792	2 300 010	2 090 782	2 487 864	1 270 647	1 217 217
15 - 19	7 209 475	3 691 218	3 518 257	4 740 001	2 485 382	2 254 619	2 469 474	1 205 836	1 263 638
20 - 24	6 690 146	3 426 714	3 263 432	4 616 663	2 412 166	2 204 497	2 073 483	1 014 548	1 058 935
25 - 29	5 895 255	2 976 430	2 918 825	4 043 777	2 043 057	2 000 720	1 851 478	933 373	918 105
30 - 34	5 009 655	2 552 370	2 457 285	3 438 737	1 744 883	1 693 854	1 570 918	807 487	763 431
35 - 39	4 854 387	2 453 579	2 400 808	3 324 212	1 671 781	1 652 431	1 530 175	781 798	748 377
40 - 44	4 068 756	2 083 531	1 985 225	2 781 023	1 424 039	1 356 984	1 287 733	659 492	1 356 984
45 - 49	3 368 769	1 710 757	1 658 012	2 251 799	1 153 832	1 097 967	1 116 970	556 925	560 045
50 - 54	2 717 349	1 356 391	1 360 958	1 724 916	874 700	850 216	992 433	481 691	510 742
55 - 59	2 058 422	1 016 254	1 042 168	1 225 906	612 521	613 385	832 516	403 733	428 783
60 - 64	1 829 288	864 299	964 989	1 030 176	484 922	545 254	799 112	379 377	419 735
65 - 69	1 645 517	794 881	850 636	883 840	417 194	466 646	761 677	377 687	383 990
70 - 74	1 172 643	517 870	654 773	635 253	270 034	365 219	537 390	247 836	289 554
75 - 79	577 597	254 443	323 154	321 179	135 075	186 104	256 418	119 368	137 050
80 - 84	246 692	98 797	147 895	137 630	52 964	84 666	109 062	45 833	63 229
85 - 89	138 361	55 298	83 063	77 087	28 707	48 380	61 274	26 591	34 683
90 - 94	52 426	18 616	33 810	28 975	9 770	19 205	23 451	8 846	14 605
95 - 99	19 504	7 402	12 102	10 919	4 100	6 819	8 585	3 302	5 283
100 +	6 209	2 256	3 953	3 183	1 118	2 065	3 026	1 138	1 888
Unknown - Inconnu	23 381	12 536	10 845	13 482	7 293	6 189	9 899	5 243	4 656

Continent, country or area, date, code and age (in years) / Continent, pays ou zone, date, code et âge (en annèes)	Total			Urban - Urbaine			Rural - Rurale		
	Both sexes Les deux sexes	Male Masculin	Female Féminin	Both sexes Les deux sexes	Male Masculin	Female Féminin	Both sexes Les deux sexes	Male Masculin	Female Féminin
ASIA - ASIE									
Turkey - Turquie									
1 VII 2004 (ESDF)[10]									
Total....................	71 152 000	35 895 000	35 255 000	...	...	...	...	...	...
0.........................	1 307 000	668 000	639 000	...	...	...	...	...	...
1 - 4.....................	5 454 000	2 782 000	2 671 000	...	...	...	...	...	...
5 - 9.....................	7 100 000	3 614 000	3 485 000	...	...	...	...	...	...
10 - 14...................	6 649 000	3 385 000	3 262 000	...	...	...	...	...	...
15 - 19...................	6 273 000	3 210 000	3 065 000	...	...	...	...	...	...
20 - 24...................	6 693 000	3 423 000	3 268 000	...	...	...	...	...	...
25 - 29...................	6 730 000	3 436 000	3 294 000	...	...	...	...	...	...
30 - 34...................	6 051 000	3 073 000	2 978 000	...	...	...	...	...	...
35 - 39...................	5 054 000	2 541 000	2 512 000	...	...	...	...	...	...
40 - 44...................	4 446 000	2 246 000	2 200 000	...	...	...	...	...	...
45 - 49...................	3 873 000	1 975 000	1 900 000	...	...	...	...	...	...
50 - 54...................	3 145 000	1 589 000	1 555 000	...	...	...	...	...	...
55 - 59...................	2 346 000	1 164 000	1 183 000	...	...	...	...	...	...
60 - 64...................	1 950 000	944 000	1 006 000	...	...	...	...	...	...
65 - 69...................	1 645 000	774 000	873 000	...	...	...	...	...	...
70 - 74...................	1 190 000	542 000	647 000	...	...	...	...	...	...
75 +.....................	1 246 000	529 000	717 000	...	...	...	...	...	...
Uzbekistan - Ouzbékistan									
1 VII 2001 (ESDF)									
Total....................	24 964 433	12 442 510	12 521 923	9 256 101	4 573 055	4 683 046	15 708 332	7 869 455	7 838 877
0.........................	513 043	263 408	249 635	158 893	81 393	77 500	354 150	182 015	172 135
1 - 4.....................	2 219 863	1 138 212	1 081 651	693 448	355 999	337 449	1 526 415	782 213	744 202
5 - 9.....................	3 237 989	1 653 776	1 584 213	1 015 989	519 360	496 629	2 222 000	1 134 416	1 087 584
10 - 14...................	3 203 022	1 627 673	1 575 349	1 049 577	533 870	515 707	2 153 445	1 093 803	1 059 642
15 - 19...................	2 821 926	1 422 296	1 399 630	984 385	497 725	486 660	1 837 541	924 571	912 970
20 - 24...................	2 296 834	1 157 998	1 138 836	841 326	425 348	415 978	1 455 508	732 650	722 858
25 - 29...................	2 030 200	1 023 174	1 007 026	788 176	397 184	390 992	1 242 024	625 990	616 034
30 - 34...................	1 749 557	861 368	888 189	726 099	372 846	353 253	1 023 458	488 522	534 936
35 - 39...................	1 672 397	816 665	855 732	660 932	323 492	337 440	1 011 465	493 173	518 292
40 - 44...................	1 479 057	728 780	750 277	612 755	297 460	315 295	866 302	431 320	434 982
45 - 49...................	1 034 628	506 734	527 894	464 375	223 425	240 950	570 253	283 309	286 944
50 - 54...................	696 648	337 634	359 014	340 008	161 069	178 939	356 640	176 565	180 075
55 - 59...................	394 997	197 700	197 297	185 073	88 314	96 759	209 924	109 386	100 538
60 - 64...................	553 697	265 428	288 269	254 409	115 715	138 694	299 288	149 713	149 575
65 - 69...................	399 550	185 653	213 897	171 869	75 277	96 592	227 681	110 376	117 305
70 - 74...................	325 230	143 466	181 764	146 702	57 100	89 602	178 528	86 366	92 162
75 - 79...................	185 449	67 568	117 881	87 515	27 439	60 076	97 934	40 129	57 805
80 - 84...................	78 794	23 459	55 335	39 138	10 729	28 409	39 656	12 730	26 926
85 - 89...................	41 343	10 761	30 582	20 793	4 904	15 889	20 550	5 857	14 693
90 - 94...................	19 195	6 220	12 975	9 150	2 774	6 376	10 045	3 446	6 599
95 - 99...................	10 114	4 171	5 943	4 954	1 461	3 493	5 160	2 710	2 450
100 +....................	900	366	534	535	171	364	365	195	170
Viet Nam									
1 IV 1999 (CDFC)									
Total....................	76 323 173	37 469 117	38 854 056	18 076 823	8 825 112	9 251 711	58 246 350	28 644 005	29 602 345
0.........................	1 263 599	647 832	615 767	232 977	120 215	112 762	1 030 622	527 617	503 005
1 - 4.....................	5 908 643	3 034 911	2 873 732	1 184 870	611 659	573 211	4 723 773	2 423 252	2 300 521
5 - 9.....................	9 033 162	4 634 400	4 398 762	1 746 284	899 731	846 553	7 286 878	3 734 669	3 552 209
10 - 14...................	9 066 562	4 654 315	4 412 247	1 775 015	913 513	861 502	7 291 547	3 740 802	3 550 745
15 - 19...................	8 222 280	4 141 058	4 081 222	1 902 373	944 176	958 197	6 319 907	3 196 882	3 123 025
20 - 24...................	6 925 387	3 430 084	3 495 303	1 787 592	869 997	917 595	5 137 795	2 560 087	2 577 708
25 - 29...................	6 568 174	3 281 300	3 286 874	1 730 659	845 461	885 198	4 837 515	2 435 839	2 401 676
30 - 34...................	6 033 706	3 003 421	3 030 285	1 582 568	776 373	806 195	4 451 138	2 227 048	2 224 090
35 - 39...................	5 586 620	2 726 540	2 860 080	1 547 320	759 866	787 454	4 039 300	1 966 674	2 072 626
40 - 44...................	4 550 060	2 180 363	2 369 697	1 317 660	641 149	676 511	3 232 400	1 539 214	1 693 186
45 - 49...................	3 137 258	1 465 289	1 671 969	872 584	405 712	466 872	2 264 674	1 059 577	1 205 097
50 - 54...................	2 104 316	964 240	1 140 076	571 834	259 517	312 317	1 532 482	704 723	827 759
55 - 59...................	1 787 007	782 143	1 004 864	463 473	209 785	253 688	1 323 534	572 358	751 176
60 - 64...................	1 747 308	759 708	987 600	409 484	179 982	229 502	1 337 824	579 726	758 098
65 - 69...................	1 646 775	725 600	921 175	367 000	164 733	202 267	1 279 775	560 867	718 908
70 - 74...................	1 211 104	500 522	710 582	262 578	111 897	150 681	948 526	388 625	559 901
75 - 79...................	821 749	307 069	514 680	170 797	63 805	106 992	650 952	243 264	407 688

7. Population by age, sex and urban/rural residence: latest available year, 1996 - 2005
Population selon l'âge, le sexe et la résidence, urbaine/rurale: dernière année disponible, 1996 - 2005 (continued - suite)

Continent, country or area, date, code and age (in years) Continent, pays ou zone, date, code et âge (en années)	Total			Urban - Urbaine			Rural - Rurale		
	Both sexes Les deux sexes	Male Masculin	Female Féminin	Both sexes Les deux sexes	Male Masculin	Female Féminin	Both sexes Les deux sexes	Male Masculin	Female Féminin
ASIA - ASIE									
Viet Nam									
1 IV 1999 (CDFC)									
80 - 84	418 244	144 203	274 041	89 323	30 036	59 287	328 921	114 167	214 754
85 +	291 219	86 119	205 100	62 432	17 505	44 927	228 787	68 614	160 173
Yemen - Yémen									
1 VII 1997 (ESDF)									
Total	16 484 000	8 227 000	8 257 000	...	...	...	...	...	...
0	712 000	363 000	349 000	...	...	...	...	...	...
1 - 4	2 446 000	1 247 000	1 199 000	...	...	...	...	...	...
5 - 9	2 384 000	1 213 000	1 171 000	...	...	...	...	...	...
10 - 14	2 203 000	1 129 000	1 074 000	...	...	...	...	...	...
15 - 19	2 024 000	1 047 000	977 000	...	...	...	...	...	...
20 - 24	1 426 000	717 000	709 000	...	...	...	...	...	...
25 - 29	957 000	456 000	501 000	...	...	...	...	...	...
30 - 34	878 000	405 000	473 000	...	...	...	...	...	...
35 - 39	821 000	377 000	444 000	...	...	...	...	...	...
40 - 44	645 000	302 000	343 000	...	...	...	...	...	...
45 - 49	495 000	240 000	255 000	...	...	...	...	...	...
50 - 54	385 000	188 000	197 000	...	...	...	...	...	...
55 - 59	297 000	146 000	151 000	...	...	...	...	...	...
60 - 64	238 000	113 000	125 000	...	...	...	...	...	...
65 - 69	198 000	99 000	99 000	...	...	...	...	...	...
70 - 74	149 000	74 000	75 000	...	...	...	...	...	...
75 +	226 000	111 000	115 000	...	...	...	...	...	...
EUROPE									
Albania - Albanie									
1 VII 2005 (ESDF)									
Total	3 142 066	1 565 316	1 576 749	...	...	...	...	...	...
0 - 4	246 463	127 821	118 642	...	...	...	...	...	...
5 - 9	270 896	139 913	130 983	...	...	...	...	...	...
10 - 14	302 149	154 740	147 410	...	...	...	...	...	...
15 - 19	315 436	160 326	155 111	...	...	...	...	...	...
20 - 24	277 778	135 198	142 581	...	...	...	...	...	...
25 - 29	221 336	105 567	115 769	...	...	...	...	...	...
30 - 34	207 119	99 110	108 009	...	...	...	...	...	...
35 - 39	208 905	100 959	107 946	...	...	...	...	...	...
40 - 44	218 753	108 514	110 239	...	...	...	...	...	...
45 - 49	202 609	102 531	100 079	...	...	...	...	...	...
50 - 54	159 236	81 420	77 816	...	...	...	...	...	...
55 - 59	128 587	65 653	62 934	...	...	...	...	...	...
60 - 64	116 574	58 662	57 913	...	...	...	...	...	...
65 - 69	101 340	51 071	50 269	...	...	...	...	...	...
70 - 74	73 879	36 068	37 811	...	...	...	...	...	...
75 - 79	49 141	22 242	26 899	...	...	...	...	...	...
80 - 84	27 101	10 534	16 567	...	...	...	...	...	...
85 - 89	10 773	3 899	6 874	...	...	...	...	...	...
90 - 94	3 496	972	2 525	...	...	...	...	...	...
95 +	498	123	376	...	...	...	...	...	...
Andorra - Andorre[37]									
1 VII 2004 (ESDJ)									
Total	74 885	38 990	35 895	...	...	...	...	...	...
0	304	151	153	...	...	...	...	...	...
1 - 4	2 983	1 546	1 437	...	...	...	...	...	...
5 - 9	3 853	1 996	1 857	...	...	...	...	...	...
10 - 14	3 631	1 881	1 750	...	...	...	...	...	...
15 - 19	3 419	1 777	1 642	...	...	...	...	...	...
20 - 24	4 401	2 201	2 200	...	...	...	...	...	...
25 - 29	6 182	3 157	3 025	...	...	...	...	...	...
30 - 34	7 312	3 674	3 638	...	...	...	...	...	...
35 - 39	7 544	3 896	3 648	...	...	...	...	...	...
40 - 44	7 113	3 787	3 326	...	...	...	...	...	...
45 - 49	6 154	3 352	2 802	...	...	...	...	...	...

7. Population by age, sex and urban/rural residence: latest available year, 1996 - 2005
Population selon l'âge, le sexe et la résidence, urbaine/rurale: dernière année disponible, 1996 - 2005 (continued - suite)

Continent, country or area, date, code and age (in years) / Continent, pays ou zone, date, code et âge (en années)	Total			Urban - Urbaine			Rural - Rurale		
	Both sexes Les deux sexes	Male Masculin	Female Féminin	Both sexes Les deux sexes	Male Masculin	Female Féminin	Both sexes Les deux sexes	Male Masculin	Female Féminin
EUROPE									
Andorra - Andorre[37]									
1 VII 2004 (ESDJ)									
50 - 54	4 974	2 783	2 191	...	...	...	...	...	...
55 - 59	4 274	2 367	1 907	...	...	...	...	...	...
60 - 64	3 329	1 759	1 570	...	...	...	...	...	...
65 - 69	2 391	1 246	1 145	...	...	...	...	...	...
70 - 74	2 298	1 174	1 124	...	...	...	...	...	...
75 - 79	1 904	952	952	...	...	...	...	...	...
80 - 84	1 399	648	751	...	...	...	...	...	...
85 - 89	735	339	396	...	...	...	...	...	...
90 - 94	410	178	232	...	...	...	...	...	...
95 - 99	169	74	95	...	...	...	...	...	...
100 +	106	52	54	...	...	...	...	...	...
Austria - Autriche									
15 V 2001 (CDJC)									
Total	8 032 926	3 889 189	4 143 737	5 368 693	2 564 828	2 803 865	2 664 233	1 324 361	1 339 872
0	77 060	39 641	37 419	50 942	26 172	24 770	26 118	13 469	12 649
1 - 4	332 964	170 439	162 525	215 492	110 553	104 939	117 472	59 886	57 586
5 - 9	469 735	240 593	229 142	296 471	151 887	144 584	173 264	88 706	84 558
10 - 14	473 723	242 791	230 932	294 674	151 245	143 429	179 049	91 546	87 503
15 - 19	483 957	247 452	236 505	300 985	153 733	147 252	182 972	93 719	89 253
20 - 24	472 777	240 171	232 606	309 267	154 636	154 631	163 510	85 535	77 975
25 - 29	539 031	268 179	270 852	364 619	178 639	185 980	174 412	89 540	84 872
30 - 34	668 281	337 121	331 160	456 030	227 926	228 104	212 251	109 195	103 056
35 - 39	704 872	358 748	346 124	473 632	239 432	234 200	231 240	119 316	111 924
40 - 44	625 783	316 280	309 503	416 601	207 478	209 123	209 182	108 802	100 380
45 - 49	525 207	261 903	263 304	352 245	172 161	180 084	172 962	89 742	83 220
50 - 54	514 535	255 906	258 629	356 937	174 415	182 522	157 598	81 491	76 107
55 - 59	452 265	220 827	231 438	326 907	157 892	169 015	125 358	62 935	62 423
60 - 64	451 057	217 191	233 866	305 628	145 952	159 676	145 429	71 239	74 190
65 - 69	332 596	152 844	179 752	215 372	97 381	117 991	117 224	55 463	61 761
70 - 74	327 321	140 193	187 128	217 723	90 939	126 784	109 598	49 254	60 344
75 - 79	290 140	97 886	192 254	202 551	66 803	135 748	87 589	31 083	56 506
80 - 84	151 242	45 800	105 442	108 554	32 170	76 384	42 688	13 630	29 058
85 - 89	96 166	25 556	70 610	70 458	18 358	52 100	25 708	7 198	18 510
90 - 94	37 255	8 413	28 842	28 193	6 138	22 055	9 062	2 275	6 787
95 +	6 959	1 255	5 704	5 412	918	4 494	1 547	337	1 210
1 VII 2005 (ESDJ)									
Total	8 233 306	4 001 861	4 231 445	...	...	...	...	...	...
0	78 891	40 437	38 454	...	...	...	...	...	...
1 - 4	319 618	164 364	155 254	...	...	...	...	...	...
5 - 9	432 662	221 520	211 142	...	...	...	...	...	...
10 - 14	486 536	249 592	236 944	...	...	...	...	...	...
15 - 19	488 584	250 435	238 149	...	...	...	...	...	...
20 - 24	526 502	266 092	260 410	...	...	...	...	...	...
25 - 29	511 823	258 364	253 459	...	...	...	...	...	...
30 - 34	584 508	290 984	293 524	...	...	...	...	...	...
35 - 39	695 523	351 911	343 612	...	...	...	...	...	...
40 - 44	704 470	357 225	347 245	...	...	...	...	...	...
45 - 49	609 532	305 728	303 804	...	...	...	...	...	...
50 - 54	507 621	251 134	256 487	...	...	...	...	...	...
55 - 59	479 696	235 800	243 896	...	...	...	...	...	...
60 - 64	468 953	225 017	243 936	...	...	...	...	...	...
65 - 69	395 348	185 770	209 578	...	...	...	...	...	...
70 - 74	308 865	136 170	172 695	...	...	...	...	...	...
75 - 79	279 923	110 578	169 345	...	...	...	...	...	...
80 - 84	220 008	66 749	153 259	...	...	...	...	...	...
85 - 89	82 288	22 221	60 067	...	...	...	...	...	...
90 - 94	42 629	9 994	32 635	...	...	...	...	...	...
95 +	9 326	1 776	7 550	...	...	...	...	...	...
Unknown - Inconnu	-	-	-	...	...	...	...	...	...
Belarus - Bélarus									
1 VII 2004 (ESDF)									
Total	9 824 568	4 596 633	5 227 935	7 050 685	3 296 800	3 753 885	2 773 883	1 299 833	1 474 050
0	88 224	45 340	42 884	64 732	33 288	31 444	23 492	12 052	11 440

7. Population by age, sex and urban/rural residence: latest available year, 1996 - 2005
Population selon l'âge, le sexe et la résidence, urbaine/rurale: dernière année disponible, 1996 - 2005 (continued - suite)

Continent, country or area, date, code and age (in years) / Continent, pays ou zone, date, code et âge (en années)	Total			Urban - Urbaine			Rural - Rurale		
	Both sexes Les deux sexes	Male Masculin	Female Féminin	Both sexes Les deux sexes	Male Masculin	Female Féminin	Both sexes Les deux sexes	Male Masculin	Female Féminin
EUROPE									
Belarus - Bélarus									
1 VII 2004 (ESDF)									
1 - 4	360 845	185 705	175 140	265 254	136 527	128 727	95 591	49 178	46 413
5 - 9	472 005	242 676	229 329	330 051	169 893	160 158	141 954	72 783	69 171
10 - 14	641 694	328 969	312 725	452 912	232 422	220 490	188 782	96 547	92 235
15 - 19	824 261	421 077	403 184	630 672	318 006	312 666	193 589	103 071	90 518
20 - 24	798 321	407 821	390 500	645 861	326 350	319 511	152 460	81 471	70 989
25 - 29	709 741	358 318	351 423	558 989	279 996	278 993	150 752	78 322	72 430
30 - 34	684 871	339 807	345 064	519 759	253 403	266 356	165 112	86 404	78 708
35 - 39	690 264	339 386	350 878	512 729	244 426	268 303	177 535	94 960	82 575
40 - 44	816 370	398 433	417 937	614 211	288 314	325 897	202 159	110 119	92 040
45 - 49	790 590	377 680	412 910	599 573	275 285	324 288	191 017	102 395	88 622
50 - 54	654 784	304 602	350 182	500 238	224 610	275 628	154 546	79 992	74 554
55 - 59	469 979	211 710	258 269	348 438	154 528	193 910	121 541	57 182	64 359
60 - 64	408 886	169 559	239 327	264 638	110 713	153 925	144 248	58 846	85 402
65 - 69	489 643	187 503	302 140	287 336	111 026	176 310	202 307	76 477	125 830
70 - 74	393 732	137 478	256 254	193 056	66 534	126 522	200 676	70 944	129 732
75 - 79	311 872	92 089	219 783	154 593	47 102	107 491	157 279	44 987	112 292
80 - 84	145 285	34 353	110 932	70 218	16 766	53 452	75 067	17 587	57 480
85 - 89	47 871	9 773	38 098	24 213	5 298	18 915	23 658	4 475	19 183
90 - 94	21 489	3 803	17 686	10 667	1 939	8 728	10 822	1 864	8 958
95 - 99	3 451	489	2 962	2 199	312	1 887	1 252	177	1 075
100 +	390	62	328	346	62	284	44	-	44
Belgium - Belgique									
1 I 2004 (ESDJ)									
Total	10 396 421	5 087 176	5 309 245	...	...	...	...	...	...
0	112 298	57 364	54 934	...	...	...	...	...	...
1 - 4	459 076	234 457	224 619	...	...	...	...	...	...
5 - 9	590 072	301 694	288 378	...	...	...	...	...	...
10 - 14	635 993	325 086	310 907	...	...	...	...	...	...
15 - 19	611 017	311 969	299 048	...	...	...	...	...	...
20 - 24	645 006	325 731	319 275	...	...	...	...	...	...
25 - 29	652 039	328 486	323 553	...	...	...	...	...	...
30 - 34	732 319	370 439	361 880	...	...	...	...	...	...
35 - 39	788 716	400 179	388 537	...	...	...	...	...	...
40 - 44	808 508	408 212	400 296	...	...	...	...	...	...
45 - 49	759 489	382 008	377 481	...	...	...	...	...	...
50 - 54	695 175	349 780	345 395	...	...	...	...	...	...
55 - 59	638 422	318 127	320 295	...	...	...	...	...	...
60 - 64	488 171	237 637	250 534	...	...	...	...	...	...
65 - 69	493 967	232 610	261 357	...	...	...	...	...	...
70 - 74	473 162	210 246	262 916	...	...	...	...	...	...
75 - 79	384 354	156 109	228 245	...	...	...	...	...	...
80 - 84	267 180	95 329	171 851	...	...	...	...	...	...
85 - 89	98 598	28 450	70 148	...	...	...	...	...	...
90 - 94	50 827	11 411	39 416	...	...	...	...	...	...
95 - 99	10 869	1 726	9 143	...	...	...	...	...	...
100 +	1 163	126	1 037	...	...	...	...	...	...
Bulgaria - Bulgarie									
1 VII 2005 (ESDF)									
Total	7 739 900	3 755 469	3 984 431	5 424 661	2 613 346	2 811 315	2 315 239	1 142 123	1 173 116
0	67 894	34 876	33 018	49 501	25 337	24 164	18 393	9 539	8 854
1 - 4	267 955	138 001	129 954	192 568	99 269	93 299	75 387	38 732	36 655
5 - 9	320 746	164 683	156 063	223 480	114 627	108 853	97 266	50 056	47 210
10 - 14	403 535	207 081	196 454	281 317	143 991	137 326	122 218	63 090	59 128
15 - 19	515 281	263 804	251 477	380 440	193 660	186 780	134 841	70 144	64 697
20 - 24	539 426	277 010	262 416	419 101	212 458	206 643	120 325	64 552	55 773
25 - 29	579 233	296 646	282 587	445 809	225 635	220 174	133 424	71 011	62 413
30 - 34	563 866	286 927	276 939	427 897	214 909	212 988	135 969	72 018	63 951
35 - 39	531 052	268 533	262 518	396 628	196 537	200 091	134 424	71 997	62 427
40 - 44	527 150	263 919	263 231	392 541	191 700	200 841	134 609	72 219	62 390
45 - 49	544 047	268 704	275 343	405 632	195 266	210 366	138 415	73 438	64 977
50 - 54	551 994	267 685	284 309	406 127	192 942	213 185	145 867	74 743	71 124
55 - 59	556 321	263 534	292 787	389 442	182 094	207 348	166 879	81 440	85 439
60 - 64	441 752	202 410	239 342	276 103	127 085	149 018	165 649	75 325	90 324

Continent, country or area, date, code and age (in years) / Continent, pays ou zone, date, code et âge (en années)	Total			Urban - Urbaine			Rural - Rurale		
	Both sexes Les deux sexes	Male Masculin	Female Féminin	Both sexes Les deux sexes	Male Masculin	Female Féminin	Both sexes Les deux sexes	Male Masculin	Female Féminin
EUROPE									
Bulgaria - Bulgarie									
1 VII 2005 (ESDF)									
65 - 69	399 093	176 270	222 823	229 234	99 662	129 572	169 859	76 608	93 251
70 - 74	389 057	165 572	223 485	213 241	87 174	126 067	175 816	78 398	97 418
75 - 79	293 118	118 294	174 824	161 823	63 431	98 392	131 295	54 863	76 432
80 - 84	178 372	66 736	111 636	96 474	34 831	61 643	81 898	31 905	49 993
85 - 89	50 061	18 056	32 005	26 976	9 378	17 598	23 085	8 678	14 407
90 - 94	17 235	5 866	11 369	8 960	2 921	6 039	8 275	2 945	5 330
95 - 99	2 463	791	1 672	1 246	406	840	1 217	385	832
100 +	249	70	179	121	33	88	128	37	91
Channel Islands: Guernsey - Îles Anglo-Normandes: Guernesey									
29 IV 2001 (CDJC)									
Total	59 807	29 138	30 669	...	...	...	...	...	...
0	612	304	308	...	...	...	...	...	...
1 - 4	2 564	1 326	1 238	...	...	...	...	...	...
5 - 9	3 452	1 798	1 654	...	...	...	...	...	...
10 - 14	3 672	1 839	1 833	...	...	...	...	...	...
15 - 19	3 544	1 858	1 686	...	...	...	...	...	...
20 - 24	3 678	1 785	1 893	...	...	...	...	...	...
25 - 29	3 996	1 976	2 020	...	...	...	...	...	...
30 - 34	4 640	2 189	2 451	...	...	...	...	...	...
35 - 39	4 785	2 382	2 403	...	...	...	...	...	...
40 - 44	4 466	2 182	2 284	...	...	...	...	...	...
45 - 49	4 068	2 072	1 996	...	...	...	...	...	...
50 - 54	4 620	2 304	2 316	...	...	...	...	...	...
55 - 59	3 291	1 655	1 636	...	...	...	...	...	...
60 - 64	3 053	1 544	1 509	...	...	...	...	...	...
65 - 69	2 591	1 252	1 339	...	...	...	...	...	...
70 - 74	2 341	1 042	1 299	...	...	...	...	...	...
75 - 79	1 928	806	1 122	...	...	...	...	...	...
80 - 84	1 282	463	819	...	...	...	...	...	...
85 - 89	801	264	537	...	...	...	...	...	...
90 - 94	325	77	248	...	...	...	...	...	...
95 +	98	20	78	...	...	...	...	...	...
Channel Islands: Jersey - Îles Anglo-Normandes: Jersey									
10 III 1996 (CDFC)									
Total	85 150	41 394	43 756	...	...	...	...	...	...
0	951	505	446	...	...	...	...	...	...
1 - 4	3 942	2 037	1 905	...	...	...	...	...	...
5 - 9	4 868	2 486	2 382	...	...	...	...	...	...
10 - 14	4 356	2 231	2 125	...	...	...	...	...	...
15 - 19	4 278	2 134	2 144	...	...	...	...	...	...
20 - 24	5 637	2 706	2 931	...	...	...	...	...	...
25 - 29	7 821	3 806	4 015	...	...	...	...	...	...
30 - 34	8 074	3 961	4 113	...	...	...	...	...	...
35 - 39	7 109	3 527	3 582	...	...	...	...	...	...
40 - 44	6 269	3 103	3 166	...	...	...	...	...	...
45 - 49	6 374	3 195	3 179	...	...	...	...	...	...
50 - 54	4 876	2 419	2 457	...	...	...	...	...	...
55 - 59	4 654	2 377	2 277	...	...	...	...	...	...
60 - 64	3 981	2 003	1 978	...	...	...	...	...	...
65 - 69	3 441	1 635	1 806	...	...	...	...	...	...
70 - 74	2 994	1 360	1 634	...	...	...	...	...	...
75 - 79	2 209	850	1 359	...	...	...	...	...	...
80 - 84	1 833	654	1 179	...	...	...	...	...	...
85 - 89	1 026	301	725	...	...	...	...	...	...
90 - 94	378	85	293	...	...	...	...	...	...
95 - 99	73	17	56	...	...	...	...	...	...
100 +	6	2	4	...	...	...	...	...	...

7. Population by age, sex and urban/rural residence: latest available year, 1996 - 2005
Population selon l'âge, le sexe et la résidence, urbaine/rurale: dernière année disponible, 1996 - 2005 (continued - suite)

Continent, country or area, date, code and age (in years) / Continent, pays ou zone, date, code et âge (en années)	Total			Urban - Urbaine			Rural - Rurale		
	Both sexes Les deux sexes	Male Masculin	Female Féminin	Both sexes Les deux sexes	Male Masculin	Female Féminin	Both sexes Les deux sexes	Male Masculin	Female Féminin
EUROPE									
Croatia - Croatie									
31 III 2001 (CDJC)									
Total	4 437 460	2 135 900	2 301 560	2 471 328	1 171 950	1 299 378	1 966 132	963 950	1 002 182
0	42 942	22 097	20 845	23 438	12 112	11 326	19 504	9 985	9 519
1 - 4	194 580	99 621	94 959	104 707	53 579	51 128	89 873	46 042	43 831
5 - 9	248 528	127 274	121 254	134 027	68 669	65 358	114 501	58 605	55 896
10 - 14	268 584	137 175	131 409	144 935	74 118	70 817	123 649	63 057	60 592
15 - 19	298 606	152 676	145 930	165 511	84 240	81 271	133 095	68 436	64 659
20 - 24	305 631	155 739	149 892	176 487	88 565	87 922	129 144	67 174	61 970
25 - 29	294 497	148 666	145 831	171 776	84 620	87 156	122 721	64 046	58 675
30 - 34	295 431	147 920	147 511	169 076	82 749	86 327	126 355	65 171	61 184
35 - 39	317 273	158 506	158 767	177 369	85 563	91 806	139 904	72 943	66 961
40 - 44	333 403	166 499	166 904	189 206	89 569	99 637	144 197	76 930	67 267
45 - 49	333 576	168 290	165 286	195 040	93 697	101 343	138 536	74 593	63 943
50 - 54	299 773	148 224	151 549	178 220	84 433	93 787	121 553	63 791	57 762
55 - 59	229 775	108 673	121 102	134 170	61 988	72 182	95 605	46 685	48 920
60 - 64	262 016	120 667	141 349	142 207	65 853	76 354	119 809	54 814	64 995
65 - 69	252 947	110 459	142 488	131 008	58 413	72 595	121 939	52 046	69 893
70 - 74	203 885	81 884	122 001	102 578	41 358	61 220	101 307	40 526	60 781
75 - 79	137 201	44 149	93 052	69 924	22 818	47 106	67 277	21 331	45 946
80 - 84	56 954	17 040	39 914	29 302	8 963	20 339	27 652	8 077	19 575
85 - 89	30 833	8 682	22 151	16 108	4 575	11 533	14 725	4 107	10 618
90 - 94	10 265	2 571	7 694	5 386	1 310	4 076	4 879	1 261	3 618
95 - 99	1 371	302	1 069	753	153	600	618	149	469
100 +	84	21	63	54	16	38	30	5	25
Unknown - Inconnu	19 305	8 765	10 540	10 046	4 589	5 457	9 259	4 176	5 083
1 VII 2005 (ESDJ)									
Total	4 441 900	2 138 600	2 303 300	...	...	...	...	...	...
0	42 700	22 000	20 700	...	...	...	...	...	...
1 - 4	163 400	84 000	79 400	...	...	...	...	...	...
5 - 9	247 700	126 800	120 900	...	...	...	...	...	...
10 - 14	254 000	130 000	124 000	...	...	...	...	...	...
15 - 19	275 500	140 300	135 200	...	...	...	...	...	...
20 - 24	308 900	157 600	151 300	...	...	...	...	...	...
25 - 29	309 900	157 200	152 700	...	...	...	...	...	...
30 - 34	295 600	148 900	146 700	...	...	...	...	...	...
35 - 39	305 800	152 800	153 000	...	...	...	...	...	...
40 - 44	320 800	159 800	161 000	...	...	...	...	...	...
45 - 49	336 500	167 300	169 200	...	...	...	...	...	...
50 - 54	327 700	163 500	164 200	...	...	...	...	...	...
55 - 59	274 600	132 800	141 800	...	...	...	...	...	...
60 - 64	230 800	106 100	124 700	...	...	...	...	...	...
65 - 69	245 200	108 000	137 200	...	...	...	...	...	...
70 - 74	220 500	89 800	130 700	...	...	...	...	...	...
75 - 79	154 700	56 200	98 500	...	...	...	...	...	...
80 - 84	88 800	25 400	63 400	...	...	...	...	...	...
85 +	38 800	10 100	28 700	...	...	...	...	...	...
Czech Republic - République tchèque									
31 XII 2005 (ESDJ)									
Total	10 251 079	5 002 648	5 248 431	7 558 795	3 660 441	3 898 354	2 692 284	1 342 207	1 350 077
0	102 414	52 534	49 880	75 540	38 859	36 681	26 874	13 675	13 199
1 - 4	376 609	193 568	183 041	275 508	141 914	133 594	101 101	51 654	49 447
5 - 9	448 338	230 322	218 016	320 094	163 940	156 154	128 244	66 382	61 862
10 - 14	573 970	294 761	279 209	411 323	211 133	200 190	162 647	83 628	79 019
15 - 19	653 519	334 212	319 307	478 848	244 339	234 509	174 671	89 873	84 798
20 - 24	698 533	357 619	340 914	513 473	262 306	251 167	185 060	95 313	89 747
25 - 29	863 320	441 069	422 251	641 764	326 785	314 979	221 556	114 284	107 272
30 - 34	865 852	442 517	423 335	640 340	324 670	315 670	225 512	117 847	107 665
35 - 39	690 452	352 753	337 699	511 633	258 245	253 388	178 819	94 508	84 311
40 - 44	689 672	350 924	338 748	512 872	257 976	254 896	176 800	92 948	83 852
45 - 49	676 111	339 996	336 115	497 998	246 643	251 355	178 113	93 353	84 760
50 - 54	775 341	383 056	392 285	574 529	279 857	294 672	200 812	103 199	97 613
55 - 59	782 568	379 521	403 047	580 111	276 506	303 605	202 457	103 015	99 442
60 - 64	597 989	280 092	317 897	450 650	208 480	242 170	147 339	71 612	75 727

213

Continent, country or area, date, code and age (in years) / Continent, pays ou zone, date, code et âge (en années)	Total			Urban - Urbaine			Rural - Rurale		
	Both sexes Les deux sexes	Male Masculin	Female Féminin	Both sexes Les deux sexes	Male Masculin	Female Féminin	Both sexes Les deux sexes	Male Masculin	Female Féminin
EUROPE									
Czech Republic - République tchèque									
31 XII 2005 (ESDJ)									
65 - 69	431 419	192 557	238 862	319 627	141 875	177 752	111 792	50 682	61 110
70 - 74	380 290	158 198	222 092	279 685	115 811	163 874	100 605	42 387	58 218
75 - 79	323 150	120 962	202 188	237 593	89 083	148 510	85 557	31 879	53 678
80 - 84	219 814	70 607	149 207	162 735	52 199	110 536	57 079	18 408	38 671
85 - 89	68 211	19 537	48 674	50 230	14 258	35 972	17 981	5 279	12 702
90 - 94	28 195	6 769	21 426	20 483	4 803	15 680	7 712	1 966	5 746
95 - 99	4 960	1 001	3 959	3 528	711	2 817	1 432	290	1 142
100 +	352	73	279	231	48	183	121	25	96
Denmark - Danemark[38]									
1 VII 2005 (ESDJ)									
Total	5 415 978	2 679 857	2 736 121	...	...	...	...	...	...
0	64 633	33 107	31 526	...	...	...	...	...	...
1 - 4	261 655	133 898	127 757	...	...	...	...	...	...
5 - 9	341 850	175 256	166 594	...	...	...	...	...	...
10 - 14	348 764	178 802	169 962	...	...	...	...	...	...
15 - 19	308 959	158 661	150 298	...	...	...	...	...	...
20 - 24	289 183	146 546	142 637	...	...	...	...	...	...
25 - 29	339 245	170 325	168 920	...	...	...	...	...	...
30 - 34	385 074	193 840	191 234	...	...	...	...	...	...
35 - 39	407 890	207 266	200 624	...	...	...	...	...	...
40 - 44	406 193	206 287	199 906	...	...	...	...	...	...
45 - 49	370 668	187 545	183 123	...	...	...	...	...	...
50 - 54	358 858	180 342	178 516	...	...	...	...	...	...
55 - 59	385 003	193 220	191 783	...	...	...	...	...	...
60 - 64	329 951	163 885	166 066	...	...	...	...	...	...
65 - 69	244 890	118 431	126 459	...	...	...	...	...	...
70 - 74	193 193	89 160	104 033	...	...	...	...	...	...
75 - 79	158 193	68 230	89 963	...	...	...	...	...	...
80 - 84	119 645	45 124	74 521	...	...	...	...	...	...
85 - 89	67 376	21 486	45 890	...	...	...	...	...	...
90 - 94	27 789	7 146	20 643	...	...	...	...	...	...
95 - 99	6 327	1 204	5 123	...	...	...	...	...	...
100 +	639	96	543	...	...	...	...	...	...
Unknown - Inconnu	-	-	-	...	...	...	...	...	...
Estonia - Estonie									
1 VII 2003 (ESDF)									
Total	1 353 557	623 705	729 852	937 201	421 605	515 596	416 356	202 100	214 256
0	12 949	6 580	6 369	8 897	4 530	4 367	4 052	2 050	2 002
1 - 4	49 812	25 678	24 134	33 726	17 414	16 312	16 086	8 264	7 822
5 - 9	63 843	32 775	31 068	40 782	20 913	19 869	23 061	11 862	11 199
10 - 14	93 635	48 076	45 559	59 553	30 541	29 012	34 082	17 535	16 547
15 - 19	106 955	54 559	52 396	70 955	36 170	34 785	36 000	18 389	17 611
20 - 24	99 349	50 628	48 721	71 999	35 501	36 498	27 350	15 127	12 223
25 - 29	93 254	46 926	46 328	70 190	34 358	35 832	23 064	12 568	10 496
30 - 34	93 929	46 614	47 315	67 271	32 744	34 527	26 658	13 870	12 788
35 - 39	88 343	42 888	45 455	61 235	29 077	32 158	27 108	13 811	13 297
40 - 44	98 240	46 937	51 303	68 180	31 354	36 826	30 060	15 583	14 477
45 - 49	95 931	44 728	51 203	67 796	30 269	37 527	28 135	14 459	13 676
50 - 54	91 007	41 400	49 607	64 793	28 202	36 591	26 214	13 198	13 016
55 - 59	71 857	31 614	40 243	49 454	20 813	28 641	22 403	10 801	11 602
60 - 64	77 210	32 372	44 838	52 993	21 214	31 779	24 217	11 158	13 059
65 - 69	70 257	27 438	42 819	48 595	18 356	30 239	21 662	9 082	12 580
70 - 74	61 866	22 077	39 789	43 078	14 993	28 085	18 788	7 084	11 704
75 - 79	45 447	13 244	32 203	31 686	9 136	22 550	13 761	4 108	9 653
80 - 84	23 475	5 632	17 843	15 601	3 763	11 838	7 874	1 869	6 005
85 - 89	10 241	2 270	7 971	6 628	1 465	5 163	3 613	805	2 808
90 - 94	4 616	877	3 739	2 888	505	2 383	1 728	372	1 356
95 - 99	852	128	724	511	73	438	341	55	286
100 +	80	16	64	46	11	35	34	5	29
Unknown - Inconnu	409	248	161	344	203	141	65	45	20

Continent, country or area, date, code and age (in years) Continent, pays ou zone, date, code et âge (en années)	Total			Urban - Urbaine			Rural - Rurale		
	Both sexes Les deux sexes	Male Masculin	Female Féminin	Both sexes Les deux sexes	Male Masculin	Female Féminin	Both sexes Les deux sexes	Male Masculin	Female Féminin
EUROPE									
Estonia - Estonie									
1 VII 2004 (ESDF)									
Total....................	1 349 290	621 525	727 765	...	...	...	...	...	...
0........................	13 438	6 859	6 580	...	...	...	...	...	...
1 - 4	50 834	26 129	24 705	...	...	...	...	...	...
5 - 9	61 951	31 816	30 136	...	...	...	...	...	...
10 - 14	85 691	44 004	41 687	...	...	...	...	...	...
15 - 19	107 161	54 763	52 398	...	...	...	...	...	...
20 - 24	101 672	51 721	49 951	...	...	...	...	...	...
25 - 29	93 641	47 275	46 366	...	...	...	...	...	...
30 - 34	93 926	46 678	47 248	...	...	...	...	...	...
35 - 39	87 976	42 763	45 214	...	...	...	...	...	...
40 - 44	96 512	46 157	50 355	...	...	...	...	...	...
45 - 49	96 374	45 012	51 363	...	...	...	...	...	...
50 - 54	90 659	41 235	49 425	...	...	...	...	...	...
55 - 59	76 646	33 674	42 972	...	...	...	...	...	...
60 - 64	71 929	30 197	41 733	...	...	...	...	...	...
65 - 69	72 302	28 125	44 177	...	...	...	...	...	...
70 - 74	60 238	21 547	38 691	...	...	...	...	...	...
75 - 79	46 836	14 073	32 763	...	...	...	...	...	...
80 - 84	25 451	6 020	19 431	...	...	...	...	...	...
85 + ...	15 707	3 271	12 436	...	...	...	...	...	...
Unknown - Inconnu	351	211	140	...	...	...	...	...	...
Finland - Finlande									
1 VII 2005 (ESDJ)									
Total....................	5 246 096	2 567 214	2 678 882	3 285 197	1 580 650	1 704 547	1 960 899	986 564	974 336
0........................	57 611	29 450	28 161	37 581	19 216	18 365	20 030	10 234	9 796
1 - 4	226 710	115 992	110 718	141 890	72 703	69 188	84 820	43 290	41 531
5 - 9	296 425	151 303	145 123	178 418	90 852	87 566	118 008	60 451	57 557
10 - 14	329 986	168 104	161 882	195 161	99 128	96 033	134 826	68 976	65 850
15 - 19	319 524	163 346	156 178	193 060	96 372	96 688	126 464	66 974	59 490
20 - 24	333 650	170 602	163 048	243 695	120 034	123 661	89 956	50 569	39 387
25 - 29	331 014	169 351	161 663	245 414	124 526	120 888	85 600	44 826	40 775
30 - 34	307 672	157 500	150 172	212 344	108 820	103 525	95 328	48 681	46 648
35 - 39	352 535	179 383	173 152	230 167	116 248	113 920	122 368	63 136	59 233
40 - 44	378 624	192 236	186 389	237 828	119 262	118 566	140 797	72 974	67 823
45 - 49	380 910	192 192	188 718	232 420	114 633	117 787	148 490	77 559	70 931
50 - 54	395 233	198 096	197 138	238 754	115 309	123 445	156 479	82 787	73 693
55 - 59	414 608	206 809	207 799	253 075	121 716	131 359	161 533	85 093	76 440
60 - 64	285 543	139 139	146 405	173 157	81 712	91 445	112 387	57 427	54 960
65 - 69	243 312	113 516	129 796	140 481	62 950	77 531	102 831	50 566	52 266
70 - 74	206 050	90 568	115 482	116 901	49 077	67 824	89 150	41 491	47 659
75 - 79	178 809	69 809	109 000	99 373	36 742	62 631	79 436	33 067	46 369
80 - 84	122 051	38 949	83 102	67 374	20 405	46 970	54 677	18 544	36 133
85 - 89	58 268	15 194	43 075	32 590	7 997	24 594	25 678	7 197	18 481
90 - 94	22 781	4 859	17 922	12 837	2 519	10 318	9 944	2 340	7 604
95 - 99	4 435	774	3 661	2 494	410	2 084	1 941	364	1 577
100 + ...	349	47	302	189	24	165	161	23	138
Unknown - Inconnu	-	-	-	-	-	-	-	-	-
France[39]									
1 VII 2005 (ESDJ)									
Total....................	60 995 911	29 638 708	31 357 203	...	...	...	...	...	...
0 - 4	3 835 224	1 960 707	1 874 517	...	...	...	...	...	...
5 - 9	3 701 394	1 895 546	1 805 848	...	...	...	...	...	...
10 - 14	3 697 811	1 893 654	1 804 157	...	...	...	...	...	...
15 - 19	3 928 586	2 003 179	1 925 407	...	...	...	...	...	...
20 - 24	3 941 630	1 989 427	1 952 203	...	...	...	...	...	...
25 - 29	3 802 373	1 911 518	1 890 855	...	...	...	...	...	...
30 - 34	4 260 328	2 136 090	2 124 238	...	...	...	...	...	...
35 - 39	4 323 356	2 150 492	2 172 864	...	...	...	...	...	...
40 - 44	4 379 410	2 160 422	2 218 988	...	...	...	...	...	...
45 - 49	4 235 177	2 077 435	2 157 742	...	...	...	...	...	...
50 - 54	4 152 086	2 040 293	2 111 793	...	...	...	...	...	...
55 - 59	4 006 477	1 978 810	2 027 667	...	...	...	...	...	...
60 - 64	2 707 046	1 324 777	1 382 269	...	...	...	...	...	...

Continent, country or area, date, code and age (in years) / Continent, pays ou zone, date, code et âge (en années)	Total			Urban - Urbaine			Rural - Rurale		
	Both sexes Les deux sexes	Male Masculin	Female Féminin	Both sexes Les deux sexes	Male Masculin	Female Féminin	Both sexes Les deux sexes	Male Masculin	Female Féminin
EUROPE									
France[39]									
1 VII 2005 (ESDJ)									
65 - 69	2 559 485	1 203 094	1 356 391	...	...	...	...	...	...
70 - 74	2 496 686	1 104 473	1 392 213	...	...	...	...	...	...
75 - 79	2 151 856	877 933	1 273 923	...	...	...	...	...	...
80 - 84	1 670 856	609 345	1 061 511	...	...	...	...	...	...
85 - 89	642 668	202 899	439 769	...	...	...	...	...	...
90 - 94	387 427	96 721	290 706	...	...	...	...	...	...
95 - 99	99 299	18 751	80 548	...	...	...	...	...	...
100 +	16 736	3 142	13 594	...	...	...	...	...	...
Unknown - Inconnu	-	-	-	...	...	...	...	...	...
Germany - Allemagne									
1 VII 2004 (ESDJ)									
Total	82 501 274	40 350 091	42 151 183	...	...	...	...	...	...
0	705 523	361 890	343 633	...	...	...	...	...	...
1 - 4	2 983 937	1 529 680	1 454 257	...	...	...	...	...	...
5 - 9	3 979 132	2 042 141	1 936 991	...	...	...	...	...	...
10 - 14	4 372 996	2 243 405	2 129 591	...	...	...	...	...	...
15 - 19	4 764 549	2 444 298	2 320 251	...	...	...	...	...	...
20 - 24	4 884 391	2 478 447	2 405 944	...	...	...	...	...	...
25 - 29	4 724 552	2 401 907	2 322 645	...	...	...	...	...	...
30 - 34	5 472 595	2 794 968	2 677 627	...	...	...	...	...	...
35 - 39	7 029 451	3 612 189	3 417 262	...	...	...	...	...	...
40 - 44	7 045 628	3 604 504	3 441 124	...	...	...	...	...	...
45 - 49	6 088 781	3 091 328	2 997 453	...	...	...	...	...	...
50 - 54	5 548 272	2 772 204	2 776 068	...	...	...	...	...	...
55 - 59	4 456 911	2 222 650	2 234 261	...	...	...	...	...	...
60 - 64	5 335 710	2 621 966	2 713 744	...	...	...	...	...	...
65 - 69	5 075 378	2 417 126	2 658 252	...	...	...	...	...	...
70 - 74	3 560 555	1 598 727	1 961 828	...	...	...	...	...	...
75 - 79	2 971 452	1 146 336	1 825 116	...	...	...	...	...	...
80 - 84	2 108 808	628 273	1 480 535	...	...	...	...	...	...
85 - 89	782 870	199 031	583 839	...	...	...	...	...	...
90 - 94	465 555	100 678	364 877	...	...	...	...	...	...
95 +	144 228	38 343	105 885	...	...	...	...	...	...
Gibraltar[40]									
12 XI 2001 (CDFC)									
Total	27 495	13 644	13 851	...	...	...	...	...	...
0	143	74	69	...	...	...	...	...	...
1 - 4	1 315	693	622	...	...	...	...	...	...
5 - 9	1 773	932	841	...	...	...	...	...	...
10 - 14	1 831	956	875	...	...	...	...	...	...
15 - 19	1 801	917	884	...	...	...	...	...	...
20 - 24	1 764	912	852	...	...	...	...	...	...
25 - 29	1 770	867	903	...	...	...	...	...	...
30 - 34	1 916	959	957	...	...	...	...	...	...
35 - 39	2 044	1 008	1 036	...	...	...	...	...	...
40 - 44	1 995	987	1 008	...	...	...	...	...	...
45 - 49	1 904	988	916	...	...	...	...	...	...
50 - 54	1 944	1 056	888	...	...	...	...	...	...
55 - 59	1 610	844	766	...	...	...	...	...	...
60 - 64	1 379	691	688	...	...	...	...	...	...
65 - 69	1 247	611	636	...	...	...	...	...	...
70 - 74	1 037	477	560	...	...	...	...	...	...
75 - 79	895	329	566	...	...	...	...	...	...
80 - 84	605	186	419	...	...	...	...	...	...
85 - 89	306	100	206	...	...	...	...	...	...
90 - 94	134	25	109	...	...	...	...	...	...
95 +	34	9	25	...	...	...	...	...	...
Unknown - Inconnu	48	23	25	...	...	...	...	...	...
Greece - Grèce[41]									
1 VII 2005 (ESDF)									
Total	11 103 929	5 497 372	5 606 557	...	...	...	...	...	...
0	106 388	54 963	51 425	...	...	...	...	...	...
1 - 4	521 113	268 931	252 182	...	...	...	...	...	...

Continent, country or area, date, code and age (in years) / Continent, pays ou zone, date, code et âge (en années)	Total			Urban - Urbaine			Rural - Rurale		
	Both sexes Les deux sexes	Male Masculin	Female Féminin	Both sexes Les deux sexes	Male Masculin	Female Féminin	Both sexes Les deux sexes	Male Masculin	Female Féminin
EUROPE									
Greece - Grèce[41]									
1 VII 2005 (ESDF)									
5 - 9	516 872	264 805	252 067	...	...	...	...	...	...
10 - 14	557 841	287 194	270 647	...	...	...	...	...	...
15 - 19	603 948	313 788	290 160	...	...	...	...	...	...
20 - 24	749 359	391 128	358 231	...	...	...	...	...	...
25 - 29	845 178	440 172	405 006	...	...	...	...	...	...
30 - 34	865 538	445 135	420 403	...	...	...	...	...	...
35 - 39	878 355	445 805	432 550	...	...	...	...	...	...
40 - 44	797 489	399 130	398 359	...	...	...	...	...	...
45 - 49	782 173	387 678	394 495	...	...	...	...	...	...
50 - 54	715 016	354 891	360 125	...	...	...	...	...	...
55 - 59	679 735	330 538	349 197	...	...	...	...	...	...
60 - 64	557 547	263 686	293 861	...	...	...	...	...	...
65 - 69	613 368	279 427	333 941	...	...	...	...	...	...
70 - 74	580 098	262 357	317 741	...	...	...	...	...	...
75 - 79	451 170	197 818	253 352	...	...	...	...	...	...
80 - 84	244 310	103 295	141 015	...	...	...	...	...	...
85 - 89	99 822	42 779	57 043	...	...	...	...	...	...
90 - 94	34 087	14 327	19 760	...	...	...	...	...	...
95 - 99	8 122	3 751	4 371	...	...	...	...	...	...
100 +	2 788	737	2 051	...	...	...	...	...	...
Hungary - Hongrie									
1 VII 2005 (ESDF)									
Total	10 087 065	4 788 847	5 298 218	6 670 187	3 125 833	3 544 354	3 416 879	1 663 014	1 753 865
0	95 109	48 904	46 206	62 344	32 024	30 320	32 765	16 880	15 886
1 - 4	383 004	196 813	186 191	244 761	125 635	119 126	138 243	71 178	67 065
5 - 9	497 027	254 861	242 166	305 352	156 399	148 953	191 676	98 463	93 213
10 - 14	591 431	302 515	288 916	367 026	187 364	179 662	224 405	115 152	109 254
15 - 19	630 776	321 943	308 833	414 832	208 938	205 894	215 944	113 006	102 939
20 - 24	681 564	347 371	334 194	459 947	231 095	228 852	221 618	116 276	105 342
25 - 29	831 831	424 876	406 955	579 226	291 923	287 303	252 605	132 953	119 652
30 - 34	770 574	391 368	379 207	525 970	264 218	261 752	244 605	127 150	117 455
35 - 39	690 277	348 475	341 802	456 101	227 778	228 323	234 176	120 697	113 479
40 - 44	609 315	302 000	307 316	390 965	189 429	201 536	218 351	112 571	105 780
45 - 49	716 492	347 059	369 433	462 231	216 694	245 538	254 261	130 366	123 895
50 - 54	785 917	373 171	412 746	528 788	243 385	285 404	257 129	129 787	127 342
55 - 59	649 063	299 912	349 152	442 098	199 703	242 395	206 966	100 209	106 757
60 - 64	570 533	250 729	319 804	387 295	169 151	218 144	183 239	81 578	101 661
65 - 69	477 356	193 061	284 296	313 112	126 760	186 353	164 244	66 301	97 943
70 - 74	423 596	163 018	260 578	274 838	106 617	168 222	148 758	56 402	92 356
75 - 79	338 985	118 569	220 416	222 580	78 435	144 145	116 405	40 134	76 271
80 - 84	225 602	70 791	154 811	149 599	46 840	102 759	76 003	23 951	52 052
85 - 89	75 419	21 737	53 682	52 497	15 226	37 271	22 922	6 511	16 411
90 +	43 199	11 678	31 522	30 629	8 224	22 405	12 570	3 454	9 117
Iceland - Islande									
1 VII 2005 (ESDJ)									
Total	295 864	148 449	147 415	275 017	137 003	138 014	20 847	11 446	9 401
0	4 194	2 131	2 063	3 990	2 022	1 968	204	109	95
1 - 4	16 741	8 504	8 237	15 836	8 023	7 813	905	481	424
5 - 9	21 486	10 965	10 521	20 107	10 266	9 841	1 379	699	680
10 - 14	22 947	11 747	11 200	21 254	10 887	10 367	1 693	860	833
15 - 19	21 799	11 176	10 623	20 080	10 241	9 839	1 719	935	784
20 - 24	21 499	10 924	10 575	19 988	10 091	9 897	1 511	833	678
25 - 29	21 439	10 839	10 600	20 267	10 175	10 092	1 172	664	508
30 - 34	21 035	10 731	10 304	19 823	10 054	9 769	1 212	677	535
35 - 39	20 671	10 430	10 241	19 276	9 659	9 617	1 395	771	624
40 - 44	21 823	10 931	10 892	20 155	9 999	10 156	1 668	932	736
45 - 49	21 032	10 730	10 302	19 498	9 876	9 622	1 534	854	680
50 - 54	18 553	9 448	9 105	17 161	8 642	8 519	1 392	806	586
55 - 59	15 815	8 138	7 677	14 605	7 437	7 168	1 210	701	509
60 - 64	12 117	6 023	6 094	11 150	5 504	5 646	967	519	448
65 - 69	9 248	4 534	4 714	8 438	4 080	4 358	810	454	356
70 - 74	8 938	4 237	4 701	8 191	3 818	4 373	747	419	328
75 - 79	7 477	3 403	4 074	6 867	3 040	3 827	610	363	247

7. Population by age, sex and urban/rural residence: latest available year, 1996 - 2005
Population selon l'âge, le sexe et la résidence, urbaine/rurale: dernière année disponible, 1996 - 2005 (continued - suite)

Continent, country or area, date, code and age (in years) / Continent, pays ou zone, date, code et âge (en années)	Total			Urban - Urbaine			Rural - Rurale		
	Both sexes Les deux sexes	Male Masculin	Female Féminin	Both sexes Les deux sexes	Male Masculin	Female Féminin	Both sexes Les deux sexes	Male Masculin	Female Féminin
EUROPE									
Iceland - Islande									
1 VII 2005 (ESDJ)									
80 - 84	5 121	2 157	2 964	4 742	1 951	2 791	379	206	173
85 - 89	2 694	1 021	1 673	2 457	902	1 555	237	119	118
90 - 94	974	317	657	892	281	611	82	36	46
95 - 99	231	51	180	215	45	170	16	6	10
100 +	30	12	18	25	10	15	5	2	3
Ireland - Irlande									
28 IV 2002 (CDFC)									
Total	3 917 203	1 946 164	1 971 039	2 334 282	1 133 507	1 200 775	1 582 921	812 657	770 264
0	54 499	27 805	26 694	34 126	17 447	16 679	20 373	10 358	10 015
1 - 4	223 131	114 235	108 896	132 464	67 852	64 612	90 667	46 383	44 284
5 - 9	264 090	135 890	128 200	148 750	76 507	72 243	115 340	59 383	55 957
10 - 14	285 708	146 114	139 594	156 518	79 813	76 705	129 190	66 301	62 889
15 - 19	313 188	160 413	152 775	180 794	90 629	90 165	132 394	69 784	62 610
20 - 24	328 334	165 292	163 042	229 323	110 629	118 694	99 011	54 663	44 348
25 - 29	312 693	156 100	156 593	218 159	106 459	111 700	94 534	49 641	44 893
30 - 34	304 676	152 377	152 299	198 557	98 235	100 322	106 119	54 142	51 977
35 - 39	290 906	144 530	146 376	175 440	85 989	89 451	115 466	58 541	56 925
40 - 44	271 984	135 301	136 683	156 586	76 632	79 954	115 398	58 669	56 729
45 - 49	249 604	124 981	124 623	139 387	67 871	71 516	110 217	57 110	53 107
50 - 54	230 843	116 585	114 258	128 125	62 642	65 483	102 718	53 943	48 775
55 - 59	197 294	99 827	97 467	109 812	53 573	56 239	87 482	46 254	41 228
60 - 64	154 252	77 559	76 693	87 940	42 559	45 381	66 312	35 000	31 312
65 - 69	133 474	65 290	68 184	75 006	34 910	40 096	58 468	30 380	28 088
70 - 74	112 129	51 719	60 410	61 997	26 751	35 246	50 132	24 968	25 164
75 - 79	89 815	37 377	52 438	48 176	18 610	29 566	41 639	18 767	22 872
80 - 84	58 857	22 283	36 574	31 005	10 617	20 388	27 852	11 666	16 186
85 - 89	29 629	9 444	20 185	15 533	4 387	11 146	14 096	5 057	9 039
90 - 94	9 871	2 617	7 254	5 329	1 201	4 128	4 542	1 416	3 126
95 - 99	1 972	379	1 593	1 115	168	947	857	211	646
100 +	254	46	208	140	26	114	114	20	94
15 IV 2005 (ESDF)									
Total	4 130 722	2 058 952	2 071 770	...	...	...	...	...	...
0	61 066	31 493	29 573	...	...	...	...	...	...
1 - 4	236 299	120 937	115 362	...	...	...	...	...	...
5 - 9	281 210	144 596	136 614	...	...	...	...	...	...
10 - 14	274 715	141 063	133 652	...	...	...	...	...	...
15 - 19	296 004	151 437	144 567	...	...	...	...	...	...
20 - 24	341 343	171 368	169 975	...	...	...	...	...	...
25 - 29	351 412	177 897	173 515	...	...	...	...	...	...
30 - 34	330 226	166 242	163 984	...	...	...	...	...	...
35 - 39	306 373	154 637	151 736	...	...	...	...	...	...
40 - 44	290 670	144 580	146 090	...	...	...	...	...	...
45 - 49	263 776	131 479	132 297	...	...	...	...	...	...
50 - 54	242 498	122 264	120 234	...	...	...	...	...	...
55 - 59	222 039	111 929	110 110	...	...	...	...	...	...
60 - 64	172 385	86 622	85 763	...	...	...	...	...	...
65 - 69	141 407	69 236	72 171	...	...	...	...	...	...
70 - 74	116 934	55 468	61 466	...	...	...	...	...	...
75 - 79	91 072	38 845	52 227	...	...	...	...	...	...
80 - 84	63 455	23 928	39 527	...	...	...	...	...	...
85 - 89	32 289	10 781	21 508	...	...	...	...	...	...
90 - 94	12 419	3 457	8 962	...	...	...	...	...	...
95 +	3 130	693	2 437	...	...	...	...	...	...
Isle of Man - Îles de Man									
30 IV 2005 (ESDJ)									
Total	77 993	38 360	39 652	...	...	...	...	...	...
0 - 4	4 262	2 212	2 052	...	...	...	...	...	...
5 - 9	4 459	2 325	2 135	...	...	...	...	...	...
10 - 14	4 879	2 514	2 366	...	...	...	...	...	...
15 - 19	4 735	2 386	2 349	...	...	...	...	...	...
20 - 24	4 492	2 244	2 249	...	...	...	...	...	...
25 - 29	4 364	2 197	2 167	...	...	...	...	...	...
30 - 34	5 181	2 523	2 661	...	...	...	...	...	...

Continent, country or area, date, code and age (in years) Continent, pays ou zone, date, code et âge (en années)	Total			Urban - Urbaine			Rural - Rurale		
	Both sexes Les deux sexes	Male Masculin	Female Féminin	Both sexes Les deux sexes	Male Masculin	Female Féminin	Both sexes Les deux sexes	Male Masculin	Female Féminin
EUROPE									
Isle of Man - Îles de Man									
30 IV 2005 (ESDJ)									
35 - 39	5 822	2 891	2 932	...	...	...	...	...	...
40 - 44	6 164	3 116	3 048	...	...	...	...	...	...
45 - 49	5 446	2 684	2 763	...	...	...	...	...	...
50 - 54	5 169	2 621	2 550	...	...	...	...	...	...
55 - 59	5 570	2 873	2 697	...	...	...	...	...	...
60 - 64	4 338	2 126	2 213	...	...	...	...	...	...
65 - 69	3 742	1 856	1 891	...	...	...	...	...	...
70 - 74	3 058	1 433	1 625	...	...	...	...	...	...
75 - 79	2 538	1 034	1 504	...	...	...	...	...	...
80 - 84	2 075	780	1 295	...	...	...	...	...	...
85 - 89	1 043	366	678	...	...	...	...	...	...
90 +	656	179	477	...	...	...	...	...	...
Italy - Italie									
1 VII 2004 (ESDJ)									
Total	58 175 310	28 222 706	29 952 604	...	...	...	...	...	...
0	547 567	280 828	266 740	...	...	...	...	...	...
1 - 4	2 163 171	1 109 737	1 053 434	...	...	...	...	...	...
5 - 9	2 671 964	1 375 453	1 296 511	...	...	...	...	...	...
10 - 14	2 840 330	1 458 787	1 381 543	...	...	...	...	...	...
15 - 19	2 888 282	1 483 714	1 404 568	...	...	...	...	...	...
20 - 24	3 226 972	1 647 804	1 579 169	...	...	...	...	...	...
25 - 29	3 990 359	2 022 724	1 967 635	...	...	...	...	...	...
30 - 34	4 613 815	2 331 991	2 281 824	...	...	...	...	...	...
35 - 39	4 816 156	2 428 326	2 387 831	...	...	...	...	...	...
40 - 44	4 483 752	2 242 154	2 241 599	...	...	...	...	...	...
45 - 49	3 955 775	1 963 059	1 992 716	...	...	...	...	...	...
50 - 54	3 710 420	1 826 050	1 884 370	...	...	...	...	...	...
55 - 59	3 688 019	1 802 812	1 885 208	...	...	...	...	...	...
60 - 64	3 324 821	1 592 418	1 732 403	...	...	...	...	...	...
65 - 69	3 210 418	1 498 987	1 711 431	...	...	...	...	...	...
70 - 74	2 856 672	1 265 721	1 590 952	...	...	...	...	...	...
75 - 79	2 354 807	957 683	1 397 124	...	...	...	...	...	...
80 - 84	1 679 797	601 537	1 078 261	...	...	...	...	...	...
85 - 89	674 998	210 658	464 341	...	...	...	...	...	...
90 - 94	389 499	104 189	285 311	...	...	...	...	...	...
95 - 99	79 292	16 616	62 676	...	...	...	...	...	...
100 +	8 429	1 465	6 964	...	...	...	...	...	...
Latvia - Lettonie									
1 VII 2005 (ESDJ)									
Total	2 300 512	1 060 101	1 240 411	1 563 372	702 490	860 882	737 140	357 611	379 529
0	20 886	10 720	10 166	14 163	7 296	6 867	6 723	3 424	3 299
1 - 4	80 525	41 184	39 341	53 357	27 210	26 147	27 168	13 974	13 194
5 - 9	95 274	48 944	46 330	60 303	30 963	29 340	34 971	17 981	16 990
10 - 14	138 296	70 462	67 834	84 957	43 187	41 770	53 339	27 275	26 064
15 - 19	183 168	93 537	89 631	116 937	59 292	57 645	66 231	34 245	31 986
20 - 24	176 913	90 064	86 849	120 049	60 031	60 018	56 864	30 033	26 831
25 - 29	158 915	80 503	78 412	111 588	55 045	56 543	47 327	25 458	21 869
30 - 34	161 828	81 305	80 523	113 246	55 313	57 933	48 582	25 992	22 590
35 - 39	156 792	77 402	79 390	106 992	51 166	55 826	49 800	26 236	23 564
40 - 44	169 270	82 119	87 151	115 477	53 913	61 564	53 793	28 206	25 587
45 - 49	169 538	80 509	89 029	117 849	53 534	64 315	51 689	26 975	24 714
50 - 54	148 100	67 876	80 224	105 203	46 088	59 115	42 897	21 788	21 109
55 - 59	131 498	57 867	73 631	94 468	39 836	54 632	37 030	18 031	18 999
60 - 64	126 107	52 419	73 688	84 876	33 975	50 901	41 231	18 444	22 787
65 - 69	129 201	50 054	79 147	89 727	33 851	55 876	39 474	16 203	23 271
70 - 74	100 039	35 088	64 951	67 629	23 377	44 252	32 410	11 711	20 699
75 - 79	82 186	24 519	57 667	57 705	17 469	40 236	24 481	7 050	17 431
80 - 84	46 470	10 220	36 250	31 893	7 205	24 688	14 577	3 015	11 562
85 - 89	16 162	3 504	12 658	10 842	2 482	8 360	5 320	1 022	4 298
90 - 94	7 564	1 460	6 104	4 932	1 016	3 916	2 632	444	2 188
95 - 99	1 589	308	1 281	1 049	213	836	540	95	445
100 +	191	37	154	130	28	102	61	9	52
Unknown - Inconnu	-	-	-	-	-	-	-	-	-

Continent, country or area, date, code and age (in years) / Continent, pays ou zone, date, code et âge (en années)	Total			Urban - Urbaine			Rural - Rurale		
	Both sexes Les deux sexes	Male Masculin	Female Féminin	Both sexes Les deux sexes	Male Masculin	Female Féminin	Both sexes Les deux sexes	Male Masculin	Female Féminin
EUROPE									
Liechtenstein									
1 VII 2005 (ESDF)									
Total	34 734	17 100	17 634	...	...	...	...	...	...
0	378	194	184	...	...	...	...	...	...
1 - 4	1 539	817	722	...	...	...	...	...	...
5 - 9	2 097	1 019	1 078	...	...	...	...	...	...
10 - 14	2 076	1 032	1 044	...	...	...	...	...	...
15 - 19	2 105	1 086	1 019	...	...	...	...	...	...
20 - 24	2 177	1 106	1 071	...	...	...	...	...	...
25 - 29	2 201	1 112	1 089	...	...	...	...	...	...
30 - 34	2 616	1 292	1 324	...	...	...	...	...	...
35 - 39	3 067	1 533	1 534	...	...	...	...	...	...
40 - 44	3 018	1 477	1 541	...	...	...	...	...	...
45 - 49	2 808	1 381	1 427	...	...	...	...	...	...
50 - 54	2 483	1 247	1 236	...	...	...	...	...	...
55 - 59	2 320	1 196	1 124	...	...	...	...	...	...
60 - 64	1 898	958	940	...	...	...	...	...	...
65 - 69	1 280	622	658	...	...	...	...	...	...
70 - 74	912	402	510	...	...	...	...	...	...
75 - 79	769	308	461	...	...	...	...	...	...
80 - 84	566	191	375	...	...	...	...	...	...
85 - 89	275	88	187	...	...	...	...	...	...
90 - 94	126	35	91	...	...	...	...	...	...
95 - 99	20	4	16	...	...	...	...	...	...
100 +	3	-	3	...	...	...	...	...	...
Lithuania - Lituanie									
1 VII 2005 (ESDJ)									
Total	3 414 304	1 592 402	1 821 902	2 275 118	1 040 296	1 234 822	1 139 186	552 106	587 080
0	30 278	15 454	14 824	19 567	9 980	9 587	10 711	5 474	5 237
1 - 4	122 810	63 117	59 693	76 961	39 521	37 440	45 849	23 596	22 253
5 - 9	182 217	93 701	88 516	116 698	59 999	56 699	65 519	33 702	31 817
10 - 14	237 454	121 430	116 024	150 048	76 593	73 455	87 406	44 837	42 569
15 - 19	272 453	139 080	133 373	174 608	88 577	86 031	97 845	50 503	47 342
20 - 24	255 731	130 233	125 498	174 468	86 455	88 013	81 263	43 778	37 485
25 - 29	225 533	113 898	111 635	163 950	79 661	84 289	61 583	34 237	27 346
30 - 34	239 203	118 658	120 545	172 569	83 639	88 930	66 634	35 019	31 615
35 - 39	249 866	122 660	127 206	172 763	82 755	90 008	77 103	39 905	37 198
40 - 44	268 992	130 812	138 180	186 177	87 090	99 087	82 815	43 722	39 093
45 - 49	250 475	118 387	132 088	174 253	78 803	95 450	76 222	39 584	36 638
50 - 54	206 812	95 480	111 332	144 044	63 298	80 746	62 768	32 182	30 586
55 - 59	179 678	78 988	100 690	122 315	51 418	70 897	57 363	27 570	29 793
60 - 64	173 379	72 710	100 669	112 604	45 873	66 731	60 775	26 837	33 938
65 - 69	165 562	64 870	100 692	104 426	39 951	64 475	61 136	24 919	36 217
70 - 74	143 539	52 044	91 495	85 666	30 859	54 807	57 873	21 185	36 688
75 - 79	112 297	35 702	76 595	67 108	21 577	45 531	45 189	14 125	31 064
80 - 84	64 566	16 898	47 668	36 998	9 537	27 461	27 568	7 361	20 207
85 - 89	21 494	5 325	16 169	12 411	2 992	9 419	9 083	2 333	6 750
90 - 94	9 229	2 047	7 182	5 658	1 189	4 469	3 571	858	2 713
95 - 99	2 355	804	1 551	1 586	472	1 114	769	332	437
100 +	381	104	277	240	57	183	141	47	94
Unknown - Inconnu	-	-	-	-	-	-	-	-	-
Luxembourg									
1 VII 2005 (ESDJ)									
Total	457 250	225 775	231 475	...	...	...	...	...	...
0	5 405	2 801	2 604	...	...	...	...	...	...
1 - 4	22 125	11 491	10 634	...	...	...	...	...	...
5 - 9	29 028	14 898	14 130	...	...	...	...	...	...
10 - 14	28 707	14 689	14 018	...	...	...	...	...	...
15 - 19	26 752	13 599	13 153	...	...	...	...	...	...
20 - 24	26 184	13 500	12 684	...	...	...	...	...	...
25 - 29	29 029	14 596	14 433	...	...	...	...	...	...
30 - 34	34 221	17 010	17 211	...	...	...	...	...	...
35 - 39	39 066	19 541	19 525	...	...	...	...	...	...
40 - 44	38 873	19 728	19 145	...	...	...	...	...	...
45 - 49	34 792	17 629	17 163	...	...	...	...	...	...

Continent, country or area, date, code and age (in years) Continent, pays ou zone, date, code et âge (en années)	Total			Urban - Urbaine			Rural - Rurale		
	Both sexes Les deux sexes	Male Masculin	Female Féminin	Both sexes Les deux sexes	Male Masculin	Female Féminin	Both sexes Les deux sexes	Male Masculin	Female Féminin
EUROPE									
Luxembourg									
1 VII 2005 (ESDJ)									
50 - 54	30 244	15 398	14 846	...	...	...	...	...	...
55 - 59	26 403	13 547	12 856	...	...	...	...	...	...
60 - 64	20 981	10 428	10 553	...	...	...	...	...	...
65 - 69	19 025	9 002	10 023	...	...	...	...	...	...
70 - 74	17 042	7 675	9 367	...	...	...	...	...	...
75 - 79	14 457	5 967	8 490	...	...	...	...	...	...
80 - 84	8 975	2 842	6 133	...	...	...	...	...	...
85 - 89	3 920	1 051	2 869	...	...	...	...	...	...
90 - 94	1 719	356	1 363	...	...	...	...	...	...
95 +	302	27	275	...	...	...	...	...	...
Unknown - Inconnu	-	-	-	...	...	...	...	...	...
Malta - Malte									
31 XII 2005 (ESDJ)									
Total	404 346	200 626	203 720	...	...	...	...	...	...
0	3 861	1 983	1 878	...	...	...	...	...	...
1 - 4	15 836	8 144	7 692	...	...	...	...	...	...
5 - 9	23 274	11 911	11 363	...	...	...	...	...	...
10 - 14	26 301	13 580	12 721	...	...	...	...	...	...
15 - 19	28 543	14 678	13 865	...	...	...	...	...	...
20 - 24	29 878	15 340	14 538	...	...	...	...	...	...
25 - 29	30 668	15 857	14 811	...	...	...	...	...	...
30 - 34	28 204	14 511	13 693	...	...	...	...	...	...
35 - 39	24 348	12 408	11 940	...	...	...	...	...	...
40 - 44	27 638	14 001	13 637	...	...	...	...	...	...
45 - 49	30 451	15 249	15 202	...	...	...	...	...	...
50 - 54	28 705	14 395	14 310	...	...	...	...	...	...
55 - 59	30 648	15 182	15 466	...	...	...	...	...	...
60 - 64	21 612	10 421	11 191	...	...	...	...	...	...
65 - 69	17 428	8 052	9 376	...	...	...	...	...	...
70 - 74	14 426	6 151	8 275	...	...	...	...	...	...
75 - 79	10 583	4 301	6 282	...	...	...	...	...	...
80 - 84	7 041	2 700	4 341	...	...	...	...	...	...
85 - 89	3 408	1 315	2 093	...	...	...	...	...	...
90 +	1 493	447	1 046	...	...	...	...	...	...
Monaco									
21 VI 2000 (CDJC)									
Total	32 020	15 544	16 476	...	...	...	...	...	...
0	145	69	76	...	...	...	...	...	...
1 - 4	1 223	644	579	...	...	...	...	...	...
5 - 9	1 462	747	715	...	...	...	...	...	...
10 - 14	1 407	746	661	...	...	...	...	...	...
15 - 19	1 337	706	631	...	...	...	...	...	...
20 - 24	1 297	661	636	...	...	...	...	...	...
25 - 29	1 638	830	808	...	...	...	...	...	...
30 - 34	2 346	1 184	1 162	...	...	...	...	...	...
35 - 39	2 386	1 205	1 181	...	...	...	...	...	...
40 - 44	2 328	1 151	1 177	...	...	...	...	...	...
45 - 49	2 178	1 107	1 071	...	...	...	...	...	...
50 - 54	2 584	1 264	1 320	...	...	...	...	...	...
55 - 59	2 405	1 163	1 242	...	...	...	...	...	...
60 - 64	2 083	1 018	1 065	...	...	...	...	...	...
65 - 69	1 794	854	940	...	...	...	...	...	...
70 - 74	1 704	803	901	...	...	...	...	...	...
75 - 79	1 598	704	894	...	...	...	...	...	...
80 - 84	937	347	590	...	...	...	...	...	...
85 - 89	669	216	453	...	...	...	...	...	...
90 - 94	374	96	278	...	...	...	...	...	...
95 - 99	96	20	76	...	...	...	...	...	...
100 +	11	2	9	...	...	...	...	...	...
Unknown - Inconnu	18	7	11	...	...	...	...	...	...

7. Population by age, sex and urban/rural residence: latest available year, 1996 - 2005
Population selon l'âge, le sexe et la résidence, urbaine/rurale: dernière année disponible, 1996 - 2005 (continued - suite)

Continent, country or area, date, code and age (in years) Continent, pays ou zone, date, code et âge (en années)	Total			Urban - Urbaine			Rural - Rurale		
	Both sexes Les deux sexes	Male Masculin	Female Féminin	Both sexes Les deux sexes	Male Masculin	Female Féminin	Both sexes Les deux sexes	Male Masculin	Female Féminin
EUROPE									
Netherlands - Pays-Bas									
1 I 2003 (ESDJ)									
Total.................	16 192 572	8 015 471	8 177 101	10 529 908	5 179 099	5 350 809	5 662 664	2 836 372	2 826 292
0....................	202 386	103 818	98 568	132 720	68 208	64 512	69 666	35 610	34 056
1 - 4.................	820 227	419 480	400 747	523 999	267 883	256 116	296 228	151 597	144 631
5 - 9.................	984 718	503 582	481 136	614 030	313 763	300 267	370 688	189 819	180 869
10 - 14...............	1 002 757	512 955	489 802	623 866	318 675	305 191	378 891	194 280	184 611
15 - 19...............	958 911	491 763	467 148	611 610	310 847	300 763	347 301	180 916	166 385
20 - 24...............	972 828	491 819	481 009	688 130	339 227	348 903	284 698	152 592	132 106
25 - 29...............	1 031 179	518 928	512 251	742 632	371 082	371 550	288 547	147 846	140 701
30 - 34...............	1 295 220	656 339	638 881	888 931	452 444	436 487	406 289	203 895	202 394
35 - 39...............	1 324 943	675 781	649 162	870 709	445 586	425 123	454 234	230 195	224 039
40 - 44...............	1 275 679	645 907	629 772	823 858	417 006	406 852	451 821	228 901	222 920
45 - 49...............	1 168 260	589 999	578 261	746 303	374 569	371 734	421 957	215 430	206 527
50 - 54...............	1 123 820	569 836	553 984	709 046	357 690	351 356	414 774	212 146	202 628
55 - 59...............	1 038 381	525 879	512 502	643 424	324 128	319 296	394 957	201 751	193 206
60 - 64...............	772 807	386 143	386 664	476 182	235 201	240 981	296 625	150 942	145 683
65 - 69...............	649 864	312 394	337 470	404 190	191 342	212 848	245 674	121 052	124 622
70 - 74...............	571 857	257 288	314 569	364 836	161 117	203 719	207 021	96 171	110 850
75 - 79...............	454 765	183 786	270 979	299 622	119 201	180 421	155 143	64 585	90 558
80 - 84...............	311 084	108 826	202 258	208 276	71 512	136 764	102 808	37 314	65 494
85 - 89...............	159 983	45 327	114 656	107 992	29 661	78 331	51 991	15 666	36 325
90 - 94...............	59 433	13 274	46 159	40 338	8 472	31 866	19 095	4 802	14 293
95 - 99...............	12 250	2 167	10 083	8 366	1 375	6 991	3 884	792	3 092
100 +................	1 220	180	1 040	848	110	738	372	70	302
1 VII 2004 (ESDJ)									
Total.................	16 281 779	8 055 947	8 225 833	...	...	...	...	...	...
0....................	197 272	101 094	96 179	...	...	...	...	...	...
1 - 4.................	818 649	418 722	399 927	...	...	...	...	...	...
5 - 9.................	987 203	505 206	481 997	...	...	...	...	...	...
10 - 14...............	1 009 016	516 177	492 839	...	...	...	...	...	...
15 - 19...............	975 618	498 999	476 619	...	...	...	...	...	...
20 - 24...............	969 108	489 828	479 280	...	...	...	...	...	...
25 - 29...............	1 001 064	502 644	498 420	...	...	...	...	...	...
30 - 34...............	1 222 582	615 729	606 853	...	...	...	...	...	...
35 - 39...............	1 315 422	668 779	646 643	...	...	...	...	...	...
40 - 44...............	1 300 617	659 038	641 579	...	...	...	...	...	...
45 - 49...............	1 192 502	601 227	591 275	...	...	...	...	...	...
50 - 54...............	1 113 562	562 984	550 578	...	...	...	...	...	...
55 - 59...............	1 099 416	556 240	543 176	...	...	...	...	...	...
60 - 64...............	809 840	405 894	403 946	...	...	...	...	...	...
65 - 69...............	670 357	324 596	345 761	...	...	...	...	...	...
70 - 74...............	575 817	261 806	314 011	...	...	...	...	...	...
75 - 79...............	457 803	187 948	269 855	...	...	...	...	...	...
80 - 84...............	330 385	116 918	213 467	...	...	...	...	...	...
85 - 89...............	159 398	45 664	113 735	...	...	...	...	...	...
90 - 94...............	62 126	14 061	48 065	...	...	...	...	...	...
95 - 99...............	12 694	2 196	10 498	...	...	...	...	...	...
100 +................	1 333	201	1 132	...	...	...	...	...	...
Norway - Norvège									
3 XI 2001 (CDJC)[42]									
Total.................	4 520 947	2 240 281	2 280 666	3 458 699	1 694 153	1 764 546	1 018 422	522 925	495 497
0....................	57 205	29 340	27 865	44 798	23 002	21 796	11 828	6 048	5 780
1 - 4.................	240 268	123 153	117 115	186 738	95 742	90 996	51 255	26 232	25 023
5 - 9.................	307 650	158 230	149 420	235 620	121 061	114 559	69 433	35 833	33 600
10 - 14...............	300 609	153 989	146 620	227 068	116 054	111 014	71 100	36 697	34 403
15 - 19...............	267 596	137 494	130 102	199 238	102 194	97 044	66 278	34 188	32 090
20 - 24...............	273 126	138 679	134 447	211 551	106 040	105 511	59 030	31 337	27 693
25 - 29...............	316 989	160 678	156 311	255 685	128 167	127 518	57 993	30 759	27 234
30 - 34...............	351 386	178 688	172 698	280 044	141 397	138 647	67 654	35 193	32 461
35 - 39...............	338 689	173 595	165 094	265 141	134 740	130 401	70 226	36 890	33 336
40 - 44...............	319 293	162 807	156 486	246 090	124 014	122 076	70 273	37 050	33 223
45 - 49...............	309 642	157 276	152 366	236 578	118 274	118 304	70 375	37 421	32 954
50 - 54...............	301 283	154 010	147 273	227 967	114 779	113 188	70 543	37 669	32 874
55 - 59...............	269 320	136 414	132 906	203 022	101 540	101 482	63 778	33 413	30 365

Continent, country or area, date, code and age (in years) / Continent, pays ou zone, date, code et âge (en années)	Total			Urban - Urbaine			Rural - Rurale		
	Both sexes Les deux sexes	Male Masculin	Female Féminin	Both sexes Les deux sexes	Male Masculin	Female Féminin	Both sexes Les deux sexes	Male Masculin	Female Féminin
EUROPE									
Norway - Norvège									
3 XI 2001 (CDJC)[42]									
60 - 64	190 808	93 953	96 855	140 947	67 923	73 024	47 966	25 008	22 958
65 - 69	163 197	77 766	85 431	119 675	55 351	64 324	41 888	21 553	20 335
70 - 74	161 097	73 389	87 708	118 670	52 350	66 320	40 811	20 243	20 568
75 - 79	151 839	63 682	88 157	111 134	44 980	66 154	38 918	17 898	21 020
80 - 84	113 628	41 784	71 844	83 558	29 286	54 272	28 500	11 877	16 623
85 - 89	60 467	18 752	41 715	44 821	12 816	32 005	14 644	5 617	9 027
90 - 94	22 093	5 668	16 425	16 645	3 797	12 848	4 988	1 744	3 244
95 - 99	4 307	849	3 458	3 333	580	2 753	872	239	633
100 +	455	85	370	376	66	310	69	16	53
1 VII 2005 (ESDJ)									
Total	4 623 291	2 293 026	2 330 266	...	...	...	...	...	...
0	57 030	29 219	27 812	...	...	...	...	...	...
1 - 4	231 235	117 995	113 240	...	...	...	...	...	...
5 - 9	306 523	157 303	149 221	...	...	...	...	...	...
10 - 14	313 277	160 998	152 279	...	...	...	...	...	...
15 - 19	294 109	150 895	143 215	...	...	...	...	...	...
20 - 24	274 457	139 322	135 136	...	...	...	...	...	...
25 - 29	289 032	145 398	143 635	...	...	...	...	...	...
30 - 34	338 638	171 159	167 479	...	...	...	...	...	...
35 - 39	355 892	181 365	174 527	...	...	...	...	...	...
40 - 44	331 974	169 464	162 511	...	...	...	...	...	...
45 - 49	318 279	161 610	156 669	...	...	...	...	...	...
50 - 54	300 648	152 710	147 938	...	...	...	...	...	...
55 - 59	300 836	152 838	147 999	...	...	...	...	...	...
60 - 64	231 269	115 671	115 599	...	...	...	...	...	...
65 - 69	174 151	83 827	90 324	...	...	...	...	...	...
70 - 74	151 366	69 689	81 677	...	...	...	...	...	...
75 - 79	140 063	60 430	79 634	...	...	...	...	...	...
80 - 84	117 954	44 651	73 303	...	...	...	...	...	...
85 - 89	66 304	21 048	45 256	...	...	...	...	...	...
90 - 94	24 630	6 316	18 314	...	...	...	...	...	...
95 - 99	5 096	1 035	4 061	...	...	...	...	...	...
100 +	533	90	443	...	...	...	...	...	...
Poland - Pologne									
1 VII 2004 (ESDF)									
Total	38 180 249	18 478 368	19 701 881	23 490 202	11 162 807	12 327 395	14 690 047	7 315 561	7 374 486
0	352 585	181 664	170 921	200 427	103 276	97 151	152 158	78 388	73 770
1 - 4	1 456 107	747 325	708 782	809 075	415 678	393 397	647 032	331 647	315 385
5 - 9	2 087 358	1 068 981	1 018 377	1 127 702	577 661	550 041	959 656	491 320	468 336
10 - 14	2 583 521	1 321 706	1 261 815	1 416 709	725 119	691 590	1 166 812	596 587	570 225
15 - 19	3 043 241	1 555 810	1 487 431	1 789 899	911 903	877 996	1 253 342	643 907	609 435
20 - 24	3 287 121	1 671 029	1 616 092	2 080 527	1 043 225	1 037 302	1 206 594	627 804	578 790
25 - 29	3 033 481	1 538 688	1 494 793	1 947 737	974 685	973 052	1 085 744	564 003	521 741
30 - 34	2 619 975	1 327 885	1 292 090	1 627 679	816 617	811 062	992 296	511 268	481 028
35 - 39	2 374 985	1 200 617	1 174 368	1 429 350	706 819	722 531	945 635	493 798	451 837
40 - 44	2 642 543	1 323 062	1 319 481	1 620 835	781 048	839 787	1 021 708	542 014	479 694
45 - 49	3 108 826	1 535 060	1 573 766	2 029 187	959 968	1 069 219	1 079 639	575 092	504 547
50 - 54	2 915 221	1 410 163	1 505 058	1 962 797	914 718	1 048 079	952 424	495 445	456 979
55 - 59	2 164 265	1 021 652	1 142 613	1 458 569	672 981	785 588	705 696	348 671	357 025
60 - 64	1 530 330	690 689	839 641	996 054	441 759	554 295	534 276	248 930	285 346
65 - 69	1 565 923	669 738	896 185	982 934	412 338	570 596	582 989	257 400	325 589
70 - 74	1 415 912	567 673	848 239	855 324	340 069	515 255	560 588	227 604	332 984
75 - 79	1 061 525	372 827	688 698	618 684	214 855	403 829	442 841	157 972	284 869
80 - 84	613 562	189 761	423 801	348 448	104 474	243 974	265 114	85 287	179 827
85 +	323 768	84 038	239 730	188 265	45 614	142 651	135 503	38 424	97 079
Portugal[43]									
12 III 2001 (CDFC)									
Total	10 356 117	5 000 141	5 355 976	5 680 711	2 713 204	2 967 507	4 675 406	2 286 937	2 388 469
0	110 914	56 866	54 048	63 392	32 505	30 887	47 522	24 361	23 161
1 - 4	428 577	219 103	209 474	238 914	122 152	116 762	189 663	96 951	92 712
5 - 9	537 521	275 199	262 322	291 377	149 224	142 153	246 144	125 975	120 169
10 - 14	579 590	296 385	283 205	306 265	156 159	150 106	273 325	140 226	133 099
15 - 19	688 686	351 422	337 264	364 989	185 544	179 445	323 697	165 878	157 819

7. Population by age, sex and urban/rural residence: latest available year, 1996 - 2005
Population selon l'âge, le sexe et la résidence, urbaine/rurale: dernière année disponible, 1996 - 2005 (continued - suite)

Continent, country or area, date, code and age (in years) Continent, pays ou zone, date, code et âge (en années)	Total			Urban - Urbaine			Rural - Rurale		
	Both sexes Les deux sexes	Male Masculin	Female Féminin	Both sexes Les deux sexes	Male Masculin	Female Féminin	Both sexes Les deux sexes	Male Masculin	Female Féminin
EUROPE									
Portugal[43]									
12 III 2001 (CDFC)									
20 - 24	790 901	400 087	390 814	446 459	222 820	223 639	344 442	177 267	167 175
25 - 29	814 661	409 243	405 418	477 253	237 314	239 939	337 408	171 929	165 479
30 - 34	761 457	379 363	382 094	436 577	215 220	221 357	324 880	164 143	160 737
35 - 39	770 781	378 783	391 998	431 579	208 353	223 226	339 202	170 430	168 772
40 - 44	728 518	357 528	370 990	410 550	197 035	213 515	317 968	160 493	157 475
45 - 49	686 134	333 382	352 752	392 185	186 726	205 459	293 949	146 656	147 293
50 - 54	642 516	309 484	333 032	373 939	178 079	195 860	268 577	131 405	137 172
55 - 59	571 452	268 899	302 553	320 755	151 997	168 758	250 697	116 902	133 795
60 - 64	550 916	256 179	294 737	289 014	133 942	155 072	261 902	122 237	139 665
65 - 69	538 165	244 230	293 935	271 583	120 482	151 101	266 582	123 748	142 834
70 - 74	453 962	196 615	257 347	225 235	93 945	131 290	228 727	102 670	126 057
75 - 79	348 066	143 439	204 627	169 460	66 449	103 011	178 606	76 990	101 616
80 - 84	201 706	76 014	125 692	96 249	33 700	62 549	105 457	42 314	63 143
85 - 89	108 419	36 167	72 252	53 184	16 295	36 889	55 235	19 872	35 363
90 - 94	36 063	10 241	25 822	18 088	4 583	13 505	17 975	5 658	12 317
95 - 99	6 523	1 417	5 106	3 350	639	2 711	3 173	778	2 395
100 +	589	95	494	314	41	273	275	54	221
1 VII 2005 (ESDJ)									
Total	10 549 424	5 105 041	5 444 383	...	...	...	...	...	...
0	108 786	56 106	52 680	...	...	...	...	...	...
1 - 4	444 443	229 520	214 923	...	...	...	...	...	...
5 - 9	539 074	275 645	263 429	...	...	...	...	...	...
10 - 14	553 532	282 871	270 661	...	...	...	...	...	...
15 - 19	594 471	303 557	290 914	...	...	...	...	...	...
20 - 24	715 838	363 814	352 025	...	...	...	...	...	...
25 - 29	818 043	413 170	404 874	...	...	...	...	...	...
30 - 34	826 531	414 394	412 137	...	...	...	...	...	...
35 - 39	779 430	387 467	391 963	...	...	...	...	...	...
40 - 44	782 947	385 116	397 832	...	...	...	...	...	...
45 - 49	726 263	355 777	370 486	...	...	...	...	...	...
50 - 54	679 233	328 667	350 567	...	...	...	...	...	...
55 - 59	629 106	299 540	329 567	...	...	...	...	...	...
60 - 64	551 410	256 452	294 959	...	...	...	...	...	...
65 - 69	531 564	242 277	289 287	...	...	...	...	...	...
70 - 74	485 920	212 595	273 326	...	...	...	...	...	...
75 - 79	374 923	152 670	222 253	...	...	...	...	...	...
80 - 84	248 765	94 111	154 654	...	...	...	...	...	...
85 - 89	110 267	37 135	73 132	...	...	...	...	...	...
90 - 94	41 142	12 266	28 876	...	...	...	...	...	...
95 - 99	6 916	1 697	5 220	...	...	...	...	...	...
100 +	825	199	626	...	...	...	...	...	...
Unknown - Inconnu	-	-	-	...	...	...	...	...	...
Republic of Moldova - République de Moldova[44]									
1 VII 2004 (ESDJ)									
Total	3 603 940	1 726 630	1 877 310	1 476 980	712 971	764 009	2 126 960	1 013 659	1 113 301
0	36 877	19 090	17 787	13 251	6 923	6 328	23 626	12 167	11 459
1 - 4	143 995	74 342	69 653	49 886	25 835	24 051	94 109	48 507	45 602
5 - 9	221 693	113 541	108 152	74 221	38 378	35 843	147 472	75 163	72 309
10 - 14	295 893	151 224	144 669	107 949	55 401	52 548	187 944	95 823	92 121
15 - 19	362 381	183 936	178 445	139 027	70 616	68 411	223 354	113 320	110 034
20 - 24	337 280	170 114	167 166	131 354	67 581	63 773	205 926	102 533	103 393
25 - 29	299 930	152 278	147 652	122 441	61 696	60 745	177 489	90 582	86 907
30 - 34	241 227	118 787	122 440	120 222	60 665	59 557	121 005	58 122	62 883
35 - 39	224 152	108 717	115 435	107 025	52 573	54 452	117 127	56 144	60 983
40 - 44	275 531	130 836	144 695	126 893	59 454	67 439	148 638	71 382	77 256
45 - 49	277 178	130 988	146 190	127 779	58 985	68 794	149 399	72 003	77 396
50 - 54	251 003	116 414	134 589	115 459	53 521	61 938	135 544	62 893	72 651
55 - 59	143 825	64 282	79 543	67 195	31 125	36 070	76 630	33 157	43 473
60 - 64	137 484	58 675	78 809	52 501	23 969	28 532	84 983	34 706	50 277
65 - 69	130 621	53 395	77 226	49 105	20 889	28 216	81 516	32 506	49 010
70 - 74	99 564	38 008	61 556	31 056	12 167	18 889	68 508	25 841	42 667
75 - 79	73 553	25 863	47 690	24 184	8 280	15 904	49 369	17 583	31 786

7. Population by age, sex and urban/rural residence: latest available year, 1996 - 2005
Population selon l'âge, le sexe et la résidence, urbaine/rurale: dernière année disponible, 1996 - 2005 (continued - suite)

Continent, country or area, date, code and age (in years) / Continent, pays ou zone, date, code et âge (en années)	Total			Urban - Urbaine			Rural - Rurale		
	Both sexes Les deux sexes	Male Masculin	Female Féminin	Both sexes Les deux sexes	Male Masculin	Female Féminin	Both sexes Les deux sexes	Male Masculin	Female Féminin
EUROPE									
Republic of Moldova - République de Moldova[44]									
1 VII 2004 (ESDJ)									
80 - 84	35 820	11 769	24 051	11 362	3 314	8 048	24 458	8 455	16 003
85 + ...	15 933	4 371	11 562	6 070	1 599	4 471	9 863	2 772	7 091
Romania - Roumanie									
1 VII 2005 (ESDJ)									
Total....................	21 623 849	10 543 518	11 080 331	11 879 897	5 692 516	6 187 381	9 743 952	4 851 002	4 892 950
0	215 597	110 720	104 877	113 777	58 540	55 237	101 820	52 180	49 640
1 - 4	838 292	431 118	407 174	405 639	208 636	197 003	432 653	222 482	210 171
5 - 9	1 108 895	568 389	540 506	513 126	263 253	249 873	595 769	305 136	290 633
10 - 14	1 209 921	619 434	590 487	602 157	307 724	294 433	607 764	311 710	296 054
15 - 19	1 727 418	881 000	846 418	988 973	499 409	489 564	738 445	381 591	356 854
20 - 24	1 618 002	827 513	790 489	976 086	490 011	486 075	641 916	337 502	304 414
25 - 29	1 786 029	915 862	870 167	1 054 488	526 377	528 111	731 541	389 485	342 056
30 - 34	1 678 743	855 635	823 108	938 798	460 620	478 178	739 945	395 015	344 930
35 - 39	1 761 497	890 199	871 298	1 048 640	498 163	550 477	712 857	392 036	320 821
40 - 44	1 238 076	618 597	619 479	767 250	357 184	410 066	470 826	261 413	209 413
45 - 49	1 525 338	750 091	775 247	985 345	462 420	522 925	539 993	287 671	252 322
50 - 54	1 509 522	730 222	779 300	950 642	458 654	491 988	558 880	271 568	287 312
55 - 59	1 241 759	589 008	652 751	690 647	331 448	359 199	551 112	257 560	293 552
60 - 64	973 314	445 157	528 157	476 442	218 530	257 912	496 872	226 627	270 245
65 - 69	1 089 704	475 236	614 468	491 285	213 746	277 539	598 419	261 490	336 929
70 - 74	907 414	381 704	525 710	382 269	157 674	224 595	525 145	224 030	301 115
75 - 79	665 075	266 285	398 790	274 437	107 337	167 100	390 638	158 948	231 690
80 - 84	374 155	135 770	238 385	152 069	51 498	100 571	222 086	84 272	137 814
85 - 89	103 294	34 236	69 058	44 588	13 921	30 667	58 706	20 315	38 391
90 - 94	43 159	14 382	28 777	19 643	6 229	13 414	23 516	8 153	15 363
95 - 99	7 545	2 628	4 917	3 186	1 030	2 156	4 359	1 598	2 761
100 + ...	1 100	332	768	410	112	298	690	220	470
Russian Federation - Fédération de Russie									
1 I 2005 (ESDJ)									
Total....................	143 474 219	66 602 762	76 871 457	104 719 359	48 150 424	56 568 935	38 754 860	18 452 338	20 302 522
0 - 4	6 866 644	3 521 369	3 345 275	4 801 628	2 465 337	2 336 291	2 065 016	1 056 032	1 008 984
5 - 9	6 535 725	3 342 598	3 193 127	4 410 677	2 258 194	2 152 483	2 125 048	1 084 404	1 040 644
10 - 14	8 468 928	4 328 547	4 140 381	5 690 688	2 908 495	2 782 193	2 778 240	1 420 052	1 358 188
15 - 19	12 241 805	6 224 129	6 017 676	8 744 915	4 403 711	4 341 204	3 496 890	1 820 418	1 676 472
20 - 24	12 267 572	6 201 309	6 066 263	9 535 761	4 788 470	4 747 291	2 731 811	1 412 839	1 318 972
25 - 29	10 880 964	5 437 719	5 443 245	8 331 485	4 128 253	4 203 232	2 549 479	1 309 466	1 240 013
30 - 34	10 211 514	5 086 937	5 124 577	7 770 592	3 850 412	3 920 180	2 440 922	1 236 525	1 204 397
35 - 39	9 411 668	4 626 583	4 785 085	6 914 523	3 359 486	3 555 037	2 497 145	1 267 097	1 230 048
40 - 44	11 665 400	5 641 140	6 024 260	8 532 332	4 041 099	4 491 233	3 133 068	1 600 041	1 533 027
45 - 49	11 884 591	5 601 116	6 283 475	8 745 822	4 010 484	4 735 338	3 138 769	1 590 632	1 548 137
50 - 54	10 517 576	4 800 441	5 717 135	7 921 819	3 526 701	4 395 118	2 595 757	1 273 740	1 322 017
55 - 59	7 655 682	3 361 177	4 294 505	5 901 561	2 543 529	3 358 032	1 754 121	817 648	936 473
60 - 64	5 178 964	2 086 473	3 092 491	3 777 371	1 510 352	2 267 019	1 401 593	576 121	825 472
65 - 69	7 509 925	2 834 177	4 675 748	5 299 985	1 967 176	3 332 809	2 209 940	867 001	1 342 939
70 - 74	4 895 982	1 678 793	3 217 189	3 310 035	1 105 720	2 204 315	1 585 947	573 073	1 012 874
75 - 79	4 370 371	1 260 426	3 109 945	2 994 424	867 390	2 127 034	1 375 947	393 036	982 911
80 - 84	1 874 948	387 006	1 487 942	1 318 816	278 684	1 040 132	556 132	108 322	447 810
85 + ...	1 035 960	182 822	853 138	716 925	136 931	579 994	319 035	45 891	273 144
San Marino - Saint-Marin									
1 VII 2004 (ESDF)									
Total....................	29 457	14 442	15 015	...	...	...	...	...	...
0	308	160	149	...	...	...	...	...	...
1 - 4	1 274	678	596	...	...	...	...	...	...
5 - 9	1 508	800	708	...	...	...	...	...	...
10 - 14	1 383	707	676	...	...	...	...	...	...
15 - 19	1 292	672	620	...	...	...	...	...	...
20 - 24	1 519	779	740	...	...	...	...	...	...
25 - 29	2 038	983	1 055	...	...	...	...	...	...
30 - 34	2 559	1 256	1 304	...	...	...	...	...	...
35 - 39	2 863	1 385	1 478	...	...	...	...	...	...
40 - 44	2 617	1 297	1 320	...	...	...	...	...	...

Continent, country or area, date, code and age (in years) / Continent, pays ou zone, date, code et âge (en années)	Total			Urban - Urbaine			Rural - Rurale		
	Both sexes Les deux sexes	Male Masculin	Female Féminin	Both sexes Les deux sexes	Male Masculin	Female Féminin	Both sexes Les deux sexes	Male Masculin	Female Féminin

EUROPE

San Marino - Saint-Marin
1 VII 2004 (ESDF)

45 - 49	2 067	1 054	1 013	...	...	...	...	...	...
50 - 54	1 876	932	944	...	...	...	...	...	...
55 - 59	1 819	892	927	...	...	...	...	...	...
60 - 64	1 526	751	775	...	...	...	...	...	...
65 - 69	1 383	688	696	...	...	...	...	...	...
70 - 74	1 207	553	655	...	...	...	...	...	...
75 - 79	946	413	533	...	...	...	...	...	...
80 - 84	765	290	475	...	...	...	...	...	...
85 - 89	321	102	219	...	...	...	...	...	...
90 - 94	163	47	116	...	...	...	...	...	...
95 - 99	29	9	20	...	...	...	...	...	...
100 +	2	-	2	...	...	...	...	...	...

Serbia and Montenegro - Serbie-et-Montenegro[45]
1 VII 2003 (ESDJ)

Total	8 152 676	3 967 478	4 185 198	4 654 786	2 227 301	2 427 485	3 497 890	1 740 177	1 757 713
0	86 200	44 418	41 782	53 075	27 382	25 693	33 125	17 036	16 089
1 - 4	322 645	165 351	157 294	179 618	92 485	87 133	143 027	72 866	70 161
5 - 9	436 106	223 992	212 114	242 286	124 688	117 598	193 820	99 304	94 516
10 - 14	480 951	246 133	234 818	271 988	138 937	133 051	208 963	107 196	101 767
15 - 19	545 363	278 862	266 501	319 785	162 663	157 122	225 578	116 199	109 379
20 - 24	566 129	288 126	278 003	345 516	172 893	172 623	220 613	115 233	105 380
25 - 29	564 788	284 287	280 501	344 243	168 823	175 420	220 545	115 464	105 081
30 - 34	527 060	262 928	264 132	315 022	152 942	162 080	212 038	109 986	102 052
35 - 39	527 572	261 214	266 358	310 687	148 625	162 062	216 885	112 589	104 296
40 - 44	572 083	282 742	289 341	340 255	160 766	179 489	231 828	121 976	109 852
45 - 49	638 825	317 636	321 189	382 135	181 958	200 177	256 690	135 678	121 012
50 - 54	641 777	316 623	325 154	388 500	184 676	203 824	253 277	131 947	121 330
55 - 59	452 198	216 784	235 414	266 384	125 067	141 317	185 814	91 717	94 097
60 - 64	448 403	209 575	238 828	243 343	111 780	131 563	205 060	97 795	107 265
65 - 69	477 449	217 450	259 999	247 469	112 948	134 521	229 980	104 502	125 478
70 - 74	415 625	180 416	235 209	194 198	82 361	111 837	221 427	98 055	123 372
75 - 79	273 821	106 855	166 966	128 316	49 350	78 966	145 505	57 505	88 000
80 - 84	129 139	47 320	81 819	58 647	20 866	37 781	70 492	26 454	44 038
85 - 89	28 929	10 415	18 514	14 159	4 888	9 271	14 770	5 527	9 243
90 - 94	14 093	5 099	8 994	7 039	2 435	4 604	7 054	2 664	4 390
95 - 99	2 603	936	1 667	1 492	550	942	1 111	386	725
100 +	917	316	601	629	218	411	288	98	190

Slovakia - Slovaquie
25 V 2001 (CDJC)

Total	5 379 455	2 612 515	2 766 940	3 022 106	1 453 638	1 568 468	2 357 349	1 158 877	1 198 472
0	52 468	26 946	25 522	26 392	13 568	12 824	26 076	13 378	12 698
1 - 4	225 241	115 451	109 790	112 913	57 815	55 098	112 328	57 636	54 692
5 - 9	338 772	173 426	165 346	179 016	91 507	87 509	159 756	81 919	77 837
10 - 14	399 012	203 773	195 239	228 288	116 408	111 880	170 724	87 365	83 359
15 - 19	440 003	224 835	215 168	256 798	131 346	125 452	183 205	93 489	89 716
20 - 24	466 328	237 744	228 584	268 502	136 866	131 636	197 826	100 878	96 948
25 - 29	432 649	219 862	212 787	242 797	121 583	121 214	189 852	98 279	91 573
30 - 34	359 200	181 495	177 705	201 867	98 460	103 407	157 333	83 035	74 298
35 - 39	380 054	190 953	189 101	222 722	107 092	115 630	157 332	83 861	73 471
40 - 44	398 966	200 264	198 702	240 260	115 581	124 679	158 706	84 683	74 023
45 - 49	410 780	202 899	207 881	250 543	120 025	130 518	160 237	82 874	77 363
50 - 54	343 768	166 384	177 384	203 207	96 510	106 697	140 561	69 874	70 687
55 - 59	255 423	117 483	137 940	142 222	64 660	77 562	113 201	52 823	60 378
60 - 64	218 344	96 088	122 256	112 957	49 628	63 329	105 387	46 460	58 927
65 - 69	197 491	82 476	115 015	98 867	41 737	57 130	98 624	40 739	57 885
70 - 74	175 488	68 061	107 427	84 220	33 073	51 147	91 268	34 988	56 280
75 - 79	135 913	48 248	87 665	63 749	22 917	40 832	72 164	25 331	46 833
80 - 84	57 718	19 332	38 386	26 894	9 218	17 676	30 824	10 114	20 710
85 - 89	31 757	9 824	21 933	14 602	4 513	10 089	17 155	5 311	11 844
90 - 94	10 537	2 896	7 641	4 724	1 255	3 469	5 813	1 641	4 172
95 - 99	1 811	461	1 350	868	229	639	943	232	711

Continent, country or area, date, code and age (in years) / Continent, pays ou zone, date, code et âge (en années)	Total			Urban - Urbaine			Rural - Rurale		
	Both sexes Les deux sexes	Male Masculin	Female Féminin	Both sexes Les deux sexes	Male Masculin	Female Féminin	Both sexes Les deux sexes	Male Masculin	Female Féminin

EUROPE

Slovakia - Slovaquie
25 V 2001 (CDJC)

100 +	208	72	136	116	44	72	92	28	64
Unknown - Inconnu	47 524	23 542	23 982	39 582	19 603	19 979	7 942	3 939	4 003

1 VII 2005 (ESDJ)

Total	5 387 285	2 614 912	2 772 373	...	...	...	...	...	...
0	53 834	27 665	26 169	...	...	...	...	...	...
1 - 4	206 505	106 015	100 490	...	...	...	...	...	...
5 - 9	287 495	147 322	140 173	...	...	...	...	...	...
10 - 14	358 989	183 450	175 539	...	...	...	...	...	...
15 - 19	412 893	210 711	202 182	...	...	...	...	...	...
20 - 24	449 093	229 317	219 776	...	...	...	...	...	...
25 - 29	471 448	240 188	231 260	...	...	...	...	...	...
30 - 34	420 494	213 209	207 285	...	...	...	...	...	...
35 - 39	362 358	182 544	179 814	...	...	...	...	...	...
40 - 44	384 393	192 630	191 763	...	...	...	...	...	...
45 - 49	402 804	200 201	202 603	...	...	...	...	...	...
50 - 54	397 540	193 898	203 642	...	...	...	...	...	...
55 - 59	311 487	146 761	164 726	...	...	...	...	...	...
60 - 64	237 025	105 075	131 950	...	...	...	...	...	...
65 - 69	193 786	80 645	113 141	...	...	...	...	...	...
70 - 74	171 848	66 875	104 973	...	...	...	...	...	...
75 - 79	134 684	47 659	87 025	...	...	...	...	...	...
80 - 84	88 990	28 348	60 642	...	...	...	...	...	...
85 - 89	26 288	8 007	18 281	...	...	...	...	...	...
90 - 94	12 077	3 398	8 679	...	...	...	...	...	...
95 - 99	2 714	791	1 923	...	...	...	...	...	...
100 +	540	203	337	...	...	...	...	...	...

Slovenia - Slovénie
1 VII 2005 (ESDJ)

Total	2 001 114	980 070	1 021 044	965 538[46]	457 869[46]	507 669[46]	987 547[46]	488 268[46]	499 279[46]
0	18 069	9 250	8 819	8 502[46]	4 341[46]	4 161[46]	9 387[46]	4 815[46]	4 572[46]
1 - 4	71 282	36 650	34 632	33 045[46]	17 041[46]	16 004[46]	37 243[46]	19 078[46]	18 165[46]
5 - 9	92 568	47 778	44 790	41 944[46]	21 696[46]	20 248[46]	49 521[46]	25 534[46]	23 987[46]
10 - 14	102 957	52 777	50 180	46 443[46]	23 747[46]	22 696[46]	55 474[46]	28 489[46]	26 985[46]
15 - 19	123 507	63 419	60 088	57 858[46]	29 543[46]	28 315[46]	64 051[46]	32 958[46]	31 093[46]
20 - 24	141 356	72 515	68 841	66 975[46]	34 014[46]	32 961[46]	70 653[46]	36 181[46]	34 472[46]
25 - 29	153 502	79 417	74 085	72 696[46]	37 055[46]	35 641[46]	75 198[46]	38 657[46]	36 541[46]
30 - 34	145 499	74 883	70 616	67 969[46]	33 864[46]	34 105[46]	71 742[46]	37 028[46]	34 714[46]
35 - 39	149 973	75 993	73 980	69 934[46]	33 689[46]	36 245[46]	74 185[46]	37 955[46]	36 230[46]
40 - 44	155 302	78 677	76 625	74 762[46]	35 668[46]	39 094[46]	74 555[46]	38 331[46]	36 224[46]
45 - 49	156 060	79 846	76 214	76 234[46]	36 369[46]	39 865[46]	74 326[46]	39 005[46]	35 321[46]
50 - 54	155 623	80 214	75 409	78 733[46]	38 418[46]	40 315[46]	72 516[46]	38 230[46]	34 286[46]
55 - 59	122 423	61 325	61 098	62 545[46]	29 776[46]	32 769[46]	57 291[46]	29 544[46]	27 747[46]
60 - 64	103 456	49 543	53 913	52 507[46]	23 802[46]	28 705[46]	49 492[46]	24 655[46]	24 837[46]
65 - 69	95 847	43 800	52 047	48 113[46]	21 653[46]	26 460[46]	46 775[46]	21 570[46]	25 205[46]
70 - 74	85 872	34 939	50 933	43 021[46]	17 322[46]	25 699[46]	42 286[46]	17 338[46]	24 948[46]
75 - 79	65 759	22 914	42 845	32 825[46]	11 367[46]	21 458[46]	32 550[46]	11 379[46]	21 171[46]
80 - 84	41 018	11 229	29 789	20 686[46]	5 921[46]	14 765[46]	20 109[46]	5 227[46]	14 882[46]
85 - 89	12 860	3 163	9 697	6 613[46]	1 692[46]	4 921[46]	6 188[46]	1 452[46]	4 736[46]
90 - 94	6 784	1 474	5 310	3 393[46]	759[46]	2 634[46]	3 358[46]	710[46]	2 648[46]
95 - 99	1 280	245	1 035	672[46]	122[46]	550[46]	599[46]	123[46]	476[46]
100 +	117	19	98	68[46]	10[46]	58[46]	48[46]	9[46]	39[46]
Unknown - Inconnu	-	-	-	-[46]	-[46]	-[46]	-[46]	-[46]	-[46]

Spain - Espagne
1 VII 2005 (ESDJ)

Total	43 398 190	21 367 297	22 030 893	...	...	...	...	...	...
0	454 922	234 489	220 433	...	...	...	...	...	...
1 - 4	1 747 789	898 694	849 095	...	...	...	...	...	...
5 - 9	2 004 100	1 028 644	975 456	...	...	...	...	...	...
10 - 14	2 084 266	1 070 743	1 013 523	...	...	...	...	...	...
15 - 19	2 310 815	1 186 713	1 124 102	...	...	...	...	...	...
20 - 24	2 926 423	1 497 253	1 429 170	...	...	...	...	...	...
25 - 29	3 693 600	1 902 956	1 790 644	...	...	...	...	...	...

Continent, country or area, date, code and age (in years) Continent, pays ou zone, date, code et âge (en années)	Total			Urban - Urbaine			Rural - Rurale		
	Both sexes Les deux sexes	Male Masculin	Female Féminin	Both sexes Les deux sexes	Male Masculin	Female Féminin	Both sexes Les deux sexes	Male Masculin	Female Féminin
EUROPE									
Spain - Espagne									
1 VII 2005 (ESDJ)									
30 - 34	3 767 262	1 942 009	1 825 253	...	...	...	...	...	...
35 - 39	3 594 532	1 832 716	1 761 816	...	...	...	...	...	...
40 - 44	3 374 442	1 698 758	1 675 684	...	...	...	...	...	...
45 - 49	3 015 773	1 503 879	1 511 894	...	...	...	...	...	...
50 - 54	2 607 062	1 289 814	1 317 248	...	...	...	...	...	...
55 - 59	2 439 838	1 191 770	1 248 068	...	...	...	...	...	...
60 - 64	2 108 925	1 016 766	1 092 159	...	...	...	...	...	...
65 - 69	1 879 394	879 117	1 000 277	...	...	...	...	...	...
70 - 74	1 936 605	871 928	1 064 677	...	...	...	...	...	...
75 - 79	1 568 033	661 015	907 018	...	...	...	...	...	...
80 - 84	1 071 747	410 156	661 591	...	...	...	...	...	...
85 - 89	537 908	175 166	362 742	...	...	...	...	...	...
90 - 94	217 592	60 528	157 064	...	...	...	...	...	...
95 - 99	51 862	12 893	38 969	...	...	...	...	...	...
100 +	5 300	1 290	4 010	...	...	...	...	...	...
Sweden - Suède									
1 VII 2005 (ESDJ)									
Total	9 029 572	4 476 431	4 553 142	...	...	...	...	...	...
0	101 323	52 086	49 237	...	...	...	...	...	...
1 - 4	389 629	199 856	189 774	...	...	...	...	...	...
5 - 9	474 303	243 312	230 992	...	...	...	...	...	...
10 - 14	606 924	311 177	295 747	...	...	...	...	...	...
15 - 19	586 539	301 144	285 395	...	...	...	...	...	...
20 - 24	524 790	268 036	256 755	...	...	...	...	...	...
25 - 29	544 890	277 358	267 533	...	...	...	...	...	...
30 - 34	611 457	310 784	300 673	...	...	...	...	...	...
35 - 39	644 584	328 919	315 665	...	...	...	...	...	...
40 - 44	625 965	319 498	306 467	...	...	...	...	...	...
45 - 49	585 646	297 179	288 467	...	...	...	...	...	...
50 - 54	581 202	293 241	287 962	...	...	...	...	...	...
55 - 59	636 584	319 785	316 800	...	...	...	...	...	...
60 - 64	555 883	279 549	276 334	...	...	...	...	...	...
65 - 69	414 755	202 412	212 343	...	...	...	...	...	...
70 - 74	347 104	161 037	186 068	...	...	...	...	...	...
75 - 79	313 248	136 022	177 226	...	...	...	...	...	...
80 - 84	262 452	104 408	158 044	...	...	...	...	...	...
85 - 89	148 845	51 293	97 552	...	...	...	...	...	...
90 - 94	59 223	16 437	42 787	...	...	...	...	...	...
95 - 99	12 921	2 705	10 217	...	...	...	...	...	...
100 +	1 310	199	1 111	...	...	...	...	...	...
Switzerland - Suisse[47]									
1 VII 2005 (ESDJ)									
Total	7 437 116	3 640 600	3 796 516	...	...	...	...	...	...
0	72 690	37 299	35 391	...	...	...	...	...	...
1 - 4	292 435	150 489	141 946	...	...	...	...	...	...
5 - 9	399 198	205 256	193 942	...	...	...	...	...	...
10 - 14	435 040	223 383	211 657	...	...	...	...	...	...
15 - 19	437 213	223 932	213 281	...	...	...	...	...	...
20 - 24	442 142	222 852	219 290	...	...	...	...	...	...
25 - 29	465 600	231 056	234 544	...	...	...	...	...	...
30 - 34	527 139	262 088	265 051	...	...	...	...	...	...
35 - 39	612 427	305 906	306 521	...	...	...	...	...	...
40 - 44	627 340	316 270	311 070	...	...	...	...	...	...
45 - 49	556 384	281 271	275 113	...	...	...	...	...	...
50 - 54	493 913	247 410	246 503	...	...	...	...	...	...
55 - 59	478 655	239 008	239 647	...	...	...	...	...	...
60 - 64	414 374	203 888	210 486	...	...	...	...	...	...
65 - 69	325 445	153 155	172 290	...	...	...	...	...	...
70 - 74	286 869	128 297	158 572	...	...	...	...	...	...
75 - 79	238 456	97 530	140 926	...	...	...	...	...	...
80 - 84	180 521	66 388	114 133	...	...	...	...	...	...
85 - 89	95 183	31 003	64 180	...	...	...	...	...	...

7. Population by age, sex and urban/rural residence: latest available year, 1996 - 2005
Population selon l'âge, le sexe et la résidence, urbaine/rurale: dernière année disponible, 1996 - 2005 (continued - suite)

Continent, country or area, date, code and age (in years) / Continent, pays ou zone, date, code et âge (en années)	Total			Urban - Urbaine			Rural - Rurale		
	Both sexes Les deux sexes	Male Masculin	Female Féminin	Both sexes Les deux sexes	Male Masculin	Female Féminin	Both sexes Les deux sexes	Male Masculin	Female Féminin
EUROPE									
Switzerland - Suisse[47]									
1 VII 2005 (ESDJ)									
90 - 94	44 216	11 723	32 493	...	...	...	...	...	...
95 +	11 876	2 396	9 480	...	...	...	...	...	...
The Former Yugoslav Rep. of Macedonia - L'ex-République yougoslave de Macédoine									
1 VII 2005 (ESDF)									
Total	2 036 855	1 021 772	1 015 083	...	...	...	...	...	...
0	22 610	11 625	10 985	...	...	...	...	...	...
1 - 4	94 848	48 971	45 877	...	...	...	...	...	...
5 - 9	130 446	67 429	63 017	...	...	...	...	...	...
10 - 14	153 315	78 786	74 529	...	...	...	...	...	...
15 - 19	163 234	83 889	79 345	...	...	...	...	...	...
20 - 24	165 241	84 844	80 397	...	...	...	...	...	...
25 - 29	157 384	81 001	76 383	...	...	...	...	...	...
30 - 34	149 620	75 983	73 637	...	...	...	...	...	...
35 - 39	148 942	75 662	73 280	...	...	...	...	...	...
40 - 44	147 428	74 962	72 466	...	...	...	...	...	...
45 - 49	144 902	73 954	70 948	...	...	...	...	...	...
50 - 54	134 376	67 505	66 871	...	...	...	...	...	...
55 - 59	110 410	53 592	56 818	...	...	...	...	...	...
60 - 64	89 234	42 809	46 425	...	...	...	...	...	...
65 - 69	81 499	38 221	43 278	...	...	...	...	...	...
70 - 74	68 735	31 218	37 517	...	...	...	...	...	...
75 - 79	42 936	18 475	24 461	...	...	...	...	...	...
80 - 84	22 249	9 135	13 114	...	...	...	...	...	...
85 - 89	6 036	2 489	3 547	...	...	...	...	...	...
90 - 94	2 060	844	1 216	...	...	...	...	...	...
95 +	424	149	275	...	...	...	...	...	...
Unknown - Inconnu	926	229	697	...	...	...	...	...	...
Ukraine									
5 XII 2001 (CDFC)									
Total	48 240 902	22 316 317	25 924 585	32 290 729	14 903 592	17 387 137	15 950 173	7 412 725	8 537 448
0	358 166	183 728	174 438	219 819	112 829	106 990	138 347	70 899	67 448
1 - 4	1 616 029	828 496	787 533	971 165	498 793	472 372	644 864	329 703	315 161
5 - 9	2 559 107	1 311 943	1 247 164	1 566 939	804 013	762 926	992 168	507 930	484 238
10 - 14	3 416 561	1 750 539	1 666 022	2 233 242	1 145 140	1 088 102	1 183 319	605 399	577 920
15 - 19	3 891 568	1 989 538	1 902 030	2 843 968	1 451 113	1 392 855	1 047 600	538 425	509 175
20 - 24	3 489 588	1 766 985	1 722 603	2 502 035	1 257 873	1 244 162	987 553	509 112	478 441
25 - 29	3 402 010	1 700 516	1 701 494	2 372 359	1 174 123	1 198 236	1 029 651	526 393	503 258
30 - 34	3 204 103	1 586 043	1 618 060	2 195 441	1 060 601	1 134 840	1 008 662	525 442	483 220
35 - 39	3 417 079	1 660 397	1 756 682	2 372 481	1 117 635	1 254 846	1 044 598	542 762	501 836
40 - 44	3 828 331	1 833 438	1 994 893	2 704 764	1 254 682	1 450 082	1 123 567	578 756	544 811
45 - 49	3 470 419	1 623 194	1 847 225	2 491 185	1 132 099	1 359 086	979 234	491 095	488 139
50 - 54	3 182 588	1 454 550	1 728 038	2 279 654	1 022 278	1 257 376	902 934	432 272	470 662
55 - 59	2 062 711	892 852	1 169 859	1 362 264	590 267	771 997	700 447	302 585	397 862
60 - 64	3 364 050	1 398 332	1 965 718	2 160 327	898 221	1 262 106	1 203 723	500 111	703 612
65 - 69	2 158 171	868 633	1 289 538	1 283 340	522 241	761 099	874 831	346 392	528 439
70 - 74	2 239 064	806 587	1 432 477	1 292 298	475 502	816 796	946 766	331 085	615 681
75 - 79	1 500 920	416 155	1 084 765	845 122	240 075	605 047	655 798	176 080	479 718
80 - 84	618 819	147 952	470 867	340 633	86 630	254 003	278 186	61 322	216 864
85 - 89	324 697	65 475	259 222	177 221	38 841	138 380	147 476	26 634	120 842
90 - 94	100 593	18 643	81 950	49 709	9 981	39 728	50 884	8 662	42 222
95 - 99	15 119	2 419	12 700	7 261	1 255	6 006	7 858	1 164	6 694
100 +	1 549	199	1 350	661	106	555	888	93	795
Unknown - Inconnu	19 660	9 703	9 957	18 841	9 294	9 547	819	409	410
1 VII 2004 (ESDJ)									
Total	47 271 271	21 840 401	25 430 870	...	...	...	...	...	...
0	414 634	213 119	201 515	...	...	...	...	...	...
1 - 4	1 533 811	789 224	744 587	...	...	...	...	...	...
5 - 9	2 225 162	1 139 772	1 085 390	...	...	...	...	...	...
10 - 14	2 944 446	1 509 276	1 435 170	...	...	...	...	...	...
15 - 19	3 757 321	1 920 789	1 836 532	...	...	...	...	...	...

Continent, country or area, date, code and age (in years) / Continent, pays ou zone, date, code et âge (en années)	Total			Urban - Urbaine			Rural - Rurale		
	Both sexes Les deux sexes	Male Masculin	Female Féminin	Both sexes Les deux sexes	Male Masculin	Female Féminin	Both sexes Les deux sexes	Male Masculin	Female Féminin
EUROPE									
Ukraine									
1 VII 2004 (ESDJ)									
20 - 24	3 709 786	1 889 845	1 819 941	...	...	...	...	...	...
25 - 29	3 410 477	1 710 972	1 699 506	...	...	...	...	...	...
30 - 34	3 291 742	1 631 230	1 660 512	...	...	...	...	...	...
35 - 39	3 142 690	1 532 714	1 609 977	...	...	...	...	...	...
40 - 44	3 680 850	1 759 871	1 920 979	...	...	...	...	...	...
45 - 49	3 575 003	1 670 590	1 904 414	...	...	...	...	...	...
50 - 54	3 304 191	1 501 526	1 802 665	...	...	...	...	...	...
55 - 59	2 410 760	1 051 150	1 359 610	...	...	...	...	...	...
60 - 64	2 432 159	995 315	1 436 844	...	...	...	...	...	...
65 - 69	2 811 124	1 107 662	1 703 462	...	...	...	...	...	...
70 - 74	1 801 864	653 321	1 148 544	...	...	...	...	...	...
75 - 79	1 661 403	504 979	1 156 424	...	...	...	...	...	...
80 - 84	770 993	181 430	589 563	...	...	...	...	...	...
85 - 89	264 206	54 641	209 565	...	...	...	...	...	...
90 - 94	112 772	20 434	92 338	...	...	...	...	...	...
95 - 99	14 144	2 305	11 840	...	...	...	...	...	...
100 +	1 738	240	1 498	...	...	...	...	...	...
United Kingdom - Royaume-Uni									
29 IV 2001 (CDFC)									
Total	58 789 194	28 579 869	30 209 325	47 007 427	22 769 606	24 237 821	11 781 767	5 810 263	5 971 504
0	660 025	337 154	322 871	545 015	278 159	266 856	115 010	58 995	56 015
1 - 4	2 826 228	1 448 534	1 377 694	2 305 860	1 181 014	1 124 846	520 368	267 520	252 848
5 - 9	3 738 042	1 914 727	1 823 315	3 009 441	1 541 475	1 467 966	728 601	373 252	355 349
10 - 14	3 880 557	1 987 606	1 892 951	3 103 939	1 588 218	1 515 721	776 618	399 388	377 230
15 - 19	3 663 782	1 870 508	1 793 274	2 968 710	1 505 467	1 463 243	695 072	365 041	330 031
20 - 24	3 545 984	1 765 257	1 780 727	3 041 392	1 493 532	1 547 860	504 592	271 725	232 867
25 - 29	3 867 015	1 895 469	1 971 546	3 299 342	1 610 026	1 689 316	567 673	285 443	282 230
30 - 34	4 493 532	2 199 767	2 293 765	3 723 844	1 824 665	1 899 179	769 688	375 102	394 586
35 - 39	4 625 777	2 277 678	2 348 099	3 727 542	1 835 623	1 891 919	898 235	442 055	456 180
40 - 44	4 151 613	2 056 545	2 095 068	3 290 231	1 629 251	1 660 980	861 382	427 294	434 088
45 - 49	3 735 986	1 851 391	1 884 595	2 911 582	1 441 854	1 469 728	824 404	409 537	414 867
50 - 54	4 040 576	2 003 158	2 037 418	3 082 777	1 526 738	1 556 039	957 799	476 420	481 379
55 - 59	3 339 004	1 651 396	1 687 608	2 514 831	1 238 414	1 276 417	824 173	412 982	411 191
60 - 64	2 880 074	1 409 684	1 470 390	2 203 267	1 070 975	1 132 292	676 807	338 709	338 098
65 - 69	2 596 939	1 241 382	1 355 557	2 005 735	948 325	1 057 410	591 204	293 057	298 147
70 - 74	2 339 319	1 059 156	1 280 163	1 821 307	812 938	1 008 369	518 012	246 218	271 794
75 - 79	1 967 088	817 738	1 149 350	1 542 567	632 032	910 535	424 521	185 706	238 815
80 - 84	1 313 592	482 707	830 885	1 030 404	373 231	657 173	283 188	109 476	173 712
85 - 89	752 035	226 520	525 515	589 543	174 135	415 408	162 492	52 385	110 107
90 - 94	293 961	68 682	225 279	229 205	52 178	177 027	64 756	16 504	48 252
95 - 99	68 655	12 920	55 735	53 532	9 866	43 666	15 123	3 054	12 069
100 +	9 410	1 890	7 520	7 361	1 490	5 871	2 049	400	1 649
1 VII 2005 (ESDF)									
Total	60 209 452	29 479 150	30 730 302	...	...	...	...	...	...
0	715 940	366 945	348 995	...	...	...	...	...	...
1 - 4	3 427 520	1 755 631	1 671 889	...	...	...	...	...	...
5 - 9	3 560 453	1 823 229	1 737 224	...	...	...	...	...	...
10 - 14	3 821 333	1 961 857	1 859 476	...	...	...	...	...	...
15 - 19	3 964 725	2 038 195	1 926 530	...	...	...	...	...	...
20 - 24	3 906 247	1 980 008	1 926 239	...	...	...	...	...	...
25 - 29	3 734 556	1 867 257	1 867 299	...	...	...	...	...	...
30 - 34	4 162 024	2 065 728	2 096 296	...	...	...	...	...	...
35 - 39	4 643 204	2 305 000	2 338 204	...	...	...	...	...	...
40 - 44	4 602 430	2 273 840	2 328 590	...	...	...	...	...	...
45 - 49	4 042 163	2 001 396	2 040 767	...	...	...	...	...	...
50 - 54	3 670 285	1 815 239	1 855 046	...	...	...	...	...	...
55 - 59	3 911 695	1 929 362	1 982 333	...	...	...	...	...	...
60 - 64	3 114 098	1 519 032	1 595 066	...	...	...	...	...	...
65 - 69	2 711 373	1 305 862	1 405 511	...	...	...	...	...	...
70 - 74	2 337 015	1 083 226	1 253 789	...	...	...	...	...	...
75 - 79	1 947 120	839 039	1 108 081	...	...	...	...	...	...
80 - 84	1 477 351	563 628	913 723	...	...	...	...	...	...

Continent, country or area, date, code and age (in years) / Continent, pays ou zone, date, code et âge (en années)	Total			Urban - Urbaine			Rural - Rurale		
	Both sexes Les deux sexes	Male Masculin	Female Féminin	Both sexes Les deux sexes	Male Masculin	Female Féminin	Both sexes Les deux sexes	Male Masculin	Female Féminin
EUROPE									
United Kingdom - Royaume-Uni									
1 VII 2005 (ESDF)									
85 - 89	756 447	248 175	508 272	...	...	...	...	...	...
90 +	419 413	103 446	315 967	...	...	...	...	...	...
OCEANIA - OCÉANIE									
American Samoa - Samoas américaines[12]									
1 IV 2000 (CDJC)									
Total	57 291	29 264	28 027	...	...	...	...	...	...
0 - 4	7 820	4 008	3 812	...	...	...	...	...	...
5 - 9	7 788	4 058	3 730	...	...	...	...	...	...
10 - 14	6 604	3 389	3 215	...	...	...	...	...	...
15 - 19	5 223	2 747	2 476	...	...	...	...	...	...
20 - 24	4 476	2 328	2 148	...	...	...	...	...	...
25 - 29	4 356	2 218	2 138	...	...	...	...	...	...
30 - 34	4 351	2 167	2 184	...	...	...	...	...	...
35 - 39	4 059	1 980	2 079	...	...	...	...	...	...
40 - 44	3 302	1 654	1 648	...	...	...	...	...	...
45 - 49	2 660	1 331	1 329	...	...	...	...	...	...
50 - 54	2 073	1 071	1 002	...	...	...	...	...	...
55 - 59	1 474	817	657	...	...	...	...	...	...
60 - 64	1 204	636	568	...	...	...	...	...	...
65 - 69	790	407	383	...	...	...	...	...	...
70 - 74	555	231	324	...	...	...	...	...	...
75 +	556	222	334	...	...	...	...	...	...
Australia - Australie[11]									
1 VII 2004 (ESDJ)									
Total	20 091 504	9 990 513	10 100 991	17 503 103	8 639 350	8 863 753	2 588 401	1 351 163	1 237 238
0	251 036	129 234	121 802	222 393	114 395	107 998	28 643	14 839	13 804
1 - 4	1 010 211	517 728	492 483	881 579	451 566	430 013	128 632	66 162	62 470
5 - 9	1 330 019	682 309	647 710	1 136 867	582 674	554 193	193 152	99 635	93 517
10 - 14	1 387 485	711 924	675 561	1 172 804	600 885	571 919	214 681	111 039	103 642
15 - 19	1 370 457	702 012	668 445	1 192 373	607 108	585 265	178 084	94 904	83 180
20 - 24	1 392 312	714 044	678 268	1 268 089	643 828	624 261	124 223	70 216	54 007
25 - 29	1 356 280	683 704	672 576	1 232 918	618 820	614 098	123 362	64 884	58 478
30 - 34	1 520 727	755 563	765 164	1 355 177	672 600	682 577	165 550	82 963	82 587
35 - 39	1 461 412	726 262	735 150	1 275 056	632 721	642 335	186 356	93 541	92 815
40 - 44	1 542 629	768 574	774 055	1 324 389	657 550	666 839	218 240	111 024	107 216
45 - 49	1 433 616	712 380	721 236	1 222 978	603 512	619 466	210 638	108 868	101 770
50 - 54	1 322 701	657 973	664 728	1 122 002	553 221	568 781	200 699	104 752	95 947
55 - 59	1 202 826	606 481	596 345	1 015 645	506 936	508 709	187 181	99 545	87 636
60 - 64	904 894	456 836	448 058	765 208	381 157	384 051	139 686	75 679	64 007
65 - 69	746 382	368 410	377 972	641 997	310 767	331 230	104 385	57 643	46 742
70 - 74	628 410	301 416	326 994	553 263	259 877	293 386	75 147	41 539	33 608
75 - 79	549 695	247 588	302 107	494 997	218 486	276 511	54 698	29 102	25 596
80 - 84	384 810	154 502	230 308	351 763	138 502	213 261	33 047	16 000	17 047
85 +	295 602	93 573	202 029	273 605	84 745	188 860	21 997	8 828	13 169
Cook Islands - Îles Cook[48]									
1 XII 2001 (CDFC)									
Total	18 027	...	...	...	...	...	...	...	...
0 - 4	1 722	...	...	...	...	...	...	...	...
5 - 9	1 895	...	...	...	...	...	...	...	...
10 - 14	1 798	...	...	...	...	...	...	...	...
15 - 19	1 460	...	...	...	...	...	...	...	...
20 - 24	1 227	...	...	...	...	...	...	...	...
25 - 29	1 385	...	...	...	...	...	...	...	...
30 - 34	1 431	...	...	...	...	...	...	...	...
35 - 39	1 367	...	...	...	...	...	...	...	...
40 - 44	1 194	...	...	...	...	...	...	...	...
45 - 49	925	...	...	...	...	...	...	...	...
50 - 54	906	...	...	...	...	...	...	...	...

7. Population by age, sex and urban/rural residence: latest available year, 1996 - 2005
Population selon l'âge, le sexe et la résidence, urbaine/rurale: dernière année disponible, 1996 - 2005 (continued - suite)

Continent, country or area, date, code and age (in years) / Continent, pays ou zone, date, code et âge (en années)	Total			Urban - Urbaine			Rural - Rurale		
	Both sexes Les deux sexes	Male Masculin	Female Féminin	Both sexes Les deux sexes	Male Masculin	Female Féminin	Both sexes Les deux sexes	Male Masculin	Female Féminin
OCEANIA - OCÉANIE									
Cook Islands - Îles Cook[48]									
1 XII 2001 (CDFC)									
55 - 59	799	...	...	...	...	...	...	...	...
60 - 64	730	...	...	...	...	...	...	...	...
65 - 69	538	...	...	...	...	...	...	...	...
70 - 74	324	...	...	...	...	...	...	...	...
75 - 79	195	...	...	...	...	...	...	...	...
80 +	131	...	...	...	...	...	...	...	...
Fiji - Fidji									
25 VIII 1996 (CDFC)									
Total	775 077	393 931	381 146	359 495	180 119	179 376	415 582	213 812	201 770
0	18 239	9 282	8 957	8 136	4 213	3 923	10 103	5 069	5 034
1 - 4	75 975	39 281	36 694	32 702	16 877	15 825	43 273	22 404	20 869
5 - 9	87 095	44 937	42 158	35 977	18 271	17 706	51 118	26 666	24 452
10 - 14	92 855	47 709	45 146	40 497	20 644	19 853	52 358	27 065	25 293
15 - 19	83 682	42 829	40 853	41 404	20 748	20 656	42 278	22 081	20 197
20 - 24	66 955	34 444	32 511	35 678	17 936	17 742	31 277	16 508	14 769
25 - 29	61 660	31 283	30 377	30 706	15 554	15 152	30 954	15 729	15 225
30 - 34	60 841	30 727	30 114	28 905	14 318	14 587	31 936	16 409	15 527
35 - 39	55 779	28 525	27 254	26 975	13 523	13 452	28 804	15 002	13 802
40 - 44	44 180	22 341	21 839	21 863	10 765	11 098	22 317	11 576	10 741
45 - 49	37 081	18 482	18 599	18 007	8 913	9 094	19 074	9 569	9 505
50 - 54	28 683	14 286	14 397	13 300	6 567	6 733	15 383	7 719	7 664
55 - 59	22 245	10 857	11 388	9 562	4 560	5 002	12 683	6 297	6 386
60 - 64	15 459	7 605	7 854	6 389	3 039	3 350	9 070	4 566	4 504
65 - 69	10 761	5 138	5 623	4 191	1 941	2 250	6 570	3 197	3 373
70 - 74	6 357	3 054	3 303	2 473	1 129	1 344	3 884	1 925	1 959
75 - 79	4 152	1 881	2 271	1 558	654	904	2 594	1 227	1 367
80 - 84	1 938	843	1 095	782	339	443	1 156	504	652
85 - 89	772	290	482	266	97	169	506	193	313
90 - 94	265	100	165	82	23	59	183	77	106
95 +	103	37	66	42	8	34	61	29	32
French Polynesia - Polynésie française									
1 I 1999 (ESDF)									
Total	227 525	117 738	109 787	...	...	...	...	...	...
0	4 268	2 177	2 091	...	...	...	...	...	...
1 - 4	18 470	9 604	8 866	...	...	...	...	...	...
5 - 9	25 518	13 178	12 340	...	...	...	...	...	...
10 - 14	25 533	13 055	12 478	...	...	...	...	...	...
15 - 19	22 126	11 290	10 836	...	...	...	...	...	...
20 - 24	19 077	9 884	9 193	...	...	...	...	...	...
25 - 29	19 574	10 141	9 433	...	...	...	...	...	...
30 - 34	19 667	10 179	9 488	...	...	...	...	...	...
35 - 39	17 032	8 941	8 091	...	...	...	...	...	...
40 - 44	14 421	7 640	6 781	...	...	...	...	...	...
45 - 49	11 037	5 830	5 207	...	...	...	...	...	...
50 - 54	9 001	4 790	4 211	...	...	...	...	...	...
55 - 59	7 202	3 845	3 357	...	...	...	...	...	...
60 - 64	5 518	2 899	2 619	...	...	...	...	...	...
65 - 69	3 998	2 042	1 956	...	...	...	...	...	...
70 - 74	2 600	1 244	1 356	...	...	...	...	...	...
75 - 79	1 365	585	780	...	...	...	...	...	...
80 +	1 118	414	704	...	...	...	...	...	...
Guam[12]									
1 IV 2000 (CDJC)									
Total	154 805	79 181	75 624	...	...	...	...	...	...
0	3 535	1 862	1 673	...	...	...	...	...	...
1 - 4	13 250	6 945	6 305	...	...	...	...	...	...
5 - 9	16 090	8 270	7 820	...	...	...	...	...	...
10 - 14	14 281	7 232	7 049	...	...	...	...	...	...
15 - 19	12 379	6 273	6 106	...	...	...	...	...	...
20 - 24	11 989	6 140	5 849	...	...	...	...	...	...
25 - 29	12 944	6 584	6 360	...	...	...	...	...	...
30 - 34	12 906	6 727	6 179	...	...	...	...	...	...

7. Population by age, sex and urban/rural residence: latest available year, 1996 - 2005
Population selon l'âge, le sexe et la résidence, urbaine/rurale: dernière année disponible, 1996 - 2005 (continued - suite)

Continent, country or area, date, code and age (in years) / Continent, pays ou zone, date, code et âge (en années)	Total			Urban - Urbaine			Rural - Rurale		
	Both sexes Les deux sexes	Male Masculin	Female Féminin	Both sexes Les deux sexes	Male Masculin	Female Féminin	Both sexes Les deux sexes	Male Masculin	Female Féminin
OCEANIA - OCÉANIE									
Guam[12]									
1 IV 2000 (CDJC)									
35 - 39	12 751	6 692	6 059	...	...	...	...	...	...
40 - 44	10 390	5 344	5 046	...	...	...	...	...	...
45 - 49	9 042	4 608	4 434	...	...	...	...	...	...
50 - 54	7 506	3 813	3 693	...	...	...	...	...	...
55 - 59	4 993	2 548	2 445	...	...	...	...	...	...
60 - 64	4 534	2 190	2 344	...	...	...	...	...	...
65 - 69	3 399	1 628	1 771	...	...	...	...	...	...
70 - 74	2 461	1 287	1 174	...	...	...	...	...	...
75 - 79	1 384	681	703	...	...	...	...	...	...
80 - 84	616	234	382	...	...	...	...	...	...
85 - 89	248	83	165	...	...	...	...	...	...
90 - 94	79	30	49	...	...	...	...	...	...
95 - 99	22	9	13	...	...	...	...	...	...
100 + ...	6	1	5	...	...	...	...	...	...
Kiribati									
7 XI 2000 (CDFC)									
Total..................	84 494	41 646	42 848	...	...	...	...	...	...
0 - 4	11 980	6 085	5 895	...	...	...	...	...	...
5 - 9	11 270	5 872	5 398	...	...	...	...	...	...
10 - 14	10 522	5 429	5 093	...	...	...	...	...	...
15 - 19	8 929	4 444	4 485	...	...	...	...	...	...
20 - 24	6 791	3 396	3 395	...	...	...	...	...	...
25 - 29	5 577	2 613	2 964	...	...	...	...	...	...
30 - 34	6 607	3 131	3 476	...	...	...	...	...	...
35 - 39	5 591	2 701	2 890	...	...	...	...	...	...
40 - 44	4 543	2 150	2 393	...	...	...	...	...	...
45 - 49	3 394	1 659	1 735	...	...	...	...	...	...
50 - 54	2 803	1 361	1 442	...	...	...	...	...	...
55 - 59	2 044	961	1 083	...	...	...	...	...	...
60 - 64	1 638	730	908	...	...	...	...	...	...
65 + ...	2 805	1 114	1 691	...	...	...	...	...	...
Marshall Islands - Îles Marshall									
1 VII 2001 (ESDF)									
Total..................	54 584	27 960	26 624	...	...	...	...	...	...
0 - 4	9 016	4 684	4 332	...	...	...	...	...	...
5 - 9	6 653	3 391	3 262	...	...	...	...	...	...
10 - 14	7 272	3 745	3 527	...	...	...	...	...	...
15 - 19	6 998	3 576	3 422	...	...	...	...	...	...
20 - 24	5 190	2 594	2 596	...	...	...	...	...	...
25 - 29	3 982	1 991	1 991	...	...	...	...	...	...
30 - 34	3 407	1 736	1 671	...	...	...	...	...	...
35 - 39	2 996	1 538	1 458	...	...	...	...	...	...
40 - 44	2 558	1 276	1 282	...	...	...	...	...	...
45 - 49	2 174	1 155	1 019	...	...	...	...	...	...
50 - 54	1 618	883	735	...	...	...	...	...	...
55 - 59	957	514	443	...	...	...	...	...	...
60 - 64	623	318	305	...	...	...	...	...	...
65 - 69	478	236	242	...	...	...	...	...	...
70 - 74	289	159	130	...	...	...	...	...	...
75 + ...	373	164	209	...	...	...	...	...	...
Micronesia, Federated States of - Micronésie, États Fédérés de La									
1 IV 2000 (CDJC)									
Total..................	107 008	54 191	52 817	...	...	...	...	...	...
0	2 906	1 528	1 378	...	...	...	...	...	...
1 - 4	11 877	6 051	5 826	...	...	...	...	...	...
5 - 9	14 169	7 310	6 859	...	...	...	...	...	...
10 - 14	14 220	7 481	6 739	...	...	...	...	...	...
15 - 19	13 237	6 754	6 483	...	...	...	...	...	...
20 - 24	9 525	4 886	4 639	...	...	...	...	...	...
25 - 29	7 603	3 695	3 908	...	...	...	...	...	...

Continent, country or area, date, code and age (in years) / Continent, pays ou zone, date, code et âge (en années)	Total			Urban - Urbaine			Rural - Rurale		
	Both sexes Les deux sexes	Male Masculin	Female Féminin	Both sexes Les deux sexes	Male Masculin	Female Féminin	Both sexes Les deux sexes	Male Masculin	Female Féminin
OCEANIA - OCÉANIE									
Micronesia, Federated States of - Micronésie, États Fédérés de La									
1 IV 2000 (CDJC)									
30 - 34	6 489	3 124	3 365	...	...	...	...	...	...
35 - 39	6 015	2 994	3 021	...	...	...	...	...	...
40 - 44	5 559	2 801	2 758	...	...	...	...	...	...
45 - 49	4 647	2 393	2 254	...	...	...	...	...	...
50 - 54	3 209	1 654	1 555	...	...	...	...	...	...
55 - 59	1 898	899	999	...	...	...	...	...	...
60 - 64	1 733	830	903	...	...	...	...	...	...
65 - 69	1 487	699	788	...	...	...	...	...	...
70 - 74	993	457	536	...	...	...	...	...	...
75 - 79	727	310	417	...	...	...	...	...	...
80 - 84	328	138	190	...	...	...	...	...	...
85 +	386	187	199	...	...	...	...	...	...
New Caledonia - Nouvelle-Calédonie									
1 I 2004 (ESDF)									
Total	221 958	112 716	109 242	...	...	...	...	...	...
0	4 067	2 105	1 962	...	...	...	...	...	...
1 - 4	17 225	8 761	8 464	...	...	...	...	...	...
5 - 9	21 083	10 821	10 262	...	...	...	...	...	...
10 - 14	21 016	10 924	10 092	...	...	...	...	...	...
15 - 19	19 551	10 040	9 511	...	...	...	...	...	...
20 - 24	18 594	9 255	9 339	...	...	...	...	...	...
25 - 29	18 367	8 862	9 505	...	...	...	...	...	...
30 - 34	17 999	9 236	8 763	...	...	...	...	...	...
35 - 39	16 479	8 464	8 015	...	...	...	...	...	...
40 - 44	14 964	7 604	7 360	...	...	...	...	...	...
45 - 49	12 255	6 221	6 034	...	...	...	...	...	...
50 - 54	10 517	5 523	4 994	...	...	...	...	...	...
55 - 59	9 394	5 105	4 289	...	...	...	...	...	...
60 - 64	7 220	3 717	3 503	...	...	...	...	...	...
65 - 69	5 226	2 605	2 621	...	...	...	...	...	...
70 - 74	3 788	1 768	2 020	...	...	...	...	...	...
75 - 79	2 441	1 053	1 388	...	...	...	...	...	...
80 +	1 772	652	1 120	...	...	...	...	...	...
New Zealand - Nouvelle-Zélande									
1 VII 2005 (ESDJ)									
Total	4 098 900	2 017 100	2 081 800	3 530 500	1 724 600	1 805 900	567 400	291 900	275 400
0 - 4	...	...	...	245 360	125 560	119 810	36 530	18 590	17 940
0	56 890	29 200	27 690	...	...	...	...	...	...
1 - 4	225 040	114 980	110 070	...	...	...	...	...	...
5 - 9	289 560	148 990	140 570	246 330	126 720	119 610	43 180	22 240	20 940
10 - 14	308 560	159 060	149 490	258 000	132 740	125 260	50 510	26 300	24 210
15 - 19	305 630	156 300	149 320	264 730	134 750	129 980	40 860	21 540	19 320
20 - 24	289 600	148 050	141 550	265 690	134 410	131 280	23 840	13 590	10 250
25 - 29	253 950	125 420	128 530	230 230	112 860	117 370	23 650	12 510	11 130
30 - 34	287 880	137 630	150 250	255 100	121 400	133 700	32 720	16 190	16 520
35 - 39	303 000	145 740	157 260	262 250	126 100	136 150	40 680	19 600	21 090
40 - 44	319 520	155 110	164 400	270 730	131 030	139 700	48 710	24 030	24 670
45 - 49	292 830	144 040	148 790	245 200	119 650	125 550	47 550	24 340	23 210
50 - 54	254 700	126 050	128 650	212 530	104 090	108 440	42 060	21 900	20 160
55 - 59	233 560	116 010	117 550	194 120	95 580	98 550	39 350	20 380	18 970
60 - 64	180 510	89 140	91 370	149 110	72 820	76 290	31 330	16 280	15 050
65 - 69	145 710	70 710	75 000	121 560	57 890	63 680	24 110	12 800	11 310
70 - 74	120 110	57 470	62 650	102 630	47 900	54 730	17 450	9 550	7 900
75 - 79	102 230	46 590	55 640	89 730	39 920	49 810	12 480	6 660	5 820
80 - 84	72 900	29 000	43 900	65 620	25 500	40 110	7 270	3 490	3 780
85 +	...	...	...	51 550	15 640	35 920	5 080	1 950	3 130
85 - 89	37 960	12 630	25 330	...	...	...	...	...	...
90 +	18 690	4 960	13 730	...	...	...	...	...	...

Continent, country or area, date, code and age (in years) / Continent, pays ou zone, date, code et âge (en années)	Total			Urban - Urbaine			Rural - Rurale		
	Both sexes Les deux sexes	Male Masculin	Female Féminin	Both sexes Les deux sexes	Male Masculin	Female Féminin	Both sexes Les deux sexes	Male Masculin	Female Féminin

OCEANIA - OCÉANIE

Niue - Nioué
7 IX 2001 (CDFC)

Total.....................	1 788	897	891	...	...	...	...	...	...
0	36	15	21	...	...	...	...	...	...
1 - 4	119	57	62	...	...	...	...	...	...
5 - 9	164	85	79	...	...	...	...	...	...
10 - 14	210	114	96	...	...	...	...	...	...
15 - 19	160	74	86	...	...	...	...	...	...
20 - 24	109	56	53	...	...	...	...	...	...
25 - 29	114	63	51	...	...	...	...	...	...
30 - 34	106	54	52	...	...	...	...	...	...
35 - 39	111	60	51	...	...	...	...	...	...
40 - 44	110	59	51	...	...	...	...	...	...
45 - 49	124	56	68	...	...	...	...	...	...
50 - 54	83	39	44	...	...	...	...	...	...
55 - 59	82	43	39	...	...	...	...	...	...
60 - 64	93	44	49	...	...	...	...	...	...
65 - 69	75	35	40	...	...	...	...	...	...
70 - 74	37	23	14	...	...	...	...	...	...
75 - 79	24	10	14	...	...	...	...	...	...
80 - 84	22	6	16	...	...	...	...	...	...
85 - 89	5	2	3	...	...	...	...	...	...
90 + ...	4	2	2	...	...	...	...	...	...

Norfolk Island - Île Norfolk
7 VIII 2001 (CDFC)

Total.....................	2 037	1 017	1 020	...	...	...	...	...	...
0 - 4	146	74	72	...	...	...	...	...	...
5 - 9	136	69	67	...	...	...	...	...	...
10 - 14	129	72	57	...	...	...	...	...	...
15 - 19	90	41	49	...	...	...	...	...	...
20 - 24	83	45	38	...	...	...	...	...	...
25 - 29	122	61	61	...	...	...	...	...	...
30 - 34	149	71	78	...	...	...	...	...	...
35 - 39	170	83	87	...	...	...	...	...	...
40 - 44	173	87	86	...	...	...	...	...	...
45 - 49	165	87	78	...	...	...	...	...	...
50 - 54	162	73	89	...	...	...	...	...	...
55 - 59	139	68	71	...	...	...	...	...	...
60 - 64	107	55	52	...	...	...	...	...	...
65 - 69	83	36	47	...	...	...	...	...	...
70 + ...	179	93	86	...	...	...	...	...	...
Unknown - Inconnu	4	2	2	...	...	...	...	...	...

Northern Mariana Islands - Îles Mariannes septentrionales
1 IV 2000 (CDFC)

Total.....................	69 221	31 984	37 237	...	...	...	...	...	...
0 - 4	5 792	...	...	...	...	...	...	...	...
5 - 9	5 420	...	...	...	...	...	...	...	...
10 - 14	4 377	...	...	...	...	...	...	...	...
15 - 19	3 943	...	...	...	...	...	...	...	...
20 - 24	7 566	...	...	...	...	...	...	...	...
25 - 34	20 181	...	...	...	...	...	...	...	...
35 - 44	12 651	...	...	...	...	...	...	...	...
45 - 54	6 208	...	...	...	...	...	...	...	...
55 - 59	1 199	...	...	...	...	...	...	...	...
60 - 64	837	...	...	...	...	...	...	...	...
65 - 74	748	...	...	...	...	...	...	...	...
75 - 84	233	...	...	...	...	...	...	...	...
85 + ...	66	...	...	...	...	...	...	...	...

Palau - Palaos
15 IV 2000 (CDFC)

Total.....................	19 129	10 450	8 679	...	...	...	...	...	...
0	179	99	80	...	...	...	...	...	...
1 - 4	1 129	591	538	...	...	...	...	...	...

Continent, country or area, date, code and age (in years) / Continent, pays ou zone, date, code et âge (en années)	Total			Urban - Urbaine			Rural - Rurale		
	Both sexes Les deux sexes	Male Masculin	Female Féminin	Both sexes Les deux sexes	Male Masculin	Female Féminin	Both sexes Les deux sexes	Male Masculin	Female Féminin
OCEANIA - OCÉANIE									
Palau - Palaos									
15 IV 2000 (CDFC)									
5 - 9	1 700	856	844	...	...	...	...	...	...
10 - 14	1 555	794	761	...	...	...	...	...	...
15 - 19	1 382	738	644	...	...	...	...	...	...
20 - 24	1 342	731	611	...	...	...	...	...	...
25 - 29	1 910	1 106	804	...	...	...	...	...	...
30 - 34	2 169	1 219	950	...	...	...	...	...	...
35 - 39	1 891	1 104	787	...	...	...	...	...	...
40 - 44	1 651	976	675	...	...	...	...	...	...
45 - 49	1 272	750	522	...	...	...	...	...	...
50 - 54	886	510	376	...	...	...	...	...	...
55 - 59	563	306	257	...	...	...	...	...	...
60 - 64	463	230	233	...	...	...	...	...	...
65 - 69	318	161	157	...	...	...	...	...	...
70 - 74	274	115	159	...	...	...	...	...	...
75 - 79	212	78	134	...	...	...	...	...	...
80 - 84	113	48	65	...	...	...	...	...	...
85 - 89	60	15	45	...	...	...	...	...	...
90 - 94	17	2	15	...	...	...	...	...	...
95 +	43	21	22	...	...	...	...	...	...
Papua New Guinea - Papouasie-Nouvelle-Guinée									
9 VII 2000 (CDFC)									
Total	5 190 786	2 691 744	2 499 042	686 301	372 453	313 848	4 504 485	2 319 291	2 185 194
0	125 718	65 539	60 179	16 930	8 991	7 939	108 788	56 548	52 240
1 - 4	600 962	312 237	288 725	71 219	37 178	34 041	529 743	275 059	254 684
5 - 9	727 370	381 339	346 031	86 078	45 216	40 862	641 292	336 123	305 169
10 - 14	620 874	330 965	289 909	75 022	39 374	35 648	545 852	291 591	254 261
15 - 19	554 481	293 277	261 204	78 912	41 679	37 233	475 569	251 598	223 971
20 - 24	474 801	239 863	234 938	79 915	43 166	36 749	394 886	196 697	198 189
25 - 29	448 414	219 680	228 734	70 866	37 802	33 064	377 548	181 878	195 670
30 - 34	384 260	191 662	192 598	57 156	30 983	26 173	327 104	160 679	166 425
35 - 39	330 337	166 656	163 681	48 585	26 512	22 073	281 752	140 144	141 608
40 - 44	252 368	128 910	123 458	36 195	20 956	15 239	216 173	107 954	108 219
45 - 49	198 757	104 867	93 890	25 337	15 595	9 742	173 420	89 272	84 148
50 - 54	151 013	79 899	71 114	16 428	10 414	6 014	134 585	69 485	65 100
55 - 59	108 708	59 308	49 400	9 692	6 131	3 561	99 016	53 177	45 839
60 - 64	89 503	48 530	40 973	6 723	4 247	2 476	82 780	44 283	38 497
65 - 69	57 221	31 351	25 870	3 641	2 141	1 500	53 580	29 210	24 370
70 - 74	35 134	19 657	15 477	1 930	1 105	825	33 204	18 552	14 652
75 - 79	16 864	9 782	7 082	880	498	382	15 984	9 284	6 700
80 - 84	8 669	5 041	3 628	489	295	194	8 180	4 746	3 434
85 - 89	3 315	1 984	1 331	176	99	77	3 139	1 885	1 254
90 +	2 017	1 197	820	127	71	56	1 890	1 126	764
Samoa									
5 XI 2001 (CDFC)									
Total	176 710	92 050	84 660	...	...	...	...	...	...
0 - 4	26 028	13 631	12 397	...	...	...	...	...	...
5 - 9	24 917	13 024	11 893	...	...	...	...	...	...
10 - 14	20 985	10 948	10 037	...	...	...	...	...	...
15 - 19	17 608	9 488	8 120	...	...	...	...	...	...
20 - 24	14 281	7 549	6 732	...	...	...	...	...	...
25 - 29	13 197	6 910	6 287	...	...	...	...	...	...
30 - 34	12 258	6 545	5 713	...	...	...	...	...	...
35 - 39	10 385	5 378	5 007	...	...	...	...	...	...
40 - 44	8 855	4 628	4 227	...	...	...	...	...	...
45 - 49	6 833	3 538	3 295	...	...	...	...	...	...
50 - 54	5 081	2 538	2 543	...	...	...	...	...	...
55 - 59	4 417	2 217	2 200	...	...	...	...	...	...
60 - 64	3 659	1 835	1 824	...	...	...	...	...	...
65 - 69	2 975	1 452	1 523	...	...	...	...	...	...
70 - 74	2 272	1 036	1 236	...	...	...	...	...	...
75 +	2 656	1 147	1 509	...	...	...	...	...	...
Unknown - Inconnu	303	186	117	...	...	...	...	...	...

Continent, country or area, date, code and age (in years) / Continent, pays ou zone, date, code et âge (en annèes)	Total			Urban - Urbaine			Rural - Rurale		
	Both sexes Les deux sexes	Male Masculin	Female Féminin	Both sexes Les deux sexes	Male Masculin	Female Féminin	Both sexes Les deux sexes	Male Masculin	Female Féminin
OCEANIA - OCÉANIE									
Tokelau - Tokélaou									
11 X 2001 (CDFC)									
Total	1 537	761	776	...	...	...	...	...	...
0 - 4	218	112	106	...	...	...	...	...	...
5 - 9	206	118	88	...	...	...	...	...	...
10 - 14	202	102	100	...	...	...	...	...	...
15 - 19	144	71	73	...	...	...	...	...	...
20 - 24	85	42	43	...	...	...	...	...	...
25 - 29	95	43	52	...	...	...	...	...	...
30 - 34	100	50	50	...	...	...	...	...	...
35 - 39	88	43	45	...	...	...	...	...	...
40 - 44	84	41	43	...	...	...	...	...	...
45 - 49	63	28	35	...	...	...	...	...	...
50 - 54	52	20	32	...	...	...	...	...	...
55 - 59	54	26	28	...	...	...	...	...	...
60 - 64	49	21	28	...	...	...	...	...	...
65 +	97	44	53	...	...	...	...	...	...
Tonga									
31 XII 2002 (ESDF)									
Total	101 002	51 473	49 528	...	...	...	...	...	...
0 - 4	12 179	6 295	5 884	...	...	...	...	...	...
5 - 9	12 686	6 577	6 109	...	...	...	...	...	...
10 - 14	11 795	6 303	5 492	...	...	...	...	...	...
15 - 19	11 980	6 241	5 739	...	...	...	...	...	...
20 - 24	9 942	5 111	4 831	...	...	...	...	...	...
25 - 29	7 057	3 564	3 493	...	...	...	...	...	...
30 - 34	6 284	3 207	3 077	...	...	...	...	...	...
35 - 39	5 382	2 723	2 659	...	...	...	...	...	...
40 - 44	4 541	2 186	2 355	...	...	...	...	...	...
45 - 49	4 029	1 908	2 121	...	...	...	...	...	...
50 - 54	3 397	1 572	1 825	...	...	...	...	...	...
55 - 59	3 105	1 467	1 638	...	...	...	...	...	...
60 - 64	2 775	1 393	1 382	...	...	...	...	...	...
65 - 69	2 277	1 167	1 110	...	...	...	...	...	...
70 - 74	1 668	840	828	...	...	...	...	...	...
75 +	1 904	919	985	...	...	...	...	...	...
Tuvalu									
1 XI 2002 (CDFC)									
Total	9 561	4 729	4 832	...	...	...	...	...	...
0	182	92	90	...	...	...	...	...	...
1 - 4	996	528	468	...	...	...	...	...	...
5 - 9	1 201	612	589	...	...	...	...	...	...
10 - 14	1 079	591	488	...	...	...	...	...	...
15 - 19	826	474	352	...	...	...	...	...	...
20 - 24	682	326	356	...	...	...	...	...	...
25 - 29	523	245	278	...	...	...	...	...	...
30 - 34	545	278	267	...	...	...	...	...	...
35 - 39	684	331	353	...	...	...	...	...	...
40 - 44	697	310	387	...	...	...	...	...	...
45 - 49	580	261	319	...	...	...	...	...	...
50 - 54	467	199	268	...	...	...	...	...	...
55 - 59	276	129	147	...	...	...	...	...	...
60 - 64	280	131	149	...	...	...	...	...	...
65 - 69	207	84	123	...	...	...	...	...	...
70 - 74	167	75	92	...	...	...	...	...	...
75 - 79	101	40	61	...	...	...	...	...	...
80 - 84	56	20	36	...	...	...	...	...	...
85 - 89	10	1	9	...	...	...	...	...	...
90 - 94	2	2	-	...	...	...	...	...	...
95 +	-	-	-	...	...	...	...	...	...
Vanuatu [49]									
1 VII 2004 (ESDF)									
Total	215 541	110 141	105 399	...	...	...	...	...	...
0 - 4	33 815	17 435	16 380	...	...	...	...	...	...
5 - 9	27 846	14 474	13 372	...	...	...	...	...	...

Continent, country or area, date, code and age (in years) / Continent, pays ou zone, date, code et âge (en années)	Total			Urban - Urbaine			Rural - Rurale		
	Both sexes Les deux sexes	Male Masculin	Female Féminin	Both sexes Les deux sexes	Male Masculin	Female Féminin	Both sexes Les deux sexes	Male Masculin	Female Féminin
OCEANIA - OCÉANIE									
Vanuatu[49]									
1 VII 2004 (ESDF)									
10 - 14	*27 125*	*14 025*	*13 100*	...	...	...	...	...	...
15 - 19	*23 437*	*12 132*	*11 305*	...	...	...	...	...	...
20 - 24	*18 951*	*9 684*	*9 267*	...	...	...	...	...	...
25 - 29	*16 235*	*8 027*	*8 207*	...	...	...	...	...	...
30 - 34	*14 670*	*7 175*	*7 494*	...	...	...	...	...	...
35 - 39	*12 560*	*6 214*	*6 346*	...	...	...	...	...	...
40 - 44	*10 429*	*5 221*	*5 208*	...	...	...	...	...	...
45 - 49	*8 303*	*4 221*	*4 082*	...	...	...	...	...	...
50 - 54	*6 476*	*3 333*	*3 143*	...	...	...	...	...	...
55 - 59	*5 083*	*2 632*	*2 452*	...	...	...	...	...	...
60 - 64	*3 824*	*1 996*	*1 828*	...	...	...	...	...	...
65 - 69	*2 714*	*1 417*	*1 296*	...	...	...	...	...	...
70 - 74	*1 810*	*957*	*854*	...	...	...	...	...	...
75 + ...	*2 265*	*1 198*	*1 066*	...	...	...	...	...	...
Wallis and Futuna Islands - Îles Wallis et Futuna									
3 X 1996 (CDFC)									
Total.................	14 166	6 984	7 182	...	...	...	...	...	...
0.................	293	156	137	...	...	...	...	...	...
1 - 4.................	1 399	719	680	...	...	...	...	...	...
5 - 9.................	1 814	923	891	...	...	...	...	...	...
10 - 14.................	1 894	1 006	888	...	...	...	...	...	...
15 - 19.................	1 675	823	852	...	...	...	...	...	...
20 - 24.................	1 082	491	591	...	...	...	...	...	...
25 - 29.................	960	438	522	...	...	...	...	...	...
30 - 34.................	758	341	417	...	...	...	...	...	...
35 - 39.................	836	381	455	...	...	...	...	...	...
40 - 44.................	715	365	350	...	...	...	...	...	...
45 - 49.................	637	325	312	...	...	...	...	...	...
50 - 54.................	531	293	238	...	...	...	...	...	...
55 - 59.................	508	251	257	...	...	...	...	...	...
60 - 64.................	324	146	178	...	...	...	...	...	...
65 - 69.................	271	103	168	...	...	...	...	...	...
70 - 74.................	184	85	99	...	...	...	...	...	...
75 - 79.................	185	94	91	...	...	...	...	...	...
80 - 84.................	83	37	46	...	...	...	...	...	...
85 - 89.................	15	7	8	...	...	...	...	...	...
90 +.................	2	-	2	...	...	...	...	...	...

FOOTNOTES - NOTES

Italics: estimates which are less reliable. -
Italiques: estimations moins sûres.

'Code' indicates the source of data, as follows:
CDFS - Census, de facto, sample tabulation
CDJC - Census, de jure, complete tabulation
CDJS - Census, de jure, sample tabulation
SSDF - Sample survey, de facto
SSDJ - Sample survey, de jure
ESDF - Estimates, de facto
ESDJ - Estimates, de jure

Le 'Code' indique la source des données, comme suit:
CDFC - Recensement, population de fait, tabulation complète
CDFS - Recensement, population de fait, tabulation par sondage
CDJC - Recensement, population de droit, tabulation complète
CDJS - Recensement, population de droit, tabulation par sondage
SSDF - Enquête par sondage, population de fait
SSDJ - Enquête par sondage, population de droit

ESDF - Estimations, population de fait
ESDJ - Estimations, population de droit

[1] Urban and rural data were reported in different years and do not add up to the total. - Les données concernant la population urbaine et la population rurale portent sur des années différentes et leur somme ne correspond pas au total cité.

[2] Data as reported by national statistical authorities. Figures for urban and rural do not add up to the total. - Données comme déclarées par les autorités statistiques nationales. Les données pour la population urbaine et la population rurale ne s'ajoutent pas au total.

[3] Data refer to national projections. - Les données se réfèrent aux projections nationales.

[4] The number of males and/or females excludes persons whose sex is not stated (18 urban, 19 rural). - Il n'est pas tenu compte dans le nombre d'hommes et de femmes des personnes dont le sexe n'est pas indiqué (18 en zone urbaine et 19 en zone rurale).

[5] Data as reported by national statistical authorities. Figures for male and female do not add up to the total. - Données comme déclarées par les autorités statistiques nationales. Les données pour la population masculine et la population féminine ne s'ajoutent pas au total.

[6] Data have been adjusted for underenumeration estimated at 6.8 per cent. - Les données ont été ajustées pour compenser les lacunes du dénombrement estimées à 6,8 p. 100.

[7] For 2004, data refer to estimated population after considering HIV. - Pour 2004, les données portent sur la population estimée après prise en compte du VIH.

[8] Total population excludes persons who were not contacted at the time of the census. - La population non comprend pas les personnes qui n'ont pas été contactées à l'heure du recensement.

[9] Excluding the institutional population. - Non compris la population dans les institutions.

[10] Because of rounding, totals are not in all cases the sum of the parts. - Les chiffres étant arrondis, les totaux ne correspondent pas toujours rigoureusement à la somme des chiffres partiels.

[11] Unrevised data. - Les données n'ont pas été révisées.

[12] Including armed forces stationed in the area. - Y compris les militaires en garnison sur le territoire.

[13] Data exclude adjustment for underenumeration. Excluding persons residing in institutions. - Les données n'ont pas été ajustées pour compenser les lacunes du dénombrement. Non compris les personnes dans les institutions.

[14] Excluding armed forces overseas and civilian citizens absent from country for an extended period of time. - Non compris les militaires à l'étranger, et les civils hors du pays pendant une période prolongée.

[15] Data include persons in remote areas, military personnel outside the country, merchant seamen at sea, civilian seasonal workers outside the country, and other civilians outside the country, and exclude nomads, foreign military, civilian aliens temporarily in the country, transients on ships and Indian jungle population. - Y compris les personnes vivant dans des régions éloignées, le personel militaire en dehors du pays, les marins marchands, les ouvriers saisonniers en dehors du pays, et autres civils en dehors du pays, et non compris les nomades, les militaires étrangers, les étrangers civils temporairement dans le pays, les transiteurs sur des bateaux et les Indiens de la jungle.

[16] Total in this table is different from population estimates presented in other tables due to differences in methodology. - Le total figurant dans ce tableau est différent des chiffres de population présentés dans d'autres tableaux, ayant été obtenus par des méthodes différentes.

[17] Excluding nomadic Indian tribes. - Non compris les tribus d'Indiens nomades.

[18] Excluding Indian jungle population. - Non compris les Indiens de la jungle.

[19] Mid-year estimates have been adjusted for underenumeration, at latest census. - Les estimations au millieu de l'année tiennent compte d'un ajustement destiné à compenser les lacunes du dénombrement lors du dernier recensement.

[20] The population for the year 2005 corresponds to the population actually enumerated in the census conducted between 18 July and 20 August 2005. The total (adjusted) population is 27 219 264 inhabitants. - La population pour 2005 correspond à la population effectivement dénombrée lors du recensement réalisé entre le 18 juillet et le 20 août 2005. La population totale (après ajustement) compte 27 219 264 habitants.

[21] Figures for male and female population do not add up to the figure for total population, because they exclude 365 persons of unknown sex. - Les chiffres relatifs à la population masculine et féminine ne correspondent pas au chiffre de la population totale, parce que l'on en a exclu 365 personnes de sexe inconnu.

[22] Based on Cambodia Intercensal Population Survey. Data exclude institutional, homeless households and transient poulation. - Les données ne comprennent pas la population des institutions, les ménages sans abri et la population de passage.

[23] For statistical purposes, the data for China do not include those for the Hong Kong Special Administrative Region (Hong Kong SAR), Macao Special Administrative Region (Macao SAR) and Taiwan province of China. - Pour la présentation des statistiques, les données pour la Chine ne comprennent pas la Région Administrative Spéciale de Hong Kong (Hong Kong RAS), la Région Administrative Spéciale de Macao (Macao RAS) et Taïwan province de Chine.

[24] Data refer to government controlled areas. - Les données se rapportent aux zones contrôlées par le Gouvernement.

[25] Including data for the Indian-held part of Jammu and Kashmir, the final status of which has not yet been determined. Data exclude Mao-Maram, Paomata and Purul sub-divisions of Senapati district of Manipur. The population of Manipur including the estimated population of the three sub-divisions of Senapati district is 2,291,125 (Males 1,161,173 and females 1,129,952). - Y compris les données pour la partie du Jammu et du Cachemire occupée par l'Inde dont le statut définitif n'a pas encore été déterminé. Non compris les subdivisions Mao-Maram Paomata et Purul du district de Senapati dans l'État du Manipur. Cet État compte 2 291 125 habitants (1 161 173 hommes et 1 129 952 femmes), y compris la population estimative des trois subdivisions du district de Senapati.

[26] Data exclude adjustment for underenumeration. - Les données n'ont pas été ajustées pour compenser les lacunes du dénombrement.

[27] Data relate to the population for the Iranian Year 1384 (21 March 2005-20 March 2006). - Les données concernent la population pour l'année iranienne 1384 (21 mars 2005-20 mars 2006).

[28] Because of rounding, totals are not in all cases the sum of the parts. Including data for East Jerusalem and Israeli residents in certain other territories under occupation by Israeli military forces since June 1967. - Les chiffres étant arrondis, les totaux ne correspondent pas toujours rigoureusement à la somme des chiffres partiels. Y compris les données pour Jérusalem-Est et les résidents israéliens dans certains autres territoires occupés depuis 1967 par les forces armées israéliennes.

[29] Excluding diplomatic personnel outside the country and foreign military and civilian personnel and their dependants stationed in the area. - Non compris le personnel diplomatique hors du pays ni les militaires et agents civils étrangers en poste sur le territoire et les membres de leur famille les accompagnant.

[30] Excluding data for Jordanian territory under occupation since June 1967 by Israeli military forces. Excluding foreigners, including registered Palestinian refugees. - Non compris les données pour le territoire jordanien occupé depuis juin 1967 par les forces armées israéliennes. Non compris les étrangers, mais y compris les réfugiés de Palestine enregistrés.

[31] Excluding alien armed forces, civilian aliens employed by armed forces, foreign diplomatic personnel and their dependants and Korean diplomatic personnel and their dependants outside the country. - Non compris les militaires étrangers, les civils étrangers employés par les forces armées, le personnel diplomatique étranger et les membres de leur famille les accompagnant et le personnel diplomatique coréen hors du pays et les membres de leurs familles les accompagnant.

[32] Excluding foreigners. - Non compris étrangers.

[33] Data refer to constant population as reported by national statistical authorities, meaning that it does not include migrant population. - Les données se rapportent à la population constante déclarée par les autorités statistiques nationales; la population migrante n'est donc pas comprise.

[34] Excluding Malaysian citizens and permanent residents who were away or intended to be away from the country for more than six months. Excluding Malaysian military, naval and diplomatic personnel and their families outside the country, and tourists, businessman who intended to be in Malaysia for less than six months. Census results have been adjusted for underenumeration. - Non compris les citoyens malaisiens et les résidents permanents qui étaient ou qui ont prévu d'être hors du pays pour six mois ou plus. Non compris le personnel militaire Malaisien, le personnel naval ou diplomatique et leurs familles hors du pays, et les touristes et les hommes d'affaires qui avaient l'intention de rester en Malaisie moins de six mois. Les résultats du recensement ont été ajustées pour compenser les lacunes du dénombrement

[35] Excluding data for the Pakistan-held part of Jammu and Kashmir, the final status of which has not yet been determined. Data based on Pakistan Demographic Survey 2003. These estimates do not reflect completely accurately the actual population and vital events of the country. - Non compris les données concernant la partie du Jammu et Cachemire occupée par le Pakistan dont le statut définitif n'a pas été déterminé. D'après les résultats de Pakistan démographique par sondage 2003. Ces estimations ne dénotent pas d'une manière complètement ponctuelle la population actuelle et les statistiques de l'état civil du pays.

[36] Including Palestinian refugees. - Y compris les réfugiés de Palestine.

[37] Population statistics are compiled from registers. - Les statistiques de la population sont compilées à partir des registres.

[38] Excluding Faeroe Islands and Greenland. Population statistics are compiled from registers. - Non compris les Iles Féroé et le Gröenland. Les statistiques de la population sont compilées à partir des registres.

[39] Excluding diplomatic personnel outside the country and including members of alien armed forces not living in military camps and foreign diplomatic personnel not living in embassies or consulates. Excluding Overseas Departments, namely, French Guiana, Guadeloupe, Martinique and Reunion, shown separately. - Non compris le personnel diplomatique hors du pays et y compris les militaires étrangers ne vivant pas dans des camps militaires et le personnel diplomatique étranger ne vivant pas dans les ambassades ou les consulats. Non compris les départements d'outre mer, c'est-à-dire la Guyane française, la Guadeloupe, la Martinique et la Réunion, qui font l'objet de rubriques distinctes.

[40] Excluding families of military personnel, visitors and transients. - Non compris les familles des militaires, ni les visiteurs et transients.

[41] Mid-year population excludes armed forces stationed outside the country, but includes alien armed forces stationed in the area. - Les estimations au millieu de l'année non compris les militaires en garnison hors du pays, mais y compris les militaires étrangers en garnison sur le territoire.

[42] Including residents temporarily outside the country. - Y compris les résidents se trouvant temporairement hors du pays.

[43] Including the Azores and Madeira Islands. - Y compris les Açores et Madère.

[44] Data do not include information for Transnistria and the municipality of Bender. - Les données ne tiennent pas compte de l'information sur la Transnistrie et la municipalité de Bender.

[45] Without data for Kosovo and Metohia. - Sans les données pour le Kosovo and Metohie.

[46] Because the data by urban/rural residence are available only for citizens of the Republic of Slovenia, excluding citizens temporarily residing abroad, the sum by urban and rural does not add up to the total. - Les données concernant la résidence en zone urbaine ou rurale sont disponibles seulement pour les nationaux slovènes, mais les nationaux se trouvant provisoirement à l'étranger ne sont pas pris en compte. La somme des chiffres disponibles pour les zones urbaines et rurales ne correspond donc pas au total.

[47] As reported by the country. Reasons for discrepancy with other tables not ascertained. - Données comme déclarées par le pays. On ne sait pas comment s'explique la divergence entre ces chiffres et les chiffres correspondants indiqués ailleurs.

[48] Excluding Niue, shown separately, which is part of Cook Islands, but because of remoteness is administered separately. - Non compris Nioué, qui fait l'objet d'une rubrique distincte et qui fait partie des îles Cook, mais qui, en raison de son éloignement, est administrée séparément.

[49] Data refer to national projections. Figures for male and female do not add up to the total, reason for discrepancy not ascertained. - Les données se réfèrent aux projections nationales. La some des données pour la population masculine et pour la population féminine n'est pas égale au total, les raisons de cette différence ne sont pas expliquées.

Table 8

Table 8 presents population of capital cities and cities of 100 000 or more inhabitants for the latest available year from 1986 – 2005.

Description of variables: Since the way in which cities are delimited differs from one country or area to another, the table not only presents data for the so-called city proper, but also for the urban agglomeration, if available.

City proper is defined as a locality with legally fixed boundaries and an administratively recognized urban status, usually characterized by some form of local government.

Urban agglomeration has been defined as comprising the city or town proper and also the suburban fringe or densely settled territory lying outside of, but adjacent to, the city boundaries.

For some countries or areas, however, the data relate to entire administrative divisions known, for example, as shi or municipalities (municipios) which are composed of a populated centre and adjoining territory, some of which may contain other, often separate urban localities or may be distinctively rural in character. For this group of countries or areas the type of civil division is given in a footnote.

The surface area of the city or urban agglomeration is presented, when available.

City names are presented in the original language of the country or area in which the cities are located. In cases where the original names are not in the Roman alphabet, they have been Romanized. Cities are listed in English alphabetical order.

Capital cities are shown in the table regardless of their population size. The names of the capital cities are printed in capital letters. The designation of any specific city as a capital city is as reported by the country or area.

The table also covers cities whose urban agglomeration's population exceeds 100 000; that is, while the urban agglomeration should have a population of 100 000 or more to be included in the table, the city proper may be of a smaller population size.

The reference date of each population figure appears in the stub of the table. Estimates based on results of sample surveys and city censuses as well as those derived from other sources are noted in the "code" column.

Reliability of data: Specific information is generally not available on the reliability of the estimates of the population of cities or urban agglomerations presented in this table.

In the absence of such quality assessment, data from population censuses, sample surveys and city censuses are considered to be reliable and, therefore, set in roman type. Other estimates are considered to be reliable if they are based on a complete census (or a sample survey), and have been adjusted by a continuous population register or adjusted on the basis of the calculated balance of births, deaths, and migration.

Limitations: Statistics on the population of capital cities and cities of 100 000 or more inhabitants are subject to the same qualifications as have been set forth for population statistics in general as discussed in section 3 of the Technical Notes.

International comparability of data on city population is limited to a great extent by variations in national concepts and definitions. Although an effort is made to reduce the sources of non-comparability somewhat by presenting the data for both city proper and urban agglomeration, many serious problems of comparability remain.

Data presented in the "city proper" column for some countries represent an urban administrative area legally distinguished from surrounding rural territory, while for other countries these data represent a commune or an equally small administrative unit. In still other countries, the administrative units may be relatively extensive and thereby include considerable territories beyond the urban centre itself.

City data are also especially affected by whether the data refer to *de facto* or *de jure* population, as well as variations among countries in how each of these concepts is applied. With reference to the total population, the difference between the *de facto* and *de jure* population is discussed at length in section 3.1.1 of the Technical Notes.

Data on city populations based on intercensal estimates present additional problems: comparability is impaired by the different methods used in making the estimates and by the loss of precision in applying to selected segments of the population, methods best suited for the whole population. For example, it is far more difficult to apply the component method of estimating population growth to cities than it is to the entire country.

Births and deaths occurring in the cities do not all originate in the population present in or resident of that area. Therefore, the use of natural increase to estimate the probable size of the city population is a potential source of error. Internal migration is another component of population change that cannot be measured with accuracy in many areas. Because of these factors, estimates in this table may be less valuable in general and in particular limited for purposes of international comparison.

City data, even when set in roman type, are often not as reliable as estimates for the total population of the country or area. Furthermore, because the sources of these data include censuses (national or city), surveys and estimates, the years to which they refer vary widely. In addition, because city boundaries may alter over time, comparisons covering different years should be carried out with caution.

Earlier data: Population of capital cities and cities with a population of 100 000 or more have been shown in previous issues of the *Demographic Yearbook*. For more information on specific topics and years for which data are reported, readers should consult the Historical Index.

Tableau 8

Le tableau 8 présente les données les plus récentes (1986 – 2005) dont on dispose sur la population des capitales et des villes de 100 000 habitants ou plus.

Description des variables : Étant donné que les villes ne sont pas délimitées de la même manière dans tous les pays ou zones, on s'est efforcé de donner, dans ce tableau, des chiffres correspondant non seulement aux villes proprement dites, mais aussi, le cas échéant, aux agglomérations urbaines.

On entend par villes proprement dites les localités qui ont des limites juridiquement définies et sont administrativement considérées comme villes, ce qui se caractérise généralement par l'existence d'une autorité locale.

L'agglomération urbaine comprend, par définition, la ville proprement dite ainsi que la proche banlieue, c'est-à-dire la zone fortement peuplée qui est extérieure, mais contiguë aux limites de la ville.

En outre, dans certains pays ou zones, les données se rapportent à des divisions administratives entières, connues par exemple sous le nom de shi ou de municipios, qui comportent une agglomération et le territoire avoisinant, lequel peut englober d'autres agglomérations urbaines tout à fait distinctes ou être à caractère essentiellement rural. Pour ce groupe de pays ou zones, le type de division administrative est indiqué en note.

On trouvera à la fin du tableau la superficie de la ville ou agglomération urbaine chaque fois que possible.

Les noms des villes sont indiqués dans la langue du pays ou zone où ces villes sont situées. Les noms de villes qui ne sont pas à l'origine libellés en caractères latins ont été romanisés. Les villes sont énumérées dans l'ordre alphabétique anglais.

Les capitales figurent dans le tableau quel que soit le chiffre de leur population et leur nom a été imprimé en lettres majuscules. Ne sont indiquées comme capitales que les villes ainsi désignées par le pays ou zone intéressé.

En ce qui concerne les autres villes, le tableau indique celles dont la population est égale ou supérieure à 100 000 habitants. Ce chiffre limite s'applique à l'agglomération urbaine et non à la ville proprement dite, dont la population peut être moindre.

L'année à laquelle se réfère le chiffre correspondant à chaque population figure dans la colonne de gauche du tableau. La colonne « Code » permet de savoir si les estimations sont fondées sur les résultats d'enquêtes par sondage ou de recensements municipaux ou sont tirées d'autres sources.

Fiabilité des données : on ne possède généralement pas de renseignements précis sur la fiabilité des estimations de la population des villes ou agglomérations urbaines présentées dans ce tableau.

Les données provenant de recensements de la population, d'enquêtes par sondage ou de recensements municipaux sont jugées sûres et figurent par conséquent en caractères romains. D'autres estimations sont considérées comme sûres si elles sont fondées sur un recensement complet (ou une enquête par sondage) et ont été ajustées en fonction des données provenant d'un registre permanent de population ou en fonction de la balance, établie par le calcul des naissances, des décès et des migrations.

Insuffisance des données : les statistiques portant sur la population des capitales et des villes de 100 000 habitants ou plus appellent toutes les réserves qui ont été formulées à la section 3 des Notes techniques à propos des statistiques de la population en général.

La comparabilité internationale des données portant sur la population des villes est compromise dans une large mesure par la diversité des définitions nationales. Bien que l'on se soit efforcé de réduire les facteurs de non-comparabilité en présentant à la fois dans le tableau les données relatives aux villes proprement dites et celles concernant les agglomérations urbaines, de graves problèmes de comparabilité n'en subsistent pas moins.

Pour certains pays, les données figurant dans la colonne intitulée « Ville proprement dite » correspondent à une zone administrative urbaine juridiquement distincte du territoire rural environnant, tandis que pour d'autres pays ces données correspondent à une commune ou petite unité administrative analogue. Pour d'autres encore, les unités administratives en cause peuvent être relativement étendues et englober par conséquent un vaste territoire au-delà du centre urbain lui-même.

L'emploi de données se rapportant tantôt à la population de fait, tantôt à la population de droit, ainsi que les différences de traitement de ces deux notions d'un pays à l'autre influent particulièrement sur les statistiques urbaines. En ce qui concerne la population totale, la différence entre population de fait et population de droit est expliquée en détail à la section 3.1.1 des Notes techniques.

Les statistiques relatives à la population urbaine qui sont fondées sur des estimations intercensitaires posent encore plus de problèmes que les données issues de recensement. Leur comparabilité est compromise par la diversité des méthodes employées pour établir les estimations et par l'imprécision qui résulte de l'application de certaines méthodes à telles ou telles composantes de la population alors qu'elles sont conçues pour être appliquées à l'ensemble de la population. La méthode des composantes, par exemple, est beaucoup plus difficile à appliquer en vue de l'estimation de l'accroissement de la population lorsqu'il s'agit de villes que lorsqu'il s'agit d'un pays tout entier.

Les naissances et décès qui surviennent dans les villes ne correspondent pas tous à la population présente ou résidente. En conséquence, des erreurs peuvent se produire si l'on établit pour les villes des estimations fondées sur l'accroissement naturel de la population. Les migrations intérieures constituent un second élément d'estimation que, dans bien des régions, on ne peut pas toujours mesurer avec exactitude. Pour ces raisons, les estimations présentées dans ce tableau risquent dans l'ensemble d'être peu fiables et leur valeur est particulièrement limitée du point de vue des comparaisons internationales.

Même lorsqu'elles figurent en caractères romains, il arrive souvent que les statistiques urbaines ne soient pas aussi fiables que les estimations concernant la population totale de la zone ou du pays considéré. De surcroît, comme ces statistiques proviennent aussi bien de recensements (nationaux ou municipaux) que d'enquêtes ou d'estimations, les années auxquelles elles se rapportent sont extrêmement variables. Enfin, comme les limites urbaines varient parfois d'une époque à une autre, il y a lieu d'être prudent lorsque l'on compare des données se rapportant à des années différentes.

Données publiées antérieurement : des statistiques concernant la population des capitales et des villes de 100 000 habitants ou plus ont été présentées dans des éditions antérieures de l'*Annuaire démographique*. Pour plus de précisions concernant les années et les sujets pour lesquels des données ont été publiées, se reporter à l'index.

8. Population of capital cities and cities of 100 000 or more inhabitants: latest available year, 1986 - 2005
Population des capitales et des villes de 100 000 habitants ou plus: dernière année disponible, 1986 - 2005

Continent, country or area, date and city / Continent, pays ou zone, date et ville	Code[1]	City proper — Ville proprement dite Population				Urban agglomeration — Agglomération urbaine Population			
		Both sexes Les deux sexes	Male Masculin	Female Féminin	Surface area Superficie (km²)	Both sexes Les deux sexes	Male Masculin	Female Féminin	Surface area Superficie (km²)
AFRICA — AFRIQUE									
Algeria — Algérie									
25 VI 1998									
ALGER (EL DJAZAIR)	CDJC	1 569 897	...	...	...	...	...	...	...
Annaba	CDJC	352 523	...	...	...	...	...	...	...
Batna	CDJC	246 800	...	...	...	...	...	...	...
Béchar	CDJC	134 523	...	...	...	...	...	...	...
Bejaïa	CDJC	144 405	...	...	...	...	...	...	...
Biskra	CDJC	177 060	...	...	...	...	...	...	...
Blida (El Boulaïda)	CDJC	229 788	...	...	...	...	...	...	...
Bordj Bou Arreridj	CDJC	129 004	...	...	...	...	...	...	...
Bordj el Kiffan	CDJC	103 690	...	...	...	...	...	...	...
Chlef (Ech Cheliff)	CDJC	174 314	...	...	...	...	...	...	...
Constantine (Qacentina)	CDJC	465 021	...	...	...	...	...	...	...
El Djelfa	CDJC	158 679	...	...	...	...	...	...	...
El Eulma	CDJC	104 758	...	...	...	...	...	...	...
El Oued (El Wad)	CDJC	105 151	...	...	...	...	...	...	...
Ghardaïa	CDJC	127 959	...	...	...	...	...	...	...
Guelma	CDJC	108 682	...	...	...	...	...	...	...
Jijel	CDJC	106 306	...	...	...	...	...	...	...
Medea (Lemdiyya)	CDJC	128 427	...	...	...	...	...	...	...
Mostaganem	CDJC	125 911	...	...	...	...	...	...	...
M'Sila	CDJC	102 151	...	...	...	...	...	...	...
Oran (Wahran)	CDJC	705 335	...	...	...	...	...	...	...
Ouargla (Wargla)	CDJC	139 381	...	...	...	...	...	...	...
Relizane	CDJC	104 644	...	...	...	...	...	...	...
Saïda	CDJC	113 533	...	...	...	...	...	...	...
Sétif (Stif)	CDJC	214 842	...	...	...	...	...	...	...
Sidi-bel-Abbès	CDJC	183 931	...	...	...	...	...	...	...
Skikda	CDJC	153 531	...	...	...	...	...	...	...
Souk Ahras	CDJC	114 512	...	...	...	...	...	...	...
Tebessa	CDJC	154 335	...	...	...	...	...	...	...
Tiaert	CDJC	148 850	...	...	...	...	...	...	...
Tlemcen (Tilimsen)	CDJC	156 258	...	...	...	...	...	...	...
Tougourt	CDJC	114 183	...	...	...	...	...	...	...
Angola									
1 VII 1993									
Huambo	ESDF	...	...	...	...	*400 000*	...	...	...
LUANDA	ESDF	...	...	...	...	*1 822 407*	*855 676*	*936 731*	...
Benin — Bénin									
1 VII 2000									
Cotonou	ESDF	*650 660*	*318 752*	*331 908*	*79*	...	...	...	...
Parakou	ESDF	*144 627*	*73 603*	*71 024*	*441*	...	...	...	...
PORTO-NOVO	ESDF	*232 756*	*113 737*	*119 019*	*50*	...	...	...	...
Botswana									
17 VIII 2001									
Francistown	CDFC	83 023	40 147	42 876	79	113 315	...	...	...
GABORONE	CDFC	186 007	91 851	94 156	169	282 150	...	...	...
Burkina Faso									
1 VII 2005									
Bobo Dioulasso	ESDF	399 068	...	...	...	...	...	...	...
OUAGADOUGOU	ESDF	973 522	...	...	...	1 029 297	...	...	...
Burundi									
16 VIII 1990									
BUJUMBURA	CDFC	235 440	129 195	106 245	...	...	...	...	...
Cameroon — Cameroun									
1 VII 1998									
Bafoussam	ESDF	*205 620*	...	...	...	...	...	...	...
Bamenda	ESDF	*252 083*	...	...	...	...	...	...	...
Bertoua	ESDF	*129 067*	...	...	...	...	...	...	...
Douala	ESDF	*1 382 900*	...	...	...	...	...	...	...
Edéa	ESDF	*101 200*	...	...	...	...	...	...	...
Garoua	ESDF	*293 081*	...	...	...	...	...	...	...
Kousséri	ESDF	*233 280*	...	...	...	...	...	...	...

8. Population of capital cities and cities of 100 000 or more inhabitants: latest available year, 1986 - 2005
Population des capitales et des villes de 100 000 habitants ou plus: dernière année disponible, 1986 - 2005
(continued — suite)

Continent, country or area, date and city / Continent, pays ou zone, date et ville	Code[1]	City proper — Ville proprement dite Population				Urban agglomeration — Agglomération urbaine Population			
		Both sexes Les deux sexes	Male Masculin	Female Féminin	Surface area Superficie (km²)	Both sexes Les deux sexes	Male Masculin	Female Féminin	Surface area Superficie (km²)
AFRICA — AFRIQUE									
Cameroon — Cameroun									
1 VII 1998									
Kumba	ESDF	110 860	...	...	...	...	...	...	...
Loum	ESDF	115 781	...	...	...	...	...	...	...
Maroua	ESDF	225 469	...	...	...	...	...	...	...
Ngaoundéré	ESDF	156 804	...	...	...	...	...	...	...
Nkongsamba	ESDF	104 908	...	...	...	...	...	...	...
YAOUNDE	ESDF	1 293 000	...	...	...	...	...	...	...
Cape Verde — Cap-Vert									
23 VI 1990									
PRAIA	CDFC	61 644	...	...	...	...	...	...	...
Central African Republic — République centrafricaine									
8 XII 1988									
BANGUI	CDFC	451 690	...	...	...	...	...	...	...
Chad — Tchad									
8 IV 1993									
N'DJAMENA	CDFC	530 965	...	...	...	...	...	...	...
Comoros — Comores									
15 IX 1991									
MORONI	CDFC	30 365	...	...	...	...	...	...	...
Côte d'Ivoire									
1 III 1988									
Abidjan	CDFC	1 929 079	...	...	...	...	...	...	...
Bouake	CDFC	329 850	...	...	...	362 192	...	...	...
Daloa	CDFC	121 842	...	...	...	127 923	...	...	...
Korhogo	CDFC	109 445	...	...	...	112 888	...	...	...
YAMOUSSOUKRO	CDFC	106 786	...	...	...	126 191	...	...	...
Djibouti									
1 VII 1995									
DJIBOUTI	ESDF	383 000	...	...	...	...	...	...	...
Egypt — Égypte									
19 XI 1996									
Alexandria	CDFC	3 339 076	1 707 477	1 631 599	...	...	...	...	...
Al Orizah	CDFC	100 482	53 081	47 401	...	...	...	...	...
Assyût	CDFC	343 662	182 151	161 511	...	...	...	...	...
Aswan	CDFC	219 541	111 640	107 901	...	...	...	...	...
Banha	CDFC	135 892	69 154	66 738	...	...	...	...	...
Beni-Suef	CDFC	171 734	87 105	84 629	...	...	...	...	...
CAIRO	CDFC	6 800 992	3 486 260	3 314 732	...	...	...	...	...
Damanhûr	CDFC	209 423	107 965	101 458	...	...	...	...	...
El-Mahalla El-Kubra	CDFC	394 924	199 100	195 824	...	...	...	...	...
Faiyûm	CDFC	260 830	134 462	126 368	...	...	...	...	...
Giza	CDFC	2 221 817	1 139 665	1 082 152	...	...	...	...	...
Imbaba	CDFC	523 265	266 793	256 472	...	...	...	...	...
Ismailia	CDFC	255 134	129 004	126 130	...	...	...	...	...
Kafr-El-Dwar	CDFC	101 056	51 491	49 565	...	...	...	...	...
Kena	CDFC	155 382	79 038	76 344	...	...	...	...	...
Luxer	CDFC	153 758	79 753	74 005	...	...	...	...	...
Mansûra	CDFC	369 409	187 622	181 787	...	...	...	...	...
Menia	CDFC	201 440	103 428	98 012	...	...	...	...	...
Port Said	CDFC	472 335	242 502	229 833	...	...	...	...	...
Shebin-El-Kom	CDFC	156 794	79 868	76 926	...	...	...	...	...
Shubra-El-Khema	CDFC	870 776	449 271	421 505	...	...	...	...	...
Sohag	CDFC	170 417	85 918	84 499	...	...	...	...	...
Suez	CDFC	417 527	214 133	203 394	...	...	...	...	...
Tanta	CDFC	372 893	188 594	184 299	...	...	...	...	...
Zagazig	CDFC	267 469	136 094	131 375	...	...	...	...	...
Eritrea — Érythrée									
1 VII 1990									
ASMARA	ESDF	358 100	...	...	...	...	...	...	...

8. Population of capital cities and cities of 100 000 or more inhabitants: latest available year, 1986 - 2005
Population des capitales et des villes de 100 000 habitants ou plus: dernière année disponible, 1986 - 2005
(continued — suite)

Continent, country or area, date and city / Continent, pays ou zone, date et ville	Code[1]	City proper — Ville proprement dite Population				Urban agglomeration — Agglomération urbaine Population			
		Both sexes Les deux sexes	Male Masculin	Female Féminin	Surface area Superficie (km²)	Both sexes Les deux sexes	Male Masculin	Female Féminin	Surface area Superficie (km²)
AFRICA — AFRIQUE									
Ethiopia — Ethiopie									
1 VII 2002									
ADDIS ABABA	ESDF	2 646 000	1 273 000	1 373 000	...	...	...	...	...
Awassa	ESDF	103 725	52 308	51 417	...	...	...	...	...
Bahir Dar	ESDF	140 084	72 736	67 348	28	...	...	...	...
Debre Zeit	ESDF	108 632	53 648	54 984	...	...	...	...	...
Dessie	ESDF	141 616	72 578	69 038	15	...	...	...	...
Dire Dawa	ESDF	237 012	118 880	118 132	18	...	...	...	...
Gondar	ESDF	163 097	82 229	80 868	40	...	...	...	...
Harar	ESDF	105 000	53 000	52 000	...	...	...	...	...
Jimma	ESDF	131 708	67 138	64 570	...	...	...	...	...
Mekele	ESDF	141 433	71 990	69 443	24	...	...	...	...
Nazareth	ESDF	189 362	94 822	94 540	...	...	...	...	...
Gabon									
31 VII 1993									
LIBREVILLE	CDFC	362 386	184 192	178 194	...	418 616	212 383	206 233	...
Gambia — Gambie									
15 IV 1993									
BANJUL	CDFC	42 326	22 268	20 058	12	...	...	...	...
Ghana									
26 III 2000									
ACCRA	CDFC	1 658 937	817 404	841 533	...	...	...	...	...
Kumasi	CDFC	1 170 270	587 012	583 258	...	...	...	...	...
Sekondi	CDFC	114 157	56 697	57 460	...	...	...	...	...
Takoradi	CDFC	175 436	86 794	88 642	...	...	...	...	...
Tamale	CDFC	202 317	100 854	101 463	...	...	...	...	...
Tema	CDFC	141 479	68 467	73 012	...	...	...	...	...
Guinea — Guinée									
1 XII 1996									
CONAKRY	CDFC	1 091 500	...	...	...	...	...	...	...
Kankan	CDFC	...	...	...	...	261 341	...	...	...
Kindia	CDFC	...	...	...	...	287 607	...	...	...
Labé	CDFC	...	...	...	...	249 515	...	...	...
Nzérékoré	CDFC	...	...	...	...	282 772	...	...	...
Guinea-Bissau — Guinée-Bissau									
1 XII 1991									
BISSAU	CDFC	197 600	...	...	...	...	...	...	...
Kenya									
1 VII 2003									
Eldoret	ESDF	194 456	101 117	93 339	151	...	...	...	...
Kisumu	ESDF	226 088	113 044	113 044	475	...	...	...	...
Mombasa	ESDF	767 454	403 923	363 531	230	...	...	...	...
NAIROBI	ESDF	2 656 997	1 347 255	1 309 742	696	...	...	...	...
Nakuru	ESDF	255 645	130 379	125 266	290	...	...	...	...
Lesotho									
12 IV 1986									
MASERU	CDFC	109 382	...	...	...	...	...	...	...
Libyan Arab Jamahiriya — Jamahiriya arabe libyenne									
1 VII 1990									
Al Khums	ESDJ	200 000	...	...	...	...	...	...	...
BENGHAZI[2]	ESDJ	800 000	...	...	...	...	...	...	...
Misurata	ESDJ	360 000	...	...	...	...	...	...	...
Sebha	ESDJ	150 000	...	...	...	...	...	...	...
TRIPOLI[2]	ESDJ	1 500 000	...	...	...	...	...	...	...
Zuwarah	ESDJ	280 000	...	...	...	...	...	...	...
Madagascar									
1 VII 2005									
ANTANANARIVO[3]	ESDF	1 015 140	495 393	519 747	...	...	...	...	...
Antsirabe	ESDF	...	...	...	...	180 180	87 691	92 489	...
Fianarantsoa	ESDF	...	...	...	...	165 220	80 410	84 810	...
Mahajanga	ESDF	...	...	...	...	152 785	74 359	78 426	...
Toamasina	ESDF	...	...	...	...	203 469	99 026	104 443	...

8. Population of capital cities and cities of 100 000 or more inhabitants: latest available year, 1986 - 2005
Population des capitales et des villes de 100 000 habitants ou plus: dernière année disponible, 1986 - 2005
(continued — suite)

Continent, country or area, date and city / Continent, pays ou zone, date et ville	Code[1]	City proper — Ville proprement dite Population				Urban agglomeration — Agglomération urbaine Population			
		Both sexes Les deux sexes	Male Masculin	Female Féminin	Surface area Superficie (km²)	Both sexes Les deux sexes	Male Masculin	Female Féminin	Surface area Superficie (km²)
AFRICA — AFRIQUE									
Madagascar									
1 VII 2005									
Toliara	ESDF	...	...	...	...	*113 993*	*55 479*	*58 514*	...
Malawi									
1 VII 2003									
Blantyre City	ESDJ	*678 381*	*350 493*	*327 888*	...	*349 427*	*171 614*	*177 813*	...
LILONGWE	ESDJ	*632 867*	*328 154*	*304 713*	...	*1 087 917*	*532 131*	*555 786*	...
Mali									
1 IV 1998									
BAMAKO	CDJC	1 016 167	520 688	495 479	252	...	...	...	...
Mauritania — Mauritanie									
1 XI 2000									
NOUAKCHOTT	CDFC	558 195	...	...	...	...	...	...	...
Mauritius — Maurice									
1 VII 2005									
Beau Bassin-Rose Hill	ESDJ	108 339	52 827	55 512	20	...	...	...	...
PORT LOUIS	ESDJ	148 565	73 717	74 848	46	...	...	...	...
Vacoas - Phoenix	ESDJ	105 196	51 841	53 355	54	...	...	...	...
Morocco — Maroc[4]									
1 VII 2003									
Agadir	ESDF	*494 000*	...	...	...	...	...	...	...
Béni-Mellal	ESDF	*998 000*	...	...	...	...	...	...	...
Casablanca (Dar-el-Beida)[5]	ESDF	*3 389 000*	...	...	...	...	...	...	...
El-Jadida	ESDF	*1 102 000*	...	...	...	...	...	...	...
Fès	ESDF	*1 185 000*	...	...	...	...	...	...	...
Kénitra	ESDF	*598 000*	...	...	...	...	...	...	...
Khouribga	ESDF	*336 000*	...	...	...	...	...	...	...
Marrakech[5]	ESDF	*1 068 000*	...	...	...	...	...	...	...
Meknès[5]	ESDF	*680 000*	...	...	...	...	...	...	...
Mohammedia	ESDF	*223 000*	...	...	...	...	...	...	...
Oujda	ESDF	*486 000*	...	...	...	...	...	...	...
RABAT	ESDF	*673 000*	...	...	...	...	...	...	...
Safi	ESDF	*906 000*	...	...	...	...	...	...	...
Salé	ESDF	*880 000*	...	...	...	...	...	...	...
Tanger	ESDF	*782 000*	...	...	...	...	...	...	...
Tétouan	ESDF	*652 000*	...	...	...	...	...	...	...
Mozambique									
1 VIII 1997									
Beira	CDFC	397 368	...	...	...	...	...	...	...
Chimoio	CDFC	171 056	...	...	...	...	...	...	...
MAPUTO	CDFC	966 837	...	...	...	1 391 499	...	...	...
Matola	CDFC	424 662	...	...	...	...	...	...	...
Mocuba	CDFC	124 650	...	...	...	...	...	...	...
Nacala	CDFC	158 248	...	...	...	...	...	...	...
Nampula	CDFC	303 346	...	...	...	...	...	...	...
Quelimane	CDFC	150 116	...	...	...	...	...	...	...
Tete	CDFC	101 984	...	...	...	...	...	...	...
Namibia — Namibie									
27 VIII 2001									
WINDHOEK	CDFC	...	...	...	...	233 529	117 306	116 222	...
Niger[6]									
20 V 2001									
NIAMEY	CDJC	707 951	358 500	349 451	...	...	...	...	...
Nigeria — Nigéria									
26 XI 1991									
Aba	CDFC	500 183	...	...	...	...	...	...	...
Abeokuta	CDFC	352 735	...	...	...	...	...	...	...
ABUJA	CDFC	107 069	...	...	...	378 671	...	...	...
Ado-Ekiti	CDFC	156 122	...	...	...	...	...	...	...
Akure	CDFC	239 124	...	...	...	...	...	...	...
Awka	CDFC	104 682	...	...	...	...	...	...	...
Bauchi	CDFC	206 537	...	...	...	...	...	...	...
Benin City	CDFC	762 719	...	...	...	...	...	...	...

8. Population of capital cities and cities of 100 000 or more inhabitants: latest available year, 1986 - 2005
Population des capitales et des villes de 100 000 habitants ou plus: dernière année disponible, 1986 - 2005
(continued — suite)

Continent, country or area, date and city / Continent, pays ou zone, date et ville	Code[1]	City proper — Ville proprement dite Population				Urban agglomeration — Agglomération urbaine Population			
		Both sexes Les deux sexes	Male Masculin	Female Féminin	Surface area Superficie (km²)	Both sexes Les deux sexes	Male Masculin	Female Féminin	Surface area Superficie (km²)
AFRICA — AFRIQUE									
Nigeria — Nigéria									
26 XI 1991									
Bida	CDFC	111 245	...	...	...	...	...	...	...
Calabar	CDFC	310 839	...	...	...	...	...	...	...
Damaturu	CDFC	141 897	...	...	...	...	...	...	...
Ede	CDFC	142 363	...	...	...	...	...	...	...
Effon-Alaiye	CDFC	158 977	...	...	...	...	...	...	...
Enugu	CDFC	407 756	...	...	...	...	...	...	...
Gboko	CDFC	101 281	...	...	...	...	...	...	...
Gombe	CDFC	163 604	...	...	...	...	...	...	...
Gusau	CDFC	132 393	...	...	...	...	...	...	...
Ibadan	CDFC	1 835 300	...	...	...	...	...	...	...
Ife	CDFC	186 856	...	...	...	...	...	...	...
Ijebu-Ode	CDFC	124 313	...	...	...	...	...	...	...
Ikare	CDFC	103 843	...	...	...	...	...	...	...
Ikire	CDFC	111 435	...	...	...	...	...	...	...
Ikorodu	CDFC	184 674	...	...	...	...	...	...	...
Ikot Ekpene	CDFC	119 402	...	...	...	...	...	...	...
Ilawe-Ekiti	CDFC	104 049	...	...	...	...	...	...	...
Ilesha	CDFC	139 445	...	...	...	...	...	...	...
Ilorin	CDFC	532 089	...	...	...	...	...	...	...
Ise	CDFC	108 136	...	...	...	...	...	...	...
Iseyin	CDFC	170 936	...	...	...	...	...	...	...
Iwo	CDFC	125 645	...	...	...	...	...	...	...
Jimeta	CDFC	141 724	...	...	...	...	...	...	...
Jos	CDFC	510 300	...	...	...	...	...	...	...
Kaduna	CDFC	993 642	...	...	...	...	...	...	...
Kano	CDFC	2 166 554	...	...	...	...	...	...	...
Katsina	CDFC	259 315	...	...	...	...	...	...	...
Lagos	CDFC	5 195 247	...	...	...	...	...	...	...
Maiduguri	CDFC	618 278	...	...	...	...	...	...	...
Makurdi	CDFC	151 515	...	...	...	...	...	...	...
Minna	CDFC	189 191	...	...	...	...	...	...	...
Mubi	CDFC	128 900	...	...	...	...	...	...	...
Nnewi	CDFC	121 065	...	...	...	...	...	...	...
Ogbomosho	CDFC	433 030	...	...	...	...	...	...	...
Okene	CDFC	312 775	...	...	...	...	...	...	...
Okpogho	CDFC	105 127	...	...	...	...	...	...	...
Ondo	CDFC	146 051	...	...	...	...	...	...	...
Onitsha	CDFC	350 280	...	...	...	...	...	...	...
Oshogbo	CDFC	250 951	...	...	...	...	...	...	...
Owerri	CDFC	119 711	...	...	...	...	...	...	...
Owo	CDFC	157 181	...	...	...	...	...	...	...
Oyo	CDFC	369 894	...	...	...	...	...	...	...
Port Harcourt	CDFC	703 421	...	...	...	...	...	...	...
Sagamu	CDFC	127 513	...	...	...	...	...	...	...
Sango Otta	CDFC	103 332	...	...	...	...	...	...	...
Sapele	CDFC	109 576	...	...	...	...	...	...	...
Sokoto	CDFC	329 639	...	...	...	...	...	...	...
Suleja	CDFC	105 075	...	...	...	...	...	...	...
Ugep	CDFC	134 773	...	...	...	...	...	...	...
Umuahia	CDFC	147 167	...	...	...	...	...	...	...
Warri	CDFC	363 382	...	...	...	...	...	...	...
Zaria	CDFC	612 257	...	...	...	...	...	...	...
Réunion									
1 VII 2002									
SAINT-DENIS[7]	ESDF	134 042	63 922	70 120	143	...	...	...	...
Rwanda									
15 VIII 1991									
KIGALI	CDJC	233 640	125 550	108 090	...	...	...	...	...

8. Population of capital cities and cities of 100 000 or more inhabitants: latest available year, 1986 - 2005
Population des capitales et des villes de 100 000 habitants ou plus: dernière année disponible, 1986 - 2005
(continued — suite)

Continent, country or area, date and city / Continent, pays ou zone, date et ville	Code[1]	City proper — Ville proprement dite Population				Urban agglomeration — Agglomération urbaine Population			
		Both sexes Les deux sexes	Male Masculin	Female Féminin	Surface area Superficie (km²)	Both sexes Les deux sexes	Male Masculin	Female Féminin	Surface area Superficie (km²)
AFRICA — AFRIQUE									
Saint Helena ex. dep. — Sainte-Hélène sans dép.									
8 III 1998									
JAMESTOWN	CDFC	884	452	432	4	...	...	...	...
Sao Tome and Principe — Sao Tomé-et-Principe									
25 VIII 2001									
SAO TOME	CDJC	...	...	...		49 957	24 003	25 954	
Senegal — Sénégal									
1 VII 1999									
DAKAR	ESDF	879 703	...	...	500	1 976 533	...	...	...
Kaolack	ESDF	227 915	...	...	...	...	...	...	...
Mbour	ESDF	135 619	...	...	...	...	...	...	...
Pikine-Guediawaye[8]	ESDF	1 096 830	...	...	...	...	...	...	...
Saint Louis	ESDF	147 961	...	...	...	...	...	...	...
Thiès	ESDF	256 113	...	...	...	...	...	...	...
Ziguinchor	ESDF	199 871	...	...	...	...	...	...	...
Seychelles									
29 VIII 1997									
VICTORIA	CDFC	...	...	...	...	24 701	...	...	
Somalia — Somalie									
1 VII 2001									
MOGADISHU	ESDF	*1 212 000*	...	...	...	...	...	...	...
South Africa — Afrique du Sud									
10 X 1996									
Alexandra	CDFC	171 284	...	...	...	...	...	...	...
Benoni	CDFC	366 343	...	...	...	...	...	...	...
Bloemfontein	CDFC	350 504	...	...	...	...	...	...	...
Boksburg	CDFC	263 179	...	...	...	...	...	...	...
Botshabelo	CDFC	177 971	...	...	...	...	...	...	...
CAPE TOWN[9]	CDFC	987 007	...	...	...	...	...	...	...
Durban	CDFC	669 242	...	...	...	...	...	...	...
Germiston	CDFC	164 252	...	...	...	...	...	...	...
Johannesburg	CDFC	752 349	...	...	...	...	...	...	...
Kathlehong	CDFC	344 803	...	...	...	...	...	...	...
Kempton Park	CDFC	344 426	...	...	...	...	...	...	...
Khayelitsa	CDFC	314 239	...	...	...	...	...	...	...
Kimberley	CDFC	206 070	...	...	...	...	...	...	...
Mangaung	CDFC	176 525	...	...	...	...	...	...	...
Pietermaritzburg	CDFC	405 385	...	...	...	...	...	...	...
Port Elizabeth	CDFC	775 255	...	...	...	...	...	...	...
PRETORIA[9]	CDFC	692 348	340 363	351 985	...	...	...	...	...
Roodepoort	CDFC	279 340	...	...	...	...	...	...	...
Soweto	CDFC	904 165	...	...	...	...	...	...	...
Springs	CDFC	163 304	...	...	...	...	...	...	...
Tembisa	CDFC	237 676	...	...	...	...	...	...	...
Umlazi	CDFC	339 715	...	...	...	...	...	...	...
Vereeniging	CDFC	379 638	...	...	...	...	...	...	...
Sudan — Soudan									
15 IV 1993									
Al-Fasher	CDFC	141 884	...	...	...	...	...	...	...
Al-Gadarif	CDFC	191 164	...	...	...	...	...	...	...
Al-Gezira	CDFC	211 362	...	...	...	...	...	...	...
Al-Obeid	CDFC	229 425	...	...	...	...	...	...	...
Juba	CDFC	114 980	...	...	...	...	...	...	...
Kassala	CDFC	234 622	...	...	...	...	...	...	...
KHARTOUM	CDFC	947 483	...	...	...	2 919 773	...	...	...
Khartoum North	CDFC	700 887	...	...	...	...	...	...	...
Kosti	CDFC	173 599	...	...	...	...	...	...	...
Nyala	CDFC	227 183	...	...	...	...	...	...	...
Omdurman	CDFC	1 271 403	...	...	...	...	...	...	...
Port Sudan	CDFC	308 195	...	...	...	...	...	...	...

8. Population of capital cities and cities of 100 000 or more inhabitants: latest available year, 1986 - 2005
Population des capitales et des villes de 100 000 habitants ou plus: dernière année disponible, 1986 - 2005
(continued — suite)

| Continent, country or area, date and city | Code[1] | City proper — Ville proprement dite Population | | | | Urban agglomeration — Agglomération urbaine Population | | | |
Continent, pays ou zone, date et ville		Both sexes Les deux sexes	Male Masculin	Female Féminin	Surface area Superficie (km²)	Both sexes Les deux sexes	Male Masculin	Female Féminin	Surface area Superficie (km²)
AFRICA — AFRIQUE									
Swaziland									
25 VIII 1986									
MBABANE	CDFC	38 290	...	...	...	...	...	...	...
Togo									
1 VII 1990									
LOME	ESDF	*450 000*	...	...	...	...	...	...	...
Tunisia — Tunisie									
1 VII 1998									
Bizerte	ESDF	*105 520*	...	...	...	...	...	...	...
Gabes	ESDF	*104 950*	...	...	...	...	...	...	...
Kairouan	ESDF	*110 280*	...	...	...	...	...	...	...
Sfax	ESDF	*248 800*	...	...	...	...	...	...	...
TUNIS	ESDF	*702 330*	...	...	...	...	...	...	...
Uganda — Ouganda									
12 IX 2002									
Gulu	CDFC	113 144	...	...	...	...	...	...	...
KAMPALA	CDFC	1 208 544	588 433	620 111	...	...	...	...	...
United Republic of Tanzania — République Unie de Tanzanie									
28 VIII 1988									
Arusha	CDFC	134 708	69 875	64 833	...	...	...	...	...
Dar es Salaam	CDFC	1 360 850	715 925	644 925	...	...	...	...	...
DODOMA	CDFC	203 833	101 437	102 396	...	...	...	...	...
Mbeya	CDFC	152 844	74 259	78 585	...	...	...	...	...
Morogoro	CDFC	117 760	59 144	58 616	...	...	...	...	...
Mwanza	CDFC	223 013	113 779	109 234	...	...	...	...	...
Shinyanga	CDFC	100 724	50 117	50 607	...	...	...	...	...
Tanga	CDFC	187 455	96 259	91 196	...	...	...	...	...
Zanzibar	CDFC	157 634	77 787	79 847	...	...	...	...	...
Western Sahara — Sahara occidental									
1 VII 1999									
EL AAIUN	ESDF	*169 000*	...	...	...	...	...	...	...
Zambia — Zambie									
1 VII 2000									
Chingola	ESDF	164 964	82 643	82 321	1 678	...	...	...	...
Kabwe	ESDF	170 387	84 041	86 346	1 572	...	...	...	...
Kitwe	ESDF	362 423	180 865	181 558	777	...	...	...	...
Luanshya	ESDF	144 009	72 449	71 560	811	...	...	...	...
LUSAKA	ESDF	1 057 212	528 891	528 321	360	...	...	...	...
Mufulira	ESDF	137 272	68 253	69 019	1 637	...	...	...	...
Ndola	ESDF	371 221	185 043	186 178	1 103	...	...	...	...
Zimbabwe									
17 VIII 2002									
Bulawayo	CDFC	676 650	323 550	353 100	479	...	...	...	...
Gweru	CDFC	140 806	67 689	73 117	...	...	...	...	...
HARARE	CDFC	1 435 784	720 021	715 763	872	...	...	...	...
Mutare	CDFC	170 466	85 006	85 460	...	...	...	...	...
AMERICA, NORTH — AMERIQUE DU NORD									
Anguilla									
1 VII 2001									
THE VALLEY	ESDF	4 904	...	...	...	...	...	...	...
Antigua and Barbuda — Antigua-et-Barbuda									
28 V 1991									
ST. JOHN	CDFC	22 342	...	...	...	...	...	...	...
Aruba									
6 X 1991									
ORANJESTAD	CDJC	20 045	9 441	10 604	...	...	...	...	...

8. Population of capital cities and cities of 100 000 or more inhabitants: latest available year, 1986 - 2005
Population des capitales et des villes de 100 000 habitants ou plus: dernière année disponible, 1986 - 2005
(continued — suite)

Continent, country or area, date and city / Continent, pays ou zone, date et ville	Code[1]	City proper — Ville proprement dite Population				Urban agglomeration — Agglomération urbaine Population			
		Both sexes Les deux sexes	Male Masculin	Female Féminin	Surface area Superficie (km²)	Both sexes Les deux sexes	Male Masculin	Female Féminin	Surface area Superficie (km²)
AMERICA, NORTH — AMERIQUE DU NORD									
Bahamas									
1 V 2000									
NASSAU	CDFC	...	...	...	...	210 832	...	...	...
Belize									
1 VII 2000									
BELMOPAN	ESDF	*8 305*	*4 050*	*4 255*	...	...	...	...	...
Bermuda — Bermudes[10]									
20 V 2000									
HAMILTON	CDJC	969	508	461	0	...	...	...	...
British Virgin Islands — Iles Vierges britanniques									
1 VII 1992									
ROAD TOWN	ESDF	*3 500*	...	...	...	...	...	...	...
Canada									
1 VII 2005									
Abbotsford	ESDJ	...	...	...	...	162 789	81 939	80 850	626
Calgary	ESDJ	...	...	...	...	1 060 297	533 894	526 403	5 083
Chicoutimi-Jonquière	ESDJ	...	...	...	...	152 950	75 791	77 159	1 754
Edmonton	ESDJ	...	...	...	...	1 016 007	509 072	506 935	9 419
Halifax	ESDJ	...	...	...	...	380 844	186 051	194 793	5 496
Hamilton	ESDJ	...	...	...	...	714 935	352 069	362 866	1 372
Kingston	ESDJ	...	...	...	...	156 217	77 405	78 812	1 907
Kitchener	ESDJ	...	...	...	...	458 552	228 668	229 884	827
London	ESDJ	...	...	...	...	464 304	227 427	236 877	2 333
Montréal	ESDJ	...	...	...	...	3 635 733	1 779 863	1 855 870	4 047
Oshawa	ESDJ	...	...	...	...	340 287	168 654	171 633	903
OTTAWA	ESDJ	...	...	...	...	1 148 785	564 708	584 077	5 318
Québec	ESDJ	...	...	...	...	717 641	349 481	368 160	3 154
Regina	ESDJ	...	...	...	...	199 041	97 499	101 542	3 408
St. Catharines	ESDJ	...	...	...	...	396 933	194 177	202 756	1 406
St. John's	ESDJ	...	...	...	...	182 485	88 199	94 286	805
Saint John	ESDJ	...	...	...	...	126 708	61 567	65 141	3 360
Saskatoon	ESDJ	...	...	...	...	235 840	115 513	120 327	5 192
Sherbrooke	ESDJ	...	...	...	...	163 713	80 065	83 648	1 108
Sudbury	ESDJ	...	...	...	...	161 081	79 096	81 985	3 536
Thunder Bay	ESDJ	...	...	...	...	126 519	62 585	63 934	2 548
Toronto	ESDJ	...	...	...	...	5 304 090	2 609 483	2 694 607	5 903
Trois-Rivières	ESDJ	...	...	...	...	142 201	68 813	73 388	880
Vancouver	ESDJ	...	...	...	...	2 208 333	1 091 964	1 116 369	2 879
Victoria	ESDJ	...	...	...	...	334 670	161 621	173 049	695
Windsor	ESDJ	...	...	...	...	332 334	165 382	166 952	1 023
Winnipeg	ESDJ	...	...	...	...	706 854	348 008	358 846	4 151
Cayman Islands — Iles Caïmanes									
10 X 1999									
GEORGE TOWN	CDFC	20 626	10 191	10 435	...	...	...	...	...
Costa Rica									
1 VII 2003									
Alajuela	ESDJ	241 177	122 986	118 191	388	...	...	...	...
Cartago	ESDJ	142 442	71 889	70 553	288	...	...	...	...
Heredia	ESDJ	112 461	55 422	57 039	283	...	...	...	...
Puntarenas	ESDJ	111 458	57 716	53 742	1 842	...	...	...	...
SAN JOSE	ESDJ	334 780	165 046	169 734	45	...	...	...	...
Cuba									
1 VII 2005									
Bayamo	ESDF	145 475	...	...	...	...	...	...	...
Camagüey	ESDF	307 169	...	...	...	...	...	...	...
Ciego de Avila	ESDF	108 711	...	...	...	...	...	...	...
Cienfuegos	ESDF	142 145	...	...	...	...	...	...	...
Guantánamo	ESDF	208 615	...	...	...	...	...	...	...
Holguín	ESDF	273 239	...	...	...	...	...	...	...
LA HABANA	ESDF	2 186 909	...	...	727	...	...	...	...

8. Population of capital cities and cities of 100 000 or more inhabitants: latest available year, 1986 - 2005
Population des capitales et des villes de 100 000 habitants ou plus: dernière année disponible, 1986 - 2005
(continued — suite)

Continent, country or area, date and city Continent, pays ou zone, date et ville	Code[1]	City proper — Ville proprement dite Population				Urban agglomeration — Agglomération urbaine Population			
		Both sexes Les deux sexes	Male Masculin	Female Féminin	Surface area Superficie (km²)	Both sexes Les deux sexes	Male Masculin	Female Féminin	Surface area Superficie (km²)
AMERICA, NORTH — AMERIQUE DU NORD									
Cuba									
1 VII 2005									
Las Tunas	ESDF	147 569	...	...	...	...	...	...	...
Matanzas	ESDF	129 064	...	...	...	...	...	...	...
Pinar del Río	ESDF	138 013	...	...	...	...	...	...	...
Santa Clara	ESDF	209 327	...	...	...	...	...	...	...
Santiago de Cuba	ESDF	425 343	...	...	...	...	...	...	...
Dominica — Dominique									
12 V 1991									
ROSEAU	CDFC	16 243	...	...	...	...	...	...	...
Dominican Republic — République dominicaine									
1 VII 2001									
San Pedro de Macoris	ESDF	*266 629*	...	...	...	...	...	...	...
Santiago de los Caballeros	ESDF	*836 614*	...	...	...	...	...	...	...
SANTO DOMINGO	ESDF	*2 677 056*	...	...	...	...	...	...	...
El Salvador[11]									
1 VII 2003									
Ahuachapan	ESDF	115 521	57 593	57 928	245	...	...	...	...
Apopa	ESDF	192 728	91 699	100 830	52	...	...	...	...
Ciudad Delgado	ESDF	164 069	78 063	85 837	33	...	...	...	...
Cuscatancingo	ESDF	104 640	49 787	54 745	5	...	...	...	...
Ilopango	ESDF	144 985	68 983	75 852	35	...	...	...	...
Mejicanos	ESDF	200 917	95 596	105 114	22	...	...	...	...
Nueva San Salvador	ESDF	175 286	86 161	89 097	112	...	...	...	...
SAN SALVADOR	ESDF	497 844	236 873	261 836	886	...	...	...	...
San Martin	ESDF	123 663	58 838	64 697	56	...	...	...	...
San Miguel	ESDF	259 197	128 026	131 171	594	...	...	...	...
Santa Ana	ESDF	261 568	129 155	132 413	400	...	...	...	...
Sonsonate	ESDF	103 490	51 402	52 088	233	...	...	...	...
Soyapango	ESDF	290 412	138 177	152 739	30	...	...	...	...
Greenland — Groenland									
1 VII 2000									
NUUK (GODTHAB)	ESDJ	13 552	7 265	6 287	...	...	...	...	...
Guadeloupe									
8 III 1999									
BASSE-TERRE	CDJC	12 377	5 687	6 690	...	44 747	21 252	23 495	...
Pointe-à-Pitre	CDJC	...	...	...	...	171 773	...	...	...
Guatemala									
1 VII 2001									
GUATEMALA	ESDF	*1 022 001*	*491 891*	*530 110*	*228*	...	...	...	...
Escuintla	ESDF	*114 626*	*57 893*	*56 733*	*332*	...	...	...	...
Mixco	ESDF	*452 134*	*221 928*	*230 206*	*99*	...	...	...	...
Quetzaltenango	ESDF	*152 223*	*76 272*	*75 951*	*120*	...	...	...	...
Villa Nueva	ESDF	*390 329*	*192 238*	*198 091*	*114*	...	...	...	...
Haiti — Haïti									
1 VII 1999									
Cap-Haitien	ESDJ	*113 555*	*50 064*	*63 491*	10	...	...	...	...
Carrefour	ESDJ	*336 222*	*146 838*	*189 384*	23	...	...	...	...
Delmas	ESDJ	*284 079*	*124 774*	*159 305*	26	...	...	...	...
PORT-AU-PRINCE	ESDJ	*990 558*	*436 170*	*554 388*	21	...	...	...	...
Honduras									
1 VII 2003									
La Ceiba	ESDF	137 815	67 691	70 124	...	...	...	...	...
San Pedro Sula	ESDF	518 736	251 514	267 222	...	...	...	...	...
TEGUCIGALPA	ESDF	858 437	411 687	446 749	...	...	...	...	...
Jamaica — Jamaïque									
10 IX 2001									
KINGSTON	CDJC	579 006	272 472	306 534	22	...	...	...	...
Portmore	CDJC	156 467	72 292	84 175	...	...	...	...	...
Spanish Town	CDJC	131 510	63 791	67 719	...	...	...	...	...

8. Population of capital cities and cities of 100 000 or more inhabitants: latest available year, 1986 - 2005
Population des capitales et des villes de 100 000 habitants ou plus: dernière année disponible, 1986 - 2005
(continued — suite)

Continent, country or area, date and city / Continent, pays ou zone, date et ville	Code[1]	City proper — Ville proprement dite Population				Urban agglomeration — Agglomération urbaine Population			
		Both sexes Les deux sexes	Male Masculin	Female Féminin	Surface area Superficie (km²)	Both sexes Les deux sexes	Male Masculin	Female Féminin	Surface area Superficie (km²)
AMERICA, NORTH — AMERIQUE DU NORD									
Martinique									
8 III 1999									
FORT-DE-FRANCE	CDJC	94 152	42 812	51 340	...	134 796	61 705	73 091	...
Mexico — Mexique[12,13]									
1 VII 2003									
Acapulco (de Juárez)	ESDJ	...	...	...	...	819 517	...	...	...
Acayucan	ESDJ	...	...	...	...	106 713	...	...	...
Aguascalientes	ESDJ	...	...	...	...	766 312	...	...	...
Apizaco	ESDJ	...	...	...	...	174 619	...	...	...
Campeche	ESDJ	206 337	...	...	...	...	...	...	...
Cancun	ESDJ	...	...	...	...	510 950	...	...	...
Celaya	ESDJ	299 398	...	...	...	...	...	...	...
Chetumal	ESDJ	130 952	...	...	...	...	...	...	...
Chihuahua	ESDJ	...	...	...	...	738 855	...	...	...
Chilpacingo (de los Bravo)	ESDJ	154 030	...	...	...	...	...	...	...
Ciudad Acuña	ESDJ	129 834	...	...	...	...	...	...	...
Ciudad Del Carmen	ESDJ	139 352	...	...	...	...	...	...	...
Ciudad Obregón	ESDJ	264 166	...	...	...	...	...	...	...
Ciudad Valles	ESDJ	109 420	...	...	...	...	...	...	...
Ciudad Victoria	ESDJ	271 873	...	...	...	...	...	...	...
Coatzacoalcos	ESDJ	...	...	...	...	323 509	...	...	...
Colimas	ESDJ	...	...	...	...	226 495	...	...	...
Córdoba	ESDJ	...	...	...	...	289 122	...	...	...
Cuautla	ESDJ	...	...	...	...	387 840	...	...	...
Cuernavaca	ESDJ	...	...	...	...	804 140	...	...	...
Culiacán Rosales	ESDJ	584 280	...	...	...	...	...	...	...
Delicias	ESDJ	103 886	...	...	...	...	...	...	...
Durango (Victoria de Durango) ...	ESDJ	454 565	...	...	...	...	...	...	...
Ensenada	ESDJ	...	...	...	...	261 128	...	...	...
Fresnillo	ESDJ	103 013	...	...	...	...	...	...	...
Guadalajara	ESDJ	...	...	...	...	3 944 094	...	...	...
Guanajuato	ESDJ	...	...	...	...	102 195	...	...	...
Guaynas	ESDJ	...	...	...	...	191 201	...	...	...
Hermosillo	ESDJ	594 299	...	...	...	...	...	...	...
Hidalgo del Parral	ESDJ	103 716	...	...	...	...	...	...	...
Iguala (de la Independencia)	ESDJ	111 043	...	...	...	...	...	...	...
Irapuato	ESDJ	344 194	...	...	...	...	...	...	...
Juárez	ESDJ	...	...	...	...	1 379 589	...	...	...
La Paz	ESDJ	...	...	...	...	178 101	...	...	...
La Piedad	ESDJ	...	...	...	...	243 555	...	...	...
Lázaro Cárdenas	ESDJ	...	...	...	...	137 065	...	...	...
León (de los Aldama)	ESDJ	...	...	...	...	1 379 851	...	...	...
Los Mochis	ESDJ	213 964	...	...	...	...	...	...	...
Manzanillo	ESDJ	101 536	...	...	...	...	...	...	...
Matamoros	ESDJ	...	...	...	...	474 667	...	...	...
Mazatlán	ESDJ	352 409	...	...	...	...	...	...	...
Mérida	ESDJ	...	...	...	...	863 756	...	...	...
Mexicali	ESDJ	...	...	...	...	609 714	...	...	...
MEXICO, CIUDAD DE	ESDJ	...	...	...	...	19 493 540	...	...	...
Minatitlán	ESDJ	...	...	...	...	336 240	...	...	...
Monclova	ESDJ	...	...	...	...	299 265	...	...	...
Monterrey	ESDJ	...	...	...	...	3 542 979	...	...	...
Morelia	ESDJ	...	...	...	...	709 941	...	...	...
Moroleón - Uriangato	ESDJ	...	...	...	...	107 767	...	...	...
Navojoa	ESDJ	104 947	...	...	...	...	...	...	...
Nogales	ESDJ	179 415	...	...	...	...	...	...	...
Nuevo Laredo	ESDJ	...	...	...	...	354 372	...	...	...
Oaxaca de Juárez	ESDJ	...	...	...	...	495 241	...	...	...
Ocotlán	ESDJ	...	...	...	...	133 569	...	...	...
Orizaba	ESDJ	...	...	...	...	391 620	...	...	...
Pachuca (de Soto)	ESDJ	...	...	...	...	404 861	...	...	...

8. Population of capital cities and cities of 100 000 or more inhabitants: latest available year, 1986 - 2005
Population des capitales et des villes de 100 000 habitants ou plus: dernière année disponible, 1986 - 2005
(continued — suite)

Continent, country or area, date and city / Continent, pays ou zone, date et ville	Code[1]	City proper — Ville proprement dite Population				Urban agglomeration — Agglomération urbaine Population			
		Both sexes Les deux sexes	Male Masculin	Female Féminin	Surface area Superficie (km²)	Both sexes Les deux sexes	Male Masculin	Female Féminin	Surface area Superficie (km²)
AMERICA, NORTH — AMERIQUE DU NORD									
Mexico — Mexique[12,13]									
1 VII 2003									
Piedras Negras	ESDJ	...	...	...	...	167 994	...	...	...
Poza Rica de Hidalgo	ESDJ	...	...	...	...	460 733	...	...	...
Puebla de Zaragoza	ESDJ	...	...	...	...	2 016 956	...	...	...
Puerto Vallarta	ESDJ	...	...	...	...	276 378	...	...	...
Querétaro	ESDJ	...	...	...	...	877 837	...	...	...
Reynosa	ESDJ	...	...	...	...	603 335	...	...	...
Rioverde - Ciudad Fernández	ESDJ	...	...	...	...	131 505	...	...	...
Salamanca	ESDJ	146 432	...	...	...		...	...	...
Saltillo	ESDJ	...	...	...	...	697 652	...	...	...
San Cristobal de las Casas	ESDJ	124 404	...	...	...	...	...	...	...
San Francisco del Rincón	ESDJ	...	...	...	...	159 788	...	...	...
San Juan del Río	ESDJ	112 166	...	...	...	...	...	...	...
San Luis Potosí	ESDJ	...	...	...	...	895 602	...	...	...
San Luis Rio Colorado	ESDJ	144 593	...	...	...		...	...	...
San Martín Texmelucan	ESDJ	...	...	...	...	155 376	...	...	...
Tampico	ESDJ	...	...	...	...	806 919	...	...	...
Tapachula (de Cordova y Ordoñez)	ESDJ	196 951	...	...	...	...	...	...	...
Tecomán	ESDJ	...	...	...	...	134 285	...	...	...
Tehuacán	ESDJ	223 497	...	...	...	...	...	...	...
Tepic	ESDJ	...	...	...	...	369 582	...	...	...
Tijuana	ESDJ	...	...	...	...	1 437 729	...	...	...
Tlaxcala	ESDJ	...	...	...	...	269 457	...	...	...
Toluca (de Lerdo)	ESDJ	...	...	...	...	1 567 750	...	...	...
Torreón	ESDJ	...	...	...	...	1 082 616	...	...	...
Tula	ESDJ	...	...	...	...	179 635	...	...	...
Tulancingo	ESDJ	...	...	...	...	204 684	...	...	...
Tuxtla Gutiérrez	ESDJ	...	...	...	...	545 105	...	...	...
Uruapan	ESDJ	...	...	...	...	245 080	...	...	...
Veracruz	ESDJ	...	...	...	...	656 100	...	...	...
Villahermosa	ESDJ	...	...	...	...	648 819	...	...	...
Xalapa-Enriquez	ESDJ	...	...	...	...	545 706	...	...	...
Zacatecas	ESDJ	...	...	...	...	245 244	...	...	...
Zamora de Hidalgo	ESDJ	...	...	...	...	228 914	...	...	...
Netherlands Antilles — Antilles néerlandaises									
27 I 1992									
WILLEMSTAD	CDJC	2 345	...	...		...	...	...	
Nicaragua									
03 VI 2005									
Leon	CDJC	...	...	...	...	139 433	64 973	74 460	...
MANAGUA	CDJC	...	...	...	...	908 892	430 389	478 503	...
Panama									
1 VII 2000									
PANAMA[14]	ESDF	484 261	230 747	253 514	107	...	...	...	...
San Miguelito	ESDF	331 692	161 901	169 791	50	...	...	...	...
Puerto Rico — Porto Rico[15]									
1 VII 2005									
Arecibo	ESDJ	101 920	...	...	327	...	...	...	...
Bayamón	ESDJ	222 195	...	...	115	...	...	...	...
Caguas	ESDJ	142 378	...	...	152	...	...	...	...
Carolina	ESDJ	187 472	...	...	118	...	...	...	...
Guaynabo	ESDJ	102 287	...	...	70	...	...	...	...
Ponce	ESDJ	182 387	...	...	301	...	...	...	...
SAN JUAN	ESDJ	428 591	...	...	124	...	...	...	...
Saint Lucia — Sainte-Lucie									
22 V 2001									
CASTRIES	CDFC	11 092	5 238	5 854	...	...	...	...	...

8. Population of capital cities and cities of 100 000 or more inhabitants: latest available year, 1986 - 2005
Population des capitales et des villes de 100 000 habitants ou plus: dernière année disponible, 1986 - 2005
(continued — suite)

Continent, country or area, date and city / Continent, pays ou zone, date et ville	Code[1]	City proper — Ville proprement dite Population				Urban agglomeration — Agglomération urbaine Population			
		Both sexes Les deux sexes	Male Masculin	Female Féminin	Surface area Superficie (km²)	Both sexes Les deux sexes	Male Masculin	Female Féminin	Surface area Superficie (km²)
AMERICA, NORTH — AMERIQUE DU NORD									
Saint Pierre and Miquelon — Saint Pierre-et-Miquelon									
8 III 1999									
SAINT-PIERRE	CDFC	5 618	...	...	...	...	...	...	...
Saint Vincent and the Grenadines — Saint Vincent-et-les Grenadines									
12 V 1991									
KINGSTOWN	CDFC	15 466	...	...	...	...	...	...	...
Trinidad and Tobago — Trinité-et-Tobago									
1 VII 1996									
PORT-OF-SPAIN	ESDF	43 396	20 739	22 657	12	...	...	...	...
Turks and Caicos Islands — Iles Turques et Caïques									
31 V 1990									
GRAND TURK	CDFC	3 691	...	...	...	...	...	...	...
United States — Etats-Unis[16,17]									
1 VII 2005									
Abilene (TX)	ESDJ	114 757	...	...	273	...	...	...	...
Akron (OH)	ESDJ	210 795	...	...	161	...	...	...	...
Albuquerque (NM)	ESDJ	494 236	...	...	479	...	...	...	...
Alexandria (VA)[18]	ESDJ	135 337	...	...	39	...	...	...	...
Allentown (PA)	ESDJ	106 992	...	...	45	...	...	...	...
Amarillo (TX)	ESDJ	183 021	...	...	243	...	...	...	...
Anaheim (CA)[19]	ESDJ	331 804	...	...	127	...	...	...	...
Anchorage (AK)	ESDJ	275 043	...	...	4 396	...	...	...	...
Ann Arbor (MI)	ESDJ	113 271	...	...	70	...	...	...	...
Antioch (CA)	ESDJ	100 631	...	...	70	...	...	...	...
Arlington (TX)[20]	ESDJ	362 805	...	...	246	...	...	...	...
Arlington (VA)[18]	ESDJ	195 965	...	...	67	...	...	...	...
Arvada (CO)[21]	ESDJ	103 966	...	...	90	...	...	...	...
Athens (GA)	ESDJ	103 238	...	...	301	...	...	...	...
Atlanta (GA)	ESDJ	470 688	...	...	341	...	...	...	...
Augusta-Richmond (GA)	ESDJ	190 782	...	...	783	...	...	...	...
Aurora (CO)[21]	ESDJ	297 235	...	...	379	...	...	...	...
Aurora (IL)[22]	ESDJ	168 181	...	...	107	...	...	...	...
Austin (TX)	ESDJ	690 252	...	...	688	...	...	...	...
Bakersfield (CA)	ESDJ	295 536	...	...	304	...	...	...	...
Baltimore (MD)	ESDJ	635 815	...	...	210	...	...	...	...
Baton Rouge (LA)	ESDJ	222 064	...	...	199	...	...	...	...
Beaumont (TX)	ESDJ	111 799	...	...	214	...	...	...	...
Bellevue (WA)[23]	ESDJ	117 137	...	...	82	...	...	...	...
Berkeley (CA)[24]	ESDJ	100 744	...	...	27	...	...	...	...
Birmingham (AL)	ESDJ	231 483	...	...	388	...	...	...	...
Boise City (ID)	ESDJ	193 161	...	...	176	...	...	...	...
Boston (MA)	ESDJ	559 034	...	...	125	...	...	...	...
Bridgeport (CT)	ESDJ	139 008	...	...	41	...	...	...	...
Brownsville (TX)	ESDJ	167 493	...	...	340	...	...	...	...
Buffalo (NY)	ESDJ	279 745	...	...	105	...	...	...	...
Burbank (CA)[19]	ESDJ	104 108	...	...	45	...	...	...	...
Cambridge (MA)[25]	ESDJ	100 135	...	...	17	...	...	...	...
Cape Coral (FL)	ESDJ	140 010	...	...	273	...	...	...	...
Carrollton (TX)[20]	ESDJ	118 870	...	...	93	...	...	...	...
Cary (NC)	ESDJ	106 439	...	...	122	...	...	...	...
Cedar Rapids (IA)	ESDJ	123 119	...	...	174	...	...	...	...
Chandler (AZ)[26]	ESDJ	234 939	...	...	165	...	...	...	...
Charleston (SC)	ESDJ	106 712	...	...	262	...	...	...	...
Charlotte (NC)	ESDJ	610 949	...	...	697	...	...	...	...
Chattanooga (TN)	ESDJ	154 762	...	...	349	...	...	...	...
Chesapeake (VA)[27]	ESDJ	218 968	...	...	883	...	...	...	...
Chicago (IL)	ESDJ	2 842 518	...	...	588	...	...	...	...

8. **Population of capital cities and cities of 100 000 or more inhabitants: latest available year, 1986 - 2005**
Population des capitales et des villes de 100 000 habitants ou plus: dernière année disponible, 1986 - 2005
(continued — suite)

Continent, country or area, date and city / Continent, pays ou zone, date et ville	Code[1]	City proper — Ville proprement dite Population				Urban agglomeration — Agglomération urbaine Population			
		Both sexes Les deux sexes	Male Masculin	Female Féminin	Surface area Superficie (km²)	Both sexes Les deux sexes	Male Masculin	Female Féminin	Surface area Superficie (km²)
AMERICA, NORTH — AMERIQUE DU NORD									
United States — Etats-Unis[16,17]									
1 VII 2005									
Chula Vista (CA)[28]	ESDJ	210 497	...	...	130	...	...	...	...
Cincinnati (OH)	ESDJ	308 728	...	...	202	...	...	...	...
Clarksville (TN)	ESDJ	112 878	...	...	246	...	...	...	...
Clearwater (FL)[29]	ESDJ	108 687	...	...	66	...	...	...	...
Cleveland (OH)	ESDJ	452 208	...	...	201	...	...	...	...
Colorado Springs (CO)	ESDJ	369 815	...	...	493	...	...	...	...
Columbia (SC)	ESDJ	117 088	...	...	324	...	...	...	...
Columbus (GA)	ESDJ	185 271	...	...	560	...	...	...	...
Columbus (OH)	ESDJ	730 657	...	...	563	...	...	...	...
Concord (CA)	ESDJ	123 252	...	...	79	...	...	...	...
Coral Springs (FL)[30]	ESDJ	128 804	...	...	62	...	...	...	...
Corona (CA)[31]	ESDJ	149 387	...	...	98	...	...	...	...
Corpus Christi (TX)	ESDJ	283 474	...	...	412	...	...	...	...
Costa Mesa (CA)[19]	ESDJ	109 830	...	...	41	...	...	...	...
Dallas (TX)	ESDJ	1 213 825	...	...	881	...	...	...	...
Daly City (CA)[24]	ESDJ	100 339	...	...	20	...	...	...	...
Dayton (OH)	ESDJ	158 873	...	...	144	...	...	...	...
Denton (TX)	ESDJ	104 153	...	...	176	...	...	...	...
Denver (CO)	ESDJ	557 917	...	...	397	...	...	...	...
Des Moines (IA)	ESDJ	194 163	...	...	204	...	...	...	...
Detroit (MI)	ESDJ	886 671	...	...	359	...	...	...	...
Downey (CA)[19]	ESDJ	109 718	...	...	32	...	...	...	...
Durham (NC)	ESDJ	204 845	...	...	266	...	...	...	...
El Monte (CA)[19]	ESDJ	122 513	...	...	25	...	...	...	...
El Paso (TX)	ESDJ	598 590	...	...	645	...	...	...	...
Elizabeth (NJ)[32]	ESDJ	125 809	...	...	32	...	...	...	...
Elk Grove (CA)	ESDJ	112 338	...	...	108	...	...	...	...
Erie (PA)	ESDJ	102 612	...	...	49	...	...	...	...
Escondido (CA)[28]	ESDJ	134 085	...	...	95	...	...	...	...
Eugene (OR)	ESDJ	144 515	...	...	107	...	...	...	...
Evansville (IN)	ESDJ	115 918	...	...	106	...	...	...	...
Fairfield (CA)	ESDJ	104 476	...	...	98	...	...	...	...
Fayetteville (NC)	ESDJ	129 928	...	...	164	...	...	...	...
Flint (MI)	ESDJ	118 551	...	...	87	...	...	...	...
Fontana (CA)[31]	ESDJ	163 860	...	...	95	...	...	...	...
Fort Collins (CO)	ESDJ	128 026	...	...	133	...	...	...	...
Fort Lauderdale (FL)[30]	ESDJ	167 380	...	...	83	...	...	...	...
Fort Wayne (IN)	ESDJ	223 341	...	...	245	...	...	...	...
Fort Worth (TX)[20]	ESDJ	624 067	...	...	864	...	...	...	...
Fremont (CA)[24]	ESDJ	200 468	...	...	199	...	...	...	...
Fresno (CA)	ESDJ	461 116	...	...	277	...	...	...	...
Fullerton (CA)[19]	ESDJ	132 787	...	...	58	...	...	...	...
Gainesville (FL)	ESDJ	108 184	...	...	137	...	...	...	...
Garden Grove (CA)[19]	ESDJ	166 075	...	...	47	...	...	...	...
Garland (TX)[20]	ESDJ	216 346	...	...	148	...	...	...	...
Gilbert (AZ)[26]	ESDJ	173 989	...	...	146	...	...	...	...
Glendale (AZ)[26]	ESDJ	239 435	...	...	149	...	...	...	...
Glendale (CA)[19]	ESDJ	200 065	...	...	79	...	...	...	...
Grand Prairie (TX)[20]	ESDJ	144 337	...	...	186	...	...	...	...
Grand Rapids (MI)	ESDJ	193 780	...	...	115	...	...	...	...
Green Bay (WI)	ESDJ	101 203	...	...	118	...	...	...	...
Greensboro (NC)	ESDJ	231 962	...	...	285	...	...	...	...
Hampton (VA)[27]	ESDJ	145 579	...	...	134	...	...	...	...
Hartford (CT)	ESDJ	124 397	...	...	45	...	...	...	...
Hayward (CA)[24]	ESDJ	140 293	...	...	115	...	...	...	...
Henderson (NV)[33]	ESDJ	232 146	...	...	251	...	...	...	...
Hialeah (FL)[30]	ESDJ	220 485	...	...	55	...	...	...	...
Hollywood (FL)[30]	ESDJ	145 629	...	...	71	...	...	...	...
Honolulu (HI)	ESDJ	377 379	...	...	222	...	...	...	...

8. Population of capital cities and cities of 100 000 or more inhabitants: latest available year, 1986 - 2005
Population des capitales et des villes de 100 000 habitants ou plus: dernière année disponible, 1986 - 2005
(continued — suite)

Continent, country or area, date and city — Continent, pays ou zone, date et ville	Code[1]	City proper — Ville proprement dite Population				Urban agglomeration — Agglomération urbaine Population			
		Both sexes Les deux sexes	Male Masculin	Female Féminin	Surface area Superficie (km²)	Both sexes Les deux sexes	Male Masculin	Female Féminin	Surface area Superficie (km²)
AMERICA, NORTH — AMERIQUE DU NORD									
United States — Etats-Unis[16,17]									
1 VII 2005									
Houston (TX)	ESDJ	2 016 582	...	...	1 524	...	...	...	...
Huntington Beach (CA)[19]	ESDJ	194 457	...	...	68	...	...	...	...
Huntsville (AL)	ESDJ	166 313	...	...	479	...	...	...	...
Independence (MO)[34]	ESDJ	110 208	...	...	201	...	...	...	...
Indianapolis (IN)	ESDJ	784 118	...	...	936	...	...	...	...
Inglewood (CA)[19]	ESDJ	114 467	...	...	24	...	...	...	...
Irvine (CA)[19]	ESDJ	186 852	...	...	126	...	...	...	...
Irving (TX)[20]	ESDJ	193 649	...	...	173	...	...	...	...
Jackson (MS)	ESDJ	177 977	...	...	272	...	...	...	...
Jacksonville (FL)	ESDJ	782 623	...	...	1 934	...	...	...	...
Jersey City (NJ)[32]	ESDJ	239 614	...	...	39	...	...	...	...
Joliet (IL)[22]	ESDJ	136 208	...	...	118	...	...	...	...
Kansas City (KS)[34]	ESDJ	144 210	...	...	323	...	...	...	...
Kansas City (MO)	ESDJ	444 965	...	...	813	...	...	...	...
Killeen (TX)[35]	ESDJ	100 233	...	...	94	...	...	...	...
Knoxville (TN)	ESDJ	180 130	...	...	253	...	...	...	...
Lafayette (LA)	ESDJ	112 030	...	...	125	...	...	...	...
Lakewood	ESDJ	140 671	...	...	108	...	...	...	...
Lancaster (CA)	ESDJ	134 032	...	...	243	...	...	...	...
Lansing (MI)	ESDJ	115 518	...	...	93	...	...	...	...
Laredo (TX)	ESDJ	208 754	...	...	216	...	...	...	...
Las Vegas (NV)	ESDJ	545 147	...	...	344	...	...	...	...
Lexington-Fayette (KY)	ESDJ	268 080	...	...	737	...	...	...	...
Lincoln (NE)	ESDJ	239 213	...	...	210	...	...	...	...
Little Rock (AR)	ESDJ	184 564	...	...	303	...	...	...	...
Long Beach (CA)[19]	ESDJ	474 014	...	...	132	...	...	...	...
Los Angeles (CA)	ESDJ	3 844 829	...	...	1 217	...	...	...	...
Louisville (KY)	ESDJ	556 429	...	...	842	...	...	...	...
Lowell (MA)[25]	ESDJ	103 111	...	...	36	...	...	...	...
Lubbock (TX)	ESDJ	209 737	...	...	298	...	...	...	...
Madison (WI)	ESDJ	221 551	...	...	195	...	...	...	...
Manchester (NH)	ESDJ	109 691	...	...	86	...	...	...	...
McAllen (TX)	ESDJ	123 622	...	...	122	...	...	...	...
Memphis (TN)	ESDJ	672 277	...	...	787	...	...	...	...
Mesa (AZ)[26]	ESDJ	442 780	...	...	336	...	...	...	...
Mesquite (TX)[20]	ESDJ	129 902	...	...	113	...	...	...	...
Miami (FL)	ESDJ	386 417	...	...	93	...	...	...	...
Milwaukee (WI)	ESDJ	578 887	...	...	249	...	...	...	...
Minneapolis (MN)	ESDJ	372 811	...	...	142	...	...	...	...
Miramar (FL)	ESDJ	106 623	...	...	77	...	...	...	...
Mobile (AL)	ESDJ	191 544	...	...	305	...	...	...	...
Modesto (CA)	ESDJ	207 011	...	...	93	...	...	...	...
Montgomery (AL)	ESDJ	200 127	...	...	406	...	...	...	...
Moreno Valley (CA)[31]	ESDJ	178 367	...	...	132	...	...	...	...
Naperville (IL)[22]	ESDJ	141 579	...	...	100	...	...	...	...
Nashville-Davidson (TN)	ESDJ	549 110	...	...	1 224	...	...	...	...
New Haven (CT)	ESDJ	124 791	...	...	49	...	...	...	...
New Orleans (LA)	ESDJ	454 863	...	...	438	...	...	...	...
New York (NY)	ESDJ	8 143 197	...	...	783	...	...	...	...
Newark (NJ)[32]	ESDJ	280 666	...	...	62	...	...	...	...
Newport News (VA)[27]	ESDJ	179 899	...	...	177	...	...	...	...
Norfolk (VA)[27]	ESDJ	231 954	...	...	139	...	...	...	...
Norman (OK)	ESDJ	101 719	...	...	460	...	...	...	...
North Las Vegas (NV)[33]	ESDJ	176 635	...	...	206	...	...	...	...
Norwalk (CA)[19]	ESDJ	105 834	...	...	25	...	...	...	...
Oakland (CA)[24]	ESDJ	395 274	...	...	145	...	...	...	...
Oceanside (CA)[28]	ESDJ	166 108	...	...	105	...	...	...	...
Oklahoma City (OK)	ESDJ	531 324	...	...	1 572	...	...	...	...
Olathe (KS)	ESDJ	111 334	...	...	144	...	...	...	...

8. Population of capital cities and cities of 100 000 or more inhabitants: latest available year, 1986 - 2005
Population des capitales et des villes de 100 000 habitants ou plus: dernière année disponible, 1986 - 2005
(continued — suite)

Continent, country or area, date and city / Continent, pays ou zone, date et ville	Code[1]	City proper — Ville proprement dite Population				Urban agglomeration — Agglomération urbaine Population			
		Both sexes Les deux sexes	Male Masculin	Female Féminin	Surface area Superficie (km²)	Both sexes Les deux sexes	Male Masculin	Female Féminin	Surface area Superficie (km²)
AMERICA, NORTH — AMERIQUE DU NORD									
United States — Etats-Unis[16,17]									
1 VII 2005									
Omaha (NE)	ESDJ	414 521	...	...	304	...	...	...	...
Ontario (CA)[19]	ESDJ	172 679	...	...	129	...	...	...	...
Orange (CA)[19]	ESDJ	134 950	...	...	62	...	...	...	...
Orlando (FL)	ESDJ	213 223	...	...	260	...	...	...	...
Overland Park (KS)[34]	ESDJ	164 811	...	...	161	...	...	...	...
Oxnard (CA)	ESDJ	183 628	...	...	70	...	...	...	...
Palmdale (CA)[36]	ESDJ	134 570	...	...	274	...	...	...	...
Pasadena (CA)[19]	ESDJ	143 731	...	...	60	...	...	...	...
Pasadena (TX)[37]	ESDJ	143 852	...	...	117	...	...	...	...
Paterson (NJ)[32]	ESDJ	149 843	...	...	22	...	...	...	...
Pembroke Pines (FL)[30]	ESDJ	150 380	...	...	85	...	...	...	...
Peoria (AZ)[26]	ESDJ	138 200	...	...	456	...	...	...	...
Peoria (IL)	ESDJ	112 685	...	...	119	...	...	...	...
Philadelphia (PA)	ESDJ	1 463 281	...	...	347	...	...	...	...
Phoenix (AZ)	ESDJ	1 461 575	...	...	1 328	...	...	...	...
Pittsburgh (PA)	ESDJ	316 718	...	...	144	...	...	...	...
Plano (TX)[20]	ESDJ	250 096	...	...	186	...	...	...	...
Pomona (CA)[19]	ESDJ	153 787	...	...	59	...	...	...	...
Pompano Beach (FL)	ESDJ	104 179	...	...	62	...	...	...	...
Port St. Lucie (FL)	ESDJ	131 692	...	...	288	...	...	...	...
Portland (OR)	ESDJ	533 427	...	...	348	...	...	...	...
Portsmouth (VA)[27]	ESDJ	100 169	...	...	86	...	...	...	...
Providence (RI)	ESDJ	176 862	...	...	48	...	...	...	...
Provo (UT)	ESDJ	113 459	...	...	103	...	...	...	...
Pueblo (CO)	ESDJ	103 495	...	...	120	...	...	...	...
Raleigh (NC)	ESDJ	341 530	...	...	339	...	...	...	...
Rancho Cucamonga (CA)[19]	ESDJ	169 353	...	...	100	...	...	...	...
Reno (NV)	ESDJ	203 550	...	...	187	...	...	...	...
Richmond (CA)	ESDJ	102 186	...	...	78	...	...	...	...
Richmond (VA)	ESDJ	193 777	...	...	156	...	...	...	...
Riverside (CA)	ESDJ	290 086	...	...	205	...	...	...	...
Rochester (NY)	ESDJ	211 091	...	...	93	...	...	...	...
Rockford (IL)	ESDJ	152 916	...	...	151	...	...	...	...
Roseville (CA)	ESDJ	105 940	...	...	81	...	...	...	...
Sacramento (CA)	ESDJ	456 441	...	...	252	...	...	...	...
St. Louis (MO)	ESDJ	344 362	...	...	160	...	...	...	...
St. Paul (MN)[38]	ESDJ	275 150	...	...	135	...	...	...	...
St. Petersburg (FL)[29]	ESDJ	249 079	...	...	159	...	...	...	...
Salem (OR)	ESDJ	148 751	...	...	120	...	...	...	...
Salinas (CA)	ESDJ	146 431	...	...	50	...	...	...	...
Salt Lake City (UT)	ESDJ	178 097	...	...	283	...	...	...	...
San Antonio (TX)	ESDJ	1 256 509	...	...	1 088	...	...	...	...
San Bernardino (CA)[31]	ESDJ	198 550	...	...	153	...	...	...	...
San Buenaventura (CA)[39]	ESDJ	104 017	...	...	56	...	...	...	...
San Diego (CA)	ESDJ	1 255 540	...	...	844	...	...	...	...
San Francisco (CA)	ESDJ	739 426	...	...	121	...	...	...	...
San Jose (CA)	ESDJ	912 332	...	...	456	...	...	...	...
Santa Ana (CA)[19]	ESDJ	340 368	...	...	70	...	...	...	...
Santa Clara (CA)[40]	ESDJ	105 402	...	...	48	...	...	...	...
Santa Clarita (CA)	ESDJ	168 253	...	...	133	...	...	...	...
Santa Rosa (CA)	ESDJ	153 158	...	...	105	...	...	...	...
Savannah (GA)	ESDJ	128 453	...	...	223	...	...	...	...
Scottsdale (AZ)[26]	ESDJ	226 013	...	...	479	...	...	...	...
Seattle (WA)	ESDJ	573 911	...	...	217	...	...	...	...
Shreveport (LA)	ESDJ	198 874	...	...	273	...	...	...	...
Simi Valley (CA)	ESDJ	118 687	...	...	109	...	...	...	...
Sioux Falls (SD)	ESDJ	139 517	...	...	163	...	...	...	...
South Bend (IN)	ESDJ	105 262	...	...	104	...	...	...	...
Spokane (WA)	ESDJ	196 818	...	...	150	...	...	...	...

8. Population of capital cities and cities of 100 000 or more inhabitants: latest available year, 1986 - 2005
Population des capitales et des villes de 100 000 habitants ou plus: dernière année disponible, 1986 - 2005
(continued — suite)

Continent, country or area, date and city / Continent, pays ou zone, date et ville	Code[1]	City proper — Ville proprement dite Population				Urban agglomeration — Agglomération urbaine Population			
		Both sexes Les deux sexes	Male Masculin	Female Féminin	Surface area Superficie (km²)	Both sexes Les deux sexes	Male Masculin	Female Féminin	Surface area Superficie (km²)
AMERICA, NORTH — AMERIQUE DU NORD									
United States — Etats-Unis[16,17]									
1 VII 2005									
Springfield (IL)	ESDJ	115 668	...	...	145	...	...	...	...
Springfield (MA)	ESDJ	151 732	...	...	83	...	...	...	...
Springfield (MO)	ESDJ	150 298	...	...	203	...	...	...	...
Stamford (CT)[41]	ESDJ	120 045	...	...	98	...	...	...	...
Sterling Heights (MI)[42]	ESDJ	128 034	...	...	95	...	...	...	...
Stockton (CA)	ESDJ	286 926	...	...	147	...	...	...	...
Sunnyvale (CA)[40]	ESDJ	128 902	...	...	57	...	...	...	...
Syracuse (NY)	ESDJ	141 683	...	...	65	...	...	...	...
Tacoma (WA)[23]	ESDJ	195 898	...	...	130	...	...	...	...
Tallahassee (FL)	ESDJ	158 500	...	...	256	...	...	...	...
Tampa (FL)	ESDJ	325 989	...	...	303	...	...	...	...
Tempe (AZ)[26]	ESDJ	161 143	...	...	104	...	...	...	...
Thornton (CO)	ESDJ	105 182	...	...	78	...	...	...	...
Thousand Oaks (CA)	ESDJ	124 359	...	...	142	...	...	...	...
Toledo (OH)	ESDJ	301 285	...	...	209	...	...	...	...
Topeka (KS)	ESDJ	121 946	...	...	148	...	...	...	...
Torrance (CA)[19]	ESDJ	142 384	...	...	53	...	...	...	...
Tucson (AZ)	ESDJ	515 526	...	...	583	...	...	...	...
Tulsa (OK)	ESDJ	382 457	...	...	509	...	...	...	...
Vallejo (CA)	ESDJ	117 483	...	...	78	...	...	...	...
Vancouver (WA)[43]	ESDJ	157 493	...	...	112	...	...	...	...
Virginia Beach (VA)	ESDJ	438 415	...	...	643	...	...	...	...
Visalia (CA)	ESDJ	108 669	...	...	84	...	...	...	...
Waco (TX)	ESDJ	120 465	...	...	225	...	...	...	...
Warren (MI)[42]	ESDJ	135 311	...	...	89	...	...	...	...
WASHINGTON (DC)	ESDJ	550 521	...	...	158	...	...	...	...
Waterbury (CT)	ESDJ	107 902	...	...	74	...	...	...	...
West Covina (CA)[19]	ESDJ	108 185	...	...	42	...	...	...	...
West Valley City (UT)[44]	ESDJ	113 300	...	...	92	...	...	...	...
Westminster (CO)[21]	ESDJ	105 084	...	...	84	...	...	...	...
Wichita (KS)	ESDJ	354 865	...	...	391	...	...	...	...
Winston-Salem (NC)	ESDJ	193 755	...	...	284	...	...	...	...
Worcester (MA)	ESDJ	175 898	...	...	97	...	...	...	...
Yonkers (NY)[32]	ESDJ	196 425	...	...	47	...	...	...	...
United States Virgin Islands — Iles Vierges américaines[15]									
1 IV 2000									
CHARLOTTE AMALIE	CDFC	11 004	...	...	...	18 914	...	...	...
AMERICA, SOUTH — AMERIQUE DU SUD									
Argentina — Argentine									
15 V 1991									
Avellaneda	CDFC	344 024	...	...	...	...	...	...	...
Bahía Blanca	CDFC	260 096	...	...	...	...	...	...	...
BUENOS AIRES	CDFC	2 965 403	...	...	...	11 298 030	...	...	...
Catamarca	CDFC	109 882	...	...	...	132 626	...	...	...
Comodoro Rivadavia	CDFC	124 104	...	...	...	...	...	...	...
Concordia	CDFC	116 485	...	...	...	...	...	...	...
Córdoba	CDFC	1 157 507	...	...	...	1 208 554	...	...	...
Corrientes	CDFC	258 103	...	...	...	...	...	...	...
Formosa	CDFC	147 636	...	...	...	...	...	...	...
General San Martín	CDFC	406 809	...	...	...	...	...	...	...
La Matanza	CDFC	1 120 088	...	...	...	...	...	...	...
Lanus	CDFC	468 561	...	...	...	...	...	...	...
La Plata	CDFC	521 936	...	...	...	642 979	...	...	...
Lomas de Zamora	CDFC	574 330	...	...	...	...	...	...	...
Mar del Plata	CDFC	512 880	...	...	...	...	...	...	...

8. Population of capital cities and cities of 100 000 or more inhabitants: latest available year, 1986 - 2005
Population des capitales et des villes de 100 000 habitants ou plus: dernière année disponible, 1986 - 2005
(continued — suite)

Continent, country or area, date and city / Continent, pays ou zone, date et ville	Code[1]	City proper — Ville proprement dite Population				Urban agglomeration — Agglomération urbaine Population			
		Both sexes Les deux sexes	Male Masculin	Female Féminin	Surface area Superficie (km²)	Both sexes Les deux sexes	Male Masculin	Female Féminin	Surface area Superficie (km²)
AMERICA, SOUTH — AMERIQUE DU SUD									
Argentina — Argentine									
15 V 1991									
Mendoza	CDFC	121 620	...	...	...	773 113	...	...	...
Morón	CDFC	643 553	...	...	...	...	...	...	...
Neuquén	CDFC	167 296	...	...	...	183 579	...	...	...
Paraná	CDFC	207 041	...	...	...	211 936	...	...	...
Posadas	CDFC	201 273	...	...	...	210 755	...	...	...
Quilmes	CDFC	511 234	...	...	...	...	...	...	...
Resistencia	CDFC	229 212	...	...	...	292 287	...	...	...
Río Cuarto	CDFC	134 355	...	...	...	138 853	...	...	...
Rosario	CDFC	907 718	...	...	...	1 118 905	...	...	...
Salta	CDFC	367 550	...	...	...	370 904	...	...	...
San Fernando	CDFC	141 063	...	...	...	...	...	...	...
San Isidro	CDFC	299 023	...	...	...	...	...	...	...
San Juan	CDFC	119 423	...	...	...	352 691	...	...	...
San Miguel de Tucumán	CDFC	470 809	...	...	...	622 324	...	...	...
San Nicolás	CDFC	119 302	...	...	...	...	...	...	...
San Salvador de Jujuy	CDFC	178 748	...	...	...	180 102	...	...	...
Santa Fé	CDFC	353 063	...	...	...	406 388	...	...	...
Santiago del Estero	CDFC	189 947	...	...	...	263 471	...	...	...
Vicente López	CDFC	289 505	...	...	...	...	...	...	...
Bolivia — Bolivie									
1 VII 2005									
Cochabamba	ESDF	578 151	276 054	302 097	...	...	...	...	...
El Alto	ESDF	795 740	390 388	405 352	...	...	...	...	...
LA PAZ[45]	ESDF	834 848	397 496	437 352	...	...	...	...	...
Oruro	ESDF	216 459	104 275	112 184	...	...	...	...	...
Potosí	ESDF	147 672	70 939	76 733	...	...	...	...	...
Santa Cruz	ESDF	1 344 626	654 254	690 372	...	...	...	...	...
SUCRE[45]	ESDF	238 374	114 590	123 785	...	...	...	...	...
Tarija	ESDF	165 050	79 517	85 534	...	...	...	...	...
Brazil — Brésil[11]									
1 VII 2005									
Abaeteluba	ESDF	133 316	...	...	1 090	...	...	...	...
Açailândia	ESDF	106 357	...	...	...	...	...	...	...
Aguas Lindas de Goiás	ESDF	168 919	...	...	...	...	...	...	...
Alagoinhas	ESDF	139 818	...	...	761	...	...	...	...
Almirante Tamandaré	ESDF	113 589	...	...	...	...	...	...	...
Alvorada	ESDF	214 953	...	...	...	...	...	...	...
Americana	ESDF	203 845	...	...	...	...	...	...	...
Ananindeua	ESDF	498 095	...	...	485	...	...	...	...
Anápolis	ESDF	318 808	...	...	...	...	...	...	...
Angra dos Reis	ESDF	144 137	...	...	...	...	...	...	...
Aparecida de Goiania	ESDF	453 104	...	...	...	...	...	...	...
Apucarana	ESDF	117 260	...	...	556	...	...	...	...
Aracaju	ESDF	505 286	...	...	151	...	...	...	...
Araçatuba	ESDF	181 598	...	...	2 668	...	...	...	...
Araguaina	ESDF	130 105	...	...	...	...	...	...	...
Araguario	ESDF	109 876	...	...	...	...	...	...	...
Arapiraca	ESDF	202 390	...	...	...	...	...	...	...
Arapongas	ESDF	100 855	...	...	...	...	...	...	...
Araraquara	ESDF	199 657	...	...	...	...	...	...	...
Araras	ESDF	116 566	...	...	...	...	...	...	...
Araruama	ESDF	110 378	...	...	...	...	...	...	...
Araucária	ESDF	118 313	...	...	...	...	...	...	...
Atibaia	ESDF	129 751	...	...	...	...	...	...	...
Bagé	ESDF	122 461	...	...	7 185	...	...	...	...
Barbacena	ESDF	124 601	...	...	...	...	...	...	...
Barueri	ESDF	265 549	...	...	...	...	...	...	...
Barra Mansa	ESDF	176 151	...	...	830	...	...	...	...
Barreiras	ESDF	138 037	...	...	...	...	...	...	...

8. Population of capital cities and cities of 100 000 or more inhabitants: latest available year, 1986 - 2005
Population des capitales et des villes de 100 000 habitants ou plus: dernière année disponible, 1986 - 2005
(continued — suite)

Continent, country or area, date and city Continent, pays ou zone, date et ville	Code[1]	City proper — Ville proprement dite Population				Urban agglomeration — Agglomération urbaine Population			
		Both sexes Les deux sexes	Male Masculin	Female Féminin	Surface area Superficie (km²)	Both sexes Les deux sexes	Male Masculin	Female Féminin	Surface area Superficie (km²)
AMERICA, SOUTH — AMERIQUE DU SUD									
Brazil — Brésil[11]									
1 VII 2005									
Barretos	ESDF	110 195	...	...	...	...	...	...	...
Bauru	ESDF	356 680	...	...	702	...	...	...	...
Belém	ESDF	1 428 368	...	...	736	...	...	...	...
Belford Roxo	ESDF	489 002	...	...	...	...	...	...	...
Belo Horizonte	ESDF	2 399 920	...	...	335	...	...	...	...
Bento Gonçalves	ESDF	104 423	...	...	...	...	...	...	...
Betim	ESDF	407 003	...	...	376	...	...	...	...
Birigui	ESDF	108 472	...	...	...	...	...	...	...
Blumenou	ESDF	298 603	...	...	509	...	...	...	...
Boa Vista	ESDF	249 655	...	...	...	...	...	...	...
Botucatu	ESDF	121 274	...	...	...	...	...	...	...
Bragança	ESDF	103 751	...	...	...	...	...	...	...
Bragança Paulista	ESDF	143 621	...	...	770	...	...	...	...
BRASILIA	ESDF	2 383 784	...	...	5 794	...	...	...	...
Cabo de Santo Agostinho	ESDF	172 150	...	...	...	...	...	...	...
Cabo Frio	ESDF	165 591	...	...	...	...	...	...	...
Cachoeirinha	ESDF	121 880	...	...	...	...	...	...	..
Cachoeiro de Itapemirim	ESDF	198 150	...	...	892	...	...	...	...
Camacari	ESDF	197 144	...	...	718	...	...	...	...
Camaragibe	ESDF	150 354	...	...	...	...	...	...	...
Cametá	ESDF	106 816	...	...	...	...	...	...	...
Campina Grande	ESDF	379 871	...	...	970	...	...	...	...
Campinas	ESDF	1 059 420	...	...	781	...	...	...	...
Campo Grande	ESDF	765 247	...	...	8 091	...	...	...	...
Campo Largo	ESDF	107 756	...	...	...	...	...	...	...
Campos dos Goytacazes	ESDF	429 667	...	...	4 536	...	...	...	...
Canoas	ESDF	333 322	...	...	...	...	...	...	...
Carapicuíba	ESDF	389 634	...	...	...	...	...	...	...
Cariacica	ESDF	361 058	...	...	279	...	...	...	...
Caruaru	ESDF	283 152	...	...	936	...	...	...	...
Cascavel	ESDF	284 083	...	...	2 074	...	...	...	...
Castanhal	ESDF	158 462	...	...	1 003	...	...	...	...
Catanduva	ESDF	116 984	...	...	...	...	...	...	...
Caucaia	ESDF	313 584	...	...	1 293	...	...	...	...
Caxias	ESDF	144 387	...	...	6 724	...	...	...	...
Caxias do Sul	ESDF	412 053	...	...	1 601	...	...	...	...
Chapecó	ESDF	173 262	...	...	...	...	...	...	...
Codo	ESDF	115 098	...	...	4 923	...	...	...	...
Colatina	ESDF	111 789	...	...	2 094	...	...	...	...
Colombo	ESDF	231 787	...	...	...	...	...	...	...
Conselheiro Lafaiete	ESDF	113 019	...	...	...	...	...	...	...
Contagem	ESDF	603 376	...	...	167	...	...	...	...
Coronel Fabriciano	ESDF	104 851	...	...	...	...	...	...	...
Corumbá	ESDF	101 089	...	...	...	...	...	...	...
Cotia	ESDF	179 685	...	...	...	...	...	...	...
Crato	ESDF	115 087	...	...	...	...	...	...	...
Criciúma	ESDF	188 233	...	...	...	...	...	...	...
Cubatao	ESDF	121 002	...	...	...	...	...	...	...
Cuiabá	ESDF	542 861	...	...	3 922	...	...	...	...
Curitiba	ESDF	1 788 559	...	...	427	...	...	...	...
Diadema	ESDF	395 333	...	...	...	...	...	...	...
Divinópolis	ESDF	207 983	...	...	716	...	...	...	...
Dourados	ESDF	186 357	...	...	4 082	...	...	...	...
Duque de Caxias	ESDF	855 010	...	...	463	...	...	...	...
Embu	ESDF	245 855	...	...	...	...	...	...	...
Erechim	ESDF	100 251	...	...	...	...	...	...	...
Feira de Santana	ESDF	535 820	...	...	1 344	...	...	...	...
Ferraz de Vasconcelos	ESDF	176 532	...	...	...	...	...	...	...
Florianópolis	ESDF	406 564	...	...	440	...	...	...	...

8. Population of capital cities and cities of 100 000 or more inhabitants: latest available year, 1986 - 2005
Population des capitales et des villes de 100 000 habitants ou plus: dernière année disponible, 1986 - 2005
(continued — suite)

Continent, country or area, date and city / Continent, pays ou zone, date et ville	Code[1]	City proper — Ville proprement dite Population				Urban agglomeration — Agglomération urbaine Population			
		Both sexes Les deux sexes	Male Masculin	Female Féminin	Surface area Superficie (km²)	Both sexes Les deux sexes	Male Masculin	Female Féminin	Surface area Superficie (km²)
AMERICA, SOUTH — AMERIQUE DU SUD									
Brazil — Brésil[11]									
1 VII 2005									
Fortaleza	ESDF	2 416 920	...	...	336	...	...	...	...
Foz do Iguaçu	ESDF	309 113	...	...	596	...	...	...	...
Franca	ESDF	328 121	...	...	...	...	...	...	...
Francisco Morato	ESDF	170 585	...	...	...	...	...	...	...
Franco da Rocha	ESDF	124 816	...	...	...	...	...	...	...
Garanhuns	ESDF	128 398	...	...	456	...	...	...	...
Goiânia	ESDF	1 220 412	...	...	788	...	...	...	...
Governador Valadares	ESDF	259 405	...	...	2 447	...	...	...	...
Gravatai	ESDF	270 763	...	...	...	...	...	...	...
Guaratinguetá	ESDF	113 012	...	...	...	...	...	...	...
Guaíba	ESDF	105 808	...	...	...	...	...	...	...
Guarapari	ESDF	108 120	...	...	...	...	...	...	...
Guarapuava	ESDF	169 007	...	...	5 365	...	...	...	...
Guarujá	ESDF	305 171	...	...	...	...	...	...	...
Guarulhos	ESDF	1 283 253	...	...	...	...	...	...	...
Hortolandia	ESDF	201 795	...	...	...	...	...	...	...
Ibirité	ESDF	173 617	...	...	...	...	...	...	...
Ilhéus	ESDF	220 932	...	...	1 712	...	...	...	...
Imperatriz	ESDF	232 560	...	...	6 014	...	...	...	...
Indaiatuba	ESDF	181 124	...	...	...	...	...	...	...
Ipatinga	ESDF	236 463	...	...	231	...	...	...	...
Itabiraí	ESDF	107 721	...	...	...	...	...	...	...
Itaboraí	ESDF	220 981	...	...	569	...	...	...	...
Itabuna	ESDF	205 070	...	...	...	...	...	...	...
Itajaí	ESDF	168 088	...	...	...	...	...	...	...
Itapetininga	ESDF	143 097	...	...	2 035	...	...	...	...
Itapecerica da Serra	ESDF	162 239	...	...	...	...	...	...	...
Itapevi	ESDF	202 683	...	...	...	...	...	...	...
Itapipoca	ESDF	107 012	...	...	...	...	...	...	...
Itaquaquecetuba	ESDF	352 755	...	...	...	...	...	...	...
Itu	ESDF	156 100	...	...	640	...	...	...	...
Jaboatao dos Guarapes	ESDF	651 355	...	...	...	...	...	...	...
Jacareí	ESDF	211 559	...	...	...	...	...	...	...
Jandira	ESDF	113 323	...	...	...	...	...	...	...
Jaraguá do Sul	ESDF	131 786	...	...	...	...	...	...	...
Jaú	ESDF	125 399	...	...	...	...	...	...	...
Jequié	ESDF	148 992	...	...	3 113	...	...	...	...
Ji-Paraná	ESDF	113 453	...	...	...	...	...	...	...
Joao Pessoa	ESDF	672 081	...	...	...	...	...	...	...
Joinville	ESDF	496 051	...	...	1 080	...	...	...	...
Juazeiro	ESDF	208 299	...	...	5 615	...	...	...	...
Juàzeiro do Norte	ESDF	240 638	...	...	...	...	...	...	...
Juiz de Fora	ESDF	509 125	...	...	1 424	...	...	...	...
Jundiaí	ESDF	348 621	...	...	432	...	...	...	...
Lages	ESDF	168 384	...	...	5 287	...	...	...	...
Lauro de Freitas	ESDF	146 150	...	...	...	...	...	...	...
Limeira	ESDF	279 554	...	...	...	...	...	...	...
Linhares	ESDF	123 000	...	...	4 388	...	...	...	...
Londrina	ESDF	495 696	...	...	2 129	...	...	...	...
Luziânia	ESDF	187 262	...	...	4 653	...	...	...	...
Macae	ESDF	160 725	...	...	...	...	...	...	...
Macapá	ESDF	368 367	...	...	517	...	...	...	...
Maceió	ESDF	922 458	...	...	744	...	...	...	...
Magé	ESDF	237 000	...	...	...	...	...	...	...
Manaus	ESDF	1 688 524	...	...	11 349	...	...	...	...
Maraba	ESDF	200 801	...	...	14 320	...	...	...	...
Maracanau	ESDF	196 422	...	...	...	...	...	...	...
Maranguape	ESDF	100 279	...	...	...	...	...	...	...
Marília	ESDF	224 093	...	...	1 194	...	...	...	...

8. Population of capital cities and cities of 100 000 or more inhabitants: latest available year, 1986 - 2005
Population des capitales et des villes de 100 000 habitants ou plus: dernière année disponible, 1986 - 2005
(continued — suite)

Continent, country or area, date and city / Continent, pays ou zone, date et ville	Code[1]	City proper — Ville proprement dite Population				Urban agglomeration — Agglomération urbaine Population			
		Both sexes Les deux sexes	Male Masculin	Female Féminin	Surface area Superficie (km²)	Both sexes Les deux sexes	Male Masculin	Female Féminin	Surface area Superficie (km²)
AMERICA, SOUTH — AMERIQUE DU SUD									
Brazil — Brésil[11]									
1 VII 2005									
Maringá	ESDF	324 397	...	...	490	...	...	...	...
Mauá	ESDF	413 943	...	...	...	...	...	...	...
Mesquita	ESDF	185 552	...	...	...	...	...	...	...
Moji das Cruzes	ESDF	372 419	...	...	749	...	...	...	...
Moji-Guaçu	ESDF	141 559	...	...	960	...	...	...	...
Montes Claros	ESDF	348 991	...	...	4 135	...	...	...	...
Mossoró	ESDF	229 787	...	...	2 108	...	...	...	...
Natal	ESDF	789 896	...	...	...	...	...	...	...
Nilópolis	ESDF	150 475	...	...	...	...	...	...	...
Niterói	ESDF	476 669	...	...	131	...	...	...	...
Nossa Senhora do Socorro	ESDF	179 060	...	...	...	...	...	...	...
Nova Friburgo	ESDF	178 102	...	...	930	...	...	...	...
Nova Iguaçu	ESDF	844 583	...	...	795	...	...	...	...
Nôvo Hamburgo	ESDF	258 754	...	...	...	...	...	...	...
Olinda	ESDF	387 494	...	...	...	...	...	...	...
Ourinhos	ESDF	106 350	...	...	...	...	...	...	...
Osasco	ESDF	714 950	...	...	...	...	...	...	...
Palhoça	ESDF	128 102	...	...	...	...	...	...	...
Palmas	ESDF	220 889	...	...	...	...	...	...	...
Paranaguá	ESDF	147 934	...	...	1 015	...	...	...	...
Parintins	ESDF	112 636	...	...	...	...	...	...	...
Parnaíba	ESDF	143 675	...	...	1 053	...	...	...	...
Parnamirim	ESDF	170 055	...	...	...	...	...	...	...
Passo Fundo	ESDF	188 302	...	...	1 596	...	...	...	...
Paulo Afonso	ESDF	103 776	...	...	...	...	...	...	...
Passos	ESDF	106 516	...	...	...	...	...	...	...
Patos de Minas	ESDF	139 354	...	...	3 336	...	...	...	...
Paulista	ESDF	299 744	...	...	...	...	...	...	...
Pelotas	ESDF	346 452	...	...	1 924	...	...	...	...
Petrolina	ESDF	260 004	...	...	6 116	...	...	...	...
Petrópolis	ESDF	310 216	...	...	771	...	...	...	...
Pindamonhangaba	ESDF	143 737	...	...	719	...	...	...	...
Pinhais	ESDF	123 288	...	...	...	...	...	...	...
Piracicaba	ESDF	366 442	...	...	1 426	...	...	...	...
Poços de Caldas	ESDF	154 477	...	...	533	...	...	...	...
Poà	ESDF	110 213	...	...	...	...	...	...	...
Ponta Grossa	ESDF	304 973	...	...	2 212	...	...	...	...
Porto Alegre	ESDF	1 440 939	...	...	...	...	...	...	...
Porto Seguro	ESDF	140 692	...	...	...	...	...	...	...
Porto Velho	ESDF	380 974	...	...	...	...	...	...	...
Pouso Alegre	ESDF	125 209	...	...	...	...	...	...	...
Praia Grande	ESDF	245 386	...	...	...	...	...	...	...
Presidente Prudente	ESDF	206 704	...	...	554	...	...	...	...
Queimados	ESDF	139 118	...	...	...	...	...	...	...
Recife	ESDF	1 515 052	...	...	...	...	...	...	...
Resende	ESDF	119 729	...	...	...	...	...	...	...
Ribeirao das Neves	ESDF	322 969	...	...	...	...	...	...	...
Ribeirao Prêto	ESDF	559 650	...	...	...	...	...	...	...
Ribeirao Pires	ESDF	118 864	...	...	...	...	...	...	...
Rio Branco	ESDF	314 127	...	...	...	...	...	...	...
Rio Claro	ESDF	190 373	...	...	503	...	...	...	...
Rio de Janeiro	ESDF	6 136 652	...	...	1 256	...	...	...	...
Rio Grande	ESDF	196 982	...	...	2 825	...	...	...	...
Rio Verde	ESDF	136 229	...	...	9 136	...	...	...	...
Rondonópolis	ESDF	169 814	...	...	4 594	...	...	...	...
Sabára	ESDF	134 282	...	...	...	...	...	...	...
Salvador	ESDF	2 714 018	...	...	313	...	...	...	...
Santa Bárbara D'Oeste	ESDF	188 417	...	...	...	...	...	...	...
Santa Cruz do Sul	ESDF	119 803	...	...	...	...	...	...	...

8. Population of capital cities and cities of 100 000 or more inhabitants: latest available year, 1986 - 2005
Population des capitales et des villes de 100 000 habitants ou plus: dernière année disponible, 1986 - 2005
(continued — suite)

Continent, country or area, date and city / Continent, pays ou zone, date et ville	Code[1]	City proper — Ville proprement dite Population				Urban agglomeration — Agglomération urbaine Population			
		Both sexes Les deux sexes	Male Masculin	Female Féminin	Surface area Superficie (km²)	Both sexes Les deux sexes	Male Masculin	Female Féminin	Surface area Superficie (km²)
AMERICA, SOUTH — AMERIQUE DU SUD									
Brazil — Brésil[11]									
1 VII 2005									
Santa Luzia (Minas Gerais)	ESDF	219 699	...	...	...	...	...	...	...
Santa Maria	ESDF	270 073	...	...	3 279	...	...	...	...
Salto	ESDF	108 552	...	...	...	...	...	...	...
Santa Rita	ESDF	131 684	...	...	...	...	...	...	...
Santarém	ESDF	276 074	...	...	...	...	...	...	...
Santo André	ESDF	673 234	...	...	...	...	...	...	...
Santos	ESDF	418 375	...	...	725	...	...	...	...
Sao Bernardo do Campo	ESDF	803 906	...	...	319	...	...	...	...
Sao Caetano do Sul	ESDF	133 241	...	...	...	...	...	...	...
Sao Carlo	ESDF	218 702	...	...	1 120	...	...	...	...
Sao Gonçalo	ESDF	973 372	...	...	...	...	...	...	...
Sao Joao de Meriti	ESDF	466 996	...	...	...	...	...	...	...
Sao José	ESDF	201 103	...	...	...	...	...	...	...
Sao José de Ribamar	ESDF	134 593	...	...	...	...	...	...	...
Sao José do Rio Prêto	ESDF	415 508	...	...	586	...	...	...	...
Sao José dos Campos	ESDF	610 965	...	...	1 186	...	...	...	...
Sao José dos Pinhais	ESDF	261 125	...	...	923	...	...	...	...
Sao Leopoldo	ESDF	212 498	...	...	...	...	...	...	...
Sao Luís	ESDF	998 385	...	...	822	...	...	...	...
Sao Paulo	ESDF	11 016 703	...	...	1 493	...	...	...	...
Sao Vicente	ESDF	329 370	...	...	...	...	...	...	...
Sapucaia do Sul	ESDF	135 956	...	...	...	...	...	...	...
Serra	ESDF	394 370	...	...	549	...	...	...	...
Sertaozinho	ESDF	106 407	...	...	...	...	...	...	...
Sete Lagoas	ESDF	215 069	...	...	...	...	...	...	...
Simoes Filho	ESDF	109 930	...	...	...	...	...	...	...
Sobral	ESDF	175 814	...	...	1 646	...	...	...	...
Sorocaba	ESDF	578 068	...	...	...	...	...	...	...
Sumaré	ESDF	237 900	...	...	208	...	...	...	...
Susano	ESDF	280 318	...	...	...	...	...	...	...
Taboao da Serra	ESDF	225 405	...	...	...	...	...	...	...
Taubaté	ESDF	271 660	...	...	...	...	...	...	...
Tatuí	ESDF	107 115	...	...	...	...	...	...	...
Teixeira de Freitas	ESDF	123 557	...	...	...	...	...	...	...
Teófilo Otoni	ESDF	127 530	...	...	...	...	...	...	...
Teresina	ESDF	801 971	...	...	1 356	...	...	...	...
Teresópolis	ESDF	150 921	...	...	768	...	...	...	...
Timon	ESDF	146 139	...	...	1 702	...	...	...	...
Toledo	ESDF	107 033	...	...	...	...	...	...	...
Uberaba	ESDF	285 094	...	...	4 524	...	...	...	...
Uberlândia	ESDF	600 368	...	...	4 040	...	...	...	...
Uruguaiana	ESDF	136 364	...	...	6 763	...	...	...	...
Valparaiso de Goiás	ESDF	123 921	...	...	...	...	...	...	...
Varginha	ESDF	124 502	...	...	...	...	...	...	...
Várzea Grande	ESDF	254 736	...	...	900	...	...	...	...
Várzea Paulista	ESDF	110 449	...	...	...	...	...	...	...
Viamao	ESDF	261 971	...	...	...	...	...	...	...
Vila Velha	ESDF	405 374	...	...	...	...	...	...	...
Vitória	ESDF	317 085	...	...	...	...	...	...	...
Vitória da Conquista	ESDF	290 042	...	...	3 743	...	...	...	...
Vitória de Santo Antao	ESDF	125 563	...	...	344	...	...	...	...
Volta Redonda	ESDF	258 145	...	...	...	...	...	...	...
Chile — Chili									
1 VII 2004									
Antofagasta	ESDF	262 383	129 111	133 272	...	...	...	...	...
Arica	ESDF	193 745	96 109	97 636	...	...	...	...	...
Calama	ESDF	137 128	69 271	67 857	...	...	...	...	...
Chillán	ESDF	182 342	86 873	95 469	...	...	...	...	...
Concepción	ESDF	403 238	197 691	205 547	...	...	...	...	...

8. Population of capital cities and cities of 100 000 or more inhabitants: latest available year, 1986 - 2005
Population des capitales et des villes de 100 000 habitants ou plus: dernière année disponible, 1986 - 2005
(continued — suite)

Continent, country or area, date and city Continent, pays ou zone, date et ville	Code[1]	City proper — Ville proprement dite Population				Urban agglomeration — Agglomération urbaine Population			
		Both sexes Les deux sexes	Male Masculin	Female Féminin	Surface area Superficie (km²)	Both sexes Les deux sexes	Male Masculin	Female Féminin	Surface area Superficie (km²)
AMERICA, SOUTH — AMERIQUE DU SUD									
Chile — Chili									
1 VII 2004									
Copiapó	ESDF	132 425	67 264	65 161	...	...	...	...	...
Coquimbo	ESDF	147 786	71 922	75 864	...	...	...	...	...
Iquique	ESDF	181 181	92 576	88 605	...	...	...	...	...
La Serena	ESDF	140 482	67 867	72 615	...	...	...	...	...
Los Angeles	ESDF	126 421	61 681	64 740	...	...	...	...	...
Osorno	ESDF	138 660	66 734	71 926	...	...	...	...	...
Puente Alto	ESDF	491 717	240 858	250 859	...	...	...	...	...
Puerto Montt	ESDF	151 432	74 319	77 113	...	...	...	...	...
Punta Arenas	ESDF	128 836	66 435	62 401	...	...	...	...	...
Quilpué	ESDF	128 455	60 374	68 081	...	...	...	...	...
Rancagua	ESDF	229 793	111 452	118 341	...	...	...	...	...
San Bernardo	ESDF	278 286	139 286	139 000	...	...	...	...	...
SANTIAGO[46]	ESDF	4 981 779	2 397 499	2 584 280	...	...	...	...	...
Talca	ESDF	192 414	91 773	100 641	...	...	...	...	...
Talcahuano	ESDF	296 161	145 541	150 620	...	...	...	...	...
Temuco	ESDF	301 055	144 224	156 831	...	...	...	...	...
Valdivia	ESDF	130 994	63 767	67 227	...	...	...	...	...
Valparaíso	ESDF	285 512	140 379	145 133	...	...	...	...	...
Viña del Mar	ESDF	357 522	171 396	186 126	...	...	...	...	...
Colombia — Colombie[47]									
1 VII 2005									
Apartadó	ESDF	...	...	...	...	103 170	...	...	607
Armenia	ESDF	...	...	...	...	321 378	...	...	115
Barrancabermeja	ESDF	...	...	...	...	208 501	...	...	1 274
Barranquilla	ESDF	...	...	...	...	1 386 895	...	...	166
Bello	ESDF	...	...	...	...	400 291	...	...	151
Bucaramanga	ESDF	...	...	...	...	577 347	...	...	154
Buenaventura	ESDF	...	...	...	...	278 960	...	...	6 785
Buga	ESDF	...	...	...	...	132 320	...	...	873
Cali	ESDF	...	...	...	...	2 423 381	...	...	552
Cartagena	ESDF	...	...	...	...	1 030 149	...	...	570
Cartago	ESDF	...	...	...	...	139 450	...	...	260
Ciénaga	ESDF	...	...	...	...	124 255	...	...	1 366
Cúcuta	ESDF	...	...	...	...	742 689	...	...	1 098
Dos Quebradas	ESDF	...	...	...	...	191 909	...	...	80
Duitama	ESDF	...	...	...	...	122 513	...	...	229
Envigado	ESDF	...	...	...	...	175 085	...	...	51
Facatativa	ESDF	...	...	...	...	102 355	...	...	160
Florencia (Caquetá)	ESDF	...	...	...	...	151 403	...	...	2 292
Floridablanca	ESDF	...	...	...	...	258 509	...	...	101
Fusagasuga	ESDF	...	...	...	...	113 137	...	...	206
Girardot	ESDF	...	...	...	...	133 637	...	...	130
Girón	ESDF	...	...	...	...	120 804	...	...	681
Ibagué	ESDF	...	...	...	...	449 037	...	...	1 439
Itagüi	ESDF	...	...	...	...	288 207	...	...	17
Lorica	ESDF	...	...	...	...	128 508	...	...	890
Magangué	ESDF	...	...	...	...	173 734	...	...	1 102
Maicao	ESDF	...	...	...	...	138 805	...	...	2 229
Malambo	ESDF	...	...	...	...	105 480	...	...	108
Manizales	ESDF	...	...	...	...	382 193	...	...	477
Medellín	ESDF	...	...	...	...	2 093 624	...	...	387
Montería	ESDF	...	...	...	...	348 168	...	...	3 043
Neiva	ESDF	...	...	...	...	377 480	...	...	1 468
Ocaña	ESDF	...	...	...	...	104 606	...	...	463
Palmira	ESDF	...	...	...	...	294 805	...	...	1 044
Pasto	ESDF	...	...	...	...	424 283	...	...	1 181
Pereira	ESDF	...	...	...	...	521 684	...	...	702
Piedecuesta	ESDF	...	...	...	...	105 331	...	...	481
Popayán	ESDF	...	...	...	...	239 087	...	...	464

8. Population of capital cities and cities of 100 000 or more inhabitants: latest available year, 1986 - 2005
Population des capitales et des villes de 100 000 habitants ou plus: dernière année disponible, 1986 - 2005
(continued — suite)

Continent, country or area, date and city / Continent, pays ou zone, date et ville	Code[1]	City proper — Ville proprement dite Population				Urban agglomeration — Agglomération urbaine Population			
		Both sexes Les deux sexes	Male Masculin	Female Féminin	Surface area Superficie (km²)	Both sexes Les deux sexes	Male Masculin	Female Féminin	Surface area Superficie (km²)
AMERICA, SOUTH — AMERIQUE DU SUD									
Colombia — Colombie[47]									
1 VII 2005									
Sabanalarge	ESDF	...	...	...	...	102 558	...	...	...
Sahagún	ESDF	...	...	...	...	137 527	...	...	993
SANTA FE DE BOGOTA	ESDF	...	...	...	...	7 185 889	...	...	1 635
Santa Marta	ESDF	...	...	...	...	447 860	...	...	2 369
Sincelejo	ESDF	...	...	...	...	269 010	...	...	292
Soacha	ESDF	...	...	...	...	315 880	...	...	187
Sogamoso	ESDF	...	...	...	...	166 450	...	...	214
Soledad	ESDF	...	...	...	...	344 315	...	...	67
Tuluá	ESDF	...	...	...	...	191 100	...	...	818
Tumaco	ESDF	...	...	...	...	169 454	...	...	3 778
Tunja	ESDF	...	...	...	...	126 570	...	...	118
Turbo	ESDF	...	...	...	...	126 025	...	...	3 090
Valledupar	ESDF	...	...	...	...	365 548	...	...	4 225
Villavicencio	ESDF	...	...	...	...	367 885	...	...	1 328
Zipaquira	ESDF	...	...	...	...	103 234	...	...	194
Ecuador — Equateur									
1 VII 2003									
Ambato	ESDF	169 103	...	...	27	...	...	...	...
Cuenca	ESDF	303 994	...	...	47	...	...	...	...
Durán	ESDF	183 731	...	...	...	...	...	...	...
Esmeraldas	ESDF	103 063	...	...	8	...	...	...	...
Guayaquil	ESDF	2 090 039	...	...	193	...	...	...	...
Ibarra	ESDF	118 116	...	...	39	...	...	...	...
Loja	ESDF	129 429	...	...	21	...	...	...	...
Machala	ESDF	217 266	...	...	23	...	...	...	...
Manta	ESDF	193 232	...	...	38	...	...	...	...
Milagro	ESDF	119 420	...	...	17	...	...	...	...
Portoviejo	ESDF	194 916	...	...	38	...	...	...	...
Quevedo	ESDF	128 068	...	...	20	...	...	...	...
QUITO	ESDF	1 482 447	...	...	170	...	...	...	...
Riobamba	ESDF	140 558	...	...	24	...	...	...	...
Santo Domingo de los Colorados	ESDF	211 689	...	...	43	...	...	...	...
Falkland Islands (Malvinas) — Iles Falkland (Malvinas)									
8 IV 2001									
STANLEY	CDFC	1 989	1 009	980	...	...	...	...	...
French Guiana — Guyane Française									
8 III 1999									
CAYENNE[7]	CDJC	50 395	24 496	25 899	24	65 933	32 394	33 539	70
Guyana									
1 VII 2001									
GEORGETOWN	ESDF	...	...	...	...	280 000	...	...	...
Paraguay									
28 VIII 2002									
ASUNCION[48]	CDFC	513 399	...	...	117	1 620 483	...	...	...
Capiatá	CDFC	154 469	...	...	...	...	...	...	...
Ciudad del Este	CDFC	223 350	...	...	57	333 535	...	...	...
Fernando de la Mora	CDFC	114 332	...	...	...	...	...	...	...
Lambaré	CDFC	119 984	...	...	...	...	...	...	...
Luque	CDFC	170 433	...	...	...	...	...	...	...
San Lorenzo	CDFC	202 745	...	...	91	...	...	...	...
Peru — Pérou[49]									
1 VII 2003									
Arequipa	ESDF	770 659	...	...	...	...	...	...	...
Ayacucho	ESDF	134 612	...	...	...	...	...	...	...
Cajamarca	ESDF	119 615	...	...	...	...	...	...	...
Callao	ESDF	798 875	...	...	...	...	...	...	...
Chiclayo	ESDF	494 702	...	...	...	...	...	...	...
Chimbote	ESDF	342 030	...	...	...	...	...	...	...

8. Population of capital cities and cities of 100 000 or more inhabitants: latest available year, 1986 - 2005
Population des capitales et des villes de 100 000 habitants ou plus: dernière année disponible, 1986 - 2005
(continued — suite)

Continent, country or area, date and city — Continent, pays ou zone, date et ville	Code[1]	City proper — Ville proprement dite Population				Urban agglomeration — Agglomération urbaine Population			
		Both sexes Les deux sexes	Male Masculin	Female Féminin	Surface area Superficie (km²)	Both sexes Les deux sexes	Male Masculin	Female Féminin	Surface area Superficie (km²)
AMERICA, SOUTH — AMERIQUE DU SUD									
Peru — Pérou[49]									
1 VII 2003									
Chincha Alta	ESDF	133 189	...	...	...	...	...	...	...
Cuzco	ESDF	305 039	...	...	...	...	...	...	...
Huancayo	ESDF	323 246	...	...	...	...	...	...	...
Huánuco	ESDF	159 220	...	...	...	...	...	...	...
Ica	ESDF	252 012	...	...	...	...	...	...	...
Iquitos	ESDF	323 688	...	...	...	...	...	...	...
Juliaca	ESDF	189 265	...	...	...	...	...	...	...
LIMA	ESDF	7 075 339	...	...	...	...	...	...	...
Pisco	ESDF	105 301	...	...	...	...	...	...	...
Piura	ESDF	354 109	...	...	...	...	...	...	...
Pucallpa	ESDF	232 565	...	...	...	...	...	...	...
Puno	ESDF	108 176	...	...	...	...	...	...	...
Sullana	ESDF	172 879	...	...	...	...	...	...	...
Tacna	ESDF	250 036	...	...	...	...	...	...	...
Tarapoto	ESDF	109 301	...	...	...	...	...	...	...
Trujillo	ESDF	620 410	...	...	...	...	...	...	...
Suriname									
2 VIII 2004									
PARAMARIBO	CDFC	242 946	120 292	122 405	182	...	...	...	...
Uruguay									
30 VI 2005									
MONTEVIDEO	ESDF	1 347 888	628 834	719 054	530	...	...	...	...
Venezuela (Bolivarian Republic of) - Venezuela (République bolivarienne du)									
1 VII 1998									
Acarigua-Araure	ESDF	227 684	...	...	1 065	...	...	...	...
Barcelona	ESDF	301 595	...	...	463	...	...	...	...
Barcelona-Puerto La Cruz	ESDF	484 149	...	...	707	...	...	...	...
Barinas	ESDF	221 558	...	...	848	...	...	...	...
Barquisimeto	ESDF	810 809	...	...	2 645	...	...	...	...
Cabimas	ESDF	213 290	...	...	175	...	...	...	...
CARACAS	ESDF	1 975 294	...	...	433	...	...	...	...
Carúpano	ESDF	116 107	...	...	203	...	...	...	...
Catia la Mar	ESDF	117 013	...	...	76	...	...	...	...
Ciudad Bolívar	ESDF	278 525	...	...	5 851	...	...	...	...
Ciudad Guayana	ESDF	641 998	...	...	1 612	...	...	...	...
Coro	ESDF	167 048	...	...	438	...	...	...	...
Cumaná	ESDF	265 621	...	...	405	...	...	...	...
Guarenas	ESDF	169 202	...	...	180	...	...	...	...
Los Teques	ESDF	176 292	...	...	98	...	...	...	...
Maracaibo	ESDF	1 706 547	...	...	604	...	...	...	...
Maracay	ESDF	458 761	...	...	169	...	...	...	...
Maturín	ESDF	262 167	...	...	...	...	...	...	...
Mérida	ESDF	272 437	...	...	482	...	...	...	...
Puerto Cabello	ESDF	176 347	...	...	309	...	...	...	...
Punto Fijo	ESDF	118 126	...	...	31	...	...	...	...
San Cristóbal	ESDF	272 374	...	...	248	...	...	...	...
San Fernando de Apure	ESDF	121 949	...	...	...	...	...	...	...
Turmero	ESDF	203 434	...	...	208	...	...	...	...
Valencia	ESDF	1 263 888	...	...	1 212	...	...	...	...
Valera	ESDF	121 090	...	...	55	...	...	...	...
ASIA — ASIE									
Afghanistan									
1 VII 1988									
Herat	ESDF	177 300	...	...	...	...	...	...	...
KABUL	ESDF	1 424 400	...	...	...	...	...	...	...

8. Population of capital cities and cities of 100 000 or more inhabitants: latest available year, 1986 - 2005
Population des capitales et des villes de 100 000 habitants ou plus: dernière année disponible, 1986 - 2005
(continued — suite)

Continent, country or area, date and city — Continent, pays ou zone, date et ville	Code[1]	City proper — Ville proprement dite Population				Urban agglomeration — Agglomération urbaine Population			
		Both sexes Les deux sexes	Male Masculin	Female Féminin	Surface area Superficie (km²)	Both sexes Les deux sexes	Male Masculin	Female Féminin	Surface area Superficie (km²)
ASIA — ASIE									
Afghanistan									
1 VII 1988									
Kandahar (Quandahar)	ESDF	*225 500*	...	...	...	...	...	...	...
Mazar-i-Sharif	ESDF	*130 600*	...	...	...	...	...	...	...
Armenia — Arménie									
1 VII 2004									
Gyumri (Leninakan)	ESDJ	149 200	70 700	78 500	50	...	...	...	...
Vanadzor (Kirovakan)	ESDJ	105 900	49 900	56 000	25	...	...	...	...
YEREVAN	ESDJ	1 102 427	514 398	588 029	227	...	...	...	...
Azerbaijan — Azerbaïdjan									
1 VII 2004									
BAKU	ESDF	1 847 500	901 700	945 800	2 130	...	...	...	...
Ganja	ESDF	303 800	146 100	157 700	110	...	...	...	...
Sumgayit	ESDF	291 600	143 400	148 200	80	...	...	...	...
Bahrain — Bahreïn									
7 IV 2001									
MANAMA	CDFC	153 395	98 320	55 075	27	...	...	...	...
Bangladesh									
22 I 2001									
Barisal	CDFC	...	...	...	...	192 810	103 785	89 025	20
Bogra	CDFC	...	...	...	...	154 807	82 368	72 439	11
Brahmanbaria	CDFC	...	...	...	...	129 278	66 890	62 388	18
Chittagong	CDFC	...	...	...	...	2 023 489	1 127 516	895 973	168
Comilla	CDFC	...	...	...	...	166 519	88 927	77 592	11
DHAKA	CDFC	...	...	...	...	5 333 571	3 025 395	2 308 176	154
Dinajpur	CDFC	...	...	...	...	157 914	82 068	75 846	19
Gazipur	CDFC	...	...	...	...	122 801	65 522	57 279	49
Jamalpur	CDFC	...	...	...	...	120 955	62 059	58 896	53
Jessore	CDFC	...	...	...	...	176 655	94 203	82 452	15
Kadamrasul	CDFC	...	...	...	...	128 561	66 799	61 762	6
Khulna	CDFC	...	...	...	...	770 498	412 661	357 837	60
Mymensingh	CDFC	...	...	...	...	227 204	119 172	108 032	22
Naogaon	CDFC	...	...	...	...	124 046	65 406	58 640	37
Narayanganj	CDFC	...	...	...	...	241 393	131 168	110 225	13
Narsingdi	CDFC	...	...	...	...	124 204	67 575	56 629	9
Nawabganj	CDFC	...	...	...	...	152 223	75 375	76 848	34
Pabna	CDFC	...	...	...	...	116 305	60 666	55 639	27
Rajshahi	CDFC	...	...	...	...	388 811	208 525	180 286	97
Rangpur	CDFC	...	...	...	...	241 310	124 296	117 014	51
Saidpur	CDFC	...	...	...	...	112 609	58 289	54 320	34
Sirajganj	CDFC	...	...	...	...	128 144	66 673	61 471	28
Tangail	CDFC	...	...	...	...	128 785	66 856	61 929	29
Tongi	CDFC	...	...	...	...	283 099	156 335	126 764	30
Bhutan — Bhoutan									
30 V 2005									
THIMPHU	CDFC	79 185	42 465	36 720	...	...	...	...	...
Brunei Darussalam — Brunéi Darussalam									
21 VIII 2001									
BANDAR SERI BEGAWAN	CDFC	27 285	13 639	13 646	...	...	...	...	...
Cambodia — Cambodge									
1 VII 2002									
Bat Dambang	ESDF	*171 382*	*82 785*	*88 597*	*114*	...	...	...	...
PHNOM PENH	ESDF	*703 963*	*339 763*	*364 200*	*21*	*1 234 444*	...	...	...
Seam Reab	ESDF	*140 966*	*69 052*	*71 914*	*292*	...	...	...	...
China — Chine									
1 VII 1999									
Chiayi	ESDF	264 286	133 270	131 016	...	...	...	...	...
Hsinchu	ESDF	359 087	183 682	175 405	...	...	...	...	...
Kaohsiung[50]	ESDF	1 468 586	744 243	724 343	...	...	...	...	...
Keelung	ESDF	383 272	196 952	186 320	...	...	...	...	...
Taichung	ESDF	930 175	461 069	469 106	...	...	...	...	...

8. Population of capital cities and cities of 100 000 or more inhabitants: latest available year, 1986 - 2005
Population des capitales et des villes de 100 000 habitants ou plus: dernière année disponible, 1986 - 2005
(continued — suite)

Continent, country or area, date and city — Continent, pays ou zone, date et ville	Code[1]	City proper — Ville proprement dite Population				Urban agglomeration — Agglomération urbaine Population			
		Both sexes Les deux sexes	Male Masculin	Female Féminin	Surface area Superficie (km²)	Both sexes Les deux sexes	Male Masculin	Female Féminin	Surface area Superficie (km²)
ASIA — ASIE									
China — Chine									
1 VII 1999									
Tainan	ESDF	725 445	366 061	359 384	...	...	...	...	...
Taipei[50]	ESDF	2 640 322	1 310 368	1 329 954	...	...	...	...	...
1 XI 2000									
Acheng	CDJC	638 894	327 774	311 120	...	...	...	...	...
Akesu	CDJC	561 822	295 811	266 011	...	...	...	...	...
Aletai	CDJC	178 510	91 207	87 303	...	...	...	...	...
Anda	CDJC	473 091	243 349	229 742	...	...	...	...	...
An'guo	CDJC	378 830	189 944	188 886	...	...	...	...	...
Ankang	CDJC	843 426	443 270	400 156	...	...	...	...	...
Anlu	CDJC	611 990	314 089	297 901	...	...	...	...	...
Anning	CDJC	295 173	161 481	133 692	...	...	...	...	...
Anqing	CDJC	582 751	293 884	288 867	...	...	...	...	...
Anqiu	CDJC	1 096 782	554 403	542 379	...	...	...	...	...
Anshan	CDJC	1 556 285	787 838	768 447	...	...	...	...	...
Anshun	CDJC	767 307	395 894	371 413	...	...	...	...	...
Anyang	CDJC	768 992	390 120	378 872	...	...	...	...	...
Atushi	CDJC	200 345	101 867	98 478	...	...	...	...	...
Baicheng	CDJC	484 979	244 453	240 526	...	...	...	...	...
Baise	CDJC	340 483	177 310	163 173	...	...	...	...	...
Baishan	CDJC	335 400	172 109	163 291	...	...	...	...	...
Baiyin	CDJC	460 982	243 672	217 310	...	...	...	...	...
Baoding	CDJC	902 496	455 625	446 871	...	...	...	...	...
Baoji	CDJC	600 377	308 493	291 884	...	...	...	...	...
Baoshan	CDJC	846 865	430 076	416 789	...	...	...	...	...
Baotou	CDJC	1 671 181	862 495	808 686	...	...	...	...	...
Bazhong	CDJC	1 185 862	616 323	569 539	...	...	...	...	...
Bazhou	CDJC	557 901	285 321	272 580	...	...	...	...	...
Beian	CDJC	442 474	226 743	215 731	...	...	...	...	...
Beihai	CDJC	558 635	290 544	268 091	...	...	...	...	...
BEIJING (PEKING)	CDJC	11 509 595	6 020 903	5 488 692	...	...	...	...	...
Beiliu	CDJC	1 049 035	557 967	491 068	...	...	...	...	...
Beining	CDJC	527 217	270 153	257 064	...	...	...	...	...
Beipiao	CDJC	573 836	291 584	282 252	...	...	...	...	...
Bengbu	CDJC	809 399	413 444	395 955	...	...	...	...	...
Benxi	CDJC	980 069	495 102	484 967	...	...	...	...	...
Bijie	CDJC	1 128 230	589 537	538 693	...	...	...	...	...
Binzhou	CDJC	600 883	299 952	300 931	...	...	...	...	...
Bole	CDJC	224 869	116 506	108 363	...	...	...	...	...
Botou	CDJC	550 888	280 209	270 679	...	...	...	...	...
Bozhou	CDJC	1 351 939	697 126	654 813	...	...	...	...	...
Cangzhou	CDJC	443 561	223 648	219 913	...	...	...	...	...
Cenxi	CDJC	731 623	384 212	347 411	...	...	...	...	...
Changchun	CDJC	3 225 557	1 647 216	1 578 341	...	...	...	...	...
Changde	CDJC	1 346 739	686 467	660 272	...	...	...	...	...
Changge	CDJC	646 306	332 022	314 284	...	...	...	...	...
Changji	CDJC	387 169	202 275	184 894	...	...	...	...	...
Changle	CDJC	689 815	358 963	330 852	...	...	...	...	...
Changning	CDJC	795 223	428 332	366 891	...	...	...	...	...
Changsha	CDJC	2 122 873	1 099 304	1 023 569	...	...	...	...	...
Changshu	CDJC	1 239 637	598 034	641 603	...	...	...	...	...
Changyi	CDJC	683 182	340 763	342 419	...	...	...	...	...
Changzhi	CDJC	648 981	332 246	316 735	...	...	...	...	...
Changzhou	CDJC	1 081 845	552 850	528 995	...	...	...	...	...
Chaohu	CDJC	778 864	396 961	381 903	...	...	...	...	...
Chaoyang (Guangdong)	CDJC	2 470 812	1 256 428	1 214 384	...	...	...	...	...
Chaoyang (Liaoning)	CDJC	475 038	238 128	236 910	...	...	...	...	...
Chaozhou	CDJC	363 582	181 260	182 322	...	...	...	...	...
Chengde	CDJC	437 251	221 221	216 030	...	...	...	...	...
Chengdu	CDJC	4 333 541	2 258 996	2 074 545	...	...	...	...	...
Chenghai	CDJC	860 003	428 157	431 846	...	...	...	...	...

8. Population of capital cities and cities of 100 000 or more inhabitants: latest available year, 1986 - 2005
Population des capitales et des villes de 100 000 habitants ou plus: dernière année disponible, 1986 - 2005
(continued — suite)

Continent, country or area, date and city / Continent, pays ou zone, date et ville	Code[1]	City proper — Ville proprement dite Population				Urban agglomeration — Agglomération urbaine Population			
		Both sexes Les deux sexes	Male Masculin	Female Féminin	Surface area Superficie (km²)	Both sexes Les deux sexes	Male Masculin	Female Féminin	Surface area Superficie (km²)
ASIA — ASIE									
China — Chine									
1 XI 2000									
Chenzhou	CDJC	655 014	340 799	314 215	...	...	...	...	...
Chibi	CDJC	510 926	267 233	243 693	...	...	...	...	...
Chifeng	CDJC	1 153 723	589 450	564 273	...	...	...	...	...
Chishui	CDJC	251 780	130 227	121 553	...	...	...	...	...
Chizhou	CDJC	555 489	280 395	275 094	...	...	...	...	...
Chongqing	CDJC	9 691 901	5 013 398	4 678 503	...	...	...	...	...
Chongzhou	CDJC	650 698	330 345	320 353	...	...	...	...	...
Chuxiong	CDJC	503 682	261 315	242 367	...	...	...	...	...
Chuzhou	CDJC	493 735	251 117	242 618	...	...	...	...	...
Cixi	CDJC	1 214 537	615 279	599 258	...	...	...	...	...
Conghua	CDJC	517 552	264 150	253 402	...	...	...	...	...
Daan	CDJC	430 512	219 682	210 830	...	...	...	...	...
Dafeng	CDJC	756 766	383 391	373 375	...	...	...	...	...
Dali	CDJC	521 169	262 564	258 605	...	...	...	...	...
Dalian	CDJC	3 245 191	1 641 485	1 603 706	...	...	...	...	...
Dandong	CDJC	780 414	389 277	391 137	...	...	...	...	...
Dangyang	CDJC	495 946	253 125	242 821	...	...	...	...	...
Danjiangkou	CDJC	501 126	262 922	238 204	...	...	...	...	...
Danyang	CDJC	877 232	442 296	434 936	...	...	...	...	...
Danzhou	CDJC	835 465	442 636	392 829	...	...	...	...	...
Daqing	CDJC	1 380 051	704 765	675 286	...	...	...	...	...
Dashiqiao	CDJC	714 670	370 713	343 957	...	...	...	...	...
Datong	CDJC	1 526 744	785 754	740 990	...	...	...	...	...
Daye	CDJC	873 859	460 417	413 442	...	...	...	...	...
Dazhou	CDJC	384 525	192 819	191 706	...	...	...	...	...
Dehui	CDJC	878 349	448 146	430 203	...	...	...	...	...
Dengfeng	CDJC	609 085	321 081	288 004	...	...	...	...	...
Dengta	CDJC	502 149	259 895	242 254	...	...	...	...	...
Dengzhou	CDJC	1 290 656	677 791	612 865	...	...	...	...	...
Dexing	CDJC	297 784	155 178	142 606	...	...	...	...	...
Deyang	CDJC	628 876	324 823	304 053	...	...	...	...	...
Dezhou	CDJC	552 445	277 994	274 451	...	...	...	...	...
Dingzhou	CDJC	1 107 903	559 214	548 689	...	...	...	...	...
Dongfang	CDJC	358 318	188 840	169 478	...	...	...	...	...
Donggang	CDJC	640 340	324 344	315 996	...	...	...	...	...
Dongguan	CDJC	6 445 777	3 035 742	3 410 035	...	...	...	...	...
Dongsheng	CDJC	252 566	129 512	123 054	...	...	...	...	...
Dongtai	CDJC	1 164 653	583 122	581 531	...	...	...	...	...
Dongxing	CDJC	108 131	58 939	49 192	...	...	...	...	...
Dongyang	CDJC	753 094	375 565	377 529	...	...	...	...	...
Dongying	CDJC	788 844	407 241	381 603	...	...	...	...	...
Dujiangyan	CDJC	621 980	314 845	307 135	...	...	...	...	...
Dunhua	CDJC	480 834	247 966	232 868	...	...	...	...	...
Dunhuang	CDJC	187 578	96 679	90 899	...	...	...	...	...
Duyun	CDJC	463 426	241 421	222 005	...	...	...	...	...
Enping	CDJC	464 898	240 765	224 133	...	...	...	...	...
Enshi	CDJC	755 725	397 284	358 441	...	...	...	...	...
Emeishan	CDJC	423 070	217 201	205 869	...	...	...	...	...
Ezhou	CDJC	1 023 285	533 940	489 345	...	...	...	...	...
Fangchenggang	CDJC	422 514	233 979	188 535	...	...	...	...	...
Feicheng	CDJC	948 602	476 032	472 570	...	...	...	...	...
Fengcheng (Jiangxi)	CDJC	1 216 412	644 029	572 383	...	...	...	...	...
Fengcheng (Liaoning)	CDJC	560 384	288 402	271 982	...	...	...	...	...
Fenghua	CDJC	471 558	239 252	232 306	...	...	...	...	...
Fengnan	CDJC	550 872	285 442	265 430	...	...	...	...	...
Fengzhen	CDJC	264 204	137 562	126 642	...	...	...	...	...
Fenyang	CDJC	387 046	199 129	187 917	...	...	...	...	...
Foshan	CDJC	768 656	398 973	369 683	...	...	...	...	...
Fuan	CDJC	554 057	296 379	257 678	...	...	...	...	...
Fuding	CDJC	521 070	276 419	244 651	...	...	...	...	...

8. Population of capital cities and cities of 100 000 or more inhabitants: latest available year, 1986 - 2005
Population des capitales et des villes de 100 000 habitants ou plus: dernière année disponible, 1986 - 2005
(continued — suite)

Continent, country or area, date and city / Continent, pays ou zone, date et ville	Code[1]	City proper — Ville proprement dite Population				Urban agglomeration — Agglomération urbaine Population			
		Both sexes Les deux sexes	Male Masculin	Female Féminin	Surface area Superficie (km²)	Both sexes Les deux sexes	Male Masculin	Female Féminin	Surface area Superficie (km²)
ASIA — ASIE									
China — Chine									
1 XI 2000									
Fujin	CDJC	420 579	215 650	204 929	...	...	...	...	...
Fukang	CDJC	152 965	80 372	72 593	...	...	...	...	...
Fuqing	CDJC	1 174 540	597 890	576 650	...	...	...	...	...
Fuquan	CDJC	292 720	155 972	136 748	...	...	...	...	...
Fushun	CDJC	1 434 447	722 549	711 898	...	...	...	...	...
Fuxin	CDJC	627 855	311 912	315 943	...	...	...	...	...
Fuyang (Anhui)	CDJC	628 633	324 172	304 461	...	...	...	...	...
Fuyang (Zhejiang)	CDJC	1 719 057	878 560	840 497	...	...	...	...	...
Fuzhou (Fujian)	CDJC	2 124 435	1 086 638	1 037 797	...	...	...	...	...
Fuzhou (Jiangxi)	CDJC	1 007 391	533 936	473 455	...	...	...	...	...
Gaizhou	CDJC	883 811	455 641	428 170	...	...	...	...	...
Ganzhou	CDJC	494 600	254 272	240 328	...	...	...	...	...
Gaoan	CDJC	788 329	416 678	371 651	...	...	...	...	...
Gaobeidian	CDJC	538 582	268 027	270 555	...	...	...	...	...
Gaocheng	CDJC	758 269	380 317	377 952	...	...	...	...	...
Gaomi	CDJC	842 403	420 956	421 447	...	...	...	...	...
Gaoming	CDJC	301 041	159 746	141 295	...	...	...	...	...
Gaoping	CDJC	471 671	236 439	235 232	...	...	...	...	...
Gaoyao	CDJC	625 125	314 474	310 651	...	...	...	...	...
Gaoyou	CDJC	797 752	392 863	404 889	...	...	...	...	...
Gaozhou	CDJC	1 219 132	639 497	579 635	...	...	...	...	...
Geermu	CDJC	135 897	73 572	62 325	...	...	...	...	...
Gejiu	CDJC	453 311	243 377	209 934	...	...	...	...	...
Genhe	CDJC	157 337	80 485	76 852	...	...	...	...	...
Gongyi	CDJC	777 202	395 784	381 418	...	...	...	...	...
Gongzhuling	CDJC	1 041 735	532 134	509 601	...	...	...	...	...
Guang'an	CDJC	1 093 103	561 454	531 649	...	...	...	...	...
Guanghan	CDJC	577 298	289 596	287 702	...	...	...	...	...
Guangshui	CDJC	885 936	458 607	427 329	...	...	...	...	...
Guangyuan	CDJC	905 057	467 422	437 635	...	...	...	...	...
Guangzhou	CDJC	8 524 826	4 445 052	4 079 774	...	...	...	...	...
Guigang	CDJC	1 413 128	731 298	681 830	...	...	...	...	...
Guilin	CDJC	804 571	414 004	390 567	...	...	...	...	...
Guiping	CDJC	1 359 035	716 617	642 418	...	...	...	...	...
Guixi	CDJC	535 517	282 662	252 855	...	...	...	...	...
Guiyang	CDJC	2 985 105	1 568 544	1 416 561	...	...	...	...	...
Gujiao	CDJC	205 702	110 105	95 597	...	...	...	...	...
Haerbin	CDJC	3 481 504	1 759 609	1 721 895	...	...	...	...	...
Haicheng	CDJC	1 181 130	606 805	574 325	...	...	...	...	...
Haikou	CDJC	830 192	431 774	398 418	...	...	...	...	...
Hailaer	CDJC	262 184	132 849	129 335	...	...	...	...	...
Hailin	CDJC	435 677	222 525	213 152	...	...	...	...	...
Hailun	CDJC	720 008	368 751	351 257	...	...	...	...	...
Haimen	CDJC	942 952	431 066	511 886	...	...	...	...	...
Haining	CDJC	666 080	331 349	334 731	...	...	...	...	...
Haiyang	CDJC	654 594	329 202	325 392	...	...	...	...	...
Hami	CDJC	388 714	201 005	187 709	...	...	...	...	...
Hancheng	CDJC	387 041	201 881	185 160	...	...	...	...	...
Hanchuan	CDJC	1 057 396	552 093	505 303	...	...	...	...	...
Handan	CDJC	1 329 734	693 882	635 852	...	...	...	...	...
Hangzhou	CDJC	2 451 319	1 301 103	1 150 216	...	...	...	...	...
Hanzhong	CDJC	503 871	258 142	245 729	...	...	...	...	...
Hebi	CDJC	495 336	260 212	235 124	...	...	...	...	...
Hechi	CDJC	318 348	167 526	150 822	...	...	...	...	...
Hechuan	CDJC	1 420 520	732 503	688 017	...	...	...	...	...
Hefei	CDJC	1 659 075	879 749	779 326	...	...	...	...	...
Hegang	CDJC	694 640	354 262	340 378	...	...	...	...	...
Heihe	CDJC	192 764	97 488	95 276	...	...	...	...	...
Hejian	CDJC	757 581	383 621	373 960	...	...	...	...	...
Hejin	CDJC	368 572	195 677	172 895	...	...	...	...	...

8. Population of capital cities and cities of 100 000 or more inhabitants: latest available year, 1986 - 2005
Population des capitales et des villes de 100 000 habitants ou plus: dernière année disponible, 1986 - 2005
(continued — suite)

Continent, country or area, date and city Continent, pays ou zone, date et ville	Code[1]	City proper — Ville proprement dite Population				Urban agglomeration — Agglomération urbaine Population			
		Both sexes Les deux sexes	Male Masculin	Female Féminin	Surface area Superficie (km²)	Both sexes Les deux sexes	Male Masculin	Female Féminin	Surface area Superficie (km²)
ASIA — ASIE									
China — Chine									
1 XI 2000									
Helong	CDJC	215 266	110 051	105 215	...	...	...	...	...
Hengshui	CDJC	422 761	212 417	210 344	...	...	...	...	...
Hengyang	CDJC	879 051	450 222	428 829	...	...	...	...	...
Heshan (Guangdong)	CDJC	405 779	202 461	203 318	...	...	...	...	...
Heshan (Guangxi)	CDJC	131 249	69 205	62 044	...	...	...	...	...
Hetian	CDJC	186 127	94 034	92 093	...	...	...	...	...
Heyuan	CDJC	227 773	115 330	112 443	...	...	...	...	...
Heze	CDJC	1 280 031	656 790	623 241	...	...	...	...	...
Hezhou	CDJC	850 023	446 208	403 815	...	...	...	...	...
Honghu	CDJC	877 775	459 997	417 778	...	...	...	...	...
Hongjiang	CDJC	485 061	250 434	234 627	...	...	...	...	...
Houma	CDJC	225 123	113 997	111 126	...	...	...	...	...
Huadian	CDJC	444 415	228 624	215 791	...	...	...	...	...
Huaian	CDJC	1 200 679	619 541	581 138	...	...	...	...	...
Huaibei	CDJC	741 195	382 444	358 751	...	...	...	...	...
Huaihua	CDJC	346 522	178 221	168 301	...	...	...	...	...
Huainan	CDJC	1 357 228	701 205	656 023	...	...	...	...	...
Huaiyin	CDJC	555 052	282 186	272 866	...	...	...	...	...
Huanggang	CDJC	373 568	194 607	178 961	...	...	...	...	...
Huanghua	CDJC	483 273	251 128	232 145	...	...	...	...	...
Huangshan	CDJC	406 200	208 004	198 196	...	...	...	...	...
Huangshi (Hubei)	CDJC	653 722	334 712	319 010	...	...	...	...	...
Huayin	CDJC	242 488	125 006	117 482	...	...	...	...	...
Huaying	CDJC	352 257	183 962	168 295	...	...	...	...	...
Huazhou	CDJC	1 007 796	529 550	478 246	...	...	...	...	...
Huhehaote	CDJC	1 406 955	724 328	682 627	...	...	...	...	...
Huixian	CDJC	776 326	394 763	381 563	...	...	...	...	...
Huiyang	CDJC	862 822	429 006	433 816	...	...	...	...	...
Huizhou	CDJC	591 686	292 216	299 470	...	...	...	...	...
Hulin	CDJC	311 509	160 842	150 667	...	...	...	...	...
Huludao	CDJC	900 936	456 211	444 725	...	...	...	...	...
Hunchun	CDJC	211 091	108 873	102 218	...	...	...	...	...
Huozhou	CDJC	274 955	142 316	132 639	...	...	...	...	...
Huzhou	CDJC	1 145 414	573 421	571 993	...	...	...	...	...
Jiamusi	CDJC	859 944	433 369	426 575	...	...	...	...	...
Jian (Jiangxi)	CDJC	473 113	244 476	228 637	...	...	...	...	...
Jian (Jilin)	CDJC	239 849	124 475	115 374	...	...	...	...	...
Jiande	CDJC	473 062	242 606	230 456	...	...	...	...	...
Jiangdu	CDJC	1 053 023	512 151	540 872	...	...	...	...	...
Jiangjin	CDJC	1 322 890	686 106	636 784	...	...	...	...	...
Jiangmen	CDJC	536 317	271 693	264 624	...	...	...	...	...
Jiangshan	CDJC	473 222	241 301	231 921	...	...	...	...	...
Jiangyan	CDJC	861 321	419 333	441 988	...	...	...	...	...
Jiangyin	CDJC	1 315 472	665 719	649 753	...	...	...	...	...
Jiangyou	CDJC	849 761	436 112	413 649	...	...	...	...	...
Jian'ou	CDJC	478 651	249 624	229 027	...	...	...	...	...
Jianyang (Sichuan)	CDJC	1 412 523	728 353	684 170	...	...	...	...	...
Jianyang (Fujian)	CDJC	317 848	167 066	150 782	...	...	...	...	...
Jiaohe	CDJC	474 109	243 510	230 599	...	...	...	...	...
Jiaonan	CDJC	827 771	419 331	408 440	...	...	...	...	...
Jiaozhou	CDJC	783 478	388 207	395 271	...	...	...	...	...
Jiaozuo	CDJC	747 299	384 395	362 904	...	...	...	...	...
Jiaxing	CDJC	881 923	445 646	436 277	...	...	...	...	...
Jiayuguan	CDJC	159 541	85 959	73 582	...	...	...	...	...
Jieshou	CDJC	640 878	327 384	313 494	...	...	...	...	...
Jiexiu	CDJC	372 993	190 675	182 318	...	...	...	...	...
Jieyang	CDJC	633 570	324 831	308 739	...	...	...	...	...
Jilin	CDJC	1 953 134	984 762	968 372	...	...	...	...	...
Jimo	CDJC	1 111 202	553 261	557 941	...	...	...	...	...
Ji'nan	CDJC	2 999 934	1 539 067	1 460 867	...	...	...	...	...

8. Population of capital cities and cities of 100 000 or more inhabitants: latest available year, 1986 - 2005
Population des capitales et des villes de 100 000 habitants ou plus: dernière année disponible, 1986 - 2005
(continued — suite)

Continent, country or area, date and city / Continent, pays ou zone, date et ville	Code[1]	City proper — Ville proprement dite Population				Urban agglomeration — Agglomération urbaine Population			
		Both sexes Les deux sexes	Male Masculin	Female Féminin	Surface area Superficie (km²)	Both sexes Les deux sexes	Male Masculin	Female Féminin	Surface area Superficie (km²)
ASIA — ASIE									
China — Chine									
1 XI 2000									
Jinchang	CDJC	204 902	106 725	98 177	...	...	...	...	...
Jincheng	CDJC	304 221	157 663	146 558	...	...	...	...	...
Jingdezhen	CDJC	444 720	228 747	215 973	...	...	...	...	...
Jinggangshan	CDJC	145 769	74 722	71 047	...	...	...	...	...
Jinghong	CDJC	443 672	229 846	213 826	...	...	...	...	...
Jingjiang	CDJC	639 665	316 885	322 780	...	...	...	...	...
Jingmen	CDJC	583 373	300 284	283 089	...	...	...	...	...
Jingzhou	CDJC	1 177 150	598 951	578 199	...	...	...	...	...
Jinhua	CDJC	424 859	216 773	208 086	...	...	...	...	...
Jining (Shandong)	CDJC	1 050 522	530 322	520 200	...	...	...	...	...
Jining (Inner Mongolia)	CDJC	272 448	136 913	135 535	...	...	...	...	...
Jinjiang	CDJC	1 479 259	772 066	707 193	...	...	...	...	...
Jinshi	CDJC	243 242	126 619	116 623	...	...	...	...	...
Jintan	CDJC	533 350	256 798	276 552	...	...	...	...	...
Jinzhong	CDJC	534 357	274 957	259 400	...	...	...	...	...
Jinzhou (Liaoning)	CDJC	861 991	430 777	431 214	...	...	...	...	...
Jinzhou (Hebei)	CDJC	520 942	265 012	255 930	...	...	...	...	...
Jishou	CDJC	294 297	151 422	142 875	...	...	...	...	...
Jiujiang	CDJC	551 329	280 126	271 203	...	...	...	...	...
Jiuquan	CDJC	346 258	177 943	168 315	...	...	...	...	...
Jiutai	CDJC	799 729	411 067	388 662	...	...	...	...	...
Jixi	CDJC	910 782	467 547	443 235	...	...	...	...	...
Jiyuan	CDJC	626 478	323 554	302 924	...	...	...	...	...
Jizhou	CDJC	373 825	187 005	186 820	...	...	...	...	...
Jurong	CDJC	594 316	302 713	291 603	...	...	...	...	...
Kaifeng	CDJC	796 171	398 133	398 038	...	...	...	...	...
Kaili	CDJC	433 236	230 692	202 544	...	...	...	...	...
Kaiping	CDJC	668 692	326 560	342 132	...	...	...	...	...
Kaiyuan (Liaoning)	CDJC	529 736	271 422	258 314	...	...	...	...	...
Kaiyuan (Yunnan)	CDJC	292 039	152 771	139 268	...	...	...	...	...
Kashi (Xinjiang)	CDJC	340 640	172 136	168 504	...	...	...	...	...
Kelamayi	CDJC	270 232	143 500	126 732	...	...	...	...	...
Kuerle	CDJC	381 943	199 344	182 599	...	...	...	...	...
Kuitun	CDJC	285 299	148 740	136 559	...	...	...	...	...
Kunming	CDJC	3 035 406	1 615 096	1 420 310	...	...	...	...	...
Kunshan	CDJC	750 074	377 433	372 641	...	...	...	...	...
Laiwu	CDJC	1 233 525	626 549	606 976	...	...	...	...	...
Laixi	CDJC	728 796	366 400	362 396	...	...	...	...	...
Laiyang	CDJC	897 681	453 293	444 388	...	...	...	...	...
Laizhou	CDJC	889 361	450 192	439 169	...	...	...	...	...
Langfang	CDJC	715 388	363 094	352 294	...	...	...	...	...
Langzhong	CDJC	787 809	400 390	387 419	...	...	...	...	...
Lanxi	CDJC	607 196	314 090	293 106	...	...	...	...	...
Lanzhou	CDJC	2 087 759	1 092 661	995 098	...	...	...	...	...
Laohekou	CDJC	509 468	257 204	252 264	...	...	...	...	...
Lasa	CDJC	223 001	117 004	105 997	...	...	...	...	...
Lechang	CDJC	423 444	223 788	199 656	...	...	...	...	...
Leiyang	CDJC	1 180 235	631 431	548 804	...	...	...	...	...
Leizhou	CDJC	1 268 298	674 213	594 085	...	...	...	...	...
Leling	CDJC	615 833	313 642	302 191	...	...	...	...	...
Lengshuijiang	CDJC	339 701	175 071	164 630	...	...	...	...	...
Leping	CDJC	729 639	381 937	347 702	...	...	...	...	...
Leqing	CDJC	1 162 765	605 494	557 271	...	...	...	...	...
Leshan	CDJC	1 120 158	567 028	553 130	...	...	...	...	...
Lianjiang	CDJC	1 205 764	642 214	563 550	...	...	...	...	...
Lianyuan	CDJC	996 893	521 941	474 952	...	...	...	...	...
Lianyungang	CDJC	687 242	354 350	332 892	...	...	...	...	...
Lianzhou	CDJC	409 360	212 292	197 068	...	...	...	...	...
Liaocheng	CDJC	950 319	474 976	475 343	...	...	...	...	...
Liaoyang	CDJC	728 492	365 833	362 659	...	...	...	...	...

8. Population of capital cities and cities of 100 000 or more inhabitants: latest available year, 1986 - 2005
Population des capitales et des villes de 100 000 habitants ou plus: dernière année disponible, 1986 - 2005
(continued — suite)

Continent, country or area, date and city Continent, pays ou zone, date et ville	Code[1]	City proper — Ville proprement dite Population				Urban agglomeration — Agglomération urbaine Population			
		Both sexes Les deux sexes	Male Masculin	Female Féminin	Surface area Superficie (km²)	Both sexes Les deux sexes	Male Masculin	Female Féminin	Surface area Superficie (km²)
ASIA — ASIE									
China — Chine									
1 XI 2000									
Liaoyuan	CDJC	462 233	234 701	227 532	...	...	...	...	...
Lichuan	CDJC	786 984	417 988	368 996	...	...	...	...	...
Liling	CDJC	934 396	484 127	450 269	...	...	...	...	...
Lin'an	CDJC	514 238	261 852	252 386	...	...	...	...	...
Linfen	CDJC	724 403	367 377	357 026	...	...	...	...	...
Lingbao	CDJC	722 890	377 872	345 018	...	...	...	...	...
Linghai	CDJC	647 310	332 906	314 404	...	...	...	...	...
Lingwu	CDJC	249 890	128 364	121 526	...	...	...	...	...
Lingyuan	CDJC	620 121	324 554	295 567	...	...	...	...	...
Linhai	CDJC	948 618	479 625	468 993	...	...	...	...	...
Linhe	CDJC	510 965	260 835	250 130	...	...	...	...	...
Linjiang	CDJC	184 901	94 904	89 997	...	...	...	...	...
Linqing	CDJC	694 247	348 411	345 836	...	...	...	...	...
Linxia	CDJC	202 498	104 017	98 481	...	...	...	...	...
Linxiang	CDJC	448 452	235 723	212 729	...	...	...	...	...
Linyi	CDJC	1 938 510	988 940	949 570	...	...	...	...	...
Linzhou	CDJC	982 254	501 659	480 595	...	...	...	...	...
Lishi	CDJC	235 678	121 253	114 425	...	...	...	...	...
Lishui	CDJC	348 241	178 908	169 333	...	...	...	...	...
Liuan	CDJC	1 559 037	807 902	751 135	...	...	...	...	...
Liupanshui	CDJC	995 055	523 692	471 363	...	...	...	...	...
Liuyang	CDJC	1 307 572	680 610	626 962	...	...	...	...	...
Liuzhou	CDJC	1 220 392	634 909	585 483	...	...	...	...	...
Liyang	CDJC	740 871	375 694	365 177	...	...	...	...	...
Longhai	CDJC	816 318	415 936	400 382	...	...	...	...	...
Longjing	CDJC	261 551	132 150	129 401	...	...	...	...	...
Longkou	CDJC	671 335	337 507	333 828	...	...	...	...	...
Longquan	CDJC	250 398	131 534	118 864	...	...	...	...	...
Longyan	CDJC	543 731	298 481	245 250	...	...	...	...	...
Loudi	CDJC	398 577	205 172	193 405	...	...	...	...	...
Lucheng	CDJC	213 944	111 293	102 651	...	...	...	...	...
Lufeng	CDJC	1 164 767	600 959	563 808	...	...	...	...	...
Luoding	CDJC	866 190	449 131	417 059	...	...	...	...	...
Luohe	CDJC	304 105	150 273	153 832	...	...	...	...	...
Luoyang	CDJC	1 491 680	759 425	732 255	...	...	...	...	...
Luquan	CDJC	397 449	202 340	195 109	...	...	...	...	...
Luxi (Yunnan)	CDJC	337 406	172 038	165 368	...	...	...	...	...
Luzhou	CDJC	1 252 884	636 652	616 232	...	...	...	...	...
Maanshan	CDJC	567 576	292 994	274 582	...	...	...	...	...
Macheng	CDJC	1 129 047	595 391	533 656	...	...	...	...	...
Manzhouli	CDJC	181 112	92 853	88 259	...	...	...	...	...
Maoming	CDJC	644 301	335 713	308 588	...	...	...	...	...
Meihekou	CDJC	617 674	317 226	300 448	...	...	...	...	...
Meishan	CDJC	799 309	402 889	396 420	...	...	...	...	...
Meixian	CDJC	313 821	160 925	152 896	...	...	...	...	...
Meizhou	CDJC	354 302	178 658	175 644	...	...	...	...	...
Mianyang	CDJC	1 162 962	604 414	558 548	...	...	...	...	...
Mianzhu	CDJC	515 830	263 098	252 732	...	...	...	...	...
Miluo	CDJC	658 867	342 113	316 754	...	...	...	...	...
Mingguang	CDJC	569 585	290 126	279 459	...	...	...	...	...
Miquan	CDJC	180 952	95 368	85 584	...	...	...	...	...
Mishan	CDJC	438 277	224 565	213 712	...	...	...	...	...
Mudanjiang	CDJC	1 014 206	512 000	502 206	...	...	...	...	...
Muling	CDJC	310 096	158 623	151 473	...	...	...	...	...
Nan'an	CDJC	1 385 276	700 218	685 058	...	...	...	...	...
Nanchang	CDJC	1 844 253	952 504	891 749	...	...	...	...	...
Nanchong	CDJC	1 771 920	922 452	849 468	...	...	...	...	...
Nanchuan	CDJC	631 853	326 307	305 546	...	...	...	...	...
Nan'gong	CDJC	467 356	234 978	232 378	...	...	...	...	...
Nanhai	CDJC	2 133 741	1 111 731	1 022 010	...	...	...	...	...

8. Population of capital cities and cities of 100 000 or more inhabitants: latest available year, 1986 - 2005
Population des capitales et des villes de 100 000 habitants ou plus: dernière année disponible, 1986 - 2005
(continued — suite)

Continent, country or area, date and city / Continent, pays ou zone, date et ville	Code[1]	City proper — Ville proprement dite Population				Urban agglomeration — Agglomération urbaine Population			
		Both sexes Les deux sexes	Male Masculin	Female Féminin	Surface area Superficie (km²)	Both sexes Les deux sexes	Male Masculin	Female Féminin	Surface area Superficie (km²)

ASIA — ASIE

China — Chine
1 XI 2000

Nanjing	CDJC	3 624 234	1 935 931	1 688 303	...	...	...	...	...
Nankang	CDJC	694 987	338 836	356 151	...	...	...	...	...
Nanning	CDJC	1 766 701	924 916	841 785	...	...	...	...	...
Nanping	CDJC	488 818	257 352	231 466	...	...	...	...	...
Nantong	CDJC	771 386	386 206	385 180	...	...	...	...	...
Nanxiong	CDJC	372 844	185 330	187 514	...	...	...	...	...
Nanyang	CDJC	1 584 715	814 822	769 893	...	...	...	...	...
Nehe	CDJC	672 295	343 873	328 422	...	...	...	...	...
Neijiang	CDJC	1 391 931	709 053	682 878	...	...	...	...	...
Ning'an	CDJC	437 328	223 201	214 127	...	...	...	...	...
Ningbo	CDJC	1 567 499	804 850	762 649	...	...	...	...	...
Ningde	CDJC	400 293	213 131	187 162	...	...	...	...	...
Ningguo	CDJC	381 842	199 915	181 927	...	...	...	...	...
Panjin	CDJC	602 541	309 377	293 164	...	...	...	...	...
Panshi	CDJC	530 470	273 219	257 251	...	...	...	...	...
Panzhihua	CDJC	690 739	363 585	327 154	...	...	...	...	...
Penglai	CDJC	500 408	252 726	247 682	...	...	...	...	...
Pengzhou	CDJC	770 749	389 697	381 052	...	...	...	...	...
Pingdingshan	CDJC	900 903	470 362	430 541	...	...	...	...	...
Pingdu	CDJC	1 321 975	670 685	651 290	...	...	...	...	...
Pinghu	CDJC	507 899	249 848	258 051	...	...	...	...	...
Pingliang	CDJC	454 996	236 426	218 570	...	...	...	...	...
Pingxiang (Jiangxi)	CDJC	783 445	402 198	381 247	...	...	...	...	...
Pingxiang (Guangxi)	CDJC	107 046	57 445	49 601	...	...	...	...	...
Pizhou	CDJC	1 539 922	791 332	748 590	...	...	...	...	...
Pulandian	CDJC	757 844	385 636	372 208	...	...	...	...	...
Puning	CDJC	1 856 402	954 242	902 160	...	...	...	...	...
Putian	CDJC	443 926	216 578	227 348	...	...	...	...	...
Puyang	CDJC	448 290	229 387	218 903	...	...	...	...	...
Qian'an	CDJC	632 704	323 330	309 374	...	...	...	...	...
Qianjiang	CDJC	992 438	506 290	486 148	...	...	...	...	...
Qidong	CDJC	1 057 073	495 819	561 254	...	...	...	...	...
Qingdao	CDJC	2 720 972	1 359 527	1 361 445	...	...	...	...	...
Qingtongxia	CDJC	248 640	129 121	119 519	...	...	...	...	...
Qingyuan	CDJC	506 680	258 819	247 861	...	...	...	...	...
Qingzhen	CDJC	471 305	248 079	223 226	...	...	...	...	...
Qingzhou	CDJC	894 468	450 090	444 378	...	...	...	...	...
Qinhuangdao	CDJC	817 487	411 355	406 132	...	...	...	...	...
Qinyang	CDJC	446 404	224 725	221 679	...	...	...	...	...
Qinzhou	CDJC	1 035 504	578 428	457 076	...	...	...	...	...
Qionghai	CDJC	449 845	236 560	213 285	...	...	...	...	...
Qionglai	CDJC	631 577	321 382	310 195	...	...	...	...	...
Qiongshan	CDJC	678 149	355 557	322 592	...	...	...	...	...
Qiqihaer	CDJC	1 540 089	776 191	763 898	...	...	...	...	...
Qitaihe	CDJC	486 704	254 500	232 204	...	...	...	...	...
Qixia	CDJC	651 357	331 148	320 209	...	...	...	...	...
Quanzhou	CDJC	1 192 286	616 826	575 460	...	...	...	...	...
Qufu	CDJC	625 313	317 685	307 628	...	...	...	...	...
Qujing	CDJC	648 956	333 756	315 200	...	...	...	...	...
Quzhou	CDJC	286 271	148 054	138 217	...	...	...	...	...
Renhuai	CDJC	520 759	270 091	250 668	...	...	...	...	...
Renqiu	CDJC	768 900	390 649	378 251	...	...	...	...	...
Rizhao	CDJC	1 148 190	576 050	572 140	...	...	...	...	...
Rongcheng	CDJC	732 147	368 156	363 991	...	...	...	...	...
Rugao	CDJC	1 362 533	659 720	702 813	...	...	...	...	...
Ruian	CDJC	1 207 788	627 593	580 195	...	...	...	...	...
Ruichang	CDJC	398 844	209 755	189 089	...	...	...	...	...
Ruijin	CDJC	535 499	280 328	255 171	...	...	...	...	...
Ruili	CDJC	155 210	80 532	74 678	...	...	...	...	...
Rushan	CDJC	580 326	291 047	289 279	...	...	...	...	...

8. Population of capital cities and cities of 100 000 or more inhabitants: latest available year, 1986 - 2005
Population des capitales et des villes de 100 000 habitants ou plus: dernière année disponible, 1986 - 2005
(continued — suite)

| Continent, country or area, date and city | Code[1] | City proper — Ville proprement dite Population | | | | Urban agglomeration — Agglomération urbaine Population | | | |
Continent, pays ou zone, date et ville		Both sexes Les deux sexes	Male Masculin	Female Féminin	Surface area Superficie (km²)	Both sexes Les deux sexes	Male Masculin	Female Féminin	Surface area Superficie (km²)
ASIA — ASIE									
China — Chine									
1 XI 2000									
Ruzhou	CDJC	923 245	474 090	449 155	...	...	...	...	...
Sanhe	CDJC	456 882	229 788	227 094	...	...	...	...	...
Sanmenxia	CDJC	288 746	149 846	138 900	...	...	...	...	...
Sanming	CDJC	337 105	178 031	159 074	...	...	...	...	...
Sanshui	CDJC	440 119	230 835	209 284	...	...	...	...	...
Sanya	CDJC	482 296	254 293	228 003	...	...	...	...	...
Shahe	CDJC	474 260	243 171	231 089	...	...	...	...	...
Shanghai	CDJC	14 348 535	7 414 274	6 934 261	...	...	...	...	...
Shangqiu	CDJC	1 428 983	729 319	699 664	...	...	...	...	...
Shangrao	CDJC	327 703	164 698	163 005	...	...	...	...	...
Shangyu	CDJC	722 523	354 917	367 606	...	...	...	...	...
Shangzhi	CDJC	582 764	298 966	283 798	...	...	...	...	...
Shangzhou	CDJC	530 883	279 160	251 723	...	...	...	...	...
Shantou	CDJC	1 270 112	636 189	633 923	...	...	...	...	...
Shanwei	CDJC	409 677	211 746	197 931	...	...	...	...	...
Shaoguan	CDJC	535 979	282 515	253 464	...	...	...	...	...
Shaowu	CDJC	288 401	151 117	137 284	...	...	...	...	...
Shaoxing	CDJC	633 118	310 860	322 258	...	...	...	...	...
Shaoyang	CDJC	607 868	309 563	298 305	...	...	...	...	...
Shengzhou	CDJC	671 221	345 614	325 607	...	...	...	...	...
Shenyang	CDJC	5 303 053	2 700 380	2 602 673	...	...	...	...	...
Shenzhen	CDJC	7 008 831	3 454 392	3 554 439	...	...	...	...	...
Shenzhou	CDJC	568 558	289 086	279 472	...	...	...	...	...
Shifang	CDJC	432 579	218 447	214 132	...	...	...	...	...
Shihezi	CDJC	590 115	305 253	284 862	...	...	...	...	...
Shijiazhuang	CDJC	1 969 975	1 005 476	964 499	...	...	...	...	...
Shishi	CDJC	498 786	264 700	234 086	...	...	...	...	...
Shishou	CDJC	602 649	310 486	292 163	...	...	...	...	...
Shiyan	CDJC	589 824	309 552	280 272	...	...	...	...	...
Shizuishan	CDJC	314 296	163 261	151 035	...	...	...	...	...
Shouguang	CDJC	1 081 991	548 020	533 971	...	...	...	...	...
Shuangcheng	CDJC	749 182	382 673	366 509	...	...	...	...	...
Shuangliao	CDJC	404 499	206 071	198 428	...	...	...	...	...
Shuangyashan	CDJC	487 294	248 542	238 752	...	...	...	...	...
Shulan	CDJC	660 065	340 293	319 772	...	...	...	...	...
Shunde	CDJC	1 694 152	893 580	800 572	...	...	...	...	...
Shuozhou	CDJC	563 896	290 621	273 275	...	...	...	...	...
Sihui	CDJC	409 804	209 936	199 868	...	...	...	...	...
Simao	CDJC	230 834	120 071	110 763	...	...	...	...	...
Siping	CDJC	492 841	247 416	245 425	...	...	...	...	...
Songyuan	CDJC	538 469	273 101	265 368	...	...	...	...	...
Songzi	CDJC	859 941	437 980	421 961	...	...	...	...	...
Suihua	CDJC	800 207	405 382	394 825	...	...	...	...	...
Suining	CDJC	1 355 388	696 590	658 798	...	...	...	...	...
Suizhou	CDJC	1 598 752	818 936	779 816	...	...	...	...	...
Suqian	CDJC	244 651	124 719	119 932	...	...	...	...	...
Suzhou (Anhui)	CDJC	1 601 181	819 067	782 114	...	...	...	...	...
Suzhou (Jiangsu)	CDJC	1 344 709	686 919	657 790	...	...	...	...	...
Tacheng	CDJC	149 210	76 056	73 154	...	...	...	...	...
Taian	CDJC	1 538 211	775 346	762 865	...	...	...	...	...
Taicang	CDJC	515 063	250 788	264 275	...	...	...	...	...
Taishan	CDJC	948 716	478 773	469 943	...	...	...	...	...
Taixing	CDJC	1 235 454	618 158	617 296	...	...	...	...	...
Taiyuan	CDJC	2 558 382	1 321 216	1 237 166	...	...	...	...	...
Taizhou (Zhejiang)	CDJC	1 491 963	766 497	725 466	...	...	...	...	...
Taizhou (Jiangsu)	CDJC	607 660	303 078	304 582	...	...	...	...	...
Tangshan	CDJC	1 711 311	863 091	848 220	...	...	...	...	...
Taonan	CDJC	441 096	224 878	216 218	...	...	...	...	...
Tengzhou	CDJC	1 548 817	811 999	736 818	...	...	...	...	...
Tianchang	CDJC	590 745	297 550	293 195	...	...	...	...	...

8. Population of capital cities and cities of 100 000 or more inhabitants: latest available year, 1986 - 2005
Population des capitales et des villes de 100 000 habitants ou plus: dernière année disponible, 1986 - 2005
(continued — suite)

Continent, country or area, date and city / Continent, pays ou zone, date et ville	Code[1]	City proper — Ville proprement dite Population				Urban agglomeration — Agglomération urbaine Population			
		Both sexes Les deux sexes	Male Masculin	Female Féminin	Surface area Superficie (km²)	Both sexes Les deux sexes	Male Masculin	Female Féminin	Surface area Superficie (km²)

ASIA — ASIE

China — Chine
1 XI 2000

Tianjin	CDJC	7 499 181	3 825 069	3 674 112	...	...	...	...	...
Tianmen	CDJC	1 613 739	849 283	764 456	...	...	...	...	...
Tianshui	CDJC	1 146 986	594 508	552 478	...	...	...	...	...
Tiefa	CDJC	239 636	121 471	118 165	...	...	...	...	...
Tieli	CDJC	354 601	181 024	173 577	...	...	...	...	...
Tieling	CDJC	433 799	217 795	216 004	...	...	...	...	...
Tongcheng	CDJC	660 772	321 098	339 674	...	...	...	...	...
Tongchuan	CDJC	404 257	211 294	192 963	...	...	...	...	...
Tonghua	CDJC	460 148	231 960	228 188	...	...	...	...	...
Tongjiang	CDJC	164 595	85 426	79 169	...	...	...	...	...
Tongliao	CDJC	793 913	400 930	392 983	...	...	...	...	...
Tongling	CDJC	362 477	188 130	174 347	...	...	...	...	...
Tongren	CDJC	308 583	163 632	144 951	...	...	...	...	...
Tongshi	CDJC	100 836	53 146	47 690	...	...	...	...	...
Tongxiang	CDJC	713 399	360 567	352 832	...	...	...	...	...
Tongzhou	CDJC	1 371 498	652 777	718 721	...	...	...	...	...
Tulufan	CDJC	251 652	129 183	122 469	...	...	...	...	...
Tumen	CDJC	132 368	67 067	65 301	...	...	...	...	...
Urumqi	CDJC	1 753 298	911 328	841 970	...	...	...	...	...
Wafangdian	CDJC	956 063	489 377	466 686	...	...	...	...	...
Wanning	CDJC	513 604	272 751	240 853	...	...	...	...	...
Wanyuan	CDJC	536 685	278 918	257 767	...	...	...	...	...
Weifang	CDJC	1 380 300	696 720	683 580	...	...	...	...	...
Weihai	CDJC	609 219	307 867	301 352	...	...	...	...	...
Weihui	CDJC	464 371	233 151	231 220	...	...	...	...	...
Weinan	CDJC	888 866	451 028	437 838	...	...	...	...	...
Wenchang	CDJC	509 271	260 432	248 839	...	...	...	...	...
Wendeng	CDJC	675 061	335 330	339 731	...	...	...	...	...
Wenling	CDJC	1 162 783	604 031	558 752	...	...	...	...	...
Wenzhou	CDJC	1 915 548	1 028 001	887 547	...	...	...	...	...
Wuan	CDJC	720 196	373 108	347 088	...	...	...	...	...
Wuchang	CDJC	888 782	454 587	434 195	...	...	...	...	...
Wuchuan	CDJC	822 482	429 336	393 146	...	...	...	...	...
Wudalianchi	CDJC	338 689	176 002	162 687	...	...	...	...	...
Wugang (Hunan)	CDJC	694 847	363 904	330 943	...	...	...	...	...
Wugang (Henan)	CDJC	313 089	164 347	148 742	...	...	...	...	...
Wuhai	CDJC	427 553	223 947	203 606	...	...	...	...	...
Wuhan	CDJC	8 312 700	4 306 729	4 005 971	...	...	...	...	...
Wuhu	CDJC	697 197	359 560	337 637	...	...	...	...	...
Wujiang	CDJC	857 104	426 423	430 681	...	...	...	...	...
Wujin	CDJC	1 420 204	719 200	701 004	...	...	...	...	...
Wulanhaote	CDJC	269 162	135 406	133 756	...	...	...	...	...
Wusu	CDJC	190 359	100 288	90 071	...	...	...	...	...
Wuwei	CDJC	946 506	488 872	457 634	...	...	...	...	...
Wuxi	CDJC	1 425 766	732 231	693 535	...	...	...	...	...
Wuxian	CDJC	1 128 429	557 717	570 712	...	...	...	...	...
Wuxue	CDJC	719 426	381 959	337 467	...	...	...	...	...
Wuyishan	CDJC	212 156	112 006	100 150	...	...	...	...	...
Wuzhong	CDJC	355 442	181 909	173 533	...	...	...	...	...
Wuzhou	CDJC	381 043	193 424	187 619	...	...	...	...	...
Xiamen	CDJC	2 053 070	1 061 697	991 373	...	...	...	...	...
Xi'an	CDJC	4 481 508	2 320 642	2 160 866	...	...	...	...	...
Xiangcheng	CDJC	1 052 468	546 760	505 708	...	...	...	...	...
Xiangfan	CDJC	871 388	443 899	427 489	...	...	...	...	...
Xiangtan	CDJC	707 783	363 619	344 164	...	...	...	...	...
Xiangxiang	CDJC	807 718	413 489	394 229	...	...	...	...	...
Xianning	CDJC	567 598	295 836	271 762	...	...	...	...	...
Xiantao	CDJC	1 474 078	774 487	699 591	...	...	...	...	...
Xianyang	CDJC	953 860	493 153	460 707	...	...	...	...	...
Xiaogan	CDJC	883 123	454 917	428 206	...	...	...	...	...

8. Population of capital cities and cities of 100 000 or more inhabitants: latest available year, 1986 - 2005
Population des capitales et des villes de 100 000 habitants ou plus: dernière année disponible, 1986 - 2005
(continued — suite)

Continent, country or area, date and city Continent, pays ou zone, date et ville	Code[1]	City proper — Ville proprement dite Population				Urban agglomeration — Agglomération urbaine Population			
		Both sexes Les deux sexes	Male Masculin	Female Féminin	Surface area Superficie (km²)	Both sexes Les deux sexes	Male Masculin	Female Féminin	Surface area Superficie (km²)
ASIA — ASIE									
China — Chine									
1 XI 2000									
Xiaoshan	CDJC	1 233 348	613 229	620 119	...	...	...	...	...
Xiaoyi	CDJC	414 154	215 941	198 213	...	...	...	...	...
Xichang	CDJC	615 212	318 658	296 554	...	...	...	...	...
Xifeng	CDJC	317 669	163 228	154 441	...	...	...	...	...
Xilin'haote	CDJC	173 796	89 527	84 269	...	...	...	...	...
Xingcheng	CDJC	524 527	269 567	254 960	...	...	...	...	...
Xinghua	CDJC	1 441 659	745 856	695 803	...	...	...	...	...
Xingning	CDJC	871 507	436 749	434 758	...	...	...	...	...
Xingping	CDJC	551 523	284 879	266 644	...	...	...	...	...
Xingtai	CDJC	536 282	272 661	263 621	...	...	...	...	...
Xingyang	CDJC	619 840	316 049	303 791	...	...	...	...	...
Xingyi	CDJC	719 605	375 079	344 526	...	...	...	...	...
Xinhui	CDJC	932 425	467 557	464 868	...	...	...	...	...
Xi'ning	CDJC	854 466	440 359	414 107	...	...	...	...	...
Xinji	CDJC	623 219	314 536	308 683	...	...	...	...	...
Xinle	CDJC	439 644	220 811	218 833	...	...	...	...	...
Xinmi	CDJC	779 014	406 291	372 723	...	...	...	...	...
Xinmin	CDJC	653 719	333 683	320 036	...	...	...	...	...
Xintai	CDJC	1 344 395	687 569	656 826	...	...	...	...	...
Xinxiang	CDJC	775 941	394 224	381 717	...	...	...	...	...
Xinyang	CDJC	1 255 750	644 031	611 719	...	...	...	...	...
Xinyi (Guangdong)	CDJC	907 978	464 088	443 890	...	...	...	...	...
Xinyi (Jiangsu)	CDJC	962 656	491 509	471 147	...	...	...	...	...
Xinyu	CDJC	778 391	408 940	369 451	...	...	...	...	...
Xinzheng	CDJC	609 173	315 462	293 711	...	...	...	...	...
Xinzhou	CDJC	496 608	251 708	244 900	...	...	...	...	...
Xishan	CDJC	1 181 073	599 540	581 533	...	...	...	...	...
Xuancheng	CDJC	822 707	428 470	394 237	...	...	...	...	...
Xuanwei	CDJC	1 292 825	691 846	600 979	...	...	...	...	...
Xuchang	CDJC	373 387	188 476	184 911	...	...	...	...	...
Xuzhou	CDJC	1 679 626	866 686	812 940	...	...	...	...	...
Yaan	CDJC	334 475	171 237	163 238	...	...	...	...	...
Yakeshi	CDJC	405 806	207 451	198 355	...	...	...	...	...
Yan'an	CDJC	403 868	209 240	194 628	...	...	...	...	...
Yancheng	CDJC	683 663	347 576	336 087	...	...	...	...	...
Yangchun	CDJC	840 581	440 930	399 651	...	...	...	...	...
Yangjiang	CDJC	538 069	276 769	261 300	...	...	...	...	...
Yangquan	CDJC	655 317	346 209	309 108	...	...	...	...	...
Yangzhong	CDJC	301 672	150 538	151 134	...	...	...	...	...
Yangzhou	CDJC	711 993	362 425	349 568	...	...	...	...	...
Yanji	CDJC	432 339	223 342	208 997	...	...	...	...	...
Yanshi	CDJC	816 026	414 890	401 136	...	...	...	...	...
Yantai	CDJC	1 724 404	871 452	852 952	...	...	...	...	...
Yibin	CDJC	809 099	419 397	389 702	...	...	...	...	...
Yichang	CDJC	712 738	371 510	341 228	...	...	...	...	...
Yicheng	CDJC	522 835	266 340	256 495	...	...	...	...	...
Yichun (Jiangxi)	CDJC	920 357	480 945	439 412	...	...	...	...	...
Yichun (Heilongjiang)	CDJC	814 016	413 071	400 945	...	...	...	...	...
Yidu	CDJC	385 779	196 716	189 063	...	...	...	...	...
Yima	CDJC	136 543	73 411	63 132	...	...	...	...	...
Yinchuan	CDJC	807 487	415 203	392 284	...	...	...	...	...
Yingcheng	CDJC	650 485	340 907	309 578	...	...	...	...	...
Yingde	CDJC	810 446	421 964	388 482	...	...	...	...	...
Yingkou	CDJC	698 059	353 751	344 308	...	...	...	...	...
Yingtan	CDJC	178 406	92 050	86 356	...	...	...	...	...
Yi'ning	CDJC	357 519	179 862	177 657	...	...	...	...	...
Yiwu	CDJC	912 670	461 103	451 567	...	...	...	...	...
Yixing	CDJC	1 164 275	592 095	572 180	...	...	...	...	...
Yiyang	CDJC	1 228 881	629 842	599 039	...	...	...	...	...
Yizheng	CDJC	610 356	311 144	299 212	...	...	...	...	...

8. Population of capital cities and cities of 100 000 or more inhabitants: latest available year, 1986 - 2005
Population des capitales et des villes de 100 000 habitants ou plus: dernière année disponible, 1986 - 2005
(continued — suite)

Continent, country or area, date and city / Continent, pays ou zone, date et ville	Code[1]	City proper — Ville proprement dite Population				Urban agglomeration — Agglomération urbaine Population			
		Both sexes Les deux sexes	Male Masculin	Female Féminin	Surface area Superficie (km²)	Both sexes Les deux sexes	Male Masculin	Female Féminin	Surface area Superficie (km²)
ASIA — ASIE									
China — Chine									
1 XI 2000									
Yizhou	CDJC	549 434	288 084	261 350	...	...	...	...	...
Yong'an	CDJC	334 852	180 109	154 743	...	...	...	...	...
Yongcheng	CDJC	1 264 607	654 047	610 560	...	...	...	...	...
Yongchuan	CDJC	984 730	507 848	476 882	...	...	...	...	...
Yongkang	CDJC	557 067	290 946	266 121	...	...	...	...	...
Yongji	CDJC	421 244	214 446	206 798	...	...	...	...	...
Yongzhou	CDJC	976 539	508 021	468 518	...	...	...	...	...
Yuanjiang	CDJC	700 236	363 730	336 506	...	...	...	...	...
Yuanping	CDJC	471 853	244 751	227 102	...	...	...	...	...
Yucheng	CDJC	494 301	248 103	246 198	...	...	...	...	...
Yueyang	CDJC	912 993	471 170	441 823	...	...	...	...	...
Yuhang	CDJC	817 715	419 877	397 838	...	...	...	...	...
Yulin (Shaanxi)	CDJC	451 337	232 951	218 386	...	...	...	...	...
Yulin (Guangxi)	CDJC	918 229	491 729	426 500	...	...	...	...	...
Yumen	CDJC	188 931	99 832	89 099	...	...	...	...	...
Yuncheng	CDJC	604 381	304 489	299 892	...	...	...	...	...
Yunfu	CDJC	261 636	136 789	124 847	...	...	...	...	...
Yunzhou	CDJC	598 387	303 581	294 806	...	...	...	...	...
Yushu	CDJC	1 155 670	592 213	563 457	...	...	...	...	...
Yuxi	CDJC	409 044	206 139	202 905	...	...	...	...	...
Yuyao	CDJC	852 719	429 835	422 884	...	...	...	...	...
Yuzhou	CDJC	1 122 669	587 728	534 941	...	...	...	...	...
Zaoyang	CDJC	1 054 374	538 588	515 786	...	...	...	...	...
Zaozhuang	CDJC	1 996 798	1 025 190	971 608	...	...	...	...	...
Zengcheng	CDJC	899 644	466 540	433 104	...	...	...	...	...
Zhalantun	CDJC	409 051	211 922	197 129	...	...	...	...	...
Zhangjiagang	CDJC	957 223	466 771	490 452	...	...	...	...	...
Zhangjiajie	CDJC	453 723	234 454	219 269	...	...	...	...	...
Zhangjiakou	CDJC	903 348	455 048	448 300	...	...	...	...	...
Zhangping	CDJC	264 757	140 779	123 978	...	...	...	...	...
Zhangqiu	CDJC	977 324	485 925	491 399	...	...	...	...	...
Zhangshu	CDJC	527 823	273 691	254 132	...	...	...	...	...
Zhangye	CDJC	486 688	248 469	238 219	...	...	...	...	...
Zhangzhou	CDJC	567 884	291 597	276 287	...	...	...	...	...
Zhanjiang	CDJC	1 350 665	707 187	643 478	...	...	...	...	...
Zhaodong	CDJC	832 657	424 694	407 963	...	...	...	...	...
Zhaoqing	CDJC	507 834	254 086	253 748	...	...	...	...	...
Zhaotong	CDJC	727 959	377 931	350 028	...	...	...	...	...
Zhaoyuan	CDJC	593 705	297 504	296 201	...	...	...	...	...
Zhengzhou	CDJC	2 589 387	1 347 037	1 242 350	...	...	...	...	...
Zhenjiang	CDJC	695 663	364 429	331 234	...	...	...	...	...
Zhijiang	CDJC	508 835	257 013	251 822	...	...	...	...	...
Zhongshan	CDJC	2 363 322	1 175 587	1 187 735	...	...	...	...	...
Zhongxiang	CDJC	1 021 998	516 758	505 240	...	...	...	...	...
Zhoukou	CDJC	323 738	162 443	161 295	...	...	...	...	...
Zhoushan	CDJC	715 685	362 426	353 259	...	...	...	...	...
Zhuanghe	CDJC	835 062	422 677	412 385	...	...	...	...	...
Zhucheng	CDJC	1 053 695	531 390	522 305	...	...	...	...	...
Zhuhai	CDJC	833 908	414 067	419 841	...	...	...	...	...
Zhuji	CDJC	1 070 675	535 820	534 855	...	...	...	...	...
Zhumadian	CDJC	338 036	170 485	167 551	...	...	...	...	...
Zhuozhou	CDJC	546 754	275 834	270 920	...	...	...	...	...
Zhuzhou	CDJC	879 996	454 057	425 939	...	...	...	...	...
Zibo	CDJC	2 817 479	1 429 838	1 387 641	...	...	...	...	...
Zigong	CDJC	1 051 384	532 479	518 905	...	...	...	...	...
Zixing	CDJC	351 581	181 632	169 949	...	...	...	...	...
Ziyang	CDJC	1 016 034	527 326	488 708	...	...	...	...	...
Zoucheng	CDJC	1 101 003	571 761	529 242	...	...	...	...	...
Zunhua	CDJC	683 662	348 121	335 541	...	...	...	...	...
Zunyi	CDJC	691 694	358 839	332 855	...	...	...	...	...

8. Population of capital cities and cities of 100 000 or more inhabitants: latest available year, 1986 - 2005
Population des capitales et des villes de 100 000 habitants ou plus: dernière année disponible, 1986 - 2005
(continued — suite)

Continent, country or area, date and city / Continent, pays ou zone, date et ville	Code[1]	City proper — Ville proprement dite Population				Urban agglomeration — Agglomération urbaine Population			
		Both sexes Les deux sexes	Male Masculin	Female Féminin	Surface area Superficie (km²)	Both sexes Les deux sexes	Male Masculin	Female Féminin	Surface area Superficie (km²)
ASIA — ASIE									
China : Hong Kong SAR — Chine - Hong Kong RAS									
1 VII 2005									
HONG KONG	ESDJ	6 813 200	3 264 000	3 549 200	1 099	...	...	...	
China : Macao SAR — Chine - Macao RAS									
1 VII 2005									
MACAO	ESDJ	473 457	227 600	245 857	26	...	...	...	
Cyprus — Chypre									
31 XII 2004									
LEFKOSIA[51]	ESDJ	...	...	...	...	219 200	...	...	
Lemesos[52]	ESDJ	...	...	...	...	172 500	...	...	
Georgia — Géorgie									
1 VII 2003									
Batumi	ESDF	120 200	...	...					
Kutaisi	ESDF	183 800	...	...					
Rustavi	ESDF	115 000	...	...					
TBILISI	ESDF	1 059 600	...	...					
India — Inde[53]									
1 III 2001									
Abohar	CDFC	124 303	66 434	57 869	23	...	...	...	
Achalpur	CDFC	107 304	55 678	51 626	...	...	...	...	
Adilabad	CDFC	108 233	55 023	53 210	...	128 196	64 883	63 313	...
Adityapur	CDFC	119 221	63 855	55 366	...	...	...	...	
Adoni	CDFC	155 969	78 908	77 061	30	161 125	81 577	79 548	...
Agartala	CDFC	189 327	94 398	94 929	16	...	...	...	
Agra	CDFC	1 259 979	674 902	585 077	121	1 321 410	708 622	612 788	141
Ahmedabad	CDFC	3 515 361	1 863 886	1 651 475	...	4 519 278	2 397 728	2 121 550	...
Ahmednagar	CDFC	307 455	159 409	148 046	18	347 396	184 604	162 792	30
Aizawl	CDFC	229 714	116 983	112 731	110	...	...	...	
Ajmer	CDFC	485 197	253 854	231 343	242	490 138	256 379	233 759	...
Akola	CDFC	399 978	206 433	193 545	23	...	...	...	
Alandur	CDFC	146 154	74 784	71 370	...	...	...	...	
Alappuzha	CDFC	177 079	85 708	91 371	70	282 727	137 232	145 495	84
Aligarh	CDFC	667 732	357 152	310 580	34	...	...	...	...
Alipurduar	CDFC	...	...	...	...	114 069	58 527	55 542	26
Allahabad	CDFC	990 298	549 754	440 544	...	1 049 579	581 876	467 703	...
Alwal	CDFC	106 424	56 562	49 862	...	...	...	...	
Alwar	CDFC	260 245	139 141	121 104	...	265 850	143 238	122 612	58
Ambala	CDFC	139 222	73 956	65 266	17	168 003	92 610	75 393	38
Ambala Sadar	CDFC	106 378	55 461	50 917	...	...	...	...	
Ambarnath	CDFC	203 795	107 378	96 417	...	...	...	...	
Ambattur	CDFC	302 492	156 237	146 255	...	...	...	...	
Amravati	CDFC	549 370	283 789	265 581	122	...	...	...	
Amritsar	CDFC	975 695	524 127	451 568	...	1 011 327	543 638	467 689	...
Amroha	CDFC	164 890	86 836	78 054	6	...	...	...	
Anand	CDFC	130 462	68 032	62 430	...	218 064	115 183	102 881	...
Anantapur	CDFC	220 951	112 273	108 678	...	243 359	123 976	119 383	...
Anklesvar	CDFC	...	...	...	...	112 648	60 265	52 383	...
Arcot	CDFC	...	...	...	...	126 975	62 938	64 037	19
Arrah	CDFC	203 395	109 876	93 519	31	...	...	...	
Asansol	CDFC	486 304	256 551	229 753	25	1 090 171	576 813	513 358	223
Ashoknagar Kalyangarh	CDFC	111 475	56 340	55 135	...	...	...	...	
Aurangabad	CDFC	872 667	458 869	413 798	139	891 841	468 815	423 026	148
Avadi	CDFC	230 913	119 187	111 726	...	...	...	...	
Azamgarh	CDFC	104 943	51 284	53 659	...	...	...	...	
Bahadurgarh	CDFC	119 839	65 835	54 004	...	131 924	72 851	59 073	...
Baharampur	CDFC	160 168	81 795	78 373	17	170 343	87 038	83 305	19
Bahraich	CDFC	168 376	89 532	78 844	13	...	...	...	
Baidyabati	CDFC	108 231	56 429	51 802	...	...	...	...	
Baleshwar	CDFC	106 032	55 637	50 395	...	156 274	82 034	74 240	42
Ballia	CDFC	102 226	55 123	47 103	...	...	...	...	

8. Population of capital cities and cities of 100 000 or more inhabitants: latest available year, 1986 - 2005
Population des capitales et des villes de 100 000 habitants ou plus: dernière année disponible, 1986 - 2005
(continued — suite)

Continent, country or area, date and city Continent, pays ou zone, date et ville	Code[1]	City proper — Ville proprement dite Population				Urban agglomeration — Agglomération urbaine Population			
		Both sexes Les deux sexes	Male Masculin	Female Féminin	Surface area Superficie (km²)	Both sexes Les deux sexes	Male Masculin	Female Féminin	Surface area Superficie (km²)
ASIA — ASIE									
India — Inde[53]									
1 III 2001									
Bally	CDFC	261 575	149 810	111 765	12	...	...	...	...
Balurghat	CDFC	135 516	68 822	66 694	...	143 095	72 687	70 408	8
Banda	CDFC	134 822	72 663	62 159	...	139 387	75 172	64 215	...
Bangalore	CDFC	4 292 223	2 240 956	2 051 267	...	5 686 844	2 983 926	2 702 918	446
Bangaon	CDFC	102 115	52 489	49 626	...	...	...	...	...
Bankura	CDFC	128 811	66 333	62 478	19	...	...	...	...
Bansberia	CDFC	104 453	55 403	49 050	...	...	...	...	...
Baranagar	CDFC	250 615	132 701	117 914	7	...	...	...	...
Barasat	CDFC	231 515	118 367	113 148	...	...	...	...	...
Barddhaman	CDFC	285 871	148 824	137 047	23	...	...	...	...
Bareilly	CDFC	699 839	368 022	331 817	107	729 800	386 418	343 382	124
Baripada	CDFC	...	...	...	...	100 593	53 610	46 983	...
Barrackpur	CDFC	144 331	76 268	68 063	14	...	...	...	...
Barshi	CDFC	104 786	53 894	50 892	...	...	...	...	...
Basirhat	CDFC	113 120	57 876	55 244	22	...	...	...	...
Basti	CDFC	106 985	56 813	50 172	...	...	...	...	...
Batala	CDFC	126 646	67 026	59 620	...	147 753	78 342	69 411	...
Bathinda	CDFC	217 389	117 359	100 030	97	...	...	...	...
Beawar	CDFC	123 701	64 394	59 307	...	125 923	65 569	60 354	18
Begusarai	CDFC	...	...	...	...	107 203	57 349	49 854	...
Belgaum	CDFC	399 600	204 846	194 754	142	506 235	261 862	244 373	155
Bellary	CDFC	317 000	163 082	153 918	66	...	...	...	...
Bettiah	CDFC	116 692	61 803	54 889	...	...	...	...	...
Bhadravati	CDFC	160 392	81 260	79 132	...	...	...	...	...
Bhadreswar	CDFC	105 944	57 991	47 953	...	...	...	...	...
Bhagalpur	CDFC	340 349	182 704	157 645	30	349 709	187 627	162 082	31
Bhalswa Jahangir Pur	CDFC	151 427	83 289	68 138	...	...	...	...	...
Bharatpur	CDFC	204 456	109 809	94 647	41	205 104	110 148	94 956	51
Bharuch	CDFC	148 391	76 568	71 823	...	176 531	91 273	85 258	...
Bhatpara	CDFC	441 956	243 065	198 891	16	...	...	...	...
Bhavani	CDFC	...	...	...	...	104 285	52 804	51 481	...
Bhavnagar	CDFC	510 958	267 019	243 939	...	517 578	270 458	247 120	...
Bheemavaram	CDFC	137 327	69 487	67 840	26	141 975	71 938	70 037	...
Bhilai Nagar	CDFC	553 837	289 853	263 984	89	...	...	...	...
Bhilwara	CDFC	280 185	148 642	131 543	118	...	...	...	...
Bhind	CDFC	153 768	83 009	70 759	17	...	...	...	...
Bhiwandi	CDFC	598 703	367 858	230 845	26	621 390	382 493	238 897	28
Bhiwani	CDFC	169 424	91 726	77 698	28	...	...	...	...
Bhopal	CDFC	1 433 875	755 685	678 190	285	1 454 830	766 602	688 228	...
Bhubaneswar	CDFC	647 302	360 476	286 826	125	657 477	365 848	291 629	...
Bhusawal	CDFC	172 366	89 187	83 179	13	187 524	97 192	90 332	25
Bid	CDFC	138 091	71 790	66 301	8	...	...	...	...
Bidar	CDFC	172 298	89 715	82 583	...	173 678	90 449	83 229	47
Bidhan Nagar	CDFC	167 848	85 215	82 633	...	...	...	...	...
Bihar	CDFC	231 972	121 813	110 159	24	...	...	...	...
Bijapur	CDFC	245 946	126 554	119 392	...	253 307	130 237	123 070	75
Bikaner	CDFC	529 007	282 450	246 557	166	...	...	...	...
Bilaspur	CDFC	265 178	137 273	127 905	36	330 291	170 898	159 393	46
Birnagar	CDFC	...	...	...	...	115 104	59 179	55 925	...
Bokaro Steel City	CDFC	394 173	213 044	181 129	163	497 855	268 668	229 187	183
Bommanahalli	CDFC	201 220	108 040	93 180	...	...	...	...	...
Botad	CDFC	100 059	52 668	47 391	...	...	...	...	...
Brahmapur	CDFC	289 724	150 089	139 635	80	...	...	...	...
Budaun	CDFC	148 138	78 294	69 844	4	...	...	...	...
Bulandshahr	CDFC	176 256	93 066	83 190	12	...	...	...	...
Burhanpur	CDFC	194 360	100 031	94 329	13	...	...	...	...
Byatarayanapura	CDFC	180 931	94 683	86 248	...	...	...	...	...
Chakdaha	CDFC	...	...	...	...	101 278	51 321	49 957	...
Champdani	CDFC	103 232	57 874	45 358	...	...	...	...	...
Chandan Nagar	CDFC	162 166	84 222	77 944	10	...	...	...	...

8. Population of capital cities and cities of 100 000 or more inhabitants: latest available year, 1986 - 2005
Population des capitales et des villes de 100 000 habitants ou plus: dernière année disponible, 1986 - 2005
(continued — suite)

Continent, country or area, date and city Continent, pays ou zone, date et ville	Code[1]	City proper — Ville proprement dite Population				Urban agglomeration — Agglomération urbaine Population			
		Both sexes Les deux sexes	Male Masculin	Female Féminin	Surface area Superficie (km²)	Both sexes Les deux sexes	Male Masculin	Female Féminin	Surface area Superficie (km²)
ASIA — ASIE									
India — Inde[53]									
1 III 2001									
Chandausi	CDFC	103 757	55 167	48 590	...	...	...	...	...
Chandigarh	CDFC	808 796	451 387	357 409	70	...	...	...	...
Chandrapur	CDFC	297 612	148 499	149 113	56	...	...	...	...
Chapra	CDFC	178 835	96 077	82 758	17	...	...	...	...
Chennai (Madras)	CDFC	4 216 268	2 161 605	2 054 663	174	6 424 624	3 294 328	3 130 296	612
Cherthala	CDFC	...	...	...	...	141 512	68 740	72 772	93
Chhatarpur	CDFC	...	...	...	...	109 021	58 393	50 628	...
Chhindwara	CDFC	122 309	63 583	58 726	...	153 635	79 889	73 746	...
Chikmagalur	CDFC	101 022	51 611	49 411	...	...	...	...	...
Chirala	CDFC	...	...	...	...	166 877	83 262	83 615	48
Chirkunda	CDFC	...	...	...	...	106 200	56 528	49 672	...
Chitradurga	CDFC	122 594	62 811	59 783	...	125 060	64 075	60 985	16
Chittoor	CDFC	152 966	77 044	75 922	33	...	...	...	...
Churu	CDFC	...	...	...	...	101 853	53 099	48 754	...
Coimbatore	CDFC	923 085	476 056	447 029	106	1 446 034	743 161	702 873	317
Coonoor	CDFC	...	...	...	...	101 234	51 089	50 145	...
Cuddalore	CDFC	158 569	80 113	78 456	28	...	...	...	...
Cuddapah	CDFC	125 725	63 165	62 560	42	260 899	132 297	128 602	78
Cuttack	CDFC	535 139	286 192	248 947	122	587 637	314 435	273 202	153
Dallo Pura	CDFC	132 628	71 349	61 279	...	...	...	...	...
Damoh	CDFC	112 160	58 898	53 262	...	127 939	67 244	60 695	36
Darbhanga	CDFC	266 834	142 042	124 792	19	...	...	...	...
Darjiling	CDFC	107 530	53 325	54 205	...	109 163	54 131	55 032	...
Dasarahalli	CDFC	263 636	143 225	120 411	...	...	...	...	...
Davangere	CDFC	363 780	187 603	176 177	...	...	...	...	...
Dehradun	CDFC	447 808	236 852	210 956	37	527 859	279 653	248 206	86
Dehri	CDFC	119 007	63 552	55 455	...	...	...	...	...
Delhi[54]	CDFC	9 817 439	5 378 658	4 438 781	431	12 791 458	7 021 896	5 769 562	624
Delhi Cantonment	CDFC	124 452	75 700	48 752	...	...	...	...	...
Deoghar	CDFC	...	...	...	...	112 501	61 405	51 096	...
Deoli	CDFC	119 432	66 575	52 857	...	...	...	...	...
Deoria	CDFC	104 222	54 737	49 485	...	...	...	...	...
Dewas	CDFC	230 658	120 610	110 048	100	...	...	...	...
Dhanbad	CDFC	198 963	108 400	90 563	23	1 064 357	578 602	485 755	201
Dharmavaram	CDFC	103 400	52 799	50 601	...	...	...	...	...
Dhule	CDFC	341 473	177 631	163 842	46	...	...	...	...
Dibrugarh	CDFC	122 523	65 736	56 787	15	137 879	74 239	63 640	16
Dimapur	CDFC	107 382	61 595	45 787	...	...	...	...	...
Dinapur Nizamat	CDFC	130 339	69 024	61 315	...	...	...	...	...
Dindigul	CDFC	196 619	98 969	97 650	14	...	...	...	...
Dohad	CDFC	...	...	...	...	112 087	57 765	54 322	...
Dumdum	CDFC	101 319	52 868	48 451	...	...	...	...	...
Durg	CDFC	231 182	118 896	112 286	51	...	...	...	...
Durgapur	CDFC	492 996	263 426	229 570	154	...	...	...	...
Durg-Bhilai Nagar	CDFC	...	...	...	...	923 559	480 432	443 127	183
Eluru	CDFC	189 772	92 405	97 367	15	215 343	104 987	110 356	...
English Bazar	CDFC	161 448	82 932	78 516	...	224 392	115 454	108 938	19
Erode	CDFC	151 184	76 726	74 458	8	391 169	199 306	191 863	132
Etah	CDFC	107 098	56 960	50 138	...	...	...	...	...
Etawah	CDFC	211 460	112 833	98 627	9	...	...	...	...
Faizabad	CDFC	144 924	76 078	68 846	33	208 164	114 252	93 912	63
Faridabad	CDFC	1 054 981	580 548	474 433	178	...	...	...	...
Farrukhabad-cum-Fategarh	CDFC	227 876	120 783	107 093	17	242 558	129 608	112 950	21
Fatehpur	CDFC	151 757	79 836	71 921	57	...	...	...	...
Firozabad	CDFC	278 801	147 980	130 821	9	432 213	230 477	201 736	12
Gadag-Betgeri	CDFC	154 849	78 672	76 177	35	...	...	...	...
Gajuwaka	CDFC	258 960	133 461	125 483	...	...	...	...	...
Gandhinagar	CDFC	195 891	103 814	92 077	57	...	...	...	...
Ganganagar	CDFC	210 788	115 412	95 376	21	222 833	121 877	100 956	...
Gangawati	CDFC	...	...	...	...	101 397	51 253	50 144	...

8. Population of capital cities and cities of 100 000 or more inhabitants: latest available year, 1986 - 2005
Population des capitales et des villes de 100 000 habitants ou plus: dernière année disponible, 1986 - 2005
(continued — suite)

Continent, country or area, date and city / Continent, pays ou zone, date et ville	Code[1]	City proper — Ville proprement dite Population				Urban agglomeration — Agglomération urbaine Population			
		Both sexes Les deux sexes	Male Masculin	Female Féminin	Surface area Superficie (km²)	Both sexes Les deux sexes	Male Masculin	Female Féminin	Surface area Superficie (km²)
ASIA — ASIE									
India — Inde[53]									
1 III 2001									
Gaya	CDFC	383 197	203 252	179 945	29	394 185	209 926	184 259	32
Ghatlodiya	CDFC	106 259	56 040	50 219	...	...	...	...	...
Ghaziabad	CDFC	968 521	521 408	447 113	64	...	...	...	...
Ghazipur	CDFC	...	...	...	...	103 283	54 321	48 962	...
Giridih	CDFC	...	...	...	...	105 212	55 154	50 058	...
Godhra	CDFC	121 852	63 143	58 709	...	131 144	67 933	63 211	...
Gonda	CDFC	122 164	67 400	54 764	...	...	...	...	...
Gondiya	CDFC	120 878	61 435	59 443	18	...	...	...	...
Gorakhpur	CDFC	624 570	330 450	294 120	137	...	...	...	...
Gudivada	CDFC	112 245	55 439	56 806	13	...	...	...	...
Gudiyatham	CDFC	...	...	...	...	100 021	49 822	50 199	...
Gulbarga	CDFC	427 929	222 623	205 306	...	435 631	226 848	208 783	43
Guna	CDFC	137 132	72 462	64 670	46	...	...	...	...
Guntakul	CDFC	117 403	59 364	58 039	52	...	...	...	...
Guntur	CDFC	514 707	257 939	256 768	30	...	...	...	...
Gurgaon	CDFC	173 542	92 985	80 557	15	229 243	123 370	105 873	24
Guruvayur	CDFC	...	...	...	...	138 676	64 550	74 126	50
Guwahati	CDFC	808 021	441 347	366 674	217	814 575	445 649	368 926	...
Gwalior	CDFC	826 919	442 484	384 435	290	865 800	465 388	400 412	303
Habra	CDFC	127 695	65 263	62 432	18	239 170	121 603	117 567	37
Hajipur	CDFC	119 276	63 762	55 514	...	...	...	...	...
Haldia	CDFC	170 695	89 886	80 809	69	...	...	...	...
Haldwani-cum-Kathgodam	CDFC	129 140	68 826	60 314	11	159 020	84 611	74 409	...
Halisahar	CDFC	124 479	67 124	57 355	...	...	...	...	...
Hanumangarh	CDFC	129 654	69 583	60 071	...	...	...	...	...
Haora (Howrah)	CDFC	1 008 704	547 969	460 735	52	...	...	...	...
Hapur	CDFC	211 987	112 962	99 025	14	...	...	...	...
Hardoi	CDFC	112 474	59 877	52 597	...	...	...	...	...
Hardwar	CDFC	175 010	94 650	80 360	15	220 433	119 159	101 274	42
Hassan	CDFC	117 386	60 225	57 161	...	133 317	68 337	64 980	27
Hathras	CDFC	123 243	65 908	57 335	8	126 352	67 568	58 784	...
Hazaribag	CDFC	127 243	67 905	59 338	...	135 446	72 296	63 150	...
Hindupur	CDFC	125 056	64 159	60 897	38	...	...	...	...
Hisar	CDFC	256 810	140 240	116 570	45	263 070	143 816	119 254	49
Hoshiarpur	CDFC	148 243	78 946	69 297	28	...	...	...	...
Hospet	CDFC	163 284	83 430	79 854	28	...	...	...	...
Hubli-Dharwad	CDFC	786 018	403 270	382 748	191	...	...	...	...
Hugli-Chinsurah	CDFC	170 201	86 728	83 473	17	...	...	...	...
Hyderabad	CDFC	3 449 878	1 773 899	1 675 979	...	5 533 640	2 854 938	2 678 702	...
Ichalakaranji	CDFC	257 572	135 988	121 584	30	285 795	150 934	134 861	38
Imphal	CDFC	217 275	107 593	109 682	33	245 967	121 588	124 379	37
Indore	CDFC	1 597 441	839 843	757 598	...	1 639 044	861 758	777 286	165
Itarsi	CDFC	...	...	...	...	109 288	57 118	52 170	...
Jabalpur	CDFC	951 469	496 829	454 640	154	1 117 200	588 556	528 644	224
Jagadhri	CDFC	101 300	55 910	45 390	...	...	...	...	...
Jagdalpur	CDFC	...	...	...	...	103 216	53 048	50 168	...
Jaipur	CDFC	2 324 319	1 239 711	1 084 608	200	...	...	...	...
Jalandhar	CDFC	701 223	376 925	324 298	80	709 255	381 116	328 139	...
Jalgaon	CDFC	368 579	193 464	175 115	62	...	...	...	...
Jalna	CDFC	235 529	121 728	113 801	82	...	...	...	...
Jalpaiguri	CDFC	100 212	50 570	49 642	...	...	...	...	...
Jammu	CDFC	378 431	206 061	172 370	...	607 642	330 769	276 873	...
Jamnagar	CDFC	447 734	235 093	212 641	...	558 462	292 954	265 508	...
Jamshedpur	CDFC	570 349	300 081	270 268	60	1 101 804	580 336	521 468	160
Jamuria	CDFC	129 456	68 741	60 715	...	...	...	...	...
Jaunpur	CDFC	159 996	84 179	75 817	25	...	...	...	...
Jetpur Navagadh	CDFC	104 311	54 772	49 539	...	...	...	...	...
Jhansi	CDFC	383 248	203 003	180 245	48	463 281	246 495	216 786	83
Jhunjhunun	CDFC	100 476	52 814	47 662	...	...	...	...	...
Jind	CDFC	136 089	73 557	62 532	...	...	...	...	...

8. Population of capital cities and cities of 100 000 or more inhabitants: latest available year, 1986 - 2005
Population des capitales et des villes de 100 000 habitants ou plus: dernière année disponible, 1986 - 2005
(continued — suite)

Continent, country or area, date and city / Continent, pays ou zone, date et ville	Code¹	City proper — Ville proprement dite Population				Urban agglomeration — Agglomération urbaine Population			
		Both sexes Les deux sexes	Male Masculin	Female Féminin	Surface area Superficie (km²)	Both sexes Les deux sexes	Male Masculin	Female Féminin	Surface area Superficie (km²)
ASIA — ASIE									
India — Inde[53]									
1 III 2001									
Jodhpur	CDFC	846 408	450 816	395 592	79	856 034	455 860	400 174	...
Jorhat	CDFC	...	...	...	60	135 091	71 837	63 254	69
Junagadh	CDFC	168 686	86 935	81 751	...	252 138	130 318	121 820	...
Kaithal	CDFC	117 226	63 090	54 136	...	...	...	...	...
Kakinada	CDFC	289 920	143 905	146 015	39	368 672	183 619	185 053	58
Kalol	CDFC	100 021	53 098	46 923	...	112 025	59 532	52 493	...
Kalyan	CDFC	1 193 266	633 395	559 871	225	...	...	...	...
Kamarhati	CDFC	314 334	168 633	145 701	11	...	...	...	...
Kamptee	CDFC	...	...	...	...	137 056	71 633	65 423	36
Kancheepuram	CDFC	152 984	77 058	75 926	12	188 349	94 942	93 407	40
Kanchrapara	CDFC	126 118	65 197	60 921	13	...	...	...	...
Kanhangad	CDFC	...	...	...	...	129 364	61 954	67 410	84
Kannur	CDFC	...	...	...	...	498 175	237 101	261 074	145
Kanpur	CDFC	2 532 138	1 354 581	1 177 557	267	2 690 486	1 440 140	1 250 346	299
Kapra	CDFC	159 176	82 914	76 262	...	...	...	...	...
Karaikkudi	CDFC	...	...	...	...	125 185	62 230	62 955	79
Karawal Nagar	CDFC	148 549	80 364	68 185	...	...	...	...	...
Karimnagar	CDFC	203 819	104 514	99 305	24	215 782	110 479	105 303	...
Karnal	CDFC	210 476	112 263	98 213	22	222 017	118 428	103 589	24
Karur	CDFC	...	...	...	...	153 123	77 130	75 993	19
Katihar	CDFC	175 169	93 567	81 602	25	190 862	102 126	88 736	...
Khammam	CDFC	158 022	80 072	77 950	...	196 763	100 255	96 508	26
Khandwa	CDFC	171 976	88 859	83 117	36	...	...	...	...
Khanna	CDFC	103 059	55 290	47 769	...	...	...	...	...
Kharagpur	CDFC	207 984	107 506	100 478	91	296 323	152 700	143 623	125
Khardaha	CDFC	116 252	61 254	54 998	...	...	...	...	...
Khargone	CDFC	...	...	...	...	103 980	54 236	49 744	...
Kirari Suleman Nagar	CDFC	153 874	84 908	68 966	...	...	...	...	...
Kishangarh	CDFC	116 156	61 025	55 131	...	...	...	...	...
Koch Bihar	CDFC	...	...	...	...	102 922	52 186	50 736	...
Kochi	CDFC	596 473	295 351	301 122	109	1 355 406	670 462	684 944	373
Kolar	CDFC	113 299	57 773	55 526	...	...	...	...	...
Kolhapur	CDFC	485 183	251 958	233 225	67	497 554	258 400	239 154	67
Kolkata (Calcutta)[55]	CDFC	4 580 544	2 506 029	2 074 515	185	13 216 546	7 072 114	6 144 432	897
Kollam	CDFC	361 441	177 586	183 855	41	379 975	186 842	193 133	68
Korba	CDFC	315 695	165 028	150 667	35	...	...	...	...
Kota	CDFC	695 899	369 897	326 002	221	704 731	374 570	330 161	...
Kothagudem	CDFC	...	...	...	...	105 265	52 377	52 888	35
Kottayam	CDFC	...	...	...	...	172 867	84 915	87 952	64
Kozhikode	CDFC	436 527	211 785	224 742	96	880 168	428 984	451 184	233
Krishnanagar	CDFC	139 070	70 512	68 558	16	148 645	75 381	73 264	...
Krishnarajapura	CDFC	187 453	98 107	89 346	...	...	...	...	...
Kukatpalle	CDFC	290 591	152 159	138 432	...	...	...	...	...
Kulti	CDFC	290 057	152 947	137 110	...	...	...	...	...
Kumbakonam	CDFC	140 021	69 607	70 414	13	160 827	80 012	80 815	15
Kurnool	CDFC	267 739	135 859	131 880	15	320 619	163 071	157 548	46
L.B. Nagar	CDFC	261 987	135 636	126 351	...	...	...	...	...
Lakhimpur	CDFC	120 566	64 804	55 762	...	...	...	...	...
Lalitpur	CDFC	111 810	58 901	52 909	...	...	...	...	...
Latur	CDFC	299 828	156 477	143 351	21	...	...	...	...
Loni	CDFC	120 659	64 976	55 683	...	...	...	...	...
Lucknow	CDFC	2 207 340	1 165 932	1 041 408	310	2 266 933	1 199 273	1 067 660	338
Ludhiana	CDFC	1 395 053	789 868	605 185	135	...	...	...	...
Machilipatnam	CDFC	183 370	91 400	91 970	27	...	...	...	...
Madanapalle	CDFC	...	...	...	...	107 262	54 507	52 755	...
Madhyamgram	CDFC	155 503	79 716	75 787	...	...	...	...	...
Madurai	CDFC	922 913	466 909	456 004	47	1 194 665	604 728	589 937	115
Mahadevapura	CDFC	135 597	72 803	62 794	...	...	...	...	...
Mahbubnagar	CDFC	130 849	67 019	63 830	14	139 483	71 508	67 975	...
Mahesana	CDFC	...	...	...	...	141 367	74 928	66 439	...

8. Population of capital cities and cities of 100 000 or more inhabitants: latest available year, 1986 - 2005
Population des capitales et des villes de 100 000 habitants ou plus: dernière année disponible, 1986 - 2005
(continued — suite)

Continent, country or area, date and city / Continent, pays ou zone, date et ville	Code[1]	City proper — Ville proprement dite Population				Urban agglomeration — Agglomération urbaine Population			
		Both sexes Les deux sexes	Male Masculin	Female Féminin	Surface area Superficie (km²)	Both sexes Les deux sexes	Male Masculin	Female Féminin	Surface area Superficie (km²)
ASIA — ASIE									
India — Inde[53]									
1 III 2001									
Maheshtala	CDFC	389 214	204 734	184 480	...	...	...	...	...
Mainpuri	CDFC	...	...	...		102 007	54 043	47 964	...
Malappuram	CDFC	...	...	...		170 364	83 669	86 695	111
Malegaon	CDFC	409 190	208 744	200 446	13	...	...	...	...
Malerkotla	CDFC	106 802	56 872	49 930	...	...	...	...	...
Malkajgiri	CDFC	175 000	90 000	85 000	...	...	...	...	...
Mancherial	CDFC	...	...	...		118 047	60 371	57 676	...
Mandsaur	CDFC	116 483	60 269	56 214	...	117 532	60 860	56 672	
Mandya	CDFC	131 211	66 630	64 581	17	...	...	...	...
Mangalore	CDFC	398 745	200 234	198 511	75	538 560	269 176	269 384	155
Mango	CDFC	166 091	87 322	78 769	...	...	...	...	...
Mathura	CDFC	298 827	159 249	139 578	9	319 235	171 516	147 719	22
Maunath Bhanjan	CDFC	210 071	108 696	101 375	9	...	...	...	...
Medinipur	CDFC	153 349	78 365	74 984	15	...	...	...	...
Meerut	CDFC	1 074 229	571 074	503 155	142	1 167 399	624 904	542 495	178
Mira-Bhayandar	CDFC	520 301	286 458	233 843	...	...	...	...	...
Mirzapur-cum-Vindhyachal	CDFC	205 264	109 872	95 392	39	...	...	...	...
Modinagar	CDFC	112 918	60 260	52 658	10	139 642	74 570	65 072	17
Moga	CDFC	124 624	66 843	57 781	...	134 242	71 996	62 246	...
Moradabad	CDFC	641 240	340 217	301 023	34	...	...	...	...
Morena	CDFC	150 890	82 281	68 609	96	...	...	...	...
Mormugoa	CDFC	...	...	...		104 689	55 927	48 762	...
Motihari	CDFC	101 506	54 629	46 877	...	109 250	59 517	49 733	...
Mughalsarai	CDFC	...	...	...		116 246	61 572	54 674	...
Mumbai (Bombay)	CDFC	11 914 398	6 577 902	5 336 496	466	16 368 084	8 979 172	7 388 912	1 041
Munger	CDFC	187 311	100 374	86 937	18	...	...	...	...
Murwara (Katni)	CDFC	186 738	97 666	89 072	107	...	...	...	...
Muzaffarnagar	CDFC	316 452	166 998	149 454	...	331 403	174 877	156 526	12
Muzaffarpur	CDFC	305 465	163 907	141 558	26	...	...	...	...
Mysore	CDFC	742 261	377 132	365 129	103	785 800	399 904	385 896	129
Nabadwip	CDFC	115 036	58 268	56 768	...	125 346	63 544	61 802	...
Nadiad	CDFC	192 799	100 452	92 347	...	196 679	102 469	94 210	...
Nagaon	CDFC	107 471	56 888	50 583	...	123 054	64 976	58 078	...
Nagercoil	CDFC	208 149	103 075	105 074	24	...	...	...	...
Nagpur	CDFC	2 051 320	1 058 692	992 628	217	2 122 965	1 097 723	1 025 242	229
Naihati	CDFC	215 432	113 706	101 726	4	...	...	...	...
Nala Sopara	CDFC	184 664	99 629	85 035	...	...	...	...	...
Nalgonda	CDFC	110 651	56 495	54 156	...	111 745	57 042	54 703	...
Nanded	CDFC	430 598	224 766	205 832	21	...	...	...	...
Nandyal	CDFC	151 771	76 914	74 857	15	156 216	79 145	77 071	...
Nangloi Jat	CDFC	150 371	82 358	68 013	...	...	...	...	...
Nashik	CDFC	1 076 967	579 638	497 329	259	1 152 048	619 962	532 086	322
Navghar-Manikpur	CDFC	116 700	61 806	54 894	...	...	...	...	...
Navi Mumbai (New Bombay)	CDFC	703 947	395 891	308 056	...	...	...	...	...
Navsari	CDFC	134 009	69 766	64 243	...	229 323	122 335	106 988	...
Neemuch	CDFC	107 496	56 509	50 987	...	112 691	59 250	53 441	...
Nellore	CDFC	378 947	191 283	187 664	48	404 922	204 269	200 653	...
NEW DELHI[56,57]	CDFC	294 783	161 596	133 187	...	...	...	...	...
Neyveli	CDFC	128 133	65 632	62 501	97	138 387	70 920	67 467	116
Nizamabad	CDFC	286 956	145 457	141 499	37	...	...	...	...
Noida	CDFC	293 908	162 306	131 602	90	...	...	...	...
North Barrackpur	CDFC	123 523	63 827	59 696	...	...	...	...	...
North Dumdum	CDFC	220 032	112 868	107 164	...	...	...	...	...
Ongole	CDFC	149 589	76 134	73 455	8	152 945	77 862	75 083	20
Orai	CDFC	139 444	74 974	64 470	...	...	...	...	...
Ozhukarai	CDFC	217 623	110 038	107 585	...	...	...	...	...
Palakkad	CDFC	130 736	64 293	66 443	30	197 281	96 790	100 491	59
Palanpur	CDFC	110 383	58 019	52 364	...	122 279	64 343	57 936	...
Pali	CDFC	187 571	99 258	88 313	84	...	...	...	...
Pallavaram	CDFC	143 984	73 152	70 832	...	...	...	...	...

8. Population of capital cities and cities of 100 000 or more inhabitants: latest available year, 1986 - 2005
Population des capitales et des villes de 100 000 habitants ou plus: dernière année disponible, 1986 - 2005
(continued — suite)

Continent, country or area, date and city — Continent, pays ou zone, date et ville	Code[1]	City proper — Ville proprement dite Population				Urban agglomeration — Agglomération urbaine Population			
		Both sexes Les deux sexes	Male Masculin	Female Féminin	Surface area Superficie (km²)	Both sexes Les deux sexes	Male Masculin	Female Féminin	Surface area Superficie (km²)
ASIA — ASIE									
India — Inde[53]									
1 III 2001									
Palwal	CDFC	100 528	53 577	46 951	...	...	...	...	...
Panchkula Urban Estate	CDFC	140 992	75 925	65 067	...	...	...	...	...
Panihati	CDFC	348 379	180 068	168 311	19	...	...	...	...
Panipat	CDFC	261 665	143 565	118 100	21	353 983	194 697	159 286	...
Panvel	CDFC	104 031	54 967	49 064	...	...	...	...	...
Parbhani	CDFC	259 170	133 892	125 278	58	...	...	...	...
Patan	CDFC	112 038	59 031	53 007	...	113 568	59 889	53 679	...
Pathankot	CDFC	159 559	87 505	72 054	...	168 275	91 998	76 277	...
Patiala	CDFC	302 870	162 465	140 405	...	323 309	173 412	149 897	...
Patna	CDFC	1 376 950	749 868	627 082	107	1 707 429	925 857	781 572	129
Phagwara	CDFC	...	...	...	...	102 111	55 224	46 887	...
Phusro	CDFC	...	...	...	...	174 367	93 656	80 711	84
Pilibhit	CDFC	124 082	65 824	58 258	10	...	...	...	...
Pimpri Chinchwad	CDFC	1 006 417	543 436	462 981	...	...	...	...	...
Pollachi	CDFC	...	...	...	...	127 993	64 417	63 576	43
Pondicherry	CDFC	220 749	109 386	111 363	20	505 715	253 336	252 379	67
Porbandar	CDFC	133 083	68 261	64 822	...	197 414	101 882	95 532	...
Port Blair	CDFC	100 186	55 507	44 679	...	...	...	...	...
Proddatur	CDFC	164 932	82 826	82 106	7	...	...	...	...
Pudukkottai	CDFC	108 947	54 537	54 410	...	...	...	...	...
Pune	CDFC	2 540 069	1 325 694	1 214 375	146	3 755 525	1 980 941	1 774 584	423
Puri	CDFC	157 610	82 229	75 381	17	...	...	...	...
Purnia	CDFC	171 235	92 573	78 662	45	196 757	106 051	90 706	60
Puruliya	CDFC	113 766	59 171	54 595	...	...	...	...	...
Quthbullapur	CDFC	225 816	118 463	107 353	...	...	...	...	...
Rae Bareli	CDFC	169 285	88 961	80 324	50	...	...	...	...
Raichur	CDFC	205 634	105 714	99 920	...	...	...	...	...
Raiganj	CDFC	165 222	87 489	77 733	11	175 064	92 742	82 322	15
Raigarh	CDFC	110 987	57 465	53 522	...	115 740	59 916	55 824	...
Raipur	CDFC	605 131	314 369	290 762	...	699 264	364 034	335 230	64
Rajahmundry	CDFC	313 347	158 027	155 320	52	408 341	205 655	202 686	64
Rajapalayam	CDFC	121 982	61 080	60 902	11	...	...	...	...
Rajarhat Gopalpur	CDFC	271 781	140 179	131 602	...	...	...	...	...
Rajkot	CDFC	966 642	506 915	459 727	...	1 002 160	525 797	476 363	...
Rajnandgaon	CDFC	143 727	72 964	70 763	93	...	...	...	...
Rajpur Sonarpur	CDFC	336 390	173 591	162 799	...	...	...	...	...
Ramagundam	CDFC	235 540	120 307	115 233	28	236 623	120 871	115 752	...
Rampur	CDFC	281 549	146 621	134 928	20	...	...	...	...
Ranaghat	CDFC	...	...	...	...	145 172	73 804	71 368	25
Ranchi	CDFC	846 454	450 514	395 940	177	862 850	459 251	403 599	182
Raniganj	CDFC	122 891	65 360	57 531	...	...	...	...	...
Ratlam	CDFC	221 267	113 982	107 285	39	233 480	120 473	113 007	41
Raurkela	CDFC	224 601	121 028	103 573	133	484 292	258 466	225 826	157
Rewa	CDFC	183 232	98 476	84 756	55	...	...	...	...
Rewari	CDFC	100 946	54 111	46 835	...	...	...	...	...
Rishra	CDFC	113 259	62 602	50 657	...	...	...	...	...
Robertson Pet	CDFC	141 294	70 568	70 726	...	156 961	78 574	78 387	...
Rohtak	CDFC	286 773	154 153	132 620	28	294 537	158 299	136 238	...
Roorkee	CDFC	...	...	...	...	114 811	63 861	50 950	...
S.A.S. Nagar (Mohali)	CDFC	123 284	65 570	57 714	...	...	...	...	...
Sagar	CDFC	232 321	122 491	109 830	36	309 164	163 018	146 146	52
Saharanpur	CDFC	452 925	239 456	213 469	25	...	...	...	...
Saharasa	CDFC	124 015	67 010	57 005	...	...	...	...	...
Salem	CDFC	693 236	352 770	340 466	20	748 513	381 042	367 471	93
Sambalpur	CDFC	154 164	79 914	74 250	50	226 966	117 954	109 012	90
Sambhal	CDFC	182 930	97 264	85 666	16	...	...	...	...
Sangli-Miraj-Kupwad	CDFC	436 639	224 195	212 444	...	447 632	229 852	217 780	...
Santipur	CDFC	138 195	70 084	68 111	25	...	...	...	...
Sasaram	CDFC	131 042	69 665	61 377	...	...	...	...	...
Satara	CDFC	108 043	55 935	52 108	...	...	...	...	...

8. Population of capital cities and cities of 100 000 or more inhabitants: latest available year, 1986 - 2005
Population des capitales et des villes de 100 000 habitants ou plus: dernière année disponible, 1986 - 2005
(continued — suite)

Continent, country or area, date and city / Continent, pays ou zone, date et ville	Code[1]	City proper — Ville proprement dite Population				Urban agglomeration — Agglomération urbaine Population			
		Both sexes Les deux sexes	Male Masculin	Female Féminin	Surface area Superficie (km²)	Both sexes Les deux sexes	Male Masculin	Female Féminin	Surface area Superficie (km²)
ASIA — ASIE									
India — Inde[53]									
1 III 2001									
Satna	CDFC	225 468	120 203	105 265	...	229 323	122 335	106 988	...
Sawai Madhopur	CDFC	...	...	...	...	101 994	53 942	48 052	...
Secunderabad	CDFC	204 182	103 274	100 908	...	...	...	...	...
Serampore	CDFC	197 955	105 613	92 342	6	...	...	...	...
Serilingampalle	CDFC	150 525	75 462	75 063	...	...	...	...	...
Shahjahanpur	CDFC	297 932	162 796	135 136	13	323 166	176 910	146 256	23
Shillong	CDFC	132 876	66 129	66 747	10	267 881	134 416	133 465	25
Shimla	CDFC	142 161	80 772	61 389	32	144 578	82 424	62 154	35
Shimoga	CDFC	274 105	140 107	133 998	...	...	...	...	...
Shivapuri	CDFC	146 859	78 395	68 464	81	...	...	...	...
Sikar	CDFC	184 904	96 327	88 577	23	185 506	96 646	88 860	...
Silchar	CDFC	142 393	72 727	69 666	16	184 285	94 321	89 964	...
Siliguri	CDFC	470 275	249 942	220 333	16	...	...	...	...
Singrauli	CDFC	185 580	100 342	85 238	...	...	...	...	...
Sirsa	CDFC	160 129	85 802	74 327	19	...	...	...	...
Sitapur	CDFC	151 827	79 682	72 145	26	...	...	...	...
Sivakasi	CDFC	...	...	...	...	121 312	60 923	60 389	13
Siwan	CDFC	108 172	57 223	50 949	...	...	...	...	...
Solapur	CDFC	873 037	444 885	428 152	...	...	...	...	...
Sonipat	CDFC	216 213	117 654	98 559	28	225 151	122 488	102 663	...
South Dum Dum	CDFC	392 150	200 182	191 968	11	...	...	...	...
Srikakulam	CDFC	109 666	54 788	54 878	...	117 066	58 613	58 453	...
Srinagar	CDFC	894 940	481 750	413 190	...	971 357	523 017	448 340	...
Sultan Pur Majra	CDFC	163 716	88 313	75 403	...	...	...	...	...
Sultanpur	CDFC	100 085	53 163	46 922	...	...	...	...	...
Surat	CDFC	2 433 787	1 372 307	1 061 480	...	2 811 466	1 597 093	1 214 373	...
Surendranagar Dudhrej	CDFC	156 417	81 430	74 987	...	...	...	...	...
Tadepalligudem	CDFC	102 303	50 476	51 827	...	...	...	...	...
Tambaram	CDFC	137 609	70 181	67 428	...	...	...	...	...
Tenali	CDFC	149 839	74 868	74 971	15	...	...	...	...
Thane	CDFC	1 261 517	674 660	586 857	144	...	...	...	...
Thanesar	CDFC	120 072	65 786	54 286	...	122 704	67 239	55 465	...
Thanjavur	CDFC	215 725	106 950	108 775	15	...	...	...	...
Thiruvananthapuram	CDFC	744 739	365 899	378 840	142	889 191	437 009	452 182	178
Thoothukkudi (Tuticorin)	CDFC	216 058	107 781	108 277	13	242 860	121 205	121 655	140
Thrissur	CDFC	317 474	154 188	163 286	...	330 067	160 386	169 681	88
Tinsukia	CDFC	...	...	...	...	108 102	59 515	48 587	...
Tiruchchirappalli	CDFC	746 062	373 541	372 521	23	847 131	424 541	422 590	166
Tirunelveli	CDFC	411 298	203 173	208 125	15	431 603	213 399	218 204	87
Tirupati	CDFC	227 657	117 786	109 871	16	302 678	154 845	147 833	20
Tiruppur	CDFC	346 551	180 629	165 922	44	542 787	282 872	259 915	91
Tiruvannamalai	CDFC	130 301	66 026	64 275	14	...	...	...	...
Tiruvottiyur	CDFC	211 768	108 938	102 830	...	...	...	...	...
Titagarh	CDFC	124 198	70 608	53 590	·3	...	...	...	...
Tonk	CDFC	135 663	70 135	65 528	...	...	...	...	...
Tumkur	CDFC	248 592	129 215	119 377	...	...	...	...	...
Udaipur	CDFC	389 317	205 319	183 998	64	...	...	...	...
Udupi	CDFC	113 039	55 933	57 106	...	127 060	62 644	64 416	73
Ujjain	CDFC	429 933	223 745	206 188	...	430 669	224 223	206 446	92
Ulhasnagar	CDFC	472 943	251 610	221 333	22	...	...	...	...
Uluberia	CDFC	202 095	105 735	96 360	...	...	...	...	...
Unnao	CDFC	144 917	76 474	68 443	16	...	...	...	...
Uppal Kalan	CDFC	118 259	61 299	56 960	...	...	...	...	...
Uttarpara Kotrung	CDFC	150 204	78 661	71 543	...	...	...	...	...
Vadakara	CDFC	...	...	...	...	123 965	59 743	64 222	39
Vadodara	CDFC	1 306 035	684 130	621 905	...	1 492 398	783 237	709 161	...
Valsad	CDFC	...	...	...	...	145 650	75 322	70 328	...
Vaniyambadi	CDFC	...	...	...	...	103 841	51 668	52 173	...
Varanasi	CDFC	1 100 748	584 514	516 234	83	1 211 749	644 922	566 827	105
Vasai	CDFC	...	...	...	...	174 382	91 121	83 261	...

8. Population of capital cities and cities of 100 000 or more inhabitants: latest available year, 1986 - 2005
Population des capitales et des villes de 100 000 habitants ou plus: dernière année disponible, 1986 - 2005
(continued — suite)

Continent, country or area, date and city / Continent, pays ou zone, date et ville	Code[1]	City proper — Ville proprement dite Population				Urban agglomeration — Agglomération urbaine Population			
		Both sexes Les deux sexes	Male Masculin	Female Féminin	Surface area Superficie (km²)	Both sexes Les deux sexes	Male Masculin	Female Féminin	Surface area Superficie (km²)
ASIA — ASIE									
India — Inde[53]									
1 III 2001									
Vejalpur	CDFC	113 304	58 828	54 476	...	...	...	...	...
Vellore	CDFC	177 413	88 048	89 365	12	388 211	193 779	194 432	62
Veraval	CDFC	141 207	72 074	69 133	...	157 869	80 813	77 056	...
Vidisha	CDFC	125 457	66 579	58 878	...	...	...	...	...
Vijayawada	CDFC	825 436	436 366	389 070	...	1 011 152	531 084	480 068	105
Virar	CDFC	118 945	63 762	55 183	...	...	...	...	...
Visakhapatnam	CDFC	969 608	489 038	480 570	78	1 329 472	674 080	655 392	318
Vizianagarm	CDFC	174 324	86 111	88 213	21	195 462	96 771	98 691	30
Wadhwan	CDFC	...	...	...	...	219 828	114 217	105 611	...
Warangal	CDFC	528 570	267 820	260 750	57	577 190	292 709	284 481	67
Wardha	CDFC	111 070	57 447	53 623	8	...	...	...	...
Yamunanagar	CDFC	189 587	101 888	87 699	16	306 640	166 324	140 316	42
Yavatmal	CDFC	122 906	62 838	60 068	10	141 970	72 883	69 087	13
Indonesia — Indonésie									
1 VII 2003									
Ambon	ESDF	224 160	...	...	359	...	...	...	...
Balikpapan	ESDF	429 568	...	...	503	...	...	...	...
Banda Aceh	ESDF	269 943	...	...	61	...	...	...	...
Bandar Lampung	ESDF	789 755	...	...	193	...	...	...	...
Bandjarmasin	ESDF	567 345	...	...	72	...	...	...	...
Bandung	ESDF	2 231 139	...	...	1 670	...	...	...	...
Batam	ESDF	547 550	...	...	969	...	...	...	...
Bengkulu	ESDF	254 693	...	...	145	...	...	...	...
Binjai	ESDF	226 468	...	...	9	...	...	...	...
Bitung	ESDF	163 074	...	...	304	...	...	...	...
Blitar	ESDF	123 327	...	...	33	...	...	...	...
Bogor	ESDF	816 911	...	...	119	...	...	...	...
Cirebon	ESDF	273 311	...	...	37	...	...	...	...
Denpasar	ESDF	502 873	...	...	124	...	...	...	...
Gorontalo	ESDF	145 828	...	...	65	...	...	...	...
JAKARTA	ESDF	8 640 184	...	...	740	...	...	...	...
Jambi	ESDF	444 551	...	...	205	...	...	...	...
Jayapura	ESDF	192 961	...	...	740	...	...	...	...
Kediri	ESDF	252 126	...	...	63	...	...	...	...
Madiun	ESDF	170 408	...	...	34	...	...	...	...
Magelang	ESDF	121 079	...	...	18	...	...	...	...
Makasar (Ujung Pandang)	ESDF	1 151 245	...	...	199	...	...	...	...
Malang	ESDF	770 483	...	...	145	...	...	...	...
Manado	ESDF	412 425	...	...	157	...	...	...	...
Mataram	ESDF	341 770	...	...	61	...	...	...	...
Medan	ESDF	1 983 659	...	...	265	...	...	...	...
Mojokerto	ESDF	112 137	...	...	16	...	...	...	...
Padang	ESDF	770 451	...	...	694	...	...	...	...
Pekalongan	ESDF	272 208	...	...	45	...	...	...	...
Pakanbaru	ESDF	672 480	...	...	632	...	...	...	...
Palangkaraya	ESDF	166 017	...	...	2 400	...	...	...	...
Palembang	ESDF	1 290 599	...	...	369	...	...	...	...
Pangkal Pinang	ESDF	158 163	...	...	89	...	...	...	...
Pare Pare	ESDF	113 290	...	...	99	...	...	...	...
Pasuruan	ESDF	176 987	...	...	35	...	...	...	...
Pematang Siantar	ESDF	224 446	...	...	80	...	...	...	...
Pontianak	ESDF	483 224	...	...	108	...	...	...	...
Probolinggo	ESDF	200 465	...	...	57	...	...	...	...
Salatiga	ESDF	160 592	...	...	57	...	...	...	...
Samarinda	ESDF	563 570	...	...	781	...	...	...	...
Semarang	ESDF	1 396 059	...	...	374	...	...	...	...
Sukabumi	ESDF	269 987	...	...	48	...	...	...	...
Surabaya	ESDF	2 689 728	...	...	351	...	...	...	...
Surakarta	ESDF	492 325	...	...	44	...	...	...	...
Tangerang	ESDF	1 471 396	...	...	187	...	...	...	...

8. Population of capital cities and cities of 100 000 or more inhabitants: latest available year, 1986 - 2005
Population des capitales et des villes de 100 000 habitants ou plus: dernière année disponible, 1986 - 2005
(continued — suite)

Continent, country or area, date and city — Continent, pays ou zone, date et ville	Code[1]	City proper — Ville proprement dite Population				Urban agglomeration — Agglomération urbaine Population			
		Both sexes Les deux sexes	Male Masculin	Female Féminin	Surface area Superficie (km²)	Both sexes Les deux sexes	Male Masculin	Female Féminin	Surface area Superficie (km²)
ASIA — ASIE									
Indonesia — Indonésie									
1 VII 2003									
Tanjung Balai	ESDF	145 572	...	...	68	...	...	...	...
Tebing Tinggi	ESDF	132 982	...	...	32	...	...	...	...
Tegal	ESDF	242 423	...	...	35	...	...	...	...
Yogyakarta	ESDF	392 239	...	...	33	...	...	...	...
Iran (Islamic Republic of) — Iran (République islamique d')									
1 VII 2003									
Abadan	ESDJ	277 998	...	...	...	...	...	...	...
Ahwaz	ESDJ	949 054	...	...	...	...	...	...	...
Amol	ESDJ	195 588	...	...	...	...	...	...	...
Andimeshk	ESDJ	133 932	...	...	...	...	...	...	...
Arak	ESDJ	476 568	...	...	...	...	...	...	...
Ardabil	ESDJ	390 682	...	...	...	...	...	...	...
Babol	ESDJ	196 569	...	...	...	...	...	...	...
Bandar-e-Abbas	ESDJ	315 075	...	...	...	...	...	...	...
Birjand	ESDJ	186 893	...	...	...	...	...	...	...
Bojnurd	ESDJ	182 465	...	...	...	...	...	...	...
Borujerd	ESDJ	244 205	...	...	...	...	...	...	...
Bukand	ESDJ	173 005	...	...	...	...	...	...	...
Bushehr	ESDJ	150 411	...	...	...	...	...	...	...
Dezful	ESDJ	241 544	...	...	...	...	...	...	...
Esfahan	ESDJ	1 523 006	...	...	...	...	...	...	...
Gonbad-e-Kavus	ESDJ	125 215	...	...	...	...	...	...	...
Gorgan	ESDJ	241 085	...	...	...	...	...	...	...
Hamadan	ESDJ	494 378	...	...	...	...	...	...	...
Ilam	ESDJ	141 915	...	...	...	...	...	...	...
Islam Shahr (Qasemabad)	ESDJ	273 520	...	...	...	...	...	...	...
Karaj	ESDJ	1 212 220	...	...	...	...	...	...	...
Kashan	ESDJ	244 877	...	...	...	...	...	...	...
Kerman	ESDJ	529 748	...	...	...	...	...	...	...
Kermanshah	ESDJ	816 428	...	...	...	...	...	...	...
Khomeini shahr	ESDJ	181 110	...	...	...	...	...	...	...
Khoramabad	ESDJ	313 177	...	...	...	...	...	...	...
Khoramshahr	ESDJ	142 506	...	...	...	...	...	...	...
Khoy	ESDJ	166 974	...	...	...	...	...	...	...
Mahabad	ESDJ	137 173	...	...	...	...	...	...	...
Malayer	ESDJ	169 060	...	...	...	...	...	...	...
Marvadsht	ESDJ	125 072	...	...	...	...	...	...	...
Maraqeh	ESDJ	155 350	...	...	...	...	...	...	...
Mashhad	ESDJ	2 070 604	...	...	...	...	...	...	...
Masjed Soleyman	ESDJ	132 496	...	...	...	...	...	...	...
Najafabad	ESDJ	204 637	...	...	...	...	...	...	...
Neyshabur	ESDJ	205 842	...	...	...	...	...	...	...
Orumiyeh	ESDJ	601 478	...	...	...	...	...	...	...
Qaem shahr	ESDJ	168 359	...	...	...	...	...	...	...
Qazvin	ESDJ	306 984	...	...	...	...	...	...	...
Qarchak	ESDJ	165 462	...	...	...	...	...	...	...
Qods	ESDJ	236 463	...	...	...	...	...	...	...
Qom	ESDJ	986 922	...	...	...	...	...	...	...
Rasht	ESDJ	519 481	...	...	...	...	...	...	...
Sabzewar	ESDJ	215 278	...	...	...	...	...	...	...
Sanandaj	ESDJ	327 969	...	...	...	...	...	...	...
Saqez	ESDJ	148 445	...	...	...	...	...	...	...
Sari	ESDJ	253 052	...	...	...	...	...	...	...
Shahr Kord	ESDJ	121 337	...	...	...	...	...	...	...
Shahrud	ESDJ	128 642	...	...	...	...	...	...	...
Shiraz	ESDJ	1 197 847	...	...	...	...	...	...	...
Sirjan	ESDJ	197 303	...	...	...	...	...	...	...
Tabriz	ESDJ	1 365 476	...	...	...	...	...	...	...
TEHRAN	ESDJ	7 188 936	...	...	...	...	...	...	...

8. Population of capital cities and cities of 100 000 or more inhabitants: latest available year, 1986 - 2005
Population des capitales et des villes de 100 000 habitants ou plus: dernière année disponible, 1986 - 2005
(continued — suite)

Continent, country or area, date and city Continent, pays ou zone, date et ville	Code[1]	City proper — Ville proprement dite Population				Urban agglomeration — Agglomération urbaine Population			
		Both sexes Les deux sexes	Male Masculin	Female Féminin	Surface area Superficie (km²)	Both sexes Les deux sexes	Male Masculin	Female Féminin	Surface area Superficie (km²)
ASIA — ASIE									
Iran (Islamic Republic of) — Iran (République islamique d')									
1 VII 2003									
Varamin	ESDJ	*187 178*	...	...	...	...	...	...	...
Yazd	ESDJ	*432 233*	...	...	...	...	...	...	...
Zabol	ESDJ	*118 424*	...	...	...	...	...	...	...
Zahedan	ESDJ	*534 771*	...	...	...	...	...	...	...
Zanjan	ESDJ	*346 253*	...	...	...	...	...	...	...
Iraq									
17 X 1987									
Adhamiyah	CDFC	464 151	...	...	...	...	...	...	...
Amara	CDFC	208 797	...	...	...	...	...	...	...
BAGHDAD[58]	CDFC	3 841 268	...	...	...	...	...	...	...
Basra	CDFC	406 296	...	...	...	...	...	...	...
Diwaniya	CDFC	196 519	...	...	...	...	...	...	...
Erbil	CDFC	485 968	...	...	...	...	...	...	...
Hilla	CDFC	268 834	...	...	...	...	...	...	...
Kadhimain	CDFC	521 444	...	...	...	...	...	...	...
Karradah Sharqiyah	CDFC	235 554	...	...	...	...	...	...	...
Kerbala	CDFC	296 705	...	...	...	...	...	...	...
Kirkuk	CDFC	418 624	...	...	...	...	...	...	...
Kut	CDFC	183 183	...	...	...	...	...	...	...
Majnoon	CDFC	244 545	...	...	...	...	...	...	...
Mosul	CDFC	664 221	...	...	...	...	...	...	...
Najaf	CDFC	309 010	...	...	...	...	...	...	...
Nasariya	CDFC	265 937	...	...	...	...	...	...	...
Ramadi	CDFC	192 556	...	...	...	...	...	...	...
Sulamaniya	CDFC	364 096	...	...	...	...	...	...	...
Israel — Israël									
1 VII 2005									
Ashdod	ESDJ	198 800	97 600	101 200	47	...	...	...	...
Ashqelon	ESDJ	105 800	51 500	54 300	48	...	...	...	...
Bat Yam	ESDJ	130 000	61 400	68 600	8	...	...	...	...
Be'er Sheva	ESDJ	184 800	89 900	94 900	53	...	...	...	...
Bene Beraq	ESDJ	143 700	72 000	71 700	7	...	...	...	...
Haifa	ESDJ	267 600	128 500	139 100	64	...	...	...	...
Holon	ESDJ	166 000	79 900	86 100	19	...	...	...	...
JERUSALEM[59,60]	ESDJ	713 200	355 000	358 200	125	...	...	...	...
Netanya	ESDJ	170 400	82 200	88 200	29	...	...	...	...
Petah Tiqwa	ESDJ	177 800	86 100	91 700	36	...	...	...	...
Ramat Gan	ESDJ	127 900	60 000	67 900	13	...	...	...	...
Rehovot	ESDJ	102 500	50 000	52 500	23	...	...	...	...
Rishon Leziyyon	ESDJ	218 400	106 400	112 000	59	...	...	...	...
Tel Aviv-Yafo	ESDJ	375 200	180 400	194 800	52	...	...	...	...
Japan — Japon[61,62,63]									
1 VII 2004									
Abiko	ESDF	131 630	65 294	66 336	43	...	...	...	...
Ageo	ESDF	219 072	109 631	109 441	46	...	...	...	...
Aizuwakamatsu	ESDF	116 082	55 254	60 828	315	...	...	...	...
Akashi	ESDF	292 456	142 310	150 146	49	...	...	...	...
Akishima	ESDF	109 726	55 308	54 418	17	...	...	...	...
Akita	ESDF	318 112	151 496	166 616	460	...	...	...	...
Amagasaki	ESDF	462 442	225 320	237 122	50	...	...	...	...
Anjo	ESDF	166 080	84 326	81 754	86	...	...	...	...
Aomori	ESDF	295 084	138 831	156 253	692	...	...	...	...
Asahikawa	ESDF	361 549	170 589	190 960	748	...	...	...	...
Asaka	ESDF	126 867	66 197	60 670	18	...	...	...	...
Ashikaga	ESDF	160 891	78 609	82 282	178	...	...	...	...
Atsugi	ESDF	222 070	115 526	106 544	94	...	...	...	...
Beppu	ESDF	126 804	57 119	69 685	125	...	...	...	...
Chiba	ESDF	917 917	460 985	456 932	272	...	...	...	...
Chigasaki	ESDF	227 322	112 246	115 076	36	...	...	...	...

8. Population of capital cities and cities of 100 000 or more inhabitants: latest available year, 1986 - 2005
Population des capitales et des villes de 100 000 habitants ou plus: dernière année disponible, 1986 - 2005
(continued — suite)

Continent, country or area, date and city / Continent, pays ou zone, date et ville	Code[1]	City proper — Ville proprement dite Population				Urban agglomeration — Agglomération urbaine Population			
		Both sexes Les deux sexes	Male Masculin	Female Féminin	Surface area Superficie (km²)	Both sexes Les deux sexes	Male Masculin	Female Féminin	Surface area Superficie (km²)
ASIA — ASIE									
Japan — Japon[61,62,63]									
1 VII 2004									
Chofu	ESDF	213 748	107 915	105 833	22	...	...	...	...
Daito	ESDF	128 453	64 259	64 194	18	...	...	...	...
Ebetsu	ESDF	123 912	59 752	64 160	188	...	...	...	...
Ebina	ESDF	123 051	62 624	60 427	26	...	...	...	...
Fuchu	ESDF	240 599	125 628	114 971	29	...	...	...	...
Fuji	ESDF	237 642	117 759	119 883	214	...	...	...	...
Fujieda	ESDF	129 594	63 402	66 192	141	...	...	...	...
Fujimi	ESDF	105 110	52 734	52 376	20	...	...	...	...
Fujinomiya	ESDF	122 313	60 246	62 067	315	...	...	...	...
Fujisawa	ESDF	392 679	196 632	196 047	70	...	...	...	...
Fukaya	ESDF	103 647	51 670	51 977	69	...	...	...	...
Fukui	ESDF	252 321	122 757	129 564	341	...	...	...	...
Fukuoka	ESDF	1 390 182	668 435	721 747	339	...	...	...	...
Fukushima	ESDF	290 707	140 337	150 370	746	...	...	...	...
Fukuyama	ESDF	406 221	196 371	209 850	364	...	...	...	...
Funabashi	ESDF	567 661	287 892	279 769	86	...	...	...	...
Gifu	ESDF	405 003	191 654	213 349	195	...	...	...	...
Habikino	ESDF	119 645	57 226	62 419	26	...	...	...	...
Hachinohe	ESDF	241 065	116 010	125 055	214	...	...	...	...
Hachioji	ESDF	552 927	281 167	271 760	186	...	...	...	...
Hadano	ESDF	168 472	86 783	81 689	104	...	...	...	...
Hakodate	ESDF	282 978	130 386	152 592	347	...	...	...	...
Hamamatsu	ESDF	598 038	297 989	300 049	257	...	...	...	...
Handa	ESDF	113 858	56 393	57 465	47	...	...	...	...
Higashihiroshima	ESDF	130 265	66 884	63 381	288	...	...	...	...
Higashikurume	ESDF	114 347	56 691	57 656	13	...	...	...	...
Higashimurayama	ESDF	145 654	72 000	73 654	17	...	...	...	...
Higashiosaka	ESDF	513 327	252 360	260 967	62	...	...	...	...
Hikone	ESDF	109 258	53 803	55 455	98	...	...	...	...
Himeji	ESDF	481 043	231 224	249 819	276	...	...	...	...
Hino	ESDF	174 028	89 370	84 658	28	...	...	...	...
Hirakata	ESDF	405 833	196 163	209 670	65	...	...	...	...
Hiratsuka	ESDF	256 621	130 007	126 614	68	...	...	...	...
Hirosaki	ESDF	174 159	79 928	94 231	274	...	...	...	...
Hiroshima	ESDF	1 143 463	554 241	589 222	742	...	...	...	...
Hitachi	ESDF	188 745	94 221	94 524	153	...	...	...	...
Hitachinaka	ESDF	153 114	77 021	76 093	99	...	...	...	...
Hofu	ESDF	118 496	57 269	61 227	189	...	...	...	...
Ibaraki	ESDF	266 574	131 118	135 456	77	...	...	...	...
Ichihara	ESDF	280 104	143 570	136 534	368	...	...	...	...
Ichikawa	ESDF	465 292	240 201	225 091	57	...	...	...	...
Ichinomiya	ESDF	279 524	136 650	142 874	82	...	...	...	...
Iida	ESDF	107 108	50 988	56 120	325	...	...	...	...
Ikeda	ESDF	100 987	49 444	51 543	22	...	...	...	...
Ikoma	ESDF	113 091	53 806	59 285	53	...	...	...	...
Imabari	ESDF	116 750	54 111	62 639	75	...	...	...	...
Inazawa	ESDF	101 523	50 583	50 940	48	...	...	...	...
Iruma	ESDF	150 362	74 656	75 706	45	...	...	...	...
Isehara	ESDF	100 504	51 564	48 940	56	...	...	...	...
Isesaki	ESDF	124 547	61 895	62 652	65	...	...	...	...
Ishinomaki	ESDF	117 607	56 709	60 898	137	...	...	...	...
Itami	ESDF	193 142	95 051	98 091	25	...	...	...	...
Iwaki	ESDF	356 444	173 466	182 978	1 231	...	...	...	...
Iwakuni	ESDF	104 113	49 531	54 582	221	...	...	...	...
Iwatsuki	ESDF	109 995	55 185	54 810	49	...	...	...	...
Izumi (Osaka)	ESDF	177 654	86 360	91 294	85	...	...	...	...
Joetsu	ESDF	135 624	66 150	69 474	249	...	...	...	...
Kadoma	ESDF	133 363	66 233	67 130	12	...	...	...	...
Kagoshima	ESDF	554 984	258 841	296 143	290	...	...	...	...
Kakamigahara	ESDF	133 990	65 718	68 272	80	...	...	...	...

8. Population of capital cities and cities of 100 000 or more inhabitants: latest available year, 1986 - 2005
Population des capitales et des villes de 100 000 habitants ou plus: dernière année disponible, 1986 - 2005
(continued — suite)

Continent, country or area, date and city / Continent, pays ou zone, date et ville	Code[1]	City proper — Ville proprement dite Population				Urban agglomeration — Agglomération urbaine Population			
		Both sexes Les deux sexes	Male Masculin	Female Féminin	Surface area Superficie (km²)	Both sexes Les deux sexes	Male Masculin	Female Féminin	Surface area Superficie (km²)
ASIA — ASIE									
Japan — Japon[61,62,63]									
1 VII 2004									
Kakogawa	ESDF	266 818	130 471	136 347	139	...	...	...	...
Kamagaya	ESDF	103 627	51 562	52 065	21	...	...	...	...
Kamakura	ESDF	169 597	80 926	88 671	40	...	...	...	...
Kanazawa	ESDF	456 775	222 185	234 590	468	...	...	...	...
Kariya	ESDF	138 932	72 399	66 533	50	...	...	...	...
Kashihara	ESDF	125 728	60 411	65 317	40	...	...	...	...
Kashiwa	ESDF	333 789	166 436	167 353	73	...	...	...	...
Kasuga	ESDF	108 814	53 345	55 469	14	...	...	...	...
Kasugai	ESDF	295 517	147 696	147 821	93	...	...	...	...
Kasukabe	ESDF	203 928	101 499	102 429	38	...	...	...	...
Kawachinagano	ESDF	119 029	56 503	62 526	110	...	...	...	...
Kawagoe	ESDF	335 348	169 504	165 844	109	...	...	...	...
Kawaguchi	ESDF	480 494	245 044	235 450	56	...	...	...	...
Kawanishi	ESDF	157 107	74 831	82 276	53	...	...	...	...
Kawasaki	ESDF	1 305 264	675 702	629 562	143	...	...	...	...
Kiryu	ESDF	112 125	54 200	57 925	137	...	...	...	...
Kisarazu	ESDF	122 900	61 519	61 381	139	...	...	...	...
Kishiwada	ESDF	202 209	97 528	104 681	72	...	...	...	...
Kitakyushu[64]	ESDF	1 000 490	471 789	528 701	485	...	...	...	...
Kitami	ESDF	111 049	53 800	57 249	421	...	...	...	...
Kobe	ESDF	1 519 251	722 386	796 865	550	...	...	...	...
Kochi	ESDF	332 880	155 460	177 420	145	...	...	...	...
Kodaira	ESDF	183 921	91 955	91 966	20	...	...	...	...
Kofu	ESDF	194 502	95 509	98 993	172	...	...	...	...
Koganei	ESDF	114 139	57 697	56 442	11	...	...	...	...
Kokubunji	ESDF	115 778	58 285	57 493	11	...	...	...	...
Komaki	ESDF	147 333	74 548	72 785	63	...	...	...	...
Komatsu	ESDF	108 737	52 572	56 165	371	...	...	...	...
Koriyama	ESDF	339 205	167 679	171 526	757	...	...	...	...
Koshigaya	ESDF	316 332	158 596	157 736	60	...	...	...	...
Kumagaya	ESDF	156 505	78 577	77 928	85	...	...	...	...
Kumamoto	ESDF	670 385	317 226	353 159	267	...	...	...	...
Kurashiki	ESDF	435 758	210 307	225 451	299	...	...	...	...
Kure	ESDF	211 944	102 326	109 618	146	...	...	...	...
Kurume	ESDF	239 319	113 616	125 703	125	...	...	...	...
Kusatsu	ESDF	118 384	61 070	57 314	48	...	...	...	...
Kushiro	ESDF	187 844	89 906	97 938	222	...	...	...	...
Kuwana	ESDF	110 386	54 193	56 193	57	...	...	...	...
Kyoto	ESDF	1 465 984	699 954	766 030	610	...	...	...	...
Machida	ESDF	404 124	200 023	204 101	72	...	...	...	...
Maebashi	ESDF	283 366	138 715	144 651	147	...	...	...	...
Matsubara	ESDF	129 610	62 881	66 729	17	...	...	...	...
Matsudo	ESDF	474 099	238 056	236 043	61	...	...	...	...
Matsue	ESDF	152 377	73 535	78 842	221	...	...	...	...
Matsumoto	ESDF	208 799	103 189	105 610	266	...	...	...	...
Matsusaka	ESDF	126 837	61 212	65 625	210	...	...	...	...
Matsuyama	ESDF	478 606	225 506	253 100	289	...	...	...	...
Minoh	ESDF	126 773	61 160	65 613	48	...	...	...	...
Misato	ESDF	129 266	65 874	63 392	30	...	...	...	...
Mishima	ESDF	112 036	55 020	57 016	62	...	...	...	...
Mitaka	ESDF	177 516	88 792	88 724	17	...	...	...	...
Mito	ESDF	249 206	121 133	128 073	176	...	...	...	...
Miyakonojo	ESDF	132 568	62 276	70 292	306	...	...	...	...
Miyazaki	ESDF	310 078	145 479	164 599	287	...	...	...	...
Moriguchi	ESDF	147 794	72 366	75 428	13	...	...	...	...
Morioka	ESDF	288 227	137 766	150 461	489	...	...	...	...
Muroran	ESDF	100 625	48 493	52 132	81	...	...	...	...
Musashino	ESDF	136 182	65 942	70 240	11	...	...	...	...
Nagano	ESDF	361 926	175 668	186 258	404	...	...	...	...
Nagaoka	ESDF	194 622	95 455	99 167	262	...	...	...	...

8. Population of capital cities and cities of 100 000 or more inhabitants: latest available year, 1986 - 2005
Population des capitales et des villes de 100 000 habitants ou plus: dernière année disponible, 1986 - 2005
(continued — suite)

Continent, country or area, date and city / Continent, pays ou zone, date et ville	Code[1]	City proper — Ville proprement dite Population				Urban agglomeration — Agglomération urbaine Population			
		Both sexes Les deux sexes	Male Masculin	Female Féminin	Surface area Superficie (km²)	Both sexes Les deux sexes	Male Masculin	Female Féminin	Surface area Superficie (km²)
ASIA — ASIE									
Japan — Japon[61,62,63]									
1 VII 2004									
Nagareyama	ESDF	151 901	75 289	76 612	35	...	...	...	...
Nagasaki	ESDF	417 127	192 796	224 331	241	...	...	...	...
Nagoya	ESDF	2 200 793	1 092 361	1 108 432	326	...	...	...	...
Naha	ESDF	309 955	149 194	160 761	39	...	...	...	...
Nara	ESDF	363 677	172 187	191 490	212	...	...	...	...
Narashino	ESDF	158 990	80 497	78 493	21	...	...	...	...
Neyagawa	ESDF	244 810	120 278	124 532	25	...	...	...	...
Niigata	ESDF	530 323	256 628	273 695	206	...	...	...	...
Niihama	ESDF	124 416	59 376	65 040	161	...	...	...	...
Niiza	ESDF	151 693	76 331	75 362	23	...	...	...	...
Nishio	ESDF	458 464	218 046	240 418	99	...	...	...	...
Nishinomiya	ESDF	103 226	51 944	51 282	76	...	...	...	...
Nishitokyo	ESDF	187 665	93 258	94 407	16	...	...	...	...
Nobeoka	ESDF	122 471	57 240	65 231	284	...	...	...	...
Noda	ESDF	150 676	75 421	75 255	74	...	...	...	...
Numazu	ESDF	206 910	102 115	104 795	152	...	...	...	...
Obihiro	ESDF	172 054	82 896	89 158	619	...	...	...	...
Odawara	ESDF	198 930	97 859	101 071	114	...	...	...	...
Ogaki	ESDF	150 536	72 916	77 620	80	...	...	...	...
Oita	ESDF	443 468	213 613	229 855	361	...	...	...	...
Okayama	ESDF	637 265	306 531	330 734	513	...	...	...	...
Okazaki	ESDF	349 858	175 536	174 322	227	...	...	...	...
Okinawa	ESDF	125 254	60 140	65 114	49	...	...	...	...
Ome	ESDF	142 316	71 534	70 782	103	...	...	...	...
Omuta	ESDF	133 187	60 541	72 646	82	...	...	...	...
Osaka	ESDF	2 635 405	1 287 234	1 348 171	222	...	...	...	...
Ota	ESDF	144 731	73 192	71 539	98	...	...	...	...
Otaru	ESDF	145 957	66 754	79 203	243	...	...	...	...
Otsu	ESDF	299 157	145 070	154 087	302	...	...	...	...
Oyama	ESDF	158 589	79 793	78 796	172	...	...	...	...
Saga	ESDF	166 798	78 902	87 896	104	...	...	...	...
Sagamihara	ESDF	623 361	316 022	307 339	90	...	...	...	...
Saitama	ESDF	1 064 854	535 778	529 076	168	...	...	...	...
Sakai	ESDF	794 249	383 067	411 182	137	...	...	...	...
Sakura	ESDF	172 828	84 826	88 002	104	...	...	...	...
Sanda	ESDF	113 837	55 412	58 425	210	...	...	...	...
Sapporo	ESDF	1 859 400	886 246	973 154	1 121	...	...	...	...
Sasebo	ESDF	239 319	112 748	126 571	248	...	...	...	...
Sayama	ESDF	160 994	81 447	79 547	49	...	...	...	...
Sendai	ESDF	1 024 830	500 520	524 310	784	...	...	...	...
Seto	ESDF	132 063	65 324	66 739	112	...	...	...	...
Shimonoseki	ESDF	247 464	115 728	131 736	224	...	...	...	...
Shizuoka	ESDF	702 711	342 242	360 469	1 374	...	...	...	...
Shunan	ESDF	154 403	74 523	79 880	656	...	...	...	...
Soka	ESDF	233 894	119 921	113 973	27	...	...	...	...
Suita	ESDF	353 381	173 153	180 228	36	...	...	...	...
Suzuka	ESDF	192 178	95 621	96 557	195	...	...	...	...
Tachikawa	ESDF	170 756	85 316	85 440	24	...	...	...	...
Tajimi	ESDF	104 016	50 516	53 500	78	...	...	...	...
Takamatsu	ESDF	335 257	161 827	173 430	194	...	...	...	...
Takaoka	ESDF	169 698	81 378	88 320	151	...	...	...	...
Takarazuka	ESDF	219 250	102 998	116 252	102	...	...	...	...
Takasaki	ESDF	244 173	120 905	123 268	111	...	...	...	...
Takatsuki	ESDF	353 849	171 788	182 061	105	...	...	...	...
Tama	ESDF	146 534	73 563	72 971	21	...	...	...	...
Toda	ESDF	114 601	60 027	54 574	18	...	...	...	...
Tokai	ESDF	102 601	53 300	49 301	43	...	...	...	...
Tokorozawa	ESDF	336 273	168 577	167 696	72	...	...	...	...
Tokushima	ESDF	267 559	126 830	140 729	191	...	...	...	...
TOKYO[65]	ESDF	8 397 617	4 165 782	4 231 835	621	...	...	...	...

8. Population of capital cities and cities of 100 000 or more inhabitants: latest available year, 1986 - 2005
Population des capitales et des villes de 100 000 habitants ou plus: dernière année disponible, 1986 - 2005
(continued — suite)

Continent, country or area, date and city / Continent, pays ou zone, date et ville	Code[1]	City proper — Ville proprement dite Population				Urban agglomeration — Agglomération urbaine Population			
		Both sexes Les deux sexes	Male Masculin	Female Féminin	Surface area Superficie (km²)	Both sexes Les deux sexes	Male Masculin	Female Féminin	Surface area Superficie (km²)
ASIA — ASIE									
Japan — Japon[61,62,63]									
1 VII 2004									
Tomakomai	ESDF	172 664	84 382	88 282	561	...	...	...	...
Tondabayashi	ESDF	125 842	60 027	65 815	40	...	...	...	...
Tottori	ESDF	152 470	74 539	77 931	237	...	...	...	...
Toyama	ESDF	325 977	157 791	168 186	209	...	...	...	...
Toyota	ESDF	361 054	190 539	170 515	290	...	...	...	...
Toyohashi	ESDF	372 305	184 784	187 521	261	...	...	...	...
Toyokawa	ESDF	120 500	59 880	60 620	65	...	...	...	...
Toyonaka	ESDF	388 374	187 353	201 021	36	...	...	...	...
Tsu	ESDF	164 728	80 065	84 663	102	...	...	...	...
Tsuchiura	ESDF	135 460	67 134	68 326	82	...	...	...	...
Tsukuba	ESDF	198 421	101 906	96 515	260	...	...	...	...
Ube	ESDF	172 245	82 053	90 192	210	...	...	...	...
Ueda	ESDF	125 717	61 866	63 851	177	...	...	...	...
Uji	ESDF	189 704	92 572	97 132	68	...	...	...	...
Urasoe	ESDF	105 146	51 657	53 489	19	...	...	...	...
Urayasu	ESDF	151 047	77 320	73 727	17	...	...	...	...
Utsunomiya	ESDF	451 705	225 694	226 011	312	...	...	...	...
Wakayama	ESDF	380 942	179 917	201 025	209	...	...	...	...
Yachiyo	ESDF	179 091	88 741	90 350	51	...	...	...	...
Yaizu	ESDF	120 427	58 566	61 861	46	...	...	...	...
Yamagata	ESDF	255 289	122 671	132 618	381	...	...	...	...
Yamaguchi	ESDF	143 185	68 332	74 853	357	...	...	...	...
Yamato	ESDF	220 422	111 694	108 728	27	...	...	...	...
Yao	ESDF	273 283	132 779	140 504	42	...	...	...	...
Yatsushiro	ESDF	104 245	48 691	55 554	147	...	...	...	...
Yokkaichi	ESDF	295 116	145 151	149 965	197	...	...	...	...
Yokohama	ESDF	3 552 857	1 791 547	1 761 310	437	...	...	...	...
Yokosuka	ESDF	430 354	216 531	213 823	101	...	...	...	...
Yonago	ESDF	140 932	67 063	73 869	106	...	...	...	...
Zama	ESDF	129 468	66 713	62 755	18	...	...	...	...
Jordan — Jordanie									
31 XII 2003									
AMMAN	ESDF	*1 254 284*	...	...	...	...	...	...	...
Irbid	ESDF	*272 681*	...	...	...	...	...	...	...
Russiefa	ESDF	*240 630*	...	...	...	...	...	...	...
Zarqa	ESDF	*472 830*	...	...	...	...	...	...	...
Kazakhstan									
1 I 2004									
Aktau	ESDF	154 718	75 005	79 713	...	174 357	85 054	89 303	...
Aktobe	ESDF	249 759	115 677	134 082	...	280 290	130 704	149 586	...
Almaty	ESDF	1 175 208	533 470	641 738	...	1 175 208	533 470	641 738	...
ASTANA	ESDF	510 533	248 044	262 489	...	510 533	248 044	262 489	...
Atirau	ESDF	145 100	68 174	76 926	...	196 311	93 081	103 230	...
Ekibastuz	ESDF	119 488	56 096	63 392	...	140 892	66 509	74 383	...
Karaganda	ESDF	428 867	195 342	233 525	...	429 027	195 414	233 613	...
Koktshetau	ESDF	123 640	56 343	67 297	...	135 350	61 826	73 524	...
Kustanai	ESDF	204 243	92 514	111 729	...	204 243	92 514	111 729	...
Kyzylorda	ESDF	157 719	74 857	82 862	...	196 172	94 605	101 567	...
Pavlodar	ESDF	286 538	130 681	155 857	...	304 473	139 294	165 179	...
Petropavlovsk (Severo-Kazakhstanskaya oblast)	ESDF	192 320	86 328	105 992	...	193 184	86 786	106 398	...
Rudni	ESDF	104 495	48 117	56 378	...	116 630	53 961	62 669	...
Semipalatinsk	ESDF	268 998	121 813	147 185	...	297 282	135 830	161 452	...
Shimkent	ESDF	513 110	244 003	269 107	...	513 110	244 003	269 107	...
Taldykorgan	ESDF	100 577	44 882	55 695	...	122 129	55 560	66 569	...
Taraz	ESDF	327 911	150 940	176 971	...	327 911	150 940	176 971	...
Temirtau	ESDF	159 812	73 470	86 342	...	169 335	78 087	91 248	...
Uralsk	ESDF	195 811	88 484	107 327	...	224 396	102 177	122 219	...
Ust-Kamenogorsk	ESDF	294 507	132 846	161 661	...	305 053	138 004	167 049	...

8. Population of capital cities and cities of 100 000 or more inhabitants: latest available year, 1986 - 2005
Population des capitales et des villes de 100 000 habitants ou plus: dernière année disponible, 1986 - 2005
(continued — suite)

Continent, country or area, date and city / Continent, pays ou zone, date et ville	Code[1]	City proper — Ville proprement dite Population				Urban agglomeration — Agglomération urbaine Population			
		Both sexes Les deux sexes	Male Masculin	Female Féminin	Surface area Superficie (km²)	Both sexes Les deux sexes	Male Masculin	Female Féminin	Surface area Superficie (km²)
ASIA — ASIE									
Korea (Dem. People's Republic of) — Corée (Rép. populaire dém. de)									
31 XII 1993									
Chongjin	CDFC	582 480	...	...	...	...	...	...	...
Haeju	CDFC	229 172	...	...	...	...	...	...	...
Hamhung	CDFC	709 730	...	...	...	...	...	...	...
Hyesan	CDFC	178 020	...	...	...	...	...	...	...
Kaesong	CDFC	334 433	...	...	...	...	...	...	...
Kanggye	CDFC	223 410	...	...	...	...	...	...	...
Nampho	CDFC	731 448	...	...	...	...	...	...	...
Phyongsong	CDFC	272 934	...	...	...	...	...	...	...
PYONGYANG	CDFC	2 741 260	...	...	...	...	...	...	...
Sariwon	CDFC	254 146	...	...	...	...	...	...	...
Sinuiji	CDFC	326 011	...	...	...	...	...	...	...
Wonsan	CDFC	300 148	...	...	...	...	...	...	...
Korea (Republic of) — Corée (République de)									
1 XI 2000									
Andong	CDFC	182 098	89 823	92 275	1 518	...	...	...	...
Asan	CDFC	180 763	90 812	89 951		...	...	...	...
Boryeong	CDFC	109 535	55 390	54 145		...	...	...	...
Bucheon (Puchon)	CDFC	761 389	384 935	376 454	53	...	...	...	...
Busan (Pusan)	CDFC	3 662 884	1 827 062	1 835 822	748	...	...	...	...
Changwon	CDFC	517 410	265 941	251 469	293	...	...	...	...
Cheonan	CDFC	417 835	212 874	204 961	637	...	...	...	...
Cheongju	CDFC	586 700	292 144	294 556	153	...	...	...	...
Chuncheon	CDFC	252 547	125 605	126 942	1 117	...	...	...	...
Chungju	CDFC	217 927	110 540	107 387	984	...	...	...	...
Daegu (Taegu)	CDFC	2 480 578	1 247 562	1 233 016	885	...	...	...	...
Daejeon (Taejon)	CDFC	1 368 207	690 600	677 607	539	...	...	...	...
Gangneung (Kangnung)	CDFC	228 232	113 826	114 406	1 039	...	...	...	...
Geoje	CDFC	168 022	87 169	80 853		...	...	...	...
Gimcheon	CDFC	147 855	73 629	74 226	...	...	...	...	...
Gimhae (Kimhae)	CDFC	331 979	167 255	164 724	463	...	...	...	...
Gimje	CDFC	102 589	50 067	52 522	...	...	...	...	...
Gongju	CDFC	130 376	64 537	65 839		...	...	...	...
Goyang	CDFC	763 971	381 072	382 899	...	...	...	...	...
Gumi (Kumi)	CDFC	341 550	173 253	168 297	127	...	...	...	...
Gunpo (Kunpo)	CDFC	263 760	133 013	130 747	36	...	...	...	...
Gunsan (Kunsan)	CDFC	272 715	138 537	134 178	388	...	...	...	...
Gwangju (Kwangchu)	CDFC	1 352 797	674 228	678 569	501	...	...	...	...
Gwangmyeong (Kwangmyong)	CDFC	334 089	167 115	166 974	38	...	...	...	...
Gwangyang	CDFC	132 639	67 629	65 010		...	...	...	...
Gyeongju (Kyongju)	CDFC	275 842	136 891	138 951	1 324	...	...	...	...
Gyeongsan	CDFC	228 206	114 162	114 044		...	...	...	...
Icheon	CDFC	179 719	88 460	91 259	...	...	...	...	...
Iksan (Iri)	CDFC	323 687	161 231	162 456	507	...	...	...	...
Incheon	CDFC	2 475 139	1 250 383	1 224 756	955	...	...	...	...
Jecheon (Chechon)	CDFC	143 710	72 855	70 855	882	...	...	...	...
Jeju (Cheju)	CDFC	279 996	138 932	141 064	255	...	...	...	...
Jeongeup	CDFC	129 152	62 902	66 250	...	...	...	...	...
Jeonju (Chonchu)	CDFC	616 468	306 661	309 807	206	...	...	...	...
Jinhae (Chinhae)	CDFC	127 578	64 317	63 261		...	...	...	...
Jinju (Chinju)	CDFC	339 791	168 576	171 215	712	...	...	...	...
Masan	CDFC	434 371	218 050	216 321	329	...	...	...	...
Miryang	CDFC	115 962	56 855	59 107		...	...	...	...
Mokpo	CDFC	250 480	125 922	124 558	46	...	...	...	...
Nonsan	CDFC	137 452	68 799	68 653	...	...	...	...	...
Pohang	CDFC	515 714	264 319	251 395	1 126	...	...	...	...
Sacheon	CDFC	111 078	55 285	55 793	...	...	...	...	...
Sangju	CDFC	116 493	57 152	59 341	...	...	...	...	...
Seongnam	CDFC	914 590	461 011	453 579	141	...	...	...	...

8. Population of capital cities and cities of 100 000 or more inhabitants: latest available year, 1986 - 2005
Population des capitales et des villes de 100 000 habitants ou plus: dernière année disponible, 1986 - 2005
(continued — suite)

Continent, country or area, date and city / Continent, pays ou zone, date et ville	Code[1]	City proper — Ville proprement dite Population				Urban agglomeration — Agglomération urbaine Population			
		Both sexes Les deux sexes	Male Masculin	Female Féminin	Surface area Superficie (km²)	Both sexes Les deux sexes	Male Masculin	Female Féminin	Surface area Superficie (km²)
ASIA — ASIE									
Korea (Republic of) — Corée (République de)									
1 XI 2000									
Seosan	CDFC	143 154	73 100	70 054	...	...	...	...	...
SEOUL	CDFC	9 895 217	4 966 993	4 928 224	605	...	...	...	...
Suncheon	CDFC	265 930	133 064	132 866	907	...	...	...	...
Suwon (Puwan)	CDFC	946 704	476 639	470 065	121	...	...	...	...
Tongyeong	CDFC	123 842	62 017	61 825	...	...	...	...	...
Uijeongbu (Eujeongbu)	CDFC	355 380	177 657	177 723	81	...	...	...	...
Ulsan	CDFC	1 014 428	522 062	492 366	1 055	...	...	...	...
Wonju	CDFC	268 352	134 901	133 451	865	...	...	...	...
Yangsan	CDFC	191 975	96 551	95 424	...	...	...	...	...
Yeongcheon	CDFC	111 392	55 176	56 216	...	...	...	...	...
Yeongju	CDFC	126 507	63 556	62 951	...	...	...	...	...
Yeosu	CDFC	303 233	152 836	150 397	45	...	...	...	...
1 VII 2003									
Busan (Pusan)	ESDF	*3 685 290*	*1 842 597*	*1 842 693*	*748*	...	...	...	...
Daegu (Taegu)	ESDF	*2 547 231*	*1 284 324*	*1 262 907*	*885*	...	...	...	...
Daejeon (Taejon)	ESDF	*1 463 009*	*740 406*	*722 603*	*539*	...	...	...	...
Gwangju (Kwangchu)	ESDF	*1 428 929*	*714 734*	*714 195*	*501*	...	...	...	...
Incheon	ESDF	*2 615 133*	*1 324 700*	*1 290 433*	*955*	...	...	...	...
Jeju (Cheju)	ESDF	*534 647*	*266 649*	*267 998*	*255*	...	...	...	...
SEOUL	ESDF	*10 024 308*	*5 044 617*	*4 979 691*	*605*	...	...	...	...
Ulsan	ESDF	*1 066 271*	*549 669*	*516 602*	*1 055*	...	...	...	...
Kuwait — Koweït									
1 VII 2004									
Hawalli	ESDF	*125 877*	*90 219*	*35 658*	...	...	...	...	...
KUWAIT CITY	ESDF	*44 424*	*36 947*	*7 477*	...	...	...	...	...
Salmiya	ESDF	*197 161*	*121 724*	*75 437*	...	...	...	...	...
Kyrgyzstan — Kirghizistan									
1 VII 2005									
BISHKEK	ESDJ	794 800	379 500	415 300	127	...	...	...	...
Osh	ESDJ	250 500	119 900	130 600	182	...	...	...	...
Lao People's Democratic Republic — République démocratique populaire lao									
1 III 1995									
VIENTIANE	CDFC	...	...	...	...	528 100	...	...	...
Malaysia — Malaisie									
14 VIII 1991									
Alor Setar	CDFC	124 412	...	...	...	164 444	...	...	...
George Town	CDFC	219 603	...	...	...	...	...	...	...
Ipoh	CDFC	382 853	...	...	...	468 841	...	...	...
Johore Bharu	CDFC	328 436	...	...	...	441 703	...	...	...
Klang	CDFC	243 355	...	...	...	368 379	...	...	...
Kota Bahru	CDFC	219 582	...	...	...	234 581	...	...	...
KUALA LUMPUR	CDFC	1 145 342	...	...	...	...	...	...	...
Kuala Terengganu	CDFC	228 119	...	...	...	...	...	...	...
Kuantan	CDFC	199 484	...	...	...	202 445	...	...	...
Petaling Jaya	CDFC	254 350	...	...	...	350 995	...	...	...
Seleyang Baru	CDFC	124 228	...	...	...	134 197	...	...	...
Seremban	CDFC	182 869	...	...	...	193 237	...	...	...
Shah Alam	CDFC	102 019	...	...	...	117 027	...	...	...
Sungai Petani	CDFC	114 763	...	...	...	116 977	...	...	...
Taiping	CDFC	183 261	...	...	...	200 324	...	...	...
Kota Kinabalu	CDFC	76 120	...	...	...	160 184	...	...	...
Sandakan	CDFC	125 841	...	...	...	156 675	...	...	...
Kuching	CDFC	148 059	...	...	...	277 905	...	...	...
Sibu	CDFC	126 381	...	...	...	133 479	...	...	...
Maldives									
31 III 2000									
MALE	CDFC	74 069	38 559	35 510	...	...	...	...	...

8. Population of capital cities and cities of 100 000 or more inhabitants: latest available year, 1986 - 2005
Population des capitales et des villes de 100 000 habitants ou plus: dernière année disponible, 1986 - 2005
(continued — suite)

Continent, country or area, date and city Continent, pays ou zone, date et ville	Code[1]	City proper — Ville proprement dite Population				Urban agglomeration — Agglomération urbaine Population			
		Both sexes Les deux sexes	Male Masculin	Female Féminin	Surface area Superficie (km²)	Both sexes Les deux sexes	Male Masculin	Female Féminin	Surface area Superficie (km²)
ASIA — ASIE									
Mongolia — Mongolie									
1 VII 2005									
ULAANBAATAR	ESDF	*946 907*	*457 614*	*489 293*	*201*	...	...	...	...
Nepal — Népal									
22 VI 2001									
Biratnagar	CDJC	166 674	87 664	79 010	58	...	...	...	...
Birgunj	CDJC	112 484	60 956	51 528	21	...	...	...	...
KATHMANDU	CDJC	671 846	360 103	311 743	49	...	...	...	...
Lalitpur	CDJC	162 991	84 502	78 489	15	...	...	...	...
Pokhara	CDJC	156 312	79 563	76 749	55	...	...	...	...
Occupied Palestinian Territory — Territoire palestinien occupé									
1 VII 2005									
Gaza	ESDF	*395 262*	...	...	...	...	...	...	...
Hebron	ESDF	*160 470*	...	...	...	...	...	...	...
Khan Yunis	ESDF	*125 823*	...	...	...	...	...	...	...
Nablus	ESDF	*130 326*	...	...	...	...	...	...	...
Oman									
7 VII 2003									
MUSCAT	CDFC	24 893	13 695	11 198	...	...	...	...	...
Salalah	CDFC	156 530	92 489	64 041	...	...	...	...	...
Pakistan[66]									
2 III 1998									
Abbotabad	CDFC	106 101	61 698	44 403	...	...	...	...	...
Bahawalnagar	CDFC	111 313	57 779	53 534	...	...	...	...	...
Bahawalpur	CDFC	408 395	222 228	186 167	...	...	...	...	...
Burewala	CDFC	152 097	78 726	73 371	...	...	...	...	...
Chiniot	CDFC	172 522	90 474	82 048	...	...	...	...	...
Chishtian	CDFC	102 287	52 427	49 860	...	...	...	...	...
Dadu	CDFC	102 550	53 508	49 042	...	...	...	...	...
Daska	CDFC	102 883	52 359	50 524	...	...	...	...	...
Dera Ghazi Khan	CDFC	190 542	98 738	91 804	...	...	...	...	...
Faisalabad (Lyallpur)	CDFC	2 008 861	1 053 085	955 776	...	...	...	...	...
Gojra	CDFC	117 872	60 598	57 294	...	...	...	...	...
Gujranwala	CDFC	1 132 509	588 512	543 997	...	...	...	...	...
Gujrat	CDFC	251 792	128 524	123 268	...	...	...	...	...
Hafizabad	CDFC	133 678	69 231	64 447	...	...	...	...	...
Hyderabad	CDFC	1 166 894	612 283	554 611	...	...	...	...	...
ISLAMABAD	CDFC	529 180	290 717	238 463	...	...	...	...	...
Jacobabad	CDFC	138 780	71 854	66 926	...	...	...	...	...
Jaranwala	CDFC	106 785	55 819	51 166	...	...	...	...	...
Jhang	CDFC	293 366	153 123	140 243	...	...	...	...	...
Jhelum	CDFC	147 392	79 169	68 223	...	...	...	...	...
Kamoke	CDFC	152 288	78 848	73 440	...	...	...	...	...
Karachi	CDFC	9 339 023	5 029 900	4 309 123	...	...	...	...	...
Kasur	CDFC	245 321	129 553	115 768	...	...	...	...	...
Khairpur	CDFC	105 637	55 358	50 279	...	...	...	...	...
Khanewal	CDFC	133 986	69 145	64 841	...	...	...	...	...
Khanpur	CDFC	120 382	62 371	58 011	...	...	...	...	...
Kohat	CDFC	126 627	71 505	55 122	...	...	...	...	...
Lahore	CDFC	5 143 495	2 707 220	2 436 275	...	...	...	...	...
Larkana	CDFC	270 283	140 622	129 661	...	...	...	...	...
Mangora	CDFC	173 868	91 742	82 126	...	...	...	...	...
Mardan	CDFC	245 926	129 247	116 679	...	...	...	...	...
Mirpur Khas	CDFC	189 671	97 940	91 731	...	...	...	...	...
Multan	CDFC	1 197 384	637 911	559 473	...	...	...	...	...
Muridke	CDFC	111 951	58 210	53 741	...	...	...	...	...
Muzaffargharh	CDFC	123 404	66 556	56 848	...	...	...	...	...
Nawabshah	CDFC	189 244	98 116	91 128	...	...	...	...	...
Okara	CDFC	201 815	104 245	97 570	...	...	...	...	...
Pakpattan	CDFC	109 033	56 676	52 357	...	...	...	...	...
Peshawar	CDFC	982 816	521 901	460 915	...	...	...	...	...

8. Population of capital cities and cities of 100 000 or more inhabitants: latest available year, 1986 - 2005
Population des capitales et des villes de 100 000 habitants ou plus: dernière année disponible, 1986 - 2005
(continued — suite)

Continent, country or area, date and city Continent, pays ou zone, date et ville	Code[1]	City proper — Ville proprement dite Population				Urban agglomeration — Agglomération urbaine Population			
		Both sexes Les deux sexes	Male Masculin	Female Féminin	Surface area Superficie (km²)	Both sexes Les deux sexes	Male Masculin	Female Féminin	Surface area Superficie (km²)
ASIA — ASIE									
Pakistan[66]									
2 III 1998									
Quetta	CDFC	565 137	307 759	257 378	...	...	...	...	...
Rahimyar Khan	CDFC	233 537	121 446	112 091	...	...	...	...	...
Rawalpindi	CDFC	1 409 768	750 530	659 238	...	...	...	...	...
Sadiqabad	CDFC	144 391	75 217	69 174	...	...	...	...	...
Sahiwal	CDFC	208 778	108 992	99 786	...	...	...	...	...
Sargodha	CDFC	458 440	239 837	218 603	...	...	...	...	...
Shakkarpur	CDFC	134 883	69 713	65 170	...	...	...	...	...
Sheikhu Pura	CDFC	280 263	146 739	133 524	...	...	...	...	...
Sialkote	CDFC	421 502	227 398	194 104	...	...	...	...	...
Sukkur	CDFC	335 551	175 679	159 872	...	...	...	...	...
Tandoadam	CDFC	104 907	54 670	50 237	...	...	...	...	...
Wah Cantonment	CDFC	198 891	104 230	94 661	...	...	...	...	...
Philippines									
1 V 2000									
Angeles	CDJC	267 788	132 972	134 816	60	...	...	...	...
Bacolod	CDJC	429 076	209 729	219 347	156	...	...	...	...
Bago	CDJC	141 721	72 777	68 944	402	...	...	...	...
Baguio	CDJC	252 386	124 208	128 178	58	...	...	...	...
Basilan	CDJC	332 828	166 413	166 415	...	...	...	...	...
Batangas	CDJC	247 588	123 740	123 848	283	...	...	...	...
Butuan	CDJC	267 279	135 735	131 544	816	...	...	...	...
Cabanatuan	CDJC	222 859	111 461	111 398	283	...	...	...	...
Cadiz	CDJC	141 954	72 701	69 253	467	...	...	...	...
Cagayan de Oro	CDJC	461 877	228 524	233 353	413	...	...	...	...
Calbayog	CDJC	147 187	75 157	72 030	...	...	...	...	...
Caloocan	CDJC	1 177 604	587 890	589 714	56	...	...	...	...
Cebu	CDJC	718 821	351 640	367 181	281	...	...	...	...
Cotabato	CDJC	163 849	79 853	83 996	144	...	...	...	...
Dagupan	CDJC	130 328	64 468	65 860	37	...	...	...	...
Davao	CDJC	1 147 116	573 242	573 874	1 211	...	...	...	...
Digos	CDJC	125 171	63 107	62 064	...	...	...	...	...
Dumaguete	CDJC	102 265	49 378	52 887	34	...	...	...	...
General Santos	CDJC	411 822	207 496	264 326	402	...	...	...	...
Gingoog	CDJC	102 379	52 302	50 077	...	...	...	...	...
Iligan	CDJC	285 061	141 641	143 420	673	...	...	...	...
Iloilo	CDJC	366 391	177 620	188 771	56	...	...	...	...
Kabankalan	CDJC	149 769	76 479	73 290	697	...	...	...	...
Kalookan (Caloocan)	CDJC	1 177 604	587 890	589 714	56	...	...	...	...
Kidapawan	CDJC	101 205	51 278	49 927	...	...	...	...	...
Koronadal	CDJC	133 786	67 493	66 293	...	...	...	...	...
Lapu-Lapu	CDJC	217 019	106 099	110 920	...	...	...	...	...
Las Piñas	CDJC	472 780	229 776	243 004	33	...	...	...	...
Legasp	CDJC	157 010	78 141	78 869	154	...	...	...	...
Lipa	CDJC	218 447	109 938	108 509	209	...	...	...	...
Lucena City	CDJC	196 075	97 380	98 695	80	...	...	...	...
Makati	CDJC	471 379	226 422	244 957	18	...	...	...	...
Malabalay	CDJC	123 672	63 381	60 291	969	...	...	...	...
Malabon	CDJC	338 855	168 587	170 268	...	...	...	...	...
Malolos	CDJC	175 291	86 600	88 691	67	...	...	...	...
Mandaue	CDJC	259 728	128 501	131 227	12	...	...	...	...
Mandaluyong	CDJC	278 474	135 287	143 187	9	...	...	...	...
MANILA	CDJC	1 581 082	770 491	810 591	614	...	...	...	...
Marawi	CDJC	131 090	63 110	67 980	23	...	...	...	...
Marikina	CDJC	391 170	191 585	199 585	22	...	...	...	...
Muntinlupa	CDJC	379 310	187 381	191 929	40	...	...	...	...
Naga	CDJC	137 810	68 040	69 770	84	...	...	...	...
Navotas	CDJC	230 403	115 697	114 706	...	...	...	...	...
Olongapo	CDJC	194 260	95 585	98 675	185	...	...	...	...
Ormoc	CDJC	154 297	78 612	75 685	...	...	...	...	...
Ozamis	CDJC	110 420	54 986	55 434	...	...	...	...	...

8. Population of capital cities and cities of 100 000 or more inhabitants: latest available year, 1986 - 2005
Population des capitales et des villes de 100 000 habitants ou plus: dernière année disponible, 1986 - 2005
(continued — suite)

Continent, country or area, date and city — Continent, pays ou zone, date et ville	Code[1]	City proper — Ville proprement dite Population				Urban agglomeration — Agglomération urbaine Population			
		Both sexes Les deux sexes	Male Masculin	Female Féminin	Surface area Superficie (km²)	Both sexes Les deux sexes	Male Masculin	Female Féminin	Surface area Superficie (km²)
ASIA — ASIE									
Philippines									
1 V 2000									
Pagadian	CDJC	142 585	71 009	71 576	332	...	...	...	...
Paranaque	CDJC	449 811	217 828	231 983	47	...	...	...	...
Pasay	CDJC	354 908	175 041	179 867	14	...	...	...	...
Pasig	CDJC	505 058	246 047	259 011	48	...	...	...	...
Puerto Princesa	CDJC	161 912	83 045	78 867	2 381	...	...	...	...
Quezon City	CDJC	2 173 831	1 064 780	1 109 051	172	...	...	...	...
Roxas	CDJC	126 352	62 542	63 810	95	...	...	...	...
Sagay City	CDJC	129 765	65 935	63 830	330	...	...	...	...
San Carlos (Negros Occidental)	CDJC	118 259	60 073	58 186	452	...	...	...	...
San Carlos (Pangasinan)	CDJC	154 264	77 652	76 612	...	...	...	...	...
San Fernando City	CDJC	221 857	111 798	110 059	68	...	...	...	...
San Juan	CDJC	117 680	54 604	63 076	6	...	...	...	...
San Pablo	CDJC	207 927	102 685	105 242	...	...	...	...	...
Silay	CDJC	107 722	54 419	53 303	215	...	...	...	...
Surigao	CDJC	118 534	59 253	59 281	225	...	...	...	...
Tacloban	CDJC	178 639	88 490	90 149	...	...	...	...	...
Taguig	CDJC	467 375	233 712	233 663	...	...	...	...	...
Tagum	CDJC	179 531	90 004	89 527	...	...	...	...	...
Tarlac	CDJC	262 481	132 532	129 949	...	...	...	...	...
Toledo	CDJC	141 174	71 719	69 455	...	...	...	...	...
Tuguegarao	CDJC	120 645	60 270	60 375	145	...	...	...	...
Valenzuela	CDJC	485 433	244 373	241 060	47	...	...	...	...
Zamboanga	CDJC	601 794	302 089	299 705	464	...	...	...	...
Qatar									
16 III 2004									
Al-Rayyan	CDFC	272 860	185 762	87 098	894	...	...	...	...
DOHA	CDFC	339 847	219 676	120 171	159	...	...	...	...
Saudi Arabia — Arabie saoudite									
15 IX 2004									
Abha	CDFC	201 912	113 102	88 810		...	...	...	...
Ad-Dammam	CDFC	744 321	450 494	293 827		...	...	...	...
Al-Hawiyah	CDFC	132 078	69 481	62 597		...	...	...	...
Al-Hufuf	CDFC	287 841	155 924	131 917		...	...	...	...
Al-Jubayl	CDFC	222 544	135 659	86 885		...	...	...	...
Al-Kharj	CDFC	200 958	109 112	91 846		...	...	...	...
Al-Khubar	CDFC	165 799	101 818	63 981		...	...	...	...
Al-Madinah	CDFC	918 889	493 929	424 960		...	...	...	...
Al-Mubarraz	CDFC	285 067	150 449	134 618		...	...	...	...
Al-Qurrayyat	CDFC	100 436	52 869	47 567		...	...	...	...
Ar'ar	CDFC	145 237	77 744	67 493		...	...	...	...
Ath-Thuqbah	CDFC	191 826	117 165	74 661		...	...	...	...
At-Ta'if	CDFC	521 273	274 531	246 742		...	...	...	...
Buraydah	CDFC	378 422	211 317	167 105		...	...	...	...
Hafar al-Batin	CDFC	231 978	122 781	109 197		...	...	...	...
Ha'il	CDFC	267 005	142 015	124 990		...	...	...	...
Jiddah	CDFC	2 801 481	1 619 932	1 181 549		...	...	...	...
Jizan	CDFC	100 694	57 988	42 706		...	...	...	...
Khamis Mushayt	CDFC	372 695	208 397	164 298		...	...	...	...
Makkah	CDFC	1 294 168	704 672	589 496		...	...	...	...
Najran (Aba as-Suud)	CDFC	246 880	133 405	113 475		...	...	...	...
RIYADH	CDFC	4 087 152	2 354 246	1 732 906		...	...	...	...
Sekaka	CDFC	122 686	66 672	56 014		...	...	...	...
Tabuk	CDFC	441 351	241 913	199 438		...	...	...	...
Unayzah	CDFC	128 930	71 841	57 089		...	...	...	...
Yanbu al-Bahr	CDFC	188 430	105 966	82 464		...	...	...	...
Singapore — Singapour									
1 VII 2005									
SINGAPORE	ESDF	4 341 800	...	...	...	...	...	...	...

8. Population of capital cities and cities of 100 000 or more inhabitants: latest available year, 1986 - 2005
Population des capitales et des villes de 100 000 habitants ou plus: dernière année disponible, 1986 - 2005
(continued — suite)

Continent, country or area, date and city / Continent, pays ou zone, date et ville	Code[1]	City proper — Ville proprement dite Population				Urban agglomeration — Agglomération urbaine Population			
		Both sexes Les deux sexes	Male Masculin	Female Féminin	Surface area Superficie (km²)	Both sexes Les deux sexes	Male Masculin	Female Féminin	Surface area Superficie (km²)
ASIA — ASIE									
Sri Lanka									
1 VII 1990									
COLOMBO	ESDF	615 000	...	...	...	...	...	...	...
Dehiwala-Mount Lavinia	ESDF	196 000	...	...	...	...	...	...	...
Jaffna	ESDF	129 000	...	...	...	...	...	...	...
Kandy	ESDF	104 000	...	...	...	...	...	...	...
Moratuwa	ESDF	170 000	...	...	...	...	...	...	...
Syrian Arab Republic — République arabe syrienne									
1 VII 2000									
Aleppo	ESDF	3 818 000	1 968 000	1 850 000	...	...	...	...	...
Al-Hasakeh	ESDF	1 295 000	657 000	638 000	...	...	...	...	...
Al-Kamishli	ESDF	467 120	229 542	237 578	...	...	...	...	...
Al-Rakka	ESDF	708 000	360 000	348 000	...	...	...	...	...
DAMASCUS	ESDF	1 675 000	865 000	810 000	...	...	...	...	...
Deir El-Zor	ESDF	803 000	404 000	399 000	...	...	...	...	...
Hama	ESDF	1 525 000	780 000	745 000	...	...	...	...	...
Homs	ESDF	1 365 000	698 000	667 000	...	...	...	...	...
Lattakia	ESDF	890 000	455 000	435 000	...	...	...	...	...
Tajikistan — Tadjikistan									
1 VII 1993									
DUSHANBE	ESDJ	528 600	...	...	...	...	...	...	...
Thailand — Thaïlande									
1 VII 2002									
BANGKOK	ESDJ	...	...	...	...	7 917 000	3 777 000	4 140 000	1 569
Buri Ram	ESDJ	...	...	...	...	209 422	103 236	106 186	10 323
Chachoengsao	ESDJ	...	...	...	...	136 757	66 900	69 857	5 351
Chaiyaphum	ESDJ	...	...	...	...	183 160	91 174	91 986	12 778
Chanthaburi	ESDJ	...	...	...	...	151 738	75 128	76 610	6 338
Chiang Mai	ESDJ	...	...	...	...	390 445	194 072	196 373	20 107
Chiang Rai	ESDJ	...	...	...	...	197 793	99 969	97 824	11 678
Chon Buri	ESDJ	...	...	...	...	556 545	275 351	281 194	4 363
Kalasin	ESDJ	...	...	...	...	191 744	96 148	95 596	6 947
Kanchanaburi	ESDJ	...	...	...	...	164 353	80 691	83 662	19 483
Khon Kaen	ESDJ	...	...	...	...	398 533	197 778	200 755	10 886
Lampang	ESDJ	...	...	...	...	226 503	112 418	114 085	12 534
Loei	ESDJ	...	...	...	...	101 540	51 723	49 817	11 425
Lop Buri	ESDJ	...	...	...	...	122 123	60 891	61 232	6 200
Lumphun	ESDJ	...	...	...	...	106 226	53 335	52 891	4 506
Maha Sarakham	ESDJ	...	...	...	...	120 926	58 649	62 277	5 292
Nakhon Pathom	ESDJ	...	...	...	...	243 813	117 596	126 217	2 168
Nakhon Ratchasima	ESDJ	...	...	...	...	566 104	276 925	289 179	20 494
Nakhon Sawan	ESDJ	...	...	...	...	236 163	113 951	122 212	9 598
Nakhon Si Thammarat	ESDJ	...	...	...	...	287 761	139 923	147 838	9 943
Narathiwat	ESDJ	...	...	...	...	166 081	83 082	82 999	4 475
Nong Bua Lam Phu	ESDJ	...	...	...	...	111 176	55 872	55 304	3 859
Nong Khai	ESDJ	...	...	...	...	185 556	93 325	92 231	7 332
Nonthaburi	ESDJ	...	...	...	...	564 835	273 604	291 231	622
Pathum Thani	ESDJ	...	...	...	...	280 365	136 072	144 293	1 526
Pattani	ESDJ	...	...	...	...	123 675	61 406	62 269	1 940
Phayao	ESDJ	...	...	...	...	111 195	56 311	54 884	6 335
Phetchabun	ESDJ	...	...	...	...	152 980	74 615	78 365	12 668
Phetchaburi	ESDJ	...	...	...	...	163 340	79 317	84 023	6 225
Phichit	ESDJ	...	...	...	...	120 795	57 339	63 456	4 531
Phitsanulok	ESDJ	...	...	...	...	158 628	76 015	82 613	10 816
Phra Nakhon Si Ayutthaya	ESDJ	...	...	...	...	243 518	116 101	127 417	2 557
Phrae	ESDJ	...	...	...	...	113 542	56 168	57 374	6 539
Prachuap Khiri Khan	ESDJ	...	...	...	...	163 070	79 845	83 225	6 368
Ratchaburi	ESDJ	...	...	...	...	250 650	120 854	129 796	5 197
Rayong	ESDJ	...	...	...	...	212 129	106 858	105 271	3 552
Roi Et	ESDJ	...	...	...	...	154 162	77 163	76 999	8 299
Sakon Nakhon	ESDJ	...	...	...	...	146 795	72 790	74 005	9 606

8. Population of capital cities and cities of 100 000 or more inhabitants: latest available year, 1986 - 2005
Population des capitales et des villes de 100 000 habitants ou plus: dernière année disponible, 1986 - 2005
(continued — suite)

Continent, country or area, date and city / Continent, pays ou zone, date et ville	Code[1]	City proper — Ville proprement dite Population				Urban agglomeration — Agglomération urbaine Population			
		Both sexes Les deux sexes	Male Masculin	Female Féminin	Surface area Superficie (km²)	Both sexes Les deux sexes	Male Masculin	Female Féminin	Surface area Superficie (km²)
ASIA — ASIE									
Thailand — Thaïlande									
1 VII 2002									
Samut Prakan	ESDJ	...	...	...	...	680 363	332 881	347 482	1 004
Samut Sakhon	ESDJ	...	...	...	...	190 595	91 375	99 220	872
Saraburi	ESDJ	...	...	...	...	209 274	104 501	104 773	3 577
Si Sa Ket	ESDJ	...	...	...	...	151 251	74 862	76 389	8 840
Songkhla	ESDJ	...	...	...	...	437 747	213 072	224 675.	7 394
Sukhothai	ESDJ	...	...	...	...	116 026	55 681	60 345	6 596
Suphan Buri	ESDJ	...	...	...	...	154 249	73 024	81 225	5 358
Surat Thani	ESDJ	...	...	...	...	281 161	137 869	143 292	12 892
Surin	ESDJ	...	...	...	...	106 835	51 563	55 272	8 124
Trang	ESDJ	...	...	...	...	127 194	61 557	65 637	4 918
Ubon Ratchathani	ESDJ	...	...	...	...	274 120	135 579	138 541	15 745
Udon Thani	ESDJ	...	...	...	...	403 467	202 154	201 313	11 730
Yala	ESDJ	...	...	...	...	117 076	58 502	58 574	4 521
Timor-Leste									
1 VII 2001									
DILI	ESDF	56 000	...	...	...	...	...	...	...
Turkey — Turquie									
1 VII 2003									
Adana[67]	ESDF	...	...	...	...	1 187 098	...	...	...
Adiyaman	ESDF	203 880	...	...	...	...	...	...	...
Afyon	ESDF	137 411	...	...	...	...	...	...	...
Aksaray	ESDF	141 521	...	...	...	...	...	...	...
ANKARA[68]	ESDF	...	...	...	...	3 729 453	...	...	...
Antalya	ESDF	670 229	...	...	...	...	...	...	...
Aydin	ESDF	152 918	...	...	...	...	...	...	...
Balikesir	ESDF	227 428	...	...	...	...	...	...	...
Bandirma	ESDF	102 733	...	...	...	...	...	...	...
Batman	ESDF	277 349	...	...	...	...	...	...	...
Bursa[69]	ESDF	...	...	...	...	1 305 059	...	...	...
Ceyhan	ESDF	114 956	...	...	...	...	...	...	...
Corlu	ESDF	164 431	...	...	...	...	...	...	...
Corum	ESDF	173 960	...	...	...	...	...	...	...
Denizli	ESDF	295 319	...	...	...	...	...	...	...
Derince[70]	ESDF	101 744	...	...	...	...	...	...	...
Diyarbakir	ESDF	595 951	...	...	...	...	...	...	...
Edirne	ESDF	122 932	...	...	...	...	...	...	...
Elazig	ESDF	281 560	...	...	...	...	...	...	...
Erzincan	ESDF	110 196	...	...	...	...	...	...	...
Erzurum	ESDF	396 092	...	...	...	...	...	...	...
Eskisehir	ESDF	498 836	...	...	...	...	...	...	...
Gaziantep[71]	ESDF	...	...	...	...	926 458	...	...	...
Gebze	ESDF	282 938	...	...	...	...	...	...	...
Hatay	ESDF	149 607	...	...	...	...	...	...	...
Içel	ESDF	568 388	...	...	...	...	...	...	...
Inegol	ESDF	115 096	...	...	...	...	...	...	...
Iskenderun	ESDF	158 695	...	...	...	...	...	...	...
Isparta	ESDF	157 913	...	...	...	...	...	...	...
Istanbul[72]	ESDF	...	...	...	...	9 555 719	...	...	...
Izmir[73]	ESDF	...	...	...	...	2 299 584	...	...	...
Kahramanmaras	ESDF	354 891	...	...	...	...	...	...	...
Karaman	ESDF	113 687	...	...	...	...	...	...	...
Kayseri[74]	ESDF	...	...	...	...	566 162	...	...	...
Kirikkale	ESDF	208 086	...	...	...	...	...	...	...
Kiziltepe	ESDF	130 904	...	...	...	...	...	...	...
Kocaeli	ESDF	194 055	...	...	...	...	...	...	...
Konya[75]	ESDF	...	...	...	...	810 957	...	...	...
Kütahya	ESDF	175 905	...	...	...	...	...	...	...
Malatya	ESDF	412 724	...	...	...	...	...	...	...
Manisa	ESDF	230 223	...	...	...	...	...	...	...
Nazilli	ESDF	112 269	...	...	...	...	...	...	...

8. Population of capital cities and cities of 100 000 or more inhabitants: latest available year, 1986 - 2005
    Population des capitales et des villes de 100 000 habitants ou plus: dernière année disponible, 1986 - 2005
(continued — suite)

Continent, country or area, date and city Continent, pays ou zone, date et ville	Code[1]	City proper — Ville proprement dite Population				Urban agglomeration — Agglomération urbaine Population			
		Both sexes Les deux sexes	Male Masculin	Female Féminin	Surface area Superficie (km²)	Both sexes Les deux sexes	Male Masculin	Female Féminin	Surface area Superficie (km²)
ASIA — ASIE									
Turkey — Turquie									
1 VII 2003									
Ordu	ESDF	*113 756*	...	...	...	...	...	...	...
Osmaniye	ESDF	*189 238*	...	...	...	...	...	...	...
Sakarya	ESDF	*283 516*	...	...	...	...	...	...	...
Samsun	ESDF	*377 927*	...	...	...	...	...	...	...
Sanliurfa	ESDF	*411 159*	...	...	...	...	...	...	...
Siirt	ESDF	*106 966*	...	...	...	...	...	...	...
Sivas	ESDF	*256 914*	...	...	...	...	...	...	...
Siverek	ESDF	*149 236*	...	...	...	...	...	...	...
Tarsus	ESDF	*222 693*	...	...	...	...	...	...	...
Tekirdag	ESDF	*113 285*	...	...	...	...	...	...	...
Tokat	ESDF	*121 694*	...	...	...	...	...	...	...
Trabzon	ESDF	*228 013*	...	...	...	...	...	...	...
Turhal	ESDF	*103 225*	...	...	...	...	...	...	...
Usak	ESDF	*145 758*	...	...	...	...	...	...	...
Van	ESDF	*324 352*	...	...	...	...	...	...	...
Viransehir	ESDF	*144 731*	...	...	...	...	...	...	...
Turkmenistan — Turkménistan									
1 VII 1990									
ASHKHABAD	ESDF	407 000	...	...	...	...	...	...	...
Chardzhou	ESDF	164 000	...	...	...	...	...	...	...
Tashauz	ESDF	114 000	...	...	...	...	...	...	...
United Arab Emirates — Emirats Arabes Unis									
1 VII 2002									
ABU DHABI	ESDF	*527 000*	*359 000*	*168 000*	...	...	...	...	...
Ajman	ESDF	*205 000*	*122 000*	*83 000*	...	...	...	...	...
Al-Ayn	ESDF	*328 000*	*215 000*	*113 000*	...	...	...	...	...
Al-Sharjah	ESDF	*488 000*	*317 000*	*171 000*	...	...	...	...	...
Dubai	ESDF	*1 089 000*	*759 000*	*330 000*	...	...	...	...	...
Uzbekistan — Ouzbékistan									
1 VII 2001									
Almalyk	ESDF	113 114	56 317	56 797	...	...	...	...	...
Andizhan	ESDF	338 366	165 159	173 207	...	...	...	...	...
Angren	ESDF	128 757	64 060	64 697	...	...	...	...	...
Bukhara	ESDF	237 361	118 613	118 748	...	...	...	...	...
Chirchik	ESDF	141 742	70 203	71 539	...	...	...	...	...
Banjzak	ESDF	131 512	68 441	63 071	...	...	...	...	...
Fergana	ESDF	183 037	87 142	95 895	...	...	...	...	...
Karshi	ESDF	204 690	104 159	100 531	...	...	...	...	...
Kokand	ESDF	197 450	95 872	101 578	...	...	...	...	...
Margilan	ESDF	149 646	73 899	75 747	...	...	...	...	...
Namangan	ESDF	391 297	197 962	193 335	...	...	...	...	...
Navoi	ESDF	138 082	70 577	67 505	...	...	...	...	...
Nukus	ESDF	212 012	103 918	108 094	...	...	...	...	...
Samarkand	ESDF	361 339	178 608	182 731	...	...	...	...	...
TASHKENT	ESDF	2 137 218	1 043 213	1 094 005	...	...	...	...	...
Termez	ESDF	116 467	60 031	56 436	...	...	...	...	...
Urgentch	ESDF	138 609	67 667	70 942	...	...	...	...	...
Viet Nam									
1 VII 1992									
Buonmathuot	ESDF	*282 095*	...	...	...	...	...	...	...
Campha	ESDF	*209 086*	...	...	...	...	...	...	...
Cantho	ESDF	*215 587*	...	...	...	...	...	...	...
Dalat	ESDF	*106 409*	...	...	...	...	...	...	...
Da Nang	ESDF	*382 674*	...	...	...	...	...	...	...
Haiphong	ESDF	*783 133*	...	...	22	...	...	...	...
HANOI	ESDF	*1 073 760*	...	...	46	...	...	...	...
Ho Chi Minh[76]	ESDF	*3 015 743*	...	...	140	...	...	...	...
Hon Gai	ESDF	*127 484*	...	...	...	...	...	...	...
Hué	ESDF	*219 149*	...	...	...	...	...	...	...

8. Population of capital cities and cities of 100 000 or more inhabitants: latest available year, 1986 - 2005
Population des capitales et des villes de 100 000 habitants ou plus: dernière année disponible, 1986 - 2005
(continued — suite)

Continent, country or area, date and city / Continent, pays ou zone, date et ville	Code[1]	City proper — Ville proprement dite Population				Urban agglomeration — Agglomération urbaine Population			
		Both sexes Les deux sexes	Male Masculin	Female Féminin	Surface area Superficie (km²)	Both sexes Les deux sexes	Male Masculin	Female Féminin	Surface area Superficie (km²)
ASIA — ASIE									
Viet Nam									
1 VII 1992									
Longxuyen	ESDF	132 681	...	...	...	...	...	...	...
Mytho	ESDF	108 404	...	...	...	...	...	...	...
Namdinh	ESDF	171 699	...	...	...	...	...	...	...
Nhatrang	ESDF	221 331	...	...	...	...	...	...	...
Qui Nhon	ESDF	163 385	...	...	...	...	...	...	...
Rach Gia	ESDF	141 132	...	...	...	...	...	...	...
Thai Nguyen	ESDF	127 643	...	...	...	...	...	...	...
Vinh	ESDF	112 455	...	...	...	...	...	...	...
Vungtau	ESDF	145 145	...	...	...	...	...	...	...
Yemen — Yémen									
16 XII 1994									
Adan	CDFC	398 294	...	...	...	...	...	...	...
Al-Hudaydah (Hodeidah)	CDFC	298 452	...	...	...	...	...	...	...
Al-Mukalla	CDFC	122 359	...	...	...	...	...	...	...
Ibb	CDFC	103 312	...	...	...	...	...	...	...
SANA'A	CDFC	954 448	...	...	...	...	...	...	...
Ta'izz	CDFC	317 571	...	...	...	...	...	...	...
EUROPE									
Albania — Albanie[77]									
1 VII 2003									
TIRANA	ESDF	392 863	194 006	198 857	31	...	...	...	...
Andorra — Andorre									
1 VII 2003									
ANDORRA LA VELLA	ESDJ	...	...	...	...	21 245	10 702	10 543	...
Austria — Autriche[78,79]									
01 I 2005									
Bregenz[80]	ESDJ	123 902	61 008	62 894	150	...	...	...	...
Graz	ESDJ	240 278	114 665	125 613	128	...	...	...	...
Innsbruck	ESDJ	115 498	54 526	60 972	105	...	...	...	...
Linz	ESDJ	187 112	88 638	98 474	96	...	...	...	...
Salzburg	ESDJ	146 868	68 778	78 090	66	...	...	...	...
WIEN	ESDJ	1 626 440	774 583	851 857	415	...	...	...	...
Belarus — Bélarus									
1 VII 2004									
Baranovichi	ESDF	168 312	78 242	90 070	55	...	...	...	...
Bobruisk	ESDF	220 062	102 764	117 298	90	...	...	...	...
Borisov	ESDF	150 148	70 894	79 254	47	...	...	...	...
Brest	ESDF	300 124	138 255	161 869	74	...	...	...	...
Gomel	ESDF	...	...	...	...	492 150	224 836	267 314	118
Grodno	ESDF	316 735	146 432	170 303	93	...	...	...	...
MINSK	ESDF	1 765 773	818 800	946 973	305	...	...	...	...
Mogilev	ESDF	366 873	169 565	197 308	108	...	...	...	...
Mozir	ESDF	111 724	53 631	58 093	38	...	...	...	...
Novopolotsk	ESDF	...	...	...	...	106 928	50 814	56 114	54
Orsha	ESDF	...	...	...	...	141 135	67 279	73 856	51
Pinsk	ESDF	130 268	61 057	69 211	42	...	...	...	...
Soligorsk	ESDF	101 033	47 748	53 285	9	...	...	...	...
Vitebsk	ESDF	...	...	...	...	350 820	157 345	193 475	96
Belgium — Belgique[81]									
1 VII 2000									
Antwerpen (Anvers)	ESDJ	445 570	216 319	229 251	205	...	...	...	...
Brugge	ESDJ	116 559	56 436	60 123	138	...	...	...	...
BRUXELLES (BRUSSEL)	ESDJ	964 405	461 065	503 340	161	...	...	...	...
Charleroi	ESDJ	200 233	96 214	104 019	102	...	...	...	...
Gent (Gand)	ESDJ	224 685	109 142	115 543	156	...	...	...	...
Liège (Luik)	ESDJ	184 550	89 176	95 374	69	...	...	...	...
Namur	ESDJ	105 248	50 251	54 997	176	...	...	...	...

8. Population of capital cities and cities of 100 000 or more inhabitants: latest available year, 1986 - 2005
Population des capitales et des villes de 100 000 habitants ou plus: dernière année disponible, 1986 - 2005
(continued — suite)

Continent, country or area, date and city / Continent, pays ou zone, date et ville	Code[1]	City proper — Ville proprement dite Population				Urban agglomeration — Agglomération urbaine Population			
		Both sexes Les deux sexes	Male Masculin	Female Féminin	Surface area Superficie (km²)	Both sexes Les deux sexes	Male Masculin	Female Féminin	Surface area Superficie (km²)
EUROPE									
Bosnia and Herzegovina — Bosnie-Herzégovine									
31 III 1991									
Banja Luka	ESDJ	195 994	...	...	1 239	...	...	...	...
Doboj	ESDJ	102 624	...	...	697	...	...	...	...
Mostar	ESDJ	127 034	...	...	1 227	...	...	...	...
Prijedor	ESDJ	112 635	...	...	834	...	...	...	...
SARAJEVO	ESDJ	529 021	...	...	2 095	...	...	...	...
Tuzla	ESDJ	131 866	...	...	303	...	...	...	...
Zenica	ESDJ	145 837	...	...	505	...	...	...	...
Bulgaria — Bulgarie[47,82]									
1 VII 2005									
Bourgas	ESDF	189 387	91 354	98 032	...	...	...	...	...
Pleven	ESDF	114 527	55 331	59 196	...	...	...	...	...
Plovdiv	ESDF	341 668	162 586	179 082	...	...	...	...	...
Rousse	ESDF	157 870	75 899	81 972	...	...	...	...	...
SOFIA	ESDF	1 143 690	540 749	602 940	...	...	...	...	...
Stara Zagora	ESDF	141 484	68 650	72 835	...	...	...	...	...
Varna	ESDF	311 911	151 248	160 662	...	...	...	...	...
Channel Islands: Guernsey — Iles Anglo-Normandes: Guernesey									
29 IV 2001									
ST. PETER PORT	CDJC	16 488	...	...	...	...	...	...	...
Channel Islands — Iles Anglo-Normandes: Jersey									
11 III 2001									
ST. HELIER	CDJC	28 310	13 669	14 641	9	...	...	...	...
Croatia — Croatie									
1 VII 2001									
Osijek	ESDJ	90 411	41 592	48 819	...	114 616	53 497	61 119	...
Rijeka	ESDJ	143 800	68 382	75 418	...	144 043	68 511	75 532	...
Split	ESDJ	175 140	83 720	91 420	...	188 694	90 484	98 210	...
ZAGREB	ESDJ	691 724	321 507	370 217	1 405	779 145	363 992	415 153	...
Czech Republic — République tchéque									
1 VII 2005									
Brno	ESDJ	366 904	174 257	192 647	230	...	...	...	...
Hradec Králové	ESDJ	94 436	45 015	49 421	106	...	...	...	...
Liberec	ESDJ	97 596	46 424	51 172	106	...	...	...	...
Olomouc	ESDJ	100 491	47 379	53 112	103	...	...	...	...
Ostrava	ESDJ	310 681	149 780	160 901	214	...	...	...	...
Plzen	ESDJ	162 659	78 173	84 486	138	...	...	...	...
PRAHA	ESDJ	1 176 116	563 147	612 969	496	...	...	...	...
Östí nad Labem	ESDJ	94 021	45 360	48 661	94	...	...	...	...
Denmark — Danemark									
1 VII 2005									
Ålborg	ESDJ	163 290	81 090	82 200	560	...	...	...	...
Århus	ESDJ	293 932	143 989	149 943	469	...	...	...	...
KOBENHAVN	ESDJ	500 150	246 232	253 918	88	...	...	...	...
Odense	ESDJ	185 861	90 817	95 044	304	...	...	...	...
Estonia — Estonie									
1 VII 2003									
TALLINN	ESDF	396 762	178 706	218 056	158	...	...	...	...
Tartu	ESDF	101 244	45 047	56 197	39	...	...	...	...
Faeroe Islands — Iles Féroé									
1 VII 1992									
THORSHAVN	ESDJ	14 671	...	...	63	16 218	...	...	79
Finland — Finlande									
1 VII 2005									
Espoo	ESDJ	229 588	112 326	117 262	312	...	...	...	...
HELSINKI	ESDJ	559 976	261 100	298 876	186	...	...	...	...
Oulu	ESDJ	128 094	62 450	65 644	369	...	...	...	...

8. Population of capital cities and cities of 100 000 or more inhabitants: latest available year, 1986 - 2005
Population des capitales et des villes de 100 000 habitants ou plus: dernière année disponible, 1986 - 2005
(continued — suite)

Continent, country or area, date and city / Continent, pays ou zone, date et ville	Code[1]	City proper — Ville proprement dite Population				Urban agglomeration — Agglomération urbaine Population			
		Both sexes Les deux sexes	Male Masculin	Female Féminin	Surface area Superficie (km²)	Both sexes Les deux sexes	Male Masculin	Female Féminin	Surface area Superficie (km²)
EUROPE									
Finland — Finlande									
1 VII 2005									
Tampere	ESDJ	203 634	97 431	106 204	523	...	...	...	...
Turku	ESDJ	174 846	81 648	93 198	246	...	...	...	...
Vantaa	ESDJ	186 355	91 075	95 280	241	...	...	...	...
France[83,84]									
8 III 1999									
Aix-en-Provence	CDJC	134 280	62 220	72 060	186	...	...	...	...
Amiens	CDJC	135 406	63 513	71 893	49	...	...	...	...
Angers	CDJC	151 406	69 235	82 171	43	...	...	...	...
Besançon	CDJC	117 693	54 692	63 001	65	...	...	...	...
Bordeaux	CDJC	215 277	99 637	115 640	49	...	...	...	...
Boulogne-Billancourt	CDJC	106 384	49 840	56 544	6	...	...	...	...
Brest	CDJC	149 495	71 431	78 064	50	...	...	...	...
Caen	CDJC	114 079	52 605	61 474	26	...	...	...	...
Clermont-Ferrand	CDJC	136 968	63 702	73 266	43	...	...	...	...
Dijon	CDJC	150 144	69 331	80 813	40	...	...	...	...
Grenoble	CDJC	153 531	73 311	80 220	18	...	...	...	...
Le Havre	CDJC	190 806	90 882	99 924	47	...	...	...	...
Le Mans	CDJC	145 994	68 982	77 012	53	...	...	...	...
Lille[85]	CDJC	184 445	86 196	98 249	30	...	...	...	...
Limoges	CDJC	134 055	62 106	71 949	77	...	...	...	...
Lyon[86]	CDJC	444 852	206 422	238 430	48	...	...	...	...
Marseille	CDJC	796 525	376 082	420 443	241	...	...	...	...
Metz	CDJC	123 720	59 670	64 050	42	...	...	...	...
Montpellier	CDJC	225 748	103 437	122 311	57	...	...	...	...
Mulhouse	CDJC	110 129	53 963	56 166	22	...	...	...	...
Nantes	CDJC	270 474	126 599	143 875	65	...	...	...	...
Nancy	CDJC	103 533	47 345	56 188	15	...	...	...	...
Nice	CDJC	343 166	157 148	186 018	72	...	...	...	...
Nîmes	CDJC	133 391	62 451	70 940	162	...	...	...	...
Orléans	CDJC	113 077	53 728	59 349	27	...	...	...	...
PARIS	CDJC	2 125 017	995 844	1 129 173	105	...	...	...	...
Perpignan	CDJC	105 027	47 870	57 157	68	...	...	...	...
Reims	CDJC	187 183	88 707	98 476	47	...	...	...	...
Rennes	CDJC	206 221	95 224	110 997	50	...	...	...	...
Rouen	CDJC	106 356	49 432	56 924	21	...	...	...	...
Saint-Étienne	CDJC	180 393	84 135	96 258	80	...	...	...	...
Strasbourg[85]	CDJC	263 682	124 926	138 756	78	...	...	...	...
Toulon	CDJC	160 549	74 964	85 585	43	...	...	...	...
Toulouse	CDJC	390 174	185 107	205 067	118	...	...	...	...
Tours	CDJC	132 637	60 117	72 520	34	...	...	...	...
Villeurbanne	CDJC	124 451	59 519	64 932	15	...	...	...	...
Germany — Allemagne									
1 VII 1999									
Aachen	ESDJ	243 825	121 671	122 154	161	...	...	...	...
Augsburg	ESDJ	254 867	121 846	133 021	147	...	...	...	...
Bergisch Gladbach	ESDJ	106 150	50 723	55 427	83	...	...	...	...
BERLIN	ESDJ	3 386 667	1 644 575	1 742 092	891	...	...	...	...
Bielefeld	ESDJ	321 125	152 701	168 424	258	...	...	...	...
Bochum	ESDJ	392 830	190 433	202 397	145	...	...	...	...
Bonn	ESDJ	301 048	143 416	157 632	141	...	...	...	...
Bottrop	ESDJ	121 097	58 490	62 607	101	...	...	...	...
Braunschweig	ESDJ	246 322	119 350	126 972	192	...	...	...	...
Bremen	ESDJ	540 330	259 439	280 891	327	...	...	...	...
Bremerhaven	ESDJ	122 735	59 991	62 744	78	...	...	...	...
Chemnitz	ESDJ	263 222	125 123	138 099	176	...	...	...	...
Cottbus	ESDJ	110 894	53 712	57 182	150	...	...	...	...
Darmstadt	ESDJ	137 776	67 680	70 096	122	...	...	...	...
Dortmund	ESDJ	590 213	286 880	303 333	280	...	...	...	...
Dresden	ESDJ	476 668	229 565	247 103	237	...	...	...	...
Duisburg	ESDJ	519 793	252 735	267 058	233	...	...	...	...

8. Population of capital cities and cities of 100 000 or more inhabitants: latest available year, 1986 - 2005
Population des capitales et des villes de 100 000 habitants ou plus: dernière année disponible, 1986 - 2005
(continued — suite)

Continent, country or area, date and city / Continent, pays ou zone, date et ville	Code[1]	City proper — Ville proprement dite Population				Urban agglomeration — Agglomération urbaine Population			
		Both sexes Les deux sexes	Male Masculin	Female Féminin	Surface area Superficie (km²)	Both sexes Les deux sexes	Male Masculin	Female Féminin	Surface area Superficie (km²)

EUROPE

Germany — Allemagne
  1 VII 1999

Düsseldorf	ESDJ	568 855	268 630	300 225	217	...	...	...	...
Erfurt	ESDJ	201 267	96 937	104 330	269	...	...	...	...
Erlangen	ESDJ	100 750	48 939	51 811	77	...	...	...	...
Essen	ESDJ	599 515	286 350	313 165	210	...	...	...	...
Frankfurt am Main	ESDJ	643 821	314 431	329 390	248	...	...	...	...
Freiburg im Breisgau	ESDJ	202 455	96 025	106 430	153	...	...	...	...
Fürth	ESDJ	109 771	52 773	56 998	63	...	...	...	...
Gelsenkirchen	ESDJ	281 979	135 781	146 198	105	...	...	...	...
Gera	ESDJ	114 718	55 211	59 507	152	...	...	...	...
Göttingen	ESDJ	124 775	60 334	64 441	117	...	...	...	...
Hagen	ESDJ	205 201	98 338	106 863	160	...	...	...	...
Halle	ESDJ	254 360	121 314	133 046	135	...	...	...	...
Hamburg	ESDJ	1 704 735	824 686	880 049	755	...	...	...	...
Hamm	ESDJ	181 804	89 307	92 497	226	...	...	...	...
Hannover	ESDJ	514 718	245 017	269 701	204	...	...	...	...
Heidelberg	ESDJ	139 672	65 694	73 978	109	...	...	...	...
Heilbronn	ESDJ	119 526	58 400	61 126	100	...	...	...	...
Herne	ESDJ	175 661	85 577	90 084	51	...	...	...	...
Hildesheim	ESDJ	104 013	48 910	55 103	93	...	...	...	...
Ingolstadt	ESDJ	114 826	56 417	58 409	133	...	...	...	...
Kaiserslautern	ESDJ	100 025	49 247	50 778	140	...	...	...	...
Karlsruhe	ESDJ	277 204	134 775	142 429	173	...	...	...	...
Kassel	ESDJ	196 211	93 058	103 153	107	...	...	...	...
Kiel	ESDJ	233 795	113 274	120 521	117	...	...	...	...
Koblenz	ESDJ	108 003	51 340	56 663	105	...	...	...	...
Köln	ESDJ	962 507	466 543	495 964	405	...	...	...	...
Krefeld	ESDJ	241 769	117 087	124 682	138	...	...	...	...
Leipzig	ESDJ	489 532	235 789	253 743	176	...	...	...	...
Leverkusen	ESDJ	160 841	78 116	82 725	79	...	...	...	...
Lübeck	ESDJ	213 326	101 024	112 302	214	...	...	...	...
Ludwigshafen am Rhein	ESDJ	163 771	81 257	82 514	78	...	...	...	...
Magdeburg	ESDJ	235 021	112 839	122 234	193	...	...	...	...
Mainz	ESDJ	183 134	89 093	94 041	98	...	...	...	...
Mannheim	ESDJ	307 730	151 145	156 585	145	...	...	...	...
Moers	ESDJ	106 837	51 824	55 013	68	...	...	...	...
Mönchengladbach	ESDJ	263 697	126 721	136 976	170	...	...	...	...
Mülheim an der Ruhr	ESDJ	173 895	82 677	91 218	91	...	...	...	...
München	ESDJ	1 194 560	571 363	623 197	311	...	...	...	...
Münster (Westf.)	ESDJ	264 670	123 825	140 845	303	...	...	...	...
Neuss	ESDJ	149 702	72 522	77 180	99	...	...	...	...
Nürnberg	ESDJ	486 628	233 415	253 213	186	...	...	...	...
Oberhausen	ESDJ	222 349	107 562	114 787	77	...	...	...	...
Offenbach am Main	ESDJ	116 627	57 539	59 088	45	...	...	...	...
Oldenburg	ESDJ	154 125	73 572	80 553	103	...	...	...	...
Osnabrück	ESDJ	164 539	77 981	86 558	120	...	...	...	...
Paderborn	ESDJ	137 647	67 010	70 637	179	...	...	...	...
Pforzheim	ESDJ	117 227	55 738	61 489	98	...	...	...	...
Potsdam	ESDJ	128 983	62 651	66 332	109	...	...	...	...
Recklinghausen	ESDJ	125 022	60 456	64 566	66	...	...	...	...
Regensburg	ESDJ	125 236	59 600	65 636	81	...	...	...	...
Remscheid	ESDJ	120 125	57 923	62 202	75	...	...	...	...
Reutlingen	ESDJ	110 343	53 564	56 779	87	...	...	...	...
Rostock	ESDJ	203 279	99 627	103 652	181	...	...	...	...
Saarbrücken	ESDJ	183 836	87 875	95 961	167	...	...	...	...
Salzgitter	ESDJ	112 934	54 808	58 126	224	...	...	...	...
Schwerin	ESDJ	102 878	49 428	53 450	130	...	...	...	...
Siegen	ESDJ	109 225	53 585	55 640	115	...	...	...	...
Solingen	ESDJ	165 583	79 712	85 871	89	...	...	...	...
Stuttgart	ESDJ	582 443	284 977	297 466	207	...	...	...	...
Ulm	ESDJ	116 103	56 511	59 592	119	...	...	...	...

8. Population of capital cities and cities of 100 000 or more inhabitants: latest available year, 1986 - 2005
Population des capitales et des villes de 100 000 habitants ou plus: dernière année disponible, 1986 - 2005
(continued — suite)

Continent, country or area, date and city / Continent, pays ou zone, date et ville	Code[1]	City proper — Ville proprement dite Population				Urban agglomeration — Agglomération urbaine Population			
		Both sexes Les deux sexes	Male Masculin	Female Féminin	Surface area Superficie (km²)	Both sexes Les deux sexes	Male Masculin	Female Féminin	Surface area Superficie (km²)
EUROPE									
Germany — Allemagne									
1 VII 1999									
Wiesbaden	ESDJ	268 716	129 032	139 684	204	...	...	...	...
Witten	ESDJ	103 384	49 545	53 839	72	...	...	...	...
Wolfsburg	ESDJ	121 954	59 761	62 193	204	...	...	...	...
Wuppertal	ESDJ	368 993	176 350	192 643	168	...	...	...	...
Würzburg	ESDJ	127 350	58 801	68 549	88	...	...	...	...
Zwickau	ESDJ	104 146	49 513	54 633	73	...	...	...	...
Gibraltar									
14 X 1991									
GIBRALTAR	CDFC	28 074	...	...	...	...	...	...	...
Greece — Grèce[87]									
18 III 2001									
ATHINAI	CDJC	789 166	374 900	414 266	39	...	...	...	...
Calithèa	CDJC	115 150	54 137	61 013	5	...	...	...	...
Iraclion	CDJC	135 761	66 956	68 805	52	...	...	...	...
Larissa	CDJC	131 095	64 000	67 095	88	...	...	...	...
Patrai	CDJC	168 530	82 981	85 549	57	...	...	...	...
Pésterion	CDJC	146 743	72 391	74 352	10	...	...	...	...
Pireas	CDJC	181 933	87 362	94 571	...	...	...	...	...
Thessaloniki	CDJC	385 406	180 122	205 284	...	...	...	...	...
Holy See — Saint-Siège[88]									
1 VII 1988									
VATICAN CITY	ESDF	766	...	...	...	...	...	...	...
Hungary — Hongrie									
1 VII 2005									
BUDAPEST	ESDF	1 697 724	773 850	923 874	525	...	...	...	...
Debrecen	ESDF	204 190	94 710	109 480	462	...	...	...	...
Györ	ESDF	127 936	60 257	67 680	175	...	...	...	...
Kecskemét	ESDF	108 560	50 408	58 152	321	...	...	...	...
Miskolc	ESDF	175 058	81 003	94 056	237	...	...	...	...
Nyiregyhaza	ESDF	116 145	53 866	62 279	274	...	...	...	...
Pécs	ESDF	156 342	71 864	84 478	163	...	...	...	...
Szeged	ESDF	163 074	74 848	88 226	281	...	...	...	...
Székesfehérvar	ESDF	101 382	47 682	53 700	171	...	...	...	...
Iceland — Islande[89,90]									
1 VII 2005									
REYKJAVIK	ESDJ	114 365	56 373	57 992	100	185 669	91 767	93 902	
Ireland — Irlande									
28 IV 2002									
Cork	CDFC	123 062	59 263	63 799	40	186 239	90 348	95 891	...
DUBLIN	CDFC	495 781	237 813	257 968	118	1 004 614	485 209	519 405	...
Isle of Man — Ile de Man									
29 IV 2001									
DOUGLAS	CDJC	25 347	12 460	12 887	...	...	...	...	...
Italy — Italie									
31 XII 2005									
Ancona	ESDJ	101 862	48 437	53 425	124	...	...	...	...
Bari	ESDJ	326 915	157 539	169 376	116	...	...	...	...
Bergamo	ESDJ	116 197	54 351	61 846	40	...	...	...	...
Bologna	ESDJ	373 743	174 708	199 035	141	...	...	...	...
Brescia	ESDJ	191 059	90 570	100 489	91	...	...	...	...
Cagliari	ESDJ	160 391	74 791	85 600	86	...	...	...	...
Catania	ESDJ	304 144	143 480	160 664	181	...	...	...	...
Ferrara	ESDJ	132 471	61 908	70 563	404	...	...	...	...
Firenze	ESDJ	366 901	171 544	195 357	102	...	...	...	...
Foggia	ESDJ	153 650	74 175	79 475	508	...	...	...	...
Forli	ESDJ	112 477	54 233	58 244	228	...	...	...	...
Genova	ESDJ	620 316	291 378	328 938	244	...	...	...	...
Giugliano in Campania	ESDJ	108 772	53 592	55 180	94	...	...	...	...
Latina	ESDJ	112 943	54 381	58 562	278	...	...	...	...
Livorno	ESDJ	160 534	76 729	83 805	104	...	...	...	...

8. Population of capital cities and cities of 100 000 or more inhabitants: latest available year, 1986 - 2005
Population des capitales et des villes de 100 000 habitants ou plus: dernière année disponible, 1986 - 2005
(continued — suite)

Continent, country or area, date and city Continent, pays ou zone, date et ville	Code[1]	City proper — Ville proprement dite Population				Urban agglomeration — Agglomération urbaine Population			
		Both sexes Les deux sexes	Male Masculin	Female Féminin	Surface area Superficie (km²)	Both sexes Les deux sexes	Male Masculin	Female Féminin	Surface area Superficie (km²)
EUROPE									
Italy — Italie									
31 XII 2005									
Messina	ESDJ	246 323	117 573	128 750	211	...	...	...	...
Milano	ESDJ	1 308 735	618 709	690 026	182	...	...	...	...
Modena	ESDJ	180 469	86 852	93 617	183	...	...	...	...
Monza	ESDJ	121 961	58 649	63 312	33	...	...	...	...
Napoli	ESDJ	984 242	469 033	515 209	117	...	...	...	...
Novara	ESDJ	102 817	49 330	53 487	103	...	...	...	...
Padova	ESDJ	210 985	99 314	111 671	93	...	...	...	...
Palermo	ESDJ	670 820	319 681	351 139	159	...	...	...	...
Parma	ESDJ	175 789	83 446	92 343	261	...	...	...	...
Perugia	ESDJ	161 390	76 926	84 464	450	...	...	...	...
Pescara	ESDJ	122 457	57 702	64 755	33	...	...	...	...
Prato	ESDJ	183 823	89 992	93 831	98	...	...	...	...
Ravenna	ESDJ	149 084	72 548	76 536	653	...	...	...	...
Reggio di Calabria	ESDJ	184 369	88 705	95 664	236	...	...	...	...
Reggio nell'Emilia	ESDJ	157 388	76 757	80 631	232	...	...	...	...
Rimini	ESDJ	135 682	65 433	70 249	134	...	...	...	...
ROMA	ESDJ	2 547 677	1 192 999	1 354 678	1 308	...	...	...	...
Salerno	ESDJ	134 820	63 005	71 815	59	...	...	...	...
Sassari	ESDJ	127 893	61 597	66 296	546	...	...	...	...
Siracusa	ESDJ	122 972	59 839	63 133	204	...	...	...	...
Taranto	ESDJ	197 582	94 136	103 446	210	...	...	...	...
Terni	ESDJ	109 569	51 938	57 631	212	...	...	...	...
Torino	ESDJ	900 608	429 669	470 939	130	...	...	...	...
Trento	ESDJ	111 044	53 196	57 848	158	...	...	...	...
Trieste	ESDJ	206 058	96 179	109 879	84	...	...	...	...
Venezia	ESDJ	269 780	127 838	141 942	416	...	...	...	...
Verona	ESDJ	259 380	123 448	135 932	207	...	...	...	...
Vicenza	ESDJ	114 232	54 467	59 765	81	...	...	...	...
Latvia — Lettonie[91]									
1 VII 2005									
Daugavpils	ESDF	109 931	49 317	60 614	72	...	...	...	...
RIGA	ESDF	729 670	324 718	404 952	307	...	...	...	...
Liechtenstein[92]									
30 VI 2005									
VADUZ	ESDF	5 019	2 418	2 601	17	...	...	...	...
Lithuania — Lituanie									
1 VII 2005									
Kaunas	ESDJ	362 348	162 794	199 554	157	...	...	...	...
Klaipeda	ESDJ	188 042	86 694	101 348	98	...	...	...	...
Panevezhis	ESDJ	115 781	52 774	63 007	50	...	...	...	...
Shauliai	ESDJ	129 529	58 973	70 556	81	...	...	...	...
VILNIUS	ESDJ	541 551	246 145	295 406	394	...	...	...	...
Luxembourg									
1 VII 2005									
LUXEMBOURG-VILLE	ESDJ	76 521	...	...	51	...	...	...	...
Malta — Malte[93]									
31 XII 2005									
VALLETTA	ESDJ	7 086	3 382	3 704	1	...	...	...	...
Monaco									
1 VII 2000									
MONACO	ESDJ	*32 020*	*15 544*	*16 476*	...	...	...	...	...
Netherlands — Pays-Bas[94]									
01 I 2005									
Almere	ESDJ	175 007	86 961	88 046	130	...	...	...	...
Amersfoort	ESDJ	134 906	66 021	68 885	63	163 883	80 328	83 555	122
AMSTERDAM	ESDJ	742 783	366 155	376 628	165	1 020 858	501 677	519 181	366
Apeldoorn	ESDJ	156 064	76 595	79 469	340	...	...	...	...
Arnhem	ESDJ	141 321	69 805	71 516	98	142 834	70 556	72 278	126
Breda	ESDJ	168 054	81 615	86 439	127	...	...	...	...
Dordrecht	ESDJ	119 263	58 487	60 776	80	246 318	120 913	125 405	158

8. Population of capital cities and cities of 100 000 or more inhabitants: latest available year, 1986 - 2005
Population des capitales et des villes de 100 000 habitants ou plus: dernière année disponible, 1986 - 2005
(continued — suite)

Continent, country or area, date and city / Continent, pays ou zone, date et ville	Code[1]	City proper — Ville proprement dite Population				Urban agglomeration — Agglomération urbaine Population			
		Both sexes Les deux sexes	Male Masculin	Female Féminin	Surface area Superficie (km²)	Both sexes Les deux sexes	Male Masculin	Female Féminin	Surface area Superficie (km²)
EUROPE									
Netherlands — Pays-Bas[94]									
01 I 2005									
Ede	ESDJ	106 416	52 038	54 378	318	...	...	...	...
Eindhoven	ESDJ	208 455	105 019	103 436	88	320 677	160 764	159 913	199
Emmen	ESDJ	108 617	53 687	54 930	337	...	...	...	...
Enschede	ESDJ	153 679	78 340	75 339	141	...	...	...	...
Geleen-Sittard	ESDJ	...	...	...	...	140 847	69 442	71 405	122
Groningen	ESDJ	180 604	89 304	91 300	80	199 738	98 314	101 424	125
Haarlem	ESDJ	146 739	71 237	75 502	29	189 388	91 231	98 157	76
Haarlemmermeer	ESDJ	131 816	65 755	66 061	180	...	...	...	...
Heerlen-Kerkrade	ESDJ	...	...	...	...	211 359	103 922	107 437	109
Leiden	ESDJ	118 563	57 782	60 781	22	254 387	124 276	130 111	87
Maastricht	ESDJ	121 456	58 589	62 867	57	...	...	...	...
Nijmegen	ESDJ	158 215	75 665	82 550	54	...	...	...	...
Rotterdam	ESDJ	596 407	292 790	303 617	206	999 347	490 163	509 187	330
s-Gravenhage	ESDJ	...	...	...	...	618 825	301 075	317 750	180
s-Hertogenbosch	ESDJ	133 978	65 891	68 087	85	159 217	78 281	80 936	118
The Hague	ESDJ	472 096	231 475	240 621	83	...	...	...	...
Tilburg	ESDJ	199 068	98 323	100 745	116	221 460	109 476	111 984	158
Utrecht	ESDJ	275 258	132 564	142 694	96	410 090	198 934	211 156	168
Zaanstad	ESDJ	139 817	68 938	70 879	74	...	...	...	...
Zoetermeer	ESDJ	115 792	56 683	59 109	35	...	...	...	...
Zwolle	ESDJ	111 900	54 277	57 623	112	...	...	...	...
Norway — Norvège									
1 VII 2005									
Bergen	ESDJ	240 684	118 728	121 956	445	...	...	...	...
OSLO	ESDJ	534 128	260 731	273 398	427	...	...	...	...
Stavanger	ESDJ	114 574	56 608	57 966	66	...	...	...	...
Trondheim	ESDJ	157 387	77 696	79 690	321	...	...	...	...
Poland — Pologne[95]									
1 VII 2004									
Bialystok	ESDF	291 917	137 213	154 704	94	...	...	...	...
Bielsko-Biala	ESDF	177 219	83 711	93 508	125	...	...	...	...
Bydgoszcz	ESDF	369 153	173 343	195 808	174	...	...	...	...
Bytom	ESDF	190 292	92 350	97 942	69	...	...	...	...
Chorzów	ESDF	115 505	55 203	60 302	34	...	...	...	...
Czestochowa	ESDF	248 894	117 445	131 449	160	...	...	...	...
Dabrowa Górnicza	ESDF	131 024	63 315	67 709	188	...	...	...	...
Elblag	ESDF	127 732	61 242	66 490	80	...	...	...	...
Gdansk	ESDF	460 524	218 807	241 717	262	...	...	...	...
Gdynia	ESDF	253 651	121 376	132 275	136	...	...	...	...
Gliwice	ESDF	201 086	97 175	103 911	134	...	...	...	...
Gorzów Wielkopolski	ESDF	125 787	59 972	65 815	86	...	...	...	...
Kalisz	ESDF	108 666	50 980	57 686	70	...	...	...	...
Katowice	ESDF	321 163	152 055	169 108	164	...	...	...	...
Kielce	ESDF	209 962	99 817	110 145	109	...	...	...	...
Koszalin	ESDF	107 702	51 308	56 394	83	...	...	...	...
Kraków	ESDF	757 957	354 927	403 030	327	...	...	...	...
Legnica	ESDF	106 245	50 444	55 801	56	...	...	...	...
Lódz	ESDF	776 297	354 286	422 011	294	...	...	...	...
Lublin	ESDF	355 954	164 456	191 498	148	...	...	...	...
Olsztyn	ESDF	173 350	80 328	93 022	88	...	...	...	...
Opole	ESDF	128 686	60 391	68 295	96	...	...	...	...
Plock	ESDF	127 935	61 372	66 563	88	...	...	...	...
Poznan	ESDF	573 003	266 989	306 014	261	...	...	...	...
Radom	ESDF	227 944	109 075	118 869	112	...	...	...	...
Ruda Slaska	ESDF	147 838	72 169	75 669	78	...	...	...	...
Rybnik	ESDF	141 975	69 759	72 216	148	...	...	...	...
Rzeszów	ESDF	158 987	75 081	83 906	54	...	...	...	...
Sosnowiec	ESDF	229 207	109 237	119 970	91	...	...	...	...
Szczecin	ESDF	413 294	196 547	216 747	301	...	...	...	...
Tarnów	ESDF	118 295	56 357	61 938	72	...	...	...	...

8. Population of capital cities and cities of 100 000 or more inhabitants: latest available year, 1986 - 2005
Population des capitales et des villes de 100 000 habitants ou plus: dernière année disponible, 1986 - 2005
(continued — suite)

Continent, country or area, date and city / Continent, pays ou zone, date et ville	Code[1]	City proper — Ville proprement dite Population				Urban agglomeration — Agglomération urbaine Population			
		Both sexes Les deux sexes	Male Masculin	Female Féminin	Surface area Superficie (km²)	Both sexes Les deux sexes	Male Masculin	Female Féminin	Surface area Superficie (km²)
EUROPE									
Poland — Pologne[95]									
1 VII 2004									
Torun	ESDF	208 386	96 913	111 473	116	...	...	...	...
Tychy	ESDF	131 854	64 173	67 681	82	...	...	...	...
Walbrzych	ESDF	167 498	79 219	88 279	85	...	...	...	...
WARSZAWA	ESDF	1 690 821	780 726	910 095	517	...	...	...	...
Wloclawek	ESDF	120 440	56 957	63 483	85	...	...	...	...
Wroclaw	ESDF	636 854	298 556	338 298	293	...	...	...	...
Zabrze	ESDF	193 212	93 607	99 605	80	...	...	...	...
Zielona Góra	ESDF	118 707	55 765	62 942	58	...	...	...	...
Portugal									
1 VII 2005									
Amadora	ESDF	175 865	84 208	91 657	24	...	...	...	...
LISBOA	ESDF	524 640	239 117	285 523	85	...	...	...	...
Porto	ESDF	236 210	107 099	129 111	41	...	...	...	...
Republic of Moldova — République de Moldova									
1 VII 2004									
Balti	ESDJ	144 200	...	...	...	148 900	...	...	...
KISHINEV	ESDJ	661 200	...	...	121	780 100	...	...	...
Romania — Roumanie									
01 I 2005									
Arad	ESDJ	169 327	79 291	90 036	267	...	...	...	...
Bacau	ESDJ	181 126	87 152	93 974	43	...	...	...	...
Baia Mare	ESDJ	140 885	67 802	73 083	233	...	...	...	...
Botosani	ESDJ	117 563	56 446	61 117	41	...	...	...	...
Braila	ESDJ	218 984	104 992	113 992	33	...	...	...	...
Brasov	ESDJ	283 328	135 891	147 437	267	...	...	...	...
BUCURESTI	ESDJ	1 927 448	897 217	1 030 231	238	...	...	...	...
Buzau	ESDJ	137 042	65 804	71 238	81	...	...	...	...
Cluj-Napoca	ESDJ	311 528	146 445	165 083	180	...	...	...	...
Constanta	ESDJ	306 860	145 488	161 372	127	...	...	...	...
Craiova	ESDJ	299 494	143 732	155 762	81	...	...	...	...
Drobeta Turnu-Severin	ESDJ	110 086	53 297	56 789	55	...	...	...	...
Focsani	ESDJ	101 384	48 569	52 815	...	...	...	...	...
Galati	ESDJ	299 205	145 489	153 716	246	...	...	...	...
Iasi	ESDJ	307 783	145 964	161 819	94	...	...	...	...
Oradea	ESDJ	206 463	97 738	108 725	111	...	...	...	...
Piatra Neamt	ESDJ	110 288	52 605	57 683	77	...	...	...	...
Pitesti	ESDJ	171 098	82 184	88 914	41	...	...	...	...
Ploiesti	ESDJ	234 739	110 876	123 863	58	...	...	...	...
Rimnicu Vilcea	ESDJ	112 384	54 145	58 239	90	...	...	...	...
Satu-Mare	ESDJ	115 655	54 813	60 842	150	...	...	...	...
Sibiu	ESDJ	154 543	72 492	82 051	122	...	...	...	...
Suceava	ESDJ	106 831	51 384	55 447	52	...	...	...	...
Timisoara	ESDJ	303 908	142 593	161 315	49	...	...	...	...
Tirgu-Mures	ESDJ	147 734	70 309	77 425	130	...	...	...	...
Russian Federation — Fédération de Russie[96,97]									
1 VII 2004									
Abakan	ESDJ	164 674	75 749	88 925	...	...	...	...	...
Achinsk	ESDJ	115 461	52 092	63 369	...	117 429	...	...	...
Almetievsk	ESDJ	142 173	66 319	75 854	...	153 121	...	...	...
Angarsk	ESDJ	247 931	113 963	133 968	...	...	...	...	...
Arkhangelsk	ESDJ	351 626	157 183	194 443	...	358 567	...	...	...
Armavir	ESDJ	191 679	85 826	105 853	...	210 197	...	...	...
Artem (Primorskiy Krai)	ESDJ	...	...	...	...	111 466	...	...	...
Arzamas	ESDJ	107 585	48 852		...	...	...	...	...
Astrakhan	ESDJ	501 319	229 381	271 938	...	...	...	...	...
Balakovo	ESDJ	199 572	90 680	108 892	...	200 923	...	...	...
Balashikha	ESDJ	181 481	85 083	96 398	...	...	...	...	...
Barnaul	ESDJ	631 221	281 351	349 870	...	660 101	...	...	...

8. Population of capital cities and cities of 100 000 or more inhabitants: latest available year, 1986 - 2005
Population des capitales et des villes de 100 000 habitants ou plus: dernière année disponible, 1986 - 2005
(continued — suite)

Continent, country or area, date and city — Continent, pays ou zone, date et ville	Code[1]	City proper — Ville proprement dite Population				Urban agglomeration — Agglomération urbaine Population			
		Both sexes Les deux sexes	Male Masculin	Female Féminin	Surface area Superficie (km²)	Both sexes Les deux sexes	Male Masculin	Female Féminin	Surface area Superficie (km²)
EUROPE									
Russian Federation — Fédération de Russie[96,97]									
1 VII 2004									
Bataisk	ESDJ	104 832	49 523	55 309	...	...	...	...	...
Belgorod	ESDJ	340 943	154 721	186 222	...	...	...	...	...
Berezniki	ESDJ	169 910	76 053	93 857	...	172 837	...	...	...
Biisk	ESDJ	227 640	101 852	125 788	...	230 167	...	...	...
Blagoveshchensk (Amurskaya oblast)	ESDJ	217 716	99 996	117 720	...	221 880	...	...	...
Bratsk	ESDJ	256 552	116 674	139 878	...	...	...	...	...
Bryansk	ESDJ	424 057	189 292	234 765	...	444 629	...	...	...
Cheboksary	ESDJ	442 616	198 576	244 040	...	454 011	...	...	...
Chelyabinsk	ESDJ	1 095 053	492 534	602 519	...	...	...	...	...
Cherepovets	ESDJ	309 469	141 752	167 717	...	...	...	...	...
Cherkessk	ESDJ	117 139	52 467	64 672	...	...	...	...	...
Chita	ESDJ	308 492	144 227	164 265	...	310 773	...	...	...
Derbent	ESDJ	104 844	50 304	54 540	...	...	...	...	...
Dimitrovgrad	ESDJ	129 076	60 112	68 964	...	...	...	...	...
Dzerzhinsk (Novgorodskaya oblast)	ESDJ	255 714	114 309	141 405	...	266 400	...	...	...
Ekaterinoburg	ESDJ	1 304 251	587 811	716 440	...	1 334 917	...	...	...
Elektrostal	ESDJ	146 429	65 865	80 564	...	...	...	...	...
Elets	ESDJ	114 511	51 933	62 578	...	...	...	...	...
Elista	ESDJ	103 349	46 762	56 587	...	107 754	...	...	...
Engels	ESDJ	191 953	88 098	103 855	...	227 888	...	...	...
Glazov	ESDJ	100 774	45 615	55 159	...	...	...	...	...
Groznyi	ESDJ	215 675	98 291	117 384	...	...	...	...	...
Hasaviurt	ESDJ	124 001	59 395	64 606	...	...	...	...	...
Ioshkap-Ola	ESDJ	253 407	113 966	139 441	...	279 294	...	...	...
Irkutsk	ESDJ	582 547	262 634	319 913	...	...	...	...	...
Ivanovo	ESDJ	418 248	183 744	234 504	...	...	...	...	...
Izhevsk	ESDJ	623 436	280 928	342 508	...	...	...	...	...
Kaliningrad (Kaliningradskaya oblast)	ESDJ	425 617	199 628	225 989	...	...	...	...	...
Kaliningrad (Moskovskaya oblast)	ESDJ	171 640	77 060	94 580	...	...	...	...	...
Kaluga	ESDJ	329 453	146 764	182 689	...	346 373	...	...	...
Kamensk-Uralsky	ESDJ	183 313	81 928	101 385	...	185 559	...	...	...
Kamyshin	ESDJ	123 747	59 083	64 664	...	...	...	...	...
Kansk	ESDJ	102 001	47 016	54 985	...	...	...	...	...
Kazan	ESDJ	1 110 022	494 437	615 585	...	1 108 469	...	...	...
Kemerovo	ESDJ	522 641	234 691	287 950	...	...	...	...	...
Khabarovsk	ESDJ	579 047	269 279	309 768	...	...	...	...	...
Khimki	ESDJ	179 681	81 535	98 146	...	...	...	...	...
Kirov	ESDJ	448 509	197 991	250 518	...	495 760	...	...	...
Kiselevsk	ESDJ	104 113	47 582	56 531	...	106 804	...	...	...
Kislovodsk	ESDJ	128 857	58 302	70 555	...	134 609	...	...	...
Kolomna	ESDJ	148 762	68 696	80 066	...	...	...	...	...
Komsomolsk-na-Amure	ESDJ	275 908	129 004	146 904	...	...	...	...	...
Korolev	ESDJ	171 640	77 060	94 580	...	...	...	...	...
Kostroma	ESDJ	275 949	123 576	152 373	...	...	...	...	...
Kovrov	ESDJ	152 776	70 748	82 028	...	...	...	...	...
Krasnodar	ESDJ	715 417	325 142	390 275	...	785 803	...	...	...
Krasnoyarsk	ESDJ	917 195	414 161	503 034	...	...	...	...	...
Kurgan	ESDJ	334 294	149 717	184 577	...	...	...	...	...
Kursk	ESDJ	406 410	181 690	224 720	...	...	...	...	...
Kyzyl	ESDJ	108 107	49 800	58 307	...	...	...	...	...
Leninsk-Kuznetsky	ESDJ	109 313	50 633	58 680	...	143 389	...	...	...
Lipetsk	ESDJ	503 112	229 764	273 348	...	...	...	...	...
Lyubertsy	ESDJ	157 739	70 049	87 690	...	...	...	...	...
Magadan	ESDJ	99 836	46 691	53 145	...	106 931	...	...	...
Magnitogorsk	ESDJ	416 656	190 727	225 929	...	...	...	...	...

8. Population of capital cities and cities of 100 000 or more inhabitants: latest available year, 1986 - 2005
Population des capitales et des villes de 100 000 habitants ou plus: dernière année disponible, 1986 - 2005
(continued — suite)

Continent, country or area, date and city / Continent, pays ou zone, date et ville	Code[1]	City proper — Ville proprement dite Population				Urban agglomeration — Agglomération urbaine Population			
		Both sexes Les deux sexes	Male Masculin	Female Féminin	Surface area Superficie (km²)	Both sexes Les deux sexes	Male Masculin	Female Féminin	Surface area Superficie (km²)

EUROPE

Russian Federation — Fédération de Russie[96,97]

1 VII 2004

Maikop	ESDJ	157 223	70 647	86 576	...	175 861	...	...	...
Makhachkala	ESDJ	465 026	222 449	242 577	...	548 414	...	...	...
Mezhdurechensk	ESDJ	103 040	48 229	54 811	...	...	...	...	...
Miass	ESDJ	155 707	70 503	85 204	...	169 698	...	...	...
MOSKVA	ESDJ	10 406 578	4 954 465	5 452 113	...	...	...	...	...
Murmansk	ESDJ	325 101	150 417	174 684	...	...	...	...	...
Murom	ESDJ	123 627	54 933	68 694	...	...	...	...	...
Mytishchi	ESDJ	161 517	72 366	89 151	...	...	...	...	...
Naberezhnye Tchelny	ESDJ	507 945	234 944	273 001	...	511 821	...	...	...
Nakhodka	ESDJ	173 522	84 403	89 119	...	87 299	...	...	...
Naltchik	ESDJ	272 776	122 569	150 207	...	298 756	...	...	...
Nazran	ESDJ	128 776	61 328	67 448	...	...	...	...	...
Nefteyugansk	ESDJ	111 518	54 896	56 622	...	...	...	...	...
Neftekamsk	ESDJ	119 086	55 232	63 854	...	129 848	...	...	...
Nevinnomyssk	ESDJ	130 732	61 338	69 394	...	...	...	...	...
Nizhnekamsk	ESDJ	226 998	106 266	120 732	...	...	...	...	...
Nizhenvartovsk	ESDJ	240 067	117 898	122 169	...	...	...	...	...
Nizhny Tagil	ESDJ	383 094	175 846	207 248	...	...	...	...	...
Nizhny Novgorod	ESDJ	1 289 477	570 535	718 942	...	1 301 325	...	...	...
Noginsk	ESDJ	116 913	52 671	64 242	...	...	...	...	...
Norilsk	ESDJ	131 935	65 642	66 293	...	219 578	...	...	...
Novocheboksarsk	ESDJ	125 467	58 916	66 551	...	125 682	...	...	...
Novocherkassk	ESDJ	180 808	86 037	94 771	...	...	...	...	...
Novokuybishevsk	ESDJ	111 849	50 335	61 514	...	114 188	...	...	...
Novokuznetsk	ESDJ	563 257	255 067	308 190	...	...	...	...	...
Novomoskovsk (Tulskaya oblast)	ESDJ	129 816	58 207	71 609	...	...	...	...	...
Novorossiysk	ESDJ	231 066	110 527	120 539	...	281 270	...	...	...
Novoshakhtinsk	ESDJ	116 191	53 022	63 169	...	...	...	...	...
Novosibirsk	ESDJ	1 405 569	639 747	765 822	...	...	...	...	...
Novotroitsk	ESDJ	104 891	50 087	54 804	...	112 639	...	...	...
Obninsk	ESDJ	105 264	48 450	56 814	...	...	...	...	...
Odintsovo	ESDJ	133 208	63 029	70 179	...	...	...	...	...
Oktyabrsky	ESDJ	108 158	49 884	58 274	...	...	...	...	...
Omsk	ESDJ	1 142 773	520 915	621 858	...	...	...	...	...
Orekhovo-Zuevo	ESDJ	122 226	53 462	68 764	...	...	...	...	...
Orel	ESDJ	329 352	146 629	182 723	...	...	...	...	...
Orenburg	ESDJ	538 626	246 233	292 393	...	556 176	...	...	...
Orsk	ESDJ	247 576	109 991	137 585	...	252 765	...	...	...
Penza	ESDJ	512 896	231 226	281 670	...	514 331	...	...	...
Perm	ESDJ	989 499	444 464	545 035	...	1 001 241	...	...	...
Pervouralsk	ESDJ	132 744	59 912	72 832	...	157 568	...	...	...
Petropavlovsk-Kamchatsky	ESDJ	195 982	97 965	98 017	...	...	...	...	...
Petrozavodsk	ESDJ	266 011	117 346	148 665	...	266 511	...	...	...
Podolsk	ESDJ	180 040	80 513	99 527	...	...	...	...	...
Prokopyevsk	ESDJ	218 850	99 455	119 395	...	221 300	...	...	...
Pskov	ESDJ	200 080	89 637	110 443	...	...	...	...	...
Pyatigorsk	ESDJ	139 729	62 721	77 008	...	204 773	...	...	...
Rostov-na-Donu	ESDJ	1 057 958	481 963	575 995	...	...	...	...	...
Rubtsovsk	ESDJ	160 430	76 224	84 206	...	...	...	...	...
Ryazan	ESDJ	515 938	234 131	281 807	...	...	...	...	...
Rybinsk	ESDJ	217 475	97 460	120 015	...	...	...	...	...
Salavat	ESDJ	157 932	75 767	82 165	...	...	...	...	...
Samara (Samarskaya oblast)	ESDJ	1 133 418	509 653	623 765	...	1 157 191	...	...	...
Saransk	ESDJ	299 154	133 065	166 089	...	327 597	...	...	...
Sarapyul	ESDJ	100 950	45 419	55 531	...	...	...	...	...
Saratov	ESDJ	857 961	383 697	474 264	...	...	...	...	...
Sergiev Posad	ESDJ	114 054	51 622	62 432	...	...	...	...	...
Serov	ESDJ	98 683	44 000	54 683	...	100 819	...	...	...
Serpukhov	ESDJ	126 695	57 464	69 231	...	...	...	...	...

8. Population of capital cities and cities of 100 000 or more inhabitants: latest available year, 1986 - 2005
Population des capitales et des villes de 100 000 habitants ou plus: dernière année disponible, 1986 - 2005
(continued — suite)

Continent, country or area, date and city Continent, pays ou zone, date et ville	Code[1]	City proper — Ville proprement dite Population				Urban agglomeration — Agglomération urbaine Population			
		Both sexes Les deux sexes	Male Masculin	Female Féminin	Surface area Superficie (km²)	Both sexes Les deux sexes	Male Masculin	Female Féminin	Surface area Superficie (km²)
EUROPE									
Russian Federation — Fédération de Russie[96,97]									
1 VII 2004									
Severodvinsk	ESDJ	197 363	91 111	106 252	...	200 241	...	...	...
Seversk	ESDJ	108 090	...	...	...	114 850	...	...	...
Shakhty	ESDJ	249 110	113 185	135 925	...	...	...	...	...
Shchelkovo	ESDJ	112 872	52 733	60 139	...	...	...	...	...
Smolensk	ESDJ	319 329	141 894	177 435	...	...	...	...	...
Sochi	ESDJ	328 525	149 385	179 140	...	396 997	...	...	...
Solikamsk	ESDJ	100 443	46 477	53 966	...	...	...	...	...
St. Petersburg	ESDJ	4 600 000	2 063 335	2 536 665	...	...	...	...	...
Starsy Oskol	ESDJ	217 420	99 871	117 549	...	...	...	...	...
Stavropol	ESDJ	355 914	162 896	193 018	...	355 806	...	...	...
Sterlitamak	ESDJ	264 950	120 800	144 150	...	...	...	...	...
Surgut	ESDJ	291 750	142 772	148 978	...	...	...	...	...
Syktivkar	ESDJ	228 928	104 167	124 761	...	244 354	...	...	...
Syzran	ESDJ	183 518	83 459	100 059	...	...	...	...	...
Taganrog	ESDJ	272 953	122 263	150 690	...	...	...	...	...
Tambov	ESDJ	287 216	128 199	159 017	...	...	...	...	...
Tobolsk	ESDJ	...	...	...	...	105 848	...	...	...
Tolyatti	ESDJ	704 792	330 207	374 585	...	716 759	...	...	...
Tomsk	ESDJ	487 357	225 404	261 953	...	...	...	...	...
Tula	ESDJ	406 726	178 855	227 871	...	518 393	...	...	...
Tver	ESDJ	406 726	178 855	227 871	...	...	...	...	...
Tyumen	ESDJ	538 320	248 253	290 067	...	565 397	...	...	...
Ufa	ESDJ	1 036 026	471 977	564 049	...	1 041 813	...	...	...
Uhta	ESDJ	103 064	49 036	54 028	...	126 936	...	...	...
Ulan-Ude	ESDJ	352 623	162 182	190 441	...	382 528	...	...	...
Ulyanovsk	ESDJ	623 139	284 370	338 769	...	646 996	...	...	...
Ussuriisk	ESDJ	156 029	75 380	80 649	...	...	...	...	...
Ust-Ulimsk	ESDJ	99 778	47 583	52 195	...	...	...	...	...
Uzno-Sakhalinsk	ESDJ	173 618	81 035	92 583	...	181 433	...	...	...
Velikie Luky	ESDJ	103 463	45 958	57 505	...	...	...	...	...
Velikiy Novgorod	ESDJ	218 815	95 200	123 615	...	...	...	...	...
Vladikavkaz (Osetinskaya ASSR)	ESDJ	314 483	146 638	167 845	...	331 840	...	...	...
Vladimir	ESDJ	310 496	139 885	170 611	...	332 587	...	...	...
Vladivostok	ESDJ	586 829	274 670	312 159	...	615 093	...	...	...
Volgodonsk	ESDJ	171 370	78 147	93 223	...	...	...	...	...
Volgograd	ESDJ	999 122	454 702	544 420	...	1 035 269	...	...	...
Vologda	ESDJ	288 404	128 404	160 000	...	297 508	...	...	...
Volzhsky	ESDJ	309 428	141 861	167 567	...	320 865	...	...	...
Vorkuta	ESDJ	...	...	...	...	128 805	...	...	...
Voronezh	ESDJ	848 751	380 307	468 444	...	929 340	...	...	...
Yakutsk	ESDJ	235 560	108 185	127 375	...	254 635	...	...	...
Yaroslave	ESDJ	605 219	269 038	336 181	...	...	...	...	...
Yoshkar-ola	ESDJ	253 407	113 966	139 441	...	...	...	...	...
Yuzhno-Sakhalinsk	ESDJ	173 618	81 035	92 583	...	...	...	...	...
Zelenodolsk	ESDJ	99 647	44 687	54 960	...	...	...	...	...
Zheleznodorozhny	ESDJ	115 289	52 098	63 191	...	...	...	...	...
Zhukovsky	ESDJ	101 171	46 154	55 017	...	...	...	...	...
Zlatoust	ESDJ	191 531	87 301	104 230	...	194 575	...	...	...
San Marino — Saint-Marin									
1 VII 2004									
SAN MARINO	ESDF	4 464	2 168	2 296	...	...	...	...	...
Serbia and Montenegro — Serbie-et-Montenegro[98]									
1 VII 2003									
BEOGRAD	ESDJ	1 297 142	607 363	689 779	...	1 594 977	755 857	839 120	3 224
Cacak	ESDJ	73 693	35 418	38 275	...	117 578	57 103	60 475	636
Kragujevac	ESDJ	146 568	71 069	75 499	...	175 598	85 481	90 117	835
Kraljevo	ESDJ	63 583	30 624	32 959	...	121 595	59 526	62 069	1 529
Krusevac	ESDJ	57 230	27 253	29 977	...	131 116	63 693	67 423	854

8. Population of capital cities and cities of 100 000 or more inhabitants: latest available year, 1986 - 2005
Population des capitales et des villes de 100 000 habitants ou plus: dernière année disponible, 1986 - 2005
(continued — suite)

Continent, country or area, date and city Continent, pays ou zone, date et ville	Code[1]	City proper — Ville proprement dite Population				Urban agglomeration — Agglomération urbaine Population			
		Both sexes Les deux sexes	Male Masculin	Female Féminin	Surface area Superficie (km²)	Both sexes Les deux sexes	Male Masculin	Female Féminin	Surface area Superficie (km²)
EUROPE									
Serbia and Montenegro — **Serbie-et-Montenegro**[98]									
1 VII 2003									
Leskovac	ESDJ	68 970	33 627	35 343	...	155 679	77 366	78 313	1 024
Nis	ESDJ	174 092	83 706	90 386	...	251 362	122 747	128 615	597
Novi Sad	ESDJ	243 232	113 956	129 276	...	309 608	146 734	162 874	699
Pancevo	ESDJ	93 563	44 933	48 630	...	128 447	62 363	66 084	755
Podgorica	ESDJ	...	...	...	...	168 815	82 723	86 092	1 441
Sabac	ESDJ	55 288	26 192	29 096	...	123 155	60 143	63 012	775
Smederevo	ESDJ	63 260	30 782	32 478	...	109 977	54 193	55 784	163
Subotica	ESDJ	108 714	51 513	57 201	...	149 257	71 506	77 751	1 007
Zrenjanin	ESDJ	80 162	38 156	42 006	...	132 430	64 031	68 399	1 326
Slovakia — Slovaquie									
1 VII 2005									
BRATISLAVA	ESDJ	425 293	198 915	226 378	368	...	...	...	...
Kosice	ESDJ	234 937	112 100	122 837	244	...	...	...	...
Slovenia — Slovénie									
30 VI 2005									
LJUBLJANA	ESDJ	247 167	114 727	132 440	164	248 833	115 545	133 288	171
Maribor	ESDJ	91 191	42 804	48 387	38	105 913	50 038	55 875	99
Spain — Espagne[99]									
1 VII 2001									
Albacete	ESDJ	149 434	73 118	76 316	12 431	...	...	...	...
Alicante	ESDJ	279 535	133 842	145 693	2 008	...	...	...	...
Almería	ESDJ	172 055	83 580	88 475	2 962	...	...	...	...
Badajoz	ESDJ	127 736	61 724	66 012	15 302	...	...	...	...
Barcelona	ESDJ	1 392 641	645 778	746 863	991	...	...	...	...
Bilbao	ESDJ	346 683	163 657	183 026	413	...	...	...	...
Burgos	ESDJ	161 520	77 752	83 768	1 084	...	...	...	...
Cádiz	ESDJ	132 872	63 267	69 605	112	...	...	...	...
Castellón de la Plana	ESDJ	139 009	67 626	71 383	1 075	...	...	...	...
Córdoba	ESDJ	303 874	145 870	158 004	12 533	...	...	...	...
Donostia - San Sebastián	ESDJ	177 831	83 418	94 413	615	...	...	...	...
Granada	ESDJ	231 577	107 066	124 511	882	...	...	...	...
Huelva	ESDJ	138 605	66 712	71 893	1 513	...	...	...	...
Jaén	ESDJ	106 449	51 274	55 175	4 243	...	...	...	...
La Coruña	ESDJ	235 847	109 402	126 445	376	...	...	...	...
Las Palmas de Gran Canaria	ESDJ	357 601	175 390	182 211	1 005	...	...	...	...
León	ESDJ	140 638	65 374	75 264	392	...	...	...	...
Lleida	ESDJ	110 770	53 629	57 141	2 120	...	...	...	...
Logroño	ESDJ	130 024	62 371	67 653	796	...	...	...	...
MADRID	ESDJ	2 912 705	1 353 349	1 559 356	6 058	...	...	...	...
Málaga	ESDJ	545 966	261 923	284 043	3 930	...	...	...	...
Murcia	ESDJ	353 943	171 763	182 180	8 865	...	...	...	...
Ourense	ESDJ	102 896	47 855	55 041	845	...	...	...	...
Oviedo	ESDJ	198 989	92 363	106 626	1 866	...	...	...	...
Palma de Mallorca	ESDJ	313 766	152 241	161 525	2 008	...	...	...	...
Pamplona	ESDJ	164 054	77 561	86 493	238	...	...	...	...
Salamanca	ESDJ	153 943	71 790	82 153	386	...	...	...	...
Santa Cruz de Tenerife	ESDJ	200 015	95 764	104 251	1 506	...	...	...	...
Santander	ESDJ	177 180	82 556	94 624	348	...	...	...	...
Sevilla	ESDJ	686 853	327 131	359 722	1 413	...	...	...	...
Tarragona	ESDJ	115 756	56 117	59 639	624	...	...	...	...
Valencia	ESDJ	745 216	354 340	390 876	1 346	...	...	...	...
Valladolid	ESDJ	309 116	147 960	161 156	1 975	...	...	...	...
Vitoria-Gasteiz	ESDJ	218 746	107 514	111 232	2 768	...	...	...	...
Zaragoza	ESDJ	593 204	284 834	308 370	10 631	...	...	...	...
Sweden — Suède									
1 VII 1999									
Göteborg	ESDJ	462 470	226 323	236 147	449	788 970	389 432	399 538	...
Helsingborg	ESDJ	116 870	56 377	60 493	346	...	...	...	...
Jönköping	ESDJ	116 344	56 809	59 535	1 485	...	...	...	...

8. Population of capital cities and cities of 100 000 or more inhabitants: latest available year, 1986 - 2005
Population des capitales et des villes de 100 000 habitants ou plus: dernière année disponible, 1986 - 2005
(continued — suite)

Continent, country or area, date and city / Continent, pays ou zone, date et ville	Code[1]	City proper — Ville proprement dite Population				Urban agglomeration — Agglomération urbaine Population			
		Both sexes Les deux sexes	Male Masculin	Female Féminin	Surface area Superficie (km²)	Both sexes Les deux sexes	Male Masculin	Female Féminin	Surface area Superficie (km²)
EUROPE									
Sweden — Suède									
1 VII 1999									
Linköping	ESDJ	132 500	66 412	66 088	1 431	...	...	...	...
Malmö	ESDJ	257 574	123 610	133 964	154	518 506	252 814	265 692	...
Norrköping	ESDJ	122 212	60 089	62 123	1 491	...	...	...	...
Orebro	ESDJ	123 503	59 759	63 744	1 371	...	...	...	...
STOCKHOLM	ESDJ	743 703	356 604	387 099	187	1 643 366	800 874	842 492	...
Umeå	ESDJ	103 970	51 325	52 645	2 316	...	...	...	...
Uppsala	ESDJ	188 478	91 600	96 878	2 465	...	...	...	...
Västerås	ESDJ	125 433	62 033	63 400	956	...	...	...	...
Switzerland — Suisse									
1 VII 2001									
Bâle	ESDJ	165 356	78 073	87 283	24	401 610	192 661	208 949	271
BERNE	ESDJ	122 427	56 721	65 706	52	320 058	152 617	167 441	410
Genève	ESDJ	175 403	82 201	93 202	16	467 040	223 324	243 716	436
Lausanne	ESDJ	115 208	53 701	61 507	41	290 881	139 072	151 809	275
Zürich	ESDJ	339 234	162 164	177 070	88	960 310	468 595	491 715	847
The Former Yougoslav Rep. of Macedonia — L'ex-République yougoslave de Macédoine									
1 XI 2002									
SKOPLJE	CDJC	467 257	229 485	237 772	...	...	...	...	...
Ukraine									
01 I 2005									
Alchevsk	ESDJ	116 472	53 523	62 949	30	...	...	...	...
Berdyansk	ESDJ	119 505	53 458	66 047	41	122 694	54 971	67 723	205
Bila Tserkva (Belaya Tserkov)	ESDJ	200 865	93 471	107 394	42	...	...	...	...
Cherkasy	ESDJ	290 796	133 856	156 940	60	291 570	134 262	157 308	76
Chernihiv	ESDJ	294 677	136 812	157 865	49	...	...	...	...
Chernivtsy	ESDJ	238 492	109 710	128 782	71	...	...	...	...
Dnieprodzerzhynsk	ESDJ	248 980	112 364	136 616	84	255 882	115 491	140 391	138
Dnipropetrovsk	ESDJ	1 044 094	476 165	567 929	250	1 046 365	477 278	569 087	405
Donetsk (Donestskaya oblast)	ESDJ	991 310	441 714	549 596	305	1 008 002	449 307	558 695	557
Enakievo (Yenakievo)	ESDJ	96 928	43 317	53 611	41	151 930	68 891	83 039	425
Evpotoriya	ESDJ	103 662	46 266	57 396	21	118 670	53 069	65 601	54
Horlivka	ESDJ	276 873	124 786	152 087	162	298 514	134 597	163 917	399
Ivano-Frankivsk	ESDJ	216 626	102 690	113 936	34	232 040	109 938	122 102	90
Kerch	ESDJ	153 858	69 573	84 285	43	...	...	...	...
Kharkiv	ESDJ	1 445 173	660 732	784 441	239	...	...	...	...
Kherson	ESDJ	315 676	142 769	172 907	58	353 128	160 153	192 975	304
Khmelnytskiy (Hmilnyk)	ESDJ	253 068	117 864	135 204	50	...	...	...	...
KYIV (KIEV)	ESDJ	2 625 094	1 217 865	1 407 229	834	...	...	...	...
Kirovohrad	ESDJ	245 226	111 387	133 839	59	253 256	115 031	138 225	74
Kramatorsk	ESDJ	174 440	77 909	96 531	53	208 839	93 877	114 962	349
Krasny Lutch	ESDJ	89 642	41 547	48 095	39	136 916	63 728	73 188	181
Kremenchuh	ESDJ	230 222	105 746	124 476	44	...	...	...	...
Kryviy Rig	ESDJ	695 168	316 203	378 965	243	698 599	317 925	380 674	470
Lysychansk	ESDJ	111 160	50 443	60 717	45	128 454	58 383	70 071	87
Luhansk	ESDJ	449 314	200 381	248 933	120	488 290	218 590	269 700	269
Lutsk	ESDJ	199 832	90 707	109 125	43	...	...	...	...
Lviv	ESDJ	727 061	342 015	385 046	94	752 285	353 969	398 316	168
Makyivka	ESDJ	374 301	170 162	204 139	161	415 715	189 508	226 207	460
Mariupol	ESDJ	479 045	219 290	259 755	134	501 158	229 739	271 419	200
Melitopol	ESDJ	159 135	72 385	86 750	47	...	...	...	...
Mykolayiv (Nikolaevskaya oblast)	ESDJ	504 516	229 322	275 194	112	...	...	...	...
Nikopol	ESDJ	133 828	60 310	73 518	46	...	...	...	...
Odessa	ESDJ	989 468	458 474	530 994	130	...	...	...	...
Pavlohrad	ESDJ	114 691	53 344	61 347	48	...	...	...	...
Poltava	ESDJ	302 939	139 355	163 584	77	...	...	...	...
Rivne	ESDJ	244 448	112 289	132 159	40	...	...	...	...
Sevastopol	ESDJ	338 508	154 201	184 307	55	376 645	171 922	204 723	866
Simpheropol	ESDJ	336 250	148 412	187 838	49	357 999	158 359	199 640	90

8. Population of capital cities and cities of 100 000 or more inhabitants: latest available year, 1986 - 2005
Population des capitales et des villes de 100 000 habitants ou plus: dernière année disponible, 1986 - 2005
(continued — suite)

Continent, country or area, date and city / Continent, pays ou zone, date et ville	Code[1]	City proper — Ville proprement dite Population				Urban agglomeration — Agglomération urbaine Population			
		Both sexes Les deux sexes	Male Masculin	Female Féminin	Surface area Superficie (km²)	Both sexes Les deux sexes	Male Masculin	Female Féminin	Surface area Superficie (km²)
EUROPE									
Ukraine									
01 I 2005									
Siverodonetsk	ESDJ	116 679	52 509	64 170	22	126 626	57 224	69 402	65
Slovyansk	ESDJ	119 937	52 632	67 305	59	139 740	61 742	77 998	74
Stakhanov	ESDJ	84 538	37 342	47 196	43	101 506	45 029	56 477	83
Sumy	ESDJ	281 396	128 337	153 059	62	284 227	129 661	154 566	127
Ternopil	ESDJ	219 238	102 603	116 635	34	...	...	...	...
Uzhhorod	ESDJ	115 468	53 672	61 796	23	...	...	...	...
Vinnytsya	ESDJ	358 403	165 241	193 162	56	...	...	...	...
Zaporizhya	ESDJ	795 422	360 836	434 586	169	798 034	362 008	436 026	328
Zhytomyr	ESDJ	276 618	128 194	148 424	55	...			
United Kingdom — Royaume-Uni[100]									
29 IV 2001									
Aberdeen	ESDF	...	...	...	...	212 125	103 818	108 307	...
Aberdeenshire	ESDF	...	...	...	...	226 871	112 470	114 401	...
Aldershot	ESDF	...	...	...	...	243 344	121 127	122 217	...
Angus	ESDF	...	...	...	...	108 400	52 458	55 942	...
Basildon/North Benfleet	ESDF	...	...	...	...	101 492	48 649	52 843	...
Bedford/Kempston	ESDF	...	...	...	...	101 928	50 341	51 587	...
Belfast[101]	ESDF	...	...	...	...	276 459	129 321	147 138	...
Birkenhead	ESDF	...	...	...	...	319 675	152 133	167 542	...
Blackburn/Darwen	ESDF	...	...	...	...	136 655	66 834	69 821	...
Blackpool	ESDF	...	...	...	...	261 088	124 698	136 390	...
Bournemouth	ESDF	...	...	...	...	383 713	182 875	200 838	...
Brighton/Worthing/Littlehampton	ESDF	...	...	...	...	461 181	220 275	240 906	...
Bristol	ESDF	...	...	...	...	551 066	269 689	281 377	...
Burnley/Nelson	ESDF	...	...	...	...	149 796	72 657	77 139	...
Cambridge	ESDF	...	...	...	...	131 465	65 343	66 122	...
Cardiff[102]	ESDF	...	...	...	...	327 706	156 272	171 434	...
Cheltenham/Charlton Kings	ESDF	...	...	...	...	110 320	53 526	56 794	...
Chesterfield/Staveley	ESDF	...	...	...	...	100 879	49 204	51 675	...
Colchester	ESDF	...	...	...	...	104 390	51 652	52 738	...
Coventry/Bedworth	ESDF	...	...	...	...	336 452	166 666	169 786	...
Crawley	ESDF	...	...	...	...	180 177	88 404	91 773	...
Dearne Valley	ESDF	...	...	...	...	207 726	100 992	106 734	...
Derby	ESDF	...	...	...	...	236 738	115 644	121 094	...
Doncaster	ESDF	...	...	...	...	127 851	62 127	65 724	...
Dumfries & Galloway	ESDF	...	...	...	...	147 765	71 303	76 462	...
Dundee	ESDF	...	...	...	...	145 663	69 140	76 523	...
East Ayrshire	ESDF	...	...	...	...	130 235	57 842	62 393	...
East Dunbartonshire	ESDF	...	...	...	...	108 243	52 014	56 229	...
Eastbourne	ESDF	...	...	...	...	106 562	49 369	57 193	...
Edinburgh[103]	ESDF	...	...	...	...	448 624	214 711	233 913	...
Exeter	ESDF	...	...	...	...	106 772	52 045	54 727	...
Falkirk	ESDF	...	...	...	...	145 191	70 016	75 175	...
Fife	ESDF	...	...	...	...	349 429	167 628	181 801	...
Glasgow	ESDF	...	...	...	...	577 869	272 309	305 560	...
Gloucester	ESDF	...	...	...	...	136 203	66 669	69 534	...
Grimsby/Cleethorpes	ESDF	...	...	...	...	138 842	67 360	71 482	...
Hastings/Bexhill	ESDF	...	...	...	...	126 386	59 247	67 139	...
High Wycombe	ESDF	...	...	...	...	118 229	57 857	60 372	...
Highland	ESDF	...	...	...	...	208 914	102 297	106 617	...
Ipswich	ESDF	...	...	...	...	141 658	69 468	72 190	...
Kingston-upon-Hull	ESDF	...	...	...	...	301 416	146 926	154 490	...
Leicester	ESDF	...	...	...	...	441 213	214 060	227 153	...
Lincoln	ESDF	...	...	...	...	104 221	50 794	53 427	...
Liverpool	ESDF	...	...	...	...	816 216	389 119	427 097	...
LONDON[104]	ESDF	...	...	...	...	8 278 251	4 007 297	4 270 954	...
Luton/Dunstable	ESDF	...	...	...	...	236 318	117 707	118 611	...
Manchester	ESDF	...	...	...	...	2 244 931	1 090 898	1 154 033	...
Mansfield	ESDF	...	...	...	...	158 114	76 884	81 230	...
Milton Keynes	ESDF	...	...	...	...	184 506	91 441	93 065	...

8. Population of capital cities and cities of 100 000 or more inhabitants: latest available year, 1986 - 2005
Population des capitales et des villes de 100 000 habitants ou plus: dernière année disponible, 1986 - 2005
(continued — suite)

Continent, country or area, date and city / Continent, pays ou zone, date et ville	Code[1]	City proper — Ville proprement dite Population				Urban agglomeration — Agglomération urbaine Population			
		Both sexes Les deux sexes	Male Masculin	Female Féminin	Surface area Superficie (km²)	Both sexes Les deux sexes	Male Masculin	Female Féminin	Surface area Superficie (km²)
EUROPE									
United Kingdom — Royaume-Uni[100]									
29 IV 2001									
Newport	ESDF	...	...	...	...	139 298	66 884	72 414	...
North Ayrshire	ESDF	...	...	...	...	135 817	64 238	71 579	...
North Lanarkshire	ESDF	...	...	...	...	321 067	153 966	167 101	...
Northampton	ESDF	...	...	...	...	197 199	96 670	100 529	...
Norwich	ESDF	...	...	...	...	194 839	94 523	100 316	...
Nottingham	ESDF	...	...	...	...	666 358	327 851	338 507	...
Nuneaton	ESDF	...	...	...	...	132 236	64 837	67 399	...
Oxford	ESDF	...	...	...	...	143 016	70 462	72 554	...
Perth & Kinross	ESDF	...	...	...	...	134 949	65 172	69 777	...
Peterborough	ESDF	...	...	...	...	136 292	66 139	70 153	...
Plymouth	ESDF	...	...	...	...	243 795	119 076	124 719	...
Portsmouth	ESDF	...	...	...	...	442 252	216 341	225 911	...
Preston	ESDF	...	...	...	...	264 601	129 665	134 936	...
Reading/Wokingham	ESDF	...	...	...	...	369 804	185 475	184 329	...
Renfrewshire	ESDF	...	...	...	...	172 867	82 525	90 342	...
Scottish Borders	ESDF	...	...	...	...	106 764	51 361	55 403	...
Sheffield	ESDF	...	...	...	...	640 720	312 619	328 101	...
Slough	ESDF	...	...	...	...	141 848	70 286	71 562	...
South Ayrshire	ESDF	...	...	...	...	112 097	53 406	58 691	...
South Lanarkshire	ESDF	...	...	...	...	302 216	144 206	158 010	...
Southampton	ESDF	...	...	...	...	304 400	151 534	152 866	...
Southend	ESDF	...	...	...	...	269 415	129 650	139 765	...
Southport/Formby	ESDF	...	...	...	...	115 882	54 337	61 545	...
St Albans/Hatfield	ESDF	...	...	...	...	114 710	56 585	58 125	...
Sunderland	ESDF	...	...	...	...	182 974	88 892	94 082	...
Swansea	ESDF	...	...	...	...	270 506	130 648	139 858	...
Swindon	ESDF	...	...	...	...	155 432	77 551	77 881	...
Teesside	ESDF	...	...	...	...	365 323	176 475	188 848	...
Telford	ESDF	...	...	...	...	138 241	67 770	70 471	...
Thanet	ESDF	...	...	...	...	119 144	56 266	62 878	...
The Medway Towns	ESDF	...	...	...	...	231 659	114 069	117 590	...
The Potteries	ESDF	...	...	...	...	362 403	176 467	185 936	...
Torbay	ESDF	...	...	...	...	110 366	52 551	57 815	...
Tyneside	ESDF	...	...	...	...	879 996	425 119	454 877	...
Warrington	ESDF	...	...	...	...	158 195	77 334	80 861	...
West Lothian	ESDF	...	...	...	...	158 714	76 701	82 013	...
West Midlands	ESDF	...	...	...	...	2 284 093	1 109 397	1 174 696	...
West Yorkshire	ESDF	...	...	...	...	1 499 465	724 818	774 647	...
Wigan	ESDF	...	...	...	...	166 840	81 254	85 586	...
York	ESDF	...	...	...	...	137 505	66 142	71 363	...
OCEANIA — OCEANIE									
American Samoa — Samoa américaines[15]									
1 IV 2000									
PAGO PAGO	CDJC	4 278	2 086	2 192	...	...	...	...	...
Australia — Australie[105]									
30 VI 2005									
Adelaide[106]	ESDJ	1 129 145	554 962	574 183	1 830	...	...	...	...
Albury-Wodonga[107]	ESDJ	100 175	49 498	50 677	4 410	...	...	...	...
Brisbane[106]	ESDJ	1 790 921	888 980	901 941	5 900	...	...	...	...
Cairns[107]	ESDJ	123 775	62 490	61 285	490	...	...	...	...
CANBERRA[106]	ESDJ	325 405	161 193	164 212	810	...	...	...	...
Darwin[106]	ESDJ	111 179	59 093	52 086	3 120	...	...	...	...
Geelong[107]	ESDJ	165 827	80 851	84 976	390	...	...	...	...
Gold Coast-Tweed[107]	ESDJ	540 115	267 325	272 790	1 320	...	...	...	...
Wollongong[107]	ESDJ	274 838	137 510	137 328	1 090	...	...	...	...
Greater Hobart[106]	ESDJ	203 527	99 485	104 042	1 360	...	...	...	...
Launceston[107]	ESDJ	103 221	50 357	52 864	800	...	...	...	...

8. Population of capital cities and cities of 100 000 or more inhabitants: latest available year, 1986 - 2005
Population des capitales et des villes de 100 000 habitants ou plus: dernière année disponible, 1986 - 2005
(continued — suite)

Continent, country or area, date and city / Continent, pays ou zone, date et ville	Code[1]	City proper — Ville proprement dite Population				Urban agglomeration — Agglomération urbaine Population			
		Both sexes Les deux sexes	Male Masculin	Female Féminin	Surface area Superficie (km²)	Both sexes Les deux sexes	Male Masculin	Female Féminin	Surface area Superficie (km²)
OCEANIA — OCEANIE									
Australia — Australie[105]									
30 VI 2005									
Melbourne[106]	ESDJ	3 635 508	1 792 547	1 842 961	7 690	...	...	...	...
Newcastle[107]	ESDJ	508 597	251 625	256 972	4 050	...	...	...	...
Perth[106]	ESDJ	1 478 039	733 953	744 086	5 390	...	...	...	...
Sunshine Coast[107]	ESDJ	215 059	105 235	109 824	460	...	...	...	...
Sydney[106]	ESDJ	4 255 954	2 115 723	2 140 231	12 140	...	...	...	...
Toowoomba[107]	ESDJ	119 486	57 923	61 563	550	...	...	...	...
Townsville[107]	ESDJ	149 207	75 645	73 562	460	...	...	...	...
Cook Islands — Iles Cook									
1 XII 2001									
RAROTONGA	CDFC	12 188	...	...	...	...	...	...	...
Fiji — Fidji									
31 VIII 1996									
SUVA	CDFC	77 366	38 518	38 848	...	167 975	83 910	84 065	...
French Polynesia — Polynésie francaise									
7 XI 2002									
PAPEETE	CDFC	26 181	...	...	...	124 864	...	...	...
Guam[15]									
1 IV 2000									
AGANA	CDJC	1 100	672	428	3	...	...	...	...
Kiribati									
7 XI 2000									
TARAWA	CDFC	...	...	...	...	36 717	...	...	...
Marshall Islands — Iles Marshall									
1 VI 1999									
MAJURO	CDFC	23 676	12 075	11 601	...	...	...	...	...
Micronesia, Federated States of — Micronésie, États fédérés de									
1 IV 2000									
PALIKIR	CDJC	6 227	...	...	...	...	...	...	...
Nauru									
17 IV 1992									
YAREN	CDFC	672	...	...	...	...	...	...	...
New Caledonia — Nouvelle-Calédonie									
16 IV 1996									
NOUMEA	CDFC	76 293	38 443	37 850	46	118 823	60 327	58 496	1 643
New Zealand — Nouvelle-Zélande[108,109,110]									
1 VII 2005									
Auckland	ESDJ	425 400	211 000	214 400	633	1 241 700	610 500	631 200	1 085
Christchurch	ESDJ	347 700	168 700	179 000	452	367 800	178 700	189 100	608
Dunedin[111]	ESDJ	122 500	58 700	63 800	3 342	114 800	54 900	59 900	255
Hamilton	ESDJ	131 400	64 000	67 300	98	185 100	90 200	94 900	1 099
Lower hutt	ESDJ	100 500	49 700	50 800	377	...	...	...	...
Manukau	ESDJ	332 900	164 000	168 900	683	...	...	...	...
Northshore	ESDJ	212 200	104 100	108 100	129	...	...	...	...
Tauranga	ESDJ	103 900	49 400	54 500	168	109 100	51 900	57 200	178
Waitakere	ESDJ	191 900	92 700	99 100	367	...	...	...	...
WELLINGTON	ESDJ	185 100	90 500	94 700	290	370 100	182 200	187 900	444
Niue — Nioué									
13 IX 2001									
ALOFI	CDFC	615	...	...	...	...	...	...	...
Norfolk Island — Ile Norfolk									
1 VII 1997									
KINGSTON	ESDF	*800*	...	...	...	...	...	...	...
Northern Mariana Islands — Iles Mariannes du Nord									
1 IV 2000									
GARAPAN	CDFC	3 588	...	...	...	...	...	...	...

8. Population of capital cities and cities of 100 000 or more inhabitants: latest available year, 1986 - 2005
Population des capitales et des villes de 100 000 habitants ou plus: dernière année disponible, 1986 - 2005
(continued — suite)

Continent, country or area, date and city Continent, pays ou zone, date et ville	Code[1]	City proper — Ville proprement dite Population				Urban agglomeration — Agglomération urbaine Population			
		Both sexes Les deux sexes	Male Masculin	Female Féminin	Surface area Superficie (km²)	Both sexes Les deux sexes	Male Masculin	Female Féminin	Surface area Superficie (km²)
OCEANIA — OCEANIE									
Palau — Palaos									
15 IV 2000									
KOROR	CDFC	10 600	...	...	...	...	...	...	...
Papua New Guinea —									
Papouasie-Nouvelle-Guinée									
9 VII 2000									
PORT MORESBY	CDFC	254 158	138 974	115 184	...	...	...	...	...
Pitcairn									
1 VII 1993									
ADAMSTOWN	ESDF	53	...	...	5	...	...	...	...
Samoa									
1 XI 2001									
APIA	CDFC	38 836	...	...	...	...	...	...	...
Solomon Islands — Iles Salomon									
21 XI 1999									
HONIARA	CDFC	49 107	...	...	...	...	...	...	...
Tonga									
1 VII 2000									
NUKU'ALOFA	ESDF	21 538	10 625	10 913	...	30 336	15 115	15 221	...
Tuvalu									
1 XI 2002									
FUNAFUTI	CDFC	4 492	2 281	2 211	...	...	...	...	...
Vanuatu									
16 XI 1999									
PORT VILA	CDFC	29 356	...	...	...	...	...	...	...
Wallis and Futuna Islands — Iles									
Wallis et Futuna									
3 X 1996									
META-UTU	CDFC	1 137	...	...	...	...	...	...	...

GENERAL NOTES - NOTES GENERALES

The capital city of each country is shown in capital letters. Figures in italics are estimates of questionable reliability. For definition of city proper and urban agglomeration, method of evaluation and limitations of data see Technical Notes for this table. — Le nom de la capitale de chaque pays est imprimé en majuscules. Les chiffres en italique sont des estimations dont la fiabilité n'est pas assurée. Pour la définition de la ville proprement dite et de l'agglomération urbaine, et pour les méthodes d'évaluation et les insuffisances de données, voir les notes techniques pour ce tableau.

FOOTNOTES - NOTES

[1] 'Code' indicates the source of data, as follows:
CDFC - Census, de facto, complete tabulation
CDFS - Census, de facto, sample tabulation
CDJC - Census, de jure, complete tabulation
CDJS - Census, de jure, sample tabulation
SSDF - Sample survey, de facto
SSDJ - Sample survey, de jure
ESDF - Estimates, de facto
ESDJ - Estimates, de jure
Le 'Code' indique la source des données, comme suit:
CDFC - Recensement, population de fait, tabulation complète
CDFS - Recensement, population de fait, tabulation par sondage
CDJC - Recensement, population de droit, tabulation complète
CDJS - Recensement, population de droit, tabulation par sondage
SSDF - Enquête par sondage, population de fait
SSDJ - Enquête par sondage, population de droit
ESDF - Données estimées, population de fait

ESDJ - Données estimées, population de droit
[2] Dual capitals. — Le pays a deux capitales.
[3] For the urban commune of Antananarivo. — Pour la commune urbaine d'Antananarivo.
[4] Data for city proper refer to population in municipalities. - Les données concernant la ville proprement dite se rapportent a la population des municipalités.
[5] Data include those for two or more cities. - Les données présentées concernent deux villes ou plus.
[6] Data for cities proper refer to communes. — Les données pour les villes se réfèrent aux communes.
[7] For communes which may contain rural areas as well as urban centre. — Commune(s) pouvant comprendre un centre urbain et une zone rurale.
[8] Included in urban agglomeration of Dakar. — Comprise dans l'agglomération urbaine de Dakar.
[9] Pretoria is the administrative capital, Cape Town the legislative capital. — Pretoria est la capitale administrative, Le Cap la capitale législative.
[10] Excluding persons residing in institutions. — Non compris les personnes dans les institutions.
[11] For municipalities which may contain an urban centre as well as a rural area. — Pour les municipalités qui peuvent comprendre un centre urbain et aussi une zone rurale.
[12] The definition of locality is based on the 2000 Population census. - La localité est définie suivant le recensement général de la population de 2000.
[13] Urban agglomeration (Metropolitan area) refers to 2 or more municipalities where there is only one urban concentration. - L'agglomération urbaine (zone métropolitaine) se rapporte à 2 municipalités ou plus où il y a seulement une concentration urbaine.
[14] Including municipalities of Bella Vista, Betania, Calidonia, Curundu, El Chorillo, Juan Diaz, Parque Lefevre, Pedregal, Pueblo Nuevo, Rio Abajo, San Felipe, San Francisco and Santa Ana. — Y compris les municipalités de Bella Vista, Betania, Calidonia, Curundu, El Chorillo, Juan Diaz, Parque Lefevre, Pedregal, Pueblo Nuevo, Rio Abajo, San Felipe, San Francisco et

Santa Ana.

15 Including armed forces stationed in the area. — Y compris les militaires en garnison sur le territoire.

16 Excluding armed forces overseas and civilian citizens absent from country for extended period of time. — Non compris les militaires à l'étranger et les civils hors du pays pendant une période prolongée.

17 City refers to a type of incorporated place in 49 states and the District of Columbia, that has an elected government and provides a range of government functions and services. Also included are Honolulu, Hawaii Census Designated Place (CDP), for which the Census Bureau reports data under agreement with the State of Hawaii (instead of the combined city and county of Honolulu), and Arlington, VA CDP (which is coextensive with Arlington County - an entirely urban county that provides the same levels of services and functions as a municipality. - Par ville, on entend un lieu doté de la personnalité morale dans 49 États et dans le district de Columbia, qui a un gouvernement élu et fournit tout un ensemble de fonctions et de services publics. Sont également inclus Honolulu, lieu chargé du recensement pour Hawaii, pour lequel le Census Bureau établit les données en accord avec l'État de Hawaii (au lieu de la ville et du comté d'Honolulu), et Arlington, lieu chargé du recensement pour la Virginie, qui est de même étendue que le comté d'Arlington, lequel est un comté entièrement urbain qui offre les mêmes niveaux de services et de fonctions qu'une municipalité.

18 Included in urban agglomeration of Washington, DC--VA--MD. — Comprise dans l'agglomération urbaine de Washington, DC--VA--MD

19 Included in urban agglomeration of Los Angeles--Long Beach--Santa Ana, CA. — Comprise dans l'agglomération urbaine de Los Angeles--Long Beach--Santa Ana, CA.

20 Included in urban agglomeration of Dallas--Fort Worth--Arlington, TX. — Comprise dans l'agglomération urbaine de Dallas--Fort Worth--Arlington, TX.

21 Included in urban agglomeration of Denver--Aurora, CO. — Comprise dans l'agglomération urbaine de Denver--Aurora, CO.

22 Included in urban agglomeration of Chicago, IL--IN. — Comprise dans l'agglomération urbaine de Chicago, IL--IN.

23 Included in urban agglomeration of Seattle, WA. — Comprise dans l'agglomération urbaine de Seattle, WA.

24 Included in urban agglomeration of San Francisco--Oakland, CA. — Comprise dans l'agglomération urbaine de San Francisco--Oakland, CA.

25 Included in urban agglomeration of Boston, MA--NH--RI. — Comprise dans l'agglomération urbaine de Boston, MA--NH--RI.

26 Included in urban agglomeration of Phoenix--Mesa, AZ. — Comprise dans l'agglomération urbaine de Phoenix--Mesa, AZ.

27 Included in urban agglomeration of Virginia Beach, VA. — Comprise dans l'agglomération urbaine de Virginia Beach, VA.

28 Included in urban agglomeration of San Diego, CA. — Comprise dans l'agglomération urbaine de San Diego, CA.

29 Included in urban agglomeration of Tampa--St. Petersburg, FL. — Comprise dans l'agglomération urbaine de Tampa--St. Petersburg, FL.

30 Included in urban agglomeration of Miami, FL. — Comprise dans l'agglomération urbaine de Miami, FL.

31 Included in urban agglomeration of Riverside--San Bernardino, CA. — Comprise dans l'agglomération urbaine de Riverside--San Bernardino, CA.

32 Included in urban agglomeration of New York--Newark, NY--NJ--CT. — Comprise dans l'agglomération urbaine de New York--Newark, NY--NJ--CT.

33 Included in urban agglomeration of Las Vegas, NV. — Comprise dans l'agglomération urbaine de Las Vegas, NV.

34 Included in urban agglomeration of Kansas City, MO--KS. — Comprise dans l'agglomération urbaine de Kansas City, MO--KS.

35 Data for urban agglomeration refer to Killeen-Temple 'metropolitan statistical area'. — Les données pour l'agglomération urbaine se rapportent à la 'zone métropolitaine statistique' de Killeen-Temple.

36 Included in urban agglomeration of Lancaster--Palmdale, CA. — Comprise dans l'agglomération urbaine de Lancaster--Palmdale, CA.

37 Included in urban agglomeration of Houston, TX. — Comprise dans l'agglomération urbaine de Houston, TX.

38 Included in urban agglomeration of Minneapolis--St. Paul, MN. — Comprise dans l'agglomération urbaine de Minneapolis--St. Paul, MN.

39 Included in urban agglomeration of Oxnard, CA. — Comprise dans l'agglomération urbaine de Oxnard, CA.

40 Included in urban agglomeration of San Jose, CA. — Comprise dans l'agglomération urbaine de San Jose, CA.

41 Included in urban agglomeration of Bridgeport--Stamford, CT--NY. — Comprise dans l'agglomération urbaine de Bridgeport--Stamford, CT--NY.

42 Included in urban agglomeration of Detroit, MI. — Comprise dans l'agglomération urbaine de Detroit, MI.

43 Included in urban agglomeration of Portland, OR--WA. — Comprise dans l'agglomération urbaine de Portland, OR--WA.

44 Included in urban agglomeration of Salt Lake City, UT. — Comprise dans l'agglomération urbaine de Salt Lake City, UT.

45 La Paz is the actual capital and the seat of the Government but Sucre is the legal capital and the seat of the judiciary. — La Paz est la capitale effective et le siège du gouvernement, mais Sucre est la capitale constitutionnelle et la siège du pouvoir judiciaire.

46 'Metropolitan area' Grand Santiago. — 'Zone métropolitaine' Grand Santiago.

47 Urban agglomeration refers to the urban part of the municipality with a proper city center. - L'agglomération urbaine se rapporte à la partie urbaine de la municipalité avec un centre de la ville.

48 Data for urban agglomeration refer to 'metropolitan area', comprising Asuncion proper and localities of Trinidad, Zeballos Cué, Campo Grande and Lamboré. — Les données pour l'agglomération urbaine se rapportent à la 'zone métropolitaine' comprenant la ville d'Asuncion proprement dite et les localités de Trinidad, Zeballos Cué, Campo Grande et Lamboré.

49 City population refers to urban population of districts within the city. - La population des villes se rapporte à la population urbaine des districts compris dans la ville.

50 For municipalities which may contain rural area as well as urban centre. — Pour les municipalités qui peuvent comprendre un centre urbaine et une zone rurale.

51 Lefkosia urban agglomeration is composed of Lefkosia municipality, Agios Dometios, Egkomi, Strovolos, Aglangia, Lakatameia, Anthoupoli, Latsia and Geri. — L'agglomération urbaine de Lefkosia comprend la municipalité de Lefkosia et Agios Dometios, Egkomi, Strovolos, Aglangia, Lakatameia, Anthoupoli, Latsia et Geri.

52 Lemesos urban agglomeration is composed of Lemesos municipality, Mesa Geitonia, Agios Athanasios, Germasogeia, Pano Polemidia, Ypsonas, Kato Polemidia, and parts of Mouttagiaka, Agios Tychon, Parekklisia, Monagrouli, Moni, Pyrgos and Tserkezoi. — L'agglomération urbaine de Lemesos comprend la municipalité de Lemesos et Mesa Geitonia, Agios Athanasios, Germasogeia, Pano Polemidia, Ypsonas, Kato Polemidia, et certaines parties des Mouttagiaka, Agios Tychon, Parekklisia, Monagrouli, Moni, Pyrgos et Tserkezoi.

53 Including data for the India-held part of Jammu and Kashmir, the final status of which has not yet been determined. Excluding cities for Assam state. — Y compris les données concernant la partie de Jammu-et-Cachemire occupée par l'Inde, dont le statut définitif n'a pas encore été déterminé. Non compris les villes de l'état d'Assam.

54 Data for urban agglomeration includes New Delhi. — Les données pour l'agglomération urbaine y compris New Delhi.

55 Data for urban agglomeration include Bally, Baranagar, Barrackpur, Bhatpara, Calcutta Municipal Corporation, Chandan Nagar, Garden Reach, Houghly-Chinsura, Howrah, Jadarpur, Kamarhati, Naihati, Panihati, Serampore, South Dum Dum, South Suburban, and Titagarh. — Les données pour l'agglomération urbaine y compris Bally, Baranagar, Barrackpur, Bhatpara, Calcutta Municipal Corporation, Chandan Nagar, Garden Reach, Houghly Chinsura, Howrah, Jadarpur, Kamarhati, Naihati, Panihati, Serampopre, South Dum Dum, South Suburban et Titagarh.

56 Included in urban agglomeration of Delhi. — Comprise dans l'agglomération urbaine de Delhi.

57 Data refer to the New Delhi Municipal Council. — Les données se rapportent au New Delhi Municipal Council.

58 Including Karkh, Rassaiah, Adhamiya and Kadhimain Qadha Centres and Maamoon, Mansour and Karradah-Sharqiyah Nahlyas. — Y compris les cazas de Karkh, Adhamiya et Kadhimain ainsi que les nahiyas de Maamoon, Mansour et Karradah-Sharqiyah.

59 Designation and data provided by Israel. The position of the United Nations on the question of Jerusalem is contained in General Assembly resolution 181 (II) and subsequent resolutions of the General Assembly and the Security Council concerning this question. — Appellation et données fournies par Israel. La position des Nations Unies concernant la question de Jérusalem est décrite dans la résolution 181 (II) de l'Assemblée générale et résolutions ultérieures de l'Assemblée générale et du Conseil de sécurité sur cette question.

60 Including East Jerusalem. — Y compris Jérusalem-Est.

61 Excluding diplomatic personnel outside country and foreign military and civilian personnel and their dependants stationed in the area. — Non compris le personnel diplomatique hors du territoire, les militaires et agents civils étrangers en poste sur le territoire et les membres de leur famille les accompagnant.

62 Except for Tokyo, all data refer to shi, a minor division which may include some scattered or rural population as well as an urban centre. — Sauf pour Tokyo, toutes les données se rapportent à des shi, petites divisions administratives qui peuvent comprendre des peuplements dispersés ou ruraux en plus d'un centre urbain.

63 Data excluding Hokkaido region. — Non compris la région de Hokkaido.

64 Including Kokura, Moji, Tobata, Wakamatsu and Yahata (Yawata). — Y compris Kokura, Moji, Tobata, Wakamatsu et Yahata (Yawata).

65 Data for city proper refer to 23 wards (ku) of the old city. The urban agglomeration figures refer to Tokyo-to (Tokyo Prefecture), comprising the 23 wards plus 14 urban counties (shi), 18 towns (machi) and 8 villages (mura). The 'Tokyo Metropolitan Area' comprises the 23 wards of Tokyo-to plus 21 cities, 20 towns and 2 villages. The 'Keihin Metropolitan Area' (Tokyo-Yokohama Metropolitan Area) plus 9 cities (one of which is Yokohama City) and two towns, with a total population of 20 485 542 on 1 October 1965. — Les données concernant la ville proprement dite se rapportent aux 23 circonscriptions de la vieille ville. Les chiffres pour l'agglomération urbaine se rapportent à Tokyo-to (préfecture de Tokyo), comprenant les 23 circonscriptions plus 14 cantons urbains (Shi), 18 villes

(machi) et 8 villages (mura). La 'zone métropolitaine de Tokyo' comprend les 23 circonscriptions de Tokyo-to plus 21 municipalités, 20 villes et 2 villages. La 'zone métropolitaine de Keihin' (zone métropolitaine de Tokyo-Yokohama) comprend la zone métropolitaine de Tokyo, plus 9 municipalités, dont l'une est Yokohama et 2 villes, elle comptait 20 485 542 habitants au 1er octobre 1965.

66 Excluding data for the Pakistan-held part of Jammu and Kashmir, the final status of which has not yet been determined, and for Junagadh, Manavadar, Gilgit and Baltistan. — Non compris les données pour la partie de Jammu-Cachemire occupée par le Pakistan dont le status definitif n'a pas encore été déterminé, et le Junagardh, le Manavadar, le Gilgit et le Baltistan.

67 Covers Seyhan and Yuregir districts in Adana. - Y compris la population des districts de Seyhan et de Yuregir.

68 Covers Altindag, Cankaya, Etimesgut, Golbasi, Kecioren, Mamak, Sincan, and Yenimahalle districts in Ankara. - Y compris la population des districts de Altindag, de Cankaya, de Etimesgut, de Golbasi, de Kecioren, de Mamak, de Sincan, et de Yenimahalle.

69 Covers Nilufer, Osmangazi and Yildirim districts in Bursa. - Y compris la population des districts de Nilufer, de Osmangazi et de Yildirim.

70 District centre. — Le centre du district.

71 Covers Sahinbey and Sehitkamil districts in Gaziantep. - Y compris la population des districts de Sahinbey et de Sehitkamil.

72 Covers Adalar, Avcilar, Bagcilar, Bahcelievler, Bakirkoy, Bayrampasa, Besiktas, Beykoz, Beyoglu, Eminonu, Esenler, Eyup, Fatih, Gaziosmanpasa, Gungoren, Kadikoy, Kagithane, Kartal, Kucukcekmece, Maltepe, Pendik, Sariyer, Sisli, Sultanbeyli, Tuzla, Umraniye, Uskudar, Zentinburnu districts in Istanbul. - Y compris la population des districts de Adalar, de Avcilar, de Bagcilar, de Bahcelievler, de Bakirkoy, de Bayrampasa, de Besiktas, de Beykoz, de Beyoglu, de Eminonu, de Esenler, de Eyup, de Fatih, de Gaziosmanpasa, de Gungoren, de Kadikoy, de Kagithane, de Kartal, de Kucukcekmece, de Maltepe, de Pendik, de Sariyer, de Sisli, de Sultanbeyli, de Tuzla, de Umraniye, de Uskudar, et de Zentinburnu.

73 Covers Bolcova, Bornova, Buca, Cigli, Gaziemir, Guzelbahce, Karsiyaka, Konak and Narlidere districts in Izmir. - Y compris la population des districts de Bolcova, de Bornova, de Buca, de Cigli, de Gaziemir, de Guzelbahce, de Karsiyaka, de Konak et de Narlidere.

74 Covers Kocasinan and Melikgazi districts in Kayseri. - Y compris la population des districts de Kocasinan et de Melikgazi.

75 Covers Karatay, Meram and Selcuklu districts Konya. - Y compris la population des districts de Karatay, de Meram et de Selcuklu.

76 Including Cholon. — Y compris Cholon.

77 City is defined as a residential center that has a zoning and urbanisation plan approved by law. - Une ville est définie comme centre résidentiel soumis à un règlement de zonage et à un plan d'urbanisation approuvés par voie législative.

78 City proper refers to commune or municipality. - La ville proprement dite se rapporte à la commune ou à la municipalité

79 Urban agglomeration refers to core area of an urban region. The core area consists of a densely inhabited area and of urban localities in short distance as well as of next situated urban localities, agglomerated in case of mutual commuting to work (at least 35 index points). - Par agglomération urbaine, on entend la zone centrale d'une région urbaine, qui est constituée d'une zone de peuplement dense et des localités urbaines avoisinantes, ainsi que des localités urbaines situées un peu plus loin, les habitants des unes allant travailler dans les autres (35 points d'indice au minimum).

80 Political district.-District électoral.

81 Data for cities proper refer to communes which may contain an urban centre and a rural area. — Les données concernant les villes proprement dites se rapportent à des communes qui peuvent comprendre un centre urbain et une zone rurale.

82 City is a settlement with a status of city according to the administrative-territorial division of the country at the end of the respective year. - La ville est une agglomération avec un statut de ville selon la division administratif-territoriale du pays à la fin de l'année respective.

83 Data for cities proper refer to communes which are centres for urban agglomeration. — Les données concernant les villes proprement dites se rapportent à des communes qui sont des centres d'agglomérations urbaines.

84 De jure population, but excluding diplomatic personnel outside the country and including foreign diplomatic personnel not living in embassies or consulates. — Population de droit, mais non compris le personnel diplomatique hors du pays et y compris le personnel diplomatique étranger qui ne vit pas dans les ambassades ou les consulats.

85 Data refer to French territory of this international agglomeration. — Les données se rapportent aux habitants de cette agglomération internationale qui vivent en territoire francais.

86 Including Villeurbanne. — Y compris Villeurbanne.

87 Including armed forces stationed outside the country but excluding alien armed forces stationed in the area. — Y compris les militaires en garnison hors du pays, mais non compris les militaires étrangers en garnison sur le territoire.

88 Data refer to the Vatican City State. — Les données se rapportent à l'Etat de la cité du Vatican.

89 The boundaries of a city are related to the boundaries of a commune. - Les limites d'une ville correspondent aux limites d'une commune.

90 The urban agglomeration of the capital area is much bigger and includes the following communes: Bessastaðahreppur, Garðabær, Hafnarfjörður, Kjósarhreppur, Kópavogur, Mosfellsbær, Reykjavík, Seltjarnarnes. - L'agglomération urbaine de la capitale est beaucoup plus étendue et comprend les communes suivantes : Bessastaðahreppur, Garðabær, Hafnarfjörður, Kjósarhreppur, Kópavogur, Mosfellsbær ,Reykjavík ,Seltjarnarnes.

91 City is populated area with no less than 2 000 resident population, which is approved by the Cabinet of Ministers'. - Une ville est une zone de peuplement comptant au moins 2 000 habitants, selon une réglementation approuvée par le Cabinet ministériel.

92 Population is not classified as 'urban' or 'rural'. About 95% of the population in Liechtenstein are living in a community with a population of 2000 and more. - La population n'est pas classée en 'urbaine' et 'rurale'. Environ 95 % de la population du Liechtenstein vit en agglomération comptant plus de 2 000 habitants.

93 Including civilian nationals temporarily outside the country. — Y compris les civils nationaux temporairement hors du pays.

94 Data for cities proper refer to administrative units (municipalities). — Les données concernant les villes proprement dites se rapportent à des unités administratives (municipalités).

95 City is defined as administratively separated area entitled to civil (municipal) rights. Urban agglomeration is not defined. - Une ville est définie comme une zone administrativement distincte dotée de droits municipaux. Il n'y a pas de définition de l'agglomération urbaine.

96 City is defined as industrial and cultural centers according to the legislation. - Une ville est définie comme centre culturel et industriel, conformément à la législation.

97 Urban agglomeration includes the city and its populated localities subordinated to its authority. - Une agglomération urbaine comprend la ville et les localités peuplées qui relèvent de la même autorité.

98 Data for Urban agglomeration refer to communes which are administrative division.- Les données pour l'agglomération urbaine se rapportent aux communes qui sont des divisions administrative.

99 2001 data refer to municipals with 100 000 + population. - Les données de 2001 font référence aux municipalités de plus de 100 000 habitants.

100 Data to urban areas with 100,000+ residents. — Les données se rapportent aux zones urbaines avec plus de 100 000 résidents.

101 Capital of Northern Ireland. — Capitale de l'Irlande du Nord.

102 Capital of Wales for certain purposes. — Considérée à certains égards comme la capitale du pays de Galles.

103 Capital of Scotland. — Capitale de l'Ecosse.

104 'Greater London' conurbation as reconstituted in 1965 and comprising 32 new Greater London Boroughs. — Ensemble urbain du 'Grand Londres', tel qu'il a été reconstitué en 1965, comprenant 32 nouveaux Greater London Boroughs.

105 For all regions it is not possible to distinguish between 'city proper' and 'urban agglomeration' areas, therefore data has been include under 'city proper'. - Il n'est pas possible de distinguer pour toutes les régions entre 'ville proprement dite' et 'agglomération urbaine', et les données sont donc présentées sous 'ville proprement dite'.

106 Statistical division, which is a relatively stable area that includes a large buffer around each city to reduce the need to change boundaries as the city grows. - Division statistique, définie comme zone relativement stable comprenant une zone-tampon assez étendue autour de chaque ville, ce qui permet de ne pas avoir à en modifier aussi souvent les limites à mesure que la ville s'étend.

107 Statistical district, which includes a much smaller buffer and basically just represent the urban area of that city. - District statistique, comprenant une zone-tampon beaucoup plus restreinte, et représentant pour l'essentiel la seule zone urbaine de la ville considérée.

108 Excludes inland water and oceanic areas. - Exclut les eaux intérieures et les zones océaniques.

109 A city is a territorial authority which is a distinct entity, is predominantly urban in character, has a minimum population of 50,000 and is a major centre of activity within its parent region. - Une ville est une collectivité territoriale qui constitue une entité distincte, est à prédominance urbaine, compte au moins 50 000 habitants et est un grand centre d'activité dans la région où elle est située.

110 Urban agglomerations refer to main urban areas that are centres with populations of 30,000 or more. - Les agglomérations urbaines désignent les principales zones urbaines qui sont des centres de population comptant au moins 30 000 habitants.

111 The Territorial Authority of Dunedin City (3341.53 sq km) includes a large hinterland of rural area. The Dunedin 'Urban Area' (255.13 sq km) is the area of Dunedin City that is urban. - La collectivité territoriale de Dunedin (3 341,53 kilomètres carrés) comprend de vastes étendues rurales. La 'zone urbaine' de Dunedin (255,13 kilomètres carrés) correspond à la zone urbanisée de la ville de Dunedin.

Table 9

Table 9 presents live births and live-birth rates by urban/rural residence for as many years as possible between 2001 and 2005.

Description of variables: Live birth is defined as the complete expulsion or extraction from its mother of a product of conception, irrespective of the duration of pregnancy, which after such separation, breathes or shows any other evidence of life such as beating of the heart, pulsation of the umbilical cord, or definite movements of voluntary muscles, whether or not the umbilical cord has been cut or the placenta is attached; each product of such a birth is considered live-born[1].

Statistics on the number of live births are obtained from civil registers unless otherwise noted. For those countries or areas where civil registration statistics on live births are considered reliable (estimated completeness of 90 per cent or more) the birth rates shown have been calculated on the basis of registered live births. However, for countries or areas where civil registration of live births is non-existent or considered unreliable (estimated completeness of less than 90 per cent or of unknown completeness), estimates provided by national statistical authorities are presented and are identified by the code "|" in the first column.

Rate computation: Crude live-birth rates are the annual number of live births per 1 000 mid-year population.

Rates by urban/rural residence are the annual number of live births, in the appropriate urban or rural category, per 1 000 corresponding mid-year population. Rates are calculated only for data considered complete, that is, coded with a "C" and for estimates, coded "|". These rates have been calculated by the Statistics Division of the United Nations Department for Economic and Social Affairs.

Rates presented in this table are limited to those countries or areas having a minimum number of 30 live births in a given year.

In addition, some rates were obtained from sample surveys, using different methods[2]; to distinguish them from civil registration data, estimated rates are identified by a footnote.

Reliability of data: Each country or area has been asked to indicate the estimated completeness of the live births recorded in its civil register. These national assessments are indicated by the quality codes (C) and (U) that appear in the first column of this table.

"C" indicates that the data are estimated to be virtually complete, that is, representing at least 90 per cent of the live births occurring each year, while "U" indicates that data are estimated to be incomplete, that is, representing less than 90 per cent of the live births occurring each year. A third code (...) indicates that no information was provided regarding completeness.

Data from civil registers that are reported as incomplete or of unknown completeness (coded "U" or "...") are considered unreliable. They appear in italics in this table and rates are not calculated for these data.

These quality codes apply only to data from civil registers. If data from other sources are presented, the symbol (|) is shown instead of the quality code. For more information about the quality of vital statistics data in general, and the information available on the basis of the completeness estimates in particular, see section 4.2 of the Technical Notes.

Limitations: Statistics on live births are subject to the same qualifications as have been set forth for vital statistics in general and birth statistics in particular as discussed in section 4 of the Technical Notes.

The reliability of data, an indication of which is described above, is an important factor in considering the limitations. In addition, some live births are tabulated by date of registration and not by date of occurrence; these have been indicated by a plus sign "+". Whenever the lag between the date of occurrence and date of registration is prolonged and, therefore, a large proportion of the live-birth registrations are delayed, birth statistics for any given year may be seriously affected.

Another factor that limits international comparability is the practice of some countries or areas not to include in live-birth statistics infants who were born alive but died before the registration of the birth or within the first 24 hours of life, thus underestimating the total number of life births. Statistics of this type are footnoted.

In addition, it should be noted that rates are affected also by the quality and limitations of the population estimates that are used in their computation. The problems of under-enumeration or over-enumeration and, to some extent, the differences in definition of total population have been discussed in section 3 of the Technical Notes dealing with population data in general, and specific information pertaining to individual countries or areas is given in the footnotes to table 3.

The rates estimated from the results of sample surveys are subject to possibilities of considerable error as a result of omissions in reporting of births, or as a result of erroneous reporting of births that occurred outside the reference period. However, rates estimated from sample surveys have the advantage of the availability of a built-in and strictly corresponding population base.

It should be emphasized that crude birth rates - like crude death, marriage and divorce rates - may be seriously affected by the age-sex structure of the populations to which they relate. Nevertheless, they do provide a simple measure of the level of and changes in natality.

The urban/rural classification of birth may refer to the residence of mother or the place of delivery, as the national practices vary and is provided by each country or area. In addition, the comparability of data by urban/rural residence is affected by the national definition of urban and rural used in tabulating these data. It is assumed, in the absence of specific information to the contrary, that the definitions of urban and rural used in connection with the national population census were also used in the compilation of the vital statistics for each country or area. However, it cannot be ruled out that, for a given country or area, different definitions of urban and rural are used for the vital statistics data and the population census data respectively. When known, the definitions of urban used in national population census are presented at the end of the technical notes to table 6. As discussed in detail in the technical notes to table 6, these definitions vary considerably from one area or country to another. Urban/rural differentials in vital rates may also be affected by whether the vital events have been tabulated in terms of place of occurrence or place of usual residence. This problem is discussed in more detail in section 4.1.4.1 of the Technical notes.

Earlier data: Live births have been shown in each issue of the *Demographic Yearbook*. Data included in this table update the series covering a period of years as follows:

Issue	Years Covered
Special Edition on Natality, CD, 1999	
- Numbers	1980 - 1999
- Rates	1985 - 1999
Historical Supplement, CD, 1997	1948 – 1997
1992	1983 – 1992
1986	1967 – 1986
1981	1962 – 1981
Historical Supplement, 1979	1948 - 1977

For further information on years covered prior to 1948, readers should consult the Historical Index.

NOTES

[1] *Principles and Recommendations for a Vital Statistics System Revision 2*, Sales No. E. 01.XVII.10, United Nations, New York, 2001.
[2] *Manual X: Indirect Techniques for Demographic Estimation*, United Nations publication, Sales No. E.83.XIII.2, United Nations, New York, 1983.

Tableau 9

Le tableau 9 présente des données sur les naissances vivantes et les taux bruts de natalité selon le lieu de résidence (zone urbaine ou rurale) pour le plus grand nombre d'années possible entre 2001 et 2005.

Description des variables : La naissance vivante est l'expulsion ou l'extraction complète du corps de la mère, indépendamment de la durée de gestation, d'un produit de la conception qui, après cette séparation, respire ou manifeste tout autre signe de vie, tel que battement de cœur, pulsation du cordon ombilical ou contraction effective d'un muscle soumis à l'action de la volonté, que le cordon ombilical ait été coupé ou non et que le placenta soit ou non demeuré attaché ; tout produit d'une telle naissance est considéré comme « enfant né vivant »[1].

Sauf indication contraire, les statistiques relatives au nombre de naissances vivantes sont établies sur la base des registres de l'état civil. Pour les pays ou zones où les statistiques obtenues auprès des services de l'état civil sont jugées sûres (complétude estimée à 90 p. 100 ou plus), les taux de natalité indiqués ont été calculés par la Division de statistique de l'ONU d'après les naissances vivantes enregistrées. En revanche, pour les pays ou zones où les services de l'état civil n'enregistrent pas les naissances vivantes et ceux où l'enregistrement des naissances vivantes est de qualité douteuse (complétude estimée à moins de 90 p. 100 ou degré de complétude inconnu), on a présenté, autant que possible, des taux estimatifs nationaux signalés par le code '|'.

Calcul des taux : Les taux bruts de natalité représentent le nombre annuel de naissances vivantes pour 1 000 habitants au milieu de l'année.

Les taux selon le lieu de résidence (zone urbaine ou rurale) représentent le nombre annuel de naissances vivantes, classées selon la catégorie urbaine ou rurale appropriée pour 1 000 habitants au milieu de l'année. Les taux ont été calculés seulement pour les données considérées complètes, c'est-à-dire celles associées au code 'C'. Ces taux ont été calculés par la Division de statistique du Département des affaires économiques et sociales.

Les taux présentés dans ce tableau se rapportent seulement aux pays ou zones où l'on a enregistré un nombre minimal de 30 naissances vivantes au cours d'une année donnée.

Dans certains cas, les données ont été calculées à partir d'enquêtes par sondage, en utilisant différentes techniques indirectes d'estimation démographique[2]. Pour les distinguer des données qui proviennent des registres de l'état civil, les taux estimatifs ont été signalés par une note.

Fiabilité des données : Il a été demandé à chaque pays ou zone d'indiquer le degré estimatif de complétude des données sur les naissances vivantes figurant dans ses registres d'état civil. Ces évaluations nationales sont signalées par les codes de qualité 'C' et 'U' qui apparaissent dans la deuxième colonne du tableau.

La lettre 'C' indique que les données sont jugées à peu près complètes, c'est-à-dire qu'elles représentent au moins 90 p. 100 des naissances vivantes survenues chaque année ; la lettre 'U' signifie que les données sont jugées incomplètes, c'est-à-dire qu'elles représentent moins de 90 p. 100 des naissances vivantes survenues chaque année. Un troisième code, '...', indique qu'aucun renseignement n'a été communiqué quant à la complétude des données.

Les données provenant des registres de l'état civil qui sont déclarées incomplètes ou dont le degré de complétude n'est pas connu (code 'U' ou '...') sont jugées douteuses. Elles apparaissent en italique dans le tableau. Les taux pour ces données ne sont pas calculés.

Les codes de qualité ne s'appliquent qu'aux données provenant des registres de l'état civil. Si l'on présente des données autres que celles de l'état civil, le signe '|' est utilisé à la place du code de qualité. Pour plus de précisions sur la qualité des données reposant sur les statistiques de l'état civil en général et les estimations de complétude en particulier, voir la section 4.2 des Notes techniques.

Insuffisance des données : Les statistiques concernant les naissances vivantes appellent toutes les réserves qui ont été formulées à propos des statistiques de l'état civil en général et des statistiques des naissances en particulier (voir la section 4 des Notes techniques).

La fiabilité des données, au sujet de laquelle des indications ont été fournies plus haut, est un facteur important. Il faut également tenir compte du fait que, dans certains cas, les données relatives aux naissances vivantes sont exploitées selon la date de l'enregistrement et non selon la date de l'événement ; ces cas ont été signalés par le signe '+'. Chaque fois que le décalage entre l'événement et son enregistrement est grand et qu'une forte proportion des naissances vivantes fait l'objet d'un enregistrement tardif, les statistiques des naissances vivantes pour une année donnée peuvent être considérablement faussées.

Un autre facteur qui nuit à la comparabilité internationale est la pratique de certains pays ou zones qui consiste à ne pas inclure dans les statistiques des naissances vivantes les enfants nés vivants mais décédés avant l'enregistrement de leur naissance ou dans les 24 heures qui ont suivi la naissance, pratique qui conduit à sous-estimer le nombre total de naissances vivantes. Lorsque ce facteur a joué, cela a été signalé en note à la fin du tableau.

La qualité et les limitations des estimations concernant la population ont également une incidence sur le calcul des taux. Les problèmes liés au sur-dénombrement ou au sous-dénombrement et, dans une certaine mesure, aux différences dans la définition de la population totale ont été abordés à la section 3 des Notes techniques relative aux données sur la population en général et des précisions sur certains pays ou zones sont données dans les notes se rapportant au tableau 3.

Les taux estimatifs fondés sur les résultats d'enquêtes par sondage comportent des possibilités d'erreurs considérables dues soit à des omissions dans les déclarations, soit au fait que l'on a déclaré à tort des naissances survenues en réalité hors de la période considérée. Toutefois, les taux estimatifs fondés sur les résultats d'enquêtes par sondage présentent un gros avantage : le chiffre de population utilisé comme base est, par définition, rigoureusement correspondant.

Il faut souligner que les taux bruts de natalité, de même que les taux bruts de mortalité, de nuptialité et de divortialité, peuvent varier très sensiblement selon la structure par âge et par sexe de la population à laquelle ils se rapportent. Ils offrent néanmoins un moyen simple de mesurer le niveau et l'évolution de la natalité.

La classification des naissances selon le lieu de résidence (zone urbaine ou rurale) peut se rapporter au lieu de résidence de la mère ou au lieu d'occurrence et correspond à celle indiquée par chaque pays ou zone. En outre, la comparabilité des données selon le lieu de résidence (zone urbaine ou rurale) peut être limitée par les définitions nationales des termes « urbain » et « rural » utilisées pour la mise en tableaux de ces données. En l'absence d'indications contraires, on a supposé que les mêmes définitions avaient servi pour le recensement national de la population et pour l'établissement des statistiques de l'état civil pour chaque pays ou zone. Toutefois, il n'est pas exclu que, pour une zone ou un pays donné, des définitions différentes aient été retenues. Les définitions du terme « urbain » utilisées pour les recensements nationaux de population ont été présentées à la fin des notes techniques du tableau 6 lorsqu'elles étaient connues. Comme on l'a précisé dans les notes techniques relatives au tableau 6, ces définitions varient considérablement d'un pays ou d'une zone à l'autre. La différence entre ces taux pour les zones urbaines et rurales pourra aussi être faussée selon que les faits d'état civil auront été classés d'après le lieu de l'événement ou le lieu de résidence habituel. Ce problème est examiné plus en détail à la section 4.1.4.1 des Notes techniques.

Données publiées antérieurement : Les différentes éditions de l'*Annuaire démographique* contiennent des données sur les naissances vivantes. Les données qui figurent dans le tableau 9 actualisent les données qui portaient sur les périodes suivantes :

Éditions	Années considérées
Édition spéciale sur les statistiques de la natalité (CD-ROM), 1999	
- Nombre	1980 – 1999
- Taux	1985 – 1999
Supplément historique (CD-ROM), 1997	1948 – 1997

1992	1983 – 1992
1986	1967 – 1986
1981	1962 – 1981
Supplément rétrospectif, 1979	1948 – 1977

Pour plus de détails concernant les années antérieures à 1948, se reporter à l'index historique.

NOTES

[1] *Principes et recommandations pour un système de statistique de l'état civil, deuxième révision*, numéro de vente : F.01.XVII.10, publication des Nations Unies, New York, 2003.
[2] *Manuel X, techniques indirectes d'estimation démographique*, numéro de vente : F.83.XIII.2, publication des Nations Unies, New York, 1984.

9. Live births and crude birth rates, by urban/rural residence: 2001 - 2005
Naissances vivantes et taux bruts de natalité selon la résidence, urbaine/rurale: 2001 - 2005

Continent, country or area and urban/rural residence / Continent, pays ou zone et résidence urbaine/rurale	Code[1]	Number - Nombre					Rate - Taux				
		2001	2002	2003	2004	2005	2001	2002	2003	2004	2005
AFRICA — AFRIQUE											
Algeria - Algérie[2,3]											
Total	C	618 380	616 963	...	...	...	20.0	19.7	...	...	...
Benin - Bénin[4]											
Total	I	263 726	...	...	...	...	41.1	...	...	...	...
Botswana[4]											
Total	I	53 735	...	...	...	...	32.0	...	...	...	...
Cape Verde - Cap-Vert											
Total	C	12 926	13 123	13 334	...	...	29.1	29.0	28.9	...	...
Chad - Tchad											
Total	...	397 896	...	...	...	...	...	...	...	...	...
Congo[5]											
Total	+U	41 312	40 708	44 132	44 473		...	...	...	...	...
Egypt - Égypte											
Total	C	1 741 308	1 766 589	1 777 418	1 779 500	1 800 972	26.7	26.5	26.1	25.0	25.0
Ghana											
Total	...	433 202	...	...	...	...	...	...	...	...	...
Kenya											
Total	U	468 249	494 941	495 433	...		...	...	...	...	...
Libyan Arab Jamahiriya - Jamahiriya arabe libyenne											
Total	C	99 187	111 053	...		...	18.7	20.2	...		...
Malawi[4]											
Total	I	555 558	567 241	578 978	...	...	51.4	50.8	50.1	...	...
Mali											
Total	U	525 685	...	...	...	...	...	...	...	...	...
Mauritius - Maurice											
Total	+C	19 696	19 983	19 343	19 230	18 820	16.4	16.5	15.8	15.6	15.1
Urban-Urbaine	+C	7 768	7 930	7 580	7 268	7 115	15.2	15.4	14.6	13.9	13.6
Rural-Rurale	+C	11 928	12 053	11 763	11 962	11 705	17.3	17.3	16.7	16.8	16.3
Morocco - Maroc[6]											
Total	C	541 298	...	...	...	...	18.6	...	...	...	...
Urban-Urbaine	C	282 380	...	...	...	...	17.3	...	...	...	...
Rural-Rurale	C	258 297	...	...	...	...	20.1	...	...	...	...
Mozambique[4]											
Total	I	753 252	...	...	...	...	42.7	...	...	...	...
Namibia - Namibie[7]											
Total	I	45 157	...	...	...	...	...	...	...	...	...
Urban-Urbaine	I	15 352	...	...	...	...	...	...	...	...	...
Rural-Rurale	I	29 805	...	...	...	...	...	...	...	...	...
Réunion[2]											
Total	C	14 541	14 789	14 427	14 545	*14 799	19.8	19.8	18.9	18.9	*19.0
Saint Helena ex. dep. - Sainte-Hélène sans dép.											
Total	C	36	39	37	34	34	...	...	...	...	...
Seychelles											
Total	+C	1 440	1 481	1 498	1 435	*1 536	17.7	17.7	18.1	17.4	*18.5
South Africa - Afrique du Sud											
Total	U	896 200	899 286	875 748	897 514	848 043	...	...	...	...	...
Tunisia - Tunisie											
Total	C	*163 300	...	...	...	...	*16.9	...	...	...	...
AMERICA, NORTH — AMERIQUE DU NORD											
Anguilla											
Total	+C	183	169	139	164	167	15.8	14.2	11.4	13.1	12.2
Aruba											
Total	C	1 263	1 228	1 244	1 193	1 234	13.7	13.2	13.1	12.2	12.3
Bahamas											
Total	U	5 353	...	5 054	...	...	...	...	...	...	...
Barbados - Barbade											
Total	+C	...	*3 812	...	...	...	...	*14.1	...	...	...
Belize											
Total	U	7 215	7 553	7 440	8 083	8 396	...	...	...	...	...

9. Live births and crude birth rates, by urban/rural residence: 2001 - 2005
Naissances vivantes et taux bruts de natalité selon la résidence, urbaine/rurale: 2001 - 2005
(continued — suite)

Continent, country or area and urban/rural residence / Continent, pays ou zone et résidence urbaine/rurale	Code[1]	Number - Nombre					Rate - Taux				
		2001	2002	2003	2004	2005	2001	2002	2003	2004	2005
AMERICA, NORTH — AMERIQUE DU NORD											
Bermuda - Bermudes											
Total	C	831	830	834	831	*835	13.3	13.2	13.2	13.1	*13.1
British Virgin Islands - Îles Vierges britanniques											
Total	C	314	253	269	318	...	15.2	12.1	12.6	14.7	...
Canada[8]											
Total	C	333 744	328 802	335 202	337 422	342 176	10.8	10.5	10.6	10.5	10.6
Cayman Islands - Îles Caïmanes											
Total	C	622	583	623	611	699	15.0	13.7	14.3	13.8	14.5
Costa Rica											
Total	C	76 401	71 144	72 938	72 247	*71 548	19.6	17.8	17.8	17.3	*16.8
Urban-Urbaine	C	...	...	...	31 203	*30 602	...	...	...	12.7	*12.2
Rural-Rurale	C	...	...	...	41 044	*40 946	...	...	...	24.0	*23.4
Cuba											
Total	C	138 718	141 276	136 795	127 192	120 716	12.4	12.6	12.2	11.3	10.7
Urban-Urbaine	C	102 285	103 994	100 429	92 129	88 922	12.1	12.3	11.8	10.8	10.5
Rural-Rurale	C	36 433	37 282	36 366	35 063	31 794	13.5	13.8	13.4	12.8	11.6
Dominica - Dominique											
Total	+C	1 213	1 081	...	...	...	17.1	15.4	...	...	...
Dominican Republic - République dominicaine											
Total	+U	161 733	147 027	142 051	112 630	...	...	...	...	...	...
El Salvador											
Total	C	138 354	129 363	124 476	119 710	112 769	21.6	19.8	18.8	17.7	16.4
Urban-Urbaine	C	83 478	77 779	73 311	...	...	22.2	20.2	18.6	...	...
Rural-Rurale	C	54 876	51 584	51 165	...	...	20.8	19.3	18.9	...	...
Greenland - Groenland											
Total	C	937	940	895	893	887	16.6	16.6	15.8	15.7	...
Urban-Urbaine	C	780	745	717	...	...	16.9	16.0	15.3	...	...
Rural-Rurale	C	157	195	178	...	...	15.3	19.2	17.8	...	...
Grenada - Grenade											
Total	+C	1 899	...	...	...	...	18.8	...	...	...	...
Guadeloupe[2]											
Total	C	7 503	6 995	7 047	7 273	7 551	17.3	16.0	16.1	16.4	16.9
Guatemala											
Total	C	415 338	387 287	375 092	383 704	*374 066	35.6	32.3	31.0	31.0	*29.5
Jamaica - Jamaïque[9]											
Total	C	48 065	44 331	43 407	42 448	41 836	18.5	16.9	16.5	16.2	15.7
Martinique[2]											
Total	C	5 908	5 446	5 430	5 255	5 032	15.3	14.0	13.9	13.3	12.7
Mexico - Mexique[6]											
Total	+U	2 767 610	2 699 084	2 655 894	2 625 056	2 567 906	...	...	...	...	...
Urban-Urbaine	+U	1 749 126	1 762 883	1 684 413	1 762 959	1 776 726	...	...	...	...	...
Rural-Rurale	+U	748 772	718 257	721 339	683 866	643 618	...	...	...	...	...
Netherlands Antilles - Antilles néerlandaises[10]											
Total	C	2 705	2 442	2 488	2 357	...	15.5	14.0	13.9	12.9	...
Nicaragua											
Total	+U	121 310	121 361	120 784	121 402	121 380	...	...	...	...	...
Urban-Urbaine	+U	67 373	65 465	63 105	62 412	62 960	...	...	...	...	...
Rural-Rurale	+U	53 937	55 896	57 679	58 990	58 420	...	...	...	...	...
Panama											
Total	C	63 900	61 671	61 753	62 743	*63 645	22.1	20.2	19.8	19.8	*19.7
Urban-Urbaine	C	39 800	38 167	38 568	38 797	...	...	...	...	...	...
Rural-Rurale	C	24 100	23 504	23 185	23 946	...	...	...	...	...	...
Puerto Rico - Porto Rico[6]											
Total	C	55 982	52 871	50 803	...	50 687	14.6	13.7	13.1	...	13.0
Saint Kitts and Nevis - Saint-Kitts-et-Nevis											
Total	+C	803	...	...	...	...	17.4	...	...	...	...
Saint Lucia - Sainte-Lucie											
Total	C	2 788	2 598	2 486	*2 322	...	17.7	16.3	15.5	*14.3	...

9. Live births and crude birth rates, by urban/rural residence: 2001 - 2005
Naissances vivantes et taux bruts de natalité selon la résidence, urbaine/rurale: 2001 - 2005
(continued — suite)

Continent, country or area and urban/rural residence / Continent, pays ou zone et résidence urbaine/rurale	Code[1]	Number - Nombre					Rate - Taux				
		2001	2002	2003	2004	2005	2001	2002	2003	2004	2005
AMERICA, NORTH — AMERIQUE DU NORD											
Saint Vincent and the Grenadines - Saint Vincent-et-les Grenadines											
Total	+C	2 109	1 985	1 923	1 804	1 779	19.3	18.4	18.3	17.3	17.1
Trinidad and Tobago - Trinité-et-Tobago											
Total	C	18 078	16 990	...	...	...	14.3	13.3	...	...	...
Turks Caicos Islands - Îles Turques et Caïques											
Total	C	271	153	213	300	318	13.6	7.3	8.5	10.9	10.4
United States - États-Unis											
Total	C	4 025 933	4 021 726	4 089 950	*4 115 590	4 138 349	14.1	14.0	14.1	*14.0	14.0
AMERICA, SOUTH — AMERIQUE DU SUD											
Argentina - Argentine											
Total	C	683 495	694 684	697 952	736 261	712 220	18.4	18.5	18.4	19.3	18.5
Brazil - Brésil[11]											
Total	U	2 509 354	2 581 055	2 822 462	2 813 704	2 874 542	...	...	...	...	...
Chile - Chili											
Total	C	246 116	238 981	234 486	230 352	...	15.8	15.2	14.7	14.3	...
Urban-Urbaine	C	216 015	213 171	209 572	...	...	16.0	15.6	15.2	...	...
Rural-Rurale	C	30 101	25 810	24 914	...	...	14.5	12.3	11.8	...	...
Colombia - Colombie[6,12]											
Total	U	724 319	700 455	710 702	723 099	719 533	...	...	...	...	...
Urban-Urbaine	U	552 445	539 729	546 406	554 045	554 145	...	...	...	...	...
Rural-Rurale	U	154 404	148 599	149 345	154 369	152 218	...	...	...	...	...
Ecuador - Équateur[13]											
Total	U	192 786	183 792	178 549	168 893	168 324	...	...	...	...	...
Urban-Urbaine	U	148 551	143 377	137 189	132 618	131 539	...	...	...	...	...
Rural-Rurale	U	44 235	40 415	41 360	36 275	36 785	...	...	...	...	...
French Guiana - Guyane française[2]											
Total	C	5 114	5 249	5 553	5 312	5 998	30.1	29.9	30.7	28.4	30.0
Paraguay											
Total	U	...	...	45 669	49 857	51 444	...	...	...	...	...
Peru - Pérou[11,14]											
Total	+U	354 618	355 870	373 600	...	...	...	...	...	...	...
Suriname[6,15]											
Total	C	9 717	10 188	9 634	9 062	8 657	20.7	21.4	20.0	18.6	17.3
Urban-Urbaine	C	6 016	6 298	...	...	...	...	...	...	...	...
Rural-Rurale	C	3 490	3 670	...	...	...	...	...	...	...	...
Uruguay											
Total	C	51 959	51 953	*50 631	*50 052	47 334	15.7	15.7	*15.3	*15.2	14.3
Venezuela (Bolivarian Republic of) - Venezuela (République bolivarienne du)[11]											
Total	C	529 552	492 678	555 614	637 799	665 997	21.4	19.5	21.6	24.4	25.1
ASIA — ASIE											
Armenia - Arménie[16]											
Total	C	32 065	32 229	35 793	37 520	37 499	10.0	10.0	11.1	11.7	11.7
Urban-Urbaine	C	20 328	20 804	22 629	23 628	23 762	9.8	10.1	11.0	11.5	11.5
Rural-Rurale	C	11 737	11 425	13 164	13 892	13 737	10.3	10.0	11.5	12.1	11.9
Azerbaijan - Azerbaïdjan[16]											
Total	+C	110 356	110 715	113 467	131 609	141 901	13.6	13.5	13.8	15.8	16.9
Urban-Urbaine	+C	49 676	49 733	51 057	59 026	...	12.1	12.0	12.0	13.8	...
Rural-Rurale	+C	60 680	60 982	62 410	72 583	...	15.2	15.1	15.6	18.0	...
Bahrain - Bahreïn											
Total	C	13 468	13 576	14 560	14 968	15 198	20.6	20.2	21.1	21.2	21.0

9. Live births and crude birth rates, by urban/rural residence: 2001 - 2005
Naissances vivantes et taux bruts de natalité selon la résidence, urbaine/rurale: 2001 - 2005
(continued — suite)

Continent, country or area and urban/rural residence / Continent, pays ou zone et résidence urbaine/rurale	Code[1]	Number - Nombre					Rate - Taux				
		2001	2002	2003	2004	2005	2001	2002	2003	2004	2005
ASIA — ASIE											
Bangladesh[17]											
Total		...	...	...	...	...	18.9	20.1	20.9	20.8	...
Bhutan - Bhoutan[18]											
Total	I	...	...	...	...	12 538	...	...	...	...	19.7
Urban-Urbaine	I	...	...	...	...	3 845	...	...	...	...	...
Rural-Rurale	I	...	...	...	...	8 693	...	...	...	...	...
Brunei Darussalam - Brunéi Darussalam											
Total	+C	7 363	7 464	7 047	7 163	*6 933	22.1	21.7	20.2	19.9	*18.7
Cambodia - Cambodge											
Total	U	*359 678*	*367 569*	*375 799*	*384 267*	...	...	...	...	...	...
China - Chine[19,20,21]											
Total	I	17 020 000	16 470 000	15 990 000	15 930 000	16 170 000	13.4	12.9	12.4	12.3	12.4
China: Hong Kong SAR - Chine: Hong Kong RAS											
Total	C	48 219	48 209	46 965	49 796	57 098	7.2	7.1	7.0	7.3	8.4
China: Macao SAR - Chine: Macao RAS											
Total	C	3 241	3 162	3 212	3 308	3 671	7.5	7.2	7.2	7.3	7.8
Cyprus - Chypre[6,22]											
Total	C	8 167	7 883	8 088	8 309	8 243	11.6	11.1	11.2	11.3	10.9
Urban-Urbaine	C	4 760	4 806	4 854	5 366	5 672	...	...	...	...	...
Rural-Rurale	C	2 926	2 637	2 692	2 863	2 512	...	...	...	...	...
Georgia - Géorgie[16,23]											
Total	C	47 589	46 605	46 194	49 572	46 512	10.8	10.7	10.7	11.5	10.7
Urban-Urbaine	C	25 078	...	34 589	...	...	11.0	...	15.3	...	...
Rural-Rurale	C	15 338	...	11 605	...	...	7.3	...	5.6	...	...
India - Inde[24,25]											
Total		...	...	...	...	...	25.4	25.0	24.8	24.1	23.8
Urban-Urbaine		...	...	...	...	...	20.3	20.0	19.8	19.0	19.1
Rural-Rurale		...	...	...	...	...	27.1	26.6	26.4	25.9	25.6
Iran (Islamic Republic of) - Iran (République islamique d')[26]											
Total	C	1 112 193	1 122 104	1 171 573	1 154 368	1 233 873	17.2	17.1	17.6	17.1	18.0
Urban-Urbaine	C	724 072	734 332	768 845	759 162	815 445	17.2	17.1	17.5	17.2	17.9
Rural-Rurale	C	388 121	387 772	402 728	395 206	418 428	17.4	17.2	17.8	17.0	18.3
Iraq											
Total	U	...	...	*691 269	*840 257	*896 340	...	...	...	...	...
Israel - Israël[6,27]											
Total	C	136 638	139 535	144 936	145 207	143 913	21.2	21.2	21.7	21.3	20.8
Urban-Urbaine	C	124 640	126 795	131 658	131 794	130 294	21.1	21.1	21.5	21.2	20.5
Rural-Rurale	C	11 998	12 738	13 272	13 404	13 517	22.3	23.1	23.4	23.0	23.7
Japan - Japon[6,28]											
Total	C	1 170 662	1 153 855	1 123 610	1 110 721	1 062 530	9.2	9.1	8.8	8.7	8.3
Urban-Urbaine	C	947 755	939 091	917 627	916 299	917 831	...	...	...	...	...
Rural-Rurale	C	222 709	214 569	205 813	194 246	144 529	...	...	...	...	...
Jordan - Jordanie[29,30]											
Total	C	142 956	146 077	148 294	150 248	152 276	28.7	28.7	28.4	28.1	27.8
Kazakhstan[16]											
Total	C	221 487	227 171	247 946	273 028	278 977	14.9	15.3	16.6	18.2	18.4
Urban-Urbaine	C	115 316	122 151	138 680	155 997	...	13.7	14.5	16.3	18.2	...
Rural-Rurale	C	106 171	105 020	109 266	117 031	...	16.5	16.4	17.0	18.2	...
Korea (Republic of) - Corée (République de)[31]											
Total	C	557 228	494 625	493 471	476 052	438 062	11.8	10.4	10.3	9.9	9.1
Urban-Urbaine	C	453 431	404 409	...	...	...	...	...	...	...	...
Rural-Rurale	C	103 797	90 216	...	...	...	...	...	...	...	...
Kuwait - Koweït											
Total	C	41 342	43 490	43 982	47 274	50 941	18.9	19.2	18.9	19.8	20.7
Kyrgyzstan - Kirghizistan[16]											
Total	C	98 138	101 012	105 490	109 939	109 839	19.8	20.2	20.9	21.6	21.4
Urban-Urbaine	C	28 491	30 195	31 866	37 381	35 600	16.2	17.1	17.8	20.6	19.4
Rural-Rurale	C	69 647	70 817	73 624	72 558	74 239	21.8	21.9	22.6	22.1	22.4

9. Live births and crude birth rates, by urban/rural residence: 2001 - 2005
Naissances vivantes et taux bruts de natalité selon la résidence, urbaine/rurale: 2001 - 2005
(continued — suite)

Continent, country or area and urban/rural residence / Continent, pays ou zone et résidence urbaine/rurale	Code[1]	Number - Nombre					Rate - Taux				
		2001	2002	2003	2004	2005	2001	2002	2003	2004	2005
ASIA — ASIE											
Lebanon - Liban											
Total	C	83 693	76 405	71 465	73 900	73 770	...	...	...	19.7	...
Malaysia - Malaisie[2]											
Total	C	516 000	482 600	*516 300	*514 500	*512 700	21.5	19.7	*20.6	*20.1	*19.6
Maldives											
Total	C	4 897	5 003	5 154	5 198	5 518	17.7	17.8	18.1	18.0	18.8
Urban-Urbaine	C	1 636	1 877	1 965	2 145	2 456	21.6	24.4	25.1	27.0	...
Rural-Rurale	C	3 261	3 125	3 189	3 053	3 062	16.3	15.3	15.4	14.5	...
Mongolia - Mongolie											
Total	C	49 685	46 922	45 723	45 501	45 326	20.5	19.1	18.4	18.1	17.8
Urban-Urbaine	C	24 691	24 067	24 315	25 812	26 462	17.9	17.1	16.9	17.4	17.5
Rural-Rurale	C	24 994	22 855	21 408	19 689	18 864	24.0	21.7	20.4	19.0	19.1
Occupied Palestinian Territory - Territoire palestinien occupé											
Total	U	*103 780*	*106 511*	*106 355*	*111 245*	*109 439*	...	...	...	...	...
Oman[32]											
Total	U	*39 297*	*40 222*	*40 062*	*40 584*	*42 065*	...	...	...	...	...
Pakistan[33,34]											
Total	I	3 719 694	...	3 683 290	...	3 772 494	26.2	...	25.0	...	24.6
Urban-Urbaine	I	1 192 190	...	1 194 081	...	1 226 151	...	...	...	...	...
Rural-Rurale	I	2 527 504	...	2 489 209	...	2 546 343	...	...	...	...	...
Philippines											
Total	C	1 714 093	1 666 773	1 669 442	...	...	22.0	21.0	20.6	...	...
Qatar											
Total	C	12 118	12 200	12 856	13 190	13 401	18.7	17.9	17.9	17.4	16.8
Saudi Arabia - Arabie saoudite											
Total	...	*559 680*	*564 483*	*569 326*	*574 211*	*582 582*	...	...	...	...	...
Singapore - Singapour											
Total	C	41 451	40 760	37 485	37 174	37 492	10.0	9.8	9.0	8.8	8.6
Sri Lanka											
Total	+C	358 583	*363 549	*363 343	*360 220	...	19.1	*19.1	*18.9	*18.5	...
Syrian Arab Republic - République arabe syrienne[2,35]											
Total	U	*524 212*	*471 970*	*492 639*	*491 476*	...	...	...	...	...	...
Tajikistan - Tadjikistan[16,36]											
Total	I	171 623	175 599	177 938	179 600	180 800	27.2	27.3	27.1	26.8	26.4
Urban-Urbaine	I	45 454	42 823	45 182	...	...	27.1	25.1	26.0	...	...
Rural-Rurale	I	126 169	132 776	132 756	...	...	27.2	28.0	27.5	...	...
Thailand - Thaïlande											
Total	+U	*790 425*	*782 911*	*742 183*	*813 069*	*809 485*	...	...	...	...	...
Turkey - Turquie[37]											
Total	I	1 486 000	1 362 000	1 361 000	1 360 000	1 361 000	21.7	19.7	19.4	19.1	18.9
Uzbekistan - Ouzbékistan[16]											
Total	C	512 950	...	...	...	...	20.5	...	...	...	...
Urban-Urbaine	C	159 492	...	...	...	...	17.2	...	...	...	...
Rural-Rurale	C	353 458	...	...	...	...	22.5	...	...	...	...
Yemen - Yémen											
Total	...	...	*189 341*	*130 112*	*153 945*	*152 792*	...	...	...	...	...
EUROPE											
Albania - Albanie											
Total	C	54 283	45 515	47 012	43 022	39 612	17.7	14.7	15.1	13.8	12.6
Andorra - Andorre											
Total	C	777	749	721	814	828	11.8	11.3	10.3	10.9	10.5
Austria - Autriche											
Total	C	75 458	78 399	76 944	78 968	78 190	9.4	9.7	9.5	9.7	9.5
Belarus - Bélarus[16]											
Total	C	91 720	88 743	88 512	88 943	90 508	9.2	8.9	9.0	9.1	9.3
Urban-Urbaine	C	66 612	65 091	64 814	65 038	66 259	9.5	9.3	9.2	9.2	9.4
Rural-Rurale	C	25 108	23 652	23 698	23 905	24 249	8.5	8.2	8.4	8.6	8.9

9. Live births and crude birth rates, by urban/rural residence: 2001 - 2005
Naissances vivantes et taux bruts de natalité selon la résidence, urbaine/rurale: 2001 - 2005
(continued — suite)

Continent, country or area and urban/rural residence / Continent, pays ou zone et résidence urbaine/rurale	Code[1]	Number - Nombre					Rate - Taux				
		2001	2002	2003	2004	2005	2001	2002	2003	2004	2005
EUROPE											
Belgium - Belgique[38]											
Total	C	114 014	111 225	112 591	116 048	117 799	11.1	10.8	10.9	11.1	11.2
Bosnia and Herzegovina - Bosnie-Herzégovine											
Total	C	37 717	35 587	35 234	35 151	34 627	9.9	9.3	9.2	9.1	9.0
Bulgaria - Bulgarie											
Total	C	68 180	66 499	67 359	69 886	71 075	8.6	8.5	8.6	9.0	9.2
Urban-Urbaine	C	48 567	47 779	48 597	50 390	52 280	8.9	8.7	8.9	9.3	9.6
Rural-Rurale	C	19 613	18 720	18 762	19 496	18 795	8.1	7.8	7.9	8.3	8.1
Channel Islands: Jersey - Îles Anglo-Normandes: Jersey											
Total	+C	973	930	1 005	971	969	11.2	10.6	11.5	11.1	11.0
Croatia - Croatie											
Total	C	40 993	40 094	39 668	40 307	42 492	9.2	9.0	8.9	9.1	9.6
Urban-Urbaine	C	22 938	22 539	21 837	22 420	23 421	9.3	...	...	...	...
Rural-Rurale	C	18 055	17 555	17 831	17 887	19 071	9.2	...	...	...	...
Czech Republic - République tchèque											
Total	C	90 715	97 878	93 685	97 664	102 211	8.9	9.6	9.2	9.6	10.0
Urban-Urbaine	C	67 081	73 482	69 120	72 231	75 719	8.9	9.8	9.2	9.6	10.0
Rural-Rurale	C	23 634	24 396	24 565	25 433	26 492	8.9	9.2	9.2	9.5	9.9
Denmark - Danemark[39]											
Total	C	65 458	64 075	64 599	64 609	64 282	12.2	11.9	12.0	12.0	11.9
Estonia - Estonie											
Total	C	12 632	13 001	13 036	13 992	14 350	9.3	9.6	9.6	10.4	10.7
Urban-Urbaine	C	8 645	8 840	9 049	9 892	10 233	9.2	9.4	9.7	10.6	11.0
Rural-Rurale	C	3 987	4 161	3 987	4 100	4 117	9.5	10.0	9.6	9.9	10.0
Faeroe Islands - Îles Féroé											
Total	C	632	709	705	713	712	13.6	15.0	14.7	14.8	14.8
Finland - Finlande[40]											
Total	C	56 189	55 555	56 630	57 758	57 745	10.8	10.7	10.9	11.0	11.0
Urban-Urbaine	C	36 191	36 263	37 303	37 816	38 181	11.4	11.3	11.5	11.7	11.6
Rural-Rurale	C	19 998	19 292	19 327	19 942	19 564	10.0	9.7	9.8	10.1	10.0
France[41,42]											
Total	C	770 945	761 630	761 464	767 816	774 355	13.0	12.7	12.6	12.7	12.7
Urban-Urbaine	C	585 317	577 724	574 477	578 024	581 681	...	...	...	...	...
Rural-Rurale	C	184 112	182 454	185 572	188 475	191 223	...	...	...	...	...
Germany - Allemagne											
Total	C	734 475	719 250	706 721	705 622	685 795	8.9	8.7	8.6	8.6	8.3
Gibraltar[43]											
Total	+C	374	371	372	421	418	13.6	13.0	13.0	14.7	14.5
Greece - Grèce											
Total	C	102 282	103 838	104 420	105 655	107 545	9.3	9.5	9.5	9.6	9.7
Urban-Urbaine	C	...	...	...	...	73 816	...	...	...	...	...
Rural-Rurale	C	...	...	...	...	33 729	...	...	...	...	...
Hungary - Hongrie[6]											
Total	C	97 047	96 804	94 647	95 137	97 496	9.5	9.5	9.3	9.4	9.7
Urban-Urbaine	C	59 119	60 753	59 280	60 331	63 785	9.0	9.2	9.0	9.2	9.6
Rural-Rurale	C	37 019	35 248	34 465	33 983	32 860	10.2	9.9	9.7	9.6	9.6
Iceland - Islande											
Total	C	4 091	4 049	4 143	4 234	4 280	14.4	14.1	14.3	14.5	14.5
Urban-Urbaine	C	3 849	3 823	3 906	...	4 054	14.6	14.4	14.6	...	14.7
Rural-Rurale	C	242	226	237	...	226	11.2	10.5	11.1	...	10.8
Ireland - Irlande[44]											
Total	+C	57 854	60 521	61 529	*61 684	*61 042	15.0	15.5	15.5	*15.3	*14.8
Isle of Man - Îles de Man											
Total	+C	863	903	860	862	901	11.3	11.7	11.1	11.1	11.6
Italy - Italie											
Total	C	535 282	530 443	544 063	562 599	554 022	9.4	9.3	9.4	9.7	9.5
Latvia - Lettonie[16]											
Total	C	19 664	20 044	21 006	20 334	21 497	8.3	8.6	9.0	8.8	9.3
Urban-Urbaine	C	12 531	12 938	13 891	13 820	14 591	7.8	8.2	8.8	8.8	9.3
Rural-Rurale	C	7 133	7 106	7 115	6 514	6 906	9.4	9.4	9.5	8.8	9.4

9. Live births and crude birth rates, by urban/rural residence: 2001 - 2005
Naissances vivantes et taux bruts de natalité selon la résidence, urbaine/rurale: 2001 - 2005
(continued — suite)

Continent, country or area and urban/rural residence / Continent, pays ou zone et résidence urbaine/rurale	Code[1]	Number - Nombre					Rate - Taux				
		2001	2002	2003	2004	2005	2001	2002	2003	2004	2005
EUROPE											
Liechtenstein											
Total	C	401	395	347	372	*381	12.1	11.7	10.2	10.8	*11.0
Lithuania - Lituanie[16]											
Total	C	31 546	30 014	30 598	30 419	30 541	9.1	8.7	8.9	8.9	8.9
Urban-Urbaine	C	19 672	18 697	19 140	19 464	19 914	8.4	8.1	8.3	8.5	8.8
Rural-Rurale	C	11 874	11 317	11 458	10 955	10 627	10.3	9.9	10.0	9.6	9.3
Luxembourg											
Total	C	5 459	5 345	5 303	5 452	5 371	12.4	12.0	11.8	12.0	11.7
Malta - Malte[45]											
Total	C	3 859	3 805	4 036	3 887	3 858	10.0	9.8	10.1	9.7	9.6
Monaco											
Total	C	748	771	842	825	894	...	...	...	...	...
Netherlands - Pays-Bas[46]											
Total	C	202 603	202 083	200 297	194 007	187 910	12.6	12.5	12.3	11.9	11.5
Urban-Urbaine	C	132 295	132 825	132 805	130 945	128 353	12.7	12.7	12.5	12.2	11.9
Rural-Rurale	C	70 308	69 258	67 492	63 062	59 557	12.4	12.2	12.0	11.3	10.7
Norway - Norvège											
Total	C	56 696	55 434	56 458	56 951	56 756	12.6	12.2	12.4	12.4	12.3
Poland - Pologne											
Total	C	368 205	353 765	351 072	356 131	364 383	9.6	9.3	9.2	9.3	9.5
Urban-Urbaine	C	205 708	197 434	199 583	204 898	211 200	8.7	8.4	8.5	8.7	9.0
Rural-Rurale	C	162 497	156 331	151 489	151 233	153 183	11.1	10.7	10.3	10.3	10.4
Portugal											
Total	C	112 774	114 383	112 515	109 298	109 399	11.0	11.0	10.8	10.4	10.4
Republic of Moldova - République de Moldova[16]											
Total	C	36 448	35 705	36 471	38 272	37 695	10.0	9.9	10.1	10.6	10.5
Urban-Urbaine	C	12 542	12 747	12 788	14 060	13 583	8.4	8.6	8.6	9.5	9.2
Rural-Rurale	C	23 906	22 958	23 683	24 212	24 112	11.1	10.7	11.1	11.4	11.4
Romania - Roumanie											
Total	C	220 368	210 529	212 459	216 261	221 020	9.8	9.7	9.8	10.0	10.2
Urban-Urbaine	C	102 432	98 190	100 915	111 348	117 780	8.4	8.5	8.7	9.4	9.9
Rural-Rurale	C	117 936	112 339	111 544	104 913	103 240	11.6	11.0	11.0	10.7	10.6
Russian Federation - Fédération de Russie[16]											
Total	C	1 311 604	1 396 967	1 477 301	1 502 477	*1 457 400	9.0	9.6	10.2	10.4	*10.2
Urban-Urbaine	C	928 642	998 056	1 050 565	1 074 247	...	8.7	9.4	9.9	10.2	...
Rural-Rurale	C	382 962	398 911	426 736	428 230	...	9.8	10.3	11.1	11.1	...
San Marino - Saint-Marin											
Total	+C	315	295	300	306	284	11.4	10.4	10.3	10.4	9.2
Serbia and Montenegro - Serbie-et-Montenegro[47]											
Total	C	130 194	86 600	87 370	*88 406	...	12.2	10.7	10.7	*10.9	...
Urban-Urbaine	C	69 491	54 356	54 296	...	...	12.6	11.8	11.7	...	...
Rural-Rurale	C	60 703	32 244	33 074	...	...	11.8	9.2	9.5	...	...
Slovakia - Slovaquie											
Total	C	51 136	50 841	51 713	53 747	54 430	9.5	9.5	9.6	10.0	10.1
Urban-Urbaine	C	26 106	26 321	26 798	28 399	28 816	8.7	8.7	8.9	9.5	9.6
Rural-Rurale	C	25 030	24 520	24 915	25 348	25 614	10.6	10.4	10.5	10.6	10.7
Slovenia - Slovénie											
Total	C	17 477	17 501	17 321	17 961	18 157	8.8	8.8	8.7	9.0	9.1
Urban-Urbaine	C	8 039	8 400	8 425	8 745	8 869	...	8.6	8.7	9.0	9.2
Rural-Rurale	C	9 438	9 101	8 896	9 216	9 288	...	9.3	9.1	9.4	9.4
Spain - Espagne											
Total	C	406 380	418 846	441 881	454 591	*465 616	10.0	10.1	10.5	10.6	*10.7
Sweden - Suède[48]											
Total	C	91 466	95 815	99 157	100 928	101 346	10.3	10.7	11.1	11.2	11.2
Switzerland - Suisse											
Total	C	73 509	72 372	71 848	73 082	72 903	10.1	9.9	9.8	9.9	9.8
Urban-Urbaine	C	49 292	52 869	52 727	53 795	53 976	9.3	9.9	9.8	9.9	9.9
Rural-Rurale	C	24 217	19 503	19 121	19 287	18 927	12.4	10.0	9.7	9.7	9.5

9. Live births and crude birth rates, by urban/rural residence: 2001 - 2005
Naissances vivantes et taux bruts de natalité selon la résidence, urbaine/rurale: 2001 - 2005
(continued — suite)

Continent, country or area and urban/rural residence / Continent, pays ou zone et résidence urbaine/rurale	Code[1]	Number - Nombre					Rate - Taux				
		2001	2002	2003	2004	2005	2001	2002	2003	2004	2005
EUROPE											
The Former Yugoslav Rep. of Macedonia - L'ex-République yougoslave de Macédoine											
Total	C	27 010	27 761	27 011	23 361	22 482	13.3	13.7	13.3	11.5	11.0
Urban-Urbaine	C	14 761	14 909	...	...	12 519	...	...	...	...	...
Rural-Rurale	C	12 249	12 852	...	...	9 963	...	...	...	...	...
Ukraine[16]											
Total	C	376 478	390 688	408 589	427 259	426 086	7.7	8.1	8.5	9.0	9.1
Urban-Urbaine	C	237 228	248 877	266 415	284 361	284 257	7.3	7.7	8.3	...	...
Rural-Rurale	C	139 250	141 811	142 174	142 898	141 829	8.7	8.9	9.1	...	...
United Kingdom - Royaume-Uni[49,50]											
Total	C	669 123	668 777	695 549	*715 996	722 600	11.3	11.3	11.7	*12.0	12.0
OCEANIA — OCEANIE											
American Samoa - Samoas américaines											
Total	C	1 655	1 629	1 608	1 713	1 720	27.9	26.8	25.7	26.7	26.3
Australia - Australie											
Total	+C	246 394	250 988	251 161	254 246	259 791	12.7	12.8	12.6	12.6	12.7
Urban-Urbaine	+C	147 379	165 041	166 906	169 901	176 079	9.4	...	...	9.7	...
Rural-Rurale	+C	99 015	85 947	84 255	84 345	83 712	27.0	...	...	32.6	...
Cook Islands - Îles Cook											
Total	+C	313	292	298	295	...	17.2	15.9	16.2	14.5	...
Fiji - Fidji											
Total	+C	16 689	16 990	17 701	...	...	20.5	20.7	21.4	...	...
French Polynesia - Polynésie française											
Total	C	4 874	4 763	4 501	4 431	4 469	20.4	19.6	18.2	17.7	17.6
Guam[51]											
Total	C	3 583	3 222	3 298	*3 427	*3 203	22.6	20.0	20.2	*20.6	*19.0
Marshall Islands - Îles Marshall											
Total	+U	*1 511	...	...	...	...	...	...	...	...	...
Micronesia, Federated States of - Micronésie, États Fédérés de La											
Total	U	2 620	2 446	2 483	...	...	...	...	...	...	...
Nauru											
Total	C	296	219	...	...	...	25.3	...	...	...	...
New Caledonia - Nouvelle-Calédonie											
Total	C	4 326	4 194	4 102	3 978	...	19.9	18.9	18.2	17.3	...
New Zealand - Nouvelle-Zélande[6]											
Total	+C	55 799	54 021	56 134	58 073	57 745	14.4	13.7	14.0	14.3	14.1
Urban-Urbaine	+C	48 745	47 068	49 166	50 933	50 300	14.6	13.9	14.3	14.6	14.2
Rural-Rurale	+C	6 986	6 896	6 878	7 060	7 391	12.7	12.5	12.3	12.5	13.0
Niue - Nioué[52]											
Total	C	23	25	33	18	...	...	...	...	...	...
Northern Mariana Islands - Îles Mariannes septentrionales											
Total	U	1 451	1 289	1 355	1 439	1 335	...	...	...	...	...
Palau - Palaos											
Total	C	300	259	312	259	279	15.3	13.0	15.4	12.6	14.0
Papua New Guinea - Papouasie-Nouvelle-Guinée											
Total	U	182 619	187 645	192 817	...	...	...	...	...	...	...
Samoa											
Total	C	*3 516	*2 826	*2 070	*1 679	...	...	*19.9	*15.8	*11.5	*9.2	...

9. Live births and crude birth rates, by urban/rural residence: 2001 - 2005
Naissances vivantes et taux bruts de natalité selon la résidence, urbaine/rurale: 2001 - 2005
(continued — suite)

Continent, country or area and urban/rural residence / Continent, pays ou zone et résidence urbaine/rurale	Code[1]	Number - Nombre					Rate - Taux				
		2001	2002	2003	2004	2005	2001	2002	2003	2004	2005
OCEANIA — OCEANIE											
Tokelau - Tokélaou											
Total	...	*19*	*20*	...	...	...	...	...	...	...	...
Tonga											
Total	+C	2 546	2 662	2 781	*2 628	...	25.3	26.4	27.4	...	...
Tuvalu											
Total	U	*197*	*156*	*185*	*190*	*231*	...	...	...	...	...
Wallis and Futuna Islands - Îles Wallis et Futuna											
Total	C	266	262	290	241	223	...	...	19.4	...	...

FOOTNOTES - NOTES

Italics: data from civil registers that are incomplete or of unknown completeness. — Italiques: données incomplètes ou dont le degré de complétude n'est pas connu provenant des registres de l'état civil.

* Provisional. — Données provisoires.

[1] 'Code' indicates the source of data, as follows:
C - Civil registration, estimated over 90% complete
U - Civil registration, estimated less than 90% complete
| - Other source, estimated reliable
+ - Data tabulated by date of registration rather than occurence.
... - Information not available

Le 'Code' indique la source des données, comme suit:
C - Registres de l'état civil considérés complèts à 90 p. 100 au moins.
U - Registres de l'état civil qui ne sont pas considérés complèts à 90 p. 100 au moins.
| - Autre source, considérée fiable.
+ - Données exploitées selon la date de l'enregistrement et non la date de l'événement.
... - Information non disponible.

[2] Excluding live-born infants who died before their birth was registered. -Non compris les enfants nés vivants décédés avant l'enregistrement de leur naissance.

[3] For Algerian population only. -Pour la population algérienne seulement.

[4] Data refer to national projections. -Les données se réfèrent aux projections nationales.

[5] Data from civil registration centers of Brazzaville, Pointe-Noire, Dolisie, Nkayi, Mossendijo and Ouesso communes. -Données issues des centers d'enregistrement des faits d'état-civil des communes de Brazzaville, Pointe-Noire, Dolisie, Nkayi, Mossendijo et Ouesso.

[6] Figures for urban and rural areas do not add up to the total, since they do not include the category 'Unknown residence'. -La somme des données pour la résidence urbaine et rurale n'est pas égale au total parce qu'elle n'inclue pas la catégorie 'Résidence inconnue'.

[7] For 2001, data refer to last twelve months preceding census in August 2001. -Pour 2001, les données se rapportent aux douze mois précédant le recensement d'août 2001.

[8] Including Canadian residents temporarily in the United States, but excluding United States residents temporarily in Canada. -Y compris les résidents canadiens se trouvant temporairement aux Etats-Unis, mais ne comprenant pas les résidents des Etats-Unis se trouvant temporairement au Canada.

[9] Including births to non-resident mothers. -Y compris les naissances chez des mères non résidentes.

[10] Data refer to births to mothers resident in the Netherlands Antilles (including births outside the Netherlands Antilles to resident mothers, excluding births to non-resident mothers). -Ces données concernent les enfants nés de femmes qui résidaient aux Antilles néerlandaises (y compris ceux qui sont nés hors des Antilles néerlandaises). Elles ne concernent pas les enfants nés de non-résidentes.

[11] Excluding Indian jungle population. -Non compris les Indiens de la jungle.

[12] Data on live births and deaths are based on a civil registration system put in place in January 1998. -Les données sur les naissances et les décès sont basées sur un système d'enregistrement des faits d'état civil mis en place en janvier 1998.

[13] Excluding nomadic Indian tribes. -Non compris les tribus d'Indiens nomades.

[14] Data refer to registered live births only. -Les données concernent les naissances vivantes enregistrées seulement.

[15] Data for urban refer to the total of the district of Paramaribo (capital) and Wanica district. -Les données relatives aux zones urbaines correspondent au total pour le district de Paramaribo (capitale) et le district de Wanica.

[16] Excluding infants born alive of less than 28 weeks' gestation, of less than 1 000 grams in weight and 35 centimeters in length, who die within seven days of birth. -Non compris les enfants nés vivants après moins de 28 semaines de gestations, pesant moins de 1 000 grammes, mesurant moins de 35 centimètres et décédés dans les sept jours qui ont suivi leur naissance.

[17] Rates were obtained by the Sample Vital Registration System 2004 of Bangladesh. -Taux obtenus au moyen du Sample Vital Registration System 2004 du Bangladesh.

[18] For 2005, data refer to last twelve months preceding census on May 2005. -Pour 2005, les données se rapportent aux douze mois précédant le recensement mai 2005.

[19] For statistical purposes, the data for China do not include those for the Hong Kong Special Administrative Region (Hong Kong SAR), Macao Special Administrative Region (Macao SAR) and Taiwan province of China. -Pour la présentation des statistiques, les données pour la Chine ne comprennent pas la Région Administrative Spéciale de Hong Kong (Hong Kong RAS), la Région Administrative Spéciale de Macao (Macao RAS) et Taïwan province de Chine.

[20] Data from 2001 to 2004 have been estimated on the basis of the annual National Sample Surveys on Population Changes. -Les données de 2001 à 2004 ont été estimées sur la base de l'enquête annuelle "National Sample Survey on Population Changes".

[21] Data for 2005 are estimated from the National Sample Survey of 1 Per cent population. -Les données pour 2005 ont été estimées à partir de l'enquête nationale qui a porté sur un échantillon de 1 % de la population.

[22] Data refer to government controlled areas. -Les données se rapportent aux zones contrôlées par le Gouvernement.

[23] For certain years, data for urban and rural areas were not revised, as opposed to data for the whole. -Pour certaines années, les données selon la résidence urbaine/rurale n'ont pas été révisées, ce qui a été le cas avec les données pour l'ensemble du pays.

[24] Including data for the Indian-held part of Jammu and Kashmir, the final status of which has not yet been determined. - Y compris les données pour la partie du Jammu et du Cachemire occupée par l'Inde dont le statut définitif n'a pas encore été déterminé.

[25] Rates were obtained by the Sample Registration System of India, actually a large demographic survey. - Les taux ont été obtenus par le Système de l'enregistrement par échantillon de l'Inde qui est au fait une large enquête démographique.

[26] Data relate to the Iranian Year which begins on 21 March and ends on 20 March of the following year. -Les données concernent l'année iranienne, qui commence le 21 mars et se termine le 20 mars de l'année suivante.

[27] Including data for East Jerusalem and Israeli residents in certain other territories under occupation by Israeli military forces since June 1967. -Y compris les données pour Jérusalem-Est et les résidents israéliens dans certains autres

territoires occupés depuis 1967 par les forces armées israéliennes.

[28] For Japanese nationals in Japan only; however, rates computed on population including foreigners except foreign military and civilian personnel and their dependants stationed in the area. - Pour les nationaux japonais au Japon seulement; toutefois, les taux sont calculés sur la base d'une population comprenant les étrangers, mais ne comprenant ni les militaires et agents civils étrangers en poste sur le territoire ni les membres de leur famille les accompagnant.

[29] Excluding data for Jordanian territory under occupation since June 1967 by Israeli military forces. Excluding foreigners, including registered Palestinian refugees. -Non compris les données pour le territoire jordanien occupé depuis juin 1967 par les forces armées israéliennes. Non compris les étrangers, mais y compris les réfugiés de Palestine enregistrés.

[30] For 2004, data Published by the United Nations Economic and Social Commission for Western Asia. -Pour 2004, informations Publié par la Commission économique et sociale des Nations Unies pour l'Asie occidentale.

[31] Excluding alien armed forces, civilian aliens employed by armed forces, and foreign diplomatic personnel and their dependants. -Non compris les militaires étrangers, les civils étrangers employés par les forces armées ni le personnel diplomatique étranger et les membres de leur famille les accompagnant.

[32] Data refer to the recorded events in Ministry of Health hospitals and health centres only. -Les données se rapportent aux faits d'état civil enregistrés dans les hôpitaux et les dispensaires du Ministère de la santé seulement.

[33] Excluding data for the Pakistan-held part of Jammu and Kashmir, the final status of which has not yet been determined. -Non compris les données concernant la partie du Jammu et Cachemire occupée par le Pakistan dont le statut définitif n'a pas été déterminé.

[34] Data based on Pakistan Demographic Survey . -Données extraites de l'enquête démographique effectuée par le Pakistan.

[35] Excluding nomad population and Palestinian refugees. -Non compris la population nomade et les réfugiés de Palestine.

[36] Including an upward adjustment for under-registration. -Y compris un ajustement pour sous-enregistrement.

[37] Based on the results of the Population Demographic Survey. -D'après les résultats de la Population Demographic Survey.

[38] Including armed forces stationed outside the country, but excluding alien armed forces stationed in the area. -Y compris les militaires nationaux hors du pays, mais non compris les militaires étrangers en garnison sur le territoire.

[39] Excluding Faeroe Islands and Greenland. -Non compris les Iles Féroé et le Gröenland.

[40] Including nationals temporarily outside the country. -Y compris les nationaux se trouvant temporairement hors du pays.

[41] Including armed forces stationed outside the country. -Y compris les militaires nationaux hors du pays.

[42] The difference between 'Total' and the sum of 'urban' and 'rural' is due to the cases of unknown place of residence or residence abroad. -La différence entre le 'Total' et la somme des données selon la résidence urbaine/rurale se rapporte à la situation ou on ignore la résidence ou si la résidence est à l'étranger.

[43] Excluding armed forces. -Non compris les militaires en garnison.

[44] Events registered within one year of occurrence. -Evénements enregistrés dans l'année qui suit l'événement.

[45] Live births to Maltese parents only; however, rates computed on population including work and resident permit holders and foreigners residing in Malta.- - Naissances vivantes aux parents maltais seulement; toutefois, les taux sont calculés sur la base d'une population comprenant les titulaires de permis de travail et de permis de séjour et les étrangers résidant à Malte.

[46] Including residents outside the country if listed in a Netherlands population register. -Y compris les résidents hors du pays, s'ils sont inscrits sur un registre de population néerlandais.

[47] From 2002, without data for Kosovo and Metohia. -Après 2002, sans les données pour le Kosovo and Metohie.

[48] Based on the results of the Total Population Register. -Selon les résultats du recensement complet de la population.

[49] Data tabulated by date of occurrence for England and Wales, and by date of registration for Northern Ireland and Scotland. -Données exploitées selon la date de l'événement pour l'Angleterre et le pays de Galles, et selon la date de l'enregistrement pour l'Irlande du Nord et l'Ecosse.

[50] Data revised to exclude births in Northern Ireland to non-residents of Northern Ireland. -Données révisées non compris des naissances en Irlande du Nord aux non-résidents de l'Irlande du Nord.

[51] Including United States military personnel, their dependants and contract employees. -Y compris les militaires des Etats-Unis, les membres de leur famille les accompagnant et les agents contractuels des Etats-Unis.

[52] Includes children born in New Zealand to women resident in Niue who chose to travel to New Zealand to give birth. -Y compris les enfants nés en Nouvelle-Zélande de femmes résidant à Nioué qui ont choisi de se rendre en Nouvelle-Zélande pour accoucher.

Rates computed on population including civilian nationals temporarily outside the country. -Les taux sont calculés sur la base d'un chiffre de population qui comprend les civils nationaux temporairement hors du pays.

Data exclude Kosovo and Metohia. -Les données ne comprennent pas le Kosovo-Metohija.

337

Table 10

Table 10 presents live births by age of mother, sex of the child and urban/rural residence for the latest available year.

Description of variables: Age is defined as age at last birthday, that is, the difference between the date of birth and the date of the occurrence of the event, expressed in completed solar years. The age classification used in this table is the following: under 15 years, 5-year age groups through 45-49 years, and 50 years and over.

Reliability of data: Data from civil registers of live births which are reported as incomplete (less than 90 per cent completeness) or of unknown completeness are considered unreliable and are set in *italics* rather than in roman type. Table 9 and the technical notes for that table provide more detailed information on the completeness of live-birth registration. For more information about the quality of vital statistics data in general, see section 4.2 of the Technical Notes.

Limitations: Statistics on live births by age of mother are subject to the same qualifications as have been set forth for vital statistics in general and birth statistics in particular as discussed in section 4 of the Technical Notes.

The reliability of the data described above, is an important factor in considering the limitations. In addition, some live births are tabulated by date of registration and not by date of occurrence; these are indicated in the table by a plus sign "+". Whenever the lag between the date of occurrence and date of registration is prolonged and, therefore, a large proportion of the live-birth registrations are delayed, birth statistics for any given year may be seriously affected. For example, the age of the mother will almost always refer to the date of registration rather than to the date of birth of the child. Hence, in those countries or areas where registration of births is delayed, possibly for years, statistics on births by age of mother should be used with caution.

Another factor which limits international comparability is the practice of some countries or areas of not including in live-birth statistics infants who were born alive but died before the registration of the birth or within the first 24 hours of life, thus underestimating the total number of live births. Statistics of this type are footnoted.

Because these statistics are classified according to age, they are subject to the limitations with respect to accuracy of age reporting similar to those already discussed in connection with section 3.1.3 of the Technical Notes. The factors influencing the accuracy of reporting may be somewhat dissimilar in vital statistics (because of the differences in the method of taking a census and registering a birth) but, in general, the same errors can be observed. The absence of frequencies in the unknown age group does not necessarily indicate completely accurate reporting and tabulation of the age item. It is often an indication that the unknowns have been eliminated by assigning ages to them before tabulation, or by proportionate distribution after tabulation.

On the other hand, large frequencies in the unknown age category may indicate that a large proportion of the births are born outside of wedlock, the records for which tend to be incomplete in so far as characteristics of the parents are concerned.

Another limitation of age reporting may result from calculating age of mother at birth of child (or at time of registration) from year of birth rather than from day, month and year of birth. Information on this factor is given in footnotes when known.

In few countries, data by age refer to deliveries rather than to live births causing under-enumeration in the event of a multiple birth. This practice leads to lack of strict comparability, both among countries or areas relying on this practice and between data shown in this table and table 9.

The comparability of data by urban/rural residence is affected by the national definitions of urban and rural used in tabulating these data. It is assumed, in the absence of specific information to the contrary, that the definitions of urban and rural used in connection with the national population census were also used in the compilation of the vital statistics for each country or area. However, the possibility cannot be excluded that, for a given country or area, the same definitions of urban and rural are not used for both the vital statistics data and the population census data. When known, the definitions of urban used in national population censuses are presented at the end of table 6. As discussed in detail in the technical notes for table 6, these definitions vary considerably from one country or area to another.

Earlier data: Live births by age of mother have been shown for the latest available year in each issue of the Yearbook. Data included in this table update the series covering period of years as follows:

Issue	Years Covered
Special Edition on Natality, CD, 1999	1990 – 1998
Historical Supplement CD, 1997	1948 – 1997
1992	1983 – 1992
1986	1977 – 1988
1981	1972 – 1980
Historical Supplement, 1979	1948 - 1977

For further information on years covered prior to 1948, readers should consult the Historical Index.

Tableau 10

Le tableau 10 présente les données les plus récentes dont on dispose sur les naissances vivantes selon l'âge de la mère, le sexe de l'enfant et le lieu de résidence (zone urbaine ou rurale).

Description des variables : L'âge désigne l'âge au dernier anniversaire, c'est-à-dire la différence entre la date de naissance et la date de l'événement exprimée en années solaires révolues. La classification par âge utilisée dans ce tableau comprend les catégories suivantes : moins de 15 ans, groupes quinquennaux jusqu'à 45-49 ans, 50 ans et plus, et âge inconnu.

Fiabilité des données : Les données sur les naissances vivantes provenant des registres de l'état civil qui sont déclarées incomplètes (degré de complétude inférieur à 90 p. 100) ou dont le degré de complétude n'est pas connu sont jugées douteuses et apparaissent en italique et non en caractères romains. Le tableau 9 et les notes techniques qui s'y rapportent présentent des renseignements plus détaillés sur le degré de complétude de l'enregistrement des naissances vivantes. Pour plus de précisions sur la qualité des statistiques de l'état civil en général, voir la section 4.2 des Notes techniques.

Insuffisance des données : Les statistiques relatives aux naissances vivantes selon l'âge de la mère appellent toutes les réserves qui ont été formulées à propos des statistiques de l'état civil en général et des statistiques de naissances en particulier (voir la section 4 des Notes techniques).

La fiabilité des données, au sujet de laquelle des indications ont été données plus haut, est un facteur important. Il faut également tenir compte du fait que, dans certains cas, les données relatives aux naissances vivantes sont exploitées selon la date de l'enregistrement et non la date de l'événement ; ces cas ont été signalés dans le tableau par le signe '+'. Chaque fois que le décalage entre l'événement et son enregistrement est grand et qu'une forte proportion des naissances vivantes fait l'objet d'un enregistrement tardif, les statistiques des naissances vivantes pour une année donnée peuvent être considérablement faussées. Par exemple, l'âge de la mère représente presque toujours son âge à la date de l'enregistrement et non à la date de la naissance de l'enfant. Ainsi, dans les pays ou zones où l'enregistrement des naissances est tardif, le retard atteignant parfois plusieurs années, il faut utiliser avec prudence les statistiques concernant les naissances selon l'âge de la mère.

Un autre facteur qui nuit à la comparabilité internationale est la pratique de certains pays ou zones qui consiste à ne pas inclure dans les statistiques des naissances vivantes les enfants nés vivants mais décédés avant l'enregistrement de leur naissance ou dans les 24 heures qui ont suivi la naissance, pratique qui conduit à sous-estimer le nombre total de naissances vivantes. Quand pareil facteur a joué, cela a été signalé en note à la fin du tableau.

Étant donné que les statistiques du tableau 10 sont classées selon l'âge, elles appellent les mêmes réserves concernant l'exactitude des déclarations d'âge que celles formulées à la section 3.1.3 des Notes techniques. Dans le cas des statistiques de l'état civil, les facteurs qui interviennent à cet égard sont parfois différents, étant donné que le recensement de la population et l'enregistrement des naissances se font par des méthodes différentes, mais, d'une manière générale, les erreurs observées seront les mêmes. Si aucun nombre ne figure dans la rangée réservée aux âges inconnus, cela ne signifie pas nécessairement que les déclarations d'âge et l'exploitation des données par âge ont été tout à fait exactes. C'est souvent une indication que l'on a attribué un âge aux personnes d'âge inconnu avant l'exploitation des données ou qu'elles ont été réparties proportionnellement entre les différents groupes après cette opération.

À l'inverse, lorsque le nombre des personnes d'âge inconnu est important, cela peut signifier que la proportion de naissances parmi les mères célibataires est élevée, étant donné qu'en pareil cas l'acte de naissance ne contient pas tous les renseignements concernant les parents.

Les déclarations par âge peuvent comporter des distorsions, du fait que l'âge de la mère au moment de la naissance d'un enfant (ou de la déclaration de naissance) est donné par année de naissance et non par date exacte (jour, mois et année).

Dans quelques pays, la classification par âges se réfère aux accouchements, et non aux naissances vivantes, ce qui conduit à un sous-dénombrement en cas de naissances gémellaires. Cette pratique nuit à la comparabilité des données, à la fois entre pays ou zones qui recourent à cette méthode et entre les données présentées dans le tableau 10 et celles du tableau 9.

La comparabilité des données selon le lieu de résidence (zone urbaine ou rurale) peut être limitée par les définitions nationales des termes « urbain » et « rural » utilisées pour la mise en tableaux de ces données. En l'absence d'indications contraires, on a supposé que les mêmes définitions avaient servi pour le recensement national de la population et pour l'établissement des statistiques de l'état civil pour chaque pays ou zone. Toutefois, il n'est pas exclu que, pour une zone ou un pays donné, des définitions différentes aient été retenues. Les définitions du terme « urbain » utilisées pour les recensements nationaux de population ont été présentées à la fin des notes techniques du tableau 6 lorsqu'elles étaient connues. Comme on l'a précisé dans les notes techniques relatives au tableau 6, ces définitions varient considérablement d'un pays ou d'une zone à l'autre.

Données publiées antérieurement : Les différentes éditions de l'*Annuaire démographique* regroupent les dernières statistiques dont on disposait à l'époque sur les naissances vivantes selon l'âge de la mère. Les données qui figurent dans le tableau 10 actualisent les données qui portaient sur les périodes suivantes :

Éditions	Années considérées
Édition spéciale sur les statistiques de la natalité (CD-ROM), 1999	1990 – 1998
Supplément historique (CD-ROM), 1997	1948 – 1997
1992	1983 – 1992
1986	1977 – 1988
1981	1972 – 1980
Supplément rétrospectif, 1979	1948 – 1977

Pour plus de détails concernant les années antérieures à 1948, se reporter à l'index historique.

10. Live births by age of mother, sex of the child and urban/rural residence: latest available year, 1996 - 2005
Naissances vivantes selon l'âge de la mère, le sexe de l'enfant et la résidence, urbaine/rurale: dernière année disponible, 1996 - 2005

Continent, country or area, date, code and age (in years) / Continent, pays ou zone, code, date et âge (en années)	Total			Urban - Urbaine			Rural - Rurale		
	Both sexes Les deux sexes	Male Masculin	Female Féminin	Both sexes Les deux sexes	Male Masculin	Female Féminin	Both sexes Les deux sexes	Male Masculin	Female Féminin
AFRICA - AFRIQUE									
Egypt - Égypte									
1999 (C)									
Total....................	1 693 025	870 195	822 830	657 902	338 638	319 264	1 035 123	531 557	503 566
0 - 19..................	58 512	29 955	28 557	20 778	10 785	9 993	37 734	19 170	18 564
20 - 24..................	449 584	231 642	217 942	169 931	87 629	82 302	279 653	144 013	135 640
25 - 29..................	491 555	252 991	238 564	187 184	96 644	90 540	304 371	156 347	148 024
30 - 34..................	309 972	159 186	150 786	124 244	63 653	60 591	185 728	95 533	90 195
35 - 39..................	163 663	83 988	79 675	61 243	31 423	29 820	102 420	52 565	49 855
40 - 44..................	38 298	19 828	18 470	13 614	7 005	6 609	24 684	12 823	11 861
45 +....................	8 219	4 201	4 018	2 341	1 193	1 148	5 878	3 008	2 870
Unknown - Inconnu.......	173 222	88 404	84 818	78 567	40 306	38 261	94 655	48 098	46 557
Kenya									
2000 (U)									
Total....................	470 712	...	...	...	...	...	...	...	...
0 - 14..................	1 033	...	...	...	...	...	...	...	...
15 - 19..................	72 510	...	...	...	...	...	...	...	...
20 - 24..................	151 037	...	...	...	...	...	...	...	...
25 - 29..................	117 804	...	...	...	...	...	...	...	...
30 - 34..................	76 286	...	...	...	...	...	...	...	...
35 - 39..................	33 301	...	...	...	...	...	...	...	...
40 - 44..................	9 096	...	...	...	...	...	...	...	...
45 - 49..................	1 571	...	...	...	...	...	...	...	...
50 +....................	218	...	...	...	...	...	...	...	...
Unknown - Inconnu.......	7 856	...	...	...	...	...	...	...	...
Libyan Arab Jamahiriya - Jamahiriya arabe libyenne									
2002 (C)									
Total....................	111 053	57 722	53 331	...	...	...	...	...	...
0 - 19..................	1 196	592	604	...	...	...	...	...	...
20 - 24..................	15 018	7 845	7 173	...	...	...	...	...	...
25 - 29..................	32 713	16 877	15 836	...	...	...	...	...	...
30 - 34..................	33 325	17 384	15 941	...	...	...	...	...	...
35 - 39..................	18 702	9 777	8 925	...	...	...	...	...	...
40 - 44..................	6 422	3 296	3 126	...	...	...	...	...	...
45 +....................	676	364	312	...	...	...	...	...	...
Unknown - Inconnu.......	3 001	1 587	1 414	...	...	...	...	...	...
Mauritius - Maurice									
2005 (C)									
Total....................	18 578	9 468	9 110	...	...	...	...	...	...
0 - 14..................	26	13	13	...	...	...	...	...	...
15 - 19..................	1 534	771	763	...	...	...	...	...	...
20 - 24..................	4 902	2 503	2 399	...	...	...	...	...	...
25 - 29..................	5 706	2 899	2 807	...	...	...	...	...	...
30 - 34..................	3 094	1 560	1 534	...	...	...	...	...	...
35 - 39..................	1 403	709	694	...	...	...	...	...	...
40 - 44..................	418	224	194	...	...	...	...	...	...
45 - 49..................	18	7	11	...	...	...	...	...	...
50 +....................	-	-	-	...	...	...	...	...	...
Unknown - Inconnu.......	1 477	782	695	...	...	...	...	...	...
Morocco - Maroc									
2001 (C)									
Total....................	541 298	277 242	264 056	282 380[1]	144 818[1]	137 562[1]	258 297[1]	132 082[1]	126 215[1]
0 - 14..................	1 016	525	491	457[1]	234[1]	223[1]	559[1]	291[1]	268[1]
15 - 19..................	45 049	23 151	21 898	19 695[1]	10 164[1]	9 531[1]	25 327[1]	12 973[1]	12 354[1]
20 - 24..................	131 163	67 353	63 810	62 623[1]	32 254[1]	30 369[1]	68 480[1]	35 068[1]	33 412[1]
25 - 29..................	136 599	69 989	66 610	73 246[1]	37 596[1]	35 650[1]	63 288[1]	32 360[1]	30 928[1]
30 - 34..................	117 851	60 300	57 551	66 841[1]	34 234[1]	32 607[1]	50 954[1]	26 040[1]	24 914[1]
35 - 39..................	75 484	38 586	36 898	43 396[1]	22 230[1]	21 166[1]	32 054[1]	16 336[1]	15 718[1]
40 - 44..................	27 453	13 958	13 495	13 819[1]	6 959[1]	6 860[1]	13 624[1]	6 991[1]	6 633[1]
45 - 49..................	3 974	1 998	1 976	1 445[1]	713[1]	732[1]	2 528[1]	1 284[1]	1 244[1]
50 +....................	1 105	556	549	313[1]	157[1]	156[1]	791[1]	399[1]	392[1]
Unknown - Inconnu.......	1 604	826	778	545[1]	277[1]	268[1]	692[1]	340[1]	352[1]

10. Live births by age of mother, sex of the child and urban/rural residence: latest available year, 1996 - 2005
Naissances vivantes selon l'âge de la mère, le sexe de l'enfant et la résidence, urbaine/rurale: dernière année disponible, 1996 - 2005 (continued - suite)

Continent, country or area, date, code and age (in years) / Continent, pays ou zone, code, date et âge (en annèes)	Total			Urban - Urbaine			Rural - Rurale		
	Both sexes Les deux sexes	Male Masculin	Female Féminin	Both sexes Les deux sexes	Male Masculin	Female Féminin	Both sexes Les deux sexes	Male Masculin	Female Féminin
AFRICA - AFRIQUE									
Namibia - Namibie[2]									
2001 (|)									
Total.	45 157	22 643	22 514	15 352	7 678	7 674	29 805	14 965	14 840
12 - 14	74	37	37	16	4	12	58	33	25
15 - 19	5 278	2 638	2 640	1 377	665	712	3 901	1 973	1 928
20 - 24	11 964	5 997	5 967	3 827	1 930	1 897	8 137	4 067	4 070
25 - 29	11 056	5 563	5 493	4 389	2 231	2 158	6 667	3 332	3 335
30 - 34	8 429	4 259	4 170	3 217	1 621	1 596	5 212	2 638	2 574
35 - 39	5 292	2 636	2 656	1 793	882	911	3 499	1 754	1 745
40 - 44	2 383	1 187	1 196	613	297	316	1 770	890	880
45 +	681	326	355	120	48	72	561	278	283
Réunion[3]									
2003 (C)									
Total.	14 427	7 412	7 015	...	...	...	...	...	...
0 - 19.	1 241	596	645	...	...	...	...	...	...
20 - 24	3 054	1 596	1 458	...	...	...	...	...	...
25 - 29	3 925	2 046	1 879	...	...	...	...	...	...
30 - 34	3 478	1 788	1 690	...	...	...	...	...	...
35 - 39	2 110	1 064	1 046	...	...	...	...	...	...
40 - 44	596	309	287	...	...	...	...	...	...
45 +	23	13	10	...	...	...	...	...	...
Saint Helena ex. dep. - Sainte-Hélène sans dép.									
2000 (C)									
Total.	56	32	24	...	...	...	...	...	...
15 - 19	7	3	4	...	...	...	...	...	...
20 - 24	16	10	6	...	...	...	...	...	...
25 - 29	12	5	7	...	...	...	...	...	...
30 - 34	13	9	4	...	...	...	...	...	...
35 - 39	7	4	3	...	...	...	...	...	...
40 - 44	1	1	-	...	...	...	...	...	...
South Africa - Afrique du Sud									
1999 (U)									
Total.	1 363 800	...	...	...	...	...	...	...	...
15 - 19	195 560	...	...	...	...	...	...	...	...
20 - 24	362 872	...	...	...	...	...	...	...	...
25 - 29	339 586	...	...	...	...	...	...	...	...
30 - 34	246 119	...	...	...	...	...	...	...	...
35 - 39	140 344	...	...	...	...	...	...	...	...
40 - 44	52 428	...	...	...	...	...	...	...	...
45 - 49	13 437	...	...	...	...	...	...	...	...
50 +	4 439	...	...	...	...	...	...	...	...
Unknown - Inconnu	9 015	...	...	...	...	...	...	...	...
Swaziland[4]									
1997 (|)									
Total.	31 087	...	...	6 915	...	...	24 172	...	...
15 - 19	4 192	...	...	897	...	...	3 295	...	...
20 - 24	8 927	...	...	2 107	...	...	6 820	...	...
25 - 29	7 537	...	...	1 895	...	...	5 642	...	...
30 - 34	4 893	...	...	1 021	...	...	3 872	...	...
35 - 39	3 413	...	...	664	...	...	2 749	...	...
40 - 44	1 247	...	...	194	...	...	1 053	...	...
45 - 49	564	...	...	78	...	...	486	...	...
50 +	230	...	...	32	...	...	198	...	...
Unknown - Inconnu	84	...	...	27	...	...	57	...	...
Tunisia - Tunisie									
1998 (C)									
Total.	166 718	...	...	...	...	...	...	...	...
15 - 19	3 650	...	...	...	...	...	...	...	...
20 - 24	28 802	...	...	...	...	...	...	...	...
25 - 29	44 260	...	...	...	...	...	...	...	...
30 - 34	39 518	...	...	...	...	...	...	...	...
35 - 39	19 869	...	...	...	...	...	...	...	...
40 - 44	5 327	...	...	...	...	...	...	...	...

10. Live births by age of mother, sex of the child and urban/rural residence: latest available year, 1996 - 2005
Naissances vivantes selon l'âge de la mère, le sexe de l'enfant et la résidence, urbaine/rurale: dernière année disponible, 1996 - 2005 (continued - suite)

Continent, country or area, date, code and age (in years) / Continent, pays ou zone, code, date et âge (en années)	Total			Urban - Urbaine			Rural - Rurale		
	Both sexes Les deux sexes	Male Masculin	Female Féminin	Both sexes Les deux sexes	Male Masculin	Female Féminin	Both sexes Les deux sexes	Male Masculin	Female Féminin
AFRICA - AFRIQUE									
Tunisia - Tunisie									
1998 (C)									
45 +......................	650	...	...	...	...	...	...	...	...
Unknown - Inconnu.......	2 446	...	...	...	...	...	...	...	...
AMERICA, NORTH - AMÉRIQUE DU NORD									
Anguilla									
2004 (+C)									
Total......................	164	...	...	...	...	...	...	...	...
0 - 14......................	1	...	...	...	...	...	...	...	...
15 - 19....................	25	...	...	...	...	...	...	...	...
20 - 24....................	47	...	...	...	...	...	...	...	...
25 - 29....................	35	...	...	...	...	...	...	...	...
30 - 34....................	26	...	...	...	...	...	...	...	...
35 - 39....................	25	...	...	...	...	...	...	...	...
40 +......................	5	...	...	...	...	...	...	...	...
Aruba									
2004 (C)									
Total......................	1 193	592	601	...	...	...	...	...	...
0 - 14......................	8	3	5	...	...	...	...	...	...
15 - 19....................	127	62	65	...	...	...	...	...	...
20 - 24....................	256	119	137	...	...	...	...	...	...
25 - 29....................	322	168	154	...	...	...	...	...	...
30 - 34....................	283	139	144	...	...	...	...	...	...
35 - 39....................	162	82	80	...	...	...	...	...	...
40 - 44....................	33	17	16	...	...	...	...	...	...
45 - 49....................	2	2	-	...	...	...	...	...	...
50 +......................	-	-	-	...	...	...	...	...	...
Bahamas									
2001 (U)									
Total......................	4 495	2 305	2 190	...	...	...	...	...	...
0 - 14......................	5	3	2	...	...	...	...	...	...
15 - 19....................	568	282	286	...	...	...	...	...	...
20 - 24....................	1 120	567	553	...	...	...	...	...	...
25 - 29....................	1 154	602	552	...	...	...	...	...	...
30 - 34....................	904	460	444	...	...	...	...	...	...
35 - 39....................	601	319	282	...	...	...	...	...	...
40 - 44....................	125	63	62	...	...	...	...	...	...
45 - 49....................	10	5	5	...	...	...	...	...	...
Unknown - Inconnu.......	8	4	4	...	...	...	...	...	...
Belize									
1997 (U)									
Total......................	5 738	2 921	2 817	2 354	1 152	1 202	3 384	1 769	1 615
0 - 14......................	17	8	9	4	2	2	13	6	7
15 - 19....................	993	504	489	392	202	190	601	302	299
20 - 24....................	1 762	907	855	759	368	391	1 003	539	464
25 - 29....................	1 350	660	690	566	271	295	784	389	395
30 - 34....................	804	419	385	327	161	166	477	258	219
35 - 39....................	422	228	194	159	85	74	263	143	120
40 - 44....................	105	55	50	37	21	16	68	34	34
45 +......................	15	6	9	5	2	3	10	4	6
Unknown - Inconnu.......	270	134	136	105	40	65	165	94	71
2002 (U)									
Total......................	7 356	...	...	...	...	...	...	...	...
0 - 14......................	22	...	...	...	...	...	...	...	...
15 - 19....................	1 237	...	...	...	...	...	...	...	...
20 - 24....................	2 233	...	...	...	...	...	...	...	...
25 - 29....................	1 712	...	...	...	...	...	...	...	...
30 - 34....................	1 106	...	...	...	...	...	...	...	...
35 - 39....................	566	...	...	...	...	...	...	...	...
40 - 44....................	165	...	...	...	...	...	...	...	...

Continent, country or area, date, code and age (in years) / Continent, pays ou zone, code, date et âge (en années)	Total			Urban - Urbaine			Rural - Rurale		
	Both sexes Les deux sexes	Male Masculin	Female Féminin	Both sexes Les deux sexes	Male Masculin	Female Féminin	Both sexes Les deux sexes	Male Masculin	Female Féminin
AMERICA, NORTH - AMÉRIQUE DU NORD									
Belize									
2002 (U)									
45 +	17	...	...	...	...	...	...	...	...
Unknown - Inconnu	298	...	...	...	...	...	...	...	...
Bermuda - Bermudes									
2003 (C)									
Total	834	...	...	...	...	...	...	...	...
15 - 19	79	...	...	...	...	...	...	...	...
20 - 24	116	...	...	...	...	...	...	...	...
25 - 29	203	...	...	...	...	...	...	...	...
30 - 34	250	...	...	...	...	...	...	...	...
35 - 39	148	...	...	...	...	...	...	...	...
40 +	38	...	...	...	...	...	...	...	...
Canada[5]									
2004 (C)									
Total	337 072	173 154	163 918	...	...	...	...	...	...
0 - 14	111	66	45	...	...	...	...	...	...
15 - 19	14 705	7 274	6 801	...	...	...	...	...	...
20 - 24	55 383	28 526	26 857	...	...	...	...	...	...
25 - 29	103 743	53 135	50 608	...	...	...	...	...	...
30 - 34	105 705	54 377	51 328	...	...	...	...	...	...
35 - 39	48 130	24 676	23 454	...	...	...	...	...	...
40 - 44	9 376	4 826	4 550	...	...	...	...	...	...
45 - 49	413	196	217	...	...	...	...	...	...
50 +	13	6	7	...	...	...	...	...	...
Unknown - Inconnu	123	72	51	...	...	...	...	...	...
Costa Rica									
2004 (C)									
Total	72 247	...	...	...	...	...	...	...	...
0 - 14	446	...	...	...	...	...	...	...	...
15 - 19	14 346	...	...	...	...	...	...	...	...
20 - 24	21 779	...	...	...	...	...	...	...	...
25 - 29	16 900	...	...	...	...	...	...	...	...
30 - 34	11 141	...	...	...	...	...	...	...	...
35 - 39	5 760	...	...	...	...	...	...	...	...
40 - 44	1 483	...	...	...	...	...	...	...	...
45 +	110	...	...	...	...	...	...	...	...
Unknown - Inconnu	282	...	...	...	...	...	...	...	...
Cuba									
2005 (C)									
Total	120 716	62 219	58 497	88 922	45 802	43 120	31 794	16 417	15 377
0 - 14	422	223	199	240	129	111	182	94	88
15 - 19	18 030	9 220	8 810	11 815	6 019	5 796	6 215	3 201	3 014
20 - 24	32 584	16 885	15 699	23 720	12 274	11 446	8 864	4 611	4 253
25 - 29	29 052	14 972	14 080	21 845	11 303	10 542	7 207	3 669	3 538
30 - 34	26 740	13 755	12 985	20 529	10 521	10 008	6 211	3 234	2 977
35 - 39	11 733	6 057	5 676	9 099	4 696	4 403	2 634	1 361	1 273
40 - 44	2 081	1 071	1 010	1 620	835	785	461	236	225
45 - 49	58	29	29	41	21	20	17	8	9
50 +	10	5	5	8	3	5	2	2	-
Unknown - Inconnu	6	2	4	5	1	4	1	1	-
Dominican Republic - République dominicaine									
1999 (+U)									
Total	193 418	99 127	94 291	...	...	...	...	...	...
0 - 14	1 665	909	756	...	...	...	...	...	...
15 - 19	23 353	11 880	11 473	...	...	...	...	...	...
20 - 24	53 145	27 213	25 932	...	...	...	...	...	...
25 - 29	51 520	26 568	24 952	...	...	...	...	...	...
30 - 34	32 644	16 649	15 995	...	...	...	...	...	...
35 - 39	15 335	7 867	7 468	...	...	...	...	...	...
40 - 44	6 015	3 124	2 891	...	...	...	...	...	...
45 - 49	2 624	1 388	1 236	...	...	...	...	...	...

10. Live births by age of mother, sex of the child and urban/rural residence: latest available year, 1996 - 2005
Naissances vivantes selon l'âge de la mère, le sexe de l'enfant et la résidence, urbaine/rurale: dernière année disponible, 1996 - 2005 (continued - suite)

Continent, country or area, date, code and age (in years) / Continent, pays ou zone, code, date et âge (en années)	Total			Urban - Urbaine			Rural - Rurale		
	Both sexes Les deux sexes	Male Masculin	Female Féminin	Both sexes Les deux sexes	Male Masculin	Female Féminin	Both sexes Les deux sexes	Male Masculin	Female Féminin
AMERICA, NORTH - AMÉRIQUE DU NORD									
Dominican Republic - République dominicaine									
1999 (+U)									
50 +	*2 558*	*1 238*	*1 320*	...	...	...	...	...	...
Unknown - Inconnu	*4 559*	*2 291*	*2 268*	...	...	...	...	...	...
El Salvador									
2003 (C)									
Total	124 476	64 988	59 488	73 311	38 272	35 039	51 165	26 716	24 449
0 - 14	1 161	595	566	646	316	330	515	279	236
15 - 19	24 405	12 797	11 608	13 289	6 951	6 338	11 116	5 846	5 270
20 - 24	38 372	20 075	18 297	23 252	12 114	11 138	15 120	7 961	7 159
25 - 29	30 333	15 914	14 419	18 882	9 909	8 973	11 451	6 005	5 446
30 - 34	17 680	9 087	8 593	10 737	5 570	5 167	6 943	3 517	3 426
35 - 39	9 033	4 740	4 293	4 979	2 613	2 366	4 054	2 127	1 927
40 - 44	2 797	1 426	1 371	1 236	654	582	1 561	772	789
45 - 49	299	145	154	116	59	57	183	86	97
50 +	49	31	18	19	12	7	30	19	11
Unknown - Inconnu	347	178	169	155	74	81	192	104	88
Greenland - Groenland									
2003 (C)									
Total	895	480	415	717	386	331	178	94	84
0 - 14	1	1	-	-	-	-	1	1	-
15 - 19	100	52	48	83	40	43	17	12	5
20 - 24	262	144	118	208	123	85	54	21	33
25 - 29	203	104	99	158	77	81	45	27	18
30 - 34	179	93	86	142	75	67	37	18	19
35 - 39	128	72	56	107	57	50	21	15	6
40 - 44	20	13	7	18	13	5	2	-	2
45 - 49	2	1	1	1	1	-	1	-	1
Grenada - Grenade									
2000 (+C)									
Total	1 883	...	...	...	...	...	...	...	...
0 - 14	9	...	...	...	...	...	...	...	...
15 - 19	310	...	...	...	...	...	...	...	...
20 - 24	490	...	...	...	...	...	...	...	...
25 - 29	452	...	...	...	...	...	...	...	...
30 - 34	339	...	...	...	...	...	...	...	...
35 - 39	208	...	...	...	...	...	...	...	...
40 - 44	73	...	...	...	...	...	...	...	...
45 +	2	...	...	...	...	...	...	...	...
Guadeloupe									
2003 (C)									
Total	7 047	3 543	3 504	...	...	...	...	...	...
0 - 14	7	2	5	...	...	...	...	...	...
15 - 19	431	215	216	...	...	...	...	...	...
20 - 24	1 148	588	560	...	...	...	...	...	...
25 - 29	1 815	912	903	...	...	...	...	...	...
30 - 34	2 001	1 005	996	...	...	...	...	...	...
35 - 39	1 280	637	643	...	...	...	...	...	...
40 - 44	352	177	175	...	...	...	...	...	...
45 +	13	7	6	...	...	...	...	...	...
Guatemala									
1999 (C)									
Total	360 759	183 621	177 138	140 491	...	...	220 268	...	...
0 - 14	1 776	892	884	677	...	...	1 099	...	...
15 - 19	65 999	33 808	32 191	25 674	...	...	40 325	...	...
20 - 24	108 223	54 947	53 276	44 487	...	...	63 736	...	...
25 - 29	79 683	40 608	39 075	32 492	...	...	47 191	...	...
30 - 34	53 921	27 473	26 448	20 520	...	...	33 401	...	...
35 - 39	34 730	17 623	17 107	11 694	...	...	23 036	...	...
40 - 44	13 305	6 722	6 583	3 955	...	...	9 350	...	...
45 - 49	1 981	973	1 008	502	...	...	1 479	...	...
50 +	557	288	269	119	...	...	438	...	...
Unknown - Inconnu	584	287	297	371	...	...	213	...	...

Continent, country or area, date, code and age (in years) Continent, pays ou zone, code, date et âge (en années)	Total			Urban - Urbaine			Rural - Rurale		
	Both sexes Les deux sexes	Male Masculin	Female Féminin	Both sexes Les deux sexes	Male Masculin	Female Féminin	Both sexes Les deux sexes	Male Masculin	Female Féminin
AMERICA, NORTH -									
AMÉRIQUE DU NORD									
Jamaica - Jamaïque[6]									
2004 (C)									
Total.....................	42 448	...	...	...	...	...	...	...	...
0 - 14....................	278	...	...	...	...	...	...	...	...
15 - 19....................	7 956	...	...	...	...	...	...	...	...
20 - 24....................	11 596	...	...	...	...	...	...	...	...
25 - 29....................	9 407	...	...	...	...	...	...	...	...
30 - 34....................	7 367	...	...	...	...	...	...	...	...
35 - 39....................	4 448	...	...	...	...	...	...	...	...
40 - 44....................	1 307	...	...	...	...	...	...	...	...
45 - 49....................	66	...	...	...	...	...	...	...	...
50 +.....................	1	...	...	...	...	...	...	...	...
Unknown - Inconnu........	22	...	...	...	...	...	...	...	...
Martinique[7]									
2003 (C)									
Total.....................	5 430	2 774	2 656	...	...	...	...	...	...
0 - 14....................	6	3	3	...	...	...	...	...	...
15 - 19....................	397	217	180	...	...	...	...	...	...
20 - 24....................	812	397	415	...	...	...	...	...	...
25 - 29....................	1 330	698	632	...	...	...	...	...	...
30 - 34....................	1 554	759	795	...	...	...	...	...	...
35 - 39....................	1 038	541	497	...	...	...	...	...	...
40 - 44....................	283	155	128	...	...	...	...	...	...
45 +.....................	10	4	6	...	...	...	...	...	...
Mexico - Mexique[8]									
2005 (+U)									
Total.....................	2 567 906	1 284 304	1 283 009	1 776 726	897 076	879 449	643 618	323 483	319 958
0 - 14....................	9 880	4 956	4 919	5 639	2 863	2 775	3 516	1 728	1 785
15 - 19....................	412 368	209 771	202 518	283 530	144 396	139 106	116 089	58 980	57 072
20 - 24....................	728 815	369 979	358 729	518 046	263 334	254 662	192 744	97 615	95 082
25 - 29....................	618 381	313 455	304 839	453 543	230 481	223 017	151 824	76 472	75 315
30 - 34....................	417 702	211 594	206 045	311 310	158 100	153 181	98 322	49 405	48 889
35 - 39....................	187 204	93 965	93 205	132 917	66 791	66 114	50 304	25 218	25 068
40 - 44....................	49 220	24 697	24 514	30 919	15 555	15 355	17 026	8 511	8 515
45 - 49....................	6 225	3 071	3 152	3 296	1 625	1 671	2 690	1 332	1 356
50 +.....................	1 873	928	945	815	391	424	833	435	398
Unknown - Inconnu........	136 238	51 888	84 143	36 711	13 540	23 144	10 270	3 787	6 478
Montserrat									
1999 (+C)									
Total.....................	45	19	26	...	...	...	...	...	...
0 - 14....................	-	-	-	...	...	...	...	...	...
15 - 19....................	7	5	2	...	...	...	...	...	...
20 - 24....................	10	4	6	...	...	...	...	...	...
25 - 29....................	11	4	7	...	...	...	...	...	...
30 - 34....................	12	4	8	...	...	...	...	...	...
35 - 39....................	5	2	3	...	...	...	...	...	...
40 - 44....................	-	-	-	...	...	...	...	...	...
45 - 49....................	-	-	-	...	...	...	...	...	...
50 +.....................	-	-	-	...	...	...	...	...	...
Unknown - Inconnu........	-	-	-	...	...	...	...	...	...
Netherlands Antilles -									
Antilles néerlandaises									
2004 (C)									
Total.....................	2 357	1 230	1 127	...	...	...	...	...	...
0 - 14....................	6	1	5	...	...	...	...	...	...
15 - 19....................	259	129	130	...	...	...	...	...	...
20 - 24....................	447	239	208	...	...	...	...	...	...
25 - 29....................	558	296	262	...	...	...	...	...	...
30 - 34....................	601	308	293	...	...	...	...	...	...
35 - 39....................	362	190	172	...	...	...	...	...	...
40 - 44....................	86	44	42	...	...	...	...	...	...
45 - 49....................	7	3	4	...	...	...	...	...	...
50 +.....................	-	-	-	...	...	...	...	...	...
Unknown - Inconnu........	31	20	11	...	...	...	...	...	...

10. Live births by age of mother, sex of the child and urban/rural residence: latest available year, 1996 - 2005
Naissances vivantes selon l'âge de la mère, le sexe de l'enfant et la résidence, urbaine/rurale: dernière année disponible, 1996 - 2005 (continued - suite)

Continent, country or area, date, code and age (in years) / Continent, pays ou zone, code, date et âge (en années)	Total			Urban - Urbaine			Rural - Rurale		
	Both sexes Les deux sexes	Male Masculin	Female Féminin	Both sexes Les deux sexes	Male Masculin	Female Féminin	Both sexes Les deux sexes	Male Masculin	Female Féminin
AMERICA, NORTH - AMÉRIQUE DU NORD									
Nicaragua									
2005 (+U)									
Total....................	121 380	63 001	58 379	62 960	32 687	30 273	58 420	30 314	28 106
0 - 14...................	1 441	753	688	689	360	329	752	393	359
15 - 19.................	31 846	16 476	15 370	15 932	8 267	7 665	15 914	8 209	7 705
20 - 24.................	39 579	20 696	18 883	21 308	11 191	10 117	18 271	9 505	8 766
25 - 29.................	25 244	13 065	12 179	13 667	7 031	6 636	11 577	6 034	5 543
30 - 34.................	14 126	7 348	6 778	7 283	3 754	3 529	6 843	3 594	3 249
35 - 39.................	7 034	3 634	3 400	3 263	1 687	1 576	3 771	1 947	1 824
40 - 44.................	1 832	901	931	740	361	379	1 092	540	552
45 - 49.................	245	114	131	71	34	37	174	80	94
50 +....................	33	14	19	7	2	5	26	12	14
Panama									
1999 (C)									
Total....................	64 248	33 077	31 171	32 724	16 894	15 830	31 524	16 183	15 341
0 - 14...................	537	290	247	205	114	91	332	176	156
15 - 19.................	12 126	6 288	5 838	5 594	2 893	2 701	6 532	3 395	3 137
20 - 24.................	18 281	9 435	8 846	9 344	4 846	4 498	8 937	4 589	4 348
25 - 29.................	15 488	7 964	7 524	8 369	4 321	4 048	7 119	3 643	3 476
30 - 34.................	10 451	5 314	5 137	5 822	2 989	2 833	4 629	2 325	2 304
35 - 39.................	4 925	2 581	2 344	2 553	1 309	1 244	2 372	1 272	1 100
40 - 44.................	1 076	528	548	448	226	222	628	302	326
45 - 49.................	95	46	49	14	9	5	81	37	44
50 +....................	23	9	14	1	-	1	22	9	13
Unknown - Inconnu......	1 246	622	624	374	187	187	872	435	437
2003 (C)									
Total....................	61 753	...	...	...	...	...	...	...	...
0 - 14...................	487	...	...	...	...	...	...	...	...
15 - 19.................	11 434	...	...	...	...	...	...	...	...
20 - 24.................	17 693	...	...	...	...	...	...	...	...
25 - 29.................	14 652	...	...	...	...	...	...	...	...
30 - 34.................	10 843	...	...	...	...	...	...	...	...
35 - 39.................	5 023	...	...	...	...	...	...	...	...
40 - 44.................	1 199	...	...	...	...	...	...	...	...
45 - 49.................	88	...	...	...	...	...	...	...	...
50 +....................	3	...	...	...	...	...	...	...	...
Unknown - Inconnu......	331	...	...	...	...	...	...	...	...
Puerto Rico - Porto Rico									
2000 (C)									
Total....................	59 460	30 593	28 867	30 464[1]	15 589[1]	14 875[1]	28 967[1]	14 991[1]	13 976[1]
0 - 14...................	272	155	117	115[1]	62[1]	53[1]	156[1]	93[1]	63[1]
15 - 19.................	11 118	5 735	5 383	4 972[1]	2 552[1]	2 420[1]	6 140[1]	3 181[1]	2 959[1]
20 - 24.................	19 423	10 005	9 418	9 360[1]	4 804[1]	4 556[1]	10 057[1]	5 197[1]	4 860[1]
25 - 29.................	15 152	7 806	7 346	8 167[1]	4 169[1]	3 998[1]	6 983[1]	3 637[1]	3 346[1]
30 - 34.................	8 902	4 515	4 387	5 123[1]	2 586[1]	2 537[1]	3 779[1]	1 929[1]	1 850[1]
35 - 39.................	3 762	1 974	1 788	2 243[1]	1 176[1]	1 067[1]	1 518[1]	797[1]	721[1]
40 - 44.................	748	362	386	437[1]	218[1]	219[1]	311[1]	144[1]	167[1]
45 - 49.................	29	14	15	18[1]	7[1]	11[1]	10[1]	7[1]	3[1]
Unknown - Inconnu......	54	27	27	29[1]	15[1]	14[1]	13[1]	6[1]	7[1]
2005 (C)									
Total....................	50 687	25 999	24 688	...	...	...	...	...	...
0 - 14...................	206	99	107	...	...	...	...	...	...
15 - 19.................	8 934	4 660	4 274	...	...	...	...	...	...
20 - 24.................	16 049	8 218	7 831	...	...	...	...	...	...
25 - 29.................	13 447	6 843	6 604	...	...	...	...	...	...
30 - 34.................	7 965	4 083	3 882	...	...	...	...	...	...
35 - 39.................	3 300	1 691	1 609	...	...	...	...	...	...
40 - 44.................	738	377	361	...	...	...	...	...	...
45 - 49.................	35	21	14	...	...	...	...	...	...
50 +....................	2	2	-	...	...	...	...	...	...
Unknown - Inconnu......	11	5	6	...	...	...	...	...	...

10. Live births by age of mother, sex of the child and urban/rural residence: latest available year, 1996 - 2005
Naissances vivantes selon l'âge de la mère, le sexe de l'enfant et la résidence, urbaine/rurale: dernière année disponible, 1996 - 2005 (continued - suite)

Continent, country or area, date, code and age (in years) Continent, pays ou zone, code, date et âge (en années)	Total			Urban - Urbaine			Rural - Rurale		
	Both sexes Les deux sexes	Male Masculin	Female Féminin	Both sexes Les deux sexes	Male Masculin	Female Féminin	Both sexes Les deux sexes	Male Masculin	Female Féminin
AMERICA, NORTH - AMÉRIQUE DU NORD									
Saint Kitts and Nevis - Saint-Kitts-et-Nevis									
2001 (+C)									
Total..............	803	...	...	...	...	...	...	...	...
10 - 14	3	...	...	...	...	...	...	...	...
15 - 19	164	...	...	...	...	...	...	...	...
20 - 24	241	...	...	...	...	...	...	...	...
25 - 29	166	...	...	...	...	...	...	...	...
30 - 34	148	...	...	...	...	...	...	...	...
35 - 39	67	...	...	...	...	...	...	...	...
40 + ...	14	...	...	...	...	...	...	...	...
Saint Lucia - Sainte-Lucie[9]									
2002 (C)									
Total..............	2 529	1 299	1 230	...	...	...	...	...	...
0 - 14..............	8	5	3	...	...	...	...	...	...
15 - 19	447	223	224	...	...	...	...	...	...
20 - 24	686	356	330	...	...	...	...	...	...
25 - 29	569	284	285	...	...	...	...	...	...
30 - 34	469	238	231	...	...	...	...	...	...
35 - 39	277	156	121	...	...	...	...	...	...
40 - 44	71	36	35	...	...	...	...	...	...
45 - 49	2	1	1	...	...	...	...	...	...
Saint Vincent and the Grenadines - Saint Vincent-et-les Grenadines									
2003 (+C)									
Total..............	1 923	975	948	...	...	...	...	...	...
0 - 14..............	10	4	6	...	...	...	...	...	...
15 - 19	388	193	195	...	...	...	...	...	...
20 - 24	547	286	261	...	...	...	...	...	...
25 - 29	430	208	222	...	...	...	...	...	...
30 - 34	304	163	141	...	...	...	...	...	...
35 - 39	182	82	100	...	...	...	...	...	...
40 - 44	55	34	21	...	...	...	...	...	...
45 - 49	4	2	2	...	...	...	...	...	...
50 + ...	-	-	-	...	...	...	...	...	...
Unknown - Inconnu	3	3	-	...	...	...	...	...	...
Trinidad and Tobago - Trinité-et-Tobago									
2002 (C)									
Total..............	16 990	8 613	8 377	...	...	...	...	...	...
0 - 14..............	28	16	12	...	...	...	...	...	...
15 - 19	2 377	1 257	1 120	...	...	...	...	...	...
20 - 24	5 275	2 706	2 569	...	...	...	...	...	...
25 - 29	4 328	2 195	2 133	...	...	...	...	...	...
30 - 34	2 919	1 426	1 493	...	...	...	...	...	...
35 - 39	1 652	812	840	...	...	...	...	...	...
40 - 44	364	175	189	...	...	...	...	...	...
45 + ...	11	8	3	...	...	...	...	...	...
Unknown - Inconnu	36	18	18	...	...	...	...	...	...
Turks Caicos Islands - Îles Turques et Caïques									
2005 (C)									
Total..............	318	158	160	...	...	...	...	...	...
0 - 14..............	1	-	1	...	...	...	...	...	...
15 - 19	28	13	15	...	...	...	...	...	...
20 - 24	65	29	36	...	...	...	...	...	...
25 - 29	83	40	43	...	...	...	...	...	...
30 - 34	76	47	29	...	...	...	...	...	...
35 - 39	52	23	29	...	...	...	...	...	...
40 - 44	11	5	6	...	...	...	...	...	...
45 + ...	2	1	1	...	...	...	...	...	...

10. Live births by age of mother, sex of the child and urban/rural residence: latest available year, 1996 - 2005
Naissances vivantes selon l'âge de la mère, le sexe de l'enfant et la résidence, urbaine/rurale: dernière année disponible, 1996 - 2005 (continued - suite)

Continent, country or area, date, code and age (in years) / Continent, pays ou zone, code, date et âge (en années)	Total			Urban - Urbaine			Rural - Rurale		
	Both sexes Les deux sexes	Male Masculin	Female Féminin	Both sexes Les deux sexes	Male Masculin	Female Féminin	Both sexes Les deux sexes	Male Masculin	Female Féminin
AMERICA, NORTH - AMÉRIQUE DU NORD									
United States - États-Unis									
2004* (C)									
Total	4 115 590	...	...	...	...	...	...	...	...
10 - 14	6 789	...	...	...	...	...	...	...	...
15 - 19	415 408	...	...	...	...	...	...	...	...
20 - 24	1 034 834	...	...	...	...	...	...	...	...
25 - 29	1 105 297	...	...	...	...	...	...	...	...
30 - 34	967 008	...	...	...	...	...	...	...	...
35 - 39	476 123	...	...	...	...	...	...	...	...
40 - 44	103 917	...	...	...	...	...	...	...	...
45 +	6 214	...	...	...	...	...	...	...	...
United States Virgin Islands - Îles Vierges américaines									
1997 (C)									
Total[10]	2 124	...	...	...	...	...	...	...	...
0 - 14	5	...	...	...	...	...	...	...	...
15 - 19	349	...	...	...	...	...	...	...	...
20 - 24	555	...	...	...	...	...	...	...	...
25 - 29	568	...	...	...	...	...	...	...	...
30 - 34	413	...	...	...	...	...	...	...	...
35 - 39	190	...	...	...	...	...	...	...	...
40 - 44	44	...	...	...	...	...	...	...	...
45 +	-	...	...	...	...	...	...	...	...
AMERICA, SOUTH - AMÉRIQUE DU SUD									
Argentina - Argentine									
2005 (C)									
Total	712 220	...	...	...	...	...	...	...	...
0 - 14	2 699	...	...	...	...	...	...	...	...
15 - 19	104 410	...	...	...	...	...	...	...	...
20 - 24	177 813	...	...	...	...	...	...	...	...
25 - 29	182 778	...	...	...	...	...	...	...	...
30 - 34	141 689	...	...	...	...	...	...	...	...
35 - 39	73 194	...	...	...	...	...	...	...	...
40 - 44	21 382	...	...	...	...	...	...	...	...
45 - 49	1 488	...	...	...	...	...	...	...	...
50 +	87	...	...	...	...	...	...	...	...
Unknown - Inconnu	6 680	...	...	...	...	...	...	...	...
Brazil - Brésil[9]									
2005 (U)									
Total	2 880 637	1 475 807	1 404 830	...	...	...	...	...	...
0 - 14	21 320	10 993	10 327	...	...	...	...	...	...
15 - 19	574 484	295 517	278 967	...	...	...	...	...	...
20 - 24	875 615	448 843	426 772	...	...	...	...	...	...
25 - 29	689 359	352 800	336 559	...	...	...	...	...	...
30 - 34	429 018	219 398	209 620	...	...	...	...	...	...
35 - 39	208 757	106 385	102 372	...	...	...	...	...	...
40 - 44	56 364	28 480	27 884	...	...	...	...	...	...
45 - 49	4 129	2 127	2 002	...	...	...	...	...	...
50 +	279	152	127	...	...	...	...	...	...
Unknown - Inconnu	21 312	11 112	10 200	...	...	...	...	...	...
Chile - Chili									
2003 (C)									
Total	234 486	119 963	114 523	...	...	...	...	...	...
0 - 14	994	502	492	...	...	...	...	...	...
15 - 19	33 838	17 390	16 448	...	...	...	...	...	...
20 - 24	54 536	27 926	26 610	...	...	...	...	...	...
25 - 29	56 443	28 775	27 668	...	...	...	...	...	...
30 - 34	50 557	25 945	24 612	...	...	...	...	...	...
35 - 39	29 662	15 211	14 451	...	...	...	...	...	...
40 - 44	8 087	4 026	4 061	...	...	...	...	...	...

10. Live births by age of mother, sex of the child and urban/rural residence: latest available year, 1996 - 2005
Naissances vivantes selon l'âge de la mère, le sexe de l'enfant et la résidence, urbaine/rurale: dernière année disponible, 1996 - 2005 (continued - suite)

Continent, country or area, date, code and age (in years) / Continent, pays ou zone, code, date et âge (en années)	Total			Urban - Urbaine			Rural - Rurale		
	Both sexes Les deux sexes	Male Masculin	Female Féminin	Both sexes Les deux sexes	Male Masculin	Female Féminin	Both sexes Les deux sexes	Male Masculin	Female Féminin
AMERICA, SOUTH - AMÉRIQUE DU SUD									
Chile - Chili									
2003 (C)									
45 - 49	362	185	177	...	...	...	...	...	...
50 + ...	7	3	4	...	...	...	...	...	...
Colombia - Colombie[11]									
2005 (U)									
Total....................	719 533	370 426	349 107	554 145[1]	285 398[1]	268 747[1]	152 218[1]	78 159[1]	74 059[1]
0 - 14..................	6 452	3 338	3 114	4 210[1]	2 219[1]	1 991[1]	2 066[1]	1 028[1]	1 038[1]
15 - 19	154 478	80 002	74 476	112 407[1]	58 288[1]	54 119[1]	38 918[1]	20 068[1]	18 850[1]
20 - 24	215 258	110 316	104 942	166 075[1]	85 017[1]	81 058[1]	45 665[1]	23 466[1]	22 199[1]
25 - 29	160 539	82 752	77 787	128 026[1]	66 028[1]	61 998[1]	30 073[1]	15 478[1]	14 595[1]
30 - 34	102 659	52 723	49 936	82 336[1]	42 340[1]	39 996[1]	18 793[1]	9 596[1]	9 197[1]
35 - 39	58 426	30 074	28 352	46 117[1]	23 754[1]	22 363[1]	11 394[1]	5 857[1]	5 537[1]
40 - 44	16 338	8 363	7 975	12 252[1]	6 329[1]	5 923[1]	3 814[1]	1 886[1]	1 928[1]
45 - 49	1 271	659	612	804[1]	413[1]	391[1]	432[1]	225[1]	207[1]
50 + ...	186	96	90	125[1]	61[1]	64[1]	54[1]	30[1]	24[1]
Unknown - Inconnu	3 926	2 103	1 823	1 793[1]	949[1]	844[1]	1 009[1]	525[1]	484[1]
Ecuador - Équateur[12]									
2004 (U)									
Total....................	168 893	85 999	82 894	132 618	67 598	65 020	36 275	18 401	17 874
0 - 14..................	1 908	981	927	1 555	796	759	353	185	168
15 - 19	29 145	14 987	14 158	22 490	11 555	10 935	6 655	3 432	3 223
20 - 24	50 760	25 781	24 979	39 743	20 159	19 584	11 017	5 622	5 395
25 - 29	38 133	19 409	18 724	30 697	15 660	15 037	7 436	3 749	3 687
30 - 34	25 313	12 915	12 398	20 023	10 264	9 759	5 290	2 651	2 639
35 - 39	13 869	6 991	6 878	10 633	5 374	5 259	3 236	1 617	1 619
40 - 44	4 953	2 531	2 422	3 449	1 792	1 657	1 504	739	765
45 - 49	662	311	351	446	203	243	216	108	108
50 + ...	-	-	-	-	-	-	-	-	-
Unknown - Inconnu	4 150	2 093	2 057	3 582	1 795	1 787	568	298	270
2005 (U)									
Total....................	168 324	...	...	...	...	...	...	...	...
0 - 14..................	614	...	...	...	...	...	...	...	...
15 - 19	29 030	...	...	...	...	...	...	...	...
20 - 24	50 551	...	...	...	...	...	...	...	...
25 - 29	39 315	...	...	...	...	...	...	...	...
30 - 34	25 284	...	...	...	...	...	...	...	...
35 - 39	13 978	...	...	...	...	...	...	...	...
40 - 44	4 761	...	...	...	...	...	...	...	...
45 - 49	682	...	...	...	...	...	...	...	...
50 + ...	-	...	...	...	...	...	...	...	...
Unknown - Inconnu	4 109	...	...	...	...	...	...	...	...
French Guiana - Guyane française									
2003 (C)									
Total....................	5 553	2 842	2 711	...	...	...	...	...	...
0 - 14..................	62	32	30	...	...	...	...	...	...
15 - 19	830	431	399	...	...	...	...	...	...
20 - 24	1 292	695	597	...	...	...	...	...	...
25 - 29	1 405	705	700	...	...	...	...	...	...
30 - 34	1 157	596	561	...	...	...	...	...	...
35 - 39	624	299	325	...	...	...	...	...	...
40 - 44	173	78	95	...	...	...	...	...	...
45 - 49	10	6	4	...	...	...	...	...	...
50 + ...	-	-	-	...	...	...	...	...	...
Peru - Pérou[13]									
2002 (+U)									
Total....................	355 870	...	...	...	...	...	...	...	...
0 - 14..................	986	...	...	...	...	...	...	...	...
15 - 19	48 340	...	...	...	...	...	...	...	...
20 - 24	95 905	...	...	...	...	...	...	...	...
25 - 29	88 304	...	...	...	...	...	...	...	...
30 - 34	65 196	...	...	...	...	...	...	...	...
35 - 39	39 100	...	...	...	...	...	...	...	...

10. Live births by age of mother, sex of the child and urban/rural residence: latest available year, 1996 - 2005
Naissances vivantes selon l'âge de la mère, le sexe de l'enfant et la résidence, urbaine/rurale: dernière année disponible, 1996 - 2005 (continued - suite)

Continent, country or area, date, code and age (in years) / Continent, pays ou zone, code, date et âge (en années)	Total			Urban - Urbaine			Rural - Rurale		
	Both sexes Les deux sexes	Male Masculin	Female Féminin	Both sexes Les deux sexes	Male Masculin	Female Féminin	Both sexes Les deux sexes	Male Masculin	Female Féminin
AMERICA, SOUTH - AMÉRIQUE DU SUD									
Peru - Pérou[13]									
2002 (+U)									
40 - 44	12 899	...	...	...	...	...	...	...	...
45 - 49	1 441	...	...	...	...	...	...	...	...
50 +	210	...	...	...	...	...	...	...	...
Unknown - Inconnu	3 489	...	...	...	...	...	...	...	...
Suriname									
2003 (C)									
Total[14]	9 450	...	...	...	...	...	...	...	...
0 - 14	80	...	...	...	...	...	...	...	...
15 - 19	1 431	...	...	...	...	...	...	...	...
20 - 24	2 609	...	...	...	...	...	...	...	...
25 - 29	2 302	...	...	...	...	...	...	...	...
30 - 34	1 702	...	...	...	...	...	...	...	...
35 - 39	901	...	...	...	...	...	...	...	...
40 - 44	241	...	...	...	...	...	...	...	...
45 +	15	...	...	...	...	...	...	...	...
Unknown - Inconnu	169	...	...	...	...	...	...	...	...
Uruguay									
2002 (C)									
Total	51 997	...	...	...	...	...	...	...	...
0 - 14	207	...	...	...	...	...	...	...	...
15 - 19	8 226	...	...	...	...	...	...	...	...
20 - 24	13 117	...	...	...	...	...	...	...	...
25 - 29	13 033	...	...	...	...	...	...	...	...
30 - 34	9 954	...	...	...	...	...	...	...	...
35 - 39	5 395	...	...	...	...	...	...	...	...
40 - 44	1 473	...	...	...	...	...	...	...	...
45 - 49	79	...	...	...	...	...	...	...	...
50 +	4	...	...	...	...	...	...	...	...
Unknown - Inconnu	508	...	...	...	...	...	...	...	...
Venezuela (Bolivarian Republic of) - Venezuela (République bolivarienne du)[15]									
2002 (C)									
Total	492 678	254 969	237 709	...	...	...	...	...	...
0 - 14	5 148	2 660	2 488	...	...	...	...	...	...
15 - 19	100 062	51 874	48 188	...	...	...	...	...	...
20 - 24	146 417	75 965	70 452	...	...	...	...	...	...
25 - 29	110 318	56 888	53 430	...	...	...	...	...	...
30 - 34	73 522	38 081	35 441	...	...	...	...	...	...
35 - 39	36 756	18 951	17 805	...	...	...	...	...	...
40 - 44	10 443	5 408	5 035	...	...	...	...	...	...
45 - 49	1 376	685	691	...	...	...	...	...	...
50 +	412	186	226	...	...	...	...	...	...
Unknown - Inconnu	8 224	4 271	3 953	...	...	...	...	...	...
ASIA - ASIE									
Armenia - Arménie[16]									
2004 (C)									
Total	37 520	...	...	23 628	...	...	13 892	...	...
15 - 19	4 717	...	...	2 397	...	...	2 320	...	...
20 - 24	18 734	...	...	11 310	...	...	7 424	...	...
25 - 29	9 315	...	...	6 510	...	...	2 805	...	...
30 - 34	3 245	...	...	2 343	...	...	902	...	...
35 - 39	1 195	...	...	861	...	...	334	...	...
40 - 44	298	...	...	197	...	...	101	...	...
45 - 49	16	...	...	10	...	...	6	...	...
50 +	-	...	...	-	...	...	-	...	...

10. Live births by age of mother, sex of the child and urban/rural residence: latest available year, 1996 - 2005
Naissances vivantes selon l'âge de la mère, le sexe de l'enfant et la résidence, urbaine/rurale: dernière année disponible,
1996 - 2005 (continued - suite)

Continent, country or area, date, code and age (in years) / Continent, pays ou zone, code, date et âge (en années)	Total			Urban - Urbaine			Rural - Rurale		
	Both sexes Les deux sexes	Male Masculin	Female Féminin	Both sexes Les deux sexes	Male Masculin	Female Féminin	Both sexes Les deux sexes	Male Masculin	Female Féminin
ASIA - ASIE									
Azerbaijan - Azerbaïdjan[16]									
2004 (+C)									
Total.....................	131 609	71 009	60 600	59 026	32 047	26 979	72 583	38 962	33 621
15 - 19	13 739	7 115	6 624	4 695	2 432	2 263	9 044	4 683	4 361
20 - 24	54 902	28 884	26 018	23 512	12 400	11 112	31 390	16 484	14 906
25 - 29	35 916	19 610	16 306	17 555	9 515	8 040	18 361	10 095	8 266
30 - 34	16 846	9 599	7 247	8 361	4 826	3 535	8 485	4 773	3 712
35 - 39	7 790	4 504	3 286	3 696	2 200	1 496	4 094	2 304	1 790
40 - 44	2 189	1 189	1 000	1 088	617	471	1 101	572	529
45 - 49	204	96	108	104	51	53	100	45	55
50 + ...	23	12	11	15	6	9	8	6	2
Bahrain - Bahreïn									
2005 (C)									
Total......................	15 198	...	...	...	...	...	...	...	...
0 - 14...................	4	...	...	...	...	...	...	...	...
15 - 19	485	...	...	...	...	...	...	...	...
20 - 24	3 508	...	...	...	...	...	...	...	...
25 - 29	4 852	...	...	...	...	...	...	...	...
30 - 34	3 508	...	...	...	...	...	...	...	...
35 - 39	2 076	...	...	...	...	...	...	...	...
40 - 44	681	...	...	...	...	...	...	...	...
45 - 49	69	...	...	...	...	...	...	...	...
50 + ...	7	...	...	...	...	...	...	...	...
Unknown - Inconnu	8	...	...	...	...	...	...	...	...
Bhutan - Bhoutan[17]									
2005 (|)									
Total.....................	12 538	6 306	6 232	3 845	1 943	1 902	8 693	4 363	4 330
15 - 19	1 376	711	665	309	158	151	1 067	553	514
20 - 24	4 211	2 156	2 055	1 388	702	686	2 823	1 454	1 369
25 - 29	3 677	1 814	1 863	1 332	670	662	2 345	1 144	1 201
30 - 34	1 753	880	873	518	265	253	1 235	615	620
35 - 39	960	463	497	215	110	105	745	353	392
40 - 44	434	207	227	64	30	34	370	177	193
45 - 49	127	75	52	19	8	11	108	67	41
Brunei Darussalam - Brunéi Darussalam									
2002 (+C)									
Total.....................	7 464	3 818	3 646	...	...	...	...	...	...
0 - 14...................	7	4	3	...	...	...	...	...	...
15 - 19	387	187	200	...	...	...	...	...	...
20 - 24	1 585	819	766	...	...	...	...	...	...
25 - 29	2 125	1 072	1 053	...	...	...	...	...	...
30 - 34	1 967	994	973	...	...	...	...	...	...
35 - 39	1 052	560	492	...	...	...	...	...	...
40 - 44	317	169	148	...	...	...	...	...	...
45 - 49	21	12	9	...	...	...	...	...	...
50 + ...	-	-	-	...	...	...	...	...	...
Unknown - Inconnu	3	1	2	...	...	...	...	...	...
Cambodia - Cambodge									
2004 (U)									
Total.....................	320 594[9]	...	...	40 790[18]	...	...	279 843[18]	...	...
15 - 19	23 238	...	...	2 097	...	...	21 140	...	...
20 - 24	106 787	...	...	11 172	...	...	95 615	...	...
25 - 29	66 573	...	...	9 448	...	...	57 125	...	...
30 - 34	57 861	...	...	8 609	...	...	49 252	...	...
35 - 39	43 391	...	...	6 945	...	...	36 446	...	...
40 - 44	19 386	...	...	2 066	...	...	17 320	...	...
45 - 49	3 358	...	...	453	...	...	2 945	...	...
China: Hong Kong SAR - Chine: Hong Kong RAS									
2005 (C)									
Total.....................	57 098	29 880	27 218	...	...	...	...	...	...
0 - 14...................	7	4	3	...	...	...	...	...	...
15 - 19	821	442	379	...	...	...	...	...	...
20 - 24	8 130	4 169	3 961	...	...	...	...	...	...

Continent, country or area, date, code and age (in years) / Continent, pays ou zone, code, date et âge (en années)	Total			Urban - Urbaine			Rural - Rurale		
	Both sexes Les deux sexes	Male Masculin	Female Féminin	Both sexes Les deux sexes	Male Masculin	Female Féminin	Both sexes Les deux sexes	Male Masculin	Female Féminin
ASIA - ASIE									
China: Hong Kong SAR - Chine: Hong Kong RAS									
2005 (C)									
25 - 29	16 146	8 409	7 737	...	...	...	...	...	...
30 - 34	20 274	10 586	9 688	...	...	...	...	...	...
35 - 39	9 897	5 303	4 594	...	...	...	...	...	...
40 - 44	1 732	926	806	...	...	...	...	...	...
45 - 49	81	37	44	...	...	...	...	...	...
50 +	6	3	3	...	...	...	...	...	...
Unknown - Inconnu	4	1	3	...	...	...	...	...	...
China: Macao SAR - Chine: Macao RAS									
2005 (C)									
Total	3 671	1 892	1 779	...	...	...	...	...	...
0 - 14	-	-	-	...	...	...	...	...	...
15 - 19	74	52	22	...	...	...	...	...	...
20 - 24	558	266	292	...	...	...	...	...	...
25 - 29	1 010	525	485	...	...	...	...	...	...
30 - 34	1 292	665	627	...	...	...	...	...	...
35 - 39	635	316	319	...	...	...	...	...	...
40 - 44	95	62	33	...	...	...	...	...	...
45 - 49	7	6	1	...	...	...	...	...	...
50 +	-	-	-	...	...	...	...	...	...
Cyprus - Chypre[19]									
2005 (C)									
Total	8 243	4 225	4 018	5 672[20]	2 890	2 782	2 512[20]	1 303	1 209
0 - 14	-	-	-	-	-	-	-	-	-
15 - 19	180	90	90	123	61	62	55	27	28
20 - 24	1 439	718	721	897	457	440	537	261	276
25 - 29	2 972	1 549	1 423	1 967	996	971	996	545	451
30 - 34	2 416	1 232	1 184	1 791	911	880	617	317	300
35 - 39	939	488	451	702	372	330	233	114	119
40 - 44	179	90	89	134	65	69	44	25	19
45 - 49	23	7	16	13	4	9	10	3	7
50 +	-	-	-	-	-	-	-	-	-
Unknown - Inconnu	95	51	44	45	24	21	20	11	9
Georgia - Géorgie[16]									
2001 (C)									
Total	40 416	21 906	18 510	25 078	13 427	11 651	15 338	8 479	6 859
0 - 14	86	45	41	53	31	22	33	14	19
15 - 19	4 814	2 557	2 257	2 769	1 440	1 329	2 045	1 117	928
20 - 24	15 733	8 392	7 341	9 193	4 883	4 310	6 540	3 509	3 031
25 - 29	9 640	5 334	4 306	6 397	3 501	2 896	3 243	1 833	1 410
30 - 34	5 992	3 291	2 701	3 896	2 098	1 798	2 096	1 193	903
35 - 39	3 058	1 686	1 372	2 046	1 097	949	1 012	589	423
40 - 44	809	449	360	535	287	248	274	162	112
45 - 49	146	80	66	89	42	47	57	38	19
50 +	38	17	21	26	11	15	12	6	6
Unknown - Inconnu	100	55	45	74	37	37	26	18	8
2005 (C)									
Total	46 512	...	...	...	...	...	...	...	...
0 - 19	6 903	...	...	...	...	...	...	...	...
20 - 24	16 703	...	...	...	...	...	...	...	...
25 - 29	12 110	...	...	...	...	...	...	...	...
30 - 34	6 896	...	...	...	...	...	...	...	...
35 - 39	2 870	...	...	...	...	...	...	...	...
40 - 44	752	...	...	...	...	...	...	...	...
45 +	278	...	...	...	...	...	...	...	...
Iraq[21]									
2000 (U)									
Total	471 886	...	...	...	...	...	...	...	...
15 - 19	21 367	...	...	...	...	...	...	...	...
20 - 24	115 973	...	...	...	...	...	...	...	...
25 - 29	149 287	...	...	...	...	...	...	...	...
30 - 34	110 981	...	...	...	...	...	...	...	...

10. Live births by age of mother, sex of the child and urban/rural residence: latest available year, 1996 - 2005
Naissances vivantes selon l'âge de la mère, le sexe de l'enfant et la résidence, urbaine/rurale: dernière année disponible, 1996 - 2005 (continued - suite)

Continent, country or area, date, code and age (in years) / Continent, pays ou zone, code, date et âge (en annèes)	Total Both sexes Les deux sexes	Total Male Masculin	Total Female Féminin	Urban - Urbaine Both sexes Les deux sexes	Urban - Urbaine Male Masculin	Urban - Urbaine Female Féminin	Rural - Rurale Both sexes Les deux sexes	Rural - Rurale Male Masculin	Rural - Rurale Female Féminin
ASIA - ASIE									
Iraq[21]									
2000 (U)									
35 - 39	*52 196*	...	...	...	...	...	...	...	...
40 - 44	*16 717*	...	...	...	...	...	...	...	...
45 +	*5 365*	...	...	...	...	...	...	...	...
Israel - Israël[22]									
2005 (C)									
Total	143 913	73 956	69 957	130 294[1]	66 886[1]	63 408[1]	13 517[1]	7 010[1]	6 507[1]
0 - 14	3	3	-	3[1]	3[1]	-[1]	-[1]	-[1]	-[1]
15 - 19	4 101	2 070	2 031	3 849[1]	1 945[1]	1 904[1]	250[1]	123[1]	127[1]
20 - 24	29 117	14 983	14 134	26 961[1]	13 836[1]	13 125[1]	2 127[1]	1 129[1]	998[1]
25 - 29	45 989	23 747	22 242	41 960[1]	21 677[1]	20 283[1]	3 995[1]	2 053[1]	1 942[1]
30 - 34	40 150	20 573	19 577	35 781[1]	18 338[1]	17 443[1]	4 348[1]	2 222[1]	2 126[1]
35 - 39	19 232	9 877	9 355	16 985[1]	8 690[1]	8 295[1]	2 238[1]	1 181[1]	1 057[1]
40 - 44	4 564	2 329	2 235	4 052[1]	2 051[1]	2 001[1]	508[1]	275[1]	233[1]
45 - 49	370	176	194	346[1]	164[1]	182[1]	24[1]	12[1]	12[1]
50 +	64	30	34	59[1]	28[1]	31[1]	5[1]	2[1]	3[1]
Unknown - Inconnu	323	168	155	298[1]	154[1]	144[1]	22[1]	13[1]	9[1]
Japan - Japon[23]									
2005 (C)									
Total	1 062 530	545 032	517 498	917 831[1]	471 118[1]	446 713[1]	144 529[1]	73 821[1]	70 708[1]
0 - 14	42	20	22	37[1]	17[1]	20[1]	5[1]	3[1]	2[1]
15 - 19	16 531	8 581	7 950	13 887[1]	7 175[1]	6 712[1]	2 643[1]	1 405[1]	1 238[1]
20 - 24	128 135	65 498	62 637	106 306[1]	54 535[1]	51 771[1]	21 827[1]	10 962[1]	10 865[1]
25 - 29	339 328	174 571	164 757	290 173[1]	149 473[1]	140 700[1]	49 111[1]	25 073[1]	24 038[1]
30 - 34	404 700	207 444	197 256	354 261[1]	181 521[1]	172 740[1]	50 356[1]	25 875[1]	24 481[1]
35 - 39	153 440	78 597	74 843	135 277[1]	69 309[1]	65 968[1]	18 131[1]	9 274[1]	8 857[1]
40 - 44	19 750	10 035	9 715	17 369[1]	8 845[1]	8 524[1]	2 374[1]	1 186[1]	1 188[1]
45 - 49	564	265	299	483[1]	222[1]	261[1]	81[1]	43[1]	38[1]
50 +	34	18	16	33[1]	18[1]	15[1]	1[1]	-[1]	1[1]
Unknown - Inconnu	6	3	3	5[1]	3[1]	2[1]	-[1]	-[1]	-[1]
Kazakhstan[16]									
2003 (C)									
Total	247 946	127 610	120 336	138 680	71 549	67 131	109 266	56 061	53 205
0 - 14	...	...	...	...	18	14	...	9	11
0 - 19	19 744	10 101	9 643	10 911	...	...	8 833	...	...
15 - 19	...	...	...	...	5 520	5 358	...	4 551	4 260
20 - 24	87 391	44 819	42 572	47 811	24 612	23 200	39 580	20 208	19 373
25 - 29	71 825	37 138	34 687	40 920	21 293	19 628	30 905	15 847	15 059
30 - 34	42 848	22 078	20 770	24 359	12 557	11 802	18 489	9 521	8 968
35 - 39	20 811	10 768	10 043	11 675	6 024	5 650	9 136	4 743	4 393
40 - 44	4 739	2 404	2 335	2 589	1 321	1 268	2 150	1 084	1 066
45 - 49	228	126	102	109	60	49	119	66	53
50 +	17	10	7	9	4	5	8	6	2
Unknown - Inconnu	343	166	177	297	140	157	46	26	20
2004 (C)									
Total	273 028	140 549	132 479	155 997	...	...	117 031	...	...
0 - 19	21 068	10 890	10 178	11 895	...	...	9 173	...	...
20 - 24	94 209	48 746	45 463	52 469	...	...	41 740	...	...
25 - 29	79 360	40 694	38 666	45 976	...	...	33 384	...	...
30 - 34	48 835	25 037	23 798	28 714	...	...	20 121	...	...
35 - 39	23 577	12 085	11 492	13 553	...	...	10 024	...	...
40 - 44	5 459	2 833	2 626	3 026	...	...	2 433	...	...
45 - 49	234	130	104	116	...	...	118	...	...
50 +	27	10	17	18	...	...	9	...	...
Unknown - Inconnu	259	124	135	230	...	...	29	...	...
Korea (Republic of) - Corée (République de)[24]									
2004 (C)									
Total	476 052	247 399	228 653	...	...	...	...	...	...
0 - 14	27	18	9	...	...	...	...	...	...
15 - 19	3 412	1 885	1 527	...	...	...	...	...	...
20 - 24	39 498	20 591	18 907	...	...	...	...	...	...
25 - 29	199 075	102 389	96 686	...	...	...	...	...	...

10. Live births by age of mother, sex of the child and urban/rural residence: latest available year, 1996 - 2005
Naissances vivantes selon l'âge de la mère, le sexe de l'enfant et la résidence, urbaine/rurale: dernière année disponible, 1996 - 2005 (continued - suite)

Continent, country or area, date, code and age (in years) / Continent, pays ou zone, code, date et âge (en années)	Total			Urban - Urbaine			Rural - Rurale		
	Both sexes Les deux sexes	Male Masculin	Female Féminin	Both sexes Les deux sexes	Male Masculin	Female Féminin	Both sexes Les deux sexes	Male Masculin	Female Féminin
ASIA - ASIE									
Korea (Republic of) - Corée (République de)[24]									
2004 (C)									
30 - 34	187 566	98 097	89 469	...	...	...	...	...	...
35 - 39	39 778	20 984	18 794	...	...	...	...	...	...
40 - 44	5 388	2 765	2 623	...	...	...	...	...	...
45 - 49	373	184	189	...	...	...	...	...	...
50 +	26	13	13	...	...	...	...	...	...
Unknown - Inconnu	909	473	436	...	...	...	...	...	...
Kuwait - Koweït									
2005 (C)									
Total	50 941	25 922	25 019	...	...	...	...	...	...
0 - 14	-	-	-	...	...	...	...	...	...
15 - 19	1 244	637	607	...	...	...	...	...	...
20 - 24	10 827	5 484	5 343	...	...	...	...	...	...
25 - 29	15 842	8 112	7 730	...	...	...	...	...	...
30 - 34	12 297	6 185	6 112	...	...	...	...	...	...
35 - 39	6 719	3 415	3 304	...	...	...	...	...	...
40 - 44	1 877	993	884	...	...	...	...	...	...
45 - 49	200	107	93	...	...	...	...	...	...
50 +	-	-	-	...	...	...	...	...	...
Unknown - Inconnu	1 935	989	946	...	...	...	...	...	...
Kyrgyzstan - Kirghizistan[16]									
2005 (C)									
Total	109 839	56 534	53 305	35 600	18 434	17 166	74 239	38 100	36 139
0 - 14	1	1	-	-	-	-	1	1	-
15 - 19	7 512	3 813	3 699	2 217	1 110	1 107	5 295	2 703	2 592
20 - 24	40 832	21 211	19 621	12 603	6 638	5 965	28 229	14 573	13 656
25 - 29	30 415	15 494	14 921	9 985	5 123	4 862	20 430	10 371	10 059
30 - 34	18 525	9 583	8 942	6 279	3 290	2 989	12 246	6 293	5 953
35 - 39	9 176	4 694	4 482	3 285	1 652	1 633	5 891	3 042	2 849
40 - 44	2 661	1 378	1 283	915	465	450	1 746	913	833
45 - 49	387	187	200	114	57	57	273	130	143
50 +	93	57	36	23	11	12	70	46	24
Unknown - Inconnu	237	116	121	179	88	91	58	28	30
Maldives									
2003 (C)									
Total	5 154	2 686	2 468	1 965	1 037	928	3 189	1 649	1 540
0 - 14	2	2	-	-	-	-	2	2	-
15 - 19	278	130	148	86	45	41	192	85	107
20 - 24	1 704	906	798	698	375	323	1 006	531	475
25 - 29	1 460	753	707	632	337	295	828	416	412
30 - 34	1 023	529	494	375	191	184	648	338	310
35 - 39	556	301	255	146	78	68	410	223	187
40 - 44	112	57	55	25	11	14	87	46	41
45 - 49	11	4	7	2	-	2	9	4	5
50 +	3	1	2	1	-	1	2	1	1
Mongolia - Mongolie									
1998 (C)									
Total	49 256	24 999	24 257	22 393	11 320	11 073	26 863	13 679	13 184
0 - 14	50	19	31	16	8	8	34	11	23
15 - 19	3 658	1 811	1 847	1 451	734	717	2 207	1 077	1 130
20 - 24	17 857	9 078	8 779	7 720	3 906	3 814	10 137	5 172	4 965
25 - 29	14 919	7 613	7 306	6 876	3 479	3 397	8 043	4 134	3 909
30 - 34	7 893	3 987	3 906	3 950	1 988	1 962	3 943	1 999	1 944
35 - 39	3 678	1 854	1 824	1 873	948	925	1 805	906	899
40 - 44	982	518	464	424	215	209	558	303	255
45 - 49	188	104	84	71	36	35	117	68	49
50 +	31	15	16	12	6	6	19	9	10
2005 (C)									
Total	45 326	23 002	22 324	26 462	...	...	18 864	...	...
0 - 14	29	15	14	11	...	...	18	...	...
15 - 19	2 233	1 138	1 095	1 040	...	...	1 193	...	...
20 - 24	14 831	7 433	7 398	8 303	...	...	6 528	...	...
25 - 29	14 605	7 461	7 144	8 668	...	...	5 937	...	...

10. Live births by age of mother, sex of the child and urban/rural residence: latest available year, 1996 - 2005
Naissances vivantes selon l'âge de la mère, le sexe de l'enfant et la résidence, urbaine/rurale: dernière année disponible, 1996 - 2005 (continued - suite)

Continent, country or area, date, code and age (in years) Continent, pays ou zone, code, date et âge (en années)	Total			Urban - Urbaine			Rural - Rurale		
	Both sexes Les deux sexes	Male Masculin	Female Féminin	Both sexes Les deux sexes	Male Masculin	Female Féminin	Both sexes Les deux sexes	Male Masculin	Female Féminin
ASIA - ASIE									
Mongolia - Mongolie									
2005 (C)									
30 - 34	8 505	4 357	4 148	5 289	...	...	3 216	...	...
35 - 39	3 972	2 045	1 927	2 519	...	...	1 453	...	...
40 - 44	916	432	484	499	...	...	417	...	...
45 - 49	206	104	102	115	...	...	91	...	...
50 + ...	29	17	12	18	...	...	11	...	...
Oman[21]									
1999 (U)									
Total.	44 067	...	...	...	...	...	...	...	...
15 - 19	4 096	...	...	...	...	...	...	...	...
20 - 24	13 224	...	...	...	...	...	...	...	...
25 - 29	11 504	...	...	...	...	...	...	...	...
30 - 34	7 759	...	...	...	...	...	...	...	...
35 - 39	5 563	...	...	...	...	...	...	...	...
40 - 44	1 739	...	...	...	...	...	...	...	...
45 + ...	182	...	...	...	...	...	...	...	...
Pakistan[25]									
2005 (I)									
Total.	3 772 494	1 993 492	1 779 002	1 226 151	653 480	572 671	2 546 343	1 340 012	1 206 331
15 - 19	161 490	90 049	71 441	32 480	16 115	16 365	129 010	73 934	55 076
20 - 24	1 050 830	556 310	494 520	338 217	172 425	165 792	712 613	383 885	328 728
25 - 29	1 166 365	611 186	555 179	399 554	214 071	185 483	766 811	397 115	369 696
30 - 34	754 513	395 425	359 088	262 585	142 356	120 229	491 928	253 069	238 859
35 - 39	425 352	222 186	203 166	142 496	80 113	62 383	282 856	142 073	140 783
40 - 44	161 914	86 273	75 641	38 358	21 167	17 191	123 556	65 106	58 450
45 + ...	52 030	32 063	19 967	12 461	7 233	5 228	39 569	24 830	14 739
Philippines									
2003 (C)									
Total.	1 669 442	868 749	800 693	...	...	...	...	...	...
0 - 14.	829	422	407	...	...	...	...	...	...
15 - 19	123 036	64 147	58 889	...	...	...	...	...	...
20 - 24	472 211	246 027	226 184	...	...	...	...	...	...
25 - 29	458 341	239 200	219 141	...	...	...	...	...	...
30 - 34	340 211	177 132	163 079	...	...	...	...	...	...
35 - 39	193 825	100 206	93 619	...	...	...	...	...	...
40 - 44	68 400	35 260	33 140	...	...	...	...	...	...
45 - 49	8 124	4 145	3 979	...	...	...	...	...	...
50 + ...	728	346	382	...	...	...	...	...	...
Unknown - Inconnu	3 737	1 864	1 873	...	...	...	...	...	...
Qatar									
2005 (C)									
Total.	13 401	6 839	6 562	...	...	...	...	...	...
15 - 19	345	184	161	...	...	...	...	...	...
20 - 24	2 591	1 287	1 304	...	...	...	...	...	...
25 - 29	4 197	2 173	2 024	...	...	...	...	...	...
30 - 34	3 538	1 827	1 711	...	...	...	...	...	...
35 - 39	2 017	1 007	1 010	...	...	...	...	...	...
40 - 44	614	314	300	...	...	...	...	...	...
45 - 49	77	36	41	...	...	...	...	...	...
50 + ...	22	11	11	...	...	...	...	...	...
Unknown - Inconnu	-	-	-	...	...	...	...	...	...
Saudi Arabia - Arabie saoudite									
2005 (...)									
Total.	582 582	298 396	284 186	...	...	...	...	...	...
15 - 19	25 652	13 139	12 513	...	...	...	...	...	...
20 - 24	153 901	78 827	75 074	...	...	...	...	...	...
25 - 29	194 252	99 495	94 757	...	...	...	...	...	...
30 - 34	135 325	69 313	66 012	...	...	...	...	...	...
35 - 39	57 941	29 677	28 264	...	...	...	...	...	...
40 - 44	14 373	7 362	7 011	...	...	...	...	...	...
45 - 49	1 137	583	555	...	...	...	...	...	...

10. Live births by age of mother, sex of the child and urban/rural residence: latest available year, 1996 - 2005
Naissances vivantes selon l'âge de la mère, le sexe de l'enfant et la résidence, urbaine/rurale: dernière année disponible, 1996 - 2005 (continued - suite)

Continent, country or area, date, code and age (in years) Continent, pays ou zone, code, date et âge (en années)	Total			Urban - Urbaine			Rural - Rurale		
	Both sexes Les deux sexes	Male Masculin	Female Féminin	Both sexes Les deux sexes	Male Masculin	Female Féminin	Both sexes Les deux sexes	Male Masculin	Female Féminin
ASIA - ASIE									
Singapore - Singapour									
2005 (C)									
Total	37 492	19 351[26]	18 140[26]	...	...	...	...	...	...
0 - 14	11	6	5	...	...	...	...	...	...
15 - 19	842	433	409	...	...	...	...	...	...
20 - 24	3 723	1 943	1 780	...	...	...	...	...	...
25 - 29	11 114	5 737	5 377	...	...	...	...	...	...
30 - 34	14 593	7 521	7 072	...	...	...	...	...	...
35 - 39	6 101	3 128	2 973	...	...	...	...	...	...
40 - 44	1 067	563	504	...	...	...	...	...	...
45 - 49	40	20	20	...	...	...	...	...	...
50 +	-	-	-	...	...	...	...	...	...
Unknown - Inconnu	1	-	-	...	...	...	...	...	...
Sri Lanka									
1996 (+C)									
Total	340 649	173 603	167 046	234 715	119 540	115 175	105 934	54 063	51 871
0 - 14	139	73	66	109	59	50	30	14	16
15 - 19	28 271	14 483	13 788	18 849	9 594	9 255	9 422	4 889	4 533
20 - 24	83 244	42 548	40 696	54 727	27 881	26 846	28 517	14 667	13 850
25 - 29	101 510	51 840	49 670	70 277	35 933	34 344	31 233	15 907	15 326
30 - 34	76 096	38 601	37 495	55 159	27 969	27 190	20 937	10 632	10 305
35 - 39	42 130	21 467	20 663	28 886	14 765	14 121	13 244	6 702	6 542
40 - 44	8 378	4 168	4 210	6 143	3 076	3 067	2 235	1 092	1 143
45 - 49	804	386	418	534	250	284	270	136	134
50 +	77	37	40	31	13	18	46	24	22
Tajikistan - Tadjikistan[16]									
1999 (U)									
Total	114 015	60 552	53 463	23 602	12 650	10 952	90 413	47 902	42 511
15 - 19	10 026	5 239	4 787	2 207	1 156	1 051	7 819	4 083	3 736
20 - 24	38 400	20 275	18 125	8 093	4 355	3 738	30 307	15 920	14 387
25 - 29	30 752	16 431	14 321	6 394	3 414	2 980	24 358	13 017	11 341
30 - 34	20 245	10 744	9 501	4 144	2 223	1 921	16 101	8 521	7 580
35 - 39	10 957	5 873	5 084	2 116	1 153	963	8 841	4 720	4 121
40 - 44	2 819	1 532	1 287	441	226	215	2 378	1 306	1 072
45 - 49	234	128	106	31	17	14	203	111	92
50 +	37	25	12	5	4	1	32	21	11
Unknown - Inconnu	545	305	240	171	102	69	374	203	171
Thailand - Thaïlande									
1999 (+U)									
Total	772 604	398 608	373 996	116 268	59 796	56 472	656 336	338 812	317 524
0 - 14	1 525	817	708	161	77	84	1 364	740	624
15 - 19	91 785	47 478	44 307	9 485	4 984	4 501	82 300	42 494	39 806
20 - 24	215 558	111 265	104 293	25 069	12 898	12 171	190 489	98 367	92 122
25 - 29	217 409	112 172	105 237	30 889	15 857	15 032	186 520	96 315	90 205
30 - 34	146 305	75 426	70 879	25 943	13 219	12 724	120 362	62 207	58 155
35 - 39	63 192	32 560	30 632	11 438	5 914	5 524	51 754	26 646	25 108
40 - 44	15 125	7 746	7 379	2 031	1 049	982	13 094	6 697	6 397
45 - 49	1 748	893	855	129	67	62	1 619	826	793
50 +	227	124	103	7	3	4	220	121	99
Unknown - Inconnu	19 730	10 127	9 603	11 116	5 728	5 388	8 614	4 399	4 215
2005 (+U)									
Total	809 485	416 474	393 011	...	...	...	...	...	...
0 - 14	2 549	1 301	1 248	...	...	...	...	...	...
15 - 19	113 048	58 207	54 841	...	...	...	...	...	...
20 - 24	207 269	106 613	100 656	...	...	...	...	...	...
25 - 29	220 696	113 676	107 020	...	...	...	...	...	...
30 - 34	164 735	84 673	80 062	...	...	...	...	...	...
35 - 39	78 749	40 531	38 218	...	...	...	...	...	...
40 - 44	18 809	9 667	9 142	...	...	...	...	...	...
45 - 49	1 364	667	697	...	...	...	...	...	...
50 +	78	43	35	...	...	...	...	...	...
Unknown - Inconnu	2 188	1 096	1 092	...	...	...	...	...	...

10. Live births by age of mother, sex of the child and urban/rural residence: latest available year, 1996 - 2005
Naissances vivantes selon l'âge de la mère, le sexe de l'enfant et la résidence, urbaine/rurale: dernière année disponible, 1996 - 2005 (continued - suite)

Continent, country or area, date, code and age (in years) Continent, pays ou zone, code, date et âge (en années)	Total			Urban - Urbaine			Rural - Rurale		
	Both sexes Les deux sexes	Male Masculin	Female Féminin	Both sexes Les deux sexes	Male Masculin	Female Féminin	Both sexes Les deux sexes	Male Masculin	Female Féminin
ASIA - ASIE									
Turkey - Turquie[27]									
1997 (I)									
Total...............	1 377 000	...	...	...	...	...	...	...	...
0 - 14...............	-	...	...	...	...	...	...	...	...
15 - 19...............	165 000	...	...	...	...	...	...	...	...
20 - 24...............	531 000	...	...	...	...	...	...	...	...
25 - 29...............	387 000	...	...	...	...	...	...	...	...
30 - 34...............	182 000	...	...	...	...	...	...	...	...
35 - 39...............	79 000	...	...	...	...	...	...	...	...
40 - 44...............	28 000	...	...	...	...	...	...	...	...
45 +...............	5 000	...	...	...	...	...	...	...	...
Uzbekistan - Ouzbékistan[16]									
2000 (C)									
Total...............	527 580	...	...	163 834	...	...	363 746	...	...
15 - 19...............	28 179	...	...	10 217	...	...	17 962	...	...
20 - 24...............	228 743	...	...	69 369	...	...	159 374	...	...
25 - 29...............	160 082	...	...	48 315	...	...	111 767	...	...
30 - 34...............	78 316	...	...	25 084	...	...	53 232	...	...
35 - 39...............	26 866	...	...	9 095	...	...	17 771	...	...
40 - 44...............	4 979	...	...	1 639	...	...	3 340	...	...
45 - 49...............	348	...	...	96	...	...	252	...	...
50 +...............	67	...	...	19	...	...	48	...	...
EUROPE									
Albania - Albanie									
2004 (C)									
Total...............	43 022	22 859	20 163	18 859	10 001	8 858	24 163	12 858	11 305
15 - 19...............	2 249	1 213	1 036	1 001	539	462	1 248	674	574
20 - 24...............	13 516	7 006	6 510	5 508	2 849	2 659	8 008	4 157	3 851
25 - 29...............	14 476	7 669	6 807	6 269	3 311	2 958	8 207	4 358	3 849
30 - 34...............	8 491	4 597	3 894	3 991	2 161	1 830	4 500	2 436	2 064
35 - 39...............	3 239	1 800	1 439	1 532	855	677	1 707	945	762
40 - 44...............	736	419	317	346	185	161	390	234	156
45 - 49...............	64	38	26	36	22	14	28	16	12
50 +...............	12	7	5	5	2	3	7	5	2
Unknown - Inconnu.......	239	110	129	171	77	94	68	33	35
2005 (C)									
Total...............	39 612	...	...	...	...	...	...	...	...
0 - 19...............	2 513	...	...	...	...	...	...	...	...
20 - 24...............	13 099	...	...	...	...	...	...	...	...
25 - 29...............	12 843	...	...	...	...	...	...	...	...
30 - 34...............	7 489	...	...	...	...	...	...	...	...
35 - 39...............	2 827	...	...	...	...	...	...	...	...
40 - 44...............	585	...	...	...	...	...	...	...	...
45 - 49...............	62	...	...	...	...	...	...	...	...
50 +...............	17	...	...	...	...	...	...	...	...
Unknown - Inconnu.......	177	...	...	...	...	...	...	...	...
Andorra - Andorre									
2004 (C)									
Total...............	814	418	396	...	...	...	...	...	...
15 - 19...............	9	6	3	...	...	...	...	...	...
20 - 24...............	79	47	32	...	...	...	...	...	...
25 - 29...............	209	102	107	...	...	...	...	...	...
30 - 34...............	309	156	153	...	...	...	...	...	...
35 - 39...............	169	82	87	...	...	...	...	...	...
40 - 44...............	36	24	12	...	...	...	...	...	...
45 - 49...............	3	1	2	...	...	...	...	...	...
Austria - Autriche									
2005 (C)									
Total...............	78 190	39 878	38 312	...	...	...	...	...	...
0 - 14...............	3	2	1	...	...	...	...	...	...
15 - 19...............	3 059	1 574	1 485	...	...	...	...	...	...
20 - 24...............	14 395	7 281	7 114	...	...	...	...	...	...

10. Live births by age of mother, sex of the child and urban/rural residence: latest available year, 1996 - 2005
Naissances vivantes selon l'âge de la mère, le sexe de l'enfant et la résidence, urbaine/rurale: dernière année disponible, 1996 - 2005 (continued - suite)

Continent, country or area, date, code and age (in years) / Continent, pays ou zone, code, date et âge (en années)	Total			Urban - Urbaine			Rural - Rurale		
	Both sexes Les deux sexes	Male Masculin	Female Féminin	Both sexes Les deux sexes	Male Masculin	Female Féminin	Both sexes Les deux sexes	Male Masculin	Female Féminin
EUROPE									
Austria - Autriche									
2005 (C)									
25 - 29	23 804	12 147	11 657	...	...	...	...	...	...
30 - 34	23 271	11 894	11 377	...	...	...	...	...	...
35 - 39	11 414	5 804	5 610	...	...	...	...	...	...
40 - 44	2 149	1 125	1 024	...	...	...	...	...	...
45 - 49	89	48	41	...	...	...	...	...	...
50 + ...	6	3	3	...	...	...	...	...	...
Belarus - Bélarus[16]									
2004 (C)									
Total....................	88 943	45 668	43 275	65 038	33 461	31 577	23 905	12 207	11 698
0 - 14....................	10	6	4	5	3	2	5	3	2
15 - 19	8 858	4 572	4 286	5 605	2 903	2 702	3 253	1 669	1 584
20 - 24	34 823	17 840	16 983	25 195	12 925	12 270	9 628	4 915	4 713
25 - 29	26 187	13 459	12 728	19 953	10 217	9 736	6 234	3 242	2 992
30 - 34	13 416	6 895	6 521	10 205	5 289	4 916	3 211	1 606	1 605
35 - 39	4 525	2 328	2 197	3 270	1 698	1 572	1 255	630	625
40 - 44	963	490	473	678	360	318	285	130	155
45 - 49	48	23	25	33	17	16	15	6	9
Unknown - Inconnu	113	55	58	94	49	45	19	6	13
Bosnia and Herzegovina - Bosnie-Herzégovine									
2005 (C)									
Total....................	34 627	...	...	...	...	...	...	...	...
0 - 14....................	9	...	...	...	...	...	...	...	...
15 - 19	2 082	...	...	...	...	...	...	...	...
20 - 24	10 464	...	...	...	...	...	...	...	...
25 - 29	11 562	...	...	...	...	...	...	...	...
30 - 34	6 765	...	...	...	...	...	...	...	...
35 - 39	2 660	...	...	...	...	...	...	...	...
40 - 44	549	...	...	...	...	...	...	...	...
45 - 49	27	...	...	...	...	...	...	...	...
50 + ...	1	...	...	...	...	...	...	...	...
Unknown - Inconnu	510	...	...	...	...	...	...	...	...
Bulgaria - Bulgarie									
2005 (C)									
Total....................	71 075	36 478	34 597	52 280	26 748	25 532	18 795	9 730	9 065
0 - 14....................	399	199	200	248	127	121	151	72	79
15 - 19	9 679	4 975	4 704	5 695	2 897	2 798	3 984	2 078	1 906
20 - 24	20 628	10 563	10 065	13 762	7 004	6 758	6 866	3 559	3 307
25 - 29	22 871	11 767	11 104	18 028	9 265	8 763	4 843	2 502	2 341
30 - 34	13 113	6 760	6 353	10 939	5 629	5 310	2 174	1 131	1 043
35 - 39	3 796	1 892	1 904	3 153	1 580	1 573	643	312	331
40 - 44	550	298	252	423	228	195	127	70	57
45 - 49	18	10	8	14	7	7	4	3	1
50 + ...	1	1	-	-	-	-	1	1	-
Unknown - Inconnu	20	13	7	18	11	7	2	2	-
Channel Islands: Guernsey - Îles Anglo-Normandes: Guernesey									
2000 (C)									
Total....................	644	336	308	...	...	...	...	...	...
15 - 19	42	15	27	...	...	...	...	...	...
20 - 24	84	49	35	...	...	...	...	...	...
25 - 29	192	101	91	...	...	...	...	...	...
30 - 34	200	102	98	...	...	...	...	...	...
35 - 39	106	60	46	...	...	...	...	...	...
40 - 44	20	9	11	...	...	...	...	...	...
Croatia - Croatie									
2005 (C)									
Total....................	42 492	21 750	20 742	23 421	12 034	11 387	19 071	9 716	9 355
0 - 14....................	6	3	3	2	1	1	4	2	2
15 - 19	1 886	953	933	710	342	368	1 176	611	565
20 - 24	9 929	5 014	4 915	4 266	2 169	2 097	5 663	2 845	2 818
25 - 29	14 965	7 711	7 254	8 280	4 278	4 002	6 685	3 433	3 252

10. Live births by age of mother, sex of the child and urban/rural residence: latest available year, 1996 - 2005
Naissances vivantes selon l'âge de la mère, le sexe de l'enfant et la résidence, urbaine/rurale: dernière année disponible, 1996 - 2005 (continued - suite)

Continent, country or area, date, code and age (in years) / Continent, pays ou zone, code, date et âge (en années)	Total			Urban - Urbaine			Rural - Rurale		
	Both sexes Les deux sexes	Male Masculin	Female Féminin	Both sexes Les deux sexes	Male Masculin	Female Féminin	Both sexes Les deux sexes	Male Masculin	Female Féminin
EUROPE									
Croatia - Croatie									
2005 (C)									
30 - 34	10 672	5 508	5 164	6 896	3 542	3 354	3 776	1 966	1 810
35 - 39	4 208	2 135	2 073	2 745	1 427	1 318	1 463	708	755
40 - 44	740	381	359	471	249	222	269	132	137
45 - 49	44	25	19	23	12	11	21	13	8
50 +	2	...	2	2	-	2	-	-	-
Unknown - Inconnu	40	20	20	26	14	12	14	6	8
Czech Republic - République tchèque									
2005 (C)									
Total	102 211	52 453	49 758	75 719	38 978	36 741	26 492	13 475	13 017
0 - 14	19	15	4	12	9	3	7	6	1
15 - 19	3 483	1 824	1 659	2 676	1 428	1 248	807	396	411
20 - 24	16 716	8 609	8 107	11 600	5 972	5 628	5 116	2 637	2 479
25 - 29	43 354	22 242	21 112	31 520	16 251	15 269	11 834	5 991	5 843
30 - 34	29 699	15 175	14 524	22 902	11 715	11 187	6 797	3 460	3 337
35 - 39	7 664	3 939	3 725	6 006	3 101	2 905	1 658	838	820
40 - 44	1 228	629	599	966	487	479	262	142	120
45 - 49	46	18	28	36	14	22	10	4	6
50 +	2	2	-	1	1	-	1	1	-
Unknown - Inconnu	-	-	-	-	-	-	-	-	-
Denmark - Danemark[28]									
2005 (C)									
Total	64 282	32 827	31 455	...	...	...	...	...	...
0 - 14	6	2	4	...	...	...	...	...	...
15 - 19	839	453	386	...	...	...	...	...	...
20 - 24	6 252	3 202	3 050	...	...	...	...	...	...
25 - 29	21 317	10 890	10 427	...	...	...	...	...	...
30 - 34	24 293	12 334	11 959	...	...	...	...	...	...
35 - 39	9 868	5 041	4 827	...	...	...	...	...	...
40 - 44	1 654	876	778	...	...	...	...	...	...
45 - 49	51	28	23	...	...	...	...	...	...
50 +	2	1	1	...	...	...	...	...	...
Unknown - Inconnu	-	-	-	...	...	...	...	...	...
Estonia - Estonie									
2005 (C)									
Total	14 350	7 486	6 864	10 233	5 365	4 868	4 117	2 121	1 996
0 - 14	3	1	2	2	1	1	1	-	1
15 - 19	1 113	597	516	660	372	288	453	225	228
20 - 24	3 583	1 924	1 659	2 488	1 341	1 147	1 095	583	512
25 - 29	4 542	2 356	2 186	3 428	1 776	1 652	1 114	580	534
30 - 34	3 315	1 675	1 640	2 437	1 249	1 188	878	426	452
35 - 39	1 501	781	720	1 011	524	487	490	257	233
40 - 44	282	146	136	200	99	101	82	47	35
45 - 49	11	6	5	7	3	4	4	3	1
50 +	-	-	-	-	-	-	-	-	-
Unknown - Inconnu	-	-	-	-	-	-	-	-	-
Faeroe Islands - Îles Féroé									
2005 (C)									
Total	713	...	...	...	...	...	...	...	...
0 - 14	-	...	...	...	...	...	...	...	...
15 - 19	24	...	...	...	...	...	...	...	...
20 - 24	119	...	...	...	...	...	...	...	...
25 - 29	229	...	...	...	...	...	...	...	...
30 - 34	196	...	...	...	...	...	...	...	...
35 - 39	124	...	...	...	...	...	...	...	...
40 - 44	19	...	...	...	...	...	...	...	...
45 - 49	2	...	...	...	...	...	...	...	...
50 +	-	...	...	...	...	...	...	...	...
Finland - Finlande[29]									
2005 (C)									
Total	57 745	29 400	28 345	38 181	19 419	18 762	19 564	9 981	9 583
0 - 14	5	4	1	2	1	1	3	3	-
15 - 19	1 605	856	749	1 041	537	504	564	319	245

10. Live births by age of mother, sex of the child and urban/rural residence: latest available year, 1996 - 2005
Naissances vivantes selon l'âge de la mère, le sexe de l'enfant et la résidence, urbaine/rurale: dernière année disponible, 1996 - 2005 (continued - suite)

Continent, country or area, date, code and age (in years) / Continent, pays ou zone, code, date et âge (en années)	Total			Urban - Urbaine			Rural - Rurale		
	Both sexes Les deux sexes	Male Masculin	Female Féminin	Both sexes Les deux sexes	Male Masculin	Female Féminin	Both sexes Les deux sexes	Male Masculin	Female Féminin
EUROPE									
Finland - Finlande[29]									
2005 (C)									
20 - 24	9 364	4 716	4 648	6 107	3 055	3 052	3 257	1 661	1 596
25 - 29	18 794	9 566	9 228	12 494	6 341	6 153	6 300	3 225	3 075
30 - 34	16 949	8 656	8 293	11 372	5 804	5 568	5 577	2 852	2 725
35 - 39	8 915	4 522	4 393	5 815	2 991	2 824	3 100	1 531	1 569
40 - 44	2 002	1 019	983	1 286	651	635	716	368	348
45 - 49	111	61	50	64	39	25	47	22	25
50 +	-	-	-	-	-	-	-	-	-
Unknown - Inconnu	-	-	-	-	-	-	-	-	-
France[30]									
2005 (C)									
Total	774 355	396 346	378 009	581 681[31]	297 599[31]	284 082[31]	191 223[31]	97 971[31]	93 252[31]
0 - 14	47	28	19	34[31]	20[31]	14[31]	13[31]	8[31]	5[31]
15 - 19	14 946	7 635	7 311	12 661[31]	6 439[31]	6 222[31]	2 265[31]	1 181[31]	1 084[31]
20 - 24	107 288	54 761	52 527	86 187[31]	43 985[31]	42 202[31]	20 982[31]	10 723[31]	10 259[31]
25 - 29	242 272	124 726	117 546	178 890[31]	92 140[31]	86 750[31]	63 017[31]	32 387[31]	30 630[31]
30 - 34	257 933	131 520	126 413	188 194[31]	95 834[31]	92 360[31]	69 187[31]	35 394[31]	33 793[31]
35 - 39	121 735	62 284	59 451	91 686[31]	46 917[31]	44 769[31]	29 720[31]	15 188[31]	14 532[31]
40 - 44	28 525	14 538	13 987	22 664[31]	11 532[31]	11 132[31]	5 800[31]	2 969[31]	2 831[31]
45 - 49	1 564	833	731	1 320[31]	711[31]	609[31]	239[31]	121[31]	118[31]
50 +	45	21	24	45[31]	21[31]	24[31]	-[31]	-[31]	-[31]
Unknown - Inconnu	-	-	-	-[31]	-[31]	-[31]	-[31]	-[31]	-[31]
Germany - Allemagne									
2005 (C)									
Total	685 795	351 757	334 038	...	...	...	...	...	...
0 - 14	162	84	78	...	...	...	...	...	...
15 - 19	24 798	12 650	12 148	...	...	...	...	...	...
20 - 24	113 647	58 494	55 153	...	...	...	...	...	...
25 - 29	197 865	101 204	96 661	...	...	...	...	...	...
30 - 34	207 095	106 275	100 820	...	...	...	...	...	...
35 - 39	119 969	61 673	58 296	...	...	...	...	...	...
40 - 44	21 495	10 966	10 529	...	...	...	...	...	...
45 - 49	743	402	341	...	...	...	...	...	...
50 +	21	9	12	...	...	...	...	...	...
Unknown - Inconnu	-	-	-	...	...	...	...	...	...
Gibraltar									
2002 (C)									
Total	375	...	...	...	...	...	...	...	...
15 - 19	25	...	...	...	...	...	...	...	...
20 - 24	59	...	...	...	...	...	...	...	...
25 - 29	120	...	...	...	...	...	...	...	...
30 - 34	115	...	...	...	...	...	...	...	...
35 - 39	46	...	...	...	...	...	...	...	...
40 - 44	10	...	...	...	...	...	...	...	...
Greece - Grèce									
2005 (C)									
Total	107 545	55 539	52 006	73 816	38 030	35 786	33 729	17 509	16 220
0 - 14	60	23	37	45	18	27	15	5	10
15 - 19	3 031	1 574	1 457	1 734	876	858	1 297	698	599
20 - 24	14 969	7 761	7 208	8 517	4 390	4 127	6 452	3 371	3 081
25 - 29	33 532	17 403	16 129	22 029	11 487	10 542	11 503	5 916	5 587
30 - 34	35 891	18 566	17 325	26 198	13 533	12 665	9 693	5 033	4 660
35 - 39	16 940	8 595	8 345	12 919	6 497	6 422	4 021	2 098	1 923
40 - 44	2 825	1 484	1 341	2 127	1 114	1 013	698	370	328
45 - 49	263	114	149	221	100	121	42	14	28
50 +	34	19	15	26	15	11	8	4	4
Unknown - Inconnu	-	-	-	-	-	-	-	-	-
Hungary - Hongrie[1]									
2005 (C)									
Total	97 496	50 327	47 169	63 785	32 876	30 909	32 860	17 011	15 849
0 - 14	121	54	67	56	26	30	65	28	37
15 - 19	6 165	3 153	3 012	2 969	1 523	1 446	3 150	1 602	1 548
20 - 24	16 723	8 506	8 217	9 179	4 610	4 569	7 305	3 779	3 526
25 - 29	36 291	18 877	17 414	24 223	12 648	11 575	11 768	6 070	5 698

Continent, country or area, date, code and age (in years) / Continent, pays ou zone, code, date et âge (en années)	Total			Urban - Urbaine			Rural - Rurale		
	Both sexes Les deux sexes	Male Masculin	Female Féminin	Both sexes Les deux sexes	Male Masculin	Female Féminin	Both sexes Les deux sexes	Male Masculin	Female Féminin
EUROPE									
Hungary - Hongrie[1]									
2005 (C)									
30 - 34	27 343	14 117	13 226	19 713	10 119	9 594	7 444	3 900	3 544
35 - 39	9 326	4 794	4 532	6 621	3 397	3 224	2 639	1 369	1 270
40 - 44	1 462	797	665	978	534	444	471	253	218
45 - 49	63	28	35	44	18	26	18	10	8
50 +	2	1	1	2	1	1	-	-	-
Unknown - Inconnu	-	-	-	-	-	-	-	-	-
Iceland - Islande									
2005 (C)									
Total	4 280	2 183	2 097	4 054	2 056	1 998	226	127	99
0 - 14	-	-	-	-	-	-	-	-	-
15 - 19	151	69	82	139	66	73	12	3	9
20 - 24	867	436	431	827	410	417	40	26	14
25 - 29	1 373	702	671	1 316	669	647	57	33	24
30 - 34	1 174	586	588	1 107	544	563	67	42	25
35 - 39	589	330	259	546	307	239	43	23	20
40 - 44	117	53	64	110	53	57	7	-	7
45 - 49	9	7	2	9	7	2	-	-	-
50 +	-	-	-	-	-	-	-	-	-
Unknown - Inconnu	-	-	-	-	-	-	-	-	-
Ireland - Irlande									
1999 (+C)[32]									
Total	53 354	27 508	25 846	30 827	15 973	14 854	22 527	11 535	10 992
0 - 14	11	3	8	8	1	7	3	2	1
15 - 19	3 290	1 732	1 558	2 152	1 146	1 006	1 138	586	552
20 - 24	7 503	3 937	3 566	4 780	2 542	2 238	2 723	1 395	1 328
25 - 29	13 576	6 942	6 634	7 850	4 046	3 804	5 726	2 896	2 830
30 - 34	17 614	9 049	8 565	9 888	5 096	4 792	7 726	3 953	3 773
35 - 39	9 377	4 850	4 527	5 146	2 651	2 495	4 231	2 199	2 032
40 - 44	1 638	828	810	846	413	433	792	415	377
45 - 49	72	34	38	35	18	17	37	16	21
50 +	1	1	-	1	1	-	-	-	-
Unknown - Inconnu	272	132	140	121	59	62	151	73	78
2005* (+C)									
Total	61 042	31 369	29 673	...	...	...	...	...	...
0 - 14	7	3	4	...	...	...	...	...	...
15 - 19	2 420	1 265	1 155	...	...	...	...	...	...
20 - 24	7 785	3 946	3 839	...	...	...	...	...	...
25 - 29	13 650	6 928	6 722	...	...	...	...	...	...
30 - 34	21 335	11 040	10 295	...	...	...	...	...	...
35 - 39	13 208	6 830	6 378	...	...	...	...	...	...
40 - 44	2 452	1 258	1 194	...	...	...	...	...	...
45 - 49	72	35	37	...	...	...	...	...	...
50 +	2	1	1	...	...	...	...	...	...
Unknown - Inconnu	111	63	48	...	...	...	...	...	...
Italy - Italie									
2004 (C)									
Total	553 770	284 311	269 459	...	...	...	...	...	...
0 - 14	11	6	5	...	...	...	...	...	...
15 - 19	9 730	5 011	4 719	...	...	...	...	...	...
20 - 24	52 429	26 992	25 437	...	...	...	...	...	...
25 - 29	143 476	73 686	69 790	...	...	...	...	...	...
30 - 34	202 272	103 905	98 367	...	...	...	...	...	...
35 - 39	115 961	59 471	56 490	...	...	...	...	...	...
40 - 44	21 898	11 157	10 741	...	...	...	...	...	...
45 - 49	819	416	403	...	...	...	...	...	...
50 +	95	45	50	...	...	...	...	...	...
Unknown - Inconnu	7 079	3 622	3 457	...	...	...	...	...	...
Latvia - Lettonie[16]									
2005 (C)									
Total	21 497	10 987	10 510	14 591	7 542	7 049	6 906	3 445	3 461
0 - 14	-	-	-	-	-	-	-	-	-
15 - 19	1 429	733	696	801	407	394	628	326	302
20 - 24	5 848	3 030	2 818	3 699	1 963	1 736	2 149	1 067	1 082

Continent, country or area, date, code and age (in years) Continent, pays ou zone, code, date et âge (en années)	Total			Urban - Urbaine			Rural - Rurale		
	Both sexes Les deux sexes	Male Masculin	Female Féminin	Both sexes Les deux sexes	Male Masculin	Female Féminin	Both sexes Les deux sexes	Male Masculin	Female Féminin
EUROPE									
Latvia - Lettonie[16]									
2005 (C)									
25 - 29	6 612	3 338	3 274	4 731	2 410	2 321	1 881	928	953
30 - 34	4 871	2 523	2 348	3 506	1 822	1 684	1 365	701	664
35 - 39	2 202	1 099	1 103	1 509	766	743	693	333	360
40 - 44	495	248	247	319	165	154	176	83	93
45 - 49	34	15	19	20	8	12	14	7	7
50 + ...	-	-	-	-	-	-	-	-	-
Unknown - Inconnu	6	1	5	6	1	5	...	...	...
Liechtenstein									
2005* (C)									
Total..........	381	187	194	...	...	...	...	...	...
0 - 14.	-	-	-	...	...	...	...	...	...
15 - 19	7	1	6	...	...	...	...	...	...
20 - 24	35	16	19	...	...	...	...	...	...
25 - 29	84	38	46	...	...	...	...	...	...
30 - 34	149	73	76	...	...	...	...	...	...
35 - 39	89	53	36	...	...	...	...	...	...
40 - 44	17	6	11	...	...	...	...	...	...
45 - 49	-	-	-	...	...	...	...	...	...
50 + ...	-	-	-	...	...	...	...	...	...
Lithuania - Lituanie[16]									
2005 (C)									
Total..........	30 541	15 621	14 920	19 914	10 181	9 733	10 627	5 440	5 187
0 - 14.	6	3	3	4	2	2	2	1	1
15 - 19	2 488	1 273	1 215	1 233	636	597	1 255	637	618
20 - 24	8 361	4 249	4 112	4 931	2 494	2 437	3 430	1 755	1 675
25 - 29	10 042	5 120	4 922	7 030	3 610	3 420	3 012	1 510	1 502
30 - 34	6 409	3 300	3 109	4 572	2 340	2 232	1 837	960	877
35 - 39	2 624	1 351	1 273	1 754	890	864	870	461	409
40 - 44	583	306	277	371	195	176	212	111	101
45 + ...	26	18	8	17	13	4	9	5	4
Unknown - Inconnu	2	1	1	2	1	1	-	-	-
Luxembourg									
2005 (C)									
Total..........	5 371	2 784	2 587	...	...	...	...	...	...
0 - 14.	-	-	-	...	...	...	...	...	...
15 - 19	158	76	82	...	...	...	...	...	...
20 - 24	723	358	365	...	...	...	...	...	...
25 - 29	1 555	812	743	...	...	...	...	...	...
30 - 34	1 820	937	883	...	...	...	...	...	...
35 - 39	935	505	430	...	...	...	...	...	...
40 - 44	166	86	80	...	...	...	...	...	...
45 - 49	5	3	2	...	...	...	...	...	...
50 + ...	-	-	-	...	...	...	...	...	...
Unknown - Inconnu	9	7	2	...	...	...	...	...	...
Malta - Malte[33]									
2005 (C)									
Total..........	3 858	1 984	1 874	...	...	...	...	...	...
0 - 19.	230	119	111	...	...	...	...	...	...
20 - 24	661	327	334	...	...	...	...	...	...
25 - 29	1 438	744	694	...	...	...	...	...	...
30 - 34	1 111	582	529	...	...	...	...	...	...
35 - 39	327	172	155	...	...	...	...	...	...
40 - 44	83	34	49	...	...	...	...	...	...
45 - 49	5	4	1	...	...	...	...	...	...
50 + ...	3	2	1	...	...	...	...	...	...
Unknown - Inconnu	-	-	-	...	...	...	...	...	...
Netherlands - Pays-Bas[34]									
2005 (C)									
Total..........	189 075	96 957	92 118	129 134	66 213	62 921	59 941	30 744	29 197
0 - 14.	-	-	-	-	-	-	-	-	-
15 - 19	2 023	1 069	954	1 598	844	754	425	225	200
20 - 24	16 813	8 599	8 214	12 664	6 531	6 133	4 149	2 068	2 081
25 - 29	49 112	25 295	23 817	33 095	16 965	16 130	16 017	8 330	7 687

10. Live births by age of mother, sex of the child and urban/rural residence: latest available year, 1996 - 2005
Naissances vivantes selon l'âge de la mère, le sexe de l'enfant et la résidence, urbaine/rurale: dernière année disponible, 1996 - 2005 (continued - suite)

Continent, country or area, date, code and age (in years) / Continent, pays ou zone, code, date et âge (en années)	Total			Urban - Urbaine			Rural - Rurale		
	Both sexes Les deux sexes	Male Masculin	Female Féminin	Both sexes Les deux sexes	Male Masculin	Female Féminin	Both sexes Les deux sexes	Male Masculin	Female Féminin
EUROPE									
Netherlands - Pays-Bas[34]									
2005 (C)									
30 - 34	74 260	38 026	36 234	49 239	25 177	24 062	25 021	12 849	12 172
35 - 39	40 262	20 599	19 663	27 721	14 261	13 460	12 541	6 338	6 203
40 - 44	6 365	3 253	3 112	4 630	2 345	2 285	1 735	908	827
45 - 49	234	113	121	181	87	94	53	26	27
50 +	6	3	3	6	3	3	-	-	-
Norway - Norvège[35]									
2005 (C)									
Total	56 756	29 053	27 703	...	...	...	...	...	...
0 - 14	1	-	1	...	...	...	...	...	...
15 - 19	1 152	586	566	...	...	...	...	...	...
20 - 24	7 924	4 050	3 874	...	...	...	...	...	...
25 - 29	17 869	9 121	8 748	...	...	...	...	...	...
30 - 34	19 860	10 156	9 704	...	...	...	...	...	...
35 - 39	8 487	4 368	4 119	...	...	...	...	...	...
40 - 44	1 404	744	660	...	...	...	...	...	...
45 - 49	58	27	31	...	...	...	...	...	...
50 +	1	1	-	...	...	...	...	...	...
Unknown - Inconnu	-	-	-	...	...	...	...	...	...
Poland - Pologne									
2005 (C)									
Total	364 383	187 385	176 998	211 200	108 880	102 320	153 183	78 505	74 678
0 - 14	46	27	19	30	18	12	16	9	7
15 - 19	19 249	9 885	9 364	10 246	5 322	4 924	9 003	4 563	4 440
20 - 24	95 533	49 089	46 444	49 074	25 349	23 725	46 459	23 740	22 719
25 - 29	137 307	70 573	66 734	82 831	42 616	40 215	54 476	27 957	26 519
30 - 34	79 152	40 722	38 430	49 983	25 689	24 294	29 169	15 033	14 136
35 - 39	26 654	13 771	12 883	15 555	8 118	7 437	11 099	5 653	5 446
40 - 44	6 116	3 144	2 972	3 309	1 681	1 628	2 807	1 463	1 344
45 - 49	323	173	150	170	87	83	153	86	67
50 +	3	1	2	2	-	2	1	1	-
Portugal									
2005 (C)									
Total	109 399	56 612	52 787	...	...	...	...	...	...
0 - 14	72	43	29	...	...	...	...	...	...
15 - 19	5 443	2 820	2 623	...	...	...	...	...	...
20 - 24	16 760	8 649	8 111	...	...	...	...	...	...
25 - 29	34 119	17 838	16 281	...	...	...	...	...	...
30 - 34	35 144	18 078	17 066	...	...	...	...	...	...
35 - 39	14 745	7 597	7 148	...	...	...	...	...	...
40 - 44	2 947	1 494	1 453	...	...	...	...	...	...
45 - 49	158	88	70	...	...	...	...	...	...
50 +	8	4	4	...	...	...	...	...	...
Unknown - Inconnu	3	1	2	...	...	...	...	...	...
Republic of Moldova - République de Moldova[16]									
2004 (C)									
Total	38 272	19 827	18 445	14 060	7 376	6 684	24 212	12 451	11 761
0 - 14	10	8	2	3	3	-	7	5	2
15 - 19	5 207	2 675	2 532	1 273	688	585	3 934	1 987	1 947
20 - 24	15 247	7 907	7 340	5 238	2 745	2 493	10 009	5 162	4 847
25 - 29	10 562	5 476	5 086	4 390	2 285	2 105	6 172	3 191	2 981
30 - 34	5 061	2 657	2 404	2 222	1 196	1 026	2 839	1 461	1 378
35 - 39	1 744	893	851	761	373	388	983	520	463
40 - 44	408	194	214	154	76	78	254	118	136
45 - 49	15	7	8	7	3	4	8	4	4
50 +	5	2	3	1	-	1	4	2	2
Unknown - Inconnu	13	8	5	11	7	4	2	1	1
Romania - Roumanie									
2005 (C)									
Total	221 020	113 884	107 136	117 780	60 654	57 126	103 240	53 230	50 010
0 - 14	527	266	261	190	89	101	337	177	160
15 - 19	28 356	14 594	13 762	10 152	5 132	5 020	18 204	9 462	8 742
20 - 24	57 908	29 988	27 920	26 125	13 641	12 484	31 783	16 347	15 436

10. Live births by age of mother, sex of the child and urban/rural residence: latest available year, 1996 - 2005
Naissances vivantes selon l'âge de la mère, le sexe de l'enfant et la résidence, urbaine/rurale: dernière année disponible, 1996 - 2005 (continued - suite)

Continent, country or area, date, code and age (in years) / Continent, pays ou zone, code, date et âge (en annèes)	Total			Urban - Urbaine			Rural - Rurale		
	Both sexes Les deux sexes	Male Masculin	Female Féminin	Both sexes Les deux sexes	Male Masculin	Female Féminin	Both sexes Les deux sexes	Male Masculin	Female Féminin
EUROPE									
Romania - Roumanie									
2005 (C)									
25 - 29	72 990	37 512	35 478	43 296	22 196	21 100	29 694	15 316	14 378
30 - 34	42 606	21 887	20 719	26 653	13 723	12 930	15 953	8 164	7 789
35 - 39	16 298	16 298	7 857	10 138	5 236	4 902	6 160	3 205	2 955
40 - 44	2 205	2 205	1 081	1 168	606	562	1 037	518	519
45 - 49	129	129	57	57	31	26	72	41	31
50 +	1	-	1	1	-	1	-	-	-
Russian Federation - Fédération de Russie[16]									
2004 (C)									
Total	1 502 477	...	...	1 074 247	...	...	428 230	...	...
0 - 14	382	...	...	217	...	...	165	...	...
15 - 19	171 558	...	...	106 897	...	...	64 661	...	...
20 - 24	557 843	...	...	389 798	...	...	168 045	...	...
25 - 29	434 067	...	...	325 418	...	...	108 649	...	...
30 - 34	232 411	...	...	175 507	...	...	56 904	...	...
35 - 39	85 038	...	...	61 502	...	...	23 536	...	...
40 - 44	18 073	...	...	12 340	...	...	5 733	...	...
45 - 49	837	...	...	559	...	...	278	...	...
50 +	25	...	...	22	...	...	3	...	...
Unknown - Inconnu	2 243	...	...	1 987	...	...	256	...	...
San Marino - Saint-Marin									
2004 (+C)									
Total	306	...	...	...	...	...	...	...	...
15 - 19	1	...	...	...	...	...	...	...	...
20 - 24	15	...	...	...	...	...	...	...	...
25 - 29	69	...	...	...	...	...	...	...	...
30 - 34	134	...	...	...	...	...	...	...	...
35 - 39	75	...	...	...	...	...	...	...	...
40 - 44	11	...	...	...	...	...	...	...	...
45 - 49	1	...	...	...	...	...	...	...	...
Serbia and Montenegro - Serbie-et-Montenegro[36]									
2003 (C)									
Total	87 370	45 154	42 216	54 296	28 063	26 233	33 074	17 091	15 983
0 - 14	46	32	14	25	16	9	21	16	5
15 - 19	6 443	3 354	3 089	3 037	1 551	1 486	3 406	1 803	1 603
20 - 24	26 073	13 386	12 687	14 387	7 472	6 915	11 686	5 914	5 772
25 - 29	29 178	15 091	14 087	18 740	9 686	9 054	10 438	5 405	5 033
30 - 34	17 338	8 975	8 363	12 186	6 288	5 898	5 152	2 687	2 465
35 - 39	6 326	3 267	3 059	4 587	2 342	2 245	1 739	925	814
40 - 44	1 308	700	608	905	480	425	403	220	183
45 - 49	69	33	36	48	19	29	21	14	7
50 +	12	7	5	6	5	1	6	2	4
Unknown - Inconnu	577	309	268	375	204	171	202	105	97
Slovakia - Slovaquie									
2005 (C)									
Total	54 430	27 979	26 451	28 816	14 916	13 900	25 614	13 063	12 551
0 - 14	35	18	17	11	6	5	24	12	12
15 - 19	4 080	2 096	1 984	1 673	864	809	2 407	1 232	1 175
20 - 24	13 397	6 888	6 509	5 959	3 095	2 864	7 438	3 793	3 645
25 - 29	20 354	10 417	9 937	11 387	5 854	5 533	8 967	4 563	4 404
30 - 34	12 151	6 252	5 899	7 267	3 768	3 499	4 884	2 484	2 400
35 - 39	3 688	1 936	1 752	2 095	1 112	983	1 593	824	769
40 - 44	691	353	338	407	208	199	284	145	139
45 - 49	34	19	15	17	9	8	17	10	7
50 +	-	-	-	-	-	-	-	-	-
Slovenia - Slovénie									
2005 (C)									
Total	18 157	9 355	8 802	8 869	4 578	4 291	9 288	4 777	4 511
0 - 14	4	4	-	1	1	-	3	3	-
15 - 19	368	177	191	173	78	95	195	99	96
20 - 24	2 783	1 447	1 336	1 185	605	580	1 598	842	756
25 - 29	7 135	3 656	3 479	3 281	1 686	1 595	3 854	1 970	1 884

10. Live births by age of mother, sex of the child and urban/rural residence: latest available year, 1996 - 2005
Naissances vivantes selon l'âge de la mère, le sexe de l'enfant et la résidence, urbaine/rurale: dernière année disponible, 1996 - 2005 (continued - suite)

Continent, country or area, date, code and age (in years) / Continent, pays ou zone, code, date et âge (en années)	Total			Urban - Urbaine			Rural - Rurale		
	Both sexes Les deux sexes	Male Masculin	Female Féminin	Both sexes Les deux sexes	Male Masculin	Female Féminin	Both sexes Les deux sexes	Male Masculin	Female Féminin
EUROPE									
Slovenia - Slovénie									
2005 (C)									
30 - 34	5 588	2 897	2 691	2 946	1 541	1 405	2 642	1 356	1 286
35 - 39	1 935	999	936	1 092	578	514	843	421	422
40 - 44	324	164	160	183	84	99	141	80	61
45 - 49	20	11	9	8	5	3	12	6	6
Spain - Espagne									
2003 (C)									
Total.....................	441 881	227 584	214 297	...	...	...	...	...	...
0 - 14..................	168	82	86	...	...	...	...	...	...
15 - 19	12 338	6 374	5 964	...	...	...	...	...	...
20 - 24	43 890	22 657	21 233	...	...	...	...	...	...
25 - 29	115 454	59 541	55 913	...	...	...	...	...	...
30 - 34	171 294	88 202	83 092	...	...	...	...	...	...
35 - 39	84 974	43 581	41 393	...	...	...	...	...	...
40 - 44	13 137	6 829	6 308	...	...	...	...	...	...
45 - 49	593	299	294	...	...	...	...	...	...
50 +..................	33	19	14	...	...	...	...	...	...
Sweden - Suède									
2005 (C)									
Total.....................	101 341	52 034	49 307	...	...	...	...	...	...
0 - 14..................	-	-	-	...	...	...	...	...	...
15 - 19	1 681	891	790	...	...	...	...	...	...
20 - 24	11 983	6 190	5 793	...	...	...	...	...	...
25 - 29	29 361	15 075	14 286	...	...	...	...	...	...
30 - 34	37 508	19 244	18 264	...	...	...	...	...	...
35 - 39	17 388	8 962	8 426	...	...	...	...	...	...
40 - 44	3 271	1 605	1 666	...	...	...	...	...	...
45 - 49	144	65	79	...	...	...	...	...	...
50 +..................	5	2	3	...	...	...	...	...	...
Unknown - Inconnu	-	-	-	...	...	...	...	...	...
Switzerland - Suisse									
2005 (C)									
Total.....................	72 903	37 569	35 334	53 976	27 773	26 203	18 927	9 796	9 131
0 - 14..................	7	4	3	6	3	3	1	1	-
15 - 19	1 084	568	516	812	420	392	272	148	124
20 - 24	8 298	4 243	4 055	6 186	3 161	3 025	2 112	1 082	1 030
25 - 29	20 024	10 283	9 741	14 349	7 350	6 999	5 675	2 933	2 742
30 - 34	26 327	13 619	12 708	19 382	10 094	9 288	6 945	3 525	3 420
35 - 39	14 499	7 503	6 996	11 156	5 714	5 442	3 343	1 789	1 554
40 - 44	2 580	1 314	1 266	2 025	1 005	1 020	555	309	246
45 - 49	79	33	46	56	24	32	23	9	14
50 +..................	5	2	3	4	2	2	1	-	1
The Former Yugoslav Rep. of Macedonia - L'ex-République yougoslave de Macédoine									
2005 (C)									
Total.....................	22 482	11 451	11 031	12 519	6 355	6 164	9 963	5 096	4 867
0 - 14..................	21	13	8	15	8	7	6	5	1
15 - 19	1 722	905	817	878	461	417	844	444	400
20 - 24	6 631	3 351	3 280	3 369	1 699	1 670	3 262	1 652	1 610
25 - 29	8 025	4 066	3 959	4 618	2 324	2 294	3 407	1 742	1 665
30 - 34	4 454	2 265	2 189	2 684	1 372	1 312	1 770	893	877
35 - 39	1 370	721	649	800	414	386	570	307	263
40 - 44	244	126	118	143	75	68	101	51	50
45 - 49	10	1	9	9	1	8	1	-	1
50 +..................	3	2	1	1	...	1	2	2	-
Unknown - Inconnu	2	1	1	2	1	1	-	-	-
Ukraine[37]									
2004 (C)									
Total.....................	427 259	...	...	284 361	...	...	142 898	...	...
0 - 14..................	136	...	...	64	...	...	72	...	...
15 - 19	53 874	...	...	30 163	...	...	23 711	...	...
20 - 24	169 505	...	...	110 532	...	...	58 973	...	...

10. Live births by age of mother, sex of the child and urban/rural residence: latest available year, 1996 - 2005
Naissances vivantes selon l'âge de la mère, le sexe de l'enfant et la résidence, urbaine/rurale: dernière année disponible, 1996 - 2005 (continued - suite)

Continent, country or area, date, code and age (in years) / Continent, pays ou zone, code, date et âge (en annèes)	Total			Urban - Urbaine			Rural - Rurale		
	Both sexes Les deux sexes	Male Masculin	Female Féminin	Both sexes Les deux sexes	Male Masculin	Female Féminin	Both sexes Les deux sexes	Male Masculin	Female Féminin
EUROPE									
Ukraine[37]									
2004 (C)									
25 - 29	119 641	...	...	83 835	...	...	35 806	...	...
30 - 34	58 746	...	...	42 023	...	...	16 723	...	...
35 - 39	19 696	...	...	13 749	...	...	5 947	...	...
40 - 44	4 148	...	...	2 722	...	...	1 426	...	...
45 - 49	194	...	...	126	...	...	68	...	...
50 +	3	...	...	3	...	...	...	...	...
Unknown - Inconnu	1 316	...	...	1 144	...	...	172	...	...
United Kingdom - Royaume-Uni[38]									
2004 (C)									
Total	715 996	...	...	...	...	...	...	...	...
10 - 14	226	...	...	...	...	...	...	...	...
15 - 19	50 525	...	...	...	...	...	...	...	...
20 - 24	134 615	...	...	...	...	...	...	...	...
25 - 29	179 050	...	...	...	...	...	...	...	...
30 - 34	213 619	...	...	...	...	...	...	...	...
35 - 39	114 852	...	...	...	...	...	...	...	...
40 - 44	22 107	...	...	...	...	...	...	...	...
45 - 49	923	...	...	...	...	...	...	...	...
Unknown - Inconnu	26	...	...	...	...	...	...	...	...
OCEANIA - OCÉANIE									
American Samoa - Samoas américaines									
2005 (C)									
Total	1 720	...	...	...	...	...	...	...	...
0 - 14	-	...	...	...	...	...	...	...	...
15 - 19	101	...	...	...	...	...	...	...	...
20 - 24	406	...	...	...	...	...	...	...	...
25 - 29	517	...	...	...	...	...	...	...	...
30 - 34	371	...	...	...	...	...	...	...	...
35 - 39	248	...	...	...	...	...	...	...	...
40 - 44	75	...	...	...	...	...	...	...	...
45 - 49	2	...	...	...	...	...	...	...	...
50 +	-	...	...	...	...	...	...	...	...
Australia - Australie[39]									
2005 (+C)									
Total	259 791	133 428	126 363	176 079	90 505	85 574	83 712	42 923	40 789
0 - 14	85	45	40	47	23	24	38	22	16
15 - 19	10 659	5 479	5 180	6 258	3 182	3 076	4 401	2 297	2 104
20 - 24	36 482	18 821	17 661	22 608	11 568	11 040	13 874	7 253	6 621
25 - 29	69 420	35 750	33 670	45 320	23 381	21 939	24 100	12 369	11 731
30 - 34	89 158	45 594	43 564	62 622	32 143	30 479	26 536	13 451	13 085
35 - 39	44 873	23 028	21 845	32 563	16 741	15 822	12 310	6 287	6 023
40 - 44	8 376	4 297	4 079	6 124	3 169	2 955	2 252	1 128	1 124
45 - 49	335	187	148	243	134	109	92	53	39
50 +	23	11	12	19	9	10	4	3	3
Unknown - Inconnu	380	216	164	275	155	120	105	61	44
Guam[40]									
2003 (C)									
Total	3 298	1 682	1 616	...	...	...	...	...	...
0 - 14	3	2	1	...	...	...	...	...	...
15 - 19	355	179	176	...	...	...	...	...	...
20 - 24	883	462	421	...	...	...	...	...	...
25 - 29	854	450	404	...	...	...	...	...	...
30 - 34	717	347	370	...	...	...	...	...	...
35 - 39	389	184	205	...	...	...	...	...	...
40 - 44	87	53	34	...	...	...	...	...	...
45 - 49	6	2	4	...	...	...	...	...	...
50 +	1	1	-	...	...	...	...	...	...
Unknown - Inconnu	3	2	1	...	...	...	...	...	...

10. Live births by age of mother, sex of the child and urban/rural residence: latest available year, 1996 - 2005
Naissances vivantes selon l'âge de la mère, le sexe de l'enfant et la résidence, urbaine/rurale: dernière année disponible, 1996 - 2005 (continued - suite)

Continent, country or area, date, code and age (in years) / Continent, pays ou zone, code, date et âge (en années)	Total			Urban - Urbaine			Rural - Rurale		
	Both sexes Les deux sexes	Male Masculin	Female Féminin	Both sexes Les deux sexes	Male Masculin	Female Féminin	Both sexes Les deux sexes	Male Masculin	Female Féminin
OCEANIA - OCÉANIE									
Kiribati									
1996 (U)									
Total.....................	2 299	...	...	...	...	...	...	...	...
0 - 14....................	1	...	...	...	...	...	...	...	...
15 - 19	131	...	...	...	...	...	...	...	...
20 - 24	469	...	...	...	...	...	...	...	...
25 - 29	631	...	...	...	...	...	...	...	...
30 - 34	616	...	...	...	...	...	...	...	...
35 - 39	363	...	...	...	...	...	...	...	...
40 - 44	74	...	...	...	...	...	...	...	...
45 - 49	14	...	...	...	...	...	...	...	...
Marshall Islands - Îles Marshall[41]									
1999 (+U)									
Total.....................	1 478	...	...	...	...	...	...	...	...
0 - 14....................	3	...	...	...	...	...	...	...	...
15 - 19	279	...	...	...	...	...	...	...	...
20 - 24	482	...	...	...	...	...	...	...	...
25 - 29	373	...	...	...	...	...	...	...	...
30 - 34	211	...	...	...	...	...	...	...	...
35 - 39	108	...	...	...	...	...	...	...	...
40 - 44	19	...	...	...	...	...	...	...	...
Micronesia, Federated States of - Micronésie, États Fédérés de La									
2003 (U)									
Total[42]..................	2 485	...	...	...	...	...	...	...	...
10 - 14	10	...	...	...	...	...	...	...	...
15 - 19	329	...	...	...	...	...	...	...	...
20 - 24	675	...	...	...	...	...	...	...	...
25 - 29	649	...	...	...	...	...	...	...	...
30 - 34	401	...	...	...	...	...	...	...	...
35 - 39	275	...	...	...	...	...	...	...	...
40 - 44	108	...	...	...	...	...	...	...	...
45 + ...	11	...	...	...	...	...	...	...	...
Unknown - Inconnu	27	...	...	...	...	...	...	...	...
New Caledonia - Nouvelle-Calédonie									
2003 (C)									
Total.....................	4 102	...	...	...	...	...	...	...	...
0 - 14....................	-	...	...	...	...	...	...	...	...
15 - 19	190	...	...	...	...	...	...	...	...
20 - 24	1 017	...	...	...	...	...	...	...	...
25 - 29	1 215	...	...	...	...	...	...	...	...
30 - 34	1 030	...	...	...	...	...	...	...	...
35 - 39	518	...	...	...	...	...	...	...	...
40 - 44	130	...	...	...	...	...	...	...	...
45 - 49	2	...	...	...	...	...	...	...	...
New Zealand - Nouvelle-Zélande[43]									
2005 (+C)									
Total.....................	57 745	29 546	28 199	50 300[1]	25 804[1]	24 496[1]	7 391[1]	3 718[1]	3 673[1]
0 - 14....................	37	17	20	37[1]	17[1]	20[1]	-[1]	-[1]	-[1]
15 - 19	4 099	2 136	1 963	3 670[1]	1 902[1]	1 768[1]	425[1]	233[1]	192[1]
20 - 24	9 709	4 941	4 768	8 659[1]	4 392[1]	4 267[1]	1 032[1]	544[1]	488[1]
25 - 29	13 798	7 127	6 671	12 033[1]	6 214[1]	5 819[1]	1 756[1]	905[1]	851[1]
30 - 34	17 977	9 177	8 800	15 505[1]	7 982[1]	7 523[1]	2 457[1]	1 188[1]	1 269[1]
35 - 39	10 029	5 088	4 941	8 625[1]	4 396[1]	4 229[1]	1 397[1]	689[1]	708[1]
40 - 44	2 003	1 011	992	1 694[1]	859[1]	835[1]	308[1]	152[1]	156[1]
45 - 49	90	47	43	74[1]	40[1]	34[1]	16[1]	7[1]	9[1]
50 + ...	3	2	1	3[1]	2[1]	1[1]	-[1]	-[1]	-[1]
Unknown - Inconnu	-	-	-	-[1]	-[1]	-[1]	-[1]	-[1]	-[1]

10. Live births by age of mother, sex of the child and urban/rural residence: latest available year, 1996 - 2005
Naissances vivantes selon l'âge de la mère, le sexe de l'enfant et la résidence, urbaine/rurale: dernière année disponible, 1996 - 2005 (continued - suite)

Continent, country or area, date, code and age (in years) / Continent, pays ou zone, code, date et âge (en années)	Total			Urban - Urbaine			Rural - Rurale		
	Both sexes Les deux sexes	Male Masculin	Female Féminin	Both sexes Les deux sexes	Male Masculin	Female Féminin	Both sexes Les deux sexes	Male Masculin	Female Féminin
OCEANIA - OCÉANIE									
Northern Mariana Islands - Îles Mariannes septentrionales									
2002 (U)									
Total..............	*1 289*	...	...	...	...	...	...	...	...
0 - 19...................	*110*	...	...	...	...	...	...	...	...
20 - 24...............	*298*	...	...	...	...	...	...	...	...
25 - 29...............	*347*	...	...	...	...	...	...	...	...
30 - 34...............	*317*	...	...	...	...	...	...	...	...
35 - 39...............	*182*	...	...	...	...	...	...	...	...
40 +.....................	*35*	...	...	...	...	...	...	...	...
Unknown - Inconnu.......	-	...	...	...	...	...	...	...	...
Palau - Palaos									
1999 (C)									
Total..............	250	...	...	...	...	...	...	...	...
15 - 19...............	20	...	...	...	...	...	...	...	...
20 - 24...............	40	...	...	...	...	...	...	...	...
25 - 29...............	70	...	...	...	...	...	...	...	...
30 - 34...............	77	...	...	...	...	...	...	...	...
35 - 39...............	33	...	...	...	...	...	...	...	...
40 - 44...............	10	...	...	...	...	...	...	...	...
Tonga									
2000 (+C)									
Total..............	2 471	...	...	...	...	...	...	...	...
0 - 14.................	2	...	...	...	...	...	...	...	...
15 - 19...............	101	...	...	...	...	...	...	...	...
20 - 24...............	528	...	...	...	...	...	...	...	...
25 - 29...............	695	...	...	...	...	...	...	...	...
30 - 34...............	688	...	...	...	...	...	...	...	...
35 - 39...............	314	...	...	...	...	...	...	...	...
40 - 44...............	122	...	...	...	...	...	...	...	...
45 - 49...............	14	...	...	...	...	...	...	...	...
Unknown - Inconnu.......	7	...	...	...	...	...	...	...	...
Tuvalu									
2003 (U)									
Total..............	*239*	...	...	...	...	...	...	...	...
15 - 19...............	*17*	...	...	...	...	...	...	...	...
20 - 24...............	*76*	...	...	...	...	...	...	...	...
25 - 29...............	*53*	...	...	...	...	...	...	...	...
30 - 34...............	*35*	...	...	...	...	...	...	...	...
35 - 39...............	*37*	...	...	...	...	...	...	...	...
40 - 44...............	*20*	...	...	...	...	...	...	...	...
45 - 49...............	-	...	...	...	...	...	...	...	...
Wallis and Futuna Islands - Îles Wallis et Futuna									
2005 (C)									
Total..............	223	...	...	...	...	...	...	...	...
15 - 19...............	10	...	...	...	...	...	...	...	...
20 - 24...............	52	...	...	...	...	...	...	...	...
25 - 29...............	68	...	...	...	...	...	...	...	...
30 - 34...............	58	...	...	...	...	...	...	...	...
35 - 39...............	26	...	...	...	...	...	...	...	...
40 - 44...............	9	...	...	...	...	...	...	...	...

FOOTNOTES - NOTES

Italics: estimates which are less reliable. - Italiques: estimations moins sûres.

* Provisional. - Données provisoires.

'Code' indicates the source of data, as follows:
C - Civil registration, estimated over 90% complete
U - Civil registration, estimated less than 90% complete
| - Other source, estimated reliable

+ - Data tabulated by date of registration rather than occurrence.
... - Information not available

Le 'Code' indique la source des données, comme suit:
C - Registres de l'état civil considérés complets à 90 p. 100 au moins.
U - Registres de l'état civil qui ne sont pas considérés complets à 90 p. 100 au moins.
| - Autre source, considérée fiable.
+ - Données exploitées selon la date de l'enregistrement et non la date de l'événement.

... - Information non disponible.

[1] Figures for urban and rural areas do not add up to the total, since they do not include the category 'Unknown residence'. - La somme des données pour la résidence urbaine et rurale n'est pas égale au total parce qu'elle n'inclue pas la catégorie 'Résidence inconnue'.

[2] For 2001, data refer to last twelve months preceding census in August 2001. - Pour 2001, les données se rapportent aux douze mois précédant le recensement d'août 2001.

[3] Excluding live-born infants who died before their birth was registered. - Non compris les enfants nés vivants décédés avant l'enregistrement de leur naissance.

[4] Data for 1997 refer to last twelve months preceding population and housing census of 1997. - Les données pour 1997 se réfèrent au douze mois précédant le recensement de population et de l'habitat de 1997.

[5] Including Canadian residents temporarily in the United States, but excluding United States residents temporarily in Canada. - Y compris les résidents canadiens se trouvant temporairement aux Etats-Unis, mais ne comprenant pas les résidents des Etats-Unis se trouvant temporairement au Canada.

[6] Including births to non-resident mothers. - Y compris les naissances chez des mères non résidentes.

[7] Excluding live-born infants who died before their birth was registered. Age classification is based on year of birth of mother rather than the exact age of mother at birth of child. - Non compris les enfants nés vivants décédés avant l'enregistrement de leur naissance. Le classement selon l'âge est basé sur l'année de naissance de la mère et non sur l'age exacte de la mère au moment de naissance de l'enfant.

[8] Figures for urban and rural areas do not add up to the total, since they do not include the category 'Unknown residence'. Data for born in wedlock considers live births to women in marriage. Live births to women in consensual unions are excluded. - La somme des données pour la résidence urbaine et rurale n'est pas égale au total parce qu'elle n'inclue pas la catégorie 'Résidence inconnue'. Les données pour nés dans le mariage considèrent des naissances aux femmes mariées. Des naissances aux femmes dans des unions consensuels sont exclues.

[9] Data as reported by national statistical authorities; they may differ from data presented in other tables. - Les données comme elles ont été déclarées par l'institut national de la statistique; elles peuvent être différentes de celles présentées dans d'autres tableaux.

[10] Reason for discrepancy between these figures and corresponding figures shown elsewhere not ascertained. - On ne sait pas comment s'explique la divergence entre ces chiffres et les chiffres correspondants indiqués ailleurs.

[11] Data on live births and deaths are based on a civil registration system put in place in January 1998. - Les données sur les naissances et les décès sont basées sur un système d'enregistrement des faits d'état civil mis en place en janvier 1998.

[12] Excluding nomadic Indian tribes. - Non compris les tribus d'Indiens nomades.

[13] Excluding Indian jungle population. Data refer to registered live births only. - Non compris les Indiens de la jungle. Les données concernent les naissances vivantes enregistrées seulement.

[14] For 2003, data excluding 184 live births of non-resident mothers. - Pour 2003, les données comprennent 184 naissances vivantes de mères non résidentes.

[15] Excluding Indian jungle population. - Non compris les Indiens de la jungle.

[16] Excluding infants born alive of less than 28 weeks' gestation, of less than 1 000 grams in weight and 35 centimeters in length, who die within seven days of birth. - Non compris les enfants nés vivants après moins de 28 semaines de gestations, pesant moins de 1 000 grammes, mesurant moins de 35 centimètres et décédés dans les sept jours qui ont suivi leur naissance.

[17] For 2005, data refer to last twelve months preceding census in May 2005. - Pour 2005, les données se rapportent aux douze mois précédant le recensement de mai 2005.

[18] Figures for urban and rural areas do not add up to the total; reason for discrepancy not ascertained. - La somme des données pour la résidence urbaine et rurale n'est pas égale au total; on ne sait pas comment s'explique la divergence.

[19] Data refer to government controlled areas. - Les données se rapportent aux zones contrôlées par le Gouvernement.

[20] Data for urban and rural residence excluded 59 births of unknown residence. - Les données pour la résidence urbaine/rurale ne comprennent pas 59 naissances d'enfants dont on ignore la résidence.

[21] Published by the United Nations Economic and Social Commission for Western Asia. - Publié par la Commission économique et sociale des Nations Unies pour l'Asie occidentale.

[22] Including data for East Jerusalem and Israeli residents in certain other territories under occupation by Israeli military forces since June 1967. - Y compris les données pour Jérusalem-Est et les résidents israéliens dans certains autres territoires occupés depuis 1967 par les forces armées israéliennes.

[23] Data refer to Japanese nationals in Japan only. - Les données se raportent aux nationaux japonais au Japon seulement.

[24] Excluding alien armed forces, civilian aliens employed by armed forces, and foreign diplomatic personnel and their dependants. - Non compris les militaires étrangers, les civils étrangers employés par les forces armées ni le personnel diplomatique étranger et les membres de leur famille les accompagnant.

[25] Excluding data for the Pakistan-held part of Jammu and Kashmir, the final status of which has not yet been determined. Data based on Pakistan Demographic Survey (PDS 2005). - Non compris les données concernant la partie du Jammu et Cachemire occupée par le Pakistan dont le statut définitif n'a pas été déterminé. Données extraites de l'enquête démographique effectuée par le Pakistan en 2005.

[26] Figures for male and female categories do not add up to the total, since they do not include the category "Unknown". - La somme des chiffres indiqués pour les sexes masculin et féminin n'est pas égale au total parce qu'elle n'inclut pas la catégorie " inconnue ".

[27] Based on the results of the Population Growth Survey. Data as reported by national statistical authorities; they may differ from data presented in other tables. - D'après les résultats de la 'Population Growth Survey.' Les données comme elles ont été déclarées par l'institut national de la statistique; elles peuvent être différentes de celles présentées dans d'autres tableaux.

[28] Excluding Faeroe Islands and Greenland. - Non compris les Iles Féroé et le Groenland.

[29] Including nationals temporarily outside the country. - Y compris les nationaux se trouvant temporairement hors du pays.

[30] Excluding Overseas Departments, namely, French Guiana, Guadeloupe, Martinique and Reunion, shown separately. Including armed forces stationed outside the country. Age classification is based on year of birth of mother rather than the exact age of mother at birth of child. - Non compris les départements d'outre mer, c'est-à-dire la Guyane française, la Guadeloupe, la Martinique et la Réunion, qui font l'objet de rubriques distinctes. Y compris les militaires nationaux hors du pays. Le classement selon l'âge est basé sur l'année de naissance de la mère et non sur l'age exacte de la mère au moment de naissance de l'enfant.

[31] The difference between 'Total' and the sum of 'urban' and 'rural' is due to the cases of unknown place of residence or residence abroad. - La différence entre le 'Total' et la somme des données selon la résidence urbaine/rurale se rapporte à la situation ou on ignore la résidence ou si la résidence est à l'étranger.

[32] Births registered within one year of occurrence. - Naissances enregistrées dans l'année qui suit l'événement.

[33] Live births to Maltese parents only. - Naissances vivantes aux parents maltais seulement.

[34] Including residents outside the country if listed in a Netherlands population register. - Y compris les résidents hors du pays, s'ils sont inscrits sur un registre de population néerlandais.

[35] Age classification is based on year of birth of mother rather than the exact age of mother at birth of child. - Le classement selon l'âge est basé sur l'année de naissance de la mère et non sur l'age exacte de la mère au moment de naissance de l'enfant.

[36] Without data for Kosovo and Metohia. - Sans les données pour le Kosovo and Metohie.

[37] Age classification based on year of birth rather than on completed years of age. Excluding infants born alive of less than 28 weeks' gestation, of less than 1 000 grams in weight and 35 centimeters in length, who die within seven days of birth. - La classification par âge est fondée sur l'année de naissance et non sur l'âge en années révolues. Non compris les enfants nés vivants après moins de 28 semaines de gestations, pesant moins de 1 000 grammes, mesurant moins de 35 centimètres et décédés dans les sept jours qui ont suivi leur naissance.

[38] Data tabulated by date of occurrence for England and Wales, and by date of registration for Northern Ireland and Scotland. Data for the United Kingdom and Northern Ireland excludes births to non-resident mothers of Northern Ireland. - Données exploitées selon la date de l'événement pour l'Angleterre et le pays de Galles, et selon la date de l'enregistrement pour l'Irlande du Nord et l'Ecosse. Les données concernant le Royaume-Uni de Grande-Bretagne et d'Irlande du Nord ne tiennent pas compte des enfants nés de mères non résidentes en Irlande du Nord.

[39] Data is referred to in Australia as 'nuptial' births. Data includes; births born in wedlock where age of father is unknown and ; births born out of wedlock and where the father has not acknowledged the bith and age of father is therefore unknown. - L'Australie utilise le terme « nuptial » pour qualifier ces naissances. Les données se rapportent aux enfants légitimes pour lesquels l'âge du père n'est pas connu et aux naissances hors mariage non reconnues par le père et pour lesquelles l'âge du père n'est par conséquent pas connu.

[40] Including United States military personnel, their dependants and contract employees. - Y compris les militaires des Etats-Unis, les membres de leur famille les accompagnant et les agents contractuels des Etats-Unis.

[41] Excluding United States military personnel, their dependants and contract employees. - Non compris les militaires des Etats-Unis, les membres de leur famille les accompagnant et les agents contractuels des Etats-Unis.

[42] The total births by year may not match due to late births report coming from the Outer Islands of Yap. - Le total des naissances annuelles peut ne pas correspondre, les îles extérieures de Yap ayant communiqué leurs données tardivement.

[43] For resident population only. - Pour la population résidante seulement.

Table 11

Table 11 presents live-birth rates by age of mother and urban/rural residence for the latest available year.

Description of variables: Age is defined as age at last birthday preceding the live birth, that is, the difference between the date of birth and the date of the occurrence of the event, expressed in completed solar years. The age classification used in this table is the following: under 20 years, 5-year age groups through 40-44 years, and 45 years or over.

Rate computation: Live-birth rates specific to age of mother are the annual number of births to women in each age group (as shown in table 10) per 1 000 female population in the same age group.

Birth rates by age of mother and urban/rural residence are the annual number of live births that occurred to a specific age-urban/rural group (as shown in table 10) per 1 000 females in the corresponding age-urban/rural group. These rates are calculated by the Statistics Division of the United Nations.

Since relatively few births occur to women below 15 or above 50 years of age, birth rates for women under 20 years of age and for those 45 years of age or over are computed on the female population aged 15-19 and 45-49, respectively. Similarly, the rate for women of "All ages" is based on all live births irrespective of age of mother, and is computed on the female population aged 15-49 years. This rate for "All ages" is known as the general fertility rate.

Births to mothers of unknown age are distributed proportionately across the age groups, by the Statistics Division of the United Nations, in accordance with the distribution of births by age of mother prior to the calculation of the rates.

The population used in computing the rates is the estimated or enumerated distribution of females by age. First priority is given to an estimate for the mid-point of the same year (as shown in table 7), second priority to census returns of the year to which the births referred, and third priority to an estimate for some other point of time in the year.

Rates presented in this table are limited to those for countries or areas having at least a total of 100 live births in a given year.

Reliability of data: Rates are not computed if the data on live births from civil registers are reported as incomplete (less than 90 per cent completeness) or of unknown completeness. Table 9 and the technical notes for that table provide more detailed information on the completeness of live-birth registration. For more information about the quality of vital statistics data in general, and the information available on the basis of the completeness of estimates in particular, see section 4.2 of the Technical Notes.

Limitations: Rates shown in this table are subject to the same limitations that affect the corresponding frequencies and are set forth in the technical notes for table 10. These include differences in the completeness of registration, the treatment of infants who were born alive but died before the registration of the birth or within the first 24 hours of life, the method used to determine age of mother and the quality of the reported information relating to age of mother. In addition, some rates are based on births tabulated by date of registration and not by date of occurrence; these have been indicated by a plus sign "+".

The effect of including delayed registration on the distribution of births by age of mother may be noted in the age-specific fertility rates for women at older ages. In some cases, high age-specific rates for women aged 45 years and over may reflect age of mother at registration of birth and not fertility at these older ages.

The comparability of data by urban/rural residence is affected by the national definitions of urban and rural used in tabulating these data. It is assumed, in the absence of specific information to the contrary, that the definitions of urban and rural used in connection with the national population census were also used in the compilation of the vital statistics for each country or area. However, it is possible that, for a given country or area, the definitions of urban and rural used for both the vital statistics data and the population census data are not the same. When known, the definitions of urban used in national population censuses are presented at the end of the technical notes for table 6. As discussed in detail in the technical notes for table 6, these definitions vary considerably from one country or area to another.

In addition to problems of comparability, vital rates classified by urban/rural residence are also subject to certain special types of bias. If, when calculating vital rates, different definitions of urban are used in connection with the vital events and the population data and if this results in a net difference between the numerator and denominator of the rate in the population at risk, then the vital rates would be biased. Urban/rural differentials in vital rates may also be affected by whether the vital events have been tabulated in terms of place of occurrence or place of usual residence. This problem is discussed in more detail in section 4.1.4.1 of the Technical Notes.

Earlier data: Live-birth rates specific for age of mother have been shown for the latest available year in each issue of the Yearbook. Data included in this table update the series covering a period of years as follows:

Issue	Years Covered
Special Topic on Natality, CD, 1999	1990 – 1998
Historical Supplement CD, 1997	1948 – 1997
1992	1983 – 1992
1986	1977 – 1985
1981	1972 – 1980
Historical Supplement, 1979	1948 - 1977

Tableau 11

Le tableau 11 présente les taux des naissances vivantes selon l'âge de la mère et selon le lieu de résidence (zone urbaine ou rurale) correspondant aux données les plus récentes dont on dispose.

Description des variables : L'âge désigne l'âge au dernier anniversaire précédant la naissance, c'est-à-dire la différence entre la date de naissance et la date de l'événement, exprimée en années solaires révolues. La classification par âge utilisée dans le tableau 11 comprend les catégories suivantes : moins de 20 ans, groupes quinquennaux jusqu'à 40-44 ans, et 45 et plus.

Calcul des taux : Les taux des naissances vivantes selon l'âge de la mère représentent le nombre annuel de naissances dans chaque groupe d'âge (voir tableau 10) pour 1 000 femmes des mêmes groupes d'âge.

Les taux de natalité selon l'âge de la mère et le lieu de résidence (zone urbaine ou rurale) représentent le nombre annuel de naissances vivantes intervenues dans un groupe d'âge donné parmi la population urbaine ou rurale (comme il est indiqué au tableau 10) pour 1 000 femmes du groupe d'âge correspondant parmi la population urbaine ou rurale. Ces taux ont été calculés par la Division de statistique de l'ONU.

Étant donné que le nombre de naissances parmi les femmes de moins de 15 ans ou de plus de 50 ans est relativement peu élevé, les taux de natalité parmi les femmes âgées de moins de 20 ans et celles de 45 ans et plus ont été calculés sur la base des populations féminines âgées de 15 à 19 ans et de 45 à 49 ans, respectivement. De même, le taux pour les femmes de « tous âges » est fondé sur la totalité des naissances vivantes, indépendamment de l'âge de la mère et ce chiffre est rapporté à l'effectif de la population féminine âgée de 15 à 49 ans. Ce taux « tous âges » est le taux global de fécondité.

Les naissances pour lesquelles l'âge de la mère était inconnu ont été réparties par la Division de statistique de l'ONU, avant le calcul des taux, suivant les proportions observées pour celles où l'âge de la mère était connu.

Les chiffres de population utilisés pour le calcul des taux proviennent de dénombrements ou de répartitions estimatives de la population féminine selon l'âge. On a utilisé de préférence les estimations de la population au milieu de l'année considérée selon les chiffres du tableau 7 ; à défaut, on s'est contenté des données censitaires se rapportant à l'année des naissances et, si ces données manquaient également, d'estimations établies à un autre moment de l'année.

Les taux présentés dans ce tableau ne concernent que les pays ou zones où l'on a enregistré un total d'au moins 100 naissances vivantes dans une année donnée.

Fiabilité des données : On a choisi de ne pas faire figurer dans le tableau 11 des taux calculés à partir de données sur les naissances vivantes issues de registres de l'état civil qui sont déclarées incomplètes (degré de complétude inférieur à 90 p. 100) ou dont le degré de complétude n'est pas connu. Le tableau 9 et les notes techniques qui s'y rapportent présentent des renseignements plus détaillés sur le degré de complétude de l'enregistrement des naissances vivantes. Pour plus de précisions sur la qualité des données reposant sur les statistiques de l'état civil en général et les estimations de complétude en particulier, voir la section 4.2 des Notes techniques.

Insuffisance des données : Les taux du tableau 11 appellent les mêmes réserves que celles concernant les fréquences correspondantes (voir à ce sujet les notes techniques relatives au tableau 10). Leurs imperfections tiennent notamment au degré de complétude de l'enregistrement, au classement des enfants nés vivants décédés avant l'enregistrement de leur naissance ou dans les 24 heures qui ont suivi la naissance, à la méthode utilisée pour déterminer l'âge de la mère et à l'exactitude des renseignements concernant l'âge de la mère. En outre, dans certains cas, les données relatives aux naissances sont exploitées selon la date de l'enregistrement et non selon la date de l'événement ; ces cas ont été signalés par le signe '+'.

On peut se rendre compte, d'après les taux relatifs aux groupes d'âge les plus avancés, des conséquences que peut avoir l'inclusion, dans les statistiques des naissances selon l'âge de la mère, des naissances enregistrées tardivement. Dans certains cas, il se peut que des taux élevés pour le groupe d'âge 45 ans et plus ne traduisent pas le niveau de fécondité de ce groupe d'âge, mais l'âge de la mère au moment où la naissance a été enregistrée.

La comparabilité des données selon le lieu de résidence (zone urbaine ou rurale) peut être limitée par les définitions nationales des termes « urbain » et « rural » utilisées pour le classement de ces données. En l'absence d'indications contraires, on a supposé que les mêmes définitions avaient servi pour le recensement national de la population et pour l'établissement des statistiques de l'état civil pour chaque pays ou zone. Toutefois, il n'est pas exclu que, pour une zone ou un pays donné, des définitions différentes aient été retenues. Les définitions du terme « urbain » utilisées pour les recensements nationaux de population ont été présentées à la fin du tableau 6 lorsqu'elles étaient connues. Comme on l'a précisé dans les notes techniques relatives au tableau 6, ces définitions varient considérablement d'un pays ou d'une zone à l'autre.

Outre les problèmes de comparabilité, les taux démographiques classés selon le lieu de résidence (zone urbaine ou rurale) sont également sujets à des distorsions particulières. Si l'on utilise des définitions différentes du terme « urbain » pour classer les faits d'état civil et les données relatives à la population lors du calcul des taux et qu'il en résulte une différence nette entre le numérateur et le dénominateur pour le taux de la population exposée au risque, les taux démographiques s'en trouveront faussés. La différence entre ces taux pour les zones urbaines et rurales pourra aussi être faussée selon que les faits d'état civil auront été classés d'après le lieu de l'événement ou d'après le lieu de résidence habituel. Ce problème est examiné plus en détail à la section 4.1.4.1 des Notes techniques.

Données publiées antérieurement : Les différentes éditions de l'*Annuaire démographique* regroupent les statistiques les plus récentes dont on disposait à l'époque sur les taux de naissances vivantes selon l'âge de la mère. Les données qui figurent dans le tableau 11 actualisent les données qui portaient sur les périodes suivantes :

Éditions	Années considérées
Édition spéciale sur les statistiques de la natalité (CD-ROM), 1999	1990 – 1998
Supplément historique (CD-ROM), 1997	1948 – 1997
1992	1983 – 1992
1986	1977 – 1985
1981	1972 – 1980
Supplément rétrospectif, 1979	1948 - 1977

11. Live-birth rates by age of mother and urban/rural residence: latest available year, 1996 - 2005
Naissances vivantes, taux selon l'âge de la mère et la résidence, urbaine/rurale: dernière année disponible, 1996 - 2005

Continent, country or area, year and urban/rural residence / Continent, pays ou zone, année, et résidence urbaine/rurale	All ages Tous âges[1]	Age of mother (in years) - Age de la mère (en années)						
		-20[2]	20-24	25-29	30-34	35-39	40-44	45+[3]
AFRICA — AFRIQUE								
Egypt - Égypte								
1999								
Total	108.4	18.5	192.8	226.3	162.8	87.7	25.7	6.7
Mauritius - Maurice								
2005								
Total	53.9	34.9	105.2	110.7	71.2	30.7	9.0	0.4
Morocco - Maroc								
2001								
Total	66.7	28.9	88.3	102.3	104.4	73.6	32.1	7.6
Urban - Urbaine	57.5	23.8	74.5	90.2	89.9	63.4	24.9	4.2
Rural - Rurale	80.5	34.7	106.0	120.9	132.0	93.7	45.4	13.1
Namibia - Namibie[4]								
2001								
Total	100.1	51.2	135.8	144.6	137.3	103.1	59.8	22.1
Urban - Urbaine	84.8	45.2	106.0	120.8	113.0	79.5	37.9	10.9
Rural - Rurale	110.4	53.8	156.5	166.0	158.2	121.6	74.7	28.3
Réunion[5]								
1999								
Total	72.0	35.1	115.9	143.0	107.1	61.3	15.1	1.3
Swaziland[6]								
1997								
Total	133.2	73.0	193.4	199.4	162.6	130.8	64.7	50.0
Urban - Urbaine	106.6	65.3	147.1	157.0	115.9	92.6	39.2	31.0
Rural - Rurale	143.5	75.4	214.3	219.4	182.0	145.4	73.4	55.5
Tunisia - Tunisie								
1998								
Total	67.8	7.5	66.0	112.3	110.3	64.7	21.2	3.4
AMERICA, NORTH — AMERIQUE DU NORD								
Anguilla+								
2001								
Total	57.6	61.7	136.3	102.2	49.8	37.7	15.6	...
Bermuda - Bermudes								
2000								
Total	49.1	25.5	81.1	83.4	97.3	51.3	5.1	...
Canada[7]								
2004								
Total	41.4	14.3	51.0	97.4	96.0	40.2	6.9	0.3
Costa Rica								
2004								
Total	62.8	69.5	112.1	99.5	73.5	37.3	10.3	0.9
Cuba								
2005								
Total	40.1	44.9	93.0	81.3	53.2	21.9	4.1	0.2
Urban - Urbaine	38.7	39.2	90.0	82.6	54.6	22.2	4.0	0.2
Rural - Rurale	44.5	61.9	102.1	77.3	49.0	21.0	4.4	0.3
El Salvador								
2003								
Total	70.8	78.6	117.5	95.1	67.4	43.5	16.6	2.4
Urban - Urbaine	67.0	77.5	122.0	96.3	62.6	35.1	10.7	1.4
Rural - Rurale	77.0	79.9	111.3	93.2	76.5	61.3	29.6	4.4
Greenland - Groenland								
2000								
Total	62.4	60.9	154.8	126.0	75.9	35.9	7.3	0.6
Urban - Urbaine	58.7	52.8	153.3	118.8	72.5	33.1	6.9	0.7
Rural - Rurale	81.6	106.2	162.8	153.6	93.0	51.3	9.5	0.0
Grenada - Grenade+								
2000								
Total	76.5	54.7	107.0	132.7	113.8	64.1	26.7	1.1
Guadeloupe								
2003								
Total	60.4	25.9	81.3	132.3	108.6	64.6	19.3	0.8
Guatemala								
1999								
Total	141.4	110.3	211.2	193.4	162.6	128.3	60.1	13.8
Jamaica - Jamaïque[8]								
2004								
Total	61.5	64.8	103.3	86.2	70.4	45.2	16.3	1.1

11. Live-birth rates by age of mother and urban/rural residence: latest available year, 1996 - 2005
Naissances vivantes, taux selon l'âge de la mère et la résidence, urbaine/rurale: dernière année disponible, 1996 - 2005 (continued — suite)

Continent, country or area, year and urban/rural residence / Continent, pays ou zone,année, et résidence urbaine/rurale	All ages Tous âges[1]	-20[2]	20-24	25-29	30-34	35-39	40-44	45+[3]
AMERICA, NORTH — AMERIQUE DU NORD								
Martinique[5,9]								
2003								
Total	52.3	26.2	67.7	116.7	99.2	57.2	16.7	0.7
Netherlands Antilles - Antilles néerlandaises								
2004								
Total	47.0	41.2	95.5	103.6	80.6	42.4	9.5	0.9
Panama								
1999								
Total	86.6	97.4	148.3	128.8	95.0	51.0	13.3	1.8
Urban - Urbaine	71.7	81.1	127.1	109.7	81.7	40.3	8.5	0.3
Rural - Rurale	110.6	117.3	179.0	161.1	118.7	70.7	22.0	4.4
2003								
Total	75.1	83.6	132.6	112.7	86.0	44.7	12.6	1.2
Puerto Rico - Porto Rico								
2005								
Total	51.3	62.4	109.7	92.7	58.3	24.1	5.3	0.3
Saint Kitts and Nevis - Saint-Kitts-et-Nevis[+]								
2000								
Total	80.0	86.6	140.2	123.1	80.0	57.4	20.0	1.0
Saint Lucia - Sainte-Lucie								
2002								
Total	72.8	...	96.1	83.9	76.4	45.9	14.1	0.6
Saint Vincent and the Grenadines - Saint Vincent-et-les Grenadines[+]								
2001								
Total	76.4	74.5	121.3	120.7	97.2	53.9	14.2	0.9
Trinidad and Tobago - Trinité-et-Tobago								
1997								
Total	52.2	43.3	97.0	88.0	70.0	35.3	9.4	0.6
United States - États-Unis								
2004								
Total	56.2	41.8	101.8	115.3	95.5	45.3	9.0	0.6
AMERICA, SOUTH — AMERIQUE DU SUD								
Argentina - Argentine								
2005								
Total	73.5	65.3	112.5	113.4	104.8	61.4	18.9	1.5
Chile - Chili								
2003								
Total	55.0	50.3	87.5	94.8	81.7	47.3	13.4	0.7
French Guiana - Guyane française[5]								
2003								
Total	118.5	111.8	201.8	236.5	144.0	84.7	27.3	2.1
Suriname								
2003								
Total	75.7	74.0	132.7	122.0	85.2	52.2	17.0	1.2
Uruguay								
2002								
Total	64.4	65.5	103.2	107.0	90.0	49.7	13.9	0.9
Venezuela (Bolivarian Republic of) - Venezuela (République bolivarienne du)[10]								
2002								
Total	74.3	84.8	129.0	109.9	80.1	42.9	14.1	2.9
ASIA — ASIE								
Armenia - Arménie[11]								
2004								
Total	41.0	29.8	128.4	76.1	30.4	10.6	2.1	0.1

11. Live-birth rates by age of mother and urban/rural residence: latest available year, 1996 - 2005
Naissances vivantes, taux selon l'âge de la mère et la résidence, urbaine/rurale: dernière année disponible, 1996 - 2005 (continued — suite)

Continent, pays ou zone,année, et résidence urbaine/rurale	All ages Tous âges[1]	-20[2]	20-24	25-29	30-34	35-39	40-44	45+[3]
ASIA — ASIE								
Armenia - Arménie[11]								
2004								
Urban - Urbaine	39.0	24.4	116.0	78.4	33.0	12.0	2.1	0.1
Rural - Rurale	44.9	38.5	153.6	71.2	25.1	8.2	2.1	0.2
Azerbaijan - Azerbaïdjan[11],+								
2004								
Total	53.0	31.0	144.4	107.2	51.5	22.0	6.0	0.8
Urban - Urbaine	44.8	20.5	118.0	100.7	49.7	19.9	5.4	0.7
Rural - Rurale	62.4	42.2	173.4	114.2	53.4	24.2	6.8	0.9
Bahrain - Bahreïn								
2005								
Total	82.9	17.7	118.0	162.9	113.6	72.6	30.6	5.3
Bhutan - Bhoutan[12]								
2005								
Total	79.4	36.5	138.9	141.6	89.4	54.5	31.3	9.9
Urban - Urbaine	71.5	22.1	115.3	138.8	78.1	39.5	18.8	7.1
Rural - Rurale	83.5	44.9	154.4	143.2	95.3	61.3	35.3	10.7
Brunei Darussalam - Brunéi Darussalam+								
2001								
Total	73.7	29.9	90.9	125.0	108.1	68.0	24.5	1.8
China: Hong Kong SAR - Chine: Hong Kong RAS								
2005								
Total	27.5	3.9	33.3	60.7	64.4	29.6	4.7	0.3
China: Macao SAR - Chine: Macao RAS								
2005								
Total	23.8	3.2	27.8	58.4	61.2	27.9	3.6	0.3
Cyprus - Chypre[13]								
2005								
Total	41.0	6.5	46.8	102.5	86.2	33.9	6.3	0.8
Georgia - Géorgie[11]								
2000								
Total	31.3	30.9	82.5	59.5	30.2	12.9	3.9	0.7
Urban - Urbaine	32.5	31.6	86.7	64.2	34.2	14.4	4.4	0.8
Rural - Rurale	29.4	30.0	77.0	52.1	24.1	10.5	3.1	0.6
2004								
Total	42.2	36.3	101.0	75.0	47.5	21.6	5.6	2.6
Israel - Israël[14]								
2005								
Total	85.6	14.7	106.6	169.9	159.7	90.8	23.2	2.2
Urban - Urbaine	84.3	15.2	107.1	167.4	153.8	87.7	22.5	2.2
Rural - Rurale	99.1	9.5	99.1	199.9	232.3	124.2	30.7	1.9
Japan - Japon[15]								
2005								
Total	37.7	5.1	34.4	81.1	83.4	35.3	4.9	0.2
Kazakhstan[11]								
2004								
Total	64.1	27.1	142.7	131.0	86.0	43.6	9.3	0.5
Urban - Urbaine	61.0	28.8	134.3	124.1	81.7	40.5	8.2	0.4
Rural - Rurale	68.7	25.2	154.9	141.8	93.1	48.7	11.0	0.7
Korea (Republic of) - Corée (République de)[16]								
2004								
Total	35.4	2.3	20.6	107.3	86.9	19.7	2.6	0.2
Kuwait - Koweït								
2005								
Total	83.0	16.0	118.6	142.3	119.9	73.9	27.0	4.1
Kyrgyzstan - Kirghizistan[11]								
2005								
Total	77.3	26.0	164.9	144.6	98.5	53.7	15.9	3.3
Urban - Urbaine	64.5	24.6	136.9	108.6	80.0	46.1	13.6	2.3
Rural - Rurale	85.4	26.6	181.6	172.6	111.7	59.1	17.5	4.0
Maldives								
2003								
Total	67.9	14.5	116.3	133.4	103.2	63.4	15.4	2.8

11. Live-birth rates by age of mother and urban/rural residence: latest available year, 1996 - 2005
Naissances vivantes, taux selon l'âge de la mère et la résidence, urbaine/rurale: dernière année disponible, 1996 - 2005 (continued — suite)

Continent, pays ou zone,année, et résidence urbaine/rurale	All ages Tous âges[1]	-20[2]	20-24	25-29	30-34	35-39	40-44	45+[3]
ASIA — ASIE								
Mongolia - Mongolie								
2005								
Total	62.7	15.4	110.4	123.3	83.7	42.5	11.9	4.5
Pakistan[17,18]								
2003								
Total	114.5	23.7	163.1	229.6	190.0	112.7	49.0	18.8
Urban - Urbaine	97.9	14.2	137.1	219.3	169.2	93.4	34.2	11.2
Rural - Rurale	124.5	29.7	178.9	236.1	201.6	124.5	57.8	23.7
Philippines								
2003								
Total	79.4	30.2	125.7	135.3	113.1	74.0	30.6	4.7
Qatar								
2005								
Total	84.8	16.1	123.1	159.6	118.8	79.3	29.8	7.3
Saudi Arabia - Arabie saoudite[19]								
2004								
Total	93.4	14.7	66.1	228.3	117.5	97.9	58.7	30.0
Singapore - Singapour								
2005								
Total	37.8	7.4	33.8	83.8	93.0	38.9	6.5	0.3
Sri Lanka+								
1996								
Total	72.6	29.1	88.7	129.1	110.9	81.8	20.0	2.4
Turkey - Turquie								
1997								
Total	81.1	50.0	173.6	144.9	73.3	36.1	15.5	3.4
Uzbekistan - Ouzbékistan[11]								
2000								
Total	82.7	21.1	205.4	161.4	89.7	31.5	7.0	0.8
Urban - Urbaine	65.7	21.8	167.9	123.6	73.0	26.6	5.4	0.5
Rural - Rurale	93.6	20.7	227.5	185.9	100.6	34.7	8.2	1.1
EUROPE								
Albania - Albanie								
2005								
Total	47.2	16.3	92.3	111.4	69.6	26.3	5.3	0.8
Andorra - Andorre								
2004								
Total	40.1	5.5	35.9	69.1	84.9	46.3	10.8	1.1
Austria - Autriche								
2005								
Total	38.3	12.9	55.3	93.9	79.3	33.2	6.2	0.3
Belarus - Bélarus[11]								
2004								
Total	33.3	22.0	89.3	74.6	38.9	12.9	2.3	0.1
Urban - Urbaine	31.0	18.0	79.0	71.6	38.4	12.2	2.1	0.1
Rural - Rurale	41.5	36.0	135.7	86.1	40.8	15.2	3.1	0.2
Bulgaria - Bulgarie								
2005								
Total	37.9	40.1	78.6	81.0	47.4	14.5	2.1	0.1
Urban - Urbaine	36.4	31.8	66.6	81.9	51.4	15.8	2.1	0.1
Rural - Rurale	43.0	63.9	123.1	77.6	34.0	10.3	2.0	0.1
Channel Islands: Guernsey - Îles Anglo-Normandes: Guernesey								
1996								
Total	43.5	24.0	37.4	91.6	89.1	41.0	5.5	...
Croatia - Croatie								
2005								
Total	39.7	14.0	65.7	98.1	72.8	27.5	4.6	0.3
Czech Republic - République tchèque								
2005								
Total	40.6	11.0	49.0	102.7	70.2	22.7	3.6	0.1
Urban - Urbaine	40.4	11.5	46.2	100.1	72.6	23.7	3.8	0.1
Rural - Rurale	41.2	9.6	57.0	110.3	63.1	19.7	3.1	0.1

11. Live-birth rates by age of mother and urban/rural residence: latest available year, 1996 - 2005
Naissances vivantes, taux selon l'âge de la mère et la résidence, urbaine/rurale: dernière année disponible, 1996 - 2005 (continued — suite)

Continent, pays ou zone, année, et résidence urbaine/rurale	All ages Tous âges[1]	-20[2]	20-24	25-29	30-34	35-39	40-44	45+[3]
EUROPE								
Denmark - Danemark[20]								
2005								
Total	52.0	5.6	43.8	126.2	127.0	49.2	8.3	0.3
Finland - Finlande[21]								
2005								
Total	49.0	10.3	57.4	116.3	112.9	51.5	10.7	0.6
Urban - Urbaine	48.0	10.8	49.4	103.4	109.8	51.0	10.8	0.5
Rural - Rurale	50.9	9.5	82.7	154.5	119.6	52.3	10.6	0.7
France[9,22]								
2005								
Total	53.6	7.8	55.0	128.1	121.4	56.0	12.9	0.7
Germany - Allemagne								
2004								
Total	36.0	11.0	49.5	86.4	81.5	35.5	5.8	0.2
Gibraltar								
2001								
Total	60.9	24.9	77.5	168.3	110.8	43.4	7.9	...
Greece - Grèce								
2005								
Total	39.8	10.7	41.8	82.8	85.4	39.2	7.1	0.8
Hungary - Hongrie								
2005								
Total	39.8	20.4	50.0	89.2	72.1	27.3	4.8	0.2
Urban - Urbaine	38.4	14.7	40.1	84.3	75.3	29.0	4.9	0.2
Rural - Rurale	41.7	31.2	69.3	98.4	63.4	23.3	4.5	0.1
Iceland - Islande								
2005								
Total	58.2	14.2	82.0	129.5	113.9	57.5	10.7	0.9
Urban - Urbaine	58.8	14.1	83.6	130.4	113.3	56.8	10.8	0.9
Rural - Rurale	49.7	15.3	59.0	112.2	125.2	68.9	9.5	0.0
Ireland - Irlande[23,+]								
2005								
Total	56.4	16.8	45.9	78.8	130.3	87.2	16.8	0.6
Italy - Italie								
2004								
Total	40.0	7.0	33.6	73.9	89.8	49.2	9.9	0.5
Latvia - Lettonie[11]								
2005								
Total	36.4	15.9	67.4	84.3	60.5	27.7	5.7	0.4
Urban - Urbaine	35.3	13.9	61.7	83.7	60.5	27.0	5.2	0.3
Rural - Rurale	39.0	19.6	80.1	86.0	60.4	29.4	6.9	0.6
Liechtenstein								
2005								
Total	42.3	6.9	32.7	77.1	112.5	58.0	11.0	0.0
Lithuania - Lituanie[11]								
2005								
Total	34.4	18.7	66.6	90.0	53.2	20.6	4.2	0.2
Urban - Urbaine	31.5	14.4	56.0	83.4	51.4	19.5	3.7	0.2
Rural - Rurale	41.4	26.6	91.5	110.1	58.1	23.4	5.4	0.2
Luxembourg								
2005								
Total	47.4	12.0	57.1	107.9	105.9	48.0	8.7	0.3
Malta - Malte[24]								
2005								
Total	39.5	16.6	45.5	97.1	81.1	27.4	6.1	0.5
Netherlands - Pays-Bas[25]								
2004								
Total	49.2	4.6	36.3	99.0	130.2	61.3	9.7	0.4
Norway - Norvège[9]								
2005								
Total	52.4	8.1	58.6	124.4	118.6	48.6	8.6	0.4
Poland - Pologne								
2004								
Total	35.8	13.8	60.9	89.1	55.5	21.9	4.8	0.2
Urban - Urbaine	32.4	12.6	49.1	82.4	54.6	20.4	4.1	0.2
Rural - Rurale	41.7	15.4	82.0	101.4	56.9	24.4	6.1	0.3
Portugal								
2005								
Total	41.8	19.0	47.6	84.3	85.3	37.6	7.4	0.4

Continent, country or area, year and urban/rural residence / Continent, pays ou zone, année, et résidence urbaine/rurale	All ages Tous âges[1]	-20[2]	20-24	25-29	30-34	35-39	40-44	45+[3]
EUROPE								
Republic of Moldova - République de Moldova[11] 2004								
Total	37.4	29.2	91.2	71.6	41.3	15.1	2.8	0.1
Urban - Urbaine	31.7	18.7	82.2	72.3	37.3	14.0	2.3	0.1
Rural - Rurale	41.8	35.8	96.8	71.0	45.2	16.1	3.3	0.2
Romania - Roumanie 2005								
Total	39.5	34.1	73.3	83.9	51.8	18.7	3.6	0.2
Urban - Urbaine	34.0	21.1	53.7	82.0	55.7	18.4	2.8	0.1
Rural - Rurale	48.5	52.0	104.4	86.8	46.2	19.2	5.0	0.3
Russian Federation - Fédération de Russie[11] 2004								
Total	37.7	28.2	93.4	80.2	45.9	17.6	2.9	0.1
Urban - Urbaine	35.6	24.0	83.4	77.7	45.3	17.1	2.7	0.1
Rural - Rurale	44.3	39.8	129.1	88.5	47.9	19.0	3.7	0.2
San Marino - Saint-Marin+ 2004								
Total	40.6	1.6	20.3	65.4	102.8	50.7	8.3	1.0
Serbia and Montenegro - Serbie-et-Montenegro[26] 2003								
Total	44.4	24.5	94.4	104.7	66.1	23.9	4.6	0.3
Urban - Urbaine	44.9	19.6	83.9	107.6	75.7	28.5	5.1	0.3
Rural - Rurale	43.7	31.5	111.6	99.9	50.8	16.8	3.7	0.2
Slovakia - Slovaquie 2005								
Total	37.9	20.4	61.0	88.0	58.6	20.5	3.6	0.2
Slovenia - Slovénie 2005								
Total	36.3	6.2	40.4	96.3	79.1	26.2	4.2	0.3
Urban - Urbaine	36.0	6.1	36.0	92.1	86.4	30.1	4.7	0.2
Rural - Rurale	38.0	6.4	46.4	105.5	76.1	23.3	3.9	0.3
Spain - Espagne 2003								
Total	40.8	10.8	29.3	65.6	99.0	50.2	8.3	0.4
Sweden - Suède 2005								
Total	50.1	5.9	46.7	109.7	124.7	55.1	10.7	0.5
Switzerland - Suisse 2005								
Total	39.9	5.1	37.8	85.4	99.3	47.3	8.3	0.3
The Former Yugoslav Rep. of Macedonia - L'ex-République yougoslave de Macédoine 2005								
Total	42.7	22.0	82.5	105.1	60.5	18.7	3.4	0.2
Ukraine[11,27] 2004								
Total	34.3	29.5	93.4	70.6	35.5	12.3	2.2	0.1
United Kingdom - Royaume-Uni[28,29] 2004								
Total	49.8	26.8	71.5	97.6	97.5	48.5	9.8	0.5
OCEANIA — OCEANIE								
American Samoa - Samoas américaines 2000								
Total	123.6	57.4	199.3	238.5	180.4	102.0	26.7	0.0
Australia - Australie+ 2004								
Total	50.7	16.3	53.4	102.5	114.4	57.4	10.6	0.5

11. Live-birth rates by age of mother and urban/rural residence: latest available year, 1996 - 2005
Naissances vivantes, taux selon l'âge de la mère et la résidence, urbaine/rurale: dernière année disponible, 1996 - 2005 (continued — suite)

Continent, country or area, year and urban/rural residence / Continent, pays ou zone,année, et résidence urbaine/rurale	Age of mother (in years) - Age de la mère (en années)							
	All ages Tous âges[1]	-20[2]	20-24	25-29	30-34	35-39	40-44	45+[3]
OCEANIA — OCEANIE								
New Caledonia - Nouvelle-Calédonie								
2003								
Total	71.2	20.3	109.2	129.5	118.9	64.8	18.3	0.3
New Zealand - Nouvelle-Zélande+								
2005								
Total	55.5	27.7	68.6	107.4	119.6	63.8	12.2	0.6
Urban - Urbaine	55.0	28.5	66.0	102.5	116.0	63.3	12.1	0.6
Rural - Rurale	58.6	22.0	100.7	157.8	148.7	66.2	12.5	0.7
Tonga+								
1999								
Total	110.2	28.3	128.3	220.2	201.6	128.2	49.3	3.2
Wallis and Futuna Islands - Îles Wallis et Futuna								
1996								
Total	86.0	17.7	93.4	153.8	206.9	99.2	45.9	9.6

FOOTNOTES - NOTES

+ Data tabulated by date of registration rather than occurrence. — Données exploitées selon la date de l'enregistrement et non la date de l'événement.

[1] Rates computed on female population aged 15-49. — Taux calculés sur la base de la population féminine de 15 à 49 ans.
[2] Rates computed on female population aged 15-19. — Taux calculés sur la base de la population féminine de 15 à 19 ans.
[3] Rates computed on female population aged 45-49. — Taux calculés sur la base de la population féminine de 45 à 49 ans.
[4] For 2001, data refer to last twelve months preceding census in August 2001. -Pour 2001, les données se rapportent aux douze mois précédant le recensement d'août 2001.
[5] Excluding live-born infants who died before their birth was registered. -Non compris les enfants nés vivants décédés avant l'enregistrement de leur naissance.
[6] Data for 1997 refer to last twelve months preceding population and housing census of 1997. -Les données pour 1997 se réfèrent au douze mois précédant le recensement de population et de l'habitat de 1997.
[7] Including Canadian residents temporarily in the United States, but excluding United States residents temporarily in Canada. -Y compris les résidents canadiens se trouvant temporairement aux Etats-Unis, mais ne comprenant pas les résidents des Etats-Unis se trouvant temporairement au Canada.
[8] Including births to non-resident mothers. -Y compris les naissances chez des mères non résidentes.
[9] Age classification is based on year of birth of mother rather than the exact age of mother at birth of child. -Le classement selon l'âge est basé sur l'année de naissance de la mère et non sur l'age exacte de la mère au moment de naissance de l'enfant.
[10] Excluding Indian jungle population. -Non compris les Indiens de la jungle.
[11] Excluding infants born alive of less than 28 weeks' gestation, of less than 1 000 grams in weight and 35 centimeters in length, who die within seven days of birth. -Non compris les enfants nés vivants après moins de 28 semaines de gestations, pesant moins de 1 000 grammes, mesurant moins de 35 centimètres et décédés dans les sept jours qui ont suivi leur naissance.
[12] For 2005, data refer to last twelve months preceding census on May 2005. -Pour 2005, les données se rapportent aux douze mois précédant le recensement mai 2005.
[13] Data refer to government controlled areas. -Les données se rapportent aux zones contrôlées par le Gouvernement.
[14] Beginning 1970, including data for East Jerusalem and Israeli residents in certain other territories under occupation by Israeli military forces since 1967. -A partir de 1970, y compris les données pour Jérusalem-Est et les résidents israéliens dans certains autres territoires occupés depuis juin 1967 par les forces armées israéliennes.

[15] For Japanese nationals in Japan only; however, rates computed on population including foreigners except foreign military and civilian personnel and their dependants stationed in the area. - Pour les nationaux japonais au Japon seulement; toutefois, les taux sont calculés sur la base d'une population comprenant les étrangers, mais ne comprenant ni les militaires et agents civils étrangers en poste sur le territoire ni les membres de leur famille les accompagnant.
[16] Excluding alien armed forces, civilian aliens employed by armed forces, and foreign diplomatic personnel and their dependants. -Non compris les militaires étrangers, les civils étrangers employés par les forces armées ni le personnel diplomatique étranger et les membres de leur famille les accompagnant.
[17] Data based on Pakistan Demographic Survey (PDS 2005). - Données extraites de l'enquête démographique effectuée par le Pakistan en 2005.
[18] Excluding data for the Pakistan-held part of Jammu and Kashmir, the final status of which has not yet been determined. -Non compris les données concernant la partie du Jammu et Cachemire occupée par le Pakistan dont le statut définitif n'a pas été déterminé.
[19] For 2004, data refer to last twelve months preceding the census in September 2004. -Pour 2004, les données se rapportent pour la dernière fois à douze mois précédant le recensement septembre 2004.
[20] Excluding Faeroe Islands and Greenland. -Non compris les Iles Féroé et le Gröenland.
[21] Including nationals temporarily outside the country. -Y compris les nationaux se trouvant temporairement hors du pays.
[22] Including armed forces stationed outside the country. -Y compris les militaires nationaux hors du pays.
[23] Births registered within one year of occurrence. -Naissances enregistrées dans l'année qui suit l'événement.
[24] Live births to Maltese parents only; however, rates computed on population including work and resident permit holders and foreigners residing in Malta.- Naissances vivantes aux parents maltais seulement; toutefois, les taux sont calculés sur la base d'une population comprenant les titulaires de permis de travail et de permis de séjour et les étrangers résidant à Malte.
[25] Including residents outside the country if listed in a Netherlands population register. -Y compris les résidents hors du pays, s'ils sont inscrits sur un registre de population néerlandais.
[26] Without data for Kosovo and Metohia. -Sans les données pour le Kosovo and Metohie.
[27] Age classification based on year of birth rather than on completed years of age. -La classification par âge est fondée sur l'année de naissance et non sur l'âge en années révolues.
[28] Data tabulated by date of occurrence for England and Wales, and by date of registration for Northern Ireland and Scotland. -Données exploitées selon la date de l'événement pour l'Angleterre et le pays de Galles, et selon la date de l'enregistrement pour l'Irlande du Nord et l'Ecosse.
[29] Data revised to exclude births in Northern Ireland to non-residents of Northern Ireland. -Données révisées non compris des naissances en Irlande du Nord aux non-résidents de l'Irlande du Nord.

Table 12

Table 12 presents late foetal deaths and late foetal-death ratios by urban/rural residence for as many years as possible between 2001 and 2005.

Description of variables: Late foetal deaths are foetal deaths[i] of 28 or more completed weeks of gestation. Foetal deaths of unknown gestational age are included with those 28 or more weeks.

Statistics on the number of late foetal deaths are obtained from civil registers unless otherwise noted.

The urban/rural classification of late foetal deaths is as provided by each country or area; it is presumed to be based on the national census definitions of urban population that have been set forth at the end of the technical notes for table 6.

Ratio computation: Late foetal-death ratios are the annual number of late foetal deaths per 1 000 live births (as shown in table 9) in the same year. The live-birth base was adopted because it is assumed to be more comparable from one country or area to another than the sum of live births and foetal deaths.

Ratios by urban/rural residence are the annual number of late foetal deaths, in the appropriate urban or rural category, per 1 000 corresponding live births (as shown in table 9). These ratios are calculated by the Statistics Division of the United Nations.

Ratios presented in this table are limited to those for countries or areas and urban/rural areas having at least a total of 30 late foetal deaths in a given year.

Reliability of data: Each country or area is asked to indicate the estimated completeness of the late foetal deaths recorded in its civil register. These national assessments are indicated by the quality codes, C and U that appear in the first column of this table.

C indicates that the data are estimated to be virtually complete, that is, representing at least 90 per cent of the late foetal deaths occurring each year, while U indicates that data are estimated to be incomplete, that is, representing less than 90 per cent of the late foetal deaths occurring each year. The code ... indicates that no information was provided regarding completeness.

Data from civil registers which are reported as incomplete or of unknown completeness (coded U or ...) are considered unreliable. They appear in italics in this table. Ratios are not computed for data so coded.

For more information about the quality of vital statistics data in general, see section 4.2 of the Technical Notes.

Limitations: Statistics on late foetal deaths are subject to the same qualifications as have been set forth for vital statistics in general and foetal-death statistics in particular as discussed in section 4 of the Technical Notes.

The reliability of the data is a very important factor. Of all vital statistics, the registration of foetal deaths is probably the most incomplete.

Variation in the definition of foetal deaths, and in particular late foetal deaths, also limits international comparability. The criterion of 28 or more completed weeks of gestation to distinguish late foetal deaths is not universally used; some countries or areas use different durations of gestation or other criteria such as size of the foetus. In addition, the difficulty of accurately determining gestational age further reduces comparability. However, to promote comparability, late foetal deaths shown in this table are restricted to those of at least 28 or more completed weeks of gestation. Wherever this is not possible a footnote is provided.

Another factor introducing variation in the definition of late foetal deaths is the practice by some countries or areas of including in late foetal-death statistics infants who were born alive but died before the registration of the birth or within the first 24 hours of life, thus overestimating the total number of late foetal deaths. This has also the effect of inflating the late foetal-death ratios unduly by decreasing the birth denominator and increasing the foetal-death numerator. Statistics of this type are footnoted.

In addition, late foetal-death ratios are subject to the limitations of the data on live births with which they have been calculated. These have been set forth in the technical notes for table 9.

Regarding the computation of the ratios, it must be pointed out that when late foetal deaths and live births are both under registered, the resulting ratios may be of reasonable magnitude. For the countries or areas where live-birth registration is poorest, the late foetal-death ratios may be the largest, effectively masking the completeness of the base data. For this reason, possible variations in birth-registration completeness as well as the reported completeness of late foetal deaths must always be borne in mind in evaluating late foetal-death ratios.

In addition to the indirect effect of live-birth under-registration, late foetal-death ratios may be seriously affected by date-of-registration tabulation of live births. When the annual number of live births registered and reported fluctuates over a wide range due to changes in legislation or to special needs for proof of birth on the part of large segments of the population, then the late foetal-death ratios will also fluctuate, but inversely. Because of these effects, data for countries or areas known to tabulate live births by date of registration should be used with caution.

Finally, it may be noted that the counting of live-born infants as late foetal deaths, because they died before the registration of the birth or within the first 24 hours of life, has the effect of inflating the late foetal-death ratios unduly by decreasing the birth denominator and increasing the foetal-death numerator. This factor should not be overlooked in using data from this table.

The comparability of data by urban/rural residence is affected by the national definitions of urban and rural used in tabulating these data. It is assumed, in the absence of specific information to the contrary, that the definitions of urban and rural used in connection with the national population census were also used in the compilation of the vital statistics for each country or area. However, it cannot be excluded that, for a given country or area, different definitions of urban and rural are used for the vital statistics data and the population census data respectively. When known, the definitions of urban used in national population censuses are presented at the end of the technical notes for table 6. As discussed in detail in the technical notes for table 6, these definitions vary considerably from one country or area to another.

Urban/rural differentials in late foetal death ratios may also be affected by whether the late foetal deaths and live births have been tabulated in terms of place of occurrence or place of usual residence. This problem is discussed in more detail in section 4.1.4.1 of the Technical Notes.

Earlier data: Late foetal deaths and late foetal-death ratios have been shown in each issue of the Demographic Yearbook beginning with the 1951 issue. A special topic CD on natality published in 2001 presents the data for all available years from 1990 to 1998. For more information on specific topics, and years for which data are reported, readers should consult the Historical Index.

NOTES

[i] For definition, see section 4.1.1.3 of the Technical Notes.

Tableau 12

Le tableau 12 présente des données sur les morts fœtales tardives et les rapports de mortinatalité selon le lieu de résidence (zone urbaine ou rurale) pour le plus grand nombre d'années possible entre 2001 et 2005.

Description des variables : Par mort fœtale tardive, on entend le décès d'un fœtus[1] survenu après 28 semaines complètes de gestation au moins. Les morts fœtales pour lesquelles la durée de la période de gestation n'est pas connue sont comprises dans cette catégorie.

Sauf indication contraire, les statistiques du nombre de morts fœtales tardives sont établies sur la base des registres de l'état civil.

La classification des morts fœtales tardives selon le lieu de résidence (zone urbaine ou rurale) est celle qui a été communiquée par chaque pays ou zone ; on part du principe qu'elle repose sur les définitions de la population urbaine utilisées pour les recensements nationaux, telles qu'elles sont reproduites à la fin des notes techniques du tableau 6.

Calcul des rapports : Les rapports de mortinatalité représentent le nombre annuel de morts fœtales tardives pour 1 000 naissances vivantes (telles qu'elles sont présentées au tableau 9) survenues pendant la même année. On a pris pour base de calcul les naissances vivantes parce que l'on pense qu'elle sont plus facilement comparables d'un pays ou d'une zone à l'autre que la somme des naissances vivantes et des morts fœtales.

Les rapports selon le lieu de résidence (zone urbaine ou rurale) représentent le nombre annuel de morts fœtales tardives, classées selon la catégorie urbaine ou rurale appropriée pour 1 000 naissances vivantes (telles qu'elles sont présentées au tableau 9) survenues parmi la population correspondante. Ces rapports ont été calculés par la Division de statistique de l'ONU.

Les rapports présentés dans le tableau 12 ne concernent que les pays ou zones où l'on a enregistré un total d'au moins 1 000 morts fœtales tardives pendant une année donnée.

Fiabilité des données : Il a été demandé à chaque pays ou zone d'indiquer le degré estimatif de complétude des données sur les morts fœtales tardives figurant dans ses registres d'état civil. Ces évaluations nationales sont signalées par les codes de qualité 'C', 'U' et '...' qui apparaissent dans la deuxième colonne du tableau.

La lettre 'C' indique que les données sont jugées à peu près complètes, c'est-à-dire qu'elles représentent au moins 90 p. 100 des morts fœtales tardives survenues chaque année ; la lettre 'U' signifie que les données sont jugées incomplètes, c'est-à-dire qu'elles représentent moins de 90 p.100 des morts fœtales tardives survenues chaque année. Le code '...' indique qu'aucun renseignement n'a été communiqué quant à la complétude des données.

Les données provenant des registres de l'état civil qui sont déclarées incomplètes ou dont le degré de complétude n'est pas connu (code 'U' ou '...') sont jugées douteuses. Elles apparaissent en italique dans le tableau ; les rapports, dans ces cas, n'ont pas été calculés.

Pour plus de précisions sur la qualité des données reposant sur les statistiques de l'état civil en général, voir la section 4.2 des Notes techniques.

Insuffisance des données : Les statistiques des morts fœtales tardives appellent toutes les réserves qui ont été formulées à propos des statistiques de l'état civil en général et des statistiques concernant les morts fœtales en particulier (voir la section 4 des Notes techniques).

La fiabilité des données est un facteur très important. Les statistiques concernant les morts fœtales sont probablement les moins complètes de toutes les statistiques de l'état civil.

L'hétérogénéité des définitions de la mort fœtale et, en particulier, de la mort fœtale tardive nuit aussi à la comparabilité internationale des données. Le critère des 28 semaines complètes de gestation au moins n'est pas universellement utilisé ; certains pays ou zones retiennent des critères différents pour la durée de la période de gestation ou d'autres critères tels que la taille du fœtus. De surcroît, la comparabilité est rendue malaisée par le fait qu'il est difficile d'établir avec précision l'âge gestationnel. Pour faciliter les comparaisons, les morts fœtales tardives considérées ici sont exclusivement celles qui sont survenues au terme de 28 semaines de gestation au moins. Les exceptions sont signalées en note.

Un autre facteur d'hétérogénéité dans la définition de la mort fœtale tardive est la pratique de certains pays ou zones qui consiste à inclure dans les statistiques des morts fœtales tardives les enfants nés vivants mais décédés avant l'enregistrement de leur naissance ou dans les 24 heures qui ont suivi la naissance, pratique qui conduit à surestimer le nombre total des morts fœtales tardives. Cela donne aussi des rapports de mortinatalité exagérés parce que le dénominateur (nombre de naissances) se trouve alors diminué et le numérateur (morts fœtales) augmenté. Quand pareil facteur a joué, cela a été signalé en note.

Les rapports de mortinatalité appellent en outre toutes les réserves qui ont été formulées à propos des statistiques des naissances vivantes qui ont servi à leur calcul (voir à ce sujet les notes techniques relatives au tableau 9).

En ce qui concerne le calcul des rapports, il convient de noter que, si l'enregistrement des morts fœtales tardives et celui des naissances vivantes sont loin d'être exhaustifs, les rapports de mortinatalité peuvent être raisonnables. C'est parfois pour les pays ou zones où l'enregistrement des naissances vivantes laisse le plus à désirer que les rapports de mortinatalité sont les plus élevés, ce qui masque le caractère incomplet des données de base. Aussi, pour porter un jugement sur la qualité des rapports de mortinatalité, il ne faut jamais oublier que la complétude de l'enregistrement des naissances comme celle de l'enregistrement des morts fœtales tardives peuvent varier sensiblement.

Hormis les effets indirects des lacunes de l'enregistrement des naissances vivantes, il arrive que les rapports de mortinatalité soient considérablement faussés lorsque l'exploitation des données relatives aux naissances se fait d'après la date de l'enregistrement. Si le nombre des naissances vivantes enregistrées vient à varier notablement d'une année à l'autre par suite de modifications de la législation ou parce que de très nombreuses personnes ont besoin de se procurer une attestation de naissance, les rapports de mortinatalité varient également, mais en sens inverse. Il convient donc d'utiliser avec prudence le données des pays ou zones où les statistiques sont établies d'après la date de l'enregistrement.

Enfin, on notera que l'inclusion parmi les morts fœtales tardives des décès d'enfants nés vivants qui sont décédés avant l'enregistrement de leur naissance ou dans les 24 heures qui ont suivi la naissance conduit à des rapports de mortinatalité exagérés parce que le dénominateur (nombre de naissances) se trouve alors diminué et le numérateur (morts fœtales) augmenté. Il importe de ne pas négliger ce facteur lorsque l'on utilise les données du tableau 12.

La comparabilité des données selon le lieu de résidence (zone urbaine ou rurale) peut être limitée par les définitions nationales des termes « urbain » et « rural » utilisées pour la mise en tableaux de ces données. En l'absence d'indications contraires, on a supposé que les mêmes définitions avaient servi pour le recensement national de la population et pour l'établissement des statistiques de l'état civil pour chaque pays ou zone. Toutefois, il n'est pas exclu que, pour une zone ou un pays donné, des définitions différentes aient été retenues. Les définitions du terme « urbain » utilisées pour les recensements nationaux de population ont été présentées à la fin des notes techniques du tableau 6 lorsqu'elles étaient connues. Comme on l'a précisé dans les notes techniques relatives au tableau 6, ces définitions varient considérablement d'un pays ou d'une zone à l'autre.

La différence entre les rapports de mortinatalité pour les zones urbaines et rurales pourra aussi être faussée selon que les morts fœtales tardives et les naissances vivantes auront été classées d'après le lieu de l'événement ou le lieu de résidence habituel. Ce problème est examiné plus en détail à la section 4.1.4.1 des Notes techniques.

Données publiées antérieurement : Les éditions de l'*Annuaire démographique* parues à partir de 1951 contiennent des statistiques concernant les morts fœtales tardives et les rapports de mortinatalité. Un CD-ROM sur la natalité paru en 2001 présente les données pour toutes les années disponibles de 1990 à 1998. Pour plus de précisions concernant les années et les sujets pour lesquels des données ont été publiées, se reporter à l'index.

---

[1] Pour la définition, voir la section 4.1.1.3 des Notes techniques.

12. Late foetal deaths and late foetal death ratios, by urban/rural residence; 2001 - 2005
Morts foetales tardives et rapports de mortinatalité, selon la résidence, urbaine/rurale: 2001 - 2005

Continent, country or area and urban/rural residence Continent, pays ou zone et résidence, urbaine/rurale	Code[1]	Number - Nombre					Ratio - Rapport				
		2001	2002	2003	2004	2005	2001	2002	2003	2004	2005
AFRICA — AFRIQUE											
Algeria - Algérie											
Total	+C	15 654	17 135	...	...	...	25.3	27.8	...	...	...
Egypt - Égypte											
Total	+U	5 393	4 745	4 605	4 201	4 218	...	...	...	...	...
Urban - Urbaine	+U	4 550	3 842	3 567	3 436	3 549	...	...	...	...	...
Rural - Rurale	+U	843	903	1 038	765	669	...	...	...	...	...
Mauritius - Maurice											
Total	+C	244	203	220	191	185	12.4	10.2	11.4	9.9	9.8
Urban - Urbaine	+C	83	86	79	70	65	10.7	10.8	10.4	9.6	9.1
Rural - Rurale	+C	161	117	141	121	120	13.5	9.7	12.0	10.1	10.3
Réunion											
Total	C	...	...	...	159	170	...	...	...	10.9	11.5
AMERICA, NORTH — AMERIQUE DU NORD											
Bermuda - Bermudes											
Total	C	-	-	...	...	...	...	...	...	...	...
Canada[2]											
Total	C	1 097	1 028	1 027	972	...	3.3	3.1	3.1	2.9	...
Costa Rica											
Total	C	510	465	471	524	503	6.7	6.5	6.5	7.3	7.0
Cuba[3]											
Total	C	1 982	1 983	1 868	1 675	1 642	14.3	14.0	13.7	13.2	13.6
El Salvador											
Total	C	706	617	535	...	...	5.1	4.8	4.3	...	...
Urban - Urbaine	C	611	550	461	...	...	7.3	7.1	6.3	...	...
Rural - Rurale	C	95	67	74	...	...	1.7	1.3	1.4	...	...
Guadeloupe											
Total	C	77	118	151	140	157	10.3	16.9	21.4	19.2	20.8
Guatemala											
Total	C	5 686	5 631	5 318	...	...	13.7	14.5	14.2	...	...
Martinique											
Total	C	60	89	118	98	88	10.2	16.3	21.7	18.6	17.5
Mexico - Mexique[4]											
Total	+U	15 270	14 971	14 513	14 098	13 641	...	...	...	...	...
Urban - Urbaine	+U	11 398	10 951	10 734	10 391	10 101	...	...	...	...	...
Rural - Rurale	+U	3 795	3 696	3 556	3 422	3 385	...	...	...	...	...
Panama[5]											
Total	U	394	...	...	...	...	...	...	...	...	...
Puerto Rico - Porto Rico[4]											
Total	C	584	234	206	...	189	10.4	4.4	4.1	...	3.7
Urban - Urbaine	C	361	138	...	...	...	12.3	...	...	...	...
Rural - Rurale	C	220	90	...	...	...	8.3	...	...	...	...
Saint Lucia - Sainte-Lucie											
Total	C	32	51	36	39		11.5	19.6	14.5	16.8	
Saint Vincent and the Grenadines - Saint Vincent-et-les Grenadines											
Total	+C	18	16	...	...	...	...	...	...	...	...
Turks Caicos Islands - Îles Turques et Caïques[6,7]											
Total	C	1	2	5	1	...	...	...	...	...	...
United States - États-Unis											
Total	C	13 704	13 285	...	...	...	3.4	3.3	...	...	...
AMERICA, SOUTH — AMERIQUE DU SUD											
Argentina - Argentine											
Total	C	4 833	4 850	4 663	3 812	5 048	7.1	7.0	6.7	5.2	7.1
Brazil - Brésil[8]											
Total	U	18 341	...	30 201	28 852	26 257	...	...	...	...	...
Chile - Chili											
Total	C	1 278	1 197	1 404	1 510	...	5.2	5.0	6.0	6.6	...

12. Late foetal deaths and late foetal death ratios, by urban/rural residence; 2001 - 2005
Morts foetales tardives et rapports de mortinatalité, selon la résidence, urbaine/rurale: 2001 - 2005
(continued — suite)

Continent, country or area and urban/rural residence Continent, pays ou zone et résidence, urbaine/rurale	Code[1]	Number - Nombre					Ratio - Rapport				
		2001	2002	2003	2004	2005	2001	2002	2003	2004	2005
AMERICA, SOUTH — AMERIQUE DU SUD											
Chile - Chili											
Urban - Urbaine	C	1 095	1 044	1 220	...	...	5.1	4.9	5.8	...	...
Rural - Rurale	C	183	153	184	...	...	6.1	5.9	7.4	...	...
Colombia - Colombie[4,9]											
Total	...	6 399	6 121	8 542	8 897	10 604	...	...	...	...	...
Urban - Urbaine	...	4 144	3 951	6 119	6 400	7 699	...	...	...	...	...
Rural - Rurale	...	1 678	1 705	1 886	1 798	2 277	...	...	...	...	...
Ecuador - Équateur[10]											
Total	...	2 751	2 685	2 298	2 098	...	...	...	...	...	...
Urban - Urbaine	...	2 384	2 372	1 992	1 879	...	...	...	...	...	...
Rural - Rurale	...	367	313	306	219	...	...	...	...	...	...
French Guiana - Guyane française											
Total	C	51	72	69	60	63	10.0	13.7	12.4	11.3	10.5
Uruguay											
Total	C	...	...	...	458		...	...	...	9.2	
Venezuela (Bolivarian Republic of) - Venezuela (République bolivarienne du)[8]											
Total	...	4 149	3 852	...	...	...	...	...	...	...	...
ASIA — ASIE											
Armenia - Arménie											
Total	C	269	236	289	290	358	8.4	7.3	8.1	7.7	9.5
Urban - Urbaine	C	224	196	227	224	284	11.0	9.4	10.0	9.5	12.0
Rural - Rurale	C	45	40	62	66	74	3.8	3.5	4.7	4.8	5.4
Azerbaijan - Azerbaïdjan											
Total	+C	425	443	431	479	...	3.9	4.0	3.8	3.6	...
Bahrain - Bahreïn											
Total	...	17	19	15	34	35	...	...	...	...	...
China: Hong Kong SAR - Chine: Hong Kong RAS											
Total	...	221	308	189	164	218	...	...	...	...	...
China: Macao SAR - Chine: Macao RAS											
Total	C	8	8	8	4	5	...	...	...	...	...
Georgia - Géorgie											
Total	C	746	726	811	...	...	15.7	15.6	17.6	...	...
Urban - Urbaine	C	...	...	791	...	...	...	...	22.9	...	...
Rural - Rurale	C	...	...	20	...	...	...	...	...	...	...
Israel - Israël[4,11,12,13]											
Total	C	595	549	560	420	...	4.4	3.9	3.9	2.9	...
Urban - Urbaine	C	532	498	503	378	...	4.3	3.9	3.8	2.9	...
Rural - Rurale	C	43	46	53	34	...	3.6	3.6	4.0	2.5	...
Japan - Japon[4,14,15]											
Total	C	2 876	2 850	2 692	2 487	2 401	2.5	2.5	2.4	2.2	2.3
Urban - Urbaine	C	2 342	2 288	2 161	2 057	2 083	2.5	2.4	2.4	2.2	2.3
Rural - Rurale	C	531	561	529	430	318	2.4	2.6	2.6	2.2	2.2
Kazakhstan											
Total	C	1 719	1 748	1 768	1 729	...	7.8	7.7	7.1	6.3	...
Urban - Urbaine	C	1 059	1 050	1 169	1 196	...	9.2	8.6	8.4	7.7	...
Rural - Rurale	C	660	698	599	533	...	6.2	6.6	5.5	4.6	...
Kuwait - Koweït											
Total	C	286	325	307	355	375	6.9	7.5	7.0	7.5	7.4
Kyrgyzstan - Kirghizistan[16]											
Total	C	617	759	879	1 437	1 586	6.3	7.5	8.3	13.1	14.4
Urban - Urbaine	C	335	395	470	962	1 022	11.8	13.1	14.7	25.7	28.7
Rural - Rurale	C	282	364	409	475	564	4.0	5.1	5.6	6.5	7.6
Maldives[17]											
Total	...	53	61	71	...	...	...	...	...	...	...
Urban - Urbaine	...	20	27	28	...	...	...	...	...	...	...
Rural - Rurale	...	33	34	43	...	...	...	...	...	...	...

12. Late foetal deaths and late foetal death ratios, by urban/rural residence; 2001 - 2005
Morts foetales tardives et rapports de mortinatalité, selon la résidence, urbaine/rurale: 2001 - 2005
(continued — suite)

Continent, country or area and urban/rural residence / Continent, pays ou zone et résidence, urbaine/rurale	Code[1]	Number - Nombre					Ratio - Rapport				
		2001	2002	2003	2004	2005	2001	2002	2003	2004	2005
ASIA — ASIE											
Oman[18]											
Total	U	365	376	381	346	387	...	...	...	...	...
Philippines											
Total	...	4 765	4 645	4 386	...	...	...	...	...	...	...
Qatar											
Total	C	75	62	81	64	97	6.2	5.1	6.3	4.9	7.2
Singapore - Singapour											
Total	+C	107	114	95	115	102	2.6	2.8	2.5	3.1	2.7
Tajikistan - Tadjikistan											
Total	C	1 057	1 096	1 043	...	...	6.2	6.2	5.9	...	...
Urban - Urbaine	C	915	940	899	...	...	20.1	22.0	19.9	...	...
Rural - Rurale	C	142	156	144	...	...	1.1	1.2	1.1	...	...
Uzbekistan - Ouzbékistan											
Total	C	2 902	...	...	...	...	5.7	...	...	...	...
Urban - Urbaine	C	1 138	...	...	...	...	7.1	...	...	...	...
Rural - Rurale	C	1 764	...	...	...	...	5.0	...	...	...	...
EUROPE											
Andorra - Andorre											
Total	C	1	-	3	5	...	...	...	...	...	...
Austria - Autriche											
Total	C	278	338	307	313	289	3.7	4.3	4.0	4.0	3.7
Belgium - Belgique											
Total	C	583	...	493	437	442	5.1	...	4.4	3.8	3.8
Bosnia and Herzegovina - Bosnie-Herzégovine											
Total	C	193	138	150	168	147	5.1	3.9	4.3	4.8	4.2
Bulgaria - Bulgarie											
Total	C	500	539	549	...	565	7.3	8.1	8.2	...	7.9
Urban - Urbaine	C	246	323	348	...	363	5.1	6.8	7.2	...	6.9
Rural - Rurale	C	254	216	201	...	202	13.0	11.5	10.7	...	10.7
Croatia - Croatie[19]											
Total	C	216	189	180	179	186	5.3	4.7	4.5	4.4	4.4
Urban - Urbaine	C	111	108	94	107	105	4.8	4.8	4.3	4.8	4.5
Rural - Rurale	C	105	81	86	72	81	5.8	4.6	4.8	4.0	4.2
Czech Republic - République tchèque											
Total	C	263	261	272	265	287	2.9	2.7	2.9	2.7	2.8
Urban - Urbaine	C	200	207	209	238	195	3.0	2.8	3.0	3.3	2.6
Rural - Rurale	C	63	54	63	27	92	2.7	2.2	2.6	...	3.5
Denmark - Danemark											
Total	C	277	224	239	316	...	4.2	3.5	3.7	4.9	...
Estonia - Estonie											
Total	C	63	74	63	63	88	5.0	5.7	4.8	4.5	6.1
Urban - Urbaine	C	42	47	45	49	60	4.9	5.3	5.0	5.0	5.9
Rural - Rurale	C	21	27	18	14	28	...	...	...	...	...
Finland - Finlande[20]											
Total	C	185	134	133	117	113	3.3	2.4	2.3	2.0	2.0
Urban - Urbaine	C	94	82	84	73	77	2.6	2.3	2.3	1.9	2.0
Rural - Rurale	C	91	52	49	44	36	4.6	2.7	2.5	2.2	1.8
France[21,22,23]											
Total	C	3 741	6 259	6 862	7 054	6 964	4.9	8.2	9.0	9.2	9.0
Urban - Urbaine	C	2 959	4 840	5 309	5 469	5 370	5.1	8.4	9.2	9.5	9.2
Rural - Rurale	C	754	1 373	1 477	1 510	1 518	4.1	7.5	8.0	8.0	7.9
Germany - Allemagne											
Total	C	2 881	2 700	2 699	2 728	2 487	3.9	3.8	3.8	3.9	3.6
Greece - Grèce											
Total	C	588	...	504	...	421	5.7	...	4.8	...	3.9
Urban - Urbaine	C	...	...	...	...	293	...	...	...	...	4.0
Rural - Rurale	C	...	...	...	...	128	...	...	...	...	3.8
Hungary - Hongrie[4,24]											
Total	C	550	523	530	476	506	5.7	5.4	5.6	5.0	5.2
Urban - Urbaine	C	304	306	291	268	305	5.1	5.0	4.9	4.4	4.8

12. Late foetal deaths and late foetal death ratios, by urban/rural residence; 2001 - 2005
Morts foetales tardives et rapports de mortinatalité, selon la résidence, urbaine/rurale: 2001 - 2005
(continued — suite)

Continent, country or area and urban/rural residence Continent, pays ou zone et résidence, urbaine/rurale	Code[1]	Number - Nombre					Ratio - Rapport				
		2001	2002	2003	2004	2005	2001	2002	2003	2004	2005
EUROPE											
Hungary - Hongrie[4,24]											
Rural - Rurale	C	244	208	237	208	201	6.6	5.9	6.9	6.1	6.1
Iceland - Islande											
Total	C	10	7	4	15	8	...	...	...	...	...
Urban - Urbaine	C	9	7	4	...	7	...	...	...	...	...
Rural - Rurale	C	1	-	-	...	1	...	...	...	...	...
Ireland - Irlande											
Total	+C	259	274	258	...	...	4.5	4.5	4.2	...	...
Italy - Italie[17]											
Total	C	...	1 721	1 702	...	...	...	3.2	3.1	...	...
Latvia - Lettonie											
Total	C	138	130	130	136	132	7.0	6.5	6.2	6.7	6.1
Urban - Urbaine	C	88	108	76	90	79	7.0	8.3	5.5	6.5	5.4
Rural - Rurale	C	50	68	54	46	53	7.0	9.6	7.6	7.1	7.7
Lithuania - Lituanie[25]											
Total	C	167	193	168	150	152	5.3	6.4	5.5	4.9	5.0
Urban - Urbaine	C	90	125	106	81	86	4.6	6.7	5.5	4.2	4.3
Rural - Rurale	C	77	68	62	69	66	6.5	6.0	5.4	6.3	6.2
Luxembourg											
Total	C	23	20	17	16	21	...	...	...	...	...
Malta - Malte											
Total	C	...	...	18	15	8	...	...	...	...	...
Netherlands - Pays-Bas											
Total	C	...	945	928	795	760	...	4.7	4.6	4.1	4.0
Urban - Urbaine	C	...	617	631	527	517	...	4.6	4.8	4.0	4.0
Rural - Rurale	C	...	328	297	268	243	...	4.7	4.4	4.2	4.1
Norway - Norvège											
Total	C	241	197	213	210	182	4.3	3.6	3.8	3.7	3.2
Poland - Pologne											
Total	C	1 574	1 372	1 322	1 342	1 283	4.3	3.9	3.8	3.8	3.5
Urban - Urbaine	C	797	703	687	715	687	3.9	3.6	3.4	3.5	3.3
Rural - Rurale	C	777	669	635	627	596	4.8	4.3	4.2	4.1	3.9
Portugal											
Total	C	390	388	349	293	...	3.5	3.4	3.1	2.7	...
Romania - Roumanie											
Total	C	1 282	1 319	1 290	...	1 262	5.8	6.3	6.1	...	5.7
Urban - Urbaine	C	567	602	569	...	589	5.5	6.1	5.6	...	5.0
Rural - Rurale	C	715	717	721	...	673	6.1	6.4	6.5	...	6.5
Russian Federation - Fédération de Russie											
Total	C	8 711	8 998	9 043	8 745	...	6.6	6.4	6.1	5.8	...
Urban - Urbaine	C	6 416	6 687	6 624	6 416	...	6.9	6.7	6.3	6.0	...
Rural - Rurale	C	2 295	2 311	2 419	2 329	...	6.0	5.8	5.7	5.4	...
San Marino - Saint-Marin											
Total	+C	1	-	2	-	...	...	...	...	...	...
Serbia and Montenegro - Serbie-et-Monténégro[26]											
Total	C	741	479	453	431	...	5.7	5.5	5.2	4.9	...
Urban - Urbaine	C	415	308	286	...	...	6.0	5.7	5.3	...	...
Rural - Rurale	C	356	171	167	...	...	5.9	5.3	5.0	...	...
Slovakia - Slovaquie											
Total	C	207	194	217	211	195	4.0	3.8	4.2	3.9	3.6
Urban - Urbaine	C	100	95	114	92	93	3.8	3.6	4.3	3.2	3.2
Rural - Rurale	C	107	99	103	119	102	4.3	4.0	4.1	4.7	4.0
Slovenia - Slovénie											
Total	C	85	93	94	62	76	4.9	5.3	5.4	3.5	4.2
Urban - Urbaine	C	38	43	45	32	...	4.7	5.1	5.3	3.7	...
Rural - Rurale	C	46	50	49	30	...	4.9	5.5	5.5	3.3	...
Spain - Espagne											
Total	C	1 541	1 470	1 494	1 438	1 546	3.8	3.5	3.4	3.2	3.3
Sweden - Suède											
Total	C	349	352	359	333	301	3.8	3.7	3.6	3.3	3.0
Switzerland - Suisse											
Total	C	279	255	306	276	307	3.8	3.5	4.3	3.8	4.2

12. Late foetal deaths and late foetal death ratios, by urban/rural residence; 2001 - 2005
Morts foetales tardives et rapports de mortinatalité, selon la résidence, urbaine/rurale: 2001 - 2005
(continued — suite)

Continent, country or area and urban/rural residence — Continent, pays ou zone et résidence, urbaine/rurale	Code[1]	Number - Nombre					Ratio - Rapport				
		2001	2002	2003	2004	2005	2001	2002	2003	2004	2005
EUROPE											
Switzerland - Suisse											
Urban - Urbaine	C	176	186	232	206	210	3.6	3.5	4.4	3.8	3.9
Rural - Rurale	C	103	69	74	70	97	4.3	3.5	3.9	3.6	5.1
The Former Yugoslav Rep. of Macedonia - L'ex-République yougoslave de Macédoine											
Total	C	284	291	232	258	215	10.5	10.5	8.6	11.0	9.6
Urban - Urbaine	C	182	187	...	...	102	12.3	12.5	...	...	8.1
Rural - Rurale	C	102	104	...	...	113	8.3	8.1	...	...	11.3
Ukraine											
Total	C	1 830	1 837	1 969	1 986	...	4.9	4.7	4.8	4.6	...
Urban - Urbaine	C	1 214	1 270	1 361	1 398	...	5.1	5.1	5.1	4.9	...
Rural - Rurale	C	616	567	608	588	...	4.4	4.0	4.3	4.1	...
United Kingdom - Royaume-Uni											
Total	C	3 572	3 772	3 989	3 962	...	5.3	5.6	5.7	5.5	...
OCEANIA — OCEANIE											
Australia - Australie[9,27]											
Total	+C	778	728	759	732	757	3.2	2.9	3.0	2.9	2.9
Urban - Urbaine	+C	433	472	504	439	513	2.9	2.9	3.0	2.6	2.9
Rural - Rurale	+C	345	256	255	293	244	3.5	3.0	3.0	3.5	2.9
French Polynesia - Polynésie française											
Total	C	31	17	35	...	...	6.4	...	7.8	...	...
New Caledonia - Nouvelle-Calédonie											
Total	+C	36	30	25	...	...	8.3	7.2	...	...	...
New Zealand - Nouvelle-Zélande[28]											
Total	+C	157	167	169	228	174	2.8	3.1	3.0	3.9	3.0
Urban - Urbaine	+C	138	150	150	210	156	2.8	3.2	3.1	4.1	3.1
Rural - Rurale	+C	19	17	19	18	18	...	...	...	...	...
Palau - Palaos											
Total	C	47	2	2	18	5	156.7	...	...	...	...
Papua New Guinea - Papouasie-Nouvelle-Guinée											
Total	U	*922*	*1 080*	*991*	...	...	...	...	...	...	...

FOOTNOTES - NOTES

Italics: data from civil registers which are incomplete or of unknown completeness. — *Italiques:* données incomplètes ou dont le degré d'exactitude n'est pas connu, provenant des registres de l'état civil.

[1] 'Code' indicates the source of data, as follows:
C - Civil registration, estimated over 90% complete
U - Civil registration, estimated less than 90% complete
| - Other source, estimated reliable
+ - Data tabulated by date of registration rather than occurence.
... - Information not available

Le 'Code' indique la source des données, comme suit:
C - Registres de l'état civil considérés complèts à 90 p. 100 au moins.
U - Registres de l'état civil qui ne sont pas considérés complèts à 90 p. 100 au moins.
| - Autre source, considérée pas douteuses.
+ - Données exploitées selon la date de l'enregistrement et non la date de l'événement.
... - Information pas disponible.

[2] Including Canadian residents temporarily in the United States, but excluding United States residents temporarily in Canada. -Y compris les résidents canadiens se trouvant temporairement aux Etats-Unis, mais ne comprenant pas les résidents des Etats-Unis se trouvant temporairement au Canada.

[3] Late foetal death is indicated by the fact that the foetus is at least 500 grams or more in weight. -Les décès foetaux tardifs sont caractérisés par le fait que le foetus pèse au moins 500 grammes

[4] Figures for urban and rural areas do not add up to the total, since they do not include the category 'Unknown residence'. -La somme des données pour la residence urbaine et rurale n'est pas égale au total parce qu'elle n'inclue pas la catégorie 'Residence inconnue'.

[5] Excluding tribal Indian population. -Non compris les Indiens vivant en tribus.

[6] Includes some underreporting of foetal deaths especially among those under 28 weeks gestational age. -Des décès intra-utérins n'ont sans doute pas été déclarés, surtout parmi ceux qui sont survenus à moins de 28 semaines de gestation.

[7] For 2003, two of the 5 still births are to non Turks and Caicos nationals. -Pour 2003, deux des cinq mortinaissances concernent des personnes qui n'étaient pas ressortissantes des Îles Turques et Caïques.

[8] Excluding Indian jungle population. -Non compris les Indiens de la jungle.

[9] Data include unknown gestational weeks. -Les données comprennnent les cas où le nombre de semaines de gestation n'est pas connu.

[10] Excluding nomadic Indian tribes. -Non compris les tribus d'Indiens nomades.

[11] Including data for East Jerusalem and Israeli residents in certain other

territories under occupation by Israeli military forces since June 1967. -Y compris les données pour Jérusalem-Est et les résidents israéliens dans certains autres territoires occupés depuis 1967 par les forces armées israéliennes.

[12] For 2001 and 2004, data include 8 foetal deaths of unknown gestational age and weight over 1000 grams. -Pour 2001 et 2004, y compris huit décès intra-utérins pour lesquels l'âge gestationnel est inconnu et le poids est supérieur à 1 000 grammes.

[13] For 2002, data include 9 foetal deaths of unknown gestational age and weight over 1000 grams. -Pour 2002, y compris neuf décès intra-utérins pour lesquels l'âge gestationnel est inconnu et le poids est supérieur à 1 000 grammes.

[14] Data refer to Japanese nationals in Japan only. -Les données se raportent aux nationaux japonais au Japon seulement.

[15] Data exclude the unknown duration of pregnancy. -Exception faite des grossesses dont la durée n'est pas connue.

[16] Since 2004, WHO criteria have been adopted in the country. -Depuis 2004, le pays a adopté les critères de l'OMS.

[17] Data refer to total foetal deaths. -Y compris toutes les morts foetales.

[18] Data refer to the recorded events in Ministry of Health hospitals and health centres only. -Les données se rapportent aux faits d'état civil enregistrés dans les hôpitaux et les dispensaires du Ministère de la santé seulement.

[19] From 2001 a late foetal death (stillbirth) is considered a death of foetus of at least 22 completed weeks of gestation as well as more than 500 grams of weight. -Depuis 2001, pour qu'il y ait mort fœtale tardive (mort né), il faut que le décès d'un fœtus survienne après 22 semaines complètes de gestation au moins et que le fœtus ait atteint un poids de 500 grammes.

[20] Including nationals temporarily outside the country. -Y compris les nationaux se trouvant temporairement hors du pays.

[21] Foetal deaths after at least 180 days (6 calendar months or 26 weeks) of gestation. -Morts foetales survenues après 180 jours (6 mois civils ou 26 semaines) au moins de gestation.

[22] The difference between 'Total' and the sum of 'urban' and 'rural' is due to the cases of unknown place of residence or residence abroad. -La différence entre le 'Total' et la somme des données selon la résidence urbaine/rurale se rapporte à la situation ou on ignore la résidence ou si la résidence est à l'étranger.

[23] The strong increase in still births number is due to a legislative change: according to a circular of November 2001, a still birth bulletin is now drawn up after 22 weeks of amenorrhea or for a 500 g weight. These new criteria take the place of the 180 days of gestation, existing in the registry declaration. -La forte évolution du nombre d'enfants sans vie est liée à un changement législatif: selon une circulaire de novembre 2001, un acte d'enfant sans vie correspond désormais au terme de vingt-deux semaines d'aménorrhée ou à un poids de 500 grammes. Ces critères se substituent au délai de 180 jours de gestation prévu dans l'état civil.

[24] Late foetal death is indicated by the fact that the foetus is at least 24 (it has been 28 weeks until 1996) completed weeks of gestational and does not show any sign of life after the separation from its mother; the foetus has to be 30 cm or more in length or 500 grams or more in weight if its gestational age cannot be determined. -Pour qu'il y ait mort foetale tardive, il faut que le décès d'un foetus survienne après 24 semaines complètes de gestation au moins (28 semaines jusqu'en 1996), que le foetus n'ait pas donné signe de vie après avoir été séparé de la mère, qu'il mesure 30 centimètres au moins ou pèse 500 grammes si la durée de la période de gestation n'est pas connue.

[25] Late foetal death is defined as an infant born without any signs of life, weighing at least 500 grams, after during of pregnancy of at least 22 weeks. -On dit qu'il y a mort intra-utérine tardive lorsqu'un enfant pesant au minimum 500 grammes naît sans donner aucun signe de vie au terme d'une grossesse qui a duré au moins 22 semaines.

[26] From 2002, without data for Kosovo and Metohia. -Après 2002, sans les données pour le Kosovo and Metohie.

[27] Where the sex is indeterminate the death is coded to 'Males'. -Lorsque le sexe n'est pas connu, le décès est porté dans la catégorie « Hommes ».

[28] For resident population only. -Pour la population résidante seulement.

Table 13

Table 13 presents legally induced abortions for as many years as possible between 1996 and 2005.

Description of variables: There are two major categories of abortion: spontaneous and induced. Induced abortions are those initiated by deliberate action undertaken with the intention of terminating pregnancy; all other abortions are considered spontaneous.

The induction of abortion is subject to governmental regulation in most, if not all, countries or areas. This regulation varies from complete prohibition in some countries or areas to abortion on request, with services provided by governmental health authorities, in others. More generally, governments have attempted to define the conditions under which a pregnancy may lawfully be terminated and have established procedures for authorizing abortion in individual cases.

In an effort to provide more complete interpretation of these statistics, countries or areas providing data on legally induced abortions have been requested to communicate grounds for legally induced abortions in their country or area. This information is presented in table 13-1 below.

Reliability of data: Unlike data on live births and foetal deaths, which are generally collected through systems of vital registration, data on abortion are collected from a variety of sources. Because of this, the quality specification, showing the completeness of civil registers, which is presented for other tables, does not appear here.

Limitations: With regard to the collection of information on abortions, a variety of sources are used, but hospital records are the most common source of information. This implies that most cases that have no contact with hospitals are missed. Data from other sources are probably also incomplete. The data in the present table are limited to legally induced abortions, which, by their nature, might be assumed to be more complete than data on all induced abortions.

Earlier data: Legally induced abortions have been shown previously in all issues of the *Demographic Yearbook* since the 1971 issue.

13-1 Grounds for legally induced abortions

Country	Grounds for abortion					
	(a) Continuation of pregnancy would involve risk to the life of the pregnant woman greater than if the pregnancy were terminated.	(b) Continuation of pregnancy would involve risk of injury to the physical health of the pregnant woman greater than if the pregnancy were terminated.	(c) Continuation of pregnancy would involve risk of injury to the mental health of the pregnant woman greater than if the pregnancy were terminated.	(d) Continuation of pregnancy would involve risk of injury to the mental or physical health of any existing children of the family greater than if the pregnancy were terminated.	(e) There is a substantial risk that if the child were born it would suffer from such physical or mental abnormalities as to be seriously handicapped.	(f) Other
Canada	x	x	x			
Mexico		x				
China Hong Kong SAR	x	x	x	x	x	
Israel	x	x	x		x	x
Japan	x	x				x
Singapore	x	x	x	x	x	x
Czech Rep.	x	x	x		x	
Denmark	x	x	x	x	x	
Estonia	x	x	x	x	x	
Finland	x	x	x		x	x

Country	Grounds for abortion					
	(a) Continuation of pregnancy would involve risk to the life of the pregnant woman greater than if the pregnancy were terminated.	(b) Continuation of pregnancy would involve risk of injury to the physical health of the pregnant woman greater than if the pregnancy were terminated.	(c) Continuation of pregnancy would involve risk of injury to the mental health of the pregnant woman greater than if the pregnancy were terminated.	(d) Continuation of pregnancy would involve risk of injury to the mental or physical health of any existing children of the family greater than if the pregnancy were terminated.	(e) There is a substantial risk that if the child were born it would suffer from such physical or mental abnormalities as to be seriously handicapped.	(f) Other
Germany	x	x	x			x
Greece	x	x	x	x	x	
Hungary	x	x	x	x	x	
Iceland	x	x	x	x	x	x
Italy	x	x	x		x	
Latvia	x	x	x			
Lithuania						x
Netherlands	x	x	x		x	
Norway	x	x	x	x	x	x
Poland	x	x			x	x
Republic of Moldova	x	x	x	x	x	
United Kingdom	x	x	x	x	x	
New Zealand	x	x	x		x	x

Tableau 13

Ce tableau présente des données relatives aux avortements provoqués légalement, pour le plus grand nombre d'années possible entre 1996 et 2005.

Description des variables : L'avortement peut être spontané ou provoqué. L'avortement provoqué est celui qui résulte de manœuvres délibérées, entreprises afin d'interrompre la grossesse ; tous les autres avortements sont considérés comme spontanés.

L'interruption délibérée de la grossesse fait l'objet d'une réglementation officielle dans la plupart des pays ou zones, sinon dans tous. Cette réglementation va de l'interdiction totale à l'autorisation de l'avortement sur demande, pratiqué par des services de santé publique. Le plus souvent, les gouvernements se sont efforcés de définir les circonstances dans lesquelles la grossesse peut être interrompue licitement et de fixer une procédure d'autorisation.

Dans un effort de fournir une interprétation plus complète de ces statistiques, les pays ou les zones fournissant des données sur des avortements légalement induits ont été demandés pour communiquer des raisons pour des avortements légalement induits dans leur pays ou zone. Cette information est présentée dans le tableau 13-1 ci-dessous.

Fiabilité des données : À la différence des données sur les naissances vivantes et les morts fœtales, qui proviennent généralement des registres d'état civil, les données sur l'avortement sont tirées de sources diverses. Aussi ne trouve-t-on pas ici une évaluation de la qualité des données semblable à celle qui indique, pour les autres tableaux, le degré d'exhaustivité des données de l'état civil.

Insuffisance des données : En ce qui concerne les renseignements sur l'avortement, un grand nombre de sources sont utilisées, les relevés hospitaliers restant cependant la source la plus commune. Il s'ensuit que la plupart des cas qui ne passent pas par les hôpitaux sont ignorés. Il faut aussi tenir compte du fait que les données provenant d'autres sources sont probablement incomplètes. Les données du tableau 13 se limitent aux avortements provoqués pour raisons légales dont on peut supposer, en raison de leur nature même, que les statistiques sont plus complètes que les données concernant l'ensemble des avortements provoqués.

Données publiées antérieurement : Des statistiques concernant les avortements provoqués pour raisons légales sont publiées dans *l'Annuaire démographique* depuis 1971.

13-1 Motifs d'autorisation pour avortements provoqués légalement

Pays ou zone	Motifs d'autorisation					
	(a) La non-interruption de la grossesse comporterait, pour la vie de la femme enceinte, un risque plus grave que celui de l'avortement.	(b) La non-interruption de la grossesse comporterait, pour la santé physique de la femme enceinte, un risque plus grave que celui de l'avortement.	(c) La non-interruption de la grossesse comporterait, pour la santé mentale de la femme, un risque plus grave que celui de l'avortement.	(d) La non-interruption de la grossesse comporterait, pour la santé mentale ou physique d'un enfant déjà né dans la famille, un risque plus grave que celui de l'avortement.	(e) L'enfant né à terme courrait un risque important de souffrir d'anomalies physiques ou mentales entraînant pour lui un grave handicap.	(f) Autres motifs.
Canada	x	x	x			
Mexique		x				
Chine: Hong Kong RAS	x	x	x	x	x	
Israël	x	x	x		x	x
Japon	x	x				x
Singapour	x	x	x	x	x	x
République tchèque	x	x	x		x	

Pays ou zone	Motifs d'autorisation					
	(a) La non-interruption de la grossesse comporterait, pour la vie de la femme enceinte, un risque plus grave que celui de l'avortement.	(b) La non-interruption de la grossesse comporterait, pour la santé physique de la femme enceinte, un risque plus grave que celui de l'avortement.	(c) La non-interruption de la grossesse comporterait, pour la santé mentale de la femme, un risque plus grave que celui de l'avortement.	(d) La non-interruption de la grossesse comporterait, pour la santé mentale ou physique d'un enfant déjà né dans la famille, un risque plus grave que celui de l'avortement.	(e) L'enfant né à terme courrait un risque important de souffrir d'anomalies physiques ou mentales entraînant pour lui un grave handicap.	(f) Autres motifs.
Danemark	x	x	x	x	x	
Estonie	x	x	x	x	x	
Finlande	x	x	x		x	x
Allemagne	x	x	x			x
Grèce	x	x	x	x	x	
Hongrie	x	x	x	x	x	
Islande	x	x	x	x	x	x
Italie	x	x	x		x	x
Lettonie	x	x	x		x	
Lituanie						x
Pays-Bas	x	x	x		x	
Norvège	x	x	x	x	x	x
Pologne	x	x			x	x
République de Moldova	x	x	x	x	x	
Royaume-Uni	x	x	x	x	x	
Nouvelle Zélande	x	x	x		x	x

13. Legally induced abortions: 1996 - 2005
Avortements provoqués légalement: 1996 - 2005

Continent and country or area Continent et pays ou zone	Number - Nombre									
	1996	1997	1998	1999	2000	2001	2002	2003	2004	2005
AFRICA — AFRIQUE										
Réunion	4 567	4 729	4 652	4 522	4 404	4 339	4 385	...	...	...
Seychelles	...	...	...	536	495	461	460	440	...	...
South Africa - Afrique du Sud[1]	...	...	28 978	...	...	...	...	...	...	...
AMERICA, NORTH — AMERIQUE DU NORD										
Anguilla	...	...	...	...	...	...	...	24	...	...
Canada	111 659	111 709	110 331	105 666	105 427	106 418	105 154	103 768	...	...
Costa Rica	9 009	8 705	8 850	9 160	9 711	8 220	8 332	8 967	8 074	7 974
Cuba	83 827	80 097	75 109	80 037	76 293	69 563	70 823	65 628	67 277	62 530
Dominican Republic - République dominicaine	20 852	22 911	31 068	...	...	20 187	28 091	24 899	26 438	29 167
Greenland - Groenland	862	843	915	842	944	809	821	869	...	...
Mexico - Mexique[2]	540	561	596	614	541	574	593	676	752	735
Panama[3]	...	...	...	...	11	...	...	...	...	...
Puerto Rico - Porto Rico	...	...	...	...	...	1 229	...	7 781	9 215	6 713
Turks Caicos Islands - Îles Turques et Caïques[4]	...	...	...	...	...	...	39	32	43	32
ASIA — ASIE										
Armenia - Arménie	31 323	25 266	18 286	14 403	11 769	10 419	9 372	10 290	10 487	10 925
Azerbaijan - Azerbaïdjan	28 375	25 182	24 914	20 878	17 501	18 332	16 606	16 903	19 798	...
Bahrain - Bahreïn	...	1 592	1 680	1 658	1 655	1 747	1 749	...	...	...
China: Hong Kong SAR - Chine: Hong Kong RAS	25 041	23 939	22 086	20 891	21 375	20 235	18 651	17 420	15 880	14 190
Israel - Israël[5,6]	17 447	19 210	18 500	18 372	18 689	19 131	19 126	19 671	19 712	18 806
Japan - Japon[7]	338 867	337 799	333 220	337 288	341 146	341 588	329 326	319 831	301 673	289 127
Kazakhstan	193 462	156 222	148 799	137 808	...	...	...	...	...	...
Kyrgyzstan - Kirghizistan	34 113	31 598	28 090	25 790	22 044	23 390	18 995	19 225	19 984	20 035
Mongolia - Mongolie	15 588	12 870	...	...	...	...	...	...	...	...
Qatar	76	97	71	124	177	127	121	131	172	169
Singapore - Singapour	14 362	13 827	13 838	13 753	13 734	13 140	12 749	12 272	12 070	11 482
Tajikistan - Tadjikistan	...	...	...	21 234	22 066	19 087	21 104	18 822	20 500	19 400
Uzbekistan - Ouzbékistan	104 620	...	...	...	...	...	...	...	...	...
EUROPE										
Albania - Albanie	32 538	22 103	18 944	19 930	21 004	17 125	17 500	12 087	10 517	9 403
Belarus - Bélarus	174 098	152 660	145 339	135 824	121 895	101 402	89 895	80 174	71 700	64 655
Belgium - Belgique	...	...	11 999	12 734	13 762	14 775	14 791	15 595	...	...
Bulgaria - Bulgarie	98 566	87 896	79 842	72 382	61 378	51 165	50 824	48 035	47 223	41 795
Channel Islands: Guernsey - Îles Anglo-Normandes: Guernesey	...	57	104	92	89	...	...	...	...	...
Croatia - Croatie	12 339	10 036	8 907	8 064	7 534	6 574	6 191	5 923	5 232	4 563
Czech Republic - République tchèque	48 086	45 022	42 959	39 382	34 623	32 528	31 142	29 298	27 574	26 453
Denmark - Danemark[8]	18 135	17 152	16 592	16 271	15 681	15 315	14 991	15 622	14 674	15 103
Estonia - Estonie[9]	16 887	16 615	15 798	14 503	12 743	11 653	10 834	10 619	10 074	9 610
Faeroe Islands - Îles Féroé	48	38	59	47	49	42	49	37	44	29
Finland - Finlande	10 423	10 250	10 751	10 837	10 932	10 738	10 974	10 767	11 162	10 969
France[10]	186 752	188 477	195 368	196 295	...	201 434	204 931	202 594	209 907	...
Germany - Allemagne	130 899	130 890	131 795	130 471	134 609	134 964	130 387	123 030	129 650	124 023
Greece - Grèce	12 542	12 853	11 838	11 824	18 015	22 223	16 173	15 782	...	...
Hungary - Hongrie	76 600	74 564	68 971	65 981	59 249	56 404	56 075	53 789	52 539	48 689
Iceland - Islande	854	921	...	935	987	984	926	951	...	...
Italy - Italie	138 925	140 166	138 354	138 708	...	132 073	131 039	124 118	...	...
Latvia - Lettonie	24 227	21 768	19 964	18 031	17 240	15 647	14 685	14 508	13 723	12 785
Lithuania - Lituanie[11]	27 832	22 680	21 022	18 846	16 259	13 677	12 495	11 513	10 644	9 972
Netherlands - Pays-Bas	22 441	...	24 141	...	...	...	...	...	...	...
Norway - Norvège	...	...	14 028	14 251	14 635	13 887	13 557	13 888	14 071	13 989
Poland - Pologne[12,13]	491	3 171	312	151	138	123	159	174	199	225
Republic of Moldova - République de Moldova	46 010	...	31 293	27 908	20 395	16 028	15 739	17 551	17 965	16 642
Romania - Roumanie	456 221	347 126	271 496	259 888	257 865	254 855	247 608	224 807	191 038	163 459
Russian Federation - Fédération de Russie	...	...	...	...	...	...	...	...	1 797 567	...

13. Legally induced abortions: 1996 - 2005
Avortements provoqués légalement: 1996 - 2005 (continued — suite)

Continent and country or area	Number - Nombre									
Continent et pays ou zone	1996	1997	1998	1999	2000	2001	2002	2003	2004	2005

EUROPE

Serbia and Montenegro - Serbie-et-Montenegro	83 577	64 099	58 739	...	...	...	17 382	16 222	15 307	...
Slovakia - Slovaquie	...	...	21 109	19 949	...	18 026				14 427
Slovenia - Slovénie	10 218	9 712	9 116	8 707	8 429	7 799	7 327	6 873	6 403	5 851
Spain - Espagne	51 002	46 902	53 847	58 399	63 756	69 857	77 125	79 788	84 985	91 664
Sweden - Suède	32 117	31 433	31 008	30 712	30 980	31 772	33 365	34 473	34 454	34 978
The Former Yugoslav Rep. of Macedonia - L'ex-République yougoslave de Macédoine	...	12 028	...	...	...	...	...	...	...	...
Ukraine	687 035	596 740	525 329	495 760	434 223	369 750	345 367	315 835	289 065	263 590
United Kingdom - Royaume-Uni[14]	189 473	191 855	199 887	195 394	197 366	197 913	...	...	...	...

OCEANIA — OCEANIE

New Caledonia - Nouvelle-Calédonie	...	1 528	1 466	...	...	...	...	...	...	...
New Zealand - Nouvelle-Zélande	14 805	15 208	15 029	15 501	16 103	16 410	17 380	18 511	18 211	17 531

FOOTNOTES - NOTES

* Provisional. — Données provisoires.

[1] Data refer to both 1997 and 1998. -Les données se rapportent à 1997 et à 1998.

[2] Data refer to 'Therapeutic Abortions'. According to the Mexican law, only the induced abortions, prescribed by medical reasons and induced because of pregnancy coming from sexual agression, are considered as legal. -Les données se rapportent aux « interruptions volontaires de grossesse pour des motifs thérapeutiques ». D'après la loi mexicaine, seuls sont considérés légaux les avortements déclenchés pour des raisons médicales ou parce que la grossesse est le résultat d'une agression sexuelle.

[3] Data refer to abortions granted for medical reasons by the Comision Multidisciplinaria Nacional de Aborto Terapéutico. -Les données se réfèrent aux avortements autorisés pour des raisons médicales par la Comision Multidisciplinaria Nacional de Aborto Terapéutico.

[4] For abortions performed in hospitals at Grand Turk and Providenciales. -Pour des avortements exécutés dans les hôpitaux dans Grand Turk et Providenciales.

[5] Including data for East Jerusalem and Israeli residents in certain other territories under occupation by Israeli military forces since June 1967. -Y compris les données pour Jérusalem-Est et les résidents israéliens dans certains autres territoires occupés depuis 1967 par les forces armées israéliennes.

[6] Legally induced abortions are applications to commissions for termination of pregnancy and not authorizations. -Les données relatives aux avortements provoqués légalement se rapportent aux demandes d'autorisation et non aux autorisations elles-mêmes.

[7] Data refer to Japanese nationals in Japan only. -Les données se raportent aux nationaux japonais au Japon seulement.

[8] Excluding Faeroe Islands and Greenland. -Non compris les Iles Féroé et le Gröenland.

[9] 2005 data includes 47 legally induced abortions where the place of residence of woman was unknown -Les données de 2005 comprennent 47 avortements provoqués légalement pour lesquels on ne connaît pas le lieu de résidence de la femme.

[10] Total only contains women between 15 and 49 years old. -Le total se rapporte uniquement aux femmes dont l'âge est compris entre 15 et 49 ans.

[11] Data refer to requested abortions only and exclude abortions due to therapeutic reasons. -Les données se rapportent seulement aux interruptions volontaires de grossesse et excluent les avortements effectués pour des rasions thérapeutiques.

[12] Based on hospital and polyclinic records. -D'après les registres des hôpitaux et des polycliniques.

[13] From 1993 a restrictive legal adjustment binds in Poland, in 1997 regulations were moderated briefly and only this year women were able to have an abortion if they had difficult life conditions -Depuis 1993, un ajustement légal restrictif lie en Pologne. En 1997 le règlement a été modéré brièvement et seulement cette année les femmes pouvaient avoir un avortement si elles avaient des conditions difficiles de vie

[14] For residents only. -Pour les résidents seulement.

Table 14

Table 14 presents legally induced abortions by age and number of previous live births of women for the latest available year.

Description of variables: Age is defined as age at last birthday, that is, the difference between the date of birth and the date of the occurrence of the event, expressed in complete solar years. The age classification used in this table is the following: under 15 years, 5-year age groups through 45-49 years and 50 years and over.

Except where otherwise indicated, eight categories are used in classifying the number of previous live births: 0 through 5, 6 or more live births, and, if required, number of live births unknown.

In an effort to provide more complete interpretation of these statistics, countries or areas providing data on legally induced abortions have been requested to communicate grounds for legally induced abortions in their country or area. This information is presented in table 13-1 above.

Reliability of data: Unlike data on live births and foetal deaths, which are generally collected through systems of vital registration, data on abortion are collected from a variety of sources. Because of this, the quality specification, showing the completeness of civil registers, which is presented for other tables, does not appear here.

Limitations: With regard to the collection of information on abortions, a variety of sources are used, but hospital records are the most common source of information. This implies that most cases that have no contact with hospitals are missed. Data from other sources are probably also incomplete. The data in the present table are limited to legally induced abortions, which, by their nature, might be assumed to be more complete than data on all induced abortions.

In addition, deficiencies in the reporting of age and number of previous live births of the woman, differences in the method used for obtaining the age of the woman, and the proportion of abortions for which age or previous live births of the woman are unknown must all be taken into account in using these data.

Earlier data: Legally induced abortions by age and previous live births of women have been shown previously in most issues of the *Demographic Yearbook* since the 1971 issue. For more information on specific topics and years for which data are reported, readers should consult the Index.

Tableau 14

Le tableau 14 présente les données les plus récentes dont on dispose sur les avortements provoqués pour des raisons légales, selon l'âge de la mère et le nombre de naissances vivantes précédentes.

Description des variables : Les notes techniques du tableau 13 contiennent une classification des avortements provoqués légalement. L'âge considéré est l'âge au dernier anniversaire, c'est-à-dire la différence entre la date de naissance et la date de l'avortement, exprimée en années solaires révolues. La classification par âge utilisée dans le tableau 14 est la suivante : moins de 15 ans, groupes quinquennaux jusqu'à 45-49 ans, 50 ans et plus, et âge inconnu.

Sauf indication contraire, les naissances vivantes antérieures sont classées dans les huit catégories suivantes: 0 à 5 naissances vivantes, 6 naissances vivantes ou plus et, le cas échéant, nombre de naissances vivantes inconnu.

Afin de fournir une interprétation plus complète de ces statistiques, il a été demande aux pays ou zones fournissant des données de communiquer les motifs d'avortement autorisés par la loi. Cette information est présentée dans le tableau 13-1.

Fiabilité des données : à la différence des données sur les naissances vivantes et les morts fœtales, qui proviennent généralement des registres d'état civil, les données sur l'avortement sont tirées de sources diverses. Aussi ne trouve-t-on pas ici une évaluation de la qualité des données semblable à celle qui indique, pour les autres tableaux, le degré d'exhaustivité des données de l'état civil.

Insuffisance des données : en ce qui concerne les renseignements sur l'avortement, un grand nombre de sources sont utilisées, les relevés hospitaliers restant cependant la source la plus commune. Il s'ensuit que la plupart des cas qui ne passent pas par les hôpitaux sont ignorés. Il faut aussi tenir compte du fait que les données provenant d'autres sources sont probablement incomplètes. Les données du tableau 14 se limitent aux avortements provoqués pour raisons légales dont on peut supposer, en raison de leur nature même, que les statistiques sont plus complètes que les données concernant l'ensemble des avortements provoqués.

En outre, on doit tenir compte, lorsque l'on utilise ces données, des erreurs de déclaration de l'âge de la mère et du nombre des naissances vivantes précédentes, de l'hétérogénéité des méthodes de calcul de l'âge de la mère et de la proportion d'avortements pour lesquels l'âge de la mère ou le nombre des naissances vivantes ne sont pas connus.

Données publiées antérieurement : Depuis 1971, la plupart des éditions de l'*Annuaire démographique* contiennent des statistiques concernant les avortements provoqués pour raisons légales, selon l'âge de la mère et le nombre de naissances vivantes antérieures. Pour plus de précisions concernant les années et les sujets pour lesquels des données ont été publiées, se reporter à l'index.

14. Legally induced abortions by age and number of previous live births of women: latest available year, 1996 - 2005
Avortments provoqués légalement selon l'âge de la femme et selon le nombre des naissances vivantes précédentes: dernière année disponible, 1996 - 2005

Continent, country or area, year and age / Continent, pays ou zone, année et âge	Total	0	1	2	3	4	5	6+	Unknown Inconnu
AMERICA, NORTH — AMERIQUE DU NORD									
Canada									
2001									
Total	106 418	...	...	...	...	...	...	...	...
0 - 14	412	...	...	...	...	...	...	...	...
15 - 19	19 968	...	...	...	...	...	...	...	...
20 - 24	32 730	...	...	...	...	...	...	...	...
25 - 29	22 012	...	...	...	...	...	...	...	...
30 - 34	16 243	...	...	...	...	...	...	...	...
35 - 39	10 977	...	...	...	...	...	...	...	...
40+	4 043	...	...	...	...	...	...	...	...
Unknown	33	...	...	...	...	...	...	...	...
Mexico - Mexique[1]									
2005									
Total	735	133	206	174	74	19	9	9	111
10 - 14	2	1	-	-	-	-	-	-	1
15 - 19	91	33	22	6	-	-	-	-	30
20 - 24	180	34	64	39	9	1	-	-	33
25 - 29	166	21	54	47	19	3	1	-	21
30 - 34	146	28	32	41	27	5	7	1	5
35 - 39	79	8	15	26	11	6	1	2	10
40 - 44	20	-	5	1	5	4	-	4	1
45 - 49	1	1	-	-	-	-	-	-	-
50 - 54	-	-	-	-	-	-	-	-	-
Unknown	50	7	14	14	3	-	-	2	10
Panama[2]									
2000									
Total	11	7	3	-	-	-	-	1	-
15 - 19	2	2	-	-	-	-	-	-	-
20 - 24	4	3	1	-	-	-	-	-	-
25 - 29	2	1	1	-	-	-	-	-	-
30 - 34	2	-	1	-	-	-	-	1	-
35+	1	1	-	-	-	-	-	-	-
Puerto Rico - Porto Rico									
2005									
Total	6 713	...	...	...	...	...	...	...	...
0 - 14	7	...	...	...	...	...	...	...	...
15 - 19	787	...	...	...	...	...	...	...	...
20 - 24	2 158	...	...	...	...	...	...	...	...
25 - 29	1 485	...	...	...	...	...	...	...	...
30 - 34	881	...	...	...	...	...	...	...	...
35 - 39	257	...	...	...	...	...	...	...	...
40 - 44	94	...	...	...	...	...	...	...	...
45 - 49	3	...	...	...	...	...	...	...	...
50+	-	...	...	...	...	...	...	...	...
Unknown	1 041	...	...	...	...	...	...	...	...
Turks Caicos Islands - Îles Turques et Caïques[3]									
2005									
Total	32	...	...	...	...	...	...	...	...
15 - 19	4	...	...	...	...	...	...	...	...
20 - 24	7	...	...	...	...	...	...	...	...
25 - 29	9	...	...	...	...	...	...	...	...
30 - 34	6	...	...	...	...	...	...	...	...
35 - 39	4	...	...	...	...	...	...	...	...
40 - 44	1	...	...	...	...	...	...	...	...
45+	1	...	...	...	...	...	...	...	...

14. Legally induced abortions by age and number of previous live births of women: latest available year, 1996 - 2005
Avortments provoqués légalement selon l'âge de la femme et selon le nombre des naissances vivantes précédentes: dernière année disponible, 1996 - 2005 (continued — suite)

Continent, country or area, year and age / Continent, pays ou zone, année et âge	Total	0	1	2	3	4	5	6+	Unknown Inconnu
ASIA — ASIE									
Azerbaijan - Azerbaïdjan									
2004									
Total	19 798	...	...	...	...	...	...	...	...
0 - 14	-	...	...	...	...	...	...	...	...
15 - 19	725	...	...	...	...	...	...	...	...
20 - 24	4 552	...	...	...	...	...	...	...	...
25 - 29	6 681	...	...	...	...	...	...	...	...
30 - 34	4 830	...	...	...	...	...	...	...	...
35+	3 010	...	...	...	...	...	...	...	...
China: Hong Kong SAR - Chine: Hong Kong RAS[4]									
2005									
Total	14 190	7 995	2 764	2 774	547	110	...	...	-
0 - 14	28	28	-	-	-	-	-	-	-
15 - 19	1 260	1 215	41	4	-	-	-	-	-
20 - 24	3 258	2 924	259	58	15	2	-	-	-
25 - 29	2 883	2 007	554	281	35	6	-	...	-
30 - 34	2 740	1 136	786	701	103	14	...	...	-
35 - 39	2 518	516	735	1 012	208	47	...	...	-
40 - 44	1 353	159	354	644	162	34	...	...	-
45+	150	10	35	74	24	7	...	...	-
Unknown	-	-	-	-	-	-	-	...	-
Israel - Israël[5,6]									
2005									
Total	18 806	7 903	2 932	3 725	2 372	985	362	314	213
0 - 14	60	57	-	1	-	2	-	-	-
15 - 19	2 616	2 505	71	8	3	-	1	-	28
20 - 24	3 827	2 906	549	240	63	13	2	-	54
25 - 29	3 825	1 574	965	771	334	98	26	13	44
30 - 34	4 003	631	852	1 387	689	260	95	59	30
35 - 39	2 825	144	365	873	815	344	137	130	17
40 - 44	1 405	43	114	401	415	238	84	99	11
45 - 49	154	11	10	36	44	24	16	10	3
50+	8	4	-	-	2	1	-	1	-
Unknown	83	28	6	8	7	5	1	2	26
Japan - Japon[7]									
2005									
Total	289 127	...	...	...	...	...	...	...	...
0 - 14	308	...	...	...	...	...	...	...	...
15 - 19	29 811	...	...	...	...	...	...	...	...
20 - 24	72 217	...	...	...	...	...	...	...	...
25 - 29	59 911	...	...	...	...	...	...	...	...
30 - 34	59 748	...	...	...	...	...	...	...	...
35 - 39	46 038	...	...	...	...	...	...	...	...
40 - 44	19 319	...	...	...	...	...	...	...	...
45 - 49	1 663	...	...	...	...	...	...	...	...
50+	28	...	...	...	...	...	...	...	...
Unknown	84	...	...	...	...	...	...	...	...
Kazakhstan									
1999									
Total	137 808	...	...	...	...	...	...	...	...
0 - 14	177	...	...	...	...	...	...	...	...
15 - 18	8 971	...	...	...	...	...	...	...	...
19 - 35	105 204	...	...	...	...	...	...	...	...
36+	23 456	...	...	...	...	...	...	...	...
Unknown	-	...	...	...	...	...	...	...	...
Kyrgyzstan - Kirghizistan									
2005									
Total	20 035	...	...	...	...	...	...	...	...
0 - 14	5	...	...	...	...	...	...	...	...
15 - 19	1 827	...	...	...	...	...	...	...	...
20 - 24	4 463	...	...	...	...	...	...	...	...

14. Legally induced abortions by age and number of previous live births of women: latest available year, 1996 - 2005
Avortments provoqués légalement selon l'âge de la femme et selon le nombre des naissances vivantes précédentes: dernière année disponible, 1996 - 2005 (continued — suite)

Continent, country or area, year and age Continent, pays ou zone, année et âge	Total	Number of previous live births - Nombre des naissances vivantes précédentes							
		0	1	2	3	4	5	6+	Unknown Inconnu
ASIA — ASIE									
Kyrgyzstan - Kirghizistan									
2005									
25 - 29	4 779	...	...	...	...	...	...	...	...
30 - 34	4 455	...	...	...	...	...	...	...	...
35 - 39	3 025	...	...	...	...	...	...	...	...
40 - 44	1 349	...	...	...	...	...	...	...	...
45+	132	...	...	...	...	...	...	...	...
Singapore - Singapour[4]									
2005									
Total	11 482	5 777	1 952	2 341	1 019	393	...	...	...
0 - 14	16	16	-	-	-	-	...	...	...
15 - 19	1 263	1 168	86	9	-	-	...	...	...
20 - 24	3 090	2 418	414	188	57	13	...	...	...
25 - 29	2 557	1 405	543	427	123	59	...	...	...
30 - 34	2 229	504	536	754	327	108	...	...	...
35 - 39	1 557	200	265	640	324	128	...	...	...
40 - 44	697	63	102	293	168	71	...	...	...
45+	73	3	6	30	20	14	...	...	...
Tajikistan - Tadjikistan									
2003									
Total	18 822	...	...	...	...	...	...	...	...
0 - 14	2	...	...	...	...	...	...	...	...
15 - 19	1 493	...	...	...	...	...	...	...	...
20 - 34	11 830	...	...	...	...	...	...	...	...
35+	5 497	...	...	...	...	...	...	...	...
EUROPE									
Belarus - Bélarus									
2004									
Total	71 700	...	...	...	...	...	...	...	...
0 - 14	20	...	...	...	...	...	...	...	...
15 - 19	6 721	...	...	...	...	...	...	...	...
20 - 24	18 405	...	...	...	...	...	...	...	...
25 - 29	18 141	...	...	...	...	...	...	...	...
30 - 34	13 976	...	...	...	...	...	...	...	...
35 - 39	9 453	...	...	...	...	...	...	...	...
40 - 44	4 508	...	...	...	...	...	...	...	...
45+	476	...	...	...	...	...	...	...	...
Belgium - Belgique									
2003									
Total	15 595	...	...	...	...	...	...	...	...
0 - 14	65	...	...	...	...	...	...	...	...
15 - 19	2 097	...	...	...	...	...	...	...	...
20 - 24	4 032	...	...	...	...	...	...	...	...
25 - 29	3 411	...	...	...	...	...	...	...	...
30 - 34	3 001	...	...	...	...	...	...	...	...
35 - 39	2 107	...	...	...	...	...	...	...	...
40 - 44	810	...	...	...	...	...	...	...	...
45 - 49	67	...	...	...	...	...	...	...	...
50+	1	...	...	...	...	...	...	...	...
Unknown	4	...	...	...	...	...	...	...	...
Bulgaria - Bulgarie									
2005									
Total	41 795	...	...	...	...	...	...	...	...
0 - 14	211	...	...	...	...	...	...	...	...
15 - 19	3 679	...	...	...	...	...	...	...	...
20 - 24	10 660	...	...	...	...	...	...	...	...
25 - 29	11 518	...	...	...	...	...	...	...	...
30 - 34	8 805	...	...	...	...	...	...	...	...
35 - 39	5 350	...	...	...	...	...	...	...	...
40 - 44	1 499	...	...	...	...	...	...	...	...

14. Legally induced abortions by age and number of previous live births of women: latest available year, 1996 - 2005
Avortments provoqués légalement selon l'âge de la femme et selon le nombre des naissances vivantes précédentes: dernière année disponible, 1996 - 2005 (continued — suite)

Continent, country or area, year and age / Continent, pays ou zone, année et âge	Total	0	1	2	3	4	5	6+	Unknown Inconnu
EUROPE									
Bulgaria - Bulgarie									
2005									
45 - 49	71	...	...	...	...	...	...	...	...
50+	2	...	...	...	...	...	...	...	...
Unknown	-	...	...	...	...	...	...	...	...
Channel Islands: Guernsey - Îles Anglo-Normandes: Guernesey									
2000									
Total	89	46	21	11	9	1	1	-	-
0 - 14	1	1	-	-	-	-	-	-	-
15 - 19	12	11	1	-	-	-	-	-	-
20 - 24	30	17	13	-	-	-	-	-	-
25 - 29	18	11	3	3	1	-	-	-	-
30 - 34	15	4	3	4	2	1	1	-	-
35 - 39	10	1	1	4	4	-	-	-	-
40 - 44	3	1	-	-	2	-	-	-	-
Croatia - Croatie									
2005									
Total	4 563	...	...	...	...	...	...	...	...
0 - 14	5	...	...	...	...	...	...	...	...
15 - 19	350	...	...	...	...	...	...	...	...
20 - 29	1 687	...	...	...	...	...	...	...	...
30 - 39	1 901	...	...	...	...	...	...	...	...
40 - 49	475	...	...	...	...	...	...	...	...
50+	1	...	...	...	...	...	...	...	...
Unknown	144	...	...	...	...	...	...	...	...
Czech Republic - République tchèque									
2005									
Total	26 453	7 170	6 957	9 136	2 355	563	163	109	-
0 - 14	45	45	-	-	-	-	-	-	-
15 - 19	2 405	2 091	279	35	-	-	-	-	-
20 - 24	4 891	2 756	1 490	520	103	16	4	2	-
25 - 29	6 218	1 588	2 209	1 905	368	94	34	20	-
30 - 34	6 505	509	1 802	3 174	764	174	54	28	-
35 - 39	4 293	138	848	2 321	731	171	47	37	-
40 - 44	1 911	41	306	1 064	355	100	23	22	-
45 - 49	177	2	21	112	33	8	1	-	-
50+	8	-	2	5	1	-	-	-	-
Unknown	-	-	-	-	-	-	-	-	-
Denmark - Danemark[8]									
2005									
Total	15 103	...	...	...	...	...	...	...	...
0 - 14	-	...	...	...	...	...	...	...	...
15 - 19	2 372	...	...	...	...	...	...	...	...
20 - 24	3 015	...	...	...	...	...	...	...	...
25 - 29	2 905	...	...	...	...	...	...	...	...
30 - 34	3 107	...	...	...	...	...	...	...	...
35 - 39	2 604	...	...	...	...	...	...	...	...
40 - 44	1 018	...	...	...	...	...	...	...	...
45 - 49	82	...	...	...	...	...	...	...	...
50+	-	...	...	...	...	...	...	...	...
Unknown	-	...	...	...	...	...	...	...	...
Estonia - Estonie									
2005									
Total	9 610	2 657	3 389	2 546	741	174	60	32	11
0 - 14	12	12	-	-	-	-	-	-	-
15 - 19	1 345	1 150	183	12	-	-	-	-	-
20 - 24	2 374	1 069	1 041	237	21	2	-	-	4
25 - 29	1 961	296	929	577	121	27	7	2	2
30 - 34	1 895	91	672	832	216	49	21	12	2

14. Legally induced abortions by age and number of previous live births of women:
latest available year, 1996 - 2005
Avortments provoqués légalement selon l'âge de la femme et selon le nombre des naissances vivantes précédentes: dernière année disponible, 1996 - 2005 (continued — suite)

Continent, country or area, year and age Continent, pays ou zone, année et âge	Total	0	1	2	3	4	5	6+	Unknown Inconnu
EUROPE									
Estonia - Estonie									
2005									
35 - 39	1 361	24	429	586	237	55	17	10	3
40 - 44	602	14	128	268	132	39	14	7	-
45 - 49	60	1	7	34	14	2	1	1	-
50+	-	-	-	-	-	-	-	-	-
Unknown	-		-			-		-	-
Finland - Finlande									
2005									
Total	10 931	4 416	1 983	1 612	1 245	792	434	449	-
0 - 14	55	54	1	-					-
15 - 19	2 268	1 846	329	74	18	-	1		-
20 - 24	2 964	1 532	734	407	177	77	23	14	-
25 - 29	2 059	598	446	364	311	177	97	66	-
30 - 34	1 553	226	211	315	326	215	124	136	-
35 - 39	1 364	116	177	304	254	216	133	164	-
40 - 44	624	40	80	140	150	98	54	62	-
45 - 49	44	4	5	8	9	9	2	7	-
50+	-	-	-	-	-	-	-	-	-
Unknown	-	-	-	-	-	-	-	-	-
France									
2004									
Total	209 907	...	...	...	...	...	...	...	...
0 - 14		...	...	...	...	...	...	...	...
15 - 19	28 925	...	...	...	...	...	...	...	...
20 - 24	52 929	...	...	...	...	...	...	...	...
25 - 29	44 001	...	...	...	...	...	...	...	...
30 - 34	40 512	...	...	...	...	...	...	...	...
35 - 39	29 706	...	...	...	...	...	...	...	...
40 - 44	12 521	...	...	...	...	...	...	...	...
45 - 49	1 313	...	...	...	...	...	...	...	...
50+	-	...	...	...	...	...	...	...	...
Germany - Allemagne									
2005									
Total	124 023	50 357	32 657	28 629	8 911	2 394	684	391	...
0 - 14	659	659	-	-	-	-	-	-	...
15 - 19	15 753	14 250	1 350	142	8	2	-	1	...
20 - 24	29 212	17 995	7 859	2 731	509	94	18	6	...
25 - 29	26 534	9 279	8 804	6 329	1 584	394	107	37	...
30 - 34	22 790	4 369	6 924	7 932	2 565	702	204	94	...
35 - 39	19 978	2 782	5 542	7 794	2 748	771	202	139	...
40 - 44	8 419	942	2 060	3 416	1 362	394	138	107	...
45 - 49	659	80	117	275	132	34	14	7	...
50+	19	1	1	10	3	3	1	-	...
Greece - Grèce									
2003									
Total	15 782	...	...	...	...	...	...	...	...
0 - 14	8	...	...	...	...	...	...	...	...
15 - 19	569	...	...	...	...	...	...	...	...
20 - 29	5 934	...	...	...	...	...	...	...	...
30 - 39	7 557	...	...	...	...	...	...	...	...
40 - 49	1 345	...	...	...	...	...	...	...	...
50+	48	...	...	...	...	...	...	...	...
Unknown	321	...	...	...	...	...	...	...	...
Hungary - Hongrie									
2005									
Total	48 689	12 976	11 388	12 832	7 078	2 683	957	775	...
0 - 14	195	192	3	-	-	-	-	-	...
15 - 19	5 588	4 261	1 065	216	41	4	1	-	...
20 - 24	9 786	4 297	2 733	1 644	841	221	41	9	...
25 - 29	11 967	2 839	3 216	2 965	1 808	740	272	127	...
30 - 34	10 712	1 028	2 549	3 627	2 058	827	320	303	...

14. Legally induced abortions by age and number of previous live births of women: latest available year, 1996 - 2005

Avortments provoqués légalement selon l'âge de la femme et selon le nombre des naissances vivantes précédentes: dernière année disponible, 1996 - 2005 (continued — suite)

Continent, country or area, year and age / Continent, pays ou zone, année et âge	Total	\- Nombre des naissances vivantes précédentes							
	Total	0	1	2	3	4	5	6+	Unknown Inconnu
EUROPE									
Hungary - Hongrie									
2005									
35 - 39	7 531	282	1 393	3 037	1 697	655	227	240	...
40 - 44	2 679	69	394	1 226	588	221	91	90	...
45 - 49	224	5	33	117	44	15	5	5	...
50+	7	3	2	-	1	-	-	1	...
Iceland - Islande									
2003									
Total	951	...	...	...	...	...	...	...	...
0 - 14	8	...	...	...	...	...	...	...	...
15 - 19	185	...	...	...	...	...	...	...	...
20 - 24	258	...	...	...	...	...	...	...	...
25 - 29	168	...	...	...	...	...	...	...	...
30 - 34	171	...	...	...	...	...	...	...	...
35 - 39	109	...	...	...	...	...	...	...	...
40 - 44	49	...	...	...	...	...	...	...	...
45 - 49	3	...	...	...	...	...	...	...	...
Italy - Italie									
2003									
Total	124 118	52 804	28 193	30 616	9 001	2 007	464	216	817
0 - 14	255	242	3	1	-	-	-	-	9
15 - 19	9 725	8 722	744	114	13	2	1	-	129
20 - 24	24 074	17 042	4 694	1 757	251	47	4	3	276
25 - 29	28 656	13 633	7 686	5 655	1 212	217	44	11	198
30 - 34	27 794	7 948	7 527	9 078	2 470	502	107	52	110
35 - 39	22 877	3 840	5 299	9 387	3 273	734	180	95	69
40 - 44	9 580	1 147	2 016	4 191	1 604	449	113	46	14
45 - 49	760	76	133	333	149	47	12	9	1
50+	36	9	9	12	4	1	1	-	-
Unknown	361	145	82	88	25	8	2	-	11
Latvia - Lettonie									
2005									
Total	12 785	...	...	...	...	...	...	...	...
0 - 14	11	...	...	...	...	...	...	...	...
15 - 19	1 427	...	...	...	...	...	...	...	...
20 - 24	3 216	...	...	...	...	...	...	...	...
25 - 29	2 924	...	...	...	...	...	...	...	...
30 - 34	2 517	...	...	...	...	...	...	...	...
35 - 39	1 853	...	...	...	...	...	...	...	...
40 - 44	762	...	...	...	...	...	...	...	...
45 - 49	75	...	...	...	...	...	...	...	...
50+	-	...	...	...	...	...	...	...	...
Unknown	-	...	...	...	...	...	...	...	...
Lithuania - Lituanie[9]									
2005									
Total	9 972	...	...	...	...	...	...	...	...
0 - 14	8	...	...	...	...	...	...	...	...
15 - 19	820	...	...	...	...	...	...	...	...
20 - 24	2 235	...	...	...	...	...	...	...	...
25 - 29	2 317	...	...	...	...	...	...	...	...
30 - 34	2 112	...	...	...	...	...	...	...	...
35 - 39	1 643	...	...	...	...	...	...	...	...
40 - 44	760	...	...	...	...	...	...	...	...
45+	77	...	...	...	...	...	...	...	...
Norway - Norvège									
2005									
Total	13 989	...	...	...	...	...	...	...	...
0 - 14	45	...	...	...	...	...	...	...	...
15 - 19	2 166	...	...	...	...	...	...	...	...
20 - 24	3 699	...	...	...	...	...	...	...	...
25 - 29	2 942	...	...	...	...	...	...	...	...
30 - 34	2 526	...	...	...	...	...	...	...	...

14. Legally induced abortions by age and number of previous live births of women: latest available year, 1996 - 2005
Avortments provoqués légalement selon l'âge de la femme et selon le nombre des naissances vivantes précédentes: dernière année disponible, 1996 - 2005 (continued — suite)

Continent, country or area, year and age / Continent, pays ou zone, année et âge	Number of previous live births - Nombre des naissances vivantes précédentes								
	Total	0	1	2	3	4	5	6+	Unknown Inconnu

EUROPE

Norway - Norvège
2005

35 - 39	1 921	...	...	...	...	...	...	...	...
40 - 44	644	...	...	...	...	...	...	...	...
45 - 49	46	...	...	...	...	...	...	...	...
50+	-	...	...	...	...	...	...	...	...
Unknown	-	...	...	...	...	...	...	...	...

Poland - Pologne
2005

Total	225	...	...	...	...	...	...	...	...
15 - 19	9	...	...	...	...	...	...	...	...
20 - 24	34	...	...	...	...	...	...	...	...
25 - 29	53	...	...	...	...	...	...	...	...
30 - 34	65	...	...	...	...	...	...	...	...
35 - 39	64	...	...	...	...	...	...	...	...
Unknown	-	...	...	...	...	...	...	...	...

Republic of Moldova - République de Moldova
2004

Total	17 965	...	...	...	...	...	...	...	...
0 - 14	10	...	...	...	...	...	...	...	...
15 - 19	1 605	...	...	...	...	...	...	...	...
20 - 34	13 498	...	...	...	...	...	...	...	...
35+	2 852	...	...	...	...	...	...	...	...

Romania - Roumanie
2003

Total	224 807	...	...	...	...	...	...	...	...
0 - 14	868	...	...	...	...	...	...	...	...
15 - 19	19 489	...	...	...	...	...	...	...	...
20 - 24	50 508	...	...	...	...	...	...	...	...
25 - 29	58 781	...	...	...	...	...	...	...	...
30 - 34	52 343	...	...	...	...	...	...	...	...
35 - 39	32 749	...	...	...	...	...	...	...	...
40 - 44	9 044	...	...	...	...	...	...	...	...
45 - 49	1 000	...	...	...	...	...	...	...	...
50+	25	...	...	...	...	...	...	...	...

Russian Federation - Fédération de Russie
2004

Total	1 797 567	...	...	...	...	...	...	...	...
0 - 14	1 127	...	...	...	...	...	...	...	...
15 - 19	176 906	...	...	...	...	...	...	...	...
20 - 24	427 330	...	...	...	...	...	...	...	...
25 - 29	405 815	...	...	...	...	...	...	...	...
30 - 34	311 048	...	...	...	...	...	...	...	...
35 - 39	199 322	...	...	...	...	...	...	...	...
40 - 44	90 740	...	...	...	...	...	...	...	...
45 - 49	8 789	...	...	...	...	...	...	...	...
50+	277	...	...	...	...	...	...	...	...
Unknown	176 213	...	...	...	...	...	...	...	...

Serbia and Montenegro - Serbie-et-Montenegro[4]
1998

Total	58 739	6 941	10 691	31 998	7 022	2 085	...	...	2
0 - 14	10	...	...	...	...	...	...	...	...
15 - 19	9 725	...	...	...	...	...	...	...	...
20 - 24	28 223	...	...	...	...	...	...	...	...
25 - 29	19 649	...	...	...	...	...	...	...	...
30 - 34	1 121	...	...	...	...	...	...	...	...
35 - 39	4	...	...	...	...	...	...	...	...
40+	7	...	...	...	...	...	...	...	...

14. Legally induced abortions by age and number of previous live births of women: latest available year, 1996 - 2005
Avortments provoqués légalement selon l'âge de la femme et selon le nombre des naissances vivantes précédentes: dernière année disponible, 1996 - 2005 (continued — suite)

Continent, country or area, year and age / Continent, pays ou zone, année et âge	Total	Number of previous live births - Nombre des naissances vivantes précédentes							
		0	1	2	3	4	5	6+	Unknown Inconnu

EUROPE

Slovakia - Slovaquie
2005

Age	Total	0	1	2	3	4	5	6+	Unknown
Total	14 427	3 964	3 728	4 538	1 469	427	164	137	...
0 - 14	14	14	-	-	-	-	-	-	...
15 - 19	1 255	1 069	153	27	6	-	-	-	...
20 - 24	2 827	1 534	834	365	70	20	3	1	...
25 - 29	3 578	902	1 231	1 048	280	80	29	8	...
30 - 34	3 345	296	921	1 454	429	140	52	53	...
35 - 39	2 285	117	426	1 118	438	99	45	42	...
40 - 44	1 034	30	152	480	226	78	35	33	...
45 - 49	86	1	11	46	19	9	-	-	...
50+	3	1	-	-	1	1	-	-	...

Slovenia - Slovénie
2005

Age	Total	0	1	2	3	4	5	6+	Unknown
Total	5 851	1 815	1 373	2 010	526	87	21	15	4
0 - 14	4	4	-	-	-	-	-	-	-
15 - 19	460	427	25	6	1	-	-	-	1
20 - 24	1 073	749	234	82	7	-	1	-	-
25 - 29	1 248	404	405	360	67	9	-	2	1
30 - 34	1 293	150	348	598	158	25	7	6	1
35 - 39	1 146	57	239	609	199	32	6	3	1
40 - 44	573	21	113	322	86	20	7	4	-
45 - 49	51	2	8	32	8	1	-	-	-
50+	3	1	1	1	-	-	-	-	-

Spain - Espagne[10]
2004

Age	Total	0	1	2	3	4	5	6+	Unknown
Total	84 985	42 757	19 962	15 023	4 772	1 400	741	...	330
0 - 14	369	365	1	-	-	-	-	...	3
15 - 19	11 677	10 415	1 057	145	16	4	-	...	40
20 - 24	22 461	15 193	5 127	1 680	353	33	13	...	62
25 - 29	20 309	9 931	5 541	3 457	981	239	77	...	83
30 - 34	15 212	4 630	4 381	4 186	1 329	424	195	...	67
35 - 39	10 572	1 777	2 846	3 757	1 373	476	288	...	55
40 - 44	4 072	414	949	1 665	661	211	153	...	19
45 - 49	313	32	60	133	59	13	15	...	1

Sweden - Suède[11]
2005

Age	Total	0	1	2	3	4	5	6+	Unknown
Total	34 978	18 158	5 584	6 852	2 900	842	235	95	312
0 - 14	255	253	-	-	-	-	-	-	2
15 - 19	6 686	6 374	207	19	4	-	-	1	81
20 - 24	8 067	6 259	1 260	394	47	10	2	1	94
25 - 29	6 514	3 181	1 552	1 280	364	65	15	3	54
30 - 34	5 965	1 347	1 308	2 169	833	215	43	15	35
35 - 39	5 052	530	881	2 051	1 083	332	100	38	37
40 - 44	2 215	180	350	868	510	198	66	35	8
45 - 49	203	23	23	69	54	22	9	2	1
50+	2	-	-	-	2	-	-	-	-
Unknown	19	11	3	2	3	-	-	-	-

Ukraine
2004

Age	Total	0	1	2	3	4	5	6+	Unknown
Total	289 065	...	...	...	...	...	...	...	...
0 - 14	141	...	...	...	...	...	...	...	...
15 - 17	6 951	...	...	...	...	...	...	...	...
18 - 34	234 195	...	...	...	...	...	...	...	...
35+	47 778	...	...	...	...	...	...	...	...

United Kingdom - Royaume-Uni[12]
2000

Age	Total	0	1	2	3	4	5	6+	Unknown
Total	197 366	105 328	37 645	33 532	13 982	4 683	1 414	753	29
0 - 14	1 170	1 165	4	1	-	-	-	-	-
15 - 19	40 225	35 254	4 393	528	40	4	-	-	6
20 - 24	53 590	35 263	11 732	5 183	1 150	222	25	9	6

14. Legally induced abortions by age and number of previous live births of women: latest available year, 1996 - 2005
Avortments provoqués légalement selon l'âge de la femme et selon le nombre des naissances vivantes précédentes: dernière année disponible, 1996 - 2005 (continued — suite)

Continent, country or area, year and age / Continent, pays ou zone, année et âge	Total	Number of previous live births - Nombre des naissances vivantes précédentes							Unknown Inconnu
		0	1	2	3	4	5	6+	
EUROPE									
United Kingdom - Royaume-Uni[12]									
2000									
25 - 29	42 680	20 273	9 640	8 295	3 212	953	231	71	5
30 - 34	31 928	8 925	7 004	9 504	4 339	1 491	455	205	5
35 - 39	20 684	3 562	3 711	7 438	3 771	1 433	485	279	5
40 - 44	6 526	794	1 081	2 375	1 359	542	203	171	1
45 - 49	490	62	66	189	108	36	14	15	-
50+	25	4	4	9	2	2	1	3	-
Unknown	48	26	10	10	1	-	-	-	1
2001									
Total	197 913	...	...	...	...	...	...	...	...
0 - 14	1 157	...	...	...	...	...	...	...	...
15 - 19	40 387	...	...	...	...	...	...	...	...
20 - 24	54 878	...	...	...	...	...	...	...	...
25 - 29	41 126	...	...	...	...	...	...	...	...
30 - 34	31 921	...	...	...	...	...	...	...	...
35 - 39	21 096	...	...	...	...	...	...	...	...
40 - 44	6 833	...	...	...	...	...	...	...	...
45 - 49	513	...	...	...	...	...	...	...	...
Unknown	2	...	...	...	...	...	...	...	...
OCEANIA — OCEANIE									
New Zealand - Nouvelle-Zélande									
2005									
Total	17 531	11 210	4 345	1 394	427	116	23	16	...
0 - 14	92	90	2	-	-	-	-	-	...
15 - 19	3 718	3 147	493	71	7	-	-	-	...
20 - 24	5 203	3 465	1 276	366	82	12	1	1	...
25 - 29	3 491	1 870	1 050	395	126	38	6	6	...
30 - 34	2 520	1 280	794	305	98	31	8	4	...
35 - 39	1 773	974	515	167	80	28	7	2	...
40 - 44	687	358	203	84	33	6	1	2	...
45+	47	26	12	6	1	1	-	1	...

FOOTNOTES - NOTES

* Provisional. — Données provisoires.

[1] Data refer to 'Therapeutic Abortions'. According to the Mexican law, only the induced abortions, prescribed by medical reasons and induced because of pregnancy coming from sexual agression, are considered as legal. -Les données se rapportent aux « interruptions volontaires de grossesse pour des motifs thérapeutiques ». D'après la loi mexicaine, seuls sont considérés légaux les avortements déclenchés pour des raisons médicales ou parce que la grossesse est le résultat d'une agression sexuelle.

[2] Data refer to abortions granted for medical reasons by the Comision Multidisciplinaria Nacional de Aborto Terapéutico. -Les données se réfèrent aux avortements autorisés pour des raisons médicales par la Comision Multidisciplinaria Nacional de Aborto Terapéutico.

[3] For abortions performed in hospitals at Grand Turk and Providenciales. -Pour des avortements exécutés dans les hôpitaux dans Grand Turk et Providenciales.

[4] Column '4' includes '5' and over. -Colonne '4' compris '5' plus.

[5] Including data for East Jerusalem and Israeli residents in certain other territories under occupation by Israeli military forces since June 1967. -Y compris les données pour Jérusalem-Est et les résidents israéliens dans certains autres territoires occupés depuis 1967 par les forces armées israéliennes.

[6] Legally induced abortions are applications to commissions for termination of pregnancy and not authorizations. -Les données relatives aux avortements provoqués légalement se rapportent aux demandes d'autorisation et non aux autorisations elles-mêmes.

[7] Data refer to Japanese nationals in Japan only. -Les données se raportent aux nationaux japonais au Japon seulement.

[8] Excluding Faeroe Islands and Greenland. -Non compris les Iles Féroé et le Gröenland.

[9] Data refer to requested abortions only and exclude abortions due to therapeutic reasons. -Les données se rapportent seulement aux interruptions volontaires de grossesse et excluent les avortements effectués pour des rasions thérapeutiques.

[10] Column '5' includes '6' and over. -Colonne '5' compris 6 plus.

[11] Abortion by previous deliveries of mother rather than previous live births of mother. -Avortements selon les accouchements précédents de la mère plutôt que selon les naissances vivantes de la mère.

[12] For residents only. -Pour les résidents seulement.

Table 15

Table 15 presents infant deaths and infant mortality rates by urban/rural residence for as many years as possible between 2001 and 2005.

Description of variables: Infant deaths are deaths of live-born infants under one year of age.

Statistics on the number of infant deaths are obtained from civil registers unless otherwise noted. Infant mortality rates are, in most instances, calculated from data on registered infant deaths and registered live births for a country or area where civil registration is considered reliable (that is, with an estimated completeness of 90 per cent or more).

The urban/rural classification of infant deaths is that provided by each reporting country or area; it is presumed to be based on the national census definitions of urban population that have been set forth at the end of the technical notes of table 6.

Rate computation: Infant mortality rates are the annual number of deaths of infants under one year of age per 1 000 live births (as shown in table 9) in the same year.

Rates by urban/rural residence are the annual number of infant deaths, in the appropriate urban or rural category, per 1 000 corresponding live births (as shown in table 9). These rates have been calculated by the Statistics Division of the United Nations.

Rates presented in this table have been limited to those for countries or areas having at least a total of 100 infant deaths in a given year and for which the quality code is represented by a C or a symbol |.

Reliability of data: Each country or area has been asked to indicate the estimated completeness of the infant deaths recorded in its civil register. These national assessments are indicated by the quality codes C, U and | that appear in the first column of this table.

C indicates that the data are estimated to be virtually complete, that is, representing at least 90 per cent of the infant deaths occurring each year, while U indicates that data are estimated to be incomplete that is, representing less than 90 per cent of the infant deaths occurring each year. The code | indicates that the source of data is not civil registration, but is still considered reliable. The code ... indicates that no information was provided regarding completeness.

Data from civil registers that are reported as incomplete or of unknown completeness (coded U or ...) are considered unreliable. They appear in italics in this table; rates are not computed for data so coded.

Limitations: Statistics on infant deaths are subject to the same qualifications as have been set forth for vital statistics in general and death statistics in particular as discussed in section 4 of the Technical Notes.

The reliability of the data, an indication of which is described above, is an important factor in considering the limitations. In addition, some infant deaths are tabulated by date of registration and not by date of occurrence; these have been indicated by a plus sign (+). Whenever the lag between the date of occurrence and date of registration is prolonged and, therefore, a large proportion of the infant-death registrations are delayed, infant-death statistics for any given year may be seriously affected.

Another factor that limits international comparability is the practice of some countries or areas not to include in infant-death statistics infants who were born alive but died before the registration of the birth or within the first 24 hours of life, thus underestimating the total number of infant deaths. Statistics of this type are footnoted.

The method of reckoning age at death for infants may also introduce non-comparability. If year alone, rather than completed minutes, hours, days and months elapsed since birth, is used to calculate age at time of death, many of the infants who died during the eleventh month of life and some of those who died at younger ages will be classified as having completed one year of age and thus be excluded. The effect would be to underestimate the number of infant deaths. Information on this factor is given in footnotes when known. Reckoning of infant age is further discussed in the technical notes for table 16.

In addition, infant mortality rates are subject to the limitations of the data on live births with which they have been calculated. These have been set forth in the technical notes for table 9.

Because the two components of the infant mortality rate, infant deaths in the numerator and live births in the denominator, are both obtained from systems of civil registration, the limitations which affect live-birth statistics are very similar to those which have been mentioned above in connection with the infant-death statistics. It is important to consider the reliability of the data (the completeness of registration) and the method of tabulation (by date of occurrence or by date of registration) of live-birth statistics as well as infant-death statistics, both of which are used to calculate infant mortality rates. The quality code and use of italics to indicate unreliable data presented in this table refer only to infant deaths. Similarly, the indication of the basis of tabulation (the use of the symbol (+) to indicate data tabulated by date of registration) presented in this table also refers only to infant deaths. Table 9 provides the corresponding information for live births.

If the registration of infant deaths is more complete than the registration of live births, then infant mortality rates would be biased upwards. If, however, the registration of live births is more complete than registration of infant deaths, infant mortality rates would be biased downwards. If both infant deaths and live births are tabulated by registration, it should be noted that deaths tend to be more promptly reported than births.

Infant mortality rates may be seriously affected by the practice of some countries or areas of not considering infants that were born alive but died before the registration of the birth or within the first 24 hours of life as live-birth and subsequently infant death. Although this practice results in both the number of infant deaths in the numerator and the number of live births in the denominator being underestimated, its impact is greater on the numerator of the infant mortality rate. As a result this practice causes infant mortality rates to be biased downwards.

Infant mortality rates will also be underestimated if the method of reckoning age at death results in an underestimation of the number of infant deaths. This point has been discussed above.

Because of all these factors care should be taken in comparing and rank ordering infant mortality rates.

With respect to the method of calculating infant mortality rates used in this table, it should be noted that no adjustment was made to take account of the fact that a proportion of the infant deaths that occur during a given year are deaths of infants that were born during the preceding year and hence are not taken from the universe of births used to compute the rates. However, unless the number of live births or infant deaths is changing rapidly, the error involved is insignificant.

The comparability of data by urban/rural residence is affected by the national definitions of urban and rural used in tabulating these data. It is assumed, in the absence of specific information to the contrary, that the definitions of urban and rural used in connection with the national population census were also used in the compilation of the vital statistics for each country or area. However, it cannot be denied that, for some countries or areas, different definitions of urban and rural may be used for the vital statistics data and the population census data respectively. When known, the definitions of urban used in national population censuses are presented at the end of the technical notes for table 6. As discussed in detail in the technical notes for table 6, these definitions vary considerably from one country or area to another.

Urban/rural differentials in infant mortality rates may also be affected by whether the infant deaths and live births have been tabulated in terms of place of occurrence or place of usual residence. This problem is discussed in more detail in section 4.1.4.1 of the Technical Notes.

Earlier data: Infant deaths and infant mortality rates have been shown in previous issues of the *Demographic Yearbook*. For more information on specific topics and years for which data are reported, readers should consult the Historical Index.

Tableau 15

Le tableau 15 présente des données sur les décès d'enfants de moins d'un an et les taux de mortalité infantile selon le lieu de résidence (zone urbaine ou rurale) pour le plus grand nombre d'années possible entre 2001 et 2005.

Description des variables : Les chiffres se rapportent aux décès d'enfants de moins d'un an.

Sauf indication contraire, les statistiques concernant le nombre de décès d'enfants de moins d'un an sont établies à partir des registres de l'état civil. Dans la plupart des cas, les taux de mortalité infantile sont calculés à partir des données relatives aux décès enregistrés d'enfants de moins d'un an et aux naissances vivantes enregistrées dans un pays ou une zone lorsque les registres de l'état civil sont jugés fiables (exhaustivité estimée à 90 p. 100 ou plus).

La classification des décès d'enfants de moins d'un an selon le lieu de résidence (zone urbaine ou rurale) est celle qui a été communiquée par chaque pays ou zone ; on part du principe qu'elle repose sur les définitions de la population urbaine utilisées pour les recensements nationaux, telles qu'elles sont reproduites à la fin des notes techniques du tableau 6.

Calcul des taux : Les taux de mortalité infantile représentent le nombre annuel de décès d'enfants de moins d'un an pour 1 000 naissances vivantes (fréquences du tableau 9) survenues pendant la même année.

Les taux selon le lieu de résidence (zone urbaine ou rurale) représentent le nombre annuel de décès d'enfants de moins d'un an, classés selon la catégorie urbaine ou rurale appropriée pour 1 000 naissances vivantes survenues parmi la population correspondante (fréquences du tableau 9). Ces taux ont été calculés par la Division de statistique de l'ONU.

Les taux présentés dans ce tableau se rapportent seulement aux pays ou zones où l'on a enregistré au moins un total de 100 décès d'enfants de moins d'un an au cours d'une année donnée et pour lesquels le code de qualité est soit 'C', soit 'I'.

Fiabilité des données : Il a été demandé à chaque pays ou zone d'indiquer le degré estimatif de complétude des données sur les décès d'enfants de moins d'un an figurant dans ses registres d'état civil. Ces évaluations nationales sont signalées par les codes de qualité 'C', 'U' et 'I' qui apparaissent dans la deuxième colonne du tableau.

La lettre 'C' indique que les données sont jugées à peu près complètes, c'est-à-dire qu'elles représentent au moins 90 p. 100 des décès d'enfants de moins d'un an survenus chaque année ; la lettre 'U' signifie que les données sont jugées incomplètes, c'est-à-dire qu'elles représentent moins de 90 p.100 des décès d'enfants de moins d'un an survenus chaque année. Le symbole 'I' indique que la source des données n'est pas un registre de l'état civil, mais est quand même considérée fiable. Le code '...' dénote qu'aucun renseignement n'a été communiqué quant à la complétude des données.

Les données provenant des registres de l'état civil qui sont déclarées incomplètes ou dont le degré de complétude n'est pas connu (code 'U' ou '...') sont jugées douteuses. Elles apparaissent en italique dans le tableau ; les taux, dans ces cas là, n'ont pas été calculés.

Insuffisance des données : Les statistiques des décès d'enfants de moins d'un an appellent toutes les réserves qui ont été formulées à propos des statistiques de l'état civil en général et des statistiques concernant les décès en particulier (voir la section 4 des notes techniques).

La fiabilité des données, au sujet de laquelle des indications ont été fournies plus haut, est un facteur important. Il faut également tenir compte du fait que, dans certains cas, les données relatives aux décès d'enfants de moins d'un an sont exploitées selon la date de l'enregistrement et non la date de l'événement ; ces cas ont été signalés par le signe '+'. Chaque fois que le décalage entre l'événement et son enregistrement est grand et qu'une forte proportion des décès d'enfants de moins d'un an fait l'objet d'un enregistrement tardif, les statistiques des décès d'enfants de moins d'un an pour une année donnée peuvent être considérablement faussées.

Un autre facteur qui nuit à la comparabilité internationale est la pratique de certains pays ou zones qui consiste à ne pas inclure dans les statistiques des décès d'enfants de moins d'un an les enfants nés vivants mais décédés avant l'enregistrement de leur naissance ou dans les 24 heures qui ont suivi la naissance, pratique qui conduit à sous-estimer le nombre total de décès d'enfants de moins d'un an. Quand pareil facteur a joué, cela a été signalé en note.

Les méthodes appliquées pour calculer l'âge au moment du décès peuvent également nuire à la comparabilité des données. Si l'on utilise à cet effet l'année seulement, et non pas les minutes, heures, jours et mois qui se sont écoulés depuis la naissance, de nombreux enfants décédés au cours du onzième mois qui a suivi leur naissance et certains enfants décédés encore plus jeunes seront classés comme décédés à un an révolu et donc exclus des données. Cette pratique conduit à sous-estimer le nombre de décès d'enfants de moins d'un an. Les renseignements dont on dispose sur ce facteur apparaissent en note à la fin du tableau. La question du calcul de l'âge au moment du décès est examinée plus en détail dans les notes techniques se rapportant au tableau 16.

Les taux de mortalité infantile appellent en outre toutes les réserves qui ont été formulées à propos des statistiques des naissances vivantes qui ont servi à leur calcul (voir à ce sujet les notes techniques relatives au tableau 9).

Les deux composantes du taux de mortalité infantile - décès d'enfants de moins d'un an au numérateur et naissances vivantes au dénominateur - étant obtenues à partir des registres de l'état civil, les statistiques des naissances vivantes appellent des réserves presque identiques à celles qui ont été formulées plus haut à propos des statistiques des décès d'enfants de moins d'un an. Il importe de prendre en considération la fiabilité des données (complétude de l'enregistrement) et le mode d'exploitation (selon la date de l'événement ou selon la date de l'enregistrement) dans le cas des statistiques des naissances vivantes tout comme dans le cas de celles des décès d'enfants de moins d'un an, puisque les unes et les autres servent au calcul des taux de mortalité infantile. Dans le tableau 15, le code de qualité et l'emploi de caractères italiques pour signaler les données moins sûres ne concernent que les décès d'enfants de moins d'un an. L'indication du mode d'exploitation des données (emploi du signe '+' pour signaler les données exploitées selon la date de l'enregistrement) ne porte là aussi que sur les décès d'enfants de moins d'un an. Le tableau 9 contient les renseignements correspondants pour les naissances vivantes.

Si l'enregistrement des décès d'enfants de moins d'un an est plus complet que l'enregistrement des naissances vivantes, les taux de mortalité infantile seront entachés d'une erreur par excès. En revanche, si l'enregistrement des naissances vivantes est plus complet que l'enregistrement des décès d'enfants de moins d'un an, les taux de mortalité infantile seront entachés d'une erreur par défaut. Si les décès d'enfants de moins d'un an et les naissances vivantes sont exploitées selon la date de l'enregistrement, il convient de ne pas perdre de vue que les décès sont, en règle générale, déclarés plus rapidement que les naissances.

Les taux de mortalité infantile peuvent être gravement faussés par la pratique de certains pays ou zones qui consiste à ne pas classer dans les naissances vivantes et ensuite dans les décès d'enfants de moins d'un an les enfants nés vivants mais décédés soit avant l'enregistrement de leur naissance, soit dans les 24 heures qui ont suivi la naissance. Cette pratique conduit à sous-estimer aussi bien le nombre des décès d'enfants de moins d'un an, qui constitue le numérateur, que le nombre des naissances vivantes, qui constitue le dénominateur, mais c'est pour le numérateur du taux de mortalité infantile que la distorsion est la plus marquée. Ce système a pour effet d'introduire une erreur par défaut dans les taux de mortalité infantile.

Les taux de mortalité infantile seront également sous-estimés si la méthode utilisée pour calculer l'âge au moment du décès conduit à sous-estimer le nombre de décès d'enfants de moins d'un an. Cette question a été examinée plus haut.

Tous ces facteurs sont importants et il faut donc en tenir compte lorsque l'on compare et classe les taux de mortalité infantile.

En ce qui concerne la méthode de calcul des taux de mortalité infantile utilisée dans le tableau, il convient de noter qu'il n'a pas été tenu compte du fait qu'une partie des décès survenus pendant une année donnée sont des décès d'enfants nés l'année précédente et ne correspondent donc pas à l'ensemble des naissances utilisé pour le calcul des taux. Toutefois, l'erreur n'est pas grave, à moins que le nombre des naissances vivantes ou des décès d'enfants de moins d'un an ne varie rapidement.

La comparabilité des données selon le lieu de résidence (zone urbaine ou rurale) peut être limitée par les définitions nationales des termes « urbain » et « rural » utilisées pour la mise en tableaux de ces données. En l'absence d'indications contraires, on a supposé que les mêmes définitions avaient servi pour le recensement national de la population et pour l'établissement des statistiques de l'état civil pour chaque pays ou zone. Toutefois, il n'est pas exclu que, pour une zone ou un pays donné, des définitions différentes aient été retenues. Les définitions du terme « urbain » utilisées pour les recensements nationaux de population ont été présentées à la fin des notes techniques du tableau 6 lorsqu'elles étaient connues. Comme on l'a précisé dans les notes techniques relatives au tableau 6, ces définitions varient considérablement d'un pays ou d'une zone à l'autre.

La différence entre les taux de mortalité infantile pour les zones urbaines et rurales pourra aussi être faussée selon que les décès d'enfants de moins d'un an et les naissances vivantes auront été classés d'après le lieu de l'événement ou le lieu de résidence habituel. Ce problème est examiné plus en détail à la section 4.1.4.1 des Notes techniques.

Données publiées antérieurement : Des statistiques concernant les décès d'enfants de moins d'un an et les taux de mortalité infantile ont déjà été présentées dans des éditions antérieures de l'*Annuaire démographique*. Pour plus de précisions concernant les années et les sujets pour lesquels des données ont été publiées, se reporter à l'index historique.

15. Infant deaths and infant mortality rates, by urban/rural residence: 2001 - 2005
Décès d'enfants de moins d'un an et taux de mortalité infantile, selon la résidence, urbaine/rurale: 2001 - 2005

Continent, country or area and urban/rural residence / Continent, pays ou zone et résidence, urbaine/rurale	Code[1]	Number - Nombre					Rate - Taux				
		2001	2002	2003	2004	2005	2001	2002	2003	2004	2005
AFRICA — AFRIQUE											
Algeria - Algérie[2,3]											
Total	U	21 622	19 850	...	...	...	...	...	...	...	...
Benin - Bénin[4]											
Total	I	25 001	...	...	...	...	94.8	...	...	...	...
Botswana[5]											
Total	I	1 576	...	...	...	...	29.3	...	...	...	...
Egypt - Égypte											
Total	C	49 149	37 904	38 859	40 177	36 146	28.2	21.5	21.9	22.6	20.1
Urban-Urbaine	C	21 436	15 825	17 021	16 954	16 676	28.7	20.6	22.1	23.8	23.1
Rural-Rurale	C	27 713	22 079	21 838	23 223	19 470	27.9	22.1	21.7	21.8	18.1
Ghana											
Total	...	51 639	34 293	...	...	...	...	...	...	...	...
Kenya											
Total	U	36 289	35 940	35 515	35 321	35 252	...	...	...	...	...
Libyan Arab Jamahiriya - Jamahiriya arabe libyenne											
Total	U	2 568	...	...	...	...	...	...	...	...	...
Mauritius - Maurice											
Total	+C	282	297	250	277	248	14.3	14.9	12.9	14.4	13.2
Urban-Urbaine	+C	114	102	93	90	92	14.7	12.9	...	...	...
Rural-Rurale	+C	168	195	157	187	156	14.1	16.2	13.3	15.6	13.3
Morocco - Maroc[6]											
Total	U	7 379	...	...	...	...	...	...	...	...	...
Urban-Urbaine	U	2 804	...	...	...	...	...	...	...	...	...
Rural-Rurale	U	4 569	...	...	...	...	...	...	...	...	...
Mozambique[4]											
Total	I	99 164	...	...	...	...	131.6	...	...	...	...
Réunion											
Total	C	103	91	*107	...	...	7.1	...	*7.4	...	...
Saint Helena ex. dep. - Sainte-Hélène sans dép.											
Total	C	-	...	1	...	1	...	...	...	...	...
Seychelles											
Total	+C	19	26	25	17	*16	...	...	...	...	...
AMERICA, NORTH — AMERIQUE DU NORD											
Anguilla											
Total	+C	-	2	2	-	3	...	...	...	...	...
Aruba											
Total	+U	4	3	3	3	6	...	...	...	...	...
Bahamas											
Total	C	37	...	87	...	...	...	...	...	...	...
Barbados - Barbade											
Total	+C	...	*54	...	...	...	...	...	...	...	...
Belize											
Total	U	120	145	...	112	137	...	...	...	...	...
Bermuda - Bermudes											
Total	C	3	-	2	...	*2	...	...	...	...	...
Canada[7]											
Total	C	1 739	1 762	1 765	1 775	...	5.2	5.4	5.3	5.3	...
Costa Rica											
Total	C	827	793	737	668	*700	10.8	11.1	10.1	9.2	*9.8
Cuba[6]											
Total	C	861	922	859	*736	746	6.2	6.5	6.3	*5.8	6.2
Urban-Urbaine	C	649	719	671	...	584	6.3	6.9	6.7	...	6.6
Rural-Rurale	C	212	203	188	...	162	5.8	5.4	5.2	...	5.1
Dominica - Dominique											
Total	+C	24	...	...	...	...	...	...	...	...	...
El Salvador											
Total	C	1 682	1 284	1 322	1 255	...	12.2	9.9	10.6	10.5	...
Urban-Urbaine	C	1 091	821	847	...	...	13.1	10.6	11.6	...	...
Rural-Rurale	C	591	463	475	...	...	10.8	9.0	9.3	...	...

416

15. Infant deaths and infant mortality rates, by urban/rural residence: 2001 - 2005
Décès d'enfants de moins d'un an et taux de mortalité infantile, selon la résidence, urbaine/rurale: 2001 - 2005 (continued — suite)

Continent, country or area and urban/rural residence / Continent, pays ou zone et résidence, urbaine/rurale	Code[1]	Number - Nombre					Rate - Taux				
		2001	2002	2003	2004	2005	2001	2002	2003	2004	2005
AMERICA, NORTH — AMERIQUE DU NORD											
Greenland - Groenland											
Total	C	10	10	8	...	...	...	...	...	...	...
Urban-Urbaine	C	10	7	8	...	...	...	...	...	...	...
Rural-Rurale	C	-	3	-	...	...	...	...	...	...	...
Grenada - Grenade											
Total	+C	33	...	...	...	...	...	...	...	...	...
Guadeloupe[2]											
Total	C	49	45	56	50	...	...	...	...	...	...
Guatemala											
Total	C	...	...	11 022	10 038	*9 947	...	...	29.4	26.2	*26.6
Jamaica - Jamaïque											
Total	U	833	809	753	695	...	...	...	...	...	...
Martinique											
Total	C	43	33	33	27	...	...	...	...	...	...
Mexico - Mexique[6]											
Total	+U	35 911	36 567	33 355	32 764	32 603	...	...	...	...	...
Urban-Urbaine	+U	27 056	27 207	25 073	24 433	24 372	...	...	...	...	...
Rural-Rurale	+U	8 503	8 498	7 714	7 671	7 639	...	...	...	...	...
Netherlands Antilles - Antilles néerlandaises											
Total	C	24	17	19	20	...	...	...	...	...	...
Nicaragua											
Total	+U	2 031	2 217	2 008	1 827	1 970	...	...	...	...	...
Urban-Urbaine	+U	1 023	1 168	1 091	1 073	934	...	...	...	...	...
Rural-Rurale	+U	1 008	1 049	917	754	1 036	...	...	...	...	...
Panama											
Total	U	1 053	885	940	932	980	...	...	...	...	...
Urban-Urbaine	U	556	488	500	772	...	...	...	...	...	...
Rural-Rurale	U	497	397	440	160	...	...	...	...	...	...
Puerto Rico - Porto Rico[6]											
Total	C	515	516	498	...	472	9.2	9.8	9.8	...	9.3
Urban-Urbaine	C	311	...	297	...	...	10.6	...	11.1	...	...
Rural-Rurale	C	204	...	199	...	...	7.7	...	8.2	...	...
Saint Lucia - Sainte-Lucie											
Total	C	37	36	37	*45	...	...	...	...	...	...
Saint Vincent and the Grenadines - Saint Vincent-et-les Grenadines											
Total	+C	39	35	35	33	29	...	...	...	...	...
Trinidad and Tobago - Trinité-et-Tobago											
Total	C	335	412	...	...	...	18.5	24.2	...	...	...
Turks Caicos Islands - Îles Turques et Caïques											
Total	C	2	2	2	-	1	...	...	...	...	...
United States - États-Unis											
Total	C	27 568	28 034	28 025	*27 838	...	6.8	7.0	6.9	*6.8	...
AMERICA, SOUTH — AMERIQUE DU SUD											
Argentina - Argentine											
Total	C	11 111	11 703	11 494	*10 576	9 507	16.3	16.8	16.5	*14.4	13.3
Brazil - Brésil[8]											
Total	U	47 171	45 243	48 039	41 851	39 259	...	...	...	...	...
Chile - Chili											
Total	C	2 159	1 964	1 935	2 034	...	8.8	8.2	8.3	8.8	...
Urban-Urbaine	C	1 855	1 715	1 691	...	...	8.6	8.0	8.1	...	...
Rural-Rurale	C	304	249	244	...	...	10.1	9.6	9.8	...	...
Colombia - Colombie[6,9]											
Total	U	14 430	12 640	12 335	11 772	11 441	...	...	...	...	...
Urban-Urbaine	U	10 458	8 970	8 894	8 445	8 147	...	...	...	...	...
Rural-Rurale	U	3 163	2 922	2 755	2 664	2 640	...	...	...	...	...

15. Infant deaths and infant mortality rates, by urban/rural residence: 2001 - 2005
Décès d'enfants de moins d'un an et taux de mortalité infantile, selon la résidence, urbaine/rurale: 2001 - 2005 (continued — suite)

Continent, country or area and urban/rural residence / Continent, pays ou zone et résidence, urbaine/rurale	Code[1]	Number - Nombre					Rate - Taux				
		2001	2002	2003	2004	2005	2001	2002	2003	2004	2005
AMERICA, SOUTH — AMERIQUE DU SUD											
Ecuador - Équateur[10]											
Total	U	4 800	4 530	3 985	3 942	3 717	...	...	...	...	...
Urban-Urbaine	U	3 544	3 420	3 085	3 121	...	...	...	...	...	...
Rural-Rurale	U	1 256	1 110	900	821	...	...	...	...	...	...
French Guiana - Guyane française[2]											
Total	C	70	52	58	55	...	...	...	...	...	...
Paraguay[11,12,13]											
Total	I	3 898	...	674	647	539	...	...	...	...	...
Urban-Urbaine	I	2 076	...	...	...	...	...	...	...	...	...
Rural-Rurale	I	1 822	...	...	...	...	...	...	...	...	...
Peru - Pérou[8,14]											
Total	+U	6 604	6 511	7 122	...	...	...	...	...	...	...
Suriname											
Total	C	133	148	109	120	...	13.7	14.5	11.3	13.2	...
Urban-Urbaine	C	70	84	...	...	...	...	...	...	...	...
Rural-Rurale	C	62	64	...	...	...	...	...	...	...	...
Uruguay											
Total	C	721	708	*757	*660	*601	13.9	13.6	*15.0	*13.2	*12.7
Venezuela (Bolivarian Republic of) - Venezuela (République bolivarienne du)[8]											
Total	C	8 158	7 645	...	...	...	15.4	15.5	...	...	...
ASIA — ASIE											
Armenia - Arménie[15]											
Total	C	497	450	422	430	460	15.5	14.0	11.8	11.5	12.3
Urban-Urbaine	C	333	300	311	311	351	16.4	14.4	13.7	13.2	14.8
Rural-Rurale	C	164	150	111	119	109	14.0	13.1	8.4	8.6	7.9
Azerbaijan - Azerbaïdjan[15]											
Total	+C	1 382	1 422	1 451	1 287	1 321	12.5	12.8	12.8	9.8	9.3
Urban-Urbaine	+C	558	554	633	605	...	11.2	11.1	12.4	10.2	...
Rural-Rurale	+C	824	868	818	682	...	13.6	14.2	13.1	9.4	...
Bahrain - Bahreïn											
Total	C	117	94	107	135	134	8.7	...	7.3	9.0	8.8
Bangladesh[16]											
Total	...	...	...	...	...	...	56.0	53.0	53.0	52.0	...
Urban-Urbaine	...	...	...	...	...	...	43.0	37.0	40.0	41.0	...
Rural-Rurale	...	...	...	...	...	...	60.0	57.0	57.0	55.0	...
Bhutan - Bhoutan[17]											
Total	I	...	...	...	...	503	...	...	...	...	40.1
Urban-Urbaine	I	...	...	...	...	126	...	...	...	...	32.8
Rural-Rurale	I	...	...	...	...	377	...	...	...	...	43.4
Brunei Darussalam - Brunéi Darussalam											
Total	+C	50	62	67	63	*51	...	...	...	...	...
Cambodia - Cambodge											
Total	...	87	83	80	76	...	...	...	...	...	...
China: Hong Kong SAR - Chine: Hong Kong RAS											
Total	C	124	110	109	132	131	2.6	2.3	2.3	2.7	2.3
China: Macao SAR - Chine: Macao RAS											
Total	C	14	11	2	10	12	...	...	...	...	...
Cyprus - Chypre[18]											
Total	C	37	37	33	29	33	...	...	...	...	...
Georgia - Géorgie[15]											
Total	C	1 098	1 102	1 144	1 178	916	23.1	23.6	24.8	23.8	19.7
Urban-Urbaine	C	...	...	1 057	...	...	...	...	30.6	...	...
Rural-Rurale	C	...	...	87	...	...	...	...	...	...	...

15. Infant deaths and infant mortality rates, by urban/rural residence: 2001 - 2005
Décès d'enfants de moins d'un an et taux de mortalité infantile, selon la résidence, urbaine/rurale: 2001 - 2005 (continued — suite)

Continent, country or area and urban/rural residence / Continent, pays ou zone et résidence, urbaine/rurale	Code[1]	Number - Nombre					Rate - Taux				
		2001	2002	2003	2004	2005	2001	2002	2003	2004	2005
ASIA — ASIE											
India - Inde[19,20]											
Total	...	...	...	...	...	...	66.0	63.0	60.0	58.0	58.0
Urban-Urbaine	...	...	...	...	...	...	42.0	40.0	38.0	40.0	40.0
Rural-Rurale	...	...	...	...	...	...	72.0	69.0	66.0	64.0	64.0
Iraq											
Total	U	...	...	...	*10 972	*12 460	...	...	...	...	...
Israel - Israël[6,21,22]											
Total	C	700	752	717	670	627	5.1	5.4	4.9	4.6	4.4
Urban-Urbaine	C	632	678	641	597	550	5.1	5.3	4.9	4.5	4.2
Rural-Rurale	C	67	73	74	73	76	...	...	...	...	...
Japan - Japon[6,23]											
Total	C	3 599	3 497	3 364	3 122	2 958	3.1	3.0	3.0	2.8	2.8
Urban-Urbaine	C	2 896	2 815	2 728	2 591	2 544	3.1	3.0	3.0	2.8	2.8
Rural-Rurale	C	698	672	631	529	407	3.1	3.1	3.1	2.7	2.8
Kazakhstan[15]											
Total	C	4 239	3 850	3 824	3 901	4 213	19.1	16.9	15.4	14.3	15.1
Urban-Urbaine	C	2 371	2 203	2 349	2 418	...	20.6	18.0	16.9	15.5	...
Rural-Rurale	C	1 868	1 647	1 475	1 483	...	17.6	15.7	13.5	12.7	...
Korea (Republic of) - Corée (République de)[24]											
Total	C	3 008	2 545	2 470	2 209	...	5.4	5.1	5.0	4.6	...
Kuwait - Koweït											
Total	C	420	418	412	422	420	10.2	9.6	9.4	8.9	8.2
Kyrgyzstan - Kirghizistan[15,25]											
Total	C	2 123	2 128	2 186	2 812	3 258	21.6	21.1	20.7	25.6	29.7
Urban-Urbaine	C	785	852	880	1 427	1 617	27.6	28.2	27.6	38.2	45.4
Rural-Rurale	C	1 338	1 276	1 306	1 385	1 641	19.2	18.0	17.7	19.1	22.1
Malaysia - Malaisie											
Total	C	2 900	3 100	*3 000	*2 700	*2 600	5.6	6.4	*5.8	*5.2	*5.1
Maldives											
Total	C	85	89	72	76	67	...	...	...	...	...
Urban-Urbaine	C	22	28	16	21	...	...	...	...	...	...
Rural-Rurale	C	63	61	56	55	...	...	...	...	...	...
Mongolia - Mongolie											
Total	C	1 464	1 390	1 051	1 016	938	29.5	29.6	23.0	22.3	20.7
Urban-Urbaine	C	710	626	520	531	520	28.8	26.0	21.4	20.6	19.7
Rural-Rurale	C	754	764	531	485	418	30.2	33.4	24.8	24.6	22.2
Nepal - Népal[26]											
Total	I	13 037	...	...	...	...	...	...	...	...	...
Occupied Palestinian Territory - Territoire palestinien occupé											
Total	U	1 138	1 126	1 150	1 103	1 057	...	...	...	...	...
Oman[27]											
Total	U	335	332	335	336	315	...	...	...	...	...
Pakistan[28,29]											
Total	I	286 609	...	280 729	...	289 169	77.1	...	76.2	...	76.7
Urban-Urbaine	I	82 185	...	80 199	...	82 299	68.9	...	67.2	...	67.1
Rural-Rurale	I	204 424	...	200 530	...	206 870	80.9	...	80.6	...	81.2
Philippines											
Total	C	26 129	23 778	22 844	...	...	15.2	14.3	13.7	...	...
Qatar											
Total	C	111	107	137	113	110	9.2	8.8	10.7	8.6	8.2
Saudi Arabia - Arabie saoudite											
Total	...	11 669	11 498	11 330	11 164	11 078	...	...	...	...	...
Singapore - Singapour											
Total	+C	100	123	100	82	95	2.4	3.0	2.7	...	...
Sri Lanka											
Total	+C	*4 323	...	...	...	...	*12.1	...	...	...	...
Thailand - Thaïlande											
Total	+U	5 105	5 105	5 349	6 061	6 183	...	...	...	...	...

Continent, country or area and urban/rural residence / Continent, pays ou zone et résidence, urbaine/rurale	Code[1]	Number - Nombre					Rate - Taux				
		2001	2002	2003	2004	2005	2001	2002	2003	2004	2005
ASIA — ASIE											
Turkey - Turquie[30,31]											
Total	I	60 332	36 365	34 842	33 456	...	40.6	26.7	25.6	24.6	...
Urban-Urbaine	I	14 947	...	...	...	...	...	...	...	...	...
Rural-Rurale	I	45 385	...	...	...	...	...	...	...	...	...
Uzbekistan - Ouzbékistan[15]											
Total	C	9 427	...	...	...	...	18.4	...	...	...	...
Urban-Urbaine	C	3 399	...	...	...	...	21.3	...	...	...	...
Rural-Rurale	C	6 028	...	...	...	...	17.1	...	...	...	...
EUROPE											
Albania - Albanie											
Total	C	603	466	395	336	303	11.1	10.2	8.4	7.8	7.6
Andorra - Andorre											
Total	C	2	-	-	2	5	...	...	...	...	...
Austria - Autriche											
Total	C	365	318	343	353	327	4.8	4.1	4.5	4.5	4.2
Belarus - Bélarus[15]											
Total	C	839	695	685	614	640	9.1	7.8	7.7	6.9	7.1
Urban-Urbaine	C	535	454	440	386	398	8.0	7.0	6.8	5.9	6.0
Rural-Rurale	C	304	241	245	228	242	12.1	10.2	10.3	9.5	10.0
Belgium - Belgique											
Total	C	518	551	538	549	515	4.5	5.0	4.8	4.7	4.4
Bosnia and Herzegovina - Bosnie-Herzégovine											
Total	C	287	335	268	253	233	7.6	9.4	7.6	7.2	6.7
Bulgaria - Bulgarie											
Total	C	982	887	831	814	739	14.4	13.3	12.3	11.6	10.4
Urban-Urbaine	C	625	571	522	516	464	12.9	12.0	10.7	10.2	8.9
Rural-Rurale	C	357	316	309	298	275	18.2	16.9	16.5	15.3	14.6
Croatia - Croatie											
Total	C	315	282	251	245	242	7.7	7.0	6.3	6.1	5.7
Urban-Urbaine	C	179	144	135	132	151	7.8	6.4	6.2	5.9	6.4
Rural-Rurale	C	136	138	116	113	91	7.5	7.9	6.5	6.3	...
Czech Republic - République tchèque											
Total	C	360	385	365	366	347	4.0	3.9	3.9	3.7	3.4
Urban-Urbaine	C	266	288	266	268	261	4.0	3.9	3.8	3.7	3.4
Rural-Rurale	C	94	97	99	98	86	...	...	...	...	...
Denmark - Danemark[32]											
Total	C	320	284	286	283	280	4.9	4.4	4.4	4.4	4.4
Estonia - Estonie[6]											
Total	C	111	74	91	90	78	8.8	...	...	...	...
Urban-Urbaine	C	81	53	59	58	51	...	...	...	...	...
Rural-Rurale	C	30	21	32	32	27	...	...	...	...	...
Finland - Finlande[33]											
Total	C	181	168	176	191	174	3.2	3.0	3.1	3.3	3.0
Urban-Urbaine	C	112	109	107	121	103	3.1	3.0	2.9	3.2	2.7
Rural-Rurale	C	69	59	69	70	71	...	...	...	...	...
France[34,35]											
Total	C	3 438	3 114	3 053	2 988	2 775	4.5	4.1	4.0	3.9	3.6
Urban-Urbaine	C	2 694	2 437	2 403	2 321	2 139	4.6	4.2	4.2	4.0	3.7
Rural-Rurale	C	725	657	625	633	610	3.9	3.6	3.4	3.4	3.2
Germany - Allemagne											
Total	C	3 163	3 036	2 990	2 918	2 696	4.3	4.2	4.2	4.1	3.9
Gibraltar											
Total	C	...	...	2	...	...	...	...	...	...	...
Greece - Grèce											
Total	C	522	600	420	429	409	5.1	5.8	4.0	4.1	3.8
Urban-Urbaine	C	...	...	...	319	302	...	...	...	...	4.1
Rural-Rurale	C	...	...	...	110	107	...	...	...	...	3.2
Hungary - Hongrie[6]											
Total	C	789	693	690	628	607	8.1	7.2	7.3	6.6	6.2
Urban-Urbaine	C	471	421	375	384	369	8.0	6.9	6.3	6.4	5.8

15. Infant deaths and infant mortality rates, by urban/rural residence: 2001 - 2005
Décès d'enfants de moins d'un an et taux de mortalité infantile, selon la résidence, urbaine/rurale: 2001 - 2005 (continued — suite)

Continent, country or area and urban/rural residence / Continent, pays ou zone et résidence, urbaine/rurale	Code[1]	Number - Nombre					Rate - Taux				
		2001	2002	2003	2004	2005	2001	2002	2003	2004	2005
EUROPE											
Hungary - Hongrie[6]											
Rural-Rurale	C	311	269	308	236	228	8.4	7.6	8.9	6.9	6.9
Iceland - Islande											
Total	C	11	9	10	12	10	...	...	...	...	...
Urban-Urbaine	C	9	9	10	...	10	...	...	...	...	...
Rural-Rurale	C	2	-	-	...	-	...	...	...	...	...
Ireland - Irlande[36]											
Total	+C	331	306	326	*300	*244	5.7	5.1	5.3	*4.9	*4.0
Isle of Man - Îles de Man											
Total	+C	-	3	6	2	...	...	...	...	...	...
Italy - Italie											
Total	C	2 482	2 337	2 482	*2 289	*2 554	4.6	4.4	4.6	*4.1	*4.6
Latvia - Lettonie[15]											
Total	C	217	197	198	191	168	11.0	9.8	9.4	9.4	7.8
Urban-Urbaine	C	139	105	129	117	102	11.1	8.1	9.3	8.5	7.0
Rural-Rurale	C	78	92	69	74	66	...	...	...	...	...
Liechtenstein											
Total	C	-	1	1	1	*1	...	...	...	...	...
Lithuania - Lituanie[15]											
Total	C	250	238	206	240	209	7.9	7.9	6.7	7.9	6.8
Urban-Urbaine	C	148	128	108	133	135	7.5	6.8	5.6	6.8	6.8
Rural-Rurale	C	102	110	98	107	74	8.6	9.7	...	9.8	...
Luxembourg											
Total	C	32	27	26	21	14	...	...	...	...	...
Malta - Malte											
Total	C	17	23	23	23	23	...	...	...	...	...
Netherlands - Pays-Bas[37]											
Total	C	1 088	1 014	962	852	928	5.4	5.0	4.8	4.4	4.9
Urban-Urbaine	C	...	670	627	554	647	...	5.0	4.7	4.2	5.0
Rural-Rurale	C	...	344	335	298	281	...	5.0	5.0	4.7	4.7
Norway - Norvège[38]											
Total	C	223	192	190	185	175	3.9	3.5	3.4	3.2	3.1
Poland - Pologne											
Total	C	2 823	2 662	2 470	2 423	2 340	7.7	7.5	7.0	6.8	6.4
Urban-Urbaine	C	1 575	1 551	1 446	1 462	1 339	7.7	7.9	7.2	7.1	6.3
Rural-Rurale	C	1 248	1 111	1 024	961	1 001	7.7	7.1	6.8	6.4	6.5
Portugal											
Total	C	567	574	466	418	382	5.0	5.0	4.1	3.8	3.5
Republic of Moldova - République de Moldova[15]											
Total	C	597	528	522	464	468	16.4	14.8	14.3	12.1	12.4
Urban-Urbaine	C	212	192	178	167	177	16.9	15.1	13.9	11.9	13.0
Rural-Rurale	C	385	336	344	297	291	16.1	14.6	14.5	12.3	12.1
Romania - Roumanie											
Total	C	4 057	3 648	3 546	3 641	3 310	18.4	17.3	16.7	16.8	15.0
Urban-Urbaine	C	1 594	1 426	1 381	1 555	1 458	15.6	14.5	13.7	14.0	12.4
Rural-Rurale	C	2 463	2 222	2 165	2 086	1 852	20.9	19.8	19.4	19.9	17.9
Russian Federation - Fédération de Russie[15]											
Total	C	19 104	18 407	18 142	17 339	...	14.6	13.2	12.3	11.5	...
Urban-Urbaine	C	12 899	12 511	12 235	11 596	...	13.9	12.5	11.6	10.8	...
Rural-Rurale	C	6 205	5 896	5 907	5 743	...	16.2	14.8	13.8	13.4	...
San Marino - Saint-Marin											
Total	+C	1	2	2	1	-	...	...	...	...	...
Serbia and Montenegro - Serbie-et-Montenegro[39]											
Total	C	1 709	882	803	*660	...	13.1	10.2	9.2	*7.5	...
Urban-Urbaine	C	1 006	616	537	...	...	14.5	11.3	9.9	...	...
Rural-Rurale	C	703	266	266	...	...	11.6	8.2	8.0	...	...
Slovakia - Slovaquie											
Total	C	319	388	406	365	392	6.2	7.6	7.9	6.8	7.2
Urban-Urbaine	C	147	191	176	171	188	5.6	7.3	6.6	6.0	6.5
Rural-Rurale	C	172	197	230	194	204	6.9	8.0	9.2	7.7	8.0

Continent, country or area and urban/rural residence / Continent, pays ou zone et résidence, urbaine/rurale	Code[1]	Number - Nombre					Rate - Taux				
		2001	2002	2003	2004	2005	2001	2002	2003	2004	2005
EUROPE											
Slovenia - Slovénie											
Total	C	74	67	69	66	75	...	...	...	...	...
Urban-Urbaine	C	33	37	37	34	26	...	...	...	...	...
Rural-Rurale	C	41	30	32	32	49	...	...	...	...	...
Spain - Espagne											
Total	C	1 657	1 737	1 733	1 813	*1 765	4.1	4.1	3.9	4.0	*3.8
Sweden - Suède											
Total	C	334	313	308	314	246	3.7	3.3	3.1	3.1	2.4
Switzerland - Suisse											
Total	C	365	326	311	309	308	5.0	4.5	4.3	4.2	4.2
Urban-Urbaine	C	248	242	225	219	223	5.0	4.6	4.3	4.1	4.1
Rural-Rurale	C	117	84	86	90	85	4.8	...	...	...	...
The Former Yugoslav Rep. of Macedonia - L'ex-République yougoslave de Macédoine											
Total	C	321	283	305	308	287	11.9	10.2	11.3	13.2	12.8
Urban-Urbaine	C	182	157	...	...	151	12.3	10.5	...	...	12.1
Rural-Rurale	C	139	126	...	...	136	11.3	9.8	...	...	13.7
Ukraine[15]											
Total	C	4 283	4 023	3 882	4 024	4 259	11.4	10.3	9.5	9.4	10.0
Urban-Urbaine	C	2 690	2 543	2 531	2 584	2 675	11.3	10.2	9.5	9.1	9.4
Rural-Rurale	C	1 593	1 480	1 351	1 440	1 584	11.4	10.4	9.5	10.1	11.2
United Kingdom - Royaume-Uni											
Total	C	3 664	3 499	3 686	3 606	*3 670	5.5	5.2	5.3	5.0	*5.1
OCEANIA — OCEANIE											
American Samoa - Samoas américaines											
Total	C	14	27	20	26	12	...	...	...	...	...
Australia - Australie											
Total	+C	1 309	1 264	1 199	1 184	1 302	5.3	5.0	4.8	4.7	5.0
Urban-Urbaine	+C	733	779	740	766	858	5.0	4.7	4.4	4.5	4.9
Rural-Rurale	+C	576	485	459	418	444	5.8	5.6	5.4	5.0	5.3
Cook Islands - Îles Cook											
Total	+C	4	2	4	5		...	...	...	...	...
Fiji - Fidji											
Total	+C	342	320	304	...	...	20.5	18.8	17.2	...	...
French Polynesia - Polynésie française											
Total	C	36	32	31	20	28	...	...	...	...	...
Guam[40]											
Total	C	35	20	37	*41	...	...	...	...	...	...
Marshall Islands - Îles Marshall											
Total	+U	40	...	...	...	...	...	...	...	...	...
New Caledonia - Nouvelle-Calédonie											
Total	C	24	29	24	25		...	...	...	...	...
New Zealand - Nouvelle-Zélande[6,41]											
Total	+C	296	300	277	324	295	5.3	5.6	4.9	5.6	5.1
Urban-Urbaine	+C	253	255	231	274	246	5.2	5.4	4.7	5.4	4.9
Rural-Rurale	+C	26	24	27	33	26	...	...	...	...	...
Northern Mariana Islands - Îles Mariannes septentrionales											
Total	U	11	10	...	...	...	...	...	...	...	...
Palau - Palaos											
Total	C	5	6	2	7	6	...	...	...	...	...

15. Infant deaths and infant mortality rates, by urban/rural residence: 2001 - 2005
Décès d'enfants de moins d'un an et taux de mortalité infantile, selon la résidence, urbaine/rurale: 2001 - 2005 (continued — suite)

Continent, country or area and urban/rural residence — Continent, pays ou zone et résidence, urbaine/rurale	Code[1]	Number - Nombre					Rate - Taux				
		2001	2002	2003	2004	2005	2001	2002	2003	2004	2005
OCEANIA — OCEANIE											
Papua New Guinea - Papouasie-Nouvelle-Guinée											
Total	U	*1 841*	*2 230*	*2 082*	...	...	...	...	...	...	...
Tonga											
Total	+C	33	26	34	*35	...	...	...	...	...	...
Tuvalu											
Total	U	*5*	*4*	*4*	*5*	*6*	...	...	...	...	...

FOOTNOTES - NOTES

GENERAL NOTES - NOTES GENERALES

Data exclude foetal deaths. Rates are the number of deaths of infants under one year of age per 1000 live births. Rates are shown only for countries or areas having at least a total of 100 infant deaths in a given year. For definitions of 'urban', see end of Technical Notes for table 6. For method of evaluation and limitations of data, see Technical Notes for this table. — Les données ne comprennent pas les morts foetales. Les taux représentent le nombre de décès d'enfants de moins d'un an pour 1000 naissances vivantes. Les taux présentés ne se rapportent qu'aux pays ou zones où l'on a enregistré un total d'au moins 100 décès d'enfants de moins d'un an dans un année donnée. Pour les définitions des 'régions urbaines', se reporter à la fin des Notes techniques du tableau 6. Pour la méthode d'évaluation et les insuffisances des données, voir Notes techniques pour ce tableau.

Italics: data from civil registers which are incomplete or of unknown completeness. — *Italiques:* données incomplètes ou dont le degré d'exactitude n'est pas connu provenant des registres de l'état civil.

* Provisional. — Données provisoires.
[1] 'Code' indicates the source of data, as follows:
C - Civil registration, estimated over 90% complete
U - Civil registration, estimated less than 90% complete
| - Other source, estimated reliable
+ - Data tabulated by date of registration rather than occurence.
... - Information not available

Le 'Code' indique la source des données, comme suit:
C - Registres de l'état civil considérés complèts à 90 p. 100 au moins.
U - Registres de l'état civil qui ne sont pas considérés complèts à 90 p. 100 au moins.
| - Autre source, considérée fiable.
+ - Données exploitées selon la date de l'enregistrement et non la date de l'événement.
... - Information non disponible.

[2] Excluding live-born infants who died before their birth was registered. -Non compris les enfants nés vivants décédés avant l'enregistrement de leur naissance.
[3] For Algerian population only. -Pour la population algérienne seulement.
[4] Data refer to national projections. -Les données se réfèrent aux projections nationales.
[5] For 2001, data refer to last twelve months preceding census in August 2001. -Pour 2001, les données se rapportent aux douze mois précédant le recensement d'août 2001.
[6] Figures for urban and rural areas do not add up to the total, since they do not include the category 'Unknown residence'. -La somme des données pour la résidence urbaine et rurale n'est pas égale au total parce qu'elle n'inclue pas la catégorie 'Résidence inconnue'.

[7] Including Canadian residents temporarily in the United States, but excluding United States residents temporarily in Canada. -Y compris les résidents canadiens se trouvant temporairement aux Etats-Unis, mais ne comprenant pas les résidents des Etats-Unis se trouvant temporairement au Canada.
[8] Excluding Indian jungle population. -Non compris les Indiens de la jungle.
[9] Data on live births and deaths are based on a civil registration system put in place in January 1998. -Les données sur les naissances et les décès sont basées sur un système d'enregistrement des faits d'état civil mis en place en janvier 1998.
[10] Excluding nomadic Indian tribes. -Non compris les tribus d'Indiens nomades.
[11] For 2001, data were collected from population census held on August 2002, referring to events in calendar year 2001. -Pour 2001, les données sont tirées du recensement de la population réalisé en août 2002, concernant des événements de l'année civile 2001.
[12] For 2004, based on the general office for civil registration. -En 2004, d'après la direction générale du registre de l'état civil.
[13] The code shown refers to 2001 data only. -Le code mentionné fait référence aux informations de 2001 uniquement.
[14] Data refer to registered infant deaths only. -Les données se rapportent aux décès enregistrés d'enfants de moins de 1 an seulement.
[15] Excluding infants born alive of less than 28 weeks' gestation, or less than 1 000 grams in weight and 35 centimeters in length, who die within seven days of birth. -Non compris les enfants nés vivants après moins de 28 semaines de gestations, pesant moins de 1 000 grammes, mesurant moins de 35 centimètres et décédés dans les sept jours qui ont suivi leur naissance.
[16] Rates were obtained by the Sample Vital Registration System 2004 of Bangladesh. -Taux obtenus au moyen du Sample Vital Registration System 2004 du Bangladesh.
[17] For 2005, data refer to last twelve months preceding census on May 2005. -Pour 2005, les données se rapportent pour la dernière fois aux douze mois précédant le recensement mai 2005.
[18] Data refer to government controlled areas. -Les données se rapportent aux zones contrôlées par le Gouvernement.
[19] Including data for the Indian-held part of Jammu and Kashmir, the final status of which has not yet been determined. -Y compris les données pour la partie du Jammu et du Cachemire occupée par l'Inde dont le statut définitif n'a pas encore été déterminé.
[20] Rates were obtained by the Sample Registration System of India, actually a large demographic survey. -Les taux ont été obtenus par le Système de l'enregistrement par échantillon de l'Inde qui est au fait une large enquête démographique.
[21] Including data for East Jerusalem and Israeli residents in certain other territories under occupation by Israeli military forces since June 1967. -Y compris les données pour Jérusalem-Est et les résidents israéliens dans certains autres territoires occupés depuis 1967 par les forces armées israéliennes.
[22] Data include deaths abroad of Israeli residents who were out of the country for less than a year. -Y compris les décès à l'étranger de résidents israéliens qui ont quitté le pays depuis moins d'un an.
[23] Data refer to Japanese nationals in Japan only. -Les données se raportent aux nationaux japonais au Japon seulement.
[24] Excluding alien armed forces, civilian aliens employed by armed forces, and foreign diplomatic personnel and their dependants. -Non

compris les militaires étrangers, les civils étrangers employés par les forces armées ni le personnel diplomatique étranger et les membres de leur famille les accompagnant.

[25] Since 2004, WHO criteria have been adopted in the country. -Depuis 2004, le pays a adopté les critères de l'OMS.

[26] For 2001, data refer to last twelve months preceding census on June 2001. -Pour 2001, les données se rapportent aux douze mois précédant le recensement de juin 2001.

[27] Data refer to the recorded events in Ministry of Health hospitals and health centres only. -Les données se rapportent aux faits d'état civil enregistrés dans les hôpitaux et les dispensaires du Ministère de la santé seulement.

[28] Excluding data for the Pakistan-held part of Jammu and Kashmir, the final status of which has not yet been determined. -Non compris les données concernant la partie du Jammu et Cachemire occupée par le Pakistan dont le statut définitif n'a pas été déterminé.

[29] Data based on Pakistan Demographic Survey. -Données extraites de l'enquête démographique effectuée par le Pakistan.

[30] Based on the results of the Population Demographic Survey. -D'après les résultats de la Population Demographic Survey.

[31] Reason for discrepancy between the figures for 2001 and the figures for 2002-2004 not ascertained. -On ne sait pas comment s'explique la divergence entre les chiffres pour 2001 et les chiffres pour 2002-2004.

[32] Excluding Faeroe Islands and Greenland. -Non compris les Iles Féroé et le Grôenland.

[33] Including nationals temporarily outside the country. -Y compris les nationaux se trouvant temporairement hors du pays.

[34] Excluding Overseas Departments, namely, French Guiana, Guadeloupe, Martinique and Reunion, shown separately. -Non compris les départements d'outre-mer, c'est-à-dire la Guyane française, la Guadeloupe, la Martinique et la Réunion, qui font l'objet de rubriques distinctes.

[35] Urban/rural figures, excluding nationals outside the country. -Les chiffres urbaine/rurale, non compris les nationaux hors du pays.

[36] Events registered within one year of occurrence. -Evénements enregistrés dans l'année qui suit l'événement.

[37] Including residents outside the country if listed in a Netherlands population register. -Y compris les résidents hors du pays, s'ils sont inscrits sur un registre de population néerlandais.

[38] Including residents temporarily outside the country: -Y compris les résidents se trouvant temporairement hors du pays.

[39] From 2002, without data for Kosovo and Metohia. -2002 et après sans les données pour le Kosovo and Metohie.

[40] Including United States military personnel, their dependants and contract employees. -Y compris les militaires des Etats-Unis, les membres de leur famille les accompagnant et les agents contractuels des Etats-Unis.

[41] For resident population only. -Pour la population résidante seulement.

Table 16

Table 16 presents infant deaths and infant mortality rates by age and sex for latest available year.

Description of variables: Age is defined as hours, days and months of life completed, based on the difference between the hour, day, month and year of birth and the hour, day, month and year of death. The age classification used in this table is the following: under 1 day, 1-6 days, 7-27 days and 28-364 days. For some countries or areas the statistics presented are for several years, and include those years for which data only recently become available and were therefore not published in previous issues of the *Demographic Yearbook*.

Rate computation: Infant mortality rates are the annual number of deaths of infants under one year of age per 1 000 live births (as shown in table 9) in the same year.

Infant mortality rates by age and sex are the annual number of infant deaths that occurred in a specific age-sex group per 1 000 live births in the corresponding sex group (as shown in table 9). These rates have been calculated by the Statistics Division of the United Nations. The denominator for all these rates, regardless of age of infant at death, is the number of live births by sex.

Infant deaths of unknown age are included only in the rate for under one year of age. Deaths under the category of sex "unknown" are included in the rate for the total and, hence, these rates, shown in the first column of the table, should agree with the infant mortality rates shown in table 15. Discrepancies are explained in footnotes.

Rates presented in this table have been limited to those for countries or areas having at least a total of 1 000 deaths in a given year. Moreover, rates specific for individual sub-categories based on 30 or fewer infant deaths are identified by the symbol (♦).

Reliability of data: Data from civil registers of infant deaths which are reported as incomplete (less than 90 percent completeness) or of unknown completeness are considered unreliable and are set in italics rather than in roman type. Rates on these data are not computed. Tables 9 and 15 and the technical notes for these tables provide more detailed information on the completeness of infant death registration. For more information about the quality of vital statistics data in general, and the information available on the basis of the completeness of estimates in particular, see section 4.2 of the Technical Notes.

Limitations: Statistics on infant deaths by age and sex are subject to the same qualifications as have been set forth for vital statistics in general and death statistics in particular as discussed in section 4 of the Technical Notes.

The reliability of the data, an indication of which is described above, is an important factor in considering the limitations. In addition, some infant deaths are tabulated by date of registration and not by date of occurrence; these have been indicated by a plus sign (+). Whenever the lag between the date of occurrence and date of registration is prolonged and, therefore, a large proportion of the infant-death registrations are delayed, infant-death statistics for any given year may be seriously affected.

Another factor that limits international comparability is the practice of some countries or areas of not including in infant-death statistics infants who were born alive but died before the registration of the birth or within the first 24 hours of life, thus underestimating the total number of infant deaths. Statistics of this type are footnoted. In this table in particular, this practice may contribute to the lack of comparability among deaths under one year, under 28 days, under one week and under one day.

Variation in the method of reckoning age at the time of death may also introduce non-comparability. Although it is to some degree a limiting factor throughout the age span, it is an especially important consideration with respect to deaths at ages under one day and under one week (early neonatal deaths) and under 28 days (neonatal deaths). As noted above, the recommended method of reckoning infant age at death is to calculate duration of life in minutes, hours and days, as appropriate. This gives age in completed units of time. In some countries or areas, however, infant age is calculated to the nearest day only, that is, age at death for an infant is the difference between the day, month and year of birth and the day, month and year of death. The result of this procedure is to classify as deaths at age one day, many deaths of infants that occurred before the infants had completed 24 hours of life. The under-one-day class is thus understated while the frequency in the 1-6-day age group is inflated.

425

A special limitation on comparability of neonatal (under 28 days) deaths is the variation in the classification of infant age used. It is evident from the footnotes that some countries or areas continue to report infant age in calendar, rather than lunar month (4-week or 28- day) periods. This failure to tabulate infant deaths under 4 weeks of age in terms of completed days introduces another source of variation between countries or areas. Deaths classified as occurring under one month usually connote deaths within any one calendar month; these frequencies are not strictly comparable with those referring to deaths within 4 weeks or 27 completed days.

In addition, infant mortality rates by age and sex are subject to the limitations of the data on live births with which they have been calculated. These have been set forth in the technical notes for table 9. These limitations have also been discussed in the technical notes for table 15.

In addition, it should be noted that infant mortality rates by age are affected by the problems related to the practice of excluding infants who were born alive but died before the registration of the birth or within the first 24 hours of life from both infant-death and live-birth statistics and the problems related to the reckoning of infant age at death. These factors, which have been described above, may affect certain age groups more than others. In so far as the numbers of infant deaths for the various age groups are underestimated or overestimated, the corresponding rates for the various age groups will also be underestimated or overestimated. The youngest age groups are more likely to be underestimated than other age groups; the youngest age group (under one day) is likely to be the most seriously affected.

Earlier data: Infant deaths and infant mortality rates by age and sex have been shown in previous issues of the *Demographic Yearbook*. For information on specific years covered, readers should consult the Historical Index.

Tableau 16

Le tableau 16 présente les données les plus récentes dont on dispose sur les décès d'enfants de moins d'un an et les taux de mortalité infantile selon l'âge et le sexe.

Description des variables : l'âge est exprimé en heures, jours et mois révolus et est calculé en retranchant la date de la naissance (heure, jour, mois et année) de celle du décès (heure, jour, mois et année). La classification par âge utilisée dans le tableau est la suivante : moins d'un jour, 1 à 6 jours, 7 à 27 jours et 28 à 364 jours. Pour certains pays et zones, les statistiques portent sur plusieurs années. Cela s'explique par le fait qu'elles ne sont disponibles que depuis peu et n'ont donc pas pu être publiées dans les éditions précédentes de l'*Annuaire démographique*.

Calcul des taux : les taux de mortalité infantile selon l'âge et le sexe représentent le nombre annuel de décès d'enfants de moins d'un an selon l'âge et le sexe pour 1 000 naissances vivantes d'enfants du même sexe (fréquences du tableau 9) survenues au cours de l'année considérée.

Les taux de mortalité infantile selon l'âge et le sexe représentent le nombre annuel de décès d'enfants de moins d'un an intervenu dans un groupe d'âge donné parmi la population de sexe masculin ou féminin (fréquences du tableau 9) pour 1 000 naissances vivantes survenues parmi la population du même sexe. Ces taux ont été calculés par la Division de statistique de l'ONU. Le dénominateur de tous ces taux, quel que soit l'âge de l'enfant au moment du décès, est le nombre de naissances vivantes selon le sexe.

Il n'est tenu compte des décès d'enfants d'âge « inconnu » que pour le calcul du taux relatif à l'ensemble des décès de moins d'un an. Étant donné que les décès d'enfants de sexe inconnu sont compris dans le numérateur des taux concernant le total qui figurent dans la deuxième colonne du tableau 16, les chiffres obtenus devraient concorder avec les taux de mortalité infantile du tableau 15. Les divergences sont expliquées en note.

Les taux présentés dans le tableau 16 ne concernent que les pays ou zones où l'on a enregistré un total d'au moins 1 000 décès au cours d'une année donnée. Les taux relatifs à des sous-catégories qui sont fondées sur un nombre égal ou inférieur à 30 décès d'enfants âgés de moins d'un an sont signalés par le signe '♦'.

Fiabilité des données : les données relatives aux décès d'enfants de moins d'un an provenant de registres de l'état civil qui sont déclarées incomplètes (degré de complétude inférieur à 90 p.100) ou dont le degré de complétude n'est pas connu sont jugées douteuses et apparaissent en italique et non en caractères romains. Les taux à partir de ces données n'ont pas été calculés. Les tableaux 9 et 15 et les notes techniques se rapportant à ces tableaux comportent des renseignements plus détaillés sur le degré de complétude de l'enregistrement des décès d'enfants de moins d'un an. Pour plus de précisions sur la qualité des données reposant sur les statistiques de l'état civil en général et les estimations de complétude en particulier, voir la section 4.2 des Notes techniques.

Insuffisance des données : les statistiques des décès d'enfants de moins d'un an selon l'âge et le sexe appellent toutes les réserves qui ont été formulées à propos des statistiques de l'état civil en général et des statistiques concernant les décès en particulier (voir la section 4 des Notes techniques).

La fiabilité des données, au sujet de laquelle des indications ont été fournies plus haut, est un facteur important. Il faut également tenir compte du fait que, dans certains cas, les données relatives aux décès d'enfants de moins d'un an sont exploitées selon la date de l'enregistrement et non la date de l'événement ; ces cas ont été signalés par le signe '+'. Chaque fois que le décalage entre l'événement et son enregistrement est grand et qu'une forte proportion des décès d'enfants de moins d'un an fait l'objet d'un enregistrement tardif, les statistiques des décès d'enfants de moins d'un an pour une année donnée peuvent être considérablement faussées.

Un autre facteur qui nuit à la comparabilité internationale est la pratique de certains pays ou zones qui consiste à ne pas inclure dans les statistiques des décès d'enfants de moins d'un an les enfants nés vivants mais décédés soit avant l'enregistrement de leur naissance, soit dans les 24 heures qui ont suivi la naissance, pratique qui conduit à sous-estimer le nombre total de décès d'enfants de moins d'un an. Quand pareil facteur a joué, cela a été signalé en note. Dans le tableau 16 en particulier, ce système peut limiter la comparabilité des données concernant les décès d'enfants de moins d'un an, de moins de 28 jours, de moins d'une semaine et de moins d'un jour.

Le manque d'uniformité des méthodes suivies pour calculer l'âge au moment du décès nuit également à la comparabilité des données. Ce facteur influe dans une certaine mesure sur les données relatives à la mortalité à tous les âges, mais il a des répercussions particulièrement marquées sur les statistiques des décès de moins d'un jour et de moins d'une semaine (mortalité néo-natale précoce) et de moins de 28 jours (mortalité néo-natale). Comme on l'a dit, l'âge d'un enfant de moins d'un an à son décès est calculé, selon la méthode recommandée, en évaluant la durée de vie en minutes, heures et jours, selon le cas. L'âge est ainsi exprimé en unités de temps révolues. Toutefois, dans certains pays ou zones, l'âge de ces enfants est ramené au jour le plus proche en retranchant la date de la naissance (jour, mois et année) de celle du décès (jour, mois et année). Il s'ensuit que de nombreux décès survenus dans les vingt-quatre heures qui suivent la naissance sont classés comme décès d'un jour. Dans ces conditions, les données concernant les décès de moins d'un jour sont entachées d'une erreur par défaut et celles qui se rapportent aux décès de 1 à 6 jours d'une erreur par excès.

La comparabilité des données relatives à la mortalité néo-natale (moins de 28 jours) est influencée par un facteur spécial : l'hétérogénéité de la classification par âge utilisée pour les enfants de moins d'un an. Les notes figurant à la fin des tableaux montrent que, dans un certain nombre de pays ou zones, on continue d'utiliser le mois civil au lieu du mois lunaire (4 semaines ou 28 jours).

Lorsque les données relatives aux décès de moins de 4 semaines ne sont pas exploitées sur la base de l'âge en jours révolus, il existe une nouvelle cause de non-comparabilité internationale. Les décès de moins d'un mois sont généralement ceux qui se produisent au cours d'un mois civil ; les taux calculés sur la base de ces données ne sont pas strictement comparables à ceux qui sont établis à partir des données concernant les décès survenus dans les 4 semaines ou 27 jours révolus qui suivent la naissance.

Les taux de mortalité infantile selon l'âge et le sexe appellent en outre toutes les réserves qui ont été formulées à propos des statistiques des naissances vivantes qui ont servi à leur calcul (voir à ce sujet les notes techniques relatives au tableau 9). Ces insuffisances ont également été examinées dans les notes techniques relatives au tableau 15.

Il convient de signaler aussi que les taux de mortalité infantile selon l'âge peuvent être gravement faussés par la pratique qui consiste à ne pas classer dans les naissances vivantes et ensuite dans les décès d'enfants de moins d'un an les enfants nés vivants mais décédés soit avant l'enregistrement de leur naissance, soit dans les 24 heures qui ont suivi la naissance, et par les problèmes que pose le calcul de l'âge de l'enfant au moment du décès. Ces facteurs, qui ont été décrits plus haut, peuvent fausser les statistiques concernant certains groupes d'âge plus que d'autres. Si le nombre des décès d'enfants de moins d'un an pour chaque groupe d'âge est sous-estimé ou surestimé, les taux correspondants pour chacun de ces groupes d'âge seront eux aussi sous-estimés ou surestimés. Les risques de sous-estimation sont plus grands pour les groupes les plus jeunes ; c'est pour le groupe d'âge le plus jeune de tous (moins d'un jour) que les données risquent de comporter les plus grosses erreurs.

Données publiées antérieurement : Des statistiques des décès d'enfants de moins d'un an et des taux de mortalité infantile selon l'âge et le sexe ont déjà été présentées dans des éditions antérieures de l'*Annuaire démographique*. Pour plus de précisions concernant les années pour lesquelles ces données ont été publiées, se reporter à l'index.

16. Infant deaths and infant mortality rates by age and sex: latest available year, 1996 - 2005
Décès d'enfants de moins d'un an et taux de mortalité infantile selon l'âge et le sexe: dernière année disponible, 1996 - 2005

Continent, country or area, year, age (in days) and urban/rural residence / Continent, pays ou zone, année, âge (en jours) et résidence,urbaine/rurale	Number - Nombre			Rate - Taux		
	Both sexes Les deux sexes	Male Masculin	Female Féminin	Both sexes Les deux sexes	Male Masculin	Female Féminin
AFRICA — AFRIQUE						
Egypt - Égypte						
2005						
Total	36 146	19 695	16 451	20.1	21.4	18.7
0-6	7 930	4 863	3 067	4.4	5.3	3.5
7-27	7 598	4 302	3 296	4.2	4.7	3.7
28-364	19 708	10 026	9 682	10.9	10.9	11.0
Unknown - Inconnu	910	504	406	0.5	0.5	0.5
Mauritius - Maurice+						
2005						
Total	248	146	102	...	...	...
Under 1 day - Moins d'un jour	40	24	16	...	...	...
1-6	87	51	36	...	...	...
7-27	59	40	19	...	...	...
28-364	62	31	31	...	...	...
Unknown - Inconnu	-	-	-	...	...	...
Morocco - Maroc						
2001						
Total	7 379	4 022	3 357	...	...	...
0-27	1 638	912	726	...	...	...
28-364	5 729	3 103	2 626	...	...	...
Unknown - Inconnu	12	7	5	...	...	...
Réunion						
2003						
Total	107	59	48	...	...	...
Under 1 day - Moins d'un jour	43	26	17	...	...	...
1-6	19	12	7	...	...	...
7-27	16	7	9	...	...	...
28-364	29	14	15	...	...	...
Saint Helena ex. dep. - Sainte-Hélène sans dép.						
2005						
Total	1	1	-	...	...	...
Under 1 day - Moins d'un jour	-	-	-	...	...	...
1-6	1	1	-	...	...	...
7-27	-	-	-	...	...	...
28-364	-	-	-	...	...	...
Unknown - Inconnu	-	-	-	...	...	...
South Africa - Afrique du Sud						
1996						
Total	24 560	12 979	11 581	...	...	...
Under 1 day - Moins d'un jour	3 795	2 098	1 697	...	...	...
1-6	4 542	2 427	2 115	...	...	...
7-27	2 415	1 288	1 127	...	...	...
28-364	13 808	7 166	6 642	...	...	...
Tunisia - Tunisie						
1998						
Total	3 098	1 775	1 323	...	...	...
Under 1 day - Moins d'un jour	464	281	183	...	...	...
1-6	847	485	362	...	...	...
7-27	559	332	227	...	...	...
28-364	1 227	677	550	...	...	...
Unknown - Inconnu	1	-	1	...	...	...
AMERICA, NORTH — AMERIQUE DU NORD						
Bahamas						
2001						
Total	37	23	14	...	...	...
0-6	8	7	1	...	...	...
7-27	15	8	7	...	...	...
28-364	14	8	6	...	...	...
Bermuda - Bermudes						
1996						
Total	3	1	2	...	...	...
Under 1 day - Moins d'un jour	1	1	-	...	...	...
1-6	1	-	1	...	...	...

16. Infant deaths and infant mortality rates by age and sex: latest available year, 1996 - 2005
Décès d'enfants de moins d'un an et taux de mortalité infantile selon l'âge et le sexe: dernière année disponible, 1996 - 2005 (continued — suite)

Continent, country or area, year, age (in days) and urban/rural residence / Continent, pays ou zone, année, âge (en jours) et résidence,urbaine/rurale	Number - Nombre			Rate - Taux		
	Both sexes Les deux sexes	Male Masculin	Female Féminin	Both sexes Les deux sexes	Male Masculin	Female Féminin
AMERICA, NORTH — AMERIQUE DU NORD						
Bermuda - Bermudes						
1996						
7-27	-	-	-	...	...	...
28-364	1	-	1	...	...	...
Canada[1]						
2004						
Total	1 775	953	822	5.3	5.5	5.0
Under 1 day - Moins d'un jour	907	467	440	2.7	2.7	2.7
1-6	227	126	101	0.7	0.7	0.6
7-27	210	119	91	0.6	0.7	0.6
28-364	431	241	190	1.3	1.4	1.2
Cayman Islands - Îles Caïmanes						
1996						
Total	6	3	3	...	...	...
Under 1 day - Moins d'un jour	4	1	3	...	...	...
1-6	-	-	-	...	...	...
7-27	-	-	-	...	...	...
28-364	2	2	-	...	...	...
Costa Rica						
2005						
Total	700	383	317	...	...	...
Under 1 day - Moins d'un jour	207	118	89	...	...	...
1-6	190	103	87	...	...	...
7-27	111	63	48	...	...	...
28-364	192	99	93	...	...	...
Cuba						
2005						
Total	746	412	334	...	...	...
Under 1 day - Moins d'un jour	75	35	40	...	...	...
1-6	183	107	76	...	...	...
7-27	151	78	73	...	...	...
28-364	337	192	145	...	...	...
El Salvador						
2003						
Total	1 322	747	575	10.6	11.5	9.7
Under 1 day - Moins d'un jour	147	83	64	1.2	1.3	1.1
1-6	193	110	83	1.6	1.7	1.4
7-27	184	99	85	1.5	1.5	1.4
28-364	798	455	343	6.4	7.0	5.8
Greenland - Groenland						
2003						
Total	8	6	2	...	...	...
Under 1 day - Moins d'un jour	3	3	-	...	...	...
1-6	2	1	1	...	...	...
7-27	-	-	-	...	...	...
28-364	3	2	1	...	...	...
Guadeloupe[2]						
2003						
Total	56	34	22	...	...	...
Under 1 day - Moins d'un jour	13	5	8	...	...	...
1-6	8	4	4	...	...	...
7-27	19	12	7	...	...	...
28-364	16	13	3	...	...	...
Unknown - Inconnu	-	-	-	...	...	...
Guatemala						
1999						
Total	13 161	7 349	5 812	32.2	...	...
Under 1 day - Moins d'un jour	999	570	429	2.4	...	...
1-6	2 180	1 286	894	5.3	...	...
7-27	1 741	949	792	4.3	...	...
28-364	8 241	4 544	3 697	20.1	...	...
Martinique						
2003						
Total	33	14	19	...	...	...

16. Infant deaths and infant mortality rates by age and sex: latest available year, 1996 - 2005
Décès d'enfants de moins d'un an et taux de mortalité infantile selon l'âge et le sexe: dernière année disponible, 1996 - 2005 (continued — suite)

Continent, country or area, year, age (in days) and urban/rural residence / Continent, pays ou zone, année, âge (en jours) et résidence,urbaine/rurale	Number - Nombre			Rate - Taux		
	Both sexes Les deux sexes	Male Masculin	Female Féminin	Both sexes Les deux sexes	Male Masculin	Female Féminin
AMERICA, NORTH — AMERIQUE DU NORD						
Martinique						
2003						
Under 1 day - Moins d'un jour	9	4	5	...	...	...
1-6	11	5	6	...	...	...
7-27	4	1	3	...	...	...
28-364	9	4	5	...	...	...
Unknown - Inconnu	-	-	-	...	...	...
Mexico - Mexique+						
2005						
Total	32 603	18 214	14 318	...	...	...
Under 1 day - Moins d'un jour	6 763	3 777	2 938	...	...	...
1-6	8 009	4 575	3 421	...	...	...
7-27	5 456	3 074	2 378	...	...	...
28-364	12 374	6 787	5 581	...	...	...
Unknown - Inconnu	1	1	-	...	...	...
Montserrat+						
1996						
Total	1	1	-	...	...	...
Under 1 day - Moins d'un jour	1	1	-	...	...	...
1-6	-	-	-	...	...	...
7-27	-	-	-	...	...	...
28-364	-	-	-	...	...	...
Netherlands Antilles - Antilles néerlandaises						
2004						
Total	20	13	7	...	...	...
Under 1 day - Moins d'un jour	4	3	1	...	...	...
1-6	5	2	3	...	...	...
7-27	3	2	1	...	...	...
28-364	8	6	2	...	...	...
Nicaragua+						
2005						
Total	1 970	1 125	845	...	...	...
Under 1 day - Moins d'un jour	291	159	132	...	...	...
1-6	765	449	316	...	...	...
7-27	310	179	131	...	...	...
28-364	604	338	266	...	...	...
Panama						
1999						
Total	1 005	571	434	...	...	...
Under 1 day - Moins d'un jour	147	78	69	...	...	...
1-6	253	145	108	...	...	...
7-27	207	127	80	...	...	...
28-364	398	221	177	...	...	...
2003						
Total	940	...	...	...	...	...
0-27	499	...	...	...	...	...
28-364	441	...	...	...	...	...
Puerto Rico - Porto Rico						
2005						
Total	472	252	220	...	...	...
Under 1 day - Moins d'un jour	100	46	54	...	...	...
1-6	144	87	57	...	...	...
7-27	93	43	50	...	...	...
28-364	134	75	59	...	...	...
Unknown - Inconnu	1	1	-	...	...	...
Saint Lucia - Sainte-Lucie						
2002						
Total	36	17	19	...	...	...
Under 1 day - Moins d'un jour	11	5	6	...	...	...
1-6	16	6	10	...	...	...
7-27	2	1	1	...	...	...
28-364	7	5	2	...	...	...

16. Infant deaths and infant mortality rates by age and sex: latest available year, 1996 - 2005
Décès d'enfants de moins d'un an et taux de mortalité infantile selon l'âge et le sexe: dernière année disponible, 1996 - 2005 (continued — suite)

Continent, country or area, year, age (in days) and urban/rural residence — Continent, pays ou zone, année, âge (en jours) et résidence, urbaine/rurale	Number - Nombre			Rate - Taux		
	Both sexes Les deux sexes	Male Masculin	Female Féminin	Both sexes Les deux sexes	Male Masculin	Female Féminin
AMERICA, NORTH — AMERIQUE DU NORD						
Saint Vincent and the Grenadines - Saint Vincent-et-les Grenadines[+]						
2005						
Total	29	17	12	...	...	...
Under 1 day - Moins d'un jour	6	3	3	...	...	...
1-6	11	6	5	...	...	...
7-27	3	2	1	...	...	...
28-364	9	6	3	...	...	...
Trinidad and Tobago - Trinité-et-Tobago						
2002						
Total	412	247	165	...	...	...
Under 1 day - Moins d'un jour	91	51	40	...	...	...
1-6	148	92	56	...	...	...
7-27	105	71	34	...	...	...
28-364	68	33	35	...	...	...
Unknown - Inconnu	-	-	-	...	...	...
United States - États-Unis						
2003						
Total	28 025	15 902	12 123	6.9	7.6	6.1
Under 1 day - Moins d'un jour	11 469	6 387	5 082	2.8	3.1	2.5
1-6	3 664	2 123	1 541	0.9	1.0	0.8
7-27	3 760	2 126	1 634	0.9	1.0	0.8
28-364	9 132	5 266	3 866	2.2	2.5	1.9
AMERICA, SOUTH — AMERIQUE DU SUD						
Argentina - Argentine						
2005						
Total	9 507	5 402	4 088	13.3	14.8	11.8
0-6	4 641	2 660	1 967	6.5	7.3	5.7
7-27	1 666	931	732	2.3	2.5	2.1
28-364	3 200	1 811	1 389	4.5	5.0	4.0
Brazil - Brésil[3,4]						
2004						
Total	46 072	27 014	19 000	...	...	...
Under 1 day - Moins d'un jour	9 866	5 608	4 222	...	...	...
1-6	10 694	6 269	4 412	...	...	...
7-27	6 783	3 730	3 050	...	...	...
28-364	14 508	8 084	6 418	...	...	...
Unknown - Inconnu	4 221	3 323	898	...	...	...
Chile - Chili						
2003						
Total	1 935	1 061	874	8.3	8.8	7.6
Under 1 day - Moins d'un jour	605	315	290	2.6	2.6	2.5
1-6	332	187	145	1.4	1.6	1.3
7-27	275	168	107	1.2	1.4	0.9
28-364	723	391	332	3.1	3.3	2.9
Colombia - Colombie[5]						
2005						
Total	11 441	6 480	4 960	...	...	...
Under 1 day - Moins d'un jour	2 466	1 386	1 080	...	...	...
1-6	2 452	1 432	1 020	...	...	...
7-27	1 845	1 046	799	...	...	...
28-364	4 317	2 415	1 901	...	...	...
Unknown - Inconnu	361	201	160	...	...	...
Ecuador - Équateur[6]						
2004						
Total	3 942	2 241	1 701	...	...	...
Under 1 day - Moins d'un jour	760	420	340	...	...	...
1-6	829	498	331	...	...	...
7-27	568	331	237	...	...	...
28-364	1 785	992	793	...	...	...

16. Infant deaths and infant mortality rates by age and sex: latest available year, 1996 - 2005
Décès d'enfants de moins d'un an et taux de mortalité infantile selon l'âge et le sexe: dernière année
disponible, 1996 - 2005 (continued — suite)

Continent, country or area, year, age (in days) and urban/rural residence — Continent, pays ou zone, année, âge (en jours) et résidence,urbaine/rurale	Number - Nombre			Rate - Taux		
	Both sexes Les deux sexes	Male Masculin	Female Féminin	Both sexes Les deux sexes	Male Masculin	Female Féminin
AMERICA, SOUTH — AMERIQUE DU SUD						
French Guiana - Guyane française[2]						
2003						
Total	58	32	26	...	...	...
Under 1 day - Moins d'un jour	10	3	7	...	...	...
1-6	15	10	5	...	...	...
7-27	16	12	4	...	...	...
28-364	17	7	10	...	...	...
Peru - Pérou[+,4,7,8]						
2003						
Total	7 122	3 886	3 233	...	...	...
Under 1 day - Moins d'un jour	1 256	701	553	...	...	...
1-6	1 503	836	667	...	...	...
7-27	1 160	647	513	...	...	...
28-364	3 203	1 702	1 500	...	...	...
Uruguay						
2000						
Total	742	434	304	...	...	...
Under 1 day - Moins d'un jour	152	87	61	...	...	...
1-6	124	74	50	...	...	...
7-27	142	90	52	...	...	...
28-364	324	183	141	...	...	...
Venezuela (Bolivarian Republic of) - Venezuela (République bolivarienne du)[4]						
2001						
Total	8 158	4 710	3 448	15.4	17.1	13.5
0-27	5 657	3 288	2 369	10.7	12.0	9.3
28-364	2 501	1 422	1 079	4.7	5.2	4.2
ASIA — ASIE						
Armenia - Arménie[9]						
2005						
Total	460	272	188	...	...	...
Under 1 day - Moins d'un jour	67	37	30	...	...	...
1-6	213	134	79	...	...	...
7-27	40	24	16	...	...	...
28-364	140	77	63	...	...	...
Azerbaijan - Azerbaïdjan[+,9]						
2004						
Total	1 287	757	530	9.8	10.7	8.7
Under 1 day - Moins d'un jour	111	69	42	0.8	1.0	0.7
1-6	192	139	53	1.5	2.0	0.9
7-27	56	31	25	0.4	0.4	♦0.4
28-364	928	518	410	7.1	7.3	6.8
Bahrain - Bahreïn						
2002						
Total	94	48	46	...	...	...
0-6	29	14	15	...	...	...
7-27	22	9	13	...	...	...
28-364	43	25	18	...	...	...
2005						
Total	134	...	...	...	...	...
0-6	43	...	...	...	...	...
7-27	33	...	...	...	...	...
28-364	58	...	...	...	...	...
China: Hong Kong SAR - Chine: Hong Kong RAS						
2005						
Total	131	78	53	...	...	...
Under 1 day - Moins d'un jour	21	13	8	...	...	...
1-6	39	24	15	...	...	...
7-27	27	10	17	...	...	...
28-364	44	31	13	...	...	...
Unknown - Inconnu	-	-	-	...	...	...

16. Infant deaths and infant mortality rates by age and sex: latest available year, 1996 - 2005
Décès d'enfants de moins d'un an et taux de mortalité infantile selon l'âge et le sexe: dernière année disponible, 1996 - 2005 (continued — suite)

Continent, country or area, year, age (in days) and urban/rural residence Continent, pays ou zone, année, âge (en jours) et résidence,urbaine/rurale	Number - Nombre			Rate - Taux		
	Both sexes Les deux sexes	Male Masculin	Female Féminin	Both sexes Les deux sexes	Male Masculin	Female Féminin
ASIA — ASIE						
China: Macao SAR - Chine: Macao RAS						
2005						
Total	12	5	7	...	...	...
Under 1 day - Moins d'un jour	6	4	2	...	...	...
1-6	1	-	1	...	...	...
7-27	1	-	1	...	...	...
28-364	4	1	3	...	...	...
Cyprus - Chypre[10]						
2005						
Total	33	19	14	...	...	...
Under 1 day - Moins d'un jour	9	5	4	...	...	...
1-6	9	5	4	...	...	...
7-27	4	3	1	...	...	...
28-364	11	6	5	...	...	...
Georgia - Géorgie[9]						
2005						
Total	916	482	434	19.7	...	...
Under 1 day - Moins d'un jour	635	317	318	13.7	...	...
1-6	190	116	74	4.1	...	...
7-27	33	20	13	0.7	...	...
28-364	58	29	29	1.2	...	...
Israel - Israël[7,11,12]						
2005						
Total	627	342	284	...	...	...
Under 1 day - Moins d'un jour	130	63	66	...	...	...
1-6	138	83	55	...	...	...
7-27	114	64	50	...	...	...
28-364	245	132	113	...	...	...
Japan - Japon[13]						
2005						
Total	2 958	1 641	1 317	2.8	3.0	2.5
Under 1 day - Moins d'un jour	691	375	316	0.7	0.7	0.6
1-6	400	233	167	0.4	0.4	0.3
7-27	419	215	204	0.4	0.4	0.4
28-364	1 448	818	630	1.4	1.5	1.2
Kazakhstan[9]						
2004						
Total	3 901	2 280	1 621	14.3	16.2	12.2
Under 1 day - Moins d'un jour	344	199	145	1.3	1.4	1.1
1-6	1 560	935	625	5.7	6.7	4.7
7-27	569	310	259	2.1	2.2	2.0
28-364	1 426	835	591	5.2	5.9	4.5
Unknown - Inconnu	2	1	1	0.0	0.0	0.0
Kuwait - Koweït						
2005						
Total	420	223	197	...	...	...
Under 1 day - Moins d'un jour	110	66	44	...	...	...
1-6	95	52	43	...	...	...
7-27	68	30	38	...	...	...
28-364	147	75	72	...	...	...
Kyrgyzstan - Kirghizistan[9,14]						
2005						
Total	3 258	1 830	1 428	29.7	32.4	26.8
Under 1 day - Moins d'un jour	902	478	424	8.2	8.5	8.0
1-6	1 104	648	456	10.1	11.5	8.6
7-27	291	168	123	2.6	3.0	2.3
28-364	961	536	425	8.7	9.5	8.0
Malaysia - Malaisie						
2000						
Total	3 578	2 026	1 552	6.6	7.2	5.9
Under 1 day - Moins d'un jour	115	69	46	0.2	0.2	0.2
1-6	1 353	777	576	2.5	2.8	2.2
7-27	584	319	265	1.1	1.1	1.0
28-364	1 526	861	665	2.8	3.1	2.5

16. Infant deaths and infant mortality rates by age and sex: latest available year, 1996 - 2005
Décès d'enfants de moins d'un an et taux de mortalité infantile selon l'âge et le sexe: dernière année disponible, 1996 - 2005 (continued — suite)

Continent, country or area, year, age (in days) and urban/rural residence / Continent, pays ou zone, année, âge (en jours) et résidence,urbaine/rurale	Number - Nombre			Rate - Taux		
	Both sexes Les deux sexes	Male Masculin	Female Féminin	Both sexes Les deux sexes	Male Masculin	Female Féminin
ASIA — ASIE						
Maldives						
2005						
Total	67	32	35	...	...	...
0-6	40	19	21	...	...	...
7-27	6	4	2	...	...	...
28-364	21	9	12	...	...	...
Occupied Palestinian Territory - Territoire palestinien occupé						
2005						
Total	*1 057*	*519*	*538*	...	...	...
Under 1 day - Moins d'un jour	*56*	*34*	*22*	...	...	...
1-6	*246*	*130*	*116*	...	...	...
7-27	*231*	*121*	*110*	...	...	...
28-364	*524*	*234*	*290*	...	...	...
Pakistan[15,16]						
2005						
Total	289 169	168 960	120 209	76.7	84.8	67.6
Under 1 day - Moins d'un jour	30 052	18 699	11 353	8.0	9.4	6.4
1-6	113 531	68 118	45 413	30.1	34.2	25.5
7-27	38 734	23 374	15 359	10.3	11.7	8.6
28-364	106 852	58 768	48 084	28.3	29.5	27.0
Philippines						
2003						
Total	22 844	13 329	9 515	13.7	15.3	11.9
Under 1 day - Moins d'un jour	4 466	2 560	1 906	2.7	2.9	2.4
1-6	5 936	3 619	2 317	3.6	4.2	2.9
7-27	2 742	1 637	1 105	1.6	1.9	1.4
28-364	9 700	5 513	4 187	5.8	6.3	5.2
Qatar						
2004						
Total	113	60	53	...	...	...
Under 1 day - Moins d'un jour	-	-	-	...	...	...
1-6	51	26	25	...	...	...
7-27	29	15	14	...	...	...
28-364	33	19	14	...	...	...
Singapore - Singapour[+]						
2005						
Total	95	57	38	...	...	...
Under 1 day - Moins d'un jour	16	8	8	...	...	...
1-6	23	14	9	...	...	...
7-27	21	12	9	...	...	...
28-364	35	23	12	...	...	...
Sri Lanka[+]						
1996						
Total	5 879	3 271	2 608	17.3	18.8	15.6
Under 1 day - Moins d'un jour	1 630	899	731	4.8	5.2	4.4
1-6	1 818	1 072	746	5.3	6.2	4.5
7-27	952	526	426	2.8	3.0	2.6
28-364	1 479	774	705	4.3	4.5	4.2
Thailand - Thaïlande[+]						
2005						
Total	*6 183*	*3 450*	*2 733*	...	...	...
Under 1 day - Moins d'un jour	*711*	*378*	*333*	...	...	...
1-6	*1 813*	*1 041*	*772*	...	...	...
7-27	*1 121*	*644*	*477*	...	...	...
28-364	*2 538*	*1 387*	*1 151*	...	...	...
Turkey - Turquie[17,18]						
1999						
Urban - Urbaine						
Total	15 870	8 931	6 939	...	...	...
0-6	8 483	4 876	3 607	...	...	...
7-27	1 978	1 093	885	...	...	...
28-364	5 409	2 962	2 447	...	...	...

16. Infant deaths and infant mortality rates by age and sex: latest available year, 1996 - 2005
Décès d'enfants de moins d'un an et taux de mortalité infantile selon l'âge et le sexe: dernière année disponible, 1996 - 2005 (continued — suite)

Continent, country or area, year, age (in days) and urban/rural residence Continent, pays ou zone, année, âge (en jours) et résidence,urbaine/rurale	Number - Nombre			Rate - Taux		
	Both sexes Les deux sexes	Male Masculin	Female Féminin	Both sexes Les deux sexes	Male Masculin	Female Féminin
ASIA — ASIE						
Uzbekistan - Ouzbékistan[9]						
2000						
Total	10 091	5 805	4 286	19.1	21.4	16.7
Under 1 day - Moins d'un jour	607	355	252	1.2	1.3	1.0
1-6	2 179	1 352	827	4.1	5.0	3.2
7-27	1 279	731	548	2.4	2.7	2.1
28-364	6 026	3 367	2 659	11.4	12.4	10.4
EUROPE						
Albania - Albanie						
2005						
Total	303	167	136	...	...	...
Under 1 day - Moins d'un jour	15	10	5	...	...	...
1-6	37	23	14	...	...	...
7-27	26	17	9	...	...	...
28-364	225	117	108	...	...	...
Andorra - Andorre						
2004						
Total	2	1	1	...	...	...
Under 1 day - Moins d'un jour	-	-	-	...	...	...
1-6	-	-	-	...	...	...
7-27	-	-	-	...	...	...
28-364	2	1	1	...	...	...
Austria - Autriche						
2005						
Total	327	175	152	...	...	...
Under 1 day - Moins d'un jour	118	49	69	...	...	...
1-6	54	33	21	...	...	...
7-27	58	31	27	...	...	...
28-364	97	62	35	...	...	...
Unknown - Inconnu	-	-	-	...	...	...
Belarus - Bélarus[9]						
2004						
Total	614	364	250	...	...	...
Under 1 day - Moins d'un jour	74	48	26	...	...	...
1-6	119	76	43	...	...	...
7-27	80	45	35	...	...	...
28-364	341	195	146	...	...	...
Belgium - Belgique						
2000						
Total	554	305	249	...	...	...
Under 1 day - Moins d'un jour	91	46	45	...	...	...
1-6	153	85	68	...	...	...
7-27	90	56	34	...	...	...
28-364	220	118	102	...	...	...
Bosnia and Herzegovina - Bosnie-Herzégovine						
2005						
Total	233	133	100	...	...	...
Under 1 day - Moins d'un jour	50	29	31	...	...	...
1-6	101	62	39	...	...	...
7-27	31	14	17	...	...	...
28-364	51	31	20	...	...	...
Unknown - Inconnu	-	-	-	...	...	...
Bulgaria - Bulgarie						
2005						
Total	739	429	310	...	...	...
Under 1 day - Moins d'un jour	133	75	58	...	...	...
1-6	163	100	63	...	...	...
7-27	148	85	63	...	...	...
28-364	295	169	126	...	...	...
Unknown - Inconnu	-	-	-	...	...	...

16. Infant deaths and infant mortality rates by age and sex: latest available year, 1996 - 2005
Décès d'enfants de moins d'un an et taux de mortalité infantile selon l'âge et le sexe: dernière année disponible, 1996 - 2005 (continued — suite)

Continent, country or area, year, age (in days) and urban/rural residence	Number - Nombre			Rate - Taux		
Continent, pays ou zone, année, âge (en jours) et résidence,urbaine/rurale	Both sexes Les deux sexes	Male Masculin	Female Féminin	Both sexes Les deux sexes	Male Masculin	Female Féminin
EUROPE						
Croatia - Croatie						
2005						
Total	242	125	117	...	...	...
Under 1 day - Moins d'un jour	82	43	39	...	...	...
1-6	64	34	30	...	...	...
7-27	26	9	17	...	...	...
28-364	70	39	31	...	...	...
Unknown - Inconnu	-	-	-	...	...	...
Czech Republic - République tchèque						
2005						
Total	347	211	136	...	...	...
Under 1 day - Moins d'un jour	35	16	19	...	...	...
1-6	81	60	21	...	...	...
7-27	90	53	37	...	...	...
28-364	141	82	59	...	...	...
Unknown - Inconnu	-	-	-	...	...	...
Denmark - Danemark[19]						
2005						
Total	280	167	113	...	...	...
Under 1 day - Moins d'un jour	106	60	46	...	...	...
1-6	71	39	32	...	...	...
7-27	38	23	15	...	...	...
28-364	65	45	20	...	...	...
Unknown - Inconnu	-	-	-	...	...	...
Estonia - Estonie						
2005						
Total	78	43	35	...	...	...
Under 1 day - Moins d'un jour	15	8	7	...	...	...
1-6	14	10	4	...	...	...
7-27	18	9	9	...	...	...
28-364	37	20	17	...	...	...
Unknown - Inconnu	-	-	-	...	...	...
Finland - Finlande[20]						
2005						
Total	174	95	79	...	...	...
Under 1 day - Moins d'un jour	58	26	32	...	...	...
1-6	42	20	22	...	...	...
7-27	20	15	5	...	...	...
28-364	54	34	20	...	...	...
Unknown - Inconnu	-	-	-	...	...	...
France[21]						
2004						
Total	2 988	1 683	1 305	3.9	4.3	3.5
Under 1 day - Moins d'un jour	689	382	307	0.9	1.0	0.8
1-6	681	407	274	0.9	1.0	0.7
7-27	598	340	258	0.8	0.9	0.7
28-364	981	534	447	1.3	1.4	1.2
Germany - Allemagne						
2004						
Total	2 918	1 629	1 289	4.1	4.5	3.8
Under 1 day - Moins d'un jour	813	440	373	1.2	1.2	1.1
1-6	633	366	267	0.9	1.0	0.8
7-27	446	263	183	0.6	0.7	0.5
28-364	1 026	560	466	1.5	1.5	1.4
Greece - Grèce						
2005						
Total	409	220	189	...	...	...
Under 1 day - Moins d'un jour	55	30	25	...	...	...
1-6	124	64	60	...	...	...
7-27	94	53	41	...	...	...
28-364	125	63	62	...	...	...
Unknown - Inconnu	11	10	1	...	...	...

16. Infant deaths and infant mortality rates by age and sex: latest available year, 1996 - 2005
Décès d'enfants de moins d'un an et taux de mortalité infantile selon l'âge et le sexe: dernière année disponible, 1996 - 2005 (continued — suite)

Continent, country or area, year, age (in days) and urban/rural residence Continent, pays ou zone, année, âge (en jours) et résidence,urbaine/rurale	Number - Nombre			Rate - Taux		
	Both sexes Les deux sexes	Male Masculin	Female Féminin	Both sexes Les deux sexes	Male Masculin	Female Féminin
EUROPE						
Hungary - Hongrie						
2005						
Total	607	354	253	...	...	...
Under 1 day - Moins d'un jour	116	69	47	...	...	...
1-6	146	92	54	...	...	...
7-27	133	79	54	...	...	...
28-364	212	114	98	...	...	...
Unknown - Inconnu	-	-	-	...	...	...
Iceland - Islande						
2005						
Total	10	6	4	...	...	...
Under 1 day - Moins d'un jour	3	-	3	...	...	...
1-6	3	3	-	...	...	...
7-27	1	1	-	...	...	...
28-364	3	2	1	...	...	...
Unknown - Inconnu	-	-	-	...	...	...
Ireland - Irlande[+,22]						
2005						
Total	244	114	130	...	...	...
Under 1 day - Moins d'un jour	85	40	45	...	...	...
1-6	62	30	32	...	...	...
7-27	30	15	15	...	...	...
28-364	67	29	38	...	...	...
Unknown - Inconnu	-	-	-	...	...	...
Isle of Man - Îles de Man[+]						
2004						
Total	2	1	1	...	...	...
Under 1 day - Moins d'un jour	-	-	-	...	...	...
1-6	-	-	-	...	...	...
7-27	1	-	1	...	...	...
28-364	1	1	-	...	...	...
Italy - Italie						
2003						
Total	2 482	1 370	1 112	4.6	4.9	4.2
Under 1 day - Moins d'un jour	660	378	282	1.2	1.4	1.1
1-6	663	363	300	1.2	1.3	1.1
7-27	493	277	216	0.9	1.0	0.8
28-364	666	352	314	1.2	1.3	1.2
Latvia - Lettonie[9]						
2005						
Total	168	87	81	...	...	...
Under 1 day - Moins d'un jour	17	9	8	...	...	...
1-6	64	35	29	...	...	...
7-27	40	17	23	...	...	...
28-364	47	26	21	...	...	...
Unknown - Inconnu	-	-	-	...	...	...
Lithuania - Lituanie[9]						
2005						
Total	209	120	89	...	...	...
Under 1 day - Moins d'un jour	32	19	13	...	...	...
1-6	47	26	21	...	...	...
7-27	45	29	16	...	...	...
28-364	85	46	39	...	...	...
Unknown - Inconnu	-	-	-	...	...	...
Luxembourg						
2005						
Total	14	5	9	...	...	...
Under 1 day - Moins d'un jour	1	-	1	...	...	...
1-6	4	2	2	...	...	...
7-27	3	1	2	...	...	...
28-364	6	2	4	...	...	...
Unknown - Inconnu	-	-	-	...	...	...

16. Infant deaths and infant mortality rates by age and sex: latest available year, 1996 - 2005
Décès d'enfants de moins d'un an et taux de mortalité infantile selon l'âge et le sexe: dernière année disponible, 1996 - 2005 (continued — suite)

Continent, country or area, year, age (in days) and urban/rural residence Continent, pays ou zone, année, âge (en jours) et résidence,urbaine/rurale	Number - Nombre			Rate - Taux		
	Both sexes Les deux sexes	Male Masculin	Female Féminin	Both sexes Les deux sexes	Male Masculin	Female Féminin
EUROPE						
Malta - Malte						
2001						
Total	17	12	5	...	...	...
0-6	10	7	3	...	...	...
7-27	2	1	1	...	...	...
28-364	5	4	1	...	...	...
Netherlands - Pays-Bas[23]						
2003						
Total	962	562	400	...	...	...
Under 1 day - Moins d'un jour	320	192	128	...	...	...
1-6	235	145	90	...	...	...
7-27	170	83	87	...	...	...
28-364	237	142	95	...	...	...
Norway - Norvège[24]						
2005						
Total	175	96	79	...	...	...
Under 1 day - Moins d'un jour	42	24	18	...	...	...
1-6	48	25	23	...	...	...
7-27	30	14	16	...	...	...
28-364	55	33	22	...	...	...
Unknown - Inconnu	-	-	-	...	...	...
Poland - Pologne						
2005						
Total	2 340	1 304	1 036	6.4	7.0	5.9
Under 1 day - Moins d'un jour	568	305	263	1.6	1.6	1.5
1-6	665	385	280	1.8	2.1	1.6
7-27	400	227	173	1.1	1.2	1.0
28-364	707	387	320	1.9	2.1	1.8
Portugal						
2004						
Total	413	243	170	...	...	...
Under 1 day - Moins d'un jour	90	50	40	...	...	...
1-6	97	56	41	...	...	...
7-27	92	63	29	...	...	...
28-364	134	74	60	...	...	...
Republic of Moldova - République de Moldova[9]						
2004						
Total	464	269	195	...	...	...
Under 1 day - Moins d'un jour	49	29	20	...	...	...
1-6	150	93	57	...	...	...
7-27	64	33	31	...	...	...
28-364	201	114	87	...	...	...
Unknown - Inconnu	-	-	-	...	...	...
Romania - Roumanie						
2003						
Total	3 546	2 060	1 486	16.7	18.8	14.4
Under 1 day - Moins d'un jour	255	147	108	1.2	1.3	1.0
1-6	1 006	608	398	4.7	5.6	3.9
7-27	604	362	242	2.8	3.3	2.4
28-364	1 681	943	738	7.9	8.6	7.2
Russian Federation - Fédération de Russie[9]						
2004						
Total	17 339	10 090	7 249	11.5	13.1	9.9
Under 1 day - Moins d'un jour	2 200	1 251	949	1.5	1.6	1.3
1-6	5 079	3 100	1 979	3.4	4.0	2.7
7-27	2 945	1 709	1 236	2.0	2.2	1.7
28-364	7 091	4 013	3 078	4.7	5.2	4.2
Unknown - Inconnu	24	17	7	0.0	0.0	0.0
San Marino - Saint-Marin+						
2003						
Total	2	1	1	...	...	...
Under 1 day - Moins d'un jour	1	-	1	...	...	...
1-6	-	-	-	...	...	...
7-27	1	1	-	...	...	...

16. Infant deaths and infant mortality rates by age and sex: latest available year, 1996 - 2005
Décès d'enfants de moins d'un an et taux de mortalité infantile selon l'âge et le sexe: dernière année disponible, 1996 - 2005 (continued — suite)

Continent, country or area, year, age (in days) and urban/rural residence / Continent, pays ou zone, année, âge (en jours) et résidence,urbaine/rurale	Number - Nombre			Rate - Taux		
	Both sexes Les deux sexes	Male Masculin	Female Féminin	Both sexes Les deux sexes	Male Masculin	Female Féminin
EUROPE						
San Marino - Saint-Marin[+]						
2003						
28-364	-	-	-	...	...	...
Serbia and Montenegro - Serbie-et-Montenegro[25]						
2003						
Total	803	442	361	...	...	...
Under 1 day - Moins d'un jour	170	104	66	...	...	...
1-6	281	152	129	...	...	...
7-27	128	66	62	...	...	...
28-364	224	120	104	...	...	...
Slovakia - Slovaquie						
2005						
Total	392	225	167	...	...	...
Under 1 day - Moins d'un jour	56	29	27	...	...	...
1-6	97	59	38	...	...	...
7-27	72	42	30	...	...	...
28-364	167	95	72	...	...	...
Slovenia - Slovénie						
2005						
Total	75	41	34	...	...	...
Under 1 day - Moins d'un jour	24	10	14	...	...	...
1-6	21	11	10	...	...	...
7-27	9	5	4	...	...	...
28-364	14	10	4	...	...	...
Spain - Espagne						
2003						
Total	1 733	964	769	3.9	4.2	3.6
Under 1 day - Moins d'un jour	322	180	142	0.7	0.8	0.7
1-6	368	211	157	0.8	0.9	0.7
7-27	416	234	182	0.9	1.0	0.8
28-364	627	339	288	1.4	1.5	1.3
Sweden - Suède						
2005						
Total	246	131	115	...	...	...
Under 1 day - Moins d'un jour	55	30	25	...	...	...
1-6	60	33	27	...	...	...
7-27	35	16	19	...	...	...
28-364	96	52	44	...	...	...
Switzerland - Suisse						
2005						
Total	308	179	129	...	...	...
Under 1 day - Moins d'un jour	136	81	55	...	...	...
1-6	60	34	26	...	...	...
7-27	36	23	13	...	...	...
28-364	76	41	35	...	...	...
The Former Yugoslav Rep. of Macedonia - L'ex-République yougoslave de Macédoine						
2005						
Total	287	156	131	...	...	...
Under 1 day - Moins d'un jour	83	50	33	...	...	...
1-6	81	44	37	...	...	...
7-27	50	24	26	...	...	...
28-364	73	38	35	...	...	...
Ukraine[9]						
2004						
Total	4 024	2 347	1 677	9.4	10.7	8.1
Under 1 day - Moins d'un jour	362	214	148	0.8	1.0	0.7
1-6	1 063	636	427	2.5	2.9	2.1
7-27	759	467	292	1.8	2.1	1.4
28-364	1 840	1 030	810	4.3	4.7	3.9
United Kingdom - Royaume-Uni						
2003						
Total	3 686	2 029	1 657	5.3	5.7	4.9

16. Infant deaths and infant mortality rates by age and sex: latest available year, 1996 - 2005
Décès d'enfants de moins d'un an et taux de mortalité infantile selon l'âge et le sexe: dernière année disponible, 1996 - 2005 (continued — suite)

Continent, country or area, year, age (in days) and urban/rural residence Continent, pays ou zone, année, âge (en jours) et résidence,urbaine/rurale	Number - Nombre			Rate - Taux		
	Both sexes Les deux sexes	Male Masculin	Female Féminin	Both sexes Les deux sexes	Male Masculin	Female Féminin
EUROPE						
United Kingdom - Royaume-Uni						
2003						
Under 1 day - Moins d'un jour	1 073	593	480	1.5	1.7	1.4
1-6	873	483	390	1.3	1.4	1.2
7-27	583	300	283	0.8	0.8	0.8
28-364	1 157	653	504	1.7	1.8	1.5
OCEANIA — OCEANIE						
Australia - Australie+,26						
2005						
Total	1 302	714	588	5.0	5.4	4.7
Under 1 day - Moins d'un jour	565	311	255	2.2	2.3	2.0
1-6	198	111	87	0.8	0.8	0.7
7-27	170	93	77	0.7	0.7	0.6
28-364	368	199	169	1.4	1.5	1.3
New Caledonia - Nouvelle-Calédonie						
2003						
Total	24	14	10	...	...	...
Under 1 day - Moins d'un jour	5	2	3	...	...	...
1-6	4	3	1	...	...	...
7-27	3	2	1	...	...	...
28-364	12	7	5	...	...	...
New Zealand - Nouvelle-Zélande+,27						
2005						
Total	295	172	123	...	...	...
Under 1 day - Moins d'un jour	95	52	43	...	...	...
1-6	52	37	15	...	...	...
7-27	35	21	14	...	...	...
28-364	113	62	51	...	...	...
Unknown - Inconnu	-	-	-	...	...	...
Tonga+						
1997						
Total	20	...	...	...	...	...
Under 1 day - Moins d'un jour	4	...	...	...	...	...
1-6	2	...	...	...	...	...
7-27	2	...	...	...	...	...
28-364	12	...	...	...	...	...
1998						
Total	29	22	7	...	...	...

FOOTNOTES - NOTES

Italics: data from civil registers that are incomplete or of unknown completeness. — *Italiques:* données incomplètes ou dont le degré d'exactitude n'est pas connu provenant des registres de l'état civil.

+ Data tabulated by date of registration rather than occurrence. — Données exploitées selon la date de l'enregistrement et non la date de l'événement.

♦ Rates based on 30 or fewer infant deaths. — Taux basés sur 30 décès d'enfants ou moins.

[1] Including Canadian residents temporarily in the United States, but excluding United States residents temporarily in Canada. -Y compris les résidents canadiens se trouvant temporairement aux Etats-Unis, mais ne comprenant pas les résidents des Etats-Unis se trouvant temporairement au Canada.

[2] Excluding live-born infants who died before their birth was registered. -Non compris les enfants nés vivants décédés avant l'enregistrement de leur naissance.

[3] Reason for discrepancy between these figures and corresponding figures shown elsewhere not ascertained. -On ne sait pas comment s'explique la divergence entre ces chiffres et les chiffres correspondants indiqués ailleurs.

[4] Excluding Indian jungle population. -Non compris les Indiens de la jungle.

[5] Data on live births and deaths are based on a civil registration system put in place in January 1998. -Les données sur les naissances et les décès sont basées sur un système d'enregistrement des faits d'état civil mis en place en janvier 1998.

[6] Excluding nomadic Indian tribes. -Non compris les tribus d'Indiens nomades.

[7] Data for male and female categories exclude infant deaths of unknown sex. -Il n'est pas tenu compte dans les données classées par sexe des décès d'enfant de moins d'un an de sexe inconnu.

[8] Data refer to registered infant deaths only. -Les données se rapportent aux décès enregistrés d'enfants de moins de 1 an seulement.

[9] Excluding infants born alive of less than 28 weeks' gestation, of less than 1 000 grams in weight and 35 centimeters in length, who die within several days of birth. -Non compris les enfants nés vivants après moins de 28 semaines de gestations, pesant moins de 1 000 grammes, mesurant moins de 35 centimètres et décédés dans les sept jours qui ont suivi leur naissance.

[10] Data refer to government controlled areas. -Les données se

rapportent aux zones contrôlées par le Gouvernement.

[11] Including data for East Jerusalem and Israeli residents in certain other territories under occupation by Israeli military forces since June 1967. -Y compris les données pour Jérusalem-Est et les résidents israéliens dans certains autres territoires occupés depuis 1967 par les forces armées israéliennes.

[12] Data include deaths abroad of Israeli residents who were out of the country for less than a year. -Y compris les décès à l'étranger de résidents israéliens qui ont quitté le pays depuis moins d'un an.

[13] Data refer to Japanese nationals in Japan only. -Les données se raportent aux nationaux japonais au Japon seulement.

[14] Since 2004, WHO criteria have been adopted in the country. -Depuis 2004, le pays a adopté les critères de l'OMS.

[15] Data based on Pakistan Demographic Survey. -Données extraites de l'enquête démographique effectuée par le Pakistan.

[16] Excluding data for the Pakistan-held part of Jammu and Kashmir, the final status of which has not yet been determined. -Non compris les données concernant la partie du Jammu et Cachemire occupée par le Pakistan dont le statut définitif n'a pas été déterminé.

[17] Based on the results of the Population Demographic Survey. -D'après les résultats de la Population Demographic Survey.

[18] Deaths in province and district centers. -Les décès aux centres des provinces et des zones seulement.

[19] Excluding Faeroe Islands and Greenland. -Non compris les Iles Féroé et le Gröenland.

[20] Including nationals temporarily outside the country. -Y compris les nationaux se trouvant temporairement hors du pays.

[21] Excluding Overseas Departments, namely, French Guiana, Guadeloupe, Martinique and Reunion, shown separately. -Non compris les départements d'outre mer, c'est-à-dire la Guyane française, la Guadeloupe, la Martinique et la Réunion, qui font l'objet de rubriques distinctes.

[22] Events registered within one year of occurrence. -Evénements enregistrés dans l'année qui suit l'événement.

[23] Including residents outside the country if listed in a Netherlands population register. -Y compris les résidents hors du pays, s'ils sont inscrits sur un registre de population néerlandais.

[24] Including residents temporarily outside the country. -Y compris les résidents se trouvant temporairement hors du pays.

[25] Without data for Kosovo and Metohia. -Sans les données pour le Kosovo and Metohie.

[26] Total includes not stated days and months -Le total comprend les cas pour lesquels l'âge en jours et en mois n'a pas été précisé.

[27] For resident population only. -Pour la population résidante seulement.

Table 17

Table 17 presents maternal deaths and maternal mortality rates for as many years as possible between 1995 and 2004. This table is a reprint of table 17 in the Demographic Yearbook 2004.

Description of variables: Maternal deaths are defined for the purposes of the Demographic Yearbook as those caused by deliveries and complications of pregnancy, childbirth and the puerperium, within 42 days of termination of pregnancy. They are usually defined as deaths coded "38-41" for ICD-9 Basic Tabulation List or as deaths coded "A34", "O00-O95", "O98-O99" for ICD-10, respectively. However, data for ICD-10 shown in this table include deaths due to "O96" and "O97" which refer to deaths from any obstetric cause occurring more than 42 days but less than one year after delivery and death from sequelae of direct obstetric causes occurring one year or more after delivery. For details on causes and corresponding ICD codes, see technical notes for Table 21.

For further information on the definition of maternal mortality from the tenth revisions of the *International Statistical Classification of Diseases and Related Health Problems*[1], see also section 4.3 of the Technical Notes.

Statistics on maternal death presented in this table are provided by the World Health Organisation. They are limited to countries or areas that meet the criterion that cause-of-death statistics are either classified by or convertible to the ninth or tenth revisions mentioned above. Data that are classified by the tenth revision are set in bold in the table.

Rate computation: Maternal mortality rates are the annual number of maternal deaths per 100 000 live births (table 9) in the same year. These rates have been calculated by the Statistics Division of the United Nations. Rates based on 30 or fewer maternal deaths are identified by the symbol (♦).

Reliability of data: In general the quality code for deaths shown in table 18 is used to determine whether data on deaths in other tables appear in roman or *italic* type. However, the reliability of data for the completeness of cause of death data is provided by the World Health Organisation; it may differ from the reliability of data for the total number of deaths. Therefore, there are cases when the quality code in table 18 does not correspond with the typeface used in this table.

Countries and areas that have incomplete (less than 90 per cent completeness) or of unknown completeness of cause of deaths data coverage are considered unreliable and are set in italics rather than in roman type. Rates on these data are not computed.

In addition, when it is known that registration of cause of death does not cover certain areas of a country, rates are not computed. Those countries are Republic of Moldova and Russian Federation, as indicated in footnotes 6 and 7, respectively. All other footnotes pertaining to the inclusion or exclusion of certain population of a country refer only to the live births in the denominator.

Limitations: Statistics on maternal deaths are subject to the same qualifications that have been set forth for vital statistics in general and death statistics in particular as discussed in section 4 of the Technical Notes. The reliability of the data, an indication of which is described above, is an important factor in considering the limitations. In addition, maternal-death statistics are subject to all the qualifications relating to cause-of-death statistics. These have been set forth in section 4 of the Technical Notes.

Maternal mortality rates are subject to the limitations of the data on live births with which they have been calculated. These have been set forth in the technical notes for table 9. Specific information pertaining to individual countries or areas is given in the footnotes to table 9.

The calculation of the maternal mortality rates based on the total number of live births approximates the risk of dying from complications of pregnancy, childbirth or puerperium. Ideally this rate should be based on the number of women exposed to the risk of pregnancy, in other words, the number of women conceiving. Since it is impossible to know how many women have conceived, the total number of live births is used in calculating this rate.

NOTES

[1] *International Statistical Classification of Diseases and Related Health Problems*, Tenth Revision, Volume 2, World Health Organization, Geneva, 1992.

Earlier data: Maternal deaths and maternal mortality rates have been shown in previous issues of the *Demographic Yearbook*. For information on specific years covered, the reader should consult the Index.

It should however be noted that in issues prior to 1975, maternal mortality rates were calculated using the female population rather than live births. Therefore, maternal mortality rates published since 1975 are not comparable to the earlier maternal death rates.

Tableau 17

Ce tableau présente des statistiques et des taux de mortalité liée à la maternité pour le plus grand nombre d'années possible entre 1995 et 2004. Ce tableau est une réimpression du tableau 17 de l'Annuaire Démographique 2004.

Description des variables : aux fins de l'*Annuaire démographique*, les décès liés à la maternité sont ceux entraînés par l'accouchement ou les complications de la grossesse, de l'accouchement et des suites de couches dans un délai de 42 jours après la terminaison de la grossesse. Ils sont généralement associés aux codes 38 à 41 dans le cas de la liste de base pour la mise en tableaux de la CIM-9 et aux codes A34, O00 à O95 et O98 et O99 dans le cas de la CIM-10. Les statistiques associées à des codes correspondant à la CIM-10 englobent des décès de type O96 et O97, qui désignent les décès liés à des causes obstétriques se produisant après 42 jours mais moins d'un an après l'accouchement et les décès entraînés par les séquelles de complications obstétriques directes qui se produisent un an ou plus après l'accouchement. Pour plus de précisions sur les causes des décès et les codes correspondants de la CIM, voir les notes techniques correspondant au tableau 21.

Pour plus de précisions concernant les définitions de la mortalité liée à la maternité dans la dixième révision de la *Classification statistique internationale des maladies et des problèmes de santé connexes*[1], se reporter également à la section 4.3 des Notes techniques.

Les statistiques de mortalité liée à la maternité présentées dans le tableau 17 émanent de l'Organisation mondiale de la santé. Elles ne se rapportent qu'aux pays ou zones qui répondent aux critères selon lesquels les statistiques relatives à la cause des décès sont conformes à la liste de la neuvième ou de la dixième révision de la CIM ou peuvent être aisément comparées aux catégories de cette liste. Les données conformes à la dixième révision sont indiquées en gras dans le tableau.

Calcul des taux : Les taux de mortalité liée à la maternité représentent le nombre annuel de décès dus à la maternité pour 100 000 naissances vivantes (fréquences du tableau 9) de la même année. Ces taux ont été calculés par la Division de statistique de l'ONU. Les taux fondés sur 30 décès liés à la maternité ou moins sont signalés par le signe '♦'.

Fiabilité des données : en général, les code de qualité associés aux données sur les décès indiqués au tableau 18 servent à déterminer si, dans les autres tableaux, les données relatives à la mortalité apparaissent en caractères romains ou italiques. Toutefois, les renseignements relatifs à la fiabilité des données concernant l'exhaustivité des données classées en fonction de la cause des décès émanent de l'Organisation mondiale de la santé et il est possible qu'ils ne correspondent pas avec le degré de fiabilité des données portant sur le nombre total des décès. Il y a donc des cas où les codes de qualité figurant dans le tableau 18 ne coïncident pas avec les caractères utilisés dans le présent tableau.

Les statistiques relatives aux pays et aux zones pour lesquels la couverture des données concernant les causes des décès est incomplète (degré de complétude inférieur à 90 p. 100) ou dont le degré de complétude n'est pas connu sont jugées douteuses et apparaissent en italique et non en caractères romains. Les taux correspondants ne sont pas calculés.

En outre, lorsque l'on sait que l'enregistrement des causes des décès ne couvre pas certaines zones d'un pays, les taux ne sont pas non plus calculés. Cela est le cas de la République de Moldova et de la Fédération de Russie, comme indiqué dans les notes 6 et 7 respectivement. En ce qui concerne toutes les autres notes qui portent sur l'inclusion ou l'exclusion de certaines populations dans un pays, ce sont les naissances vivantes qui figurent au dénominateur.

Insuffisance des données : les statistiques de la mortalité liée à la maternité appellent toutes les réserves qui ont été formulées à propos des statistiques de l'état civil en général et des statistiques relatives à la mortalité en particulier (voir la section 4 des Notes techniques). La fiabilité des données, au sujet de laquelle des indications ont été fournies plus haut, est un facteur important. En outre, les statistiques de la mortalité liée à la maternité appellent les mêmes réserves que celles exposées à la section 4 des Notes techniques en ce qui concerne les statistiques des causes de décès.

Les taux de mortalité liée à la maternité appellent également toutes les réserves formulées à propos des statistiques des naissances vivantes qui ont servi à leur calcul (voir à ce sujet les notes techniques relatives au tableau 9). Des précisions sur certains pays ou zones sont données dans les notes se rapportant au tableau 9.

En prenant le nombre total des naissances vivantes comme base pour le calcul des taux de mortalité liée à la maternité, on obtient une mesure approximative de la probabilité de décès dus aux complications de la grossesse, de l'accouchement et des suites de couches. Idéalement, ces taux devraient être calculés sur la base du nombre de femmes exposées aux risques liés à la grossesse, c'est-à-dire sur la base du nombre de femmes qui conçoivent. Étant donné qu'il est impossible de connaître le nombre de femmes ayant conçu, c'est le nombre total de naissances vivantes que l'on utilise pour calculer ces taux.

Données publiées antérieurement : des statistiques concernant les décès liés à la maternité (nombre de décès et taux) ont déjà été présentées dans des éditions antérieures de l'*Annuaire démographique*. Pour plus de précisions concernant les années pour lesquelles ces données ont été publiées, se reporter à l'index.

Il faut souligner que, avant 1975, les taux de mortalité liée à la maternité étaient calculés sur la base de la population féminine et non sur celle du nombre de naissances vivantes. Ils ne sont donc pas comparables à ceux qui figurent dans les éditions de l'*Annuaire démographique* parues après 1975.

NOTE

[1] *Classification statistique internationale des maladies et des problèmes de santé connexes*, dixième révision, volume 2. Genève, Organisation mondiale de la santé, 1992.

17. Maternal deaths and maternal death rates: 1995 - 2004
Mortalité liée à la maternité nombre de décès et taux: 1995 - 2004

Continent and country or area Continent et pays ou zone	1995	1996	1997	1998	1999	2000	2001	2002	2003	2004
AFRICA — AFRIQUE										
Egypt - Égypte										
Number - Nombre	...	...	...	...	...	*492*	...	...	...	...
Mauritius - Maurice										
Number - Nombre	12	6	10	4	7	3	4	1	4	3
Rate — Taux	◆58.2	◆29.3	◆50.0	◆20.6	◆34.5	◆14.8	◆20.3	◆5.0	◆20.7	◆16.1
Réunion										
Number - Nombre	...	...	...	...	...	...	-	...	...	...
South Africa - Afrique du Sud										
Number - Nombre	*499*	*606*	...	...	...	...	...	...	...	*1 158*
AMERICA, NORTH — AMERIQUE DU NORD										
Anguilla										
Number - Nombre	-	...	...	...	...	-	-	...	...	-
Antigua and Barbuda - Antigua-et-Barbuda										
Number - Nombre	*2*	...	...	...	...	-	...	-	...	...
Bahamas										
Number - Nombre	*4*	-	*7*	*1*	*1*	*2*	...	...	...	...
Barbados - Barbade										
Number - Nombre	-	...	...	...	...	*1*	-	...	...	...
Rate — Taux	-	...	...	...	...	◆*26.6*	-	...	...	...
Belize										
Number - Nombre	1	-	3	9	3	5	3	...	...	...
Rate — Taux	◆15.1	-	◆40.8	◆150.4	◆48.2	◆68.4	◆42.4	...	...	...
Bermuda - Bermudes										
Number - Nombre	...	-	-	-	-	-	...	...	...	...
British Virgin Islands - Îles Vierges britanniques										
Number - Nombre	-	-	-	-	-	...	...	...	...	...
Canada										
Number - Nombre	17	18	19	13	8	**11**	**26**	**15**	**23**	...
Rate — Taux	◆4.5	◆4.9	◆5.5	◆3.8	◆2.4	◆3.4	◆7.8	◆4.6	◆6.9	...
Cayman Islands - Îles Caïmanes										
Number - Nombre	-	-	-	-	-	*1*	...	...	...	...
Costa Rica										
Number - Nombre	*16*	*23*	*29*	*14*	*15*	*28*	*24*	*27*	*24*	*22*
Cuba										
Number - Nombre	70	51	59	59	66	58	**57**	**65**	**62**	**56**
Rate — Taux	47.6	36.4	38.6	39.1	43.8	40.4	**41.1**	**46.0**	**45.3**	**44.0**
Dominica - Dominique										
Number - Nombre	1	-	-	1	-	-	1	1	-	...
Rate — Taux	◆66.6	-	-	◆81.3	-	-	◆82.4	◆92.5	-	...
Dominican Republic - République dominicaine										
Number - Nombre	*77*	*43*	*74*	*64*	*69*	*51*	*64*	...	...	...
El Salvador										
Number - Nombre	*55*	*42*	*42*	*42*	*23*	*31*	*28*	*32*	*27*	...
Grenada - Grenade										
Number - Nombre	-	-	...	...	...	...	...	...	...	...
Guadeloupe										
Number - Nombre	...	...	...	...	...	*3*	*2*	...	...	...
Guatemala										
Number - Nombre	*360*	*335*	*342*	*324*	*316*	*346*	*278*	*280*	*293*	...
Haiti - Haïti										
Number - Nombre	...	...	...	...	...	...	*180*	*135*	*124*	...
Martinique										
Number - Nombre	...	...	...	...	...	*2*	*1*	...	...	...
Mexico - Mexique										
Number - Nombre	1 454	1 291	1 266	**1 430**	**1 411**	**1 325**	**1 268**	**1 324**	**1 332**	...
Rate — Taux	52.9	47.7	46.9	**53.6**	**51.0**	**47.3**	**45.8**	**49.1**	**50.2**	...
Nicaragua										
Number - Nombre		*123*	*127*	*113*	*138*	*97*	*124*	*114*	*88*	...
Panama										
Number - Nombre	...	*35*	*28*	*30*	*31*	*30*	*37*	*38*	*34*	...
Puerto Rico - Porto Rico										
Number - Nombre	*9*	*11*	*13*	*8*	*10*	*14*	*6*	*5*	...	...

17. Maternal deaths and maternal death rates: 1995 - 2004
Mortalité liée à la maternité nombre de décès et taux: 1995 - 2004 (continued — suite)

Continent and country or area / Continent et pays ou zone	1995	1996	1997	1998	1999	2000	2001	2002	2003	2004
AMERICA, NORTH — AMERIQUE DU NORD										
Saint Kitts and Nevis - Saint-Kitts-et-Nevis										
Number - Nombre	1	2	-	...	...	...	...	...	...	...
Rate — Taux	◆125.5	◆240.1	-	...	...	...	...	...	...	...
Saint Lucia - Sainte-Lucie										
Number - Nombre	-	1	-	-	1	3	1	1	...	...
Rate — Taux	-	◆31.8	-	-	◆33.4	◆103.3	◆35.9	◆38.5	...	...
Saint Vincent and the Grenadines - Saint Vincent-et-les Grenadines										
Number - Nombre	4	2	1	-	1	1	-	-	-	...
Rate — Taux	◆153.0	◆85.5	◆43.3	-	◆46.1	◆46.5	-	-	-	...
Trinidad and Tobago - Trinité-et-Tobago										
Number - Nombre	13	7	13	8	7	10	...	...	...	...
Rate — Taux	◆67.5	◆38.9	◆70.5	...	◆38.2	◆55.1	...	...	...	...
Turks Caicos Islands - Îles Turques et Caïques										
Number - Nombre	-	-	-	-	-	-	1	...	...	...
United States - États-Unis										
Number - Nombre	277	294	327	281	406	404	416	379	...	...
Rate — Taux	7.1	7.6	8.4	7.1	10.3	10.0	10.3	9.4	...	...
United States Virgin Islands - Îles Vierges américaines										
Number - Nombre	...	...	1	-	-	1	2	-	...	...
AMERICA, SOUTH — AMERIQUE DU SUD										
Argentina - Argentine										
Number - Nombre	290	317	265	260	287	245	309	356	321	...
Rate — Taux	44.0	46.9	38.3	38.1	41.8	34.9	45.2	51.2	46.0	...
Brazil - Brésil										
Number - Nombre	1 632	1 465	1 791	1 937	1 823	1 648	...	1 648	...	...
Chile - Chili										
Number - Nombre	86	63	61	55	60	49	45	42	33	...
Rate — Taux	30.7	23.8	23.5	21.4	23.9	19.7	18.3	17.6	14.1	...
Colombia - Colombie										
Number - Nombre	411	430	420	721	676	...	...	...	...	...
Ecuador - Équateur										
Number - Nombre	170	194	162	153	209	232	187	149	139	129
French Guiana - Guyane française										
Number - Nombre	...	...	...	...	...	...	2	...	...	...
Guyana										
Number - Nombre	35	26	...	...	...	...	17	20	21	...
Paraguay										
Number - Nombre	104	109	89	96	103	140	132	...	150	...
Peru - Pérou										
Number - Nombre	301	337	246	279	261	263	...	...	...	...
Suriname										
Number - Nombre	1	3	5	7	4	9	...	...	...	...
ASIA — ASIE										
Armenia - Arménie										
Number - Nombre	17	10	17	10	12	18	7	3	8	...
Rate — Taux	◆34.7	◆20.8	◆38.7	◆25.4	◆32.9	◆52.5	◆21.8	◆9.3	◆22.4	...
Azerbaijan - Azerbaïdjan										
Number - Nombre	53	56	41	51	51	44	27	22	...	...
Bahrain - Bahreïn										
Number - Nombre	...	...	2	2	3	2	...	...	...	...
Rate — Taux	...	...	◆14.9	◆14.9	◆21.0	◆14.3	...	...	...	...
Brunei Darussalam - Brunéi Darussalam										
Number - Nombre	...	1	2	3	-	2	...	...	...	...
Rate — Taux	...	◆13.1	◆26.8	◆40.5	-	◆26.7	...	...	...	...

17. Maternal deaths and maternal death rates: 1995 - 2004
Mortalité liée à la maternité nombre de décès et taux: 1995 - 2004 (continued — suite)

Continent and country or area Continent et pays ou zone	1995	1996	1997	1998	1999	2000	2001	2002	2003	2004
ASIA — ASIE										
China: Hong Kong SAR - Chine: Hong Kong RAS										
Number - Nombre	5	2	1	1	1	3	1	1	2	2
Georgia - Géorgie										
Number - Nombre	17	9	13	15	9	4	4	...	...	...
Israel - Israël[1]										
Number - Nombre	7	9	12	11	9	5	9	...	3	...
Rate — Taux	♦6.0	♦7.4	♦9.6	♦8.5	♦6.8	♦3.7	♦6.6	...	♦2.1	...
Japan - Japon[2]										
Number - Nombre	90	80	81	89	79	84	79	90	74	56
Rate — Taux	7.6	6.6	6.8	7.4	6.7	7.1	6.7	7.8	6.6	5.0
Kazakhstan										
Number - Nombre	159	134	137	122	98	94	87	80	67	63
Korea (Republic of) - Corée (République de)										
Number - Nombre	88	75	66	63	77	62	70	71	58	59
Kuwait - Koweït										
Number - Nombre	1	3	7	3	3	2	1	3	...	...
Kyrgyzstan - Kirghizistan										
Number - Nombre	52	27	64	35	44	44	43	54	52	56
Philippines										
Number - Nombre	1 485	1 549	1 513	1 579	...	...	...	...	...	...
Qatar										
Number - Nombre	-	...	...	...						
Singapore - Singapour										
Number - Nombre	2	2	1	5	2	8	4	4	2	...
Sri Lanka										
Number - Nombre	81	...	...	...	...	...	...	...		
Tajikistan - Tadjikistan										
Number - Nombre	95	58	38	57	45	36	40	...	...	...
Thailand - Thaïlande										
Number - Nombre	96	120	87	63	93	102	...	114	...	...
Turkmenistan - Turkménistan										
Number - Nombre	63	49	21	16	...	...	...	...	...	...
EUROPE										
Albania - Albanie										
Number - Nombre	9	8	5	8	2	8	2	5	1	...
Austria - Autriche										
Number - Nombre	1	4	2	4	1	2	5	2	2	3
Rate — Taux	♦1.1	♦4.5	♦2.4	♦4.9	♦1.3	♦2.6	♦6.6	♦2.6	♦2.6	♦3.8
Belarus - Bélarus										
Number - Nombre	14	21	23	26	19	20	13	17	18	...
Rate — Taux	♦13.8	♦21.9	♦25.7	♦28.1	♦20.4	...	...	♦19.2	♦20.3	...
Belgium - Belgique										
Number - Nombre	11	6	10	...	...	...	...	...	...	...
Rate — Taux	♦9.5	♦5.3	♦8.6	...	...	...	...	...	...	...
Bulgaria - Bulgarie										
Number - Nombre	10	14	12	10	16	13	13	11	4	7
Rate — Taux	♦13.9	♦19.4	♦18.7	♦15.3	♦22.1	♦17.6	♦19.1	♦16.5	♦5.9	♦10.0
Croatia - Croatie										
Number - Nombre	6	1	6	3	5	3	1	4	3	3
Rate — Taux	♦12.0	♦1.9	♦10.8	♦6.4	♦11.1	♦6.9	♦2.4	♦10.0	♦7.6	♦7.4
Czech Republic - République tchèque										
Number - Nombre	2	5	2	5	6	5	3	3	4	5
Rate — Taux	♦2.1	♦5.5	♦2.2	♦5.5	♦6.7	♦5.5	♦3.3	♦3.1	♦4.3	♦5.1
Denmark - Danemark[3]										
Number - Nombre	7	4	5	2	4	-	2	...	...	...
Rate — Taux	♦10.0	♦5.9	♦7.4	♦3.0	♦6.0	-	♦3.1	...	...	...
Estonia - Estonie										
Number - Nombre	7	-	2	2	2	5	1	1	4	4
Rate — Taux	♦51.6	-	♦15.8	♦16.4	♦15.9	♦38.2	♦7.9	♦7.7	♦30.7	♦28.5
Finland - Finlande										
Number - Nombre	1	2	3	3	2	3	3	3	2	7
Rate — Taux	♦1.6	♦3.3	♦5.1	♦5.3	♦3.5	♦5.3	♦5.3	♦5.4	♦3.5	♦12.1

17. Maternal deaths and maternal death rates: 1995 - 2004
Mortalité liée à la maternité nombre de décès et taux: 1995 - 2004 (continued — suite)

Continent and country or area / Continent et pays ou zone	1995	1996	1997	1998	1999	2000	2001	2002	2003	2004
EUROPE										
France[4]										
Number - Nombre	70	97	70	75	55	50	56	67	56	...
Rate — Taux	9.6	13.2	9.6	10.2	7.4	6.5	7.3	8.8	7.4	...
Germany - Allemagne										
Number - Nombre	41	51	49	44	37	43	27	21	30	37
Rate — Taux	5.4	6.4	6.0	5.5	4.8	5.6	♦3.7	♦2.9	♦4.2	5.2
Greece - Grèce										
Number - Nombre	-	4	-	7	6	-	4	1	2	3
Rate — Taux	-	♦4.0	-	♦6.9	♦5.2	-	♦3.9	♦1.0	♦1.9	...
Hungary - Hongrie										
Number - Nombre	17	12	21	6	4	10	5	8	7	...
Rate — Taux	♦15.2	♦11.4	♦20.9	♦6.2	♦4.2	♦10.2	♦5.2	♦8.3	♦7.4	...
Iceland - Islande										
Number - Nombre	-	-	-	-	-	-	1	-	-	...
Rate — Taux	-	-	-	-	-	-	♦24.4	-	-	...
Ireland - Irlande										
Number - Nombre	-	3	3	2	1	1	3	5	-	...
Rate — Taux	-	♦6.0	♦5.7	♦3.7	♦1.9	♦1.8	♦5.2	♦8.3	-	...
Italy - Italie										
Number - Nombre	17	20	23	18	14	16	11	17	...	...
Rate — Taux	♦3.2	♦3.8	♦4.3	♦3.5	♦2.7	♦2.9	♦2.1	♦3.2	...	...
Latvia - Lettonie										
Number - Nombre	5	4	8	9	8	5	5	1	3	2
Rate — Taux	♦23.2	♦20.2	♦42.5	♦48.9	♦41.2	♦24.7	♦25.4	♦5.0	♦14.3	♦9.8
Lithuania - Lituanie										
Number - Nombre	7	5	6	5	5	3	4	6	1	5
Rate — Taux	♦17.0	♦12.8	♦15.9	♦13.5	♦13.7	♦8.8	♦12.7	♦20.0	♦3.3	♦16.4
Luxembourg										
Number - Nombre	1	-	-	1	-	1	-	-	-	1
Rate — Taux	♦18.4	-	-	♦18.6	-	♦17.5	-	-	-	♦18.3
Malta - Malte										
Number - Nombre	1	1	-	1	1	-	2	-	-	-
Rate — Taux	♦21.7	♦20.2	-	♦22.3	♦23.2	-	♦51.8	-	-	-
Netherlands - Pays-Bas										
Number - Nombre	14	23	15	23	19	18	14	20	8	10
Rate — Taux	♦7.3	♦12.1	♦7.8	♦11.5	♦9.5	♦8.7	♦6.9	♦9.9	♦4.0	♦5.2
Norway - Norvège										
Number - Nombre	4	1	1	4	5	2	3	2	7	-
Rate — Taux	♦6.6	♦1.6	♦1.7	♦6.9	♦8.4	♦3.4	♦5.3	♦3.6	♦12.4	-
Poland - Pologne										
Number - Nombre	43	21	...	...	20	30	13	19	14	17
Rate — Taux	9.9	♦4.9	...	...	♦5.2	♦7.9	♦3.5	♦5.4	♦4.0	♦4.8
Portugal[5]										
Number - Nombre	9	6	6	9	6	3	6	8	8	...
Rate — Taux	♦8.4	♦5.4	♦5.3	♦7.9	♦5.2	♦2.5	♦5.3	♦7.0	♦7.1	...
Republic of Moldova - République de Moldova[6]										
Number - Nombre	23	22	23	15	11	10	16	11	8	9
Romania - Roumanie										
Number - Nombre	113	95	98	96	98	75	75	47	65	52
Rate — Taux	47.8	41.1	41.4	40.5	41.8	32.0	34.0	22.3	30.6	...
Russian Federation - Fédération de Russie[7]										
Number - Nombre	727	636	633	565	537	503	479	469	463	352
Rate — Taux	...	...	...	...	...	...	...	...	...	23.4
San Marino - Saint-Marin										
Number - Nombre	-						...		...	...
Serbia and Montenegro - Serbie-et-Monténégro										
Number - Nombre	...	...	18	12	7	7	8	1	...	...
Rate — Taux	...	...	♦13.7	♦9.3	♦5.6	♦5.6	♦6.1	♦1.2	...	...
Slovakia - Slovaquie										
Number - Nombre	5	3	1	5	5	1	7	4	...	...
Rate — Taux	♦8.1	♦5.0	♦1.7	♦8.7	♦8.9	♦1.8	♦13.7	♦7.9	...	...
Slovenia - Slovénie										
Number - Nombre	1	3	2	-	2	2	3	-	-	2
Rate — Taux	♦5.3	♦16.0	♦11.0	-	♦11.4	♦11.0	♦17.2	-	-	♦11.1

Continent and country or area Continent et pays ou zone	1995	1996	1997	1998	1999	2000	2001	2002	2003	2004
EUROPE										
Spain - Espagne[8]										
Number - Nombre	11	11	8	10	**14**	**14**	**17**	**14**	**20**	**21**
Rate — Taux	♦3.0	♦3.0	♦2.2	♦2.7	♦**3.7**	♦**3.5**	♦**4.2**	♦**3.3**	♦**4.5**	♦**4.6**
Sweden - Suède										
Number - Nombre	4	5	3	7	1	4	**3**	**4**	...	...
Rate — Taux	♦3.9	♦5.3	♦3.3	♦7.9	♦1.1	♦4.4	♦**3.3**	♦**4.2**	...	...
Switzerland - Suisse										
Number - Nombre	7	3	3	3	6	5	**1**	**3**	**4**	**4**
Rate — Taux	♦8.5	♦3.6	♦3.7	♦3.8	♦7.7	♦6.4	♦**1.4**	♦**4.1**	♦**5.6**	♦**5.5**
The Former Yugoslav Rep. of Macedonia - L'ex-République yougoslave de Macédoine										
Number - Nombre	7	-	1	1	2	**4**	**4**	**3**	**1**	...
Rate — Taux	♦21.8	-	♦3.4	♦3.4	♦7.3	♦**13.6**	♦**14.8**	♦**10.8**	♦**3.7**	...
Ukraine										
Number - Nombre	159	142	111	114	98	95	90	85	71	56
Rate — Taux	32.3	30.4	25.1	27.2	...	24.7	23.9	21.8	17.4	13.1
United Kingdom - Royaume-Uni										
Number - Nombre	51	48	39	49	37	92	**50**	**40**	**53**	**55**
Rate — Taux	7.0	6.5	5.4	6.8	5.3	13.5	**7.5**	**6.0**	**7.6**	**7.7**
OCEANIA — OCEANIE										
Australia - Australie										
Number - Nombre	21	13	12	**5**	**13**	**13**	**12**	**13**	**8**	...
Rate — Taux	♦8.2	♦5.1	♦4.8	♦**2.0**	♦**5.2**	♦**5.2**	♦**4.9**	♦**5.2**	♦**3.2**	...
Fiji - Fidji										
Number - Nombre	...	...	...	...	*1*	...	...	...	...	...
New Zealand - Nouvelle-Zélande[9]										
Number - Nombre	2	4	3	3	4	**5**	**3**	**8**	**4**	...
Rate — Taux	♦3.5	♦7.0	♦5.2	♦5.4	♦7.0	♦**8.8**	♦**5.4**	♦**14.8**	♦**7.1**	...

FOOTNOTES - NOTES

Data in bold refer to maternal deaths based on ICD-10 Classification, otherwise data refer to maternal deaths based on ICD-9 Classification. - Les données en typographie gras se rapportent aux décès maternelles basées sur la classification CIM-10, autrement les données se rapportent aux décès maternelles basées sur la classification CIM-9.

Italics: data from civil registers that are incomplete or of unknown completeness. — *Italiques:* données incomplètes ou dont le degré d'exactitude n'est pas connu, provenant des registres de l'état civil.

♦ Rates based on 30 or fewer deaths. — Taux basés sur 30 décès ou moins.

[1] Including data for East Jerusalem and Israeli residents in certain other territories under occupation by Israeli military forces since June 1967. — Y compris les données pour Jérusalem-Est et les résidents israéliens dans certains autres territoires occupés depuis 1967 par les forces.

[2] For Japanese nationals in Japan only. — Pour les nationaux japonais au Japon seulement.

[3] Excluding Faeroe Islands and Greenland. — Non compris les îles Féroé et le Gröenland.

[4] Excluding Overseas Departments, namely French Guiana, Guadeloupe, Martinique and Reunion, shown separately. - Non compris les départements d'outre-mer, c'est-à-dire la Guyane française, la Guadeloupe, la Martinique et la Réunion, qui font l'objet de rubriques distinctes.

[5] Including the Azores and Madeira Islands. - Y compris les Açores et Madère.

[6] Data on cause of deaths do not include those in the Transnistria region; therefore rates are not computed. - Les données sur la cause des décès ne comprennent pas ceux de la région de Transnistria, en conséquence, les taux n'ont pas étés calcules.

[7] For 2003 and before, data on cause of deaths do not include those in the Chechnya region; therefore rates are not computed. - Pour 2003 et avant, les données sur la cause des décès ne comprennent pas ceux de la région de Chechnya, en conséquence, les taux n'ont pas étés calcules.

[8] Including the Balearic and Canary Islands, and Alhucemas, Ceuta, Chafarinas, Melilla and Penon de Vélez de la Gomera. - Y compris les Baléares et les Canaries, Al Hoceima, Ceuta, les îles Zaffarines, Melilla et Penon de Vélez de la Gomera.

[9] Including Campbell and Kermadec Islands (population 20 in 1961, surface area 148 km2) as well as Antipodes, Auckland, Bounty, Snares, Solander and Three Kings island, all of which are uninhabited. - Y compris les îles Campbell et Kermadec (20 habitants en 1961, superficie: 148 km2) ainsi que les îles Antipodes, Auckland, Bounty, Snares, Solander et Three Kings, qui sont toutes inhabitées.

Table 18

Table 18 presents deaths and crude death rates by urban/rural residence for as many years as possible between 2001 and 2005.

Description of variables: Death is defined as the permanent disappearance of all evidence of life at any time after live birth has taken place (post-natal cessation of vital functions without capability of resuscitation).

Statistics on the number of deaths are obtained from civil registers unless otherwise noted. For those countries or areas where civil registration statistics on deaths are considered reliable (estimated completeness of 90 per cent or more), the death rates shown have been calculated on the basis of registered deaths.

The urban/rural classification of deaths is that provided by each country or area; it is presumed to be based on the national census definitions of urban population that have been set forth at the end of the technical notes for table 6.

For certain countries, there is a discrepancy between the total number of deaths shown in this table and those shown in subsequent tables for the same year. Usually this discrepancy arises because the total number of deaths occurring in a given year is revised although the remaining tabulations are not.

Rate computation: Crude death rates are the annual number of deaths per 1 000 mid-year population.

Rates by urban/rural residence are the annual number of deaths, in the appropriate urban or rural category, per 1 000 corresponding mid-year population. These rates are calculated by the Statistics Division of the United Nations.

Rates presented in this table are limited to those countries or areas with a minimum number of 30 deaths in a given year.

Reliability of data: Each country or area has been asked to indicate the estimated completeness of the deaths recorded in its civil register. These national assessments are indicated by the quality codes (C), (U) and (I) that appear in the first column of this table. C indicates that the data are estimated to be virtually complete, that is, representing at least 90 per cent of the deaths occurring each year, while U indicates that data are estimated to be incomplete that is, representing less than 90 per cent of the deaths occurring each year. The code (I) indicates that the source of data is different than civil registration, but still considered reliable and explained by footnote. The code (...) indicates that no information was provided regarding completeness or no assessment has been done in the country.

Data from civil registers that are reported as incomplete or of unknown completeness (code U or ...) are considered unreliable. They appear in italics in this table; rates based on these data are not computed.

Limitations: Statistics on deaths are subject to the same qualifications as have been set forth for vital statistics in general and death statistics in particular as discussed in section 4 of the Introduction.

The reliability of the data, an indication of which is described above, is an important factor in considering the limitations. In addition, some deaths are tabulated by date of registration and not by date of occurrence; these have been indicated with a plus sign (+). Whenever the lag between the date of occurrence and date of registration is prolonged and, therefore, a large proportion of the death registrations are delayed, death statistics for any given year may be seriously affected. However, delays in the registration of deaths are less common and shorter than in the registration of live births.

International comparability in mortality statistics may also be affected by the exclusion of deaths of infants who were born alive but died before the registration of the birth or within the first 24 hours of life. Statistics of this type are footnoted.

In addition, it should be noted that rates are affected also by the quality and limitations of the population estimates that are used in their computation. The problems of under-enumeration or over-enumeration and, to some extent, the differences in definition of total population have been discussed in section 3 of the Introduction dealing with population data in general, and specific information pertaining to individual countries or areas is given in the footnotes to table 3.

Estimated rates based directly on the results of sample surveys are subject to considerable error as a result of omissions in reporting deaths or as a result of erroneous reporting of those that occurred outside the period of reference. However, such rates do have the advantage of having a "built-in" and corresponding base.

It should be emphasized that crude death rates -- like other crude rates, such as of birth, marriage and divorce -- may be seriously affected by the age-sex structure of the populations to which they relate. Nevertheless, they do provide a simple measure of the level and changes in mortality.

The comparability of data by urban/rural residence is affected by the national definitions of urban and rural used in tabulating these data. It is assumed, in the absence of specific information to the contrary, that the definitions of urban and rural used in connection with the national population census were also used in the compilation of the vital statistics for each country or area. However, it cannot be excluded that, for a given country or area, different definitions of urban and rural are used for the vital statistics data and the population census data respectively. When known, the definitions of urban used in national population censuses are presented at the end of the technical notes for table 6. As discussed in detail in the technical notes for table 6, these definitions vary considerably from one country or area to another.

In addition to problems of comparability, vital rates classified by urban/rural residence are also subject to certain types of bias. If, when calculating vital rates, different definitions of urban are used in connection with the vital events and the population data and if this results in a net difference between the numerator and denominator of the rate in the population at risk, then the vital rates would be biased. Urban/rural differentials in vital rates may also be affected by whether the vital events have been tabulated in terms of place of occurrence or place of usual residence. This problem is discussed in more detail in section 4.1.4.1 of the Introduction.

Earlier data: Deaths and crude death rates have been shown in each issue of the Demographic Yearbook. Data included in this table update the series covering a period of years as follows:

Issue	Years Covered
Historical Supplement CD, 1997	1948 – 1997
1992	1983 – 1992
1985	1976 – 1985
1980	1971 – 1980
Historical Supplement, 1979	1948 – 1977

Tableau 18

Le tableau 18 présente le nombre des décès et les taux bruts de mortalité selon le lieu de résidence (zone urbaine ou rurale) pour le plus grand nombre d'années possible entre 2001 et 2005.

Description des variables : Le décès est défini comme la disparition permanente de tout signe de vie à un moment quelconque postérieur à la naissance vivante (cessation des fonctions vitales après la naissance sans possibilité de réanimation).

Sauf indication contraire, les statistiques relatives au nombre de décès sont établies sur la base des registres d'état civil. Pour les pays ou zones où les données concernant l'enregistrement des décès par les services de l'état civil sont jugées sûres (complétude estimée à 90 p. 100 ou plus), les taux de mortalité ont été calculés d'après les décès enregistrés.

La répartition des décès entre zones urbaines et zones rurales est celle qui a été communiquée par chaque pays ou zone ; on part du principe qu'elle repose sur les définitions de la population urbaine utilisées pour les recensements nationaux, qui sont reproduites à la fin des notes techniques du tableau 6.

Pour quelques pays il y a une discordance entre le nombre total des décès présenté dans ce tableau et ceux présentés après pour la même année. Habituellement ces différences apparaissent lorsque le nombre total des décès pour une certaine année a été révisé alors que les autres tabulations ne l'ont pas été.

Calcul des taux : Les taux bruts de mortalité représentent le nombre annuel de décès pour 1 000 habitants en milieu d'année.

Les taux selon le lieu de résidence (zone urbaine ou rurale) représentent le nombre annuel de décès, classés selon la catégorie urbaine ou rurale appropriée, pour 1 000 habitants en milieu d'année. Ces taux ont été calculés par la Division de statistique de l'ONU.

Les taux présentés dans ce tableau se rapportent seulement aux pays ou zones où l'on a enregistré un nombre minimal de 30 décès au cours d'une année donnée.

Fiabilité des données : Il a été demandé à chaque pays ou zone d'indiquer le degré estimatif de complétude des données sur les décès d'enfants de moins d'un an figurant dans ses registres d'état civil. Ces évaluations nationales sont signalées par les codes de qualité 'C', 'U' et 'I' qui apparaissent dans la deuxième colonne du tableau.

La lettre 'C' indique que les données sont jugées à peu près complètes, c'est-à-dire qu'elles représentent au moins 90 p. 100 des décès d'enfants de moins d'un an survenus chaque année ; la lettre 'U' signifie que les données sont jugées incomplètes, c'est-à-dire qu'elles représentent moins de 90 p.100 des décès d'enfants de moins d'un an survenus chaque année. Le symbole 'I' indique que la source des données est fiable mais n'est pas un registre de l'état civil ; le symbole, dans ce cas, est accompagné par une note explicative. Le code '...' dénote qu'aucun renseignement n'a été communiqué quant à la complétude des données.

Les données provenant des registres de l'état civil qui sont déclarées incomplètes ou dont le degré de complétude n'est pas connu (code 'U' ou '...') sont jugées douteuses. Elles apparaissent en italique dans le présent tableau et les taux correspondants n'ont pas été calculés.

Insuffisance des données : Les statistiques relatives à la mortalité appellent les mêmes réserves que celles qui ont été formulées à propos des statistiques de l'état civil en général et des statistiques relatives aux décès en particulier (voir la section 4 des Introduction).

La fiabilité des données, au sujet de laquelle des indications ont été fournies plus haut, est un facteur important. Il faut également tenir compte du fait que, dans certains cas, les décès sont classés par date d'enregistrement et non par date d'occurrence ; ces cas ont été signalés par le signe '+'. Chaque fois que le décalage entre le décès et son enregistrement est grand et qu'une forte proportion des décès fait l'objet d'un enregistrement tardif, les statistiques relatives aux décès survenus pendant l'année peuvent être considérablement faussées.

En règle générale, toutefois, les décès sont enregistrés beaucoup plus rapidement que les naissances vivantes, et les retards prolongés sont rares.

Un autre facteur qui nuit à la comparabilité internationale est la pratique qui consiste à ne pas inclure dans les statistiques de la mortalité les enfants nés vivants mais décédés avant l'enregistrement de leur naissance ou dans les 24 heures qui ont suivi la naissance. Quand pareil facteur a joué, cela a été signalé en note à la fin du tableau.

Il convient de noter par ailleurs que l'exactitude des taux dépend également de la qualité et des limitations des estimations de la population qui sont utilisées pour leur calcul. Le problème des erreurs par excès ou par défaut commises lors du dénombrement et, dans une certaine mesure, le problème de l'hétérogénéité des définitions de la population totale ont été examinés à la section 3 de l'Introduction, relative à la population en général ; des indications concernant certains pays ou zones sont données en note à la fin du tableau 3.

Les taux estimatifs fondés directement sur les résultats d'enquêtes par sondage comportent des possibilités d'erreurs considérables dues soit à des omissions dans les déclarations des décès, soit au fait que l'on a déclaré à tort des décès survenus en réalité hors de la période considérée. Toutefois, ces taux présentent un avantage : le chiffre de population utilisé comme base est connu par définition et rigoureusement correspondant.

Il faut souligner que les taux bruts de mortalité, de même que les taux bruts de natalité, de nuptialité et de divortialité, peuvent varier très sensiblement selon la composition par âge et par sexe de la population à laquelle ils se rapportent. Ils offrent néanmoins un moyen simple de mesurer le niveau et l'évolution de la mortalité.

La comparabilité des données selon le lieu de résidence (zone urbaine ou rurale) peut être limitée par les définitions nationales des termes « urbain » et « rural » utilisées pour le classement de ces données. En l'absence d'indications contraires, on a supposé que les mêmes définitions avaient servi pour le recensement national de la population et pour l'établissement des statistiques de l'état civil pour chaque pays ou zone. Toutefois, il n'est pas exclu que, pour une zone ou un pays donné, des définitions différentes aient été retenues. Les définitions du terme « urbain » utilisées pour les recensements nationaux de population ont été présentées à la fin du tableau 6 lorsqu'elles étaient connues. Comme on l'a précisé dans les notes techniques relatives au tableau 6, ces définitions varient considérablement d'un pays ou d'une zone à l'autre.

Outre les problèmes de comparabilité, les taux démographiques classés selon le lieu de résidence « urbaine » ou « rurale » sont également sujets à des distorsions particulières. Si l'on utilise des définitions différentes du terme « urbain » pour classer les faits d'état civil et les données relatives à la population lors du calcul des taux et qu'il en résulte une différence nette entre le numérateur et le dénominateur pour le taux de la population exposée au risque, les taux démographiques s'en trouveront faussés. La différence entre ces taux pour les zones urbaines et rurales pourra aussi être faussée selon que les faits d'état civil auront été classés d'après le lieu où ils se sont produits ou d'après le lieu de résidence habituel. Ce problème est examiné plus en détail à la section 4.1.4.1 de l'Introduction.

Données publiées antérieurement : les différentes éditions de l'*Annuaire démographique* contiennent des statistiques des décès et des taux bruts de mortalité. Les données qui figurent dans le tableau 18 actualisent les données qui portaient sur les périodes suivantes :

Éditions	**Années considérées**
Supplément historique (CD-ROM), 1997	1948 – 1997
1992	1983 – 1992
1985	1976 – 1985
1980	1971 – 1980
Supplément rétrospectif, 1979	1948 – 1977

18. Deaths and crude death rates, by urban/rural residence: 2001 - 2005
Décès et taux bruts de mortalité, selon la résidence, urbaine/rurale: 2001 - 2005

Continent, country or area, and urban/rural residence / Continent, pays ou zone et résidence, urbaine/rurale	Co-de[1]	Number - Nombre					Rate - Taux				
		2001	2002	2003	2004	2005	2001	2002	2003	2004	2005
AFRICA — AFRIQUE											
Algeria - Algérie[2,3]											
Total	U	*129 092*	*126 557*	...	...	...	...	...	...	...	...
Benin - Bénin[4]											
Total	I	83 417	...	...	...	...	13.0	...	...	...	...
Botswana[5]											
Total	I	20 823					12.4				
Urban - Urbaine	I	10 041		...			11.0				
Rural - Rurale	I	10 782					14.0				
Chad - Tchad											
Total	...	*138 025*									
Egypt - Égypte											
Total	C	404 531	424 034	440 149	440 790	450 646	6.2	6.4	6.5	6.2	6.3
Urban - Urbaine	C	196 099	204 377	211 719	195 491	198 588	...	...	7.3	...	...
Rural - Rurale	C	208 432	219 657	228 430	245 299	252 058	...	...	5.8	...	...
Ghana											
Total	...	*52 332*	*34 682*								
Kenya											
Total	U	*168 500*	*171 800*	*174 950*	*178 051*	*168 919*	...	...	...	...	...
Libyan Arab Jamahiriya - Jamahiriya arabe libyenne											
Total	U	*18 334*	*19 362*	...	...	...	...	...	...	...	...
Malawi[4]											
Total	I	221 963	217 205	213 705	...	...	20.5	19.4	18.5	...	...
Mauritius - Maurice											
Total	+C	7 983	8 310	8 520	8 475	8 646	6.7	6.9	7.0	6.9	7.0
Urban - Urbaine	+C	3 634	3 702	3 942	3 914	3 988	7.1	7.2	7.6	7.5	7.6
Rural - Rurale	+C	4 349	4 608	4 578	4 561	4 658	6.3	6.6	6.5	6.4	6.5
Morocco - Maroc[6]											
Total	U	*95 612*	...	...	...	...	...	...	...	...	...
Urban - Urbaine	U	*55 745*									
Rural - Rurale	U	*39 787*									
Mozambique[4]											
Total	I	331 162					18.8				
Namibia - Namibie[7]											
Total	I	37 592					20.5				
Réunion[2]											
Total	C	3 829	4 004	*4 022	3 884	4 357	5.2	5.4	*5.3	5.1	5.6
Saint Helena ex. dep. - Sainte-Hélène sans dép.											
Total	C	41	52	44	33	39	...	...	...	...	...
Seychelles											
Total	+C	554	647	668	611	*673	6.8	7.7	8.1	7.4	*8.1
South Africa - Afrique du Sud[8]											
Total	...	*451 279*	*497 577*	*550 904*	*565 954*	...	...	...	...	...	...
Tunisia - Tunisie											
Total	U	*53 300*	...				...	...			
Zimbabwe[9]											
Total	I	...	200 294	...	...	...	...	17.2	...	...	...
Urban - Urbaine	I	...	50 364	...	...	...	...	12.5	...	...	...
Rural - Rurale	I	...	149 930	...	...	...	...	19.7	...	...	...
AMERICA, NORTH — AMERIQUE DU NORD											
Anguilla											
Total	+C	50	52	65	53	62	4.3	4.4	5.3	4.2	4.5
Antigua and Barbuda - Antigua-et-Barbuda[10]											
Total	+C	462	444				6.0	5.7	...	...	...
Aruba											
Total	C	435	492	501	502	482	4.7	5.3	5.3	5.1	4.8

Continent, country or area, and urban/rural residence / Continent, pays ou zone et résidence, urbaine/rurale	Co-de[1]	Number - Nombre					Rate - Taux				
		2001	2002	2003	2004	2005	2001	2002	2003	2004	2005
AMERICA, NORTH — AMERIQUE DU NORD											
Bahamas											
Total	C	1 609	...	1 649	...	...	5.2	...	5.2	...	...
Barbados - Barbade[11]											
Total	+C	1 712	*2 285	...	...	...	6.3	*8.4	...	...	...
Belize											
Total	U	1 261	1 284	1 277	1 298	1 369	...	...	...	...	...
Bermuda - Bermudes											
Total	C	442	404	434	406	*437	7.1	6.4	6.9	6.4	*6.9
British Virgin Islands - Îles Vierges britanniques											
Total	C	101	97	104	120	...	4.9	4.6	4.9	5.5	...
Canada[12]											
Total	C	219 538	223 603	226 169	226 584	231 240	7.1	7.1	7.1	7.1	7.2
Cayman Islands - Îles Caïmanes											
Total	C	132	120	153	196	170	3.2	2.8	3.5	4.4	3.5
Costa Rica											
Total	C	15 609	15 004	15 800	15 949	*16 139	4.0	3.8	3.9	3.8	*3.8
Cuba[6]											
Total	C	79 395	73 882	78 434	*81 095	84 824	7.1	6.6	7.0	*7.2	7.5
Urban - Urbaine	C	64 579	60 167	64 200	*68 587	69 969	7.6	7.1	7.6	*8.1	8.2
Rural - Rurale	C	14 794	13 697	14 224	*12 508	14 855	5.5	5.1	5.2	*4.6	5.4
Dominica - Dominique[13]											
Total	+C	510	594	557	...	...	7.2	8.4	...	...	...
Dominican Republic - République dominicaine											
Total	+U	26 636	26 166	28 343	30 118	...	...	...	...	...	...
El Salvador											
Total	C	29 559	27 458	29 377	30 058	...	4.6	4.2	4.4	4.4	...
Urban - Urbaine	C	20 921	19 595	20 856	...	...	5.6	5.1	5.3	...	...
Rural - Rurale	C	8 638	7 863	8 521	...	...	3.3	2.9	3.1	...	...
Greenland - Groenland											
Total	C	438	435	412	...	...	7.8	7.7	7.3	...	...
Urban - Urbaine	C	361	344	340	...	...	7.8	7.4	7.3	...	...
Rural - Rurale	C	77	91	72	...	...	7.5	9.0	7.2	...	...
Grenada - Grenade											
Total	+C	727	...	...	...	...	7.2	...	...	...	...
Guadeloupe[2]											
Total	C	2 765	2 584	2 636	2 676	2 904	6.4	5.9	6.0	6.0	6.5
Guatemala											
Total	C	68 041	66 089	66 695	66 991	*71 039	5.8	5.5	5.5	5.4	*5.6
Haiti - Haïti[10]											
Total	U	9 599	7 657	8 011	...	...	...	...	...	...	...
Jamaica - Jamaïque											
Total	U	14 473	15 711	15 581	15 389	15 523	...	...	...	...	...
Martinique[2]											
Total	C	2 754	2 681	2 725	2 647	2 610	7.1	6.9	7.0	6.7	6.6
Mexico - Mexique[6]											
Total	+C	443 127	459 687	472 140	473 417	495 240	4.4	4.6	4.6	4.6	4.8
Urban - Urbaine	+C	336 551	342 331	354 633	353 951	370 267	4.4	4.4	4.5	4.5	...
Rural - Rurale	+C	100 670	107 345	109 167	110 999	116 657	4.0	4.2	4.2	4.3	...
Netherlands Antilles - Antilles néerlandaises[14]											
Total	C	1 215	1 220	1 374	1 412	...	7.0	7.0	7.7	7.7	...
Nicaragua											
Total	+U	14 236	15 070	15 379	14 975	16 770	...	...	...	...	...
Urban - Urbaine	+U	9 149	9 805	10 180	10 489	10 931	...	...	...	...	...
Rural - Rurale	+U	5 087	5 265	5 199	4 486	5 839	...	...	...	...	...

Continent, country or area, and urban/rural residence / Continent, pays ou zone et résidence, urbaine/rurale	Code[1]	Number - Nombre					Rate - Taux				
		2001	2002	2003	2004	2005	2001	2002	2003	2004	2005
AMERICA, NORTH — AMERIQUE DU NORD											
Panama											
Total	U	12 442	12 428	13 248	13 475	14 180	...	...	...	...	...
Urban - Urbaine	U	8 079	8 214	8 638	9 815	...	...	...	...	...	...
Rural - Rurale	U	4 363	4 214	4 610	3 660	...	...	...	...	...	...
Puerto Rico - Porto Rico[6]											
Total	C	28 794	28 098	28 356	...	29 701	7.5	7.3	7.3	...	7.6
Urban - Urbaine	C	15 406	15 026	15 038	...	...	...	...	...	...	...
Rural - Rurale	C	13 367	13 009	13 283	...	...	...	...	...	...	...
Saint Kitts and Nevis - Saint-Kitts-et-Nevis											
Total	+C	352	...	...	...	...	7.6	...	...	...	...
Saint Lucia - Sainte-Lucie											
Total	C	998	960	1 046	*1 114	...	6.3	6.0	6.5	*6.9	...
Saint Vincent and the Grenadines - Saint Vincent-et-les Grenadines											
Total	+C	765	766	790	812	813	7.0	7.1	7.5	7.8	7.8
Trinidad and Tobago - Trinité-et-Tobago											
Total	C	9 753	9 797	...	...	...	7.7	7.7	...	...	...
Turks Caicos Islands - Îles Turques et Caïques											
Total	C	69	48	61	46	53	3.5	2.3	2.4	1.7	1.7
United States - États-Unis											
Total	C	2 416 425	2 443 387	2 448 288	*2 398 343	...	8.5	8.5	8.4	*8.2	...
United States Virgin Islands - Îles Vierges américaines[10]											
Total	C	605	617	...	...	...	5.6	5.7	...	...	...
AMERICA, SOUTH — AMERIQUE DU SUD											
Argentina - Argentine											
Total	C	285 941	291 190	302 064	*294 051	293 529	7.7	7.8	8.0	*7.7	7.6
Brazil - Brésil[15]											
Total	U	931 017	958 475	977 717	998 725	979 854	...	...	...	...	...
Chile - Chili											
Total	C	81 873	81 079	83 672	86 138	...	5.3	5.1	5.3	5.4	...
Urban - Urbaine	C	68 884	69 209	72 647	...	...	5.1	5.1	5.3	...	...
Rural - Rurale	C	12 989	11 870	11 025	...	...	6.3	5.7	5.2	...	...
Colombia - Colombie[6,16]											
Total	U	191 513	192 262	193 267	188 933	188 795	...	...	...	...	...
Urban - Urbaine	U	143 333	143 237	145 545	144 135	146 017	...	...	...	...	...
Rural - Rurale	U	38 610	38 094	38 028	36 720	36 053	...	...	...	...	...
Ecuador - Équateur[17]											
Total	U	55 214	55 549	53 521	54 729	56 825	...	...	...	...	...
Urban - Urbaine	U	40 423	42 236	40 585	41 783	...	...	...	...	...	...
Rural - Rurale	U	14 791	13 313	12 936	12 946	...	...	...	...	...	...
French Guiana - Guyane française[2]											
Total	C	668	656	692	719	705	3.9	3.7	3.8	3.8	3.5
Guyana											
Total	+C	4 629	5 003	4 986	5 141	...	6.2	6.7	6.6	6.8	...
Paraguay[11]											
Total	U	18 400	...	19 593	20 283	17 360	...	...	...	...	...

18. Deaths and crude death rates, by urban/rural residence: 2001 - 2005
Décès et taux bruts de mortalité, selon la résidence, urbaine/rurale: 2001 - 2005 (continued — suite)

Continent, country or area, and urban/rural residence / Continent, pays ou zone et résidence, urbaine/rurale	Code[1]	Number - Nombre					Rate - Taux				
		2001	2002	2003	2004	2005	2001	2002	2003	2004	2005
AMERICA, SOUTH — AMERIQUE DU SUD											
Peru - Pérou[15,18]	+U										
Total		*79 966*	*80 862*	*85 198*	*94 149*	...	...	...	...	...	...
Suriname[6,19]	C										
Total		3 099	3 125	3 154	3 319	3 392	6.6	6.6	6.6	6.8	6.8
Urban - Urbaine	C	...	2 218	...	...	...	...	...	...	...	...
Rural - Rurale	C	...	871	...	...	...	...	...	...	...	...
Uruguay	C										
Total		31 228	31 628	32 587	*32 222	*33 319	9.4	9.6	9.9	*9.8	*10.1
Venezuela (Bolivarian Republic of) - Venezuela (République bolivarienne du)[15]	C										
Total		107 867	105 388	118 562	110 946	110 301	4.4	4.2	4.6	4.2	4.2
ASIA — ASIE											
Armenia - Arménie[20]	C										
Total		24 003	25 554	26 014	25 679	26 379	7.5	8.0	8.1	8.0	8.2
Urban - Urbaine	C	15 654	16 737	16 870	16 531	17 128	7.6	8.1	8.2	8.0	8.3
Rural - Rurale	C	8 349	8 817	9 144	9 148	9 251	7.3	7.7	8.0	7.9	8.0
Azerbaijan - Azerbaïdjan[20]											
Total	+C	45 284	46 522	49 001	49 568	51 962	5.6	5.7	6.0	6.0	6.2
Urban - Urbaine	+C	23 382	23 605	24 999	25 867	...	5.7	5.7	5.9	6.0	...
Rural - Rurale	+C	21 902	22 917	24 002	23 701	...	5.5	5.7	6.0	5.9	...
Bahrain - Bahreïn	C										
Total		1 979	2 035	2 114	2 215	2 222	3.0	3.0	3.1	3.1	3.1
Bangladesh[21]											
Total		...	...	...	...	...	4.8	5.1	5.9	5.8	...
Urban - Urbaine		...	...	...	...	...	3.4	3.8	4.7	4.4	...
Rural - Rurale		...	...	...	...	...	5.2	5.4	6.2	6.1	...
Bhutan - Bhoutan[22]											
Total	I	...	...	...	...	4 498	...	...	...	...	7.1
Urban - Urbaine	I	...	...	...	...	1 048	...	...	...	...	...
Rural - Rurale	I	...	...	...	...	3 450	...	...	...	...	...
Brunei Darussalam - Brunéi Darussalam											
Total	+C	1 014	1 041	1 010	1 010	*1 072	3.0	3.0	2.9	2.8	*2.9
Cambodia - Cambodge	U										
Total		*126 257*	*125 617*	*124 981*	*124 391*	...	...	...	...	...	...
China - Chine[23,24,25]	I										
Total		8 180 000	8 210 000	8 250 000	8 320 000	8 490 000	6.4	6.4	6.4	6.4	6.5
China: Hong Kong SAR - Chine: Hong Kong RAS	C										
Total		33 378	34 267	36 971	36 918	38 830	5.0	5.1	5.5	5.4	5.7
China: Macao SAR - Chine: Macao RAS	C										
Total		1 327	1 415	1 474	1 533	1 615	3.1	3.2	3.3	3.4	3.4
Cyprus - Chypre[26]	C										
Total		4 827	5 168	5 200	5 225	5 425	6.9	7.3	7.2	7.1	7.2
Georgia - Géorgie[20]	C										
Total		46 218	46 446	46 055	48 793	42 984	10.5	10.7	10.6	11.3	9.9
Urban - Urbaine	C	...	...	28 887	...	...	...	...	12.8	...	...
Rural - Rurale	C	...	...	17 168	...	...	...	...	8.3	...	...
India - Inde[27,28]											
Total		...	...	...	...	...	8.4	8.1	8.0	7.5	7.6
Urban - Urbaine		...	...	...	...	...	6.3	6.1	6.0	5.8	6.0
Rural - Rurale		...	...	...	...	...	9.1	8.7	8.7	8.2	8.1

Continent, country or area, and urban/rural residence — Continent, pays ou zone et résidence, urbaine/rurale	Code[1]	Number - Nombre					Rate - Taux				
		2001	2002	2003	2004	2005	2001	2002	2003	2004	2005
ASIA — ASIE											
Iran (Islamic Republic of) - Iran (République islamique d')[29]											
Total	C	421 525	337 237	368 518	355 213	361 326	6.5	5.1	5.5	5.3	5.3
Urban - Urbaine	C	243 435	234 091	265 239	240 872	238 235	5.8	5.4	6.0	5.5	5.2
Rural - Rurale	C	178 090	103 146	103 279	114 341	123 091	8.0	4.6	4.6	4.9	5.4
Iraq											
Total	U	...	...	*95 935	*101 820	*115 775	...	...	...	...	...
Israel - Israël[6,30,31]											
Total	C	37 186	38 409	38 499	37 939	38 911	5.8	5.8	5.8	5.6	5.6
Urban - Urbaine	C	34 753	35 962	36 086	35 527	36 478	5.9	6.0	5.9	5.7	5.7
Rural - Rurale	C	2 429	2 442	2 407	2 411	2 424	4.5	4.4	4.2	4.1	4.3
Japan - Japon[6,32]											
Total	C	970 331	982 379	1 014 951	1 028 602	1 083 796	7.6	7.7	7.9	8.1	8.5
Urban - Urbaine	C	712 639	724 274	750 810	773 413	877 007	...	...	...	...	...
Rural - Rurale	C	255 462	256 004	261 979	253 197	204 723	...	...	...	...	...
Jordan - Jordanie[33,34]											
Total	U	16 164	17 220	16 937	17 896	17 883	...	...	...	...	...
Kazakhstan[20]											
Total	C	147 876	149 381	155 277	152 250	157 121	10.0	10.1	10.4	10.1	10.4
Urban - Urbaine	C	94 166	95 470	99 595	98 025	...	11.2	11.3	11.7	11.4	...
Rural - Rurale	C	53 710	53 911	55 682	54 225	...	8.3	8.4	8.7	8.4	...
Korea (Republic of) - Corée (République de)[35]											
Total	C	242 730	246 515	245 817	245 771	245 511	5.1	5.2	5.1	5.1	5.1
Urban - Urbaine	C	154 230	157 755	...	...	...	...	...	...	...	...
Rural - Rurale	C	88 500	88 760	...	...	...	...	...	...	...	...
Kuwait - Koweït											
Total	C	4 364	4 342	4 424	4 793	4 784	2.0	1.9	1.9	2.0	1.9
Kyrgyzstan - Kirghizistan[20]											
Total	C	32 677	35 235	35 941	35 061	36 992	6.6	7.1	7.1	6.9	7.2
Urban - Urbaine	C	12 783	13 583	13 943	14 108	14 526	7.3	7.7	7.8	7.8	7.9
Rural - Rurale	C	19 894	21 652	21 998	20 953	22 466	6.2	6.7	6.8	6.4	6.8
Lebanon - Liban											
Total	C	17 568	17 294	17 187	17 774	18 012	...	...	...	4.7	...
Malaysia - Malaisie											
Total	C	104 600	105 900	*111 700	*113 900	*116 200	4.4	4.3	*4.5	*4.5	*4.4
Maldives											
Total	C	1 081	1 113	1 026	1 007	1 015	3.9	4.0	3.6	3.5	3.5
Urban - Urbaine	C	288	347	297	294	326	3.8	4.5	3.8	3.7	...
Rural - Rurale	C	793	766	729	713	689	4.0	3.8	3.5	3.4	...
Mongolia - Mongolie											
Total	C	15 999	15 857	16 006	16 404	16 480	6.6	6.4	6.4	6.5	6.5
Urban - Urbaine	C	9 215	8 981	9 480	10 183	10 148	6.7	6.4	6.6	6.9	6.7
Rural - Rurale	C	6 784	6 876	6 526	6 221	6 332	6.5	6.5	6.2	6.0	6.4
Nepal - Népal[36]											
Total	I	106 789	...	...	...	...	4.6	...	...	...	...
Occupied Palestinian Territory - Territoire palestinien occupé											
Total	U	9 177	10 316	10 207	10 029	9 645	...	...	...	...	...
Oman[37]											
Total	U	2 550	2 564	2 701	2 743	2 849	...	...	...	...	...
Pakistan[38,39]											
Total	I	*956 515	...	970 428	...	1 019 467	6.7	...	6.6	...	6.6
Urban - Urbaine	I	302 482	...	309 451	...	321 394	...	...	...	...	...
Rural - Rurale	I	654 033	...	660 977	...	698 073	...	...	...	...	...
Philippines											
Total	C	381 834	396 297	396 331	...	...	4.9	5.0	4.9	...	...
Qatar											
Total	C	1 210	1 220	1 311	1 341	1 545	1.9	1.8	1.8	1.8	1.9

18. Deaths and crude death rates, by urban/rural residence: 2001 - 2005
Décès et taux bruts de mortalité, selon la résidence, urbaine/rurale: 2001 - 2005 (continued — suite)

Continent, country or area, and urban/rural residence / Continent, pays ou zone et résidence, urbaine/rurale	Co-de[1]	Number - Nombre					Rate - Taux				
		2001	2002	2003	2004	2005	2001	2002	2003	2004	2005
ASIA — ASIE											
Saudi Arabia - Arabie saoudite											
Total	...	87 125	88 476	89 849	91 243	92 487	...	...	...	...	...
Singapore - Singapour											
Total	+C	15 367	15 820	16 036	15 860	16 215	3.7	3.8	3.8	3.7	3.7
Sri Lanka											
Total	+C	112 858	*110 637	*114 310	*112 568	...	6.0	*5.8	*5.9	*5.8	...
Syrian Arab Republic - République arabe syrienne[2,40]											
Total	U	60 814	53 252	53 778	57 855		...	...	...	...	...
Tajikistan - Tadjikistan[20]											
Total	C	32 015	31 142	33 185	29 700	31 500	5.1	4.8	5.0	4.4	4.6
Urban - Urbaine	C	9 452	9 274	9 722	...	...	5.6	5.4	5.6	...	...
Rural - Rurale	C	22 563	21 868	23 463	...	...	4.9	4.6	4.9	...	...
Thailand - Thaïlande											
Total	+U	369 493	380 364	384 131	393 592	395 374	...	...	...	...	...
Turkey - Turquie[41]											
Total	I	485 000	429 000	436 000	443 000	450 000	7.1	6.2	6.2	6.2	6.2
Urban - Urbaine	I	175 137	...	...	...	...	4.3	...	...	...	...
Rural - Rurale	I	309 863	...	...	...	...	11.2	...	...	...	...
Uzbekistan - Ouzbékistan[20]											
Total	C	132 542	...	...	...	...	5.3	...	...	...	...
Urban - Urbaine	C	59 743	...	...	...	...	6.5	...	...	...	...
Rural - Rurale	C	72 799	...	...	...	...	4.6	...	...	...	...
Yemen - Yémen											
Total	...	...	21 157	20 346	22 255	19 653	...	...	...	...	...
EUROPE											
Albania - Albanie											
Total	C	15 813	16 248	17 967	17 749	17 427	5.1	5.3	5.8	5.7	5.5
Urban - Urbaine	C	...	8 560	8 923	9 248	7 040	...	6.4	6.5	6.6	4.8
Rural - Rurale	C	...	7 688	9 044	8 501	10 387	...	4.4	5.2	4.9	6.2
Andorra - Andorre											
Total	C	237	218	221	281	276	3.6	3.3	3.2	3.8	3.5
Austria - Autriche											
Total	C	74 767	76 131	77 209	74 292	75 189	9.3	9.4	9.5	9.1	9.1
Belarus - Bélarus[20]											
Total	C	140 299	146 655	143 200	140 064	141 857	14.1	14.8	14.5	14.3	14.5
Urban - Urbaine	C	72 875	77 020	75 420	74 486	76 452	10.4	10.9	10.7	10.6	10.8
Rural - Rurale	C	67 424	69 635	67 780	65 578	65 405	22.9	24.1	23.9	23.6	24.1
Belgium - Belgique[42]											
Total	C	103 447	105 642	107 628	101 929	102 963	10.1	10.2	10.4	9.8	9.8
Bosnia and Herzegovina - Bosnie-Herzégovine											
Total	C	30 325	30 155	31 757	32 616	34 402	8.0	7.9	8.3	8.5	9.0
Bulgaria - Bulgarie											
Total	C	112 368	112 617	111 927	110 110	113 374	14.2	14.3	14.3	14.2	14.6
Urban - Urbaine	C	62 778	63 765	64 495	64 638	65 309	11.5	11.7	11.8	11.9	12.0
Rural - Rurale	C	49 590	48 852	47 432	45 472	48 065	20.4	20.3	20.1	19.4	20.8
Channel Islands: Jersey - Îles Anglo-Normandes: Jersey											
Total	+C	784	841	760	748	752	9.0	9.6	8.7	8.5	8.6
Croatia - Croatie											
Total	C	49 552	50 569	52 575	49 756	51 790	11.2	11.4	11.8	11.2	11.7
Urban - Urbaine	C	24 838	24 984	25 976	24 418	25 899	10.1	...	...	...	...
Rural - Rurale	C	24 714	25 585	26 599	25 338	25 891	12.6	...	...	...	...

18. Deaths and crude death rates, by urban/rural residence: 2001 - 2005
Décès et taux bruts de mortalité, selon la résidence, urbaine/rurale: 2001 - 2005 (continued — suite)

Continent, country or area, and urban/rural residence / Continent, pays ou zone et résidence, urbaine/rurale	Code[1]	Number - Nombre					Rate - Taux				
		2001	2002	2003	2004	2005	2001	2002	2003	2004	2005
EUROPE											
Czech Republic - République tchèque											
Total	C	107 755	108 243	111 288	107 177	107 938	10.5	10.6	10.9	10.5	10.5
Urban - Urbaine	C	77 649	78 023	80 561	77 674	78 141	10.3	10.4	10.7	10.3	10.3
Rural - Rurale	C	30 106	30 220	30 727	29 503	29 797	11.3	11.3	11.5	11.0	11.1
Denmark - Danemark[43]											
Total	C	58 338	58 610	57 574	55 806	54 962	10.9	10.9	10.7	10.3	10.1
Estonia - Estonie[6]											
Total	C	18 516	18 355	18 152	17 685	17 316	13.6	13.5	13.4	13.1	12.9
Urban - Urbaine	C	12 119	12 309	12 106	11 432	11 053	12.8	13.1	12.9	12.2	11.8
Rural - Rurale	C	6 240	5 920	6 037	6 250	6 262	14.9	14.2	14.5	15.1	15.2
Faeroe Islands - Îles Féroé											
Total	C	358	392	404	379	419	7.7	8.3	8.4	7.9	8.7
Finland - Finlande[44]											
Total	C	48 550	49 418	48 996	47 600	47 928	9.4	9.5	9.4	9.1	9.1
Urban - Urbaine	C	26 928	27 591	27 156	26 715	27 009	8.5	8.6	8.4	8.2	8.2
Rural - Rurale	C	21 622	21 827	21 840	20 885	20 919	10.8	11.0	11.0	10.5	10.7
France[45,46]											
Total	C	531 073	535 144	552 339	509 429	527 533	8.9	8.9	9.2	8.4	8.6
Urban - Urbaine	C	375 209	379 292	393 958	360 779	373 576	...	...	...	...	...
Rural - Rurale	C	153 959	153 896	156 493	146 823	152 218	...	...	...	...	...
Germany - Allemagne											
Total	C	828 541	841 686	853 946	818 271	830 227	10.1	10.2	10.3	9.9	10.1
Gibraltar[47]											
Total	C	249	242	234	242	249	9.1	8.5	8.2	8.4	8.7
Greece - Grèce											
Total	C	102 559	103 915	105 529	104 942	105 091	9.4	9.5	9.6	9.5	9.5
Urban - Urbaine	C	53 558	57 288	58 197	58 300	58 022	...	...	...	...	...
Rural - Rurale	C	49 001	46 627	47 332	46 642	47 069	...	...	...	...	...
Hungary - Hongrie[48]											
Total	C	132 183	132 833	135 823	132 492	135 732	13.0	13.1	13.4	13.1	13.5
Urban - Urbaine	C	81 673	83 112	84 106	82 363	85 546	12.5	12.6	12.8	12.5	12.8
Rural - Rurale	C	49 857	49 128	51 086	49 473	49 479	13.7	13.8	14.3	14.0	14.5
Iceland - Islande											
Total	C	1 725	1 821	1 827	1 824	1 838	6.1	6.3	6.3	6.2	6.2
Urban - Urbaine	C	1 555	1 658	1 676	1 672	1 693	5.9	6.2	6.3	6.2	6.2
Rural - Rurale	C	170	163	151	152	145	7.9	7.6	7.1	7.0	7.0
Ireland - Irlande[49]											
Total	+C	30 212	29 348	29 074	*28 151	*27 441	7.9	7.5	7.3	*7.0	*6.6
Isle of Man - Îles de Man											
Total	+C	855	877	852	798	775	11.2	11.4	11.0	10.3	9.9
Italy - Italie											
Total	C	556 892	560 390	586 468	545 051	567 304	9.8	9.8	10.2	9.4	9.7
Latvia - Lettonie[20]											
Total	C	32 991	32 498	32 437	32 024	32 777	14.0	13.9	13.9	13.8	14.2
Urban - Urbaine	C	21 460	21 059	21 038	20 814	21 186	13.4	13.3	13.3	13.3	13.6
Rural - Rurale	C	11 531	11 439	11 399	11 210	11 591	15.3	15.2	15.2	15.1	15.7
Liechtenstein											
Total	C	220	215	217	198	*215	6.6	6.4	6.4	5.7	*6.2
Lithuania - Lituanie[20]											
Total	C	40 399	41 072	40 990	41 340	43 799	11.6	11.8	11.9	12.0	12.8
Urban - Urbaine	C	22 962	23 175	23 082	23 550	25 067	9.9	10.0	10.0	10.3	11.0
Rural - Rurale	C	17 437	17 897	17 908	17 790	18 732	15.1	15.6	15.6	15.5	16.4
Luxembourg											
Total	C	3 719	3 744	4 053	3 578	3 621	8.4	8.4	9.0	7.9	7.9
Malta - Malte[50]											
Total	C	2 935	3 031	3 072	2 903	3 130	7.6	7.8	7.7	7.2	7.8
Monaco											
Total	C	636	564	617	525	601	...	...	...	...	...

18. Deaths and crude death rates, by urban/rural residence: 2001 - 2005
Décès et taux bruts de mortalité, selon la résidence, urbaine/rurale: 2001 - 2005 (continued — suite)

Continent, country or area, and urban/rural residence / Continent, pays ou zone et résidence, urbaine/rurale	Co-de[1]	Number - Nombre					Rate - Taux				
		2001	2002	2003	2004	2005	2001	2002	2003	2004	2005
EUROPE											
Netherlands - Pays-Bas[51]											
Total	C	140 377	142 355	141 936	136 553	136 402	8.7	8.8	8.7	8.4	8.4
Urban - Urbaine	C	93 616	94 926	94 744	91 388	91 060	9.0	9.1	8.9	8.5	8.5
Rural - Rurale	C	46 761	47 429	47 192	45 165	45 342	8.3	8.4	8.4	8.1	8.2
Norway - Norvège[52]											
Total	C	43 981	44 465	42 478	41 200	41 232	9.7	9.8	9.3	9.0	8.9
Poland - Pologne											
Total	C	363 220	359 486	365 230	363 522	368 285	9.5	9.4	9.6	9.5	9.7
Urban - Urbaine	C	215 615	213 629	216 349	216 515	219 403	9.1	9.0	9.2	9.2	9.4
Rural - Rurale	C	147 605	145 857	148 881	147 007	148 882	10.1	10.0	10.2	10.0	10.1
Portugal											
Total	C	105 092	106 258	108 795	102 010	107 462	10.2	10.2	10.4	9.7	10.2
Republic of Moldova - République de Moldova[20]											
Total	C	40 075	41 852	43 079	41 668	44 689	11.0	11.6	11.9	11.6	12.4
Urban - Urbaine	C	12 844	13 229	13 650	13 319	14 199	8.6	8.9	9.2	9.0	9.6
Rural - Rurale	C	27 231	28 623	29 429	28 349	30 490	12.7	13.4	13.8	13.3	14.4
Romania - Roumanie											
Total	C	259 603	269 666	266 575	258 890	262 101	11.6	12.4	12.3	11.9	12.1
Urban - Urbaine	C	110 063	113 225	112 283	...	116 809	9.0	9.8	9.7	...	9.8
Rural - Rurale	C	149 540	156 441	154 292	...	145 292	14.7	15.4	15.2	...	14.9
Russian Federation - Fédération de Russie[20]											
Total	C	2 254 856	2 332 272	2 365 826	2 295 402	2 303 935	15.4	16.1	16.4	16.0	16.1
Urban - Urbaine	C	1 592 254	1 638 822	1 657 569	1 606 894	...	14.9	15.4	15.6	15.3	...
Rural - Rurale	C	662 602	693 450	708 257	688 508	...	17.0	17.9	18.4	17.9	...
San Marino - Saint-Marin											
Total	+C	195	203	216	185	219	7.1	7.1	7.5	6.3	7.1
Serbia and Montenegro - Serbie-et-Montenegro[53]											
Total	C	113 063	108 298	109 650	*110 148	...	10.6	13.3	13.4	*13.5	...
Urban - Urbaine	C	57 280	55 129	55 615	...	...	10.4	12.0	11.9	...	...
Rural - Rurale	C	55 783	53 169	54 035	...	...	10.8	15.2	15.4	...	...
Slovakia - Slovaquie											
Total	C	51 980	51 532	52 230	51 852	53 475	9.7	9.6	9.7	9.6	9.9
Urban - Urbaine	C	24 520	24 737	25 272	25 041	26 111	8.1	8.2	8.4	8.4	8.7
Rural - Rurale	C	27 460	26 795	26 958	26 811	27 364	11.6	11.3	11.3	11.2	11.4
Slovenia - Slovénie											
Total	C	18 508	18 701	19 451	18 523	18 825	9.3	9.4	9.7	9.3	9.4
Urban - Urbaine	C	8 277	8 684	8 983	8 725	8 791	...	8.9	9.2	9.0	9.1
Rural - Rurale	C	10 231	10 017	10 468	9 798	10 034	...	10.3	10.7	10.0	10.2
Spain - Espagne											
Total	C	360 131	368 618	384 828	371 934	387 355	8.8	8.9	9.2	8.7	8.9
Sweden - Suède											
Total	C	93 752	95 009	92 961	90 532	91 710	10.5	10.6	10.4	10.1	10.2
Switzerland - Suisse											
Total	C	61 287	61 768	63 070	60 180	61 124	8.4	8.4	8.6	8.1	8.2
Urban - Urbaine	C	42 157	45 108	46 062	43 925	44 515	7.9	8.4	8.5	8.1	8.1
Rural - Rurale	C	19 130	16 660	17 008	16 255	16 609	9.8	8.5	8.6	8.2	8.3
The Former Yugoslav Rep. of Macedonia - L'ex-République yougoslave de Macédoine											
Total	C	16 919	17 962	18 006	17 944	18 406	8.3	8.8	8.9	8.8	9.0
Urban - Urbaine	C	9 939	10 452	10 597	...	10 645	...	...	...	...	...
Rural - Rurale	C	6 980	7 510	7 409	...	7 761	...	...	...	...	...

18. Deaths and crude death rates, by urban/rural residence: 2001 - 2005
Décès et taux bruts de mortalité, selon la résidence, urbaine/rurale: 2001 - 2005 (continued — suite)

Continent, country or area, and urban/rural residence / Continent, pays ou zone et résidence, urbaine/rurale	Co-de[1]	Number - Nombre					Rate - Taux				
		2001	2002	2003	2004	2005	2001	2002	2003	2004	2005
EUROPE											
Ukraine[20]											
Total	C	745 952	754 911	765 408	761 261	781 961	15.3	15.7	16.0	16.1	16.6
Urban - Urbaine	C	450 329	454 406	459 965	460 492	471 561	13.9	14.1	14.4	...	...
Rural - Rurale	C	295 623	300 505	305 443	300 769	310 400	18.5	19.0	19.5	...	...
United Kingdom - Royaume-Uni											
Total	C	602 268	606 283	*611 188	*584 600	*582 900	10.2	10.2	*10.3	*9.8	*9.7
OCEANIA — OCEANIE											
American Samoa - Samoas américaines											
Total	C	239	295	257	289	279	4.0	4.9	4.1	4.5	4.3
Australia - Australie											
Total	+C	128 544	133 707	132 292	132 508	130 714	6.6	6.8	6.6	6.6	6.4
Urban - Urbaine	+C	76 843	85 378	84 753	84 569	84 311	4.9	...	...	4.8	...
Rural - Rurale	+C	51 701	48 329	47 539	47 939	46 403	14.1	...	...	18.5	...
Cook Islands - Îles Cook											
Total	+C	88	97	86	99	...	4.8	5.3	4.7	4.9	...
Fiji - Fidji											
Total	+C	4 929	5 133	5 068	...	...	6.1	6.3	6.1	...	...
French Polynesia - Polynésie française											
Total	C	1 171	1 127	1 122	1 130	1 265	4.9	4.6	4.5	4.5	5.0
Guam[54]											
Total	C	691	658	700	*691	*697	4.4	4.1	4.3	*4.2	*4.1
Marshall Islands - Îles Marshall											
Total	+U	271	...	...	...	...	...	...	...	...	...
Micronesia, Federated States of - Micronésie, États Fédérés de La											
Total	U	482	539	427	...	...	...	...	...	...	...
Nauru											
Total	C	92	75	...	...	...	7.9	...	...	...	...
New Caledonia - Nouvelle-Calédonie											
Total	C	1 131	1 121	1 121	1 116	...	5.2	5.1	5.0	4.9	...
New Zealand - Nouvelle-Zélande[6,55]											
Total	+C	27 825	28 065	28 010	28 419	27 034	7.2	7.1	7.0	7.0	6.6
Urban - Urbaine	+C	25 093	25 390	25 279	25 684	24 275	7.5	7.5	7.3	7.3	6.9
Rural - Rurale	+C	2 677	2 611	2 654	2 653	2 628	4.9	4.7	4.7	4.7	4.6
Niue - Nioué[56]											
Total	C	14	13	16	18	...	...	...	...	...	...
Northern Mariana Islands - Îles Mariannes septentrionales											
Total	U	150	164	...	...	...	...	...	...	...	...
Palau - Palaos											
Total	C	138	134	136	142	134	7.0	6.7	6.7	6.9	6.7
Papua New Guinea - Papouasie-Nouvelle-Guinée											
Total	U	6 737	7 573	7 054	...	...	...	...	...	...	...
Samoa											
Total	U	339	*355	*551	*547	...	...	...	...	...	...
Tonga											
Total	+C	579	591	617	*559	...	5.8	5.9	6.1	...	...
Tuvalu											
Total	U	86	87	83	89	64	...	...	...	...	...

Continent, country or area, and urban/rural residence Continent, pays ou zone et résidence, urbaine/rurale	Co-de[1]	Number - Nombre					Rate - Taux				
		2001	2002	2003	2004	2005	2001	2002	2003	2004	2005
OCEANIA — OCEANIE											
Wallis and Futuna Islands - Îles Wallis et Futuna											
Total	C	69	67	88	72	65	...	...	5.9	...	...

FOOTNOTES - NOTES

Italics: data from civil registers which are incomplete or of unknown completeness. — *Italiques:* données incomplètes ou dont le degré d'exactitude n'est pas connu, provenant des registres de l'état civil.

* Provisional. — Données provisoires.

[1] 'Code' indicates the source of data, as follows:
C - Civil registration, estimated over 90% complete
U - Civil registration, estimated less than 90% complete
| - Other source, estimated reliable
+ - Data tabulated by date of registration rather than occurence.
... - Information not available

Le 'Code' indique la source des données, comme suit:
C - Registres de l'état civil considérés complets à 90 p. 100 au moins.
U - Registres de l'état civil qui ne sont pas considérés complets à 90 p. 100 au moins.
| - Autre source, considérée pas douteuses.
+ - Données exploitées selon la date de l'enregistrement et non la date de l'événement.
... - Information pas disponible.

[2] Excluding live-born infants who died before their birth was registered. - Non compris les enfants nés vivants décédés avant l'enregistrement de leur naissance.

[3] For Algerian population only. -Pour la population algérienne seulement.

[4] Data refer to national projections. -Les données se réfèrent aux projections nationales.

[5] For 2001, data refer to last twelve months preceding census in August 2001. -Pour 2001, les données se rapportent aux douze mois précédant le recensement d'août 2001.

[6] Figures for urban and rural areas do not add up to the total, since they do not include the category 'Unknown residence'. -La somme des données pour la residence urbaine et rurale n'est pas égale au total parce qu'elle n'inclue pas la catégorie 'Residence inconnue'.

[7] For 2001, figure is estimated by country on the basis of the deaths reported for January to August in the census in August 2001. -Pour 2001, le chiffre est estimé par pays à partir des décès signalés pour la période janvier à août dans le recensement d'août 2001.

[8] Excluding deaths of unknown sex. -Non compris les décès dont on ignore le sexe.

[9] Data are for 12 months preceding the census date. -Les données portent sur les 12 mois précédant la date du recensement.

[10] Source: World Health Organization. -Source : Organisation mondiale de la santé.

[11] For 2001, Source: World Health Organization -Pour 2001, Source : Organisation mondiale de la santé

[12] Including Canadian residents temporarily in the United States, but excluding United States residents temporarily in Canada. -Y compris les résidents canadiens se trouvant temporairement aux Etats-Unis, mais ne comprenant pas les résidents des Etats-Unis se trouvant temporairement au Canada.

[13] For 2002 and 2003, Source: World Health Organization - Pour 2002 et 2003, Source : Organisation mondiale de la santé

[14] Data refer to deaths of residents of the Netherlands Antilles (including those that died outside the Netherlands Antilles). Data exclude deaths by non-residents. -Ces données concernent les décès de résidents des Antilles néerlandaises (y compris ceux survenus hors des Antilles néerlandaises). Elles ne concernent pas les décès des non-résidents.

[15] Excluding Indian jungle population. -Non compris les Indiens de la jungle.

[16] Data on live births and deaths are based on a civil registration system put in place in January 1998. -Les données sur les naissances et les décès sont basées sur un système d'enregistrement des faits d'état civil mis en place en janvier 1998.

[17] Excluding nomadic Indian tribes. -Non compris les tribus d'Indiens nomades.

[18] Data refer to registered deaths only. -Les données se rapportent aux décès enregistrés seulement.

[19] Data for urban refer to the total of the district of Paramaribo (capital) and Wanica district. -Les données relatives aux zones urbaines correspondent au total pour le district de Paramaribo (capitale) et le district de Wanica.

[20] Excluding infants born alive of less than 28 weeks' gestation, of less than 1 000 grams in weight and 35 centimeters in length, who die within seven days of birth. -Non compris les enfants nés vivants après moins de 28 semaines de gestations, pesant moins de 1 000 grammes, mesurant moins de 35 centimètres et décédés dans les sept jours qui ont suivi leur naissance.

[21] Rates were obtained by the Sample Vital Registration System 2004 of Bangladesh. -Taux obtenus au moyen du Sample Vital Registration System 2004 du Bangladesh.

[22] For 2005, data refer to last twelve months preceding census on May 2005. -Pour 2005, les données se rapportent pour la dernière fois à douze mois précédant le recensement de mai 2005.

[23] For statistical purposes, the data for China do not include those for the Hong Kong Special Administrative Region (Hong Kong SAR), Macao Special Administrative Region (Macao SAR) and Taiwan province of China. -Pour la présentation des statistiques, les données pour la Chine ne comprennent pas la Région Administrative Spéciale de Hong Kong (Hong Kong RAS), la Région Administrative Spéciale de Macao (Macao RAS) et Taïwan province de Chine.

[24] Data from 2001 to 2004 have been estimated on the basis of the annual National Sample Surveys on Population Changes. -Les données de 2001 à 2004 ont été estimées sur la base de l'enquête annuelle "National Sample Survey on Population Changes".

[25] Data for 2005 are estimated from the National Sample Survey of 1 Per cent population. -Les données pour 2005 ont été estimées à partir de l'enquête nationale qui a porté sur un échantillon de 1 % de la population.

[26] Data refer to government controlled areas. -Les données se rapportent aux zones contrôlées par le Gouvernement.

[27] Including data for the Indian-held part of Jammu and Kashmir, the final status of which has not yet been determined. -Y compris les données pour la partie du Jammu et du Cachemire occupée par l'Inde dont le statut définitif n'a pas encore été déterminé.

[28] Rates were obtained by the Sample Registration System of India, actually a large demographic survey. -Les taux ont été obtenus par le Système de l'enregistrement par échantillon de l'Inde qui est une large enquête démographique.

[29] Data relate to the Iranian Year which begins on 21 March and ends on 20 March of the following year. -Les données concernent l'année iranienne, qui commence le 21 mars et se termine le 20 mars de l'année suivante.

[30] Including data for East Jerusalem and Israeli residents in certain other territories under occupation by Israeli military forces since June 1967. -Y compris les données pour Jérusalem-Est et les résidents israéliens dans

certains autres territoires occupés depuis 1967 par les forces armées israéliennes.

[31] As of 2002, data on deaths include deaths abroad of Israeli residents who were out of the country for less than a year (there were 109 deaths of Israelis abroad in 2002, 182(2003), 183(2004) and *30(2005)). -Depuis 2002, les données sur les décès comprennent les décès à l'étranger de résidents israéliens qui ont quitté le pays depuis moins d'un an (en 2002, 109 Israéliens sont morts à l'étranger, 182(2003) 182(2004) et *30 (2005)).

[32] For Japanese nationals in Japan only; however, rates computed on population including foreigners except foreign military and civilian personnel and their dependants stationed in the area. -Pour les nationaux japonais au Japon seulement; toutefois, les taux sont calculés sur la base d'une population comprenant les étrangers, mais ne comprenant ni les militaires et agents civils étrangers en poste sur le territoire ni les membres de leur famille les accompagnant.

[33] Excluding data for Jordanian territory under occupation since June 1967 by Israeli military forces. Excluding foreigners, including registered Palestinian refugees. -Non compris les données pour le territoire jordanien occupé depuis juin 1967 par les forces armées israéliennes. Non compris les étrangers, mais y compris les réfugiés de Palestine enregistrés.

[34] For 2004 and 2005, published by the United Nations Economic and Social Commission for Western Asia. -Pour 2004 et 2005, publié par la Commission économique et sociale des Nations Unies pour l'Asie occidentale.

[35] Excluding alien armed forces, civilian aliens employed by armed forces, and foreign diplomatic personnel and their dependants. -Non compris les militaires étrangers, les civils étrangers employés par les forces armées ni le personnel diplomatique étranger et les membres de leur famille les accompagnant.

[36] For 2001, data refer to last twelve months preceding census on June 2001. -Pour 2001, les données se rapportent aux douze mois précédant le recensement juin 2001.

[37] Data refer to the recorded events in Ministry of Health hospitals and health centres only. -Les données se rapportent aux faits d'état civil enregistrés dans les hôpitaux et les dispensaires du Ministère de la santé seulement.

[38] Excluding data for the Pakistan-held part of Jammu and Kashmir, the final status of which has not yet been determined. -Non compris les données concernant la partie du Jammu et Cachemire occupée par le Pakistan dont le statut définitif n'a pas été déterminé.

[39] Data based on Pakistan Demographic Survey. -Données extraites de l'enquête démographique effectuée par le Pakistan.

[40] Excluding nomad population and Palestinian refugees. -Non compris la population nomade et les réfugiés de Palestine.

[41] Based on the results of the Population Demographic Survey. -D'après les résultats de la Population Demographic Survey.

[42] Including armed forces stationed outside the country, but excluding alien armed forces stationed in the area. -Y compris les militaires nationaux hors du pays, mais non compris les militaires étrangers en garnison sur le territoire.

[43] Excluding Faeroe Islands and Greenland. -Non compris les Iles Féroé et le Gröenland.

[44] Including nationals temporarily outside the country. -Y compris les nationaux se trouvant temporairement hors du pays.

[45] Including armed forces stationed outside the country. -Y compris les militaires nationaux hors du pays.

[46] The difference between 'Total' and the sum of 'urban' and 'rural' is due to the cases of unknown place of residence or residence abroad. -La différence entre le 'Total' et la somme des données selon la résidence urbaine/rurale se rapporte à la situation ou on ignore la résidence ou si la résidence est à l'étranger.

[47] Excluding armed forces. -Non compris les militaires en garnison.

[48] Data for urban/rural residence, for the de jure population. -Les données selon la résidence urbaine/rurale, pour la population de droit.

[49] Events registered within one year of occurrence. -Evénements enregistrés dans l'année qui suit l'événement.

[50] For Maltese population only; however, rates computed on population including work and resident permit holders and foreigners residing in Malta. -Pour population Maltaise seulement; toutefois, les taux sont calculés sur la base d'une population comprenant les titulaires de permis de travail et de permis de séjour et les étrangers résident à Malte.

[51] Including residents outside the country if listed in a Netherlands population register. -Y compris les résidents hors du pays, s'ils sont inscrits sur un registre de population néerlandais.

[52] Including residents temporarily outside the country. -Y compris les résidents se trouvant temporairement hors du pays.

[53] From 2002, without data for Kosovo and Metohia. -Après 2002, sans les données pour le Kosovo and Metohie.

[54] Including United States military personnel, their dependants and contract employees. -Y compris les militaires des Etats-Unis, les membres de leur famille les accompagnant et les agents contractuels des Etats-Unis.

[55] For resident population only. -Pour la population résidante seulement.

[56] Includes deaths occurred in New Zealand but buried in Niue and deaths occurred in Niue but buried elsewhere. -Y compris les personnes décédées en Nouvelle-Zélande qui sont enterrées à Nioué et les personnes décédées à Nioué qui sont enterrées ailleurs.

Table 19

Table 19 presents deaths by age, sex and urban/rural residence for latest available year.

Description of variables: Age is defined as age at last birthday, that is, the difference between the date of birth and the date of the occurrence of the event, expressed in completed solar years. The age classification used in this table is the following: under 1 year, 1-4 years, 5-year age groups through 95-99 years, and 100 years or over.

The urban/rural classification of deaths is that provided by each country or area; it is presumed to be based on the national census definitions of urban population that have been set forth at the end of the technical notes for table 6.

Reliability of data: Data from civil registers of deaths that are reported as incomplete (less than 90 per cent completeness) or of unknown completeness are considered unreliable and are set in italics rather than in roman type. Table 18 and the technical notes for that table provide more detailed information on the completeness of death registration. For more information about the quality of vital statistics data in general and the information available on the basis of the completeness estimates in particular, see section 4.2 of the Introduction.

Limitations: Statistics on deaths by age and sex are subject to the same qualifications as are set forth for vital statistics in general and death statistics in particular as discussed in section 4 of the Introduction.

The reliability of the data is an important factor in considering the limitations. In addition, some deaths are tabulated by date of registration and not by date of occurrence; these have been indicated by a plus sign (+). Whenever the lag between the date of occurrence and date of registration is prolonged and, therefore, a large proportion of the death registrations are delayed, death statistics for any given year may be seriously affected. However, delays in the registration of deaths are less common and shorter than in the registration of live births.

International comparability in mortality statistics may also be affected by the exclusion of deaths of infants who were born alive but died before the registration of the birth or within the first 24 hours of life. Statistics of this type are footnoted.

Because these statistics are classified according to age, they are subject to the limitations with respect to accuracy of age reporting similar to those already discussed in connection with section 3.1.3 of the Introduction. The factors influencing the accuracy of reporting may be somewhat dissimilar in vital statistics (because of the differences in the method of taking a census and registering a death) but, in general, the same errors can be observed.

The absence of frequencies in the unknown age group does not necessarily indicate completely accurate reporting and tabulation of the age item. It is often an indication that the unknowns have been eliminated by assigning ages to them before tabulation, or by proportionate distribution after tabulation.

International comparability of statistics on deaths by age is also affected by the use of different methods to determine age at death. If age is obtained from an item that simply requests age at death in completed years or is derived from information on year of birth and death rather than from information on complete date (day, month and year) of birth and death, the number of deaths classified in the under-one-year age group will tend to be reduced and the number of deaths in the next age group will tend to be somewhat increased. A similar bias may affect other age groups but its impact is usually negligible. Information on this factor is given in the footnotes when known.

The comparability of data by urban/rural residence is affected by the national definitions of urban and rural used in tabulating these data. It is assumed, in the absence of specific information to the contrary, that the definitions of urban and rural used in connection with the national population census were also used in the compilation of the vital statistics for each country or area. However, it cannot be excluded that, for a given country or area, different definitions of urban and rural are used for the vital statistics data and the population census data respectively. When known, the definitions of urban used in national population censuses are presented at the end of the technical notes for table 6. As discussed in detail in the technical notes for table 6, these definitions vary considerably from one country or area to another.

Earlier data: Deaths by age and sex have been shown for the latest available year in each issue of the Yearbook since the 1955 issue. Data included in this table update the series covering a period of years as follows:

Issue	Years Covered
Historical Supplement CD, 1997	1948 – 1997
1996	1987 – 1995
1992	1983 – 1992
1985	1976 – 1984
1980	1971 – 1979
Historical Supplement, 1979	1948 - 1977

Data have been presented by urban/rural residence in each regular issue of the Yearbook since the 1967 issue.

Tableau 19

Le tableau 19 présente les données les plus récentes dont on dispose sur les décès selon l'âge, le sexe et le lieu de résidence (zone urbaine ou rurale).

Description des variables : L'âge considéré est l'âge au dernier anniversaire, c'est-à-dire la différence entre la date de naissance et la date du décès, exprimée en années solaires révolues. La classification par âge est la suivante : moins d'un an, 1 à 4 ans, groupes quinquennaux jusqu'à 95-99 ans et 100 ans et plus.

La classification des décès selon le lieu de résidence (zone urbaine ou rurale) est celle qui a été communiquée par chaque pays ou zone ; on part du principe qu'elle repose sur les définitions de la population urbaine utilisées pour les recensements nationaux, qui sont reproduites à la fin des notes techniques du tableau 6.

Fiabilité des données : Les données sur les décès issues des registres d'état civil qui sont déclarées incomplètes (degré d'exhaustivité inférieur à 90 p.100) ou dont le degré d'exhaustivité n'est pas connu sont jugées douteuses et apparaissent en italique et non en caractères romains. Le tableau 18 et les notes techniques s'y rapportant présentent des renseignements plus détaillés sur le degré d'exhaustivité de l'enregistrement des décès. Pour plus de précisions sur la qualité des statistiques de l'état civil en général et le degré de complétude en particulier, voir la section 4.2 des Introduction.

Insuffisance des données : Les statistiques des décès selon l'âge et le sexe appellent les mêmes réserves que les statistiques de l'état civil en général et les statistiques relatives à la mortalité en particulier (voir la section 4 des Introduction).

La fiabilité des données est un facteur important. Il faut également tenir compte du fait que, dans certains cas, les données relatives aux décès sont classées par date d'enregistrement et non par date d'occurrence ; ces cas ont été signalés par le signe '+'. Chaque fois que le décalage entre le décès et son enregistrement est grand et qu'une forte proportion des décès fait l'objet d'un enregistrement tardif, les statistiques des décès de l'année peuvent être considérablement faussées.

En règle générale, toutefois, les décès sont enregistrés beaucoup plus rapidement que les naissances vivantes, et les retards prolongés sont rares.

Un autre facteur qui nuit à la comparabilité internationale est la pratique de certains pays ou zones qui consiste à ne pas inclure dans les statistiques des décès les enfants nés vivants mais décédés avant l'enregistrement de leur naissance ou dans les 24 heures qui ont suivi la naissance, pratique qui conduit à sous-évaluer le nombre de décès à moins d'un an. Quand pareil facteur a joué, cela a été signalé en note à la fin du tableau.

Étant donné que les statistiques relatives à la mortalité sont classées selon l'âge, elles appellent les mêmes réserves concernant l'exactitude des déclarations d'âge que celles qui ont été formulées à la section 3.1.3 des Introduction. Dans le cas des données d'état civil, les facteurs qui interviennent à cet égard sont parfois un peu différents, du fait que le recensement et l'enregistrement des décès se font par des méthodes différentes, mais, d'une manière générale, les erreurs observées sont les mêmes.

Si aucun nombre ne figure dans la rangée réservée aux âges inconnus, cela ne signifie pas nécessairement que les déclarations d'âge et le classement par âge sont tout à fait exacts. C'est souvent une indication que l'on a attribué un âge aux personnes d'âge inconnu avant l'exploitation des données ou qu'elles ont été réparties proportionnellement entre les différents groupes après cette opération.

Le manque d'uniformité des méthodes suivies pour obtenir l'âge au moment du décès nuit également à la comparabilité internationale des données. Si l'âge est connu, soit d'après la réponse à une simple question sur l'âge du décès en années révolues, soit d'après l'année de la naissance et l'année du décès, et non d'après des renseignements concernant la date exacte (jour, mois et année) de la naissance et du décès, le nombre de décès classés dans la catégorie « moins d'un an » sera entaché d'une erreur par défaut et le chiffre figurant dans la catégorie suivante d'une erreur par excès.

Les données pour les autres groupes d'âge pourront être entachées d'une distorsion analogue, mais les répercussions seront généralement négligeables. Les imperfections, lorsqu'elles étaient connues, ont été signalées en note à la fin du tableau.

La comparabilité des données selon le lieu de résidence (zone urbaine ou rurale) peut être limitée par les définitions nationales des termes « urbain » et « rural » utilisées pour le classement de ces données. En l'absence d'indications contraires, on a supposé que les mêmes définitions avaient servi pour le recensement national de la population et pour l'établissement des statistiques de l'état civil pour chaque pays ou zone. Toutefois, il n'est pas exclu que, pour une zone ou un pays donné, des définitions différentes aient été retenues. Les définitions du terme « urbain » utilisées pour les recensements nationaux de population ont été présentées à la fin du tableau 6 lorsqu'elles étaient connues. Comme on l'a précisé dans les notes techniques relatives au tableau 6, ces définitions varient considérablement d'un pays ou d'une zone à l'autre.

Données publiées antérieurement : Les éditions de l'*Annuaire démographique* parues depuis 1955 présentent les statistiques les plus récentes dont on disposait à l'époque sur les décès selon l'âge et le sexe. Les données qui figurent dans le tableau 19 actualisent les données qui portaient sur les périodes suivantes :

Éditions	Années considérées
Supplément historique (CD-ROM), 1997	1948 – 1997
1996	1987 – 1995
1992	1983 – 1992
1985	1976 – 1984
1980	1971 – 1979
Supplément rétrospectif, 1979	1948 - 1977

Des données selon le lieu de résidence (zone urbaine ou rurale) ont été présentées dans toutes les éditions de l'*Annuaire* depuis celle de 1967, exception faite des éditions spéciales.

19. Deaths by age, sex and urban/rural residence: latest available year, 1996 - 2005
Décès selon l'âge, le sexe et la résidence, urbaine/rurale: dernière année disponible, 1996 - 2005

Continent, country or area, date, code and age (in years) / Continent, pays ou zone, date, code et âge (en années)	Total			Urban - Urbaine			Rural - Rurale		
	Both sexes Les deux sexes	Male Masculin	Female Féminin	Both sexes Les deux sexes	Male Masculin	Female Féminin	Both sexes Les deux sexes	Male Masculin	Female Féminin

AFRICA - AFRIQUE

Algeria - Algérie[1]
1998 (+U)

Total	131 708	73 352	58 356	...	...	...	...	...	...
0	21 169	12 009	9 160	...	...	...	...	...	...
1 - 4	4 475	2 378	2 097	...	...	...	...	...	...
5 - 9	2 759	1 592	1 167	...	...	...	...	...	...
10 - 14	2 272	1 373	899	...	...	...	...	...	...
15 - 19	3 017	1 947	1 070	...	...	...	...	...	...
20 - 24	3 425	2 335	1 090	...	...	...	...	...	...
25 - 29	3 508	2 355	1 153	...	...	...	...	...	...
30 - 34	3 216	1 958	1 258	...	...	...	...	...	...
35 - 39	3 195	1 770	1 425	...	...	...	...	...	...
40 - 44	3 468	1 959	1 509	...	...	...	...	...	...
45 - 49	3 771	2 135	1 636	...	...	...	...	...	...
50 - 54	3 777	2 184	1 593	...	...	...	...	...	...
55 - 59	5 113	2 908	2 205	...	...	...	...	...	...
60 - 64	7 616	4 227	3 389	...	...	...	...	...	...
65 - 69	8 962	4 937	4 025	...	...	...	...	...	...
70 - 74	10 320	5 732	4 588	...	...	...	...	...	...
75 - 79	11 346	6 241	5 105	...	...	...	...	...	...
80 +	30 299	15 312	14 987	...	...	...	...	...	...

Botswana[2]
2001 (|)

Total	20 823	10 800	10 023	10 041	5 204	4 837	10 782	5 596	5 186
0	1 576	815	761	718	364	354	858	451	407
1 - 4	1 187	637	550	551	294	257	636	343	293
5 - 9	484	251	233	210	118	92	274	133	141
10 - 14	249	114	135	112	51	61	137	63	74
15 - 19	386	179	207	192	88	104	194	91	103
20 - 24	1 090	388	702	520	197	323	570	191	379
25 - 29	2 091	848	1 243	1 056	443	613	1 035	405	630
30 - 34	2 376	1 235	1 141	1 208	631	577	1 168	604	564
35 - 39	2 039	1 132	907	997	550	447	1 042	582	460
40 - 44	1 595	910	685	842	483	359	753	427	326
45 - 49	1 334	814	520	702	422	280	632	392	240
50 - 54	858	529	329	418	253	165	440	276	164
55 - 59	669	416	253	333	208	125	336	208	128
60 - 64	638	386	252	316	197	119	322	189	133
65 - 69	673	374	299	308	154	154	365	220	145
70 - 74	601	322	279	261	131	130	340	191	149
75 - 79	569	315	254	256	144	112	313	171	142
80 +	1 634	740	894	762	329	433	872	411	461
Unknown - Inconnu	774	395	379	279	147	132	495	248	247

Egypt - Égypte
2005 (C)

Total	450 646	246 751	203 895	198 588	115 027	83 561	252 058	131 724	120 334
0	36 146	19 695	16 451	16 676	9 784	6 892	19 470	9 911	9 559
1 - 4	4 844	2 431	2 413	1 461	826	635	3 383	1 605	1 778
5 - 9	2 632	1 476	1 156	944	557	387	1 688	919	769
10 - 14	1 788	998	790	765	441	324	1 023	557	466
15 - 19	1 471	832	639	621	359	262	850	473	377
20 - 24	4 694	2 801	1 893	2 033	1 235	798	2 661	1 566	1 095
25 - 29	3 912	2 408	1 504	1 829	1 166	663	2 083	1 242	841
30 - 34	6 266	4 023	2 243	3 275	2 143	1 132	2 991	1 880	1 111
35 - 39	6 574	4 152	2 422	3 607	2 459	1 148	2 967	1 693	1 274
40 - 44	6 438	3 916	2 522	3 473	2 245	1 228	2 965	1 671	1 294
45 - 49	6 275	3 710	2 565	3 202	2 001	1 201	3 073	1 709	1 364
50 - 54	8 445	5 103	3 342	4 242	2 663	1 579	4 203	2 440	1 763
55 - 59	12 750	8 162	4 588	6 211	3 977	2 234	6 539	4 185	2 354
60 - 64	19 335	13 022	6 313	9 584	6 408	3 176	9 751	6 614	3 137
65 - 69	31 368	19 981	11 387	15 330	9 893	5 437	16 038	10 088	5 950
70 - 74	35 682	22 055	13 627	17 415	10 966	6 449	18 267	11 089	7 178
75 - 79	37 685	21 808	15 877	18 033	10 801	7 232	19 652	11 007	8 645
80 - 84	44 494	24 810	19 684	19 875	11 575	8 300	24 619	13 235	11 384
85 - 89	49 889	25 961	23 928	21 152	11 607	9 545	28 737	14 354	14 383

Continent, country or area, date, code and age (in years) / Continent, pays ou zone, date, code et âge (en années)	Total			Urban - Urbaine			Rural - Rurale		
	Both sexes Les deux sexes	Male Masculin	Female Féminin	Both sexes Les deux sexes	Male Masculin	Female Féminin	Both sexes Les deux sexes	Male Masculin	Female Féminin
AFRICA - AFRIQUE									
Egypt - Égypte									
2005 (C)									
90 - 94	46 951	23 677	23 274	18 593	9 829	8 764	28 358	13 848	14 510
95 - 99	36 906	16 714	20 192	13 620	6 588	7 032	23 286	10 126	13 160
100 + ...	33 923	12 512	21 411	11 745	4 742	7 003	22 178	7 770	14 408
Unknown - Inconnu	12 178	6 504	5 674	4 902	2 762	2 140	7 276	3 742	3 534
Kenya									
2002 (U)									
Total..................	206 089	107 108	98 981	...	...	...	...	...	...
0	32 459	16 735	15 724	...	...	...	...	...	...
1 - 4..................	22 623	12 166	10 457	...	...	...	...	...	...
5 - 14.................	11 035	5 889	5 146	...	...	...	...	...	...
15 - 24................	15 157	6 083	9 074	...	...	...	...	...	...
25 - 34................	29 921	13 485	16 436	...	...	...	...	...	...
35 - 44................	27 720	14 714	13 006	...	...	...	...	...	...
45 - 54................	19 896	11 770	8 126	...	...	...	...	...	...
55 - 74................	26 196	15 183	11 013	...	...	...	...	...	...
75 + ...	21 082	11 083	9 999	...	...	...	...	...	...
Libyan Arab Jamahiriya - Jamahiriya arabe libyenne									
2002 (U)									
Total..................	19 362	11 278	8 084	...	...	...	...	...	...
0	2 194	1 190	1 004	...	...	...	...	...	...
1 - 4..................	891	546	345	...	...	...	...	...	...
5 - 9..................	267	142	125	...	...	...	...	...	...
10 - 19................	670	432	238	...	...	...	...	...	...
20 - 29................	1 100	824	276	...	...	...	...	...	...
30 - 39................	1 287	820	467	...	...	...	...	...	...
40 - 49................	1 118	621	497	...	...	...	...	...	...
50 - 59................	1 492	860	632	...	...	...	...	...	...
60 - 69................	2 936	1 754	1 182	...	...	...	...	...	...
70 - 79................	3 812	2 254	1 558	...	...	...	...	...	...
80 + ...	3 595	1 835	1 760	...	...	...	...	...	...
Malawi[3]									
1998 (I)									
Total..................	208 040	113 856	94 184	22 186	12 404	9 782	185 854	101 452	84 402
0	44 928	24 977	19 951	5 241	2 968	2 273	39 687	22 009	17 678
1 - 4..................	59 930	32 821	27 109	6 180	3 435	2 745	53 750	29 386	24 364
5 - 9..................	16 717	9 200	7 517	1 628	926	702	15 089	8 274	6 815
10 - 14................	9 638	4 849	4 789	801	440	361	8 837	4 409	4 428
15 - 19................	7 130	3 427	3 703	672	336	336	6 458	3 091	3 367
20 - 24................	11 710	6 947	4 763	1 240	629	611	10 470	6 318	4 152
25 - 29................	9 290	4 853	4 437	1 168	548	620	8 122	4 305	3 817
30 - 34................	8 797	4 481	4 316	1 168	621	547	7 629	3 860	3 769
35 - 39................	7 036	3 678	3 358	969	553	416	6 067	3 125	2 942
40 - 44................	6 338	3 713	2 625	822	527	295	5 516	3 186	2 330
45 - 49................	5 639	3 705	1 934	587	388	199	5 052	3 317	1 735
50 - 54................	3 677	2 160	1 517	461	310	151	3 216	1 850	1 366
55 - 59................	3 872	1 739	2 133	335	200	135	3 537	1 539	1 998
60 - 64................	2 921	1 620	1 301	259	152	107	2 662	1 468	1 194
65 - 69................	2 695	1 257	1 438	156	90	66	2 539	1 167	1 372
70 - 74................	2 228	1 358	870	131	76	55	2 097	1 282	815
75 - 79................	1 599	942	657	104	64	40	1 495	878	617
80 - 84................	1 516	842	674	92	52	40	1 424	790	634
85 + ...	2 379	1 287	1 092	172	89	83	2 207	1 198	1 009
Mauritius - Maurice									
2005 (+C)									
Total..................	8 646	4 863	3 783	...	...	...	...	...	...
0	248	146	102	...	...	...	...	...	...
1 - 4..................	50	27	23	...	...	...	...	...	...
5 - 9..................	21	12	9	...	...	...	...	...	...
10 - 14................	22	10	12	...	...	...	...	...	...
15 - 19................	43	24	19	...	...	...	...	...	...
20 - 24................	77	54	23	...	...	...	...	...	...
25 - 29................	107	82	25	...	...	...	...	...	...

19. Deaths by age, sex and urban/rural residence: latest available year, 1996 - 2005
Décès selon l'âge, le sexe et la résidence, urbaine/rurale: dernière année disponible, 1996 - 2005 (continued - suite)

Continent, country or area, date, code and age (in years) / Continent, pays ou zone, date, code et âge (en années)	Total			Urban - Urbaine			Rural - Rurale		
	Both sexes Les deux sexes	Male Masculin	Female Féminin	Both sexes Les deux sexes	Male Masculin	Female Féminin	Both sexes Les deux sexes	Male Masculin	Female Féminin
AFRICA - AFRIQUE									
Mauritius - Maurice									
2005 (+C)									
30 - 34	127	87	40	...	...	...	...	...	...
35 - 39	225	161	64	...	...	...	...	...	...
40 - 44	332	236	96	...	...	...	...	...	...
45 - 49	465	309	156	...	...	...	...	...	...
50 - 54	606	412	194	...	...	...	...	...	...
55 - 59	728	469	259	...	...	...	...	...	...
60 - 64	722	427	295	...	...	...	...	...	...
65 - 69	800	463	337	...	...	...	...	...	...
70 - 74	937	544	393	...	...	...	...	...	...
75 - 79	1 078	555	523	...	...	...	...	...	...
80 - 84	1 008	474	534	...	...	...	...	...	...
85 +	1 044	365	679	...	...	...	...	...	...
Unknown - Inconnu	6	6	-	...	...	...	...	...	...
Morocco - Maroc									
2001 (U)									
Total	95 612	62 023	33 589	55 745[4]	34 330[4]	21 415[4]	39 787[4]	27 639[4]	12 148[4]
0	7 379	4 022	3 357	2 804[4]	1 566[4]	1 238[4]	4 569[4]	2 453[4]	2 116[4]
1 - 4	3 066	1 590	1 476	965[4]	521[4]	444[4]	2 100[4]	1 068[4]	1 032[4]
5 - 9	1 300	787	513	518[4]	323[4]	195[4]	782[4]	464[4]	318[4]
10 - 14	1 346	805	541	617[4]	381[4]	236[4]	727[4]	423[4]	304[4]
15 - 19	1 954	1 174	780	1 064[4]	664[4]	400[4]	889[4]	509[4]	380[4]
20 - 24	2 721	1 734	987	1 522[4]	991[4]	531[4]	1 195[4]	740[4]	455[4]
25 - 29	2 685	1 679	1 006	1 491[4]	959[4]	532[4]	1 189[4]	716[4]	473[4]
30 - 34	2 784	1 685	1 099	1 689[4]	1 051[4]	638[4]	1 093[4]	632[4]	461[4]
35 - 39	2 884	1 716	1 168	1 821[4]	1 094[4]	727[4]	1 058[4]	619[4]	439[4]
40 - 44	3 683	2 272	1 411	2 400[4]	1 479[4]	921[4]	1 279[4]	791[4]	488[4]
45 - 49	3 798	2 476	1 322	2 538[4]	1 635[4]	903[4]	1 255[4]	837[4]	418[4]
50 - 54	4 385	2 925	1 460	2 899[4]	1 899[4]	1 000[4]	1 484[4]	1 024[4]	460[4]
55 - 59	4 949	3 229	1 720	3 244[4]	1 998[4]	1 246[4]	1 698[4]	1 228[4]	470[4]
60 - 64	8 122	5 290	2 832	5 114[4]	3 093[4]	2 021[4]	3 003[4]	2 194[4]	809[4]
65 - 69	9 255	6 243	3 012	5 926[4]	3 671[4]	2 255[4]	3 322[4]	2 568[4]	754[4]
70 - 74	11 272	7 590	3 682	6 932[4]	4 182[4]	2 750[4]	4 337[4]	3 406[4]	931[4]
75 - 79	9 110	6 417	2 693	5 560[4]	3 552[4]	2 008[4]	3 543[4]	2 859[4]	684[4]
80 +	14 063	9 896	4 167	8 111[4]	5 022[4]	3 089[4]	5 942[4]	4 868[4]	1 074[4]
Unknown - Inconnu	856	493	363	530[4]	249[4]	281[4]	322[4]	240[4]	82[4]
Mozambique[5]									
1997 (I)									
Total	385 754	206 737	179 017	70 750	39 060	31 690	315 004	167 677	147 327
0	99 947	54 065	45 882	16 506	9 132	7 374	83 441	44 933	38 508
1 - 4	123 644	66 656	56 988	16 230	8 766	7 464	107 414	57 890	49 524
5 - 9	31 778	17 034	14 744	4 267	2 367	1 900	27 511	14 667	12 844
10 - 14	14 914	8 144	6 770	2 407	1 337	1 070	12 507	6 807	5 700
15 - 19	12 169	5 896	6 273	2 624	1 379	1 245	9 545	4 517	5 028
20 - 24	10 633	4 883	5 750	2 691	1 328	1 363	7 942	3 555	4 387
25 - 29	9 556	4 643	4 913	2 606	1 378	1 228	6 950	3 265	3 685
30 - 34	8 691	4 610	4 081	2 490	1 454	1 036	6 201	3 156	3 045
35 - 39	8 180	4 411	3 769	2 340	1 350	990	5 840	3 061	2 779
40 - 44	7 276	4 092	3 184	2 158	1 289	869	5 118	2 803	2 315
45 - 49	7 208	4 194	3 014	2 130	1 307	823	5 078	2 887	2 191
50 - 54	7 386	4 227	3 159	2 191	1 299	892	5 195	2 928	2 267
55 - 59	5 300	3 090	2 210	1 484	890	594	3 816	2 200	1 616
60 - 64	7 853	4 380	3 473	2 309	1 293	1 016	5 544	3 087	2 457
65 - 69	5 348	2 962	2 386	1 608	911	697	3 740	2 051	1 689
70 - 74	5 008	2 897	2 111	1 536	855	681	3 472	2 042	1 430
75 - 79	3 440	1 918	1 522	1 054	589	465	2 386	1 329	1 057
80 +	6 610	3 512	3 098	1 751	894	857	4 859	2 618	2 241
Unknown - Inconnu	10 813	5 123	5 690	2 368	1 242	1 126	8 445	3 881	4 564
Namibia - Namibie[6]									
2001 (I)									
Total	25 061	12 338[7]	12 137[7]	6 529	3 354[7]	3 175[7]	18 532	9 063[7]	8 962[7]
0 - 4	4 631	2 180[7]	2 343[7]	1 084	487[7]	582[7]	3 547	1 693[7]	1 761[7]
5 - 9	938	461[7]	447[7]	174	90[7]	83[7]	764	371[7]	364[7]

Continent, country or area, date, code and age (in years) / Continent, pays ou zone, date, code et âge (en années)	Total			Urban - Urbaine			Rural - Rurale		
	Both sexes Les deux sexes	Male Masculin	Female Féminin	Both sexes Les deux sexes	Male Masculin	Female Féminin	Both sexes Les deux sexes	Male Masculin	Female Féminin
AFRICA - AFRIQUE									
Namibia - Namibie[6]									
2001 (I)									
10 - 14	508	246[7]	256[7]	110	48[7]	60[7]	398	198[7]	196[7]
15 - 19	658	317[7]	330[7]	173	81[7]	88[7]	485	236[7]	242[7]
20 - 24	1 240	492[7]	740[7]	334	149[7]	184[7]	906	343[7]	556[7]
25 - 29	1 791	799[7]	989[7]	502	228[7]	274[7]	1 289	571[7]	715[7]
30 - 34	2 032	1 029[7]	988[7]	545	278[7]	264[7]	1 487	751[7]	724[7]
35 - 39	1 845	1 003[7]	837[7]	532	290[7]	241[7]	1 313	713[7]	596[7]
40 - 44	1 370	753[7]	615[7]	406	220[7]	186[7]	964	533[7]	429[7]
45 - 49	1 099	609[7]	485[7]	323	181[7]	142[7]	776	428[7]	343[7]
50 - 54	866	547[7]	317[7]	289	182[7]	107[7]	577	365[7]	210[7]
55 - 59	699	419[7]	279[7]	208	121[7]	87[7]	491	298[7]	192[7]
60 - 64	761	431[7]	315[7]	244	137[7]	105[7]	517	294[7]	210[7]
65 - 69	576	310[7]	260[7]	160	89[7]	69[7]	416	221[7]	191[7]
70 - 74	729	405[7]	322[7]	203	100[7]	101[7]	526	305[7]	221[7]
75 - 79	571	266[7]	291[7]	147	71[7]	73[7]	424	195[7]	218[7]
80 - 84	539	228[7]	299[7]	139	54[7]	84[7]	400	174[7]	215[7]
85 - 89	361	162[7]	189[7]	92	40[7]	50[7]	269	122[7]	139[7]
90 - 94	246	102[7]	138[7]	50	22[7]	28[7]	196	80[7]	110[7]
95 +	373	131[7]	242[7]	52	23[7]	29[7]	321	108[7]	213[7]
Unknown - Inconnu	3 228	1 448[7]	1 455[7]	762	384[7]	338[7]	2 466	1 064[7]	1 117[7]
Réunion[8]									
2003* (C)									
Total	4 022	2 311	1 711	...	...	...	...	...	...
0	107	59	48	...	...	...	...	...	...
1 - 4	19	11	8	...	...	...	...	...	...
5 - 9	9	4	5	...	...	...	...	...	...
10 - 14	14	8	6	...	...	...	...	...	...
15 - 19	38	30	8	...	...	...	...	...	...
20 - 24	44	34	10	...	...	...	...	...	...
25 - 29	36	26	10	...	...	...	...	...	...
30 - 34	81	52	29	...	...	...	...	...	...
35 - 39	126	93	33	...	...	...	...	...	...
40 - 44	159	118	41	...	...	...	...	...	...
45 - 49	196	144	52	...	...	...	...	...	...
50 - 54	222	162	60	...	...	...	...	...	...
55 - 59	234	165	69	...	...	...	...	...	...
60 - 64	267	178	89	...	...	...	...	...	...
65 - 69	396	258	138	...	...	...	...	...	...
70 - 74	425	264	161	...	...	...	...	...	...
75 - 79	478	268	210	...	...	...	...	...	...
80 - 84	482	220	262	...	...	...	...	...	...
85 +	689	217	472	...	...	...	...	...	...
Saint Helena ex. dep. - Sainte-Hélène sans dép.									
2005 (C)									
Total	39	21	18	...	...	...	...	...	...
0	1	1	-	...	...	...	...	...	...
1 - 4	-	-	-	...	...	...	...	...	...
5 - 9	-	-	-	...	...	...	...	...	...
10 - 14	-	-	-	...	...	...	...	...	...
15 - 19	-	-	-	...	...	...	...	...	...
20 - 24	-	-	-	...	...	...	...	...	...
25 - 29	-	-	-	...	...	...	...	...	...
30 - 34	-	-	-	...	...	...	...	...	...
35 - 39	-	-	-	...	...	...	...	...	...
40 - 44	-	-	-	...	...	...	...	...	...
45 - 49	2	2	-	...	...	...	...	...	...
50 - 54	1	1	-	...	...	...	...	...	...
55 - 59	2	2	-	...	...	...	...	...	...
60 - 64	1	-	1	...	...	...	...	...	...
65 - 69	3	2	1	...	...	...	...	...	...
70 - 74	4	2	2	...	...	...	...	...	...
75 - 79	8	7	1	...	...	...	...	...	...

19. Deaths by age, sex and urban/rural residence: latest available year, 1996 - 2005
Décès selon l'âge, le sexe et la résidence, urbaine/rurale: dernière année disponible, 1996 - 2005 (continued - suite)

Continent, country or area, date, code and age (in years) / Continent, pays ou zone, date, code et âge (en années)	Total			Urban - Urbaine			Rural - Rurale		
	Both sexes Les deux sexes	Male Masculin	Female Féminin	Both sexes Les deux sexes	Male Masculin	Female Féminin	Both sexes Les deux sexes	Male Masculin	Female Féminin

AFRICA - AFRIQUE

Saint Helena ex. dep. - Sainte-Hélène sans dép.									
2005 (C)									
80 - 84	8	-	8	...	...	...	...	...	...
85 - 89	3	1	2	...	...	...	...	...	...
90 - 94	3	2	1	...	...	...	...	...	...
95 - 99	2	1	1	...	...	...	...	...	...
100 + ...	1	-	1	...	...	...	...	...	...
Unknown - Inconnu	-	-	-	...	...	...	...	...	...
Seychelles									
2001 (+C)									
Total	554	330	224	...	...	...	...	...	...
0	19	8	11	...	...	...	...	...	...
1 - 4	3	2	1	...	...	...	...	...	...
5 - 9	1	-	1	...	...	...	...	...	...
10 - 14	1	1	-	...	...	...	...	...	...
15 - 19	2	1	1	...	...	...	...	...	...
20 - 24	8	8	-	...	...	...	...	...	...
25 - 29	10	10	-	...	...	...	...	...	...
30 - 34	13	11	2	...	...	...	...	...	...
35 - 39	17	11	6	...	...	...	...	...	...
40 - 44	32	25	7	...	...	...	...	...	...
45 - 49	27	21	6	...	...	...	...	...	...
50 - 54	26	20	6	...	...	...	...	...	...
55 - 59	28	22	6	...	...	...	...	...	...
60 - 64	44	29	15	...	...	...	...	...	...
65 - 69	59	33	26	...	...	...	...	...	...
70 - 74	57	35	22	...	...	...	...	...	...
75 - 79	61	35	26	...	...	...	...	...	...
80 - 84	68	36	32	...	...	...	...	...	...
85 + ...	78	22	56	...	...	...	...	...	...
South Africa - Afrique du Sud									
2004 (...)									
Total	565 954[9]	287 113	278 841	...	...	...	...	...	...
0 - 4	55 734[9]	29 454	26 280	...	...	...	...	...	...
5 - 9	5 894[9]	3 129	2 765	...	...	...	...	...	...
10 - 14	3 849[9]	2 105	1 744	...	...	...	...	...	...
15 - 19	9 135[9]	4 602	4 533	...	...	...	...	...	...
20 - 24	24 947[9]	10 188	14 759	...	...	...	...	...	...
25 - 29	46 457[9]	19 479	26 978	...	...	...	...	...	...
30 - 34	58 017[9]	27 977	30 040	...	...	...	...	...	...
35 - 39	52 389[9]	27 751	24 638	...	...	...	...	...	...
40 - 44	46 168[9]	26 034	20 134	...	...	...	...	...	...
45 - 49	38 657[9]	22 702	15 955	...	...	...	...	...	...
50 - 54	34 618[9]	20 778	13 840	...	...	...	...	...	...
55 - 59	29 600[9]	17 756	11 844	...	...	...	...	...	...
60 - 64	29 897[9]	16 712	13 185	...	...	...	...	...	...
65 - 69	28 584[9]	14 973	13 611	...	...	...	...	...	...
70 - 74	28 476[9]	13 277	15 199	...	...	...	...	...	...
75 - 79	25 527[9]	11 638	13 889	...	...	...	...	...	...
80 - 84	20 331[9]	8 533	11 798	...	...	...	...	...	...
85 - 89	14 342[9]	4 969	9 373	...	...	...	...	...	...
90 + ...	10 634[9]	3 248	7 386	...	...	...	...	...	...
Unknown - Inconnu	2 698[9]	1 808	890	...	...	...	...	...	...
Swaziland[5]									
1997 (|)									
Total	8 480	4 714	3 766	1 370	753	617	7 110	3 961	3 149
0 - 4	2 043	1 068	975	301	165	136	1 742	903	839
5 - 9	191	104	87	29	15	14	162	89	73
10 - 14	143	74	69	23	12	11	120	62	58
15 - 19	258	123	135	42	20	22	216	103	113
20 - 24	455	199	256	86	39	47	369	160	209
25 - 29	603	317	286	112	62	50	491	255	236
30 - 34	577	321	256	97	54	43	480	267	213

19. Deaths by age, sex and urban/rural residence: latest available year, 1996 - 2005
Décès selon l'âge, le sexe et la résidence, urbaine/rurale: dernière année disponible, 1996 - 2005 (continued - suite)

Continent, country or area, date, code and age (in years) / Continent, pays ou zone, date, code et âge (en années)	Total			Urban - Urbaine			Rural - Rurale		
	Both sexes Les deux sexes	Male Masculin	Female Féminin	Both sexes Les deux sexes	Male Masculin	Female Féminin	Both sexes Les deux sexes	Male Masculin	Female Féminin
AFRICA - AFRIQUE									
Swaziland[5]									
1997 (|)									
35 - 39	529	315	214	95	49	46	434	266	168
40 - 44	489	309	180	86	54	32	403	255	148
45 - 49	434	287	147	81	49	32	353	238	115
50 - 54	439	274	165	78	48	30	361	226	135
55 - 59	358	235	123	64	40	24	294	195	99
60 - 64	365	237	128	50	25	25	315	212	103
65 - 69	305	195	110	43	31	12	262	164	98
70 - 74	315	189	126	41	22	19	274	167	107
75 +	745	341	404	97	41	56	648	300	348
Unknown - Inconnu	231	126	105	45	27	18	186	99	87
Tunisia - Tunisie									
1998 (U)									
Total	*42 571*	*25 319*	*17 252*	...	...	...	...	...	...
0	*3 098*	*1 775*	*1 323*	...	...	...	...	...	...
1 - 4	*2 096*	*1 196*	*900*	...	...	...	...	...	...
5 - 9	*412*	*252*	*160*	...	...	...	...	...	...
10 - 14	*382*	*236*	*146*	...	...	...	...	...	...
15 - 19	*578*	*408*	*170*	...	...	...	...	...	...
20 - 24	*653*	*459*	*194*	...	...	...	...	...	...
25 - 29	*612*	*425*	*187*	...	...	...	...	...	...
30 - 34	*801*	*528*	*273*	...	...	...	...	...	...
35 - 39	*812*	*519*	*293*	...	...	...	...	...	...
40 - 44	*998*	*631*	*367*	...	...	...	...	...	...
45 - 49	*1 161*	*737*	*424*	...	...	...	...	...	...
50 - 54	*1 267*	*805*	*462*	...	...	...	...	...	...
55 - 59	*1 833*	*1 152*	*681*	...	...	...	...	...	...
60 - 64	*2 920*	*1 843*	*1 077*	...	...	...	...	...	...
65 - 69	*4 337*	*2 673*	*1 664*	...	...	...	...	...	...
70 - 74	*4 918*	*2 943*	*1 975*	...	...	...	...	...	...
75 - 79	*5 201*	*2 930*	*2 271*	...	...	...	...	...	...
80 +	*10 199*	*5 681*	*4 518*	...	...	...	...	...	...
Unknown - Inconnu	*293*	*126*	*167*	...	...	...	...	...	...
Zimbabwe[10]									
2002 (|)									
Total	200 294	103 741	96 553	50 364	26 779	23 585	149 930	76 962	72 968
0	23 672	12 887	10 785	6 770	3 697	3 073	16 902	9 190	7 712
1 - 4	16 231	8 688	7 543	3 523	1 943	1 580	12 708	6 745	5 963
5 - 9	5 166	2 793	2 373	1 160	641	519	4 006	2 152	1 854
10 - 14	3 599	1 946	1 653	896	488	408	2 703	1 458	1 245
15 - 19	4 165	1 802	2 363	940	417	523	3 225	1 385	1 840
20 - 24	9 623	3 440	6 183	2 366	882	1 484	7 257	2 558	4 699
25 - 29	17 414	6 930	10 484	4 464	1 788	2 676	12 950	5 142	7 808
30 - 34	21 358	10 286	11 072	5 763	2 897	2 866	15 595	7 389	8 206
35 - 39	19 611	10 176	9 435	5 549	3 046	2 503	14 062	7 130	6 932
40 - 44	15 322	8 608	6 714	4 223	2 448	1 775	11 099	6 160	4 939
45 - 49	11 993	6 907	5 086	3 327	2 003	1 324	8 666	4 904	3 762
50 - 54	8 845	5 029	3 816	2 354	1 360	994	6 491	3 669	2 822
55 - 59	6 229	3 857	2 372	1 555	959	596	4 674	2 898	1 776
60 - 64	5 910	3 649	2 261	1 410	865	545	4 500	2 784	1 716
65 - 69	4 504	2 682	1 822	1 051	626	425	3 453	2 056	1 397
70 - 74	4 638	2 810	1 828	954	587	367	3 684	2 223	1 461
75 +	11 781	6 066	5 715	2 048	1 091	957	9 733	4 975	4 758
Unknown - Inconnu	10 233	5 185	5 048	2 011	1 041	970	8 222	4 144	4 078
AMERICA, NORTH - AMÉRIQUE DU NORD									
Anguilla									
2004 (+C)									
Total	53	25	28	...	...	...	...	...	...
0	-	-	-	...	...	...	...	...	...
1 - 4	-	-	-	...	...	...	...	...	...

Continent, country or area, date, code and age (in years) / Continent, pays ou zone, date, code et âge (en annèes)	Total			Urban - Urbaine			Rural - Rurale		
	Both sexes Les deux sexes	Male Masculin	Female Féminin	Both sexes Les deux sexes	Male Masculin	Female Féminin	Both sexes Les deux sexes	Male Masculin	Female Féminin
AMERICA, NORTH - AMÉRIQUE DU NORD									
Anguilla									
2004 (+C)									
5 - 9	-	-	-	...	...	...	...	...	...
10 - 14	-	-	-	...	...	...	...	...	...
15 - 19	-	-	-	...	...	...	...	...	...
20 - 24	1	1	-	...	...	...	...	...	...
25 - 29	-	-	-	...	...	...	...	...	...
30 - 34	1	-	1	...	...	...	...	...	...
35 - 39	3	2	1	...	...	...	...	...	...
40 - 44	2	1	1	...	...	...	...	...	...
45 - 49	2	2	-	...	...	...	...	...	...
50 - 54	3	1	2	...	...	...	...	...	...
55 - 59	-	-	-	...	...	...	...	...	...
60 - 64	2	2	-	...	...	...	...	...	...
65 - 69	5	2	3	...	...	...	...	...	...
70 - 74	6	1	5	...	...	...	...	...	...
75 - 79	5	2	3	...	...	...	...	...	...
80 - 84	4	2	2	...	...	...	...	...	...
85 +	19	9	10	...	...	...	...	...	...
Antigua and Barbuda - Antigua-et-Barbuda[11]									
2002 (+C)									
Total	444	234	210	...	...	...	...	...	...
0	21	14	7	...	...	...	...	...	...
1 - 4	3	2	1	...	...	...	...	...	...
5 - 9	1	-	1	...	...	...	...	...	...
10 - 14	2	1	1	...	...	...	...	...	...
15 - 19	2	2	-	...	...	...	...	...	...
20 - 24	9	6	3	...	...	...	...	...	...
25 - 29	3	3	-	...	...	...	...	...	...
30 - 34	11	8	3	...	...	...	...	...	...
35 - 39	10	8	2	...	...	...	...	...	...
40 - 44	13	5	8	...	...	...	...	...	...
45 - 49	13	6	7	...	...	...	...	...	...
50 - 54	16	7	9	...	...	...	...	...	...
55 - 59	18	9	9	...	...	...	...	...	...
60 - 64	24	15	9	...	...	...	...	...	...
65 - 69	28	17	11	...	...	...	...	...	...
70 - 74	52	27	25	...	...	...	...	...	...
75 - 79	48	30	18	...	...	...	...	...	...
80 - 84	64	32	32	...	...	...	...	...	...
85 - 89	54	25	29	...	...	...	...	...	...
90 - 94	30	10	20	...	...	...	...	...	...
95 +	22	7	15	...	...	...	...	...	...
Aruba									
2004 (C)									
Total	510[12]	289	221	...	...	...	...	...	...
0	1	-	1	...	...	...	...	...	...
1 - 4	1	1	-	...	...	...	...	...	...
5 - 14	3	1	2	...	...	...	...	...	...
15 - 24	10	8	2	...	...	...	...	...	...
25 - 44	36	28	8	...	...	...	...	...	...
45 - 64	124	81	43	...	...	...	...	...	...
65 +	335	170	165	...	...	...	...	...	...
Bahamas									
2001 (C)									
Total	1 609	879	730	...	...	...	...	...	...
0	37	23	14	...	...	...	...	...	...
1 - 4	14	6	8	...	...	...	...	...	...
5 - 9	7	5	2	...	...	...	...	...	...
10 - 14	7	3	4	...	...	...	...	...	...
15 - 19	22	17	5	...	...	...	...	...	...
20 - 24	25	17	8	...	...	...	...	...	...
25 - 29	62	40	22	...	...	...	...	...	...

Continent, country or area, date, code and age (in years) / Continent, pays ou zone, date, code et âge (en années)	Total			Urban - Urbaine			Rural - Rurale		
	Both sexes Les deux sexes	Male Masculin	Female Féminin	Both sexes Les deux sexes	Male Masculin	Female Féminin	Both sexes Les deux sexes	Male Masculin	Female Féminin
AMERICA, NORTH - AMÉRIQUE DU NORD									
Bahamas									
2001 (C)									
30 - 34	86	55	31	...	...	...	...	...	...
35 - 39	97	58	39	...	...	...	...	...	...
40 - 44	118	78	40	...	...	...	...	...	...
45 - 49	106	64	42	...	...	...	...	...	...
50 - 54	91	53	38	...	...	...	...	...	...
55 - 59	108	63	45	...	...	...	...	...	...
60 - 64	111	71	40	...	...	...	...	...	...
65 - 69	145	80	65	...	...	...	...	...	...
70 - 74	126	64	62	...	...	...	...	...	...
75 - 79	120	60	60	...	...	...	...	...	...
80 - 84	141	72	69	...	...	...	...	...	...
85 - 89	108	37	71	...	...	...	...	...	...
90 - 94	52	7	45	...	...	...	...	...	...
95 - 99	19	6	13	...	...	...	...	...	...
100 +	7	-	7	...	...	...	...	...	...
Barbados - Barbade[11]									
2001 (+C)									
Total	1 712	784	928	...	...	...	...	...	...
0	32	15	17	...	...	...	...	...	...
1 - 4	5	2	3	...	...	...	...	...	...
5 - 9	2	1	1	...	...	...	...	...	...
10 - 14	1	1	-	...	...	...	...	...	...
15 - 19	9	7	2	...	...	...	...	...	...
20 - 24	16	12	4	...	...	...	...	...	...
25 - 29	26	18	8	...	...	...	...	...	...
30 - 34	32	16	16	...	...	...	...	...	...
35 - 39	31	16	15	...	...	...	...	...	...
40 - 44	51	29	22	...	...	...	...	...	...
45 - 49	45	31	14	...	...	...	...	...	...
50 - 54	53	33	20	...	...	...	...	...	...
55 - 59	66	34	32	...	...	...	...	...	...
60 - 64	84	39	45	...	...	...	...	...	...
65 - 69	107	55	52	...	...	...	...	...	...
70 - 74	175	82	93	...	...	...	...	...	...
75 - 79	192	89	103	...	...	...	...	...	...
80 - 84	285	137	148	...	...	...	...	...	...
85 - 89	260	106	154	...	...	...	...	...	...
90 - 94	145	46	99	...	...	...	...	...	...
95 +	92	14	78	...	...	...	...	...	...
Unknown - Inconnu	3	1	2	...	...	...	...	...	...
Belize									
2001 (U)									
Total	1 261	...	...	...	...	...	...	...	...
0	120	...	...	...	...	...	...	...	...
1 - 4	32	...	...	...	...	...	...	...	...
5 - 9	15	...	...	...	...	...	...	...	...
10 - 14	12	...	...	...	...	...	...	...	...
15 - 19	35	...	...	...	...	...	...	...	...
20 - 24	41	...	...	...	...	...	...	...	...
25 - 29	54	...	...	...	...	...	...	...	...
30 - 34	51	...	...	...	...	...	...	...	...
35 - 39	56	...	...	...	...	...	...	...	...
40 - 44	53	...	...	...	...	...	...	...	...
45 - 49	62	...	...	...	...	...	...	...	...
50 - 54	53	...	...	...	...	...	...	...	...
55 - 59	57	...	...	...	...	...	...	...	...
60 - 64	68	...	...	...	...	...	...	...	...
65 - 69	98	...	...	...	...	...	...	...	...
70 - 74	122	...	...	...	...	...	...	...	...
75 - 79	87	...	...	...	...	...	...	...	...
80 +	239	...	...	...	...	...	...	...	...
Unknown - Inconnu	6	...	...	...	...	...	...	...	...

19. Deaths by age, sex and urban/rural residence: latest available year, 1996 - 2005
Décès selon l'âge, le sexe et la résidence, urbaine/rurale: dernière année disponible, 1996 - 2005 (continued - suite)

Continent, country or area, date, code and age (in years)	Total			Urban - Urbaine			Rural - Rurale		
Continent, pays ou zone, date, code et âge (en années)	Both sexes Les deux sexes	Male Masculin	Female Féminin	Both sexes Les deux sexes	Male Masculin	Female Féminin	Both sexes Les deux sexes	Male Masculin	Female Féminin
AMERICA, NORTH - AMÉRIQUE DU NORD									
Bermuda - Bermudes									
2003 (C)									
Total....................	434	...	...	...	...	...	...	...	...
0 - 14.................	2	...	...	...	...	...	...	...	...
15 - 24.................	2	...	...	...	...	...	...	...	...
25 - 44.................	31	...	...	...	...	...	...	...	...
45 - 64.................	81	...	...	...	...	...	...	...	...
65 - 84.................	197	...	...	...	...	...	...	...	...
85 +.................	121	...	...	...	...	...	...	...	...
British Virgin Islands - Îles Vierges britanniques[11]									
1998 (C)									
Total....................	85	50	35	...	...	...	...	...	...
0....................	3	2	1	...	...	...	...	...	...
1 - 4....................	-	-	-	...	...	...	...	...	...
5 - 9....................	1	1	-	...	...	...	...	...	...
10 - 14....................	-	-	-	...	...	...	...	...	...
15 - 19....................	2	2	-	...	...	...	...	...	...
20 - 24....................	2	2	-	...	...	...	...	...	...
25 - 29....................	2	2	-	...	...	...	...	...	...
30 - 34....................	1	1	-	...	...	...	...	...	...
35 - 39....................	5	1	4	...	...	...	...	...	...
40 - 44....................	2	1	1	...	...	...	...	...	...
45 - 49....................	5	3	2	...	...	...	...	...	...
50 - 54....................	6	6	-	...	...	...	...	...	...
55 - 59....................	3	1	2	...	...	...	...	...	...
60 - 64....................	1	1	-	...	...	...	...	...	...
65 - 69....................	3	2	1	...	...	...	...	...	...
70 - 74....................	11	7	4	...	...	...	...	...	...
75 - 79....................	15	8	7	...	...	...	...	...	...
80 - 84....................	9	5	4	...	...	...	...	...	...
85 - 89....................	8	3	5	...	...	...	...	...	...
90 - 94....................	3	1	2	...	...	...	...	...	...
95 +....................	3	1	2	...	...	...	...	...	...
Canada[13]									
2004 (C)									
Total....................	226 584	114 513	112 071	...	...	...	...	...	...
0....................	1 775	953	822	...	...	...	...	...	...
1 - 4....................	286	154	132	...	...	...	...	...	...
5 - 9....................	195	126	69	...	...	...	...	...	...
10 - 14....................	259	157	102	...	...	...	...	...	...
15 - 19....................	934	666	268	...	...	...	...	...	...
20 - 24....................	1 287	938	349	...	...	...	...	...	...
25 - 29....................	1 228	873	355	...	...	...	...	...	...
30 - 34....................	1 490	1 009	481	...	...	...	...	...	...
35 - 39....................	2 268	1 468	800	...	...	...	...	...	...
40 - 44....................	3 709	2 376	1 333	...	...	...	...	...	...
45 - 49....................	5 676	3 454	2 222	...	...	...	...	...	...
50 - 54....................	7 829	4 742	3 087	...	...	...	...	...	...
55 - 59....................	10 611	6 477	4 134	...	...	...	...	...	...
60 - 64....................	13 139	8 071	5 068	...	...	...	...	...	...
65 - 69....................	16 499	9 961	6 538	...	...	...	...	...	...
70 - 74....................	23 763	14 061	9 702	...	...	...	...	...	...
75 - 79....................	31 831	17 561	14 270	...	...	...	...	...	...
80 - 84....................	37 974	18 453	19 521	...	...	...	...	...	...
85 - 89....................	32 997	13 394	19 603	...	...	...	...	...	...
90 +....................	32 830	9 615	23 215	...	...	...	...	...	...
Unknown - Inconnu......	4	4	-	...	...	...	...	...	...
Cayman Islands - Îles Caïmanes[11]									
2000 (C)									
Total....................	137	80	57	...	...	...	...	...	...
0....................	-	-	-	...	...	...	...	...	...
1 - 4....................	-	-	-	...	...	...	...	...	...

Continent, country or area, date, code and age (in years) / Continent, pays ou zone, date, code et âge (en années)	Total			Urban - Urbaine			Rural - Rurale		
	Both sexes Les deux sexes	Male Masculin	Female Féminin	Both sexes Les deux sexes	Male Masculin	Female Féminin	Both sexes Les deux sexes	Male Masculin	Female Féminin
AMERICA, NORTH - AMÉRIQUE DU NORD									
Cayman Islands - Îles Caïmanes[11]									
2000 (C)									
5 - 9	1	-	1	...	...	...	...	...	...
10 - 14	-	-	-	...	...	...	...	...	...
15 - 19	1	1	-	...	...	...	...	...	...
20 - 24	2	2	-	...	...	...	...	...	...
25 - 29	4	2	2	...	...	...	...	...	...
30 - 34	4	4	-	...	...	...	...	...	...
35 - 39	4	2	2	...	...	...	...	...	...
40 - 44	6	6	-	...	...	...	...	...	...
45 - 49	10	5	5	...	...	...	...	...	...
50 - 54	5	3	2	...	...	...	...	...	...
55 - 59	6	6	-	...	...	...	...	...	...
60 - 64	14	10	4	...	...	...	...	...	...
65 - 69	10	8	2	...	...	...	...	...	...
70 - 74	17	9	8	...	...	...	...	...	...
75 - 79	13	7	6	...	...	...	...	...	...
80 - 84	17	7	10	...	...	...	...	...	...
85 - 89	12	3	9	...	...	...	...	...	...
90 - 94	8	4	4	...	...	...	...	...	...
95 +	3	1	2	...	...	...	...	...	...
Costa Rica									
2004 (C)									
Total	15 949	9 047	6 902	...	...	...	...	...	...
0	668	373	295	...	...	...	...	...	...
1 - 4	109	59	50	...	...	...	...	...	...
5 - 9	76	47	29	...	...	...	...	...	...
10 - 14	99	51	48	...	...	...	...	...	...
15 - 19	227	166	61	...	...	...	...	...	...
20 - 24	291	225	66	...	...	...	...	...	...
25 - 29	298	216	82	...	...	...	...	...	...
30 - 34	323	231	92	...	...	...	...	...	...
35 - 39	367	263	104	...	...	...	...	...	...
40 - 44	546	363	183	...	...	...	...	...	...
45 - 49	643	412	231	...	...	...	...	...	...
50 - 54	703	449	254	...	...	...	...	...	...
55 - 59	838	521	317	...	...	...	...	...	...
60 - 64	971	581	390	...	...	...	...	...	...
65 - 69	1 254	745	509	...	...	...	...	...	...
70 - 74	1 532	840	692	...	...	...	...	...	...
75 - 79	1 895	1 025	870	...	...	...	...	...	...
80 - 84	1 824	948	876	...	...	...	...	...	...
85 +	3 264	1 515	1 749	...	...	...	...	...	...
Unknown - Inconnu	21	17	4	...	...	...	...	...	...
Cuba									
2005 (C)									
Total	84 824	45 878	38 946	69 969	37 055	32 914	14 855	8 823	6 032
0	746	412	334	584	325	259	162	87	75
1 - 4	219	126	93	168	94	74	51	32	19
5 - 9	146	102	44	113	79	34	33	23	10
10 - 14	200	122	78	149	93	56	51	29	22
15 - 19	415	264	151	322	205	117	93	59	34
20 - 24	497	332	165	397	268	129	100	64	36
25 - 29	625	416	209	501	337	164	124	79	45
30 - 34	964	642	322	738	490	248	226	152	74
35 - 39	1 469	912	557	1 155	728	427	314	184	130
40 - 44	2 009	1 227	782	1 645	1 015	630	364	212	152
45 - 49	2 314	1 395	919	1 886	1 142	744	428	253	175
50 - 54	3 359	2 004	1 355	2 792	1 673	1 119	567	331	236
55 - 59	4 707	2 789	1 918	3 908	2 326	1 582	799	463	336
60 - 64	6 087	3 609	2 478	5 125	3 035	2 090	962	574	388
65 - 69	7 298	4 223	3 075	6 112	3 538	2 574	1 186	685	501
70 - 74	9 002	5 107	3 895	7 466	4 173	3 293	1 536	934	602

Continent, country or area, date, code and age (in years) / Continent, pays ou zone, date, code et âge (en années)	Total			Urban - Urbaine			Rural - Rurale		
	Both sexes Les deux sexes	Male Masculin	Female Féminin	Both sexes Les deux sexes	Male Masculin	Female Féminin	Both sexes Les deux sexes	Male Masculin	Female Féminin
AMERICA, NORTH - AMÉRIQUE DU NORD									
Cuba									
2005 (C)									
75 - 79	11 165	6 099	5 066	9 290	4 935	4 355	1 875	1 164	711
80 - 84	11 860	6 103	5 757	9 884	4 901	4 983	1 976	1 202	774
85 - 89	10 835	5 207	5 628	8 938	4 119	4 819	1 897	1 088	809
90 - 94	7 300	3 213	4 087	5 921	2 418	3 503	1 379	795	584
95 - 99	2 918	1 279	1 639	2 352	958	1 394	566	321	245
100 +	682	289	393	520	200	320	162	89	73
Unknown - Inconnu	7	6	1	3	3	-	4	3	1
Dominica - Dominique[11]									
2003 (+C)									
Total	557	297	260	...	...	...	...	...	...
0	20	11	9	...	...	...	...	...	...
1 - 4	3	1	2	...	...	...	...	...	...
5 - 9	-	-	-	...	...	...	...	...	...
10 - 14	2	2	-	...	...	...	...	...	...
15 - 19	3	3	-	...	...	...	...	...	...
20 - 24	8	6	2	...	...	...	...	...	...
25 - 29	9	9	-	...	...	...	...	...	...
30 - 34	7	4	3	...	...	...	...	...	...
35 - 39	11	8	3	...	...	...	...	...	...
40 - 44	19	16	3	...	...	...	...	...	...
45 - 49	18	8	10	...	...	...	...	...	...
50 - 54	20	8	12	...	...	...	...	...	...
55 - 59	18	9	9	...	...	...	...	...	...
60 - 64	25	16	9	...	...	...	...	...	...
65 - 69	41	24	17	...	...	...	...	...	...
70 - 74	64	38	26	...	...	...	...	...	...
75 - 79	59	37	22	...	...	...	...	...	...
80 - 84	81	37	44	...	...	...	...	...	...
85 - 89	67	35	32	...	...	...	...	...	...
90 - 94	43	12	31	...	...	...	...	...	...
95 +	24	3	21	...	...	...	...	...	...
Unknown - Inconnu	15	10	5	...	...	...	...	...	...
Dominican Republic - République dominicaine									
2004 (+U)									
Total	30 118	17 688[7]	12 377[7]	...	...	...	...	...	...
0	2 551	1 342[7]	1 200[7]	...	...	...	...	...	...
1 - 4	456	246[7]	209[7]	...	...	...	...	...	...
5 - 9	238	138[7]	100[7]	...	...	...	...	...	...
10 - 14	258	149[7]	108[7]	...	...	...	...	...	...
15 - 19	538	379[7]	157[7]	...	...	...	...	...	...
20 - 24	877	647[7]	228[7]	...	...	...	...	...	...
25 - 29	972	689[7]	282[7]	...	...	...	...	...	...
30 - 34	1 141	793[7]	348[7]	...	...	...	...	...	...
35 - 39	1 149	775[7]	368[7]	...	...	...	...	...	...
40 - 44	1 199	746[7]	449[7]	...	...	...	...	...	...
45 - 49	1 217	764[7]	450[7]	...	...	...	...	...	...
50 - 54	1 454	894[7]	557[7]	...	...	...	...	...	...
55 - 59	1 555	968[7]	585[7]	...	...	...	...	...	...
60 - 64	1 859	1 132[7]	727[7]	...	...	...	...	...	...
65 - 69	2 219	1 381[7]	838[7]	...	...	...	...	...	...
70 - 74	2 856	1 603[7]	1 252[7]	...	...	...	...	...	...
75 - 79	2 586	1 457[7]	1 127[7]	...	...	...	...	...	...
80 - 84	2 583	1 399[7]	1 182[7]	...	...	...	...	...	...
85 +	3 910	1 888[7]	2 017[7]	...	...	...	...	...	...
Unknown - Inconnu	500	298[7]	193[7]	...	...	...	...	...	...
El Salvador									
2003 (C)									
Total	29 377	17 040	12 337	20 856	11 916	8 940	8 521	5 124	3 397
0	1 322	747	575	847	475	372	475	272	203
1 - 4	477	263	214	282	160	122	195	103	92

Continent, country or area, date, code and age (in years) / Continent, pays ou zone, date, code et âge (en années)	Total			Urban - Urbaine			Rural - Rurale		
	Both sexes Les deux sexes	Male Masculin	Female Féminin	Both sexes Les deux sexes	Male Masculin	Female Féminin	Both sexes Les deux sexes	Male Masculin	Female Féminin
AMERICA, NORTH - AMÉRIQUE DU NORD									
El Salvador									
2003 (C)									
5 - 9	218	126	92	135	73	62	83	53	30
10 - 14	265	163	102	181	107	74	84	56	28
15 - 19	756	562	194	538	408	130	218	154	64
20 - 24	1 194	957	237	866	698	168	328	259	69
25 - 29	1 252	1 012	240	907	740	167	345	272	73
30 - 34	1 056	827	229	754	592	162	302	235	67
35 - 39	1 155	845	310	839	606	233	316	239	77
40 - 44	1 109	766	343	798	565	233	311	201	110
45 - 49	1 215	814	401	849	578	271	366	236	130
50 - 54	1 329	817	512	958	583	375	371	234	137
55 - 59	1 512	950	562	1 061	656	405	451	294	157
60 - 64	1 867	1 025	842	1 348	738	610	519	287	232
65 - 69	2 156	1 173	983	1 509	792	717	647	381	266
70 - 74	2 475	1 298	1 177	1 740	896	844	735	402	333
75 - 79	2 735	1 384	1 351	1 980	991	989	755	393	362
80 - 84	2 792	1 321	1 471	1 977	895	1 082	815	426	389
85 +	4 492	1 990	2 502	3 287	1 363	1 924	1 205	627	578
Greenland - Groenland									
2003 (C)									
Total	412	235	177	340	197	143	72	38	34
0	8	6	2	8	6	2	-	-	-
1 - 4	4	2	2	3	2	1	1	-	1
5 - 9	1	-	1	1	-	1	-	-	-
10 - 14	2	2	-	2	2	-	-	-	-
15 - 19	12	7	5	11	7	4	1	-	1
20 - 24	17	13	4	15	11	4	2	2	-
25 - 29	5	3	2	5	3	2	-	-	-
30 - 34	10	5	5	5	2	3	5	3	2
35 - 39	16	12	4	13	10	3	3	2	1
40 - 44	15	11	4	13	10	3	2	1	1
45 - 49	21	13	8	17	9	8	4	4	-
50 - 54	23	13	10	18	10	8	5	3	2
55 - 59	36	25	11	31	21	10	5	4	1
60 - 64	32	18	14	26	16	10	6	2	4
65 - 69	61	40	21	48	34	14	13	6	7
70 - 74	64	29	35	50	23	27	14	6	8
75 - 79	38	19	19	34	17	17	4	2	2
80 - 84	32	13	19	27	11	16	5	2	3
85 +	15	4	11	13	3	10	2	1	1
Grenada - Grenade									
2000 (+C)									
Total	716	365	351	...	...	...	...	...	...
0	27	10	17	...	...	...	...	...	...
1 - 4	1	1	-	...	...	...	...	...	...
5 - 9	1	1	-	...	...	...	...	...	...
10 - 14	4	4	-	...	...	...	...	...	...
15 - 19	8	2	6	...	...	...	...	...	...
20 - 24	11	9	2	...	...	...	...	...	...
25 - 29	17	13	4	...	...	...	...	...	...
30 - 34	21	11	10	...	...	...	...	...	...
35 - 39	17	7	10	...	...	...	...	...	...
40 - 44	14	9	5	...	...	...	...	...	...
45 - 49	21	13	8	...	...	...	...	...	...
50 - 54	27	15	12	...	...	...	...	...	...
55 - 59	24	17	7	...	...	...	...	...	...
60 - 64	50	30	20	...	...	...	...	...	...
65 - 69	61	35	26	...	...	...	...	...	...
70 - 74	81	52	29	...	...	...	...	...	...
75 - 79	96	50	46	...	...	...	...	...	...
80 - 84	69	27	42	...	...	...	...	...	...
85 - 89	84	34	50	...	...	...	...	...	...
90 - 94	52	16	36	...	...	...	...	...	...

Continent, country or area, date, code and age (in years) Continent, pays ou zone, date, code et âge (en années)	Total			Urban - Urbaine			Rural - Rurale		
	Both sexes Les deux sexes	Male Masculin	Female Féminin	Both sexes Les deux sexes	Male Masculin	Female Féminin	Both sexes Les deux sexes	Male Masculin	Female Féminin
AMERICA, NORTH - AMÉRIQUE DU NORD									
Grenada - Grenade									
2000 (+C)									
95 - 99	24	8	16	...	...	...	...	...	...
100 +	6	1	5	...	...	...	...	...	...
Guadeloupe[8]									
2003 (C)									
Total	2 636	1 405	1 231	...	...	...	...	...	...
0	56	34	22	...	...	...	...	...	...
1 - 4	9	5	4	...	...	...	...	...	...
5 - 9	5	4	1	...	...	...	...	...	...
10 - 14	5	3	2	...	...	...	...	...	...
15 - 19	21	18	3	...	...	...	...	...	...
20 - 24	23	19	4	...	...	...	...	...	...
25 - 29	23	17	6	...	...	...	...	...	...
30 - 34	39	31	8	...	...	...	...	...	...
35 - 39	60	40	20	...	...	...	...	...	...
40 - 44	76	47	29	...	...	...	...	...	...
45 - 49	102	71	31	...	...	...	...	...	...
50 - 54	112	87	25	...	...	...	...	...	...
55 - 59	128	85	43	...	...	...	...	...	...
60 - 64	177	96	81	...	...	...	...	...	...
65 - 69	213	126	87	...	...	...	...	...	...
70 - 74	257	141	116	...	...	...	...	...	...
75 - 79	316	180	136	...	...	...	...	...	...
80 - 84	356	185	171	...	...	...	...	...	...
85 - 89	329	124	205	...	...	...	...	...	...
90 - 94	205	65	140	...	...	...	...	...	...
95 - 99	96	19	77	...	...	...	...	...	...
100 +	28	8	20	...	...	...	...	...	...
Guatemala[11]									
2003 (C)									
Total	66 612	38 383	28 229	...	...	...	...	...	...
0	11 016	6 114	4 902	...	...	...	...	...	...
1 - 4	4 533	2 334	2 199	...	...	...	...	...	...
5 - 9	1 005	540	465	...	...	...	...	...	...
10 - 14	874	525	349	...	...	...	...	...	...
15 - 19	2 004	1 370	634	...	...	...	...	...	...
20 - 24	2 720	1 985	735	...	...	...	...	...	...
25 - 29	2 559	1 852	707	...	...	...	...	...	...
30 - 34	2 367	1 711	656	...	...	...	...	...	...
35 - 39	2 436	1 708	728	...	...	...	...	...	...
40 - 44	2 694	1 801	893	...	...	...	...	...	...
45 - 49	2 620	1 677	943	...	...	...	...	...	...
50 - 54	2 947	1 762	1 185	...	...	...	...	...	...
55 - 59	2 881	1 629	1 252	...	...	...	...	...	...
60 - 64	3 130	1 697	1 433	...	...	...	...	...	...
65 - 69	3 755	2 016	1 739	...	...	...	...	...	...
70 - 74	4 447	2 417	2 030	...	...	...	...	...	...
75 - 79	4 802	2 506	2 296	...	...	...	...	...	...
80 - 84	4 306	2 165	2 141	...	...	...	...	...	...
85 - 89	3 059	1 452	1 607	...	...	...	...	...	...
90 - 94	1 606	680	926	...	...	...	...	...	...
95 +	587	251	336	...	...	...	...	...	...
Unknown - Inconnu	264	191	73	...	...	...	...	...	...
Haiti - Haïti[11]									
2003 (U)									
Total	8 011	4 135	3 876	...	...	...	...	...	...
0	724	388	336	...	...	...	...	...	...
1 - 4	501	270	231	...	...	...	...	...	...
5 - 9	161	85	76	...	...	...	...	...	...
10 - 14	135	66	69	...	...	...	...	...	...
15 - 19	216	114	102	...	...	...	...	...	...
20 - 24	324	158	166	...	...	...	...	...	...
25 - 29	371	179	192	...	...	...	...	...	...

Continent, country or area, date, code and age (in years) / Continent, pays ou zone, date, code et âge (en années)	Total			Urban - Urbaine			Rural - Rurale		
	Both sexes Les deux sexes	Male Masculin	Female Féminin	Both sexes Les deux sexes	Male Masculin	Female Féminin	Both sexes Les deux sexes	Male Masculin	Female Féminin
AMERICA, NORTH -									
AMÉRIQUE DU NORD									
Haiti - Haïti[11]									
2003 (U)									
30 - 34	442	229	213	...	...	...	...	...	...
35 - 39	392	215	177	...	...	...	...	...	...
40 - 44	434	234	200	...	...	...	...	...	...
45 - 49	363	190	173	...	...	...	...	...	...
50 - 54	346	177	169	...	...	...	...	...	...
55 - 59	316	176	140	...	...	...	...	...	...
60 - 64	397	205	192	...	...	...	...	...	...
65 - 69	378	196	182	...	...	...	...	...	...
70 - 74	460	245	215	...	...	...	...	...	...
75 - 79	416	223	193	...	...	...	...	...	...
80 - 84	417	208	209	...	...	...	...	...	...
85 - 89	266	110	156	...	...	...	...	...	...
90 - 94	162	57	105	...	...	...	...	...	...
95 +	132	48	84	...	...	...	...	...	...
Unknown - Inconnu	658	362	296	...	...	...	...	...	...
Jamaica - Jamaïque									
2004 (U)									
Total	15 388	8 486	6 902	...	...	...	...	...	...
0	695	374	321	...	...	...	...	...	...
1 - 4	111	56	55	...	...	...	...	...	...
5 - 9	72	32	40	...	...	...	...	...	...
10 - 14	63	42	21	...	...	...	...	...	...
15 - 19	226	162	64	...	...	...	...	...	...
20 - 24	450	357	93	...	...	...	...	...	...
25 - 29	502	373	129	...	...	...	...	...	...
30 - 34	538	403	135	...	...	...	...	...	...
35 - 39	578	400	178	...	...	...	...	...	...
40 - 44	569	346	223	...	...	...	...	...	...
45 - 49	551	316	235	...	...	...	...	...	...
50 - 54	558	325	233	...	...	...	...	...	...
55 - 59	634	383	251	...	...	...	...	...	...
60 - 64	922	546	376	...	...	...	...	...	...
65 - 69	1 078	593	485	...	...	...	...	...	...
70 - 74	1 480	866	614	...	...	...	...	...	...
75 - 79	1 597	842	755	...	...	...	...	...	...
80 - 84	1 723	844	879	...	...	...	...	...	...
85 - 89	1 409	640	769	...	...	...	...	...	...
90 - 94	1 078	414	664	...	...	...	...	...	...
95 - 99	395	129	266	...	...	...	...	...	...
100 +	159	43	116	...	...	...	...	...	...
Martinique[8]									
2003 (C)									
Total	2 725	1 421	1 304	...	...	...	...	...	...
0	33	14	19	...	...	...	...	...	...
1 - 4	8	3	5	...	...	...	...	...	...
5 - 9	6	3	3	...	...	...	...	...	...
10 - 14	5	4	1	...	...	...	...	...	...
15 - 19	20	16	4	...	...	...	...	...	...
20 - 24	20	14	6	...	...	...	...	...	...
25 - 29	21	16	5	...	...	...	...	...	...
30 - 34	40	29	11	...	...	...	...	...	...
35 - 39	42	27	15	...	...	...	...	...	...
40 - 44	53	36	17	...	...	...	...	...	...
45 - 49	81	50	31	...	...	...	...	...	...
50 - 54	91	55	36	...	...	...	...	...	...
55 - 59	97	58	39	...	...	...	...	...	...
60 - 64	137	84	53	...	...	...	...	...	...
65 - 69	189	118	71	...	...	...	...	...	...
70 - 74	267	156	111	...	...	...	...	...	...
75 - 79	360	213	147	...	...	...	...	...	...
80 - 84	439	221	218	...	...	...	...	...	...
85 - 89	386	178	208	...	...	...	...	...	...

Continent, country or area, date, code and age (in years) / Continent, pays ou zone, date, code et âge (en années)	Total			Urban - Urbaine			Rural - Rurale		
	Both sexes Les deux sexes	Male Masculin	Female Féminin	Both sexes Les deux sexes	Male Masculin	Female Féminin	Both sexes Les deux sexes	Male Masculin	Female Féminin
AMERICA, NORTH - AMÉRIQUE DU NORD									
Martinique[8]									
2003 (C)									
90 - 94	273	85	188	...	...	...	...	...	...
95 - 99	129	35	94	...	...	...	...	...	...
100 +	28	6	22	...	...	...	...	...	...
Mexico - Mexique									
2005 (C)									
Total	495 240	273 126[7]	221 968[7]	370 267[4]	200 629[14]	169 568[14]	116 657[4]	66 697[14]	49 933[14]
0	32 603	18 214[7]	14 318[7]	24 372[4]	13 635[14]	10 684[14]	7 639[4]	4 237[14]	3 389[14]
1 - 4	6 469	3 514[7]	2 953[7]	4 088[4]	2 288[14]	1 800[14]	2 272[4]	1 174[14]	1 096[14]
5 - 9	3 176	1 774[7]	1 400[7]	2 135[4]	1 178[14]	956[14]	985[4]	566[14]	418[14]
10 - 14	3 644	2 145[7]	1 499[7]	2 429[4]	1 403[14]	1 026[14]	1 137[4]	702[14]	435[14]
15 - 19	7 498	5 142[7]	2 355[7]	5 248[4]	3 593[14]	1 655[14]	2 085[4]	1 437[14]	648[14]
20 - 24	9 825	7 147[7]	2 676[7]	7 063[4]	5 125[14]	1 937[14]	2 464[4]	1 810[14]	654[14]
25 - 29	10 909	7 943[7]	2 965[7]	7 849[4]	5 716[14]	2 132[14]	2 681[4]	1 938[14]	743[14]
30 - 34	12 539	9 097[7]	3 442[7]	9 245[4]	6 722[14]	2 523[14]	2 859[4]	2 043[14]	816[14]
35 - 39	14 062	9 953[7]	4 108[7]	10 446[4]	7 367[14]	3 079[14]	3 079[4]	2 154[14]	925[14]
40 - 44	17 048	11 366[7]	5 681[7]	12 796[4]	8 466[14]	4 330[14]	3 758[4]	2 490[14]	1 267[14]
45 - 49	20 839	13 074[7]	7 764[7]	15 834[4]	9 803[14]	6 031[14]	4 544[4]	2 908[14]	1 635[14]
50 - 54	24 758	14 997[7]	9 760[7]	19 039[4]	11 407[14]	7 632[14]	5 264[4]	3 250[14]	2 013[14]
55 - 59	29 706	17 098[7]	12 607[7]	23 211[4]	13 206[14]	10 004[14]	6 066[4]	3 577[14]	2 489[14]
60 - 64	35 371	19 621[7]	15 748[7]	27 002[4]	14 870[14]	12 132[14]	7 829[4]	4 398[14]	3 430[14]
65 - 69	40 938	22 211[7]	18 724[7]	31 288[4]	16 714[14]	14 574[14]	9 152[4]	5 161[14]	3 989[14]
70 - 74	47 028	24 994[7]	22 034[7]	35 722[4]	18 712[14]	17 010[14]	10 831[4]	5 992[14]	4 839[14]
75 - 79	49 394	25 374[7]	24 018[7]	37 413[4]	18 708[14]	18 704[14]	11 532[4]	6 385[14]	5 146[14]
80 - 84	49 602	24 789[7]	24 810[7]	37 282[4]	18 067[14]	19 214[14]	11 902[4]	6 482[14]	5 418[14]
85 - 89	36 239	16 645[7]	19 594[7]	27 156[4]	11 914[14]	15 242[14]	8 799[4]	4 569[14]	4 230[14]
90 - 94	25 788	10 688[7]	15 098[7]	18 915[4]	7 444[14]	11 470[14]	6 693[4]	3 152[14]	3 540[14]
95 - 99	11 678	4 443[7]	7 235[7]	8 250[4]	2 897[14]	5 353[14]	3 324[4]	1 489[14]	1 835[14]
100 +	4 007	1 385[7]	2 622[7]	2 624[4]	831[14]	1 793[14]	1 341[4]	542[14]	799[14]
Unknown - Inconnu	2 119	1 512[7]	557[7]	860[4]	563[14]	287[14]	421[4]	241[14]	179[14]
Montserrat									
1999 (+C)									
Total	59	39	20	...	...	...	...	...	...
0	-	-	-	...	...	...	...	...	...
1 - 4	-	-	-	...	...	...	...	...	...
5 - 9	-	-	-	...	...	...	...	...	...
10 - 14	-	-	-	...	...	...	...	...	...
15 - 19	1	-	1	...	...	...	...	...	...
20 - 24	-	-	-	...	...	...	...	...	...
25 - 29	-	-	-	...	...	...	...	...	...
30 - 34	-	-	-	...	...	...	...	...	...
35 - 39	-	-	-	...	...	...	...	...	...
40 - 44	-	-	-	...	...	...	...	...	...
45 - 49	1	1	-	...	...	...	...	...	...
50 - 54	1	1	-	...	...	...	...	...	...
55 - 59	2	2	-	...	...	...	...	...	...
60 - 64	3	2	1	...	...	...	...	...	...
65 - 69	3	2	1	...	...	...	...	...	...
70 - 74	7	6	1	...	...	...	...	...	...
75 - 79	5	4	1	...	...	...	...	...	...
80 - 84	15	8	7	...	...	...	...	...	...
85 - 89	11	5	6	...	...	...	...	...	...
90 +	9	7	2	...	...	...	...	...	...
Unknown - Inconnu	1	1	-	...	...	...	...	...	...
Netherlands Antilles - Antilles néerlandaises[15]									
2004 (C)									
Total	1 412	753	659	...	...	...	...	...	...
0	20	13	7	...	...	...	...	...	...
1 - 4	2	1	1	...	...	...	...	...	...
5 - 9	2	2	-	...	...	...	...	...	...
10 - 14	3	3	-	...	...	...	...	...	...

Continent, country or area, date, code and age (in years) Continent, pays ou zone, date, code et âge (en années)	Total			Urban - Urbaine			Rural - Rurale		
	Both sexes Les deux sexes	Male Masculin	Female Féminin	Both sexes Les deux sexes	Male Masculin	Female Féminin	Both sexes Les deux sexes	Male Masculin	Female Féminin
AMERICA, NORTH - **AMÉRIQUE DU NORD**									
Netherlands Antilles - **Antilles néerlandaises**[15] 2004 (C)									
15 - 19	13	10	3	...	...	...	...	...	...
20 - 24	11	8	3	...	...	...	...	...	...
25 - 29	18	11	7	...	...	...	...	...	...
30 - 34	26	19	7	...	...	...	...	...	...
35 - 39	32	23	9	...	...	...	...	...	...
40 - 44	41	26	15	...	...	...	...	...	...
45 - 49	57	32	25	...	...	...	...	...	...
50 - 54	75	45	30	...	...	...	...	...	...
55 - 59	83	54	29	...	...	...	...	...	...
60 - 64	109	63	46	...	...	...	...	...	...
65 - 69	135	77	58	...	...	...	...	...	...
70 - 74	165	86	79	...	...	...	...	...	...
75 - 79	164	94	70	...	...	...	...	...	...
80 - 84	161	79	82	...	...	...	...	...	...
85 - 89	144	56	88	...	...	...	...	...	...
90 - 94	91	34	57	...	...	...	...	...	...
95 - 99	49	15	34	...	...	...	...	...	...
100 +	11	2	9	...	...	...	...	...	...
Nicaragua 2005 (+U)									
Total	16 770	9 717	7 053	10 931	6 214	4 717	5 839	3 503	2 336
0	1 970	1 124	846	934	520	414	1 036	604	432
1 - 4	369	189	180	153	77	76	216	112	104
5 - 9	167	102	65	71	43	28	96	59	37
10 - 14	214	123	91	97	58	39	117	65	52
15 - 19	470	323	147	293	218	75	177	105	72
20 - 24	631	467	164	383	287	96	248	180	68
25 - 29	543	390	153	343	255	88	200	135	65
30 - 34	563	425	138	349	267	82	214	158	56
35 - 39	583	402	181	391	282	109	192	120	72
40 - 44	642	424	218	439	296	143	203	128	75
45 - 49	808	518	290	551	360	191	257	158	99
50 - 54	823	508	315	572	363	209	251	145	106
55 - 59	868	475	393	613	327	286	255	148	107
60 - 64	969	561	408	652	379	273	317	182	135
65 - 69	1 179	658	521	834	457	377	345	201	144
70 - 74	1 277	722	555	912	490	422	365	232	133
75 - 79	1 386	711	675	997	497	500	389	214	175
80 +	3 308	1 595	1 713	2 347	1 038	1 309	961	557	404
Panama 1999 (U)									
Total	11 938	6 978	4 960	7 108	4 042	3 066	4 830	2 936	1 894
0	1 005	571	434	490	284	206	515	287	228
1 - 4	302	157	145	81	42	39	221	115	106
5 - 9	122	76	46	49	25	24	73	51	22
10 - 14	95	58	37	30	17	13	65	41	24
15 - 19	222	154	68	117	84	33	105	70	35
20 - 24	302	224	78	159	119	40	143	105	38
25 - 29	332	246	86	190	139	51	142	107	35
30 - 34	369	261	108	225	163	62	144	98	46
35 - 39	329	222	107	197	128	69	132	94	38
40 - 44	396	260	136	239	158	81	157	102	55
45 - 49	411	272	139	265	178	87	146	94	52
50 - 54	496	329	167	301	210	91	195	119	76
55 - 59	514	322	192	319	198	121	195	124	71
60 - 64	663	405	258	413	251	162	250	154	96
65 - 69	817	489	328	468	268	200	349	221	128
70 - 74	1 012	594	418	620	360	260	392	234	158
75 - 79	1 255	693	562	796	415	381	459	278	181
80 - 84	1 324	704	620	860	449	411	464	255	209
85 - 89	1 066	548	518	690	328	362	376	220	156

Continent, country or area, date, code and age (in years) / Continent, pays ou zone, date, code et âge (en années)	Total			Urban - Urbaine			Rural - Rurale		
	Both sexes Les deux sexes	Male Masculin	Female Féminin	Both sexes Les deux sexes	Male Masculin	Female Féminin	Both sexes Les deux sexes	Male Masculin	Female Féminin
AMERICA, NORTH - AMÉRIQUE DU NORD									
Panama									
1999 (U)									
90 - 94	553	241	312	376	142	234	177	99	78
95 - 99	210	75	135	141	45	96	69	30	39
100 +	49	24	25	38	17	21	11	7	4
Unknown - Inconnu	94	53	41	44	22	22	50	31	19
2003 (U)									
Total	13 248	7 763	5 485	...	...	...	...	...	...
0	940	517	423	...	...	...	...	...	...
1 - 4	345	200	145	...	...	...	...	...	...
5 - 9	133	69	64	...	...	...	...	...	...
10 - 14	104	58	46	...	...	...	...	...	...
15 - 19	241	164	77	...	...	...	...	...	...
20 - 24	327	240	87	...	...	...	...	...	...
25 - 29	333	244	89	...	...	...	...	...	...
30 - 34	352	239	113	...	...	...	...	...	...
35 - 39	377	264	113	...	...	...	...	...	...
40 - 44	422	275	147	...	...	...	...	...	...
45 - 49	433	251	182	...	...	...	...	...	...
50 - 54	505	316	189	...	...	...	...	...	...
55 - 59	629	408	221	...	...	...	...	...	...
60 - 64	763	460	303	...	...	...	...	...	...
65 - 69	957	584	373	...	...	...	...	...	...
70 - 74	1 155	679	476	...	...	...	...	...	...
75 - 79	1 330	783	547	...	...	...	...	...	...
80 - 84	1 433	792	641	...	...	...	...	...	...
85 +	2 408	1 177	1 231	...	...	...	...	...	...
Unknown - Inconnu	61	43	18	...	...	...	...	...	...
Puerto Rico - Porto Rico									
2003 (C)									
Total	28 356	15 758	12 598	15 038[4]	8 095[4]	6 943[4]	13 283[4]	7 633[4]	5 650[4]
0	498	288	210	294[4]	168[4]	126[4]	198[4]	114[4]	84[4]
1 - 4	47	26	21	27[4]	15[4]	12[4]	19[4]	10[4]	9[4]
5 - 9	32	16	16	13[4]	6[4]	7[4]	19[4]	10[4]	9[4]
10 - 14	47	31	16	16[4]	11[4]	5[4]	31[4]	20[4]	11[4]
15 - 19	201	161	40	106[4]	89[4]	17[4]	95[4]	72[4]	23[4]
20 - 24	419	359	60	238[4]	204[4]	34[4]	179[4]	153[4]	26[4]
25 - 29	414	345	69	228[4]	188[4]	40[4]	185[4]	156[4]	29[4]
30 - 34	404	304	100	217[4]	163[4]	54[4]	187[4]	141[4]	46[4]
35 - 39	526	382	144	275[4]	191[4]	84[4]	249[4]	189[4]	60[4]
40 - 44	661	453	208	341[4]	232[4]	109[4]	320[4]	221[4]	99[4]
45 - 49	898	580	318	471[4]	302[4]	169[4]	426[4]	277[4]	149[4]
50 - 54	1 221	781	440	613[4]	378[4]	235[4]	608[4]	403[4]	205[4]
55 - 59	1 627	1 035	592	807[4]	518[4]	289[4]	819[4]	517[4]	302[4]
60 - 64	2 006	1 206	800	1 027[4]	614[4]	413[4]	979[4]	592[4]	387[4]
65 - 69	2 311	1 410	901	1 165[4]	703[4]	462[4]	1 145[4]	706[4]	439[4]
70 - 74	2 869	1 589	1 280	1 507[4]	833[4]	674[4]	1 360[4]	754[4]	606[4]
75 - 79	3 450	1 894	1 556	1 846[4]	975[4]	871[4]	1 602[4]	917[4]	685[4]
80 - 84	3 882	1 956	1 926	2 120[4]	1 016[4]	1 104[4]	1 761[4]	939[4]	822[4]
85 +	6 822	2 924	3 898	3 720[4]	1 482[4]	2 238[4]	3 099[4]	1 440[4]	1 659[4]
Unknown - Inconnu	21	18	3	7[4]	7[4]	-[4]	2[4]	2[4]	-[4]
2005 (C)									
Total	29 702	16 479	13 223	...	...	...	...	...	...
0	471	251	220	...	...	...	...	...	...
1 - 4	42	22	20	...	...	...	...	...	...
5 - 9	30	12	18	...	...	...	...	...	...
10 - 14	38	27	11	...	...	...	...	...	...
15 - 19	192	157	35	...	...	...	...	...	...
20 - 24	436	362	74	...	...	...	...	...	...
25 - 29	403	330	73	...	...	...	...	...	...
30 - 34	436	333	103	...	...	...	...	...	...
35 - 39	519	366	153	...	...	...	...	...	...
40 - 44	663	469	194	...	...	...	...	...	...

19. Deaths by age, sex and urban/rural residence: latest available year, 1996 - 2005
Décès selon l'âge, le sexe et la résidence, urbaine/rurale: dernière année disponible, 1996 - 2005 (continued - suite)

Continent, country or area, date, code and age (in years) / Continent, pays ou zone, date, code et âge (en annèes)	Total			Urban - Urbaine			Rural - Rurale		
	Both sexes Les deux sexes	Male Masculin	Female Féminin	Both sexes Les deux sexes	Male Masculin	Female Féminin	Both sexes Les deux sexes	Male Masculin	Female Féminin
AMERICA, NORTH - AMÉRIQUE DU NORD									
Puerto Rico - Porto Rico									
2005 (C)									
45 - 49	884	599	285	...	...	...	...	...	...
50 - 54	1 196	801	395	...	...	...	...	...	...
55 - 59	1 673	1 091	582	...	...	...	...	...	...
60 - 64	2 116	1 312	804	...	...	...	...	...	...
65 - 69	2 479	1 495	984	...	...	...	...	...	...
70 - 74	3 070	1 746	1 324	...	...	...	...	...	...
75 - 79	3 490	1 878	1 612	...	...	...	...	...	...
80 - 84	4 107	1 979	2 128	...	...	...	...	...	...
85 - 89	3 599	1 645	1 954	...	...	...	...	...	...
90 - 94	2 537	1 091	1 446	...	...	...	...	...	...
95 - 99	1 000	399	601	...	...	...	...	...	...
100 +	274	79	195	...	...	...	...	...	...
Unknown - Inconnu	47	35	12	...	...	...	...	...	...
Saint Kitts and Nevis - Saint-Kitts-et-Nevis									
2001 (+C)									
Total	352	181	171	...	...	...	...	...	...
0	10	3	7	...	...	...	...	...	...
1 - 4	6	1	5	...	...	...	...	...	...
5 - 9	3	3	-	...	...	...	...	...	...
10 - 14	2	1	1	...	...	...	...	...	...
15 - 19	2	1	1	...	...	...	...	...	...
20 - 24	2	1	1	...	...	...	...	...	...
25 - 29	6	4	2	...	...	...	...	...	...
30 - 34	5	3	2	...	...	...	...	...	...
35 - 39	8	6	2	...	...	...	...	...	...
40 - 44	9	6	3	...	...	...	...	...	...
45 - 49	22	16	6	...	...	...	...	...	...
50 - 54	9	4	5	...	...	...	...	...	...
55 - 59	12	8	4	...	...	...	...	...	...
60 - 64	13	9	4	...	...	...	...	...	...
65 - 69	19	9	10	...	...	...	...	...	...
70 - 74	29	17	12	...	...	...	...	...	...
75 - 79	63	31	32	...	...	...	...	...	...
80 - 84	56	25	31	...	...	...	...	...	...
85 +	76	33	43	...	...	...	...	...	...
Saint Lucia - Sainte-Lucie									
2003 (C)									
Total	1 046	584	462	...	...	...	...	...	...
0	37	16	21	...	...	...	...	...	...
1 - 4	12	9	3	...	...	...	...	...	...
5 - 9	4	4	-	...	...	...	...	...	...
10 - 14	5	3	2	...	...	...	...	...	...
15 - 19	14	11	3	...	...	...	...	...	...
20 - 24	15	11	4	...	...	...	...	...	...
25 - 29	22	18	4	...	...	...	...	...	...
30 - 34	30	18	12	...	...	...	...	...	...
35 - 39	30	20	10	...	...	...	...	...	...
40 - 44	30	20	10	...	...	...	...	...	...
45 - 49	37	22	15	...	...	...	...	...	...
50 - 54	34	22	12	...	...	...	...	...	...
55 - 59	53	35	18	...	...	...	...	...	...
60 - 64	55	27	28	...	...	...	...	...	...
65 - 69	94	46	48	...	...	...	...	...	...
70 - 74	102	62	40	...	...	...	...	...	...
75 - 79	141	75	66	...	...	...	...	...	...
80 - 84	125	77	48	...	...	...	...	...	...
85 +	196	83	113	...	...	...	...	...	...
Unknown - Inconnu	10	5	5	...	...	...	...	...	...

Continent, country or area, date, code and age (in years) / Continent, pays ou zone, date, code et âge (en annèes)	Total			Urban - Urbaine			Rural - Rurale		
	Both sexes Les deux sexes	Male Masculin	Female Féminin	Both sexes Les deux sexes	Male Masculin	Female Féminin	Both sexes Les deux sexes	Male Masculin	Female Féminin
AMERICA, NORTH - AMÉRIQUE DU NORD									
Saint Vincent and the Grenadines - Saint Vincent-et-les Grenadines									
2003 (+C)									
Total	790	434	356	...	...	...	...	...	...
0	35	19	16	...	...	...	...	...	...
1 - 4	7	4	3	...	...	...	...	...	...
5 - 9	5	2	3	...	...	...	...	...	...
10 - 14	3	2	1	...	...	...	...	...	...
15 - 19	6	6	-	...	...	...	...	...	...
20 - 24	8	7	1	...	...	...	...	...	...
25 - 29	13	12	1	...	...	...	...	...	...
30 - 34	20	12	8	...	...	...	...	...	...
35 - 39	31	18	13	...	...	...	...	...	...
40 - 44	23	14	9	...	...	...	...	...	...
45 - 49	27	19	8	...	...	...	...	...	...
50 - 54	33	21	12	...	...	...	...	...	...
55 - 59	45	28	17	...	...	...	...	...	...
60 - 64	50	37	13	...	...	...	...	...	...
65 - 69	69	40	29	...	...	...	...	...	...
70 - 74	85	42	43	...	...	...	...	...	...
75 - 79	89	38	51	...	...	...	...	...	...
80 - 84	99	49	50	...	...	...	...	...	...
85 +	137	59	78	...	...	...	...	...	...
Unknown - Inconnu	5	5	-	...	...	...	...	...	...
Trinidad and Tobago - Trinité-et-Tobago									
2002 (C)									
Total	9 797	5 564	4 233	...	...	...	...	...	...
0	412	247	165	...	...	...	...	...	...
1 - 4	53	22	31	...	...	...	...	...	...
5 - 9	23	10	13	...	...	...	...	...	...
10 - 14	36	22	14	...	...	...	...	...	...
15 - 19	118	77	41	...	...	...	...	...	...
20 - 24	196	138	58	...	...	...	...	...	...
25 - 29	211	127	84	...	...	...	...	...	...
30 - 34	244	165	79	...	...	...	...	...	...
35 - 39	342	220	122	...	...	...	...	...	...
40 - 44	354	229	125	...	...	...	...	...	...
45 - 49	467	301	166	...	...	...	...	...	...
50 - 54	558	354	204	...	...	...	...	...	...
55 - 59	678	420	258	...	...	...	...	...	...
60 - 64	792	472	320	...	...	...	...	...	...
65 - 69	866	499	367	...	...	...	...	...	...
70 - 74	1 028	583	445	...	...	...	...	...	...
75 - 79	1 037	575	462	...	...	...	...	...	...
80 - 84	977	521	456	...	...	...	...	...	...
85 +	1 394	572	822	...	...	...	...	...	...
Unknown - Inconnu	11	10	1	...	...	...	...	...	...
Turks Caicos Islands - Îles Turques et Caïques									
2005 (C)									
Total	53	32	21	...	...	...	...	...	...
0	1	1	-	...	...	...	...	...	...
1 - 4	-	-	-	...	...	...	...	...	...
5 - 9	-	-	-	...	...	...	...	...	...
10 - 14	1	1	-	...	...	...	...	...	...
15 - 19	1	1	-	...	...	...	...	...	...
20 - 24	-	-	-	...	...	...	...	...	...
25 - 29	2	2	-	...	...	...	...	...	...
30 - 34	8	5	3	...	...	...	...	...	...
35 - 39	3	2	1	...	...	...	...	...	...
40 - 44	3	1	2	...	...	...	...	...	...
45 - 49	1	1	-	...	...	...	...	...	...

19. Deaths by age, sex and urban/rural residence: latest available year, 1996 - 2005
Décès selon l'âge, le sexe et la résidence, urbaine/rurale: dernière année disponible, 1996 - 2005 (continued - suite)

Continent, country or area, date, code and age (in years) / Continent, pays ou zone, date, code et âge (en années)	Total			Urban - Urbaine			Rural - Rurale		
	Both sexes Les deux sexes	Male Masculin	Female Féminin	Both sexes Les deux sexes	Male Masculin	Female Féminin	Both sexes Les deux sexes	Male Masculin	Female Féminin
AMERICA, NORTH - AMÉRIQUE DU NORD									
Turks Caicos Islands - Îles Turques et Caïques									
2005 (C)									
50 - 54	2	-	2	...	...	...	...	...	...
55 - 59	2	2	-	...	...	...	...	...	...
60 - 64	2	2	-	...	...	...	...	...	...
65 - 69	-	-	-	...	...	...	...	...	...
70 - 74	3	3	-	...	...	...	...	...	...
75 - 79	6	1	5	...	...	...	...	...	...
80 - 84	5	3	2	...	...	...	...	...	...
85 +	11	5	6	...	...	...	...	...	...
Unknown - Inconnu	2	2	-	...	...	...	...	...	...
United States - États-Unis									
2004* (C)									
Total	2 398 343	1 179 995	1 218 348	...	...	...	...	...	...
0	27 838	15 690	12 149	...	...	...	...	...	...
1 - 4	4 801	2 635	2 166	...	...	...	...	...	...
5 - 9	2 856	1 623	1 233	...	...	...	...	...	...
10 - 14	3 900	2 310	1 590	...	...	...	...	...	...
15 - 19	13 521	9 528	3 993	...	...	...	...	...	...
20 - 24	19 499	14 732	4 767	...	...	...	...	...	...
25 - 29	18 474	13 332	5 142	...	...	...	...	...	...
30 - 34	21 770	14 572	7 199	...	...	...	...	...	...
35 - 39	31 507	20 136	11 371	...	...	...	...	...	...
40 - 44	52 803	32 731	20 072	...	...	...	...	...	...
45 - 49	77 158	48 097	29 060	...	...	...	...	...	...
50 - 54	98 947	62 160	36 787	...	...	...	...	...	...
55 - 59	120 141	72 621	47 520	...	...	...	...	...	...
60 - 64	143 273	84 347	58 926	...	...	...	...	...	...
65 - 69	171 738	98 340	73 398	...	...	...	...	...	...
70 - 74	228 103	124 739	103 364	...	...	...	...	...	...
75 - 79	311 754	160 756	150 998	...	...	...	...	...	...
80 - 84	374 538	173 659	200 880	...	...	...	...	...	...
85 +	675 296	227 684	447 612	...	...	...	...	...	...
Unknown - Inconnu	426	302	124	...	...	...	...	...	...
United States Virgin Islands - Îles Vierges américaines[11]									
2002 (C)									
Total	617	371	246	...	...	...	...	...	...
0	8	1	7	...	...	...	...	...	...
1 - 4	1	-	1	...	...	...	...	...	...
5 - 9	-	-	-	...	...	...	...	...	...
10 - 14	1	-	1	...	...	...	...	...	...
15 - 19	11	10	1	...	...	...	...	...	...
20 - 24	13	11	2	...	...	...	...	...	...
25 - 29	13	9	4	...	...	...	...	...	...
30 - 34	13	10	3	...	...	...	...	...	...
35 - 39	26	19	7	...	...	...	...	...	...
40 - 44	15	10	5	...	...	...	...	...	...
45 - 49	25	16	9	...	...	...	...	...	...
50 - 54	28	17	11	...	...	...	...	...	...
55 - 59	50	34	16	...	...	...	...	...	...
60 - 64	57	39	18	...	...	...	...	...	...
65 - 69	57	41	16	...	...	...	...	...	...
70 - 74	57	32	25	...	...	...	...	...	...
75 - 79	66	37	29	...	...	...	...	...	...
80 - 84	66	32	34	...	...	...	...	...	...
85 - 89	62	32	30	...	...	...	...	...	...
90 - 94	36	17	19	...	...	...	...	...	...
95 +	11	3	8	...	...	...	...	...	...
Unknown - Inconnu	1	1	-	...	...	...	...	...	...

Continent, country or area, date, code and age (in years) / Continent, pays ou zone, date, code et âge (en années)	Total			Urban - Urbaine			Rural - Rurale		
	Both sexes Les deux sexes	Male Masculin	Female Féminin	Both sexes Les deux sexes	Male Masculin	Female Féminin	Both sexes Les deux sexes	Male Masculin	Female Féminin
AMERICA, SOUTH - AMÉRIQUE DU SUD									
Argentina - Argentine									
2005 (C)									
Total	293 529	155 604[7]	137 670[7]	...	...	...	...	...	...
0	9 507	5 402[7]	4 088[7]	...	...	...	...	...	...
1 - 4	1 539	808[7]	728[7]	...	...	...	...	...	...
5 - 9	901	536[7]	365[7]	...	...	...	...	...	...
10 - 14	1 028	624[7]	401[7]	...	...	...	...	...	...
15 - 19	2 370	1 660[7]	706[7]	...	...	...	...	...	...
20 - 24	2 991	2 221[7]	766[7]	...	...	...	...	...	...
25 - 29	3 050	2 169[7]	869[7]	...	...	...	...	...	...
30 - 34	3 089	2 062[7]	1 027[7]	...	...	...	...	...	...
35 - 39	3 629	2 295[7]	1 329[7]	...	...	...	...	...	...
40 - 44	5 157	3 174[7]	1 980[7]	...	...	...	...	...	...
45 - 49	7 916	4 963[7]	2 953[7]	...	...	...	...	...	...
50 - 54	11 863	7 622[7]	4 235[7]	...	...	...	...	...	...
55 - 59	15 829	10 327[7]	5 499[7]	...	...	...	...	...	...
60 - 64	20 497	13 412[7]	7 075[7]	...	...	...	...	...	...
65 - 69	25 203	16 049[7]	9 146[7]	...	...	...	...	...	...
70 - 74	32 784	19 790[7]	12 977[7]	...	...	...	...	...	...
75 - 79	40 544	21 795[7]	18 740[7]	...	...	...	...	...	...
80 - 84	42 559	19 598[7]	22 946[7]	...	...	...	...	...	...
85 +	62 311	20 695[7]	41 598[7]	...	...	...	...	...	...
Unknown - Inconnu	762	402[7]	242[7]	...	...	...	...	...	...
Brazil - Brésil[16]									
2005 (U)									
Total	979 854	570 399	409 455	...	...	...	...	...	...
0	39 259	22 135	17 124	...	...	...	...	...	...
1 - 4	7 724	4 246	3 478	...	...	...	...	...	...
5 - 9	4 616	2 658	1 958	...	...	...	...	...	...
10 - 14	5 658	3 542	2 116	...	...	...	...	...	...
15 - 19	18 004	14 207	3 797	...	...	...	...	...	...
20 - 24	25 564	20 731	4 833	...	...	...	...	...	...
25 - 29	25 585	19 784	5 801	...	...	...	...	...	...
30 - 34	26 137	19 377	6 760	...	...	...	...	...	...
35 - 39	31 160	21 942	9 218	...	...	...	...	...	...
40 - 44	39 178	26 494	12 684	...	...	...	...	...	...
45 - 49	48 931	32 075	16 856	...	...	...	...	...	...
50 - 54	57 274	36 810	20 464	...	...	...	...	...	...
55 - 59	63 816	40 215	23 601	...	...	...	...	...	...
60 - 64	71 499	43 724	27 775	...	...	...	...	...	...
65 - 69	87 202	51 261	35 941	...	...	...	...	...	...
70 - 74	96 416	54 592	41 824	...	...	...	...	...	...
75 - 79	104 668	55 486	49 182	...	...	...	...	...	...
80 - 84	93 215	45 700	47 515	...	...	...	...	...	...
85 - 89	71 063	30 571	40 492	...	...	...	...	...	...
90 - 94	41 051	15 714	25 337	...	...	...	...	...	...
95 - 99	15 035	5 220	9 815	...	...	...	...	...	...
100 +	2 922	824	2 098	...	...	...	...	...	...
Unknown - Inconnu	3 877	3 091	786	...	...	...	...	...	...
Chile - Chili									
2003 (C)									
Total	83 672	45 482	38 190	72 647	38 782	33 865	11 025	6 700	4 325
0	1 935	1 061	874	1 691	936	755	244	125	119
1 - 4	396	218	178	329	179	150	67	39	28
5 - 9	250	147	103	207	120	87	43	27	16
10 - 14	318	205	113	265	170	95	53	35	18
15 - 19	616	460	156	502	373	129	114	87	27
20 - 24	999	790	209	838	661	177	161	129	32
25 - 29	1 051	827	224	903	713	190	148	114	34
30 - 34	1 300	981	319	1 114	837	277	186	144	42
35 - 39	1 690	1 223	467	1 418	1 012	406	272	211	61
40 - 44	2 233	1 489	744	1 901	1 241	660	332	248	84
45 - 49	2 845	1 833	1 012	2 491	1 582	909	354	251	103

19. Deaths by age, sex and urban/rural residence: latest available year, 1996 - 2005
Décès selon l'âge, le sexe et la résidence, urbaine/rurale: dernière année disponible, 1996 - 2005 (continued - suite)

Continent, country or area, date, code and age (in years) / Continent, pays ou zone, date, code et âge (en années)	Total			Urban - Urbaine			Rural - Rurale		
	Both sexes Les deux sexes	Male Masculin	Female Féminin	Both sexes Les deux sexes	Male Masculin	Female Féminin	Both sexes Les deux sexes	Male Masculin	Female Féminin
AMERICA, SOUTH - AMÉRIQUE DU SUD									
Chile - Chili									
2003 (C)									
50 - 54	3 631	2 287	1 344	3 187	1 992	1 195	444	295	149
55 - 59	4 812	3 038	1 774	4 224	2 644	1 580	588	394	194
60 - 64	6 177	3 783	2 394	5 420	3 289	2 131	757	494	263
65 - 69	7 299	4 410	2 889	6 324	3 775	2 549	975	635	340
70 - 74	10 073	5 816	4 257	8 768	4 968	3 800	1 305	848	457
75 - 79	10 875	5 884	4 991	9 418	5 003	4 415	1 457	881	576
80 - 84	10 676	5 049	5 627	9 255	4 259	4 996	1 421	790	631
85 - 89	9 082	3 713	5 369	7 887	3 123	4 764	1 195	590	605
90 - 94	5 383	1 756	3 627	4 691	1 466	3 225	692	290	402
95 - 99	1 720	446	1 274	1 538	385	1 153	182	61	121
100 +	284	63	221	253	51	202	31	12	19
Unknown - Inconnu	27	3	24	23	3	20	4	-	4
2004 (C)									
Total	86 138	46 549	39 589	...	...	...	...	...	...
0	2 034	1 161	873	...	...	...	...	...	...
1 - 4	388	209	179	...	...	...	...	...	...
5 - 9	235	147	88	...	...	...	...	...	...
10 - 14	317	185	132	...	...	...	...	...	...
15 - 19	721	524	197	...	...	...	...	...	...
20 - 24	983	751	232	...	...	...	...	...	...
25 - 29	1 025	754	271	...	...	...	...	...	...
30 - 34	1 291	989	302	...	...	...	...	...	...
35 - 39	1 670	1 170	500	...	...	...	...	...	...
40 - 44	2 307	1 574	733	...	...	...	...	...	...
45 - 49	2 878	1 865	1 013	...	...	...	...	...	...
50 - 54	3 609	2 326	1 283	...	...	...	...	...	...
55 - 59	4 664	2 961	1 703	...	...	...	...	...	...
60 - 64	6 118	3 752	2 366	...	...	...	...	...	...
65 - 69	7 439	4 416	3 023	...	...	...	...	...	...
70 - 74	10 100	5 917	4 183	...	...	...	...	...	...
75 - 79	11 508	6 155	5 353	...	...	...	...	...	...
80 - 84	11 007	5 225	5 782	...	...	...	...	...	...
85 +	17 844	6 468	11 376	...	...	...	...	...	...
Colombia - Colombie[17]									
2005 (U)									
Total	188 795	109 389[7]	79 381[7]	146 017[4]	81 959[14]	64 055[14]	36 053[4]	22 463[14]	13 587[14]
0	11 441	6 480[7]	4 960[7]	8 147[4]	4 592[4]	3 555[4]	2 640[4]	1 505[14]	1 134[14]
1 - 4	2 521	1 361	1 160	1 557[4]	861[4]	696[4]	881[4]	455[4]	426[4]
5 - 9	1 298	768	530	862[4]	503[4]	359[4]	409[4]	249[4]	160[4]
10 - 14	1 397	828[7]	568[7]	909[4]	536[4]	373[4]	436[4]	265[4]	171[4]
15 - 19	4 467	3 326	1 141	3 133[4]	2 381[4]	752[4]	1 054[4]	737[4]	317[4]
20 - 24	7 098	5 766	1 332	4 991[4]	4 022[4]	969[4]	1 529[4]	1 247[4]	282[4]
25 - 29	6 643	5 437[7]	1 204[7]	4 647[4]	3 770[14]	875[14]	1 358[4]	1 106[4]	252[4]
30 - 34	5 915	4 582[7]	1 331[7]	4 229[4]	3 207[4]	1 022[4]	1 203[4]	942[4]	261[4]
35 - 39	6 112	4 408	1 704	4 383[4]	3 063[4]	1 320[4]	1 280[4]	963[4]	317[4]
40 - 44	6 445	4 310	2 135	4 891[4]	3 179[4]	1 712[4]	1 236[4]	858[4]	378[4]
45 - 49	7 009	4 396	2 613	5 385[4]	3 242[4]	2 143[4]	1 323[4]	912[4]	411[4]
50 - 54	8 263	5 028	3 235	6 484[4]	3 853[4]	2 631[4]	1 489[4]	962[4]	527[4]
55 - 59	9 206	5 356[7]	3 849[7]	7 301[4]	4 129[4]	3 172[4]	1 650[4]	1 055[14]	594[14]
60 - 64	11 115	6 427[7]	4 686[7]	8 852[4]	5 028[14]	3 823[14]	2 026[4]	1 241[14]	784[14]
65 - 69	14 696	8 223	6 473	11 795[4]	6 463[4]	5 332[4]	2 608[4]	1 568[4]	1 040[4]
70 - 74	18 399	10 022	8 377	14 763[4]	7 827[4]	6 936[4]	3 311[4]	1 996[4]	1 315[4]
75 - 79	20 508	10 845	9 663	16 510[4]	8 503[4]	8 007[4]	3 681[4]	2 144[4]	1 537[4]
80 - 84	18 774	9 275	9 499	14 998[4]	7 156[4]	7 842[4]	3 495[4]	1 967[4]	1 528[4]
85 +	26 360	11 648	14 712	21 787[4]	9 357[4]	12 430[4]	4 235[4]	2 130[4]	2 105[4]
Unknown - Inconnu	1 128	903[7]	209[7]	393[4]	287[4]	106[4]	209[4]	161[4]	48[4]
Ecuador - Équateur[18]									
2004 (U)									
Total	54 729	31 292	23 437	41 783	23 947	17 836	12 946	7 345	5 601
0	3 942	2 241	1 701	3 121	1 789	1 332	821	452	369
1 - 4	1 595	885	710	1 067	605	462	528	280	248

19. Deaths by age, sex and urban/rural residence: latest available year, 1996 - 2005
Décès selon l'âge, le sexe et la résidence, urbaine/rurale: dernière année disponible, 1996 - 2005 (continued - suite)

Continent, country or area, date, code and age (in years) / Continent, pays ou zone, date, code et âge (en annèes)	Total			Urban - Urbaine			Rural - Rurale		
	Both sexes Les deux sexes	Male Masculin	Female Féminin	Both sexes Les deux sexes	Male Masculin	Female Féminin	Both sexes Les deux sexes	Male Masculin	Female Féminin
AMERICA, SOUTH - AMÉRIQUE DU SUD									
Ecuador - Équateur[18]									
2004 (U)									
5 - 14................	1 327	788	539	948	564	384	379	224	155
15 - 49................	12 277	8 441	3 836	9 549	6 643	2 906	2 728	1 798	930
50 - 64................	8 296	4 875	3 421	6 473	3 768	2 705	1 823	1 107	716
65 +..................	27 239	14 025	13 214	20 587	10 549	10 038	6 652	3 476	3 176
Unknown - Inconnu.......	53	37	16	38	29	9	15	8	7
2005 (U)									
Total..................	56 825	32 621	24 204	...	...	...	...	...	...
0.....................	3 717	2 122	1 595	...	...	...	...	...	...
1 - 4..................	1 431	794	637	...	...	...	...	...	...
5 - 14.................	1 316	774	542	...	...	...	...	...	...
15 - 49................	13 028	9 059	3 969	...	...	...	...	...	...
50 - 64................	8 684	5 193	3 491	...	...	...	...	...	...
65 +..................	28 600	14 639	13 961	...	...	...	...	...	...
Unknown - Inconnu.......	49	40	9	...	...	...	...	...	...
French Guiana - Guyane française[8]									
2003 (C)									
Total..................	692	435	257	...	...	...	...	...	...
0.....................	58	32	26	...	...	...	...	...	...
1 - 4..................	17	10	7	...	...	...	...	...	...
5 - 9..................	3	1	2	...	...	...	...	...	...
10 - 14................	6	5	1	...	...	...	...	...	...
15 - 19................	15	10	5	...	...	...	...	...	...
20 - 24................	17	11	6	...	...	...	...	...	...
25 - 29................	31	25	6	...	...	...	...	...	...
30 - 34................	26	18	8	...	...	...	...	...	...
35 - 39................	38	28	10	...	...	...	...	...	...
40 - 44................	34	24	10	...	...	...	...	...	...
45 - 49................	38	26	12	...	...	...	...	...	...
50 - 54................	44	33	11	...	...	...	...	...	...
55 - 59................	36	25	11	...	...	...	...	...	...
60 - 64................	45	29	16	...	...	...	...	...	...
65 - 69................	43	28	15	...	...	...	...	...	...
70 - 74................	47	36	11	...	...	...	...	...	...
75 - 79................	50	37	13	...	...	...	...	...	...
80 - 84................	49	19	30	...	...	...	...	...	...
85 - 89................	53	24	29	...	...	...	...	...	...
90 - 94................	23	8	15	...	...	...	...	...	...
95 - 99................	15	4	11	...	...	...	...	...	...
100 +.................	4	2	2	...	...	...	...	...	...
Guyana[11]									
2003 (+C)									
Total..................	4 986	2 898	2 088	...	...	...	...	...	...
0.....................	290	157	133	...	...	...	...	...	...
1 - 4..................	72	40	32	...	...	...	...	...	...
5 - 9..................	33	21	12	...	...	...	...	...	...
10 - 14................	43	24	19	...	...	...	...	...	...
15 - 19................	64	39	25	...	...	...	...	...	...
20 - 24................	148	97	51	...	...	...	...	...	...
25 - 29................	175	120	55	...	...	...	...	...	...
30 - 34................	263	169	94	...	...	...	...	...	...
35 - 39................	274	188	86	...	...	...	...	...	...
40 - 44................	277	195	82	...	...	...	...	...	...
45 - 49................	305	197	108	...	...	...	...	...	...
50 - 54................	338	207	131	...	...	...	...	...	...
55 - 59................	339	212	127	...	...	...	...	...	...
60 - 64................	377	228	149	...	...	...	...	...	...
65 - 69................	401	226	175	...	...	...	...	...	...
70 - 74................	418	214	204	...	...	...	...	...	...
75 - 79................	441	224	217	...	...	...	...	...	...
80 - 84................	291	145	146	...	...	...	...	...	...
85 - 89................	220	97	123	...	...	...	...	...	...

Continent, country or area, date, code and age (in years) Continent, pays ou zone, date, code et âge (en années)	Total			Urban - Urbaine			Rural - Rurale		
	Both sexes Les deux sexes	Male Masculin	Female Féminin	Both sexes Les deux sexes	Male Masculin	Female Féminin	Both sexes Les deux sexes	Male Masculin	Female Féminin
AMERICA, SOUTH - AMÉRIQUE DU SUD									
Guyana[11]									
2003 (+C)									
90 - 94	104	39	65	...	...	...	...	...	...
95 - 99	36	12	24	...	...	...	...	...	...
100 +	77	47	30	...	...	...	...	...	...
Paraguay									
2001 (I)[19]									
Total	38 514	20 073[7]	15 948[7]	23 907	12 238[7]	10 148[7]	14 607	7 835[7]	5 800[7]
0	3 898	2 219[7]	1 662[7]	2 076	1 156[7]	911[7]	1 822	1 063[7]	751[7]
1 - 4	1 666	939[7]	720[7]	745	419[7]	322[7]	921	520[7]	398[7]
5 - 9	554	308[7]	242[7]	289	163[7]	123[7]	265	145[7]	119[7]
10 - 14	446	255[7]	189[7]	213	104[7]	108[7]	233	151[7]	81[7]
15 - 19	1 019	640[7]	379[7]	582	380[7]	202[7]	437	260[7]	177[7]
20 - 24	1 208	863[7]	340[7]	675	488[7]	183[7]	533	375[7]	157[7]
25 - 29	1 061	754[7]	302[7]	641	461[7]	177[7]	420	293[7]	125[7]
30 - 34	927	626[7]	297[7]	581	401[7]	177[7]	346	225[7]	120[7]
35 - 39	1 115	664[7]	449[7]	681	405[7]	275[7]	434	259[7]	174[7]
40 - 44	1 222	730[7]	489[7]	781	465[7]	314[7]	441	265[7]	175[7]
45 - 49	1 550	929[7]	619[7]	1 035	632[7]	402[7]	515	297[7]	217[7]
50 - 54	1 765	999[7]	763[7]	1 176	658[7]	516[7]	589	341[7]	247[7]
55 - 59	1 703	997[7]	702[7]	1 134	668[7]	463[7]	569	329[7]	239[7]
60 - 64	2 378	1 333[7]	1 039[7]	1 560	882[7]	674[7]	818	451[7]	365[7]
65 - 69	2 373	1 278[7]	1 093[7]	1 622	848[7]	774[7]	751	430[7]	319[7]
70 - 74	2 996	1 744[7]	1 246[7]	2 026	1 162[7]	860[7]	970	582[7]	386[7]
75 - 79	2 793	1 483[7]	1 300[7]	1 740	877[7]	860[7]	1 053	606[7]	440[7]
80 - 84	2 846	1 377[7]	1 465[7]	1 889	876[7]	1 010[7]	957	501[7]	455[7]
85 - 89	2 220	1 006[7]	1 209[7]	1 485	652[7]	831[7]	735	354[7]	378[7]
90 +	1 912	670[7]	1 227[7]	1 236	394[7]	835[7]	676	276[7]	392[7]
Unknown - Inconnu	2 862	259[7]	216[7]	1 740	147[7]	131[7]	1 122	112[7]	85[7]
2005 (U)									
Total	17 360	9 658[7]	7 614[7]	...	...	...	...	...	...
0	539	294[7]	240[7]	...	...	...	...	...	...
1 - 4	272	160[7]	111[7]	...	...	...	...	...	...
5 - 9	150	89[7]	60[7]	...	...	...	...	...	...
10 - 14	161	107[7]	54[7]	...	...	...	...	...	...
15 - 19	338	228[7]	109[7]	...	...	...	...	...	...
20 - 24	477	355[7]	122[7]	...	...	...	...	...	...
25 - 29	392	268[7]	123[7]	...	...	...	...	...	...
30 - 34	401	274[7]	127[7]	...	...	...	...	...	...
35 - 39	431	277[7]	151[7]	...	...	...	...	...	...
40 - 44	585	359[7]	220[7]	...	...	...	...	...	...
45 - 49	687	420[7]	261[7]	...	...	...	...	...	...
50 - 54	922	563[7]	356[7]	...	...	...	...	...	...
55 - 59	974	574[7]	399[7]	...	...	...	...	...	...
60 - 64	1 203	705[7]	491[7]	...	...	...	...	...	...
65 - 69	1 334	746[7]	587[7]	...	...	...	...	...	...
70 - 74	1 603	887[7]	705[7]	...	...	...	...	...	...
75 - 79	1 925	1 044[7]	871[7]	...	...	...	...	...	...
80 - 84	1 792	891[7]	892[7]	...	...	...	...	...	...
85 +	2 930	1 269[7]	1 647[7]	...	...	...	...	...	...
Unknown - Inconnu	244	148[7]	88[7]	...	...	...	...	...	...
Peru - Pérou[20]									
2003 (+U)									
Total	85 198	45 261[7]	39 909[7]	...	...	...	...	...	...
0	7 122	3 886[7]	3 233[7]	...	...	...	...	...	...
1 - 4	1 914	990[7]	923[7]	...	...	...	...	...	...
5 - 9	887	523	364	...	...	...	...	...	...
10 - 14	854	486	368	...	...	...	...	...	...
15 - 19	1 440	849	591	...	...	...	...	...	...
20 - 24	2 009	1 251	758	...	...	...	...	...	...
25 - 29	2 030	1 276	754	...	...	...	...	...	...

19. Deaths by age, sex and urban/rural residence: latest available year, 1996 - 2005
Décès selon l'âge, le sexe et la résidence, urbaine/rurale: dernière année disponible, 1996 - 2005 (continued - suite)

Continent, country or area, date, code and age (in years) / Continent, pays ou zone, date, code et âge (en années)	Total			Urban - Urbaine			Rural - Rurale		
	Both sexes Les deux sexes	Male Masculin	Female Féminin	Both sexes Les deux sexes	Male Masculin	Female Féminin	Both sexes Les deux sexes	Male Masculin	Female Féminin
AMERICA, SOUTH - AMÉRIQUE DU SUD									
Peru - Pérou[20]									
2003 (+U)									
30 - 34	2 221	1 424	797	...	...	...	...	...	...
35 - 39	2 468	1 486[7]	981[7]	...	...	...	...	...	...
40 - 44	2 696	1 601[7]	1 094[7]	...	...	...	...	...	...
45 - 49	2 984	1 669	1 315	...	...	...	...	...	...
50 - 54	3 630	2 013	1 617	...	...	...	...	...	...
55 - 59	3 993	2 230[7]	1 762[7]	...	...	...	...	...	...
60 - 64	5 041	2 734	2 307	...	...	...	...	...	...
65 - 69	6 123	3 325	2 798	...	...	...	...	...	...
70 - 74	7 853	4 308	3 545	...	...	...	...	...	...
75 - 79	8 488	4 602[7]	3 885[7]	...	...	...	...	...	...
80 - 84	8 679	4 397[7]	4 281[7]	...	...	...	...	...	...
85 - 89	7 160	3 277	3 883	...	...	...	...	...	...
90 - 94	4 589	1 869	2 720	...	...	...	...	...	...
95 - 99	2 258	752	1 506	...	...	...	...	...	...
100 +	460	145	315	...	...	...	...	...	...
Unknown - Inconnu	299	168[7]	112[7]	...	...	...	...	...	...
Suriname									
2002 (C)									
Total	3 125	1 783	1 342	2 218[21]	1 266[21]	952[21]	871[4]	493[4]	378[4]
0	148	84	64	112[21]	68[21]	44[21]	34[4]	14[4]	20[4]
1 - 4	53	27	26	31[21]	17[21]	14[21]	22[4]	10[4]	12[4]
5 - 9	10	5	5	7[21]	2[21]	5[21]	3[4]	3[4]	-[4]
10 - 14	23	12	11	17[21]	10[21]	7[21]	6[4]	2[4]	4[4]
15 - 19	37	23	14	23[21]	12[21]	11[21]	14[4]	11[4]	3[4]
20 - 24	74	44	30	44[21]	27[21]	17[21]	29[4]	17[4]	12[4]
25 - 29	70	49	21	52[21]	38[21]	14[21]	16[4]	10[4]	6[4]
30 - 34	105	73	32	68[21]	50[21]	18[21]	37[4]	23[4]	14[4]
35 - 39	127	88	39	94[21]	66[21]	28[21]	29[4]	20[4]	9[4]
40 - 44	171	106	65	125[21]	79[21]	46[21]	42[4]	23[4]	19[4]
45 - 49	143	78	65	112[21]	61[21]	51[21]	31[4]	17[4]	14[4]
50 - 54	153	87	66	121[21]	66[21]	55[21]	31[4]	20[4]	11[4]
55 - 59	199	127	72	141[21]	87[21]	54[21]	56[4]	38[4]	18[4]
60 - 64	256	151	105	182[21]	110[21]	72[21]	69[4]	38[4]	31[4]
65 - 69	359	195	164	257[21]	143[21]	114[21]	99[4]	50[4]	49[4]
70 - 74	334	197	137	221[21]	134[21]	87[21]	108[4]	60[4]	48[4]
75 - 79	304	170	134	211[21]	112[21]	99[21]	90[4]	55[4]	35[4]
80 - 84	233	107	126	158[21]	74[21]	84[21]	74[4]	33[4]	41[4]
85 - 89	184	97	87	133[21]	64[21]	69[21]	49[4]	32[4]	17[4]
90 - 94	104	54	50	78[21]	39[21]	39[21]	26[4]	15[4]	11[4]
95 - 99	27	8	19	21[21]	7[21]	14[21]	5[4]	1[4]	4[4]
100 +	11	1	10	10[21]	-[21]	10[21]	1[4]	1[4]	-[4]
2004 (C)									
Total	3 319	1 894	1 425	...	...	...	...	...	...
0	120	78	42	...	...	...	...	...	...
1 - 4	56	34	22	...	...	...	...	...	...
5 - 9	18	8	10	...	...	...	...	...	...
10 - 14	27	17	10	...	...	...	...	...	...
15 - 19	41	28	13	...	...	...	...	...	...
20 - 24	70	42	28	...	...	...	...	...	...
25 - 29	97	68	29	...	...	...	...	...	...
30 - 34	110	71	39	...	...	...	...	...	...
35 - 39	142	97	45	...	...	...	...	...	...
40 - 44	164	107	57	...	...	...	...	...	...
45 - 49	197	117	80	...	...	...	...	...	...
50 - 54	159	97	62	...	...	...	...	...	...
55 - 59	223	124	99	...	...	...	...	...	...
60 - 64	259	143	116	...	...	...	...	...	...
65 - 69	333	196	137	...	...	...	...	...	...
70 - 74	369	210	159	...	...	...	...	...	...
75 - 79	343	199	144	...	...	...	...	...	...

Continent, country or area, date, code and age (in years) / Continent, pays ou zone, date, code et âge (en années)	Total			Urban - Urbaine			Rural - Rurale		
	Both sexes Les deux sexes	Male Masculin	Female Féminin	Both sexes Les deux sexes	Male Masculin	Female Féminin	Both sexes Les deux sexes	Male Masculin	Female Féminin
AMERICA, SOUTH - AMÉRIQUE DU SUD									
Suriname									
2004 (C)									
80 - 84	293	149	144	...	...	...	...	...	...
85 - 89	161	65	96	...	...	...	...	...	...
90 - 94	99	35	64	...	...	...	...	...	...
95 - 99	32	7	25	...	...	...	...	...	...
100 +	6	2	4	...	...	...	...	...	...
Uruguay									
2002 (C)									
Total	31 628	16 796[7]	14 819[7]	...	...	...	...	...	...
0	708	401[7]	304[7]	...	...	...	...	...	...
1 - 4	104	69	35	...	...	...	...	...	...
5 - 9	63	31	32	...	...	...	...	...	...
10 - 14	67	42	25	...	...	...	...	...	...
15 - 19	182	139	43	...	...	...	...	...	...
20 - 24	249	199	50	...	...	...	...	...	...
25 - 29	260	196	64	...	...	...	...	...	...
30 - 34	301	200	101	...	...	...	...	...	...
35 - 39	339	218[7]	120[7]	...	...	...	...	...	...
40 - 44	494	273	221	...	...	...	...	...	...
45 - 49	754	467	287	...	...	...	...	...	...
50 - 54	1 108	724	384	...	...	...	...	...	...
55 - 59	1 501	990	511	...	...	...	...	...	...
60 - 64	2 095	1 422	673	...	...	...	...	...	...
65 - 69	2 842	1 818	1 024	...	...	...	...	...	...
70 - 74	3 938	2 395[7]	1 542[7]	...	...	...	...	...	...
75 +	16 534	7 149[7]	9 381[7]	...	...	...	...	...	...
Unknown - Inconnu	89	63[7]	22[7]	...	...	...	...	...	...
Venezuela (Bolivarian Republic of) - Venezuela (République bolivarienne du)[16]									
2002 (C)									
Total	105 388	64 917	40 471	...	...	...	...	...	...
0	7 645	4 406	3 239	...	...	...	...	...	...
1 - 4	1 937	1 077	860	...	...	...	...	...	...
5 - 9	829	493	336	...	...	...	...	...	...
10 - 14	1 061	668	393	...	...	...	...	...	...
15 - 19	3 540	2 929	611	...	...	...	...	...	...
20 - 24	5 301	4 579	722	...	...	...	...	...	...
25 - 29	4 293	3 578	715	...	...	...	...	...	...
30 - 34	3 957	3 002	955	...	...	...	...	...	...
35 - 39	3 621	2 586	1 035	...	...	...	...	...	...
40 - 44	4 168	2 795	1 373	...	...	...	...	...	...
45 - 49	4 878	3 164	1 714	...	...	...	...	...	...
50 - 54	5 518	3 549	1 969	...	...	...	...	...	...
55 - 59	5 802	3 719	2 083	...	...	...	...	...	...
60 - 64	6 494	4 032	2 462	...	...	...	...	...	...
65 - 69	7 964	4 746	3 218	...	...	...	...	...	...
70 - 74	9 145	5 339	3 806	...	...	...	...	...	...
75 - 79	9 369	5 076	4 293	...	...	...	...	...	...
80 - 84	8 247	4 164	4 083	...	...	...	...	...	...
85 - 89	6 270	2 793	3 477	...	...	...	...	...	...
90 - 94	3 518	1 463	2 055	...	...	...	...	...	...
95 - 99	1 201	420	781	...	...	...	...	...	...
100 +	364	133	231	...	...	...	...	...	...
Unknown - Inconnu	266	206	60	...	...	...	...	...	...

19. Deaths by age, sex and urban/rural residence: latest available year, 1996 - 2005
Décès selon l'âge, le sexe et la résidence, urbaine/rurale: dernière année disponible, 1996 - 2005 (continued - suite)

Continent, country or area, date, code and age (in years) Continent, pays ou zone, date, code et âge (en années)	Total			Urban - Urbaine			Rural - Rurale		
	Both sexes Les deux sexes	Male Masculin	Female Féminin	Both sexes Les deux sexes	Male Masculin	Female Féminin	Both sexes Les deux sexes	Male Masculin	Female Féminin

ASIA - ASIE

Armenia - Arménie[22]
2005 (C)

Total	26 379	13 752	12 627	17 128	8 976	8 152	9 251	4 776	4 475
0	460	272	188	351	217	134	109	55	54
1 - 4	56	32	24	35	20	15	21	12	9
5 - 9	46	27	19	25	15	10	21	12	9
10 - 14	47	33	14	27	20	7	20	13	7
15 - 19	131	101	30	85	65	20	46	36	10
20 - 24	132	97	35	87	65	22	45	32	13
25 - 29	162	120	42	113	82	31	49	38	11
30 - 34	220	161	59	167	125	42	53	36	17
35 - 39	334	236	98	219	159	60	115	77	38
40 - 44	646	427	219	416	272	144	230	155	75
45 - 49	968	644	324	666	440	226	302	204	98
50 - 54	1 265	858	407	941	625	316	324	233	91
55 - 59	1 301	860	441	987	658	329	314	202	112
60 - 64	1 367	859	508	963	588	375	404	271	133
65 - 69	3 682	2 143	1 539	2 480	1 431	1 049	1 202	712	490
70 - 74	4 275	2 357	1 918	2 688	1 463	1 225	1 587	894	693
75 - 79	5 639	2 694	2 945	3 410	1 597	1 813	2 229	1 097	1 132
80 - 84	3 113	1 096	2 017	1 968	680	1 288	1 145	416	729
85 - 89	1 331	394	937	826	251	575	505	143	362
90 +	1 204	341	863	674	203	471	530	138	392

Azerbaijan - Azerbaïdjan[22]
2004 (+C)

Total	49 568	26 039	23 529	25 867	13 797	12 070	23 701	12 242	11 459
0	1 287	757	530	605	385	220	682	372	310
1 - 4	726	405	321	139	69	70	587	336	251
5 - 9	336	191	145	130	68	62	206	123	83
10 - 14	315	200	115	126	75	51	189	125	64
15 - 19	438	279	159	228	139	89	210	140	70
20 - 24	586	393	193	304	213	91	282	180	102
25 - 29	647	429	218	332	231	101	315	198	117
30 - 34	931	659	272	518	361	157	413	298	115
35 - 39	1 264	858	406	696	488	208	568	370	198
40 - 44	1 873	1 255	618	1 077	749	328	796	506	290
45 - 49	2 270	1 557	713	1 384	953	431	886	604	282
50 - 54	2 431	1 557	874	1 549	1 011	538	882	546	336
55 - 59	2 323	1 491	832	1 493	979	514	830	512	318
60 - 64	3 493	2 108	1 385	2 057	1 246	811	1 436	862	574
65 - 69	7 684	4 301	3 383	3 924	2 249	1 675	3 760	2 052	1 708
70 - 74	8 158	4 225	3 933	4 008	2 025	1 983	4 150	2 200	1 950
75 - 79	6 696	3 114	3 582	3 455	1 500	1 955	3 241	1 614	1 627
80 - 84	3 703	1 208	2 495	1 928	573	1 355	1 775	635	1 140
85 - 89	1 983	532	1 451	1 000	263	737	983	269	714
90 - 94	1 379	334	1 045	587	147	440	792	187	605
95 - 99	501	113	388	182	42	140	319	71	248
100 +	544	73	471	145	31	114	399	42	357

Bahrain - Bahreïn
2005 (C)

Total	2 222	1 327	895	...	...	...	...	...	...
0	134	72	62	...	...	...	...	...	...
1 - 4	31	17	14	...	...	...	...	...	...
5 - 9	26	15	11	...	...	...	...	...	...
10 - 14	9	4	5	...	...	...	...	...	...
15 - 19	37	28	9	...	...	...	...	...	...
20 - 24	58	40	18	...	...	...	...	...	...
25 - 29	65	51	14	...	...	...	...	...	...
30 - 34	68	51	17	...	...	...	...	...	...
35 - 39	87	66	21	...	...	...	...	...	...
40 - 44	94	73	21	...	...	...	...	...	...
45 - 49	123	90	33	...	...	...	...	...	...
50 - 54	127	93	34	...	...	...	...	...	...
55 - 59	103	63	40	...	...	...	...	...	...
60 - 64	120	71	49	...	...	...	...	...	...

Continent, country or area, date, code and age (in years) / Continent, pays ou zone, date, code et âge (en années)	Total			Urban - Urbaine			Rural - Rurale		
	Both sexes Les deux sexes	Male Masculin	Female Féminin	Both sexes Les deux sexes	Male Masculin	Female Féminin	Both sexes Les deux sexes	Male Masculin	Female Féminin
ASIA - ASIE									
Bahrain - Bahreïn									
2005 (C)									
65 - 69	221	111	110	...	...	...	...	...	...
70 - 74	235	118	117	...	...	...	...	...	...
75 +	684	364	320	...	...	...	...	...	...
Bhutan - Bhoutan[23]									
2005 (I)									
Total	4 498	2 390	2 108	1 048	568	480	3 450	1 822	1 628
0	503	270	233	126	60	66	377	210	167
1 - 4	269	143	126	77	45	32	192	98	94
5 - 9	139	85	54	49	36	13	90	49	41
10 - 14	88	46	42	14	4	10	74	42	32
15 - 19	126	65	61	19	13	6	107	52	55
20 - 24	123	65	58	28	15	13	95	50	45
25 - 29	133	74	59	36	22	14	97	52	45
30 - 34	145	79	66	32	19	13	113	60	53
35 - 39	182	107	75	60	40	20	122	67	55
40 - 44	174	95	79	42	21	21	132	74	58
45 - 49	250	129	121	71	36	35	179	93	86
50 - 54	204	113	91	41	26	15	163	87	76
55 - 59	239	126	113	66	30	36	173	96	77
60 - 64	291	145	146	57	28	29	234	117	117
65 - 69	331	163	168	76	35	41	255	128	127
70 - 74	368	188	180	59	29	30	309	159	150
75 +	933	497	436	195	109	86	738	388	350
Brunei Darussalam - Brunéi Darussalam									
2004 (+C)									
Total	1 010	559	451	...	...	...	...	...	...
0 - 4	70	37	33	...	...	...	...	...	...
5 - 9	12	10	2	...	...	...	...	...	...
10 - 14	10	6	4	...	...	...	...	...	...
15 - 19	12	8	4	...	...	...	...	...	...
20 - 24	19	14	5	...	...	...	...	...	...
25 - 29	21	15	6	...	...	...	...	...	...
30 - 34	36	19	17	...	...	...	...	...	...
35 - 39	37	20	17	...	...	...	...	...	...
40 - 44	47	26	21	...	...	...	...	...	...
45 - 49	55	33	22	...	...	...	...	...	...
50 - 54	52	31	21	...	...	...	...	...	...
55 - 59	62	25	37	...	...	...	...	...	...
60 - 64	54	31	23	...	...	...	...	...	...
65 - 69	98	55	43	...	...	...	...	...	...
70 +	425	229	196	...	...	...	...	...	...
China - Chine[24]									
1999 (...)									
Total	7 420 000	4 140 000	3 280 000	...	...	...	...	...	...
0 - 4	474 000	237 000	237 000	...	...	...	...	...	...
5 - 9	40 000	22 000	18 000	...	...	...	...	...	...
10 - 14	33 000	20 000	13 000	...	...	...	...	...	...
15 - 19	72 000	38 000	34 000	...	...	...	...	...	...
20 - 24	104 000	59 000	45 000	...	...	...	...	...	...
25 - 29	165 000	87 000	78 000	...	...	...	...	...	...
30 - 34	180 000	112 000	68 000	...	...	...	...	...	...
35 - 39	147 000	93 000	54 000	...	...	...	...	...	...
40 - 44	229 000	150 000	79 000	...	...	...	...	...	...
45 - 49	306 000	199 000	107 000	...	...	...	...	...	...
50 - 54	286 000	177 000	109 000	...	...	...	...	...	...
55 - 59	414 000	242 000	172 000	...	...	...	...	...	...
60 - 64	673 000	432 000	241 000	...	...	...	...	...	...
65 - 69	906 000	540 000	366 000	...	...	...	...	...	...
70 - 74	1 028 000	594 000	434 000	...	...	...	...	...	...
75 - 79	947 000	528 000	419 000	...	...	...	...	...	...
80 - 84	799 000	381 000	418 000	...	...	...	...	...	...

Continent, country or area, date, code and age (in years) / Continent, pays ou zone, date, code et âge (en années)	Total			Urban - Urbaine			Rural - Rurale		
	Both sexes Les deux sexes	Male Masculin	Female Féminin	Both sexes Les deux sexes	Male Masculin	Female Féminin	Both sexes Les deux sexes	Male Masculin	Female Féminin
ASIA - ASIE									
China - Chine[24]									
1999 (...)									
85 - 89	*423 000*	*174 000*	*249 000*	...	...	...	...	...	...
90 + ...	*193 000*	*54 000*	*139 000*	...	...	...	...	...	...
China: Hong Kong SAR - Chine: Hong Kong RAS									
2005 (C)									
Total.....................	38 830	21 606[7]	17 222[7]	...	...	...	...	...	...
0	131	78	53	...	...	...	...	...	...
1 - 4	30	15	15	...	...	...	...	...	...
5 - 9	27	16	11	...	...	...	...	...	...
10 - 14	35	22	13	...	...	...	...	...	...
15 - 19	91	57	34	...	...	...	...	...	...
20 - 24	145	93	52	...	...	...	...	...	...
25 - 29	218	130	88	...	...	...	...	...	...
30 - 34	296	185	111	...	...	...	...	...	...
35 - 39	456	282	174	...	...	...	...	...	...
40 - 44	757	454	303	...	...	...	...	...	...
45 - 49	1 106	721	385	...	...	...	...	...	...
50 - 54	1 423	917	506	...	...	...	...	...	...
55 - 59	1 683	1 185	498	...	...	...	...	...	...
60 - 64	1 774	1 261	513	...	...	...	...	...	...
65 - 69	3 050	2 160	890	...	...	...	...	...	...
70 - 74	4 896	3 189	1 707	...	...	...	...	...	...
75 - 79	6 149	3 746	2 403	...	...	...	...	...	...
80 - 84	6 641	3 469	3 172	...	...	...	...	...	...
85 + ...	9 889	3 598	6 291	...	...	...	...	...	...
Unknown - Inconnu	33	28[7]	3[7]	...	...	...	...	...	...
China: Macao SAR - Chine: Macao RAS									
2005 (C)									
Total.....................	1 615	909	706	...	...	...	...	...	...
0	12	5	7	...	...	...	...	...	...
1 - 4	3	1	2	...	...	...	...	...	...
5 - 9	2	1	1	...	...	...	...	...	...
10 - 14	6	5	1	...	...	...	...	...	...
15 - 19	4	4	-	...	...	...	...	...	...
20 - 24	17	10	7	...	...	...	...	...	...
25 - 29	14	8	6	...	...	...	...	...	...
30 - 34	18	14	4	...	...	...	...	...	...
35 - 39	26	14	12	...	...	...	...	...	...
40 - 44	41	26	15	...	...	...	...	...	...
45 - 49	94	63	31	...	...	...	...	...	...
50 - 54	94	69	25	...	...	...	...	...	...
55 - 59	85	68	17	...	...	...	...	...	...
60 - 64	84	65	19	...	...	...	...	...	...
65 - 69	107	68	39	...	...	...	...	...	...
70 - 74	163	102	61	...	...	...	...	...	...
75 - 79	222	123	99	...	...	...	...	...	...
80 - 84	248	114	134	...	...	...	...	...	...
85 + ...	375	149	226	...	...	...	...	...	...
Cyprus - Chypre[25]									
2005 (C)									
Total.....................	5 425	2 835	2 590	...	...	...	...	...	...
0	38	19	19	...	...	...	...	...	...
1 - 4	12	5	7	...	...	...	...	...	...
5 - 9	20	10	10	...	...	...	...	...	...
10 - 14	15	7	8	...	...	...	...	...	...
15 - 19	34	25	9	...	...	...	...	...	...
20 - 24	46	35	11	...	...	...	...	...	...
25 - 29	47	33	14	...	...	...	...	...	...
30 - 34	54	36	18	...	...	...	...	...	...
35 - 39	61	42	19	...	...	...	...	...	...
40 - 44	67	40	27	...	...	...	...	...	...
45 - 49	91	52	39	...	...	...	...	...	...

19. Deaths by age, sex and urban/rural residence: latest available year, 1996 - 2005
Décès selon l'âge, le sexe et la résidence, urbaine/rurale: dernière année disponible, 1996 - 2005 (continued - suite)

Continent, country or area, date, code and age (in years) Continent, pays ou zone, date, code et âge (en années)	Total			Urban - Urbaine			Rural - Rurale		
	Both sexes Les deux sexes	Male Masculin	Female Féminin	Both sexes Les deux sexes	Male Masculin	Female Féminin	Both sexes Les deux sexes	Male Masculin	Female Féminin
ASIA - ASIE									
Cyprus - Chypre[25]									
2005 (C)									
50 - 54	123	83	40	...	...	...	...	...	...
55 - 59	217	142	75	...	...	...	...	...	...
60 - 64	279	186	93	...	...	...	...	...	...
65 - 69	421	253	168	...	...	...	...	...	...
70 - 74	520	299	221	...	...	...	...	...	...
75 - 79	834	419	415	...	...	...	...	...	...
80 - 84	960	464	496	...	...	...	...	...	...
85 + ...	1 559	670	889	...	...	...	...	...	...
Unknown - Inconnu	27	15	12	...	...	...	...	...	...
Georgia - Géorgie[22]									
2001 (C)									
Total....................	39 339	19 569	19 770	21 600	11 077	10 523	17 739	8 492	9 247
0	478	301	177	439	280	159	39	21	18
1 - 4	58	26	32	29	10	19	29	16	13
5 - 9	40	29	11	27	21	6	13	8	5
10 - 14	74	53	21	50	36	14	24	17	7
15 - 19	183	114	69	99	66	33	84	48	36
20 - 24	208	137	71	134	88	46	74	49	25
25 - 29	370	271	99	231	169	62	139	102	37
30 - 34	463	350	113	270	204	66	193	146	47
35 - 39	668	506	162	427	327	100	241	179	62
40 - 44	953	711	242	629	484	145	324	227	97
45 - 49	1 156	857	299	778	584	194	378	273	105
50 - 54	1 294	924	370	890	635	255	404	289	115
55 - 59	1 311	877	434	823	568	255	488	309	179
60 - 64	3 440	1 980	1 460	2 067	1 242	825	1 373	738	635
65 - 69	5 046	2 936	2 110	2 693	1 560	1 133	2 353	1 376	977
70 - 74	7 055	3 787	3 268	3 703	1 965	1 738	3 352	1 822	1 530
75 - 79	6 361	2 713	3 648	3 381	1 361	2 020	2 980	1 352	1 628
80 - 84	4 249	1 361	2 888	2 177	676	1 501	2 072	685	1 387
85 - 89	3 498	997	2 501	1 775	512	1 263	1 723	485	1 238
90 - 94	1 558	413	1 145	636	175	461	922	238	684
95 - 99	487	97	390	165	37	128	322	60	262
100 + ...	301	75	226	93	25	68	208	50	158
Unknown - Inconnu	88	54	34	84	52	32	4	2	2
2003 (C)									
Total....................	46 055	22 829	23 226	...	...	...	...	...	...
0	1 144	657	487	...	...	...	...	...	...
1 - 4	131	79	52	...	...	...	...	...	...
5 - 9	35	20	15	...	...	...	...	...	...
10 - 14	66	28	38	...	...	...	...	...	...
15 - 19	107	70	37	...	...	...	...	...	...
20 - 24	212	141	71	...	...	...	...	...	...
25 - 29	319	195	124	...	...	...	...	...	...
30 - 34	415	326	89	...	...	...	...	...	...
35 - 39	551	358	193	...	...	...	...	...	...
40 - 44	885	558	327	...	...	...	...	...	...
45 - 49	1 246	886	360	...	...	...	...	...	...
50 - 54	1 970	1 337	633	...	...	...	...	...	...
55 - 59	1 899	1 188	711	...	...	...	...	...	...
60 - 64	3 188	1 891	1 297	...	...	...	...	...	...
65 - 69	5 393	3 204	2 189	...	...	...	...	...	...
70 - 74	7 115	3 720	3 395	...	...	...	...	...	...
75 - 79	8 841	3 988	4 853	...	...	...	...	...	...
80 - 84	5 716	2 146	3 570	...	...	...	...	...	...
85 + ...	6 822	2 037	4 785	...	...	...	...	...	...
Israel - Israël[26]									
2005 (C)									
Total....................	38 911[27]	19 340[28]	19 570[28]	36 478[4]	18 121[14]	18 356[14]	2 424[4]	1 213[4]	1 211[4]
0	627[27]	342[28]	284[28]	550[4]	300[14]	249[14]	76[4]	41[4]	35[4]
1 - 4	160[27]	94[27]	66[27]	139	77	62	21	17	4
5 - 9	60[27]	34[27]	26[27]	55	30	25	5	4	1
10 - 14	81[27]	49[27]	32[27]	73	46	27	8	3	5

Continent, country or area, date, code and age (in years) / Continent, pays ou zone, date, code et âge (en années)	Total			Urban - Urbaine			Rural - Rurale		
	Both sexes Les deux sexes	Male Masculin	Female Féminin	Both sexes Les deux sexes	Male Masculin	Female Féminin	Both sexes Les deux sexes	Male Masculin	Female Féminin
ASIA - ASIE									
Israel - Israël[26]									
2005 (C)									
15 - 19	173[27]	115[27]	58[27]	154	101	53	19	14	5
20 - 24	308[27]	235[27]	73[27]	282[4]	214[4]	68[4]	25[4]	20[4]	5[4]
25 - 29	263[27]	193[27]	70[27]	234	172	62	29	21	8
30 - 34	296[27]	210[27]	86[27]	272	190	82	24	20	4
35 - 39	340[27]	215[27]	125[27]	320	203	117	20	12	8
40 - 44	516[27]	337[27]	179[27]	481	318	163	35	19	16
45 - 49	810[27]	507[27]	303[27]	760	478	282	50	29	21
50 - 54	1 232[27]	771[27]	461[27]	1 155[4]	724[4]	431[4]	76[4]	46[4]	30[4]
55 - 59	1 628[27]	988[27]	640[27]	1 538[4]	936[4]	602[4]	89[4]	51[4]	38[4]
60 - 64	1 744[27]	1 068[27]	676[27]	1 651	1 013	638	93	55	38
65 - 69	2 750[27]	1 604[27]	1 146[27]	2 610	1 528	1 082	140	76	64
70 - 74	3 828[27]	2 116[27]	1 712[27]	3 638[4]	2 012[4]	1 626[4]	189[4]	104[4]	85[4]
75 - 79	5 614[27]	2 786[27]	2 828[27]	5 334	2 644	2 690	280	142	138
80 - 84	7 067[27]	3 159[27]	3 908[27]	6 664[4]	2 959[4]	3 705[4]	400[4]	199[4]	201[4]
85 +	11 414[27]	4 517[27]	6 897[27]	10 568[4]	4 176[4]	6 392[4]	845[4]	340[4]	505[4]
Japan - Japon[29]									
2005 (C)									
Total	1 083 796	584 970	498 826	...	...	...	...	...	...
0	2 958	1 641	1 317	...	...	...	...	...	...
1 - 4	1 144	650	494	...	...	...	...	...	...
5 - 9	655	409	246	...	...	...	...	...	...
10 - 14	590	361	229	...	...	...	...	...	...
15 - 19	1 802	1 220	582	...	...	...	...	...	...
20 - 24	3 370	2 303	1 067	...	...	...	...	...	...
25 - 29	4 170	2 887	1 283	...	...	...	...	...	...
30 - 34	5 952	3 915	2 037	...	...	...	...	...	...
35 - 39	7 469	4 915	2 554	...	...	...	...	...	...
40 - 44	10 238	6 806	3 432	...	...	...	...	...	...
45 - 49	15 754	10 577	5 177	...	...	...	...	...	...
50 - 54	28 964	19 546	9 418	...	...	...	...	...	...
55 - 59	49 579	34 233	15 346	...	...	...	...	...	...
60 - 64	62 258	43 403	18 855	...	...	...	...	...	...
65 - 69	80 829	55 261	25 568	...	...	...	...	...	...
70 - 74	120 825	80 198	40 627	...	...	...	...	...	...
75 - 79	159 362	99 338	60 024	...	...	...	...	...	...
80 - 84	174 185	89 502	84 683	...	...	...	...	...	...
85 - 89	165 385	70 110	95 275	...	...	...	...	...	...
90 - 94	127 573	42 590	84 983	...	...	...	...	...	...
95 - 99	50 503	12 825	37 678	...	...	...	...	...	...
100 +	9 578	1 736	7 842	...	...	...	...	...	...
Unknown - Inconnu	653	544	109	...	...	...	...	...	...
Kazakhstan[22]									
2003 (C)									
Total	155 277	87 216	68 061	99 595	56 357	43 238	55 682	30 859	24 823
0	3 824	2 234	1 590	2 349	1 409	940	1 475	825	650
1 - 4	1 022	564	458	414	223	191	608	341	267
5 - 9	544	328	216	281	172	109	263	156	107
10 - 14	679	410	269	347	210	137	332	200	132
15 - 19	1 688	1 155	533	973	643	330	715	512	203
20 - 24	2 737	2 010	727	1 606	1 192	414	1 131	818	313
25 - 29	3 609	2 718	891	2 317	1 742	575	1 292	976	316
30 - 34	4 337	3 312	1 025	2 817	2 165	652	1 520	1 147	373
35 - 39	5 232	3 895	1 337	3 462	2 586	876	1 770	1 309	461
40 - 44	8 082	5 973	2 109	5 443	4 032	1 411	2 639	1 941	698
45 - 49	9 576	6 898	2 678	6 593	4 775	1 818	2 983	2 123	860
50 - 54	10 981	7 651	3 330	7 512	5 329	2 183	3 469	2 322	1 147
55 - 59	8 618	5 807	2 811	5 752	3 926	1 826	2 866	1 881	985
60 - 64	15 291	9 592	5 699	9 534	6 014	3 520	5 757	3 578	2 179
65 - 69	18 206	10 922	7 284	11 265	6 772	4 493	6 941	4 150	2 791
70 - 74	17 766	9 251	8 515	11 258	5 740	5 518	6 508	3 511	2 997
75 - 79	18 518	7 409	11 109	12 002	4 655	7 347	6 516	2 754	3 762
80 - 84	10 584	3 204	7 380	6 688	1 997	4 691	3 896	1 207	2.689

19. Deaths by age, sex and urban/rural residence: latest available year, 1996 - 2005
Décès selon l'âge, le sexe et la résidence, urbaine/rurale: dernière année disponible, 1996 - 2005 (continued - suite)

Continent, country or area, date, code and age (in years) Continent, pays ou zone, date, code et âge (en années)	Total			Urban - Urbaine			Rural - Rurale		
	Both sexes Les deux sexes	Male Masculin	Female Féminin	Both sexes Les deux sexes	Male Masculin	Female Féminin	Both sexes Les deux sexes	Male Masculin	Female Féminin
ASIA - ASIE									
Kazakhstan[22]									
2003 (C)									
85 + ...	12 649	2 793	9 856	7 667	1 701	5 966	4 982	1 092	3 890
Unknown - Inconnu	1 334	1 090	244	1 315	1 074	241	19	16	3
2004 (C)									
Total.....................	152 250	86 304	65 946	...	...	...	...	...	...
0	3 901	2 280	1 621	...	...	...	...	...	...
1 - 4	932	541	391	...	...	...	...	...	...
5 - 9	501	319	182	...	...	...	...	...	...
10 - 14	643	401	242	...	...	...	...	...	...
15 - 19	1 698	1 175	523	...	...	...	...	...	...
20 - 24	2 988	2 279	709	...	...	...	...	...	...
25 - 29	4 074	3 157	917	...	...	...	...	...	...
30 - 34	4 775	3 669	1 106	...	...	...	...	...	...
35 - 39	5 444	4 057	1 387	...	...	...	...	...	...
40 - 44	8 187	6 006	2 181	...	...	...	...	...	...
45 - 49	9 808	7 135	2 673	...	...	...	...	...	...
50 - 54	11 187	7 867	3 320	...	...	...	...	...	...
55 - 59	9 821	6 658	3 163	...	...	...	...	...	...
60 - 64	12 306	7 671	4 635	...	...	...	...	...	...
65 - 69	18 980	11 278	7 702	...	...	...	...	...	...
70 - 74	15 416	8 012	7 404	...	...	...	...	...	...
75 - 79	18 335	7 509	10 826	...	...	...	...	...	...
80 - 84	10 742	3 070	7 672	...	...	...	...	...	...
85 + ...	11 597	2 469	9 128	...	...	...	...	...	...
Unknown - Inconnu	915	751	164	...	...	...	...	...	...
Korea (Republic of) - Corée (République de)[30]									
2004 (C)									
Total.....................	245 771	136 249	109 522	...	...	...	...	...	...
0	2 209	1 211	998	...	...	...	...	...	...
1 - 4	727	411	316	...	...	...	...	...	...
5 - 9	649	405	244	...	...	...	...	...	...
10 - 14	518	317	201	...	...	...	...	...	...
15 - 19	1 007	703	304	...	...	...	...	...	...
20 - 24	1 780	1 197	583	...	...	...	...	...	...
25 - 29	2 190	1 475	715	...	...	...	...	...	...
30 - 34	3 303	2 203	1 100	...	...	...	...	...	...
35 - 39	5 315	3 724	1 591	...	...	...	...	...	...
40 - 44	8 899	6 489	2 410	...	...	...	...	...	...
45 - 49	11 824	8 882	2 942	...	...	...	...	...	...
50 - 54	12 146	9 159	2 987	...	...	...	...	...	...
55 - 59	14 094	10 461	3 633	...	...	...	...	...	...
60 - 64	20 655	14 682	5 973	...	...	...	...	...	...
65 - 69	27 028	17 916	9 112	...	...	...	...	...	...
70 - 74	29 835	17 039	12 796	...	...	...	...	...	...
75 - 79	32 429	15 511	16 918	...	...	...	...	...	...
80 - 84	33 335	13 681	19 654	...	...	...	...	...	...
85 - 89	22 895	7 375	15 520	...	...	...	...	...	...
90 - 94	11 179	2 756	8 423	...	...	...	...	...	...
95 + ...	3 745	650	3 095	...	...	...	...	...	...
Unknown - Inconnu	9	2	7	...	...	...	...	...	...
Kuwait - Koweït									
2005 (C)									
Total.....................	4 784	3 137	1 647	...	...	...	...	...	...
0	420	223	197	...	...	...	...	...	...
1 - 4	84	46	38	...	...	...	...	...	...
5 - 9	50	29	21	...	...	...	...	...	...
10 - 14	50	31	19	...	...	...	...	...	...
15 - 19	100	80	20	...	...	...	...	...	...
20 - 24	128	107	21	...	...	...	...	...	...
25 - 29	227	189	38	...	...	...	...	...	...
30 - 34	197	151	46	...	...	...	...	...	...
35 - 39	222	178	44	...	...	...	...	...	...
40 - 44	266	215	51	...	...	...	...	...	...

19. Deaths by age, sex and urban/rural residence: latest available year, 1996 - 2005
Décès selon l'âge, le sexe et la résidence, urbaine/rurale: dernière année disponible, 1996 - 2005 (continued - suite)

Continent, country or area, date, code and age (in years) / Continent, pays ou zone, date, code et âge (en années)	Total			Urban - Urbaine			Rural - Rurale		
	Both sexes Les deux sexes	Male Masculin	Female Féminin	Both sexes Les deux sexes	Male Masculin	Female Féminin	Both sexes Les deux sexes	Male Masculin	Female Féminin
ASIA - ASIE									
Kuwait - Koweït									
2005 (C)									
45 - 49	305	250	55	...	...	...	...	...	...
50 - 54	314	237	77	...	...	...	...	...	...
55 - 59	332	224	108	...	...	...	...	...	...
60 - 64	317	200	117	...	...	...	...	...	...
65 - 69	425	269	156	...	...	...	...	...	...
70 - 74	381	191	190	...	...	...	...	...	...
75 - 79	320	177	143	...	...	...	...	...	...
80 - 84	202	111	91	...	...	...	...	...	...
85 + ...	281	136	145	...	...	...	...	...	...
Unknown - Inconnu	163	93	70	...	...	...	...	...	...
Kyrgyzstan - Kirghizistan[22]									
2005 (C)									
Total....................	36 992	20 399	16 593	14 526	7 935	6 591	22 466	12 464	10 002
0	3 258	1 830	1 428	1 617	914	703	1 641	916	725
1 - 4	579	333	246	98	51	47	481	282	199
5 - 9	151	85	66	22	14	8	129	71	58
10 - 14	191	119	72	51	37	14	140	82	58
15 - 19	369	220	149	102	63	39	267	157	110
20 - 24	569	381	188	158	118	40	411	263	148
25 - 29	795	564	231	290	221	69	505	343	162
30 - 34	1 118	824	294	422	311	111	696	513	183
35 - 39	1 331	970	361	552	408	144	779	562	217
40 - 44	1 692	1 216	476	645	461	184	1 047	755	292
45 - 49	1 976	1 385	591	793	561	232	1 183	824	359
50 - 54	2 121	1 441	680	931	646	285	1 190	795	395
55 - 59	2 106	1 349	757	948	621	327	1 158	728	430
60 - 64	1 896	1 185	711	788	481	307	1 108	704	404
65 - 69	3 872	2 290	1 582	1 528	903	625	2 344	1 387	957
70 - 74	4 087	2 205	1 882	1 407	718	689	2 680	1 487	1 193
75 - 79	4 819	2 189	2 630	1 789	729	1 060	3 030	1 460	1 570
80 - 84	2 993	1 044	1 949	1 166	350	816	1 827	694	1 133
85 - 89	1 632	435	1 197	697	178	519	935	257	678
90 - 94	811	196	615	358	81	277	453	115	338
95 - 99	307	67	240	87	24	63	220	43	177
100 + ...	271	32	239	29	6	23	242	26	216
Unknown - Inconnu	48	39	9	48	39	9	-	-	-
Malaysia - Malaisie									
2000 (C)									
Total....................	104 859	60 793	44 066	...	...	...	...	...	...
0	3 578	2 026	1 552	...	...	...	...	...	...
1 - 4	1 282	694	588	...	...	...	...	...	...
5 - 9	836	500	336	...	...	...	...	...	...
10 - 14	961	597	364	...	...	...	...	...	...
15 - 19	1 966	1 480	486	...	...	...	...	...	...
20 - 24	2 229	1 677	552	...	...	...	...	...	...
25 - 29	2 281	1 746	535	...	...	...	...	...	...
30 - 34	2 669	2 000	669	...	...	...	...	...	...
35 - 39	3 249	2 337	912	...	...	...	...	...	...
40 - 44	4 078	2 793	1 285	...	...	...	...	...	...
45 - 49	4 728	3 090	1 638	...	...	...	...	...	...
50 - 54	6 106	3 901	2 205	...	...	...	...	...	...
55 - 59	7 070	4 485	2 585	...	...	...	...	...	...
60 - 64	9 943	6 103	3 840	...	...	...	...	...	...
65 - 69	11 029	6 257	4 772	...	...	...	...	...	...
70 - 74	12 160	6 622	5 538	...	...	...	...	...	...
75 - 79	11 807	5 874	5 933	...	...	...	...	...	...
80 - 84	9 179	4 272	4 907	...	...	...	...	...	...
85 + ...	9 571	4 276	5 295	...	...	...	...	...	...
Unknown - Inconnu	137	63	74	...	...	...	...	...	...
Maldives									
2005 (C)									
Total....................	1 015	606	409	326	183	143	689	423	266
0	67	32	35	29	10	19	38	22	16

19. Deaths by age, sex and urban/rural residence: latest available year, 1996 - 2005
Décès selon l'âge, le sexe et la résidence, urbaine/rurale: dernière année disponible, 1996 - 2005 (continued - suite)

Continent, country or area, date, code and age (in years) Continent, pays ou zone, date, code et âge (en années)	Total			Urban - Urbaine			Rural - Rurale		
	Both sexes Les deux sexes	Male Masculin	Female Féminin	Both sexes Les deux sexes	Male Masculin	Female Féminin	Both sexes Les deux sexes	Male Masculin	Female Féminin
ASIA - ASIE									
Maldives									
2005 (C)									
1 - 4	20	8	12	4	2	2	16	6	10
5 - 9	13	7	6	3	1	2	10	6	4
10 - 14	12	9	3	6	5	1	6	4	2
15 - 19	13	10	3	4	3	1	9	7	2
20 - 24	10	6	4	3	1	2	7	5	2
25 - 29	10	9	1	5	4	1	5	5	-
30 - 34	9	4	5	4	2	2	5	2	3
35 - 39	13	6	7	10	4	6	3	2	1
40 - 44	17	7	10	8	2	6	9	5	4
45 - 49	28	16	12	12	4	8	16	12	4
50 - 54	28	17	11	15	10	5	13	7	6
55 - 59	42	25	17	21	12	9	21	13	8
60 - 64	92	58	34	34	19	15	58	39	19
65 - 69	142	85	57	40	23	17	102	62	40
70 +	499	307	192	128	81	47	371	226	145
Mongolia - Mongolie									
1998 (C)									
Total	15 860	8 535	7 325	8 779	4 714	4 044	7 081	3 790	3 251
0	1 741	960	781	936	506	409	805	423	342
1 - 4	767	405	362	367	194	173	400	211	189
5 - 9	143	83	60	62	36	26	81	47	34
10 - 14	150	89	61	82	49	33	68	40	28
15 - 19	236	142	94	143	86	57	93	56	37
20 - 24	398	215	183	257	139	118	141	76	65
25 - 29	454	297	157	270	177	93	184	120	64
30 - 34	543	332	211	338	207	131	205	125	80
35 - 39	712	433	279	436	265	171	276	168	108
40 - 44	644	386	258	401	240	161	243	146	97
45 - 49	730	414	316	442	251	191	288	163	125
50 - 54	850	454	396	513	274	239	337	180	157
55 - 59	1 113	637	476	620	355	265	493	282	211
60 - 64	1 299	720	579	645	339	306	654	381	273
65 - 69	1 605	849	756	889	470	419	716	379	337
70 +	4 475	2 119	2 356	2 378	1 126	1 252	2 097	993	1 104
2003 (C)									
Total	16 006	9 499	6 507	9 480	...	...	6 526	...	...
0	1 051	602	449	520	...	...	531	...	...
1 - 4	356	202	154	138	...	...	218	...	...
5 - 9	116	66	50	61	...	...	55	...	...
10 - 14	112	69	43	61	...	...	51	...	...
15 - 19	210	139	71	135	...	...	75	...	...
20 - 24	327	235	92	174	...	...	153	...	...
25 - 29	455	321	134	275	...	...	180	...	...
30 - 34	552	385	167	351	...	...	201	...	...
35 - 39	716	515	201	499	...	...	217	...	...
40 - 44	989	676	313	663	...	...	326	...	...
45 - 49	1 076	693	383	701	...	...	375	...	...
50 - 54	1 044	664	380	645	...	...	399	...	...
55 - 59	1 123	699	424	704	...	...	419	...	...
60 - 64	1 513	927	586	867	...	...	646	...	...
65 - 69	1 530	940	590	882	...	...	648	...	...
70 - 74	1 589	879	710	904	...	...	685	...	...
75 - 79	1 200	620	580	722	...	...	478	...	...
80 - 84	1 042	504	538	605	...	...	437	...	...
85 - 89	641	242	399	376	...	...	265	...	...
90 - 94	275	89	186	139	...	...	136	...	...
95 - 99	72	29	43	49	...	...	23	...	...
100 +	17	3	14	9	...	...	8	...	...
Nepal - Népal[31]									
2001 (I)									
Total	106 789	59 544	47 245	...	...	...	...	...	...
0	13 037	6 956	6 081	...	...	...	...	...	...
1 - 4	9 790	5 590	4 200	...	...	...	...	...	...

19. Deaths by age, sex and urban/rural residence: latest available year, 1996 - 2005
Décès selon l'âge, le sexe et la résidence, urbaine/rurale: dernière année disponible, 1996 - 2005 (continued - suite)

Continent, country or area, date, code and age (in years) Continent, pays ou zone, date, code et âge (en annèes)	Total			Urban - Urbaine			Rural - Rurale		
	Both sexes Les deux sexes	Male Masculin	Female Féminin	Both sexes Les deux sexes	Male Masculin	Female Féminin	Both sexes Les deux sexes	Male Masculin	Female Féminin
ASIA - ASIE									
Nepal - Népal[31]									
2001 (I)									
5 - 9	3 320	1 726	1 594	...	...	...	...	...	...
10 - 14	2 304	1 332	972	...	...	...	...	...	...
15 - 19	2 523	1 293	1 230	...	...	...	...	...	...
20 - 24	2 747	1 449	1 298	...	...	...	...	...	...
25 - 29	2 688	1 429	1 259	...	...	...	...	...	...
30 - 34	2 474	1 303	1 172	...	...	...	...	...	...
35 - 39	2 839	1 594	1 244	...	...	...	...	...	...
40 - 44	2 970	1 828	1 142	...	...	...	...	...	...
45 - 49	3 553	2 027	1 526	...	...	...	...	...	...
50 - 54	4 662	2 771	1 891	...	...	...	...	...	...
55 - 59	6 115	3 612	2 503	...	...	...	...	...	...
60 - 64	8 337	4 710	3 626	...	...	...	...	...	...
65 - 69	8 667	4 764	3 903	...	...	...	...	...	...
70 - 74	9 606	5 512	4 093	...	...	...	...	...	...
75 - 79	8 113	4 657	3 456	...	...	...	...	...	...
80 +	13 042	6 990	6 052	...	...	...	...	...	...
Occupied Palestinian Territory - Territoire palestinien occupé									
2005 (U)									
Total	9 645	5 415	4 230	...	...	...	...	...	...
0	1 057	519	538	...	...	...	...	...	...
1 - 4	327	173	154	...	...	...	...	...	...
5 - 9	173	107	66	...	...	...	...	...	...
10 - 14	139	87	52	...	...	...	...	...	...
15 - 19	224	184	40	...	...	...	...	...	...
20 - 24	172	133	39	...	...	...	...	...	...
25 - 29	165	127	38	...	...	...	...	...	...
30 - 34	187	133	54	...	...	...	...	...	...
35 - 39	179	113	66	...	...	...	...	...	...
40 - 44	186	114	72	...	...	...	...	...	...
45 - 49	292	192	100	...	...	...	...	...	...
50 - 54	386	264	122	...	...	...	...	...	...
55 - 59	539	336	203	...	...	...	...	...	...
60 - 64	660	351	309	...	...	...	...	...	...
65 - 69	922	494	428	...	...	...	...	...	...
70 - 74	1 075	574	501	...	...	...	...	...	...
75 - 79	1 205	606	599	...	...	...	...	...	...
80 - 84	791	412	379	...	...	...	...	...	...
85 - 89	547	264	283	...	...	...	...	...	...
90 - 94	220	123	97	...	...	...	...	...	...
95 - 99	141	73	68	...	...	...	...	...	...
100 +	58	36	22	...	...	...	...	...	...
Oman[32]									
2005 (U)									
Total	2 849	...	...	...	...	...	...	...	...
0	315	...	...	...	...	...	...	...	...
1 - 4	63	...	...	...	...	...	...	...	...
5 - 14	62	...	...	...	...	...	...	...	...
15 - 44	372	...	...	...	...	...	...	...	...
45 +	2 037	...	...	...	...	...	...	...	...
Pakistan[33]									
2005 (I)									
Total	1 019 467	579 377	440 090	321 394	182 358	139 036	698 073	397 019	301 054
0 - 4	368 059	211 759	156 300	103 537	60 612	42 925	264 522	151 147	113 375
5 - 9	23 661	12 863	10 798	3 115	420	2 695	20 547	12 443	8 103
10 - 14	15 408	8 412	6 996	4 014	1 556	2 458	11 394	6 856	4 538
15 - 19	16 574	7 309	9 266	2 963	687	2 276	13 612	6 622	6 990
20 - 24	23 454	10 197	13 257	8 416	5 008	3 407	15 038	5 188	9 850
25 - 29	19 050	9 934	9 116	4 741	3 192	1 549	14 309	6 742	7 568
30 - 34	16 415	8 425	7 990	4 961	2 235	2 725	11 454	6 190	5 264
35 - 39	20 240	10 672	9 568	6 092	2 948	3 145	14 148	7 724	6 424
40 - 44	24 539	14 051	10 488	8 858	5 001	3 857	15 682	9 050	6 631

19. Deaths by age, sex and urban/rural residence: latest available year, 1996 - 2005
Décès selon l'âge, le sexe et la résidence, urbaine/rurale: dernière année disponible, 1996 - 2005 (continued - suite)

Continent, country or area, date, code and age (in years) / Continent, pays ou zone, date, code et âge (en années)	Total			Urban - Urbaine			Rural - Rurale		
	Both sexes Les deux sexes	Male Masculin	Female Féminin	Both sexes Les deux sexes	Male Masculin	Female Féminin	Both sexes Les deux sexes	Male Masculin	Female Féminin
ASIA - ASIE									
Pakistan[33]									
2005 (I)									
45 - 49	28 193	17 196	10 997	13 154	8 650	4 504	15 039	8 546	6 493
50 - 54	45 835	23 314	22 521	17 065	8 785	8 280	28 770	14 529	14 241
55 - 59	45 765	27 898	17 867	17 794	9 419	8 375	27 970	18 479	9 492
60 - 64	65 863	40 859	25 003	24 394	15 594	8 800	41 469	25 265	16 203
65 - 69	53 933	26 352	27 581	18 842	7 971	10 871	35 091	18 382	16 710
70 - 74	66 763	37 156	29 607	21 605	13 187	8 418	45 159	23 970	21 187
75 - 79	48 494	24 009	24 486	18 834	11 345	7 489	29 660	12 663	16 997
80 - 84	44 377	24 463	22 915	13 818	6 549	7 269	30 559	14 913	15 646
85 + ...	92 843	67 508	25 334	29 193	19 199	9 994	63 650	48 310	15 340
Philippines									
2003 (C)									
Total....................	396 331	233 739	162 592	...	...	...	...	...	...
0	22 844	13 329	9 515	...	...	...	...	...	...
1 - 4....................	10 327	5 595	4 732	...	...	...	...	...	...
5 - 9....................	5 335	3 113	2 222	...	...	...	...	...	...
10 - 14....................	4 630	2 671	1 959	...	...	...	...	...	...
15 - 19....................	6 631	4 312	2 319	...	...	...	...	...	...
20 - 24....................	9 841	6 847	2 994	...	...	...	...	...	...
25 - 29....................	10 870	7 502	3 368	...	...	...	...	...	...
30 - 34....................	12 702	8 721	3 981	...	...	...	...	...	...
35 - 39....................	15 020	10 182	4 838	...	...	...	...	...	...
40 - 44....................	17 829	12 035	5 794	...	...	...	...	...	...
45 - 49....................	21 461	14 449	7 012	...	...	...	...	...	...
50 - 54....................	25 767	17 325	8 442	...	...	...	...	...	...
55 - 59....................	26 793	17 975	8 818	...	...	...	...	...	...
60 - 64....................	31 406	20 380	11 026	...	...	...	...	...	...
65 - 69....................	34 964	21 379	13 585	...	...	...	...	...	...
70 - 74....................	35 452	20 286	15 166	...	...	...	...	...	...
75 - 79....................	33 900	17 752	16 148	...	...	...	...	...	...
80 - 84....................	31 292	14 336	16 956	...	...	...	...	...	...
85 - 89....................	21 895	8 939	12 956	...	...	...	...	...	...
90 - 94....................	11 996	4 541	7 455	...	...	...	...	...	...
95 +....................	4 624	1 621	3 003	...	...	...	...	...	...
Unknown - Inconnu.......	752	449	303	...	...	...	...	...	...
Qatar									
2005 (C)									
Total....................	1 545	1 108	437	...	...	...	...	...	...
0	110	60	50	...	...	...	...	...	...
1 - 4....................	30	20	10	...	...	...	...	...	...
5 - 9....................	14	9	5	...	...	...	...	...	...
10 - 14....................	14	6	8	...	...	...	...	...	...
15 - 19....................	42	37	5	...	...	...	...	...	...
20 - 24....................	78	70	8	...	...	...	...	...	...
25 - 29....................	77	69	8	...	...	...	...	...	...
30 - 34....................	77	67	10	...	...	...	...	...	...
35 - 39....................	72	64	8	...	...	...	...	...	...
40 - 44....................	94	81	13	...	...	...	...	...	...
45 - 49....................	109	89	20	...	...	...	...	...	...
50 - 54....................	127	107	20	...	...	...	...	...	...
55 - 59....................	108	81	27	...	...	...	...	...	...
60 - 64....................	97	66	31	...	...	...	...	...	...
65 - 69....................	120	65	55	...	...	...	...	...	...
70 - 74....................	116	69	47	...	...	...	...	...	...
75 - 79....................	92	53	39	...	...	...	...	...	...
80 - 84....................	97	55	42	...	...	...	...	...	...
85 - 89....................	36	21	15	...	...	...	...	...	...
90 - 94....................	18	13	5	...	...	...	...	...	...
95 +....................	8	2	6	...	...	...	...	...	...
Unknown - Inconnu.......	9	4	5	...	...	...	...	...	...

Continent, country or area, date, code and age (in years) / Continent, pays ou zone, date, code et âge (en années)	Total			Urban - Urbaine			Rural - Rurale		
	Both sexes Les deux sexes	Male Masculin	Female Féminin	Both sexes Les deux sexes	Male Masculin	Female Féminin	Both sexes Les deux sexes	Male Masculin	Female Féminin
ASIA - ASIE									
Saudi Arabia - Arabie saoudite									
2005 (...)									
Total...........	92 486	54 253	38 233	...	...	...	...	...	...
0 - 4....................	12 889	6 692	6 197	...	...	...	...	...	...
5 - 9....................	977	524	453	...	...	...	...	...	...
10 - 14..................	977	566	411	...	...	...	...	...	...
15 - 19..................	1 350	791	559	...	...	...	...	...	...
20 - 24..................	1 695	998	697	...	...	...	...	...	...
25 - 29..................	2 248	1 371	877	...	...	...	...	...	...
30 - 34..................	2 750	1 681	1 069	...	...	...	...	...	...
35 - 39..................	3 309	2 131	1 178	...	...	...	...	...	...
40 - 44..................	3 997	2 698	1 299	...	...	...	...	...	...
45 - 49..................	4 754	3 266	1 488	...	...	...	...	...	...
50 - 54..................	5 285	3 629	1 656	...	...	...	...	...	...
55 - 59..................	5 538	3 658	1 880	...	...	...	...	...	...
60 - 64..................	6 116	3 756	2 360	...	...	...	...	...	...
65 - 69..................	6 924	3 985	2 939	...	...	...	...	...	...
70 - 74..................	8 082	4 448	3 634	...	...	...	...	...	...
75 - 79..................	8 176	4 484	3 692	...	...	...	...	...	...
80 +....................	17 419	9 575	7 844	...	...	...	...	...	...
Singapore - Singapour									
2005 (+C)									
Total....................	16 215	8 963	7 252	...	...	...	...	...	...
0........................	95	57	38	...	...	...	...	...	...
1 - 4....................	39	22	17	...	...	...	...	...	...
5 - 9....................	31	13	18	...	...	...	...	...	...
10 - 14..................	31	15	16	...	...	...	...	...	...
15 - 19..................	70	47	23	...	...	...	...	...	...
20 - 24..................	141	95	46	...	...	...	...	...	...
25 - 29..................	136	94	42	...	...	...	...	...	...
30 - 34..................	204	130	74	...	...	...	...	...	...
35 - 39..................	287	190	97	...	...	...	...	...	...
40 - 44..................	426	271	155	...	...	...	...	...	...
45 - 49..................	654	418	236	...	...	...	...	...	...
50 - 54..................	938	605	333	...	...	...	...	...	...
55 - 59..................	1 185	788	397	...	...	...	...	...	...
60 - 64..................	1 155	710	445	...	...	...	...	...	...
65 - 69..................	1 709	1 103	606	...	...	...	...	...	...
70 - 74..................	1 978	1 160	818	...	...	...	...	...	...
75 - 79..................	2 174	1 159	1 015	...	...	...	...	...	...
80 - 84..................	2 034	1 001	1 033	...	...	...	...	...	...
85 +....................	2 919	1 078	1 841	...	...	...	...	...	...
Unknown - Inconnu.......	9	7	2	...	...	...	...	...	...
Sri Lanka									
1996 (+C)									
Total....................	122 161	79 784	42 377	60 131	39 546	20 585	62 030	40 238	21 792
0........................	5 879	3 271	2 608	5 062	2 816	2 246	817	455	362
1 - 4....................	1 237	667	570	805	432	373	432	235	197
5 - 9....................	924	514	410	551	301	250	373	213	160
10 - 14..................	990	550	440	562	292	270	428	258	170
15 - 19..................	3 320	2 487	833	1 512	1 015	497	1 808	1 472	336
20 - 24..................	6 180	5 241	939	2 828	2 279	549	3 352	2 962	390
25 - 29..................	5 875	4 966	909	2 557	2 041	516	3 318	2 925	393
30 - 34..................	4 712	3 875	837	2 177	1 673	504	2 535	2 202	333
35 - 39..................	4 838	3 793	1 045	2 467	1 853	614	2 371	1 940	431
40 - 44..................	4 607	3 585	1 022	2 650	2 048	602	1 957	1 537	420
45 - 49..................	5 819	4 309	1 510	3 514	2 649	865	2 305	1 660	645
50 - 54..................	6 387	4 511	1 876	3 883	2 806	1 077	2 504	1 705	799
55 - 59..................	6 904	4 867	2 037	4 015	2 896	1 119	2 889	1 971	918
60 - 64..................	8 431	5 529	2 902	4 598	3 143	1 455	3 833	2 386	1 447
65 - 69..................	10 699	6 751	3 948	5 491	3 530	1 961	5 208	3 221	1 987
70 - 74..................	12 549	7 424	5 125	5 884	3 538	2 346	6 665	3 886	2 779
75 - 79..................	10 704	6 080	4 624	4 489	2 569	1 920	6 215	3 511	2 704

Continent, country or area, date, code and age (in years) / Continent, pays ou zone, date, code et âge (en années)	Total			Urban - Urbaine			Rural - Rurale		
	Both sexes Les deux sexes	Male Masculin	Female Féminin	Both sexes Les deux sexes	Male Masculin	Female Féminin	Both sexes Les deux sexes	Male Masculin	Female Féminin
ASIA - ASIE									
Sri Lanka									
1996 (+C)									
80 - 84	10 071	5 404	4 667	3 609	1 950	1 659	6 462	3 454	3 008
85 + ...	12 035	5 960	6 075	3 477	1 715	1 762	8 558	4 245	4 313
2001 (+C)									
Total....................	112 858	70 646	42 212	...	...	...	...	...	...
0	4 519	2 576	1 943	...	...	...	...	...	...
1 - 4	919	493	426	...	...	...	...	...	...
5 - 14	1 436	825	611	...	...	...	...	...	...
15 - 24	4 706	3 395	1 311	...	...	...	...	...	...
25 - 34	5 593	4 345	1 248	...	...	...	...	...	...
35 - 44	7 977	6 261	1 716	...	...	...	...	...	...
45 - 54	12 524	9 239	3 285	...	...	...	...	...	...
55 - 64	15 854	10 890	4 964	...	...	...	...	...	...
65 - 74	23 552	14 220	9 332	...	...	...	...	...	...
75 + ...	35 778	18 402	17 376	...	...	...	...	...	...
Thailand - Thaïlande									
1999 (+U)									
Total....................	362 593	213 427	149 166	36 796	21 674	15 122	325 797	191 753	134 044
0	5 003	2 765	2 238	711	359	352	4 292	2 406	1 886
1 - 4	5 948	3 193	2 755	451	246	205	5 497	2 947	2 550
5 - 9	3 040	1 804	1 236	184	106	78	2 856	1 698	1 158
10 - 14	2 162	1 300	862	181	112	69	1 981	1 188	793
15 - 19	6 504	4 861	1 643	553	408	145	5 951	4 453	1 498
20 - 24	11 727	8 192	3 535	1 280	972	308	10 447	7 220	3 227
25 - 29	22 108	16 139	5 969	1 860	1 447	413	20 248	14 692	5 556
30 - 34	23 928	18 116	5 812	2 242	1 715	527	21 686	16 401	5 285
35 - 39	20 640	15 414	5 226	2 120	1 607	513	18 520	13 807	4 713
40 - 44	18 982	13 089	5 893	2 120	1 480	640	16 862	11 609	5 253
45 - 49	18 489	12 071	6 418	2 107	1 380	727	16 382	10 691	5 691
50 - 54	18 660	11 727	6 933	2 017	1 267	750	16 643	10 460	6 183
55 - 59	21 563	13 072	8 491	2 322	1 419	903	19 241	11 653	7 588
60 - 64	27 435	16 057	11 378	3 029	1 810	1 219	24 406	14 247	10 159
65 - 69	31 442	17 504	13 938	3 299	1 895	1 404	28 143	15 609	12 534
70 - 74	32 171	17 261	14 910	3 202	1 660	1 542	28 969	15 601	13 368
75 - 79	30 537	15 485	15 052	2 971	1 449	1 522	27 566	14 036	13 530
80 - 84	26 406	11 901	14 505	2 803	1 203	1 600	23 603	10 698	12 905
85 + ...	32 613	12 063	20 550	3 292	1 118	2 174	29 321	10 945	18 376
Unknown - Inconnu	3 235	1 413	1 822	52	21	31	3 183	1 392	1 791
2005 (+U)									
Total....................	395 374	225 622	169 752	...	...	...	...	...	...
0	6 183	3 450	2 733	...	...	...	...	...	...
1 - 4	2 536	1 453	1 083	...	...	...	...	...	...
5 - 9	2 419	1 472	947	...	...	...	...	...	...
10 - 14	2 492	1 529	963	...	...	...	...	...	...
15 - 19	6 287	4 957	1 330	...	...	...	...	...	...
20 - 24	8 297	6 475	1 822	...	...	...	...	...	...
25 - 29	11 749	8 344	3 405	...	...	...	...	...	...
30 - 34	15 442	10 951	4 491	...	...	...	...	...	...
35 - 39	18 012	12 832	5 180	...	...	...	...	...	...
40 - 44	20 102	14 078	6 024	...	...	...	...	...	...
45 - 49	22 061	14 915	7 146	...	...	...	...	...	...
50 - 54	24 397	15 701	8 696	...	...	...	...	...	...
55 - 59	25 976	15 856	10 120	...	...	...	...	...	...
60 - 64	28 431	16 649	11 782	...	...	...	...	...	...
65 - 69	36 414	20 539	15 875	...	...	...	...	...	...
70 - 74	41 607	22 090	19 517	...	...	...	...	...	...
75 - 79	42 417	21 262	21 155	...	...	...	...	...	...
80 - 84	35 484	16 111	19 373	...	...	...	...	...	...
85 + ...	43 689	16 454	27 235	...	...	...	...	...	...
Unknown - Inconnu	1 379	504	875	...	...	...	...	...	...
Uzbekistan - Ouzbékistan[22]									
2000 (C)									
Total....................	135 598	70 794	64 804	61 130	32 195	28 935	74 468	38 599	35 869
0	10 091	5 805	4 286	3 703	2 136	1 567	6 388	3 669	2 719

Continent, country or area, date, code and age (in years) / Continent, pays ou zone, date, code et âge (en annèes)	Total			Urban - Urbaine			Rural - Rurale		
	Both sexes Les deux sexes	Male Masculin	Female Féminin	Both sexes Les deux sexes	Male Masculin	Female Féminin	Both sexes Les deux sexes	Male Masculin	Female Féminin
ASIA - ASIE									
Uzbekistan - Ouzbékistan[22]									
2000 (C)									
1 - 4	5 417	2 925	2 492	1 177	645	532	4 240	2 280	1 960
5 - 9	1 474	886	588	423	251	172	1 051	635	416
10 - 14	1 436	852	584	442	260	182	994	592	402
15 - 19	2 001	1 289	712	709	475	234	1 292	814	478
20 - 24	2 849	1 758	1 091	1 155	789	366	1 694	969	725
25 - 29	3 427	2 177	1 250	1 501	1 023	478	1 926	1 154	772
30 - 34	3 660	2 403	1 257	1 657	1 185	472	2 003	1 218	785
35 - 39	4 181	2 759	1 422	1 993	1 407	586	2 188	1 352	836
40 - 44	5 086	3 277	1 809	2 584	1 789	795	2 502	1 488	1 014
45 - 49	5 290	3 445	1 845	2 797	1 924	873	2 493	1 521	972
50 - 54	5 765	3 647	2 118	3 140	2 052	1 088	2 625	1 595	1 030
55 - 59	6 104	3 794	2 310	3 056	1 990	1 066	3 048	1 804	1 244
60 - 64	12 287	7 257	5 030	5 897	3 603	2 294	6 390	3 654	2 736
65 - 69	14 077	7 757	6 320	6 312	3 601	2 711	7 765	4 156	3 609
70 - 74	17 094	8 713	8 381	8 142	4 010	4 132	8 952	4 703	4 249
75 - 79	12 547	4 824	7 723	6 043	2 111	3 932	6 504	2 713	3 791
80 - 84	8 807	2 836	5 971	4 430	1 285	3 145	4 377	1 551	2 826
85 - 89	7 198	2 312	4 886	3 747	1 011	2 736	3 451	1 301	2 150
90 - 94	3 782	1 295	2 487	1 515	421	1 094	2 267	874	1 393
95 - 99	1 963	579	1 384	511	167	344	1 452	412	1 040
100 +	1 062	204	858	196	60	136	866	144	722
EUROPE									
Albania - Albanie									
2004 (C)									
Total	17 749	9 950	7 799	9 248	5 267	3 981	8 501	4 683	3 818
0	336	181	155	124	67	57	212	114	98
1 - 4	237	132	105	76	43	33	161	89	72
5 - 9	164	108	56	51	35	16	113	73	40
10 - 14	140	86	54	49	32	17	91	54	37
15 - 19	157	106	51	65	50	15	92	56	36
20 - 24	219	147	72	96	66	30	123	81	42
25 - 29	181	140	41	94	71	23	87	69	18
30 - 34	225	159	66	112	83	29	113	76	37
35 - 39	244	160	84	128	86	42	116	74	42
40 - 44	365	249	116	223	153	70	142	96	46
45 - 49	469	313	156	277	183	94	192	130	62
50 - 54	586	397	189	366	245	121	220	152	68
55 - 59	676	451	225	386	261	125	290	190	100
60 - 64	1 248	820	428	706	458	248	542	362	180
65 - 69	1 720	1 158	562	973	658	315	747	500	247
70 - 74	2 428	1 478	950	1 328	811	517	1 100	667	433
75 - 79	2 608	1 462	1 146	1 429	801	628	1 179	661	518
80 - 84	2 768	1 256	1 512	1 419	641	778	1 349	615	734
85 - 89	1 652	719	933	750	325	425	902	394	508
90 - 94	936	298	638	430	140	290	506	158	348
95 - 99	300	103	197	127	43	84	173	60	113
100 +	90	27	63	39	15	24	51	12	39
Andorra - Andorre									
2005 (C)									
Total	276	157	119	...	...	...	...	...	...
0	5	3	2	...	...	...	...	...	...
1 - 4	2	1	1	...	...	...	...	...	...
5 - 9	-	-	-	...	...	...	...	...	...
10 - 14	-	-	-	...	...	...	...	...	...
15 - 19	1	1	-	...	...	...	...	...	...
20 - 24	1	1	-	...	...	...	...	...	...
25 - 29	1	1	-	...	...	...	...	...	...
30 - 34	3	3	-	...	...	...	...	...	...
35 - 39	3	3	-	...	...	...	...	...	...
40 - 44	3	-	3	...	...	...	...	...	...

19. Deaths by age, sex and urban/rural residence: latest available year, 1996 - 2005
Décès selon l'âge, le sexe et la résidence, urbaine/rurale: dernière année disponible, 1996 - 2005 (continued - suite)

Continent, country or area, date, code and age (in years) / Continent, pays ou zone, date, code et âge (en années)	Total			Urban - Urbaine			Rural - Rurale		
	Both sexes Les deux sexes	Male Masculin	Female Féminin	Both sexes Les deux sexes	Male Masculin	Female Féminin	Both sexes Les deux sexes	Male Masculin	Female Féminin
EUROPE									
Andorra - Andorre									
2005 (C)									
45 - 49	7	6	1	...	...	...	...	...	...
50 - 54	6	5	1	...	...	...	...	...	...
55 - 59	19	14	5	...	...	...	...	...	...
60 - 64	17	12	5	...	...	...	...	...	...
65 - 69	13	9	4	...	...	...	...	...	...
70 - 74	31	19	12	...	...	...	...	...	...
75 - 79	20	14	6	...	...	...	...	...	...
80 - 84	46	25	21	...	...	...	...	...	...
85 - 89	49	20	29	...	...	...	...	...	...
90 - 94	36	15	21	...	...	...	...	...	...
95 - 99	12	4	8	...	...	...	...	...	...
100 +	1	1	-	...	...	...	...	...	...
Austria - Autriche									
1999 (C)									
Total	78 200	35 880	42 320	46 752	20 596	26 156	31 448	15 284	16 164
0	341	176	165	191	100	91	150	76	74
1 - 4	98	67	31	51	37	14	47	30	17
5 - 9	51	28	23	25	11	14	26	17	9
10 - 14	72	36	36	38	17	21	34	19	15
15 - 19	276	197	79	116	78	38	160	119	41
20 - 24	330	257	73	177	136	41	153	121	32
25 - 29	348	251	97	183	132	51	165	119	46
30 - 34	512	352	160	313	201	112	199	151	48
35 - 39	806	550	256	472	324	148	334	226	108
40 - 44	1 075	714	361	621	406	215	454	308	146
45 - 49	1 433	922	511	848	523	325	585	399	186
50 - 54	2 251	1 468	783	1 425	916	509	826	552	274
55 - 59	3 554	2 373	1 181	2 238	1 464	774	1 316	909	407
60 - 64	3 939	2 654	1 285	2 194	1 461	733	1 745	1 193	552
65 - 69	6 004	3 939	2 065	3 267	2 091	1 176	2 737	1 848	889
70 - 74	8 963	5 084	3 879	5 131	2 793	2 338	3 832	2 291	1 541
75 - 79	12 409	5 726	6 683	7 297	3 256	4 041	5 112	2 470	2 642
80 - 84	10 218	3 965	6 253	6 134	2 373	3 761	4 084	1 592	2 492
85 +	25 520	7 121	18 399	16 031	4 277	11 754	9 489	2 844	6 645
2005 (C)									
Total	75 189	34 986	40 203	...	...	...	...	...	...
0	327	175	152	...	...	...	...	...	...
1 - 4	68	34	34	...	...	...	...	...	...
5 - 9	56	33	23	...	...	...	...	...	...
10 - 14	56	35	21	...	...	...	...	...	...
15 - 19	239	178	61	...	...	...	...	...	...
20 - 24	315	237	78	...	...	...	...	...	...
25 - 29	283	209	74	...	...	...	...	...	...
30 - 34	362	260	102	...	...	...	...	...	...
35 - 39	639	425	214	...	...	...	...	...	...
40 - 44	951	634	317	...	...	...	...	...	...
45 - 49	1 437	924	513	...	...	...	...	...	...
50 - 54	2 024	1 352	672	...	...	...	...	...	...
55 - 59	3 130	2 089	1 041	...	...	...	...	...	...
60 - 64	4 362	2 901	1 461	...	...	...	...	...	...
65 - 69	5 247	3 407	1 840	...	...	...	...	...	...
70 - 74	6 989	4 213	2 776	...	...	...	...	...	...
75 - 79	10 760	5 614	5 146	...	...	...	...	...	...
80 - 84	15 311	5 948	9 363	...	...	...	...	...	...
85 - 89	10 035	3 234	6 801	...	...	...	...	...	...
90 - 94	9 367	2 468	6 899	...	...	...	...	...	...
95 - 99	2 846	560	2 286	...	...	...	...	...	...
100 +	385	56	329	...	...	...	...	...	...
Belarus - Bélarus[22]									
2005 (C)									
Total	141 857	75 532	66 325	76 452	42 341	34 111	65 405	33 191	32 214
0	640	389	251	398	238	160	242	151	91
1 - 4	197	108	89	98	50	48	99	58	41

19. Deaths by age, sex and urban/rural residence: latest available year, 1996 - 2005
Décès selon l'âge, le sexe et la résidence, urbaine/rurale: dernière année disponible, 1996 - 2005 (continued - suite)

Continent, country or area, date, code and age (in years) / Continent, pays ou zone, date, code et âge (en années)	Total			Urban - Urbaine			Rural - Rurale		
	Both sexes Les deux sexes	Male Masculin	Female Féminin	Both sexes Les deux sexes	Male Masculin	Female Féminin	Both sexes Les deux sexes	Male Masculin	Female Féminin
EUROPE									
Belarus - Bélarus[22]									
2005 (C)									
5 - 9	122	85	37	66	46	20	56	39	17
10 - 14	138	91	47	86	63	23	52	28	24
15 - 19	549	411	138	321	235	86	228	176	52
20 - 24	1 141	908	233	725	563	162	416	345	71
25 - 29	1 601	1 282	319	999	792	207	602	490	112
30 - 34	2 250	1 775	475	1 368	1 058	310	882	717	165
35 - 39	2 931	2 334	597	1 669	1 294	375	1 262	1 040	222
40 - 44	4 744	3 717	1 027	2 900	2 167	733	1 844	1 550	294
45 - 49	7 022	5 381	1 641	4 413	3 286	1 127	2 609	2 095	514
50 - 54	8 394	6 265	2 129	5 516	4 047	1 469	2 878	2 218	660
55 - 59	9 486	6 642	2 844	6 316	4 383	1 933	3 170	2 259	911
60 - 64	9 984	6 802	3 182	6 001	4 120	1 881	3 983	2 682	1 301
65 - 69	16 946	10 520	6 426	9 500	5 902	3 598	7 446	4 618	2 828
70 - 74	18 484	9 896	8 588	8 989	4 746	4 243	9 495	5 150	4 345
75 - 79	23 205	9 952	13 253	11 308	4 938	6 370	11 897	5 014	6 883
80 - 84	17 794	5 260	12 534	8 430	2 534	5 896	9 364	2 726	6 638
85 - 89	8 561	2 081	6 480	4 147	1 079	3 068	4 414	1 002	3 412
90 - 94	5 527	1 120	4 407	2 307	519	1 788	3 220	601	2 619
95 - 99	1 598	313	1 285	627	132	495	971	181	790
100 +	367	55	312	111	20	91	256	35	221
Unknown - Inconnu	176	145	31	157	129	28	19	16	3
Belgium - Belgique[34]									
2002 (C)									
Total	105 642	52 436	53 206	...	...	...	...	...	...
0	492	288	204	...	...	...	...	...	...
1 - 4	127	74	53	...	...	...	...	...	...
5 - 9	87	53	34	...	...	...	...	...	...
10 - 14	88	46	42	...	...	...	...	...	...
15 - 19	282	200	82	...	...	...	...	...	...
20 - 24	450	348	102	...	...	...	...	...	...
25 - 29	498	361	137	...	...	...	...	...	...
30 - 34	595	406	189	...	...	...	...	...	...
35 - 39	921	610	311	...	...	...	...	...	...
40 - 44	1 400	905	495	...	...	...	...	...	...
45 - 49	2 239	1 462	777	...	...	...	...	...	...
50 - 54	3 232	2 062	1 170	...	...	...	...	...	...
55 - 59	4 095	2 683	1 412	...	...	...	...	...	...
60 - 64	5 057	3 291	1 766	...	...	...	...	...	...
65 - 69	7 919	5 125	2 794	...	...	...	...	...	...
70 - 74	12 038	7 409	4 629	...	...	...	...	...	...
75 - 79	17 080	9 516	7 564	...	...	...	...	...	...
80 - 84	17 439	8 112	9 327	...	...	...	...	...	...
85 - 89	15 974	5 672	10 302	...	...	...	...	...	...
90 - 94	11 457	3 021	8 436	...	...	...	...	...	...
95 - 99	3 645	718	2 927	...	...	...	...	...	...
100 +	527	74	453	...	...	...	...	...	...
Bosnia and Herzegovina - Bosnie-Herzégovine									
2004 (C)									
Total	31 825	16 373	15 452	...	...	...	...	...	...
0	253	151	102	...	...	...	...	...	...
1 - 4	39	24	15	...	...	...	...	...	...
5 - 9	29	16	13	...	...	...	...	...	...
10 - 14	27	15	12	...	...	...	...	...	...
15 - 19	105	74	31	...	...	...	...	...	...
20 - 24	144	100	44	...	...	...	...	...	...
25 - 29	152	114	38	...	...	...	...	...	...
30 - 34	205	135	70	...	...	...	...	...	...
35 - 39	304	207	97	...	...	...	...	...	...
40 - 44	565	378	187	...	...	...	...	...	...
45 - 49	1 044	677	367	...	...	...	...	...	...
50 - 54	1 393	910	483	...	...	...	...	...	...
55 - 59	1 714	1 121	593	...	...	...	...	...	...

19. Deaths by age, sex and urban/rural residence: latest available year, 1996 - 2005
Décès selon l'âge, le sexe et la résidence, urbaine/rurale: dernière année disponible, 1996 - 2005 (continued - suite)

Continent, country or area, date, code and age (in years) / Continent, pays ou zone, date, code et âge (en années)	Total			Urban - Urbaine			Rural - Rurale		
	Both sexes Les deux sexes	Male Masculin	Female Féminin	Both sexes Les deux sexes	Male Masculin	Female Féminin	Both sexes Les deux sexes	Male Masculin	Female Féminin
EUROPE									
Bosnia and Herzegovina - Bosnie-Herzégovine									
2004 (C)									
60 - 64	2 711	1 637	1 074	...	...	...	...	...	...
65 - 69	4 692	2 678	2 014	...	...	...	...	...	...
70 - 74	6 125	3 243	2 882	...	...	...	...	...	...
75 - 79	5 738	2 598	3 140	...	...	...	...	...	...
80 - 84	4 079	1 489	2 590	...	...	...	...	...	...
85 - 89	1 366	422	944	...	...	...	...	...	...
90 - 94	907	310	597	...	...	...	...	...	...
95 - 99	176	50	126	...	...	...	...	...	...
100 +	26	5	21	...	...	...	...	...	...
Unknown - Inconnu	31	19	12	...	...	...	...	...	...
Bulgaria - Bulgarie									
2005 (C)									
Total	113 374	60 761	52 613	65 309	35 164	30 145	48 065	25 597	22 468
0	739	429	310	464	271	193	275	158	117
1 - 4	149	91	58	94	59	35	55	32	23
5 - 9	93	52	41	55	31	24	38	21	17
10 - 14	124	75	49	81	48	33	43	27	16
15 - 19	226	135	91	155	88	67	71	47	24
20 - 24	396	290	106	280	204	76	116	86	30
25 - 29	503	354	149	372	268	104	131	86	45
30 - 34	630	444	186	466	328	138	164	116	48
35 - 39	967	659	308	656	438	218	311	221	90
40 - 44	1 617	1 139	478	1 110	775	335	507	364	143
45 - 49	2 873	1 987	886	1 997	1 340	657	876	647	229
50 - 54	4 580	3 313	1 267	3 121	2 206	915	1 459	1 107	352
55 - 59	6 936	4 984	1 952	4 671	3 308	1 363	2 265	1 676	589
60 - 64	8 025	5 418	2 607	4 940	3 271	1 669	3 085	2 147	938
65 - 69	10 842	6 801	4 041	6 337	3 961	2 376	4 505	2 840	1 665
70 - 74	16 755	9 344	7 411	9 270	5 069	4 201	7 485	4 275	3 210
75 - 79	21 018	10 202	10 816	11 680	5 611	6 069	9 338	4 591	4 747
80 - 84	21 344	9 155	12 189	11 438	4 838	6 600	9 906	4 317	5 589
85 - 89	9 444	3 762	5 682	5 038	1 973	3 065	4 406	1 789	2 617
90 - 94	5 101	1 803	3 298	2 573	911	1 662	2 528	892	1 636
95 - 99	917	298	619	460	151	309	457	147	310
100 +	95	26	69	51	15	36	44	11	33
Channel Islands: Guernsey - Îles Anglo-Normandes: Guernesey									
2000 (C)									
Total	565	264	301	...	...	...	...	...	...
0	4	3	1	...	...	...	...	...	...
1 - 4	1	-	1	...	...	...	...	...	...
15 - 19	4	3	1	...	...	...	...	...	...
20 - 24	1	-	1	...	...	...	...	...	...
25 - 29	1	1	-	...	...	...	...	...	...
30 - 34	2	1	1	...	...	...	...	...	...
35 - 39	2	2	-	...	...	...	...	...	...
40 - 44	4	4	-	...	...	...	...	...	...
45 - 49	7	5	2	...	...	...	...	...	...
50 - 54	13	9	4	...	...	...	...	...	...
55 - 59	13	7	6	...	...	...	...	...	...
60 - 64	30	15	15	...	...	...	...	...	...
65 - 69	45	29	16	...	...	...	...	...	...
70 - 74	57	27	30	...	...	...	...	...	...
75 - 79	71	38	33	...	...	...	...	...	...
80 - 84	103	55	48	...	...	...	...	...	...
85 - 89	108	45	63	...	...	...	...	...	...
90 - 94	68	14	54	...	...	...	...	...	...
95 - 99	24	3	21	...	...	...	...	...	...
100 +	5	2	3	...	...	...	...	...	...
Unknown - Inconnu	2	1	1	...	...	...	...	...	...

Continent, country or area, date, code and age (in years) / Continent, pays ou zone, date, code et âge (en années)	Total			Urban - Urbaine			Rural - Rurale		
	Both sexes Les deux sexes	Male Masculin	Female Féminin	Both sexes Les deux sexes	Male Masculin	Female Féminin	Both sexes Les deux sexes	Male Masculin	Female Féminin
EUROPE									
Croatia - Croatie									
2005 (C)									
Total	51 790	26 066	25 724	25 899	13 040	12 859	25 891	13 026	12 865
0	242	125	117	151	73	78	91	52	39
1 - 4	38	24	14	20	12	8	18	12	6
5 - 9	31	21	10	11	6	5	20	15	5
10 - 14	35	23	12	13	9	4	22	14	8
15 - 19	144	103	41	69	49	20	75	54	21
20 - 24	181	144	37	91	71	20	90	73	17
25 - 29	235	190	45	139	109	30	96	81	15
30 - 34	250	190	60	146	110	36	104	80	24
35 - 39	367	256	111	181	118	63	186	138	48
40 - 44	636	457	179	306	210	96	330	247	83
45 - 49	1 235	874	361	614	401	213	621	473	148
50 - 54	2 022	1 470	552	1 038	720	318	984	750	234
55 - 59	2 468	1 792	676	1 351	959	392	1 117	833	284
60 - 64	3 242	2 229	1 013	1 731	1 159	572	1 511	1 070	441
65 - 69	5 449	3 514	1 935	2 830	1 812	1 018	2 619	1 702	917
70 - 74	8 006	4 587	3 419	3 881	2 226	1 655	4 125	2 361	1 764
75 - 79	9 419	4 405	5 014	4 503	2 115	2 388	4 916	2 290	2 626
80 - 84	9 508	3 265	6 243	4 655	1 608	3 047	4 853	1 657	3 196
85 - 89	4 293	1 323	2 970	2 149	701	1 448	2 144	622	1 522
90 - 94	3 113	876	2 237	1 563	469	1 094	1 550	407	1 143
95 - 99	800	183	617	410	94	316	390	89	301
100 +	64	7	57	41	6	35	23	1	22
Unknown - Inconnu	12	8	4	6	3	3	6	5	1
Czech Republic - République tchèque									
2005 (C)									
Total	107 938	54 072	53 866	78 141	38 724	39 417	29 797	15 348	14 449
0	347	211	136	261	166	95	86	45	41
1 - 4	69	34	35	46	25	21	23	9	14
5 - 9	57	32	25	38	24	14	19	8	11
10 - 14	107	56	51	67	37	30	40	19	21
15 - 19	274	188	86	181	119	62	93	69	24
20 - 24	434	345	89	303	234	69	131	111	20
25 - 29	556	420	136	403	306	97	153	114	39
30 - 34	697	512	185	489	358	131	208	154	54
35 - 39	798	562	236	577	409	168	221	153	68
40 - 44	1 274	883	391	913	606	307	361	277	84
45 - 49	2 486	1 704	782	1 823	1 230	593	663	474	189
50 - 54	4 458	3 086	1 372	3 236	2 199	1 037	1 222	887	335
55 - 59	7 089	4 878	2 211	5 192	3 516	1 676	1 897	1 362	535
60 - 64	8 192	5 489	2 703	6 043	3 957	2 086	2 149	1 532	617
65 - 69	8 856	5 538	3 318	6 431	3 964	2 467	2 425	1 574	851
70 - 74	12 913	7 292	5 621	9 303	5 151	4 152	3 610	2 141	1 469
75 - 79	18 111	8 712	9 399	13 024	6 186	6 838	5 087	2 526	2 561
80 - 84	21 094	8 265	12 829	15 275	6 017	9 258	5 819	2 248	3 571
85 - 89	10 071	3 324	6 747	7 285	2 413	4 872	2 786	911	1 875
90 - 94	8 022	2 086	5 936	5 778	1 498	4 280	2 244	588	1 656
95 - 99	1 851	423	1 428	1 335	284	1 051	516	139	377
100 +	182	32	150	138	25	113	44	7	37
Denmark - Danemark[35]									
2004 (C)									
Total	55 806	27 497	28 309	...	...	...	...	...	...
0	283	153	130	...	...	...	...	...	...
1 - 4	61	27	34	...	...	...	...	...	...
5 - 9	34	20	14	...	...	...	...	...	...
10 - 14	52	37	15	...	...	...	...	...	...
15 - 19	105	73	32	...	...	...	...	...	...
20 - 24	161	115	46	...	...	...	...	...	...
25 - 29	171	124	47	...	...	...	...	...	...
30 - 34	278	200	78	...	...	...	...	...	...
35 - 39	469	317	152	...	...	...	...	...	...
40 - 44	707	454	253	...	...	...	...	...	...

19. Deaths by age, sex and urban/rural residence: latest available year, 1996 - 2005
Décès selon l'âge, le sexe et la résidence, urbaine/rurale: dernière année disponible, 1996 - 2005 (continued - suite)

Continent, country or area, date, code and age (in years) / Continent, pays ou zone, date, code et âge (en années)	Total			Urban - Urbaine			Rural - Rurale		
	Both sexes Les deux sexes	Male Masculin	Female Féminin	Both sexes Les deux sexes	Male Masculin	Female Féminin	Both sexes Les deux sexes	Male Masculin	Female Féminin
EUROPE									
Denmark - Danemark[35]									
2004 (C)									
45 - 49	1 126	698	428	...	...	...	...	...	...
50 - 54	1 774	1 099	675	...	...	...	...	...	...
55 - 59	2 788	1 705	1 083	...	...	...	...	...	...
60 - 64	3 555	2 189	1 366	...	...	...	...	...	...
65 - 69	4 278	2 491	1 787	...	...	...	...	...	...
70 - 74	5 865	3 253	2 612	...	...	...	...	...	...
75 - 79	7 823	4 202	3 621	...	...	...	...	...	...
80 - 84	9 610	4 598	5 012	...	...	...	...	...	...
85 - 89	8 397	3 386	5 011	...	...	...	...	...	...
90 - 94	5 945	1 844	4 101	...	...	...	...	...	...
95 - 99	2 023	455	1 568	...	...	...	...	...	...
100 +	301	57	244	...	...	...	...	...	...
Estonia - Estonie									
2005 (C)									
Total	17 316	8 834	8 482	11 053[4]	5 593[4]	5 460[4]	6 262[4]	3 240[4]	3 022[4]
0	78	43	35	51	32	19	27	11	16
1 - 4	24	10	14	15	6	9	9	4	5
5 - 9	18	11	7	11	6	5	7	5	2
10 - 14	13	7	6	5	3	2	8	4	4
15 - 19	65	47	18	43	28	15	22	19	3
20 - 24	126	100	26	92	75	17	34	25	9
25 - 29	145	127	18	106	92	14	39	35	4
30 - 34	157	117	40	113	82	31	44	35	9
35 - 39	227	172	55	163	121	42	64	51	13
40 - 44	398	301	97	264	197	67	134	104	30
45 - 49	609	450	159	408	281	127	201	169	32
50 - 54	911	657	254	626	440	186	285	217	68
55 - 59	1 096	756	340	720[4]	496[4]	224[4]	375[4]	259[4]	116[4]
60 - 64	1 227	873	354	732	487	245	495	386	109
65 - 69	1 815	1 176	639	1 132	711	421	683	465	218
70 - 74	2 132	1 225	907	1 365	770	595	767	455	312
75 - 79	2 675	1 243	1 432	1 828	843	985	847	400	447
80 - 84	2 421	734	1 687	1 496	434	1 062	925	300	625
85 - 89	1 542	416	1 126	918	262	656	624	154	470
90 - 94	1 213	259	954	710	148	562	503	111	392
95 - 99	331	57	274	184	31	153	147	26	121
100 +	45	11	34	23	6	17	22	5	17
Unknown - Inconnu	48	42	6	48	42	6	-	-	-
Finland - Finlande[36]									
2005 (C)									
Total	47 928	24 057	23 871	27 009	13 261	13 748	20 919	10 796	10 123
0	174	95	79	103	52	51	71	43	28
1 - 4	65	40	25	42	26	16	23	14	9
5 - 9	65	35	30	44	21	23	21	14	7
10 - 14	54	28	26	34	19	15	20	9	11
15 - 19	127	81	46	75	44	31	52	37	15
20 - 24	205	151	54	137	95	42	68	56	12
25 - 29	206	156	50	150	117	33	56	39	17
30 - 34	272	197	75	193	136	57	79	61	18
35 - 39	473	332	141	305	207	98	168	125	43
40 - 44	755	540	215	482	342	140	273	198	75
45 - 49	1 233	848	385	761	521	240	472	327	145
50 - 54	1 989	1 373	616	1 194	811	383	795	562	233
55 - 59	3 023	2 097	926	1 856	1 240	616	1 167	857	310
60 - 64	2 818	1 940	878	1 694	1 158	536	1 124	782	342
65 - 69	3 419	2 302	1 117	1 928	1 265	663	1 491	1 037	454
70 - 74	4 613	2 796	1 817	2 574	1 476	1 098	2 039	1 320	719
75 - 79	6 781	3 795	2 986	3 718	2 004	1 714	3 063	1 791	1 272
80 - 84	8 242	3 488	4 754	4 370	1 807	2 563	3 872	1 681	2 191
85 - 89	6 935	2 181	4 754	3 764	1 102	2 662	3 171	1 079	2 092
90 - 94	4 829	1 260	3 569	2 660	647	2 013	2 169	613	1 556
95 - 99	1 453	298	1 155	814	158	656	639	140	499
100 +	197	24	173	111	13	98	86	11	75

Continent, country or area, date, code and age (in years) Continent, pays ou zone, date, code et âge (en années)	Total			Urban - Urbaine			Rural - Rurale		
	Both sexes Les deux sexes	Male Masculin	Female Féminin	Both sexes Les deux sexes	Male Masculin	Female Féminin	Both sexes Les deux sexes	Male Masculin	Female Féminin
EUROPE									
France[37]									
2004 (C)									
Total	509 429	263 087	246 342	360 779	182 597	178 182	146 823	79 291	67 532
0	2 988	1 683	1 305	2 321	1 309	1 012	633	355	278
1 - 4	636	386	250	478	294	184	144	85	59
5 - 9	346	193	153	257	144	113	79	42	37
10 - 14	454	271	183	301	177	124	141	85	56
15 - 19	1 525	1 087	438	945	652	293	548	415	133
20 - 24	2 323	1 768	555	1 605	1 218	387	675	520	155
25 - 29	2 264	1 669	595	1 652	1 196	456	564	435	129
30 - 34	3 365	2 362	1 003	2 474	1 728	746	841	603	238
35 - 39	5 138	3 446	1 692	3 803	2 535	1 268	1 252	846	406
40 - 44	8 374	5 531	2 843	6 175	4 070	2 105	2 092	1 389	703
45 - 49	13 054	8 842	4 212	9 656	6 486	3 170	3 284	2 281	1 003
50 - 54	19 238	13 178	6 060	14 154	9 648	4 506	4 928	3 434	1 494
55 - 59	23 540	16 350	7 190	17 105	11 732	5 373	6 280	4 517	1 763
60 - 64	23 180	15 960	7 220	16 536	11 215	5 321	6 451	4 608	1 843
65 - 69	32 432	21 814	10 618	22 744	15 022	7 722	9 494	6 650	2 844
70 - 74	49 837	31 618	18 219	34 618	21 539	13 079	15 042	9 953	5 089
75 - 79	69 374	40 220	29 154	48 083	27 201	20 882	21 131	12 920	8 211
80 - 84	92 103	45 818	46 285	64 202	31 107	33 095	27 781	14 637	13 144
85 - 89	58 830	23 479	35 351	42 257	16 502	25 755	16 506	6 943	9 563
90 - 94	69 200	21 055	48 145	48 853	14 446	34 407	20 304	6 595	13 709
95 - 99	26 504	5 671	20 833	19 066	3 890	15 176	7 424	1 779	5 645
100 +	4 724	686	4 038	3 494	486	3 008	1 229	199	1 030
Germany - Allemagne									
2004 (C)									
Total	818 271	383 388	434 883	...	...	...	...	...	...
0	2 464	1 379	1 085	...	...	...	...	...	...
1 - 4	1 021	551	470	...	...	...	...	...	...
5 - 9	398	222	176	...	...	...	...	...	...
10 - 14	430	260	170	...	...	...	...	...	...
15 - 19	1 524	1 044	480	...	...	...	...	...	...
20 - 24	2 371	1 732	639	...	...	...	...	...	...
25 - 29	2 284	1 648	636	...	...	...	...	...	...
30 - 34	3 028	2 123	905	...	...	...	...	...	...
35 - 39	5 993	4 088	1 905	...	...	...	...	...	...
40 - 44	10 767	7 331	3 436	...	...	...	...	...	...
45 - 49	16 104	10 605	5 499	...	...	...	...	...	...
50 - 54	23 124	15 310	7 814	...	...	...	...	...	...
55 - 59	27 625	18 193	9 432	...	...	...	...	...	...
60 - 64	48 438	32 496	15 942	...	...	...	...	...	...
65 - 69	73 812	48 563	25 249	...	...	...	...	...	...
70 - 74	86 326	53 234	33 092	...	...	...	...	...	...
75 - 79	118 996	62 965	56 031	...	...	...	...	...	...
80 - 84	148 184	57 806	90 378	...	...	...	...	...	...
85 - 89	98 048	30 618	67 430	...	...	...	...	...	...
90 - 94	106 282	25 802	80 480	...	...	...	...	...	...
95 - 99	35 990	6 740	29 250	...	...	...	...	...	...
100 +	5 062	678	4 384	...	...	...	...	...	...
Greece - Grèce									
2005 (C)									
Total	105 091	55 435	49 656	58 022	30 215	27 807	47 069	25 220	21 849
0	409	220	189	302	164	138	107	56	51
1 - 4	84	41	43	57	29	28	27	12	15
5 - 9	88	48	40	60	32	28	28	16	12
10 - 14	90	51	39	57	31	26	33	20	13
15 - 19	259	197	62	144	112	32	115	85	30
20 - 24	577	468	109	409	327	82	168	141	27
25 - 29	652	501	151	436	339	97	216	162	54
30 - 34	618	449	169	422	309	113	196	140	56
35 - 39	875	621	254	580	401	179	295	220	75
40 - 44	1 116	741	375	748	476	272	368	265	103
45 - 49	1 730	1 184	546	1 119	739	380	611	445	166
50 - 54	2 561	1 787	774	1 693	1 135	558	868	652	216

19. Deaths by age, sex and urban/rural residence: latest available year, 1996 - 2005
Décès selon l'âge, le sexe et la résidence, urbaine/rurale: dernière année disponible, 1996 - 2005 (continued - suite)

Continent, country or area, date, code and age (in years) / Continent, pays ou zone, date, code et âge (en années)	Total			Urban - Urbaine			Rural - Rurale		
	Both sexes Les deux sexes	Male Masculin	Female Féminin	Both sexes Les deux sexes	Male Masculin	Female Féminin	Both sexes Les deux sexes	Male Masculin	Female Féminin
EUROPE									
Greece - Grèce									
2005 (C)									
55 - 59	3 771	2 664	1 107	2 437	1 690	747	1 334	974	360
60 - 64	4 360	3 042	1 318	2 608	1 795	813	1 752	1 247	505
65 - 69	7 631	5 076	2 555	4 284	2 837	1 447	3 347	2 239	1 108
70 - 74	12 509	7 740	4 769	6 809	4 133	2 676	5 700	3 607	2 093
75 - 79	18 604	10 091	8 513	10 350	5 400	4 950	8 254	4 691	3 563
80 - 84	18 731	8 700	10 031	10 204	4 550	5 654	8 527	4 150	4 377
85 - 89	15 349	6 233	9 116	8 136	3 157	4 979	7 213	3 076	4 137
90 - 94	11 022	4 218	6 804	5 381	2 007	3 374	5 641	2 211	3 430
95 - 99	3 437	1 191	2 246	1 542	481	1 061	1 895	710	1 185
100 +	618	172	446	244	71	173	374	101	273
Hungary - Hongrie									
2005 (C)									
Total	135 732	69 781	65 951	85 546[38]	42 914[38]	42 632[38]	49 479[38]	26 337[38]	23 142[38]
0	607	354	253	369[38]	219[38]	150[38]	228[38]	130[38]	98[38]
1 - 4	123	73	50	73[38]	43[38]	30[38]	48[38]	29[38]	19[38]
5 - 9	80	47	33	40[38]	23[38]	17[38]	37[38]	22[38]	15[38]
10 - 14	76	43	33	40[38]	19[38]	21[38]	36[38]	24[38]	12[38]
15 - 19	253	168	85	155[38]	101[38]	54[38]	93[38]	64[38]	29[38]
20 - 24	372	281	91	193[38]	153[38]	40[38]	156[38]	112[38]	44[38]
25 - 29	620	459	161	376[38]	268[38]	108[38]	210[38]	166[38]	44[38]
30 - 34	739	530	209	436[38]	310[38]	126[38]	282[38]	202[38]	80[38]
35 - 39	1 350	944	406	788[38]	532[38]	256[38]	532[38]	389[38]	143[38]
40 - 44	2 381	1 679	702	1 325[38]	917[38]	408[38]	1 007[38]	724[38]	283[38]
45 - 49	5 171	3 724	1 447	2 975[38]	2 075[38]	900[38]	2 129[38]	1 592[38]	537[38]
50 - 54	8 212	5 779	2 433	5 040[38]	3 406[38]	1 634[38]	3 074[38]	2 288[38]	786[38]
55 - 59	9 008	6 239	2 769	5 617[38]	3 831[38]	1 786[38]	3 309[38]	2 343[38]	966[38]
60 - 64	10 667	7 146	3 521	6 678[38]	4 386[38]	2 292[38]	3 918[38]	2 701[38]	1 217[38]
65 - 69	12 533	7 564	4 969	7 738[38]	4 554[38]	3 184[38]	4 751[38]	2 976[38]	1 775[38]
70 - 74	16 763	9 106	7 657	10 527[38]	5 674[38]	4 853[38]	6 189[38]	3 401[38]	2 788[38]
75 - 79	21 216	9 872	11 344	13 278[38]	6 197[38]	7 081[38]	7 894[38]	3 649[38]	4 245[38]
80 - 84	22 977	8 916	14 061	14 548[38]	5 549[38]	8 999[38]	8 390[38]	3 347[38]	5 043[38]
85 - 89	11 812	3 934	7 878	7 890[38]	2 635[38]	5 255[38]	3 908[38]	1 293[38]	2 615[38]
90 - 94	8 484	2 362	6 122	5 810[38]	1 630[38]	4 180[38]	2 662[38]	726[38]	1 936[38]
95 - 99	2 045	502	1 543	1 481[38]	355[38]	1 126[38]	561[38]	145[38]	416[38]
100 +	234	51	183	169[38]	37[38]	132[38]	65[38]	14[38]	51[38]
Unknown - inconnu	9	8	1	-[38]	-[38]	-[38]	-[38]	-[38]	-[38]
Iceland - Islande									
2005 (C)									
Total	1 838	945	893	1 693	855	838	145	90	55
0	10	6	4	10	6	4	-	-	-
1 - 4	3	2	1	3	2	1	-	-	-
5 - 9	1	-	1	1	-	1	-	-	-
10 - 14	1	-	1	1	-	1	-	-	-
15 - 19	11	9	2	10	8	2	1	1	-
20 - 24	10	8	2	9	7	2	1	1	-
25 - 29	6	5	1	6	5	1	-	-	-
30 - 34	7	5	2	7	5	2	-	-	-
35 - 39	11	7	4	11	7	4	-	-	-
40 - 44	15	10	5	15	10	5	-	-	-
45 - 49	37	17	20	36	16	20	1	1	-
50 - 54	52	28	24	48	25	23	4	3	1
55 - 59	76	47	29	70	43	27	6	4	2
60 - 64	95	67	28	90	64	26	5	3	2
65 - 69	110	64	46	101	60	41	9	4	5
70 - 74	169	101	68	156	90	66	13	11	2
75 - 79	249	137	112	236	127	109	13	10	3
80 - 84	372	195	177	337	171	166	35	24	11
85 - 89	311	133	178	278	114	164	33	19	14
90 - 94	193	69	124	179	64	115	14	5	9
95 - 99	81	29	52	73	27	46	8	2	6
100 +	18	6	12	16	4	12	2	2	-

Continent, country or area, date, code and age (in years) / Continent, pays ou zone, date, code et âge (en années)	Total			Urban - Urbaine			Rural - Rurale		
	Both sexes Les deux sexes	Male Masculin	Female Féminin	Both sexes Les deux sexes	Male Masculin	Female Féminin	Both sexes Les deux sexes	Male Masculin	Female Féminin
EUROPE									
Ireland - Irlande[39]									
1999 (+C)									
Total............	31 683	16 480	15 203	17 288	8 599	8 689	14 395	7 881	6 514
0..................	293	160	133	195	108	87	98	52	46
1 - 4..............	68	39	29	37	25	12	31	14	17
5 - 9..............	41	28	13	20	14	6	21	14	7
10 - 14............	56	37	19	31	19	12	25	18	7
15 - 19............	171	123	48	90	64	26	81	59	22
20 - 24............	233	179	54	130	103	27	103	76	27
25 - 29............	196	149	47	109	83	26	87	66	21
30 - 34............	222	153	69	141	94	47	81	59	22
35 - 39............	279	174	105	178	111	67	101	63	38
40 - 44............	406	243	163	232	143	89	174	100	74
45 - 49............	637	392	245	409	249	160	228	143	85
50 - 54............	888	553	335	514	301	213	374	252	122
55 - 59............	1 226	777	449	747	460	287	479	317	162
60 - 64............	1 675	1 065	610	1 003	626	377	672	439	233
65 - 69............	2 606	1 630	976	1 485	897	588	1 121	733	388
70 - 74............	3 961	2 375	1 586	2 224	1 300	924	1 737	1 075	662
75 - 79............	5 492	3 005	2 487	2 877	1 499	1 378	2 615	1 506	1 109
80 - 84............	5 601	2 666	2 935	2 823	1 221	1 602	2 778	1 445	1 333
85 +...............	7 632	2 732	4 900	4 043	1 282	2 761	3 589	1 450	2 139
2005* (+C)									
Total............	27 441	13 904	13 537	...	...	...	...	...	...
0..................	244	114	130	...	...	...	...	...	...
1 - 4..............	48	25	23	...	...	...	...	...	...
5 - 9..............	27	16	11	...	...	...	...	...	...
10 - 14............	35	17	18	...	...	...	...	...	...
15 - 19............	133	97	36	...	...	...	...	...	...
20 - 24............	211	161	50	...	...	...	...	...	...
25 - 29............	195	150	45	...	...	...	...	...	...
30 - 34............	236	161	75	...	...	...	...	...	...
35 - 39............	257	159	98	...	...	...	...	...	...
40 - 44............	388	237	151	...	...	...	...	...	...
45 - 49............	574	337	237	...	...	...	...	...	...
50 - 54............	838	499	339	...	...	...	...	...	...
55 - 59............	1 176	721	455	...	...	...	...	...	...
60 - 64............	1 587	990	597	...	...	...	...	...	...
65 - 69............	2 105	1 260	845	...	...	...	...	...	...
70 - 74............	2 969	1 812	1 157	...	...	...	...	...	...
75 - 79............	4 002	2 167	1 835	...	...	...	...	...	...
80 - 84............	5 003	2 392	2 611	...	...	...	...	...	...
85 - 89............	4 167	1 655	2 512	...	...	...	...	...	...
90 - 94............	2 441	759	1 682	...	...	...	...	...	...
95 - 99............	710	157	553	...	...	...	...	...	...
100 +..............	95	18	77	...	...	...	...	...	...
Isle of Man - Îles de Man									
2004 (+C)									
Total............	798	390	408	...	...	...	...	...	...
0..................	2	1	1	...	...	...	...	...	...
1 - 4..............	-	-	-	...	...	...	...	...	...
5 - 9..............	-	-	-	...	...	...	...	...	...
10 - 14............	1	1	-	...	...	...	...	...	...
15 - 19............	3	3	-	...	...	...	...	...	...
20 - 24............	5	4	1	...	...	...	...	...	...
25 - 29............	3	3	-	...	...	...	...	...	...
30 - 34............	3	1	2	...	...	...	...	...	...
35 - 39............	6	5	1	...	...	...	...	...	...
40 - 44............	7	4	3	...	...	...	...	...	...
45 - 49............	11	5	6	...	...	...	...	...	...
50 - 54............	17	8	9	...	...	...	...	...	...
55 - 59............	31	18	13	...	...	...	...	...	...
60 - 64............	33	19	14	...	...	...	...	...	...
65 - 69............	60	45	15	...	...	...	...	...	...
70 - 74............	82	46	36	...	...	...	...	...	...

Continent, country or area, date, code and age (in years) Continent, pays ou zone, date, code et âge (en annèes)	Total			Urban - Urbaine			Rural - Rurale		
	Both sexes Les deux sexes	Male Masculin	Female Féminin	Both sexes Les deux sexes	Male Masculin	Female Féminin	Both sexes Les deux sexes	Male Masculin	Female Féminin
EUROPE									
Isle of Man - Îles de Man									
2004 (+C)									
75 - 79	118	59	59	...	...	...	...	...	...
80 - 84	169	77	92	...	...	...	...	...	...
85 - 89	111	43	68	...	...	...	...	...	...
90 - 94	96	36	60	...	...	...	...	...	...
95 + ...	40	12	28	...	...	...	...	...	...
Italy - Italie									
2003 (C)									
Total..............	588 897	289 826	299 071	...	...	...	...	...	...
0	2 134	1 146	988	...	...	...	...	...	...
1 - 4	389	208	181	...	...	...	...	...	...
5 - 9	276	158	118	...	...	...	...	...	...
10 - 14	366	224	142	...	...	...	...	...	...
15 - 19	1 131	859	272	...	...	...	...	...	...
20 - 24	1 765	1 375	390	...	...	...	...	...	...
25 - 29	2 389	1 824	565	...	...	...	...	...	...
30 - 34	2 906	2 074	832	...	...	...	...	...	...
35 - 39	4 234	2 869	1 365	...	...	...	...	...	...
40 - 44	5 596	3 569	2 027	...	...	...	...	...	...
45 - 49	7 872	4 968	2 904	...	...	...	...	...	...
50 - 54	12 267	7 825	4 442	...	...	...	...	...	...
55 - 59	18 623	12 178	6 445	...	...	...	...	...	...
60 - 64	28 336	18 640	9 696	...	...	...	...	...	...
65,- 69	41 819	26 904	14 915	...	...	...	...	...	...
70 - 74	63 728	39 105	24 623	...	...	...	...	...	...
75 - 79	91 628	50 840	40 788	...	...	...	...	...	...
80 - 84	104 270	48 917	55 353	...	...	...	...	...	...
85 - 89	93 506	35 681	57 825	...	...	...	...	...	...
90 - 94	78 224	24 282	53 942	...	...	...	...	...	...
95 - 99	23 865	5 574	18 291	...	...	...	...	...	...
100 + ...	3 573	606	2 967	...	...	...	...	...	...
Latvia - Lettonie[22]									
2005 (C)									
Total..............	32 777	16 601	16 176	21 186	10 740	10 446	11 591	5 861	5 730
0	168	87	81	102	54	48	66	33	33
1 - 4	36	22	14	22	17	5	14	5	9
5 - 9	30	20	10	12	9	3	18	11	7
10 - 14	40	29	11	22	14	8	18	15	3
15 - 19	103	72	31	59	41	18	44	31	13
20 - 24	218	165	53	129	100	29	89	65	24
25 - 29	243	200	43	171	143	28	72	57	15
30 - 34	360	278	82	228	169	59	132	109	23
35 - 39	541	441	100	373	307	66	168	134	34
40 - 44	848	632	216	592	439	153	256	193	63
45 - 49	1 159	851	308	787	569	218	372	282	90
50 - 54	1 639	1 199	440	1 103	790	313	536	409	127
55 - 59	2 003	1 393	610	1 407	960	447	596	433	163
60 - 64	2 636	1 816	820	1 611	1 079	532	1 025	737	288
65 - 69	3 568	2 294	1 274	2 301	1 435	866	1 267	859	408
70 - 74	4 127	2 264	1 863	2 556	1 393	1 163	1 571	871	700
75 - 79	5 013	2 252	2 761	3 320	1 500	1 820	1 693	752	941
80 - 84	4 717	1 364	3 353	3 072	916	2 156	1 645	448	1 197
85 - 89	2 723	687	2 036	1 737	457	1 280	986	230	756
90 - 94	1 895	402	1 493	1 137	265	872	758	137	621
95 - 99	614	114	500	387	74	313	227	40	187
100 + ...	93	17	76	55	7	48	38	10	28
Unknown - Inconnu	3	2	1	3	2	1	-	-	-
Liechtenstein									
2005* (C)									
Total..............	215	113	102	...	...	...	...	...	...
0 - 9	3	2	1	...	...	...	...	...	...
10 - 19	1	1	-	...	...	...	...	...	...
20 - 29	2	1	1	...	...	...	...	...	...
30 - 39	3	2	1	...	...	...	...	...	...

Continent, country or area, date, code and age (in years) / Continent, pays ou zone, date, code et âge (en années)	Total			Urban - Urbaine			Rural - Rurale		
	Both sexes Les deux sexes	Male Masculin	Female Féminin	Both sexes Les deux sexes	Male Masculin	Female Féminin	Both sexes Les deux sexes	Male Masculin	Female Féminin
EUROPE									
Liechtenstein									
2005* (C)									
40 - 49	12	10	2	...	...	...	...	...	...
50 - 59	22	16	6	...	...	...	...	...	...
60 - 69	29	22	7	...	...	...	...	...	...
70 - 79	44	22	22	...	...	...	...	...	...
80 - 89	62	26	36	...	...	...	...	...	...
90 - 99	37	11	26	...	...	...	...	...	...
100 +	-	-	-	...	...	...	...	...	...
Lithuania - Lituanie[22]									
2005 (C)									
Total	43 799	23 384	20 415	25 067	13 407	11 660	18 732	9 977	8 755
0	209	120	89	135	73	62	74	47	27
1 - 4	52	36	16	23	15	8	29	21	8
5 - 9	58	43	15	38	29	9	20	14	6
10 - 14	56	39	17	28	20	8	28	19	9
15 - 19	216	161	55	138	100	38	78	61	17
20 - 24	350	296	54	209	175	34	141	121	20
25 - 29	451	374	77	265	214	51	186	160	26
30 - 34	614	493	121	339	271	68	275	222	53
35 - 39	887	705	182	505	401	104	382	304	78
40 - 44	1 333	1 025	308	801	613	188	532	412	120
45 - 49	1 905	1 442	463	1 154	851	303	751	591	160
50 - 54	2 291	1 697	594	1 393	1 014	379	898	683	215
55 - 59	2 746	1 925	821	1 664	1 145	519	1 082	780	302
60 - 64	3 508	2 451	1 057	2 091	1 441	650	1 417	1 010	407
65 - 69	4 338	2 826	1 512	2 524	1 611	913	1 814	1 215	599
70 - 74	5 308	2 944	2 364	3 026	1 655	1 371	2 282	1 289	993
75 - 79	6 274	2 817	3 457	3 657	1 663	1 994	2 617	1 154	1 463
80 - 84	6 139	2 099	4 040	3 366	1 145	2 221	2 773	954	1 819
85 - 89	3 494	964	2 530	1 828	494	1 334	1 666	470	1 196
90 - 94	2 461	572	1 889	1 311	294	1 017	1 150	278	872
95 - 99	919	299	620	485	151	334	434	148	286
100 +	189	55	134	86	31	55	103	24	79
Unknown - Inconnu	1	1	-	1	1	-	-	-	-
Luxembourg									
2005 (C)									
Total	3 621	1 780	1 841	...	...	...	...	...	...
0	14	5	9	...	...	...	...	...	...
1 - 4	4	2	2	...	...	...	...	...	...
5 - 9	5	2	3	...	...	...	...	...	...
10 - 14	4	4	-	...	...	...	...	...	...
15 - 19	3	2	1	...	...	...	...	...	...
20 - 24	22	17	5	...	...	...	...	...	...
25 - 29	17	11	6	...	...	...	...	...	...
30 - 34	19	15	4	...	...	...	...	...	...
35 - 39	49	31	18	...	...	...	...	...	...
40 - 44	46	30	16	...	...	...	...	...	...
45 - 49	74	52	22	...	...	...	...	...	...
50 - 54	117	78	39	...	...	...	...	...	...
55 - 59	170	108	62	...	...	...	...	...	...
60 - 64	221	153	68	...	...	...	...	...	...
65 - 69	273	174	99	...	...	...	...	...	...
70 - 74	419	256	163	...	...	...	...	...	...
75 - 79	574	305	269	...	...	...	...	...	...
80 - 84	601	234	367	...	...	...	...	...	...
85 - 89	479	172	307	...	...	...	...	...	...
90 - 94	371	99	272	...	...	...	...	...	...
95 - 99	126	27	99	...	...	...	...	...	...
100 +	13	3	10	...	...	...	...	...	...
Malta - Malte[40]									
2004 (C)									
Total	2 903	1 436	1 467	...	...	...	...	...	...
0	23	14	9	...	...	...	...	...	...
1 - 4	8	3	5	...	...	...	...	...	...

19. Deaths by age, sex and urban/rural residence: latest available year, 1996 - 2005
Décès selon l'âge, le sexe et la résidence, urbaine/rurale: dernière année disponible, 1996 - 2005 (continued - suite)

Continent, country or area, date, code and age (in years) / Continent, pays ou zone, date, code et âge (en années)	Total			Urban - Urbaine			Rural - Rurale		
	Both sexes Les deux sexes	Male Masculin	Female Féminin	Both sexes Les deux sexes	Male Masculin	Female Féminin	Both sexes Les deux sexes	Male Masculin	Female Féminin
EUROPE									
Malta - Malte[40]									
2004 (C)									
5 - 9	1	1	-	...	...	...	...	...	...
10 - 14	4	1	3	...	...	...	...	...	...
15 - 19	11	9	2	...	...	...	...	...	...
20 - 24	15	9	6	...	...	...	...	...	...
25 - 29	13	11	2	...	...	...	...	...	...
30 - 34	12	6	6	...	...	...	...	...	...
35 - 39	13	10	3	...	...	...	...	...	...
40 - 44	24	17	7	...	...	...	...	...	...
45 - 49	42	20	22	...	...	...	...	...	...
50 - 54	82	52	30	...	...	...	...	...	...
55 - 59	152	84	68	...	...	...	...	...	...
60 - 64	133	91	42	...	...	...	...	...	...
65 - 69	257	146	111	...	...	...	...	...	...
70 - 74	374	215	159	...	...	...	...	...	...
75 - 79	501	242	259	...	...	...	...	...	...
80 - 84	547	251	296	...	...	...	...	...	...
85 - 89	390	164	226	...	...	...	...	...	...
90 +	301	90	211	...	...	...	...	...	...
Netherlands - Pays-Bas[41]									
2005 (C)									
Total	136 402	66 362	70 040	91 060	43 321	47 739	45 342	23 041	22 301
0	834	450	384	581	321	260	253	129	124
1 - 4	276	154	122	186	109	77	90	45	45
5 - 9	99	61	38	78	51	27	21	10	11
10 - 14	119	64	55	60	30	30	59	34	25
15 - 19	241	159	82	137	82	55	104	77	27
20 - 24	345	223	122	228	141	87	117	82	35
25 - 29	385	259	126	278	179	99	107	80	27
30 - 34	576	341	235	419	245	174	157	96	61
35 - 39	1 010	589	421	709	413	296	301	176	125
40 - 44	1 647	910	737	1 125	625	500	522	285	237
45 - 49	2 516	1 394	1 122	1 721	968	753	795	426	369
50 - 54	3 883	2 218	1 665	2 557	1 455	1 102	1 326	763	563
55 - 59	6 176	3 622	2 554	4 105	2 405	1 700	2 071	1 217	854
60 - 64	7 199	4 496	2 703	4 702	2 897	1 805	2 497	1 599	898
65 - 69	9 614	6 090	3 524	6 267	3 851	2 416	3 347	2 239	1 108
70 - 74	13 760	8 396	5 364	8 908	5 296	3 612	4 852	3 100	1 752
75 - 79	19 542	10 983	8 559	13 046	7 198	5 848	6 496	3 785	2 711
80 - 84	24 670	11 982	12 688	16 430	7 798	8 632	8 240	4 184	4 056
85 - 89	22 234	8 422	13 812	15 038	5 604	9 434	7 196	2 818	4 378
90 - 94	15 107	4 305	10 802	10 230	2 857	7 373	4 877	1 448	3 429
95 - 99	5 265	1 099	4 166	3 614	705	2 909	1 651	394	1 257
100 +	904	145	759	641	91	550	263	54	209
Norway - Norvège[42]									
2004* (C)									
Total	41 200	19 991	21 209	...	...	...	...	...	...
0	185	99	86	...	...	...	...	...	...
1 - 4	46	29	17	...	...	...	...	...	...
5 - 9	30	11	19	...	...	...	...	...	...
10 - 14	37	16	21	...	...	...	...	...	...
15 - 19	123	86	37	...	...	...	...	...	...
20 - 24	192	146	46	...	...	...	...	...	...
25 - 29	209	150	59	...	...	...	...	...	...
30 - 34	230	153	77	...	...	...	...	...	...
35 - 39	328	214	114	...	...	...	...	...	...
40 - 44	425	266	159	...	...	...	...	...	...
45 - 49	641	373	268	...	...	...	...	...	...
50 - 54	1 011	632	379	...	...	...	...	...	...
55 - 59	1 591	970	621	...	...	...	...	...	...
60 - 64	1 760	1 107	653	...	...	...	...	...	...
65 - 69	2 284	1 425	859	...	...	...	...	...	...
70 - 74	3 484	2 136	1 348	...	...	...	...	...	...
75 - 79	5 459	2 994	2 465	...	...	...	...	...	...

19. Deaths by age, sex and urban/rural residence: latest available year, 1996 - 2005
Décès selon l'âge, le sexe et la résidence, urbaine/rurale: dernière année disponible, 1996 - 2005 (continued - suite)

Continent, country or area, date, code and age (in years) — Continent, pays ou zone, date, code et âge (en années)	Total			Urban - Urbaine			Rural - Rurale		
	Both sexes Les deux sexes	Male Masculin	Female Féminin	Both sexes Les deux sexes	Male Masculin	Female Féminin	Both sexes Les deux sexes	Male Masculin	Female Féminin
EUROPE									
Norway - Norvège[42]									
2004* (C)									
80 - 84	8 425	4 139	4 286	...	...	...	...	...	...
85 - 89	7 795	3 039	4 756	...	...	...	...	...	...
90 - 94	5 056	1 539	3 517	...	...	...	...	...	...
95 - 99	1 573	369	1 204	...	...	...	...	...	...
100 +	228	49	179	...	...	...	...	...	...
Unknown - Inconnu	89	49	40	...	...	...	...	...	...
Poland - Pologne									
2005 (C)									
Total	368 285	196 776	171 509	219 403	115 737	103 666	148 882	81 039	67 843
0	2 340	1 304	1 036	1 339	754	585	1 001	550	451
1 - 4	387	212	175	191	97	94	196	115	81
5 - 9	320	166	154	164	86	78	156	80	76
10 - 14	426	264	162	218	134	84	208	130	78
15 - 19	1 378	1 029	349	717	519	198	661	510	151
20 - 24	2 298	1 885	413	1 274	1 030	244	1 024	855	169
25 - 29	2 427	1 954	473	1 454	1 138	316	973	816	157
30 - 34	2 929	2 277	652	1 712	1 283	429	1 217	994	223
35 - 39	4 218	3 240	978	2 463	1 819	644	1 755	1 421	334
40 - 44	7 393	5 542	1 851	4 488	3 232	1 256	2 905	2 310	595
45 - 49	15 259	11 163	4 096	9 663	6 801	2 862	5 596	4 362	1 234
50 - 54	22 342	16 090	6 252	14 767	10 239	4 528	7 575	5 851	1 724
55 - 59	25 884	18 081	7 803	17 254	11 686	5 568	8 630	6 395	2 235
60 - 64	23 080	15 784	7 296	15 293	10 184	5 109	7 787	5 600	2 187
65 - 69	34 466	22 417	12 049	21 652	13 679	7 973	12 814	8 738	4 076
70 - 74	46 777	27 268	19 509	27 831	15 898	11 933	18 946	11 370	7 576
75 - 79	57 119	27 991	29 128	32 959	15 851	17 108	24 160	12 140	12 020
80 - 84	56 750	21 909	34 841	31 601	11 903	19 698	25 149	10 006	15 143
85 - 89	32 101	10 530	21 571	17 199	5 348	11 851	14 902	5 182	9 720
90 - 94	22 973	6 012	16 961	12 836	3 141	9 695	10 137	2 871	7 266
95 - 99	6 561	1 494	5 067	3 813	812	3 001	2 748	682	2 066
100 +	857	164	693	515	103	412	342	61	281
Portugal									
2005 (C)									
Total	107 462	55 493	51 969	...	...	...	...	...	...
0	382	198	184	...	...	...	...	...	...
1 - 4	94	63	31	...	...	...	...	...	...
5 - 9	96	58	38	...	...	...	...	...	...
10 - 14	84	52	32	...	...	...	...	...	...
15 - 19	285	213	72	...	...	...	...	...	...
20 - 24	459	345	114	...	...	...	...	...	...
25 - 29	579	434	145	...	...	...	...	...	...
30 - 34	926	698	228	...	...	...	...	...	...
35 - 39	1 197	875	322	...	...	...	...	...	...
40 - 44	1 731	1 252	479	...	...	...	...	...	...
45 - 49	2 292	1 575	717	...	...	...	...	...	...
50 - 54	3 048	2 098	950	...	...	...	...	...	...
55 - 59	3 956	2 717	1 239	...	...	...	...	...	...
60 - 64	4 911	3 252	1 659	...	...	...	...	...	...
65 - 69	7 899	5 025	2 874	...	...	...	...	...	...
70 - 74	11 954	7 190	4 764	...	...	...	...	...	...
75 - 79	17 055	9 207	7 848	...	...	...	...	...	...
80 - 84	20 576	9 697	10 879	...	...	...	...	...	...
85 - 89	16 142	6 306	9 836	...	...	...	...	...	...
90 - 94	10 409	3 420	6 989	...	...	...	...	...	...
95 - 99	2 958	739	2 219	...	...	...	...	...	...
100 +	429	79	350	...	...	...	...	...	...
Republic of Moldova - République de Moldova[22]									
2005 (C)									
Total	44 689	23 277	21 412	14 199	7 714	6 485	30 490	15 563	14 927
0	468	247	221	177	96	81	291	151	140
1 - 4	122	73	49	32	17	15	90	56	34
5 - 9	76	40	36	19	13	6	57	27	30

19. Deaths by age, sex and urban/rural residence: latest available year, 1996 - 2005
Décès selon l'âge, le sexe et la résidence, urbaine/rurale: dernière année disponible, 1996 - 2005 (continued - suite)

Continent, country or area, date, code and age (in years) / Continent, pays ou zone, date, code et âge (en années)	Total			Urban - Urbaine			Rural - Rurale		
	Both sexes Les deux sexes	Male Masculin	Female Féminin	Both sexes Les deux sexes	Male Masculin	Female Féminin	Both sexes Les deux sexes	Male Masculin	Female Féminin
EUROPE									
Republic of Moldova - République de Moldova[22] **2005 (C)**									
10 - 14	92	61	31	21	14	7	71	47	24
15 - 19	202	152	50	69	51	18	133	101	32
20 - 24	315	233	82	129	89	40	186	144	42
25 - 29	386	293	93	146	110	36	240	183	57
30 - 34	581	428	153	235	171	64	346	257	89
35 - 39	801	586	215	313	223	90	488	363	125
40 - 44	1 552	1 137	415	572	427	145	980	710	270
45 - 49	2 576	1 820	756	946	657	289	1 630	1 163	467
50 - 54	3 318	2 272	1 046	1 277	907	370	2 041	1 365	676
55 - 59	3 129	1 978	1 151	1 258	851	407	1 871	1 127	744
60 - 64	3 731	2 107	1 624	1 212	736	476	2 519	1 371	1 148
65 - 69	5 232	2 813	2 419	1 675	963	712	3 557	1 850	1 707
70 - 74	6 118	3 010	3 108	1 639	797	842	4 479	2 213	2 266
75 - 79	6 565	2 820	3 745	1 904	803	1 101	4 661	2 017	2 644
80 - 84	5 472	1 974	3 498	1 499	494	1 005	3 973	1 480	2 493
85 - 89	2 437	795	1 642	668	190	478	1 769	605	1 164
90 - 94	1 215	361	854	341	90	251	874	271	603
95 - 99	252	63	189	59	13	46	193	50	143
100 +	49	14	35	8	2	6	41	12	29
Romania - Roumanie 2005 (C)									
Total	262 101	138 461	123 640	116 809	62 256	54 553	145 292	76 205	69 087
0	3 310	1 912	1 398	1 458	856	602	1 852	1 056	796
1 - 4	559	316	243	238	134	104	321	182	139
5 - 9	361	209	152	162	94	68	199	115	84
10 - 14	392	233	159	173	95	78	219	138	81
15 - 19	1 006	645	361	477	299	178	529	346	183
20 - 24	973	722	251	509	367	142	464	355	109
25 - 29	1 409	1 006	403	712	500	212	697	506	191
30 - 34	1 979	1 446	533	943	672	271	1 036	774	262
35 - 39	3 273	2 318	955	1 606	1 087	519	1 667	1 231	436
40 - 44	4 296	3 076	1 220	2 206	1 500	706	2 090	1 576	514
45 - 49	9 099	6 464	2 635	5 169	3 522	1 647	3 930	2 942	988
50 - 54	13 024	9 131	3 893	7 522	5 239	2 283	5 502	3 892	1 610
55 - 59	15 271	10 375	4 896	8 303	5 616	2 687	6 968	4 759	2 209
60 - 64	17 432	11 405	6 027	8 539	5 590	2 949	8 893	5 815	3 078
65 - 69	29 265	17 785	11 480	13 343	8 113	5 230	15 922	9 672	6 250
70 - 74	38 043	20 691	17 352	16 178	8 677	7 501	21 865	12 014	9 851
75 - 79	45 218	21 680	23 538	18 384	8 835	9 549	26 834	12 845	13 989
80 - 84	42 795	17 263	25 532	16 692	6 361	10 331	26 103	10 902	15 201
85 - 89	18 981	6 694	12 287	7 750	2 597	5 153	11 231	4 097	7 134
90 - 94	12 522	4 155	8 367	5 209	1 717	3 492	7 313	2 438	4 875
95 - 99	2 627	841	1 786	1 116	345	771	1 511	496	1 015
100 +	266	94	172	120	40	80	146	54	92
Russian Federation - Fédération de Russie[22] **2004 (C)**									
Total	2 295 402	1 240 142	1 055 260	1 606 894	871 433	735 461	688 508	368 709	319 799
0	17 339	10 090	7 249	11 596	6 666	4 930	5 743	3 424	2 319
1 - 4	3 991	2 247	1 744	2 342	1 321	1 021	1 649	926	723
5 - 9	2 731	1 698	1 033	1 661	1 037	624	1 070	661	409
10 - 14	3 946	2 563	1 383	2 454	1 584	870	1 492	979	513
15 - 19	14 602	10 483	4 119	9 358	6 633	2 725	5 244	3 850	1 394
20 - 24	29 601	23 633	5 968	20 611	16 361	4 250	8 990	7 272	1 718
25 - 29	41 179	32 754	8 425	29 906	23 743	6 163	11 273	9 011	2 262
30 - 34	49 524	38 773	10 751	36 209	28 154	8 055	13 315	10 619	2 696
35 - 39	61 000	47 292	13 708	43 111	33 192	9 919	17 889	14 100	3 789
40 - 44	104 966	80 979	23 987	74 833	57 266	17 567	30 133	23 713	6 420
45 - 49	143 011	108 186	34 825	102 629	77 040	25 589	40 382	31 146	9 236
50 - 54	173 291	126 701	46 590	126 903	92 452	34 451	46 388	34 249	12 139
55 - 59	152 017	105 379	46 638	113 444	78 399	35 045	38 573	26 980	11 593
60 - 64	166 951	109 347	57 604	116 074	75 908	40 166	50 877	33 439	17 438

19. Deaths by age, sex and urban/rural residence: latest available year, 1996 - 2005
Décès selon l'âge, le sexe et la résidence, urbaine/rurale: dernière année disponible, 1996 - 2005 (continued - suite)

Continent, country or area, date, code and age (in years) / Continent, pays ou zone, date, code et âge (en années)	Total Both sexes Les deux sexes	Total Male Masculin	Total Female Féminin	Urban - Urbaine Both sexes Les deux sexes	Urban - Urbaine Male Masculin	Urban - Urbaine Female Féminin	Rural - Rurale Both sexes Les deux sexes	Rural - Rurale Male Masculin	Rural - Rurale Female Féminin
EUROPE									
Russian Federation - Fédération de Russie[22]									
2004 (C)									
65 - 69	269 030	160 960	108 070	184 150	109 190	74 960	84 880	51 770	33 110
70 - 74	273 326	139 336	133 990	182 625	91 007	91 618	90 701	48 329	42 372
75 - 79	335 600	131 978	203 622	232 549	91 450	141 099	103 051	40 528	62 523
80 - 84	203 445	51 094	152 351	142 879	36 300	106 579	60 566	14 794	45 772
85 - 89	132 373	26 755	105 618	91 873	19 520	72 353	40 500	7 235	33 265
90 - 94	81 070	13 222	67 848	54 014	9 557	44 457	27 056	3 665	23 391
95 - 99	16 513	2 161	14 352	10 654	1 546	9 108	5 859	615	5 244
100 +	2 379	296	2 083	1 229	182	1 047	1 150	114	1 036
Unknown - Inconnu	17 517	14 215	3 302	15 790	12 925	2 865	1 727	1 290	437
San Marino - Saint-Marin									
2004 (+C)									
Total	185	94	91	...	...	...	...	...	...
1 - 14	-	-	-	...	...	...	...	...	...
15 - 19	2	2	-	...	...	...	...	...	...
20 - 24	2	2	-	...	...	...	...	...	...
25 - 29	-	-	-	...	...	...	...	...	...
30 - 34	1	-	1	...	...	...	...	...	...
35 - 39	-	-	-	...	...	...	...	...	...
40 - 44	3	-	3	...	...	...	...	...	...
45 - 49	2	-	2	...	...	...	...	...	...
50 - 54	7	5	2	...	...	...	...	...	...
55 - 59	9	6	3	...	...	...	...	...	...
60 - 64	8	6	2	...	...	...	...	...	...
65 - 69	12	7	5	...	...	...	...	...	...
70 - 74	14	9	5	...	...	...	...	...	...
75 - 79	22	13	9	...	...	...	...	...	...
80 - 84	35	16	19	...	...	...	...	...	...
85 - 89	34	16	18	...	...	...	...	...	...
90 - 94	27	7	20	...	...	...	...	...	...
95 - 99	5	4	1	...	...	...	...	...	...
100 +	1	-	1	...	...	...	...	...	...
Serbia and Montenegro - Serbie-et-Montenegro[43]									
2003 (C)									
Total	109 650	55 999	53 651	55 615	28 201	27 414	54 035	27 798	26 237
0	803	442	361	537	286	251	266	156	110
1 - 4	121	71	50	75	43	32	46	28	18
5 - 9	70	41	29	42	26	16	28	15	13
10 - 14	90	62	28	47	30	17	43	32	11
15 - 19	247	178	69	139	100	39	108	78	30
20 - 24	345	254	91	214	157	57	131	97	34
25 - 29	422	307	115	246	177	69	176	130	46
30 - 34	481	299	182	295	183	112	186	116	70
35 - 39	820	552	268	481	313	168	339	239	100
40 - 44	1 519	975	544	913	549	364	606	426	180
45 - 49	3 066	2 008	1 058	1 829	1 158	671	1 237	850	387
50 - 54	5 186	3 449	1 737	3 123	1 999	1 124	2 063	1 450	613
55 - 59	5 451	3 637	1 814	3 228	2 099	1 129	2 223	1 538	685
60 - 64	8 251	5 120	3 131	4 604	2 800	1 804	3 647	2 320	1 327
65 - 69	14 008	8 185	5 823	7 649	4 458	3 191	6 359	3 727	2 632
70 - 74	20 020	10 570	9 450	9 551	4 866	4 685	10 469	5 704	4 765
75 - 79	21 577	9 561	12 016	10 272	4 454	5 818	11 305	5 107	6 198
80 - 84	16 222	6 333	9 889	7 240	2 755	4 485	8 982	3 578	5 404
85 - 89	5 976	2 213	3 763	2 861	1 006	1 855	3 115	1 207	1 908
90 - 94	4 020	1 392	2 628	1 826	588	1 238	2 194	804	1 390
95 - 99	743	250	493	316	91	225	427	159	268
100 +	104	35	69	48	14	34	56	21	35
Unknown - Inconnu	108	65	43	79	49	30	29	16	13
Slovakia - Slovaquie									
2005 (C)									
Total	53 475	28 151	25 324	26 111	13 676	12 435	27 364	14 475	12 889
0	392	225	167	188	115	73	204	110	94

19. Deaths by age, sex and urban/rural residence: latest available year, 1996 - 2005
Décès selon l'âge, le sexe et la résidence, urbaine/rurale: dernière année disponible, 1996 - 2005 (continued - suite)

Continent, country or area, date, code and age (in years) / Continent, pays ou zone, date, code et âge (en années)	Total			Urban - Urbaine			Rural - Rurale		
	Both sexes Les deux sexes	Male Masculin	Female Féminin	Both sexes Les deux sexes	Male Masculin	Female Féminin	Both sexes Les deux sexes	Male Masculin	Female Féminin
EUROPE									
Slovakia - Slovaquie									
2005 (C)									
1 - 4	73	40	33	41	20	21	32	20	12
5 - 9	61	40	21	26	14	12	35	26	9
10 - 14	40	27	13	22	12	10	18	15	3
15 - 19	170	115	55	84	56	28	86	59	27
20 - 24	263	206	57	140	110	30	123	96	27
25 - 29	307	229	78	168	131	37	139	98	41
30 - 34	401	301	100	228	161	67	173	140	33
35 - 39	577	422	155	296	205	91	281	217	64
40 - 44	992	719	273	502	351	151	490	368	122
45 - 49	1 948	1 422	526	1 033	716	317	915	706	209
50 - 54	2 930	2 141	789	1 618	1 151	467	1 312	990	322
55 - 59	3 459	2 473	986	1 863	1 276	587	1 596	1 197	399
60 - 64	3 927	2 656	1 271	2 003	1 310	693	1 924	1 346	578
65 - 69	4 756	2 965	1 791	2 282	1 408	874	2 474	1 557	917
70 - 74	6 653	3 689	2 964	3 181	1 731	1 450	3 472	1 958	1 514
75 - 79	8 453	4 015	4 438	4 025	1 913	2 112	4 428	2 102	2 326
80 - 84	9 578	3 793	5 785	4 434	1 764	2 670	5 144	2 029	3 115
85 - 89	4 431	1 523	2 908	2 102	718	1 384	2 329	805	1 524
90 - 94	3 231	954	2 277	1 467	426	1 041	1 764	528	1 236
95 - 99	753	180	573	367	81	286	386	99	287
100 +	80	16	64	41	7	34	39	9	30
Slovenia - Slovénie									
2005 (C)									
Total	18 825	9 413	9 412	8 791	4 337	4 454	10 034	5 076	4 958
0	75	41	34	26	16	10	49	25	24
1 - 4	21	11	10	8	4	4	13	7	6
5 - 9	9	3	6	4	2	2	5	1	4
10 - 14	15	8	7	8	5	3	7	3	4
15 - 19	46	38	8	15	13	2	31	25	6
20 - 24	101	77	24	51	38	13	50	39	11
25 - 29	124	104	20	55	46	9	69	58	11
30 - 34	124	84	40	59	42	17	65	42	23
35 - 39	157	106	51	68	44	24	89	62	27
40 - 44	302	214	88	137	95	42	165	119	46
45 - 49	522	369	153	266	170	96	256	199	57
50 - 54	805	566	239	389	256	133	416	310	106
55 - 59	913	622	291	458	307	151	455	315	140
60 - 64	1 216	842	374	573	382	191	643	460	183
65 - 69	1 675	1 112	563	809	524	285	866	588	278
70 - 74	2 432	1 432	1 000	1 070	630	440	1 362	802	560
75 - 79	3 118	1 561	1 557	1 440	706	734	1 678	855	823
80 - 84	3 221	1 157	2 064	1 509	538	971	1 712	619	1 093
85 - 89	1 818	540	1 278	815	256	559	1 003	284	719
90 - 94	1 635	422	1 213	794	215	579	841	207	634
95 - 99	453	96	357	217	46	171	236	50	186
100 +	43	8	35	20	2	18	23	6	17
Spain - Espagne									
2003 (C)									
Total	384 828	199 897	184 931	...	...	...	...	...	...
0	1 733	964	769	...	...	...	...	...	...
1 - 4	442	245	197	...	...	...	...	...	...
5 - 9	254	154	100	...	...	...	...	...	...
10 - 14	341	201	140	...	...	...	...	...	...
15 - 19	1 032	741	291	...	...	...	...	...	...
20 - 24	1 746	1 336	410	...	...	...	...	...	...
25 - 29	2 136	1 604	532	...	...	...	...	...	...
30 - 34	2 872	2 148	724	...	...	...	...	...	...
35 - 39	3 933	2 757	1 176	...	...	...	...	...	...
40 - 44	5 545	3 880	1 665	...	...	...	...	...	...
45 - 49	7 193	4 894	2 299	...	...	...	...	...	...
50 - 54	9 401	6 658	2 743	...	...	...	...	...	...
55 - 59	13 294	9 548	3 746	...	...	...	...	...	...
60 - 64	15 972	11 387	4 585	...	...	...	...	...	...

Continent, country or area, date, code and age (in years) / Continent, pays ou zone, date, code et âge (en années)	Total			Urban - Urbaine			Rural - Rurale		
	Both sexes Les deux sexes	Male Masculin	Female Féminin	Both sexes Les deux sexes	Male Masculin	Female Féminin	Both sexes Les deux sexes	Male Masculin	Female Féminin
EUROPE									
Spain - Espagne									
2003 (C)									
65 - 69	26 636	18 199	8 437	...	...	...	...	...	...
70 - 74	41 879	26 930	14 949	...	...	...	...	...	...
75 - 79	57 377	33 001	24 376	...	...	...	...	...	...
80 - 84	68 007	33 043	34 964	...	...	...	...	...	...
85 - 89	63 748	24 046	39 702	...	...	...	...	...	...
90 - 94	44 198	13 752	30 446	...	...	...	...	...	...
95 - 99	14 609	3 891	10 718	...	...	...	...	...	...
100 +	2 480	518	1 962	...	...	...	...	...	...
Sweden - Suède									
2005 (C)									
Total	91 710	44 788	46 922	...	...	...	...	...	...
0	246	131	115	...	...	...	...	...	...
1 - 4	83	46	37	...	...	...	...	...	...
5 - 9	49	33	16	...	...	...	...	...	...
10 - 14	62	38	24	...	...	...	...	...	...
15 - 19	153	107	46	...	...	...	...	...	...
20 - 24	247	178	69	...	...	...	...	...	...
25 - 29	271	203	68	...	...	...	...	...	...
30 - 34	300	194	106	...	...	...	...	...	...
35 - 39	452	278	174	...	...	...	...	...	...
40 - 44	685	443	242	...	...	...	...	...	...
45 - 49	1 071	668	403	...	...	...	...	...	...
50 - 54	1 832	1 084	748	...	...	...	...	...	...
55 - 59	3 239	1 933	1 306	...	...	...	...	...	...
60 - 64	4 418	2 682	1 736	...	...	...	...	...	...
65 - 69	5 520	3 376	2 144	...	...	...	...	...	...
70 - 74	7 531	4 501	3 030	...	...	...	...	...	...
75 - 79	11 706	6 575	5 131	...	...	...	...	...	...
80 - 84	17 909	9 064	8 845	...	...	...	...	...	...
85 - 89	18 281	7 843	10 438	...	...	...	...	...	...
90 - 94	12 756	4 278	8 478	...	...	...	...	...	...
95 - 99	4 262	1 040	3 222	...	...	...	...	...	...
100 +	637	93	544	...	...	...	...	...	...
Switzerland - Suisse									
2005 (C)									
Total	61 124	29 705	31 419	44 515	21 218	23 297	16 609	8 487	8 122
0	308	179	129	223	129	94	85	50	35
1 - 4	55	35	20	43	27	16	12	8	4
5 - 9	45	29	16	28	19	9	17	10	7
10 - 14	50	32	18	32	19	13	18	13	5
15 - 19	150	95	55	100	64	36	50	31	19
20 - 24	234	174	60	157	115	42	77	59	18
25 - 29	213	138	75	153	100	53	60	38	22
30 - 34	284	189	95	215	141	74	69	48	21
35 - 39	499	323	176	386	254	132	113	69	44
40 - 44	739	473	266	526	346	180	213	127	86
45 - 49	1 104	679	425	778	460	318	326	219	107
50 - 54	1 456	965	491	1 081	709	372	375	256	119
55 - 59	2 241	1 460	781	1 646	1 064	582	595	396	199
60 - 64	3 061	1 964	1 097	2 236	1 394	842	825	570	255
65 - 69	3 706	2 357	1 349	2 774	1 724	1 050	932	633	299
70 - 74	5 297	3 221	2 076	3 848	2 290	1 558	1 449	931	518
75 - 79	7 606	4 259	3 347	5 543	3 047	2 496	2 063	1 212	851
80 - 84	10 957	5 282	5 675	7 863	3 716	4 147	3 094	1 566	1 528
85 - 89	10 766	4 308	6 458	7 716	3 039	4 677	3 050	1 269	1 781
90 - 94	8 707	2 722	5 985	6 390	1 964	4 426	2 317	758	1 559
95 - 99	3 169	749	2 420	2 402	541	1 861	767	208	559
100 +	477	72	405	375	56	319	102	16	86

19. Deaths by age, sex and urban/rural residence: latest available year, 1996 - 2005
Décès selon l'âge, le sexe et la résidence, urbaine/rurale: dernière année disponible, 1996 - 2005 (continued - suite)

Continent, country or area, date, code and age (in years) / Continent, pays ou zone, date, code et âge (en années)	Total			Urban - Urbaine			Rural - Rurale		
	Both sexes Les deux sexes	Male Masculin	Female Féminin	Both sexes Les deux sexes	Male Masculin	Female Féminin	Both sexes Les deux sexes	Male Masculin	Female Féminin
EUROPE									
The Former Yugoslav Rep. of Macedonia - L'ex-République yougoslave de Macédoine									
2005 (C)									
Total.....................	18 406	9 815	8 591	10 645	5 685	4 960	7 761	4 130	3 631
0......................	287	156	131	151	83	68	136	73	63
1 - 4...................	36	22	14	19	9	10	17	13	4
5 - 9...................	15	9	6	8	5	3	7	4	3
10 - 14................	31	23	8	20	14	6	11	9	2
15 - 19................	59	40	19	37	25	12	22	15	7
20 - 24................	76	51	25	42	27	15	34	24	10
25 - 29................	100	71	29	66	43	23	34	28	6
30 - 34................	99	67	32	52	36	16	47	31	16
35 - 39................	155	101	54	90	62	28	65	39	26
40 - 44................	252	161	91	170	109	61	82	52	30
45 - 49................	511	323	188	318	196	122	193	127	66
50 - 54................	924	610	314	644	421	223	280	189	91
55 - 59................	1 055	717	338	689	466	223	366	251	115
60 - 64................	1 297	825	472	801	518	283	496	307	189
65 - 69................	2 092	1 202	890	1 241	732	509	851	470	381
70 - 74................	3 039	1 618	1 421	1 774	922	852	1 265	696	569
75 - 79................	3 276	1 608	1 668	1 838	879	959	1 438	729	709
80 - 84................	2 976	1 315	1 661	1 622	700	922	1 354	615	739
85 +..................	2 123	896	1 227	1 060	438	622	1 063	458	605
Unknown - Inconnu.......	3	-	3	3	-	3	-	-	-
Ukraine[22]									
2005 (C)									
Total.....................	781 961	403 440	378 521	471 561	249 101	222 460	310 400	154 339	156 061
0......................	4 259	2 467	1 792	2 675	1 546	1 129	1 584	921	663
1 - 4...................	1 179	696	483	619	345	274	560	351	209
5 - 9...................	819	518	301	451	280	171	368	238	130
10 - 14................	880	560	320	496	298	198	384	262	122
15 - 19................	2 808	2 037	771	1 741	1 258	483	1 067	779	288
20 - 24................	5 606	4 391	1 215	3 734	2 884	850	1 872	1 507	365
25 - 29................	9 236	7 089	2 147	6 418	4 863	1 555	2 818	2 226	592
30 - 34................	13 174	10 151	3 023	9 055	6 812	2 243	4 119	3 339	780
35 - 39................	17 104	13 108	3 996	11 408	8 520	2 888	5 696	4 588	1 108
40 - 44................	26 610	20 380	6 230	17 727	13 281	4 446	8 883	7 099	1 784
45 - 49................	37 169	28 128	9 041	24 781	18 424	6 357	12 388	9 704	2 684
50 - 54................	46 481	33 967	12 514	31 364	22 601	8 763	15 117	11 366	3 751
55 - 59................	50 494	34 255	16 239	34 043	23 117	10 926	16 451	11 138	5 313
60 - 64................	56 082	36 514	19 568	33 648	21 915	11 733	22 434	14 599	7 835
65 - 69................	103 054	61 244	41 810	63 151	37 268	25 883	39 903	23 976	15 927
70 - 74................	87 560	45 515	42 045	50 307	26 151	24 156	37 253	19 364	17 889
75 - 79................	129 834	54 476	75 358	76 267	32 323	43 944	53 567	22 153	31 414
80 - 84................	99 406	28 718	70 688	54 734	15 866	38 868	44 672	12 852	31 820
85 - 89................	49 504	11 479	38 025	27 694	6 885	20 809	21 810	4 594	17 216
90 - 94................	32 663	6 280	26 383	17 289	3 602	13 687	15 374	2 678	12 696
95 - 99................	6 972	1 199	5 773	3 392	657	2 735	3 580	542	3 038
100 +..................	882	129	753	394	76	318	488	53	435
Unknown - Inconnu.......	185	139	46	173	129	44	12	10	2
United Kingdom - Royaume-Uni									
2003* (C)									
Total.....................	611 188	288 604	322 584	...	...	...	...	...	...
0......................	3 686	2 029	1 657	...	...	...	...	...	...
1 - 4...................	663	351	312	...	...	...	...	...	...
5 - 9...................	390	214	176	...	...	...	...	...	...
10 - 14................	510	289	221	...	...	...	...	...	...
15 - 19................	1 393	969	424	...	...	...	...	...	...
20 - 24................	2 006	1 467	539	...	...	...	...	...	...
25 - 29................	2 222	1 556	666	...	...	...	...	...	...
30 - 34................	3 403	2 267	1 136	...	...	...	...	...	...
35 - 39................	4 923	3 156	1 767	...	...	...	...	...	...

19. Deaths by age, sex and urban/rural residence: latest available year, 1996 - 2005
Décès selon l'âge, le sexe et la résidence, urbaine/rurale: dernière année disponible, 1996 - 2005 (continued - suite)

Continent, country or area, date, code and age (in years) / Continent, pays ou zone, date, code et âge (en années)	Total			Urban - Urbaine			Rural - Rurale		
	Both sexes Les deux sexes	Male Masculin	Female Féminin	Both sexes Les deux sexes	Male Masculin	Female Féminin	Both sexes Les deux sexes	Male Masculin	Female Féminin
EUROPE									
United Kingdom - Royaume-Uni									
2003* (C)									
40 - 44	6 967	4 252	2 715	...	...	...	...	...	...
45 - 49	9 689	5 783	3 906	...	...	...	...	...	...
50 - 54	14 830	8 906	5 924	...	...	...	...	...	...
55 - 59	23 399	14 181	9 218	...	...	...	...	...	...
60 - 64	30 388	18 644	11 744	...	...	...	...	...	...
65 - 69	43 916	26 366	17 550	...	...	...	...	...	...
70 - 74	65 022	37 208	27 814	...	...	...	...	...	...
75 - 79	91 979	48 365	43 614	...	...	...	...	...	...
80 - 84	114 112	52 568	61 544	...	...	...	...	...	...
85 - 89	95 959	35 532	60 427	...	...	...	...	...	...
90 - 94	68 030	19 423	48 607	...	...	...	...	...	...
95 - 99	23 708	4 600	19 108	...	...	...	...	...	...
100 + ...	3 990	476	3 514	...	...	...	...	...	...
Unknown - Inconnu	3	2	1	...	...	...	...	...	...
OCEANIA - OCÉANIE									
American Samoa - Samoas américaines									
2005 (C)									
Total	279	177	102	...	...	...	...	...	...
0	12	6	6	...	...	...	...	...	...
1 - 4	6	2	4	...	...	...	...	...	...
5 - 9	5	5	-	...	...	...	...	...	...
10 - 14	2	1	1	...	...	...	...	...	...
15 - 19	2	2	-	...	...	...	...	...	...
20 - 24	3	2	1	...	...	...	...	...	...
25 - 29	3	2	1	...	...	...	...	...	...
30 - 34	5	3	2	...	...	...	...	...	...
35 - 39	15	12	3	...	...	...	...	...	...
40 - 44	9	6	3	...	...	...	...	...	...
45 - 49	12	6	6	...	...	...	...	...	...
50 - 54	19	14	5	...	...	...	...	...	...
55 - 59	30	23	7	...	...	...	...	...	...
60 - 64	24	21	3	...	...	...	...	...	...
65 - 69	30	18	12	...	...	...	...	...	...
70 - 74	28	17	11	...	...	...	...	...	...
75 - 79	26	15	11	...	...	...	...	...	...
80 - 84	24	9	15	...	...	...	...	...	...
85 + ...	24	13	11	...	...	...	...	...	...
Australia - Australie									
2005 (+C)									
Total	130 714	67 241	63 473	84 311	42 585	41 726	46 403	24 656	21 747
0	1 302	714	588	858	459	399	444	255	189
1 - 4	243	139	104	132	71	61	111	68	43
5 - 9	145	86	59	86	57	29	59	29	30
10 - 14	141	81	60	83	47	36	58	34	24
15 - 19	497	347	150	291	209	82	206	138	68
20 - 24	812	612	200	491	369	122	321	243	78
25 - 29	864	644	220	527	403	124	337	241	96
30 - 34	1 141	814	327	723	522	201	418	292	126
35 - 39	1 364	895	469	800	527	273	564	368	196
40 - 44	2 059	1 313	746	1 245	792	453	814	521	293
45 - 49	2 813	1 759	1 054	1 724	1 054	670	1 089	705	384
50 - 54	3 796	2 352	1 444	2 369	1 413	956	1 427	939	488
55 - 59	5 356	3 385	1 971	3 414	2 159	1 255	1 942	1 226	716
60 - 64	6 669	4 167	2 502	4 017	2 496	1 521	2 652	1 671	981
65 - 69	8 843	5 606	3 237	5 501	3 449	2 052	3 342	2 157	1 185
70 - 74	11 885	7 244	4 641	7 448	4 462	2 986	4 437	2 782	1 655
75 - 79	18 197	10 597	7 600	11 532	6 575	4 957	6 665	4 022	2 643
80 - 84	23 264	11 752	11 512	15 348	7 699	7 649	7 916	4 053	3 863

Continent, country or area, date, code and age (in years) / Continent, pays ou zone, date, code et âge (en années)	Total			Urban - Urbaine			Rural - Rurale		
	Both sexes Les deux sexes	Male Masculin	Female Féminin	Both sexes Les deux sexes	Male Masculin	Female Féminin	Both sexes Les deux sexes	Male Masculin	Female Féminin
OCEANIA - OCÉANIE									
Australia - Australie									
2005 (+C)									
85 - 89	20 855	8 597	12 258	13 794	5 719	8 075	7 061	2 878	4 183
90 - 94	14 651	4 774	9 877	9 920	3 177	6 743	4 731	1 597	3 134
95 - 99	4 916	1 210	3 706	3 385	824	2 561	1 531	386	1 145
100 + ...	876	141	735	622	102	521	253	39	214
Unknown - Inconnu	25	12	13	-	-	-	25	12	13
Marshall Islands - Îles Marshall									
1997 (+U)									
Total....................	243	135	108	...	...	...	...	...	...
0	49	17	32	...	...	...	...	...	...
1 - 4	7	1	6	...	...	...	...	...	...
5 - 9	2	1	1	...	...	...	...	...	...
10 - 14	2	1	1	...	...	...	...	...	...
15 - 19	8	6	2	...	...	...	...	...	...
20 - 24	10	9	1	...	...	...	...	...	...
25 - 29	9	6	3	...	...	...	...	...	...
30 - 34	8	2	6	...	...	...	...	...	...
35 - 39	6	5	1	...	...	...	...	...	...
40 - 44	10	5	5	...	...	...	...	...	...
45 - 49	18	12	6	...	...	...	...	...	...
50 - 54	13	9	4	...	...	...	...	...	...
55 - 59	17	10	7	...	...	...	...	...	...
60 - 64	17	13	4	...	...	...	...	...	...
65 - 69	19	12	7	...	...	...	...	...	...
70 - 74	13	6	7	...	...	...	...	...	...
75 + ...	35	20	15	...	...	...	...	...	...
Micronesia, Federated States of - Micronésie, États Fédérés de La									
2003 (U)									
Total....................	427	...	...	...	...	...	...	...	...
0	21	...	...	...	...	...	...	...	...
1 - 4	20	...	...	...	...	...	...	...	...
5 - 9	8	...	...	...	...	...	...	...	...
10 - 14	4	...	...	...	...	...	...	...	...
15 - 19	14	...	...	...	...	...	...	...	...
20 - 24	8	...	...	...	...	...	...	...	...
25 - 29	13	...	...	...	...	...	...	...	...
30 - 34	6	...	...	...	...	...	...	...	...
35 - 39	10	...	...	...	...	...	...	...	...
40 - 44	19	...	...	...	...	...	...	...	...
45 - 49	21	...	...	...	...	...	...	...	...
50 - 54	47	...	...	...	...	...	...	...	...
55 - 59	33	...	...	...	...	...	...	...	...
60 - 64	32	...	...	...	...	...	...	...	...
65 - 69	50	...	...	...	...	...	...	...	...
70 + ...	121	...	...	...	...	...	...	...	...
New Caledonia - Nouvelle-Calédonie									
2003 (C)									
Total....................	1 121	666	455	...	...	...	...	...	...
0	24	14	10	...	...	...	...	...	...
1 - 4	10	9	1	...	...	...	...	...	...
5 - 9	8	4	4	...	...	...	...	...	...
10 - 14	5	2	3	...	...	...	...	...	...
15 - 19	12	7	5	...	...	...	...	...	...
20 - 24	30	22	8	...	...	...	...	...	...
25 - 29	22	13	9	...	...	...	...	...	...
30 - 34	28	22	6	...	...	...	...	...	...
35 - 39	27	16	11	...	...	...	...	...	...
40 - 44	36	26	10	...	...	...	...	...	...
45 - 49	47	29	18	...	...	...	...	...	...
50 - 54	56	32	24	...	...	...	...	...	...

Continent, country or area, date, code and age (in years) / Continent, pays ou zone, date, code et âge (en années)	Total			Urban - Urbaine			Rural - Rurale		
	Both sexes Les deux sexes	Male Masculin	Female Féminin	Both sexes Les deux sexes	Male Masculin	Female Féminin	Both sexes Les deux sexes	Male Masculin	Female Féminin
OCEANIA - OCÉANIE									
New Caledonia - Nouvelle-Calédonie									
2003 (C)									
55 - 59	101	65	36	...	...	...	...	...	...
60 - 64	89	60	29	...	...	...	...	...	...
65 - 69	136	82	54	...	...	...	...	...	...
70 - 74	142	92	50	...	...	...	...	...	...
75 - 79	134	74	60	...	...	...	...	...	...
80 - 84	91	42	49	...	...	...	...	...	...
85 - 89	72	32	40	...	...	...	...	...	...
90 - 94	35	21	14	...	...	...	...	...	...
95 +	16	2	14	...	...	...	...	...	...
New Zealand - Nouvelle-Zélande[44]									
2005 (+C)									
Total	27 034	13 431	13 603	24 275[4]	11 824[4]	12 451[4]	2 628[4]	1 529[4]	1 099[4]
0	295	172	123	246[4]	143[4]	103[4]	26[4]	14[4]	12[4]
1 - 4	60	31	29	46[4]	24[4]	22[4]	14[4]	7[4]	7[4]
5 - 9	45	20	25	36[4]	17[4]	19[4]	9[4]	3[4]	6[4]
10 - 14	50	32	18	42[4]	27[4]	15[4]	8[4]	5[4]	3[4]
15 - 19	201	141	60	164[4]	116[4]	48[4]	36[4]	25[4]	11[4]
20 - 24	213	157	56	174[4]	125[4]	49[4]	35[4]	29[4]	6[4]
25 - 29	166	126	40	137[4]	103[4]	34[4]	26[4]	20[4]	6[4]
30 - 34	229	141	88	202[4]	123[4]	79[4]	24[4]	17[4]	7[4]
35 - 39	318	196	122	276[4]	167[4]	109[4]	38[4]	25[4]	13[4]
40 - 44	486	297	189	407[4]	243[4]	164[4]	78[4]	53[4]	25[4]
45 - 49	641	349	292	538[4]	295[4]	243[4]	98[4]	50[4]	48[4]
50 - 54	830	493	337	711[4]	416[4]	295[4]	115[4]	73[4]	42[4]
55 - 59	1 222	729	493	1 022[4]	607[4]	415[4]	191[4]	117[4]	74[4]
60 - 64	1 499	881	618	1 276[4]	750[4]	526[4]	211[4]	123[4]	88[4]
65 - 69	1 908	1 134	774	1 612[4]	947[4]	665[4]	284[4]	178[4]	106[4]
70 - 74	2 551	1 507	1 044	2 227[4]	1 303[4]	924[4]	319[4]	199[4]	120[4]
75 - 79	3 654	2 048	1 606	3 307[4]	1 829[4]	1 478[4]	340[4]	214[4]	126[4]
80 - 84	4 704	2 275	2 429	4 345[4]	2 083[4]	2 262[4]	343[4]	186[4]	157[4]
85 - 89	4 063	1 627	2 436	3 824[4]	1 507[4]	2 317[4]	229[4]	117[4]	112[4]
90 - 94	2 826	866	1 960	2 662[4]	809[4]	1 853[4]	155[4]	56[4]	99[4]
95 - 99	911	192	719	866[4]	174[4]	692[4]	42[4]	17[4]	25[4]
100 +	162	17	145	155[4]	16[4]	139[4]	7[4]	1[4]	6[4]
Northern Mariana Islands - Îles Mariannes septentrionales									
2002 (U)									
Total	164	96	59	...	...	...	...	...	...
0	10	...	...	...	...	...	...	...	...
1 - 4	2	1	1	...	...	...	...	...	...
5 - 14	4	3	1	...	...	...	...	...	...
15 - 19	5	4	1	...	...	...	...	...	...
20 - 24	4	4	-	...	...	...	...	...	...
25 - 44	31	20	11	...	...	...	...	...	...
45 - 64	52	33	19	...	...	...	...	...	...
65 - 74	26	16	10	...	...	...	...	...	...
75 - 84	21	11	11	...	...	...	...	...	...
85 +	9	4	5	...	...	...	...	...	...
Palau - Palaos									
1999 (C)									
Total	131	78	53	...	...	...	...	...	...
1 - 14	4	2	2	...	...	...	...	...	...
15 - 24	3	3	-	...	...	...	...	...	...
25 - 44	22	16	6	...	...	...	...	...	...
45 - 64	41	27	14	...	...	...	...	...	...
65 +	56	27	29	...	...	...	...	...	...

Continent, country or area, date, code and age (in years) / Continent, pays ou zone, date, code et âge (en années)	Total			Urban - Urbaine			Rural - Rurale		
	Both sexes Les deux sexes	Male Masculin	Female Féminin	Both sexes Les deux sexes	Male Masculin	Female Féminin	Both sexes Les deux sexes	Male Masculin	Female Féminin
OCEANIA - OCÉANIE									
Tonga									
2000 (+C)									
Total	653	334	319	...	...	...	...	...	...
1 - 9	23	10	13	...	...	...	...	...	...
10 - 19	14	10	4	...	...	...	...	...	...
20 - 29	21	10	11	...	...	...	...	...	...
30 - 39	16	5	11	...	...	...	...	...	...
40 - 49	33	20	13	...	...	...	...	...	...
50 - 59	78	37	41	...	...	...	...	...	...
60 - 69	116	67	49	...	...	...	...	...	...
70 +	299	151	148	...	...	...	...	...	...
Unknown - Inconnu	25	12	13	...	...	...	...	...	...
Tuvalu									
2005 (U)									
Total	*59*	*33*	*26*	...	...	...	...	...	...
0	*6*	*5*	*1*	...	...	...	...	...	...
1 - 4	*2*	*1*	*1*	...	...	...	...	...	...
5 - 9	*-*	*-*	*-*	...	...	...	...	...	...
10 - 14	*-*	*-*	*-*	...	...	...	...	...	...
15 - 19	*-*	*-*	*-*	...	...	...	...	...	...
20 - 24	*1*	*1*	*-*	...	...	...	...	...	...
25 - 29	*-*	*-*	*-*	...	...	...	...	...	...
30 - 34	*1*	*1*	*-*	...	...	...	...	...	...
35 - 39	*2*	*2*	*-*	...	...	...	...	...	...
40 - 44	*2*	*2*	*-*	...	...	...	...	...	...
45 - 49	*3*	*3*	*-*	...	...	...	...	...	...
50 - 54	*6*	*3*	*3*	...	...	...	...	...	...
55 - 59	*4*	*3*	*1*	...	...	...	...	...	...
60 - 64	*7*	*2*	*5*	...	...	...	...	...	...
65 - 69	*6*	*2*	*4*	...	...	...	...	...	...
70 - 74	*1*	*-*	*1*	...	...	...	...	...	...
75 - 79	*8*	*4*	*4*	...	...	...	...	...	...
80 - 84	*8*	*3*	*5*	...	...	...	...	...	...
85 - 89	*2*	*1*	*1*	...	...	...	...	...	...
Wallis and Futuna Islands - Îles Wallis et Futuna									
2005 (C)									
Total	65	27	38	...	...	...	...	...	...
0	1	-	1	...	...	...	...	...	...
1 - 4	1	1	-	...	...	...	...	...	...
5 - 9	-	-	-	...	...	...	...	...	...
10 - 14	1	1	-	...	...	...	...	...	...
15 - 19	1	1	-	...	...	...	...	...	...
20 - 24	3	2	1	...	...	...	...	...	...
25 - 29	-	-	-	...	...	...	...	...	...
30 - 34	-	-	-	...	...	...	...	...	...
35 - 39	-	-	-	...	...	...	...	...	...
40 - 44	1	-	1	...	...	...	...	...	...
45 - 49	2	2	-	...	...	...	...	...	...
50 - 54	6	-	6	...	...	...	...	...	...
55 - 59	5	3	2	...	...	...	...	...	...
60 - 64	4	3	1	...	...	...	...	...	...
65 - 69	6	2	4	...	...	...	...	...	...
70 - 74	4	2	2	...	...	...	...	...	...
75 - 79	10	3	7	...	...	...	...	...	...
80 - 84	5	3	2	...	...	...	...	...	...
85 - 89	13	4	9	...	...	...	...	...	...
90 - 94	2	-	2	...	...	...	...	...	...
95 +	-	-	-	...	...	...	...	...	...

FOOTNOTES - NOTES

Italics: estimates which are less reliable. - Italiques: estimations moins sûres.

* Provisional. -
Données provisoires.

'Code' indicates the source of data, as follows:
C - Civil registration, estimated over 90% complete
U - Civil registration, estimated less than 90% complete
| - Other source, estimated reliable
+ - Data tabulated by date of registration rather than occurence.
... - Information not available

Le 'Code' indique la source des données, comme suit:
C - Registres de l'état civil considérés complets à 90 p. 100 au moins.
U - Registres de l'état civil qui ne sont pas considérés complets à 90 p. 100 au moins.
| - Autre source, considérée pas douteuses.
+ - Données exploitées selon la date de l'enregistrement et non la date de l'événement.
... - Information pas disponible.

[1] Excluding live-born infants who died before their birth was registered. For Algerian population only. - Non compris les enfants nés vivants décédés avant l'enregistrement de leur naissance. Pour la population algérienne seulement.

[2] For 2001, data refer to last twelve months preceding census in August 2001. - Pour 2001, les données se rapportent aux douze mois précédant le recensement d'août 2001.

[3] Based on the results of the population census. - D'après les résultats du recensement de la population.

[4] Figures for urban and rural areas do not add up to the total, since they do not include the category 'Unknown residence'. - La somme des données pour la résidence urbaine et rurale n'est pas égale au total parce qu'elle n'inclue pas la catégorie 'Résidence inconnue'.

[5] Data for 1997 refer to last twelve months preceding population and housing census of 1997. - Les données pour 1997 se réfèrent au douze mois précédant le recensement de population et de l'habitat de 1997.

[6] Deaths for 2001 refer to the period January-August 2001. - Le chiffre des décès de 2001 correspond à la période allant de janvier à août 2001.

[7] Figures for male and female categories do not add up to the total, since they do not include the category "Unknown". - La somme des chiffres indiqués pour les sexes masculin et féminin n'est pas égale au total parce qu'elle n'inclut pas la catégorie " inconnue ".

[8] Excluding live-born infants who died before their birth was registered. - Non compris les enfants nés vivants décédés avant l'enregistrement de leur naissance.

[9] Excluding deaths of unknown sex. - Non compris les décès dont on ignore le sexe.

[10] Data are for 12 months preceding the census date. - Les données portent sur les 12 mois précédant la date du recensement.

[11] Source: World Health Organization. - Source : Organisation mondiale de la santé.

[12] Data as reported by national statistical authorities; they may differ from data presented in other tables. - Les données comme elles ont été déclarées par l'institut national de la statistique; elles peuvent être différentes de celles présentées dans d'autres tableaux.

[13] Including Canadian residents temporarily in the United States, but excluding United States residents temporarily in Canada. - Y compris les résidents canadiens se trouvant temporairement aux Etats-Unis, mais ne comprenant pas les résidents des Etats-Unis se trouvant temporairement au Canada.

[14] Figures for urban and rural areas do not add up to the total, since they do not include the category 'Unknown residence'. Figures for male and female categories do not add up to the total, since they do not include the category "Unknown". - La somme des données pour la résidence urbaine et rurale n'est pas égale au total parce qu'elle n'inclue pas la catégorie 'Résidence inconnue'. La somme des chiffres indiqués pour les sexes masculin et féminin n'est pas égale au total parce qu'elle n'inclut pas la catégorie " inconnue ".

[15] Data refer to deaths of residents of the Netherlands Antilles (including those that died outside the Netherlands Antilles). Data exclude deaths by non-residents. - Ces données concernent les décès de résidents des Antilles néerlandaises (y compris ceux survenus hors des Antilles néerlandaises). Elles ne concernent pas les décès des non-résidents.

[16] Excluding Indian jungle population. - Non compris les Indiens de la jungle.

[17] Data on live births and deaths are based on a civil registration system put in place in January 1998. - Les données sur les naissances et les décès sont basées sur un système d'enregistrement des faits d'état civil mis en place en janvier 1998.

[18] Excluding nomadic Indian tribes. - Non compris les tribus d'Indiens nomades.

[19] For 2001, data were collected from population census held on August 2002, referring to events in calendar year 2001. - Pour 2001, les données sont tirées du recensement de la population réalisé en août 2002, concernant des événements de l'année civile 2001.

[20] Excluding Indian jungle population. Data refer to registered deaths only. - Non compris les Indiens de la jungle. Les données se rapportent aux décès enregistrés seulement.

[21] Figures for urban and rural areas do not add up to the total, since they do not include the category 'Unknown residence'. Data for urban refer to the total of the district of Paramaribo (capital) and Wanica district. - La somme des données pour la résidence urbaine et rurale n'est pas égale au total parce qu'elle n'inclue pas la catégorie 'Résidence inconnue'. Les données relatives aux zones urbaines correspondent au total pour le district de Paramaribo (capitale) et le district de Wanica.

[22] Excluding infants born alive of less than 28 weeks' gestation, of less than 1 000 grams in weight and 35 centimeters in length, who die within seven days of birth. - Non compris les enfants nés vivants après moins de 28 semaines de gestations, pesant moins de 1 000 grammes, mesurant moins de 35 centimètres et décédés dans les sept jours qui ont suivi leur naissance.

[23] For 2005, data refer to last twelve months preceding census in May 2005. - Pour 2005, les données se rapportent aux douze mois précédant le recensement de mai 2005.

[24] For statistical purposes, the data for China do not include those for the Hong Kong Special Administrative Region (Hong Kong SAR), Macao Special Administrative Region (Macao SAR) and Taiwan province of China. - Pour la présentation des statistiques, les données pour la Chine ne comprennent pas la Région Administrative Spéciale de Hong Kong (Hong Kong RAS), la Région Administrative Spéciale de Macao (Macao RAS) et Taïwan province de Chine.

[25] Data refer to government controlled areas. - Les données se rapportent aux zones contrôlées par le Gouvernement.

[26] Including data for East Jerusalem and Israeli residents in certain other territories under occupation by Israeli military forces since June 1967. - Y compris les données pour Jérusalem-Est et les résidents israéliens dans certains autres territoires occupés depuis 1967 par les forces armées israéliennes.

[27] Data include 30 (preliminary figure) deaths abroad of Israeli residents who were out of the country for less than a year. - Y compris les décès à l'étranger de 30 résidents israéliens (chiffres préliminaires) qui ont quitté le pays depuis moins d'un an.

[28] Figures for male and female categories do not add up to the total, since they do not include the category "Unknown". Data include 30 (preliminary figure) deaths abroad of Israeli residents who were out of the country for less than a year. - La somme des chiffres indiqués pour les sexes masculin et féminin n'est pas égale au total parce qu'elle n'inclut pas la catégorie " inconnue ". Y compris les décès à l'étranger de 30 résidents israéliens (chiffres préliminaires) qui ont quitté le pays depuis moins d'un an.

[29] Data refer to Japanese nationals in Japan only. - Les données se rapportent aux nationaux japonais au Japon seulement.

[30] Excluding alien armed forces, civilian aliens employed by armed forces, and foreign diplomatic personnel and their dependants. - Non compris les militaires étrangers, les civils étrangers employés par les forces armées ni le personnel diplomatique étranger et les membres de leur famille les accompagnant.

[31] For 2001, data refer to last twelve months preceding census on June 2001. - Pour 2001, les données se rapportent aux douze mois précédant le recensement juin 2001.

[32] Data refer to the recorded events in Ministry of Health hospitals and health centres only. - Les données se rapportent aux faits d'état civil enregistrés dans les hôpitaux et les dispensaires du Ministère de la santé seulement.

[33] Excluding data for the Pakistan-held part of Jammu and Kashmir, the final status of which has not yet been determined. Data based on Pakistan Demographic Survey (PDS 2005). - Non compris les données concernant la partie du Jammu et Cachemire occupée par le Pakistan dont le statut définitif n'a pas été déterminé. Données extraites de l'enquête démographique effectuée par le Pakistan en 2005.

[34] Including armed forces stationed outside the country, but excluding alien armed forces stationed in the area. - Y compris les militaires nationaux hors du pays, mais non compris les militaires étrangers en garnison sur le territoire.

[35] Excluding Faeroe Islands and Greenland. - Non compris les Iles Féroé et le Gröenland.

[36] Including nationals temporarily outside the country. - Y compris les nationaux se trouvant temporairement hors du pays.

[37] Excluding Overseas Departments, namely, French Guiana, Guadeloupe, Martinique and Reunion, shown separately. Including armed forces stationed outside the country. For ages five years and over, age classification based on year of birth rather than exact date of birth. The difference between 'Total' and the sum of 'urban' and 'rural' is due to the cases of unknown place of residence or residence abroad. - Non compris les départements d'outre mer, c'est-à-dire la Guyane française, la Guadeloupe, la Martinique et la Réunion, qui font l'objet de rubriques distinctes. Y compris les militaires nationaux hors du pays. A partir de cinq ans, le classement selon l'âge est basé sur l'année de naissances et non sur la date exacte de naissance. La différence entre le 'Total' et la somme des

données selon la résidence urbaine/rurale se rapporte à la situation ou on ignore la résidence ou si la résidence est à l'étranger.

[38] Data for urban/rural residence, for the de jure population. - Les données selon la résidence urbaine/rurale, pour la population de droit.

[39] Events registered within one year of occurrence. - Evénements enregistrés dans l'année qui suit l'événement.

[40] Maltese population only. - Population Maltaise seulement.

[41] Including residents outside the country if listed in a Netherlands population register. - Y compris les résidents hors du pays, s'ils sont inscrits sur un registre de population néerlandais.

[42] Including residents temporarily outside the country. - Y compris les résidents se trouvant temporairement hors du pays.

[43] Without data for Kosovo and Metohia. - Sans les données pour le Kosovo and Metohie.

[44] For resident population only. - Pour la population résidante seulement.

Table 20

Table 20 presents death rates by age, sex and urban/rural residence for the latest available year.

Description of variables: Age is defined as age at last birthday, that is, the difference between the date of birth and the date of the occurrence of the event, expressed in completed solar years. The age classification used in this table is the following: under 1 year, 1-4 years, 5-year age groups through 95-99, and 100 years or over.

The urban/rural classification of deaths is that provided by each country or area; it is presumed to be based on the national census definition of urban population that have been set forth at the end of the technical notes for table 6.

Rate computation: Death rates specific for age and sex are the annual number of deaths in each age-sex group (as shown in table 19) per 1 000 population in the same age-sex group.

Death rates by age, sex and urban/rural residence are the annual number of deaths that occurred in a specific age-sex-urban/rural group (as shown in table 19) per 1 000 population in the corresponding age-sex-urban/rural group (as shown in table 7). These rates are calculated by the Statistics Division of the United Nations.

Deaths at unknown age and the population of unknown age are excluded from age-specific rate calculations but are part of the death rate for all ages combined.

Death rates for infants under one year of age in this table differ from the infant mortality rates shown elsewhere, because the latter are computed per 1 000 live births rather than per 1 000 population.

The population used in computing the rates is estimated or enumerated distributions by age and sex. First priority was given to an estimate for the mid-point of the same year (as shown in table 7), second priority to census returns of the year to which the deaths referred and third priority to an estimate for some other point of time in the year.

Rates presented in this table have been limited to those for countries or areas having at least a total of 1 000 deaths in a given year. Moreover, rates specific for individual sub-categories that are based on 30 or fewer deaths are identified by the symbol (♦).

Reliability of data: Rates are not computed if data from civil registers of deaths are reported as incomplete (less than 90 per cent completeness) or of unknown completeness, and therefore deemed unreliable. Table 18 and the technical notes for that table provide more detailed information on the completeness of death registration. For more information about the quality of vital statistics, see section 4.2 of the Introduction.

Limitations: Rates shown in this table are subject to all the same limitations that affect the corresponding frequencies and are set forth in the technical notes for table 19. These include differences in the completeness of registration, the treatment of infants who were born alive but died before the registration of their birth or within the first 24 hours of life, the method used to determine age at death and the quality of the reported information relating to age at death. In addition, some rates are based on deaths tabulated by date of registration and not by date of occurrence; these have been indicated with a plus sign (+).

The problem of obtaining precise correspondence between deaths (numerator) and population (denominator) as regards the inclusion or exclusion of armed forces, refugees, displaced persons and other special groups is particularly difficult where age-specific death rates are concerned. This is the case for Japan and Malta. For Japan, deaths refer to Japanese nationals only while the population include foreigners except foreign military and civilian personnel and their dependants stationed in the area. Similarly for Malta, deaths are for Maltese nationals only while the population include foreigners who hold work and resident permit and reside in the country. One should also note that male rates in the age range 20 to 40 years may be especially affected by this non-correspondence, and care should be exercised in using these rates for comparative purposes.

Even when deaths and population do correspond conceptually, comparability of the rates may be affected by abnormal conditions such as absence from the country or area of large numbers of young men in the military forces or working abroad as temporary workers. Death rates may appear high in the younger ages, simply because a large section of the able-bodied members of the age group, whose death rates under normal conditions might be less than the average for persons of their age, is not included.

Also, in a number of cases the rates shown here for all ages combined differ from crude death rates shown elsewhere, because in this table they are computed on the population for which an appropriate age-sex distribution was available, while the crude death rates shown elsewhere may utilize a different total population. The population by age and sex might refer to a census date within the year rather than to the mid-point, or it might be more or less inclusive as regards ethnic groups, armed forces and so forth. In a few instances, the difference is attributable to the fact that the rates in this table were computed on the mean population whereas the corresponding rates in other tables were computed on an estimate for 1 July.

The comparability of data by urban/rural residence is affected by the national definitions of urban and rural used in tabulating these data. It is assumed, in the absence of specific information to the contrary, that the definitions of urban and rural used in connection with the national population census were also used in the compilation of the vital statistics for each country or area. However, it cannot be excluded that, for a given country or area, different definitions of urban and rural are used for the vital statistics data and the population census data respectively. When known, the definitions of urban used in national population censuses are presented at the end of the technical notes for table 6. As discussed in detail in the technical notes for table 6, these definitions vary considerably from one country or area to another.

In addition to problems of comparability, vital rates classified by urban/rural residence are also subject to certain special types of bias. If, when calculating vital rates, different definitions of urban are used in connection with the vital events and the population data and if this results in a net difference between the numerator and denominator of the rate in the population at risk, then the vital rates would be biased. Urban/rural differentials in vital rates may also be affected by whether the vital events have been tabulated in terms of place of occurrence or place of usual residence. This problem is discussed in more detail in section 4.1.4.1 of the Introduction.

Earlier data: Death rates specific for age and sex have been shown for the latest available year in many of the issues of the Yearbook since the 1955 issue. Data included in this table update the series shown in the Yearbook and in the Special Supplements covering a period of years as follows:

Issue	Years Covered
Historical Supplement CD, 1997	1948 – 1997
1996	1987 - 1995
1992	1983 – 1992
1985	1976 – 1984
1980	1971 – 1979
Historical Supplement, 1979	1948 - 1977

Tableau 20

Le tableau 20 présente les taux de mortalité selon l'âge et le sexe et selon le lieu de résidence (zone urbaine ou rurale) correspondant à la dernière année disponible.

Description des variables : L'âge considéré est l'âge au dernier anniversaire, c'est-à-dire la différence entre la date de naissance et la date du décès, exprimée en années solaires révolues. La classification par âge est la suivante : moins d'un an, 1 à 4 ans, groupes quinquennaux jusqu'à 95-99 ans et 100 ans et plus.

La classification des décès selon le lieu de résidence (zone urbaine ou rurale) est celle qui a été communiquée par chaque pays ou zone ; on part du principe qu'elle repose sur les définitions de la population urbaine utilisées pour les recensements nationaux, qui sont reproduites à la fin des notes techniques du tableau 6.

Calcul des taux : les taux de mortalité selon l'âge et le sexe représentent le nombre annuel de décès survenus pour chaque sexe et chaque groupe d'âge (fréquences du tableau 19) pour 1 000 personnes du même groupe.

Les taux de mortalité selon l'âge, le sexe et le lieu de résidence (zone urbaine ou rurale) représentent le nombre annuel de décès survenus dans un groupe d'âge et de sexe donné parmi la population urbaine ou rurale (fréquences du tableau 19) pour 1 000 personnes du même groupe parmi la population urbaine ou rurale. Ces taux ont été calculés par la Division de statistique de l'ONU.

On n'a pas tenu compte des décès à un âge inconnu ni de la population d'âge inconnu, sauf dans les taux de mortalité pour tous les âges combinés.

Il convient de noter que, dans ce tableau, les taux de mortalité des groupes de moins d'un an sont différents des taux de mortalité infantile qui figurent dans d'autres tableaux, ces derniers ayant été établis pour 1 000 naissances vivantes et non pour 1 000 habitants.

Les chiffres de population utilisés pour le calcul des taux proviennent de dénombrements ou de répartitions estimatives de la population selon l'âge et le sexe. On a utilisé de préférence les estimations de la population au milieu de l'année considérée selon les chiffres du tableau 7 ; à défaut, on s'est contenté des données censitaires se rapportant à l'année des décès et, si ces données manquaient également, d'estimations établies à un autre moment de l'année.

Les taux présentés dans le tableau 20 ne se rapportent qu'aux pays ou zones où l'on a enregistré un total d'au moins 1 000 décès pendant l'année. Les taux relatifs à des sous-catégories, qui sont fondés sur 30 décès ou moins, sont signalés par le signe '♦'.

Fiabilité des données : on a choisi de ne pas faire figurer dans le tableau 20 des taux calculés à partir de données sur les décès issues de registres d'état civil qui sont déclarées incomplètes (degré d'exhaustivité inférieur à 90 p. 100) ou dont le degré d'exhaustivité n'est pas connu. Le tableau 18 et les notes techniques s'y rapportant présentent des renseignements plus détaillés sur le degré d'exhaustivité de l'enregistrement des décès. Pour plus de précisions sur la qualité des statistiques de l'état civil, voir la section 4.2 de l'introduction.

Insuffisance des données : les taux présentés dans le tableau 20 appellent les mêmes réserves que celles formulées à propos des fréquences correspondantes (voir à ce sujet les notes techniques se rapportant au tableau 19). Leurs imperfections tiennent notamment aux différences d'exhaustivité de l'enregistrement, au classement des enfants nés vivants mais décédés avant l'enregistrement de leur naissance ou dans les 24 heures qui ont suivi la naissance, à la méthode utilisée pour obtenir l'âge au moment du décès, et à la qualité des déclarations concernant l'âge au moment du décès. En outre, dans certains cas, les données relatives aux décès sont classées par date d'enregistrement et non par date de l'événement ; ces cas ont été signalés par le signe '+'.

S'agissant des taux de mortalité par âge, il est particulièrement difficile d'établir une correspondance exacte entre les décès (numérateur) et la population (dénominateur) du fait de l'inclusion ou de l'exclusion des militaires, des réfugiés, des personnes déplacées et d'autres groupes spéciaux. C'est le cas pour le Japon et Malte. Pour le Japon, les décès se rapportent aux seuls citoyens japonais alors que la population inclut les étrangers à l'exception des militaires étrangers et des personnels civils ainsi que leurs familles stationnés dans le pays. De même, pour Malte, les décès se rapportent aux nationaux alors que la population inclut les étrangers titulaires d'un permis de séjour et de travail qui résident dans le pays. Les taux de mortalité pour le sexe masculin dans les groupes d'âge de 20 à 40 ans peuvent être tout particulièrement influencés par ce manque de correspondance, et il importe d'être prudent quand on les utilise dans des comparaisons. Il convient d'ajouter que, même lorsque population et décès correspondent, la comparabilité des taux peut être compromise par des conditions anormales telles que l'absence du pays ou de la zone d'un grand nombre de jeunes gens qui sont sous les drapeaux ou qui travaillent à l'étranger comme travailleurs temporaires. Il arrive ainsi que les taux de mortalité paraissent élevés parmi les groupes les plus jeunes simplement parce que l'on en a exclu un grand nombre d'individus en bonne santé pour lesquels le taux de mortalité pourrait être, dans des conditions normales, inférieur à la moyenne observée pour les personnes du même âge.

De même, les taux indiqués pour tous les âges combinés diffèrent dans plusieurs cas des taux bruts de mortalité qui figurent dans d'autres tableaux, parce qu'ils se rapportent à une population pour laquelle on disposait d'une répartition par âge et par sexe appropriée, tandis que les taux bruts de mortalité indiqués ailleurs peuvent avoir été calculés sur la base d'un chiffre de population totale différent. Ainsi, il est possible que les chiffres de population par âge et par sexe proviennent d'un recensement effectué dans le courant de l'année et non au milieu de l'année, et qu'ils se différencient des autres chiffres de population en excluant ou en incluant certains groupes ethniques, les militaires, etc. Quelquefois, la différence tient à ce que les taux du tableau 20 ont été calculés sur la base de la population moyenne, alors que les taux correspondants des autres tableaux reposent sur une estimation au 1er juillet. Les écarts de cet ordre sont insignifiants, mais il n'en a pas été tenu compte dans le tableau.

La comparabilité des données selon le lieu de résidence (zone urbaine ou rurale) peut être limitée par les définitions nationales des termes « urbain » et « rural » utilisées pour le classement de ces données. En l'absence d'indications contraires, on a supposé que les mêmes définitions avaient servi pour le recensement national de la population et pour l'établissement des statistiques de l'état civil pour chaque pays ou zone. Toutefois, il n'est pas exclu que, pour une zone ou un pays donné, des définitions différentes aient été retenues. Les définitions du terme « urbain » utilisées pour les recensements nationaux de population ont été présentées à la fin du tableau 6 lorsqu'elles étaient connues. Comme on l'a précisé dans les notes techniques relatives au tableau 6, ces définitions varient considérablement d'un pays ou d'une zone à l'autre.

Outre les problèmes de comparabilité, les taux démographiques classés selon le lieu de résidence (zone urbaine ou rurale) sont également sujets à des distorsions particulières. Si l'on utilise des définitions différentes du terme « urbain » pour classer les faits d'état civil et les données relatives à la population lors du calcul des taux et qu'il en résulte une différence nette entre le numérateur et le dénominateur pour le taux de la population exposée au risque, les taux démographiques s'en trouveront faussés. La différence entre ces taux pour les zones urbaines et rurales pourra aussi être faussée selon que les faits d'état civil auront été classés d'après le lieu où ils se sont produits ou d'après le lieu de résidence habituel.

Ce problème est examiné plus en détail à la section 4.1.4.1 de l'introduction.

Données publiées antérieurement : un certain nombre d'éditions de l'*Annuaire* parues depuis 1955 présentent les statistiques les plus récentes dont on disposait à l'époque sur les taux de mortalité selon l'âge et le sexe. Les données du tableau 20 actualisent celles qui figuraient dans les éditions de l'*Annuaire démographique* et dans les *Suppléments spéciaux* qui portaient sur les périodes suivantes :

Éditions	Années considérées
Supplément historique (CD-ROM), 1997	1948 – 1997
1996	1987 - 1995
1992	1983 – 1992
1985	1976 – 1984
1980	1971 – 1979
Supplément rétrospectif, 1979	1948 - 1977

Continent, country or area, date, code and age (in years) / Continent, pays ou zone, date, code et âge (en années)	Total			Urban - Urbaine			Rural - Rurale		
	Both sexes Les deux sexes	Male Masculin	Female Féminin	Both sexes Les deux sexes	Male Masculin	Female Féminin	Both sexes Les deux sexes	Male Masculin	Female Féminin
AFRICA - AFRIQUE									
Botswana[1]									
2001 (I)									
Total	12.4	13.3	11.6	...	...	...	...	...	...
0	36.8	37.5	36.1	...	...	...	...	...	...
1 - 4	7.8	8.3	7.2	...	...	...	...	...	...
5 - 9	2.3	2.4	2.2	...	...	...	...	...	...
10 - 14	1.2	1.1	1.3	...	...	...	...	...	...
15 - 19	1.9	1.8	2.0	...	...	...	...	...	...
20 - 24	6.4	4.8	7.8	...	...	...	...	...	...
25 - 29	14.2	11.8	16.4	...	...	...	...	...	...
30 - 34	20.9	22.5	19.4	...	...	...	...	...	...
35 - 39	21.4	25.4	17.9	...	...	...	...	...	...
40 - 44	20.9	25.8	16.7	...	...	...	...	...	...
45 - 49	21.0	27.5	15.3	...	...	...	...	...	...
50 - 54	19.0	24.5	14.0	...	...	...	...	...	...
55 - 59	20.1	26.5	14.3	...	...	...	...	...	...
60 - 64	22.3	28.9	16.5	...	...	...	...	...	...
65 - 69	26.4	33.7	20.8	...	...	...	...	...	...
70 - 74	28.4	36.2	22.8	...	...	...	...	...	...
75 +	60.1	73.2	51.6	...	...	...	...	...	...
Egypt - Égypte									
1996 (C)									
Total	6.4	6.7	6.1	6.9	7.7	6.2	6.0	6.0	6.0
0	85.0	84.3	85.7	79.3	85.2	73.1	89.3	83.7	95.2
1 - 4	2.7	2.6	2.8	2.3	2.4	2.2	3.0	2.8	3.2
5 - 9	0.9	0.9	0.8	0.9	1.1	0.8	0.8	0.9	0.8
10 - 14	0.7	0.8	0.6	0.8	1.0	0.6	0.6	0.7	0.6
15 - 19	1.0	1.1	0.8	1.2	1.5	0.9	0.8	0.8	0.7
20 - 24	1.1	1.3	0.9	1.5	1.9	1.0	0.8	0.9	0.8
25 - 29	1.3	1.6	1.1	1.7	2.2	1.3	1.0	1.1	0.9
30 - 34	1.7	2.1	1.3	2.0	2.6	1.4	1.4	1.7	1.2
35 - 39	2.2	2.6	1.7	2.4	3.0	1.9	1.9	2.3	1.6
40 - 44	3.4	4.4	2.4	3.7	4.7	2.7	3.1	4.0	2.1
45 - 49	5.6	6.8	4.2	6.2	7.5	4.8	4.9	6.1	3.7
50 - 54	9.3	11.4	7.3	10.3	12.3	8.2	8.4	10.5	6.5
55 - 59	16.0	18.6	13.0	17.9	20.5	14.9	14.2	16.9	11.4
60 - 64	23.8	26.9	20.6	25.6	28.4	22.6	22.1	25.4	18.9
65 - 69	41.9	43.2	40.4	45.9	46.3	45.3	38.9	40.6	37.0
70 - 74	69.3	70.9	67.5	72.7	73.2	72.0	66.6	69.0	64.3
75 +	186.5	161.1	213.8	185.3	163.6	210.5	187.5	159.2	216.0
1999 (C)									
Total	6.4	6.8	6.0	...	...	...	...	...	...
0	34.3	35.4	33.2	...	...	...	...	...	...
1 - 4	2.4	2.4	2.4	...	...	...	...	...	...
5 - 9	0.7	0.8	0.6	...	...	...	...	...	...
10 - 14	0.6	0.7	0.6	...	...	...	...	...	...
15 - 19	0.8	1.0	0.7	...	...	...	...	...	...
20 - 24	1.2	1.4	0.9	...	...	...	...	...	...
25 - 29	1.2	1.6	0.9	...	...	...	...	...	...
30 - 34	1.4	1.8	1.1	...	...	...	...	...	...
35 - 39	2.1	2.6	1.6	...	...	...	...	...	...
40 - 44	3.3	4.2	2.3	...	...	...	...	...	...
45 - 49	5.8	7.3	4.3	...	...	...	...	...	...
50 - 54	10.3	12.9	7.8	...	...	...	...	...	...
55 - 59	15.5	17.9	12.7	...	...	...	...	...	...
60 - 64	22.9	26.1	19.6	...	...	...	...	...	...
65 - 69	43.1	44.4	41.5	...	...	...	...	...	...
70 - 74	71.3	72.7	69.7	...	...	...	...	...	...
75 +	199.5	175.9	224.8	...	...	...	...	...	...
Malawi[2]									
1998 (I)									
Total	20.9	23.4	18.6	15.5	16.7	14.1	21.9	24.6	19.3
0	122.0	136.9	107.4	106.9	120.9	92.9	124.3	139.3	109.6
1 - 4	46.4	51.2	41.6	37.2	41.4	33.1	47.7	52.7	42.9
5 - 9	11.6	12.9	10.4	8.9	10.3	7.5	12.0	13.2	10.8

20. Death rates specific for age, sex and urban/rural residence: latest available year, 1996 - 2005
Taux de mortalité selon l'âge, le sexe et la résidence, urbaine/rurale: dernière année disponible, 1996 - 2005 (continued - suite)

Continent, country or area, date, code and age (in years) / Continent, pays ou zone, date, code et âge (en années)	Total			Urban - Urbaine			Rural - Rurale		
	Both sexes Les deux sexes	Male Masculin	Female Féminin	Both sexes Les deux sexes	Male Masculin	Female Féminin	Both sexes Les deux sexes	Male Masculin	Female Féminin
AFRICA - AFRIQUE									
Malawi[2]									
1998 (|)									
10 - 14	7.8	7.9	7.8	4.4	5.2	3.8	8.4	8.3	8.5
15 - 19	6.6	6.5	6.6	3.7	3.8	3.7	7.1	7.0	7.2
20 - 24	12.0	16.0	8.8	6.7	7.0	6.4	13.2	18.3	9.3
25 - 29	11.7	12.3	11.1	7.7	6.4	9.3	12.7	14.0	11.5
30 - 34	14.6	14.8	14.5	11.1	10.2	12.3	15.4	15.9	14.9
35 - 39	14.5	15.4	13.7	12.9	12.9	12.9	14.8	15.9	13.8
40 - 44	17.6	20.6	14.5	16.3	17.5	14.6	17.8	21.2	14.5
45 - 49	16.9	22.3	11.6	15.2	16.7	12.9	17.2	23.2	11.5
50 - 54	15.4	18.0	12.8	18.6	20.4	15.8	15.0	17.6	12.5
55 - 59	22.1	19.3	25.0	22.5	21.8	23.5	22.1	19.1	25.1
60 - 64	19.1	22.4	16.1	24.9	25.4	24.1	18.7	22.1	15.6
65 - 69	19.3	19.1	19.5	20.0	21.3	18.4	19.3	19.0	19.6
70 - 74	22.7	30.0	16.5	26.5	31.6	21.7	22.5	29.9	16.2
75 - 79	24.4	29.3	19.7	35.4	43.0	27.6	23.9	28.6	19.3
80 - 84	33.2	41.1	26.8	46.7	59.6	36.5	32.6	40.3	26.4
85 +	51.7	60.6	44.1	89.6	104.8	77.6	50.1	58.8	42.6
Mauritius - Maurice									
2005 (+C)									
Total	7.0	7.9	6.0	...	...	...	...	...	...
0	13.3	15.4	11.0	...	...	...	...	...	...
1 - 4	0.6	◆0.7	◆0.6	...	...	...	...	...	...
5 - 9	◆0.2	◆0.2	◆0.2	...	...	...	...	...	...
10 - 14	◆0.2	◆0.2	◆0.2	...	...	...	...	...	...
15 - 19	0.4	◆0.5	0.4	...	...	...	...	...	...
20 - 24	0.8	1.0	◆0.5	...	...	...	...	...	...
25 - 29	1.0	1.5	◆0.4	...	...	...	...	...	...
30 - 34	1.4	1.9	0.9	...	...	...	...	...	...
35 - 39	2.3	3.3	1.3	...	...	...	...	...	...
40 - 44	3.3	4.7	1.9	...	...	...	...	...	...
45 - 49	5.3	7.0	3.5	...	...	...	...	...	...
50 - 54	8.0	11.0	5.1	...	...	...	...	...	...
55 - 59	13.5	18.2	9.2	...	...	...	...	...	...
60 - 64	19.4	24.7	14.8	...	...	...	...	...	...
65 - 69	27.4	35.6	20.9	...	...	...	...	...	...
70 - 74	43.7	58.8	32.3	...	...	...	...	...	...
75 - 79	65.8	83.5	53.7	...	...	...	...	...	...
80 - 84	101.0	129.3	84.5	...	...	...	...	...	...
85 +	189.6	235.0	171.8	...	...	...	...	...	...
Mozambique[3]									
1997 (|)									
Total	25.2	28.2	22.5	15.9	17.7	14.1	29.1	32.8	25.8
0	186.7	205.1	168.9	119.1	132.8	105.6	210.4	230.7	190.8
1 - 4	56.0	61.2	51.0	29.1	31.6	26.5	65.2	71.2	59.3
5 - 9	14.3	15.3	13.2	6.9	7.8	6.1	17.1	18.2	16.0
10 - 14	8.2	8.6	7.7	4.0	4.4	3.6	10.2	10.5	9.8
15 - 19	7.5	7.6	7.3	4.6	4.8	4.5	9.0	9.3	8.7
20 - 24	7.3	7.7	6.9	5.8	6.1	5.6	7.9	8.5	7.5
25 - 29	8.2	9.1	7.5	7.5	8.6	6.6	8.5	9.4	7.8
30 - 34	9.8	11.2	8.5	8.8	10.5	7.1	10.3	11.6	9.2
35 - 39	10.2	11.8	8.8	9.5	10.7	8.2	10.5	12.4	9.0
40 - 44	12.7	15.2	10.5	12.5	14.2	10.5	12.8	15.6	10.5
45 - 49	13.4	16.3	10.7	15.2	18.0	12.2	12.7	15.6	10.2
50 - 54	18.9	23.6	14.9	22.9	27.0	18.8	17.6	22.4	13.8
55 - 59	15.8	19.1	12.7	19.4	22.8	15.8	14.7	17.9	11.8
60 - 64	32.8	38.3	27.8	40.4	46.7	34.4	30.4	35.6	25.7
65 - 69	25.5	29.5	21.8	36.1	44.9	28.8	22.6	25.6	19.9
70 - 74	51.1	61.1	41.7	71.8	89.6	57.5	45.3	53.9	36.9
75 - 79	40.8	46.2	35.5	63.2	82.8	48.7	35.2	38.6	31.7
80 +	98.3	110.3	87.4	143.7	184.7	116.7	88.2	97.0	79.8
Namibia - Namibie[4]									
2001 (|)									
Total	13.7	13.9[5]	12.9[5]	10.8	11.2[5]	10.5[5]	15.1	15.4[5]	14.0[5]
0 - 4	19.2	18.2[5]	19.3[5]	16.1	14.5[5]	17.1[5]	20.4	19.6[5]	20.2[5]

20. Death rates specific for age, sex and urban/rural residence: latest available year, 1996 - 2005
Taux de mortalité selon l'âge, le sexe et la résidence, urbaine/rurale: dernière année disponible, 1996 - 2005 (continued - suite)

Continent, country or area, date, code and age (in years) / Continent, pays ou zone, date, code et âge (en années)	Total			Urban - Urbaine			Rural - Rurale		
	Both sexes Les deux sexes	Male Masculin	Female Féminin	Both sexes Les deux sexes	Male Masculin	Female Féminin	Both sexes Les deux sexes	Male Masculin	Female Féminin
AFRICA - AFRIQUE									
Namibia - Namibie[4]									
2001 (|)									
5 - 9	3.8	3.8[5]	3.6[5]	2.9	3.1[5]	2.7[5]	4.1	4.0[5]	3.8[5]
10 - 14	2.2	2.2[5]	2.2[5]	2.0	1.9[5]	2.0[5]	2.3	2.3[5]	2.2[5]
15 - 19	3.3	3.2[5]	3.2[5]	3.1	3.2[5]	2.9[5]	3.3	3.2[5]	3.3[5]
20 - 24	7.1	5.7[5]	8.4[5]	4.7	4.3[5]	5.1[5]	8.7	6.6[5]	10.7[5]
25 - 29	11.9	10.8[5]	12.9[5]	6.8	6.1[5]	7.5[5]	16.7	15.4[5]	17.8[5]
30 - 34	17.1	18.0[5]	16.1[5]	9.3	9.3[5]	9.3[5]	24.7	27.5[5]	22.0[5]
35 - 39	19.1	22.2[5]	16.3[5]	11.5	12.3[5]	10.7[5]	26.1	33.1[5]	20.7[5]
40 - 44	18.5	22.0[5]	15.4[5]	12.2	13.0[5]	11.5[5]	23.6	31.0[5]	18.1[5]
45 - 49	19.0	22.6[5]	15.7[5]	13.7	14.3[5]	13.0[5]	22.7	29.9[5]	17.3[5]
50 - 54	18.1	24.9[5]	12.3[5]	17.2	19.8[5]	14.1[5]	18.6	28.5[5]	11.6[5]
55 - 59	19.9	25.2[5]	15.0[5]	19.1	20.5[5]	17.4[5]	20.2	27.8[5]	14.1[5]
60 - 64	22.1	27.7[5]	16.7[5]	28.7	32.7[5]	24.3[5]	20.0	25.8[5]	14.5[5]
65 - 69	22.8	27.2[5]	18.8[5]	29.3	34.3[5]	24.1[5]	21.0	25.1[5]	17.4[5]
70 - 74	33.1	43.5[5]	25.3[5]	54.8	61.8[5]	48.4[5]	28.7	39.6[5]	20.7[5]
75 - 79	35.7	41.7[5]	30.2[5]	58.1	66.5[5]	49.9[5]	31.5	36.7[5]	26.7[5]
80 - 84	39.0	42.5[5]	35.3[5]	79.3	79.4[5]	78.3[5]	33.2	37.2[5]	29.1[5]
85 - 89	66.8	79.7[5]	56.0[5]	94.6	117.3[5]	79.1[5]	60.7	72.1[5]	50.7[5]
90 - 94	96.3	110.0[5]	84.8[5]	133.0	♦144.7[5]	♦125.0[5]	89.9	103.2[5]	78.3[5]
95 +	137.5	146.0[5]	133.3[5]	198.5	♦207.2[5]	♦192.1[5]	131.0	137.4[5]	128.0[5]
Réunion[6]									
1999 (C)									
Total	5.4	6.5	4.4	...	...	...	...	...	...
0	35.7	40.1	31.4	...	...	...	...	...	...
1 - 4	♦0.5	♦0.6	♦0.4	...	...	...	...	...	...
5 - 9	♦0.2	♦0.2	♦0.1	...	...	...	...	...	...
10 - 14	♦0.3	♦0.3	♦0.3	...	...	...	...	...	...
15 - 19	0.5	♦0.9	♦0.2	...	...	...	...	...	...
20 - 24	0.9	1.6	♦0.3	...	...	...	...	...	...
25 - 29	1.0	1.3	♦0.6	...	...	...	...	...	...
30 - 34	1.6	2.3	♦0.9	...	...	...	...	...	...
35 - 39	1.5	2.4	♦0.7	...	...	...	...	...	...
40 - 44	3.2	4.8	1.5	...	...	...	...	...	...
45 - 49	4.7	6.7	2.7	...	...	...	...	...	...
50 - 54	7.3	11.1	3.4	...	...	...	...	...	...
55 - 59	9.9	14.6	5.3	...	...	...	...	...	...
60 - 64	14.8	20.5	9.6	...	...	...	...	...	...
65 - 69	21.0	29.1	14.1	...	...	...	...	...	...
70 - 74	31.5	45.8	20.4	...	...	...	...	...	...
75 - 79	46.6	64.2	34.9	...	...	...	...	...	...
80 - 84	77.9	106.5	63.3	...	...	...	...	...	...
85 - 89	108.9	134.4	98.2	...	...	...	...	...	...
90 - 94	160.1	183.5	151.5	...	...	...	...	...	...
95 - 99	180.8	♦123.7	203.3	...	...	...	...	...	...
100 +	♦321.4	♦400.0	♦304.3	...	...	...	...	...	...
Swaziland[3]									
1997 (|)									
Total	9.1	10.7	7.7	6.4	7.1	5.7	9.9	11.9	8.3
0 - 4	15.0	15.8	14.2	12.1	13.5	10.8	15.6	16.3	14.9
5 - 9	1.4	1.5	1.2	♦1.3	♦1.4	♦1.2	1.4	1.5	1.2
10 - 14	1.0	1.1	1.0	♦1.0	♦1.2	♦0.9	1.0	1.1	1.0
15 - 19	2.3	2.2	2.3	1.7	♦1.9	♦1.6	2.5	2.3	2.6
20 - 24	5.3	5.1	5.5	3.2	3.0	3.3	6.4	6.2	6.6
25 - 29	8.9	10.5	7.5	4.5	4.9	4.1	11.3	14.5	9.2
30 - 34	11.1	14.6	8.5	5.4	5.8	4.9	14.1	21.0	10.0
35 - 39	11.5	16.0	8.2	6.3	6.2	6.4	14.1	22.5	8.9
40 - 44	13.8	19.1	9.3	7.8	8.8	6.4	16.5	25.4	10.3
45 - 49	14.3	19.8	9.2	9.4	9.7	9.0	16.2	25.3	9.3
50 - 54	18.8	25.4	13.2	13.6	14.1	♦12.8	20.6	30.6	13.3
55 - 59	20.0	26.8	13.4	17.0	17.6	♦16.2	20.8	30.1	12.9
60 - 64	26.3	37.5	17.0	21.3	♦19.3	♦23.8	27.4	42.2	15.9
65 - 69	30.0	42.0	20.0	32.1	43.7	♦19.0	29.7	41.7	20.1

20. Death rates specific for age, sex and urban/rural residence: latest available year, 1996 - 2005
Taux de mortalité selon l'âge, le sexe et la résidence, urbaine/rurale: dernière année disponible, 1996 - 2005 (continued - suite)

Continent, country or area, date, code and age (in years) / Continent, pays ou zone, date, code et âge (en années)	Total			Urban - Urbaine			Rural - Rurale		
	Both sexes Les deux sexes	Male Masculin	Female Féminin	Both sexes Les deux sexes	Male Masculin	Female Féminin	Both sexes Les deux sexes	Male Masculin	Female Féminin
AFRICA - AFRIQUE									
Swaziland[3]									
1997 (|)									
70 - 74	43.1	64.6	28.8	53.5	♦64.1	♦44.9	41.9	64.7	27.1
75 + ...	63.1	72.9	56.7	91.3	83.8	97.7	60.3	71.6	53.1
Zimbabwe[7]									
2002 (|)									
Total.....................	17.2	18.4	16.1	12.5	13.5	11.6	19.7	21.1	18.4
0	69.6	75.8	63.3	57.5	62.6	52.4	75.9	82.8	69.1
1 - 4.....................	12.2	13.0	11.3	8.3	9.2	7.4	13.9	14.7	13.1
5 - 9	3.4	3.7	3.1	2.7	3.1	2.4	3.6	3.9	3.4
10 - 14	2.4	2.6	2.2	2.3	2.7	2.0	2.4	2.5	2.2
15 - 19	2.8	2.4	3.1	1.8	1.9	1.8	3.3	2.7	3.9
20 - 24	7.9	6.1	9.4	4.2	3.4	4.8	11.1	8.4	13.3
25 - 29	17.6	14.6	20.4	9.4	7.4	11.5	25.2	22.2	27.7
30 - 34	29.3	27.8	30.7	16.7	15.1	18.6	40.6	41.4	39.8
35 - 39	38.9	43.2	35.1	25.0	26.1	23.7	49.8	59.9	42.5
40 - 44	35.3	44.2	28.0	25.1	27.9	22.1	41.7	57.6	31.0
45 - 49	33.6	41.8	26.6	25.9	28.3	22.9	38.0	51.7	28.2
50 - 54	29.4	39.3	22.0	26.9	28.2	25.3	30.4	46.0	21.1
55 - 59	29.5	39.2	21.1	28.0	30.7	24.6	30.1	43.1	20.1
60 - 64	30.5	38.6	22.7	33.1	37.0	28.4	29.7	39.2	21.4
65 - 69	34.1	41.7	26.9	39.3	44.0	34.0	32.8	41.1	25.2
70 - 74	37.8	46.6	29.3	46.8	55.4	37.6	36.0	44.7	27.7
75 + ...	35.9	42.2	31.0	86.5	102.9	73.1	69.2	81.1	60.1
AMERICA, NORTH - AMÉRIQUE DU NORD									
Bahamas									
2000 (C)									
Total.....................	5.4	6.1	4.7	...	...	...	...	...	...
0	8.8	♦8.9	♦8.7	...	...	...	...	...	...
1 - 4.....................	♦0.8	♦0.9	♦0.8	...	...	...	...	...	...
5 - 9	♦0.4	♦0.6	♦0.3	...	...	...	...	...	...
10 - 14	♦0.4	♦0.4	♦0.4	...	...	...	...	...	...
15 - 19	♦0.6	♦0.9	♦0.3	...	...	...	...	...	...
20 - 24	1.6	♦2.1	♦1.1	...	...	...	...	...	...
25 - 29	2.9	3.3	2.5	...	...	...	...	...	...
30 - 34	2.9	3.7	♦2.2	...	...	...	...	...	...
35 - 39	4.1	5.5	2.8	...	...	...	...	...	...
40 - 44	5.1	7.2	3.3	...	...	...	...	...	...
45 - 49	6.3	8.1	4.5	...	...	...	...	...	...
50 - 54	8.4	11.3	5.8	...	...	...	...	...	...
55 - 59	10.5	14.3	7.1	...	...	...	...	...	...
60 - 64	14.2	18.1	10.8	...	...	...	...	...	...
65 - 69	22.2	27.2	18.1	...	...	...	...	...	...
70 - 74	29.2	33.7	26.0	...	...	...	...	...	...
75 - 79	43.6	50.0	39.3	...	...	...	...	...	...
80 - 84	71.4	72.8	70.5	...	...	...	...	...	...
85 - 89	102.8	146.8	82.1	...	...	...	...	...	...
90 + ...	184.0	248.2	156.1	...	...	...	...	...	...
Canada[8]									
2004 (C)									
Total.....................	7.1	7.2	6.9	...	...	...	...	...	...
0	5.4	5.6	5.1	...	...	...	...	...	...
1 - 4.....................	0.2	0.2	0.2	...	...	...	...	...	...
5 - 9	0.1	0.1	0.1	...	...	...	...	...	...
10 - 14	0.1	0.1	0.1	...	...	...	...	...	...
15 - 19	0.4	0.6	0.3	...	...	...	...	...	...
20 - 24	0.6	0.8	0.3	...	...	...	...	...	...
25 - 29	0.6	0.8	0.3	...	...	...	...	...	...
30 - 34	0.7	0.9	0.4	...	...	...	...	...	...
35 - 39	0.9	1.2	0.7	...	...	...	...	...	...
40 - 44	1.4	1.7	1.0	...	...	...	...	...	...

20. Death rates specific for age, sex and urban/rural residence: latest available year, 1996 - 2005
Taux de mortalité selon l'âge, le sexe et la résidence, urbaine/rurale: dernière année disponible, 1996 - 2005 (continued - suite)

Continent, country or area, date, code and age (in years) / Continent, pays ou zone, date, code et âge (en années)	Total			Urban - Urbaine			Rural - Rurale		
	Both sexes Les deux sexes	Male Masculin	Female Féminin	Both sexes Les deux sexes	Male Masculin	Female Féminin	Both sexes Les deux sexes	Male Masculin	Female Féminin
AMERICA, NORTH - AMÉRIQUE DU NORD									
Canada[8]									
2004 (C)									
45 - 49	2.2	2.7	1.7	...	...	...	...	...	...
50 - 54	3.5	4.3	2.7	...	...	...	...	...	...
55 - 59	5.5	6.8	4.2	...	...	...	...	...	...
60 - 64	9.0	11.3	6.8	...	...	...	...	...	...
65 - 69	14.1	17.7	10.8	...	...	...	...	...	...
70 - 74	22.8	28.8	17.5	...	...	...	...	...	...
75 - 79	37.5	47.8	29.6	...	...	...	...	...	...
80 - 84	62.1	78.6	51.8	...	...	...	...	...	...
85 - 89	108.2	133.7	95.7	...	...	...	...	...	...
90 +	201.8	225.7	193.3	...	...	...	...	...	...
Costa Rica									
2004 (C)									
Total	3.8	4.2	3.3	...	...	...	...	...	...
0 - 4	2.0	2.2	1.8	...	...	...	...	...	...
5 - 9	0.2	0.2	♦0.1	...	...	...	...	...	...
10 - 14	0.2	0.2	0.2	...	...	...	...	...	...
15 - 19	0.5	0.7	0.3	...	...	...	...	...	...
20 - 24	0.7	1.1	0.3	...	...	...	...	...	...
25 - 29	0.9	1.2	0.5	...	...	...	...	...	...
30 - 34	1.0	1.5	0.6	...	...	...	...	...	...
35 - 39	1.2	1.6	0.7	...	...	...	...	...	...
40 - 44	1.8	2.4	1.3	...	...	...	...	...	...
45 - 49	2.6	3.3	1.9	...	...	...	...	...	...
50 - 54	3.8	4.8	2.8	...	...	...	...	...	...
55 - 59	6.1	7.7	4.6	...	...	...	...	...	...
60 - 64	9.5	11.6	7.5	...	...	...	...	...	...
65 - 69	15.4	18.9	12.1	...	...	...	...	...	...
70 - 74	24.6	28.4	21.1	...	...	...	...	...	...
75 - 79	41.0	47.8	35.1	...	...	...	...	...	...
80 - 84	67.4	78.9	58.2	...	...	...	...	...	...
85 +	143.3	154.2	135.1	...	...	...	...	...	...
Cuba									
2005 (C)									
Total	7.5	8.1	6.9	8.2	8.9	7.6	5.4	6.1	4.7
0	6.1	6.5	5.6	6.5	7.0	6.0	4.9	5.1	4.6
1 - 4	0.4	0.4	0.4	0.4	0.5	0.4	0.3	0.4	♦0.3
5 - 9	0.2	0.3	0.1	0.2	0.3	0.1	0.2	♦0.2	♦0.1
10 - 14	0.3	0.3	0.2	0.3	0.3	0.2	0.2	♦0.3	♦0.2
15 - 19	0.5	0.6	0.4	0.5	0.6	0.4	0.4	0.5	0.3
20 - 24	0.7	0.9	0.5	0.7	1.0	0.5	0.5	0.7	0.4
25 - 29	0.8	1.1	0.6	0.9	1.2	0.6	0.6	0.8	0.5
30 - 34	0.9	1.2	0.6	1.0	1.3	0.7	0.9	1.1	0.6
35 - 39	1.4	1.7	1.0	1.4	1.8	1.0	1.2	1.3	1.0
40 - 44	2.0	2.4	1.5	2.1	2.6	1.6	1.6	1.8	1.4
45 - 49	3.4	4.2	2.6	3.6	4.5	2.7	2.7	3.1	2.4
50 - 54	5.2	6.3	4.1	5.5	6.9	4.2	4.0	4.4	3.6
55 - 59	8.0	9.8	6.3	8.5	10.7	6.5	6.3	6.9	5.6
60 - 64	12.0	14.5	9.6	12.9	16.2	10.0	8.6	9.4	7.6
65 - 69	10.3	12.3	8.4	11.2	14.0	8.7	7.4	7.6	7.2
70 - 74	23.1	28.3	18.7	24.7	32.0	19.1	17.8	18.7	16.4
75 +	305.6	354.6	269.1	325.5	398.2	279.3	237.5	251.0	220.1
El Salvador									
2003 (C)									
Total	4.4	5.2	3.7	5.3	6.3	4.4	3.1	3.7	2.5
0	8.1	9.0	7.2	9.7	10.7	8.7	6.3	7.1	5.5
1 - 4	0.7	0.8	0.7	0.8	0.9	0.7	0.6	0.7	0.6
5 - 9	0.3	0.3	0.2	0.3	0.3	0.3	0.2	0.3	♦0.2
10 - 14	0.4	0.4	0.3	0.4	0.5	0.4	0.3	0.3	♦0.2
15 - 19	1.1	1.7	0.6	1.5	2.3	0.7	0.7	1.0	0.4
20 - 24	1.8	2.9	0.7	2.3	3.8	0.9	1.1	1.7	0.5
25 - 29	2.0	3.2	0.8	2.4	4.0	0.9	1.3	2.0	0.6
30 - 34	2.1	3.4	0.9	2.3	3.9	0.9	1.6	2.5	0.7

541

Continent, country or area, date, code and age (in years) / Continent, pays ou zone, date, code et âge (en années)	Total			Urban - Urbaine			Rural - Rurale		
	Both sexes Les deux sexes	Male Masculin	Female Féminin	Both sexes Les deux sexes	Male Masculin	Female Féminin	Both sexes Les deux sexes	Male Masculin	Female Féminin
AMERICA, NORTH - AMÉRIQUE DU NORD									
El Salvador									
2003 (C)									
35 - 39	3.0	4.7	1.5	3.2	5.2	1.6	2.5	3.9	1.2
40 - 44	3.6	5.4	2.0	3.8	6.0	2.0	3.1	4.4	2.1
45 - 49	4.5	6.6	2.8	4.8	7.2	2.8	4.0	5.3	2.7
50 - 54	5.9	7.7	4.3	6.7	8.8	4.9	4.6	5.9	3.3
55 - 59	8.1	10.8	5.7	9.1	12.2	6.5	6.5	8.6	4.4
60 - 64	12.8	14.9	10.9	14.9	17.9	12.3	9.4	10.5	8.3
65 - 69	17.6	20.8	14.8	19.8	23.4	16.8	14.0	16.8	11.2
70 - 74	25.5	30.0	21.9	28.3	33.9	24.0	20.7	23.8	17.9
75 - 79	42.2	50.5	36.2	46.4	56.4	39.5	34.2	39.9	29.5
80 + ...	132.9	162.9	115.2	119.5	137.8	108.6	187.8	267.3	141.9
Guadeloupe[6]									
2003 (C)									
Total	6.0	6.7	5.4	...	...	...	...	...	...
0	8.1	9.7	♦6.5	...	...	...	...	...	...
1 - 4	♦0.3	♦0.3	♦0.3	...	...	...	...	...	...
5 - 9	♦0.1	♦0.2	♦0.1	...	...	...	...	...	...
10 - 14	♦0.1	♦0.2	♦0.1	...	...	...	...	...	...
15 - 19	♦0.6	♦1.0	♦0.2	...	...	...	...	...	...
20 - 24	♦0.8	♦1.3	♦0.3	...	...	...	...	...	...
25 - 29	♦0.9	♦1.3	♦0.4	...	...	...	...	...	...
30 - 34	1.1	2.0	♦0.4	...	...	...	...	...	...
35 - 39	1.6	2.4	♦1.0	...	...	...	...	...	...
40 - 44	2.2	2.8	♦1.6	...	...	...	...	...	...
45 - 49	3.5	5.3	2.0	...	...	...	...	...	...
50 - 54	4.5	7.5	♦1.9	...	...	...	...	...	...
55 - 59	6.3	8.7	4.1	...	...	...	...	...	...
60 - 64	10.9	12.7	9.3	...	...	...	...	...	...
65 - 69	14.9	19.1	11.2	...	...	...	...	...	...
70 - 74	22.7	28.5	18.2	...	...	...	...	...	...
75 - 79	34.1	45.4	25.6	...	...	...	...	...	...
80 - 84	53.8	68.2	43.8	...	...	...	...	...	...
85 - 89	96.8	98.9	95.6	...	...	...	...	...	...
90 + ...	148.6	142.2	151.2	...	...	...	...	...	...
Guatemala									
1999 (C)									
Total	5.8	6.6	5.0	...	...	...	...	...	...
0 - 4	10.1	10.8	9.3	...	...	...	...	...	...
5 - 9	0.7	0.7	0.7	...	...	...	...	...	...
10 - 14	0.7	0.8	0.5	...	...	...	...	...	...
15 - 19	1.4	1.7	1.0	...	...	...	...	...	...
20 - 24	2.1	2.9	1.3	...	...	...	...	...	...
25 - 29	2.6	3.7	1.5	...	...	...	...	...	...
30 - 34	3.4	4.8	2.1	...	...	...	...	...	...
35 - 39	4.4	6.2	2.7	...	...	...	...	...	...
40 - 44	5.4	7.1	3.7	...	...	...	...	...	...
45 - 49	6.9	9.0	4.8	...	...	...	...	...	...
50 - 54	8.8	10.9	6.7	...	...	...	...	...	...
55 - 59	10.8	12.3	9.3	...	...	...	...	...	...
60 - 64	15.2	17.5	12.9	...	...	...	...	...	...
65 + ...	52.5	56.5	48.8	...	...	...	...	...	...
Martinique[6]									
2003 (C)									
Total	7.0	7.7	6.3	...	...	...	...	...	...
0	6.2	♦5.2	♦7.3	...	...	...	...	...	...
1 - 4	♦0.4	♦0.3	♦0.5	...	...	...	...	...	...
5 - 9	♦0.2	♦0.2	♦0.2	...	...	...	...	...	...
10 - 14	♦0.2	♦0.2	♦0.1	...	...	...	...	...	...
15 - 19	♦0.6	♦1.0	♦0.3	...	...	...	...	...	...
20 - 24	♦0.8	♦1.1	♦0.5	...	...	...	...	...	...
25 - 29	♦1.0	♦1.6	♦0.4	...	...	...	...	...	...
30 - 34	1.4	♦2.2	♦0.7	...	...	...	...	...	...
35 - 39	1.3	♦1.8	♦0.8	...	...	...	...	...	...

Continent, country or area, date, code and age (in years) Continent, pays ou zone, date, code et âge (en années)	Total			Urban - Urbaine			Rural - Rurale		
	Both sexes Les deux sexes	Male Masculin	Female Féminin	Both sexes Les deux sexes	Male Masculin	Female Féminin	Both sexes Les deux sexes	Male Masculin	Female Féminin
AMERICA, NORTH - AMÉRIQUE DU NORD									
Martinique[6]									
2003 (C)									
40 - 44	1.7	2.4	♦1.0	...	...	...	...	...	...
45 - 49	3.0	4.1	2.2	...	...	...	...	...	...
50 - 54	4.0	5.3	2.9	...	...	...	...	...	...
55 - 59	5.2	6.7	3.9	...	...	...	...	...	...
60 - 64	8.7	11.6	6.2	...	...	...	...	...	...
65 - 69	12.2	16.7	8.4	...	...	...	...	...	...
70 - 74	22.1	29.3	16.4	...	...	...	...	...	...
75 - 79	36.8	52.1	25.8	...	...	...	...	...	...
80 - 84	65.0	84.5	52.7	...	...	...	...	...	...
85 - 89	107.2	137.0	90.4	...	...	...	...	...	...
90 + ...	187.0	186.1	187.3	...	...	...	...	...	...
Mexico - Mexique[9]									
2003 (+C)									
Total.................	4.5	5.0[5]	4.0[5]	4.3	4.7	3.9	4.9	5.7	4.1
0	16.8	18.7	14.6	16.6	18.5	14.6	16.1	18.2	13.9
1 - 4	0.8	0.9	0.8	0.7	0.8	0.6	1.1	1.2	1.0
5 - 9	0.3	0.3	0.2	0.3	0.3	0.2	0.3	0.4	0.3
10 - 14	0.3	0.4	0.3	0.3	0.4	0.2	0.4	0.5	0.3
15 - 19	0.7	0.9	0.4	0.6	0.8	0.4	0.8	1.1	0.5
20 - 24	1.0	1.4	0.5	0.8	1.2	0.5	1.2	1.8	0.7
25 - 29	1.2	1.8	0.6	1.1	1.6	0.6	1.5	2.3	0.8
30 - 34	1.5	2.2	0.8	1.3	1.9	0.7	1.9	2.8	1.1
35 - 39	1.9	2.7	1.1	1.7	2.4	1.0	2.4	3.5	1.5
40 - 44	2.7	3.6	1.8	2.4	3.2	1.6	3.3	4.5	2.1
45 - 49	3.9	5.1	2.8	3.7	4.8	2.7	4.4	5.9	3.0
50 - 54	6.0	7.4	4.7	5.8	7.1	4.7	6.0	7.5	4.6
55 - 59	9.3	11.2	7.4	9.2	11.0	7.5	8.8	10.8	7.0
60 - 64	14.0	16.5	11.8	14.0	16.2	12.0	13.2	15.8	10.8
65 - 69	21.0	24.5	17.9	21.3	24.5	18.5	19.1	23.1	15.5
70 - 74	32.4	37.8	27.8	32.6	37.4	28.6	30.3	37.3	24.3
75 - 79	49.3	57.1	43.0	49.9	56.3	44.8	45.6	57.0	36.3
80 - 84	79.0	90.2	70.4	78.7	87.0	72.3	77.3	96.6	62.3
85 - 89	117.8	126.5	111.4	118.5	121.5	116.3	112.3	137.1	93.7
90 - 94	177.4	180.1	175.4	176.6	171.2	180.5	174.9	200.4	156.3
95 - 99	243.8	226.5	255.7	247.4	219.1	267.2	229.0	239.1	221.3
100 + ...	522.7	471.6	557.9	511.5	439.6	560.7	534.5	523.3	542.4
Netherlands Antilles - Antilles néerlandaises[10]									
2004 (C)									
Total.................	7.7	8.8	6.7	...	...	...	...	...	...
0	♦8.2	♦10.4	♦5.8	...	...	...	...	...	...
1 - 4	♦0.2	♦0.2	♦0.2	...	...	...	...	...	...
5 - 9	♦0.1	♦0.3	-	...	...	...	...	...	...
10 - 14	♦0.2	♦0.4	-	...	...	...	...	...	...
15 - 19	♦1.0	♦1.5	♦0.5	...	...	...	...	...	...
20 - 24	♦1.2	♦1.9	♦0.6	...	...	...	...	...	...
25 - 29	♦1.8	♦2.3	♦1.3	...	...	...	...	...	...
30 - 34	♦1.9	♦3.0	♦0.9	...	...	...	...	...	...
35 - 39	2.0	♦3.2	♦1.0	...	...	...	...	...	...
40 - 44	2.5	♦3.5	♦1.6	...	...	...	...	...	...
45 - 49	3.9	4.9	♦3.1	...	...	...	...	...	...
50 - 54	6.0	8.0	♦4.4	...	...	...	...	...	...
55 - 59	8.3	11.7	♦5.4	...	...	...	...	...	...
60 - 64	14.9	19.1	11.5	...	...	...	...	...	...
65 - 69	22.2	27.9	17.4	...	...	...	...	...	...
70 - 74	35.9	42.9	30.5	...	...	...	...	...	...
75 - 79	52.9	73.3	38.5	...	...	...	...	...	...
80 - 84	79.2	105.2	64.0	...	...	...	...	...	...
85 - 89	128.6	148.9	118.3	...	...	...	...	...	...
90 - 94	197.8	274.2	169.6	...	...	...	...	...	...
95 - 99	392.0	♦384.6	395.3	...	...	...	...	...	...
100 + ...	♦392.9	♦200.0	♦500.0	...	...	...	...	...	...

20. Death rates specific for age, sex and urban/rural residence: latest available year, 1996 - 2005
Taux de mortalité selon l'âge, le sexe et la résidence, urbaine/rurale: dernière année disponible, 1996 - 2005 (continued - suite)

Continent, country or area, date, code and age (in years) / Continent, pays ou zone, date, code et âge (en années)	Total			Urban - Urbaine			Rural - Rurale		
	Both sexes Les deux sexes	Male Masculin	Female Féminin	Both sexes Les deux sexes	Male Masculin	Female Féminin	Both sexes Les deux sexes	Male Masculin	Female Féminin
AMERICA, NORTH - AMÉRIQUE DU NORD									
Puerto Rico - Porto Rico									
2005 (C)									
Total....................	7.6	8.8	6.5	...	...	...	...	...	...
0 - 4....................	2.0	2.1	1.9	...	...	...	...	...	...
5 - 9....................	♦0.1	♦0.1	♦0.1	...	...	...	...	...	...
10 - 14..................	0.1	♦0.2	♦0.1	...	...	...	...	...	...
15 - 19..................	0.6	1.0	0.2	...	...	...	...	...	...
20 - 24..................	1.5	2.5	0.5	...	...	...	...	...	...
25 - 29..................	1.4	2.4	0.5	...	...	...	...	...	...
30 - 34..................	1.6	2.6	0.8	...	...	...	...	...	...
35 - 39..................	2.0	2.9	1.1	...	...	...	...	...	...
40 - 44..................	2.5	3.8	1.4	...	...	...	...	...	...
45 - 49..................	3.5	5.1	2.1	...	...	...	...	...	...
50 - 54..................	5.1	7.5	3.1	...	...	...	...	...	...
55 - 59..................	7.3	10.4	4.7	...	...	...	...	...	...
60 - 64..................	11.3	15.4	7.9	...	...	...	...	...	...
65 - 69..................	16.1	21.3	11.7	...	...	...	...	...	...
70 - 74..................	25.0	32.1	19.4	...	...	...	...	...	...
75 - 79..................	38.5	48.4	31.0	...	...	...	...	...	...
80 +....................	94.1	106.6	85.8	...	...	...	...	...	...
Saint Lucia - Sainte-Lucie									
2003 (C)									
Total....................	6.5	7.4	5.6	...	...	...	...	...	...
0	15.7	♦14.0	♦17.3	...	...	...	...	...	...
1 - 4	♦1.1	♦1.6	♦0.5	...	...	...	...	...	...
5 - 9	♦0.2	♦0.5	-	...	...	...	...	...	...
10 - 14	♦0.3	♦0.3	♦0.2	...	...	...	...	...	...
15 - 19	♦0.8	♦1.3	♦0.3	...	...	...	...	...	...
20 - 24	♦1.0	♦1.5	♦0.5	...	...	...	...	...	...
25 - 29	♦1.7	♦2.8	♦0.6	...	...	...	...	...	...
30 - 34	♦2.5	♦3.1	♦1.9	...	...	...	...	...	...
35 - 39	♦2.6	♦3.5	♦1.7	...	...	...	...	...	...
40 - 44	♦2.9	♦4.0	♦1.9	...	...	...	...	...	...
45 - 49	4.8	♦5.6	♦3.9	...	...	...	...	...	...
50 - 54	5.8	♦7.4	♦4.1	...	...	...	...	...	...
55 - 59	11.3	15.8	♦7.3	...	...	...	...	...	...
60 - 64	13.9	♦14.5	♦13.3	...	...	...	...	...	...
65 - 69	25.8	26.5	25.2	...	...	...	...	...	...
70 - 74	35.1	44.6	26.4	...	...	...	...	...	...
75 - 79	70.9	80.7	62.3	...	...	...	...	...	...
80 +....................	103.3	124.1	88.6	...	...	...	...	...	...
Trinidad and Tobago - Trinité-et-Tobago									
1997 (C)									
Total....................	7.2	7.9	6.5	...	...	...	...	...	...
0	19.8	21.4	18.2	...	...	...	...	...	...
1 - 4	0.8	0.8	♦0.7	...	...	...	...	...	...
5 - 9	0.3	♦0.4	♦0.2	...	...	...	...	...	...
10 - 14	0.4	♦0.4	♦0.3	...	...	...	...	...	...
15 - 19	0.7	0.8	0.6	...	...	...	...	...	...
20 - 24	1.4	1.8	0.9	...	...	...	...	...	...
25 - 29	1.6	1.9	1.2	...	...	...	...	...	...
30 - 34	2.5	3.2	1.9	...	...	...	...	...	...
35 - 39	3.0	3.7	2.3	...	...	...	...	...	...
40 - 44	3.9	4.8	2.9	...	...	...	...	...	...
45 - 49	5.4	6.6	4.3	...	...	...	...	...	...
50 - 54	8.3	10.3	6.3	...	...	...	...	...	...
55 - 59	13.6	16.6	10.9	...	...	...	...	...	...
60 - 64	22.1	24.2	20.2	...	...	...	...	...	...
65 - 69	31.7	36.0	27.8	...	...	...	...	...	...
70 - 74	44.7	60.6	32.8	...	...	...	...	...	...
75 - 79	62.6	82.7	47.8	...	...	...	...	...	...
80 +....................	146.2	154.8	139.3	...	...	...	...	...	...

20. Death rates specific for age, sex and urban/rural residence: latest available year, 1996 - 2005
Taux de mortalité selon l'âge, le sexe et la résidence, urbaine/rurale: dernière année disponible, 1996 - 2005 (continued - suite)

Continent, country or area, date, code and age (in years) / Continent, pays ou zone, date, code et âge (en annèes)	Total			Urban - Urbaine			Rural - Rurale		
	Both sexes Les deux sexes	Male Masculin	Female Féminin	Both sexes Les deux sexes	Male Masculin	Female Féminin	Both sexes Les deux sexes	Male Masculin	Female Féminin
AMERICA, NORTH - AMÉRIQUE DU NORD									
United States - États-Unis									
2004* (C)									
Total...................	8.2	8.2	8.2	...	...	...	...	...	...
0......................	6.9	7.6	6.2	...	...	...	...	...	...
1 - 4..................	0.3	0.3	0.3	...	...	...	...	...	...
5 - 9..................	0.1	0.2	0.1	...	...	...	...	...	...
10 - 14................	0.2	0.2	0.2	...	...	...	...	...	...
15 - 19................	0.7	0.9	0.4	...	...	...	...	...	...
20 - 24................	0.9	1.4	0.5	...	...	...	...	...	...
25 - 29................	0.9	1.3	0.5	...	...	...	...	...	...
30 - 34................	1.1	1.4	0.7	...	...	...	...	...	...
35 - 39................	1.5	1.9	1.1	...	...	...	...	...	...
40 - 44................	2.3	2.9	1.7	...	...	...	...	...	...
45 - 49................	3.5	4.4	2.6	...	...	...	...	...	...
50 - 54................	5.1	6.5	3.7	...	...	...	...	...	...
55 - 59................	7.3	9.1	5.6	...	...	...	...	...	...
60 - 64................	11.4	14.0	8.9	...	...	...	...	...	...
65 - 69................	17.3	21.3	13.8	...	...	...	...	...	...
70 - 74................	26.8	32.9	21.9	...	...	...	...	...	...
75 - 79................	42.1	52.0	35.1	...	...	...	...	...	...
80 - 84................	68.1	82.8	59.0	...	...	...	...	...	...
85 +...................	138.5	149.8	133.4	...	...	...	...	...	...
AMERICA, SOUTH - AMÉRIQUE DU SUD									
Argentina - Argentine									
2005 (C)									
Total...................	7.6	8.2[5]	7.0[5]	...	...	...	...	...	...
0 - 4..................	3.3	3.7[5]	2.9[5]	...	...	...	...	...	...
5 - 9..................	0.3	0.3[5]	0.2[5]	...	...	...	...	...	...
10 - 14................	0.3	0.4[5]	0.2[5]	...	...	...	...	...	...
15 - 19................	0.7	1.0[5]	0.4[5]	...	...	...	...	...	...
20 - 24................	0.9	1.4[5]	0.5[5]	...	...	...	...	...	...
25 - 29................	0.9	1.3[5]	0.5[5]	...	...	...	...	...	...
30 - 34................	1.1	1.5[5]	0.8[5]	...	...	...	...	...	...
35 - 39................	1.5	1.9[5]	1.1[5]	...	...	...	...	...	...
40 - 44................	2.3	2.8[5]	1.7[5]	...	...	...	...	...	...
45 - 49................	3.7	4.8[5]	2.7[5]	...	...	...	...	...	...
50 - 54................	6.0	8.0[5]	4.1[5]	...	...	...	...	...	...
55 - 59................	9.2	12.6[5]	6.1[5]	...	...	...	...	...	...
60 - 64................	14.1	19.7[5]	9.2[5]	...	...	...	...	...	...
65 - 69................	20.6	29.2[5]	13.6[5]	...	...	...	...	...	...
70 - 74................	31.7	45.1[5]	21.8[5]	...	...	...	...	...	...
75 - 79................	49.8	68.3[5]	37.9[5]	...	...	...	...	...	...
80 +...................	130.6	152.6[5]	119.8[5]	...	...	...	...	...	...
Chile - Chili									
2003 (C)									
Total...................	5.3	5.8	4.8	5.3	5.7	4.8	5.2	6.0	4.4
0......................	7.8	8.4	7.2	7.8	8.5	7.1	7.9	8.0	7.9
1 - 4..................	0.4	0.4	0.4	0.4	0.4	0.3	0.5	0.6	♦0.4
5 - 9..................	0.2	0.2	0.2	0.2	0.2	0.1	0.2	♦0.3	♦0.2
10 - 14................	0.2	0.3	0.2	0.2	0.3	0.2	0.3	0.3	♦0.2
15 - 19................	0.4	0.6	0.2	0.4	0.6	0.2	0.6	0.9	♦0.3
20 - 24................	0.8	1.2	0.3	0.8	1.2	0.3	1.1	1.5	0.5
25 - 29................	0.9	1.4	0.4	0.9	1.3	0.4	1.0	1.5	0.5
30 - 34................	1.0	1.6	0.5	1.0	1.6	0.5	1.2	1.7	0.6
35 - 39................	1.4	2.0	0.7	1.3	1.9	0.7	1.6	2.4	0.8
40 - 44................	1.9	2.5	1.2	1.8	2.4	1.2	2.1	2.8	1.2
45 - 49................	2.8	3.7	2.0	2.9	3.7	2.0	2.7	3.4	1.8
50 - 54................	4.5	5.8	3.3	4.6	6.0	3.3	4.2	5.0	3.2
55 - 59................	7.3	9.5	5.2	7.4	9.8	5.2	6.4	7.8	4.7

Continent, country or area, date, code and age (in years) / Continent, pays ou zone, date, code et âge (en années)	Total			Urban - Urbaine			Rural - Rurale		
	Both sexes Les deux sexes	Male Masculin	Female Féminin	Both sexes Les deux sexes	Male Masculin	Female Féminin	Both sexes Les deux sexes	Male Masculin	Female Féminin
AMERICA, SOUTH - AMÉRIQUE DU SUD									
Chile - Chili									
2003 (C)									
60 - 64	11.6	15.1	8.5	12.0	15.8	8.7	9.5	11.5	7.2
65 - 69	17.6	23.3	12.8	18.1	24.6	13.1	14.6	17.8	10.9
70 - 74	30.4	40.5	22.7	31.5	42.9	23.4	24.7	30.6	18.2
75 - 79	46.1	61.3	35.6	47.1	64.6	36.1	40.1	47.5	32.3
80 +	116.7	134.0	107.1	119.6	141.1	108.9	100.1	106.0	95.0
2004 (C)									
Total	5.4	5.8	4.9	...	...	...	...	...	...
0	8.3	9.3	7.2	...	...	...	...	...	...
1 - 4	0.4	0.4	0.4	...	...	...	...	...	...
5 - 9	0.2	0.2	0.1	...	...	...	...	...	...
10 - 14	0.2	0.2	0.2	...	...	...	...	...	...
15 - 19	0.5	0.7	0.3	...	...	...	...	...	...
20 - 24	0.8	1.1	0.4	...	...	...	...	...	...
25 - 29	0.9	1.3	0.5	...	...	...	...	...	...
30 - 34	1.0	1.6	0.5	...	...	...	...	...	...
35 - 39	1.3	1.9	0.8	...	...	...	...	...	...
40 - 44	1.9	2.6	1.2	...	...	...	...	...	...
45 - 49	2.7	3.6	1.9	...	...	...	...	...	...
50 - 54	4.3	5.7	3.0	...	...	...	...	...	...
55 - 59	6.8	9.0	4.8	...	...	...	...	...	...
60 - 64	11.0	14.3	8.1	...	...	...	...	...	...
65 - 69	17.5	22.8	13.1	...	...	...	...	...	...
70 - 74	29.7	40.1	21.8	...	...	...	...	...	...
75 - 79	46.7	61.2	36.7	...	...	...	...	...	...
80 +	118.9	135.9	109.6	...	...	...	...	...	...
Suriname									
2004 (C)									
Total	6.7	7.6	5.8	...	...	...	...	...	...
0	12.2	15.6	8.7	...	...	...	...	...	...
1 - 4	1.3	1.6	♦1.1	...	...	...	...	...	...
5 - 9	♦0.4	♦0.3	♦0.4	...	...	...	...	...	...
10 - 14	♦0.6	♦0.7	♦0.4	...	...	...	...	...	...
15 - 19	0.9	♦1.2	♦0.6	...	...	...	...	...	...
20 - 24	1.6	1.9	♦1.3	...	...	...	...	...	...
25 - 29	2.6	3.6	♦1.5	...	...	...	...	...	...
30 - 34	2.8	3.6	2.0	...	...	...	...	...	...
35 - 39	3.8	5.1	2.5	...	...	...	...	...	...
40 - 44	4.8	6.1	3.5	...	...	...	...	...	...
45 - 49	7.7	9.3	6.2	...	...	...	...	...	...
50 - 54	7.8	9.8	5.9	...	...	...	...	...	...
55 - 59	14.9	17.8	12.3	...	...	...	...	...	...
60 - 64	19.5	23.1	16.4	...	...	...	...	...	...
65 - 69	31.4	38.1	25.1	...	...	...	...	...	...
70 - 74	42.6	51.2	34.9	...	...	...	...	...	...
75 - 79	66.6	82.3	52.7	...	...	...	...	...	...
80 - 84	102.7	120.6	89.0	...	...	...	...	...	...
85 - 89	149.8	165.8	141.8	...	...	...	...	...	...
90 - 94	215.2	190.2	231.9	...	...	...	...	...	...
95 +	294.6	♦264.7	♦305.3	...	...	...	...	...	...
Uruguay									
2002 (C)									
Total	9.6	10.5[5]	8.7[5]	...	...	...	...	...	...
0	14.0	15.4[5]	12.3[5]	...	...	...	...	...	...
1 - 4	0.5	0.6	0.3	...	...	...	...	...	...
5 - 9	0.2	0.2	0.2	...	...	...	...	...	...
10 - 14	0.2	0.3	♦0.2	...	...	...	...	...	...
15 - 19	0.7	1.0	0.3	...	...	...	...	...	...
20 - 24	1.0	1.5	0.4	...	...	...	...	...	...
25 - 29	1.1	1.6	0.5	...	...	...	...	...	...
30 - 34	1.4	1.8	0.9	...	...	...	...	...	...
35 - 39	1.6	2.1[5]	1.1[5]	...	...	...	...	...	...
40 - 44	2.4	2.7	2.1	...	...	...	...	...	...

20. Death rates specific for age, sex and urban/rural residence: latest available year, 1996 - 2005
Taux de mortalité selon l'âge, le sexe et la résidence, urbaine/rurale: dernière année disponible, 1996 - 2005 (continued - suite)

Continent, country or area, date, code and age (in years) / Continent, pays ou zone, date, code et âge (en années)	Total			Urban - Urbaine			Rural - Rurale		
	Both sexes Les deux sexes	Male Masculin	Female Féminin	Both sexes Les deux sexes	Male Masculin	Female Féminin	Both sexes Les deux sexes	Male Masculin	Female Féminin
AMERICA, SOUTH - AMÉRIQUE DU SUD									
Uruguay									
2002 (C)									
45 - 49	4.0	5.1	2.9	...	...	...	...	...	...
50 - 54	6.5	8.8	4.3	...	...	...	...	...	...
55 - 59	9.9	13.8	6.4	...	...	...	...	...	...
60 - 64	15.0	22.0	9.0	...	...	...	...	...	...
65 - 69	22.0	31.8	14.3	...	...	...	...	...	...
70 - 74	33.3	47.7[5]	22.7[5]	...	...	...	...	...	...
75 +	88.5	105.3[5]	78.9[5]	...	...	...	...	...	...
Venezuela (Bolivarian Republic of) - Venezuela (République bolivarienne du)[11]									
2002 (C)									
Total	4.2	5.1	3.2	...	...	...	...	...	...
0	13.5	15.2	11.7	...	...	...	...	...	...
1 - 4	0.9	0.9	0.8	...	...	...	...	...	...
5 - 9	0.3	0.4	0.3	...	...	...	...	...	...
10 - 14	0.4	0.5	0.3	...	...	...	...	...	...
15 - 19	1.4	2.2	0.5	...	...	...	...	...	...
20 - 24	2.3	3.9	0.6	...	...	...	...	...	...
25 - 29	2.1	3.5	0.7	...	...	...	...	...	...
30 - 34	2.1	3.2	1.0	...	...	...	...	...	...
35 - 39	2.1	3.0	1.2	...	...	...	...	...	...
40 - 44	2.8	3.7	1.8	...	...	...	...	...	...
45 - 49	3.9	5.0	2.7	...	...	...	...	...	...
50 - 54	5.3	6.8	3.8	...	...	...	...	...	...
55 - 59	7.2	9.4	5.1	...	...	...	...	...	...
60 - 64	11.0	14.0	8.1	...	...	...	...	...	...
65 - 69	17.7	22.1	13.7	...	...	...	...	...	...
70 - 74	26.5	33.3	20.7	...	...	...	...	...	...
75 - 79	40.2	48.6	33.4	...	...	...	...	...	...
80 +	117.7	128.1	110.2	...	...	...	...	...	...
ASIA - ASIE									
Armenia - Árménie[12]									
2004 (C)									
Total	8.0	8.6	7.5	8.0	8.8	7.3	7.9	8.2	7.7
0	11.8	14.3	9.0	13.6	17.2	9.5	8.9	9.5	8.1
1 - 4	0.4	♦0.4	♦0.4	0.4	♦0.2	♦0.5	♦0.4	♦0.5	♦0.3
5 - 9	0.2	♦0.2	♦0.1	♦0.2	♦0.2	♦0.1	♦0.2	♦0.3	♦0.1
10 - 14	0.2	0.2	♦0.2	0.2	♦0.2	♦0.1	♦0.2	♦0.2	♦0.2
15 - 19	0.3	0.5	♦0.1	0.3	0.5	♦0.1	0.4	0.6	♦0.1
20 - 24	0.5	0.6	0.3	0.5	0.7	♦0.3	0.4	♦0.5	♦0.3
25 - 29	0.6	0.9	0.4	0.6	0.9	0.4	0.6	0.8	0.4
30 - 34	1.0	1.5	0.6	1.1	1.7	0.6	1.0	1.3	♦0.7
35 - 39	1.6	2.2	1.0	1.5	2.2	1.0	1.6	2.2	1.1
40 - 44	2.4	3.5	1.5	2.5	3.8	1.4	2.3	3.1	1.5
45 - 49	4.1	5.9	2.5	4.3	6.3	2.7	3.6	5.2	2.0
50 - 54	6.4	9.2	4.0	6.4	9.2	4.1	6.3	9.1	3.7
55 - 59	10.2	14.8	6.4	10.8	16.0	6.6	8.5	11.5	6.0
60 - 64	17.1	23.8	11.9	17.8	25.1	12.2	15.3	20.8	11.2
65 - 69	28.0	38.1	20.3	29.0	39.1	21.4	26.2	36.3	18.4
70 - 74	43.7	56.8	34.0	45.7	59.3	35.8	40.8	53.3	31.2
75 - 79	72.9	89.4	63.1	74.2	89.5	65.3	71.2	89.2	59.8
80 - 84	122.9	137.8	116.7	124.4	138.0	118.8	120.4	137.4	113.1
85 +	255.9	268.3	251.4	242.6	244.3	241.9	274.4	305.9	264.1
2005 (C)									
Total	8.2	8.9	7.6	...	...	...	...	...	...
0 - 4	2.9	3.1	2.5	...	...	...	...	...	...
5 - 9	0.2	♦0.2	♦0.2	...	...	...	...	...	...
10 - 14	0.2	0.2	♦0.1	...	...	...	...	...	...

Continent, country or area, date, code and age (in years) / Continent, pays ou zone, date, code et âge (en années)	Total			Urban - Urbaine			Rural - Rurale		
	Both sexes Les deux sexes	Male Masculin	Female Féminin	Both sexes Les deux sexes	Male Masculin	Female Féminin	Both sexes Les deux sexes	Male Masculin	Female Féminin
ASIA - ASIE									
Armenia - Arménie[12]									
2005 (C)									
15 - 19	0.4	0.6	♦0.2	...	...	...	...	...	...
20 - 24	0.4	0.6	0.2	...	...	...	...	...	...
25 - 29	0.6	1.0	0.3	...	...	...	...	...	...
30 - 34	1.1	1.6	0.5	...	...	...	...	...	...
35 - 39	1.6	2.4	0.9	...	...	...	...	...	...
40 - 44	2.5	3.5	1.6	...	...	...	...	...	...
45 - 49	3.8	5.4	2.4	...	...	...	...	...	...
50 - 54	6.7	9.8	4.0	...	...	...	...	...	...
55 - 59	10.4	15.2	6.4	...	...	...	...	...	...
60 - 64	16.1	23.3	10.6	...	...	...	...	...	...
65 - 69	27.1	36.9	19.8	...	...	...	...	...	...
70 - 74	44.8	57.9	35.1	...	...	...	...	...	...
75 - 79	75.0	93.4	63.6	...	...	...	...	...	...
80 - 84	120.1	141.2	111.0	...	...	...	...	...	...
85 +	257.2	289.4	246.1	...	...	...	...	...	...
Azerbaijan - Azerbaïdjan[12]									
2004 (+C)									
Total	6.0	6.4	5.6	6.0	6.6	5.5	5.9	6.1	5.6
0	10.5	11.4	9.4	11.0	12.9	8.8	10.1	10.2	9.9
1 - 4	1.6	1.7	1.6	0.7	0.6	0.8	2.4	2.6	2.2
5 - 9	0.5	0.5	0.5	0.4	0.4	0.4	0.6	0.6	0.5
10 - 14	0.3	0.4	0.3	0.3	0.3	0.2	0.4	0.5	0.3
15 - 19	0.5	0.6	0.4	0.5	0.6	0.4	0.5	0.6	0.3
20 - 24	0.8	1.0	0.5	0.8	1.0	0.5	0.8	1.0	0.6
25 - 29	1.0	1.4	0.7	1.0	1.4	0.6	1.0	1.3	0.7
30 - 34	1.5	2.2	0.8	1.7	2.6	0.9	1.3	1.9	0.7
35 - 39	1.9	2.7	1.1	2.0	3.1	1.1	1.7	2.3	1.2
40 - 44	2.7	3.8	1.7	2.8	4.1	1.6	2.6	3.4	1.8
45 - 49	4.2	5.9	2.6	4.4	6.2	2.7	3.9	5.5	2.4
50 - 54	7.0	9.3	4.9	7.3	9.8	4.9	6.5	8.5	4.7
55 - 59	11.4	15.5	7.8	11.8	16.2	7.8	10.8	14.3	7.7
60 - 64	19.1	25.3	13.9	20.1	26.4	14.7	17.9	23.9	13.0
65 - 69	30.9	39.3	24.3	31.6	41.0	24.2	30.2	37.6	24.4
70 - 74	48.8	57.6	41.9	50.9	60.1	44.0	46.9	55.6	40.0
75 - 79	72.3	82.4	65.4	74.6	82.0	69.8	70.0	82.8	60.7
80 - 84	96.7	97.4	96.3	100.4	91.0	105.0	92.9	104.1	87.7
85 - 89	143.7	140.0	145.1	158.7	131.5	171.4	131.1	149.4	125.3
90 - 94	191.5	196.5	190.0	209.6	183.8	220.0	180.0	207.8	172.9
95 - 99	200.4	188.3	204.2	227.5	210.0	233.3	187.6	177.5	190.8
100 +	388.6	243.3	428.2	241.7	155.0	285.0	498.8	420.0	510.0
Bahrain - Bahreïn									
2005 (C)									
Total	3.1	3.2	2.9	...	...	...	...	...	...
0 - 4	2.7	2.9	2.4	...	...	...	...	...	...
5 - 9	♦0.4	♦0.4	♦0.3	...	...	...	...	...	...
10 - 14	♦0.1	♦0.1	♦0.2	...	...	...	...	...	...
15 - 19	0.6	♦0.9	♦0.3	...	...	...	...	...	...
20 - 24	0.9	1.1	♦0.6	...	...	...	...	...	...
25 - 29	0.8	1.1	♦0.5	...	...	...	...	...	...
30 - 34	0.8	1.0	♦0.6	...	...	...	...	...	...
35 - 39	1.2	1.5	♦0.7	...	...	...	...	...	...
40 - 44	1.5	1.8	♦0.9	...	...	...	...	...	...
45 - 49	2.9	3.2	2.3	...	...	...	...	...	...
50 - 54	5.3	5.9	4.2	...	...	...	...	...	...
55 - 59	7.5	7.9	7.0	...	...	...	...	...	...
60 - 64	11.3	12.8	9.6	...	...	...	...	...	...
65 - 69	30.8	31.4	30.3	...	...	...	...	...	...
70 - 74	43.0	42.2	43.9	...	...	...	...	...	...
75 +	120.2	123.1	117.0	...	...	...	...	...	...
Bhutan - Bhoutan[13]									
2005 (I)									
Total	7.1	7.2	7.0	5.3	5.4	5.3	7.9	8.0	7.7
0	40.8	44.3	37.5	30.7	29.3	32.1	45.9	51.9	40.1

20. Death rates specific for age, sex and urban/rural residence: latest available year, 1996 - 2005
Taux de mortalité selon l'âge, le sexe et la résidence, urbaine/rurale: dernière année disponible, 1996 - 2005 (continued - suite)

Continent, country or area, date, code and age (in years) / Continent, pays ou zone, date, code et âge (en années)	Total			Urban - Urbaine			Rural - Rurale		
	Both sexes Les deux sexes	Male Masculin	Female Féminin	Both sexes Les deux sexes	Male Masculin	Female Féminin	Both sexes Les deux sexes	Male Masculin	Female Féminin
ASIA - ASIE									
Bhutan - Bhoutan[13]									
2005 (I)									
1 - 4	5.4	5.6	5.1	5.1	5.9	4.3	5.5	5.5	5.4
5 - 9	2.0	2.4	1.5	2.5	3.8	♦1.3	1.8	1.9	1.6
10 - 14	1.1	1.2	1.1	♦0.6	♦0.4	♦0.9	1.4	1.5	1.2
15 - 19	1.7	1.7	1.6	♦0.7	♦1.0	♦0.4	2.2	2.2	2.3
20 - 24	1.7	1.6	1.9	♦1.0	♦0.9	♦1.1	2.3	2.1	2.5
25 - 29	2.3	2.4	2.3	1.7	♦1.8	♦1.5	2.7	2.7	2.7
30 - 34	3.4	3.4	3.4	2.1	♦2.2	♦2.0	4.1	4.1	4.1
35 - 39	4.7	5.1	4.3	4.6	5.3	♦3.7	4.8	5.0	4.5
40 - 44	5.8	5.9	5.7	5.0	♦4.1	♦6.2	6.2	6.8	5.5
45 - 49	9.0	8.7	9.5	10.7	9.0	13.1	8.5	8.5	8.5
50 - 54	9.3	9.6	8.9	9.1	♦9.4	♦8.6	9.3	9.7	8.9
55 - 59	14.6	14.4	14.8	24.4	♦19.6	30.8	12.6	13.3	11.9
60 - 64	20.0	19.2	20.8	26.7	♦25.8	♦27.6	18.8	18.1	19.6
65 - 69	29.1	27.2	31.3	46.9	41.4	52.8	26.2	24.8	27.7
70 - 74	42.1	41.8	42.4	47.9	♦50.1	♦45.9	41.2	40.6	41.7
75 +	96.8	102.7	90.8	134.7	169.5	106.8	90.1	92.5	87.5
Brunei Darussalam - Brunéi Darussalam									
2004 (+C)									
Total	2.8	3.0	2.6	...	...	...	...	...	...
0 - 4	1.3	1.3	1.3	...	...	...	...	...	...
5 - 9	♦0.3	♦0.6	♦0.1	...	...	...	...	...	...
10 - 14	♦0.3	♦0.4	♦0.3	...	...	...	...	...	...
15 - 19	♦0.4	♦0.6	♦0.3	...	...	...	...	...	...
20 - 24	♦0.6	♦0.9	♦0.3	...	...	...	...	...	...
25 - 29	♦0.6	♦0.8	♦0.3	...	...	...	...	...	...
30 - 34	1.0	♦1.0	♦1.0	...	...	...	...	...	...
35 - 39	1.2	♦1.3	♦1.2	...	...	...	...	...	...
40 - 44	1.9	♦1.8	♦1.9	...	...	...	...	...	...
45 - 49	3.1	3.4	♦2.8	...	...	...	...	...	...
50 - 54	4.8	5.3	♦4.1	...	...	...	...	...	...
55 - 59	10.0	♦7.6	12.8	...	...	...	...	...	...
60 - 64	10.8	12.4	♦9.2	...	...	...	...	...	...
65 - 69	27.2	32.4	22.6	...	...	...	...	...	...
70 +	96.6	99.6	93.3	...	...	...	...	...	...
China: Hong Kong SAR - Chine: Hong Kong RAS									
2005 (C)									
Total	5.7	6.6[5]	4.9[5]	...	...	...	...	...	...
0	3.3	3.8	2.8	...	...	...	...	...	...
1 - 4	♦0.2	♦0.2	♦0.2	...	...	...	...	...	...
5 - 9	♦0.1	♦0.1	♦0.1	...	...	...	...	...	...
10 - 14	0.1	♦0.1	♦0.1	...	...	...	...	...	...
15 - 19	0.2	0.3	0.2	...	...	...	...	...	...
20 - 24	0.3	0.4	0.2	...	...	...	...	...	...
25 - 29	0.4	0.6	0.3	...	...	...	...	...	...
30 - 34	0.5	0.8	0.4	...	...	...	...	...	...
35 - 39	0.8	1.1	0.5	...	...	...	...	...	...
40 - 44	1.1	1.4	0.8	...	...	...	...	...	...
45 - 49	1.7	2.3	1.2	...	...	...	...	...	...
50 - 54	2.8	3.6	2.0	...	...	...	...	...	...
55 - 59	4.3	6.0	2.6	...	...	...	...	...	...
60 - 64	7.5	10.1	4.7	...	...	...	...	...	...
65 - 69	12.4	17.1	7.4	...	...	...	...	...	...
70 - 74	21.4	28.3	14.8	...	...	...	...	...	...
75 - 79	36.2	48.4	26.0	...	...	...	...	...	...
80 - 84	61.7	81.4	48.7	...	...	...	...	...	...
85 +	119.6	140.0	110.4	...	...	...	...	...	...
China: Macao SAR - Chine: Macao RAS									
2005 (C)									
Total	3.4	4.0	2.9	...	...	...	...	...	...
0 - 4	♦0.9	♦0.7	♦1.1	...	...	...	...	...	...

20. Death rates specific for age, sex and urban/rural residence: latest available year, 1996 - 2005
Taux de mortalité selon l'âge, le sexe et la résidence, urbaine/rurale: dernière année disponible, 1996 - 2005 (continued - suite)

Continent, country or area, date, code and age (in years) / Continent, pays ou zone, date, code et âge (en années)	Total			Urban - Urbaine			Rural - Rurale		
	Both sexes Les deux sexes	Male Masculin	Female Féminin	Both sexes Les deux sexes	Male Masculin	Female Féminin	Both sexes Les deux sexes	Male Masculin	Female Féminin
ASIA - ASIE									
China: Macao SAR - Chine: Macao RAS									
2005 (C)									
5 - 9	◆0.1	◆0.1	◆0.1	...	...	...	...	...	...
10 - 14	◆0.2	◆0.3	◆0.1	...	...	...	...	...	...
15 - 19	◆0.1	◆0.2	-	...	...	...	...	...	...
20 - 24	◆0.4	◆0.6	◆0.3	...	...	...	...	...	...
25 - 29	◆0.4	◆0.6	◆0.3	...	...	...	...	...	...
30 - 34	◆0.5	◆0.9	◆0.2	...	...	...	...	...	...
35 - 39	◆0.7	◆0.9	◆0.5	...	...	...	...	...	...
40 - 44	0.8	◆1.2	◆0.6	...	...	...	...	...	...
45 - 49	2.0	2.6	1.3	...	...	...	...	...	...
50 - 54	2.7	3.8	◆1.5	...	...	...	...	...	...
55 - 59	3.6	5.4	◆1.6	...	...	...	...	...	...
60 - 64	6.8	10.1	◆3.2	...	...	...	...	...	...
65 - 69	11.1	13.9	8.2	...	...	...	...	...	...
70 - 74	17.7	25.9	11.6	...	...	...	...	...	...
75 +	52.9	63.4	46.5	...	...	...	...	...	...
Cyprus - Chypre[14]									
2005 (C)									
Total	7.2	7.6	6.7	...	...	...	...	...	...
0	4.6	◆4.5	◆4.7	...	...	...	...	...	...
1 - 4	◆0.4	◆0.3	◆0.4	...	...	...	...	...	...
5 - 9	◆0.4	◆0.4	◆0.4	...	...	...	...	...	...
10 - 14	◆0.3	◆0.2	◆0.3	...	...	...	...	...	...
15 - 19	0.6	◆0.9	◆0.3	...	...	...	...	...	...
20 - 24	0.7	1.1	◆0.4	...	...	...	...	...	...
25 - 29	0.8	1.1	◆0.5	...	...	...	...	...	...
30 - 34	1.0	1.3	◆0.6	...	...	...	...	...	...
35 - 39	1.1	1.6	◆0.7	...	...	...	...	...	...
40 - 44	1.2	1.4	◆0.9	...	...	...	...	...	...
45 - 49	1.7	2.0	1.4	...	...	...	...	...	...
50 - 54	2.6	3.5	1.7	...	...	...	...	...	...
55 - 59	5.1	6.9	3.4	...	...	...	...	...	...
60 - 64	8.1	11.1	5.2	...	...	...	...	...	...
65 - 69	14.1	17.7	10.8	...	...	...	...	...	...
70 - 74	22.2	28.0	17.4	...	...	...	...	...	...
75 - 79	46.8	54.2	41.2	...	...	...	...	...	...
80 - 84	84.1	96.2	75.2	...	...	...	...	...	...
85 +	185.8	203.6	174.2	...	...	...	...	...	...
Georgia - Géorgie[12]									
2000 (C)									
Total	8.4	8.6	8.1	7.8	8.4	7.3	9.1	8.8	9.3
0	14.2	15.9	12.2	21.0	23.7	17.8	3.1	◆3.2	◆3.0
1 - 4	0.4	0.4	◆0.3	0.4	◆0.4	◆0.3	◆0.3	◆0.4	◆0.3
5 - 9	0.1	◆0.2	◆0.1	◆0.1	◆0.2	◆0.1	◆0.1	◆0.1	◆0.1
10 - 14	0.1	0.2	◆0.1	0.1	◆0.2	◆0.1	◆0.1	◆0.1	◆0.1
15 - 19	0.4	0.4	0.3	0.3	0.4	◆0.2	0.4	0.5	0.4
20 - 24	0.6	0.9	0.3	0.7	1.1	0.3	0.5	0.7	◆0.4
25 - 29	1.0	1.4	0.4	1.0	1.6	0.4	0.9	1.2	0.6
30 - 34	1.2	1.9	0.6	1.3	2.1	0.6	1.1	1.7	0.6
35 - 39	1.8	2.8	0.9	1.9	3.1	0.9	1.6	2.3	0.9
40 - 44	2.6	4.2	1.2	2.7	4.6	1.2	2.5	3.7	1.2
45 - 49	3.8	6.0	1.8	4.1	6.7	2.0	3.1	4.8	1.4
50 - 54	5.6	8.5	3.1	6.0	9.3	3.2	4.9	7.2	2.9
55 - 59	6.8	10.2	4.1	7.5	11.8	4.3	5.7	8.1	3.7
60 - 64	13.4	17.9	9.7	14.2	20.2	9.5	12.3	15.2	9.9
65 - 69	21.6	30.3	15.2	22.2	32.1	15.2	21.0	28.5	15.1
70 - 74	35.2	46.6	27.8	36.5	50.2	28.4	33.8	43.3	27.1
75 - 79	54.1	68.8	47.5	55.5	67.5	50.4	52.6	70.1	44.6
80 - 84	77.9	57.6	92.5	79.6	54.3	99.0	76.3	61.1	86.5
85 +	164.4	109.3	204.4	146.4	96.7	181.0	182.6	121.3	228.9
2003 (C)									
Total	10.6	11.2	10.2	...	...	...	...	...	...
0	25.4	27.5	23.0	...	...	...	...	...	...

20. Death rates specific for age, sex and urban/rural residence: latest available year, 1996 - 2005
Taux de mortalité selon l'âge, le sexe et la résidence, urbaine/rurale: dernière année disponible, 1996 - 2005 (continued - suite)

Continent, country or area, date, code and age (in years) / Continent, pays ou zone, date, code et âge (en années)	Total			Urban - Urbaine			Rural - Rurale		
	Both sexes Les deux sexes	Male Masculin	Female Féminin	Both sexes Les deux sexes	Male Masculin	Female Féminin	Both sexes Les deux sexes	Male Masculin	Female Féminin
ASIA - ASIE									
Georgia - Géorgie[12]									
2003 (C)									
1 - 4	0.7	0.8	0.6	...	...	...	...	...	...
5 - 9	0.1	◆0.1	◆0.1	...	...	...	...	...	...
10 - 14	0.2	◆0.2	0.2	...	...	...	...	...	...
15 - 19	0.3	0.4	0.2	...	...	...	...	...	...
20 - 24	0.6	0.8	0.4	...	...	...	...	...	...
25 - 29	1.0	1.2	0.8	...	...	...	...	...	...
30 - 34	1.4	2.3	0.6	...	...	...	...	...	...
35 - 39	1.8	2.5	1.2	...	...	...	...	...	...
40 - 44	2.7	3.6	1.9	...	...	...	...	...	...
45 - 49	4.0	6.1	2.2	...	...	...	...	...	...
50 - 54	7.4	10.9	4.4	...	...	...	...	...	...
55 - 59	11.7	16.3	8.0	...	...	...	...	...	...
60 - 64	14.7	20.0	10.6	...	...	...	...	...	...
65 - 69	26.7	37.0	18.9	...	...	...	...	...	...
70 - 74	40.5	51.8	32.7	...	...	...	...	...	...
75 - 79	76.4	95.9	65.5	...	...	...	...	...	...
80 - 84	113.2	146.0	99.7	...	...	...	...	...	...
85 +	264.4	345.3	240.5	...	...	...	...	...	...
Israel - Israël[15]									
2005 (C)									
Total	5.6[16]	5.6[17]	5.6[17]	5.7[9]	5.8[18]	5.7[18]	4.3[9]	4.2[9]	4.4[9]
0	4.4[16]	4.6[17]	4.1[17]	4.2[9]	4.5[18]	3.9[18]	5.9[9]	6.2[9]	5.6[9]
1 - 4	0.3[16]	0.3[16]	0.2[16]	0.3	0.3	0.2	◆0.4	◆0.6	◆0.2
5 - 9	0.1[16]	0.1[16]	◆0.1[16]	0.1	◆0.1	◆0.1	◆0.1	◆0.1	-
10 - 14	0.1[16]	0.2[16]	0.1[16]	0.1	0.2	◆0.1	◆0.1	◆0.1	◆0.2
15 - 19	0.3[16]	0.4[16]	0.2[16]	0.3	0.4	0.2	◆0.3	◆0.5	◆0.2
20 - 24	0.6[16]	0.8[16]	0.3[16]	0.6[9]	0.8[9]	0.3[9]	◆0.5[9]	◆0.8[9]	◆0.2[9]
25 - 29	0.5[16]	0.7[16]	0.3[16]	0.5	0.7	0.2	◆0.7	◆1.0	◆0.4
30 - 34	0.6[16]	0.8[16]	0.3[16]	0.6	0.8	0.4	◆0.6	◆1.0	◆0.2
35 - 39	0.8[16]	1.0[16]	0.6[16]	0.8	1.1	0.6	◆0.6	◆0.7	◆0.4
40 - 44	1.3[16]	1.8[16]	0.9[16]	1.4	1.8	0.9	1.1	◆1.1	◆1.0
45 - 49	2.1[16]	2.8[16]	1.5[16]	2.2	2.9	1.6	1.6	◆1.8	◆1.4
50 - 54	3.3[16]	4.3[16]	2.4[16]	3.4[9]	4.4[9]	2.4[9]	2.6[9]	3.1[9]	◆2.2[9]
55 - 59	4.9[16]	6.2[16]	3.7[16]	5.0[9]	6.4[9]	3.7[9]	3.8[9]	4.3[9]	3.4[9]
60 - 64	8.5[16]	11.0[16]	6.3[16]	8.7	11.4	6.4	6.2	7.2	5.2
65 - 69	13.4[16]	17.1[16]	10.2[16]	13.5	17.4	10.2	11.8	12.5	11.1
70 - 74	23.0[16]	29.0[16]	18.4[16]	23.2[9]	29.3[9]	18.4[9]	20.1[9]	23.7[9]	16.9[9]
75 - 79	39.6[16]	47.8[16]	33.9[16]	39.7	48.0	34.0	37.0	43.9	31.8
80 - 84	67.8[16]	76.5[16]	62.0[16]	67.8[9]	76.4[9]	62.2[9]	67.3[9]	77.5[9]	59.5[9]
85 +	164.8[16]	168.3[16]	162.5[16]	163.7[9]	167.3[9]	161.3[9]	179.9[9]	180.9[9]	179.2[9]
Japan - Japon[19]									
2005 (C)									
Total	8.5	9.4	7.6	...	...	...	...	...	...
0 - 4	0.7	0.8	0.7	...	...	...	...	...	...
5 - 9	0.1	0.1	0.1	...	...	...	...	...	...
10 - 14	0.1	0.1	0.1	...	...	...	...	...	...
15 - 19	0.3	0.4	0.2	...	...	...	...	...	...
20 - 24	0.4	0.6	0.3	...	...	...	...	...	...
25 - 29	0.5	0.7	0.3	...	...	...	...	...	...
30 - 34	0.6	0.8	0.4	...	...	...	...	...	...
35 - 39	0.9	1.1	0.6	...	...	...	...	...	...
40 - 44	1.3	1.7	0.9	...	...	...	...	...	...
45 - 49	2.0	2.7	1.3	...	...	...	...	...	...
50 - 54	3.3	4.4	2.1	...	...	...	...	...	...
55 - 59	4.9	6.9	3.0	...	...	...	...	...	...
60 - 64	7.3	10.5	4.3	...	...	...	...	...	...
65 - 69	10.9	15.8	6.6	...	...	...	...	...	...
70 - 74	18.4	26.7	11.4	...	...	...	...	...	...
75 - 79	30.7	44.7	20.2	...	...	...	...	...	...
80 - 84	51.8	74.8	39.2	...	...	...	...	...	...
85 +	122.7	157.9	109.1	...	...	...	...	...	...

20. Death rates specific for age, sex and urban/rural residence: latest available year, 1996 - 2005
Taux de mortalité selon l'âge, le sexe et la résidence, urbaine/rurale: dernière année disponible, 1996 - 2005 (continued - suite)

Continent, country or area, date, code and age (in years) — Continent, pays ou zone, date, code et âge (en années)	Total			Urban - Urbaine			Rural - Rurale		
	Both sexes Les deux sexes	Male Masculin	Female Féminin	Both sexes Les deux sexes	Male Masculin	Female Féminin	Both sexes Les deux sexes	Male Masculin	Female Féminin
ASIA - ASIE									
Kazakhstan[12]									
2003 (C)									
Total	10.4	12.1	8.8	11.8	14.3	9.6	8.6	9.6	7.7
0	16.3	18.6	13.9	18.3	21.3	15.0	14.0	15.3	12.6
1 - 4	1.2	1.3	1.1	0.9	1.0	0.9	1.5	1.6	1.3
5 - 9	0.5	0.5	0.4	0.5	0.6	0.4	0.4	0.5	0.3
10 - 14	0.5	0.5	0.4	0.5	0.6	0.4	0.5	0.5	0.4
15 - 19	1.1	1.5	0.7	1.2	1.6	0.8	1.0	1.4	0.6
20 - 24	2.1	3.0	1.1	2.1	3.2	1.1	2.1	2.8	1.2
25 - 29	3.0	4.6	1.5	3.4	5.3	1.6	2.6	3.7	1.3
30 - 34	3.9	6.0	1.8	4.3	7.0	1.9	3.3	4.8	1.7
35 - 39	4.9	7.5	2.4	5.5	8.7	2.6	4.1	5.9	2.2
40 - 44	7.1	10.9	3.6	7.9	12.6	3.8	5.9	8.6	3.1
45 - 49	10.2	15.6	5.4	11.4	18.1	5.8	8.3	12.0	4.7
50 - 54	14.4	22.0	8.0	15.7	25.1	8.2	12.2	17.1	7.7
55 - 59	20.1	30.4	11.8	21.5	34.0	12.0	17.6	24.9	11.3
60 - 64	29.3	44.2	18.6	30.9	49.1	18.9	26.9	37.8	18.2
65 - 69	40.5	59.2	27.5	41.3	63.3	27.0	39.5	53.5	28.4
70 - 74	59.7	83.8	45.5	60.2	86.9	45.6	58.8	79.2	45.2
75 - 79	83.5	110.0	72.0	84.4	112.3	72.9	82.0	106.2	70.3
80 - 84	124.8	151.5	115.9	125.2	153.6	116.1	124.0	148.1	115.6
85 +	241.0	262.5	235.6	245.9	257.8	242.7	233.9	270.3	225.4
2004 (C)									
Total	10.1	11.9	8.5	...	...	...	...	...	...
0	15.2	17.2	13.0	...	...	...	...	...	...
1 - 4	1.1	1.2	0.9	...	...	...	...	...	...
5 - 9	0.4	0.5	0.3	...	...	...	...	...	...
10 - 14	0.4	0.5	0.3	...	...	...	...	...	...
15 - 19	1.1	1.5	0.7	...	...	...	...	...	...
20 - 24	2.2	3.4	1.1	...	...	...	...	...	...
25 - 29	3.4	5.2	1.5	...	...	...	...	...	...
30 - 34	4.3	6.6	1.9	...	...	...	...	...	...
35 - 39	5.2	7.9	2.6	...	...	...	...	...	...
40 - 44	7.2	11.1	3.7	...	...	...	...	...	...
45 - 49	10.0	15.5	5.2	...	...	...	...	...	...
50 - 54	14.2	22.0	7.7	...	...	...	...	...	...
55 - 59	19.6	30.0	11.3	...	...	...	...	...	...
60 - 64	27.9	42.1	17.9	...	...	...	...	...	...
65 - 69	38.4	56.3	26.2	...	...	...	...	...	...
70 - 74	56.5	78.6	43.3	...	...	...	...	...	...
75 - 79	78.8	104.0	67.5	...	...	...	...	...	...
80 - 84	114.6	131.9	109.0	...	...	...	...	...	...
85 +	227.7	234.7	225.8	...	...	...	...	...	...
Korea (Republic of) - Corée (République de)[20]									
2004 (C)									
Total	5.1	5.6	4.6	...	...	...	...	...	...
0	4.6	4.8	4.3	...	...	...	...	...	...
1 - 4	0.3	0.4	0.3	...	...	...	...	...	...
5 - 9	0.2	0.2	0.2	...	...	...	...	...	...
10 - 14	0.2	0.2	0.1	...	...	...	...	...	...
15 - 19	0.3	0.4	0.2	...	...	...	...	...	...
20 - 24	0.4	0.6	0.3	...	...	...	...	...	...
25 - 29	0.6	0.7	0.4	...	...	...	...	...	...
30 - 34	0.7	1.0	0.5	...	...	...	...	...	...
35 - 39	1.3	1.7	0.8	...	...	...	...	...	...
40 - 44	2.1	3.0	1.1	...	...	...	...	...	...
45 - 49	3.1	4.6	1.6	...	...	...	...	...	...
50 - 54	4.5	6.8	2.3	...	...	...	...	...	...
55 - 59	6.4	9.4	3.3	...	...	...	...	...	...
60 - 64	10.7	16.1	5.9	...	...	...	...	...	...
65 - 69	16.3	23.9	10.0	...	...	...	...	...	...
70 - 74	25.6	36.1	18.5	...	...	...	...	...	...
75 - 79	44.6	59.8	36.1	...	...	...	...	...	...
80 - 84	81.4	104.9	70.5	...	...	...	...	...	...

20. Death rates specific for age, sex and urban/rural residence: latest available year, 1996 - 2005
Taux de mortalité selon l'âge, le sexe et la résidence, urbaine/rurale: dernière année disponible, 1996 - 2005 (continued - suite)

Continent, country or area, date, code and age (in years) / Continent, pays ou zone, date, code et âge (en années)	Total			Urban - Urbaine			Rural - Rurale		
	Both sexes Les deux sexes	Male Masculin	Female Féminin	Both sexes Les deux sexes	Male Masculin	Female Féminin	Both sexes Les deux sexes	Male Masculin	Female Féminin
ASIA - ASIE									
Korea (Republic of) - Corée (République de)[20]									
2004 (C)									
85 - 89	138.1	169.7	126.8	...	...	...	...	...	...
90 - 94	243.5	300.1	229.3	...	...	...	...	...	...
95 +	427.5	566.2	406.5	...	...	...	...	...	...
Kuwait - Koweït									
2005 (C)									
Total	1.9	2.1	1.7	...	...	...	...	...	...
0	10.3	11.0	9.7	...	...	...	...	...	...
1 - 4	0.5	0.6	0.5	...	...	...	...	...	...
5 - 9	0.3	♦0.3	♦0.2	...	...	...	...	...	...
10 - 14	0.3	0.4	♦0.2	...	...	...	...	...	...
15 - 19	0.6	1.0	♦0.2	...	...	...	...	...	...
20 - 24	0.6	0.9	♦0.2	...	...	...	...	...	...
25 - 29	0.7	0.9	0.3	...	...	...	...	...	...
30 - 34	0.6	0.7	0.4	...	...	...	...	...	...
35 - 39	0.8	1.0	0.5	...	...	...	...	...	...
40 - 44	1.3	1.6	0.7	...	...	...	...	...	...
45 - 49	2.0	2.5	1.1	...	...	...	...	...	...
50 - 54	3.3	3.8	2.5	...	...	...	...	...	...
55 - 59	6.1	6.5	5.4	...	...	...	...	...	...
60 - 64	10.0	10.8	9.0	...	...	...	...	...	...
65 - 69	20.7	23.6	17.1	...	...	...	...	...	...
70 - 74	33.9	33.9	33.8	...	...	...	...	...	...
75 - 79	53.6	61.7	46.1	...	...	...	...	...	...
80 - 84	69.3	86.0	56.0	...	...	...	...	...	...
85 +	137.7	149.9	128.0	...	...	...	...	...	...
Kyrgyzstan - Kirghizistan[12]									
2005 (C)									
Total	7.2	8.1	6.4	8.1	9.3	7.0	6.8	7.5	6.1
0	30.5	33.4	27.5	46.6	51.2	41.7	22.8	24.8	20.7
1 - 4	1.5	1.7	1.3	0.8	0.8	0.8	1.8	2.0	1.5
5 - 9	0.3	0.3	0.3	♦0.2	♦0.2	♦0.1	0.4	0.4	0.3
10 - 14	0.3	0.4	0.2	0.3	0.4	♦0.2	0.3	0.4	0.3
15 - 19	0.6	0.7	0.5	0.6	0.7	0.4	0.7	0.8	0.6
20 - 24	1.1	1.5	0.8	0.9	1.4	0.4	1.3	1.6	1.0
25 - 29	1.9	2.6	1.1	1.6	2.5	0.7	2.1	2.7	1.4
30 - 34	3.0	4.3	1.6	2.8	4.3	1.4	3.1	4.4	1.7
35 - 39	3.9	5.7	2.1	4.0	6.1	2.0	3.8	5.4	2.2
40 - 44	5.2	7.6	2.8	5.0	7.6	2.7	5.2	7.6	2.9
45 - 49	7.1	10.2	4.1	7.2	11.0	4.0	7.0	9.8	4.2
50 - 54	10.8	15.3	6.6	11.9	17.9	6.7	10.0	13.8	6.5
55 - 59	16.0	22.0	10.8	17.1	24.8	10.7	15.3	20.0	10.9
60 - 64	26.6	35.9	18.5	28.2	39.9	19.3	25.5	33.7	17.9
65 - 69	37.0	50.7	26.6	37.7	54.6	26.1	36.6	48.5	26.9
70 - 74	55.7	72.8	43.7	55.4	75.2	43.5	55.9	71.7	43.8
75 - 79	78.0	91.0	69.8	81.0	100.0	71.6	76.4	87.0	68.6
80 - 84	107.6	118.2	102.6	111.3	122.3	107.2	105.3	116.2	99.6
85 - 89	163.7	172.8	160.6	184.9	177.5	187.6	150.8	169.6	144.7
90 - 94	203.9	209.9	202.0	246.7	228.8	252.5	179.3	198.3	173.6
95 - 99	184.8	153.7	195.9	188.7	♦166.7	198.7	183.3	147.3	194.9
100 +	521.2	240.6	617.6	♦135.5	♦142.9	♦133.7	790.8	♦285.7	1004.7
Malaysia - Malaisie									
2000 (C)									
Total	4.5	5.1	3.9	...	...	...	...	...	...
0 - 4	1.9	2.0	1.7	...	...	...	...	...	...
5 - 9	0.3	0.4	0.3	...	...	...	...	...	...
10 - 14	0.4	0.5	0.3	...	...	...	...	...	...
15 - 19	0.8	1.2	0.4	...	...	...	...	...	...
20 - 24	1.1	1.6	0.5	...	...	...	...	...	...
25 - 29	1.2	1.8	0.6	...	...	...	...	...	...
30 - 34	1.5	2.2	0.8	...	...	...	...	...	...
35 - 39	1.9	2.7	1.1	...	...	...	...	...	...
40 - 44	2.7	3.7	1.8	...	...	...	...	...	...

Continent, country or area, date, code and age (in years) / Continent, pays ou zone, date, code et âge (en années)	Total			Urban - Urbaine			Rural - Rurale		
	Both sexes Les deux sexes	Male Masculin	Female Féminin	Both sexes Les deux sexes	Male Masculin	Female Féminin	Both sexes Les deux sexes	Male Masculin	Female Féminin
ASIA - ASIE									
Malaysia - Malaisie									
2000 (C)									
45 - 49	4.0	5.1	2.9	...	...	...	...	...	...
50 - 54	6.6	8.1	5.0	...	...	...	...	...	...
55 - 59	11.5	14.0	8.7	...	...	...	...	...	...
60 - 64	18.0	22.3	13.9	...	...	...	...	...	...
65 - 69	31.8	37.9	26.3	...	...	...	...	...	...
70 - 74	46.0	52.6	40.1	...	...	...	...	...	...
75 + ...	105.4	112.6	99.8	...	...	...	...	...	...
Maldives									
2005 (C)									
Total.	3.5	4.1	2.8	...	...	...	...	...	...
0 - 4	3.2	2.9	3.5	...	...	...	...	...	...
5 - 9	♦0.4	♦0.4	♦0.4	...	...	...	...	...	...
10 - 14	♦0.3	♦0.5	♦0.2	...	...	...	...	...	...
15 - 19	♦0.3	♦0.5	♦0.1	...	...	...	...	...	...
20 - 24	♦0.3	♦0.4	♦0.2	...	...	...	...	...	...
25 - 29	♦0.4	♦0.8	♦0.1	...	...	...	...	...	...
30 - 34	♦0.4	♦0.4	♦0.5	...	...	...	...	...	...
35 - 39	♦0.7	♦0.7	♦0.8	...	...	...	...	...	...
40 - 44	♦1.1	♦0.9	♦1.3	...	...	...	...	...	...
45 - 49	♦2.3	♦2.6	♦2.0	...	...	...	...	...	...
50 - 54	♦3.8	♦4.3	♦3.2	...	...	...	...	...	...
55 - 59	7.2	♦8.5	♦6.0	...	...	...	...	...	...
60 - 64	16.1	19.6	12.4	...	...	...	...	...	...
65 - 69	24.7	28.0	21.0	...	...	...	...	...	...
70 + ...	65.5	69.2	60.3	...	...	...	...	...	...
Mongolia - Mongolie									
2003 (C)									
Total.	6.4	7.6	5.2	...	...	...	...	...	...
0	24.9	28.8	21.0	...	...	...	...	...	...
1 - 4	1.9	2.1	1.6	...	...	...	...	...	...
5 - 9	0.4	0.5	0.4	...	...	...	...	...	...
10 - 14	0.4	0.4	0.3	...	...	...	...	...	...
15 - 19	0.7	0.9	0.5	...	...	...	...	...	...
20 - 24	1.2	1.8	0.7	...	...	...	...	...	...
25 - 29	2.0	2.8	1.2	...	...	...	...	...	...
30 - 34	2.8	3.9	1.7	...	...	...	...	...	...
35 - 39	3.9	5.7	2.2	...	...	...	...	...	...
40 - 44	6.7	9.2	4.2	...	...	...	...	...	...
45 - 49	10.6	13.7	7.5	...	...	...	...	...	...
50 - 54	15.0	19.6	10.7	...	...	...	...	...	...
55 - 59	19.3	24.6	14.2	...	...	...	...	...	...
60 - 64	30.6	40.1	22.2	...	...	...	...	...	...
65 - 69	41.8	56.0	29.8	...	...	...	...	...	...
70 + ...	94.1	111.8	81.7	...	...	...	...	...	...
Nepal - Népal[21]									
2001 (I)									
Total.	4.7	5.2	4.2	...	...	...	...	...	...
0	26.3	27.5	25.1	...	...	...	...	...	...
1 - 4	4.3	4.9	3.8	...	...	...	...	...	...
5 - 9	1.0	1.1	1.0	...	...	...	...	...	...
10 - 14	0.8	0.9	0.7	...	...	...	...	...	...
15 - 19	1.1	1.1	1.0	...	...	...	...	...	...
20 - 24	1.4	1.5	1.2	...	...	...	...	...	...
25 - 29	1.6	1.7	1.4	...	...	...	...	...	...
30 - 34	1.7	1.8	1.5	...	...	...	...	...	...
35 - 39	2.2	2.4	1.9	...	...	...	...	...	...
40 - 44	2.7	3.4	2.1	...	...	...	...	...	...
45 - 49	3.8	4.3	3.4	...	...	...	...	...	...
50 - 54	6.1	7.1	5.1	...	...	...	...	...	...
55 - 59	10.2	11.3	8.8	...	...	...	...	...	...
60 - 64	16.0	18.0	14.0	...	...	...	...	...	...
65 - 69	22.4	24.3	20.4	...	...	...	...	...	...
70 - 74	35.1	38.9	31.0	...	...	...	...	...	...

20. Death rates specific for age, sex and urban/rural residence: latest available year, 1996 - 2005
Taux de mortalité selon l'âge, le sexe et la résidence, urbaine/rurale: dernière année disponible, 1996 - 2005 (continued - suite)

Continent, country or area, date, code and age (in years) / Continent, pays ou zone, date, code et âge (en années)	Total			Urban - Urbaine			Rural - Rurale		
	Both sexes Les deux sexes	Male Masculin	Female Féminin	Both sexes Les deux sexes	Male Masculin	Female Féminin	Both sexes Les deux sexes	Male Masculin	Female Féminin
ASIA - ASIE									
Nepal - Népal[21]									
2001 (|)									
75 - 79	48.9	56.6	41.4	...	...	...	...	...	...
80 +	100.6	111.8	90.1	...	...	...	...	...	...
Pakistan[22]									
2003 (|)									
Total	7.0	7.5	6.4	6.2	6.8	5.6	7.4	7.9	6.9
0 - 4	19.9	21.5	18.2	16.5	17.5	15.4	21.5	23.3	19.5
5 - 9	0.8	1.1	0.6	0.5	0.7	0.3	1.0	1.3	0.7
10 - 14	0.4	0.7	0.1	0.2	0.4	-	0.5	0.8	0.1
15 - 19	0.9	0.6	1.3	0.6	0.4	0.9	1.1	0.7	1.5
20 - 24	1.7	1.4	1.9	1.5	1.2	2.0	1.8	1.6	1.9
25 - 29	1.8	1.9	1.6	0.9	1.4	0.3	2.3	2.3	2.4
30 - 34	2.0	2.3	1.7	1.3	2.2	0.4	2.4	2.4	2.4
35 - 39	2.6	2.7	2.6	1.8	2.4	1.2	3.1	2.8	3.4
40 - 44	3.5	3.8	3.1	4.0	4.3	3.6	3.1	3.5	2.8
45 - 49	4.8	5.6	4.1	5.3	5.0	5.5	4.6	5.9	3.2
50 - 54	11.4	10.0	12.9	13.9	13.3	14.7	9.9	8.1	12.0
55 - 59	15.8	16.7	14.7	20.4	24.8	15.5	13.0	11.9	14.3
60 - 64	23.7	26.3	20.7	22.7	28.6	15.5	24.3	25.0	23.3
65 - 69	27.2	21.0	35.0	25.7	19.5	33.3	28.0	21.9	35.9
70 - 74	47.1	43.2	52.3	57.1	53.4	61.6	42.1	38.2	47.3
75 - 79	65.2	71.5	57.5	71.1	82.0	59.0	62.2	66.5	56.6
80 - 84	98.5	85.2	116.3	98.3	97.8	98.9	98.5	79.3	125.5
85 +	195.5	247.0	128.8	230.4	312.5	136.1	180.7	221.3	125.4
Philippines									
2003 (C)									
Total	4.9	5.7	4.0	...	...	...	...	...	...
0 - 4	3.4	3.8	3.0	...	...	...	...	...	...
5 - 9	0.6	0.6	0.5	...	...	...	...	...	...
10 - 14	0.5	0.6	0.4	...	...	...	...	...	...
15 - 19	0.8	1.0	0.6	...	...	...	...	...	...
20 - 24	1.3	1.8	0.8	...	...	...	...	...	...
25 - 29	1.6	2.2	1.0	...	...	...	...	...	...
30 - 34	2.1	2.9	1.3	...	...	...	...	...	...
35 - 39	2.9	3.9	1.8	...	...	...	...	...	...
40 - 44	4.0	5.4	2.6	...	...	...	...	...	...
45 - 49	5.7	7.7	3.7	...	...	...	...	...	...
50 - 54	8.5	11.4	5.5	...	...	...	...	...	...
55 - 59	11.1	15.0	7.2	...	...	...	...	...	...
60 - 64	17.1	22.8	11.7	...	...	...	...	...	...
65 - 69	25.7	32.8	19.1	...	...	...	...	...	...
70 - 74	37.1	45.8	29.5	...	...	...	...	...	...
75 - 79	54.5	64.6	46.6	...	...	...	...	...	...
80 +	138.5	140.4	137.2	...	...	...	...	...	...
Qatar									
2005 (C)									
Total	1.9	2.1	1.6	...	...	...	...	...	...
0	8.1	8.6	7.6	...	...	...	...	...	...
1 - 4	♦0.6	♦0.8	♦0.4	...	...	...	...	...	...
5 - 9	♦0.2	♦0.3	♦0.2	...	...	...	...	...	...
10 - 14	♦0.2	♦0.2	♦0.3	...	...	...	...	...	...
15 - 19	0.9	1.6	♦0.2	...	...	...	...	...	...
20 - 24	1.2	1.6	♦0.4	...	...	...	...	...	...
25 - 29	0.9	1.1	♦0.3	...	...	...	...	...	...
30 - 34	0.8	0.9	♦0.3	...	...	...	...	...	...
35 - 39	0.8	1.0	♦0.3	...	...	...	...	...	...
40 - 44	1.2	1.3	♦0.6	...	...	...	...	...	...
45 - 49	1.7	1.8	♦1.5	...	...	...	...	...	...
50 - 54	3.2	3.4	♦2.4	...	...	...	...	...	...
55 - 59	5.1	4.8	♦6.1	...	...	...	...	...	...
60 - 64	9.9	9.1	12.3	...	...	...	...	...	...
65 - 69	29.2	26.1	34.2	...	...	...	...	...	...
70 - 74	42.6	39.8	47.5	...	...	...	...	...	...
75 - 79	75.0	73.2	77.7	...	...	...	...	...	...

20. Death rates specific for age, sex and urban/rural residence: latest available year, 1996 - 2005
Taux de mortalité selon l'âge, le sexe et la résidence, urbaine/rurale: dernière année disponible, 1996 - 2005 (continued - suite)

Continent, country or area, date, code and age (in years) / Continent, pays ou zone, date, code et âge (en années)	Total			Urban - Urbaine			Rural - Rurale		
	Both sexes Les deux sexes	Male Masculin	Female Féminin	Both sexes Les deux sexes	Male Masculin	Female Féminin	Both sexes Les deux sexes	Male Masculin	Female Féminin
ASIA - ASIE									
Qatar									
2005 (C)									
80 - 84	143.9	144.7	142.9	...	...	...	...	...	...
85 - 89	140.1	◆181.0	◆106.4	...	...	...	...	...	...
90 - 94	◆142.9	◆166.7	◆104.2	...	...	...	...	...	...
95 +	◆133.3	◆50.0	◆300.0	...	...	...	...	...	...
Saudi Arabia - Arabie saoudite[23]									
2004 (I)									
Total	3.3	3.7	2.9	...	...	...	...	...	...
0	18.4	17.7	19.0	...	...	...	...	...	...
1 - 4	0.5	0.4	0.6	...	...	...	...	...	...
5 - 9	0.9	1.0	0.8	...	...	...	...	...	...
10 - 14	0.7	0.8	0.5	...	...	...	...	...	...
15 - 19	1.3	2.1	0.5	...	...	...	...	...	...
20 - 24	1.5	2.4	0.5	...	...	...	...	...	...
25 - 29	0.8	1.0	0.4	...	...	...	...	...	...
30 - 34	0.6	0.6	0.5	...	...	...	...	...	...
35 - 39	0.8	0.7	0.8	...	...	...	...	...	...
40 - 44	1.4	1.4	1.5	...	...	...	...	...	...
45 - 49	2.3	2.6	1.8	...	...	...	...	...	...
50 - 54	4.5	4.4	4.7	...	...	...	...	...	...
55 - 59	6.2	6.5	5.9	...	...	...	...	...	...
60 - 64	18.5	21.4	15.3	...	...	...	...	...	...
65 - 69	21.8	28.7	14.2	...	...	...	...	...	...
70 - 74	57.4	75.8	39.8	...	...	...	...	...	...
75 - 79	51.5	57.3	43.7	...	...	...	...	...	...
80 +	114.6	115.7	113.3	...	...	...	...	...	...
Singapore - Singapour									
2005 (+C)									
Total	4.6	5.1	4.1	...	...	...	...	...	...
0 - 4	0.7	0.8	0.6	...	...	...	...	...	...
5 - 9	0.1	◆0.1	◆0.2	...	...	...	...	...	...
10 - 14	0.1	◆0.1	◆0.1	...	...	...	...	...	...
15 - 19	0.3	0.4	◆0.2	...	...	...	...	...	...
20 - 24	0.6	0.8	0.4	...	...	...	...	...	...
25 - 29	0.5	0.8	0.3	...	...	...	...	...	...
30 - 34	0.7	0.9	0.5	...	...	...	...	...	...
35 - 39	0.9	1.3	0.6	...	...	...	...	...	...
40 - 44	1.3	1.6	0.9	...	...	...	...	...	...
45 - 49	2.1	2.6	1.5	...	...	...	...	...	...
50 - 54	3.6	4.6	2.6	...	...	...	...	...	...
55 - 59	5.9	7.8	3.9	...	...	...	...	...	...
60 - 64	9.6	12.1	7.2	...	...	...	...	...	...
65 - 69	16.5	22.3	11.2	...	...	...	...	...	...
70 - 74	25.1	32.1	19.2	...	...	...	...	...	...
75 - 79	39.3	48.1	32.5	...	...	...	...	...	...
80 - 84	68.3	81.4	59.0	...	...	...	...	...	...
85 +	125.3	138.2	118.8	...	...	...	...	...	...
Sri Lanka									
1996 (+C)									
Total	6.7	8.5	4.7	...	...	...	...	...	...
0 - 4	3.1	3.4	2.8	...	...	...	...	...	...
5 - 9	0.4	0.5	0.4	...	...	...	...	...	...
10 - 14	0.5	0.5	0.4	...	...	...	...	...	...
15 - 19	1.7	2.5	0.9	...	...	...	...	...	...
20 - 24	3.3	5.5	1.0	...	...	...	...	...	...
25 - 29	3.7	6.3	1.2	...	...	...	...	...	...
30 - 34	3.4	5.5	1.2	...	...	...	...	...	...
35 - 39	4.7	7.3	2.0	...	...	...	...	...	...
40 - 44	5.3	8.1	2.4	...	...	...	...	...	...
45 - 49	7.7	11.3	4.1	...	...	...	...	...	...
50 - 54	9.6	12.9	6.0	...	...	...	...	...	...
55 - 59	13.2	17.7	8.2	...	...	...	...	...	...
60 - 64	20.1	24.5	15.0	...	...	...	...	...	...

Continent, country or area, date, code and age (in years) / Continent, pays ou zone, date, code et âge (en années)	Total			Urban - Urbaine			Rural - Rurale		
	Both sexes Les deux sexes	Male Masculin	Female Féminin	Both sexes Les deux sexes	Male Masculin	Female Féminin	Both sexes Les deux sexes	Male Masculin	Female Féminin
ASIA - ASIE									
Sri Lanka									
1996 (+C)									
65 - 69	34.5	41.2	27.0	...	...	...	...	...	...
70 - 74	56.3	61.9	49.8	...	...	...	...	...	...
75 - 79	81.7	88.1	74.6	...	...	...	...	...	...
80 +	176.8	177.6	176.1	...	...	...	...	...	...
Uzbekistan - Ouzbékistan[12]									
2000 (C)									
Total	5.5	5.8	5.2	6.6	7.1	6.2	4.8	5.0	4.6
0	19.1	21.4	16.6	22.6	25.4	19.6	17.5	19.6	15.3
1 - 4	2.3	2.4	2.2	1.6	1.7	1.5	2.6	2.8	2.5
5 - 9	0.4	0.5	0.4	0.4	0.5	0.3	0.5	0.6	0.4
10 - 14	0.5	0.5	0.4	0.4	0.5	0.4	0.5	0.6	0.4
15 - 19	0.7	0.9	0.5	0.7	1.0	0.5	0.7	0.9	0.5
20 - 24	1.3	1.6	1.0	1.4	1.9	0.9	1.2	1.4	1.0
25 - 29	1.7	2.2	1.3	1.9	2.5	1.2	1.6	1.9	1.3
30 - 34	2.1	2.9	1.4	2.4	3.3	1.4	2.0	2.5	1.5
35 - 39	2.5	3.4	1.7	3.0	4.3	1.7	2.2	2.7	1.6
40 - 44	3.6	4.8	2.6	4.4	6.3	2.6	3.1	3.7	2.5
45 - 49	5.4	7.2	3.7	6.2	8.9	3.7	4.7	5.8	3.6
50 - 54	9.4	12.2	6.7	10.2	14.1	6.7	8.5	10.4	6.6
55 - 59	14.2	17.6	10.8	15.3	20.9	10.2	13.2	15.0	11.3
60 - 64	22.3	27.5	17.5	23.3	31.4	16.5	21.5	24.5	18.4
65 - 69	35.9	43.2	29.7	37.2	49.2	28.2	34.8	39.0	30.9
70 - 74	52.7	61.0	46.2	54.6	69.8	45.0	51.2	55.1	47.4
75 - 79	72.9	80.3	68.9	73.8	84.7	69.0	72.1	77.2	68.8
80 - 84	114.2	129.9	108.1	115.6	127.9	111.3	112.9	131.6	104.7
85 - 89	164.0	194.7	152.6	166.2	183.1	160.8	161.7	204.8	143.4
90 - 94	195.5	192.3	197.2	171.3	152.4	179.9	215.8	219.9	213.3
95 +	316.6	202.4	394.2	156.3	168.0	151.3	460.7	220.9	700.6
EUROPE									
Albania - Albanie									
2004 (C)									
Total	5.7	6.4	5.0	...	...	...	...	...	...
0	6.9	7.2	6.6	...	...	...	...	...	...
1 - 4	1.2	1.2	1.1	...	...	...	...	...	...
5 - 9	0.6	0.7	0.4	...	...	...	...	...	...
10 - 14	0.5	0.5	0.4	...	...	...	...	...	...
15 - 19	0.5	0.7	0.3	...	...	...	...	...	...
20 - 24	0.8	1.2	0.5	...	...	...	...	...	...
25 - 29	0.8	1.3	0.4	...	...	...	...	...	...
30 - 34	1.1	1.6	0.6	...	...	...	...	...	...
35 - 39	1.2	1.6	0.8	...	...	...	...	...	...
40 - 44	1.6	2.2	1.0	...	...	...	...	...	...
45 - 49	2.4	3.1	1.6	...	...	...	...	...	...
50 - 54	3.8	5.0	2.5	...	...	...	...	...	...
55 - 59	5.6	7.3	3.8	...	...	...	...	...	...
60 - 64	10.4	13.7	7.1	...	...	...	...	...	...
65 - 69	17.5	22.9	11.7	...	...	...	...	...	...
70 - 74	33.8	42.5	25.7	...	...	...	...	...	...
75 - 79	56.9	72.9	44.4	...	...	...	...	...	...
80 - 84	100.3	114.3	91.1	...	...	...	...	...	...
85 - 89	182.5	212.1	164.8	...	...	...	...	...	...
90 - 94	266.4	305.2	251.4	...	...	...	...	...	...
95 +	781.6	1070.0	688.7	...	...	...	...	...	...
Austria - Autriche									
2005 (C)									
Total	9.1	8.7	9.5	...	...	...	...	...	...
0	4.1	4.3	4.0	...	...	...	...	...	...
1 - 4	0.2	0.2	0.2	...	...	...	...	...	...
5 - 9	0.1	0.1	♦0.1	...	...	...	...	...	...
10 - 14	0.1	0.1	♦0.1	...	...	...	...	...	...

Continent, country or area, date, code and age (in years) / Continent, pays ou zone, date, code et âge (en annèes)	Total			Urban - Urbaine			Rural - Rurale		
	Both sexes Les deux sexes	Male Masculin	Female Féminin	Both sexes Les deux sexes	Male Masculin	Female Féminin	Both sexes Les deux sexes	Male Masculin	Female Féminin
EUROPE									
Austria - Autriche									
2005 (C)									
15 - 19	0.5	0.7	0.3	...	...	...	...	...	...
20 - 24	0.6	0.9	0.3	...	...	...	...	...	...
25 - 29	0.6	0.8	0.3	...	...	...	...	...	...
30 - 34	0.6	0.9	0.3	...	...	...	...	...	...
35 - 39	0.9	1.2	0.6	...	...	...	...	...	...
40 - 44	1.3	1.8	0.9	...	...	...	...	...	...
45 - 49	2.4	3.0	1.7	...	...	...	...	...	...
50 - 54	4.0	5.4	2.6	...	...	...	...	...	...
55 - 59	6.5	8.9	4.3	...	...	...	...	...	...
60 - 64	9.3	12.9	6.0	...	...	...	...	...	...
65 - 69	13.3	18.3	8.8	...	...	...	...	...	...
70 - 74	22.6	30.9	16.1	...	...	...	...	...	...
75 - 79	38.4	50.8	30.4	...	...	...	...	...	...
80 - 84	69.6	89.1	61.1	...	...	...	...	...	...
85 - 89	121.9	145.5	113.2	...	...	...	...	...	...
90 - 94	219.7	246.9	211.4	...	...	...	...	...	...
95 +	346.5	346.8	346.4	...	...	...	...	...	...
Belarus - Bélarus[12]									
2004 (C)									
Total	14.3	16.1	12.6	10.6	12.5	8.9	23.6	25.3	22.1
0	7.0	8.0	5.8	6.0	6.8	5.1	9.7	11.4	8.0
1 - 4	0.6	0.6	0.5	0.4	0.4	0.3	1.1	1.4	0.8
5 - 9	0.2	0.3	0.2	0.2	0.2	♦0.2	0.4	0.4	♦0.3
10 - 14	0.2	0.3	0.2	0.2	0.2	♦0.1	0.3	0.4	♦0.2
15 - 19	0.7	1.1	0.4	0.6	0.9	0.3	1.2	1.7	0.7
20 - 24	1.4	2.2	0.6	1.1	1.7	0.4	2.8	4.3	1.0
25 - 29	2.1	3.3	0.9	1.7	2.6	0.7	3.7	5.7	1.6
30 - 34	3.0	4.8	1.2	2.4	3.8	1.0	4.9	7.7	1.7
35 - 39	4.1	6.5	1.9	3.4	5.2	1.7	6.4	9.7	2.6
40 - 44	6.0	9.5	2.6	4.9	7.9	2.2	9.3	13.8	3.9
45 - 49	8.7	13.9	4.0	7.4	12.0	3.5	12.9	19.0	5.7
50 - 54	12.2	19.4	6.0	10.6	17.1	5.3	17.4	25.7	8.5
55 - 59	18.1	28.3	9.8	16.3	25.7	8.8	23.4	35.3	12.9
60 - 64	26.7	44.0	14.4	24.1	39.0	13.4	31.3	53.3	16.2
65 - 69	33.8	54.1	21.1	32.1	51.2	20.0	36.2	58.3	22.7
70 - 74	50.0	76.2	36.0	48.1	73.3	34.8	51.9	79.0	37.1
75 - 79	71.8	101.1	59.5	70.8	97.3	59.1	72.8	105.1	59.9
80 - 84	114.9	146.0	105.3	108.0	135.9	99.2	121.4	155.6	111.0
85 - 89	174.7	207.7	166.3	159.3	193.8	149.6	190.5	224.1	182.7
90 - 94	271.7	309.8	263.5	220.4	280.0	207.1	322.3	340.7	318.5
95 - 99	452.6	654.4	419.3	265.6	397.4	243.8	781.2	1107.3	727.4
100 +	1043.6	1338.7	987.8	361.3	♦451.6	341.5	6409.1	...	5159.1
Belgium - Belgique[24]									
2002 (C)									
Total	10.2	10.4	10.1	...	...	...	...	...	...
0 - 4	1.1	1.2	0.9	...	...	...	...	...	...
5 - 9	0.1	0.2	0.1	...	...	...	...	...	...
10 - 14	0.1	0.1	0.1	...	...	...	...	...	...
15 - 19	0.5	0.6	0.3	...	...	...	...	...	...
20 - 24	0.7	1.1	0.3	...	...	...	...	...	...
25 - 29	0.8	1.1	0.4	...	...	...	...	...	...
30 - 34	0.8	1.1	0.5	...	...	...	...	...	...
35 - 39	1.1	1.5	0.8	...	...	...	...	...	...
40 - 44	1.8	2.2	1.3	...	...	...	...	...	...
45 - 49	3.0	3.9	2.1	...	...	...	...	...	...
50 - 54	4.7	5.9	3.4	...	...	...	...	...	...
55 - 59	6.9	9.1	4.7	...	...	...	...	...	...
60 - 64	10.2	13.7	6.9	...	...	...	...	...	...
65 - 69	16.0	22.0	10.6	...	...	...	...	...	...
70 - 74	25.6	35.7	17.6	...	...	...	...	...	...
75 - 79	44.5	61.6	33.0	...	...	...	...	...	...
80 - 84	76.0	99.9	63.0	...	...	...	...	...	...
85 +	181.3	210.9	171.0	...	...	...	...	...	...

20. Death rates specific for age, sex and urban/rural residence: latest available year, 1996 - 2005
Taux de mortalité selon l'âge, le sexe et la résidence, urbaine/rurale: dernière année disponible, 1996 - 2005 (continued - suite)

Continent, country or area, date, code and age (in years) Continent, pays ou zone, date, code et âge (en années)	Total			Urban - Urbaine			Rural - Rurale		
	Both sexes Les deux sexes	Male Masculin	Female Féminin	Both sexes Les deux sexes	Male Masculin	Female Féminin	Both sexes Les deux sexes	Male Masculin	Female Féminin
EUROPE									
Bulgaria - Bulgarie									
2005 (C)									
Total	14.6	16.2	13.2	12.0	13.5	10.7	20.8	22.4	19.2
0	10.9	12.3	9.4	9.4	10.7	8.0	15.0	16.6	13.2
1 - 4	0.6	0.7	0.4	0.5	0.6	0.4	0.7	0.8	♦0.6
5 - 9	0.3	0.3	0.3	0.2	0.3	♦0.2	0.4	♦0.4	♦0.4
10 - 14	0.3	0.4	0.2	0.3	0.3	0.2	0.4	♦0.4	♦0.3
15 - 19	0.4	0.5	0.4	0.4	0.5	0.4	0.5	0.7	0.4
20 - 24	0.7	1.0	0.4	0.7	1.0	0.4	1.0	1.3	♦0.5
25 - 29	0.9	1.2	0.5	0.8	1.2	0.5	1.0	1.2	0.7
30 - 34	1.1	1.5	0.7	1.1	1.5	0.6	1.2	1.6	0.8
35 - 39	1.8	2.5	1.2	1.7	2.2	1.1	2.3	3.1	1.4
40 - 44	3.1	4.3	1.8	2.8	4.0	1.7	3.8	5.0	2.3
45 - 49	5.3	7.4	3.2	4.9	6.9	3.1	6.3	8.8	3.5
50 - 54	8.3	12.4	4.5	7.7	11.4	4.3	10.0	14.8	4.9
55 - 59	12.5	18.9	6.7	12.0	18.2	6.6	13.6	20.6	6.9
60 - 64	18.2	26.8	10.9	17.9	25.7	11.2	18.6	28.5	10.4
65 - 69	27.2	38.6	18.1	27.6	39.7	18.3	26.5	37.1	17.9
70 - 74	43.1	56.4	33.2	43.5	58.1	33.3	42.6	54.5	33.0
75 - 79	71.7	86.2	61.9	72.2	88.5	61.7	71.1	83.7	62.1
80 - 84	119.7	137.2	109.2	118.6	138.9	107.1	121.0	135.3	111.8
85 - 89	188.6	208.4	177.5	186.8	210.4	174.2	190.9	206.2	181.6
90 - 94	296.0	307.4	290.1	287.2	311.9	275.2	305.5	302.9	306.9
95 - 99	372.3	376.7	370.2	369.2	371.9	367.9	375.5	381.8	372.6
100 +	381.5	♦371.4	385.5	421.5	♦454.5	409.1	343.8	♦297.3	362.6
Croatia - Croatie									
2001 (C)									
Total	11.2	11.7	10.6	10.1	10.8	9.4	12.6	12.9	12.3
0	7.3	7.6	7.1	7.6	7.8	7.4	7.0	7.2	6.7
1 - 4	0.3	0.4	♦0.2	♦0.3	♦0.3	♦0.2	0.4	♦0.5	♦0.2
5 - 9	0.2	♦0.2	♦0.1	♦0.1	♦0.2	♦0.1	♦0.2	♦0.2	♦0.2
10 - 14	0.2	♦0.2	♦0.1	♦0.1	♦0.2	♦0.1	♦0.2	♦0.3	♦0.1
15 - 19	0.5	0.8	0.3	0.5	0.7	♦0.3	0.5	0.9	♦0.2
20 - 24	0.8	1.2	0.3	0.8	1.3	♦0.3	0.7	1.1	♦0.3
25 - 29	0.7	1.1	0.3	0.7	1.0	♦0.3	0.7	1.2	♦0.2
30 - 34	0.9	1.2	0.5	0.9	1.2	0.6	0.9	1.2	♦0.5
35 - 39	1.4	2.1	0.8	1.3	1.9	0.8	1.5	2.2	0.7
40 - 44	2.4	3.5	1.3	2.1	3.0	1.2	2.9	4.2	1.5
45 - 49	4.0	5.9	2.1	3.6	5.5	1.9	4.7	6.6	2.4
50 - 54	6.5	9.4	3.7	5.9	8.5	3.7	7.4	10.6	3.9
55 - 59	9.8	14.4	5.6	9.5	13.9	5.6	10.2	15.0	5.6
60 - 64	15.2	22.4	9.1	14.5	21.0	8.8	16.1	24.1	9.4
65 - 69	24.2	34.9	16.0	23.3	33.0	15.5	25.2	37.0	16.4
70 - 74	39.4	54.0	29.5	38.9	53.7	28.9	39.8	54.3	30.2
75 - 79	62.9	80.2	54.7	60.9	75.0	54.0	65.1	85.7	55.5
80 - 84	106.1	126.4	97.4	100.2	122.5	90.3	112.4	130.7	104.8
85 - 89	168.2	191.2	159.2	155.3	182.5	144.5	182.5	201.1	175.3
90 - 94	275.0	318.6	260.5	254.2	322.9	232.1	298.2	314.8	292.4
95 - 99	394.6	404.0	392.0	355.9	405.2	343.3	441.7	402.7	454.2
100 +	607.1	♦761.9	555.6	♦425.9	♦312.5	♦473.7	♦833.3	♦1800.0	♦640.0
2005 (C)									
Total	11.7	12.2	11.2	...	...	...	...	...	...
0	5.7	5.7	5.7	...	...	...	...	...	...
1 - 4	0.2	♦0.3	♦0.2	...	...	...	...	...	...
5 - 9	0.1	♦0.2	♦0.1	...	...	...	...	...	...
10 - 14	0.1	♦0.2	♦0.1	...	...	...	...	...	...
15 - 19	0.5	0.7	0.3	...	...	...	...	...	...
20 - 24	0.6	0.9	0.2	...	...	...	...	...	...
25 - 29	0.8	1.2	0.3	...	...	...	...	...	...
30 - 34	0.8	1.3	0.4	...	...	...	...	...	...
35 - 39	1.2	1.7	0.7	...	...	...	...	...	...
40 - 44	2.0	2.9	1.1	...	...	...	...	...	...
45 - 49	3.7	5.2	2.1	...	...	...	...	...	...
50 - 54	6.2	9.0	3.4	...	...	...	...	...	...
55 - 59	9.0	13.5	4.8	...	...	...	...	...	...

20. Death rates specific for age, sex and urban/rural residence: latest available year, 1996 - 2005
Taux de mortalité selon l'âge, le sexe et la résidence, urbaine/rurale: dernière année disponible, 1996 - 2005 (continued - suite)

Continent, country or area, date, code and age (in years) Continent, pays ou zone, date, code et âge (en années)	Total			Urban - Urbaine			Rural - Rurale		
	Both sexes Les deux sexes	Male Masculin	Female Féminin	Both sexes Les deux sexes	Male Masculin	Female Féminin	Both sexes Les deux sexes	Male Masculin	Female Féminin
EUROPE									
Croatia - Croatie									
2005 (C)									
60 - 64	14.0	21.0	8.1	...	...	...	...	...	...
65 - 69	22.2	32.5	14.1	...	...	...	...	...	...
70 - 74	36.3	51.1	26.2	...	...	...	...	...	...
75 - 79	60.9	78.4	50.9	...	...	...	...	...	...
80 - 84	107.1	128.5	98.5	...	...	...	...	...	...
85 + ...	213.1	236.5	204.9	...	...	...	...	...	...
Czech Republic - République tchèque									
2005 (C)									
Total....................	10.5	10.8	10.3	10.3	10.6	10.1	11.1	11.4	10.7
0	3.4	4.0	2.7	3.5	4.3	2.6	3.2	3.3	3.1
1 - 4	0.2	0.2	0.2	0.2	◆0.2	◆0.2	◆0.2	◆0.2	◆0.3
5 - 9	0.1	0.1	◆0.1	0.1	◆0.1	◆0.1	◆0.1	◆0.1	◆0.2
10 - 14	0.2	0.2	◆0.2	0.2	0.2	◆0.1	0.2	◆0.2	◆0.3
15 - 19	0.4	0.6	0.3	0.4	0.5	0.3	0.5	0.8	◆0.3
20 - 24	0.6	1.0	0.3	0.6	0.9	0.3	0.7	1.2	◆0.2
25 - 29	0.6	1.0	0.3	0.6	0.9	0.3	0.7	1.0	0.4
30 - 34	0.8	1.2	0.4	0.8	1.1	0.4	0.9	1.3	0.5
35 - 39	1.2	1.6	0.7	1.1	1.6	0.7	1.2	1.6	0.8
40 - 44	1.8	2.5	1.2	1.8	2.3	1.2	2.0	3.0	1.0
45 - 49	3.7	5.0	2.3	3.7	5.0	2.4	3.7	5.1	2.2
50 - 54	5.7	8.1	3.5	5.6	7.9	3.5	6.1	8.6	3.4
55 - 59	9.1	12.9	5.5	9.0	12.7	5.5	9.4	13.2	5.4
60 - 64	13.7	19.6	8.5	13.4	19.0	8.6	14.6	21.4	8.1
65 - 69	20.5	28.8	13.9	20.1	27.9	13.9	21.7	31.1	13.9
70 - 74	34.0	46.1	25.3	33.3	44.5	25.3	35.9	50.5	25.2
75 - 79	56.0	72.0	46.5	54.8	69.4	46.0	59.5	79.2	47.7
80 - 84	96.0	117.1	86.0	93.9	115.3	83.8	101.9	122.1	92.3
85 - 89	147.6	170.1	138.6	145.0	169.2	135.4	154.9	172.6	147.6
90 - 94	284.5	308.2	277.0	282.1	311.9	273.0	291.0	299.1	288.2
95 - 99	373.2	422.6	360.7	378.4	399.4	373.1	360.3	479.3	330.1
100 + ...	517.0	438.4	537.6	597.4	◆520.8	617.5	363.6	◆280.0	385.4
Denmark - Danemark[25]									
2004 (C)									
Total....................	10.3	10.3	10.4	...	...	...	...	...	...
0	4.3	4.6	4.1	...	...	...	...	...	...
1 - 4	0.2	◆0.2	0.3	...	...	...	...	...	...
5 - 9	0.1	◆0.1	◆0.1	...	...	...	...	...	...
10 - 14	0.2	0.2	◆0.1	...	...	...	...	...	...
15 - 19	0.4	0.5	0.2	...	...	...	...	...	...
20 - 24	0.5	0.8	0.3	...	...	...	...	...	...
25 - 29	0.5	0.7	0.3	...	...	...	...	...	...
30 - 34	0.7	1.0	0.4	...	...	...	...	...	...
35 - 39	1.1	1.5	0.7	...	...	...	...	...	...
40 - 44	1.8	2.3	1.3	...	...	...	...	...	...
45 - 49	3.0	3.7	2.3	...	...	...	...	...	...
50 - 54	4.9	6.1	3.8	...	...	...	...	...	...
55 - 59	7.1	8.6	5.5	...	...	...	...	...	...
60 - 64	11.5	14.3	8.8	...	...	...	...	...	...
65 - 69	17.9	21.7	14.4	...	...	...	...	...	...
70 - 74	30.7	37.1	25.3	...	...	...	...	...	...
75 - 79	48.9	61.4	39.6	...	...	...	...	...	...
80 - 84	79.7	102.0	66.4	...	...	...	...	...	...
85 - 89	129.8	165.4	113.3	...	...	...	...	...	...
90 - 94	214.9	259.4	199.5	...	...	...	...	...	...
95 - 99	332.0	399.1	316.5	...	...	...	...	...	...
100 + ...	527.1	633.3	507.3	...	...	...	...	...	...
Estonia - Estonie									
2003 (C)									
Total....................	13.4	14.7	12.3	12.9[9]	14.5[9]	11.6[9]	14.5[9]	15.2[9]	13.8[9]
0	7.0	8.5	5.5	6.6	7.9	◆5.3	7.9	◆9.8	◆6.0
1 - 4	◆0.5	◆0.5	◆0.5	◆0.5	◆0.5	◆0.5	◆0.6	◆0.6	◆0.5
5 - 9	◆0.2	◆0.2	◆0.1	◆0.2	◆0.2	◆0.2	◆0.1	◆0.3	-

20. Death rates specific for age, sex and urban/rural residence: latest available year, 1996 - 2005
Taux de mortalité selon l'âge, le sexe et la résidence, urbaine/rurale: dernière année disponible, 1996 - 2005 (continued - suite)

Continent, country or area, date, code and age (in years) / Continent, pays ou zone, date, code et âge (en années)	Total			Urban - Urbaine			Rural - Rurale		
	Both sexes Les deux sexes	Male Masculin	Female Féminin	Both sexes Les deux sexes	Male Masculin	Female Féminin	Both sexes Les deux sexes	Male Masculin	Female Féminin
EUROPE									
Estonia - Estonie									
2003 (C)									
10 - 14	0.3	♦0.4	♦0.3	♦0.3	♦0.4	♦0.2	♦0.4	♦0.3	♦0.5
15 - 19	0.7	1.0	♦0.4	0.7	1.0	♦0.4	♦0.6	♦0.9	♦0.3
20 - 24	1.2	2.0	♦0.5	1.2	1.9	♦0.5	1.5	2.3	♦0.4
25 - 29	1.6	2.6	♦0.6	1.5	2.4	♦0.6	2.1	3.0	♦1.0
30 - 34	1.8	3.1	♦0.5	1.8	3.2	♦0.6	1.7	2.7	♦0.5
35 - 39	3.0	4.6	1.5	2.8	4.4	1.4	3.4	5.1	♦1.5
40 - 44	5.1	8.1	2.4	5.4	8.7	2.6	4.5	6.8	♦1.9
45 - 49	6.7	10.8	3.1	6.7	11.0	3.3	6.7	10.4	2.8
50 - 54	10.5	16.7	5.3	10.4[9]	17.1[9]	5.3	10.5[9]	15.8[9]	5.1
55 - 59	14.7	22.5	8.5	14.9	23.2	8.9	14.1	21.1	7.7
60 - 64	19.9	31.9	11.2	18.9	30.3	11.3	21.9	35.0	10.7
65 - 69	26.5	43.2	15.9	25.0	40.6	15.6	29.9	48.3	16.5
70 - 74	39.7	62.1	27.2	38.6	62.0	26.2	42.0	62.5	29.6
75 - 79	59.1	85.0	48.5	58.6	83.5	48.5	60.3	88.4	48.4
80 - 84	95.8	125.4	86.4	94.4	123.6	85.1	98.6	128.9	89.1
85 - 89	163.5	188.1	156.4	163.4	206.1	151.3	163.6	155.3	166.0
90 - 94	261.9	315.8	249.3	240.7	306.9	226.6	297.5	328.0	289.1
95 - 99	363.8	414.1	355.0	364.0	♦411.0	356.2	363.6	♦418.2	353.1
100 +	512.5	♦375.0	546.9	♦478.3	♦272.7	♦542.9	♦558.8	♦600.0	♦551.7
Finland - Finlande[26]									
2005 (C)									
Total	9.1	9.4	8.9	8.2	8.4	8.1	10.7	10.9	10.4
0	3.0	3.2	2.8	2.7	2.7	2.8	3.5	4.2	♦2.9
1 - 4	0.3	0.3	♦0.2	0.3	♦0.4	♦0.2	♦0.3	♦0.3	♦0.2
5 - 9	0.2	0.2	♦0.2	0.2	♦0.2	♦0.3	♦0.2	♦0.2	♦0.1
10 - 14	0.2	♦0.2	♦0.2	0.2	♦0.2	♦0.2	♦0.1	♦0.1	♦0.2
15 - 19	0.4	0.5	0.3	0.4	0.5	0.3	0.4	0.6	♦0.3
20 - 24	0.6	0.9	0.3	0.6	0.8	0.3	0.8	1.1	♦0.3
25 - 29	0.6	0.9	0.3	0.6	0.9	0.3	0.7	0.9	♦0.4
30 - 34	0.9	1.3	0.5	0.9	1.2	0.6	0.8	1.3	♦0.4
35 - 39	1.3	1.9	0.8	1.3	1.8	0.9	1.4	2.0	0.7
40 - 44	2.0	2.8	1.2	2.0	2.9	1.2	1.9	2.7	1.1
45 - 49	3.2	4.4	2.0	3.3	4.5	2.0	3.2	4.2	2.0
50 - 54	5.0	6.9	3.1	5.0	7.0	3.1	5.1	6.8	3.2
55 - 59	7.3	10.1	4.5	7.3	10.2	4.7	7.2	10.1	4.1
60 - 64	9.9	13.9	6.0	9.8	14.2	5.9	10.0	13.6	6.2
65 - 69	14.1	20.3	8.6	13.7	20.1	8.6	14.5	20.5	8.7
70 - 74	22.4	30.9	15.7	22.0	30.1	16.2	22.9	31.8	15.1
75 - 79	37.9	54.4	27.4	37.4	54.5	27.4	38.6	54.2	27.4
80 - 84	67.5	89.6	57.2	64.9	88.6	54.6	70.8	90.6	60.6
85 - 89	119.0	143.5	110.4	115.5	137.8	108.2	123.5	149.9	113.2
90 - 94	212.0	259.3	199.1	207.2	256.9	195.1	218.1	262.0	204.6
95 - 99	327.7	385.3	315.5	326.4	385.8	314.8	329.2	384.6	316.4
100 +	564.5	♦510.6	572.8	588.9	♦541.7	595.7	535.8	♦478.3	545.5
France[27]									
2004 (C)									
Total	8.4	8.9	7.9	...	...	...	...	...	...
0	3.9	4.3	3.5	...	...	...	...	...	...
1 - 4	0.2	0.2	0.2	...	...	...	...	...	...
5 - 9	0.1	0.1	0.1	...	...	...	...	...	...
10 - 14	0.1	0.1	0.1	...	...	...	...	...	...
15 - 19	0.4	0.5	0.2	...	...	...	...	...	...
20 - 24	0.6	0.9	0.3	...	...	...	...	...	...
25 - 29	0.6	0.9	0.3	...	...	...	...	...	...
30 - 34	0.8	1.1	0.5	...	...	...	...	...	...
35 - 39	1.2	1.6	0.8	...	...	...	...	...	...
40 - 44	1.9	2.6	1.3	...	...	...	...	...	...
45 - 49	3.1	4.3	2.0	...	...	...	...	...	...
50 - 54	4.6	6.4	2.9	...	...	...	...	...	...
55 - 59	6.3	8.8	3.8	...	...	...	...	...	...
60 - 64	8.8	12.4	5.3	...	...	...	...	...	...
65 - 69	12.5	18.0	7.7	...	...	...	...	...	...
70 - 74	19.9	28.6	13.0	...	...	...	...	...	...

20. Death rates specific for age, sex and urban/rural residence: latest available year, 1996 - 2005
Taux de mortalité selon l'âge, le sexe et la résidence, urbaine/rurale: dernière année disponible, 1996 - 2005 (continued - suite)

Continent, country or area, date, code and age (in years) / Continent, pays ou zone, date, code et âge (en annèes)	Total			Urban - Urbaine			Rural - Rurale		
	Both sexes Les deux sexes	Male Masculin	Female Féminin	Both sexes Les deux sexes	Male Masculin	Female Féminin	Both sexes Les deux sexes	Male Masculin	Female Féminin
EUROPE									
France[27]									
2004 (C)									
75 - 79	32.6	46.7	23.1	...	...	...	...	...	...
80 - 84	57.2	78.0	45.3	...	...	...	...	...	...
85 - 89	101.5	131.6	88.2	...	...	...	...	...	...
90 - 94	176.6	215.2	163.7	...	...	...	...	...	...
95 - 99	282.1	319.2	273.4	...	...	...	...	...	...
100 +	314.4	252.2	328.2	...	...	...	...	...	...
Germany - Allemagne									
2004 (C)									
Total	9.9	9.5	10.3	...	...	...	...	...	...
0	3.5	3.8	3.2	...	...	...	...	...	...
1 - 4	0.3	0.4	0.3	...	...	...	...	...	...
5 - 9	0.1	0.1	0.1	...	...	...	...	...	...
10 - 14	0.1	0.1	0.1	...	...	...	...	...	...
15 - 19	0.3	0.4	0.2	...	...	...	...	...	...
20 - 24	0.5	0.7	0.3	...	...	...	...	...	...
25 - 29	0.5	0.7	0.3	...	...	...	...	...	...
30 - 34	0.6	0.8	0.3	...	...	...	...	...	...
35 - 39	0.9	1.1	0.6	...	...	...	...	...	...
40 - 44	1.5	2.0	1.0	...	...	...	...	...	...
45 - 49	2.6	3.4	1.8	...	...	...	...	...	...
50 - 54	4.2	5.5	2.8	...	...	...	...	...	...
55 - 59	6.2	8.2	4.2	...	...	...	...	...	...
60 - 64	9.1	12.4	5.9	...	...	...	...	...	...
65 - 69	14.5	20.1	9.5	...	...	...	...	...	...
70 - 74	24.2	33.3	16.9	...	...	...	...	...	...
75 - 79	40.0	54.9	30.7	...	...	...	...	...	...
80 - 84	70.3	92.0	61.0	...	...	...	...	...	...
85 - 89	125.2	153.8	115.5	...	...	...	...	...	...
90 - 94	228.3	256.3	220.6	...	...	...	...	...	...
95 +	284.6	193.5	317.6	...	...	...	...	...	...
Greece - Grèce									
2005 (C)									
Total	9.5	10.1	8.9	...	...	...	...	...	...
0	3.8	4.0	3.7	...	...	...	...	...	...
1 - 4	0.2	0.2	0.2	...	...	...	...	...	...
5 - 9	0.2	0.2	0.2	...	...	...	...	...	...
10 - 14	0.2	0.2	0.1	...	...	...	...	...	...
15 - 19	0.4	0.6	0.2	...	...	...	...	...	...
20 - 24	0.8	1.2	0.3	...	...	...	...	...	...
25 - 29	0.8	1.1	0.4	...	...	...	...	...	...
30 - 34	0.7	1.0	0.4	...	...	...	...	...	...
35 - 39	1.0	1.4	0.6	...	...	...	...	...	...
40 - 44	1.4	1.9	0.9	...	...	...	...	...	...
45 - 49	2.2	3.1	1.4	...	...	...	...	...	...
50 - 54	3.6	5.0	2.1	...	...	...	...	...	...
55 - 59	5.5	8.1	3.2	...	...	...	...	...	...
60 - 64	7.8	11.5	4.5	...	...	...	...	...	...
65 - 69	12.4	18.2	7.7	...	...	...	...	...	...
70 - 74	21.6	29.5	15.0	...	...	...	...	...	...
75 - 79	41.2	51.0	33.6	...	...	...	...	...	...
80 - 84	76.7	84.2	71.1	...	...	...	...	...	...
85 - 89	153.8	145.7	159.8	...	...	...	...	...	...
90 - 94	323.3	294.4	344.3	...	...	...	...	...	...
95 - 99	423.2	317.5	513.8	...	...	...	...	...	...
100 +	221.7	233.4	217.5	...	...	...	...	...	...
Hungary - Hongrie									
2005 (C)									
Total	13.5	14.6	12.4	12.8[28]	13.7[28]	12.0[28]	14.5[28]	15.8[28]	13.2[28]
0	6.4	7.2	5.5	5.9[28]	6.8[28]	4.9[28]	7.0[28]	7.7[28]	6.2[28]
1 - 4	0.3	0.4	0.3	0.3[28]	0.3[28]	♦0.3[28]	0.3[28]	♦0.4[28]	♦0.3[28]
5 - 9	0.2	0.2	0.1	0.1[28]	♦0.1[28]	♦0.1[28]	0.2[28]	♦0.2[28]	♦0.2[28]
10 - 14	0.1	0.1	0.1	0.1[28]	♦0.1[28]	♦0.1[28]	0.2[28]	♦0.2[28]	♦0.1[28]
15 - 19	0.4	0.5	0.3	0.4[28]	0.5[28]	0.3[28]	0.4[28]	0.6[28]	♦0.3[28]

20. Death rates specific for age, sex and urban/rural residence: latest available year, 1996 - 2005
Taux de mortalité selon l'âge, le sexe et la résidence, urbaine/rurale: dernière année disponible, 1996 - 2005 (continued - suite)

Continent, country or area, date, code and age (in years) / Continent, pays ou zone, date, code et âge (en années)	Total			Urban - Urbaine			Rural - Rurale		
	Both sexes Les deux sexes	Male Masculin	Female Féminin	Both sexes Les deux sexes	Male Masculin	Female Féminin	Both sexes Les deux sexes	Male Masculin	Female Féminin
EUROPE									
Hungary - Hongrie									
2005 (C)									
20 - 24	0.5	0.8	0.3	0.4[28]	0.7[28]	0.2[28]	0.7[28]	1.0[28]	0.4[28]
25 - 29	0.7	1.1	0.4	0.6[28]	0.9[28]	0.4[28]	0.8[28]	1.2[28]	0.4[28]
30 - 34	1.0	1.4	0.6	0.8[28]	1.2[28]	0.5[28]	1.2[28]	1.6[28]	0.7[28]
35 - 39	2.0	2.7	1.2	1.7[28]	2.3[28]	1.1[28]	2.3[28]	3.2[28]	1.3[28]
40 - 44	3.9	5.6	2.3	3.4[28]	4.8[28]	2.0[28]	4.6[28]	6.4[28]	2.7[28]
45 - 49	7.2	10.7	3.9	6.4[28]	9.6[28]	3.7[28]	8.4[28]	12.2[28]	4.3[28]
50 - 54	10.4	15.5	5.9	9.5[28]	14.0[28]	5.7[28]	12.0[28]	17.6[28]	6.2[28]
55 - 59	13.9	20.8	7.9	12.7[28]	19.2[28]	7.4[28]	16.0[28]	23.4[28]	9.0[28]
60 - 64	18.7	28.5	11.0	17.2[28]	25.9[28]	10.5[28]	21.4[28]	33.1[28]	12.0[28]
65 - 69	26.3	39.2	17.5	24.7[28]	35.9[28]	17.1[28]	28.9[28]	44.9[28]	18.1[28]
70 - 74	39.6	55.9	29.4	38.3[28]	53.2[28]	28.8[28]	41.6[28]	60.3[28]	30.2[28]
75 - 79	62.6	83.3	51.5	59.7[28]	79.0[28]	49.1[28]	67.8[28]	90.9[28]	55.7[28]
80 - 84	101.8	125.9	90.8	97.2[28]	118.5[28]	87.6[28]	110.4[28]	139.7[28]	96.9[28]
85 - 89	156.6	181.0	146.8	150.3[28]	173.1[28]	141.0[28]	170.5[28]	198.6[28]	159.3[28]
90 +	249.1	249.6	249.0	243.6[28]	245.9[28]	242.7[28]	261.6[28]	256.3[28]	263.6[28]
Iceland - Islande									
2005 (C)									
Total	6.2	6.4	6.1	6.2	6.2	6.1	7.0	7.9	5.9
0	♦2.4	♦2.8	♦1.9	♦2.5	♦3.0	♦2.0	-	-	-
1 - 4	♦0.2	♦0.2	♦0.1	♦0.2	♦0.2	♦0.1	-	-	-
5 - 9	-	-	♦0.1	-	-	♦0.1	-	-	-
10 - 14	-	-	♦0.1	-	-	♦0.1	-	-	-
15 - 19	♦0.5	♦0.8	♦0.2	♦0.5	♦0.8	♦0.2	♦0.6	♦1.1	-
20 - 24	♦0.5	♦0.7	♦0.2	♦0.5	♦0.7	♦0.2	♦0.7	♦1.2	-
25 - 29	♦0.3	♦0.5	♦0.1	0.3	♦0.5	♦0.1	-	-	-
30 - 34	♦0.3	♦0.5	♦0.2	♦0.4	♦0.5	♦0.2	-	-	-
35 - 39	♦0.5	♦0.7	♦0.4	♦0.6	♦0.7	♦0.4	-	-	-
40 - 44	♦0.7	♦0.9	♦0.5	♦0.7	♦1.0	♦0.5	-	-	-
45 - 49	1.8	♦1.6	♦1.9	1.8	♦1.6	♦2.1	♦0.7	♦1.2	-
50 - 54	2.8	♦3.0	♦2.6	2.8	♦2.9	♦2.7	♦2.9	♦3.7	♦1.7
55 - 59	4.8	5.8	♦3.8	4.8	5.8	♦3.8	♦5.0	♦5.7	♦3.9
60 - 64	7.8	11.1	♦4.6	8.1	11.6	♦4.6	♦5.2	♦5.8	♦4.5
65 - 69	11.9	14.1	9.8	12.0	14.7	9.4	♦11.1	♦8.8	♦14.0
70 - 74	18.9	23.8	14.5	19.0	23.6	15.1	♦17.4	♦26.3	♦6.1
75 - 79	33.3	40.3	27.5	34.4	41.8	28.5	♦21.3	♦27.5	♦12.1
80 - 84	72.6	90.4	59.7	71.1	87.6	59.5	92.3	♦116.5	♦63.6
85 - 89	115.4	130.3	106.4	113.1	126.4	105.5	139.2	♦159.7	♦118.6
90 - 94	198.2	217.7	188.7	200.7	227.8	188.2	♦170.7	♦138.9	♦195.7
95 - 99	350.6	♦568.6	288.9	339.5	♦600.0	270.6	♦500.0	♦333.3	♦600.0
100 +	♦600.0	♦500.0	♦666.7	♦640.0	♦400.0	♦800.0	♦400.0	♦1000.0	-
Ireland - Irlande[29]									
1996 (+C)									
Total	8.8	9.2	8.3	8.1	8.4	7.8	9.7	10.4	9.0
0	5.7	6.2	5.2	6.1	6.6	5.5	5.2	5.6	4.9
1 - 4	0.3	0.3	0.3	0.3	♦0.3	♦0.3	0.4	♦0.4	♦0.4
5 - 9	0.1	♦0.2	♦0.1	♦0.1	♦0.2	♦0.1	♦0.1	♦0.2	-
10 - 14	0.2	0.2	♦0.1	0.2	♦0.2	♦0.1	♦0.2	♦0.2	♦0.1
15 - 19	0.5	0.6	0.3	0.4	0.5	♦0.2	0.6	0.8	♦0.4
20 - 24	0.8	1.3	0.3	0.6	1.0	♦0.2	1.3	1.9	♦0.5
25 - 29	0.8	1.2	0.4	0.7	1.1	♦0.3	1.0	1.5	♦0.6
30 - 34	0.8	1.1	0.5	0.8	1.1	0.5	0.8	1.2	♦0.5
35 - 39	1.0	1.4	0.6	1.0	1.3	0.7	1.1	1.5	0.6
40 - 44	1.6	2.0	1.2	1.5	2.0	1.1	1.7	2.0	1.4
45 - 49	2.5	3.0	1.9	2.8	3.5	2.1	2.1	2.5	1.6
50 - 54	4.6	5.5	3.6	4.6	5.7	3.5	4.5	5.2	3.7
55 - 59	7.4	9.5	5.3	8.1	10.7	5.6	6.5	8.0	4.8
60 - 64	13.2	17.1	9.3	14.0	18.6	9.8	12.2	15.3	8.7
65 - 69	23.1	30.9	16.1	24.1	32.9	17.0	21.9	28.8	14.8
70 - 74	38.2	49.6	29.0	40.6	54.6	30.8	35.5	45.0	26.8
75 - 79	63.2	81.2	50.3	66.1	89.6	52.0	60.3	74.4	48.3
80 - 84	106.1	135.3	88.3	103.3	140.5	85.2	108.8	131.3	92.0
85 +	202.3	239.5	185.9	196.8	247.4	179.4	208.6	233.2	194.7

Continent, country or area, date, code and age (in years) Continent, pays ou zone, date, code et âge (en années)	Total			Urban - Urbaine			Rural - Rurale		
	Both sexes Les deux sexes	Male Masculin	Female Féminin	Both sexes Les deux sexes	Male Masculin	Female Féminin	Both sexes Les deux sexes	Male Masculin	Female Féminin
EUROPE									
Ireland - Irlande[29]									
2005* (+C)									
Total	6.6	6.8	6.5	...	...	...	...	...	...
0	4.0	3.6	4.4	...	...	...	...	...	...
1 - 4	0.2	♦0.2	♦0.2	...	...	...	...	...	...
5 - 9	♦0.1	♦0.1	♦0.1	...	...	...	...	...	...
10 - 14	0.1	♦0.1	♦0.1	...	...	...	...	...	...
15 - 19	0.4	0.6	0.2	...	...	...	...	...	...
20 - 24	0.6	0.9	0.3	...	...	...	...	...	...
25 - 29	0.6	0.8	0.3	...	...	...	...	...	...
30 - 34	0.7	1.0	0.5	...	...	...	...	...	...
35 - 39	0.8	1.0	0.6	...	...	...	...	...	...
40 - 44	1.3	1.6	1.0	...	...	...	...	...	...
45 - 49	2.2	2.6	1.8	...	...	...	...	...	...
50 - 54	3.5	4.1	2.8	...	...	...	...	...	...
55 - 59	5.3	6.4	4.1	...	...	...	...	...	...
60 - 64	9.2	11.4	7.0	...	...	...	...	...	...
65 - 69	14.9	18.2	11.7	...	...	...	...	...	...
70 - 74	25.4	32.7	18.8	...	...	...	...	...	...
75 - 79	43.9	55.8	35.1	...	...	...	...	...	...
80 - 84	78.8	100.0	66.1	...	...	...	...	...	...
85 - 89	129.1	153.5	116.8	...	...	...	...	...	...
90 - 94	196.6	219.6	187.7	...	...	...	...	...	...
95 +	257.2	252.5	258.5	...	...	...	...	...	...
Italy - Italie									
2003 (C)									
Total	10.2	10.4	10.1	...	...	...	...	...	...
0	4.0	4.2	3.8	...	...	...	...	...	...
1 - 4	0.2	0.2	0.2	...	...	...	...	...	...
5 - 9	0.1	0.1	0.1	...	...	...	...	...	...
10 - 14	0.1	0.2	0.1	...	...	...	...	...	...
15 - 19	0.4	0.6	0.2	...	...	...	...	...	...
20 - 24	0.5	0.8	0.2	...	...	...	...	...	...
25 - 29	0.6	0.9	0.3	...	...	...	...	...	...
30 - 34	0.6	0.9	0.4	...	...	...	...	...	...
35 - 39	0.9	1.2	0.6	...	...	...	...	...	...
40 - 44	1.3	1.7	0.9	...	...	...	...	...	...
45 - 49	2.0	2.6	1.5	...	...	...	...	...	...
50 - 54	3.3	4.3	2.3	...	...	...	...	...	...
55 - 59	5.3	7.0	3.6	...	...	...	...	...	...
60 - 64	8.3	11.5	5.5	...	...	...	...	...	...
65 - 69	13.3	18.4	8.9	...	...	...	...	...	...
70 - 74	22.5	31.3	15.5	...	...	...	...	...	...
75 - 79	39.3	54.1	29.3	...	...	...	...	...	...
80 - 84	68.1	89.5	56.3	...	...	...	...	...	...
85 - 89	129.1	157.5	116.2	...	...	...	...	...	...
90 - 94	210.7	245.2	198.1	...	...	...	...	...	...
95 - 99	329.9	370.7	319.2	...	...	...	...	...	...
100 +	480.4	484.6	479.6	...	...	...	...	...	...
Latvia - Lettonie[12]									
2005 (C)									
Total	14.2	15.7	13.0	13.6	15.3	12.1	15.7	16.4	15.1
0	8.0	8.1	8.0	7.2	7.4	7.0	9.8	9.6	10.0
1 - 4	0.4	♦0.5	♦0.4	♦0.4	♦0.6	♦0.2	♦0.5	♦0.4	♦0.7
5 - 9	♦0.3	♦0.4	♦0.2	♦0.2	♦0.3	♦0.1	♦0.5	♦0.6	♦0.4
10 - 14	0.3	♦0.4	♦0.2	♦0.3	♦0.3	♦0.2	♦0.3	♦0.5	♦0.1
15 - 19	0.6	0.8	0.3	0.5	0.7	♦0.3	0.7	0.9	♦0.4
20 - 24	1.2	1.8	0.6	1.1	1.7	♦0.5	1.6	2.2	♦0.9
25 - 29	1.5	2.5	0.5	1.5	2.6	♦0.5	1.5	2.2	♦0.7
30 - 34	2.2	3.4	1.0	2.0	3.1	1.0	2.7	4.2	♦1.0
35 - 39	3.5	5.7	1.3	3.5	6.0	1.2	3.4	5.1	1.4
40 - 44	5.0	7.7	2.5	5.1	8.1	2.5	4.8	6.8	2.5
45 - 49	6.8	10.6	3.5	6.7	10.6	3.4	7.2	10.5	3.6
50 - 54	11.1	17.7	5.5	10.5	17.1	5.3	12.5	18.8	6.0
55 - 59	15.2	24.1	8.3	14.9	24.1	8.2	16.1	24.0	8.6

Continent, country or area, date, code and age (in years) Continent, pays ou zone, date, code et âge (en années)	Total			Urban - Urbaine			Rural - Rurale		
	Both sexes Les deux sexes	Male Masculin	Female Féminin	Both sexes Les deux sexes	Male Masculin	Female Féminin	Both sexes Les deux sexes	Male Masculin	Female Féminin
EUROPE									
Latvia - Lettonie[12]									
2005 (C)									
60 - 64	20.9	34.6	11.1	19.0	31.8	10.5	24.9	40.0	12.6
65 - 69	27.6	45.8	16.1	25.6	42.4	15.5	32.1	53.0	17.5
70 - 74	41.3	64.5	28.7	37.8	59.6	26.3	48.5	74.4	33.8
75 - 79	61.0	91.8	47.9	57.5	85.9	45.2	69.2	106.7	54.0
80 - 84	101.5	133.5	92.5	96.3	127.1	87.3	112.8	148.6	103.5
85 - 89	168.5	196.1	160.8	160.2	184.1	153.1	185.3	225.0	175.9
90 - 94	250.5	275.3	244.6	230.5	260.8	222.7	288.0	308.6	283.8
95 - 99	386.4	370.1	390.3	368.9	347.4	374.4	420.4	421.1	420.2
100 +	486.9	♦459.5	493.5	423.1	♦250.0	470.6	623.0	♦1111.1	♦538.5
Lithuania - Lituanie[12]									
2005 (C)									
Total	12.8	14.7	11.2	11.0	12.9	9.4	16.4	18.1	14.9
0	6.9	7.8	6.0	6.9	7.3	6.5	6.9	8.6	♦5.2
1 - 4	0.4	0.6	♦0.3	♦0.3	♦0.4	♦0.2	♦0.6	♦0.9	♦0.4
5 - 9	0.3	0.5	♦0.2	0.3	♦0.5	♦0.2	♦0.3	♦0.4	♦0.2
10 - 14	0.2	0.3	♦0.1	♦0.2	♦0.3	♦0.1	♦0.3	♦0.4	♦0.2
15 - 19	0.8	1.2	0.4	0.8	1.1	0.4	0.8	1.2	♦0.4
20 - 24	1.4	2.3	0.4	1.2	2.0	0.4	1.7	2.8	♦0.5
25 - 29	2.0	3.3	0.7	1.6	2.7	0.6	3.0	4.7	♦1.0
30 - 34	2.6	4.2	1.0	2.0	3.2	0.8	4.1	6.3	1.7
35 - 39	3.5	5.7	1.4	2.9	4.8	1.2	5.0	7.6	2.1
40 - 44	5.0	7.8	2.2	4.3	7.0	1.9	6.4	9.4	3.1
45 - 49	7.6	12.2	3.5	6.6	10.8	3.2	9.9	14.9	4.4
50 - 54	11.1	17.8	5.3	9.7	16.0	4.7	14.3	21.2	7.0
55 - 59	15.3	24.4	8.2	13.6	22.3	7.3	18.9	28.3	10.1
60 - 64	20.2	33.7	10.5	18.6	31.4	9.7	23.3	37.6	12.0
65 - 69	26.2	43.6	15.0	24.2	40.3	14.2	29.7	48.8	16.5
70 - 74	37.0	56.6	25.8	35.3	53.6	25.0	39.4	60.8	27.1
75 - 79	55.9	78.9	45.1	54.5	77.1	43.8	57.9	81.7	47.1
80 - 84	95.1	124.2	84.8	91.0	120.1	80.9	100.6	129.6	90.0
85 - 89	162.6	181.0	156.5	147.3	165.1	141.6	183.4	201.5	177.2
90 - 94	266.7	279.4	263.0	231.7	247.3	227.6	322.0	324.0	321.4
95 - 99	390.2	371.9	399.7	305.8	319.9	299.8	564.4	445.8	654.5
100 +	496.1	528.8	483.8	358.3	543.9	300.5	730.5	♦510.6	840.4
Luxembourg									
2005 (C)									
Total	7.9	7.9	8.0	...	...	...	...	...	...
0	♦2.6	♦1.8	♦3.5	...	...	...	...	...	...
1 - 4	♦0.2	♦0.2	♦0.2	...	...	...	...	...	...
5 - 9	♦0.2	♦0.1	♦0.2	...	...	...	...	...	...
10 - 14	♦0.1	♦0.3	-	...	...	...	...	...	...
15 - 19	♦0.1	♦0.1	♦0.1	...	...	...	...	...	...
20 - 24	♦0.8	♦1.3	♦0.4	...	...	...	...	...	...
25 - 29	♦0.6	♦0.8	♦0.4	...	...	...	...	...	...
30 - 34	♦0.6	♦0.9	♦0.2	...	...	...	...	...	...
35 - 39	1.3	1.6	♦0.9	...	...	...	...	...	...
40 - 44	1.2	♦1.5	♦0.8	...	...	...	...	...	...
45 - 49	2.1	2.9	♦1.3	...	...	...	...	...	...
50 - 54	3.9	5.1	2.6	...	...	...	...	...	...
55 - 59	6.4	8.0	4.8	...	...	...	...	...	...
60 - 64	10.5	14.7	6.4	...	...	...	...	...	...
65 - 69	14.3	19.3	9.9	...	...	...	...	...	...
70 - 74	24.6	33.4	17.4	...	...	...	...	...	...
75 - 79	39.7	51.1	31.7	...	...	...	...	...	...
80 - 84	67.0	82.3	59.8	...	...	...	...	...	...
85 - 89	122.2	163.7	107.0	...	...	...	...	...	...
90 - 94	215.8	278.1	199.6	...	...	...	...	...	...
95 +	460.3	♦1111.1	396.4	...	...	...	...	...	...
Malta - Malte[30]									
2004 (C)									
Total	7.2	7.2	7.2	...	...	...	...	...	...
0	♦5.8	♦7.0	♦4.6	...	...	...	...	...	...
1 - 4	♦0.5	♦0.4	♦0.6	...	...	...	...	...	...

Continent, country or area, date, code and age (in years) Continent, pays ou zone, date, code et âge (en années)	Total			Urban - Urbaine			Rural - Rurale		
	Both sexes Les deux sexes	Male Masculin	Female Féminin	Both sexes Les deux sexes	Male Masculin	Female Féminin	Both sexes Les deux sexes	Male Masculin	Female Féminin
EUROPE									
Malta - Malte[30]									
2004 (C)									
5 - 9	-	♦0.1	-	...	...	...	...	...	...
10 - 14	♦0.1	♦0.1	♦0.2	...	...	...	...	...	...
15 - 19	♦0.4	♦0.6	♦0.1	...	...	...	...	...	...
20 - 24	♦0.5	♦0.6	♦0.4	...	...	...	...	...	...
25 - 29	♦0.4	♦0.7	♦0.1	...	...	...	...	...	...
30 - 34	♦0.5	♦0.4	♦0.5	...	...	...	...	...	...
35 - 39	♦0.5	♦0.8	♦0.2	...	...	...	...	...	...
40 - 44	♦0.8	♦1.2	♦0.5	...	...	...	...	...	...
45 - 49	1.4	♦1.3	♦1.5	...	...	...	...	...	...
50 - 54	2.8	3.6	♦2.1	...	...	...	...	...	...
55 - 59	5.0	5.6	4.4	...	...	...	...	...	...
60 - 64	7.3	10.4	4.4	...	...	...	...	...	...
65 - 69	14.8	18.3	11.8	...	...	...	...	...	...
70 - 74	26.8	36.5	19.7	...	...	...	...	...	...
75 - 79	48.3	56.7	42.4	...	...	...	...	...	...
80 - 84	79.9	94.8	70.5	...	...	...	...	...	...
85 - 89	139.0	158.3	127.8	...	...	...	...	...	...
90 +	199.6	192.3	202.9	...	...	...	...	...	...
Netherlands - Pays-Bas[31]									
2003 (C)									
Total	8.8	8.6	8.9	9.0	8.7	9.3	8.3	8.5	8.2
0	4.3	4.9	3.7	4.3	4.9	3.6	4.3	4.9	3.8
1 - 4	0.3	0.4	0.3	0.3	0.4	0.3	0.3	0.3	0.3
5 - 9	0.2	0.2	0.1	0.2	0.2	0.1	0.2	0.2	♦0.1
10 - 14	0.1	0.2	0.1	0.1	0.2	0.1	0.1	♦0.1	♦0.1
15 - 19	0.3	0.4	0.2	0.3	0.4	0.2	0.3	0.3	0.3
20 - 24	0.4	0.5	0.2	0.3	0.4	0.2	0.6	0.8	0.3
25 - 29	0.5	0.6	0.3	0.5	0.6	0.3	0.5	0.6	0.3
30 - 34	0.5	0.7	0.4	0.6	0.7	0.4	0.5	0.7	0.4
35 - 39	0.8	0.9	0.7	0.8	0.9	0.7	0.7	0.9	0.6
40 - 44	1.4	1.6	1.2	1.5	1.8	1.3	1.3	1.5	1.2
45 - 49	2.4	2.6	2.1	2.6	2.8	2.3	2.0	2.2	1.9
50 - 54	3.8	4.3	3.2	4.1	4.6	3.5	3.3	3.8	2.8
55 - 59	6.1	7.3	4.8	6.4	7.6	5.2	5.6	7.0	4.2
60 - 64	9.5	11.8	7.1	9.9	12.4	7.4	8.8	11.0	6.6
65 - 69	15.5	20.4	11.0	16.3	21.4	11.8	14.1	18.7	9.7
70 - 74	26.2	35.3	18.8	26.8	35.7	19.8	25.2	34.8	17.0
75 - 79	44.8	61.4	33.6	45.5	62.2	34.5	43.5	59.8	31.8
80 - 84	81.3	111.9	64.8	81.9	112.8	65.8	79.9	110.3	62.6
85 - 89	142.4	185.6	125.3	141.9	186.1	125.1	143.5	184.5	125.8
90 - 94	258.5	323.4	239.8	257.5	325.7	239.4	260.4	319.5	240.6
95 - 99	435.0	496.5	421.8	431.1	496.7	418.3	443.4	496.2	429.8
100 +	701.6	844.4	676.9	706.4	818.2	689.7	690.9	885.7	645.7
2004 (C)									
Total	8.4	8.2	8.5	...	...	...	...	...	...
0	3.8	4.3	3.4	...	...	...	...	...	...
1 - 4	0.3	0.4	0.3	...	...	...	...	...	...
5 - 9	0.1	0.1	0.1	...	...	...	...	...	...
10 - 14	0.1	0.1	0.1	...	...	...	...	...	...
15 - 19	0.3	0.4	0.2	...	...	...	...	...	...
20 - 24	0.4	0.5	0.2	...	...	...	...	...	...
25 - 29	0.4	0.6	0.3	...	...	...	...	...	...
30 - 34	0.5	0.6	0.4	...	...	...	...	...	...
35 - 39	0.8	0.9	0.6	...	...	...	...	...	...
40 - 44	1.3	1.5	1.1	...	...	...	...	...	...
45 - 49	2.3	2.4	2.1	...	...	...	...	...	...
50 - 54	3.7	4.2	3.2	...	...	...	...	...	...
55 - 59	5.7	6.9	4.5	...	...	...	...	...	...
60 - 64	9.1	11.3	6.8	...	...	...	...	...	...
65 - 69	14.5	18.9	10.3	...	...	...	...	...	...
70 - 74	25.2	33.8	18.0	...	...	...	...	...	...
75 - 79	41.9	56.8	31.5	...	...	...	...	...	...
80 - 84	76.1	101.0	62.4	...	...	...	...	...	...

20. Death rates specific for age, sex and urban/rural residence: latest available year, 1996 - 2005
Taux de mortalité selon l'âge, le sexe et la résidence, urbaine/rurale: dernière année disponible, 1996 - 2005 (continued - suite)

Continent, country or area, date, code and age (in years) Continent, pays ou zone, date, code et âge (en années)	Total			Urban - Urbaine			Rural - Rurale		
	Both sexes Les deux sexes	Male Masculin	Female Féminin	Both sexes Les deux sexes	Male Masculin	Female Féminin	Both sexes Les deux sexes	Male Masculin	Female Féminin
EUROPE									
Netherlands - Pays-Bas[31]									
2004 (C)									
85 - 89	134.1	175.2	117.5	...	...	...	...	...	...
90 - 94	236.4	288.0	221.3	...	...	...	...	...	...
95 - 99	399.6	476.3	383.5	...	...	...	...	...	...
100 +	631.7	711.4	617.5	...	...	...	...	...	...
Norway - Norvège[32]									
2004* (C)									
Total	9.0	8.8	9.2	...	...	...	...	...	...
0	3.3	3.4	3.1	...	...	...	...	...	...
1 - 4	0.2	♦0.2	♦0.1	...	...	...	...	...	...
5 - 9	♦0.1	♦0.1	♦0.1	...	...	...	...	...	...
10 - 14	0.1	♦0.1	♦0.1	...	...	...	...	...	...
15 - 19	0.4	0.6	0.3	...	...	...	...	...	...
20 - 24	0.7	1.0	0.3	...	...	...	...	...	...
25 - 29	0.7	1.0	0.4	...	...	...	...	...	...
30 - 34	0.7	0.9	0.5	...	...	...	...	...	...
35 - 39	0.9	1.2	0.7	...	...	...	...	...	...
40 - 44	1.3	1.6	1.0	...	...	...	...	...	...
45 - 49	2.0	2.3	1.7	...	...	...	...	...	...
50 - 54	3.4	4.2	2.6	...	...	...	...	...	...
55 - 59	5.3	6.4	4.2	...	...	...	...	...	...
60 - 64	8.1	10.3	6.0	...	...	...	...	...	...
65 - 69	13.6	17.7	9.8	...	...	...	...	...	...
70 - 74	22.6	30.1	16.2	...	...	...	...	...	...
75 - 79	38.4	49.3	30.3	...	...	...	...	...	...
80 - 84	71.2	93.2	57.9	...	...	...	...	...	...
85 - 89	122.5	152.3	108.8	...	...	...	...	...	...
90 - 94	212.2	251.7	198.6	...	...	...	...	...	...
95 - 99	327.4	375.0	315.2	...	...	...	...	...	...
100 +	452.4	583.3	426.2	...	...	...	...	...	...
Poland - Pologne									
2004 (C)									
Total	9.5	10.5	8.6	9.2	10.3	8.3	10.0	11.0	9.1
0	6.9	7.5	6.2	7.3	8.0	6.5	6.3	6.8	5.8
1 - 4	0.3	0.3	0.2	0.2	0.2	0.2	0.3	0.3	0.2
5 - 9	0.2	0.2	0.1	0.1	0.2	0.1	0.2	0.2	0.1
10 - 14	0.2	0.2	0.1	0.2	0.2	0.1	0.2	0.2	0.2
15 - 19	0.4	0.6	0.3	0.4	0.6	0.2	0.5	0.7	0.3
20 - 24	0.7	1.1	0.3	0.6	1.0	0.3	0.8	1.3	0.3
25 - 29	0.8	1.3	0.3	0.7	1.2	0.3	0.9	1.5	0.3
30 - 34	1.1	1.7	0.5	1.0	1.6	0.5	1.2	1.9	0.5
35 - 39	1.8	2.7	0.8	1.7	2.6	0.8	1.9	2.9	0.7
40 - 44	2.9	4.3	1.5	2.9	4.3	1.6	2.9	4.4	1.3
45 - 49	5.0	7.3	2.7	4.9	7.3	2.8	5.1	7.4	2.4
50 - 54	7.6	11.2	4.2	7.5	11.1	4.3	7.9	11.5	4.0
55 - 59	10.8	16.1	6.0	10.6	15.7	6.2	11.2	16.8	5.6
60 - 64	15.7	23.8	9.0	15.7	23.5	9.5	15.6	24.3	8.0
65 - 69	22.5	34.0	13.9	22.3	33.6	14.2	22.7	34.7	13.3
70 - 74	34.3	49.8	23.9	34.0	48.5	24.4	34.8	51.7	23.3
75 - 79	53.1	72.4	42.6	52.7	71.5	42.7	53.6	73.6	42.5
80 - 84	88.6	112.3	78.0	86.2	110.3	75.8	91.8	114.8	80.9
85 +	184.4	206.0	176.9	174.3	195.4	167.6	198.5	218.5	190.6
Portugal									
2005 (C)									
Total	10.2	10.9	9.5	...	...	...	...	...	...
0	3.5	3.5	3.5	...	...	...	...	...	...
1 - 4	0.2	0.3	0.1	...	...	...	...	...	...
5 - 9	0.2	0.2	0.1	...	...	...	...	...	...
10 - 14	0.2	0.2	0.1	...	...	...	...	...	...
15 - 19	0.5	0.7	0.2	...	...	...	...	...	...
20 - 24	0.6	0.9	0.3	...	...	...	...	...	...
25 - 29	0.7	1.1	0.4	...	...	...	...	...	...
30 - 34	1.1	1.7	0.6	...	...	...	...	...	...
35 - 39	1.5	2.3	0.8	...	...	...	...	...	...

20. Death rates specific for age, sex and urban/rural residence: latest available year, 1996 - 2005
Taux de mortalité selon l'âge, le sexe et la résidence, urbaine/rurale: dernière année disponible, 1996 - 2005 (continued - suite)

Continent, country or area, date, code and age (in years) / Continent, pays ou zone, date, code et âge (en années)	Total			Urban - Urbaine			Rural - Rurale		
	Both sexes Les deux sexes	Male Masculin	Female Féminin	Both sexes Les deux sexes	Male Masculin	Female Féminin	Both sexes Les deux sexes	Male Masculin	Female Féminin
EUROPE									
Portugal									
2005 (C)									
40 - 44	2.2	3.3	1.2	...	...	...	...	...	...
45 - 49	3.2	4.4	1.9	...	...	...	...	...	...
50 - 54	4.5	6.4	2.7	...	...	...	...	...	...
55 - 59	6.3	9.1	3.8	...	...	...	...	...	...
60 - 64	8.9	12.7	5.6	...	...	...	...	...	...
65 - 69	14.9	20.7	9.9	...	...	...	...	...	...
70 - 74	24.6	33.8	17.4	...	...	...	...	...	...
75 - 79	45.5	60.3	35.3	...	...	...	...	...	...
80 - 84	82.7	103.0	70.3	...	...	...	...	...	...
85 - 89	146.4	169.8	134.5	...	...	...	...	...	...
90 - 94	253.0	278.8	242.0	...	...	...	...	...	...
95 - 99	427.7	435.6	425.1	...	...	...	...	...	...
100 +	520.0	397.0	559.1	...	...	...	...	...	...
Republic of Moldova - République de Moldova[12]									
2004 (C)									
Total	11.6	12.5	10.7	9.0	10.1	8.0	13.3	14.3	12.5
0	12.6	14.1	11.0	12.6	15.2	9.8	12.6	13.5	11.6
1 - 4	0.9	0.9	0.8	0.7	◆0.6	◆0.7	1.0	1.0	0.9
5 - 9	0.3	0.4	◆0.2	◆0.4	◆0.4	◆0.3	0.3	0.5	◆0.2
10 - 14	0.3	0.4	0.3	◆0.3	◆0.3	◆0.3	0.3	0.4	◆0.3
15 - 19	0.6	0.8	0.4	0.5	0.6	◆0.4	0.7	1.0	0.4
20 - 24	0.9	1.4	0.4	0.8	1.3	◆0.3	0.9	1.4	0.4
25 - 29	1.3	1.9	0.7	1.3	1.9	0.6	1.3	1.9	0.7
30 - 34	2.0	2.8	1.2	1.7	2.4	1.0	2.2	3.3	1.3
35 - 39	3.5	5.4	1.8	2.9	4.4	1.5	4.1	6.4	2.0
40 - 44	5.3	8.1	2.8	4.1	6.4	2.2	6.3	9.5	3.4
45 - 49	8.0	12.1	4.3	6.5	9.8	3.6	9.2	13.9	4.8
50 - 54	12.2	17.7	7.3	10.5	15.8	6.1	13.5	19.4	8.4
55 - 59	16.4	22.3	11.6	14.7	20.9	9.5	17.9	23.7	13.4
60 - 64	28.7	37.6	22.1	25.2	33.5	18.3	30.9	40.5	24.3
65 - 69	39.5	53.3	29.9	33.1	44.3	24.8	43.3	59.0	32.9
70 - 74	58.0	76.3	46.7	49.9	63.8	41.0	61.7	82.2	49.2
75 - 79	83.7	99.4	75.2	75.0	88.5	68.0	88.0	104.6	78.8
80 - 84	140.5	156.9	132.5	118.6	128.8	114.4	150.7	167.9	141.6
85 +	224.4	255.8	212.6	162.1	182.6	154.8	262.8	298.0	249.0
Romania - Roumanie									
2005 (C)									
Total	12.1	13.1	11.2	9.8	10.9	8.8	14.9	15.7	14.1
0	15.4	17.3	13.3	12.8	14.6	10.9	18.2	20.2	16.0
1 - 4	0.7	0.7	0.6	0.6	0.6	0.5	0.7	0.8	0.7
5 - 9	0.3	0.4	0.3	0.3	0.4	0.3	0.3	0.4	0.3
10 - 14	0.3	0.4	0.3	0.3	0.3	0.3	0.4	0.4	0.3
15 - 19	0.6	0.7	0.4	0.5	0.6	0.4	0.7	0.9	0.5
20 - 24	0.6	0.9	0.3	0.5	0.7	0.3	0.7	1.1	0.4
25 - 29	0.8	1.1	0.5	0.7	0.9	0.4	1.0	1.3	0.6
30 - 34	1.2	1.7	0.6	1.0	1.5	0.6	1.4	2.0	0.8
35 - 39	1.9	2.6	1.1	1.5	2.2	0.9	2.3	3.1	1.4
40 - 44	3.5	5.0	2.0	2.9	4.2	1.7	4.4	6.0	2.5
45 - 49	6.0	8.6	3.4	5.2	7.6	3.1	7.3	10.2	3.9
50 - 54	8.6	12.5	5.0	7.9	11.4	4.6	9.8	14.3	5.6
55 - 59	12.3	17.6	7.5	12.0	16.9	7.5	12.6	18.5	7.5
60 - 64	17.9	25.6	11.4	17.9	25.6	11.4	17.9	25.7	11.4
65 - 69	26.9	37.4	18.7	27.2	38.0	18.8	26.6	37.0	18.5
70 - 74	41.9	54.2	33.0	42.3	55.0	33.4	41.6	53.6	32.7
75 - 79	68.0	81.4	59.0	67.0	82.3	57.1	68.7	80.8	60.4
80 - 84	114.4	127.1	107.1	109.8	123.5	102.7	117.5	129.4	110.3
85 - 89	183.8	195.5	177.9	173.8	186.6	168.0	191.3	201.7	185.8
90 - 94	290.1	288.9	290.8	265.2	275.6	260.3	311.0	299.0	317.3
95 - 99	348.2	320.0	363.2	350.3	335.0	357.6	346.6	310.4	367.6
100 +	241.8	283.1	224.0	292.7	357.1	268.5	211.6	245.5	195.7

20. Death rates specific for age, sex and urban/rural residence: latest available year, 1996 - 2005
Taux de mortalité selon l'âge, le sexe et la résidence, urbaine/rurale: dernière année disponible, 1996 - 2005 (continued - suite)

Continent, country or area, date, code and age (in years) Continent, pays ou zone, date, code et âge (en annèes)	Total			Urban - Urbaine			Rural - Rurale		
	Both sexes Les deux sexes	Male Masculin	Female Féminin	Both sexes Les deux sexes	Male Masculin	Female Féminin	Both sexes Les deux sexes	Male Masculin	Female Féminin
EUROPE									
Russian Federation - Fédération de Russie[12]									
2004 (C)									
Total.....................	16.0	18.6	13.7	15.3	18.0	12.9	17.9	20.1	15.8
0........................	11.8	13.3	10.1	11.1	12.4	9.7	13.5	15.7	11.2
1 - 4....................	0.8	0.8	0.7	0.6	0.7	0.6	1.0	1.1	0.9
5 - 9....................	0.4	0.5	0.3	0.4	0.5	0.3	0.5	0.6	0.4
10 - 14..................	0.4	0.6	0.3	0.4	0.5	0.3	0.5	0.7	0.4
15 - 19..................	1.2	1.7	0.7	1.0	1.5	0.6	1.5	2.2	0.9
20 - 24..................	2.4	3.9	1.0	2.2	3.5	0.9	3.3	5.2	1.3
25 - 29..................	3.8	6.0	1.6	3.6	5.8	1.5	4.5	7.0	1.8
30 - 34..................	4.9	7.7	2.1	4.7	7.4	2.1	5.5	8.7	2.3
35 - 39..................	6.4	10.1	2.8	6.1	9.7	2.7	7.1	11.0	3.1
40 - 44..................	8.8	14.0	3.9	8.6	13.8	3.8	9.5	14.6	4.2
45 - 49..................	12.0	19.3	5.5	11.7	19.1	5.4	13.1	19.9	6.1
50 - 54..................	16.6	26.5	8.2	16.0	26.1	7.8	18.3	27.4	9.4
55 - 59..................	21.6	34.0	11.8	20.8	33.2	11.3	24.3	36.6	13.7
60 - 64..................	28.9	47.0	16.7	27.7	45.3	16.0	32.2	51.3	18.8
65 - 69..................	37.1	58.5	24.0	36.0	57.3	23.3	39.7	61.4	25.6
70 - 74..................	53.7	79.8	40.1	53.1	79.0	40.0	55.1	81.3	40.3
75 - 79..................	77.7	107.6	65.9	78.2	107.4	66.5	76.7	108.2	64.5
80 - 84..................	114.5	139.6	108.0	114.0	136.8	107.8	115.9	146.9	108.5
85 - 89..................	186.0	205.3	181.7	185.0	200.5	181.3	188.3	219.7	182.6
90 - 94..................	280.8	284.3	280.1	275.5	273.9	275.8	292.2	315.4	288.8
95 - 99..................	386.1	355.1	391.3	373.1	339.0	379.6	412.2	403.5	413.3
100 +....................	236.5	196.5	243.5	213.0	164.3	224.6	268.1	286.4	266.2
Serbia and Montenegro - Serbie-et-Montenegro[33]									
2003 (C)									
Total.....................	13.4	14.1	12.8	11.9	12.7	11.3	15.4	16.0	14.9
0........................	9.3	10.0	8.6	10.1	10.4	9.8	8.0	9.2	6.8
1 - 4....................	0.4	0.4	0.3	0.4	0.5	0.4	0.3	◆0.4	◆0.3
5 - 9....................	0.2	0.2	◆0.1	0.2	◆0.2	◆0.1	◆0.1	◆0.2	◆0.1
10 - 14..................	0.2	0.3	◆0.1	0.2	◆0.2	◆0.1	0.2	0.3	◆0.1
15 - 19..................	0.5	0.6	0.3	0.4	0.6	0.2	0.5	0.7	◆0.3
20 - 24..................	0.6	0.9	0.3	0.6	0.9	0.3	0.6	0.8	0.3
25 - 29..................	0.7	1.1	0.4	0.7	1.0	0.4	0.8	1.1	0.4
30 - 34..................	0.9	1.1	0.7	0.9	1.2	0.7	0.9	1.1	0.7
35 - 39..................	1.6	2.1	1.0	1.5	2.1	1.0	1.6	2.1	1.0
40 - 44..................	2.7	3.4	1.9	2.7	3.4	2.0	2.6	3.5	1.6
45 - 49..................	4.8	6.3	3.3	4.8	6.4	3.4	4.8	6.3	3.2
50 - 54..................	8.1	10.9	5.3	8.0	10.8	5.5	8.1	11.0	5.1
55 - 59..................	12.1	16.8	7.7	12.1	16.8	8.0	12.0	16.8	7.3
60 - 64..................	18.4	24.4	13.1	18.9	25.0	13.7	17.8	23.7	12.4
65 - 69..................	29.3	37.6	22.4	30.9	39.5	23.7	27.7	35.7	21.0
70 - 74..................	48.2	58.6	40.2	49.2	59.1	41.9	47.3	58.2	38.6
75 - 79..................	78.8	89.5	72.0	80.1	90.3	73.7	77.7	88.8	70.4
80 - 84..................	125.6	133.8	120.9	123.5	132.0	118.7	127.4	135.3	122.7
85 - 89..................	206.6	212.5	203.3	202.1	205.8	200.1	210.9	218.4	206.4
90 - 94..................	285.2	273.0	292.2	259.4	241.5	268.9	311.0	301.8	316.6
95 - 99..................	285.4	267.1	295.7	211.8	165.5	238.9	384.3	411.9	369.7
100 +....................	113.4	110.8	114.8	76.3	◆64.2	82.7	194.4	◆214.3	184.2
Slovakia - Slovaquie									
2001 (C)									
Total.....................	9.7	10.6	8.8	8.1	8.9	7.4	11.6	12.8	10.6
0........................	6.1	6.9	5.3	5.6	6.0	5.1	6.6	7.7	5.4
1 - 4....................	0.4	0.5	0.3	0.4	◆0.4	◆0.4	0.4	0.7	◆0.2
5 - 9....................	0.2	0.3	◆0.1	0.2	◆0.3	◆0.1	0.2	◆0.3	◆0.1
10 - 14..................	0.2	0.3	◆0.1	0.2	0.3	◆0.1	0.2	◆0.3	◆0.2
15 - 19..................	0.4	0.6	0.3	0.4	0.5	0.3	0.5	0.6	0.3
20 - 24..................	0.6	0.9	0.2	0.5	0.8	◆0.2	0.7	1.1	◆0.3
25 - 29..................	0.8	1.2	0.4	0.8	1.1	0.4	0.9	1.4	0.4
30 - 34..................	1.1	1.7	0.5	1.0	1.5	0.5	1.3	1.9	0.6
35 - 39..................	1.7	2.5	0.8	1.4	2.1	0.9	2.0	3.0	0.8
40 - 44..................	2.9	4.3	1.6	2.4	3.5	1.5	3.7	5.4	1.8

Continent, country or area, date, code and age (in years) / Continent, pays ou zone, date, code et âge (en années)	Total			Urban - Urbaine			Rural - Rurale		
	Both sexes Les deux sexes	Male Masculin	Female Féminin	Both sexes Les deux sexes	Male Masculin	Female Féminin	Both sexes Les deux sexes	Male Masculin	Female Féminin
EUROPE									
Slovakia - Slovaquie									
2001 (C)									
45 - 49	4.9	7.2	2.7	4.3	6.1	2.7	5.9	8.8	2.7
50 - 54	7.7	11.5	4.1	6.8	10.2	3.7	9.0	13.5	4.6
55 - 59	11.6	17.6	6.6	10.5	15.5	6.3	13.1	20.1	6.9
60 - 64	18.3	28.3	10.4	16.8	25.2	10.2	19.8	31.6	10.5
65 - 69	27.0	40.5	17.2	25.9	37.8	17.3	28.0	43.3	17.2
70 - 74	41.7	59.7	30.3	40.5	55.5	30.8	42.8	63.7	29.9
75 - 79	65.1	83.4	55.1	63.3	79.9	54.0	66.7	86.6	56.0
80 - 84	106.5	131.3	94.1	103.4	126.3	91.4	109.3	135.9	96.3
85 - 89	174.9	198.7	164.3	170.7	196.1	159.3	178.5	200.9	168.5
90 - 94	274.0	293.2	266.7	266.7	278.1	262.6	279.9	304.7	270.1
95 - 99	339.0	318.9	345.9	326.0	262.0	349.0	351.0	375.0	343.2
100 +	259.6	♦125.0	330.9	275.9	♦90.9	♦388.9	♦239.1	♦178.6	♦265.6
2005 (C)									
Total	9.9	10.8	9.1	...	...	...	...	...	...
0	7.3	8.1	6.4	...	...	...	...	...	...
1 - 4	0.4	0.4	0.3	...	...	...	...	...	...
5 - 9	0.2	0.3	♦0.1	...	...	...	...	...	...
10 - 14	0.1	♦0.1	♦0.1	...	...	...	...	...	...
15 - 19	0.4	0.5	0.3	...	...	...	...	...	...
20 - 24	0.6	0.9	0.3	...	...	...	...	...	...
25 - 29	0.7	1.0	0.3	...	...	...	...	...	...
30 - 34	1.0	1.4	0.5	...	...	...	...	...	...
35 - 39	1.6	2.3	0.9	...	...	...	...	...	...
40 - 44	2.6	3.7	1.4	...	...	...	...	...	...
45 - 49	4.8	7.1	2.6	...	...	...	...	...	...
50 - 54	7.4	11.0	3.9	...	...	...	...	...	...
55 - 59	11.1	16.9	6.0	...	...	...	...	...	...
60 - 64	16.6	25.3	9.6	...	...	...	...	...	...
65 - 69	24.5	36.8	15.8	...	...	...	...	...	...
70 - 74	38.7	55.2	28.2	...	...	...	...	...	...
75 - 79	62.8	84.2	51.0	...	...	...	...	...	...
80 - 84	107.6	133.8	95.4	...	...	...	...	...	...
85 - 89	168.6	190.2	159.1	...	...	...	...	...	...
90 - 94	267.5	280.8	262.4	...	...	...	...	...	...
95 - 99	277.5	227.6	298.0	...	...	...	...	...	...
100 +	148.1	♦78.8	189.9	...	...	...	...	...	...
Slovenia - Slovénie									
2005 (C)									
Total	9.4	9.6	9.2	9.1	9.5	8.8	10.2	10.4	9.9
0	4.2	4.4	3.9	♦3.1	♦3.7	♦2.4	5.2	♦5.2	♦5.2
1 - 4	♦0.3	♦0.3	♦0.3	♦0.2	♦0.2	♦0.2	♦0.3	♦0.4	♦0.3
5 - 9	♦0.1	♦0.1	♦0.1	♦0.1	♦0.1	♦0.1	♦0.1	-	♦0.2
10 - 14	♦0.1	♦0.2	♦0.1	♦0.1	♦0.2	♦0.1	♦0.1	♦0.1	♦0.1
15 - 19	0.4	0.6	♦0.1	♦0.3	♦0.4	♦0.1	0.5	♦0.8	♦0.2
20 - 24	0.7	1.1	♦0.3	0.8	1.1	♦0.4	0.7	1.1	♦0.3
25 - 29	0.8	1.3	♦0.3	0.8	1.2	♦0.3	0.9	1.5	♦0.3
30 - 34	0.9	1.1	0.6	0.9	1.2	♦0.5	0.9	1.1	♦0.7
35 - 39	1.0	1.4	0.7	1.0	1.3	♦0.7	1.2	1.6	♦0.7
40 - 44	1.9	2.7	1.1	1.8	2.7	1.1	2.2	3.1	1.3
45 - 49	3.3	4.6	2.0	3.5	4.7	2.4	3.4	5.1	1.6
50 - 54	5.2	7.1	3.2	4.9	6.7	3.3	5.7	8.1	3.1
55 - 59	7.5	10.1	4.8	7.3	10.3	4.6	7.9	10.7	5.0
60 - 64	11.8	17.0	6.9	10.9	16.0	6.7	13.0	18.7	7.4
65 - 69	17.5	25.4	10.8	16.8	24.2	10.8	18.5	27.3	11.0
70 - 74	28.3	41.0	19.6	24.9	36.4	17.1	32.2	46.3	22.4
75 - 79	47.4	68.1	36.3	43.9	62.1	34.2	51.6	75.1	38.9
80 - 84	78.5	103.0	69.3	72.9	90.9	65.8	85.1	118.4	73.4
85 - 89	141.4	170.7	131.8	123.2	151.3	113.6	162.1	195.6	151.8
90 - 94	241.0	286.3	228.4	234.0	283.3	219.8	250.4	291.5	239.4
95 - 99	353.9	391.8	344.9	322.9	377.0	310.9	394.0	406.5	390.8
100 +	367.5	♦421.1	357.1	♦294.1	♦200.0	♦310.3	♦479.2	♦666.7	♦435.9

Continent, country or area, date, code and age (in years) / Continent, pays ou zone, date, code et âge (en années)	Total			Urban - Urbaine			Rural - Rurale		
	Both sexes Les deux sexes	Male Masculin	Female Féminin	Both sexes Les deux sexes	Male Masculin	Female Féminin	Both sexes Les deux sexes	Male Masculin	Female Féminin
EUROPE									
Spain - Espagne									
2003 (C)									
Total	9.2	9.7	8.7	...	...	...	...	...	...
0	4.1	4.4	3.7	...	...	...	...	...	...
1 - 4	0.3	0.3	0.2	...	...	...	...	...	...
5 - 9	0.1	0.2	0.1	...	...	...	...	...	...
10 - 14	0.2	0.2	0.1	...	...	...	...	...	...
15 - 19	0.4	0.6	0.3	...	...	...	...	...	...
20 - 24	0.6	0.9	0.3	...	...	...	...	...	...
25 - 29	0.6	0.9	0.3	...	...	...	...	...	...
30 - 34	0.8	1.2	0.4	...	...	...	...	...	...
35 - 39	1.1	1.6	0.7	...	...	...	...	...	...
40 - 44	1.7	2.4	1.1	...	...	...	...	...	...
45 - 49	2.6	3.5	1.6	...	...	...	...	...	...
50 - 54	3.8	5.4	2.2	...	...	...	...	...	...
55 - 59	5.7	8.4	3.1	...	...	...	...	...	...
60 - 64	8.2	12.2	4.5	...	...	...	...	...	...
65 - 69	13.5	19.8	8.0	...	...	...	...	...	...
70 - 74	22.1	31.7	14.3	...	...	...	...	...	...
75 - 79	38.6	53.1	28.1	...	...	...	...	...	...
80 - 84	70.2	91.2	57.6	...	...	...	...	...	...
85 - 89	130.1	155.5	118.4	...	...	...	...	...	...
90 - 94	225.7	248.7	216.6	...	...	...	...	...	...
95 - 99	348.8	363.6	343.8	...	...	...	...	...	...
100 +	440.1	341.5	476.4	...	...	...	...	...	...
Sweden - Suède									
2005 (C)									
Total	10.2	10.0	10.3	...	...	...	...	...	...
0	2.4	2.5	2.3	...	...	...	...	...	...
1 - 4	0.2	0.2	0.2	...	...	...	...	...	...
5 - 9	0.1	0.1	◆0.1	...	...	...	...	...	...
10 - 14	0.1	0.1	◆0.1	...	...	...	...	...	...
15 - 19	0.3	0.4	0.2	...	...	...	...	...	...
20 - 24	0.5	0.7	0.3	...	...	...	...	...	...
25 - 29	0.5	0.7	0.3	...	...	...	...	...	...
30 - 34	0.5	0.6	0.4	...	...	...	...	...	...
35 - 39	0.7	0.8	0.6	...	...	...	...	...	...
40 - 44	1.1	1.4	0.8	...	...	...	...	...	...
45 - 49	1.8	2.2	1.4	...	...	...	...	...	...
50 - 54	3.2	3.7	2.6	...	...	...	...	...	...
55 - 59	5.1	6.0	4.1	...	...	...	...	...	...
60 - 64	7.9	9.6	6.3	...	...	...	...	...	...
65 - 69	13.3	16.7	10.1	...	...	...	...	...	...
70 - 74	21.7	28.0	16.3	...	...	...	...	...	...
75 - 79	37.4	48.3	29.0	...	...	...	...	...	...
80 - 84	68.2	86.8	56.0	...	...	...	...	...	...
85 - 89	122.8	152.9	107.0	...	...	...	...	...	...
90 - 94	215.4	260.3	198.1	...	...	...	...	...	...
95 - 99	329.9	384.5	315.4	...	...	...	...	...	...
100 +	486.4	468.5	489.6	...	...	...	...	...	...
Switzerland - Suisse									
2005 (C)									
Total	8.2	8.2	8.3	...	...	...	...	...	...
0	4.2	4.8	3.6	...	...	...	...	...	...
1 - 4	0.2	0.2	◆0.1	...	...	...	...	...	...
5 - 9	0.1	◆0.1	◆0.1	...	...	...	...	...	...
10 - 14	0.1	0.1	◆0.1	...	...	...	...	...	...
15 - 19	0.3	0.4	0.3	...	...	...	...	...	...
20 - 24	0.5	0.8	0.3	...	...	...	...	...	...
25 - 29	0.5	0.6	0.3	...	...	...	...	...	...
30 - 34	0.5	0.7	0.4	...	...	...	...	...	...
35 - 39	0.8	1.1	0.6	...	...	...	...	...	...
40 - 44	1.2	1.5	0.9	...	...	...	...	...	...
45 - 49	2.0	2.4	1.5	...	...	...	...	...	...
50 - 54	2.9	3.9	2.0	...	...	...	...	...	...

20. Death rates specific for age, sex and urban/rural residence: latest available year, 1996 - 2005
Taux de mortalité selon l'âge, le sexe et la résidence, urbaine/rurale: dernière année disponible, 1996 - 2005 (continued - suite)

Continent, country or area, date, code and age (in years) / Continent, pays ou zone, date, code et âge (en années)	Total			Urban - Urbaine			Rural - Rurale		
	Both sexes Les deux sexes	Male Masculin	Female Féminin	Both sexes Les deux sexes	Male Masculin	Female Féminin	Both sexes Les deux sexes	Male Masculin	Female Féminin
EUROPE									
Switzerland - Suisse									
2005 (C)									
55 - 59	4.7	6.1	3.3	...	...	...	...	...	...
60 - 64	7.4	9.6	5.2	...	...	...	...	...	...
65 - 69	11.4	15.4	7.8	...	...	...	...	...	...
70 - 74	18.5	25.1	13.1	...	...	...	...	...	...
75 - 79	31.9	43.7	23.8	...	...	...	...	...	...
80 - 84	60.7	79.6	49.7	...	...	...	...	...	...
85 - 89	113.1	139.0	100.6	...	...	...	...	...	...
90 - 94	196.9	232.2	184.2	...	...	...	...	...	...
95 +	307.0	342.7	298.0	...	...	...	...	...	...
The Former Yugoslav Rep. of Macedonia - L'ex-République yougoslave de Macédoine									
2005 (C)									
Total	9.0	9.6	8.5	...	...	...	...	...	...
0	12.7	13.4	11.9	...	...	...	...	...	...
1 - 4	0.4	♦0.4	♦0.3	...	...	...	...	...	...
5 - 9	♦0.1	♦0.1	♦0.1	...	...	...	...	...	...
10 - 14	0.2	♦0.3	♦0.1	...	...	...	...	...	...
15 - 19	0.4	0.5	♦0.2	...	...	...	...	...	...
20 - 24	0.5	0.6	♦0.3	...	...	...	...	...	...
25 - 29	0.6	0.9	♦0.4	...	...	...	...	...	...
30 - 34	0.7	0.9	0.4	...	...	...	...	...	...
35 - 39	1.0	1.3	0.7	...	...	...	...	...	...
40 - 44	1.7	2.1	1.3	...	...	...	...	...	...
45 - 49	3.5	4.4	2.6	...	...	...	...	...	...
50 - 54	6.9	9.0	4.7	...	...	...	...	...	...
55 - 59	9.6	13.4	5.9	...	...	...	...	...	...
60 - 64	14.5	19.3	10.2	...	...	...	...	...	...
65 - 69	25.7	31.4	20.6	...	...	...	...	...	...
70 - 74	44.2	51.8	37.9	...	...	...	...	...	...
75 - 79	76.3	87.0	68.2	...	...	...	...	...	...
80 - 84	133.8	144.0	126.7	...	...	...	...	...	...
85 +	249.2	257.3	243.5	...	...	...	...	...	...
Ukraine[34]									
2001 (C)									
Total	15.5	16.9	14.2	13.9	15.9	12.3	18.5	19.0	18.1
0	12.0	13.5	10.3	12.2	13.7	10.7	11.5	13.3	9.6
1 - 4	0.9	1.0	0.8	0.7	0.8	0.6	1.2	1.3	1.0
5 - 9	0.4	0.5	0.3	0.4	0.5	0.3	0.4	0.5	0.3
10 - 14	0.4	0.5	0.3	0.4	0.5	0.2	0.4	0.5	0.3
15 - 19	0.9	1.2	0.5	0.8	1.1	0.5	1.2	1.7	0.7
20 - 24	1.8	2.8	0.8	1.7	2.6	0.8	2.1	3.2	0.8
25 - 29	2.6	4.0	1.1	2.5	4.0	1.1	2.6	4.1	1.0
30 - 34	3.4	5.3	1.5	3.4	5.3	1.6	3.4	5.3	1.3
35 - 39	4.7	7.6	2.0	4.6	7.6	2.0	4.9	7.6	2.0
40 - 44	6.4	10.3	2.8	6.2	10.3	2.7	6.8	10.5	2.9
45 - 49	9.2	14.9	4.3	8.9	14.7	4.1	10.0	15.4	4.6
50 - 54	12.5	19.8	6.4	12.3	19.6	6.3	13.2	20.2	6.8
55 - 59	17.9	28.1	10.1	17.5	27.6	9.8	18.7	29.2	10.7
60 - 64	24.6	38.5	14.7	24.3	38.0	14.6	25.1	39.4	14.9
65 - 69	33.3	48.9	22.8	33.6	48.9	23.1	32.8	48.9	22.2
70 - 74	51.2	72.3	39.3	52.7	73.2	40.7	49.2	70.9	37.5
75 - 79	72.6	95.5	63.8	73.0	93.9	64.7	72.1	97.8	62.7
80 - 84	116.0	139.5	108.7	117.5	138.4	110.3	114.3	141.0	106.7
85 - 89	206.8	236.7	199.3	202.8	229.2	195.4	211.6	247.7	203.6
90 - 94	310.2	344.3	302.4	315.9	343.1	309.0	304.6	345.8	296.1
95 - 99	421.3	438.2	418.1	411.0	420.7	408.9	430.9	457.0	426.4
100 +	584.9	758.8	559.3	574.9	735.8	544.1	592.3	784.9	569.8
2004 (C)									
Total	16.1	17.9	14.5	...	...	...	...	...	...
0	9.7	11.0	8.3	...	...	...	...	...	...
1 - 4	0.7	0.8	0.7	...	...	...	...	...	...

20. Death rates specific for age, sex and urban/rural residence: latest available year, 1996 - 2005
Taux de mortalité selon l'âge, le sexe et la résidence, urbaine/rurale: dernière année disponible, 1996 - 2005 (continued - suite)

Continent, country or area, date, code and age (in years) / Continent, pays ou zone, date, code et âge (en années)	Total			Urban - Urbaine			Rural - Rurale		
	Both sexes Les deux sexes	Male Masculin	Female Féminin	Both sexes Les deux sexes	Male Masculin	Female Féminin	Both sexes Les deux sexes	Male Masculin	Female Féminin
EUROPE									
Ukraine[34]									
2004 (C)									
5 - 9	0.4	0.4	0.3	...	...	...	...	...	...
10 - 14	0.3	0.4	0.2	...	...	...	...	...	...
15 - 19	0.7	1.0	0.4	...	...	...	...	...	...
20 - 24	1.5	2.3	0.7	...	...	...	...	...	...
25 - 29	2.6	4.0	1.2	...	...	...	...	...	...
30 - 34	3.7	5.8	1.7	...	...	...	...	...	...
35 - 39	5.3	8.2	2.4	...	...	...	...	...	...
40 - 44	7.2	11.7	3.2	...	...	...	...	...	...
45 - 49	10.0	16.2	4.7	...	...	...	...	...	...
50 - 54	13.9	22.1	7.0	...	...	...	...	...	...
55 - 59	18.1	28.5	10.1	...	...	...	...	...	...
60 - 64	25.6	40.6	15.2	...	...	...	...	...	...
65 - 69	34.5	52.3	23.0	...	...	...	...	...	...
70 - 74	50.5	71.8	38.4	...	...	...	...	...	...
75 - 79	75.5	101.1	64.4	...	...	...	...	...	...
80 - 84	116.5	141.7	108.8	...	...	...	...	...	...
85 - 89	190.7	214.7	184.5	...	...	...	...	...	...
90 - 94	289.6	305.3	286.2	...	...	...	...	...	...
95 - 99	468.3	505.5	461.0	...	...	...	...	...	...
100 +	452.9	538.6	439.3	...	...	...	...	...	...
United Kingdom - Royaume-Uni									
2003* (C)									
Total	10.3	9.9	10.6	...	...	...	...	...	...
0	5.4	5.8	5.0	...	...	...	...	...	...
1 - 4	0.2	0.3	0.2	...	...	...	...	...	...
5 - 9	0.1	0.1	0.1	...	...	...	...	...	...
10 - 14	0.1	0.1	0.1	...	...	...	...	...	...
15 - 19	0.4	0.5	0.2	...	...	...	...	...	...
20 - 24	0.5	0.8	0.3	...	...	...	...	...	...
25 - 29	0.6	0.9	0.4	...	...	...	...	...	...
30 - 34	0.8	1.0	0.5	...	...	...	...	...	...
35 - 39	1.0	1.4	0.7	...	...	...	...	...	...
40 - 44	1.6	2.0	1.2	...	...	...	...	...	...
45 - 49	2.5	3.0	2.0	...	...	...	...	...	...
50 - 54	4.0	4.8	3.1	...	...	...	...	...	...
55 - 59	6.1	7.5	4.8	...	...	...	...	...	...
60 - 64	10.3	13.0	7.8	...	...	...	...	...	...
65 - 69	16.5	20.6	12.7	...	...	...	...	...	...
70 - 74	27.7	34.6	21.9	...	...	...	...	...	...
75 - 79	47.6	59.0	39.2	...	...	...	...	...	...
80 - 84	77.7	95.5	67.0	...	...	...	...	...	...
85 - 89	136.0	162.0	124.3	...	...	...	...	...	...
90 +	240.2	261.5	233.6	...	...	...	...	...	...
OCEANIA - OCÉANIE									
Australia - Australie									
2004 (+C)									
Total	6.6	6.8	6.3	...	...	...	...	...	...
0	4.7	5.2	4.2	...	...	...	...	...	...
1 - 4	0.3	0.3	0.2	...	...	...	...	...	...
5 - 9	0.1	0.1	0.1	...	...	...	...	...	...
10 - 14	0.1	0.1	0.1	...	...	...	...	...	...
15 - 19	0.4	0.5	0.3	...	...	...	...	...	...
20 - 24	0.6	0.8	0.3	...	...	...	...	...	...
25 - 29	0.7	0.9	0.4	...	...	...	...	...	...
30 - 34	0.8	1.2	0.4	...	...	...	...	...	...
35 - 39	0.9	1.2	0.6	...	...	...	...	...	...
40 - 44	1.3	1.7	0.9	...	...	...	...	...	...
45 - 49	2.0	2.4	1.6	...	...	...	...	...	...
50 - 54	2.9	3.6	2.1	...	...	...	...	...	...

Continent, country or area, date, code and age (in years) / Continent, pays ou zone, date, code et âge (en années)	Total			Urban - Urbaine			Rural - Rurale		
	Both sexes Les deux sexes	Male Masculin	Female Féminin	Both sexes Les deux sexes	Male Masculin	Female Féminin	Both sexes Les deux sexes	Male Masculin	Female Féminin
OCEANIA - OCÉANIE									
Australia - Australie									
2004 (+C)									
55 - 59	4.4	5.4	3.4	...	...	...	...	...	...
60 - 64	7.4	9.3	5.4	...	...	...	...	...	...
65 - 69	12.0	15.2	9.0	...	...	...	...	...	...
70 - 74	20.4	26.7	14.7	...	...	...	...	...	...
75 - 79	35.2	44.8	27.2	...	...	...	...	...	...
80 - 84	61.3	76.4	51.1	...	...	...	...	...	...
85 +	137.6	156.4	128.9	...	...	...	...	...	...
New Caledonia - Nouvelle-Calédonie									
2003 (C)									
Total	5.1	6.0	4.2	...	...	...	...	...	...
0	♦5.8	♦6.5	♦5.0	...	...	...	...	...	...
1 - 4	♦0.6	♦1.0	♦0.1	...	...	...	...	...	...
5 - 9	♦0.4	♦0.4	♦0.4	...	...	...	...	...	...
10 - 14	♦0.2	♦0.2	♦0.3	...	...	...	...	...	...
15 - 19	♦0.6	♦0.7	♦0.5	...	...	...	...	...	...
20 - 24	♦1.6	♦2.4	♦0.9	...	...	...	...	...	...
25 - 29	♦1.2	♦1.4	♦1.0	...	...	...	...	...	...
30 - 34	♦1.6	♦2.4	♦0.7	...	...	...	...	...	...
35 - 39	♦1.6	♦1.9	♦1.4	...	...	...	...	...	...
40 - 44	2.5	♦3.6	♦1.4	...	...	...	...	...	...
45 - 49	4.0	♦4.8	♦3.1	...	...	...	...	...	...
50 - 54	5.3	5.7	♦4.9	...	...	...	...	...	...
55 - 59	11.3	13.4	8.8	...	...	...	...	...	...
60 - 64	12.6	16.7	♦8.4	...	...	...	...	...	...
65 - 69	27.7	33.5	22.0	...	...	...	...	...	...
70 - 74	38.4	52.4	25.7	...	...	...	...	...	...
75 - 79	59.8	74.6	48.0	...	...	...	...	...	...
80 +	121.0	149.2	104.7	...	...	...	...	...	...
New Zealand - Nouvelle-Zélande[35]									
2005 (+C)									
Total	6.6	6.7	6.5	6.9^9	6.9^9	6.9^9	4.6^9	5.2^9	4.0^9
0 - 4	1.3	1.4	1.1	1.2^9	1.3^9	1.0^9	1.1^9	$♦1.1^9$	$♦1.1^9$
0	5.2	5.9	4.4	...	...	...	...	...	...
1 - 4	0.3	0.3	♦0.3	...	...	...	...	...	...
5 - 9	0.2	♦0.1	♦0.2	0.1^9	$♦0.1^9$	$♦0.2^9$	$♦0.2^9$	$♦0.1^9$	$♦0.3^9$
10 - 14	0.2	0.2	♦0.1	0.2^9	$♦0.2^9$	$♦0.1^9$	$♦0.2^9$	$♦0.2^9$	$♦0.1^9$
15 - 19	0.7	0.9	0.4	0.6^9	0.9^9	0.4^9	0.9^9	$♦1.2^9$	$♦0.6^9$
20 - 24	0.7	1.1	0.4	0.7^9	0.9^9	0.4^9	1.5^9	$♦2.1^9$	$♦0.6^9$
25 - 29	0.7	1.0	0.3	0.6^9	0.9^9	0.3^9	$♦1.1^9$	$♦1.6^9$	$♦0.5^9$
30 - 34	0.8	1.0	0.6	0.8^9	1.0^9	0.6^9	$♦0.7^9$	$♦1.1^9$	$♦0.4^9$
35 - 39	1.0	1.3	0.8	1.1^9	1.3^9	0.8^9	0.9^9	$♦1.3^9$	$♦0.6^9$
40 - 44	1.5	1.9	1.1	1.5^9	1.9^9	1.2^9	1.6^9	2.2^9	$♦1.0^9$
45 - 49	2.2	2.4	2.0	2.2^9	2.5^9	1.9^9	2.1^9	2.1^9	2.1^9
50 - 54	3.3	3.9	2.6	3.3^9	4.0^9	2.7^9	2.7^9	3.3^9	2.1^9
55 - 59	5.2	6.3	4.2	5.3^9	6.4^9	4.2^9	4.9^9	5.7^9	3.9^9
60 - 64	8.3	9.9	6.8	8.6^9	10.3^9	6.9^9	6.7^9	7.6^9	5.8^9
65 - 69	13.1	16.0	10.3	13.3^9	16.4^9	10.4^9	11.8^9	13.9^9	9.4^9
70 - 74	21.2	26.2	16.7	21.7^9	27.2^9	16.9^9	18.3^9	20.8^9	15.2^9
75 - 79	35.7	44.0	28.9	36.9^9	45.8^9	29.7^9	27.2^9	32.1^9	21.6^9
80 - 84	64.5	78.4	55.3	66.2^9	81.7^9	56.4^9	47.2^9	53.3^9	41.5^9
85 +[9]	...	...	...	145.6	160.2	139.2	85.2	97.9	77.3
85 - 89	107.0	128.8	96.2	...	...	...	...	...	...
90 +	208.6	216.7	205.7	...	...	...	...	...	...

FOOTNOTES - NOTES

♦ Rates based on 30 or fewer deaths. - Taux basés sur 30 décès ou moins.

* Provisional. - Données provisoires.

'Code' indicates the source of data, as follows:
C - Civil registration, estimated over 90% complete
U - Civil registration, estimated less than 90% complete
| - Other source, estimated reliable

+ - Data tabulated by date of registration rather than occurence.
... - Information not available

Le 'Code' indique la source des données, comme suit:
C - Registres de l'état civil considérés complets à 90 p. 100 au moins.
U - Registres de l'état civil qui ne sont pas considérés complets à 90 p. 100 au moins.
| - Autre source, considérée pas douteuses.
+ - Données exploitées selon la date de l'enregistrement et non la date de l'événement.
... - Information pas disponible.

[1] For 2001, data refer to last twelve months preceding census in August 2001. - Pour 2001, les données se rapportent aux douze mois précédant le recensement d'août 2001.

[2] Based on the results of the population census. - D'après les résultats du recensement de la population.

[3] Data for 1997 refer to last twelve months preceding population and housing census of 1997. - Les données pour 1997 se réfèrent au douze mois précédant le recensement de population et de l'habitat de 1997.

[4] Deaths for 2001 refer to the period January-August 2001. - Le chiffre des décès de 2001 correspond à la période allant de janvier à août 2001.

[5] Figures for male and female categories do not add up to the total, since they do not include the category "Unknown". - La somme des chiffres indiqués pour les sexes masculin et féminin n'est pas égale au total parce qu'elle n'inclut pas la catégorie " inconnue ".

[6] Excluding live-born infants who died before their birth was registered. - Non compris les enfants nés vivants décédés avant l'enregistrement de leur naissance.

[7] Data are for 12 months preceding the census date. - Les données portent sur les 12 mois précédant la date du recensement.

[8] Including Canadian residents temporarily in the United States, but excluding United States residents temporarily in Canada. - Y compris les résidents canadiens se trouvant temporairement aux Etats-Unis, mais ne comprenant pas les résidents des Etats-Unis se trouvant temporairement au Canada.

[9] Figures for urban and rural areas do not add up to the total, since they do not include the category 'Unknown residence'. - La somme des données pour la résidence urbaine et rurale n'est pas égale au total parce qu'elle n'inclue pas la catégorie 'Résidence inconnue'.

[10] Data refer to deaths of residents of the Netherlands Antilles (including those that die outside the Netherlands Antilles). Data exclude deaths by non-residents. - Ces données concernent les décès de résidents des Antilles néerlandaises (y compris ceux survenus hors des Antilles néerlandaises). Elles ne concernent pas les décès des non-résidents.

[11] Excluding Indian jungle population. - Non compris les Indiens de la jungle.

[12] Excluding infants born alive of less than 28 weeks' gestation, of less than 1 000 grams in weight and 35 centimeters in length, who die within seven days of birth. - Non compris les enfants nés vivants après moins de 28 semaines de gestations, pesant moins de 1 000 grammes, mesurant moins de 35 centimètres et décédés dans les sept jours qui ont suivi leur naissance.

[13] For 2005, data refer to last twelve months preceding census in May 2005. - Pour 2005, les données se rapportent aux douze mois précédant le recensement de mai 2005.

[14] Data refer to government controlled areas. - Les données se rapportent aux zones contrôlées par le Gouvernement.

[15] Including data for East Jerusalem and Israeli residents in certain other territories under occupation by Israeli military forces since June 1967. - Y compris les données pour Jérusalem-Est et les résidents israéliens dans certains autres territoires occupés depuis 1967 par les forces armées israéliennes.

[16] Data include 30 (preliminary figure) deaths abroad of Israeli residents who were out of the country for less than a year. - Y compris les décès à l'étranger de 30 résidents israéliens (chiffres préliminaires) qui ont quitté le pays depuis moins d'un an.

[17] Figures for male and female categories do not add up to the total, since they do not include the category "Unknown". Data include 30 (preliminary figure) deaths abroad of Israeli residents who were out of the country for less than a year. - La somme des chiffres indiqués pour les sexes masculin et féminin n'est pas égale au total parce qu'elle n'inclut pas la catégorie " inconnue ". Y compris les décès à l'étranger de 30 résidents israéliens (chiffres préliminaires) qui ont quitté le pays depuis moins d'un an.

[18] Figures for urban and rural areas do not add up to the total, since they do not include the category 'Unknown residence'. Figures for male and female categories do not add up to the total, since they do not include the category "Unknown". - La somme des données pour la résidence urbaine et rurale n'est pas égale au total parce qu'elle n'inclue pas la catégorie 'Résidence inconnue'. La somme des chiffres indiqués pour les sexes masculin et féminin n'est pas égale au total parce qu'elle n'inclut pas la catégorie " inconnue ".

[19] Data refer to Japanese nationals in Japan only. - Les données se raportent aux nationaux japonais au Japon seulement.

[20] Excluding alien armed forces, civilian aliens employed by armed forces, and foreign diplomatic personnel and their dependants. - Non compris les militaires étrangers, les civils étrangers employés par les forces armées ni le personnel diplomatique étranger et les membres de leur famille les accompagnant.

[21] For 2001, data refer to last twelve months preceding census on June 2001. - Pour 2001, les données se rapportent aux douze mois précédant le recensement juin 2001.

[22] Excluding data for the Pakistan-held part of Jammu and Kashmir, the final status of which has not yet been determined. Data based on Pakistan Demographic Survey (PDS 2003). - Non compris les données concernant la partie du Jammu et Cachemire occupée par le Pakistan dont le statut définitif n'a pas été déterminé. Données extraites de l'enquête démographique effectuée par le Pakistan en 2003.

[23] For 2004, data refer to last twelve months preceding the census in September 2004. - Pour 2004, les données se rapportent aux douze mois précédant le recensement septembre 2004.

[24] Including armed forces stationed outside the country, but excluding alien armed forces stationed in the area. - Y compris les militaires nationaux hors du pays, mais non compris les militaires étrangers en garnison sur le territoire.

[25] Excluding Faeroe Islands and Greenland. - Non compris les Iles Féroé et le Gröenland.

[26] Including nationals temporarily outside the country. - Y compris les nationaux se trouvant temporairement hors du pays.

[27] Excluding Overseas Departments, namely, French Guiana, Guadeloupe, Martinique and Reunion, shown separately. Including armed forces stationed outside the country. For ages five years and over, age classification based on year of birth rather than exact date of birth. The difference between 'Total' and the sum of 'urban' and 'rural' is due to the cases of unknown place of residence or residence abroad. - Non compris les départements d'outre mer, c'est-à-dire la Guyane française, la Guadeloupe, la Martinique et la Réunion, qui font l'objet de rubriques distinctes. Y compris les militaires nationaux hors du pays. A partir de cinq ans, le classement selon l'âge est basé sur l'année de naissances et non sur la date exacte de naissance. La différence entre le 'Total' et la somme des données selon la résidence urbaine/rurale se rapporte à la situation ou on ignore la résidence ou si la résidence est à l'étranger.

[28] Data for urban/rural residence, for the de jure population. - Les données selon la résidence urbaine/rurale, pour la population de droit.

[29] Events registered within one year of occurrence. - Evénements enregistrés dans l'année qui suit l'événement.

[30] Maltese population only. - Population Maltaise seulement.

[31] Including residents outside the country if listed in a Netherlands population register. - Y compris les résidents hors du pays, s'ils sont inscrits sur un registre de population néerlandais.

[32] Including residents temporarily outside the country. - Y compris les résidents se trouvant temporairement hors du pays.

[33] Without data for Kosovo and Metohia. - Sans les données pour le Kosovo and Metohie.

[34] Age classification based on year of birth rather than on completed years of age. Excluding infants born alive of less than 28 weeks' gestation, of less than 1 000 grams in weight and 35 centimeters in length, who die within seven days of birth. - La classification par âge est fondée sur l'année de naissance et non sur l'âge en années révolues. Non compris les enfants nés vivants après moins de 28 semaines de gestations, pesant moins de 1 000 grammes, mesurant moins de 35 centimètres et décédés dans les sept jours qui ont suivi leur naissance.

[35] For resident population only. - Pour la population résidante seulement.

Table 21

Table 21 presents deaths by month of occurrence for as many years as possible between 2001 and 2005.

Description of variables: Death is defined as the permanent disappearance of all evidence of life at any time after live birth has taken place (post-natal cessation of vital functions without capability of resuscitation).

Month of death is the calendar month when death occurred, rather than the month when the event was registered.

Statistics on the number of deaths are obtained from civil registers unless otherwise specified.

Reliability of data: Each country or area has been asked to indicate the estimated completeness of the deaths recorded in its civil register. These national assessments are indicated by the quality codes C and U that appear in the first column of this table.

C indicates that the data are estimated to be virtually complete, that is, representing at least 90 per cent of the deaths occurring each year, while U indicates that data are estimated to be incomplete, that is, representing less than 90 per cent of the deaths occurring each year. The code (...) indicates that no information was provided regarding completeness. The code (|) indicates that the source of data is not a civil register, but still reliable.

Data from civil registers which are reported as incomplete or of unknown completeness (code U or ...) are considered unreliable. They appear in italics in this table.

These quality codes apply only to data from civil registers. If a series of data for a country or area contains both data from a civil register and estimated data from, for example, a sample survey, then the code applies only to the registered data. For more information about the quality of vital statistics data in general, and the information available on the basis of the completeness estimates in particular, see section 4.2 of the Introduction.

Limitations: Statistics on deaths by month are subject to the same qualifications as have been set forth for vital statistics in general and death statistics in particular as discussed in section 4 of the Introduction.

The reliability of the data is an important factor in considering the limitations. In addition, some deaths are tabulated by date of registration and not by date of occurrence; these have been indicated by a plus sign (+). Whenever the lag between the date of occurrence and date of registration is prolonged and, therefore, a large proportion of the death registrations are delayed, death statistics for any given year may be seriously affected.

As a rule, however, delays in the registration of deaths are less common and shorter than in the registration of live births.

International comparability in mortality statistics may also be affected by the exclusion of deaths of infants who were born alive but died before the registration of the birth or within the first 24 hours of life. Statistics of this type are footnoted.

Earlier data: Deaths by month have been shown in previous issues of the Demographic Yearbook featuring mortality as the special topic. Data included in this table update the series covering the period of years as follows:

Issue	Years Covered
2001	1985-2000
1985	1976-1984
1980	1971-1979
1974	1965-1973
1967	1962-1966
1951	1946-1950

Tableau 21

Le tableau 21 présente des statistiques des décès par mois pour le plus grand nombre d'années possible entre 2001 et 2005.

Description des variables: le décès est défini comme la disparition permanente de tout signe de vie à un moment quelconque postérieur à la naissance vivante (cessation des fonctions vitales après la naissance sans possibilité de réanimation).

Le mois du décès est le mois civil du décès effectif et non de son enregistrement.

Sauf indication contraire, les statistiques du nombre de décès sont établies sur la base des registres d'état civil.

Fiabilité des données : il a été demandé à chaque pays ou zone d'indiquer le degré estimé d'exhaustivité des données sur les décès figurant dans ses registres d'état civil. Ces évaluations nationales sont désignées par les codes de qualité C et U qui apparaissent dans la première colonne du tableau.

La lettre C indique que les données sont jugées à peu près complètes, c'est-à-dire qu'elles représentent au moins 90 p. 100 des décès survenus chaque année; la lettre U indique que les données sont jugées incomplètes, c'est-à-dire qu'elles représentent moins de 90 p. 100 des décès survenus chaque année. Le code (...) indique qu'aucun renseignement n'a été fourni quant à l'exhaustivité des données. Le code (|) indique que les données ne proviennent pas des registres de l'état civil mais qu'elles sont néanmoins fiables.

Les données provenant des registres d'état civil qui sont déclarées incomplètes ou dont le degré d'exhaustivité n'est pas connu (code U ou...) sont jugées douteuses. Elles apparaissent en italique dans le présent tableau.

Ces codes de qualité ne s'appliquent qu'aux données tirées des registres d'état civil. Si une série de données pour un pays ou zone contient à la fois des données provenant de ces registres et des estimations calculées, par exemple sur la base d'enquêtes par sondage, le code s'applique uniquement aux données de l'état civil. Pour plus de précisions sur la qualité des données d'état civil en général, et sur les estimations de l'exhaustivité en particulier, voir la section 4.2 de l'introduction.

Insuffisance des données : les statistiques des décès par mois appellent toutes les réserves qui ont été faites à propos des statistiques de l'état civil en général et des statistiques des décès en particulier (voir explications à la section 4 de l'introduction.).

La fiabilité des données est un facteur important en l'occurrence. Il faut également tenir compte du fait que, dans certains cas, les décès sont classés par date d'enregistrement et non par date effective; ces cas ont été identifiés par le signe(+). Lorsque le décalage entre le décès et son enregistrement est grand, c'est-à-dire qu'une forte proportion des décès fait l'objet d'un enregistrement tardif, les statistiques des décès dans l'année peuvent être sérieusement faussées.

En règle générale, toutefois, les décès sont enregistrés beaucoup plus rapidement que les naissances vivantes, et les retards sont rares.

Un autre facteur qui nuit à la comparabilité internationale des statistiques de la mortalité est la pratique qui consiste à ne pas y inclure les enfants nés vivants mais décédés avant l'enregistrement de leur naissance ou dans les 24 heures qui ont suivi la naissance. Quand tel était le cas, on l'a signalé en note à la fin du tableau.

Données publiées antérieurement: des statistiques de la mortalité mensuelle figurent déjà dans des éditions antérieures de l'Annuaire présentant mortalité comme sujet spécial. Les données présentées dans ce tableau mettent à jour les périodes d'années suivantes :

Edition	Années considérées
2001	1985-2000
1985	1976-1984
1980	1971-1979
1974	1965-1973
1967	1962-1966
1951	1946-1950

21. Deaths by month of occurence: 2001 - 2005
Décès selon le mois de décès: 2001 - 2005

Continent, country or area and year / Continent, pays ou zone et année	Code [1]	Total	Jan Jan	Feb Fév	Mar Mar	Apr Avr	May Mai	Jun Jun	Jul Jui	Aug Aoû	Sep Sep	Oct Oct	Nov Nov	Dec Déc
AFRICA — AFRIQUE														
Algeria - Algérie [2,3]														
2002	U	126 557	12 728	10 470	11 579	10 476	9 547	9 099	9 891	10 227	9 728	10 331	10 635	11 846
Egypt - Égypte														
2003	C	440 149	43 203	37 971	38 195	33 968	34 139	34 900	35 801	36 093	34 252	34 395	37 950	39 282
2004	C	440 790	44 292	39 523	37 252	33 265	35 157	33 554	35 198	35 516	34 334	36 097	36 807	39 795
2005	C	450 646	46 693	36 943	36 604	35 114	36 759	35 145	37 126	38 908	35 098	36 373	37 275	38 608
Ghana														
2002	...	34 682	4 066	3 665	3 771	3 673	4 094	3 937	4 448	3 081	2 564	805	283	295
Libyan Arab Jamahiriya - Jamahiriya arabe libyenne														
2002	U	19 362	1 728	1 452	1 541	1 482	1 371	1 434	1 658	1 688	1 640	1 713	1 749	1 906
Mauritius - Maurice														
2001	+C	7 983	740	580	587	575	607	692	783	727	690	687	639	676
2002	+C	8 310	705	593	764	734	679	676	713	776	725	674	677	594
2003	+C	8 520	736	632	649	721	642	697	866	854	685	720	624	694
2004	+C	8 475	661	653	703	679	704	753	786	780	686	766	656	648
2005	+C	8 646	759	637	750	671	700	682	784	806	748	747	664	698
Réunion [2]														
2001	C	3 829	358	279	341	275	297	336	359	318	315	335	324	292
2002	C	4 004	329	321	383	319	315	331	338	342	346	315	323	342
2003	C	4 022	372	306	311	310	301	310	365	405	335	368	330	309
Saint Helena ex. dep. - Sainte-Hélène sans dép.														
2001	C	41	3	3	3	1	2	2	4	6	3	5	5	4
2002	C	52	4	4	10	3	5	1	6	4	4	5	4	2
2003	C	44	2	5	3	1	5	5	5	4	3	8	1	2
2004	C	33	3	2	4	3	2	3	1	2	3	3	5	2
2005	C	39	3	6	3	2	3	4	4	4	4	1	2	3
AMERICA, NORTH — AMERIQUE DU NORD														
Aruba														
2002	C	489	47	30	52	39	31	26	46	52	35	43	42	46
2003	C	501	44	35	51	38	40	45	38	33	34	42	47	54
2004	C	502	41	40	52	43	34	46	51	34	37	32	36	56
2005	C	482	41	37	38	52	28	36	47	26	41	39	41	56
Bahamas														
2001	C	1 609	169	113	135	120	139	135	140	139	120	127	124	148
Barbados - Barbade														
2002	+C	2 285	253	203	184	213	220	171	186	169	154	204	164	164
Canada [4]														
2001	C	219 538	20 429	18 046	19 511	18 170	18 215	17 602	17 541	17 676	16 942	18 524	17 872	19 010
2002	C	223 603	20 165	18 546	20 088	18 314	18 542	17 274	18 448	17 983	17 010	18 414	18 733	20 086
2003	C	226 169	20 621	17 850	19 919	18 414	18 575	17 852	17 922	17 961	17 528	19 291	18 984	21 252
2004	C	226 584	21 796	19 343	19 913	18 935	18 152	17 752	17 921	17 313	17 547	19 204	18 507	20 201
Costa Rica														
2003	C	15 800	1 397	1 242	1 192	1 296	1 218	1 332	1 375	1 405	1 274	1 367	1 365	1 337
2004	C	15 949	1 443	1 293	1 333	1 228	1 286	1 271	1 311	1 320	1 322	1 415	1 331	1 396
2005	C	16 139	1 442	1 223	1 335	1 333	1 377	1 345	1 412	1 332	1 224	1 342	1 362	1 412
Cuba														
2001	C	79 395	8 807	5 898	6 292	5 922	6 163	7 498	7 516	6 589	5 792	6 028	6 301	6 589
2002	C	73 882	8 193	5 489	5 855	5 510	5 735	6 977	6 995	6 132	5 389	5 610	5 864	6 133
2003	C	78 434	7 864	6 224	6 265	6 231	6 320	6 245	6 803	6 674	6 169	6 335	6 122	7 182
2004	C	81 095	7 345	6 373	6 544	6 421	6 103	6 642	6 736	7 387	6 807	6 717	6 735	7 285
2005	C	84 824	7 943	7 417	6 765	6 331	6 356	6 262	7 546	8 105	7 210	7 179	6 695	7 015
Dominican Republic - République dominicaine [5]														
2001	+U	26 636	2 537	2 214	2 332	1 977	1 933	2 294	2 327	2 399	2 125	2 017	2 169	2 310
2002	+U	26 166	2 338	2 089	2 221	2 065	2 097	2 150	2 324	2 280	2 262	2 193	1 973	2 174
2003	+U	28 343	2 347	2 147	2 556	2 377	2 433	2 334	2 181	2 302	2 221	2 371	2 456	2 618
2004	+U	30 119	2 947	2 640	2 614	2 699	2 848	2 662	2 570	2 455	2 276	2 111	2 051	2 245
El Salvador														
2001	C	29 559	2 857	2 240	2 211	2 374	2 359	2 526	2 946	2 737	2 345	2 356	2 293	2 315
2002	C	27 458	2 254	2 048	2 265	2 183	2 272	2 415	2 310	2 290	2 383	2 321	2 271	2 446
2003	C	29 377	2 399	2 203	2 352	2 191	2 556	2 853	2 696	2 544	2 254	2 316	2 404	2 609

Continent, country or area and year / Continent, pays ou zone et année	Code[1]	Total	Jan	Feb Fév	Mar	Apr Avr	May Mai	Jun	Jul Jui	Aug Aoû	Sep	Oct	Nov	Dec Déc
AMERICA, NORTH — AMERIQUE DU NORD														
Greenland - Groenland														
2001	C	438	30	26	34	38	39	42	45	41	45	37	23	38
2002	C	435	43	46	30	38	37	37	33	35	31	40	36	29
2003	C	412	42	24	34	31	43	38	41	39	33	33	26	28
Guadeloupe[2]														
2001	C	2 765	228	217	263	157	304	237	231	273	229	201	212	213
2002	C	2 584	226	204	174	207	230	235	232	229	232	218	201	196
2003	C	2 636	240	215	196	229	221	201	240	230	228	227	200	209
Jamaica - Jamaïque														
2001	U	14 476	1 446	1 060	1 249	1 212	1 254	1 355	1 361	1 292	1 117	1 157	1 132	840
2002	+U	14 931	1 492	1 195	1 170	1 285	1 220	1 177	1 407	1 240	1 087	1 293	1 143	1 222
2003	+U	14 939	1 560	1 294	1 286	1 220	1 214	1 156	1 280	1 105	1 154	1 252	1 068	1 350
2004	+U	14 050	1 442	1 148	1 249	1 198	1 073	1 240	1 169	1 160	1 089	1 147	1 155	980
Martinique[2]														
2001	C	2 754	192	219	212	210	227	252	231	251	257	235	232	236
2002	C	2 681	243	220	219	202	209	201	228	260	238	228	202	231
2003	C	2 725	199	193	222	218	263	194	249	238	233	243	233	240
Mexico - Mexique[5]														
2001	+C	443 127	43 096	35 369	36 836	34 944	35 456	33 544	35 384	35 069	34 241	37 004	37 812	44 076
2002	+C	459 687	47 844	38 458	39 938	35 441	36 380	33 907	35 878	36 148	34 841	36 730	39 307	44 557
2003	+C	472 140	44 759	37 290	39 554	38 021	39 379	35 949	37 020	36 955	35 890	37 751	38 527	50 823
2004	+C	473 417	49 221	41 430	39 434	36 863	37 849	35 444	36 808	37 343	36 023	37 897	39 320	45 489
2005	+C	495 240	47 199	39 551	42 511	38 956	39 487	39 085	39 501	39 244	38 645	39 716	42 405	48 741
Netherlands Antilles - Antilles néerlandaises[6]														
2002	C	1 220	94	96	109	80	126	82	108	113	112	94	109	97
2003	C	1 374	104	120	113	97	125	100	126	107	117	117	126	122
2004	C	1 412	129	92	120	102	106	114	112	105	151	127	123	131
Nicaragua[7]														
2001	+U	12 789	1 191	1 034	1 101	1 201	1 144	1 107	1 127	1 217	1 158	1 119	1 001	389
2002	+U	15 061	1 267	1 088	1 262	1 212	1 251	1 368	1 307	1 179	1 251	1 329	1 378	1 169
2003	+U	15 379	1 228	1 055	1 241	1 261	1 347	1 298	1 348	1 395	1 293	1 312	1 270	1 331
2004	+U	15 821	1 352	1 236	1 167	1 332	1 239	1 285	1 392	1 378	1 323	1 413	1 378	1 326
2005	+U	16 770	1 162	1 263	1 411	1 313	1 409	1 559	1 646	1 475	1 391	1 429	1 326	1 386
Panama														
2001	U	12 442	1 055	934	984	948	939	975	1 091	1 069	1 163	1 138	1 075	1 071
2003	U	13 248	1 078	1 005	1 085	1 088	1 104	1 025	1 156	1 172	1 173	1 130	1 088	1 144
Puerto Rico - Porto Rico														
2002	C	28 098	2 506	2 278	2 507	2 253	2 369	2 244	2 339	2 375	2 298	2 270	2 336	2 323
2003	C	28 356	2 530	2 212	2 407	2 245	2 410	2 344	2 342	2 306	2 366	2 297	2 266	2 631
2005	C	29 701	2 947	2 569	2 590	2 395	2 469	2 440	2 355	2 391	2 383	2 362	2 340	2 460
Saint Lucia - Sainte-Lucie														
2001	C	998	91	66	93	78	72	77	69	81	86	72	87	126
2002	C	957	105	101	74	87	81	84	73	64	66	86	60	76
Saint Vincent and the Grenadines - Saint Vincent-et-les Grenadines														
2001	+C	765	57	51	86	72	72	64	53	53	69	61	62	65
2002	+C	770	64	50	60	63	77	60	76	72	63	69	59	57
2003	+C	790	67	48	73	61	67	63	64	71	64	63	59	90
2004	+C	812	82	68	55	66	76	57	58	76	57	79	59	79
2005	+C	813	67	44	68	64	77	69	76	76	76	62	60	74
Trinidad and Tobago - Trinité-et-Tobago														
2002	C	9 797	861	718	799	791	785	798	874	826	783	861	849	852
Turks Caicos Islands - Îles Turques et Caïques[5]														
2004	C	46	3	3	2	2	3	4	2	5	6	3	4	8
2005	C	53	4	2	2	3	2	3	6	8	10	2	4	7
United States - États-Unis[8]														
2001	C	2 419 960	226 976	198 968	215 850	203 027	200 929	191 547	191 578	191 284	189 107	202 679	197 400	210 615

Continent, country or area and year / Continent, pays ou zone et année	C-o-d-e[1]	Total	Jan / Jan	Feb / Fév	Mar / Mar	Apr / Avr	May / Mai	Jun / Jun	Jul / Jui	Aug / Aoû	Sep / Sep	Oct / Oct	Nov / Nov	Dec / Déc
AMERICA, NORTH — AMERIQUE DU NORD														
United States - États-Unis[8]														
2002	C	2 443 387	225 981	209 433	226 471	199 782	199 866	187 688	193 274	191 023	187 561	199 975	202 310	220 023
2003	C	2 448 288	224 122	200 529	213 548	199 379	199 161	191 526	193 630	192 520	188 503	202 794	201 078	241 498
AMERICA, SOUTH — AMERIQUE DU SUD														
Brazil - Brésil[9,10]														
2001	U	928 345	79 101	70 648	76 632	74 158	80 813	79 188	86 707	83 229	79 016	79 259	74 469	65 125
2003	U	977 717	80 490	75 103	81 489	81 149	85 495	84 162	91 368	87 134	83 658	82 074	77 186	68 409
2004	U	990 953	79 916	77 742	85 992	82 163	86 990	88 638	89 269	89 367	82 187	83 127	76 805	68 757
2005	U	977 105	81 891	74 831	82 666	80 048	86 265	84 181	91 335	86 175	79 947	83 463	77 200	69 103
Chile - Chili														
2001	C	81 873	6 349	5 758	6 217	6 176	7 000	7 696	8 478	7 521	7 151	6 760	6 146	6 621
2002	C	81 079	6 581	5 639	6 178	6 409	6 862	7 261	7 798	7 334	7 338	6 832	6 359	6 488
2003	C	83 672	6 736	5 779	6 297	6 516	7 405	7 155	8 246	8 239	7 163	6 942	6 577	6 617
Colombia - Colombie[11]														
2001	U	191 513	16 828	14 691	16 254	15 826	16 242	15 816	16 087	16 165	15 468	15 835	15 621	16 680
2002	U	192 262	17 133	14 721	15 940	15 503	16 312	16 281	16 279	16 377	15 223	16 012	15 905	16 576
2003	U	193 267	17 239	14 158	15 851	15 243	16 388	16 333	16 816	16 166	15 263	16 000	16 466	17 344
2004	U	188 933	16 611	14 649	15 340	15 076	16 127	15 793	16 058	16 213	15 232	15 722	15 575	16 537
2005	U	188 795	16 529	14 022	15 781	14 795	15 787	15 578	16 026	15 537	15 216	15 989	16 252	17 283
French Guiana - Guyane française[2]														
2001	C	668	56	55	50	55	40	62	62	51	52	64	65	56
2002	C	656	63	61	57	29	41	66	70	46	62	56	57	48
2003	C	692	62	56	63	46	62	66	75	59	61	57	47	38
Paraguay														
2003	U	19 593	1 678	1 445	1 577	1 701	1 568	1 600	1 776	1 809	1 822	1 626	1 476	1 515
2004	U	20 283	1 683	1 347	1 580	1 614	1 931	2 060	1 878	1 979	1 639	1 515	1 564	1 493
2005	U	17 360	1 677	1 358	1 427	1 302	1 452	1 424	1 678	1 590	1 550	1 331	1 319	1 252
Peru - Pérou[9,12]														
2001	+U	79 901	9 417	6 030	6 620	6 346	6 507	6 498	6 472	6 889	6 750	6 401	6 282	5 689
Suriname														
2001	C	3 099	263	270	262	254	262	222	263	265	266	213	263	296
2002	C	3 125	273	214	264	220	260	274	286	272	270	263	284	245
2003	C	3 154	278	218	244	264	261	265	263	309	264	266	253	269
2004	C	3 319	293	246	283	248	261	273	298	313	257	294	249	304
2005	C	3 392	285	257	274	310	319	297	275	277	272	296	275	255
Uruguay														
2004	C	32 154	2 556	2 210	2 411	2 472	2 825	3 303	3 636	3 086	2 701	2 561	2 467	1 926
ASIA — ASIE														
Armenia - Arménie[13]														
2001	C	24 003	2 340	3 015	2 564	2 005	2 780	1 659	1 815	1 955	1 436	1 874	1 217	1 343
2003	C	26 014	3 664	3 124	2 385	3 930	2 103	1 805	1 926	1 535	1 358	1 372	1 349	1 463
2004	C	25 679	2 475	3 025	2 658	4 864	1 950	1 802	1 777	1 519	1 359	1 460	1 378	1 412
2005	C	26 379	2 593	3 006	2 217	5 552	2 030	1 676	1 759	1 563	1 468	1 560	1 454	1 501
Azerbaijan - Azerbaïdjan[13]														
2002	+C	46 522	4 559	3 946	4 089	4 315	3 737	3 610	4 004	3 559	3 426	4 030	4 035	3 212
2003	+C	49 001	5 004	4 260	4 885	4 969	4 175	3 717	3 811	3 544	3 568	3 676	3 601	3 791
2004	+C	49 568	4 813	4 624	4 586	4 266	3 869	3 805	3 877	3 822	3 782	3 744	3 971	4 409
2005	+C	51 962	4 958	4 592	4 944	4 534	4 109	4 000	4 126	4 337	3 826	3 974	4 179	4 383
Brunei Darussalam - Brunéi Darussalam														
2001	+C	1 014	89	64	77	93	71	84	78	99	87	104	84	84
2002	+C	1 041	87	73	81	105	87	81	85	95	93	88	76	90
2003	+C	1 010	67	63	84	101	67	88	97	79	93	98	69	104
2004	+C	1 010	70	50	98	87	82	99	91	89	99	94	70	81
China: Hong Kong SAR - Chine: Hong Kong RAS[5]														
2001	C	33 378	2 984	2 830	2 870	2 763	2 773	2 598	2 695	2 732	2 581	2 740	2 721	3 091
2002	C	34 267	3 263	3 127	2 979	2 772	2 924	2 638	2 758	2 667	2 576	2 699	2 734	3 074

21. Deaths by month of occurence: 2001 - 2005
Décès selon le mois de décès: 2001 - 2005 (continued — suite)

Continent, country or area and year / Continent, pays ou zone et année	C-o-d-e[1]	Total	Jan / Jan	Feb / Fév	Mar / Mar	Apr / Avr	May / Mai	Jun / Jun	Jul / Jui	Aug / Aoû	Sep / Sep	Oct / Oct	Nov / Nov	Dec / Déc
ASIA — ASIE														
China: Hong Kong SAR - Chine: Hong Kong RAS[5]														
2003	C	36 971	3 617	3 114	3 267	3 458	3 222	2 845	2 800	2 641	2 785	2 939	2 827	3 423
2004	C	36 918	3 717	3 551	3 142	3 032	2 882	2 783	3 038	2 919	2 827	2 934	2 868	3 203
2005	C	38 830	3 822	3 257	3 976	3 312	3 342	3 147	2 980	2 781	2 768	2 941	2 882	3 596
China: Macao SAR - Chine: Macao RAS														
2001	C	1 327	136	102	116	103	131	94	101	103	113	117	99	112
2002	C	1 415	152	124	106	122	106	109	103	102	113	122	106	150
2003	C	1 474	153	124	137	130	116	117	114	102	108	122	104	147
2004	C	1 533	151	170	112	105	115	116	119	136	138	120	125	126
2005	C	1 615	167	122	165	143	135	121	131	125	114	107	136	149
Cyprus - Chypre[5,14]														
2002	C	5 168	520	423	484	408	433	398	470	388	368	372	420	484
2003	C	5 200	457	454	512	437	414	388	381	382	330	399	388	526
2004	C	5 225	543	479	488	408	431	393	428	394	399	350	422	490
2005	C	5 425	537	509	496	434	450	352	407	476	405	437	478	444
Iran (Islamic Republic of) - Iran (République islamique d')														
2001	C	432 291	38 172	35 557	31 139	25 378	40 458	31 660	48 288	48 972	34 471	30 490	34 437	33 269
2002	C	340 920	35 410	31 483	27 209	25 790	29 811	28 006	29 082	28 793	25 354	26 543	27 088	26 351
2003	C	340 946	32 273	30 979	27 167	27 196	28 344	27 317	28 415	27 329	28 037	27 120	26 577	30 192
2004	C	382 290	38 365	45 088	34 544	28 809	32 260	29 708	28 448	28 293	27 813	28 781	28 265	31 916
Israel - Israël[15,16]														
2001	C	37 184	3 439	3 277	3 394	3 051	2 982	2 685	2 840	2 999	2 817	3 125	3 109	3 466
2002	C	38 376	4 039	3 681	3 433	3 072	3 058	2 917	2 897	3 034	2 893	2 964	3 090	3 298
2003	C	38 499	3 528	3 261	3 644	3 118	3 137	2 907	2 960	2 940	2 939	3 045	3 272	3 748
2004	C	37 939	3 776	3 312	3 437	3 032	2 974	2 828	2 907	2 890	2 894	3 046	2 993	3 850
2005	C	38 911	4 536	3 695	3 464	3 205	3 040	2 868	2 895	2 991	2 854	3 023	3 184	3 156
Japan - Japon[17]														
2001	C	970 331	93 575	80 999	88 804	82 137	79 085	72 163	75 403	73 598	72 692	78 782	83 546	89 547
2002	C	982 379	93 827	83 225	88 232	79 637	79 132	73 275	76 520	75 725	73 617	80 087	87 069	92 033
2003	C	1 014 951	108 157	88 456	91 686	83 671	82 229	74 833	76 508	77 476	74 733	82 664	82 878	91 660
2004	C	1 028 602	99 908	92 415	91 961	83 574	82 730	75 575	79 403	79 135	76 086	85 774	86 762	95 279
2005	C	1 083 796	103 215	95 754	108 113	91 577	86 307	78 091	80 430	82 140	78 716	85 391	90 964	103 098
Kazakhstan[5,13]														
2001	C	147 876	13 531	11 828	12 574	12 343	12 947	11 816	11 777	11 248	11 502	12 544	11 897	13 869
2002	C	149 381	14 524	11 579	12 622	12 174	13 151	12 057	12 437	12 078	11 369	12 482	11 745	13 094
2003	C	155 277	15 784	13 858	13 543	12 616	13 018	12 394	12 224	12 133	11 648	13 008	12 172	12 813
2004	C	152 250	13 984	12 517	13 194	12 288	12 858	12 066	12 441	12 038	11 825	13 242	12 273	13 257
Korea (Republic of) - Corée (République de)[18]														
2001	C	242 730	21 068	19 660	22 125	20 927	20 384	18 696	19 432	19 303	19 122	20 965	20 573	20 475
2002	C	246 515	20 623	18 365	21 203	20 549	20 377	18 922	19 283	19 714	19 849	21 432	22 248	23 950
2003	C	245 817	21 875	19 446	20 685	20 080	20 506	18 937	19 407	19 950	20 224	21 967	21 280	21 460
2004	C	245 771	21 395	20 483	22 420	20 971	20 737	18 992	19 613	19 890	19 241	21 100	20 165	20 764
Kuwait - Koweït														
2001	C	4 364	418	382	388	333	331	338	361	347	343	372	337	414
2002	C	4 342	387	339	354	381	401	357	325	312	343	390	368	385
2003	C	4 424	403	381	377	343	294	329	338	373	345	378	426	437
2004	C	4 793	477	494	459	374	409	337	328	387	362	348	396	422
2005	C	4 784	473	371	389	368	427	380	382	372	356	411	415	440
Kyrgyzstan - Kirghizistan[5,13]														
2001	C	32 677	3 169	2 942	2 949	2 770	2 776	2 621	2 456	2 373	2 501	2 661	2 559	2 896
2002	C	35 235	3 381	3 098	3 022	2 902	3 050	2 755	2 785	2 753	2 626	2 839	2 877	3 143
2003	C	35 941	3 412	3 441	3 224	3 004	3 049	2 893	2 833	2 695	2 554	2 843	2 842	3 142
2004	C	35 061	3 365	3 049	3 139	2 984	2 915	2 754	2 621	2 689	2 496	2 953	2 965	3 127
2005	C	36 992	3 462	3 058	3 147	3 024	3 068	2 972	3 011	2 886	2 736	2 978	3 156	3 493
Lebanon - Liban														
2001	C	17 568	1 994	1 453	1 585	1 331	1 565	1 316	1 349	1 411	1 399	1 494	1 362	1 309
2002	C	17 294	1 687	1 434	1 426	1 717	1 363	1 287	1 254	1 408	1 449	1 449	1 305	1 515
2003	C	17 187	1 696	1 241	1 803	1 470	1 482	1 242	1 357	1 225	1 334	1 417	1 208	1 712
2004	C	17 774	1 882	1 490	1 781	1 355	1 203	1 358	1 416	1 450	1 464	1 351	1 354	1 670
2005	C	18 012	1 761	1 477	1 896	1 455	1 457	1 326	1 353	1 541	1 350	1 423	1 469	1 504

Continent, country or area and year / Continent, pays ou zone et année	Code[1]	Total	Jan Jan	Feb Fév	Mar Mar	Apr Avr	May Mai	Jun Jun	Jul Jui	Aug Aoû	Sep Sep	Oct Oct	Nov Nov	Dec Déc
ASIA — ASIE														
Maldives														
2001	C	1 081	80	84	98	103	78	97	93	76	95	88	83	106
2002	C	1 113	85	73	89	92	93	76	95	126	89	100	80	115
2003	C	1 022	92	86	76	84	97	85	88	88	82	85	69	90
2004	C	1 007	73	82	114	74	75	62	83	70	59	84	66	165
2005	C	1 015	101	80	91	79	87	88	89	96	75	70	81	78
Mongolia - Mongolie[19]														
2001	C	14 589	1 159	1 093	1 241	1 288	1 332	1 199	1 087	1 105	1 237	1 197	1 137	1 514
2002	C	14 933	1 343	1 246	1 185	1 344	1 292	1 295	1 226	1 067	1 187	1 237	1 213	1 298
2003	C	15 130	1 147	1 291	1 319	1 368	1 280	1 279	1 262	1 091	1 188	1 257	1 225	1 423
Occupied Palestinian Territory - Territoire palestinien occupé														
2001	U	*8 910*	*878*	*770*	*774*	*649*	*682*	*593*	*728*	*684*	*661*	*721*	*790*	*980*
2002	U	*10 265*	*1 054*	*917*	*1 033*	*983*	*774*	*663*	*728*	*809*	*692*	*816*	*797*	*999*
2003	U	*10 207*	*945*	*928*	*984*	*828*	*775*	*695*	*739*	*778*	*752*	*904*	*926*	*953*
2004	U	*10 029*	*935*	*900*	*867*	*744*	*773*	*736*	*783*	*754*	*798*	*829*	*783*	*1 127*
2005	U	*9 645*	*1 139*	*962*	*831*	*723*	*698*	*690*	*775*	*721*	*713*	*743*	*811*	*839*
Pakistan[20,21]														
2003	I	970 428	102 813	68 692	49 396	52 735	69 643	68 164	81 689	80 935	72 489	96 181	96 606	131 085
2005	I	1 019 467	82 963	93 534	80 393	58 503	66 622	72 215	85 779	80 842	83 798	103 176	76 594	135 049
Philippines														
2001	C	381 834	34 436	28 818	31 256	30 852	30 965	29 924	32 622	32 883	32 211	33 041	32 312	32 514
2002	C	396 297	36 457	29 986	31 882	30 356	31 623	30 338	37 825	38 851	32 629	32 894	31 755	31 701
2003	C	396 331	33 427	29 522	31 975	31 692	32 709	30 640	34 052	35 457	33 737	34 712	33 567	34 841
Qatar														
2001	C	1 210	108	104	91	104	97	95	97	93	96	105	103	117
2002	C	1 220	108	94	79	121	107	99	87	96	105	105	108	111
2003	C	1 311	125	102	102	104	102	106	104	96	113	123	115	119
2004	C	1 341	119	96	101	109	102	95	107	124	123	118	131	116
2005	C	1 545	141	107	132	140	128	125	109	123	125	141	124	150
Singapore - Singapour														
2001	+C	15 367	1 384	1 206	1 330	1 220	1 361	1 245	1 322	1 257	1 257	1 218	1 241	1 326
2002	+C	15 820	1 382	1 254	1 427	1 277	1 494	1 326	1 276	1 313	1 229	1 301	1 180	1 361
2003	+C	16 036	1 498	1 246	1 340	1 343	1 544	1 388	1 302	1 222	1 208	1 313	1 263	1 369
2004	+C	15 860	1 357	1 250	1 283	1 428	1 464	1 362	1 321	1 250	1 194	1 345	1 256	1 350
2005	+C	16 215	1 416	1 249	1 395	1 363	1 420	1 383	1 435	1 346	1 251	1 354	1 249	1 354
Thailand - Thaïlande														
2003	+U	*384 131*	*34 112*	*31 269*	*33 231*	*34 020*	*32 993*	*30 754*	*32 147*	*32 811*	*30 915*	*31 111*	*30 087*	*30 681*
2004	+U	*393 592*	*34 266*	*32 326*	*35 358*	*34 401*	*31 707*	*31 687*	*32 941*	*32 620*	*30 525*	*32 816*	*31 662*	*33 283*
2005	+U	*395 374*	*35 531*	*30 577*	*34 276*	*33 961*	*33 266*	*31 156*	*32 777*	*33 124*	*31 232*	*32 904*	*33 104*	*33 466*
Yemen - Yémen														
2003	...	*20 346*	*863*	*1 766*	*1 490*	*1 498*	*2 437*	*2 273*	*1 473*	*1 269*	*1 147*	*1 954*	*2 131*	*2 045*
EUROPE														
Albania - Albanie														
2004	C	17 749	2 218	1 840	1 954	1 761	1 960	1 406	1 326	1 305	1 149	1 103	761	966
Andorra - Andorre														
2004	C	281	19	21	23	21	26	20	17	28	24	29	31	22
2005	C	276	28	30	30	29	25	21	21	13	21	21	14	23
Austria - Autriche														
2001	C	74 767	6 866	5 955	6 456	6 317	6 155	5 772	5 950	6 149	5 634	6 240	6 290	6 983
2002	C	76 131	7 017	6 193	6 672	6 290	6 234	6 297	6 031	5 930	5 774	6 322	6 320	7 051
2003	C	77 209	7 162	6 932	7 680	6 206	6 214	5 935	6 184	6 178	5 785	6 297	6 118	6 518
2004	C	74 292	7 471	6 531	6 521	5 992	5 899	5 705	5 913	5 718	5 523	6 169	6 150	6 700
2005	C	75 189	7 011	7 147	7 214	6 044	6 190	5 599	5 804	5 725	5 523	6 232	6 123	6 577
Belarus - Bélarus[5,13]														
2002	C	146 655	13 840	11 781	14 414	12 424	12 201	10 725	11 523	10 154	10 770	12 751	11 854	14 202
2003	C	143 200	14 245	11 377	12 556	11 999	12 036	10 625	11 253	10 391	11 489	12 654	11 680	12 875
2004	C	140 064	14 333	11 263	11 786	11 534	11 890	10 943	10 735	10 532	10 775	12 125	11 774	12 355
2005	C	141 789	11 598	12 073	13 614	11 552	12 725	11 032	10 375	11 012	10 792	11 555	12 240	11 775
Belgium - Belgique[22]														
2001	C	103 447	10 102	8 463	9 114	8 563	8 872	8 301	8 301	8 278	7 736	7 973	8 268	9 476
2002	C	105 642	11 100	8 962	9 173	8 738	8 459	8 078	8 411	8 291	7 810	8 616	8 312	9 692
2003	C	107 628	9 997	8 956	9 419	9 319	8 479	8 401	8 423	8 521	8 421	8 659	8 554	10 479
2004	C	101 929	10 346	8 577	9 071	8 336	7 916	8 138	7 974	7 865	7 714	8 278	8 329	9 385

21. Deaths by month of occurence: 2001 - 2005
Décès selon le mois de décès: 2001 - 2005 (continued — suite)

Continent, country or area and year / Continent, pays ou zone et année	Code¹	Total	Jan Jan	Feb Fév	Mar Mar	Apr Avr	May Mai	Jun Jun	Jul Jui	Aug Août	Sep Sep	Oct Oct	Nov Nov	Dec Déc
EUROPE														
Belgium - Belgique[22]														
2005	C	102 963	9 950	9 363	10 465	8 478	8 497	8 126	7 534	7 641	7 508	8 229	8 146	9 026
Bosnia and Herzegovina - Bosnie-Herzégovine														
2003	C	31 757	2 921	2 468	3 080	2 799	2 620	2 566	2 474	2 441	2 335	2 696	2 634	2 723
2004	C	31 825	3 193	2 938	2 808	2 603	2 689	2 461	2 494	2 353	2 343	2 584	2 586	2 773
2005	C	34 402	3 191	3 148	3 545	2 874	2 947	2 614	2 570	2 608	2 424	2 753	2 892	2 836
Bulgaria - Bulgarie														
2001	C	112 368	10 508	9 134	10 133	9 700	9 361	8 681	9 032	8 276	7 769	8 774	9 774	11 226
2002	C	112 617	11 535	8 935	9 819	9 328	9 140	8 841	8 751	8 206	8 129	9 281	9 630	11 022
2003	C	111 927	10 898	10 503	11 524	9 600	9 158	8 619	8 175	8 082	7 528	8 823	8 857	10 160
2004	C	110 110	11 563	10 064	9 747	9 055	9 103	8 663	8 352	8 016	7 779	8 968	9 117	9 683
2005	C	113 374	10 001	10 758	10 807	9 488	9 392	8 375	8 560	8 306	8 042	9 348	9 579	10 718
Croatia - Croatie														
2001	C	49 552	4 410	3 916	4 269	4 008	4 084	4 006	4 067	4 011	3 789	3 972	4 197	4 823
2002	C	50 569	4 877	4 027	4 616	4 218	4 095	4 109	3 821	3 892	3 766	4 321	4 091	4 736
2003	C	52 575	4 731	4 255	5 335	4 691	4 183	4 174	4 108	4 216	3 922	4 232	4 153	4 575
2004	C	49 756	5 111	4 585	4 381	4 010	4 097	3 856	3 819	3 811	3 627	4 051	4 036	4 372
2005	C	51 790	4 672	4 688	5 285	4 301	4 328	4 020	3 925	3 821	3 697	4 132	4 208	4 713
Czech Republic - République tchèque														
2001	C	107 755	9 675	8 546	9 431	8 982	8 770	8 552	8 645	8 587	8 737	8 950	9 015	9 865
2002	C	108 243	9 768	8 390	9 385	9 401	8 773	8 667	8 595	8 792	8 458	9 208	9 013	9 793
2003	C	111 288	10 291	9 893	10 833	9 132	8 806	8 749	8 884	8 729	8 449	9 238	8 669	9 615
2004	C	107 177	10 152	9 121	9 242	8 610	8 681	8 468	8 724	8 398	8 406	9 027	8 810	9 538
2005	C	107 938	9 568	9 821	10 855	8 847	8 810	8 169	8 640	8 472	8 306	8 841	8 504	9 105
Denmark - Danemark[23]														
2001	C	58 338	5 338	4 737	5 277	5 064	4 895	4 490	4 697	4 639	4 493	4 603	4 770	5 335
2002	C	58 610	5 478	4 645	5 438	5 235	4 733	4 361	4 646	4 656	4 488	4 786	4 814	5 330
2003	C	57 574	5 492	4 732	5 400	4 884	4 617	4 369	4 475	4 501	4 408	4 747	4 466	5 483
2004	C	55 806	5 613	4 712	4 901	4 495	4 572	4 185	4 449	4 527	4 297	4 542	4 606	4 907
2005	C	54 962	4 934	4 610	5 402	4 654	4 596	4 220	4 436	4 423	4 137	4 404	4 352	4 794
Estonia - Estonie														
2001	C	18 516	1 651	1 517	1 638	1 505	1 528	1 503	1 510	1 379	1 499	1 466	1 600	1 720
2002	C	18 355	1 714	1 420	1 577	1 554	1 557	1 438	1 443	1 370	1 391	1 648	1 517	1 726
2003	C	18 152	1 869	1 441	1 709	1 532	1 443	1 364	1 460	1 310	1 374	1 499	1 442	1 709
2004	C	17 685	1 797	1 598	1 497	1 439	1 515	1 432	1 330	1 301	1 320	1 450	1 445	1 561
2005	C	17 316	1 627	1 438	1 678	1 432	1 408	1 324	1 328	1 332	1 368	1 414	1 412	1 555
Finland - Finlande[24]														
2001	C	48 550	4 143	3 865	4 173	4 127	4 087	4 135	4 034	3 885	3 908	3 922	3 978	4 293
2002	C	49 418	4 532	4 029	4 550	4 383	4 044	3 808	4 026	3 896	3 744	4 107	3 908	4 391
2003	C	48 996	4 811	3 818	4 092	4 025	3 916	3 723	3 949	3 942	3 856	3 990	3 866	5 008
2004	C	47 600	4 621	3 892	4 085	3 867	3 925	3 930	3 823	3 816	3 796	3 968	3 748	4 129
2005	C	47 928	4 205	3 866	4 598	4 017	4 160	3 831	3 895	3 707	3 804	3 850	3 768	4 227
France[25,26]														
2001	C	531 073	49 529	42 513	46 133	43 594	44 212	41 846	43 230	42 518	40 973	43 132	44 583	48 810
2002	C	535 144	55 663	45 849	46 785	44 009	42 973	42 132	42 319	40 461	40 322	44 243	43 166	47 222
2003	C	552 339	50 920	44 667	47 177	44 479	42 928	42 604	43 760	56 550	41 137	43 786	43 954	50 377
2004	C	509 429	50 377	43 446	44 993	41 464	41 337	39 021	39 975	39 091	39 360	42 660	41 530	46 175
2005	C	527 533	48 186	50 324	53 401	43 365	42 433	40 712	39 780	38 870	38 973	42 551	41 991	46 947
Germany - Allemagne														
2001	C	828 541	74 828	65 680	73 293	69 121	69 384	65 240	68 517	66 829	64 468	68 300	68 452	74 429
2003	C	853 946	79 116	72 341	83 497	70 144	68 225	66 029	68 133	73 767	64 519	68 806	66 955	72 414
2004	C	818 271	75 332	68 300	73 288	67 638	66 532	64 477	65 155	65 784	63 510	68 406	66 827	73 022
2005	C	830 227	73 561	72 275	83 271	68 245	69 328	64 485	64 725	64 075	62 261	67 033	67 339	73 629
Gibraltar[27]														
2002	C	242	18	32	33	19	18	21	15	21	12	14	15	24
2003	C	234	21	23	19	21	21	19	19	23	8	18	20	22
2004	C	242	26	17	27	18	31	16	15	19	21	14	16	22
2005	C	249	39	18	31	27	16	17	13	20	9	16	22	21
Hungary - Hongrie														
2001	C	132 183	11 721	10 398	11 150	10 730	10 863	10 542	10 794	10 476	10 430	11 084	11 275	12 720
2002	C	132 833	12 307	10 219	11 280	11 366	10 886	11 014	10 750	10 089	10 141	11 543	10 899	12 339
2003	C	135 823	12 402	11 011	14 308	11 977	10 886	10 530	10 460	10 428	10 127	11 255	10 672	11 767
2004	C	132 492	12 783	11 915	11 605	10 808	10 751	10 300	10 447	10 158	10 117	11 087	10 798	11 723
2005	C	135 732	11 710	11 322	14 198	11 651	11 318	10 469	10 719	10 177	9 992	11 237	11 015	11 924

Continent, country or area and year / Continent, pays ou zone et année	Code[1]	Total	Jan / Jan	Feb / Fév	Mar / Mar	Apr / Avr	May / Mai	Jun / Jun	Jul / Jui	Aug / Aoû	Sep / Sep	Oct / Oct	Nov / Nov	Dec / Déc
EUROPE														
Iceland - Islande														
2001	C	1 725	156	129	141	143	138	146	132	156	145	153	145	141
2002	C	1 821	143	144	202	178	146	173	122	146	136	140	153	138
2003	C	1 827	171	140	141	145	201	130	141	148	160	129	138	183
2004	C	1 824	194	155	174	145	150	132	148	161	134	126	151	154
2005	C	1 836	191	194	157	140	150	134	138	126	165	136	163	142
Ireland - Irlande[28]														
2001	+C	30 212	2 909	2 529	2 872	2 525	2 493	2 262	2 426	2 306	2 293	2 388	2 425	2 784
2002	+C	29 381	2 786	2 354	2 751	2 556	2 365	2 309	2 368	2 142	2 215	2 400	2 342	2 793
2003	+C	28 823	3 182	2 393	2 493	2 457	2 567	2 260	2 400	1 970	2 222	2 317	2 461	2 101
2004	+C	28 151	2 933	2 454	2 758	2 413	2 297	2 219	2 284	2 086	2 136	1 992	2 658	1 921
2005	+C	27 441	2 761	2 372	2 614	2 441	2 354	2 164	2 025	2 013	2 071	2 134	2 070	2 422
Italy - Italie														
2001	C	556 892	50 055	45 223	47 933	45 475	45 785	43 698	44 804	46 847	41 848	44 885	46 508	53 831
2002	C	560 390	56 705	47 666	50 142	47 549	45 036	48 567	43 077	41 023	40 353	45 969	45 244	49 059
2003	C	586 468	54 590	50 524	57 805	48 300	46 902	45 949	49 299	50 650	44 617	46 607	44 669	46 556
2004	C	545 051	51 925	49 715	49 927	44 252	44 238	42 552	43 227	41 153	39 451	44 465	44 951	49 195
2005	C	588 897	56 589	59 343	56 028	44 795	44 964	43 026	43 257	41 790	39 787	44 793	44 639	50 332
Latvia - Lettonie[13]														
2001	C	32 991	2 981	2 716	2 807	2 789	2 616	2 653	2 712	2 446	2 437	2 770	2 867	3 197
2002	C	32 498	2 982	2 622	3 019	2 891	2 755	2 433	2 516	2 410	2 442	2 858	2 597	2 973
2003	C	32 437	3 056	2 554	3 015	2 732	2 719	2 539	2 563	2 277	2 565	2 929	2 727	2 761
2004	C	32 024	3 222	2 873	2 757	2 617	2 696	2 585	2 451	2 332	2 392	2 692	2 565	2 842
2005	C	32 777	2 928	2 664	3 160	2 828	2 777	2 538	2 463	2 466	2 437	2 712	2 744	3 060
Liechtenstein														
2001	C	220	16	12	18	31	19	12	18	19	27	17	13	18
2002	C	215	18	15	24	24	17	16	16	18	14	17	20	16
2003	C	217	22	16	23	16	21	20	18	19	19	12	17	14
2004	C	198	20	13	18	11	8	19	22	15	13	16	15	28
2005	C	215	20	24	12	24	23	24	15	11	14	18	14	16
Lithuania - Lituanie[13]														
2001	C	40 399	3 724	3 203	3 449	3 314	3 316	3 240	3 223	2 940	3 078	3 593	3 415	3 904
2002	C	41 072	3 753	3 222	3 714	3 620	3 401	3 028	3 187	3 048	3 074	3 579	3 448	3 998
2003	C	40 990	3 915	3 148	3 886	3 547	3 461	3 090	3 203	2 974	3 040	3 578	3 383	3 765
2004	C	41 340	4 000	3 526	3 494	3 336	3 390	3 234	3 253	3 125	3 160	3 657	3 446	3 719
2005	C	43 799	3 789	3 436	4 208	3 724	3 823	3 413	3 392	3 387	3 310	3 720	3 668	3 929
Luxembourg														
2001	C	3 719	356	297	325	322	298	296	283	295	274	331	312	330
2002	C	3 744	354	327	323	339	308	317	293	271	265	317	310	320
2003	C	4 053	359	331	359	302	346	316	334	368	320	319	333	366
2004	C	3 578	375	315	321	284	306	268	273	282	278	293	281	302
2005	C	3 621	336	315	379	322	316	269	285	258	265	267	290	319
Malta - Malte[29]														
2001	C	2 935	282	293	260	263	230	203	237	237	190	226	232	282
2002	C	3 031	359	268	293	270	241	263	231	217	191	217	203	278
2003	C	3 072	293	294	320	255	216	245	276	225	224	181	230	313
2004	C	2 903	356	266	270	226	222	213	231	219	208	215	216	261
2005	C	3 130	319	366	351	262	242	212	234	214	208	211	211	300
Netherlands - Pays-Bas[30]														
2001	C	140 377	13 102	11 115	12 572	11 557	12 059	11 420	11 185	11 113	10 706	11 523	11 391	12 634
2002	C	142 355	13 469	11 735	13 281	11 968	11 623	11 084	11 509	11 134	10 438	11 530	11 491	13 093
2003	C	141 936	13 106	11 305	13 113	12 203	11 309	11 088	11 234	11 619	10 942	11 445	11 291	13 281
2004	C	136 553	13 726	11 300	11 983	11 092	11 093	10 692	10 786	11 166	10 553	11 103	10 969	12 090
2005	C	136 402	12 544	12 264	13 783	11 214	11 453	10 883	10 381	10 348	10 024	10 805	10 796	11 907
Norway - Norvège[31]														
2001	C	43 981	4 021	3 617	3 870	3 748	3 722	3 468	3 545	3 473	3 446	3 536	3 524	4 011
2002	C	44 465	4 194	3 691	3 989	3 492	3 614	3 331	3 587	3 385	3 472	3 654	3 815	4 241
2003	C	42 478	4 234	3 372	3 694	3 474	3 292	3 208	3 438	3 296	3 362	3 454	3 537	4 117
2004	C	41 200	4 148	3 455	3 550	3 270	3 282	3 217	3 317	3 220	3 216	3 415	3 388	3 722
2005	C	41 232	3 721	3 368	4 043	3 571	3 370	3 182	3 239	3 247	3 169	3 283	3 213	3 826
Poland - Pologne														
2001	C	363 220	33 011	28 798	31 086	29 627	29 931	28 565	29 603	28 598	28 458	30 626	30 353	34 564
2002	C	359 486	31 732	27 391	31 619	30 899	30 006	28 222	29 074	28 097	27 453	31 545	29 661	33 787
2003	C	365 230	33 809	31 147	36 552	30 275	29 207	27 953	28 804	27 654	27 781	30 855	29 529	31 664
2004	C	363 522	33 960	30 874	30 796	29 540	29 828	28 906	29 176	28 802	28 145	31 082	29 845	32 568
2005	C	368 285	32 946	30 965	35 667	30 863	31 303	28 583	29 274	28 369	27 948	30 754	29 822	31 791
Portugal														
2001	C	105 092	10 240	9 032	9 475	8 509	8 883	7 795	7 696	7 956	7 509	8 150	8 962	10 885

Continent, country or area and year / Continent, pays ou zone et année	Code[1]	Total	Jan	Feb Fév	Mar	Apr Avr	May Mai	Jun	Jul Jui	Aug Août	Sep	Oct	Nov	Dec Déc
EUROPE														
Portugal														
2002	C	106 258	11 960	10 336	9 876	8 712	8 113	7 824	8 063	7 834	7 432	8 005	8 319	9 784
2003	C	108 795	10 618	9 162	9 475	8 422	8 789	8 014	7 920	10 110	7 528	8 148	9 573	11 036
2004	C	102 010	10 330	8 913	9 591	8 508	8 119	7 732	8 005	7 441	7 354	7 814	8 462	9 741
2005	C	107 462	11 891	12 426	11 106	8 180	7 920	7 506	7 516	7 830	7 211	7 728	8 388	9 760
Republic of Moldova - République de Moldova[13]														
2001	C	40 075	4 195	3 404	3 586	3 366	3 375	2 958	2 818	2 659	2 639	3 261	3 737	4 077
2002	C	41 852	4 646	3 598	3 667	3 583	3 415	2 948	3 031	2 525	2 860	3 745	3 858	3 976
2003	C	43 079	4 948	3 775	4 036	3 767	3 479	2 987	2 875	2 818	3 104	3 702	3 792	3 796
2004	C	41 668	4 621	3 950	3 600	3 485	3 171	3 119	2 831	2 581	2 966	3 353	3 900	4 091
2005	C	44 689	4 142	3 993	4 448	3 870	3 748	3 373	2 999	3 212	3 234	3 510	3 945	4 215
Romania - Roumanie														
2001	C	259 603	24 207	20 448	23 194	22 433	21 364	19 500	19 839	18 497	18 557	21 381	23 297	26 886
2002	C	269 666	26 466	22 037	27 474	24 750	21 893	20 297	19 349	18 292	18 786	22 273	22 180	25 869
2003	C	266 575	26 020	22 649	24 821	23 901	21 785	19 965	19 156	18 214	18 347	22 166	21 890	27 661
2004	C	258 890	28 855	22 823	22 806	21 918	21 175	19 525	19 280	18 429	18 050	21 348	21 290	23 391
2005	C	262 101	23 493	22 353	25 223	22 658	23 110	20 116	20 329	18 855	18 508	21 853	22 319	23 284
Russian Federation - Fédération de Russie[5,13]														
2001	C	2 254 856	210 964	174 237	185 729	179 292	198 162	180 683	194 110	179 207	168 168	200 837	186 448	193 977
2004	C	2 295 402	220 196	187 239	191 245	186 719	197 313	184 080	182 229	180 430	178 991	196 239	188 174	200 811
2005	C	2 303 935	208 864	191 169	207 440	191 545	201 266	182 151	187 810	178 561	179 976	195 917	184 207	193 286
San Marino - Saint-Marin														
2003	+C	216	20	25	24	12	13	19	17	19	14	23	18	12
2004	+C	185	11	14	21	17	22	11	21	9	11	9	15	24
2005	+C	219	18	14	14	15	14	19	20	23	18	20	18	26
Serbia and Montenegro - Serbie-et-Montenegro[32]														
2001	C	113 063	10 409	9 205	9 763	9 227	9 376	8 846	8 929	8 450	8 628	9 485	9 843	10 902
2002	C	108 298	10 831	9 252	9 610	9 160	8 972	8 761	8 216	7 936	7 807	9 123	8 761	9 869
2003	C	109 650	9 929	9 162	11 234	9 666	8 926	8 597	8 217	8 275	8 118	9 123	8 852	9 551
Slovakia - Slovaquie														
2001	C	51 980	4 591	3 979	4 267	4 374	4 370	4 177	4 385	4 199	4 208	4 354	4 379	4 697
2002	C	51 532	4 593	3 948	4 413	4 307	4 344	4 208	4 307	4 051	4 085	4 410	4 128	4 738
2003	C	52 230	4 645	4 141	4 950	4 393	4 213	4 189	4 117	4 084	4 016	4 523	4 343	4 616
2004	C	51 852	4 905	4 277	4 431	4 098	4 286	4 104	4 215	4 041	4 045	4 467	4 319	4 664
2005	C	53 475	4 664	4 334	5 108	4 594	4 518	4 123	4 197	4 187	4 101	4 596	4 417	4 636
Slovenia - Slovénie														
2001	C	18 508	1 657	1 501	1 576	1 559	1 588	1 442	1 513	1 515	1 456	1 480	1 540	1 681
2002	C	18 701	1 764	1 420	1 574	1 542	1 544	1 596	1 468	1 465	1 542	1 661	1 504	1 621
2003	C	19 451	1 768	1 595	1 893	1 709	1 547	1 467	1 533	1 596	1 517	1 602	1 500	1 724
2004	C	18 523	1 916	1 638	1 616	1 448	1 498	1 449	1 485	1 406	1 388	1 579	1 477	1 623
2005	C	18 825	1 723	1 983	1 778	1 433	1 462	1 445	1 455	1 414	1 474	1 519	1 514	1 625
Spain - Espagne														
2001	C	360 131	32 621	29 053	31 221	28 799	30 478	28 599	29 056	29 887	26 314	28 770	30 211	35 122
2002	C	368 618	40 049	33 242	33 129	30 379	29 044	28 851	28 793	27 270	26 486	29 112	29 275	32 988
2003	C	384 828	35 814	31 863	32 431	30 596	30 332	31 816	31 288	34 729	27 569	29 859	32 370	36 161
2004	C	371 934	36 484	31 233	33 655	30 515	30 218	28 163	29 360	28 895	26 830	29 896	30 941	35 744
2005	C	387 355	48 081	37 467	37 528	30 311	29 837	28 559	28 647	27 687	26 456	29 144	29 657	33 981
Sweden - Suède[5]														
2001	C	93 752	8 693	7 471	8 313	7 970	7 900	7 471	7 643	7 320	7 282	7 583	7 705	8 401
2002	C	95 009	8 471	7 447	9 010	8 148	7 569	7 054	7 531	7 610	7 181	8 070	7 720	8 797
2003	C	92 961	9 317	7 609	8 304	7 699	7 271	6 879	7 456	7 266	7 222	7 641	7 387	8 495
2004	C	90 532	9 054	7 363	7 860	7 249	7 426	6 976	7 170	7 208	6 999	7 494	7 435	8 298
2005	C	91 710	8 217	7 868	9 333	7 968	7 430	7 142	7 186	7 112	6 892	7 147	7 143	8 066
Switzerland - Suisse														
2001	C	61 287	5 581	4 988	5 367	4 956	5 097	4 839	4 958	4 893	4 785	5 194	5 104	5 525
2003	C	63 070	5 833	5 160	6 068	5 188	4 967	5 037	4 981	5 253	4 853	5 240	4 919	5 571
2004	C	60 180	6 404	5 044	5 307	4 961	4 781	4 581	4 597	4 600	4 645	4 960	4 975	5 325
2005	C	61 124	5 752	5 948	5 872	4 816	4 823	4 703	4 529	4 581	4 502	4 856	5 066	5 676

21. Deaths by month of occurence: 2001 - 2005
Décès selon le mois de décès: 2001 - 2005 (continued — suite)

Continent, country or area and year / Continent, pays ou zone et année	Code[1]	Total	Jan Jan	Feb Fév	Mar Mar	Apr Avr	May Mai	Jun Jun	Jul Jui	Aug Aoû	Sep Sep	Oct Oct	Nov Nov	Dec Déc
EUROPE														
The Former Yugoslav Rep. of Macedonia - L'ex-République yougoslave de Macédoine														
2001	C	16 919	1 569	1 339	1 399	1 419	1 400	1 350	1 412	1 359	1 244	1 336	1 426	1 666
2002	C	17 962	1 709	1 551	1 551	1 448	1 417	1 465	1 362	1 285	1 396	1 616	1 560	1 602
2003	C	18 006	1 610	1 586	1 912	1 501	1 522	1 479	1 395	1 378	1 241	1 536	1 388	1 458
2004	C	17 944	1 746	1 627	1 574	1 519	1 491	1 403	1 429	1 344	1 277	1 436	1 491	1 607
2005	C	18 406	1 726	1 795	1 635	1 463	1 563	1 436	1 407	1 412	1 295	1 550	1 500	1 624
Ukraine[13]														
2001	C	745 952	69 876	59 100	63 213	61 380	63 504	55 222	63 417	53 863	52 655	64 998	65 815	72 909
2003	C	765 408	78 635	64 810	74 245	66 297	64 418	52 980	58 700	51 601	58 492	64 181	62 101	68 948
2004	C	761 261	77 057	63 325	67 388	62 357	58 988	59 989	56 219	55 161	56 689	63 915	67 986	72 187
2005	C	781 961	70 462	70 127	77 167	68 112	69 048	58 486	57 191	60 008	55 790	62 682	66 386	66 502
United Kingdom - Royaume-Uni														
2001	C	602 268	59 632	50 275	55 100	49 937	49 439	46 211	47 127	45 785	45 841	48 274	49 246	55 399
2002	C	606 216	62 449	49 740	52 620	49 608	48 579	46 378	47 922	45 922	45 835	50 957	49 374	56 829
2003	C	611 184	58 731	50 525	53 223	50 856	49 258	45 657	46 727	47 903	46 056	50 807	53 229	58 212
2004	C	583 082	59 283	48 731	51 698	47 407	46 681	45 191	45 345	45 395	44 362	47 665	47 052	54 269
2005	C	582 963	57 668	50 305	56 771	49 147	46 811	47 359	42 257	45 512	43 839	44 539	47 900	50 855
OCEANIA — OCEANIE														
American Samoa - Samoas américaines														
2001	C	239	14	23	30	17	14	22	15	28	18	20	16	22
2002	C	295	27	22	26	25	24	26	30	23	29	25	19	19
2003	C	257	18	21	17	27	23	25	16	24	14	27	18	27
2004	C	289	32	23	26	31	27	29	21	22	12	19	23	24
2005	C	279	32	17	24	24	22	22	20	19	29	16	20	34
Australia - Australie[33]														
2001	+C	128 758	10 035	9 131	10 007	9 911	10 893	11 299	12 131	12 000	11 096	11 222	10 463	10 570
2002	+C	133 118	10 286	9 227	10 147	10 042	11 140	11 884	13 304	13 021	11 816	11 279	10 451	10 521
2003	+C	131 866	10 039	9 097	10 369	10 163	11 033	11 272	12 083	13 263	12 405	11 293	10 445	10 404
2004	+C	132 230	10 350	9 735	10 212	10 274	11 135	11 594	12 470	12 435	11 835	11 219	10 519	10 452
2005	+C	125 351	10 143	9 223	10 067	10 260	11 017	11 470	12 372	12 720	11 309	11 088	10 063	5 619
New Caledonia - Nouvelle-Calédonie														
2001	C	1 131	112	72	85	91	97	97	103	116	94	87	93	84
2002	C	1 121	90	92	90	86	95	109	104	90	101	100	78	86
2003	C	1 121	93	83	94	88	102	97	86	105	113	86	75	99
New Zealand - Nouvelle-Zélande[33,34]														
2001	+C	27 825	2 055	1 903	2 110	2 188	2 335	2 540	2 786	2 794	2 430	2 404	2 121	2 159
2002	+C	28 065	2 256	1 997	2 171	2 142	2 402	2 481	2 688	2 716	2 535	2 360	2 143	2 174
2003	+C	28 010	2 087	1 834	2 103	2 215	2 406	2 546	2 968	2 598	2 417	2 407	2 093	2 336
2004	+C	28 419	2 109	2 050	2 228	2 129	2 258	2 425	2 657	2 645	2 981	2 555	2 132	2 250
2005	+C	27 034	2 204	1 919	2 241	2 087	2 314	2 374	2 418	2 493	2 386	2 253	2 199	2 146
Northern Mariana Islands - Îles Mariannes septentrionales														
2001	U	*150*	*10*	*11*	*16*	*8*	*18*	*12*	*13*	*15*	*15*	*10*	*11*	*11*
2002	U	*164*	*18*	*12*	*13*	*12*	*20*	*11*	*16*	*12*	*14*	*14*	*7*	*15*
Tuvalu[35]														
2001	U	*86*	*25*	*...*	*...*	*28*	*...*	*...*	*14*	*...*	*...*	*19*	*...*	*...*
2002	U	*87*	*25*	*...*	*...*	*28*	*...*	*...*	*21*	*...*	*...*	*13*	*...*	*...*
2003	U	*83*	*7*	*6*	*7*	*5*	*4*	*6*	*10*	*5*	*4*	*11*	*9*	*9*
2004	U	*89*	*21*	*...*	*...*	*30*	*...*	*...*	*20*	*...*	*...*	*18*	*...*	*...*
2005	U	*59*	*11*	*3*	*8*	*5*	*9*	*7*	*8*	*3*	*2*	*2*	*-*	*1*

FOOTNOTES - NOTES

Italics: data from civil registers which are incomplete or of unknown completeness. — *Italiques:* données incomplètes ou dont le degré d'exactitude n'est pas connu, provenant des registres de l'état civil.

[1] 'Code' indicates the source of data, as follows:
C - Civil registration, estimated over 90% complete
U - Civil registration, estimated less than 90% complete
| - Other source, estimated reliable
+ - Data tabulated by date of registration rather than occurence.

... - Information not available

Le 'Code' indique la source des données, comme suit:
C - Registres de l'état civil considérés complets à 90 p. 100 au moins.
U - Registres de l'état civil qui ne sont pas considérés complets à 90 p. 100 au moins.
| - Autre source, considérée non douteuse.
+ - Données exploitées selon la date de l'enregistrement et non la date de l'événement.
... - Information non disponible.

[2] Excluding live-born infants who died before their birth was registered. -Non compris les enfants nés vivants décédés avant l'enregistrement de leur naissance.

[3] For Algerian population only. -Pour la population algérienne seulement.

[4] Including Canadian residents temporarily in the United States, but excluding United States residents temporarily in Canada. -Y compris les résidents canadiens se trouvant temporairement aux Etats-Unis, mais ne comprenant pas les résidents des Etats-Unis se trouvant temporairement au Canada.

[5] Total includes deaths of unknown month. -Le total compris les décès dont on ignore le mois du naissance.

[6] Data refer to deaths of residents of the Netherlands Antilles (including those that died outside the Netherlands Antilles). Data exclude deaths by non-residents. -Ces données concernent les décès de résidents des Antilles néerlandaises (y compris ceux survenus hors des Antilles néerlandaises). Elles ne concernent pas les décès des non-résidents.

[7] Reason for discrepancy between these figures and corresponding figures shown elsewhere not ascertained. -On ne sait pas comment s'explique la divergence entre ces chiffres et les chiffres correspondants indiqués ailleurs.

[8] For 2001, unrevised data. -Pour 2001, les données n'ont pas été révisées.

[9] Excluding Indian jungle population. -Non compris les Indiens de la jungle.

[10] Excluding unknown sex. -Non compris sexe inconnu.

[11] Data on live births and deaths are based on a civil registration system put in place in January 1998. -Les données sur les naissances et les décès sont basées sur un système d'enregistrement des faits d'état civil mis en place en janvier 1998.

[12] Data refer to registered deaths only. -Les données se rapportent aux décès enregistrés seulement.

[13] Excluding infants born alive of less than 28 weeks' gestation, of less than 1 000 grams in weight and 35 centimeters in length, who die within seven days of birth. -Non compris les enfants nés vivants après moins de 28 semaines de gestations, pesant moins de 1 000 grammes, mesurant moins de 35 centimètres et décédés dans les sept jours qui ont suivi leur naissance.

[14] Data refer to government controlled areas. -Les données se rapportent aux zones contrôlées par le Gouvernement.

[15] Including data for East Jerusalem and Israeli residents in certain other territories under occupation by Israeli military forces since June 1967. -Y compris les données pour Jérusalem-Est et les résidents israéliens dans certains autres territoires occupés depuis 1967 par les forces armées israéliennes.

[16] As of 2002, data on deaths include deaths abroad of Israeli residents who were out of the country for less than a year (there were 109 deaths of Israelis abroad in 2002, 182(2003), 183(2004) and *30(2005)). -Depuis 2002, les données sur les décès comprennent les décès à l'étranger de résidents israéliens qui ont quitté le pays depuis moins d'un an (en 2002, 109 Israéliens sont morts à l'étranger, 182(2003) 182(2004) et *30 (2005)).

[17] Data refer to Japanese nationals in Japan only. -Les données se raportent aux nationaux japonais au Japon seulement.

[18] Excluding alien armed forces, civilian aliens employed by armed forces, and foreign diplomatic personnel and their dependants. -Non compris les militaires étrangers, les civils étrangers employés par les forces armées ni le personnel diplomatique étranger et les membres de leur famille les accompagnant.

[19] Source: Ministry of health reports. -Source: Rapports du Ministère de Santé

[20] Excluding data for the Pakistan-held part of Jammu and Kashmir, the final status of which has not yet been determined. -Non compris les données concernant la partie du Jammu et Cachemire occupée par le Pakistan dont le statut définitif n'a pas été déterminé.

[21] Data based on Pakistan Demographic Survey . -Données extraites de l'enquête démographique effectuée par le Pakistan.

[22] Including armed forces stationed outside the country, but excluding alien armed forces stationed in the area. -Y compris les militaires nationaux hors du pays, mais non compris les militaires étrangers en garnison sur le territoire.

[23] Excluding Faeroe Islands and Greenland. -Non compris les Iles Féroé et le Gröenland.

[24] Including nationals temporarily outside the country. -Y compris les nationaux se trouvant temporairement hors du pays.

[25] Excluding Overseas Departments, namely, French Guiana, Guadeloupe, Martinique and Reunion, shown separately. -Non compris les départements d'outre mer, c'est-à-dire la Guyane française, la Guadeloupe, la Martinique et la Réunion, qui font l'objet de rubriques distinctes.

[26] Including armed forces stationed outside the country. -Y compris les militaires nationaux hors du pays.

[27] Excluding armed forces. -Non compris les militaires en garnison.

[28] Events registered within one year of occurrence. -Evénements enregistrés dans l'année qui suit l'événement.

[29] Maltese population only. -Population Maltaise seulement.

[30] Including residents outside the country if listed in a Netherlands population register. -Y compris les résidents hors du pays, s'ils sont inscrits sur un registre de population néerlandais.

[31] Including residents temporarily outside the country. -Y compris les résidents se trouvant temporairement hors du pays.

[32] From 2002, without data for Kosovo and Metohia. -Après 2002, sans les données pour le Kosovo and Metohie.

[33] Data are tabulated by year and month of occurrence on data registered to 31 December of a given year. -Données exploitées selon la date de l'événement, registrées jusque le 31 Decembre.

[34] For resident population only. Data are tabulated by year and month of occurrence on data registered to 31 December of a given year. -Pour la population résidante seulement. Données exploitées selon la date de l'événement, registrées jusque le 31 Decembre.

[35] For 2001, 2002 and 2004 data for January refer to "January - March"; data for April refer to "April - June"; data for July refer to "July - September"; data for October refer to "October - December". -Pour 2001, 2002 et 2004 les données pour janvier se rapportent à "janvier - mars" ; les données pour avril se rapportent à "avril - juin" ; les données pour juillet se rapportent à "juillet - septembre" ; les données pour octobre se rapportent à "octobre - décembre".

Table 22

Table 22 presents expectation of life at specified ages for each sex for the latest available year.

Description of variables: Expectation of life, e_x is defined as the average number of years of life remaining to persons reaching age x if they continued to be subject to the mortality conditions of the period indicated in the table.

Male and female expectations are shown separately for selected ages beginning at birth (age 0) and proceeding with ages 5, 10, 15, 20, 25, 30, 35, 40, 45, 50, 55, 60, 65, 70, 75, 85, 90, 95 and 100 years.

The table shows life expectancy derived from an abridged or full life table as reported by the country or area.

Data are shown with one decimal regardless of the number of digits provided in the original computation.

Life table computation: From the demographic point of view, a life table is regarded as a theoretical model of a population that is continuously replenished by births and depleted by deaths. The model gives a complete picture of the mortality experience of a population based on the assumption that the theoretical cohort is subject, throughout its existence, to the age-specific mortality rates observed at a particular time. Thus levels of mortality prevailing at the time a life table is constructed are assumed to remain unchanged into the future until all members of the cohort have died.

Reliability of data: The values shown in this table come from official life tables. It is assumed that, if necessary, the basic data (population and deaths classified by age and sex) have been adjusted for deficiencies before their use in constructing the life tables.

Limitations: Expectation-of-life values are subject to the same qualifications as have been set forth for population statistics in general and death statistics in particular, as discussed in sections 3 and 4, respectively, of the Technical Notes. They must be interpreted strictly using the underlying assumption that surviving cohorts are subjected to the same age-specific mortality rates of the period to which the life table refers.

Earlier data: Expectation of life at specified ages for each sex has been shown in previous issues of the *Demographic Yearbook*. Data included in this table update the series covering a period of years as follows:

Issue	Years Covered
Historical Supplement CD, 1997	1948 – 1997
Special Issue on Population Ageing and the Situation of Elderly Persons, 1991	1950 – 1990
Historical Supplement, 1979	1948 – 1977
1948	1896 – 1947

Tableau 22

Le tableau 22 présente les espérances de vie à des âges déterminés, pour chaque sexe, qui correspondent à la dernière année pour laquelle on dispose de données.

Description des variables : L'espérance de vie, e_x, se définit comme le nombre moyen d'années restant à vivre aux hommes et aux femmes qui ont atteint l'âge x, à supposer qu'ils continuent de connaître les mêmes conditions de mortalité observées pendant la période sur laquelle porte le tableau.

Les chiffres sont présentés séparément pour chaque sexe à partir de la naissance (âge 0) et pour les âges suivants : 5,10, 15, 20, 25, 30, 35, 40, 45, 50, 55, 60, 65, 70, 75, 80, 85, 90, 95 et 100 ans.

Dans le tableau figurent les espérances de vie calculées selon les tables de mortalité abrégées ou complètes communiquées par les pays et les zones.

Les données sont arrondies à la première décimale, indépendamment du nombre de décimales qui figurent dans le calcul initial.

Calcul des tables de mortalité : du point de vue démographique, les tables de mortalité sont considérées comme des modèles théoriques représentant une population constamment reconstituée par les naissances et réduite par les décès. Ces modèles donnent un aperçu complet de la mortalité d'une population et reposent sur l'hypothèse que chaque cohorte théoriquement distinguée connaît, pendant toute son existence, le taux de mortalité par âge observé à un moment donné. Les mortalités correspondant à l'époque à laquelle sont calculées les tables de mortalité sont ainsi censées demeurer inchangées dans l'avenir jusqu'au décès de tous les membres de la cohorte.

Fiabilité des donnés : étant donné que les chiffres figurant dans ce tableau proviennent de tables officielles de mortalité, elles sont toutes présumées sûres. En ce qui concerne les chiffres extraits de tables officielles de mortalité, on part du principe que les données de base (effectif de la population et nombre de décès selon l'âge et le sexe) ont été ajustées, en tant que de besoin, avant de servir à l'établissement de la table de mortalité.

Insuffisance des données : les espérances de vie appellent les mêmes réserves que celles qui ont été formulées à propos des statistiques de la population en général et des statistiques de mortalité en particulier (voir les sections 3 et 4 des Notes techniques). Lorsque l'on interprète les données, il ne faut jamais perdre de vue que, par hypothèse, les cohortes de survivants sont soumises, pour chaque âge, aux conditions de mortalité de la période visée par la table de mortalité.

Données publiées antérieurement : les espérances de vie à des âges déterminés pour chaque sexe figuraient déjà dans des éditions antérieures de l'*Annuaire démographique*. Les données présentées dans le tableau 22 actualisent les données qui portaient sur les périodes suivantes :

Éditions	Années considérées
Supplément historique (CD-ROM), 1997	1948 – 1997
Édition spéciale sur le vieillissement de la population et la situation des personnes âgées, 1991	1950 – 1990
Supplément rétrospectif, 1979	1948 – 1977
1948	1896 – 1947

22. Expectation of life at specified ages for each sex: latest available year, 1996 - 2005
Espérance de vie à un âge donné pour chaque sexe: dernière année disponible, 1996 - 2005

Continent, country or area and date / Continent, pays ou zone et date	At birth - A la naissance	5	10	15	20	25	30	35	40	45	50	55	60	65	70	75	80	85	90	95	100
AFRICA - AFRIQUE																					
Algeria - Algérie[1] 2000																					
Male - Hommes	72.5	70.6	65.8	61.0	56.3	51.6	46.9	42.2	37.6	33.0	28.5	24.1	19.9	16.1	12.4	9.0	5.9	...	...	...	...
Female - Femmes	74.2	72.1	67.3	62.5	57.7	52.9	48.1	43.3	38.6	34.0	29.5	25.1	20.7	16.6	12.8	9.3	6.1	...	...	...	...
Botswana[2] 1999																					
Male - Hommes	65.7	...	...	...	...	...	...	...	...	...	...	...	...	...	...	...	...	...	...	...	...
Female - Femmes	69.0	...	...	...	...	...	...	...	...	...	...	...	...	...	...	...	...	...	...	...	...
Burkina Faso 1996																					
Male - Hommes	53.8	59.9	56.3	52.0	47.7	43.6	39.6	35.5	31.6	27.6	23.7	20.0	16.4	13.0	10.0	7.3	4.8	3.8	2.9	2.0	...
Female - Femmes	54.1	60.2	56.7	52.5	48.3	44.2	40.2	36.2	32.3	28.4	24.5	20.8	17.1	13.8	10.8	8.3	6.1	4.3	3.0	2.0	...
Djibouti 1998																					
Male - Hommes	49.0	...	...	...	...	...	...	...	...	...	...	...	...	...	...	...	...	...	...	...	...
Female - Femmes	52.0	...	...	...	...	...	...	...	...	...	...	...	...	...	...	...	...	...	...	...	...
Egypt - Égypte 2001																					
Male - Hommes	65.6	64.7	59.9	55.1	50.4	45.6	40.9	36.2	31.6	27.2	22.9	18.9	15.4	12.1	9.2	6.8	5.2	4.0	...	...	...
Female - Femmes	67.4	66.8	62.0	57.2	52.3	47.5	42.7	37.9	33.1	28.4	23.9	19.5	15.5	11.7	8.6	5.7	4.0	2.8	...	...	...
2003																					
Male - Hommes	67.9	...	...	...	...	...	...	...	...	...	...	...	...	...	...	...	...	...	...	...	...
Female - Femmes	72.3	...	...	...	...	...	...	...	...	...	...	...	...	...	...	...	...	...	...	...	...
Kenya 1989 - 1999																					
Male - Hommes	52.9	54.8	51.1	46.6	42.3	38.3	34.5	21.0	27.7	24.4	21.0	17.7	14.5	11.6	8.9	6.7	5.0	3.8	3.1	2.5	...
Female - Femmes	60.4	63.0	59.0	54.3	49.9	45.9	42.2	38.6	34.8	30.9	27.0	23.1	19.3	15.6	12.2	9.2	6.7	4.8	3.6	2.5	...
Lesotho 2001																					
Male - Hommes	48.7	...	...	...	...	...	...	...	...	...	...	...	...	...	...	...	...	...	...	...	...
Female - Femmes	56.3	...	...	...	...	...	...	...	...	...	...	...	...	...	...	...	...	...	...	...	...
Malawi 1992 - 1997																					
Male - Hommes	43.5	52.1	49.5	45.7	41.9	38.4	34.8	31.2	27.6	24.0	20.6	17.3	14.1	11.2	8.6	6.3	4.4	...	...	...	...
Female - Femmes	46.8	54.5	52.0	48.2	44.4	40.6	36.9	33.2	29.6	25.9	22.2	18.6	15.1	11.9	9.2	6.8	4.6	...	...	...	...
2003[3]																					
Male - Hommes	43.4	...	...	...	...	...	...	...	...	...	...	...	...	...	...	...	...	...	...	...	...
Female - Femmes	46.0	...	...	...	...	...	...	...	...	...	...	...	...	...	...	...	...	...	...	...	...
Mauritius - Maurice 2002 - 2004																					
Male - Hommes	68.4	64.7	59.8	54.9	50.1	45.4	40.7	36.1	31.6	27.3	23.3	19.6	16.2	13.2	10.6	8.5	6.5	5.2	...	...	...
Female - Femmes	75.3	71.4	66.5	61.5	56.7	51.8	47.0	42.2	37.4	32.8	28.3	24.0	20.1	16.7	13.3	10.5	8.1	6.1	...	...	...
Réunion 2003																					
Male - Hommes	71.3	...	...	...	...	...	...	...	...	...	...	...	...	...	...	...	...	...	...	...	...
Female - Femmes	79.8	...	...	...	...	...	...	...	...	...	...	...	...	...	...	...	...	...	...	...	...
Saint Helena ex. dep. - Sainte-Hélène sans dép. 1995 - 2004																					
Male - Hommes	71.9	68.3	63.3	...	53.6	...	44.3	...	34.6	...	25.9	...	17.7	...	10.8	...	7.5	...	...	...	...
Female - Femmes	79.1	74.4	69.8	...	60.0	...	50.0	...	40.1	...	30.8	...	22.1	...	14.7	...	8.5	...	...	...	...
South Africa - Afrique du Sud 2004																					
Male - Hommes	49.9	...	...	...	...	...	...	...	...	...	...	...	...	...	...	...	...	...	...	...	...
Female - Femmes	52.9	...	...	...	...	...	...	...	...	...	...	...	...	...	...	...	...	...	...	...	...
Swaziland[4] 1997																					
Male - Hommes	58.0	...	...	...	...	...	...	...	...	...	...	...	...	...	...	...	...	...	...	...	...
Female - Femmes	63.0	...	...	...	...	...	...	...	...	...	...	...	...	...	...	...	...	...	...	...	...
Zimbabwe 2001 - 2002																					
Male - Hommes	42.7	43.3	39.1	34.7	30.0	25.8	22.6	20.6	20.0	19.3	18.3	16.7	14.8	12.5	9.8	6.8	4.0	...	...	...	...
Female - Femmes	45.9	46.0	41.6	37.0	32.5	28.9	26.7	25.7	25.2	25.0	23.2	20.6	17.7	14.5	11.2	7.6	4.5	...	...	...	...

22. Expectation of life at specified ages for each sex: latest available year, 1996 - 2005
Espérance de vie à un âge donné pour chaque sexe: dernière année disponible, 1996 - 2005 (continued - suite)

Continent, country or area and date / Continent, pays ou zone et date	At birth - A la naissance	5	10	15	20	25	30	35	40	45	50	55	60	65	70	75	80	85	90	95	100
AMERICA, NORTH - AMÉRIQUE DU NORD																					
Aruba																					
2000																					
Male - Hommes	70.0	65.4	60.5	55.6	50.9	46.7	42.3	37.7	33.0	28.5	24.2	20.1	16.3	13.1	10.4	8.1	5.7	3.9	4.0	3.2	...
Female - Femmes	76.0	71.9	67.0	62.0	57.2	52.5	47.7	43.0	38.3	33.6	28.9	24.4	20.5	16.7	13.1	10.4	7.5	5.5	4.7	3.6	...
British Virgin Islands - Îles Vierges britanniques																					
2004																					
Male - Hommes	69.9	...	...	...	...	...	...	...	...	...	...	...	...	...	...	...	...	...	...	...	...
Female - Femmes	78.5	...	...	...	...	...	...	...	...	...	...	...	...	...	...	...	...	...	...	...	...
Canada																					
2004																					
Male - Hommes	77.8	73.3	68.3	63.4	58.6	53.8	49.0	44.2	39.5	34.8	30.2	25.8	21.6	17.7	14.1	10.9	8.1	5.9	4.3	...	...
Female - Femmes	82.6	78.0	73.1	68.1	63.2	58.3	53.4	48.5	43.6	38.8	34.2	29.6	25.2	21.0	17.0	13.3	10.0	7.2	5.1	...	...
Cuba																					
2001 - 2003																					
Male - Hommes	75.1	70.8	65.9	61.0	56.2	51.5	46.7	42.0	37.4	32.9	28.5	24.3	20.4	16.7	13.3	10.3	7.7	5.3	...	...	...
Female - Femmes	79.0	74.5	69.6	64.7	59.8	54.9	50.1	45.2	40.5	35.8	31.3	26.9	22.6	18.6	14.9	11.5	8.6	5.8	...	...	...
Dominican Republic - République dominicaine																					
1995 - 2000																					
Male - Hommes	69.9	67.7	62.9	58.1	53.4	48.8	44.2	39.7	35.2	30.8	26.5	22.4	18.5	15.0	11.8	9.1	7.1	...	...	...	...
Female - Femmes	73.1	71.2	66.4	61.6	56.8	52.1	47.3	42.7	38.1	33.5	29.1	24.8	20.7	16.9	13.3	10.3	7.9	...	...	...	...
El Salvador																					
1995 - 2000																					
Male - Hommes	66.5	64.6	59.9	55.1	50.5	46.2	42.0	37.8	33.8	29.7	25.8	22.0	18.3	14.9	11.7	8.9	6.6	...	...	...	...
Female - Femmes	72.5	70.3	65.5	60.7	56.0	51.4	46.8	42.3	37.9	33.6	29.3	25.2	21.2	17.4	13.9	10.8	8.1	...	...	...	...
2000 - 2005																					
Male - Hommes	67.7	...	...	...	...	...	...	...	...	...	...	...	...	...	...	...	...	...	...	...	...
Female - Femmes	73.7	...	...	...	...	...	...	...	...	...	...	...	...	...	...	...	...	...	...	...	...
Greenland - Groenland																					
1999 - 2003																					
Male - Hommes	64.1	60.7	55.9	51.3	47.5	43.7	39.5	35.2	30.7	26.4	22.3	18.1	14.7	11.5	9.1	7.1	5.9	5.2	...	...	...
Female - Femmes	69.5	65.5	60.6	55.9	51.4	46.9	42.4	37.8	33.1	28.6	24.4	20.4	16.4	13.4	10.5	7.8	6.2	5.3	...	...	...
Guadeloupe																					
2002																					
Male - Hommes	74.6	70.2	65.3	60.5	55.7	51.2	46.8	42.2	37.7	33.2	29.0	24.8	20.9	17.3	13.8	10.6	7.9	5.1	2.0	0.5	...
Female - Femmes	81.5	77.0	72.1	67.1	62.1	57.3	52.4	47.6	42.9	38.2	33.5	28.8	24.4	20.3	16.4	12.7	9.0	5.7	2.3	0.5	...
Guatemala																					
1995 - 2000																					
Male - Hommes	61.4	60.6	56.0	51.2	46.8	42.7	38.8	34.9	31.2	27.4	23.7	20.1	16.8	13.6	10.7	8.2	6.1	...	...	...	...
Female - Femmes	67.2	66.2	62.6	56.9	52.3	47.7	43.3	38.9	34.6	30.4	26.3	22.3	18.6	15.2	12.0	9.2	6.9	...	...	...	...
Jamaica - Jamaïque																					
2003																					
Male - Hommes	71.3	67.8	62.9	58.1	53.5	49.3	45.2	41.1	36.9	32.6	28.4	24.2	20.4	17.0	13.8	11.1	8.7	7.0	5.5	...	...
Female - Femmes	77.1	73.7	68.8	63.9	59.0	54.3	49.7	45.0	40.5	36.0	31.6	27.4	23.3	19.6	16.0	12.9	10.1	7.8	5.8	...	...
Martinique																					
2002																					
Male - Hommes	75.4	71.0	66.0	61.1	56.3	51.7	47.1	42.5	37.9	33.4	28.9	24.7	20.4	16.5	13.0	10.0	7.5	4.8	2.0	0.5	...
Female - Femmes	82.2	77.7	72.8	67.9	62.9	58.0	53.0	48.1	43.3	38.6	34.0	29.3	24.8	20.3	16.3	12.3	8.9	5.5	2.3	0.5	...
Mexico - Mexique																					
2005																					
Male - Hommes	71.9	68.5	63.6	58.7	53.9	49.3	44.8	40.3	35.9	31.6	27.4	23.5	19.8	16.4	13.4	10.7	8.4	6.4	4.8	3.4	2.5
Female - Femmes	77.4	73.7	68.7	63.8	58.9	54.1	49.2	44.4	39.7	35.1	30.6	26.3	22.2	18.4	14.9	11.8	9.1	6.8	5.0	3.5	2.5
Netherlands Antilles - Antilles néerlandaises																					
2002 - 2004																					
Male - Hommes	70.6	67.5	62.6	57.7	53.1	48.9	44.6	40.1	35.5	31.1	26.9	22.9	19.1	15.7	12.5	9.8	7.5	5.6	4.1	2.9	2.3
Female - Femmes	79.0	75.3	70.3	65.3	60.4	55.5	50.6	45.8	41.0	36.4	31.8	27.5	23.3	19.4	15.8	12.6	9.7	7.3	5.4	4.0	3.1
Nicaragua																					
2000 - 2005																					
Male - Hommes	67.2	65.3	60.6	55.7	51.2	46.8	42.5	38.2	34.0	29.9	25.9	22.1	18.5	15.2	12.1	9.4	6.9	...	...	...	...
Female - Femmes	71.9	69.5	64.8	60.0	55.3	50.6	45.9	41.3	36.8	32.4	28.1	24.0	20.2	16.6	13.3	10.3	7.5	...	...	...	...

Continent, country or area and date / Continent, pays ou zone et date	At birth - A la naissance	5	10	15	20	25	30	35	40	45	50	55	60	65	70	75	80	85	90	95	100
AMERICA, NORTH - AMÉRIQUE DU NORD																					
Panama[5]																					
2000																					
Male - Hommes	72.2	69.2	64.4	59.5	54.8	50.2	45.7	41.0	36.4	31.9	27.5	23.3	19.3	15.6	12.4	9.5	7.1	...	...	...	...
Female - Femmes	76.8	73.7	68.9	64.0	59.2	54.3	49.5	44.8	40.1	35.4	30.9	26.5	22.2	18.1	14.3	10.9	7.9	...	...	...	...
Puerto Rico - Porto Rico																					
2002 - 2004																					
Male - Hommes	73.7	69.5	64.5	59.6	54.9	50.6	46.2	41.7	37.3	33.0	28.8	24.8	21.0	17.4	14.1	11.1	8.6	6.5	4.8	3.4	2.4
Female - Femmes	81.1	76.9	71.9	67.0	62.1	57.2	52.3	47.5	42.8	38.1	33.5	29.0	24.7	20.6	16.7	13.1	10.0	7.4	5.2	3.6	2.4
Saint Kitts and Nevis - Saint-Kitts-et-Nevis																					
1998																					
Male - Hommes	68.2	65.0	60.1	55.3	50.5	45.8	41.1	36.5	32.7	28.5	24.3	20.6	16.6	13.3	11.0	9.1	6.6	4.7	3.4	2.2	0.4
Female - Femmes	70.7	67.5	62.5	57.6	52.7	48.0	43.4	38.8	34.4	29.8	25.4	21.3	17.6	14.3	11.3	8.9	6.3	4.6	3.3	2.2	0.4
Saint Lucia - Sainte-Lucie																					
2002																					
Male - Hommes	72.0	68.1	63.2	58.3	53.6	49.2	44.7	40.3	35.8	31.5	27.4	23.7	20.4	16.9	13.6	11.3	9.3	7.2	...	...	...
Female - Femmes	76.7	73.0	68.1	63.2	58.3	53.5	48.6	43.8	39.1	34.5	30.2	26.0	21.9	18.5	15.0	12.1	9.9	6.9	...	...	...
Saint Vincent and the Grenadines - Saint Vincent-et-les Grenadines																					
2001																					
Male - Hommes	66.9	63.9	59.2	54.3	49.6	45.1	40.7	36.5	32.3	28.2	24.1	19.9	16.2	12.8	9.7	7.3	4.3	4.1	...	...	...
Female - Femmes	72.9	69.3	64.5	59.5	54.7	49.8	45.2	40.7	36.1	31.7	27.3	23.0	19.0	14.6	10.8	7.3	4.1	3.6	...	...	...
Turks Caicos Islands - Îles Turques et Caïques																					
2001																					
Male - Hommes	79.0	75.3	70.3	65.3	60.3	55.8	50.8	46.0	41.2	37.1	33.0	28.4	24.3	20.8	17.5	12.5	7.5	4.1	...	...	...
Female - Femmes	77.4	72.5	67.5	62.5	57.5	52.9	48.2	43.4	38.6	33.8	29.6	25.0	20.0	17.0	13.2	11.7	10.3	8.8	...	...	...
United States - États-Unis																					
2003																					
Male - Hommes	74.8	70.4	65.5	60.6	55.8	51.2	46.5	41.9	37.3	32.8	28.5	24.4	20.4	16.8	13.5	10.5	8.0	6.0	4.4	3.2	2.3
Female - Femmes	80.1	75.7	70.7	65.8	60.9	56.0	51.2	46.4	41.6	37.0	32.4	28.0	23.8	19.8	16.0	12.6	9.6	7.2	5.2	3.7	2.6
AMERICA, SOUTH - AMÉRIQUE DU SUD																					
Argentina - Argentine																					
2000 - 2001																					
Male - Hommes	70.0	66.6	61.7	56.8	52.1	47.4	42.8	38.2	33.7	29.3	25.0	21.1	17.4	14.1	11.1	8.6	6.5	4.9	3.7	2.9	...
Female - Femmes	77.5	73.9	69.0	64.1	59.2	54.4	49.5	44.7	40.0	35.4	30.9	26.5	22.3	18.4	14.7	11.3	8.4	6.2	4.6	3.5	...
Bolivia - Bolivie																					
1995 - 2000																					
Male - Hommes	59.8	60.8	56.7	52.2	48.0	43.7	39.5	35.3	31.2	27.1	23.2	19.5	15.9	12.7	9.8	7.5	5.9	...	...	...	...
Female - Femmes	63.2	63.8	59.7	55.2	50.8	46.5	42.1	37.8	33.6	29.4	25.3	21.4	17.6	14.0	10.8	8.3	6.5	...	...	...	...
Brazil - Brésil[6]																					
2005																					
Male - Hommes	68.1	65.6	60.8	55.9	51.4	47.1	42.8	38.5	34.3	30.3	26.3	22.6	19.2	16.0	13.1	10.8	8.8	...	...	...	...
Female - Femmes	75.8	72.8	67.9	63.0	58.2	53.4	48.6	43.9	39.3	34.7	30.4	26.2	22.3	18.6	15.2	12.2	9.7	...	...	...	...
Chile - Chili																					
2001 - 2002																					
Male - Hommes	74.4	70.3	65.4	60.4	55.7	51.0	46.4	41.8	37.2	32.6	28.2	24.1	20.1	16.5	13.3	10.5	8.1	6.2	4.9	4.5	8.5
Female - Femmes	80.4	76.2	71.2	66.3	61.4	56.5	51.6	46.8	41.9	37.2	32.5	28.0	23.7	19.7	15.9	12.5	9.5	7.1	5.2	3.9	2.9
Colombia - Colombie																					
2002 - 2007																					
Male - Hommes	69.6	67.0	62.2	57.3	52.8	48.5	44.2	39.8	35.5	31.1	26.8	22.7	18.8	15.3	12.2	9.6	7.5	...	...	...	...
Female - Femmes	75.7	72.9	68.0	63.2	58.3	53.6	48.8	44.0	39.3	34.7	30.2	25.9	21.8	17.9	14.5	11.5	9.2	...	...	...	...

22. Expectation of life at specified ages for each sex: latest available year, 1996 - 2005
Espérance de vie à un âge donné pour chaque sexe: dernière année disponible, 1996 - 2005 (continued - suite)

Continent, country or area and date Continent, pays ou zone et date	At birth - A la naissance	5	10	15	20	25	30	35	40	45	50	55	60	65	70	75	80	85	90	95	100
AMERICA, SOUTH -																					
AMÉRIQUE DU SUD																					
Ecuador - Équateur[7]																					
2000 - 2005																					
Male - Hommes	71.3	68.8	64.1	59.3	54.8	50.5	46.3	42.1	37.8	33.6	29.6	25.5	21.6	17.9	14.4	11.2	8.1	...	...	...	...
Female - Femmes	77.2	74.2	69.4	64.5	59.8	55.1	50.4	45.7	41.1	36.6	32.2	27.8	23.7	19.7	15.8	12.2	8.8	...	...	...	...
French Guiana -																					
Guyane française																					
2002																					
Male - Hommes	72.5	68.7	63.8	58.9	54.2	49.7	45.0	40.7	36.3	32.1	27.9	23.8	19.8	16.4	12.8	9.7	7.3	4.8	2.0	0.5	...
Female - Femmes	79.2	75.3	70.6	65.7	60.8	55.9	51.1	46.4	41.9	37.1	32.7	28.1	23.8	19.8	15.6	12.1	8.4	4.9	2.3	0.5	...
2003																					
Male - Hommes	71.3	...	...	...	...	...	...	...	...	...	...	...	...	...	...	...	...	...	...	...	...
Female - Femmes	79.7	...	...	...	...	...	...	...	...	...	...	...	...	...	...	...	...	...	...	...	...
Paraguay																					
2000 - 2005																					
Male - Hommes	68.6	...	...	...	...	...	...	...	...	...	...	...	...	...	...	...	...	...	...	...	...
Female - Femmes	73.1	...	...	...	...	...	...	...	...	...	...	...	...	...	...	...	...	...	...	...	...
Peru - Pérou[6]																					
1995 - 2000																					
Male - Hommes	65.9	65.9	61.4	56.6	52.0	47.4	42.9	38.5	34.1	29.8	25.7	21.7	18.1	14.7	11.7	9.2	7.0	...	...	...	...
Female - Femmes	70.9	70.2	65.6	60.7	55.9	51.2	46.5	41.9	37.3	32.9	28.5	24.3	20.3	16.5	13.3	10.4	7.8	...	...	...	...
Uruguay																					
2004																					
Male - Hommes	71.7	68.1	63.2	58.3	53.5	48.8	44.1	39.4	34.7	30.1	25.7	21.6	17.9	14.5	11.5	8.8	6.6	4.7	3.3	2.5	1.8
Female - Femmes	78.9	75.3	70.3	65.4	60.5	55.6	50.8	45.9	41.2	36.5	31.9	27.5	23.3	19.2	15.3	11.6	8.6	6.0	4.2	2.9	2.2
Venezuela (Bolivarian																					
Republic of) -																					
Venezuela																					
(République																					
bolivarienne du)[6]																					
1995 - 2000																					
Male - Hommes	68.6	66.6	61.8	56.9	52.3	47.8	43.3	38.8	34.3	29.9	25.6	21.6	17.9	14.5	11.4	8.6	5.9	...	...	...	...
Female - Femmes	74.5	72.1	67.2	62.3	57.5	52.6	47.8	43.1	38.4	33.7	29.2	24.9	20.8	16.9	13.3	9.9	6.9	...	...	...	...
2002																					
Male - Hommes	70.8	...	...	...	...	...	...	...	...	...	...	...	...	...	...	...	...	...	...	...	...
Female - Femmes	76.6	...	...	...	...	...	...	...	...	...	...	...	...	...	...	...	...	...	...	...	...
ASIA - ASIE																					
Afghanistan																					
2002																					
Male - Hommes	43.0	...	...	...	...	...	...	...	...	...	...	...	...	...	...	...	...	...	...	...	...
Female - Femmes	43.0	...	...	...	...	...	...	...	...	...	...	...	...	...	...	...	...	...	...	...	...
Armenia - Arménie																					
2004																					
Male - Hommes	70.3	66.3	61.4	56.5	51.6	46.8	42.0	37.3	32.7	28.2	24.0	19.9	16.2	13.0	10.3	8.0	5.8	3.7	2.4	1.4	1.4
Female - Femmes	76.4	72.2	67.3	62.3	57.4	52.5	47.6	42.7	37.9	33.2	28.5	24.1	19.7	15.8	12.2	9.1	6.5	4.2	2.3	1.4	0.6
2005																					
Male - Hommes	70.3	...	...	...	...	...	...	...	...	...	...	...	...	...	...	...	...	...	...	...	...
Female - Femmes	76.5	...	...	...	...	...	...	...	...	...	...	...	...	...	...	...	...	...	...	...	...	...
Azerbaijan -																					
Azerbaïdjan																					
2004																					
Male - Hommes	69.6	66.1	61.3	56.4	51.5	46.8	42.1	37.5	33.0	28.6	24.4	20.4	16.7	13.7	11.2	9.1	7.5	5.5	3.9	2.7	0.9
Female - Femmes	75.2	70.9	66.1	61.2	56.3	51.4	46.6	41.8	37.0	32.3	27.7	23.3	19.0	15.3	11.9	9.1	6.8	4.8	3.2	2.0	0.8
2005																					
Male - Hommes	69.6	...	...	...	...	...	...	...	...	...	...	...	...	...	...	...	...	...	...	...	...
Female - Femmes	75.2	...	...	...	...	...	...	...	...	...	...	...	...	...	...	...	...	...	...	...	...	...
Bahrain - Bahreïn																					
2001																					
Male - Hommes	73.2	...	64.4	59.5	54.7	49.9	45.2	40.4	35.6	30.9	26.4	22.0	17.8	14.1	11.3	9.5	...	...	...	...	...
Female - Femmes	76.2	...	67.1	62.1	57.2	52.3	47.4	42.5	37.7	32.9	28.2	23.7	19.6	15.9	12.9	10.9	...	...	...	...	...
2005																					
Male - Hommes	73.1	...	...	...	...	...	...	...	...	...	...	...	...	...	...	...	...	...	...	...	...
Female - Femmes	77.3	...	...	...	...	...	...	...	...	...	...	...	...	...	...	...	...	...	...	...	...

Continent, country or area and date / Continent, pays ou zone et date	At birth - A la naissance	5	10	15	20	25	30	35	40	45	50	55	60	65	70	75	80	85	90	95	100
ASIA - ASIE																					
Bangladesh																					
2005																					
Male - Hommes	64.5	...	...	...	...	...	...	...	...	...	...	...	...	...	...	...	...	...	...	...	...
Female - Femmes	65.7	...	...	...	...	...	...	...	...	...	...	...	...	...	...	...	...	...	...	...	...
China - Chine[8,9]																					
2000																					
Male - Hommes	69.6	...	...	...	...	...	...	...	...	...	...	...	...	...	...	...	...	...	...	...	...
Female - Femmes	73.3	...	...	...	...	...	...	...	...	...	...	...	...	...	...	...	...	...	...	...	...
China: Hong Kong SAR - Chine: Hong Kong RAS																					
2005																					
Male - Hommes	78.8	74.0	69.1	64.1	59.2	54.3	49.4	44.6	39.9	35.1	30.5	26.0	21.7	17.7	14.1	10.8	8.1	6.0	4.3	3.1	2.1
Female - Femmes	84.6	79.8	74.8	69.9	64.9	60.0	55.1	50.2	45.3	40.5	35.7	31.0	26.4	21.9	17.7	13.8	10.4	7.6	5.4	3.7	2.6
China: Macao SAR - Chine: Macao RAS																					
2002 - 2005																					
Male - Hommes	77.6	73.1	68.2	63.2	58.3	53.5	48.8	44.1	39.4	34.7	30.2	25.7	21.3	17.1	13.2	9.8	7.1	4.7	2.8	1.5	1.3
Female - Femmes	82.3	77.7	72.7	67.8	62.8	57.9	53.0	48.1	43.3	38.5	33.7	28.9	24.2	19.7	15.2	11.2	8.1	5.7	3.7	2.3	2.7
Cyprus - Chypre[10]																					
2004 - 2005																					
Male - Hommes	77.0	72.4	67.5	62.5	57.8	53.0	48.3	43.6	38.8	34.1	29.5	25.0	20.7	16.7	13.1	9.7	6.9	4.8	3.3	2.3	...
Female - Femmes	81.7	77.0	72.1	67.2	62.2	57.3	52.4	47.6	42.7	37.8	33.1	28.3	23.8	19.3	15.2	11.3	8.1	5.6	4.5	3.4	...
Georgia - Géorgie																					
2004																					
Male - Hommes	67.8	64.7	59.9	55.0	50.1	45.3	40.6	36.1	31.8	27.5	23.4	19.4	16.0	12.4	9.6	6.7	4.9	2.6	...	...	...
Female - Femmes	74.9	71.9	67.0	62.1	57.1	52.2	47.4	42.6	37.8	33.1	28.5	23.9	19.7	15.5	12.1	8.7	6.1	3.8	...	...	...
2005																					
Male - Hommes	69.3	...	...	...	...	...	...	...	...	...	...	...	...	...	...	...	...	...	...	...	...
Female - Femmes	76.7	...	...	...	...	...	...	...	...	...	...	...	...	...	...	...	...	...	...	...	...
India - Inde[11]																					
2000 - 2004																					
Male - Hommes	62.1	63.3	58.8	54.1	49.5	45.0	40.5	36.1	31.8	27.6	23.6	19.9	16.5	13.4	10.8	...	...	...	...	...	...
Female - Femmes	63.7	66.7	62.2	57.6	53.1	48.7	44.2	39.7	35.3	30.8	26.5	22.4	18.6	15.2	12.2	...	...	...	...	...	...
Iran (Islamic Republic of) - Iran (République islamique d')																					
1996																					
Male - Hommes	66.1	64.6	59.9	55.1	50.5	46.0	41.4	36.8	32.3	27.9	23.7	19.8	16.2	12.9	10.1	7.7	5.7	4.2	3.1	...	...
Female - Femmes	68.4	66.8	62.1	57.3	52.7	48.0	43.5	39.0	34.5	30.1	25.8	21.7	17.8	14.3	11.1	8.4	6.2	4.5	3.2	...	...
2001																					
Male - Hommes	67.6	...	...	...	...	...	...	...	...	...	...	...	...	...	...	...	...	...	...	...	...
Female - Femmes	70.4	...	...	...	...	...	...	...	...	...	...	...	...	...	...	...	...	...	...	...	...
Iraq																					
1997																					
Male - Hommes	58.0	...	...	...	...	...	...	...	...	...	...	...	...	...	...	...	...	...	...	...	...
Female - Femmes	59.0	...	...	...	...	...	...	...	...	...	...	...	...	...	...	...	...	...	...	...	...
Israel - Israël[12]																					
2005																					
Male - Hommes	78.3	73.8	68.8	63.9	59.0	54.2	49.4	44.6	39.8	35.1	30.6	26.2	21.9	18.0	14.4	11.3	8.6	6.5	...	...	...
Female - Femmes	82.3	77.7	72.7	67.7	62.8	57.9	53.0	48.0	43.2	38.4	33.6	29.0	24.5	20.2	16.1	12.4	9.2	6.7	...	...	...
Japan - Japon[13]																					
2005																					
Male - Hommes	78.5	73.9	68.9	63.9	59.1	54.2	49.4	44.6	39.8	35.1	30.6	26.2	22.1	18.1	14.4	11.1	8.2	5.9	4.2	3.1	2.2
Female - Femmes	85.5	80.8	75.8	70.8	65.9	61.0	56.1	51.2	46.4	41.5	36.8	32.2	27.6	23.2	18.9	14.8	11.1	8.0	5.6	3.9	2.8
Jordan - Jordanie[14]																					
2005																					
Male - Hommes	70.6	...	...	...	...	...	...	...	...	...	...	...	...	...	...	...	...	...	...	...	...
Female - Femmes	72.4	...	...	...	...	...	...	...	...	...	...	...	...	...	...	...	...	...	...	...	...
Kazakhstan																					
2004																					
Male - Hommes	60.6	56.9	52.1	47.2	42.6	38.2	34.2	30.2	26.4	22.7	19.4	16.3	13.6	11.1	9.1	7.3	5.8	4.3	3.1	2.2	1.7
Female - Femmes	72.0	68.1	63.2	58.4	53.5	48.8	44.2	39.6	35.1	30.6	26.4	22.3	18.5	15.0	11.8	9.0	6.7	4.8	3.4	2.3	1.7
2005																					
Male - Hommes	60.3	...	...	...	...	...	...	...	...	...	...	...	...	...	...	...	...	...	...	...	...
Female - Femmes	71.8	...	...	...	...	...	...	...	...	...	...	...	...	...	...	...	...	...	...	...	...

22. Expectation of life at specified ages for each sex: latest available year, 1996 - 2005
Espérance de vie à un âge donné pour chaque sexe: dernière année disponible, 1996 - 2005 (continued - suite)

Continent, country or area and date / Continent, pays ou zone et date	At birth - A la naissance	5	10	15	20	25	30	35	40	45	50	55	60	65	70	75	80	85	90	95	100
ASIA - ASIE																					
Korea (Republic of) - Corée (République de)																					
2003																					
Male - Hommes	73.9	69.4	64.5	59.5	54.7	49.8	45.0	40.3	35.6	31.1	26.8	22.7	18.8	15.1	11.8	9.0	6.7	5.0	3.7	2.9	2.4
Female - Femmes	80.8	76.3	71.4	66.4	61.5	56.6	51.7	46.8	42.0	37.2	32.5	27.9	23.3	19.0	14.9	11.2	8.2	5.8	4.2	3.1	2.5
Kyrgyzstan - Kirghizistan																					
2005																					
Male - Hommes	64.2	61.7	56.8	51.9	47.1	42.4	37.9	33.7	29.5	25.6	21.8	18.2	15.0	12.3	10.1	8.1	6.5	4.8	3.5	3.0	1.5
Female - Femmes	71.9	69.2	64.3	59.4	54.5	49.7	45.0	40.3	35.7	31.2	26.8	22.6	18.7	15.1	11.9	9.1	6.8	4.8	3.5	2.9	1.4
Lao People's Democratic Republic - République démocratique populaire lao[15]																					
2005																					
Male - Hommes	55.0	...	...	...	...	...	...	...	...	...	...	...	...	...	...	...	...	...	...	...	...
Female - Femmes	63.0	...	...	...	...	...	...	...	...	...	...	...	...	...	...	...	...	...	...	...	...
Malaysia - Malaisie																					
2005																					
Male - Hommes	70.6	66.2	...	...	51.9	...	...	...	33.7	...	...	20.8	16.9	...	...	...	...	...	...	...	...
Female - Femmes	76.4	71.9	...	...	57.2	...	...	...	37.9	...	...	24.1	19.8	...	...	...	...	...	...	...	...
Maldives																					
2005																					
Male - Hommes	71.7	68.0	63.2	58.3	53.5	48.6	43.7	38.9	34.1	29.4	24.7	20.2	16.2	12.7	9.1	6.4	...	...	...	...	...
Female - Femmes	72.7	69.0	64.1	59.2	54.3	49.4	44.5	39.6	34.8	30.1	25.3	20.9	16.5	12.8	8.9	6.0	...	...	...	...	...
Mongolia - Mongolie																					
1997 - 2006																					
Male - Hommes	62.6	61.2	56.4	51.5	46.8	42.2	37.9	33.6	29.6	25.8	22.2	18.9	15.8	13.4	11.7	...	...	...	...	...	...
Female - Femmes	69.4	67.6	62.7	57.8	53.0	48.2	43.6	39.0	34.5	30.1	26.0	22.1	18.5	15.6	13.3	...	...	...	...	...	...
Nepal - Népal																					
2005																					
Male - Hommes	62.3	...	...	...	...	...	...	...	...	...	...	...	...	...	...	...	...	...	...	...	...
Female - Femmes	63.1	...	...	...	...	...	...	...	...	...	...	...	...	...	...	...	...	...	...	...	...
Occupied Palestinian Territory - Territoire palestinien occupé																					
2001																					
Male - Hommes	70.5	67.5	62.7	57.8	53.1	48.4	43.6	38.9	34.2	29.6	25.2	21.1	17.2	13.8	10.7	8.1	6.1	...	...	...	...
Female - Femmes	73.6	70.3	65.5	60.5	55.7	50.9	46.1	41.3	36.6	32.0	27.5	23.2	19.0	15.2	11.7	8.8	6.4	...	...	...	...
Oman																					
2005																					
Male - Hommes	73.2	...	...	...	...	...	...	...	...	...	...	...	...	...	...	...	...	...	...	...	...
Female - Femmes	74.4	...	...	...	...	...	...	...	...	...	...	...	...	...	...	...	...	...	...	...	...
Pakistan[16,17]																					
2003																					
Male - Hommes	64.7	66.6	61.9	57.1	52.4	47.7	43.1	38.6	34.1	29.7	25.6	21.8	18.5	15.4	11.9	...	...	...	...	...	...
Female - Femmes	65.6	67.2	62.4	57.4	52.6	48.0	43.5	38.9	34.4	30.0	25.7	21.8	18.5	15.4	12.9	...	...	...	...	...	...
Qatar																					
2003 - 2005																					
Male - Hommes	75.1	71.1	66.2	61.3	56.7	52.1	47.3	42.5	37.7	32.9	28.2	23.5	19.0	14.8	11.4	8.2	5.6	...	...	...	...
Female - Femmes	75.6	71.4	66.5	61.5	56.6	51.7	46.8	41.8	36.9	32.0	27.2	22.6	18.3	14.4	11.5	8.8	7.3	...	...	...	...
Singapore - Singapour																					
2005																					
Male - Hommes	77.9	73.1	68.1	63.2	58.3	53.4	48.5	43.7	38.9	34.2	29.5	25.1	20.9	17.0	13.5	10.4	7.4	4.6	...	...	...
Female - Femmes	81.6	76.8	71.9	66.9	62.0	57.0	52.1	47.2	42.3	37.5	32.7	28.1	23.6	19.3	15.3	11.4	7.9	4.7	...	...	...
Turkey - Turquie[18]																					
2004																					
Male - Hommes	68.8	...	...	...	...	...	...	...	...	...	...	...	...	...	...	...	...	...	...	...	...
Female - Femmes	73.6	...	...	...	...	...	...	...	...	...	...	...	...	...	...	...	...	...	...	...	...
Yemen - Yémen																					
2004																					
Male - Hommes	60.2	...	...	...	...	...	...	...	...	...	...	...	...	...	...	...	...	...	...	...	...
Female - Femmes	62.0	...	...	...	...	...	...	...	...	...	...	...	...	...	...	...	...	...	...	...	...

22. Expectation of life at specified ages for each sex: latest available year, 1996 - 2005
Espérance de vie à un âge donné pour chaque sexe: dernière année disponible, 1996 - 2005 (continued - suite)

Continent, country or area and date / Continent, pays ou zone et date	At birth - A la naissance	5	10	15	20	25	30	35	40	45	50	55	60	65	70	75	80	85	90	95	100
EUROPE																					
Albania - Albanie 2000																					
Male - Hommes	72.5	69.5	64.8	59.9	55.1	50.4	45.8	41.1	36.4	31.8	27.3	22.9	18.6	14.8	11.3	8.4	6.0	3.8	...	...	...
Female - Femmes	77.3	74.4	69.5	64.7	59.8	54.9	50.0	45.2	40.3	35.5	30.8	26.1	21.6	17.3	13.2	9.6	6.4	3.8	...	...	...
Austria - Autriche 2005																					
Male - Hommes	75.5	72.1	67.1	62.2	57.4	52.6	47.8	43.0	38.3	33.6	29.1	24.8	20.8	17.0	13.4	10.2	7.5	5.3	3.7	2.9	...
Female - Femmes	81.5	77.6	72.7	67.7	62.8	57.9	53.0	48.1	43.2	38.4	33.7	29.1	24.7	20.3	16.2	12.3	8.9	6.1	4.1	2.9	...
Belarus - Bélarus 2004																					
Male - Hommes	63.2	58.9	53.9	49.0	44.3	39.7	35.3	31.1	27.1	23.2	19.8	16.5	13.7	11.4	9.2	7.3	5.6	4.2	3.1	2.2	1.5
Female - Femmes	75.0	70.5	65.6	60.7	55.8	50.9	46.2	41.4	36.8	32.2	27.8	23.6	19.7	15.9	12.4	9.3	6.8	4.8	3.3	2.2	1.4
Belgium - Belgique 2004																					
Male - Hommes	76.5	71.8	66.9	61.9	57.1	52.4	47.6	42.8	38.1	33.4	29.0	24.7	20.6	16.8	13.2	10.0	7.3	5.1	3.6	2.5	2.1
Female - Femmes	82.4	77.7	72.8	67.8	62.9	57.9	53.0	48.1	43.3	38.5	33.9	29.4	25.0	20.7	16.5	12.6	9.2	6.4	4.4	3.1	2.2
Bosnia and Herzegovina - Bosnie-Herzégovine 2003																					
Male - Hommes	71.3	...	...	...	...	...	...	...	...	...	...	...	...	...	...	...	...	...	...	...	...
Female - Femmes	76.7	...	...	...	...	...	...	...	...	...	...	...	...	...	...	...	...	...	...	...	...
Bulgaria - Bulgarie 2003 - 2005																					
Male - Hommes	69.0	65.1	60.2	55.3	50.5	45.8	41.0	36.3	31.8	27.4	23.3	19.6	16.2	13.1	10.4	7.9	5.8	4.3	3.0	2.0	0.5
Female - Femmes	76.3	72.3	67.3	62.4	57.5	52.6	47.7	42.9	38.2	33.5	29.0	24.6	20.3	16.3	12.6	9.3	6.7	4.9	3.4	2.2	0.5
Czech Republic - République tchèque 2005																					
Male - Hommes	72.9	68.2	63.3	58.3	53.5	48.7	43.9	39.2	34.5	29.9	25.6	21.5	17.8	14.4	11.3	8.5	6.1	4.2	2.8	1.8	1.2
Female - Femmes	79.1	74.4	69.4	64.5	59.6	54.6	49.7	44.8	40.0	35.2	30.6	26.0	21.7	17.6	13.7	10.1	7.1	4.6	2.8	1.7	1.0
Denmark - Danemark[19] 2004 - 2005																					
Male - Hommes	75.6	71.1	66.1	61.2	56.3	51.5	46.7	41.9	37.2	32.5	28.1	23.8	19.8	16.0	12.5	9.5	7.0	5.0	3.5	2.5	1.7
Female - Femmes	80.2	75.6	70.7	65.7	60.8	55.8	50.9	46.0	41.2	36.4	31.8	27.3	23.0	19.0	15.1	11.8	8.8	6.3	4.3	2.9	2.1
Estonia - Estonie 2005																					
Male - Hommes	67.2	62.7	57.8	52.9	48.1	43.5	39.1	34.5	30.2	26.1	22.3	19.0	15.8	13.1	10.5	8.2	6.3	4.4	...	...	...
Female - Femmes	78.1	73.7	68.8	63.8	58.9	54.1	49.2	44.4	39.6	35.0	30.5	26.2	22.1	18.0	14.2	10.7	7.6	5.2	...	...	...
Finland - Finlande 2005																					
Male - Hommes	75.5	70.9	65.9	61.0	56.1	51.4	46.6	41.9	37.2	32.7	28.4	24.3	20.4	16.7	13.3	10.0	7.4	5.3	3.5	2.5	2.0
Female - Femmes	82.3	77.6	72.7	67.7	62.8	57.9	53.0	48.1	43.3	38.6	33.9	29.4	25.0	20.7	16.5	12.6	9.1	6.3	4.3	2.9	1.8
France[20] 2004																					
Male - Hommes	76.7	72.1	67.2	62.2	57.4	52.6	47.9	43.1	38.4	33.9	29.6	25.4	21.5	17.7	14.1	10.9	8.1	5.8	4.1	3.2	3.4
Female - Femmes	83.8	79.2	74.2	69.3	64.3	59.4	54.5	49.6	44.8	40.1	35.5	30.9	26.5	22.1	17.9	13.9	10.3	7.2	4.9	3.4	2.8
Germany - Allemagne 2003 - 2005																					
Male - Hommes	76.2	71.6	66.7	61.7	56.8	52.0	47.2	42.4	37.6	33.0	28.6	24.3	20.3	16.5	13.0	10.0	7.3	5.3	3.7	2.7	2.0
Female - Femmes	81.8	77.1	72.2	67.2	62.3	57.4	52.4	47.5	42.7	37.9	33.2	28.7	24.3	19.9	15.8	12.0	8.7	6.1	4.0	2.8	2.0
Gibraltar 2001																					
Male - Hommes	78.5	73.5	68.5	63.5	58.5	53.5	...	43.5	...	33.9	...	25.8	...	17.9	...	11.3	...	...	...	...	...
Female - Femmes	83.3	79.5	75.0	70.0	65.0	60.0	...	50.3	...	40.3	...	30.3	...	20.6	...	13.7	...	...	...	...	...
Greece - Grèce 2005																					
Male - Hommes	76.8	72.2	67.2	62.3	57.5	52.8	48.1	43.3	38.6	34.0	29.5	25.1	21.1	17.2	13.6	10.4	7.7	5.7	4.3	3.2	2.3
Female - Femmes	81.7	77.1	72.2	67.2	62.3	57.4	52.5	47.6	42.7	37.9	33.2	28.5	23.9	19.4	15.1	11.2	7.9	5.6	4.1	3.0	2.1
Hungary - Hongrie 2005																					
Male - Hommes	68.6	64.2	59.2	54.3	49.4	44.6	39.8	35.1	30.5	26.3	22.6	19.2	16.0	13.1	10.4	8.0	6.0	4.1	2.6	1.5	0.6
Female - Femmes	76.9	72.4	67.5	62.5	57.6	52.7	47.8	42.9	38.1	33.5	29.1	24.9	20.9	16.9	13.2	9.9	7.0	4.6	2.8	1.6	0.6

598

22. Expectation of life at specified ages for each sex: latest available year, 1996 - 2005
Espérance de vie à un âge donné pour chaque sexe: dernière année disponible, 1996 - 2005 (continued - suite)

Continent, country or area and date / Continent, pays ou zone et date	At birth - A la naissance	5	10	15	20	25	30	35	40	45	50	55	60	65	70	75	80	85	90	95	100
EUROPE																					
Iceland - Islande																					
2004 - 2005																					
Male - Hommes	79.2	74.4	69.4	64.5	59.7	54.9	50.1	45.2	40.3	35.5	30.9	26.3	21.9	18.0	14.1	10.6	7.7	5.4	3.5	2.2	1.5
Female - Femmes	83.3	78.5	73.5	68.5	63.6	58.7	53.7	48.7	43.8	38.9	34.2	29.7	25.2	20.7	16.6	12.6	9.1	6.5	4.4	2.9	1.5
Ireland - Irlande																					
2002																					
Male - Hommes	75.1	70.7	65.7	60.8	56.0	51.3	46.5	41.8	37.0	32.3	27.8	23.4	19.2	15.4	11.9	8.9	6.5	4.6	3.3	2.4	1.7
Female - Femmes	80.3	75.7	70.8	65.8	60.9	56.0	51.1	46.2	41.4	36.6	31.9	27.4	22.9	18.7	14.8	11.2	8.2	5.8	4.1	2.9	2.1
Isle of Man - Îles de Man																					
1996																					
Male - Hommes	73.7	68.7	65.7	58.7	53.7	49.2	44.8	40.3	35.9	31.3	26.7	22.4	18.5	15.2	12.1	9.4	7.5	5.6	...	...	...
Female - Femmes	79.8	75.0	70.0	65.0	60.0	55.0	50.0	45.0	40.1	35.3	30.6	26.1	21.9	18.3	14.4	11.3	8.6	6.1	...	...	...
Italy - Italie																					
2003																					
Male - Hommes	77.2	72.6	67.6	62.7	57.8	53.1	48.3	43.5	38.7	34.0	29.4	25.0	20.8	16.8	13.2	10.0	7.3	5.1	3.7	2.6	1.8
Female - Femmes	82.8	78.2	73.2	68.3	63.3	58.4	53.5	48.6	43.7	38.9	34.1	29.5	25.0	20.6	16.4	12.5	9.1	6.2	4.3	2.9	2.0
Latvia - Lettonie																					
2005																					
Male - Hommes	65.6	61.3	56.4	51.5	46.7	42.0	37.5	33.2	29.0	25.2	21.5	18.1	15.0	12.2	9.7	7.5	5.7	4.2	3.1	...	...
Female - Femmes	77.4	73.1	68.2	63.3	58.4	53.6	48.7	43.9	39.2	34.6	30.1	25.8	21.8	18.0	14.6	11.6	9.0	6.8	5.1	...	...
Lithuania - Lituanie																					
2005																					
Male - Hommes	65.4	61.0	56.1	51.2	46.5	42.0	37.6	33.4	29.3	25.4	21.8	18.6	15.7	13.1	10.6	8.3	6.3	4.6	3.4	2.6	1.9
Female - Femmes	77.4	73.0	68.0	63.1	58.2	53.3	48.5	43.7	39.0	34.4	30.0	25.7	21.7	17.7	13.9	10.4	7.4	5.1	3.5	2.4	2.1
Luxembourg																					
2000 - 2002																					
Male - Hommes	74.8	70.4	65.4	60.5	55.7	51.0	46.3	41.6	36.9	32.3	27.8	23.6	19.5	15.8	12.5	9.5	7.0	5.0	3.4	2.1	1.5
Female - Femmes	81.0	76.5	71.5	66.6	61.6	56.7	51.9	47.0	42.2	37.5	32.8	28.2	23.8	19.7	15.8	12.2	9.1	6.5	4.3	2.6	1.5
Malta - Malte																					
2005																					
Male - Hommes	77.7	73.2	68.2	63.3	58.4	53.6	48.8	44.0	39.1	34.3	29.5	25.1	20.7	16.7	13.2	10.3	8.0	6.8	...	...	...
Female - Femmes	81.4	77.4	72.4	67.5	62.5	57.5	52.6	47.6	42.7	37.9	33.2	28.6	24.1	19.8	15.7	12.0	8.9	6.9	...	...	...
Netherlands - Pays-Bas																					
2005																					
Male - Hommes	77.2	72.7	67.7	62.8	57.9	53.0	48.1	43.3	38.5	33.7	29.1	24.6	20.4	16.4	12.8	9.6	7.0	4.9	3.4	2.4	...
Female - Femmes	81.6	77.0	72.1	67.1	62.2	57.2	52.3	47.4	42.6	37.8	33.2	28.7	24.3	20.0	15.9	12.2	8.9	6.2	4.2	2.8	...
Norway - Norvège																					
2005																					
Male - Hommes	77.7	73.1	68.1	63.2	58.3	53.6	48.8	44.0	39.3	34.5	29.9	25.5	21.2	17.1	13.4	10.1	7.3	5.1	3.6	2.6	...
Female - Femmes	82.5	77.8	72.8	67.9	62.9	58.1	53.2	48.3	43.4	38.6	33.9	29.4	24.9	20.6	16.5	12.7	9.3	6.4	4.3	2.9	...
Poland - Pologne																					
2005																					
Male - Hommes	70.8	66.4	61.4	56.5	51.7	47.0	42.2	37.6	33.0	28.7	24.7	21.0	17.5	14.4	11.5	9.0	6.9	5.2	...	...	...
Female - Femmes	79.4	74.9	70.0	65.0	60.1	55.2	50.3	45.4	40.6	35.8	31.3	26.9	22.7	18.6	14.7	11.2	8.2	5.9	...	...	...
Portugal																					
2004 - 2005																					
Male - Hommes	74.9	70.3	65.4	60.4	55.6	50.9	46.1	41.5	37.0	32.5	28.2	24.0	20.0	16.2	12.6	9.5	7.0	...	...	...	...
Female - Femmes	81.4	76.7	71.8	66.8	61.9	57.0	52.1	47.3	42.4	37.7	33.0	28.4	23.9	19.6	15.4	11.6	8.3	...	...	...	...
Republic of Moldova - République de Moldova																					
2004																					
Male - Hommes	64.5	60.8	56.0	51.0	46.2	41.5	36.9	32.4	28.2	24.3	20.7	17.3	14.1	11.5	9.2	7.3	5.5	4.2	3.4	2.4	0.0
Female - Femmes	72.2	68.4	63.5	58.6	53.7	48.8	43.9	39.2	34.5	30.0	25.5	21.4	17.5	14.3	11.2	8.5	6.2	4.8	3.0	2.1	0.0
Romania - Roumanie																					
2005																					
Male - Hommes	68.2	64.7	59.8	54.9	50.1	45.4	40.6	35.9	31.4	27.2	23.3	19.7	16.4	13.3	10.6	8.1	6.1	4.5	3.3	2.4	1.8
Female - Femmes	75.5	71.8	66.8	61.9	57.1	52.2	47.3	42.4	37.7	33.0	28.6	24.2	20.1	16.1	12.5	9.2	6.6	4.6	3.2	2.3	1.6
Russian Federation - Fédération de Russie																					
2004																					
Male - Hommes	58.9	54.9	50.0	45.1	40.5	36.2	32.3	28.5	24.8	21.4	18.4	15.7	13.2	11.0	8.9	7.1	5.7	4.3	3.2	2.5	1.4
Female - Femmes	72.3	68.2	63.3	58.4	53.6	48.9	44.2	39.7	35.2	30.8	26.6	22.7	18.9	15.3	11.9	9.0	6.5	4.7	3.3	2.4	1.8

22. Expectation of life at specified ages for each sex: latest available year, 1996 - 2005
Espérance de vie à un âge donné pour chaque sexe: dernière année disponible, 1996 - 2005 (continued - suite)

Continent, country or area and date / Continent, pays ou zone et date	At birth - A la naissance	5	10	15	20	25	30	35	40	45	50	55	60	65	70	75	80	85	90	95	100
EUROPE																					
2005																					
Male - Hommes	58.9	...	...	...	...	...	...	...	...	...	...	...	...	...	...	...	...	...	...	...	...
Female - Femmes	72.4	...	...	...	...	...	...	...	...	...	...	...	...	...	...	...	...	...	...	...	...
San Marino - Saint-Marin																					
2000																					
Male - Hommes	77.4	73.0	68.0	63.1	58.5	53.8	49.1	44.3	39.5	34.7	30.1	25.6	21.4	17.2	13.5	10.5	7.7	5.7	3.8	2.3	0.5
Female - Femmes	84.0	79.6	74.6	69.6	64.7	59.7	54.8	49.9	45.0	40.2	35.4	30.7	26.0	21.6	17.1	13.1	9.3	6.3	4.3	2.7	0.5
Serbia and Montenegro - Serbie-et-Montenegro[21]																					
2003																					
Male - Hommes	70.0	65.8	60.9	56.0	51.1	46.4	41.6	36.9	32.2	27.7	23.5	19.7	16.2	13.0	10.2	7.9	5.9	4.2	...	...	...
Female - Femmes	75.2	70.9	66.0	61.1	56.1	51.2	46.3	41.5	36.7	32.0	27.5	23.2	19.0	15.1	11.6	8.7	6.3	4.4	...	...	...
Slovakia - Slovaquie																					
2005																					
Male - Hommes	70.1	65.7	60.8	55.9	51.0	46.2	41.4	36.7	32.1	27.7	23.6	19.8	16.3	13.2	10.4	7.9	5.8	4.1	...	...	...
Female - Femmes	77.9	73.4	68.5	63.5	58.6	53.6	48.7	43.8	39.0	34.3	29.7	25.2	20.9	16.8	13.0	9.6	6.7	4.5	...	...	...
Slovenia - Slovénie																					
2004 - 2005																					
Male - Hommes	74.1	69.5	64.5	59.6	54.8	50.1	45.3	40.6	35.8	31.3	27.0	22.9	19.1	15.5	12.2	9.5	7.3	5.4	3.9	2.9	1.0
Female - Femmes	81.3	76.7	71.8	66.8	61.9	57.0	52.0	47.2	42.3	37.6	33.0	28.5	24.1	19.9	15.8	12.0	8.8	6.3	4.5	3.1	1.0
Spain - Espagne																					
2003 - 2004																					
Male - Hommes	76.7	72.1	67.1	62.2	57.4	52.6	47.8	43.0	38.3	33.7	29.3	25.0	20.9	17.0	13.5	10.3	7.5	5.4	3.7	2.1	0.5
Female - Femmes	83.2	78.6	73.6	68.7	63.7	58.8	53.9	49.0	44.1	39.4	34.6	30.0	25.4	20.9	16.7	12.7	9.1	6.2	4.1	2.3	0.5
Sweden - Suède																					
2005																					
Male - Hommes	78.4	73.7	68.7	63.8	58.9	54.1	49.3	44.4	39.6	34.9	30.2	25.7	21.4	17.4	13.7	10.3	7.4	5.2	3.5	2.5	1.8
Female - Femmes	82.8	78.0	73.1	68.1	63.1	58.2	53.3	48.4	43.5	38.7	33.9	29.3	24.9	20.6	16.6	12.7	9.3	6.5	4.4	3.1	2.2
Switzerland - Suisse																					
2004 - 2005																					
Male - Hommes	78.6	74.1	69.1	64.1	59.3	54.5	49.7	44.9	40.1	35.4	30.8	26.3	22.1	18.1	14.3	10.9	8.0	5.7	4.0	3.0	...
Female - Femmes	83.7	79.1	74.1	69.2	64.2	59.3	54.4	49.5	44.6	39.8	35.1	30.5	25.9	21.5	17.3	13.3	9.7	6.8	4.7	3.4	...
The Former Yugoslav Rep. of Macedonia - L'ex-République yougoslave de Macédoine																					
2004																					
Male - Hommes	71.4	67.6	62.6	57.7	52.9	48.0	43.2	38.5	33.7	29.1	24.8	20.7	17.0	13.4	10.3	7.6	5.5	3.9	2.8	2.2	1.3
Female - Femmes	75.9	71.9	66.9	62.0	57.1	52.1	47.2	42.3	37.5	32.7	28.1	23.6	19.3	15.3	11.6	8.5	6.1	4.3	3.2	2.3	0.9
Ukraine																					
2003 - 2004																					
Male - Hommes	62.6	58.5	53.6	48.7	44.0	39.4	35.1	31.0	27.1	23.5	20.2	17.2	14.3	11.8	9.5	7.4	5.7	4.2	3.0	2.0	0.8
Female - Femmes	74.1	69.9	65.0	60.0	55.2	50.4	45.6	41.0	36.4	31.9	27.6	23.4	19.5	15.7	12.3	9.2	6.6	4.7	3.2	2.1	0.8
United Kingdom - Royaume-Uni																					
2000																					
Male - Hommes	75.3	70.9	65.9	61.0	56.1	51.4	46.6	41.9	37.1	32.5	27.9	23.6	19.5	15.7	12.3	9.4	7.0	5.0	3.7	2.7	2.0
Female - Femmes	80.1	75.6	70.6	65.7	60.8	55.9	51.0	46.1	41.2	36.5	31.8	27.3	23.0	18.8	15.0	11.5	8.6	6.1	4.3	3.0	2.2
OCEANIA - OCÉANIE																					
Australia - Australie																					
2003 - 2005																					
Male - Hommes	78.5	74.0	69.0	64.1	59.2	54.5	49.7	45.0	40.2	35.6	31.0	26.5	22.2	18.1	14.4	11.0	8.2	5.9	4.2	3.2	2.5
Female - Femmes	83.3	78.8	73.8	68.9	63.9	59.0	54.1	49.3	44.4	39.6	34.9	30.3	25.7	21.4	17.2	13.4	9.9	7.1	4.9	3.6	2.8
Fiji - Fidji																					
1996																					
Male - Hommes	64.5	...	...	...	...	42.4	...	...	...	...	...	...	10.7	...	...	...	...	...	...	...	...
Female - Femmes	68.7	...	...	...	...	46.4	...	...	...	...	...	...	13.0	...	...	...	...	...	...	...	...

22. Expectation of life at specified ages for each sex: latest available year, 1996 - 2005
Espérance de vie à un âge donné pour chaque sexe: dernière année disponible, 1996 - 2005 (continued - suite)

Continent, country or area and date / Continent, pays ou zone et date	At birth - A la naissance	5	10	15	20	25	30	35	40	45	50	55	60	65	70	75	80	85	90	95	100
OCEANIA - OCÉANIE																					
Kiribati 1995 - 2000																					
Male - Hommes	58.2	...	...	...	...	...	...	...	...	...	...	...	...	...	...	...	...	...	...	...	...
Female - Femmes	67.3	...	...	...	...	...	...	...	...	...	...	...	...	...	...	...	...	...	...	...	...
Marshall Islands - Îles Marshall 1999																					
Male - Hommes	65.7	...	...	...	...	...	...	...	...	...	...	...	...	...	...	...	...	...	...	...	...
Female - Femmes	69.4	...	...	...	...	...	...	...	...	...	...	...	...	...	...	...	...	...	...	...	...
Nauru 2000																					
Male - Hommes	57.0	...	...	...	...	...	...	...	...	...	...	...	...	...	...	...	...	...	...	...	...
Female - Femmes	64.0	...	...	...	...	...	...	...	...	...	...	...	...	...	...	...	...	...	...	...	...
New Caledonia - Nouvelle-Calédonie 2003																					
Male - Hommes	71.3	67.0	62.1	57.2	52.4	48.0	43.3	38.8	34.2	29.7	25.4	21.2	17.4	13.8	11.0	9.0	7.1	5.1	3.8	9.8	...
Female - Femmes	77.3	72.7	67.8	62.9	58.1	53.3	48.5	43.8	39.0	34.3	29.8	25.4	21.5	17.4	14.3	10.9	8.5	6.4	5.0	2.7	...
New Zealand - Nouvelle-Zélande 2004 - 2006																					
Male - Hommes	77.9	73.4	68.4	63.5	58.8	54.1	49.3	44.5	39.8	35.1	30.6	26.1	21.8	17.8	14.2	10.9	8.1	5.8	4.3	...	...
Female - Femmes	81.9	77.4	72.4	67.5	62.6	57.7	52.8	48.0	43.1	38.4	33.7	29.2	24.7	20.5	16.5	12.8	9.5	6.7	4.6	...	...
Palau - Palaos 2000																					
Male - Hommes	66.6	...	...	...	...	...	...	...	...	...	...	...	...	...	...	...	...	...	...	...	...
Female - Femmes	74.5	...	...	...	...	...	...	...	...	...	...	...	...	...	...	...	...	...	...	...	...
Papua New Guinea - Papouasie-Nouvelle-Guinée 2000																					
Male - Hommes	53.7	54.1	50.2	45.7	41.6	37.7	33.7	29.8	25.9	22.1	18.5	15.0	11.9	9.2	6.9	5.0	3.6	2.6	1.7	0.6	...
Female - Femmes	54.8	54.7	50.8	46.3	42.1	38.1	34.1	30.1	26.2	22.3	18.6	15.2	12.0	9.2	6.8	5.0	3.6	2.5	1.6	0.6	...
Tonga 1998																					
Male - Hommes	69.8	66.5	61.6	56.7	52.0	47.2	42.5	37.8	33.1	28.5	24.1	20.0	16.3	13.0	10.4	7.2	5.5	...	...	...	...
Female - Femmes	71.8	68.3	63.5	58.6	53.7	48.9	44.2	39.4	34.8	30.2	25.8	21.6	17.7	14.1	11.2	7.8	5.9	...	...	...	...
Tuvalu 1997 - 2002																					
Male - Hommes	61.7	59.5	54.8	50.0	45.2	40.6	35.9	32.1	28.0	24.1	20.0	17.1	13.7	10.8	9.0	6.9	5.4	...	...	...	...
Female - Femmes	65.1	62.6	57.7	53.7	50.0	45.3	40.9	36.6	32.2	28.1	23.8	20.3	16.9	13.2	10.6	7.9	6.4	...	...	...	...
Vanuatu 1999																					
Male - Hommes	65.6	...	...	...	...	...	...	...	...	...	...	...	...	...	...	...	...	...	...	...	...
Female - Femmes	69.0	...	...	...	...	...	...	...	...	...	...	...	...	...	...	...	...	...	...	...	...

FOOTNOTES - NOTES

[1] For Algerian population only. - Pour la population algérienne seulement.

[2] Data refer to national projections. - Les données se réfèrent aux projections nationales.

[3] Projections based on the 1998 Malawi Population and Housing Census. - Les projections sont basées sur les résultats du recensement de la population et de l'habitat de Malawi de 1998.

[4] Data for 1997 refer to last twelve months preceding population and housing census of 1997. - Les données pour 1997 se réfèrent au douze mois précédant le recensement de population et de l'habitat de 1997.

[5] Excluding tribal Indian population. - Non compris les Indiens vivant en tribus.

[6] Excluding Indian jungle population. - Non compris les Indiens de la jungle.

[7] Excluding nomadic Indian tribes. - Non compris les tribus d'Indiens nomades.

[8] Life expectancy in 2000 is calculated by the death data of 2000's Population Census, which modified by the mortality rates from the annual national sample surveys on population changes since 1990 . - L'espérance de vie en 2000 par est calculée en se fondant sur les données relatives aux décès issues du recensement de la population de 2000 modifiées par les taux de mortalité extraits des enquêtes nationales annuelles par sondage concernant l'évolution de la population depuis 1990.

[9] For statistical purposes, the data for China do not include those for the Hong Kong Special Administrative Region (Hong Kong SAR), Macao Special Administrative Region (Macao SAR) and Taiwan province of China. - Pour présentation des statistiques, les données pour la Chine ne comprennent pas la Région Administrative Spéciale de Hong Kong (Hong Kong RAS), la Région Administrative Spéciale de Macao (Macao RAS) et Taïwan province de Chine.

[10] Data refer to government controlled areas. - Les données se rapportent aux zones contrôlées par le Gouvernement.

[11] Including data for the Indian-held part of Jammu and Kashmir, the final status of which has not yet been determined. - Y compris les données pour la partie du Jammu et du Cachemire occupée par l'Inde dont le statut définitif n'a pas encore été déterminé.

[12] Including data for East Jerusalem and Israeli residents in certain other territories under occupation by Israeli military forces since June 1967. - Y compris les données pour Jérusalem-Est et les résidents israéliens dans certains autres territoires occupés depuis 1967 par les forces armées israéliennes.

[13] Data refer to Japanese nationals in Japan only. - Les données se raportent aux nationaux japonais au Japon seulement.

¹⁴ Excluding data for Jordanian territory under occupation since June 1967 by Israeli military forces. Excluding foreigners, including registered Palestinian refugees. - Non compris les données pour le territoire jordanien occupé depuis juin 1967 par les forces armées israéliennes. Non compris les étrangers, mais y compris les réfugiés de Palestine enregistrés.

¹⁵ Data estimated from population and housing census 2005. - Données dérivées du recensement de population et du logement de 2005.

¹⁶ Data based on Pakistan Demographic Survey (PDS 2003) . - Données extraites de l'enquête démographique effectuée par le Pakistan en 2003.

¹⁷ Excluding data for the Pakistan-held part of Jammu and Kashmir, the final status of which has not yet been determined. - Non compris les données concernant la partie du Jammu et Cachemire occupée par le Pakistan dont le statut définitif n'a pas été déterminé.

¹⁸ Based on the results of the Population Demographic Survey. - D'après les résultats de la Population Demographic Survey.

¹⁹ Excluding Faeroe Islands and Greenland. - Non compris les Iles Féroé et le Gröenland.

²⁰ Excluding Overseas Departments, namely, French Guiana, Guadeloupe, Martinique and Reunion, shown separately. - Non compris les départements d'outre mer, c'est-à-dire la Guyane française, la Guadeloupe, la Martinique et la Réunion, qui font l'objet de rubriques distinctes.

²¹ Without data for Kosovo and Metohia. - Sans les données pour le Kosovo and Metohie.

Table 23

Table 23 presents number of marriages and crude marriage rates by urban/rural residence for every year with available data between 2001 and 2005.

Description of variables: Marriage is defined as the act, ceremony or process by which the legal relationship of husband and wife is constituted. The legality of the union may be established by civil, religious or other means as recognized by the laws of each country. [i]

Marriage statistics in this table, therefore, include both first marriages and remarriages after divorce, widowhood or annulment. They do not, unless otherwise noted, include resumption of marriage ties after legal separation. These statistics refer to the number of marriages performed, and not to the number of persons marrying.

Statistics shown are obtained from civil registers of marriage. Exceptions, such as data from church registers, are identified in footnotes.

The urban/rural classification of marriages is that provided by each country or area; it is presumed to be based on the national census definitions of urban population which have been set forth at the end of the technical notes for table 6.

For certain countries, there is a discrepancy between the total number of marriages shown in this table and those shown in subsequent tables for the same year. Usually this discrepancy arises because the total number of marriages occurring in a given year is revised although the remaining tabulations are not.

Rate computation: Crude marriage rates are the annual number of marriages per 1 000 mid-year population. Rates by urban/rural residence are the annual number of marriages, in the appropriate urban or rural category, per 1 000 corresponding mid-year population. These rates are calculated by the Statistics Division of the United Nations. Rates presented in this table have been limited to those for countries or areas having at least a total of 30 marriages in a given year.

Reliability of data: Each country or area has been asked to indicate the estimated completeness of the number of marriages recorded in its civil register. These national assessments are indicated by the quality codes C and U that appear in the first column of this table.

C indicates that the data are estimated to be virtually complete, that is, representing at least 90 per cent of the marriages occurring each year, while U indicates that data are estimated to be incomplete, that is, representing less than 90 per cent of the marriages occurring each year. The code ... indicates that no information was provided regarding completeness.

Data from civil registers which are reported as incomplete or of unknown completeness (coded U or ...) are considered unreliable. They appear in italics in this table; rates are not computed for these data.

These quality codes apply only to data from civil registers. For more information about the quality of vital statistics data in general, see section 4.2 of the Technical Notes.

Limitations: Statistics on marriages are subject to the same qualifications that have been set forth for vital statistics in general and marriage statistics in particular as discussed in section 4 of the Technical Notes.

The fact that marriage is a legal event, unlike birth and death that are biological events, has implications for international comparability of data. Marriage has been defined, for statistical purposes, in terms of the laws of individual countries or areas. These laws vary throughout the world. In addition, comparability is further limited because some countries or areas compile statistics only for civil marriages although religious marriages may also be legally recognized; in other countries or areas, the only available records are church registers and, therefore, the statistics may not reflect marriages that are civil marriages only.

Because in many countries or areas marriage is a civil legal contract which, to establish its legality, must be celebrated before a civil officer, it follows that for these countries or areas registration would tend to be almost automatic at the time of, or immediately following, the marriage ceremony. This factor should be kept in mind when considering the reliability of data, described above. For this reason the practice of tabulating data by date of registration does not generally pose serious problems of comparability as it does in the case of birth and death statistics.

As indicators of family formation, the statistics on the number of marriages presented in this table are bound to be deficient to the extent that they do not include either customary unions, which are not registered even though they are considered legal and binding under customary law, or consensual unions (also known as extra-legal or de facto unions). In general, lower marriage rates over a period of years are an indication of higher incidence of customary or consensual unions.

In addition, rates are affected also by the quality and limitations of the population estimates that are used in their computation. The problems of under-enumeration or over-enumeration and, to some extent, the differences in definition of total population have been discussed in section 3 of the Technical Notes dealing with population data in general, and specific information pertaining to individual countries or areas is given in the footnotes to table 3.

Strict correspondence between the numerator of the rate and the denominator is not always obtained; for example, marriages among civilian and military segments of the population may be related to civilian population. The effect of this may be to increase the rates, but, in most cases, this effect is negligible.

It should be emphasized that crude marriage rates like crude birth, death and divorce rates, may be seriously affected by the age-sex-marital structure of the population to which they relate. Crude marriage rates do, however, provide a simple measure of the level and changes in marriage.

The comparability of data by urban/rural residence is affected by the national definitions of urban and rural used in tabulating these data. It is assumed, in the absence of specific information to the contrary, that the definitions of urban and rural used in connection with the national population census were also used in the compilation of the vital statistics for each country or area. However, it cannot be excluded that, for a given country or area, different definitions of urban and rural are used for the vital statistics data and the population census data respectively. When known, the definitions of urban in national population censuses are presented at the end of the technical notes for table 6. As discussed in detail in the notes, these definitions vary considerably from one country or area to another.

In addition to problems of comparability, marriage rates classified by urban/rural residence are also subject to certain special types of bias. If, when calculating marriage rates, different definitions of urban are used in connection with the vital events and the population data, and if this results in a net difference between the numerator and denominator of the rate in the population at risk, then the marriage rates would be biased. Urban/rural differentials in marriage rates may also be affected by whether the vital events have been tabulated in terms of place of occurrence or place of usual residence. This problem is discussed in more detail in section 4.1.4.1. of the Technical Notes.

Earlier data: Marriages and crude marriage rates have been shown in each issue of the *Demographic Yearbook*. For more information on specific topics, and years for which data are reported, readers should consult the Historical Index.

NOTES

[i] *Principles and Recommendations for a Vital Statistics System Revision 2.* Sales No. E. 01.XVII.10, United Nations, New York, 2001

Tableau 23

Le tableau 23 présente des données sur les mariages et les taux bruts de nuptialité selon le lieu de résidence (zone urbaine ou rurale) pour les années où l'information est disponible entre 2001 et 2005.

Description des variables : le mariage désigne l'acte, la cérémonie ou la procédure qui établit un rapport légal entre mari et femme. L'union peut être rendue légale par une procédure civile ou religieuse, ou par toute autre procédure, conformément à la législation du pays[1].

Les statistiques de la nuptialité présentées dans ce tableau comprennent donc les premiers mariages et les remariages faisant suite à un divorce, un veuvage ou une annulation. Toutefois, sauf indication contraire, elles ne comprennent pas les unions reconstituées après une séparation légale. Ces statistiques se rapportent au nombre de mariages célébrés, non au nombre de personnes qui se marient.

Les statistiques présentées reposent sur l'enregistrement des mariages par les services de l'état civil. Les exceptions (données provenant des registres des églises, par exemple) font l'objet d'une note à la fin du tableau.

La classification des mariages selon le lieu de résidence (zone urbaine ou rurale) est celle qui a été communiquée par chaque pays ou zone ; on part du principe qu'elle repose sur les définitions de la population urbaine utilisées pour les recensements nationaux telles qu'elles sont reproduites à la fin des notes techniques se rapportant au tableau 6.

Pour quelques pays il y a une discordance entre le nombre total de mariages présenté dans ce tableau et ceux présentés après pour la même année. Habituellement ces différences apparaissent lorsque le nombre total des mariages pour une certaine année a été révisé alors que les autres tabulations ne l'ont pas été.

Calcul des taux : les taux bruts de nuptialité représentent le nombre annuel de mariages pour 1 000 habitants au milieu de l'année. Les taux selon le lieu de résidence (zone urbaine ou rurale) représentent le nombre annuel de mariages, classés selon la catégorie urbaine ou rurale appropriée, pour 1 000 habitants au milieu de l'année. Ces taux ont été calculés par la Division de statistique de l'ONU. Les taux du tableau 23 ne se rapportent qu'aux pays ou zones où l'on a enregistré un total d'au moins 30 mariages pendant une année donnée.

Fiabilité des données : il a été demandé à chaque pays ou zone d'indiquer le degré estimatif de complétude des données sur les mariages figurant dans ses registres d'état civil. Ces évaluations nationales sont signalées par les codes de qualité 'C' et 'U' qui apparaissent dans la deuxième colonne du tableau.

La lettre 'C' indique que les données sont jugées à peu près complètes, c'est-à-dire qu'elles représentent au moins 90 p. 100 des mariages survenus chaque année ; la lettre 'U' signale que les données sont jugées incomplètes, c'est-à-dire qu'elles représentent moins de 90 p. 100 des mariages survenus chaque année. Le code '...' indique qu'aucun renseignement n'a été communiqué quant à la complétude des données.

Les données issues des registres de l'état civil qui sont déclarées incomplètes ou dont le degré de complétude n'est pas connu (code 'U' ou '...') sont jugées douteuses. Elles apparaissent en italique dans le tableau et les taux correspondants n'ont pas été calculés.

Les codes de qualité ne s'appliquent qu'aux données provenant des registres de l'état civil. Pour plus de précisions sur la qualité des données reposant sur les statistiques de l'état civil en général, voir la section 4.2 des Notes techniques.

Insuffisance des données : les statistiques relatives aux mariages appellent les mêmes réserves que celles qui ont été formulées à propos des statistiques de l'état civil en général et des statistiques concernant la nuptialité en particulier (voir la section 4 des Notes techniques).

Le fait que le mariage soit un acte juridique, à la différence de la naissance et du décès, qui sont des faits biologiques, a des répercussions sur la comparabilité internationale des données. Aux fins de la statistique, le mariage est défini par la législation de chaque pays ou zone. Cette législation varie d'un pays à l'autre. La comparabilité est limitée en outre du fait que certains pays ou zones ne réunissent des statistiques que pour les mariages civils, bien que les mariages religieux y soient également reconnus par la loi ; dans d'autres, les seuls relevés disponibles sont les registres des églises et, en conséquence, les statistiques peuvent ne pas rendre compte des mariages exclusivement civils.

Étant donné que, dans de nombreux pays ou zones, le mariage est un contrat juridique civil qui, pour être légal, doit être conclu devant un officier d'état civil, il s'ensuit que dans ces pays ou zones l'enregistrement se fait à peu près systématiquement au moment de la cérémonie ou immédiatement après. Il faut tenir compte de cet élément lorsque l'on évalue la fiabilité des données, dont il est question plus haut. C'est pourquoi la pratique consistant à exploiter les données selon la date de l'enregistrement ne pose généralement pas les graves problèmes de comparabilité auxquels on se heurte dans le cas des statistiques concernant les naissances et les décès.

Les statistiques relatives au nombre des mariages présentées dans ce tableau donnent une idée forcément trompeuse de la formation des familles, dans la mesure où elles ne tiennent compte ni des mariages coutumiers, qui ne sont pas enregistrés bien qu'ils soient considérés comme légaux et créateurs d'obligations en vertu du droit coutumier, ni des unions consensuelles (appelées également unions non légalisées ou unions de fait). En général, une diminution du taux de nuptialité pendant un certain nombre d'années indique une augmentation des mariages coutumiers ou des unions consensuelles.

L'exactitude des taux dépend également de la qualité et des insuffisances des estimations de population qui sont utilisées pour leur calcul. Le problème des erreurs par excès ou par défaut commises lors du dénombrement et, dans une certaine mesure, le problème de l'hétérogénéité des définitions de la population totale ont été examinés à la section 3 des Notes techniques relative à la population en général ; des indications concernant les différents pays ou zones sont données en note à la fin du tableau 3.

Il n'a pas toujours été possible d'obtenir une correspondance rigoureuse entre le numérateur et le dénominateur pour le calcul des taux. Par exemple, les mariages parmi la population civile et les militaires sont parfois rapportés à la population civile. Cela peut avoir pour effet d'accroître les taux, mais, dans la plupart des cas, il est probable que la différence sera négligeable.

Il faut souligner que les taux bruts de nuptialité, de même que les taux bruts de natalité, de mortalité et de divortialité, peuvent varier sensiblement selon la structure par âge et par sexe de la population à laquelle ils se rapportent. Les taux bruts de nuptialité offrent néanmoins un moyen simple de mesurer la fréquence et l'évolution des mariages.

La comparabilité des données selon le lieu de résidence (zone urbaine ou rurale) peut être limitée par les définitions nationales des termes « urbain » et « rural » utilisées pour le classement de ces données. En l'absence d'indications contraires, on a supposé que les mêmes définitions avaient servi pour le recensement national de la population et pour l'établissement des statistiques de l'état civil pour chaque pays ou zone. Toutefois, il n'est pas exclu que, pour une zone ou un pays donné, des définitions différentes aient été retenues. Les définitions du terme « urbain » utilisées pour les recensements nationaux de population ont été présentées à la fin des notes techniques du tableau 6 lorsqu'elles étaient connues. Comme on l'a précisé dans les notes techniques relatives au tableau 6, ces définitions varient considérablement d'un pays ou d'une zone à l'autre.

Outre les problèmes de comparabilité, les taux de nuptialité classés selon le lieu de résidence (zone urbaine ou rurale) sont également sujets à des distorsions particulières. Si l'on utilise des définitions différentes du terme « urbain » pour classer les faits d'état civil et les données relatives à la population lors du calcul des taux et qu'il en résulte une différence nette entre le numérateur et le dénominateur pour le taux de la population exposée au risque, les taux de nuptialité s'en trouveront faussés. La différence entre ces taux pour les zones urbaines et rurales pourra aussi être faussée selon que les faits d'état civil auront été classés d'après le lieu où ils se sont produits ou d'après le lieu de résidence habituel. Ce problème est examiné plus en détail à la section 4.1.4.1 des Notes techniques.

Données publiées antérieurement : les différentes éditions de *l'Annuaire démographique* regroupent des données sur le nombre des mariages. Pour plus de précisions concernant les années et les sujets pour lesquels des données ont été publiées, se reporter à l'index historique.

NOTE

[1] *Principes et recommandations pour un système de statistiques de l'état civil, deuxième révision*, numéro de vente : F.01.XVII.10, publication des Nations Unies, New York, 2003.

23. Marriages and crude marriage rates, by urban/rural residence: 2001 - 2005
Mariages et taux bruts de nuptialité, selon la résidence, urbaine/rurale: 2001 - 2005

Continent, country or area and urban/rural residence / Continent, pays ou zone et résidence, urbaine/rurale	Code[1]	Marriages - Mariages					Rate - Taux				
		2001	2002	2003	2004	2005	2001	2002	2003	2004	2005
AFRICA — AFRIQUE											
Algeria - Algérie[2]											
Total	...	194 273	218 620	...	...	...	...	...	...	...	...
Egypt - Égypte[3]											
Total	+...	457 534	510 517	537 092	550 709	522 751	...	...	...	...	...
Urban-Urbaine	+...	167 616	183 538	185 880	175 361	170 556	...	...	...	...	...
Rural-Rurale	+...	289 918	326 979	351 212	375 348	352 195	...	...	...	...	...
Libyan Arab Jamahiriya - Jamahiriya arabe libyenne[4]											
Total	U	28 661	33 323	...	...	...	...	...	...	...	...
Mauritius - Maurice											
Total	+C	10 635	10 484	10 812	11 385	11 294	8.9	8.7	8.8	9.2	9.1
Urban-Urbaine	+C	3 423	3 295	3 298	3 422	3 551	6.7	6.4	6.4	6.6	6.8
Rural-Rurale	+C	7 212	7 189	7 514	7 963	7 743	10.5	10.3	10.7	11.2	10.8
Réunion											
Total	C	3 508	3 284	*3 212	*3 269	*3 115	4.8	4.4	*4.2	*4.3	*4.0
Saint Helena ex. dep. - Sainte-Hélène sans dép.											
Total	C	20	13	20	10	10	...	...	...	...	...
Seychelles											
Total	+C	790	865	823	...	...	9.7	10.3	9.9	...	...
South Africa - Afrique du Sud											
Total	...	134 581	177 202	178 689	176 521	180 657	...	...	...	...	...
Tunisia - Tunisie											
Total	...	61 800	...	...	...	...	...	...	...	...	...
AMERICA, NORTH — AMERIQUE DU NORD											
Anguilla[5]											
Total	C	51	53	75	70	*89	4.4	4.4	6.1	5.6	*6.5
Aruba[6]											
Total	C	845	728	663	606	572	9.2	7.8	7.0	6.2	5.7
Bahamas											
Total	C	1 787	...	...	...	...	5.8	...	...	...	...
Belize											
Total	+C	1 558	1 622	...	...	...	6.1	6.1	...	...	...
Bermuda - Bermudes											
Total	C	923	937	861	...	...	14.8	14.9	13.7	...	...
British Virgin Islands - Îles Vierges britanniques											
Total	C	435	384	475	426	...	21.1	18.3	22.3	19.6	...
Canada											
Total	C	146 618	146 738	147 391	...	...	4.7	4.7	4.7	...	...
Cayman Islands - Îles Caïmanes											
Total	C	341	321	344	920	810	8.2	7.6	7.9	20.8	16.8
Costa Rica											
Total	C	23 790	23 926	24 448	25 370	*25 631	6.1	6.0	6.0	6.1	*6.0
Cuba											
Total	C	54 345	56 876	54 739	50 878	51 831	4.9	5.1	4.9	4.5	4.6
Urban-Urbaine	C	49 429	51 728	50 103	46 655	48 335	5.8	6.1	5.9	5.5	5.7
Rural-Rurale	C	4 916	5 148	4 636	4 223	3 496	1.8	1.9	1.7	1.5	1.3
Dominican Republic - République dominicaine											
Total	+C	24 470	*24 467	*29 467	*23 094	...	2.8	*2.9	*3.4	*2.6	...
El Salvador											
Total	+C	29 216	25 998	24 972	...	...	4.6	4.0	3.8	...	...
Urban-Urbaine	+C	23 668	22 102	20 836	...	...	6.3	5.7	5.3	...	...
Rural-Rurale	+C	5 548	3 896	4 136	...	...	2.1	1.5	1.5	...	...
Grenada - Grenade											
Total	+C	509	...	...	...	...	5.0	...	...	...	...
Guadeloupe											
Total	C	1 929	1 809	1 701	1 771	1 727	4.5	4.1	3.9	4.0	3.9
Guatemala											
Total	C	54 722	51 857	51 247	...	...	4.7	4.3	4.2	...	...

Continent, country or area and urban/rural residence / Continent, pays ou zone et résidence, urbaine/rurale	Code[1]	Marriages - Mariages					Rate - Taux				
		2001	2002	2003	2004	2005	2001	2002	2003	2004	2005
AMERICA, NORTH — AMERIQUE DU NORD											
Jamaica - Jamaïque											
Total	C	22 308	23 070	22 476	21 670	...	8.6	8.8	8.6	8.2	...
Martinique											
Total	C	1 572	1 524	1 414	1 425	1 453	4.1	3.9	3.6	3.6	3.7
Mexico - Mexique[7]											
Total	+C	665 434	616 654	584 142	600 563	595 713	6.7	6.1	5.7	5.8	5.7
Urban-Urbaine	+C	501 426	469 962	436 825	447 840	446 557	6.6	6.1	5.6	5.6	...
Rural-Rurale	+C	145 362	134 326	132 873	134 918	132 052	5.7	5.3	5.2	5.2	...
Netherlands Antilles - Antilles néerlandaises[8]											
Total	C	887	677	748	710	...	5.1	3.9	4.2	3.9	...
Nicaragua											
Total	+U	21 140	21 037	21 390	18 679	23 069	...	...	...	...	...
Panama[9]											
Total	C	9 687	9 558	10 310	10 290	*10 512	3.3	3.1	3.3	3.2	*3.3
Urban-Urbaine	C	...	...	8 622	...	...	...	...	...	...	...
Rural-Rurale	C	...	...	1 688	...	...	...	...	...	...	...
Puerto Rico - Porto Rico											
Total	C	28 598	25 645	25 236	23 650	23 511	7.4	6.6	6.5	6.1	6.0
Saint Lucia - Sainte-Lucie											
Total	C	513	500	540	*459	...	3.2	3.1	3.4	*2.8	...
Saint Vincent and the Grenadines - Saint Vincent-et-les Grenadines											
Total	+C	506	509	491	526	576	4.8	4.7	4.7	5.0	5.6
Trinidad and Tobago - Trinité-et-Tobago											
Total	C	7 139	7 434	...	...	...	5.6	5.8	...	...	...
Turks Caicos Islands - Îles Turques et Caïques											
Total	C	520	593	491	499	489	26.1	28.4	19.5	18.1	16.0
United States - États-Unis											
Total	C	2 345 000	2 254 000	2 245 000	2 279 000	...	8.2	7.8	7.7	7.8	...
AMERICA, SOUTH — AMERIQUE DU SUD											
Argentina - Argentine											
Total	C	130 533	122 343	129 049	128 212	132 720	3.5	3.3	3.4	3.4	3.4
Brazil - Brésil[10]											
Total	U	710 121	715 166	748 981	806 968	835 846	...	...	...	...	...
Chile - Chili											
Total	+C	64 088	60 971	56 659	53 403	53 842	4.1	3.9	3.6	3.3	3.3
Urban-Urbaine	+C	56 427	54 730	51 807	...	...	4.2	4.0	3.8	...	...
Rural-Rurale	+C	7 661	6 241	4 852	...	...	3.7	3.0	2.3	...	...
Ecuador - Équateur[11]											
Total	U	67 741	66 208	65 393	...	66 612	...	...	...	...	...
French Guiana - Guyane française											
Total	C	547	522	524	539	596	3.2	3.0	2.9	2.9	3.0
Paraguay											
Total	U	17 950	16 100	17 717	17 763	19 826	...	...	...	...	...
Suriname											
Total	C	2 006	2 005	1 936	1 951	...	4.3	4.2	4.0	4.0	...
Uruguay											
Total	C	13 988	14 073	14 147	13 123	13 075	4.2	4.3	4.3	4.0	4.0
Venezuela (Bolivarian Republic of) - Venezuela (République bolivarienne du)[10]											
Total	C	81 516	73 163	74 562	74 103	86 093	3.3	2.9	2.9	2.8	3.2

Continent, country or area and urban/rural residence / Continent, pays ou zone et résidence, urbaine/rurale	Code[1]	Marriages - Mariages					Rate - Taux				
		2001	2002	2003	2004	2005	2001	2002	2003	2004	2005
ASIA — ASIE											
Armenia - Arménie											
Total	C	12 302	13 682	15 463	16 975	16 624	3.8	4.3	4.8	5.3	5.2
Urban-Urbaine	C	8 340	9 207	10 174	11 164	10 975	4.0	4.5	4.9	5.4	5.3
Rural-Rurale	C	3 962	4 475	5 289	5 811	5 649	3.5	3.9	4.6	5.0	4.9
Azerbaijan - Azerbaïdjan											
Total	+C	41 861	41 661	56 091	62 177	71 643	5.2	5.1	6.8	7.5	8.5
Urban-Urbaine	+C	22 927	22 438	26 935	30 873	...	5.6	5.4	6.3	7.2	...
Rural-Rurale	+C	18 934	19 223	29 156	31 304	...	4.7	4.8	7.3	7.8	...
Bahrain - Bahreïn[12]											
Total	...	*4 504*	*4 909*	*5 373*	*4 667*		...	...	...	...	...
Brunei Darussalam - Brunéi Darussalam											
Total	...	*2 091*	*2 288*	*2 262*	*2 027*		...	...	...	...	...
China - Chine[13]											
Total	+C	8 050 000	7 860 000	8 114 000	8 672 000	8 231 000	6.3	6.1	6.3	6.7	6.3
China: Hong Kong SAR - Chine: Hong Kong RAS											
Total	C	32 825	32 070	35 439	41 376	43 018	4.9	4.8	5.3	6.1	6.3
China: Macao SAR - Chine: Macao RAS											
Total	+C	1 222	1 209	1 309	1 737	1 734	2.8	2.8	3.0	3.8	3.7
Cyprus - Chypre[14,15]											
Total	C	10 574	10 284	10 810	5 349	5 881	15.1	14.5	15.0	7.3	7.8
Urban-Urbaine	C	...	6 641	9 563	4 275	...	...	...	...	...	...
Rural-Rurale	C	...	3 643	1 247	1 074	...	...	...	...	...	...
Georgia - Géorgie											
Total	C	13 336	12 535	12 696	14 866	18 012	3.0	2.9	2.9	3.4	4.1
Urban-Urbaine	C	8 027	...	8 161	...	...	3.5	...	3.6	...	...
Rural-Rurale	C	5 309	...	4 535	...	...	2.5	...	2.2	...	...
Iran (Islamic Republic of) - Iran (République islamique d')[16]											
Total	C	640 710	650 960	681 034	723 976	787 671	9.9	9.9	10.2	10.7	11.5
Urban-Urbaine	C	495 629	513 772	522 160	527 337	558 424	11.8	11.9	11.9	11.9	12.2
Rural-Rurale	C	145 081	137 188	158 874	196 639	229 247	6.5	6.1	7.0	8.4	10.0
Iraq											
Total	U	...	...	...	*262 554*		...	...	...	...	...
Israel - Israël[17]											
Total	C	38 924	39 718	39 154	39 860	...	6.0	6.0	5.9	5.9	...
Japan - Japon[18]											
Total	+C	799 999	757 331	740 191	720 417	714 265	6.3	5.9	5.8	5.6	5.6
Urban-Urbaine	+C	663 506	629 906	617 978	606 934	627 290	...	...	...	...	...
Rural-Rurale	+C	136 493	127 425	122 213	113 483	86 975	...	...	...	...	...
Jordan - Jordanie[12,19]											
Total	+C	49 794	46 873	48 784	53 754	56 418	10.0	9.2	9.3	10.0	10.3
Kazakhstan											
Total	C	92 852	98 986	110 414	114 685	123 045	6.2	6.7	7.4	7.6	8.1
Urban-Urbaine	C	54 395	58 529	66 794	69 794	...	6.5	6.9	7.9	8.1	...
Rural-Rurale	C	38 457	40 457	43 620	44 891	...	6.0	6.3	6.8	7.0	...
Korea (Republic of) - Corée (République de)											
Total	+C	320 063	306 573	304 932	310 944	316 375	6.8	6.4	6.4	6.5	6.6
Urban-Urbaine	+C	261 575	252 808	251 873	257 035	261 346	...	...	...	...	...
Rural-Rurale	+C	58 488	53 765	53 059	53 909	55 029	...	...	...	...	...
Kuwait - Koweït											
Total	C	11 916	11 973	12 246	12 359	12 419	5.5	5.3	5.3	5.2	5.1
Kyrgyzstan - Kirghizistan											
Total	C	27 455	31 240	34 266	34 542	37 321	5.5	6.3	6.8	6.8	7.3
Urban-Urbaine	C	8 258	9 065	9 953	11 039	11 651	4.7	5.1	5.6	6.1	6.4
Rural-Rurale	C	19 197	22 175	24 313	23 503	25 670	6.0	6.9	7.5	7.2	7.7
Lebanon - Liban											
Total	C	32 225	31 653	30 636	30 014	29 705	...	...	...	8.0	...
Maldives											
Total	...	*3 202*	*2 594*	*3 088*	*3 400*	*4 932*	...	...	...	...	...
Urban-Urbaine	...	*1 159*	*1 121*	*1 376*	*1 626*	*2 123*	...	...	...	...	...

Continent, country or area and urban/rural residence — Continent, pays ou zone et résidence, urbaine/rurale	Code[1]	Marriages - Mariages					Rate - Taux				
		2001	2002	2003	2004	2005	2001	2002	2003	2004	2005
ASIA — ASIE											
Maldives											
Rural-Rurale	...	*2 043*	*1 473*	*1 712*	*1 774*	*2 809*	...	...	...	...	...
Mongolia - Mongolie											
Total	C	12 393	13 514	14 572	11 242	14 993	5.1	5.5	5.9	4.5	5.9
Urban-Urbaine	C	6 091	7 206	8 374	6 195	8 242	4.4	5.1	5.8	4.2	5.5
Rural-Rurale	C	6 302	6 308	6 198	5 047	6 751	6.0	6.0	5.9	4.9	6.8
Occupied Palestinian Territory - Territoire palestinien occupé											
Total	C	24 635	22 611	26 267	27 634	28 876	7.5	6.7	7.5	7.6	7.7
Philippines											
Total	U	*559 162*	*583 167*	*593 553*	...	...	...	...	...	...	...
Qatar											
Total	C	2 194	2 351	2 550	2 649	2 734	3.4	3.4	3.6	3.5	3.4
Saudi Arabia - Arabie saoudite											
Total	...	*81 576*	*90 982*	*98 343*	*111 063*	*105 066*	...	...	...	...	...
Singapore - Singapour[20,21]											
Total	+C	22 280	23 198	21 962	22 189	22 992	5.4	5.6	5.2	5.2	5.3
Sri Lanka											
Total	+U	*186 698*	*190 832*	*193 387*	*191 985*	...	...	...	...	...	...
Syrian Arab Republic - République arabe syrienne[22]											
Total	+U	*153 842*	*174 449*	...	*178 166*	...	...	...	...	...	...
Tajikistan - Tadjikistan											
Total	C	28 827	32 262	39 143	47 320	52 352	4.6	5.0	6.0	7.1	7.6
Urban-Urbaine	C	8 587	9 721	11 190	...	...	5.1	5.7	6.4	...	...
Rural-Rurale	C	20 240	22 541	27 953	...	...	4.4	4.8	5.8	...	...
Turkey - Turquie[23]											
Total	+U	*453 213*	*447 820*	*477 451*	477 451	...	...	...	...	6.7	...
Urban-Urbaine	+U	*296 295*	*299 930*	*322 926*	...	...	...	...	...	...	...
Rural-Rurale	+U	*156 918*	*147 890*	*154 525*	...	...	...	...	...	...	...
Uzbekistan - Ouzbékistan											
Total	C	170 101	...	...	...	...	6.8	...	...	...	...
Urban-Urbaine	C	64 302	...	...	...	...	6.9	...	...	...	...
Rural-Rurale	C	105 799	...	...	...	...	6.7	...	...	...	...
Viet Nam											
Total	C	...	*964 701	...	...	...	...	*12.1	...	...	...
Urban-Urbaine	C	...	*254 281	...	...	...	...	*12.7	...	...	...
Rural-Rurale	C	...	*710 420	...	...	...	...	*11.9	...	...	...
Yemen - Yémen											
Total	...	*9 120*	*10 934*	...	...	...	...	...	...	...	...
EUROPE											
Albania - Albanie											
Total	C	25 717	26 202	27 342	20 949	21 795	8.4	8.5	8.8	6.7	6.9
Urban-Urbaine	C	...	12 171	11 785	9 679	...	...	9.0	8.6	6.9	...
Rural-Rurale	C	...	14 031	15 557	11 270	...	...	8.0	9.0	6.5	...
Andorra - Andorre											
Total	C	213	186	197	218	224	3.2	2.8	2.8	2.9	2.8
Austria - Autriche[24]											
Total	C	34 213	36 570	37 195	38 528	39 153	4.3	4.5	4.6	4.7	4.8
Belarus - Bélarus											
Total	C	68 697	66 652	69 905	60 265	...	6.9	6.7	7.1	6.1	...
Urban-Urbaine	C	...	53 838	57 028	49 001	...	...	7.7	8.1	6.9	...
Rural-Rurale	C	...	12 814	12 877	11 264	...	...	4.4	4.5	4.1	...
Belgium - Belgique[25]											
Total	C	42 110	40 434	41 777	43 326	43 182	4.1	3.9	4.0	4.2	4.1
Bosnia and Herzegovina - Bosnie-Herzégovine											
Total	C	20 302	20 122	20 733	22 252	21 698	5.3	5.3	5.4	5.8	5.6
Bulgaria - Bulgarie[26]											
Total	C	31 974	29 218	30 645	31 038	33 501	4.0	3.7	3.9	4.0	4.3
Urban-Urbaine	C	24 466	23 085	24 543	...	26 658	4.5	4.2	4.5	...	4.9

Continent, country or area and urban/rural residence / Continent, pays ou zone et résidence, urbaine/rurale	Code[1]	Marriages - Mariages					Rate - Taux				
		2001	2002	2003	2004	2005	2001	2002	2003	2004	2005
EUROPE											
Bulgaria - Bulgarie[26]											
Rural-Rurale	C	7 508	6 133	6 102	...	6 843	3.1	2.6	2.6	...	3.0
Channel Islands: Jersey - Îles Anglo-Normandes:											
Jersey											
Total	+C	664	...	...	...	...	7.6	...	...	...	...
Croatia - Croatie											
Total	C	22 076	22 806	22 337	22 700	22 138	5.0	5.1	5.0	5.1	5.0
Urban-Urbaine	C	12 380	12 918	12 375	12 713	12 326	5.0	...	...	...	...
Rural-Rurale	C	9 696	9 888	9 962	9 987	9 812	4.9	...	...	...	...
Czech Republic - République tchèque											
Total	C	52 374	52 732	48 943	51 447	51 829	5.1	5.2	4.8	5.0	5.1
Urban-Urbaine	C	39 666	40 014	37 134	38 999	39 392	5.2	5.3	4.9	5.2	5.2
Rural-Rurale	C	12 708	12 718	11 809	12 448	12 437	4.8	4.8	4.4	4.6	4.6
Denmark - Danemark[27]											
Total	C	36 567	37 210	35 041	37 711	36 148	6.8	6.9	6.5	7.0	6.7
Estonia - Estonie[28]											
Total	C	5 647	5 853	5 699	6 009	6 121	4.1	4.3	4.2	4.5	4.5
Urban-Urbaine	C	...	4 020	3 933	4 183	...	...	4.3	4.2	4.5	...
Rural-Rurale	C	...	1 491	1 491	1 582	...	...	3.6	3.6	3.8	...
Finland - Finlande[29]											
Total	C	24 830	26 969	25 815	29 342	29 283	4.8	5.2	5.0	5.6	5.6
Urban-Urbaine	C	17 843	19 398	18 534	20 957	20 961	5.6	6.0	5.7	6.5	6.4
Rural-Rurale	C	6 987	7 571	7 281	8 385	8 322	3.5	3.8	3.7	4.2	4.2
France[30,31,32]											
Total	C	288 255	279 087	275 963	271 598	276 303	4.8	4.7	4.6	4.5	4.5
Urban-Urbaine	C	222 689	214 125	210 905	205 239	206 846	...	...	...	...	...
Rural-Rurale	C	61 111	60 099	59 503	60 768	63 658	...	...	...	...	...
Germany - Allemagne											
Total	C	389 591	391 967	382 911	395 992	388 451	4.7	4.8	4.6	4.8	4.7
Gibraltar											
Total	C	164	166	179	159	182	6.0	5.8	6.3	5.5	6.3
Greece - Grèce											
Total	C	58 491	57 872	61 081	51 377	61 043	5.3	5.3	5.5	4.6	5.5
Urban-Urbaine	C	...	...	...	...	43 099	...	...	...	...	...
Rural-Rurale	C	...	...	...	...	17 944	...	...	...	...	...
Hungary - Hongrie[32]											
Total	C	43 583	46 008	45 398	43 791	44 234	4.3	4.5	4.5	4.3	4.4
Urban-Urbaine	C	28 876	31 207	30 703	29 682	30 759	4.4	4.7	4.7	4.5	4.6
Rural-Rurale	C	13 769	13 912	13 702	12 963	12 471	3.8	3.9	3.8	3.7	3.6
Iceland - Islande[33]											
Total	C	1 484	1 652	*1 473	1 515	*1 607	5.2	5.7	*5.1	5.2	*5.4
Urban-Urbaine	C	1 406	1 581	*1 400	1 428	*1 528	5.3	5.9	*5.2	5.3	*5.6
Rural-Rurale	C	78	71	*73	87	*79	3.6	3.3	*3.4	4.0	*3.8
Ireland - Irlande											
Total	+C	19 246	20 556	*20 302	*20 619	*21 355	5.0	5.2	*5.1	*5.1	*5.2
Isle of Man - Îles de Man											
Total	+C	392	430	413	399	...	5.1	5.6	5.3	5.1	...
Italy - Italie											
Total	C	264 026	270 013	264 097	248 969	247 740	4.6	4.7	4.6	4.3	4.2
Latvia - Lettonie											
Total	C	9 258	9 738	9 989	10 370	12 544	3.9	4.2	4.3	4.5	5.5
Urban-Urbaine	C	6 755	7 115	7 373	7 664	9 081	4.2	4.5	4.7	4.9	5.8
Rural-Rurale	C	2 503	2 623	2 616	2 706	3 463	3.3	3.5	3.5	3.6	4.7
Liechtenstein											
Total	C	199	175	149	164	*188	6.0	5.2	4.4	4.8	*5.4
Lithuania - Lituanie											
Total	C	15 764	16 151	16 975	19 130	19 938	4.5	4.7	4.9	5.6	5.8
Urban-Urbaine	C	11 036	11 637	12 066	13 239	14 156	4.7	5.0	5.2	5.8	6.2
Rural-Rurale	C	4 728	4 514	4 909	5 891	5 782	4.1	3.9	4.3	5.1	5.1
Luxembourg[33]											
Total	C	1 983	2 020	2 001	1 999	2 032	4.5	4.5	4.4	4.4	4.4
Malta - Malte											
Total	C	2 194	2 240	2 350	2 402	2 374	5.7	5.8	5.9	6.0	5.9

23. Marriages and crude marriage rates, by urban/rural residence: 2001 - 2005
Mariages et taux bruts de nuptialité, selon la résidence, urbaine/rurale: 2001 - 2005 (continued — suite)

Continent, country or area and urban/rural residence / Continent, pays ou zone et résidence, urbaine/rurale	Code[1]	Marriages - Mariages					Rate - Taux				
		2001	2002	2003	2004	2005	2001	2002	2003	2004	2005
EUROPE											
Malta - Malte											
Urban-Urbaine	C	...	...	...	2 210	...	...	...	...	...	...
Rural-Rurale	C	...	...	...	192	...	...	...	...	...	...
Monaco											
Total	C	175	175	183	171	161	...	...	...	...	...
Netherlands - Pays-Bas[34,35,36]											
Total	C	82 091	85 808	80 427	73 441	72 263	5.1	5.3	5.0	4.5	4.4
Urban-Urbaine	C	45 261	47 645	45 295	42 102	41 480	4.4	4.5	4.3	3.9	3.9
Rural-Rurale	C	27 847	28 671	26 897	24 698	24 351	4.9	5.1	4.8	4.4	4.4
Norway - Norvège[37]											
Total	C	22 967	24 069	22 361	22 354	22 392	5.1	5.3	4.9	4.9	4.8
Poland - Pologne											
Total	C	195 122	191 935	195 446	191 824	206 916	5.1	5.0	5.1	5.0	5.4
Urban-Urbaine	C	118 210	115 816	118 709	116 407	125 630	5.0	4.9	5.0	5.0	5.4
Rural-Rurale	C	76 912	76 119	76 737	75 417	81 286	5.3	5.2	5.2	5.1	5.5
Portugal											
Total	C	58 390	56 457	53 735	49 178	48 671	5.7	5.4	5.1	4.7	4.6
Republic of Moldova - République de Moldova											
Total	C	21 065	21 685	24 961	25 164	...	5.8	6.0	6.9	7.0	...
Urban-Urbaine	C	9 727	10 194	11 520	11 160	...	6.5	6.9	7.8	7.6	...
Rural-Rurale	C	11 338	11 491	13 441	14 004	...	5.3	5.4	6.3	6.6	...
Romania - Roumanie											
Total	C	129 930	129 018	133 953	143 304	141 832	5.8	5.9	6.2	6.6	6.6
Urban-Urbaine	C	77 231	76 547	81 483	90 179	92 651	6.3	6.6	7.0	7.6	7.8
Rural-Rurale	C	52 699	52 471	52 470	53 125	49 181	5.2	5.2	5.2	5.4	5.0
Russian Federation - Fédération de Russie											
Total	C	1 001 589	1 019 762	1 091 778	979 667	*1 066 400	6.9	7.0	7.6	6.8	*7.4
San Marino - Saint-Marin											
Total	+C	174	208	200	207	223	6.3	7.3	6.9	7.0	7.2
Serbia and Montenegro - Serbie-et-Montenegro[38]											
Total	C	57 165	45 741	45 964	*46 341	...	5.4	5.6	5.6	*5.7	...
Urban-Urbaine	C	32 572	28 262	28 866	...	...	5.9	6.1	6.2	...	...
Rural-Rurale	C	24 593	17 479	17 098	...	...	4.8	5.0	4.9	...	...
Slovakia - Slovaquie											
Total	C	23 795	25 062	26 002	27 885	26 149	4.4	4.7	4.8	5.2	4.9
Urban-Urbaine	C	13 591	14 370	15 068	15 986	15 180	4.5	4.8	5.0	5.3	5.1
Rural-Rurale	C	10 204	10 692	10 934	11 899	10 969	4.3	4.5	4.6	5.0	4.6
Slovenia - Slovénie											
Total	C	6 935	7 064	6 756	6 558	5 769	3.5	3.5	3.4	3.3	2.9
Urban-Urbaine	C	3 569	3 768	3 624	3 521	2 971	...	3.9	3.7	3.6	3.1
Rural-Rurale	C	3 366	3 296	3 132	3 037	2 798	...	3.4	3.2	3.1	2.8
Spain - Espagne[39]											
Total	C	208 057	211 522	212 300	216 149	*209 125	5.1	5.1	5.1	5.1	*4.8
Sweden - Suède											
Total	C	35 778	38 012	39 041	43 088	44 381	4.0	4.3	4.4	4.8	4.9
Switzerland - Suisse											
Total	C	35 987	40 213	40 056	39 460	40 139	5.0	5.5	5.4	5.3	5.4
Urban-Urbaine	C	25 668	31 057	30 870	30 120	30 781	4.8	5.8	5.7	5.5	5.6
Rural-Rurale	C	10 319	9 156	9 186	9 340	9 358	5.3	4.7	4.7	4.7	4.7
The Former Yugoslav Rep. of Macedonia - L'ex-République yougoslave de Macédoine											
Total	C	13 267	14 522	*14 402	*14 073	14 500	6.5	7.1	*7.1	*6.9	7.1
Urban-Urbaine	C	7 584	7 905	...	...	7 709	...	...	...	...	...
Rural-Rurale	C	5 683	6 617	...	...	6 791	...	...	...	...	...
Ukraine											
Total	C	309 602	317 228	370 966	278 225	...	6.4	6.6	7.8	5.9	...
Urban-Urbaine	C	223 638	231 532	277 014	209 369	...	6.9	7.2	8.7	...	...
Rural-Rurale	C	85 964	85 696	93 952	68 856	...	5.4	5.4	6.0	...	...

23. Marriages and crude marriage rates, by urban/rural residence: 2001 - 2005
Mariages et taux bruts de nuptialité, selon la résidence, urbaine/rurale: 2001 - 2005 (continued — suite)

Continent, country or area and urban/rural residence / Continent, pays ou zone et résidence, urbaine/rurale	Code[1]	Marriages - Mariages					Rate - Taux				
		2001	2002	2003	2004	2005	2001	2002	2003	2004	2005
EUROPE											
United Kingdom - Royaume-Uni											
Total	C	286 129	293 021	306 214	...	...	4.8	4.9	5.1	...	...
OCEANIA — OCEANIE											
American Samoa - Samoas américaines											
Total	C	254	292	285	287	202	4.3	4.8	4.6	4.5	3.1
Australia - Australie[40]											
Total	+C	103 130	105 435	106 394	110 958	109 323	5.3	5.4	5.3	5.5	5.4
Cook Islands - Îles Cook[41]											
Total	+C	578	604	623	645	755	31.8	32.8	33.9	31.8	37.4
Fiji - Fidji											
Total	+C	7 276	7 584	7 440	...	...	9.0	9.2	9.0	...	...
French Polynesia - Polynésie française											
Total	C	964	1 042	1 047	...	...	4.0	4.3	4.2	...	...
Guam[42]											
Total	C	1 418	1 288	1 334	...	...	9.0	8.0	8.2	...	...
New Caledonia - Nouvelle-Calédonie											
Total	C	925	905	873	895	...	4.3	4.1	3.9	3.9	...
Urban-Urbaine	C	592	621	594	...	...	...	...	...	...	...
Rural-Rurale	C	333	284	279	...	...	...	...	...	...	...
New Zealand - Nouvelle-Zélande											
Total	+C	19 972	20 690	21 419	21 006	20 470	5.1	5.3	5.3	5.2	5.0
Niue - Nioué											
Total	C	8	15	12	14	...	...	...	...	...	...
Samoa											
Total	...	*821*	...	...	...	...	...	...	...	...	...
Tonga											
Total	+C	771	750	697	...	...	7.7	7.4	6.9	...	...

FOOTNOTES - NOTES

Italics: data from civil registers which are incomplete or of unknown completeness.
-Italiques: données incomplètes ou dont le degré d'exactitude n'est pas connu, provenant des registres de l'état civil.

* Provisional. — Données provisoires.

[1] 'Code' indicates the source of data, as follows:
C - Civil registration, estimated over 90% complete
U - Civil registration, estimated less than 90% complete
+ - Data tabulated by date of registration rather than occurence.
... - Information not available

Le 'Code' indique la source des données, comme suit:
C - Registres de l'état civil considérés complèts à 90 p. 100 au moins.
U - Registres de l'état civil qui ne sont pas considérés complèts à 90 p. 100 au moins.
+ - Données exploitées selon la date de l'enregistrement et non la date de l'événement.
... - Information pas disponible.

[2] For Algerian population only. -Pour la population algérienne seulement.
[3] Including marriages resumed after 'revocable divorce' (among Moslem population), which approximates legal separation. -Y compris les unions reconstituées après un 'divorce révocable' (parmi la population musulmane), qui est à peu près l'équivalent d'une séparation légale.
[4] Data refer to Libyan nationals only. -Les données se raportent aux nationaux libyens seulement.
[5] Data exclude visitors. -Les données non compris des visiteurs.

[6] For residents only. -Pour les résidents seulement.
[7] Urban and rural distribution of marriages are displayed by place of residence of bride. The difference between 'Total' and the sum of urban and rural is due to the unknown place of residence of the bride. -La distribution des mariages entre zones urbaines et rurales est montrée selon le lieu de résidence de la mariée. La différence entre le 'Total' et la somme des chiffres pour les zones urbaines et rurales est due aux cas où le lieu de résidence de la mariée n'est pas connu.
[8] Number of marriages of which at least one person was resident of the Netherlands Antilles (marital tourism is excluded). -Nombre de couples mariés dont l'un des membres au moins résidait aux Antilles néerlandaises (le tourisme conjugal n'est pas pris en compte).
[9] Excluding tribal Indian population. -Non compris les Indiens vivant en tribus.
[10] Excluding Indian jungle population. -Non compris les Indiens de la jungle.
[11] Excluding nomadic Indian tribes. -Non compris les tribus d'Indiens nomades.
[12] For 2004, published by the United Nations Economic and Social Commission for Western Asia. -Pour 2004, publié par la Commission économique et sociale des Nations Unies pour l'Asie occidentale.
[13] For statistical purposes, the data for China do not include those for the Hong Kong Special Administrative Region (Hong Kong SAR), Macao Special Administrative Region (Macao SAR) and Taiwan province of China. -Pour la présentation des statistiques, les données pour la Chine ne comprennent pas la Région Administrative Spéciale de Hong Kong (Hong Kong RAS), la Région Administrative Spéciale de Macao (Macao RAS) et Taïwan province de Chine.
[14] Data refer to government controlled areas. -Les données se rapportent aux zones contrôlées par le Gouvernement.
[15] After 2004, figures refer to marriages of residents only. -Après 2004, chiffres se rapportent exclusivement aux mariages de résidents.
[16] Data relate to the Iranian Year which begins on 21 March and ends on 20 March of the following year. -Les données concernent l'année iranienne, qui commence le 21 mars et se termine le 20 mars de l'année suivante.
[17] Including data for East Jerusalem and Israeli residents in certain other

territories under occupation by Israeli military forces since June 1967. -Y compris les données pour Jérusalem-Est et les résidents israéliens dans certains autres territoires occupés depuis 1967 par les forces armées israéliennes.

[18] Data refer to Japanese nationals in Japan only. -Les données se raportent aux nationaux japonais au Japon seulement.

[19] Excluding data for Jordanian territory under occupation since June 1967 by Israeli military forces. Excluding foreigners, including registered Palestinian refugees. -Non compris les données pour le territoire jordanien occupé depuis juin 1967 par les forces armées israéliennes. Non compris les étrangers, mais y compris les réfugiés de Palestine enregistrés.

[20] Registration of Kandyan marriages is complete; registration of Moslem and general marriages is incomplete. -Tous les mariages des Kandyens sont enregistrés; l'enregistrement des mariages musulmans et des autres mariages est incomplet.

[21] Figures exclude marriages previously officiated outside Singapore or under religious and customary rites. -Les figures excluent les mariages célébrés précédemment au dehors de Singapour ou sous les rites réligieuse ou accoutumés.

[22] Excluding nomads. -Non compris les nomades.

[23] Data refer to provincial capitals and district centres only. -Les données se rapportent aux capitales des provinces et les chefs-lieux de districts seulement.

[24] Excluding aliens temporarily in the area. -Non compris les étrangers se trouvant temporairement le territoire.

[25] Including armed forces stationed outside the country, but excluding alien armed forces in the area unless marriage performed by local foreign authority. -Y compris les militaires nationaux hors du pays et les militaires étrangers en garnison sur le territoire, sauf si le mariage a été célébré pour l'autorité locale.

[26] Including Bulgarian nationals outside the country, but excluding aliens in the area. -Y compris les nationaux bulgares à l'étranger, mais non compris les étrangers sur le territoire.

[27] Excluding Faeroe Islands and Greenland. -Non compris les Iles Féroé et le Gröenland.

[28] Urban and rural distribution of marriages and divorces is displayed by place of residence of groom/husband. The difference between 'Total' and the sum of urban and rural is due to the unknown place of residence of grooms/husbands and to grooms/husbands living outside Estonia. -Les mariages et divorces sont classés par rapport à la résidence urbaine/rurale de l'époux. La somme des mariages et divorces par résidence urbaine/rurale est différente du 'total' car elle ne tient pas compte ni des résidences inconnues de l'époux ni des mariages et divorces d'époux vivant à l'étranger.

[29] Only marriages in which the bride was resident in Finland. -Seulement mariages où l'épouse réside en Finlande.

[30] Excluding Overseas Departments, namely, French Guiana, Guadeloupe, Martinique and Reunion, shown separately. -Non compris les départements d'outre mer, c'est-à-dire la Guyane française, la Guadeloupe, la Martinique et la Réunion, qui font l'objet de rubriques distinctes.

[31] Including armed forces stationed outside the country. -Y compris les militaires nationaux hors du pays.

[32] The difference between 'Total' and the sum of 'urban' and 'rural' is due to the cases of unknown place of residence or residence abroad. -La différence entre le 'Total' et la somme des données selon la résidence urbaine/rurale se rapporte à la situation ou on ignore la résidence ou si la résidence est à l'étranger.

[33] Data refer to de jure population. -Les données se raportent a la population de droit.

[34] Including same sex marriages. -Y compris les mariages entre personnes du même sexe.

[35] Marriages of couples of which at least one partner is recorded in a Dutch municipal register, irrespective of the country where the marriage was performed. -Mariages où un des conjoints au moins est inscrit dans un registre municipal néerlandais, quel que soit le pays où le mariage a été contracté.

[36] The difference between 'Total' and the sum of 'urban' and 'rural' is due to marriages (of which at least one partner recorded in a Dutch municipal register) contracted abroad. -La différence entre le Total et la somme des zones urbaines et des zones rurales est due aux mariages contractés à l'étranger (dont un des conjoints au moins est inscrit dans un registre municipal néerlandais).

[37] Only marriages in which the groom was resident in Norway. -Seulement mariages où l'époux réside en Norvège.

[38] Without data for Kosovo and Metohia. -Sans les données pour le Kosovo and Metohie.

[39] For 2005, including same sex marriages. -Pour 2005, y compris les mariages entre personnes du même sexe.

[40] In 2004, marriage registrations were sampled for the states for the states of New South Wales, Victoria, Queensland and South Australia, while the other states and territories were fully enumerated. -En 2004, on a procédé à des enquêtes par échantillonnage concernant les enregistrements de mariages dans les états de New South Wales, Victoria, Queenslands et South Australia et à un dénombrement complet dans les autres états et territoires.

[41] Excluding Niue, shown separately, which is part of Cook Islands, but because of remoteness is administered separately. -Non compris Nioué, qui fait l'objet d'une rubrique distincte et qui fait partie des îles Cook, mais qui, en raison de son éloignement, est administrée séparément.

[42] Including United States military personnel, their dependants and contract employees. -Y compris les militaires des Etats-Unis, les membres de leur famille les accompagnant et les agents contractuels des Etats-Unis.

Table 24

Table 24 presents the marriages by age of groom and age of bride for every year with available data between 2001 and 2005.

Description of variables: Marriage is defined as the act, ceremony or process by which the legal relationship of husband and wife is constituted. The legality of the union may be established by civil, religious or other means as recognized by the laws of each country.[i]

Marriage statistics in this table, therefore, include both first marriages and remarriages after divorce, widowhood or annulment. They do not, unless otherwise noted, include resumption of marriage ties after legal separation. These statistics refer to the number of marriages performed, and not to the number of persons marrying.

Age is defined as age at last birthday, that is, the difference between the date of birth and the date of the occurrence of the event, expressed in completed solar years. The age classification generally used in this table is the following: under 15 years, 5-year age groups through 90-94, and 100 years and over. The same classification is used for both grooms and brides.

In an effort to provide interpretation of these statistics, countries or areas providing data on marriages by age of bride and groom have been requested to specify "the minimum legal age at which marriage can take place with and without parental consent". This information is presented in the table 24-1 below.

Reliability of data: Data from civil registers of marriages that are reported as incomplete (less than 90 per cent completeness) or of unknown completeness are considered unreliable and are set in *italics* rather than in roman type. Table 23 and the technical notes for that table provide more detailed information on the completeness of marriage registration. For more information about the quality of vital statistics data in general, see section 4.2 of the Technical Notes.

Limitations: Statistics on marriages by age of groom and age of bride are subject to the same qualifications as have been set forth for vital statistics in general and marriage statistics in particular as discussed in Section 4 of the Technical Notes.

The fact that marriage is a legal event, unlike birth and death that are biological events, has implications for international comparability of data. Marriage has been defined, for statistical purposes, in terms of the laws of individual countries or areas. These laws vary throughout the world. In addition, comparability is further limited because some countries or areas compile statistics only for civil marriages although religious marriages may also be legally recognized; in other countries or areas, the only available records are church registers and, therefore, the statistics may not reflect to marriages that are civil marriages only.

Because in many countries or areas marriage is a civil legal contract which, to establish its legality, must be celebrated before a civil officer, it follows that for these countries or areas registration would tend to be almost automatic at the time of, or immediately following, the marriage ceremony. This factor should be kept in mind when considering the reliability of data, described above. For this reason the practice of tabulating data by date of registration does not generally pose serious problems of comparability as it does in the case of birth and death statistics.

Because these statistics are classified according to age, they are subject to the limitations with respect to accuracy of age reporting similar to those already discussed in connection with Section 3.1.3 of the Technical Notes. It is probable that biases are less pronounced in marriage statistics, because information is obtained from the persons concerned and since marriage is a legal act, the participants are likely to give correct information. However, in some countries or areas, there appears to be a concentration of marriages at the legal minimum age for marriage and at the age at which valid marriage may be contracted without parental consent, indicating perhaps an overstatement in some cases to comply with the law.

Aside from the possibility of age misreporting, it should be noted that marriage patterns at younger ages, that is, for ages up to 24 years, are influenced to a large extent by laws regarding the minimum age for marriage

Factors that may influence age reporting, particularly at older ages include an inclination to understate the age of the bride in order that it may be equal to or less than that of the groom.

The absence of frequencies in the unknown age group does not necessarily indicate completely accurate reporting and tabulation of the age item. It is sometimes an indication that the unknowns have been eliminated by assigning ages to them before tabulation, or by proportionate distribution after tabulation.

Another age-reporting factor that must be kept in mind in using these data is the variation that may result from calculating age at marriage from year of birth rather than from day, month and year of birth. Information on this factor is given in footnotes when known.

Earlier data: Marriages by age of groom and age of bride have been shown for the latest available year in most issues of the *Demographic Yearbook*. In addition, issues, including those featuring marriage and divorce statistics, have presented data covering a period of years. For information on the specific topics and the years covered, readers should consult the Historical Index.

24-1 Minimum legal age at which marriage can take place

Country or area	With parental consent		Without parental consent	
	Groom	Bride	Groom	Bride
Africa				
Egypt	18	16	...	...
Mauritius	16	16	18	18
America, North				
Anguilla	...	...	18	18
Bahamas	..	..	..	..
Bermuda	16	16	18	18
Canada	16	16	16	16
Costa Rica	16	16	18	18
Cuba	14	14	16	16
El Salvador	15	14	15	14
Mexico	16	14	18	18
Panama	16	14	18	18
Puerto Rico	16	14	18	16
America, South				
Brazil	14	12	...	...
Chile	14	12	18	18
Ecuador	14	12	...	...
Uruguay	14	12	18	18
Venezuela	21	18	...	...
Asia				
Armenia	18	17	...	...
Azerbaijan	18	17	...	...
Bahrain	15	...	...	...
China: Hong Kong SAR	16	16	21	21

Country or area	With parental consent		Without parental consent	
	Groom	*Bride*	*Groom*	*Bride*
China: Macao SAR	16	16	18	18
Israel	…	17	…	17
Japan	18	16	20	20
Kazakhstan	16	16	18	17
Korea (Republic of)	18	16	20	20
Kyrgyzstan	18	18	18	18
Occupied Palestinian Territory	15.5	14.5	…	…
Philippines	18-20	18-20	21	21
Singapore	16 (Muslim marriages) 18 (Civil marriages)	16 (Muslim marriages) 18 (Civil marriages)	21 (Muslim marriages) 21 (Civil marriages)	.. (Muslim marriages) 21 (Civil marriage) 18 if person has previously been married
Tajikistan	17	17	16	16
Turkey	15	14	18	18
Uzbekistan	17	17	17	17
Europe				
Albania	18	16	…	…
Austria	18	16	18	16
Belarus	18	18	18	18
Belgium	17	15	18	18
Bosnia and Herzegovina	18	18	18	18
Bulgaria	16	16	18	18
Croatia	16	16	18	18
Czech Republic	16	16	18	18
Denmark	18	15	18	18
Estonia	15	15	18	18
Finland	Under 18 consent of Ministry of Justice necessary	Under 18, consent of Ministry of Justice necessary	18	18
France	16	14	18	18
Hungary	16	16	18	18
Iceland	18	18	18	18
Ireland	…	…	18	18
Italy	16	16	…	…

Country or area	With parental consent		Without parental consent	
	Groom	Bride	Groom	Bride
Latvia	16	16	18	18
Lithuania	15 (by judgment)	15 (by judgment)	18	18
Luxembourg	...	...	18	18
Malta	16	16	18	18
Netherlands	16	16	18	18
Norway	16	16	18	18
Poland	-	16, 17	18	18
Portugal	16	16	18	18
Republic of Moldova	16	14	18	16
Romania	17	16	18	18
Russian Federation	16	16	18	18
Serbia and Montenegro	16	16	18	18
Slovakia	16	16	18	18
Slovenia	15	15	18	18
Spain	...	...	18	18
Sweden	18	18	18	18
Switzerland	...	...	18	18
The Former Yugoslav Rep. of Macedonia	16	16	18	18
Ukraine	14	14	18	17
United Kingdom	16	16	18	18
Oceania				
Australia	16	16	18	16
New Zealand	16	16	16	16

NOTES

[1] *Principles and Recommendations for a Vital Statistics System Revision 2*, Sales No. E. 01.XVII.10, United Nations, New York, 2001

Tableau 24

Le tableau 24 présente des statistiques concernant les mariages classés selon l'âge de l'époux et selon l'âge de l'épouse pour les années où les données sont disponibles entre 2001 et 2005.

Description des variables : le mariage désigne l'acte, la cérémonie ou la procédure qui établit un rapport légal entre mari et femme. L'union peut être rendue légale par une procédure civile ou religieuse, ou par toute autre procédure, conformément à la législation du pays[1].

Les statistiques de la nuptialité présentées dans ce tableau comprennent donc les premiers mariages et les remariages faisant suite à un divorce, un veuvage ou une annulation. Toutefois, sauf indication contraire, elles ne comprennent pas les unions reconstituées après une séparation légale. Ces statistiques se rapportent au nombre de mariages célébrés, non au nombre de personnes qui se marient.

L'âge désigne l'âge au dernier anniversaire, c'est-à-dire la différence entre la date de naissance et la date de l'événement, exprimée en années solaires révolues. Le classement par âge utilisé dans le tableau 24 comprend les groupes suivants : moins de 15 ans, groupes quinquennaux jusqu'à 90-94 ans, 100 ans et plus. On a adopté la même classification pour les deux sexes.

Dans un effort de fournir l'interprétation de ces statistiques, les pays ou les zones fournissant des données sur les mariages par l'âge de l'épouse et de par l'âge de mari ont été demandés d'indiquer "l'âge légal minimum avec auquel le mariage peut avoir lieu avec et sans consentement parental". Cette information est présentée dans le tableau 24-1 ci-dessous.

Fiabilité des données : les données sur les mariages issues des registres de l'état civil qui sont déclarées incomplètes (degré de complétude inférieur à 90 p. 100) ou dont le degré de complétude n'est pas connu sont jugées douteuses et apparaissent en italique et non en caractères romains. Le tableau 23 et les notes techniques s'y rapportant présentent des renseignements plus détaillés sur le degré de complétude de l'enregistrement des mariages. Pour plus de précisions sur la qualité des données reposant sur les statistiques de l'état civil en général, voir la section 4.2 des notes techniques.

Insuffisance des données : les statistiques des mariages selon l'âge de l'époux et selon l'âge de l'épouse appellent les mêmes réserves que celles formulées à propos des statistiques de l'état civil en général et des statistiques de la nuptialité en particulier (voir la section 4 des Notes techniques).

Le fait que le mariage soit un acte juridique, à la différence de la naissance et du décès, qui sont des faits biologiques, a des répercussions sur la comparabilité internationale des données. Aux fins de la statistique, le mariage est défini par la législation de chaque pays ou zone. Cette législation varie d'un pays à l'autre. La comparabilité est limitée en outre du fait que certains pays et zones ne réunissent des statistiques que pour les mariages civils, bien que les mariages religieux y soient également reconnus par la loi ; dans d'autres, les seuls relevés disponibles sont les registres des églises et, en conséquence, les statistiques peuvent ne pas rendre compte des mariages exclusivement civils.

Le mariage étant, dans de nombreux pays ou zones, un contrat juridique civil qui, pour être légal, doit être conclu devant un officier d'état civil, il s'ensuit que, dans ces pays ou zones, l'enregistrement se fait à peu près systématiquement au moment de la cérémonie ou immédiatement après. Il faut tenir compte de cet élément lorsque l'on évalue la fiabilité des données, dont il est question plus haut. C'est pourquoi la pratique consistant à exploiter les données selon la date de l'enregistrement ne pose généralement pas les graves problèmes de comparabilité auxquels on se heurte dans le cas des statistiques des naissances et des décès.

Étant donné que ces statistiques sont classées selon l'âge, elles appellent les mêmes réserves concernant l'exactitude des déclarations d'âge que celles dont il a déjà été question à la section 3.1.3 des Notes techniques. Il est probable que les statistiques de la nuptialité sont moins faussées par ce genre d'erreur, car les renseignements sont donnés par les intéressés eux-mêmes, et, comme le mariage est un acte juridique, il y a toutes chances que leurs déclarations soient exactes. Toutefois, dans certains pays ou zones, il semble y avoir une concentration de mariages à l'âge minimal légal de nubilité ainsi qu'à l'âge auquel le mariage peut être valablement contracté sans le consentement des parents, ce qui peut indiquer que certains déclarants se vieillissent pour se conformer à la loi.

Outre la possibilité d'erreurs dans les déclarations d'âge, il convient de noter que la législation fixant l'âge minimal de nubilité influe notablement sur les caractéristiques de la nuptialité pour les premiers âges, c'est-à-dire jusqu'à 24 ans.

Parmi les facteurs pouvant exercer une influence sur les déclarations d'âge, en particulier celles qui sont faites par des personnes plus âgées, il faut citer la tendance à diminuer l'âge de l'épouse de façon qu'il soit égal ou inférieur à celui de l'époux.

Si aucun nombre ne figure dans la rangée réservée aux âges inconnus, cela ne signifie pas nécessairement que les déclarations d'âge et l'exploitation des données par âge aient été tout à fait exactes. C'est parfois une indication que l'on a attribué un âge aux personnes d'âge inconnu avant l'exploitation des données ou qu'elles ont été réparties proportionnellement entre les différents groupes après cette opération.

Il importe de ne pas oublier non plus, lorsque l'on utilisera ces données, que l'on calcule parfois l'âge des conjoints au moment du mariage sur la base de l'année de naissance seulement et non d'après la date exacte (jour, mois et année) de naissance. Des renseignements à ce sujet sont donnés en note chaque fois que possible.

Donnés publiées antérieurement : on trouve dans la plupart des éditions de l'*Annuaire démographique* des statistiques concernant les mariages selon l'âge de l'époux et selon l'âge de l'épouse qui ont été établies à partir des données les plus récentes dont on disposait à l'époque. En outre, certaines éditions, y compris celles qui étaient plus particulièrement consacrées aux statistiques de la nuptialité et de la divortialité, présentaient des séries chronologiques. Pour plus de précisions concernant les années et les sujets pour lesquels des données ont été publiées, se reporter à l'index historique.

24-1 L'âge légal minimum avec auquel le mariage peut avoir lieu

Pays ou zone	Avec consentement parental		Sans consentement parental	
	Epoux	Epouse	Epoux	Epouse
Afrique				
Egypte	18	16	...	...
Maurice	16	16	18	18
Amérique du Nord				
Anguilla	...	...	18	18
Bahamas	..	..	..	..
Bermudes	16	16	18	18
Canada	16	16	16	16
Costa Rica	16	16	18	18
Cuba	14	14	16	16
El Salvador	15	14	15	14
Mexique	16	14	18	18
Panama	16	14	18	18
Porto Rico	16	14	18	16
Amérique du Sud				
Brésil	14	12	...	...
Chili	14	12	18	18
Equateur	14	12	...	...
Uruguay	14	12	18	18

Pays ou zone	Avec consentement parental		Sans consentement parental	
	Epoux	*Epouse*	*Epoux*	*Epouse*
Venezuela	21	18	…	…
Asie				
Arménie	18	17	…	…
Azerbaïdjan	18	17	…	…
Bahreïn	15	…	…	…
Chine: Hong Kong RAS	16	16	21	21
Chine: Macao RAS	16	16	18	18
Israël	…	17	…	17
Japon	18	16	20	20
Kazakhstan	16	16	18	17
Corée (République de)	18	16	20	20
Kirghizistan	18	18	18	18
Territoire palestinien occupé	15.5	14.5	…	…
Philippines	18-20	18-20	21	21
Singapour	16 (mariages musulmans) 18 (mariages civils)	16 (mariages musulmans) 18 (mariages civils)	21 (mariages musulmans) 21 (mariages civils)	.. (mariages musulmans) 21 (mariages civils) 18 si le mariage n'est pas le premier
Tadjikistan	17	17	16	16
Turquie	15	14	18	18
Ouzbékistan	17	17	17	17
Europe				
Albanie	18	16	…	…
Autriche	18	16	18	16
Bélarus	18	18	18	18
Belgique	17	15	18	18
Bosnie-Herzégovine	18	18	18	18
Bulgarie	16	16	18	18
Croatie	16	16	18	18
République tchèque	16	16	18	18
Danemark	18	15	18	18
Estonie	15	15	18	18

Pays ou zone	Avec consentement parental		Sans consentement parental	
	Epoux	*Epouse*	*Epoux*	*Epouse*
Finlande	Agrément du Ministère de la justice requis de moins de 18	Agrément du Ministère de la justice requis de moins de 18	18	18
France	16	14	18	18
Hongrie	16	16	18	18
Islande	18	18	18	18
Irlande	...	...	18	18
Italie	16	16	...	...
Lettonie	16	16	18	18
Lituanie	15 (en vertu d'une décision de justice)	15 (en vertu d'une décision de justice)	18	18
Luxembourg	...	...	18	18
Malte	16	16	18	18
Pays-Bas	16	16	18	18
Norvège	16	16	18	18
Pologne	-	16, 17	18	18
Portugal	16	16	18	18
République de Moldova	16	14	18	16
Roumanie	17	16	18	18
Fédération de Russie	16	16	18	18
Serbie-et-Montenegro	16	16	18	18
Slovaque	16	16	18	18
Slovénie	15	15	18	18
Espagne	...	...	18	18
Suede	18	18	18	18
Suisse	...	...	18	18
L'ex-République yougoslave de Macédoine	16	16	18	18
Ukraine	14	14	18	17
Royaume-Uni	16	16	18	18
Océanie				
Australie	16	16	18	16
Nouvelle-Zélande	16	16	16	16

NOTE

[1] *Principes et recommandations pour un système de statistiques de l'état civil, deuxième révision,* numéro de vente F.01.XVII.10, publication des Nations Unies, New York, 2003.

24. Marriages by age of bridegroom and by age of bride: 2001 - 2005
Mariages selon l'âge de l'époux et selon l'âge de l'épouse: 2001 - 2005

Continent, country or area and age / Continent, pays ou zone et âge	2001 Groom Epoux	2001 Bride Epouse	2002 Groom Epoux	2002 Bride Epouse	2003 Groom Epoux	2003 Bride Epouse	2004 Groom Epoux	2004 Bride Epouse	2005 Groom Epoux	2005 Bride Epouse
AFRICA — AFRIQUE										
Mauritius - Maurice[+]										
All ages - Tous âges	10 635	10 635	10 484	10 484	10 812	10 812	...	...	11 294	11 294
0-14	-	1	-	-	-	-	...	...	-	17
15-19	167	1 819	134	1 666	147	1 531	...	...	143	1 429
20-24	2 131	4 025	2 130	4 078	2 111	4 040	...	...	1 770	3 742
25-29	3 587	2 152	3 599	2 162	3 717	2 416	...	...	4 030	2 900
30-34	2 206	1 184	2 109	1 156	2 141	1 230	...	...	2 392	1 364
35-39	1 148	675	1 129	687	1 221	726	...	...	1 262	795
40-44	548	352	579	338	587	435	...	...	712	507
45-49	345	227	357	210	378	228	...	...	423	278
50-54	246	108	201	97	253	126	...	...	246	144
55-59	119	50	123	46	129	51	...	...	152	52
60-64	58	22	59	27	67	15	...	...	...	...
60+	...	...	...	...	...	...	...	...	144	41
65-69	35	9	41	11	35	5	...	...	...	...
70-74	23	7	15	3	14	4	...	...	...	...
75+	22	4	8	3	12	4	...	...	...	...
Unknown - Inconnu	-	-	-	-	-	1	...	...	20	25
Réunion										
All ages - Tous âges	...	...	3 284	3 284	...	...	...	...	...	...
15-19	...	...	...	148	...	...	...	...	...	...
18-19	...	...	16	...	...	...	...	...	...	...
20-24	...	...	402	823	...	...	...	...	...	...
25-29	...	...	908	921	...	...	...	...	...	...
30-34	...	...	761	551	...	...	...	...	...	...
35-39	...	...	428	372	...	...	...	...	...	...
40-44	...	...	294	229	...	...	...	...	...	...
45-49	...	...	192	99	...	...	...	...	...	...
50-54	...	...	120	65	...	...	...	...	...	...
55-59	...	...	62	38	...	...	...	...	...	...
60+	...	...	101	38	...	...	...	...	...	...
Seychelles[+]										
All ages - Tous âges	790	790	...	...	...	...	...	...	...	...
15-19	7	26	...	...	...	...	...	...	...	...
20-24	66	136	...	...	...	...	...	...	...	...
25-29	149	198	...	...	...	...	...	...	...	...
30-34	210	196	...	...	...	...	...	...	...	...
35-39	156	103	...	...	...	...	...	...	...	...
40-44	92	62	...	...	...	...	...	...	...	...
45-49	43	35	...	...	...	...	...	...	...	...
50-54	27	19	...	...	...	...	...	...	...	...
55+	40	15	...	...	...	...	...	...	...	...
AMERICA, NORTH — AMERIQUE DU NORD										
Anguilla										
All ages - Tous âges	...	...	...	...	75	75	...	...	...	...
18-23	...	...	...	...	9	13	...	...	...	...
24-29	...	...	...	...	24	24	...	...	...	...
30-35	...	...	...	...	17	17	...	...	...	...
36-41	...	...	...	...	9	9	...	...	...	...
42-47	...	...	...	...	10	6	...	...	...	...
48-53	...	...	...	...	1	3	...	...	...	...
54-58	...	...	...	...	1	1	...	...	...	...
59-64	...	...	...	...	2	1	...	...	...	...
65+	...	...	...	...	2	1	...	...	...	...
Unknown - Inconnu	...	...	...	...	-	-	...	...	...	...
Aruba[1]										
All ages - Tous âges	...	...	...	...	...	...	...	...	572	572
0-14	...	...	...	...	...	...	...	...	-	-
15-19	...	...	...	...	...	...	...	...	8	24
20-24	...	...	...	...	...	...	...	...	55	99
25-29	...	...	...	...	...	...	...	...	102	117
30-34	...	...	...	...	...	...	...	...	128	100
35-39	...	...	...	...	...	...	...	...	83	87
40-44	...	...	...	...	...	...	...	...	58	52

24. Marriages by age of bridegroom and by age of bride: 2001 - 2005
Mariages selon l'âge de l'époux et selon l'âge de l'épouse: 2001 - 2005 (continued — suite)

Continent, country or area and age / Continent, pays ou zone et âge	2001 Groom Epoux	2001 Bride Epouse	2002 Groom Epoux	2002 Bride Epouse	2003 Groom Epoux	2003 Bride Epouse	2004 Groom Epoux	2004 Bride Epouse	2005 Groom Epoux	2005 Bride Epouse
AMERICA, NORTH — AMERIQUE DU NORD										
Aruba[1]										
45-49	...	...	...	...	...	...	...	...	44	49
50-54	...	...	...	...	...	...	...	...	33	31
55-59	...	...	...	...	...	...	...	...	36	8
60-64	...	...	...	...	...	...	...	...	10	1
65-69	...	...	...	...	...	...	...	...	10	3
70-74	...	...	...	...	...	...	...	...	4	-
75+	...	...	...	...	...	...	...	...	1	1
Bahamas										
All ages - Tous âges	1 787	1 787	...	...	...	...	...	...	...	...
15-19	11	82	...	...	...	...	...	...	...	...
20-24	254	430	...	...	...	...	...	...	...	...
25-29	490	474	...	...	...	...	...	...	...	...
30-34	406	333	...	...	...	...	...	...	...	...
35-39	247	197	...	...	...	...	...	...	...	...
40-44	120	132	...	...	...	...	...	...	...	...
45-49	97	61	...	...	...	...	...	...	...	...
50-54	64	41	...	...	...	...	...	...	...	...
55-59	36	12	...	...	...	...	...	...	...	...
60+	51	14	...	...	...	...	...	...	...	...
Unknown - Inconnu	11	11	...	...	...	...	...	...	...	...
Bermuda - Bermudes										
All ages - Tous âges	...	...	937	937	861	861	...	...	...	...
0-19	...	...	2	8	-	9	...	...	...	...
20-29	...	...	206	302	191	256	...	...	...	...
30-39	...	...	423	397	386	380	...	...	...	...
40-49	...	...	165	146	162	152	...	...	...	...
50-59	...	...	97	65	91	52	...	...	...	...
60+	...	...	44	19	31	12	...	...	...	...
Canada										
All ages - Tous âges	146 618	146 618	146 738	146 738	...	...	...	...	...	...
15-19	976	3 674	919	3 504	...	...	...	...	...	...
20-24	19 912	32 479	19 421	31 526	...	...	...	...	...	...
25-29	43 787	45 073	43 355	45 377	...	...	...	...	...	...
30-34	30 309	25 056	30 788	25 579	...	...	...	...	...	...
35-39	18 172	14 550	18 266	14 675	...	...	...	...	...	...
40-44	11 308	9 481	11 497	9 526	...	...	...	...	...	...
45-49	7 580	6 728	7 711	6 827	...	...	...	...	...	...
50-54	5 670	4 345	5 667	4 349	...	...	...	...	...	...
55-59	3 466	2 295	3 686	2 372	...	...	...	...	...	...
60-64	2 053	1 190	2 101	1 254	...	...	...	...	...	...
65-69	1 386	791	1 362	807	...	...	...	...	...	...
70-74	965	501	910	481	...	...	...	...	...	...
75+	970	426	974	431	...	...	...	...	...	...
Unknown - Inconnu	64	29	81	30	...	...	...	...	...	...
Costa Rica										
All ages - Tous âges	23 790	23 790	...	...	24 448	24 448	25 370	25 370	25 631	25 631
0-14	-	81	...	...	-	30	-	32	-	17
15-19	1 328	4 907	...	...	1 110	4 335	1 112	4 230	977	3 775
20-24	6 934	7 629	...	...	6 642	7 642	6 655	7 637	6 041	7 461
25-29	6 101	4 669	...	...	6 362	5 105	6 651	5 456	6 782	5 741
30-34	3 667	2 444	...	...	3 809	2 609	3 969	2 868	4 045	2 986
35-39	2 015	1 394	...	...	2 227	1 607	2 301	1 705	2 385	1 666
40-44	1 184	923	...	...	1 420	1 013	1 409	1 106	1 613	1 220
45-49	807	530	...	...	825	668	1 008	757	1 065	769
50+	...	...	...	...	1 524	837	1 652	900	1 865	1 034
50-54	444	294	...	...	...	...	...	...	...	...
55-59	300	162	...	...	...	...	...	...	...	...
60-64	227	105	...	...	...	...	...	...	...	...
65+	562	127	...	...	...	...	...	...	...	...
Unknown - Inconnu	441	525	...	...	529	602	613	679	858	962
Cuba										
All ages - Tous âges	...	...	...	...	...	...	50 878	50 878	51 831	51 831
0-14	...	...	...	...	...	...	1	150	4	124
15-19	...	...	...	...	...	...	1 432	5 844	1 369	5 702

Continent, country or area and age / Continent, pays ou zone et âge	2001 Groom Epoux	2001 Bride Epouse	2002 Groom Epoux	2002 Bride Epouse	2003 Groom Epoux	2003 Bride Epouse	2004 Groom Epoux	2004 Bride Epouse	2005 Groom Epoux	2005 Bride Epouse
AMERICA, NORTH — AMERIQUE DU NORD										
Cuba										
20-24	...	...	...	...	...	...	6 571	9 816	6 989	10 276
25-29	...	...	...	...	...	...	9 037	7 863	8 638	8 060
30-34	...	...	...	...	...	...	9 211	8 091	9 514	8 122
35-39	...	...	...	...	...	...	7 604	6 522	7 873	6 527
40-44	...	...	...	...	...	...	5 448	4 732	5 942	5 214
45-49	...	...	...	...	...	...	3 136	2 627	3 188	2 795
50-54	...	...	...	...	...	...	2 552	2 124	2 549	1 960
55-59	...	...	...	...	...	...	2 013	1 335	1 977	1 331
60-64	...	...	...	...	...	...	1 527	776	1 550	801
65-69	...	...	...	...	...	...	999	448	939	423
70-74	...	...	...	...	...	...	609	226	555	210
75+	...	...	...	...	...	...	651	261	657	225
Unknown - Inconnu	...	...	...	...	...	...	87	63	87	61
El Salvador[+]										
All ages - Tous âges	29 287	29 287	26 077	26 077	25 071	25 071	...	...	...	...
0-14	-	85	-	42	-	45	...	...	...	...
15-19	1 272	4 262	1 026	3 446	928	3 283	...	...	...	...
20-24	7 999	9 207	6 609	7 790	6 394	7 568	...	...	...	...
25-29	7 211	6 369	6 601	6 012	6 451	5 900	...	...	...	...
30-34	4 547	3 628	4 048	3 247	3 923	3 195	...	...	...	...
35-39	2 712	2 113	2 539	2 040	2 415	1 818	...	...	...	...
40-44	1 742	1 322	1 626	1 302	1 516	1 157	...	...	...	...
45-49	1 225	935	1 043	820	1 028	833	...	...	...	...
50-54	806	570	845	588	750	516	...	...	...	...
55-59	599	358	612	331	576	328	...	...	...	...
60-64	512	206	478	231	413	199	...	...	...	...
65+	662	232	650	228	677	229	...	...	...	...
Guadeloupe										
All ages - Tous âges	...	...	1 809	1 809	1 701	1 701	...	...	...	...
0-14	...	...	-	-	-	-	...	...	...	...
15-19	...	...	-	35	3	28	...	...	...	...
20-24	...	...	91	223	49	226	...	...	...	...
25-29	...	...	377	523	320	423	...	...	...	...
30-34	...	...	503	401	437	412	...	...	...	...
35-39	...	...	369	255	328	238	...	...	...	...
40-44	...	...	204	165	197	122	...	...	...	...
45-49	...	...	99	89	121	94	...	...	...	...
50-54	...	...	68	45	74	61	...	...	...	...
55-59	...	...	44	29	63	35	...	...	...	...
60-64	...	...	19	23	41	29	...	...	...	...
65-69	...	...	34	10	30	11	...	...	...	...
70+	...	...	1	11	38	22	...	...	...	...
Jamaica - Jamaïque										
All ages - Tous âges	...	...	...	...	22 476	22 476	...	...	...	...
15-19	...	...	...	...	58	363	...	...	...	...
20-24	...	...	...	...	2 159	3 873	...	...	...	...
25-29	...	...	...	...	5 278	5 978	...	...	...	...
30-34	...	...	...	...	5 264	4 771	...	...	...	...
35-39	...	...	...	...	3 631	3 090	...	...	...	...
40-44	...	...	...	...	2 399	2 054	...	...	...	...
45-49	...	...	...	...	1 543	1 173	...	...	...	...
50-54	...	...	...	...	874	622	...	...	...	...
55-59	...	...	...	...	536	266	...	...	...	...
60-64	...	...	...	...	316	139	...	...	...	...
65+	...	...	...	...	418	147	...	...	...	...
Martinique										
All ages - Tous âges	...	...	1 524	1 524	1 414	1 414	...	...	...	...
15-19	...	...	1	6	1	11	...	...	...	...
20-24	...	...	42	140	46	144	...	...	...	...
25-29	...	...	321	432	235	328	...	...	...	...
30-34	...	...	366	340	340	353	...	...	...	...
35-39	...	...	281	236	273	203	...	...	...	...
40-44	...	...	176	142	185	144	...	...	...	...
45-49	...	...	95	88	114	83	...	...	...	...

24. Marriages by age of bridegroom and by age of bride: 2001 - 2005
Mariages selon l'âge de l'époux et selon l'âge de l'épouse: 2001 - 2005 (continued — suite)

Continent, country or area and age / Continent, pays ou zone et âge	2001 Groom Epoux	2001 Bride Epouse	2002 Groom Epoux	2002 Bride Epouse	2003 Groom Epoux	2003 Bride Epouse	2004 Groom Epoux	2004 Bride Epouse	2005 Groom Epoux	2005 Bride Epouse
AMERICA, NORTH — AMERIQUE DU NORD										
Martinique										
50-54	...	...	92	65	83	60	...	...	...	...
55-59	...	...	55	25	48	38	...	...	...	...
60-64	...	...	41	26	31	17	...	...	...	...
65-69	...	...	23	13	24	17	...	...	...	...
70+	...	...	31	11	...	16	...	...	...	...
70-74	...	...	...	...	29	...	...	...	...	...
75-79	...	...	...	...	4	...	...	...	...	...
80+	...	...	...	...	1	...	...	...	...	...
Unknown - Inconnu	...	...	...	...	-	-	...	...	...	...
Mexico - Mexique+										
All ages - Tous âges	665 434	665 434	616 654	616 654	584 142	584 142	600 563	600 563	595 713	595 713
0-14	466	7 245	791	6 498	651	5 767	684	5 686	119	4 366
15-19	86 922	188 887	79 473	172 569	72 248	159 789	71 804	158 523	68 082	151 639
20-24	236 321	226 389	217 228	210 334	204 677	198 599	205 552	201 349	199 676	198 189
25-29	176 987	134 343	165 299	126 194	156 597	120 060	157 519	123 279	156 104	122 770
30-34	76 429	51 129	73 322	49 124	71 657	48 765	77 228	53 071	78 893	55 394
35-39	33 917	23 267	31 711	21 304	30 433	20 718	33 181	23 221	34 734	24 753
40-44	18 618	12 735	16 727	11 403	16 217	11 282	18 126	13 046	18 829	13 647
45-49	10 920	7 939	9 918	7 101	9 716	7 144	10 981	8 206	11 627	8 843
50+	24 854	13 500	22 185	12 127	...	...	25 488	14 182	...	...
50-54	...	...	...	...	6 274	4 483			7 803	5 636
55-59	...	...	...	...	4 707	3 046			5 803	3 905
60-64	...	...	...	...	4 412	2 094			5 435	2 664
65-69	...	...	...	...	2 892	1 260			3 474	1 587
70-74	...	...	...	...	1 788	696			2 293	824
75-79	...	...	...	...	1 088	305			1 273	424
80-84	...	...	...	...	520	106			668	160
85-89	...	...	...	...	174	19	...	...	227	34
90-94	...	...	...	...	74	5	...	...	86	6
95+					17	4	...	...	31	8
Unknown - Inconnu	...	...	...	...	-	-	...	...	556	864
Panama[2]										
All ages - Tous âges	...	...	9 558	9 558	10 310	10 310	10 290	10 290	10 512	10 512
0-14	...	...	-	15	-	12	-	7	-	15
15-19	...	...	119	600	124	620	117	643	111	619
20-24	...	...	1 505	2 232	1 516	2 397	1 491	2 290	1 485	2 377
25-29	...	...	2 487	2 562	2 706	2 733	2 673	2 778	2 709	2 826
30-34	...	...	1 989	1 612	2 123	1 698	2 042	1 691	2 187	1 754
35-39	...	...	1 098	836	1 203	943	1 223	992	1 307	1 054
40-49	...	...	1 079	860	1 253	1 059	1 413	1 061	1 384	1 071
50-59	...	...	614	498	695	481	664	492	666	474
60-69	...	...	410	158	440	194	460	194	453	189
70+	...	...	169	44	176	51	166	50	178	55
Unknown - Inconnu	...	...	88	141	74	122	41	92	32	78
Puerto Rico - Porto Rico										
All ages - Tous âges	28 598	28 598	25 645	25 645	25 236	25 236	23 650	23 650	23 511	23 511
0-14	-	98	-	74	-	53	-	44	-	33
15-19	1 788	4 196	1 445	3 401	1 275	3 256	1 192	2 952	1 134	2 817
20-24	7 893	8 554	6 861	7 500	6 572	7 149	5 648	6 212	5 286	6 040
25-29	6 899	6 009	6 209	5 508	6 071	5 481	5 741	5 343	5 945	5 321
30-34	4 039	3 326	3 590	3 073	3 585	3 067	3 498	3 028	3 480	3 148
35-39	2 535	2 218	2 162	1 987	2 240	1 985	2 205	1 934	2 249	1 906
40-44	1 705	1 579	1 545	1 383	1 590	1 415	1 582	1 388	1 553	1 387
45-49	1 179	1 021	1 158	1 022	1 130	1 078	1 078	992	1 207	1 074
50-54	853	678	860	672	903	714	853	690	864	726
55+	1 706	917	1 815	1 025	1 869	1 038	1 853	1 067	...	...
55-59	...	...	...	...	...	...	...	...	648	496
60-64	...	...	...	...	...	...	...	...	526	303
65-69	...	...	...	...	...	...	...	...	266	139
70-74	...	...	...	...	...	...	...	...	179	77
75-79	...	...	...	...	...	...	...	...	113	29
80-84	...	...	...	...	...	...	...	...	39	10
85-89	...	...	...	...	...	...	...	...	16	5
90-94	...	...	...	...	...	...	...	...	6	-

Continent, country or area and age / Continent, pays ou zone et âge	2001 Groom Epoux	2001 Bride Epouse	2002 Groom Epoux	2002 Bride Epouse	2003 Groom Epoux	2003 Bride Epouse	2004 Groom Epoux	2004 Bride Epouse	2005 Groom Epoux	2005 Bride Epouse
AMERICA, NORTH — AMERIQUE DU NORD										
Puerto Rico - Porto Rico										
95-99	...	...	...	...	...	...	...	...	-	-
100+	...	...	...	...	...	...	...	...	-	-
Unknown - Inconnu	...	...	-	-	1	...	...	...	-	-
Saint Lucia - Sainte-Lucie										
All ages - Tous âges	513	513	472	472	489	489	...	...	...	...
0-14	-	-	-	-	-	-	...	...	...	...
15-19	1	8	1	12	1	8	...	...	...	...
20-24	41	98	34	74	31	84	...	...	...	...
25-29	114	141	104	121	114	128	...	...	...	...
30-34	110	85	107	90	103	102	...	...	...	...
35-39	84	73	74	76	95	71	...	...	...	...
40-44	70	47	58	44	61	41	...	...	...	...
45-49	34	25	30	20	34	23	...	...	...	...
50-54	16	7	21	12	18	13	...	...	...	...
55-59	12	15	13	12	9	8	...	...	...	...
60-64	11	5	8	5	8	4	...	...	...	...
65+	20	9	22	6	15	7	...	...	...	...
Trinidad and Tobago - Trinité-et-Tobago										
All ages - Tous âges	...	...	7 434	7 434	...	...	...	...	...	...
0-14	...	...	-	9	...	...	...	...	...	...
15-19	...	...	113	769	...	...	...	...	...	...
20-24	...	...	1 316	2 176	...	...	...	...	...	...
25-29	...	...	2 147	1 832	...	...	...	...	...	...
30-34	...	...	1 401	1 063	...	...	...	...	...	...
35-39	...	...	969	691	...	...	...	...	...	...
40-44	...	...	586	404	...	...	...	...	...	...
45-49	...	...	301	228	...	...	...	...	...	...
50-54	...	...	258	116	...	...	...	...	...	...
55-59	...	...	143	74	...	...	...	...	...	...
60-64	...	...	76	28	...	...	...	...	...	...
65+	...	...	124	44	...	...	...	...	...	...
Turks Caicos Islands - Îles Turques et Caïques										
All ages - Tous âges	...	...	593	593	491	491	499	499	489	489
0-14	...	...	-	-	-	-	-	-	-	-
15-19	...	...	1	2	-	3	-	5	-	3
20-24	...	...	20	52	19	48	24	49	19	40
25-29	...	...	130	148	123	163	104	130	88	120
30-34	...	...	164	193	130	131	126	136	149	142
35-39	...	...	116	93	96	59	95	96	95	103
40-44	...	...	80	56	52	47	72	42	69	37
45-49	...	...	47	30	30	24	36	29	34	31
50-54	...	...	19	15	23	9	22	5	20	8
55-59	...	...	10	2	14	5	13	7	6	3
60-64	...	...	...	-	...	...	4	-	7	1
60+	...	...	4	-	2	1	...	...	...	...
65+	...	...	...	...	...	...	3	-	1	-
Unknown - Inconnu	...	...	2	2	2	1	-	-	1	1
AMERICA, SOUTH — AMERIQUE DU SUD										
Brazil - Brésil[3]										
All ages - Tous âges	710 121	710 121	715 166	715 166	748 981	748 981	806 941	806 941	835 846	835 846
0-14	68	1 270	83	1 155	41	884	22	792	15	588
15-19	29 709	150 034	27 315	139 577	26 963	127 944	34 454	150 948	34 078	148 950
20-24	219 990	238 056	214 682	238 639	207 172	244 922	233 547	261 180	232 400	263 575
25-29	208 510	154 755	209 394	159 174	221 444	176 401	233 369	184 215	245 699	198 241
30-34	114 045	75 584	116 803	79 327	130 217	91 134	130 030	92 088	136 927	98 180
35-39	55 806	38 510	58 383	40 970	65 892	45 887	67 668	48 177	71 343	51 434
40-44	28 223	20 246	30 669	22 171	34 914	25 050	37 570	27 733	40 009	29 645
45-49	16 104	12 624	17 364	13 450	19 764	15 014	21 717	16 812	23 695	18 079
50-54	11 121	7 971	11 606	8 594	12 881	9 420	14 181	10 450	15 462	11 283

24. Marriages by age of bridegroom and by age of bride: 2001 - 2005
Mariages selon l'âge de l'époux et selon l'âge de l'épouse: 2001 - 2005 (continued — suite)

Continent, country or area and age / Continent, pays ou zone et âge	2001 Groom Epoux	2001 Bride Epouse	2002 Groom Epoux	2002 Bride Epouse	2003 Groom Epoux	2003 Bride Epouse	2004 Groom Epoux	2004 Bride Epouse	2005 Groom Epoux	2005 Bride Epouse
AMERICA, SOUTH — AMERIQUE DU SUD										
Brazil - Brésil[3]										
55-59	7 659	4 688	8 450	5 204	8 899	5 675	10 271	6 088	10 997	6 741
60-64	6 132	2 803	6 664	3 078	6 895	3 163	7 720	3 396	7 830	3 672
65+	12 294	3 051	13 179	3 214	13 798	3 365	14 898	3 570	15 920	3 968
Unknown - Inconnu	460	529	574	613	101	122	1 494	1 492	1 471	1 490
Chile - Chili[+]										
All ages - Tous âges	64 088	64 088	60 971	60 971	56 659	56 659	53 403	53 403	53 842	53 842
0-14	-	94	-	91	-	66	-	44	-	1
15-19	2 262	8 781	1 757	7 169	1 445	5 905	1 205	5 009	1 075	4 690
20-24	16 638	20 837	14 876	19 574	13 323	18 150	12 004	16 785	11 486	16 227
25-29	22 788	18 679	21 636	18 399	19 540	17 082	18 145	16 354	18 326	16 893
30-34	11 571	7 916	11 669	7 767	11 520	7 735	11 399	7 803	11 898	8 262
35-39	4 920	3 458	4 797	3 365	4 615	3 191	4 618	3 048	4 775	3 340
40-44	2 129	1 674	2 209	1 806	2 199	1 723	2 140	1 621	2 335	1 600
45-49	1 071	970	1 151	972	1 210	1 037	1 170	1 038	1 205	1 030
50-54	708	612	758	671	717	590	693	633	673	629
55-59	506	400	550	441	543	455	576	392	542	431
60-64	419	264	442	297	463	308	419	297	443	306
65-69	389	185	375	193	361	188	344	197	354	196
70-74	323	135	318	138	305	131	300	110	299	143
75+	364	83	433	88	418	98	390	72	431	94
Ecuador - Équateur[4]										
All ages - Tous âges	67 741	67 741	66 208	66 208	65 393	65 393	63 299	63 299	66 612	66 612
0-14	22	801	41	676	30	626	30	532	...	...
0-19	...	...	...	...	...	...	...	...	6 549	16 487
15-19	8 147	19 164	7 701	18 148	7 147	17 214	6 442	15 666	...	...
20-24	24 263	23 643	23 466	23 091	22 867	22 924	21 199	21 715	21 650	22 379
25-29	16 320	11 909	16 284	12 147	16 072	12 073	15 879	12 299	17 113	13 407
30-34	8 266	5 491	8 059	5 285	8 242	5 514	8 408	5 681	8 952	6 170
35-39	4 224	2 832	4 162	2 903	4 310	2 792	4 248	2 959	4 720	3 290
40-44	2 410	1 623	2 314	1 592	2 432	1 728	2 524	1 737	2 786	1 965
45-49	1 478	951	1 523	999	1 529	1 058	1 585	1 047	1 726	1 155
50+	...	...	...	...	...	...	...	...	3 080	1 692
50-54	971	560	942	563	960	605	1 019	677	...	...
55-59	562	302	605	333	611	336	655	353	...	...
60-64	391	187	409	178	414	211	436	232	...	...
65-69	284	124	263	141	320	160	325	170	...	...
70+	403	154	439	152	459	152	520	182	...	...
Unknown - Inconnu	...	...	-	-	-	-	29	49	36	67
French Guiana - Guyáne française										
All ages - Tous âges	...	...	522	522	524	524	...	...	...	...
0-14	...	...	-	-	...	...	...	...	...	...
15-19	...	...	3	22	4	25	...	...	...	...
20-24	...	...	39	101	34	90	...	...	...	...
25-29	...	...	101	118	100	128	...	...	...	...
30-34	...	...	113	97	131	117	...	...	...	...
35-39	...	...	90	68	86	64	...	...	...	...
40-44	...	...	55	54	54	30	...	...	...	...
45-49	...	...	50	24	38	34	...	...	...	...
50-54	...	...	28	15	25	22	...	...	...	...
55-59	...	...	15	16	29	7	...	...	...	...
60-64	...	...	14	3	8	3	...	...	...	...
65-69	...	...	7	3	4	3	...	...	...	...
70-74	...	...	7	1	6	1	...	...	...	...
75-79	...	...	-	-	1	-	...	...	...	...
80+	...	...	-	-	4	-	...	...	...	...
Paraguay										
All ages - Tous âges	17 950	17 950	16 100	16 100	17 717	17 717	17 763	17 763	19 826	19 826
0-14	-	34	1	12	-	19	-	29	-	33
15-19	643	4 690	501	3 873	612	4 377	638	4 320	670	4 107
20-24	5 841	6 105	5 280	5 849	5 632	6 362	5 872	6 510	5 831	6 861
25-29	5 154	3 322	4 817	3 143	5 405	3 358	5 311	3 427	6 058	4 312
30-34	2 892	1 668	2 506	1 431	2 779	1 555	2 757	1 542	3 196	2 022
35-39	1 422	837	1 236	741	1 337	803	1 340	796	1 699	1 013

Continent, country or area and age / Continent, pays ou zone et âge	2001 Groom Epoux	2001 Bride Epouse	2002 Groom Epoux	2002 Bride Epouse	2003 Groom Epoux	2003 Bride Epouse	2004 Groom Epoux	2004 Bride Epouse	2005 Groom Epoux	2005 Bride Epouse
AMERICA, SOUTH — AMERIQUE DU SUD										
Paraguay										
40-44	789	507	694	392	765	496	738	468	928	594
45-49	415	316	385	259	413	296	406	276	530	350
50-54	272	178	216	157	256	175	232	164	326	208
55-59	149	90	146	105	162	93	132	82	186	111
60-64	110	79	115	56	108	73	113	60	127	80
65-69	86	45	76	31	92	39	72	33	103	52
70-74	66	35	40	16	39	28	51	22	55	32
75+	104	29	82	23	110	27	92	22	104	30
Unknown - Inconnu	7	15	5	12	7	16	9	12	13	21
Suriname										
All ages - Tous âges	2 006	2 006	2 005	2 005	...	...	...	...	...	...
0-14	-	7	-	6	...	...	...	...	...	...
15-19	24	377	23	382	...	...	...	...	...	...
20-24	393	535	421	596	...	...	...	...	...	...
25-29	520	383	542	333	...	...	...	...	...	...
30-34	390	277	367	233	...	...	...	...	...	...
35-39	215	168	208	187	...	...	...	...	...	...
40-44	151	110	142	113	...	...	...	...	...	...
45-49	105	70	101	72	...	...	...	...	...	...
50-54	80	38	65	36	...	...	...	...	...	...
55+	128	41	136	47	...	...	...	...	...	...
Uruguay										
All ages - Tous âges	13 988	13 988	14 073	14 073	...	...	...	...	...	...
0-19	524	2 160	453	1 728	...	...	...	...	...	...
20-24	3 388	3 868	3 015	3 618	...	...	...	...	...	...
25-29	4 164	3 492	4 227	3 900	...	...	...	...	...	...
30-34	2 140	1 816	2 292	1 890	...	...	...	...	...	...
35-39	1 184	812	1 209	972	...	...	...	...	...	...
40-49	1 176	872	1 335	1 011	...	...	...	...	...	...
50+	1 412	968	1 542	954	...	...	...	...	...	...
Unknown - Inconnu	-	-	-	-	...	...	...	...	...	...
Venezuela (Bolivarian Republic of) - Venezuela (République bolivarienne du)[3]										
All ages - Tous âges	81 516	81 516	73 163	73 163	...	...	...	...	86 093	86 093
0-14	38	886	38	673	...	...	...	...	6	518
15-19	4 977	15 993	4 233	13 452	...	...	...	...	3 710	12 708
20-24	23 441	25 634	20 114	22 819	...	...	...	...	20 499	25 155
25-29	22 958	18 632	21 009	17 730	...	...	...	...	25 752	22 982
30-34	13 084	9 450	12 435	8 786	...	...	...	...	15 480	11 079
35-39	6 904	4 827	6 253	4 277	...	...	...	...	8 079	5 693
40-44	3 992	2 655	3 569	2 344	...	...	...	...	4 673	3 288
45-49	2 491	1 585	2 168	1 380	...	...	...	...	2 972	1 984
50-54	1 449	833	1 292	789	...	...	...	...	1 878	1 225
55-59	786	406	750	368	...	...	...	...	1 133	700
60+	1 396	615	1 302	545	...	...	...	...	1 911	761
ASIA — ASIE										
Azerbaijan - Azerbaïdjan+										
All ages - Tous âges	41 861	41 861	41 661	41 661	56 091	56 091	62 177	62 177	...	...
0-17	15	2 348	12	2 140	21	2 556	25	3 214	...	...
18-19	470	7 661	405	7 024	461	9 704	545	10 706	...	...
20-24	11 123	19 299	10 507	19 338	14 363	26 394	16 957	29 324	...	...
25-29	17 230	7 334	17 081	7 779	23 063	10 422	25 009	11 404	...	...
30-34	8 162	2 656	8 425	2 627	11 126	3 458	11 732	3 681	...	...
35-39	2 525	1 306	2 706	1 312	3 710	1 738	4 182	1 867	...	...
40-44	952	727	1 023	805	1 361	997	1 538	1 063	...	...
45-49	404	281	461	324	648	474	746	539	...	...
50-54	276	112	299	142	377	183	429	188	...	...
55-59	136	54	146	64	217	69	269	76	...	...
60+	568	83	596	106	744	96	745	115	...	...
Bahrain - Bahreïn										
All ages - Tous âges	...	...	4 909	4 909	...	...	...	...	...	...

Continent, country or area and age / Continent, pays ou zone et âge	2001 Groom Epoux	2001 Bride Epouse	2002 Groom Epoux	2002 Bride Epouse	2003 Groom Epoux	2003 Bride Epouse	2004 Groom Epoux	2004 Bride Epouse	2005 Groom Epoux	2005 Bride Epouse
ASIA — ASIE										
Bahrain - Bahreïn										
0-14	...	...	-	23	...	...	...	...	...	...
15-19	...	...	78	972	...	...	...	...	...	...
20-24	...	...	1 476	2 191	...	...	...	...	...	...
25-29	...	...	1 809	968	...	...	...	...	...	...
30-34	...	...	724	366	...	...	...	...	...	...
35-39	...	...	355	214	...	...	...	...	...	...
40-44	...	...	194	115	...	...	...	...	...	...
45-49	...	...	112	41	...	...	...	...	...	...
50+	...	...	158	17	...	...	...	...	...	...
Unknown - Inconnu	...	...	3	2	...	...	...	...	...	...
Brunei Darussalam - Brunéi Darussalam										
All ages - Tous âges	...	...	...	...	2 262	2 262	2 027	2 027	...	...
0-14	...	...	...	...	-	13	1	10	...	...
15-19	...	...	...	...	82	314	45	227	...	...
20-24	...	...	...	...	658	844	414	635	...	...
25-29	...	...	...	...	828	713	701	626	...	...
30-34	...	...	...	...	351	216	478	308	...	...
35-39	...	...	...	...	164	87	191	118	...	...
40-44	...	...	...	...	67	36	99	53	...	...
45-49	...	...	...	...	46	22	47	28	...	...
50-54	...	...	...	...	26	13	21	16	...	...
55-59	...	...	...	...	19	2	12	5	...	...
60-64	...	...	...	...	12	2	6	1	...	...
65-69	...	...	...	...	3	-	9	-	...	...
70+	...	...	...	...	6	-	3	-	...	...
China: Hong Kong SAR - Chine: Hong Kong RAS										
All ages - Tous âges	32 825	32 825	32 070	32 070	35 439	35 439	41 376	41 376	43 018	43 018
15-19	208	947	211	865	178	858	208	839	...	...
16-19	...	...	...	...	...	...	...	...	220	935
20-24	3 169	7 164	2 930	6 898	2 832	7 364	3 089	8 096	3 525	8 114
25-29	10 373	13 143	9 275	12 105	9 855	13 331	10 608	14 923	9 948	14 231
30-34	8 546	6 773	8 124	6 895	9 502	8 120	11 157	10 014	10 834	10 208
35-39	4 891	2 664	4 784	2 881	5 172	3 207	6 226	3 961	6 056	4 687
40-44	2 300	1 027	2 690	1 195	3 080	1 334	3 837	1 857	4 099	2 492
45-49	1 256	486	1 511	577	1 809	630	2 272	889	2 978	1 198
50-54	721	211	907	285	1 138	302	1 467	392	1 938	612
55-59	377	99	522	132	607	126	799	175	1 247	252
60-64	330	110	336	88	438	57	544	97	687	113
65-69	281	104	333	74	349	51	457	55	624	73
70-74	208	61	235	51	264	37	386	46	435	64
75+	165	36	212	24	215	22	326	32	427	39
China: Macao SAR - Chine: Macao RAS+										
All ages - Tous âges	1 222	1 222	1 209	1 209	1 309	1 309	1 737	1 737	1 734	1 734
15-19	10	52	9	45	20	53	19	52	24	71
20-24	129	233	126	247	121	305	217	424	259	491
25-29	392	480	388	462	444	511	533	684	523	601
30-34	298	200	290	243	366	265	487	345	468	304
35-39	156	109	165	88	160	97	203	118	188	145
40-44	88	55	79	54	77	41	118	59	106	70
45-49	48	28	77	34	72	21	84	36	75	23
50-54	28	26	30	16	15	5	34	8	44	12
55-59	21	16	14	8	10	3	16	3	12	5
60-64	16	5	8	1	5	2	6	2	10	4
65-69	16	9	8	6	9	2	10	2	9	4
70+	20	9	15	5	10	4	10	4	...	...
70-74	...	...	...	...	...	...	...	...	6	-
75+	...	...	...	...	...	...	...	...	10	4
Cyprus - Chypre[5,6]										
All ages - Tous âges	...	...	10 284	10 284	10 810	10 810	5 349	5 349	5 881	5 881
15-19	...	...	73	477	41	392	37	210	38	228
20-24	...	...	1 497	2 742	1 352	2 642	826	1 516	923	1 722
25-29	...	...	3 187	3 306	3 362	3 626	1 838	1 865	2 154	2 056

24. Marriages by age of bridegroom and by age of bride: 2001 - 2005
Mariages selon l'âge de l'époux et selon l'âge de l'épouse: 2001 - 2005 (continued — suite)

Continent, country or area and age / Continent, pays ou zone et âge	2001 Groom Epoux	2001 Bride Epouse	2002 Groom Epoux	2002 Bride Epouse	2003 Groom Epoux	2003 Bride Epouse	2004 Groom Epoux	2004 Bride Epouse	2005 Groom Epoux	2005 Bride Epouse
ASIA — ASIE										
Cyprus - Chypre[5,6]										
30-34	...	...	2 467	1 845	2 691	2 107	1 116	874	1 247	951
35-39	...	...	1 275	833	1 443	933	593	418	633	396
40-44	...	...	658	457	743	529	360	208	335	257
45-49	...	...	395	273	464	252	210	131	180	129
50-54	...	...	281	180	283	164	130	67	121	78
55-59	...	...	183	80	175	89	87	42	82	35
60+	...	...	226	48	243	61	147	14	166	27
Unknown - Inconnu	...	...	42	43	13	15	5	4	2	2
Georgia - Géorgie										
All ages - Tous âges	13 336	13 336	12 535	12 535	12 696	12 696	14 866	14 866	18 012	18 012
16-19	740	2 443	651	2 311	635	2 513	614	2 298	724	3 009
20-24	3 969	5 772	3 667	5 155	3 479	4 848	3 851	5 907	4 655	6 885
25-29	3 587	2 521	3 524	2 494	3 607	2 667	4 515	3 351	5 102	4 035
30-34	2 305	1 207	2 202	1 268	2 269	1 291	2 706	1 619	3 422	1 991
35-39	1 258	600	1 139	575	1 249	586	1 389	748	1 892	946
40-44	673	348	625	318	666	361	863	386	1 075	487
45-49	287	184	301	172	301	181	366	224	471	278
50-54	172	99	164	110	165	101	184	139	231	165
55-59	77	46	78	39	88	33	97	48	145	94
60+	262	99	181	89	196	96	254	139	274	109
Unknown - Inconnu	6	17	3	4	41	19	27	7	21	13
Israel - Israël[7]										
All ages - Tous âges	38 924	38 924	39 718	39 718	39 154	39 154	39 860	39 860	...	...
0-19	1 284	7 014	1 347	7 271	1 350	6 804	1 292	6 964	...	...
20-24	11 008	15 716	10 977	15 596	10 383	14 997	10 063	14 556	...	...
25-29	16 273	11 135	16 533	11 497	16 507	11 995	16 521	12 203	...	...
30-34	6 106	2 870	6 572	3 177	6 760	3 304	7 296	3 749	...	...
35-39	1 940	956	1 998	979	2 067	985	2 226	1 136	...	...
40-44	897	463	926	477	828	432	956	496	...	...
45-49	542	291	479	268	430	267	518	288	...	...
50-54	295	217	313	189	301	149	340	189	...	...
55-59	185	73	188	84	183	97	230	132	...	...
60-64	144	71	144	58	122	48	142	44	...	...
65-69	108	46	108	38	102	41	109	50	...	...
70-74	71	20	63	30	54	20	83	31	...	...
75+	71	20	58	14	67	15	84	22	...	...
Unknown - Inconnu	-	32	12	40	-	-	-	-	...	...
Japan - Japon[+,8]										
All ages - Tous âges	709 864	709 864	671 602	671 602	651 544	651 544	627 329	627 329	618 100	618 100
0-19	10 894	22 216	9 946	20 818	8 821	19 126	7 639	17 503	6 806	15 572
20-24	113 415	169 807	102 377	151 931	93 122	138 832	86 481	128 632	81 691	123 109
25-29	290 929	322 253	268 111	298 966	249 134	281 696	229 599	263 321	219 019	253 127
30-34	163 873	124 696	163 467	127 802	166 485	134 448	165 572	137 249	166 113	140 488
35-39	63 731	37 556	63 537	38 848	67 240	42 337	68 758	44 978	71 736	48 630
40-44	25 989	12 848	25 743	13 138	27 081	14 385	28 826	14 983	30 247	16 150
45-49	15 241	7 573	14 130	7 187	14 241	7 227	14 807	7 599	15 656	7 795
50-54	12 530	6 750	11 232	6 376	10 919	6 321	10 654	5 668	10 588	5 499
55-59	6 457	3 214	6 109	3 361	6 937	3 695	7 343	3 818	8 121	4 070
60-64	3 545	1 700	3 660	1 842	4 063	1 987	4 054	2 102	4 278	2 062
65-69	1 831	778	1 780	789	1 886	924	1 921	905	2 031	926
70-74	876	289	866	367	947	367	1 031	371	1 041	431
75+	547	184	639	177	664	193	644	197	770	237
Unknown - Inconnu	6	-	5	-	4	6	-	3	3	4
Kazakhstan										
All ages - Tous âges	...	...	...	...	110 414	110 414	114 685	114 685	...	...
0-14	...	...	...	...	-	-	...	...	...	...
0-17	...	...	...	...	...	...	129	1 629	...	...
15-19	...	...	...	...	3 769	17 568	...	...	...	...
18-19	...	...	...	...	...	...	3 548	15 887	...	...
20-24	...	...	...	...	39 569	53 270	40 037	55 161	...	...
25-29	...	...	...	...	36 302	21 459	38 314	23 049	...	...
30-34	...	...	...	...	15 021	8 367	16 150	8 886	...	...
35-39	...	...	...	...	6 483	3 795	6 863	4 027	...	...
40-44	...	...	...	...	3 659	2 256	3 877	2 343	...	...
45-49	...	...	...	...	2 021	1 363	2 222	1 493	...	...

Continent, country or area and age / Continent, pays ou zone et âge	2001 Groom Epoux	2001 Bride Epouse	2002 Groom Epoux	2002 Bride Epouse	2003 Groom Epoux	2003 Bride Epouse	2004 Groom Epoux	2004 Bride Epouse	2005 Groom Epoux	2005 Bride Epouse
ASIA — ASIE										
Kazakhstan										
50-54	...	...	...	...	1 320	964	1 380	933	...	...
55-59	...	...	...	...	639	453	763	498	...	...
60-64	...	...	...	...	668	420	...	...	...	...
60+	...	...	...	...	...	...	1 397	777	...	...
65-69	...	...	...	...	503	298	...	...	...	...
70-74	...	...	...	...	237	120	...	...	...	...
75-79	...	...	...	...	165	52	...	...	...	...
80-84	...	...	...	...	42	10	...	...	...	...
85-89	...	...	...	...	14	3	...	...	...	...
90-94	...	...	...	...	1	3	...	...	...	...
Unknown - Inconnu	...	...	...	...	1	13	5	2	...	...
Korea (Republic of) - Corée (République de)[+]										
All ages - Tous âges	320 063	320 063	306 573	306 573	304 932	304 932	310 944	310 944	316 375	316 375
0-14	6	41	1	28	1	34	2	30	-	13
15-19	1 899	6 895	1 553	5 742	1 333	5 140	1 173	5 060	1 013	5 882
20-24	21 914	74 009	19 169	65 388	17 249	59 210	16 215	53 777	14 913	48 974
25-29	147 192	158 129	133 725	151 349	124 030	148 493	113 432	146 356	109 387	147 243
30-34	91 070	41 655	94 321	44 525	97 149	48 702	102 894	53 620	104 734	57 570
35-39	26 123	17 687	25 568	17 110	27 655	17 902	31 301	20 499	35 399	22 190
40-44	14 404	11 577	14 316	11 673	15 774	12 814	18 328	14 924	20 036	15 646
45-49	7 615	5 579	8 080	6 051	9 906	7 187	12 569	9 673	14 275	10 721
50-54	4 611	2 523	4 687	2 622	5 511	3 110	7 124	4 214	8 094	5 070
55+	5 223	1 963	5 133	2 042	6 311	2 309	7 906	2 791	8 524	3 066
Unknown - Inconnu	6	5	20	43	13	31	-	-	-	-
Kuwait - Koweït										
All ages - Tous âges	...	...	...	...	...	...	12 359	12 359	12 419	12 419
0-14	...	...	...	...	...	...	...	66	...	54
0-19	...	...	...	...	...	...	690	...	430	...
15-19	...	...	...	...	...	...	...	2 697	...	2 750
20-24	...	...	...	...	...	...	4 638	4 375	3 990	4 839
25-29	...	...	...	...	...	...	3 574	2 241	3 492	2 298
30-34	...	...	...	...	...	...	1 442	1 262	1 668	1 088
35-39	...	...	...	...	...	...	819	755	941	654
40-44	...	...	...	...	...	...	441	461	591	370
45-49	...	...	...	...	...	...	240	227	316	166
50-54	...	...	...	...	...	...	120	92	195	49
55-59	...	...	...	...	...	...	74	41	81	13
60-64	...	...	...	...	...	...	39	...	42	...
60+	...	...	...	...	...	...	...	51	...	12
65-69	...	...	...	...	...	...	20	...	36	...
70-74	...	...	...	...	...	...	8	15	...	...
75+	...	...	...	...	...	...	5	14	...	...
Unknown - Inconnu	...	...	...	...	...	...	249	91	608	126
Kyrgyzstan - Kirghizistan										
All ages - Tous âges	27 455	27 455	31 240	31 240	34 266	34 266	34 542	34 542	37 321	37 321
0-14	-	-	-	-	-	-	-	-	-	-
15-19	830	6 666	768	6 953	815	7 015	726	6 402	713	6 494
20-24	10 746	13 596	11 206	15 498	11 942	17 470	12 049	18 234	12 729	19 644
25-29	9 753	4 050	11 657	5 106	13 164	5 751	13 245	5 840	14 330	6 597
30-34	3 196	1 407	4 294	1 728	4 743	2 036	4 931	2 099	5 392	2 402
35-39	1 179	646	1 422	793	1 595	866	1 602	823	1 979	958
40-44	669	403	727	452	803	461	768	493	922	542
45-49	358	273	401	268	457	245	464	276	490	284
50-54	251	171	262	170	256	170	291	168	301	172
55-59	91	57	107	70	111	75	190	91	188	121
60-64	163	96	166	95	142	68	81	34	83	23
65-69	90	44	101	48	111	65	85	52	98	51
70-74	73	30	57	39	60	23	58	17	45	21
75+	56	16	72	20	-	21	52	13	-	12
Unknown - Inconnu	-	-	-	-	67	-	-	-	51	-
Mongolia - Mongolie										
All ages - Tous âges	12 393	12 393	...	...	...	...	...	...	...	...
18-19	473	1 177	...	...	...	...	...	...	...	...
20-24	4 917	5 813	...	...	...	...	...	...	...	...

Continent, country or area and age / Continent, pays ou zone et âge	2001 Groom Epoux	2001 Bride Epouse	2002 Groom Epoux	2002 Bride Epouse	2003 Groom Epoux	2003 Bride Epouse	2004 Groom Epoux	2004 Bride Epouse	2005 Groom Epoux	2005 Bride Epouse
ASIA — ASIE										
Mongolia - Mongolie										
25-29	4 135	3 335	...	...	...	...	...	...	...	...
30-34	1 580	1 196	...	...	...	...	...	...	...	...
35-39	839	620	...	...	...	...	...	...	...	...
40-44	302	175	...	...	...	...	...	...	...	...
45-49	78	54	...	...	...	...	...	...	...	...
50+	69	23	...	...	...	...	...	...	...	...
Occupied Palestinian Territory - Territoire palestinien occupé										
All ages - Tous âges	24 635	24 635	22 611	22 611	26 267	26 267	27 634	27 634	28 876	28 876
0-14	3	926	3	810	3	920	4	903	2	845
15-19	2 396	13 168	2 093	11 893	2 099	13 470	2 148	13 959	2 121	14 512
20-24	10 255	6 963	9 505	6 640	10 628	8 085	11 126	8 752	11 435	9 241
25-29	7 426	2 046	6 982	1 930	8 655	2 278	9 259	2 449	9 948	2 568
30-34	2 222	804	1 942	685	2 532	817	2 643	826	2 824	880
35-39	841	481	769	381	892	406	933	446	935	457
40-44	427	145	413	183	485	201	484	200	541	252
45-49	304	60	270	58	286	57	306	66	326	74
50-54	235	30	200	20	225	20	228	15	227	34
55-59	191	7	132	7	154	9	160	9	161	8
60-64	126	3	107	1	105	3	...	...	...	...
60+	...	...	...	...	...	...	343	9	356	5
65-69	104	1	97	3	95	1	...	...	...	...
70-74	57	1	63	-	62	-	...	...	...	...
75+	48	-	35	-	46	-	...	...	...	...
Unknown - Inconnu	-	-	-	-	-	-	...	...	-	...
Philippines										
All ages - Tous âges	...	...	583 167	583 167	593 553	593 553	...	...		
0-19	...	...	20 425	80 800	19 799	80 045	...	...		
20-24	...	...	185 224	232 790	185 610	235 351	...	...		
25-29	...	...	185 828	146 876	191 627	152 719	...	...		
30-34	...	...	94 770	62 664	97 265	63 908	...	...		
35-39	...	...	42 505	28 343	43 067	28 845	...	...		
40-44	...	...	22 041	14 589	22 826	15 000	...	...		
45-49	...	...	12 584	7 906	12 903	8 124	...	...		
50+	...	...	19 655	9 036	20 216	9 288	...	...		
Unknown - Inconnu	...	...	135	163	240	273	...	...		
Qatar										
All ages - Tous âges	2 194	2 194	2 351	2 351	2 550	2 550	2 649	2 649	2 734	2 734
0-14	...	9	...	8	...	5	...	7	...	9
0-19	34	...	36	...	35	...	30	...	51	...
15-19	...	374	...	374	...	346	...	350	...	426
20-24	563	970	610	1 037	611	1 096	632	1 109	706	1 162
25-29	858	494	882	582	966	653	958	718	996	660
30-34	420	173	469	197	515	259	541	233	520	261
35-39	145	101	171	89	200	97	222	137	205	112
40-44	81	56	94	42	105	62	147	66	112	61
45-49	46	9	44	17	64	24	64	21	69	33
50-54	22	7	17	2	27	6	37	8	35	6
55-59	9	1	9	-	11	1	9	-	21	3
60-64	10	-	11	...	10	...	5	...	8	...
60+	...	...	...	1	...	...	...	...	...	1
65-69	2	...	5	...	1	...	3	...	5	...
70-74	3	...	2	...	4	...	1	...	5	...
75+	-	...	1	...	1	...	-	...	1	...
Unknown - Inconnu	1	-	-	2	...	1	-	...	...	...
Singapore - Singapour[+,9,10]										
All ages - Tous âges	22 280	22 280	23 198	23 198	21 962	21 962	...	...	22 992	22 992
0-14	1	-	-	-	-	-	...	...	-	-
15-19	194	821	157	747	139	620	...	...	120	731
20-24	2 464	6 450	2 371	6 399	2 103	5 639	...	...	2 056	5 331
25-29	9 235	9 420	9 830	10 270	8 923	9 798	...	...	7 936	9 634
30-34	5 185	3 223	5 595	3 470	5 613	3 539	...	...	5 960	4 216
35-39	2 535	1 342	2 629	1 243	2 476	1 254	...	...	2 873	1 645
40-44	1 352	587	1 297	592	1 323	616	...	...	1 795	770
45-49	669	260	693	295	714	318	...	...	1 108	398

Continent, country or area and age / Continent, pays ou zone et âge	2001 Groom Epoux	2001 Bride Epouse	2002 Groom Epoux	2002 Bride Epouse	2003 Groom Epoux	2003 Bride Epouse	2004 Groom Epoux	2004 Bride Epouse	2005 Groom Epoux	2005 Bride Epouse
ASIA — ASIE										
Singapore - Singapour[+,9,10]										
50-54	341	107	306	112	373	114	...	...	607	165
55-59	145.	35	175	51	179	49	...	...	314	69
60+	159	35	145	19	119	15	...	...	223	33
Turkey - Turquie[+,11]										
All ages - Tous âges	...	...	447 820	447 820	477 451	477 451	...	...	...	...
0-14	...	...	-	56	-	41	...	...	...	...
15-19	...	...	12 791	89 528	15 893	107 391	...	...	...	...
20-24	...	...	146 045	215 165	156 240	211 468	...	...	...	...
25-29	...	...	196 070	95 032	199 876	104 470	...	...	...	...
30-34	...	...	51 744	24 599	60 267	29 557	...	...	...	...
35-39	...	...	17 915	10 906	20 107	11 153	...	...	...	...
40-44	...	...	7 998	5 479	9 141	6 070	...	...	...	...
45-49	...	...	4 802	2 992	5 013	3 150	...	...	...	...
50-54	...	...	3 171	1 876	3 511	1 940	...	...	...	...
55-59	...	...	2 049	871	2 285	976	...	...	...	...
60-64	...	...	1 840	614	1 883	628	...	...	...	...
65-69	...	...	1 635	391	1 384	299	...	...	...	...
70-74	...	...	1 210	211	1 229	200	...	...	...	...
75+	...	...	550	100	622	108	...	...	...	...
EUROPE										
Albania - Albanie										
All ages - Tous âges	25 717	25 717	26 202	26 202	27 342	27 342	20 949	20 949		
0-19	141	4 557	374	7 491	342	7 833	...	...		
15-19	...	...	...	...	...	...	186	4 696	...	...
20-24	3 721	12 433	5 855	11 881	6 062	12 388	4 326	10 275	...	...
25-29	11 128	5 865	11 350	4 497	12 061	4 689	9 011	3 863	...	...
30-34	7 069	1 776	5 759	1 401	5 892	1 472	4 864	1 283	...	...
35-39	1 981	519	1 661	537	1 705	557	1 520	468	...	...
40-44	694	249	649	228	688	223	540	199	...	...
45-49	262	96	261	108	299	124	240	99	...	...
50+	303	70	293	59	293	56	262	66	...	...
Unknown - Inconnu	418	152	-	-	-	-	-	-	...	...
Austria - Autriche[12]										
All ages - Tous âges	34 213	34 213	36 570	36 570	37 195	37 195	38 528	38 528	39 153	39 153
0-14	-	-	-	-	-	-	-	-	-	-
15-19	389	1 334	449	1 420	447	1 396	441	1 456	382	1 330
20-24	3 852	7 261	4 020	7 565	4 080	7 373	4 137	7 312	3 812	7 180
25-29	9 019	10 063	9 182	10 528	8 904	10 564	8 963	10 477	8 809	10 562
30-34	8 795	7 063	9 343	7 368	9 358	7 625	9 332	7 863	9 592	8 036
35-39	5 118	3 740	5 662	4 290	5 874	4 399	6 393	4 731	6 529	4 921
40-44	2 704	2 151	3 143	2 423	3 417	2 641	3 667	2 907	3 981	3 130
45-49	1 527	1 233	1 767	1 369	1 935	1 504	2 140	1 825	2 358	1 905
50-54	1 148	740	1 213	830	1 211	902	1 307	943	1 394	1 104
55-59	823	365	859	490	953	485	1 031	586	1 080	577
60-64	478	165	581	190	637	192	675	303	701	260
65-69	169	46	160	48	178	69	237	85	300	95
70-74	94	30	101	28	98	29	107	17	95	30
75+	97	22	...	...	...	...	...	...	...	...
75-79	...	...	55	13	59	12	56	14	65	10
80-84	...	...	27	7	33	2	30	8	36	11
85-89	...	...	5	-	11	1	9	1	13	1
90-94	...	...	2	1	-	1	2	-	5	1
95+	...	...	1	-	-	-	1	-	1	-
Unknown - Inconnu	...	...	...	...	...	...	...	...	...	...
Belarus - Bélarus										
All ages - Tous âges	68 697	68 697	66 652	66 652	69 905	69 905	60 265	60 265	...	...
0-17	179	1 662	174	1 473	112	1 368	114	1 124	...	...
18-19	2 366	11 234	2 205	10 378	2 229	9 977	1 741	7 769	...	...
20-24	30 286	30 583	28 696	29 986	29 274	32 120	24 573	27 339	...	...
25-29	17 134	11 096	17 032	10 687	18 453	11 695	15 980	10 542	...	...
30-34	6 876	4 944	6 658	4 851	7 349	5 288	6 366	4 676	...	...
35-39	4 042	3 058	3 779	2 901	3 941	2 857	3 478	2 670	...	...
40-44	2 776	2 172	2 820	2 205	2 915	2 222	2 718	1 989	...	...

Continent, country or area and age / Continent, pays ou zone et âge	2001		2002		2003		2004		2005	
	Groom Epoux	Bride Epouse	Groom Epoux	Bride Epouse	Groom Epoux	Bride Epouse	Groom Epoux	Bride Epouse	Groom Epoux	Bride Epouse
EUROPE										
Belarus - Bélarus										
45-49	1 704	1 416	1 853	1 572	2 018	1 667	1 888	1 609	...	...
50-54	1 255	1 008	1 317	1 074	1 362	1 133	1 259	1 046	...	...
55-59	552	460	638	502	779	575	822	600	...	...
60+	1 527	1 064	1 480	1 023	1 473	1 003	1 326	901	...	...
Bosnia and Herzegovina - Bosnie-Herzégovine										
All ages - Tous âges	20 302	20 302	20 122	20 122	20 733	20 733	21 470	21 470	21 698	21 698
0-14	-	1	-	1	-	1	-	1	-	-
15-19	277	3 571	273	3 364	275	3 260	288	3 260	280	3 147
20-24	5 877	8 316	5 698	8 186	5 694	8 541	5 755	8 762	5 716	8 707
25-29	6 704	4 211	6 721	4 402	7 111	4 587	7 505	4 969	7 586	5 184
30-34	3 361	1 800	3 408	1 810	3 446	1 865	3 689	2 010	3 816	2 076
35-39	1 741	949	1 756	880	1 778	958	1 784	916	1 772	991
40-44	...	...	833	527	927	578	981	580	1 004	590
40-49	1 399	861	...	...	...	...	...	...	...	...
45-49	...	...	462	369	536	382	486	382	516	356
50+	935	573	...	...	...	...	...	...	...	...
50-54	...	...	293	225	281	231	321	252	303	293
55-59	...	...	175	114	194	113	177	134	231	149
60-64	...	...	170	85	159	93	155	90	141	84
65-69	...	...	159	64	151	68	136	59	162	62
70-74	...	...	106	23	94	19	98	21	103	22
75+	...	...	52	17	68	12	86	16	63	13
Unknown - Inconnu	8	20	16	55	19	25	9	18	5	24
Bulgaria - Bulgarie[13]										
All ages - Tous âges	31 974	31 974	29 218	29 218	30 645	30 645	31 038	31 038	33 501	33 501
0-14	...	...	-	-	-	-	-	-	-	-
15-19	...	...	401	3 579	358	3 077	316	2 631	332	2 722
16-19	473	3 523	...	...	...	...	...	...	...	...
20-24	8 292	13 287	7 033	11 713	6 614	11 719	6 130	11 509	5 898	11 581
25-29	12 363	8 848	11 817	8 854	12 355	9 970	12 266	10 153	12 940	11 116
30-34	5 387	2 654	5 347	2 624	5 940	3 070	6 356	3 589	7 480	4 359
35-39	2 128	1 068	1 944	957	2 238	1 121	2 496	1 308	2 975	1 642
40-44	1 147	690	1 013	569	1 198	655	1 313	684	1 420	743
45-49	748	469	584	359	709	415	793	477	892	560
50-54	528	360	419	266	487	309	513	334	570	377
55-59	320	194	263	139	303	160	329	175	427	210
60-64	209	134	149	72	147	62	225	86	252	94
65-69	180	87	107	52	130	47	134	50	135	54
70-74	98	33	73	17	79	26	93	24	103	31
75+	101	31	68	17	87	14	74	18	77	12
Croatia - Croatie										
All ages - Tous âges	22 076	22 076	22 806	22 806	22 337	22 337	22 700	22 700	22 138	22 138
0-14	-	-	-	-	-	-	-	-	-	-
15-19	224	2 456	211	2 263	223	2 017	228	1 903	181	1 664
20-24	5 251	8 414	5 160	8 661	4 728	8 212	4 810	8 104	4 310	7 612
25-29	8 529	6 558	8 789	6 895	8 638	7 061	8 609	7 335	8 552	7 507
30-34	4 117	2 230	4 394	2 446	4 502	2 563	4 750	2 820	4 901	2 918
35-39	1 677	907	1 838	933	1 894	956	1 929	1 025	1 894	983
40-44	781	478	835	523	831	498	842	491	816	501
45-49	459	329	505	400	490	366	490	374	500	327
50-54	309	265	361	276	324	269	338	273	318	253
55-59	196	170	190	154	195	147	208	124	205	172
60-64	157	136	168	119	156	103	147	103	129	84
65-69	145	79	139	71	148	86	142	79	141	60
70-74	127	28	103	37	104	39	92	30	90	28
75+	94	14	104	16	...	...	...	...	...	...
75-79	...	...	...	...	66	13	60	17	59	13
80-84	...	...	...	...	24	2	41	4	24	5
85-89	...	...	...	...	5	-	9	-	8	-
90-94	...	...	...	...	1	-	-	-	1	-
95-99	...	...	...	...	...	-	...	-	-	-
100+	...	...	...	...	...	-	...	-	-	-
Unknown - Inconnu	10	12	9	12	8	5	5	18	9	6

Continent, country or area and age / Continent, pays ou zone et âge	2001 Groom Époux	2001 Bride Epouse	2002 Groom Époux	2002 Bride Epouse	2003 Groom Époux	2003 Bride Epouse	2004 Groom Époux	2004 Bride Epouse	2005 Groom Époux	2005 Bride Epouse
EUROPE										
Czech Republic - République tchèque										
All ages - Tous âges	52 374	52 374	52 732	52 732	48 943	48 943	51 447	51 447	51 829	51 829
0-14	-	-	-	-	-	-	-	-	-	-
15-19	482	2 404	414	1 960	274	1 504	266	1 393	221	1 218
20-24	11 569	19 971	9 629	17 782	7 380	14 570	6 463	13 205	5 372	12 107
25-29	20 343	17 486	21 160	19 285	19 674	19 069	20 192	21 044	19 921	21 290
30-34	8 195	4 717	8 941	5 495	9 414	5 729	11 320	7 001	12 695	8 138
35-39	4 053	2 356	4 389	2 573	4 250	2 538	4 626	2 785	4 618	2 915
40-44	2 234	1 699	2 436	1 707	2 275	1 697	2 502	1 824	2 811	1 941
45-49	1 973	1 662	2 058	1 720	1 946	1 610	2 022	1 642	1 974	1 586
50-54	1 651	1 144	1 669	1 165	1 666	1 117	1 718	1 310	1 762	1 277
55-59	929	560	1 081	638	1 073	669	1 217	749	1 261	813
60-64	444	189	457	229	486	243	624	268	617	316
65-69	227	85	237	95	231	114	226	126	283	139
70-74	129	61	153	53	142	53	143	56	164	49
75+	145	40	...	...	...	...	...	...	...	...
75-79	...	...	75	22	86	25	71	30	76	34
80-84	...	...	26	5	40	5	50	14	39	6
85-89	...	...	3	1	4	-	5	-	12	-
90-94	...	...	3	2	2	-	2	-	3	-
95+	...	...	1	-	-	-	-	-	-	-
Denmark - Danemark[14]										
All ages - Tous âges	...	...	37 210	37 210	35 041	35 041	37 711	37 711	36 148	36 148
0-14	...	...	-	2	-	5	-	-	-	1
15-19	...	...	207	845	95	438	89	386	72	348
20-24	...	...	2 026	3 941	1 503	3 170	1 487	3 204	1 369	3 131
25-29	...	...	9 034	11 196	8 195	10 348	8 510	10 778	7 907	10 220
30-34	...	...	8 844	7 788	8 782	7 893	9 323	8 489	9 262	8 265
35-39	...	...	6 143	4 639	5 786	4 608	6 281	5 152	5 935	4 752
40-44	...	...	3 389	2 761	3 324	2 599	3 861	2 987	3 665	2 910
45-49	...	...	2 317	1 910	2 318	1 846	2 554	2 104	2 429	2 056
50-54	...	...	1 745	1 294	1 605	1 317	1 893	1 504	1 864	1 450
55-59	...	...	1 367	793	1 388	855	1 553	955	1 414	917
60-64	...	...	603	384	696	417	749	466	824	490
65-69	...	...	309	180	272	190	291	188	352	201
70-74	...	...	142	72	152	76	140	89	152	96
75-79	...	...	62	42	73	39	83	45	84	37
80-84	...	...	38	12	31	11	39	16	37	14
85-89	...	...	3	7	12	11	13	8	10	7
90-94	...	...	2	-	4	-	4	-	3	1
95-99	...	...	-	-	-	-	-	-	1	-
100+	...	...	-	-	-	-	-	-	-	-
Unknown - Inconnu	...	...	979	1 344	805	1 218	841	1 340	768	1 252
Estonia - Estonie										
All ages - Tous âges	5 647	5 647	5 853	5 853	5 699	5 699	6 009	6 009	6 121	6 121
0-14	-	-	-	-	-	-	-	-	-	-
15-19	107	475	78	414	84	407	90	388	65	369
20-24	1 258	1 737	1 151	1 751	1 153	1 706	1 102	1 737	1 111	1 772
25-29	1 567	1 426	1 762	1 604	1 682	1 563	1 720	1 626	1 813	1 679
30-34	1 002	705	1 132	864	1 102	835	1 255	925	1 172	889
35-39	540	423	590	414	623	423	662	474	712	527
40-44	390	312	388	274	367	289	408	305	438	327
45-49	272	240	292	237	245	191	291	220	316	216
50-54	188	148	197	151	170	118	178	172	205	163
55-59	131	75	114	65	107	75	147	80	140	91
60-64	87	54	86	43	82	45	68	41	64	44
65-69	44	28	30	21	36	26	46	26	48	26
70-74	36	15	20	11	27	13	23	11	23	9
75+	25	9	...	...	...	...	...	...	14	9
75-79	...	...	9	3	13	7	14	3	...	...
80-84	...	...	3	1	5	1	4	1	...	...
85-89	...	...	-	-	2	-	-	-	...	...
90-94	...	...	1	-	1	-	1	-	...	...
95-99	...	...	-	-	-	-	-	-	...	...
100+	...	...	-	-	-	-	-	-	...	...

Continent, country or area and age / Continent, pays ou zone et âge	2001 Groom Epoux	2001 Bride Epouse	2002 Groom Epoux	2002 Bride Epouse	2003 Groom Epoux	2003 Bride Epouse	2004 Groom Epoux	2004 Bride Epouse	2005 Groom Epoux	2005 Bride Epouse
EUROPE										
Estonia - Estonie										
Unknown - Inconnu	-	-	-	-	-	-	-	-	-	-
Finland - Finlande[15]										
All ages - Tous âges	24 830	24 830	26 969	26 969	25 815	25 815	29 342	29 342	29 283	29 283
0-14	-	-	-	-	-	-	-	-	-	-
15-19	275	813	237	779	224	704	261	779	265	773
20-24	3 130	5 100	3 144	5 047	2 859	4 663	3 035	4 826	3 110	5 002
25-29	7 088	7 340	7 646	8 262	7 393	8 110	7 963	8 876	8 148	8 892
30-34	5 382	4 518	5 852	4 756	5 587	4 587	6 214	5 175	6 220	5 358
35-39	3 356	2 614	3 635	2 956	3 646	2 878	4 177	3 598	4 081	3 300
40-44	2 027	1 673	2 263	1 851	2 153	1 798	2 715	2 148	2 640	2 168
45-49	1 437	1 308	1 738	1 597	1 593	1 420	2 012	1 818	2 010	1 784
50-54	1 027	791	1 172	876	1 072	825	1 303	1 023	1 188	974
55-59	548	361	676	469	695	489	926	666	934	609
60-64	298	178	340	209	329	191	400	240	356	242
65-69	136	71	116	89	134	78	180	105	175	95
70-74	72	38	95	42	65	49	90	51	76	46
75+	54	25	...	...	...	...	...	...	...	...
75-79	...	...	29	23	42	18	45	25	55	28
80-84	...	...	21	11	17	5	16	12	15	7
85-89	...	...	4	2	6	-	5	-	10	3
90-94	...	...	1	-	-	-	-	-	-	2
95-99	...	...	-	-	-	-	-	-	-	-
100+	...	...	-	-	-	-	-	-	-	-
Unknown - Inconnu	...	...	-	-	-	-	-	-	-	-
France[16,17,18]										
All ages - Tous âges	288 255	288 255	279 087	279 087	275 963	275 963	271 598	271 598	276 303	276 303
0-14	-	2	-	2	-	7	-	3	-	1
15-19	483	4 107	439	4 086	461	4 296	409	3 420	382	3 320
20-24	22 678	53 545	21 762	50 412	21 076	48 687	19 555	45 221	18 315	42 404
25-29	99 067	104 580	90 060	96 470	84 253	90 850	78 963	88 182	77 617	88 348
30-34	70 827	54 222	70 534	55 112	71 136	55 781	69 869	54 744	69 218	55 183
35-39	36 875	29 423	36 562	29 272	36 436	29 848	36 651	29 804	38 666	31 466
40-44	21 853	17 595	21 989	17 721	22 848	18 707	22 953	19 464	24 498	20 734
45-49	14 180	11 233	14 186	11 532	14 752	12 086	15 331	13 003	16 407	13 897
50-54	10 649	7 627	10 757	7 866	10 986	8 242	11 841	9 006	12 713	10 049
55-59	5 451	3 178	6 289	3 740	6 928	4 206	8 058	5 006	9 416	6 284
60-64	2 886	1 366	3 102	1 421	3 286	1 653	3 838	1 964	4 412	2 504
65-69	1 567	713	1 526	787	1 698	814	1 913	898	2 229	1 130
70-74	873	396	968	397	1 045	437	1 100	499	1 217	558
75-79	514	167	540	171	610	203	600	237	673	264
80-84	239	74	248	76	314	107	335	93	351	104
85-89	87	22	100	17	86	29	122	47	135	42
90-94	18	2	21	4	37	7	47	3	43	13
95-99	8	3	4	1	11	3	13	4	11	2
100+	-	-	-	-	-	-	-	-	-	-
Unknown - Inconnu	-	-	-	-	-	-	-	-	-	-
Germany - Allemagne										
All ages - Tous âges	389 591	389 591	391 963	391 963	382 911	382 911	395 992	395 992	...	...
0-19	2 735	13 192	2 500	11 956	2 161	10 516	1 743	9 284	...	...
20-24	37 803	72 260	37 476	73 339	35 275	69 839	33 321	67 172	...	...
25-29	86 177	101 124	85 360	103 382	82 823	101 913	83 007	103 853	...	...
30-34	101 703	83 802	104 548	86 395	97 185	81 411	94 724	81 546	...	...
35-39	62 305	46 298	68 134	49 747	68 384	49 685	74 074	54 988	...	...
40-44	33 238	26 763	35 557	27 524	36 953	28 256	42 886	33 473	...	...
45-49	21 448	18 186	21 180	17 182	21 847	17 978	24 942	20 451	...	...
50-54	15 820	12 632	14 880	10 996	15 309	11 529	16 755	12 603	...	...
55-59	11 101	6 998	9 303	5 300	9 392	5 672	10 174	6 160	...	...
60-64	9 279	5 172	7 092	3 799	7 339	3 673	7 586	3 790	...	...
65-69	3 811	1 893	3 060	1 433	3 229	1 548	3 760	1 788	...	...
70-74	2 242	822	1 471	543	1 482	547	1 497	536	...	...
75-79	1 113	328	808	259	926	233	896	243	...	...
80+	816	121	594	108	606	111	627	105	...	...
Greece - Grèce										
All ages - Tous âges	58 491	58 491	57 872	57 872	61 081	61 081	51 377	51 377	61 043	61 043
0-14	2	53	11	76	6	68	5	48	2	54

Continent, country or area and age / Continent, pays ou zone et âge	2001		2002		2003		2004		2005	
	Groom Epoux	Bride Epouse	Groom Epoux	Bride Epouse	Groom Epoux	Bride Epouse	Groom Epoux	Bride Epouse	Groom Epoux	Bride Epouse
EUROPE										
Greece - Grèce										
15-19	419	3 134	418	2 583	379	2 414	381	2 065	348	1 945
20-24	5 194	14 715	4 870	13 686	4 674	13 219	3 738	10 184	3 765	11 144
25-29	19 243	21 877	18 264	21 947	18 972	23 787	15 444	19 637	18 086	23 767
30-34	17 882	11 095	17 991	11 606	19 080	12 801	16 180	11 575	19 886	14 443
35-39	7 850	3 832	8 131	4 025	9 417	4 651	8 180	4 234	10 095	5 283
40-44	3 517	1 645	3 553	1 737	3 889	1 872	3 209	1 635	3 997	2 062
45-49	1 650	945	1 782	955	1 823	1 027	1 740	898	2 023	1 080
50-54	990	587	1 009	599	1 001	618	907	519	1 094	626
55-59	579	258	662	339	736	319	585	315	713	334
60-64	437	205	436	164	391	162	366	133	378	166
65-69	344	84	367	92	323	86	300	81	310	75
70-74	243	47	219	47	201	30	170	35	185	40
75+	141	14	159	16	189	27	172	18	...	...
75-79	...	...	...	...	...	...	...	...	107	18
80-84	...	...	...	...	...	...	...	...	41	5
85-89	...	...	...	...	...	...	...	...	11	1
90-94	...	...	...	...	...	...	...	...	2	-
95-99	...	...	...	...	...	...	...	...	-	-
100+	...	...	...	...	...	...	...	...	-	-
Unknown - Inconnu	-	-	-	-	-	-	-	-	-	-
Hungary - Hongrie										
All ages - Tous âges	43 583	43 583	46 008	46 008	45 398	45 398	43 791	43 791	44 234	44 234
0-14	-	-	-	-	-	-	-	-	-	-
15-19	667	2 978	559	2 631	441	2 160	401	1 838	383	1 716
20-24	9 409	15 230	8 253	14 639	6 942	12 974	5 644	11 245	4 848	10 402
25-29	16 383	14 216	18 422	16 561	18 553	17 643	17 559	17 504	17 538	17 780
30-34	7 629	4 959	8 770	5 708	9 475	6 139	9 723	6 503	10 818	7 378
35-39	3 158	2 074	3 437	2 177	3 609	2 246	4 041	2 415	4 320	2 681
40-44	2 028	1 337	1 975	1 361	1 843	1 304	1 895	1 300	1 871	1 316
45-49	1 663	1 236	1 763	1 260	1 705	1 261	1 587	1 205	1 428	1 119
50-54	1 089	769	1 161	869	1 131	868	1 188	911	1 298	963
55-59	663	392	718	402	751	431	791	469	755	480
60-64	371	216	416	197	465	173	458	229	487	238
65-69	233	102	233	111	170	109	234	103	213	98
70-74	153	49	163	59	153	57	126	49	154	41
75+	137	25	...	...	...	...	...	...	...	...
75-79	...	...	71	24	96	27	89	19	78	13
80-84	...	...	48	8	53	6	45	1	36	8
85-89	...	...	15	-	7	-	8	-	5	-
90-94	...	...	3	1	2	-	2	-	1	1
95-99	...	...	1	-	2	-	-	-	1	-
100+	...	...	-	-	-	-	-	-	-	-
Unknown - Inconnu	...	...	-	-	-	-	-	-	-	-
Iceland - Islande[19]										
All ages - Tous âges	1 484	1 484	1 619	1 619	1 473	1 473	1 515	1 515	1 607	1 607
0-14	-	-	-	-	-	-	-	-	-	-
15-19	4	25	3	28	3	11	2	14	2	8
20-24	113	240	118	224	108	205	109	193	83	186
25-29	419	505	433	495	344	456	347	427	379	511
30-34	356	291	399	363	386	338	366	350	425	357
35-39	225	175	259	220	258	217	248	202	269	209
40-44	127	112	161	133	161	109	168	131	163	136
45-49	92	65	102	70	81	59	119	98	105	81
50-54	56	35	56	36	57	32	78	53	79	56
55-59	42	13	49	28	32	22	41	25	47	36
60-64	...	...	15	13	25	16	...	...	19	11
60+	48	23	...	...	...	...	34	21	...	...
65-69	...	...	14	6	10	4	...	...	20	7
70-74	...	...	4	1	5	1	...	...	11	5
75+	...	...	...	2	...	...	...	...	...	...
75-79	...	...	3	-	2	1	...	...	4	3
80-84	...	...	1	-	1	1	...	...	1	1
85+	...	...	2	...	-	1	...	...	-	-
Unknown - Inconnu	2	-	-	-	-	-	3	1	-	-

24. Marriages by age of bridegroom and by age of bride: 2001 - 2005
Mariages selon l'âge de l'époux et selon l'âge de l'épouse: 2001 - 2005 (continued — suite)

Continent, country or area and age / Continent, pays ou zone et âge	2001 Groom Epoux	2001 Bride Epouse	2002 Groom Epoux	2002 Bride Epouse	2003 Groom Epoux	2003 Bride Epouse	2004 Groom Epoux	2004 Bride Epouse	2005 Groom Epoux	2005 Bride Epouse
EUROPE										
Ireland - Irlande										
All ages - Tous âges	...	...	20 556	20 556	...	...	...	...	21 355	21 355
0-14	...	...	-	-	...	...	...	...	-	-
15-19	...	...	135	251	...	...	...	...	116	246
20-24	...	...	1 119	2 409	...	...	...	...	1 025	2 052
25-29	...	...	7 102	8 810	...	...	...	...	6 475	8 481
30-34	...	...	7 172	5 798	...	...	...	...	7 903	6 733
35-39	...	...	2 790	1 920	...	...	...	...	3 145	2 208
40-44	...	...	1 013	670	...	...	...	...	1 289	780
45-49	...	...	524	317	...	...	...	...	598	404
50-54	...	...	308	168	...	...	...	...	358	223
55-59	...	...	173	106	...	...	...	...	209	120
60-64	...	...	113	39	...	...	...	...	120	58
65-69	...	...	36	21	...	...	...	...	70	21
70-74	...	...	25	8	...	...	...	...	27	9
75-79	...	...	11	3	...	...	...	...	11	5
80-84	...	...	6	-	...	...	...	...	2	-
85-89	...	...	-	-	...	...	...	...	2	1
90-94	...	...	-	-	...	...	...	...	-	1
95-99	...	...	-	-	...	...	...	...	-	-
100+	...	...	-	-	...	...	...	...	-	-
Unknown - Inconnu	...	...	29	36	...	...	...	...	5	13
Isle of Man - Îles de Man										
All ages - Tous âges	...	...	...	...	...	...	399	399	...	...
0-14	...	...	...	...	...	...	-	-	...	...
15-19	...	...	...	...	...	...	1	6	...	...
20-24	...	...	...	...	...	...	34	64	...	...
25-29	...	...	...	...	...	...	89	95	...	...
30-34	...	...	...	...	...	...	108	103	...	...
35-39	...	...	...	...	...	...	52	55	...	...
40-44	...	...	...	...	...	...	49	28	...	...
45-49	...	...	...	...	...	...	22	17	...	...
50-54	...	...	...	...	...	...	16	11	...	...
55-59	...	...	...	...	...	...	12	10	...	...
60-64	...	...	...	...	...	...	8	5	...	...
65-69	...	...	...	...	...	...	5	3	...	...
70-74	...	...	...	...	...	...	1	2	...	...
75-79	...	...	...	...	...	...	2	-	...	...
80-84	...	...	...	...	...	...	-	-	...	...
85-89	...	...	...	...	...	...	-	-	...	...
90-94	...	...	...	...	...	...	-	-	...	...
95-99	...	...	...	...	...	...	-	-	...	...
100+	...	...	...	...	...	...	-	-	...	...
Italy - Italie										
All ages - Tous âges	264 026	264 026	270 013	270 013	264 097	264 097	...	...	...	...
0-14	-	-	-	-	-	-	...	...	...	...
15-19	1 021	7 962	1 003	7 522	873	6 517	...	...	...	...
20-24	21 476	55 768	19 910	51 865	17 658	47 202	...	...	...	...
25-29	92 579	107 362	89 013	107 614	83 086	103 560	...	...	...	...
30-34	84 554	56 763	88 595	61 938	88 858	64 176	...	...	...	...
35-39	34 221	19 808	37 579	22 508	38 780	23 417	...	...	...	...
40-44	12 620	7 649	14 267	8 405	14 903	8 751	...	...	...	...
45-49	6 382	3 703	7 122	4 388	7 258	4 656	...	...	...	...
50-54	4 314	2 349	4 592	2 747	4 619	2 841	...	...	...	...
55-59	2 572	1 285	3 041	1 460	3 152	1 490	...	...	...	...
60-64	1 887	727	2 157	881	2 166	860	...	...	...	...
65-69	1 087	339	1 279	367	1 358	339	...	...	...	...
70-74	705	193	733	204	724	198	...	...	...	...
75-79	386	91	441	83	406	56	...	...	...	...
80-84	135	20	190	28	175	30	...	...	...	...
85-89	69	7	68	2	66	4	...	...	...	...
90-94	17	-	22	1	15	-	...	...	...	...
95-99	1	-	1	-	-	-	...	...	...	...
Latvia - Lettonie										
All ages - Tous âges	9 258	9 258	9 738	9 738	...	...	10 370	10 370	12 544	12 544
0-14	-	-	-	-	...	...	-	-	-	-

640

Continent, country or area and age / Continent, pays ou zone et âge	2001 Groom Epoux	2001 Bride Epouse	2002 Groom Epoux	2002 Bride Epouse	2003 Groom Epoux	2003 Bride Epouse	2004 Groom Epoux	2004 Bride Epouse	2005 Groom Epoux	2005 Bride Epouse
EUROPE										
Latvia - Lettonie										
15-19	174	719	158	655	...	...	128	632	138	670
20-24	2 585	3 407	2 465	3 366	...	...	2 503	3 562	2 733	4 036
25-29	2 843	2 326	3 044	2 618	...	...	3 195	2 834	3 778	3 430
30-34	1 387	1 069	1 664	1 286	...	...	1 804	1 355	2 314	1 754
35-39	689	558	743	593	...	...	966	692	1 164	923
40-44	504	394	509	380	...	...	596	448	822	531
45-49	327	275	362	302	...	...	376	292	543	440
50-54	268	210	277	207	...	...	267	219	346	285
55-59	161	103	154	120	...	...	207	146	260	-210
60-64	149	103	138	111	...	...	155	82	164	98
65-69	66	47	97	55	...	...	78	63	139	109
70-74	67	32	63	31	...	...	45	29	64	30
75+	38	15	...	...	...	...	...	...	...	...
75-79	...	...	43	12	...	...	28	12	48	21
80-84	...	...	13	2	...	...	12	4	18	6
85+	...	...	8	-	...	...	...	...	...	...
85-89	...	...	...	...	...	...	9	-	13	1
90+	...	...	...	...	...	...	1	-	-	-
Lithuania - Lituanie										
All ages - Tous âges	15 764	15 764	16 151	16 151	16 975	16 975	19 130	19 130	19 938	19 938
0-14	-	2	-	1	-	4	-	4	-	1
15-19	459	1 976	391	1 786	390	1 718	399	1 779	399	1 784
20-24	5 460	6 759	5 352	6 901	5 334	7 037	5 467	7 531	5 497	7 817
25-29	4 694	3 472	5 011	3 754	5 367	4 283	6 337	5 032	6 722	5 262
30-34	1 991	1 396	2 110	1 478	2 399	1 633	2 925	2 017	3 021	2 065
35-39	1 060	744	1 119	768	1 144	797	1 402	973	1 516	1 078
40-44	682	470	758	533	828	534	886	642	935	719
45-49	455	350	433	340	482	395	594	463	650	455
50-54	335	254	332	245	382	233	387	264	389	299
55-59	247	134	222	150	222	138	262	170	304	191
60-64	147	96	212	94	205	101	218	120	226	142
65-69	117	58	98	61	104	62	103	68	152	74
70-74	61	38	49	29	59	26	74	41	66	34
75+	56	15	64	11	59	14	76	26	61	17
Luxembourg[19]										
All ages - Tous âges	1 983	1 983	2 022	2 022	2 001	2 001	1 999	1 999	2 032	2 032
0-14	-	-	-	-	-	-	-	-	-	-
15-19	6	59	7	62	9	50	3	31	7	29
20-24	206	346	191	389	163	371	143	343	131	296
25-29	521	660	562	592	532	569	511	632	489	655
30-34	541	452	521	479	502	496	530	449	559	489
35-39	284	203	302	229	335	240	358	241	349	265
40-44	161	115	183	124	170	125	187	148	208	131
45-49	130	81	120	75	117	74	115	83	119	92
50-54	69	39	65	39	75	44	79	41	83	34
55-59	36	13	28	18	49	20	43	15	51	29
60-64	11	10	19	7	24	8	19	11	22	7
65-69	10	2	14	4	15	1	8	5	8	1
70-74	5	1	5	2	5	2	-	-	4	3
75+	3	1	...	...	...	...	...	...	...	...
75-79	...	...	3	-	4	-	2	-	1	-
80-84	...	...	2	1	1	-	1	-	-	1
85+	...	...	1	1	1	-	-	1	1	-
Malta - Malte										
All ages - Tous âges	2 194	2 194	2 240	2 240	...	...	2 402	2 402	2 374	2 374
16-19	31	148	22	120	...	...	16	94	8	51
20-24	578	959	478	193	...	...	385	799	303	715
25-29	963	738	1 007	766	...	...	1 080	924	1 060	978
30-34	332	192	381	223	...	...	464	282	525	338
35-39	148	68	169	116	...	...	194	138	218	123
40-44	61	26	83	42	...	...	92	63	96	72
45-49	27	28	36	32	...	...	65	44	66	38
50-54	18	16	29	10	...	...	40	29	34	30
55-59	14	6	15	15	...	...	33	16	27	13
60-64	7	8	11	3	...	...	17	6	22	10

Continent, country or area and age / Continent, pays ou zone et âge	2001 Groom Epoux	2001 Bride Epouse	2002 Groom Epoux	2002 Bride Epouse	2003 Groom Epoux	2003 Bride Epouse	2004 Groom Epoux	2004 Bride Epouse	2005 Groom Epoux	2005 Bride Epouse
EUROPE										
Malta - Malte										
65+	15	5	9	6	...	...	16	7	15	6
Netherlands - Pays-Bas[20,21]										
All ages - Tous âges	79 677	79 677	83 970	83 970	...	...	72 231	72 231	71 113	71 113
0-19	321	2 073	320	2 192	...	...	...	...	...	...
15-19	...	...	...	...	...	...	174	1 290	102	837
20-24	6 351	13 982	6 629	14 193	...	...	5 252	11 516	4 980	11 227
25-29	21 217	25 922	20 914	26 550	...	...	16 776	21 879	16 445	21 306
30-34	24 441	18 785	25 985	20 328	...	...	20 981	17 237	19 552	16 206
35-39	11 410	7 840	12 769	8 907	...	...	11 761	8 219	11 786	8 674
40-44	5 789	4 280	6 414	4 669	...	...	6 440	4 762	6 540	4 938
45-49	3 523	2 759	3 782	2 836	...	...	3 831	2 950	4 161	3 146
50-54	2 736	1 983	2 866	2 053	...	...	2 713	1 915	2 887	2 157
55-59	1 744	1 031	1 995	1 166	...	...	2 045	1 272	2 186	1 385
60-64	1 001	513	1 170	567	...	...	1 094	577	1 198	630
65-69	606	297	638	317	...	...	633	374	731	379
70-74	305	122	295	116	...	...	300	145	295	144
75+	233	90	...	...	...	...	...	...	...	...
75-79	...	...	124	53	...	...	145	65	154	61
80-84	...	...	53	18	...	...	58	22	72	15
85-89	...	...	15	5	...	...	24	6	16	5
90+	...	...	1	-	...	...	4	2	8	3
Norway - Norvège[22,23]										
All ages - Tous âges	22 967	22 967	24 069	24 069	22 361	22 361	22 354	22 354	22 392	22 392
0-14	-	-	-	-	-	1	-	-	-	-
15-19	114	551	104	558	81	484	88	444	74	444
20-24	1 641	3 706	1 641	3 792	1 518	3 478	1 421	3 324	1 389	3 103
25-29	5 932	7 459	6 037	7 697	5 294	6 898	4 853	6 641	4 672	6 440
30-34	6 114	5 149	6 440	5 470	5 926	5 173	6 018	5 307	5 753	5 244
35-39	3 565	2 622	3 879	2 919	3 718	2 786	3 799	2 828	4 009	3 053
40-44	2 028	1 413	2 199	1 565	2 094	1 462	2 269	1 563	2 339	1 684
45-49	1 417	1 025	1 472	1 027	1 424	1 003	1 504	1 050	1 557	1 124
50-54	1 087	574	1 090	585	1 090	565	1 084	651	1 103	656
55-59	578	282	733	287	676	318	747	321	833	339
60-64	309	97	266	95	326	122	340	120	384	193
65-69	99	52	101	47	127	44	135	58	152	71
70-74	42	22	64	15	52	11	53	25	71	27
75+	41	15	...	...	...	...	...	...	...	...
75-79	...	...	31	6	25	9	30	6	31	9
80-84	...	...	10	5	10	6	11	10	21	3
85+	...	...	...	...	-	1	...	...	...	...
85-89	...	...	2	1	...	...	1	-	3	1
90-94	...	...	...	...	...	...	1	-	1	1
95+	...	...	...	...	...	...	1	-	...	...
Unknown - Inconnu	-	-	-	-	...	-	-	6	-	-
Poland - Pologne										
All ages - Tous âges	...	...	...	...	195 446	195 446	191 824	191 824	206 916	206 916
15-19	...	...	...	...	...	...	...	...	2 244	13 356
16-19	...	...	...	...	...	16 821	...	13 863	...	...
18-19	...	...	...	...	3 263	...	2 559	...	...	...
20-24	...	...	...	...	63 180	92 635	57 297	88 365	57 645	90 633
25-29	...	...	...	...	81 258	57 236	83 392	60 575	91 052	69 534
30-34	...	...	...	...	23 048	12 220	24 548	13 239	29 900	16 512
35-39	...	...	...	...	7 977	4 304	7 941	4 033	9 237	4 890
40-44	...	...	...	...	4 509	2 953	4 145	2 661	4 551	2 800
45-49	...	...	...	...	3 405	2 923	3 314	2 891	3 544	2 869
50-54	...	...	...	...	2 748	2 545	2 598	2 500	2 756	2 525
55-59	...	...	...	...	1 700	1 495	1 905	1 494	2 004	1 624
60-64	...	...	...	...	1 336	984	1 263	922	1 202	898
65-69	...	...	...	...	1 171	720	1 147	744	1 109	740
70-74	...	...	...	...	927	415	806	358	796	357
75-79	...	...	...	...	589	151	572	136	528	129
80-84	...	...	...	...	250	39	245	38	251	40
85+	...	...	...	...	85	5	92	5	97	9
Portugal										
All ages - Tous âges	58 390	58 390	56 457	56 457	53 735	53 735	49 178	49 178	48 671	48 671

24. Marriages by age of bridegroom and by age of bride: 2001 - 2005
Mariages selon l'âge de l'époux et selon l'âge de l'épouse: 2001 - 2005 (continued — suite)

Continent, country or area and age / Continent, pays ou zone et âge	2001		2002		2003		2004		2005	
	Groom Epoux	Bride Epouse	Groom Epoux	Bride Epouse	Groom Epoux	Bride Epouse	Groom Epoux	Bride Epouse	Groom Epoux	Bride Epouse
EUROPE										
Portugal										
0-16	24	492	10	396	9	305	...	...	2	197
15-19	...	...	...	...	...	...	682	3 386	...	...
17-19	1 256	5 234	1 058	4 520	888	3 679	...	...	549	2 608
20-24	15 079	19 551	13 087	17 580	11 252	15 705	9 798	13 779	8 769	12 815
25-29	23 394	20 079	23 541	20 663	22 041	19 889	19 829	18 326	19 067	18 243
30-34	9 488	6 519	9 979	7 007	10 291	7 378	9 791	7 088	10 555	7 827
35-39	3 495	2 559	3 469	2 610	3 644	2 761	3 509	2 636	3 893	2 825
40-44	1 797	1 378	1 770	1 362	1 866	1 540	1 868	1 489	1 965	1 554
45-49	1 140	956	1 093	842	1 193	940	1 076	894	1 199	1 019
50-54	806	591	740	612	833	641	830	669	810	657
55-59	609	400	580	352	567	377	574	408	625	408
60-64	437	282	406	240	368	219	410	227	418	234
65-69	399	175	329	146	336	153	348	147	371	154
70-74	235	108	175	79	220	79	222	83	224	79
75+	...	...	...	...	...	...	...	...	224	51
75-79	132	49	129	38	141	52	142	28	...	...
80-84	65	13	60	9	60	13	74	13	...	...
85-89	25	3	28	-	20	3	18	4	...	...
90-94	8	1	2	1	4	1	...	...	...	...
90+							7	1		
95-99	1	-	1	-	2	-	...	...	...	...
100+	-	-	-	-	-	-	...	...	...	...
Unknown - Inconnu	-	-	...	...	-	-	...	...	...	...
Republic of Moldova - République de Moldova[24]										
All ages - Tous âges	16 076	16 076	16 663	16 663	18 970	18 970	18 775	18 775	...	...
0-15	-	28	-	13	-	9	-	10	...	...
16-19	838	5 572	863	5 183	905	5 444	821	5 153	...	...
20-24	9 176	8 344	9 145	8 961	10 065	10 455	9 581	10 293	...	...
25-29	4 676	1 619	5 148	1 915	6 142	2 401	6 349	2 578	...	...
30-34	887	267	984	299	1 286	430	1 373	477	...	...
35-39	251	80	233	85	317	102	366	135	...	...
40-44	90	38	93	40	133	42	133	52	...	...
45-49	26	13	28	20	36	16	74	25	...	...
50-54	19	9	27	11	21	16	34	21	...	...
55-59	8	9	5	6	10	6	13	9	...	...
60-64	14	10	11	12	4	2	9	3	...	...
65-69	9	13	9	8	9	8	3	3	...	...
70-74	7	15	12	30	6	11	4	6	...	...
75+	72	56	105	80	35	27	14	10	...	...
Unknown - Inconnu	3	3	-	-	1	1	1	-	...	...
Romania - Roumanie										
All ages - Tous âges	129 930	129 930	129 018	129 018	133 953	133 953	143 304	143 304	141 832	141 832
0-19							1 698	20 566	1 773	19 336
15-19	1 604	21 434	1 566	20 325	1 515	20 460	...	...	...	...
20-24	41 940	56 394	38 798	54 046	36 495	52 913	33 144	51 779	29 764	48 526
25-29	47 305	28 671	48 987	30 400	52 997	34 460	56 633	39 054	56 000	40 106
30-34	20 085	12 196	20 420	12 549	21 152	12 685	24 033	15 076	25 464	15 905
35-39	6 179	3 485	6 734	4 102	8 687	5 523	11 793	7 628	12 532	8 538
40-44	4 561	2 781	4 345	2 556	4 467	2 745	5 489	3 179	5 371	3 181
45-49	3 191	2 168	3 259	2 179	3 351	2 331	4 093	2 697	4 159	2 672
50-54	1 990	1 273	2 016	1 368	2 290	1 442	2 763	1 674	2 813	1 808
55-59	1 143	616	1 051	645	1 140	627	1 449	801	1 760	895
60+	1 932	912	1 842	848	1 859	767	2 209	850	2 196	865
Russian Federation - Fédération de Russie										
All ages - Tous âges	1 001 589	1 001 589	1 019 762	1 019 762	1 091 778	1 091 778	979 667	979 667	...	...
0-17	3 576	28 438	3 316	25 795	3 415	26 428	2 812	23 428	...	...
18-24	432 766	561 093	421 283	560 025	437 321	596 181	376 343	519 606	...	...
25-34	354 058	250 614	374 513	267 911	417 253	297 448	381 937	276 317	...	...
35+	210 925	161 208	220 447	165 936	233 633	171 623	218 344	160 167	...	...
Unknown - Inconnu	264	236	203	95	156	98	231	149	...	...
San Marino - Saint-Marin										
All ages - Tous âges	...	...	...	...	200	200	207	207	...	...
15-19	...	...	...	...	1	1	-	-	...	...

24. Marriages by age of bridegroom and by age of bride: 2001 - 2005
Mariages selon l'âge de l'époux et selon l'âge de l'épouse: 2001 - 2005 (continued — suite)

Continent, country or area and age / Continent, pays ou zone et âge	2001 Groom Epoux	2001 Bride Epouse	2002 Groom Epoux	2002 Bride Epouse	2003 Groom Epoux	2003 Bride Epouse	2004 Groom Epoux	2004 Bride Epouse	2005 Groom Epoux	2005 Bride Epouse
EUROPE										
San Marino - Saint-Marin										
20-24	...	...	...	...	8	20	9	16	...	...
25-29	...	...	...	...	58	52	56	63	...	...
30-34	...	...	...	...	56	31	59	37	...	...
35-39	...	...	...	...	35	17	30	11	...	...
40-44	...	...	...	...	15	5	14	5	...	...
45-49	...	...	...	...	3	1	7	4	...	...
50-54	...	...	...	...	4	1	3	2	...	...
55-59	...	...	...	...	2	2	8	1	...	...
60-64	...	...	...	...	2	1	2	-	...	...
65-69	...	...	...	...	2	-	1	-	...	...
70-74	...	...	...	...	-	-	1	-	...	...
75+	...	...	...	...	1	-	-	-	...	...
Unknown - Inconnu	...	...	...	...	13	69	17	68	...	...
Serbia and Montenegro - Serbie-et-Monténégro[25]										
All ages - Tous âges	...	...	45 741	45 741	45 964	45 964	...	...	...	...
15-19	...	...	560	5 238	567	5 036	...	...	...	...
20-24	...	...	9 372	16 223	9 055	15 822	...	...	...	...
25-29	...	...	15 982	12 604	16 469	13 192	...	...	...	...
30-34	...	...	9 046	5 217	9 342	5 506	...	...	...	...
35-39	...	...	3 985	2 125	4 016	2 205	...	...	...	...
40-44	...	...	2 176	1 322	2 136	1 260	...	...	...	...
45-49	...	...	1 346	1 030	1 220	1 030	...	...	...	...
50-54	...	...	991	725	953	742	...	...	...	...
55-59	...	...	529	410	581	361	...	...	...	...
60-64	...	...	483	279	431	266	...	...	...	...
65-69	...	...	402	183	353	186	...	...	...	...
70-74	...	...	286	98	278	80	...	...	...	...
75+	...	...	283	63	258	54	...	...	...	...
Unknown - Inconnu	...	...	300	224	305	224	...	...	...	...
Slovakia - Slovaquie										
All ages - Tous âges	23 795	23 795	25 062	25 062	...	...	27 885	27 885	26 149	26 149
0-14	-	-	-	-	...	...				
15-19	614	2 830	565	2 606	...	...	724	2 355	520	1 752
20-24	7 949	11 251	7 258	10 975	...	...	6 772	10 876	5 055	9 027
25-29	9 078	6 331	10 020	7 577	...	...	11 309	9 584	10 582	9 586
30-34	2 950	1 545	3 510	1 872	...	...	4 811	2 650	5 239	3 294
35-39	1 282	666	1 521	759	...	...	1 789	966	1 971	998
40-44	668	438	783	472	...	...	891	511	1 025	515
45-49	469	368	559	381	...	...	583	384	675	401
50-54	343	179	357	218	...	...	423	272	447	280
55-59	171	87	198	104	...	...	256	162	293	158
60-64	124	51	131	52	...	...	152	64	159	90
65-69	81	35	83	32	...	...	76	38	93	34
70-74	38	11	36	8	...	...	43	17	41	8
75+	28	3	...	...	...	...	...	...	...	...
75-79	...	...	30	4	...	...	31	3	32	3
80-84	...	...	9	2	...	...	21	2	13	3
85+	...	...	2	-	...	...	4	1	4	-
Slovenia - Slovénie										
All ages - Tous âges	6 935	6 935	7 064	7 064	6 756	6 756	6 558	6 558	5 769	5 769
0-14	-	1	-	1	-	-	-	-	-	-
15-19	34	225	29	189	36	194	37	180	22	138
20-24	976	1 988	865	1 874	839	1 695	692	1 477	521	1 123
25-29	2 770	2 799	2 666	2 790	2 503	2 725	2 402	2 712	2 067	2 527
30-34	1 646	997	1 756	1 162	1 733	1 176	1 774	1 196	1 656	1 091
35-39	683	380	793	422	752	401	763	428	659	382
40-44	281	194	354	249	331	218	336	205	300	183
45-49	200	127	227	159	200	141	191	129	177	132
50-54	129	97	136	111	150	106	146	104	143	91
55-59	78	53	87	47	81	52	78	61	83	45
60-64	42	33	59	29	57	24	47	39	55	31
65-69	38	25	39	18	28	13	35	12	50	12
70-74	30	11	24	5	20	5	24	9	19	4
75+	28	5	...	...	...	...	...	...	...	...

Continent, country or area and age	2001		2002		2003		2004		2005	
Continent, pays ou zone et âge	Groom Epoux	Bride Epouse	Groom Epoux	Bride Epouse	Groom Epoux	Bride Epouse	Groom Epoux	Bride Epouse	Groom Epoux	Bride Epouse
EUROPE										
Slovenia - Slovénie										
75-79	...	...	18	7	12	2	13	5	10	10
80-84	...	...	9	1	8	3	17	1	4	-
85-89	...	...	1	-	5	-	2	-	3	-
90-94	...	...	1	-	1	-	1	-	-	-
95+	...	...	-	-	-	-	-	-	-	-
Spain - Espagne										
All ages - Tous âges	...	...	211 522	211 522	212 300	212 300	216 149	216 149	208 146	208 146
0-14	...	...	1	13	-	4	2	13	-	3
15-19	...	...	836	3 244	670	2 893	625	2 741	534	2 460
20-24	...	...	17 400	36 913	16 019	34 086	14 169	31 039	12 424	27 386
25-29	...	...	88 281	99 837	84 887	97 843	81 650	96 225	74 928	90 353
30-34	...	...	64 248	45 707	66 015	48 796	69 428	52 832	68 597	53 802
35-39	...	...	21 289	13 922	23 163	15 396	25 412	17 562	25 882	17 561
40-44	...	...	8 334	5 567	9 077	6 382	10 597	7 644	10 832	7 870
45-49	...	...	4 180	2 912	4 849	3 284	5 685	4 062	5 856	4 388
50-54	...	...	2 640	1 606	2 895	1 776	3 400	2 093	3 588	2 226
55-59	...	...	1 696	852	1 935	909	2 189	1 081	2 330	1 084
60-64	...	...	981	419	1 123	409	1 256	429	1 450	524
65-69	...	...	754	291	686	256	734	207	764	246
70-74	...	...	458	120	476	150	495	122	486	140
75-79	...	...	218	72	283	75	264	55	254	70
80-84	...	...	125	34	149	30	150	32	150	27
85-89	...	...	61	9	56	8	69	9	47	6
90-94	...	...	15	4	...	...	23	3	24	-
90+	...	...	...	...	17	3	...	...	...	...
95+	...	...	5	-	...	...	1	-	-	-
Unknown - Inconnu	...	...	-	-	-	-	-	-	-	-
Sweden - Suède										
All ages - Tous âges	35 778	35 778	38 012	38 012	39 041	39 041	43 088	43 088	44 381	44 381
0-14	-	-	-	-	-	-	-	-	-	-
15-19	70	359	421	328	58	743	60	775	60	739
20-24	1 519	3 118	2 268	3 120	1 449	3 834	1 464	4 068	1 414	3 907
25-29	7 699	10 240	8 061	10 264	7 150	10 437	7 158	10 677	7 120	10 597
30-34	9 267	8 314	10 300	8 760	9 864	9 798	10 815	10 858	11 220	11 494
35-39	5 595	4 468	6 524	5 023	6 684	5 787	7 467	6 611	7 681	6 866
40-44	3 050	2 345	3 596	2 645	3 590	3 081	4 195	3 731	4 829	4 036
45-49	2 095	1 763	2 393	1 902	2 334	2 176	2 768	2 574	2 854	2 630
50-54	1 694	1 309	1 892	1 443	1 789	1 494	2 057	1 790	2 158	1 835
55-59	1 183	698	1 474	868	1 542	1 042	1 727	1 199	1 814	1 286
60-64	514	250	603	300	684	413	843	449	1 004	594
65-69	186	113	239	131	269	130	349	209	366	252
70-74	111	58	132	55	117	72	147	79	163	81
75+	94	42	...	...	...	...	...	...	...	...
75-79	...	...	67	34	48	27	88	38	75	34
80-84	...	...	32	13	25	7	29	22	35	23
85+	...	...	...	...	...	...	...	8	...	...
85-89	...	...	10	2	5	-	12	...	16	4
90-94	...	...	-	1	-	-	2	...	5	2
95-99	...	...	-	-	-	-	-	...	-	1
100+	...	...	-	-	-	-	1	...	-	-
Unknown - Inconnu	2 701	3 379	-	3 123	3 433	-	3 906	-	3 567	-
Switzerland - Suisse										
All ages - Tous âges	35 987	35 987	...	...	...	...	39 460	39 460	40 139	40 139
0-14	-	1	...	...	...	...	-	-	-	-
15-19	189	950	...	...	...	...	229	1 036	212	1 018
20-24	3 040	6 486	...	...	...	...	3 525	6 407	3 564	6 412
25-29	8 939	11 398	...	...	...	...	9 287	11 495	9 035	11 748
30-34	10 100	8 476	...	...	...	...	10 427	9 495	10 738	9 753
35-39	5 641	4 035	...	...	...	...	6 565	4 893	6 742	4 976
40-44	2 905	1 883	...	...	...	...	3 483	2 422	3 716	2 589
45-49	1 812	1 208	...	...	...	...	2 178	1 642	2 257	1 646
50-54	1 425	851	...	...	...	...	1 481	1 102	1 489	1 013
55-59	1 041	457	...	...	...	...	1 110	568	1 196	579
60-64	479	149	...	...	...	...	678	262	664	242
65-69	230	47	...	...	...	...	253	81	275	88

Continent, country or area and age / Continent, pays ou zone et âge	2001 Groom Epoux	2001 Bride Epouse	2002 Groom Epoux	2002 Bride Epouse	2003 Groom Epoux	2003 Bride Epouse	2004 Groom Epoux	2004 Bride Epouse	2005 Groom Epoux	2005 Bride Epouse
EUROPE										
Switzerland - Suisse										
70-74	102	26	...	...	...	...	113	29	130	48
75+	84	20	...	...	...	...	...	...	...	...
75-79	...	...	...	...	...	...	74	20	64	16
80-84	...	...	...	...	...	...	43	6	41	8
85-89	...	...	...	...	...	...	11	2	15	3
90-94	...	...	...	...	...	...	2	-	1	-
95+	...	...	...	...	...	...	1	-	-	-
The Former Yugoslav Rep. of Macedonia - L'ex-République yougoslave de Macédoine										
All ages - Tous âges	13 267	13 267	14 522	14 522	14 402	14 402	14 073	14 073	14 500	14 500
0-14	-	-								
15-19	458	2 759	472	2 869	446	2 648	421	2 626	405	2 508
20-24	4 397	5 719	4 955	6 398	4 348	6 078	4 273	5 680	4 102	5 788
25-29	5 109	3 152	5 516	3 459	5 536	3 632	5 235	3 610	5 406	3 736
30-34	1 946	869	2 111	908	2 399	1 056	2 283	1 139	2 415	1 261
35-39	674	319	774	380	859	413	934	456	1 083	569
40-44	270	172	296	194	347	231	424	230	500	265
45-49	153	114	134	137	181	128	204	157	242	200
50-54	84	71	89	74	90	98	106	79	123	92
55-59	45	23	37	29	63	51	58	48	89	43
60-64	42	33	40	30	47	17	42	24	32	19
65-69	33	16	46	20	44	13	40	17	43	9
70-74	32	6	29	5	21	8	25	5	29	7
75+	24	4	23	19	21	5	28	2	31	3
Unknown - Inconnu	-	10	-	-	-	24	-	-	-	-
Ukraine[22]										
All ages - Tous âges	309 602	309 602	317 228	317 228	370 966	370 966	278 225	278 225	...	...
0-14	...	...	10	710	...	...	...	...	...	...
0-15	14	807	...	...	9	684	7	319	...	...
15-19	...	...	13 757	72 094	...	...	...	...	...	...
16-19	13 624	71 888	...	...	14 358	77 711	10 148	55 233	...	...
20-24	127 627	124 256	127 476	128 996	148 115	156 493	107 035	115 168	...	...
25-29	76 809	45 768	82 161	48 021	99 431	59 132	73 515	45 059	...	...
30-34	31 069	20 755	33 096	21 994	40 198	26 153	31 079	20 398	...	...
35-39	17 747	12 487	17 852	12 341	20 264	14 112	15 889	10 754	...	...
40-44	12 662	9 876	13 239	9 911	15 203	11 153	11 483	8 514	...	...
45-49	8 662	7 514	8 797	7 430	10 515	8 711	8 389	7 159	...	...
50-54	6 798	5 820	6 845	5 852	7 823	6 626	6 439	5 703	...	...
55-59	3 486	2 811	3 615	2 970	4 413	3 211	4 272	3 332	...	...
60+	11 104	7 620	10 380	6 909	10 637	6 980	9 969	6 586	...	...
United Kingdom - Royaume-Uni										
All ages - Tous âges	...	...	293 021	293 021	...	...	...	...	...	...
15-19	...	...	2 023	7 505	...	...	...	...	...	...
20-24	...	...	28 666	51 478	...	...	...	...	...	...
25-29	...	...	74 858	82 892	...	...	...	...	...	...
30-34	...	...	72 592	62 279	...	...	...	...	...	...
35-39	...	...	44 189	35 978	...	...	...	...	...	...
40-44	...	...	25 558	21 019	...	...	...	...	...	...
45-49	...	...	15 910	13 232	...	...	...	...	...	...
50-54	...	...	11 891	8 955	...	...	...	...	...	...
55-59	...	...	8 055	4 903	...	...	...	...	...	...
60-64	...	...	4 324	2 366	...	...	...	...	...	...
65-69	...	...	2 451	1 251	...	...	...	...	...	...
70-74	...	...	1 328	662	...	...	...	...	...	...
75-79	...	...	746	328	...	...	...	...	...	...
80-84	...	...	316	128	...	...	...	...	...	...
85-89	...	...	113	44	...	...	...	...	...	...
90-94	...	...	1	1	...	...	...	...	...	...
Unknown - Inconnu	...	...	-	-	...	...	...	...	...	...

24. Marriages by age of bridegroom and by age of bride: 2001 - 2005
Mariages selon l'âge de l'époux et selon l'âge de l'épouse: 2001 - 2005 (continued — suite)

Continent, country or area and age / Continent, pays ou zone et âge	2001		2002		2003		2004		2005	
	Groom Epoux	Bride Epouse	Groom Epoux	Bride Epouse	Groom Epoux	Bride Epouse	Groom Epoux	Bride Epouse	Groom Epoux	Bride Epouse
OCEANIA — OCEANIE										
Australia - Australie+,26,27										
All ages - Tous âges	103 130	103 130	105 435	105 435	106 394	106 394	110 958	110 958	109 323	109 323
0-14	-	-								
15-19	609	2 778	573	2 654	562	2 523	568	2 275	327	1 590
20-24	14 440	23 853	14 190	23 369	13 401	22 712	13 414	22 874	11 413	20 149
25-29	33 091	33 938	31 875	33 425	31 761	33 333	32 496	35 435	30 721	34 568
30-34	22 390	18 845	24 136	20 546	25 210	21 467	26 815	22 577	27 577	23 717
35-39	12 067	9 038	12 518	9 671	12 682	9 949	13 659	10 396	14 517	11 403
40-44	7 136	5 462	7 554	5 807	7 865	6 101	8 166	6 423	8 424	6 391
45-49	4 693	3 881	5 062	4 124	5 128	4 177	5 574	4 449	5 666	4 549
50-54	3 680	2 535	3 853	2 734	3 813	2 785	3 959	2 952	4 073	3 231
55-59	2 115	1 262	2 522	1 439	2 703	1 563	2 966	1 756	3 106	1 869
60-64	1 224	688	1 289	718	1 407	766	1 447	894	1 653	909
65-69	741	393	817	422	760	463	919	431	874	496
70-74	447	241	511	296	517	300	434	264	454	241
75+	497	216	...	...	...	...	...	...	...	...
75-79	...	...	326	153	361	170	326	146	315	135
80-84	...	...	159	59	171	62	163	59	140	54
85-89	...	...	41	14	46	18	-	18	...	21
90-94	...	...	8	4	7	5	-	8	11	-
95-99	...	...	-	-	-	-	-	-	...	-
100+	...	...	-	-	-	-	-	-	-	-
Unknown - Inconnu	...	...	-	-	-	-	-	-	-	-
New Caledonia - Nouvelle-Calédonie										
All ages - Tous âges	...	...	...	...	873	873	...	...	...	...
0-19	...	...	...	...	1	24	...	...	...	...
20-24	...	...	...	...	65	146	...	...	...	...
25-29	...	...	...	...	199	255	...	...	...	...
30-34	...	...	...	...	228	184	...	...	...	...
35-39	...	...	...	...	139	105	...	...	...	...
40-49	...	...	...	...	125	109	...	...	...	...
50-59	...	...	...	...	85	35	...	...	...	...
60+	...	...	...	...	31	15	...	...	...	...
New Zealand - Nouvelle-Zélande+,28										
All ages - Tous âges	...	...	20 690	20 690	21 419	21 419	21 006	21 006	20 470	20 470
0-14	...	...	-	-	-	-	-	-	-	-
15-19	...	...	225	639	212	599	167	496	157	482
20-24	...	...	2 776	4 178	2 890	4 417	2 541	3 978	2 441	3 802
25-29	...	...	5 417	5 849	5 487	5 932	5 222	5 776	4 989	5 534
30-34	...	...	4 583	4 199	4 810	4 372	4 866	4 416	4 770	4 280
35-39	...	...	2 651	2 256	2 740	2 270	2 790	2 308	2 731	2 334
40-44	...	...	1 760	1 377	1 775	1 486	1 832	1 556	1 799	1 529
45-49	...	...	1 182	929	1 246	1 012	1 252	1 028	1 233	1 019
50-54	...	...	845	614	870	630	889	660	922	692
55-59	...	...	539	283	649	348	637	377	635	398
60-64	...	...	307	169	355	172	375	199	369	188
65-69	...	...	182	91	188	84	210	106	198	125
70-74	...	...	119	50	107	55	116	56	126	46
75+	...	...	104	56	90	42	109	50	100	41
Unknown - Inconnu	...	...	-	-	-	-	-	-	-	-
Samoa										
All ages - Tous âges	821	821	...	...	...	...	...	...	...	...
15-19	10	71	...	...	...	...	...	...	...	...
20-24	149	285	...	...	...	...	...	...	...	...
25-29	223	177	...	...	...	...	...	...	...	...
30-34	165	114	...	...	...	...	...	...	...	...
35-39	116	83	...	...	...	...	...	...	...	...
40-44	60	39	...	...	...	...	...	...	...	...
45-49	40	23	...	...	...	...	...	...	...	...
50-54	25	12	...	...	...	...	...	...	...	...
55-59	9	11	...	...	...	...	...	...	...	...
60-64	12	1	...	...	...	...	...	...	...	...
65-69	7	2	...	...	...	...	...	...	...	...
70-74	1	-	...	...	...	...	...	...	...	...

24. Marriages by age of bridegroom and by age of bride: 2001 - 2005
Mariages selon l'âge de l'époux et selon l'âge de l'épouse: 2001 - 2005 (continued — suite)

Continent, country or area and age / Continent, pays ou zone et âge	2001		2002		2003		2004		2005	
	Groom Epoux	Bride Epouse	Groom Epoux	Bride Epouse	Groom Epoux	Bride Epouse	Groom Epoux	Bride Epouse	Groom Epoux	Bride Epouse
OCEANIA — OCEANIE										
Samoa										
75+	-	-	...	...	...	...	...	...	...	...
Unknown - Inconnu	*4*	*3*	...	...	...	...	...	...	...	...

FOOTNOTES - NOTES

Italics: data from civil registers which are incomplete or of unknown completeness. — *Italiques:* données incomplètes ou dont le degré d'exactitude n'est pas connu, provenant des registres de l'état civil.

+ Data tabulated by date of registration rather than occurrence. — Données exploitées selon la date de l'enregistrement et non la date de l'événement.

1 For residents only. -Pour les résidents seulement.
2 Excluding tribal Indian population. -Non compris les Indiens vivant en tribus.
3 Excluding Indian jungle population. -Non compris les Indiens de la jungle.
4 Excluding nomadic Indian tribes. -Non compris les tribus d'Indiens nomades.
5 Data refer to government controlled areas. -Les données se rapportent aux zones contrôlées par le Gouvernement.
6 After 2004, figures refer to marriages of residents only. -Après 2004, chiffres se rapportent exclusivement aux mariages de résidents.
7 Including data for East Jerusalem and Israeli residents in certain other territories under occupation by Israeli military forces since June 1967. -Y compris les données pour Jérusalem-Est et les résidents israéliens dans certains autres territoires occupés depuis 1967 par les forces armées israéliennes.
8 Data refer to Japanese nationals in Japan only; and to grooms and brides married for the first time whose marriages occurred and were registered in the same year. -Les données se raportent aux nationaux japonais au Japon seulement; et aux époux et épouses mariés pour la première fois, dont le mariage a été célébré et enregistré la même année.
9 Figures exclude marriages previously officiated outside Singapore or under religious and customary rites. -Les figures excluent les mariages célébrés précédemment au dehors de Singapour ou sous les rites réligieuse ou accoutumés.
10 Registration of Kandyan marriages is complete; registration of Moslem and general marriages is incomplete. -Tous les mariages des Kandyens sont enregistrés; l'enregistrement des mariages musulmans et des autres mariages est incomplet.
11 Data refer to provincial capitals and district centres only. -Les données se rapportent aux capitales des provinces et les chefs-lieux de districts seulement.
12 Excluding aliens temporarily in the area. -Non compris les étrangers se trouvant temporairement le territoire.

13 Including Bulgarian nationals outside the country, but excluding aliens in the area. -Y compris les nationaux bulgares à l'étranger, mais non compris les étrangers sur le territoire.
14 Excluding Faeroe Islands and Greenland. -Non compris les Iles Féroé et le Gröenland.
15 Only marriages in which the bride was resident in Finland. -Seulement mariages où l'épouse réside en Finlande.
16 Age classification based on year of birth rather than exact date of birth. -Le classement selon l'âge est basé sur l'année de naissances et non sur la date exacte de naissance.
17 Including armed forces stationed outside the country. -Y compris les militaires nationaux hors du pays.
18 Excluding Overseas Departments, namely, French Guiana, Guadeloupe, Martinique and Reunion, shown separately. -Non compris les départements d'outre mer, c'est-à-dire la Guyane française, la Guadeloupe, la Martinique et la Réunion, qui font l'objet de rubriques distinctes.
19 Data refer to de jure population. -Les données se raportent a la population de droit.
20 Including residents outside the country if listed in a Netherlands population register. -Y compris les résidents hors du pays, s'ils sont inscrits sur un registre de population néerlandais.
21 Excluding same sex marriages. -À l'exclusion des mariages entre personnes du même sexe.
22 Age classification based on year of birth rather than on completed years of age. -La classification par âge est fondée sur l'année de naissance et non sur l'âge en années révolues.
23 Only marriages in which the groom was resident in Norway. -Seulement mariages où l'époux réside en Norvège.
24 Data refer to first marriages only. -Données se rapportent aux premiers mariages seulement.
25 Without data for Kosovo and Metohia. -Sans les données pour le Kosovo and Metohie.
26 Data for certain cells suppressed by national statistical office for confidentiality reasons. -Les données pour certaines cases ont été supprimées par le bureau national de statistiques pour des raisons de confidentialité.
27 In 2004, marriage registrations were sampled for the states of New South Wales, Victoria, Queensland and South Australia, while the other states and territories were fully enumerated. -En 2004, on a procédé à des enquêtes par échantillonnage concernant les enregistrements de mariages dans les états de New South Wales, Victoria, Queenslands et South Australia et à un dénombrement complet dans les autres états et territoires.
28 For resident population only. -Pour la population résidante seulement.

Table 25

Table 25 presents number of divorces and crude divorce rates for as many years as possible between 2001 and 2005.

Description of variables: Divorce is defined as a final legal dissolution of a marriage, that is, that separation of husband and wife which confers on the parties the right to remarriage under civil, religious and/or other provisions, according to the laws of each country[1].

Unless otherwise noted, divorce statistics exclude legal separations that do not allow remarriage. These statistics refer to the number of divorces granted, and not to the number of persons divorcing.

Divorce statistics are obtained from court records and/or civil registers according to national practice. The actual compilation of these statistics may be the responsibility of the civil registrar, the national statistical office or other government offices.

The urban/rural classification of divorces is that provided by each country or area; it is presumed to be based on the national census definitions of urban population, which have been set forth at the end of the technical notes for table 6.

Rate computation: Crude divorce rates by urban/rural residence are the annual number of divorces per 1 000 mid-year population. Rates presented in this table have been limited to those countries or areas having at least a total of 30 divorces in a given year. These rates are calculated by the Statistics Division of the United Nations.

Reliability of data: Each country or area has been asked to indicate the estimated completeness of the divorces recorded in its civil register. These national assessments are indicated by the quality codes C and U that appear in the first column of this table.

C indicates that the data are estimated to be virtually complete, that is, representing at least 90 per cent of the divorces that occur each year, while U indicates that data are estimated to be incomplete, that is, representing less than 90 per cent of the divorces occurring each year. The code ... indicates that no information was provided regarding completeness.

Data from civil registers that are reported as incomplete or of unknown completeness (coded U or ...) are considered unreliable. They appear in *italics* in this table and the rates were not computed on data so coded. These quality codes apply only to data from civil registers. For more information about the quality of vital statistics data in general, see section 4.2 of the Technical Notes.

Limitations: Statistics on divorces are subject to the same qualifications as have been set forth for vital statistics in general and divorce statistics in particular as discussed in section 4 of the Technical Notes.

Divorce, like marriage, is a legal event, and this has implications for international comparability of data. Divorce has been defined, for statistical purposes, in terms of the laws of individual countries or areas. The laws pertaining to divorce vary considerably from one country or area to another. This variation in the legal provision for divorce also affects the incidence of divorce, which is relatively low in countries or areas where divorce decrees are difficult to obtain.

Since divorces are granted by courts and statistics on divorce refer to the actual divorce decree, effective as of the date of the decree, marked year-to-year fluctuations may reflect court delays and clearances rather than trends in the incidence of divorce. The comparability of divorce statistics may also be affected by tabulation procedures. In some countries or areas annulments and/or legal separations may be included. This practice is more common for countries or areas in which the number of divorces is small. Information on this practice is given in the footnotes when known.

Because the registration of a divorce in many countries or areas is the responsibility solely of the court or the authority which granted it, and since the registration recording such cases is part of the records of the court proceedings, it follows that divorces are likely to be registered soon after the decree is granted. For this reason the practice of tabulating data by date of registration does not generally pose serious problems of comparability as it does in the case of birth and death statistics.

As noted briefly above, the incidence of divorce is affected by the relative ease or difficulty of obtaining a divorce according to the laws of individual countries or areas. The incidence of divorce is also affected by the ability of individuals to meet financial and other costs of the court procedures. Connected with this aspect is the influence of certain religious faiths on the incidence of divorce. For all these reasons, divorce statistics are not strictly comparable as measures of family dissolution by legal means. Furthermore, family dissolution by other than legal means, such as separation, is not measured in statistics for divorce.

For certain countries or areas there is or was no legal provision for divorce in the sense used here, and therefore no data for these countries or areas appear in this table.

In addition, it should be noted that rates are affected also by the quality and limitations of the population estimates that are used in their computation. The problems of under-enumeration or over-enumeration, and to some extent, the differences in definition of total population, have been discussed in section 3 of the Technical Notes dealing with population data in general, and specific information pertaining to individual countries or areas is given in the footnotes to table 3.

As will be seen from the footnotes, strict correspondence between the numerator of the rate and the denominator is not always obtained; for example, divorces among civilian plus military segments of the population may be related to civilian population only. The effect of this may be to increase the rates but, in most cases, the effect is negligible.

As mentioned above, data for some countries or areas may include annulments and/or legal separations. This practice affects the comparability of the crude divorce rates. For example, inclusion of annulments in the numerator of the rates produces a negligible effect on the rates, but inclusion of legal separations may have a measurable effect on the level.

It should be emphasized that crude divorce rates like crude birth, death and marriage rates may be seriously affected by age-sex structure of the populations to which they relate. Like crude marriage rates, they are also affected by the existing distribution of the population by marital status. Nevertheless, crude divorce rates provide a simple measure of the level and changes in divorces.

The comparability of data by urban/rural residence is affected by the national definitions of urban and rural used in tabulating these data. It is assumed, in the absence of specific information to the contrary, that the definitions of urban and rural used in connection with the national population census were also used in the compilation of the vital statistics for each country or area. However, it cannot be excluded that, for a given country or area, different definitions of urban and rural are used for the vital statistics data and the population census data respectively. When known, the definitions of urban in national population censuses are presented at the end of the technical notes for table 6. As discussed in detail in the notes, these definitions vary considerably from one country or area to another.

In addition to problems of comparability, divorce rates classified by urban/rural residence are also subject to certain special types of bias. If, when calculating divorce rates, different definitions of urban are used in connection with the vital events and the population data, and if this results in a net difference between the numerator and denominator of the rate in the population at risk, then the divorce rates would be biased. Urban/rural differentials in divorce rates may also be affected by whether the vital events have been tabulated in terms of place of occurrence or place of usual residence. This problem is discussed in more detail in section 4.1.4.1. of the Technical Notes.

Earlier data: Divorces have been shown in previous issues of the Demographic Yearbook. The earliest data, which were for 1935, appeared in the 1951 issue. For more information on specific topics and years for which data are reported, readers should consult the Historical Index.

NOTES

[i] For definition, please see section 4.1.1 of the Technical Notes.

Tableau 25

Le tableau 25 présente des statistiques concernant les divorces et les taux bruts de divortialité pour le plus grand nombre d'années possible entre 2001 et 2005.

Description des variables : le divorce est la dissolution légale et définitive des liens du mariage, c'est-à-dire la séparation de l'époux et de l'épouse qui confère aux parties le droit de se remarier civilement ou religieusement, ou selon toute autre procédure, conformément à la législation du pays[1].

Sauf indication contraire, les statistiques de la divortialité n'englobent pas les séparations légales qui excluent un remariage. Ces statistiques se rapportent aux jugements de divorce prononcés, non aux personnes divorcées.

Les statistiques de la divortialité proviennent, selon la pratique suivie par chaque pays, des actes des tribunaux et/ou des registres de l'état civil. L'officier d'état civil, les services nationaux de statistique ou d'autres services gouvernementaux peuvent être chargés d'établir ces statistiques.

La classification des divorces selon le lieu de résidence (zone urbaine ou rurale) est celle qui a été communiquée par chaque pays ou zone ; on part du principe qu'elle repose sur les définitions de la population urbaine utilisées pour les recensements nationaux, qui sont reproduites à la fin des notes techniques du tableau 6.

Calcul des taux : Les taux bruts de divortialité selon le lieu de résidence (zone urbaine ou rurale) représentent le nombre annuel de divorces enregistrés pour 1 000 habitants au milieu de l'année. Les taux du tableau 25 ne se rapportent qu'aux pays ou zones où l'on a enregistré un total d'au moins 30 divorces pendant une année donnée. Ces taux sont calculés par la division de statistique de l'ONU.

Fiabilité des données : Il a été demandé à chaque pays ou zone d'indiquer le degré estimatif de complétude des données sur les divorces figurant dans ses registres d'état civil. Ces évaluations nationales sont désignées par les codes de qualité 'C' et 'U' qui apparaissent dans la deuxième colonne du tableau.

La lettre 'C' indique que les données sont jugées à peu près complètes, c'est-à-dire qu'elles représentent au moins 90 p. 100 des divorces survenus chaque année ; la lettre 'U' signale que les données sont jugées incomplètes, c'est-à-dire qu'elles représentent moins de 90 p. 100 des divorces survenus chaque année. Le code '...' indique qu'aucun renseignement n'a été communiqué quant à la complétude des données.

Les données issues des registres de l'état civil qui sont déclarées incomplètes ou dont le degré de complétude n'est pas connu (code 'U' ou '...') sont jugées douteuses. Elles apparaissent en italique dans le tableau et les taux correspondants n'ont pas été calculés. Les codes de qualité ne s'appliquent qu'aux données extraites des registres de l'état civil. Pour plus de précisions sur la qualité des données reposant sur les statistiques de l'état civil en général, voir la section 4.2 des notes techniques.

Insuffisance des données : Les statistiques des divorces appellent les mêmes réserves que celles formulées à propos des statistiques de l'état civil en général et des statistiques de divortialité en particulier (voir la section 4 des notes techniques).

Le divorce est, comme le mariage, un acte juridique, et ce fait influe sur la comparabilité internationale des données. Aux fins de la statistique, le divorce est défini par la législation de chaque pays ou zone. La législation sur le divorce varie considérablement d'un pays ou d'une zone à l'autre, ce qui influe aussi sur la fréquence des divorces, laquelle est relativement faible dans les pays ou zones où le jugement de divorce est difficile à obtenir.

Du fait que les divorces sont prononcés par les tribunaux et que les statistiques de la divortialité se rapportent aux jugements de divorce proprement dits, qui prennent effet à la date où ces jugements sont rendus, il se peut que des fluctuations annuelles accusées traduisent le rythme plus ou moins rapide auquel les affaires sont jugées plutôt que l'évolution de la fréquence des divorces. Les méthodes d'exploitation des données peuvent aussi influer sur la comparabilité des statistiques de la divortialité. Dans certains pays ou zones, ces statistiques peuvent comprendre les annulations et/ou les séparations légales. C'est notamment le cas dans les pays ou zones où les divorces sont peu nombreux. Lorsqu'ils sont connus, des renseignements à ce propos sont donnés en note à la fin du tableau.

Étant donné que dans de nombreux pays ou zones, le tribunal ou l'autorité qui a prononcé le divorce est seul habilité à enregistrer cet acte, et, comme l'acte d'enregistrement figure alors sur les registres du tribunal, l'enregistrement suit généralement de peu le jugement. C'est pourquoi la pratique consistant à exploiter les données selon la date de l'enregistrement ne pose généralement pas les graves problèmes de comparabilité auxquels on se heurte dans le cas des statistiques des naissances et des décès.

Comme on l'a brièvement mentionné ci-dessus, la fréquence des divorces est fonction notamment de la facilité relative avec laquelle la législation de chaque pays ou zone permet d'obtenir le divorce. Elle dépend également de la capacité des intéressés à supporter les frais de procédure. Il faut aussi citer l'influence de certaines religions sur la fréquence des divorces. Pour toutes ces raisons, les statistiques de divortialité ne sont pas rigoureusement comparables et ne permettent pas de mesurer exactement la fréquence des dissolutions légales des mariages. De plus, elles ne rendent pas compte des cas de dissolution extrajudiciaire du mariage, comme la séparation.

Dans certains pays ou zones, il n'existe ou il n'existait pas de législation sur le divorce selon l'acception retenue aux fins du tableau 25, si bien que l'on ne dispose pas de données les concernant.

De surcroît, il convient de noter que l'exactitude des taux dépend également de la qualité et des insuffisances des estimations de population qui sont utilisées pour leur calcul. Le problème des erreurs par excès ou par défaut commises lors du dénombrement et, dans une certaine mesure, le problème de l'hétérogénéité des définitions de la population totale ont été examinés à la section 3 des notes techniques, relative à la population en général ; des explications concernant les différents pays ou zones sont données en note à la fin du tableau 3.

Comme on le verra dans les notes, il n'a pas toujours été possible d'obtenir une correspondance rigoureuse entre le numérateur et le dénominateur pour le calcul des taux. Par exemple, les divorces parmi la population civile et les militaires sont parfois rapportés à la population civile seulement. Cela peut avoir pour effet d'accroître les taux, mais, dans la plupart des cas, il est probable que la différence sera négligeable.

Comme indiqué plus haut, les données concernant certains pays ou zones peuvent comprendre les annulations et/ou les séparations légales. Cette pratique influe sur la comparabilité des taux bruts de divortialité. Par exemple, l'inclusion des annulations dans le numérateur a une influence négligeable, mais l'inclusion des séparations légales peut avoir un effet appréciable.

Il faut souligner que les taux bruts de divortialité, de même que les taux bruts de natalité, de mortalité et de nuptialité, peuvent varier sensiblement selon la structure par âge et par sexe. Comme les taux bruts de nuptialité, ils peuvent également varier en raison de la répartition de la population selon l'état matrimonial. Les taux bruts de divortialité offrent néanmoins un moyen simple de mesurer la fréquence et l'évolution des divorces.

La comparabilité des données selon le lieu de résidence (zone urbaine ou rurale) peut être limitée par les définitions nationales des termes « urbain » et « rural » utilisées pour la mise en tableaux de ces données. En l'absence d'indications contraires, on a supposé que les mêmes définitions avaient servi pour le recensement national de la population et pour l'établissement des statistiques de l'état civil pour chaque pays ou zone. Toutefois, il n'est pas exclu que, pour une zone ou un pays donné, des définitions différentes aient été retenues. Les définitions du terme « urbain » utilisées pour les recensements nationaux de population ont été présentées à la fin des notes techniques du tableau 6 lorsqu'elles étaient connues. Comme on l'a précisé dans les notes techniques relatives au tableau 6, ces définitions varient considérablement d'un pays ou d'une zone à l'autre.

Outre les problèmes de comparabilité, les taux de divortialité classés selon le lieu de résidence (zone urbaine ou rurale) sont également sujets à des distorsions particulières. Si l'on utilise des définitions différentes du terme « urbain » pour classer les faits d'état civil et les données relatives à la population lors du calcul des taux et qu'il en résulte une différence nette entre le numérateur et le dénominateur pour le taux de la population exposée au risque, les taux de divortialité s'en trouveront faussés. La différence entre ces taux pour les zones urbaines et rurales pourra aussi être faussée selon que les faits d'état civil auront été classés d'après le lieu de l'événement ou d'après le lieu de résidence habituel. Ce problème est examiné plus en détail à la section 4.1.4.1 des notes techniques.

Données publiées antérieurement : des statistiques concernant les divorces ont déjà été présentées dans des éditions antérieures de l'*Annuaire démographique*. Les plus anciennes, qui portaient sur 1935, ont été publiées dans l'édition de 1951. Pour plus de précisions concernant les années et les sujets pour lesquels des données ont été publiées, se reporter à l'index historique.

NOTE

[1] Pour la définition, voir la section 4.1.1 des Notes techniques.

25. Divorces and crude divorce rates by urban/rural residence: 2001 - 2005
Divorces et taux bruts de divortialité selon la résidence, urbaine/rurale: 2001 - 2005

Continent and country or area and urban/rural residence / Continent et pays ou zone et résidence urbaine/rurale	Code[1]	Divorces					Rate - Taux				
		2001	2002	2003	2004	2005	2001	2002	2003	2004	2005
AFRICA — AFRIQUE											
Egypt - Égypte[2]											
Total	U	*70 279*	*70 069*	*69 867*	...	...	...	...	...	...	...
Libyan Arab Jamahiriya - Jamahiriya arabe libyenne[3]											
Total	C	1 662	1 740	...	...	...	0.31	0.32	...	...	...
Mauritius - Maurice											
Total	+C	1 512	1 291	1 190	1 162	1 133	1.26	1.07	0.97	0.94	0.91
Réunion											
Total	C	904	940	*844	...	...	1.23	1.26	*1.10	...	...
Saint Helena ex. dep. - Sainte-Hélène sans dép.											
Total	C	4	13	12	8	...	...	...	...	...	...
Seychelles											
Total	+C	109	112	126	...	...	1.34	1.34	1.52	...	...
South Africa - Afrique du Sud[4]											
Total	...	*34 045*	*31 370*	*31 566*	*31 768*	*32 484*	...	...	...	...	...
AMERICA, NORTH — AMERIQUE DU NORD											
Anguilla											
Total	+C	2	11	9	18	...	...	...	...	...	...
Aruba											
Total	C	325	498	480	484	444	3.54	5.34	5.05	4.96	4.41
Belize											
Total	+C	36	45	...	...	...	0.14	0.17	...	...	...
Bermuda - Bermudes											
Total	C	150	230	185	...	...	2.40	3.67	2.93	...	...
British Virgin Islands - Îles Vierges britanniques											
Total	C	70	56	77	60	...	3.39	2.67	3.61	2.77	...
Canada											
Total	C	71 110	70 155	70 828	...	...	2.29	2.24	2.24	...	...
Costa Rica											
Total	C	7 084	7 786	9 442	9 467	9 887	1.81	1.95	2.31	2.27	2.32
Cuba											
Total	C	37 260	35 590	33 851	35 594	34 359	3.34	3.18	3.02	3.17	3.06
Urban	C	35 069	32 966	31 130	33 017	32 251	4.14	3.89	3.66	3.88	3.80
Rural	C	2 191	2 624	2 721	2 577	2 108	0.81	0.97	1.00	0.94	0.77
Dominican Republic - République dominicaine											
Total	C	8 358	*8 810	*10 657	*11 071	...	0.96	*1.03	*1.22	*1.25	...
El Salvador											
Total	C	2 662	4 253	4 220	...	...	0.42	0.65	0.64	...	...
Grenada - Grenade											
Total	C	114	...	...	...	...	1.13	...	...	...	...
Guadeloupe											
Total	C	904	...	...	...	...	2.09	...	...	...	...
Jamaica - Jamaïque											
Total	C	1 691	1 745	1 600	1 739	...	0.65	0.67	0.61	0.67	...
Martinique											
Total	C	*453	...	...	...	...	*1.17	...	...	...	...
Mexico - Mexique[5]											
Total	+C	57 370	60 641	64 248	67 575	70 184	0.58	0.60	0.63	0.66	0.68
Urban	+C	50 221	52 589	55 272	58 689	61 926	0.66	0.68	0.70	0.74	...
Rural	+C	2 448	2 626	2 908	2 907	2 964	0.10	0.10	0.11	0.11	...
Netherlands Antilles - Antilles néerlandaises											
Total	C	547	510	540	513	...	3.14	2.92	3.02	2.80	...
Nicaragua											
Total	+U	*3 348*	*3 051*	*3 170*	*2 779*	*3 916*	...	...	...	...	...
Panama[6]											
Total	C	2 309	2 313	*2 732	...	...	0.80	0.76	*0.88	...	...
Urban	C	1 987	...	...	...	...	...	...	...	...	...
Rural	C	322	...	...	...	...	...	...	...	...	...

25. Divorces and crude divorce rates by urban/rural residence: 2001 - 2005
Divorces et taux bruts de divortialité selon la résidence, urbaine/rurale: 2001 - 2005 (continued — suite)

Continent and country or area and urban/rural residence / Continent et pays ou zone et résidence urbaine/rurale	Code[1]	Divorces					Rate - Taux				
		2001	2002	2003	2004	2005	2001	2002	2003	2004	2005
AMERICA, NORTH — AMERIQUE DU NORD											
Puerto Rico - Porto Rico											
Total	C	13 870	14 578	14 225	15 197	...	3.61	3.78	3.67	3.90	...
Saint Lucia - Sainte-Lucie											
Total	C	76	45	113	*114	...	0.48	0.28	0.70	*0.70	...
Saint Vincent and the Grenadines - Saint Vincent-et-les Grenadines											
Total	+C	61	45	93	85	92	0.56	0.42	0.88	0.81	0.89
Trinidad and Tobago - Trinité-et-Tobago											
Total	C	1 340	1 565	...	...	...	1.06	1.23	...	...	...
Turks Caicos Islands - Îles Turques et Caïques											
Total	C	24	46	9	16	24	...	2.20	...	...	...
AMERICA, SOUTH — AMERIQUE DU SUD											
Brazil - Brésil[7]											
Total	U	*122 791*	...	*135 564*	*130 527*	*153 839*	...	...	...	...	...
Ecuador - Équateur[8]											
Total	+...	*11 068*	*10 987*	*10 912*	*11 251*		...	...	...	...	...
French Guiana - Guyane française											
Total	C	120	...	...	...	...	0.71	...	...	...	...
Suriname											
Total	C	567	797	629	607	...	1.21	1.67	1.31	1.25	...
Uruguay											
Total	+C	7 409	6 761	*14 003	*14 300	...	2.24	2.04	*4.24	*4.33	...
Venezuela (Bolivarian Republic of) - Venezuela (République bolivarienne du)[7]											
Total	...	*16 939*	*16 627*	*20 077*	*21 260*	*21 451*	...	...	...	...	...
ASIA — ASIE											
Armenia - Arménie											
Total	C	1 776	1 684	1 820	1 968	2 466	0.55	0.52	0.57	0.61	0.77
Urban	C	1 525	1 456	1 536	1 658	2 019	0.74	0.71	0.74	0.80	0.98
Rural	C	251	228	284	310	447	0.22	0.20	0.25	0.27	0.39
Azerbaijan - Azerbaïdjan											
Total	+C	5 382	5 738	6 671	6 914	8 895	0.66	0.70	0.81	0.83	1.06
Urban	+C	4 341	4 726	5 555	5 606	...	1.05	1.14	1.31	1.31	...
Rural	+C	1 041	1 012	1 116	1 308	...	0.26	0.25	0.28	0.32	...
Bahrain - Bahreïn[9]											
Total	...	*801*	*838*	*923*	*1 031*		...	...	...	...	...
Brunei Darussalam - Brunéi Darussalam											
Total	...	*332*	*328*	*349*	*392*		...	...	...	...	...
Cambodia - Cambodge											
Total	...	...	...	...	*158 011*	...	...	...	...	...	...
Urban	...	...	...	...	*24 778*	...	...	...	...	...	...
Rural	...	...	...	...	*133 233*	...	...	...	...	...	...
China - Chine[10]											
Total	+C	1 250 000	1 177 000	1 330 000	1 665 000	1 785 000	0.98	0.92	1.03	1.28	1.37
China: Hong Kong SAR - Chine: Hong Kong RAS											
Total	...	*13 425*	*12 943*	*13 829*	*15 604*	*14 873*	...	...	...	...	...
China: Macao SAR - Chine: Macao RAS											
Total	C	348	385	440	475	573	0.80	0.88	0.99	1.04	1.21
Cyprus - Chypre[5,11,12]											
Total	C	1 197	1 320	1 472	1 614	1 514	1.71	1.86	2.04	2.19	2.00

25. Divorces and crude divorce rates by urban/rural residence: 2001 - 2005
Divorces et taux bruts de divortialité selon la résidence, urbaine/rurale: 2001 - 2005 (continued — suite)

Continent and country or area and urban/rural residence / Continent et pays ou zone et résidence urbaine/rurale	Code[1]	Divorces					Rate - Taux				
		2001	2002	2003	2004	2005	2001	2002	2003	2004	2005
ASIA — ASIE											
Cyprus - Chypre[5,11,12]											
Urban	C	...	1 023	1 162	1 293	1 208	...	...	...	...	...
Rural	C	...	247	267	258	254	...	...	...	...	...
Georgia - Géorgie											
Total	C	1 987	1 836	1 825	1 793	1 928	0.45	0.42	0.42	0.42	0.44
Urban	C	1 964	...	1 802	...	...	0.86	...	0.80	...	...
Rural	C	23	...	23			...	...	...	...	...
Iran (Islamic Republic of) - Iran (République islamique d')[13]											
Total	C	60 559	67 256	72 359	73 882	84 243	0.94	1.03	1.09	1.09	1.23
Urban	C	54 603	61 074	64 213	63 406	70 024	1.29	1.42	1.46	1.43	1.53
Rural	C	5 956	6 182	8 146	10 476	14 219	0.27	0.27	0.36	0.45	0.62
Israel - Israël[14]											
Total	C	11 164	10 939	10 689	11 185	...	1.73	1.67	1.60	1.64	...
Japan - Japon[15]											
Total	+C	285 911	289 836	283 854	270 804	261 917	2.25	2.27	2.22	2.12	2.05
Urban	+C	235 968	238 811	234 304	224 699	227 275	...	...	...	...	...
Rural	+C	49 943	51 025	49 550	46 105	34 642	...	...	...	...	...
Jordan - Jordanie[9,16]											
Total	+C	9 017	9 032	9 022	9 791	*10 200	1.81	1.77	1.73	1.83	*1.86
Kazakhstan											
Total	C	29 599	31 236	31 717	31 492	...	1.99	2.10	2.13	2.10	...
Urban	C	24 227	25 563	26 451	26 288	...	2.88	3.03	3.12	3.07	...
Rural	C	5 372	5 673	5 266	5 204	...	0.83	0.88	0.82	0.81	...
Korea (Republic of) - Corée (République de)[17]											
Total	+C	135 014	145 324	167 096	139 365	128 468	2.85	3.05	3.49	2.90	2.66
Urban	+C	110 825	119 788	138 207	114 297	105 408	...	...	...	...	...
Rural	+C	24 189	25 536	28 889	25 068	23 060	...	...	...	...	...
Kuwait - Koweït											
Total	C	4 002	3 891	3 998	4 899	4 538	1.83	1.72	1.72	2.05	1.85
Kyrgyzstan - Kirghizistan											
Total	C	5 861	6 104	5 367	5 311	6 097	1.18	1.22	1.07	1.04	1.19
Urban	C	3 756	3 780	3 280	3 441	3 543	2.13	2.14	1.84	1.89	1.94
Rural	C	2 105	2 324	2 087	1 870	2 554	0.66	0.72	0.64	0.57	0.77
Lebanon - Liban											
Total	+C	4 480	4 060	4 328	4 372	4 746	...	...	...	1.16	...
Maldives											
Total	...	1 529	836	1 135	1 161	1 757	...	...	...	...	...
Urban	...	641	431	530	589	935	...	...	...	...	...
Rural	...	888	405	605	572	822	...	...	...	...	...
Mongolia - Mongolie											
Total	C	650	688	884	1 098	1 622	0.27	0.28	0.36	0.44	0.64
Urban	C	577	583	813	1 032	1 508	0.42	0.42	0.56	0.70	1.00
Rural	C	73	105	71	66	114	0.07	0.10	0.07	0.06	0.12
Occupied Palestinian Territory - Territoire palestinien occupé											
Total	C	3 687	3 046	3 909	3 961	4 211	1.13	0.90	1.11	1.09	1.12
Qatar											
Total	C	566	732	790	787	643	0.87	1.07	1.10	1.04	0.81
Saudi Arabia - Arabie saoudite											
Total	U	16 425	18 765	20 794	...	...	...	...	...	...	...
Singapore - Singapour											
Total	+C	4 838	5 538	6 293	6 047	...	1.17	1.33	1.50	1.43	...
Syrian Arab Republic - République arabe syrienne[18]											
Total	U	13 077	14 314	...	17 336	...	...	...	...	...	...
Tajikistan - Tadjikistan											
Total	C	2 266	2 283	2 390	2 587	2 885	0.36	0.35	0.36	0.39	0.42
Urban	C	1 820	1 822	1 860	...	...	1.09	1.07	1.07	...	...
Rural	C	446	461	530	...	...	0.10	0.10	0.11	...	...
Turkey - Turquie											
Total	U	50 402	51 096	50 108	...	...	...	...	...	...	...

Continent and country or area and urban/rural residence / Continent et pays ou zone et résidence urbaine/rurale	Code[1]	Divorces					Rate - Taux				
		2001	2002	2003	2004	2005	2001	2002	2003	2004	2005
ASIA — ASIE											
Turkey - Turquie											
Urban	U	...	35 862	42 614	...	...	...	...	...	...	...
Rural	U	...	15 234	7 494	...	...	...	...	...	...	...
Uzbekistan - Ouzbékistan											
Total	C	15 646	...	...	...	...	0.63	...	...	...	...
Urban	C	9 777	...	...	...	...	1.06	...	...	...	...
Rural	C	5 869	...	...	...	...	0.37	...	...	...	...
Viet Nam											
Total	C	...	*39 829	...	...	...	...	*0.50	...	...	...
Urban	C	...	*14 542	...	...	...	...	*0.73	...	...	...
Rural	C	...	*25 287	...	...	...	...	*0.42	...	...	...
Yemen - Yémen											
Total	...	617	998	104	...	...	...	...	...	...	...
EUROPE											
Albania - Albanie											
Total	C	2 462	3 494	3 634	2 968	3 929	0.80	1.13	1.17	0.95	1.25
Austria - Autriche[19]											
Total	C	20 582	19 918	19 066	19 590	19 453	2.56	2.46	2.35	2.40	2.36
Belarus - Bélarus											
Total	C	...	37 386	31 679	29 133	...	...	3.77	3.21	2.97	...
Urban	C	...	31 066	26 453	24 597	...	...	4.42	3.76	3.49	...
Rural	C	...	6 320	5 226	4 536	...	...	2.19	1.84	1.64	...
Belgium - Belgique[20]											
Total	C	29 314	30 628	31 355	31 418	30 844	2.85	2.96	3.02	3.01	2.94
Bosnia and Herzegovina - Bosnie-Herzégovine											
Total	C	2 126	2 272	1 918	1 523	1 763	0.56	0.59	0.50	0.40	0.46
Bulgaria - Bulgarie[21,22]											
Total	C	10 275	10 197	12 000	14 657	14 663	1.30	1.30	1.53	1.88	1.89
Urban	C	8 765	8 613	9 973	11 803	11 801	1.60	1.58	1.83	2.17	2.18
Rural	C	1 503	1 584	2 027	2 854	2 862	0.62	0.66	0.86	1.22	1.24
Channel Islands: Jersey - Îles Anglo-Normandes: Jersey											
Total	+C	276	...	...	...	...	3.17	...	...	...	...
Croatia - Croatie											
Total	C	4 670	4 496	4 935	4 985	4 883	1.05	1.01	1.11	1.12	1.10
Urban	C	3 445	3 241	3 554	3 509	3 533	1.39	...	...	...	...
Rural	C	1 225	1 255	1 381	1 476	1 350	0.62	...	...	...	...
Czech Republic - République tchèque											
Total	C	31 586	31 758	32 824	33 060	31 288	3.09	3.11	3.22	3.24	3.06
Urban	C	26 044	26 070	26 569	26 841	25 233	3.45	3.46	3.53	3.57	3.34
Rural	C	5 542	5 688	6 255	6 219	6 055	2.08	2.13	2.34	2.32	2.26
Denmark - Danemark[23]											
Total	C	14 597	15 304	15 763	15 774	15 300	2.72	2.85	2.93	2.92	2.82
Estonia - Estonie[24]											
Total	C	4 312	4 074	3 973	4 158	4 054	3.16	3.00	2.94	3.08	3.01
Urban	C	3 204	3 030	2 865	2 997	2 882	3.39	3.22	3.06	3.21	3.09
Rural	C	931	907	970	1 016	1 056	2.22	2.17	2.33	2.45	2.56
Faeroe Islands - Îles Féroé											
Total	C	36	53	57	48	67	0.77	1.12	1.19	0.99	1.39
Finland - Finlande[25]											
Total	C	13 568	13 336	13 475	13 234	13 383	2.62	2.56	2.58	2.53	2.55
Urban	C	9 624	9 561	9 613	9 344	9 451	3.03	2.97	2.97	2.88	2.88
Rural	C	3 944	3 775	3 862	3 890	3 932	1.96	1.90	1.95	1.96	2.01
France											
Total	C	112 631	115 861	125 175	131 335	152 020	1.89	1.94	2.08	2.17	2.49
Germany - Allemagne											
Total	C	197 498	204 214	213 975	213 691	201 693	2.40	2.48	2.59	2.59	2.45
Gibraltar											
Total	C	129	150	159	119	97	4.69	5.26	5.57	4.15	3.37
Greece - Grèce											
Total	C	11 184	11 080	12 033	12 307	13 494	1.02	1.01	1.09	1.11	1.22

25. Divorces and crude divorce rates by urban/rural residence: 2001 - 2005
Divorces et taux bruts de divortialité selon la résidence, urbaine/rurale: 2001 - 2005 (continued — suite)

Continent and country or area and urban/rural residence / Continent et pays ou zone et résidence urbaine/rurale	Code[1]	Divorces					Rate - Taux				
		2001	2002	2003	2004	2005	2001	2002	2003	2004	2005
EUROPE											
Hungary - Hongrie[5]											
Total	C	24 376	25 493	25 040	24 633	24 795	2.39	2.51	2.47	2.44	2.46
Urban	C	17 547	18 528	18 135	17 567	17 685	2.68	2.80	2.76	2.67	2.65
Rural	C	6 653	6 797	6 770	6 850	6 863	1.83	1.91	1.90	1.94	2.01
Iceland - Islande[26]											
Total	C	551	529	*531	560	*560	1.93	1.84	*1.84	1.91	*1.89
Urban	C	522	504	*508	524	*529	1.98	1.89	*1.90	1.93	*1.92
Rural	C	29	25	*23	36	*31	...	...	...	1.66	*1.49
Ireland - Irlande											
Total	C	2 838	2 591	2 970	3 347	3 411	0.74	0.66	0.75	0.83	0.83
Isle of Man - Îles de Man											
Total	+C	353	402	338	...	...	4.63	5.21	4.36	...	...
Italy - Italie											
Total	C	40 051	41 835	43 856	45 097	...	0.70	0.73	0.76	0.78	...
Latvia - Lettonie											
Total	C	5 740	5 952	4 828	5 271	6 341	2.44	2.55	2.08	2.28	2.76
Urban	C	4 639	4 769	3 774	4 117	4 870	2.90	3.01	2.39	2.62	3.12
Rural	C	1 101	1 183	1 054	1 154	1 471	1.46	1.57	1.41	1.55	2.00
Liechtenstein											
Total	C	82	99	84	101	93	2.48	2.94	2.47	2.93	2.68
Lithuania - Lituanie											
Total	C	11 024	10 579	10 599	10 997	11 097	3.17	3.05	3.07	3.20	3.25
Urban	C	8 598	8 398	8 377	8 106	8 105	3.69	3.62	3.63	3.54	3.56
Rural	C	2 426	2 181	2 222	2 891	2 992	2.11	1.90	1.94	2.52	2.63
Luxembourg											
Total	C	1 028	1 092	1 026	1 055	1 046	2.33	2.45	2.28	2.33	2.29
Monaco											
Total	C	77	69	73	82	69	...	...	...	...	...
Netherlands - Pays-Bas[27]											
Total	C	37 104	33 179	31 479	31 098	31 905	2.31	2.05	1.94	1.91	1.95
Urban	C	26 193	23 582	22 700	20 918	21 298	2.52	2.25	2.14	1.95	1.98
Rural	C	10 354	8 999	8 245	8 192	8 547	1.83	1.59	1.47	1.47	1.54
Norway - Norvège											
Total	C	10 308	10 450	10 757	11 045	11 040	2.28	2.30	2.36	2.41	2.39
Poland - Pologne[28]											
Total	C	45 243	45 414	48 632	56 332	67 578	1.18	1.19	1.27	1.48	1.77
Urban	C	38 209	38 254	40 876	45 954	53 611	1.62	1.62	1.74	1.96	2.29
Rural	C	7 034	7 072	7 669	10 288	13 846	0.48	0.48	0.52	0.70	0.94
Portugal											
Total	C	18 851	27 960	22 818	23 348	22 853	1.83	2.70	2.19	2.22	2.17
Republic of Moldova - République de Moldova											
Total	C	10 808	12 698	14 672	14 918	14 521	2.98	3.50	4.06	4.14	4.04
Urban	C	7 309	8 947	10 565	11 015	10 816	4.92	6.03	7.13	7.46	7.34
Rural	C	3 499	3 751	4 107	3 903	3 705	1.63	1.75	1.93	1.84	1.75
Romania - Roumanie											
Total	C	31 135	31 790	33 073	35 225	33 193	1.39	1.46	1.52	1.63	1.54
Urban	C	22 362	22 675	23 542	25 134	23 709	1.83	1.95	2.03	2.11	2.00
Rural	C	8 773	9 115	9 531	10 091	9 484	0.86	0.89	0.94	1.03	0.97
Russian Federation - Fédération de Russie											
Total	C	763 493	853 647	798 824	635 835	*604 900	5.23	5.87	5.53	4.42	*4.23
San Marino - Saint-Marin											
Total	+C	49	45	45	62	...	1.77	1.58	1.55	2.11	...
Serbia and Montenegro - Serbie-et-Montenegro[29]											
Total	C	8 723	10 488	8 432	*9 047	...	0.82	1.29	1.03	*1.11	...
Urban	C	5 949	7 312	5 750	...	...	1.08	1.59	1.24	...	...
Rural	C	2 774	3 176	2 682	...	...	0.54	0.91	0.77	...	...
Slovakia - Slovaquie											
Total	C	9 817	10 960	10 716	10 889	11 553	1.82	2.04	1.99	2.02	2.14
Urban	C	7 172	7 782	7 720	7 700	8 209	2.38	2.58	2.57	2.57	2.75
Rural	C	2 645	3 178	2 996	3 189	3 344	1.12	1.34	1.26	1.34	1.39
Slovenia - Slovénie											
Total	C	2 274	2 457	2 461	2 411	2 647	1.14	1.23	1.23	1.21	1.32

25. Divorces and crude divorce rates by urban/rural residence: 2001 - 2005
Divorces et taux bruts de divortialité selon la résidence, urbaine/rurale: 2001 - 2005 (continued — suite)

Continent and country or area and urban/rural residence / Continent et pays ou zone et résidence urbaine/rurale	Code[1]	Divorces					Rate - Taux				
		2001	2002	2003	2004	2005	2001	2002	2003	2004	2005
EUROPE											
Slovenia - Slovénie											
Urban	C	1 433	1 533	1 533	1 442	1 623	...	1.57	1.58	1.49	1.68
Rural	C	841	924	928	969	1 024	...	0.95	0.95	0.99	1.04
Spain - Espagne											
Total	C	39 242	41 621	45 448	50 974	72 848	0.96	1.01	1.08	1.19	1.68
Sweden - Suède											
Total	C	21 022	21 322	21 130	20 106	20 000	2.36	2.39	2.36	2.24	2.21
Switzerland - Suisse											
Total	C	15 778	16 363	16 799	17 949	21 332	2.17	2.24	2.28	2.42	2.86
Urban	C	11 707	12 953	13 180	14 069	16 799	2.21	2.42	2.44	2.59	3.07
Rural	C	4 071	3 410	3 619	3 880	4 533	2.09	1.74	1.84	1.96	2.28
The Former Yugoslav Rep. of Macedonia - L'ex-République yougoslave de Macédoine											
Total	C	1 448	1 310	1 405	1 645	1 552	0.71	0.64	0.69	0.81	0.76
Urban	C	...	...	...	...	1 009	...	...	...	...	...
Rural	C	...	...	...	...	543	...	...	...	...	...
Ukraine											
Total	C	181 334	183 538	177 183	173 163	183 455	3.72	3.81	3.71	3.66	3.90
Urban	C	147 877	145 457	138 053	134 372	141 971	4.56	4.52	4.32	...	...
Rural	C	33 457	38 081	39 130	38 791	41 484	2.09	2.40	2.50	...	...
United Kingdom - Royaume-Uni											
Total	C	156 562	160 528	166 536	...	...	2.65	2.71	2.80	...	...
OCEANIA — OCEANIE											
Australia - Australie											
Total	+C	55 330	54 004	53 145	52 747	52 399	2.85	2.75	2.67	2.62	2.57
New Caledonia - Nouvelle-Calédonie[30]											
Total	C	230	219	246	...	...	1.06	0.99	1.09	...	...
Urban	C	148	129	139	...	...	...	...	...	...	...
Rural	C	25	17	25	...	...	...	...	...	...	...
New Zealand - Nouvelle-Zélande											
Total	+C	9 683	10 292	10 491	10 609	9 972	2.50	2.61	2.62	2.61	2.43
Niue - Nioué											
Total	C	...	-	...	...	...	...	...	...	...	...
Samoa											
Total	...	*24*	*44*	*34*	*38*	**44*	...	...	...	...	**0.24*
Tonga											
Total	+C	89	109	103	...	...	0.88	1.08	1.02	...	...

FOOTNOTES - NOTES

Italics: data from civil registers which are incomplete or of unknown completeness. — *Italiques:* données incomplètes ou dont le degré d'exactitude n'est pas connu, provenant des registres de l'état civil.

* Provisional. — Données provisoires.

[1] 'Code' indicates the source of data, as follows:
C - Civil registration, estimated over 90% complete
U - Civil registration, estimated less than 90% complete
+ - Data tabulated by date of registration rather than occurence.
... - Information not available

Le 'Code' indique la source des données, comme suit:
C - Registres de l'état civil considérés complèts à 90 p. 100 au moins.
U - Registres de l'état civil qui ne sont pas considérés complèts à 90 p. 100 au moins.
+ - Données exploitées selon la date de l'enregistrement et non la date de l'événement.
... - Information pas disponible.

[2] Including 'revocable divorces' (among Moslem population), which approximate legal separations. -Y compris les 'divorces révocables' (parmi la population musulmane), qui sont à peu près l'équivalent des séparations légales.
[3] Data refer to Libyan nationals only. -Les données se raportent aux nationaux libyens seulement.
[4] Including annulments and legal separations. -Y compris les annulations et séparations légales.
[5] Figures for urban and rural areas do not add up to the total, since they do not include the category 'Unknown residence'. -La somme des donées pour la residence urbaine et rurale n'est pas égale au total parce qu'elle n'inclue pas la catégorie 'Residence inconnue'.
[6] Excluding tribal Indian population. -Non compris les Indiens vivant en tribus.
[7] Excluding Indian jungle population. -Non compris les Indiens de la jungle.
[8] Excluding nomadic Indian tribes. -Non compris les tribus d'Indiens nomades.
[9] Published by the United Nations Economic and Social Commission for Western Asia. -Publié par la Commission économique et sociale des Nations Unies pour l'Asie occidentale.
[10] For statistical purposes, the data for China do not include those for the

Hong Kong Special Administrative Region (Hong Kong SAR), Macao Special Administrative Region (Macao SAR) and Taiwan province of China. -Pour la présentation des statistiques, les données pour Chine ne comprend pas la Région Administrative Spéciale de Hong Kong (Hong Kong RAS), la Région Administrative Spéciale de Macao (Macao RAS) et Taïwan province de Chine.

[11] Data refer to government controlled areas. -Les données se rapportent aux zones contrôlées par le Gouvernement.

[12] Data according to the place of usual residence of husband. -Données correspondant au lieu de résidence habituelle du mari.

[13] Data relate to the Iranian Year which begins on 21 March and ends on 20 March of the following year. -Les données concernent l'année iranienne, qui commence le 21 mars et se termine le 20 mars de l'année suivante.

[14] Including data for East Jerusalem and Israeli residents in certain other territories under occupation by Israeli military forces since June 1967. -Y compris les données pour Jérusalem-Est et les résidents israéliens dans certains autres territoires occupés depuis 1967 par les forces armées israéliennes.

[15] Data refer to Japanese nationals in Japan only. -Les données se raportent aux nationaux japonais au Japon seulement.

[16] Excluding data for Jordanian territory under occupation since June 1967 by Israeli military forces. Excluding foreigners, including registered Palestinian refugees. -Non compris les données pour le territoire jordanien occupé depuis juin 1967 par les forces armées israéliennes. Non compris les étrangers, mais y compris les réfugiés de Palestine enregistrés.

[17] Excluding alien armed forces, civilian aliens employed by armed forces, and foreign diplomatic personnel and their dependants. -Non compris les militaires étrangers, les civils étrangers employés par les forces armées ni le personnel diplomatique étranger et les membres de leur famille les accompagnant.

[18] Excluding nomads. -Non compris les nomades.

[19] Excluding aliens temporarily in the area. -Non compris les étrangers se trouvant temporairement le territoire.

[20] Including divorces among armed forces stationed outside the country and alien armed forces in the area. -Y compris les divorces de militaires nationaux hors du pays et les militaires étrangers en garnison sur le territoire.

[21] Including Bulgarian nationals outside the country, but excluding foreigners in the country. -Y compris les nationaux bulgares à l'étranger, mais non compris les étrangers sur le territoire.

[22] For certain years, data for urban and rural areas were not revised, as opposed to data for the whole. -Pour certaines années, les données selon la résidence urbaine/rurale n'ont pas été révisées, ce qui a été le cas avec les données pour l'ensemble du pays.

[23] Excluding Faeroe Islands and Greenland. -Non compris les Iles Féroé et le Gröenland.

[24] Urban and rural distribution of marriages and divorces is displayed by place of residence of groom/husband. The difference between 'Total' and the sum of urban and rural is due to the unknown place of residence of grooms/husbands and to grooms/husbands living outside Estonia. -Les mariages et divorces sont classés par rapport à la résidence urbaine/rurale de l'époux. La somme des mariages et divorces par résidence urbaine/rurale est différente du 'total' car elle ne tient pas compte ni des résidences inconnues de l'époux ni des mariages et divorces d'époux vivant à l'étranger.

[25] Including nationals temporarily outside the country. -Y compris les nationaux se trouvant temporairement hors du pays.

[26] Data refer to de jure population. -Les données se raportent a la population de droit.

[27] The difference between 'Total' and the sum of 'urban' and 'rural' is due to divorces contracted abroad. -L'écart entre le chiffre total de la population et la somme des chiffres de la population urbaine et de la population rurale est imputable aux divorces prononcés à l'étranger.

[28] Data by teritorial division exclude divorces if both persons live abroad. -Les données par division territoriale ne comprennent pas les divorces si l'une et l'autre personnes vivent à l'étranger.

[29] From 2002, without data for Kosovo and Metohia. -Après 2002, sans les données pour le Kosovo and Metohie.

[30] Divorces are based on place of residence at marriage not at divorce. -Les divorces sont comptés en fonction du lieu de résidence au mariage, et non pas au divorce.

Annex I: United Nations Annual interpolated mid-year population, estimates 1996 - 2005
Annexe I: Population au milieu de l'année interpolée, estimations 1996 - 2005

Continent and country or area Continent et pays ou zone	Population estimates (in thousands) - Estimations (en milliers)[1]									
	1996	1997	1998	1999	2000	2001	2002	2003	2004	2005
AFRICA — AFRIQUE										
Algeria - Algérie	28 760	29 216	29 646	30 072	30 506	30 954	31 414	31 885	32 366	32 854
Angola	12 644	12 953	13 257	13 578	13 930	14 318	14 737	15 180	15 636	16 095
Benin - Bénin	6 410	6 607	6 804	7 009	7 227	7 460	7 706	7 962	8 224	8 490
Botswana	1 603	1 638	1 671	1 701	1 729	1 753	1 775	1 795	1 815	1 836
Burkina Faso	10 571	10 876	11 192	11 526	11 882	12 262	12 664	13 082	13 507	13 933
Burundi	6 315	6 378	6 447	6 539	6 668	6 839	7 049	7 294	7 566	7 859
Cameroon - Cameroun	14 418	14 774	15 130	15 491	15 861	16 240	16 627	17 019	17 409	17 795
Cape Verde - Cap-Vert	411	420	430	440	451	461	472	484	495	507
Central African Republic - République centrafricaine	3 538	3 625	3 709	3 789	3 864	3 933	3 997	4 060	4 123	4 191
Chad - Tchad	7 387	7 633	7 893	8 169	8 465	8 783	9 119	9 465	9 810	10 146
Comoros - Comores	625	643	661	680	699	718	738	758	778	798
Congo	2 873	2 955	3 037	3 120	3 203	3 285	3 367	3 449	3 530	3 610
Côte d'Ivoire	15 422	15 856	16 279	16 679	17 049	17 385	17 691	17 982	18 275	18 585
Democratic Republic of the Congo - République démocratique du Congo	46 509	47 532	48 495	49 517	50 689	52 036	53 537	55 175	56 918	58 741
Djibouti	642	663	687	709	730	747	763	777	790	804
Egypt - Égypte	61 784	62 941	64 119	65 316	66 529	67 757	69 004	70 268	71 550	72 850
Equatorial Guinea - Guinée équatoriale	391	401	411	420	431	441	451	462	473	484
Eritrea - Érythrée	3 266	3 341	3 437	3 553	3 684	3 833	3 999	4 176	4 354	4 527
Ethiopia - Éthiopie	62 122	63 934	65 738	67 552	69 388	71 250	73 134	75 046	76 995	78 986
Gabon	1 083	1 109	1 134	1 158	1 182	1 205	1 228	1 249	1 270	1 291
Gambia - Gambie	1 202	1 247	1 292	1 338	1 384	1 431	1 477	1 524	1 571	1 617
Ghana	18 341	18 790	19 237	19 688	20 148	20 617	21 094	21 575	22 057	22 535
Guinea - Guinée	7 535	7 722	7 889	8 047	8 203	8 359	8 514	8 671	8 833	9 003
Guinea-Bissau - Guinée-Bissau	1 226	1 261	1 295	1 332	1 370	1 412	1 456	1 502	1 549	1 597
Kenya	28 150	28 914	29 678	30 455	31 252	32 071	32 913	33 780	34 675	35 599
Lesotho	1 754	1 788	1 823	1 856	1 886	1 911	1 932	1 950	1 966	1 981
Liberia - Libéria	2 282	2 476	2 698	2 906	3 071	3 181	3 247	3 292	3 348	3 442
Libyan Arab Jamahiriya - Jamahiriya arabe libyenne	4 930	5 030	5 133	5 238	5 346	5 456	5 568	5 683	5 799	5 918
Madagascar	14 371	14 809	15 259	15 719	16 187	16 662	17 145	17 636	18 135	18 643
Malawi	10 318	10 607	10 941	11 288	11 623	11 945	12 260	12 574	12 894	13 226
Mali	8 970	9 211	9 462	9 726	10 004	10 298	10 607	10 930	11 265	11 611
Mauritania - Mauritanie	2 289	2 354	2 422	2 493	2 566	2 642	2 721	2 801	2 882	2 963
Mauritius - Maurice[2]	1 138	1 150	1 162	1 174	1 186	1 197	1 209	1 220	1 231	1 241
Morocco - Maroc	27 346	27 733	28 109	28 475	28 827	29 166	29 495	29 821	30 152	30 495
Mozambique	16 426	16 878	17 311	17 745	18 194	18 660	19 134	19 610	20 078	20 533
Namibia - Namibie	1 704	1 752	1 798	1 841	1 879	1 913	1 942	1 969	1 994	2 020
Niger	9 626	9 981	10 350	10 732	11 124	11 527	11 941	12 367	12 808	13 264
Nigeria - Nigéria	112 079	115 193	118 348	121 542	124 773	128 039	131 336	134 659	138 001	141 356
Réunion	676	688	700	712	724	737	749	761	774	785
Rwanda	5 869	6 363	7 015	7 660	8 176	8 530	8 762	8 912	9 052	9 234
Saint Helena - Sainte-Hélène[3]	5	5	6	6	6	6	6	6	6	6
Sao Tome and Principe - Sao Tomé-et-Principe	130	133	135	138	140	143	145	148	150	153
Senegal - Sénégal	9 299	9 548	9 803	10 065	10 334	10 609	10 891	11 179	11 472	11 770
Seychelles	77	78	79	80	81	82	83	84	85	86
Sierra Leone	4 172	4 216	4 284	4 384	4 521	4 703	4 924	5 163	5 390	5 586
Somalia - Somalie	6 300	6 433	6 622	6 837	7 055	7 272	7 494	7 721	7 954	8 196
South Africa - Afrique du Sud	42 401	43 236	44 009	44 729	45 398	46 017	46 581	47 089	47 541	47 939
Sudan - Soudan	30 261	31 044	31 830	32 602	33 349	34 063	34 752	35 436	36 145	36 900
Swaziland	978	999	1 020	1 040	1 058	1 075	1 089	1 102	1 114	1 125
Togo	4 671	4 846	5 033	5 221	5 403	5 576	5 744	5 907	6 071	6 239
Tunisia - Tunisie	9 104	9 226	9 341	9 453	9 564	9 672	9 780	9 888	9 996	10 105
Uganda - Ouganda	21 908	22 576	23 252	23 953	24 690	25 467	26 284	27 139	28 028	28 947
United Republic of Tanzania - République Unie de Tanzanie	30 715	31 492	32 254	33 031	33 849	34 712	35 615	36 551	37 508	38 478
Western Sahara - Sahara occidental	267	276	286	298	315	337	362	389	416	440
Zambia - Zambie	9 498	9 742	9 986	10 224	10 451	10 665	10 870	11 069	11 270	11 478
Zimbabwe	12 001	12 195	12 369	12 524	12 656	12 767	12 859	12 941	13 025	13 120

Annex I: United Nations Annual interpolated mid-year population, estimates 1996 - 2005
Annexe I: Population au milieu de l'année interpolée, estimations 1996 - 2005
(continued — suite)

Continent and country or area / Continent et pays ou zone	Population estimates (in thousands) - Estimations (en milliers)[1]									
	1996	1997	1998	1999	2000	2001	2002	2003	2004	2005
AMERICA, NORTH — AMERIQUE DU NORD										
Anguilla	11	11	11	11	11	11	12	12	12	12
Antigua and Barbuda - Antigua-et-Barbuda	70	72	73	75	77	78	80	81	82	83
Aruba	85	87	88	89	90	93	96	99	101	103
Bahamas	285	290	294	299	303	307	311	315	319	323
Barbados - Barbade	281	283	284	285	286	288	289	290	291	292
Belize	220	226	232	238	245	251	257	263	269	276
Bermuda - Bermudes	62	62	62	63	63	63	63	64	64	64
British Virgin Islands - Îles Vierges britanniques	19	19	20	20	21	21	21	21	22	22
Canada	29 586	29 859	30 127	30 402	30 689	30 992	31 308	31 632	31 955	32 271
Cayman Islands - Îles Caïmanes	34	36	37	39	40	41	43	44	45	46
Costa Rica	3 563	3 655	3 748	3 840	3 929	4 014	4 097	4 176	4 253	4 327
Cuba	10 980	11 026	11 068	11 107	11 142	11 174	11 203	11 227	11 247	11 260
Dominica - Dominique	69	69	69	69	68	68	68	68	68	68
Dominican Republic - République dominicaine	8 159	8 305	8 452	8 598	8 744	8 890	9 035	9 180	9 325	9 470
El Salvador	5 746	5 862	5 976	6 088	6 195	6 297	6 392	6 485	6 576	6 668
Greenland - Groenland	56	56	56	56	56	56	57	57	57	57
Grenada - Grenade	99	99	99	100	100	101	102	104	105	105
Guadeloupe	409	412	415	418	421	425	428	432	435	438
Guatemala	10 235	10 471	10 714	10 966	11 229	11 505	11 793	12 090	12 397	12 710
Haiti - Haïti	7 983	8 131	8 279	8 427	8 573	8 718	8 861	9 005	9 149	9 296
Honduras	5 699	5 825	5 949	6 072	6 196	6 320	6 446	6 573	6 702	6 834
Jamaica - Jamaïque	2 508	2 529	2 549	2 569	2 589	2 609	2 628	2 647	2 665	2 682
Martinique	378	380	382	384	386	388	390	392	394	396
Mexico - Mexique	93 497	95 204	96 870	98 401	99 735	100 834	101 734	102 525	103 338	104 266
Montserrat	9	8	7	6	5	5	5	5	5	6
Netherlands Antilles - Antilles néerlandaises	189	186	184	182	181	180	181	182	184	186
Nicaragua	4 762	4 855	4 944	5 028	5 108	5 184	5 256	5 325	5 394	5 463
Panama	2 725	2 781	2 837	2 893	2 950	3 006	3 063	3 119	3 175	3 232
Puerto Rico - Porto Rico	3 727	3 756	3 783	3 809	3 834	3 858	3 881	3 903	3 925	3 947
Saint Kitts and Nevis - Saint-Kitts-et-Nevis	44	44	45	45	46	47	47	48	49	49
Saint Lucia - Sainte-Lucie	147	149	150	151	153	154	156	158	159	161
Saint Pierre and Miquelon - Saint Pierre-et-Miquelon	6	6	6	6	6	6	6	6	6	6
Saint Vincent and the Grenadines - Saint Vincent-et-les Grenadines	114	114	115	115	116	117	117	118	118	119
Trinidad and Tobago - Trinité-et-Tobago	1 277	1 284	1 290	1 295	1 301	1 305	1 310	1 315	1 319	1 324
Turks Caicos Islands - Îles Turques et Caïques	16	17	17	18	19	20	21	22	24	24
United States - États-Unis	273 138	276 043	278 961	281 898	284 857	287 837	290 832	293 837	296 844	299 846
United States Virgin Islands - Îles Vierges américaines	108	109	109	110	110	111	111	111	111	111
AMERICA, SOUTH — AMERIQUE DU SUD										
Argentina - Argentine	35 266	35 689	36 102	36 504	36 896	37 274	37 642	38 005	38 372	38 747
Bolivia - Bolivie	7 648	7 813	7 980	8 147	8 317	8 488	8 661	8 835	9 009	9 182
Brazil - Brésil	164 073	166 566	169 087	171 622	174 161	176 702	179 246	181 787	184 318	186 831
Chile - Chili	14 617	14 828	15 029	15 223	15 412	15 596	15 776	15 951	16 124	16 295
Colombia - Colombie	38 945	39 633	40 320	41 004	41 683	42 354	43 019	43 675	44 317	44 946
Ecuador - Équateur	11 596	11 786	11 966	12 139	12 306	12 466	12 621	12 771	12 917	13 061
Falkland Islands (Malvinas) - Îles Falkland (Malvinas)	3	3	3	3	3	3	3	3	3	3
French Guiana - Guyane française	144	149	154	160	165	171	176	182	187	192
Guyana	739	738	736	735	734	735	736	738	739	739
Paraguay	4 909	5 019	5 129	5 239	5 349	5 460	5 571	5 682	5 793	5 904
Peru - Pérou	24 242	24 613	24 973	25 322	25 663	25 995	26 321	26 641	26 959	27 274
Suriname	420	424	428	432	436	440	443	447	450	452
Uruguay	3 242	3 265	3 287	3 305	3 318	3 325	3 326	3 325	3 324	3 326

Annex I: United Nations Annual interpolated mid-year population, estimates 1996 - 2005
Annexe I: Population au milieu de l'année interpolée, estimations 1996 - 2005
(continued — suite)

Continent and country or area Continent et pays ou zone	Population estimates (in thousands) - Estimations (en milliers)[1]									
	1996	1997	1998	1999	2000	2001	2002	2003	2004	2005
AMERICA, SOUTH — AMERIQUE DU SUD										
Venezuela (Bolivarian Republic of) - Venezuela (République bolivarienne du)	22 544	23 009	23 474	23 938	24 402	24 867	25 331	25 795	26 260	26 726
ASIA — ASIE										
Afghanistan	18 983	19 476	19 837	20 220	20 737	21 414	22 214	23 115	24 076	25 067
Armenia - Arménie	3 178	3 143	3 119	3 100	3 082	3 065	3 050	3 038	3 027	3 018
Azerbaijan - Azerbaïdjan	7 882	7 961	8 030	8 090	8 143	8 189	8 229	8 266	8 306	8 352
Bahrain - Bahreïn	593	608	622	636	650	665	680	695	710	725
Bangladesh	128 921	131 524	134 127	136 757	139 434	142 167	144 943	147 741	150 528	153 281
Bhutan - Bhoutan	509	517	529	543	559	574	591	607	623	637
Brunei Darussalam - Brunéi Darussalam	303	310	318	326	333	341	349	358	366	374
Cambodia - Cambodge	11 700	11 989	12 264	12 526	12 780	13 024	13 259	13 489	13 720	13 956
China - Chine[4]	1 225 680	1 237 431	1 248 852	1 259 740	1 269 962	1 279 486	1 288 401	1 296 838	1 304 983	1 312 979
China - Hong Kong SAR - Chine - Hong Kong RAS[5]	6 305	6 399	6 489	6 577	6 662	6 746	6 826	6 905	6 982	7 057
China - Macao SAR - Chine - Macao RAS[6]	418	424	429	435	441	448	454	461	468	473
Cyprus - Chypre	742	753	764	776	786	797	807	817	827	836
Timor-Leste	847	833	816	809	819	849	896	954	1 013	1 067
Georgia - Géorgie	4 954	4 887	4 829	4 774	4 720	4 666	4 614	4 564	4 517	4 473
India - Inde	972 968	991 513	1 009 905	1 028 145	1 046 235	1 064 156	1 081 899	1 099 494	1 116 985	1 134 403
Indonesia - Indonésie	200 271	203 122	205 970	208 825	211 693	214 575	217 466	220 355	223 225	226 063
Iran (Islamic Republic of) - Iran (République islamique d')	63 083	63 916	64 700	65 435	66 125	66 770	67 383	68 001	68 669	69 421
Iraq	22 317	23 013	23 709	24 392	25 052	25 687	26 301	26 892	27 456	27 996
Israel - Israël	5 534	5 682	5 821	5 954	6 084	6 212	6 335	6 455	6 574	6 692
Japan - Japon	125 816	126 150	126 469	126 765	127 034	127 273	127 483	127 659	127 798	127 897
Jordan - Jordanie	4 441	4 541	4 620	4 700	4 799	4 919	5 055	5 207	5 371	5 544
Kazakhstan	15 704	15 474	15 253	15 072	14 954	14 910	14 933	15 008	15 107	15 211
Korea (Dem. People's Republic of) - Corée (Rép. populaire dém. de)	22 000	22 269	22 518	22 745	22 946	23 122	23 272	23 401	23 514	23 616
Korea (Republic of) - Corée (République de)	45 405	45 786	46 146	46 479	46 780	47 047	47 282	47 490	47 684	47 870
Kuwait - Koweït	1 753	1 839	1 966	2 103	2 228	2 339	2 439	2 531	2 617	2 700
Kyrgyzstan - Kirghizistan	4 652	4 724	4 802	4 878	4 946	5 005	5 057	5 105	5 153	5 204
Lao People's Democratic Republic - République démocratique populaire lao	4 808	4 919	5 025	5 127	5 224	5 316	5 402	5 487	5 574	5 664
Lebanon - Liban	3 569	3 631	3 681	3 726	3 772	3 821	3 869	3 918	3 965	4 011
Malaysia - Malaisie	21 125	21 668	22 214	22 752	23 274	23 775	24 258	24 728	25 191	25 653
Maldives	253	259	264	268	273	277	282	286	291	295
Mongolia - Mongolie	2 409	2 426	2 439	2 454	2 470	2 488	2 509	2 533	2 557	2 581
Myanmar	43 713	44 288	44 850	45 385	45 884	46 343	46 768	47 170	47 565	47 967
Nepal - Népal	22 216	22 767	23 321	23 873	24 419	24 958	25 491	26 021	26 554	27 094
Oman	2 228	2 281	2 329	2 369	2 402	2 427	2 444	2 459	2 479	2 507
Pakistan	131 001	134 395	137 845	141 202	144 360	147 289	150 036	152 680	155 333	158 081
Philippines	70 081	71 579	73 092	74 633	76 213	77 834	79 490	81 172	82 868	84 566
Qatar	539	553	569	590	617	649	687	727	764	796
Saudi Arabia - Arabie saoudite	18 700	19 193	19 718	20 260	20 807	21 357	21 916	22 481	23 047	23 612
Singapore - Singapour	3 588	3 703	3 817	3 923	4 017	4 097	4 164	4 221	4 274	4 327
Sri Lanka	18 234	18 373	18 498	18 611	18 714	18 805	18 887	18 964	19 040	19 121
Syrian Arab Republic - République arabe syrienne	14 978	15 342	15 712	16 099	16 511	16 949	17 411	17 893	18 389	18 894
Tajikistan - Tadjikistan	5 855	5 937	6 018	6 097	6 173	6 246	6 318	6 391	6 467	6 550
Thailand - Thaïlande	58 175	58 830	59 475	60 091	60 666	61 192	61 675	62 127	62 565	63 003
Turkey - Turquie	63 837	64 941	66 039	67 115	68 158	69 164	70 136	71 084	72 025	72 970
Turkmenistan - Turkménistan	4 270	4 334	4 390	4 445	4 502	4 564	4 630	4 698	4 766	4 833
United Arab Emirates - Émirats arabes unis	2 577	2 734	2 900	3 072	3 247	3 424	3 603	3 779	3 947	4 104
Uzbekistan - Ouzbékistan	23 320	23 688	24 034	24 375	24 724	25 083	25 452	25 828	26 209	26 593
Viet Nam	74 575	75 741	76 857	77 964	79 094	80 256	81 440	82 640	83 839	85 029

Annex I: United Nations Annual interpolated mid-year population, estimates 1996 - 2005
Annexe I: Population au milieu de l'année interpolée, estimations 1996 - 2005
(continued — suite)

Continent and country or area Continent et pays ou zone	Population estimates (in thousands) - Estimations (en milliers)[1]									
	1996	1997	1998	1999	2000	2001	2002	2003	2004	2005
ASIA — ASIE										
Occupied Palestinian Territory - Territoire palestinien occupé	2 718	2 821	2 927	3 036	3 149	3 266	3 387	3 510	3 636	3 762
Yemen - Yémen	16 099	16 635	17 145	17 655	18 182	18 730	19 295	19 877	20 478	21 096
EUROPE										
Albania - Albanie	3 122	3 101	3 088	3 081	3 080	3 085	3 098	3 115	3 134	3 154
Andorra - Andorre	66	66	66	66	66	68	69	71	72	73
Austria - Autriche	8 076	8 088	8 092	8 097	8 111	8 137	8 172	8 212	8 253	8 292
Belarus - Bélarus	10 237	10 198	10 152	10 103	10 052	10 001	9 951	9 899	9 848	9 795
Belgium - Belgique	10 106	10 125	10 143	10 165	10 193	10 229	10 271	10 316	10 360	10 398
Bosnia and Herzegovina - Bosnie-Herzégovine	3 402	3 463	3 575	3 694	3 787	3 846	3 881	3 897	3 905	3 915
Bulgaria - Bulgarie	8 272	8 196	8 127	8 063	8 003	7 946	7 894	7 844	7 795	7 745
Channel Islands - Îles Anglo-Normandes	144	145	146	146	147	147	148	148	148	149
Croatia - Croatie	4 654	4 618	4 572	4 531	4 506	4 498	4 506	4 522	4 540	4 551
Czech Republic - République tchèque	10 297	10 279	10 257	10 237	10 220	10 209	10 202	10 197	10 195	10 192
Denmark - Danemark	5 249	5 271	5 294	5 315	5 335	5 354	5 372	5 388	5 403	5 417
Estonia - Estonie	1 418	1 401	1 389	1 379	1 370	1 363	1 357	1 352	1 348	1 344
Faeroe Islands - Îles Féroé	44	44	45	46	46	47	47	48	48	48
Finland - Finlande	5 125	5 140	5 152	5 164	5 176	5 189	5 203	5 217	5 231	5 246
France	58 411	58 585	58 750	58 943	59 187	59 492	59 849	60 236	60 624	60 991
Germany - Allemagne	81 911	82 070	82 165	82 235	82 309	82 395	82 485	82 568	82 628	82 652
Gibraltar	27	27	27	27	27	28	28	28	29	29
Greece - Grèce	10 740	10 813	10 876	10 929	10 975	11 011	11 038	11 060	11 079	11 100
Holy See - Saint-Siège[7]	1	1	1	1	1	1	1	1	1	1
Hungary - Hongrie	10 314	10 293	10 267	10 240	10 214	10 189	10 164	10 139	10 113	10 086
Iceland - Islande	270	273	275	278	281	284	287	290	293	296
Ireland - Irlande	3 639	3 672	3 709	3 753	3 804	3 862	3 926	3 995	4 068	4 143
Isle of Man - Îles de Man	73	74	75	76	77	77	78	78	78	78
Italy - Italie	57 382	57 441	57 497	57 575	57 692	57 856	58 055	58 271	58 475	58 646
Latvia - Lettonie	2 459	2 435	2 415	2 397	2 379	2 361	2 345	2 330	2 315	2 302
Liechtenstein	31	32	32	32	33	33	34	34	34	35
Lithuania - Lituanie	3 605	3 578	3 551	3 525	3 503	3 483	3 468	3 454	3 440	3 425
Luxembourg	414	420	426	432	437	441	445	449	452	457
Malta - Malte	380	383	385	387	389	392	394	397	400	403
Monaco	32	32	32	32	32	32	32	32	32	33
Netherlands - Pays-Bas	15 556	15 651	15 743	15 834	15 924	16 014	16 103	16 188	16 264	16 328
Norway - Norvège	4 384	4 409	4 435	4 461	4 489	4 518	4 547	4 578	4 609	4 639
Poland - Pologne	38 604	38 582	38 538	38 485	38 433	38 384	38 338	38 294	38 247	38 196
Portugal	10 057	10 091	10 130	10 176	10 227	10 284	10 346	10 410	10 472	10 528
Republic of Moldova - République de Moldova	4 347	4 305	4 255	4 201	4 145	4 089	4 033	3 978	3 925	3 877
Romania - Roumanie	22 561	22 450	22 345	22 242	22 138	22 032	21 928	21 826	21 726	21 628
Russian Federation - Fédération de Russie	148 926	148 667	148 339	147 927	147 423	146 828	146 159	145 438	144 696	143 953
San Marino - Saint-Marin	26	26	26	27	27	28	28	29	30	30
Slovakia - Slovaquie	5 375	5 382	5 385	5 387	5 388	5 388	5 388	5 387	5 387	5 387
Slovenia - Slovénie	1 969	1 973	1 977	1 980	1 984	1 987	1 991	1 994	1 997	1 999
Spain - Espagne	39 473	39 549	39 663	39 877	40 229	40 742	41 388	42 103	42 795	43 397
Sweden - Suède	8 848	8 855	8 855	8 857	8 868	8 889	8 920	8 957	8 998	9 038
Switzerland - Suisse	7 170	7 197	7 219	7 239	7 263	7 292	7 324	7 358	7 392	7 424
The Former Yugoslav Rep. of Macedonia - L'ex-République yougoslave de Macédoine	1 973	1 983	1 993	2 002	2 009	2 016	2 022	2 026	2 030	2 034
Ukraine	50 678	50 260	49 791	49 313	48 854	48 428	48 027	47 649	47 282	46 918
United Kingdom - Royaume-Uni	58 117	58 280	58 454	58 648	58 868	59 116	59 388	59 676	59 965	60 245
OCEANIA — OCEANIE										
American Samoa - Samoas américaines	53	54	55	56	57	58	60	61	63	64
Australia - Australie[8]	18 291	18 502	18 709	18 920	19 139	19 367	19 604	19 844	20 081	20 310
Cook Islands - Îles Cook	18	17	17	16	16	16	15	15	14	14
Fiji - Fidji	776	783	790	796	802	807	813	818	823	828

Annex I: United Nations Annual interpolated mid-year population, estimates 1996 - 2005
Annexe I: Population au milieu de l'année interpolée, estimations 1996 - 2005
(continued — suite)

Continent and country or area Continent et pays ou zone	Population estimates (in thousands) - Estimations (en milliers)[1]									
	1996	1997	1998	1999	2000	2001	2002	2003	2004	2005
OCEANIA — OCEANIE										
French Polynesia - Polynésie française	220	224	228	232	236	240	244	248	252	256
Guam	147	149	151	153	155	158	160	163	166	169
Kiribati	78	80	81	83	84	86	87	89	90	92
Marshall Islands - Îles Marshall	51	51	52	52	52	53	54	54	56	57
Micronesia, Federated States of - Micronésie, États Fédérés de La	108	108	108	107	107	107	108	109	109	110
Nauru	10	10	10	10	10	10	10	10	10	10
New Caledonia - Nouvelle-Calédonie	198	202	207	211	215	219	223	227	230	234
New Zealand - Nouvelle-Zélande	3 715	3 750	3 782	3 815	3 854	3 899	3 948	4 000	4 050	4 097
Niue - Nioué	2	2	2	2	2	2	2	2	2	2
Northern Mariana Islands - Îles Mariannes septentrionales	60	62	65	67	69	71	74	76	78	80
Palau - Palaos	18	18	18	19	19	20	20	20	20	20
Papua New Guinea - Papouasie-Nouvelle-Guinée	4 837	4 970	5 105	5 243	5 381	5 520	5 659	5 798	5 935	6 070
Pitcairn	-	-	-	-	-	-	-	-	-	-
Samoa	170	172	174	176	177	179	180	181	183	184
Solomon Islands - Îles Salomon	372	383	393	404	415	427	438	449	461	472
Tokelau - Tokélaou	1	1	2	2	2	2	1	1	1	1
Tonga	98	98	98	98	98	98	98	99	99	99
Tuvalu	10	10	10	10	10	10	10	10	10	10
Vanuatu	176	179	182	186	190	194	199	204	210	215
Wallis and Futuna Islands - Îles Wallis et Futuna	14	15	15	15	15	15	15	15	15	15

FOOTNOTES - NOTES

[1] For 1996-2005 all data refer to annual interpolated estimates of mid-year population. All estimates are produced by the United Nations, Department of Economic and Social Affairs, Population Division (2007) and published in *World Population Prospects: The 2006 Revision.*CD-ROM Edition - Extended Dataset in Excel and ASCII formats (United Nations publication, Sales No. E.07.XIII.7). — Les données pour 1996-2005 sont des estimations de population au milieu de l'année interpolée. Toutes ces données sont produites par Les Nations Unies, Département des Affaires Sociales et Économiques, Division de Population (2007)et ont été publiées dans *World Population Prospects: The 2006 Revision. CD-ROM Edition - Extended Dataset in Excel and ASCII formats* (United Nations publication, Sales No. E.07.XIII.7).

[2] Including Agalega, Rodrigues and Saint Brandon. — Y compris Agalega, Rodrigues et Saint Brandon.

[3] Including Ascension and Tristan da Cunha. — Y compris Ascension et Tristan da Cunha.

[4] For statistical purposes, the data for China do not include Hong Kong and Macao Special Administrative Regions (SAR) of China. — A des fins statistiques, les données pour la Chine ne comprennent pas les Régions Administratives Spéciales (SAR) de Hong Kong et Macao.

[5] As of 1 July 1997, Hong Kong became a Special Administrative Region (SAR) of China. — A partir du 1 juillet 1997, Hong Kong est devenue une Région Administrative Spéciale (SAR) de la Chine.

[6] As of 20 December 1999, Macao became a Special Administrative Region (SAR) of China. — A partir du 20 décembre 1999, Macao est devenue une Région Administrative Spéciale (SAR) de la Chine.

[7] Refers to the Vatican City State. — Ce rapport à l'état du Vatican.

[8] Including Christmas Island, Cocos (Keeling) Islands and Norfolk Island. — Y compris Christmas Island, Cocos (Keeling) Islands et Norfolk Island.

Annex II: United Nations Medium Variant Population Projections - Vital statistics summary and expectation of life at birth: 2000 - 2005
Annexe II: Projections de la population de variante moyenne de l'ONU - Aperçu des statistiques de l'état civil et espérance de vie à la naissance: 2000 - 2005

Continent, country or area Continent, pays ou zone	Crude birth rate — Taux bruts de natalité[1]	Crude death rate — Taux bruts de mortalité[1]	Infant mortality rate — Décès d'enfants de moins d'un an[1]	Expectation of life at birth — Espérance de vie à la naissance[1]		Total fertility rate— Indice synthétique de fécondité[1]	Natural increase — Accroissement naturel[1]
				Male — Masculin	Female — Féminin		
AFRICA — AFRIQUE							
Algeria - Algérie	20.7	5.0	37.4	69.7	72.2	2.53	1.57
Angola	48.6	22.1	140.8	39.3	42.7	6.75	2.65
Benin - Bénin	42.2	12.6	106.0	53.0	55.7	5.87	2.96
Botswana	26.0	16.3	58.9	45.7	47.4	3.18	0.98
Burkina Faso	45.9	15.7	109.9	49.0	52.2	6.36	3.02
Burundi	44.2	16.7	106.5	45.9	48.7	6.80	2.75
Cameroon - Cameroun	37.9	15.0	90.0	49.3	50.3	4.92	2.29
Cape Verde - Cap-Vert	30.9	5.3	29.8	66.8	73.0	3.77	2.56
Central African Republic - République centrafricaine	37.9	19.4	102.1	41.7	44.8	4.96	1.85
Chad - Tchad	47.4	16.0	124.3	49.1	52.0	6.54	3.14
Comoros - Comores	36.5	7.4	57.7	60.9	65.1	4.89	2.91
Congo	37.2	12.7	75.1	51.7	54.2	4.78	2.45
Côte d'Ivoire	37.5	16.5	121.8	45.9	48.0	5.06	2.10
Democratic Republic of the Congo - République démocratique du Congo	49.6	19.3	119.6	43.5	46.4	6.70	3.03
Djibouti	31.4	12.0	95.0	51.9	54.9	4.52	1.94
Egypt - Égypte	25.5	5.9	35.9	67.7	72.0	3.17	1.96
Equatorial Guinea - Guinée équatoriale	39.8	16.4	100.8	48.0	50.7	5.64	2.34
Eritrea - Érythrée	40.5	10.6	62.7	52.5	57.8	5.53	2.99
Ethiopia - Éthiopie	40.7	14.4	95.4	49.4	52.1	5.78	2.63
Gabon	27.7	11.7	61.8	55.7	57.8	3.39	1.60
Gambia - Gambie	38.1	11.2	79.9	56.8	59.3	5.16	2.69
Ghana	32.2	10.0	63.4	58.0	58.9	4.39	2.23
Guinea - Guinée	42.0	13.5	113.2	52.0	55.4	5.84	2.85
Guinea-Bissau - Guinée-Bissau	49.9	19.5	121.2	43.8	47.3	7.10	3.04
Kenya	39.1	13.2	70.0	49.9	52.1	5.00	2.59
Lesotho	31.3	17.7	74.2	43.2	45.7	3.79	1.36
Liberia - Libéria	49.9	19.8	142.8	42.8	44.8	6.80	3.01
Libyan Arab Jamahiriya - Jamahiriya arabe libyenne	24.0	4.1	20.9	70.5	75.7	3.03	2.00
Madagascar	39.3	11.0	74.8	55.7	58.9	5.28	2.83
Malawi	43.8	17.5	101.1	44.4	45.7	6.03	2.63
Mali	48.6	16.4	138.1	49.5	54.0	6.71	3.22
Mauritania - Mauritanie	35.3	8.7	68.0	60.5	64.0	4.83	2.65
Mauritius - Maurice[2]	15.9	6.8	15.2	68.6	75.5	1.91	0.91
Morocco - Maroc	20.9	6.0	37.5	67.5	71.8	2.52	1.50
Mozambique	43.5	19.2	107.7	42.8	45.3	5.52	2.44
Namibia - Namibie	27.4	12.9	55.0	50.3	52.5	3.58	1.45
Niger	51.2	15.6	118.9	55.4	53.6	7.45	3.56
Nigeria - Nigéria	42.7	17.5	115.5	45.9	47.3	5.85	2.52
Réunion	19.9	5.1	14.9	71.5	80.0	2.46	1.48
Rwanda	41.7	18.4	117.7	41.7	45.0	6.01	2.33
Sao Torne and Principe - Sao Tomé-et-Principe	34.9	8.2	76.9	62.5	66.1	4.34	2.66
Senegal - Sénégal	37.6	9.8	69.1	59.7	63.6	5.22	2.78
Sierra Leone	46.9	23.5	165.6	39.3	42.8	6.50	2.35
Somalia - Somalie	45.8	18.5	127.3	44.8	47.1	6.43	2.73
South Africa - Afrique du Sud	24.1	13.5	51.9	51.2	55.6	2.80	1.06
Southern Africa - Afrique méridionale	24.7	13.8	54.2	50.6	54.5	2.90	1.08
Sudan - Soudan	34.4	11.2	72.6	55.0	57.8	4.82	2.32
Swaziland	30.4	17.2	87.3	42.6	45.1	3.91	1.33
Togo	39.6	10.8	93.9	55.6	59.5	5.37	2.88
Tunisia - Tunisie	17.1	5.5	22.5	71.1	75.1	2.04	1.16
Uganda - Ouganda	47.3	15.5	84.2	47.3	48.2	6.75	3.18
United Republic of Tanzania - République Unie de Tanzanie	42.1	14.6	78.2	48.7	50.6	5.66	2.75
Western Sahara - Sahara occidental	25.1	6.5	53.1	62.3	65.8	3.01	1.86
Zambia - Zambie	41.9	21.7	101.6	38.9	39.4	5.65	2.02
Zimbabwe	28.9	20.5	64.4	40.2	39.7	3.56	0.84
AMERICA, NORTH — AMERIQUE DU NORD							
Aruba	16.2	6.9	18.8	70.5	76.4	2.12	0.93
Bahamas	18.1	6.5	15.3	68.5	73.6	2.11	1.16

Annex II: United Nations Medium Variant Population Projections - Vital statistics summary and expectation of life at birth: 2000 - 2005

Annexe II: Projections de la population de variante moyenne de l'ONU - Aperçu des statistiques de l'état civil et espérance de vie à la naissance: 2000 - 2005

(continued — suite)

Continent, country or area / Continent, pays ou zone	Crude birth rate — Taux bruts de natalité[1]	Crude death rate — Taux bruts de mortalité[1]	Infant mortality rate — Décès d'enfants de moins d'un an[1]	Expectation of life at birth — Espérance de vie à la naissance[1] Male — Masculin	Female — Féminin	Total fertilty rate— Indice synthétique de fécondité[1]	Natural increase — Accroissement naturel[1]
AMERICA, NORTH — AMERIQUE DU NORD							
Barbados - Barbade	11.9	7.3	12.3	72.8	78.8	1.50	0.47
Belize	28.3	3.8	18.5	72.8	78.8	3.35	2.45
Canada	10.7	7.2	5.1	77.3	82.3	1.52	0.34
Costa Rica	19.1	3.9	10.5	75.8	80.6	2.28	1.52
Cuba	12.0	7.6	6.1	75.3	79.1	1.63	0.44
Dominican Republic - République dominicaine	25.2	6.0	34.9	67.9	74.2	2.95	1.92
El Salvador	25.1	5.9	26.4	67.7	73.7	2.88	1.92
Grenada - Grenade	18.4	8.8	37.7	66.1	69.3	2.43	0.96
Guadeloupe	15.7	6.2	7.3	75.1	81.5	2.06	0.96
Guatemala	35.8	6.0	38.6	65.5	72.5	4.60	2.97
Haiti - Haïti	29.8	10.5	56.3	56.4	59.9	4.00	1.93
Honduras	30.2	6.0	31.6	64.8	72.6	3.72	2.42
Jamaica - Jamaïque	21.8	7.1	14.6	69.5	74.7	2.63	1.47
Martinique	14.3	7.1	7.0	75.7	81.6	1.98	0.71
Mexico - Mexique	21.4	4.7	20.5	72.4	77.4	2.40	1.67
Netherlands Antilles - Antilles néerlandaises	14.5	7.5	15.0	71.2	78.7	2.06	0.70
Nicaragua	26.3	5.0	26.4	68.0	73.8	3.00	2.14
Panama	22.7	5.0	20.6	72.3	77.4	2.70	1.77
Puerto Rico - Porto Rico	13.7	7.4	8.1	73.7	82.0	1.84	0.63
Saint Lucia - Sainte-Lucie	19.1	7.0	14.6	70.7	74.4	2.24	1.22
Saint Vincent and the Grenadines - Saint Vincent-et-les Grenadines	20.8	6.9	26.7	68.5	72.8	2.30	1.39
Trinidad and Tobago - Trinité-et-Tobago	14.5	7.9	15.1	66.8	71.1	1.61	0.66
United States - États-Unis	14.1	8.3	6.8	74.7	80.0	2.04	0.58
United States Virgin Islands - Îles Vierges américaines	14.6	5.8	9.4	74.6	82.6	2.23	0.89
AMERICA, SOUTH — AMERIQUE DU SUD							
Argentina - Argentine	18.0	7.7	15.0	70.6	78.1	2.35	1.03
Bolivia - Bolivie	30.2	8.2	55.6	61.8	66.0	3.96	2.21
Brazil - Brésil	20.6	6.3	27.3	67.3	74.9	2.35	1.43
Chile - Chili	15.7	5.0	8.0	74.8	80.8	2.00	1.08
Colombia - Colombie	21.2	5.6	20.5	68.0	75.4	2.47	1.56
Ecuador - Équateur	23.2	5.0	24.9	71.3	77.2	2.82	1.82
French Guiana - Guyane française	27.1	3.7	14.8	71.9	79.1	3.68	2.34
Guyana	21.3	9.1	49.4	60.6	66.5	2.43	1.22
Paraguay	26.9	5.6	35.5	68.7	72.9	3.48	2.13
Peru - Pérou	22.2	6.2	30.3	67.5	72.5	2.70	1.60
Suriname	21.2	6.8	31.8	66.0	72.5	2.60	1.44
Uruguay	16.0	9.3	14.4	71.6	78.9	2.20	0.67
Venezuela (Bolivarian Republic of) - Venezuela (République bolivarienne du)	22.9	5.0	18.9	69.9	75.8	2.72	1.79
ASIA — ASIE							
Afghanistan	49.7	21.6	168.1	42.2	42.1	7.48	2.81
Armenia - Arménie	11.2	8.9	30.3	67.9	74.6	1.35	0.23
Azerbaijan - Azerbaïdjan	14.3	6.9	75.6	63.2	70.5	1.67	0.75
Bahrain - Bahreïn	19.3	3.1	12.7	73.5	76.5	2.51	1.62
Bangladesh	27.8	8.2	61.3	61.3	62.8	3.22	1.96
Bhutan - Bhoutan	22.4	7.8	52.7	61.8	65.2	2.91	1.45
Brunei Darussalam - Brunéi Darussalam ...	23.6	2.8	6.1	74.2	78.9	2.50	2.08
Cambodia - Cambodge	27.5	10.0	72.8	53.7	59.5	3.64	1.74
China - Chine[3]	13.6	6.6	25.7	70.5	73.7	1.70	0.70
China - Hong Kong SAR - Chine - Hong Kong RAS[4]	8.1	5.3	3.8	78.6	84.5	0.94	0.28
China - Macao SAR - Chine - Macao RAS[5]	7.4	4.3	7.7	77.6	82.2	0.84	0.31
Cyprus - Chypre	12.1	7.0	5.9	76.6	81.3	1.63	0.52
Georgia - Géorgie	11.1	11.1	40.5	66.5	74.3	1.48	0.01
India - Inde	25.1	8.7	62.5	61.7	64.2	3.11	1.64
Indonesia - Indonésie	20.7	6.6	34.2	66.7	70.5	2.38	1.40

Annex II: United Nations Medium Variant Population Projections - Vital statistics summary and expectation of life at birth: 2000 - 2005

Annexe II: Projections de la population de variante moyenne de l'ONU - Aperçu des statistiques de l'état civil et espérance de vie à la naissance: 2000 - 2005

(continued — suite)

Continent, country or area Continent, pays ou zone	Crude birth rate — Taux bruts de natalité[1]	Crude death rate — Taux bruts de mortalité[1]	Infant mortality rate — Décès d'enfants de moins d'un an[1]	Expectation of life at birth — Espérance de vie à la naissance[1]		Total fertilty rate— Indice synthétique de fécondité[1]	Natural increase — Accroissement naturel[1]
				Male — Masculin	Female — Féminin		
ASIA — ASIE							
Iran (Islamic Republic of) - Iran (République islamique d')	19.0	5.5	37.2	68.0	71.0	2.12	1.34
Iraq	35.6	10.6	94.3	54.9	59.3	4.86	2.50
Israel - Israël	21.1	5.6	5.1	77.6	81.7	2.91	1.54
Japan - Japon	9.0	8.0	3.2	78.3	85.2	1.29	0.09
Jordan - Jordanie	27.9	4.1	23.2	69.7	73.1	3.53	2.38
Kazakhstan	16.7	10.6	32.0	59.5	70.6	2.01	0.61
Korea (Dem. People's Republic of) - Corée (Rép. populaire dém. de)	15.1	9.3	50.0	64.2	68.8	1.92	0.58
Korea (Republic of) - Corée (République de)	10.4	5.4	4.7	73.5	80.6	1.24	0.49
Kuwait - Koweït	18.6	1.7	8.6	75.3	79.2	2.30	1.68
Kyrgyzstan - Kirghizistan	21.0	7.9	55.1	61.4	69.4	2.50	1.31
Lao People's Democratic Republic - République démocratique populaire lao	28.4	8.0	62.2	60.7	63.1	3.59	2.04
Lebanon - Liban	19.3	7.0	25.2	68.9	73.2	2.32	1.23
Malaysia - Malaisie	22.7	4.5	10.1	70.8	75.5	2.87	1.82
Maldives	22.2	6.5	45.8	65.6	65.6	2.81	1.57
Mongolia - Mongolie	19.7	6.9	44.7	61.9	68.4	2.07	1.28
Myanmar	19.5	10.2	74.9	56.7	63.4	2.25	0.93
Nepal - Népal	30.2	8.7	64.5	61.0	61.6	3.68	2.15
Oman	23.5	2.8	15.2	72.9	75.9	3.70	2.08
Pakistan	27.5	7.7	75.4	63.3	63.9	3.99	1.98
Philippines	28.1	5.1	27.8	68.2	72.5	3.54	2.30
Qatar	17.8	2.6	9.7	73.7	75.3	2.93	1.52
Saudi Arabia - Arabie saoudite	26.5	3.8	22.4	69.8	74.0	3.81	2.27
Singapore - Singapour	10.1	4.9	3.0	76.8	80.8	1.35	0.53
Sri Lanka	16.3	7.3	12.4	67.0	75.0	2.02	0.90
Syrian Arab Republic - République arabe syrienne	28.2	3.6	18.6	71.2	74.9	3.48	2.47
Tajikistan - Tadjikistan	29.4	6.6	63.0	63.4	68.6	3.81	2.27
Thailand - Thaïlande	15.4	8.6	11.9	63.7	74.0	1.83	0.68
Timor - Leste	41.7	10.2	78.5	57.5	59.1	6.96	3.16
Turkey - Turquie	19.5	5.8	31.4	68.5	73.3	2.23	1.37
Turkmenistan - Turkménistan	22.9	8.3	78.3	58.2	66.7	2.76	1.46
United Arab Emirates - Émirats arabes unis	16.7	1.4	9.0	76.3	80.5	2.52	1.52
Uzbekistan - Ouzbékistan	23.7	6.8	58.0	63.3	69.7	2.74	1.69
Viet Nam	20.2	5.2	22.3	71.2	74.9	2.32	1.50
Occupied Palestinian Territory - Territoire palestinien occupé	39.1	4.2	20.9	70.8	73.9	5.63	3.48
Yemen - Yémen	39.3	8.6	69.2	58.8	61.8	6.02	3.07
EUROPE							
Albania - Albanie	17.2	5.5	21.7	72.6	79.0	2.25	1.18
Austria - Autriche	9.5	9.5	4.6	75.9	81.7	1.38	...
Belarus - Bélarus	9.3	14.5	9.7	62.5	74.6	1.24	...
Belgium - Belgique	10.8	10.3	4.4	75.1	81.2	1.64	0.05
Bosnia and Herzegovina - Bosnie-Herzégovine	9.4	8.7	13.4	71.4	76.7	1.28	0.07
Bulgaria - Bulgarie	8.7	14.2	12.6	68.9	76.0	1.26	...
Channel Islands - Îles Anglo-Normandes ...	10.5	9.9	5.5	75.9	80.8	1.41	0.06
Croatia - Croatie	9.1	11.5	6.9	71.3	78.4	1.35	...
Czech Republic - République tchèque	9.0	10.8	3.9	72.1	78.7	1.18	...
Denmark - Danemark	12.0	10.7	4.6	75.0	79.6	1.76	0.13
Estonia - Estonie	9.8	13.7	7.4	65.1	76.7	1.39	...
Finland - Finlande	11.0	9.5	3.9	74.9	81.7	1.75	0.14
France	12.8	9.2	4.4	76.0	83.2	1.88	0.36
Germany - Allemagne	8.7	10.3	4.5	75.7	81.5	1.35	...
Greece - Grèce	9.4	9.9	7.7	76.4	80.1	1.28	...
Hungary - Hongrie	9.5	13.3	7.2	68.3	76.6	1.30	...
Iceland - Islande	14.4	6.1	3.1	79.3	82.7	1.99	0.83
Ireland - Irlande	15.2	7.6	5.4	75.3	80.3	1.97	0.76
Italy - Italie	9.4	9.9	5.2	76.9	82.9	1.29	...

**Annex II: United Nations Medium Variant Population Projections - Vital statistics summary and expectation of life at birth:
2000 - 2005**
**Annexe II: Projections de la population de variante moyenne de l'ONU - Aperçu des statistiques de l'état civil et espérance
de vie à la naissance: 2000 - 2005**

(continued — suite)

Continent, country or area / Continent, pays ou zone	Crude birth rate — Taux bruts de natalité[1]	Crude death rate — Taux bruts de mortalité[1]	Infant mortality rate — Décès d'enfants de moins d'un an[1]	Expectation of life at birth — Espérance de vie à la naissance[1]		Total fertility rate— Indice synthétique de fécondité[1]	Natural increase — Accroissement naturel[1]
				Male — Masculin	Female — Féminin		
EUROPE							
Latvia - Lettonie	8.7	13.6	11.6	65.7	76.8	1.25	...
Lithuania - Lituanie	9.0	11.8	9.5	66.4	77.7	1.28	...
Luxembourg	12.0	8.9	4.7	75.1	81.1	1.67	0.32
Malta - Malte	10.0	7.7	6.9	76.2	80.8	1.46	0.24
Netherlands - Pays-Bas	12.4	8.7	5.0	76.3	81.0	1.73	0.36
Norway - Norvège	12.3	9.5	3.8	76.7	81.8	1.80	0.29
Poland - Pologne	9.4	9.6	7.2	70.4	78.8	1.25	...
Portugal	10.9	10.4	5.5	73.9	80.5	1.45	0.05
Republic of Moldova - République de Moldova	11.4	12.4	16.7	64.3	71.5	1.50	...
Romania - Roumanie	10.0	12.2	16.8	67.8	75.0	1.29	...
Russian Federation - Fédération de Russie	9.9	15.9	17.2	58.5	71.8	1.30	...
Slovakia - Slovaquie	9.7	9.8	7.4	69.8	77.8	1.22	...
Slovenia - Slovénie	8.9	9.4	5.3	72.9	80.4	1.23	...
Spain - Espagne	10.2	8.7	4.4	76.6	83.4	1.29	0.15
Sweden - Suède	10.9	10.5	3.3	77.8	82.3	1.67	0.04
Switzerland - Suisse	9.8	8.1	4.4	77.9	83.2	1.42	0.17
The Former Yugoslav Rep. of Macedonia - L'ex-République yougoslave de Macédoine	12.0	8.6	16.5	71.1	75.9	1.56	0.34
Ukraine	8.4	15.8	13.5	62.0	73.4	1.15	...
United Kingdom - Royaume-Uni	11.6	10.2	5.2	76.1	80.7	1.70	0.14
OCEANIA — OCEANIE							
Australia - Australie[6]	12.7	6.8	4.8	77.9	82.9	1.76	0.59
Fiji - Fidji	23.1	6.4	21.6	65.7	70.1	2.98	1.68
French Polynesia - Polynésie française	19.3	4.9	8.8	70.6	75.8	2.39	1.44
Guam	20.7	5.1	10.1	72.4	77.0	2.74	1.56
Micronesia, Federated States of - Micronésie, États Fédérés de La	24.6	5.3	28.8	68.7	72.8	3.01	1.93
New Caledonia - Nouvelle-Calédonie	18.0	5.2	6.6	71.9	78.7	2.23	1.28
New Zealand - Nouvelle-Zélande	14.2	7.1	5.6	77.0	81.3	1.96	0.71
Papua New Guinea - Papouasie-Nouvelle-Guinée	34.0	9.9	65.3	54.1	59.9	4.32	2.41
Samoa	29.4	5.7	25.7	67.1	73.5	4.42	2.37
Solomon Islands - Îles Salomon	33.6	7.9	60.1	61.6	63.0	4.36	2.57
Tonga	24.3	5.7	20.7	71.3	73.3	3.73	1.87
Vanuatu	31.0	5.7	34.3	66.8	70.4	4.15	2.53

FOOTNOTES - NOTES

[1] All data are medium variant projections, produced by the United Nations, Department of Economic and Social Affairs, Population Division (2007) and published in *World Population Prospects: The 2006 Revision*. CD-ROM Edition - Extended Dataset in Excel and ASCII formats (United Nations publication, Sales No. E.07.XIII.7). — Toutes ces données sont des projections de la population au milieu de l'année de variante moyenne; elles sont produites par Les Nations Unies, Département des Affaires Sociales et Économiques, ont été publiées dans *World Population Prospects: The 2006 Revision. CD-ROM Edition - Extended Dataset in Excel and ASCII formats* (United Nations publication, Sales No. E.07.XIII.7).

[2] Including Agalega, Rodrigues and Saint Brandon. — Y compris Agalega, Rodrigues et Saint Brandon.

[3] For statistical purposes, the data for China do not include Hong Kong and Macao Special Administrative Regions (SAR) of China. — A des fins statistiques, les données pour la Chine ne comprennent pas les Régions Administratives Spéciales (SAR) de Hong Kong et Macao.

[4] As of 1 July 1997, Hong Kong became a Special Administrative Region (SAR) of China. — A partir du 1 juillet 1997, Hong Kong est devenue une Région Administrative Spéciale (SAR) de la Chine.

[5] As of 20 December 1999, Macao became a Special Administrative Region (SAR) of China. — A partir du 20 décembre 1999, Macao est devenue une Région Administrative Spéciale (SAR) de la Chine.

[6] Including Christmas Island, Cocos (Keeling) Islands and Norfolk Island. — Y compris Christmas Island, Cocos (Keeling) Islands et Norfolk Island.

Subject-matter	Year of issue	Time coverage	Subject-matter	Year of issue	Time coverage
	1993	1989-93		1998-99	Latest
	1994	1990-94		1999CD[iv]	1990-98
	1995	1991-95		2000-2005	Latest
	1996	1992-96	- by age of mother and birth order	1949/50	1936-47
	1997	1993-97		1954	Latest
	1997HS[iii]	1948-97		1959	1949-58
	1998	1994-98		1965	1955-64
	1999	1995-99		1969	1963-68
	1999CD[iv]	1980-99		1975	1966-74
	2000	1996-00		1981	1972-80
	2001	1997-01		1986	1977-85
	2002	1998-02		1999CD[iv]	1990-98
	2003	1999-03	- by age of mother and sex	1965-1968	Latest
	2004	2000-04		1969	1963-68
	2005	2001-05		1970-1974	Latest
- by age of father	1949/50	1942-49		1975	1966-74
	1954	1936-53		1976-1978	Latest
	1959	1949-58		1978HS[ii]	1948-77
	1965	1955-64		1979-1980	Latest
	1969	1963-68		1981	1972-80
	1975	1966-74		1982-1985	Latest
	1981	1972-80		1986	1977-85
	1999CD[iv]	1990-98		1987-1991	Latest
- by age of mother	1948	1936-47		1992	1983-92
	1949/50	1936-49		1993-1997	Latest
	1954	1936-53		1997HS[iii]	1948-96
	1955-1956	Latest		1998-99	Latest
	1958	Latest		1999CD[iv]	1990-98
	1959	1949-58		2000-2005	Latest
	1960-1964	Latest	- by age of mother and urban/rural residence (see: by urban/rural residence, below)		
	1965	1955-64			
	1966-1968	Latest			
	1969	1963-68			
	1970-1974	Latest			
	1975	1966-74	- by birth order	1948	1936-47
	1976-1978	Latest		1949/50	1936-49
	1978HS[ii]	1948-77		1954	1936-53
	1979-1980	Latest		1955	Latest
	1981	1972-80		1959	1949-58
	1982-1985	Latest		1965	1955-64
	1986	1977-85		1969	1963-68
	1987-1991	Latest		1975	1966-74
	1992	1983-92		1981	1972-80
	1993-1997	Latest		1986	1977-85
	1997HS[iii] [3]	1948-96		1999CD[iv]	1990-98

Subject-matter	Year of issue	Time coverage	Subject-matter	Year of issue	Time coverage
- living, by age of mother and urban/rural residence				1990	1986-90
				1991	1987-91
				1992	1983-92
	1971	1962-71		1993	1989-93
	1973	1965-73		1994	1990-94
	1975	1965-74		1995	1991-95
	1981	1972-80		1996	1987-96
	1986	1977-85		1997	1993-97
	1997HS[iii]	1948-96		1997HS[iii]	1948-97
				1998	1994-98
Cities (see: Population)				1999	1995-99
				2000	1996-00
D				2001	1997-01
				2002	1998-02
Deaths.....................................	1948	1932-47		2003	1999-03
	1949/50	1934-49		2004	2000-04
	1951	1935-50		2005	2001-05
	1952	1936-51			
	1953	1950-52	- by age and sex	1948	1936-47
	1954	1946-53		1951	1936-50
	1955	1946-54		1955-1956	Latest
	1956	1947-55		1957	1948-56
	1957	1940-56		1958-1960	Latest
	1958	1948-57		1961	1955-60
	1959	1949-58		1962-1965	Latest
	1960	1950-59		1966	1961-65
	1961	1952-61		1967-1973	Latest
	1962	1953-62		1974	1965-73
	1963	1954-63		1975-1979	Latest
	1964	1960-64		1978HS[ii]	1948-77
	1966	1947-66		1980	1971-79
	1967	1963-67		1981-1984	Latest
	1968	1964-68		1985	1976-84
	1969	1965-69		1986-1991	Latest
	1970	1966-70		1992	1983-92
	1971	1967-71		1993-1995	Latest
	1972	1968-72		1996	1987-95
	1973	1969-73		1997	Latest
	1974	1965-74		1997HS[iii]	1948-96
	1975	1971-75		1998-2005	Latest
	1976	1972-76			
	1977	1973-77	- by age and sex and urban/rural residence		
	1978	1974-78			
	1978HS[ii]	1948-78		1967-1973	Latest
	1979	1975-79		1974	1965-73
	1980	1971-80		1975-1979	Latest
	1981	1977-81		1980	1971-79
	1982	1978-82		1981-1984	Latest
	1983	1979-83		1985	1976-84
	1984	1980-84		1986-1991	Latest
	1985	1976-85		1992	1983-92
	1986	1982-86		1993-1995	Latest
	1987	1983-87		1996	1987-95
	1988	1984-88		1997	Latest
	1989	1985-89		1997HS[iii]	1948-96
				1998-2005	Latest

Subject-matter	Year of issue	Time coverage	Subject-matter	Year of issue	Time coverage
- by age and sex and urban/rural residence				1974	Latest
				1980	Latest
	1967	Latest		1985	Latest
	1972	Latest		1996	Latest
	1974	1965-73	- by occupation, age and sex	1957	Latest
	1975-1979	Latest			
	1980	1971-79			
	1981-1984	Latest	- by occupation and age, males	1961	Latest
	1985	1976-84		1967	Latest
	1986-1991	Latest	- by urban/rural residence		
	1991PA[vii]	1950-1990		1967	Latest
	1992	1983-1992		1968	1964-68
	1993-1995	Latest		1969	1965-69
	1996	1987-95		1970	1966-70
	1997	Latest		1971	1967-71
	1997HS[iii]	1948-96		1972	1968-72
	1998-2005	Latest		1973	1969-73
				1974	1965-74
- by cause	1951	1947-49		1975	1971-75
	1952	1947-51[vi]		1976	1972-76
	1953	1947-52		1977	1973-77
	1954	1945-53		1978	1974-78
	1955-1956	Latest		1979	1975-79
	1957	1952-56		1980	1971-80
	1958-1960	Latest		1981	1977-81
	1961	1955-60		1982	1978-82
	1962-1965	Latest		1983	1979-83
	1966	1960-65		1984	1980-84
	1967-1973	Latest		1985	1976-85
	1974	1965-73		1986	1982-86
	1975-1979	Latest		1987	1983-87
	1980	1971-79		1988	1984-88
	1981-1984	Latest		1989	1985-89
	1985	1976-84		1990	1986-90
	1986-1991	Latest		1991	1987-91
	1991PA[vii]	1960-90		1992	1983-92
	1992-1995	Latest		1993	1989-93
	1996	1987-95		1994	1990-94
	1997-2000	Latest		1995	1991-95
	2002	1995-02		1996	1987-96
	2004	1995-04		1997	1993-97
- by cause, age and sex	1957	Latest		1998	1994-98
				1999	1995-99
	1961	Latest		1987	1983-87
	1991PA[vii]	1960-90		1988	1984-88
				1989	1985-89
- by cause and sex	1967	Latest		1990	1986-90
	1974	Latest		1991	1987-91
	1980	Latest		1992	1983-92
	1985	Latest		1993	1989-93
	1996	Latest		1994	1990-94
- by marital status, age and sex				1995	1991-95
	1961	Latest		1996	1987-96
	1967	Latest		1997	1993-97

Subject-matter	Year of issue	Time coverage	Subject-matter	Year of issue	Time coverage
	1963	1954-63		1990	1980-89
	1964	1960-64	- by age of wife classified by age of husband		
	1965	1961-65			
	1966	1962-66		1958	1946-57
	1967	1963-67		1968	Latest
	1968	1949-68		1976	Latest
	1969	1965-69		1982	Latest
	1970	1966-70		1982	Latest
	1971	1967-71		1990	Latest
	1972	1968-72	- by duration of marriage		
	1973	1969-73		1958	1948-57
	1974	1970-74		1968	1958-67
	1975	1971-75		1976	1966-75
	1976	1957-76		1982	1972-81
	1977	1973-77		1990	1980-89
	1978	1974-78	- by duration of marriage and age of husband, wife		
	1979	1975-79			
	1980	1976-80		1958	1946-57
	1981	1977-81		1968	Latest
	1982	1963-82		1976	Latest
	1983	1979-83		1982	Latest
	1984	1980-84		1990	Latest
	1985	1981-85	- by number of children involved		
	1986	1982-86		1958	1948-57
	1987	1983-87		1968	1958-67
	1988	1984-88		1976	1966-75
	1989	1985-89		1982	1972-81
	1990	1971-90		1990	1980-89
	1991	1987-91			
	1992	1988-92	Divorce rates	1952	1935-51
	1993	1989-93		1953	1936-52
	1994	1990-94		1954	1946-53
	1995	1991-95		1955	1946-54
	1996	1992-96		1956	1947-55
	1997	1993-97		1957	1948-56
	1998	1994-98		1958	1930-57
	1999	1995-99		1959	1949-58
	2000	1996-00		1960	1950-59
	2001	1997-01		1961	1952-61
	2002	1998-02		1962	1953-62
	2003	1999-03		1963	1954-63
	2004	2000-04		1964	1960-64
	2005	2001-05		1965	1961-65
- by age of husband				1966	1962-66
	1968	1958-67		1967	1963-67
	1976	1966-75		1968	1920-64ᵛ
	1982	1972-81			1953-68
	1987	1975-86		1969	1965-69
	1990	1980-89		1970	1966-70
- by age of wife	1968	1958-67		1971	1967-71
	1976	1966-75		1972	1968-72
	1982	1972-81		1973	1969-73
	1987	1975-86		1974	1970-74
				1975	1971-75
				1976	1957-76
				1977	1973-77

Subject-matter	Year of issue	Time coverage	Subject-matter	Year of issue	Time coverage
	1992	1987-91		1981	1972-80
	1993	1988-92		1986	1977-85
	1994	1989-93	- by urban/rural residence		
	1995	1990-94		1971	1966-70
	1996	1987-95		1972	1967-71
	1997	1992-96		1973	1968-72
	1998	1993-97		1974	1965-73
	1999	1994-98		1975	1966-74
	1999CD[iv]	1990-98		1976	1971-75
	2000	1995-99		1977	1972-76
	2001	1997-01		1978	1973-77
	2002	1998-02		1979	1974-78
	2003	1999-03		1980	1971-79
	2004	2000-04		1981	1972-80
	2005	2001-05		1982	1977-81
				1983	1978-82
- by age of mother	1954	1936-53		1984	1979-83
	1959	1949-58		1985	1975-84
	1965	1955-64		1986	1977-85
	1969	1963-68		1987	1982-86
	1975	1966-74		1988	1983-87
	1981	1972-80		1989	1984-88
	1986	1977-85		1990	1985-89
				1991	1986-90
- by age of mother and birth order	1954	Latest		1992	1987-91
	1959	1949-58		1993	1988-92
	1965	3-Latest		1994	1989-93
	1969	1963-68		1995	1990-94
	1975	1966-74		1996	1987-95
	1981	1972-80		1997	1992-96
	1986	1977-85		1998	1993-97
- by period of gestation	1957	1950-56		1999	1994-98
	1959	1949-58		1999CD[iv]	1990-98
	1961	1952-60		2000	1995-99
	1965	5-Latest		2001	1997-01
	1966	1956-65		2002	1998-02
	1967-1968	Latest		2003	1999-03
	1969	1963-68		2004	2000-04
	1974	1965-73		2005	2001-05
	1975	1966-74	- illegitimate	1961	1952-60
	1980	1971-79		1965	5-Latest
	1981	1972-80		1969	1963-68
	1985	1976-84		1975	1966-74
	1986	1977-85		1981	1972-80
	1996	1987-95		1986	1977-85
- by sex	1961	1952-60	- illegitimate, percent	1961	1952-60
	1965	5 Latest		1965	5-Latest
	1969	1963-68		1969	1963-68
	1975	1966-74			

Subject-matter	Year of issue	Time coverage	Subject-matter	Year of issue	Time coverage
- by age of mother	1954	1936-53		1988	1983-87
	1959	1949-58		1989	1984-88
	1965	1955-64		1990	1985-89
	1969	1963-68		1991	1986-90
	1975	1966-74		1992	1987-91
	1981	1972-80		1993	1988-92
	1986	1977-85		1994	1989-93
	1996	1987-95		1995	1990-94
	1999CD[iv]	1990-98		1996	1987-95
- by age of mother and birth order	1954	Latest		1997	1992-96
	1959	1949-58		1998	1993-97
	1965	3-Latest		1999	1994-98
	1969	1963-68		1999CD[iv]	1990-98
	1975	1966-74		2000	1995-99
	1981	1972-80		2001	1997-01
	1986	1977-85		2002	1998-02
	1999CD[iv]	1990-98		2003	1999-03
- by period of gestation	1957	1950-56		2004	2000-04
	1959	1949-58		2005	2001-05
	1961	1952-60	- illegitimate	1961	1952-60
	1965	5-Latest		1965	5-Latest
	1966	1956-65			
	1967-1968	Latest	- legitimate	1959	1949-58
	1969	1963-68		1965	1955-64
	1974	1965-73		1969	1963-68
	1975	1966-74		1975	1966-74
	1980	1971-79		1981	1972-80
	1981	1972-80		1986	1977-85
	1985	1976-84			
	1986	1977-85	- legitimate by age of mother	1959	1949-58
- by urban/rural residence	1971	1966-70		1965	1955-64
	1972	1967-71		1969	1963-68
	1973	1968-72		1975	1966-74
	1974	1965-73		1981	1972-80
	1975	1966-74		1986	1977-85
	1976	1971-75			
	1977	1972-76			
	1978	1973-77			
	1979	1974-78			
	1980	1971-79			
	1981	1972-80			
	1982	1977-81			
	1983	1978-82			
	1984	1979-83			
	1985	1975-84			
	1986	1977-85			
	1987	1982-86			

G

Gestational age of foetal deaths (see: Foetal deaths)

Gross reproduction rates (see: Reproduction rates)

H

Homeless (see: Population)

Subject-matter	Year of issue	Time coverage	Subject-matter	Year of issue	Time coverage
	1975	1971-75		1975-1979	Latest
	1976	1972-76		1980	1971-79
	1977	1973-77		1981-1984	Latest
	1978	1974-78		1985	1976-84
	1978HS[ii]	1948-78		1986-1991	Latest
	1979	1975-79		1992	1983-92
	1980	1971-80		1993-1995	Latest
	1981	1977-81		1996	1987-95
	1982	1978-82		1997-1999	Latest
	1983	1979-83	- by urban/rural residence		
	1984	1980-84		1967	Latest
	1985	1976-85		1968	1964-68
	1986	1982-86		1969	1965-69
	1987	1983-87		1970	1966-70
	1988	1984-88		1971	1967-71
	1989	1985-89		1972	1968-72
	1990	1986-90		1973	1969-73
	1991	1987-91		1974	1965-74
	1992	1983-92		1975	1971-75
	1993	1989-93		1976	1972-76
	1994	1990-94		1977	1973-77
	1995	1991-95		1978	1974-78
	1996	1987-96		1979	1975-79
	1997	1993-97		1980	1971-80
	1997HS[iii]	1948-97		1981	1977-81
	1998	1994-98		1982	1978-82
	1999	1995-99		1983	1979-83
	2000	1996-00		1984	1980-84
	2001	1997-01		1985	1976-85
	2002	1998-02		1986	1982-86
	2003	1999-03		1987	1983-87
	2004	2000-04		1988	1984-88
	2005	2001-05		1989	1985-89
				1990	1986-90
- by age and sex	1948	1936-47		1991	1987-91
	1951	1936-49		1992	1983-92
	1957	1948-56		1993	1989-93
	1961	1952-60		1994	1990-94
	1966	1956-65		1995	1991-95
	1967	1962-66		1996	1987-96
	1971-1973	Latest		1997	1993-97
	1974	1965-73		1998	1994-98
	1975-1979	Latest		1999	1995-99
	1980	1971-79		2000	1996-00
	1981-1984	Latest		2001	1997-01
	1985	1976-84		2002	1998-02
	1986-1991	Latest		2003	1999-03
	1992	1983-92		2004	2000-04
	1993-1995	Latest		2005	2001-05
	1996	1987-95	**Intercensal rates of population increase**	1948	1900-48
	1997-2005	Latest		1949/50	1900-50
- by age and sex and urban/rural residence				1951	1900-51
				1952	1850-1952
	1971-1973	Latest		1953	1850-1953
	1974	1965-73			

Subject-matter	Year of issue	Time coverage	Subject-matter	Year of issue	Time coverage
	1953	1950-52	- by age of bride	1948	1936-47
	1954	1946-53		1949/50	1936-49
	1955	1946-54		1958	1948-57
	1956	1947-55		1959-1967	Latest
	1957	1948-56		1968	1958-67
	1958	1940-57		1969-1975	Latest
	1959	1949-58		1976	1966-75
	1960	1950-59		1977-1981	Latest
	1961	1952-61		1982	1972-81
	1962	1953-62		1983-1986	Latest
	1963	1954-63		1987	1975-86
	1964	1960-64		1988-1989	Latest
	1965	1956-65		1990	1980-1989
	1966	1962-66		1991-1997	Latest
	1967	1963-67		1998	1993-97
	1968	1949-68		1999	1994-98
	1969	1965-69		2000	1995-99
	1970	1966-70		2001	1997-01
	1971	1967-71		2002	1998-02
	1972	1968-72		2003	1999-03
	1973	1969-73		2004	2000-04
	1974	1970-74		2005	2001-05
	1975	1971-75	- by age of bride classified by age of groom		
	1976	1957-76		1958	1948-57
	1977	1973-77		1968	Latest
	1978	1974-78		1976	Latest
	1979	1975-79		1982	Latest
	1980	1976-80		1990	Latest
	1981	1977-81			
	1982	1963-82	- by age of bride and previous marital status		
	1983	1979-83		1958	1948-57
	1984	1980-84		1968	Latest
	1985	1981-85		1976	Latest
	1986	1982-86		1982	Latest
	1987	1983-87		1990	Latest
	1988	1984-88	- by age of groom	1948	1936-47
	1989	1985-89		1949/50	1936-49
	1990	1971-90		1958	1948-57
	1991	1987-91		1959-1967	Latest
	1992	1988-92		1968	1958-67
	1993	1989-93		1969-1975	Latest
	1994	1990-94		1976	1966-75
	1995	1991-95		1977-1981	Latest
	1996	1992-96		1982	1972-81
	1997	1993-97		1983-1986	Latest
	1998	1994-98		1987	1975-86
	1999	1995-99		1988-1989	Latest
	2000	1996-00		1990	1980-1989
	2001	1997-01		1990-1997	Latest
	2002	1998-02		1998	1993-97
	2003	1999-03		1999	1994-98
	2004	2000-04		2000	1995-99
	2005	2001-05		2001	1997-01

Subject-matter	Year of issue	Time coverage	Subject-matter	Year of issue	Time coverage
	1956	1947-55		1953	1936-51
	1957	1948-56		1954	1936-52
	1958	1930-57		1958	1935-56
	1959	1949-58		1968	1955-67
	1960	1950-59		1976	1966-75
	1961	1952-61		1982	1972-81
	1962	1953-62		1987	1975-86
	1963	1954-63		1990	1980-89
	1964	1960-64	- by sex among marriageable population		
	1965	1956-65			
	1966	1962-66		1958	1935-56
	1967	1963-67		1968	1935-67
	1968	1920-64[v]		1976	1966-75
		1953-68		1982	1972-81
	1969	1965-69		1990	1980-89
	1970	1966-70	- by urban/rural residence		
	1971	1967-71		1968	Latest
	1972	1968-72		1969	1965-69
	1973	1969-73		1970	1966-70
	1974	1970-74		1971	1967-71
	1975	1971-75		1972	1968-72
	1976	1957-76		1973	1969-73
	1977	1973-77		1974	1970-74
	1978	1974-78		1975	1971-75
	1979	1975-79		1976	1957-76
	1980	1976-80		1977	1973-77
	1981	1977-81		1978	1974-78
	1982	1963-82		1979	1975-79
	1983	1979-83		1980	1976-80
	1984	1980-84		1981	1977-81
	1985	1981-85		1982	1963-82
	1986	1982-86		1983	1979-83
	1987	1983-87		1984	1980-84
	1988	1984-88		1985	1981-85
	1989	1985-89		1986	1982-86
	1990	1971-90		1987	1983-87
	1991	1987-91		1988	1984-88
	1992	1988-92		1989	1985-89
	1993	1989-93		1990	1971-90
	1994	1990-94		1991	1987-91
	1995	1991-95		1992	1988-92
	1996	1992-96		1993	1989-93
	1997	1993-97		1994	1990-94
	1998	1994-98		1995	1991-95
	1999	1995-99		1996	1992-96
	2000	1996-00		1997	1993-97
	2001	1997-01		1998	1994-98
	2002	1998-02		1999	1995-99
	2003	1999-03		2000	1996-00
	2004	2000-04		2001	1997-01
	2005	2001-05		2002	1998-02
				2003	1999-03
				2004	2000-04
- by age and sex	1948	1936-46		2005	2001-05
	1949/50	1936-49			

Subject-matter	Year of issue	Time coverage	Subject-matter	Year of issue	Time coverage
	1989	1979-88		1962	1958-61
	1996	1986-95		1966	1960-65
	1972	1965-71		1970	1962-69
	1974	1967-73		1977	1967-76
	1976	1969-75		1989	1975-88
- arrivals, by major categories	1949/50	1945-49	by country or area of intended residence	1948	1945-47
	1951	1946-50		1949/50	1945-48
	1952	1947-51		1951	1948-50
	1954	1948-53		1952	1949-51
	1957	1951-56		1954	1950-53
	1959	1953-58		1957	1953-56
	1962	1956-61		1959	1956-58
	1966	1960-65		1977	1958-76
	1968	1966-67		1989	1975-88
	1977	1967-76	- immigrants, long term		
	1985	1975-84	by age and sex	1948	1945-47
	1989	1979-88		1949/50	1946-48
	1996	1986-95		1951	1948-50
- continental and inter-continental	1948	1936-47		1952	1949-51
	1977	1967-76		1954	1950-53
				1957	1953-56
- departures	1970	1963-69		1959	1955-58
	1972	1965-71		1962	1958-61
	1974	1967-73		1966	1960-65
	1976	1969-75		1970	1962-69
	1977	1967-76		1977	1967-76
	1985	1975-84		1989	1975-88
	1989	1979-88	by country or area of last residence	1948	1945-47
	1996	1986-95		1949/50	1945-48
- departures, by major categories	1949/50	1945-49		1951	1948-50
	1951	1946-50		1952	1949-51
	1952	1947-51		1954	1950-53
	1954	1948-53		1957	1953-56
	1957	1951-56		1959	1956-58
	1959	1953-58		1977	1958-76
	1962	1956-61		1989	1975-88
	1966	1960-65		1948	1945-47
	1968	1966-67		1949/50	1945-48
	1977	1967-76	- refugees, by country or area of destination:		
	1985	1975-84	repatriated by the International Refugee Organization	1952	1947-51
	1989	1979-88			
	1996	1986-95			
- emigrants, long term:			resettled by the International	1952	1947-51
by age and sex	1948	1945-47			
	1949/50	1946-48			
	1951	1948-50			
	1952	1949-51			
	1954	1950-53			
	1957	1953-56			
	1959	1955-58			

Subject-matter	Year of issue	Time coverage	Subject-matter	Year of issue	Time coverage
	1983	1974-83	- civil division (see: by major civil divisions, above)		
	1988	1980-88[vi]			
	1993	1985-93			
- by sex:			- density (see: Density)		
enumerated	1948-1952	Latest			
	1953	1950-52	- Disabled	1991PA[vii]	Latest
	1954-1959	Latest	- economically active:		
	1960	1900-61	by age and sex	1945	1945-54
	1961	Latest		1956	1945-55
	1962	1900-62		1964	1955-64
	1963	1955-63		1972	1962-72
	1964	1955-64	by age and sex and urban/rural residence		
	1965-1969	Latest			
	1970	1950-70			
	1971	1962-71		1973	1965-73[vi]
	1972	Latest		1979	1970-79[vi]
	1973	1965-73		1984	1974-84
	1974-1978	Latest		1988	1980-88[vi]
	1978HS[ii]	1948-78		1994	1985-94
	1979-1982	Latest	by age and sex, per cent	1949/50	1930-48
	1983	1974-83		1954	Latest
	1984-1997	Latest		1955	1945-54
	1997HS[iii]	1948-97		1956	1945-55
	1998-2003	Latest		1964	1955-64
estimated	1948-1949/50	1945and latest		1972	1962-72
	1951-1954	Latest	by age and sex, per cent and urban/rural residence		
	1955-1959	Latest			
	1960	1940-60			
	1961-1969	Latest			
	1970	1950-70		1973	1965-73[vi]
	1971	1962-71		1979	1970-79[vi]
	1972	Latest		1984	1974-84
	1973	1965-73		1988	1980-88[vi]
	1974-1997	Latest		1994	1985-94
	1997HS[iii]	1948-97	by industry, age and sex	1956	1945-55
	1998-1999	Latest		1964	1955-64
	2000	1991-00		1972	1962-72
	2001	1992-01	by industry, age, sex and urban/rural residence		
	2002	1993-02			
	2003	1994-03			
	2004	1995-04		1973	1965-74[vi]
	2005	1996-05		1979	1970-79[vi]
- by single years of age and sex	1955	1945-54		1984	1974-84
	1962	1955-62		1988	1980-88[vi]
	1963	1955-63[vi]		1994	1985-94
	1971	1962-71	by industry, status and sex		
	1973	1965-73[vi]		1948	Latest
	1979	1970-79[vi]		1949/50	Latest
	1983	1974-83		1955	1945-54
	1988	1980-88[vi]		1964	1955-64
	1993	1985-93		1972	1962-72
- cities (see: of cities, below)					

Subject-matter	Year of issue	Time coverage	Subject-matter	Year of issue	Time coverage
by industry, status and sex and urban/rural residence				1973	1965-73[vi]
				1979	1970-79[vi]
				1984	1974-84
	1973	1965-73[vi]		1994	1985-94
	1979	1970-79[vi]	by status, age and sex		
	1984	1974-84		1956	1945-55
	1988	1980-88[vi]		1964	1955-64
	1994	1985-94		1972	1962-72
by living arrangements, age, sex and urban/rural residence			by status, age and sex and urban/rural residence		
	1987	1975-86		1973	1965-73[vi]
	1995	1985-95		1979	1970-79[vi]
by occupation, age and sex				1984	1974-84
	1956	1945-55		1988	1980-88[vi]
	1964	1955-64		1994	1985-94
	1972	1962-72	by status, industry and sex	1948	Latest
by occupation, age and sex and urban/rural residence				1949/50	Latest
				1955	1945-54
				1964	1955-64
	1973	1965-73[vi]		1972	1962-72
	1979	1970-79[vi]	by status, industry, and sex and urban/rural residence		
	1984	1974-84			
	1988	1980-88[vi]			
	1994	1985-94		1973	1965-73[vi]
by occupation, status and sex				1979	1970-79[vi]
				1984	1974-84
	1956	1945-55		1988	1980-88[vi]
	1964	1955-64		1994	1985-94
	1972	1962-72	by status, occupation and sex	1956	1945-55
by occupation, status and sex and urban/rural residence				1964	1955-64
				1972	1962-72
	1973	1965-73[vi]	by status, occupation and sex and urban/rural residence		
	1979	1970-7vi[vi]			
	1984	1974-84			
	1988	1980-88[vi]		1973	1965-73[vi]
	1994	1985-94		1979	1970-79[vi]
by sex	1948	Latest		1984	1974-84
	1949/50	1926-48		1988	1980-88[vi]
	1955	1945-54		1994	1985-94
	1956	1945-55	female, by marital status and age		
	1960	1920-60			
	1963	1955-63		1956	1945-55
	1964	1955-64		1964	1955-64
	1970	1950-70		1968	Latest
	1972	1962-72		1972	1962-72

Subject-matter	Year of issue	Time coverage	Subject-matter	Year of issue	Time coverage
	1969	1963-69		1968	1960-68
	1970	1963-70			1963-68
	1971	1963-71		1969	1960-69
	1972	1963-72			1963-69
	1973	1970-73		1970	1963-70
	1974	1970-74			1965-70
	1975	1970-75		1971	1963-71
	1976	1970-76			1965-71
	1977	1970-77		1972	1963-72
	1978	1975-78			1965-72
	1979	1975-79		1973	1965-73
	1980	1975-80			1970-73
	1981	1975-81		1974	1965-74
	1982	1975-82			1970-74
	1983	1980-83		1975	1965-75
	1984	1980-84			1970-75
	1985	1980-85		1976	1965-76
	1986	1980-86			1970-76
	1987	1980-87		1977	1965-77
	1988	1985-88			1970-77
	1989	1985-89		1978-1979	1970-75
	1990	1985-90		1980-1983	1975-80
	1991	1985-91		1984-1986	1980-85
	1992	1985-92		1987-1992	1985-90
	1993	1990-93		1993-1997	1990-95
	1994	1990-94		1998-2000	1995-00
	1995	1990-95		2001-2005	2000-05
	1996	1990-96	- Homeless by age and sex		
	1997	1990-97		1991PA[vii]	Latest
	1998	1993-98	- illiteracy rates by sex		
	1999	1995-99		1948	Latest
	2000	1995-00		1955	1945-54
	2001-2005	2000-05		1960	1920-60
average annual for the world, macro-regions (continents) and regions				1963	1955-63[vi]
				1964	1955-64[vi]
				1970	1950-70
			- illiteracy rates by sex and urban/rural residence		
	1957	1950-56		1973	1965-73
	1958	1950-57		1979	1970-79[vi]
	1959	1950-58		1983	1974-83
	1960	1950-59		1988	1980-88[vi]
	1961	1950-60		1993	1985-93
	1962	1950-61			
	1963	1958-62	- illiterate, by sex	1948	Latest
		1960-62		1955	1945-54
	1964	1958-63		1960	1920-60
		1960-63		1963	1955-63
	1965	1958-64		1964	1955-64
		1960-64		1970	1950-70
	1966	1958-66	- illiterate, by sex and age		
		1960-66		1948	Latest
	1967	1960-67		1955	1945-54
		1963-67		1963	1955-63

Subject-matter	Year of issue	Time coverage	Subject-matter	Year of issue	Time coverage
	1964	1955-64[vi]		1987	1975-86
	1970	1950-70	- living arrangements	1991PA[vii]	1950-90
- illiterate, by sex and age and urban/rural residence				1995	1985-95
	1973	1965-73	- localities (see: by localities, above)		
	1979	1970-79[vi]			
	1983	1974-83	- major civil divisions (see: by major civil divisions, above)		
	1988	1980-88[vi]			
	1993	1985-93			
- illiterate, by sex and urban/rural residence			- married by age and sex (see also: by marital status, above): numbers and percent		
	1973	1965-73		1954	1926-52
	1979	1970-79[vi]		1960	1920-60
	1983	1974-83		1970	1950-70
	1988	1980-88[vi]	- married female by percentage and duration of marriage		
	1993	1985-93			
- in collective living quarters and homeless	1991PA[vii]	Latest		1968	Latest
			- never married proportion by sex, selected ages		
- in households (see: by household type, above, also: Households)				1976	1966-75
				1978HS[ii]	1948-77
				1982	1972-81
- in localities (see: by localities and by locality size-classes, above)				1990	1980-89
			- not economically active	1972	1962-72
- increase rates (see: growth rates, above)			- not economically active by urban/rural residence		
				1973	1965-73[vi]
				1979	1970-79[vi]
- literacy rates: by sex (see also: illiteracy rates, above)				1984	1974-84
	1955	1945-54		1988	1980-88[vi]
				1994	1985-94
- literacy rates, by sex and age	1955	1945-54	- of cities: capital city	1952	Latest
				1955	1945-54
- literate, by sex and age (see also: illiterate, above)				1957	Latest
	1948	Latest		1960	1939-61
	1955	1945-54		1962	1955-62
	1963	1955-63		1963	1955-63
	1964	1955-64[vi]		1964-1969	Latest
- literate, by sex and age by urban/rural residence				1970	1950-70
				1971	1962-71
	1971	1962-71		1972	Latest
	1973	1965-73[vi]		1973	1965-73
	1979	1970-74[vi]		1974-2005	Latest
	1983	1974-83	of 100000+ inhabitants	1952	Latest
	1988	1980-88[vi]		1955	1945-54
	1993	1985-93		1957	Latest
				1960	1939-61

Subject-matter	Year of issue	Time coverage	Subject-matter	Year of issue	Time coverage
	1962	1955-62		1974	1965-74
	1963	1955-63		1975	1966-75
	1964-1969	Latest		1976	1967-76
	1970	1950-70		1977	1968-77
	1971	1962-71		1978	1969-78
	1972	Latest		1978HS[ii]	1948-78
	1973	1965-73		1979	1970-79
	1974-2005	Latest		1980	1971-80
- of continents				1981	1972-81
(see: of macro				1982	1973-82
regions, below)				1983	1974-83
- of countries or				1984	1975-84
areas (totals):				1985	1976-85
enumerated	1948	1900-48		1986	1977-86
	1949/50	1900-50		1987	1978-87
	1951	1900-51		1988	1979-88
	1952	1850-1952		1989	1980-89
	1953	1850-1953		1990	1981-90
	1954	Latest		1991	1982-91
	1955	1850-1954		1992	1983-92
	1956-1961	Latest		1993	1984-93
	1962	1900-62		1994	1985-94
	1963	Latest		1995	1986-95
	1964	1955-64		1996	1987-96
	1965-1978	Latest		1997	1988-97
	1978HS[ii]	1948-78		1997HS[iii]	1948-97
	1979-1997	Latest		1998	1989-98
	1997HS[iii]	1948-97		1999	1990-99
	1998-2005	Latest		2000	1991-00
				2001	1992-01
estimated	1948	1932-47		2002	1993-02
	1949/50	1932-49		2003	1994-03
	1951	1930-50		2004	1995-04
	1952	1920-51		2005	1996-05
	1953	1920-53				
	1954	1920-54	- of major regions	1949/50	1920-49
	1955	1920-55		1951	1950
	1956	1920-56		1952	1920-51
	1957	1940-57		1953	1920-52
	1958	1939-58		1954	1920-53
	1959	1940-59		1955	1920-54
	1960	1920-60		1956	1920-55
	1961	1941-61		1957	1920-56
	1962	1942-62		1958	1920-57
	1963	1943-63		1959	1920-58
	1964	1955-64		1960	1920-59
	1965	1946-65		1961	1920-60
	1966	1947-66		1962	1920-61
	1967	1958-67		1963	1930-62
	1968	1959-68		1964	1930-63
	1969	1960-69		1965	1930-65
	1970	1950-70		1966	1930-66
	1971	1962-71		1967	1930-67
	1972	1963-72		1968	1930-68
	1973	1964-73				

Subject-matter	Year of issue	Time coverage	Subject-matter	Year of issue	Time coverage
	1969	1930-69		1968	1930-68
	1970	1950-70		1969	1930-69
	1971	1950-71		1970	1950-70
	1972	1950-72		1971	1950-71
	1973	1950-73		1972	1950-72
	1974	1950-74		1973	1950-73
	1975	1950-75		1974	1950-74
	1976	1950-76		1975	1950-75
	1977	1950-77		1976	1950-76
	1978	1950-78		1977	1950-77
	1979	1950-79		1978	1950-78
	1980	1950-80		1979	1950-79
	1981	1950-81		1980	1950-80
	1982	1950-82		1981	1950-81
	1983	1950-83		1982	1950-82
	1984	1950-84		1983	1950-83
	1985	1950-85		1984	1950-84
	1986	1950-86		1985	1950-85
	1987	1950-87		1986	1950-86
	1988	1950-88		1987	1950-87
	1989	1950-89		1988	1950-88
	1990	1950-90		1989	1950-89
	1991	1950-91		1990	1950-90
	1992	1950-92		1991	1950-91
	1993	1950-93		1992	1950-92
	1994	1950-94		1993	1950-93
	1995	1950-95		1994	1950-94
	1996	1950-96		1995	1950-95
	1997	1950-97		1996	1950-96
	1998-1999	1950-00		1997	1950-97
	2000	1950-00		1998-1999	1950-00
	2001	1950-01		2000	1950-00
	2002	1950-02		2001	1950-01
	2003	1950-03		2002	1950-02
	2004	1950-04		2003	1950-03
	2005	1950-05		2004	1950-04
				2005	1950-05
- of regions	1949/50	1920-49	- of the world	1949/50	1920-49
	1952	1920-51		1951	1950
	1953	1920-52		1952	1920-51
	1954	1920-53		1953	1920-52
	1955	1920-54		1954	1920-53
	1956	1920-55		1955	1920-54
	1957	1920-56		1956	1920-55
	1958	1920-57		1957	1920-56
	1959	1920-58		1958	1920-57
	1960	1920-59		1959	1920-58
	1961	1920-60		1960	1920-59
	1962	1920-61		1961	1920-60
	1963	1930-62		1962	1920-61
	1964	1930-63		1963	1930-62
	1965	1930-65		1964	1930-63
	1966	1930-66		1965	1930-65
	1967	1930-67			

Subject-matter	Year of issue	Time coverage	Subject-matter	Year of issue	Time coverage
	1988	1979-88		2001	1992-01
	1989	1980-89		2002	1993-02
	1990	1981-90		2003	1994-03
	1991	1982-91		2004	1995-04
	1992	1983-92		2005	1996-05
	1993	1984-93	by single		
	1994	1985-94	years of age		
	1995	1986-95	and sex	1971	1962-71
	1996	1987-96		1973	1965-73[vi]
	1997	1988-97		1979	1970-79[vi]
	1998	1989-98		1983	1974-83
	1999	1990-99		1993	1985-93
	2000	1991-00	female:		
	2001	1992-01	by number of		
	2002	1993-02	children		
	2003	1994-03	born alive and		
	2004	1995-04	age	1971	1962-71
	2005	1996-05		1973	1965-73[vi]
				1975	1965-74
percent	1948	Latest		1978HS[ii]	1948-77
	1952	1900-51		1981	1972-80
	1955	1945-54		1986	1977-85
	1960	1920-60		1997HS[iii]	1948-96
	1962	1955-62	female:		
	1970	1950-70	by number of		
	1971	1962-71	children		
	1973	1965-73	living and age	1971	1962-71
	1974	1966-74		1973	1965-73[vi]
	1975	1967-75		1975	1965-74
	1976	1967-76		1978HS[ii]	1948-77
	1977	1968-77		1981	1972-80
	1978	1969-78		1986	1977-85
	1979	1970-79		1997HS[iii]	1948-96
	1980	1971-80			
	1981	1972-81	**Post-neo-natal deaths:**		
	1982	1973-82	- by sex	1948	1936-47
	1983	1974-83		1951	1936-50
	1984	1975-84		1957	1948-56
	1985	1976-85		1961	1952-60
	1986	1977-86		1963-1965	Latest
	1987	1978-87		1966	1961-65
	1988	1979-88		1967	1962-66
	1989	1980-89		1968-1970	Latest
	1990	1981-90		2000-2004	Latest
	1991	1982-91	- by age and sex	2000-2004	Latest
	1992	1983-92	- by sex and		
	1993	1984-93	urban/rural		
	1994	1985-94	residence	1971-1973	Latest
	1995	1986-95		1974	1965-73
	1996	1987-96		1975-1979	Latest
	1997	1988-97		1980	1971-79
	1998	1989-98		1981-1984	Latest
	1999	1990-99		1985	1976-84
	2000	1991-00		1986-1991	Latest
				1992	1983-92
				1993-1995	Latest

Subject-matter	Year of issue	Time coverage
	1996	1987-95
	1997-1999	Latest
Post-neo-natal mortality rates:		
- by sex	1948	1936-47
	1951	1936-50
	1957	1948-56
	1961	1952-60
	1966	1956-65
	1967	1962-66
	1968-1970	Latest
	2000-2004	Latest
- by age and sex	2000-2004	Latest
- by sex and urban/rural residence	1971-1973	Latest
	1974	1965-73
	1975-1979	Latest
	1980	1971-79
	1981-1984	Latest
	1985	1976-84
	1986-1991	Latest
	1992	1983-92
	1993-1995	Latest
	1996	1987-95
	1997-1999	Latest

R

Rates (see under following subject-matter headings: Annulments, Births, Deaths, Divorces, Fertility, Illiteracy, Infant Mortality, Intercensal, Life Tables, Literacy Marriages, Maternal mortality, Natural increase, Neo-natal mortality, Population growth, Post-neo-natal mortality, Reproduction)

Ratios (see under following subject matter headings: Births, Child-woman, Fertility, Foetal deaths, Perinatal mortality)

Refugees, by country or area of destination:

Subject-matter	Year of issue	Time coverage
- repatriated by the International Refugee Organization	1952	1947-51
- resettled by the International	1952	1947-51

Subject-matter	Year of issue	Time coverage
Refugee Organization		

Religion and sex (see: Population)

Subject-matter	Year of issue	Time coverage
Reproduction rates, gross and net	1948	1920-47
	1949/50	1900-48
	1954	1920-53
	1965	1930-64
	1969	1963-68
	1975	1966-74
	1978HS[ii]	1948-77
	1981	1962-80
	1986	1967-85
	1997HS[iii]	1948-96
	1999CD[iv]	1980-99

Rural/urban births [see: Birth(s)]

Rural/urban population (see: Population: urban/rural residence)

S

Sex (see appropriate subject entry, e.g., Births, Death rates, Migration, Population, etc.)

Size of (living) family:

Subject-matter	Year of issue	Time coverage
- female population by age (see also: Children)	1949/50	Latest
	1954	1930-53
	1955	1945-54
	1959	1949-58
	1963	1955-63
	1965	1955-65
	1968	1955-67
	1969	Latest
	1971	1962-71
	1973	1965-73[vi]
	1975	1965-74
	1978HS[ii]	1948-77
	1981	1972-80
	1986	1977-85
	1997HS[iii]	1948-96

Special text (see separate listing in Appendix to this Index)

Special topic (see: Topic of each Demographic

Subject-matter	Year of issue	Time coverage	Subject-matter	Year of issue	Time coverage
Yearbook)					-1953
			- Historical Supplement	1978HS[ii]	1948-78
Still birth(s) [see: Foetal death(s), late)]				1997HS[iii]	1948-97
			- Marriage and Divorce	1958	1930-57
Surface area				1968	1920-68
- of continents	1949/50			1976	1957-76
	1999	Latest		1982	1963-82
	2000	2000		1990	1971-90
	2001	2001	- Migration (international)	1977	1958-76
	2002	2002		1989	1975-88
	2003	2003	- Mortality	1951	1905-50
	2004	2004		1957	1930-56
	2005	2005		1961	1945-61
- of countries or areas	1948-2005	Latest		1966	1920-66
- of macro-regions	1964-1999	Latest		1967	1900-67
	2000	2000		1974	1965-74
	2001	2001		1980	1971-80
	2002	2002		1985	1976-85
	2003	2003		1992	1983-92
	2004	2004		1996	1987-96
	2005	2005			
- of regions	1952-1999	Latest	- Natality	1949/50	1932-49
	2000	2000		1954	1920-53
	2001	2001		1959	1920-58
	2002	2002		1965	1920-65
	2003	2003		1969	1925-69
	2004	2004		1975	1956-75
	2005	2005		1981	1962-81
- of the world	1949/50			1986	1967-86
	1999	Latest		1992	1983-92
	2000	2000		1999CD[iv]	1980-99
	2001	2001	- Nuptiality (see: Marriage and Divorce, above)		
	2002	2002			
	2003	2003			
	2004	2004			
	2005	2005	- Population Ageing and the Situation of Elderly Persons	1991PA[vii]	1950-90
Survivors (see: Life tables)					
			- Population Census: Economic characteristics	1956	1945-55
T				1964	1955-64
				1972	1962-72
Text (see separate listing in Appendix to this Index)				1973	1965-73[vi]
				1979	1970-79[vi]
				1984	1974-84
Topic of each Demographic Yearbook				1988	1980-88[vi]
- Divorce (see: Marriage and Divorce, below)				1994	1985-94
			Educational characteristics	1955	1945-54
- General demography	1948	1900-48		1956	1945-55
	1953	1850			

APPENDIX

Special text of each Demographic Yearbook:

Divorce:

'Uses of Marriage and Divorce Statistics', 1958.

Marriage:

'Uses of Marriage and Divorce Statistics', 1958.

Households:

'Concepts and definitions of households, householder and institutional population', 1987.

Migration:

'Statistics of International Migration', 1977.

Mortality:

'Recent Mortality Trends', 1951.
'Development of Statistics of Causes of Death', 1951.
'Factors in Declining Mortality', 1957.
'Notes on Methods of Evaluating the Reliability of Conventional Mortality Statistics', 1961.
'Recent Trends of Mortality', 1966.
'Mortality Trends among Elderly Persons', 1991PA[vii].

Natality:

'Graphic Presentation of Trends in Fertility', 1959.
'Recent Trends in Birth Rates', 1965.
'Recent Changes in World Fertility', 1969.

Population

'World Population Trends, 1920-1949', 1949/50.
'Urban Trends and Characteristics', 1952.
'Background to the1950 Censuses of Population', 1955.
'The World Demographic Situation', 1956.
'How Well Do We Know the Present Size and Trend of the World's Population?', 1960.
'Notes on Availability of National Population Census Data and Methods of Estimating their Reliability', 1962.
'Availability and Adequacy of Selected Data Obtained from Population Censuses Taken 1955-1963', 1963.
'Availability of Selected Population Census Statistics: 1955-1964', 1964.
'Statistical Concepts and Definitions of Urban and Rural Population', 1967.
'Statistical Concepts and Definitions of Household', 1968.
'How Well Do We Know the Present Size and Trend of the World's Population?', 1970.
'United Nations Recommendations on Topics to be Investigated in a Population Census
Compared with Country Practice in National Censuses taken 1965-1971', 1971.
'Statistical Definitions of Urban Population and their Use in Applied Demography', 1972.
'Dates of National Population and Housing Census carried out during the decade1965-1974', 1974.
'Dates of National Population and/or Housing Censuses taken or anticipated during the decade 1975-1984', 1979.
'Dates of National Population and/or Housing Censuses taken during the decade1965-1974 and taken or anticipated during the decade 1975-1984', 1983.
'Dates of National Population and/or Housing Censuses taken during the decade1975-1984 and taken or anticipated during the decade 1985-1994', 1988 and 1993.
'Statistics Concerning the Economically Active Population: An Overview', 1984.

'Disability', 1991PA[vii].
'Population Ageing', 1991PA[vii].
'Special Needs for the Study of Population Ageing and Elderly Persons', 1991PA[vii].

General Notes

This cumulative index covers the contents of each of the 52 issues of the Demographic Yearbook. 'Year of issue' stands for the particular issue in which the indicated subject-matter appears. Unless otherwise specified, 'Time coverage' designates the years for which annual statistics are shown in the Demographic Yearbook referred to in 'Year of issue' column. 'Latest' or '2-Latest' indicates that data are for latest available year(s) only.

---

[i] Only titles not available for preceding bibliography.

[ii] Historical Supplement to the 30th DYB published in a separate volume in year 1979.

[iii] Historical Supplement to the 49th DYB published in a separate volume (CD-ROM) in year 2000.

[iv] Supplement to the 51st DYB focusing on natality published in a separate volume (CD-ROM) in year 2002.

[v] Five-year average rates.

[vi] Only data not available for preceding issue.

[vii] Population ageing published in separate volume.

Index
Index historique (suite)
(Voir notes à la fin de l'index)

Index
Index historique (suite)
(Voir notes à la fin de l'index)

Sujet	Année de l'édition	Période considérée	Sujet	Année de l'édition	Période considérée
C				1999	1995-99
				2000	1996-00
				2001	1997-01
				2002	1998-02
Cause de décès (voir: Décès)				2003	1999-03
				2004	2000-04
Chômeurs (voir: Population)				2005	2001-05
			-d'enfants de moins d'un an (voir: Mortalité infantile)		
Composition ethnique (voir: Population)			-selon l'âge et le sexe	1948	1936-47
				1951	1936-50
Décès	1948	1932-47		1955-1956	Dernière
	1949/50	1934-49		1957	1948-56
	1951	1935-50		1958-1960	Dernière
	1952	1936-51		1961	1955-60
	1953	1950-52		1962-1965	Dernière
	1954	1946-53		1966	1961-65
	1955	1946-54		1967-1973	Dernière
	1956	1947-55		1974	1965-73
	1957	1940-56		1975-1979	Dernière
	1958	1948-57		1978 SR [i]	1948-77
	1959	1949-58		1980	1971-79
	1960	1950-59		1981-1984	Dernière
	1961	1952-61		1985	1976-84
	1962	1953-62		1986-1991	Dernière
	1963	1954-63		1992	1983-92
	1964	1960-64		1993-1995	Dernière
	1965	1961-65		1996	1987-95
	1966	1947-66		1997	Dernière
	1967	1963-67		1997SR [ii]	1948-96
	1968	1964-68		1998-2005	Dernière
	1969	1965-69	-selon l'âge et le sexe et la résidence (urbaine/rurale)	1967-1973	Dernière
	1970	1966-70		1974	1965-73
	1971	1967-71		1975-1979	Dernière
	1972	1968-72		1980	1971-79
	1973	1969-73		1981-1984	Dernière
	1974	1965-74		1985	1976-84
	1975	1971-75		1986-1991	Dernière
	1976	1972-76		1992	1983-92
	1977	1973-77		1993-1995	Dernière
	1978	1974-78		1996	1987-95
	1978SR [i]	1948-78		1997	Dernière
	1979	1975-79		1997SR [ii]	1948-96
	1980	1971-80		1998-2005	Dernière
	1981	1977-81	-selon la cause	1951	1947-50
	1982	1978-82		1952	1947-51 [iii]
	1983	1979-83		1953	Dernière
	1984	1980-84		1954	1945-53
	1985	1976-85		1955-1956	Dernière
	1986	1982-86		1957	1952-56
	1987	1983-87		1958-1960	Dernière
	1988	1984-88		1961	1955-60
	1989	1985-89		1962-1965	Dernière
	1990	1986-90		1966	1960-65
	1991	1987-91		1967-1973	Dernière
	1992	1983-92		1974	1965-73
	1993	1989-93		1975-1979	Dernière
	1994	1990-94		1980	1971-79
	1995	1991-95		1981-1984	Dernière
	1996	1987-96		1985	1976-84
	1997	1993-97		1986-1995	Dernière
	1997SR [ii]	1948-97			
	1998	1994-98			

Index
Index historique (suite)
(Voir notes à la fin de l'index)

Index
Index historique (suite)
(Voir notes à la fin de l'index)

Index
Index historique (suite)
(Voir notes à la fin de l'index)

Index
Index historique (suite)
(Voir notes à la fin de l'index)

Index
Index historique (suite)
(Voir notes à la fin de l'index)

Index
Index historique (suite)
(Voir notes à la fin de l'index)

Sujet	Année de l'édition	Période considérée	Sujet	Année de l'édition	Période considérée
	1978SR [i]	1948-77	**Mariages**	1948	1932-47
	1979-1980	Dernière		1949/50	1934-49
	1981	1962-80		1951	1935-50
	1982-1985	Dernière		1952	1936-51
	1986	1977-85		1953	1950-52
	1987-1991	Dernière		1954	1946-53
	1992	1983-92		1955	1946-54
	1993-1997	Dernière		1956	1947-55
	1997SR [ii]	1948-96		1957	1948-56
	1998-2004	Dernière		1958	1940-57
	2005	2001-05		1959	1949-58
				1960	1950-59
				1961	1952-61
				1962	1953-62
				1963	1954-63
				1964	1960-64
I				1965	1956-65
				1966	1962-66
Illégitime (voir également: Naissances et morts fœtales tardives):				1967	1963-67
				1968	1949-68
-morts fœtales tardives	1961	1952-60		1969	1965-69
	1965	5-Dernières		1970	1966-70
	1969	1963-68		1971	1967-71
	1975	1966-74		1972	1968-72
	1981	1972-80		1973	1969-73
	1986	1977-85		1974	1970-74
-morts fœtales tardives, rapports de	1961	1952-60		1975	1971-75
	1965	5-Dernières		1976	1957-76
	1969	1963-68		1977	1973-77
	1975	1966-74		1978	1974-78
	1981	1972-80		1979	1975-79
	1986	1977-85		1980	1976-80
-naissances	1959	1949-58		1981	1977-81
	1965	1955-64		1982	1963-82
	1969	1963-68		1983	1979-83
	1975	1966-74		1984	1980-84
	1981	1972-80		1985	1981-85
	1986	1977-85		1986	1982-86
	1999CD [vii]	1990-98		1987	1983-87
-naissances, rapports de	1959	1949-58		1988	1984-88
	1965	1955-64		1989	1985-89
	1969	1963-68		1990	1971-90
	1975	1966-74		1991	1987-91
	1981	1972-80		1992	1988-92
	1986	1977-85		1993	1989-93
	1999CD [vii]	1990-98		1994	1990-94
Immigrants (voir: Migration internationale)				1995	1991-95
				1996	1992-96
Instruction, degré d' (voir: Population)				1997	1993-97
				1998	1994-98
				1999	1995-99
L				2000	1996-00
				2001	1997-01
				2002	1998-02
				2003	1999-03
Langue et sexe (voir: Population)				2004	2000-04
				2005	2001-05
Localités (voir: Population)			-selon l'âge de l'épouse		
				1948	1936-47
M				1949/50	1936-49
				1958	1948-57
				1959-1967	Dernière

Index
Index historique (suite)
(Voir notes à la fin de l'index)

Index
Index historique (suite)
(Voir notes à la fin de l'index)

Index
Index historique (suite)
(Voir notes à la fin de l'index)

Index
Index historique (suite)
(Voir notes à la fin de l'index)

Sujet	Année de l'édition	Période considérée	Sujet	Année de l'édition	Période considérée
Mortalité fœtale, rapports de				1984	1979-83
-selon la période de gestation				1985	1975-84
	1957	1950-56		1986	1977-85
	1959	1949-58		1987	1982-86
	1961	1952-60		1988	1983-87
	1965	5-Dernières		1989	1984-88
	1966	1956-65		1964	1959-63
	1967-1968	Dernière		1990	1985-89
	1969	1963-68		1991	1986-90
	1974	1965-73		1992	1987-91
	1975	1966-74		1993	1988-92
	1980	1971-79		1994	1989-93
	1981	1972-80		1995	1990-94
	1985	1976-84		1996	1987-95
	1986	1977-85		1997	1992-96
	1996	1987-95		1998	1993-97
	1999CD [vii]	1990-98		1999	1994-98
				1999CD [vii]	1990-98
Mortalité fœtale tardive (voir: Morts fœtales tardives)				2000	1995-99
				2001	1997-01
				2002	1998-02
Mortalité fœtale tardive, rapports de				2003	1999-03
	1951	1935-50		2004	2000-04
	1952	1935-51		2005	2001-05
	1953	1936-52	-illégitimes	1961	1952-60
	1954	1938-53		1965	5-Dernières
	1955	1946-54	-légitimes	1959	1949-58
	1956	1947-55		1965	1955-64
	1957	1948-56		1969	1963-68
	1958	1948-57		1975	1966-74
	1959	1920-54 [vi]		1981	1972-80
		1953-58		1986	1977-85
	1960	1950-59	-légitimes selon l'âge de la mère		
	1961	1945-49 [vi]		1959	1949-58
		1952-60		1965	1955-64
	1962	1945-54 [vi]		1969	1963-68
		1952-61		1975	1966-74
	1963	1945-59 [vi]		1981	1972-80
		1953-62		1986	1977-85
	1964	1959-63	-selon l'âge de la mère	1954	1936-53
	1965	1950-64 [vi]		1959	1949-58
		1955-64		1965	1955-64
	1966	1950-64 [vi]		1969	1963-68
		1956-65		1975	1966-74
	1967	1962-66		1981	1972-80
	1968	1963-67		1986	1977-85
	1969	1950-64 [vi]		1999CD [vii]	1990-98
	1969	1959-68	-selon l'âge de la mère et le rang de naissance		
	1970	1965-69		1954	Dernière
	1971	1966-70		1959	1949-58
	1972	1967-71		1965	3-Dernières
	1973	1968-72		1969	1963-68
	1974	1965-73		1975	1966-74
	1975	1966-74		1981	1972-80
	1976	1971-75		1986	1977-85
	1977	1972-76		1999CD [vii]	1990-98
	1978	1973-77	-selon la période de gestation		
	1979	1974-78		1957	1950-56
	1980	1971-79		1959	1949-58
	1981	1972-80		1961	1952-60
	1982	1977-81		1965	5-Dernières
	1983	1978-82		1966	1956-65

Index
Index historique (suite)
(Voir notes à la fin de l'index)

Index
Index historique (suite)
(Voir notes à la fin de l'index)

Sujet	Année de l'édition	Période considérée	Sujet	Année de l'édition	Période considérée
	1998-1999	Dernière			1952-61
-selon la résidence	1967	Dernière		1962	1945-59 [vi]
(urbaine/rurale)	1968	1964-68			1952-62
	1969	1965-69		1963	1945-59 [vi]
	1970	1966-70			1954-63
	1971	1967-71		1964	1960-64
	1972	1968-72		1965	1961-65
	1973	1969-73		1966	1920-64 [vi]
	1974	1965-74			1951-66
	1975	1971-75		1967	1963-67
	1976	1972-76		1968	1964-68
	1977	1973-77		1969	1965-69
	1978	1974-78		1970	1966-70
	1979	1975-79		1971	1967-71
	1980	1971-80		1972	1968-72
	1981	1977-81		1973	1969-73
	1982	1978-82		1974	1965-74
	1983	1979-83		1975	1971-75
	1984	1980-84		1976	1972-76
	1985	1976-85		1977	1973-77
	1986	1982-86		1978	1974-78
	1987	1983-87		1978SR [i]	1948-78
	1988	1984-88		1979	1975-79
	1989	1985-89		1980	1971-80
	1990	1986-90		1981	1977-81
	1991	1987-91		1982	1978-82
	1992	1983-92		1983	1979-83
	1993	1989-93		1984	1980-84
	1994	1990-94		1985	1976-85
	1995	1991-95		1986	1982-86
	1996	1987-96		1987	1983-87
	1997	1993-97		1988	1984-88
	1998	1994-98		1989	1985-89
	1999	1995-99		1990	1986-90
	2000	1996-00		1991	1987-91
	2001	1997-01		1992	1983-92
	2002	1998-02		1993	1989-93
	2003	1999-03		1994	1990-94
	2004	2000-04		1995	1991-95
	2005	2001-05		1996	1987-96
-selon le mois	1967	1962-66		1997	1993-97
	1974	1965-73		1997SR [ii]	1948-97
	1980	1971-79		1998	1994-98
	1985	1976-84		1999	1995-99
				2000	1996-00
Mortalité infantile, taux de	1948	1932-47		2001	1997-01
	1949/50	1932-49		2002	1998-02
	1951	1930-50		2003	1999-03
	1952	1920-34 [vi]		2004	2000-04
		1934-51		2005	2001-05
	1953	1920-39 [vi]	-selon l'âge et le sexe	1948	1936-47
		1940-52		1951	1936-49
	1954	1920-39 [vi]		1957	1948-56
		1946-53		1961	1952-60
	1955	1920-34 [vi]		1966	1956-65
		1946-54		1997-2005	Latest
	1956	1947-55	-selon l'âge et le sexe et la		
	1957	1948-56	résidence (urbaine/rurale)	1971-1973	Dernière
	1958	1948-57		1974	1965-73
	1959	1949-58		1975-1979	Dernière
	1960	1950-59		1980	1971-79
	1961	1945-59 [vi]		1981-1984	Dernière

Index
Index historique (suite)
(Voir notes à la fin de l'index)

Index
Index historique (suite)
(Voir notes à la fin de l'index)

Index
Index historique (suite)
(Voir notes à la fin de l'index)

Index
Index historique (suite)
(Voir notes à la fin de l'index)

Sujet	Année de l'édition	Période considérée	Sujet	Année de l'édition	Période considérée
	1998-2005	Dernière		1974	1965-74
-taux de mortalité à un âge				1975	1971-75
donné selon le sexe	1948	1891-1945		1976	1972-76
	1951	1891-1950		1977	1973-77
	1952	1891-1951 [iii]		1978	1974-78
	1953	1891-1952		1978SR [i]	1948-78
	1954	1891-1953 [iii]		1979	1975-79
	1957	1900-56		1980	1971-80
	1961	1940-60		1981	1977-81
	1966	2-Dernières		1982	1978-82
	1974	2-Dernières		1983	1979-83
	1980	2-Dernières		1984	1980-84
	1985	2-Dernières		1985	1976-85
	1996	2-Dernières		1986	1982-86
-survivants à un âge donné				1987	1983-87
selon le sexe	1948	1891-1945		1988	1984-88
	1951	1891-1950		1989	1985-89
	1952	1891-1951 [iii]		1990	1986-90
	1953	1891-1952		1991	1987-91
	1954	1891-1953 [iii]		1992	1983-92
	1957	1900-56		1993	1989-93
	1961	1940-60		1994	1990-94
	1966	2-Dernières		1995	1991-95
	1974	2-Dernières		1996	1987-96
	1980	2-Dernières		1997	1993-97
	1985	2-Dernières		1997SR [ii]	1948-96
	1996	2-Dernières		1998	1994-98
				1999	1995-99
Mortalité, taux de	1948	1932-47		2000	1996-00
	1949/50	1932-49		2001	1997-01
	1951	1905-30 [vi]		2002	1998-02
		1930-50		2003	1999-03
	1952	1920-34 [vi]		2004	2000-04
		1934-51		2005	2001-05
	1953	1920-39 [vi]	-estimatifs:		
		1940-52	pour les continents	1949/50	1947
	1954	1920-39 [vi]		1956-1977	Dernière
		1946-53		1978-1979	1970-75
	1955	1920-34 [vi]		1980-1983	1975-80
		1946-54		1984-1986	1980-85
	1956	1947-55		1987-1992	1985-90
	1957	1930-56		1993-1997	1990-95
	1958	1948-57		1998-2000	1995-00
	1959	1949-58		2001-2005	2000-05
	1960	1950-59	pour les grandes régions		
	1961	1945-59 [vi]	(continentales)	1964-1977	Dernière
		1952-61		1978-1970	1970-75
	1962	1945-54 [vi]		1980-1983	1975-80
		1952-62		1984-1986	1980-85
	1963	1945-59 [vi]		1987-1992	1985-90
		1954-63		1993-1997	1990-95
	1964	1960-64		1998-2000	1995-00
	1965	1961-65		2001-2005	2000-05
	1966	1920-64 [vi]	pour les régions	1949/50	1947
		1951-66		1956-1977	Dernière
	1967	1963-67		1978-1979	1970-75
	1968	1964-68		1980-1983	1975-80
	1969	1965-69		1984-1986	1980-85
	1970	1966-70		1987-1992	1985-90
	1971	1967-71		1993-1997	1990-95
	1972	1968-72		1998-2000	1995-00
	1973	1969-73		2001-2005	2000-05

Index
Index historique (suite)
(Voir notes à la fin de l'index)

Sujet	Année de l'édition	Période considérée	Sujet	Année de l'édition	Période considérée
pour l'ensemble du monde	1949/50	1947	-selon la cause, l'âge et le sexe	1957	Dernière
	1956-1977	Dernière		1961	Dernière
	1978-1979	1970-75		1991 VP [v]	1960-90
	1980-1983	1975-80	-selon la cause et le sexe	1967	Dernière
	1984-1986	1980-85		1974	Dernière
	1987-1992	1985-90		1980	Dernière
	1993-1997	1990-95		1985	Dernière
	1998-2000	1995-00		1991 VP [v]	1960-90
	2001-2005	2000-05		1996	Dernière
-selon l'âge et le sexe	1948	1935-47	-selon l'état matrimonial, l'âge et le sexe	1961	Dernière
	1949/50	1936-49		1967	Dernière
	1951	1936-50		1974	Dernière
	1952	1936-51		1980	Dernière
	1953	1940-52		1985	Dernière
	1954	1946-53		1996	Dernière
	1955-1956	Dernière		2003	Dernière
	1957	1948-1956	-selon la profession, l'âge et le sexe	1957	Dernière
	1961	1952-60	-selon la profession et l'âge (sexe masculin)		
	1966	1950-65		1961	Dernière
	1978SR [i]	1948-77		1967	Dernière
	1998-2005	Dernière	-selon la résidence (urbaine/rurale)	1967	Dernière
-selon l'âge et le sexe et la résidence (urbaine/rurale)	1967	Dernière		1968	1964-68
	1972	Dernière		1969	1965-69
	1974	1965-73		1970	1966-70
	1975-1978	Dernière		1971	1967-71
	1979	Dernière		1972	1968-72
	1980	1971-79		1973	1969-73
	1981-1984	Dernière		1974	1965-74
	1985	1976-84		1975	1971-75
	1986-1991	Dernière		1976	1972-76
	1991 VP [v]	1950-90		1977	1973-77
	1992	1983-92		1978	1974-78
	1993-1995	Dernière		1979	1975-79
	1996	1987-95		1980	1971-80
	1997	Dernière		1981	1977-81
	1997SR [ii]	1948-96		1982	1978-82
	1998-2005	Dernière		1983	1979-83
-selon la cause	1951	1947-49		1984	1980-84
	1952	1947-51 [iii]		1985	1976-85
	1953	1947-52		1986	1982-86
	1954	1945-53		1987	1983-87
	1955-1956	Dernière		1988	1984-88
	1957	1952-56		1989	1985-89
	1958-1960	Dernière		1990	1986-90
	1961	1955-60		1991	1987-91
	1962-1965	Dernière		1992	1983-92
	1966	1960-65		1993	1989-93
	1967-1973	Dernière		1994	1990-94
	1974	1965-73		1995	1991-95
	1975-1979	Dernière		1996	1987-96
	1980	1971-79		1997	1993-97
	1981-1984	Dernière		1998	1994-98
	1985	1976-84		1999	1995-99
	1986-1991	Dernière		2000	1996-00
	1991 VP [v]	1960-90		2001	1997-01
	1992-1995	Dernière		2002	1998-02
	1996	1987-95		2003	1999-03
	1997-2000	Dernière			
	2002	1995-02			
	2004	1995-04			

Index
Index historique (suite)
(Voir notes à la fin de l'index)

Sujet	Année de l'édition	Période considérée
	2004	2000-04
	2005	2001-05
Mort-nés (voir: Morts fœtales tardives)		
Morts fœtales:		
-selon la période de gestation	1957	1950-56
	1959	1949-58
	1961	1952-60
	1965	5-Dernières
	1966	1956-65
	1967-1968	Dernière
	1969	1963-68
	1974	1965-73
	1975	1966-74
	1980	1971-79
	1981	1972-80
	1985	1976-84
	1986	1977-85
	1996	1987-95
	1999CD [vii]	1990-98
Morts fœtales tardives	1951	1935-50
	1952	1936-51
	1953	1936-52
	1954	1938-53
	1955	1946-54
	1956	1947-55
	1957	1948-56
	1958	1948-57
	1959	1949-58
	1960	1950-59
	1961	1952-60
	1962	1953-61
	1963	1953-62
	1964	1959-63
	1965	1955-64
	1966	1947-65
	1967	1962-66
	1968	1963-67
	1969	1959-68
	1970	1965-69
	1971	1966-70
	1972	1967-71
	1973	1968-72
	1974	1965-73
	1975	1966-74
	1976	1971-75
	1977	1972-76
	1978	1973-77
	1979	1974-78
	1980	1971-79
	1981	1972-80
	1982	1977-81
	1983	1978-82
	1984	1979-83
	1985	1975-84
	1986	1977-85
	1987	1982-86
	1988	1983-87

Sujet	Année de l'édition	Période considérée
	1989	1984-88
	1990	1985-89
	1991	1986-90
	1992	1987-91
	1993	1988-92
	1994	1989-93
	1995	1990-94
	1996	1987-95
	1997	1992-96
	1998	1993-97
	1999	1994-98
	1999CD [vii]	1990-98
	2000	1995-99
	2001	1997-01
	2002	1998-02
	2003	1999-03
	2004	2000-04
	2005	2001-05
-illégitimes	1961	1952-60
	1965	5-Dernières
	1969	1963-68
	1975	1966-74
	1981	1972-80
	1986	1977-85
-illégitimes, en pourcentage	1961	1952-60
	1965	5-Dernières
	1969	1963-68
	1975	1966-74
	1981	1972-80
	1986	1977-85
-légitimes	1959	1949-58
	1965	1955-64
	1969	1963-68
	1975	1966-74
	1981	1972-80
	1986	1977-85
-légitimes selon l'âge de la mère	1959	1949-58
	1965	1955-64
	1969	1963-68
	1975	1966-74
	1981	1972-80
	1986	1977-85
-selon l'âge de la mère	1954	1936-53
	1959	1949-58
	1965	1955-64
	1969	1963-68
	1975	1966-74
	1981	1972-80
	1986	1977-85
	1999CD [vii]	1990-98
-selon l'âge de la mère et le rang de naissance	1954	Dernière
	1959	1949-58
	1965	3-Dernières
	1969	1963-68
	1975	1966-74
	1981	1972-80
	1986	1977-85
	1999CD [vii]	1990-98
-selon la période de gestation	1957	1950-56

Index
Index historique (suite)
(Voir notes à la fin de l'index)

Index
Index historique (suite)
(Voir notes à la fin de l'index)

Index
Index historique (suite)
(Voir notes à la fin de l'index)

Index
Index historique (suite)
(Voir notes à la fin de l'index)

Index
Index historique (suite)
(Voir notes à la fin de l'index)

Index
Index historique (suite)
(Voir notes à la fin de l'index)

Index
Index historique (suite)
(Voir notes à la fin de l'index)

Sujet	Année de l'édition	Période considérée	Sujet	Année de l'édition	Période considérée
	1972	1968-72		1966	1958-66
	1973	1969-73		1967	1963-67
	1974	1970-74		1968	1963-68
	1975	1971-75		1969	1963-69
	1976	1957-76		1970	1963-70
	1977	1973-77		1971	1963-71
	1978	1974-78		1972	1963-72
	1979	1975-79		1973	1970-73
	1980	1976-80		1974	1970-74
	1981	1977-81		1975	1970-75
	1982	1963-82		1976	1970-76
	1983	1979-83		1977	1970-77
	1984	1980-84		1978	1975-78
	1985	1981-85		1979	1975-79
	1986	1982-86		1980	1975-80
	1987	1983-87		1981	1975-81
	1988	1984-88		1982	1975-82
	1989	1985-89		1983	1980-83
	1990	1971-90		1984	1980-84
	1991	1987-91		1985	1980-85
	1992	1988-92		1986	1980-86
	1993	1989-93		1987	1980-87
	1994	1990-94		1988	1985-88
	1995	1991-95		1989	1985-89
	1996	1992-96		1990	1985-90
	1997	1993-97		1991	1985-91
	1998	1994-98		1992	1985-92
	1999	1995-99		1993	1990-93
	2000	1996-00		1994	1990-94
	2001	1997-01		1995	1990-95
	2002	1998-02		1996	1990-96
	2003	1999-03		1997	1990-97
	2004	2000-04		1998	1993-98
	2005	2001-05		1999	1995-99
-selon le sexe et la population mariable				2000	1996-00
	1958	1935-56		2001	1997-01
	1968	1935-67		2002	1998-02
	1976	1966-75		2003	1999-03
	1982	1972-81		2004	2000-04
	1990	1980-89		2001-2005	2000-05
Nuptialité au premier mariage, taux de, classification détaillée selon l'âge de l'épouse et de l'époux	1982	1972-81	annuels moyens pour le monde, les grandes régions (continentes) et les régions		
	1990	1980-89	géographiques	1957	1950-56
				1958	1950-57
P				1959	1950-58
				1960	1950-59
				1961	1950-60
Population:				1962	1950-61
-accroissement, taux d'......: annuels moyens pour les				1963	1958-62
pays ou zones	1957	1953-56			1960-62
	1958	1953-57		1964	1958-63
	1959	1953-58			1960-63
	1960	1953-59		1965	1958-64
	1961	1953-60			1960-64
	1962	1958-61		1966	1958-66
	1963	1958-62			1960-66
	1964	1958-63		1967	1960-67
	1965	1958-64			1963-67
				1968	1960-68

Index
Index historique (suite)
(Voir notes à la fin de l'index)

Index
Index historique (suite)
(Voir notes à la fin de l'index)

Index
Index historique (suite)
(Voir notes à la fin de l'index)

Sujet	Année de l'édition	Période considérée	Sujet	Année de l'édition	Période considérée
	1993	1985-93 [iii]		1965	1930-65
-analphabète selon le sexe				1966	1930-66
et l'âge, taux d'......	1948	Dernière		1967	1930-67
	1955	1945-54		1968	1930-68
	1960	1920-60		1969	1930-69
	1963	1955-63 [iii]		1970	1950-70
	1964	1955-64 [iii]		1971	1950-71
	1970	1950-70		1972	1950-72
-analphabète selon le sexe				1973	1950-73
et l'âge, taux d'...... et la				1974	1950-74
résidence (urbaine/rurale)	1973	1965-73		1975	1950-75
	1979	1970-79 [iii]		1976	1950-76
	1983	1974-83		·1977	1950-77
	1988	1980-88 [iii]		1978	1950-78
	1993	1985-93 [iii]		1979	1950-79
-célibataire selon l'âge et le				1980	1950-80
sexe (voir également: selon				1981	1950-81
l'état matrimonial, ci-				1982	1950-82
dessous):				1983	1950-83
nombres	1960	1920-60		1984	1950-84
	1970	1950-70		1985	1950-85
pourcentages	1949/50	1926-48		1986	1950-86
	1960	1920-60		1987	1950-87
	1970	1950-70		1988	1950-88
-chômeurs selon l'âge et le				1989	1950-89
sexe	1949/50	1946-49		1990	1950-90
-dans les localités (voir:				1991	1950-91
selon l'importance des				1992	1950-92
localités, ci-dessous)				1993	1950-93
des collectivités, âge et				1994	1950-94
sexe et résidence				1995	1950-95
urbaine/rurale	1987	1975-86		1996	1950-96
	1995	1985-95		1997	1950-97
-dans les ménages selon le				1998-2000	1950-00
type et la dimension des				2001	1950-01
ménages privés (voir				2002	1950-02
également: Ménages)	1955	1945-54		2003	1950-03
	1962	1955-62		2004	1950-04
	1963	1955-63 [iii]		2005	1950-05
-dans les logements			-des pays ou zones (total):		
collectifs et sans abri	1991VP [v]	Dernière	dénombrée	1948	1900-48
-dans les villes (voir: des				1949/50	1900-50
grandes régions)				1951	1900-51
-des continents (voir: des				1952	1850-1952
grandes régions				1953	1850-1953
(continentales))				1954	Dernière
-des grandes régions				1955	1850-1954
(continentales)	1949/50	1920-49		1956-1961	Dernière
	1951	1950		1962	1900-62
	1952	1920-51		1963	Dernière
	1953	1920-52		1964	1955-64
	1954	1920-53		1965-1978	Dernière
	1955	1920-54		1978SR [i]	1948-78
	1956	1920-55		1979-1997	Dernière
	1957	1920-56		1979SR [ii]	1948-78
	1958	1920-57		1998-2005	Dernière
	1959	1920-58	estimée	1948	1932-47
	1960	1920-59		1949/50	1932-49
	1961	1920-60		1951	1930-50
	1962	1920-61		1952	1920-51
	1963	1930-62		1953	1920-53
	1964	1930-63		1954	1920-54

Index
Index historique (suite)
(Voir notes à la fin de l'index)

Sujet	Année de l'édition	Période considérée	Sujet	Année de l'édition	Période considérée
	1955	1920-55		1988	1980-88 [iii]
	1956	1920-56		1993	1985-93
	1957	1940-57	-des régions	1949/50	1920-49
	1958	1939-58		1952	1920-51
	1959	1940-59		1953	1920-52
	1960	1920-60		1954	1920-53
	1961	1941-61		1955	1920-54
	1962	1942-62		1956	1920-55
	1963	1943-63		1957	1920-56
	1964	1955-64		1958	1920-57
	1965	1946-65		1959	1920-58
	1966	1947-66		1960	1920-59
	1967	1958-67		1961	1920-60
	1968	1959-68		1962	1920-61
	1969	1960-69		1963	1930-62
	1970	1950-70		1964	1930-63
	1971	1962-71		1965	1930-65
	1972	1963-72		1966	1930-66
	1973	1964-73		1967	1930-67
	1974	1965-74		1968	1930-68
	1975	1966-75		1969	1930-69
	1976	1967-76		1970	1950-70
	1977	1968-77		1971	1950-71
	1978	1969-78		1972	1950-72
	1978SR [i]	1948-78		1973	1950-73
	1979	1970-79		1974	1950-74
	1980	1971-80		1975	1950-75
	1981	1972-81		1976	1950-76
	1982	1973-82		1977	1950-77
	1983	1974-83		1978	1950-78
	1984	1975-84		1979	1950-79
	1985	1976-85		1980	1950-80
	1986	1977-86		1981	1950-81
	1987	1978-87		1982	1950-82
	1988	1979-88		1983	1950-83
	1989	1980-89		1984	1950-84
	1990	1981-90		1985	1950-85
	1991	1982-91		1986	1950-86
	1992	1983-92		1987	1950-87
	1993	1984-93		1988	1950-88
	1994	1985-94		1989	1950-89
	1995	1986-95		1990	1950-90
	1996	1987-96		1991	1950-91
	1997	1988-97		1992	1950-92
	1997SR [ii]	1948-97		1993	1950-93
	1998	1989-98		1994	1950-94
	1999	1990-99		1995	1950-95
	2000	1991-00		1996	1950-96
	2001	1992-01		1997	1950-97
	2002	1993-02		1998-2000	1950-00
	2003	1994-03		2001	1950-01
	2004	1995-04		2002	1950-02
	2005	1996-05		2003	1950-03
-des principales divisions administratives	1952	Dernière		2004	1950-04
	1955	1945-54		2005	1950-05
	1962	1955-62	-des villes:		
	1963	1955-63 [iii]	capitale	1952	Dernière
	1971	1962-71		1955	1945-54
	1973	1965-73 [iii]		1957	Dernière
	1979	1970-79 [iii]		1960	1939-61
	1983	1974-83		1962	1955-62
				1963	1955-63

Index
Index historique (suite)
(Voir notes à la fin de l'index)

Index
Index historique (suite)
(Voir notes à la fin de l'index)

Index
Index historique (suite)
(Voir notes à la fin de l'index)

Index
Index historique (suite)
(Voir notes à la fin de l'index)

Index
Index historique (suite)
(Voir notes à la fin de l'index)

Sujet	Année de l'édition	Période considérée	Sujet	Année de l'édition	Période considérée
	1993	1985-93		1974	1966-74
	1971	1962-71		1975	1967-75
selon l'état matrimonial, l'âge et le sexe	1971	1962-71		1976	1967-76
	1973	1965-73 [iii]		1977	1968-77
selon la langue et le sexe	1971	1962-71		1978	1969-78
	1973	1965-73 [iii]		1979	1970-79
	1979	1970-79 [iii]		1980	1971-80
	1983	1974-83		1981	1972-81
	1988	1980-88 [iii]		1982	1973-82
	1993	1985-93		1983	1974-83
selon la nationalité juridique et le sexe	1971	1962-71		1984	1975-84
	1973	1965-73 [iii]		1985	1976-85
selon la nationalité juridique et le sexe et l'âge	1977	Dernière		1986	1977-86
	1983	1974-83		1987	1978-87
	1989	1980-88		1988	1979-88
selon le niveau d'instruction, l'âge et le sexe	1971	1962-71		1989	1980-89
	1973	1965-73 [iii]		1990	1981-90
	1979	1970-79 [iii]		1991	1982-91
	1983	1974-83		1992	1983-92
	1988	1980-88 [iii]		1993	1984-93
	1993	1985-93		1994	1985-94
selon le pays ou zone de naissance et le sexe	1971	1962-71		1995	1986-95
	1973	1965-73 [iii]		1996	1987-96
selon le pays ou zone de naissance et le sexe et l'âge	1977	Dernière		1997	1988-97
	1983	1974-83		1998	1989-98
	1989	1980-88		1999	1990-99
				2000	1991-00
				2001	1992-01
				2002	1993-02
				2003	1994-03
selon les principales divisions administratives	1971	1962-71		2004	1995-04
	1973	1965-73 [iii]		2005	1996-05
	1979	1970-79 [iii]	pourcentage	1948	Dernière
	1983	1974-83		1952	1900-51
	1988	1980-88 [iii]		1955	1945-54
	1993	1985-93		1960	1920-60
selon la religion et le sexe	1971	1962-71		1962	1955-62
	1973	1965-73 [iii]		1970	1950-70
	1979	1970-79 [iii]		1971	1962-71
	1983	1974-83		1973	1965-73
	1988	1980-88 [iii]		1974	1966-74
	1993	1985-93		1975	1967-75
selon le sexe: nombres	1948	Dernière		1976	1967-76
	1952	1900-51		1977	1968-77
	1955	1945-54		1978	1969-78
	1960	1920-60		1979	1970-79
	1962	1955-62		1980	1971-80
	1963	1955-63		1981	1972-81
	1964	1955-64 [iii]		1982	1973-82
	1967	Dernière		1983	1974-83
	1970	1950-70		1984	1975-84
	1971	1962-71		1985	1976-85
	1972	Dernière		1986	1977-86
	1973	1965-73		1987	1978-87
				1988	1979-88
				1989	1980-89
				1990	1981-90
				1991	1982-91
				1992	1983-92
				1993	1984-93
				1994	1985-94
				1995	1986-95

Index
Index historique (suite)
(Voir notes à la fin de l'index)

Index
Index historique (suite)
(Voir notes à la fin de l'index)

Survivants (voir: Mortalité, tables de)

T

Tables de mortalité (voir: Mortalité, tables de)

Taux (voir: Accroissement intercensitaire de la population; Accroissement naturel; Alphabétisme; Analphabétisme; Annulation; Divortialité; Fécondité Intercensitaire; Mortalité Infantile, Mortalité maternelle; Mortalité néonatale; Mortalité post-néonatale; Mortalité, tables de; Mortalité; Natalité; Nuptialité; Reproduction; taux bruts et nets de)

Taux bruts de reproduction (voir: Reproduction)

Taux nets de reproduction (voir: Reproduction)

Texte spécial (voir liste détaillée dans l'Appendice de cet index)

Index
Index historique (suite)
(Voir notes à la fin de l'index)

Index
Index historique (suite)
(Voir notes à la fin de l'index)

Index
Index historique (suite)
(Voir notes à la fin de l'index)

1965-1974", 1974.

"Dates des recensements nationaux de la population et de l'habitation effectués ou prévus, au cours de la décennie 1975-1984",1979.

"Dates des recensements nationaux de la population et/ou de l'habitation effectués au cours de la décennie 1965-1974 et effectués ou prévus au cours de la décennie1975-1984",1983.

"Définitions et concepts statistiques du ménage",1968.

"Dates des recensements nationaux de la population et/ou de l'habitation effectués au cours de la décennie 1975-1984 et effectués ou prévus au cours de la décennie1985-1994", 1988, 1993.

"Statistiques concernant la population active: un aperçu",1984.

"'Etude du vieillissement et de la situation des personnes âgées: Besoins particuliers",1991VP [v].

"Les incapacités", 1991VP [v].

"Le vieillissement", 1991VP [v].

Notes générales

Cet index alphabétique donne la liste des sujets traités dans chacune de 51 éditions de l'Annuaire démographique. La colonne "Année de l'édition" indique l'édition spécifique dans laquelle le sujet a été traité. Sauf indication contraire, la colonne "Période considérée" désigne les années pour lesquelles les statistiques annuelles apparaissant dans l'Annuaire démographique sont indiquées sous la colonne "Année de l'édition". La rubrique "Dernière" ou " 2-Dernières" indique que les données représentent la ou les dernières années disponibles seulement.

---

[i] Le Supplément rétrospectif du 30ème Annuaire Démographique fait l'objet d'un tirage spécial publié en 1979.

[ii] Le Supplément rétrospectif du 49ème Annuaire Démographique fait l'objet d'un tirage spécial (CD-ROM) publié en 2000

[iii] Données non disponibles dans l'édition précédente seulement.

[iv] Titres non disponibles dans la bibliographie précédente seulement.

[v] Taux moyens pour 5 ans.

[vi] Vieillissement de la population.

[vii] Le Supplément du 51 Annuaire Démographique, ayant comme suject la natalité, fait l'objet d'un tirage spécial (CD-ROM) publié en 2002.